Oxford Dictionary of National Biography

Volume 10

Oxford Dictionary of National Biography

IN ASSOCIATION WITH

The British Academy

From the earliest times to the year 2000

Edited by

H. C. G. Matthew

and

Brian Harrison

Volume 10

Cappe–Chancellor

OXFORD

UNIVERSITY PRESS

OXFORD
UNIVERSITY PRESS

Great Clarendon Street, Oxford OX2 6DP

Oxford University Press is a department of the University of Oxford.
It furthers the University's objective of excellence in research, scholarship,
and education by publishing worldwide in

Oxford New York

Auckland Bangkok Buenos Aires Cape Town
Chennai Dar es Salaam Delhi Hong Kong Istanbul Karachi
Kolkata Kuala Lumpur Madrid Melbourne Mexico City Mumbai Nairobi
São Paulo Shanghai Taipei Tokyo Toronto

Oxford is a registered trade mark of Oxford University Press
in the UK and in certain other countries

Published in the United States
by Oxford University Press Inc., New York

British Library Cataloguing in Publication Data
Data available

Library of Congress Cataloging in Publication Data
Data available: for details see volume 1, p. iv

ISBN 0-19-861360-1 (this volume)
ISBN 0-19-861411-X (set of sixty volumes)

Text captured by Alliance Phototypesetters, Pondicherry
Illustrations reproduced and archived by
Alliance Graphics Ltd, UK
Typeset in OUP Swift by Interactive Sciences Limited, Gloucester
Printed in Great Britain on acid-free paper by
Butler and Tanner Ltd,
Frome, Somerset

LIST OF ABBREVIATIONS

1 General abbreviations

AB	bachelor of arts
ABC	Australian Broadcasting Corporation
ABC TV	ABC Television
act.	active
A$	Australian dollar
AD	*anno domini*
AFC	Air Force Cross
AIDS	acquired immune deficiency syndrome
AK	Alaska
AL	Alabama
A level	advanced level [examination]
ALS	associate of the Linnean Society
AM	master of arts
AMICE	associate member of the Institution of Civil Engineers
ANZAC	Australian and New Zealand Army Corps
appx *pl.* appxs	appendix(es)
AR	Arkansas
ARA	associate of the Royal Academy
ARCA	associate of the Royal College of Art
ARCM	associate of the Royal College of Music
ARCO	associate of the Royal College of Organists
ARIBA	associate of the Royal Institute of British Architects
ARP	air-raid precautions
ARRC	associate of the Royal Red Cross
ARSA	associate of the Royal Scottish Academy
art.	article / item
ASC	Army Service Corps
Asch	Austrian Schilling
ASDIC	Antisubmarine Detection Investigation Committee
ATS	Auxiliary Territorial Service
ATV	Associated Television
Aug	August
AZ	Arizona
b.	born
BA	bachelor of arts
BA (Admin.)	bachelor of arts (administration)
BAFTA	British Academy of Film and Television Arts
BAO	bachelor of arts in obstetrics
bap.	baptized
BBC	British Broadcasting Corporation / Company
BC	before Christ
BCE	before the common (*or* Christian) era
BCE	bachelor of civil engineering
BCG	bacillus of Calmette and Guérin [inoculation against tuberculosis]
BCh	bachelor of surgery
BChir	bachelor of surgery
BCL	bachelor of civil law
BCnL	bachelor of canon law
BCom	bachelor of commerce
BD	bachelor of divinity
BEd	bachelor of education
BEng	bachelor of engineering
bk *pl.* bks	book(s)
BL	bachelor of law / letters / literature
BLitt	bachelor of letters
BM	bachelor of medicine
BMus	bachelor of music
BP	before present
BP	British Petroleum
Bros.	Brothers
BS	(1) bachelor of science; (2) bachelor of surgery; (3) British standard
BSc	bachelor of science
BSc (Econ.)	bachelor of science (economics)
BSc (Eng.)	bachelor of science (engineering)
bt	baronet
BTh	bachelor of theology
bur.	buried
C.	command [identifier for published parliamentary papers]
c.	*circa*
c.	*capitulum pl. capitula*: chapter(s)
CA	California
Cantab.	Cantabrigiensis
cap.	*capitulum pl. capitula*: chapter(s)
CB	companion of the Bath
CBE	commander of the Order of the British Empire
CBS	Columbia Broadcasting System
cc	cubic centimetres
C$	Canadian dollar
CD	compact disc
Cd	command [identifier for published parliamentary papers]
CE	Common (*or* Christian) Era
cent.	century
cf.	compare
CH	Companion of Honour
chap.	chapter
ChB	bachelor of surgery
CI	Imperial Order of the Crown of India
CIA	Central Intelligence Agency
CID	Criminal Investigation Department
CIE	companion of the Order of the Indian Empire
Cie	Compagnie
CLit	companion of literature
CM	master of surgery
cm	centimetre(s)

m. *pl.* mm.	membrane(s)	ND	North Dakota
MA	(1) Massachusetts; (2) master of arts	n.d.	no date
MAI	master of engineering	NE	Nebraska
MB	bachelor of medicine	*nem. con.*	*nemine contradicente*: unanimously
MBA	master of business administration	new ser.	new series
MBE	member of the Order of the British Empire	NH	New Hampshire
MC	Military Cross	NHS	National Health Service
MCC	Marylebone Cricket Club	NJ	New Jersey
MCh	master of surgery	NKVD	[Soviet people's commissariat for internal affairs]
MChir	master of surgery		
MCom	master of commerce	NM	New Mexico
MD	(1) doctor of medicine; (2) Maryland	nm	nanometre(s)
MDMA	methylenedioxymethamphetamine	no. *pl.* nos.	number(s)
ME	Maine	Nov	November
MEd	master of education	n.p.	no place [of publication]
MEng	master of engineering	NS	new style
MEP	member of the European parliament	NV	Nevada
MG	Morris Garages	NY	New York
MGM	Metro-Goldwyn-Mayer	NZBS	New Zealand Broadcasting Service
Mgr	Monsignor	OBE	officer of the Order of the British Empire
MI	(1) Michigan; (2) military intelligence	obit.	obituary
MI1c	[secret intelligence department]	Oct	October
MI5	[military intelligence department]	OCTU	officer cadets training unit
MI6	[secret intelligence department]	OECD	Organization for Economic Co-operation and Development
MI9	[secret escape service]		
MICE	member of the Institution of Civil Engineers	OEEC	Organization for European Economic Co-operation
MIEE	member of the Institution of Electrical Engineers		
		OFM	order of Friars Minor [Franciscans]
min.	minute(s)	OFMCap	Ordine Frati Minori Cappucini: member of the Capuchin order
Mk	mark		
ML	(1) licentiate of medicine; (2) master of laws	OH	Ohio
MLitt	master of letters	OK	Oklahoma
Mlle	Mademoiselle	O level	ordinary level [examination]
mm	millimetre(s)	OM	Order of Merit
Mme	Madame	OP	order of Preachers [Dominicans]
MN	Minnesota	op. *pl.* opp.	opus *pl.* opera
MO	Missouri	OPEC	Organization of Petroleum Exporting Countries
MOH	medical officer of health	OR	Oregon
MP	member of parliament	orig.	original
m.p.h.	miles per hour	OS	old style
MPhil	master of philosophy	OSB	Order of St Benedict
MRCP	member of the Royal College of Physicians	OTC	Officers' Training Corps
MRCS	member of the Royal College of Surgeons	OWS	Old Watercolour Society
MRCVS	member of the Royal College of Veterinary Surgeons	Oxon.	Oxoniensis
		p. *pl.* pp.	page(s)
MRIA	member of the Royal Irish Academy	PA	Pennsylvania
MS	(1) master of science; (2) Mississippi	p.a.	per annum
MS *pl.* MSS	manuscript(s)	para.	paragraph
MSc	master of science	PAYE	pay as you earn
MSc (Econ.)	master of science (economics)	pbk *pl.* pbks	paperback(s)
MT	Montana	*per.*	[during the] period
MusB	bachelor of music	PhD	doctor of philosophy
MusBac	bachelor of music	pl.	(1) plate(s); (2) plural
MusD	doctor of music	priv. coll.	private collection
MV	motor vessel	pt *pl.* pts	part(s)
MVO	member of the Royal Victorian Order	pubd	published
n. *pl.* nn.	note(s)	PVC	polyvinyl chloride
NAAFI	Navy, Army, and Air Force Institutes	q. *pl.* qq.	(1) question(s); (2) quire(s)
NASA	National Aeronautics and Space Administration	QC	queen's counsel
NATO	North Atlantic Treaty Organization	R	rand
NBC	National Broadcasting Corporation	R.	Rex / Regina
NC	North Carolina	*r*	recto
NCO	non-commissioned officer	r.	reigned / ruled
		RA	Royal Academy / Royal Academician

RAC	Royal Automobile Club
RAF	Royal Air Force
RAFVR	Royal Air Force Volunteer Reserve
RAM	[member of the] Royal Academy of Music
RAMC	Royal Army Medical Corps
RCA	Royal College of Art
RCNC	Royal Corps of Naval Constructors
RCOG	Royal College of Obstetricians and Gynaecologists
RDI	royal designer for industry
RE	Royal Engineers
repr. *pl.* reprs.	reprint(s) / reprinted
repro.	reproduced
rev.	revised / revised by / reviser / revision
Revd	Reverend
RHA	Royal Hibernian Academy
RI	(1) Rhode Island; (2) Royal Institute of Painters in Water-Colours
RIBA	Royal Institute of British Architects
RIN	Royal Indian Navy
RM	Reichsmark
RMS	Royal Mail steamer
RN	Royal Navy
RNA	ribonucleic acid
RNAS	Royal Naval Air Service
RNR	Royal Naval Reserve
RNVR	Royal Naval Volunteer Reserve
RO	Record Office
r.p.m.	revolutions per minute
RRS	royal research ship
Rs	rupees
RSA	(1) Royal Scottish Academician; (2) Royal Society of Arts
RSPCA	Royal Society for the Prevention of Cruelty to Animals
Rt Hon.	Right Honourable
Rt Revd	Right Reverend
RUC	Royal Ulster Constabulary
Russ.	Russian
RWS	Royal Watercolour Society
S4C	Sianel Pedwar Cymru
s.	shilling(s)
s.a.	*sub anno*: under the year
SABC	South African Broadcasting Corporation
SAS	Special Air Service
SC	South Carolina
ScD	doctor of science
S$	Singapore dollar
SD	South Dakota
sec.	second(s)
sel.	selected
sen.	senior
Sept	September
ser.	series
SHAPE	supreme headquarters allied powers, Europe
SIDRO	Société Internationale d'Énergie Hydro-Électrique
sig. *pl.* sigs.	signature(s)
sing.	singular
SIS	Secret Intelligence Service
SJ	Society of Jesus
Skr	Swedish krona
Span.	Spanish
SPCK	Society for Promoting Christian Knowledge
SS	(1) Santissimi; (2) Schutzstaffel; (3) steam ship
STB	bachelor of theology
STD	doctor of theology
STM	master of theology
STP	doctor of theology
supp.	supposedly
suppl. *pl.* suppls.	supplement(s)
s.v.	*sub verbo / sub voce*: under the word / heading
SY	steam yacht
TA	Territorial Army
TASS	[Soviet news agency]
TB	tuberculosis (*lit.* tubercle bacillus)
TD	(1) *teachtaí dála* (member of the Dáil); (2) territorial decoration
TN	Tennessee
TNT	trinitrotoluene
trans.	translated / translated by / translation / translator
TT	tourist trophy
TUC	Trades Union Congress
TX	Texas
U-boat	*Unterseeboot*: submarine
Ufa	Universum-Film AG
UMIST	University of Manchester Institute of Science and Technology
UN	United Nations
UNESCO	United Nations Educational, Scientific, and Cultural Organization
UNICEF	United Nations International Children's Emergency Fund
unpubd	unpublished
USS	United States ship
UT	Utah
v	verso
v.	versus
VA	Virginia
VAD	Voluntary Aid Detachment
VC	Victoria Cross
VE-day	victory in Europe day
Ven.	Venerable
VJ-day	victory over Japan day
vol. *pl.* vols.	volume(s)
VT	Vermont
WA	Washington [state]
WAAC	Women's Auxiliary Army Corps
WAAF	Women's Auxiliary Air Force
WEA	Workers' Educational Association
WHO	World Health Organization
WI	Wisconsin
WRAF	Women's Royal Air Force
WRNS	Women's Royal Naval Service
WV	West Virginia
WVS	Women's Voluntary Service
WY	Wyoming
¥	yen
YMCA	Young Men's Christian Association
YWCA	Young Women's Christian Association

2 Institution abbreviations

All Souls Oxf.	All Souls College, Oxford
AM Oxf.	Ashmolean Museum, Oxford
Balliol Oxf.	Balliol College, Oxford
BBC WAC	BBC Written Archives Centre, Reading
Beds. & Luton ARS	Bedfordshire and Luton Archives and Record Service, Bedford
Berks. RO	Berkshire Record Office, Reading
BFI	British Film Institute, London
BFI NFTVA	British Film Institute, London, National Film and Television Archive
BGS	British Geological Survey, Keyworth, Nottingham
Birm. CA	Birmingham Central Library, Birmingham City Archives
Birm. CL	Birmingham Central Library
BL	British Library, London
BL NSA	British Library, London, National Sound Archive
BL OIOC	British Library, London, Oriental and India Office Collections
BLPES	London School of Economics and Political Science, British Library of Political and Economic Science
BM	British Museum, London
Bodl. Oxf.	Bodleian Library, Oxford
Bodl. RH	Bodleian Library of Commonwealth and African Studies at Rhodes House, Oxford
Borth. Inst.	Borthwick Institute of Historical Research, University of York
Boston PL	Boston Public Library, Massachusetts
Bristol RO	Bristol Record Office
Bucks. RLSS	Buckinghamshire Records and Local Studies Service, Aylesbury
CAC Cam.	Churchill College, Cambridge, Churchill Archives Centre
Cambs. AS	Cambridgeshire Archive Service
CCC Cam.	Corpus Christi College, Cambridge
CCC Oxf.	Corpus Christi College, Oxford
Ches. & Chester ALSS	Cheshire and Chester Archives and Local Studies Service
Christ Church Oxf.	Christ Church, Oxford
Christies	Christies, London
City Westm. AC	City of Westminster Archives Centre, London
CKS	Centre for Kentish Studies, Maidstone
CLRO	Corporation of London Records Office
Coll. Arms	College of Arms, London
Col. U.	Columbia University, New York
Cornwall RO	Cornwall Record Office, Truro
Courtauld Inst.	Courtauld Institute of Art, London
CUL	Cambridge University Library
Cumbria AS	Cumbria Archive Service
Derbys. RO	Derbyshire Record Office, Matlock
Devon RO	Devon Record Office, Exeter
Dorset RO	Dorset Record Office, Dorchester
Duke U.	Duke University, Durham, North Carolina
Duke U., Perkins L.	Duke University, Durham, North Carolina, William R. Perkins Library
Durham Cath. CL	Durham Cathedral, chapter library
Durham RO	Durham Record Office
DWL	Dr Williams's Library, London
Essex RO	Essex Record Office
E. Sussex RO	East Sussex Record Office, Lewes
Eton	Eton College, Berkshire
FM Cam.	Fitzwilliam Museum, Cambridge
Folger	Folger Shakespeare Library, Washington, DC
Garr. Club	Garrick Club, London
Girton Cam.	Girton College, Cambridge
GL	Guildhall Library, London
Glos. RO	Gloucestershire Record Office, Gloucester
Gon. & Caius Cam.	Gonville and Caius College, Cambridge
Gov. Art Coll.	Government Art Collection
GS Lond.	Geological Society of London
Hants. RO	Hampshire Record Office, Winchester
Harris Man. Oxf.	Harris Manchester College, Oxford
Harvard TC	Harvard Theatre Collection, Harvard University, Cambridge, Massachusetts, Nathan Marsh Pusey Library
Harvard U.	Harvard University, Cambridge, Massachusetts
Harvard U., Houghton L.	Harvard University, Cambridge, Massachusetts, Houghton Library
Herefs. RO	Herefordshire Record Office, Hereford
Herts. ALS	Hertfordshire Archives and Local Studies, Hertford
Hist. Soc. Penn.	Historical Society of Pennsylvania, Philadelphia
HLRO	House of Lords Record Office, London
Hult. Arch.	Hulton Archive, London and New York
Hunt. L.	Huntington Library, San Marino, California
ICL	Imperial College, London
Inst. CE	Institution of Civil Engineers, London
Inst. EE	Institution of Electrical Engineers, London
IWM	Imperial War Museum, London
IWM FVA	Imperial War Museum, London, Film and Video Archive
IWM SA	Imperial War Museum, London, Sound Archive
JRL	John Rylands University Library of Manchester
King's AC Cam.	King's College Archives Centre, Cambridge
King's Cam.	King's College, Cambridge
King's Lond.	King's College, London
King's Lond., Liddell Hart C.	King's College, London, Liddell Hart Centre for Military Archives
Lancs. RO	Lancashire Record Office, Preston
L. Cong.	Library of Congress, Washington, DC
Leics. RO	Leicestershire, Leicester, and Rutland Record Office, Leicester
Lincs. Arch.	Lincolnshire Archives, Lincoln
Linn. Soc.	Linnean Society of London
LMA	London Metropolitan Archives
LPL	Lambeth Palace, London
Lpool RO	Liverpool Record Office and Local Studies Service
LUL	London University Library
Magd. Cam.	Magdalene College, Cambridge
Magd. Oxf.	Magdalen College, Oxford
Man. City Gall.	Manchester City Galleries
Man. CL	Manchester Central Library
Mass. Hist. Soc.	Massachusetts Historical Society, Boston
Merton Oxf.	Merton College, Oxford
MHS Oxf.	Museum of the History of Science, Oxford
Mitchell L., Glas.	Mitchell Library, Glasgow
Mitchell L., NSW	State Library of New South Wales, Sydney, Mitchell Library
Morgan L.	Pierpont Morgan Library, New York
NA Canada	National Archives of Canada, Ottawa
NA Ire.	National Archives of Ireland, Dublin
NAM	National Army Museum, London
NA Scot.	National Archives of Scotland, Edinburgh
News Int. RO	News International Record Office, London
NG Ire.	National Gallery of Ireland, Dublin

NG Scot.	National Gallery of Scotland, Edinburgh
NHM	Natural History Museum, London
NL Aus.	National Library of Australia, Canberra
NL Ire.	National Library of Ireland, Dublin
NL NZ	National Library of New Zealand, Wellington
NL NZ, Turnbull L.	National Library of New Zealand, Wellington, Alexander Turnbull Library
NL Scot.	National Library of Scotland, Edinburgh
NL Wales	National Library of Wales, Aberystwyth
NMG Wales	National Museum and Gallery of Wales, Cardiff
NMM	National Maritime Museum, London
Norfolk RO	Norfolk Record Office, Norwich
Northants. RO	Northamptonshire Record Office, Northampton
Northumbd RO	Northumberland Record Office
Notts. Arch.	Nottinghamshire Archives, Nottingham
NPG	National Portrait Gallery, London
NRA	National Archives, London, Historical Manuscripts Commission, National Register of Archives
Nuffield Oxf.	Nuffield College, Oxford
N. Yorks. CRO	North Yorkshire County Record Office, Northallerton
NYPL	New York Public Library
Oxf. UA	Oxford University Archives
Oxf. U. Mus. NH	Oxford University Museum of Natural History
Oxon. RO	Oxfordshire Record Office, Oxford
Pembroke Cam.	Pembroke College, Cambridge
PRO	National Archives, London, Public Record Office
PRO NIre.	Public Record Office for Northern Ireland, Belfast
Pusey Oxf.	Pusey House, Oxford
RA	Royal Academy of Arts, London
Ransom HRC	Harry Ransom Humanities Research Center, University of Texas, Austin
RAS	Royal Astronomical Society, London
RBG Kew	Royal Botanic Gardens, Kew, London
RCP Lond.	Royal College of Physicians of London
RCS Eng.	Royal College of Surgeons of England, London
RGS	Royal Geographical Society, London
RIBA	Royal Institute of British Architects, London
RIBA BAL	Royal Institute of British Architects, London, British Architectural Library
Royal Arch.	Royal Archives, Windsor Castle, Berkshire [by gracious permission of her majesty the queen]
Royal Irish Acad.	Royal Irish Academy, Dublin
Royal Scot. Acad.	Royal Scottish Academy, Edinburgh
RS	Royal Society, London
RSA	Royal Society of Arts, London
RS Friends, Lond.	Religious Society of Friends, London
St Ant. Oxf.	St Antony's College, Oxford
St John Cam.	St John's College, Cambridge
S. Antiquaries, Lond.	Society of Antiquaries of London
Sci. Mus.	Science Museum, London
Scot. NPG	Scottish National Portrait Gallery, Edinburgh
Scott Polar RI	University of Cambridge, Scott Polar Research Institute
Sheff. Arch.	Sheffield Archives
Shrops. RRC	Shropshire Records and Research Centre, Shrewsbury
SOAS	School of Oriental and African Studies, London
Som. ARS	Somerset Archive and Record Service, Taunton
Staffs. RO	Staffordshire Record Office, Stafford

Suffolk RO	Suffolk Record Office
Surrey HC	Surrey History Centre, Woking
TCD	Trinity College, Dublin
Trinity Cam.	Trinity College, Cambridge
U. Aberdeen	University of Aberdeen
U. Birm.	University of Birmingham
U. Birm. L.	University of Birmingham Library
U. Cal.	University of California
U. Cam.	University of Cambridge
UCL	University College, London
U. Durham	University of Durham
U. Durham L.	University of Durham Library
U. Edin.	University of Edinburgh
U. Edin., New Coll.	University of Edinburgh, New College
U. Edin., New Coll. L.	University of Edinburgh, New College Library
U. Edin. L.	University of Edinburgh Library
U. Glas.	University of Glasgow
U. Glas. L.	University of Glasgow Library
U. Hull	University of Hull
U. Hull, Brynmor Jones L.	University of Hull, Brynmor Jones Library
U. Leeds	University of Leeds
U. Leeds, Brotherton L.	University of Leeds, Brotherton Library
U. Lond.	University of London
U. Lpool	University of Liverpool
U. Lpool L.	University of Liverpool Library
U. Mich.	University of Michigan, Ann Arbor
U. Mich., Clements L.	University of Michigan, Ann Arbor, William L. Clements Library
U. Newcastle	University of Newcastle upon Tyne
U. Newcastle, Robinson L.	University of Newcastle upon Tyne, Robinson Library
U. Nott.	University of Nottingham
U. Nott. L.	University of Nottingham Library
U. Oxf.	University of Oxford
U. Reading	University of Reading
U. Reading L.	University of Reading Library
U. St Andr.	University of St Andrews
U. St Andr. L.	University of St Andrews Library
U. Southampton	University of Southampton
U. Southampton L.	University of Southampton Library
U. Sussex	University of Sussex, Brighton
U. Texas	University of Texas, Austin
U. Wales	University of Wales
U. Warwick Mod. RC	University of Warwick, Coventry, Modern Records Centre
V&A	Victoria and Albert Museum, London
V&A NAL	Victoria and Albert Museum, London, National Art Library
Warks. CRO	Warwickshire County Record Office, Warwick
Wellcome L.	Wellcome Library for the History and Understanding of Medicine, London
Westm. DA	Westminster Diocesan Archives, London
Wilts. & Swindon RO	Wiltshire and Swindon Record Office, Trowbridge
Worcs. RO	Worcestershire Record Office, Worcester
W. Sussex RO	West Sussex Record Office, Chichester
W. Yorks. AS	West Yorkshire Archive Service
Yale U.	Yale University, New Haven, Connecticut
Yale U., Beinecke L.	Yale University, New Haven, Connecticut, Beinecke Rare Book and Manuscript Library
Yale U. CBA	Yale University, New Haven, Connecticut, Yale Center for British Art

3 Bibliographic abbreviations

Adams, *Drama*   W. D. Adams, *A dictionary of the drama*, 1: *A–G* (1904); 2: *H–Z* (1956) [vol. 2 microfilm only]

AFM   J O'Donovan, ed. and trans., *Annala rioghachta Eireann / Annals of the kingdom of Ireland by the four masters*, 7 vols. (1848–51); 2nd edn (1856); 3rd edn (1990)

Allibone, *Dict.*   S. A. Allibone, *A critical dictionary of English literature and British and American authors*, 3 vols. (1859–71); suppl. by J. F. Kirk, 2 vols. (1891)

ANB   J. A. Garraty and M. C. Carnes, eds., *American national biography*, 24 vols. (1999)

Anderson, *Scot. nat.*   W. Anderson, *The Scottish nation, or, The surnames, families, literature, honours, and biographical history of the people of Scotland*, 3 vols. (1859–63)

Ann. mon.   H. R. Luard, ed., *Annales monastici*, 5 vols., Rolls Series, 36 (1864–9)

Ann. Ulster   S. Mac Airt and G. Mac Niocaill, eds., *Annals of Ulster (to AD 1131)* (1983)

APC   *Acts of the privy council of England*, new ser., 46 vols. (1890–1964)

APS   *The acts of the parliaments of Scotland*, 12 vols. in 13 (1814–75)

Arber, *Regs. Stationers*   F. Arber, ed., *A transcript of the registers of the Company of Stationers of London, 1554–1640 AD*, 5 vols. (1875–94)

ArchR   *Architectural Review*

ASC   D. Whitelock, D. C. Douglas, and S. I. Tucker, ed. and trans., *The Anglo-Saxon Chronicle: a revised translation* (1961)

AS chart.   P. H. Sawyer, *Anglo-Saxon charters: an annotated list and bibliography*, Royal Historical Society Guides and Handbooks (1968)

AusDB   D. Pike and others, eds., *Australian dictionary of biography*, 16 vols. (1966–2002)

Baker, *Serjeants*   J. H. Baker, *The order of serjeants at law*, SeldS, suppl. ser., 5 (1984)

Bale, *Cat.*   J. Bale, *Scriptorum illustrium Maioris Brytannie, quam nunc Angliam et Scotiam vocant: catalogus*, 2 vols. in 1 (Basel, 1557–9); facs. edn (1971)

Bale, *Index*   J. Bale, *Index Britanniae scriptorum*, ed. R. L. Poole and M. Bateson (1902); facs. edn (1990)

BBCS   *Bulletin of the Board of Celtic Studies*

BDMBR   J. O. Baylen and N. J. Gossman, eds., *Biographical dictionary of modern British radicals*, 3 vols. in 4 (1979–88)

Bede, *Hist. eccl.*   *Bede's Ecclesiastical history of the English people*, ed. and trans. B. Colgrave and R. A. B. Mynors, OMT (1969); repr. (1991)

Bénézit, *Dict.*   E. Bénézit, *Dictionnaire critique et documentaire des peintres, sculpteurs, dessinateurs et graveurs*, 3 vols. (Paris, 1911–23); new edn, 8 vols. (1948–66), repr. (1966); 3rd edn, rev. and enl., 10 vols. (1976); 4th edn, 14 vols. (1999)

BIHR   *Bulletin of the Institute of Historical Research*

Birch, *Seals*   W. de Birch, *Catalogue of seals in the department of manuscripts in the British Museum*, 6 vols. (1887–1900)

Bishop Burnet's History   *Bishop Burnet's History of his own time*, ed. M. J. Routh, 2nd edn, 6 vols. (1833)

Blackwood   *Blackwood's [Edinburgh] Magazine*, 328 vols. (1817–1980)

Blain, Clements & Grundy, *Feminist comp.*   V. Blain, P. Clements, and I. Grundy, eds., *The feminist companion to literature in English* (1990)

BL cat.   *The British Library general catalogue of printed books* [in 360 vols. with suppls., also CD-ROM and online]

BMJ   *British Medical Journal*

Boase & Courtney, *Bibl. Corn.*   G. C. Boase and W. P. Courtney, *Bibliotheca Cornubiensis: a catalogue of the writings … of Cornishmen*, 3 vols. (1874–82)

Boase, *Mod. Eng. biog.*   F. Boase, *Modern English biography: containing many thousand concise memoirs of persons who have died since the year 1850*, 6 vols. (privately printed, Truro, 1892–1921); repr. (1965)

Boswell, *Life*   *Boswell's Life of Johnson: together with Journal of a tour to the Hebrides and Johnson's Diary of a journey into north Wales*, ed. G. B. Hill, enl. edn, rev. L. F. Powell, 6 vols. (1934–50); 2nd edn (1964); repr. (1971)

Brown & Stratton, *Brit. mus.*   J. D. Brown and S. S. Stratton, *British musical biography* (1897)

Bryan, *Painters*   M. Bryan, *A biographical and critical dictionary of painters and engravers*, 2 vols. (1816); new edn, ed. G. Stanley (1849); new edn, ed. R. E. Graves and W. Armstrong, 2 vols. (1886–9); [4th edn], ed. G. C. Williamson, 5 vols. (1903–5) [various reprs.]

Burke, *Gen. GB*   J. Burke, *A genealogical and heraldic history of the commoners of Great Britain and Ireland*, 4 vols. (1833–8); new edn as *A genealogical and heraldic dictionary of the landed gentry of Great Britain and Ireland*, 3 vols. [1843–9] [many later edns]

Burke, *Gen. Ire.*   J. B. Burke, *A genealogical and heraldic history of the landed gentry of Ireland* (1899); 2nd edn (1904); 3rd edn (1912); 4th edn (1958); 5th edn as *Burke's Irish family records* (1976)

Burke, *Peerage*   J. Burke, *A general* [later edns *A genealogical*] *and heraldic dictionary of the peerage and baronetage of the United Kingdom* [later edns *the British empire*] (1829–)

Burney, *Hist. mus.*   C. Burney, *A general history of music, from the earliest ages to the present period*, 4 vols. (1776–89)

Burtchaell & Sadleir, *Alum. Dubl.*   G. D. Burtchaell and T. U. Sadleir, *Alumni Dublinenses: a register of the students, graduates, and provosts of Trinity College* (1924); [2nd edn], with suppl., in 2 pts (1935)

Calamy rev.   A. G. Matthews, *Calamy revised* (1934); repr. (1988)

CCI   *Calendar of confirmations and inventories granted and given up in the several commissariots of Scotland* (1876–)

CClR   *Calendar of the close rolls preserved in the Public Record Office*, 47 vols. (1892–1963)

CDS   J. Bain, ed., *Calendar of documents relating to Scotland*, 4 vols., PRO (1881–8); suppl. vol. 5, ed. G. G. Simpson and J. D. Galbraith [1986]

CEPR letters   W. H. Bliss, C. Johnson, and J. Twemlow, eds., *Calendar of entries in the papal registers relating to Great Britain and Ireland: papal letters* (1893–)

CGPLA   *Calendars of the grants of probate and letters of administration* [in 4 ser.: *England & Wales, Northern Ireland, Ireland*, and *Éire*]

Chambers, *Scots.*   R. Chambers, ed., *A biographical dictionary of eminent Scotsmen*, 4 vols. (1832–5)

Chancery records   chancery records pubd by the PRO

Chancery records (RC)   chancery records pubd by the Record Commissions

CIPM	Calendar of inquisitions post mortem, [20 vols.], PRO (1904–); also Henry VII, 3 vols. (1898–1955)
Clarendon, Hist. rebellion	E. Hyde, earl of Clarendon, The history of the rebellion and civil wars in England, 6 vols. (1888); repr. (1958) and (1992)
Cobbett, Parl. hist.	W. Cobbett and J. Wright, eds., Cobbett's Parliamentary history of England, 36 vols. (1806–1820)
Colvin, Archs.	H. Colvin, A biographical dictionary of British architects, 1600–1840, 3rd edn (1995)
Cooper, Ath. Cantab.	C. H. Cooper and T. Cooper, Athenae Cantabrigienses, 3 vols. (1858–1913); repr. (1967)
CPR	Calendar of the patent rolls preserved in the Public Record Office (1891–)
Crockford	Crockford's Clerical Directory
CS	Camden Society
CSP	Calendar of state papers [in 11 ser.: domestic, Scotland, Scottish series, Ireland, colonial, Commonwealth, foreign, Spain [at Simancas], Rome, Milan, and Venice]
CYS	Canterbury and York Society
DAB	Dictionary of American biography, 21 vols. (1928–36), repr. in 11 vols. (1964); 10 suppls. (1944–96)
DBB	D. J. Jeremy, ed., Dictionary of business biography, 5 vols. (1984–6)
DCB	G. W. Brown and others, Dictionary of Canadian biography, [14 vols.] (1966–)
Debrett's Peerage	Debrett's Peerage (1803–) [sometimes Debrett's Illustrated peerage]
Desmond, Botanists	R. Desmond, Dictionary of British and Irish botanists and horticulturists (1977); rev. edn (1994)
Dir. Brit. archs.	A. Felstead, J. Franklin, and L. Pinfield, eds., Directory of British architects, 1834–1900 (1993); 2nd edn, ed. A. Brodie and others, 2 vols. (2001)
DLB	J. M. Bellamy and J. Saville, eds., Dictionary of labour biography, [10 vols.] (1972–)
DLitB	Dictionary of Literary Biography
DNB	Dictionary of national biography, 63 vols. (1885–1900), suppl., 3 vols. (1901); repr. in 22 vols. (1908–9); 10 further suppls. (1912–96); Missing persons (1993)
DNZB	W. H. Oliver and C. Orange, eds., The dictionary of New Zealand biography, 5 vols. (1990–2000)
DSAB	W. J. de Kock and others, eds., Dictionary of South African biography, 5 vols. (1968–87)
DSB	C. C. Gillispie and F. L. Holmes, eds., Dictionary of scientific biography, 16 vols. (1970–80); repr. in 8 vols. (1981); 2 vol. suppl. (1990)
DSBB	A. Slaven and S. Checkland, eds., Dictionary of Scottish business biography, 1860–1960, 2 vols. (1986–90)
DSCHT	N. M. de S. Cameron and others, eds., Dictionary of Scottish church history and theology (1993)
Dugdale, Monasticon	W. Dugdale, Monasticon Anglicanum, 3 vols. (1655–72); 2nd edn, 3 vols. (1661–82); new edn, ed. J. Caley, J. Ellis, and B. Bandinel, 6 vols. in 8 pts (1817–30); repr. (1846) and (1970)
DWB	J. E. Lloyd and others, eds., Dictionary of Welsh biography down to 1940 (1959) [Eng. trans. of Y bywgraffiadur Cymreig hyd 1940, 2nd edn (1954)]
EdinR	Edinburgh Review, or, Critical Journal
EETS	Early English Text Society
Emden, Cam.	A. B. Emden, A biographical register of the University of Cambridge to 1500 (1963)
Emden, Oxf.	A. B. Emden, A biographical register of the University of Oxford to AD 1500, 3 vols. (1957–9); also A biographical register of the University of Oxford, AD 1501 to 1540 (1974)
EngHR	English Historical Review
Engraved Brit. ports.	F. M. O'Donoghue and H. M. Hake, Catalogue of engraved British portraits preserved in the department of prints and drawings in the British Museum, 6 vols. (1908–25)
ER	The English Reports, 178 vols. (1900–32)
ESTC	English short title catalogue, 1475–1800 [CD-ROM and online]
Evelyn, Diary	The diary of John Evelyn, ed. E. S. De Beer, 6 vols. (1955); repr. (2000)
Farington, Diary	The diary of Joseph Farington, ed. K. Garlick and others, 17 vols. (1978–98)
Fasti Angl. (Hardy)	J. Le Neve, Fasti ecclesiae Anglicanae, ed. T. D. Hardy, 3 vols. (1854)
Fasti Angl., 1066–1300	[J. Le Neve], Fasti ecclesiae Anglicanae, 1066–1300, ed. D. E. Greenway and J. S. Barrow, [8 vols.] (1968–)
Fasti Angl., 1300–1541	[J. Le Neve], Fasti ecclesiae Anglicanae, 1300–1541, 12 vols. (1962–7)
Fasti Angl., 1541–1857	[J. Le Neve], Fasti ecclesiae Anglicanae, 1541–1857, ed. J. M. Horn, D. M. Smith, and D. S. Bailey, [9 vols.] (1969–)
Fasti Scot.	H. Scott, Fasti ecclesiae Scoticanae, 3 vols. in 6 (1871); new edn, [11 vols.] (1915–)
FO List	Foreign Office List
Fortescue, Brit. army	J. W. Fortescue, A history of the British army, 13 vols. (1899–1930)
Foss, Judges	E. Foss, The judges of England, 9 vols. (1848–64); repr. (1966)
Foster, Alum. Oxon.	J. Foster, ed., Alumni Oxonienses: the members of the University of Oxford, 1715–1886, 4 vols. (1887–8); later edn (1891); also Alumni Oxonienses … 1500–1714, 4 vols. (1891–2); 8 vol. repr. (1968) and (2000)
Fuller, Worthies	T. Fuller, The history of the worthies of England, 4 pts (1662); new edn, 2 vols., ed. J. Nichols (1811); new edn, 3 vols., ed. P. A. Nuttall (1840); repr. (1965)
GEC, Baronetage	G. E. Cokayne, Complete baronetage, 6 vols. (1900–09); repr. (1983) [microprint]
GEC, Peerage	G. E. C. [G. E. Cokayne], The complete peerage of England, Scotland, Ireland, Great Britain, and the United Kingdom, 8 vols. (1887–98); new edn, ed. V. Gibbs and others, 14 vols. in 15 (1910–98); microprint repr. (1982) and (1987)
Genest, Eng. stage	J. Genest, Some account of the English stage from the Restoration in 1660 to 1830, 10 vols. (1832); repr. [New York, 1965]
Gillow, Lit. biog. hist.	J. Gillow, A literary and biographical history or bibliographical dictionary of the English Catholics, from the breach with Rome, in 1534, to the present time, 5 vols. [1885–1902]; repr. (1961); repr. with preface by C. Gillow (1999)
Gir. Camb. opera	Giraldi Cambrensis opera, ed. J. S. Brewer, J. F. Dimock, and G. F. Warner, 8 vols., Rolls Series, 21 (1861–91)
GJ	Geographical Journal

Gladstone, *Diaries* — *The Gladstone diaries: with cabinet minutes and prime-ministerial correspondence*, ed. M. R. D. Foot and H. C. G. Matthew, 14 vols. (1968–94)

GM — *Gentleman's Magazine*

Graves, *Artists* — A. Graves, ed., *A dictionary of artists who have exhibited works in the principal London exhibitions of oil paintings from 1760 to 1880* (1884); new edn (1895); 3rd edn (1901); facs. edn (1969); repr. [1970], (1973), and (1984)

Graves, *Brit. Inst.* — A. Graves, *The British Institution, 1806–1867: a complete dictionary of contributors and their work from the foundation of the institution* (1875); facs. edn (1908); repr. (1969)

Graves, *RA exhibitors* — A. Graves, *The Royal Academy of Arts: a complete dictionary of contributors and their work from its foundation in 1769 to 1904*, 8 vols. (1905–6); repr. in 4 vols. (1970) and (1972)

Graves, *Soc. Artists* — A. Graves, *The Society of Artists of Great Britain, 1760–1791, the Free Society of Artists, 1761–1783: a complete dictionary* (1907); facs. edn (1969)

Greaves & Zaller, *BDBR* — R. L. Greaves and R. Zaller, eds., *Biographical dictionary of British radicals in the seventeenth century*, 3 vols. (1982–4)

Grove, *Dict. mus.* — G. Grove, ed., *A dictionary of music and musicians*, 5 vols. (1878–90); 2nd edn, ed. J. A. Fuller Maitland (1904–10); 3rd edn, ed. H. C. Colles (1927); 4th edn with suppl. (1940); 5th edn, ed. E. Blom, 9 vols. (1954); suppl. (1961) [see also *New Grove*]

Hall, *Dramatic ports.* — L. A. Hall, *Catalogue of dramatic portraits in the theatre collection of the Harvard College library*, 4 vols. (1930–34)

Hansard — *Hansard's parliamentary debates*, ser. 1–5 (1803–)

Highfill, Burnim & Langhans, *BDA* — P. H. Highfill, K. A. Burnim, and E. A. Langhans, *A biographical dictionary of actors, actresses, musicians, dancers, managers, and other stage personnel in London, 1660–1800*, 16 vols. (1973–93)

Hist. U. Oxf. — T. H. Aston, ed., *The history of the University of Oxford*, 8 vols. (1984–2000) [1: *The early Oxford schools*, ed. J. I. Catto (1984); 2: *Late medieval Oxford*, ed. J. I. Catto and R. Evans (1992); 3: *The collegiate university*, ed. J. McConica (1986); 4: *Seventeenth-century Oxford*, ed. N. Tyacke (1997); 5: *The eighteenth century*, ed. L. S. Sutherland and L. G. Mitchell (1986); 6–7: *Nineteenth-century Oxford*, ed. M. G. Brock and M. C. Curthoys (1997–2000); 8: *The twentieth century*, ed. B. Harrison (2000)]

HJ — *Historical Journal*

HMC — Historical Manuscripts Commission

Holdsworth, *Eng. law* — W. S. Holdsworth, *A history of English law*, ed. A. L. Goodhart and H. L. Hanbury, 17 vols. (1903–72)

HoP, *Commons* — *The history of parliament: the House of Commons* [1386–1421, ed. J. S. Roskell, L. Clark, and C. Rawcliffe, 4 vols. (1992); 1509–1558, ed. S. T. Bindoff, 3 vols. (1982); 1558–1603, ed. P. W. Hasler, 3 vols. (1981); 1660–1690, ed. B. D. Henning, 3 vols. (1983); 1690–1715, ed. D. W. Hayton, E. Cruickshanks, and S. Handley, 5 vols. (2002); 1715–1754, ed. R. Sedgwick, 2 vols. (1970); 1754–1790, ed. L. Namier and J. Brooke, 3 vols. (1964), repr. (1985); 1790–1820, ed. R. G. Thorne, 5 vols. (1986); in draft (used with permission): 1422–1504, 1604–1629, 1640–1660, and 1820–1832]

IGI — *International Genealogical Index*, Church of Jesus Christ of the Latterday Saints

ILN — *Illustrated London News*

IMC — Irish Manuscripts Commission

Irving, *Scots.* — J. Irving, ed., *The book of Scotsmen eminent for achievements in arms and arts, church and state, law, legislation and literature, commerce, science, travel and philanthropy* (1881)

JCS — *Journal of the Chemical Society*

JHC — *Journals of the House of Commons*

JHL — *Journals of the House of Lords*

John of Worcester, *Chron.* — *The chronicle of John of Worcester*, ed. R. R. Darlington and P. McGurk, trans. J. Bray and P. McGurk, 3 vols., OMT (1995–) [vol. 1 forthcoming]

Keeler, *Long Parliament* — M. F. Keeler, *The Long Parliament, 1640–1641: a biographical study of its members* (1954)

Kelly, *Handbk* — *The upper ten thousand: an alphabetical list of all members of noble families*, 3 vols. (1875–7); continued as *Kelly's handbook of the upper ten thousand for 1878* [1879], 2 vols. (1878–9); continued as *Kelly's handbook to the titled, landed and official classes*, 94 vols. (1880–1973)

LondG — *London Gazette*

LP Henry VIII — J. S. Brewer, J. Gairdner, and R. H. Brodie, eds., *Letters and papers, foreign and domestic, of the reign of Henry VIII*, 23 vols. in 38 (1862–1932); repr. (1965)

Mallalieu, *Watercolour artists* — H. L. Mallalieu, *The dictionary of British watercolour artists up to 1820*, 3 vols. (1976–90); vol. 1, 2nd edn (1986)

Memoirs FRS — *Biographical Memoirs of Fellows of the Royal Society*

MGH — Monumenta Germaniae Historica

MT — *Musical Times*

Munk, *Roll* — W. Munk, *The roll of the Royal College of Physicians of London*, 2 vols. (1861); 2nd edn, 3 vols. (1878)

N&Q — *Notes and Queries*

New Grove — S. Sadie, ed., *The new Grove dictionary of music and musicians*, 20 vols. (1980); 2nd edn, 29 vols. (2001) [also online edn; see also Grove, *Dict. mus.*]

Nichols, *Illustrations* — J. Nichols and J. B. Nichols, *Illustrations of the literary history of the eighteenth century*, 8 vols. (1817–58)

Nichols, *Lit. anecdotes* — J. Nichols, *Literary anecdotes of the eighteenth century*, 9 vols. (1812–16); facs. edn (1966)

Obits. FRS — *Obituary Notices of Fellows of the Royal Society*

O'Byrne, *Naval biog. dict.* — W. R. O'Byrne, *A naval biographical dictionary* (1849); repr. (1990); [2nd edn], 2 vols. (1861)

OHS — Oxford Historical Society

Old Westminsters — *The record of Old Westminsters*, 1–2, ed. G. F. R. Barker and A. H. Stenning (1928); suppl. 1, ed. J. B. Whitmore and G. R. Y. Radcliffe [1938]; 3, ed. J. B. Whitmore, G. R. Y. Radcliffe, and D. C. Simpson (1963); suppl. 2, ed. F. E. Pagan (1978); 4, ed. F. E. Pagan and H. E. Pagan (1992)

OMT — Oxford Medieval Texts

Ordericus Vitalis, *Eccl. hist.* — *The ecclesiastical history of Orderic Vitalis*, ed. and trans. M. Chibnall, 6 vols., OMT (1969–80); repr. (1990)

Paris, *Chron.* — *Matthaei Parisiensis, monachi sancti Albani, chronica majora*, ed. H. R. Luard, Rolls Series, 7 vols. (1872–83)

Parl. papers — *Parliamentary papers* (1801–)

PBA — *Proceedings of the British Academy*

Pepys, *Diary*	*The diary of Samuel Pepys*, ed. R. Latham and W. Matthews, 11 vols. (1970–83); repr. (1995) and (2000)	Symeon of Durham, *Opera*	*Symeonis monachi opera omnia*, ed. T. Arnold, 2 vols., Rolls Series, 75 (1882–5); repr. (1965)
Pevsner	N. Pevsner and others, Buildings of England series	Tanner, *Bibl. Brit.-Hib.*	T. Tanner, *Bibliotheca Britannico-Hibernica*, ed. D. Wilkins (1748); repr. (1963)
PICE	*Proceedings of the Institution of Civil Engineers*	Thieme & Becker, *Allgemeines Lexikon*	U. Thieme, F. Becker, and H. Vollmer, eds., *Allgemeines Lexikon der bildenden Künstler von der Antike bis zur Gegenwart*, 37 vols. (Leipzig, 1907–50); repr. (1961–5), (1983), and (1992)
Pipe rolls	*The great roll of the pipe for . . .*, PRSoc. (1884–)		
PRO	Public Record Office		
PRS	*Proceedings of the Royal Society of London*	Thurloe, *State papers*	*A collection of the state papers of John Thurloe*, ed. T. Birch, 7 vols. (1742)
PRSoc.	Pipe Roll Society		
PTRS	*Philosophical Transactions of the Royal Society*	*TLS*	*Times Literary Supplement*
QR	*Quarterly Review*	Tout, *Admin. hist.*	T. F. Tout, *Chapters in the administrative history of mediaeval England: the wardrobe, the chamber, and the small seals*, 6 vols. (1920–33); repr. (1967)
RC	Record Commissions		
Redgrave, *Artists*	S. Redgrave, *A dictionary of artists of the English school* (1874); rev. edn (1878); repr. (1970)		
		TRHS	*Transactions of the Royal Historical Society*
Reg. Oxf.	C. W. Boase and A. Clark, eds., *Register of the University of Oxford*, 5 vols., OHS, 1, 10–12, 14 (1885–9)	*VCH*	H. A. Doubleday and others, eds., *The Victoria history of the counties of England*, [88 vols.] (1900–)
Reg. PCS	J. H. Burton and others, eds., *The register of the privy council of Scotland*, 1st ser., 14 vols. (1877–98); 2nd ser., 8 vols. (1899–1908); 3rd ser., [16 vols.] (1908–70)	Venn, *Alum. Cant.*	J. Venn and J. A. Venn, *Alumni Cantabrigienses: a biographical list of all known students, graduates, and holders of office at the University of Cambridge, from the earliest times to 1900*, 10 vols. (1922–54); repr. in 2 vols. (1974–8)
Reg. RAN	H. W. C. Davis and others, eds., *Regesta regum Anglo-Normannorum, 1066–1154*, 4 vols. (1913–69)	Vertue, *Note books*	[G. Vertue], *Note books*, ed. K. Esdaile, earl of Ilchester, and H. M. Hake, 6 vols., Walpole Society, 18, 20, 22, 24, 26, 30 (1930–55)
RIBA Journal	*Journal of the Royal Institute of British Architects* [later *RIBA Journal*]	*VF*	*Vanity Fair*
RotP	J. Strachey, ed., *Rotuli parliamentorum ut et petitiones, et placita in parliamento*, 6 vols. (1767–77)	Walford, *County families*	E. Walford, *The county families of the United Kingdom, or, Royal manual of the titled and untitled aristocracy of Great Britain and Ireland* (1860)
RotS	D. Macpherson, J. Caley, and W. Illingworth, eds., *Rotuli Scotiae in Turri Londinensi et in domo capitulari Westmonasteriensi asservati*, 2 vols., RC, 14 (1814–19)	Walker rev.	A. G. Matthews, *Walker revised: being a revision of John Walker's Sufferings of the clergy during the grand rebellion, 1642–60* (1948); repr. (1988)
RS	Record(s) Society	Walpole, *Corr.*	*The Yale edition of Horace Walpole's correspondence*, ed. W. S. Lewis, 48 vols. (1937–83)
Rymer, *Foedera*	T. Rymer and R. Sanderson, eds., *Foedera, conventiones, literae et cuiuscunque generis acta publica inter reges Angliae et alios quosvis imperatores, reges, pontifices, principes, vel communitates*, 20 vols. (1704–35); 2nd edn, 20 vols. (1726–35); 3rd edn, 10 vols. (1739–45), facs. edn (1967); new edn, ed. A. Clarke, J. Caley, and F. Holbrooke, 4 vols., RC, 50 (1816–30)	Ward, *Men of the reign*	T. H. Ward, ed., *Men of the reign: a biographical dictionary of eminent persons of British and colonial birth who have died during the reign of Queen Victoria* (1885); repr. (Graz, 1968)
		Waterhouse, *18c painters*	E. Waterhouse, *The dictionary of 18th century painters in oils and crayons* (1981); repr. as *British 18th century painters in oils and crayons* (1991), vol. 2 of *Dictionary of British art*
Sainty, *Judges*	J. Sainty, ed., *The judges of England, 1272–1990*, SeldS, suppl. ser., 10 (1993)	Watt, *Bibl. Brit.*	R. Watt, *Bibliotheca Britannica, or, A general index to British and foreign literature*, 4 vols. (1824) [many reprs.]
Sainty, *King's counsel*	J. Sainty, ed., *A list of English law officers and king's counsel*, SeldS, suppl. ser., 7 (1987)		
SCH	Studies in Church History	Wellesley index	W. E. Houghton, ed., *The Wellesley index to Victorian periodicals, 1824–1900*, 5 vols. (1966–89); new edn (1999) [CD-ROM]
Scots peerage	J. B. Paul, ed. *The Scots peerage, founded on Wood's edition of Sir Robert Douglas's Peerage of Scotland, containing an historical and genealogical account of the nobility of that kingdom*, 9 vols. (1904–14)	Wing, *STC*	D. Wing, ed., *Short-title catalogue of . . . English books . . . 1641–1700*, 3 vols. (1945–51); 2nd edn (1972–88); rev. and enl. edn, ed. J. J. Morrison, C. W. Nelson, and M. Seccombe, 4 vols. (1994–8) [see also *STC, 1475–1640*]
SeldS	Selden Society	*Wisden*	*John Wisden's Cricketer's Almanack*
SHR	*Scottish Historical Review*	Wood, *Ath. Oxon.*	A. Wood, *Athenae Oxonienses . . . to which are added the Fasti*, 2 vols. (1691–2); 2nd edn (1721); new edn, 4 vols., ed. P. Bliss (1813–20); repr. (1967) and (1969)
State trials	T. B. Howell and T. J. Howell, eds., *Cobbett's Complete collection of state trials*, 34 vols. (1809–28)		
STC, 1475–1640	A. W. Pollard, G. R. Redgrave, and others, eds., *A short-title catalogue of . . . English books . . . 1475–1640* (1926); 2nd edn, ed. W. A. Jackson, F. S. Ferguson, and K. F. Pantzer, 3 vols. (1976–91) [see also Wing, *STC*]	Wood, *Vic. painters*	C. Wood, *Dictionary of Victorian painters* (1971); 2nd edn (1978); 3rd edn as *Victorian painters*, 2 vols. (1995), vol. 4 of *Dictionary of British art*
		WW	*Who's who* (1849–)
STS	Scottish Text Society	*WWBMP*	M. Stenton and S. Lees, eds., *Who's who of British members of parliament*, 4 vols. (1976–81)
SurtS	Surtees Society	*WWW*	*Who was who* (1929–)

Cappe, Catharine (1744–1821). *See under* Cappe, Newcome (1733–1800).

Cappe, Newcome (1733–1800), Unitarian minister and preacher, was born at Leeds on 21 February 1733. He was the eldest son of Joseph Cappe, minister of Mill Hill Dissenting Chapel in Leeds, and his wife, who was the daughter of Mr Newcome of Waddington, Lincolnshire. From his mother's side of the family he appears to have inherited considerable property. He studied at two of the best dissenting academies—under John Aikin at Kibworth (1748–9) and under Philip Doddridge at Northampton (1749–52)—and under William Leechman at Glasgow University (1752–5).

In 1755 Cappe became co-pastor to the Revd John Hotham at the dissenting chapel in St Saviourgate, York; he was ordained in that city on 26 May 1756 and in the same month became sole minister on Hotham's death. He quickly established himself as one of York's leading citizens, founding a literary club in 1771, taking part in the Yorkshire Association for economical and parliamentary reform in 1779, and helping to distribute material in favour of the repeal of the Test and Corporation Acts in 1787. His large residence in Upper Ousegate became a centre for the local intelligentsia, particularly those of reforming persuasions. He never sought a permanent move from York for, according to William Wood, who preached Cappe's funeral sermon,

> he carried an aversion to public life, and a love of studious retirement, to a somewhat blameable excess. With natural and acquired capacities for extensive usefulness, in the course of five-and-forty years he was seldom absent from this city. (Wood, 18)

This was partly the result of his domestic circumstances. In October 1759 he married Sarah Turner, the daughter of a Hull merchant. They had six children, but she died of consumption in 1773. His second wife was Catharine [*see below*], daughter of an Anglican clergyman, Jeremiah Harrison, vicar of Catterick; the marriage took place at Barwick in Elmet on 19 February 1788. It is due to her subsequent career as a writer that so much about Cappe himself is known.

Cappe published several biblical commentaries and other religious discourses, together with a number of individual sermons. In 1757 his sermon celebrating the victory of Frederick the Great at Rossbach was well received and rapidly passed through thirteen editions. During the War of American Independence he preached several fast-day sermons which stressed national degeneracy and divine retribution; his tone was distinctly pro-American. Notable among such discourses was his *Sermon Preached on the Thirteenth of December, the Late Day of National Humiliation, etc* (1776). His *Discourses on the Providence and Government of God*, which was first published in 1795, had reached a third edition by 1818. His theological affinities were unitarian, and he was associated in politics as well as religion with such luminaries of rational dissent as Joseph Priestley and Theophilus Lindsey. Cappe was plagued by poor health and in 1791 suffered a paralytic stroke, followed by others later in the decade. He died at York on 24

December 1800. Two of his sons became medical practitioners; the elder, Joseph Cappe, predeceased his father, and the younger, Robert Cappe, died at sea while travelling to Leghorn in 1802.

Catharine Cappe (1744–1821) was born on 3 June 1744 at Long Preston, in the West Riding of Yorkshire. On her mother's side she was related to the family of Sir Rowland Winn, bt, of Nostel. She survived a severe attack of smallpox at the age of three. She was educated at York for the purpose, in her own words, of 'attending the dancing school and learning the sort of ornamental needle-work then in fashion' (*Memoirs of the Life*, 38). At the age of thirteen she was placed at a boarding-school at York, where there was a French master and where she received an education of a fairly high quality. Her father died on 22 July 1763 and was succeeded as vicar of Catterick by Theophilus Lindsey, with whose family Catharine Harrison became friendly. Lindsey himself was a formative intellectual influence upon her, and his resignation, on theological grounds, from the Church of England in 1773 and his decision to establish a separate Unitarian chapel in London led her from the Anglicanism of her father into rational dissenting circles. Newcome Cappe was a representative of that tradition in York, and after their marriage in 1788 she joined in his literary and theological endeavours, subsequently becoming his memorialist and expositor. They had no children.

After the death of her husband, Catharine Cappe pursued a literary and philanthropic career of her own. She carried out extensive work for charity schools and published on the subject. She edited and republished several of Newcome Cappe's works and prefaced two of them with memoirs of him, in addition to collecting several of his shorter essays into one volume entitled *Discourses Chiefly on Devotional Subjects* (1805). Her most important production, however, was her volume of memoirs, first published in 1822, with a third edition in 1826. It presents a valuable account of the experiences and educational opportunities of a woman from a clerical and modestly propertied family in the later eighteenth century and has interesting reflections on the female role. It also contains much helpful biographical information about some of the leading dissenters of the period. Catharine Cappe died suddenly at York on 27 July 1821.   G. M. DITCHFIELD

Sources *Discourses chiefly on devotional subjects, by … Newcome Cappe, to which are prefixed memoirs of his life, by Catharine Cappe* (1805) • W. Wood, *A sermon preached … immediately after the interment of the Rev. Newcome Cappe* (1801) • *Memoirs of the life of the late Mrs Catharine Cappe, written by herself*, ed. M. Cappe (1822) • T. Belsham, *Memoirs of the late Reverend Theophilus Lindsey*, new edn (1873) • *Life and correspondence of Joseph Priestley*, ed. J. T. Rutt, 2 vols. (1831–2) • *GM*, 1st ser., 70 (1800), 1299 • *GM*, 1st ser., 71 (1801), 181–2 • *Monthly Review*, new ser., 34 (1801), 81–4 • J. E. Bradley, *Religion, revolution and English radicalism: nonconformity in eighteenth-century politics and society* (1990) • J. Seed, 'Gentlemen dissenters: the social and political meanings of rational dissent in the 1770s', *HJ*, 28 (1985), 299–325 • R. Davies, *A memoir of the York press: with notices of authors, printers, and stationers, in the sixteenth, seventeenth, and eighteenth centuries* (1868), 266, 274, 295–8, 303 • will, Borth. Inst., prog. March 1801 • will, Borth. Inst. [Catharine Cappe], prog. Dec 1821

Archives Borth Inst. · DWL | BL, biographical notice of Catharine Cappe, Add. MS 36527 · BL, letters of Catharine Cappe, Add. MS 18204 · DWL, letters of Catharine Cappe · Sheffield Central Library, Fitzwilliam MSS · Sheffield Central Library, Wentworth Woodhouse MSS · York City Library, Yorkshire Association MSS **Likenesses** attrib. W. Staveley, portrait, 1799, DWL; repro. in Rutt, *Memoirs*, 1, 60 · W. Bond, engraving (Catharine Cappe; after miniature), repro. in Cappe, ed., *Memoirs*, frontispiece

Cappel, Aaron (1560–1620), Reformed minister, was born on 9 October 1560 in London, the son of Anthoine Cappel, an immigrant silkweaver who had arrived from Antwerp in 1559, and who went on to be one of the first and longest-serving elders of the French church of London, and his wife, Barbara. Cappel was a pensioner at Peterhouse, Cambridge, from an unknown date until 1581, and then went on to study at Geneva from 1583 to 1585, funded by the French church of London, to which he had promised his services upon the completion of his studies. He spent a few more years on the continent, studying at Heidelberg in 1586, but was recalled by the French church of London in September 1590. On 28 May 1591 he was accepted as a full minister of the church, joining Robert le Maçon de la Fontaine and Jean Castol. On 10 October that year he married, in the French church of Canterbury, Esther (or Hester) Maurois, the daughter of one of the elders of that church. He also had connections with the other principal francophone refugee church in England, in Norwich, which he temporarily served as minister from November 1597 to June 1598.

As a pastor, Cappel gained the approval of Isaac Casaubon for his theology and preaching. Outside the immediate concerns of his own church, he was involved in larger protestant causes through his friendship and correspondence with Andrew Melville, the Scottish presbyterian leader. He supported in England the request of the Huguenot grandee the duc de Bouillon to have Melville freed from the Tower of London to take up a position at the Academy of Sedan. In a letter of 1611, after he had finally been permitted to go to Sedan, Melville commented in passing on this friendship to his son James, writing, 'The excellent Cappel has in the most friendly manner recommended you by letter to the Duke of Bouillon, but has as yet received no answer. … In the mean time write to me frequently by Cappel concerning every thing' (M'Crie, 1.275).

Cappel died in 1620, and was buried in his London parish of St Katharine Coleman on 1 February, survived by his wife, Esther (who was still living in January 1626), and several of his children, including Aaron (*d.* 1625) and Hester (*d.* after 1645). CHARLES G. D. LITTLETON

Sources F. de Schickler, *Les églises du réfuge en Angleterre*, 3 vols. (Paris, 1892) · consistory minutes, 1589–1680, French Protestant Church of London, Soho Square, MSS 4–5 · *The registers of the French church, Threadneedle Street, London*, 1, ed. W. J. C. Moens, Huguenot Society of London, 9 (1896) · S. Stelling-Michaud, ed., *Le livre du recteur de l'Académie de Genève, 1559–1878*, 6 vols. (Geneva, 1959–80), vol. 2 · J. H. Hessels, ed., *Ecclesiae Londino-Batavae archivum*, 3 vols. (1887–97) · parish register, St Katherine Coleman Street, GL, MS 17832/1 · will, archdeaconry court of London, GL, MS 9051/6 [Aaron Cappell, jnr], fol. 232r–v · T. M'Crie, *The life of Andrew Melville*, 2nd edn, 2 vols. (1824) · D. C. A. Agnew, *Protestant exiles from France, chiefly in the reign of Louis XIV, or, The Huguenot refugees and their descendants in Great Britain and Ireland*, 3rd edn, 1 (1886), 16, 100 · W. J. C. Moens, *The Walloons and their church at Norwich: their history and registers, 1565–1832*, Huguenot Society of London, 1 (1887–8) · F. W. Cross, *History of the Walloon and Huguenot church at Canterbury*, Huguenot Society of London, 15 (1898)

Capper, Francis (1735–1818), Church of England clergyman, was born on 24 August 1735, the second son of Francis Capper, a bencher of Lincoln's Inn, and his wife, Mary Bennet. He was educated at Westminster School (1742–53) and then at Christ Church, Oxford, where he graduated BA in 1757. He proceeded MA in 1760, by which time he was in holy orders and the rector of Monk Soham (October 1759) and Earl Soham (December 1759), Suffolk, benefices which he retained until his death. On 6 November 1759 he married Elizabeth (*d.* 1816), daughter of Peter Pierson; they had two sons and three daughters.

A faithful minister and an upright magistrate, Capper's only contribution to literature was a small tract, which he wrote for the use of his younger parishioners, entitled *The faith and belief of every sincere Christian, proved by references to various texts of holy scripture* (1829). Capper died at Earl Soham on 13 November 1818. An obituary in the *Gentleman's Magazine* noted that in him was exemplified 'a piety without ostentation, and a zeal tempered with judgement' (*GM*, 476).

C. J. ROBINSON, *rev.* ROBERT BROWN

Sources *GM*, 1st ser., 88/2 (1818), 476 · Foster, *Alum. Oxon.* · *Old Westminsters*, vols. 1–2

Capper, James (1743–1825), army officer and meteorologist, was born on 15 December 1743, a son of Francis Capper, a bencher at Lincoln's Inn, and his wife, Mary Bennet. His younger brother was Francis *Capper. He was educated at Harrow School (*c.*1755–*c.*1761) and served thereafter in His Majesty's Train of Artillery in the East Indies, first as a soldier cadet and later as an officer. He was then for a while a free merchant in Bengal before becoming in 1768 a captain in the Madras army and in 1769 senior writer for the presidency of Bengal. He was repatriated on grounds of ill health after becoming unwell on active service but returned to India in 1773, when appointed the East India Company's commissary-general upon the coast of Coromandel, with the brevet rank of colonel. He found on arrival that the governor's son had taken charge and a power struggle ensued, the outcome being that Capper became in April 1774 commissioner of musters and auditor of military accounts in the Madras army. Senior officials of the company insisted on his reinstatement, and this was effected in April 1775. Some time before this Capper married Mary Johnson. Two daughters were born in India, Eliza Henrietta in 1775 and Louisa *Capper in 1776. Both were baptized in Fort St George, Madras. The eldest daughter, Marianne, married Robert Clutterbuck. She and Louisa survived their father.

Capper was sent home with dispatches in early 1777 and remained in England until the autumn of 1778 when, to explore the feasibility of opening a new channel for transmitting intelligence between Europe and India, he returned to Madras by way of Aleppo, the Arabian desert, and Basrah. Details of his journey from India to England in early 1777 (via Ceylon and Suez) and his return journey in 1778–9 are contained in his *Observations on the passage to India through Egypt and across the great desert, with occasional remarks on the adjacent countries and also sketches of the different routes* (1783; 3rd edn 1785). After the revolt of Haidar Ali in July 1780 Capper rejected advice to go home (though he sent his family back) and eventually became acting commandant of artillery at Madras before returning again, in 1782 or 1783, to England. Capper's fifty-two-page *Memorial Addressed to the Honourable the Court of Directors of the East India Company* (dated 3 October 1784) shows that he considered himself to have been shabbily treated by the company over many years. In this memorial he summarized the many complaints he had sent to the company's head office and delivered a scathing attack on the company's lax and corrupt civilian management in India. Despite this he resumed his career in India in 1785, when he became comptroller-general of the army and fortification accompts on the coast of Coromandel, charged with reducing expenditure in Madras. He resigned in 1791 and returned to Britain. The East India Company twice thereafter refused him a pension.

After his return to Britain in 1791 Capper settled in Cardiff, where for many years he lived in Cathays House, near Cardiff Castle. In his *Observations on the Winds and Monsoons* (1801), Capper stated that he had for many years kept weather records wherever he resided. The observations he made twice daily from 1800 to 1807 were recorded in his manuscript 'Meteorological journal kept at Cathays near Cardiff, Glamorganshire, commencing May 1st, 1800' and summarized in his *Meteorological and miscellaneous tracts, applicable to navigation, gardening and farming, with calendars of flora for Greece, France, England and Sweden* (1809). Though a keen observer of the weather, he made no great contribution to meteorological knowledge. His attempts to correlate weather changes with lunar cycles were unsuccessful and the theories he put forward to explain meteorological phenomena were flawed. In his *Observations on the cultivation of waste lands, addressed to the gentlemen and farmers of Glamorganshire* (1805), Capper pressed an idea which had met much opposition since he first proposed it in 1798, namely his plan for the establishment of a 'School of industry for the employment of poor children of Cardiff', a feature of which was that children of the labouring classes should work on the turnpike roads or dig in the fields without shoes or stockings. Otherwise, he appears to have been an uncontroversial and respected figure. He was appointed a burgess of Cardiff in 1783 although he appears also to have had a London address at this date, capital burgess in 1793, alderman in 1794, bailiff nine times between 1794 and 1813, scavenger in 1800, deputy lieutenant-colonel of Glamorgan in 1803, and turnpike trust commissioner in 1805. He served as a magistrate for many years and helped train the Cardiff cavalry volunteers. He was also in the late 1790s a member of the Cardiff Sympathetic Society, which provided financial benefits to widows. In the early hours of 5 September 1800 he was one

of only two witnesses when the remains of the marchioness of Bute and two of her offspring were reinterred in the newly built mausoleum at St Margaret's Church, Roath, near Cardiff.

Why Capper left south Wales about 1814 is not known. A letter of 29 July 1814 comments on the 'present derangement of Col. Capper's affairs and the probable sale of his property' (J. Hunt to H. Hollier, Bute L99/56, NL Wales) and *Cardiff Records* note that in December 1816 Cardiff's town clerk had been ordered to 'take the necessary steps to recover possession of the Corporation lands in the occupation of James Capper' and that one Peter Taylor Walker had been made an Alderman 'in the room of James Capper who had removed to some place unknown and was therefore disfranchised' (Matthews). Rumours that Capper died in disgrace or penury have proved impossible to substantiate. He died apparently intestate at Ditchingham Lodge, near Bungay, Norfolk, on 6 September 1825, and was buried on 12 September at Ditchingham.

J. MALCOLM WALKER and DIANE A. WALKER

Sources BL OIOC, L/MIL/9/85; E/4/865; E/4/866; E/4/864; E/4/879 · J. H. Matthews, ed., *Cardiff records: being materials for a history of the county borough from the earliest times*, 6 vols. (1898–1911), vols. 2–4 · J. Capper, *Memorial addressed to the honourable the court of directors of the East India Company* (1784) · J. Capper, *Observations on the passage to India* (1783); 3rd edn (1785) · Harrow School archives · *GM*, 1st ser., 95/2 (1825), 381 · *GM*, 1st ser., 101/1 (1831), 565–6 · [J. Bird], *The diaries of John Bird, 1790–1803*, ed. H. M. Thomas (1987) · P. Rogers, 'The weather theories and records of Colonel Capper', *Weather*, 11 (1956), 326–9 · parish register, Ditchingham, Norfolk County Archives · [J. Watkins and F. Shoberl], *A biographical dictionary of the living authors of Great Britain and Ireland* (1816) · Watt, *Bibl. Brit.* · J. F. Waller, ed., *The imperial dictionary of universal biography*, 3 vols. in 16 pts (1857–63) · *DNB* · 'Clutterbuck, Robert', *DNB* · parish register, Cardiff, St John [marriage] · BL OIOC, N/2/1, fols. 365, 381 [baptism of Eliza and Louisa]

Archives BL, corresp., MS 19242 Plut. CLXXVII. B. · Cardiff Central Library, meteorological journal, MS 2.298

Capper, James (1829–1895), ironworker and trade unionist, was probably born in the heavily industrialized part of south Staffordshire known as the Black Country. Nothing is known of his family background or early life except that he started work at the age of eight in the Toll End ironworks, Tipton, where he eventually became an underhand puddler. As a young man he spent six years in the United States but in 1862 he returned home, apparently disillusioned, and found work as a forehand puddler with the Patent Shaft and Axletree Company, Wednesbury.

Capper's return to Britain coincided with the beginnings of trade union organization among the ironworkers. In 1862 and 1863 three unions were formed: an inclusive organization in the north-east, led by John Kane, and separate associations for puddlers and rollers in the Black Country. Capper played a leading role in organizing his fellow puddlers but this was really the limit of his commitment to unionism: like Black Countrymen generally, he was very wary of associating with outsiders. This brought him into conflict with Kane, who wanted to establish his union, the National Association of Ironworkers, in all ironmaking districts, and there were some angry clashes between the two men and their organizations. The feuding came to an end in 1868 when depression in the iron industry brought about the collapse of both Black Country unions. Capper then reluctantly threw in his lot with the National Association but as the price of his allegiance Kane had to concede a large measure of regional autonomy by sanctioning the appointment of paid district agents and local control of funds. Capper himself was the paid agent for the south Staffordshire district from 1872 until 1877, when union organization in the area again collapsed and his own membership lapsed.

Appropriately for someone who was so contrary, Capper's best service for the union was performed while he was not a member. Kane and his successor as leader of the National Association, Edward Trow, believed implicitly in sliding scales of wages backed by conciliation machinery as the best means of securing acceptable settlements from the ironmasters. Capper's experience of 'brutal' strikes and lock-outs in the Black Country led him to the same conclusion, and despite this uneasy relationship with Kane and Trow he was able to give his full support to such arrangements. He was one of the prime movers in establishing *ad hoc* conciliation machinery for the Black Country industry in 1872 and when this was formalized and made permanent in 1876 as the South Staffordshire mill and forge wages board he became the paid secretary to the workmen's panel. He held this position for twelve years and his dedicated work was an important factor in preserving peace in the industry.

Capper's position on the wages board eventually led him to rejoin the union, albeit under compulsion. This came about following the relaunch of the union as the Associated Iron and Steel Workers in 1887. Capper would not join at first but he was forced to change his mind, ironically because the employers refused to allow union representation on the board. Trow then secured its *de facto* representation by getting all the workmen's panel to join the union and since Capper owed his position to them he had to follow suit. Capper's return to the union, particularly in these circumstances, threatened a revival of internecine squabbling, but this was averted when his health broke down. He was left partly paralysed by a stroke and at the end of 1888 he resigned from the union and the wages board. His condition gradually deteriorated but his fighting spirit and physical strength kept him alive for another seven years. Capper died on 29 December 1895 at his home in Bloxwich Road, Walsall, survived by his wife and five sons. He was buried in Walsall old cemetery on 2 January 1896.   ERIC TAYLOR

Sources *Wolverhampton Express & Star* (31 Dec 1895) · *Wolverhampton Chronicle* (1 Jan 1896) · *Midland Advertiser* (4 Jan 1896) · *Midland Sun* (4 Jan 1896) · *Walsall Observer* (4 Jan 1896) · *Walsall Advertiser* (4 Jan 1896) · *Wolverhampton Chronicle* (8 Jan 1896) · *Ironworkers' Journal* (1869–89) · *Labour Tribune* (1886–9) · E. Taylor, 'Capper, James', *DLB*, vol. 2 · E. Taylor, 'The working class movement in the Black Country, 1863–1914', PhD diss., University of Keele, 1974 · E. Taylor, *The better temper: a commemorative history of the midland iron and steel wages board, 1876–1976* (1976), chaps. 1, 2 · J. H. Porter, 'Management, competition and industrial relations: the midlands manufactured iron trade, 1873–1914', *Business History*, 11 (1969), 37–47 · A. Fox, 'Industrial relations in Birmingham and the Black Country, 1860–1914', BLitt diss., U. Oxf., 1952 · D. Jones, 'The midland iron and steel wages board', *British industries*, ed. W. J. Ashley (1903), 38–67 · A. Pugh, *Men of steel, by one of them: a chronicle of eighty-eight years of trade unionism in the British iron and steel industry* (1951) · J. C. Carr and W. Taplin, *History of the British steel industry* (1962) · G. C. Allen, *The industrial development of Birmingham and the Black Country, 1860–1927* (1929)

Capper, Sir John Edward (1861–1955), army officer, was born at Lucknow, India, on 7 December 1861, the second son of William Copeland Capper of the Bengal civil service and his wife, Sarah, the daughter of William Taylor *Copeland. His younger brother, Major-General Sir Thompson *Capper, was killed at Loos in September 1915. John Capper was educated at Wellington College and commissioned lieutenant in the Royal Engineers on 2 July 1880; he was promoted captain on 1 November 1889 and major on 1 April 1899, after being employed primarily on military and public works in India and Burma. However, he did also see active service in the Tirah campaign on the north-west frontier in 1897. On 10 October 1895 he married Edith Mary (1868/9–1942), the daughter of Joseph Beausire of Noctorum, Birkenhead: they had one son, killed in action in 1916, and one daughter.

From October to December 1899 Capper was deputy assistant director of railways in South Africa, and on 29 November 1900 he received a brevet lieutenant-colonelcy. Capper then remained in South Africa until February 1903, commanding locally raised units before becoming commandant of Johannesburg; he received the CB in 1902. Having received his substantive lieutenant-colonelcy on 7 October 1905 and a brevet colonelcy on 28 January 1906, Capper was posted to command the Balloon School at Aldershot on 27 May 1906; he remained commandant until October 1910. Capper piloted the army's first airship, *Nulli Secundus*, in a flight over London in 1907. Having been promoted substantive colonel on leaving Aldershot on 7 October 1910, and after a brief period of half pay, Capper became commandant of the School of Military Engineering at Chatham, a position he held from 7 April 1911 to 28 September 1914. He was then posted to France as deputy inspector-general on the lines of communication as a temporary brigadier-general. On 9 May 1915 he became chief engineer of the 3rd corps, and two months later he became chief engineer of the Third Army, having received promotion to major-general on 3 July 1915. However, on 3 October 1915 he received command of the 24th division. In May 1917 he moved to command the machine-gun corps training centre but on 28 July he took up the appointment of director-general of the tank corps and on 1 September director-general of the War Office tank directorate, having also been considered as a possible director-general of military aeronautics.

Capper was both intelligent and technologically aware. Consequently he was readily convinced of the tank's potential for large-scale operations. Indeed he was to present a more practical version of J. F. C. Fuller's 'Plan 1919' to the general staff in July 1918, by which tanks would have played a major role had the war persisted into 1919. Unfortunately, however, Capper's poor communication skills and pomposity gave his subordinates at tank corps head-quarters the entirely opposite impression that he was unreceptive to their ideas, to the extent that they nicknamed him the Stone Age. Capper was appointed KCB in 1917; he left the War Office in July 1918, before commanding the 64th division in Britain from November 1918 to April 1919, and number one area in France and Flanders from June to September 1919. He became lieutenant-governor and commander-in-chief on Guernsey on 1 July 1920, and retired on 1 July 1925, having been appointed KCVO in 1921. He was colonel commandant of the Royal Tank Corps from September 1923 and a governor of Wellington College from 1928 until 1946. Capper died on 24 May 1955 at the Esperance Nursing Home, Eastbourne.

IAN F. W. BECKETT

Sources J. P. Harris, *Men, ideas and tanks: British military thought and armoured forces, 1903–1939* (1995) · B. H. Liddell Hart, *The tanks: the history of the royal tank regiment and its predecessors*, 2 vols. (1959) · T. Travers, *How the war was won: command and technology in the British army on the western front, 1917–1918* (1992) · *Army List* · *WWW* · A. D. Harvey, *Collision of empires* (1992) · Burke, *Peerage* (1939) · *CGPLA Eng. & Wales* (1955) · BL OIOC, N/1/100, fol. 403 · m. cert.
Archives King's Lond., Liddell Hart C., papers | King's Lond., Liddell Hart C., Fuller MSS · King's Lond., Liddell Hart C., Liddell Hart MSS
Likenesses photographs, IWM · photographs, Tank Museum, Bovington
Wealth at death £13,852 5s. 0d.: probate, 10 Aug 1955, *CGPLA Eng. & Wales*

Capper, Joseph (1726/7–1804), eccentric, was born in Cheshire to unknown parents in humble circumstances. At an early age he travelled to London, and, after serving his apprenticeship to a grocer, set up a shop on his own account in Whitechapel. With good business connections Capper soon prospered in his trade, and, having been fortunate in various speculations, eventually retired from business, probably in the late 1770s. He then spent several days walking in London, searching for lodgings. At The Horns tavern in Kennington he asked for a bed, and, being curtly refused, determined to stop in order to torment the landlord. Though for many years he talked about leaving the place the next day, he lived there for some twenty-five years until his death.

Capper's habits were very methodical, drinking tea only out of his favourite cup and sitting only in his favourite chair in the parlour of The Horns. He would not allow anyone to poke the fire without his permission. He called himself the champion of government, and nothing angered him more than to hear anyone declaiming against the British constitution. His favourite amusement was killing flies with his cane, before doing which he generally told a story about the treachery of all Frenchmen, 'whom', he said, 'I hate and detest, and would knock down just the same as these flies' (*Kirby's … Museum*, 2.477). Capper died, aged seventy-seven, at the tavern on 6 September 1804, and was buried in St Botolph's, Aldgate. In his will, which was made on the back of a sheet of banker's cheques and dated five years before his death, he left the bulk of his property, then upwards of £30,000, to his poor relations, whom he had always refused to see in

Joseph Capper (1726/7–1804), by unknown engraver, pubd 1804

his lifetime. To his nephews, whom he appointed his executors, he bequeathed £8000 to be divided between them, although there appears to have been considerable doubt whether this will had been properly witnessed or not.

G. F. R. BARKER, *rev.* DAVID TURNER

Sources *Kirby's wonderful … museum*, 6 vols. (1803–20), vols. 1–3 · *St James's Chronicle* (13 Sept 1804) · W. Granger and others, *The new wonderful museum, and extraordinary magazine*, 3 (1805), 1692–6
Likenesses G. Scott, stipple, pubd 1804, NPG · aquatint, pubd 1804, NPG [*see illus.*] · portrait, repro. in Granger, *The new wonderful museum*, 3 (1805)
Wealth at death over £30,000: *Kirby's wonderful … museum*, vol. 2, p. 478

Capper [*married name* Coningham], **Louisa** (1776–1840), author, was born on 15 November 1776, and baptized on 14 January 1777 at Fort St George, Madras, India; she was the youngest daughter of Colonel James *Capper (1743–1825), meteorologist and travel writer, and his wife, Mary Johnson. Her uncle was the clergyman and magistrate Francis Capper (1735–1818). On 16 October 1811, at Northwood on the Isle of Wight, she married the Revd Robert Coningham.

The slim volume *A Poetical History of England* (1810) is attributed to Louisa Capper (by a pencilled note on the fly-leaf of the copy in the British Library) although the author is referred to, in the preface, as 'he'. The text is supposed to have been written not for publication but for the instruction of the 'young ladies' at Rothbury House School. It begins with the Roman empire in Britain and ends with the house of Brunswick; that is to say, with George I's accession in 1714. The verse is not of an especially high quality but conveys the essential facts clearly and in an easily remembered form. A second edition was published in 1815.

Louisa Capper's book *An Abridgment of Locke's 'Essay Concerning Human Understanding'* (1811) was published in the year of her marriage. She is critical of Locke's 'prolix' style, and makes some 'alteration' in his chapters 'Of power' and 'Of the association of ideas'. She nevertheless defends the 'rational Metaphysics' in which she believes him to be engaged. Once again her interest in education is shown by the inferences which she draws on this subject from his work.

Louisa Capper died on 25 May 1840 at Chorleywood, Hertfordshire, her husband having predeceased her, and was buried in nearby Rickmansworth. A sister, Marianne, married the Hertfordshire topographer Robert Clutterbuck. MARY ANNE PERKINS

Sources GM, 1st ser., 81/2 (1811), 383, 441–2 · GM, 2nd ser., 14 (1840), 110 · Watt, *Bibl. Brit.* · DNB · IGI · GM, 1st ser., 95/2 (1825), 381

Capper, Sir Thompson (1863–1915), army officer, was born in Lucknow, India, on 20 October 1863. He was the third son of William Copeland Capper of the Bengal civil service and his wife, Sarah, the daughter of William Taylor *Copeland. His older brother was Sir John *Capper. Thompson Capper was commissioned lieutenant in the East Lancashire regiment on 9 September 1882, and was promoted captain on 22 April 1891. He served in the Chitral relief expedition in 1895 and attended the Staff College at Camberley in 1896–7, where he was regarded as an original and imaginative student. He then served with the Egyptian army in the Sudan from December 1897 to July 1899, being present at the battles of the Atbara and Omdurman. Capper received a brevet majority on 16 November 1898. After a brief attachment to the War Office as staff captain for intelligence, Capper went to South Africa in November 1899 as deputy assistant adjutant-general on the staff of the Natal army during the operations for the relief of Ladysmith and the subsequent advance into the Transvaal. From June 1901 to May 1902 he commanded a mobile column in Cape Colony. For his services he received the DSO and was promoted brevet lieutenant-colonel on 29 November 1900.

Capper's next employment was as professor and then deputy assistant adjutant-general at the Staff College from December 1902 to December 1905, in the course of which he received a brevet colonelcy in December 1904. It would appear that Sir Henry Hughes Wilson feared that Capper rather than himself would succeed to the command at Camberley and, at Wilson's suggestion, Capper was then selected first commandant of the Indian Staff College at Quetta, a position he held from March 1906 with the rank of colonel, and from May 1906 to January 1911 as temporary brigadier-general. In his teaching at Camberley, and especially at Quetta, where he lectured extensively on the Russo-Japanese War, Capper was a powerful exponent of the 'offensive spirit', arguing that 'attacking dash' was the best means of overcoming entrenched positions defended by modern firepower. He thus placed particular emphasis on courage. A fellow instructor at Camberley, Hubert Gough, recalled that Capper 'always inculcated a spirit of self-sacrifice and duty, instead of the idea of playing for safety and seeking only to avoid getting into trouble' (Gough, 93). Similarly John Charteris recorded during the first battle of Ypres that Capper told him, 'No good officer has a right to be alive during a fight like this', and that Capper had also supposedly ordered his staff to the front with the words, 'What! Nobody on the Staff wounded today; that won't do!' (Charteris, 58). It is difficult to assess Capper's precise influence on his audiences, and Douglas Haig, who came into contact with him at Quetta, believed Capper 'too full of nerves and too much of a crank to get the best out of officers' (Haig to Kiggell, Kiggell MSS, 1/27, 22 Oct 1911), while George Barrow also considered that the geniality that had marked Capper's personality at Camberley had given way to a darker intensity of outlook at Quetta.

On 15 October 1908 Capper married Winifride Mary, the eldest daughter of the Hon. Robert Joseph Gerard-Dicconson of Wrightington Hall, Wigan; they had one son. Two years later he received the CB, and after a brief period of half pay he was appointed to command the 13th infantry brigade at Dublin on 19 February 1911. Capper's abilities as a trainer of troops were much in evidence, and he was appointed inspector of infantry in February 1914, and promoted major-general on 12 May. He had strongly supported Hubert Gough during the Curragh incident in March. On 27 August 1914 he was appointed to command the 7th division, and he took it to Belgium in October. Capper covered the Belgian retreat to the Yser and then took a leading role in the first battle of Ypres, his division losing over 10,000 of its infantry in just three weeks but holding its ground. One obituarist later commented that 'no one but Capper himself could, night after night, by the sheer force of his personality, have reconstituted from the shattered fragments of battalions a fighting line that could last through tomorrow' (*The Times*, 1 Oct 1915).

Capper was created KCMG for his services at Ypres but was accidentally wounded during experiments with hand grenades in April 1915 and did not return to his division until shortly before the battle of Loos. Indeed Capper had been appointed to a corps but received permission to remain with his division until after the battle. On 25 September 1915 the division took its first objectives but was heavily counter-attacked. Accounts vary as to whether Capper was trying to encourage his men or to urge forward a 'sticky' unit and whether or not he was riding his horse in full view of the enemy. He was hit by a sniper and died on the following day, 26 September 1915. He was buried in Lillers communal cemetery, Pas-de-Calais.

Capper had been true to the principles he had set out in one of his lectures in June 1908: that wars could not be won 'unless the individuals composing an army set out to fight with the determined spirit that they will conquer, or they will die in the attempt to do so' (Capper MSS, II/4/16).

IAN F. W. BECKETT

Sources K. Simpson, 'Capper and the offensive spirit', *Journal of the Royal United Service Institute for Defence Studies*, 118/2 (1973), 51–5 · B. Bond, *The Victorian army and the Staff College, 1854–1914* (1972) ·

G. Barrow, *Fire of life* (1942) • H. Gough, *Soldiering on* (1954) • J. Charteris, *At GHQ* (1931) • I. F. W. Beckett, ed., *The army and the Curragh incident, 1914* (1986) • T. Travers, *The killing ground* (1987) • *Army List* • WWW • Burke, *Gen. GB* (1914) • *CGPLA Eng. & Wales* (1916) • King's Lond., Liddell Hart C., Capper MSS • King's Lond., Liddell Hart C., Kiggell MSS • *DNB* • m. cert.
Archives King's Lond., Liddell Hart C., papers, incl. research notes on Russo-Japanese War | King's Lond., Liddell Hart C., Kiggell MSS • NL Scot., Haig MSS
Likenesses photographs, IWM
Wealth at death £1149 10s. 10d.: probate, 4 Jan 1916, *CGPLA Eng. & Wales*

Captal de Buch. *See* Grailly, Jean (III) de (*d.* 1377).

Caraboo, Princess. *See* Baker, Mary (*bap.* 1791, *d.* 1864).

Caracalla (188–217). *See under* Septimius Severus, Lucius (145/6–211).

Caraccioli, Charles (*b.* 1722?), topographer, was probably the individual born at Le Mans on 12 May 1722 and baptized Joseph Jean-Baptiste Charles, the son of Marc-Antoine Caraccioli Caraffa, marquis d'Ortonomar (*c.*1680–1735), and his wife, Espérance Marie Bouvet, on 17 June 1722. The family, of Neapolitan origin, had been settled in France since the fifteenth century. Caraccioli's elder brother Louis-Antoine (1719–1803), who succeeded to their father's title in 1735, was a prolific author.

It seems likely that as a young man Charles left for the French colony at Pondicherry, but moved to Britain during the hostilities of the 1750s. In 1775 he published the first volume of *The Life of Robert, Lord Clive*, which was followed in 1777 by three further volumes. The work, a virulent attack on its subject, was described in the *Monthly Review* as 'a slovenly jumble' (*Monthly Review*, 53, 1775, 80) and 'ill-digested, worse connected, and similarly printed' (*Monthly Review*, 55, 1776, 480). It includes what appear to be eye-witness accounts of military engagements, although the reviewer suspected that the later volumes had been pirated from a work published in Cambridge in 1776. *An Historical Account of Sturbridge, Bury and the most Famous Fairs* is attributed to Caraccioli in the British Library catalogue and *Chiron, or, The Mental Optician* (1758), by Richard Gough. Gough's interest in Caraccioli arose from the appearance, in 1766, of the *Antiquities of Arundel*, the subscription list of which shows signs of East Indies connections. The author, who describes himself as the master of the grammar school, states that 'he was educated, and, till within these few years, has lived abroad, totally unconversant in the English Tongue', and a random paragraph of the work is indeed printed in French (Caraccioli, 216). Arundel had no grammar school, but Caraccioli did live at substantial houses in the town between 1764 and 1769 and probably taught at the school conducted in the Fitzalan chapel in the parish church. Although *Arundel* was the first historical monograph on a Sussex town and would remain so for almost thirty years, it was a false dawn. Arundel's antiquities are dispatched in twenty-two pages, the remaining 254 being dedicated to the lives of the earls. Gough's description was scathing, correcting Caraccioli's reading of 'the only epitaph he has printed'

and describing the whole as 'most awkwardly compiled from printed books' (Gough, 288).

In 1771, as Charles Alexander Caraccioli and describing himself as a man of letters, Caraccioli published in London *Considerations sur l'origine ... et les conquestes de l'empire de Russie*, dedicated to Catherine the Great. Part of the work, supposedly based on a stay in Russia, deals with Poland, where Caraccioli's brother had been tutor to the children of Prince Rewski between 1754 and 1761. Again as Charles Alexander Caraccioli, in 1772 he invited subscriptions for a two-volume history of the French provinces under the dominion of the English monarchs. The author attributed his interest in the subject to Andrew Ducarel, and claimed to have visited monastic sites and examined manuscripts in the course of his research. The work does not appear to have been published. In 1775 appeared *Anecdotes of New Hall*, attributed to Caraccioli. Published at Chelmsford and dedicated to Lady Waltham, the work is little more than a prurient discussion of the *amours* of former residents of the Essex mansion. Caraccioli may have returned to France after the peace of 1783, although his brother's *Letters ... by an Indian at Paris* was published at Colchester in 1790 and at Dublin the following year, possibly by Charles's means. It is not known when or where he died.   CHRISTOPHER WHITTICK

Sources C. Caraccioli, *History and antiquities of Arundel* (1766) • M. D. Rebut, 'La vie et les œuvres du Marquis Louis-Antione Caraccioli', *Bulletin de la Société d'Agriculture de la Sarthe* (1905) • N. H. F. Desportes, *Bibliographie de Maine* (1844) • parish register, St Vincent, Le Mans archives • BL OIOC • *Monthly Review*, 18 (1758) • *Monthly Review*, 53 (1775), 80–81 • *Monthly Review*, 55 (1776) • R. G. [R. Gough], *British topography*, [new edn], 2 (1780) • S. Sokol, *The Polish biographical dictionary* (1992) • BM, department of prints and drawings, Heal 17.27 • S. Halkett and J. Laing, *Dictionary of anonymous and pseudonymous English literature*, ed. J. Kennedy and others, new edn, 1 (1926)

Caractacus. *See* Caratacus (*fl.* AD 40–51).

Caradoc [*formerly* Cradock], **John Francis**, **first Baron Howden** (1762–1839), army officer, the only son of the Most Revd John *Cradock (1707/8–1778), archbishop of Dublin, and his wife, Mary, widow of Richard St George of Kilrush, co. Kilkenny, and daughter of William Blaydwin of Boston, Lincolnshire, was born on 11 August 1762 in Henrietta Street, Dublin, when his father was bishop of Kilmore.

Cradock was admitted to Trinity College, Dublin, on 31 October 1774. His father's political influence was considerable, and he rose quickly in the army, having entered it in 1777 as a cornet in the 4th regiment of horse. In 1779 he transferred as ensign to the 2nd (Coldstream) guards. In 1781 he was promoted lieutenant and captain, and in 1785 major in the 12th light dragoons. In 1786 he exchanged into the 13th regiment, in 1789 he was promoted lieutenant-colonel and in the following year commanded the regiment when it was ordered to the West Indies at the time of the Nootka Sound affair.

In 1791 Cradock returned to England on being appointed acting quartermaster-general in Ireland (he became quartermaster-general in September 1792), but in 1793 he accompanied Sir Charles Grey to the West Indies as aide-de-camp and was given command of two picked battalions selected for dangerous services. At their head he served throughout the campaign in which Grey seized the islands of the French West Indies, and he was wounded at the capture of Martinique. At its conclusion he received the thanks of parliament and was promoted colonel of the 127th regiment. On 1 October 1795 he was appointed assistant quartermaster-general, and on 1 January 1798 was promoted major-general. In 1798 his local knowledge was invaluable to Lord Cornwallis in the suppression of the Irish uprising. Cradock was present at the battle of Vinegar Hill and the capture of Wexford, accompanied Cornwallis against the French general Humbert, and was wounded in the affair at Ballinahinch. He sat in the Irish House of Commons as MP for Clogher, co. Tyrone (1785–90), Castlebar, co. Mayo (1790–97), Midleton, co. Cork, from 1799 to April 1800, and Thomastown, co. Kilkenny, in May 1800. In parliament he was a staunch supporter of the government, and on 17 February 1800 acted as second to the Rt Hon. Isaac Corry, chancellor of the Irish exchequer, in his famous duel with Henry Grattan in Phoenix Park, Dublin. At the same time, he strengthened his political connections by marrying, on 17 November 1798, Lady Theodosia Sarah Frances Meade (d. 1853), third daughter of John Meade, first earl of Clanwilliam.

At the Union in 1800 Cradock lost his seat in parliament, but he was appointed to the staff of Sir Ralph Abercromby in the Mediterranean. He joined the army at Minorca, commanded the 2nd brigade, and was colonel 2nd battalion 54th foot (1801–2). He fought in the battles of 8, 13, and 21 March 1801 in Egypt, and after Abercromby's death accompanied General Hutchinson in the advance on Cairo as second in command. He was present at the surrender of Cairo, but then fell ill with fever and was unable to assist in the capture of Alexandria. At the conclusion of the Egyptian campaign he was appointed commander-in-chief of a corps of 7000 men and ordered to capture Corsica. The peace of Amiens put an end to the expedition, but he was made a KB (16 February 1803) and colonel of the 71st Highland light infantry (a post he held until 1809), and on 21 December 1803 he was appointed commander-in-chief at Madras as a local lieutenant-general.

Cradock's command at Madras was marked by the mutiny at Vellore. Shortly after his arrival he decided to reduce the chaotic mass of regulations for the army under his command into something like a regular code. In 1805 the new code was issued under the sanction of the governor, Lord William Bentinck, and as it was particularly inflexible on questions of uniform it greatly offended the sepoys. The family of Tipu Sahib took advantage of the discontent to foment a conspiracy among the Muslims in the Sepoy army, and on 10 July 1806 a mutiny broke out at Vellore. When it was suppressed there were mutual recriminations among the authorities at Fort George as to its cause; Cradock blamed his subalterns for advising the changes, and the governor for sanctioning them. The governor declared it all the commander-in-chief's fault, and finally, in 1807, the court of directors recalled both Cradock and Bentinck.

The ministers at once appointed Cradock commander of a division in Ireland, but his mind was 'soured by ill-treatment' (A. Wellesley, *Civil Correspondence and Memoranda of … Arthur, Duke of Wellington*, 1860, vol. 5 of *Supplementary despatches, correspondence and memoranda*, 261), and he resigned his division and applied for active service. In December 1808 Cradock, who had been promoted lieutenant-general on 1 January 1805, arrived in Lisbon to take command of the troops which Sir John Moore had left in Portugal. His position was a difficult one: he had not more than 10,000 men under his command, including wounded and sick, and could not put more than 5000 in the field. This was soon complicated by Moore's retreat; the Portuguese regency wished him to advance to Oporto, and the people became furious and insulted and even murdered English soldiers in the streets of Lisbon. Cradock knew that it was impossible to protect Oporto against Maréchal Soult's victorious army, and he prepared instead to defend Lisbon, threatened by both Soult and Victor in the east. Instructions arrived for him to prepare to evacuate Portugal, but the British ministers suddenly resolved to defend Lisbon at all costs, and Cradock was ordered to advance from Lisbon and take up a central position. He moved reluctantly from Passa d'Arcos to Leiria, and there formed his small army in order of battle to await the advance of Soult from Oporto. He had time to reorganize his army, and, after receiving reinforcements, had begun an advance against Soult, when news arrived that he was to be promoted to the governorship of Gibraltar and superseded in Portugal by Arthur Wellesley (the duke of Wellington). However, he was not given the governorship. Wellesley tried to soften Cradock's disappointment, but to the end of his life he felt that he had been badly treated.

In 1809 Cradock was appointed colonel of the 43rd regiment, and in 1811 he was promoted to the governorship of the Cape of Good Hope, which, however, he retained only until 1814. In 1814 he was promoted general and on 2 January 1815 was made a GCB; nevertheless, he remained a disappointed man. Wellington appointed his only son, John Hobart, to his personal staff, and through the duke's influence Cradock was created Baron Howden in the peerage of Ireland on 19 October 1819. In 1820, claiming descent from Caradoc (prince of north Wales), he exchanged the name Cradock for Caradoc. He was further favoured by the duke, and on 10 September 1831 was created a peer of the United Kingdom as Baron Howden of Howden and Grimston, on the coronation of William IV. He died at 13 Hertford Street, Park Lane, London, on 26 July 1839 and was buried on 1 August at Kensal Green, Middlesex. He was succeeded as baron by his only son, John Hobart *Caradoc (1799–1873), at whose death the baronies became extinct.

H. M. STEPHENS, *rev.* STEWART M. FRASER

Sources W. F. P. Napier, *History of the war in the Peninsula and in the south of France*, 3 vols. (1878) • J. Philippart, ed., *The royal military calendar*, 3 vols. (1815–16) • *Asiatic Annual Register*, 9 (1807) • J. Mill, *The history of British India*, ed. H. H. Wilson, 4th edn, 9 vols. (1840–48) •

C. W. C. Oman, *A history of the Peninsular War*, 7 vols. (1902–30); repr. (1995–7) · T. Pakenham, *The year of liberty: the story of the great Irish rebellion of 1798* (1972) · P. Moon, *The British conquest and dominion of India* (1989) · GEC, *Peerage* · Burke, *Peerage* · GM, 2nd ser., 12 (1839), 310, 670

Archives Bodl. Oxf., corresp. and papers | BL, corresp. with lords Holland and Wellesley and letters to Sir Robert Wilson, Add. MSS 51614, 37283–37310, 30111–30112
Likenesses W. Say, mezzotint, pubd 1805 (after T. Lawrence), BM · M. Stewart, oils (after T. Lawrence), Government House, Cape Town, South Africa

Caradoc [*formerly* Cradock], **John Hobart**, **second Baron Howden** (1799–1873), diplomatist, only child of John Francis *Caradoc, first Baron Howden (1762–1839), and Lady Theodosia Sarah Frances Meade (*d.* 1853), third daughter of the first earl of Clanwilliam, was born John Hobart Cradock at St Stephen's Green, Dublin, on 16 October 1799. His father changed the family name from Cradock to Caradoc in 1820. He was educated at Eton College *c.*1812–1815, was gazetted an ensign in the Grenadier Guards on 13 July 1815, and was soon afterwards appointed an aide-de-camp to the duke of Wellington at Paris, where he remained until the dispersion of the army of occupation in 1818. On 22 October 1818 he was promoted lieutenant and captain in the Grenadier Guards, and then proceeded to Lisbon, as aide-de-camp to Marshal Beresford; in 1820 he was appointed aide-de-camp to Sir Thomas Maitland, the governor of Malta. In 1823 he exchanged to the 29th regiment, but in 1824 he determined to enter the diplomatic service, and was appointed an attaché at Berlin. In 1825 he joined the embassy at Paris. He was famous for his amorous exploits, living up to his nickname, 'Beauty Caradoc': his duel in Paris over the duchesse d'Esclaux infuriated Canning, and his liaison with Emily Cowper (later Lady Palmerston) was notorious (Bourne, 199).

In 1827 Caradoc was ordered to Egypt in order to try to prevent Mehmet Ali from intervening in the struggle between Turkey and Greece. In this he failed, and he was then ordered to join Sir Edward Codrington, the admiral commanding the Mediterranean Fleet, as military commissioner, with instructions to force Mehmet Ali to withdraw the army with which he had occupied the Morea. At Navarino he was wounded, and he had afterwards no difficulty in securing the withdrawal of the Egyptian army.

On 11 January 1830 Caradoc married Catherine, daughter of Paul, Count Skavronsky, and widow of Prince Bagration of Russia. They had no children, and Caradoc obtained a separation from her. She died in Venice on 2 June 1857. In 1830 he was elected MP for Dundalk, but he did not seek re-election in 1831, and in 1832 was appointed military commissioner with the French army under Marshal Gérard, which was besieging Antwerp. Here he was again wounded, and was made, for his services, a commander of the Légion d'honneur, and of the Order of Leopold of Belgium. His wound at Antwerp gave rise to the fashion of the 'manche à la Caradoc', as women imitated his ribboned sleeve. In August 1834 he was appointed military commissioner with the Spanish army, and observed the wars of the 1830s, being rewarded for his services with the Order of San Fernando. In 1839 he succeeded his father

as second Baron Howden, and returned to England. He was promoted colonel in the army in 1841, and made an equerry to the duchess of Kent, a post which he held until her death in 1861. On 25 January 1847 he was appointed minister at Rio de Janeiro with a special mission to the Argentine confederation and the republic of Uruguay. He was ordered to act in conjunction with Count Walewski, the French minister-plenipotentiary, and also not to allow the British fleet to do more than blockade Buenos Aires and Montevideo. When Count Walewski showed himself favourably inclined towards General Rosas, governor of Buenos Aires, and when Rosas himself paid no attention to the ultimatum of the two powers, Howden decided to leave the questions at issue unsettled, and raised the blockade of Buenos Aires on 2 July 1847. He returned to Rio de Janeiro by way of Montevideo, arriving on 7 August, and remained in Brazil until 1850, when he was appointed minister-plenipotentiary at Madrid. In 1854 he was promoted major-general, and on 23 February 1852 made a KCB. At Madrid he was both well-known and popular, and had thus a great advantage over his predecessor, Sir Henry Bulwer. Alarmed at the implications of a tory government in Britain for his position in Spain, he retired in March 1858 without a pension, and was made a GCB and a knight grand cross of the order of Charles III of Spain. In 1859 he was promoted lieutenant-general, in 1861 he left the army, and after the death of the duchess of Kent in that year he lived in retirement at his castle, named Caradoc, near Bayonne; he died there on 8 October 1873 (his probate certificate gives 9 October 1873), and was buried on 11 October in the Castle's mausoleum. His titles became extinct.

H. M. STEPHENS, *rev.* H. C. G. MATTHEW

Sources FO List (1872) · GEC, *Peerage* · K. Bourne, *Palmerston: the early years, 1784–1841* (1982) · A. R. Pfeil, *The Anglo-French intervention in the River Plate considered* (1847) · J. H. Caradoc, *Two letters addressed to the Rt. Hon. Lord Howden* (1847) · Lord Lamington, 'In the days of the dandies', *Blackwood*, 147 (1890), 1–16, 169–84, 313–30; pubd separately (1890) · CGPLA Eng. & Wales (1874)
Archives Bodl. Oxf., corresp. and dispatches · PRO, corresp. and papers | BL, corresp. with Lord Aberdeen, Add. MS 43124 · BL, corresp. with Lord Holland, Add. MS 51614 · Bodl. Oxf., letters to earl of Clarendon · Hants. RO, corresp. with Lord Malmesbury · NL Scot., letters to second earl of Minto · Norfolk RO, letters to Sir Henry Bulwer · PRO, corresp. with earls Granville, PRO 30/29 · PRO, corresp. with Lord John Russell, PRO 30/22 · U. Southampton L., corresp. with Lord Palmerston
Wealth at death under £180,000 in England: probate, 22 May 1874, CGPLA Eng. & Wales

Caradog (1060x75–1124), hermit and monk, was the son of noble parents from Brycheiniog (Brecon). The principal source for his life is an account in Capgrave's *Nova legenda Angliae* which probably derives from a life, now lost, written by Gerald of Wales as part of his unsuccessful attempt to secure the hermit's canonization by Pope Innocent III. After studying letters Caradog joined the court of Rhys ap Tewdwr, king of Deheubarth in south Wales, where he was placed in charge of two of the king's hounds and was also an accomplished harpist. One day, however, he lost the hounds, and Rhys threatened to mutilate and kill him; this prompted Caradog to leave the court and vow himself to a celibate and monastic life. He made his way with some companions to the church of Llandaff, whose bishop, Herewald, tonsured him a cleric. After a while he decided to escape the crowds at Llandaff and moved to the deserted church of St Cenydd at Llangynydd in Gower, which he restored and where, according to the Book of Llandaff, Herewald ordained him a monk. Thence he went to St David's, and was soon ordained a priest.

Caradog continued to follow his religious vocation, establishing a community at 'Ary', probably the peninsula of Barry near Llanrhian in the cantref of Pebidiog, but Norse raids eventually compelled him to abandon the site. About 1105 the bishop of St David's gave him the church at St Ishmaels in the cantref of Rhos (alternatively identified by J. E. Lloyd as Haroldston East near Haverfordwest, whose church is also dedicated to St Ishmael). His new location was not entirely peaceful, for the Flemings settled by Henry I in Rhos c.1108, especially Tancard, castellan of Haverfordwest, tried in vain to expel him from the church. However, it appears that Tancard and his wife later warmed to the hermit, for, according to Gerald of Wales, they frequently sent their young son Richard to him with gifts of food.

It is doubtful whether Caradog is to be identified with the Master Caradog who visited another hermit, Elgar (d. 1120), on Bardsey Island off the Llŷn peninsula in north Wales, perhaps about 1115. Caradog died on 13 or 14 April 1124 and, despite Tancard's attempt to prevent the removal of his body from Rhos, was buried in St David's Cathedral. HUW PRYCE

Sources J. E. Lloyd, *A history of Wales from the earliest times to the Edwardian conquest*, 3rd edn, 2 vols. (1939) • F. G. Cowley, *The monastic order in south Wales, 1066-1349* (1977) • C. Horstman, ed., *Nova legenda Anglie, as collected by John of Tynemouth, J. Capgrave, and others*, 2 vols. (1901) • J. G. Evans and J. Rhys, eds., *The text of the Book of Llan Dâv reproduced from the Gwysaney manuscript* (1893) • *Gir. Camb. opera* • Giraldus Cambrensis, 'De invectionibus', ed. W. S. Davies, *Y Cymmrodor*, 30 (1920) • *Acta sanctorum: Aprilis*, 2 (Antwerp, 1675), 150–52 • S. Baring-Gould and J. Fisher, *The lives of the British saints*, 4 vols., Honourable Society of Cymmrodorion, Cymmrodorion Record Series (1907–13)

Caradog ab Iestyn (d. before 1175). *See under* Iestyn ap Gwrgant (*fl. c.*1081–*c.*1120).

Caradog ap Gruffudd ap Rhydderch (d. 1081), king in Wales, who in Upper Gwent (Gwent Uwchcoed) faced the Norman incursions in south-east Wales, was the representative of a dynasty first brought to prominence by Rhydderch ab Iestyn. The family had close links with Gwynllŵg, Upper Gwent, and Ergyng. In 1023 Rhydderch broke the direct hereditary succession to the major kingdom of Deheubarth and established himself as ruler of south Wales. He was killed in an encounter with pirates from Ireland in 1033, and Deheubarth reverted to the old dynasty under Hywel ab Edwin and his brother, Maredudd.

Rhydderch's sons, **Gruffudd ap Rhydderch** (d. 1055), **Caradog ap Rhydderch** (d. 1035), and Rhys remained active in south-east Wales. In 1034 they were defeated in battle at Hiraethwy by Hywel ab Edwin and Maredudd, but they had considerable success in border warfare against English forces. Two of them died at the hands of their English enemies, Caradog in battle in 1035, and Rhys many years later in 1053. Gruffudd ap Rhydderch ruled his territories for more than twenty years and was the leading figure of his generation. When Hywel ab Edwin died in 1044, and the annexation of Deheubarth by the prince of Gwynedd, Gruffudd ap Llywelyn, seemed imminent, he moved swiftly, took control of Deheubarth, and maintained the integrity of the southern kingdom. Within a year, the *Brut y tywysogyon* recorded that there was 'great deceit and treachery between Gruffudd and Rhys, sons of Rhydderch, and Gruffudd ap Llywelyn'. The *Brenhinedd y Saesson* described the clash as a massacre. The following year, Gruffudd ap Llywelyn allied with English forces under Earl Swein, son of Earl Godwine, and it is generally assumed that this represented an attempt—in the event, patently unsuccessful—to dislodge his rival. During these years changes in the balance of power in Gwent were taking place; in the 1040s the ruling dynasty of Morgannwg extended its influence eastward into the coastal area of Gwent south of the forest of Wentwood (Gwent Is Coed). For Gruffudd ap Rhydderch and his successors this was at the least a political irritant. A fortunate chance enabled Gruffudd to pursue his ambitions on the English border when in 1047 his northern rival Gruffudd ap Llywelyn suffered a crippling set-back which gave south Wales a long respite. In 1049 Gruffudd ap Rhydderch made allies of an Irish Scandinavian force which sailed up the Usk, and together they inflicted much damage in Gwent Is Coed; part of the force moved further east and attacked English border lands. Ealdred, bishop of Worcester, was responsible at that time for the defence of the border, but his men were taken by surprise and suffered heavy casualties. Gruffudd was raiding in Herefordshire again in 1052, advancing as far as Leominster. On this occasion, English soldiers were supported by a contingent of French fighting men, but they were no match for the Welsh raiders. Gruffudd and Rhys were still working in close co-operation; in 1053 Edward the Confessor and his advisers took counsel and decided that 'Rhys, the Welsh king's brother, should be killed, because he was causing injuries' (*ASC*, s.a. 1053 (text D)), and his head was taken to Gloucester on 5 January. Later in the year, perhaps as a reprisal, a Welsh raiding party attacked Westbury-on-Severn and inflicted heavy casualties among the men serving on patrols there. Gruffudd himself died in 1055; for south Wales he had been a forceful ruler, and for the English borders a dangerous enemy. His death paved the way for the conquest of the south by Gruffudd ap Llywelyn, whose influence impinged directly on Morgannwg and Gwent.

Gruffudd ap Rhydderch's son and eventual successor, Caradog, in eclipse until the death of Gruffudd ap Llywelyn in 1063, emerged as the dominant figure in south Wales. He made his mark in 1065. Harold, earl of Wessex, carried out a military sweep in Gwent, and began to build a hunting lodge at Portskewett. Before the work was completed Caradog raided the site and destroyed the buildings. Within a few years he had to face the Norman infiltration and settlement of Gwent, which was well advanced before the death of William fitz Osbern in 1071. Their main thrust was in Is Coed, with Chepstow, Caldicot, and Caerleon as their key strongholds.

It has been argued that Caradog's strength limited the scale of Norman advance in northern Gwent. His main ambitions seem to have been centred on Morgannwg, and his influence there to have been opposed vigorously but unsuccessfully by the princes of Deheubarth. In 1072, fighting with Norman knights as his allies, he defeated and killed Maredudd ab Owain of Deheubarth, and was acknowledged as ruler of Morgannwg. There was further conflict in 1075 and 1076, and in a winter campaign two years later he killed Rhys ab Owain and his brother, Hywel. These campaigns lie behind the claim that he was anxious to regain Deheubarth for his family. In 1078, however, that kingdom passed to Rhys ap Tewdwr. A critical element in Caradog's career is his relationship with the Normans. He could not prevent their advance, especially in southern Gwent; he was glad to use them as allies in 1072. When in 1075 Roger, earl of Hereford, was forced into submission after rebelling against William the Conqueror, some of his knightly tenants were said to have taken refuge from William I's officials with Caradog, in Morgannwg. Caradog died fighting Rhys ap Tewdwr and Gruffudd ap Cynan at the battle of Mynydd Carn in 1081. His heirs survived in Gwynllŵg, and were later established in Caerleon. They did not succeed to Morgannwg, where one of his associates, Iestyn ap Gwrgant, assumed power, and his line survived the Norman infiltration of his kingdom in the 1090s. DAVID WALKER

Sources T. Jones, ed. and trans., *Brut y tywysogyon, or, The chronicle of the princes: Peniarth MS 20* (1952) · J. E. Lloyd, *A history of Wales from the earliest times to the Edwardian conquest*, 3rd edn, 2 vols. (1939); repr. (1988) · J. B. Smith, 'The kingdom of Morgannwg and the Norman conquest of Glamorgan', *Glamorgan county history*, ed. G. Williams, 3: *The middle ages*, ed. T. B. Pugh (1971), 1–43 · D. Crouch, 'The slow death of kingship in Glamorgan, 1067–1158', *Morgannwg*, 29 (1985), 20–41 · D. Walker, *Medieval Wales* (1990) · ASC, s.a. 1053 [text D]

Caradog ap Rhydderch (d. 1035). *See under* Caradog ap Gruffudd ap Rhydderch (d. 1081).

Caradog of Llancarfan (d. after 1138), hagiographer, was identified as a writer of note by Geoffrey of Monmouth, who announced in his *Historia regum Britanniae* (perhaps with mock solemnity) that he would leave the history of Welsh kings since the time of Cadwaladr (d. 664/682) to Caradog, and the history of English kings to William of Malmesbury and Henry of Huntingdon. In 1584 David Powell confidently identified Caradog as the author of the *Brut y tywysogyon* down to the year 1156, an ascription that misled subsequent editors for more than three hundred years until, in 1928, J. E. Lloyd established that Caradog had no part in compiling the *Brut*. Caradog wrote two hagiographical books. In a twelfth-century life of Gildas and in one manuscript of a life of St Cadog he is identified in a couplet which preserves an archaic form of the name Llancarfan:

> Nancarbanensis dictamina sunt Carotoci:
> qui legat, emendat; placet illi compositori.

The life of Gildas shows a sound knowledge of Llancarfan, where Caradog was educated in a monastic community, and, more surprisingly, of Glastonbury suggesting that at some time he took refuge at Glastonbury or, less probably, that he was engaged as a professional to produce the life for the monks there. His style has been identified in a fragment of a life of St Cyngar. Claims linking him with a life of St Illtud and with the production of the Book of Llandaff have not been sustained. Caradog was alive when the *Historia regum Britanniae* was issued c.1136–8; the date of his death is not known. DAVID WALKER

Sources 'Vita Gildae', *Chronica minora saec. IV. V. VI. VII.*, 3, ed. T. Mommsen, MGH Auctores Antiquissimi, 13 (Berlin, 1898) · P. Grosjean, ed., 'Vita S. Cadoci', *Analecta Bollandiana*, 58 (1940), 156–61; 60 (1942), 35–67 · 'Vie de Saint Cadoc par Caradoc de Llancarfan', ed. P. Grosjean, *Analecta Bollandiana*, 60 (1942), 35–67 · T. Jones, introduction, *Brut y tywysogyon, or, The chronicle of the princes: Peniarth MS 20*, ed. and trans. T. Jones (1952) · J. E. Lloyd, 'The Welsh chronicles', *PBA*, 14 (1928), 369–91 · C. W. Lewis, 'The literary tradition of Morgannwg down to the middle of the sixteenth century', *Glamorgan county history*, ed. G. Williams, 3: *The middle ages*, ed. T. B. Pugh (1971), 449–554 · C. Brooke, 'The archbishops of St David's, Llandaff, and Caerleon-on-Usk', in N. K. Chadwick and others, *Studies in the early British church* (1958)

Caradon. For this title name *see* Foot, Hugh Mackintosh, Baron Caradon (1907–1990).

Caratacus [Caractacus] (*fl.* AD 40–51), king in Britain, was a son of *Cunobelinus, the greatest king in Iron Age Britain. After the death of their father about AD 40, Caratacus (this form of the name is to be preferred to Caractacus) and his brother *Togodumnus [*see under* Roman Britain, British leaders in (*act.* 55 BC–AD 84)] were the dominant leaders among the Iron Age tribes of southern Britain. Their power base, like that of their father, lay north of the Thames among the Catuvellauni and Trinovantes, but they exercised suzerainty over most of the other peoples in the south-east of the island. For three decades before his death Cunobelinus had maintained a cautious policy towards the Roman empire (by then firmly established up to the adjacent shores of the continent), avoiding provocation and permitting the development of diplomatic and commercial relations. On his death, and probably as a direct result thereof, there was a hardening of attitude towards Rome on the part of his successors. The British prince *Adminius [*see under* Roman Britain, British leaders in], possibly another of Cunobelinus's sons, fled to the emperor Gaius (Caligula) in or about AD 40, thereby inclining that unstable young man towards a plan (which came to naught) for an invasion of Britain. Verica, king of the Atrebates in the region of the middle Thames, was expelled from Britain by the new masters of the south-east; he found refuge at the court of Claudius in 41, thus providing a plausible *casus belli* for an emperor who needed a decisive and early military success. In the Roman invasion of Britain which followed in 43, Caratacus and Togodumnus were the leaders of British resistance. No other ruler or war leader is mentioned as playing any part in military operations at that time. Togodumnus died in the events immediately after the invasion, leaving Caratacus as the sole spearhead of those British tribes which could still face up to the Roman forces. For the next eight years, he provided the only effective military opposition to the advance of the Roman army in Britain.

The early activities of Caratacus and Togodumnus after the Roman landings achieved little. In two small-scale engagements, probably in Cantium (Kent), the brothers were outfought and fell back to a river line (perhaps the Medway) to regroup and recruit a larger force of warriors. When the Roman attack was launched across the river, the British fought fiercely against their disciplined opponents and carried the battle into the following day. But the end then came quickly and Caratacus was compelled to fall back to the Thames. In the running battles which ensued Togodumnus died and Caratacus decided at that stage that there was no future in resistance in south-eastern Britain. He is next heard of among the tribe of the Silures in south Wales, over whom he achieved military overlordship. In the years from AD 44 to 51 he inspired a highly successful guerrilla campaign against Roman forces under the general command of, first, Aulus Plautius and later Ostorius Scapula, successive governors of Britain.

When the latter became governor in AD 47, he found the security of western Britain seriously impaired by the tribes of Wales, one of which had actually raided Roman territory, perhaps in the Severn valley. The country in which Caratacus was now operating was ideally suited to the kind of warfare in which British warriors excelled. Broken hill-country seamed by wooded valleys offered ample scope for ambushes and rapid raids. For five more years Caratacus kept up the struggle against the steady advance of Roman arms. In AD 51 he withdrew into the remoter regions of central Wales as the Roman grip on the border regions tightened. There he changed tactics. Choosing a strong natural position on steep-sided hills, further protected by walls of boulders, he hoped to inflict a crushing defeat on a Roman force sent against him. The site of this battle has been long discussed. The area west of Caersŵs in the upper Severn valley has been favoured by many. More recently, a complex of Roman military works has been identified at Llanymynech, south of Oswestry, and this position seems to satisfy the main requirements of the text of Tacitus which supplies the only account of the episode. After a struggle, Roman troops scaled the hilltop stronghold and overran the British position. The family of Caratacus was captured but he himself escaped and fled to the Brigantes of northern Britain, hoping there to continue the fight. The Brigantian queen Cartimandua, however, remained loyal to her alliance with Rome and handed Caratacus over to his enemies. He was dispatched to Rome and there appeared in a public spectacle before the emperor Claudius, in which he cut an impressive and dignified figure. He is reported to have addressed the emperor, remarking that his resistance had contributed largely to the conqueror's glory. If killed now he would be quickly forgotten, but if spared would become a monument to the emperor's clemency. Caratacus and his family were granted their lives. It was on this occasion that he is said to have expressed wonderment that the Romans who possessed such palaces should have envied the British their poor huts. It is unknown how long he survived his time in Rome and where he ended his days. The tradition recorded in Welsh legend that he lived for four years after his capture and that his children became Christians and brought the Christian faith to Britain is mere fantasy.

The resistance of this British leader of the Roman conquest left no lasting memorial in legend or myth. The name Caradog was carried by some of the medieval kings of Gwynedd and Gwynllŵg, but none seems to have claimed Caratacus as a remote ancestor. In the archaeological record the only slight trace of him is a small series of coins bearing the legend CARA, found south of the Thames and presumably dating from the brief period of rule before the Roman invasion.   MALCOLM TODD

Sources C. Tacitus, *The histories [and] the annals*, ed. and trans. C. H. Moore and J. Jackson, 3 (1937), bk 12, pp. 33–40 · *Dio's Roman history*, ed. and trans. E. Cary, 7 (1924), lx.20–21 · Suetonius, 'Vita divi Claudii', *Lives of the Caesars*, trans. R. Graves (1957) · S. S. Frere, *Britannia: a history of Roman Britain*, 3rd edn (1987) · P. Salway, *Roman Britain* (1981)

Carausius [Marcus Aurelius Mausaeus Carausius] (*d.* 293), Roman emperor in Britain and Gaul, revolted against the joint emperors Diocletian and Maximian and successfully maintained a separatist regime in Britain, and parts of Gaul, in the years 286 to 293. His name Mausaeus is a modern reconstruction; ancient sources give it only in abbreviated form: 'M.' on his coins, and 'MAVS.' in his only surviving inscription. Born in Menapia, the coastal region of northern Gaul which includes modern Belgium and Holland, Carausius is said to have been of very humble origins and to have followed the profession of sailor in his youth. Aurelius Victor describes him as *gubernandi gnarus* (literally a helmsman, although *gubernator* also has a technical meaning of non-commissioned second-in-command of a ship in the fleet). Carausius's naval expertise is cited as the qualification for his later naval command: possibly he served in some naval capacity in the campaigns of the emperor Carinus (*r.* 282–5) which resulted in the emperor adopting the title *Britannicus Maximus*. The suggestion that he was commander of the *Classis Britannica*, or Channel Fleet, is refuted by the archaeological evidence showing that both the continental and British bases of this fleet had been abandoned by *c.*270. Although his date of birth is unknown, to judge by his coin portraits and the careers of contemporaries of similar military rank he was probably aged about forty at the time of his revolt.

Following distinguished service in Maximian's campaign to suppress a peasant revolt in Gaul, Carausius was, in 285 or 286, promoted to the command of a fleet, based on Gesoriacum (Boulogne), whose task was to rid the North Sea from the Rhine to Brittany of Frankish and Saxon pirates. In this capacity he is credited with successes. Aurelius Victor says that 'he killed many of the barbarians' (*Liber de caesaribus*, v.39.20) while Eutropius

Carausius (*d.* 293), coin

itself in the manner of a legitimate Roman administration. Detailed knowledge of the distribution of forces in Britain is lacking, though neglected forts in Wales were recommissioned and additions made to the defences of the south coast. One of its earliest acts was to issue a prolific, and much needed, coinage. Initially a number of mints were operated, eventually consolidated to two establishments located at London and Camulodunum (Colchester). A study of coin types offers an insight into the aspirations and activities of the emperor. Specific claims are made for Carausius to be the 'Restorer of Rome' and 'Restorer of Britain'; the legend *Expectate veni* ('come, expected one') suggests a delay in Gaul before the new emperor actually made his appearance in Britain itself. The bulk of coinage was issued with the legend *Pax Aug(usti)*, an aspiration rather than a statement of fact. Commemorative coins and medals indicate that Carausius celebrated consulships in 286 and 289—honours that were not recognized by the legitimate emperors.

Having dislodged Carausius from Gaul, Maximian constructed a fleet to replace that now in the hands of the usurper and, between 288 and 290, embarked on a full-scale attempt to recover Britain. This campaign was a failure, the fleet being destroyed either in a storm, or, more likely, by enemy action. Maximian's failure resulted in the recovery by Carausius of his former holdings in northern Gaul; archaeological evidence shows that Gesoriacum was now heavily defended, while the distribution of the usurper's coins dating to this period indicates that his rule extended to Rouen.

Attempts by Carausius to achieve legitimacy can be traced through the coinage. In 292 the usurper's mints produced a series of coins in the names of Diocletian and Maximian, including gold issues. The claim to equal constitutional status was made explicit by the issue of a coin bearing portraits of the three emperors and the inscription CARAUSIUS ET FRATRES SUI ('Carausius and his brothers'). The coinage may be taken as evidence that diplomatic overtures were being made on behalf of Carausius in the period immediately before the constitutional reforms which created a second tier of imperial administration by the appointment of Caesars, or heirs apparent, to the emperors. It may be assumed that Carausius was bidding for legitimization as co-ruler with Maximian in the west. There was no reciprocal numismatic gesture by the emperors and Carausian coins no longer acknowledged Diocletian and Maximian after the promotion of the western Caesar, Constantius.

Campaigning against the usurper began immediately upon the appointment of the Caesar. A swift move against Gesoriacum, the Carausian naval base, took the garrison by surprise and the city fell after a siege. A blockading of the River Liane by a mole, which was swept away by the tide immediately after the capitulation, prevented a relieving fleet from reaching the garrison. On seeing this failure the garrison surrendered. Carausius himself is not recorded as having participated in these events.

Carausius's death in 293, at the hands of Allectus, his

records that 'he often captured many barbarians' (Eutropius, ix.13). According to the literary sources this success was gained at the expense of the territory he was supposed to protect. Accused of intercepting the pirates only on their return from their raids and of keeping their booty for himself, he was condemned to death by the emperor Maximian. Alerted to the threat, Carausius fled with 'the fleet that used to protect Gaul' and 'usurped the imperial power and seized Britain' (*Liber de caesaribus*, v.39.20).

To a very considerable extent archaeological and numismatic studies have supplemented and amended the ancient literary narrative. Coins now established as having been struck at Rouen early in the reign suggest that the early stages of the revolt were based in Gaul and centred on Rotomagus (Rouen), rather than Britain, and that the expulsion of the usurper from Gaul was neither immediate nor easily accomplished. A further series of coins struck in Britain early in the reign commemorates the legions of Germany, Britain, and the Balkans. The coins may be interpreted as honouring those legions which were represented by contingents (vexillations) assigned to Carausius for land-based operations integral with his seaborne command, which supported his coup. Control of the coast of Gaul and possession of a fleet account for the swift capitulation of Britain to the usurper's cause, especially since two of the legions of Britain, II Augusta and XX Valeria Victrix, had contingents in his army in Gaul. That Carausius enjoyed civilian support, and possibly financial backing, may be deduced from the appearance of Gallic merchants among the list of his adherents (*Panegyrici Latini*, viii(v).12). The same source notes that 'considerable forces of barbarians were seduced by the loot of the very provinces' (ibid.), and that 'several units of non-Roman soldiers were secured'. These forces presumably formed part of the army at his disposal while in command in Gaul.

Once established in Britain the new regime conducted

'chief minister', is normally associated with the fall of Gesoriacum, but the ambiguity of the sources is such that his fall may have preceded that of the city. The loss, or imminent loss, of Gesoriacum may have been the catalyst, implying dissatisfaction in the army with the conduct of the war. On the other hand Aurelius Victor credits Allectus with some unspecified misdeed for which he feared punishment by Carausius. Other sources state that Allectus 'thought his actions would be rewarded with imperial power' (*Panegyrici Latini* viii(v).12). Whether the negotiation with Diocletian and Maximian implied by this statement was the 'misdeed' specified by Aurelius Victor is unclear. The replacement of Carausius by Allectus, and the latter's tenure of power for three years, suggests that dissatisfaction with Carausius was widespread by the time of his assassination.

Carausius's limited success depended on the maintenance of an effective navy and he was active in increasing this force: a panegyric declares that 'many ships were built in our style' (*Panegyrici Latini*, viii(v).12). Archaeological evidence suggests that fleets operated in conjunction with a series of coastal defences, later known as the Saxon Shore forts, which extended from the Wash to the Severn. Although detailed study shows that this defence system was not inaugurated by Carausius, the earliest forts dating to the first half of the third century, coin evidence shows that full military use was made of it during his reign. At least one fort, Portchester Castle, has good claim to be of Carausian construction. A similar claim may be advanced for Pevensey Castle. The fort at Richborough was probably completed in the Carausian period. The single epigraphic record of the reign is a milestone from Gallows Hill, Carlisle.

In the medieval period Carausius became a figure of romance, largely through the fictions of Geoffrey of Monmouth, and he was credited by Scottish historians with having validated by treaty the Scottish claims to Northumbria and Cumbria. In the eighteenth century he enjoyed a vogue, during a period of national naval success, as the founder of the British navy, parallels being drawn between Carausius's activities in the channel and contemporary hostilities with France. His coins and medals, which began to be collected systematically, encouraged his elevation to a British national stereotype, since they show a broad-chested, thick-necked, and full-of-face portrait reminiscent of the traditional figure of John Bull. In the same century the Carausian episode was the subject of a great deal of uninformed scholarly debate. This debate mostly centred around the writings of William Stukeley whose elaborations on the inventions of Geoffrey of Monmouth found their way into accounts of the period well into the nineteenth century.   P. J. CASEY

Sources R. A. B. Mynors, ed., *XII panegyrici Latini* (1964), x(ii), xi(iii), viii(v), vi(vii) · *Sexti Aurelii Victoris liber de caesaribus*, ed. F. Pichlmayr, rev. edn, rev. R. Gruendel (Leipzig, 1961) · Eutropius, *Breviarium ab urbe condita*, ed. C. Santini (Leipzig, 1979) · P. H. Webb, *Probus to Diocletian*, ed. H. Mattingly and E. A. Sydenham (1933), vol. 5/2 of *The Roman imperial coinage*, ed. H. Mattingly and others (1923–94) · C. H. V. Sutherland, *From Diocletian's reform AD 294 to the death of Maximinus AD 313* (1967), vol. 6 of *The Roman imperial coinage*, ed. H. Mattingly and others (1923–94) · P. J. Casey, *Carausius and Allectus: the British usurpers* (1994)

Likenesses coin, BM [*see illus.*] · coins, repro. in Webb, *Probus to Diocletian*

Carbery. For this title name *see* Vaughan, John, first earl of Carbery (1574/5–1634); Vaughan, Richard, second earl of Carbery (1600?–1686); Vaughan, John, third earl of Carbery (*bap.* 1639, *d.* 1713).

Carbery, Ethna. *See* MacManus, Anna Isabel (1866–1902).

Carbonell, William Leycester Rouse (1912–1993), police officer in Malaya, was born on 14 August 1912 at 150 Albert Palace Mansions, Battersea, London, the youngest of three sons and fourth of five children of John Carbonell, owner of a small engineering firm, and his wife, Barbara Madelaine Honor, daughter of Ezekiel Rouse, medical practitioner. He was educated at Shrewsbury School, from which he won a place at St Catharine's College, Cambridge, to read anthropology, matriculating in 1931. Always a keen rower he had been captain of boats at school and earned a blue in the bow seat of the victorious 1933 Cambridge team in the boat race. After graduating he decided to join the colonial police and went on to the School of Oriental and African Studies in London to learn Malay. When, at his police board interview, Winston Churchill questioned the (then unfashionable) choice of Malaya, Carbonell replied—with typical forthright honesty—that the Malay police were equipped with motorcycles, while those elsewhere rode horses, which 'kick at one end and bite at the other, and the middle might do anything' (private information).

After training at the police academy in Kuala Lumpur Carbonell gained experience working at a variety of police stations, often in the less accessible regions of the country. During a stay in hospital he was treated by an Australian nurse, Elsa Agnes (Dargen) Curdie (1906–1999), daughter of John William Curdie of Victoria. They married on 6 November 1937 in Kuala Lumpur, and had two sons.

The outbreak of the Second World War prevented any further promotion for the time being and ultimately led to Carbonell's imprisonment by Japanese forces. From 1942 he was held in the infamous Changi gaol, moving in 1943 to the Sime Road camp, where prisoners were kept short of food and were denied access to new clothes and even the most basic medicines. But the worst torment applied was mental—they were allowed no information about the outside world except fortnight-old Japanese newspapers. Certainly Carbonell's survival owed much to his determination and deep-rooted good humour, but he also insisted that the Japanese had made a great mistake in putting all the colonial service staff together. 'You can go under on your own, but you can't let [the others] down', he said afterwards (private information). As the war came to an end the tension among the prisoners became worse, if anything. Preparations were made to install weapons around the camp, using the internees as a human shield in case of allied attack. Much relief greeted the news of Japan's surrender when it arrived at Sime Road on 29 August 1945, communications having been totally severed after the dropping of the first atomic bomb.

After a period spent recuperating in Australia, Carbonell returned to Malaya in 1946 as the battered states pulled gradually out of their wartime devastation and moved towards federation in January 1948. The new local government machinery and slowly recovering police force were not given much time to reconstitute themselves, however, before the first prolonged attack of the communist guerrilla army triggered a state of emergency. Carbonell, as assistant superintendent (promoted superintendent early in 1949) in the state of Kedah, was necessarily responsible for both collecting intelligence and conducting active missions against the insurgents.

The initial attack was eventually repulsed with much loss of life, and the communists retreated to the jungle for part of 1949, giving much needed time for plans to be laid—and extra police and troops recruited. They soon returned to the field better equipped than before, and in February 1952 General Sir Gerald Templer was appointed high commissioner and director of operations in Malaya. Carbonell was then assistant commissioner in Kelantan, but was rapidly recalled to Kuala Lumpur and promoted to senior commissioner, to take charge of the newly formed special branch. This was to be the primary agent for gathering intelligence about the enemy, as well as a vital part of the actual combat forces. It was in this role that he attracted the attention of Templer, who was impressed by his efficiency and diplomacy, as well as his earlier practice of leading armed sorties in the jungle personally—never asking a subordinate to do something he would not have undertaken himself, and earning both the king's police medal and the colonial service medal in the process.

Carbonell was promoted to commissioner of police in 1954, shortly before the British government guaranteed the Malay Federation's independence once the emergency was successfully over. This, in turn, ensured the continued assistance of the local population, who were understandably wary of the Chinese-backed communists. The battle continued to rage for several more years, but there was now no doubt about the eventual victors. Carbonell was appointed CMG in 1956 and oversaw the celebrations of Merdeka (independence) on 31 August 1957. These were conducted with genuine goodwill on all sides, with many British officials staying on to ensure a smooth handover to the new authorities. 'Not a bad start for a new nation', Carbonell put it—'and not a bad swan song for the much maligned British Imperialist, either' (private information). He carried on as commissioner for another year, receiving the high Malay honour of the Panglima Mangku Negara shortly before taking early retirement in 1958, when he returned to Britain.

Still under fifty Carbonell pursued a second career as a successful business headhunter through the 1960s before retiring again and settling down for a quiet life, first in Hampshire and then in Surrey. Always helpful to those around him he suffered a series of strokes in his last years

which rendered him unable to maintain his active lifestyle and eventually resulted in his death, at Frimley Park Hospital, Frimley, Surrey, on 30 September 1993. He was survived by his wife, Dargen, and their two sons, John and Pete.   C. J. B. JOSEPH

Sources *The Times* (14 Oct 1993) · *WWW* · A. Short, *The communist insurrection in Malaya, 1948–1960* (1975) · A. J. Stockwell, *British policy and Malay politics during the Malayan emergency* (1995) · personal knowledge (2004) · private information (2004) · b. cert. · d. cert. · *CGPLA Eng. & Wales* (1993)

Likenesses photograph, 1958, repro. in *The Times*

Wealth at death £2041: probate, 25 Nov 1993, *CGPLA Eng. & Wales*

Carbutt [*married name* Herford], **Louisa** (1832–1907), schoolmistress and educational pioneer, was born on 25 September 1832 at Altona, near Hamburg, Germany, the daughter of Francis Carbutt (1792–1874) and his wife, Louise Petronella, daughter of George Henry Penecke of Copenhagen. Sir Edward Hamer Carbutt, first baronet (1838–1905), an engineer, twice mayor of Leeds, and Liberal MP for Monmouth from 1880 to 1886, was her younger brother. Her father was a merchant who supported the Anti-Corn Law League and became mayor of Leeds in 1847. Originally a Quaker, he withdrew from the Society of Friends to become one of the Unitarian congregation of the Mill Hill Chapel, Leeds. On his death his property was distributed equally among his seven surviving sons and daughters.

Louisa Carbutt's parents believed in giving their daughters as good an education as they could afford for their sons, and she attended a boarding-school at Hamburg until 1847, acquiring a fluency in four languages. A trip to the USA at the age of twenty-five inspired her to seek an independent, unmarried vocation, earning her own living, and she left the parental home in Leeds in 1859 to become a teacher of German in the large boarding-school for girls, Rawdon House, Hertfordshire, run by Sarah Stickney Ellis. There she was disappointed at the limited intellectual horizons opened to the daughters of the middle classes; she herself studied astronomy and botany. Her reading of Friedrich Froebel's works inspired an interest in new educational methods, which was encouraged by W. B. Hodgson, professor of education at St Andrews University, who introduced her to the works of Herbert Spencer.

In 1860 Carbutt went to Knutsford, Cheshire, where two Unitarian families were seeking a governess for their daughters. She proposed, instead, to establish a school, taking both day-girls and boarders. Brook House opened in August 1860, taking girls aged between nine and fourteen. Although never a large school, Brook House was notable for its pioneering methods, principally the development of girls' intellectual, moral, and spiritual faculties without recourse to rewards or punishments. There was close companionship between teachers and pupils, who were allowed more freedom than was usual at that time. Much emphasis was laid on hygiene, fresh air, exercise, and wholesome diet. The curriculum, which was enlightened, included science teaching. Ill health caused Carbutt to give up the school in 1870 and she returned to Leeds where she was one of the first women to be elected a poor-law guardian. She was particularly concerned to promote the integration of pauper children, ensuring that they were educated with other children in ordinary board schools rather than segregated in workhouse schools. In 1884 she married William Henry *Herford (1820–1908), who had taught at Brook House and shared her educational ideals. In 1886 they settled at Paignton, Devon, where their Unitarian beliefs shocked some of the more genteel residents. She died there, at Torbay Lodge, on 4 May 1907. M. C. CURTHOYS

Sources W. H. Herford, ed., *In memoriam: Louisa Carbutt and Brook House, 1860–1870* (privately printed, Manchester, 1907) · P. Hollis, *Ladies elect: women in English local government, 1865–1914* (1987)
Likenesses photograph, 1886 (with W. H. Herford), repro. in Herford, *In memoriam*, frontispiece
Wealth at death £15,587 19s.: probate, 31 May 1907, *CGPLA Eng. & Wales*

Card, Henry (1779–1844), writer, born at Egham, Surrey, was educated at Westminster School and at Pembroke College, Oxford, where he entered in 1797; he proceeded BA 1800, MA 1805, and BD and DD 1823. In 1799 he married Marianna Bulkeley of South Lambeth. He resided for some years at Margate. In 1815 he was presented to the vicarage of Great Malvern, Worcestershire, and in 1832 to that of Dormington, Herefordshire. He was elected a fellow of the Royal Society on 2 March 1820 and was also fellow of the Society of Antiquaries and of the Royal Historical Society. He died at Great Malvern on 4 August 1844 after an illness, having had his left leg amputated following an accident. Card's historical works include *The History of the Revolutions of Russia to the Accession of Catherine the First* (2nd edn 1804); *Historical Outlines of the Rise and Establishment of Papal Power* (1804); and a work on Charlemagne. In addition he published sermons and essays on points of religion including *A dissertation on the sacrament of the Lord's supper, or, The refutation of the Hoadlyan scheme of it* (4th edn, 1821). His other publications are miscellaneous essays on education, Church reform, and two works of fiction—a novel; *Beauford, or, A Picture of High Life* (1811) and *The Brother in Law, a Comedy* (1817).

FRANCIS WATT, *rev.* MYFANWY LLOYD

Sources *GM*, 2nd ser., 22 (1844), 651–2 · [J. Watkins and F. Shoberl], *A biographical dictionary of the living authors of Great Britain and Ireland* (1816) · Watt, *Bibl. Brit.* · J. Foster, ed., *Index ecclesiasticus, or, Alphabetical lists of all ecclesiastical dignitaries in England and Wales since the Reformation* (1890) · Foster, *Alum. Oxon.*
Archives BL, letters to Lord Grenville, Add. MS 58995 | BL, corresp. with second earl of Liverpool, Add. MSS 38269, 38275–38276, 38280, *passim*
Likenesses W. Ridley, stipple (after Harding), BM, NPG; repro. in *Monthly Mirror* (1804)

Cardale, John Bate (1802–1877), first apostle of the Catholic Apostolic church, was born at 28 Lamb's Conduit Street, Holborn, London, on 7 November 1802, the eldest of five children. His father, William Cardale, a solicitor and Worcestershire landowner, was born on 17 July 1777 and died at Harrogate on 26 September 1826, having married in 1799 Mary Anne Bennett. In 1815 their son entered Rugby School, and in 1818 was articled to his father, though he would have preferred to take holy orders. On his admission as a solicitor on 8 July 1824 his father retired, and he became the head of two partnerships, Cardale and Buxton in Holborn, and Cardale and Bromley, in Bedford Row. In September 1824 he married Emma (d. 1873), the second daughter of Thomas William Plummer of Clapham.

As a member of St John's Chapel, Bedford Row, Cardale's sympathies were evangelical, and like others of that persuasion he was excited in 1830 by the news of 'spiritual manifestations' in the form of healing and glossolalia at Port Glasgow. In August he visited Scotland with his two sisters, another unmarried lady, and two medical men, George Roe (1795–1873) and John Thompson, and on his return reported favourably on the phenomena. In October he opened his own home for meetings where prayer was made for a similar 'outpouring of the Spirit'.

In April 1831 Cardale's wife (who had not been to Scotland), followed by others (including Cardale's sister, Emily), began to prophesy and 'sing in the Spirit', but in February 1832 their Anglican minister, Baptist Noel (1798–1873), rejected the authenticity of the gifts, after which Cardale began to attend the Caledonian Church in Regent Square, where Edward Irving was more sympathetic and permitted similar manifestations to occur in his church. When Irving's trustees brought the matter before the London presbytery Cardale acted as his solicitor, but to no avail, and in October 1832 Irving's congregation began to meet in a church in Newman Street.

There was some uncertainty at first as to the constitution of this new community which, together with other similar groups, soon began to call itself the Catholic Apostolic church, but the members of which were often popularly referred to as Irvingites. From the first, however, Cardale emerged as a leader in its organization. Following the prophetic instructions in October of Henry Drummond, and then of Edward Taplin in November, the church recognized Cardale as the first of twelve apostles, the rest of whom were appointed during the next two and a half years and who were to be responsible for the new church's government. On 14 July 1835 the apostles gathered in the council chamber of their cathedral church, newly built for them by Drummond at Albury near Guildford. After deliberations lasting two and a half years the world was divided into twelve regions or tribes, for each of which an apostle would be responsible. England or Judah, the seat of apostolic government, was allocated to Cardale, the Pillar of the Apostles, who had retired from active legal work in 1834 and henceforth remained in England while his fellow apostles travelled far and wide.

When, in 1839, the authority of the apostles was questioned by charismatic elements in the movement Cardale acted with characteristic decisiveness, recalling his scattered fellows and discontinuing the regular meetings of the Council of the Churches in which critical voices had been raised. The eclipse of the prophetical element in the movement was further underlined by the church's adoption in 1843 of an elaborate new liturgy (enlarged in 1846 to include the rite of sealing) which was substantially the product of Cardale's labours, and which reflects his researches into the Eastern and Catholic offices as well as the Anglican rite of his upbringing. It is evidence of Cardale's strength of will that the movement's adherents, predominantly drawn from the evangelical ranks, accepted, apparently without demur, such a profoundly sacramentalist liturgy.

For some thirty-five years Cardale ministered to Catholic Apostolic congregations throughout the United Kingdom and wrote many anonymous works of theology and moral instruction, most of which were printed for private circulation within the movement. The most substantial product of his pen is his *Readings upon the Liturgy*, which appeared between 1848 and 1878, and which enshrines his ongoing reflection on one of the subjects closest to his heart. Of particular importance for the historian of the Restored Apostolate is his *Letters on some statements contained in some late articles in the 'Old Church Porch', entitled Irvingism*, which appeared in 1855, and its sequel published twelve years later, as they clarify the early development of the movement. With the death of the apostle Henry King-Church in 1865 Cardale accepted responsibilities in Scandinavia, taught himself Danish, and in 1867 worked for a time in Copenhagen. After a brief illness he died at his home, Cooke's Place, Albury, on 18 July 1877, and was buried in Albury churchyard.

Cardale was a natural leader and a man of decisive judgement. At times his single-mindedness bordered on the dictatorial, but his kindly and encouraging manner was a source of reassurance in a community where the light of the hope of Christ's return was liable to burn less brightly with the disillusion of succeeding years. His wife had died at Albury on 31 March 1873. Of their fourteen children, three married into the family of Jasper and Eliza (*née* Awdrey) Peck. Cardale's sister Emily, who was a prophetess in the church, married James Hore and died at Western Lodge, Albury, on 18 April 1879, aged seventy-one.   TIMOTHY C. F. STUNT

Sources J. Lancaster, 'John Bate Cardale, Pillar of Apostles', diss., U. St Andr., 1978 · D. J. Tierney, 'The Catholic Apostolic church: a study in tory millenarianism', *Historical Research*, 63 (1990), 289–313 · E. Miller, *The history and doctrines of Irvingism*, 1 (1878), 63–6, 110ff., 206, 220, 245, 314 · R. A. Davenport, *Albury Apostles*, rev. edn (1974), 36–8, 77–84, 117–18, 151–2 · S. Newman-Norton, 'A biographical index of those associated with the Lord's work', Bodl. Oxf., MS facs b.61, 11 · C. G. Flegg, *Gathered under apostles: a study of the Catholic Apostolic church* (1992) · P. E. Shaw, *The Catholic Apostolic church, sometimes called Irvingite* (1946), 33ff., 72ff., 95ff. · T. C. F. Stunt, *From awakening to secession: radical evangelicals in Switzerland and Britain, 1815–35* (2000)
Archives Catholic Apostolic church, archives, London | Alnwick Castle, Northumberland, letters to Henry Drummond, homilies, addresses, and other papers
Likenesses photograph, repro. in Davenport, *Albury Apostles*, following p. 161
Wealth at death under £25,000: probate, 3 Aug 1877, *CGPLA Eng. & Wales*

Cardale, Paul (1705–1775), Presbyterian minister and theologian, was born on 13 February 1705 at Dudley, Worcestershire, the son of Samuel Cardale, one of the original trustees of the town's meeting-house, and Jane Darby. He received his early education locally before proceeding in 1720 to the academy of Ebenezer Latham at Findern, Derbyshire. Latham encouraged habits of free enquiry among his students, many of whom as a consequence emerged from the academy with heterodox opinions. The seeds of Cardale's Socinian views were sown probably at Findern, but in his first ministerial appointment as assistant pastor to the Presbyterian congregation at Kidderminster he scarcely deviated from orthodoxy in his public utterances. The exact date of the commencement of his ministerial duties at Kidderminster is not known, but the earliest date marked on the manuscript copy of the sermons he preached there is 29 May 1726.

In 1733 Cardale accepted the invitation to become minister to the Presbyterian congregation at Evesham. At that time the meeting-house was in High Street but within a few years of his settlement in the town measures were taken to obtain a site for a new chapel, the need for which stemmed as much from the dilapidated state of the original meeting-house as from any significant increase in the size of the congregation. The new chapel was located on Oat Street, and a licence for it was granted on 11 October 1737. About the time of the opening of Oat Street Chapel, Cardale married Sarah Suffield (1702–1767), a member of his congregation and sister of Thomas Suffield, a wealthy maltster and an original trustee of the chapel. Although the marriage does not appear to have produced any children it was a happy one and no doubt added to Cardale's social standing. Cardale remained as minister at Oat Street until his death.

Cardale was not a popular preacher. One or two of the more erudite members of his congregation might have appreciated the scholarly nature of his sermons but the majority, mostly shopkeepers and market gardeners, would have preferred a more popular preaching style. Job Orton commented on him that not only did he neglect his pastoral duties but he 'ruined a fine congregation by his learned, dry and critical discourses' (*Letters to Dissenting Ministers*, 1.154). Nevertheless, he maintained good and friendly relations with neighbouring ministers, especially the liberal Anglican clergyman the Revd John Rawlins, rector of Leigh and minister of Badsey and Wickhamford. Among other ministerial friends were George Broadhurst of Alcester, and Francis and Edward Blackmore who both spent their closing years at Worcester. Outside Worcestershire his closest friend for more than forty years was Dr Caleb Fleming, who visited him frequently and encouraged him in his writing.

Cardale's accomplishments as a preacher may have been modest but his contribution to the spread of Socinianism and the development of anti-Trinitarian thought was significant, even if in his own lifetime his talents and learning brought him little fame. Through his writing he was primarily responsible for the spread of Socinianism in the midlands. Spears considers him to be one of the chief pioneers of modern unitarianism, while Aspland believes that Cardale deserves to be ranked with such unitarian luminaries as John Biddle, Thomas Emlyn, Joseph

Priestley, and Theophilus Lindsey. Priestley, who did not know him personally but corresponded with him over contributions to the *Theological Repository*, held him in high regard. In a letter to Lindsey in 1771 he described Cardale as 'a most excellent man, one after your own heart' (Aspland, 612). When in 1789 Priestley learned that Joshua Toulmin was considering writing a biography of Cardale, he wrote to Toulmin: 'I am glad you are rescuing from oblivion the memory of so valuable a man' (ibid., 613). Cardale first gave written evidence of his anti-Trinitarian thinking in such early works as *The Gospel Sanctuary* (1740) and *A New Office of Devotion* (1758) but the volume, published in 1767, on which rests his reputation as a theologian was *The True Doctrine of the New Testament Concerning Jesus Christ Considered*, to which was prefixed *Discourse upon the Right of Private Judgement in Matters of Religion*. This work is an elaborate argument against the Arian and Athanasian representations of Christ as divine, and a powerful plea for freedom of conscience in matters of religion. A corrected and enlarged version appeared in 1771 and was greeted with much approval by the Socinian notable Andrew Kippis. A third edition was planned but this never progressed beyond manuscript amendments and additions to the text of the second edition. Cardale developed his thesis for the humanity of Christ and the sole deity of the father of Jesus Christ in *A Comment upon some Remarkable Passages in Christ's Prayer at the Close of his Public Ministry* (1772) and *A Treatise on the Application of Certain Terms and Epithets to Jesus Christ* (1774). He concluded his anti-Trinitarian argument in *An enquiry whether we have any scriptural warrant for a direct address of supplication, praise or thanksgiving either to the Son or the Holy Ghost* which was completed shortly before his death and published posthumously in 1776.

Most of Cardale's publications belong to the period after the death of his wife when he sought in intense theological study a refuge from the sadness of solitary old age. In later years his health deteriorated and he was troubled by a 'painful debility of limbs and voice' (Aspland, 616). He died peacefully in his sleep during the early hours of the morning of 1 March 1775 in Evesham, and was buried next to his wife in the north aisle of All Saints' Church there. An epitaph written by his friend John Rawlins and inscribed on his tombstone describes him as a 'pious and sincere Christian' and a 'learned and indefatigable minister'.

M. J. MERCER

Sources R. B. Aspland, 'Memoir of Paul Cardale', *Christian Reformer, or, Unitarian Magazine and Review*, new ser., 8 (1852) · R. Spears, *Unitarian worthies* (1876) · Surman, index of nonconformist ministers, DWL · K. G. Smith, *The story of an old meeting house, 1737–1937: being an account of Oat Street Chapel, Evesham* (1937) · T. Davis, letter, *Monthly Repository*, 16 (1821), 527 · J. Goring, 'The break up of the old dissent', in C. G. Bolam and others, *The English presbyterians: from Elizabethan puritanism to modern unitarianism* (1968), 175–218 · W. Urwick, *Nonconformity in Worcester* (1897) · Watt, *Bibl. Brit.* · *Letters to dissenting ministers and to students for the ministry from the Rev. Job Orton*, ed. S. Palmer, 2 vols. (1806), vol. 1 · G. E. Evans, *Midland churches* (1899), 122–4, 130 · *DNB* · *IGI* · list of Dr Latham's pupils at Findern, DWL

Likenesses portrait; Oat Street Chapel, Evesham, 1937

Carden, George Frederick (1798–1874), barrister and cemetery founder, was born on 21 May 1798 in London, the second of the five children of James Carden (1758–1829), attorney, and his wife, Mary (1765–1830), daughter of John *Walter (1739?–1812), founder of *The Times*. His brother was the banker and politician Sir Robert Walter *Carden. He was educated at a private school at Twickenham, admitted to the Inner Temple in October 1821, and called to the bar in May 1829. From 1830 he practised on the Oxford and Welsh circuits, specializing in equity cases. Carden began his campaign for the establishment of London's first cemetery in the mid-1820s. There were then few cemeteries in the British Isles, and none of any size in England before the establishment of St James's, Liverpool, in 1825. During this period Carden travelled widely, familiarizing himself with cemetery design in Europe and further afield. In letters to magazines and periodicals he joined his voice to the growing number of critics of intramural burial, advocating the closure of London's overcrowded city churchyards and the establishment, at a suitable distance from the metropolis, of a large-scale 'garden' or 'botanic' cemetery, on the lines of Père Lachaise, Paris. By 1830 Carden had enlisted the support of a number of influential figures, including Viscount Milton, the banker Sir John Dean Paul, and Andrew Spottiswoode MP; and in February of that year a meeting was held at the Freemasons' Tavern for the purpose of forming a joint stock company to be known as the General Cemetery Company. In July 1831 55 acres of farmland situated in the then rural setting of Kensal Green, north of London, were purchased by the company for £9400. A year later the General Cemetery Company obtained the right by act of parliament to open a cemetery at Kensal Green. It was consecrated by the bishop of London on 24 January 1833, and the first burial took place a week later. Landscaped by Richard Forrest, head gardener to the duke of Northumberland, and with buildings in the classical manner (designed by John Griffith), mausoleums, and catacombs, Kensal Green cemetery appealed at once to the public imagination, becoming in a short period of time one of the sights of the metropolis. In the following years many prominent persons were buried there, including the duke of Sussex (1843), Princess Sophia (1848), and Sir (Marc) Isambard Brunel (1849). Within ten years six other large cemeteries, including Norwood (1837) and Highgate (1839), had opened near London, creating what was termed a 'cordon sanitaire' around the city. The problem of intramural burial, however, was finally resolved only in 1850 with the passing of the Metropolitan Interments Act, which prevented further interments in the city graveyards. To Carden was due much of the credit for initiating the move towards a more sanitary approach to the disposal of the dead. His great 'garden' cemetery at Kensal Green was the first in England and, as the precursor and prototype of all subsequent town and city cemeteries, played a leading part in redefining nineteenth-century sensibilities about death. Carden resigned from his position on the board of directors in 1838 after a series of disagreements with its chairman, Sir John Dean Paul; and in the same year he sued the company for £7000 owed him for work done on its behalf. He eventually accepted an out of court settlement of £1000. He devoted the rest of his life to his profession, and continued on the Oxford circuit until the year of his death. He died unmarried on 18 November 1874 at his home, The Grove, Hendon, Middlesex, and was buried on 22 November in the cemetery he had founded.

ROBERT J. MOULDER

Sources records of the General Cemetery Company, Kensal Green · J. S. Curl, *The Victorian celebration of death* (1972) · Law List (1830–74) · Inner Temple, London · *GM*, 1st ser., 100/1 (1830), 552 · *The Times* (June 1838) · private information (2004) · *WWBMP*, vol. 1 · Burke, *Peerage* (1889) · H. Meller, *London cemeteries: an illustrated guide and gazetteer*, 3rd edn (1994) · parish register, St Martin-in-the-Fields, London [birth, baptism] · J. S. Curl, *The origins and development of the General Cemetery of All Souls, Kensal Green, London, 1824–2001* (2001)

Wealth at death £70,000: resworn administration, Nov 1875, CGPLA Eng. & Wales

Carden, Sir John Valentine, sixth baronet (1892–1935), engineer, was born at 23 Cadogan Place, London, on 6 February 1892, the elder child and only son of Sir John Craven Carden, fifth baronet (1854–1931), and his wife, Sybil Martha (1868–1911), the younger daughter of General Valentine Baker. He grew up on his father's estate of Templemore, co. Tipperary, and entered Harrow School in 1906. In 1908 he left Harrow on account of his parents' separation, and subsequently lived with his mother while receiving private tuition. In 1913, at a workshop in Farnham, Surrey, Carden produced his first cyclecar, a sporting monocar with a 4 hp engine. In its original form the vehicle was push-started, the driver jumping aboard once it was under way; for the commercial model a hand starter and a two-speed epicyclic gear were added, and the manufacturing rights were sold to Ward and Avey of A. V. Motors.

During the First World War Carden served in the Army Service Corps. At the time of his marriage, on 18 September 1915 to Vera Madeleine (b. 1889/90), daughter of William Hervet-d'Egville, of independent means, he was stationed at the Caterpillar depot, Aldershot; he also worked on American Holt tractors at Avonmouth. He became a temporary captain, and in 1919 was appointed an MBE. In February 1919 he announced a second cyclecar model, a tandem two-seater built around proprietary components, the rights to which he sold to Edward Tamplin in November 1919. A more enterprising cyclecar incorporating a single engine and rear-axle unit of Carden's own devising appeared in 1920. Although this was the first four-wheeled car of any kind to be marketed for a sum as low as £100, few were sold. The falling prices of orthodox motorcars were making cyclecar manufacture uneconomical, and Carden's attention turned instead to tracked vehicles. In the early 1920s he joined Vivian Graham Loyd in the management of a large London garage, and established with him the firm Carden Loyd Tractors. His marriage was dissolved early in 1925, and shortly afterwards, on 13 February 1925, he married Dorothy Mary (b. 1891/2), daughter of Charles Luckraft McKinnon, of independent means; they had one son.

The appointment in February 1926 of Sir George Milne as chief of the Imperial General Staff revived the pressure towards mechanization within the British army. In 1925 Carden had produced an unarmoured tracked machine with a low silhouette, designed to propel an infantryman into battle in a prone position, and in 1926 he constructed an armoured two-man 'tankette'. Eight Carden–Loyd machines were built for a newly created mechanized force, and Carden's designs of tracked and semi-tracked vehicles were honed through several marks in the light of the force's exercises on Salisbury Plain in 1927 and 1928. On 12 March 1928 Carden and Loyd entered into an agreement with Vickers–Armstrongs Ltd, giving Vickers sole rights to manufacture and sell Carden–Loyd vehicles in return for royalties and salaries of £1000 a year. Carden, based at the existing Carden–Loyd premises at Chertsey in Surrey, proceeded to design numerous military and civil tracked vehicles. In addition to a series of tanks culminating in the Light Tank mark VI and the Infantry Tank mark I (A11), both of which entered production only after his death, these included armoured machine-gun carriers, tractors adapted for various uses, and an amphibious tank. Besides his work for Vickers, he collaborated in 1934 with Stephen Appleby to develop a Ford engine for the 'Flying Flea' home-built miniature aircraft.

Carden succeeded to the baronetcy on 16 December 1931. He was killed on 10 December 1935 in the crash, on the border of Surrey and Kent near Tatsfield, of a Sabena airliner bound from Brussels to Croydon, and was buried at Frimley parish church, Surrey, on 16 December 1935. His wife survived him.

Carden was one of several men associated with Vickers–Armstrongs companies in the 1930s who brought a brilliant practical genius to the solution of engineering problems, others being Reginald Mitchell and Barnes Wallis. Carden valued an intuitive approach to design above fine technical draughtsmanship, but his productions were thoroughly suited to commercial manufacture and made widespread use of interchangeable components. His vehicles both contributed to formulating British tactical theory between the world wars and helped to realize it in practice. His designs, and copies of them, were widely adopted by foreign armies, and Vickers light tanks equipped the majority of British armoured units in 1939. The poor showing of British armour against heavier German tanks early in the Second World War was the result of an enforced reliance on light tanks to perform the roles of medium tanks, and not of shortcomings intrinsic to Carden's vehicles. The Bren carriers developed from Carden's designs were among the most versatile and ubiquitous British weapons of the war, and over 40,000 were built.

Carden was 'tall, earnest, rather cadaverous' (*Light Car*, 20 Dec 1935, 120), and habitually informal in dress. His wholehearted enthusiasm overcame his extreme shyness to make him an effective and popular leader at Chertsey. His chief recreation was piloting a light aircraft that appeared so dilapidated to his colleagues that they generally declined offers to accompany him.   JOHN WELLS

Sources CUL, Vickers archive, historical documents 616, 619, 744, 776, 859 and 895 · E. Riddle, 'John Carden', *Light Car* [journal of the light car and Edwardian section, Vintage Sports Car Club] (spring 1996), 12–15; (summer 1996), 11–14 · P. Chamberlain and C. Ellis, *British and American tanks of World War II: the complete illustrated history of British, American and commonwealth tanks, gun motor carriages and special purpose vehicles, 1939–1945* (1969) · 'John V. Carden: pioneer', *Light Car* (20 Dec 1935), 124 · G. Le Q. Martel, *In the wake of the tank: the first eighteen years of mechanization in the British army* (1935) · C. F. Foss and P. McKenzie, *The Vickers tanks* (1988) · M. Worthington-Williams, *From cyclecar to microcar: the story of the cyclecar movement* (1981) · *The Times* (11 Dec 1935) · *The Times* (12 Dec 1935) · *The Times* (17 Dec 1935) · private information (2004) [Sir John Craven Carden, seventh baronet] · B. H. Liddell Hart, 'The new British doctrine of mechanized war', *English Review*, Dec 1929, 688–701; B. H. Liddell Hart, *The current of war* (1941), 92–107 · *Light Car* (20 Dec 1935), 120 · Burke, *Peerage* (1937) · J. H. Stogdon, ed., *The Harrow School Register, 1845–1925*, 2nd ser., vol. 2 (1925) · b. cert. · m. certs. · *Debrett's Peerage* (1941)
Archives CUL, Vickers archive
Likenesses photograph, *c.*1913, repro. in Worthington-Williams, *From cyclecar to microcar* · photograph, *c.*1932, repro. in Riddle, 'John Carden' (spring 1996), 12; formerly priv. coll. · photograph, repro. in 'John V. Carden: pioneer', *Light Car*, 124
Wealth at death £102,303 5s. 11d.—probate: 1936, CGPLA Eng. & Wales

Carden, Sir Lionel Edward Gresley (1851–1915), diplomatist, was born on 15 September 1851 at Brighton, Sussex, the son of Lionel Carden, a Church of England priest, and his wife, Lucy Lawrence, *née* Ottley. He was educated at Eton College (1862–8), and began his diplomatic career in 1877. On 15 February 1881 he married Anne Eliza (1859/60–1939), daughter of John Lefferts of New York; there were no children.

Carden's career in the diplomatic service covered a period of thirty-eight years. His overseas postings were in Cuba, Central America, and Mexico. His years as a senior diplomat coincided with the rise of American power in, and Great Britain's strategic disengagement from, the Caribbean region. This changing order naturally gave rise to complications: Great Britain had extensive economic interests in the region, and diplomatic personnel—Carden in particular—endeavoured to protect these interests while at the same time the Foreign Office sought to maintain a good relationship with the United States.

Carden's vigorous defence of British economic interests in Cuba earned him the reputation in Washington of being 'anti-American'. His continued forceful assertion of British rights following his 1905 transfer to Central America led the United States government in 1910 to request the Foreign Office to arrange Carden's 'speedy transfer' to a 'post where his peculiar views would not bring him into conflict with American interests' (Records of the Department of State, 701.4114/3A). Carden, however, remained in place as the British minister to Central America until 1913, when, at the specific request of Sir Edward Grey, he became the British minister to Mexico. One authority has observed that Carden 'served as a lightning rod to absorb the charges of "anti-Americanism" [and to deflect criticism from] the policy makers at home' (Kneer, 93). Indeed, his continued assignment to sensitive positions reflected a lingering ambivalence in the Foreign Office towards the changing political situation in the Caribbean region. His creation as KCMG in 1911 suggests, yet again, that despite Washington's disfavour, Carden still retained the support and confidence of his home government. This came to an end, however, following his posting to Mexico in 1913.

While the regime of Victoriano Huerta enjoyed British diplomatic recognition, it was openly opposed by the United States government. Carden's sustained and vocal advocacy of the Mexican strongman ultimately proved both an embarrassment to London and a major source of irritation to the United States. Accordingly, American diplomats applied constant pressure on the Foreign Office to secure Carden's removal from Mexico. His appointment, which had originally been set for one year, was interrupted, much to Washington's delight and Carden's chagrin, in January 1914 by a temporary recall of several months. This was followed in August 1914 by Carden's final recall. His anticipated assignment as minister to Brazil, however, was not forthcoming, because of the wartime freeze on diplomatic promotion. In the words of one authority, Carden thereupon resigned from the diplomatic corps 'a disappointed man' and a 'victim' of circumstances beyond his control (Calvert, 284).

After several months of physical decline Carden died at his London home, 23 Basil Mansions, Knightsbridge, on 16 October 1915 and was cremated at Golders Green on 19 October. *The Times* (18 Oct 1915) lamented the loss of 'a keenwitted, strong, and energetic representative' while noting the 'apparent injustice' of the circumstances surrounding Carden's departure from the diplomatic corps.

RICHARD V. SALISBURY

Sources general correspondence, Foreign Office, PRO · National Archives and Records Administration, Washington, DC, Records of the Department of State, Record Group 59, Decimal File 701.4114/3A · W. G. Kneer, *Great Britain and the Caribbean, 1901–1913* (1975) · P. Calvert, *The Mexican revolution, 1910–1914* (1968) · *The Times* (18 Oct 1915) · *The Times* (17 Oct 1915) · K. Grieb, *The United States and Huerta* (1969) · W. V. Scholes, 'Sir Lionel Carden's proposed agreement on Central America, 1912', *The Americas*, 15 (1959), 291–5 · *FO List* (1916) · H. E. C. Stapylton, *Appendix to the Eton school lists, comprising the years 1853–6–9* (1868) · Eton, archives · b. cert. · m. cert. · d. cert. · *New York Times* (17 Feb 1881) [marriage notice]
Archives National Archives and Records Administration, Washington, DC, Central Decimal Files · PRO, Foreign Office MSS
Wealth at death £425 15s. 6d.: probate, 25 Nov 1915, CGPLA Eng. & Wales

Carden, Sir Robert Walter, first baronet (1801–1888), banker and politician, was born in London on 7 October 1801, the youngest son of James Carden (1758–1829), a barrister, of Bedford Square, London, and Richmond, Surrey, and his wife, Mary (1765–1830), daughter of John *Walter, founder of *The Times*, a newspaper in which her son Robert retained a proprietary interest. One of his brothers was George Frederick *Carden, cemetery founder. In 1816 he took a commission in the 52nd foot and in 1822 he began a sixty-five year association with the stock exchange, becoming the 'father of the house' and remaining active until his death. He married Pamela Elizabeth Edith (d. 1874), daughter of William Smith Andrews of the 19th foot, in 1827; they had ten children.

In 1855 Carden founded the City Bank, incorporated by royal charter. It became a limited company in March 1880. By 1898 the bank had opened twenty-one branches in London and its suburbs, and had amalgamated with the London City and Midland Bank Ltd. It was renamed the London Joint City and Midland Bank in 1918 and the Midland Bank in 1923, with its headquarters in Threadneedle Street. Although he was thought of as a pillar of the City (he was also a chairman of the Royal Exchange Bank and director of the Canada Company), Carden's aspirations were relatively modest. Politically, however, his influence continued to grow. His connection with the City's Dowgate ward began in 1849, when he became, in an uncontested election, its alderman, and continued until he retired to the ward of Bridge Without in 1871. He was a commissioner for the lieutenancy of London in 1849. The following year, in December 1850, he made the first of many attempts to enter parliament, on this occasion at St Albans. It was here that, although unsuccessful, he gained his reputation for forthrightness by fighting widespread corruption in the constituency. Besides sitting for Gloucester from April 1857 to May 1859 and Barnstaple from April 1880 to 1885, he also contested Marylebone in April 1861, Reading in November 1868, and Barnstaple in February 1880.

Carden had more success in his municipal career and brought to it the same direct approach. After serving as a sheriff in 1850–51 and receiving a knighthood on 17 July 1851, he was noted as the proposer of the Indian Mutiny Fund, and he made a visit to Russia on the occasion of the coronation of Tsar Alexander II. He was lord mayor of London in 1857–8. Again, he refused to accede to bribery and corruption, this time from within the common council. Consequently, on his return to the common hall of the livery companies he was received with hooting and groans. During his mayoral year his unpopularity deepened. He was the first to abandon the water procession of the lord mayor's show and to concede the City's rights over the Thames to the Thames Conservancy Board. More crucially, however, he was seen as a 'sturdy' evangelical conservative (he attended services at Portman Chapel, under the ministry of the Revd Neville Sherbrooke) in a city that maintained its Liberal and whig mix (*City Press*, 21 Jan 1888).

His year as lord mayor was also one in which Carden widened his scope for public service, becoming a JP for Middlesex and Surrey. As a magistrate, he confined City vagrants for three weeks at a time and as a result the streets were said to have been cleared of a nuisance. At a public meeting he promised to find work for all the unemployed present, but he complained subsequently that few remained working for more than a month, and only two for a year. His experience as a teacher in the Ogle Mission, Gray's Yard ragged school, and at George Yard, Whitechapel, all institutions to which he contributed financially, also gave him a close knowledge of the unemployed. Every three years, he opened his Surrey residence, Mole Lodge in West Moulsey, to the children of the High Street Mission, thus revealing a personality that could be alternately generous and stern.

The death of his wife in 1874, a year after the death of his second son Robert, a clergyman of the Church of England, seemed to temper his outlook. In 1876–7 he undertook his third spell as master of the Cutlers' Company, this time in more favourable circumstances. In June 1887 he was rewarded with a baronetcy. He was discovered dead in his chair after dinner on 19 January 1888 at his home at 64 Wimpole Street, Marylebone, London. He was buried at Kensal Green, in the cemetery which his brother George had founded. According to one obituary he was remembered as 'frosty but kindly' (*City Press*, 21 Jan 1888), the qualities that he had shown during a life that spanned almost the whole of the nineteenth century.

PETER M. CLAUS

Sources *City Press* (21 Jan 1888) · L. S. Pressnell, J. Orbell, and others, *A guide to the historical records of British banking* (1985) · L. Richmond and B. Stockford, *Company archives: the survey of the records of 1000 of the first registered companies in England and Wales* (1986) · W. F. Crick and J. E. Wadsworth, *A hundred years of joint stock banking* (1936) · WWBMP · E. Kilmurray, *Dictionary of British portraiture*, 3 (1981) · A. B. Beaven, ed., *The aldermen of the City of London, temp. Henry III–[1912]*, 2 vols. (1908–13)

Likenesses D. J. Pound, stipple and line engraving (after photograph by Mayall), NPG · Spy [L. Ward], caricature, watercolour study, NPG; repro. in *VF* (11 Dec 1880) · two lithographs, NPG

Wealth at death £23,526 14s. 8d.: resworn probate, Jan 1889, *CGPLA Eng. & Wales* (1888)

Carden, Sir Sackville Hamilton (1857–1930), naval officer, the third son of Captain Andrew Carden, 60th rifles, and his first wife, Anne, eldest daughter of Lieutenant-General Sackville Hamilton Berkeley, was born at Templemore, co. Tipperary, on 3 May 1857. He entered the navy in 1870. He took part in the Egyptian and Sudan campaigns of 1882–4, and, under Admiral Sir Harry Holdsworth Rawson, one of the most efficient officers of his time, served in the 1897 Benin expedition. Carden was promoted captain in 1899, and rear-admiral in 1908. He was for two years on half pay, then hoisted his flag in the battleship *London* as rear-admiral in the Atlantic Fleet, an appointment tenable for only one year. This was followed by special service at the Admiralty.

In August 1912, Carden was selected to be admiral superintendent of Malta Dockyard, an appointment usually regarded as a precursor to retirement. However, upon the outbreak of war in August 1914, Carden was forced into a crucial role by the circumstances following the escape of the German warships *Goeben* and *Breslau* from the Mediterranean into Turkish waters. Although Admiral Sir Berkeley Milne, commander-in-chief in the Mediterranean, was officially held blameless for the incident, his continued presence in southern waters was incompatible, owing to his seniority, with the assumption by the French of the command of allied naval forces in the Mediterranean, in accordance with a naval convention concluded soon after the outbreak of the war. Carden, who had just attained the rank of vice-admiral, was chosen (20 September 1914) to command the British battle squadron associated with the French forces.

Sir Sackville Hamilton Carden (1857–1930), by Bassano, 1915

Following the closing of the Dardanelles by the Turks (27 September), war was declared between Great Britain and Turkey on 5 November, and simultaneously French and British warships, under Carden's command, carried out a preliminary bombardment of the outer forts of the straits. When, in January 1915, definite proposals to occupy the Gallipoli peninsula were being debated in the war council on Churchill's initiative, Churchill asked Carden (by cable) whether, in his opinion, the Dardanelles could be forced by ships alone. Carden replied that the straits could not be 'rushed', but that they 'might be forced by extended operations with large numbers of ships' (Higgins, 80)—a reply contrary to orthodox naval theory and repeated staff studies. On Churchill's orders he drew up a detailed plan (submitted 11 January), involving the systematic destruction of the fortifications by naval bombardment and a subsequent invasion of the Peninsula, but insufficiently considering crucial questions concerning both the bombardment and minefields. There were strong differences of opinion in the war council when Churchill proposed Carden's plan; but pushed by Churchill, preparations for carrying it out were nevertheless begun, with the concurrence of the French and Russian governments. This diversion of forces was subsequently strongly opposed by Fisher; but approval of the Dardanelles operations was given by the war council on 28 January. Arrangements were made for the assembly of warships, and the 29th division was eventually chosen (10 March) to co-operate with the naval forces.

The first phase of the operations against the Dardanelles, the systematic bombardment of the outer forts, was begun on 19 February with the support of a large Anglo-French force of varied ships under the supreme command of Carden. It became known later in the war that successive bombardments of both the outer and intermediate defences (25 February – 8 March) had proved ineffective as the Turks, warned by the preliminary attacks, had under German guidance greatly strengthened the defences on the Peninsula, besides developing the minefields to an effectiveness exceeding the expectations of British naval officers. The attacks were undertaken under conditions of great controversy, owing to the differences within the war council; and the full responsibility of command rested with Carden, who had failed to prepare adequately for the operations, to use his aircraft efficiently, and to improve his minesweeping. Faced with an admittedly very difficult situation, he failed to rise to the challenge. The strain on an officer who had not been employed at sea for several years and who was nearly sixty years old rapidly undermined his health. He was forced, on 16 March, to relinquish command to one of his flag officers, Rear-Admiral J. M. de Robeck, and return home.

From April until June 1915 Carden was appointed to the Admiralty on special service, and in October 1917, after being on half pay, he retired with the rank of admiral. Though controversy continued about his advice on the practicability of forcing the Dardanelles, he took no part in it.

Carden, who was created KCMG in 1916, was married twice: first, in 1879, to Maria Louisa, daughter of Captain Loftus J. Nunn (99th foot); second, in 1909, to Henrietta, daughter of William English Harrison KC of Hitchin, Hertfordshire, who survived her husband. He had one daughter, by his first marriage. He died on 6 May 1930 at his home, Highfield End, Lymington, Hampshire.

Contemporaries' opinions of Carden differed, but were largely critical. Fisher long distrusted his capabilities; Churchill—though later willing to use Carden to advance his own Dardanelles initiative—wrote in 1914 that Carden had done nothing remarkable; and General W. R. Birdwood, investigating for Kitchener in 1915, considered Carden 'very second-rate', lacking initiative, and over-optimistic. Naval historians have also criticized him. Roskill wrote that he had 'never been up to the heavy responsibility which had fortuitously fallen to his lot' (Roskill, 1.156), while Marder concluded that 'Carden was a charming man and an ideal peacetime admiral, but he had none of the qualities needed for an admiral at war in the technical age' (Marder, 15).

ARCHIBALD HURD, rev. ROGER T. STEARN

Sources J. S. Corbett, *Naval operations*, 1 (1920) · PRO, Admiralty records · *First report of the Dardanelles Commission* (1917–18), col. 8490–419 · A. J. Marder, *From the Dardanelles to Oran: studies of the Royal Navy in war and peace, 1915–1940* (1974) · S. W. Roskill, *Hankey, man of secrets*, 1 (1970) · T. Higgins, *Winston Churchill and the Dardanelles* (1963) · T. Wilson, *The myriad faces of war: Britain and the Great War, 1914–1918* (1986) · *WWW* · *CGPLA Eng. & Wales* (1930)
Archives CAC Cam., papers | PRO, Admiralty records

Likenesses Bassano, photograph, 1915, NPG [*see illus.*] · portrait, repro. in Marder, *From the Dardanelles to Oran*
Wealth at death £2829 7s. 11d.: probate, 23 June 1930, *CGPLA Eng. & Wales*

Carder, Peter (*fl.* **1577–1625**), mariner, is known only from his supposedly self-penned narrative, published by Samuel Purchas in *Purchas his Pilgrimes* in 1625. He was said to be from St Veryan, Cornwall, although the lack of relevant parish registers prevents a verification. According to his narrative, Carder was with the expedition Francis Drake led from England in 1577, bound for the south seas. Drake reached the Pacific with three ships in September 1578, but then encountered fierce storms. One ship foundered, and Drake's *Golden Hind* lost sight of the other, the *Elizabeth* under John Winter, on 8 October near the Strait of Magellan. Carder claimed that he was aboard the *Golden Hind*. After parting with Winter, Drake put Carder and seven companions in an attendant pinnace, but it was soon lost 'by foul weather suddenly arising'. However, Carder and his comrades navigated their way eastwards through the Strait of Magellan, surviving on shellfish and penguins, and reached the Atlantic. They sailed northwards along the coast of South America, but north of the River Plate natives captured or killed six of Carder's companions; the seventh died from drinking too much water after a period of deprivation, and the pinnace was wrecked.

Having reached the mainland, Carder fell in with another group of natives and spent months with them, learning their language and showing them how to make shields and clubs to use alongside their bows and arrows. He even led them to victory over a neighbouring native people. Eventually he reached the Portuguese settlement of Bahia (Brazil), where he was befriended by a merchant, Antonio de Pava. For several years Carder worked for Pava, supervising a plantation and making local voyages, but the governor of Bahia planned to send him a prisoner to Portugal, and he escaped to Pernambuco. Carder then gained passage to Europe. His ship was captured by English privateers, and he finally returned to England at the end of November 1586. He was, he said, received by Elizabeth I, who was particularly interested in Drake's execution of Thomas Doughty.

Although Carder's narrative has sometimes been uncritically reproduced, prudent historians have long regarded it with suspicion. There are no references to Carder in other accounts of Drake's expedition, and Carder's own contains no pertinent details about the enterprise that could not have been taken from material already published by Richard Hakluyt. Furthermore, Drake was careful with the lives of his crews, and it seems most unlikely that he would have set down a small boat, without a compass, in seas which had already cost him two ships. More crucially, it seems inconceivable that the loss of an eight-man pinnace at that time would not have been documented in the principal narratives of the *Golden Hind*. Weighing such matters, Sir John Knox Laughton understandably concluded in a sketch published in 1886 that it was 'probable that there was no such loss to record, and that, from beginning to end, the [Carder] story is a fiction' (*DNB*).

However, Carder's account of Brazil is fuller and fresher than the earlier portions of his narrative, and some of his details of the natives, including their longhouses, personal adornment, cannibalism, and feud with the Portuguese, are consistent with what is known about the Tupinambá people of the Bahia coastal region. The truth appears to be that Carder's account was a partial, rather than a total, fabrication. He was aboard not the *Golden Hind* but the *Elizabeth*. He did travel eastwards through the Strait of Magellan, but on the *Elizabeth* rather than in a pinnace; and although Carder was lost in a small boat, it was off Brazil and not off Chile.

All of this appears from Edward Cliffe's narrative of the homeward voyage of the *Elizabeth*. After separating from Drake, Winter headed for home, passing into the Atlantic in November 1578 and reaching England in June 1579. In December Winter had built a pinnace off the River Plate, and about 20 January 1579 it parted company near St Vincent at lat. 24°S. Cliffe records: 'Here, by reason of foule weather we lost our Pinnesse, and 8 men in her, and never saw them since' (Vaux, 281–2). This was almost certainly a reference to Carder and his seven companions. Given this, Carder's narrative must be regarded as an early example of the exaggerated traveller's tale, a form of literature which has bedevilled historians of exploration. How it came into the possession of Purchas is not known. Purchas may have rescued it from the papers of his predecessor, Richard Hakluyt; more likely he had it from Carder himself, who appears to have been alive at the time of its publication.   JOHN SUGDEN

Sources 'The relation of Peter Carder', in S. Purchas, *Hakluytus posthumus, or, Purchas his pilgrimes*, bk 16, 136–46, Hakluyt Society, extra ser., 29 (1906) · W. S. W. Vaux, ed., *The world encompassed, by Sir Francis Drake* (1854) · E. G. R. Taylor, ed., 'More light on Drake', *Mariner's Mirror*, 16 (1930), 134–51 · *DNB* · J. Hemming, *Red gold: the conquest of the Brazilian indians* (1978) · J. Sugden, *Sir Francis Drake* (1991) · L. E. Pennington, ed., *The Purchas handbook: studies of the life, time and writings of Samuel Purchas*, 2 vols., Hakluyt Society, 2nd ser., 185–6 (1997)

Cardew, (Brian) Cornelius McDonough (1936–1981), composer, was born on 7 May 1936 at 413 The Pottery, Greet, near Winchcombe, Gloucester, the second of three sons of Michael Ambrose *Cardew (1901–1983) and his wife, Mariel Russell. Both his parents worked in the arts and crafts: his mother was an artist and his father was a master potter. After the family moved from Gloucester to Cornwall, Cardew attended the Canterbury Cathedral school, where he had music lessons and sang as a chorister between 1943 and 1950. He entered the Royal Academy of Music, London, in 1953, and studied with Howard Ferguson (composition) and Percy Waller (piano). In 1957 he left the academy, played the guitar in the first British performance of Boulez's *Le marteau sans maître*, and won a scholarship to attend Karlheinz Stockhausen's electronic music studio in Cologne. After impressing Stockhausen with his outstanding musicianship, his abilities as a pianist, and his skills as an improviser, Cardew acted as his assistant between 1958 and 1960, and later collaborated on the composition of *Carré*. He was married, but the name of his wife is not known.

Cardew returned to Britain in 1961. There he organized concerts devoted to experimental music and undertook a course in graphic design, a skill that he practised intermittently until his death. But composition was his passion, and the music that he wrote in the late 1950s already showed talent and potential. While the Second Viennese School influenced some of his early works, the ideas of John Cage and David Tudor dominated his approach from 1959. In *February Pieces* for piano (1959–61), *Autumn '60* (1960), and *Octet '61* (1961), he applied their principles and created material that could be arranged variously by performers. *Treatise* (1963–7) also is an aleatoric work. Influenced by the philosophy of Frege and Wittgenstein, it juxtaposes graphic symbols with some standard music notation, a technique that encouraged some commentators to describe the score as a piece of abstract visual art. In 1964 the Italian government awarded Cardew a bursary to study with Goffredo Petrassi in Rome, and in 1966 he became involved with the free improvisation group AMM. The group's musicians responded freely to each other in performance and developed their ideas according to each other's needs and responses. Along with conventional instruments, which they used in unorthodox ways, they also experimented with portable radios and electronic amplification equipment. Cardew continued to perform with AMM until 1972.

The late 1960s was a busy period for Cardew: in 1966 he was elected a fellow of the Royal Academy of Music; in 1967 he was appointed professor of composition at the academy; between 1966 and 1971 he worked at Morley College, London, teaching experimental music; and in 1968 he composed 'Paragraph 1' of *The Great Learning*. Drawing upon Ezra Pound's translations of Confucius, the work uses a mixture of graphic notation, musical symbols, and verbal instructions. It was performed for the first time at the Cheltenham festival in 1968, and over the next two years Cardew completed six more Paragraphs. As a direct result of his work at Morley College he became a founder member of the Scratch Orchestra in 1969. A confirmed socialist, he applied his political principles when managing and directing the orchestra. The group was an amalgam of professional and amateur musicians whose reputation for innovative programmes spread quickly. It performed extensively in Britain and abroad and was invited to perform the new version of *The Great Learning* at the BBC Promenade Concerts in August 1972.

In 1971 Cardew repudiated *The Great Learning*, arguing that avant-garde music had failed to reach the masses. Influenced by the teachings of Mao Zedong, he began to compose music that was populist and politically didactic. In 1974 he famously attacked Stockhausen in *Stockhausen Serves Imperialism* (1974), and later he was involved in street protests against reactionary politics that culminated in arrest and imprisonment. After a North American tour early in 1975 he became involved with the Progressive Cultural Association, and in 1979 he was a founder member of the Revolutionary Communist Party of Britain. Two years later he composed his last work: *Boolavogue*, for two pianos.

Cardew's apologists have argued that he was a leading figure in late twentieth-century music, and that performers and administrators have largely ignored his works. But recordings of his compositions have been made, and his articles and books are readily available. That said, his works are performed rarely, and he no longer holds the iconic status that he enjoyed during the 1960s and the 1970s; his ideas and music have become an anachronism. He was the product of an age that believed passionately in ideas and their execution. He never compromised his beliefs and, as Kurt Schwertsik noted poignantly in 1982, 'He never tried … to reconcile the demands of "The New" with the desire to change them; he just wasn't concerned to please respected authorities as well as pleasing, and being, himself. He was free.' Cornelius Cardew was the victim of a hit-and-run road accident on 19 December 1981 and was dead on arrival at Whipps Cross Hospital, London.   RAYMOND HOLDEN

Sources S. Bradshaw, 'Cornelius Cardew (1936–1981)', *Tempo*, 140 (March 1982), 22 • C. Cardew and A. Jack, 'Cornelius Cardew', *Music and Musicians* (May 1975), 30–34 • B. Dennis, 'Cardew's *The great learning*', *MT*, 112 (1971), 1066–8 • B. Dennis, 'Cardew's *Treatise*': mainly the visual aspects', *Tempo*, 177 (June 1991), 10–16 • *New Grove* • *New Grove*, 2nd edn, 5 (2001) • C. Hobbs, 'Cardew as teacher', *Perspectives of New Music* (autumn/winter 1981–spring/summer 1982), 2–3 • M. Nyman, 'Cardew's *The great learning*', *London Magazine*, 10/9 (1970–71), 130 • M. Nyman, *Experimental music: Cage and beyond* (1974) • M. Parsons, 'Sounds of discovery', *MT*, 109 (1968), 429–30 • K. Schwertsik, '…for Cornelius Cardew', *Tempo*, 140 (March 1982), 23–4 • H. Skempton, 'A tribute to Cornelius Cardew', *Tempo*, 140 (March 1982), 23 • *Baker's biographical dictionary of musicians*, rev. N. Slonimsky, 8th edn (1992) • J. Tilbury and M. Parsons, 'The contemporary pianist', *MT*, 110 (1969), 150–52 • L. Vought, *All music guide* (2000) • *CGPLA Eng. & Wales* (1984) • d. cert.

Archives FILM BFI NFTVA, 'Cornelius Cardew, 1936–1981', 8 July 1992 | SOUND BL NSA, 'Cornelius Cardew', V1450/03 • BL NSA, documentary recording • BL NSA, oral history interview • BL NSA, performance recordings • BL NSA, 'Towards musical democracy', 15 Feb 1996, H6479/4

Wealth at death £71,980: administration, 9 July 1984, *CGPLA Eng. & Wales*

Cardew, Michael Ambrose (1901–1983), potter, was born on 26 May 1901 at Wimbledon, Surrey, the third son and fourth child in the family of five sons and one daughter of Arthur Cardew, a civil servant, and his wife, Alexandra Rhoda, daughter of George William *Kitchin, dean of Winchester and of Durham. He was educated at King's College School, Wimbledon, and in 1919 obtained a scholarship to Exeter College, Oxford. He obtained a second class in classical honour moderations (1921) and a third class in *literae humaniores* (1923).

From childhood Cardew was surrounded by ceramics, which filled his parents' houses in Wimbledon and at Saunton, north Devon. It was the rural pottery made by Edwin Beer Fishley to which he was deeply attracted and he used to visit him at Fremington. When Fishley died in 1911, Cardew felt a sense of deprivation from which came the realization that if pots of the generous warm nature of Fishley's were to be obtained, he would have to make

Michael Ambrose Cardew (1901–1983), by unknown photographer, 1937

them himself. In the summer of 1921 he persuaded Fishley's grandson to give him lessons in throwing. Few though these were, they confirmed Cardew's love for the craft and precipitated a crisis in his academic work. He was faced with the ultimatum: either to give up potting or to surrender his scholarship. As he had long wanted to study philosophy, Cardew reluctantly agreed to put potting aside. The study of Plato and Aristotle, and the discipline of the school, left their mark. To his innate mental qualities—an alertness and ability to master and express his thoughts in clear and vigorous language—Cardew added a knowledge of method, and 'how to be capable of going on learning'.

In January 1923 he went to St Ives to meet Bernard Leach and Shoji Hamada. Leach has described how 'he strode in, nose and brow straight, handsome as a young Greek god, eyes flashing blue, hair waving gold, and within an hour announced that this was where he wanted to work'. In July he was back. Leach found that his first and best pupil 'possessed a sense of form, the potter's prime gift'. Here he also met Katharine Pleydell-Bouverie, Norah Braden, Tsuranosuke Matsubayashi, and William Staite Murray.

In 1926 Cardew decided that he must be self-supporting and that he wanted to make slipware rather than the stoneware produced by Leach. Through S. Gordon Russell he found the disused pottery at Greet, near Winchcombe in Gloucestershire. Two years later he had confidence in his powers as a thrower, held his first exhibition in London, and was making a monthly average of 350 golden-brown pots. They were cheap and made to be used. The total value of what he made in 1928 was £293 12s. 6d. He was producing the most genuine lead-glazed slipware since the eighteenth century. In 1931 he was awarded the Kokuga prize at the National Artists' Society's annual exhibition in Japan. The section for craftsmen had been established in 1928. Cardew showed a large wide dish, a milk pan, with a combed pattern which demonstrated his fluency in slip trailing. It was filled with sushi after it won the main prize.

Cardew always lived simply, with few material comforts. He loved the music of Handel and Mozart, which he played on clarinet and recorder. In 1933 he married Mary-Ellen (Mariel), the daughter of Baron Russell, journalist and contributor to *Printer's Ink*. They had three sons: Seth, who followed his father as a potter; (Brian) Cornelius McDonough *Cardew (1936–1981), composer; and Ennis, accountant. In 1939 they bought the inn at Wenford Bridge at St Breward in Cornwall, and converted it into a pottery. It remained their home despite long periods of absence and separation. In 1946 he sold the pottery at Winchcombe to Ray Finch, who continued to work there with Sidney Tustin as assistant.

Cardew was appointed pottery instructor at Achimota College in the Gold Coast in 1942 with responsibility for the tileworks at Alajo. Here he began to make stoneware. The years between 1942 and 1945 were not only demanding—they were also unsuccessful to a degree which has subsequently been considered disastrous. Dicon Nance, who worked with him, has maintained that Cardew made endless technical mistakes and that he disregarded practical advice. On the closure of the factory, Cardew decided to move up the River Volta to open a pottery at Vüme Dugamé. Here again he was less than successful because of poor raw materials, disasters in the kilns, and ill health. He still produced pots 'among the most beautiful to come from the hands of any modern potter' aided by Clement Kofi Athey (G. Wingfield-Digby, *The Work of the Modern Potter in England*, 1952).

Cardew returned to Wenford Bridge in 1948. Two years later he was appointed pottery officer for the Nigerian government. He travelled extensively and learned Hausa. From 1952 until 1965 at Abuja, as pottery officer for the department of commerce and industries, he at last achieved success, encouraging such potters as Ladi Kwali, and himself absorbing an understanding of the techniques and decoration of the indigenous culture. He used the incised native styles on stoneware bowls, casseroles, jars, jugs, stools, and teapots, because, as at Winchcombe, his pots were always intended for use.

Cardew retired to Wenford Bridge in 1965, the year in which he was appointed MBE (CBE followed in 1981). He also received an honorary doctorate from the Royal College of Art in 1982. His hard apprenticeship in Ghana, together with his capacity for continuing to learn, bore fruit in his book *Pioneer Pottery* (1969). In addition to scientific analyses, this contains the essence of Cardew's experience and thought, showing him to have been a philosopher as well as a potter. This aspect of his thought was revealed in 1976 when he wrote:

> Ethics is about our duties to our neighbour but aesthetics is about our duty to all the things and creatures of the world we belong to. Our aesthetic conscience is therefore just as tender and just as imperious as the ethical conscience.

Cardew's thoughts were invariably challenging and well expressed, not least in his autobiography A Pioneer Potter (1988), which he had wished to call 'A potter's progress'. It encapsulates his career, his trenchant views, and his clarity in expressing them. That it leaves a number of questions unanswered, questions he might have answered but for his suffering a stroke, may be regretted but for those who wish to read between the lines, inferences can be drawn. Cardew had gifts as a teacher which found expression in the tours and demonstrations which he gave in the USA, Canada, and Australia. While he never taught in a formal sense, he taught many by example. Until his death, in Truro on 11 February 1983, he retained the energy and force of character which found expression in his pots.

A recent account of Cardew remarks that he was 'the exemplary maker of our time. His life as a potter made him alternately fiercely miserable and supremely happy. He asked himself hard questions and drove himself to the limits both physically and spiritually' (Harrod, 401). The film Mud and Water Man (1973) portrayed him 'as an essentially tragic figure, half angry, half humorous, caught between cultures, a man out of time and place' (ibid., 464), and yet at Wenford Bridge, at the end of his life, he was at home and showed himself to be a remarkable combination of his education and his skills, ever articulate, persuasive, one of the great potters of the twentieth century and one whose work has been reassessed and much appreciated since his death. In his autobiography, those who did not know him will meet the honest, invincible, unbroken Cardew. Examples of his pots can be seen in the collections of the University of Wales at Aberystwyth; the Surrey Institute of Art and Design, University College, Farnham; the City Museum and Art Gallery at Stoke-on-Trent; and the York City Art Gallery. He is also represented in the national collections, at the Victoria and Albert Museum, the British Museum, and the university museums at Oxford and Cambridge.   IAN LOWE

Sources M. Cardew, Pioneer pottery (1969) · M. Cardew, A pioneer potter (1988) · G. Clark, Michael Cardew (1978) · M. Cardew and others, Michael Cardew and pupils (1983) [exhibition catalogue, York City Art Gallery, 6 March – 4 April 1983; University College of Wales, Aberystwyth, 16 April – 14 May 1983] · DNB · T. Harrod, The crafts in Britain in the 20th century (1999) · CGPLA Eng. & Wales (1984) · The Times (16 Feb 1983)
Archives Surrey Institute of Art and Design, Farnham, Crafts Study Centre collection and archive, autobiography
Likenesses photograph, 1937, unknown collection; copyprint, NPG [see illus.] · photograph, repro. in The Spectator (31 Oct 1987)
Wealth at death £57,941: probate, 10 Jan 1984, CGPLA Eng. & Wales

Cardew, Philip (1851–1910), army officer and electrical engineer, was born on 24 September 1851 at Oakshade, near Leatherhead, Surrey, the eldest son in a family of four sons and four daughters of Captain Christopher Baldock Cardew, 74th highlanders, of East Hill, Liss (son of Lieutenant-General George Cardew, colonel-commandant Royal Engineers), and his wife, Eliza Jane, second daughter of Richard *Bethell, first Baron Westbury. Educated at Guildford grammar school, he passed first into the Royal Military Academy, Woolwich, in 1868, and left at the head of his batch. He was awarded the Pollock medal and the sword of honour, and commissioned lieutenant in the Royal Engineers on 4 January 1871. After two years at Chatham, he was sent to Aldershot and Portsmouth. From September 1873 to April 1874 he was employed at the War Office on defences, and, after a year at Glasgow, went to Bermuda in May 1875.

Cardew was placed in charge of military telegraphs and joined the Submarine Mining Service, applying electricity to military purposes, which was to be the pursuit of his life. At the end of 1876 he was transferred to Chatham, where the headquarters of the Submarine Mining Service was on board HMS Hood, lying in the Medway off Gillingham. In 1878 he was acting adjutant of the submarine miners at Portsmouth, and became in the same year (1 April) assistant instructor in electricity at Chatham. Cardew married in London, on 19 June 1879, his first cousin, Mary Annunziata, daughter of Mansfield *Parkyns, the traveller in Abyssinia. They had three sons and two daughters, and Mary survived him.

Cardew assisted in important experiments with electric searchlight apparatus for the Royal Engineers committee. The need for better instruments led him to design a galvanometer for measuring large currents of electricity (described in a paper for the Institution of Electrical Engineers, 25 May 1882). He next evolved the idea of the hot-wire galvanometer, or voltmeter, for which he was awarded the gold medal at the inventions exhibition in London of 1885. He also originated a method of finding the efficiency of a dynamo.

Cardew's invention of the vibratory transmitter for telegraphy was perhaps his most important, and in the case of faulty lines it proved useful not only on active service overseas but also during heavy snowstorms at home. He received a money reward for this from the imperial and Indian governments. The utility of the invention was greatly extended by his further invention of 'separators', consisting of a combination of choking coil and two condensers. These instruments enabled a vibrating telegraph circuit to be superimposed on an ordinary Morse circuit without interference between the two, thus doubling the message-carrying capability of the line. His apparatus for testing lightning conductors was adopted by the war department.

Promoted captain on 4 January 1883 and major on 12 April 1889, Cardew was from 1 April 1882 instructor in electricity at Chatham. On 1 April 1889 he was appointed the first electrical adviser to the Board of Trade. He held a long inquiry into the proposals for the electric lighting of London, and drew up regulations on the supply of electricity for power and light.

Cardew retired from the Royal Engineers on 24 October

1894, and from the Board of Trade in 1898. He then entered into partnership with Sir William Preece & Sons, consulting engineers, and was actively engaged on large Admiralty orders, involving an expenditure of £1,500,000. He joined the board of the London, Brighton, and South Coast Railway in 1902, and visited Sydney, New South Wales, in connection with its electrical installations. He published scientific and technical papers, served on the council of the Institution of Electrical Engineers, and was its vice-president in 1901–2. Cardew died on 17 May 1910 at his residence, Crownpits House, Godalming, Surrey, and was buried at Brookwood cemetery on the 21st.

R. H. VETCH, *rev.* JAMES LUNT

Sources Royal Engineers Records · L. Darwin and G. A. Carr, 'Major Philip Cardew', *Royal Engineers Journal*, new ser., 12 (1910), 283–92 · W. Porter, *History of the corps of royal engineers*, 2 vols. (1889) · W. B. Brown, *History of submarine mining in the British Army* (1910) · *The Times* (26 May 1910)
Archives CUL, corresp. with Lord Kelvin
Wealth at death £31,179 15s.: resworn probate, 30 June 1910, *CGPLA Eng. & Wales*

Cardigan. For this title name *see* Brudenell, James Thomas, seventh earl of Cardigan (1797–1868); Lancastre Saldanha, Adeline Louisa Maria de, Countess de Lancastre [Adeline Maria Louisa Brudenell, countess of Cardigan] (1824–1915).

Cardinan family (*per.* **1066–c.1300**), gentry, whose members were lords of Cardinham, Cornwall, was descended from Turold, a follower of Robert, count of Mortain (*d.* 1095), whose son **Richard fitz Turold** (*d.* before 1123) continued as a member of the Mortain household until the downfall of Count William in 1106. In 1086 he was holding twenty-eight manors in Cornwall and one in Devon of Count Robert, together with three Devon manors in chief, all of which his father had no doubt received shortly after 1066. Before his death, by 1123, Richard had founded on his manor of Tywardreath, Cornwall, a Benedictine priory dependent on the abbey of St Sergius and St Bacchus at Angers in France.

Richard's son, **William fitz Richard** (*d.* before 1149), had succeeded to the family estates by 1123, when, in the company of other prominent west country landholders, he witnessed Henry I's charter in favour of Exeter Cathedral. At the beginning of Stephen's reign (according to the author of the *Gesta Stephani*), he swore allegiance to the new king and in return, as the most influential landholder in Cornwall, was given custody of the royal castle of Launceston and a general responsibility for administering the county. However, in 1140, following the Angevin invasion of England, he broke faith with the king and admitted into the castle Reginald (*d.* 1175), one of Henry I's illegitimate sons and a leading partisan of the Empress Matilda. He also gave him his daughter in marriage and effectively handed over control of the county to him. Although King Stephen attempted to reverse this arrangement, Reginald's creation as earl of Cornwall later in the year confirmed his ascendancy in the county. William fitz Richard became his vassal, thereafter holding his fief of

the earl for the service of fifty-one knights. On his granting of land at Goodmansleigh, Devon, to Launceston Priory, William duly described Earl Reginald as his lord and friend. He also made grants to his father's foundation at Tywardreath.

William's successor, by 1149, was his son with his wife, Annora, **Robert fitz William** (*d. c.*1175). He was a generous benefactor of both Tywardreath and Launceston priories, like his father, acknowledging Earl Reginald's lordship. He married Agnes, supposedly the daughter but more likely the widow of Walter Hay, lord of nearby Bodardle, Cornwall, whereby he acquired control of the eighteen manors held of the count of Mortain in 1086 by Walter's predecessor, Thurstan the Sheriff. These are duly recorded in Robert's tenure in 1166, liable to the service of twenty knights. Agnes lived on until at least 1186, making grants from her Bodardle lands to Wilton Priory. About 1540 John Leland recorded Robert fitz William's tomb still in existence at Tywardreath.

Robert's son **Robert fitz Robert** (*fl.* 1175–1180), a tenant-in-chief since the death of Earl Reginald in 1175, first occurs on the pipe roll of 1176/7 and, about 1180, granted land and his mill at Cardinham to the church of St Mary there. **Robert of Cardinan** (*d. c.*1227) must have been his son for, in a charter in favour of Launceston Priory, dating from the period *c.*1190–1200, he describes Robert fitz William as his grandfather. In 1193/4 he obtained from the king the right to hold a market at Lostwithiel, Cornwall, adjoining Bodardle and his castle of Restormel. This was doubtless contemporary with his charter confirming the vill's borough status. Robert's career was unspectacular, though he maintained the family's role as principal patron of Tywardreath Priory: in particular, about 1200 he gave the rent of his mill at Bodiggo, in Luxulian, Cornwall, for the soul of his first wife, Isabell. In addition he made grants to the priories of Launceston and St Michael's Mount, and also to Lammana, Cornwall, a cell dependent on Glastonbury Abbey. During King John's reign there is some indication of royal favour and in the years leading up to the political crisis of 1215–16 Robert of Cardinan maintained his allegiance to the king, being granted custody of the county of Cornwall in May 1215. Soon after Henry III's succession he lost this position to Earl Reginald's illegitimate son, Henry fitz Count (*d.* 1222). However, he served as a royal justice on the south-western circuit in 1218–19 and, on Henry fitz Count's surrender of the county in 1220, was reappointed sheriff for a short period. He died about 1227, survived by his second wife, Emma.

Robert of Cardinan's eldest son was probably the Robert de Cardinan who is recorded as serving in King John's army in the period 1213–16. However, he must be presumed to have died childless within his father's lifetime, for Robert senior's heir was another son, **Andrew of Cardinan** (*d. c.*1253). Although, with estates now owing the service of seventy-one knights, he was one of the foremost barons of Cornwall, Andrew played little part in national affairs. This may in some measure be due to the grant of the county of Cornwall to the king's brother,

Richard (d. 1272), whereby, at least from 1242–3, the Cardinan family once again became vassals of the earls of the county. Andrew was survived by his wife, Ela: her obit was said at Tywardreath on 3 September and his on 19 September.

Andrew had no son to succeed him and his estates therefore passed to his daughter, **Isolda de Tracy** (d. in or after 1301), who married first Thomas de Tracy (d. 1263x70). During her widowhood her honour was dismantled. In 1268 the town of Lostwithiel and the castle at Restormel were acquired by Richard, earl of Cornwall, and the following year she sold the manors of Bodardle and Cardinham to Oliver de Dinham, lord of Hartland. At about the same time, she conveyed Tywardreath and Ludgvan to Henry de Campernulf and by 1275 there is evidence of further alienations. Her second husband was William de Ferrers, and she was still alive in 1301.

The Cardinan estates lay almost exclusively in Cornwall and the family, though an important one within the county, had little influence outside it. Its fortunes were also closely linked to the interests of successive earls of Cornwall, to whose lordship it was periodically subject. When the male line failed, it proved impossible to keep the honour intact in the face of the ambitions of more powerful families.   ROBERT BEARMAN

Sources Pipe rolls · Chancery records · G. Oliver, *Monasticon diocesis Exoniensis* (1846) · A. Farley, ed., *Domesday Book*, 2 vols. (1783) · P. L. Hull, ed., *The cartulary of Launceston Priory (Lambeth Palace MS. 719): a calendar*, Devon and Cornwall RS, new ser., 30 (1987) · J. H. Rowe, ed., *Cornwall feet of fines*, 2 vols., Devon and Cornwall RS, old ser., 8 (1914–50) · I. J. Sanders, *English baronies: a study of their origin and descent, 1086–1327* (1960) · [W. Illingworth], ed., *Rotuli hundredorum temp. Hen. III et Edw. I*, 2 vols., RC (1812–18) · J. H. Round, ed., *Calendar of documents preserved in France, illustrative of the history of Great Britain and Ireland* (1899) · M. Beresford, *New towns of the middle ages* (1967) · P. L. Hull, ed., *The cartulary of St Michael's Mount*, Devon and Cornwall RS, new ser., 5 (1962) · *The itinerary of John Leland in or about the years 1535–1543*, ed. L. Toulmin Smith, 11 pts in 5 vols. (1906–10)

Cardinan, Andrew of (d. c.1253). *See under* Cardinan family (*per.* 1066–c.1300).

Cardinan, Robert of (d. c.1227). *See under* Cardinan family (*per.* 1066–c.1300).

Cardmaker, John (c.1496–1555), clergyman and protestant martyr, was born at Exeter. Nothing is known of his parents and all that is recorded of his early years is that he was admitted to the Franciscan order under age. After sixteen years' study at Cambridge and Oxford he supplicated the latter university for the degree of BTh in December 1532; he received the degree in the following year. By 1534 he was the warden of the Franciscans in Exeter. After hearing Hugh Latimer preach in Exeter in 1534 Cardmaker was converted to the reformed religion. In January 1536 he received from Thomas Cromwell a vice-gerential licence to preach. In April of that year Cardmaker was assigned by John Hilsey, bishop of Rochester, to preach to the Crutched Friars in London, after the authorities had been informed that the friars were denying the royal supremacy. Cardmaker left the Franciscans in 1537 and subsequently married Katherine Testwood, a widow, thereby sealing his allegiance to the reformed cause.

From 1537 Cardmaker was awarded several scattered benefices while preaching in the London area. In one sermon, preached at St Bride's, Fleet Street, in 1540, Cardmaker asserted it was 'as profitable to heare Mass and see the Sacrament, as to kiss Judas mouth' (J. Foxe, *Actes and Monuments*, 1570, 1379). Despite, or because of, the uncompromising protestantism of this sermon, Cardmaker became vicar of St Bride's in 1543. In 1546 he was interrogated by the privy council as an associate and supporter of the evangelical preacher Edward Crome, whose sermons attacking transubstantiation had created a furore that spring. During Edward VI's reign Cardmaker was one of the leading protestant preachers in London and a lecturer at St Paul's. He continuously attacked transubstantiation and the conservative clergy, even during the dark days of Somerset's fall from power. In 1550, however, he was made prebendary and chancellor of Wells; settled in Wells and took an active role in preaching in the diocese.

Mary's accession proved disastrous for Cardmaker. On 18 April 1554 he was deprived of his livings, and in May 1554 he and his bishop, William Barlow, were arrested, and then released on bonds of £200 each. In November 1554 Barlow and Cardmaker went to London disguised as merchants and vainly attempted to escape to the continent. They were arrested and imprisoned in the Fleet, where they remained until the end of January 1555, when they were examined at St Mary Overie by a commission headed by Stephen Gardiner, the lord chancellor. Barlow submitted and later fled overseas. Cardmaker also submitted, and was remanded to the Compter in Bread Street, to await release upon formally subscribing to articles of the Catholic faith. But according to an account sent before 1559 to the martyrologist John Foxe by a well-informed protestant, Cardmaker's zeal was rekindled by a fellow prisoner, the martyr Laurence Saunders. Strenuous but unsuccessful efforts were made to win Cardmaker back to the Catholic fold, especially by Thomas Martin. Cardmaker was brought before Edmund Bonner, bishop of London, on 25 May 1555, and was condemned as a relapsed heretic. He was burnt at Smithfield, London, on 30 May 1555, along with John Warne, an upholsterer. Two spectators of the execution, namely Foxe's informant and the Venetian ambassador, described the crowd's vociferous sympathy for the condemned men.

THOMAS S. FREEMAN

Sources BL, Harley MS 425, fols. 67r–68v · J. Foxe, *Rerum in ecclesia gestarum* (1559) · J. Foxe, *Actes and monuments* (1563) · J. Foxe, *The second volume of the ecclesiasticall history, conteyning the acts and monuments of martyrs*, 2nd edn (1570) · BL, Harley MS 421, fol. 39v · Exeter city muniments, MS book 51, fol. 342r (*sub anno* 1533) · *CSP Venice, 1555–6*, 94 · J. G. Nichols, ed., *The chronicle of the grey friars of London*, CS, 53 (1852) · *CSP dom., 1547–80*, 846, 848, 850 · *The diary of Henry Machyn, citizen and merchant-taylor of London, from AD 1550 to AD 1563*, ed. J. G. Nichols, CS, 42 (1848) · *APC, 1554–6*, 20 · Emden, *Oxf.*, 4.101 ·

Fasti Angl., 1541–1857, [Bath and Wells], 12, 36, 105 • *LP Henry VIII*, 10, no. 346 • BL, Add. MS 48022, fol. 88
Archives BL, Foxe MSS • Exeter city muniments, Exeter
Likenesses woodcut, NPG; repro. in Foxe, *Actes and monuments*

Cardon, Anthony (1772–1813), engraver and print publisher, was born in Brussels on 15 May 1772, the son of Antoine Alexandre Joseph Cardon (1739–1822), a Flemish painter and engraver. He moved to London during the troubles in the Low Countries in 1792 and entered the Royal Academy Schools on 3 November of that year. His first recorded employment was to engrave, in 1794–6, under the direction of Luigi Schiavonetti, three of the successful series *Cries of London* (published by Colnaghi & Co.), after Francis Wheatley. Cardon was an enterprising and hard-working man, and established himself in Marylebone as a successful engraver and as an independent print publisher, from 1802 to 1808, at 31 Clipstone Street. He worked mainly in stipple engraving and became one of the leading exponents of this medium, signing his prints A. Cardon, or Anthy. Cardon, or occasionally with his full name. He engraved many portraits, including some later published in the *British Gallery of Contemporary Portraits* (2 vols., 1822), issued by Thomas Cadell the younger. He also frequently produced engravings of Richard Cosway's delicate portrait drawings. He engraved illustrations and vignettes for various publications, including 'The Progress of Female Virtue', after drawings by Maria Cosway, published by Rudolph Ackermann in 1800.

Cardon also produced historical engravings. In fact his most lucrative works were the engravings *Battle of Alexandria* and *Battle of Maidan*, after Philippe Jacques de Loutherbourg, which he published himself. Selling prints from these plates clearly brought him income throughout his life, since he advised in his will that they should not be sold with the rest of his printmaking equipment and plates but kept by his widow, so that prints could continue to be issued on demand. Cardon was known to Joseph Farington, who noted the former's purchase of these two paintings for engraving in his diary (4 March 1805). Cardon won a gold medal in 1807 at the Society of Arts for his engraving *Battle of Alexandria*. He frequently worked with Luigi and Niccolo Schiavonetti, the successful and famous engravers and print publishers, and owned jointly with them four large plates of the enormous panoramic history painting *The Storming of Seringapatam*, after Robert Ker Porter. He engraved and published a memorial portrait of Luigi Schiavonetti, after Henry Edridge, on Luigi's death in 1810.

Cardon married Bethania Graves on 10 February 1798; the couple had five daughters, baptized between 1799 and 1811. Cardon is said also to have had a son, **Philip Cardon** (d. c.1817), trained as an engraver, whose date of birth is unrecorded. Anthony Cardon produced a large volume of work in his lifetime and is reputed to have died as a result of overwork, at his home, London Street, Fitzroy Square.

W. C. MONKHOUSE, *rev.* RUTH COHEN

Sources D. Alexander, 'Cardon, Anthony', *The dictionary of art*, ed. J. Turner (1996) • *Engraved Brit. ports.*, vol. 6 • Thieme & Becker, *Allgemeines Lexikon*, 5.381 • Farington, *Diary*, 7.2528, 2681 • *GM*, 1st ser., 78 (1808), 323 • *GM*, 1st ser., 86/1 (1816), 62 • *GM*, 1st ser., 83/1 (1813), 119, 290 • [W. Holden], *Holden's triennial directory* (1802) • [W. Holden], *Holden's triennial directory for 1805, 1806, 1807, including the year 1808*, 2 vols. (1805–7) • Redgrave, *Artists*, 70 • parish register, St Marylebone, 10 Feb 1798, marriage • will, PRO, PROB 11/1544, fol. 174
Likenesses A. Freschi, stipple, 1815 (after A. W. Devis), BM, NPG

Cardon, Philip (d. c.1817). *See under* Cardon, Anthony (1772–1813).

Cardonnel, Adam de (1663–1719), administrator, was born in October 1663 in Southampton, and baptized there on 1 November, the second son of Adam de Cardonnel (1620–1710), a prominent citizen of French Huguenot stock, originally of Caen, and Marie, daughter of Nicholas Pescod. His father became a denizen of Southampton in 1641, was naturalized in 1656, and was rewarded at the Restoration, apparently for services to the crown, by the lucrative patents of customer and collector of customs at the port of Southampton, where his heraldic device on the Bargate shows his importance. He was an elder of the French church and one of a group of Huguenots involved, after 1685, in the important local enterprise of paper making. His influence can be seen in the early posting of his son Adam to the War Office. Nothing is known of Adam's early years or education but at the War Office he rose to be chief clerk, and in February 1693 was appointed secretary and treasurer to the commissioners for sick and wounded seamen. Initially his career developed along with England's increased involvement in continental war, but it came to be increasingly linked with that of John Churchill, earl of Marlborough. He was certainly acting as Marlborough's secretary in the early part of 1692 when the general, implicated allegedly in a Jacobite plot, needed a reliable and disinterested aide. Thenceforward Cardonnel accompanied Marlborough on his campaigns, receiving 10s. a day as his secretary.

His grasp of military administration, knowledge of French, and sympathy for the position of the many Huguenot officers who brought professionalism to the English army, all commended Cardonnel to Marlborough. He was of undoubted importance in the military hierarchy. His comments from one crucial campaign throw light on its brutal and hazardous nature. Commenting on 'the burning and destroying the Elector's country' (7 August 1704) he added: 'Our last march was all in fire and smoke … I wish to God it were well over that I might get safe out of this country' (*Bath MSS*, 3.433). Cardonnel wrote of the battle of Blenheim (13 August 1704) that the duke 'knew the necessity of battle better than any of us, for I believe that if the majority of us prevailed, we should not have been for it under our circumstances' (Trevelyan, *Select Documents*, 111). Marlborough's role in the War of the Spanish Succession required diplomatic skills. Cardonnel was the only civilian selected by Marlborough to accompany him in his crucial visit, in April 1707, to Charles XII, and when Cardonnel fell ill Marlborough wrote that his death 'would give me very great trouble, for all the business I have with the foraine courts goes thorow his hands'

(Churchill, 2.678). The tracks of the perfect secretary, discreet, loyal, and self-effacing, are hard to trace, but Marlborough valued Cardonnel sufficiently, as friend and ally, to seek high office for him. He obtained from Queen Anne a promise that Cardonnel should succeed Walpole as secretary at war. In that role Walpole had corresponded directly with Cardonnel on a wide range of military and political matters and the appointment would have been suitable in terms of experience but it fell victim to party crossfire and the duke's diminishing political prestige. Cardonnel was nominated in January 1710, but Walpole was replaced in that year by George Granville, afterwards Lord Lansdowne, the nominee of Robert Harley, the tory leader.

Harley's election victory in October 1710 was the prelude to Cardonnel's and Marlborough's downfall. A committee was appointed to examine the public accounts, and its report was called for in November 1711 and published in January 1712. Sir Solomon de Medina, a bread contractor to the army, stated in evidence that he had given, on sealing each contract, a gratuity of 500 gold ducats to Cardonnel. On 19 February 1712 the house met to consider the charge and to hear Cardonnel's defence (of which no report has survived). After prolonged debate it was resolved that the taking of a gratuity was 'unwarrantable and corrupt'. Cardonnel, who had served in parliament as member for Southampton since 1701, was expelled from the house by a majority of twenty-six. Yet few would have regarded his offence as unusual or serious; he was a pawn in a larger political game.

Meanwhile Cardonnel had married on 26 November 1711 Elizabeth, widow of Isaac Teale, apothecary-general of the army, of St Margaret's, Westminster. They had no children and she died in 1713. After 1714 he married Elizabeth (d. 1737), widow of William Frankland and daughter of René Baudowin, a London merchant. There were two children of this marriage: Adam died at Chiswick in September 1725; Mary married in February 1634 William, first Earl Talbot, bringing him, it is said, a fortune of £80,000. After his disgrace Cardonnel did not seek further parliamentary office, but he remained Marlborough's loyal secretary and lived out his years at his houses in Westminster and Chiswick. He died at St Margaret's, Westminster, on 22 February 1719 and was buried on 3 March at the parish church of Chiswick. His widow later married Frederick Frankland MP, her first husband's younger brother; she died on 27 January 1737. Cardonnel's official correspondence with George Stepney, minister at Vienna and Brussels, has survived but contains little of interest. It is his long, devoted service to Marlborough that has secured his niche in history.

Cardonnel's uncle **Philip de Cardonnel** (d. in or before 1667), poet, is of unknown parents. Nothing is known of his education or early life, but from his later writings he was presumably an enthusiastic royalist during the civil war and interregnum. On the marriage of Charles II in May 1662 to Catherine of Braganza he expressed his feelings in a series of Latin poems, whose heaviness is suggested by the title: *Tagus, sive, Epithalamium Caroli II Magnae Britanniae regis, et Catherinae infantis Portugalliae; Gallico primum carmine decantatum, deindè Latino donatum. Authore P.D.C. unà cum poëmate Fortunatarum Insularum, antehàc Gallicè pro inauguratione Caroli II conscripto*. It would appear that an enlarged edition appeared in London the same year, and both editions are as rare as the material is esoteric. The earlier has a frontispiece representing Catherine being drawn to shore by Neptune and nymphs, while Charles II, ankle deep, surveys her charms through a telescope. Cardonnel was dead before the middle of August 1667, for on the 15th of that month his widow, Catherine, administered to the estate of his brother, Peter de Cardonnel, of St Margaret's, Westminster.

GEOFFREY TREASURE

Sources W. S. Churchill, *Marlborough, his life and times*, 4 vols. (1933–8) · D. Chandler, *Marlborough as military commander* (1973) · G. M. Trevelyan, *England under Queen Anne*, 3 vols. (1930–34) · R. D. Gwynn, *Huguenot heritage* (1985) · examinations and depositions, Southampton Record Society · E. Welch, ed., *Minute book of French church at Southampton*, Southampton records ser., 23 (1979) · Huguenot Society Proceedings, quarto vol. 4, Southampton Register · *Calendar of the manuscripts of the marquis of Bath preserved at Longleat, Wiltshire*, 5 vols., HMC, 58 (1904–80), vol. 3 [Prior papers] · *JHC*, 17 (1711–14), 97 · *DNB* · G. M. Trevelyan, ed., *Select documents for Queen Anne's reign down to the union with Scotland, 1702–7* (1929) · G. A. Jacobsen, *William Blathwayt: a late seventeenth century English administrator* (1932) · P. Watson and S. M. Wynne, 'Cardonnel, Adam de', HoP, *Commons, 1690–1715*, 3.458–63

Archives BL, corresp., Add. MSS 7063–7079, 38695–38710 *passim* · BL, corresp. and papers of Cardonnel and Marlborough, Add. MSS 70938–70946 | BL, letters to John Ellis, Add. MSS 28917–28918 · BL, letters to Jean Robethon, Stowe MSS 222–224, *passim* · BL, corresp. with George Stepney, Add. MS 61412 · BL, letters to Horatio Walpole, Add. MSS 38500–38501 · BL, letters to Henry Watkins, Add. MS 42176 · BL, corresp. with Charles Whitworth, Add. MSS 37351–37362, *passim* · Bodl. Oxf., corresp. with Lord North · CAC Cam., corresp. with Thomas Erle · Harvard U., Houghton L., corresp. with George Stepney · Hunt. L., corresp. with duke of Chandos · NRA, priv. coll., corresp. with Lord Cutts

Cardonnel, Adam. *See* Lawson, Adam Mansfeldt de Cardonnel- (1746/7–1820).

Cardonnel, Philip de (d. in or before **1667**). *See under* Cardonnel, Adam de (1663–1719).

Cardross. For this title name *see* Erskine, David, second Lord Cardross (*bap.* 1627, *d.* 1671); Erskine, Henry, third Lord Cardross (1650–1693).

Cardus, Sir (John Frederick) Neville (1888–1975), writer on cricket and music critic, was born on 3 April 1888 at 4 Summer Place, Rusholme, Manchester, the illegitimate child of Ada Cardus (1870–1954). His forenames were registered as John Frederick. His father may have been John Frederick Newsham (*b.* 1867), whom the seventeen-year-old Ada married three months later, on 14 July 1888. The marriage, however, did not last long, and the description of Newsham as a 'smith' hardly fitted Cardus's own comment that his father may have been 'one of the first violins in an orchestra' (Cardus, *Autobiography*, 15). The boy lived with his maternal grandparents. Robert Cardus, his grandfather, had a policeman's pension, Ann Cardus took in washing, and the household finances were augmented through the activities of Ada (who briefly returned home) and her sister Beatrice as prostitutes.

Yet the home was not quite the slum Cardus suggested and, even for the poor, the community of Rusholme, in late nineteenth-century Manchester, offered cultural expression in its cosmopolitan nature, free libraries, and music-halls. The young Cardus took what he could from his working-class background, learning to read and write at the board school in Rusholme, using the libraries and his grandfather's *Manchester Guardian*, and getting his taste for music as a chocolate seller in the Comedy Theatre. Variously, he had delivered his grandmother's washing, boiled type in a printer's business, and driven a carpenter's handcart before, in 1904, he had become a clerk in an insurance agency with the Fleming brothers, benevolent employers who encouraged him in his self-education and would let him off to watch cricket at Old Trafford. This was the time when he acquired his deep affection for Lancashire cricket and for the game's 'golden age'. He remained indebted to the Flemings, who for eight years (1904–12) 'stood between me and destitution' (Cardus, *Autobiography*, 41).

Great literature, especially Dickens, and philosophy had their place in Cardus's grandiose pursuit of culture, but it was music which mattered most. He attended concerts at the Free Trade Hall and heard the first performance of Elgar's first symphony on 3 December 1908. He saw Sir Thomas Beecham conduct *Madama Butterfly*, and his own first musical criticism, 'Bantock and style', appeared in the monthly *Musical Opinion* in 1912.

Yet in music, unlike cricket, Cardus was no performer (though he briefly took singing lessons) and it was his cricket in that same year (1912) which gave him his first opportunity. On the strength of his figures as an off-break bowler in Manchester league cricket, he successfully applied for the post of assistant cricket coach at Shrewsbury School. When war broke out in 1914, he volunteered for service but his poor eyesight brought rejection. The headmaster, C. A. Alington, was aware of his unusual interests—he had spotted him reading Euripides in translation—and appointed him as his secretary. The idyll of Cardus's four years at Shrewsbury—'because of Alington, I call myself an Old Salopian' (Cardus, *Autobiography*, 81)— ended when Alington went to Eton. He was willing to take his secretary, but only if he could be assured that Cardus would not be conscripted.

C. P. Scott, editor of the *Manchester Guardian*, took the persistent 28-year-old into his office—just as Alington had done—as a secretary. By 1917 Cardus was learning the all-round trade of reporting and briefly writing on drama and music. Two years later he reported his first cricket match. Throughout the inter-war period readers of the 'M. G.' would be avid followers of N. C. on music and Cricketer on cricket.

Security (although all his life he was fearful of being poor again) allowed Cardus to marry, on 17 June 1921, Edith Honorine Watton King (1887/8–1968), a schoolmistress, daughter of John Thomas Sissons King, schoolmaster. He gave his father's name (perhaps for respectability) as Frederick Cardus. There were no children. At about this time Cardus, who had always been known as Fred, adopted the name Neville, which alone appeared on his marriage certificate. His twin interests, at their lowest, now ensured 'a balance at the bank' (Cardus, *Second Innings*, 87).

Cricket, even more than music, provided the medium through which Cardus could display his treasure house of literary knowledge and satisfy his aesthetic appreciation of grace and movement. Neither his account of his marriage nor that shortly afterwards, of his one great scoop— A. C. MacLaren's eleven beating the 1921 all-conquering Australians, with Cardus the only major journalist present—stands microscopic examination. Both show his abilities in embellishing the non-essentials to make a well-told tale.

Cardus was essentially a writer with a talent for handling words, presenting balanced and harmonious prose, and drawing on his deep reservoir of reading. Above all, he wrote for others' enjoyment because he enjoyed writing. Cricket and music were the chosen media through which he expressed himself. The one gave him the greater fame, the other the greater satisfaction. In his approach to both he sought to understand the emotions which lay behind the technical performances. He was a romantic in the sense that he paid more attention to the spirit and beauty of what he saw and heard than to the mechanics of endeavour and achievement.

In his cricket writing Cardus was an innovator. On what had been, in earlier hands, a descriptive and narrative enterprise, he imposed criticism. To the sights and sounds of the game he brought his own use of imagery, metaphor, and allusion, with which he created a mythology of characters and scenes. But elegance and wit redeemed him from pomposity.

Cricketers took on the guise of characters: Macartney, Figaro; MacLaren, Don Quixote; Spooner's batting matched the poetry of Herrick. Yet none of this imagery gainsaid Cardus's ability to analyse. Of Wilfred Rhodes he wrote: 'Flight was his secret, flight and the curving line, now higher, now lower, tempting, inimical … every ball a decoy and one of them—ah, which?—the master ball' (Cardus, *Autobiography*, 158).

In commercial terms Cardus was an immediate success. He doubled the summer sales of the *Manchester Guardian* and, as early as 1922, a publisher had given permanency to his reports in *A Cricketer's Book*. There followed *Days in the Sun* (1924), *The Summer Game* (1929), *Good Days* (1934), and *Australian Summer* (1937). All were distillations of his 9000 words a week. In the twenty years between the wars he wrote some 2 million of them, even submitting 1200 words on an August bank holiday totally rained off.

In 1927 Cardus succeeded Samuel Longford, as the chief music critic of the *M. G.* so holding two of the paper's major portfolios. As with cricket, he got to know the performers, notably Beecham and (later) Sir John Barbirolli. Cricket was for watching: Cardus cultivated the art of listening and the ability to interpret for his readers what he heard. The fame he had quickly acquired as a cricket writer came more slowly as a music critic. Even when he had made his name, year by year, with some 4000 words a week, from two or three concerts, he remained aware that a musical error of fact might bring two dozen letters of protest; a cricket one, possibly a thousand. Others, such as his friend and rival Ernest Newman, were already established. What made him different was his total independence of judgement. He could be out of step with his contemporaries and sometimes ahead of them. He wrote intuitively, conveying his own aesthetic delight and putting an essential truth into a telling phrase; Sibelius, for example, composed 'mainly in nouns and verbs with eloquent dashes of silence' (obituary, *Guardian*). As in much else in his life, he was 'his own man', as J. B. Priestley called him (ibid.).

Cardus was ready to champion little-known composers such as Gustav Mahler and Anton Bruckner—both of them in the central European tradition in which he delighted. Pursuit of that tradition took him to Salzburg, whose festivals provided some of his finest moments. Arturo Toscanini conducting the opera *Die Meistersinger* there in 1936 would 'remain in the mind for a lifetime because of its beauty and dignity. The banner of song opened with a width and nobility that caused happiness and sadness. Toscanini held us like children' (Brookes, 152). Perhaps in the end the danger, in both cricket and music, was that readers came to appreciate the words more than the deeds they portrayed. Yet there were no concessions to the faint-hearted and *M. G.* readers had to keep up with him. This approach would later cause problems for him in Australia.

In the early years of Cardus's work, Manchester and the Hallé Orchestra were central to his writing, though some adverse notices in the 1930s during the depression, when audiences fell, caused economic concern to performers. London came to make greater claims on him, while the outbreak of the Second World War in 1939 brought an end to his work as both cricket and music critic for the *Manchester Guardian*. In 1940 he took himself off to Australia (and there were critics of his decision) to work for the *Sydney Morning Herald*.

At first Cardus enraged his readership by the savagery of his attacks. What he viewed as a genuine attempt to raise standards was seen as arrogant and insensitive. Once he had mentally accepted that Sydney was not Salzburg he struck a balance. By 1942 his writing was acceptable and understood, while he made a major cultural impact on Australia with his Sunday evening broadcasts called *Enjoyment of Music* and a similar midweek programme for children. With fewer demands on his time and living, at first, a somewhat solitary life in Sydney, he found time to write his *Ten Composers* and *Autobiography*.

Then, in a period of uncertainty, Cardus travelled between Australia and England five times in two years before finally settling in England in 1949, for the rest of his life. Yet a post-war England was alien to him and he was conscious he had not shared its hardships: 'My exile in Australia had disqualified me' (Cardus, *Full Score*, 194).

After some false starts, notably with Beaverbrook's *Evening Standard* in 1948, he returned (1950) to the *Manchester Guardian* as its London music critic, where he wrote 'Music surveys', introducing readers to the music they might be going to hear or at least might read about later. Many of the themes remained endemic to his pre-war interests in the classical tradition, with little concession to modernism. Mahler found an undue place, as a prelude to the analytical study *Gustav Mahler: his Mind and his Music*, which he published in 1965.

Another volume of autobiography, *Second Innings* (1950), was followed by a third, *Full Score* (1970), when Cardus was over eighty. Several of his earlier cricket books were reprinted. He also wrote a biography of Beecham (1961) and edited a memoir on Kathleen Ferrier (1971). His devotion to the singer was so profound that some critics suggested that it precluded his objective judgement of her talent. With Beecham his relationship had had its ups and downs but the book allowed him to dwell on a past in which he more and more took comfort.

Cardus made few forays into the post-war cricket world, although he reported two MCC tours to Australia in the 1950s and the 'Ashes' series in England in 1953. *Wisden Cricketers' Almanack* claimed him for an article virtually every year. He took great pleasure in being elected president of Lancashire County Cricket Club in 1970–71. Other honours had already come his way. He had been appointed CBE in 1964 and became, in 1967, the first music critic to be knighted. In 1972 he was elected an honorary member of the Royal Academy of Music.

The death of Cardus's wife in 1968 ended a marriage which had lasted nearly fifty years. The couple had seldom lived in the same house and both valued the independence which their separate lives gave them. Yet the friendship—it was scarcely intimacy—was sustained by their meals together, letters, and phone calls. After her death he stopped living in his club (the National Liberal) and moved into her flat. Cardus enjoyed the company of ladies and retained to the end of his life an old-world gallantry. He was a gregarious man, with a close circle of friends of both sexes. Good food and wine, talking, and membership of several London clubs were aspects of his lifestyle.

In his final years Cardus still wrote, though the way *The Guardian* handled his copy from the Edinburgh festival in 1969 upset him. The days of expansionist writing, untouched by sub-editors, were long since past and his association with the paper of his heyday diminished in happiness at the end. It was an opinion he expressed in Robin Daniels's *Conversations with Cardus* (1976).

Sir Neville Cardus died at the Nuffield Clinic, London, on 28 February 1975 and was cremated at Golders Green crematorium. Despite living to almost eighty-seven, he had changed relatively little from the lean, ascetic figure of moderate height, with sharp features, sleek hair, and strong glasses. The tributes to him as a writer were generous. Intellectually, music had been his first string but cricket had been his passport to fulfilment. And in cricket, if not in music, he had changed the course of reporting. He would have his imitators and parodists, and no serious cricket writer would remain unaffected by him. His last entry in *Who's Who* (1975) showed something of his enigmatic approach to life: 'Recreations: anything not in the form of a game'.

GERALD M. D. HOWAT

Sources C. Brookes, *His own man: the life of Neville Cardus* (1985) · N. Cardus, *Autobiography* (1947) · N. Cardus, *Second innings* (1950) · N. Cardus, *Full score* (1970) · *Wisden* (1965) · A. Lamb, 'The truth about Cardus', *Wisden* (Dec 1985) · D. Ayerst, *Guardian: biography of a newspaper* (1971) · *The Times* (1 March 1975) · *The Guardian* (1 March 1975) · b. cert. · m. cert. · Grove, *Dict. mus.*

Archives Lancashire county cricket club, Old Trafford, Manchester · U. Reading L., corresp. and literary papers | JRL, Manchester Guardian archives, letters to the *Manchester Guardian* · U. Leeds, Brotherton L., letters to Thomas Moult | SOUND BBC WAC · BL NSA, 'Fairest isle: a passion for playing', 1995, H618813 · BL NSA, documentary recordings · BL NSA, performance recordings · BL NSA, sports recordings · Sydney, ABC, support archives, 1940s

Likenesses photograph (in later life), repro. in *Wisden* (1965) · photograph (in later life), repro. in *Wisden* (1976) · photograph, repro. in Brookes, *His own man*

Wealth at death £12,559: probate, 6 May 1975, *CGPLA Eng. & Wales*

Cardwell, Edward (1787–1861), ecclesiastical historian, was the youngest of the five sons of Richard Cardwell of Blackburn, Lancashire, and his wife, Jane, daughter of John and Margaret Hodson of Wigan. He was born in Standishgate, Wigan, on 3 August 1787 and entered Brasenose College, Oxford, in 1806, where he graduated BA in 1809, MA in 1812, BD in 1819, and DD in 1831. For several years he acted as tutor and lecturer, from 1814 to 1821 was one of the university examiners, and during part of the time had John Keble as a colleague. In 1818 he was appointed Whitehall preacher by Bishop Howley, and in 1823 select preacher to the University of Oxford. He was elected Camden professor of ancient history in 1825, and was appointed by Lord Grenville, as chancellor, to succeed Archbishop Whately in 1831 as principal of St Alban Hall, Oxford. He was consequently a member of hebdomadal council. Soon after this appointment he resigned the living of Stoke Bruerne, Northamptonshire, to which he had been presented by Brasenose College in 1828. He subsequently declined the offer of the rectory of Withyham, and in 1844 refused the deanery of Carlisle offered to him by Sir Robert Peel. He was delegate of estates, delegate of the press, and curator of university galleries. He was considered one of the best men of business in the university (as well as one of the wealthiest), and for many years had a leading share in its government. The management of the Bible department of the university press was left mainly in his hands, and by his advice the paper mill at Wolvercote was established. Lord Grenville, the duke of Wellington, and Lord Derby, as they successively became chancellors of the university, appointed him to act as their private secretary. He was a personal friend of Sir Robert Peel and of W. E. Gladstone. His nephew Edward *Cardwell, son of his brother John, was MP for Oxford City, sitting as a Peelite.

Cardwell's publications were initially classical, including an edition of Aristotle's *Ethics* (2 vols., 1828–30), and lectures on Greek and Roman coinage (1832). While maintaining this interest, he also became an authority on the

Edward Cardwell (1787–1861), by William Holl (after George Richmond, 1853)

development of the Church of England, then rarely studied historically. Prompted by the rise of church-party warfare in the late 1830s, and especially hostile to the Tractarians, he planned a synodical history and compiled several valuable documentary publications, beginning with *Documentary Annals of the Reformed Church of England* (2 vols., 1839) and *The Two Books of Common Prayer ... Compared* (1839). Of especial importance in his many publications on this topic are *Synodalia* (2 vols., 1842) and *Reformatio legum ecclesiasticarum* (1850). *Synodalia* was for long the standard work, now superseded by G. L. Bray's *The Anglican Canons, 1529–1947* (1998). Together with William Palmer of Worcester, Cardwell set new standards in church historiography.

In May 1829 Cardwell married Cecilia, youngest daughter of Henry Feilden of Witton Park, Blackburn; they had several children. He died in the principal's lodge, St Alban Hall, Oxford, on 23 May 1861.

C. W. SUTTON, rev. H. C. G. MATTHEW

Sources *GM*, 3rd ser., 11 (1861), 194, 313 · W. R. Ward, *Victorian Oxford* (1965) · *N&Q*, 12th ser., 12 (1923), 268 · Gladstone, *Diaries* · private information (1886) · *CGPLA Eng. & Wales* (1861) · Cardwell's MS lectures, Bodl. Oxf. · *Hist. U. Oxf. 6: 19th-cent. Oxf.*

Archives Bodl. Oxf., collation of Josephus MSS; lecture notes relating to ancient history | BL, corresp. with W. E. Gladstone, Add. MSS 44369–44392, *passim* · BL, corresp. with Lord Grenville,

Add. MS 69112 · Lpool RO, letters to fourteenth earl of Derby ·
U. Southampton L., letters to first duke of Wellington
Likenesses W. Holl, stipple (after G. Richmond, 1853), NPG [*see
illus.*] · lithograph, Brasenose College, Oxford
Wealth at death £45,000: probate, 1 July 1861, *CGPLA Eng. &
Wales*

Cardwell, Edward, first Viscount Cardwell (1813–1886),
politician, was born on 24 July 1813 at Liverpool, son of
John Cardwell, merchant, and his wife, Elizabeth, daughter of Richard Birley of Blackburn, Lancashire. Edward
*Cardwell, the church historian, was his uncle. He was
educated at Winchester College and at Balliol College,
Oxford, where, in 1835, he obtained first-class honours in
classics and mathematics and was elected a fellow. He was
president of the Oxford Union in 1833 and 1835.

In 1838 he married Annie, daughter of Charles Stewart
Parker (*d.* 1825) of Fairlie, Ayrshire, and his wife, Margaret.
Their marriage was childless. His wife was the aunt of
Charles Stuart *Parker, who became his secretary. Parker
was a bachelor and became something of a surrogate son.

Early political career Cardwell was called to the bar in 1838
but entered parliament in 1842 as a free-trade Conservative, returned for Clitheroe following a successful petition
against the general election result there in 1841. An associate of Sir Robert Peel, whom he resembled in character
and in his somewhat austere devotion to public service, he
was appointed secretary to the Treasury in 1845, leaving
office with Peel the following year. He became MP for Liverpool in 1847 and, as a senior Peelite, joined Aberdeen's
coalition government in 1852 as president of the Board of
Trade. In the election of 1852 he lost his Liverpool seat as a
result of voting for the repeal of the navigation laws, and
for the rest of his active political career (1853–74) he was
Liberal MP for Oxford City (he lost his seat at the election
of 1857 but regained it the same year, defeating W. M.
Thackeray). His main achievement as president of the
Board of Trade was the Merchant Shipping Act of 1854; but
his expertise in financial matters was also valued by W. E.
Gladstone as chancellor of the exchequer, whom he
declined to succeed in 1855 out of loyalty to his Peelite colleagues. He entered the cabinet in 1859 as secretary for Ireland but his efforts over the next two years failed to
improve landlord–tenant relations and, as chancellor of
the duchy of Lancaster (1861–4), his political career
seemed to be in decline. He was more successful, however,
as secretary of state for the colonies (1864–6) where he
began the process of withdrawing British battalions while
simultaneously encouraging self-defence by laying the
foundations of Canadian federation.

Cardwell's army reforms When Gladstone formed his first
ministry in December 1868 Cardwell was not the first
choice as secretary of state for war—indeed Cardwell had
recently expressed a strong dislike of that office—but he
had some knowledge of the armed services and defence
issues without having advanced controversial views
which would have made him anathema to the queen and
her cousin George, duke of Cambridge, the commander-
in-chief. Perhaps most important of all, Cardwell's financial and administrative competence was expected to

Edward Cardwell, first Viscount Cardwell (1813–1886), by
George Richmond, 1871

achieve economies in one of the great spending departments. His wide-ranging army reforms over the next five
years were to constitute his chief memorial, but the near-
impossible goal of combining reduced expenditure with
increased military efficiency created enormous tensions
within the government and provoked antagonism from
reactionary military groups which fatally undermined his
never robust health.

Few nineteenth-century governments willingly grasped
the nettle of military reform: most reforming spells were
prompted by popular alarm over continental developments and rapidly ended once the perceived threat diminished. Prussia's wars of unification of 1864 and 1866, culminating in the defeat of France in 1870–71, provided the
essential political impetus for Cardwell to take up the
numerous military issues outstanding from the last burst
of reforming activity in the late 1850s. The principal
lesson of Prussia's astonishing victories seemed to be that
henceforth military strength would be measured not so
much by the regular forces in uniform at a particular time
as by the echelons of trained reservists available to swell
the ranks after mobilization. Prussia's example demonstrated that short service, and probably also the localization of units, would be necessary to achieve these new
standards of efficiency.

Before Cardwell could attempt any positive reforms he
had to reduce the military budget which accounted for as
much as 30 per cent of government expenditure. This he
did over the two years 1869 to 1871, securing cumulative
savings of more than £2 million by withdrawing 27,709

troops from colonial service, cutting the stores vote by £641,370, and reducing the size of infantry battalion cadres to just over 500 other ranks. These measures were generally welcomed, though the duke of Cambridge rightly complained that the home infantry battalions had been rendered too weak for active service.

Cardwell's first important reform—the re-organization of the War Office in 1870—was also welcomed by the House of Commons. After the Crimean War thirteen separate military departments had been hastily amalgamated, thereby creating a structure which was officially described as chaotic. The secretary of state for war was now clearly the minister responsible for the efficiency of the army and for its civil administration, but matters of command, discipline, appointments, and promotion remained the responsibility of the commander-in-chief, the duke of Cambridge, who had held office at the pleasure of the crown since 1857 (and would continue to do so until 1895). Since the latter retained separate headquarters at the Horse Guards there was ample scope for muddle and friction: in short a cumbersome bureaucracy with double establishments and the duplication of administrative business.

The War Office Act (1870) confirmed the secretary of state's supremacy as the responsible minister, with the commander-in-chief as his principal military adviser. The War Office, to which the duke of Cambridge very reluctantly moved, was now concentrated in Pall Mall, and would contain three divisions—military, supply, and finance—the first to be headed by the commander-in-chief, and the latter two by a surveyor-general and a financial secretary, both of them eligible for election to parliament. The War Office Act strengthened Cardwell's constitutional position and considerably improved the conduct of business, notably by reducing the vast daily interchange of letters, but the duke of Cambridge's anomalous position and increasing opposition to most military reforms caused great difficulties for Cardwell and his successors. In personal terms Cardwell remained correct, patient, and conciliatory, but the duke's personality and behaviour undoubtedly increased the burdens of office.

Abolition of purchase By far the most controversial and exhausting of all Cardwell's reforms was the abolition, in 1871, of the system whereby most officers' commissions in the infantry and cavalry up to and including the rank of lieutenant-colonel could be purchased and sold like personal investments in property. Before that, however, in his Army Enlistment Bill of 1870, Cardwell introduced the concept of short service. He proposed to retain twelve years as the initial term of the engagement for the infantry (in operation since 1847), but with the innovation that only six years would be spent in the colours and the remainder in the reserve. Colour service might be reduced to as short as three years if recruiting permitted. On paper at least this measure offered attractions which made it popular with press and parliament: by reducing the periods of overseas service it should improve the quality

and numbers of recruits; it would enable a reserve to be built up; and it would reduce the pension list since few soldiers would henceforth complete twenty-one years of service. The bill passed without a division.

It used to be held that Cardwell entered office determined to abolish the purchase system, but this now seems unlikely because he was a cautious political tactician rather than a crusader. On the other hand it is hard to imagine that his positive reforms could have been implemented without at some point tackling the purchase system. Indeed it was a minor cost-cutting proposal, to abolish the ranks of cornet and ensign, which forced Cardwell and his colleagues to confront the immensely complicated issue of purchase. The system, which had developed since the seventeenth century, was obsolete by 1870, but its advantages must not be overlooked. It permitted relatively rapid promotion for those officers who could afford to buy advancement; it preserved the link between the army and the upper classes, thus ensuring the service's political stability; and it obviated the need for more realistic pay and pensions. On the debit side it constituted an obstacle to the development of more professional standards, including promotion by merit; focused attention narrowly on the regiment; and prevented full co-operation between purchase and non-purchase corps, including the non-purchase volunteers and the militia.

Predecessors of Cardwell who had contemplated the abolition of purchase had faced a daunting problem beyond the deep-seated conservatism of the politically powerful class which benefited from the system—the enormous cost of refunding the regulation prices of the commission holders, and also of confronting the prevalence of illegal over-regulation payments which had defied all previous legislation. In June 1870 a royal commission reported in favour of meeting the officers' claims in full, including over-regulation payments. Reluctant though Gladstone's government was to commit some £8 million to end the system over a period of several years, it could not condone the continuation of illegal over-regulation payments. Consequently, between February and July 1871, Cardwell undertook the onerous task of steering the Army Regulation Bill through the House of Commons. He received only lukewarm support from some of his senior colleagues, and even less from the duke of Cambridge in the House of Lords. Thwarted in the Commons, a small group of die-hards, known as 'the colonels', resumed their filibustering in committee, challenging virtually every clause in a complex bill on thirteen occasions between 8 May and 19 June. Even Gladstone came to favour compromise as the government's majority steadily declined, but Cardwell remained obdurate and the bill passed its third reading early in July. Within two weeks the House of Lords had rejected the bill, only to be promptly outmanoeuvred by the controversial issue of a royal warrant which ended the purchase, sale, and exchange of commissions with effect from 1 November 1871. The military reactionaries continued to grumble, but popular feelings were probably epitomized by the notice in *Punch* on 5 August to 'gallant and stupid young gentlemen': 'You may buy commissions in the Army up to 31st day of October next. After that you will be driven to the cruel necessity of deserving them.'

Illness and further reforms The prolonged struggle over the abolition of purchase had seriously affected Cardwell's health. Already, in January 1871, he had offered to resign should Gladstone prefer a soldier to represent the government in the House of Commons. Near the end of the year Mrs Cardwell wrote privately to the prime minister begging him to offer her husband the speakership of the Commons because his health was breaking down, adding '[he] has sacrificed himself in every way to do his utmost, and beyond his strength … It is not possible that this can go on long.' Gladstone tentatively sounded out Cardwell, but the minister, sensing that the prime minister wished him to continue, declined. Unbeknown to Cardwell, the queen had also hoped he would accept the speakership, writing to Lord Halifax of his relations with the duke: 'It *never* will work well, and Mr Cardwell is much disliked by the Army, who knows he understands nothing of military matters.' She 'had a high regard for him personally, but had never thought him fit for his present post'.

In 1872 and 1873 Cardwell introduced the final and most important positive stages of his programme of reform—the linking in pairs of the infantry battalions for the purpose of improving the system of supplying imperial garrisons, accompanied by the localization of the home battalions in association with militia and volunteer units, all now under the authority of the War Office. The basic idea was to divide the country into territorial districts (the eventual number was sixty-six), each to contain two line battalions, two militia battalions, and a quota of volunteers, formed into an administrative brigade, the whole to rest upon a brigade depot, most of which would have to be built. The purpose behind the linking of battalions was that one of each pair was normally to be at home and the other overseas, with the former supplying replacements for its partner and eventually changing places with it. By this scheme Cardwell hoped to bring order into the haphazard roster of foreign reliefs to prevent battalions serving abroad continuously for as long as twenty years. In theory, then, all Cardwell's reforms were interrelated: short service, linked battalions, and localization (not to mention additional social and disciplinary improvements in the soldier's life), were designed to make the army more popular and hence solve the chronic recruiting problem. If this worked, then there would be a considerable saving on pensions and in time a large reserve (60,000–80,000 men) would be created.

Some ingredients of success, such as substantial increases in pay, and the public's attitude to military service, lay largely beyond Cardwell's control, but in linking battalions he unwisely settled for a compromise rather than obliging the majority of formerly independent battalions (all except numbers 1–25, which were already double battalions) to amalgamate as one regiment. In practice, with encouragement from the duke of Cambridge and other conservative officers, many of the individual battalions continued to cherish their separate traditions and opposed the transfer of officers and other ranks within the brigade. In many cases also 'localization' proved to be a paper scheme rather than a reality. It fell to Cardwell's Liberal successor and supporter, Hugh Childers, in 1881, to fuse the old numbered battalions into new regiments with county designations in a system which, despite many subsequent amalgamations and a few disbandments, survived for nearly a century.

Throughout his tenure of the War Office Cardwell, though himself a firm believer in financial retrenchment, was under pressure to reduce military costs even further. He had succeeded remarkably well, considering that emergency expenditure had been unavoidable in the crisis threatened by possible British involvement in the Franco-Prussian War. Nevertheless, the attempt to square the circle of far-reaching reforms with reduced expenditure caused Cardwell great stress, as is evident in his correspondence with the prime minister. On 13 December 1872, for example, Cardwell wrote angrily that he had reduced men and money to the lowest point compatible with the good of the service, only to be told that as there was an increase in the navy he *must* make a further reduction. Eventually, in January 1874, when both Cardwell and G. J. Goschen, his colleague at the Admiralty, opposed further reductions in expenditure on the services, an impasse was reached which caused the prime minister to end the ministry and call a general election.

Retirement and death When, in February 1874, Gladstone shocked his colleagues by resigning the party leadership, Cardwell was a strong candidate for the succession, but he declined it on account of age and, after achieving re-election at Oxford, accepted a peerage as Viscount Cardwell of Ellerbeck. In the late 1870s he chaired a commission on vivisection, spoke out against slavery, and attended several functions at his old university, which had awarded him an honorary DCL in 1863. But he suffered a painful lingering illness, described in one source as 'a brain disease'. After visiting him in February 1883, Gladstone noted: 'Saw Lord Cardwell—a sad spectacle, monitory of our lot' (Gladstone, *Diaries*, 10.409). Cardwell died at the Villa Como, Torquay, on 15 February 1886 and was buried in Highgate cemetery. His wife died on 20 February 1887 and was also buried at Highgate.

Cardwell's reforms in perspective The only biography of Cardwell published in the century after his death was produced by his former military secretary, Sir Robert Biddulph, in 1904. However, since the 1960s several scholars (including the author of this entry) have reassessed Cardwell's army reforms in the perspective of military developments up to the Second South African War (1899–1902), which demonstrated that further drastic changes were necessary. While the broad consensus has been that Biddulph's claims on behalf of his revered former chief were excessive, Cardwell's substantial achievements have been confirmed.

Even during Cardwell's lifetime it was apparent that his reforms were not achieving all that had been hoped of them. The precise numerical balance of 140 linked battalions had made no allowance for the demands of small but frequent colonial campaigns which soon tilted the scales and caused the smaller number serving at home to be deprived of their best men as drafts. The brigade depot system took many years to complete and the full recruiting aims of localization could never cope with the uneven demographic distribution. Even more seriously, pay and service conditions were not improved sufficiently to compete with civil employment so that recruiting remained an unsolved problem. This in turn caused the length of service to be increased, thus delaying the formation of a reserve. Cardwell's opponents persistently argued that his short service system had ruined the army in its imperial role. In poor recruiting years the minimum age and physical standards for entrants had also to be lowered. In organizational terms, Cardwell's failure to limit the duke of Cambridge's tenure of office left a legacy of friction within the War Office and delayed the creation of a general staff until after the Second South African War. In trying to emulate the Prussian model, Cardwell had been seriously, perhaps fatally, handicapped by the absence of conscription combined with the need to garrison India and a worldwide empire. Finally, there was a reluctance in Gladstone's and succeeding administrations to press beyond the catchwords of 'economy and efficiency' to analyse for what purposes army and naval forces were maintained and how they might co-operate more closely in peace and war.

On the positive side, the Cardwell reforms did constitute a watershed in the army's development. The abolition of purchase, though it produced no rapid transformation of the social basis of the officer corps, was a vital step in preparing the way for a more professional service. This became evident, for example, in the greater prestige and influence enjoyed by the Staff College, especially from the 1890s. War Office organization, the auxiliary forces, and the place of the soldier in society all improved gradually on the foundations laid by Cardwell. Even the derided reserve did eventually produce some 80,000 trained soldiers who proved remarkably reliable when mobilized for the Second South African War. Finally, despite its shortcomings, no better system than that of the linked battalions was ever devised as a method of providing imperial garrisons in an army based on voluntary service. The 'Cardwell system' which perpetuated the minister's name disappeared only with the dismantling of the empire it had served for nearly a century.

Cardwell was not distinguished as an orator or political leader but possessed many of the fine qualities associated with his first chief, Sir Robert Peel, including devotion to the public service, personal integrity, great skill in the mastery and presentation of complex parliamentary measures, and tenacious adherence to causes which he believed to be right. But, above all, he deserves the accolade of the greatest reformer of the British army in the nineteenth century.   BRIAN BOND

Sources R. Biddulph, *Lord Cardwell at the war office: a history of his administration, 1868–1874* (1904) · A. B. Erickson, *Edward T. Cardwell: Peelite* (1959) · E. M. Spiers, *The late Victorian army, 1868–1902* (1992) · A. Bruce, 'Edward Cardwell and the abolition of purchase', *Politicians and defence: studies in the formulation of British defence policy, 1845–1970*, ed. I. Beckett and J. Gooch (1981), 24–46 · B. Bond, 'The introduction and operation of short service and localization in the British army, 1868–1892', MA diss., U. Lond., 1962 · W. S. Hamer, *The British army: civil-military relations, 1885–1905* (1970) · A. V. Tucker, 'Army and society in England, 1870–1900: a reassessment of the Cardwell reforms', *Journal of British Studies*, 2/2 (1962–3), 110–41 · E. M. Spiers, *The army and society, 1815–1914* (1980) · B. Bond, 'Edward Cardwell's army reforms, 1868–1874', *The Army Quarterly*, 84 (1962) · A. Bruce, *The purchase system in the British army, 1660–1871*, Royal Historical Society Studies in History, 20 (1980) · *The Times* (16 Feb 1886) · Gladstone, *Diaries* · GEC, *Peerage*
Archives Borth. Inst., letters to Lord Halifax · PRO, corresp. and papers, PRO 30/48 | BL, corresp. with Lord Aberdeen, Add. MS 43197 · BL, letters to Sir Henry Campbell-Bannerman, Add. MS 41212 · BL, corresp. with W. E. Gladstone, Add. MSS 44118–44120 · BL, corresp. with Sir Robert Peel, Add. MS 40538–40601 · BL, corresp. with Lord Ripon, Add. MS 43551 · BL, corresp. with Lord Stanhope, Add. MS 40615 · Bodl. Oxf., letters to Lord Clarendon · Bodl. Oxf., corresp. with Colonel Doyle · Bodl. Oxf., letters to Lord Kimberley · Bucks. RLSS, letters to Lord Cottesloe · Hove Central Library, Sussex, letters to Lord Wolseley and Lady Wolseley · LPL, corresp. with Lady Burdett-Coutts · LPL, corresp. with A. C. Tait · Lpool RO, corresp. with Parker family · New Brunswick Museum, St John, corresp. with Sir William Fenwick Williams · NL Ire., letters to Lord Monck · PRO, corresp. with Lord Granville, PRO30/29 · U. Southampton L., corresp. with Lord Palmerston · Wilts. & Swindon RO, corresp. with Sidney Herbert
Likenesses F. Sargent, pencil drawing, 1834, NPG · woodengraving, pubd 1865, NPG · G. Richmond, oils, 1871, NPG [*see illus.*] · Ape [C. Pellegrini], caricature, watercolour study, NPG; repro. in *VF* (3 April 1869) · L. Caldesi & Co., carte-de-visite, NPG · L. C. Dickinson, group portrait, oils (*Gladstone's cabinet of 1868*), NPG · W. Hall, stipple (after G. Richmond), BM, NPG · Lock & Whitfield, woodburytype photograph, NPG; repro. in T. Cooper, *Men of mark: a gallery of contemporary portraits* (1878) · J. Phillip, group portrait, oils (*House of Commons, 1860*), Palace of Westminster, London · W. Walker & Sons, carte-de-visite, NPG · J. Watkins, carte-de-visite, NPG
Wealth at death £55,431 19s. 2d.: resworn probate, May 1887, CGPLA Eng. & Wales (1886)

Care, Henry (1646/7–1688), writer and polemicist, was nicknamed Harry and known as Ingenious; he spelt his surname Care, rather than Carre, Carr, Carey, Cave, or Cane, as it sometimes appeared, but no evidence links him to others called Care of the era. Nothing is known of his parents, but an unidentified uncle was a friend of the whig printer Richard Janeway. Care married a woman named Bridget or Brigitta who died in 1699, but there is no record of children. If not a Londoner by birth, he was one by choice; slight of build with a dark beard and a love of drink, he lived in London certainly from young adulthood (excepting eighteen months in 1682 and 1683) in or near Blackfriars. Lacking formal education he acquired broad knowledge of the doctrine and discipline of the Church of England, the Roman Catholic church, dissent, Judaism, and Islam, as well as English law and European and English history. Skilled in Latin and French, he also knew

Greek. A contemporary reported that Care was 'Bred an Attorney' and he no doubt worked for lawyers before he earned his livelihood from writing (Gibbon, *Touch of the Times*, 1). He liked humour, saying that 'Everything is big with Jest, if we have but the wit to find it out' (Care, *The Female Secretary*, 145). Feisty and quick tempered, he eagerly crossed literary swords with his critics, confessing to a 'natural aversion to Knaves and Fools' and refusing to retreat 'like a snail' before his enemies (Care, *Weekly Pacquet*, 5.2; BL, Add. MS 2285, fol. 163). Aggressively ambitious, he was guilty of lying, plagiarizing, and libelling his detractors.

With a nimble intellect, a desire for recognition, and a need for money, Care suited his style and his subject to the market, and from 1670 to 1678 he wrote on non-political topics. In 1670 he translated Agrippa's *De nobilitate … sexus* ('On the excellence of women', 1529), from the Latin, dedicating the result (which he entitled *Female Preeminence*) in fulsome terms to Queen Catherine. In 1671 came *The Female Secretary*, the largest collection to date of model letters for women. After an excursion into biblical esoterica in *The Jewish Calendar* (dedicated to the Baptist William Kiffin), Care turned to medicine, writing a broadside on rickets and translating from the Latin a text by a German professor (*Practical Physick*, 1676). In an effort at self-promotion he styled himself a Student of Physick and Astrology. To advance his social status he used the title 'gent.' on the frontispiece of two tracts. Exploiting the contemporary interest in history, he produced *The Plain Englishman's Historian* (1678); he also served up pornography in *Poor Robin's Intelligence* (1676–7).

The Popish Plot and the exclusion crisis transformed Care's writing career. Capitalizing on the hysteria he inaugurated *The Weekly Pacquet of Advice from Rome*, an account of the Catholic church written in instalments and addressed to persons of 'middle or meaner Rank'. The *Pacquet*, accompanied by the *Popish Courant*, a sheet of scurrilous comments on contemporary affairs, appeared every week but one from December 1678 to July 1683. Using strident anti-popery as a cover, Care with increasing bitterness excoriated as Catholic sympathizers the bench, the Anglican church, and by implication the king and the Catholic duke of York. As a champion of dissenters, he adopted a new persona, Lover of True Protestants. His productivity soared: he wrote at least ten essays on religious, constitutional, and political subjects (notably *English Liberties*, which championed juries and was condemned as seditious); he contributed to newspapers (notably the *Impartial Protestant Mercury*); and he answered Sir Roger L'Estrange's *History of the Plot* with *The History of the Damnable Popish Plot*, said by L'Estrange's biographer to be 'as worthy a piece of invective as exists in the language' (Kitchin, 246). He continued to produce pornography, publishing in 1679 *The Snotty-Nose Gazette* and *Poor Robin's Intelligence, Newly Revived*. There were more publications by Care than by any other whig author from 1678 to 1683.

In early 1681 the government launched its own propaganda campaign led by Edward Rawlins (Heraclitus Ridens), Nathaniel Thompson, and L'Estrange; they painted whigs as radical heirs of the civil war. L'Estrange respected Care enough to order his *Weekly Pacquet* delivered 'every Friday morning Piping hot to [his] breakfast' (L'Estrange, *The Observator*, no. 8). Using dialogue, humour, irony, story-telling, myth, and name-calling, L'Estrange and Care led the way in reshaping popular political rhetoric. The *Weekly Pacquet* (like L'Estrange's *The Observator*) was popular: when Care, for unknown reasons in August 1682, dismissed Langley Curtis as publisher, the latter rejoined by bringing out a rival *Weekly Pacquet*.

Care's political pen exposed him to the wrath of state, church, and tory supporters. He was called before government authorities for seditious libel five times between 1679 and 1685, as in 1679 for libelling Lord Chief Justice Sir William Scroggs in the *Popish Courant*. Upon his arrest the Green Ribbon Club assisted him financially, and at his trial on 2 July 1680 two distinguished whig lawyers, Sir William Williams and Sir Francis Winnington, defended him. Care was found guilty and ordered to discontinue his *Weekly Pacquet*, but he defiantly ignored the order and it appeared under a thinly veiled title until parliament reconvened on 21 October when shortly thereafter the true title was restored. The next day his case was dismissed, no doubt to avoid anti-government protests at the opening of parliament. In May 1682 royalists in Norwich burned him in effigy. In May 1683 Care was fined for non-attendance at church and for non-participation in the sacrament, and he was excommunicated from St Sepulchre, Holborn. Thus threatened, he began to waver in October 1681 and July 1682, and on 13 July 1683 he ceased publishing the *Weekly Pacquet*, the longest lasting of the whig serials. In October 1683 he was plea-bargaining with the court.

James became king in 1685, and in 1687 Care joined L'Estrange and William Penn as a court propagandist, 'not all for belly's sake', as Kitchin so aptly described Care's defence (Kitchin, 324, n. 1). Fear, desire to assist dissenters, and commitment to religious liberty also moved him (Care, *Publick Occurrences*, 1, 1688; H. Care, *Draconica*, 2nd edn, 1688, postscript). Care did not convert to Catholicism, but he defended the king's policies in *Publick Occurrences* (twenty-three weeks, February–August 1688) and in eleven tracts, while also exposing the persecutory practices of the Anglican church, abstracting the penal laws (in *Draconica*), urging dissenters to support James, and championing liberty of religious conscience for all, including Catholics, as a 'natural birthright of Englishmen' (H. Care, *Animadversions on a Late Paper*, 1687, 4; Care, *Publick Occurrences*, 9, 1688). He also found time to publish *The Tutor to the True English* (1687) and *The Character and Qualifications of an Honest Loyal Merchant* (1686), and to continue to pander to prurient interests in *Poor Robins Public and Private Occurances* (12 May–4 July 1688).

Care died at home in Walters Street, Blackfriars, on 8 August 1688 of 'complicated Distempers', caused by a 'Sedentary Life' (probably drink), that 'ended in a Dropsy' (Settle, *Publick Occurrences*, 26, 1688). He was buried in the churchyard of St Ann Blackfriars, on 10 August. His wealth is unknown (no will survives), but property taxes and the

£100 secret service bounty given to his widow indicate that he prospered. His enemies vilified him for assailing the Anglican church, while his friends praised his 'Golden Pen' and Elkanah Settle continued *Publick Occurrences* until October. Defoe modelled his *Review* after the *Pacquet* and declared himself to be unworthy to carry Care's books (Defoe, 618). Care's anti-popery writings helped to embed anti-Catholic prejudice in the national consciousness. They were applauded in 1736, when a two-volume *History of Popery* appeared that drew upon and praised *The Weekly Pacquet*, and in 1851, when a correspondent of *Notes and Queries* recommended the printing of Care's *Modest Inquiry* (1687), which had questioned whether St Paul was ever in Rome. *English Liberties* spread devotion for jury trials to the colonies. Care also deserves recognition for popularizing history, restyling political rhetoric, and promoting liberty of conscience. LOIS G. SCHWOERER

Sources State trials, 7.1111–30 · JHC · JHL · CSP dom. · H. Care, *Weekly Pacquet of Advice from Rome*, 1–4 (1678–83) [except for one week] · *An elegy upon the most ingenious Mr Henry Care* [1688] [advertised in *Publick Occurrences Truely Stated*, 26 (1688)] · *Publick Occurrences Truely Stated*, nos. 1–25, ed. H. Care, nos. 26–33, ed. E. Settle (12 Feb 1687/8–2 Oct 1688) · archdeaconry of London assignation book, proceedings against dissenters, GL, fol. 97 · 10 Aug 1688, GL, MS 4510/1 · 13 Aug 1689, GL, MS 7768/5 · R. L'Estrange, *The observator in dialogue*, 3 vols. (1684) · J. Y. Akerman, ed., *Moneys received and paid for secret services of Charles II and James II from 30th March 1679 to 25th December 1688*, CS, 52 (1851) · G. Kitchin, *Sir Roger L'Estrange: a contribution to the history of the press in the seventeenth century* (1913) · T. J. Crist, 'Francis Smith and the opposition press in England, 1660–1688', PhD diss., U. Cam., 1977 · D. Defoe, 'Supplementary journal to the "Advice from the the Scandal Club"; for the month of September, 1704', *The novels and miscellaneous works of Daniel De Foe*, 7 (1840–41), 618–19 · [J. Gibbon], *Flagellum mercurii Anti-Ducalis, or, The author of the dis-ingenuous 'Touch of the Times' brought to the whipping-post, to prevent his coming to the gallows* [1679] · [J. Gibbon], *A touch of the times, or, Two letters casually intercepted: the first, from the author of a late pamphlet intituled 'Day-Fatality' to the supposed author of the 'Weekly packet of advice from Rome'. The Second, the answer thereunto* [1679] · Wood, *Ath. Oxon.*, new edn, 2.469 · Newdigate newsletter, Folger, L.c.998 · *Heraclitus Ridens*, 9, 12, 15 (1681) · [N. Thompson], *The loyal protestant and true domestick intelligence, or, News from both city and country* (1679–83) [variant titles, with interruptions] · H. Care, *The female secretary, or, Choice new letters* (1671) · Henry Care to 'Right Worshipful', 1683, Bodl. Oxf., MS Rawl. C. 732, fols. 127–8 · BL, Add. MS 2285, fols. 141v–142, 163 · W. H. Hart, *Index expurgatorius Anglicanus, or, A descriptive catalogue of the principal books printed or published in England, which have been suppressed*, 1 vol. in 5 pts (1872–8); repr. (1969) · *Seventh report*, HMC, 6 (1879), 479a, 483a · N. Luttrell, *A brief historical relation of state affairs from September 1678 to April 1714*, 1 (1857) · R. Morrice, 'Ent'ring book', DWL, 1.263 · 'Journal of the Green Ribband Club', Pepys Library, Cambridge, 2875/465–491
Archives BL, Add. MS 36988, fols. 62–86v · BL, Add. MS 5960, fols. 62–87 · BL, Sloane MS 2285, fols. 141v–142
Wealth at death £100 bounty given to widow: Akerman, ed., *Moneys received*; GL, MS 7768/5

Careless, Elizabeth [Betty] (d. 1752), actress and prostitute, was known as Mrs or Miss Betty Careless. It is probable that she was acting before her name first appeared in the extant bills for the role of Polly in John Gray's *The Beggar's Opera* at the Haymarket Theatre on 30 December 1728. During the years 1730–32 she was an active member of a range of lesser known companies, performing such parts as Cherry in Farquhar's *The Beaux' Stratagem* at the Haymarket on 18 September 1730. She acted at the Lee-Harper booth at Southwark fair on 24 September 1730, at Goodman's Fields on 26 March 1731, and at the Haymarket on 1 April 1732. It is likely that she undertook various engagements during the 1730s, such as acting the roles of Mariana in Fielding's *The Miser*, a Lady of Pleasure in *The Ridotto al' fresco*, and Miss Witless in *The Comical Humours of Sir John Falstaff* (the latter two both theatrical compilations, or 'catchpenny entertainments') in a booth operated by Hallam, Griffin, Bullock, and Cibber in August and September 1733 at Bartholomew fair.

The next notice of Betty Careless does not appear until 27 October 1741, when she was known to have danced a minuet and performed the part of Polly for her own benefit at the small theatre in James Street. Tickets could be procured from Mrs Careless's Coffee House, which was probably located in Covent Garden, where she advertised: 'Mrs Careless hopes her friends will favour her according to their promise, to relieve her from terrible fits of the vapours, proceeding from bad dreams, tho' the comfort is they generally go by contraries' (BDA). Following this she acted the role of Cherry at James Street on 31 March 1743 and an unspecified part in Thomas Baker's *Tunbridge Walks* for her own benefit on 15 April 1743.

The last theatrical notices known for Betty Careless were at Hallam's booth at May fair in 1744, when she was billed as the celebrated Mrs Careless. She acted various parts in a range of plays, which included Colombine in the theatrical compilation *Harlequin Sclavonian* on 1 May, Cherry in *The Beaux' Stratagem* on 7 June, and Rose in Farquhar's *The Recruiting Officer* on 8 June.

Betty Careless had a 'celebrated' reputation as a strumpet in the area of Covent Garden Theatre. She is depicted in a print (set in the Covent Garden piazza) by the French engraver Louis Pierre Boitard (1747):

> which showed her asleep in a [sedan] chair, attended by the rakes Captain Marcellus Laroon and Captain Montague and their link-boy, Little Cazey—persons regarded by Fielding, when Bow Street magistrate, as 'the three most troublesome and difficult to manage of all my Bow Street visitors'. (BDA)

Her name was also used by Hogarth in one of the plates of *The Rake's Progress*.

The *Scots Magazine* recorded her funeral on 22 April 1752:

> The famed Betty Careless was buried from the poor's house of St. Paul's Covent-garden. She had helped the gay gentlemen of this nation to squander above 50,000 £ though at last reduced to live on alms;—almost the certain consequence attending women of her unhappy cast of life. (*Scots Magazine*, 213)

The burial was registered as being on 22 April 1752, where she is defined as a widow. It would appear that she spent the last years of her life in the poorhouse of St Paul's Church in Covent Garden. ALISON ODDEY

Sources Highfill, Burnim & Langhans, *BDA* · *Scots Magazine*, 14 (1752), 213
Likenesses L. P. Boitard, print, 1747, BM

Wealth at death living on alms: *Scots Magazine*

Carew, Sir Alexander, second baronet (1609–1644), politician and army officer, was born on 30 August 1609 and baptized at Antony, Cornwall, on 4 September of that year, the second but first surviving son of Sir Richard *Carew, first baronet (1579/80–1643?), of Antony, experimenter and educationist, and his first wife, Bridget (*d.* 1611), daughter of John Chudleigh of Ashton, in the same county. Clarendon asserted that Carew had received a good education, but he seems not to have attended either English university. He was admitted to the Middle Temple on 18 March 1628 and in 1631 he married Jane (1605/6–1679), daughter of Robert Rolle of Heanton, Devon. His father was created a baronet on 9 August 1641 and on his death Alexander succeeded to the title.

In November 1641 Carew was elected MP for Cornwall, together with Sir Bevil Grenville. Grenville pressed him hard to oppose the final reading of the bill of attainder against the earl of Strafford, but Carew replied, 'If I were sure to be the next man that should suffer upon the same scaffold with the same axe, I would give my consent to the passing of it' (*DNB*). The vehemence of this (grimly prophetic) speech may cast doubt on Clarendon's claim that he adhered to the parliamentarian cause out of an unprincipled desire for popularity. Like several of his local colleagues, notably Francis Rous, MP for Truro, Carew was reported to be hostile to episcopacy. In July 1642 he was one of four leading Cornish members sent by the Commons to assist in raising the Cornish militia. But in August at the Launceston assizes, Carew and other parliamentarians were unsuccessful in their efforts to persuade the judge, Sir Robert Foster, to prohibit the execution of the commission of array on behalf of the king. The active support of a knight of the shire was highly valued by the parliamentary leadership; Carew sat on twenty-two parliamentary committees at Westminster and was named a member of the Cornish sequestration committee on 27 March 1643. He was also entrusted with the command of the island of St Nicholas, or Drake's Island, and its fort, which dominated the entrance of Plymouth harbour.

In July 1643 Carew was at the head of the forces which marched to the relief of Exeter, but was halted by Sir John Berkeley, commander of the royalist forces then besieging the city. In light of the fall of Bristol and the deteriorating military situation in the west, Carew began to rethink his enthusiasm for the parliamentarian cause. Through his neighbour Piers Edgcumbe MP and royalist colonel of foot, and his major, William Scawen, he contacted Berkeley with a view to changing sides; his first service would be the betrayal of the island and fort under his command. But Carew was worried, despite Berkeley's firm assurances, about the reprisals which his record might provoke from his new friends. As Clarendon alleges, he 'was so sottishly and dangerously wary of his own security ... that he would not proceed till he was sufficiently assured that his pardon was passed the Great Seal of England'. Before any such formalities could be arranged, however, he was exposed 'by the treachery of a

servant whom he trusted' (Clarendon, *Hist. rebellion*, 3.236).

According to one account, Carew was provoked into revealing his new allegiance by the arrival in the harbour of 'a great ship under the Earl of Warwick's command'. When asked how many guns should salute her, Carew answered:

> 'sink her!', which the gunner refusing to do, the governor fell to buffets with him, where upon the governor's own man took his master by the choller of his doublet, and struck up his heels, and then they bound him hand and foot and carried him aboard that great ship, where the Captain of that ship would have hanged him, but the rope being put about his neck, by the entreaty of some he was spared and sent ashore to Plymouth, where the women of the town fell upon him, and would have beaten out his brains if the Mayor of the town had not rescued him, and guarded him to safe custody. (*Certaine Informations*, 34.260)

Another version had it that 'The good women in the town, upon his first apprehending ... were about to be the executioners of justice themselves, and were very hardly intreated to forbear the hanging of him in the island' (*Perfect Diurnall*, 8.57). In fact Carew was neither beaten to death nor hanged by the women of Plymouth, but arrested on 19 August 1643 and taken by sea to London. On 4 September the Commons voted to disable him from attendance.

Carew spent many months imprisoned in the Tower of London, where he fell ill. On 10 February 1644 the Commons ordered the lieutenant of the Tower to arrange for his treatment by physicians and provided that he should be allowed £5 per week from his estate. His trial took place on Tuesday 19 November 1644, before a council of war at the Guildhall under the presidency of John Corbet. The mayor of Plymouth and several merchants, officers, and soldiers gave evidence that he had given 'outward expression' of his intentions, 'firstly by openly declaring his resolution to hold this island for the King, and then by endeavouring to put that resolution in practice' (*England's Black Tribunal*, 97). Carew was found guilty and condemned to death. His wife, Jane, lodged a petition for his reprieve which was read in the Commons on 23 November; two days later, following enquiries as to his condition, a month's stay was granted 'in regard as the House is informed he is not of sane memory; and in respect to his wife and children, that he may, in the meantime, settle his estate' (*JHC*, 3, 1642–4, 704). But on 21 December her application for a further respite was rejected.

About ten o'clock in the morning of 23 December 1644, Carew 'was brought from the Tower by the Lieutenant and his officers to Tower Hill, attended by three companies of the trained Bands of the City'. He did not seek to justify himself—'I shall rather confess as the poor publican did, God be merciful to me a sinner'—and asked that the onlookers should join him in singing the twenty-third Psalm. 'The psalm being ended, he put on his cap, and unbuttoned himself, and with much resolution laid his head on the block. The executioner at two blows severed his head from his body' (*England's Black Tribunal*, 99). Carew was buried on the same day in the church of St Augustine,

Hackney. His widow died on 25 April 1679 aged seventy-three. A monument to her memory, with an inscription recording her virtues, was erected in Antony church.

STEPHEN WRIGHT

Sources M. Coate, *Cornwall in the great civil war and interregnum, 1642–1660* (1933) • Keeler, *Long Parliament* • *Certaine Informations from Several parts of the Kingdom*, 34 (4 Sept 1643) • *A Perfect Diurnall of the Passages in Parliament*, 8 (4–11 Sept 1643) • *Mercurius Politicus* (1–8 July 1644), 657–63 • J. L. Vivian, ed., *The visitations of Cornwall, comprising the herald's visitations of 1530, 1573, and 1620* (1887) • *JHC*, 3 (1642–4) • Clarendon, *Hist. rebellion* • GEC, *Baronetage* • *England's black tribunal, set forth in the trial of Charles I* (1660) [Carew's speech upon the scaffold, esp. pp. 99–100] • E. A. Andriette, *Devon and Exeter in the civil war* (1971) • W. Robinson, *The history and antiquities of the parish of Hackney, in the county of Middlesex*, 2 vols. (1842–3)

Likenesses oils, Antony, Cornwall

Carew, Bampfylde Moore (1693–1759), impostor, was born in July 1693 at Bickley, near Tiverton, in Devon, where his father, Theodore Carew, was rector for many years. At the age of twelve he was sent to Tiverton School, where he became involved with a group of schoolboys who possessed a pack of hounds. On one occasion Carew and three companions pursued a deer across neighbouring land, for which they were criticized by local farmers. To avoid punishment the youths ran away and joined a group of Gypsies. After a year and a half Carew returned home for a time, but soon after resumed a career of swindling and imposture, which saw him deceive people to whom he had previously been well known. Eventually he embarked for Newfoundland, but stayed only a short time. On his return to England he passed as the mate of a vessel, and eloped with the daughter of a respectable apothecary from Newcastle upon Tyne, whom he later married.

Carew soon returned to the nomadic life, and when Clause Patch, a Gypsy king or chief, died Carew was elected his successor. He was convicted of being an idle vagrant, and sentenced to be transported to Maryland. On his arrival he attempted to escape, but was captured and made to wear a heavy iron collar; he escaped again, and encountered some Native Americans, who removed his shackles. On departure he travelled to Pennsylvania. He was then said to have swum the Delaware River, after which he adopted the guise of a Quaker, and made his way to Philadelphia, then to New York, and finally to Boston, where he embarked for England. He escaped impressment on board a man-of-war by pricking his hands and face, and rubbing in bay salt and gunpowder, so as to simulate smallpox.

After his landing Carew continued his impostures, traced his wife and daughter, and seems to have entered Scotland about 1745, and is said to have accompanied the Young Pretender to Carlisle and Derby. Little is known of him after this time, except that a relative, Sir Thomas Carew of Hackern, offered to provide for him if he would give up his wandering life. Apparently he refused the offer, but eventually reconsidered after he gained prizes in a lottery. Carew died at Tiverton, Devon, on 27 August 1759.

JOHN ASHTON, rev. HEATHER SHORE

Bampfylde Moore Carew (1693–1759), by Richard Phelps, 1750

Sources *The life and adventures of Bamfylde Moore Carew, the noted Devonshire stroller and dogstealer* (1745) • *An apology for the life of Bampfylde-Moore Carew (son of the Rev. Mr. Carew, of Bickley)* (1749?) • H. Wilson and J. Caulfield, *The book of wonderful characters* (1869) • M. A. Nooney, *The cant dictionary of Bampfylde-Moore Carew: a study of the contents and changes in various editions* (1969) • *N&Q*, 2nd ser., 4 (1857), 330–31, 401, 522 • *N&Q*, 2nd ser., 3 (1857), 4 • *The surprising adventures of Bampfylde Moore Carew, King of the Beggars* (1812)

Likenesses J. Faber junior, mezzotint, 1750 (after R. Phelps), BM • J. Faber junior, mezzotint, 1750 (after R. Phelps), NPG • R. Phelps, oils, 1750, NPG [*see illus.*] • R. Page, engraving, repro. in Wilson and Caulfield, *Book of wonderful characters*

Carew, Sir Benjamin Hallowell [*formerly* Benjamin Hallowell] (1760–1834), naval officer, son of Benjamin Hallowell, commissioner of the American board of customs, was born in Canada in 1760, and entered the navy at an early age. On 31 August 1781 he was appointed by Sir Samuel Hood as acting lieutenant of the *Alcide*, and served in her in the action off the Chesapeake five days later. He was shortly afterwards moved into the *Alfred*, and was in her in the engagements at St Kitts and off Dominica [*see* Bayne, William]. However, he was not confirmed in his rank until 25 April 1783. After seven years of uneventful service he was made commander on 22 November 1790. During the two following years he commanded the sloop *Scorpion* on the African coast, and in 1793 went to the Mediterranean in the storeship *Camel* from which he was made a post captain on 30 August by his appointment to the temporary command of the *Robust* (74 guns). He briefly commanded the *Courageux* during the absence of Captain Waldegrave, sent home with dispatches; and on being superseded from her, served as a volunteer in the sieges of Bastia and Calvi. Nelson's acknowledgement of his zeal, embodied in

Hood's dispatch of 5 August, contributed to his appointment to the frigate *Lowestoft* and a few months later to the *Courageux*, which he commanded in the action off the Hyères Islands on 13 July 1795. He continued in her, attached to the fleet under Sir John Jervis, during the trying year 1796. On 19 December, when the fleet was in Gibraltar Bay, the *Courageux* was blown from her anchors in a heavy gale, and was driven over to the Moroccan coast and dashed to pieces at the foot of Apes' Hill. Out of her crew of 600 only about 120 escaped. Hallowell was absent at a court martial at the time.

While waiting on board the *Victory* for an opportunity to return to England, Hallowell was present in the battle off Cape St Vincent on 14 February 1797. He was afterwards sent home with the duplicate dispatches and a strong recommendation from Jervis, which led to his being immediately appointed to command the frigate *Lively* and ordered back to the Mediterranean. He was shortly afterwards transferred to the *Swiftsure* (74 guns), one of the inshore squadron off Cadiz under Captain Troubridge. Hallowell is described as having been a man of gigantic frame and vast strength, and stories were later told of the summary manner in which he, by arm and fist, quelled symptoms of mutiny which appeared on board the *Swiftsure* during this time.

In May 1798 the *Swiftsure* was detached to join Nelson; she was thus one of the small fleet which scoured the Mediterranean during July and destroyed the French fleet in Abu Qir Bay on the night of 1–2 August. The *Swiftsure*, with the *Alexander* [see Ball, Sir Alexander John], had been detached on the evening of 31 July to look into Alexandria, and was thus rather later than the other ships in getting into action. It was already dark, and as she was sailing in she met a ship leaving the battle. Hallowell was on the point of firing into her, but he had fortunately given strict orders that not a shot was to be fired until the anchor was down and the sails clewed up; the strange ship turned out to be the British *Bellerophon*, which had been compelled to haul off for a time. The *Swiftsure* took her place and, together with the *Alexander*, devoted herself to the destruction of *L'Orient*, which blew up about two hours later.

When Nelson returned to Naples Bay, the *Swiftsure* was one of the ships left on the coast of Egypt under the command of Captain Samuel Hood, and she remained there for the next eighteen months. She rejoined Nelson at Palermo on 20 March 1799, and a couple of months later Hallowell, intent on countering the flattery then lavished on Nelson, astonished the fleet by sending him a coffin made of wood and iron from the wreck of *L'Orient*, together with a note (23 May 1799):

> My lord, herewith I send you a coffin made of part of L'Orient's mainmast, that when you are tired of this life you may be buried in one of your own trophies; but may that period be far distant is the sincere wish of your obedient and much obliged servant, Ben. Hallowell.

For the next three months the *Swiftsure* remained on the coast of Italy, where Hallowell was actively employed, under Troubridge, in the capture of Sant' Elmo, Capua,

and Civitavecchia; for which services he received from the king of Naples the orders of St Ferdinand and of Merit, and a snuffbox bearing the royal cipher in diamonds. Towards the end of the year the *Swiftsure* joined Rear-Admiral Duckworth at Minorca, and accompanied him to Lisbon, on which station and off Cadiz she remained. Hallowell married, on 17 February 1800, a daughter of Captain John Nicholson *Inglefield, for many years commissioner of the dockyard at Gibraltar; they had children.

In May 1800 Rear-Admiral Sir Richard Bickerton hoisted his flag on board the *Swiftsure*, and in November went in her to the coast of Egypt. He then transferred his flag to the *Kent*, and the following June the *Swiftsure* was sent in charge of a convoy to Malta. On the way there Hallowell, having learned of the proximity of a powerful French squadron which had been endeavouring to land troops near Tripoli, resolved to make his way to reinforce Sir John Borlase Warren, off the north African coast, and accordingly left the convoy to shift for itself. He was thus alone when, on 24 June 1801, he fell in with the French squadron and was surrounded, and captured after an obstinate resistance. Hallowell was very shortly afterwards released on parole, and on 18 August was tried at Port Mahon by a court martial, which pronounced that his leaving the convoy was dictated by sound judgement and that the loss of the *Swiftsure* was unavoidable. He was therefore honourably acquitted of all blame.

In 1802 Hallowell commanded the *Argo* (44 guns) on the African coast with a broad pennant. Touching at Barbados on his return to Europe, and learning there that war had again broken out, he placed his services at the disposal of Commodore Sir Samuel Hood, then commander-in-chief on the Leeward Islands station. He was thus engaged in the capture of St Lucia and of Tobago in June 1803, and was warmly thanked by Hood in his dispatches. On his return to England he was sent out, still in the *Argo*, on a special mission to Abu Qir. He was afterwards appointed to the *Tigre*, in which he joined the fleet off Toulon under Nelson, and under his command took part in the chase of the French fleet to the West Indies in May and June 1805. In September the *Tigre* was with the fleet off Cadiz, but was one of the ships detached to Gibraltar under Rear-Admiral Louis on 3 October, and had thus no share in Trafalgar. Continuing in the *Tigre*, Hallowell was given command of the naval part of the expedition to Alexandria in 1807; after this he was with the fleet off Toulon and on the coast of Spain until his advancement to flag rank on 1 August 1811. In January 1812 he hoisted his flag on board the *Malta* (80 guns), again in the Mediterranean, where he remained until the peace. In January 1815 he was made a KCB. Between 1816 and 1818 he was commander-in-chief on the coast of Ireland, and became vice-admiral on 12 August 1819. From 1821 to 1824 he was commander-in-chief at the Nore, with his flag in the *Prince Regent*.

On the death of his cousin, Anne Paston Gee (28 March 1828), Hallowell unexpectedly succeeded to the estates of the Carews of Beddington, near Croydon, Surrey, and as required by her will assumed the name and arms of Carew, to which family, however, he was not related. To a friend who congratulated him he answered: 'Half as much twenty years ago had indeed been a blessing; but I am now old and crank.' On 22 July 1830 he attained the rank of admiral, and on 6 June 1831 was made GCB. He died at Beddington Park, Surrey, on 2 September 1834.

J. K. LAUGHTON, rev. ROGER MORRISS

Sources J. Marshall, *Royal naval biography*, 1/2 (1823), 465–83 • *GM*, 2nd ser., 2 (1834), 537 • *United Service Journal*, 3 (1834), 374 • *United Service Journal*, 1 (1835), 95 • E. P. Brenton, *Life of Lord St Vincent* (1838), 1.302 • W. James, *The naval history of Great Britain, from the declaration of war by France in 1793, to the accession of George IV*, [5th edn], 6 vols. (1859–60), vol. 3, p. 77 • *The dispatches and letters of Vice-Admiral Lord Viscount Nelson*, ed. N. H. Nicolas, 7 vols. (1844–6), vol. 3, p. 89
Archives Duke U., Perkins L., papers • NMM, corresp. and papers • Sci. Mus., corresp. and papers • Yale U., Beinecke L. | BL, letters to Lord Spencer • U. Aberdeen L., corresp. with A. M. Fraser • U. Nott. L., corresp. with Lord William Bentinck • W. Sussex RO, naval orders to W. S. Badcock
Likenesses F. Chantrey, pencil drawing, 1815, NPG • oils, 1815–19, NMM • W. C. Ross, miniature, c.1833, Los Angeles County Museum • J. Hayter, oils, NPG • M. Thomas, oils, NMM

Carew, Sir Edmund (c.1464–1513), landowner and administrator, was the eldest of three children of Sir Nicholas Carew (c.1423–1470) of Mohun's Ottery, Devon, and his wife, Margaret (d. 1471), eldest daughter of Sir John *Dinham (1405/6–1458) [see under Dinham family] and Joan or Jane Arches. Edmund's parents were buried in the chapel of St Nicholas in Westminster Abbey, and his wardship was granted first to Anne, duchess of Exeter, and then to Dame Joan Dynham, his maternal grandmother. Through his mother he was an heir of her brother John, Lord Dinham (c.1434–1501), treasurer of England under Henry VII. His brother Sir John Carew served at court and was captain of the *Regent* when he was killed during a sea battle with the French in 1512. Their sister Jane married Robert Cary of Devon. A note of Carew's name in the records of Lincoln's Inn suggests he was educated there. He supported Henry Tudor's claim to the throne, and was knighted at about the time of Bosworth in 1485. Between 1490 and his death he served on numerous commissions including those of array for Devon and of the peace for Devon, Dorset, and Somerset. In 1492 he was among the knights appointed to meet the French ambassadors negotiating peace terms with England. In 1497 he rode with the earl of Devon, William Courtenay, to assist the citizens of Exeter under attack by Perkin Warbeck and his troops. In 1511, after the death of William Courtenay, Carew rode a courser through Exeter Cathedral to present the earl's battleaxe to the bishop. He held the shrievalty of Somerset and Dorset in 1493 and in 1511, and helped Henry VII enrich his treasury by uncovering revenues hidden from the crown in the south-western counties. In 1508 the king rewarded Carew by granting to him for life the leases of royal parks in Devon and Somerset.

Carew married Katherine, daughter of Sir William Huddesfield, attorney-general to Edward IV, and Elizabeth Bozum about 1478. Of their eight children, Anne and Isabelle became nuns while Dorothy and Catherine married men of prominent west-country families. Catherine was

grandmother of Sir Humphrey Gilbert (d. 1583) and of Sir Walter Ralegh (d. 1618). There were four sons, Sir William (c.1483–1536), father of Sir George (who drowned on the *Mary Rose* in 1545) and of Sir Peter (d. 1575); Thomas, of Bickleigh; George *Carew (1497/8–1583), dean of Exeter, whose son George became earl of Totnes; and Sir Gawen (c.1503–1585).

Carew's loyalty to the Tudors came at great cost. He borrowed money from and mortgaged family estates to the crown to finance his military obligations. The debts left his descendants financially distressed for decades. His soldiering ultimately cost him his life. In 1513 Carew was a master of the ordnance in the English force that invaded France through Calais. By midsummer, Thérouanne in Artois was under siege by the English troops. At a meeting of the military captains in the tent of Lord Herbert, the rearward commander, on 24 June, Carew was killed by a gunshot fired from the town. His body was taken to Calais where he was buried in the church of St Nicholas on 26 June.

PAMELA Y. STANTON

Sources DNB • J. L. Vivian, ed., *The visitations of the county of Devon, comprising the herald's visitations of 1531, 1564, and 1620* (privately printed, Exeter, [1895]) • *LP Henry VIII* • BL, Cotton MS Julius B i, fol. 94b; Add. MS 47192, fol. 35v • PRO, C66/610 m.8d, 7D; C614 m.5d; C618, m.1d, 3d, 4d, 5d, 6d; C142/30/88 • A. Hughes, *List of sheriffs for England and Wales: from the earliest times to AD 1831*, PRO (1898); repr. (New York, 1963) • *CPR, 1485–1509; 1550–53* • Cornwall RO, AR 37/26 • W. P. Baildon, ed., *The records of the Honorable Society of Lincoln's Inn: the black books*, 1 (1897) • [E. Halle], *The union of the two noble and illustre famelies of Lancastre and Yorke*, ed. [R. Grafton], 2nd edn (1550); facs. edn (1970) [1970] • W. A. Shaw, *The knights of England*, 2 vols. (1906); repr. (1971) • J. A. Wagner, *The Devon gentleman: the life of Sir Peter Carew* (1998)
Archives Antony, Cornwall, archives, CAD 60, PG/B2/7, PG/B2/8 [accessed through Cornwall RO]

Carew, George (1497/8–1583), dean of Exeter, was probably born at his father's seat at Mohun's Ottery, Devon. He was the third son of Sir Edmund *Carew (c.1464–1513) and his wife, Katherine, daughter of Sir William Huddesfield. The length and complexity of his career in the Tudor church over four reigns has obscured his significance as a churchman who exemplified Elizabeth's views of reformation, and has resulted in several errors. Nothing is known of Carew's early education. He supplicated for the degree of BA from Broadgates Hall, Oxford, in 1522, but there is no evidence that it was granted. Wood records that he then retired to court, and in 1533 he appears as chaplain to Henry VIII upon the occasion of his being presented by the crown to his first known living, Lydford in Devon. According to Wood, he had already married before this time, 'but soon after burying his wife to his great grief, travelled beyond seas, and improved his knowledge as to men and manners very much' (Wood, 58–9). There is no record or known child of this first marriage, but in March 1534 Carew did receive royal licence for absence from his livings to live 'beyond sea' (*LP Henry VIII*, 7, no. 419 (29)). With this began a career pattern of non-residence. In the same year he was appointed archdeacon of Totnes, and in 1536 rector of East Allington, Devon, both by the king.

In 1538 Carew was in Paris lodging with Miles Coverdale, John Berkynsaw, and other clients of Thomas Cromwell, which suggests that by this juncture he must be accounted a protestant. Successive livings granted by the king followed: Titcombe (1540), Torbryan (1542), and Carhays (1543) in Exeter diocese, and Ilfracombe (1544) in Salisbury. In 1544 Carew loaned Henry £50 for his French war, and in 1545 was presented to a prebend in Wells Cathedral by a royal warrant that overrode statutory impediments to his election. He remained a royal chaplain under Edward VI, who granted him five years' non-residence, with full emoluments, to go abroad to study. In 1548 he resigned his Totnes archdeaconry upon being appointed precentor in Exeter Cathedral and becoming a canon residentiary at Wells. Edward granted him non-residence for life for all present and future benefices in 1551, and in 1552 he was presented by William Herbert, earl of Pembroke, to the deanery of Bristol.

Like his younger brother Sir Gawen Carew (a captain in the English fleet at the time of the loss of the *Mary Rose*), and his nephew Sir Peter Carew, George Carew suffered for his protestant sympathies early in Mary's reign. He was suspended from his Wells prebend in April 1554 and between June and August was deprived of Torbryan, an Exeter prebend, and the deanery of Bristol. But like his kinsmen, he persuaded the new regime that his first loyalties were to the crown, and regained much of his status. A flurry of Marian appointments followed: in 1555 prebends at Chichester and Salisbury, and in 1556 two further Salisbury prebends and one at Wells, as well as the archdeaconry of Exeter and the Devon rectory of High Beckington. In 1557 he was presented to the rectory of Mells, Somerset, by Sir John Horner, and made precentor of Salisbury in October 1558. One week after Elizabeth's accession in November, Sir John Harrington presented him to the rectory of Kelston, Somerset.

Carew appealed to Elizabeth as a protestant untainted by radicalism, exile, or disloyalty to the Tudor succession. He was duly appointed her first and only dean of the Chapel Royal. In this capacity he celebrated her coronation mass on 15 January 1559 according to the mildly reformed rite in English and without elevation of the host, the latter a ceremonial concession that no sitting bishop was willing to make. Within a year he was also made dean of Christ Church, Oxford, and precentor of Wells, and was restored as dean of Bristol. In 1560 he became registrar of the Order of the Garter and dean and canon of Windsor, and resigned his Wells prebend and the living of Kelston; in 1561 he resigned as dean of Christ Church. He was listed among the preachers at court in Lent 1565, and was about this time custodian of Gilbert Bourne, the deprived Marian bishop of Exeter. In 1569 he resigned the archdeaconry of Exeter, but was appointed dean there (*in commendam* with that of Bristol) in 1571. In the same year the queen granted him a dispensation, on the grounds of old age, from travelling to his many distant benefices to subscribe to the articles of religion in person, as was required by statute. His declining health seems to

have prompted a gradual reduction of his benefices, as he soon resigned the Windsor deanery (1572), Tiverton (1574), and the Bristol deanery (1580). Carew did not, however, as was often later claimed through confusion with the royal deanery at Windsor, resign the deanery of the Chapel Royal; it was only at Windsor that he was succeeded by William Day. Upon Carew's death the Chapel Royal deanery was left vacant until the accession of James I.

Carew died in London on 1 June 1583, aged eighty-five, and was buried on 3 July at St Giles-in-the-Fields, London, still possessed of the deaneries of the Chapel Royal and Exeter, precentorships at Salisbury and Wells, and the rectory of Mells. Before 1552 he had married Anne (d1605), daughter of Sir Nicholas Harvey. Their eldest son, Peter (BA Oxon., 1572), who was knighted in Ireland in 1579, was killed in battle there in 1580, and their heir was their second son, George *Carew, later Baron Carew of Clopton and earl of Totnes (1555–1629). Their daughter Mary married Walter Dowrish, son and heir of Thomas Dowrish of Devon.

P. E. McCullough

Sources Foster, *Alum. Oxon., 1500–1714*, 1.236 · *LP Henry VIII*, vols. 7–21 · *CPR, 1547–1603* · *CSP dom., 1547–1625* · *Fasti Angl., 1300–1541*, [Exeter] · *Fasti Angl., 1541–1857*, [Chichester] · *Fasti Angl., 1300–1541*, [Bath and Wells] · *Fasti Angl., 1300–1541*, [Salisbury] · *Fasti Angl., 1541–1857*, [Bristol] · Wood, *Ath. Oxon.: Fasti* (1815), 58–9 · will, PRO, PROB 11/65, fol. 318v · F. W. Weaver, ed., *Somerset incumbents* (privately printed, Bristol, 1889) · J. Strype, *The life and acts of Matthew Parker*, new edn, 3 vols. (1821) · J. Strype, *Annals of the Reformation and establishment of religion … during Queen Elizabeth's happy reign*, new edn, 4 vols. (1824) · P. E. McCullough, *Sermons at court: politics and religion in Elizabethan and Jacobean preaching* (1998) [incl. CD-ROM] · D. MacCulloch, *Tudor church militant: Edward VI and the protestant Reformation* (1999) · W. P. Haugaard, 'The coronation of Elizabeth I', *Journal of Ecclesiastical History*, 19 (1968), 161–70

Wealth at death see will, PRO, PROB 11/65, fol. 318v

Carew, Sir George (c.1504–1545), soldier and naval commander, was the eldest son of Sir William Carew (c.1483–1536), landowner, of Mohun's Ottery, Devon, and his wife, Joan (d. 1554), daughter of Sir William Courtenay of Powderham, Devon, and his second wife, Mary. The adventurer Sir Peter *Carew (1514?–1575) was his brother and heir. He was perhaps the George Carewe admitted to the Middle Temple on 2 November 1519, but was otherwise educated as a gentleman in the household of Henry Courtenay, second earl of Devon and first marquess of Exeter. As the eldest son, he was restricted to a more conventional landowning and military career than Peter Carew enjoyed. He did have something of his younger brother's questing spirit, however, and journeyed to Blois, unsuccessfully seeking service with Louise of Savoy, the regent of France, in 1526; he was pardoned by Henry VIII in November. Like other members of Exeter's circle, in 1533 Carew was named in connection with the prophetess Elizabeth Barton (the Holy Maid of Kent). But these indiscretions did him little harm, and in 1536 he sat in the House of Commons as second knight of the shire for Devon. His knighthood probably dates from the same year. He served as sheriff of Devon from 1536 to 1537, and was granted the lease of Frithelstock Priory, Devon.

In 1537 Carew had his first taste of naval service under the Vice-Admiral Sir John Dudley, patrolling the English Channel against pirates. In August he was formally seised of his father's estates. He returned to Devon and became a JP in 1538, sitting on the commission of oyer and terminer for the western counties. In March 1539 he succeeded his disgraced kinsman Sir Nicholas *Carew (b. in or before 1496, d. 1539) as captain of Rysbank, one of the fortifications in the Calais pale. He judged it ill-supplied with munitions, 'as raw and bare a house of war as ever was seen, with good artillery but not half a barrel of powder and no bows and arrows' (LP Henry VIII, 14/1, no. 582). He also sat on the council headed by the deputy of Calais, Arthur Plantagenet, sixth Viscount Lisle. The Act of Six Articles (1539) threatened the protestant preachers who had found a home in Calais, but Carew supported them on the council, for which he was commended by John Foxe. He also admitted to eating meat during Lent; clearly he did not share the Catholic sympathies of his former master, Exeter. In December 1539 he participated in the reception of Anne of Cleves at Calais. On 1 May 1540 Carew was back in England, tourneying in front of the king at Durham Place, but he was taken to the Tower of London (though not imprisoned) following Lisle's arrest later that month. One of Lisle's chaplains, Gregory Botolph, had defected to Rome, where he bragged that he could deliver Calais into the hands of Cardinal Reginald Pole. Carew was presumably questioned about this claim, and about the nest of protestant sacramentarians that had recently been discovered in Calais. His replies must have satisfied the crown, since he retained his post at Rysbank.

Carew married twice, but had no children. His first wife was Thomasine, daughter of Sir Lewis Pollard of King's Nympton, Devon, and his wife, Agnes. She died on 18 December 1539. Soon afterwards he married Mary (d. 1570), daughter of Henry Norris of Bray, Berkshire, and his wife, Mary, and a member of Princess Mary's household. The couple were at court at Christmas 1540, when Mary was presented with a necklace by the king. Early in 1541 they were granted Polslo Priory outside Exeter. Further advancement came in 1542, when Carew was again pricked sheriff and granted the stewardship of Exeter's possessions, worth £30 a year. In 1544 he became lieutenant of the gentlemen pensioners, drawing a salary of £1 a day.

Carew spent the last two years of his life serving his sovereign against the French. In summer 1543 he exchanged the Rysbank command for a post as lieutenant-general of horse under Sir John Wallop in Flanders, where he sat on the army council. Accompanied by his brother Peter he skirmished with the defenders of Thérouanne and then participated in the siege of Landrecies, narrowly missing a sniper's bullet while inspecting a trench outside the town. In November he was captured while too closely pursuing a French retreat, and he spent several months in enemy hands before being released at Henry's request. Carew saw further action during the Boulogne campaign of 1544, when a muster book listed him as supplying twenty men.

In spring 1545 he took another naval command in the channel under Viscount Lisle (Dudley), now lord admiral. By early summer England was preparing for invasion.

A huge French force of 150 ships and 25 galleys entered the Solent on 19 July 1545, heading for Portsmouth and the English fleet. Henry reviewed his navy in person, dining aboard the Great Harry with his senior naval commanders, Carew (who was appointed vice-admiral during the meeting) and Lisle. Before being rowed ashore the king placed a gold whistle on a chain around Carew's neck, the insignia of his promotion. Carew took for his flagship the Mary Rose, one of the great royal carracks laid down in 1509. In 1536 she had been uprated to 700 tons and strengthened to allow for a complete gun-deck. There are several accounts of the catastrophe that befell her late in the day. The French incorrectly believed that the Mary Rose was sunk by the artillery bombardment sent up by their galleys. In fact, she foundered through a combination of poor seamanship and ill luck. Both the imperial ambassador, François van der Delft, who was relying on the report of a survivor, and the antiquary John Hooker, who had eyewitness accounts from Sir Peter and Sir Gawen Carew (c.1503–1585), agreed that the Mary Rose heeled over when her sails caught a sudden breeze. The ship was probably going about to bring her second broadside to bear on the French galleys. The sea then rushed in through her open gunports, which were only about 4 feet from the waterline, and she sank with great speed. Sir George Carew went down with his ship, as did all but two dozen of her complement of 500 men. His wife, watching from Southsea Castle a mile away, fainted at the sight and was attended by the king.

Though he shares in the blame for this naval disaster, Carew was not the captain of the Mary Rose on the day she sank; Roger Grenville was at the helm. There does seem to have been a problem with the chain of command on Carew's flagship, since he shouted across to his uncle Sir Gawen Carew on the Matthew Gonson that 'he had a sort of knaves he could not rule' (Wagner, 77). Perhaps neither Carew nor Grenville was familiar with the Solent's dangerous mixture of wind and powerful double tide. The uprate of 1536 and the overloading of the ship with additional men and cannon were important factors. The entire dramatic scene is captured in the 'Cowdray engraving', an eighteenth-century copy of a lost Tudor mural. Hans Holbein the younger's sketch of Carew is in the Royal Collection at Windsor Castle.

Carew's widow returned to court, serving both Henry's daughters before marrying Sir Arthur Champernown; she died in 1570. The remains of the Mary Rose were raised in 1982, and are preserved at Portsmouth royal dockyard. Among the many personal items recovered from the sea bed were some pewter plates stamped 'G. C.', presumably George Carew's.

J. P. D. COOPER

Sources HoP, Commons, 1509–58, 1.573–4 · LP Henry VIII, vols. 11–20 · J. A. Wagner, The Devon gentleman: the life of Sir Peter Carew (1998) · N. A. M. Rodger, The safeguard of the sea: a naval history of Britain, 1: 660–1649 (1997) · D. Starkey, ed., Henry VIII: a European court in

England (1991), 181 • private information (2004) [Mrs J. A. C. Richardson]
Likenesses H. Holbein, sketch, Royal Collection

Carew, George, earl of Totnes (1555–1629), soldier and administrator, was born on 29 May 1555, the second son of George *Carew (1497/8–1583), Church of England clergyman, and his wife, Anne (*d.* 1605), daughter of Sir Nicholas Harvey and his second wife, Bridget. He was educated at Broadgates Hall, Oxford, from 1564 to 1573 and was created MA on 17 September 1589. His elder brother, Peter Carew (*d.* 1580), served as a soldier in Ireland.

Carew married Joyce (*bap.* 1562, *d.* 1637), first daughter and coheir of William Clopton, of Clopton near Stratford upon Avon, Warwickshire, on 31 May 1580. They had one son, who predeceased them. Carew went to Ireland in 1574 and entered the service of his cousin Sir Peter *Carew, who pursued claims to land allegedly granted to his ancestors by Henry II. Carew was a volunteer in the army of Sir Henry Sidney, lord deputy, in 1575. In 1576 he was appointed lieutenant-governor of co. Carlow and vice-constable of Leighlin Castle, co. Carlow, of which his brother Peter Carew was constable. In 1577, when his brother was absent, Carew successfully defended Leighlin Castle against Rory Oge O'More.

Carew continued in military service, being a captain in the Royal Navy during Sir Humphrey Gilbert's expedition to the West Indies in 1578 and a captain in the army in Ireland in 1579–80. On the death of his brother Peter Carew in a skirmish in Glenmalure, co. Wicklow, on 25 August 1580, he was appointed constable of Leighlin Castle, a post he held until 1602. As a consequence of his brother's death Carew harboured a deep hatred towards the Irish and it perhaps says something about his character that, to the embarrassment of the Irish and English governments, he killed 'Owen O'Nasy' whom he alleged to be his brother's murderer, in Dublin in 1583.

Carew continued in government service in Ireland and later in England. In 1583 he was appointed sheriff of co. Carlow and on 24 February 1586 he was knighted by Sir John Perrott, the lord deputy. Later that year he journeyed to London to report on the state of Ireland. He was master of the ordnance in Ireland from January 1588 and was named an Irish privy councillor in 1590. Despite his absence, he was appointed JP for Kent and Middlesex in 1583 and for Devon in 1592, reflecting his wealth and status as well as his proven ability. In August 1592 Carew resigned the mastership of the ordnance in Ireland on being promoted to the post of lieutenant-general of the ordnance in England. He took part in the expeditions to Cadiz in 1596 and to the Azores in 1597 under Robert Devereux, second earl of Essex. He was elected MP for Queenborough, Kent, in 1597. In 1598 he accompanied his close friend and patron Sir Robert Cecil, principal secretary, on an embassy to France—Carew had himself been nominated ambassador to France about 1586 and ambassador to Scotland in 1594, but declined to accept either post.

With the Nine Years' War spreading throughout Ireland and increasingly becoming a serious threat to English

George Carew, earl of Totnes (1555–1629), by Robert van Voerst, pubd 1633

rule, Carew was appointed lord president of Munster on 27 January 1600, remaining in the post to 1604. Applying a mixture of skilled diplomacy and military force in his dealings with Florence MacCarthy and James fitz Thomas Fitzgerald, earl of Desmond (the so-called *súgán* earl), he succeeded in suppressing the rebellion in Munster within little over a year. He worked closely with Charles Blount, eighth Baron Mountjoy, lord deputy. When the Spanish fleet under Don Juan del Águila landed at Kinsale, co. Cork, in 1601 Carew accompanied Mountjoy there and took part in the siege. In November he was given the task of intercepting Hugh O'Donnell in order to prevent his forces from joining with those of Hugh O'Neill, third earl of Tyrone. However, a sudden frost enabled O'Donnell to cross the mountains of Slieve Phelim and escape Carew. The legend that Tyrone's planned attack on Mountjoy at Kinsale was betrayed to Carew by Brian MacHugh Oge MacMahon for a bottle of whiskey, which has been told and retold, has been exposed as false by Gerard Hayes-McCoy and John Silke. After the English victory at Kinsale in December 1601, Carew completed the reduction of Munster by capturing Dunboyne Castle, co. Meath, in 1602.

As lord president of Munster, Carew systematically attacked the political power and independence of the Old English towns. He regarded them with suspicion because of their Catholicism as well as their far-reaching privileges. Besides building new fortifications at Cork, Limerick, and Waterford, he singled out Kinsale for punishment because of its apparent welcome of the Spanish fleet. Its charter was seized and the town was forced to rebuild the destroyed castle. After Ireland had been largely pacified Carew sought to return to England, but was only allowed to do so in March 1603, shortly before Elizabeth I's death. His successor as lord president of Munster was Sir Henry Brouncker, who was appointed on 4 June 1604.

Carew became a courtier and was high in the favour of James VI and I. He was appointed to the council of Anne of Denmark, and named vice-chamberlain and receiver-general of her household in October 1603. He was elected MP for Hastings, Sussex, in 1604. He was elevated to the peerage, being created Baron Carew, of Clopton, the property of his wife, on 4 May 1605. Carew held several posts and fulfilled a variety of functions; he was master of the ordnance from 27 June 1608 to 1629, appointed keeper of Nonsuch House and Park, Surrey, and councillor for the colony of Virginia (both 1609), and governor of Guernsey (1610). He was made a member of the privy council on 20 July 1616 and of the council of war on 20 July 1624. The latter body considered the question of recovering the Palatinate, lost by James's son-in-law Frederick V at the beginning of the Thirty Years' War.

Carew's involvement in Irish politics also continued. He visited Ireland in 1611, having been commissioned to report on the condition and problems of the plantation of Ulster. He suggested the creation of new boroughs in Ulster to ensure a protestant majority in the elections to the Irish parliament of 1613–15. In 1624 he was again appointed to a commission about the plantation of Ulster, together with Sir Arthur Chichester and Oliver St John, first Viscount Grandison of Limerick.

Carew was Sir Walter Ralegh's friend and pleaded unsuccessfully with James for his life. He was also a friend and patron of the antiquaries William Camden, Sir Robert Cotton, and Sir Thomas Bodley. In spite of his hatred of the Irish, Carew was very interested in Irish history and preserved contemporary documents relating to Ireland as well as buying older ones. In his will, he bequeathed his manuscripts and books to Sir Thomas *Stafford (d. 1655), who, on insufficient evidence, has been alleged to have been his illegitimate son. Stafford used Carew's papers to put together the detailed account of the Nine Years' War entitled *Pacata Hibernia* which was published in 1633. Most of the Carew manuscripts are now in Lambeth Palace Library, London.

At the accession of Charles I, Carew was already a sick old man, but he lived long enough to receive more favour. He became a member of the king's council in the north on 19 April 1625, was appointed treasurer and receiver-general to Henrietta Maria in 1626, and on 7 February 1626 was promoted earl of Totnes. He died on 27 March 1629 at his house in the Savoy, London, and was buried in the church of Stratford upon Avon on 2 May. Carew was different from many of his New English contemporaries in Ireland in that, although he spent many years in government and military service there, he did not become a planter. In this respect he was similar to his distant kinsman Sir George Carey [see below]. His attitude towards Ireland was fundamentally ambivalent: while he hated the Gaelic Irish for the death of his brother and was more than eager to leave the country after Kinsale, he was nevertheless fascinated by Irish history, even to the point of constructing pedigrees of Irish families.

Sir George Carey [Cary] (c.1541–1616), lord deputy of Ireland, was the first son of Thomas Carey (d. 1567), landowner of Cockington, Devon, and his wife, Mary, daughter of John Southcote of Bovey Tracey, Devon, and his second wife, Joanna. He was educated at the Inner Temple from 1558. Carey married Wilmot, daughter and heir of John Gifford of Yeovil, Somerset, who had been divorced from John Bury of Colyton, Devon, about 1561. They had two sons and two daughters. He was initially prominent in Devon affairs, being one of the principal gentlemen of the county, and was captain of the militia by 1572, JP from about 1579, and deputy lieutenant from 1587. He was MP for Dartmouth in 1586 and for Devon in 1589. He was a follower of Essex by the mid-1590s and went with him to Ireland. Carey was under-treasurer of Ireland from 1 March 1598. He was knighted in 1598, served as treasurer-at-war in Ireland from 1599 to 1606, and was appointed, with Adam Loftus, archbishop of Dublin, as lord justice of Ireland on 24 September 1599, when Essex returned to England. He was responsible for introducing a new debased coinage in Ireland in 1601 and was accused of enriching himself through peculation. The case was brought before the court of the exchequer and dragged on for years but came to nothing. This perhaps explains the motto on the miniature of Carey painted by Isaac Oliver: 'free from all filthy fraud' (HoP, *Commons, 1558–1603*, 1.547).

Carey was lord deputy of Ireland from May 1603 to 16 July 1604 and dealt with reconstruction in the wake of the departure of his close friend Mountjoy. Although his father and his brother Richard (b. c.1546, d. in or after 1616), were both Catholic, Carey himself was protestant, and even recommended harsher measures against Catholics, the 'wicked rabble' to stem the Counter-Reformation (ibid.). At an unknown date he married Lettice, daughter of Robert Rich, third Baron Rich and first earl of Warwick, and his first wife, Penelope. They had no children. He died on 15 February 1616 and was buried at Cockington. His will was not proved until May 1617.

UTE LOTZ-HEUMANN

Sources J. S. Brewer and W. Bullen, eds., *Calendar of the Carew manuscripts*, 6 vols., PRO (1867–73) · *CSP Ire., 1574–1625* · R. Bagwell, *Ireland under the Tudors*, 3 vols. (1885–90); repr. (1963) · R. Bagwell, *Ireland under the Stuarts*, 3 vols. (1909–16); repr. (1963) · GEC, *Peerage* · R. C. Gabriel, 'Carew, Sir George', P. W. Hasler, 'Carey, George', HoP, *Commons, 1558–1603* · DNB · T. Stafford, *Pacata Hibernia: Ireland appeased and reduced, or, An historie of the late warres of Ireland* (1633) · Foster, *Alum. Oxon.* · C. Falls, *Elizabeth's Irish wars* (1950); repr. (1996) · J. J. Silke, *Kinsale: the Spanish intervention in Ireland at the end of the Elizabethan wars* (1970) · will of George Carew, earl of Totnes,

PRO, PROB 11/129, sig. 47; PROB 11/155, sigs. 36, 57 · V. L. Rutledge, 'The commission of Sir George Carew in 1611: a review of the exchequer and the judiciary of Ireland', PhD diss., McGill University, 1986

Archives BL, register of corresp., Add. MS 28658 · Bodl. Oxf. · LPL, collections, papers, and corresp. · University College, Oxford | BL, Harley MSS · CKS, corresp. with Lionel Cranfield · PRO, state papers, Ireland and domestic

Likenesses R. van Voerst, line engraving, pubd 1633, BM, NPG [*see illus.*] · oils (after type, *c*.1615–1620), NPG; version, Garhambury House, Hertfordshire · portrait, repro. in Stafford, *Pacata Hibernia*

Wealth at death manors (esp. Clopton House near Stratford upon Avon) and lands in Warwickshire; tenements, stables, and gardens in Drury Lane; mansion house in Savoy, London; messuages and lands in Holborn; Woodgrange farm in Essex; divers manors and lands in Devon and Cornwall; unknown amount of money, jewels, and household goods; books and manuscripts: will, PRO, PROB 11/129, sig. 47; PROB 11/155, sigs. 36, 57

Carew, Sir George (*c*.1556–1612), administrator and diplomat, was probably born at Antony, Cornwall, the second son of Thomas Carew (*c*.1527–1564), landowner, and his wife, Elizabeth, daughter of Sir Richard Edgcumbe and his second wife, Elizabeth. Richard *Carew the historian was his brother. In 1577, after university, presumably Oxford, he entered the Middle Temple, before taking the grand tour and sitting in the first of seven consecutive parliaments: for St Germans in 1584–5, 1597–8, 1601, and 1604–10; and for Saltash in 1586–7, 1589, and 1593. In 1588 he married Thomasine (*d*. *c*.1635), daughter of Sir Francis Godolphin.

Carew became Lord Chancellor Hatton's secretary in spring 1587, and retained the post under succeeding keepers of the great seal Sir John Puckering and Sir Thomas Egerton. Accumulating positions, he was indeed, as he sometimes signed to prevent confusion with namesakes, 'George Carew of the Chancery'. Protonotary from 10 October 1593, he wrote ambassadorial commissions and engrossed treaties, and was also clerk for writing supplicavits and supersedeas of the peace and pardons of outlawry. The package was envied, and his charges were criticized in 1598; but he was armoured with the good opinion of his superiors, who valued his work as an extraordinary master and, from 21 December 1599, master in chancery. With his uncle Sir Matthew *Carew, he was one of Egerton's agents in administrative reconstruction. Another was William Lambarde, whose notes Carew cast into a work entitled *Treatise of the Masters* and reports, cited as Cary. These were in circulation before their first printing in 1650, and greatly helped to establish chancery precedents. Admired by scholars, remembered by Joseph Scaliger as 'vir amplissimus et sapientia et eruditione, et pietate præstantissimus' ('a man of exceptional wisdom and learning, and exceedingly devout'), Carew's enduring legacy was Cary, mostly the work of another.

In summer 1598, trade being disrupted by disputes and expulsions, Carew was sent to Brunswick, Danzig, and Elbing with some success. But he could only maintain Elizabeth's honour 'above all things' in a fruitless visit to Poland and its king, which entailed crossing to Sigismund III's other kingdom, Sweden. In 1612 he gave an account (authorship has also been attributed to William Bruce) to Jacques-Auguste de Thou, who used it in his contemporary history.

Unlike his elder brother Richard, Carew was devoted to jostling for advancement. Positive when it suited, hissed in the 1601 Commons, his humility in pursuit of favours was abject. He had a house near Kingston, Surrey, but operated mostly from lodgings in the Strand, strategically close to a residence of Sir Robert Cecil, whom he solicited with 'sensitive pen' (Hurstfield, 232). In 1602 he became master of requests and associate bencher of his inn. Within days of Elizabeth's death he was sent north with government papers for James, who knighted him at Whitehall on 23 July 1603. In 1604, on the Commons committee to consider union, his area was 'matter of estate foreign, or matter of intercourse' (Spedding, 3.199–200).

Nominated ambassador to France in summer 1605, Carew was delayed by having to wait for travel money and then by the Gunpowder Plot; he also broke his journey to conduct an interrogation. But after his first audience in December he was treated by Henri IV with exceptional familiarity and friendship. His embassy, however, was difficult. Seeking Tyrone's arrest earned a rebuke, requests for repayment of disputed money were brushed aside, and Henri could not be turned from his belief that England inclined towards Spain, flirted with Venetian meddling, and was ruled by a nincompoop. Distinguishing between the amoral man and statesman king, Carew reported his experience in letters, and after his recall in July 1609 he wove their gist into 'A Relation' for James's eyes, written in imitation of Venetian practice. Past support of Henri was regretted. France, too strong to invade, was the most dangerous neighbour. Even so, a combination of England, Spain, and the disaffected might secure fragmentation, perhaps recovery of a few lost lands. Weaknesses included the venality of French office-holding and justice: Carew would have remembered troubles as a lessee in rue Tournon, near Porte St Germain in Paris, which forced a move next door. Strengths were Henri's frugalities and the support of Sully, who diverted tax money from embezzling officials to crown coffers. He had penned a job application, one fruit as a pensioner being £200 p.a. for life.

Resuming chancery work, Carew was still an MP in 1610, despite past non-appearance and offers to resign. His stock was rising, his wife was attached to Queen Anne, and he communed with arriving friends de Thou and Isaac Casaubon, Thomasine standing as godmother for his child in 1612. When Salisbury died, Carew replaced him as master of the wards on a temporary basis in mid-June 1612. He was also responsible for French correspondence. Once considered undistinguished, a meaner sort chosen to be a tool, he did say on inauguration on 16 June that the king would be his own master, and promised reforms that never materialized; but it might have been a good appointment. Confirmation early in August accompanied membership of a committee to augment revenue. The intent, matching his appreciation of Sully, was to channel more of the proceeds to the crown by squeezing lesser agents. In 1613 court of wards net income was up, but he did not live to see it.

An adept diplomat and institutional lawyer, Carew was distracted by versatility and robbed by death. A writer who did not publish, his scholarly promise was unfulfilled. In 1611 he secured joint grants of his writing offices for his heir, Francis, but a personal worth of £10,000, placing him 'in reasonable case' (*Letters of John Chamberlain*, 1.392), was not excessive for a careerist with another son and three daughters. He died of typhus on Friday 13 November 1612, at his new house in Tothill Street, Westminster, and was buried in nearby St Margaret's Church.

W. J. JONES

Sources H. E. Bell, *An introduction to the history and records of the court of wards and liveries* (1953) · D. Buisseret, *Henry IV* (1984) · *CSP dom., 1598–1618* · G. Carew, 'A relation of the state of France', *An historical view of the negotiations between the courts of England, France, and Brussels, from the year 1592 to 1617*, ed. T. Birch (1749), 413–529 · R. Carew, *The survey of Cornwall*, ed. F. E. Halliday (1953) · *Calendar of the manuscripts of the most hon. the marquis of Salisbury*, 7–21, HMC, 9 (1899–1970) · W. J. Jones, *The Elizabethan court of chancery* (1967) · J. W. Stoye, *English travellers abroad, 1604–1667* (1952) · Boase & Courtney, *Bibl. Corn.*, vol. 3 · *The letters of John Chamberlain*, ed. N. E. McClure, 1 (1939) · M. Lee, *James I and Henri IV* (1970) · A. G. R. Smith, *Servant of the Cecils: the life of Sir Michael Hickes, 1543–1612* (1977) · W. Camden, *The history of the most renowned and victorious Princess Elizabeth*, rev. edn (1675), 537–9 · J. Hurstfield, *The queen's wards: wardship and marriage under Elizabeth I* (1958) · *The letters and life of Francis Bacon*, ed. J. Spedding, 7 vols. (1861–74), vol. 3 · H. Zins, *England and the Baltic in the Elizabethan era*, trans. H. C. Stevens (1972), 10.28, n.18 · M. Prestwich, *Cranfield: politics and profits under the early Stuarts* (1966), 109, n.3
Archives BL, relation of the state of Polonia anno 1598, Royal MS 18.B.I · Hatfield House, Hertfordshire, corresp., MSS · Hunt. L., account of France · PRO, Chancery reports and certificates, Chancery working papers, C 38/2–5 · PRO, state papers, domestic, corresp., SP 12, 14 · PRO, state papers, foreign, diplomatic letters, SP 78 · Yale U., description of France | BL, letters to Sir Thomas Edmondes, Stowe MSS 168–171, *passim* · Hunt. L., Ellesmere collection, holograph working (legal) papers
Wealth at death £10,000: *Letters of John Chamberlain*, 1.392

Carew, Sir John (d. 1362), soldier and justiciar of Ireland, was a son of the second marriage of Sir John Carew (d. 1324), who held Carew in Pembrokeshire, Moulsford in Berkshire, lands in Devon and Hampshire, and Idrone, Carlow, and other Irish properties which the family had acquired in the late twelfth century by grants made to Odo of Carew by his brother, Raymond fitz William Fitzgerald (Raymond le Gros). John's mother was Joan, daughter of Gilbert Talbot. Known as Lady Carew, during her widowhood she entered the service of Queen Philippa, and was still living in 1360. John Carew became heir to the family estates when his half-brother, Nicholas Carew, died within a few weeks of their father. In 1331–2 he and Joan were among the absentee landholders ordered to support Edward III's projected Irish expedition, but there is little evidence of activity on his part before the outbreak of the Hundred Years' War. By 1338 he was a household knight of Edward III, serving in the Netherlands (1338–40), Scotland (1341–2), Brittany (1342–3), and at Crécy and Calais (1346–7).

Carew's career acquired an Irish emphasis as he became involved in the attempt at military recovery that gathered pace from the mid-1340s. In 1344 he went to Ireland as a leading member of the retinue of the justiciar, Ralph Ufford, and lost two horses in a campaign in Ulster in 1345. After Ufford's death in April 1346 he was appointed by the Mortimers as seneschal of Trim, and was also a keeper of the peace and negotiator with the Irish in Carlow. His career in Irish central government began on 28 August 1349, when he was appointed escheator, an office he held, with brief intervals, until 1358. From 3 October to 19 December 1349 he was deputy justiciar pending the arrival of Thomas Rokeby, and organized the defence of the county of Dublin against the raids of the Uí Bhroin of Wicklow. In 1359 he was summoned to great councils at Dublin and Waterford to discuss the defence of Ireland. His experience was harnessed during the lieutenancy of Lionel, duke of Clarence. In July 1361 he was one of the group of advisers by whose counsel the king ordered his son to act; and from 14 August 1361 to 13 May 1362, now a banneret, he served Lionel with a retinue of nine men-at-arms and ten mounted archers. He died, probably in Ireland, on 6 June 1362, leaving a widow, Elizabeth. His heir was Leonard Carew (1342–1369), his son with his first wife, Margaret Mohun, and the father of Sir Thomas *Carew (1368?–1431). At least two other sons, William and Edmund, also survived him.

ROBIN FRAME

Sources *Chancery records* · PRO, E101 · PRO, E372 · Rec. Comm. calendar of memoranda rolls, NA Ire., NAI RC8 · E. St J. Brooks, *Knights' fees in counties Wexford, Carlow and Kilkenny, 13th–15th century*, IMC (1950) · J. H. Round, 'The origin of the Carews', *The Ancestor*, 5 (1903), 19–53 · A. Ayton, *Knights and warhorses: military service and the English aristocracy under Edward III* (1994) · E. Tresham, ed., *Rotulorum patentium et clausorum cancellariae Hiberniae calendarium*, Irish Record Commission (1828) · *The wardrobe book of William de Norwell*, ed. M. Lyon and others (1983) · H. G. Richardson and G. O. Sayles, *The administration of Ireland, 1172–1377* (1963) · *VCH Berkshire* · *VCH Hampshire and the Isle of Wight* · *CIPM*, 11, no. 300
Wealth at death English and Welsh estates: *CIPM*

Carew, John (1622–1660), politician and regicide, was born on 3 July 1622, the second son of Sir Richard *Carew, first baronet (1579/80–1643?), experimenter and educationist, of Antony, Cornwall, and his second wife, Grace (1603/4–1658), daughter of Robert Rolle of Heanton Satchville, Devon. He was admitted to Gloucester Hall, Oxford, on 9 March 1638, and to the Inner Temple in November 1639, but received no formal qualifications. Elected to parliament as a recruiter MP for Tregony, Cornwall, in late February 1647, he soon emerged as an independent, although he made little impression in the house before Pride's Purge in December 1648. He was involved in preparing the trial of Charles I and, although he initially sought to avoid participating in the proceedings, supported its legitimacy, proved to be one of the most assiduous commissioners, and signed the death warrant [see also Regicides].

An energetic member of the Rump, Carew served on the army committee and the committee for plundered ministers, and was elected to the council of state in February and November 1651. His interests included the disposal of church and crown property, and cases regarding suspects and delinquents. He demonstrated enthusiasm for legal reform and was involved in selecting the Hale commission, and displayed concern for social reform and the welfare of the poor, the indebted, and the imprisoned. During the First Anglo-Dutch War he developed an expertise in both diplomatic relations and naval affairs. He also became identifiable as a leading millenarian and Fifth Monarchist, alongside his close friend Thomas Harrison. He represented Devon in Barebone's assembly of 'saints', and was reappointed to the council of state in July and November 1653, but although identifiable as a supporter of religious toleration Carew's preoccupation with his duties as a navy commissioner precluded him from an active role in the Commons.

Carew did not object to government by a single person, but soon expressed his hostility to the Cromwellian protectorate and his suspicion regarding its hereditary pretensions in a work called *The Grand Catastrophe* (January 1654). His opposition to Cromwell was reflected in his rumoured involvement in 1654 in the 'Wildman' plot with its call to arms against the protector, and in his demand for the release of two Fifth Monarchist preachers, Christopher Feake and John Rogers, in February 1655. Refusing to recognize the legitimacy of the regime, Carew declined to answer a summons from Cromwell, saying that 'when the little [Barebone's] Parliament was dissolved [Cromwell] took the crown off from the head of Christ and put it upon his own' (Firth, 2.244). This led to his imprisonment in mid-February 1655, where he remained, visited by the likes of the Fifth Monarchist Anna Trapnel, until October 1656. Carew declined to join Thomas Venner's planned Fifth Monarchist rising in 1657, and by early 1658 represented those millenarians who undertook to be baptized, and who sought an alliance with the Baptists, with whom Carew held discussions at Dorchester. He was eligible to sit in the restored Rump in May 1659, but although he was reappointed as a navy commissioner (26 May), he made no recorded impression on the proceedings, and was eventually fined £100 for his absence.

Carew did not return to the Commons before the Restoration, but neither did he flee in 1660. Nevertheless, confusion over the warrant for his arrest delayed his apprehension, and ensured that he was exempted from pardon and subjected to trial as a regicide. Indicted on 10 October 1660, he was brought to trial two days later to face witnesses who testified to his presence in the high court and identified his signature on the warrant. Carew denied being 'moved by the devil' to participate in the trial, and professed obedience to God's 'holy and righteous laws' and the authority of an act of parliament (*State trials*, 5.1052). Such speeches, together with his attempt to justify the trial in the context of the 1640s, provoked the court to claim that he aimed 'to blow the trumpet of sedition' (ibid., 5.1055). Found guilty, he was executed at Charing Cross on 15 October, although his family was granted his body for private burial rather than having to suffer the ignominy of its public display. Carew went to the scaffold expecting to receive a 'glorious crown' from Christ, and confident that his prosecutors would be destroyed by the wrath of God, and by the 'resurrection of

this cause' (Ludlow, 226). He said that his own blood would 'warm the blood that had been shed, and cause notable execution to come down upon the head of their enemy' (ibid., 217).

J. T. PEACEY

Sources B. S. Capp, *The Fifth Monarchy Men: a study in seventeenth-century English millenarianism* (1972) · *JHC*, 5–7 (1646–59) · *CSP dom.*, 1651–61 · *State trials*, vol. 5 · E. Ludlow, *A voyce from the watch tower*, ed. A. B. Worden, CS, 4th ser., 21 (1978) · Johannes Cornubiensis [J. Carew], *The grand catastrophe* (1654) · A. Woolrych, *Commonwealth to protectorate* (1982) · B. Worden, *The Rump Parliament, 1648–1653* (1974) · D. Underdown, *Pride's Purge: politics in the puritan revolution* (1971) · C. Burrage, 'The fifth monarchy insurrections', *EngHR*, 25 (1910), 722–47 · Thurloe, *State papers*, vols. 3–7 · *The Clarke papers*, ed. C. H. Firth, 4 vols., CS, new ser., 49, 54, 61–2 (1891–1901), vols. 2 and 3

Likenesses S. Cooper, miniature, watercolour, Antony, Cornwall; version, V&A · group portrait, line engraving (*The regicides executed in 1660*), BM

Carew, John Edward (*c*.1782–1868), sculptor, was born at Tramore, co. Waterford. Nothing is known about his early life, though his father was probably a sculptor. He is reputed to have received some instruction in art in Dublin before moving to London in 1809, when he became an assistant to the sculptor Richard Westmacott, with whom he remained until 1823. He established his reputation with a bust of Marquess Wellesley (exh. RA, 1813; priv. coll.) and also sculpted George III (exh. RA, 1820). During the last ten or twelve years with Westmacott he was receiving annually from £1500 to £1800, as well as £800 from private practice. From 1821 he also had a studio of his own in partnership with one of his brothers at 62 Edgware Road, London.

In 1822 or 1823 Carew was introduced to the third earl of Egremont, who purchased his marble *Arethusa* for Petworth House, Sussex, in 1823 and invited him to devote his talents almost exclusively to his service. From that year until 1831 Carew, who continued to live in London, was employed on various works for his new patron. In 1831 he established himself in Brighton, where he built a house and large studio, and was frequently at Petworth House, Lord Egremont's home. In 1835 he went to live at Grove House, near Petworth, a residence granted him by Egremont at a nominal rent, and remained there until his patron's death in November 1837. Between 1823 and 1837 he was occupied in producing various groups, statues, busts, and five chimney-pieces, many of which were made expressly for Lord Egremont for Petworth. The most important of these works were *Adonis and the Boar* (1826), *Vulcan and Venus* (1827), *The Falconer* (1829), and *Prometheus and Pandora* (1831)—all at Petworth. He also made a statue of the statesman William Huskisson (1832) for Chichester Cathedral, as well as those of the earl of Egremont (exh. RA, 1831; Petworth House, Sussex), the novelist Captain Frederick Marryat (exh. RA, 1834), and Father Theobald Mathew (exh. RA, 1844). In addition to the chimney-pieces for Petworth House, he made two in marble for Buckingham Palace in London. He also restored sculptures sent from Rome. He exhibited at the Royal Academy from 1821 to 1846, in 1830 showing *Model of a Gladiator, Bear in the*

Arena, and *Theseus and Minotaur*. In each of the years 1832, 1834, and 1835 he also sent two busts to the academy.

On Lord Egremont's death Carew, who was not mentioned in the will, made a claim upon the estate of £50,000, a sum due to him (according to his contention) for various works supplied to his patron. The cause was tried at the Sussex spring assizes held at Lewes on 18 March 1840, when Richard Westmacott and Francis Chantrey both spoke of Carew's Petworth statues as works of the highest talent. On the production of convincing evidence of payment by the defendants, plaintiff's counsel was compelled to agree to a nonsuit for his client. After the trial Carew was declared insolvent, following which his pecuniary affairs had to undergo a further searching examination in the bankruptcy court.

In 1839 Carew exhibited at the Royal Academy *The Good Samaritan*, a marble bas-relief; in 1842 an angel from a monumental group; and in 1843, 1845, and 1848 some busts. He showed three works at the British Institution, including *A Boy Playing Marbles* (1842), praised by the *Art Union*. In addition to these works, he executed a statue of the actor Edmund Kean (1835, Drury Lane Theatre, London); a well-known statue, *Sir Richard Whittington Listening to the London Bells* (1844, Royal Exchange, London); and statues of Henry Grattan (1844) and John Curran (1856), both in St Stephen's Hall in the Palace of Westminster, London. He also designed *The Death of Nelson at Trafalgar*, one of the four bronze reliefs (1850) which decorate the pedestal of Nelson's Column in Trafalgar Square. He made a number of religious pieces, including a monument to Maria Fitzherbert (1837) and the *Baptism of Christ* (1837), both for the Roman Catholic church of St John the Baptist, Brighton, Sussex; a *Descent from the Cross* (1841) and a relief of the Virgin for the Portuguese embassy chapel (now the Roman Catholic church of the Assumption of St Gregory), Warwick Street, London. The religious works show a debt mainly to the late baroque tradition.

During his latter years Carew was living in London, but failing sight interfered with his work. He was married and had several children, one of whom, F. Carew, exhibited sculpture at the Royal Academy in 1849. John Edward Carew died on 30 November 1868 at his home at 40 Cambridge Street, Hyde Park, London; he was buried in Kensal Green cemetery. He worked in the neo-classical style, though with occasional baroque influences, especially in his religious work. His portraiture could be powerful and realistic, giving his sitters a strong characterization.

W. W. WROTH, rev. JOHN TURPIN

Sources W. G. Strickland, *A dictionary of Irish artists*, 1 (1913), 152–4 · R. H. C. Finch, 'The life and work of J. E. Carew', *Quarterly Bulletin of the Irish Georgian Society*, 9/3–4 (1966), 84–96 · R. Gunnis, *Dictionary of British sculptors, 1660–1851* (1953), 78–90 · H. Potterton, *Irish church monuments, 1570–1880* (1975), 38 · *Report of the trial of the cause, Carew against Burrell* (privately printed, London, 1840) · *Report of the proceedings in the court for the relief of insolvent debtors in the matter of John Edward Carew* (privately printed, London, 1842) · Redgrave, *Artists* · Graves, *RA exhibitors* · J. Johnson, ed., *Works exhibited at the Royal Society of British Artists, 1824–1893, and the New English Art Club, 1888–1917*, 2 vols. (1975)

Likenesses G. Clint, oils, Petworth House, West Sussex · J. Simpson, oils, repro. in Finch, 'Life and work of J. E. Carew' · J. Simpson, oils, Petworth House, West Sussex
Wealth at death insolvent

Carew [*née* Denny], **Martha**, **Lady Carew** (*c*.1500–1572), recusant, was born at Cheshunt, Hertfordshire, the eldest daughter of the exchequer baron Sir Edmund Denny (*d*. 1520) and his second wife, Mary Troutbeck of Bridge Trafford, Cheshire. About 1519 Martha married the financial official Wymond *Carew (1498–1549), a native of Antony in Cornwall. Together they had nineteen children; their sons included the chancery master Sir Matthew *Carew (1531–1618). The Cornish antiquary Richard Carew was their grandson. Martha was the sister of the courtier Sir Anthony *Denny (1501–1549), and an aunt of the Elizabethan secretary Sir Francis Walsingham (1532–1590).

Martha's husband held several posts in royal financial administration, and during the early 1540s the couple lived at Bletchingley, Surrey, where Wymond served the divorced Anne of Cleves as receiver. In April 1545 he was appointed treasurer of the court of first fruits and tenths, and was knighted two years later. As well as adding to the Carew family lands in south-west England, Wymond and his wife purchased the manor of Pyshoo, Hertfordshire, and the fine estate of Brooke House at Hackney, Middlesex, where they lived from early 1548. Upon Sir Wymond Carew's death in August 1549 Martha received the Hackney and Hertfordshire properties as her widow's portion, but she also inherited debts of almost £8000 owing upon her husband's account as treasurer of first fruits and tenths. Martha quickly repaid a portion of this sum, but in 1554 the exchequer seized Hackney and other Carew lands to recover the remainder. Protesting her poverty Martha petitioned the exchequer barons for relief, and in March 1557 they appointed a commission to examine the late treasurer's accounts and determine his widow's liability. Martha did not recover Hackney, however, and she again petitioned unsuccessfully for its restoration in late 1559 (the debts were not fully discharged until 1611). By the early 1560s Martha was living in London, perhaps with her widowed sister Joyce, Lady Carey.

In contrast to her many relations who embraced protestantism, like Sir Anthony Denny and her brother-in-law Sir John *Gates, it appears that Martha Carew remained a Catholic throughout her life. This constancy was not without cost, however, for on 8 September 1562 she was arrested with others attending a mass conducted by the priest Thomas Hayward at a house in Fetter Lane, London. When examined by the bishops of London and Ely, Martha and her companions refused to swear the *ex officio* oath, a tactic designed to frustrate the authorities' investigations by preventing detailed questioning. At her trial at the Old Bailey one month later Martha was convicted and, unwilling or unable to pay a fine of 100 marks, was imprisoned for six months. This ordeal did not diminish her religious commitment, for on 4 April 1568 she was again arrested for hearing mass in a house in the London parish of St Sepulchre. On this occasion she was pardoned by the queen, perhaps on account of her advanced age. Martha Carew died, presumably in London, in January 1572.

P. R. N. CARTER

Sources CPR, 1566–9; 1555–7 · Calendar of the manuscripts of the most hon. the marquis of Salisbury, 1, HMC, 9 (1883) · PRO, E337/2, E337/8, E347/17/3/1 · P. Carter, 'Financial administration, patronage and profit in Tudor England: the career of Sir Wymond Carew (1498–1549)', Southern History, 20–21 (1998–9), 20–43 · W. R. Trimble, The Catholic laity in Elizabethan England, 1558–1603 (1964)

Carew, Sir Matthew (1531–1618), civil lawyer, was a son (the second of nineteen children) of the financial official Sir Wymond *Carew (1498–1549) of Antony, Cornwall, and his recusant wife, Martha (c.1500–1572) [see Carew, Martha], daughter of Sir Edmund Denny, chief baron of the exchequer, and sister of Sir Anthony *Denny. After Westminster School he entered Trinity College, Cambridge, in 1548 as a scholar; he graduated BA in 1551 and was made a fellow of the college. He was appointed archdeacon of Norfolk on condition that he entered the priesthood within three years. He took minor orders but failed to proceed to the diaconate or priesthood, although he seems to have remained archdeacon until succeeded by Richard Stokes in 1587.

Determining on a career as a civil lawyer, for twelve years Carew attended various continental universities: Louvain, Paris, Dôle (in the Franche Comté), Padua, Bologna, and finally Siena, where in January 1565 he took his doctorate in canon and civil law. He is described in the register at Siena as 'reverend', a Cornishman of Exeter diocese, and archdeacon of Norfolk. His exercises were on Decretals, 3.19.2 for canon law and Code, 7.53.5 for civil law. Also in 1565 he became rector of Sheviock, Cornwall, near the family seat at Antony. Carew married Alice Ingpenny (or Ingpen; d. 1638), a widow, eldest daughter of Sir John Rivers (or Ryvers), lord mayor of London. Of their numerous children only three survived, one being Thomas *Carew, a well-known but dissolute poet.

Before beginning practice Carew travelled in Italy with Henry, earl of Arundel, as an interpreter. He was admitted as an advocate of the court of arches in 1573, having already been enrolled as a member of Doctors' Commons in 1559. In 1577 he became one of the masters in chancery and in 1589 was given an honorific admission to Gray's Inn. On the accession of James I in 1603, as one of the most senior masters he was knighted and in 1604 was made a justice of the peace for Surrey and Hampshire.

Carew seems to have supplied much material on the work of the masters in chancery to his nephew, Sir George *Carew, for the latter's 'Treatise of the masters in chancery'. He was anxious to assert the jurisdiction of the court of chancery, and of the civil law component of its law, often citing civil law maxims. In a document justifying the masters' gratuities to Lord Keeper Egerton he wrote of 'our travails in matters to us referred by the court wherein our pain is great, and the laws civil permit allowance by the parties assessoribus, when no public salary is appointed to them' (Jones, 107). In his reports on cases referred to

himself he was impatient of slipshod pleading and sometimes showed himself to be pedantic to the point of cantankerousness.

Towards the end of his life Carew had accumulated substantial assets of at least £9600, but he was defrauded of most of it. He died in 1618 and on 2 August was buried in St Dunstan-in-the-West, London, where a monumental inscription composed by himself was erected. It was later transferred to the present church in Fleet Street.

PETER STEIN

Sources B. P. Levack, The civil lawyers in England, 1603–1641 (1973) · G. Minucci and P. G. Morelli, Le lauree dello studio senese nel XVI secolo (1992), 323 · E. Heward, Masters in ordinary (1990) · W. J. Jones, The Elizabethan court of chancery (1967) · F. Blomefield and C. Parkin, An essay towards a topographical history of the county of Norfolk, [2nd edn], 11 vols. (1805–10), vol. 3, p. 644 · G. D. Squibb, Doctors' Commons: a history of the College of Advocates and Doctors of Law (1977) · DNB · Venn, Alum. Cant.

Wealth at death house, field and shops in Chancery Lane value £1600; lost £8000–£12,000 by fraud in later life: Levack, Civil lawyers

Carew, Nicholas (d. 1390), administrator, of Beddington, Surrey, was probably the grandson of Sir Nicholas Carew (d. 1308), rather than the son, as was once believed. Little is known about his parentage save that he came from Berkshire. Although the senior branch of the family was old and distinguished, with a pedigree dating back to the twelfth century and extensive estates in both Ireland and Devon, Nicholas had few expectations of his own. He probably trained as a lawyer, being involved from the 1340s onwards in a number of land transactions in the home counties. Prominent among his clients were Sir Richard Willoughby, his daughter Lucy, and her first husband, Sir Thomas Huscarle. By 1356 Lucy had become Carew's wife, bringing him property in Surrey and Berkshire, which enabled him to consolidate an impressive base in the south-east. The crown, meanwhile, employed Carew locally in a wide range of administrative capacities and rewarded him, as early as 1342, with a life grant of the manor of Banstead in Surrey. To this he was able to add other holdings in Kent, purchased with the new-found wealth he enjoyed as a royal servant.

Carew represented Surrey in the parliament of 1360, and established himself over the next decade as a trusted member of Edward III's household. The crisis of the early 1370s propelled him out of local politics into national life. Anti-clerical sentiment in parliament had focused on the church's unwillingness to pay more towards the war effort, the incompetence and partiality of senior officers of state, who were themselves in holy orders, and the additional problem of accountability posed by their immunity, as clergymen, from prosecution in the royal courts. Parliamentary agitation for the removal of the chancellor, treasurer, and keeper of the privy seal, and for their replacement by laymen, led to Carew's appointment, on 26 March 1371, as keeper, in succession to Peter Lacy, a royal clerk. The first layman ever to occupy this post, he remained in office until Edward died in June 1377, his greatest achievement being to weather the political upheavals of 1376, when other ministers either fell victim to attack by the Good Parliament or were ousted once the court party regained power.

Carew's talent for survival did not impress the historian T. F. Tout, who dismissed him as a nonentity, doomed never to rise above the rank of esquire. Yet had he so wished, a knighthood would certainly have been bestowed upon him, and although the experiment of entrusting the privy seal to a layman was not soon repeated, it might be argued that Carew showed considerable acumen, at least in fostering his own interests. His membership of the small and unpopular coterie of household staff who exploited Edward's declining health by controlling access to his person and patronage is beyond question: he was, indeed, one of the first to benefit personally from the influence of William, Lord Latimer (*d.* 1381) over the king, using his friend to advance private petitions on his behalf. Nor can there be any doubt of Carew's part in the reprisals, taken in November 1376, against William Wykeham, bishop of Winchester (*d.* 1404), one of the government's harshest critics. He was present with other leading courtiers when 'secret business' concerning Wykeham's trial and the confiscation of his estates came under discussion at Westminster. Not surprisingly, Carew was named as one of the executors of Edward III's will, and as a trustee for the implementation of its terms. In this capacity he secured a seat in the parliament of October 1377; and while the session was in progress the late king's mistress, Alice Perrers, appealed to him and other courtiers for help in refuting the allegations then being made against her.

Either advancing age or the demands of executing Edward's will led Carew to withdraw gradually from public life. He drew up his own last testament in October 1387, asking to be buried at Beddington church, next to one of his brothers, a priest. He died on 17 August 1390, and was succeeded by his son Nicholas (*d.* 1432), who, like his father, represented Surrey in parliament and played an active part in local government. Carew also left two daughters, one of whom was prioress of Rusper in Sussex.   CAROLE RAWCLIFFE

Sources *Chancery records* · Tout, *Admin. hist.* · *VCH Berkshire*, vol. 3 · *VCH Surrey*, vol. 4 · O. Manning and W. Bray, *The history and antiquities of the county of Surrey*, 3 vols. (1804–14) · LPL, Reg. Courtenay [fols. 232 v–233v] · HoP, *Commons* · PRO, C136/66/10

Wealth at death approx. £91 p.a. minimum (son's income *c.*1394 from inherited lands): HoP, *Commons*

Carew, Sir Nicholas (*b.* in or before **1496**, *d.* **1539**), diplomat and courtier, was the eldest son of Sir Richard Carew (*d.* 1520) of Beddington, Surrey, and Matilda, daughter of Sir Richard Oxenbridge of Ford, Sussex. The main line of his ancient family had settled at Antony in Cornwall during the fourteenth century; a younger line acquired the manor of Beddington about 1350 and founded a dynasty that was to continue there until the eighteenth century.

Early career and advancement Sir Richard Carew, Nicholas's father, was knighted by Henry VII at the battle of Blackheath, served as sheriff of Surrey in 1501, and was captain of Calais. Born no later than 1496 Nicholas Carew was at court from an early age, being later described as of

Sir Nicholas Carew (*b.* in or before 1496, *d.* 1539), by unknown artist

Henry VIII's 'own bringing up' (Starkey, *Reign of Henry VIII*, 69). He was a groom of the privy chamber by May 1511, an esquire of the body in 1515, and a gentleman of the privy chamber in 1518. In 1513 he was joined with his father in a new grant of the office of lieutenant of Calais Castle, which they were to hold in survivorship, but Nicholas surrendered this patent on his father's death. In the same year he accompanied Henry VIII to France for the siege of Tournai. Sir Richard commanded the artillery on this campaign, with a personal retinue of 1000 men. Sir Edmund Carew, a kinsman from Devon, was killed at Thérouanne by a bullet that struck him as he sat at the council table, but Nicholas survived the campaign and was one of six favoured courtiers to be rewarded with the gift of a coat of green velvet and cloth of silver.

In December 1514 Carew married Elizabeth, the daughter of Sir Thomas Bryan of Ashridge, Hertfordshire, who was active at court as vice-chamberlain to Queen Catherine of Aragon. Elizabeth's brother Sir Francis Bryan was another prominent courtier and became one of Carew's closest friends. Another friend was Charles Brandon, duke of Suffolk, the king's brother-in-law; in March 1520, for instance, Suffolk and his wife were Carew's guests at Beddington. Carew acquired additional lands and offices at about this time. In April 1514 the king had given him several manors in Sussex, together with the advowson of Plompton church, and additional lands in Surrey were settled on him and his wife following their marriage, including estates worth 40 marks per annum at Wallington, Carshalton, Woodmansterne, Woodcote, and Mitcham. To these he added Beddington when his father died. Henceforth it was his principal residence; he largely rebuilt the mansion house about 1530. On 6 November 1515 he was named as one of the king's 'cipherers', in this context a cup-bearer, with an annuity of 50 marks, and in 1517 he served in that capacity at the banquet given by Henry VIII at Greenwich in honour of Spanish ambassadors. In the same year he was appointed keeper of the manor and park of Pleasaunce in East Greenwich.

Royal favourite In the meantime Carew had taken up jousting, according to Hall with the encouragement of Henry VIII, who supplied him with gear, until on 7 July 1517 Carew was proficient enough to star as 'the Blue Knight' in a great joust held at Greenwich for the entertainment of foreign ambassadors. These included the papal nuncio, who left an account of the events. The king himself participated, but the most notable performance was given by Carew. After the jousts, in which he took part as one of the king's aides, he came forth alone and a great lance, 9 inches in diameter and 12 feet in length, was brought in by three men and placed in his lance rest. Carew carried 'the great burden' three-quarters of the length of the lists 'to the extreme admiration and astonishment' of all (Starkey, *Henry VIII*, 40). He had ample opportunity to practise for this display, using the tilt and the arming shed which the king had given him.

Now increasingly familiar with Henry VIII, Carew frequently took part in revels and tournaments at court. At about the beginning of 1518 some courtiers objected to his intimacy with the king and Carew fell from favour, but in March Richard Pace wrote that he and his wife had returned to the king's grace, 'too soon, after mine opinion' (*LP Henry VIII*, 2/4034). A year later Carew was one of the victims of a more important court purge. Cardinal Wolsey, anxious to control Henry's privy chamber, had Henry's leading courtiers, his 'minions', charged before the council with over familiarity with the king: they had 'played such light touches with him that they forgot themselves'. Carew and Bryan, moreover, had displayed inappropriately high spirits when on a recent French embassy they 'rode disguised through Paris, throwing eggs, stones and other foolish trifles at the people' (Hall, 597–8). Like other courtiers Carew was summoned before the council at Greenwich, reprimanded, and exiled, in his case to Calais, where he was made lieutenant of the tower of Rysbank, guarding the entrance to the harbour. He arrived there on 20 May, the day of his formal appointment, having been granted an annuity of £109 6s. 8d. from the issues of the town. But although Henry VIII (at Wolsey's urging) resolved to lead a new life, and to shun the dubious company of his former favourites, his change of heart was brief, and Carew and the other minions were back at court within six months. Carew had been sheriff of Surrey and Sussex in the year 1518–19. It is a sign of his renewed favour with the king that in November 1520 a debt of £742 from his shrievalty was cancelled by letters patent. He was a JP for Surrey from 1520 until his death; in 1531 he was a named a commissioner of sewers there, and in 1535 he helped survey the tenths of spiritualities.

In 1520 Carew was part of the entourage that accompanied Henry VIII to his famous meeting with François I at the Field of Cloth of Gold. He was one of fourteen knights, both English and French, who with the two kings issued a challenge against all comers to take part in a joust, a feat of arms with full pageantry and elaborate symbolism. Later he was part of a company of English maskers which included the earl of Devon and Francis Bryan. Dressed as Eastlanders, with hose of gold satin, shoes with small spikes of white nails, doublets of crimson velvet lined with cloth of gold, hats from Danzig, and purses and girdles of sealskin, they led processions through the streets of Ardres and Guisnes, minstrels playing all the while. Subsequently Carew attended Henry VIII when he met Charles V at Gravelines. Here the ceremonies were less grand, but the diplomatic talks were of greater importance than those with François.

Diplomatic mission Carew surrendered the lieutenancy of Calais Castle in October 1520, retaining a pension of £100, while in November he relinquished his annuity as one of the cup-bearers. At the end of the year he was sent with letters to François I, hoping to dissuade him from sending troops into Italy and to solicit his influence with the Scots. He was only partly successful, but he was well entertained and on his return to England he received £100 for his expenses. In 1521 he was a member of the grand jury from Surrey that indicted the third duke of Buckingham on charges of high treason. After trial by his peers Buckingham was convicted and executed. Carew was later granted the duke's forfeited manor of Bletchingley, Surrey, together with an annual fair, and he also succeeded Buckingham as steward of the park of Brasted, Kent, with a fee of £40 per annum. In the years which followed he received several further grants of lands and honours. In June 1521 he was granted the reversion of the office of constable of Wallingford Castle, together with the stewardship of Wallingford and St Walric and four and a half hundreds of the Chilterns, all formerly held by Sir Thomas Lovell. At Christmas that year he was named one of the king's carvers. In 1528 a patent was drawn up to make Carew constable of Warwick Castle, but it does not seem to have been issued. In February 1533 Carew obtained a lease for the lifetime of Catherine of Aragon of the Surrey manors of Banstead and Walton on the Hill, which had formed part of the queen's dowry; a few months later he was given the reversion of these and other properties of Catherine's. In 1527 Carew's lands were assessed for the subsidy at £400, the third highest figure among the king's household servants.

Carew took part in the earl of Surrey's invasion of Picardy in 1522, and in the same year received his most important court appointment, when, on 18 July, he was named master of the horse to Henry VIII, succeeding Sir Henry Guildford. The fee was £40 a year. In 1527 he was again sent to France, one of a mission to present François I with the Order of the Garter. Two years later he and Richard Sampson were sent to Bologna to obtain the emperor's ratification of the Franco-imperial treaty of Cambrai (5 August 1529), to which England had been admitted as a signatory. For Henry VIII this was an important move, freeing him from his alliance with France and allowing him to try to mend fences with Charles V, whose support was vital if he was to secure the annulment of his marriage to Charles's aunt, Catherine of Aragon. Carew acquitted himself well. The embassy left Greenwich on 4 October, and after passing through France and crossing the Mont Cenis pass into Italy, reached Bologna on 2 December. There Charles ratified the treaty on the 8th, and afterwards both he and Pope Clement VII were affable, if noncommittal, in discussions of Henry's marriage. The English king was sufficiently encouraged to decide to send a further embassy. Carew left Bologna on 8 February 1530, having been given a gold chain worth 2000 ducats by the emperor. The day before he departed Girolamo Ghinucci, the Italian bishop of Worcester, wrote to tell Henry that Carew had 'managed the King's business here with so much prudence and dexterity, that he leaves with the greatest satisfaction to the Emperor and the Pope' (*LP Henry VIII*, 4/3, no. 6205). Thomas Wall, Windsor herald, who had accompanied the mission, wrote an uninformative account of it, probably to help Carew in preparing his report for Henry VIII.

Carew was returned to the Commons in the Reformation Parliament, which began in 1529, as a knight of the shire for Surrey. The other county member was his fellow courtier Sir William Fitzwilliam. Because of his service on the continent he was absent from the first session, and he may have missed part of the 1531 session as well, since the king was staying with him at Beddington in February. His name appears on a list of men who were particularly interested in a treasons bill under consideration in 1534, written on the back of a letter to Thomas Cromwell; possibly they were members of a committee to which it was referred. Otherwise there is no record of his parliamentary activities.

Court politics and the king's marriages Like a number of other courtiers Carew concealed his true feelings about Henry VIII's divorce. He was a close friend of the king, but ties of loyalty also bound him to Catherine of Aragon and Princess Mary. In terms of foreign policy he was regarded as a friend of France, but as early as 1529 he had made clear to the imperialists that he was at heart a supporter of Catherine and Mary. Nevertheless there was talk of sending him to France in March 1530, and in December he was indeed dispatched to represent England at the coronation of the new French queen. In 1533 and 1535 François asked Henry to make Carew a knight of the Garter, and even chancellor of the order. Henry replied that the king of Scots was chancellor, but he did eventually promote Carew for a vacancy; significantly, he gave him precedence over George Boleyn, Viscount Rochford. Eustache Chapuys, the imperial ambassador in England, was not entirely certain of Carew's attitude towards the divorce, but told Charles V that he was confident of his loyalty to Catherine. As he set off for France in autumn 1532 to prepare for an interview between Henry and François, Carew confided in Chapuys that he would prefer his mission to fail, perhaps because he feared its consequences for Catherine's cause. The two kings met at Boulogne late in October, amid considerable magnificence, but diplomatically little was achieved.

As the divorce proceeding continued the Carews kept in touch with Princess Mary. Lady Carew's advice to Mary to submit to the king's wishes did not spring from any goodwill towards Anne Boleyn. Indeed, her husband clearly remained committed to Catherine's cause, as an incident in 1535 made clear. When the king's fool spoke well of Catherine and Mary, but called Anne a ribald and Princess Elizabeth a bastard, Henry was so enraged that he nearly killed the jester, who thereupon took shelter with Carew. Then as Anne's position came under pressure in the following year, Carew played a leading role in the machinations which eventually destroyed her. On 29 April 1536 Chapuys reported both how Carew had won the Garter at Anne's brother's expense, and how the former was promoting Jane Seymour and communicating with Mary, telling the latter 'to be of good cheer, for shortly the opposite party would put water in their wine' (*LP Henry VIII*, 10, no. 752). An ally now of Thomas Cromwell, Carew applied himself to poisoning the king's mind against Anne, while also giving Jane lodging at his own house at Beddington, where Henry paid her regular night-time visits. His plotting having achieved its end, Carew was one of three courtiers in charge of the font at the baptism of Prince Edward on 15 October 1536. Lady Carew was one of the ladies in attendance at Queen Jane's funeral on 13 November 1537.

Fall and execution Carew remained in favour with the king until the last days of 1538. In October 1536 he was called upon to provide 200 men to serve against the Pilgrimage of Grace, and was himself summoned to attend the king with 200 more. He may have been returned to parliament in that year, but evidence is lacking. In 1537 Henry made him a substantial grant of monastic lands in Surrey, including the manors of Coulsdon, Epsom, Horley, and Sutton. In April 1538 he again entertained the king at Beddington. But his position proved less secure than it appeared. Even in 1536 Cromwell had undermined the Aragonese faction which had helped him to bring Queen Anne to the block by accusing its members of wanting to restore Mary to the succession. On that occasion Mary had saved her allies when she submitted to the king and acknowledged her own bastardy. But two years later Cromwell stage-managed another court purge, and Carew was one of its victims. He was arrested on 31 December 1538, allegedly because a letter found at the home of the marchioness of Exeter (married to a kinsman of Cardinal Reginald Pole) implicated him in the treason for which her husband, the marquess, and Pole's brother, Baron Montagu, had been executed earlier in the month. Commissioners immediately seized Carew's goods, including his wife's jewellery.

There is a family tradition, reported by Thomas Fuller, that the king had turned against Carew as the result of a personal quarrel. As the two men played bowls, Henry 'gave this knight opprobrious language, betwixt jest and earnest; to which the other returned an answer rather true than discreet'. The king, 'being no good fellow in repartees, was so highly offended thereat that Sir Nicholas fell from the top of his favour to the bottom of his displeasure, and was bruised to death thereby' (Fuller, *Worthies*, 3.234). Chapuys claimed that Carew's fall formed part of a plot to deprive Princess Mary of her friends, but it is more probable that Thomas Cromwell, already fighting to preserve his own position, saw Carew as an enemy and wished him out of the way. The charges against him included commenting to the Surrey jury considering the charges against Exeter, 'I marvel greatly that the indictment against the Lord Marquis was so secretly handled and for what purpose, for the like was never seen' (*LP Henry VIII*, 14/1, no. 290)—words highly indiscreet in themselves, and showing that he had forgotten the fate of Anne Boleyn.

Carew was tried and convicted on 14 February 1539 and beheaded on Tower Hill on 8 March. According to Hall he 'made a godly confession, both of his folly and superstitious faith', saying that he had not 'savoured the sweetness of God's holy word' until the keeper of the Tower gave him a copy of the Bible in English (Hall, 827). Other evidence, too, suggests that in his last days he was converted to an evangelical religion from his lifelong traditional Catholicism. According to Wriothesley his head was not exposed but buried with his body in the chapel of St Peter ad Vincula; his remains must have been later removed, since Stow records them as interred in the London church of St Botolph, Aldersgate. Carew was attainted during the third session of the 1539 parliament. If he was allowed to make a will it does not survive. An inventory of the goods at Beddington made during Edward's reign contains full descriptions of tapestries and furniture as well as chests full of legal documents and a substantial library, including Gower's *Confessio amantis* and the chronicles of Froissart and Monstrelet. Carew's attainder was reversed in 1547 under Edward VI, and his son, Francis, was restored in blood; he recovered his father's estates in 1554. Beddington had been seized for the crown at the time of Sir Nicholas's execution, and was occasionally used by Henry VIII before being granted to the Darcys in 1552. Eventually the Carew family recovered everything lost through Sir Nicholas's ruin except Bletchingley; the estates included lands in Lincolnshire, Northamptonshire, Northumberland, Sussex, and Kent, as well as Surrey.

Lady Carew was granted some of her husband's property in 1539. Besides his son, Francis, Sir Nicholas Carew left four daughters, one of whom married Sir Arthur Darcy. Their father's image is preserved in a portrait by Holbein. A preparatory drawing survives at Basel, but it is not certain whether the consequent oil (in the Lumley collection from at least 1590 until 1785, since then in the collection of the dukes of Buccleuch at Drumlanrig) is by Holbein's hand or that of a follower. It shows Carew in tilting armour, of the sort in vogue in the late 1520s, with his left hand on the scabbard of his sword and his right holding a pole or staff. 'His face is lean, almost ascetic. He stands proud and erect, the hero of innumerable fantastic tournaments' (Starkey, *Reign of Henry VIII*, 69).

STANFORD LEHMBERG

Sources HoP, *Commons, 1509–58*, 1.575–8 · C. G. Cruikshank, *Army royal* (1969) · J. Russell, *The Field of Cloth of Gold* (1969) · J. J. Scarisbrick, *Henry VIII* (1968) · S. E. Lehmberg, *The Reformation parliament, 1529–1536* (1970) · P. Ganz, *The paintings of Hans Holbein* (1956) · *Hall's chronicle*, ed. H. Ellis (1809) · Fuller, *Worthies* (1840) · *LP Henry VIII*, vols. 1–14 · *DNB* · D. Starkey, *Henry VIII: a European court in England* (1991) · D. Loades, *The Tudor court* (1987) · E. W. Ives, *Anne Boleyn* (1986) · S. J. Gunn, *Charles Brandon, duke of Suffolk, c.1484–1545* (1988) · D. Starkey, *The reign of Henry VIII: personalities and politics* (1991) · M. H. Dodds and R. Dodds, *The Pilgrimage of Grace, 1536–1537, and the Exeter conspiracy, 1538*, 2 vols. (1971), vol. 2 · C. Wriothesley, *A chronicle of England during the reigns of the Tudors from AD 1485 to 1559*, ed. W. D. Hamilton, 1, CS, new ser., 11 (1875) · J. Stow, *A survay of London*, rev. edn (1603); repr. with introduction by C. L. Kingsford as *A survey of London*, 2 vols. (1908); repr. with addns (1971) · T. Wall, *The voyage of Sir Nicholas Carewe*, ed. R. J. Knecht, Roxburghe Club, 225 (1959)

Likenesses H. Holbein the younger, chalk drawing, Basel Gallery, Switzerland · engraving (after oil and tempura painting by H. Holbein), repro. in D. Lysons, *The environs of London* · oil and tempera on wood, Buccleuch estates, Selkirk, Scotland [*see illus.*] · oils, Antony, Cornwall

Wealth at death lands assessed at £400 for 1527 subsidy; acquired more later: Bindoff, ed., *House of Commons*; *DNB*

Carew, Sir Peter (1514?–1575), soldier and conspirator, was the third son of Sir William Carew (*c*.1483–1536) of Mohun's Ottery, Devon, and his wife, Joan (*d*. 1554), daughter of Sir William Courtenay of Powderham and his second wife, Mary. The eldest son, Sir George *Carew (*c*.1504–1545), was a courtier and naval officer. The middle brother, Sir Philip Carew, was received into the order of St John of Jerusalem in 1528, but disappeared after killing another member of the order in a duel in Lombardy. The family of Carew, whose ancestral estates lay in Pembrokeshire and Ireland, acquired manors in Devon in the early fourteenth century and made Mohun's Ottery their home in the fifteenth. By the time that Peter was born, canny political decisions and fortunate marriages had earned the Carews a place as one of the principal families of the shire. But his paternal grandfather Sir Edmund *Carew (*c*.1464–1513) borrowed heavily to fund his military service to the young Henry VIII, leaving debts that Sir William Carew was unable to clear. There was little to spare for younger sons, and this played its part in spurring Peter Carew into a vivid and adventurous career. Character, however, was as significant as circumstance, for Carew was uncommonly energetic and ambitious. Remarkably, he was also the subject of a contemporary biography, penned by the Exeter antiquary John Hooker, Carew's legal factotum and friend.

Hooker's manuscript life of Carew is preserved at Lambeth Palace Library (MS 605). Unpublished until 1840, it was written after Carew's death, probably at the instigation of his cousins Peter Carew (*d*. 1580) and George Carew (*d*. 1629). Although little known, it is a milestone in the English biographical genre. Hooker also praised Sir Peter Carew in his edition of Holinshed's *Chronicles*, and his account of the 1549 rebellion in Devon and Cornwall. He paints Carew as a man of the Renaissance: a soldier, traveller, jouster, and patron, equally at home attending his prince at court and in the country. The two men became personally acquainted in the mid-1560s; for his subject's early exploits Hooker probably had to rely on the recollections of Carew's long-lived uncle Sir Gawen Carew, and there is some confusion over dates, especially during the

Sir Peter Carew (1514?–1575), by Gerlach Flicke

1520s and 1530s. But this hardly detracts from the significance of Hooker's achievement, which was to present the life of an English knight in the guise of the classical virtues.

Hooker states that Carew was born at Mohun's Ottery in 1514. Correctly judging that his third son was 'very pert and forward' (Wagner, 29), Sir William Carew entered him at the grammar school at Exeter. Peter Carew, however, did not take to book learning, and played truant around the streets and walls of the city. On one occasion, having been spotted by his guardian Thomas Hunt, he scaled a high turret and threatened to jump if Hunt should attempt to recapture him. The boy's father was summoned, and Peter was dragged back to Mohun's Ottery on a dog lead; he remained attached to one of Sir William's dogs for several days. His next school, St Paul's in London, fared no better in turning this froward youth into a scholar. When a friend offered to have him educated as a gentleman at the French court, his father seized the chance, and so Peter Carew began an association with France that would last through war, peace, conspiracy, and exile.

Soldier and adventurer Carew was twelve when he left England, according to Hooker. His French master treated him well at first, but—perhaps tiring of the boy's stubbornness—soon demoted him from page to stable hand. His good fortune was to be spotted and rescued by a relative,

John Carew of Haccombe, who was visiting the French court. Hooker claimed that Peter accompanied his kinsman and the army of François I into Italy, where he witnessed the 1525 battle of Pavia in the retinue of the marquess of Saluzzo, John Carew having died on the journey. Here he is mistaken. The elder Carew was still alive in 1527, when he travelled through France to Italy on a diplomatic mission for Cardinal Thomas Wolsey. Hooker was probably right about Peter Carew's birth in 1514 and departure for France aged twelve, but wrong about Pavia; he appears to have mixed up the complex international politics of 1525 and 1527–8. Peter was likely discovered by John Carew in the summer of 1527, and served Saluzzo in the French army outside Naples after his kinsman's death in spring 1528. When Saluzzo himself died later the same year, Carew took the opportunity to switch his allegiance to the imperial camp, entering the service of Philibert, prince of Orange. A tradition that he was present in 1527 at the sack of Rome in the company of Charles Bourbon, constable of France, seems to be mythical. Even so, by the time of his fifteenth birthday Carew had journeyed many leagues from his Devon gentry origins, acquiring an easy familiarity with the households and arts of war of the continental nobility.

Carew remained with Orange in Italy until the latter's death in 1530, then served his mother or sister. She commended him to Henry VIII when he decided to return to England in 1531 or 1532. The young man's battle stories and dash of European courtliness swiftly caught the king's attention. Sporting a gold chain and flanked by two servants furnished by his late employer, Carew visited his awestruck parents (who had thought him dead) before returning to the royal household as a henchman. Hooker places him in Henry's train at the summit meeting with François at Calais in 1532, though this was probably Sir Nicholas Carew of Beddington (executed in 1539), a favourite of the French king. Peter Carew apparently did cross to Calais in 1539 to receive Anne of Cleves; already a gentleman of the privy chamber, he was promoted to the new band of gentleman pensioners. He promptly used his position of favour to secure royal permission for another odyssey, which took him across France to Venice, Ragusa, and, by the spring of 1541, to Constantinople and the palace of Suleiman the Magnificent. The Ottoman sultan was easily the richest prince in Europe, and the West was fascinated by the opulence and violence of his court and its politics. Carew and his two companions, his cousin John Champernon and friend Henry Knollys, used their cover as alum merchants to visit the sultan several times. In doing so they placed themselves in real danger, but departed to Venice unscathed. The three then made their way to the siege of Buda in hope of seeing the Ottoman army in action. Having survived a bloody flux that killed Champernon, Carew returned to Henry's court in 1542, his store of anecdotes more than replenished.

Carew spent the rest of the reign in military service. In mid-1543 he campaigned against the French in Flanders with his brother George Carew and uncle Gawen Carew. Hooker has him in command of a hundred-strong 'black band' of foot soldiers, apparelled at his own expense, although this sounds like an authorial flourish given his modest income. He distinguished himself in the jousts at Thérouanne, a chivalric adjunct to the actual fighting, but saw more action during the assault on Boulogne the following year, when he was required to provide five horsemen and two archers. Carew took charge of the surrendered Hardelot Castle, but was sharply rebuked by the king for his rashness in leaving his post to deliver Henry a message. Later in 1544 he served at sea with the lord admiral, John Dudley, Viscount Lisle, captaining the 230-ton *Primrose*, and in 1545 he was given command of the 700-ton *Great Venetian*. Although in his thirties, Carew was yet untroubled by any sense of caution. Spying a flotilla of twenty enemy galleys off 'Newhaven' (either Le Havre in France or Newhaven in Sussex), he came close to engaging them on his own; and when Henry held his council of war on the *Great Harry* in Portsmouth in July, Carew it was who shinned up the mast to spot the approaching French fleet. When his brother George Carew, a vice-admiral, drowned only hours later on board the *Mary Rose*, Peter inherited the family estates in Devon.

Carew was knighted through Lisle's influence for his service at Tréport later in 1545, and was elected MP for Tavistock the same year, a seat belonging to John Russell, Baron Russell. These associations marked him out as a member of the emerging protestant élite. He was sheriff of Devon in 1546–7, and was returned as MP for Dartmouth, where he was now lord of the borough, in 1547. On 20 February 1547 he married Margaret (d. 1583), daughter of Sir William Skipwith of South Ormsby, Lincolnshire, and his second wife, Alice, and widow of George Tailboys, second Baron Tailboys. He had set his sights high, since Margaret was wealthy, and was won over only by the late king's own intercession. She would show some spirit in defending her husband's reputation, and her own right to her dower lands, following Carew's disgrace in 1554. The couple settled on her extensive estates in Lincolnshire; thus Peter was out of his native shire during the disturbances preceding the great insurrection in the west in 1549.

Rebellion, conspiracy, and exile When word came to Edward Seymour, duke of Somerset and lord protector to Edward VI, that revolt was brewing in Devon and Cornwall in June 1549, he ordered Peter and Gawen Carew to make haste for the west country. It was a bad miscalculation. The duke hoped that offer of pardon would calm the rebels; Peter Carew, however, was hardly the ideal messenger. His soldier's evangelicalism put him entirely out of sympathy with those protesting in defence of their traditional religion. Unlike the older and wiser Sir Thomas Denys, who was well respected in Devon, Carew was impatient to abandon Somerset's tried and tested policy of mediation in favour of a military solution. Outraged at the rebels' aggressive stance, he promptly charged their lines at Crediton, thus confirming him as a figure of popular loathing. Indeed, Carew was nearly shot by a smith at Clyst St Mary; such violence towards local gentry was highly unusual in Tudor England. Having accused Denys

and others of favouring the rebels, he galloped off to report to Somerset (who angrily blamed Carew for turning a demonstration into a rebellion) before returning to the fray at the end of June. Russell's bloody suppression of the uprising lasted several weeks, and both Carews played an active role in it, as they did in the commissions to inventory bells, vestments, and other church goods that followed. This reinforced Carew's association with Russell, who was the principal noble in the region.

Although rewarded with the confiscated lands of the Cornish rebel leader John Winslade, Carew shouldered an alarming burden of debt. He owed some £2100 to the crown by 1552, and most of his estates were mortgaged. This, and his childless marriage, made it easier for him to contemplate conspiracy against his sovereign early in Mary I's reign. Carew was not inherently opposed to Mary's rule: she, rather than the protestant Lady Jane Grey, was proclaimed at Dartmouth and Newton Abbot in July 1553 on his orders. He remained in the House of Commons after Mary's accession, sitting as knight of the shire for Devon in the parliament of October that petitioned her to marry within her own realm. Carew's loyalty to Henry's chosen successor only failed when her determination to marry the future Philip II became apparent. If she would not marry Edward Courtenay, earl of Devon (whose father Henry, marquess of Exeter, had been a patron of the Carews), then perhaps Princess Elizabeth would.

The plot that ensued is generally attributed to Thomas Wyatt the younger, although Carew was one of its principals from the start, and attended the meeting of the conspirators at a London inn on 26 November 1553. These men were almost all professional soldiers, who had served in the English garrisons on the continent, where protestantism had taken firmer root. He was doubly useful to the conspirators: an experienced soldier and mariner, Carew was also fluent in French, a vital consideration given Henri II's interest in undermining Spanish interests by supporting this revolt. He knew Devon's havens and harbours, one result of his stint as vice-admiral of the county from 1548, and could assist any French landing in the south-west. Carew would be supported by simultaneous uprisings in Herefordshire, Leicestershire, and Kent. According to evidence later submitted in king's bench, he was clear that the plot's intention was to depose Mary, and spoke of escorting her to the Tower. He travelled to Devon just before Christmas, but perhaps some word of the plan had leaked, for he was ordered to appear before the privy council on 2 January 1554. He ignored the summons, and recruited to him a handful of protestant gentry amid false rumours that the earl of Devon was secretly living at Carew's house. By 24 January there were about seventy armed men at Mohun's Ottery, but Thomas Denys had garrisoned Exeter against them, and there was no sign of popular support for their cause. The local populace was still smarting from its treatment in 1549 and only too happy to see Carew's predicament. The following day Carew deserted his fellows, a rare example of either pragmatism or cowardice on his part. He reached Weymouth, Dorset, disguised as a servant, and took boat to France and exile. He was immediately proclaimed traitor. Only in Kent did Wyatt's rebellion pose a major threat to the crown, and there it was very serious indeed.

Carew's role in the conspiracy raises the question of his religion. All the key plotters save Courtenay were of the reformed faith, and Carew's 1554 indictment described him as irredeemably protestant. Yet it also cited his exact words: 'If the quene wold forebeare this marriage wyth the Spanyard, and use a moderation in matters of relygion, I wold dye at her foote' (Loades, 115). This implies that his allegiance to Mary might have overcome his distaste for her Catholicism, provided she marry an Englishman. Carew protected protestants in Devon as his father had before him, and was committed to ward in 1545 for possessing forbidden books. Hooker presents him as a godly man. But he was not a Marian religious exile in the sense of John Ponet, the Edwardian bishop of Winchester, who befriended Carew when he found himself at Strasbourg. Carew was happy to dash into Ponet's burning house to save his friend's money, but did not linger as the bishop wrote his propaganda against the Marian regime. In truth, he had begun to make overtures to Mary's government within months of arriving in France, and by December 1555 his wife, Margaret, had successfully pursued Philip for a pardon. Following a possibly staged kidnapping in Flanders, Carew was returned to England in May 1556 along with Sir John Cheke. Part of the price of his restoration may have been complicity in Cheke's arrest. He repaid Philip's faith in him by serving against the French in the St Quentin campaign of 1557.

Ireland Carew fully recovered his position of trust on Elizabeth I's accession in 1558. In 1559 he surveyed the Tower of London, and he was sent to report on the English army in Scotland in 1560. Otherwise he lived the life of a west-country gentleman. He held important local authority as deputy lieutenant of Devon from about 1558, an office in the gift of the new lord lieutenant, Francis Russell, second earl of Bedford, John Russell's successor. Further prestigious offices followed, including appointment as *custos rotulorum* of Devon and membership of the quorum of the commission of the peace for Dorset from 1559. He oversaw the quarter sessions and was responsible for the records and the clerks as *custos rotulorum*. He was elected senior knight of the shire for Devon in 1559, and sat as a burgess of Exeter in 1563. In the early 1560s Carew investigated piracy in the western channel and Irish Sea, capturing one of Thomas Stucley's ships in Cork Haven in 1565. His varied service was recognized, and in 1563 his attainder was formally reversed. But this act of parliament did nothing to improve Carew's finances, and in the same year he was compelled to sell Mohun's Ottery, which he had partially rebuilt, and other Devon manors to Thomas Southcote, his niece's husband. At a time when social status was determined by land, this must have stung. The solution to his plight, he decided, lay in the long-lost Carew estates in Ireland.

Carew was deeply interested in his lineage, and had inherited the extensive family muniments that illustrated his title to lands in Ireland. What he lacked was the Latin to read them, and so he turned to John Hooker, 'a man greatly given to seek and search out old records and ancient writings' (Wagner, 285). Hooker set to work on the Carew archive, and sailed to Ireland in May 1568. Sir Peter followed in August. They quickly discovered that Carew might lay claim to extensive estates in co. Meath and co. Cork, but the jewel was the barony of Idrone in western co. Carlow: 'in all Europe not a more pleasant, sweeter, or fruitfuller land', according to Hooker (Wagner, 291). Lost to the Carews in Richard II's reign, the barony was now occupied by the Kavanaghs and their overlord, Sir Edmund Butler, brother and heir to Thomas Butler, tenth earl of Ormond. Ormond was a great favourite of the queen and one of her few consistently loyal and protestant Irish subjects. When the government conveyed Idrone to Carew in December 1568, in defiance of Gaelic title and other legal obstacles, it sent out a message that chilled the Old English and the Irish chieftains alike. Carew's success threatened a wider New English plantation in Ireland, and propelled Butler into the arms of his former enemy, the rebel James fitz Maurice Fitzgerald. By summer 1569 Carew's horsemen and Butler's galloglasses and kerne were engaged in open warfare. One report charges the former with slaughtering the women and children of Butler's castle at Clogrennan, a detail not found in Hooker, who stresses instead the good lordship dispensed by Carew to his tenants at Leighlin, in co. Carlow. Meanwhile Butler denounced Carew to Sir Henry Sidney, lord deputy, as the only cause of his resort to arms. Despite this, Carew was appointed to the Irish privy council in 1569. Elizabeth was alarmed at the disorder following in Carew's wake, and he departed for England in 1570. His vigorous pursuit of his private affairs had gravely damaged the relationship between the English administration and the native political élite in Ireland.

When not surveying the seaward fortifications of Devon and Cornwall, Carew spent the next couple of years close to the court. In August 1573 he was permitted to return to Ireland as a volunteer in the expedition of Walter Devereux, first earl of Essex, to plant English civility in Ulster, but failing health soon forced him to retire to Dublin. In July 1574 he willed Idrone to his cousins Peter and George Carew in turn. Carew died at Ross on 27 November 1575, on his way to take possession of his lands in co. Cork. He was buried with full military honours beside the altar of Waterford church on 15 December. Sidney led the mourners, and the guns of the town and the ships in the harbour fired a salute. Carew's standards and pennons, yellow with black lions, were set over the grave.

Carew's widow married Sir John Clifton in 1579, but most of her second husband's debts remained unpaid at the time of her own death on 6 May 1583. A wall monument in Exeter Cathedral depicts Carew in armour, kneeling and surrounded by sixteen shields of arms. Of his house at Mohun's Ottery, only a crumbling gateway survives. A portrait of Carew, painted by Gerlach Flicke (c.1550), and housed in the Royal Collection, presents a stout and broad-shouldered man, with an impressive dark beard. The people of Devon and Cornwall recalled his behaviour during the 'commotion time' of 1549 with little fondness. But Hooker made no attempt to conceal his affection for him: a man of noble lineage and sound religion, generous to a fault, a prodigal son who liked Cicero but preferred manly action, who loved his country and knew the value of a good servant.   J. P. D. COOPER

Sources J. A. Wagner, *The Devon gentleman: the life of Sir Peter Carew* (1998) · HoP, *Commons, 1509–58*, 1.578–81 · HoP, *Commons, 1558–1603*, 1.541–2 · PRO, SP 11/3/10 · D. Loades, *Two Tudor conspiracies*, 2nd edn (1992) · S. G. Ellis, *Ireland in the age of the Tudors* (1998) · C. Brady, *The chief governors: the rise and fall of reform government in Tudor Ireland, 1536–1588* (1994) · will, PRO, PROB 11/58, sig. 1 · private information (2004) [Mrs J. A. C. Richardson]
Likenesses G. Flicke, *c*.1550, Royal Collection · G. Flicke, oils, NG Scot. [*see illus.*] · monument, Exeter Cathedral

Carew, Richard (1555–1620), antiquary and poet, was born on 17 July 1555 at Antony House, Torpoint, Cornwall, the eldest son among the three children of Thomas Carew (*c*.1527–1564) and his wife, Elizabeth Edgcumbe. His father having died when he was eight, Richard inherited an estate that had been in the possession of his family since the late fifteenth century. By about 1566 he had gone up to Christ Church, Oxford, where he became a friend of William Camden and Philip Sidney, but does not seem to have taken a degree, afterwards proceeding to the Middle Temple, where he spent another three years studying law. The claims of his inheritance recalled him to Cornwall, where in 1577 he married Juliana (1563–1629), daughter of John *Arundell (*d*. 1580) of Trerice [*see under* Arundell family] and his first wife, Katherine Cosworth. They had ten children, born between 1579 and 1604, of whom three died in infancy and only five outlived their father.

To outward appearances Carew spent the rest of his life managing his manors, conducting government business and enjoying the life of a country gentleman—he was a bee-keeper of repute, and also a keen fisherman, who planned a banqueting house on an island in a salt-water pond below his house at Antony, with amenities that would include 'cupboards and boxes, for keeping other necessary utensils towards these fishing feasts' (Halliday, 175–6). His public service began in 1581, when he was made a JP. In 1584 he entered parliament as a burgess for Saltash, and in 1597 he represented Mitchell, where he was bailiff. In 1586 he was sheriff of Cornwall, where he was also at various times a deputy lieutenant, treasurer of the lieutenancy, and in 1596 colonel of a regiment raised to defend the coast. But Carew was also a man of varied intellectual interests and attainments. He taught himself Greek, Italian, German, Spanish, and French, and put his accomplishments to good use. In 1594 he published a translation from the Italian of Torquato Tasso's *Gerusalemme liberata* under the title *Godfrey of Bulloigne, or, The recoverie of Hierusalem*. In the same year he also published *The Examination of Men's Wits*, an elegant verse translation of Camillo Camilli's Italian version of Juan Huarte's treatise *Examen de ingenios*. Carew was probably also the author of *A Herring's Tayle*, published anonymously in 1598. Set in Tintagel, this phantasmic poem, which concerns 'the strange adventures of the hardie Snayle Who durst

Richard Carew (1555–1620), by unknown artist, 1586

(unlikely match) the weathercock assayle', combines Arthurian romance with elements of natural history derived from Pliny, and has been praised by F. E. Halliday as earning for Carew a niche in the pantheon of English prosody (Halliday, 42–4). In 1607 he turned to prose, as translator of a lurid adaptation of Henri Estienne's *Apologie pour Herodote*, issued as *A World of Wonders*.

Carew became a member of the Elizabethan Society of *Antiquaries, where his scholarship was clearly valued. He assisted Sir Henry Spelman with the latter's researches into the history of tithes, and was rewarded with the dedication of the resulting treatise. Greatly interested in language, and particularly in etymology, Carew's panegyric on 'The excellencie of the English tongue' was first published in the second edition of William Camden's *Remaines* (1614). It constituted a qualified rebuttal of Richard Verstegan's *Restitution of Decayed Intelligence of Antiquities* (1605), which rejected the British contribution to England's history and languages in favour of Germanic elements. Carew thereby became entangled in a dispute which involved (among others) Verstegan, Thomas Nashe, Edmund Spenser, and William Shakespeare, over the extent to which English should either assimilate foreign words or attempt to maintain a degree of linguistic integrity. Carew accepted Saxon as the 'natural language' of England (Jones, 220), but he was much more willing to recognize the contributions of foreign tongues and cultures than Verstegan was.

Etymology is only one of many elements in Carew's most famous book. His *Survey of Cornwall* was published in 1602 with a dedication to Sir Walter Ralegh, explaining that it had been 'long since begun' but 'a great while discontinued' (McKisack, 141). Although he had the assistance of William Camden and John Hooker, the result of Carew's labours was a work unlike theirs or anyone else's. Presented in two books, the first a general description of Cornwall and the second a perambulation of the county from east to west, it contains relatively little history, though his descriptions of the Cornish landscape show that he was alert to the historical associations of particular places. He also spoke up for King Arthur, perhaps because the latter was Cornish by birth; he was aware of increasingly widespread doubts about Arthur's historicity, but described himself as unwilling to 'shake the irrefragable authoritie of the round tables Romants' (Kendrick, 161). The *Survey* contains, too, almost none of the heraldry that bulks so large in other chorographies. Nevertheless Carew was keenly interested in the affairs of the Cornish gentry, whose relative lack of status he lamented: 'most Cornish Gentlemen can better vaunt of their pedigree, than their livelyhood' (Duffin, 22).

Carew's double role as chorographer and agent of government gave him a uniquely informed perspective, manifested in the remarkable range of his book. The *Survey* is above all a representation of Cornwall as its author saw it, in terms of the landscape and climate, and of the occupations of men and women whose lives these shaped. Such matters as the local tin mines, the fishing industry, and the games people played, including hurling, all come within the compass of his lively pen. He remains interested in languages, and provides an early account of the use of sign language by two deaf people. He defends church ales because they promote neighbourly feeling, a quality clearly close to his heart, for he was a sociable man. Not the least of the pleasures of the *Survey* lies in Carew's exuberant style, perfectly encapsulated in his remarks on Cornish rats: 'alike cumbersome through their crying and rattling, while they dance their gallop galliards in the roof at night' (Halliday, 105).

Carew concluded his *Survey* on 23 April 1602, ending with the words: 'because we are arrived, I will heere sit mee downe and rest' (Halliday, 237). His health began to fail, and between 1611 and 1615 he was almost blind. He also suffered from afflictions that included a rupture and the stone. He died in his study at Antony on 6 November 1620 and was buried in the crypt of the parish church there next day. He had first made his will in April 1619, but revised it in June 1620. Most of his estate was left to his second son, Richard (his sole executor), and his widow. His son later wrote of 'his conversation so full of sweetness as he was able to gain everybody's affection … so upright in justice that they raised a common proverb upon him' (HoP, *Commons, 1558–1603*, 1.542). The same qualities have been observed in his writings. Carew's work was later praised by Ben Jonson and admired by Sir William Dugdale and John Aubrey. A modern edition of the *Survey of Cornwall* was published by F. E. Halliday in 1953, thereby helping to maintain Carew's early reputation as 'the prince of Cornish historians' (Polsue, 1.29).

S. MENDYK

Sources W. G. V. Balchin, *The Cornish landscape* (1983) · K. Barker and J. P. Kain, eds., *Maps and history in south-west England* (1991) · A. C. Baugh, *A history of the English language* (New York, 1935) · W. Borlase, *Observations on the antiquities, historical and monumental, of the county of Cornwall* (1754) · M. Brayshay, 'Introduction: the development of topographical writing in the south west', *Topographical writers in south-west England*, ed. M. Brayshay (1996), 1–33 · M. Brayshay, ed., *Topographical writers in south-west England* (1996) · J. S. Brewer and W. Bullen, eds., *Calendar of the Carew manuscripts*, 6 vols., PRO (1867–73) · R. Carew, *The survey of Cornwall* (1602) · J. J. Daniell, *A compendium of the history and geography of Cornwall*, 3rd edn (1894) · A. Duffin, *Faction and faith: politics and religion of the Cornish gentry before the civil war* (1996) · P. Berresford Ellis, *The Cornish language and its literature* (1974) · B. C. Ewell, 'Drayton's *Polyolbion*: England's body immortalized', *Studies in Philology*, 75 (1978), 297–315 · F. Smith Fussner, *The historical revolution: English historical writing and thought, 1580–1640* (New York, 1962); reprint edn (Westport, CT, 1976) · S. A. Glass, 'The Saxonists' influence on seventeenth-century English literature', *Anglo-Saxon scholarship: the first three centuries*, ed. C. T. Berkhout and M. McC. Gatch (Boston, MA, 1982), 91–105 · S. Greenblatt, 'The land speaks: cartography, chorography, and subversion in Renaissance England', *Representing the English Renaissance*, ed. S. Greenblatt (Berkeley and Los Angeles, CA, 1988), 327–61 · F. E. Halliday, *A Cornish chronicle: the Carews of Antony from Armada to civil war* (1967) · R. Carew, *The survey of Cornwall*, ed. F. E. Halliday (1953) · F. E. Halliday, ed., *The excellency of the English tongue* (1975) · T. D. Hardy and J. S. Brewer, *Report … upon the Carte and Carew papers* (1864) · HoP, *Commons, 1558–1603*, 1.542–3 · R. Foster Jones, *The triumph of the English language* (Stanford, CA, 1966) · *The letters of Sir Walter Ralegh*, ed. A. Latham and J. Youings (1999) · F. J. Levy, *Tudor historical thought* (San Marino, 1967) · M. McKisack, *Medieval history in the Tudor age* (1971) · W. H. Mullens, *Some early British ornithologists and their works* (1908–1909?) · G. Parry, *The trophies of time: English antiquarians of the seventeenth century* (Oxford and New York, 1995) · S. Piggott, *Ancient Britons and the antiquarian imagination* (1989) · S. Piggott, *Ruins in a landscape* (1976) · J. Polsue, *Lake's Parochial history of the county of Cornwall*, 4 vols. (1867–72), vol. 1 · A. L. Rowse, *Tudor Cornwall: portrait of a society*, new edn (1969) · K. Sharpe, *Sir Robert Cotton, 1586–1631: history and politics in early modern England* (1979) · H. R. Steeves, *Learned societies and English literary scholarship in Great Britain and the United States* (New York, 1913); reprint edn (New York, 1970) · R. Tuve, 'Ancients, moderns and Saxons', *ELH: a Journal of English Literary History*, 6 (1939) · D. N. C. Wood, 'Elizabethan English and Richard Carew', *Neophilogus*, 61 (1977), 304–15 · D. R. Woolf, *The idea of history in early Stuart England* (1990) · J. Youings, 'Bowmen, billmen and hackbutters: the Elizabethan militia in the south west', *Security and defence in south-west England before 1800*, ed. R. Higham (1987), 51–68 · J. Youings, 'Some early topographers of Devon and Cornwall', *Topographical writers in south-west England*, ed. M. Brayshay (1996), 50–61 · S. A. E. Mendyk, *Speculum Britanniae: regional study, antiquarianism and science in Britain to 1700* (1989) · T. D. Kendrick, *British antiquity* (1950)

Archives BL, misc. genealogical papers and corresp., Add. MSS 4421, 29300E, 34599; Cotton MSS Julius C.iii 30b, F.xi 261 Appx 67 | Antony, Cornwall, various documents · BL, Lansdowne MS 48

Likenesses oils, 1586, Antony House, Cornwall [*see illus.*]

Wealth at death 100 marks to wife; lands, patronages, woods, goods, leases, chattels to sons: Halliday

Carew, Sir Richard, first baronet (1579/80–1643?), medical experimenter and educationist, was the eldest surviving son of the poet and antiquary Richard *Carew (1555–1620) of Antony, Cornwall, and his wife, Juliana Arundell (1563–1629). Personal information comes largely from two Antony House manuscript texts—a spiritual autobiography (1628–30), called 'Reflections' in a copy of 1802, and medical precepts (1637); they are supplemented by

Carew's pamphlet published in Samuel Hartlib's *The True and Readie Way to Learne the Latine Tongue* (1654, 45–9).

Carew was encouraged to study by his father: he speaks of being 'put to School' (Hartlib, 45), but in the 'Reflections' mentions a tutor (apparently called Robinson) who instilled in him a lifelong godliness. He matriculated at Oxford from Merton College on 10 October 1594, aged fourteen; on 27 February 1597 he was admitted to the Middle Temple. In 1598 he accompanied his uncle Sir George Carew on a mission to King Sigismund Vasa of Poland during his attempt to regain his other realm of Sweden from its regent (later King Charles IX), which ended in rout at the Stångebro by Linköping (25 September 1598 os); he notes that more men were drowned in the swollen river than slain in the battle proper, and exclaims against the horrors of war.

Latin being the only language common to all parties, Carew, almost fresh from college, was required to conduct business in it but found himself at a loss for everyday words not encountered in his reading. The next year his father, anxious he should learn French, found him a place on Sir Henry Nevill's embassy to Henri IV; after initial bafflement, 'by reading and talking, I learn'd more French in three quarters of a year then I had done Latine in above thirteen' (Hartlib, 46). He also learned a lifelong mistrust of doctors after being given too strong a purge at Orléans; thereafter he would be his own physician. The safe return of 'Richardus Caraeus' was celebrated in Latin hendecasyllables by Charles Fitzgeoffrey (*Affaniae*, 1601, sig. 12r–v).

In January 1601 Carew married Bridget, daughter of John Chudleigh of Ashton and sister of Sir George Chudleigh, bt (1582–1658); they had six children, Elizabeth, Martha, Nicholas (who died in infancy), Mary, Alexander *Carew, and Gertrude. They settled in the neighbouring parish of Sheviock, where with a £60 annuity Carew devoted himself to fruit-trees and natural history. Invited to join Sir Ferdinando Gorges's unsuccessful Kennebec expedition as a missionary, he easily secured his wife's consent (she seems to have been even godlier than he), but withdrew because 'I observed the name of God had no place' in the plan for the colony, which he took to be foredoomed. After Bridget's death on 11 April 1611 he gave his children an earnestly religious upbringing; to his other interests he would add the breeding of civet cats. He sat in parliament for Cornwall in 1614 and for the borough of Mitchell (Cornwall) in 1621; his few contributions include advocacy in 1621 of a total prohibition on tobacco imports even from Virginia. On 18 February 1621, after succeeding to Antony on his father's death (6 November 1620), he married the seventeen-year-old Grace (d. 1658), daughter of Robert Rolle of Heanton and sister of Henry *Rolle (1589/90–1656), John *Rolle (1598–1648), and Jane; their four children were John *Carew (1622–1660), regicide, Wymond, Anthony, and Sir Thomas Carew of Barley, an anti-exclusionist MP for Exeter in 1681.

Carew was a lifelong medical experimenter, concerned above all with keeping warm. He appears to be the inventor of gambadoes (large boots or gaiters attached to the saddle to keep a rider's feet dry), but his greatest pride was the 'warming stone', a heat-retaining device found beneficial since Bridget's first confinement. Commercial exploitation was undertaken by John Bartlet, whose pamphlet of September 1640, *The Warming Stone: Excellent Helps Really Found out, Tried, and had, by a Warming Stone*, advertised the stones on sale at his shop in St Paul's Churchyard. Carew's name did not appear until the posthumous edition, *Excellent Helps …* (1652; re-edited 1660, c.1667), expanded with numerous accounts of cures sent to Bartlet on 16 October 1640 along with some small tracts or 'toys'; the covering letter is preserved among Samuel Hartlib's papers. One of these tracts was published in Hartlib's *True and Readie Way* as the work of Carew senior: from his experiences abroad, Carew argues that children should learn Latin by 'much Reading and Writing, and turning their Latine Books into English, and returning the same back againe into Latine'; they should be taught according to capacity rather than age, only advanced pupils learning grammar. His proposals, made at a time of Europe-wide concern with educational reform, were reprinted in eighteenth-century editions of Tanaquil Faber's *A Compendious Way of Teaching the Learned Tongues*. In 1641 he announced a book on the growing of fruit-trees (Turnbull, 107–8).

During holy communion on Whitsunday, 24 May 1640, the parish church at East Antony was struck by lightning; Carew (whom illness had kept at home) and the minister, Arthur Bache, took the parishioners' evidence on the event on oath (the congregation included Carew's widowed daughter, Elizabeth). An account published as *A Voyce in the Temple* (1640), though speaking in Bache's name, exhibits verbal similarities with Carew's report, preserved among the state papers (SP 16/454, no. 93) and printed in the *Western Antiquary* (1, 1881, 44–5).

Despite his puritanism, Carew was not active in the Commons' quarrels with James I; his 'Reflections' display more pride in royal ancestry than concern for threatened liberties, and when in 1641 Charles I sold baronetcies cheap to fill his war-chest, Carew was a buyer (creation on 9 August). His stance caused estrangement from his parliamentarian son Alexander, whose portrait he reputedly cut out of its frame at the outbreak of war (it was restored upon its subject's return to the royalist fold). Carew probably died in 1643 but there is no record of his death or burial at Antony church, for his heir pointedly erected an inscription not to him but to Richard Carew senior, his fondly remembered grandfather; an inventory of Carew's goods and chattels was appraised on 13 April 1643.

L. A. HOLFORD-STREVENS

Sources F. E. Halliday, *A Cornish chronicle: the Carews of Antony from Armada to civil war* (1967) • A. Bache, *A voyce in the temple* (1640) • *Western Antiquary*, 1 (1881), 44–5 • G. H. Turnbull, *Hartlib, Dury and Comenius: gleanings from Hartlib's papers* (1947) • Foster, *Alum. Oxon.* • H. A. C. Sturgess, ed., *Register of admissions to the Honourable Society of the Middle Temple, from the fifteenth century to the year 1944*, 3 vols. (1949) • C. Fitzgeoffrey, *Affaniae* (1601) • HoP, *Commons* [draft] • *Reg. Oxf.*, 2/2.204 • R. Carew, 'Reflections' and medical precepts, Cornwall RO, Antony House MS CZ/EE/32 • S. Hartlib, *The true and readie way to learne the Latine tongue* (1654) • inventory, 13 April 1643, Cornwall RO, Antony House MS CW/GG/35

Archives Cornwall RO, Antony House MS CZ/EE/32 | University of Sheffield, Hartlib MSS
Wealth at death approx. £400: inventory, 13 April 1643, Cornwall RO, Antony House MS CW/GG/35

Carew [Cary], Robert (*d.* 1362), theologian, was a native of south-west England. Nothing is known of his family. A fellow of Merton College, Oxford, from 1322 to 1332 or later, on the king's recommendation he was granted the reservation of a benefice in the gift of Plympton Priory, Devon, on 26 September 1331. He dined at Exeter College, Oxford, in the long vacation of 1355, and was collated to the rectory of Bromley, Kent, in 1361 and to that of Chiselhurst, Kent, in 1362, the year of his death. His commentary on the *Sentences* of Peter Lombard was seen by Bale, who, however, gives as its incipit the beginning of the third book of the commentary of the Dominican Richard Fishacre (*d.* 1248). Covering at least the first two books and part of the third, it was cited in an anonymous Paris commentary of *c.*1360, and was in the library of the Bridgettine house of Syon about 1430; Carew's commentary on Aristotle's *Posterior Analytics* was in the libraries of the University of Oxford and Balliol College in Leland's time. Neither commentary is now extant. Bale also lists *Quaestiones ordinariae*, without incipit.   JEREMY CATTO

Sources Merton Oxf., records, 3651, 3655–3656, 3659b, 3665–3666, 4078, 4086, *Catalogus vetus* p. 5 • rector's accounts, Exeter College, Oxford [Trinity term 1355] • *CEPR letters*, 2.364 • Reg. Islip, Canterbury, LPL, fol. 225v • Reg. Whittlesey, Rochester, CKS, fols. 315v, 316, 318 • Bibliothèque Mazarine, Paris, MS 732, fol. 225 [*Sentences* commentary] • M. Bateson, ed., *Catalogue of the library of Syon Monastery, Isleworth* (1898), p. 32, D.48 • Bale, *Index*, 382 • *Commentarii de scriptoribus Britannicis, auctore Joanne Lelando*, ed. A. Hall, 2 (1709), 319 • R. A. B. Mynors, *Catalogue of the manuscripts of Balliol College, Oxford* (1963), 387 • Emden, *Oxf.*, 1.366–7
Archives Bibliothèque Mazarine, Paris, MS 732, fol. 225

Carew, Sir Thomas (1368?–1431), soldier and naval commander, was the son of Sir Leonard Carew (1342–1369), and grandson of Sir John *Carew, justiciar of Ireland (*d.* 1362). His mother was probably Alice, daughter of Sir Edmund Fitzalan. Leonard had come of age only in 1364, and at his death, five years later, his son was still an infant in the king's ward, under the guardianship of a succession of male relatives. Thomas served on Richard II's first expedition to Ireland in 1394. By this time he was married to Elizabeth (*d.* 1450/51), daughter of Sir William Bonville (*d.* 1408), and already had two daughters. He was knighted during the campaign, and chose to remain in Ireland in the service of Roger Mortimer, earl of March, for most of 1395. Nothing further is known of him until his rise to prominence in the Welsh wars of Henry IV. In October 1402 he was given custody of the castle of Narberth. In June 1403 Carew was ordered, along with Thomas Percy, earl of Worcester, to array troops in Pembrokeshire: he prevented Glyn Dŵr taking Cydweli and defeated him in battle near Laugharne on 12 July. A fortnight later, now called king's knight, he was rewarded by the right to hunt in royal forests, and in the following year he was granted lands in St Clears for life. In 1407 he served under Prince Henry at the reduction of Aberystwyth.

Returning to his manors in Devon after the Welsh war,

Carew was increasingly involved in local government as a justice of the peace, as well as being commissioned to deal with illegal captures of merchant ships and other maritime disputes: he was also personally involved in capturing enemy ships in collaboration with John Hawley of Dartmouth, whose activities verged on the piratical. Carew's obvious familiarity with naval as well as military matters led to his being commissioned on 18 February 1415 (during the absence of the admiral, Thomas Beaufort, earl of Dorset) to patrol the sea and make the channel safe in anticipation of Henry V's expedition to France. He was on the Agincourt campaign, but probably did not serve at the battle, being detailed instead to the garrison of Harfleur under Beaufort, now duke of Exeter, where he was still serving in April 1416. In January 1417 he was granted 100 marks p.a. (£66 13s. 4d.) out of the revenues of the duchy of Cornwall. As the king prepared for his second campaign in France in 1417, he turned again to Carew to command the channel patrol. Mustering at Dartmouth in March, Carew headed a fleet of ten ships, including his own barge, the *Trinité*, and a Venetian carrack, and was highly successful in his task. He took reinforcements under the earl of March to St Vaast-la-Hougue in September 1417, in June 1418 was present at the siege of Louviers, and between August and December 1418 at the siege of Rouen. By May 1419 he was back at sea in an unsuccessful attempt to prevent the Castilian fleet from carrying Scottish reinforcements to France. In the spring of 1420 he was again commissioned to serve in the safe keeping of the sea, but may have been at the siege of Melun in the second half of the year. From February to September 1422 he was in Portugal as a royal envoy charged with securing military aid.

Carew was prominent in Devon administration in the reign of Henry VI, serving as justice of the peace, on commissions of array, and on *ad hoc* commissions relating to loans and to maritime misdemeanours. In 1426 he was granted the marriage of Joan, one of the daughters of Sir Hugh Courtenay; he wedded her to his son, Sir Nicholas (*d.* 1449). Sir Thomas made his will on 16 July 1429 at Dartmouth, asking to be buried in the parish church of Luppit near Honiton, and making bequests to several of the churches of the area. He was dead by 27 January 1431. Both he and his son are frequently referred to as Baro de Carew. This seems to have been a courtesy title carried by the head of the Devon branch of the Carew family: no summons to parliament was ever made in this capacity.

ANNE CURRY

Sources exchequer accounts various, PRO, E101 • exchequer warrants of issue, PRO, E404 • exchequer issue rolls, PRO, E403 • chancery French rolls, PRO, C76 • chancery Norman rolls, PRO, C64 • *Chancery records* • E. F. Jacob, ed., *The register of Henry Chichele, archbishop of Canterbury, 1414–1443*, 2, CYS, 42 (1937) • *CIPM* • N. H. Nicolas, ed., *Proceedings and ordinances of the privy council of England*, 7 vols., RC, 26 (1834–7) • J. H. Wylie, *History of England under Henry the Fourth*, 4 vols. (1884–98) • J. H. Wylie and W. T. Waugh, eds., *The reign of Henry the Fifth*, 3 vols. (1914–29) • 'The chronicle of John Strecche for the reign of Henry V, 1414–1422', ed. F. Taylor, *Bulletin of the John Rylands University Library*, 16 (1932), 137–87 • W. P. Baildon, ed., *Select cases in chancery, AD 1364 to 1471*, SeldS, 10 (1896) • T. Walsingham, *The*

St Albans chronicle, 1406–1420, ed. V. H. Galbraith (1937) · D. M. Gardiner, ed., *A calendar of early chancery proceedings relating to west country shipping, 1388–1493*, Devon and Cornwall RS, new ser., 21 (1976) · Coll. Arms, MS 9

Carew, Thomas (*d.* 1616), Church of England clergyman, is of uncertain origins, although he claimed connections with more famous and armigerous Carews, including George Carew, successively Lord Carew and earl of Totnes, with the Norfolk family of Gawdy, and with the lord of the manor at Bildeston, John Rivett, whose grandmother was a Carew. Still less is known of his education, but there is no evidence that he was a graduate, and in the Norwich consistory court he was described as 'unskillful and unlearned in the tongues, as Latin, Greek and Hebrew'. He seems to have been ordained by Bishop Edmund Freake, either at Norwich or perhaps in Freake's original diocese of Rochester, which may tend to confirm naval connections, of which there are other stray hints.

Carew's career was that of a clerical stormy petrel in Essex and Suffolk. He is first encountered in the mid-1580s at Hatfield Peverel in Essex, this being a donative served by a curate, and as such at the disposal of the owner of the former priory, Edmund Allen. It is highly probable, though incapable of final proof, that the Essex curate was identical with the man who was later curate of St Margaret and St Nicholas, Ipswich, and rector of Bildeston, Suffolk. As a notorious nonconformist who never wore the surplice or used the sign of the cross in baptism, the circumstances of his appointment enabled Bishop John Aylmer (who was later said to have consented to it) to allege that Carew had been 'elected by the people' and practised 'a presbytery' although Carew's principal offence may have been the hard pastoral line he took with crypto-papists in the parish, 'adversaries', 'monstrous enemies', whom Aylmer was anxious to win (Peel, 2.28–35). Carew's verbal onslaught on Aylmer was extreme, and he suffered periods of imprisonment, interspersed with irregular preaching. After two years of ignoring the prayer book and promulgating presbyterian doctrine in two more donatives in Ipswich, his past caught up with him and he was again on the run. But Carew had powerful friends, including Sir Martin Frobisher, and also the third Lord Rich and Sir Robert Jermyn, who in 1591 secured the right of presentation to the relatively well-endowed Suffolk rectory of Bildeston from the earl of Essex.

At Bildeston, Carew either conformed or, more probably, found himself immune from prosecution for irregularities of that kind. His published sermons were, with one exception, typical and unremarkable Calvinist effusions, which freely plagiarized more celebrated preachers such as Richard Greenham and George Gifford. The exception was a sermon (part of a collection of *Certaine Godly and Necessarie Sermons*, 1603) to which he gave the title 'A caveat for craftsmen and clothiers'. This was an outspoken attack on clothiers, remarkable less for its rhetoric, vivid though this was, than for Carew's deployment of apparently accurate facts and figures about hours of work and levels of pay in an industry in which the distinction

between entrepreneurs and employees was already emergent. Clothiers were the most unconscionable of employers, 'considering the greatness, variety and continuance of their oppressions' (Carew, *Certaine Godly and Necessarie Sermons*, sig. T6v–7r). 'It is a thing monstrous and strange that any should be so void of religion and humanity as to defraud the poor of their wages' (ibid., sig. T3v). Carew believed that the profits of rich clothiers were made from low and exploitative wages, 'the enriching of two or three in a town', 'the impoverishing of many' (ibid., sig. V6). Having been told that the rich remembered the poor in their wills, Carew remarked: 'Therefore it might be wished that such rich men would die quickly, that there might be some good done at their deaths, for they do hurt while they live' (ibid., sig. O5v).

Although the economy of Bildeston depended on cloth, it is not certain that Carew's diatribe was delivered in his own parish or that he had his own people in his sights. The so-called 'new draperies' predominated in Bildeston, and Carew alleged that things were more tolerable in that branch of the industry, reserving his harsher criticism for the 'blue men', the manufacturers of broadcloth. Certainly he continued to live, apparently peaceably, in his comfortable rectory until his death in 1616, when his will had nothing to say about the poor but expressed a concern that his widow should not be deprived of her interest in the tithe corn which was even then being harvested. Carew and his wife, Margaret (who had little to dispose of when she herself died in 1629), had no fewer than nine children, including a son George (perhaps named for Lord Carew), who entered Merton College, Oxford, in 1604 and became a London clergyman. PATRICK COLLINSON

Sources P. Collinson, 'Christian socialism in Elizabethan Suffolk: Thomas Carew and his "Caveat for clothiers"', *Counties and communities: essays on East Anglian history presented to Hassell Smith*, ed. C. Rawcliffe, R. Virgoe, and R. Wilson (1996) · P. Collinson, 'Puritanism and the poor', *Pragmatic utopias: ideals and communities, 1200–1630*, ed. R. Horrox and S. Rees-Jones (2001), 242–58 · T. Carew, *Certaine godly and necessarie sermons* (1603) · T. Carew, *Fovre godlie and profitable sermons* (1605) · A. Peel, ed., *The seconde parte of a register*, 2 vols. (1915) · Norfolk RO, DEP 24, fols. 251v–58v · S. Andrews, *Brett Valley Histories* (1990–) · F. S. Growse, *Materials for a history of Bildeston in the county of Suffolk* (1902) · Bildeston parish register, Suffolk RO, Bury St Edmunds, FB 79/D/1 · Bildeston terrier, 24 Sept 1627, Suffolk RO, Bury St Edmunds, 806/1/16 · archdeaconry of Sudbury wills, Suffolk RO, IC 500/1/75 (119), 500/1/85 (26) · Foster, *Alum. Oxon.*, 1500–1714 [George Carew]

Carew [Carve], **Thomas** (*b. c.*1590, *d.* in or after 1672), Roman Catholic priest and historian, was born in Mobernan, co. Tipperary. His father's name is unknown, but his mother was a member of the Butlers of Ormond and he enjoyed the patronage of this powerful aristocratic clan. He spoke Irish, and regardless of his anxiety to stress his Anglo-Norman ancestry, he appears to have come from a Gaelicized background. He became a priest in the diocese of Leighlin, but soon tired of such relatively sedate duties. About 1624 he left Ireland for Germany to act as chaplain for Walter Butler who was serving as colonel of an Irish regiment in the army of Emperor Ferdinand II. He returned to Ireland on two separate occasions, between

1628 and 1630 and in 1632–3. On leaving Ireland for the final time in 1633 he began writing an itinerary of his travels and of his experiences amid the Thirty Years' War in Germany. After visiting London, Prague, and much of Germany, only narrowly avoiding capture by protestant forces on occasions, he arrived in Stuttgart in December 1634 to find that Butler had just died. He became chaplain to Butler's successor, Walter Deveroux, whom he accompanied on campaigns in Germany and Lorraine for the next five years.

The first part of Carew's *Itinerarium* was published at Mainz in April 1639 and was an immediate success, being in its fourth edition by May 1641. It includes a particularly historically valuable chapter on the 1634 assassination of the famous general Wallenstein, in which Butler and Deveroux were heavily involved. However, many of the Irish serving as imperial troops in Germany were insulted by passages in the work which described the Gaelic Irish as barbarous. Carew received letters demanding he recant his views, and pamphlets satirizing him were widely distributed among the Irish forces. In May 1641 he published the second part of his *Itinerarium* (under the title *Itinerarij*), which included vigorous and unrepentant justification of his controversial opinions. He was appointed chaplain-general to the English, Irish, and Scots troops in the imperial army in September 1641. The same year he published his *Rerum Germanicarum*, a narrative of the Thirty Years' War. About 1643 he went to reside in Vienna as notary apostolic and vicar-choral of St Stephen's Cathedral. In 1646 the third part of his *Itinerarium* was illegally published (again under the title *Itinerarij*) at Spires in an uncompleted form. It appears that Carew's enemies had prevented him from obtaining the censor's approval and may even have succeeded in destroying parts of the work.

Although Carew seems to have settled in Vienna and to have stopped travelling, he continued to publish up until his death. His *Lyra, seu, Anacephalaeosis Hibernica*, published in 1651, dealt with the early history of Ireland and the history of Europe from 1148 to 1650. The second edition of the *Lyra*, published in 1666, included additional passages on contemporary Irish affairs, which were highly critical of Giovanni Rinuccini, papal nuncio to Ireland in the 1640s, and outraged many of his fellow Irish émigrés. Towards the end of his life he was involved in a vitriolic and highly personalized controversy with Anthony Bruodin (MacBroody), an Irish Franciscan monk of the convent at Prague. Bruodin's 1669 work *Propugnaculum Catholicae veritatis*, which narrated about 200 Irish Catholic martyrdoms, also contained an attack on the *Lyra*. Carew replied in *Enchiridion apologeticum* (1670), and when Bruodin responded in *Anatomicum examen* (1671), Carew's *Responsio veridica* (1672) questioned the accuracy of the friar's lives of the Irish martyrs. Perhaps the turbulence of this at times vulgar controversy took its toll on Carew, as no more is heard of him; he died in or after 1672. His portrait, engraved by M. Vliemayr, is included in the 1666 edition of the *Lyra*.   TERRY CLAVIN

Sources *Itinerarium Thomae Carve*, ed. M. Kenny (1859) · P. Nolan, 'Irishmen in the 30 Years' War', *Irish Ecclesiastical Record*, 5th ser., 22 (July–Dec 1923), 362–9 · P. Nolan, 'Irishmen in the 30 Years' War', *Irish Ecclesiastical Record*, 5th ser., 24 (July–Dec 1924), 394–400 · *The whole works of Sir James Ware concerning Ireland*, ed. and trans. W. Harris, 3 (1746), 144 · *Father Luke Wadding: commemorative volume*, ed. Franciscan Fathers dún Mhuire, Killiney (1957), 438–62 · *DNB* · T. W. Moody and others, eds., *A new history of Ireland*, 3: *Early modern Ireland, 1534–1691* (1976); repr. with corrections (1991)
Likenesses M. Vliemayr, engraving, repro. in T. Carve, *Lyra Sulzbach*, 2nd edn (1666)

Carew, Thomas (1594/5–1640), poet, was born possibly at West Wickham, Kent, where his parents had been living for a number of years. He was a younger son of Sir Matthew *Carew (1531–1618), master in chancery, and his wife, Alice (d. 1638). Alice was the widow of Richard Ingpen (or Ingpenny), of the Middle Temple, and the daughter of Sir John Ryvers (or Rivers) and his wife, Elizabeth. Though invariably spelled Carew by the poet himself the family name was pronounced 'Carey' and frequently appears in this form, or a phonetic variant, in seventeenth-century sources. Carew should, however, be distinguished from Thomas Carey (1597–1634), second son of Robert Carey, first earl of Monmouth. Carey, a courtier of both James I and Charles I, also left several poems.

Education and early career Carew's family moved from Kent to Chancery Lane, London, about 1598. Nothing is known of his early education. He matriculated from Merton College, Oxford, on 10 June 1608, aged thirteen, and graduated BA on 31 January 1611. The choice of college was presumably influenced by the fact that Merton's warden, Henry Savile, was a kinsman by marriage. In 1612 Carew was incorporated a BA of Cambridge University, and on 6 August of that year he was admitted to the Middle Temple. However, it soon became clear that he would not follow in his father's footsteps: Sir Matthew remarked just six months later that his son 'hath a chamber and studye, but I feare studiethe the lawe very litle' (*Poems*, xviii).

Carew's father already seems to have been seeking out alternative employment for him since this comment was made in a letter to Sir Dudley Carleton, who had married Sir Matthew's niece (and Savile's stepdaughter) Anne Gerard. Carew entered Carleton's service soon afterwards; he joined him on his embassy to Venice in late 1613 and probably remained with him there, and later in Turin, until Carleton's return to London in December 1615. Carew's acquaintance with Italy appears to have had a significant impact on his poetry. A number of his lyrics are translations or imitations of Italian originals while his masque draws extensively on Giordano Bruno's *Lo spaccio de la bestia trionfante* (1584).

Carew was re-engaged by Carleton for his embassy to the Netherlands, which departed in March 1616. However, he remained in The Hague for less than six months before being abruptly dismissed. The cause appears to have been some defamatory remarks about his employer and Lady Carleton that Carew unwisely committed to paper. It is not known precisely what Carew wrote; in the surviving correspondence no one is so indelicate as to repeat the substance of the libel. Carew pursued a number of alternative patrons, including his cousin (by marriage) Lord Carew, the earl of Arundel, and Sir Henry Wotton, but with no success. In Sir Matthew's view these set-backs signified that his son was 'utterly lost' (*Poems*, xxvii). It may, however, be unwise to give too much weight to a father's jaded remarks about his son's prospects. Indeed, just before Sir Matthew wrote this letter Carew was present at the creation of Charles as prince of Wales on 4 November 1616, when he served as squire to Edward Seymour, Lord Beauchamp, and was named as one of the 'gallants flaunt-[ing] it out in their greatest bravery' (*Poems*, xxix).

Early poems There is no record of Carew's movements for the next two years. This may have been a hiatus during which he commenced writing and circulating his verse with a view to promoting his wit and verbal skill to potential patrons. Such talents may have secured his next employment, as he was retained by the philosopher and poet Sir Edward Herbert (later Lord Herbert of Cherbury), who referred to Carew as 'that excellent wit' (*Autobiography*, 106). Carew joined Herbert's embassy to Paris, departing on the day of Queen Anne's funeral (13 May 1619). Carew's work shows evidence of contact with French poetic traditions, and indeed it may be during his time in Paris, rather than in Venice, that he became especially enamoured of Italian lyrics, since Giambattista Marino was resident in the city from 1615 to 1623 and frequently attended the court. Carew's earliest datable poem is an elegy on Lady Peniston (*d.* 1620), which was 'sent to his mistress out of France'. Other poems probably datable to the same period are 'Upon some Alterations in my Mistress, after my Departure into France', 'To my Mistress in Absence', and 'To her in Absence: a Ship' (*Poems*, 19–24). Neither the identity of the mistress of these poems nor the Celia to whom many of Carew's love lyrics refer is known, which raises the possibility that the addressee had no single or actual counterpart.

It is unclear how long Carew remained in Paris. Herbert himself was recalled to England, temporarily in 1621 and permanently in 1624. The first of Carew's poems to appear in print was a commendatory piece published with Thomas May's *The Heire* (1622), which had been performed in 1620. In the early 1620s Carew appears to have been closely associated with the Crofts family. He wrote a poem to be read by John Crofts (a fellow member of Herbert's entourage) to King James on the occasion of one of the royal visits to the Crofts' family home at Little Saxham, Suffolk (1620–22). He may also have been author of a masque performed at Little Saxham, possibly for the king's visit in December 1621 (McGee, 374–6). In addition Carew wrote a poem addressed 'To Saxham', in the vein of Ben Jonson's 'To Penshurst'. He continued to compose poems for members of the Crofts family throughout the 1620s and 1630s; these included pieces celebrating the marriages of John's sister (Cecilia) to Thomas Killigrew, in 1636, and of his niece (Anne Wentworth) to Lord Lovelace in 1638.

The majority of Carew's lyrics appear to have been written during the 1620s. With a couple of unauthorized exceptions, none of them was printed during his lifetime. None the less, Carew seems to have been one of the most widely read poets of his day. His verse circulated in manuscript at the universities and the inns of court, and among members of the aristocracy and the gentry. Clarendon names Carew as a member of a literary circle that included Ben Jonson, Thomas May, and John Selden (*Life of … Clarendon*, 1.16). Carew probably frequented the various literary societies that met in the taverns of London and may have been the 'M^r: Tho: Carew' who is listed as one of the members of a 'Tityre-tu' fraternity in the early 1620s, that came under suspicion for Catholic sympathies (Raylor, 77–81).

Carew at court Carew continued to cultivate patronage through his occasional verse. In particular he appears to have achieved the favour of Christopher (Kit) Villiers, the duke of Buckingham's brother, who in March 1624 had been created Baron Villiers of Daventry and earl of Anglesey. Carew later recalls the role that he played as intermediary in Villiers's courtship of his future wife, Elizabeth Sheldon:

> When I his sighes to you, and back your teares
> Convay'd to him.
> (*Poems*, 71)

However, Carew's relationship with the family can be charted mainly by the elegies that he penned for them. He wrote two elegies for Buckingham, following his assassination in 1628; three epitaphs for (it seems) the Villiers' daughter, Mary, who died in 1630; and a further poem following the death of Kit himself, addressed to the widowed countess of Anglesey, in April 1630. In addition he wrote several poems for the earl and countess of Carlisle, the first of which appears to have been an elegy on their daughter Anne (*d.* 1629), whom Carew never met. Carew's tactics of advertising his own talents and celebrating those of potential patrons paid off when he secured a position at court. On 6 April 1630 he was appointed a gentleman of the privy chamber and shortly afterwards he was awarded the active post of sewer-in-ordinary to the king. The duty of the sewer was to taste and pass dishes to the king, which brought Carew into almost daily contact with the monarch. Clarendon recalls that this appointment was to the 'Regret even of the whole *Scotch* Nation, which united themselves in recommending another Gentleman to it' (*Life of … Clarendon*, 1.19).

About the same time Carew came under attack from Philip *Massinger in a confrontation that has been described as the 'war of the theatres'. Hostilities arose when a play by Carew's friend William Davenant, *The Just Italian*, was jeered off the stage soon after its opening at Blackfriars Theatre in October 1629. Davenant's text was printed in 1630, accompanied by a commendatory poem by Carew lamenting the fact that public taste for theatre had been debased by the sort of fare offered at the Blackfriars' main rival, the Cockpit. Massinger, who was a prominent figure at the Cockpit, responded by attacking Carew as a coterie poet composing 'servile Encomions to some great mans name' (Beal, 'Massinger', 196–203). The dispute, which appears to have rolled on for a number of years, drew in other figures such as James Shirley and Thomas Heywood.

Massinger describes Carew as the writer of 'loose raptures'. This is a reference to Carew's notorious erotic fantasy, 'A Rapture', which was probably written in the 1620s. When Carew's *Poems* appeared in print in 1640, it was one of the volumes denounced in parliament by Sir Edward Dering as being 'in disgrace of Religion, &c. to the increase of all Vice, and withdrawing of the people from reading studdying, and hearing the word of God' (Ruoff). In an anonymous poem, published in 1645, Carew (who here appears as 'Cary') is made to describe his infamous poem as the product of 'wisdomes nonage, and unriper yeares', which he has 'labour'd to expunge' (*The Great Assises Holden in Parnassus by Apollo and his Assessours*, 1645, 26).

Soon after his court appointment Carew wrote two of his most justly celebrated poems, his elegy on the death of John Donne (*d*. 1631), and his response to Ben Jonson's 'Ode to Himself', which followed the failure of *The New Inne* (published in 1631). The elegy on 'great Donne' is considered by many to remain the finest example of literary criticism in verse, imitating Donne's style in order to encapsulate and celebrate his achievement, while Carew's reply to 'deare Ben' takes up Jonsonian dictates in order to criticize Jonson himself. James Howell recounts that Carew expressed similar sentiments at a dinner given by Jonson which became dominated by the host's praise for himself:

> *T. Ca.* buzz'd me in the ear, that tho' *Ben.* had barrell'd up a great deal of knowledge, yet it seems he had not read the *Ethiques*, which, among other precepts of Morality, forbid self-commendation, declaiming it to be an ill-favour'd solecism in good manners. (Howell, 2.403–4)

After the death of Gustavus Adolphus in November 1632, Aurelian Townshend urged Carew to follow up these poems with an elegy on the protestant hero. Carew declined on the grounds that his 'lyric feet' were incapable of celebrating a martial theme (*Poems*, 74). Instead he urged Townshend to write songs and masques and thereby to celebrate peace in England rather than war on the continent. Carew followed his own advice; almost half of his lyrics were set to music by the composer Henry Lawes, who was also closely associated with the Caroline court, and Carew wrote a masque that was performed at Whitehall just over a year after his poem to Townshend, on Shrove Tuesday (18 February) 1634. For the latter he collaborated with Inigo Jones, whose sketches for the elaborate stage designs and costumes survive. The king himself performed in the masque and was reported to have been 'very well pleasd' with the production; Sir Henry Herbert, master of the revels, described it as 'the noblest masque of my time to this day, the best poetrye, best scenes, and the best habitts' (Bawcutt, 187). The masque focuses on the moral authority of the king and queen; the gods have decided to expel the existing constellations from the heavens and to replace them with the royal couple and other British heroes of exemplary merit (hence the title *Coelum Brittanicum*). However, the tone is not simply celebratory; a complicating voice is that of Momus, the god of ridicule, who mocks and undercuts the conduct of the proceedings by Mercury. In the manner of a privy chamberer Momus claims jurisdiction to venture behind the public image of the royal household and looks into 'all the privy lodgings … though it bee to the surprize of a perdu Page or Chambermaid' (*Poems*, 157). This disparity between the public image of the court as a seat of platonic love and the private reality of secret liaisons is also hinted at by an anecdote related by 'old G. Clarke, Esq., formerly Lord of the Admiralty and Secretary to Prince George of Denmark':

> Thomas Carew, Gentleman of the Privy Chamber, going to light King Charles into [the Queen's] chamber, saw Jermyn Lord St. Albans with his arm round her neck;- he stumbled and put out the light;- Jermyn escaped; Carew never told the King, and the King never knew it. The Queen heaped favours on Carew. (*Seventh Report*, HMC, 244)

The anecdote, though tantalizing, is probably spurious. On the same page it is alleged that 'Milton, the poet, died a papist'.

Carew perhaps wrote another entertainment at this time. The prologue and epilogue for 'a play at Whitehall' survive, as does a series of six songs (*Poems*, 59–64, 127–8). He remained a prominent figure in literary circles, and in the later 1630s addressed poems to Davenant, Thomas Killigrew, Walter Montagu, Henry, Lord Cary of Lepington, and George Sandys. There is also a letter, purportedly written by Carew to Suckling, but this is usually attributed to the pen of the addressee, who composed the piece prompting this 'response', in which he sought to dissuade Carew from marrying a rich (unidentified) widow (*Poems*, 211–12). Suckling, who joined Carew as a gentleman of the privy chamber in 1638, also wrote an epigram 'Upon T. C. Having the P[Ox]'. The effects of syphilis may have prompted the penitent state of mind expressed in Carew's poem to Sandys in 1638, where he declares his intention to forsake the 'verdant Bay' in favour of the 'dry leavelesse Trunke on *Golgotha*' (*Poems*, 94). It is true that Carew probably did not write any more love lyrics after this date but it is doubtful that he penned his translation of eight psalms at this time. A couple of these translations, which seem to form a series, are found in manuscript sources datable to the 1620s.

Death and publication Clarendon recounts of Carew:

> [His] Glory was, that after fifty Years of his Life, spent with less Severity or Exactness than it ought to have been, He died with the greatest Remorse for that Licence, and with the greatest Manifestation of Christianity, that his best Friends could desire. (*Life of … Clarendon*, 1.19)

According to Izaak Walton, one long-standing acquaintance not impressed by this conversion was John Hales. Hales had been a fellow of Merton while Carew was an undergraduate there and had travelled with him to The Hague as Carleton's chaplain; his brother had married Carew's sister Martha. Walton recounts that Carew had obtained Hales's absolution in an earlier fit of sickness, 'upon a promise of amendment'. However, after recovering Carew 'fell to his old company and into a more visable Scandalus life'. When taken with his final illness, he sought out Hales again, 'desyring earnestly after a confession of many of his sins to have his prayers and his absolution'. Hales offered Carew his prayers 'but wood by noe meanes give him then ether the sacrament or absolution' (Butt, 273).

A poem by Davenant is addressed to Carew at his house in King Street, Westminster, but Carew probably spent considerable periods away from this address since other poems are addressed to him at John Crofts's house at the estate of Carew Ralegh at Horsley in Sussex (a fellow gentleman of the privy chamber, whose marriage was celebrated by Carew), and at Sir Richard Leighton's house in Boswell Court. Carew's last datable poem was written while he was staying at Wrest Park in Bedfordshire, the seat of Henry de Grey, earl of Kent, and his wife, Elizabeth. In this poem, possibly addressed to Gilbert North, another gentleman of the privy chamber, Carew refers to his participation in King Charles's failed Scottish campaign of the spring of 1639. The poet here, as in his verse letter to Townshend, shows distaste for militarism and prefers the isolation of an estate whose owners are not renowned for their royalist sympathies (Parker, 172–4, 188–9). In any case, Carew died in March 1640, before any further hostilities developed. His funeral was held in London, at St Dunstan-in-the-West, on 23 March 1640; he was buried there.

On the same day Thomas Walkley (who had published *Coelum Brittanicum* in 1634) entered 'a booke called *The Workes* of Thomas Carew' in the Stationers' Register. This posthumous and unauthorized volume, which was printed later in 1640, has been the basis of every subsequent edition. It can be considered as composed of several distinct sections. The first is a collection of poems by Carew derived from a reliable manuscript source together with those commendatory poems that had appeared in print during his lifetime. The second section is the most problematic since it essentially comprises a miscellany of twenty-two poems: ten of these can be definitely rejected from Carew's canon and there is little evidence to support his authorship of any of the remaining twelve. The third and final section is a reprint of the masque. A few other poems, some of uncertain authorship, were added to the collection by the subsequent editions of 1642 and 1651. There are several large manuscript sources of Carew's poetry relating to the first section of the 1640 edition; the most important of these is a (privately owned) collection of forty-seven poems by Carew with emendations and additions in the poet's own hand (Beal, 'Poems by Carew'). The nature of these authorial annotations supports Carew's reputation as a conscious and conscientious craftsman.   SCOTT NIXON

Sources *The poems of Thomas Carew, with his masque Coelum Britannicum* [sic], ed. R. Dunlap (1949) · P. Beal and others, *Index of English literary manuscripts*, ed. P. J. Croft and others, [4 vols. in 11 pts] (1980–), vol. 2 · P. Beal, 'Massinger at Bay: unpublished verses in a war of the theatres', *Yearbook of English Studies*, 10 (1980), 190–203 · P. Beal, 'Poems by Carew: the Gower manuscript', *English Manuscript Studies, 1100–1700*, 8 (2000) · J. Butt, 'Izaak Walton's collections for Fulman's life of John Hales', *Modern Language Review*, 29 (1934), 267–73 · *The life of Edward, earl of Clarendon … written by himself*, new edn, 3 vols. (1827) · *The autobiography of Edward, Lord Herbert of Cherbury*, ed. S. Lee, 2nd edn [1906] · *The control and censorship of Caroline drama: the records of Sir Henry Herbert, master of the revels, 1623–73*, ed. N. W. Bawcutt (1996) · C. E. McGee, '"The visit of the nine goddesses": a masque at Sir John Croft's house', *English Literary Renaissance*, 21 (1991), 371–84 · M. P. Parker, '"To my friend G. N. from Wrest": Carew's secular masque', *Classic and cavalier: essays on Jonson and the sons of Ben*, ed. C. J. Summers and T. -L. Pebworth (1982), 171–91 · T. Raylor, *Cavaliers, clubs and literary culture: Sir John Mennes, James Smith, and the Order of the Fancy* (1994) · J. E. Ruoff, 'Thomas Carew's early reputation', *N&Q*, 202 (1957), 61–2 · J. Howell, *Epistolae Ho-elianae*, ed. J. Jacobs, 2 vols. (1890–92) · *Seventh report*, HMC, 6 (1879)

Archives priv. coll., MS poetry with emendations and annotations in Carew's own hand

Carew, Sir Wymond (1498–1549), administrator, was born at Antony in Cornwall, the eldest son of John Carew of Antony and Thomasin Holland of Exeter. In 1519 he married Martha (d. 1572) [see Carew, Martha], daughter of the exchequer baron Edmund Denny of Cheshunt, Hertfordshire; they had at least four sons, including the chancery master Sir Matthew *Carew. The Cornish antiquary Richard Carew was his grandson.

Carew's career in royal financial administration began in the duchy of Cornwall, where he served as deputy receiver-general and was a member of several commissions by the early 1530s. Although he retained his duchy post until 1549, the demands of other offices soon compelled him to employ a deputy. The turbulent matrimonial politics of the Henrician court offered Carew the opportunity to expand his role in royal service, for the fall of the Boleyns in 1536 was followed by a purge of officials in the queen's household. Carew profited from this turmoil, securing the post of receiver-general to the new queen, Jane Seymour, and her successor, Anne of Cleves. Following her divorce in 1540 he remained with Anne's household as receiver until 1543, but by early 1544 he had returned to court as treasurer to Henry's sixth queen, Katherine Parr, joining a group of other duchy officials also in her service.

The climax of Carew's career came in April 1545 with his appointment as treasurer of the court of first fruits and tenths, the royal revenue court responsible for receipts from clerical taxation. Like his colleagues he struggled during the mid-1540s to cope with the strains upon crown finances caused by war against France and Scotland, and regularly aroused the wrath of councillors desperate for funds. The crown relied upon men of Carew's standing for local administration as well. He served on commissions of the peace from 1536 until his death, and as a Middlesex chantry commissioner in 1546 and 1548. He was also entrusted with more sensitive duties, as in December 1546 when he was one of those secretly sent to take charge of the duke of Norfolk's property following his imprisonment in the Tower. The accession of Edward VI a month later brought formal recognition of Carew's royal service, for he was knighted and subsequently represented Peterborough in the parliament of 1547.

During the 1540s Carew's career benefited from the influence exercised in the king's privy chamber by his brothers-in-law Anthony Denny and John Gates; he pressed them to promote suits on his behalf at court (with mixed success) and often acted as a business agent for Gates. In common with many of his colleagues Carew found royal service highly lucrative, and it enabled him to accumulate considerable property. As well as enlarging the family's estates in the south-west, he purchased lands near his wife's Hertfordshire home and in 1548 acquired the manor of Hackney in Middlesex, which became his principal residence. It was here that he died intestate on 24 August 1549, bequeathing his heirs considerable debts to the crown arising from his accounts in first fruits and tenths, which were not fully discharged until 1611.

P. R. N. CARTER

Sources P. Carter, 'Financial administration, patronage and profit in Tudor England: the career of Sir Wymond Carew (1498–1549)', *Southern History*, 20–21 (1998–9), 20–43 • R. Carew, *The survey of Cornwall*, ed. F. E. Halliday (1953) • J. L. Vivian, ed., *The visitations of Cornwall, comprising the herald's visitations of 1530, 1573, and 1620* (1887) • HoP, *Commons, 1509–58* • exchequer, accounts various, PRO, E 101 • exchequer, first fruits and tenths, PRO, E 336 • state papers, Henry VIII, PRO, SP 1

Wealth at death debts of more than £4000: exchequer records

Carey, Anthony, **fifth Viscount Falkland** (1656–1694), Admiralty official, was born on 15 February 1656 at Farley Castle, Somerset, and baptized at Great Tew, Oxford, on 25 February 1656, the only son of Henry Carey, fourth Viscount Falkland (1634–1663), and his wife, Rachel (1637–1718), daughter of Anthony Hungerford of Blackbourton, Oxfordshire. He succeeded to the title on 2 April 1663 at his father's death. Falkland was educated from 1668 at Winchester College, then at Christ Church, Oxford, which he left in 1672. His marriage in 1681 to Rebecca (1662–1709), daughter of Sir Rowland Lytton of Hertfordshire, brought him a great fortune and allowed him to buy the post of treasurer of the navy from Edward Seymour for £15,000. Falkland was elected MP for Oxford county in 1685, probably as a tory, and proved a very active member. In 1687 he was part of a syndicate of eight speculators led by Christopher Monck, second duke of Albemarle, who invested money in an attempt to find the Spanish treasure ship the *Concepción*. His one-seventh investment proved highly profitable, bringing him £21,766, 'a return of about forty-seven-fold' (Earle, 201). Two subsequent expeditions were much less successful, and he lost over £19,000 on them.

Falkland was elected MP for Marlow in 1689, and then represented Great Bedwyn from 1690 until 24 May 1694; he was named to several committees and spoke frequently in debates. In 1689 Edward Russell replaced him as navy treasurer, but in September that year Falkland was suggested as an Admiralty commissioner. William III told George Savile that 'Lord Falkland did not seek the employment, but was content to have it' (Foxcroft, 2.238). In January 1691, as had long been expected, 'the Churchman Lord Falkland' (Horwitz, 66) was at last appointed to the Admiralty board. The board minutes show that from January 1691 until 15 April 1693 Falkland attended meetings four or five times a week, even when parliament was sitting.

On 27 November 1692 he vigorously defended it from parliamentary critics:

I wish your change of the Admiralty might procure a remedy for your distemper. I am afraid not but that the true cause of these mischiefs complained of proceeds from the want of cruisers and convoys, of which sort of ships there is a great want. (*Parliamentary Diary of Narcissus Luttrell*, 245)

Falkland was appointed first lord of the Admiralty in the commission issued on 15 April 1693; when an investigation was launched into the events surrounding the loss of a convoy of merchantmen bound for Smyrna in the summer he led the attack against the earl of Nottingham and the three admirals, Sir Ralph Delavall, Henry Killigrew, and Sir Cloudesley Shovell. He was on bad terms with them all, especially Killigrew, who was also one of his Admiralty colleagues, following an open quarrel with them on 19 October in the presence of the inner council. Early in 1694 Falkland was accused of bribing members of parliament out of the fund for Admiralty perquisites. He was severely reprimanded and committed to the Tower on 16 February by vote of the House of Commons, but released three days later. He attended the board for the last time on 27 February, when he chaired the meeting, though his name was not removed from the commission until 2 May 1694. King William appointed Falkland as his envoy to The Hague but before taking up the post Falkland died of smallpox, possibly at his house in Deptford, on 24 May 1694; he was buried in Westminster Abbey four days later.

Falkland also wrote a prologue for William Congreve's play *The Old Bachelor*, though it appears not to have been used. When John Evelyn heard of Falkland's death, he wrote as an epitaph: 'he was a pretty, brisk, understanding, industrious young gentleman; had formerly been faulty, but much reclaimed. He married a great fortune … had been Treasurer of the Navy, and advancing in the new court. All now gone in a moment' (Evelyn, 5.182).

PETER LE FEVRE

Sources GEC, *Peerage*, new edn, 5.241–2 • L. Naylor and G. Jagger, 'Carey, Anthony', HoP, *Commons, 1660–90*, 2.16–18 • P. Earle, *The wreck of the Almiranta: Sir William Phipps and the Hispaniola treasure* (1979), 201, 217–18 • H. Horwitz, *Parliament, policy and politics in the reign of William III* (1977), 66 • admiralty board minutes, 1691–4, PRO, ADM 3/5–10 • *The parliamentary diary of Narcissus Luttrell, 1691–1693*, ed. H. Horwitz (1972) • *The life and letters of Sir George Savile … first marquis of Halifax*, ed. H. C. Foxcroft, 2 (1898), 238 • Evelyn, *Diary*, 5.182 • J. Ehrman, *The navy in the war of William III, 1689–1697* (1953), 506

Carey, (Francis) Clive Savill (1883–1968), singer and opera producer, was born at the White House, Sible Hedingham, Essex, on 30 May 1883, the fourth child and elder son of Francis Carey (1840–1911) and his wife, Elizabeth Harrowell (1852–1930/31). Gordon Vero *Carey was his brother. Carey's parents later settled at Burgess Hill, Sussex. He was educated at King's College choir school, Sherborne School, and Clare College, Cambridge, from where he proceeded BA in 1904 and gained his MusB in 1906. He was a scholar at Sherborne and organ scholar at Clare. He was also Grove scholar at the Royal College of Music, studying composition under Sir Charles Stanford and singing under J. H. Ley.

Carey's career began at Cambridge, where he lived after graduation, in between visits to France, Italy, and Germany to study music and learn languages, for which he had remarkable talent. He was assisted by his lifelong friendship with Edward Dent, an enthusiast for opera in English translation. Their first major production was *The Magic Flute* in Cambridge in 1911, in which Carey sang Papageno. He was also active in the folk-music revival, collecting songs and dances in Sussex, Essex, and Oxfordshire. Perhaps through his sympathy with the women's suffrage movement he supported Mary Neal in opposition to Cecil Sharp. Between 1910 and 1914 Carey organized the musical activities of Neal's Espérance Morris Guild, and he remained a lifelong friend. He contributed to part 2 of the *Espérance Morris Book* (1912) and published *Ten English Folk Songs* in 1915.

During the First World War, Carey served with the Royal Army Medical Corps and the Royal Army Ordnance Corps, rising to the rank of major. After demobilization he returned to singing and opera direction at the Old Vic under Lilian Baylis, taking the title role in the 1920 *Don Giovanni*. He was also in the original group of the English Singers and toured Europe with them. The most important influence on Carey's maturity was the Polish tenor Jean de Reszke (1850–1925), under whom he studied between 1920 and 1924, later acting as his accompanist and assistant. Carey's first major teaching post was at the Elder Conservatorium, Adelaide, between 1924 and 1928. In Australia he met, and in 1929 married, Doris (c.1892–1968), daughter of Samuel Johnson of Adelaide; their marriage was a happy one. He returned through the USA and Canada with the company of *The Beggar's Opera*, in which he sang Macheath.

Back in England, Carey joined the staff of the Royal College of Music and returned to work with Lilian Baylis, producing opera, at Sadler's Wells. These included the first English production of Rimsky-Korsakov's *The Snow Maiden* in 1934 and the original version of Mussorgsky's *Boris Godunov* in 1935. In 1939 the Careys were on a personal visit to Australia and spent the war years there. Carey taught at the Adelaide Conservatorium and was later co-director of the Melbourne Conservatorium. On his return to England, he was again director at Sadler's Wells in 1945–6 and professor of singing and director of the opera school at the Royal College of Music between 1946 and 1953, where his pupils included Joan Sutherland. He was appointed CBE in 1955.

As a singer, Carey felt he owed everything to de Reszke. As opera director, he and Edward Dent were pioneers of accessible, English-language productions. Sadler's Wells was avowedly a popular theatre, aiming its productions at a mass audience. Carey was generous in more private matters: at the height of his career he was not above singing in his brother's school productions of Gilbert and Sullivan. He regretted he had not done more as a composer, and some felt that a lifelong diffidence and distrust in his own abilities prevented a more productive and creative career.

Nevertheless, he had done much. He was a man who touched many branches of music and adorned everything he touched. In appearance, he was tall and handsome of face and figure.

Clive Carey suffered a disabling stroke in 1967 and lingered for a year at his home, 85 St Mark's Road, Kensington, London, looking out on the now neglected garden, which had been among his hobbies. He died at his home on 30 April 1968, and his ashes were interred at Claygate, Surrey. Doris Carey survived him only a few weeks. They had no children.   C. J. BEARMAN

Sources *Duet for two voices: an informal biography of Edward Dent compiled from his letters to Clive Carey*, ed. H. Carey (1979) · private information (2004) · *WWW* · *The Times* (3 May 1968) · Clare College, Cambridge · Royal College of Music, London · Vaughan Williams Memorial Library, London, Clive Carey MSS · B. Pickering Pick, *The Sherborne register* (1950) · Family Records Centre, London · b. cert. · d. cert.

Archives Royal College of Music, London, folk–song and folk-dance MSS · Vaughan Williams Memorial Library, London, collected papers | CUL, letters to Edward Dent · priv. coll., corresp. with George Williams Lyttleton · Vaughan Williams Memorial Library, London, Lucy Broadwood MS collection | SOUND BL NSA, performance recordings

Likenesses C. Ewald, oils, *c.*1910, Royal College of Music, London · pencil caricature, Royal College of Music, London · photographs, repro. in Carey, ed., *Duet for two voices*

Wealth at death £8878: administration with will, 10 Dec 1968, *CGPLA Eng. & Wales*

Carey, David (1782–1824), journalist and poet, was the son of a manufacturer in Arbroath. After leaving school he was placed in his father's counting-house, but subsequently he moved to Edinburgh, where he worked for a short time in the publishing house of Archibald Constable. From there he went to London and, finding employment on the periodical press, wrote with such keenness in support of the whig government as to attract the notice of Wyndham, who offered him a foreign appointment, which, however, he declined. Instead he wrote a satire entitled *Ins and Outs, or, The State of Parties, by Chrononhotonthologos*, which sold widely. In 1804 he edited the *Poetical Magazine, or, Temple of the Muses*, which consisted chiefly of his own poems, and also published separately *Pleasures of Nature, or, The Charms of Rural Life and other Poems* (1803), *The Reign of Fancy: a Poem with Notes* (1803), *Lyric Tales* (1804), and *Poems Chiefly Amatory* (1807). In 1807 he became editor of the *Inverness Journal*, which he left in 1812 to conduct the *Boston Gazette*. In the same year he published his novel *Lochiel, or, The Field of Culloden*, and renewed his connection with the London press, which occupied most of his time thereafter, although he continued to write and publish various poetical and descriptive works. In 1822 he spent some time in Paris, and on his return published *Life in Paris*, written chiefly in a humorous vein, with coloured illustrations. His visit to Paris having failed to restore his poor health, he returned to his father's house at Arbroath, where he died of consumption after eighteen months of illness on 4 October 1824.

T. F. HENDERSON, rev. NILANJANA BANERJI

Sources Allibone, *Dict.* · Anderson, *Scot. nat.* · catalogue [BM]

Carey [Carew; *née* Spencer], **Elizabeth**, **Lady Hunsdon** (1552–1618), literary patron, was born on 29 June 1552 at Althorp, Northamptonshire, the sixth child of thirteen born to Sir John Spencer (d. 1586), of Wormleighton and Althorp, and Katherine, daughter of Sir Thomas *Kitson (1485–1540), of Hengrave, Suffolk. On 29 December 1574 she married Sir George *Carey, afterwards second Baron Hunsdon (1546/7–1603) [*see under* Carey, Henry (1526–1596)]. His will praises her as 'the sweetest Companion that ever Man hathe found in this lief'.

Edmund Spenser's sixteenth dedicatory sonnet to *The Faerie Queene* (1590) is addressed to 'the most vertuous, and beautifull Lady, the Lady Carew' and in the dedication to *Muiopotmos* (1590) he records her 'great bounty to my selfe'. In *Colin Clouts Come Home Again* (1595), Spenser refers to his kinship with the Spencers,

> the noble familie:
> Of which I meanest boast my selfe to be

and celebrates Carey as '*Phyllis* the floure of rare perfection', along with her sisters, Anne, Lady Mounteagle and Compton, afterwards countess of Dorset, and Alice, Lady Strange [*see* Spencer, Alice]. He describes Carey 'Faire spreading forth her leaves with fresh delight', perhaps implying that she is a writer (*Colin Clout*, ll. 536–71). In the dedication to *Christ's Tears over Jerusalem* (1593), Thomas Nashe praises her 'pietie, bountihood, modestie, and sobrietie' and states 'you recompence learning extraordinarilie'. In dedicating *The Terrors of the Night* to her daughter, Nashe writes of Lady Carey that 'Into the Muses' society herself she hath lately adopted, and purchased divine Petrarch another monument in England', either a reference to her patronage or to her own writing; he praises her 'extraordinary liberality'. Other dedications to Carey include Thomas Churchyard's *A Tragicall Discourse of the Haplesse Mans Life* (1593); Abraham Fleming's *The Footpath to Felicitie* (1581) and *A Monomachie of Motives* (1582); Thomas Playfere's sermon, *The Meane of Mourning* (1595); and *The First Book of Songs or Airs* (1597), where John Dowland refers to her 'singular graces towards me'. A dedicatory sonnet in Henry Lok's *Ecclesiastes* (1597) is addressed to 'the Ladie of Hunsdon'.

On 9 January 1613 Chamberlain noted that Lady Hunsdon was 'newly maried' to Ralph Eure, third Baron Eure (d. 1617) (*Letters of John Chamberlain*, 1.405). Chamberlain also recorded her death 'of a palsie as is supposed' (ibid., 2.147) on 24 or 25 February 1618. She was buried on 2 March in the Hunsdon vault in Westminster Abbey.

Carey's only surviving child, Elizabeth [**Elizabeth Chamberlain**, Lady Chamberlain (1576–1635)], was born on 24 May 1576; Queen Elizabeth was one of her godmothers. She married Sir Thomas Berkeley (1575–1611), eldest son of Henry, Lord Berkeley, on 19 February 1595, bringing a dowry of '1000 li and of land near to the value of 1000 li' (Smyth, 2.396). They had two surviving children, Theophila (b. 1596), educated 'under the sole direction of her mother' (Smyth, 2.400), and George *Berkeley, afterwards eighth Baron Berkeley (1601–1658). In 1622 Lady Berkeley married Sir Thomas Chamberlain, justice of the king's bench. Smyth describes her living in Cranford,

Middlesex, 'amongst her thousands of books' (Smyth, 2.437–8). Lady Chamberlain died on 23 April 1635 and was buried in Cranford; an inscription records her descent from the earls of Wiltshire and her relationship to Queen Elizabeth through her father who was Anne Boleyn's great-nephew. Nashe dedicated *The Terrors of the Night* (1594) to her, mentioning her wit and 'religious piety'. William Camden's *Annales* (1625) names her among many dedicatees and in Philemon Holland's translation of Camden's *Britain* (1637), Thomas Meriell praises her as the 'rare Phoenix cause of this translation'.

ELAINE V. BEILIN

Sources E. A. Strathmann, 'Lady Carey and Spenser', *ELH: a Journal of English Literary History*, 2 (1935), 33–57 · *The Yale edition of the shorter poems of Edmund Spenser*, ed. W. A. Oram and others (1989) · *The letters of John Chamberlain*, ed. N. E. McClure, 2 vols. (1939) · J. Smyth, *Lives of the Berkeleys* (1883), vol. 2 of *The Berkeley manuscripts*, ed. J. Maclean (1883–5) · E. G. S. Reilly, *Historical anecdotes of the families of the Boleynes, Careys, Mordaunts, Hamiltons, and Jocelyns: arranged as an elucidation of the genealogical chart at Tollymore Park* (1839) · Burke, *Peerage* (1970) · G. Baker, *The history and antiquities of the county of Northampton*, 1 (1822–30) · GEC, *Peerage*, 1.334; 4.280 · H. Sydney and others, *Letters and memorials of state*, ed. A. Collins, 1 (1746), 372 · 'Register of burials in Westminster Abbey', *Collectanea Topographica et Genealogica*, 7 (1841), 355–7 · *Sir John Harington's A new discourse of a stale subject, called the metamorphosis of Ajax*, ed. E. S. Donno (1962) · J. J. Howard, ed., *Miscellanea Genealogica et Heraldica*, new ser., 4 (1884), 84 · *Collins peerage of England: genealogical, biographical and historical*, ed. E. Brydges, 9 vols. (1812), vol. 3, pp. 615–16 · A. C. Judson, *The life of Edmund Spenser* (1945) · C. Stopes, *The life of Henry, third earl of Southampton* (1922)
Archives AM Oxf., Mr Napier's notes, MS 240, fols. 132b–133b · BL, 'The ages of Sr Jn Spencer (my Great Grandfathers) children transcribed from a loose paper I found: by me Jn Spenser 1704', Add. MS 29438, fol. 10
Likenesses miniature, exh. South Kensington Museum 1862
Wealth at death left 1000 livres plus lands to value of almost 1000 p.a. to only daughter: Smyth, *Lives of the Berkeleys*, 396; George Carey's will, PRO, PROB 11/102, sig. 68; abstract in *Herald and Genealogist*, vol. 4, pp. 131–2

Carey, Eustace (1791–1855), missionary, was born on 22 March 1791 at Paulerspury, Northamptonshire, third son of Thomas Carey, a non-commissioned officer in the army, and nephew of Dr William Carey, Baptist missionary in Bengal. Immersed as a child in nonconformism, in 1809 he began to study for the Baptist ministry with the Revd John Sutcliff at Olney, Buckinghamshire, and in 1812 he transferred to the Bristol Baptist college. He was of frail health and it was only reluctantly that the Baptist Missionary Society (BMS) appointed him to serve in India. On 9 December 1813 he married Miss Mary Fosbrook of Leicester and on 1 August 1814 they arrived at his uncle's celebrated mission at Serampore in Bengal.

In 1815 Carey moved to Calcutta and in 1817, following a breach with Serampore's founders, he founded with his colleagues John Lawson and William Yates a missionary family union in the north of the city. Together they established elementary schools for Hindu boys and girls and, as leading lights in the Calcutta School Book Society, issued several moral tracts and textbooks in Bengali, but Carey always maintained that the spread of God's word was the missionary's primary duty and from 1819 he concentrated on itinerant preaching in and around Calcutta. This thinking was not unconnected with the split from Serampore, which was ostensibly a dispute over property rights. Carey in particular regretted the effort that his elder brethren lavished on their prestigious college which, in including literature and other secular subjects on its syllabus, seemed to him to betray its missionary objectives.

In 1825 Carey returned to Britain. He had baptized few converts, and repeated bouts of ill health and the deaths of four children had worn him down. For the rest of his life he devoted himself to promotional work for the BMS, making extensive fund-raising tours around the country. In 1828 he published *A Vindication of the Calcutta Baptist Missionaries* and in 1831 *A Supplement to the Vindication*. In 1836, however, he also issued a eulogistic *Memoir of William Carey, D.D.*; his quarrel at Serampore had always been more with Joshua and John Clark Marshman than with his uncle. After the 1832 insurrection in Jamaica, he became an ardent campaigner for emancipation.

Carey's first wife, Mary, had died in July 1829, leaving two children, William Fosbrook and Annie. Carey and his second wife, Esther, whom he married in the spring of 1834, had one son. Carey died on 19 July 1855 at his home in Camberwell Grove, London, and was buried on 24 July at Highgate cemetery. His widow, two sons, and daughter survived him, and in 1857 Esther published a lengthy memoir, *Eustace Carey: a Missionary in India*.

[ANON.], rev. KATHERINE PRIOR

Sources E. Carey, *Eustace Carey: a missionary in India* (1857) • M. A. Laird, *Missionaries and education in Bengal, 1793–1837* (1972) • B. Stanley, *The history of the Baptist Missionary Society, 1792–1992* (1992)
Archives Regent's Park College, Oxford, letters and abstracts from his journal
Likenesses M. E. Channon, lithograph, repro. in Carey, *Eustace Carey*

Carey, Felix (1786–1822), orientalist and missionary, was born on 20 October 1786 at Moulton, Northamptonshire, the eldest son of William *Carey (1761–1834), missionary to India, and his first wife, Dorothy Plackett (1756–1807). He accompanied his parents to Bengal in 1793 and was baptized at Serampore in 1800. He became fluent in Bengali, learned Sanskrit, and studied medicine. On 23 October 1804 he married Margaret Kincey or Kinsey (*b. c.*1789); she died on 26 December 1808.

In 1807 Carey volunteered to go to Burma to help start a mission there. On 22 March 1811 he married a Miss N. Blackwall (*b.* 11 Sept 1789). He introduced vaccination and was well received at the court of Ava; however, the press which he was conveying there was lost on 30 August 1814 in a shipwreck on the Irrawaddy, which also claimed the life of his wife. He published the first Burmese grammar for English students (1814) and a Burmese translation of part of the New Testament (1815); he also compiled material for a dictionary which provided the basis for the American missionary Adoniram Judson's publication in 1826.

In 1815 King Bodawpaya sent Carey as an envoy to Calcutta, but the Bengal government refused to recognize his credentials and his mission was an embarrassing failure.

In the same year, in Burma, he married for a third time, but the name and fate of his wife are uncertain. In 1818 he returned to Serampore, where he remained until his death four years later. This time was the most fruitful period of his life: he was a pioneer in the transmission of European learning into Bengal, particularly through his Bengali textbooks. They included translations of Goldsmith's *History of England* (1820) and Bunyan's *Pilgrim's Progress* (1821–2), also *Vidyahara vali*, on anatomy (1819–20). Among his works still incomplete at his death was his translation of Mack's *Principles of Chemistry*. He is believed to have contributed the articles on science to the Bengali monthly *Dig Darshan*; indeed he has been called 'the father of scientific writing in Bengali' (Siddiq Khan, 261).

Carey married for a fourth time on 2 November 1821—his fourth wife was Amelia Pope—but died barely a year later, on 10 November 1822, at Serampore; he was buried in the Baptist mission cemetery there. He was survived by his wife (who died at the same place in 1869) and three children. His career was chequered, reflecting his somewhat unstable character, but his early death was a real loss for the development of Bengali: contemporary and modern writers concur in the opinion that he was the best Bengali scholar among the Europeans of his time.

MICHAEL LAIRD

Sources B. R. Pearn, 'Felix Carey and the English Baptist mission in Burma', *Journal of the Burma Research Society*, 28 (1938), 1–91 • M. Siddiq Khan, 'Felix Carey: a prisoner of hope', *Libri*, 16 (1966), 236–69 • S. K. Chatterjee, *Felix Carey* (1991) • D. G. E. Hall, 'Felix Carey', *Journal of Religion*, 12 (1932), 473–92 • J. C. Marshman, *The life and times of Carey, Marshman and Ward*, 2 vols. (1859) • *Friend of India* (Dec 1822) • *Periodical Accounts Relative to the Baptist Missionary Society*, 1–6 (1800–17) • *Serampore Circular Letters* (1808–22) • W. Ward, 'Missionary Journal', 1799–1811, Regent's Park College, Oxford, Angus Library [typescript] • *Reports of the Calcutta School Book Society* (1819–21) • *DNB*
Archives Regent's Park College, Oxford, Angus Library | BL OIOC, Bengal political consultations; secret consultations

Carey, Sir George (*c.*1541–1616). *See under* Carew, George, earl of Totnes (1555–1629).

Carey, George, second Baron Hunsdon (1546/7–1603). *See under* Carey, Henry, first Baron Hunsdon (1526–1596).

Carey, George Jackson (1822–1872), army officer, was born on 5 October 1822 at Rozel, Guernsey, a son of Thomas Carey of Rozel and his second wife, the daughter of Colonel George Jackson, Mayo militia, and MP for co. Mayo. He was educated at Elizabeth College, Guernsey. In July 1845 he obtained an ensigncy in the Cape mounted rifles, with which he served in the Cape frontier wars of 1846–7 and 1850–3, becoming lieutenant in April 1847, captain in October 1848, and major in January 1853, and receiving brevet rank as lieutenant-colonel in May 1853 for service in the field. He became brevet colonel in 1854, and served as military secretary to his uncle, Lieutenant-General Sir James Jackson, commanding the forces at the Cape during the frontier troubles of 1856–7. Carey married in 1861 Olivia Hester, the only daughter of W. Gordon Thompson of Clifton Gardens, Hyde Park, London, and they had four children.

Carey exchanged as major to the 2nd battalion 18th Royal Irish, and went with it to New Zealand, where he served in the war from August 1863 to August 1865 as colonel on the staff and brigadier-general, and commanded the expedition on the east coast to the Thames and to Tauranga. He also commanded at the siege and capture of the Maori stronghold at Orakau, and for this, one of the few successes of the war, Carey was made CB. On 27 May 1865 William Thompson, the great Maori chief and 'king-maker', surrendered to Carey.

Carey was appointed to command the troops in Australia in August 1865, and acted as governor and administrator of Victoria from 7 May to 16 August 1866. In December 1867 he was appointed to an infantry brigade at Aldershot. In 1868 he became major-general, and in October 1871 was transferred to the command of the northern district. He died on 12 June 1872 at his residence, Westwood, Whalley Range, Manchester, and was buried at Rozel.

H. M. CHICHESTER, rev. JAMES LUNT

Sources Fortescue, Brit. army, vol. 8 · Burke, Gen. GB · Hart's Army List · B. Williams, Record of the Cape mounted rifles (1909) · T. Gibson, The Maori wars (1974) · A. J. Smithers, The Kaffir wars (1973) · R. Cannon, ed., Historical record of the eighteenth, or the royal irish regiment of foot (1848) · Boase, Mod. Eng. biog. · CGPLA Eng. & Wales (1872)
Wealth at death under £7000: probate, 19 July 1872, CGPLA Eng. & Wales

Carey, George Saville (1743–1807), entertainer and writer, the son of Henry *Carey (1687–1743), poet, and his wife, Sarah, who had been a country schoolmistress, was born a short time after his father's suicide on 5 October 1743. Kitty Clive led a benefit performance for the destitute widow and her four small children at Drury Lane on 17 November 1743. Carey was intended to be a printer, but decided instead to become an actor, and later claimed to have been encouraged by David Garrick and Susannah Cibber. His early stage career cannot be traced. The first record of his appearance on stage is at Covent Garden on 27 April 1773, as Henry in 1 Henry IV, and he may have been Axalla in Nicholas Rowe's Tamerlane on 4 November 1773. He had a more lasting success as a public lecturer on the subject of mimicry. He is first recorded giving his lecture at the Great Room, Panton Street, in the summer of 1774, and at Marylebone Gardens in the following year. He took his programme around the provinces, visiting such places as Edinburgh, Leeds, Bath, Buxton, and York. Carey developed his entertainment, which included imitations of celebrated actors and singers and culminated in a dialogue in the manner of Samuel Foote and Thomas Weston. His vocal imitations encompassed singers from soprano to bass, and after his death he was widely praised for the respectability of his programmes: 'he was careful to exclude every thing of an immoral tendency from his entertainments' (Allibone, Dict.).

Carey was an active author throughout his life, principally of works for the stage, although, with the possible exception of the farce The Dupes of Fancy, or, Every Man his Hobby (1792), there is no evidence of any of them being performed in London theatres. They included The Inoculator (a comedy) and The Cottagers (an opera), both of which Carey published with some poetry in Flights of Fancy (1776). Liberty Chastized, or, Patriotism in Chains (1768) was a political play published under the pseudonym of Paul Tell-Truth; Shakespeare's Jubilee was a masque published in 1769. The Old Women Weatherwise (1770) was performed in Hull in 1825. Carey wrote and published several other burlettas and volumes of poetry. His Lecture on Mimicry was published in 1776, and in 1777 'A Rural Ramble, to which is Annexed a Poetical Tagg, or Brighthelmstone Guide' appeared in the Monthly Review. On 10 July 1789 he married Sarah Gillo of Salisbury, an actress. Two years earlier his daughter, Ann Carey (d. 1833), had given birth in his chambers at Gray's Inn to a son, later the celebrated actor Edmund Kean.

By 1797 Carey had come to believe the unfounded rumour that his father had been the author of 'God Save the King', and applied fruitlessly to the king for an interview to urge his claims to a pension. In 1799 he published The Balnea, or, An Impartial Description of All the Popular Watering-Places of England, which reached a third edition in 1801. This work, alongside the 'Rural Ramble', suggests that Carey continued to tour the country. He also wrote a considerable number of songs, and published One Thousand Eight Hundred, or, I Wish you a Happy New Year in 1800, and The Myrtle and Vine, or, Complete Vocal Library in 1801. In the summer of 1807 he gave a series of entertainments in London, where he died suddenly of paralysis on 14 July. He was in financial straits, and was buried at the expense of his friends.

JENNETT HUMPHREYS, rev. K. D. REYNOLDS

Sources D. E. Baker, Biographia dramatica, or, A companion to the playhouse, rev. I. Reed, new edn, rev. S. Jones, 3 vols. in 4 (1812) · GM, 1st ser., 77 (1807), 781–2 · Highfill, Burnim & Langhans, BDA · Allibone, Dict.
Likenesses Terry & Co., line engraving, pubd 1776, BM, NPG · J. Hall, stipple (after W. Sherlock), BM, NPG; repro. in Highfill, Burnim & Langhans, BDA

Carey, Gordon Vero (1886–1969), indexer and headmaster, was born on 9 October 1886 at the White House, Sible Hedingham, Essex, the youngest son of Francis Carey (1840–1911) and his wife, Elizabeth Harrowell (1852–1930/31). His eldest brother, (Francis) Clive Savill *Carey (b. 1883), was director of Sadler's Wells (1945–6) and director of the opera school at the Royal College of Music (1946–53); his sister, Margery Helen, married Sir Ivo D'Oyly Elliott, one time under-secretary to the government of India and secretary to the government, United Provinces (1925–9).

Carey was a boy chorister at King's College, Cambridge, from where he won a scholarship to Eastbourne College, Sussex, and from there he went on to Gonville and Caius College, Cambridge, again on a scholarship, where he obtained a second-class classical tripos degree. Carey was a keen rugby player and won his rugby blue at Cambridge in 1907 and 1908, then played for the Harlequins for four years in the great era of the game. On 2 October 1909 he achieved the unique distinction of taking the first kick-off at Twickenham when Harlequins and Richmond played the opening match on that ground. Fifty years later, when he was again the first to kick off at the opening of the

Stoop memorial ground, his friend U. A. Titley, rugby correspondent of *The Times*, asked him 'whether he intended to make a 50-year habit of it'. His reply is unrecorded.

In the years leading up to the First World War, Carey taught at King's College, Eastbourne College, and Trinity College, Glenalmond, but in 1913 he abandoned teaching and joined the Cambridge University Press (CUP). During the war he was commissioned in the 8th battalion, the rifle brigade, and was severely wounded at Hooge (1915), where the Germans first tried out their new flame projectors. He subsequently became a staff officer in the RAF (1918–19) and was awarded the Belgian Croix de Guerre. After the war Carey returned to CUP, first as assistant secretary and then, from 1922, as educational secretary, and it was there that he compiled the *Cambridge University War List* (1921) and part-authored *An Outline History of the Great War* (1928). One of his two collaborators, Colonel Norman Rutherford, was a convicted murderer, and since he was still serving his sentence his name could not appear on the title-page. In 1919 Carey was elected a fellow of Clare College and in the same year he married Eila Reynolds, daughter of G. W. Reynolds, with whom he had two sons, Adrian and Hugh. She died in 1932, and two years later Carey married Dorothy Armstrong, second daughter of Ernest Armstrong, with whom he had one son, Nicholas.

Carey was an upright, courteous, affectionate, and meticulously minded man whose letters were written in a distinctly beautiful hand. In 1939 he wrote *Mind the Stop*, a delightful guide to punctuation, and several years later he wrote *Making an Index* (1951), which he described as 'a measly pamphlet of mine'. His love of music, a common feature of his family, meant that he continued to sing at the annual gatherings of the King's College choir almost until his death; he also never, if he could help it, missed a varsity rugby match at Twickenham. However, instead of staying at CUP as he would have wished, he was persuaded in 1928 to become headmaster of Eastbourne College, where he stayed until 1938. 'He was headmaster for nine years only, but those few years showed prodigious development in every possible way. Music; art; scholarship; games; everything flourished under him' (private information, R. Storrs).

The Second World War saw Carey as a squadron leader in the Royal Air Force Volunteer Reserve (1941) and as librarian to the RAF Staff College (1942–5). After the war he returned to his first love of proof-reading and indexing, this time for Heinemann, and it was while there that he saw one of the letters written by Gilfred Norman Knight to the national press about the possibility of setting up a society for indexers. The information may also have come via his brother-in-law Sir Ivo Elliott, a Balliol man (like Knight). Carey was an enthusiastic member of the Society of Indexers, which came into being in March 1957. In 1962 he became the society's first president, and over the years gave numerous talks and wrote several articles for the society's journal, *The Indexer*.

Carey died on 21 November 1969 in the Victoria Hospital, Lewes, Sussex. His second wife survived him. His memorial service was held on 6 December in the beautiful chapel of Eastbourne College, and in the words of his son the Revd Adrian Carey, who wrote the bidding prayer:

> It is characteristic of his own peculiar blend of confidence with diffidence, of gaiety with gloom, that he should have both expressed doubt as to whether a memorial service would be called for, and also placed on record his choice of psalm and hymns for such a service if it were held. (private information)

In 1977 the Society of Indexers created the Carey award in memory of 'the prince of indexers'—a title conferred on Carey by an anonymous book reviewer in the *Times Literary Supplement* in 1951 on the publication of his 'measly pamphlet' on indexing. GERALDINE BEARE

Sources *WW* (1955) · *The Times* (22 Nov 1969) · V. A. Titley, *The Times* (28 Nov 1969) · *The Indexer*, 6/3 (1969) · *The Indexer*, 7/1 (1970) · private information (2004) [R. Storrs, housemaster of Eastbourne College, 1969; members of the Society of Indexers] · *CGPLA Eng. & Wales* (1970) · b. cert. · d. cert.
Archives Society of Indexers, Sheffield
Likenesses photograph, repro. in *The Indexer*, 7/1 · portraits, Society of Indexers, Sheffield
Wealth at death £20,242: probate, 5 March 1970, *CGPLA Eng. & Wales*

Carey, Henry, first Baron Hunsdon (1526–1596), courtier and administrator, was born on 4 March 1526, the only son of William *Carey (c.1500–1528), courtier, of Aldenham, Hertfordshire, and his wife, Mary [see Stafford, Mary (c.1499–1543)], royal mistress, daughter of Thomas *Boleyn, earl of Wiltshire and earl of Ormond (1476/7–1539), courtier, and his wife, Elizabeth. William Carey came from a cadet branch of the Careys of Cockington, Devon, founded by his father, Thomas Carey of Chilton Foliat, Wiltshire, who married a cousin of Lady Margaret Beaufort. William Carey had a court career and was esquire of the body to Henry VIII from 1520 to 1528. The recipient of substantial grants from the king, when he died on 23 June 1528 he left for his son lands in Essex, Hampshire, Wiltshire, and Buckinghamshire, including the borough of Buckingham.

Early career, 1526–1569 Henry Carey was a member of the royal household by 21 May 1545, when he obtained licence to marry Anne (d. 1607), daughter of Sir Thomas Morgan of Arkstone, Herefordshire, and his wife, Anne. The couple had nine sons, including: George Carey, second Baron Hunsdon [see below]; Henry (d. 1581); John Carey, third Baron Hunsdon [see below]; William (d. 1593); Edmund (d. 1637); and Robert *Carey, first earl of Monmouth (1560–1639), courtier. They also had three daughters, Katherine (d. 1603), Philadelphia (d. 1627), and Margaret (d. 1605). In 1545 Henry Carey was a captain in the force assembling under John Dudley, Viscount Lisle, at Portsmouth. In 1546 he accompanied Lisle's embassy to France and in 1551 the mission to the same court of William Parr, marquess of Northampton. He was MP for the borough of Buckingham in 1547 and carver of the privy chamber from 1553 to 1558 or later. Absent from parliament in 1553, he sat as MP for Buckingham in April and November 1554; during the latter session he departed early without leave, for which information was laid against him in king's bench but no

Henry Carey Lord Hunsdon BY MARK GERARDS. ÆTATIS SVÆ 66 AN 1591

Henry Carey, first Baron Hunsdon (1526–1596), attrib. Marcus Gheeraerts the younger, 1591

action followed. In the 1555 parliament he voted with Sir Anthony Kingston against a government bill. In 1557 Carey suffered detention in the Fleet prison for debts of £507 incurred in 1551 but was released on a new recognizance on 19 May.

Carey was a gentleman of the household of his cousin Elizabeth (1533–1603) in 1554–5 and probably earlier, in 1551–2; on her accession to the throne on 17 November 1558 he was speedily recognized, knighted soon after, and raised to the peerage as first Baron Hunsdon on 13 January 1559. In 1559 he received a substantial grant of lands in Hertfordshire, Kent, and Essex worth £4000 per annum, to sustain his new dignity. The grant included the manor of Hunsdon in Hertfordshire.

Hunsdon figured in court tilts in 1559–60 and attended Thomas Howard, fourth duke of Norfolk, in Scotland during the campaign to eject the French, returning to court in July 1560. He was appointed master of the queen's hawks with a salary of £40 a year on 31 October 1560. Nominated KG on 22 April 1561, he was installed on 18 May. In 1564 Hunsdon headed a mission to France, carrying the Order of the Garter to Charles IX and acting as witness at the signing of the treaty of Troyes. He was created MA on the queen's visit to Cambridge in 1564. Three years later he was again in France, although the purpose of his visit is unclear. He was appointed captain of the gentlemen pensioners in 1564.

The northern uprising, 1569–1570 Hunsdon's first promotion to power came when the queen appointed him governor of Berwick on 25 August 1568. In this post he was one of the senior English officials in the borders at a time

of particular sensitivity. Mary, queen of Scots, fled Scotland a few months earlier and that country was in great disorder. Hunsdon wrote in September 1568, disapproving of Elizabeth's leniency towards the Scottish queen. At the same time, he thanked Sir William Cecil, principal secretary, for his support against unnamed enemies, who contested Hunsdon's appointment. He also wrote of gossip at Bolton, Cumberland, where Mary was lodged, of a match between her and his eldest son, a notion he vehemently opposed. Sir Francis Knollys, Mary's keeper, had in fact speculated on such a match.

After a busy nine or ten months in his new post, Hunsdon sought leave and at the same time asked for and received a loan of £300 for entertainment costs. He also solicited appointment to two offices, one in the exchequer, the other, as chief justice itinerant of the royal forests north of the Trent. If those requests were refused, he could no longer serve, he claimed. He failed to receive the first and had to wait until 20 December 1591 for the second. Absent from his post in autumn 1569, when rebellion broke out in the north, he hastened back to join Thomas Radcliffe, third earl of Sussex, lord president of the queen's council of the north.

Unable to reach York by road, Hunsdon went by sea to Hull, arriving at the northern capital by 26 November. He hastened to send a letter reassuring Elizabeth of the loyalty of Sussex, which had been questioned. He moved on to meet the lord president at Durham. A few days later Thomas Percy, sixth earl of Northumberland, and Charles Neville, sixth earl of Westmorland, fled across the border into Scotland. Hunsdon had already taken the opportunity, on his way north, to solicit the stewardships of Richmond and Middlesbrough, Yorkshire, forfeited by Northumberland.

On 22 January 1570 Hunsdon wrote agitatedly of dangers still threatening the north, hinting at the greatest conspiracy there in one hundred years. He declared the queen must be bewitched and urged her need for counsel and assured friends, 'small care has she for either' (*CSP dom., addenda, 1566–79*, 194–5). He presumably thought Elizabeth underestimated the continuing danger in the north (she had just ordered the dismissal of most of the forces raised against the earls). Hunsdon was personally offended because the queen thought poorly of his services (possibly because of a letter he wrote to Anne Percy, countess of Northumberland, seeking information about her husband's whereabouts). His mood changed on hearing from his wife of Elizabeth's more favourable attitude towards him and he sought Cecil's backing for his case.

The rebel earls fled to Scotland, but Leonard Dacre holed himself up in Naworth Castle, Cumberland, and recruited a force of several thousand men. When James Stewart, earl of Moray, the Scottish regent, was assassinated on 21 January 1570, it seemed the rebel cause, with the backing of Scottish border chieftains, might be revived. The queen ordered Sussex to seize Dacre. He delegated the task to Hunsdon, who wrote to Henry Scrope, ninth Baron Scrope of Bolton, warden of the west marches and captain of Carlisle, at Carlisle, asking for a loan of ordnance, only to be told none was to be had. Since Naworth was strongly fortified, Hunsdon hesitated to move and turned his attention to Newcastle upon Tyne, where he feared a plot to place the town in rebel hands. There then came a peremptory royal order to seize Dacre.

Obliged to act, but acutely aware of the numerical weakness of his 1500-strong force, Hunsdon set off in company with Sir John Forster, the warden of the middle marches. His army was largely composed of the Berwick garrison, with large numbers of musketeers. Hunsdon and Forster planned to surprise Dacre but an intercepted letter dashed this hope. When, after a forced night march, they were faced by Dacre with a larger army, Hunsdon decided to march to Carlisle, where he could join forces with Scrope. However, Dacre blocked his way at a river crossing and on 20 January 1570 Hunsdon had to stand and fight. He responded to a fierce charge by the enemy foot with a cavalry counter-charge which scattered the rebel army. Dacre fled to Scotland; Hunsdon seized Naworth.

The queen's response to this news was prompt. To a formal letter of praise she added in her own hand, 'I doubt much, my Harry, whether that the victory was given me more joyed me or that you were by God appointed the instrument of my glory'. For the country's good the first suffices, but 'for my heart's contentment the second more pleased me' (*CSP dom.*, addenda, *1566–79*, 245–6). Hunsdon had trusted to the goodness of his cause despite his weakness in number. He declared that this letter comforted him more than a £500 land grant. Elizabeth did in fact promise an increase in his livelihood, but her promise was not immediately kept. In the next summer Hunsdon had an apologetic letter from the queen for her cool reception of him at court, declaring her outward demeanour masked her true feelings. In May 1571 there was a grant in fee simple of land forfeited by Dacre in Yorkshire and Derbyshire worth £207 per annum.

Warden of the east marches, 1571–1577 Meanwhile Hunsdon was kept busy in the north. Following the assassination of Moray, civil war broke out in Scotland between the Marians and James VI's supporters. Hunsdon immediately urged English support for the king's party. Elizabeth initially opposed the dispatch of English troops to aid James, but Sussex and Hunsdon risked her wrath by making a series of devastating raids on the Scottish borderlands between April and June 1570, laying waste to the country and seizing the principal castles. The two commanders sometimes acted jointly, sometimes separated their forces. Hunsdon was responsible for the capture of Hume Castle. In May, during an illness of Sussex, they went further in acting on their own. Hunsdon proposed, without royal consent, to respond to the request of the new Scottish regent, Matthew Stewart, thirteenth earl of Lennox, for aid by leading 1000 men into the northern kingdom, but Sussex, more cautious, reduced the force and entrusted command to a more junior officer, Sir William Drury, who marched to Edinburgh and through the Clyde valley to Glasgow in assisting the regent's forces.

The queen gave reluctant approval to their actions but halted an attempt against the Marian fortress of Dumbarton. Later, more graciously, she sent a general letter of thanks to Sussex, with a separate one for Hunsdon. In July the latter solicited Cecil's help in procuring leave. Turned down the first time, he succeeded on the second request. He remained absent from his charge for over a year, until October 1571, entertaining Elizabeth at Hunsdon in September 1570.

Hunsdon was appointed warden of the east marches on 23 October 1571, charged with heavier and more diverse responsibilities. His charge now went well beyond mere border problems. In Scotland the struggle between the regency and the Marian party focused on Edinburgh, where Sir William Maitland and Sir William Kircaldy of Grange, holed up in the castle, held it and the town in defiance of the new regent, John Erskine, first earl of Mar. Elizabeth sought to aid the latter, using as far as possible diplomatic means, but holding the threat of armed intervention in suspense. Hunsdon, from Berwick, was to carry on negotiations with both parties, using Thomas Randolph and Drury, the English agents in Edinburgh, to provide information and to act as messengers. Hunsdon's task was to induce the Marian leaders to submit to the regent and to persuade the latter to offer them reasonable terms. He was in the meantime to prepare forces to go to Leith to aid the regent if negotiations failed. A secondary goal was to procure the surrender of the fugitive Northumberland.

Hunsdon used the threat of force to bring about surrender of the castle but to no avail; the defenders hoped for succour from France while the king's party clamoured insistently for more money before they would move. He came to view both parties as equally unreliable. His recipe for success was the dispatch of an English army to Edinburgh. Given a force of 4000 men for six weeks, he could deliver the castle (he hoped the queen would not dishonour him by giving command of the expedition to anyone else). Once again his hopes of return to the battlefield were disappointed.

Months dragged in weary and fruitless negotiation. Hunsdon, deeply disillusioned, continued to assert that Elizabeth was wasting her money on the Scots. If she wanted a stable regime at Edinburgh, she must use English arms. He did, however, accomplish one part of his mission; in May 1572 the Scots handed Northumberland over in return for £2000. In the same month Hunsdon pleaded for leave; there was nothing he could do in Scotland, and the borders were quiet. In July the deadlock at Edinburgh became a truce. Even before it was signed on 31 July, Hunsdon was preparing to visit friends in Durham and Yorkshire; by mid-August he had left Berwick. He did not return for a full three years. His role as a courtier was enhanced by his appointment on 31 July 1574 as keeper of Somerset House. Hunsdon does not appear much again in the public record until summer 1575, when a quarrel between the English and Scottish wardens, resulting in the death of an English commissioner and a major cattle raid by the Scots borderers, led the queen in July to require his return to the north. He was there by September, served on a joint Anglo-Scottish commission which settled matters, and left by November.

Privy councillor, 1577–1588 Then in 1577 Hunsdon moved from the periphery to the centre of power when Elizabeth appointed him to the privy council (16 November). For the remainder of his life the privy council chamber was the focus of his political and administrative career, but he was by no means discharged of his Scottish duties. On four occasions the queen ordered him north for an extended period of service—in 1578, in 1581, in 1584–5, and finally in the Armada years, 1587–8. The first occasion arose in 1578 when the position of the new Scottish regent, James Douglas, fourth earl of Morton, was threatened by a coalition of lords. Elizabeth, anxious to support him, sent Hunsdon north to confer with the lord president, Henry Hastings, third earl of Huntingdon. The two were granted authority to enter Scotland with 2000 men, if Sir Robert Bowes, the English agent at Edinburgh, requested them to act. In fact Bowes was able to patch up a settlement between Morton and his foes which left the regent with effective power. Hunsdon remained in the north until January 1579.

Scottish affairs remained in ferment. James's French cousin, Esmé Stewart, sixth seigneur d'Aubigny, had arrived in 1579 and soon acquired an ascendancy over the young king. The English watched nervously as Morton's star fell while d'Aubigny's rose. In summer 1579 there was talk of Hunsdon's going on embassy to the Scottish court. It was not until November that the queen sent him north armed with a commission to raise an army to intervene on Morton's behalf. Actually Hunsdon had already warned Elizabeth that the regent was too weak to be worth supporting and by the time he reached Berwick, Morton was in prison. Any hope that Morton's allies might rise was extinguished when Elizabeth first promised them aid and then almost immediately withdrew her offer.

Given the bankruptcy of English policy, Hunsdon could only advocate breaking relations, both diplomatic and commercial, while wasting the Scottish countryside in order to bring the Scots to heel. He began a series of pleas for deliverance from his post, declaring there was nothing for him to do on the Scottish scene while the borders were quiet, but he met refusal. He was still at Berwick when Morton was executed on 2 June 1581. In the weeks following that event, Hunsdon refused a passport to the king's ambassador, Sir John Seton, an action approved at court. At the end of July he left for friends' houses in co. Durham. By September he was back attending meetings of the privy council.

In the following years the quicksilver changes at the Scottish court saw d'Aubigny's overthrow, the short-lived dominance of his foes, their exile to England, and the rise to influence of James Hamilton, third earl of Arran. The English court distrusted Arran and hoped to see the exiles returned home. In summer 1584 Hunsdon was sent north to interview the new favourite, carrying with him the queen's terms for repairing the damaged relations of the two countries and a demand that the exiles be allowed to return. The interview took place at Berwick on 14 August;

Arran returned pleased with the occasion, but Elizabeth was not satisfied with his answers to her questions. Hunsdon, for his part, accused the principal secretaries, Sir Francis Walsingham and William Davison, of distrusting Arran while they reciprocated with the counter-accusation that Hunsdon unwisely favoured the Scottish lord. Hunsdon at the same time pleaded with Arran to moderate his responses to Elizabeth lest he fatally damage the warden's own mission by undermining his credit with the crown. In November he urged Elizabeth to accept Arran's proposals, dropping her support of the exiles and excluding them from England.

When Arran dispatched Patrick Gray, the master of Gray, as ambassador to Elizabeth in October, Hunsdon naïvely accepted the protestations of the earl's good faith—and the double-dealing envoy's display of protestant piety. The queen, for the time being, was willing to deal with Arran. Hunsdon, his mission accomplished, returned to court in February 1585.

Hunsdon's role as an active privy councillor, who regularly attended meetings, by no means diminished his responsibilities in Scottish matters. As the privy council's Scottish expert, he became in fact a kind of minister for Scottish business. He had a determining voice in the appointment of the English agents at the Scottish court and was the recipient of a steady flow of correspondence from both English and Scottish sources. The Scottish government regarded him as their spokesman on the privy council. James wrote directly to him on many matters. The queen used him as a channel of communication, dictating letters which then went north under his signature. In the aftermath of Mary's execution in February 1587, when Elizabeth sought to restore relations with James, Hunsdon's credit at Edinburgh was very useful, although he warned the queen that, in his opinion, the Scottish king would be relentless in avenging his mother's death. Robert Carey's warm relations at the Scottish court were brought into play by his father.

In August 1587, as the Armada menace grew, Elizabeth sent Hunsdon north with a substantial force with responsibility for the eastern and middle marches. There was a scheme by which, if the invaders landed, he was to assume command of a northern army. He remained in the north until April 1588, when he was called south for other duties, first as lord lieutenant of Norfolk and Suffolk, where he had to oversee the musters, and then, as principal captain and governor (20 July 1588) of an army of 36,000, to protect the queen's person. He was also lord lieutenant of Hertfordshire from 1583 to 1585.

Statesman, 1583–1596 During the 1580s Hunsdon's role at court grew steadily. In 1583 the queen re-appointed him captain of the gentlemen pensioners and in July 1585 lord chamberlain of the household. He continued his regular attendance of privy council meetings. In 1582 he served on the committee for the abortive negotiation with Jean de Simier for the Anjou match. When François, duc d'Anjou, passed from England to the Low Countries in the same year, Robert Dudley, earl of Leicester, Charles Howard, second Baron Howard of Effingham, and Hunsdon accompanied him to Antwerp, taking with them the promised English subsidy. Then, in August 1585, Hunsdon was a member of the party, with Cecil (now Baron Burghley), Leicester, Howard, Sir Christopher Hatton, and Walsingham, to negotiate the treaty of Nonsuch with the states general.

In the post-Armada years Hunsdon was busy with varied responsibilities. The deaths of a succession of leading privy councillors between 1588 and 1591 meant that he was, with Burghley and Knollys, the last survivor of his generation. He was involved closely with Lord Treasurer Burghley in the complicated dealings with the states general and Henri of Navarre and, along with Burghley and Howard, signed the contracts with the French agents which provided for armed English assistance in Normandy and Brittany in the early 1590s. Hunsdon supported James's claim to the English succession.

At home, Hunsdon's lieutenancy in East Anglia required his intervention in local disputes while, wearing yet another hat, he sat as judge in his forest jurisdiction, Elizabeth having appointed him chief justice in eyre south of Trent in 1589. On 2 March 1592 he was named high steward of Oxford for life, adding it to his other stewardships, of Doncaster and Ipswich (1590). He was also recorder of Cambridge from 1590. Lastly, his office as lord chamberlain gave him a strategic political role, since it was to him that petitions for audience with the queen must turn. In these activities Hunsdon remained busy to the last days of his life. He attended the privy council in late June, barely a month before his death at Somerset House on 23 July 1596. Hunsdon was buried in Westminster Abbey at Elizabeth's expense on 12 August and his widow erected a fine monument over his tomb. He left an illegitimate son, Valentine *Carey (d. 1626), bishop of Exeter. Hunsdon's nuncupative will is brief and was witnessed by his heir, Sir George Carey, 'for I have alwaies founde you a kynde, and lovinge sonne'. His death was apparently sudden, although recent illness meant that 'nowe I desyer noe longer to lyve'. His choice of Carey as his sole executor was even more of an issue because he felt that his wife 'knoweth not howe to deale in suche causes soe well', especially because of the 'broken and harde estate as I shall leave' (PRO, PROB 11/88, sig. 54). Carey was to have administration of his father's estate, providing for his mother, siblings, and Hunsdon's servants, while the queen promised to remove any debt attached to it, which was mainly the result of royal service. Lady Hunsdon died on 19 January 1607 and was buried with her husband.

Hunsdon stood out in the estimate of his contemporaries by his plain speaking, forthrightness, and lack of guile. This reputation is borne out by his record. He had no hesitation in baldly pressing schemes, usually for strong measures, which ran counter to the wary caution of his devious mistress. His ambitions squared with his temperament. 'He loved sword and buckler men', in Sir Robert Naunton's words (R. Naunton, *Fragmenta regalia*, 1649, 102). He certainly craved the chance to renew the martial fame he had enjoyed in 1570, grasping hopefully but vainly at each opportunity.

Hunsdon began his career with the valuable asset of royal favour, based apparently on kinship, but he had to work hard to earn the rewards of land and office which he coveted. This he did faithfully, sometimes grumblingly. He eschewed, so far as can be seen, the intrigues of the court, working closely with Burghley, but on friendly terms with Leicester. Once admitted to the inner circle of power, he proved himself a hard-working and responsible crown servant. He enjoyed a full measure of the royal bounty. The initial grant of lands in 1559 (which augmented a very respectable inheritance) was followed by a grant in fee simple of the manor of Stratfield Mortimer, Berkshire, in 1565 and in 1568 by the honour of Ampthill with lands in Bedfordshire and Buckinghamshire. After the northern uprising Hunsdon received forfeited Dacre lands in Yorkshire and Derbyshire. He bought lands in Norfolk in 1576 and in Middlesex in 1578 and 1596. In 1589 he had a patent licensing him to transport 20,000 woollen cloths, paying only English custom. This right he sold to a group of Londoners.

The second and third barons, 1596–1617 George Carey, second Baron Hunsdon (1546/7–1603), courtier, was born in 1546 or 1547, the first son of the first Baron Hunsdon, and his wife, Anne. He matriculated as a fellow-commoner, aged thirteen, from Trinity College, Cambridge, in May 1560. Carey was sent on a mission to confer with Moray in 1569 about the marriage between Mary and Norfolk, was knighted for his military services at Berwick on 11 May 1570, and was MP for Hertfordshire in 1571. He married Elizabeth *Carey (1552–1618), patron, daughter of Sir John Spencer of Althorp, Northamptonshire, and his wife, Katherine, obtaining the licence on 29 December 1574. The couple had one daughter, Elizabeth *Chamberlain (1576–1635) [see under Carey, Elizabeth]. Carey's first court appointment was that of marshal of the household (1578). He also received the constableship of Bamburgh Castle, Northumberland, in 1583, no doubt through his father's influence as governor of Berwick. JP and of the quorum for Hertfordshire from about 1580, he also sat on the Hampshire and Middlesex benches from about 1584, and was *custos rotulorum* and lord lieutenant of Hertfordshire from about 1593 and 1599 respectively. Carey was also captain of the Isle of Wight from 1583, where he had a mixed reputation among the locals. His quarrel with a local gentleman, Anthony Dillingham, reached the privy council in 1583. He did, however, manage the enfranchisement of three parliamentary boroughs on the island—Newport, Newtown, and Yarmouth. He sat in parliament again as MP for Canterbury in 1572 (a by-election), and for Hampshire in 1584, 1586, 1589, and 1593. Carey served on numerous and important committees, including among others that for the subsidy in three sessions, the fate of Mary, slanderous words, the Scottish border, and in 1593 on the petition on purveyances.

Carey was sent on missions, to the Low Countries in 1578 and to James after the Ruthven Raid in 1582. He had military responsibilities on the Isle of Wight as war drew nearer and offered to outfit a privateer in 1585. During the Armada he dispatched munitions and ships to Howard, the lord admiral. He succeeded to his father's offices of captain of the gentlemen pensioners on 23 July 1596 and lord chamberlain and privy councillor on 14 April 1597. The second Lord Hunsdon was nominated KG on 23 April 1597. He continued his south coast responsibilities. In 1597 he was designated to lead an army in defence of the Isle of Wight and the adjacent mainland counties. In a privy council debate in 1599 he painted a lurid picture of the dangers to the kingdom's security posed by the army of Robert Devereux, second earl of Essex, in Ireland. He was host to the queen on several occasions and visited by her when she was on progress at Bath, where he was a patient. He outlived Elizabeth by only a few months. Relieved of the chamberlainship on 4 May 1603, he died on 8 September.

Hunsdon was succeeded by his younger brother, **John Carey**, third Baron Hunsdon (*d.* 1617), nobleman, the third son of the first Baron Hunsdon and his wife, Anne. Carey matriculated as a fellow-commoner from Trinity College, Cambridge, on 29 September 1566. He married Mary (*d.* 1627), daughter of Leonard Hyde of Hyde Hall, Hertfordshire, and widow of Richard Peyton, obtaining the licence on 20 December 1576. The couple had a son, Henry Carey, fourth Baron Hunsdon, first Viscount Rochford, and first earl of Dover (*c.*1580–1666), and two daughters. John Carey was principally interested in local affairs. He was a gentleman pensioner by 1573 to 1603, MP for Buckinghamshire in 1584, 1589, and 1593, chamberlain of Berwick from 1585, deputy warden of the east marches, JP for Cambridgeshire from 1594, and marshal of Berwick from 1596 to 1598 and again in 1603, when he received a life pension of £424 from James VI and I. He was knighted in 1597 or 1598. He died at Hunsdon on or after 31 March 1617 and was buried there on 7 April. His widow died at her house in St Benet Paul's Wharf, London, on 4 April 1627 and was buried at Hunsdon on 7 April.

WALLACE T. MacCAFFREY

Sources APC, 1577–96 · CPR, 1558–82 · CSP dom., 1547–1603, with addenda, 1566–1625 · CSP for., 1566–71 · CSP Scot., 1563–97 · The memoirs of Robert Carey, ed. F. H. Mares (1972) · GEC, Peerage · S. Haynes, ed., A collection of state papers … left by William Cecill Lord Burghley, 2 vols. (1740) · HoP, Commons, 1509–58, 1.582–3 · HoP, Commons, 1558–1603, 1.545–51 · M. A. S. Hume, ed., Calendar of letters and state papers relating to English affairs, preserved principally in the archives of Simancas, 4 vols., PRO (1892–9) · LP Henry VIII, vol. 3/2 · DNB
Likenesses M. Gheeraerts senior, etching (Procession of Garter knights, 1576), BM · attrib. M. Gheeraerts the younger, oils, Berkeley Castle, Gloucestershire [see illus.]

Carey, Henry, second earl of Monmouth (1596–1661), translator, eldest son of Robert *Carey, first earl of Monmouth (1560–1639), and his wife, Elizabeth (*d.* 1641), daughter of Sir Hugh Trevannion and widow of Sir Henry Widdrington of Swynburne Magna, was born at Denham, Buckinghamshire, in January 1596. He entered Exeter College, Oxford, in the Lent term of 1611 as a fellow-commoner, and graduated BA in February 1613. In 1616 he was made a knight of the Bath, and as a young nobleman attended the future Charles I before leaving England to

Henry Carey, second earl of Monmouth (1596–1661), by Samuel Cooper, 1649

travel on the continent, where he became proficient in French and Italian. In 1620 he married Martha (1601–1677), eldest daughter of Sir Lionel *Cranfield, who eventually became earl of Middlesex. They had ten children; two sons and eight daughters. Their elder son, Lionel, was killed fighting for the king at Marston Moor, and their second son, Henry, died of smallpox during his father's lifetime. Carey served four terms as a member of parliament, representing Camelford, 1621–2, Beverley, 1624–5, Tregony, 1625, and St Mawes in 1626. He succeeded to the earldom on his father's death in 1639. His one recorded speech in the House of Lords was made on 13 January 1641 on the occasion of a bill going through parliament depriving the bishops of their seats in the House of Lords. The speech was later printed as a pamphlet. It contained a plea to Charles I to return to 'this good city of London' (A Speech Made in the House of Peers by the Right Hon. Earl of Monmouth, 13 January 1641, sig. A4). His name also appears on Charles I's declaration of 1642. Carey was to remain a staunch royalist throughout the civil war but took little active part, spending his time in translating works from the Italian and the French in order to avoid idleness.

Carey's translations were relevant to the times, being concerned with wars, international and civil, and the use of power. He chose to translate works that he considered would act as examples to others. For example, Romulus and Tarquin (1637), first written in Italian by Virgilio Malvezzi, was dedicated to Charles I and was intended to act 'as a glass wherein you may see your soul'. Carey wished to show the tragedy of war and claimed that the works translated were chosen for the public good. He told his readers that he undertook translations because he had not himself written anything worthy of publication. Apart from *An History of the Civill Warres of England* (1641), a translation of the work of Giovanni Biondi, he refused to translate any other work on the English civil wars 'since they are such as I would wish buried in Oblivion' (*An History of the Late Warres*, 1648, translator's epistles). *The Complete History of the Wars of Flanders* (1654), translated from the Italian of Cardinal Bentivoglio, contained congratulatory poems by Richard Baker, William Davenant, Philip Frowde, and Edmund Waller. Davenant commended Carey's work towards peace. His last translation, *The History of France* (1676), from the Italian of Gualdo Priorato, was finished by William Brent, who dedicated it to Carey's widow.

Carey died at Moor Park, Rickmansworth, Hertfordshire, and was buried at St Mary's Church, Rickmansworth, on 13 June 1661. According to the provisions of his will, made in 1659 in Rickmansworth parish church, an allowance of £100 was made to have a monument erected in the chancel of the church where he and his family were to lie. The memorial tablet was on an altar tomb in the chancel and bore the Carey arms and an inscription with details of his family. He was survived by his wife and three daughters, Elizabeth, Lady Clanaboy, and the ladies Mary and Martha Carey. They were provided for from the rents and profits of lands in Durham, Hertfordshire, Lincolnshire, Long Acre in Middlesex, Wales, and Yorkshire. His wife received all his plate, jewellery, goods and chattels, while his friends and executors received money for mourning rings. His estate at his death was worth about £15,000.   E. LORD

Sources *Memoirs of the life of Robert Carey, first earl of Monmouth* (1759) · will, PRO, PROB 11/304 · 'Memorial tablet, St Mary's Church, Rickmansworth', J. E. Cussans, *History of Hertfordshire*, 3/2 (1881), 150–51 · *IGI* · Wood, *Ath. Oxon.*, new edn, 3.516–19
Archives CKS, letters to Lionel Cranfield
Likenesses attrib. P. Van Somer, group portrait, oils, *c.*1617 (with his family), NPG · S. Cooper, miniature, 1649, Metropolitan Museum of Art, New York [*see illus.*] · W. Faithorne, line engraving (after S. Cooper), BM, NPG; repro. in *I Ragguagli di Parnasso* (1656) · W. Marshall, line engraving, BM, NPG; repro. in Lenault, *Use of the passions* (1649)
Wealth at death approx. £15,000—rents, jewels, plate, etc.: will, PRO, PROB 11/304

Carey, Henry (1687–1743), poet and songwriter, was born on or about 26 August 1687. The *Gentleman's Magazine* for July 1795 claimed he was the illegitimate son of George *Savile, marquess of Halifax (1633–1695). Circumstantial evidence supports a Savile connection: three of Carey's sons were named Savile or Saville, and he dedicated several works to Savile family members; however, his early publications mention 'Mrs. Carey', proprietor of a boarding-school, and Henry (*d.* 1720) and Mary (*d.* 1716) Carey, schoolteachers, may have been his parents. Doubt also surrounds the posthumous claim (also made in the *Gentleman's Magazine*, and by his son in *The Balnea* of 1799) that he wrote what was to be the British national anthem; it is possible Carey sang it at a patriotic meeting in 1740 (Cummings, 51).

Carey is best-known today for his facetious dramas, but his early theatre appearances with his singing students (from 1714) bear out Hawkins's claim that 'his chief employment was teaching [music] at boarding-schools, and among people of middling rank in private families' (Hawkins, 827). Carey later named Olaus Westeinson Linnert as his first music teacher; he also thanked Thomas Roseingrave for his 'friendly Instructions', and claimed to be a 'Disciple' of Geminiani (H. Carey, *Poems*, 1729). From 1714 Carey was 'Psalm-raiser' (parish clerk) to the chapel of Lincoln's Inn, but was dismissed in 1717 for singing Psalm 124 for Robert Harley, earl of Oxford, when Harley attended that chapel after escaping trial for high treason. Harley had just been released from the Tower, and the text of the psalm includes the phrase 'the snare is broken and we are escaped'. Carey evidently also had a semi-official theatrical post, as the *Weekly Journal* explained that after setting the psalm 'to a merry Tune for Joy of his Lordship's being at Liberty, he is turn'd out of the Royal Theatre at Drury Lane' (13 July 1717).

Carey's subsequent blacklisting was badly timed—on 1 September 1717 he married Elizabeth Pearks (*d.* 1729×33)—but it no doubt reinforced his polymath creative tendencies. A Grub Street connection may have been fostered at this time: Laetitia Pilkington claimed Carey was one of James Worsdale's 'Subalterns', writing under his name (Pilkington, 1.95). Carey's first publication was the twelve-part *Records of Love* (7 January–25 March 1710), notable for targeting a female readership and for its devotion to serialized fiction. Revised versions of several of the *Records of Love* poems appeared in his first collection of *Poems on Several Occasions* (1713). His 1720 and 1729 'editions' of the *Poems* are substantially different works. Carey achieved particular success in humorous and lyrical verse; although his traditional connection with Addison and membership of Button's has been disproved, he was proud of Addison's approbation for his famous song 'Sally in our Alley' (1717) and Pope's for 'Namby Pamby' (1726), both mentioned in his *Of Stage Tyrants* (1735).

By 1723 Carey had returned to Drury Lane, composing music for pantomimes such as *Harlequin Dr Faustus* (1723). Carey's first play was a comic afterpiece, *The Contrivances* (1715), which achieved little success until he adapted it in 'ballad' opera style—writing the songs himself—in 1729. The piece's popularity, with his student Catherine Raftor—later Kitty Clive—in the leading role, must have prompted the similar treatment for his second play, the 'low Life' farce *Hanging and Marriage* (1722). It became *The Clown's Stratagem* in 1730 and *Betty, or, The Country Bumpkins* in 1732. In the 1730s he wrote or prepared many songs for other writers' ballad operas and plays, which doubtless helped support his growing family with his second wife, Sarah. He composed for the masques *Cephalus and Procris* (1730) and *The Happy Nuptials*, revised as *Britannia* (both 1734), for which he also wrote the libretto.

All editions of the *Poems* include a large number of songs, described as set by Carey and others. Carey published several song and cantata collections, both serious and humorous; *The Musical Century in one Hundred English*

Ballads (2 vols., 1737–40) was his most substantial musical publication. Charles Burney aptly summed up Carey's compositional talent: 'Honest Harry Carey ... invented many very pleasing and natural melodies, which neither obscured the sense of the words, nor required much science to hear' (Burney, *Hist. mus.*, 4.653). This propensity and his limited musical talent earned him the epithet 'Ballad-maker', which Carey complained in his *Six Songs for Conversation* (1728) his 'Enemies' had attached to him. By the end of the century, however, Carey's balladeering skills were admired; William Jackson noted that 'For one musician who can make a simple tune like Carey, there are five hundred who can compose a noisy symphony like Stamitz' (Jackson, 112).

Although he objected to the title 'Ballad-maker', Carey was proud to be the defender of native theatre. In 1734, under the pseudonym Benjamin Bounce, he produced *Chrononhotonthologos*, a satire on tragic and operatic bombast, and also wrote his highly successful 'ballad farce' *The Honest Yorkshire-Man*. Opera was a regular target. Although Carey praised Handel and subscribed to his operas, occasionally sang in Italian, and translated a book of Italian arias (*A Pocket Companion*, 1725), he repeatedly attacked the vogue for Italian opera, particularly in his 1726 satires *Faustina, or, The Roman Songstress*, and *Mocking is Catching*, about the castrato Senesino. His antipathy to foreign opera found vent in his participation in the 'English Opera' experiment of 1732–3 with his friend J. F. Lampe, the Arnes, and others, for which he wrote two serious opera librettos in English (but 'after the Italian manner'), *Amelia* and *Teraminta* (both 1732). Carey was clearly proud of the operas: they were subject to much alteration, and opened his *Dramatic Works* (1743), even though he recognized his musical limitations, and had them set by Lampe and J. C. Smith respectively.

While *Amelia* was something of a success, in keeping with his temperament, Carey's métier was satire and comedy; it was through Signor Carini and Lampe's burlesque opera *The Dragon of Wantley* (1737) and its sequel, *Margery, or, A Worse Plague than the Dragon* (1738), that he achieved deserved fame. Based on a traditional English ballad story, the all-sung *Dragon of Wantley* parodied Italian opera by debasing familiar operatic traits (such as a quasi-mythological plot and a pair of rival divas) and employed sophisticated music. Its initial run of sixty-nine performances eclipsed even *The Beggar's Opera*, and it remained popular throughout the century. Carey was also mindful of those less successful, and helped found the Fund for Decayed Musicians in 1738. Carey returned to his own ballad style compositions for his final patriotic theatre piece, *Nancy, or, The Parting Lovers* (1739), about a sailor being taken off to war against the Spanish. *Nancy*, too, proved a lasting favourite.

Despite the immense popularity of *The Dragon of Wantley* and *Nancy*, the restrictions of the 1737 Licensing Act inhibited Carey's theatrical career, and when his son Charles died in 1743, Carey hanged himself at his home at Warner Street, Coldbath Fields, Clerkenwell Green, on 5 October, leaving a pregnant wife (George Saville *Carey was born a short time after his father's suicide) and three children; he was buried at St James's, Clerkenwell. Carey's constant complaints in his prefaces and poems suggest a persecution complex: printers and other authors apparently pirated or claimed his works; playhouse managers delayed or withheld production (specifically, Charles Fleetwood with *The Honest Yorkshire-Man* and *The Dragon*); 'Enemies' labelled him a balladeer and misunderstood his patriotic operatic enterprise. In the preface to the first part of his *Musical Century* (1737) Carey complained it was 'almost incredible how much I have suffer'd by having my works Pyrated; my Loss on that Account, for many Years past, amounting to near 300.L per Annum'. Perhaps this constant sense of persecution contributed to Carey's final despair.   SUZANNE ASPDEN

Sources J. N. Gillespie, 'The life and works of Henry Carey, 1687–1743', PhD diss., U. Lond., 1982 • *The plays of Henry Carey*, ed. S. L. Macey (New York and London, 1980), with an introduction by S. L. Macey • Burney, *Hist. mus.* • J. Hawkins, *A general history of the science and practice of music*, 5 vols. (1776); new edn, 3 vols. (1875) [repr. 1875–83] • H. Carey, *Poems on several occasions* (1720) • H. Carey, *On stage tyrants* (1735) • H. Carey, *The musical century* (1737–40) [repr. 1976] • *GM*, 1st ser., 65 (1795), 544 • *Weekly Journal* (13 July 1717) • L. Pilkington, *Memoirs of Laetitia Pilkington*, ed. A. C. Elias, 2 vols. (1997) • W. Jackson, *The four ages of man* (1798) • H. Carey, *Poems*, ed. F. T. Wood (1930) [with an introduction by F. T. Wood] • W. H. Cummings, *God save the king* (1902) • A. H. Scouten, ed., *The London stage, 1660–1800*, pt 3: *1729–1747* (1961) • *London Magazine*, 12 (1743) • *GM*, 1st ser., 13 (1743) • *Country Journal, or, The Craftsman* (Oct 1743)
Likenesses J. Faber junior, mezzotint (after J. Worsdale), BM, NPG; repro. in Carey, *Poems on several occasions* • C. Grignion, engraving (after Worsdale), repro. in Hawkins, *General history*
Wealth at death received handsome annuity from Savile family: *GM*, 1st ser., 65 • suicide partly prompted by pressure of financial position: Hawkins, *General history*, 827 • widow and family left destitute: Scouten, ed., *London stage*, 17 Nov 1743, 1072

Carey, James (1837–1883), Fenian and informer, was the son of Francis Carey, a bricklayer, who migrated from Celbridge, co. Kildare, to Dublin. There his wife (whose name is not known) kept a lodging-house in James Street, where James was born to them. He had at least one brother. James followed his father's trade and for eighteen years was in the employment of Michael Glynn, a builder in Dublin. He then commenced business on his own account as a builder at Denzille Street, Dublin. In this venture he was successful; he became the leading spokesman of his trade and obtained several large building contracts.

During all this period Carey was engaged in secret nationalist activities, but to outward appearance he was one of the rising men of Dublin. One of his sources of income was the subletting of a large number of tenement houses, which he rented from his former employer. Everyone believed in his piety and public spirit; there was hardly a society of the popular or religious kind of which he did not become a member. He was prominent in the home industry movement and won much attention for himself through a campaign against Scottish contractors working on the city's sewerage system. On 21 May 1865 at Rathmines, Dublin, he married Margaret McKenny, with

James Carey
(1837–1883), by
unknown
engraver, pubd
1883

whom he had at least six children. About 1861 he had joined the Fenians and was a figure of some local importance in the movement. In 1881, with Fenian organization in disarray, he was recruited to the small, newly formed society of Irish Invincibles, at a time when passions were high owing to the land war. The object of the Invincibles was 'to remove all tyrants from the country', and several attempts, without success, were made to assassinate the lord lieutenant, the seventh Earl Cowper, and the chief secretary, W. E. Forster, before it was decided to kill Thomas Henry Burke, the under-secretary. On 6 May 1882 nine of the conspirators proceeded to Phoenix Park, where Carey pointed out Burke to the others. They at once attacked and killed him with knives, and at the same time also dispatched Lord Frederick Cavendish, the newly appointed chief secretary, who was walking with Burke. For a long time no clue could be found to the perpetrators of the act. Carey was among those arrested on suspicion in July 1882. Released without charge three months later, he assumed the mantle of a wronged patriot, which helped him to win a seat on Dublin city council in November 1882. But on 13 January 1883 he was arrested in his own house, and, with sixteen others, was charged with a conspiracy to murder public officials. When arrested he was erecting a mortuary chapel in the South Dublin Union, and the work was then carried on by his brother Peter. On 13 February, Carey turned queen's evidence and betrayed details of the Invincibles' conspiracy and of the murders in Phoenix Park. His evidence condemned five of his former associates to a public execution. His life was thus in great danger, and he and his wife and family were secretly put on board the *Kinfauns Castle*, bound for the Cape, and sailed on 6 July under the name of Power. Carey indiscreetly revealed his identity to fellow passengers, one of whom happened to be a Fenian die-hard named Patrick O'Donnell. He followed Carey on board the *Melrose* on the voyage from Cape Town to Natal, and when the vessel was 12 miles off Cape Vaccas, on 29 July 1883, shot him dead. Carey was interred in the prison burial-ground at Port Elizabeth. O'Donnell was brought to England and tried for

an ordinary murder, without any reference to his Fenian connection; he was found guilty and was executed at Newgate on 17 December 1883.

G. C. BOASE, rev. R. V. COMERFORD

Sources T. Corfe, *The Phoenix Park murders: conflict, compromise and tragedy in Ireland, 1879–1882* (1968) · J. P. J. Tynan, *The Irish national Invincibles and their times* (1894) · *Phoenix Park murders: report of the trials, April and May 1883* (1883) · *Freeman's Journal* [Dublin] (31 July 1883) · *The Times* (1 Dec 1883) · *The Times* (3 Dec 1883) · *Annual Register* (1883), 192–8 · *ILN* (24 Feb 1883), 193 · *Pall Mall Gazette* (31 July 1883), 10–12 · *The Graphic* (24 Feb 1883), 200; (17 March 1883), 273 · *The Graphic* (4 Aug 1883), 112

Likenesses engraving, NPG; repro. in *Weekly Freeman*, suppl. (5 May 1883) [*see illus.*]

Carey, John, third Baron Hunsdon (*d.* 1617). *See under* Carey, Henry, first Baron Hunsdon (1526–1596).

Carey, John (1756–1826), classical scholar, was born in Dublin, one of six sons of Christopher Carey, baker; his brothers included Mathew *Carey, publisher and author, and William Paulet *Carey, art critic. At the age of twelve he was sent to finish his education in France. He spent some time in the United States about 1789, and afterwards passed many years in London as a teacher of the classics, French, and shorthand. Carey was editor of the early numbers of the *School Magazine*, published by Phillips, and was a frequent contributor to the *Gentleman's Magazine* and *Monthly Magazine*. In the latter journal (1803) he made a suggestion for enabling persons on shore to give assistance to distressed vessels by shooting a wooden ball from a mortar, an idea subsequently conceived and carried out independently by George Manby, for which invention Manby was rewarded by government. Carey brought out a new edition of Dryden's Virgil in 1803 and again in 1819. Two editions of Robert Ainsworth's *Latin Dictionary* and five of the abridgement of the same appeared in 1824 as did an edition of the *Gradus ad Parnassum*. Two years later there came his edition of the Latin *Common Prayer* in Samuel Bagster's polyglot edition, *Ruperti commentarius in Livium*, and a revision of Johann Friedrich Schleusner's *New Testament Lexicon*. He likewise edited more than fifty volumes of the Regent Latin Classics and compiled the valuable 'General index to the *Monthly Review* from 1790 to 1816' (1818). Among his works of translation were *Batavians* (Paul Jérémie Bitaubé), *Young Emigrants* (Madame de Staël), and *Letters on Switzerland* (Lehmen). Carey's 1810 story for children, *Learning Better than House and Land*, went through several editions, while his school books including *Latin Prosody Made Easy* (1800), *Introduction to English Composition and Elocution* (1817), and *Greek* and *Latin Terminations* (both 1821), were popular in their day and generally praised for their accuracy and scholarship. He also published a small volume of poems, with a portrait prefixed. He died from calculus at Prospect Place, Lambeth, London, on 8 December 1826 after several years of ill health.

C. W. SUTTON, rev. PHILIP CARTER

Sources H. J. Rose, *A new general biographical dictionary*, ed. H. J. Rose and T. Wright, 12 vols. (1848) · [J. Watkins and F. Shoberl], *A biographical dictionary of the living authors of Great Britain and Ireland* (1816) · A. J. Webb, *A compendium of Irish biography* (1878) · Watt, *Bibl. Brit.* · Boase & Courtney, *Bibl. Corn.*

Likenesses portrait, repro. in Carey's poems

Carey, John Joseph (1919–1995), footballer and football manager, was born on 23 February 1919 at 4 Adelaide Place, Lower Baggot Street, Dublin, the son of John Carey, van driver, and his wife, Sarah, *née* Byrne. He left Ireland at the age of seventeen when he was transferred by his Dublin club, St James's Gate, to Manchester United for a sum of £200. In his first full season at Old Trafford, in 1937–8, he played at inside forward and was part of the successful team that won promotion to the first division that year. In the same season he won his first international cap for the Irish team. He played for Manchester United during the first three seasons of the Second World War, in regional football leagues, but his career was interrupted in 1943 when he took the decision to join the British army. As a citizen of Éire, Carey had the choice of not joining up, but argued that the country that gave him his living was worth fighting for. He served in the Queen's Royal Hussars and took part in the campaigns in the Middle East and Italy. While in the army he regularly coached and played in service teams.

At the end of the war Carey returned to Manchester United and was promoted to club captain by the new team manager, Matt Busby. By then he had played for the club in every position with the exception of outside left, including goalkeeper; Busby utilized him as a right back. Carey excelled, and marshalled a successful Manchester United team as captain. Between the 1946/7 and 1950/51 seasons, Manchester United finished runners-up in the league four times. The title was finally clinched in the 1951/2 season. In 1948 Carey achieved the pinnacle reserved for a select few players in the domestic game by leading his team to victory in the FA cup final. After defeating Stanley Matthews's Blackpool he was able to climb the steps at Wembley and receive the cherished trophy. In 1949 he was elected footballer of the year, and in 1950 sportsman of the year.

In addition to his successful domestic career Carey also resumed international appearances after the war. He captained the Republic of Ireland to a 2–0 victory over England at Goodison Park in 1949, thereby inflicting the first ever defeat on an England team in a full international fixture played on home soil. As a result of his military service, and the ongoing disputes between the two football associations in Ireland over player selection, Carey also qualified to play for Northern Ireland after 1945. He took the opportunity, and played for both Northern Ireland and the republic in the four years following the war. He was one of thirty-two players to be capped by both countries, winning nine caps for Northern Ireland and twenty-nine for the republic. In the space of three days in 1948 he played for both Irish teams, each time against England. His standing within international football was celebrated in 1947 when he was chosen as the captain of a Rest of Europe team against England.

In 1953 Carey finally retired as a player. Although offered a coaching post under Busby at Old Trafford, he elected to move into management. His first club was second-division Blackburn Rovers. After four successful years of development, Blackburn finally achieved promotion to the first division in 1958. In the close season Carey chose to move on, and took the management post at Everton. He rebuilt a moribund team and directed them to a credible fifth place in the league by the close of the 1961 season. Such steady progress was not enough for the Everton chairman, John Moores, and Moores sacked Carey in the back of a London taxi *en route* for the Football League annual meeting. Carey then moved to Leyton Orient, and he led the London team to the first division for the first time in their history in his first season there. In 1963, following Leyton Orient's relegation, he moved on to Nottingham Forest. In 1966/7 he had his most successful season as a manager, and led his team to second place in the first division and a place in the FA cup semi-finals. The 1968/9 season was a disaster and Carey was sacked in December 1968 at a point when Nottingham Forest were still waiting for their first home win of the season. He moved back to Blackburn in the 1969/70 season in an administrative capacity, but by 1970 had been reinstalled as team manager. The team was unsuccessful, and was relegated to the third division in 1971. This was Carey's last management job.

In 1971 Carey began work for a textile company, and then moved on to the treasurer's office of Trafford borough council, where he remained until his retirement in 1984. He returned to Old Trafford in the 1970s as a scout working for Tommy Docherty, and he retained his contacts with Manchester United until his death, which took place at Macclesfield District General Hospital, Macclesfield, Cheshire, on 23 August 1995. He was survived by his wife, Margaret.   MIKE CRONIN

Sources *The Independent* (24 Aug 1995) · *Manchester Evening News* (23 Aug 1995) · *Irish Times* (24 Aug 1995) · *The Times* (26 Aug 1995) · D. Cullen, *Ireland on the ball: international soccer matches of the Republic of Ireland soccer team* (1993) · S. McGarrigle, *The complete who's who of Irish international football, 1945–96* (1996) · b. cert. · d. cert.
Archives Old Trafford, Manchester, Manchester United archives
Likenesses photograph, repro. in *Manchester Evening News* · photograph, repro. in *The Times*
Wealth at death under £145,000: probate, 2 Nov 1995, *CGPLA Eng. & Wales*

Carey [*née* Jackson], **Mary, Lady Carey** (b. *c.*1609, d. in or after **1680**), author of verse and autobiographical meditations, was the daughter and heir of Sir John Jackson of Berwick upon Tweed, Northumberland; she wrote of her family that 'I had tenderly loving parents' (Bodl. Oxf., MS Rawl. D. 1308, fols. 15–44). In her autobiographical meditations, dated between 11 February 1650 and 12 January 1658, she described her conversion to a life of piety at the age of about eighteen after a near fatal illness. She married first, at Hunsdon, Hertfordshire, on 24 June 1630, Pelham Carey (*c.*1612–1642/3), a younger son of Henry Carey, first earl of Dover (*c.*1580–1666), and his first wife, Judith Pelham (*bap.* 1590, d. 1629); her husband was knighted in Scotland on 16 July 1633. He was living in Berwick in September 1642, but died within the next few months, apparently leaving no surviving children. On 8 June 1643, still in Berwick, Mary Carey married George Payler (d. in or before 1678), paymaster of the garrison there from 1639 to 1642, but by this time one of the officers of the ordnance and armoury in the Tower of London. Although deeply attached to her second husband Mary kept the surname of her first, presumably because of Sir Pelham's titled status.

During the civil wars Lady Carey accompanied Payler on military campaigns. Later they divided their time between the north-east and the London area, as Payler retained interests in Berwick. Admitted to Gray's Inn on 23 March 1652 he continued as surveyor of the ordnance and in 1654 was additionally appointed a navy commissioner. He was MP for Berwick in 1659. His wife wrote during that decade, 'I have liv'd in Barwick, London, Kent, Hunsdon, Edenborough, Thistleworth, Hackney, Tottridge, Greenwich, Bednall Green, Clapham, Yorke, [Nun] Monkton, St James's, Newington, Covent Garden, & deare St Katherine's' (Bodl. Oxf., MS Rawl. D. 1308, fol. 195).

Of the couple's seven children the first five died in infancy, including Robert (d. 1650) and Peregrine (d. 1652); only Bethia (1652/3–1671) and Nathaniel (1654/5–1680?) survived to adulthood. In addition to live births Lady Carey suffered at least one miscarriage, an experience which provided the inspiration for her most famous poem, 'Upon the Sight of my Abortive Birth the 31th of December 1657' (Bodl. Oxf., MS Rawl. D. 1308, fols. 215–22). The poem compares the 'little Embrio; voyd of life, and feature' to the 'dead frute', in the form of lifeless religious devotions, which Lady Carey is reproached for offering to God: 'Dead dutys; prayers; praises thou dost bring, affections dead; dead hart in every thinge … Mend now my Child, & lively frute bring me; so thou advantag'd much by this wilt be' (Greer, 159–60). She also composed other pious meditations in verse and prose, including 'A Dialogue betwixt the Soule, and the Body', dedicated to her husband (Bodl. Oxf., MS Rawl. D. 1308, fols. 1–176).

After the Restoration, Lady Carey and her husband seem to have retired to his property at Nun Monkton in Yorkshire. Bethia married James Darcy of Sedbury in the same county, but died on 19 November 1671 aged only eighteen. Payler died in or before 1678, when his widow received the first of several grants of administration of his estates. Their son also predeceased his mother: Nathaniel was admitted to Sidney Sussex College, Cambridge, in 1670, and to Gray's Inn in 1671, and had a son Nathaniel (d. 1748), but had died by 3 December 1680, when Lady Carey was granted probate of his will. The date of her death is unknown. SARA H. MENDELSON

Sources Bodl. Oxf., MS Rawl. D. 1308 · N&Q, 3rd ser., 7 (1865), 203–6, 259 · G. Greer, ed., *Kissing the rod: an anthology of seventeenth-century women's verse* (1988), 155–62 · M. C. McCabe, *Meditations upon the note book of Mary Carey, 1649–1657* (1918) · *Fifth report*, HMC, 4 (1876), 40 · *Report on manuscripts in various collections*, 8 vols., HMC, 55 (1901–14), vol. 1, p. 15 · Pepys, *Diary* · R. A. Anselment, '"A heart terrifying sorrow": an occasional piece on poetry of miscarriage', *Papers on Language and Literature: a Journal for Scholars and Critics of Language and Literature*, 33/1 (1997), 13–46 · P. A. Bolton and P. Watson, 'Paylor, Sir Watkinson', HoP, *Commons, 1660–90* · CSP dom., 1639–60 · GEC, *Peerage* · GEC, *Baronetage* · Venn, *Alum. Cant.* · J. Foster, *The register of admissions to Gray's Inn, 1521–1889, together with the register of marriages in Gray's Inn chapel, 1695–1754* (privately printed, London, 1889) · *Index of wills, administrations and probate acts in the York registry, AD 1673 to 1680*, Yorkshire Archaeological Society record series, 68 (1926), 186

Carey, Mathew [*pseud.* Scriblerus O'Pindar] (1760–1839), publisher and author, was born in Dublin on 28 January 1760, one of six sons of Christopher Carey, a prosperous baker. Among his brothers were John *Carey (1756–1826), classical scholar, and William Paulet *Carey (1759–1839), art critic. Although initially a somewhat dull boy, Mathew Carey quickly became a voracious reader of novels and romances. When he was fifteen he was apprenticed to a bookseller, but two years later began his career proper by publishing his first essay, on duelling, in the *Hibernian Journal*. His highly controversial and polemical writing, including a pamphlet urging the repeal of the penal code against Catholics, quickly landed him with a threat of prosecution, and in 1779 he was put on board the Holyhead packet bound for Paris with nothing but a little money and a letter of introduction to Dr Franklin.

On his return to Dublin, Carey resumed his journalistic career, running the *Freeman's Journal* so successfully from 1780 to 1783 that his father gave him enough money to establish his own paper, the *Volunteer's Journal*, which he edited from 1783 to 1784. Its strongly expressed views soon acquired a decided influence on public opinion, and consequently brought another legal action against Carey who was thrown into prison, charged with libel by John Foster, the then Irish chancellor of the exchequer. On being released at the end of the parliamentary session, Carey sold the newspaper, and again set sail, this time for Philadelphia.

Carey received a letter of introduction to Lafayette *en route*, and impressed him so profoundly that Lafayette loaned him $400, enabling Carey to restart his journalistic career in America, issuing on 25 January 1785 the first number of the *Pennsylvania Herald*. Carey acted as editor and, in August of that year, also undertook reporting governmental debates, which gave his paper an edge over its competitors. Carey's success and opinions, however, made him unpopular, and he was wounded in a duel with a fellow journalist, which left him debilitated for more than a year. No sooner had he recovered, however, than he co-founded in October 1786 the short-lived *Columbia Magazine*, before issuing, in January 1787, the first number of another new journal, the *American Museum*, a popular but not ultimately economically remunerative periodical which was discontinued at the end of 1792.

Carey had married Bridget Flahavan in 1791, and they went on to have nine children. He became involved in philanthropic activities around this time, sitting on the committee appointed to investigate an outbreak of yellow fever in Philadelphia in 1793, and publishing a vivid pamphlet on the epidemic in that same year, and another upon the return of the disease in 1797. In the early 1790s he also started the Hibernian Society for the Relief of Emigrants from Ireland, and, throughout his life in America, interested himself in Irish literature, culture, and political questions. In 1798 he repudiated the charge of being a 'United Irishman', but continued to contribute to the Irish debate, publishing in 1799, under the pseudonym Scriblerus O'Pindar, *The Nettle*, designed, as its subtitle suggests, *To Tickle the Nose of an English Viceroy*. He also later produced a response to the presentation in William Godwin's *Mandeville* (1817) of the alleged Irish atrocities perpetuated in 1641. Carey's *Vindiciae Hibernicae, or, Ireland Vindicated* (1819) was the result of much scholarship, and represented a sustained attempt to develop and expose errors in previous histories of Ireland, such as those by Temple, Clarendon, and Hume, among others.

Meanwhile, in 1795, Carey had been allegedly responsible for two American firsts: he had helped to form the first American Sunday school society; and he had also published the first American atlas, *Carey's American Atlas*, which was both popular and held in high critical regard. In this period, Carey's success was immense, and even a bitter newspaper war with William Cobbett could not dampen it. Cobbett was also operating in Philadelphia at this time, and extracts from his attacks upon Carey are found in Cobbett's works under the pseudonym Peter Porcupine. Carey's ripostes include *The Porcupiniad, a Hudibrastic Poem* (2nd edn, 1799) and *Plumb Pudding for the Humane, Chaste, Valiant, and Enlightened Peter Porcupine* (1797). The latter pamphlet was reprinted in 1998 in Noel Thompson's *Counterblasts to Cobbett, 1797–1835*, which forms volume seventeen of the *Collected Social and Political Writings of William Cobbett*.

In the early 1800s Carey's career continued to be both highly successful and diverse. In 1802 he was appointed as the director of the Bank of Pennsylvania. He also established an annual book fair held alternately in New York and Philadelphia. Carey's position made him an increasingly influential commentator on many public questions both in Ireland and America, where he published over the next two decades an exceptionally wide range of popular polemical treatises: on American political economy, on prison discipline, on colonization, and on the oppression of women. He also helped to form a society for the promotion of national industry, through which he circulated many of his pamphlets. His writings on economics were particularly important, constituting a major influence upon the historical development and direction of the American nationalist school of economic thought.

Carey retired from business in 1824. During the remaining years of his life, he took part in various works of public charity and utility; in campaigns to promote education, and the construction of roads and canals. In 1829 he published his *Autobiographical Sketches*, which was reprinted in New York in 1970, and in 1830 Carey's *Miscellaneous Sketches* appeared, which was reprinted in 1966. In 1832 Carey offered to endow a chair of political economy at the University of Maryland, an offer which was not, however, accepted. Carey died on 16 September 1839, partly as a result of complications of an injury suffered upon the earlier overturning of his carriage. His funeral was one of the largest seen in Philadelphia at that time.

One of his sons, Henry Charles Carey (1793–1879), went on to become his father's successor in the bookselling and publishing business, becoming a leading partner in the firm of Carey, Lea, and Carey, American publishers of Thomas Carlyle, Washington Irving, and Sir Walter Scott. He left the business in 1838, however, to continue further his father's legacy, in focusing upon research and writing in the field of political economy.

EDWARD SMITH, *rev.* JASON EDWARDS

Sources A. M. Brady and B. Cleeve, eds., *A biographical dictionary of Irish writers*, rev. edn (1985) · R. Welch, ed., *The Oxford companion to Irish literature* (1996) · *New England Magazine*, 5 (1833), 404–12, 489–96; 6 (1834), 60–67, 93–106, 227–34, 306–14, 400–08; 7 (1834), 61–70, 145–8, 239–44, 320–29, 401–6, 481–5 · *Hunt's Merchant's Magazine*, 7 (1839), 429 · E. A. Duycknick, *Cyclopaedia of American literature*, 2 vols. (1855), 1.667 · *American almanack* (1841), 275 · *Niles's register*, 20.345; 24.337 · Peter Porcupine [W. Cobbett], *The political censor*, 4, 53 · Peter Porcupine [W. Cobbett], *Porcupine's political censor*, 10, 59–60 · C. W. Janson, *The stranger in America* (1807), 418–19 · E. Smith, *William Cobbett: a biography*, 2 vols. (1878) · Lea & Febiger, *One hundred years of publishing, 1785–1885* (1885) [with a biographical sketch of Carey by Henry Charles Lea] · *Who was who in America: historical volume, 1607–1896*, rev. edn (1967) · J. F. Waller, ed., *The imperial dictionary of universal biography*, 3 vols. (1857–63); new edn (1877–84) · W. Clarkin, *Mathew Carey: a biography of his publications, 1785–1824* (1984)

Likenesses J. Thomson, stipple, pubd 1822 (after J. Neagle), NG Ire.

Carey, Robert, first earl of Monmouth (1560–1639), courtier, the youngest son of Henry *Carey, first Baron Hunsdon (1526–1596), and his wife, Ann Morgan (*d.* 1607), was probably born at the family home, Hunsdon House, Hertfordshire. He was privately educated. As a son of the first cousin of Elizabeth I, he was first selected at the age of seventeen to be in the entourage of a diplomatic mission; in December 1577 he was with Thomas Leighton, who went to the Netherlands to be a mediator between the estates general of the United Provinces and Don Juan of Austria. Two other missions followed: in early 1581 he was in a group of courtiers sent to Antwerp to attend the entry of the duke of Anjou and Alençon as lord of the Netherlands; and in August 1583 he was in the suite of Walsingham's special embassy to James VI of Scotland. He later wrote that James took 'such a liking to me' that he wrote 'earnestly to the queen … to give me leave to come back to him again' (*Memoirs*, 7), while at court 'in all triumphs I was one; either at tilt, tourney, or barriers, in masques or balls' (ibid., 145).

His father's prestige in the north assured Carey's election to parliament as burgess for Morpeth, Northumberland, in the autumn of 1586. His only diplomatic mission for the queen occurred in early 1586, when he was sent to Edinburgh to explain her innocence of the execution of Mary queen of Scots, but James did not allow him to go beyond Berwick. Afterwards he sailed, under the leadership of the earl of Cumberland, in a vain attempt to assist the English garrison at Sluys in the Netherlands, before it surrendered to the duke of Parma. Finally, in May 1588, he was allowed a brief visit by James VI to deliver the queen's message. In summer 1588 he served in one of the naval squadrons deployed against the Armada and in the following year was returned once again as MP for Morpeth. In August 1591 he joined Essex's expedition into Normandy in support of Henri IV and took part in the siege of Rouen, during which he was sent back to England to beg Elizabeth to delay orders for Essex's recall. The earl was so pleased when his wishes were met that he knighted Carey when they met again, in October 1591; ironically, it was later established that the council had already postponed Essex's return on the day before Carey's arrival. In spring 1593 Carey was elected MP from both Callington and Morpeth, but chose the former, and on 20 August that year he married Elizabeth (d. 1641), the daughter of Sir Hugh Trevannion and widow of Sir Henry Widdrington, without first asking the queen's approval. After a tempestuous interview, he was reconciled, 'by an ingenious excuse' and an expensive gift (Memoirs, 51–6), but for the next decade he was absent from the court with appointments in the north.

Carey's brother-in-law, Lord Scrope, nominated him deputy warden of the west march from 1593 to 1595 and then his father followed by obtaining for him the deputy wardenship of the east march. However, when he was passed over for the permanent position of warden there, Carey wrote to Robert Cecil: 'she thinks the office too good for me and I carry a proud mind, I think myself worthy of a better' (Salisbury MSS, 7.251). Later, by November 1597, his ambition was satisfied with the post of warden of the middle march, where his performance was commended by Robert Cecil in 1601: 'Carey takes a very good course, for he goes on with that which is best for the service [and] advertises when it is done' (Salisbury MSS, 11.345). His importance was reflected in the parliamentary elections for 1597 and 1601, when he was returned as knight of the shire of Northumberland. In the former parliament he served on the committee for an important local bill about the export of sheepskins and pelts and in the latter on the committee about new penal laws, and as a knight of the shire had the right to attend other committees as well.

When the queen died on 24 March 1603 Carey rode from Richmond Palace non-stop to Holyrood to be the first to give the news to King James on the twenty-sixth. The English privy council censored his disrespect to the queen's memory, but he preferred to quote later the king's reply: 'I know you have lost a near kinsman and a loving mistress but take my hand, I will be as good a master to you' (Memoirs, 129). At his own request Carey was appointed a gentleman of the bedchamber at that time but, after James's arrival in London in May, he was demoted to a gentleman of the privy chamber by order of a committee of English and Scottish councillors. Under the Stuart regime his career became linked to the fortunes of James's young son, the future Charles I. Carey's wife, a lady-in-waiting to Queen Anne, was chosen to take care of the sickly child in February 1605 and for seven years paid exemplary attention to him and was firm in shielding him from some of his father's ill-advised plans: 'many a battle my wife had with the king but she still prevailed' (ibid., 141). At the same time Carey presided as master of Charles's growing household. Chamberlain reported that in January 1608 Carey played cards in the prince's name and won £300 and that in March 1612 he had sold his reversion of the office of

secretary of the council of the north to Arthur Ingram for £6000. In 1611 he became the master of the robes so that, with Prince Henry's death in 1612 and his sister Elizabeth's departure with the elector palatine in 1613, any service to the heir apparent augured well for his career. He was appointed, with Queen Anne's support, chamberlain of the court of the prince of Wales in 1617, although courtiers of considerable influence had wanted it. In 1621, due to Charles's patronage in the duchy of Cornwall, Carey was elected to parliament as MP for Grampound. On 6 February 1622 he was created Baron Carey of Leppington, where he held lands, in Buckrose wapentake, East Riding, Yorkshire. After Charles and Buckingham had left 'incognito' to negotiate the Spanish match in early 1623, Carey was ordered by James to lead a number of footmen and pages, 'all well appointed' to serve the prince in Madrid and 'to see them carrie themselves civilly and religiously' (Letters of John Chamberlain, 1.485). By 30 May he had returned to London 'and delivered all he had to the king but otherwise he knowes or sayes litle' (ibid., 1.499).

When Charles came to the throne in 1625 Carey did not receive a major court appointment but there were three valuable rewards: he had a post at Whitehall, as a gentleman of the bedchamber, and a grant for life of Kenilworth Castle and other lands in fee farm valued at £500 a year; and on 5 February 1626 he became earl of Monmouth, a new title celebrating Charles's coronation three days before. On the sixth he attended the House of Lords with the proxy of Francis Lord Deincourt. On 17 July the next year he was appointed lord lieutenant of Staffordshire in place of Robert Devereux, earl of Essex, who had fallen from favour for his opposition to the forced loan. He held the post until February 1629. He attended parliament again in the spring of 1628 and early 1629, but after that his constant attendance at Whitehall did not continue. In 1631 he purchased from Philip Herbert, fourth earl of Pembroke, the mansion and park of the Moor, or More, Hertfordshire, a property not far from his close relatives at Hunsdon House. His will, dated 3 September 1635, bequeathed properties in the counties of Durham, Monmouth, and Hertford to his wife, Elizabeth, for her lifetime, and then to Henry *Carey (1596–1661), his son and heir, both of whom were his executors. He died at Moor Park on 12 April 1639 and, although he wished to be buried with his parents in Westminster Abbey, was interred at Rickmansworth parish church. His memoirs were first published in 1759 (though extracts had earlier appeared in print) and have been republished in a number of subsequent editions.

A. J. LOOMIE

Sources Memoirs of the life of Robert Carey, ed. W. Scott (1808) • N. M. Fuidge, 'Carey, Robert (c.1560–1639)', HoP, Commons, 1558–1603, vol. 1 • GEC, Peerage, new edn, vols. 6, 9 • G. M. Bell, A handlist of British diplomatic representatives, 1509–1688, Royal Historical Society Guides and Handbooks, 16 (1990) • Calendar of the manuscripts of the most hon. the marquis of Salisbury, 6–7, HMC, 9 (1895–9); 11 (1906); 15 (1930) • The letters of John Chamberlain, ed. N. E. McClure, 2 vols. (1939) • H. A. Lloyd, The Rouen campaign, 1590–1592 (1973) • CSP dom., 1625–33 • N. Cuddy, 'The revival of the entourage: the bedchamber of James I, 1603–1625', The English court: from the Wars of the Roses to the civil war, ed. D. R. Starkey and others (1987), 173–225 • C. Carlton,

Charles I: the personal monarch (1983) · *VCH Hertfordshire*, vols. 2–3 · will, PRO, PROB 11/180, fol. 243v · DNB

Archives Bodl. Oxf., autobiography [copy] · U. Nott. L., autobiography [copy]

Likenesses attrib. P. van Somer, group portrait, oils, *c.*1617 (with his family), NPG · tapestry (*Armada commanders*), Palace of Westminster, London

Wealth at death left properties in three counties to wife and son: will, PRO, PROB 11/180, fol. 243v · in debt most of his life: *Memoirs*, ed. Scott

Carey, Rosa Nouchette (1840–1909), novelist, was born at Stratford-le-Bow, London, on 24 September 1840, the sixth of the seven children (five girls and two boys) of William Henry Carey (*d.* 1867), shipbroker, and his wife, Maria Jane (*d.* 1870), daughter of Edward J. Wooddill. She was brought up in London at Tryons Road, Hackney, and in South Hampstead, and educated at home and at the Ladies' Institute, St John's Wood, where she was a contemporary and friend of Mathilde Blind (1841–1896). As a child she told stories to her younger sister, and in this way created the plot of her first novel, *Nellie's Memories* (1868). The publisher's advertisements suggest that it sold over 52,000 copies. It was followed by many other novels, marked by pious tone, domestic subject matter, and a large number of rather unmemorable characters, which were staples of the market in safe fiction for girls during the last third of the nineteenth century. Even Elizabeth Lee, whose many articles on women writers in the *Dictionary of National Biography* do not display marked feminist sympathies, commented (by implication unfavourably) on how old-fashioned and limited seemed the lives of the women who inhabit Carey's fiction. Yet, gushing and unpretending as her work is, she does depict the frustrations of such women with some sympathy, exploring the pains of living up to high ideals and the psychic cost of self-abnegation. Although she is sometimes described as a follower of Charlotte M. Yonge, in whose magazine, the *Monthly Packet*, Carey's novel *Heriot's Choice* (1879) was serialized, she is a far less intellectual writer (there is a tincture of high Anglicanism but no theological content), and a less humorous one, and where Yonge's characters belong to the landed gentry, her subject is the lives of women of the urban professional middle class. A saccharine and laudatory biographical collection, *Twelve Notable Good Women of the XIXth Century* (1899), includes among its subjects Queen Victoria, Grace Darling, and Elizabeth Fry. The bibliography by Jane Crisp (1989) argues that the British Library catalogue is wrong in attributing to Carey four thrillers which appeared late in her life under the pseudonym Le Voleur.

Carey's literary career got going after the death of her father, when she was in her late twenties. After the death of her mother in 1870 Carey and her remaining unmarried sister went to keep house for a widowed brother and look after his children; after the sister married and went to live in Kirkby Stephen, Westmorland (which provided a setting for some of Carey's fiction), the brother died and Carey was left in charge of the children. As well as writing thirty-three three-volume novels, she was on the staff of the *Girls' Own Paper*, for which she wrote eight serials. She does not seem to have moved in literary circles, although she was a close friend of the novelist Ellen Wood (Mrs Henry Wood). The poet Helen Marion Burnside, who also worked for the *Girls' Own Paper*, lived with her from about 1875, and edited *The Rosa Nouchette Carey Birthday Book* (1901). When Carey's sister was widowed she returned to keep house for the two authors. Rosa Carey died of lung cancer at her home, Sandilands, Keswick Road, Putney, London, on 19 July 1909. CHARLOTTE MITCHELL

Sources J. Crisp, *Rosa Nouchette Carey (1840–1909): a bibliography* (1989) · H. C. Black, *Notable women authors of the day* (1893) · *CGPLA Eng. & Wales* (1909) · microfilm, Royal Literary Archive [application on behalf of H. M. Burnside] · b. cert. · d. cert. · probate index, Principal Registry of the Family Division, London

Archives BL, corresp. with R. Bentley & Son, Add. MSS 46619–46626 · BL, corresp. with Macmillans, Add. MS 54954

Likenesses photograph, repro. in *The Rosa Nouchette Carey birthday book* (1901), frontispiece

Wealth at death £10,398 10*s.* 5*d.*: resworn probate, 3 Sept 1909, *CGPLA Eng. & Wales*

Carey, Valentine (*d.* 1626), bishop of Exeter, was born in Berwick upon Tweed and reputed to be 'the base son to the old earl of Hunsdon' (*Downshire MSS*, 4.260), Henry *Carey, first Baron Hunsdon (1526–1596), who was governor of Berwick from 25 August 1568. His mother's identity is unknown, but he refers in his will to 'my brother John Hodson' as well as to two sisters. He matriculated as a sizar from Christ's College, Cambridge, in Michaelmas term 1585, graduated BA early in 1589, became a fellow of St John's College in 1591, and proceeded MA in 1592. Five years later he transferred to Christ's following a controversial election. He proceeded BD in 1599 and resigned his fellowship in 1600. It may have been at this point that he married Dorothy, daughter of Richard Coke (*d.* 1582) of Trusley, Derbyshire, and sister of John Coke (1563–1644), later secretary of state, and of George Coke (1570–1646), a contemporary of Carey at St John's and later bishop of Hereford.

With the advent of the new century Carey's ecclesiastical career took off. Made a prebendary of St Paul's in 1601, he was rector of West Tilbury, Essex, from 1603 to 1608 and of Great Parndon from 1604, archdeacon of Shropshire from 1606, vicar of Epping from 1607 to 1610, and prebendary of Lincoln, also from 1607. On 20 March 1610, on the presentation of Owen Gwyn, bursar at St John's College, he was instituted to the rectory of Toft, Cambridgeshire. That year he returned to Cambridge as master of Christ's College, imposed on the fellows by James I and following dissension within the college between puritans and conformists. Once installed Carey made a forceful attempt to alter the Calvinist complexion of Christ's, once the home of William Perkins. Among those who felt this pressure were Thomas Taylor, who was forced to leave, Nicholas Rush, who was expelled, and William Ames. Carey attempted to persuade Ames, who had taken up the mantle of Perkins, to wear the surplice; Ames refused and, after an inflammatory university sermon on vice, was driven to resignation. Disappointed in his hopes of election in 1612 to the mastership of St John's, which went to Gwyn, Carey became instead vice-chancellor.

Carey's career was also advancing at court. By 1609 he was a royal chaplain. From 1611 he was rector of Orsett, Essex. Although he resigned his archdeaconry of Shropshire in 1613 on the claim that the revenue did not justify his maintaining it, the following year he became dean of St Paul's. In 1621 Gwyn's cousin John Williams, lord keeper and bishop of Lincoln, nominated Carey as bishop of Exeter. By this time a client of the marquess of Buckingham, and perhaps favoured also by Henry Carey, Viscount Rochford (grandson of the first Baron Hunsdon) and by the earl of Northampton, Carey was named bishop on 14 September. The cathedral chapter at Exeter was late in forwarding their certificate of election, and he was not consecrated until 18 November.

During his short episcopate Carey spent relatively little time in his diocese, remaining mostly in London and usually visiting Exeter only between July and September. However this did not prevent his continuing energetically the jurisdictional dispute with the city fathers which he had inherited from his predecessor, Bishop William Cotton. He opposed their efforts to build another school and lobbied to increase his authority through inclusion on the commission of the peace for the city. Yet when plague hit Exeter in the autumn and winter of 1625–6 and he was obliged to stay on in Devon to avoid being seen to risk spreading infection, he seems to have displayed some generosity and practical assistance. He wrote on 13 January 1626 to his brother-in-law Sir John Coke that he had debarred attendance at sermons to avoid contagion, 'permitting only divine service, which they have no fervent desire to frequent' (*Cowper MSS*, 1.249). This served the additional purpose of striking at the puritan civic leaders' fondness for preaching. In 1625 the Arminian Richard Mountague had described Carey as 'doctrinally sound' and 'one of the firmest against our [Puritan] faction' (Tyacke, 193) and he considered that the surplice was 'the armour of light' (Wolffe, 97), yet his visitation articles of that year, while thorough, lack the partisan and overtly anti-puritan quality of the articles issued by Mountague as bishop of Chichester in 1628. He seems to have thought he lacked friends locally, but those that he had were not evidently at the forefront of the 'Arminian' campaign. During the weeks of plague he and his family stayed at Sir George Chudleigh's house, where his wife stood godmother to Chudleigh's newborn child. In 1624 he had been the broker between Coke (who had probably introduced him to Chudleigh) and Sir John Eliot in the former's quest to be elected MP for St Germains and the latter's quest for office.

When Carey drew up his will on 4 April 1626 he was already ill. Bequests to the children of his brother John Hodson, sister Veghelman and sister Lawson of Bury St Edmunds were balanced by those to the Carey family. Rochford's eldest son, Sir John Carey, received his books by Plutarch, Aristotle, and Jerome, while Rochford's daughter Judith, Carey's goddaughter (*bap.* St James Clerkenwell on 17 October 1624) received £40. Christ's and St John's Colleges and the poor of Orsett and Exeter were also beneficiaries. Lands in Great Shelford, Cambridgeshire, were left to his wife and executor for life, and then to Ernestus Carey, whose relationship to the testator is unspecified, but who seems to have been a minor already under the couple's care. Carey died in London on 10 June 1626 and was buried in St Paul's Cathedral; a memorial was erected in Exeter Cathedral. MARC L. SCHWARZ

Sources Venn, *Alum. Cant.* · *Report on the manuscripts of the marquis of Downshire*, 6 vols. in 7, HMC, 75 (1924–95), vol. 4, p. 260 · *Report on records of the city of Exeter*, HMC, 73 (1916) · *The manuscripts of the Earl Cowper*, 3 vols., HMC, 23 (1888–9), vol. 1 · K. Fincham, ed., *Visitation articles and injunctions of the early Stuart church*, 2 (1998) · M. Wolffe, *Gentry leaders in peace and war: the gentry governors of Devon in the seventeenth century* (1997) · K. Fincham, *Prelate as pastor: the episcopate of James I* (1990) · W. MacCaffrey, *Exeter, 1540–1640* (Cambridge, MA, 1958) · J. B. Mullinger, *The University of Cambridge*, 2 vols. (1883–4) · *N&Q*, 3rd ser., 6 (1864), 174, 217, 312–13 · *N&Q*, 3rd ser., 7 (1865), 117, 205 · N. Tyacke, *Anti-Calvinists: the rise of English Arminianism, c.1590–1640* (1987) · CUL, Mm MS 1.39, p. 128

Wealth at death considerable wealth: *N&Q*, 3rd ser., 6, 174

Carey, Sir Victor Gosselin (1871–1957), bailiff of Guernsey, was born on 2 July 1871 at Petit Marché, St Peter Port, Guernsey, the third of four children of Major-General de Vic Francis Carey (1831–1908), army officer, of Le Vallon, Guernsey, and his wife, Harriet Mary (1843–1932), daughter of Thomas William Gosselin of Springfield, Guernsey, and his wife, Harriet. He was educated at Elizabeth College, Guernsey, from 1880 to 1883, and subsequently at Cothill House, Abingdon, and Marlborough College (from January 1886 to July 1887). For several years he studied civil engineering and was apprenticed to an international engineering company at Boulogne. He then read law at the University of Caen (from 1895 to 1897), graduating as *bachelier-en-droit* in 1897. He returned to Guernsey and was admitted to the island bar on 5 February 1898. On 23 March 1899 he married Adelaide Eleanor Jeffreys (1872–1936), daughter of Julius Jeffreys of Richmond, Surrey; there were two sons of the marriage.

Like many of his ancestors, Carey involved himself in service to the insular community. He was elected as a deputy of the states of Guernsey (in 1900, 1903, 1906, and 1909) and proved effective. He also had a successful legal practice. In 1912 he was appointed as his majesty's receiver-general for the bailiwick of Guernsey. As receiver-general (a part-time post) he was responsible for the collection of the crown revenues and oversight of the crown estate in the islands. When Arthur William Bell, the bailiff, died suddenly in 1935, it might have been expected that the crown would have looked to the procureur (attorney-general) to fill the post; but as Ambrose Sherwill had been in post only a few months and was only forty-five, Carey was preferred. Carey did much to re-establish the good order and dignity of his office and the royal court, and in the normal way would have bowed out after six years when he was seventy. However, events in northern Europe in the summer of 1940 decreed otherwise.

The ancient office of bailiff embraced three distinct roles: chief justice, presiding officer of the legislature (the states), and spokesman for the island authorities in dealings with his majesty's government. As the *Wehrmacht* swept through northern France in 1940, the British government vacillated and then decided to demilitarize the Channel Islands. Carey was instructed by the Home Office to discharge the combined duties of bailiff and lieutenant-governor (the personal representative of the sovereign, and commander-in-chief when the island was garrisoned) and to administer the government to the best of his abilities in the interests of the inhabitants. This was an onerous task. Dealing with enemy occupation presented problems for which there were no legal precedents. With a ratio of one German soldier for each islander, Guernsey had more in common with an *Oflag* than with occupied France.

Following the evacuation and pending the imminent arrival of the occupying forces, the states moved quickly to establish a controlling committee to co-ordinate the administration of the island. Unlike his opposite number in Jersey (A. M. Coutanche), Carey did not feature in the membership of that committee. He had lost his wife in 1936, and his elder son had evacuated at the last moment with a wife who was ill after childbirth; Carey was very much alone and perhaps was not ready to shoulder additional responsibility. However, as bailiff, and with the additional role as personal representative of the sovereign, albeit in occupied territory, he felt ultimately responsible for the well-being of the islanders. This did, on occasion, lead to some uncertainties between him and the controlling committee as to where responsibilities for government lay. Moreover, Carey was regularly asked to sign official documents. This caused him considerable difficulties. On one occasion he signed a notice that referred to the allies as 'enemy forces'; on another occasion he signed a proclamation offering a reward to those who denounced islanders who were painting the resistance 'V'. These actions should not be seen in isolation. Carey lodged a variety of protests with the occupying power and was often faced by the need to yield in one direction in order to gain a concession in another. Ambrose Sherwill commented:

> No one suffered more greatly than did the Bailiff from want of food and lack of heating … I was struck by his shrunken frame as he sat by his empty office grate huddled in a heavy rug and, at the end, his physical condition was pitiable. [In 1939 Carey had weighed thirteen stone; by 1945 he was a mere eight stone.] Month after month and year after year of the Occupation, he had no work to occupy his mind and nothing to do but worry, and he worried himself sick. Not about himself … but about Guernsey and its people.
> (Sherwill, memoirs)

After the war Carey and the Guernsey administration were criticized by some British journalists. The director of public prosecutions (DPP) visited the island and concluded that 'on one or two occasions' Carey appeared to have 'given way to strong German pressure'. The DPP thought that the administration had made mistakes but was entitled to praise rather than censure. Frank Falla levelled some criticisms against the wartime administration of the island, but called the attacks on Carey unjust (Falla,

208–9). The judgement is significant because of its origin: Falla engaged in resistance in occupied Guernsey and was imprisoned by the Germans.

Carey was knighted in December 1945 and retired in February 1946. He spent the years of his retirement at Le Vallon, St Martin's, Guernsey, a home he had inherited from his parents. He died of myocarditis at the Princess Elizabeth Hospital, Guernsey, on 28 June 1957, and was buried on 2 July at St Martin's parish church.

GREGORY COX

Sources C. Cruickshank, *The German occupation of the Channel Islands* (1975) · W. W. Carey, E. F. Carey, and S. Carey Curtis, *The history of the Careys of Guernsey* (1938) · W. M. Bell, *I beg to report … Policing in Guernsey during the German occupation* (1995) · M. Bunting, *The model occupation* (1995) · private information (2004) · memoirs of Sir Ambrose Sherwill, priv. coll. · F. Falla, *The silent war* (1967) · Royal Court, Guernsey, Greffe Records · *WWW, 1951–60* · Burke, *Peerage* · *The Star* [Guernsey] (3 July 1957)
Likenesses F. Brook, oils, 1923, offices of Carey, Langlois, advocates, St Peter Port, Guernsey · oils, *c.*1946, office of the bailiff, royal court, Guernsey

Carey, William (*c.*1500–1528), courtier, was the son of Thomas Carey (1455–1500) of Chilton Foliat, Wiltshire, and grandson of Sir William Carey of Cockington, Devon, an eminent Lancastrian who was beheaded at Tewkesbury in 1471. Thomas, who was MP for Wallingford in 1491–2, married Margaret, daughter of Sir Robert Spencer of Posbury, Devon, and his wife, Eleanor Beaufort, daughter and coheir of Edmund Beaufort, first duke of Somerset (*d.* 1455); so William Carey could claim Henry VIII as a distant cousin.

No doubt this connection assisted Carey's entry into the royal court. He was present at court by January 1519, when he was playing for money with the king and winning. He may have been introduced by the earl of Devon with whom Carey appears frequently in these years. They played tennis together on the king's court at Richmond in February 1519, and Carey was involved in the tourneys at the earl's marriage celebrations. Carey was officially part of the king's household by October 1519 when he was entitled to a livery at breakfast. He seems to have been fully involved in court life, taking part in the revels of 1519–20 and the reception of the emperor Charles V in May 1520. He was present in France later that year for the meeting at the Field of Cloth of Gold, where, in the company of his old friend, the earl of Devon, he distinguished himself in the jousting. By this time Carey had become a member of the king's privy chamber, and an esquire for the body.

Carey strengthened his career as a courtier when he married Mary Boleyn (*c.*1499–1543) [*see* Stafford, Mary], sister to the future queen, on 4 February 1520 in the king's presence. This was a useful marriage alliance for both Carey and the Boleyns. Not only did it combine Carey's Beaufort blood with the Bohun, Butler, and Howard blood of the Boleyns, but it also strengthened the Boleyn family at court, where Mary's father, Sir Thomas, was a prominent courtier and rising politician. Carey, a young favourite of the young king, was a useful ally for the Boleyn and Howard families in their struggles with Wolsey.

William Carey (c.1500–1528), by unknown artist, 1580 [original, 1526]

Carey's potential influence increased even more when his wife became Henry VIII's mistress. Historians have suggested various dates for this, but it is most likely that Mary attracted the king's attentions soon after her arrival at court as Carey's young wife. Her relationship with Henry was publicly known and both Mary's father and husband benefited. While Boleyn gained greater political influence, Carey was rewarded through grants of land, many of which had belonged to the attainted duke of Buckingham, a distant Beaufort relation. It seems that Mary had returned to her husband's bed by 1525 when she was pregnant with their son, Henry *Carey, although contemporary gossip claimed that he was a bastard son of the king. Henry was Carey's only son, and was to be elevated to the peerage as Lord Hunsdon by his cousin, Elizabeth I. Carey also had a daughter, Katherine, who married Sir Francis Knollys.

The end to Carey's cuckolding by the king did not stop his career, and he continued to increase his influence in the privy chamber. When the Eltham ordinance was issued in January 1526 Carey was named as one of the six gentlemen waiters of the privy chamber, and had lodgings on the king's side of the court. He had also been made keeper of Greenwich Palace in 1526. When it became clear that the king intended to divorce his wife to marry Carey's sister-in-law it seemed that Carey would continue to rise and rise. Instead, he died suddenly of the sweating sickness, with several others of the royal household, on 23 June 1528. At the time of his death Carey was lobbying, with the king's support, to have his sister Eleanor elected

abbess of the wealthy nunnery of Wilton, even though she proved to have a somewhat chequered past—after William's death Wolsey was able to have a rival candidate installed. The wardship of Henry Carey was granted to Anne Boleyn. His father had been having his portrait painted when he died, possibly by Holbein. It shows William Carey as an elegantly dressed young man holding a book.   MICHAEL RIORDAN

Sources LP Henry VIII, vols. 1–4 • Harrison, The Devon Carys (1920) • D. Starkey, ed., Henry VIII: a European court in England (1991) • E. W. Ives, Anne Boleyn (1986) • R. M. Warnicke, The rise and fall of Anne Boleyn (1989) • J. J. Muskett, Suffolk manorial families, 2 vols. (1908) • W. C. Metcalfe, ed., The visitations of Hertfordshire, Harleian Society, 22 (1886) • HoP, Commons, 1509–58, 1.582–3 • J. C. Wedgwood and A. D. Holt, History of parliament … 1439–1509, 2 vols. (1936–8) • DNB • D. Knowles, '"The matter of Wilton" in 1528', BIHR, 31 (1958), 92–6

Likenesses oils, 1580 (after original, 1526), priv. coll. [see illus.]

Carey, William (1761–1834), orientalist and missionary, was born on 17 August 1761 at Paulerspury, Northamptonshire, the eldest of the five children of Edmund Carey and Elizabeth Wells. His father, originally a weaver, became in 1767 parish clerk and schoolmaster, which gave Carey access to a wide range of books. At the age of about fourteen he was apprenticed to a shoemaker in the hamlet of nearby Piddington. Through the influence of a fellow apprentice, he began to attend a dissenting prayer-meeting, and, from 1779, the Independent (Congregationalist) chapel in the next village, Hackleton. He married Dorothy Plackett (1756–1807), of Hackleton, on 10 June 1781. In 1783, having been persuaded of the principles of the Baptist denomination, he was baptized by John Ryland (1753–1825), in Northampton. While continuing to practise as a shoemaker he preached to the Baptist congregation at Earls Barton, near Northampton, and in his spare time studied Latin, Greek, and Hebrew. In 1785 he moved to a residential Baptist pastorate a few miles away at Moulton, though still needing to augment his income by schoolmastering and shoe making.

Carey's interest in the non-European world was awakened by reading (probably in 1784 or 1785) the published accounts of the south sea voyages of Captain James Cook. He became intensely concerned for the spiritual condition of the populations currently being opened up to European eyes. While at Moulton he began work on a pamphlet urging the obligation of Christians to spread the gospel overseas, which he completed following his move in 1789 to a pastorate in Leicester. The pamphlet, An Enquiry into the Obligations of Christians to Use Means for the Conversion of the Heathens, was published in 1792. Although it sold poorly it led a number of the Particular (Calvinistic) Baptist ministers of the east midlands to join Carey in founding the Particular Baptist Society for Propagating the Gospel among the Heathen, at Kettering in October 1792. This society, later known as the Baptist Missionary Society, was the first evangelical missionary society, and it stimulated the formation of similar societies in Britain, Europe, and North America. In January 1793 Carey offered to go as a missionary to Bengal to accompany John Thomas, an East India Company surgeon who intended to

William Carey (1761–1834), by Robert Home, 1811 [with his chief pandit, Mritunjaya]

return to India as a missionary. Thomas and Carey and his family arrived in Bengal in November 1793. Exhaustion of funds soon compelled Carey to accept a position as manager of an indigo factory, owned by George Udny, north of Malda. He learned the Bengali and Hindi languages, and began to preach in the vernacular and to translate the Bible into Bengali.

In January 1800 Carey moved to the Danish settlement of Serampore, north of Calcutta, following the refusal of the East India Company to grant permission to reside in its territory to a party of missionary recruits who had just arrived in Bengal. Among the recruits were Joshua Marshman (1768–1837) and William Ward (1769–1823). The 'Serampore trio' of Carey, Marshman, and Ward built up the Baptist work at Serampore to a level which attracted attention in Britain as well as in India. Further mission centres were established in other parts of Bengal and northern India. The first Hindu convert, Krishna Pal, was baptized at Serampore in December 1800. Although more than 1400 baptisms had been recorded by 1821, the rate of conversion was disappointing; the caste system proved a more formidable obstacle to evangelism than Carey had anticipated. His later years at Serampore were marred by deteriorating relationships with the Baptist Missionary Society in London, which culminated in the separation of the Serampore mission from the society in 1827.

Although the Serampore missionaries invested heavily in education, Carey's principal contribution was not to educational endeavour but to Bible translation and language study. Carey and his Indian pandits were responsible for the translation of the entire Bible into six Indian

languages—Bengali, Oriya, Sanskrit, Hindi, Marathi, and Assamese—and of parts of it into a further twenty-nine languages. Carey also produced grammars of Bengali (1801), Marathi (1805), Sanskrit (1806), Punjabi (1812), Telinga (1814), and Bhotia (1826), and he compiled dictionaries of Marathi (1810), Bengali (1815), and Bhotia (1826). With Marshman he also began to translate the Hindu epic, the *Ramayana*, into English; three volumes had been published by 1810. He was working on a universal dictionary of all Indian languages derived from Sanskrit when in 1812 a fire destroyed all his manuscripts for this work and others besides.

Carey's expertise in Indian languages was recognized by his appointment in 1801 as professor of Sanskrit, Marathi, and Bengali at the East India Company's Fort William College. He was also awarded in 1807 the degree of DD by Brown University, USA. His role at Fort William College helped to give the Baptist mission a more secure status in the period before 1813, during which any activity by the missionaries within the company's territory was illegal. His encouragement of the Bengali language was of permanent significance in establishing a corpus of Bengali literature and it contributed to a Bengali cultural renaissance. Carey was also a keen botanist. He edited for publication William Roxburgh's *Hortus Bengaliensis* (a catalogue of the plants in the East India Company's Calcutta garden), published in 1814, and Roxburgh's *Flora Indica* (1832).

Carey's domestic life was marked by tragedy. Dorothy Carey had been unwilling to go to India, and in Bengal she developed acute mental illness. They had seven children. Two daughters died in infancy in England; their third son, Peter, died at Mudnabati in 1794. Four sons—Felix * Carey, William, Jabez, and Jonathan—survived. Dorothy died at Serampore on 8 December 1807. In the following year, on 9 May 1808, Carey married Charlotte Rumohr, daughter of a Danish count; she died on 20 May 1821. Carey married his third wife, Grace Hughes, a widow, in 1823; she died on 22 July 1835. Carey himself died on 9 June 1834 at Serampore, where he is buried. BRIAN STANLEY

Sources S. Pearce Carey, *William Carey, DD, fellow of Linnaean Society* [1923] · E. D. Potts, *British Baptist missionaries in India, 1793–1837* (1967) · B. Stanley, *The history of the Baptist Missionary Society, 1792–1992* (1992) · M. Drewery, *William Carey: shoemaker and missionary* (1978) · E. Carey, *Memoir of William Carey* (1836) · J. C. Marshman, *The life and times of Carey, Marshman and Ward*, 2 vols. (1859)

Archives Bristol Baptist College · Linn. Soc., drawings · N. Yorks. CRO, letter-books and journals · Regent's Park College, Oxford, Angus Library, corresp.; corresp. and papers; family corresp. | Lpool RO, corresp. with William Roscoe · Northants. RO, letters to John Ryland · U. Edin. L., corresp. with Nathaniel Wallich

Likenesses R. Home, oils, 1811, Baptist Missionary Society, Didcot, Oxon. [*see illus.*] · R. Home, portrait, 1811, Regent's Park College, Oxford · W. H. Worthington, line engraving, pubd 1813 (after R. Home), BM, NPG · J. Jenkins, stipple, pubd 1836 (after R. Home), BM, NPG · J. Jenkins, line engraving, pubd 1839 (after R. Home), BM, NPG · stipple, BM · stipple (after R. Home), BM, NPG

Carey, William (1769–1846), headmaster and bishop of Exeter and St Asaph, was born in Worcester on 18 November 1769, the son of Richard Carey, a tradesman. His talent was recognized by William Vincent, through whose aid he was admitted into Westminster School, where he passed through every grade and finally became its head. In 1784 he was elected a king's scholar, in 1788 he became the captain of the school, and in 1789 he was elected to Christ Church, Oxford, which was presided over by Cyril Jackson. He graduated BA in 1793 and MA in 1796. From 1794 to 1800 he was a tutor at Christ Church, where he also filled the office of censor from 1798 to 1802. Ordained in 1799, he held the perpetual curacy of Cowley in 1800, and in 1801 became preacher at Whitehall Chapel. He received the prebendal stalls of Barnby in 1802 and of Knaresborough-cum-Bickhill in 1804, both in York Minster.

Through the influential and zealous support of his old Oxford friend, Cyril Jackson—a support which outweighed the opposition of many who desired an older man—Carey was appointed to the headmastership of Westminster School in January 1803. He proceeded to the degree of BD in 1804, and to that of DD in 1807. On 2 January 1804 he married Mary, the only daughter of the Revd William Sheepshanks of St John's, Leeds. Carey was an efficient headmaster, who won the affection of his pupils. He showed, by later standards, an indifference to the rough amusements in which the boys indulged. He seems to have given tacit approval to the fighting which was endemic in the school—the boys sparring with each other or brawling with coal-heavers—and to have regarded this as part of a necessary 'hardening process'. One of the last headmasters to wear the three-cornered hat known as a windcutter, he was described in 1806 as 'a thick-set, bandy-legged man with puck-like nose and chin, but with a good-humoured expression of face, pleasant and affable manners' (Carleton, 43). The honourable post of sub-almoner to the king was given to him in 1808, and in March 1809 he received a piece of preferment equally honourable, and more lucrative, a prebend at Westminster. He also came to the notice of the duke of York, who placed him in charge of the Royal Military Asylum at Chelsea, and of arrangements for the education of soldiers' children.

On resigning the headmastership of Westminster in December 1814, Carey retired to his country living, Sutton on the Forest, Yorkshire, to which he had been instituted in 1813. He resided there until 1820, when he was made bishop of Exeter. His consecration took place on 12 November 1820, and on the previous day he was installed a prebendary of his cathedral. The administration of the diocese by the former occupant of the see had not been marked by an excess of zeal, and the energy with which Carey threw himself into his new labours was much praised, though his performance was later attacked by one of his clergy, Jonas Dennis, in *A Living Prelate's Diocesan Government* (1835). He was translated to the wealthier bishopric of St Asaph, being elected to his new see on 12 March 1830 and confirmed on 7 April. He died at his house in Portland Place, London, on 13 September 1846, and was survived by his wife. His body was carried to Wales and buried in the churchyard of St Asaph Cathedral on 2 October 1846. A monument to his memory was erected in his cathedral.

Carey was the author of three sermons long since forgotten: one preached before the House of Commons in 1809, another to the children of London charity schools in 1824. His name is preserved in his munificent benefaction of £20,000 in consols for the better maintenance of such bachelor students of Christ Church, duly elected from Westminster School, as, 'having their own way to make in the world', shall attend the divinity lectures and prepare themselves for holy orders. A second gift to his former school was of a different character—a new set of scenery for the Westminster play modelled on the lines of its predecessor, which had been designed by Athenian Stuart. Carey's scenery was in use for fifty years, from 1808 to 1858.   W. P. COURTNEY, *rev.* M. C. CURTHOYS

Sources J. Welch, *The list of the queen's scholars of St Peter's College, Westminster*, ed. [C. B. Phillimore], new edn (1852) · W. Jerdan, *National portrait gallery of illustrious and eminent personages of the nineteenth century, with memoires*, 5 vols. (1830–34) · *GM*, 2nd ser., 26 (1846), 533–4 · J. Sargeaunt, *Annals of Westminster School* (1898) · J. D. Carleton, *Westminster School: a history* (1965) · Foster, *Alum. Oxon.* · M. Cook, ed., *The diocese of Exeter in 1821*, Devon and Cornwall RS, 3 (1958) · *GM*, 1st ser., 74 (1804), 85

Archives NL Wales, letters to T. G. Roberts, vicar of Llanrwst

Likenesses S. W. Reynolds, oils, exh. RA 1823, Christ Church Oxf. · T. A. Dean, engraving (after S. W. Reynolds), repro. in Jerdan, *National portrait gallery of illustrations* · oils, Christ Church Oxf.

Wealth at death £40,000: *GM*, 2nd ser., 26, p. 661

Carey, William Paulet (1759–1839), art critic and dealer, was born in Redmond's Hill, Dublin, the son of Christopher Carey, a baker. He was the brother of John and Mathew *Carey. He studied drawing at the school of the Royal Dublin Society, and became an engraver. From 1786 Carey made sentimental and political prints for educated journals such as the *Sentimental and Masonic Magazine*. As a member of the Society of United Irishmen, he wrote and published the *Rights of Irishmen, or, National Evening Star*, a journal of poetry and parodies, and essays, under the respective pseudonyms of Scriblerus Murrough O'Pindar and Junius Hibernicus. After getting into trouble with this society in 1793, Carey fled to Philadelphia, where his brother Matthew published a literary compendium, *The American Museum*.

By the late 1790s Carey was a dealer in prints and paintings in London, and had discontinued engraving owing to an accident. In 1801, doubtless partly motivated by business concerns, he published the first of over twenty books and pamphlets arguing the benefits of annual fine arts exhibitions, organized by national and regional institutions, as a means of cultivating patronage of British artists and fighting foreign competition. Although he stated that such principles arose from a 'disinterested public spirit', he noted that 'manufacturing and commercial interests' were at one with a desire for a domestically inclined national consensus on taste in the fine arts (W. P. Carey, *Observations on the Primary Object of the British Institution*, 1829). Carey was also involved in the encouragement of unknown artists, most notably Francis Chantrey, in relation to employment on public monuments, and he helped to establish and publicize private collections of British art. His views were both criticized and praised in periodic literature. A contemporary described Carey's criticism as 'fervid yet discriminative', and his character as one of 'impetuosity and enthusiasm' (*N&Q*, 481–4).

Carey married a Miss Lennon, of Grafton Street, Dublin, in May 1792, and had at least one daughter, Elizabeth Sheridan Carey. He lived in Marylebone, and in Museum Street, Bloomsbury, and moved to Temple Place, Bath Row, Birmingham, in 1835, where he died on 21 May 1839.   NICHOLAS GRINDLE

Sources W. G. Strickland, *A dictionary of Irish artists*, 2 vols. (1913) · D. J. O'Donoghue, *The poets of Ireland: a biographical dictionary with bibliographical particulars*, 1 vol. in 3 pts (1892–3) · W. Bates, 'William Carey', *N&Q*, 4th ser., 5 (1870), 481–4 · J. Holland, *Memorials of Sir Francis Chantrey* [1851] · *IGI* · T. Green, 'Diary of a lover of literature', *GM*, 2nd ser., 17 (1842), 139 · *DNB*

Archives Ches. & Chester ALSS, letters to Sir John Leicester · Sheff. Arch., letters to James Montgomery

Cargill [*née* Brown], **Ann** (*c.*1760–1784), singer and actress, was the daughter of Edward Brown, a London coal merchant. She made her début as a child, singing Titania in George Colman's *The Fairy Prince*, with music by Arne (Covent Garden, 12 November 1771), and then played Sally, the naughty little sister, in Colman's *Man and Wife*. A pupil of the singer Thomas Baker, she was 'very pretty, had a good voice, and an excellent ear' (*Recollections of R. J. S. Stevens*, 9) and was soon taking leading roles in musical afterpieces, comic operas, and comedies at Covent Garden. She sang in the Bach–Abel oratorio season in 1775 and that November created the capricious runaway Clara in Sheridan's *The Duenna*. She was soon a runaway in real life. In December her affair with the playwright and gunpowder manufacturer Miles Peter *Andrews (1742–1814) became the subject of gossip in the London papers. A court order returned her to her father, but she absconded, abandoning her role in *The Duenna* on 14 December. Her father made an abortive attempt to recapture the 'run-away Siren' (*Morning Post*, 5 Jan 1776), and she did not return to Covent Garden until the autumn, when a final attempt by her father to apprehend her as she approached the theatre to play Polly in *The Beggar's Opera* was thwarted by the London crowd and members of the company.

A petite and charming brunette, Miss Brown was receiving £10 a week by the 1779–80 season, but that April she broke her contract and eloped to Edinburgh with a Mr Cargill, a young man in financial difficulties who had been using the name of Doyle. As Mrs Cargill she then appeared at the Haymarket in the summer and Drury Lane in the winter. In August 1781 she played Macheath in the highly successful production of *The Beggar's Opera* by the Haymarket manager George Colman, when the male roles were played by women and the female ones by men. The *Morning Chronicle* reported that she 'hit off the gayety of manner, easy deportment, and *degagé* air of Macheath, with singular and wonderful success' (*Morning Chronicle*, 9 Aug 1781), and audiences were much taken by her shudder

Ann Cargill (*c.*1760–1784), by Johan Zoffany [as Miranda in *The Tempest*]

at the sound of the execution bell in act III. Before the end of the season she left suddenly for Bath, with her husband according to some accounts but with the son of the manager, George Colman the younger, in others. She was back at Drury Lane that autumn, where she sang the breeches role of Patie in Allan Ramsay's *The Gentle Shepherd* and created Marinetta in the *Carnival of Venice* by Richard Tickell and Thomas Linley. Colman sued the Cargills for breach of contract, to ensure that Ann could not insist on employment at the Haymarket in future summer seasons, and when the case was heard, on 29 November 1781, it emerged that both Cargills had been under the age of twenty-one when the contract was signed in 1780.

Mrs Cargill's summer season in 1782 was in Liverpool, and she then set off for India to join her latest lover, although it was rumoured that she transferred her affections to Robert Haldane, the captain of her ship. In Calcutta she 'played all her applauded opera characters at immense prices' and her benefit yielded 'the astonishing sum of 12,000 rupees' (*Morning Post*, 9 March 1784). She left for home in December 1783 on the East India packet *Nancy*, captained by Haldane, but the ship was wrecked off the Isles of Scilly, probably on 4 March 1784. The press reported that her body was found naked with an infant clasped in her arms, later that the child was not her own, and then that her body was with the captain's in his cabin, but the enduring image of the unfortunate Mrs Cargill 'floating in her shift, and her infant in her arms' is found in the *London Chronicle* (9 March 1784). She was buried at St Mary's Church, Isles of Scilly.

OLIVE BALDWIN and THELMA WILSON

Sources G. W. Stone, ed., *The London stage, 1660–1800*, pt 4: 1747–1776 (1962) · C. B. Hogan, ed., *The London stage, 1660–1800*, pt 5: 1776–1800 (1968) · *Morning Post* (6 Dec 1775) · *Morning Post* (7 Dec 1775) · *Morning Post* (15 Dec 1775) · *Morning Post* (5 Jan 1776) · *Morning Post* (5 Oct 1776) · *Morning Post* (7–9 Oct 1776) · *Morning Post* (24 April 1780) · *Morning Post* (9 March 1784) · *Morning Post* (13 March 1784) · *Morning Chronicle* (15 Dec 1775) · *Morning Chronicle* (16 Dec 1775) · *Morning Chronicle* (29 Dec 1775) · *Morning Chronicle* (7 Oct 1776) · *Morning Chronicle* (9 Aug 1781) · *Morning Chronicle* (13 Sept 1781) · *Morning Chronicle* (15 Sept 1781) · *Morning Chronicle* (8 March 1784) · *Morning Chronicle* (9 March 1784) · *Gazetteer* (19 Aug 1780) · *Morning Herald* (13–14 Sept 1781) · *Morning Herald* (26 Sept 1782) · *Morning Herald* (8–10 March 1784) · *Public Advertiser* (1 Aug 1780) · *Public Advertiser* (9 Aug 1780) · *Public Advertiser* (1 Dec 1781) · *Public Advertiser* (8 March 1784) · *Public Advertiser* (10 March 1784) · *Whitehall Evening Post* (9 March 1784) · *London Chronicle* (9 Aug 1781) · *London Chronicle* (6 March 1784) · *London Chronicle* (9 March 1784) · *London Chronicle* (11 March 1784) · *Bath Chronicle* (11 March 1784) · *Recollections of R. J. S. Stevens: an organist in Georgian London*, ed. M. Argent (1992) · 'Histories of the tête-à-tête annexed, or, Memoirs of the combustible lover, and the eloped Clara', *Town and Country Magazine*, 8 (1776), 9–11 · 'Biographical sketch of Miles Peter Andrews, Esq., M.P.', *Monthly Mirror* (April 1797), 195–200 · M. D. Wells, *Memoirs of the life of Mrs Sumbel, late Wells*, 3 vols. (1811) · A. Pasquin [J. Williams], 'The children of Thespis', *Poems*, 2 [1789] · *The letters of Richard Brinsley Sheridan*, ed. C. Price, 3 vols. (1966) · *Memoirs of William Hickey*, ed. A. Spencer, 2 (1918) · *The diary of Sylas Neville, 1767–1788*, ed. B. Cozens-Hardy (1950) · 'A copy of verses made upon the untimely death of the beautiful Mrs. Cargill', Madden Ballads, CUL, 4.375 · *Shipwrecks around the Isles of Scilly* (1988)

Likenesses R. Dunkarton, engraving, pubd 1777 (as Clara in *The duenna*; after J. Russell), Harvard TC · C. Grignion, line engraving, pubd 1777 (as Miranda in *The tempest*; with George Mattocks; after R. Dighton), BM, Harvard TC, NPG · J. R. Smith, mezzotint, pubd 1777 (as Clara in *The duenna*; after W. Peters), BM, Harvard TC · R. Read, stipple, pubd 1778 (as Clara in *The duenna*; after J. Russell), BM · J. R. Smith, mezzotint, pubd 1778 (as Clara in *The duenna*; after J. R. Smith), BM, Harvard TC · line engraving, pubd 1778 (as Daphne in *Midas*), BM, Harvard TC, NPG · Sherwin, engraving, pubd 1787 (as Clara in *The duenna*; after J. Russell), Harvard TC · W. Angus, line engraving (as Marinetta in *The carnival of Venice*, with Charles Dubellamy and John Palmer; after D. Dodd), Harvard TC, NPG · J. Collyer, engraving (as Rosetta in *Love in a village*, with Charles Dubellamy; after D. Dodd), repro. in *New English Theatre* (1784) · J. Walker, engraving (as Polly in *The beggar's opera*, with George Mattocks; after R. Dighton), repro. in *New English Theatre* (1782) · J. Zoffany, oils, unknown collection; copyprint, NPG [*see illus.*] · engraving (*The eloped Clara*), repro. in 'Histories of the tête-à-tête', *Town and Country Magazine* · engraving (as Clara in *The duenna*; after J. Russell), Harvard TC · line engraving (as Polly in *The beggar's opera*; after J. Roberts), NPG; repro. in *British Theatre* (1777) · line engraving (as Calypso), NPG; repro. in J. Hughes, *Calypso and Telemachus* (1781) · proof before inscription, Harvard TC · stipple (as Clara in *The duenna*; after W. Peters), BM · stipple (as Clara in *The duenna*; with George Mattocks), BM

Cargill, David Sime

Cargill, David Sime (1826–1904), merchant and oil industrialist, was born at Maryton, near Montrose, on 9 April 1826, the fourth and youngest son of the nine children of James Cargill, farmer, and his wife, Helen Thomson. After a brief exposure to office life in Glasgow, he spent the years 1844 to 1861 in Ceylon, building up the trade of a Scottish firm of East India merchants and establishing a Colombo department store that became known as the 'Harrods of the East'. When he returned to Glasgow, Cargill was wealthy enough to buy out his employers, and in 1861 to marry advantageously. His wife was Margaret (1840–1872), daughter of Dr John Traill of Arbroath. Three sons and two daughters were born to them before she died in 1872.

By the 1870s Cargill had immersed himself in a venture that was to become his life's work: the commercial exploitation of Burmese oil. In 1876, after visiting Burma, he purchased the Glasgow-based Rangoon Oil Company Ltd, which had failed because the king of Upper Burma used his monopoly power to overcharge for the crude oil that was to be found in his dominions. Over the next ten years Cargill supported the loss-making downstream activities from his own pocket, to the extent of £100,000. Then, in 1886, after the Third Burmese War, the British authorities annexed Upper Burma, and granted him prospecting licences in the oilfields there. Cargill introduced machine drilling and had the Rangoon refinery modernized to cope with the increased production. When in July 1886 he founded a new company, the Burmah Oil Company, his Glasgow associates were highly sceptical about its prospects. Yet in the final year of his life, 1904, it made £264,000 net profit and sold more than 2 million barrels of oil products, two-thirds of which comprised the cheap kerosene which kept Burmese and Indian lamps burning.

People who knew Cargill attributed his achievements to his combining certain conflicting qualities rarely to be found together: great courage with great caution, and broad vision with an unquenchable passion for detail. A sufferer from chronic insomnia, he often worked far into the night. Cargill had an impressive and well-tailored presence, enhanced by a Roman nose, broad forehead, and large beard. He was an active figure in Glasgow's inner commercial and public counsels, from the chamber of commerce, the Merchants' House, and the Clyde Trust to the council of the Royal Institute of Fine Arts and the Glasgow Maternity Hospital. However, Cargill's single-mindedness and lack of consideration exacted a high price from others. His managing director, Kirkman Finlay (1847–1903), doggedly worked for seventeen years in London with no effective support, before suffering a breakdown and killing himself. Although in 1878 Cargill was married again—to Connel Elizabeth Auld, with whom he had a son and a daughter—his innate reserve and general busyness clearly stunted his family's emotional lives. Two of the sons never married, one died an alcoholic, and his second son, Sir John *Cargill, never lost the diffidence he had acquired as a child.

David Cargill died of paralysis at Carruth, Bridge of Weir, Renfrewshire, near Glasgow, on 25 May 1904. He was survived by his second wife and left a movable estate worth £943,000, two-thirds of which represented his stake in the Burmah Oil Company. T. A. B. CORLEY

Sources T. A. B. Corley, 'Cargill, David Sime', *DSBB* · T. A. B. Corley, *A history of the Burmah Oil Company*, 1: *1886–1924* (1983) · T. A. B. Corley, 'Strategic factors in the growth of a multinational enterprise: the Burmah Oil Company, 1886–1928', *The growth of international business*, ed. M. Casson (1983) · *Glasgow Herald* (27 May

1905) • *Glasgow Herald* (27 April 1905) [Annual General Meeting, Burmah Oil Company] • 'The origin of the big oil companies', *Glasgow Herald* (8 Aug 1944) • W. D. C. Thompson, letter, *Glasgow Herald* (12 Aug 1959) • General Register Office for Scotland, Edinburgh • *Shipwrecks around the Isles of Scilly* (1988)

Archives Burmah Castrol plc, Swindon, archives of the Burmah Oil Company
Likenesses photographs, Burmah Castrol Archives
Wealth at death £943,000: confirmation, 19 Aug 1904, *CCI*

Cargill, Donald [Daniel] (*c*.1627–1681), field preacher and insurgent, was born at the farmhouse of Nether Cloquhat, Perthshire, the son of Lawrence Cargill (*d*. 1657), smallholder of Nether Cloquhat, and later notary at Rattray, and his wife, Marjory Blair. Initially destined for a career in the law Donald was educated at Aberdeen grammar school before entering the university there in 1643 in order to study philosophy. However, the sack of the city by the marauding highland army of the marquess of Montrose brought his studies to an abrupt close in September 1644, and he transferred to St Salvator's College at the University of St Andrews in order to complete his education. He graduated BA in the summer of 1647 and returned to his father's home at Rattray with the intention of joining him in his profitable legal practice. Soon afterwards the already devout Cargill underwent a dramatic conversion experience while on a visit to relatives in Bothwell. Devastated by his own sense of worthlessness when compared to the might and majesty of God he contemplated suicide but, at last, concluded that he had been chosen to fulfil some great—if unknown—purpose through his ministry to the Scottish people. Consequently, in 1648 he enrolled at St Mary's College, at the University of St Andrews, in order to study divinity. While there he immersed himself in the works of both John Knox and Melville, though the greatest single influence upon him was that of his tutor, Samuel Rutherford, who stressed that for governed and governors alike duty to God was to be placed before all other considerations.

Having graduated and secured his licence to preach in 1652 Cargill applied—unsuccessfully—for cures at Dunkeld and St Andrews. Thereafter it seems likely that he served as private chaplain to the household of Andrew Beaton, laird of Blebo. Though his employment was cut short by the laird's death in June 1653 Cargill remained close to the family circle and, on 10 April 1656, married Beaton's widow, Margaret Brown. His attempts to become the minister of Strathmiglo parish faltered in the autumn of 1654, owing to fears of his political and religious radicalism, while a concerted campaign mounted by local aristocrats, led by Lord Balfour of Burleigh, led the local church elders to withdraw their initial offer of the position. However, Cargill was looked upon far more sympathetically by both the churches and the town council of Glasgow. Consequently, in March 1655 he was confirmed as the incumbent minister of the Barony Church, the crypt running underneath Glasgow Cathedral. Even then his doubts as to his gifts as a preacher and his own natural shyness combined to make him reconsider the righteousness of his calling, and it was with some difficulty that he was prevailed upon by his parishioners not to return

immediately to Perthshire. His problems mounted in August 1656, when his wife died, leaving him with massive debts from a mismanaged estate and six young stepchildren to support. However, with an increased stipend of 1300 merks per annum from the town council, and with his self-doubts seemingly resolved, Cargill quickly built up a sizeable following and became a significant moral and political force locally.

Although he initially welcomed the Restoration, Cargill quickly became one of the most outspoken opponents of the re-establishment of the prelacy in Scotland and used the second anniversary of Charles II's return to deliver at Barony a blistering attack on both the remodelling of the kirk and upon the monarch himself. 'People are this Day rejoicing, [but] their Joy will be like the Crackling of Thorns under a Pot; it will soon be turned to Mourning ... [for Charles II] will be the wo[e]fulest Sight that ever the poor Church of Scotland saw' (Carslaw, 28; Walker, *Remarkable Passages*, 8). Cargill was immediately forced into hiding in order to escape arrest, while his stipend was hastily withdrawn by a frightened town council. On 1 October 1662 the Scottish privy council numbered him among fourteen ministers to be ejected from their parishes in Glasgow and ordered that he—specifically—should be henceforth banished to the north of the River Tay on account of his seditious speeches and activities. Having no intention of abandoning his ministry Cargill maintained a lively contact with his former parishioners and embarked on covert preaching missions to Perth, Edinburgh, Dundee, and Coupar Angus. However, there is no evidence that he was involved in the Pentland rising of 1666 and by winter 1668 it appears that he was actively seeking to come to terms with Lauderdale's more moderate administration. Accordingly, on 1 September 1669 his petition against his banishment was granted by the privy council and, though he was still barred from Glasgow, he was allowed to settle his business affairs in Edinburgh. The authorities may well have hoped that these concessions would pave the way for Cargill to accept the first declaration of indulgence, but he did not and was soon flouting their restrictions, embarking on regular trips in order to renew his contacts in Glasgow.

As a fresh wave of field meetings swept the lowlands Cargill's horror at the continued persecution of fellow covenanters led him to turn down the offer of a parish at Eaglesham, near Glasgow—which had been specifically earmarked for him—and to refuse to appear before the privy council, on two separate occasions in autumn 1673 and summer 1674, in order to account for his continued unauthorized preaching. He was consequently outlawed on 16 July 1674, and further articles pronouncing him a traitor were passed on 6 August 1675. The rest of his career was spent as a hunted fugitive and stories abound of his hair's breadth escapes from government troopers. Though he continued to preach primarily in Glasgow and did not take an active part in the drafting of the Rutherglen declaration of May 1679, Cargill rushed to join the fledgeling rebel army after its victory at Drumclog on 1 June that year. However, the influence he exerted upon its councils at this crucial period was divisive and at times counter-productive. The movement was split between those who were prepared to negotiate with their presbyterian brethren who had accepted the indulgences and those who would not compromise under any circumstances. Among the latter was Cargill, who now injected an element of republicanism into his lengthy dialogues with the other insurgent ministers over their future strategy. He firmly believed that the Church of Scotland would never be secure while Charles II remained on the throne and to the dismay of the majority of his peers argued that the king should be removed at the first opportunity. Thus, it was an army bitterly divided over military, political, and religious objectives which faced the government forces at Bothwell Bridge, on 22 June 1679. Prominent in the battle, Cargill was badly wounded and left for dead on the field by the triumphant government soldiers. After slipping away at night he used the first public fast day after the battle to preach to the remnants of the covenanter movement the absolute necessity of stripping Charles II of his crown and attributed their crushing defeat to the wrath of God at their willingness to make concessions to the government.

As one of the few prominent rebels and leading ministers who had eluded capture Cargill gained in added status among his supporters but also attracted growing attention from the government forces and their spies. Consequently, in late summer 1679 he went into exile in the Netherlands and preached for a time at the Scots kirk in Rotterdam. His return to Scotland, at the end of November 1679, coincided with the ministry of Richard Cameron and the renewal of the field conventicles. Together he and Cameron launched a co-ordinated campaign of preaching missions and guerrilla warfare throughout the lowlands. Cargill based himself at South Queensferry, which offered him excellent communications between Edinburgh and Dunfermline, but he was overtaken by a party of government soldiers on the night of 3 June 1680. In the ensuing struggle Cargill was badly wounded and only narrowly escaped thanks to the self-sacrifice of his travelling companion, Henry Hall. Unfortunately the document that the two men had been carrying was seized by the soldiers. Known subsequently to the authorities as the 'Queensferry paper' and almost certainly the work of Cargill, it was a draft of a new general covenant which his supporters, and those of Cameron, could use as a manifesto and rallying call in the raising of a fresh rebellion. Among its guiding principles was an outright rejection of the prelacy, Erastianism, and all of those ministers who had accepted the indulgences, a resolution to overthrow the arbitrary power of both church and state, and an affirmation of the right and mutual obligation of the covenanters to self-defence through armed struggle.

The capture of the 'Queensferry paper' afforded the earl of Roxburghe and the Scottish privy council an enormous propaganda triumph and this blow was followed on 22 July by the death in battle of Richard Cameron; Cargill preached a funeral sermon in his honour at Shotts. At an enormous outdoor meeting at Torwood on 12 September 1680 he stamped his authority and leadership upon the fledgeling sect—known variously as the Cameronians or, more properly, as the Society People—and issued a bold series of excommunications, consigning to hell virtually the entire administration of Scotland and reserving particular censure for the king, the duke of York, the duke of Lauderdale, and General Tam Dalyell of the Binns. Given his status as a wanted man, with recourse to the protection of only a handful of safe houses and a cluster of muskets, such a provocative act attested not only to the enormity of his religious faith but also to the scope of his political radicalism. Unsurprisingly the privy council intensified its search for him and, on 22 November 1680, issued a proclamation branding him 'one of the most seditious preachers … a villanous and fanatical conspirator' and raising the price already set on his head to 5000 merks, dead or alive (*Reg. PCS*, 6.581–6).

After having had his horse shot from under him during an ambush set for him by soldiers on Linlithgow Bridge, Cargill sought a temporary respite in northern England and had settled in Northumberland by January 1681. Though he maintained a regular correspondence with his followers in the lowlands his absence caused fissures to develop among the competing factions within the Society People and in April 1681 he hurried back to Scotland in order to attempt to heal a breach with John Gibb and the Sweet Singers. Gibb held that Cargill had betrayed both his ministry and the entire Scottish nation by retiring into England, but still entertained hopes of winning his former mentor over to his own exclusive brand of apocalyptical mysticism. Attempts by Cargill to reach a compromise failed and he turned his attention, instead, towards urging those of Gibb's followers already incarcerated within the prisons of Edinburgh to return to the wider covenanter fold. This tactic appears to have paid dividends and with the Gibbite threat effectively countered Cargill returned to his punishing schedule of preaching dates throughout the lowlands. However, the net cast by government soldiers, militias, and informants was slowly closing in around him and his companions. By the spring of 1681 he was the last significant field preacher left at liberty and had to be manhandled away from the chaotic scene at Loudon Hill, on 5 May 1681, after a party of dragoons charged into the crowd which had assembled to hear his sermon. His luck finally ran out on 11 July 1681, when a dawn raid by regular troops under the command of James Irvine of Bonshaw surprised him in bed at the house of one of his supporters at Covington Mill, near Lanark, and captured him.

Confined to the Tolbooth, Cargill was brought before the duke of York and the privy council at Edinburgh, on 15 July 1681, to answer charges regarding his rejection of royal authority and his conduct during the rising of 1679. Though refusing to answer any of the council's questions directly, Cargill boldly reiterated his refusal to acknowledge Charles II as a lawful prince. This alone would have been enough to condemn him, but the council chose to interrogate him again on 19 July and to produce a series of witnesses on 22 July, who testified to having seen him bearing arms at the battle of Bothwell Bridge. Tried for treason and sentenced to death before the high court on 26 July 1681 Cargill spent his last night on earth composing a final testimony which was subsequently smuggled out of prison and distributed to his followers. In it, he admitted that his 'preaching ha[d] occasioned persecution' but that the want of it would occasion worse, and forcefully returned to his theme of the correctness of the rejection of temporal authority in favour of the divine (*Cloud of Witnesses*, 31–6). The next morning he was taken to the city's Mercat Cross. His last words to the crowd were purposely drowned out by the beating of soldiers' drums. After his body was cut down from the scaffold his head was severed and hung up from the Netherbow gate as a grim warning. However, the combination of dignity and utter conviction which he had exuded during his final minutes deeply moved the spectators and, in particular, the eighteen-year-old James Renwick, who subsequently assumed his mantle as the leader of the Society People.

JOHN CALLOW

Sources P. Walker, *Some remarkable passages in the life and death of … Mr Daniel Cargill* (1732) · P. Walker and A. Shields, *Biographia Presbyteriana*, ed. J. Stevenson, 2 vols. (1827) · M. Grant, *No king but Christ: the story of Donald Cargill* (1988) · R. B. Tweed, 'Donald Cargill, covenanter: a background study with special reference to his family connections', PhD diss., U. Edin., 1964 · *Reg. PCS*, 3rd ser., vols. 6–8 · W. H. Carslaw, *Life and times of Donald Cargill, minister of the Barony Church, Glasgow* (1900) · J. Howie, *The Scots worthies*, ed. W. H. Carlaw, [new edn] (1870) · J. Kerr, ed., *Sermons delivered in times of persecution in Scotland* (1880) · J. L. Watson, *Life of Donald Cargill* (1880) · *The life and wonderful prophecies of Donald Cargill* · R. Wodrow, *The history of the sufferings of the Church of Scotland from the Restauration to the revolution*, 2 vols. (1721–2) · *A cloud of witnesses, for the royal prerogatives of Jesus Christ, or, The last speeches and testimonies of those who suffered for the truth in Scotland, since the year 1680* (1730) · A. Smellie, *Men of the covenant* (1903) · J. Barr, *The Scottish covenanters* (1946)

Cargill, James (1565–1616?), botanist, one of several children of Thomas Cargill of Aberdeen, qualified in medicine, probably at Marischal College, Aberdeen. He then studied botany and anatomy at the University of Basel, when Caspar Bauhin, who held the chair from 1589, was professor of those sciences. He is known to have sent seeds and specimens to Bauhin as late as 1603; he likewise aided the bibliographer Conrad Gesner. The botanist Matthias de l'Obel (Lobelius) mentioned Cargill's skills in his *Methodicam Pharmaceuticam* (1605).

By his will, dated 1614, Cargill, who was apparently unmarried, bequeathed 4000 marks to the magistrates and council of Aberdeen, the income to be used to maintain four poor scholars, a proviso being that if any of these were his kin, they should have the benefit of one year's additional grant. He left smaller sums to the town's grammar school and to the hospital. Cargill probably died early in 1616; his will was proved on 13 March that year by his brother David.   G. T. BETTANY, *rev.* ANITA MCCONNELL

Sources *Fasti academiae Mariscallanae Aberdonensis: selections from the records of the Marischal College and University, MDXCIII–MDCCCLX*, 1, ed. P. J. Anderson, New Spalding Club, 4 (1889), 149–53 · E. Bonjour, *Die Universität Basel* (1971), 237 · R. Pulteney, *Historical and biographical sketches of the progress of botany in England*, 2 (1790), 2 · C. Bauhin, *Prodromo theatri botanici* (Frankfurt, 1620), 100, 155 ·

M. de l' Obel, *In G. Rondelletii methodicam pharmaceuticam officinam animadversiones* (1605), 485, 507
Wealth at death over 4000 marks

Cargill, Sir John Traill, first baronet (1867–1954), merchant and oil industrialist, was born in Glasgow on 10 January 1867, the second of three sons (there were also two daughters) of David Sime *Cargill (1826–1904) and his first wife, Margaret Traill (1840–1872). After attending Glasgow Academy (1878–83), in 1890 he entered the office of the Rangoon agents of the Burmah Oil Company, which his father had founded. He returned to the Glasgow office in 1893, and two years later married Mary Hope Walker (d. 1929), daughter of George Moncrieff Grierson, a Glasgow commission merchant, and sister of Sir James Moncrieff *Grierson; they had one daughter. In 1904, at the early age of thirty-seven, he succeeded his father as chairman of the Burmah Oil Company.

Cargill had suffered a deprived childhood (his mother died when he was five, and his father was strong-willed and much preoccupied with business concerns); Cargill never overcame a diffident manner and a deeply pessimistic outlook. These attributes were a disadvantage at a time when Burmah Oil was becoming a key element in the British government's oil strategy; however, among his able advisers were Sir Boverton Redwood and (Charles) William Wallace. In 1905 Cargill contracted with the Admiralty to supply the Royal Navy with fuel oil from Rangoon. These dealings with Whitehall led to his company's being asked to acquire the important Persian oil concession, then held by William Knox D'Arcy. After three years of arduous prospecting work, Burmah Oil's resident geologist, George Bernard Reynolds, discovered oil in Persia in 1908, and a vast oilfield was subsequently proved. In the following year a new company, the Anglo-Persian Oil Company Ltd (later British Petroleum), was registered in London.

The financial burden that Anglo-Persian began to impose on Burmah Oil soon alarmed Cargill. When in 1912 its refining and marketing problems required an injection of a further £2 million, he refused to authorize that sum. Instead, the managing director of Anglo-Persian, Charles Greenway, opened negotiations with the Admiralty for either a loan or the purchase of shares from Burmah Oil. In 1914 the government, at the instigation of Winston Churchill (then first lord of the Admiralty), acquired a controlling stake in Anglo-Persian, which in turn signed a contract to supply the Admiralty with fuel oil.

From 1914 onwards, Robert Irving Watson was head of Burmah Oil's London office. He gradually gained Cargill's trust and took over the day-to-day decisions that the latter wished to delegate. From 1920, when he became managing director, Watson was effectively in charge of the company, and he left to Cargill only the highest policy matters and other public duties normally undertaken by a non-executive chairman. In the same year Cargill was created a baronet for public services. A director of the Glasgow chamber of commerce, Cargill also held directorships of Scottish and other oil and investment companies. He was deputy lieutenant of Glasgow and on the court of

Glasgow University, which awarded him an honorary LLD in 1929.

Cargill was tall, with an impressive nose, and despite his reserve he played well his symbolic role as 'father' of Burmah Oil. He made periodic visits to Burma and to Persia, and came almost to enjoy the annual general meetings of the company in Glasgow. Having been an accomplished sportsman in his youth, he encouraged sporting and other recreational events in the East with trophies and donations. His great personal integrity made him a trusted figure in Whitehall and in Glasgow alike. He refused to lobby governments on his company's behalf, and angrily condemned underhand dealings by others. He also had a large fund of common sense, successfully arguing that because women had real influence in Burma they should be given the vote.

In 1942, while Cargill was still chairman of Burmah Oil, much of what he had worked for during his life was destroyed when the Japanese invaded Burma: on his orders, the company employees made an end of all its productive assets in Burma, to deny them to the invading armies. In 1943 Cargill handed over the chairmanship to Watson, and retired to the comfort of a nursing home at 19 Great King Street, Edinburgh, where he died on 24 January 1954. He was buried at Hillfoot cemetery, Glasgow. Before his death he had given large benefactions, including donations to universities in both Glasgow and Rangoon.

T. A. B. CORLEY

Sources T. A. B. Corley, *A history of the Burmah Oil Company*, 2 vols. (1983–8) · R. W. Ferrier, *The history of the British Petroleum Company*, 1: *The developing years, 1901–1932* (1982) · T. A. B. Corley, 'Cargill, Sir John Traill', *DBB* · T. A. B. Corley, 'Cargill, Sir John Traill', *DSBB* · *Glasgow Herald* (25 Jan 1954) · *Glasgow Herald* (28 Jan 1954) · *Journal of the Institute of Petroleum*, 40 (Feb 1954) · *The Times* (25 Jan 1954) · *The Times* (28 Jan 1954) · Burke, *Peerage* · *WWW* · *The Bailie* (20 Feb 1918) · *The Bailie* (20 March 1918) · *The Bailie* (7 Jan 1920) · C. A. Oakley, *Our illustrious forbears* (1980) · 'Men you know — no. 15', *Glasgow Weekly Herald* (9 July 1932)
Archives U. Warwick Mod. RC, BP archive
Likenesses bust, Burmah Castrol · photographs, Burmah Castrol · photographs, British Petroleum · portrait; formerly in the possession of Mrs Alison Greenlees
Wealth at death £296,765 10s. 11d.: confirmation, 14 May 1954, *CGPLA Eng. & Wales*

Carhampton. For this title name *see* Luttrell, Henry Lawes, second earl of Carhampton (1737–1821); Olmius, John Luttrell-, third earl of Carhampton (c.1740–1829) [*see under* Luttrell, James (c.1751–1788)].

Carier, Benjamin (*bap.* 1565, *d.* 1614), Church of England clergyman and Roman Catholic convert, was baptized on 6 January 1565 at Boughton Monchelsea, Kent, the third child and eldest son of the four sons and five daughters of Anthony Carier (*d.* 1580). His father was vicar of Sts Peter and Augustine (later St Peter's), Boughton Monchelsea, from 1561 until his death on 19 December 1580, leaving a young family and a reputation as a preacher. A scholar at King's School, Canterbury, from 1578 at least until his father's death, and a contemporary there of Christopher

Marlowe, Carier entered Corpus Christi College, Cambridge, on 28 February 1582 as a student-servant. He graduated BA in 1587, was elected a fellow of his college on 8 March 1589, and proceeded MA in 1590, BD in 1597, in which year he was a university preacher, and DD in 1602. In 1598 he was appointed to the living of Paddlesworth in Kent by the crypto-Catholic and future recusant Sir Edward Wotton, and vicar of Thurnham with Aldington in 1600. He became domestic chaplain to Archbishop Whitgift, who presented him to the rectory of West Tarring, Sussex (1602), and the living of Old Romney, Kent (1603). At some point a chaplain to Prince Henry, he was appointed a chaplain-in-ordinary to James I, who presented him to the next vacant prebend at Canterbury Cathedral, secured in 1608. He was named one of the first fellows of Chelsea College, established by Matthew Sutcliffe for able defenders of protestantism, in 1610. He was, however, defeated in a disputed election for the mastership of his Cambridge college in 1603; attempts to secure further preferment were unsuccessful and he appears to have experienced some financial hardship.

Even so, it has been said 'that there was scarce any clergyman in England for whom his majesty had a greater regard' than Carier (Dodd, 2.424). In the spring of 1613 he sought leave from James I to go to Spa in Germany on account of his health. He left for Spa in April 1613 and in August went on to Cologne to consult the rector of the Jesuit college, where he was reconciled to the Roman Catholic church. It was reported in England that 'Dr. Carier, the King's chaplain, is turned Papist, and more likely to follow, so many priests and Jesuits arriving and passing unpunished' (*CSP dom.*, 1611–18, 203). When the king heard of his actions he ordered Isaac Casaubon to ask him to return and it has been suggested that Carier was offered inducements, possibly promotion to the see of Lincoln. Instead he wrote to the king in Latin via Casaubon in August 1613 and, when the matter became public, wrote an open letter from Liège on 12 December. This became the basis for his *A Treatise Written by Mr Doctour Carier*, perhaps published only after his death. Towards the end of this work he noted 'I have sent you my soule in this Treatize, and if it may find entertainment, and passage, my bodie shal most gladly follow after'. Instead, apparently being of the opinion that he would be put on trial if he did not conform, he never returned to his native land. He accepted an invitation from Cardinal Du Perron to go to Paris, and may have died at the cardinal's residence there. In mid-1614 Sir Henry Wotton reported 'Out of France, we have the death of Dr Carier, whose great imaginations abroad have had but a short period' (Wotton, 438).

Various motivations have been advanced as the grounds for Carier's conversion: disillusionment born of career reverses, hostility to Calvinism, defeat of ecumenical hopes, early sympathies with Roman Catholic teaching, or an instance of one for whom the Church of England 'did not seem to have a place for their concept of evangelical zeal' (Questier, 'Crypto-Catholicism', 59). Certainly he later claimed that from about 1590 he had studied church history and the fathers, finding them in opposition to current teaching and practice in the Church of England, particularly on grace, predestination, and the sacraments, which he contrasted with that of the Book of Common Prayer. He alleged a 'Calvinist takeover of an unaligned English church' (Milton, 383) and before his conversion had denounced Calvinism, which he saw as undermining both clergy and monarchy. Instead he emphasized doctrines he believed to have been ever Catholic, and pondered the prospects for peace and unity between the Anglican church and Rome, increasingly regarding divisions as more jurisdictional than theological. His *Treatise* attacked those he considered puritans within the Anglican church but still considered the latter a true church capable of reform, and clung to hopes of reconciliation. Further editions of his *Treatise* were published in 1632, 1649, and 1687 under the titles *A Carrier to a King* and *A Missive to His Majesty of Great-Britain. A Copy of a Letter Written by M. Doctor Carier* was published in 1615.

ANTONY CHARLES RYAN

Sources B. Carier, *A missive to his majesty of Great-Britain … containing the motives of his conversion to the Catholike faith* (1649) • M. Questier, 'Crypto-Catholicism, anti-Calvinism and conversion at the Jacobean court: the enigma of Benjamin Carier', *Journal of Ecclesiastical History*, 47 (1996), 45–64 • C. Dodd [H. Tootell], *The church history of England, from the year 1500, to the year 1688*, 1 (1737), 424 • H. Wotton, *Reliquiae Wottonianae*, 4th edn (1685), 438 • *Catholic Miscellany*, 5 (1826) • *Fasti Angl., 1541–1857*, [St Paul's, London], 54 • Boughton Monchelsea, St Peter's Church: list of vicars, Canterbury Cathedral Archives, Frampton collection CCA U108/3 • A. C. W. Ryan, *The monastery and palace of St. Augustine, 597–1997* (1997), 9 • treasurers' accounts, Canterbury Cathedral, 1542–1751, new foundation, treasurer 9 and miscellaneous accounts 41, Canterbury Cathedral Archives, CCA DCc/TA9; CCA DCc/MA 41 1575–1643 • Venn, *Alum. Cant.*, 1/1.297 • Foster, *Alum. Oxon.* • *CSP dom., 1611–18*, 203 • parish register, St Peter's, Boughton Monchelsea, Kent, 6 Jan 1565 [baptism] • N. Tyacke, *Anti-Calvinists: the rise of English Arminianism, c.1590–1640* (1987) • A. Milton, *Catholic and Reformed: the Roman and protestant churches in English protestant thought, 1600–1640* (1995) • M. C. Questier, *Conversion, politics and religion in England, 1580–1625* (1996) • *DNB* • *Report on the manuscripts of the marquis of Downshire*, 6 vols. in 7, HMC, 75 (1924–95), vol. 4, p. 417

Archives Trinity Cam., 'A treatise written for the use of Prince Henry. Ad Christianum Sapientiam brevis Introductio' | BL, Harley MS 7035, p. 189

Carkeet, Samuel (*d.* 1746), Presbyterian minister and theological writer, was one of six children born to Nicholas Carkeet (*bap.* 1646, *d.* in or before 1711), yeoman, of St Ewe and Pelynt, Cornwall, and Mary, his wife. Although recorded in the Pelynt registers as a dissenter in 1704, his father held local office there as way warden (1695–7) and overseer of the poor (1699). Samuel Carkeet was probably educated for the nonconformist ministry by Joseph Hallett II, and he was examined as a candidate and licensed to preach in September 1705 by the Exeter Assembly. He supplied Bodmin from 1707, initially for one year, and there he was ordained on 19 July 1710, with James Strong, subsequently of Ilminster, Somerset. Shortly afterwards he was chosen by the Lower Meeting of Totnes, Devon, as their pastor in succession to the recently deceased Samuel Mullins (1677–1710). According to the 'Evans list', he had a congregation of 350 hearers in 1715.

On 10 June 1713 at St Neot's, Cornwall, Carkeet married Mary Flamank (*bap.* 1692, *d.* 1733) of nearby Boscarne, Bodmin. Her father, William Flamank (1663–1740), was a prominent dissenter in Bodmin whose house in Boscarne had been registered as a public meeting-house on 2 October 1694. The family were probably cloth merchants, and one of her brothers, Samuel, was engaged in the wool trade in Totnes. Her father and her brother William initially put out Mary's marriage portion of £200 at interest, but a bond dated 29 August 1724 indicates that the trust was then transferred to Carkeet because of his 'provident care and affectionate love' for his wife and their son, Samuel (*bap.* 1719, *d.* 1731) (Cornwall RO, AD 103/133/30–31). Following Mary's death—she was buried in Totnes on 1 July 1733—Carkeet on 24 August 1736 married by licence, at Bodmin, Jane May (*d.* 1780?), daughter of William May, merchant, of Bodmin and his wife, Margaret Lugger of Tredethy, Cornwall. This marriage appears to have been childless.

The Exeter controversy over the orthodoxy of a number of the city's younger ministers destroyed the doctrinal accord of old dissent. A majority of the ministers at the Exeter Assembly in September 1718 decided that a declaration on the Trinity should be made by the ministers present, but Carkeet was one of several who refused. He was subsequently accused of Arianism, to which he responded with a vigorously argued repudiation, subsequently published as *Gospel Worthiness Stated; in a Sermon Preach'd at Exon at the Young Men's Lecture, 7 May* 1719. In blunt and trenchant language he protested that he was 'as far from being an Arian as he could be without being a Tritheist or a Sabellian', but maintained that Christian worth is independent of speculative opinions and argued against any unscriptural tests (Wright, 2.2).

Carkeet continued as pastor at Totnes for thirty-six years. During his ministry the Lower Meeting built a meeting-house, the trust deed for which is dated 29 August 1724. In 1741 he also published *An Essay on the Conversion of St. Paul, as Implying a Change of his Moral Character*, which argued against Henry Grove's view that the change was simply one of opinion. Carkeet died on 17 June 1746 and was buried at Totnes two days later. Dissent had markedly declined in the aftermath of the Exeter controversy and Carkeet's death prompted the merger of the smaller Higher Meeting at Totnes with the Lower Meeting under the co-pastorship of Hancock and Reynell. Similarly, by the time of the bishop's queries of 1744–5 the meeting-house at Boscarne was recorded as being disused owing to the few adherents then remaining.

Carkeet's will, dated 8 October 1741 and proved in the archdeaconry of Totnes on 10 July 1746, named his brother Nathaniel Carkeet (1689–1760) of East Looe, Cornwall, as his executor and included his sisters, Mary and Hannah, and his nieces and nephews as beneficiaries. His second wife, Jane Carkeet, probably died in 1780 when administration was granted to her brother, William May, as next of kin.

PATRICK WOODLAND

Sources Cornwall RO, AD 103/133, 30–31 [parish registers, St Neots and Bodmin; Flamank family papers; Carkeet to Flamank 29

Aug 1724] • parish register, Totnes, Devon RO • J. Maclean, *The parochial and family history of the deanery of Trigg Minor in the county of Cornwall*, 1 (1873) • E. Bryant, enquiries re: 'Stephen Carkeet' and 'Carkeet of St Ewe, Pelynt and St-Martins-by-Looe', *Devon and Cornwall Notes and Queries*, 13 (1924–5), 349–51 • E. Bryant, enquiries re: 'Stephen Carkeet' and 'Carkeet of St Ewe, Pelynt and St-Martins-by-Looe', *Devon and Cornwall Notes and Queries*, 15 (1928–9), 297–301 • G. C. B. Davies, *The early Cornish evangelicals, 1735–60* (1951) • E. Windeatt, 'Early nonconformity in Totnes', *Report and Transactions of the Devonshire Association*, 32 (1900), 412–30 • A. Brockett, *Nonconformity in Exeter, 1650–1875* (1962) • A. Warne, *Church and society in eighteenth century Devon* • *N&Q*, 9th ser., 3 (1899), 56, 116 • *N&Q*, 148 (1925), 206, 267 • W. H. K. Wright, ed., *The western antiquary*, 2 (1882), 2, 8 • J. Evans, 'List of dissenting congregations and ministers in England and Wales, 1715–1729', DWL, MS 38.4, 26 • A. Brockett, ed., *The Exeter assembly: the minutes of the assemblies of the United Brethren of Devon and Cornwall, 1691–1717*, Devon and Cornwall RS, new ser., 6 (1963), 58, 64, 72, 79, 83, 136 • *DNB* • parish registers, baptism, 26 April 1646, St Ewe, Cornwall [Nicholas Carkeet]

Archives Cornwall RO, Flamank MSS, one letter signed by Carkeet, AD 103/133, 30–31

Carkesse, James (*b. c.*1636), poet, of Hackney, Middlesex, was the son of James Carkesse, a Turkey merchant, and Mary Beresford. In 1679 he published a volume entitled *Lucida intervalla* (period of respite and clarity) which is perhaps the first instance of poetry written and published by an inmate of an asylum: Carkesse was confined at Finsbury and at Bethlem Hospital (Bedlam) for about six months in 1678. *Lucida intervalla* is a valuable record of late seventeenth-century practice regarding the confinement of the mentally ill and an individual's reaction to it. His committal was the final stage in the demise of a career which began promisingly. He was educated at Westminster School, was elected in 1652 to a scholarship at Christ Church, Oxford, obtaining his BA in 1657 and MA in 1659, and later elected FRS in 1664. His early career included employment as instructor in grammar at Magdalen College School commencing in 1656, usher there 1662–3 (or slightly later), and headmaster 1663–4. His last school employment was as headmaster of Chelmsford School in 1683.

In 1666 Carkesse was employed as clerk to William Brouncker in the Navy Office. There he made the acquaintance of Samuel Pepys, but was dismissed from his post for a misdemeanour. His work at the ticket office involved paying off discharged seamen, though they were paid only in negotiable notes to be redeemed when funds allowed, which did little to ameliorate the condition of men who were already destitute; they rioted, badly beating Carkesse. Speculators made easy prey of the seamen who, being desperate, exchanged the notes for a fraction of their supposed value. Carkesse himself was implicated in this fraud and Pepys's investigation revealed Carkesse's involvement in this, and also that he had accepted bribes. Though he was brought before the duke of York on 8 March 1667, and found guilty, his powerful friends in the House of Commons, including Sir Edward Turnor, the speaker, were able to have him reinstated, and he continued his employment until 1672–3. He spent a period under the patronage of Edward Seymour, speaker from 1673 to 1678 and holder of several significant navy posts between 1672 and 1679.

It was after his period with the Navy Office that Carkesse believed himself to be on a religious mission against dissenters, disturbing gatherings and, as he saw it, the work of the devil: dissenters and Jesuits alike were condemned by Carkesse. Whether Carkesse was incarcerated for a specific offence is difficult to determine, though the poems refer to claims of unpaid bills later settled by friends. Though he refers to himself as 'parson' in the poems, it is doubtful if he was ever ordained. Neither is it clear whether he joined the Roman Catholic church as stated in the *Dictionary of National Biography*.

The poems of *Lucida intervalla* are by turns defiant and appreciative. The poetic language is infused with the wider public hysteria concerning the first of the popish plots, and mixes biblical and classical reference, frequently creating arresting classical allusions to lunacy in the characters of Luna and Phoebus. Carkesse condemns the cruel practices of the day meted out in the name of a cure for his insanity—the purges, vomits, bloodletting, and occasional beatings—though he is grateful for the gifts of food, money, and clothes received from visitors. Most of the irony and scorn are reserved for 'the Doctor', both an actual physician (Thomas Allen) and a metonym for the apparatus of the asylum, the porters, keepers, and surgeons, and their bid to cure him of 'lampoon', itself a metaphor for classical wit (that is, superior intelligence). At one point he refers to himself as 'self-curing poet' denying that the punishment and regression treatment (being fed on milk to restore him to a childlike state) had any effect. Yet he was lucky to have been in the care of the forward-looking Allen, who refused to allow his patients to be the subjects of quackery or barbaric experiments. The strongly defiant tone of his work clearly resembles that of William Blake and both poets maintain their goal of persuading a public of the validity of their world views and personal integrity. Carkesse is by no means an apologist nor minor in the sense of being derivative.

NICHOLAS JAGGER

Sources [J. Carkesse], *Lucida intervalla*, ed. M. V. Deporte (1979) • *Old Westminsters* • Foster, *Alum. Oxon.*, 1500–1714 [James Carkes] • Pepys, *Diary*, vol. 10

Carkett, Robert (*d.* **1780**), naval officer, seems to have entered the navy in 1734 as able seaman on the *Exeter*. In her, and afterwards in the sloops *Grampus* and *Alderney*, he served in that capacity for upwards of four years, when he was appointed midshipman to the *Plymouth*, at that time in the Mediterranean Fleet. He remained in her for nearly five years, during the latter part of the time under the command of Captain George Rodney. He passed his examination on 18 July 1743, sailed for the East Indies in the *Deptford* in May 1744, was made lieutenant in the following February, and returned to England in September 1746. During the rest of the war he served in the frigate *Surprize*, and in March 1755 he was appointed to the *Monmouth* (64 guns) which, after a spell in the channel, was sent out to the Mediterranean under the command of Captain Arthur Gardiner in early 1757. In 1758 the squadron under Vice-Admiral Henry Osborn was blockading Cartagena. On the evening of 28 February the *Monmouth* chased the French ship *Foudroyant* (80 guns) out of sight of the squadron, and single-handedly brought her to action. About nine o'clock Gardiner fell mortally wounded, and the command devolved on Carkett as first lieutenant, who continued the fight. Both ships had been beaten nearly to a standstill, when the *Swiftsure* (70 guns) came up about one o'clock in the morning, forcing *Foudroyant's* surrender. Carkett was immediately promoted to command the French ship, and a few days later he was appointed to the *Revenge*, which he took to England. His post rank was dated 12 March 1758, and he continued in command of the *Revenge*, in the Downs, until the following February. He was then appointed to the frigate *Hussar*, and commanded her at home and in the West Indies until 23 May 1762 when, the ship having struck on a reef off Cape Français of St Domingo, her officers and men became prisoners of war. Carkett and the other officers were sent to England on parole in June, but he was not exchanged until the following December. In August 1763 he commissioned the *Active*, which he commanded in the West Indies, and most of the time at Pensacola, Florida, until June 1767, when, on returning to England, she was paid off at Chatham. In July 1769 he commissioned the *Lowestoft*, and again spent the greater part of the time at Pensacola, where his duties included the promotion of the settlement's welfare and food supplies. This was interrupted for a short time in 1770 by the death of Commodore Arthur Forrest, whereupon Carkett undertook the duties of senior officer at Jamaica. On being superseded he returned to Pensacola, and remained there for the next three years. The *Lowestoft* was paid off in May 1773.

In November 1778 Carkett was appointed to command the *Stirling Castle* (64 guns), and in December he sailed for the West Indies in the squadron under Commodore Joshua Rowley. In the following summer Carkett took part in the action off Grenada (6 July 1779), and on 17 April 1780 he led the line in the action to leeward of Martinique. Debate surrounds Carkett's conduct in this action. Rodney was highly critical of someone whom he clearly considered an inexperienced tactician, a line adopted by John Laughton. Rodney certainly had a clever scheme to concentrate on part of the enemy line by an unorthodox manoeuvre. However, the failure of this proposal owed more to the inadequacy of the signal book than Carkett's lack of ability. Indeed, in order to carry out Rodney's devised manoeuvre, Carkett would have been required to disobey one of the signals flown by his superior. Carkett's unwillingness to do so was not surprising given that Rodney was notorious for breaking the careers of those who showed initiative when under his command.

After the action Rodney wrote to the Admiralty informing them that Carkett's conduct had been responsible for the failure of 17 April. This clause of Rodney's letter was not published in the *Gazette*, but Carkett learned from England that something of the sort had been sent. He accordingly wrote to Rodney desiring to see that part of it which related to him. 'All the satisfaction I received', he complained to the secretary of the Admiralty on 23 July 1780, 'was his acknowledgement that he had informed

their lordships that I had not properly obeyed his signals in attacking the enemy's rear' (Beatson, 6.222). Rodney sent another letter to Carkett on 30 July in which, in response to the latter's complaint of 23 July, he attacked Carkett in direct and violent terms (Spinney, 330–31). It is unknown whether Carkett ever received this, for the *Stirling Castle*, which had been sent to Jamaica and from there ordered home with the trade, was totally lost on the Silver Keys, north of Cap François, in a violent hurricane on 5 October. All on board perished, with the exception of a midshipman and four seamen. There is no record of Carkett's marriage, but in August 1760, then a widower, he left provision in his will of £3000 for a daughter, Mary, who at that date was not yet twenty-one, and a son, Robert, was made residual legatee (PRO, PROB 11/1081, fol. 318).

J. K. LAUGHTON, *rev.* NICHOLAS TRACY

Sources J. Charnock, ed., *Biographia navalis*, 6 (1798), 300 · will, PRO, PROB 11/1081, fol. 318 · D. Spinney, *Rodney* (1969) · PRO, passing certificate, ADM 107/3, 501 · R. Beatson, *Naval and military memoirs of Great Britain*, 2nd edn, 6 (1804), 222
Archives PRO, passing certificate, ADM 107/3, 501 · PRO, state papers, 30/20, 20/11, 21/11

Carleill, Christopher (1551?–1593), soldier and naval commander, was the second son, but heir, of Alexander Carleill (*d.* 1561), merchant, of London, and his wife, Anne (*d.* 1565), daughter of Sir George *Barne, lord mayor of London, and his wife, Alice. Anne later married Sir Francis Walsingham, Elizabeth I's principal secretary. There were three strands to the weave of Carleill's career: military service, naval service, and mercantile voyaging. During the reign of Elizabeth I soldiers had to be able to fight at sea and sailors had to be able to fight on land. Once a soldier had served at sea he might easily become involved in other voyages. The state of national finances in this era meant that it was useful for soldiers to have mercantile contacts to help cover the costs of warfare—this, too, might lead to commercial ventures. Yet often these, in turn, needed armed protection. Therefore, men frequently acted as soldiers, naval officers, and merchants and one role often blurred into another. Carleill typified this.

Carleill was educated at the University of Cambridge and then admitted to Lincoln's Inn, but his stay at the inns of court was probably brief. His taste was more adventurous. In 1573 he joined the regiment led by Thomas Morgan to the Netherlands to aid the Dutch revolt against Spain. Morgan took his regiment home in autumn 1573 after a dispute with the Dutch over unpaid wages, but Carleill stayed at his own expense and 'accompanied' the Dutch army which blockaded Middelburg (*Works of Sir Roger Williams*, 148). He distinguished himself in the fighting on inland waterways which led to the capture of the capital of Zeeland.

Carleill remained in Dutch service until 1577, when, with the Low Countries briefly at peace, he fought for the Huguenots in the sixth war of religion in France. English ships and troops sailed from Wales, the west country, and the Netherlands: it was perhaps among the latter that Carleill travelled to France. They joined in the fighting against a major Catholic offensive to capture the approaches to La Rochelle, but though the fortress of Brouage was taken, the key isle of Ré was held, thanks partly to English efforts led by Carleill and John Norris.

Peace was made and Carleill returned home. He worked for his stepfather but hostilities resumed in the Low Countries in 1578; at first just a witness of events when carrying letters for Walsingham, in 1580 Carleill returned to active service as second in command to Norris. In 1580–81 they campaigned in Friesland. Carleill's comrades thought highly of his 'minde, prowes … [and] pollicy, attayned by learning and study' (Blandy, 24*v*), while his courage and skill also won him a reputation at home. However, pay was still a vexed issue, as in 1573. In April 1580 Carleill requested reimbursement of over 5000 guilders from the states of Holland for expenditure on ammunition, while that autumn the merchant George Hoddesdon reported to Walsingham that Carleill owed £100 to English merchants in Antwerp. In 1581 Carleill returned to England, but contesting claims for money were still the subject of dispute in early 1584.

The merchants of the Muscovy Company (co-founded by Carleill's grandfather) required an escort to Russia in 1582 because of war between Ivan IV of Russia and Frederick II of Denmark. Thanks to his family connections and experience at sea Carleill was appointed commander of a squadron of eleven ships. He successfully held off a Danish fleet and returned with a Russian envoy to Elizabeth. Over the next two years he tried to raise money from the Muscovy merchants for a proposed plantation in North America, south-west of Cape Breton Island. He had a promise of £1000 from the Bristol merchant community, but in the end his plans came to nothing. In the meantime Carleill patrolled the British coasts, with some of the queen's ships and some of his own, which attacked Catholic shipping; he was accused of crossing the boundary from privateering into piracy, but this charge was false.

In 1584 Carleill was appointed commander of Coleraine in Ulster, but even in royal service he had problems with being paid and was recalled in 1585, after venomous quarrels with Sir John Perrot, lord deputy. England was now openly at war with Spain and, through the influence of his stepfather, Carleill was appointed by Sir Francis Drake, Walsingham's friend and fellow 'hot protestant', as lieutenant-general of the land forces in his forthcoming expedition to the West Indies. Carleill won distinction in the fighting around San Domingo. The desecration of Catholic churches in the town after its capture was probably due to the Calvinists Carleill and Drake. On reaching home in July 1586, however, Carleill found payment of his share of the profits slow in forthcoming. In May 1587 he was still claiming £400 (and only received £280).

Carleill did not go with Drake on his famous raid on Cadiz in 1587. Instead, that year he was appointed governor of the important fortress of Carrickfergus, co. Antrim. Due to the opposition of Perrot, he was only able to take up his post in 1588, having in the interim carried out a mission for Walsingham in Scotland. In summer of 1588 Perrot was replaced and Carleill took up his place, to which he soon added the governorship of Ulster. As a contemporary observed, Walsingham 'had procured hym a fyne and proffytable gouvernment in Irelande wurthe more than 300 pounds yerly' (LPL, MS 649, fol. 388). However, by this time the debts accrued when pay was not forthcoming were so great that he found this income inadequate. His personal life made this problem all the more pressing, as he had married Mary (*d.* in or after 1596) by 1588. In 1590 he proposed to William Cecil, Lord Burghley, lord treasurer, that the property of Spanish subjects in England be seized, under his supervision, with a share of all the profits derived therefrom to be his. By these means he hoped to restore his fortunes but his suit was not granted.

In 1589 Carleill was sent to Ostend to prepare a report on how its fortifications could be improved and still owned a privateer which raided off the Spanish coast. But by summer 1592, probably in poor health and certainly in poor spirits because of his weak financial position, he was back in England, leaving his Irish offices to a deputy. He and his wife made increasingly desperate appeals for patronage to Burghley and Elizabeth, but to no avail. Carleill died in London on 11 November 1593. The plague was raging but some at the time attributed his death to sorrow because of his debts (a cousin was later noted as melancholic, so depression may have run in the family). Mary, strangely, initially 'renounced the administration of his goods, rights and credits' (Lloyd, 180) but on 17 April 1596 she was granted administration of his estate; it was worth less than £20.

An intelligent man, whose knowledge of mathematics and languages, and literary skill, were remarked on by contemporaries, Carleill was a friend and intellectual sparring partner of Edmund Spenser. He wrote commendatory Latin verses for John Sadler's 1572 translation of the important Roman military author Vegetius. Carleill's own *Brief Summary Discourse upon a Voyage Intending to the Uttermost Parts of America* was later published by Richard Hakluyt (with whom he corresponded), and he grasped the importance of attacking the enemy's commerce as well as its armed forces, proposing to Burghley measures to disrupt 'the trade with … the King of Spaynes subjectes … who dwell at Gaunte, Bruges' and other Walloon cities (BL, Lansdowne MS 113, fol. 25*r*).

Carleill was quick-tempered, yet, as the contemporary historian Petruccio Ubaldino noted, not a 'person who practised rash and ill-considered cruelty'. Despite his hatred of Catholic Spain, he refused to execute survivors of the Spanish Armada who surrendered to him in Ulster in 1588–9, since 'it seemed to him that he should use … pity, and therefore he received them chivalrously without cruelty'. Defying instructions from the new lord deputy, Sir William Fitzwilliam, Carleill at his own expense sent them to Scotland, where they could be safe (Ubaldino, 80–81).

Carleill was physically unprepossessing: fellow soldiers in Friesland in 1580 remarked that 'in feature and limmes' he was 'something inferior to captain Corne', who himself 'was not great of bodye' (Blandy, 23*r*). It cannot have helped that at some stage in his career he lost his left eye. However, his military reputation was always high. An August 1586 'note of things to be presently put in executyon' for the defence of the realm includes 'to send for Capt Carlel' (PRO, SP 12/192/62, fol. 99r); and about the same time he was on the select list of 'marshall men to be presently imploy'd' (BL, Lansdowne MS 113, fol. 148r). In June 1589, one of Walsingham's correspondents from Paris proposed 'Mr Carleill were a good man' to lead an English army to aid the Huguenot Henri of Navarre's blockade of Paris (*CSP for., January–July 1589*, 342). On Carleill's death one chronicler remarked on his 'warlike skill', while another wrote: 'he was quicke witted, and affable, valiant and fortunate in warre ... and of good experience in Navigation, whereupon some have Registered him for a Navigator, but the trueth is his most inclination, and profession, was chiefly for lande service' (Camden, 92). It was the obituary Carleill might have chosen.   D. J. B. TRIM

Sources R. Lloyd, *Elizabethan adventurer: a life of Captain Christopher Carleill* (1974) • *The works of Sir Roger Williams*, ed. J. X. Evans (1972) • W. Blandy, *The castle, or, Picture of pollicy* (1581) • *CSP for., 1577–86; 1589* • *APC, 1587–92* • state papers domestic, Elizabeth, PRO, SP 12/192; SP 12/155; SP 12/231 • administration, PRO, PROB 6/5, fol. 164 • Nationaal Archief, The Hague, 15 • BL, Lansdowne MSS 64, 100, 113 • LPL, MS 649 • W. Camden, *The historie of the life and reigne of that famous princesse, Elizabeth: ... since the yeare of the fatall Spanish invasion, to that of her sad and ever to be deplored dissolution*, trans. T. Browne (1629) • P. Ubaldini, 'The Spanish Armada', ed. G. P. B. Naish, *The naval miscellany*, 4, Navy RS, 92 (1952) • M. J. D. Cockle, *A bibliography of military books up to 1642*, 2nd edn (1957); repr. (1978) • Venn, *Alum. Cant.*
Archives BL, Lansdowne MSS, treatises, MSS 64, 100, 113 • PRO, state papers, Holland and Holland and Flanders, letters, SP 83, SP 84 • PRO, state papers Irish, letters • PRO, state papers domestic, treatises on colonizing America, SP 12/155, fols. 87–8
Likenesses R. Boissard, line engraving, NPG; repro. in Lloyd, *Elizabethan adventurer*, facing p. 66 • Passe, line engraving, repro. in H. Holland, *Heröologia Anglica* (1620)
Wealth at death debts may have exceeded amount left (which was certainly not much): Lloyd, *Elizabethan adventurer*, 180; administration, PRO, PROB 6/5, fol. 164 • Irish office valued at £300 p.a.

Carleill [**Carliell**], **Robert** (*fl.* 1619), poet, is the author of *Britaines Glorie, or, An Allegoricall Dreame with the Exposition Thereof* (1619), in which he describes himself as a gentleman. The work consists of forty-two six-line stanzas followed by a prose exposition. This poem is a polemic which attacks the religions of the Middle East, Roman Catholicism, and protestant schismatics: they are 'odious blasphemies' like:

> that stinking weede Tabacco. For as Tabacco being suckt into the mouth, causeth men to evacuate a noysome choaking smoake, and maketh the body of Man black and uncleane within: so doth their profession and their faith in their Religion make their soules black, and cause filthy blasphemies to come out of their mouthes. (*Britaines Glorie*, 9)

In contrast 'within this Land of great Britaine ... the Gospell of Jesus Christ ... doth plentifully abound' (ibid., 19). Carleill is fiercely monarchist and totally partisan towards the Church of England. The author might be Robert Carleill, citizen and leatherseller of London,

whose will of 9 October 1622 left a legacy to his son, also Robert, despite their being estranged. The elder Robert Carleill had a wife, Frances, and, at one time, owned property in Bell Alley, in St Botolph without Bishopsgate.

SIDNEY LEE, *rev.* REAVLEY GAIR

Sources N. Carlisle, *Collections for a history of the ancient family of Carlisle* (1822), 373–4

Carlell [**Carlile**], **Lodowick** (1601/2–1675), courtier and playwright, was born in Brydekirk, Dumfriesshire, the son of Herbert Carlell (1558–1632), laird of Brydekirk, and Margaret Cunningham. Carlell's childhood was probably spent in Brydekirk. Only a fragment of the family homestead remains. Nothing is known of his education, although his plays' reworking of plot lines from French and Spanish drama indicates linguistic talents.

By 1626 Carlell appears to have been resident in London, where on 11 July, aged twenty-four, he married Joan Palmer [*see* Carlile, Joan (*c.*1606–1679)]. By 1630 he held a number of court offices. In the early 1630s he was a groom of the privy chamber, and huntsman and master of the bows as well as keeper of the royal hounds. Between 1631 and 1637 he was yeoman-harrier and by 1637 was appointed one of two keepers in the royal deer park at Richmond. Carlell took up residence in the lodge at Petersham within the park grounds. It is clear from one of his plays that this was a role he relished: the prologue to *The Passionate Lovers* declares:

> Most here knows
> This author hunts and hawks and feeds his Deer,
> Not some, but most fair days, throughout the year.

Professing himself an amateur, Carlell wrote several plays during the period of his court service. *The Deserving Favourite* was printed in 1629. First acted before the king, it was subsequently staged at the Blackfriars Theatre. *Arviragus and Philicia*, published in two parts in 1639, was revived in 1672 with a new prologue by Dryden. The two parts of *The Passionate Lovers* were published in 1655 and *The Fool would be a Favourite* with *Osmond the Turk* as *Two New Playes* in 1657. Carlell also wrote a comedy, no longer extant, entitled *The Spartan Ladies*, named in Humphrey Moseley's catalogue of plays at the end of his edition of Middleton's *More Dissemblers besides Women* in 1657. A play of that title was entered on the Stationers' register on 5 September 1640 and appears to have been produced as early as 1634 (indicated by an entry in Sir Humfrey Mildmay's diary). In 1631 Thomas Dekker dedicated his play *Match mee in London* to Carlell.

After the Restoration, Carlell translated Corneille's *Héraclius* as *Heraclius, Emperour of the East*; it was never performed. He dedicated this work in 1664 to the queen mother, an indication of his continued royalism. According to a petition by his niece Eleanor Carlisle, he did not join the king's army during the civil war but gave financial aid to the tune of £1500. He did not go into exile like many, preferring to stay in England. While there are no firm records for him between 1649 and 1660 it is possible that he remained at the lodge in Richmond throughout that time. Certainly, at the Restoration he was granted a pension of £200 per annum and a grant to keep the lodge and its attendant rights of common.

In 1663 the keepership was sold. After this Carlell resided in St Martin-in-the-Fields, London. He died there in 1675 and was buried at Petersham, Richmond, on 21 August 1675. His wife died in 1679; her will indicates that Carlell was still owed £1400 by the crown at his death. Carlell's plays have not gained much attention since their own time, but are solid examples of Caroline courtier drama, their complex plot lines echoing the 1630s vogue for pastoral and romance.   JULIE SANDERS

Sources C. H. Gray, *Lodowick Carliell: his life* (1905) · A. Harbage, *Cavalier drama: an historical and critical supplement to the study of the Elizabethan and Restoration stage* (1936) · K. Sharpe, *Criticism and compliment* (1987) · L. Carlell, *The passionate lovers* (1655) · *The original diary of Sir Humfrey Mildmay of Danbury*, BL, Harleian MSS 454 · *DNB*
Wealth at death in arrears of pension of £1400: Gray, *Lodowick Carliell*, 177

Carleton. For this title name *see* individual entries under Carleton; *see also* Boyle, Henry, Baron Carleton (1669–1725).

Carleton, Billie [*real name* Florence Leonora Stewart] (1896–1918), actress and singer, was born on 4 September 1896 at Bernard Street, off Russell Square, Bloomsbury, London, the daughter of Margaret Stewart, chorus singer; her father is unknown. She was claimed to have both French and Irish antecedents.

There was something of a fairy quality about Carleton, who was often described by contemporaries as being hardly of this world. Such an incarnation emphasized the brevity of her existence, and provided a stark contrast to her sordid end. Like her fellow actress Meggie Albanesi (who died of a botched abortion in 1923, aged twenty-four), Carleton was seen as an innocent victim of a desperate time. However, witnesses were divided over whether nature or nurture was to blame for her apparently addictive persona. The impresario C. B. Cochran claimed in his memoirs, *Secrets of a Showman* (1925), that 'her childhood had given her a positive fear of alcohol … Billie Carleton never had a chance against heredity' (Cochran, 210).

Carleton was brought up by her aunt Catherine Joliffe, who claimed that both of her parents were dead. According to Cochran, Carleton was 'well read, she spoke French and German, and was an excellent pianist' (Cochran, 210). But at fifteen she left home for the stage. Cochran gave Carleton her first major role in his 1914 Empire Theatre revue *Watch your Step*, promoting her from the chorus. 'Despite her inexperience and her tiny voice, she pleased the audiences. A more beautiful creature has never fluttered upon a stage. She seemed scarcely human, so fragile was she' (ibid., 209). Carleton's 'little girl lost' looks were counterpointed by her evident glamour, and she quickly took to the hectic life of the theatre during wartime. But the dizzying gloss of fashion, celebrity, and a certain adoration encouraged transitory pleasures. During the run of *Watch your Step* Cochran was told that Carleton 'was being influenced by some undesirable people and was going to opium parties' (ibid.). The impresario fired her.

John Marsh, Carleton's patron and her senior by twenty years, had introduced her to a life of luxury. She had a flat in Savile Row, and at one point a bank balance of over £5000, although she would never earn more than £25 a week; her money was managed by Frederick Stuart, a Knightsbridge physician. The third man in Carleton's life was Reggie de Veulle, a Bond Street theatrical costumier and dress designer whose diaphanous creations she modelled. But de Veulle was also a drug user—although Stuart claimed Carleton had been introduced to opium by Jack May, proprietor of Murray's Club, one of the 150 nightclubs to spring up in Soho during the war. There is an underlying sense that Carleton used these men as much as she was herself used.

Cochran gave Carleton a second chance in *Hoop-La* at the St Martin's Theatre in November 1916, but her performance was disappointing. Andre Charlot stepped in, engaging Carleton in the revue *Some* (*More Samples!*), which was running at the Vaudeville Theatre. The *Tatler's* critic observed on 26 September 1917: 'If only her singing and speaking voice were a little stronger I could see a very brilliant future for Miss Carleton in musical comedy' (Kohn, 74). In *The Boy* at the Adelphi in August 1917, Carleton played Joy Chatterton, a night-club flapper, a type becoming notorious in wartime London. In May 1918 she appeared in *Fair and Warmer*, a Broadway farce at the Prince of Wales's, playing a maid to Fay Compton's flapper. In August she played Phyllis Harcourt in *The Freedom of the Seas*, a comic adventure at the Haymarket, making her the youngest leading lady in the West End. But her public successes were counterpointed by a tempestuous private life.

The inquest court would later hear how Carleton and de Veulle held opium parties at the latter's flat in Dover Street, 'disgusting orgies' during which Ada Ping You, Scottish wife of their Limehouse supplier, would arrive to cook the opium:

> After dinner the party … provided themselves with cushions and pillows, placed these on the floor, and sat themselves in a circle. The men divested themselves of their clothing and got into pyjamas, and the women into chiffon nightdresses … Miss Carleton arrived later at the flat from the theatre, and she, after disrobing, took her place in this circle of degenerates. (*The Times*, 14 Dec 1918)

For the victory ball at the Albert Hall on Saturday 27 November 1918, Carleton commissioned an outfit (representing France) from de Veulle; as it was to be a 'dry' event, she also ordered some cocaine for the occasion. Having dined with Fay Compton, Carleton arrived at the ball escorted by Dr Stuart, and met Lionel Belcher (an actor and heroin addict who was supplying de Veulle), who had a silver box of cocaine for Carleton, given to him in the gentlemen's lavatory by de Veulle. Carleton, Belcher, and a friend returned to Carleton's flat at the Savoy Court in the early hours of Sunday morning, where Carleton changed into a kimono; having breakfasted, the friends left. At 10 a.m. she rang a friend. At 11.30 a.m. Carleton's maid arrived for work, and found her mistress snoring. At 3.30 the snoring stopped. The maid tried to wake

Carleton, and called for Dr Stuart. He administered artificial respiration and an injection of brandy and strychnine, to no avail.

The inquest into Carleton's death, held through December and January, provided newspapers with thrilling details of the actress's tragic end. As supplier of the cocaine on which she overdosed, de Veulle was found guilty of manslaughter and sentenced to six months' imprisonment. But as Marek Kohn convincingly demonstrates in *Dope Girls: the Birth of the British Drug Underground* (1992), depressants taken to calm her cocaine hangover were a more likely cause of death.

The case made drugs a contemporary issue, not only in the press (*The Times* pursued an anti-drugs campaign in the wake of the affair), but in the theatre: within a year there were at least three plays with drug themes running in the West End; and in the cinema, D. W. Griffith's film *Broken Blossoms* (1919) threw Lillian Gish into a Limehouse opium den. In 1924 Noël Coward, who had known both Carleton and de Veulle, acknowledged the story as inspiration for his *The Vortex*, a *succès de scandale* which featured a cocaine-taking protagonist. By then Billie Carleton had become a symbol of the drug-threatened and wronged female abused by older, usually foreign, men; behind her lurked the spectre of the opium den and the white slave trade. The more complicated story of her own manipulativeness was lost in the publicity that surrounded her very public demise.   PHILIP HOARE

Sources *The Times* (30 Nov 1918) · *The Times* (4 Dec 1918) · *The Times* (14 Dec 1918) · *The Times* (21 Dec 1918) · M. Kohn, *Dope girls: the birth of the British drug underground* (1992) · C. B. Cochran, *Secrets of a showman* (1925) · J. P. Wearing, *The London stage, 1910–1919: a calendar of plays and players*, 2 vols. (1982) · P. Hoare, *Noël Coward: a biography* (1995) · P. Hoare, *Wilde's last stand: decadence, conspiracy and the First World War* (1997) · J. Parker, ed., *Who's who in the theatre*, 10th edn (1947) · S. Heppner, *Cockie* (1969) · T. Parssinen, *Secret passions, secret remedies* (1983) · *CGPLA Eng. & Wales* (1919) · b. cert. · d. cert.
Likenesses photograph, NPG · photograph, Mansell Collection, London · photograph, Jerwood Library of the Performing Arts, London, Mander and Mitchenson Theatre Collection · photograph, BL; repro. in *The Sketch* (11 Dec 1918) · photograph, BL; repro. in *The Sketch* (24 Jan 1919) · photograph, ILN picture library; repro. in *The Tatler* (16 Feb 1915)
Wealth at death £1374 18s. 7d.: administration, 11 Sept 1919, *CGPLA Eng. & Wales*

Carleton, Dudley, Viscount Dorchester (1574–1632), diplomat and letter writer, was born on 10 March 1574, the second son of Antony Carleton of Brightwell Baldwin, Oxfordshire, and his second wife, Jocosa, daughter of John Goodwin of Winchington, Buckinghamshire. Educated first at Westminster School under William Camden, Carleton then gained a scholarship to Christ Church, Oxford; he matriculated in 1592 and graduated BA in 1595. As a younger son of lesser gentry he needed employment, and after graduating he travelled and lived intermittently on the continent, adding to his classical education a knowledge of continental languages, especially French, and seeking a diplomatic appointment. In 1598 he became secretary to the governor of Ostend, Sir Edward Norris, but he returned to England on several occasions and proceeded MA in 1600. In 1602 he became secretary to Sir

Dudley Carleton, Viscount Dorchester (1574–1632), by Michiel Janszoon van Miereveldt, *c*.1620

Thomas Parry, ambassador to France, but was unhappy, and in 1603 he became controller of the household to Henry Percy, ninth earl of Northumberland, employment bringing contact with the court and leading to election to parliament as MP for St Mawes in 1604. Carleton made his name in the Commons as a government supporter, opposing the Commons' *Apology*, but parliamentary politics was not his world. In 1605 he was admitted to Gray's Inn, but the same year accompanied the young Lord Norris to Spain in Nottingham's embassy for the ratification of the Anglo-Spanish peace, as well as being inadvertently implicated in the Gunpowder Plot and consequently imprisoned in the Tower. As a servant of the Percys he had unwittingly played a role in leasing the vault for storage of the gunpowder. Readily convinced of his innocence, Robert Cecil, earl of Salisbury, authorized his release and readmission to parliament. The episode affected Carleton for the rest of his life, encouraging his natural caution, and hindering his advancement for some years. In November 1607 Carleton married Anne, Lady Tredway (*née* Gerard; 1585/6–1627), the widowed stepdaughter of Sir Henry *Savile (1549–1622), provost of Eton. Carleton assisted Savile with his edition of St Chrysostom and was active in parliament, supporting the great contract, while still hoping for a diplomatic career.

Carleton's breakthrough came in 1610, when, assisted by Salisbury, he was knighted and appointed ambassador to Venice, where he remained for five years. The appointment boosted his career but was uncongenial. He was a protestant in a Catholic state, his Italian was imperfect, and he was often bored. Yet as an orthodox late Elizabethan he came to respect the Venetian republic which was anti-papal and anti-Habsburg. His Italian sojourn ended with a substantial achievement, the mediation of peace between Spain and Savoy, concluded at Asti in 1615. Promoted to the embassy at The Hague, Carleton came into his own. He disliked the disorder of Dutch republican politics, but the post had advantages. Representing a relatively powerful state he was an *ex officio* member of the Dutch council of state, he was living among protestants, and he was close to home. Carleton responded to challenges including Anglo-Dutch commercial rivalry, the religious strife in the United Provinces, and the coming of the Thirty Years' War. Influential within the republic his views also carried weight at home and with James I. An orthodox predestinarian Calvinist, believing in the Genevan family of churches, Carleton was a key player at the Synod of Dort (where his cousin George Carleton, bishop of Llandaff, was an English delegate) and in the Dutch Calvinist revolution. Addressing the states general in 1617 he attacked the Arminians and called for a synod, and his speech was widely circulated. He stressed the need for political stability and unity, religious conformity, and the union of church and state—views also reflected in his correspondence with Archbishop George Abbot. Carleton saw schism and faction as an invitation to external enemies: Spain, the Habsburgs, and the Counter-Reformation. He wrote in 1621 of the conquest of Bohemia: 'Thus doth the greatness of the house of Austria and the Catholic League spread itself over all Europe very fearfully to those who are nearest the danger, and who put small confidence in disarmed treaties against armed authority' (PRO, SP 84/100, fol. 148). At The Hague, Carleton became closely associated with the palatine royal refugees, Frederick and Elizabeth of Bohemia, and with the cause of German protestantism. He and Elizabeth were close confidants, and when he left The Hague the palatines considered him their representative in England.

Carleton's professional aim was a secure appointment in England. His hopes of the provostship of Eton were disappointed in the early 1620s, and the secretaryship of state became the goal of his ambition. When the failed Spanish match provoked the duke of Buckingham into war with Spain, Carleton could link his ideological outlook with his ambition. In 1625 he smoothed his way to high office with a gift to Buckingham of valuable statuary. The secretaryship went to Sir John Coke, but when Buckingham went to The Hague to conclude the anti-Habsburg alliance, Carleton made himself indispensable. After returning to England with the duke he was appointed vice-chamberlain and a privy councillor. He became active in policy making councils and high political business. In 1626 he was in France with the earl of Holland, dealing with Cardinal Richelieu and encouraging the inhabitants of La Rochelle to reach agreement with Louis XIII. The treaty was concluded but French engagement in the German war remained elusive.

Returned to parliament as MP for Hastings in 1626

Carleton made a notorious intervention in the Commons as a royal spokesman, warning the house against encroachment on the king's prerogative, lest he adopt 'new counsels'. Carleton contrasted the demise of representative estates in Christian countries with the liberties of the English parliament—still free to offer supply to the king. Charles himself wished to threaten arbitrary measures, but Carleton's was also a personal plea for the survival of parliaments in England, believer as he was in a traditional constitutional harmony. The Commons was horrified, but the same year Carleton was raised to the peerage as Baron Carleton of Imbercourt, and attained the safety of the Lords, where he strengthened the duke's supporters as he faced impeachment. Carleton's warning was prophetic: the king imposed the forced loan. Carleton took a hard line and was involved in its collection. He preferred parliamentary ways, but was dependent on the duke and knew the need for supply.

Early in 1628, again at The Hague on mission, Carleton was told by the earl of Carlisle of the king's intention to appoint him secretary of state. Charles wrote: 'You cannot return sooner than ye shall be welcome', signing himself 'your loving friend' (PRO, SP 84/137, fol. 65r). Carleton was soon a highly valued adviser to Buckingham and the king, being created Viscount Dorchester on 25 July. His preferment reflected the duke's interest in ending the French war, which Dorchester opposed in the interests of the wider anti-Habsburg cause. It was while walking to a peace conference arranged by Dorchester that Buckingham was assassinated. The new viscount lamented the loss of his patron, writing to Elizabeth of Bohemia:

> I am grieved to the very soul, as well for public as private respect, besides the horror of the impious act, which lays a scandal upon our nation, our religion, the profession of a soldier, and the blood of a gentleman. All which concurred in the actor of this tragedy.   (PRO, SP 16/114/17)

Charles appointed Dorchester to the secretaryship on 18 December 1628. Part of a reshuffle which suited Lord Treasurer Richard Weston, this pleased Elizabeth of Bohemia and was arguably a concession to those favouring war with Spain.

After Buckingham's death Dorchester had hopes of the king as a reforming ruler, a monarch who would banish the recent political disorder. In dealing with Charles he had the advantages of a tactful disposition and of shared aesthetic interests. Dorchester was a connoisseur of antiquities and Venetian painting and an associate of Rubens. He had made acquisitions for Charles abroad when the future king was building his collections. Dorchester had the advantage over the other secretary, the elderly Sir John Coke, who lacked a peerage and was a more pedestrian bureaucrat. Quick thinking, worldly, and sophisticated, Dorchester could pursue ideological aims in conjunction with reason of state. There were, however, obstacles to a meeting of minds with Charles, principally in the key areas of religion and foreign policy. While the new king was an innovator Dorchester was a traditionalist who sympathized with the Commons' attack on Arminianism in 1629, with puritan emigration, with the naval strategy of war against Spain in the West Indies, and with the European protestant cause. With the earl of Holland and the third earl of Pembroke he was an advocate of parliamentary supply for war. Dorchester was a court contact for a range of radical protestant and Francophile opinion and activity. His close links to the palatines continued until his death. His friend Sir Thomas Roe was excluded from court after 1630 because of his work as an international protestant lobbyist. Dorchester was related by marriage to the Barringtons and through his cousin Sir Francis Goodwin was linked to the Russells. He was connected to the Holles family and the earl of Warwick, and like Warwick's brother Holland he was part of a circle around the queen. Publicly he retained his optimism as to Charles's intentions longer than did his associates outside the court, such as members of the Providence Island Company, but privately he despaired of the king, the Laudian church, and the Hispanophile policy. Dorchester's was a rearguard action against the clique about the king. He wrote of them to Sir Isaac Wake as 'those he now lives with and whom he doth humour in their erroneous opinions' (PRO, SP 78/89, fol. 343r).

English political events unfolded dramatically in the months following Dorchester's appointment to the secretaryship. He held out hope to Christian IV of Denmark that the next parliamentary session would subsidize his desperately flagging war effort. With Dorchester competing against Weston for influence over foreign policy Charles was hedging his bets between war and peace. Conclusion of the Anglo-French peace suited the outlook of both ministers. The treaty of Susa (1629) made no provision for the Huguenots. Dorchester had not wished them to obstruct an anti-Habsburg crusade. The collapse of the parliamentary session of 1629 was a godsend to Weston and the Spanish faction. The treasurer excluded Dorchester from Rubens's talks in London which opened Anglo-Spanish peace negotiations. Dorchester worked to keep the northern war alive. He promoted Roe's mission to the Baltic in 1629–30 which aided the launching of Gustavus Adolphus's German campaign. Dorchester and Roe recognized the strategic threat to protestantism of Spanish ambitions in the north. At home Dorchester counselled the resummoning of parliament, and drafted the proclamation of March 1629 which officially left the door open. While protecting the royal authority he sought to conciliate both the king and the imprisoned recalcitrant members of parliament, an essentially hopeless task. Dorchester rationalized his fellow travelling for the king's arbitrary rule, writing of Sir Robert Cotton's trial: 'I have seen nothing in his Majesty's courses or commandments which may any ways offend a just mind' (PRO, SP 16/167/44). His frustration at Charles's policies found an outlet in Ireland, where with the earl of Cork he promoted a vigorous anti-Catholic agenda. Abroad Dorchester perceived the strategy of the count-duke of Olivares in seeking to dissolve the Anglo-Dutch alliance, and favoured military pressure on Spain to have the Palatinate restored. Charles, however, concluded the treaty of Madrid (1630), and Dorchester wrote to Elizabeth of Bohemia describing

England as 'this wicked land' (PRO, SP 81/36, fol. 113v). He supported the marquess of Hamilton's expedition to Germany, and when the tide of Gustavus's victories gave hope of a palatine restoration Dorchester promoted Anglo-Swedish talks, which were still in train when he died in London of a fever on 15 February 1632. Charles, however, refused to re-break with Spain, and Dorchester's passing eased the task of the peace lobby who charted the course for the foreign policy of personal rule.

Sir Thomas Roe eulogized Dorchester as one who 'walked rightly in his life, died manly, and Christianly, and rejoiced in and recommended the king of Sweden; and so like a swan sang his own funeral' (PRO, SP 16/211/74). He was buried on 19 February in Westminster Abbey, and with no heir his titles became extinct. His happy first marriage had ended with the sudden death of his wife on 18 April 1627, leaving no surviving children. On 14 June 1630 he had married Anne, widow of Paul Bayning, Viscount Bayning, and daughter of Sir Henry Glemham and Lady Anne Sackville; their daughter, born in June 1632, had died soon afterwards. Although his second wife, who herself died on 10 January 1639, was amply provided for in her own right, Dorchester had not been wealthy. To his nephews (who included Dudley Carleton, agent at The Hague and clerk of the council) and widow he left the family manor of Brightwell and another in Surrey, but his will indicates an estate worth about £600 a year. Dorchester was a successful careerist, preferred essentially for his ability, but not a venal creature or great patron. Although he sought security and accepted minor bribes he did not enrich himself through office. His historical significance lies principally in his conservative role in Caroline politics and in his parts in international affairs, particularly at The Hague. His combination of an ideological temperament with diplomatic and strategic astuteness sets him apart from many contemporaries. His monument is literary and resides in the massive body of papers in the Public Record Office, most notably in his thirty-year exchange of letters with John Chamberlain. Always a voluminous correspondent, with a felicitous style and a reflective scholarly eye, when abroad he was an excellent stimulus for Chamberlain's observations of the Jacobean scene.   L. J. REEVE

Sources *Dudley Carleton to John Chamberlain, 1603–1624: Jacobean letters*, ed. M. Lee (1972) · L. J. Reeve, 'The secretaryship of state of Viscount Dorchester, 1628–32', PhD diss., U. Cam., 1984 · L. J. Reeve, *Charles I and the road to personal rule* (1989) · L. J. Reeve, 'Quiroga's paper of 1631: a missing link in Anglo-Spanish diplomacy during the Thirty Years' War', *EngHR*, 101 (1986), 913–26 · L. J. Reeve, 'Sir Thomas Roe's prophecy of 1629', *BIHR*, 56 (1983), 115–21 · L. J. Reeve, 'Secret alliance and protestant agitation in two kingdoms: the early Caroline background to the Irish rebellion of 1641', *Soldiers, writers and statesmen of the English revolution*, ed. I. Gentles and others (1998) · *The Chamberlain letters*, ed. E. M. Thomson (New York, 1965) · L. L. Peck, *Court patronage and corruption in early Stuart England* (1990) · R. P. Cust, *The forced loan and English politics, 1626–1628* (1987) · M. Nicholls, *Investigating Gunpowder Plot* (1991) · T. Cogswell, *The blessed revolution: English politics and the coming of war, 1621–1624* (1989) · GEC, *Peerage* · will, PRO, PROB 11/161, sig. 46

Archives BL, letter-book, Add. MS 36778 · BL, letter book, Egerton MS 2813 · NYPL, letters [copies] · Yale U., Beinecke L., report from Venice | Berks. RO, Trumbull MSS · BL, letters to Sir

Walter Aston, Add. MSS 36444–36447 · BL, corresp. with Lord Carlisle, Egerton MSS 2592–2596 · BL, letters to Sir Thomas Edmondes, Stowe MSS 167–176, *passim* · BL, letters to Lord Essex, Add. MS 46188 · BL, Harley MSS, papers · Chatsworth House, Derbyshire, earl of Cork's letter-book, Hardwick MS 78 · Melbourne House, Derbyshire, Coke MSS · PRO, State Papers Domestic Elizabeth I, James I, Charles I and State Papers Foreign **Likenesses** M. J. van Miereveldt, oils, *c*.1620, NPG [*see illus.*] · studio of M. J. van Miereveldt, oils, 1625, NPG · oils, NPG; repro. in Lee, ed., *Dudley Carleton*, frontispiece **Wealth at death** approx. £600 p.a. derived from manors in Oxfordshire and Surrey: will, PRO, PROB 11/161, sig. 46

Carleton, George (1529–1590), landowner and puritan, was the second son of John Carleton of Walton-on-Thames, Surrey, and Brightwell Baldwin, Oxfordshire, and his wife, Joyce, daughter of John Welbeck of Oxenheath, Kent. His maternal grandmother was Margaret Culpepper, an aunt of Queen Katherine Howard. Carleton's father was receiver to the abbot of Westminster and later deputy receiver-general to the dean and chapter, a connection which secured his son a Westminster exhibition at Christ Church, Oxford, whence he passed to Gray's Inn in 1552. In 1557 Carleton served as a captain at St Quentin, and later in life he renewed his military career, in 1573, as treasurer to the Irish expedition of Walter Devereux, first earl of Essex. In 1559 Carleton married Audrey, widow of Sir George Harper of Sutton, Kent; but she died early the following year.

Carleton built up a sizeable estate in the eastern and midland counties, partly by inheritance and partly in, 1561, through the second of his three marriages. This was to Elizabeth (*d*. 1587), daughter of Walter Mohun of Overstone, Northamptonshire, and widow of Edward Cope of Hanwell, Oxfordshire. This marriage brought Carleton the manor of Overstone, where he mostly resided. He was a JP in Oxfordshire, Northamptonshire, Lincolnshire, and the Isle of Ely, and he sat in four sessions of parliament: for Poole in 1571 and for Dorchester in 1572, 1576, and 1581, boroughs in which Francis Russell, second earl of Bedford, had a commanding interest. Carleton employed his considerable legal and managerial powers in business partnerships, trusts, and other, sometimes disordered, financial affairs of various kinsmen and friends, and he was a persistent litigant. In the Lincolnshire fens he had public responsibilities as a commissioner for sewers, and private interests as an early 'adventurer'; he was 'one of the very first that inned any marsh in Holland', and a pioneer of windmills and other 'engines', 'toys', and 'gewgaws' (HoP, *Commons, 1558–1603*). He became superintendent of the Jesuits and other Catholic recusants imprisoned in Wisbech Castle.

Carleton's diverse interests were connected and charged with a kind of demonic energy by his ardent puritanism. In parliament most of his activity was directed towards a further reformation of the church along Presbyterian lines. He supported the successive initiatives of William Strickland, Paul Wentworth, and Wentworth's brother Peter, 'my beloved in the Lord', as well as the principles of parliamentary liberty for which these puritan

members stood. Carleton believed that hardline protestants such as himself were the queen's only reliable subjects, her very 'bowels', and that these 'servants of God' should be concentrated in the counties nearest London as a militia to protect the regime from Catholic subversion (HoP, *Commons, 1558–1603*). Alternatively, he argued, they should be encouraged to settle in Irish plantations, which in his thinking looked like blueprints for both Ulster and New England.

In the last year of his life Carleton's connections with the tightly knit puritan gentry of the midlands involved him in the puritan literary conspiracy of the Marprelate tracts. Also in 1589 he married Elizabeth *Crane, daughter of Sir Robert Hussey of Linwood, Lincolnshire, and widow of Anthony Crane of St Martin-in-the-Fields. It was at her house at East Molesey, Surrey, that the first Marprelate tracts were printed, and she was to be heavily fined in the Star Chamber for her involvement. The Marprelate press then moved to Fawsley, the Northamptonshire seat of Sir Richard Knightley, an enthusiast not entirely *compos mentis*, whose affairs were in Carleton's hands. Several elusive references in the tracts themselves suggest that Carleton's involvement in this illicit venture may have been more than merely managerial. Carleton died early in January 1590, and was survived by his third wife.

PATRICK COLLINSON, rev.

Sources P. Collinson, 'Carleton, George', HoP, *Commons, 1558–1603* · P. Collinson, *The Elizabethan puritan movement* (1967) · J. E. Neale, *Elizabeth I and her parliaments*, 1: *1559–1581* (1953) **Wealth at death** bequests to preachers and corporation of Carrickfergus to erect hospital for poor soldiers: P. W. Hasler, *The House of Commons 1558–1603* (1981)

Carleton, George (1557/8–1628), bishop of Chichester, was born at Norham in Northumberland. His father, Guy, second son of Thomas Carleton of Carleton Hall, Cumberland, was warder of Norham Castle at the time. His early education was undertaken by Bernard Gilpin, 'The Apostle of the North'. Gilpin was a fellow of Queen's College, Oxford, and Carleton was sent to its joint foundation of St Edmund Hall, where he matriculated on 20 December 1577, aged nineteen. He graduated BA on 12 February 1580, and at Michaelmas that year, along with Henry Savile, he was admitted as probationer fellow at Merton College. He proceeded MA on 14 June 1585. From 1586, when he was made *praelector grammaticus*, to 1589 the controversial *Lectionem antiquarum* of Caelius Rhodiginus (Lodovico Celio) informed his lectures. He proceeded BD on 16 May 1594 and DD on 1 December 1613.

Carleton was a noted disputant, poet, and orator, delegated by the college to salute its warden, Thomas Bickley, on his consecration as bishop of Chichester in 1586. Bickley became Carleton's first clerical patron when in 1589 he was appointed vicar of Mayfield, Sussex, a preferment he held until he obtained the third portion of the rectory of Waddesdon, Buckinghamshire, in 1605. In 1609 he became rector of Nuffield in Oxfordshire. He was so excited by this appointment that when he called at Eton College in October his cousin Dudley Carleton reported

George Carleton (1557/8–1628), by unknown artist, 1627

that he rode by 'in as great haste as yf he rode post for a bishoprick' (PRO, SP 14/48/120).

Carleton's earliest writing was a laudatory piece for Queen Elizabeth, *Carmen panegyricum*. Then in 1603 he wrote *Heroici characteres* for Sir Henry Nevile, predating by five years Joseph Hall's more celebrated work on types and virtues. As he began to bid for higher preferment Carleton wrote a series of conformist pamphlets, vindicating tithes (1606) and attacking the Church of Rome (1610, 1613), in the latter case with somewhat equivocal results. In April 1614 Dudley Carleton wrote to George from Venice, warning him that his writings were capable of being misconstrued, and also censuring him for confining ordination to bishops only. Carleton took the position—summarized in his 1615 *Directions to Know the True Church*—that the Church of Rome had remained true in doctrine until the time of Luther, a position in which he was later seconded by writers as diverse as Richard Field, John White, Francis White, Thomas Morton, Joseph Hall, and James Ussher.

Early in 1615 Carleton became a household chaplain to Prince Charles, whom he regarded as 'sober, grave, swete; in speache very advised' (PRO, SP 14/80/27). He expressed himself confident that the support of both the king and the prince would ensure his promotion, but his royal patrons failed to secure the bishopric of Carlisle for him in October 1616; the post went unexpectedly to the Villiers candidate, Robert Snoden, who had been chaplain to Prince Henry. Carleton privately recognized that King James increasingly appointed only public office holders

and heads of colleges, and lamented that his lack of advancement was due to his having 'never yet been in place of government' (PRO, SP 14/88/136). In November 1617, however, he was finally appointed to the Welsh bishopric of Llandaff, when Francis Godwin was translated to Hereford. He was consecrated on 12 July 1618. Although he claimed that he was unable to do much for the gospel in Wales, 'both for want of the tongue and for the opposition of some great men who have been there to much opposit to the truthe' (PRO, SP 14/94/38), Carleton now had his long-cherished dignity. He remained living in Islington and was soon spared the minutiae of diocesan business by being required to attend the Synod of Dort (1618), an honour he assumed he owed to the earl of Buckingham, although the two had never met. Later he realized that it was Sir Dudley Carleton who had secured him the appointment.

Although Carleton was invited only as an observer at the synod he spoke out against adopting article 31 of the Belgic confession. He maintained that bishops were *iure divino* and that Christ left behind him an imparity of ministers. In common with the Church of Rome to 1870, he believed that episcopacy was itself neither immutable nor a separate order, an opinion that the Church of England reversed in 1662 but which was not objected to at Dort. As the only bishop present Carleton was given a canopied seat, and it galled some that he had precedence equal to the president of the synod. When the articles of the Synod of Dort appeared in English in 1623, Carleton urged Archbishop Abbot to have convocation adopt them, in order to uphold the Calvinist theology of grace as the official doctrine of the Church of England. He also urged Abbot to call for a fast day and for the prayers of all the churches if war with Spain was declared, foreseeing this as the final engagement between protestantism and Catholicism.

Before he returned from Dort to England, Carleton addressed the prince of Orange and the states general of the United Provinces in November 1618. Dudley Carleton ensured that a manuscript copy of this 'Oration made at The Hague' was sent on to Bishop Lancelot Andrewes, and it was printed the following year when Carleton was translated to Andrewes's former see of Chichester in September 1619. He was the king's choice. Archbishop Abbot, no doubt relieved to have Carleton's persistent bids for preferment off his hands, wrote to Dudley Carleton rejoicing in the bishop of Llandaff's promotion. Shortly afterwards it was announced that Bishop Carleton would marry the widow of Sir Henry Nevile, his old patron.

In spite of his lack of administrative experience, Carleton took readily to his episcopal duties, residing in his diocese at Aldingbourne Manor and at the palace in Chichester. He saw his role as bishop as one more concerned with executive function than with preaching. He became an active magistrate and personally attended his three diocesan visitations (1619, 1622, and 1625), although he never attended visitations in the archdeaconry of Lewes where Dr Richard Buckenham, cousin and appointee of his predecessor Samuel Harsnett, was archdeacon. Harsnett had preferred Cambridge men from

Pembroke College, including his nephew Owen Stockton and his domestic chaplain John Hullwood, but Carleton promoted Oxford graduates, among them Thomas Vicars, a fellow of Queen's, who married Carleton's stepdaughter and became his chaplain and also prebendary of Eartham in 1624 in succession to Stockton. Carleton seems to have given little attention to the conformity or otherwise of those he appointed. Thus Robert Johnson, prebendary of Firle from 1624, was frequently censured for failing to preach and catechize and Anthony Hilton proved to be a dogged puritan who failed to use the prayer book or require communicants to kneel.

Carleton continued to write. In 1624 he published *A thankful remembrance of God's mercy in an historicall collection of the … deliverances of the church and state of England*, celebrating the defeat of the Spanish Armada in 1588 and the discovery of the Gunpowder Plot in 1605, which ran to several editions. He also published an answer to Christopher Heydon's astrological tracts and at the outset of the new reign he dedicated an anti-Armininan tract to Charles I as part of the controversy over Richard Montagu's writings. Following the fiasco of the Spanish match he warned the king that 'two other great dangers have assailed your kingdome of late, *The Plague* and the *Pelagian heresie*', convinced that Arminianism went further than Pelagianism ever had (Carleton, *Examination*, sig. A3). The controversy over Montagu's opinions lasted until Charles elevated him to be Carleton's successor as bishop of Chichester.

Carleton died on 12 May 1628 and was buried in his cathedral on the 27th. His will, which does not survive, was proved on 5 June. It is impossible to establish his personal wealth, but it was later reckoned that the woods he had felled in the diocese were worth £2381 18s.

Several of Carleton's writings appeared posthumously, including his celebrated life of his old schoolteacher Bernard Gilpin; the text of the latter's sermon of 8 January 1553 preached before Edward VI was included with the fourth edition of 1636. Before he died Carleton dedicated this biography of a godly and pious man of doubt to Sir William Bellys: it was first published in 1629. Gilpin was the great-nephew of Bishop Cuthbert Tunstall of Durham and had relied upon him for his own preferment when he had remained uncertain of the changes in the Edwardian church. Carleton used the uncertainty of Gilpin's own convictions as a mirror for his own age in the debates over churchmanship that came to the fore with Montagu. His *Testimony concerning the presbyterian discipline in the Low Countries and episcopall government here in England* was published in 1642, during the parliamentary debates over a moderate episcopacy. NICHOLAS W. S. CRANFIELD

Sources G. Carleton, *An examination of those things wherein the author of the late 'Appeale' holdeth the doctrine of the church of the Pelagians and Arminians to be the doctrines of the Church of England* (1625) • J. M. Fletcher, ed., *Registrum annalium Collegii Mertonensis, 1567–1603*, OHS, new ser., 24 (1976) • state papers domestic, James I, PRO, SP 14/77/9; 88/136; 94/38; 109/60; 109/144; 164/11; 84/87; 180/56 • state papers domestic, Charles I, PRO, SP 16/142/15 (SP 14) 48/120; 75/52; 80/27; 110/49 • Archbishop Abbot's registers, LPL • G. Carleton, *The life of Bernard Gilpin* (1629) • Foster, *Alum. Oxon., 1500–1714*, 1.238 • J. Ingamells, *The English episcopal portrait, 1559–1835: a catalogue* (privately printed, London, 1981) • A. M. Hind, *Engraving in England in the sixteenth and seventeenth centuries*, ed. M. Corbett and M. Norton, 3 vols. (1952–64) • J. Nichols, *The progresses and public processions of Queen Elizabeth*, 4 vols. (1788–1821) • W. Sussex RO, Ep. I/17/19–22 • M. Lee, ed., *Dudley Carleton to John Chamberlain, 1603–1624* (New Brunswick, 1972) • K. Fincham, *Prelate as pastor: the episcopate of James I* (1990) • administration of wills, PRO, PROB 6/13, fol. 29r • D. Marcombe, 'Bernard Gilpin: anatomy of an Elizabethan legend', *Northern History*, 16 (1980), 20–39

Likenesses oils, 1627; Sothebys, 9 May 1951, lot 59 [*see illus.*] • F. Hulsius, line engraving, 1630, BM, NPG; repro. in Hind, *Engraving in England*, pl. 182

Carleton, George (1651/2?–1728x30), army officer and memoirist, was probably born at Ewelme in Oxfordshire, the son of George Carleton. He claimed to be closely related to Sir Dudley Carleton, secretary of state to Charles I. However, until the late 1920s nothing was known about him other than what appears in the memoirs of military life ascribed to his name which was first published in 1728. As this work appeared in the lifetime of Daniel Defoe, and in style and structure closely resembled narratives written by him, he was for a long time assumed to be one of Defoe's fictional characters. However, evidence published in the 1920s suggests that Carleton was indeed a real person.

The title of the volume gives a good summary of its contents: it appeared as *The military memoirs of Captain George Carleton from the Dutch War, 1672, in which he served to the conclusion of the peace of Utrecht, 1713, illustrating some of the most remarkable transactions both by sea and land during the reigns of King Charles and King James II, hitherto unobserved by all the writers of those times* (1728). In it he recounts how at the age of twenty he entered as volunteer on board the *London*, under the command of Sir Edward Spragge, and was present at the battle of Southwold Bay of 1672.

Carleton subsequently joined the army of the prince of Orange, serving as a volunteer in the Prince's Own company of guards. After the revolution of 1688 he served with distinction in Scotland, and then in Ireland. Rather than go to the West Indies, he joined the army about to go to Spain, and was present at the capture of the citadel of Monjuich. However, he was no ordinary soldier, serving as a military engineer at a number of important sieges, including that of Barcelona. He was unfortunately a member of the garrison of Denia, which was forced to surrender to the Spaniards in 1708, and he remained a prisoner until the peace treaty which ended the War of the Spanish Succession in 1713.

Some of the most interesting parts of Carleton's memoirs are taken up with his observations on Spain and the Spaniards during his captivity. 'The merits of the book lie almost entirely in its animated descriptions of campaigning in Flanders and Spain, and in the amusing sidelights thrown on the places which the author visited', observes his most recent editor. He was 'a man of acute observation and an insatiable thirst for curious knowledge' (*Memoirs*, xiii).

It is clear from internal evidence that the book was completed between 1726 and 1728. The work was reprinted in

1741, and again in 1743. James Boswell noted that Dr Johnson read it avidly and 'found in it such an air of truth, that he could not doubt its authenticity' (Boswell, *Life*, 4.334). Boswell added that Carleton 'had obtain'd, by his long service, some knowledge of the practick part of an engineer' (ibid.). Another edition, edited by Sir Walter Scott, appeared in 1808. The memoirs were extensively used as a source by the fifth earl of Stanhope in his history of the War of the Spanish Succession published in 1832.

Documentary evidence uncovered by C. H. Hartmann, the editor of the 1929 edition of the *Military Memoirs*, although slight, confirms the bare bones of Carleton's life. His name appears in various lists of army engineers serving in Spain and Portugal at this time, and on a number of occasions he was forced to ask wealthy patrons for financial help when on half-pay. When he was court-martialled in October 1700 it was mentioned in mitigation that Carleton had a wife and three children. He is thought to have died by 1730, in which year probate of a George Carleton's estate was granted.

JOHN ORMSBY, *rev.* R. L. WINSTANLEY

Sources *Memoirs of Captain Carleton*, ed. C. H. Hartmann (1929) · P. H. Stanhope, *History of the war of the succession in Spain* (1832) · J. F. Waller, ed., *The imperial dictionary of universal biography*, 3 vols. (1857–63) · *Daniel Defoe: his life, and recently discovered writings*, ed. W. Lee, 3 vols. (1869) · J. Hill, *A history of the reign of Queen Anne*, 3 vols. (1880) · A. Parnell, *The war of the succession in Spain during the reign of Queen Anne, 1702–1711* (1888) · A. W. Secord, *Studies in the narrative method of Defoe* (1924) · A. Parnell, 'Dean Swift and the memoirs of Captain Carleton', *EngHR*, 6 (1891), 97–151 · Boswell, *Life*

Carleton, Guy (1604/5–1685), bishop of Chichester, was born of genteel but obscure parents at Bramston Foot in Gilsland, Cumberland; George Carleton (1557/8–1628), bishop of Chichester from 1619, was said to be a kinsman of his. He was educated at the free school in Carlisle under Thomas Robson and was sent as a servitor to Queen's College, Oxford, finally matriculating after four years on 20 May 1625, at the age of twenty. He was tutored by Charles Robson, son of his schoolmaster, graduating BA on 15 February 1626 and proceeding MA on 29 January 1629. By the end of October 1630 he had been elected to a fellowship; he became a junior proctor of the university in 1635.

Carleton may already have been ordained by the time of the outbreak of the civil war seven years later but this did not prevent him from playing a very active role in hostilities on the king's side. By 1645 he was one of the clergy being held prisoner by parliament in London. He seems to have been ejected from two livings, lapsing into obscurity for most of the next fifteen years. He was apparently blocked by the Cromwellian triers, who vetted candidates for livings, from entering parish ministry, indicating a perhaps surprising willingness on his part to serve in the protector's church, in the mid- to late 1650s. Sheer financial necessity may have been a factor as by 1660 he was married; his wife's name is unknown.

Carleton appears to have become involved in royalist conspiracy, as early as 1660 he was imprisoned at Lambeth and condemned to death. Before the sentence could be carried out his wife managed to get a length of cord to him, with which he let himself down from a window. Unfortunately the cord was too short and he fell, injuring himself. Yet he managed to go into hiding until he was well enough to sail for the Netherlands and join Charles II, who was pleasantly surprised to discover that he was still alive.

At the Restoration, Carleton received rapid promotion, becoming a royal chaplain. He was created DD of Oxford on 2 August 1660, appointed dean of Carlisle, and installed as a prebendary of Durham before the end of the year. He stayed in the north until 1672, when he became bishop of Bristol, being consecrated at Westminster Abbey on 11 February. Given the poverty of his see Carleton was allowed to retain the post at Durham and the rectory of Wolsingham, co. Durham, which he had acquired, *in commendam*. During his time at Bristol, Carleton was a controversial figure, intervening decisively in the contested Gloucestershire election of October 1675 by mobilizing the clergy in support of the court candidate, Lord Digby. He launched a vigorous campaign against local dissenters, which not even all the beneficed clergy supported. He further antagonized Bristol's lay rulers by attending sessions and seeking to become a JP. By 1678 he was in conflict with the corporation over a range of jurisdictional and liturgical issues and sought to organize a commission of charitable uses to probe the corporation's finances. Many in Bristol were doubtless relieved when, early in 1679, his translation to the vacant see of Chichester was confirmed.

Carleton was to prove an equally contentious figure at Chichester, however. As Anthony Wood remarked, he 'had not the name there for a scholar or liberal benefactor, as his predecessor and kinsman', George Carleton (Wood, *Ath. Oxon.*, 4.867). Beyond that, he was once again cast in the role of the scourge of dissent. During the exclusion crisis, which was beginning as he came into his new diocese, he was a scathing observer and tireless opponent of the activities of local whigs. In a letter to Archbishop William Sancroft in February 1680, which is often quoted but usually misdated to February 1679, he gave a critical report on the recent visit to Chichester of the duke of Monmouth, the whig hero and potential pretender. Carleton's very visible aloofness from these proceedings earned him abuse from the crowd as 'an old popish rogue' and some shots were even fired into his house (Bodl. Oxf., MS Tanner 38, fol. 126). Undaunted, he continued to report local whig movements to the central authorities until the end of his life.

Carleton was involved in personal feuds with members of the cathedral chapter, the chancellor of the diocese, and members of Chichester corporation, which contributed to and were further exacerbated by the partisan rivalries of the time. Early in 1684 rumours of his death were circulating, but despite his advanced age, he lived into the reign of James II and still had enough strength left to campaign vigorously for the tory candidates in the general election of 1685. The effort left him too tired to attend the coronation but his death, when it came on 6 July, was actually the result of an accident, choking on stringy beans while in London for the meeting of parliament. His body was returned to Chichester and buried in the cathedral. His marriage had produced several daughters but at least two of them had predeceased him; his daughter Hester, wife of George Vane, was granted administration of his estate. He died as Monmouth's rebels were being crushed in the west country, a development of which he would certainly have approved. In a way, he never transcended the role of soldier–clergyman which he had played in the 1640s. His life from then onwards was one long combat against those he took to be the enemies of church and crown. For him, it had always been a battle to the death.

ANDREW M. COLEBY

Sources Wood, *Ath. Oxon.*, new edn · *The life and times of Anthony Wood*, ed. A. Clark, 5 vols., OHS, 19, 21, 26, 30, 40 (1891–1900) · M. Hobbs, ed., *Chichester Cathedral: an historical survey* (1994) · Foster, *Alum. Oxon.* · Sancroft papers, Bodl. Oxf., MSS Tanner · *CSP dom.*, *Jan–June 1683* · J. R. Magrath, *The Queen's College*, 2 vols. (1921) · T. Harris, P. Seaward, and M. Goldie, eds., *The politics of religion in Restoration England* (1990) · M. Knights, *Politics and opinion in crisis, 1678–1681* (1994) · administration, PRO, PROB 6/61, fol. 113*v*
Archives Bodl. Oxf., MSS Tanner, letters to Sancroft and papers, Sancroft papers · Longleat House, Wiltshire, Longleat MSS, Coventry papers
Wealth at death see administration, PRO, PROB 6/61, fol. 113*v*

Carleton, Guy, first Baron Dorchester (1724–1808), army officer and colonial governor, was born on 3 September 1724 at Strabane, the third son of Christopher Carleton of Newry, co. Down, and his wife, Catherine, daughter of Henry Ball of co. Donegal. Upon the death of his father, after Carleton had reached the age of fourteen, he was privately educated, being particularly influenced by his mother's second husband, the Revd Thomas Skelton of Newry. The Carletons, with their Anglo-Irish connections, were powerful enough to gain valuable political patronage, including that of important figures such as the duke of Richmond and Sir Charles Saunders, which did much to help launch Carleton's military career as well as sustain him during his two periods as governor of Quebec. Into the family of one of these supporters Carleton was eventually to marry. On 21 or 22 May 1772 he married Lady Maria Howard (1753/4–1836), then not yet twenty and the third daughter of Thomas Howard, second earl of Effingham; the couple had nine sons and two daughters. Similarly it was the championing of Carleton's worth by General James Wolfe that did much to smooth his career path in the army. Having been frustrated in his desire to attach Carleton to the expedition against Louisbourg in 1758, Wolfe ultimately succeeded in allowing Carleton to play a part in the capture of Quebec in 1759. This match between man and place was to be a fateful link in the subsequent chain of events—happenings which, more often than not, were momentous and were to bind Carleton to Quebec until his final departure from Canada in July 1796.

Military career Carleton had joined the 25th foot (Rothes's) as an ensign on 21 May 1742. His progress through the military ranks was to be steady rather than spectacular. He managed to combine personal bravery, a trait which led to his being wounded at least three times

Guy Carleton, first Baron Dorchester (1724–1808), by unknown artist, *c*.1780

in his early years in the army, with excessive caution as a field officer and military commander. After becoming a lieutenant in 1745, he joined the 1st foot guards with the army rank of captain on 22 July 1751. By 1757 he had become lieutenant-colonel before, in the following year on 24 August, joining the newly formed 72nd foot and on 30 December becoming a colonel in America. During the next four years, besides his involvement in the capture of Quebec, where his contribution was creditable without being notable, he fought in other important engagements of the Seven Years' War, including the attack on Port-Andro on Belle-Ile-en-Mer off the coast of France in April 1761 and the siege of Havana in 1762. In both these engagements Carleton suffered serious wounds. In recognition of his efforts, he was promoted colonel on 19 February 1762. The year 1766 marked his transference from the 72nd foot to the 93rd as well as to his new rank of brigadier in North America.

Governor of Quebec and the Quebec Act (1774) It was also in this year, to the surprise of some contemporaries as well as later observers, that Carleton was appointed head of the government in Quebec. Initially, he was lieutenant-governor, but when it became apparent that his predecessor, James Murray, would not return, Carleton assumed the titles of captain-general and governor-in-chief on 12 April 1768. Probably Carleton's rise was due mainly to his coterie of backers in Britain, including George III, as well as to the leadership exigencies created by a long and costly war. Carleton's term of office was to last until 27 June 1778. During this period he had to face up to questions concerning the form of the government of the mainly French Canadian colony as well as to the challenge posed to Britain's future in North America by the American invasion attempt of 1775–6. It is an ironic commentary on his role as a governor with a military background that he was more successful in the former than the latter capacity. Indeed Carleton's influence upon the political course of events is attested by his four years in London prior to the passing of the Quebec Act in 1774.

Of course, it was not Carleton's advocacy alone that had the effect of deflecting British policy away from the Anglicizing assumptions and intentions of the Proclamation Act of 1763. Murray, during his time in office after 1766, had been a vigorous exponent of the view that Quebec's future would be best secured by conciliating the Roman Catholic church and other traditional elements in French Canadian society such as the seigneurs and the militia. Needless to say, to take such a stand was more than a little curious given the fact that Catholics lacked full civil and political rights within Britain itself. It can be surmised that both Murray and Carleton found it pleasing to their hierarchical pretensions to imagine that Quebec was inherently both a feudal and a deferential society. Carleton certainly came to feel a disdain for the small band of British merchants in Quebec who were vociferously demanding, among other things, the rights of holding an assembly and the adoption of English civil law. It led him to predict that climatic severity would condemn any hopes of attracting widespread immigration from the other mainland colonies. Far better then, he argued, to recognize the reality of the situation, and this was the message that he constantly advanced. Crucially, he gave testimony to the House of Commons during early June 1774, in which he swayed opinion against making the conversion from seigneurial to freehold tenure in the colony.

True to form, after returning to Quebec in September 1774, Carleton persevered with his usual tactics of disregarding instructions if they contradicted his own predilections. He also continued to rule through a clique of his own favourites. But soon the disastrous consequences of the Quebec Act upon the thirteen colonies manifested themselves; the extension of Quebec's boundaries to the Mississippi, so far as many English colonists were concerned, carried with it official recognition of the Roman Catholic church, the denial of political representation, and a snub to hopes of westward settlement. Yet it is likely that the act was more the product of the internal logic of actual and projected demography than it was an attempt to stimulate loyalty among a population which might be faced at any time by the prospect of imminent invasion.

The American War of Independence Nevertheless, the rumblings of discontent grew louder, and soon the repercussions arising from Carleton's own handiwork were to test once again his mettle as a military commander. His initial over-confidence can be gauged by the fact that he agreed to the sending of two of his five regiments to New York. This put him in extreme difficulty when the two-pronged attack of Richard Montgomery and Benedict Arnold took place in the following year. He had to concede Fort St Jean on the Richelieu River above Lake Champlain, the loss of which opened the doors to the invaders. Even though

Carleton was to gain the rank of general in North America on 1 January and his knighthood on 6 July 1776, the consensus is that he owed his success in repelling the attack more to a combination of the lack of hard currency, a depletion of American manpower, and the rigours of a northern winter than to the expected loyal reaction of the French Canadians or to his own astuteness. While personally brave, especially in courting the danger of capture in Montreal in order to head up the defence of Quebec city, Carleton, in the aftermath of the arrival of fresh British reinforcements in May 1776, let slip the opportunity to pursue the fleeing Americans as far as Fort Ticonderoga in New York.

For once, too, it was not possible to help his cause in Britain, as Carleton's petulance worsened relations between himself and Lord George Germain, who had taken over the American department in late 1775. The results were that Carleton resigned his military post on 27 June 1778 and left Canada a month later. It appeared that he had written off his North American career; he did not even bother to defend before the privy council his previous high-handed action in dismissing Peter Livius as chief justice of Quebec.

Unexpectedly, however, another turn of the political wheel meant that Carleton's eclipse was only temporary. Thus it was that on 2 March 1782 he received the posting of commander-in-chief in North America. In the wake of the surrender at Yorktown in 1781, this appointment was really concerned with effecting an orderly withdrawal from the former thirteen colonies. In this respect Carleton acquitted himself well. By his encouragement of a policy of mollifying the Americans, he practised those same skills which had marked his early years in Quebec. To his credit, he skilfully played for time to allow maximum opportunity for the refugees, most notably former slaves, to escape the country. His more grandiose hope, inspired by his budding friendship with the former chief justice of New York, William Smith, of effecting a reconciliation with the Americans via the net of a loose federal scheme was to prove delusory. In late 1783 he returned once more to England, where his reward was a pension of £1000 a year for his own life and the lives of his wife and two elder children. William Smith accompanied Carleton on his return and continued to urge the necessity of a centralized system of government for the surviving colonies with Carleton at their head.

Governor of Quebec, 1786–1794 Carleton's price for co-operation in any such plan was a peerage and the office of commander-in-chief. The former he attained on 21 August 1786 when he assumed the title of Baron Dorchester. Greater political centralization, however, was more appearance than reality since he received separate commissions to head the individual provinces of Quebec, Nova Scotia, and New Brunswick. Centralized control was soon a dead letter so far as the latter two colonies were concerned.

It has been usual to regard Carleton (until 1786) and Dorchester (thereafter) as two separate individuals with quite different, almost irreconcilable, aims and objectives. In support of this contention one can cite Dorchester's continuing rapport with Smith. Indeed Smith became chief justice in Quebec, where several of his judgments pushed forward the Anglicization of the legal system. In addition, Dorchester's time in New York had induced on his part a new sympathy for English or loyalist settlers. He lauded the United Empire loyalists and wanted to treat them as a caste apart and, moreover, to grant them land in freehold. Another indication of the new order of things was the manner in which Adam Mabane, at one time the leader of the French group in the council of both Carleton and his successor, Frederick Haldimand (governor from 1777 to 1786), became sidelined after 1786. On the other hand, it seemed that Dorchester still clung to some of his original ideas but chose not to confront their inconsistencies directly, preferring to let his earlier notions be either gradually undermined or, as the circumstances demanded, quietly maintained. For example, his solicitude for the position of the Catholic church did not waver; he made certain that permission for the entry of émigré priests after 1791 was granted. In contrast to Smith, Dorchester showed no appetite for landmark legal reform. His impact upon the main provisions of the Constitutional Act of 1791 were minimal. He remained largely unimpressed by the pleas for representative government. All in all Dorchester gave every impression of a man much more willing than before to wait upon events. He returned to England on leave between August 1791 and September 1793, during which time he became a general of the army on 12 October 1793. True, he was still capable of resenting individuals who in some way thwarted his plans. Having backed unsuccessfully his own favourite for the new post of lieutenant-governor of Upper Canada, he took an immediate dislike to John Graves Simcoe after his arrival in 1792. He went out of his way to attack Simcoe's policy towards the Indians and plans for the defence of the border posts. This antipathy might help to explain why some ill-tempered remarks of his in denunciation of American policy in the west, made worse for having taken place in the charged atmosphere of the French declaration of war against Britain in February 1793, exacerbated Anglo-American relations. When mildly rebuked by the duke of Portland for this, Dorchester asked in September 1794 to be relieved of his governorship. Although his request was granted, it was to be two more years before his successor, Lieutenant-General Robert Prescott, arrived to take over. For the remainder of his life Dorchester played the role of the country gentleman. His wealth was extensive enough to allow the purchase of three separate estates—Greywell Hill and Kempshot House near Basingstoke as well as Stubbings House near Maidenhead. It was at Stubbings House that Carleton died on 10 November 1808, aged eighty-four. The first line became extinct in 1897 and a second barony, established in 1899, ended in 1963.

Reputation An estimate of Carleton's career is hampered by the fact that, on his orders, his papers were destroyed by his widow on his death. Early accounts, such as that by A. G. Bradley, were patriotically inspired and excessively hagiographic. D. G. Creighton, on the other hand, writing in the 1930s, was highly critical of Carleton for his failure to support the merchants' wish to exploit the commercial potentialities of imperial trade. Another study by A. L. Burt was critical of Carleton's temperamental frailties and military timidity. Burt's former student Hilda Neatby portrayed a powerful Carleton whose masterpiece was the Quebec Act, designed as it was to fulfil a continental purpose. More recently, Philip Lawson has trimmed Carleton's stature somewhat and placed him and his policies more within the context of Quebec society and politics. There is little doubt that Carleton could be testy and difficult. Nevertheless, a survey of the quarrels and squabbles which marked the careers of his predecessor, his contemporaries, and his successors as governors in Quebec places Carleton in a rather more favourable light. Moreover, according to C. A. Bayly, military despotisms of the sort which Carleton erected on the St Lawrence were entirely typical of his period. Where Carleton differed, however, was in his attitude towards 'outsiders' such as the French Canadians, slaves, and native peoples, where his outlook breathed a generosity of spirit usually lacking in others of his class and background. As a military commander, while he failed to press home victory, at the same time he guarded against the likelihood of disastrous defeat. Of course, Carleton will for ever be connected with the terms of the Quebec Act, but the debate on that measure, and his influence upon it, still show no sign of clear resolution.

JAMES STURGIS

Sources DNB · G. P. Browne, 'Carleton, Guy', DCB, vol. 5 · H. Neatby, *The revolutionary age, 1760–1791* (1966) · A. G. Bradley, *Sir Guy Carleton (Lord Dorchester)* (1907) · A. G. Bradley, *Sir Guy Carleton (Lord Dorchester)*, new edn (1966) · A. L. Burt, *Guy Carleton, Lord Dorchester, 1724–1808* (1955) · P. Lawson, *The imperial challenge: Quebec and Britain in the age of the American revolution* (1989) · C. A. Bayly, *Imperial meridian: the British empire and the world* (1989) · A. L. Burt, *The old province of Quebec* (1933) · V. T. Harlow, *The founding of the second British empire, 1763–1793*, 2 vols. (1952–64) · F. Ouellet, *Histoire économique et sociale du Québec, 1760–1850* (Montreal, 1966) · H. Neatby, *The Quebec Act: protest and policy* (1972) · J. Sturgis, 'Anglicisation as a theme in Lower Canadian history, 1807–1843', *British Journal of Canadian Studies*, 3 (1988), 210–33 · M. Wade, *The French Canadians, 1760–1960* (1963)

Archives BL, corresp. and letter-books, Add. MSS 21678, 21697–21700, 21743, 21781 · NA Canada, letters and papers · NRA, priv. coll., letters and papers · PRO, corresp. and papers, PRO 30/55 | BL, Haldiman MSS, Add. MSS 21661–21892 · U. Mich., Clements L., corresp. with Thomas Gage

Likenesses portrait, c.1780, priv. coll. [*see illus.*] · line engraving, NPG

Wealth at death owned two houses and separate estate: Bradley, *Sir Guy Carleton*

Carleton, Hugh, Viscount Carleton (1739–1826), judge and politician, was born on 11 September 1739, possibly in Cork, the eldest son of Francis Carleton, a wealthy merchant known as the King of Cork, and Rebecca, daughter of Hugh Lawton of Lake March, co. Cork. After attending Kilkenny College for three years, in 1755 Carleton entered Trinity College, Dublin, where he won several prizes.

He entered the Middle Temple in 1758 and, having spared no effort to master his profession as a student, was called to the Irish bar in 1764. Efficient and noted for his mastery of legal principles, Carleton soon made his mark, becoming a king's counsel in 1768, although to achieve such a mark of professional eminence so rapidly was not unknown in Ireland at that time. On 2 August 1766 he married Elizabeth (d. 1794), daughter of Richard Mercer of Dublin.

In 1769 Carleton became recorder of Cork, and, as was customary for an ambitious barrister, soon entered parliament. He did so with the help of the lord lieutenant, George, fourth Viscount Townshend, which followed, in part at least, from the standing of his father and father-in-law. As MP for Tuam (1772–6), Philipstown (1776–83), and Naas (1783–7) he proved himself to be a steady and reliable supporter of the administration, rather than an outstanding speaker. His ability was rewarded by being appointed third serjeant-at-law in 1776, second serjeant-at-law in 1777, then solicitor-general in 1779, which office he held until his appointment as chief justice of the common pleas in 1787.

In 1789 Carleton was created Baron Carleton of Anner, co. Tipperary, because the government wished to provide additional legal expertise for the House of Lords in its recently restored capacity as the final court of appeal in Ireland, and to counter the influence of John Scott, Baron Earlsfort (later earl of Clonmell), chief justice of the king's bench, and Lord Chief Baron Yelverton. When proposing Carleton's elevation the lord lieutenant (the marquess of Buckingham) described Carleton as having been 'ever steady' towards the government, whereas Earlsfort was 'slippery', and Yelverton was a '[lord] chancellor in embryo' (Fortescue MSS, 1.469). Carleton was advanced to be Viscount Carleton of Clare, co. Tipperary, in 1797.

Although regarded by his contemporaries as an able and fair judge, his conduct of the trial of the brothers Henry and John Sheares (with whose family Carleton had been intimate in their youth) in the aftermath of the 1798 rebellion made him highly unpopular with the Catholic majority. Nevertheless, in his Rise and Fall of the Irish Nation, Sir Jonah Barrington described Carleton as an 'exemplary' judge, although in his Personal Sketches of his Own Times, Barrington also referred to Carleton's lugubrious manner in court and marked tendency towards hypochondria, which led F. E. Ball in his The Judges in Ireland, 1221–1921 to characterize him as 'a subject for frequent ridicule'.

Carleton was originally opposed to the union, but changed his mind by January 1799. In the autumn of 1800, despite being only sixty-one, he took advantage of the new provisions allowing judges to retire early on pension on the grounds of ill health. In recognition of his support for the union he was elected a representative peer with government support and went to live in London. While reluctant to speak in the House of Lords as often as his party would have liked, he sat in Irish appeals and his abilities were such that he was awarded an honorary doctorate in civil law by Oxford University in 1810.

Elected a member of the Royal Irish Academy in 1788, Carleton was a man of wide intellectual interests and an avid collector of pamphlets on legal, constitutional, political, and religious topics. His collection, now bound in 158 volumes, is to be found in the library of Lincoln's Inn, by whom it was purchased in 1842. Having been widowed in 1794, on 15 July 1795 he married Mary Buckley, the second daughter of Abednego Matthew of Handley, Dorset. She died in 1810, and as there were no children by either marriage the titles became extinct upon Carleton's death at his London home at George Street, Hanover Square, on 25 February 1826. A. R. HART

Sources F. E. Ball, The judges in Ireland, 1221–1921, 2 (1926), 174, 187, 222–3, 235 · J. Barrington, Personal sketches of his own times, 1 (1827), 385–6 · J. Barrington, Rise and fall of the Irish nation (1833), 322–3 · The manuscripts of J. B. Fortescue, 10 vols., HMC, 30 (1892–1927), vol. 1, p. 469 · Correspondence of Charles, first Marquis Cornwallis, ed. C. Ross, 3 vols. (1859), vol. 3, pp. 4, 31, 257, 268, 274 · GM, 1st ser., 96/1 (1826), 270 · J. R. O'Flanagan, The Munster circuit: tales, trials and traditions (1880), 108–14 · Burtchaell & Sadleir, Alum. Dubl., 2nd edn, 134 · E. Keane, P. Beryl Phair, and T. U. Sadleir, eds., King's Inns admission papers, 1607–1867, IMC (1982), 75 · private information (2004) [Lincoln's Inn]
Archives Lincoln's Inn, collection of pamphlets
Likenesses W. Daniell, drawing, NPG · W. Daniell, etching (after G. Dance), NPG · F. Wheatley, group portrait, oils (The Irish House of Commons, 1780), Leeds City Art Galleries, Lotherton Hall, West Yorkshire · engraving, NL Ire.; repro. in Walker's Hibernian Magazine (July 1795) · portrait, NL Ire.

Carleton [née Moders (?)], **Mary** [nicknamed the German Princess] (1634x42–1673), impostor, is recorded in contradictory texts, making the accuracy of information about her origins difficult to ascertain. She was probably born Mary Moders in 1642 and baptized on 22 January; however, she is also recorded as being born eight years earlier, while Memories of the Life of the Famous Madam Charlton (1673) gives a birth date of April 1639. After the death of her father, possibly a chorister of Canterbury Cathedral or a fiddler, her mother remarried either a fiddler or an innkeeper. With her vitality and quick-wittedness Mary charmed the well-to-do, mixing with high-ranking children and learning genteel accomplishments and speech. She married a Canterbury shoemaker, John Steadman, and had two children who died. To escape her marriage she persuaded a master's mate to carry her to Barbados but was discovered by her husband. She then married a surgeon named Day, from Dover, and was indicted for bigamy; the case was dropped when she claimed she had believed her first husband dead. According to Ultimum vale (1673) she also married a bricklayer surnamed Billing.

Mary then visited the continent, where she polished her languages. In Cologne she made a new identity when mistaken for another woman. Decking herself in jewels and finery and passing as Maria de Wolway, she came to London as a noble German lady forced to flee an unwanted marriage. Her appearance of wealth was aided by false letters from the continent attesting to estates. An innkeeper named King alerted his father-in-law, Carleton, to the prize. Carleton's son John, a lawyer's clerk of eighteen, assumed fine clothes that rivalled Mary's, won her consent, and married her in April 1663. Mary's supposed wealth never materialized and the Carletons received a letter from Canterbury disclosing Mary's past. She was dragged to prison where she was visited as a curiosity by, among others, Samuel Pepys (29 May 1663). The Carletons

Mary Carleton (1634x42–1673), by T. Thrumten

bungled the trial for bigamy at the Old Bailey, producing only one witness to the earlier marriages, James Knot. Steadman failed to appear, apparently unable to afford the fare to London from Dover—the Carletons asserted that Mary had threatened to haunt him if she were hanged. She stuck to her story, insisting on her nobility but declaring her wealth an invention of the greedy Carletons. She was acquitted, and the public was jubilant. The furore was exploited in a wooden play, *A Witty Combat, or, The Female Victor*, possibly by Thomas Porter, which presented Mary as a calculating heroine. In 1664 she played herself at the Duke's Theatre. Pepys was unimpressed: 'saw *The German Princess* acted—by the woman herself … the whole play … is very simple, unless here and there a witty sprankle or two' (15 April 1664; Pepys, *Diary*, 5.124).

For the next seven years Mary Carleton used her sexual attractions to gain lovers and her strategic abilities to fool them, sometimes two at a time. She created new identities backed by supporting documents. Her career was temporarily halted when in 1670 she was caught stealing a silver tankard and condemned to hanging, a sentence commuted to transportation to Jamaica in 1671. She returned prematurely to England and continued her petty crimes, again presenting herself as a lady of quality; she managed a supreme fraud that netted her about £600 in goods and ready money. Finally she was caught again, indicted for stealing a piece of plate, and recognized by the old turnkey from Newgate as the 'German Princess'. At the trial she wore her hair fashionably frizzled and was dressed in an Indian striped gown, silk petticoat, and white shoes laced with green. In this dress she was hanged at Tyburn

on 22 January 1673, having confessed her sins. She died a Roman Catholic.

In 1663 and 1673 Mary Carleton inspired more pamphlets than any other ordinary criminal of her time; they continued to appear until well into the eighteenth century. They made her a mythical as well as a historical figure, attracting several extra stories of transvestism and trickery to her narrative. The early pamphlets tended to vindicate one side, as two titles suggest: *The Lawyer's Clarke Trappan'd by the Crafty Whore of Canterbury* and *A Vindication of a Distressed Lady*. John and Mary Carleton claimed to have written some works themselves, John's including *Ultimum vale*, and Mary's being *An Historical Narrative of the German Princess* and *The Case of Madam Mary Carleton, lately Stiled the German Princess … in an Appeal to his Illustrious Highness Prince Rupert*. It remains unclear whether she wrote them or was ghosted, or whether she was helped by a lawyer. In *The Mary Carleton Narratives, 1663–73* (1914), Ernest Bernbaum denied her authorship, declaring that *The Case* revealed more learning than she had; yet the most detailed contemporary commentator, Francis Kirkman, in *The Counterfeit Lady Unveiled* (1673), had no doubts. She was a good linguist and skilled forger of letters and there seems no reason to dismiss her as the composer of the pamphlets, though the difference in style between the two works suggests that she had different collaborators in each case. Another rash of pamphlets occurred in 1673, trying to explain the national credulity in 1663, as well as capitalizing on the scandalous life and death. One, *Memories of the Life of the Famous Madam Charlton*, took up a refrain from 1663: that all the world was a cheat and one should not therefore wonder at impostors. In Kirkman's *Counterfeit Lady Unveiled* Mary Carleton served 'as a Looking-glass, wherein we may see the Vices of this Age Epitomized' (Kirkman, preface). Kirkman summed up the problem of the life and accounts: 'How can Truth be discovered of her who was wholly composed of Falsehood?' (ibid., 3).

JANET TODD

Sources F. Kirkman, *The counterfeit lady unveiled, being a full account of the birth, life, most remarkable actions, and untimely death of Mary Carleton, known by the name of the German Princess* (1673) • M. Carleton, *The case of Madam Mary Carleton, lately stiled the German princess, truely stated, with an historical relation of her birth, education, and fortunes; in an appeal to his illustrious highness Prince Rupert* (1663) • [J. Carleton?], *Ultimum vale of John Carleton, of the Middle Temple London, gent. being a true description of the passages of that grand imposter, late a pretended Germane-lady* (1663) • *Memories of the life of the famous Madam Charlton, commonly stiled the German princess. Setting forth the whole series of her actions, with all their intrigues, and subtile contrivances from her cradle to the fatal period of her raign at Tiburn, being an account of her penitent behaviour, in her absteining from food and rest, in the prison of Newgate, from the time of her condemnation to her execution, January 23, 1672, taken from her own relation, whilst she was prisoner in the Marshalsea, and other certain information, with her nativity astrologically handled, and an epitaph on her tomb* (1673) • *The lawyer's clarke trappan'd by the crafty whore of Canterbury, or, A true relation of the whole life of Mary Mauders, the daughter of Thomas Mauders, a fidler in Canterbury* (1663) • *A vindication of a distressed lady, in answer to a pernitious, scandalous, libellous pamphlet, intituled, 'The lawyers clarke trappan'd by the crafty whore of Canterbury'* (1663) • [J. Carleton?], *The replication, or, Certain vindicatory depositions, occasioned by way of answer, to the various aspersions, and false reports of ignorant and malicious tongues, and the printed* *sheets and pamphlets of base detractors, concerning the late acted cheat* (1663) • *The arraignment, tryal and examination of Mary Moders, otherwise Stedman, now Carleton, (stiled, the German Princess) at the sessions-house in the Old Bayly, being brought prisoner from the Gatehouse Westminster, for having two husbands* (1663) • [M. Carleton], *An historical narrative of the German Princess, containing all material passages, from her first arrivall at Graves-End, the 30th of March last past, untill she was discharged from her imprisonment, June the 6th instant … written by her self* (1663) • *The articles and charge of impeachment against the German lady, prisoner in the Gate House, to be exhibited according to the records of the city of Canterbury, in order to her trial at the session-house in the Old Bailey, with the confession of the witnesses, and her father in law, touching her strange pranks and unheard of designs, as also a true narrative of her proceedings since the 25th day of March last, to the time of the contract of marriage, betwixt this rare inchantress and that worthy gentleman Mr. Carlton* (1663) • *A true account of the tryal of Mrs Mary Carlton, at the sessions in the Old Bayly, Thursday the 4th of June, 1633, she being indicted by the name of Mary Mauders alias Stedman, sometime supposed by Mr. Carlton and others, to be a princess of Germany* (1663) • *The Westminster wedding; or, Carlton's epithalamium, to the tune of, the Spanish lady* (1663) • F. B. Gent, *Vercingetorixa: or, The Germane Princess reduc'd to an English habit* (1663) • *News from Jamaica in a letter from Port Royal written by the German Princess to her fellow collegiates and friends in New-Gate* (1671) • *An exact and true relation of the examination, tryal and condemnation of the German Princess, otherwise cal'd Mary Carlton, at Justice-Hall in the Old Bailey, January 17: 1672. Also, an account of the pretended treachery which she was to discover to the bench; and the reason of her return from Jemeca* (1672) • *An elegie on the famous and renowned lady for eloquence and wit, Madam Mary Carlton otherwise styled the German Princess* (1673) • *The deportment and carriage of the German Princess, immediately before her execution, and her last speech at Tyburn, being on Wednesday the 22th of January, 1672* (1672) • *The memoires of Mary Carleton, commonly stiled, the German Princess, being a narrative of her life and death interwoven with many strange and pleasant passages, from the time of her birth to her execution at Tyburn, being the 22th of January 1672, with her behaviour in prison, her last speech, burial and epitaph* (1673) • E. Bernbaum, *The Mary Carleton narratives 1663–1673: a missing chapter in the history of the English novel* (1914) • J. Todd and E. Spearing, eds., *Counterfeit ladies* (1994) • Pepys, *Diary*

Likenesses woodcut, 1663, repro. in *The arraignment* • woodcut, 1663, repro. in Carleton, *The case* • J. Chantry, line drawing, BM; repro. in *Memories of the life* • T. Thrumten, drawing, AM Oxf. [*see illus.*] • pen-and-ink drawing, NPG • woodcut, repro. in Carleton, *Ultimum vale*

Carleton, Richard. *See* Carlton, Richard (d. 1638?).

Carleton, Thomas (c.**1735–1817**), army officer and colonial governor, was born in Ireland, the youngest son of Christopher Carleton of Newry, co. Down, and Catherine, daughter of Henry Ball of co. Donegal. He was the brother of Guy *Carleton, first Baron Dorchester (1724–1808). Following his childhood in Ireland, Thomas Carleton joined the 20th foot in 1753, achieving the rank of lieutenant and adjutant by early 1756, and that of captain on 27 August 1759, after considerable service in Europe during the Seven Years' War. He continued his military career after the peace. Several leaves of absence allowed him to tour throughout Europe and, at times, to observe other armies in combat, such as the Russians in 1774 then battling 'with the Turks on the Lower Danube' ('Statement of the services of General T. Carleton', 8 Feb 1810, Carleton collection).

The outbreak of the American War of Independence brought Carleton, now a lieutenant-colonel in the 29th foot, to his brother's side in Quebec, where Guy Carleton was governor, to serve as quartermaster general to the British forces stationed there. Like his brother, Thomas became increasingly critical of Lord North's handling of the war effort, commenting at one point: 'this letter contains the worst kind of Treason against the Minister so I shant put my name to it' (Carleton to Lord Shelburne, 23 Oct 1779, Carleton collection). Although Carleton's patron Lord Shelburne later slipped from power, Thomas was fortunate enough to be offered, after two others had declined the office, appointment as governor of the newly created colony of New Brunswick. He took the oaths of office on 28 July 1784 and with his wife, Hannah Foy (*née* Van Horn), whom he had married in London on 2 May 1783, reached his temporary capital Parrtown, soon to be renamed St John, in November 1784. Carleton had achieved colonel's rank on 20 November 1782 and journeyed to New Brunswick with two major assumptions: that his military responsibilities would continue, since the war office promised two regiments would be stationed in New Brunswick, and that his New Brunswick appointment would be a stepping-stone to higher colonial office in Quebec. He was to be disappointed on both counts.

During the colony's first year Carleton governed by prerogative, choosing not to call any elected assembly. The governor and the appointed council, almost entirely loyalist in composition, made Fredericton, well up the St John River, the capital, dispensed land and offices, incorporated St John as a city, established the colony's boundaries to protect against American claims, and in general carefully oversaw every aspect of the colony's development. The creation of a deferential, well-ordered society, dominated by a landed gentry and without the 'American spirit of innovation' was the goal, along with the 'strengthening [of] the executive powers of Government [to] discountenance its leaning so much on the popular part of the Constitution' (25 June 1785, National Archives of Canada, M.G. 11, N.B. Ser. A, 2/132–7). Officials in England as well as rank-and-file loyalists in New Brunswick had reservations about some of Carleton's decisions and inclinations.

In St John the first election in November 1785, finally called to choose an assembly, was marked by riots and strong opposition to the governor's party, but Carleton and the loyalist élite prevailed. Recounts, arrests, and military intervention produced loyalist élite domination of the assembly until the 1790s, when an even stronger opposition to the Carleton regime emerged. Meanwhile, the French menace forced considerable focus on the defences of Britain's remaining North American colonies. In the maritimes it was the senior colony of Nova Scotia that attracted most of London's attention. Carleton witnessed the loss of both regiments within his colony. The culmination of New Brunswick's military neglect came in September 1799 when Prince Edward, duke of Kent and Strathearn, assumed command of the forces in British North America with headquarters in Halifax. Somewhat softening these blows but by no means removing Carleton's military frustrations, he had been granted a major-general's rank on 12 October 1793 as well as an appointment as colonel commandant of a battalion of the 60th foot in August 1794.

Despite his promotions Carleton remained disappointed with his shrinking military responsibilities and found his efforts as governor increasingly disconcerting and burdensome. While counties were established and substantial portions of New Brunswick were settled and developed by the loyalist newcomers and old settlers (pre-loyalists and Acadians), the political, social, and economic blueprint applied by Carleton and his supportive loyalist leaders came under heavy fire in the 1790s. A second assembly, elected in 1793, challenged the authority and decisions of the lieutenant-governor, his title as of 1786, and his appointed council. The confrontation resulted in deadlock and government ground to a halt from 1795 to 1799. Measures passed by the assembly were routinely turned back by the lieutenant-governor and council while legislation initiated at the upper levels of government suffered the same fate in the assembly. Hints from the British government concerning the need to compromise, along with divisions in the opposition faction led by James Glenie, eventually achieved concessions from both sides. Normal government resumed although assembly rights and privileges had been successfully asserted at the expense of executive authority.

Carleton did not believe that 'to reign is worth ambition tho' in Hell' (Raymond, *Winslow Papers*, Carleton to Edward Winslow, 3 Jan 1805, 530). Capitalizing upon a temporary peace between France and England, in June 1802 he requested and was granted a leave of absence to return to England. Early in October 1803, accompanied by his wife, son William, daughters Emma and Anne, and stepson Captain Nathaniel Foy, Carleton sailed for England. He never returned to New Brunswick. Carleton tried to keep informed about his colony's needs but his advice was frequently ignored, and he became increasingly aware of 'the little prospect of being able to draw the attention of Ministers towards our part of the world' (ibid., 6 July 1804, 516). At the same time, his family was quickly seduced by residence at Ramsgate, winter visits to Bath, periods with Lord Dorchester at Stubbings House, near Maidenhead, and sojourns in London. Although several times pressed to return to his colonial post, Carleton declined and was allowed to continue as absentee governor until his death on 2 February 1817. He was buried beside his brother in St Swithin's Church at Nately Scures, near Basingstoke.

Thomas Carleton's career has been overshadowed by the exploits of his brother Guy. The younger Carleton's administration of the governorship of New Brunswick also suffers in historical studies which assume that the newly arrived members of the loyalist élite shaped and directed the infant colony with the governor merely following their lead. But Thomas Carleton achieved at least some of the loyalists' aims and, while present in New Brunswick, actively directed its development. He 'deserves to be acknowledged as the key figure among the founding fathers of New Brunswick' (*DCB*) although his governorship after 1803 was largely ineffective and inactive. W. G. GODFREY

Sources NA Canada, New Brunswick ser. A, MG11, vols. 1–26 · NA Canada, Thomas Carleton collection, MG23-D3 · Provincial Archives of New Brunswick, Thomas Carleton letter-books, R.G.1, RS330, vols. A1–A8 · PRO, CO 188/1–23 · W. O. Raymond, ed., *Winslow papers, A.D.1776–1826* (1901) · W. G. Godfrey, 'Carleton, Thomas', *DCB*, vol. 5 · W. G. Godfrey, 'Glenie, James', *DCB*, vol. 5 · A. G. Condon, *The envy of the American states: the loyalist dream for New Brunswick* (1984) · D. G. Bell, *Early loyalist Saint John: the origin of New Brunswick politics, 1783–1786* (1983) · W. S. MacNutt, *New Brunswick: a history, 1784–1867* (1963) · N. MacKinnon, *This unfriendly soil: the loyalist experience in Nova Scotia, 1783–1791* (1986) · W. O. Raymond, 'A sketch of the life and administration of General Thomas Carleton', *Collections of the New Brunswick Historical Society*, 6 (1905), 439–81 · DNB

Archives Montreal Historical Society, corresp. · NA Canada, MSS, MG23-D3 · New Brunswick Museum, Saint John, New Brunswick, corresp. and papers · Provincial Archives of New Brunswick, Fredericton, New Brunswick, letter-books, vols. A1–A8, R.G.1, RS330 | priv. coll., letters to Lord Shelburne

Carleton, William (*c*.1250–1311), administrator, was probably born in the village of East Carleton in Norfolk, about 5 miles east of Wymondham. He may be the man of that name whose misconduct while bailiff of a number of different Norfolk hundreds and under-constable of Norwich is mentioned in the 1274–5 hundred rolls inquiry. It is almost certain that he is the William Carleton who acted as the attorney of a number of Norfolk litigants in the common bench between 1275 and 1277, and who in 1282 stood surety for a litigant in the same court. By 1283 he had probably entered the service of Robert of Tattershall (a Lincolnshire baron much of whose property lay in Norfolk). He was certainly sufficiently trusted by Robert to have been appointed one of his general attorneys while he was out of the country.

By the autumn of 1285 Carleton had entered the king's service and been appointed a baron of the exchequer, and to this position he seems to have added that of a justice of the Jews between October 1286 (when the existing justices were disgraced and dismissed) and late 1290 (when the exchequer of the Jews was abolished after the expulsion of England's Jewish community). By 1288 he had also become a member of the king's council, and in 1290–91 was involved in making the property arrangements for the marriage of Edward I's daughter Margaret to the son of the duke of Brabant. By 1294 he had acquired a house in London in the parish of St Mary Aldermanbury, and he was bequeathed a life interest in another house in the same parish by a fellow exchequer official (Bartholmew de Castello) in 1297. He also acquired property in Essex and Suffolk, and perhaps in Norfolk, and leased crown manors in Cambridgeshire and Norfolk. In 1297 he travelled to Antwerp to negotiate a loan for Edward I, and in 1303 was involved in planning access roads to the king's new town of Hull. In the same year he also became chief baron of the exchequer.

Carleton was allowed to go into partial retirement in October 1308, and was dead by July 1311 when his will was proved in the London hustings. Although Carleton was a beneficed clerk who held the Norfolk living of North Creake (the chancel he rebuilt still stands), the Surrey living of Beddington, and the Yorkshire living of North Cave, he is known to have had at least one child, a daughter, who is mentioned in 1290 and was then married. Before his death he had apparently founded a chantry in St Mary Aldermanbury in London supported out of his London property, but he bequeathed that property not to a relative but to his cook.   PAUL BRAND

Sources Chancery records · PRO, CP40 · PRO, E13 · PRO, E159 · CLRO, hustings deeds · CLRO, wills roll

Carleton, William (1794–1869), writer, was born in 1794, probably on 4 March, in Prillisk, Clogher, co. Tyrone, the youngest of the fourteen children (six of whom died in infancy) of James Carleton, a Catholic tenant farmer, and his wife, Mary Kelly. James Carleton was bilingual in Irish and English and gifted with such an extraordinary memory that in later life his son never heard an Irish story that was completely new to him. Carleton's mother, descended from a line of Gaelic poets, had an exquisite voice and a vast repertory of songs. If, as Carleton believed, his parents' 'natural genius' had put him in touch with the spirit of the Irish people, his own keen recollection of the community in which he grew up gave that spirit a vivid embodiment in characters and incidents that made him the first authentic Irish peasant novelist in English.

Educated at unofficial 'hedge schools', and at rather better organized, though no less brutal, classical schools, Carleton seemed destined for the priesthood, and after the death of his father actually set out for the Catholic seminary at Maynooth, but turned back after an ill-omened dream. However, a disaffection with the Catholic church, which may have been triggered by the bishop of Clogher's denying him a scholarship, deepened during a pilgrimage to Lough Derg (later the theme of his first published story), although at this time he was less concerned with religious musings than with spending his late adolescence in a happy state of *dolce far niente*, performing prodigious athletic feats, and living off various relatives until they threw him out.

Finally, inspired by La Sage's picaresque hero Gil Blas, Carleton set out to make a name for himself. Refusing to contemplate manual work of any kind, he lived on his wits, and took a number of temporary teaching jobs. While still at school he had been duped into joining a secret agrarian society, but any subversive political leanings were banished by the sight of the oozing corpses of hanged Ribbonmen in Leitrim (an incident he used in his story 'Wildgoose Lodge'), and he remained a supporter of the union throughout his life. After looking over Maynooth, which he at last managed to reach, and applying unsuccessfully for a post at the Jesuit College of Conglowes, he finally abandoned any lingering thoughts of a career in the Catholic church and, shortly after arriving in Dublin in 1818, converted to protestantism. This gave him access to a network of contacts through which he secured temporary teaching posts and then a clerkship in the Sunday School Society. The security this provided enabled him to marry Jane Anderson, the niece of a benefactor, probably in early 1822. But he soon lost his post, and she was obliged to return to her mother's house, where she

William Carleton (1794–1869), by John Kirkwood, pubd 1841 (after Charles Grey)

gave birth to their first child, a daughter, in November 1822. Through his friends Carleton obtained a job in a school in Mullingar, Westmeath (where a second daughter was born, and where he was imprisoned for debt), and he secured a further teaching post in Carlow before returning to Dublin.

Back in the capital, Carleton wrote in November 1826 to the home secretary Sir Robert Peel, offering to prove the involvement of O'Connell's Catholic Association and the Catholic priesthood in agrarian crime. He was subsequently taken up by an evangelical proselytizer, the Revd Caesar Otway, who encouraged him to submit stories and sketches to his anti-Catholic paper the *Christian Examiner*. The first of these appeared in April 1828, and the series, based on his intimate knowledge of peasant life and idiom, quickly gained him a literary reputation, especially when some of the stories were collected as *Traits and Stories of the Irish Peasantry* in 1830. Carleton ceased publishing in the *Christian Examiner* after 1831, and his work began to appear in a number of other Irish periodicals, notably the recently founded *Dublin University Magazine*. He prepared a second series of *Traits and Stories*, which appeared in three volumes in 1833 to great critical acclaim, although there were complaints that his treatment of Catholic priests was biased and too harsh. These accusations were redoubled in 1834 with the publication of *Tales of Ireland*, the anti-Catholic slant of which adversely affected its sales. At this time Carleton became friends with the poet Samuel Ferguson, whom he accompanied on walking tours, and in 1836 he began to gain European recognition with the translation of *Traits and Stories* into German. Against the advice of his friends, he now determined to attempt a full-length novel, and *Fardorough the Miser*, serialized in the *Dublin University Magazine* in 1837–8, was successfully published in book form in the following year.

Driven by his expanding family, the need to send remittances to his relatives in co. Tyrone, and his increasing capacity for drink, Carleton entered the decade of his greatest productivity. He submitted a series of sketches to the short-lived *Irish Penny Journal*, and wrote a play on Dublin poverty, *The Irish Manufacturer*, which was produced at the Theatre Royal, Dublin, in March 1841. Shortly after this he became acquainted with Charles Gavan Duffy, Thomas Davis, and other Young Irelanders, and, while he never subscribed to their nationalist policies, these contacts caused him to reflect more responsibly on his position as an Irish novelist. He made a public apology for the sectarian bias of some of his earlier work and in the late 1840s produced a burst of novels which dealt with specific Irish ills: the perils of drink in *Art Maguire* (1845), Orange bigotry in *Valentine M'Clutchy* (1845), the vicious influence of secret societies in *Rody the Rover* (1845), Irish laziness and complacency in *Parra Sastha* (which he wrote in nine days in 1845), famine and the abuses of land tenure in *The Black Prophet* (1847), emigration in *The Emigrants of Ahadarra* (1848), and agrarian violence in *The Tithe Proctor* (1849). It is uncertain how far his flirtation with the Young Irelanders was genuine, and how far it was a tactical manoeuvre to secure the pension for which he had been angling since 1842. If it was the latter, it worked; the government, reluctant to see so powerful a writer defect to the nationalist opposition (he had begun to serialize *The Evil Eye* in the radical *Irish Tribune*), awarded him an annual grant of £200 in June 1848, but, with debts of £300, an extended family, and a robust thirst, this did little to ameliorate his long-term financial situation.

In the meantime Carleton had become involved in a protracted dispute with James McGlashan, the major Dublin publisher, over the rights to a novel entitled *The Black Baronet*; Carleton refused to make the changes McGlashan demanded and brought the matter to a head by placing the book (artfully disguised as *The Red Hall*) with a London publisher. This involved a visit to London in early October 1850, where he was so lionized by publishers, editors, and literary figures (including Thackeray) that he briefly contemplated settling there.

Apart from the protracted legal struggle over its publication, *The Black Baronet* signalled a move by Carleton away from depiction of the peasant life with which he was familiar to a more genteel milieu in which he was less at home. This, and the fact that his later work was written to boil the family pot, led to writing that was often slipshod

and unconvincing, although, as in the case of the melodramatic romance *Willy Reilly and his Dear Colleen Bawn* (1855), not the less popular for that. An attempt to raise money by public readings was thwarted by increasing ill health, and Disraeli refused to raise his pension. His final year was darkened by the death of his favourite daughter, Rose, and he died at 2 Woodville, Sandford, Rathmines, Dublin, of cancer of the tongue, disgruntled and still in debt, on 30 January 1869; he was buried in Mount Jerome cemetery, Dublin, and was survived by his wife.

JOHN KELLY

Sources DNB · W. Carleton, introduction, *Traits and stories of the Irish peasantry* (1843) · B. Kiely, *Poor scholar: a study of the works and days of William Carleton* (1947) · W. Carleton, *Life of William Carleton* (1996) · www.pgil-eirdata.org/html [Princess Grace Irish Library, Monaco], 30 Aug 2002 · d. cert. · correspondence, obituaries, and news cuttings, NL Ire. · BL, Peel Papers · letters to Blackwood, NL Scot. · D. J. O'Donoghue, *The life of William Carleton*, 2 vols. (1896) · A. Boue, *William Carleton 1794–1869, romancier irlandais* (1973) · R. Wolff, *William Carleton* (1980) · T. J. Flanagan, *The Irish novelists* (1959) · *Carleton Newsletter* [University of Florida] · J. McKibbin, 'Memories of Carleton', *Weekly Sun* (8 June 1895)
Archives NL Ire., corresp. · University College, Dublin, corresp. | BL, Add. MS 40390 Peel Papers Vol. ccx, fols. 29–35 · BL, Add. MS 40480 Peel Papers Vol. ccc, fol. 99 · BL, Add. MS 40517 Peel Papers Vol. cccxxvii, fols. 171–2 · NL Ire., Gavan Duffy papers incl. letters from Carleton, 5756–5757 · NL Ire., O'Donoghue's agreement with Carleton's daughter for publication of Autobiography etc., 8058 · NL Ire., letters from and about Carleton, 10517 · NL Ire., three letters from Carleton to Dunbar re his sons' education, 10862 · NL Ire., five ALS from Carleton to Lady Wilde, Miss Wall, Faulkner, etc., 13993 · NL Scot., letters to William Blackwood & Sons
Likenesses C. Grey, ink drawing, 1840, NG Ire.; repro. in Carleton, *Traits and stories* · J. Kirkwood, etchings, pubd 1841 (after drawing by C. Grey), NPG, NG Ire. [*see illus.*] · J. W. Cook, stipple (after W. Roe), NPG · C. Grey, pen drawing, NPG · J. Hogan, plaster bust, NG Ire. · J. J. Slattery, oils, NG Ire.

Carliell, Robert. *See* Carleill, Robert (*fl.* 1619).

Carlile, Christopher (*d.* in or before **1588**), Church of England clergyman, is first recorded at Michaelmas 1538, when he graduated BA at Corpus Christi College, Cambridge; in the same year he was admitted to a fellowship at Clare. He commenced MA in 1541, and on 15 October that year he was appointed master of the Jesus College grammar school. In 1548 he was elected a proctor of the university, and in 1552 was admitted BTh; he is also said to have been awarded a doctorate of theology.

A notable Hebrew scholar, Carlile became involved in religious controversies. At a commencement at Cambridge in 1552, against the opposition of Sir John Cheke, he denied the literal truth of the proposition that Christ descended into hell. His *A Discourse of Peter's Lyfe* (1582) is dedicated to Sir Thomas Wentworth, 'by whom I have been liberally sustained these thirty years', that is, since about the time of this dispute. Carlile later published the main lines of his argument of 1552 in belated response to an attack by Richard Smyth, dean of St Peter's Church, Douai, in the latter's *De missae sacrificio* (1562). He dedicated *A Discourse Concerning Two Divine Positions*, one of them described as 'touching the descension of Christ into hell', to Henry Hastings, third earl of Huntingdon, with a preface dated 13 May 1582 which expresses something of his religious outlook: 'Idolatry and blasphemy are to be corrected by the civil magistrate, and in the like manner, corruption of manners.' Such matters they must 'examine by laws, direct by judgement and conclude by conscience, guided by the word of God'. Both the identity of the patron and the sentiments here expressed suggest that Carlile was a radical protestant and it is possible that he was the activist 'Mr Carlell' of whom John Aylmer, soon to be bishop of London, complained when archdeacon of Stowe in 1576.

Most of Carlile's life remains obscure, however. He is known to have been residing at Monk's Horton, Kent, in 1563, and to have been instituted to the sinecure rectory of Hackney, Middlesex, in 1571. His successor was instituted on 22 August 1588, the living being vacant by Carlile's death. He should be distinguished from two namesakes, the first a resident of Barham, Kent, who was subsequently a parishioner of St Botolph without Bishopgate, the second a commander of English forces in the Netherlands who in 1583 published *A Briefe Summary Discourse upon the Intended Voyage to … America*.

STEPHEN WRIGHT

Sources Venn, *Alum. Cant.*, 1/1.293 · W. Robertson, *History of Hackney* (1842) · C. Carlile, *A discourse concerning two divine positions* (1582) · J. Gray, 'Jesus College Grammar School', *Proceedings of the Cambridge Antiquarian Society*, 60 (1967), 97–105 · C. Cross, *The puritan earl: the life of Henry Hastings, third earl of Huntingdon* (1966) · G. Hennessy, *Novum repertorium ecclesiasticum parochiale Londinense, or, London diocesan clergy succession from the earliest time to the year 1898* (1898)

Carlile, Elizabeth Sharples (1803–1852), freethought lecturer and advocate of women's rights, was one of six children born to Ann and Richard Sharples, a counterpane manufacturer, in Bolton, Lancashire, probably late in 1803. The family was pious and prosperous, the children received a good education, and Eliza attended boarding-school until she was about twenty. She then remained at home, sewing and reading, not questioning her faith until the deaths of her eldest sister, father, and a brother shook her faith in providence and prepared her for the theological unorthodoxy of Richard *Carlile (1790–1843).

When Richard Carlile visited Bolton in 1827 Elizabeth Sharples thought him no better than the devil, but her curiosity was aroused when he and Robert Taylor came to dine with the father of a school friend whom she was visiting in Liverpool in 1829. About a year later she discovered her cousin reading Carlile's former paper, *The Republican*, and saw Carlile's publications in his library. She began visiting a local freethought bookseller called Hardie, and in December 1831 requested him to ask Carlile to write to her. After a rapid exchange of correspondence in which admiration turned to ardent love, she determined to share his work. On 11 January 1832 she arrived in London where Carlile, who had parted from his wife, Jane, in 1830, was in the Giltspur Street compter serving two years for sedition.

Elizabeth Sharples gave her first discourse at the Rotunda lecture theatre in Blackfriars on 29 January 1832.

The Times (18 Feb 1832) found her pretty, with a good figure and genteel manners, and thought she dressed very well. Cast in the role of the Egyptian goddess Isis, she stood on the stage of the theatre, the floor strewn with whitethorn and laurel, and delivered lectures on mystical religion and women's rights that were then printed in *The Isis*, which she edited (11 February–15 December 1832). Once the novelty had passed, though, she was unable to hold her audiences or readers, and she had no head for business.

Sharples consummated her relationship with Carlile while he was still in gaol, and a son, Richard Sharples, was born in April 1833 but died of smallpox in October. From Carlile's release in August 1833 the couple cohabited in a 'moral union' from which time Elizabeth Sharples adopted Carlile as an assumed name. The Carliles lived first at his London house and shop on the corner of Bouverie Street and Fleet Street, where another son, Julian Hibbert, was born in September 1834. In November 1835 they took a seven-year lease on a cottage in Enfield Highway, where shortly afterwards a daughter, Hypatia, was born. A fourth child, Theophila, followed a year later. Though Eliza accompanied her partner on lecture tours, she played little further part in his public work. He died intestate, thus leaving her destitute, on 10 February 1843.

At first, the family was supported by Sophia Chichester, who arranged for Eliza to take charge of the sewing-room at the Ham Common Concordium. After a few months a small legacy from an aunt enabled her to set up on her own, letting apartments and maintaining her family by her needlework. In 1849, again in dire poverty, she was helped by a public subscription to set up a coffee and discussion room at 1 Warner Place, Hackney Road, in which to advocate radical freethought and women's rights. Here she gave a temporary home to the young Charles Bradlaugh. She 'looked like a queen' but was 'no good at serving coffee' (*Literary Guide*, 1 April 1915); in a few months both her business and her health had failed, and she died on 11 January 1852 at her home, 12 George Street, Hackney.

EDWARD ROYLE

Sources T. C. Campbell, *The battle for the freedom of the press, as told in the story of the life of Richard Carlile, by his daughter* (1899), pt 2. 145–242 · 'The editress to her sister Maria', *The Isis* (20 Oct 1832), 529; (27 Oct 1832), 545 · E. S. Carlile to T. Cooper, 28 July 1849, Bradlaugh MSS, 18E · E. S. Carlile to T. Cooper, 23 April 1850, Bradlaugh MSS, 19A · E. S. Carlile to T. Cooper, Bradlaugh MSS, 19B · letters to and from E. S. Carlile, Hunt. L., Carlile papers [extracts quoted in T. C. Campbell above] · H. B. Bonner, 'An echo from the past', *Literary Guide* (April 1915), 59–60 [incl. repr. extracts from letter of 28 July 1849] · W. Hilton to H. B. Bonner, 5 April 1891, Bradlaugh MSS, 2282 · H. B. Bonner and J. M. Robertson, *Charles Bradlaugh: a record of his life and work … with an account of his parliamentary struggle, politics and teachings, by John M. Robertson*, 7th edn, 1 (1908), 9–11 [incl. portraits and appendices] · J. H. Weiner, *Radicalism and freethought in nineteenth-century Britain: the life of Richard Carlile* (1983) · d. cert. · 'First discourse', *The Isis* (11 Feb 1832), 5

Archives Hunt. L. | Bishopsgate Institute, London, Bradlaugh MSS

Likenesses photograph (after crayon copy of oil painting by Miss Standish, c.1833), repro. in Campbell, *The battle for the freedom of the press*, facing p. 145

Wealth at death died in poverty

Carlile, James (*d.* 1691), actor, playwright, and soldier, was said by Charles Gildon to have been born in Lancashire. He may have been related to the playwright Lodowick *Carlell (1601/2–1675). When London's two theatre companies combined in 1682, James Carlile and William Mountfort had 'grown to the Maturity of good *Actors*' (Downes, 82). Carlile took the minor role of Aumale in *The Duke of Guise* by John Dryden and Nathaniel Lee, premièred in November 1682, and during the 1683–4 season he played Cinna in *Julius Caesar*, Vincent in Richard Brome's *The Jovial Crew*, Lesbino in Thomas Southerne's *The Disappointment*, and Pate in Brome's *The Northern Lass*. His last known role was that of Brunetto in Nahum Tate's farce *A Duke and No Duke*, which was probably first performed in August 1684. He appears to have left the stage because of antagonism from the leading actor Thomas Betterton, for when the Drury Lane patentees were at loggerheads with Betterton in 1694 they named Carlile and Mountfort as young actors whom Alexander Davenant had allowed Betterton to 'brow beate and discountenance' (Milhous, 238).

Carlile was commissioned as an ensign in the duke of Norfolk's new regiment of foot on 20 June 1685. He moved to the earl of Lichfield's regiment in July 1686 and had become a lieutenant there by 1 April 1688. Matthew Prior, in his *Satyr on the Poets* (1687), refers to Carlile's change of career and to William Mountfort's leaving the stage (temporarily) for the household of Judge Jeffreys:

> Carlile i'th' new rais'd Troops preferr'd we see,
> And chatt'ring *Montfort* in the *Chancery*.
> (*Literary Works*, 33)

In the spring of 1689 Carlile's comedy *The Fortune-Hunters, or, Two Fools Well Met* was performed at Drury Lane, with Mountfort as the rakish Young Wealthy, Edward Kynaston as his more serious brother, and Susanna Mountfort and Charlotte Butler as the two heroines. The play reflects contemporary trends in giving prominence and sympathy to the pair of serious lovers as well as to the lively ones. It was 'Acted with Applause' (Gildon, 16) and enjoyed a number of revivals until 1729.

Carlile had become a captain in Colonel Wharton's regiment by October 1689. According to Gildon, he 'got no little Reputation in the *Irish* Expeditions under his Present Majesty, and with his Brother, lost his Life in the Bed of Honour' (Gildon, 15). His brother was presumably Lodowick (or Ludovic) Carlile, who was a lieutenant in Lord Morpeth's regiment in February 1678 and a captain in the earl of Drogheda's regiment at the siege of Limerick in 1690. On 27 August Lodowick Carlile

> run on with his Granadeers to the Counterscarp, and tho' he received two Wounds between that and the Trenches, yet he went forwards, and commanded his Men to throw in their Granades; but in the leaping into the dry Ditch below the Counterscarp, an *Irishman* below shot him dead. (Story, 129)

James Carlile was killed at Aughrim on 12 July 1691, in the final battle of the Irish campaigns.

OLIVE BALDWIN and THELMA WILSON

Sources W. Van Lennep and others, eds., *The London stage, 1660–1800*, pt 1: *1660–1700* (1965) · E. L. Avery, ed., *The London stage, 1660–1800*, pt 2: *1700–1729* (1960) · A. H. Scouten, ed., *The London stage, 1660–1800*, pt 3: *1729–1747* (1961) · [C. Gildon], *The lives and characters of the English dramatick poets ... first begun by Mr Langbain* [1699] · J. Downes, *Roscius Anglicanus*, ed. J. Milhous and R. D. Hume, new edn (1987) · *Theatrical records, or, An account of English dramatic authors, and their works* (1756) · J. Milhous, *Thomas Betterton and the management of Lincoln's Inn Fields, 1695–1708* (1979), appx B, 'The reply of the patentees' · 'Satyr on the poets', *The literary works of Matthew Prior*, ed. H. B. Wright and M. K. Spears, 1 (1959), 28–33 · A. S. Borgman, *The life and death of William Mountfort* (1935) · C. Dalton, ed., *English army lists and commission registers, 1661–1714*, 6 vols. (1892–1904), vols. 1–3 · G. Story, *An impartial history of the wars of Ireland* (1693) · C. Walton, *History of the British standing army, A.D. 1660 to 1700* (1894) · *LondG* (24–7 June 1689) · J. H. Smith, *The gay couple in Restoration comedy* (1948)

Carlile, James (1784–1854), minister of the Presbyterian Church in Ireland and educationist, was born on 5 February 1784 at Paisley, the son of James Carlile, a merchant and magistrate; his mother died in 1800. He was educated at Paisley grammar school, and after a brief business career in London studied for the ministry at Glasgow and Edinburgh universities. Licensed by the Paisley presbytery in 1811, he was ordained in the Scots' Church, Mary's Abbey, in Dublin in 1813. In 1820 he married Jane Wren (*d.* 1852) of Kendal; they had two sons.

In 1831 Carlile was appointed resident commissioner to the new Irish board of national education, to take the leading part in organizing the school system, which was founded on the principle of combined secular, and separate religious, education, to enable protestant and Roman Catholic children to be educated together. He was associated in the educational board with the two archbishops of Dublin, Richard Whately and Daniel Murray, both of whom held him in high esteem. However, the national education system was bitterly opposed by conservative churchmen both Catholic and protestant, and Carlile was involved in continual controversy. Having contributed much to establish the system on firm foundations, including the provision of school text books and a teachers' training college in Dublin, in which he served as one of the professors, he resigned in 1839, devoting the remaining years of his life to Presbyterian missionary outreach to Roman Catholics in Ireland. He had long felt that existing methods of outreach were unsatisfactory, and as early as 1825 had published a memorial in which he advocated a plan partly modelled on the Moravian missions. In 1839 he prevailed on his Dublin congregation, which was a collegiate charge, to allow him, while still maintaining his relation to it, to act as their missionary in Birr, King's county, where a large number of Roman Catholics had seceded, under the leadership of their priest, from the Catholic communion, and had been received as a Presbyterian congregation by the synod of Ulster. He took an active part in the affairs of the Presbyterian Church in Ireland, and was moderator of the synod of Ulster in 1825 and of the general assembly in 1845, when he received a DD from Glasgow University. He made his mark in the synod originally in 1816, with a forthright speech in defence of the spiritual independence of the church in response to the attempt of Lord Castlereagh to prevent the synod from recognizing the Belfast Academical Institution as an alternative to a Scottish university for the education of their ministers.

Carlile was the author of many theological and polemical works, including *Jesus Christ, the Great God and our Saviour*, published in 1828 during the Arian controversy, contending that the doctrine of the Trinity is a doctrine of inference and not direct biblical revelation, thus embarrassing Henry Cooke and the Trinitarian party in the synod. Though an evangelical, he opposed Cooke's policy of driving the Arians and non-subscribers out of the synod. W. D. Killen described Carlile as 'an original thinker and fearless advocate of what he believed to be right' (Killen, 196–7). During the Irish famine, in which his own sister died, he did much relief work, supported by his congregation in Dublin. After his wife's death in Birr in 1852 he retired to Dublin, where he died at his home, 12 Leinster Road, Rathmines, on 31 March 1854. A funeral service was held in the Scots' Church, Capel Street, Dublin, and he was buried in Birr on 5 April.   FINLAY HOLMES

Sources Presbyterian Historical Society of Ireland archives, Belfast · R. J. Rodgers, 'James Carlile, 1784–1854', PhD thesis, Queen's University, Belfast, 1973 [contains a full bibliography] · R. J. Rodgers, 'Reformation at Birr', *Presbyterian Historical Society Bulletin*, 2 (Jan 1972), 5–8 · T. Hamilton, *Irish worthies* (1875), 48–58 · J. S. Reid and W. D. Killen, *History of the Presbyterian church in Ireland*, new edn, 3 (1867), 431–3 · *Banner of Ulster* (1 April 1854) · *Banner of Ulster* (8 April 1854) · *Christian Irishman* (Nov 1899), 158 · W. D. Killen, *Reminiscences of a long life* (1901); repr. (1995), 196–200 · D. H. Akenson, *The Irish education experiment: the national system of education in the nineteenth century* (1970) · J. Armstrong, *History of the Presbyterian churches in the city of Dublin* (1829)

Archives Abbey Presbyterian Church, Dublin, accounts · Abbey Presbyterian Church, Dublin, corresp. · Abbey Presbyterian Church, Dublin, minute books · Church House, Fisherwick Place, Belfast, minutes of the presbytery of Dublin · NL Ire., minutes of the Board of National Education | U. Edin., New College, letters to Thomas Chalmers

Likenesses B. R. Haydon, group portrait, oils (*The Anti-Slavery Society convention, 1840*), NPG · portrait, Abbey Presbyterian Church, Dublin, Ireland · print, repro. in Rodgers, 'James Carlile, 1784–1854'

Carlile [Carlell; *née* Palmer], **Joan** (*c.*1606–1679), portrait painter and copyist, was the daughter of William Palmer (*d.* 1634), an official of the royal parks of St James's and the Spring Garden, and his wife, Mary. Buckeridge and the *Dictionary of National Biography* mistakenly referred to Joan Carlile as Anne. In 1626 she married Lodowick *Carlell (1601/2–1675), a minor poet and court dramatist, who was groom of the privy chamber and 'gentleman of the bows' to Charles I. They lived in the parish of St Martin-in-the-Fields, London, where five of their six known children were baptized; all but two, Penelope and James, died before 1644. Though her husband is most commonly known as Carlell, she is usually referred to as Carlile.

Carlile is one of the first recorded Englishwomen to paint professionally. Sir William Sanderson described her as a 'worthy Artist' in 'Oyl Colours' in his *Graphice* of 1658. She copied the paintings of the Italian masters 'so admirably well, that she was much in favour with king Charles I, who became her patron, and presented her and Sir

Anthony Vandyck with as much ultra marine at one time, as cost him above five hundred pounds' (Buckeridge, 361).

By 1637 Lodowick was appointed a keeper of Richmond Park and the couple moved to Petersham, Richmond, Surrey, where they supplemented their income by taking in lodgers. On 1 November 1653, however, their neighbour, Brian Duppa, bishop of Salisbury, wrote that 'the Mistress of the Family intends for London, where she meanes to make use of her skill to som more Advantage then hetherto she hath don' (Toynbee and Isham, 'Joan Carlile … an identification', 275). In 1654 they moved to Covent Garden, which was then home to a number of artists, including Mary Beale, but they returned to Petersham two years later. In 1658 Bishop Duppa wrote that he feared they were in a 'declining condition' (Isham, 153).

In September 1660, after the restoration of Charles II, Lodowick and Joan Carlile were granted 'the office of Keeper of the House or Lodge and the Walk at Petersham' (Toynbee and Isham, 'Joan Carlile … an identification', 276), and the following year they were awarded an annuity of £200. In 1663 Lodowick and their son James gave up the office, and they returned to London, where they lived in St James's Market. Lodowick died in 1675 and was buried in Petersham churchyard. Joan died in 1679, and was buried beside her husband on 27 February.

Joan Carlile's paintings are characterized by their small full-length format and depict short figures set against a landscape background. The hands are distinctive, with 'claw-like' or 'spidery' fingers (Toynbee, 1971, 186–7), often displayed with the forefingers extended in a forked position.

Among those paintings attributed to Joan Carlile are both group and individual portraits, often of people in her own social circle. The *Group of Figures at a Stag Hunt* (*c.*1649–50; Lamport Hall Trust, Northamptonshire), which includes the artist and her family, and *Sir Lionel Tollemache, his Wife Elizabeth Murray and her Sister Margaret* (*c.*1650; Ham House, Surrey) foreshadow the eighteenth-century conversation piece. Horace Walpole described the figures in the latter as 'too squab, but well finished' (Walpole, 'Journals of visits', 67). Other attributed portraits include: *Sir Thomas and Lady Browne* (*c.*1641–50; NPG); three young women, probably the daughters of Walter Overbury, Joan Carlile's first cousin (*c.*1650; Okeover Hall, Staffordshire); and *Lady Anne Wentworth*(?) (Christies, 8 July 1998, lot 92). In addition, she mentioned three paintings in her will, 'the Princesse in white sattin', 'the little St Katherine and the Mercury', and 'the Lady Bedford' (Toynbee and Isham, 276), and Vertue described a self-portrait with another lady, but the present locations of these paintings are unknown.   ARIANNE BURNETTE

Sources M. Toynbee and G. Isham, 'Joan Carlile (1606?–1679): an identification', *Burlington Magazine*, 96 (1954), 273–7 · M. Toynbee, 'Joan Carlile: some further attributions', *The Connoisseur*, 178 (1971), 186–8 · M. Toynbee and G. Isham, 'The family connections of Joan Carlile', *N&Q*, 200 (1955), 515–21 · *The correspondence of Bishop Brian Duppa and Sir Justinian Isham, 1650–1660*, ed. G. Isham, Northamptonshire RS, 17 (1951) · [B. Buckeridge], 'An essay towards an English school of painting', in R. de Piles, *The art of painting, with the lives* *and characters of above 300 of the most eminent painters*, 3rd edn (1754), 354–439 • W. Sanderson, *Graphice: the use of the pen and pensil, or, The most excellent art of painting* (1658) • H. Walpole, 'Horace Walpole's journals of visits to country seats', *Walpole Society*, 16 (1927–8), 9–80 • Vertue, *Note books*, vol. 1 • M. Toynbee, 'Portrait group by Joan Carlile', *Country Life*, 135 (1964), 1127–9 • M. Toynbee, 'Some friends of Sir Thomas Browne', *Norfolk Archaeology*, 31 (1955–7), 377–94 • J. E. Ruoff, 'The author of "Britain's glory" (1618): an identification', *N&Q*, 200 (1955), 295–6 • J. Sheeran, 'Carlile [née Palmer], Joan', *The dictionary of art*, ed. J. Turner (1996) • E. K. Waterhouse, *The dictionary of British 16th and 17th century painters* (1988) • H. Walpole, *Anecdotes of painting in England: with some account of the principal artists*, ed. R. N. Wornum, new edn, 2 (1849); repr. (1862), 381 • *DNB* • will, PRO, PROB 11/367, fols. 177r–178v

Archives PRO, Lord Chamberlain 5/134

Likenesses attrib. J. Carlile, group portrait, oils, *c.*1649–1650 (*Group of Figures at a Stag Hunt*), Lamport Hall Trust, Northamptonshire • J. Carlile, oils (with another lady)

Wealth at death in debt; royal annuity was not paid regularly (she hoped in the first instance to pay debts with the arrears); if this was not possible, she directed executors to sell pictures and 'pay and distribute the money amongst the creditors': Toynbee and Isham, 'Family connections of Joan Carlile'

Carlile, Lodowick. *See* Carlell, Lodowick (1601/2–1675).

Carlile, Richard (1790–1843), radical publisher and writer, was born on 8 December 1790 at Ashburton, Devon, the second of the three children of Richard Carlile senior and Elizabeth Carlile, *née* Brookings. His father was from a Devon family, and made his living first as a shoemaker, and then as an exciseman, a teacher, and a soldier. He published a book on mathematics, took to drink, deserted his family within a few years of Carlile's birth, and died soon after. Carlile's mother kept a shop in Lawrence Lane, Ashburton. She was a devout Anglican who gave her children a serious Christian upbringing.

Carlile was provided with an elementary education in two of the local free schools, which he attended up to the age of twelve, but he did not enter the prestigious local grammar school where the deeply conservative William Gifford, editor of the *Quarterly Review*, had been educated. Upon leaving school he went to work at Edward Lee's chemist's shop in Exeter but, soon afterwards, returned to work in his mother's shop. In 1803 he had the opportunity through connections in his father's family to become a tinplate worker, and accepted. For the next fifteen years Carlile earned his living as an itinerant tinworker, making mostly domestic articles. However, the trade was in continuous decline, and as he moved from place to place to find work in the south of England he lived in constant anxiety about his future employment. In 1812–13, while in Portsmouth, he considered entering the Church of England, having been inspired by the sermons of two moderately reforming theologians, Lant Carpenter and David Bogue, who both espoused a form of deism that they claimed was within the bounds of orthodoxy. By all accounts these were difficult years for Carlile, and the precariousness of his living was increased in 1813 when he married. Nothing is known of the former life of his wife, Jane (*d.* 1843), other than that she was of poor origins and came from Hampshire. The couple were married in Gosport, and soon after moved to London where Carlile hoped

to make a better living for himself in the pursuit of his trade. Living in Bloomsbury, he worked for two employers between 1813 and 1817: Benham & Sons, south of the Thames, and Masterman, Matthews & Co., in Holborn. In the early years of their marriage the Carliles had four children: Richard (1814–1854), Alfred (*b.* 1816), Thomas Paine (1818–1819), and Thomas Paine (*b.* 1819).

Radical publisher in London Living in London in these years it would have been impossible to remain untouched by the radical reformist zeal which was especially strong in the artisan class. A combination of necessity, a sense of injustice, and a growing realization of the power and rectitude of democratic radicalism drew Carlile to give up his trade in March 1817. He became in the first instance a hawker of pamphlets and journals and subsequently a writer of radical tracts. The same year he met William T. Sherwin, whose *Weekly Political Register* was just established (April), and they entered into a business arrangement whereby he became the journal's publisher, thereby rendering himself liable to prosecution in the event of the journal's being found seditious. Carlile's mind was set on its new course and he quickly established a reputation as a prolific writer and publisher of egalitarian and republican principles. His politics and actions were uncompromising, and when, in August 1817, he reprinted the political parodies of William Hone without the author's permission (Hone, under threat of prosecution, had offered to withdraw them) he was imprisoned awaiting trial on charges of seditious libel and blasphemy. He remained there for four months until the charges were dropped on Hone's famous acquittal.

Now began the most fertile period of Carlile's controversial life as he commenced a broad reading programme in the literature of radicalism and religious scepticism while simultaneously conversing with the speakers and activists attending the great 'free and easies' and other meetings of the London agitators. Between 1817 and 1819 he immersed himself in the writings of Tom Paine and the ideas of the Spenceans; he took a vigorous part in Orator Hunt's attempt to gain election for the city of Westminster; he took on two more newspapers, *The Gracchus* and *The Gorgon*, and he started his own journal, *The Republican*, in August 1817. His greatest contribution to the radical cause, and the most momentous, was his republishing of the writings of Tom Paine, which he did serially in the *Weekly*, individually as cheap pamphlets, and also as bound volumes. Carlile rapidly became the most successful popularizer of Paine since the 1790s, and followed this later with a biography, *The Life of Thomas Paine* (1820). In December 1818 he published as part of the *Theological Works of Paine* the *Age of Reason*, a work banned in 1797, and in doing so he provoked the combined forces of government and religious conservatism against him. In 1819 he was the subject of several prosecutions, throughout which he continued to publish despite intermittent spells in prison. In February he set up as a publisher and bookseller at 55 Fleet Street, and with prosecutions pending, succeeded through the following months in disseminating large numbers of tracts and pamphlets despite confiscations and filed prosecutions in a rising storm of publicity. His reputation resulted in his invitation to attend the meeting in August at St Peter's Fields, Manchester, where he witnessed the Peterloo massacre. On returning to London he published his eyewitness accounts in Sherwin's *Weekly Political Register* (which finished publication in August), and then in *The Republican*, thereby incurring further charges of seditious libel. Carlile's trials began in October 1819, and included his famous reading of the *Age of Reason* under the justification that the jury would have to judge whether it was blasphemous, an action that amounted to an attempt to secure its republication once again, since verbatim trial proceedings were allowed to be published (10,000 twopenny copies were subsequently sold). Despite his hopes for an acquittal he was found guilty on two charges and sentenced to six years in Dorchester prison.

Imprisonment, 1819–1825 Carlile entered prison in November 1819, and was granted some privileges on account of his political status and the financial advantages gained by drawing on his profits and money raised by his supporters. Most of his six years, however, were spent in isolation, as he was not permitted to mix with other prisoners. Turning this to his advantage, Carlile commenced an extensive reading programme, and in response to Christian tracts sent to him by evangelicals he wrote spirited, dismissive replies. He developed an obsession with a healthy regimen, abjuring meat and alcohol and recommending regular bathing, hard work, and herbal remedies. Despite attempts by the Home Office to stop him Carlile was able to continue his career as a publisher, principally through the dedicated assistance of his wife and two printer friends, Thomas Davison and Thomas Moses. His sister, Mary-Anne, and other supporters also helped out at the London shop which they managed to keep open until February 1822, when confiscation of the stock forced closure. Operating as best they could from other premises, Carlile's friends and family continued his publishing campaign, and the result was the subsequent imprisonment of Jane Carlile (February 1821) and Mary-Anne Carlile (June 1822) for two years each. They were confined with Carlile at Dorchester, and in June 1822 Jane gave birth to a daughter, Hypatia.

From 1820, when he launched his first appeal for help in *The Republican*, Carlile's publishing activities depended on the help of a broader band of political support in the provinces and in London, where radical vendors and shopmen came to his aid, and were skilfully directed by him in their campaigns for a free press. Many were imprisoned, and Carlile published accounts of the trials in *The Republican*. Support from his more famous radical associates may have dwindled during Carlile's imprisonment, but there is no doubt that among artisans and workers his reputation grew as thousands flocked to his defence, to aid in publicity ventures, or help disseminate material, pulled together by religious suspicion, republicanism, and a hatred of privilege. Organizations were formed from December 1821 to support Carlile, the first being the Edinburgh Freethinkers Zetetic Society, which met regularly for lectures and raised subscriptions for the 'victim fund'. The model was followed widely, and these associations raised significant sums from very small subscriptions of a few pence each. Between 1819 and 1825 £1400 was raised for Carlile, and up to fifty districts had groups meeting regularly to uphold his cause. This is the period at which Carlile's wide influence was firmly established in the broad network of pro-Paineite organizations. Ironically his imprisonment established him as a major rallying point, and he was regarded as a figurehead of potential revolution in this period.

Birth control and freethought Carlile was freed in November 1825, and returned to London in January 1826; he secured a new shop at 62 Fleet Street in May and set about founding a joint stock book company with the aim of promulgating radical texts at affordable prices, a financial folly which lasted only two years. With the political fervour that had characterized the second decade now significantly in decline, Carlile's career lost much of its direction and purpose; indeed, from this point on he was beset with difficulties. While he continued to serve the cause of radical, reformist politics, befriending Frances Place, supporting his shopmen in Newgate, and disputing the principles of reform with Cobbett and Hunt, he also became diverted by Place's campaign for birth control. As a serious and practical antidote to the views of Malthus, the advocacy of birth control was undoubtedly a good liberal cause, but it was also a very controversial subject. After a series of articles on sexual love in *The Republican*, Carlile published a pamphlet entitled *Every Woman's Book, or, What is Love* which argued for a rational approach to birth control, attacking the Christian demonization of sexual desire while denying the traditional chauvinist assumptions about women. An important contribution to the nineteenth-century debate on birth control, Carlile's pamphlet nevertheless damaged his support among radicals and the disaffected working class.

Simultaneously Carlile was revising his position on Christianity. Always drawn towards accounts of Christian doctrine that denied its monotheism and claims of historical authenticity, Carlile had discovered several authors who read Christianity allegorically and amalgamated it with other religions as a mythical understanding of religious life and truth. One such was Robert Taylor, with whom Carlile had begun a correspondence in 1824. By 1826 the two men were well acquainted. In his writings Carlile abandoned his stance as a rationalist and began to nominate himself as a 'Christian atheist', taking on the rhetoric of mystical Christianity as he did so. No doubt this contributed to the decline of *The Republican*, which ceased publication in December 1826 as a consequence of a dwindling circulation.

In early 1827 Carlile embarked on the first of a series of lecture tours in the southern provinces, and in July he set off for six months in the north. Well attended, his lectures nevertheless attracted hostility from reformers who objected to his allegorical religion and his position on birth control. So controversial was the reception of his lecture at Stockport in September 1827 that Carlile cut short his tour to return to London and rally support for Robert Taylor, who had been imprisoned on a charge of blasphemy. This he did with great success from his shop in Fleet Street, and partly on the rising tide of the protest he launched a new weekly, *The Lion*, in January 1828. Characterized by its attacks on religion, fiction and 'superstition', *The Lion* ran with moderate success until the end of 1829. Compared to *The Republican*, *The Lion* was a much smaller and less influential enterprise, but there was some compensation for Carlile in the other projects of this period, principally the founding of the School of Free Discussion at his shop, which also included a reading room and library. On Taylor's release in February 1829 he and Carlile planned a tour to begin what they called an infidel mission to establish a network of atheist 'chapels'. They travelled extensively to the midlands and the north, experiencing a mixed response in their audiences.

More successful in every way was Carlile's opening of the Rotunda in Blackfriars Road in May 1830, at great cost. Several times a week Carlile, Taylor, and invited speakers would deliver attacks on the superstitions of Christianity, which Carlile had now identified as the single most obdurate opposition to reform and liberation. Dramatic events were also part of the programme, as were parodies of Christian services in which the readings were taken from rationalist works. The Rotunda became an important centre for working-class infidel dissent and political reform, and Carlile's principle that free discussion should reign meant that even those radicals whose views were sharply different from his own spoke there, including Cobbett and Hunt, although inevitably schisms occurred, including quarrels with the National Union of the Working Classes, which supported universal suffrage, and the British Association for Promoting Co-operative Knowledge, which backed economic co-operation.

Further imprisonment and 'moral union' with Eliza Sharples Carlile once again found himself the target of the government late in 1830, when an indictment was issued in response to his writings in support of the Swing disturbances published in *The Prompter*, one of his journals. In January 1831 he appeared at the Old Bailey on charges of seditious libel which resulted in a sentence of two years' imprisonment and a large fine which he refused to pay, thereby extending the sentence by a further six months. He served the sentence in the Giltspur Street compter, a prison which afforded him sufficient comforts to continue writing and receive guests on a regular basis. Once again, Carlile set himself a stern regimen of reading, writing, and publishing ventures. The Rotunda continued despite his absence, but after Taylor's imprisonment in July 1831 for two years, it gradually lost its support and closed the following year. From the compter, Carlile published a tract on madness, the *New View of Insanity* (1831), and an allegorical interpretation of freemasonry, the *Manual of*

Masonry (1831) while his journalism continued in *The Union*, *The Cosmopolite*, *The Isis*, and *The Gauntlet*, launched in early 1833 as a successor to *The Prompter*, which was wound up late in 1831.

Meanwhile Carlile's financial condition was worsening. His dwindling reputation in radical circles meant that he was unable to secure the kind of financial support he had won while in Dorchester prison, and the increase in working-class movements requiring subscriptions was also unwelcome competition. The Rotunda had left him with considerable debts, and he owed money to printers. Although *The Gauntlet* afforded him some relief, establishing a good circulation in 1833, his troubles were compounded by his affair with Eliza Sharples [see Carlile, Elizabeth Sharples (1803–1852)], a speaker at the Rotunda and a disciple of his allegorical Christianity. A daily visitor to the compter in 1832, she may well have been instrumental in the formal separation of the Carliles early that year, in which Jane Carlile moved out of the Fleet Street property to start a bookshop of her own. Eliza Sharples became pregnant later in 1832, and Carlile, fearful of his reputation as a person of principle, refused to receive her as a visitor, making every attempt to keep his indiscretion secret. In April 1833 she gave birth to a son, Richard Sharples, and upon his release in September Carlile realized that he would have to acknowledge their relationship, and thereupon declared that he and Eliza were joined in a 'moral marriage'. As he feared, the publicity was most damaging, eroding further his support in working-class and reformist circles.

Lecture tours and later views on Christianity Carlile immediately set off on another provincial lecture tour, with the object of diverting his listeners away from political reform as a prime objective and towards the more fundamental transformations afforded by theological reform. In Sheffield in October 1833 he declared a new position, calling himself a new Christian, while retaining his allegorical interpretation which combined the truth of the gospels with the truth of reason and rational enquiry. This shift of position caused some to question his sanity. His tour was cut short by the news of the death of Richard Sharples, and he returned to London for a while. For the greater part of 1834 Carlile toured the provinces, lecturing to small and mostly unreceptive audiences. During this year he also took a stand against the payment of church rates, which landed him back in prison in December for a few months.

On his release from prison in February 1835 Carlile's affairs were in a sorry state. His health was poor and his finances were precarious. He had no promising publishing ventures in hand, *The Gauntlet* having been given up in March 1834 and his moderately successful *A Scourge for the Littleness of Great Men* having also collapsed in the face of an action over its unstamped status. He moved out of London to Enfield, where he rented a cottage from where he made occasional forays into the city to lecture, and here he found a simpler lifestyle, cultivating his garden and living with Eliza, with whom he had two further children: Julian Hibbert and Hypatia (*b*. 1835). In August 1836 he set off again on tour, lecturing first at Brighton and then to the north, returning home in December to start yet another short-lived weekly, *The Phoenix, or, The Christian Advocate of Equal Knowledge*. As the title suggests, Carlile's position was shifting radically. While it is clear that he never retreated to orthodoxy, his increasing use of Christian rhetoric and his own claims for himself as a Christian were a far cry from the radicalism of his early years. Carlile still propounded a sceptical, rational view of religion, but his allegorical readings had diminished to a single interpretation of Christianity in which he saw Christ and the resurrection as the rebirth of the soul of reason in humankind.

It was evident by now, however, that Carlile was behind the times. The rising powers of Chartism and socialism were far more attractive for reformists than the quasi-mystical allegories of Carlile, which smacked of the millenarianism of the 1790s. While his financial condition was relieved by the kind assistance of Sarah Chichester of Painswick, and while he succeeded in some of his tours in gathering large audiences (he spoke to 1500 people in Leeds in 1839, and 3000 people on Rodborough Common, Stroud, in 1842), for the most part he found only dwindling numbers, hostility, or at best controversy. Typically, he never gave up hope, and until his death in 1843 he continued to read omnivorously and write tracts. Increasingly isolated, and all but estranged from Eliza, who moved to Devon with the children in 1842, he lost Sarah Chichester's support in January 1843 and made one last wild attempt at launching a weekly, the *Christian Warrior*, in the same month. It ran for four issues, then flopped. Within weeks Carlile was dead, dying of a bronchial infection on 10 February 1843 in Fleet Street, London. As he had dedicated his body to science it was taken to St Thomas's Hospital before his burial at Kensal Green cemetery in London on 26 February.

The significance of Carlile's achievement lies in his contribution to the cause of free speech and a free press. While his own works are unlikely to receive much attention now, his publishing career and his championship of the oppressed, of no advantage to himself or his family, stand as testimony to the depth of commitment to be found in the artisan class of the early nineteenth century. Carlile never gave up, never became disaffected, and continuously sought to discover new opportunities of disseminating his conviction that freedom from the shackles of orthodoxy and oppression was essential for the future of his civilization.

PHILIP W. MARTIN

Sources J. H. Weiner, *Radicalism and freethought in nineteenth-century Britain: the life of Richard Carlile* (1983) · I. McCalman, *Radical underworld: prophets, revolutionaries, and pornographers in London, 1795–1840* (1988); pbk edn (1993) · D. Worrall, *Radical culture: discourse, resistance and surveillance, 1790–1820* (1992) · E. Royle and J. Walvin, *English radicals and reformers, 1760–1848* (1982) · DNB

Archives Hunt. L., letters | Co-operative Union, Manchester, Holyoake House, archive, letters to George Holyoake · W. Yorks. AS, Leeds, corresp. with Humphrey Boyle

Likenesses line engraving, 1825, BM · lithograph, BM, NPG · oils, NPG · stipple, BM

Carlile, Wilson (1847–1942), founder of the Church Army, was born on 14 January 1847 at Brixton, the eldest of the twelve children of Edward Carlile, a merchant in the City of London, where his father had settled, and whose forebears had for some generations been prominent in the civic and business life of Paisley. Wilson Carlile's mother was Maria Louisa, second daughter of Benjamin Wilson, a Yorkshireman who had come to London as a silk mercer and became master of the Haberdashers' Company. He was a second cousin of Sir R. W. Carlyle and A. J. Carlyle. Carlile's education was hampered by a spinal weakness from which he suffered throughout his long life and which prevented him from taking an active part in sports or exercises. After attending a private school at Brixton he entered his maternal grandfather's business at the age of thirteen, but shortly afterwards went for a year to school at Lille, where he became fluent in French. Of this he made good use during the Franco-Prussian War, when he travelled widely in France in order to take advantage of the unsettled state of the silk market. Later he learnt to speak German with equal facility and acquired a good knowledge of Italian. When Carlile came of age the business became his property and by 1873 he had laid the foundations of a small fortune when a slump ruined him.

A serious illness supervened and turned Carlile's thoughts to religion, in which his interest hitherto had been no more than conventional. His parents, who had been devout Congregationalists, had recently joined the Church of England in which, on recovery, Carlile was confirmed after a brief attraction to the (Plymouth) Brethren. He was now in partnership with his father, giving his spare time to mission work in the parish of Holy Trinity, Richmond, where his family had settled. Having great musical ability he also acted as deputy organist to Ira D. Sankey during the great Moody and Sankey missions of 1875, and this brought him in touch with the leading evangelists of the day. In 1878 Carlile gave up his business in order to be trained for holy orders at St John's College, Highbury. He was ordained deacon in 1880 and priest in 1881, being appointed in the former year curate at St Mary Abbots Church, Kensington. The happy association of ten or twelve curates of widely different views under Edward Carr Glyn, later bishop of Peterborough, greatly influenced Carlile when he founded the Church Army as a strictly non-party society within the Church of England. He was profoundly concerned by the lack of contact between the church and the working classes, and by the absence of opportunities for working-class Anglicans to play an active part in the church's life and mission. He began open-air meetings in which the help of working men and women was enlisted, and which eventually caused so much obstruction to traffic that in June 1882 he was asked to give them up. Indoor meetings, held in the parish school and making use of magic-lantern slides, also attracted working people.

In 1882 Carlile resigned his curacy and founded the Church Army which (like the Salvation Army begun four

Wilson Carlile (1847–1942), by Lafayette, 1928

years earlier), in its early days in the slums of Westminster, met with great violence. Two or three times Carlile was gravely injured, yet not infrequently his roughest opponents came to be his greatest helpers. Opposition came also from within the church, where many disliked his unconventional methods. But the movement grew, and the success which soon came was due in no small degree to Carlile's wise decision to devolve many responsible duties to his workers. In 1884 a Church Army training college was established at Oxford, in which working men, without cost to themselves, were trained to be full-time evangelists; in 1887 a similar college for women workers was opened in west London, where for many years women were trained by Carlile's sister, Marie Louise Carlile. Under an order of convocation made in 1897 the male students were admitted, on the successful conclusion of their training, by the bishop of London to the 'office of Evangelist in the Church of God' and by this specially created office the Church Army workers obtained an official status, which was extended to women in 1921. During the war of 1914–18 the Church Army was engaged in extensive work with British troops in the various theatres of conflict.

Carlile based his organization on the unit of the parish, in which there was a 'corps' of Church Army members who, under the guidance of Church Army officers, were required to bear private and public testimony to their faith. During a serious illness in 1926 Carlile conceived the idea that every parish, including those without any

trained Church Army officer, should organize its members into corps or news teams, and this method received official support after his death. By building up the largest lay society within the Church of England Carlile not only greatly increased opportunities for the laity to participate in the work of the church but also stimulated similar efforts inside the church, independent of the Church Army (for example, in the increasing role given to lay readers). His influence on the evangelistic side of the Church of England was therefore very great. His social work was equally influential. In 1889 he established Church Army homes for ex-prisoners, tramps, and others on the margins of society, and two or three times each winter week he would spend the night on the Thames Embankment; sometimes up to 2000 homeless men and women would gather for Church Army food and shelter. This and other aspects of his social work were criticized by committed socialists on the grounds that they were only palliatives. The fact remains that Carlile's efforts not only alleviated a great amount of misery but did much to rouse the social conscience by publicizing the plight of those suffering desperate poverty, homelessness, and unemployment to middle-class Anglicans who lived in the comfort of the suburbs. By practical help, and not by platform eloquence, he drew public attention, for instance, to the problem of overcrowding in the 1920s. As a result of his appeals for gifts of money or loans at low interest nearly 1000 houses were built for large families with small incomes by the Church Army Housing Ltd, one of the precursors of the housing association movement.

In collaboration with his eldest son, Victor, Carlile wrote *The Continental Outcast* (1906), an account of a tour of labour colonies and other establishments in Denmark, Belgium, Holland, and Germany. He also composed a simple choral communion service which was widely used. In 1891 he was presented to the rectory of St Mary-at-Hill, an empty City church which he filled to overflowing before he retired in 1926, retaining a connection as honorary curate. Meanwhile the success of the work of the Church Army brought him honours from both church and state. In 1906 he was appointed a prebendary of St Paul's Cathedral; he received an honorary DD in 1915 from the University of Oxford and in 1926 from the University of Toronto. In 1926 he was appointed CH. In 1870 Carlile had married Flora (d. 1925), daughter of Thomas Vickers, lawyer, of Brixton; they had five sons. His grandson, the Revd E. Wilson Carlile, became chief secretary of the Church Army in 1949. Wilson Carlile died at his home, Kingsbury, Coley Avenue, Woking, on 26 September 1942; his funeral on 2 October was held at St Paul's Cathedral.

A. E. REFFOLD, rev. I. T. FOSTER

Sources S. Dark, *Wilson Carlile: the laughing cavalier of Christ* (1944) · A. E. Reffold, *Seven stars: the story of a fifty years' war: a résumé of the life and work of Wilson Carlile and the Church Army, which he founded in 1882* (1931) · A. E. Reffold, *The audacity to live: a résumé of the life and work of Wilson Carlile* (1938) · A. E. Reffold, *Wilson Carlile, 1847–1942: priest, prophet, evangelist* (c.1947) · E. Rowan, *Wilson Carlile and the Church Army*, rev. A. E. Reffold, 4th edn (1933) · D. Lynch, *Chariots of the gospel: the centenary history of the Church Army* (1982) · *Debrett's Peerage*

(1940) • *Record* (2 Oct 1942) • correspondence with Church Army headquarters
Likenesses Lafayette, photograph, 1928, NPG [*see illus.*] • A. S. Cope, portrait, priv. coll. • L. R. Galesta, oils, Church Army, London • J. Russell & Sons, photograph, NPG
Wealth at death £17,845 17s. 3d.: probate, 22 Feb 1943, *CGPLA Eng. & Wales*

Carline family (*per. c.*1870–*c.*1975), painters, came to prominence with **George Francis Carline** (1855–1920), born on 11 July 1855 in Lincoln, the son of Richard Carline (1806–1863) and Jane Frances Snow (1814–1861). His father was a solicitor and three times elected mayor of Lincoln, but he numbered several painters, sculptors, and architects among his forebears. His own training as a painter began in Lincoln School of Art in the early 1870s and was pursued at Heatherley's Art School in London (1882), then in Antwerp, and finally at the Académie Julian in Paris. On his return to London in 1885 he established a studio in Fulham and exhibited regularly at the Royal Academy after scoring a critical and popular success in 1886 with *Spelling out the List* (1885; priv. coll.). In 1885, while executing a portrait commission in Essex, he met and married Annie Smith [*see below*]. The couple and their growing family (they were to have five children, of whom the three youngest also trained as painters) remained in London until 1892, when they moved to Oxford. Except for several years in Switzerland (1898–9) and Derbyshire (1899–1903), they remained there until 1916, when they settled definitively in Hampstead.

From 1903 onwards George Carline was an active member of the Royal Society of British Artists. He specialized in landscapes and in charming, somewhat sentimental genre scenes featuring women and children, but he made his living mainly through portraiture and sporadic work as an illustrator and designer of advertisements (among others, for Pears soap). Although his most characteristic work in both oils and watercolours is meticulously executed and stamped with the Victorian taste of his generation, he was no die-hard conservative: there is evidence of his appreciation of impressionism and the peasant paintings of Jules Bastien-Lepage, who exerted a considerable influence on progressive British artists towards the end of the nineteenth century, and towards the end of his life he even experimented occasionally with novel materials and an abstracted style. This inquisitive attitude to vanguard developments was inherited by his children although they, like him, ultimately rejected stylistic innovation in favour of a traditional, naturalistic approach.

George Carline's marriage is further evidence of the unconventional streak in his character. Born in Buckhurst Hill, Essex, on 15 October 1862, **Annie Carline** [*née* Smith] (1862–1945) never knew her father, John Smith, or her mother. She was adopted by a relative and was employed as a housemaid when George Carline met her. She was a forceful personality, and her matriarchal role became more pronounced after his sudden death on 28 November 1920 in Assisi, during a prolonged family painting expedition to Italy. (His ashes were buried in Sunningwell, near Abingdon, on 14 December 1920.) Thus Annie Carline is the hub of the composition of Richard Carline's ambitious group portrait of family members and artist-friends, *Gathering on the Terrace* (1925; Ferens Art Gallery, Kingston upon Hull), and the subject of some compelling individual portraits by her children, notably Hilda Carline's brooding *Portrait of the Artist's Mother* (1930; priv. coll.). In 1927 she took up painting in watercolour herself and proved to have an innate talent. Her sharply observed landscapes and figure scenes delighted the artists who foregathered in the Carlines' home, and she was persuaded to exhibit

Carline family (*per. c.*1870–*c.*1975), by Richard Carline, (1923) [left to right: George Carline, Hilda Carline, Richard Carline, Annie Carline, and Sydney Carline]

them publicly, mainly with the London Group and the Artists' International Association. The cult of naïve painting was at a height in the 1930s and in 1939, on the initiative of the cubist painter and theorist André Lhote, she held an exhibition at the Galerie Pittoresque in Paris. Until her death on 20 October 1945 she was still active as a painter. She was buried in Sunningwell cemetery.

The Carlines were indefatigable, knowledgeable, and adventurous sightseers: annual painting holidays both in the English countryside and abroad were a fixed family tradition, which Richard and Nancy Carline kept up into the 1970s. Sometimes they were joined by painter-friends, as when Stanley Spencer accompanied them to Bosnia in 1922. In this manner bonds were reinforced, and so was the family commitment to painting and drawing on the spot. The family houses in Hampstead (first at 47 Downshire Hill, and from 1936 onwards at 17 Pond Street) reflected these practices: every available wall, kitchen included, was densely hung with paintings of all periods by all the members of the family and their friends, as well as with numerous artefacts from different cultures collected on their travels abroad. A 'museum' of curiosities was installed in the basement. In this stimulating (but never luxurious or chic) setting, the Carlines and their friends met to discuss art, religion, and politics, for discussion was another fixture of their daily lives. In the 1920s and 1930s the Carline family home in Hampstead became a noted meeting place for artists, writers, and intellectuals of independent and radical tendencies, to the extent that the Carlines themselves tend to be remembered for their relationships with more prominent artists, such as Stanley Spencer, William Roberts, and Charles Ginner, rather than for their own achievements.

In 1898 George Carline had suffered severe financial losses through a disastrous speculation, and he at first tried to dissuade his son **Sydney William Carline** (1888–1929), born in London on 14 August 1888, from taking up the precarious career of painting. (Later, by contrast, he did everything to foster the precocious talent of his youngest child, Richard Cotton *Carline (1896–1980), born on 9 February 1896 at 72 Woodstock Road, Oxford.) Not to be deflected, in 1908 Sydney began his training at the Slade School of Fine Art under Henry Tonks, financing himself through commissions for portrait medallions and illustrations. (In the First World War he received several official commissions for commemorative medals.) At the Slade he met Christopher Nevinson, Edward Wadsworth, Mark Gertler, and Stanley Spencer, among others, and in 1912 he joined Nevinson in Paris. This was to be a crucial awakening as, in the wake of Roger Fry's pioneering exhibitions of 1910 and 1912, he discovered the work of the post-impressionists, fauves, and cubists. Tonks was notorious for implacably opposing modernism, and Sydney reacted against the strict training in draughtsmanship for which the Slade was renowned. He enrolled at the private academy in Paris run by the eccentric symbolist painter Percyval Tudor-Hart, who advocated reliance on memory and an abstract, harmonic system for using colour and tone which had some affinity with the theories of Wassily Kandinsky. On Sydney's urging, Richard Carline abandoned plans to study at the Slade and joined him in Paris at the start of 1913. When Tudor-Hart transferred his school to Hampstead that October, they followed him there, and were joined by their sister, **Hilda Anne Carline** (1889–1950). Born in London on 20 November 1889, Hilda Carline had hitherto painted under her father's guidance in Oxford and seems to have been more responsive than her brothers to Tudor-Hart's mystical tendencies. But all three, working and living together, strove to make their painting more expressive, bold, abstract, and 'primitive' in appearance, and more like the avant-garde continental art to which their mentor had introduced them. Richard Carline recalled that 'We were a very united family and discussed our artistic problems endlessly' (*Richard Carline: Early Drawings and Watercolours*, exhibition catalogue, Anthony d'Offay Gallery, London, 1975, no pagination). A typical product of this period is Sydney Carline's primitivist memory painting *Bank Holiday on Hampstead Heath* (1915; Tate collection), but the sense of shared goals also emerges in the searching and candid portraits they painted of themselves and each other after the war (for example, Richard Carline's *Hilda with a Red Nose*, 1918, and Hilda Carline's *Self-Portrait*, 1923; both Tate collection).

Following the outbreak of war, Sydney Carline joined the Royal Flying Corps and received his commission as a pilot in 1916. Through Nevinson, he had come into contact with Futurist theory and was thrilled by the novel experience of flying and the transformation of the landscape when viewed from the cockpit. Richard Carline also joined the corps towards the end of the war, and in 1919 they were posted to the Middle East as official war artists. They made sketches from the air of the battlefields in Palestine, Mesopotamia, Syria, and Persia in preparation for a series of oil paintings for the newly founded Imperial War Museum in London (where the paintings and the majority of studies remain). They returned to England with numerous topographical watercolours of ancient temples, palaces, and ruins, and scenes of native life, which in their restraint, objectivity, and simplification of form reflect the muted style of modernism favoured in England after the war which is detectable in the contemporary work of the Bloomsbury painters. In March 1920 they held a joint exhibition of these works at the Goupil Gallery, London, and they exhibited again together in 1926 at the Bankfield Museum, Halifax. By that stage both were teaching in Oxford at the Ruskin School of Drawing, where Sydney had been appointed drawing master in 1922. Sydney Carline's sudden death from pneumonia in Drayton St Leonard, near Dorchester, Oxfordshire, on 15 February 1929, less than a year after his marriage on 12 April 1928 to Gwendolen Harter (1904–1980), occurred only weeks after his first one-man exhibition at the Goupil Gallery. He was buried in Drayton St Leonard on 18 February 1929. On 13 June 1950 Richard Carline married, in Hampstead, Nancy Mona Carline, formerly Higgins (b. 30

November 1909), also a painter. He died in Hampstead on 18 November 1980, and was buried in Sunningwell cemetery, Oxfordshire.

During the war Hilda Carline was in the Women's Land Army and from 1916 to 1918 worked on a farm in Suffolk. This experience nourished her romantic identification with landscape and was commemorated in the nostalgic and Gauguinesque composition *Return from the Farm* (1919; priv. coll.). Determined to develop her technical skills, she embarked on five years of part-time study at the Slade, where constant work from the figure resulted in a more draughtsmanlike and realistic style. Stanley *Spencer (1891–1959), to whom she was introduced in December 1919, was impressed by her talent and intrigued by her striking looks and moody, imaginative, deeply religious personality—like her mother she was an ardent Christian Scientist—and on 23 February 1925 they were married. The years preceding her marriage were particularly productive: she benefited from the intellectual stimulus and challenge provided by the 'cercle pan-artistique of Downshire Hill', as the gatherings at the Carlines' home were dubbed by Henry Lamb (letter to Richard Carline, 1923, *The Spencers and the Carlines*, no pagination), and like her brothers she exhibited regularly with the London Group. Although influenced by Spencer's fascination with material textures and sympathetic to his visionary interpretation of outwardly banal subjects, she never imitated his stylistic mannerisms and remained a more objective observer, as in her meticulous and candid portrait of their housekeeper, *Elsie* (1929; Brighton and Hove Museum).

Like many women of her generation, Hilda Carline experienced a draining conflict between her desire to paint and her domestic obligations (her daughters, Shirin and Unity, were born in 1925 and 1930 respectively), and painting became a relatively rare activity in the late 1920s. Proximity to an artist of such idiosyncratic vision, unassailable conviction, egocentricity, and brilliance as Spencer appears to have crushed her self-confidence, and some of her best later work was done after they began to lead largely separate lives in 1932. The marriage never ran smoothly, for both were uncompromising and argumentative; it ended in divorce in May 1937. Prone throughout her life to depression, she suffered a nervous breakdown in 1942, and in 1947 the breast cancer which ultimately killed her was diagnosed. She died in Hampstead on 1 November 1950, and was buried in Cookham, Berkshire. Spencer's obsession with her seems, if anything, to have increased after their divorce, and especially after her breakdown, and she inspired an unending flow of paintings and letters which ceased only with his death in 1959. Her achievement as a painter, rather than as his muse, is being re-evaluated, and in 1999 she was the subject of an important study and touring exhibition. Works by the Carlines are held in various public collections in Great Britain, including the Tate collection and Imperial War Museum, London, and the Ashmolean Museum, Oxford, and in many private collections.

ELIZABETH COWLING

Sources A. Thomas, *The art of Hilda Carline, Mrs Stanley Spencer* (1999) [exhibition catalogue, Usher Art Gallery, Lincoln, and elsewhere] · *Richard Carline, 1896–1980* (1983) [exhibition catalogue, Camden Arts Centre, London] · *Richard and Sydney Carline* (1973) [exhibition catalogue, IWM] · *The Carline family* (1971) [exhibition catalogue, Leicester Galleries, London] · *The Ruskin Drawing School under Sydney Carline (master, 1922–1929) and his staff* (1977) [exhibition catalogue, AM Oxf., 9 July – 28 Aug 1977] · *The Spencers and the Carlines in Hampstead in the 1920s* (1973) [exhibition catalogue, Stanley Spencer Gallery, Cookham, 23 May – 2 June 1973] · J. B. Smith, ed., *Spencers and Carlines: the work of Stanley and Hilda Spencer and their families* (1980) [exhibition catalogue, Morley Gallery, London, 17 Sept – 10 Oct 1980] · personal knowledge (2004) · private information (2004) [Carline family] · A. Thomas, 'Dear Hilda', *Art Review* (March 1999), 36–7 · m. cert. [S. W. Carline] · d. cert. [S. W. Carline] · d. cert. [Gwendolyn Carline] · gravestone [Annie Carline] · *CGPLA Eng. & Wales* (1946) · *CGPLA Eng. & Wales* (1921) [George Francis Carline] · b. cert. [R. C. Carline] · m. cert. [R. C. Carline] · d. cert. [R. C. Carline] · d. cert. [Annie Carline] · b. cert. [G. F. Carline]

Archives IWM, papers [Sydney Carline] · IWM, Richard Carline papers · Tate collection, corresp. and sketchbooks [Sydney Carline] · Tate collection, Richard Carline papers; corresp., studies and photographs, sketchbooks, and diary relating to a visit to Italy

Likenesses H. A. Carline, self-portrait, 1923 (Hilda Anne Carline), Tate collection · R. Carline, family group portrait, 1923, picture destroyed; copyprint, Courtauld Inst. [see illus.] · R. Carline, family group portrait, 1925 (Gathering on the terrace), Ferens Art Gallery, Kingston upon Hull · H. A. Carline, portrait, 1930 (Annie Carline; *Portrait of the artist's mother*), priv. coll.

Wealth at death £2606 8s. 6d.: probate, 1921, *CGPLA Eng. & Wales* · £3578 11s. 8d.: administration, 1929, *CGPLA Eng. & Wales* · £213,292: probate, 1981, *CGPLA Eng. & Wales* · £3557 8s. 10d.: probate, 1946, *CGPLA Eng. & Wales*

Carline, Annie (1862–1945). *See under* Carline family (*per.* c.1870–c.1975).

Carline, George Francis (1855–1920). *See under* Carline family (*per.* c.1870–c.1975).

Carline, Hilda Anne (1889–1950). *See under* Carline family (*per.* c.1870–c.1975).

Carline, Richard Cotton (1896–1980), painter and writer, was born at 72 Woodstock Road, Oxford, on 9 February 1896, the youngest of the five children (four sons and one daughter) of George Francis *Carline (1855–1920), painter, and his wife, Annie *Carline (1862–1945) [see under Carline family], in later life also a painter, daughter of John Smith, of Buckhurst Hill. As a painter Carline also followed earlier family generations, as well as his brother Sydney *Carline (1888–1929) and only sister, Hilda *Carline (1889–1950) [see under Carline family]. After attending the Dragon and St Edward's schools in Oxford he studied art from 1913 under Percyval Tudor-Hart at his schools first in Paris and then in Hampstead, being influenced by Tudor-Hart's theories of colour and tonal value.

In 1916 Carline joined the Middlesex regiment before serving as an officer in the Royal Flying Corps, first in wireless and then in experiments in camouflage and aids to identification of enemy targets from the air. In 1918 he and Sydney were appointed official war artists, Richard recording the war from the air on the western front and then (in 1919) both brothers depicting the aerial warfare in British zones in the Middle East. Their work constitutes

Richard Cotton Carline (1896–1980), by Sir Stanley Spencer, 1923

the most comprehensive group of paintings from the air in the Imperial War Museum.

Carline studied at the Slade School of Fine Art in 1921–4. In 1916 his parents had moved to Hampstead. With all three artist children living there their home became what Gilbert Spencer described as 'a focal centre', combining hospitality with endless discussion on art and its theory. The participation in this circle of Henry Lamb, Charles Ginner, Mark Gertler, and John Nash indicates its principal characteristics—which were always Carline's: the clear but careful representation of familiar motifs, freshly seen. For a few years from as early as 1914 he achieved an unusually simple and direct realism of striking psychological concentration. Elected to the London Group in 1920, he exhibited with it until the 1970s. His work was consistently admired by Sir Stanley *Spencer, whose importance in Carline's circle was consolidated by his marriage to Hilda Carline in 1925. In 1930 a series of often vertiginous paintings of masts and rigging was the last in which, during seventeen years, Carline's work had been marked by an unusual clarity and feeling for light. Thereafter his painting was less exceptional and less continuous. Remaining a strong colourist and more interested in content than in style, he developed a controlled sensuousness of paint owing something to Gauguin and fauvism.

The change in Carline's art coincided approximately with the premature deaths of his remaining brothers (he had taught under Sydney's mastership at the Ruskin School of Drawing, Oxford, in 1924–9), with the impact of the breakup of the Spencers' marriage, with intensification in the climate of discussion to include socio-political as well as aesthetic concerns, and with an expansion in Carline's own horizons. His art was influenced by the community-orientated figurative painting he saw in four pre-war visits to the USA, and he became a strong advocate of public mural painting in Britain. In the USA he also admired schemes to improve the place of artists in society and the work of artists' own organizations.

Carline's principal achievement during his last five decades was to generate contacts and creative interaction within local, national, and international communities and across boundaries of style, genre, and culture. He was motivated by strong beliefs in peace, friendship, and freedom. Tirelessly active, he was a natural organizer, finding it difficult to say no (a trait related to his instinct always to seek what was positive in the art of others rather than to criticize it). Organizations of which he was at various times chairman included the Artists' International Association (including its important refugee and regional committees); the International Artists' Association (co-founder, 1952; chairman of the UK national committee from 1959; honorary president, 1968–80), an affiliated organization of UNESCO, for which as its first art counsellor he organized its first post-war international art exhibition in Paris; and the Hampstead Artists' Council (co-founder). A member of the Britain/China Friendship Association, he selected and accompanied to China exhibitions of British historical art and watercolours in 1957 and 1963.

Opposed to exclusiveness in selection, Carline felt that exhibitions and organizations should be broadly based and that child, naïve, and ethnic art were as worthy of serious consideration as Western fine art. Through books and exhibitions he advanced appreciation of African art and of the picture postcard, and in his work at home and overseas under Cambridge University as an adviser on art education and examiner, he contributed significantly to the establishment of more liberal criteria for conducting art examinations and judging excellence in children's art. His *Draw they Must* (1968) is a history of four centuries of art teaching in general education in Britain and of its modern extension overseas.

From 1939 to 1945 Carline did important technical and liaison work on camouflage, writing the Ministry of Aircraft Production's official report on industrial and aircraft camouflage. On 13 June 1950 Carline married Nancy Mona (b. 1909), painter, daughter of Douglas Stanley Higgins, businessman; they had a son and a daughter. They continued the tradition of broad-ranging hospitality of Carline's parents. In his last decade Carline was instrumental in the creation of several exhibitions on the art of his family circle and in twentieth-century Hampstead. His *Stanley Spencer at War* (1978) is a key account of his brother-in-law as man and artist up to 1932.

Carline's general attitude was consistently open and progressive. He preferred art of pronounced directness, a quality seen in the clarity of his own early work and in his manner of expression as writer and speaker. A certain combination of idealism with outspokenness may account for his remaining somewhat outside the establishment of his day, despite the unfailing courtesy of his approach. In the last years of his life appreciation of his early achievement as a painter increased notably. He is represented in the Tate collection, the Ashmolean Museum, Oxford, and other public collections. He died in Hampstead on 18 November 1980 and was buried in Sunningwell cemetery, Oxfordshire. A memorial retrospective was held at the Camden Arts Centre, London, June–July 1983. RICHARD MORPHET, rev.

Sources The Times (25 Nov 1980) · J. B. Smith, ed., Spencers and Carlines: the work of Stanley and Hilda Spencer and their families (1980) [exhibition catalogue, Morley Gallery, London, 17 Sept – 10 Oct 1980] · Richard Carline: early drawings and watercolours (1975) [exhibition catalogue, Anthony d'Offay Gallery, London, 17 Sept – 8 Oct 1975] · R. Morphet and E. Cowling, Richard Carline, 1896–1980 (1983) [exhibition catalogue, Camden Arts Centre, London, 29 June – 24 July 1983, Playhouse Gallery, Harlow, 22 Sept – 22 Oct 1983] · B. Loftus, ed., Richard and Sydney Carline: an exhibition of their paintings, drawings and watercolours executed for the official war artist scheme during and after the First World War (1973) [exhibition catalogue, IWM, 4 July – 9 Sept 1973] · Exhibition of works of the Corbet and Carline families (1958) [exhibition catalogue, Shrewsbury Art Gallery] · Richard and Nancy Carline and their circle (1997) [exhibition catalogue, Royal National Theatre, London] · The Ruskin Drawing School under Sydney Carline (master, 1922–1929) and his staff (1977) [exhibition catalogue, AM Oxf., 9 July – 28 Aug 1977] · CGPLA Eng. & Wales (1981) · private information (1986) · personal knowledge (1986) · b. cert. · m. cert. · d. cert.

Archives IWM, papers · Tate collection, corresp.; studies and photographs, sketchbooks and diary relating to visit to Italy

Likenesses R. Carline, self-portrait in family group, 1923, picture destroyed; copyprint, Courtauld Inst.; see illus. in Carline family (per. c.1870–c.1975) · S. Spencer, oils, 1923, Rugby Art Gallery and Museum [see illus.] · S. Spencer, oils, exh. RA 1980 (The Resurrection, Cookham, 1924–7), Tate collection

Wealth at death £213,292: probate, 16 June 1981, CGPLA Eng. & Wales

Carline, Sydney William (1888–1929). See under Carline family (per. c.1870–c.1975).

Carling, Sir Ernest Rock (1877–1960), surgeon and developer of radiotherapy, was born in Sidney Road, Guildford, Surrey, on 6 March 1877, the third son of Francis Rees Carling, master ironmonger, and his wife, Lydia Colebrook. He was educated at the Royal Grammar School, Guildford, and King's College, London, and entered the Westminster Hospital medical school at the age of eighteen. His medical training was interrupted by service in the Second South African War with the Imperial Yeomanry Field Hospital as a surgical dresser to Charles Stonham, the Westminster's senior surgeon. On 10 June 1901 Carling married Edith Petra (1872/3–1959), daughter of the Revd Edward Dennis Rock, vicar of Sutton, Woodbridge, Suffolk; they had two sons.

Carling qualified MRCS LRCP in 1901. Early in his university studies he showed both brilliance and versatility, being awarded a gold medal and an exhibition in pharmacology and therapeutics; he also won a further gold medal and scholarship in obstetrics and gynaecology in his final

MB (1902). He became BS in 1903 and FRCS in 1904. After graduation he held appointments at the Westminster Hospital, first in the pathology department and then as surgical registrar; in 1906 he was appointed to the honorary consulting staff as assistant surgeon and in 1919 he became full surgeon. On his retirement from the active staff in 1942 he became honorary consulting surgeon.

Carling was a general surgeon of more than average ability and, before the days of specialization, an orthopaedic surgeon of considerable skill. In addition to the Westminster he worked at the Royal Naval Hospital, Greenwich, the Peace Memorial Hospital, Watford, the Chislehurst Hospital, and the King Edward VII Convalescent Home for Officers at Osborne. As a member of the Territorial Army he was mobilized on the outbreak of war in 1914 and served as captain in the Royal Army Medical Corps with the 4th London Hospital, and later in France and Flanders.

In many aspects of medical thinking and practice Carling was ahead of his time. The detailed planning of the new Westminster Hospital medical school and its nurses' home in St John's Gardens was as much his as the architect's, and he waited almost five years to see the building completed in the spring of 1939. Carling retained an interest in medical education throughout his career, and remained a member of the academic council of the Westminster medical school until his death. For many years he was a member of the faculty of medicine and of the board of advanced medical studies of the University of London, and he was also a member of the court of examiners at the Royal College of Surgeons, acting for a time as its chairman. He took a wide interest in benevolent activities related to the medical profession and was a member of council of the Royal Medical Benevolent Fund, treasurer of the Society for the Relief of Widows and Orphans of Medical Men, a trustee of the Nuffield Provincial Hospitals Trust and chairman of its medical advisory committee, and president of the Medical Protection Society.

Carling's interest in the use of radium in the treatment of cancer dated from 1920 when he visited the Fondation Curie in Paris and the radium institutes in Brussels and Stockholm. It was Carling's foresight which enabled Westminster Hospital to open its radium annex in Fitzjohn's Avenue, Hampstead, later developed as the radiotherapy department of the new hospital. Carling designed the first models of mass radium units and had them built with the help of physicists; he recognized from the early years that the application of the use of X-rays and radium in medicine needed the special knowledge of physicists to achieve precision, accuracy, and safety.

This scientific approach opened for Carling the door to a second profession which he embraced with enthusiasm and which occupied most of his time after his retirement from active surgical practice. He became a member of the National Radium Commission and the Atomic Energy Commission, chairman of the international commission of radiological protection, and member and for a time chairman of the Standing Advisory Committee on Cancer and Radiotherapy of the Ministry of Health. This second career was even more rewarding for Carling and more beneficial for the country than his earlier surgical achievements. His specialized knowledge resulted in his appointment as consultant adviser to both the Home Office and the Ministry of Labour, as expert adviser to the World Health Organization, and as member of the Medical Research Council. He also became chairman of the advisory committee on medical nomenclature.

Carling was knighted in 1944, made an honorary fellow of the faculty of radiology, received an honorary LLD from Queen's University, Belfast, and was elected a fellow of the Royal College of Physicians. His chief recreation in his early years was to travel and to visit art museums, especially in Italy where for a time he kept a small house. He was a great conversationalist and a lover of books, mostly on scientific subjects. Carling died at his London home, 49 Hallam Street, Portland Place, on 15 July 1960.

STANFORD CADE, rev.

Sources *BMJ* (23 July 1960) · *BMJ* (6 Aug 1960) · *The Lancet* (23 July 1960) · *The Times* (16 July 1960) · private information (1971) · personal knowledge (1971) · b. cert. · m. cert.
Likenesses W. Stoneman, photograph, 1949, NPG · A. C. Davidson-Houston, oils, Westminster Hospital, London
Wealth at death £65,158 15s. 7d.: probate, 19 Aug 1960, CGPLA Eng. & Wales

Carlingford. For this title name *see* Taaffe, Theobald, first earl of Carlingford (*d.* 1677); Taaffe, Francis, third earl of Carlingford (1639–1704); Fortescue, Chichester Samuel Parkinson-, Baron Carlingford and second Baron Clermont (1823–1898).

Carlini, Agostino (*c.*1718–1790), sculptor, was almost certainly born and trained in Genoa. He is first recorded as working at The Hague under the architect Pieter de Swart (1709–1773) for William IV of Orange from 1748 until about 1753–4. During these years he carved decorative wood fittings for the Paleis Huis ten Bosch; two of the elaborate gilt wood guéridons he carved at this time are now in the J. Paul Getty Museum, Los Angeles. The final recorded payment made to the artist by the court was in 1753, but a wood horse-sleigh carved by him was advertised for sale on his behalf in The Hague in December 1754, and again in 1756; neither of these advertisements can have led to a purchase, as it was put up for auction in 1765. Carlini may therefore have left The Hague by the end of 1754; he is documented in London in 1760, when he exhibited at the Society of Artists a drawing for the monument to General Wolfe (*d.* 1759). This may have been a drawing now in the Victoria and Albert Museum, or perhaps one in Sir John Soane's Museum. Most of the leading sculptors working in England at that time submitted designs for the competition, funded by the government, held to decide the sculptor of the monument to Wolfe; it was eventually won by Joseph Wilton.

One of Carlini's most renowned works was begun about 1760 or 1761. This was the life-size full-length marble figure portraying Joshua Ward (*d.* 1761), a highly successful quack doctor and philanthropist. Later reports imply that the statue—formerly in the Society for the Encouragement of Arts, Manufactures, and Commerce (later the Royal Society of Arts), and now in the Victoria and Albert Museum—was intended to be part of a monument to Ward in Westminster Abbey. However, this never came to pass, and the statue seems to have remained in Carlini's possession, until it was eventually given to the Royal Society of Arts by one of Joshua Ward's original executors in 1793, after Carlini had died intestate.

Carlini was a founder member of the Royal Academy in 1768, one of only three sculptors and four Italians among the initial group; he was to become keeper, succeeding George Michael Moser in 1783. Two of his works remain in the collections of the academy: a plaster equestrian model of George III, exhibited in the first exhibition at the academy in 1769, and a marble bust of the king, wearing loose classical dress, signed and dated 1773. The model was never employed for a large-scale statue, although a contemporary print by Carlini's friend Francesco Bartolozzi shows it in a landscape as a life-size sculpture. Another print by Bartolozzi published in 1771 shows Carlini's proposed monument to Alderman William Beckford (1709–1770), lord mayor of London. In January 1771 Carlini had submitted a model to a competition for a memorial to Beckford to be erected in the Guildhall of London. The competition was eventually won by John Moore; contemporary press comment suggested the contest was not fairly conducted.

Two beechwood candlesticks each showing a seated man, now in the Plymouth Museum and Art Gallery, are the only known pieces in wood by Carlini apart from his earlier work in the Netherlands. These are small-scale decorative objects, finely worked, and seem to have been made for the collector Charles Rogers, who paid Carlini £21 for them in March 1771.

Carlini was, however, most famous for carving marble, and his three major tombs, all outside London, are important monuments, combining classical features with those of the Italian baroque tradition. The monument to Lady Sophia Petty (1745–1771) in the church of All Saints at High Wycombe, Buckinghamshire, was carried out in the early 1770s, and shows her with her two sons in a sentimental but restrained pose, evoking her youthful death. A preparatory drawing for the monument is at Bowood House, Calne, Wiltshire. Carlini may also have carved the sarcophagus of John Fitzmaurice Petty, first earl of Shelburne of the second creation (1706–1761), at Bowood, based on the designs of the architect Robert Adam during the 1760s. Carlini's monument to Harriet Benson, Lady Bingley (*c.*1705–1771), at Bramham Park chapel in Yorkshire was probably completed in 1776. This shows the mourning figure of Fame leaning against a medallion portrait of Lady Bingley with a sorrowing putto, and is noticeably more Italianate in style than the roughly contemporary monument to Lady Sophia Petty.

Perhaps Carlini's most impressive tomb is that to Lord and Lady Milton at Milton Abbey in Dorset, which is signed and dated 1775. Caroline, Lady Milton, died in 1775, and her husband, Joseph Damer, erected the monument to her in the church at Milton Abbey, an estate he had purchased in 1752. Related drawings show that Carlini collaborated with Adam, who evidently designed the base of the monument. The pose of the reclining figures, the deceased wife lying on her back, and the sorrowing husband resting his cheek on the palm of his hand to contemplate her, recalls seventeenth- and early eighteenth-century monuments, such as those by John Nost. Possibly the archaic and vernacular style was felt by Lord Milton to be appropriate for the setting.

From 1776 to 1778 Carlini worked alongside a number of other sculptors (Joseph Nollekens, Joseph Wilton, John Bacon the elder, and Giuseppe Ceracchi), under the direction of the architect Sir William Chambers, on architectural sculpture for Somerset House, London. He carved two marble figures representing Prudence and Justice (for which he was paid £240), and three keystones of river gods symbolizing the rivers Dee, Tyne, and Severn (for which he received £63). Carlini's last known works were two figures of Neptune and Mercury for the Dublin Custom House; the finished statues were sent over to Dublin, probably between 1783 and 1785. The figures were largely destroyed in an attack by the Irish Republican Army in 1921, although a fragment of Mercury was saved, and is in a garden at the north-west corner of the custom house; replicas were later installed to replace the lost figures. Carlini died in London in 1790, probably in August.

Carlini remains an enigmatic figure, and is known through a few works, his sale catalogue of 1791, which records those works left in his studio after his death, and a few contemporary references. His appearance and character are, however, evoked by the biographer J. T. Smith's posthumous description of 1828:

> When Carlini was Keeper of the Royal Academy, he used to walk from his house to Somerset-place, with a broken tobacco-pipe in his mouth, and dressed in a deplorable great coat; but when he has been going out to the Academy-dinner, I have seen him getting into a chair, and full-dressed in a purple silk coat, scarlet gold-laced waistcoat, point-lace ruffles, and a sword and bag. (Smith, 205)

MARJORIE TRUSTED

Sources M. Trusted, '"A man of talent": Agostino Carlini (c.1718–1790)', *Burlington Magazine*, 134 (1992), 776–84; 135 (1993), 190–201 · R. Baarsen, 'High rococo in Holland: William IV and Agostino Carlini', *Burlington Magazine*, 140 (1998), 172–83 · D. Bindman and M. Baker, *Roubiliac and the eighteenth-century monument: sculpture as theatre* (1995), 337, pl. 279 · J. T. Smith, *Nollekens and his times*, 2 vols. (1828) · *A catalogue of the prints, a few pictures, models of monuments, copper-plates … of Augustino Carlini* [sale catalogue]
Archives V&A, sale catalogue
Likenesses C. Maucourt, miniature on vellum, 1762, NPG · J. F. Rigaud, group portrait, oils, 1777, NPG · J. R. Smith, engraving, 1778 (after oil painting by J. F. Rigaud), repro. in Trusted, '"A man of talent": Agostino Carlini, pt. 1, fig. 11 · J. Zoffany, group portrait, oils (*Royal Academicians*, 1772), Royal Collection

Carlisle. For this title name *see* Harclay, Andrew, earl of Carlisle (c.1270–1323); Hay, James, first earl of Carlisle (c.1580–1636); Hay, Lucy, countess of Carlisle (1599–1660); Howard, Charles, first earl of Carlisle (1628–1685); Howard, Charles, third earl of Carlisle (1669–1738); Howard, Henry, fourth earl of Carlisle (1694–1758) [*see under* Howard, Charles, third earl of Carlisle (1669–1738)]; Howard, Frederick, fifth earl of Carlisle (1748–1825); Howard, George, sixth earl of Carlisle (1773–1848); Howard, George William Frederick, seventh earl of Carlisle (1802–1864); Howard, George James, ninth earl of Carlisle (1843–1911); Howard, Rosalind Frances, countess of Carlisle (1845–1921); Howard, Charles James Stanley, Viscount Morpeth and tenth earl of Carlisle (1867–1912) [*see under* Howard, George James, ninth earl of Carlisle (1843–1911)].

Carlisle, Sir Anthony (1768–1840), surgeon and anatomist, was born on 15 February 1768 at Stillington, Durham, the third son of Thomas Carlisle and his first wife Barbara (d. 1768), daughter of John and Elizabeth Hubback of Cowpen Bowley, near Stillington. Following Barbara's death in childbirth, Carlisle's father married Susannah Skottowe. Nothing is known of Carlisle's early education, but he was sent to his maternal uncle, Anthony Hubback, in York, for medical training. Following his death, Carlisle was transferred in 1784 to a surgeon, William Green, of Durham. He then went to London, probably in the late 1780s, where he attended lectures by John Hunter, Matthew Baillie, George Fordyce, and others, and became the house pupil of Henry Watson, whose post as surgeon to the Westminster Hospital Carlisle obtained in 1793, on Watson's death. The next year, Carlisle began offering lectures on surgery, part of an attempt to establish a formal medical school there.

As an anatomist, Carlisle was especially interested in the exotic and anomalous, publishing papers on the lemur and sloth, the breeding of eels, defective brain development in a lamb, and a family of human beings with polydactyly (extra fingers and toes). He chose as the subject of one of his Hunterian orations (1820) to the Royal College of Surgeons the anatomy of oysters, a topic that was publicly ridiculed. He had been active in the 1790s in securing the collections of John Hunter for the college, and helped perpetuate Hunter's memory, both as an act of piety and a vehicle of collective surgical advancement. Carlisle was one of the original members when the college received its royal charter in 1800, and he held a number of offices there, sitting on council and on the court of examiners, and serving as vice-president and twice as president (1829 and 1839). He donated a number of specimens and books to the college.

From Carlisle's early days in London, he moved in the best scientific circles, and he was elected a fellow of the Royal Society in 1804. His Croonian lectures (1804–5) to the society dealt, successively, with muscular motion and the muscles of fish. His most famous scientific contribution had been communicated to the Royal Society in 1800. Drawing on Volta's recent discovery of a chemical means of generating electricity, Carlisle and William Nicholson electrolyzed water into its constituent gases. Carlisle returned once in 1820 to his youthful experiments in electrochemistry, but, more importantly, the young Humphry Davy modified the apparatus and used it in his own fundamental researches.

Carlisle's connections helped him secure the post of

professor of anatomy (1808) at the Royal Academy, where he had also studied art (and also commented that artists and sculptors do not need a detailed knowledge of anatomy). Through his appointment as surgeon to the duke of Gloucester, he became surgeon-extraordinary to the prince regent. When the latter became George IV, Carlisle was knighted.

Carlisle was a competent surgeon who wrote several papers on surgical topics and introduced a few minor improvements to surgical technique. He had a reputation of occasional casualness with his duties at Westminster Hospital, and was investigated (but exonerated) for three cases of neglect in 1838. He managed to escape the worst of Thomas Wakley's assault in *The Lancet* (founded in 1823) on the nepotism and incompetence of London hospital surgeons. Having had only one apprentice, he could hardly have pushed his students forward. He did, however, continue to give lectures on surgery at his hospital, and advocated the systematic collection and publication of hospital statistics. He was actively involved in the rebuilding of the Westminster and published a series of lectures on cholera and other epidemic diseases (1832).

Not surprising for one with his career, Carlisle had a conservative temperament. He opposed male midwives on the grounds of modesty and incompetence, and argued for temperance and regular habits in an essay on old age (1817), an early work in geriatrics.

Carlisle married Martha, daughter of John Symmons FRS, on 23 August 1800 at Alcester, Warwickshire. He lived first at Soho Square and then in Langham Place, where he died on 2 November 1840. He was buried in Kensal Green cemetery.   W. F. BYNUM

Sources R. J. Cole, 'Sir Anthony Carlisle FRS (1768–1840)', *Annals of Science*, 8 (1952), 255–70 · J. F. Clarke, *Autobiographical recollections of the medical profession* (1874), 283–94 · J. F. Pettigrew, *Biographical memoirs of the most celebrated physicians*, 1 (1838) · S. C. Lawrence, *Charitable knowledge: hospital pupils and practitioners in eighteenth-century London* (1996) · A. Thackray, 'Carlisle, Anthony', *DSB*, 3.67–8 · *GM*, 2nd ser., 14 (1840), 660 · *IGI*

Archives RCS Eng., lecture notes and letters · Wellcome L., letters

Likenesses M. A. Shee, oils, RCS Eng. · Miss Turner, lithograph (after C. Ross), BM, NPG

Carlisle, Nicholas (1771–1847), antiquary, was born at York and probably baptized there on 8 February 1771, the son of Thomas Carlisle and his second wife, Susannah Skottowe, and the half-brother of Sir Anthony *Carlisle. He entered the naval service of the East India Company, and while a purser made the best of his opportunities to lay up considerable property. Carlisle later assisted the speaker's secretary in his work of estimating the population of Great Britain, which led him into topographical studies. He produced a series of laborious compilations, useful in their day. These included topographical dictionaries of England (2 vols., 1808), Ireland (1810), Wales (1811), and Scotland (2 vols., 1813).

In January 1807 Carlisle became secretary of the Society of Antiquaries, chosen in a competition in which T. F. Dibdin was also a candidate. Carlisle was thereafter ensconced in his official apartments at Somerset House,

and he secured in addition to his salary, which increased over the years, substantial honoraria for additional tasks such as indexing the *Archaeologia*. His exactions may be explained by a loss of his inheritance and Indian profits in unsuccessful investments; whatever the cause, they were harmful to the Society of Antiquaries. Venal within the society, he was pluralist too, and became in 1812 an under-librarian of the Royal Library, which he accompanied (part-time, for two days a week) to the British Museum after its transfer to the nation in 1823. His abuses long went unchecked by the society, until there were widespread protests, led by Sir Nicholas Harris Nicolas and others. The society's reform movement of the mid-1840s attempted to pension Carlisle off, but he survived in declining health, and occupied the official apartments at Somerset House until his death, which occurred at Margate on 27 August 1847.

In 1818 Carlisle published a useful *Concise Description of the Endowed Grammar Schools of England and Wales*, for which he compiled the material by questionnaire. His other works included *Collections* for a Carlisle family history (1822) and one for that of Bland (1826). There was *An Historical Account of Charitable Commissions* (1828), he himself having been associated with the Charity Commission. He was awarded foreign decorations for his advocacy of founding chairs of English in continental universities, and (having been preferred to that small dignity) he wrote *An inquiry into the place and quality of the gentlemen of his majesty's most honourable privy chamber* (1829). His obituary notice in the *Gentleman's Magazine* may give him the character of an amiable and worthy man, but the historian of the Society of Antiquaries viewed the forty years of his secretaryship as a harmful episode for the society, especially at a time when the other officers were inadequate.

RICHARD GARNETT, *rev.* ALAN BELL

Sources J. Evans, *A history of the Society of Antiquaries* (1956) · *GM*, 2nd ser., 30 (1848), 208–10 · *IGI*

Archives Wellcome L., notes and corresp. for 2nd edn of *Endowed grammar schools* | BL, letters to Joseph Hunter, Add. MS 24867 · Bodl. Oxf., corresp. with Sir Thomas Phillips · King's Lond., corresp. with P. H. Leathers · McGill University, Montreal, McLennan Library, letters to Daniel Lysons · Yale U., Beinecke L., letters to T. J. Pettigrew

Likenesses S. Birch, miniature, 1798, S. Antiquaries, Lond.

Carlos, Edward John (1798–1851), antiquary, was born on 12 February 1798 at Newington, Surrey, the only child of William Carlos and Grace Smith. From the evidence of a grant of arms (1651) in the family possession, he was a direct descendant of Colonel William Careless or Carlos, who saved Charles II after his flight from the battle of Worcester. Carlos was educated at Mr Colecraft's school in Newington and was articled to G. T. R. Reynal, an attorney of the lord mayor's court office, where he remained for thirty-three years as attorney and manager of Reynal's business.

Carlos's great interest was in medieval architecture and its preservation. He published extensively on the subject in the *Gentleman's Magazine* from 1822 to 1848, contributing letters and articles on antiquarian topics, descriptions of new churches erected in London, critical reviews of works of restoration, and reviews of architectural books. He signed his *Gentleman's Magazine* articles with the initials E. I. C.

Carlos first appeared as a preservationist in 1825, during the unsuccessful campaign to save the church of St Katharine by the Tower from demolition, when he wrote an impassioned plea for its survival in the *Gentleman's Magazine*. He was an active member of the committee for the restoration of Crosby Hall in 1832 and published a pamphlet, *Historical and Antiquarian Notices of Crosby Hall, London*, which was also reproduced in the *Gentleman's Magazine*. This work was referred to by W. D. Caröe as being 'of very slight character' although 'it furnishes a few useful details' (Norman, 34). He was an energetic member of the committee in the successful campaign to save the lady chapel of St Mary Overie, Southwark, in 1832, speaking at public meetings, publishing a pamphlet, and writing in the *Gentleman's Magazine* of February 1832. He also contributed to the *Gentleman's Magazine* in 1832 'An account of London Bridge with observations on its architecture during its demolition'. In 1843 he published a second edition of Joseph Skelton's *Oxonia antiqua restaurata*, with additions and the descriptive text rearranged and revised. Carlos was one of the first antiquaries to take brass rubbings and examples of these, dated 1833–6, are in the Victoria and Albert Museum's prints and drawings collection, as well as drawings of architectural details (clearly the work of an informed but amateur draughtsman) from churches in Kent, Middlesex, and Suffolk.

With his wife, Mary-Ann, Carlos had two sons and two daughters. He lived at 4 York Place, Newington, Surrey, where he died on 20 January 1851. His wife survived him.

JANET MYLES

Sources GM, 2nd ser., 35 (1851), 442 • P. Norman and W. D. Caröe, *Crosby Place* (1908), 31, 34, 41, 52, 86 • W. H. Godfrey, *The parish of Chelsea*, ed. P. Norman and others, 2, Survey of London, 4 (1913) • GM, 2nd ser., 21 (1844), 548–9 [obit. of James Carlos] • J. Myles, *L. N. Cottingham, 1787–1847, architect of the Gothic revival* (1996) • Officers' Reports (Mayor's Court), 1840–56, CLRO, vol. 2, 361 • d. cert.
Archives BL, drawings and notes of Essex, Kent, Middlesex, and Surrey churches, Add. MSS 25705–25706 • Bodl. Oxf., notebooks and papers relating to churches and cathedrals • V&A, department of prints and drawings

Carlos [*formerly* Careless], **William** (*d.* 1689), royalist army officer, was born William Careless at Broomhall farm near Brewood in Staffordshire, a younger son of John Careless and his wife, Ellen Fluit. His family had been tenants of the Giffards of Chillington, Staffordshire, since at least the mid-sixteenth century. John Careless was a modest husbandman and both he and his wife, whom he married in 1595, were Catholics. William followed them in this faith and by 1633 he had married Dorothy, daughter of Walter Fox, gentleman, of Salt, near Stafford. The couple had at least three sons: William (1633–1679), who attended the English College in Rome; a second whose name is unknown and who died in 1638; and a second William (1643–1668/9).

In 1641 Careless was a yeoman living at Chillington when he and his wife were indicted for recusancy. On the outbreak of civil war he espoused the royal cause 'out of duty, and a faithful sense of loyalty to Charles I' (Hamilton, 1.13). He first obtained a commission as captain of horse in Colonel Thomas Leveson's regiment, based in Dudley Castle; but by December 1643 he had been appointed governor of Lapley House in Staffordshire with a cavalry regiment of his own. In late April 1644 the governorship of Tong Castle in Shropshire was bestowed upon him; however, the following December he was routed in a skirmish at Wolverhampton, seriously injured, and taken captive. He was imprisoned in the High House, Stafford, for nearly a year, he and his family 'being reduced to the lowest condition by the war' (Foley, 1.180–81). On his release he still 'burned with a zeal and desire for service' and went to Ireland to fight for the king (Hamilton, 1.13). But he did not stay there long and next emigrated to Spain, continuing to pursue a military career. About 1649 he secretly returned to England but was once again forced into exile, this time taking his eldest son, William, with him as companion. After a period of service in the Low Countries father and son slipped back into England in anticipation of Charles II's invasion from Scotland. For nine months they laid low in the vicinity of Brewood and, on the approach of the Scottish army in late August 1651, Careless seized the opportunity to join forces with it, raising a small number of recruits and enlisting in Lord Talbot's cavalry troop in which he served in the capacity of major.

In the battle of Worcester on 3 September 1651 Careless fought with conspicuous gallantry, and reputedly saw the last man killed in action. Separated from his son William in the fray he sought refuge in 'his own neighbourhood' (Blount, 27), first sheltering in a cottage on Tong Heath and subsequently concealing himself in Boscobel Wood. On the evening of 5 September he linked up with the fugitive Charles II, then in a desperate state, and was so moved that he 'could not refrain from weeping' (Fea, *Flight*, 211). The following day he and the king entered into legend by climbing the boughs of an oak tree in order to hide from the pursuing Commonwealth forces:

Where Noble Carlos lent his Man-like knee,
The last support of Fainting Majestie.
(ibid., 205)

As the exhausted monarch slumbered in Careless's lap there was a tense moment when William became so numb that he had to awaken his royal charge to prevent them falling out of the tree and into the hands of the Cromwellian soldiers who were riding along the horsetrack below. That night the two men retired to nearby Boscobel House, where they had 'a pleasant jocular discourse' as Careless acted as the king's undercook in the kitchen (ibid., 215). Next day Careless separated from his royal master, fearing 'he was so well known in those parts' that his continued presence would endanger Charles's safety (Broadley, 66). Under a disguised name Careless eventually managed to escape to the Netherlands, via London, and from there journeyed on to France. In Paris in late October 1651 he had an audience with both Louis XIV and Charles II, the latter having now effected his escape from England.

From late 1651 until 1656 nothing is known of Careless but in June that year he rejoined the king in Flanders. Here he enrolled as a captain in the Royal regiment of guards, an élite corps of English royalists raised by Charles to assist the Spanish in their war against the Anglo-French alliance. On 21 May 1658 the king decided 'to confer a mark of distinction' on Careless by changing his surname to Carlos and granting him a coat of arms which featured a green oak on the main shield and an oaken garland on the crest above (Coll. Arms MS). Early the following month Carlos took part in the battle of the Dunes, outside Dunkirk, an action in which he was taken prisoner by the French, though he secured his release shortly afterwards. At the Restoration he sought financial relief as a loyal and indigent former royalist army officer, and obtained in January 1661 the proceeds of a levy on all hay and straw brought into London and Westminster, together with the office of inspector of livery horsekeepers. The following February he secured a grant to sell ballast for ships on the Thames, a sinecure he was ultimately forced to surrender after tedious legal disputes with Trinity House and a compensatory award of 1000 marks. Significantly, when listed about this time as one of the intended knights of the Royal Oak, his rank was given as esquire and his income as £800 per annum. Carlos shared the royal bounty with the five Penderel brothers who had also played a pivotal role in the king's escape after Worcester, and on one occasion distributed among them an award of £400. During the Popish Plot hysteria in September 1678 recusancy proceedings were initiated against him but were subsequently overruled by an order in council of January 1679, a move personally sanctioned by the king 'in remembrance of his former fidelity and service' (Fea, *Flight*, 229–30).

In James II's reign Carlos continued to bask in royal favour, receiving £300 from the secret service fund in January 1688. His Catholicism now became more overt, as shown by the £5 he contributed to the new Catholic church erected in Birmingham in 1687–8; and even at the height of the revolution in December 1688, when making his will, he bequeathed 10s. apiece to five Catholic priests. He spent his last year in Worcestershire and died in May 1689. He was buried in his native Brewood on Oak Apple day, 29 May. He made his adopted son, Edward Carlos (a nephew), the sole executor of his estate, bequeathing him property in Worcester and Stafford. To judge from two of Isaak Fuller's depictions of Carlos, executed after the Restoration and probably drawn from life, he was a burly, clean-shaven man with a thick crop of light brown hair. Carlos won the plaudits of his contemporaries, one praising his 'noble endowments' (Fea, *Flight*, 203), another hailing him as 'the Gallant, Loyal Carles' (A. Cowley, *Six Books of Plants*, 1689, 160), though the most handsome tribute came from Charles II himself. He described Carlos as a subject of 'singular fidelity ... with an ever generous heart' (Coll. Arms MS).   JOHN SUTTON

Sources T. Blount, *Boscobel* (1660), 15, 27–8, 40 • *An exact narrative and relation of his most sacred majesties miraculous escape from Worcester on the third of September, 1651 till his arrivall at Paris* (1660) • S. Pepys, *Charles II's escape from Worcester*, ed. W. Matthews (1967), 87, 91–4 • grant of arms to Colonel William Carlos, 21 March 1658, Coll. Arms • H. Foley, ed., *Records of the English province of the Society of Jesus*, 1 (1877), 180–81 • BL, Harley MS 6804, fol. 197 • will, PRO, PROB 11/217/42 • 'Minor queries with answers', *N&Q*, 9 (1854), 305 • J. Gwynne, *Military memoirs of the great civil war*, ed. W. Scott (1822), 110–12, 133–4 • Clarendon, *Hist. rebellion*, 5.195–7 • F. W. Hamilton, *The origin and history of the first or grenadier guards*, 1 (1874), 9, 12–14; 3 (1874), 426, 497 • A. Fea, *The flight of the king* (1897), 56–7, 202, 205, 211–12, 214–6, 335–6 • A. Fea, *After Worcester fight* (1904), 246–9, 257 • A. M. Broadley, ed., *The royal miracle* (1912), 44–5, 60–65, 70, 79, 123–4 • *VCH Staffordshire*, 5.27–8 • D. Horovitz, *Brewood* (1988), 37, 44, 143 • parish registers, Brewood, Staffs. RO • Staffs. RO, Giffard papers, D590

Likenesses miniature, c.1656, V&A • I. Fuller, oils, 1670?, NPG • Stent, engraving

Carlton, Richard (*d.* 1638?), composer, matriculated as Richard Charlton from Clare College, Cambridge, in the Easter term of 1574 and graduated BA early in 1578; he subsequently took the degree of BMus. Having been ordained he became vicar of St Stephen's, Norwich, a minor canon of the cathedral from 1591 to at least 1609, and master of the choristers from 1591 to 1605. A number of other Carltons were involved in the cathedral's music in the late sixteenth and early seventeenth centuries.

In 1601 Carlton contributed to *The Triumphs of Oriana*, the collection of madrigals in praise of the aged Queen Elizabeth, and also published his own *Madrigals to Five Voices*. He defined his own creative position clearly in the preface to the collection: 'I ... cannot forget that I am an English man'. Unlike Thomas Morley, whom he must have known personally through their common Norwich associations, Carlton accepted only conditionally the light, flexible, and volatile Italian madrigal idiom which Morley introduced into English music in the 1590s; indeed, at least four of the twenty-one items in his 1601 collection are clearly very archaic viol-accompanied solo songs with words added to the instrumental lines. Carlton's characteristic style is stiffer rhythmically, yet at the same time contrapuntally more vigorous and expansive, than that of the typical Morleyan madrigal, the whole being less marked by the detailed expressive or representational response to individual words and phrases characteristic of the true madrigalist. Its most arresting individual feature is perhaps its moments of strikingly strong dissonance. Four of Carlton's madrigals set stanzas from Spenser's *Faerie Queene*.

Surprisingly, no church music by Carlton is known to exist. He was a minor figure, but his straddling of the divide between the sturdier native tradition and that of the imported madrigalian style gives his music a certain individuality. In 1612 he became rector of Bawsey-cum-Glosthorpe, Norfolk. His successor there was instituted to the living in 1638, probably following Carlton's death.

DAVID BROWN

Sources New Grove • E. H. Fellowes, *The English madrigal composers*, 2nd edn (1950) • H. W. Shaw, *The succession of organists of the Chapel Royal and the cathedrals of England and Wales from c.1538* (1991) • R. Carlton, *Madrigals to five voices* (1601), preface • Venn, *Alum. Cant.* • I. Atherton and others, eds., *Norwich Cathedral: church, city and diocese, 1096–1996* (1996), 520, 692–3 • F. Blomefield and C. Parkin, *An essay towards a topographical history of the county of Norfolk*, [2nd edn], 11 vols. (1805–10), vol. 8, p. 347

Carlyle, Alexander (1722–1805), Church of Scotland minister and memorialist, was born on 26 January 1722, the eldest child of the Revd William Carlyle (1689–1765) and Janet Robeson (1700–1779). He was descended on his father's side from a distinguished Cumberland family who had long before crossed over the Scottish border and established themselves in Dumfriesshire. Alexander was born in the parish of Cummertrees, where his father was the minister from 1720; his mother was the daughter of the minister of Tinwald, Alexander Robeson, whom he revered. Throughout his youth he maintained close ties with his mother's family in Dumfriesshire, which he always regarded as 'my native country' (Carlyle, 33–4), and he would have been raised there had not the general assembly denied, on procedural grounds, his father's call to yet another Dumfriesshire parish, Lochmaben, in 1724. Later that year William Carlyle exchanged the Solway Firth for the Firth of Forth when he was translated to Prestonpans, 8 miles east of Edinburgh in Haddingtonshire, where he had worked as a tutor and chaplain in the households of two eminent families after receiving his MA from the University of Edinburgh in 1715. Glimpses of Alexander's childhood there are recorded in a remarkable, and as yet unpublished, memoir entitled 'Recollections', as well as in his well-known *Autobiography*.

Education and early years Carlyle records that he was taught to read English at the age of five or six by a devout old woman in the parish, but he learned to speak it 'with just pronunciation and a very tolerable accent' when he was about seven, during an extended visit by an aunt from London (Carlyle, 4). He was formally educated in the parish school at Prestonpans, where he studied not only Latin but also Greek. Entering the University of Edinburgh at the age of thirteen, as was customary at the time, he passed through the arts and divinity curricula and became intimate with a number of classmates who would later become his associates in the moderate party of the Church of Scotland, including William Robertson, Adam Ferguson, and John Home. The ministry was not his first career choice, but lacking the necessary funds for success in the army and law, he selected it over an apprenticeship in surgery in deference to the views of his grandfather. He received an MA from the University of Edinburgh in 1743, and with a bursary from the duke of Hamilton continued his studies for two more years at the University of Glasgow, under Francis Hutcheson and William Leechman, and for another year in Leiden. Before going abroad he served as a volunteer in the college company that was formed to defend Edinburgh against the Jacobite forces of Charles Edward Stuart, and after the city was taken without a fight in mid-September 1745 he assisted General Cope's army at the battle of Prestonpans.

After returning from the Netherlands, Carlyle was licensed to preach by the presbytery of Haddington on 8 July 1746, and the following autumn he was presented to Cockburnspath in Berwickshire by John Hay of Spot, who had been tutored as a boy by his father. Through a stroke of good luck, as he believed, Carlyle was saved from that

Alexander Carlyle (1722–1805), by Sir Henry Raeburn, 1796

distant parish by news of an impending vacancy at Inveresk (including Musselburgh), scarcely 5 miles south-east of Edinburgh; on 24 February 1747 he was presented there by the duke of Buccleuch, though opposition by some parishioners who questioned his piety delayed his ordination until 2 August 1748. He remained at Inveresk until his death and his thorough knowledge of the parish is evident from his remarkable account of Inveresk in volume 16 of Sir John Sinclair's *Statistical Account of Scotland* (1795). Tall and strikingly handsome, with a fine voice and presence, Carlyle was a good preacher and left evidence of diligent pastoral service, including letters on the establishment of a Sunday school towards the end of his life (reprinted in Cairns, 103–6). Yet he never escaped the imputation of infidelity in the eyes of the most orthodox members of his church.

Moderate churchman Carlyle was a quintessential moderate in his support for ecclesiastical patronage and politically conservative issues, as well as in his endorsement of Enlightenment cultural principles, including liberal education, polite learning, and religious toleration. He published numerous sermons and pamphlets but no work of renown during his lifetime, which accounts for his friend Tobias Smollett remarking in *Humphry Clinker* (1771) that Carlyle, 'whose humour and conversation inflamed me with a desire of being better acquainted with his person … wants nothing but inclination to figure with the rest upon paper'. By 'the rest' Smollett meant well-known authors such as William Robertson, John Home, Adam Ferguson, David Hume, Adam Smith, and Hugh Blair, who caused him to exclaim that 'Edinburgh is a hot-bed of genius' (Smollett, 227). Alongside such men Carlyle was a familiar figure in the cultural life of what has come to be known as the Scottish Enlightenment. He was an early member of the famous Edinburgh debating club, the Select Society (1754–64), and one of the driving forces behind the Poker Club, which was established in 1762 to advance the cause of a Scots militia, but had the additional effect of fostering conviviality and fellow-feeling among clergymen of letters and members of the gentry. In later life he was a fellow of the literary branch of the Royal Society of Edinburgh, where, on 19 April 1784, he read William Collins's 'Ode on the Popular Superstitions of the Highlanders', which was published, with an introductory letter of Carlyle's own composition, in that society's first volume of *Transactions* (1788). Carlyle's extensive range of connections, coupled with his prodigious memory and acute observations, account for the enduring reputation of his *Autobiography* as one of the most important first-hand accounts of cultural activity in eighteenth-century Scotland.

Carlyle's first publication may have been an anonymous pamphlet of 1748 supporting the campaign to raise the stipends of Scottish ministers. Whether or not he wrote that particular work, he certainly cared a great deal about the stipend augmentation issue, and in 1793 he strenuously advocated that cause after pressure from landowners obliged the government to retreat from it. His own low stipend was undoubtedly one reason for his position on this matter—even after it was augmented in 1781 he received just £62 in cash, in addition to eight chalders of wheat, barley, and oats at market value—but on 14 October 1760 he greatly improved his financial situation by marrying a young woman from Northumberland worth more than £3000. His new wife, Mary Roddam (1743–1804), was then only seventeen years old, while he was thirty-eight. The marriage was successful despite the age disparity, and Carlyle outlived his wife by a little more than a year. In their effort to build a family, however, the Carlyles suffered greatly, since all four of their children died between the ages of three and thirteen.

Carlyle loved poetry and theatre, but usually perceived them through the prism of national and party ideology and personal interest. In 1754 he penned the prologue to Charles Hart's *Herminus and Espansia: a Tragedy*, as acted in Edinburgh, and turned it into a patriotic plea for the 'Scotian muse' to find a home after long years of wandering. The prologue concludes:

> The muse once cherish'd, happier Bards shall rise,
> And future Shakespears light our northern skies!

A frequent guest at nearby Dalkeith Palace, Carlyle regularly marked special occasions there with his poems, one of which was published in the *Scots Magazine*: *Verses on his Grace the Duke of Buccleugh's Birthday, September, 1767*. With the exception of *An Ode to the Memory of Colonel Gardiner, in Imitation of Milton*, which has been attributed to him (Cairns, 107), the rest of his poetry remains unpublished, despite his own wishes for a posthumous volume.

In late 1756 and early 1757 Carlyle became embroiled in the controversy over the tragedy of *Douglas* by his friend John Home. He played the hero's adopted father, Old

Norval, in a private rehearsal in Edinburgh, attended a professional performance of the play at the Canongate Theatre on 14 December 1756, and published anonymously both a broadside designed to promote attendance and, early in 1757, an ironic pamphlet intended to ridicule religious opponents of the theatre, *An argument to prove that the tragedy of Douglas ought to be publickly burnt by the hands of the hangman*. At a time when the playhouse was widely considered immoral by Calvinist Presbyterians, his involvement provoked the presbytery of Dalkeith to slap him with a libel, which was overturned by the moderates at the synod of Lothian and Tweeddale on 10 May and was finally quashed by them at the general assembly two weeks later. Carlyle remained an unrepentant promoter of his friend's plays and contributed a laudatory review of Home's next tragedy, *Agis*, to the March 1758 number of the *Critical Review*. His actions took their toll, however, and when Carlyle was nominated to preach before the general assembly in 1760 he became the first such nominee whose appointment was not unanimous. Late in life he could not resist recollecting 'with what a fit of zeal and hypocrisy, (for they were mingled), the minds of great numbers were seized, when the tragedy of Douglas was first acted in Edinburgh, in December 1756' (Sinclair, 16.313).

Political commentator In 1759 Carlyle published, under the name O. M. Haberdasher, a witty squib in support of Pitt the elder, followed the next year by his most successful pamphlet, *The Question Relating to a Scots Militia Considered*, which passed through four anonymous editions. His support for the Scots militia cause never wavered. He promoted it in newspaper letters, some of which appeared in the *Caledonian Mercury* in 1779, 1780, and 1782, and he attacked the apparent opposition to militias in Adam Smith's *Wealth of Nations* in an anonymous pamphlet published in London in 1778: *A Letter to his Grace the Duke of Buccleugh, on National Defence*. The militia issue brought out his Scottish patriotism but, like his friend Adam Ferguson, he also argued for a Scots militia on grounds of civic virtue and the need for a strong national defence during times of foreign conflict, such as the American War of Independence, which he enthusiastically supported. A fast day sermon that he preached against the American revolution in December 1776 was published the following January as *The Justice and Necessity of the War with our American Colonies Examined*. During the French Revolution he was equally conservative, in regard both to domestic issues such as political reform and repeal of the Test Act, which he opposed, and to foreign issues such as the war with France, which he exalted as a divinely sanctioned cause and a test of British virtue and resolve in three published sermons: *Sermon on the Death of Sir David Dalrymple, Bart. Lord Hailes* (1792), *National Depravity the Cause of National Calamities* (1793), and *The Love of our Country, Explained and Enforced in a Sermon from Psalm CXXXVII.5.6* (1797). Yet in his account of his parish he tempered his conservatism by holding the door open for cautious political reform 'in times of tranquillity' (Sinclair, 16.48), and when speaking on behalf of Roman Catholic relief in the general assembly of 1779 he declared himself to be 'a Revolution Whig; and, consequently, to have the greatest respect for the people' (Erskine, 32).

Carlyle was a passionate advocate of the Church of Scotland and its clergy, whom he wished to see cultured, tolerant, well ordered, and financially well off. Like other moderates he viewed the law of patronage as a means of achieving those ends by putting the power of presenting ministers to vacant parishes in the hands of an educated élite. In 1762 he wrote an anonymous pamphlet, *Faction Detected*, in support of the moderates' advocacy of the right of the town council of Edinburgh, as the legal patron, to present the Revd John Drysdale to one of the town's churches. A sermon that Carlyle published in 1767, *The tendency of the constitution of the Church of Scotland to form the temper, spirit, and character of her ministers* (reprinted in vol. 2 of the *Scots Preacher* in 1776), and another that appeared in 1793, *The Usefulness and Necessity of a Liberal Education for Clergymen*, articulated his belief that the Church of Scotland could and should compensate for its lack of wealth with excellence in other areas, including above all polite learning. He believed that too much poverty worked against his ideal of an enlightened clergy, however, and besides campaigning for augmenting stipends he set an example as an agricultural improver—being the first in his parish to use 'the wheel plough with two horses, held and driven by one man' (Sinclair, 16.290)—and spoke out against subjecting the Scottish clergy to the window tax. In 1769 he published a polemical pamphlet, *Essay upon Taxes*, on the window tax question and was appointed the Church of Scotland's commissioner to argue that cause in London and Westminster; thirteen years later he attained his goal when parliament granted his brethren relief from that tax.

Later years By the early 1780s Carlyle was one of the leaders of the moderate party, and therefore of the church. In 1770 he had been elected moderator of the general assembly, and it was with high hopes that he stood for election as principal clerk of the general assembly in 1789. He was apparently elected in a turnout of unprecedented proportions, 145 to 142, after which he took his place as clerk and delivered a victory speech, but when a hotly contested recount seemed to show that he had actually been defeated by his opponent, Professor Andrew Dalzel of Edinburgh University, he withdrew from the contest in a moment of supreme humiliation.

In 1760 Carlyle was given an honorary DD degree by King's College, Aberdeen. Two years later he was appointed his majesty's almoner, a £42-a-year sinecure that he owed to Lord Bute, and on 2 December 1779 Henry Dundas enabled him to exchange that position for a deanery worth £200 per annum. According to Sir Walter Scott, Carlyle was 'the grandest demigod I ever saw' and was 'commonly called *Jupiter Carlyle*' for that reason (Lockhart, 5.291), though there is actually more evidence that he was known to his friends as Sandy, the traditional Scottish nickname for an Alexander. His majestic appearance caused him to be much sought after by painters, and surviving portraits by David Martin, Sir Henry Raeburn, and Archibald Skirving convey something of his commanding physical presence.

After fifty-seven years as minister at Inveresk, Carlyle died on 25 August 1805, shortly before completion of the new church at Inveresk near which he was buried. Shortly before his death he left strict instructions that his nephew and executor, Carlyle Bell, and four other trustees (Henry Grieve, James Finlayson, John Lee, and John Hamilton) were to publish under his own name not only his memoirs but also his poems, sermons, pamphlets, and materials relating to the controversy over John Home's *Douglas*. After much soul-searching and debate among themselves, the trustees decided upon a more limited programme that relied upon Lee's editing of the memoirs, but in the end Lee did not deliver, and none of Carlyle's writings were published by the trustees. His surviving manuscripts remained unpublished, with only three exceptions: the *Autobiography*, which first appeared more than fifty years after Carlyle's death in John Hill Burton's splendidly edited edition of 1860, later revised in the standard 'new edition' of 1910; a comparison of William Robertson and Hugh Blair that was appended to James Kinsley's 1973 edition of the *Autobiography*, published as *Anecdotes and Characters of the Times*; and the brief *Journal of a Tour to the North of Scotland* that dates from 1765 and was separately published in Aberdeen in 1981. Indeed, most of them were not even accessible to scholars until the late 1980s, when they were finally deposited in the National Library of Scotland by a descendant of Carlyle Bell. They include much correspondence; several journals; nearly one hundred sermons; numerous notes, speeches, and book reviews; two bundles and a bound volume of occasional poetry, which complement another manuscript volume of his occasional poetry in Edinburgh University Library; and accounts of William Robertson, Henry Dundas, the highland clans, ecclesiastical affairs, and many other topics.

RICHARD B. SHER

Sources W. Adam, *Sequel to the gift of a grandfather* (1836) • W. T. Cairns, 'Jupiter Carlyle and the Scottish moderates', *The religion of Dr Johnson, and other essays* (1946), 81–110 • D. L. Carver, 'Collins and Alexander Carlyle', *Review of English Studies*, 15 (1939), 35–44 • G. M. Ditchfield, 'The Scottish campaign against the Test Act, 1790–1791', *HJ*, 23 (1980), 37–61 • R. L. Emerson, 'The social composition of Enlightened Edinburgh: the Select Society of Edinburgh, 1754–1764', *Studies on Voltaire and the Eighteenth Century*, 114 (1973), 291–329 • [J. Erskine], *A narrative of the debate in the general assembly of the Church of Scotland, May 25, 1779, occasioned by apprehensions of an intended repeal of the penal statutes against papists* (1780) • J. G. Lockhart, *The life of Sir Walter Scott*, [new edn], 10 vols. (1902) • J. Robertson, *The Scottish Enlightenment and the militia issue* (1985) • *Fasti Scot.*, new edn • R. B. Sher, 'Moderates, managers and popular politics in mid-eighteenth-century Edinburgh: the Drysdale "bustle" of the 1760s', *New perspectives on the politics and culture of early modern Scotland*, ed. J. Dwyer, R. A. Mason, and A. Murdoch (1982), 179–209 • R. B. Sher, *Church and university in the Scottish Enlightenment: the moderate literati of Edinburgh* (1985) • *The autobiography of Dr Alexander Carlyle of Inveresk, 1722–1805*, ed. J. H. Burton (1910); facs. edn with introduction by R. B. Sher (1990) • T. Smollett, *The expedition of Humphry Clinker*, ed. O. M. Brack and T. R. Preston (1990) • J. Sinclair, *Statistical account of Scotland, 1791–1799*, [new edn], ed. J. Withrington and I. R. Grant, 20 vols. (1977–83)

Archives NL Scot., biographical material; corresp.; documents relating to the *Douglas* playhouse affair; journals; letters and papers on the poor house in Musselburgh; notebooks; papers; prayers and devotional phrases; sermons · U. Edin. L., poems and papers relating to libel, Dc.4.42 | BL, corresp. with John Douglas, bishop of Salisbury, Add. MS 2185 · NL Scot., corresp. with Robert Douglas, MS 3116 · NL Scot., corresp. with Sir Gilbert Elliot · NL Scot., corresp. with Lord Milton · NRA Scotland, priv. coll., corresp. with William Creech · U. Edin. L., papers relating to libel against A. Carlyle for attending *Douglas* · U. Mich., Clements L., corresp. with Charles Townshend

Likenesses D. Martin, portrait, 1770, repro. in A. Carlyle, *Anecdotes and characters*, ed. Kinsley (1973), frontispiece; priv. coll. · D. Martin, portrait, 1770, repro. in A. Carlyle, *Anecdotes and characters*, ed. Kinsley (1973), facing p. 184; priv. coll. · J. Kay, two caricatures, etchings, 1789, BM, NPG · H. Raeburn, oils, 1796, Scot. NPG [*see illus.*] · H. Raeburn, portrait, 1796, repro. in Sher, *Church and university*; priv. coll. · J. Henning, porcelain medallion, 1805, Scot. NPG; plaster replica, Scot. NPG · J. Brown, pencil drawing, Scot. NPG · W. Roffe, stipple (after D. Martin, 1770), NPG · A. Skirving, chalk drawing, Scot. NPG · A. Skirving, oils, Scot. NPG

Carlyle, Alexander James (1861–1943), historian and social reformer, was born in Bombay on 24 July 1861, the second of three children and younger son of the Revd James Edward Carlyle (1821–1893), minister of the Free Church of Scotland in Bombay, and his wife, Jessie Margaret, daughter of James Milne of Huntly, Aberdeenshire. His elder brother was Sir Robert Warrand *Carlyle. His father, who returned to Scotland when Alexander was a month old, was compelled for reasons of health to take charge of Presbyterian churches abroad, so that Alexander's boyhood was passed in Rome, Paris, Berlin, and South Africa. His knowledge of foreign languages and literature, and his enjoyment of foreign travel, were the outcome of this experience.

Carlyle had no regular schooling, and apart from two years at Glasgow University (1876–8) his systematic studies began when in 1883 he entered Exeter College, Oxford, as an exhibitioner. He obtained a first-class in modern history in 1886 and a second-class in theology in 1888. In the latter year he was president of the Oxford Union and ordained to a curacy at St Stephen's, Westminster, where his sympathies as a social reformer were first aroused. He served as general secretary of the SPCK in 1890–91. In 1893 he was elected to a fellowship at University College, Oxford; although he had to vacate his fellowship in 1895 on his marriage to Rebecca Monteith Smith (d. 1941), daughter of the Scottish poet and preacher Walter Chalmers *Smith, he continued to serve the college as lecturer in politics and economics and as chaplain. In 1935 he was elected an honorary fellow.

From 1895 to 1919, however, Carlyle's centre in Oxford was the city church of St Martin and All Saints, of which he was rector. During these years he took a leading part, as a liberal thinker and Christian socialist formally attached to no political party, in the social life of the city and in religious movements. His friendship with Sidney and Beatrice Webb and other reformers, his co-operation with the high-church Anglicans associated with Charles Gore—for whom, although he did not share his ecclesiastical and theological opinions, he had a deep regard—and his close alliance with his old Exeter College friend John Carter

testify to his breadth of outlook. He was one of the early advocates of planned social reform, the unity of the churches, and better-informed relations between the city and the university of Oxford. He was a mainstay of the Christian Social Union, which was largely sustained by disciples of Gore and Henry Scott Holland; a friend and adviser of local trade unionism; a promoter of interdenominational summer schools of theology, which for a number of years were held in Oxford; and he was in close touch with liberal leaders of religious life and thought abroad—such as Lars Olof Jonathan (Nathan) Söderblom, archbishop of Uppsala—as well as with men of such various outlook as Baron Friedrich von Hügel and the leaders in England of the free churches.

Carlyle's resignation of the living of the city church in 1919 enabled him to give more time to his work as writer and teacher. He had never neglected these interests and had owed much to the inspiration of William Sanday, whose seminars he attended, and to co-operation with Hastings Rashdall, whose theological views he largely shared. He had published a life of Hugh Latimer, with his wife, in 1899; an essay on the church in the composite volume *Contentio veritatis* (1902); the short books *The Influence of Christianity upon Social and Political Ideas* and *Wages* in 1912; and, with J. V. Bartlet, *Christianity in History* (1917).

Since 1895 Carlyle's main preoccupation had been his *History of Mediaeval Political Theory in the West*, which he had then planned with his elder brother. Although Sir Robert Carlyle was able to contribute only to the fifth volume of the book (1928)—the volume on the thirteenth century, which represents more or less what in 1895 they had first thought to produce—the two men discussed the work continuously, and the sixth and last volume (1936) was dedicated by Alexander to Robert's memory. As the work proceeded (1903–36) it gradually won a high place in historical literature both on the continent and in the English-speaking world. Written with lucidity and with a simplicity that is apt to be misleading, it remains an invaluable guide to an immense series of texts ranging from the early Roman law books and the writings of the church fathers to the works of Bodin and Althusius. Its main theme is the rule of law, firmly rooted in the nature of things, as the basis of the search for and maintenance of justice and liberty. It was followed, in 1941, by *Political Liberty*, which was concerned with the seventeenth century. The Political Philosophy and Science Club, which Carlyle founded in 1909 primarily for teachers in the universities of Oxford, Cambridge, and London, was the practical expression of his wide political and social interests.

Apart from four years (1930–34) as a canon of Worcester Cathedral, Carlyle lived continuously in Oxford from 1895 until his death. Throughout this period he was an active teacher and lecturer working for several colleges, including the women's colleges, as a tutor in history, economics, politics, and modern languages. His diversity of interests and his unconventional manner of speech provoked criticism in some quarters but his inspiration as a teacher and his influence upon many who in later life attained distinction are indisputable, and confirm the impression that his incisive and provocative table talk made on all who knew him. At different times he was the close and valued friend of such men as Rashdall, Sidney Ball, J. A. Smith, and H. H. Joachim. His home, where his wife and his two daughters supported him with an independent devotion, was a delightful social centre. He was an urbane, cultivated man who, though he rarely talked about it and was unclerical in demeanour, was in the words of one of his younger friends 'dominated by religion'. As a curate in Westminster he was so much impressed by the evil social effects of intemperance that he became a total abstainer; but he never 'preached', although he was a good and forthright preacher, and was a living example to others by his belief that complete frankness and generous tolerance are not incompatible. In a word he expressed in action his belief in personal liberty.

Carlyle was in some ways more successful abroad than in England, whether in lecturing tours in Scandinavia or at juristic conferences in Rome. He gave the Olaus Petri lectures in Uppsala (1918) and the Lowell lectures in Boston (1924), as well as the Birkbeck lectures in ecclesiastical history at Trinity College, Cambridge (1925–7). In 1936 he was elected FBA. He received the honorary degree of DD from Glasgow University (1934) and was a foreign member of the Royal Academy of Naples. He died in Oxford on 27 May 1943. His daughter made a bequest to the University of Oxford in 1972 that provides the Carlyle lectures on medieval political theory.

F. M. POWICKE, *rev.* K. D. REYNOLDS

Sources F. M. Powicke, 'Alexander James Carlyle, 1861–1943', *PBA*, 29 (1943), 313–27 · *The Times* (29 May 1943) · *The Times* (7 June 1943) · private information (1959) · personal knowledge (1959) · *WWW* · C. W. Boase, ed., *Registrum Collegii Exoniensis*, new edn, OHS, 27 (1894) · Crockford (1902)
Archives Bodl. Oxf., corresp. and papers | BL, corresp. with Macmillans, Add. MS 55033 · BLPES, corresp. with Lord Beveridge · NL Scot., corresp. with Blackwoods
Likenesses A. Sinclair, drawing, 1919; in possession of family in 1959 · A. Sinclair, oils, 1919; in possession of family in 1959
Wealth at death £2715 4s. 5d.: probate, 31 Aug 1943, *CGPLA Eng. & Wales*

Carlyle, Benjamin Fearnley [*name in religion* Aelred] (1874–1955), Benedictine monk, was born at 8 Ashmount, Broomhill, Ecclesall Bierlow, a suburb of Sheffield, on 7 February 1874, the eldest of six children of James Fearnley Carlyle and Anna Maria Champion Kelly. He was baptized at St Mark's Church in the city on 13 March 1874, receiving the Christian names of his grandfather, a Church of England clergyman, one time rector of Badgeworth in Gloucestershire. His father was a railway engineer who worked in England and Argentina, but died unexpectedly when Carlyle was sixteen.

Carlyle entered St Bartholomew's Hospital, London, in 1892 as a medical student. But on his own confession 'most of my interest at St. Barts was given to the care of neglected cases of sick children instead of being concentrated on the actual work of taking my degree in medicine and surgery' (Carlyle, diaries, 3 Dec 1948). He wanted 'to help the poor lads in the slums' (ibid.). He also had an idea to revive the Benedictine order in the Church of England. He believed that the monastic system was 'the great solution of many social problems' (Carlyle to Green, 10 Sept 1897, Elmore Abbey Archives). He therefore made a personal profession to live according to the rule of St Benedict on 22 February 1892. His knowledge of monastic life was derived from visits to the Roman Catholic abbey of Buckfast in Devon. The prior, Benedict Gariador, gave him a copy of the rule. He read the life of the English Cistercian abbot, St Ailred, by J. D. Dalgairns, in 1893 and began calling himself Brother Aelred OSB. He joined a group of Church of England Benedictine oblates in Ealing and was chosen as their superior in 1894.

Carlyle's first attempt to found his own Benedictine community was in 1896 in the East End of London at Glengall Road, Isle of Dogs. There he kept open house for the poor and ministered to the local Boys' Brigade in a black habit. He moved to Lower Guiting in Gloucestershire in February 1898 to find a place 'where some of our poor lads might be sent' (Carlyle to Green, 8 Dec 1897). He wanted 'to lead the strict Religious life and train men for Rescue Work' (Carlyle to Green, 4 Dec 1897). Part of the divine office was recited in Latin from a monastic breviary, but the communal life was minimal. It all ended when an angry mob forced them out of the village.

Carlyle's second attempt began at Milton Abbas in Dorset in 1899, this time in white habits. He moved to Caldey Island off south Wales, where his seven disciples elected him their abbot on 23 February 1902. In the same year they all moved to Painsthorpe, on Lord Halifax's estate in Yorkshire. It was here that the community first established itself on a regular basis. Numbers passed double figures. A magazine called *Pax* was begun in 1904, to which Aelred contributed a 'Community letter' fairly regularly, and other occasional pieces. An account of the community's ideals called 'Our purpose and method' appeared under his name (1905–6). He also got himself ordained in America by C. C. Grafton, bishop of Fond du Lac, on 15 November 1904.

He returned in triumph to Caldey in 1906. With little money but great enthusiasm he now embarked on an elaborate building programme for a monastery of the purely contemplative life. Only a few of the buildings planned by his architect, J. Coates Carter, were ever completed. They were described as 'exotic and eclectic and quite without parallel' (Anson, 159). Aelred devised an equally elaborate liturgy, based on monastic ritual, with many modern Roman Catholic feasts and practices, but with devotions of his own. For a period between 1906 and 1913 Caldey became a focus of public attention. Anglo-Catholics flocked to the island. The young Ronald Knox came for his ordination retreat and stayed eleven weeks. He described Caldey as having 'something of fairyland about it' and Aelred as the 'magician who had called all this into being, as with a stroke of Prospero's wand' (*Pax*, 277, 1956, 31). But others questioned his position as an abbot and even as a validly ordained minister in the Church of England. Aelred argued that Frederick Temple, archbishop of Canterbury, had approved of his vocation and enterprise from the beginning; but he also claimed that Caldey was extra-diocesan and that he was free to do as he wished.

In order to regularize his position in the Church of England Carlyle invited Charles Gore, bishop of Oxford, to carry out a visitation. Gore, however, laid down a number of conditions before formal accession to the Church of England would be possible. Aelred replied on behalf of the community in February 1913 that 'we can not conscientiously submit to the demands you make of us' (Carlyle to Gore, 19 Feb 1913, Prinknash Abbey Archives). On 5 March he led nineteen of his monks into the Roman Catholic church.

Carlyle now had no status as a monk, priest, or abbot. He therefore went to the monastery of Maredsous in Belgium to begin a canonical noviciate. He completed it on 29 June 1914, a day after the assassination of Archduke Franz Ferdinand in Sarajevo. He was informed of the news on the morning of his profession. He was ordained by the bishop of Namur on 5 July and returned to Caldey four days before the outbreak of the First World War. Although he was reinstalled as abbot of Caldey, the legal superior, appointed by Rome for ten years, was now Francis Mostyn, the bishop of Menevia. Financial and other difficulties forced Aelred to leave Caldey in 1920. He resigned the following year and began a new career as a priest in British Columbia. At Bear Creek, 1921–30, he ministered to Okanagan Indians. In 1930 he was made parish priest of the mining town of Princeton. He still hankered after religious life. In 1933, therefore, he returned to Europe to enter the Carthusian noviciate at Miraflores near Burgos in Spain. On the way he stayed two days with his former community now at Prinknash Park in Gloucestershire. The Carthusian vocation did not materialize and he returned to Canada. In 1937 he moved to Vancouver and acted as prison chaplain to Okalla provincial gaol. In recognition of outstanding service there he received the freedom of the city of Vancouver on 1 May 1951.

On his retirement Carlyle accepted an invitation to settle with his former brethren at Prinknash. He was clothed in a white habit on arrival and was allowed to re-make his solemn vows privately on 3 November 1953. He died at St Teresa's Hospital, Corston, Somerset, on 14 October 1955 and was buried five days later under the high altar of the new abbey church at Prinknash.

At the time of Carlyle's death tributes were paid to his charm, his ability to fire young people with enthusiasm, and his greatest virtue, 'compassion for the unfortunate' (*Pax*, 277, 1956, 35). Ronald Knox, while admiring his enthusiasm, said that 'he was one of those men whose minds are too preoccupied to read the other man's thoughts in a conversation … It was not easy to tell Abbot Aelred things'. Knox found a 'faint air of make-believe' about the whole period at Caldey (*Pax*, 215, 1940, 84). Peter Anson extended this criticism to other periods of Aelred's life. But there is no denying the solid achievements of his pastoral ministry—and the community he created survived and prospered.

There are two biographies of Aelred based on personal knowledge. One, *Abbot Extraordinary*, is by Peter Anson, who was a member of the Caldey community. The other (unpublished) is by the Benedictine Michael Hanbury, who came to know Aelred well after his return to the community in 1951. The two works agree upon the facts of Aelred's life but differ sharply on the estimate of his character.   AELRED BAKER

Sources A. Carlyle, diaries, Prinknash Abbey, Prinknash, Gloucestershire, archives · letters of B. F. Carlyle to Rev. J. Green, Elmore Abbey, Newbury, Berkshire, archives · annals of Caldey, Prinknash Abbey, Prinknash, Gloucestershire, archive · M. Hanbury, 'Biography of Aelred', Prinknash Abbey, Prinknash, Gloucestershire, archives · B. F. Carlyle to C. Gore, 9 Feb 1913, Prinknash Abbey, Prinknash, Gloucestershire, archives · P. F. Anson, *Abbot extraordinary: a memoir of Aelred Carlyle, monk and missionary, 1874–1955* (1958) · R. Kollar, *Abbot Aelred Carlyle: Caldey Island and the Anglo-Catholic revival in England* (1995) · *Pax*, 277 (spring 1956) [copy in Prinknash Abbey, Gloucestershire archives] · *Pax*, 215 (1940) [copy in Prinknash Abbey, Gloucestershire archives] · b. cert. · parish register (baptism), St Mark, Sheffield, 13 March 1874 · d. cert.
Archives Elmore Abbey, Newbury, Berkshire · Prinknash Abbey, Prinknash, Gloucestershire, archives, corresp. diaries, etc. | Borth. Inst., corresp. with second Viscount Halifax · Elmore Abbey, Newbury, Berkshire, corresp. with J. Green · LPL, letters to Samuel Gurney
Likenesses G. Brown, drawing, 1918, repro. in Anson, *Abbot extraordinary*, facing p. 257

Carlyle, Jane Baillie Welsh (1801–1866), letter writer, was born on 14 July 1801 in Haddington, Scotland, the only child of Dr John Welsh (1776–1819) and Grace, or Grizel, *née* Welsh (1782–1842). She was named Jane Baillie after her grandmother. Her parents were Scottish. Her father romantically claimed descent from John Knox's family, and the Baillies from William Wallace, and a famous border Gypsy horse thief.

Early life and marriage An account of Jane Welsh's childhood is given in Thomas Carlyle's *Reminiscences*: her time at Haddington, her learning Latin, her wish (shared by other women at the time) to be educated like a boy, and her private tuition by the future church leader Edward Irving. Though Irving left to teach in Kirkcaldy in 1812, they kept in touch when she attended a school in Edinburgh about 1817, thinking themselves in love. But Irving then engaged himself to the eldest daughter of a minister in Kirkcaldy who refused to release him. Jane may never have recovered from the death in 1819 of her revered father. She and her mother stayed at the Haddington home, Jane unavailingly courted by various suitors. All seemed unsuitable, none more so to her mother than Thomas *Carlyle, who was introduced to them by Irving in 1821; but a new courtship began as Carlyle offered to guide her studies.

After this Jane Welsh's life was inextricably involved with Carlyle's and though her attachment was sorely tested, and not without exasperation and pain, their mutual admiration and often tender affection kept them together. This was partly because she knew that she had made the choice of a 'genius' to remove her from the dull sobriety and provincialism of Haddington, and that he aroused in her the 'slumbering … ambitions' her father 'first kindled there' (*Collected Letters*, 2.196). All this is brilliantly illuminated in her letters, still not fully published, and mainly in selections inevitably chosen to show their editors' predetermined interpretations.

Jane Welsh and Thomas Carlyle married on 17 October 1826. Whether their marriage was normally consummated can never be proved; the alleged evidence of Frank Harris is completely untrustworthy, and a tale that Jane once prepared baby clothes is uncertain. When Thomas left her for London in 1831 she wrote not only of being 'ever thine' but of crying and kissing his red nightcap on waking alone (6–9 August), and wishing she were in his arms, where 'I shall feel so safe so blessed' (27 September). Yet the impression left by their childless marriage with its tense affection, best expressed in their letters, is that it progressed under difficulties.

The Carlyles had two reasonably happy years in Edinburgh (1826–8), followed by a move to the Welshes' old hill farm at Craigenputtoch in Dumfriesshire, where Jane Carlyle was desperately lonely, though Thomas was productive. Apart from brief excursions, including a month with Francis Jeffrey in 1829 at his home near Edinburgh, they remained at Craigenputtoch until 1831, when they had a six-month stay in London full of interest and variety, followed by a return to Craigenputtoch relieved only by some months in Edinburgh in 1833. It was apparently during their second stay at Craigenputtoch that (as Jane Carlyle dramatically told Ellen Twisleton in the mid-1850s) she felt the full misery of their solitary life, when she found Carlyle no fit companion, and regularly went to bed in tears.

London life However idyllic their stay later seemed to Carlyle, it had to end, and in June 1834 they came to conquer London from 5 Cheyne Row. For eleven years or so Jane Carlyle presided over their circle, sometimes suffering from ill health, but sharing years of triumph. She was shocked in February 1842 by the death of her mother, to whom she had been strongly devoted if occasionally impatient. Jane's love for her had been shown in letters of deep concern for her mother's loneliness at Thornhill in Dumfriesshire, and in her dispatch of amusing news, including irritated but proud accounts of Thomas and vivid verbal sketches of men such as Lord Jeffrey, the posturing Lord Brougham, and the dandy Count d'Orsay. Meanwhile she conducted a sparkling tea-table salon, attended by European refugees, American visitors, radicals, journalists, politicians, men about town, and their joint friends, rising women critics, and novelists. Visitors included Geraldine Jewsbury, Martha Lamont, and Anna Jameson, as well as such established figures as Dickens, Thackeray, Tennyson, and Browning. They were also visited by John Forster, the actor–manager William Macready, and the Irish nationalists Gavan Duffy and John Mitchel who admired Jane Carlyle as much as or more than her husband, and who were joined by the poet and critic John Sterling, Edward, his father, of *The Times*, the Wedgwood family and their relation Erasmus Alvey Darwin, the German radical Richard Plattnauer, Mazzini and companions, the formerly Indian Bullers and Stracheys, and countless writers and thinkers who came to wonder

at Carlyle and returned because drawn to them both. Yet there was an almost unbearable exception.

In 1843, when Jane was at the peak of her social activity and enjoyment, and recently recovered from her mother's death, her attention was first called to the attraction her husband felt for the company of Lady Harriet, later the second Lady Ashburton, wife of William Bingham Baring. They met, and Jane was forced to recognize that—although she had accompanied her husband through years of upward struggle and attainment, including rewriting *The French Revolution*, helping him through his public lectures, and enduring his grim work on *Cromwell*—he now turned for stimulus to the Barings at their grand houses in Piccadilly or in the country at The Grange.

Controversy apart, all concerned behaved fairly well; but Jane's resentment was understandable since the attraction struck at her union with Carlyle by robbing her of the 'genius' who had come to dominate any society in which they found themselves and on whose achievements she had staked so much. Lady Harriet enjoyed her role as literary lion tamer, and felt an affection for her greatest capture; and, bizarre as it may seem, Carlyle was bemused by her and delighted in an almost rapturous correspondence. To Jane she seemed 'the woman of largest intellect I have ever seen—how *she* can reconcile herself to a life which is after all a mere dramatic representation … fills me with astonishment and *a certain* sorrow' (24 April 1846). Between the three of them, there were times of steady friendship, punctuated by jealous outbreaks when Lady Harriet's letters were clearly unwelcome at Cheyne Row. It dragged on because Jane Carlyle generally fought down her feelings, while Carlyle was unwilling to give up his circle of acquaintances with the Ashburtons, including many of his closest friends.

Dark years If the story is foreshortened it can be dramatized, as by Froude in his life of Carlyle and other writings, but he over-simplifies. Jane was vulnerable because in immediate terms she was weak: her health was poor, she suffered from insomnia, she lacked the Ashburtons' resources, and she was forced to see her husband going off to them at 'that eternal Bath House', where, as she wrote in her diary in 1855, she was usually not expected to accompany him. She was in fact stronger than Lady Harriet, whose health was weaker still. Yet, while Jane doped herself with morphine, Carlyle drugged himself with work, escaping to his overlong and least-liked biography of *Frederick the Great*. The full text of a tale Jane wrote in 1852, 'The Simple Story of my Own First Love' (Edinburgh, 2001), shows her seeking, rather helplessly, to define herself. But her resource lay in her inner spirit, dramatized and expressed in her letters and journal. The full text of the journal of 1855–6 shows the depth of her bitterness at that time, after it had been slowly mounting. She was isolated by her pride. It remains for discussion how far her suffering was self-inflicted, and it is difficult to generalize about her whole life from this period alone.

There is no doubt who wins most sympathy. For while

her husband did much as he pleased, Jane laid few restrictions on herself in writing, and, as she sometimes realized later, her remarks about their married life could be misinterpreted. As their friends saw, he never reproached her in letters or in any other way. But her letters display the apparently (and even actually) spontaneous Jane Carlyle as someone who could attract delighted admiration. She was ambitious, though maybe mainly for Carlyle. She was a good linguist, brilliant in conversation, utterly independent, spirited, a hero-worshipper if there ever was one, and ready to take up the women's cause:

> She could do anything well to which she chose to give herself. She was fond of Logic—too much so; and she had a keen clear incisive faculty of seeing through things, and hating all that was make-believe or pretentious. She had good sense that amounted to genius. She loved to learn and she cultivated all her faculties to the utmost of her power. She was always witty ... in a word she was fascinating and everybody fell in love with her.   (Carlyle, *Reminiscences*, 45)

Lady Harriet died in 1857 and Jane felt her death more than she admitted; Elizabeth and Edward Twisleton noted her tears as those of the 'true' rather than the 'false friend' Jane Brookfield (Harvard U., Houghton L.). Life changed in little over a year when Lord Ashburton married Louisa Stewart-Mackenzie, the third Lady Ashburton. She soon won over Jane Carlyle: 'Oh my Dearest, my Beautifulest! my Best!' (7 April 1857). They exchanged letters, with ecstatic cooings over Louisa's baby; and Jane's continued existence in the shadow of *Frederick* also saw the emergence of a gentler side shown in friendships with younger women such as John Sterling's children, and Lady Airlie.

Letters to both groups show the attraction Jane had. Where men had once turned to her for an intelligent response and possibly sympathy, younger women looked to her for advice. She looked for a free intelligence in her correspondents, some of whom were dropped—her niece Jeannie Welsh, for example, obviously no longer needed after the death of her beloved uncle John Welsh, Jane's mother's brother. There is often a lively interest in her accounts of daily life at Cheyne Row; but her endless problems with servants, bedbugs, and running the house, which took much of her time, are not the chief reason for enjoying her. The Haddington house and 5 (now 24) Cheyne Row, where she lived from 1834 until her death, and on which she expended so much of her practical genius, are both open to the public, and bring both Jane herself and the scenes she describes close to the visitor. Even so, although she was less of a traveller than her husband, some of her most evocative letters (and an account called 'Much Ado about Nothing') are about times when she returned to her birthplace, to Edinburgh, Fife, or even Dumfriesshire. Like Thomas she can be thought of, by upbringing and outlook, as a distinctly Scottish writer.

The dark years of *Frederick* lasted until 1865. Jane's life continued with diminished vitality, and she was further weakened by a dramatic fall in the street, when she almost died, as Thomas painfully records in the *Reminiscences*. She recovered only after staying with friends near her mother's old home, in the familiar surroundings of Templand, near Thornhill.

Peace restored   A last phase was relatively calm, with *Frederick* finished, domestic peace restored, and Carlyle frightened into attentiveness and ready to write of the period as entirely 'beautiful'. By selection it has sometimes been made to seem even calmer. It led up to the final scenes of Carlyle's leaving to give his rectorial address at Edinburgh in 1866, and Jane's festive dinner with Dickens, John Forster, and others, when they celebrated his triumph. It was almost as she would have wished: a few days later, on 21 April 1866, she died on a carriage drive in Hyde Park.

A final drama began after Jane's death and burial, on 26 April, with her father in St Mary's Abbey, Haddington, apart from her husband as they had agreed. At once he began his reminiscences of her, to give the fame which she had not won for herself. That account, with its chapter on her loving admirers Irving and Lord Jeffrey, did not appear until 1881, clumsily edited by J. A. Froude. It came out in the month that Carlyle died. It was followed by a truncated version of Carlyle's lovingly edited *Letters and Memorials*, in three volumes (1882–4), the *New Letters and Memorials* (1903), a succession of further selections, and a continuing controversy about the marriage.

Jane was dark and slender, and extremely pretty as a girl, though not showing to advantage in most of her portraits or many photographs. She had an exceptional fascination for men, who appreciated her wit, charm, and intelligence. Edward Sterling and his two sons, John and Anthony, were devoted; Mazzini liked to unwind in conversation with her; she nursed her old companion or fiancé George Rennie when he was dying, and rejoiced to see another, John Stodart, on his reappearance in the 1850s; Francis Jeffrey and Erasmus Darwin were fascinated by her. Of later years Carlyle writes of her 'timid modesty and graceful bashfulness' (Carlyle, *Reminiscences*, 187). Yet not everyone found her delightful: some, such as David Masson, 'Snow' Wedgwood, Harriet Martineau, and G. S. Venables, saw her as too biting and sarcastic. In addition to the younger women who were drawn to her, there were new friends such as Lady Harriet's mother the dowager Lady Sandwich, Margaret Oliphant, and Lady William Russell, who declared, 'Mr. Carlyle is a great man, yes: but Mrs. Carlyle, let me inform you is no less great as a woman' (ibid., 187). Her strange friendship with the outstanding American actress Charlotte Cushman remains to be more fully investigated. Cushman is noted for her passionately romantic attachments to mainly younger women, but her friendship with Jane is extremely unlikely to have been as unconventional as Cushman wished.

Above all there was Geraldine Jewsbury, whose surviving letters to Jane Carlyle are full of interest, particularly in their concern for the status of women, though ruthlessly cut and then destroyed by Mrs Alexander Ireland, their editor. Jewsbury burnt most of Jane's letters to her, and she is another enigma. She was Jane Carlyle's most steadfast friend, though often out of favour. Endlessly patient, often jealous, and unfailingly reliable, yet sometimes scorned for that reason, she wrote perceptively to Froude about Jane: 'Not heartless', but with 'a genuine preference for herself', needing but entirely lacking a religious faith, her unbending pride left her 'warped' and as if 'cracked, broken and disfigured'. Yet her account ends with an appeal for 'forgiveness', not clearly saying for whom (MS, priv. coll.). Jewsbury certainly included in her best novel, *The Half Sisters* (1848), many ideas about women's rights that they had discussed, and even a sharp glance at Jane herself, to whom the novel was jointly dedicated with their feminist friend Elizabeth Paulet.

The greatest woman letter writer in English Carlyle's *Reminiscences* have only recently appeared as written, and his wife's letters are being published in the ongoing and complete *Carlyle Letters*. Yet it is hardly disputed that she is the greatest woman letter writer in English. Her skill often lay in the immediacy of her letters; their appeal lies partly in the story that emerges from her self-dramatization. Short excerpts can barely do them justice. Their effectiveness has nothing to do with elegant prose, to which she could always rise, much to do with her sympathetic imagination, clear head, alertness, and a quick eye and ear for entirely natural expression. Thomas had enjoined her to write letters, 'as long and careless and garrulous and true-hearted' as they 'can be made' (18 Feb 1823). He liked it 'when you begin writing without a word to say' (10 Aug 1823), yet he also appreciated her sharp sense of telling incident and character.

Though she believed her life was dull, Jane's letters suggest the contrary. Unexpectedly alone with Tennyson, she writes:

> I did just as Carlyle would have done had he been there; got out *pipes* and TOBACCO—and *brandy and water* … he *professed* to be *ashamed* of polluting my room … but he smoked on all the same—for *three* mortal hours!—talking like an angel—only exactly as if he were talking with a clever *man*. (31 Jan 1845)

Of Emerson she reported to Lady Harriet, 'The man has *two* faces to begin with which are continually changing into one another like "*dissolving views*," the one young, refined, almost beautiful … the other decidedly old, hatchet-like, crotchety, inconclusive—like an incarnation of his own *poems*!' (28 Oct 1847). The industrial inventor

> Mr Whitworth of Manchester dropt into tea, as from the moon. An *interesting* man, for *once*; thank God for all his mercies! … still the *mechanic* in appearance and bearing; all the perfumes of—the Bank of England cannot wash *that* out of him. And besides he looks cousin once removed to a Baboon; but … is lucid as spring-water and natural as a *gowan*. (Journal, 18 Nov 1855)

After watching the teetotal campaigner Father Mathew administer the pledge at a rally, she admits that 'when I went to bed I could not sleep—the pale faces I had seen haunted me' (9 Aug 1843). Nearer home she has an encounter with their alcoholic servant Helen Mitchell, whom she found lying on the kitchen floor 'dead drunk—spread out like the three legs of Man—with a chair upset beside her and in the midst of a perfect chaos of dirty dishes and fragments of broken crockery' (27 Oct 1840). Mazzini's political views puzzle her: 'I never saw a mortal man who so completely made himself into "minced meat" for the universe!' (28 May 1843); Ruskin seems

equally enigmatic. He 'goes to sleep with, every night, a different Turner's picture on a chair opposite his bed "that he may have something beautiful to look at on first opening his eyes of a morning"' (23 Feb 1856).

Jane's letters often served to compensate for her unhappy marriage. In the pointed and elaborate 'Budget of a *Femme* incomprise' (7 Feb 1855), which she addressed to Thomas as if he were the chancellor of the exchequer, she complains bitterly about her household allowance and his unfairness. In the same period her resentment deepens in her journal, and in her forceful account to Ellen Twisleton of her early married life at Craigenputtoch, when she might end the evening by playing 'Scotch tunes' for her husband, 'till he went to bed,—oftenest with the tears running down my face, the while I played' (November 1856).

Yet her letters should not be treated simply as autobiography. She was an artist, with a keen and critical eye for the weaknesses and strengths of others. She had a strong and alert intellect, and her insights, whether sceptical or irreverent, are always direct. Her companionship with Carlyle was an education itself, as his with her. She should be judged not only by her own comments, but by those correspondents such as Amalie Bölte who knew them both, and understood the part Thomas played in her life. His unheard-of decision to publish her letters so completely was justified; he was convinced that they give 'such an electric-shower of all-illuminating brilliancy, penetration, wise discernment, just enthusiasm, humour, grace, patience, courage, love—and in fine of spontaneous *nobleness* of mind and intellect' surpassing 'whatever of best I know to exist in that kind' (Carlyle, *Reminiscences*, 161). Her other writings show no such power. She was unwilling to make the effort to express herself in other forms, and probably unable. Nevertheless she was a great writer.   KENNETH FIELDING and DAVID SORENSEN

Sources *The collected letters of Thomas and Jane Welsh Carlyle*, ed. C. R. Sanders, K. J. Fielding, and others, [30 vols.] (1970-) · T. Carlyle, *Reminiscences*, ed. K. J. Fielding and I. Campbell, new edn (1997) · archival sources, NL Scot. · *Letters and memorials of Jane Welsh Carlyle*, ed. T. Carlyle and J. A. Froude, 3 vols. (1883) · A. Carlyle, ed., *New letters and memorials of Jane Welsh Carlyle*, 2 vols. (1903) · L. Hanson and E. Hanson, *Necessary evil: the life of Jane Welsh Carlyle* [1952] · *Jane Welsh Carlyle: a new selection of her letters*, ed. T. Bliss (1949) · *I too am here, selections from the letters of Jane Welsh Carlyle*, ed. A. McQueen Simpson and M. McQueen Simpson (1977) · V. Surtees, *Jane Welsh Carlyle* (1986) · N. Clarke, *Ambitious heights: writing, friendship, love* (1990) · R. Ashton, *Thomas and Jane Carlyle: portrait of a marriage* (2002) · *Jane Carlyle, newly selected letters*, ed. K. J. Fielding and D. Sorenson (2003)

Archives Bodl. Oxf., papers · Carlyle's House, Kensington and Chelsea, London, corresp. and papers · Duke U., Perkins L., corresp. and papers · Harvard U., corresp. · Hornel Library, Broughton House, Kirkcudbright, letters · NL Scot., corresp. and papers · U. Edin. L., corresp. | Chelsea Library, London, letters to Charlotte Southam · L. Cong., Charlotte Cushman papers · NL Scot., letters to Mrs Stirling · priv. coll., papers · U. Cal., Santa Cruz, Strouse collection, corresp. and papers · V&A NAL, Forster Collection

Likenesses K. Macleay, miniature, watercolour on ivory, 1826, Scot. NPG · S. Laurence, crayon, 1838, Carlyle's House, Kensington and Chelsea, London · S. Gambardella, oils, 1843, priv. coll. · K. Hartmann, watercolour, 1849, priv. coll. · S. Laurence, oils, 1849, priv. coll. • S. Laurence, miniature, oils, 1852, NPG • A. Sterling, photograph album, NPG • photographs, NPG • photographs, Col. U.

Carlyle, John, first Lord Carlyle (d. 1501), administrator, came from a family of Annandale gentry. His father, William, acquired the Dumfriesshire barony of Torthorwald through marriage, but John was the first of his line to gain real prominence. First recorded in 1433, he received formal ownership of Torthorwald in 1449 (although tenancy did not follow until his father's death in 1463), was knighted in 1449 or 1450, and enjoyed royal favour from the late 1450s. His early career was probably the result of Douglas patronage, but following their collapse in 1452–5 he emerged as an important royal agent in the south-west. He was keeper of Threave Castle in 1458, captain of Lochmaben Castle in 1460–64, and justiciar in Annandale for the duke of Albany in 1465, while he also maintained his position at court, becoming master of the queen's stable in 1460–61.

Carlyle was one of James III's closest supporters in the 1470s. He was created Lord Carlyle between October 1473 and July 1474, probably close to 3 December 1473, when Torthorwald was erected into a free burgh of barony. On 31 October 1477 the king granted him Drumcoll, Dumfriesshire, in one of his few major grants of patronage in that decade. This was in reward for Carlyle's services, particularly in France in 1473–4 at the time of the Anglo-Scottish peace. In the period 1476–81 he was very active in central and local crown administration as a regular witness to charters under the great seal, an auditor of exchequer, a member of the lords of council, a parliamentarian, and a custumar of Kirkcudbright and Wigtown. Importantly, he was involved in receiving Edward IV's dowry payments to James III for the proposed marriage and alliance negotiated in 1474, which suggests sympathy for this controversial policy. Following the crisis of 1482, however, he was less prominent in the 1480s, though he returned to court in 1487 and was probably in James III's army at Sauchieburn in 1488. His loyalty to the defeated monarch may explain his apparent absence from public affairs in the next reign. Carlyle died between 12 January and 3 March 1501, probably at Torthorwald. He was married three times: first to Elizabeth Kirkpatrick (marriage contract of 1433); second to Janet, of unknown family, from before 1476 to c.1484; and third to Margaret Douglas (d. after 22 Dec 1509), widow of Herbert Maxwell, from before February 1493. He had six children and was succeeded by his grandson, William.   ROLAND J. TANNER

Sources N. Macdougall, *James III: a political study* (1982) • *The manuscripts of his grace the duke of Buccleuch and Queensberry ... preserved at Drumlanrig Castle*, 2 vols., HMC, 44 (1897–1903), vol. 1 • G. Burnett and others, eds., *The exchequer rolls of Scotland*, 6–10 (1883–7) • J. M. Thomson and others, eds., *Registrum magni sigilli regum Scotorum / The register of the great seal of Scotland*, 11 vols. (1882–1914), vol. 2 • *CDS*, vol. 4 • *APS*, 1424–1567 • [T. Thomson], ed., *The acts of the lords of council in civil causes, 1478–1495*, 1, RC, 41 (1839) • *Scots peerage*, vol. 6
Wealth at death eight oxen and £100 left to Torthorwald church; left £40 for his burial; also owned six silver cups: *The manuscripts of*

his grace the duke of Buccleuch and Queensberry ... preserved at Drumlanrig Castle, 2 vols., HMC, 44 (1897–1903)

Carlyle, John Aitken [Jack] (1801–1879), physician and writer, was born on 7 July 1801 at Ecclefechan, Annandale, Dumfriesshire, the third son among the nine children of James Carlyle (1757–1832), a stonemason, and his second wife, Margaret Aitken (1771–1853). He was known in the family as Jack, or as Lord Moon because of the shape of his face. From his parents he was said by his elder brother Thomas *Carlyle (1795–1881) to have inherited 'a good head and an honest heart', though the sibling relationship was often tested over the years (Froude, 216).

At an early age Jack succeeded Thomas as a teacher at Annan Academy. While a tutor to the two sons of Isabella and Charles Buller, Thomas devoted a portion of his salary to enable John to study medicine at the University of Edinburgh. He graduated MD in 1826. Thomas also sent John to complete his medical education in Germany, and supported him financially for several years in London, where he tried to obtain a practice as a physician. Failing in this, John attempted to make a living by writing, contributing to *Fraser's Magazine* and other periodicals, while also helping his brother translate Legendre's work on geometry. Thomas, however, tried to dissuade John from the literary life, arguing that he had a calling as a physician and warning him against 'wavering and waiting' with regard to seeking employment (Froude, 118).

John Carlyle attended William Hazlitt in his final illness in September 1830, and in 1831—with only 7 s. to his name and on the recommendation of his brother's friend Francis Jeffrey—he was appointed travelling physician to the countess of Clare. His salary of 300 guineas a year plus his expenses allowed him to give money to his mother and to pay off his debt to Thomas. Occasionally visiting England and Scotland, he spent nearly seven years in Italy with Lady Clare. In the intervals of his attendance he practised for some time on his own account as a physician in Rome, where, during an outbreak of cholera, he gave his medical services gratuitously to the poor. He wrote to his brother Alexander (Alick), however, that he fell into a 'state of stagnation', lulled into a monotonous routine among the wealthy English travellers who associated with Lady Clare (*Letters*, 452). After his return to England in 1837 he became in 1838 travelling physician to the duke of Buccleuch, with whom he revisited the continent. Thomas's wife, Jane Carlyle, had earlier written to her cousin Helen Walsh that she did not believe that John would be successful among the London set, for whom 'vapours and something that goes by the name of a "checked perspiration"' were matters for urgent medical attention (Ashton, 176). By 1843 he had resigned this position and, with moderate savings, abandoned the practice of medicine almost entirely, declining an invitation from Lady Holland to become her personal physician in attendance. He lived for several years in lodgings near the Chelsea home of Thomas and Jane Carlyle. Jane was blunt about what she saw as John's idleness, selfishness, and refusals of work. That he also tended to be dismissive of her ailments and on a number of occasions told her that they 'might be cured if she would only find something to do' (ibid., 176) did nothing to sweeten their relationship. While her letters to him are often full of warmth, 'she could scarcely bear his company for more than a few hours' (ibid., 350).

In August 1845 John wrote to Thomas that he was again looking for medical employment, but entreated his elder brother not to assert 'any of the old scorn; for I sincerely want some wholesome work' (Ashton, 250). The first instalment of what he intended to be a great English prose translation of the whole of Dante's *Divina commedia* appeared in 1849 as *Dante's divine comedy, the 'Inferno', with the text of the original collated from the best editions, and explanatory notes*. The preface contains an estimate of Dante as a man and a poet, and the influence of Thomas Carlyle is very conspicuous. Two appendices were regarded as useful contributions to the critical biography of the *Divina commedia*, its commentators, and translators.

On 2 November 1852 Carlyle married Phoebe Elizabeth Hough Watts, *née* Fowler (1814?–1854), a rich widow with four sons, and the daughter of John Fowler of Horton Hall in north Staffordshire. On 26 August 1854 Phoebe gave birth prematurely to a dead child, just days after she and John had been in a minor railway accident. Phoebe herself died only a few hours after her baby. The court of chancery appointed John guardian of her sons, and he was by all accounts devoted to the boys. He spent much of his time in his later years looking after them and studying Icelandic language and literature. In 1861 he edited the posthumous *History of Scottish Poetry* of his friend Dr Irving, adding notes and appending a brief glossary of the Scots words that appeared in the volume. A second, revised, edition of Carlyle's Dante appeared in 1867, with a prefatory notice, in which Carlyle spoke of issuing two volumes more, containing translations of the *Purgatorio* and the *Paradiso*. But the hope was not fulfilled, though he had completed a considerable portion of the task. A reprint of the second edition was issued in 1882.

On the death of Jane Carlyle in 1866 John offered to live with his bereaved brother, but Thomas declined the offer. While at times exasperated by John's tendency to idleness, procrastination, and 'careless, helter-skelter ways' (*DNB*), Thomas Carlyle was enormously fond of his 'truly loving Brother' who 'from me has forgiven innumerable provocations, and superficial irritations from an old date!' (*Letters*, 718). He affectionately referred to Jack's 'jolly presence' and asserted that 'He is certainly a prime honest "Lord Moon", with all his faults' (Froude, 216).

In 1878 John Carlyle endowed £1600 to found two medical bursaries in his name at the University of Edinburgh. In his will Thomas Carlyle left his brother a life interest in the lease of the house at Chelsea, with his books and the fragments of his history of James I. He made him, too, his chief executor, and asked him to superintend the execution of the instructions in his will: 'I wish him to be regarded as my second self, my surviving self' (*DNB*). John Carlyle, however, did not survive his brother. He died of

an abdominal tumour at the home of his sister Jean, The Hill, Dumfries, on 15 September 1879 and was buried in Ecclefechan cemetery.

FRANCIS ESPINASSE, *rev.* JANE POTTER

Sources R. Ashton, *Thomas and Jane Carlyle: portrait of a marriage* (2002) · *Letters of Thomas Carlyle to his brother Alexander*, ed. E. W. Marrs (1968) · J. A. Froude, *Carlyle's early life* (1890) · www.hawk37. demon.co.uk/cemeteries/ecclefechan_cem.html, 19 Aug 2002 · d. cert.
Archives NL Scot., corresp. · NL Scot., Italian journal and family corresp. · NL Scot., journal | Bodl. Oxf., letters to Gudbrandr Vigfusson · NL Scot., letters to J. S. Blackie · U. Edin. L., letters to Charles Butler
Likenesses woodcut, NPG
Wealth at death no value given: confirmation, 25 Oct 1879, CGPLA Eng. & Wales

Carlyle, Joseph Dacre (1758–1804), Arabic scholar, was born on 4 June 1758 at Carlisle, where his father practised as a physician. He was educated at Mr Wilson's school at Kirkby Lonsdale and at the Carlisle grammar school. On 13 January 1775 he entered Christ's College, Cambridge, from where he moved to Queens' College in February 1778, proceeding BA in 1779. He was elected a fellow of Queens', and proceeded MA in 1783, and BD in 1793. During his residence at Cambridge he profited from the instructions of a native of Baghdad, who passed in Britain under the name David Zamio. As a result, Carlyle became so proficient in oriental languages that he was appointed professor of Arabic on the resignation of Dr Craven in 1795. In 1793 he had succeeded William Paley as chancellor of Carlisle. In 1792 he published *Rerum Aegyptiacarum annales*, translated from the Arabic of Yusuf ibn Taghri Birdi. Four years later there appeared his well-respected translation, *Specimens of Arabian Poetry* (which included biographical sketches of selected authors).

In 1799 Carlyle was appointed chaplain to Lord Elgin's mission to Constantinople, with the special duties of learned referee; and he made a tour through Asia Minor, Palestine, Greece, and Italy, collecting Greek and Syriac manuscripts for a proposed new version of the New Testament, which unfortunately he did not live to accomplish. After returning to England in September 1801 he was presented to the living of Newcastle upon Tyne; but his health had been seriously impaired by the fatigues of travel. He died after an illness on 12 April 1804. His *Poems Suggested Chiefly by Scenes in Asia Minor, Syria, and Greece*, together with some translations from the Arabic, were published posthumously in 1805, as well as extracts from his journal and a preface by his sister. Carlyle had also almost completed an account of his tour through the Troad, which was never published, and had advanced so far in his Arabic Bible, revised from Walton's text, that it was issued in 1811 at Newcastle, edited by Henry Ford, professor of Arabic at Oxford.

STANLEY LANE-POOLE, *rev.* PHILIP CARTER

Sources GM, 1st ser., 74 (1804), 390 · J. D. Carlyle, *Specimens of Arabian poetry* (1796), preface
Archives BL, diary of visit to Mount Athos and catalogue of MSS there, Add. MSS 27604, 27234 · LPL, manuscript collection · LPL, papers relating to New Testament | BL, corresp. with Shute

Barrington, Dep 9389 · Suffolk RO, Ipswich, letters to Shute Barrington relating to MSS in Greek monasteries

Carlyle, Sir Robert Warrand (1859–1934), administrator in India and writer on medieval subjects, was born at Brechin on 11 July 1859, the elder son of James Edward Carlyle (1821–1893), minister of the Free church at Brechin, and his wife, Jessie Margaret, daughter of James Milne, of Huntly, Aberdeenshire. His father was subsequently Free Church of Scotland chaplain in Bombay, Berlin, and Pietermaritzburg. The original spelling of the family name, Carlile, had been altered by Robert's grandfather, a kinsman of Thomas Carlyle.

Robert was educated privately and at Glasgow University. In 1878 he passed the open competition for the Indian Civil Service, and in December 1880, having spent his two years' probation at Balliol College, Oxford, was posted to Midnapore, Bengal, as assistant magistrate. His early career included several stints as an under-secretary to the governments of both Bengal and India. Appointed magistrate of Tippera in August 1894, in March 1896 he was transferred to Darbhanga, Bihar, just as the famine of 1896–7 was beginning to bite. The commissioner of Patna, J. A. Bourdillon, praised without reservation his 'heart and soul' relief effort, and in 1898 he was created CIE for his famine work.

In 1902 Carlyle was appointed inspector-general of the Bengal police. In the following year, on 29 September, he married Isabel Jane, daughter of James Barton, of Farndreg, Dundalk, co. Louth. In 1904 he became chief secretary to the government of Bengal. In 1907 he was further promoted to revenue and agriculture secretary to the government of India and in 1910 became head of that department on appointment to the executive council. An advocate of lighter revenue demands, he presided over increased investment in agriculture and an expansion of the fledgeling co-operative rural credit movement. As his council portfolio also included public works, from 1911 he bore responsibility for the planning and initial construction of the new imperial capital at Delhi. He was renowned in the government for his downright, uncompromising expression of opinion, but secretariat work was not particularly congenial to him, nor did he have much liking for the debates in the legislative council. He was appointed CSI in 1910 and KCSI in 1911.

In 1915 Carlyle retired to Essex and thereafter collaborated with his younger brother Alexander James *Carlyle on volumes 3, 4, and 5 of *A History of Mediaeval Political Theory in the West* (6 vols., 1903–36). An earlier publication, 'The political theories of St. Thomas Aquinas' (*Scottish Review*, January 1896), had been erroneously attributed to Alexander.

From 1916 to 1918 Carlyle served on the central tribune which determined adjustments between war service and industrial activities, and in 1919 he became a trustee of the king's fund. In 1916 Lady Carlyle was awarded the kaisar-i-Hind gold medal for her work in organizing comfort packages for the troops in Mesopotamia. In retirement both took a great interest in the work of Carlyle's cousin Prebendary Wilson Carlile, founder of the Church Army.

Carlyle died at via Alfieri 10, Florence, on 23 May 1934. He was survived by his wife. There were no children of the marriage.   KATHERINE PRIOR

Sources *The Times* · *DNB* · E. Hilliard, ed., *The Balliol College register, 1832–1914* (privately printed, Oxford, 1914) · I. Elliott, ed., *The Balliol College register, 1833–1933*, 2nd edn (privately printed, Oxford, 1934) · *History of services of gazetted and other officers serving under the government of Bengal* (1905) · BL OIOC, Elgin MSS
Archives CUL, corresp. with Lord Hardinge, etc.
Likenesses W. Stoneman, photograph, 1918, NPG
Wealth at death £1596 19s. 2d.: resworn probate, 9 Aug 1934, CGPLA Eng. & Wales

Carlyle, Thomas (1795–1881), author, biographer, and historian, was born on 4 December 1795 in the Arched House, Ecclefechan, Annandale, Dumfriesshire. He was the eldest son of James Carlyle (1757–1832), a hard-working stonemason whose father, Thomas (1722–1806), the husband of Mary Gillespie (1727–1797), had been a carpenter and tenant farmer; beyond that, the Carlyle family's genealogy cannot be accurately determined. James Carlyle married his second wife, Margaret Aitken (1771–1853), the child of a bankrupt Dumfriesshire farmer, in 1794; she gave birth to eight children after Thomas: Alexander (1797–1876), Janet (1799–1801), John Aitken *Carlyle (1801–1879), Margaret (1803–1830), James (1805–1890), Mary (1808–1888), Jane (1810–1888), and a second Janet (1813–1897).

Early years and education, 1795–1814 Thomas's father pushed his children into literacy and propelled two sons into professional careers. While a young man, James Carlyle, with his brothers, was notorious for brawls; as an adult he attempted to live as if salvation could be approached only within the rules and spirit of the Burgher Secession church. Margaret Aitken's voice also resonated with the tones of the Old Testament prophets in terms appropriate to the daily needs of rural Calvinism. Combining within herself the theology of her church and the strong love of a devoted mother, she was 'the truest Christian Believer' her son had 'ever met with'. Born in the Arched House, Ecclefechan, a building designed and constructed by his father and uncle, Thomas soon discovered that his parents' world was circular, enclosing home, fields, family, meeting-house: the rural arches of Christian Annandale, the interwoven community of Presbyterian Scotland. As a boy he learned reading from his mother, arithmetic from his father; he attended a private school in Ecclefechan and then, at the age of six, the nearby Hoddam parish school. He immediately became the pride of the schoolmaster, the young person on whom approving adults and jealous schoolmates place the burden of differentness. For his parents that quality had its rightful place in the circle of tradition. If their son was to be a man of learning, he would be a minister of the Lord; within their society the alternative was either madness or apostasy. For the young boy there was worry, confusion, and resentment: growing up in the shadow of the local meeting-house he was taught to repress physical instincts, which came from the devil not from God. And he understood the essential message of his parents' example: 'A man's religion consists not of the many

Thomas Carlyle (1795–1881), by George Frederic Watts, 1868

things he is in doubt of and tries to believe, but of the few he is assured of, and has no need of effort for believing' (*Latter-Day Pamphlets*, in *The Works of Thomas Carlyle*, Centenary Edition, 1896–9, 313).

His mother argued against sending Carlyle to Annan Academy. His father simply said that his son would go, and on '26 May 1806, a bright sunny morning' James Carlyle walked with his son the 6 miles to Annan. His mother had extracted a reaffirmation of her son's promise that he would never fight, but she did not forbid him to fight back with his tongue. He soon became expert at defending himself verbally, developing his talent for sarcastic retorts whose aggressive defensiveness became his most effective way of dealing with a hostile world. And, finally, when he fought back physically, the beatings decreased. Annan Academy specialized in training large classes, at low cost, for university entrance at the age of fourteen, the basic subjects being French, Latin, arithmetic, algebra, and geography. Mathematics soon became Thomas's strongest academic subject; he also found modern languages attractive, and in the next decades taught himself Spanish, Italian, and German. Turning increasingly to books, he discovered an extensive lending library of novels and romances. He soon read through Defoe, Fielding, Smollett, Sterne, Congreve, and the *Arabian Nights*. In 1808, his third year at the academy, he started to reap the rewards of academic effort. Soon the assumption that had been implicit in James Carlyle's decision to send Thomas to Annan became explicit: he was to continue his education at the University of Edinburgh. In November 1809 his parents accompanied their son to the edge of town; his

mother gave him a Bible. It took the traveller three days to make the 80 mile journey to Edinburgh. By the beginning of the second day he had travelled further from Annandale than his father was ever to do in his life.

Carlyle was as unhappy and withdrawn in his first year at Edinburgh as he had been at Annan. His friends were the books he borrowed; his readiest defence was sarcasm and a retreat to reading. Nervous about sex, he later wrote that his emotional training 'forbade him to participate' in the 'amusements, too often riotous and libertine' of his generally coarse colleagues (T. Carlyle, *Last Words*, 1892 edn, 21–2). He now stood a little under 6 feet; a thin adolescent with light blue eyes, clearing complexion, small, recessive top lip, and thrusting jaw. In his second year he felt less emotionally vulnerable. Active distaste kept him awake in Professor Ritchie's class in logic: the worldly minister taught a combination of mechanistic philosophy and elementary logic inconsistent with the religious beliefs of Carlyle's parents. His mathematics class with Professor John Leslie was a different matter: an absentminded eccentric who lectured brilliantly and taught mathematics as part of a holistic system of natural forces, Leslie devoted particular attention to his bright students. By the next session, when he enrolled in his newly found mentor's advanced mathematics course, Carlyle had glimpsed the possibility that in mathematics he might find a vocation that would help him support himself during his preparation for the ministry or as a substitute for it. In Leslie's mathematics, which appealed to Carlyle's problem-solving enthusiasm, one reasoned by comparison and analogy rather than by mechanical logic.

During 1812–13, his last year in the faculty of arts, Carlyle devoted his academic time to mathematics and his personal time to intensive reading. Though his lodgings were uncomfortable and the city unwholesome, he found himself growing used to the rhythmic movement between urban tensions and rural withdrawal. Since he did not accompany his family to the meeting-house, his parents became aware that their eldest son no longer shared their conception of religious duties. They assumed, however, that he was still preparing to attend divinity school, preferably the Burgher Divinity Hall in Selkirk. Carlyle preferred Edinburgh, where he had friends, associations, and challenges; at Selkirk he would be a lonely novice restricted by a parochial library. It made more sense, he thought, to go to the Divinity Hall of the Church of Scotland in Edinburgh, where his personal life would be more rewarding and where he would have access to alternative academic and professional training. In November 1813, without completing the arts course, he enrolled in three classes in the Divinity Hall: making haste slowly, he chose the more drawn-out of two curricular alternatives, six years of unsupervised study after his residence with six annual appearances to present trial sermons. In 1813, and for several years thereafter, he read extensively in science, history, and literature.

Teaching in Annan and Kirkcaldy, 1814–1818 Carlyle's only alternative to earning his living as a minister was employment as a schoolmaster. Geometry still fascinated him; in the winter of 1813–14 he discovered that he could demonstrate his mathematical and literary skill by responding to articles on mathematics that appeared in newspapers such as the *Dumfries Courier*, in whose columns he engaged in a spirited mathematical controversy. The main attraction was not the objective discussion of geometrical problems but the satiric jousting of intellectual rivals: finally the editor expressed regret for having to suppress Carlyle's 'severe retaliation' (*Collected Letters*, 1.8–9). When he left Edinburgh for Dumfries in June 1814 he had neither an arts degree nor a theological vocation. At Dumfries, with a strong recommendation from Professor Leslie, he applied for the position of mathematics master at Annan Academy. The examiner found him superior to the only other candidate and offered him the job at £70 per annum. From the start Carlyle anticipated that he would dislike teaching. Moreover, he had to face the irony that Annan Academy was where he had been unhappy for most of his schooldays. One evening in late 1815 in Edinburgh he was introduced to a man he remembered having seen before, a native of Annan named Edward Irving, to whom the rest of the company seemed to defer. Intimately familiar with Annan, the dark-haired, handsome inquisitor, with a disquieting, uncontrollable squint, plied his new acquaintance with questions about recent events there. Insulted, Carlyle exploded: 'I have had no interest to inform myself about the births in Annan; and care not if the process of birth and generation there should cease and determine altogether!' (Carlyle, *Reminiscences*, 183–4). Irving's companion remarked, provoking general laughter, that such a development would soon put Carlyle out of business.

As he laboured in Annan at his teaching duties through the winter and spring of 1815–16 Carlyle felt that he was stuck in place, struggling with difficulties of both vocation and spirit. In May he was recommended for a teaching position at Kirkcaldy, which had the advantage of being only an hour's ferry ride from Edinburgh. Irving had recently moved there, but Carlyle was assured that 'Mr. Irving has the Academy, not the parish school … in a town and neighbourhood so populous there is field enough for you both' (Kirkcaldy town minutes, 1816). He was told that there would be no duties except those of teaching Latin, French, arithmetic, book-keeping, geometry, navigation, geography, and mensuration, with some Greek occasionally. Agreeing to take the position, Carlyle returned to Annandale to spend the summer of 1816 with his family. Unfortunately, his mother was seriously ill from a 'fever' which seemed to threaten 'the extinction of her reason' (John Martin to Carlyle, 14 June 1816). By late summer Margaret Carlyle had sufficiently recovered from the worst of her breakdowns for Thomas to reveal to his parents that he had not enrolled and would never enrol at Divinity Hall.

Aimless in Edinburgh, 1818–1821 In November 1818, after a tedious, unhappy year at Kirkcaldy, Carlyle resigned and returned to Edinburgh. Soon he was preoccupied with his health: sometimes he could not digest food, while at other times he was constipated. That his health should become a problem seemed both unwarrantedly punitive and at the same time consistent with his pervasive difficulties. He felt better during the summer of 1819. Exercise, parental concern, and rural air were partial antidotes. In the autumn in Edinburgh he began to wonder if it would be possible for him to maintain a sound mind, a sound body, or even life itself. His vocationally aimless days of study and solitude depressed him. He regularly took medicines for his stomach; he assured his family that there was nothing wrong organically, that the 'digestive apparatus' was simply unpredictable, sometimes quite satisfactory, other times refusing 'to perform its functions'. He tentatively began to study German, making slow progress, working laboriously with a dictionary. Suddenly he discovered that he could read Goethe and J. G. Fichte, whose idealism appealed to him partly because of its apparent similarity to the idealism of his mother's beliefs. Goethe, of course, could hardly pass serious muster as a Christian, his European reputation being that of a humanist whose spiritual commitments flowed out of creative pilgrimage rather than authoritative theology. The vague Christianity that seemed to 'live again' in Goethe was the Christianity of heightened spiritual sensitivity to the patterns of human experience. Immediately identifying with Goethe the man rather than the philosopher, Carlyle warned Irving that if they were together he would talk of *Faustus* for hours not because of its aesthetic attractions or its religious doctrine but because Faust's pilgrimage was the very one that he himself had been experiencing. Disappointed in almost every aspect of his life, Carlyle felt as if Goethe were reading his soul.

Courting Jane Welsh, 1821–1824 In late May 1821 Irving proposed that Carlyle accompany him to Haddington to spend a few days with his friends the recently widowed Grace Welsh (1782–1842) and her nineteen-year-old daughter Jane (1801–1866) [*see* Carlyle, Jane Baillie Welsh]. He was welcomed for his friend's sake and for the enlivenment of a residence that both women found comfortable but boring. John Welsh, a competent, widely respected physician, had died of typhus less than two years before, leaving his wife to come to terms with loneliness and straitened circumstances. A sentimental, capricious woman, Grace Welsh was unable to organize her complex situation now that her dominant husband was dead. A 'tall aquiline figure, of elegant carriage and air' (Carlyle, *Reminiscences*, 98–9), she seemed the embodiment of a middle-class hauteur that Carlyle had never encountered before. The cherished only child of an assertive father, Jane Welsh could not hide her feeling that the parent who had loved her most was gone. His influence had determined that she be schooled; his confidence had elevated her sense of special merit. Since his death she was confronting the likelihood that, despite her talent and education, marriage was the only outlet for her energy. She desired to be learned and famous, but devoted a great deal of time to parties, suitors, and excursions. To her visitor she claimed that she 'was intent on literature as the highest aim in life' (Froude, *Letters and Memorials*, 1.129). Carlyle spoke that evening of his own reading, writing, and literary ambitions. Jane listened intently, impressed by his learning and amused by his Annandale accent and country awkwardness. An excellent mimic and storyteller, she refrained from exercising her natural bent for sarcasm.

Carlyle's imagination worked full force on Jane, and in June he sent her an aggressive, intimate letter. With his constant complaints about health, rustic manners, and lack of a practical vocation, he had little to recommend him except his 'genius' and his desire to serve. Frightened of marriage because, among other reasons, she was frightened of sex, Jane Welsh could not imagine that such a man could become her husband. Although Carlyle realized that she did not consider him a serious suitor, she concealed from him the extent of her pursuit by other suitors and the nature of her relationship with Edward Irving, from whom she expected to receive a proposal of marriage. Soon after assuming the mathematics tutorship at Haddington in 1810, Irving had been employed by Dr Welsh as special tutor to his precocious ten-year-old daughter, who idolized her teacher. After he had left Haddington—and despite an implied commitment to marry the daughter of a Kirkcaldy minister—he had not forgotten her and took every opportunity to visit her at a cousin's house in Edinburgh, while she was at finishing school there.

Corresponding with Carlyle against her mother's wishes, Jane Welsh felt 'as nervous as if I were committing a murder' (*Collected Letters*, 1.142). She concluded the year by inviting him to visit her at Haddington when he had finished a new review essay that he was writing and at least two dozen pages of the original book which he had been proclaiming he would start soon; as an additional proviso she demanded that he learn to write a letter which would not anger her mother. Several weeks later she reminded him of a lesson in life which she was to relearn from him during their marriage, especially during his years of fame: 'Patient suffering ... is the first lesson to be learned by one of the parties in a Romantic Friendship' (ibid., 2.21). Living on his savings and on occasional tutoring, Carlyle was offered and accepted the opportunity to tutor the two sons of Isabella and Charles Buller. Irving had proposed that the boys be enrolled in the University of Edinburgh under Carlyle's guidance. Much as he hated teaching, he could not turn down the prospect of bright students on a well-paid and regular basis (£200 per annum, about twice as much as his father had ever earned in one year). Despite Jane's warning that he would repent of it, Carlyle went to Haddington the first weekend in February 1822. The visit was a painful disaster: both mother and daughter resented the brash appearance of a young man who did not qualify as a suitor and who was too assertive to be welcomed as a friend. But his health, despite the regimen of assorted purgatives, was as good as it had been in years, and in his pursuit of Jane he managed to avoid complete failure, a testimony to his tenaciousness and to her interest in him.

Still, Carlyle felt restless and unhappy; he was angry with himself for being miserable and frightened, and his mood intensified. Going down Leith Walk in Edinburgh on a blazing afternoon in August 1822 he realized that he had been mistaken all along in believing that 'it was with Work alone, and not also with Folly and Sin, in myself and others, that I had been appointed to struggle' (T. Carlyle, *Sartor Resartus*, in *The Works of Thomas Carlyle*, Centenary Edition, 1896–9, 99). The purpose of work was to create a visible structure that would articulate the quality of the inner spiritual life. But it was his own 'inarticulate Self-consciousness ... which only our Works can render articulate and decisively discernible' which needed to be discovered and affirmed (ibid., 132). The search did not depend on logic or reason, and since the struggle was not with external problems but with inner states, could he not choose through some effort of the will to create both himself and at the same time a work expressive of himself? Unable to find emotional security in an act of traditional belief, Carlyle suspected that the world belonged to the devil, to matter and materialism. But, he argued, if man is free, he is free to deny both doubt and logic, on the essential ground of his trust in his own feelings: such a denial confirms that he has the freedom to deny whatever contradicts his spiritual needs, to reject the life-demeaning elements within himself and the external world. Such control over his own self-definition would, Carlyle came to see, enable him to defy whatever obstacles the world raised and to oppose any attempts to define him in terms which contradicted his basic sense of himself. 'And as I so thought', he wrote ten years later in *Sartor Resartus*, his fictionalized account of these experiences, 'there rushed ... a stream of fire over my whole soul; and I shook base Fear away from me forever. I was strong, of unknown strength; a spirit, almost a god.' What religious belief had lost, personal will could provide.

Early literary contacts, 1824–1825 The Bullers, who had decided to return with their sons to London, gave Carlyle three months' leave before he was to join them there in spring 1824. In the spring of 1823 Carlyle's German studies had taken on a new dimension. Asked to write a short biographical sketch of Schiller for the *London Magazine*, he had successfully proposed to an Edinburgh publisher that he also undertake a translation of Goethe's *Wilhelm Meister*. It was published in 1824, and before leaving Edinburgh, Carlyle arranged to have copies sent to family and friends. On a visit to Haddington, he counselled Jane Welsh to 'be true to me and to yourself'. As he waited in early June 1824 for his boat to sail from Scotland on the five-day voyage to London, he wrote to her impetuously, for which she called him a 'rash, headstrong Man' who had forgotten to keep in mind that 'the continuance of our correspondence depends upon your appearing as my friend and not my Lover' (*Collected Letters*, 3.79). In London Carlyle's new friends were determined that the young genius should have the advantages of the best literary society. At a series of dinners and visits hosted by the Montagus, Stracheys, Bullers, and Irvings, Carlyle met Henry Crabb Robinson, who had studied German at Weimar, and Charles Lamb, among others. On a June morning he went to Highgate to be introduced to Coleridge, the reigning deity of the Montagu household. He followed along the garden paths as Coleridge talked about 'all conceivable and inconceivable things'. Coleridge's very presence awakened an antagonism that Carlyle struggled to cover with ordinary civility. Coleridge embodied characteristics which Carlyle had been taught to despise and which he fought against within himself, particularly lassitude, dependence, and self-pity. That much of the world worshipped Coleridge proved the dangerous tendency of the fallen individual and the fallen society to create one another in their own image. In his hostile response to Coleridge, Carlyle expressed the emotional patterns instilled in him by his judgemental, pietistic parents. Late in the month, his disappointing visit to the 'Sage of Highgate' still fresh in his mind, he sent an effusive letter and a copy of his translation of *Wilhelm Meister* to the 'Sage of Weimar'; the greater his disappointment in Coleridge, the more he turned to Goethe.

Marriage, life at Craigenputtoch, and *Sartor Resartus*, 1826–1833 By the beginning of 1825 Carlyle's desire to return to Scotland merged with his desire to establish a permanent home with Jane Welsh. His proposal that they keep house at Craigenputtoch, a small farm 20 miles from Dumfries which she had inherited from her father, seemed to her insane: the prospect of keeping house with him anywhere disturbed her. She brooded about whether she loved him in the way that a woman hopes to love the man she marries. Also, she had practical objections: she did not want to decrease her standard of living; and the prospect of such rural isolation seemed impossibly burdensome. At the end of May 1825, accompanied by his brother Alick, his sister Jean, and his mother, Thomas Carlyle went to live at a small farmhouse called Hoddam Hill, where he remained for almost a year. At the end of January 1826 he thought that he and Jane would soon be married. Two crucial matters remained unresolved—where they would live and what living arrangements would be made for Grace Welsh. Jane insisted on turning over to her mother the annual rent of about £200 from Craigenputtoch. Still, the matter of where the couple would reside remained to be settled: Carlyle urged Edinburgh or Haddington. Late in May 1826 Grace Welsh took the decisive step, renting for them a small house on Comely Bank in a north-western suburb of Edinburgh. On 9 October 1826 Thomas Carlyle received 'the last Speech and marrying words of that unfortunate young woman Jane Baillie Welsh' and sent in response his 'last blessing as a Lover … my last letter to Jane Welsh: my first blessing as a Husband, my first kiss to Jane Carlyle is at hand! O my darling! I willst always love thee' (*Collected Letters*, 4.150–51). They were married on the morning of the 17th. Unescorted by family or servants, they arrived that day at Comely Bank to spend the first night of a marriage that was to endure for just a few months short of forty years.

Carlyle awakened on his wedding morning in a 'sullen' mood, 'sick with sleeplessness, quite nervous, billus, splenetic and all the rest of it' (*Collected Letters*, 4.152). Clearly, puritanical inhibitions and romantic idealizations were in the 7 foot-wide bed with two sexual innocents. Fragile evidence suggests that though they were able to express affection with whispers and embraces their sexual relationship did not provide physical satisfaction to either of them, despite their efforts during the first half-dozen or so years of the marriage. In December 1826 Carlyle confided to his private notebook both his bewilderment about his married state and his determination to get on with his work. Before the year was out he thought he had found a vehicle for those urgent voices. He proudly announced to his mother, 'I fairly began—a Book!', at the same time apologizing that it was 'only a novel'. Within six months of their marriage Carlyle again proposed that he and Jane move to Craigenputtoch, mainly because he fantasized that his ill health could be cured only by living in the countryside. They had no special need to reduce their expenses, and to go to Craigenputtoch because he felt lonely in Edinburgh was hardly a rational act. When the decision was tentatively made in the spring of 1827 they were even more secure financially, for he had been commissioned to write an article for the *Edinburgh Review*, which paid well. In January 1827 Bryan Procter, Mrs Montagu's son-in-law, had sent him a sealed letter of introduction to the editor of the *Review*, Francis Jeffrey. Carlyle's brief essay, ostensibly a review of a new life of C. F. Richter, was an impressive début in June 1827, one that Jeffrey and some of the readers of the *Review* recognized as an occasion.

Life at Craigenputtoch, where the couple resided for six years, was no more lonely than rural life in general. From the outset Carlyle intended to relieve the isolation with long excursions to Edinburgh, London, and even Weimar. The visit to Weimar never occurred; of the six years at Craigenputtoch, two winters were spent in more social locations, a nine-month visit to London in 1831–2 and a four-month residence in Edinburgh in the winter and spring of 1833. Still, if space, as Carlyle argued, is 'a mode of our Sense', then Craigenputtoch should be no more than an extension of the moral and imaginative strength of its inhabitants. And if time also is a 'mode of our Sense', a proposition to which he was attracted, then 'this solid world, after all, is but an air-image; our Me is the only reality, "and all is Godlike or God"' (*Two Notebooks of Thomas Carlyle*, ed. C. E. Norton, 1898, 161). He quite aptly identified his feelings with his reading of the quintessential English public myths. We are, 'as it were, a sort of Crusoe's Island, where the whole happiness or sorrow depends on the Islander himself' (*Collected Letters*, 4.427–8). Carlyle soon wrote articles on Voltaire and Novalis for the *Foreign Review* and then on Burns and Tasso, as well as 'Signs of the times', for the *Edinburgh Review* (June 1829). In a strikingly calm, controlled, and precise manner, he argues in 'Signs' for a balance between the dynamical and mechanical in an age in which the mechanical was dominant and in which the spiritual basis of the most important achievements of Western culture had been obscured by substituting external machinery for underlying 'spiritual Truth'. Revolutions that did not lead towards individual inner reformations had failed to do their most important work. In October 1830 he wrote what he had at first intended to be an article; it soon seemed too long unless divided into two sections; as he continued to write 'with impetuosity' on 'the strangest of all things' it appeared as if it would 'swell into a Book'. It was 'a very singular piece' that 'glances from Heaven to Earth & back again in a strange satirical frenzy' (*Collected Letters*, 5.175). By early November he had written to Fraser about publishing 'Teufelsdreck' as two articles. Soon he again changed his mind about the structure and length and decided it should be a full-length book. Snowbound for much of February 1831, he began to revise and lengthen it, extending the biographical section dealing with the fictional Professor Teufelsdreck's life and amplifying the sections on religion and society. He soon changed the title to *Sartor Resartus* ('The Tailor Retailored'), a philosophical play on the notion that clothes either do or do not make the man, on Carlyle devising a new, better garment for contemporary society, and on the relationship between the material and the spiritual.

For some years Carlyle had been recommending Goethe and God to his countrymen; with the completion of *Sartor*, for which he now sought a London publisher, he had reason to hope people would listen to his message. Irving urged him to come to London and 'purify' the literary world. The prospect excited Jane Carlyle, and, with the product of his most sustained period of writing, Carlyle left Craigenputtoch for London in early August 1831. At thirty-six his youthful, energetic, and idiosyncratically handsome figure—with his full shock of light brown hair, and aquiline, clean-shaven face—impressively embodied a personality that for all its inner struggles seemed to his London contemporaries bright with genius. Goethe's disciple was eager to become a master himself, but the London visit was disappointing. He stayed for much of nine months, renewing some old and beginning some new friendships, but he did not find a publisher for *Sartor* and London literary society did not seem congenial. Still, by October 1831 he had two new writing projects in hand, one of them an extraordinarily revealing and influential review essay for the *Edinburgh Review* (December 1831) to which he gave the title 'Characteristics'. Carlyle thought of it as 'a sort of second Signs of the Times'. It epitomized the controversial and 'Germanic' prose style that he had devised for his essays and for *Sartor*, which was to some degree an extension of his lifelong strategy of evading or obscuring crucial problems or questions by a stylistic code. It now seemed the appropriate garment for a radical message which, even in disguised form, was likely to provoke pained and painful responses. Out of his experience with physical illness Carlyle constructed a metaphor for the psychological, social, and spiritual illness that he considered characteristic of the modern world. Deep in man's unconsciousness, he believed, lie the roots of life, concealed in darkness by a beneficent nature that will try us constantly with death and pain. If the mind could be accepted in its true nature—mysterious, spontaneous, unconscious, in vital touch with both light and darkness—then man would be defined by how he accepts and manifests in all his activities the battle between faith and doubt. In modern society the balance has been tipped in favour of doubt, the disease of enquiry being so widespread that it threatens to triumph and destroy the dialectic between light and darkness.

The move to London, 1834   Soon after new year's day 1833 the Carlyles moved from Craigenputtoch to rented rooms in Edinburgh. But further residence in Edinburgh now seemed irrelevant to Carlyle's work, and early in May they moved back to Craigenputtoch. Late in August a completely unexpected visitor, bearing a letter of introduction from John Stuart Mill through Gustav d'Eichthal, 'found the house amid desolate heathery hills'. Ralph Waldo Emerson later described his host as 'tall and gaunt, with a cliff-like brow … clinging to his northern accent with evident relish; full of lively anecdote, and with a streaming humour which floated everything he looked upon' (R. W. Emerson, *English Traits*, in *The Complete Works of Ralph Waldo Emerson*, 1903–4, 2.165). Eager for companionship, Carlyle was at his entertaining best: he impressed Emerson with his wide range of literary and philosophic knowledge and with the broad motifs of his non-sectarian spiritualism. Like Mill, who had met Carlyle in London, Emerson felt that Carlyle's charismatic presence and power for spiritual good overrode their differences of personality and belief.

The Carlyles turned toward London again. The strongest hold on them in Scotland was his family; Craigenputtoch now seemed a desert. In February 1834, as they were about to make up their minds to go, their servant announced that she would leave at the beginning of summer, regardless of their plans. Suddenly their long-deliberated and deeply felt desire to move to London became a settled decision. Thomas went at the beginning of May: as he entered London he hummed the defiant words of a ballad that his mother had frequently sung to him when he was a boy. With Leigh Hunt's assistance, he narrowed their choice of houses, after three weeks of searching, to one in Kensington and one in unfashionable Chelsea, the latter available for only £35 a year. When Jane Carlyle arrived early in June she found that the virtues of the house at 5 (now 24) Cheyne Row, Chelsea, had triumphed.

The French Revolution, 1834–1837   In September 1834 Carlyle began writing a book on the French Revolution that would occupy his energies for three years. The one volume which he had imagined would be finished by spring 1835 expanded into three. More than anything else he wanted to create a work of art rather than of expository logic or historical fact, a visionary and revelatory book that expressed the power of the supernatural within the natural, the patterns of providence within the facts of history. If he could deal effectively with both the drama and the significance of the French Revolution he would make a contribution that the world would have to notice. The patterns of that revolution were, after all, woven into the living fabric of contemporary society. Modern European man had had his clothes burned off by the revolution; he could be seen in his nakedness without the outworn symbols of the past, struggling in his contemporary affairs to find new symbols to express his changing condition.

Within the powers of language, Carlyle felt, were the resources to create the purgative drama that would persuade society that the old could never be revived and that the new was in the process of being born. Since belief systems and the institutions that clothed them were at issue, it was not a matter of thought and logic but of feeling and faith. For Carlyle, history had become the sanction of the seer and the prophet: it enabled him to address the realities of the present and future while discussing the 'realities' of the past. For the Romantic artist, sanction came from personal rebellion; for the new Victorian seer, sanction was grounded in social involvement and historical fact. Until 1834 Carlyle felt he had 'absolutely no permission to speak!' (*Collected Letters*, 7.25). But the sustaining energy that came from his new certainty that the ultimate poetry was within history gave him the courage to believe that by writing a history of the French Revolution he could make a contribution that would authenticate the role he had chosen for himself.

When Carlyle began writing *The French Revolution* he saw developing under his pen a very personal and passionate narrative. His wife commented that what he had done so far seemed more readable than *Sartor*, and this encouraged him. He showed small sections of the first volume in progress to Mill, who had become his closest London friend. Mill had an influence on the book and a stake in it beyond that of anyone but the Carlyles. He had first suggested the topic, and over a number of years he had provided information and encouragement. Through his discussions with Carlyle he had actually helped to shape its imaginative contours. On the night of 6 March 1835 there was a knock on the door at Cheyne Row: Mill appeared, distraught—'The very picture of despair'. He told the Carlyles what seemed almost inconceivable: Carlyle's 'poor manuscript, all except some four tattered leaves, was annihilated!' Having been mistaken by a servant for waste paper, it had been put into the fire, where it made an ironic blaze of its own. Where the fire blazed was—and remains—unclear. If the accident occurred at the home of Harriet Taylor, the wife of John Taylor and Mill's intimate friend and adviser, it was most likely the result of leaving the manuscript beside her bed where it was mistaken for scrap paper and either tossed into a fire or used as kindling. Mill's account was that he had inadvertently allowed it to be used as waste paper in the kitchen at his home in Westminster. Mill's sister claimed to remember a search and her brother's extreme distress; she thought that some pages were found. The unattributable accusation that Mrs Taylor purposely destroyed the manuscript has not been substantiated. That Mill would have been eager to protect Mrs Taylor and take the blame himself, if there had been any need to do so, would have been as clear to Carlyle as to modern readers. When Mill left at midnight the strain of keeping up an appearance of good spirits for his sake had brought both Carlyles to the edge of nervous collapse. It seemed doubtful that the loss could be repaired, that he could go on with the book. In the morning he decided to try again. Except for some charred fragments the book now existed only in Carlyle's memory. Before the end of

March 1836 he had finished the first section of volume 2 and returned to write volume 1 anew from the beginning. After a visit to Scotland he was back at his desk in November, and the work was soon almost complete. His target was new year's day 1837, with publication in March, two years to the month later than he had originally hoped. At ten o'clock in the evening of 12 January he finished, 'ready both to weep and to pray' (*Collected Letters*, 9.116). Instead he went out for a walk in the darkness. Published by James Fraser, the book appeared later that year.

Carlyle and London life With the death of Edward Irving in 1836 an epoch came to an end for Carlyle. The friends of his youth were gone, but his need for company and conversation was greater than he usually admitted. Although he idealized fellowship, he often simply needed to avoid loneliness. London was a place where he could always find people with whom to talk; and in the small world of literary London he was a man of whom others were aware. In the winter of 1834–5 Henry Taylor fulfilled his promise to introduce him to Southey and Wordsworth; in March and April 1835 the now aged Francis Jeffrey visited frequently. But it was to Mill that Carlyle owed his introduction to the man who became his most cherished friend of the next decade: he met John Sterling, a young clergyman and writer, much influenced by Coleridge, and the son of the editor of *The Times*, at Mill's India House office in February 1835. Soon the Carlyles saw 'a good deal' of Sterling and some of Sterling's friends, among them Frederick Denison Maurice; though Carlyle bewailed that 'Coleridge is the Father of all these', he was delighted to have their acquaintance (*The Correspondence of Emerson and Carlyle*, 1964, 176). Another treasure came to Carlyle directly through Mill: Godefroy Cavaignac, a young Frenchman 'intense in everything', a volatile republican whose opposition to Louis Philippe had brought him into exile in England (*Collected Letters*, 8.337). Late in November 1836 Harriet Martineau made the first of her many visits to Cheyne Row.

Having imagined at various times in his life that his health was shattered, Carlyle realized with moderate surprise that he had few reasons to complain about it between 1834 and 1841. Still, he kept a sensitive emotional thermometer always in his mouth. Perhaps the very recognition that much of his past illness had emotional causes helped him to find the strength to incorporate into his conscious life the conviction that the unconscious was the dominating force in determining health. As his own health improved, Jane's declined. As Carlyle lost his conviction that he was ill, Jane apparently caught the idea. She too, at frank moments, ascribed her frequent sickness to 'a bad nervous system, keeping me in a state of greater or less physical suffering' (Froude, *Letters and Memorials*, 1.96). Except for the most serious bouts of influenza, and in later years a mental as well as physical collapse, her health was never so bad that she could not function and never so good that she could function without tiredness and pain. Hardly a winter passed without a siege of flu and then a number of serious relapses. Sickness and insomnia exhausted her, and, like her mother, she had frequent migraine headaches and heavy menstrual bleeding. Aware of his wife's abilities, especially as a letter writer, Carlyle was ambivalently conscious of what they both had lost by Jane's illnesses and her lack of vocation. 'It is a pity, and perhaps not a pity, that so lively a pen did not turn itself to writing of Books … My coagitor too might become a distinguished female' (*Collected Letters*, 9.259).

Carlyle as lecturer, 1836–1840 Carlyle had long flirted with the idea of gaining bread and influence by lecturing. When in December 1836 friends suggested that a lecture series be arranged for him in London, he responded positively. By March 1837 it had been settled that, starting in May, he would speak between three and four in the afternoon on two days each week at a rented hall until his six lectures were completed. Since he had little time to prepare, it struck him that he could make effective use of his unpublished history of German literature. He had spent years studying and writing about the subject. He had made some effort to dissociate himself from an exclusive identification with German literature, and the success of that effort, which he expected to be crowned by the publication of *The French Revolution*, encouraged him to feel that he could now lecture on German literature without increasing his public connection with a foreign culture. He had already praised the high virtues of Teutonic culture and personality to the British public; the lectures provided an opportunity to elaborate on his insistence that the glories of British culture were basically Teutonic, not Celtic. Carlyle would remind his audience that the strength and energy of Britain derived from this tradition. The lectures were moderately successful. Curiosity-seekers, cultural enthusiasts, and the well-to-do who either found it *de rigueur* to attend such occasions or had been alerted to the peculiarities of the speaker were apparently entertained by his mannerisms. Scattered in the audience were friends and disciples, some of them young men who found the message as exciting as the presentation was testing. If he seemed nervous, eccentric, somewhat foreign, even extravagant, he was still clearly on their side and one of them: it was Britain he was praising. Both *The Times* and *The Spectator* reported favourably. Although he preferred not to suffer the torment of lecturing again, it was his only secure source of money, and the new literary star still had minor financial problems. *Sartor* was at last published in England in 1838, and an American edition of *Critical and Miscellaneous Essays* and American and English editions of *The French Revolution* were out by the end of the year. Still, the only money he received was from Emerson, who acted as his literary agent in America. Much as he disliked lecturing, the reward and the need were large enough to impel him to do so again. At the end of April 1838 he gave the first of twelve lectures on European literature; he lectured again in the spring of 1839 and the spring of 1840.

Hero-worship, 1841 In the autumn of 1839 Carlyle worked on an 'Article on the working people' (published as *Chartism* in 1841) that he had been long contemplating. Two other projects absorbed his energy: organizing a committee to create the London Library and preparing for the delivery in the spring of 1840 of what he vowed would be his last lecture series. Working through the winter and spring, he had sensed that 'Heroes and the heroic' would synthesize ideas and feelings he had been developing for a long time. Having in mind perhaps the writing of a full-scale biography of Oliver Cromwell, he thought that the section of the lectures devoted to Cromwell might provide an occasion to articulate the central ideas of a new book, *On Heroes, Hero-Worship, and the Heroic in History* (1841). Drawing his heroic figures from disparate cultures, he would have the opportunity to delineate the underlying forces of personality and nature whose basis was the unconscious and the mysterious. Always fascinated by the relationship between spiritual and secular power, Carlyle believed that men such as Napoleon and Cromwell had succeeded as leaders to the extent that they had incorporated in their conscious and unconscious acts the central spiritual truths. Might did not make right in any simple sense; political and military power might be used for good or for evil. To the extent that such leaders had an element of God within them, their power would be in the service of right. But whatever had been built on wickedness was, in Carlyle's eyes, neither lasting nor right. If there was a providential God, then why doubt that in the long run all visible and invisible things would finally manifest the goodness and justice of that divine power? Stripped of sectarian and theological matters, the premise of Carlyle's religion (which some of his contemporaries would not call religion at all) was that there is an element of divinity in each human being. In some the conflict between the divine and the anti-divine force plays itself out in personal anguish and public disaster; in others the divine force triumphs and shows itself in great works. For the vast majority of mankind, without the energy and the character of greatness, the supreme victory is its recognition of the divinity within such God-inspired human beings as Jesus, Muhammad, Shakespeare, and Cromwell.

Carlyle in the 1840s Having broken the closed circle of his parents' world, Carlyle felt with new force the challenge of his own precarious position and the broad threat to traditional European culture. In the revolutionary decade of the 1840s the Victorian Carlyle emerged, an explosive paradox: the visionary radical, tortured by personal and public misery, and the visionary conservative, furious at what seemed solutions which could only make matters worse. No matter how hard he 'studied to remain silent' he often found that an inner urgency forced him to speak out in ever more controversial public statements, culminating in 1850 in *Latter-Day Pamphlets*, a shriek of satiric and Swiftian despair. Carlyle feared that at some level 'progress' was a bargain with the devil, and he vaguely sensed that part of his anxiety stemmed from his suspicion that, in rejecting his parents' religion and embracing a literary career, he had himself entered into a Faustian agreement. But power could be used for good as well as for evil ends, and his pen had the potential to influence others for good, perhaps even directly. Although he feared both the misuse of his power and the dangers inherent in political commitment, he even flirted several times in the next decade with direct involvement in government, hoping that he would be offered a government position supervising educational reforms. Underlying his ambivalence was his pervasive fear that, whatever they did, whether speaking from the sidelines or actively engaged, he and his contemporaries would be the victims of power. None the less he began the decade with at least some hope that they might yet be able to beat the devil.

To Carlyle one of the immediate answers to poverty and overpopulation was emigration. But the radical party opposed emigration, for reasons that seemed to him narrow and ideological. For over six years he was to watch the badly led workers of the Chartist movement search for effective political leadership. Their energy, however, proved sufficient only to help persuade the government to repeal the corn laws, not to give positive shape to new policies for a new age. Carlyle believed that without effective leadership mass movements could do nothing more than clear away the old. For 'a man willing to work, and unable to work, is perhaps the saddest sight that Fortune's inequality exhibits under the sun' (T. Carlyle, *Chartism*, in *The Works of Thomas Carlyle*, Centenary Edition, 4.135). And if work were not available in Great Britain, because the government foolishly declined to create jobs, then it should be sought in the colonies, with the active support of the government. But in his personal life he wanted as little government assistance and interference as possible. He did not see why he should even vote in such a corrupt society; it would only lend support to a partisan and materialistic system. But, for the country as a whole, *laissez-faire* seemed to Carlyle a disastrous policy; the present social and economic problems were so serious and widespread that only national programmes funded by the government could provide effective solutions. At the same time he doubted that the corrupt web of business, bureaucracy, aristocracy, and government would support practical solutions. He increasingly felt that he was looking down a deep, widening, and magnetic chasm into which everything was destined to be pulled or to fall.

In his Romantic idealization of the power of the individual Carlyle looked to particular leaders and the concept of élite leadership rather than to the common denominator and the compromises of democracy. A new friend, with complicated problems of his own, saw the dilemma clearly. Giuseppe Mazzini, the Italian revolutionary, had been introduced to the Carlyles in 1837. Both Carlyles liked Mazzini for his innocence, his virtue, and his courage; Jane found him especially attractive. Carlyle and Mazzini argued, on good terms, aware of the distance that separated them. Between 1839 and 1841 the intimacy increased, Mazzini being more troubled by Carlyle's ideas than Carlyle by Mazzini's. Jane Carlyle and Mazzini developed an increasing intimacy during the first half of the 1840s. Sensitive to her emotional needs, Mazzini treated her with warm admiration; she was a comforting presence who could provide him with both affection and consolation. The unhappy wife and the lonely exile engaged in the amorous rhetorical disguise of brother and sister, confiding in one another during long walks around London and quiet evenings by the Carlyle fireplace. Whether Jane expected more from Mazzini is unclear. The relationship changed suddenly and its intensity declined in the summer of 1846, the moment when the Carlyle marriage faced its most threatening crisis: Jane asked her friend's advice about whether or not to leave her husband, and Mazzini strongly advised her not to.

Cromwell and *Past and Present*, 1843 Cromwell had been much on Carlyle's mind from 1839 onwards, but his proposed biography seemed to him a less interesting subject than the French Revolution had been. In November 1842 he began to write, though much of his work went into the fire at first. But it was a book about the nineteenth, not the seventeenth century. By December 1842 he was writing intensely: England's pursuit of 'money, money, and one folly and another' took on dramatic form, a literary expression of his urgent call, 'Let us all repent, and amend. Let each of us for himself do it:—that is the grand secret!' (*The Letters of Thomas Carlyle to his Brother Alexander*, ed. E. W. Marrs, 1968, 543). By the end of December much of the book was done. It seemed comparatively easy to confess that 'no Cromwell will ever come out of me in this world. I dare not even try Cromwell' (Froude, *Thomas Carlyle*, 3.280). When Jane glanced at his confusing 'hieroglyphics' and saw what seemed to her a biography of someone called Abbot Samson, she asked him 'what on earth *has* all this to do with Cromwell—and learned that Cromwell was not begun … He lets everybody go on questioning him of Cromwell and answers so as to leave them in the persuasion he is very busy with that and nothing else' (*Jane Welsh Carlyle: Letters to her Family, 1839–1863*, ed. L. Huxley, 1924, 79). *Past and Present* (1843) seemed to the author a product of the searing, furnace-like intensity in which he flourished as a writer. Rather than admit that it had satisfied the political and emotional needs that had previously been invested in the prospect of writing a biography of Cromwell, he still wondered whether or not he should return to his original intention. By late October 1843 his dilemma was still unresolved. 'A book on Cromwell is impossible! Literally so' (*Collected Letters*, 17.164). But he needed to try. The compulsion hardly seemed rational; his stubbornness, though, was intensified by his awareness that he could never write the book which he had originally planned. Through November and part of December 1843 he either faced a blank sheet or wrote unsatisfactory sentences. Shortly after the middle of December he gathered together everything he had written about Cromwell and committed it 'at one fell swoop to the fire' in the same room in which Jane was peacefully darning stockings. Once he had been the victim (and perhaps partly the beneficiary) of an accidental burning of his work; now he had deliberately put his own manuscript into the fire. Since he could not do as a biography what he believed he had to do in some form, he decided to produce an edition of Cromwell's speeches and letters. The puritan leader's words would speak for themselves. With much anxiety and complaint, Carlyle devoted the next three years to this edition: it proved the best strategy for dealing with failure.

Lady Harriet Baring Carlyle met Lady Harriet Baring in late 1839. The wealthy and forceful Lady Harriet soon invited him to be an active member of the circle that she was attracting to her father-in-law's mansion, Bath House in Piccadilly, and gathering for holidays in Hampshire. During the next year Carlyle's relationship with Lady Harriet deepened. His friendship with Bingham Baring provided a normalizing background; the quiet, proud husband eagerly supported his wife's social extravagances. Despite Jane Carlyle's claim that she was incapable of jealousy, her resentment at 'how marvellously that *liaison* has gone on' (*Collected Letters*, 16.182–3) was certainly an emotion that could hardly be distinguished from jealousy. She had no reason to fear that her husband would have an affair with Lady Harriet: her position, his sexual reticence, and his puritanical sense of duty prevented that. But that Lady Harriet seemed to have no interest in her and that her husband had an extraordinary interest in Lady Harriet left her feeling rejected by both. Although Jane was seriously ill through much of 1844–5 Carlyle's frequent visits to Bath House continued. Unknown to his wife, Carlyle was writing extraordinary notes to Lady Harriet: he was the dark man of dross, dirt, and confusion; she was radiant with light. Associating himself with winter, failure, sin, and excremental dirt, one of his lifelong metaphors of anxiety, Carlyle found it comforting and exciting to play his exaggerated darkness off against her imaginary brightness. Jane wished herself rid of the whole matter—her jealousy, her resentment, her pain, and the pervasive unhappiness which closed in on her with the threat of madness, the hope of self-extinction. Late in June 1846 she told her husband how she felt and insisted that he could not have them both: he was astonished by and resentful of the depth and bitterness of her anger. In the end she made the best of Lady Harriet, though the best was often painful.

Carlyle's *Cromwell* and other works, 1845–1849 Friendship and work were Carlyle's shield against middle-age fears: neither proved totally satisfactory. For a man who tended to think of himself as alone and friendless, he had managed by the beginning of the 1840s to create a number of lifelong friendships. The record is deeply impressive and often moving: Milnes, Sterling, Thackeray, Browning, Tennyson, Forster, Dickens, soon Edward FitzGerald, and later John Ruskin—together with Carlyle they wove a rich texture of experience, talent, achievement, and mutual affection which created a family connectiveness of the sort that Carlyle thought essential for human relations. By early 1845 he had basically completed his work on Cromwell, which was published later that year as *The Life and Letters of Oliver Cromwell*. Between 1845 and 1849 he wrote very little for publication. With sufficient income from royalties, he felt liberated from the need to write or lecture. The

problems of leadership and change still preoccupied him. For Carlyle, all public revolutions were questionable; what the individual could not do for himself it seemed doubtful that society could do for him. During the 1840s his hope that society would become better through sudden changes diminished considerably. The most demanding challenge was to confront and make the most of the inevitable changes. Some of the public changes he confronted with keen perceptiveness, others with blunt hostility. Having grown up in a tradition of spiritual and intellectual élitism he did not see any wisdom in compromises that only made misery and the fallen state of mankind more bearable. Inevitably, he feared, the government of the lowest common denominator would be dedicated to materialism—to the 'good life' as defined in material terms.

Carlyle had published *The French Revolution* at forty-two. It was not a young man's book, but it was the work of a Romantic visionary who had seen both the beauty and the terror of chaos. In 1849 he was fifty-four years old; the accumulated wear and tear of the years of psychogenic dyspepsia and the self-punishing compulsions of work and duty showed more in his emotional tenseness than in his physical presence. He usually dressed in dark clothes, softened by his distinctive wide-brimmed hats. He retained the strong frame and striking facial features of his youth. An artist whose expressiveness was inseparable from constant involvement with and comment on a rapidly changing society, Carlyle, from 1845 to 1849, gave much thought and energy to the Irish problem, partly because he was searching for a topic to write on. In September 1846 he made a lightning trip to Ireland, and in 1848 and early 1849 he seemed to be honing his pen to write at length on the topic. He published a number of brief newspaper articles in *The Spectator* and *The Examiner*, mainly attacking the maladministration of Ireland by the English landowners and by Lord John Russell's government, emphasizing that England had to solve the problem of Ireland or sink itself. By November 1849 he had finished an essay called 'Occasional discourse on the nigger question', which *Fraser's Magazine* published before the end of the year. By December he felt in the writing vein again, though not about Ireland. His subjects were democracy, work, labour, and modern government: his vision of the interplay between unalterable 'facts' and human manipulation. The main question was whether he ought to write a book or a series of pamphlets. By the new year, he had not only decided but had already begun what he conceived of as his own Tracts for the Times, a series of twelve pamphlets to be published in monthly instalments over the next year.

Latter-Day Pamphlets, 1850 To many of Carlyle's contemporaries *Latter-Day Pamphlets* (1850) represented a dividing point in his career. The sermon form and the serial procedure heightened the intensity of the separate parts and extended the period during which the work was the focus of excited attention. Whatever its actual qualities, the exaggerated response to the book was unfortunate for

Carlyle's future stature as a writer. Some of the fault, of course, was the author's. *Latter-Day Pamphlets* has much sense in it and many merits: its failure is not that of substance but of literary form. In *Latter-Day Pamphlets* Carlyle's anger overwhelmed his artistry. But the deeper source of Carlyle's failure to make an artistic success of *Latter-Day Pamphlets* was the fatigue, anxiety, indecision, and anger that had brought him at the age of fifty-five to think that much of life was behind him, that satisfying human relationships were difficult if not impossible, and that neither his own frame of mind nor the condition of his culture permitted him the liberality of imagination and the concentration of intellect which great works of art demand. It seemed clear to Carlyle that the defeat of Presbyterian values at the end of the seventeenth century and the general victory of Counter-Reformation attitudes had marked the beginning of Britain's gradual descent into materialism and all that followed. With biting sarcasm he called it the 'Pig Philosophy'. The inevitable result, he insisted, was the unsatisfying pursuit of that which, if it could ever be realized, would prove abysmally unsatisfying. Whatever man's material and technological accomplishments, they would never answer, even for 'pigs', the need for spiritual achievement and communal harmony.

John Sterling, 1851　For some years Carlyle had been brooding about the significance of the life of John Sterling, who had died in 1844. In early 1851 he decided that he would put into practice his lifelong preoccupation with the nature of biography and write an appropriate evaluation and memorial. In comparison with *Cromwell* and *Latter-Day Pamphlets* this seemed a small, sweet task. At the end of March Jane Carlyle read it. Her friendship with Sterling had been particularly close, her relationship with the entire Sterling family intense: she warmly voted for immediate printing. The proof sheets were done in the late spring and early summer, completed just before the Carlyles left for the 'water cure' at Malvern and an extended summer holiday. Significantly, *The Life of John Sterling* (1851) contains a memorably vivid but hostile pen-portrait of Coleridge, based on Carlyle's visit to Highgate in 1824. The hostility was not entirely personal: it proceeded partly from Carlyle's need as an artist to make clear the grounds for Sterling's rejection of Coleridge's influence, as well as from Carlyle's need to put his own rejection of Coleridge in a favourable light. In order to elucidate the relationship between Sterling and Coleridge, Carlyle had to reveal his views on the church and Christianity. To some it came as a shock; to others it was also an affront. Despite the Christian resonances of Carlyle's prose there was no Christian substance, if substance was to be defined theologically. In the eyes of many Christians such a position was hardly to be distinguished from atheism.

Frederick the Great and Collected Works, 1851–1865　When Carlyle celebrated his fifty-sixth birthday in 1851 his major concern was finding some work that would sustain him

through his remaining years. First he mulled over and dismissed as subjects William the Conqueror and the Norman episode in English history. The clear direction of his intention was to write a substantial work on some major figure in British or European history which would fulfil the intent of his never-realized biography of Cromwell. A book on Frederick the Great of Prussia had begun to seem a potential answer to his problem. Carlyle began serious reading on the subject in the late autumn of 1851. He had actually considered Frederick as early as 1830, when he had proposed to an Edinburgh publisher that he write a single-volume biography of the 'brave Fritz'. In the summer of 1852 he visited Germany for the first time; fortunately, despite his litany of regrets, the trip was a success, though it did not result in substantial progress in the writing of *Frederick*. For Carlyle, German culture was embodied in the piety of Luther, the sacred necessity of the Reformation, and the creation, by Goethe in particular, of Romantic idealism, a literary antidote to both eighteenth-century rationalism and modern materialism. He believed that the Anglo-Saxon hegemony would be based, like Britain itself, on Teutonic virtues of the kind which were best represented by his own father and which were deeply rooted in the racial inheritance of northern Europeans: piety, courage, reverence for work and legitimate authority, and the intuitive intelligence that recognizes and attempts to realize in daily life the consonance between man's needs and the facts of nature and the universe.

During the 1850s Carlyle gradually came to think of his new writing commitment as an inescapable misfortune; by 1854 he felt that 'enormous rubbish-mountains' surrounded him. Finally, in June 1858, volumes 1 and 2 were completed; they were published in the autumn, while their author glumly faced what he realized were at least two or three years' more work. From the beginning of his research on *Frederick* he had recognized that compulsion had triumphed over reason. With the death of his mother at the end of 1853 his tentative commitment to pursue the project to the boundaries of common sense and just a little beyond became an irreversible emotional necessity. Though the eighteenth-century world of Frederick II had none of the religious intensity of Luther's century, the subject was clearly an extension of his earlier attempts to contrast the corruption of modern Europe with Reformation spirituality. For Carlyle such work exemplified the values that his mother embodied: whereas she had found relief from painful grief in contemplating God and eternity, her son found it in work and history.

With individual titles of the 1857–8 edition of the *Collected Works* coming out a volume a month and overlapping with the first two of *Frederick*, even hostile critics, such as Herman Merivale, granted that Carlyle 'had become, while yet alive and at work among us, something of a classic' (*Quarterly Review*, July 1865). In an anonymous review George Eliot claimed in 1855 that 'it is not as a theorist, but as a great and beautiful human nature, that Carlyle influences us' (*Leader*, 27 Oct 1855, 1034–5); in October 1856, in the *National Review*, James Martineau, Harriet's influential brother, joined Carlyle to Coleridge and John Henry Newman as one of the three major influences on the religious spirit of the age. George Henry Lewes emphasized the power of genius to transcend its limitations, though 'our eyes ache a little in gazing at this constant glowing ... white heat' (G. H. Lewes, 'Carlyle's Frederick the Great', *Fraser's Magazine*, Dec 1858, 633–5). With much of the new *Collected Works* in his hands, James Fitzjames Stephen dismissed the question of politics and theology:

> Regarded as works of art, we should put the best of Mr. Carlyle's writings at the very head of contemporary literature ... If he is the most indignant and least cheerful of living writers, he is also one of the wittiest and the most humane. (J. F. Stephen, 'Mr. Carlyle', *Saturday Review*, 19 June 1858, 638)

He is 'one of the greatest wits and poets, but the most unreliable moralist and politician, of our age and nation' (ibid., 640). Stephen's calm conclusion that 'no one but a man of real and great genius could have done this' (ibid., 638) aptly crystallizes that remarkable process whereby at some point in his career a great writer's reputation transcends the limitations of his individual works. Stephen was himself a historian, and for a long time under-secretary for the colonies, and his praise in the *Saturday Review* gave Carlyle the imprimatur of the establishment. By late 1858 the writer who for years could not find a publisher for *Sartor Resartus* and who just eight years before shocked the public with what were felt to be the mad barbarities of *Latter-Day Pamphlets* had been elevated to the Parnassus where classics reside.

During the later years of Carlyle's work on *Frederick*, Jane went through the most serious crisis of her life. The death of Harriet Baring in 1857 relieved her of one emotional burden. But the habit of suffering had become entrenched; and there were other causes for pain. Carlyle's monomaniacal devotion to his work outlasted his devotion to Lady Ashburton, and Jane's own disappointments were complex and pervasive. Not only did she feel unloved but a series of neglects and deaths had left her without a sufficient number of people to love. In September 1863 she stepped off the pavement and fell heavily, tearing sinews in her thigh. Improvement came very slowly. She felt more than weak and physically ill: she felt deeply wounded as a person, as if her lifelong sense of guilt in regard to her parents and her own aborted career as a writer and her life as a woman now found its most physically symbolic residence. 'The malady is in my womb ... It is the consequence of that unlucky fall; no disease there, the doctors say, but some nervous derangement' (Froude, *Letters and Memorials*, 2.286). Jane struggled through, and in the last days of 1864 Carlyle realized that what seemed the worst year of his life had at least been merciful enough to return his wife to him alive and to bring him within moments of finishing the book which had made them both miserable for so long. Exhaustion and depression overwhelmed him. Despite all his efforts to like the Prussian king, he had been able to muster no more than respect; and his struggle to create order, both as a historian and as an artist, had been undermined by

serious doubts as to whether order itself existed and whether efforts such as his had any value. Nevertheless *Frederick* pulsed with a vital energy that few of his contemporaries and fewer modern readers have had the perception or the patience to experience. At the edge of his own strength and certain that his own death was imminent, he could not help but accentuate the autobiographical impulse and track himself towards the grave as he described Frederick's old age. Early in 1865, after thirteen years of work, Carlyle finally completed the book. He did not plan to write anything more.

Jane Carlyle's death and its aftermath, 1866–1873 With the completion of *Frederick* at the beginning of 1865 Carlyle sank into lassitude, mingling relief with depression. In November he became preoccupied with the latest indication of his high status as a hero of culture. After serving two terms Gladstone had retired from the position of rector of the University of Edinburgh; a new rector was to be elected by the students. Two names were proposed, Carlyle and Disraeli. To his surprise Carlyle was elected to the office by better than a two-to-one margin. Speaking in his inaugural address to 'Young Scotland', Carlyle concluded with his favourite poem by Goethe. Tumultuous applause burst from the enthusiastic students: everyone was on his feet, arms waving, caps flying. A few days later, still in Scotland, he received the news that Jane was dead. About three in the afternoon the previous Saturday (21 April 1866) she had gone for her regular afternoon carriage ride in Hyde Park; after several circuits of the park the driver, alarmed by Mrs Carlyle's lack of response to his request for further instructions, asked a lady to look into the carriage. Jane 'was leaning back in one corner of the carriage, rugs spread over her knees; her eyes were closed, and her upper lip slightly, slightly opened' (Froude, *Letters and Memorials*, 2.391). She seemed dead, and a few minutes later medical authority confirmed the obvious.

Carlyle managed to be remarkably involved in literature and politics during the four years that followed his wife's death. His emotional depression and trembling right hand hardly kept him from work; and certainly the reminiscences that he wrote of his wife, Irving, Southey, Wordsworth, the Skirvings, John Wilson (Christopher North), and William Hamilton, the last three done in the winter of 1868, the annotations of Althaus, and the extensive annotations of Jane's letters, are among the most bold, vivid, and revealing writing he had ever done. Between 1866 and 1869 he became deeply involved in a controversy which developed when James Eyre, the governor of Jamaica, brutally suppressed a minor slave rebellion: it was further proof that Carlyle was still capable of vigorous engagement. In August 1867 he published in *Macmillan's Magazine* 'Shooting Niagara: and after?'. With scattered energy and in the Carlylean voice of visionary rhetoric and personal despair, it spoke against the 'leap in the dark', the Reform Bill of 1867. In 1870 the outbreak of the Franco-Prussian War, whose issues touched directly on his lifelong concerns, stirred the ageing 'Sage of Chelsea' into a public statement of his views expressed with much of the vigour that had characterized his comments on social issues during his most active years. With the help of David Masson, and with James Anthony Froude and John Forster as witnesses, he bequeathed Craigenputtoch to the University of Edinburgh for a scholarship fund for needy students. With the help of a new American friend, Charles Eliot Norton, he gave to Harvard University all his books on Cromwell and Frederick. In 1873 he inserted into his will the clause that 'since I cannot be laid in the grave at Haddington, I shall be placed beside or between my father and mother in the Churchyard of Ecclefechan'.

Last years, Froude's biography, and death, 1874–1881 Far from an invalid, Carlyle entered the last decade of his life with a strong constitution that sometimes seemed an ironic insult to his real desires: he talked with Froude about the nobility of the Roman style of suicide. In September 1874 he had a new literary task in hand, the last essay of his life, 'The portraits of John Knox'. On his eightieth birthday, in 1875, his contemporaries tried to draw the final lines of Carlyle's portrait, to memorialize for the last time—other than the funereal occasion itself—the great man who had been among them for so long. Over forty years before, Carlyle had been instrumental in having a medallion engraved and a collective letter sent to Goethe on the Sage of Weimar's eightieth birthday. His own friends now did the same for him, the medal by Jacob Boehm a handsome representation of the Sage of Chelsea, the testimonial letter signed by 119 of the great and near-great of Victorian intellectual society. Even in his old age, though, neither public memorials nor disappointment about his spiritual works could prevent him from perceiving and expressing the constant battle with self-identity which had been one of the great struggles of his life. One morning, getting out of his bath and drying himself, he looked into the mirror of self and exclaimed, 'What the devil then am I, at all, at all? After all these eighty years I know nothing about it' (W. Allingham, *A Diary*, 1907, 248).

While Carlyle's friends and family waited for the inevitable, two people in particular had a practical interest in his death. Neither Mary Aitken, his niece, nor James Anthony Froude expected anything beyond what they justly deserved. Mary, who had devoted over ten years to attending to her uncle, had no competence except that which he would provide. Froude had not only agreed to publish an edition of Jane Carlyle's letters but had also begun working on an edition of Carlyle's reminiscences and a full-scale biography, an immense investment of time and energy. By 1878 Carlyle had turned over to Froude most of his literary papers, particularly letters, for two express purposes—editing for publication Jane's letters and writing his biography. Froude's *Letters and Memorials of Jane Welsh Carlyle*, with Carlyle's biographical annotations, was essentially ready for publication. In Froude's mind the only unanswered question was whether or not the volume should be prefaced with Carlyle's reminiscence of his wife, which was clearly Froude's property. In the next two years Froude completed most of the first two volumes of what was to be a four-volume biography, incorporating in part or in whole much of the material

from the other letters and biographical writings. Whether or not a separate volume containing the various reminiscences of family, friends, and literary personalities should be published had been left to Froude's judgement, as had the decision whether such a volume should contain the memoir of Jane Carlyle. The reminiscences other than Jane's were clearly understood to be Mary Aitken's property, but the decision whether or not to publish them was to be left to Froude. When, after Carlyle's death, Mary Aitken (with her husband, Alexander Carlyle) and Froude sharply disagreed about how best to serve Carlyle's posthumous reputation, a series of publications brought to light claims and counter-claims about Carlyle's personality and his treatment of his wife. The Froude–Carlyle controversy, as it was called, damaged Carlyle's reputation among the late Victorians. After the First World War Carlyle's reputation suffered for other reasons: his criticisms of democracy along with widespread misunderstanding of his views about the nature of political leadership alienated many; twentieth century readers found uncongenial the intricacies and dramatic flourishes of his prose style. The widely read Victorian prose master came to belong mostly to professional students of literature, language, and history. Among them, his reputation recovered and by the late twentieth century the Carlyles had become a major point of scholarly interest, exemplified by Duke University Press's edition of the letters of Thomas and Jane Welsh Carlyle.

Carlyle spent the summer of 1878 in Scotland, first at a rented house near Dumfries and then visiting near Ecclefechan. Early in the spring of 1879 he suddenly 'broke down altogether' into lassitude and loss of interest. Surprisingly, he had so improved by May that he was out of imminent danger. His brother Jack died on 15 September 1879, but through the autumn Carlyle was in calm spirits and, on his eighty-fourth birthday, Browning and Ruskin visited him. Though he made efforts to walk, his mobility suddenly decreased, as if his legs were retiring after a lifetime of service. Each afternoon a carriage ride provided gentle exercise and some relief from the desultory reading which was his main amusement. By March 1880 he had almost lost interest even in looking out of the carriage window. At the beginning of the next year he was too weak to dress himself, even to move. He soon sank into 'a deep heavy sleep', from which the constant ringing of the doorbell by newspaper reporters, eager to be timely with the news that the nation expected at any moment, could not disturb him. On Friday 4 February 1881 Mary Aitken thought she heard him saying to himself, 'So this is Death: well …' (W. Allingham, *A Diary*, 1907, 308–9). At about half past eight the next morning, at 5 Cheyne Row, Chelsea, he quietly, almost imperceptibly, drifted off into the complete silence that he had for so long thought of as the highest blessing. On 9 February the body was conveyed on the overnight train to Scotland and brought to Ecclefechan the next day. The funeral was at noon: on the hour 'the Presbyterian kirk bells tolled mournfully' and the hearse arrived, followed by five funeral coaches and about a hundred villagers. No one spoke. As was the custom, the coffin was lowered into the earth without a eulogy or a prayer.   FRED KAPLAN

Sources *The collected letters of Thomas and Jane Welsh Carlyle*, ed. C. R. Sanders and K. J. Fielding, 1–2 (1970) · J. A. Froude, *Thomas Carlyle*, 4 vols. (1882–4) · F. Kaplan, *Thomas Carlyle: a biography* (1983) · L. Hanson and E. Hanson, *Necessary evil: the life of Jane Welsh Carlyle* [1952] · *Letters and memorials of Jane Welsh Carlyle*, ed. T. Carlyle and J. A. Froude, 3 vols. (1883) · T. Carlyle, *Reminiscences*, ed. C. E. Norton, 2 vols. (1887) · R. L. Tarr, *Thomas Carlyle: a descriptive bibliography* (1989) · *Thomas Carlyle: the critical heritage*, ed. J. P. Seigel (1971) · W. H. Dunn, *Froude and Carlyle* (1930) · C. F. Harrold, *Carlyle and German thought, 1819–1834* (1934) · C. R. Sanders, *Carlyle's friendships and other studies* (1977) · *Carlyle and his contemporaries*, ed. J. Clubbe (1976) · R. W. Dillon, *A centenary bibliography of Carlylean studies* (1981–5) · Kirkcaldy town minutes, 1816

Archives BL, corresp., RP 392, 402 [copies] · Bodl. Oxf., pocket books · Duke U., Perkins L., letters and papers · Edinburgh Central Reference Library, letters · Harvard U., letters and literary MSS · Hornel Library, Broughton House, Kirkcudbright, family letters and letters · Hunt. L., corresp., literary MSS, and papers · JRL, letters · London Library, letters · Morgan L., corresp. and papers · NL Scot., corresp.; corresp. and papers; family corresp. and papers · NL Scot., MSS · U. Edin., letters · University of Toronto, Thomas Fisher Rare Book Library, family corresp. · V&A, letters, manuscripts, and proofs · Yale U., Beinecke L., letters, papers | BL, letters to James Marshall, Egerton MS 3032 · BL, letters to Macvey Napier, Add. MSS 34614–34615, 34621, 34622, *passim* · BL, letters as sponsor to Royal Literary Fund, loan no. 96 · BL, letters to Mr and Mrs R. Smith, Add. MS 44885 A · CUL, corresp. with Edward Fitzgerald · Harvard U., Houghton L., corresp. with Ralph Waldo Emerson · JRL, letters to John Ruskin and John James Ruskin · Kircaldy Art Gallery and Museum, papers relating to Kirkcaldy · McMaster University, Hamilton, Ontario, corresp. with Alexander Carlyle and others · Mitchell L., Glas., Glasgow City Archives, letters to William Stirling-Maxwell · NA Scot., corresp. with Robert Mitchell and family · NL Aus., letters to Alfred Deakin · NL Ire., letters to Charles Gavin Duffy · NL NZ, Turnbull L., corresp. with Geraldine Jewsbury · NL Scot., letters to William Allingham · NL Scot., letters to Baring family · NL Scot., letters to Arthur Helps · NL Scot., letters to Robert Horn · NL Scot., letters to David Hyde · NL Scot., letters to Thomas Murray · NL Scot., letters to Lady Sandwich · NRA Scotland, priv. coll., letters to John Swinton · priv. coll., Mirchouse, Keswick, corresp. with Thomas Spedding · Royal Institution of Great Britain, London, corresp. with John Tyndall · Ruskin Library, Lancaster, corresp. with John Ruskin · Som. ARS, letters to Sir Edward Strachey · Trinity Cam., letters to Lord Houghton · U. Edin. L., letters to Charles Butler · U. Edin. L., letters to J. Johnstone · U. Edin. L., letters to David Laing · V&A NAL, letters to John Forster

Likenesses D. Maclise, pencil drawing, 1832, V&A; repro. in *Fraser's Magazine*, 7 (1833) · D. Maclise, lithograph, pubd 1833, BM, NPG · S. Laurence, drawing, 1838, Carlyle's House, Kensington and Chelsea, London · R. J. Lane, lithograph, pubd 1839 (after Count D'Orsay), NPG · J. Linnell, oils, 1844, Scot. NPG · R. S. Tait, two salt prints, 1851, NPG · R. S. Tait, oils, 1855, Carlyle's House, Kensington and Chelsea, London · T. Woolner, plaster medallion, 1855, NPG; version, Scot. NPG · R. S. Tait, double portrait, oils, 1857–8 (with his wife), Carlyle's House, Kensington and Chelsea, London · F. M. Brown, group portrait, oils, c.1860 (*Work*), Man. City Gall. · T. Woolner, marble bust, 1866, U. Edin. L. · G. F. Watts, oils, c.1868, V&A · G. F. Watts, oils, 1868, NPG [*see illus.*] · W. Greaves, pencil and wash drawing, 1870, Scot. NPG · J. M. Whistler, oils, 1873, Glasgow Art Gallery and Museum · J. E. Boehm, terracotta bust, 1875, NPG · R. Herdman, oils, 1875, Scot. NPG · aquatint, 1875, NPG · A. Legros, oils, 1877, Scot. NPG · J. E. Millais, oils, 1877, NPG · H. Allingham, watercolour, 1879, Scot. NPG · W. Brodie, bronzed plaster bust, 1879, Scot. NPG · W. Greaves, oils, c.1879, Scot. NPG · H. Allingham, two drawings, 1881 (posthumous), Carlyle's House, Kensington

and Chelsea, London · J. E. Boehm, marble statue, 1881, Scot. NPG; related bronze statue, Chelsea Embankment, London · A. Gilbert, plaster death mask, 1881, NPG · photographs, Carlyle's House, Kensington and Chelsea, London · photographs, Carlyle's birthplace, Ecclefechan, Dumfries and Galloway · photographs, NPG · woodcut (after watercolour by H. Allingham), BM, NPG

Wealth at death under £40,000: resworn probate, April 1882, *CGPLA Eng. & Wales* (1881)

Carlyle, Thomas (1803–1855), apostle of the Catholic Apostolic church and German scholar, was born on 17 July 1803 at King's Grange, near Castle Douglas, Kirkcudbrightshire, of an old Dumfriesshire family. His father, William Carlyle (1759–1824), a lawyer, married in 1802 Margaret Heriot, widow of William McMurdo of Savannah, Georgia, a merchant in Jamaica. Their only son Thomas was educated at the Annan Academy together with Edward Irving, and later at the Dumfries Academy. After studying at Edinburgh University he was called to the Scottish bar on 14 December 1824, in which year also the claim to the dormant title of Baron Carlyle had devolved on him. On 7 September 1826 he married Frances Wallace (d. 1874) whose father was the Revd Archibald Laurie, minister of Loudoun, Ayrshire.

For about ten years Carlyle practised as a lawyer in Edinburgh, but his real interest was in religious matters, witnessed by his preaching in the streets of Edinburgh, which in 1833 resulted in police intervention. His anonymous publication *The Word Made Flesh* (1829) is an indication of Carlyle's sympathy for the unorthodox teaching associated with the circle around Edward Irving, and it was Carlyle who in 1831 defended the Revd John McLeod Campbell, minister of Row, Argyllshire, and Alexander Scott, Irving's assistant, when they were charged and eventually deposed in the Scottish church assembly on account of their Christological teaching. In 1832 Irving established a new London congregation in Newman Street (later known as the Catholic Apostolic church), where charismatic utterances called for the recognition of apostles. Three years later, on 1 May 1835, in the Edinburgh home of Walter Tait, Carlyle was named as the ninth of these apostles and soon after, in London on 14 July, was 'separated' for the work. Carlyle now moved with his wife to Albury, Surrey, close to the home of another apostle, Henry Drummond, where in 1838 Prussia and north Germany were identified as the Tribe of Simeon and were made Carlyle's special responsibility. The Apostle of North Germany, as he was soon to be known, was a competent German scholar and now spent much of his time in that country, which became one of the few areas outside England where the Catholic Apostolic church can be said to have had some real measure of success.

The unfair accusation made by Thomas Carlyle, the historian, that Carlyle, the advocate, took advantage of his more famous namesake and profited (especially in Germany) from the inevitable occasions of mistaken identity have been demonstrated to be without foundation. Carlyle's attractively frank manner and his quietly dignified learning made a favourable impression, and German converts to the movement included some scholars, such as the church historian H. W. J. Thiersch. Frederick William

IV was interested in Carlyle's *Moral Phenomena of Germany* (English edn, 1845) and was introduced to the author by Baron von Bunsen, who commented favourably on Carlyle's understanding of the Germans and reckoned that his 'censure is worth more than others' praise' (Brash, 38). Bunsen's wife, on the other hand, suggested that his intelligent sincerity was marred by 'the common English distemper of *half-learning*' (*Life and Letters*, 2.77). Carlyle's book was a thoughtfully moderate blend of social and theological conservatism (with a whiff of antisemitism) which questioned much of the liberalism that had become fashionable in the years before 1848. Significantly, the first sixty members of the new church in Berlin were 'sealed' by Carlyle in a hotel, when the chaos of revolution had closed most of the city's churches during March 1848. The Catholic Apostolic community in Berlin was soon to be more numerous than in any other city in the world.

In addition to his labours in Germany, Carlyle continued to publish a series of religious works, all of which questioned from his special ecclesiastical standpoint the religious assumptions of the day. Possibly the best-known of his publications is *Pleadings with my Mother, the Church in Scotland* (1854), which is included in his *Collected Writings* (1878). This volume, however, does not contain his earlier works or his *Short History of the Apostolic Work* (1851), which is an important source for any study of the movement with which he was associated.

Exhausted by his labours Carlyle died at Heath House, Albury, on 28 January 1855, and was buried in Albury parish church. His daughter Alice married the Scottish historian Henry Grey Graham. Mrs Carlyle, whose sister Harrietta married the sixth apostle, Francis Valentine Woodhouse, died at Pau on 22 February 1874.

TIMOTHY C. F. STUNT

Sources E. Miller, *The history and doctrines of Irvingism*, 1 (1878), 88, 157, 192–3, 267, 271 · H. G. Graham, 'The two Carlyles', *The Athenaeum* (14 May 1881), 654 · S. Newman-Norton, 'A biographical index of those associated with the Lord's work', Bodl. Oxf., MS facs b.61 · T. Brash, *Thomas Carlyle's double-goer and his connection with the parish of Row* (1904) · F. Krämer, *Thomas Carlyle of the Scottish bar (1803–1855)* (1966) [in Ger.] · C. C. Schwartz, 'Chronicle of the setting up of the church in Berlin', 1951 [duplicated typescript in the writer's possession] · R. A. Davenport, *Albury Apostles*, rev. edn (1974), 142 · N. Carlisle, *Collections for a history of the ancient family of Carlisle* (1822), 114–15, 139–41 · S. Hall, 'The two Thomas Carlyles', *Nineteenth Century and After*, 73 (1913), 829–33 · C. G. Flegg, *Gathered under apostles: a study of the Catholic Apostolic church* (1992) · *The life and letters of Frances, Baroness Bunsen*, ed. A. J. C. Hare, 2 vols. (1879) · T. C. F. Stunt, *From awakening to secession: radical evangelicals in Switzerland and Britain, 1815–35* (2000)

Archives NL Scot., letters and notes

Likenesses photograph, repro. in Davenport, *Albury Apostles* (1974), following p. 161

Carlyon, Clement (1777–1864), physician, was born at Truro on 14 April 1777, the fourth son of the Revd John Carlyon (1722–1798), rector of Bradwell in Essex. He was educated at Truro grammar school, where Humphry Davy and Henry Martyn were among his schoolfellows. He took his degree at Pembroke College, Cambridge, in 1798 and was appointed a travelling bachelor on the Worts foundation which allowed him to travel to Germany. There he met Samuel Taylor Coleridge and joined him on a walking tour in the Harz. After completing his medical studies at Edinburgh and London, Carlyon returned to his home town in 1806 and lived there for the rest of his life. He was mayor of Truro five times and a practising physician until 1861. His autobiography, *Early Years and Late Reflections*, was published in four volumes between 1836 and 1858. The interesting and lively reminiscences of the first two volumes are replaced in the third and fourth by reams of dreary theology. The work's most valuable aspect was Carlyon's perceptive account of Coleridge, whose high intelligence and performativeness Carlyon understood very well. It is a pity that he never wrote a full-scale biography of him. Carlyon published *Observations on the Endemic Typhus Fever of Cornwall* in 1827. These were highly regarded and brought about beneficial changes to sanitation. In later life Carlyon published *Precepts for the Preservation of Health* (1859) and several tracts, intervening in contemporary debates about the governance of the Church of England and the role of the Book of Common Prayer. Carlyon died in Truro on 5 March 1864.

RICHARD GARNETT, *rev.* RALPH PITE

Sources Allibone, *Dict.* · Boase, *Mod. Eng. biog.*

Carman, (William) Bliss (1861–1929), poet and essayist, was born on 15 April 1861, in Fredericton, New Brunswick, Canada, the eldest son of William Carman, a barrister: his mother, Sophia Mary, daughter of George Bliss, was related to Ralph Waldo Emerson. Carman's family background was United Empire loyalist. He wrote a few poems while studying at the collegiate school in Fredericton, and his first published efforts appeared in the monthly journal of the University of New Brunswick in 1879. He graduated from the university with an honours BA in Greek and Latin in 1881, spent an academic year visiting Oxford University and Edinburgh University in 1882–3, and completed an MA degree in English literature at the University of New Brunswick in 1884. He studied for two years (1886–8) at Harvard College, where he met Richard Hovey, a fellow poet who became an editorial collaborator and lifelong friend. At Harvard he studied under and was greatly influenced by Francis Child, Josiah Royce, and George Santayana, and he began publishing poems in magazines such as the *Harvard Monthly* and the *Atlantic Monthly*.

In the time between leaving Harvard and the publication of his first and very successful volume of poetry, *Low Tide on Grand Pré: a Book of Lyrics* (1893), Carman moved continually between New York, Washington, D.C., Boston, Massachusetts, Fredericton, and Windsor, Nova Scotia—and this became quite typical of his vagabond lifestyle. He made a modest income by performing editorial tasks for such publications as *The Independent*, *Current Literature*, *Cosmopolitan*, the *Boston Transcript*, the *Atlantic Monthly*, and *The Chap-Book*, the last of which he co-founded in 1894 with Hovey. He was alert to the literary issues of his time, and he wrote many literary, social commentary, and philosophical columns. Some of his work is gathered together in his prose selections, *The Kinship of Nature* (1903), The

Friendship of Art (1904), *The Poetry of Life* (1905), and *The Making of Personality* (1906). These selections clearly display some of the marks of his late-Romantic biases, his interest in symbolist experimentation, his regard for traditional poetic forms, and his enthusiasm for the spiritually curative value of the unitarianism of François Delsarte (1811–1870).

With the success of *Low Tide*, Carman was established as essentially a nature mystic and poet of the open road in the tradition of Walt Whitman, and he went on to publish more than thirty titles over the next twenty-five years, most of them exquisitely rendered perceptions of nature. Carman's many volumes include *Songs from Vagabondia* (1894), and *More Songs from Vagabondia* (1896), both collaborations with Richard Hovey. He also published *Ballads and Lyrics* (1902); *From the Book of Myths* (1902); *Sappho: one Hundred Lyrics* (1905); *Pipes of Pan* (definitive edition, 1906); *Later Poems* (1921); *Sanctuary: Sunshine House Sonnets* (1929); and *Wild Garden* (1929).

Carman spent much of his life in New England, travelled extensively across the North American continent, and in Europe, and in 1908 settled in New Canaan, Connecticut. He was unmarried, and his saint-like appearance and gentle character won for him many readers and advocates during his lifetime. It was at New Canaan that he died suddenly of heart failure on 8 June 1929. He was cremated, and his ashes interred on 20 August 1929 in Forest Hill cemetery, Fredericton, New Brunswick.

All of Carman's poetry is tissued through with a spiritual optimism, as he managed to avoid being overwhelmed by the ironic harvest of much modern verse. This in part accounts for the waning of his more learned readership during the early decades of the century, and the fact that only in the last decades of the twentieth century have a number of critics come to appreciate his strange uniqueness as an early twentieth-century poet, his musical brilliance, and his savvy as a social commentator.

TERRY WHALEN

Sources T. Whalen, *Bliss Carman and his works* (1983) · G. Lynch, ed., *Bliss Carman: a reappraisal* (1990) · J. Cappon, *Bliss Carman and the literary currents and influences of his time* (1930) · O. Shepard, *Bliss Carman* (1923) · M. Miller, *Bliss Carman: quest and revolt* (1985) · D. Stephens, *Bliss Carman* (1966)
Archives Queen's University, Kingston, Ontario, Lorne Pierce collection · University of New Brunswick, Rufus Hathaway collection
Likenesses photographs, Queen's University, Kingston, Ontario, Lorne Pierce collection, archives

Carmeliano [Carmigliano], **Pietro** [Petrus Carmelianus, Peter Carmelian] (*c*.1451–1527), poet and royal official, was the son of Giovanni (Zanino) Fava of Valle Sabbia near Brescia. He assumed the name Carmelianus at an indeterminate date, possibly to recall the Latin *carmen* (poem) and accord with the otherwise undocumented claim to the style of *poeta laureatus* which he makes in the dedicatory preface to his first extant work and repeats elsewhere. He may have first embarked on a commercial career but, according to the same preface, he was schooled in the *studia humanitatis* before beginning ten years of travel, which extended as far as the Orient. In 1481 he travelled

from Rome to France and Brittany, and thence to England, with the intention of going on to Germanic lands. He remained in London, however, staying there for all or almost all his remaining life. Carmeliano was among the first of the Italians whose command of a humanist Latinity superior to that of their English contemporaries made them valuable to the regime in their adopted country, as well as influential in establishing the new style in court and intellectual circles there. Aided by English ecclesiastical preferments, he lived comfortably under five monarchs and kept Venice, in particular, valuably informed about English relations with the papacy.

Carmeliano looks soon to have secured official secretarial employment, since his first extant attempt to win royal patronage was dated from Rolls House on 7 April (Easter day) 1482. This is the Latin poem *De vere* ('On spring'): 148 elegiac couplets, full of learned mythological and natural-historical allusion, concluding with an unequivocal appeal for help, and dedicated to Edward, prince of Wales. Grateful verses added by Carmeliano at the end of the provincially illuminated presentation copy, which is written in his own accomplished rather sloping Roman script (BL, Royal MS 12 A. XXIX), suggest that his wishes were fulfilled. An apparently earlier attempt on Edward IV was the presentation of a copy of the edition of Cicero's *De oratore* printed at Venice in 1478, to which Carmeliano had added, in manuscript, marginal comments and a dedicatory poem; once in Ely Cathedral Library (Tanner, *Bibl. Brit.-hib.*, 154–5), this has since disappeared. On 13 December 1491 Carmeliano acquired for two nobles in London, on his own account, a manuscript of Juvenal and Persius written in Padua (Bodl. Oxf., Auct. MS F. 54).

After Edward V's death Carmeliano lost no time in transferring his allegiance to Richard III, with a flattering preface to a six-hundred-hexameter *Vita B. Katherinae*, written some time between 1483 and 1485. No royal copy survives, but there remain autographs, indifferently illuminated, with dedicatory epistles in praise of Richard, seeking assistance in obtaining favour from such a virtuous king, for Sir Richard Brackenbury (Bodl. Oxf., Laud MS misc. 501) and for John Russell, bishop of Lincoln (Cambridge, Gonville and Caius College, MS 196/102). In 1486 he felt able to contribute a Latin *Suasoria laeticiae* ('Invitation to delight'), addressed to Henry VII, denigrating Richard, and celebrating the cessation of civil war and the birth of Prince Arthur (illuminated autograph presentation copy: BL, Add. MS 33736). On 27 September 1486 he was awarded the right to a pension by Henry VII, who provided further for him in 1488 with the grant of a corrody in the priory of Christ Church, Canterbury (15 February) and the right to another pension (8 April); on 23 April 1488 he obtained a patent of denization. By 1502 he was notary public by apostolic and imperial authority.

In 1490 Carmeliano joined with other expatriate courtier–poets, Bernard André, Giovanni Gigli, and Cornelio Vitelli, in answering the satirical attack on the English by the Frenchman Robert Gaguin. At an indeterminate date Gaguin addressed a complimentary poem to Carmeliano and an uncomplimentary one to Vitelli (*Epistolae et orationes*, no extant edition before 1505). By 1500, when he went to Calais in Henry's train for the meeting with the Archduke Philip, Carmeliano was one of the king's chaplains. It is not clear whether this appointment lasted into the succeeding reign. His last recorded act for Henry VII was to celebrate the betrothal at the palace of Richmond on 17 December 1508 of Henry's daughter Mary to Prince Charles (later the emperor Charles V). His compositions for the occasion were issued by the king's printer, Richard Pynson, in *Pro sponsalibus et matrimonio inter principem Karolum, & dominam Mariam* ([1508]); the preliminary and concluding poems are certainly Carmeliano's and the prose narrative may also be his (cf. STC 17558, an English version without the poems).

Probably by 1490 Carmeliano had become Henry VII's Latin secretary. He still figures in that capacity at Henry's funeral in 1509; in the pardon roll at Henry VIII's accession he is described as 'late Latin secretary'. Although formally replaced in July 1511 by Andrea Ammonio, he continued to write letters on the new king's behalf until 1513. For Henry VII he had written to Ferdinand and Isabella of Spain concerning the marriage of Prince Arthur on 2 July 1496; but his first extant royal letter was to Giangaleazzo Sforza on 21 December 1490; on 4 August 1496 he offered himself as an informant to Lodovico il Moro. He remained in official contact with Milan until at least 17 November 1498. It is not clear when Carmeliano put his tacit services at the disposal of his native republic of Venice, but it must have been by the 1490s: he is documented in this capacity as late as the 1520s. No direct financial reward is recorded for any of this; various privileges, however, were conferred at request by Venice on his relatives in Italy, beginning on 22 February 1499 with Brescian citizenship for his father and his father's descendants and continuing until at least 1517. Luca Valaresso, a Venetian merchant resident in London who was one of those acting as a blind for him, was warned by Carmeliano on 1 September 1504 that he had fallen foul of Pope Julius II; on the 24th of the same month he divulged to the doge the hostile intentions towards Venice expressed in a papal letter to Henry VII and in 1508–9 he was warmly thanked by the republic.

Under Henry VIII Carmeliano remained in close contact with the Venetian ambassador and continued to provide dispatches for Venice. The diarist Marin Sanudo records that letters from 'Camarian' were read to the Venetian senate, who received them gratefully, between 1510 and August 1520. A manuscript, 'Reports from Venice, extracted from the most reliable authors in 1517 by Pietro Carmeliano' ('Rumores e Venetiis allati fidelissimis auctoribus anno salutis nostre 1517, scribente Petro Carmeliano'), is bound with other works in a volume in the Free Library of Philadelphia. Carmeliano's final mention in state papers is on 15 April 1529, when he is cited as having been Latin secretary at the time when a papal dispensation was being sought thirty years before for Henry's marriage.

Soon after arrival in England, Carmeliano had begun to contribute to English humanist printed publications, editing the correspondence between Pope Sixtus IV and Giovanni Mocenigo, doge of Venice, concerning the war with Ferrara of 1482–4, to which he contributed a prose preface. The whole was printed by William Caxton at Westminster, probably in 1484 (*Finiunt sex quam elegantissime epistole*); it has been suggested both that financial assistance had been provided by the Venetians and that the letters were intended for stylistic imitation. During the 1480s Carmeliano possibly moved to Oxford and taught there. He supplied prefatory Latin verses, addressed to the author and to William Waynflete, bishop of Winchester, for the editions of grammatical works based on Italian models by John Anwykyll of Magdalen College School (*c.*1483); and he wrote brief sets of verses for Francesco Griffolini's edition of the *Epistles* of pseudo-Phalaris (1485). A transcript in his hand of pseudo-Phalaris, including Griffolini's prologue and text as well as his own contributions, is now Trinity College, Dublin, MS 429. A slim volume of Latin poems, reported by Guerrini as by Carmeliano (1498), is by Valerand de Varennes and belongs to 1501.

Carmeliano's status began to decline under the influence of the newer Erasmian humanism of the reign of Henry VIII; what Erasmus himself has to say of him passes from suavely self-deprecatory thanks for compliment or favour (*c.*1507–1512) to acid exchange with Ammonio about the literary capacities of this 'monster', 'cursed by the Muses' (1513). He may well have met Erasmus for the first time on Erasmus's second visit to England in 1505: about then Erasmus acknowledged a gift from Carmeliano in ten fulsome hendecasyllables (*Poems*, no. 35; published 7 Jan 1507); on 9 May 1512 he asked Ammonio to thank Carmeliano for recommending him as 'the most learned of learned men' (*doctorum doctissimus*) to John Bryan, then student and later fellow of King's College, Cambridge (*Correspondence*, no. 262); and, at the end of 1513, he and Ammonio joined in deriding the womanish abuse and a false quantity in the use of the word 'pullulare' in Carmeliano's Latin epitaph for James IV of Scotland, killed at Flodden (*Correspondence*, nos. 280, 282–3; 25 November–2 December). Printed by Pynson, this last is extant only in a late sixteenth-century transcript (BL, Add. MS. 29506), in which the offending word does not occur. Carmeliano had previously been satirized for a blunder in sense in his poem on the betrothal of Princess Mary by another member of the Erasmian circle, Thomas More, in a Latin epigram written presumably at the end of 1508. By the time it was published in March 1518 (More, 3/2, no. 147), a better-disposed More was inclined to forgive a Carmeliano who had given evidence of right thinking. In a covering letter from London of 3 September 1516, to go with his *Utopia*, More tells Erasmus how the copy of his *Novum instrumentum* intended for the Venetian ambassador had been intercepted by Carmeliano and was being zealously studied by him (*Correspondence*, no. 461); he also describes their exchange of compliments and Carmeliano's high opinion of Erasmus, and expresses his own approval of Carmeliano. The only extant original composition by Carmeliano from later than this is a Latin epigram on Domenico Mancini's poem *De quattuor virtutibus* (*c*.1518–1520); in the English version of Mancini by Alexander Barclay, Carmeliano's verses are printed in Latin and in Barclay's English version, as they are with the 1570 edition of Barclay's translation of Sebastian Brant's *Stultifera navis*.

Ordained subdeacon on 18 April 1489, deacon on 13 June, and priest on 10 April 1490, Carmeliano amassed so much from preferment that, in 1522, he was assessed among the spiritualty for the French war loan at the large sum of £333 6s. 8d. On 28 February 1522 he bought from Stephen Coope an estate named Hartcombe, in the parishes of Kingston and Ditton in Surrey, which he sold on 20 May 1524 to Roger Pynchestre, citizen and grocer of London. He was rector of St George's, Southwark (from 6 March 1490 until his death); canon and prebendary of St Stephen's Chapel, Westminster (by 30 January 1493 and perhaps until death); canon of Wells and prebendary of Compton Bishop (from 7 March 1496 to at least 1513); canon of Salisbury and prebendary of Chisenbury and Chute (from 30 November 1498); canon of York and prebendary of Ampleforth (from 7 April 1501 until death); archdeacon of Llandaff and prebendary of Consumpta per Mare (from 20 June 1504); canon of Hereford and prebendary of Cublington (perhaps from 1504 and perhaps until death); rector of Bredon, Worcestershire (from 1505); archdeacon of Gloucester (from 1511 until at least 1517); canon of Winchester (perhaps from 1512); and canon of St Paul's and prebendary of Ealdland (from September 1519 to 26 November 1526). In 1526 he was named as one of those holding livings within the provostship of Beverley in the East Riding of Yorkshire.

Carmeliano died, presumably in London, on 18 August 1527. It is possible that 'Peter de Brecia', lutenist, a royal pensioner from 17 October 1512 to after 1527, who was licensed on 13 October 1526 to import 200 tuns of Gascon wine and Toulouse woad and received a new year's gift on 1 January 1528, was related to Carmeliano. The same may be true of 'Alice Carmillian' (Ellis Carmyllyan), who enjoyed a modest stipend as a painter in Henry VIII's household in 1529–30.   J. B. TRAPP

Sources J. Gairdner, ed., *Letters and papers illustrative of the reigns of Richard III and Henry VII*, 2 vols., Rolls Series, 24 (1861–3), 1.100–02; 2.89, 369 · *CPR, 1485–94*, 189, 232, 412; *1494–1509*, 242 · W. Campbell, ed., *Materials for a history of the reign of Henry VII*, 2, Rolls Series, 60 (1877), 38, 244, 289 · *LP Henry VIII*, 1, nos. 20, 169, 280, 322, 413, 430, 438(4), 463(ii), 1188, 1970(ii), 2053(2), 2246(5.ii), 2457, 2468, 2519; 3, no. 2483; 4, nos. 348, 2001, 5465 · *CSP Venice, 1202–1509*, 771, 776, 915, 918–20, 922, 929, 941; *1509–19*, 25, 30, 61, 64, 67, 251, 963, 1331; *1520–26*, 107n., 111, 1482, 1484, 1489 · *CSP Milan*, nos. 499, 525, 561, 584, 594 · *CEPR letters*, 15.375; 18.383; 19.1017, 1153, 1350, 1431 · M. Sanudo [M. Sanuto], *I diarii*, 87 vols. (Venice, 1879–1902), vol. 10, cols. 407, 413, 542; vol. 16, col. 449; vol. 29, col. 115 · *Fasti Angl., 1300–1541*, [Hereford], 20 · *Fasti Angl., 1300–1541*, [Salisbury], 45 · *Fasti Angl., 1300–1541*, [Monastic cathedrals], 62 · *Fasti Angl., 1300–1541*, [St Paul's, London], 34 · *Fasti Angl., 1300–1541*, [York], 29 · *Fasti Angl., 1300–1541*, [Bath and Wells], 40 · *Opus epistolarum Des. Erasmi Roterodami*, ed. P. S. Allen and others, 12 vols. (1906–58), vols. 1–2, nos. 262, 280, 282–3, 461 · *The correspondence of Erasmus*, ed. and trans. R. A. B. Mynors and others, 22 vols. (1974–94), nos. 262, 280, 282–3, 461 · *Collected works of Erasmus*, ed. W. K. Ferguson and others, [86 vols.] (1974–), vols. 85, 86; no. 35 · St Thomas More, *Latin poems*, ed. C. H. Miller and others (1984), vol. 3/2 of *The Yale edition of the complete works of St Thomas More*, no. 147 · M. Firpo, 'Carmeliano, Pietro', *Dizionario biografico degli Italiani*, ed. A. M. Ghisalberti, 20 (Rome, 1977), 410–413 · G. Tournoy, 'Carmeliano', *Contemporaries of Erasmus: a biographical register*, ed. P. G. Bietenholz, 1 (1985), 270–71 · D. R. Carlson, *English humanist books: writers and patrons, manuscript and print, 1475–1525* (Toronto &c, 1993), 37–59, appxs 3, 5; and articles by Carlson listed in his bibliography · A. Modigliani, 'Un nuovo manoscritto di Pietro Carmeliano: le *Epistolae* dello pseudo-Falaride nella Trinity College Library di Dublino', *Humanistica Lovaniensia*, 33 (1984), 86–102 · R. Gaguin, *Epistole et orationes*, ed. L. Thuasne (Paris, 1903–4), 1.84; 2.258 · P. Guerrini, 'Pietro Carmeliano da Brescia segretario reale d'Inghilterra', *Brixia Sacra*, 9 (1918), 33–40 · *Emden, Oxf.*, 1.358–9 · F. B. Williams, *Index of dedications and commendatory verses in English books before 1641* (1962) · R. Weiss, *Humanism in England during the fifteenth century*, 3rd edn (1967), 169–72 · W. Nelson, *John Skelton, laureate* (New York, 1939); repr. (1964)

Archives Biblioteca Nazionale Marciana, Venice, Sanuto diaries · BL, Add. MS 24844, fol. 64 · BL, Cotton MS Faustina B. VIII, 5v (death) · BL, Egerton MS 616, fol. 4 · BL, Harley MS 1757, fol. 361v · Morgan L., letters to Sforza

Carmichael, Alexander (1832–1912), folklorist, was born on 1 December 1832 and baptized on 8 December on the island of Lismore, in western Argyllshire; his parents were Hugh Carmichael and his wife, Betty, *née* MacColl. The Carmichaels were a family of long standing in Lismore, and an earlier Bishop Carmichael, known as An t-Easbaig Bàn ('the fair-haired bishop'), is referred to as a remote relative. Carmichael entered the civil service, and worked in the customs and excise division, with periods of service in Greenock, Dublin, Islay, Cornwall, Skye, Uist, Oban, Uist again, and finally Edinburgh.

Carmichael seems to have been deeply interested in collecting Gaelic lore from his early years, and he continued to make collecting expeditions well into his seventies. Several of his main working locations provided excellent opportunities for his collecting, and he made expeditions to other Gaelic areas (such as Lewis and Sutherland). He married Mary Frances MacBean (*b*. 1841) on 13 January 1868, and they lived on South Uist in the outer isles until 1882, when they moved to Edinburgh. Mary Carmichael was greatly supportive of her husband's work, and contributed to the artistic presentation of his main work, *Carmina Gadelica*. She was not a Gaelic speaker but their children were.

During the family's Edinburgh years the Carmichael home was regarded as a centre of Gaelic-related activity, and Carmichael was widely admired by younger contemporaries such as the Revd Donald Lamont and the Revd Kenneth MacLeod, both well known for their Gaelic literary work. Part of MacLeod's vivid portrait of Carmichael may be quoted:

> Year in year out, for nearly sixty years, Dr Carmichael was on pilgrimage throughout Gaeldom. To many of us he seemed, both in temperament and in activity, as one of the Iona brethren re-born in the nineteenth century. His very appearance was suggestive of Iona: the stately and venerable figure undoubtedly was, while the Scots bonnet might easily be mistaken for a biretta, the shepherd's crook for a pastoral staff, and the long dark cloak half-concealing the kilt, for a monk's habit. (*Celtic Review*, October 1912)

Carmichael's daughter Elizabeth Catherine (Ella) [**Elizabeth Catherine Watson** (1870–1928)] was born on 9 August 1870 and played an important part in the Edinburgh Gaelic world, helping to found Gaelic societies and a Gaelic choir. Donald Lamont recalls her as a very attractive fellow student in the 1890s, and she acted as editor of the *Celtic Review* from 1904 to 1916. In 1906 she married William John *Watson, who became professor of Celtic at Edinburgh University; their son, James Carmichael Watson, succeeded his father in 1938, but was killed in 1942 during the Second World War. Ella herself died on 30 November 1928. The Carmichael dynasty in Edinburgh was a distinguished one, but all too brief.

It is notable that Alexander Carmichael contributed at an early stage to the collections of J. F. Campbell of Islay, including his *Popular Tales of the West Highlands* (1860–62) and his collection of heroic and Ossianic balladry, *Leabhar na Fèinne* (1872). He supplied Gaelic proverbs for Sheriff Nicolson's collection (1881) and contributed several papers to the *Transactions of the Society of Antiquaries of Scotland* (with drawings by Mary Carmichael). For W. F. Skene's *Celtic Scotland* he wrote a chapter on old highland land customs, and was later asked to write a more elaborate paper for the crofter royal commission report. He contributed frequently to periodicals and papers such as *An Gaidheal*, *The Highlander*, the *Celtic Review*, and the *Inverness Courier*. Alexander Carmichael died at his home, 15 Barnton Terrace, Edinburgh, on 6 June 1912, and was buried on Lismore.

Carmichael's overwhelming achievement was the collection of material which resulted in the volumes of *Carmina Gadelica*. The central core of this work is an extensive collection of runes, prayers, invocations, work songs, and so on, which touch on virtually all aspects of Gaelic communal and private life. Some aspects of that life were, of course, affected, undermined, or lost before Carmichael's time, but his patient and intimate searches often brought him into contact with some of the last repositories of ancient tradition, especially in the outer isles. This body of lore had many different aspects and sources. Some of it was securely embedded in Christian belief, often related to the early Celtic church and its saints; other items have a pagan resonance, and many grew out of the natural habitat, with its flowers, herbs, animals, weather, and seasonal changes. A short summary of the categories of the collection gives some idea of its range and flavour: prayers; seasonal hymns; addresses to the saints; blessings for household or other tasks, such as reaping, milking, and herding; incantations or charms to cure ailments such as toothache, jaundice, and indigestion; prayers to the sun and moon; blessings on stock; and waulking songs.

Only a very small number of these verses have ascribed authors, but it is clear from internal evidence that they originated in different parts of Gaelic Scotland, and were of both oral and literary origin. Some were presumably composed by clerics, and many by ordinary members of the community. A number of the hymns are Gaelic versions of well-known Catholic hymns. It is likely that some of the pieces had their origins in the middle ages and probably earlier. The highest rate of survival seems to have been in Catholic communities which in Carmichael's day still retained an undiluted Gaelic ethos.

The first two volumes of *Carmina Gadelica* appeared in 1900, with translations and annotations by Alexander Carmichael. They have a high incidence of unusual words and expressions, and some of the translations are guesswork. There is also some suspicion that the Gaelic texts were over-edited by Carmichael, and supplemented where there were gaps. These two volumes were reissued in 1928, with some light editing by Ella Carmichael, and volumes 3 and 4 appeared in 1940–41, edited by J. C. Watson, the collector's grandson. Volume 5, consisting of songs rather than runes and prayers, appeared in 1954 and was edited by Angus Matheson, who also edited volume 6 (1971), consisting mainly of glossaries and indexes. In 1992 a volume was published that consisted of the translations only, with an informative preface by John Macinnes. In the later part of the twentieth century the translated versions developed a cult following.

Soon after the publication of the first two volumes suspicions arose that Carmichael, evidently an admirer of James MacPherson's Ossianic work, was prone to polishing and perhaps romanticizing some of the *Carmina*. In 1976 Hamish Robertson published 'Studies in Carmichael's *Carmina Gadelica*' in *Scottish Gaelic Studies*, volume 12. This exposes some of Carmichael's dubious practices, and suggests that Watson was less rigorous than might have been expected in dealing with this problem. John L. Campbell, in an article in the same journal (vol. 13, 1978), rebuts some of Robertson's criticism, and John Macinnes gives his assessment in his preface to the 1992 edition. In sum, there appears to have been interference with both Gaelic texts and translations, but this does not seem to undermine crucially the wide-ranging and fascinating collection of verse lore which Carmichael rescued in the final decades of its secure existence.

DERICK S. THOMSON

Sources *Celtic Review*, 8 (1912–13), 112–29 · J. Macinnes, preface, *Charms of the Gaels: hymns and incantations / Ortha nan Gaidheal: urnan agus ubagan*, trans. A. Carmichael (1992) · H. Robertson, 'Studies in Carmichael's *Carmina Gadelica*', *Scottish Gaelic Studies*, 12/2 (1976) · J. L. Campbell, 'Studies in Carmichael's *Carmina Gadelica*', *Scottish Gaelic Studies*, 13/1 (1978) · baptism cert. · b. cert. [Elizabeth Catherine Watson] · d. cert. · d. cert. [Elizabeth Catherine Watson]
Archives NL Scot., J. F. Campbell of Islay MSS
Likenesses photograph, repro. in *Celtic Review* (Oct 1912)
Wealth at death £531 17s. 6d.: confirmation, 25 Nov 1912, CGPLA Eng. & Wales

Carmichael, Amy Beatrice (1867–1951), missionary, was born on 16 December 1867 in Millisle, co. Down, Ireland, the daughter of prosperous middle-class Presbyterian parents, David Carmichael (*d.* 1885), flour miller, and his wife, Catherine Jane Filson (*d.* 1913). She received her education from a succession of governesses, Marlborough House, Harrogate—a Wesleyan Methodist boarding-school in Yorkshire—and at Victoria College, Belfast. However, a financial crisis in the family business and the death of her father in April 1885 put an end to her academic prospects.

Religion played an important part in the Carmichael family household, and from an early age Amy became involved in both spiritual and practical work in Belfast, holding prayer and Bible meetings for neighbourhood children and schoolfriends. She organized classes for the mill girls of Belfast which were so successful that a new hall was built to accommodate them. The Welcome, as it became known, was a lively and innovative centre of evangelistic endeavour. In 1889 both she and her mother were invited to Manchester to work for the city mission there, but ill health brought Amy's part in this endeavour to a speedy conclusion. At this stage Robert Wilson, a Quaker and co-founder of the Keswick Convention, became a major influence in her life. It was while staying at his home in Cumberland, deeply engaged with the religious work of her host, that Amy received the 'call' to missionary work.

Carmichael arrived in south India in 1895, via Japan and Ceylon, sustained always by the certainty of a divine purpose guiding her life, and, like so many evangelists of the period, believed that her religious mission transcended denominational labels. At first attached to the Church of England Zenana Mission, she later joined forces with a Church Missionary Society missionary, and, forming her own band of sisters, spent a total of seven years itinerating in the Tinnevelly district, before settling in Dohnavur, Tinnevelly district, south India, which was to be her home until the end of her life.

A central concern of the Christian community which Carmichael established there was the fate of young girls (*devadasis*), ceremonially married to the deity in the temple, an ancient ritual which seems to have degenerated into prostitution. These girls and, from 1918, boys, who were vulnerable to exploitation, were a central focus of her mission which provided such children with a Christian home, and education and training which would equip them for adult life. The settlement gradually expanded, with outposts in the village, nurseries, schools, a hospital, and a house of prayer added as needed; within forty years the community at Dohnavur numbered more than 600. Despite growing numbers, however, the pattern of life was that of a family, not an institution, with the evangelists sharing in the practical work of teaching, doctoring, nursing, engineering, and farming. Financially too, the institutional approach was rejected; no fundraising appeals were launched or authorized, instead 'Indian and European, men and women, live and work together … each contributing what each has for the help of all' (Carmichael, *Gold by Moonlight*, 183).

Amy was a prolific writer, particularly after a fall in 1931 which severely restricted her movement. She published thirty-eight books in the course of her life, mostly on the work at Dohnavur. Her books, frequently reprinted and translated into many languages, were important, not only in spreading the word about the work at Dohnavur, but in inspiring and influencing later generations of young Christians. Passionately committed, and unconventional

by any standards, the intensity of her faith and her frankness about the difficulties of missionary work in India often attracted the hostility of other Europeans, as did her behaviour. She adopted Indian dress, for example, and insisted that those who worked at Dohnavur would do so without expectation of a salary since no appeals for money were ever made, except through prayer. Knowledge of her work was spreading, however, and others were more appreciative of the Dohnavur initiative. In 1919 she was awarded the kaisar-i-Hind medal for services to the people of India. A greater cause for celebration was the passing of the 1947 act of the Madras state parliament which made it illegal to dedicate young girls to temple service—a cause given wide publicity by Amy's intervention and in works such as *Lotus Buds* (1909) and *Things as They Are* (1903).

In 1927 the Dohnavur Fellowship was legally established as an independent body, thus ending the loose association with the Church of England Zenana Mission, already diluted as workers joined from a variety of countries and backgrounds. The ethos of Amy Carmichael's mission was by then quite unique. The celebration of 'coming days' (when a new child arrived at the community), the 'meetings of vision' between Christmas and the new year, and the triumphant funeral processions clearly bear the imprint of its founder, in particular her close knowledge of the local way of life and her love of nature. An abundance of flowers, the study of birds and insects, and a great deal of singing seem to have been the hallmarks of a community deeply concerned with the happiness and well-being of children, although the founder herself always maintained a strict discipline. Perhaps the greatest testimony to her leadership, however, is the fact that the community survived both the ending of British rule in India and her own death in 1951. Continuity was ensured by adapting both the ethos and the work of Dohnavur to the India of the late twentieth century, and although the fellowship members are now all of Indian nationality, the work still continues today. Amy Carmichael died at Dohnavur on 18 January 1951, and was buried there the same day.   MYRTLE HILL

Sources F. L. Houghton, *Amy Carmichael of Dohnavur* (1992) · E. Elliot, *The life and legacy of Amy Carmichael* (1987) · M. Wilkinson, *At BBC corner: I remember Amy Carmichael* (1996) · A. Carmichael, *Gold cord* (1932) · A. Carmichael, *Lotus buds* (1909) · A. Carmichael, *Gold by moonlight* (1935), 183

Archives PRO NIre., D 4061 | Dohnavur Fellowship, 15 Elm Drive, North Harrow, Middlesex · Dohnavur Fellowship, Tirunelveli district, Tamil Nadu, India

Likenesses photographs, repro. in Elliot, *Life and legacy of Amy Carmichael* · photographs, PRO NIre., family papers, D4061

Carmichael, Frederick (1708–1751), Church of Scotland minister, was the son of Gershom *Carmichael (1672–1729), professor of moral philosophy at the University of Glasgow, and his wife, Christian Ingles. He attended Glasgow University, graduating MA on 4 May 1725. In 1727 an acrimonious rectorial election rendered Andrew Ross, professor of humanity, *non compos mentis*. In his absence Carmichael taught the Latin class. Following his father's death in 1729 Carmichael contested the chair of moral philosophy but Francis Hutcheson of Dublin was appointed by a majority of one vote. Entering the ministry of the Church of Scotland, Carmichael was licensed by Glasgow presbytery in September 1733. On 31 March 1737 he was ordained to Monimail in Fife and translated to Inveresk on 15 April 1741, being succeeded in Monimail by his brother Gershom. Another brother, Patrick, was a Dutch army surgeon and later a Glasgow physician. Carmichael's presentation to Inveresk by his patron the duke of Buccleuch was deeply unpopular. Among their grievances the kirk session complained he 'has so weak a voice that some of our number who attended when he preacht at Prestonpans' Kirk could not hear him, although they were not at the greatest distance from the pulpit' (Stirling, 170). On 7 August 1743 he married Isobel (d. 1790), daughter of John Lauder, surgeon. In November of the following year Carmichael declined the chair of divinity at Marischal College, Aberdeen, and moved to New Greyfriars, Edinburgh, in December 1747. He died at New Greyfriars on 17 October 1751, after which there appeared posthumous publications of his sermon 'Christian zeal' and a collection of *Sermons on Several Important Subjects* (both 1753).

STUART W. MᶜDONALD

Sources *Fasti Scot.*, new edn · R. McD. Stirling, *Inveresk parish lore* (1894) · C. Innes, ed., *Munimenta alme Universitatis Glasguensis / Records of the University of Glasgow from its foundation till 1727*, 4 vols., Maitland Club, 72 (1854) · Watt, *Bibl. Brit.* · D. Murray, *Memories of the old college of Glasgow: some chapters in the history of the university* (1927) · R. Wodrow, *Analecta, or, Materials for a history of remarkable providences, mostly relating to Scotch ministers and Christians*, ed. [M. Leishman], 4 vols., Maitland Club, 60 (1842–3) · *The autobiography of Dr Alexander Carlyle of Inveresk, 1722–1805*, ed. J. H. Burton (1910) · J. Coutts, *A history of the University of Glasgow* (1909) · J. D. Mackie, *The University of Glasgow, 1451–1951: a short history* (1954) · W. R. Scott, *Francis Hutcheson: his life, teaching and position in the history of philosophy* (1900)

Carmichael, Gershom (1672–1729), philosopher, was born in London, the son of Alexander Carmichael (d. 1677), a Scottish presbyterian clergyman who had been deprived of his church in Scotland (at Pittenain) 'for keeping of conventicles' (*Reg. PCS*, 3.464, 22 Feb 1672). Alexander Carmichael was transported to England where he was the first minister of the Founders' Hall congregation of Scottish presbyterians in London. He was the author of *Believers mortification of sin by the spirit or gospel—holiness advanced by the power of the Holy Ghost* (1677). Gershom Carmichael's mother, Christian (d. 1694/5), was the daughter of John Inglis, minister of Hamilton. She subsequently married the noted Scottish theologian James Fraser of Brae.

Gershom Carmichael enrolled at the University of Edinburgh in 1687 and graduated MA in 1691. He was appointed regent of humanity at St Andrews in March 1693 and resigned in October of the same year to obtain an MA from Glasgow, where he was appointed regent in 1694. On 19 September 1695 he married Christian Ingles; they had six sons. Carmichael remained regent or professor of philosophy at Glasgow until the termination of the regenting system in 1727. He was then elected the first professor of moral philosophy at the University of Glasgow.

As a regent Carmichael was responsible for teaching all parts of the philosophy curriculum: logic, metaphysics, moral philosophy, and natural philosophy. His publications derive from the lectures or dictates given to his students: a short introduction to logic, *Breviuscula introductio ad logicam* (1720, 1722), which was designed as a commentary on the Port Royal logic or *The Art of Thinking*; a succinct exposition of Reformed theology, *Synopsis theologiae naturalis* (1729), written to supplement and in part replace the texts he assigned students in metaphysics, the ontology and pneumatology of the Dutch metaphysician, Gerard de Vries; and his most important publication, an extended commentary on Samuel Pufendorf's work on the duty of man and citizen, *S[amuelis] Pufendorfii de officio hominis et civis juxta legem naturalem, libri duo. Supplementis et observationibus in academicae juventutis usum auxit et illustravit Gerschomus Carmichael* (1724; first edn, 1718). Carmichael's edition of Pufendorf's work was highly regarded by jurists and moral philosophers in Europe: Jean Barbeyrac, professor of law in Groningen, acknowledged his debt to Carmichael in many passages of his translations and commentaries on the writings of Grotius, Pufendorf, and Cumberland; Everard Otto, professor of law in Utrecht, described Carmichael as a man worthy of esteem by all students of natural jurisprudence. In Scotland, Francis Hutcheson, Carmichael's successor as professor of moral philosophy in Glasgow, judged his commentary on Pufendorf's work to be 'of much more value than the text' (*A Short Introduction to Moral Philosophy*, 1747, i).

Carmichael's moral philosophy was remarkable particularly for its emphasis upon the natural rights of mankind. He argued (against Samuel Pufendorf, but in agreement with Hugo Grotius and John Locke) that every individual has a right of self-defence. He insisted (again, against Pufendorf and more unequivocally than Locke) that no man has the right to enslave another, 'for men are not among the objects which God has allowed the human race to enjoy dominion over'. He defended the theory of all the early modern natural jurists, that civil or political societies have their beginnings in an original contract, a theory which appealed to post-revolutionary Scottish thinkers, inasmuch as it excluded any claim to political power on the grounds of hereditary right. He believed that the liberty of the Scottish people had been secured by the limitations insisted on in the treaty of union and by the accession of the house of Hanover.

Carmichael justified the natural rights of men and citizens on grounds consistent with his natural theology in which all men long for beatitude or a lasting happiness that can be found only in reverence for or veneration of God. Such reverence may be expressed directly (but also indirectly) in respect for God's creation and, more specifically, in self-respect and respect for others. And he held that there was no more appropriate way of signifying respect for persons than to acknowledge that every individual enjoys certain natural rights. His theory of moral motivation, while consistent with Reformed scholastic theology, presented problems for his successors—Francis Hutcheson, Adam Smith, and Thomas Reid, among others. In their disagreements with Carmichael and with one another they generated those fruitful speculations concerning the moral experience of men in society that have come to be called the Scottish Enlightenment.

Carmichael's career at the University of Glasgow was characterized by intermittent controversy. Robert Wodrow, who had been his student in the 1690s and who remained his friend, described him as 'a little warm in his temper, but a most affectionate, friendly man' (Wodrow, 4.95–6). Carmichael was inclined to be impatient with colleagues who continued to teach in accordance with the principles of scholastic Aristotelianism: 'foolish Gershom spues out much venom against me', his fellow regent, John Tran, complained to the principal, John Stirling (letter, 27 March 1704, Glasgow University Library Gen MS 205, 67). He opposed the autocratic style of the principal on different occasions. He was suspended from teaching in 1704, for protesting against the principal's administration of the finances of the university. The suspension was rescinded following interventions on his behalf by the duchess of Hamilton, the duke of Montrose, and others. In 1717 Carmichael and other masters objected to the annual renewal of the rector by the principal and faculty without vote by the students as the statutes of the university required ('Memorial for the scholars and other matriculated members of the University of Glasgow', 21 Dec 1717, NL Scot., Pamph. 1.10, 142). Their initiative failed, although the right of the students to elect the rector was confirmed by a commission of visitation in 1727. It was the termination of the regenting system by the same commission that led to the establishment of the chair in moral philosophy which Carmichael held for only two years before his death, in his house in the college of Glasgow, on 26 November 1729.

Of Carmichael's sons, Alexander graduated MA in 1716 and was licensed university printer in 1730; James enrolled in the university in 1712 and was later appointed to administer his father's estate; and John graduated MA in 1718 and was King William's bursar in theology. Frederick *Carmichael taught the humanity class at the university (1726–8) during the illness of Professor Andrew Ross; he was then a candidate for his father's chair in moral philosophy but was defeated in a very close vote by Francis Hutcheson. Gershom, MA in 1733, was librarian at the university in 1737–9 and was subsequently minister at Monomail and South Church, Dundee; he also studied at the University of Leiden. Patrick, an army surgeon in the Dutch service before returning to Scotland, is described by Dugald Stewart as 'a younger son of Professor Gershom Carmichael … who, after a long residence in Holland, where he practised medicine, retired to Glasgow'; he married the daughter of Thomas Reid.

Gershom Carmichael died intestate. A 'testament dative' was 'faithfully made and drawn up by James Carmichael, son lawfull and Exec. dative qua nearest in kin decerned to the defunct by decret of the Commissar(y) of Glasgow' (NA Scot., CC 9/7/53, 2 June 1730). The testament dative records sums of money owing to the estate by the university; the total of these sums of money is reckoned

£54 8s. 6d. The commissary of Glasgow later recorded the amount of £444 8s. 10d. made out in favour of Elizabeth Stewart, relict of John Inglis (his wife's mother) in her lifetime and to Professor Gershom Carmichael. The bond is dated 14 February 1727. Again James Carmichael is 'decerned' to be executor dative and Alexander Carmichael signs as caution or surety for his brother James.

JAMES MOORE and MICHAEL SILVERTHORNE

Sources R. Wodrow, *Analecta, or, Materials for a history of remarkable providences, mostly relating to Scotch ministers and Christians*, ed. [M. Leishman], 4 vols., Maitland Club, 60 (1842–3) · *Fasti Scot.*, new edn · C. Innes, ed., *Munimenta alme Universitatis Glasguensis / Records of the University of Glasgow from its foundation till 1727*, 4 vols., Maitland Club, 72 (1854) · [G. Carmichael], *Natural rights on the threshold of the Scottish Enlightenment: the writings of Gershom Carmichael*, ed. J. Moore, ed. and trans. M. Silverthorne (2002) · J. Moore and M. Silverthorne, 'Gershom Carmichael and the natural jurisprudence tradition in eighteenth century Scotland', *Wealth and virtue: the shaping of political economy in the Scottish Enlightenment*, ed. I. Hont and M. Ignatieff (1983), 73–87 · J. Coutts, *A history of the University of Glasgow* (1909), 197–209 · D. Murray, *Memories of the old college of Glasgow* (1927), 506–8 · D. Stewart, 'Account of the life and writings of Thomas Reid', in *The works of Thomas Reid*, ed. W. Hamilton, 7th edn, 1 (1872) · U. Glas. L., MSS Gen 205; Murray 650 · U. Glas., 47390, 26635 · NA Scot., CC/9/7/53; CC/9/7/54 · *Reg. PCS*, 3rd ser., 3.464 · parish register, county of Lanark, Mitchell L., Glas., Glasgow City Archives, OPR 644/24 · D. Murray, *Robert and Andrew Foulis and the Glasgow press* (1913) · 'Memorial for the scholars and other matriculated members of the University of Glasgow', 21 Dec 1717, NL Scot., pamphlet 1.10, 142 · D. Murray, 'Notes on Glasgow', 1864, U. Glas. L., special collections department, David Murray collection, 2075, 832–7 · *Transactions of the Historic Society of Lancashire and Cheshire*, 36 (1884), 15–32 · D. Laing, ed., *A catalogue of the graduates … of the University of Edinburgh*, Bannatyne Club, 106 (1858) · G. du Rieu, ed., *Album studiosorum academiae Lugduno Batavae, MDLXXV–MDCCCLXXV: accedunt nomina curatorum et professorum per eadem secula* (The Hague, 1875)
Archives Mitchell L., Glas., annotations on Port Royal logic, Glasgow MS 90 · U. Glas., Archives and Business Records Centre, account of his teaching, 43170 · U. Glas. L., 2075 · U. Glas. L., letters, MS Gen 204, 205 · U. Glas. L., letters, Murray MS, 650 | NA Scot., records of money owing to him, CC/9/7/53; CC/9/7/54 · U. Glas., Archives and Business Records Centre, minutes of meetings of the faculty, 26630–26635 · U. Glas., Archives and Business Records Centre, 27038 · U. Glas., Archives and Business Records Centre, 27140
Wealth at death £54 8s. 6d. owed to him by University of Glasgow; bond of £444 8s. 10d. made out in favour of his mother-in-law, in her lifetime, and Gershom Carmichael assigned to James Carmichael: NA Scot., CC/9/7/53; CC/9/7/54; U. Glas., special collections, 2075, 834

Carmichael, James (1542/3–1628), Church of Scotland minister and scholar, is first recorded as matriculating in the University of St Andrews as a student in St Leonard's College in the session 1560–61. Of his parents and earlier education nothing is known. Among his contemporaries in the university were Andrew Melville and James Lawson, with whom his life was later to be intimately connected. It may reasonably be conjectured that Carmichael graduated MA in 1564. Subsequently he became master of the grammar school of St Andrews, a position which he held until the summer of 1570. In the latter year Carmichael and some of his colleagues at St Leonard's became involved in a controversy with the minister of the town, Robert Hamilton, whom they accused of failing to speak out against the assassins of the earl of Moray. The dispute escalated to the extent of reaching the general assembly of the kirk and coming under the consideration of the crown's legal officers. But by this time arrangements for Carmichael's translation to Haddington were well advanced, and consequently the matter seems to have been allowed to lapse.

Early ministry On 25 August 1570 Carmichael entered upon his ministry in Haddington, which, apart from some three years spent in exile in England between 1584 and 1587, extended to almost sixty years. Within two years of his induction the magistrates and town council appointed him burgh schoolmaster, a post he held until November 1576. In 1575 the privy council decided that one form of Latin grammar should be taught in all schools and that that form should be agreed by common consent. It is indicative of Carmichael's academic standing that he was one of the six scholars invited to give their advice.

From the outset of his ministry in Haddington, Carmichael took a 'somewhat prominent share in various matters connected with the Church and with general literature' (Laing, *Miscellany*, 412). He was one of the ministers who attended the convention of Leith in January 1572, and during the following decade regularly attended meetings of the general assembly and was frequently appointed to serve on its commissions. He was behind the recommendation that the acts of assemblies be extracted from the records and a copy given to every presbytery to guide it in decision making. He was likewise a natural choice to carry out this work. About the same time he was appointed to oversee the printing and publishing of the Bible in English, proposed by Alexander Arbuthnot and Thomas Bassandyne.

After the assembly had completed its work on the *Second Book of Discipline*, Carmichael was one of those appointed to examine and 'revise … according to the originall' the copy which was to be presented to the regent (Thomson, 1.398). Among the earliest known individual copies of the *Second Book of Discipline* still extant are two preserved among the state papers in the Public Record Office, London; both are recorded as 'Maister James Carmichels Booke' (Kirk, *Second Book*, 154). Not only was Carmichael a diligent member of general assemblies, he also kept his own record of their proceedings. David Calderwood in his *History of the Kirk of Scotland* acknowledges that where the register he used had pages 'reavin out', he was able to discover the missing material from the 'observations' of Carmichael (Calderwood, 3.475). In 1581 the assembly appointed Carmichael a commissioner for establishing presbyteries, and in the following year he played a part in the church's opposition to the crown's nomination of Robert Montgomery, minister of Stirling, to be archbishop of Glasgow.

Exile in England In February 1584 Andrew Melville, charged with sedition and fearing for his life, fled the country and sought refuge in England. It is not surprising that Carmichael, as one of his associates and an active supporter of the presbyterian polity, should have followed him into exile. Arrangements for their reception in London were facilitated by Sir Francis Walsingham, the secretary of state. Soon after the exiled ministers had arrived in London they were sent for by Walsingham, with whom Carmichael subsequently had regular meetings. On one occasion Carmichael presented to him 'the buik', which, Laing considered, set out 'the charges brought against the Duke of Lennox and the Earl of Arran in 1585' (Laing, *Miscellany*, 412). Its text, entitled 'Notes Proving that the Duke of Lennox and Arran', was incorporated by Calderwood in his *History of the Kirk* (4.393–448).

Walsingham reacted favourably to much of the contents of 'the buik', and promised to help in its completion. Now the apologist for the presbyterian cause, Carmichael was bent on having his work printed, and to this end requested through English diplomatic channels that John Craig, the king's chaplain, be urged to send him 'the last collection of the discipline and actis of the Generall Assemblies' (*CSP Scot.*, 1584–5, 225). He also wanted to have the history of events since 1579 written by his friend and former colleague David Hume of Godscroft, which formed the first part of the latter's *History of the Houses of Douglas and Angus* (1644), and also 'Mr Knoxes historie' and the secret acts of the last parliament. How far William Davison, the English ambassador in Scotland, was able to fulfil these requests is not easy to judge, but it may be that the two copies of the *Second Book of Discipline* preserved among the English state papers furnish evidence for his co-operation.

Carmichael at this time was also acting to further the cause of the exiled ministers on the continent. In a letter to the earl of Angus, he informed him that the ministers in London had written 'ane common letter, subscryvit with our hands' to the churches in Geneva and to Zürich (Laing, *Miscellany*, 416). The original Latin autographs, preserved in both cities and dated 1 July 1584, confirm that it was a common letter and that the exiled ministers, who had now been joined by James Lawson, had all signed it, including Carmichael. It gives a detailed account of recent events in Scotland, paying particular attention to the part played in them by Patrick Adamson, archbishop of St Andrews, and to his recent letters to the church in Zürich defending events in Scotland. This accounts for the letter sent to Zürich being much longer than that sent to Geneva. It may be reasonably conjectured that Carmichael played a significant part in the composition of this letter. In the late summer of 1584 Carmichael probably accompanied Melville and Lawson on a visit to the universities of Oxford and Cambridge. Soon after they had returned to London, Lawson took ill and died, on 12 October. His will, written out by Carmichael at Lawson's request, and witnessed by him, also named him as one of the executors. Along with Melville and others he was made responsible for revising Lawson's 'writts, bookes, and papers' (Calderwood, 4.207).

In January 1586 the changed political and ecclesiastical situation brought about by the fall from power of the earl of Arran in the previous November allowed some of the exiled ministers, among them Andrew Melville, to return home. Carmichael's reasons for remaining in London are not known. He may have done so in order to negotiate on behalf of the church in Scotland, but it is also possible that he hoped to advance the cause of his presbyterian brethren in England and abroad, and that he was still collecting material to discredit the Scottish king and the previous government. Carmichael probably remained in England until late in 1587, spending much of that time in London. He was also seeing through the press his *Grammaticae Latinae, de etymologia, liber secundus*, which was published by the press of the Cambridge University printer, Thomas Thomas, in 1587. The dedication to James VI was dated at Cambridge that September. This work may be regarded as Carmichael's contribution to the Latin grammar that the Scottish privy council had proposed in 1575. It is a Latin–Scots grammar and contains, after the manner of the day, a number of congratulatory verses addressed to the author by his friends. Several copies survive in English and Scottish libraries.

Church historian The Act of Indemnity passed by the Scottish parliament on 29 July 1587 enabled the exiled ministers still in England to return to their charges, and by December, Haddington had welcomed home its minister. From 1588 until his death Carmichael played a continuously significant role in the affairs of the church. He was one of the ministers appointed to hear the earl of Morton's confession. He was intimately involved in the trial of witches, and is said to have compiled a history of their depositions. General assemblies regularly appointed him to undertake specific responsibilities. In 1589 he was appointed a judge and commissioner in ecclesiastical causes, while in July 1591 he was on a commission to examine a work by Robert Bruce and decide on its suitability for publication.

Particularly important to Carmichael was the decision taken by the general assembly in June 1595, that 'the acts of Assembly be sighted, and speciallie acts serving for practise be extracted, and joyned with the Booke of Discipline, to be published ather in writt or in print, that none pretend ignorance' (Thomson, 3.856). Following the assembly's similar decision in 1575 Carmichael had now been at work on this for twenty years, while from 1592 he was more than once requested by lower ecclesiastical courts to 'put an end to his travellis begun by him in collecting the actis of generall assemblies' (Kirk, *Records*, 47). He was even suspended from his ministry for a while for spending so much time on this project to the neglect of his parochial responsibilities. Undeterred, in April 1595 Carmichael presented to the synod the 'twa warkis' which he had completed. He was then encouraged to do all in his power to 'perfyte the haill wark' before the next meeting (ibid., 89), but had not done so by the following October, when two fellow ministers were appointed to assist him. Carmichael's compilation of the acts of assembly from 1560 to 1597 now forms manuscript 227 in Aberdeen University Library. Carmichael's reputation as one of the

ablest literary apologists of the church was further demonstrated in 1596 by his appointment with another minister to collect 'all the conferences, acts of counsell and parliament past in favour of the kirk, and libertie and discipline thereof' (Calderwood, 5.453).

Last years In the years immediately following King James's departure to England in 1603, Carmichael continued to take a significant part with his fellow ministers in their attempts to assert the freedom of assemblies. In 1606 he returned to London with Andrew Melville, and played his part in setting forth a defence of the presbyterian polity in opposition to the royal policy towards the church. In the following year, however, his wife's illness led to his being allowed to return to Scotland, and there he continued to be recognized as one who would maintain— as he did in 1610—that nothing prejudicial to the acts of former assemblies should be countenanced. Nevertheless, at the age of sixty-seven his resolve seems to have begun to weaken, so that he showed signs of unwilling compliance with the king's policy. A slight moderation in his presbyterian stance may be detected in his acceptance of appointment as constant moderator of the presbytery of Haddington (an office created to increase the crown's control of the church) in 1606. Even so he continued to uphold the freedom of the church and wished to see some restraint placed on the power of the newly appointed bishops.

That Carmichael's scholarship continued to be greatly respected is shown by his appointment in 1608 by the privy council to examine before publication the printer's proofs of Sir John Skene's edition of the fourteenth-century legal treatise *Regiam majestatem*, a task for which he was temporarily relieved of parochial responsibilities. It was published in the following year. A Latin poem printed at the end of this work demonstrates Carmichael's gifts in the field of neo-Latin poetry. At his death he also left a manuscript collection of proverbs in the Scottish vernacular. Now in Edinburgh University Library, it was published in 1957 in an edition by M. L. Anderson.

In 1611 Andrew Melville, who had at various times referred to Carmichael as 'the profound Dreamer' and 'our Corydon of Haddington', expressed in a letter from Sedan his deep respect for his old friend's scholarship, but regretted that he had not so far produced a work of scholarly significance (M'Crie, 324). Five years later Melville expressed similar views, and also enquired if Carmichael was still alive. In fact Carmichael lived until 1628, when he died between 28 May and 24 September, aged eighty-five. He had married at the time he entered on his ministry at Haddington. His wife, Violet Simson, who predeceased him, was the daughter of Andrew Simson, minister of Dalkeith, and he was therefore the brother-in-law of Archibald and Patrick Simson, two ardent presbyterian ministers. Their son James became minister at Athelstaneford, while their eldest daughter married Archibald Livingston, minister at Broughton.

A century after Carmichael's death the ecclesiastical historian Robert Wodrow wrote of him as 'a person of very great naturall and acquired abilities, a sufficient person for business; and a great strain of both piety and strong learning runs through his letters and papers' (Laing, *Miscellany*, 412). In more recent times, too, Carmichael has continued to be highly regarded, his twentieth-century editor describing him as 'talented, scholarly and highly educated' (Anderson, *Carmichael Collection*, 29).   JAMES K. CAMERON

Sources acta rectorum, U. St Andr., 2.74 · D. Calderwood, *The history of the Kirk of Scotland*, ed. T. Thomson and D. Laing, 8 vols., Wodrow Society, 7 (1842–9) · D. Laing, ed., *The miscellany of the Wodrow Society*, Wodrow Society, [9] (1844) · J. Kirk, *The Second Book of Discipline* (1980) · T. Thomson, ed., *Acts and proceedings of the general assemblies of the Kirk of Scotland*, 3 pts, Bannatyne Club, 81 (1839–45) · J. Kirk, ed., *The records of the synod of Lothian and Tweeddale, 1589–1596, 1640–1649*, Stair Society, 30 (1977) · M. L. Anderson, ed., *The James Carmichael collection of proverbs in Scots* (1957) · *The autobiography and diary of Mr James Melvill*, ed. R. Pitcairn, Wodrow Society (1842) · G. Donaldson, 'Scottish Presbyterian exiles in England, 1584–8', *Records of the Scottish Church History Society*, 14 (1960–62), 67–80 · T. M'Crie, *The life of Andrew Melville*, new edn (1856) · D. H. Fleming, ed., *Register of the minister, elders and deacons of the Christian congregation of St Andrews*, 1, Scottish History Society, 4 (1889) · J. M. Anderson, ed., *Early records of the University of St Andrews*, Scottish History Society, 3rd ser., 8 (1926) · J. Miller, *The lamp of Lothian, or, The history of Haddington* (1844) · *Fasti Scot.*, new edn, 1.369 · J. Kirk, 'The development of the Melvillian movement in late sixteenth century Scotland', PhD diss., U. Edin., 1972 · *Original letters relating to the ecclesiastical affairs of Scotland: chiefly written by … King James the Sixth*, ed. D. Laing, 2 vols., Bannatyne Club, 92 (1851) · *The memoirs of Sir James Melville of Halhill*, ed. G. Donaldson (1969) · T. M. Cooper, ed., *Regiam majestatem and Quoniam attachiamenta*, Stair Society, 11 (1947) · *Reg. PCS*, 1st ser., vols. 2–5 · *CSP Scot. ser.* · *CSP Scot.*, 1584–5 · J. Durkan, 'Education: the laying of fresh foundations', *Humanism in Renaissance Scotland*, ed. J. MacQueen (1990), 123–60
Archives U. Aberdeen · U. Edin.

Carmichael, James, first Lord Carmichael (1579–1672), judge and government official, was the third son of Walter Carmichael of Hyndford (d. 1625), and Grizel, daughter of Sir John Carmichael of Meadowflat. He was originally designated of Hyndford, but on purchasing the lands of Westeraw took his title from them, until, on succeeding his cousin Sir John Carmichael of Carmichael, he adopted the designation of the older branch of the family. As a youth he was introduced by the earl of Dunbar at the court of James VI, and moved to the household of Prince Charles in 1615. He was created a baronet of Nova Scotia on 17 July 1627, and the following year he subscribed the submission to Charles I.

Carmichael was appointed sheriff-principal of Lanarkshire on 5 September 1632, and in 1634 lord justice clerk, which office he resigned in 1636, on being made treasurer-depute. He has been described as a 'moderate' man 'anxious to avoid trouble, supporting neither the king nor his opponents with any vigour when the troubles began' in 1637 (Stevenson, *Scottish Revolution*, 54). He was admitted an ordinary lord of session on 6 March 1639 and was one of Charles I's commissioners to the parliament of 1639, prorogation of which led to the presentation of a remonstrance against the same as illegal. On 13 November 1641 he was named as one of the commissioners for executing the office of lord high treasurer, and was appointed treasurer-depute, privy councillor, and lord of session, to be held *ad vitam aut culpam*. For his services to Charles I during the civil war, especially in lending him money, he received a patent on 27 December 1647 raising him to the peerage as Lord Carmichael. This was not made public until 3 January 1651, when it was ratified by Charles II. For his adherence to the engagement Carmichael submitted to the presbytery of Lanark on 28 December, but was deprived of his offices by the Act of Classes on 16 March 1649, one of 'only three officers of state who had, by judicious trimming managed to remain in office' since before 1637 (Stevenson, *Revolution and Counter-Revolution*, 134). Charles I had requested Carmichael's presence to discuss the Scottish situation but the regime objected and instead sent his second son, Sir Daniel Carmichael, upon whom the office of treasurer-depute was bestowed. In 1654 Carmichael was fined £2000 by the Westminster parliament, but this was remitted in 1655. He was not, as sometimes stated, sworn of the privy council and reappointed lord justice clerk by Charles II, the latter office having been bestowed on Sir John Campbell of Lundy.

With his wife, Agnes, sixth daughter of John Wilkie of Foulden, whom he had married on 1 November 1603, Carmichael had three sons and four daughters. His eldest son, Sir William, after serving as one of the *gens d'armes* of Louis XIII, joined the committee of estates in Scotland, and commanded the Clydesdale regiment against the marquess of Montrose at the battle of Philiphaugh in 1646. He predeceased his father, dying in 1657, leaving a son, John *Carmichael, who became second Lord Carmichael and first earl of Hyndford. The first Lord Carmichael died on 29 December 1672, aged ninety-three.

T. F. HENDERSON, *rev.* ALAN R. MACDONALD

Sources *Scots peerage*, 4.583–8 · G. Brunton and D. Haig, *An historical account of the senators of the college of justice, from its institution in MDXXXII* (1832), 298–9 · G. V. Irving and A. Murray, *The upper ward of Lanarkshire described and delineated*, 2 (1864), 17–21 · *APS*, 1625–51 · D. Stevenson, *The Scottish revolution, 1637–44: the triumph of the covenanters* (1973) · D. Stevenson, *Revolution and counter-revolution in Scotland, 1644–1651*, Royal Historical Society Studies in History, 4 (1977)
Likenesses oils, Parliament Hall, Edinburgh

Carmichael, Sir John, of that ilk (c.1542–1600), administrator, was the eldest son of John Carmichael (d. c.1585) and Elizabeth, third daughter of Hugh Somerville, fourth Lord Somerville. By a contract dated 5 September 1561 he married Margaret, illegitimate daughter of James Douglas, fourth earl of Morton and later regent of Scotland. They had two sons, including Sir Hugh Carmichael, and two daughters. Sir John's early career was closely tied to his father-in-law, Morton. In 1566 he was among those summoned before the privy council to be questioned concerning the murder of David Riccio. He fought for Mary, queen of Scots, at the battle of Langside in 1568, but returned to the Douglas fold to fight on the king's side during the civil war of 1570–73. Once Morton became regent, Carmichael was given crown appointments and patronage. In 1581 he was convicted of treason for trying to aid

Morton, who had been executed in that year for complicity in killing the king's father. He was associated with the Ruthven raiders who seized King James VI in August 1582, and in 1584 was again convicted of treason and exiled for participating in the raid of Stirling. He took refuge in England.

After he was restored in November 1585 with the other banished lords Carmichael began to work directly for and with the crown. On 2 December 1585 he was appointed the king's master stabler. King James made use of his talents in a variety of areas. Carmichael's military skills were employed in August 1588, when he was made captain-general of the light horsemen being raised to defend the country against a possible Spanish invasion. In 1592 he was appointed captain of the king's guard to defend James against the earl of Bothwell. He was also employed on foreign missions. He accompanied the king to Norway in October 1589 to meet Anne of Denmark, the future queen, and was knighted at her coronation. In 1590 he was sent as an ambassador to England and was intermittently sent on English missions after this. He attended parliament in 1591, 1593, 1594, 1596, 1597, and 1598. In 1588 he was appointed a privy councillor, a position which he retained until his death. He was one of the most assiduous attenders of council meetings, especially during the period from 1592 to 1599 when he was not working on the borders.

It is, indeed, as a border official that Carmichael is best remembered. He began his career as keeper of Liddesdale from 1574 to 1580, during Morton's regency. On 7 July 1575 he was involved in the so-called 'raid of Reidswire', an outbreak of disorder at a day of truce on the border in which several people were killed and others taken prisoner. In January 1588 he was appointed to a border commission that dealt with outstanding grievances between England and Scotland. On 13 September 1588 he became warden of the west march, an office which he held until July 1592. On 18 September 1599 he was reappointed as west march warden, but the earl of Angus, who had been warden and continued as lieutenant of the borders, blocked the appointment by refusing to proclaim him. Carmichael was, however, appointed again, and this time effectively, on 15 December. His reputation as a border official, both among contemporaries like Lord Scrope, warden of the English west march, and among modern scholars like T. I. Rae, was that of an efficient and conscientious man. His effectiveness made him enemies, and following a conspiracy at a football match, Carmichael was murdered by a branch of the Armstrong clan on 16 June 1600, as he was riding from Annan to Langholm to attend a warden court. According to Scrope he was 'cruelly murdered … for his good service and agreeing with me to keep them in order' (Bain, 2.664). Several Armstrongs were executed for this murder over the next six years. Carmichael's wife survived him, and died in 1625. Nigel Tranter's novel *A Rage of Regents* (1996) is loosely based on Carmichael's early career.

MICHAEL WASSER

Sources *Scots peerage* · *Reg. PCS*, 1st ser., vols. 1–6 · J. Bain, ed., *The border papers: calendar of letters and papers relating to the affairs of the*

borders of England and Scotland, 2 vols. (1894–6) · T. I. Rae, *The administration of the Scottish frontier, 1513–1603* (1966) · *APS, 1567–1625*, index with suppl. · commissary court of Edinburgh, NA Scot., CC8/8/35; CC8/8/59 · *CSP Scot., 1589–93* · M. Wasser, 'The pacification of the Scottish borders, 1598–1612', MA diss., McGill University, 1986 · J. M. Thomson and others, eds., *Registrum magni sigilli regum Scotorum / The register of the great seal of Scotland*, 11 vols. (1882–1914), vols. 3–6 · M. Livingstone, D. Hay Fleming, and others, eds., *Registrum secreti sigilli regum Scotorum / The register of the privy seal of Scotland*, 2–8 (1921–82) · D. L. W. Tough, *The last years of a frontier* (1928)

Wealth at death £1810 13s. 4d. Scots—in moveable goods; excl. lands: NA Scot., CC8/8/35, 4 March 1601

Carmichael, John, first earl of Hyndford (1638–1710), politician, was born on 28 February 1638, the son of William Carmichael, master of Carmichael (d. 1657), and Lady Grizel, third daughter of William Douglas, first marquess of Douglas. He succeeded his grandfather James *Carmichael, first Lord Carmichael (1579–1672), on 29 December 1672. His name appears in a list of those present in the fourth session of Charles II's second parliament in November 1673, although his name is not recorded on the sederunt in the acts of the parliaments of Scotland. In May 1675 he was appointed a commissioner of excise for Lanarkshire, and in July 1678 was named as a commissioner of supply for the same shire—an office he would hold again in 1689, 1690, and 1704. However, his presbyterian sympathies undoubtedly explain his limited appearance in the public record before the revolution of 1688.

After the revolution Carmichael took a more active part in national affairs. He attended the convention of estates in March 1689, and was named as one of the committee for contraverted elections. He signed both the acts declaring the convention a lawful meeting of the estates, and the letter of congratulation addressed to King William. In April, as part of an act concerning the election of town councils in the royal burghs, he was appointed overseer of the municipal election in Lanark—an important office facilitating Williamite reforms in local government—and elected a member of the committee of estates, charged with governing the country in the interval between the convention becoming a parliament on King William's instruction. In May he was named as a member of the privy council, and in January 1690 was designated a commissioner for the office of lord privy seal. It would appear from correspondence of this period that he supported the court interest, joining the earl of Melville's party in opposition to Montgomerie of Skelmorlie's 'club', in the parliament from 1689 to 1690. Throughout William's reign Carmichael regularly attended both parliament and council, commanded the militia belonging to the Nether ward of Lanarkshire, was chancellor of the University of Glasgow from 1692, and a member of various parliamentary committees—most notably the committee for settling church government (May 1690), the committees for fines and forfeitures and for visiting schools and universities (both in July 1690), the committee for trade (1696), and the committee for the security of the kingdom (1693, 1695, 1698, 1700, and 1702). In September 1696, consistent with his former conduct, he subscribed the Association whose members pledged themselves to the defence of King William's person.

In October 1690 Carmichael was appointed William's commissioner to the general assembly of the Church of Scotland—an office he was to hold again in 1694 and 1699. In a letter from Sir James Dalrymple to the earl of Melville, dated 13 October, he states he was 'glade of the good chise his Majestie hath made of Carmichaell to be his Commissioner to this Assembly, who is acceptable to all so far as I can learne' (Melville, 545–6). In late 1691 or early 1692 he was offered the position of one of the secretaries of state. However, following a lengthy delay he declined the office, stating he was not capable of being a secretary. Nevertheless, on 31 January 1699 he accepted the office of joint secretary along with James Ogilvy, Viscount Seafield, and granted a pension of £1000. By a patent dated 5 June 1701 he was created earl of Hyndford, viscount of Inglisberry and Nemphlar, and Lord Carmichael of Carmichael, being granted a further pension of £400 in May 1702—undoubtedly as a reward for his loyal service.

On the accession of Queen Anne, Hyndford was sworn a privy councillor and continued in his office of secretary of state. He was named one of the commissioners for the treaty of union and, from the approval of the first article in November 1706, consistently registered his support for this venture. He had married Beatrix, the second daughter of David Drummond, third Lord Maderty, on 9 December 1669, with whom he had seven sons and three daughters. He died on 20 September 1710 and was succeeded by his eldest son, James, second earl of Hyndford.

DEREK JOHN PATRICK

Sources *Scots peerage* · G. V. Irving and A. Murray, *The upper ward of Lanarkshire described and delineated*, 2 (1864) · APS, 1670–86, 1689–1707 · *Reg. PCS*, 3rd ser., vols. 5–6, 8, 13–16 · N. Luttrell, *A brief historical relation of state affairs from September 1678 to April 1714*, 2–5 (1857) · W. H. L. Melville, ed., *Leven and Melville papers: letters and state papers chiefly addressed to George, earl of Melville … 1689–1691*, Bannatyne Club, 77 (1843) · P. W. J. Riley, *King William and the Scottish politicians* (1979)

Carmichael, John, third earl of Hyndford (1701–1767), diplomatist, son of James Carmichael, second earl of Hyndford (d. 1737), army officer, and Lady Elizabeth Maitland (1681/2–1753), only daughter of John Maitland, fifth earl of Lauderdale, was born at Edinburgh on 15 March 1701. He was styled Lord Carmichael from 1710 until he succeeded to his father's title and estates on 16 August 1737. He entered the 3rd regiment of foot guards, in which he became captain in 1733. In September 1732 he married Elizabeth (1692–1750), eldest daughter of Admiral Sir Cloudesley Shovell and widow of Robert Marsham, first Lord Romney; they had a son, Frederick, who died of smallpox in 1736.

First chosen as a representative peer on 14 March 1738, Hyndford sat again in 1741, 1747, 1754, and 1761, retaining that status until his death. Also in March 1738 he was appointed one of the lords of police, and on 9 April 1739 constituted sheriff-principal and lord lieutenant of Lanark. In 1739 and 1740 he acted as lord high commissioner to the general assembly of the Church of Scotland.

Following Frederick II's invasion of Silesia in 1741, Hyndford was sent by George II to Berlin to mediate between the Prussian king and the Austrian empress Maria Theresa. He was to arrange an alliance between Prussia, Austria, and the maritime powers that would safeguard the pragmatic sanction, satisfy Prussia's territorial interests, and maintain the balance of power on the continent. Shrewd and persistent, but still inexperienced, Hyndford managed to negotiate the convention of Klein-Schnellendorf, which temporarily reconciled Austria and Prussia without, however, pledging either party to a more permanent agreement. As a result, once the military tide turned in favour of France, Frederick II swiftly repudiated the convention and resumed hostilities against Austria. These continued until 1742, when unexpected Austrian successes forced Frederick to readjust his diplomatic strategy and reopen negotiations through Hyndford; this resulted in the treaty of Breslau, which was signed on 11 June 1742. The treaty, which detached Prussia from the coalition against Austria, was a major turning point in the war and a notable triumph for British diplomacy.

On the conclusion of the treaty Hyndford was nominated a knight of the Thistle, and on 29 August 1742 was invested with the insignia of that order at Charlottenburg by the king of Prussia, in virtue of a commission from George II. From Frederick he received the gift of a silver dinner service and a royal grant that allowed him to add to his coat of arms the eagle of Silesia with the motto 'Ex bene merito'.

In 1744 Hyndford was sent on a special mission to Russia, where his skilful negotiations greatly accelerated the peace of Aix-la-Chapelle. He left Moscow on 8 October 1749, and after his return to Britain was sworn of the privy council, on 29 March 1750. On 17 November his wife, a lady of the bedchamber to the princess of Orange, died of apoplexy in The Hague. In 1752 Hyndford was appointed one of the lords of the bedchamber, and in the same year he was dispatched to Vienna as a colleague for Robert Keith, the British ambassador, to promote the ultimately unsuccessful imperial election plan. On 22 December 1756 he married his second wife, Jean Vigor (1726–1807), daughter of Benjamin Vigor of Fulham, Middlesex. He returned to Britain in 1764 and was appointed vice-admiral of Scotland, when he gave up his office at the board of police.

The remainder of Hyndford's life was spent at his seat in Lanarkshire, where he devoted his attention to the improvement and adornment of his estate. To encourage his tenants in the improvement of their lands, he granted them leases of fifty-seven years' duration. While occupied with his diplomatic duties abroad, he had taken a constant interest in agricultural affairs, and he used seeds brought from Russia to begin plantations on his estate. He died at his home, Carmichael House, near Tankerton, Lanarkshire, on 19 July 1767, and was buried there on 25 July. He was survived by his wife, who died on 8 February 1807. As his second marriage was childless, the title passed to his cousin John Carmichael, and became extinct on the death of the sixth earl in 1817.

T. F. HENDERSON, *rev.* KARL WOLFGANG SCHWEIZER

Sources GEC, *Peerage*, new edn · R. Lodge, *Great Britain and Prussia in the eighteenth century* (1923) · D. B. Horn, ed., *British diplomatic representatives, 1689–1789*, CS, 3rd ser., 46 (1932) · R. Browning, 'The duke of Newcastle and the imperial election plan, 1749–1754', *Journal of British Studies*, 7/1 (1967–8), 28–47 · R. Browning, *The war of the Austrian succession* (1993) · R. Douglas, *The peerage of Scotland* (1764)
Archives BL, corresp., Egerton MS 3417 · BL, corresp. and papers, Add. MSS 11365–11387 · Niedersächsisches Hauptstaatsarchiv, Hanover | BL, corresp. with duke of Newcastle, etc., Add. MSS 32691–33056, *passim* · BL, corresp. with Sir Thomas Robinson, Add. MSS 23807–23827 · BL, letters to earl of Stair, etc., Add. MSS 35452–35492, *passim* · BL, letters to Lord Tyrawly, Add. MSS 23630–23631 · Hunt. L., letters to Lord Loudoun · NMM, letters to Lord Sandwich · PRO NIre. · U. Nott. L., corresp. with duke of Newcastle
Likenesses J. Richardson, oils, 1726, Gov. Art Coll. · J. Richardson, oils, 1726, Scot. NPG · attrib. C. Alexander, oils, Gov. Art Coll.

Carmichael, John Wilson (1799–1868), marine painter, was born on 9 June 1799 in Tyne Street, Newcastle upon Tyne, the eldest of the three children of William Carmichael, a shipwright, and Mary, daughter of James Johnson, a mariner. After spending some three of his early teenage years at sea, he was apprenticed in his father's trade to Richard Farrington & Brothers, shipbuilders at North Shore in Newcastle. The Farringtons were supporters of Newcastle's early art institutions and encouraged Carmichael's artistic talent during his employment, which lasted until about 1825. His artistic development was also fostered by Newcastle's leading artist, the landscape painter Thomas Miles Richardson, and exposure to the works shown from 1822 in the exhibitions of the Northumberland Institution for the Promotion of the Fine Arts and its successors.

From 1825 Carmichael himself exhibited regularly at these exhibitions, having settled in New Road, Newcastle. Later he was to have residential and studio addresses in Blackett Street, Percy Street, Grainger Street, and Hood Street, Newcastle. He first attracted the interest of influential patrons with *Barge Day—Morning* (1828, priv. coll.), sold to the Northumberland landowner and collector Major George Anderson. Anderson's two important Canalettos inspired Carmichael's spectacular response, *Ascension Day on the Tyne* (priv. coll.) of 1829, also bought by the collector. This ambitious work, dramatic in scale, detail, and theatricality, directly compared Newcastle's celebration of its control of the River Tyne with Venice's relationship with the sea. Two series of topographical views, published as engravings in 1828–30 and 1832, further enhanced his reputation. He found a ready market for less ambitious seascapes, 'essentially all the same', as William Bell Scott later recalled, '—representing mid-day, a fresh sea, blue openings of sky amidst breezy white and gray clouds, a yacht, and a fishing boat tacking or going before the wind to the right or left' (*Autobiographical Notes*, 2.210). Carmichael's compositional devices, shared by his contemporaries Clarkson Stanfield, John Callow, and James Webb, derived from the example of J. M. W. Turner and the Dutch sea painters of the seventeenth century. He was most admired by his contemporaries for his mastery of the technical details of ships. Despite his extensive researches, he was less convincing when depicting romantic subjects, such as whaling and polar exploration, of which he had no first-hand experience.

Apart from maritime subjects, Carmichael also recorded the monuments of the industrial revolution. Engravings of *Views on the Newcastle and Carlisle Railway* were published (1836–8) and views commissioned of the London and Brighton Railway, and of new bridges, docks, and collieries. He collaborated with his friend the Newcastle architect John Dobson on the latter's presentation drawings (several of which are now in the Laing Art Gallery in Newcastle). He depicted many other contemporary events, including the visit of Queen Victoria to Edinburgh in 1842 (drawings exh. RA, 1843) and *The Naval Review, Spithead, 1853* (Museum and Art Gallery, South Shields). From 1835 he exhibited in London: at the Royal Academy (twenty-one paintings from 1835 to 1859), at the Society of British Artists (six works from 1838 to 1847), and at the British Institution (twenty-one works from 1846 to 1862). This metropolitan success encouraged him to move to the capital in April 1846, after an emotional farewell dinner and a gift of silver plate.

Carmichael had married Mary Sweet (*c.*1804–1881) on 20 March 1826; by 1846 they had had eight children. The family settled in Bloomsbury, at 20 Howland Street, Fitzroy Square, moving in 1853 to 8 Milton Street, Dorset Square. Although Carmichael's confidence was affected by the increased competition he found in London, he continued to work prolifically, combining potboilers with ambitious historical and contemporary subjects such as the voyages of Sir John Franklin, including, for instance, *'Erebus' and 'Terror' at Anchor off New Zealand* (1847, National Maritime Museum, Greenwich). Despite his many foreign subjects (mostly based on others' sketches), there is no evidence of travel beyond the North Sea and channel ports, with the exception of the period from May to August 1855 spent recording the Baltic campaign of the Crimean War for the *Illustrated London News*; this trip also resulted in several paintings.

In recognition of his technical competence, Winsor and Newton commissioned two small but popular handbooks from Carmichael, *The Art of Marine Painting in Water Colours*, published in 1859, and *The Art of Marine Painting in Oil Colours*, in 1864. About 1865, due to ill health, he moved to Scarborough, a favourite subject of his, and lived at 18 Mulgrave Terrace. This period was, however, no retirement: there is evidence of ambitious paintings, and a series of watercolour views of the north-east coast was produced for publication. He died there on 2 May 1868 of 'epileptic seizure' (probably a stroke) and on 5 May was buried in Dean Road cemetery in Scarborough. He was survived by his wife. Carmichael's work is well represented in the Laing Art Gallery, Newcastle, and other galleries in the north-east of England; the Laing Art Gallery also has an extensive collection of his sketches and working drawings. Portraits of him show a handsome dark-haired man with thick hair and a shapely mouth.   Andrew Greg

Sources D. Villar, *John Wilson Carmichael, 1799–1868* (1995) · [A. Greg], *John Wilson Carmichael, 1799–1868: paintings, watercolours and drawings* (1982) [exhibition catalogue, Laing Gallery, Newcastle upon Tyne, 15 Oct – 28 Nov 1982] • A. Watson, 'Memoir of J. W. Carmichael', in J. W. Carmichael, *Pictures of Tyneside* (1881), ix–xiv • *Autobiographical notes of the life of William Bell Scott: and notices of his artistic and poetic circle of friends, 1830 to 1882*, ed. W. Minto, 2 (1892), 185, 209–11 • Graves, *RA exhibitors*, 1 (1905), 395–6 • Graves, *Brit. Inst.*, 86–7 • J. Johnson, ed., *Works exhibited at the Royal Society of British Artists, 1824–1893, and the New English Art Club, 1888–1917*, 2 vols. (1975), 75 • E. Mackenzie, *A descriptive and historical account of the town and county of Newcastle upon Tyne*, 2 (1827), 581 • parish register, Newcastle upon Tyne, All Saints, 31/7/1799 [baptism] • d. cert.

Archives NMM, diary [copy]

Likenesses T. Ellerby, oils, 1839, Laing Art Gallery, Newcastle upon Tyne • J. Crawhall, pencil and watercolour, *c.*1840–1849, NPG • portraits, *c.*1840–1849, repro. in Villar, *John Wilson Carmichael* • engraving, *c.*1860, repro. in Villar, *John Wilson Carmichael*

Wealth at death under £1000: probate, 18 July 1868, *CGPLA Eng. & Wales*

Carmichael, Mary Grant (1850/51–1935), pianist and composer, was born in Birkenhead, Cheshire, the daughter of John Carmichael of Corosal. Her youngest brother, Montague (1857–1936), entered the diplomatic service and was the author of a number of belletristic books on Italy. Mary was educated in Aix-la-Chapelle, Bonn, and Lausanne, and studied the piano with Heinrich Porges in Munich and composition and harmony with Ebenezer Prout in London. She had a successful career accompanying singers and violinists, and was the accompanist at the Monday Popular Concerts in 1884–5. She composed a considerable quantity of music, including songs, piano works, and an operetta, *The Snow Queen*. Her song cycle *The Stream* was performed at the Lyric Club in November 1887, while her mass in E♭ for men's and boys' voices was considered her most ambitious project. She also composed marches for military bands, dedicated to lords Kitchener and Roberts. She was a convert to the Roman Catholic church, and retired in April 1926. She died unmarried on 17 March 1935 at her home, 18 Steele's Road, Haverstock Hill, Hampstead, at the age of eighty-four. Unexceptionable in musical terms, she is a good example of a woman who, nevertheless, sustained herself as a professional musician for some forty years.   K. D. REYNOLDS

Sources Brown & Stratton, *Brit. mus.* • *WWW* • F. C. Burnand, ed., *The Catholic who's who and yearbook* (1910) • O. Ebel, *Women composers: a biographical handbook of woman's work in music*, 3rd edn (1913) • d. cert. • *CGPLA Eng. & Wales* (1935)

Wealth at death £1977 3s. 3d.: probate, 22 May 1935, *CGPLA Eng. & Wales*

Carmichael, Richard (1779–1849), surgeon and educationist, was born in Bishop Street, Dublin, on 6 February 1779, the fourth son of Hugh Carmichael, solicitor, who was closely related to the Scottish family of the earls of Hyndford, and his wife, Sarah (*née* Rogers). After apprenticeship to Robert Moore Peile, and study at the Schools of Surgery, Dublin, Carmichael passed the requisite examination and in 1795 was appointed assistant surgeon (and ensign) to the Wexford militia, a position he held until 1802, when the army establishment was reduced after the peace of Amiens. Carmichael had become a member of the Royal College of Surgeons in Ireland in 1800, and in

Richard Carmichael (1779–1849), by Edward Francis Finden (after Sir Frederic William Burton)

1803 he commenced practice in Cumberland Street, Dublin. In the same year he was appointed to St George's Hospital and Dispensary, and in 1810 he became surgeon to the Lock Hospital, where he studied venereal diseases. In 1816 he was appointed to the Richmond Hospital, and in the following year (on 14 December 1817) he undertook a parotidectomy, a challenging operation which he performed successfully. Carmichael had already served as president of the College of Surgeons in Ireland in 1813, at the early age of thirty-four, and he held the position again in 1826 and 1846. He was one of the founders of the Richmond Hospital school of medicine, later called the Carmichael school. In addition to donations in his lifetime, he bequeathed £8000 for its improvement. His books included *An Essay on the Effects of Carbonate of Iron upon Cancer* (1806), *Observations on the Symptoms and Specific Distinctions of Venereal Diseases* (1818), and *An Essay on the Nature of Tuberculosis and Cancerous Diseases* (1836); he opposed the use of mercury for syphilis. There is a list of his writings in the *Dublin Quarterly Journal of Medical Science* (1850, ix.497–9).

Having become wealthy Carmichael moved to 24 Rutland Square; in addition he usually leased a summer residence by the sea. He married a distant cousin, Jane Bourne; there were no children. His generosity could manifest itself in forms other than the financial. When a vacancy on the staff of the Richmond Hospital attracted two first-class applicants, Robert Adams and John McDonnell, and it would have required the judgment of Solomon to decide between them, Carmichael tendered his own resignation, creating a second vacancy to permit the appointment of both. 'Erinensis', *The Lancet*'s Dublin correspondent, whose pen was readier to disparage than to praise, referred to Carmichael as a name 'synonymous with many excellent qualities of the head and the heart' (Fallon, 110). According to this critic he was 'a man of very plain manners, unpretending address, unostentatious habits, and on every subject of liberal opinions'. His success had 'grown out of the fertility of his own mind, unwatered by a rill of lordly patronage' (ibid., 115). Many prominent persons were his patients, and he had occasion to bleed Lord Norbury by opening his temporal artery. During the operation the judge remarked: 'Carmichael, I believe you were never called to the Bar.' 'No, my Lord,' Carmichael replied, 'I never was.' 'Well, doctor,' said Norbury, 'I'm sure I can safely say that you have cut a figure in the Temple' (Cameron, 427).

A member of the established church until 1825, Carmichael then joined a unitarian church. He was handsome, with a grave cast of countenance. In the late 1820s his health declined, and he withdrew temporarily from practice. He rested in the south of France, returning to his commitments in Dublin in 1829. He was elected a corresponding member of the French Academy of Medicine in 1835, the first Irishman to be so honoured. He said his reputation would, like an Isle of Man penny, rest upon three legs—syphilis, scrofula, and cancer—but he is remembered for his passion for medical reform, and his generosity to the Medical Benevolent Fund. A piece of plate was presented to him by 410 of his professional brethren, with an address expressing their appreciation of his zeal for the interests of his profession. During the last ten years of his life he supported the Medical Association of Ireland, and was its president from its formation. He demanded a good preliminary and professional education for students, uniform examinations by universities and medical colleges, and the separation of apothecary's work from medicine and surgery. He donated £500 to the Medical Association to promote its aims, but finding the money not needed he transferred it to the Medical Benevolent Fund, to which he left a further £4000 at his death.

On 8 June 1849 Carmichael set out on horseback for his seaside house in Sutton at about 6.30 p.m. He took a short cut, crossing the north strand of Dublin Bay, and by some ill-understood accident he was drowned. His body was recovered four days later. He was buried in the new cemetery of St George's parish, and John McDonnell paid a tribute, which is inscribed on his tomb:

> His bright example will long light congenial spirits in his profession to tread the path he trod and encourage them to emulate the energy, the perseverance, the virtues that made him an ornament to the profession, a credit to his country and an honour to human nature itself.

Carmichael's legacies included one of £3000, left in trust to the Royal College of Surgeons in Ireland to provide two prizes, given every four years, for the best essays on medical education.   J. B. LYONS

Sources C. A. Cameron, *History of the Royal College of Surgeons in Ireland*, 2nd edn (1916) • M. Fallon, ed., *The sketches of Erinensis: selections of Irish medical satire, 1824–1836* (1979) • 'Memoir of the late Richard Carmichael', *Dublin Quarterly Journal of Medical Science*, 9 (1850), 493– 504 • R. W. Fearon, 'The commonwealth of medicine: yesterday', *Irish Journal of Medical Science*, 122 (1936), 49–58 • *Dublin Medical Press* (4 July 1849) [obituary]

Likenesses C. Moore, marble bust, *c.*1853 (after C. Moore, 1847), Royal College of Surgeons in Ireland, Dublin • E. F. Finden, engraving (after F. W. Burton), AM Oxf. [*see illus.*] • engraving (after drawing by F. W. Burton), NL Ire.

Wealth at death over £15,000; legacies incl. £3000 to Royal College of Surgeons in Ireland, £8000 to the Carmichael School, £4000 to the Medical Benevolent Fund

Carmichael, Thomas David Gibson, Baron Carmichael (1859–1926), administrator in India and art collector, was born at Castlecraig, near Edinburgh, on 18 March 1859, the eldest son of the Revd Sir William Henry Gibson Carmichael, tenth baronet (1827–1891), and his wife, Eleanora Anne (*d.* 1861), eldest daughter of David Anderson, of St Germains, East Lothian. He was educated at the Revd Cowley Powles's school, Wixenford, in Wokingham, where the local rector, Charles Kingsley, inspired in him a passion for natural history. In 1877 he entered St John's College, Cambridge, graduating BA with second-class honours in history in 1881, his first choice of natural science having been vetoed by his father. A visit to Italy in 1881–2 sparked a lifelong interest in Italian art and art collecting.

After university Carmichael turned his attention to politics. His father, however, in spite of a family tradition of whiggism and the entreaties of Lord Rosebery, forbade him from standing for parliament and in 1885 he accepted instead the post of private secretary to Lord Dalhousie, secretary of state for Scotland, and afterwards to his successor, Sir George Trevelyan.

On 1 July 1886 Carmichael married Mary Helen Elizabeth (*d.* 1947), eldest of the seven children of Albert Llewellyn Nugent, younger brother of the second Baron Nugent. They settled at Chiefswood, former residence of Sir Walter Scott, near Melrose, where Carmichael began experiments in commercial apiarism. In 1891 he founded the Scottish Bee-Keepers' Association.

In 1891 Carmichael was appointed to the Prison Commission and from 1894 until 1897 chaired the general board of lunacy for Scotland. In December 1891 he succeeded to the baronetcy and with his wife moved to the family estate at Castlecraig. With his father now dead, he stood unsuccessfully for the Liberals in a by-election for Peebles and Selkirk in 1892, and was eventually returned for Midlothian in succession to W. E. Gladstone in 1895, in which year he also became a freemason. He subsequently held the office of grand master in Scotland, Victoria, and Bengal. In 1900 financial difficulties caused him to retire from parliament and later to sell his house and art collection. He continued, however, as chairman of the Scottish Liberal Association (1892–1903), whose anti-imperial tone during the Second South African War of 1899–1902 he was unable to prevent. He was a councillor of the Liberal League. In 1904 he was appointed by parliament to the Scottish churches commission. In 1908 he had just settled in as the first chairman of the newly constituted board of

Thomas David Gibson Carmichael, Baron Carmichael (1859–1926), by Sir Benjamin Stone, 1897

education, but he preferred to leave the larger issues to others. Underlying some of his diffidence was a recognition that, as foreigners, Britons could never provide a government wholly acceptable to Indians. He left India in mid-1917 at the expiry of his five-year term.

Back in Britain Carmichael immersed himself in the art world again. He had previously served as a trustee of the National Portrait Gallery (1904–8) and of the National Gallery (1906–8). Now, in 1918, he became a trustee of the Wallace Collection, in which capacity he served until his death in 1926, and also again of the National Gallery (1923–6). The sales in 1902 and 1926 of his collections, which observed few limits in class, school, or period, were events in the art world. His numerous public gifts included a bequest of a *Virgin and Child* by Piero di Lorenzo to the National Gallery.

Carmichael had a shrewd understanding of people and a whimsical sense of humour, and appears to have been happier as an observer of humankind than as a leader or administrator. He was created KCMG in 1908, GCIE in 1911, and GCSI in 1917, and appointed lord lieutenant of Peeblesshire in 1921. In February 1912 he was raised to the peerage as Baron Carmichael of Skirling. He died at his home, 13 Portman Street, Oxford Street, London, on 16 January 1926, after four years of failing health. He was buried in Skirling churchyard. He was survived by his wife, who in 1929 published an affectionate memoir, *Lord Carmichael of Skirling*. They had no children (although they had brought up two of Carmichael's nieces and a nephew) and the peerage became extinct on Carmichael's death. He was succeeded in the baronetcy by his cousin, Henry Thomas Gibson-Craig (-Carmichael).

KATHERINE PRIOR

Sources M. Carmichael, ed., *Lord Carmichael of Skirling: a memoir prepared by his wife* [1929] · DNB · *Dod's Peerage* · Burke, *Peerage* (1959) · H. C. G. Matthew, *The liberal imperialists: the ideas and politics of a post-Gladstonian élite* (1973)
Archives CUL, corresp. and papers · NL Aus., letters to Alfred Deakin · NL Scot., corresp., incl. Lord Rosebery · U. Birm. L., letters to Austen Chamberlain
Likenesses B. Stone, photograph, 1897, NPG [*see illus.*] · J. Guthrie, portrait, 1908, priv. coll.; repro. in Carmichael, *Lord Carmichael of Skirling* · Russell, photograph, 1923, repro. in Carmichael, *Lord Carmichael of Skirling*
Wealth at death £35,005 5s. 8d.: probate, 30 March 1926, CGPLA Eng. & Wales

trustees of the National Galleries of Scotland when he was offered the governorship of Victoria, Australia.

In December 1908, four months into his term in Victoria, Carmichael was embroiled in a constitutional controversy. The sitting Conservative ministry was defeated in a vote of no confidence and, rather than call on either of the leaders of the minority parties to form a government, Carmichael dissolved the state parliament and called for fresh elections, a decision which generated considerable unpopularity in the local press and boosted the agitation for local men to be appointed as governors. The rest of his term in Victoria was less eventful, although the Carmichaels found the social routine expected of an Australian governor and his wife exhausting—all the more so as Carmichael took seriously his obligation to visit outlying parts of the state. He calculated that during his time in Victoria he delivered an average of two speeches a day; his wife, patroness of numerous associations for children's and women's welfare, did not lag far behind.

In May 1911 Carmichael was appointed governor of Madras. He took office in the following November, but five months later, in April 1912, was appointed the first governor of the newly reconstituted state of Bengal.

Bengal was a difficult office. To the upheaval of the territorial readjustment and removal of the capital from Calcutta to Delhi were added a wartime economy and local revolutionary movement. Carmichael's administration achieved some progress in matters of public hygiene and

Carmyllyan [Carmylyon], **Ellis** (*fl.* 1511–1542), painter, was of unknown parentage. Between 1511 and 1542 he was one of several Italian painters in the employment of Henry VIII whose work was mainly decorative in nature. The earliest reference, to 'Alexe of myllen, paynter' (PRO, E36/1), might indicate his place of birth and some subsequent references call him 'myllyner' or 'Italian'. It was suggested by J. G. Nichols that Carmyllan might be a woman. He was not: a payment in 1532 for tiles for Westminster records 'elis carmenelle of london peynto[r] ... by hym delyverd' (PRO, E36/252). Moreover, records of payments to Levina Teerlinc refer to 'Mistress' and 'paintrix', neither term being used in connection with Carmyllyan. It has also been suggested (*DNB*) that he might be related to the poet Peter Carmeliano of Brescia, but no connection has been established. It has been stated that Carmyllyan was a miniaturist, but no documentary references support this. With few exceptions, payments to Carmyllyan were made in conjunction with those to the Neapolitan painter Vincent Volpe and they seem to have worked closely together; they are also referred to as 'Guylders'. Both worked on the temporary banqueting house erected at Greenwich in 1527 for the entertainment of the French ambassadors, as did Hans Holbein the younger. In addition, Carmyllyan supplied perfumes and some 'greate stone pottys' in 1527, which may be connected with a further visit by French ambassadors in that autumn. Carmyllyan was paid 33s. 4d. a quarter in 1529, the same rate as Gerard Horenbout, although Volpe had received a pay rise. Carmyllyan was paid for decorative works at Whitehall in 1532, where the roof of the new gallery was decorated with the king's arms and 'bullions and buddis of tymbre' which were painted and gilded by him and Andrew Wright, sergeant painter (PRO, E36/252). After 1542 Carmyllyan disappears from the accounts and it is assumed that he had died.   SUSAN BRACKEN

Sources PRO, E36/252 · PRO, E36/1 · PRO, E36/227 · E. Auerbach, *Tudor artists* (1954) · *LP Henry VIII*, vols. 4/2, 5–6, 17 · J. G. Nichols, 'Notices of the contemporaries and successors of Holbein', *Archaeologia*, 39 (1863), 19–46 · A. B. Chamberlain, *Hans Holbein the younger*, 2 vols. (1913) · T. F. Tout and H. Johnstone, eds., *State trials of the reign of Edward the First, 1289–1293*, CS, 3rd ser., 9 (1906) [and corrections made in vol. 84, 1863] · S. Anglo, *Spectacle, pageantry, and early Tudor policy* (1969); repr. (1989)
Archives PRO, E36/1 · PRO, E36/227 · PRO, E36/252

Carmylyon, Alice. *See* Carmyllyan, Ellis (*fl.* 1511–1542).

Carnaby, William (1772–1839), organist and composer, was born in London and educated at the Chapel Royal as a chorister under James Nares and Edmund Ayrton. He was later an organist in Eye, Suffolk, and in Huntingdon. In 1805 he took the degree of MusB at Trinity Hall, Cambridge, and in July 1808 was awarded the degree of MusD, for which he wrote an exercise described as 'a grand musical piece'; this was performed at Great St Mary's Church on Sunday 7 July. Carnaby by then had left Huntingdon and settled in London, where he lived, at various times, at 18 Winchester Row and 31 Red Lion Square. In 1823 he was appointed organist of the newly opened Hanover Chapel, Regent Street, at a salary of £50 per annum. He occupied this post until his death. In 1827 Carnaby published *The singing primer, or, Rudiments of solfeggi, with exercises in the principal major and minor keys*. He also wrote a considerable amount of music, including *Six Songs* (1798) dedicated to Lady Templetown; two books of songs dedicated to W. Knyvett; *Six Canzonetts* (1794) for two voices to words by Shenstone; a collection of vocal music dedicated to Viscountess Mahon; and many piano works and arrangements of pieces by Beethoven, Handel, Haydn, and Purcell. He died at his home, 7 Middlesex Place, New Road, London, on 7 November 1839.

W. B. SQUIRE, *rev.* DAVID J. GOLBY

Sources *Musical World* (14 Nov 1839), 456 · Brown & Stratton, *Brit. mus.* · Grove, *Dict. mus.* · Venn, *Alum. Cant.* · d. cert.

Likenesses A. Cardon, stipple (after J. T. Barber), BM

Carnac, Sir James Rivett, first baronet (1784–1846), administrator in India and governor of Bombay, eldest son of James Rivett, a member of the council of Bombay, and his wife, Henrietta, daughter of James Fisher of Yarmouth, Norfolk, was born in Bombay on 11 November 1784. He entered the East India Company's service in 1801 as a cadet in the Madras native infantry, the year in which his father assumed the surname of Carnac under the terms of the will of his brother-in-law General John Carnac.

In 1802, as a result of his father's influence, Carnac was appointed aide-de-camp to the governor of Bombay, Jonathan Duncan. In August of the same year he was appointed first assistant to the resident at the court of the Maharaja Gaikwar of Baroda and from that time until 1819, when compelled by ill health to leave India, he was employed in a political capacity, holding for the last two years of that period the post of resident at Baroda. During his years in western India, Carnac expended much diplomatic energy on persuading numerous petty chiefs to outlaw female infanticide. On 3 June 1815 he married Anna Maria (d. 1859), eldest daughter of William Richardes of Penglais, Cardiganshire, with whom he had four sons and four daughters.

In 1822, holding the rank of major, Carnac retired from the Indian service and went to England. In 1827 he was elected a director of the East India Company, and in 1835–6 served as deputy chairman, followed by two consecutive terms as chairman in 1836–7 and 1837–8. As chairman he helped secure for Lord Wellesley a grant of £20,000 which was designed belatedly to compensate him for the ignominy of his recall from India in 1805.

An ardent whig, Carnac was made a baronet in 1836 during Lord Melbourne's government, and in 1837 was elected MP for Sandwich. In 1838 he was offered the governorship of Bombay and resigned his seat in parliament.

Carnac arrived in Bombay at the end of May 1839 just as Lord Auckland was preparing to reinstate the ousted Shah Shuja in Afghanistan with a view to securing Afghanistan as a friendly buffer state between India and Russia. In triumphalist letters to John Cam Hobhouse, president of the Board of Control, Carnac repeatedly congratulated Hobhouse on the brilliance of the scheme and additionally advocated the annexation of Herat and Sind. He scorned the policy of non-interference with India's surviving princes, believing that this only encouraged them in intrigues, and looked forward to the time when British expansion would have absorbed them all and Britain could properly develop her empire's vast resources. On local matters, which engaged his interest rather less than questions of territorial aggrandizement, Carnac supported Bombay's Hindus and Parsis in their complaints against missionary endeavours and called for legislation to prohibit the conversion of minors to Christianity. He planned a series of major revenue surveys for the presidency but was unable to get Auckland's approval for them, and was likewise thwarted in his hopes of obtaining government funds for extensive road construction. In November 1840, less than two years into his post, Carnac's health faltered again and in April 1841 he resigned the governorship and left India for good. A scholarship was founded in his name at Elphinstone College.

Carnac died at Rockliffe, near Lymington, Hampshire, on 28 January 1846 after several months' severe illness. His widow, Anna, died on 2 January 1859. Their eldest son, Sir John Rivett Carnac (1818–1883), MP for Lymington from 1852 until 1860, succeeded to the baronetcy.

A. J. ARBUTHNOT, rev. KATHERINE PRIOR

Sources WWBMP, vol. 1 · Burke, *Peerage* (1959) · BL OIOC, Broughton MSS · GM, 2nd ser., 25 (1846) · J. H. Rivett-Carnac, *Notes on the family of Rivett-Carnac and its descent from Revett of Stowmarket and Brandeston Hall, Suffolk* (c.1909) · ecclesiastical records, BL OIOC · BL, Wellesley MSS · DNB
Archives BL OIOC, papers and corresp. relating to administration of India, Eur MSS D 556 | BL, Wellesley MSS · BL OIOC, corresp. with J. C. Hobhouse, Eur MSS F 213
Likenesses F. Chantrey, pencil drawing, 1839, NPG · P. MacDowell, marble bust, NPG · H. W. Pickersgill, oils, Oriental Club, London
Wealth at death £4000 funded property and personalty in England; £2500 in Guatemala bonds; £5000 in Spanish bonds; valuable service of plate presented by inhabitants of Bombay: GM, 659

Carnac, John (1721–1800), army officer in the East India Company, was baptized in London on 12 April 1721, the son of Peter Carnac (1665–1756), an army captain of French extraction, and his wife, Andrienne, *née* Lelonte (d. c.1762). The family moved to Dublin and in May 1736 he entered Trinity College; he received a BA degree in 1740 and then embarked upon a military career in the marines as a second lieutenant, rising to lieutenant in 1745. In 1754 he went to India as a lieutenant in the 39th foot and served at Madras as secretary and aide-de-camp to the colonel of the regiment, John Adlercron. When, in 1758, the regiment returned to England, he entered the service of the East India Company's army with the rank of captain and accompanied Francis Forde, who had also served with the 39th foot, to Bengal as his secretary. Shortly after his arrival in Bengal he became secretary and aide-de-camp to Robert Clive, governor of Bengal, and joined him in an expedition against the shahzada, son of the Mughal emperor, in February 1759. Carnac's relationship with Clive was both a professional and a personal one and he was also close to Clive's wife, Margaret.

In February 1760 Carnac sailed for England with Clive but at St Helena discovered that he had been appointed major of the company's forces in Bengal with a seat in the council. He therefore returned to India and, having taken up command of the army, proceeded to engage and defeat the Mughal emperor (formerly the shahzada) in early 1761. He now found himself caught up in the factional politics that dominated the company's relations with the nawabs of Bengal in this period and was motivated by his connection with Clive, whom he described as 'the person to whom I owe everything' (HoP, *Commons, 1754–90*, 2.194). He supported the political system established by Clive in Bengal and opposed Henry Vansittart, the governor since 1760, who had recently engineered the accession of Mir

Kasim as nawab. At the same time he was under instructions to obtain confirmation of Clive's right to his *jagir*, or income. In 1763 he was involved in the military action when fighting commenced between Mir Kasim and the British; while he seems to have distinguished himself in one of the early battles, his performance after he took command of the army again in March 1764 and his conduct at Patna, when his forces repulsed those of Shuja ud-Daula of Oudh, has been criticized (Mason, 104–6).

Carnac's opposition to Vansittart earned him dismissal from the company's service, which took effect in June 1764; this was, however, soon revoked and he was appointed to the rank of brigadier-general and made colonel of the 1st battalion. In August 1765 he participated with Clive, reappointed governor of Bengal in May, in the negotiations with Shuja ud-Daula and the Mughal emperor that resulted in both the grant of the *diwani* of Bengal, Bihar, and Orissa to the company and a diplomatic settlement that established peace. Carnac was an important part of Clive's plan to reform the activities of the company's servants in Bengal. He was a member of the council and also of the select committee, a small but powerful body which was at the heart of Clive's strategy, and in 1766 he helped Clive to deal successfully with a mutiny among the army officers. Despite his position he was able to profit financially from his service in India; in 1765 he accepted a present, made at Clive's invitation, of £22,000 from the Mughal emperor. This was in addition to gifts totalling about £15,000 made by Mir Kasim's successor, Mir Jafar, and the raja of Benares. His wealth at this time was estimated at £80,000.

Carnac resigned from the company's service in January 1767 and returned to England. His fortune was used to purchase an estate near Ringwood in Hampshire and was also employed to finance Carnac's involvement in the largely unsuccessful Polygon housing development in Southampton. In common with other nabobs he sought election to parliament and was elected as MP for Leominster in 1768 on the interest of Chase Price. In the House of Commons he supported George Grenville and spoke on matters related to India. He gave evidence to the select committee of 1772–3 which inquired into events there and in particular he defended Clive.

By 1773 Carnac's financial position was precarious owing to a failure to remit all of his fortune to England, and he subsequently returned to India as a member of the council at Bombay. He was, however, dismissed from the company's service in 1780 on account of his part in the humiliating convention of Wadgaon, which had been concluded with the Marathas following an unsuccessful expedition against their stronghold at Poona. Despite his dismissal he remained in India, his English estate being sold in 1783. Carnac, who had married Elizabeth Woollaston (d. 1767) in 1765 and Elizabeth Rivett (1752–1780) in 1769, died at Mangalore in 1800 with no surviving children. Under the terms of his will James Rivett, Carnac's brother-in-law and father of a future governor of Bombay, assumed the additional name of Carnac. D. L. PRIOR

Sources K. K. Datta and others, eds., *Fort William–India House correspondence*, 2–4 (1957–68) • M. Bence-Jones, *Clive of India* (1974) • P. Mason, *A matter of honour: an account of the Indian army, its officers and men* (1974) • P. J. Marshall, *East Indian fortunes: the British in Bengal in the eighteenth century* (1976) • J. M. Holzman, *The nabobs in England* (1926) • HoP, *Commons, 1754–90*, vol. 2 • D. L. Prior, 'The career of Robert, first Baron Clive, with special reference to his political and administrative career', MPhil diss., U. Wales, 1993 • BL OIOC, L/AG/34/29/342 • A. Temple Patterson, *A history of Southampton, 1700–1914: an oligarchy in decline* (1966) • Bengal marriages, BL OIOC, N/1/2 • Burtchaell & Sadleir, *Alum. Dubl.* • IGI • *Asiatic Annual Register*, 3 (1801)
Archives BL OIOC, corresp. and journal, Eur. Orme MSS • BL OIOC, corresp. and papers, MSS Eur F 128 • BL OIOC, home misc. series, corresp. relating to India • NL Wales, corresp. and papers | BL, letters to W. Hastings and others, Add. MSS 29133–29168, *passim* • BL OIOC, corresp. with Harry Verelst, MSS Eur F 218
Likenesses O. Humphry, miniature, 1786, NPG
Wealth at death see will and inventory, BL OIOC, L/AG/34/29/342, L/AG/34/27/387

Carnan, Thomas (1737–1788), printer and bookseller, was born in Reading, the younger son of **William Carnan** (d. 1737), printer, of the Bible and Crown in the Market Place and Minster Street, Reading, and his wife, Mary, the eldest daughter of Martin Hounshill, of Ringwood, Hampshire. William Carnan was briefly the proprietor of the *Reading Mercury*, but died shortly after Thomas's birth and left his estate jointly to his brother Charles Carnan, a linen draper of Reading, and his journeyman John *Newbery. Mary Carnan married Newbery in 1739, and the family moved to 65 St Paul's Churchyard, London, in 1744, leaving the Reading business in the charge of the elder son, John, and a journeyman, C. Mickelwright. A daughter, Anna Maria Carnan, later married the poet Christopher *Smart.

Thomas worked in the London business, during the 1750s and 1760s, latterly with his stepfather's nephew Francis Newbery (1743–1818). However, John Newbery appears to have used Carnan's name as a means of disguising his own involvement in controversial works—notably Christopher Smart's *The Midwife*, and the *Ladies Complete Pocket-Book* for 1750. In 1755 Thomas applied for the freedom of the Stationers' Company, but was refused. Following John Newbery's death in 1767, Thomas and Francis continued publishing in partnership, but in 1779 they quarrelled openly over the sale of patent medicines and from 1782 Carnan continued publishing alone.

Carnan is best remembered for challenging the profitable monopoly, held by the Stationers' Company, for the publication of almanacs. Although he was named as the publisher of the annual *Ladies Complete Pocket-Book* for 1750, John Newbery published later editions until his death. Thereafter the work was continued by Carnan and Francis Newbery, together with *The Gardeners and Planters Calendar*. These were among a group of annual publications the contents of which began to erode the almanac monopoly. The popularity of such 'diaries' was such that in 1772 the company sought counsel's opinion as to whether they were technically almanacs, and issued a warning to publishers of future prosecutions. Carnan responded by also publishing a new work, Reuben Burrow's *Ladies and Gentleman's Diary*. The company obtained an injunction, to restrain him from selling this work, which he duly answered in court by asserting that King James I had no power to grant such a perpetual monopoly in almanacs. This challenge fortunately coincided with the House of Lords' judgment upon Alexander Donaldson's appeal against an injunction to prevent him from publishing James Thomson's *Seasons*, a judgment which had the effect of seeming to undermine the legal basis for perpetual copyright. Carnan was permitted to continue selling those almanacs he had published, albeit with the profits frozen, pending a final decision by the court of common pleas.

In May 1775 the court decided in Carnan's favour, and the Stationers' Company responded by trying to buy him off from seeking dissolution of the existing injunction—an offer that he scornfully rejected. The legal expenses for the suit appear to have been shared with the publisher George Robinson (who was willing to take advantage of the company's offer). Carnan and Robinson jointly published the three almanacs in the following year, but the differing temperaments of the two men precluded a lasting business relationship. The company subsequently persuaded Lord North to bring in a bill to legalize the monopoly, against which Carnan petitioned, and which was defeated. According to William West, Carnan celebrated his success by driving his coach 'repeatedly, in triumph, round St Paul's Churchyard and through Paternoster Row' past the entrance to Stationers' Hall (West, 21). However, a subsequent petition by Carnan against a plan to raise stamp duty on sheet almanacs in 1781 was not successful. This had the effect of limiting new competition in this field. An attempt to challenge the monopoly of Eyre and Strahan, the king's printers, by printing a form of prayer in the same year, likewise failed.

Carnan was described by West as 'an eccentric and singular character' (West, 21) and by Timperley as 'a very honourable and worthy bookseller' (Timperley, 762). According to Roscoe, he was 'litigious, cantankerous, a born rebel and fighter against the "establishment", but brave and tenacious of purpose in a high degree' (Roscoe, 18). He remained unmarried and childless. Following his death on 29 July 1788 at Hornsey Lane, Highgate, Middlesex, his estate was administered by Francis Newbery and Anna Smart, who sold his almanac interests to the Stationers' Company. DAVID STOKER

Sources C. Blagden, 'Thomas Carnan and the almanac monopoly', *Studies in Bibliography*, 14 (1961), 21–39 • M. M. Stewart, 'Smart, Kenrick, Carnan and Newbery: new evidence on the paper war, 1750–51', *The Library*, 6th ser., 5 (1983), 32–43 • I. Maxted, *The London book trades, 1775–1800: a preliminary checklist of members* (1977) • H. R. Plomer and others, *A dictionary of the printers and booksellers who were at work in England, Scotland, and Ireland from 1726 to 1775* (1932) • H. R. Plomer and others, *A dictionary of the printers and booksellers who were at work in England, Scotland, and Ireland from 1668 to 1725* (1922) • W. West, *Fifty years' recollections of an old bookseller* (privately printed, Cork, 1835) • C. Knight, *Shadows of old booksellers* (1865) • C. H. Timperley, *A dictionary of printers and printing* (1839) • R. M. Wiles, *Freshest advice: early provincial newspapers in England* (1965) • G. A. Cranfield, *The development of the provincial newspaper press, 1700–1760* (1962) • K. G. Burton, *The early newspaper press in Berkshire, 1723–1855*

(1954) · S. Roscoe, *John Newbery and his successors, 1740–1814: a bibliography* (1973)

Carnan, William (d. **1737**). *See under* Carnan, Thomas (1737–1788).

Carnarvon. For this title name *see* Dormer, Robert, first earl of Carnarvon (1610?–1643); Herbert, Henry John George, third earl of Carnarvon (1800–1849); Herbert, Henry Howard Molyneux, fourth earl of Carnarvon (1831–1890); Herbert, George Edward Stanhope Molyneux, fifth earl of Carnarvon (1866–1923).

Carne, Sir Edward (*c*.1496–1561), diplomat, was the son of Howell Carne (*fl.* 1490–1497) of Cowbridge, Glamorgan, and his wife, Cicely or Sibyl, daughter of William Kemys of Newport, Monmouthshire. He claimed descent from the kings of Gwent. Carne was educated at Oxford, where he received a bachelor's degree in civil law in July 1519, and a doctorate in the same faculty in August 1524. He became principal of Greek Hall, Oxford, in July 1521 and was admitted to the College of Advocates in London in November 1525.

Carne's abilities reached the notice of Henry VIII, who employed him in the matter of his divorce from Katherine of Aragon. Once it was clear that the ruling on the divorce was to come from Rome rather than England, Henry sent Carne to Pope Clement VII with the explicit order to delay proceedings. In early November 1530 he was instructed to appear before the rota, the papal court of appeal, not as a representative of the king but instead as a private citizen. There he was to complain about the unseemliness of the order for the king himself to leave his kingdom and his princely duties and travel to Rome. Carne, as Henry's *excusator*, was extraordinarily effective, for the wrangling over his specific status and his capacity to be heard in court succeeded in stalling proceedings for two years. A spectacular example of Carne's delaying tactics occurred in February 1532, when he put forward twenty-five propositions and urged that each one be argued for a day. Katherine's advocates, wishing for the suit to progress, strenuously opposed the motion. Nevertheless, this tactic secured an eight-month postponement, as the pope ordered that the process be suspended until October, at which time the king was required to present an appropriate representative other than Carne to speak on his behalf. By delaying the process in this fashion Carne first gave Henry the opportunity to plunder Europe's universities for arguments favourable to his cause, and secondly afforded the king more time to prepare England for the break with Rome. Once the adverse verdict was handed down, Carne withdrew to Bologna.

Carne's service to the crown did not go unacknowledged. He had been rector of 'Meither' (Matharn?) in the diocese of Llandaff, since August 1517. In the 1530s he received further preferment, being appointed chancellor of Salisbury, rector of Swinbrook, Oxfordshire, rector of Marnhull, Dorset, vicar of Melksham, Wiltshire, and rector of Snailwell, Cambridgeshire. He vacated all of these posts by March 1537. In that year he married Anne, the widow of Sir John Raglan. They had one son.

In October 1538 Carne was sent with Thomas Wriothesley and Stephen Vaughan to Brussels to treat with Mary, regent of the Netherlands and sister to Charles V. Their ostensible mission was to open negotiations for two marriages, the first of Henry to Christina, duchess of Milan, and the second of the princess Mary Tudor to Dom Luis of Portugal. Of equal importance, however, was the need to stem the growing entente between France and the empire. With François I and Charles once again at peace, England was faced by the very real prospect of a Catholic alliance committed to the overthrow of the Reformation in England. The English envoys arrived at Calais on 28 September and first met with the regent in Brussels on 5 October. The mission was fraught with tension, especially after the sudden withdrawal of both the French and the imperial ambassadors from the English court. Wriothesley and Carne only just escaped arrest before receiving permission to leave for Calais in March 1539.

Carne also acted as a royal commissioner during the dissolution of the monasteries. In December 1539 he acquired property and a house in Bristol for his wife since he was unable to maintain her at court. He also purchased Colwynston Manor and Ewenni Priory in his native county of Glamorgan.

In 1538 Henry VIII again called upon Carne for help regarding his matrimonial affairs, this time to conclude a marriage rather than to annul one. Carne travelled to the court of the duke of Cleves with Dr Nicholas Wotton and Richard Berde, to propose a double marriage, the first between Mary and the duke's son, and the other between Henry and Cleves's sister Anne. Carne's instructions also bade him to procure both a picture of Henry's prospective bride and 100 well-trained cannoneers. Although a persistent legend holds that Charles V knighted Carne in 1540, it was Henry who did so in appreciation for the Welshman's continued service.

Carne was sent again with Stephen Vaughan to Mary, regent of the Netherlands, in June 1541 to settle a commercial dispute. The two men arrived in Brussels on 26 June. They lacked royal authority to make concessions, and this inability inevitably caused the talks to stall. Carne and Vaughan, recognizing the futility of further discussion, finally took leave from the imperial court in January 1542. It was Carne who left the better impression, as most considered him more 'dexterous and honest' than Vaughan (*LP Henry VIII*, 18/1, no. 259). Upon his return he became sheriff of Glamorgan. Carne's expertise in the Low Countries resulted in his appointment in June 1544 as resident ambassador with a salary of £672. His tenure ended in July 1548. He was an active administrator during Edward VI's reign, being appointed of the quorum of the commissions of the peace for Cheshire, Gloucestershire, Herefordshire, Shropshire, and Worcestershire from 1547 to 1554 (PRO, C 66/801, membranes 12d, 14d, 19d, 22d, 23d). He was on various commissions for English and Welsh counties during these years. He was a member of the council in the marches of Wales by 1551, probably through the patronage of William Herbert, first earl of Pembroke and lord president of that council. He testified during the trial of

Stephen Gardiner, bishop of Winchester, and had the integrity and bravery to speak in his favour. Consequently, he was less active during the remainder of the reign. He was returned for the county of Glamorgan to parliament in November 1554, and, according to Browne Willis, he was re-elected the following year (the official list states that the return is defaced).

In May 1555 Mary I sent an embassy consisting of Carne, Anthony Browne, Viscount Montagu, and William Thirlby, bishop of Ely, to Pope Paul IV to announce formally England's return to the Catholic faith. While Thirlby and Montagu returned to England, Carne remained in Rome as resident ambassador, the last one until the reign of Charles II. Carne, while certainly an able man, proved recalcitrant during this embassy. Upon his arrival he became embroiled in a dispute over precedence with the Portuguese ambassador that lasted for over a year and which caused the pope to banish them twice from his presence.

As the English ambassador to Rome, Carne became entangled in the threatened heresy charges made against Reginald Pole, papal legate, archbishop of Canterbury, and cousin to Mary. Pole was summoned to Rome in the summer of 1557 to clear his name, moving Carne to warn him to stay away from the Holy See or risk imprisonment. A furious Mary instructed her ambassador to insist that any heresy charges against Pole be investigated in England and, if the pope refused, to leave Rome. In the end, the charges were not made.

In 1557 Carne became deeply involved in a lawsuit that also had substantial political and religious ramifications. The case was a contested decision regarding a marriage between Richard Chetwood and Agnes Woodhall, who was a ward of a protestant branch of the Suffolk family. In 1556 the Catholic Charles Tyrrell argued at the consistory court of St Paul's that he had been betrothed previously to Agnes and was therefore entitled to marry her and receive her substantial dowry. The court under the influence of the papal legate, Pole, ruled in Tyrrell's favour and annulled the marriage. Because Catholic England was again under papal jurisdiction, Agnes and Chetwood appealed to Rome for a further hearing and engaged Thomas Wilson to act as their advocate in the matter. Carne, concerned about the repercussions of the case on English sovereignty over her own ecclesiastical affairs, petitioned at length for the case to be returned to England. While Wilson enjoyed considerable access to the pope, Carne became enraged that he had difficulty arranging a papal audience; it was Carne's son who eventually met with the pope and presented his father's views.

Carne's meddling in the Chetwood case was less palatable to Queen Elizabeth, and shortly after her accession the privy council sent him a mandate forbidding him 'to use his authority in soliciting or procuring of anything in the matter of matrimony depending between Mr. Chetwood and Mr. Tyrrille' (CSP for., 1558–9, no. 56). A month later, in February 1559, Elizabeth recalled Carne from Rome. Pope Pius IV, however, stopped Carne from leaving by appointing him warden of the English College in Rome. It is more than likely that Carne's subsequent entreaties to Elizabeth's ministers for help in returning home were attempts to safeguard his English properties rather than heartfelt nostalgia for his homeland—sources indicate that Carne did not want to quit Rome and had enlisted the help of the papacy in that regard. On 20 April 1560 Carne was relieved of the wardenship, although he still retained a pension from the college. He died in Rome on 19 January 1561. Friends erected a monument to Carne, and it is located just outside the entrance to the church of San Gregorio Magno in Rome. The monument was defaced by the French in 1798 during their occupation of Rome, and it was repaired in the mid-nineteenth century at the behest of the antiquary John Montgomery Traherne (1788–1860).

L. E. HUNT

Sources LP Henry VIII · CSP for., 1553–9 · CSP Venice, 1527–33; 1556–7 · J. M. Cleary, 'The Carne memorial in Rome', Reports and Transactions of the Cardiff Naturalists Society, 80 (1948–50) · The English Hospice in Rome: the venerabile sexcentenary issue, 21 (1962) · G. de C. Parmiter, The king's Great Matter (1967) · W. C. Richardson, Stephen Vaughan, financial agent of Henry VIII: a study of financial relations with the Low Countries [1953] · DNB · R. Williams, Enwogion Cymru: a biographical dictionary of eminent Welshmen (1852) · Emden, Oxf., 4.103–4 · J. J. Scarisbrick, Henry VIII (1968) · CSP Spain, 1554–8 · HoP, Commons, 1509–58 · will, PRO, PROB 11/44, fols. 167r–168r
Archives PRO, state papers
Wealth at death see will, PRO, PROB 11/44, fols. 167r–168r

Carne, Elizabeth Catherine Thomas

Carne, Elizabeth Catherine Thomas (1817–1873), geologist and author, was born at Riviere House, Phillack, in Cornwall, on 16 December 1817, the fifth of six children of the industrialist Joseph *Carne (1782–1858), and his wife, Mary (1777–1835), daughter of William Thomas of Haverfordwest. Her father, a Methodist, was a noted local geologist and Elizabeth Carne shared his interests; he probably taught her most of the geology she knew. In his will, he left her 'all my minerals with the cases which contain them solely because she knows more of and is more attached to the science of mineralogy than my other daughters'. She also inherited from him £22,000 and the family house, in Chapel Street, Penzance, and took over as head of the family bank, Batten, Carne, and Carne. Generous donations to schools in and around Penzance came from her inheritance, and in 1861, when the Royal Geological Society of Cornwall decided to build a new museum and offices, she gave £200 in memory of her father, for the land on which the new building would stand. Most exceptionally for a woman she was elected a member of the Royal Geological Society of Cornwall, her name first appearing on the list of members in 1865, although her first paper had been read to the society in 1860. In 1869 Miss Carne made a further offer to the society, to build a new wing to house her father's collection, but the members did not find her conditions acceptable. Nor did they approve of another offer, that she should have a 99-year lease on the front room of the museum to display the minerals, in return for the installation of galleries and heating in the building. The society therefore never had access to the Carne collection, which later went to the Sedgwick Museum of the University of Cambridge.

Miss Carne made a number of visits to places in Europe,

including Pau (described in her book, *Three Months Rest at Pau in the Winter and Spring of 1859*) and Menton, where she took the opportunity to examine parts of the geology of the French Alps, later described in her paper 'Enquiry into the age of that part of the district of the Maritime Alps which surrounds Mentone', *Transactions of the Royal Geological Society of Cornwall* 7 (1865) 433–41. She also wrote three more papers for the society, published in its *Transactions*: two continued her father's work on granites and raised beaches, and a third was on the metamorphic rocks of Cornwall. Her papers show acute observation, wide reading of geological literature, and a willingness to put forward new ideas. In her later years, Miss Carne and an elder sister spent many hours in the museum, arranging and labelling the existing collection. She was also the author of a number of books and many papers for the *London Quarterly Review* (some under the pseudonym John Altrayd Wittitterly). She died at 6 Coulson's Terrace, Penzance, of typhoid fever, on 7 September 1873, and was buried on 12 September at Phillack churchyard.

DENISE CROOK

Sources Boase & Courtney, *Bibl. Corn.* · A. C. Todd, 'The Royal Geological Society of Cornwall', *Present views of some aspects of the geology of Cornwall and Devon*, ed. K. F. G. Hosking and G. J. Shrimpton (1964), 1–23 · *60th annual report of the Royal Geological Society of Cornwall* (1873), 31 · E. Carne, 'Enquiry into the age of that part of the district of the Maritime Alps which surrounds Mentone', *Transactions of the Royal Geological Society of Cornwall*, 7 (1865), 433–41 · E. Carne, 'Enquiry into the nature of the forces that have acted on the formation and elevation of the Land's End granite', *Transactions of the Royal Geological Society of Cornwall*, 9 (1878), 132–51 · d. cert.
Archives Cornwall RO, sketches of places in Europe and Isles of Scilly
Wealth at death under £35,000: probate, 20 Oct 1873, *CGPLA Eng. & Wales*

Carne, James Power (1906–1986), army officer, was born on 11 April 1906 at 8 Cambridge Place, Falmouth, Cornwall, the son of George Newby Carne, manager of the Falmouth Brewery, and his wife, Annie Emily, *née* Power. He was educated at the Imperial Service College, Windsor (later merged with Haileybury College) and the Royal Military College, Sandhurst, and was commissioned into the Gloucestershire regiment in 1925. He was seconded to the King's African rifles from 1930 to 1936 but returned to become adjutant of the 1st battalion, the Gloucestershire regiment, from 1937 to 1940. After the outbreak of the Second World War he returned to the King's African rifles, then served on the staff in Madagascar. He commanded the 6th and 26th battalions of the King's African rifles between 1943 and 1946, and served in Burma in 1944. On 20 December 1946 he married Jean Gibson (1908/9–1992), daughter of William Harry Ferguson, businessman, and widow of Lieutenant-Colonel J. T. Gibson, of the Welch regiment. There was one son from her first marriage, but no children of her marriage to Carne.

Carne commanded the 5th (TA) battalion of the Gloucestershire regiment from 1947 to 1950, but when the 1st battalion was ordered to Korea in August 1950 he was appointed to command it. At the end of the Second World War,

Korea, which had been annexed by Japan in 1905, was divided at the 38th parallel, leaving Soviet forces dominating the northern zone and the United States the southern. North Korea then became a Soviet-influenced communist state and South Korea a democracy under United States tutelage. On 25 June 1950 North Korean troops invaded South Korea and thus produced a reaction from the United Nations, which mustered an intervention force; although this was largely American, it contained elements from many other countries. After initial setbacks the UN force, commanded by General Douglas MacArthur, made a brilliant counter-attack, destroying the North Korean army, and advanced into North Korea with the intention of unifying the country. This move alarmed the Chinese who, after issuing warnings, intervened with large numbers of fanatical, experienced troops, and drove the UN forces back over the 38th parallel.

Carne was awarded a DSO for his handling of his troops in the early stages of the war, and was awarded the Victoria Cross for his part in the Gloucesters' heroic stand on the Imjin River between 22 and 24 April 1951. For three days and nights the Gloucesters were attacked by Chinese forces, who outnumbered them by twenty to one. The Gloucesters, who began the battle with fewer than 800 men, were trying to hold a front of 12,000 yards. The Imjin itself was not a formidable obstacle to the attackers. In these circumstances Carne, a quiet, almost inarticulate officer, led by example, moving about the battlefield with unruffled calm, often smoking a pipe, although the enemy machine-gun and mortar fire were unrelenting. Air support and reinforcements failed to reach him, and his task as a commander of an infantry battalion in a precarious situation was not helped by misleading and often inexplicable orders from the higher command. On several occasions he took command of small assault parties himself in order to recover positions which had been lost. With ammunition almost all expended, a huge number of casualties (only 169 of the original strength were still on their feet) and with the Chinese bypassing on either side, Carne was told that, as he could not be relieved, he should divide his remaining troops into small groups and order them to make for the UN line further back. He himself was captured while commanding one of those smaller groups. The Chinese had by then taken such heavy losses that they never again attempted a similar frontal assault.

Captivity in North Korea proved very different from internment in Germany or Italy in the Second World War, and was similar to the sadistic treatment experienced by the prisoners who fell into Japanese hands in 1942. Starvation, torture, and back-breaking hard work were routine procedures to break the spirits of prisoners and to make them convert to communism. Political lectures were delivered, but the main inducement was that conversion would be followed by freedom—in Korea or China. Successes were very few and this fact owed much to the steadfastness and resilience shown by Carne and others, although they were weakened by disease and dismayed by the increasing number of deaths among the prisoners. (However, one convert was George Blake, who later became an important Soviet agent working in the Foreign Office.) At one stage Carne and a fellow officer were convicted of having a 'generally hostile' attitude towards communism, forced to read out bogus confessions, and put in solitary confinement. Carne preserved his sanity by making stone carvings. He and his fellow prisoners were eventually released after more than two years of captivity, and returned to a heroes' welcome at Southampton on 15 October 1953.

In addition to the VC and DSO, Carne was awarded the American Distinguished Service Cross (in 1953). He retired from the army in 1957, settling in Cranham, Gloucestershire, was granted the freedom of Gloucester in 1953 and of Falmouth in 1954, and was deputy lieutenant for Gloucester in 1960. His only comment on his captivity was: 'I have gained an added pride in being British and have lost a little weight' (The Times). He died of bronchopneumonia and carcinoma of the pharynx at the Cotswold Nuffield Nursing Home, Talbot Road, Cheltenham, Gloucestershire, on 19 April 1986. He was survived by his wife and stepson. He was buried at Cranham, and the stone cross which he carved for use at prison camp services was placed in Gloucester Cathedral.

PHILIP WARNER

Sources D. Harvey, Monuments to courage: VC headstones and memorials, 2 (1999) · Gloucestershire regimental records · M. Hastings, The Korean War (1987) · A. Farrar-Hockley, The edge of the sword (1954) · D. S. Daniell [A. S. Daniell], Cap of honour: the story of the Gloucestershire regiment, new edn (1975) · E. J. Khan, The Gloucesters [1951] · M. Page, A history of the king's African rifles and east African forces (1998) · WWW, 1981–90 · The Times (23 April 1986) · b. cert. · m. cert. · d. cert.
Likenesses photograph, repro. in The Times · photograph, repro. in Register of the Victoria Cross, 3rd edn (1997), 54

Carne, John (1789–1844), traveller and author, was born on 18 June 1789, probably at Truro. His father, William Carne (1754–1836), was a partner in the Angarrack tin smelting works near Hayle and a partner in the bank of Batten and Carne; he married in 1780 Miss Anna Cock (d. 8 November 1822). John was the second son of the marriage: his elder brother was Joseph *Carne, and he had a younger brother, John James. Carne was a member of Queens' College, Cambridge, at different times after 1812, both before and after his journey to the East, but he never resided long enough for a degree. In 1824 he married Ellen (d. 1868), daughter of Mr Lane, a poor drawing-master of Worcester. Her brother, Theodore Lane, an artist of much promise and an exhibitioner at the Royal Academy, met with an untimely fate by falling through a skylight at the horse bazaar in Gray's Inn Lane on 21 May 1828, when his daughter Emma was adopted by her uncle. Carne was admitted in 1826 to deacon's orders but, except during a few months' residence at Vevey in Switzerland, he never officiated as a clergyman.

Carne's father, a strict man of business, wanted his son to follow in his footsteps, as had his elder brother, but after a short trial of business allowed him to follow his literary inclinations. His first literary attempt was the anonymous Poems Containing the Indian and Lazarus (1820). Carne resolved to visit the holy places, and accordingly

left England on 26 March 1821. He visited Constantinople, Greece, the Levant, Egypt, and Palestine. In Palestine, while returning from St Catherine's Monastery on Mount Sinai, he was imprisoned for a few days by Bedouin. Back in England he published in the New Monthly Magazine an account of his travels entitled 'Letters from the East', which was in 1826 reproduced in a volume dedicated to Sir Walter Scott, which went to a third edition. This work and his talents for society brought him into the company of Scott, Southey, Campbell, Lockhart, Jerdan, and other men of letters. His friends rated him more as a story-teller than as a writer, and he often captivated audiences by his tales.

In later life Carne lived chiefly in Penzance. He aged prematurely and he ceased to write some years before his death. While preparing to set out for the Mediterranean he was attacked by a sudden illness and died at Penzance on 19 April 1844, and was buried in Gulval churchyard. He was survived by his wife, who subsequently remarried.

Carne wrote prolifically, based largely on his travels to the East (1826, 1830, 1831) and to Switzerland and Italy (1834), and on missionary activity (1833, 1844, 1852). His books were well reviewed at the time for their content and style, but passed relatively quickly into obscurity.

G. C. BOASE, rev. ELIZABETH BAIGENT

Sources Boase, Mod. Eng. biog. · W. R. Dawson and E. P. Uphill, Who was who in Egyptology, 3rd edn, rev. M. L. Bierbrier (1995) · Venn, Alum. Cant. · Allibone, Dict. · D. Gilbert, almanac, Cornwall RO, DG/24A

Carne, Joseph (1782–1858), geologist and industrialist, was born on 17 April 1782 at Penzance, Cornwall, the eldest son of William Carne (1754–1836), a banker and a partner in the Angarrack tin smelting works near Hayle. A Methodist throughout his life, Carne was educated at the Wesleyan school, Keynsham, near Bristol. He was involved with a number of local businesses; in 1807 he was appointed manager of the Cornish Copper Company at Hayle, the only company to attempt to smelt copper ore in Cornwall, and remained in this post until the company ceased smelting in 1819. On 23 March 1808 he married Mary (1777–1835), daughter of William Thomas, physician, of Haverfordwest, Pembrokeshire. They had one son and five daughters, including Elizabeth Catherine Thomas *Carne (1817–1873).

In 1819 the Cornish Copper Company was renamed Sandys, Carne, and Vivian, and continued to produce iron products. Carne became a partner and on behalf of the company played a leading role in pursuing a legal dispute, over ownership of some land at Hayle harbour, against Harvey & Co. of Hayle between 1813 and 1832. In 1823 he joined the bank of Batten, Carne, and Carne in which his father was a senior partner. Carne was involved in many public activities in Penzance. He was the first secretary of the Penzance Dispensary (founded in 1809), treasurer of the Royal Geological Society of Cornwall from 1827 to 1858, secretary of the Penzance Library in 1824, and president of the same institution from 1834 until his death; in 1839 he was elected president of the Penzance Natural History Society. He also served as a justice of the peace from 1836. He was noted for his benevolence to Methodist causes, donating 500 guineas to the Methodist centenary fund for the Cornish district in 1839, and facilitating purchases of land for Methodist chapels and Sunday schools.

From an early age Carne took an interest in geology, perhaps learning through other Cornish men of science or from working miners. He was elected an honorary member of the Geological Society of London at its foundation in 1807, and in 1814 was a founder member of the Cornwall Geological Society (later the Royal Geological Society of Cornwall). He read a total of thirty-six papers to this latter society, of which nine were published. The majority of his papers reflect his interests in the economic geology of Cornwall. He contributed annual reports of the quantities of tin ore mined and smelted in the county; a paper summarizing these reports was published in the *Journal of the Statistical Society* (1839). Two of his papers published in the *Transactions of the Royal Geological Society of Cornwall* were particularly important. In the first, 'On the relative ages of the veins of Cornwall' (1822), he showed that the mineralized veins of Cornwall had been formed later than the rocks in which they were to be found. He classified veins into three groups: contemporaneous (formed at the same time as the containing rocks), doubtful (possibly formed contemporaneously), and true veins (formed after the rocks). For the last and most important group, he found that there were eight stages of vein formation, not all of which produced minerals; he also showed that some of the later veins had displaced earlier ones by faulting. His paper 'On the mineral productions and geology of the parish of St Just' (1822) was accompanied by a map of the St Just area showing the geology and the main mineral veins and the location of mines and stream-tin works, both active and closed. He also located, with some assistance from R. W. Fox (1789–1877), the areas where minerals of interest to geologists and collectors might be found.

In 1830 Carne made a study of stream (diluvial) tin, the most valuable tin ore then found in Cornwall, and argued that it had been eroded from tin veins by a powerful flood; he suggested that the evidence from these stream-tin deposits was 'most decidedly opposed to the doctrine that "all the changes which have taken place on the earth's surface have arisen from causes which are still in operation"' (J. Carne, 'A description of the stream-work at drift mine near Penzance', *Transactions of the Royal Geological Society of Cornwall*, 4, 1834, 55), a reference to the theories of Charles Lyell, then recently published. Carne read further papers to the Royal Geological Society of Cornwall on the history of silver and copper mining in Cornwall (1818), on recent improvements in copper mining (1822), the origin of the sands of north Cornwall (1827), the granite of the west of Cornwall (1827) and of the Isles of Scilly (1828), and raised beaches (1838).

Carne had an important collection of Cornish minerals, made during his visits to mines throughout the county, which he left to his daughter Elizabeth on his death, and which is now in the Sedgwick Museum, Cambridge. In his later years, he spent much of his time in the Penzance Library, cataloguing its collection of books, many of which

he had himself purchased. He died of bronchitis at his home in Chapel Street, Penzance, on 12 October 1858, and was buried at Phillack churchyard, near Hayle, four days later.   DENISE CROOK

Sources Boase & Courtney, *Bibl. Corn.* · E. Sparrow and M. Smelt, eds., *The Penzance Library: celebration essays* (1988) · W. H. Pascoe, *CCC: the history of the Cornish Copper Company* (1981) · E. Vale, *The Harveys of Hayle: engine builders, shipwrights and merchants of Cornwall* (1966), 72–4 · J. Carne, 'On the relative age of the veins of Cornwall', *Transactions of the Royal Geological Society of Cornwall*, 2 (1822), 49–128 · J. Carne, 'On the mineral productions and geology of the parish of St Just', *Transactions of the Royal Geological Society of Cornwall*, 2 (1822), 290–358 · J. Carne, 'An account of the discovery of some varieties of tin-ore in a vein … with remarks on diluvial tin in general', *Transactions of the Royal Geological Society of Cornwall*, 4 (1832), 95–112 · G. C. Boase, *Collectanea Cornubiensia: a collection of biographical and topographical notes relating to the county of Cornwall* (1890) · J. Carne, 'Statistics of the tin mines in Cornwall, and of the consumption of tin in Great Britain', *Journal of the Statistical Society*, 2 (1839), 260–68 · *46th annual report of the Royal Geological Society of Cornwall* (1859), 5–6
Archives Royal Institution of Cornwall, Truro, papers, mainly legal and associated · U. Cam., Sedgwick Museum of Earth Sciences, mineral collection
Likenesses oils (after R. Pentreath), Penzance Library
Wealth at death under £120,000: probate, 29 Oct 1858, *CGPLA Eng. & Wales*

Carne, Robert Harkness (*bap.* 1784, *d.* 1844), Calvinist minister, was the fourth child and only son of John Carne (1750–1820), of St Austell, Cornwall, mercer, and his wife, Jenepher. His exact date of birth is not known; he was baptized at Holy Trinity Church, St Austell, on 10 October 1784. Educated privately, he matriculated at Exeter College, Oxford, on 15 January 1803, taking his BA on 19 November 1806. He was ordained deacon by John Fisher, bishop of Exeter, on 21 February 1807 in London, and priest by George Pelham, bishop of Exeter, on 28 August 1808 in Exeter Cathedral. He was licensed successively as assistant curate to the parishes of Crediton (August 1808; £40 a year); Drewsteignton (October 1809, 80 guineas a year, plus surplice fees and use of the parsonage house and garden); and Torbryan (1815, £75 a year).

Some time after 1815, and as the result of Carne's advancing Calvinistic doctrines, his licence to preach was withdrawn by Bishop Pelham. He then served briefly as curate in another parish in the diocese of Exeter without licence, until the incumbent received a caution from the bishop. Shortly afterwards, Carne was elected to the lectureship of Marazion Chapel, Mount's Bay, Cornwall, by the local corporation, the mayor writing to the bishop announcing the result. Bishop Pelham replied:

> Mr Carne knows that to his moral conduct I have nothing to object, indeed I have every reason to believe it exemplary, but to my conception the doctrines he maintains are not those of the Church of England, nor are they, as I conceive, according to its discipline. I therefore cannot conscientiously license him, and without a license no clergyman is authorized to preach. (Carne)

Carne then moved to Berkshire where he served—unlicensed and unmolested by John Fisher, by then bishop of Salisbury—as curate of an unidentified parish;

his health soon declined, however, and after twelve months he was compelled to resign. During 1820 he seceded from the Church of England, objecting to the recent violence inflicted upon his conscience and right to private judgement by the bishop of Exeter.

Although an outspoken Calvinist, Carne publicly opposed the excesses of the so-called Western Schism, an antinomian group secession from the church, whose leaders, 'inflated with self-conceit' (Carne), had lapsed into heterodoxy. He could not stomach their claim that sanctification was so complete at the moment of conversion that it inoculated the believer against the eternal effects of sin; nor could he accept the ideas that forgiveness and pardon were unnecessary (since believers were already forgiven and pardoned), that the Lord's prayer was erroneous, and that confession was gratuitous. Between 1821 and 1822 Carne served as minister of the Whitefield Calvinistic Tabernacle, Coombe Street, Exeter. In 1822 he formed High Street Chapel, Musgrave's Alley, Exeter, which operated along the lines of the Countess of Huntingdon's Connexion. His relationship with the chapel continued until about 1835 when, under his successor, a new building was constructed in Grosvenor Place. In retirement he lived in Jersey, where he died from apoplexy at St Helier on 12 July 1844. He was buried at St Helier four days later.

Carne was the author of a large number of published works touching upon the major doctrinal controversies of the day, including *All the Elect Children of God Contemplated as Members of One Body* (1817); *The proper deity, and distinct personality, agency, and worship of the Holy Spirit vindicated against the recent evils of Mssrs Baring, Bevan, Cowan … (1818)*, and *Apostasy of Mr Huyshe, Exposed* (1821). His *Reasons for Withdrawing from the National Establishment* (1820) contains a number of biographical details. His influence in westcountry nonconformist circles was considerable.

GRAYSON CARTER

Sources A. Brockett, *Nonconformity in Exeter, 1650–1875* (1962) · Devon RO, Exeter diocesan records · R. H. Carne, *Reasons for withdrawing from the national establishment* (1820) · G. Carter, 'Evangelical seceders from the Church of England, c.1800–1850', DPhil diss., U. Oxf., 1990 · *Chronique de Jersey* (20 July 1844) · Boase & Courtney, *Bibl. Corn.*, 1.61–2, 3.1114 · IGI

Carnegie, Andrew (1835–1919), steelmaker and philanthropist, was born in Moodie Street, Dunfermline, Fife, on 25 November 1835, the eldest of three children of William Carnegie (d. 1855), a damask linen weaver, and his wife, Margaret. After the age of eight he was educated at a Lancastrian school. Other influences on him—aside from his parents' poverty—were his family's nonconformity (his father was a Swedenborgian) and its Chartist sympathies.

From rags to riches In 1848 the depression in the linen trade prompted the Carnegies to emigrate to the United States, where they joined relatives in Pittsburgh in the picturesquely named district of Slabtown, Allegheny. Andrew Carnegie began work at the age of thirteen as a bobbin-boy in a cotton factory at a weekly wage of $1.20, thus beginning a classic rise from 'rags to riches'. The

Andrew Carnegie (1835–1919), by unknown photographer

early phase of his career, up to about 1863—by which time he had already acquired the income of a dollar millionaire—was characterized by his energy, his ability to attract the attention and help of those in authority, and his unerring knack of being in the right industry at the right time. By 1850 he had become a messenger-boy at the O'Reilly Telegraph Company in Pittsburgh. Three years later he was appointed clerk and telegraph operator to Thomas A. Scott, assistant superintendent of the Pennsylvania Railroad Company. According to Carnegie, 'the great aim of every boy should be to do something beyond the sphere of his abilities—something which attracts the attention of those over him' (Wall, 126). Carnegie did just that, and Scott rewarded him with ever greater authority and also loaned his assistant the capital to invest in the Adams Express stock, the dividends from which gave Carnegie his first taste of capitalism. Another investment soon after, in the Woodruff Sleeping Car Company, proved the basis of his great fortune. In 1859 Scott became vice-president of the Pennsylvania Railroad Company and appointed Andy (as Carnegie was known) to take his former post as superintendent of the western division of the line. A short man—only 5 feet 3 inches tall—Carnegie grew a beard to disguise his youth, as he was at the time only twenty-four. A hard taskmaster, he quickly proved himself a most effective manager on one of the busiest divisions of what was then the nation's best-managed railroad.

By the time of the American Civil War, Carnegie's interests had diversified: besides the Woodruff Sleeping Car Company (ultimately absorbed by the Pullman Car Company, a deal which he helped negotiate), he had interests in the Columbia Oil Company, a scheme for building telegraph lines, a project for establishing a sutler's business for the army, a horse-trading concern, a bridge-building company, a locomotive works, and several other ventures. Nearly all of these made money and by 1868, when he had moved to New York, he had assets of $400,000 and an annual income of over $56,000. He seriously considered retiring at the age of thirty-five, declaring in a private note to himself that: 'No idol was more debasing than the worship of money' (Wall, 225). However, by then wider horizons beckoned.

Carnegie's railroad experience convinced him that an even greater fortune could be made in the iron and steel industry. It was one of the reasons why after the civil war he had organized the Keystone Bridge Company in Pittsburgh. Having become even more convinced of the potential of the new Bessemer process on a visit to England in 1872, he decided to commit himself more fully to the iron and steel business during the depression of 1873. His key decision was to invest $250,000 in the Edgar Thomson Steel Company, formed in 1874 with a capital of $1 million. The Bessemer plant at the company's site at Braddock's Field, near Pittsburgh—laid out by the engineer Alexander Holley—was designed to manufacture rails. Carnegie's huge success with this venture was due first to his commitment to technological change and second to his previous experience with the railroads. He wanted to have the most modern equipment available and was willing, if necessary, to scrap expensive machinery after only a short time if better technology could be had. The administrative structure he put together at the Edgar Thomson works was similar to the one he had worked in at the Pennsylvania Railroad Company. He appointed the country's most talented steel engineer, Captain William Jones, as general superintendent to oversee the daily work of the managers in charge of the blast furnaces, Bessemer converters, and other departments of the works.

Business attitudes and tactics As general manager, Carnegie selected William P. Shinn, a highly competent railroad executive who had been appointed the general agent of the Pennsylvania company when it was formed in 1871. Shinn introduced methods (copied from the railroads) of generating statistical data, which allowed Carnegie to become an early exponent of cost accounting. He insisted on knowing the exact expense of every operation and did his best to reduce costs. His maxim was: watch the costs and the profits will take care of themselves. He also appreciated the need to control raw materials in order to assure continuous operations and minimize costs. He purchased ore lands in the Lake Superior region, acquired boats and ore-handling facilities, and joined forces in 1884 with Henry Clay Frick (1849–1919), who controlled the great Connesville coal beds. Carnegie Bros. & Co.—the head of this large vertical combine—was formed in 1881 with a capital of $5 million; its chairman was Tom Carnegie

(1843–1886), Andrew's brother, though after 1889 Frick held the post. Andrew Carnegie himself had no title, though he controlled 55 per cent of the capital in the partnership, which made a profit of $2 million in its first year. In 1887, a year after the death of his mother, he married, on 22 April, Louise Whitfield (d. 1946), daughter of John W. Whitfield, a prosperous merchant; they had one daughter, Margaret.

Carnegie had a remarkable talent for picking men from the ranks and he gave a good deal of freedom to his youthful executives (his 'young geniuses', as he liked to refer to them). Besides Jones and Frick, Charles Schwab, who later became president of the United States Steel Corporation, was another notable recruit. But there was a cost: job security was poor and managers were expended as ruthlessly as old machinery if they did not perform. Tom, Carnegie's brother, was driven to drink by the pressure of running the company and died prematurely. Carnegie's attitude to labour was equally unsentimental: like most American steelmasters, he regarded labour as primarily an item of cost. Although the introduction of machinery had reduced much of the employees' toil in the furnaces, compared to European workers, American labourers in Carnegie's mills (and in other steelworks) soon found their wages reduced and their unions undermined. Carnegie's (and Frick's) policies led in 1892 to a bloody showdown with the unions at the company's works in Homestead, Pennsylvania, when both sides suffered injury. (Even Frick was shot and stabbed, though he soon recovered.) Carnegie's reputation with the public was also harmed by the débâcle, especially so since his book *Triumphant Democracy* (1886) expounded his theories of philanthropy and democracy. Nevertheless, he and Frick had removed steel unionism from their steelworks.

Carnegie's ruthless business tactics paid dividends during the bitter depression years of the 1890s, when the recurrent price wars and the economies of scale possessed by large-scale production resulted in many of his rivals failing to survive. Meanwhile, Carnegie thrived. By the end of the 1890s his business had profits of $20 million. For the year 1900 they stood at $40 million. After the mergers of the 1890s, however, the Carnegie company itself began to face stiff competition in selling ingots to specialized producers. When Carnegie threatened to enter the market for finished products—thus raising the spectre of another vicious price war—a number of his rivals persuaded the New York banker J. P. Morgan to arrange a massive consolidation that would absorb Carnegie's interests and those of other competitors. After much negotiation (during which Carnegie succeeded in forcing out Frick), the United States Steel Corporation was formed—the world's first billion-dollar company—and Carnegie sold out his interest. As John D. Rockefeller had done in oil, Carnegie had accumulated one of the greatest fortunes the world had ever seen: his share from the transaction was a staggering $447 million.

The philanthropist of Skibo At the age of sixty-five Carnegie went into 'retirement', with his wife and daughter, to his 30,000 acre estate at Skibo in Sutherland, Scotland. Now a white-bearded and kind-faced patriarch, he could play the Scottish laird at his estate, and guests were led into dinner by a piper. However, his main interests after 1900 lay in other directions. No longer a businessman, he still retained his energy, wealth, and desire to make things happen in the world. This was to be achieved by his second career as America's first great philanthropist and a new role as an international pacifist.

Like many men of influence and wealth, Carnegie was unable to resist trying to put the world to rights. He was largely self-taught and an avid reader, especially of Herbert Spencer, whose social Darwinism appealed to him. However, his actions were not always consistent with Spencer's ideas (a writer he never entirely understood). A friend of Spencer and also of Matthew Arnold, he was closely associated with such Liberal statesmen as W. E. Gladstone and John Morley. Like Cecil Rhodes, he helped to finance the Gladstonian Liberal Party after the split over home rule in 1886 and he offered Gladstone an interest-free loan of any size to set him up privately; the offer was declined. Through Gladstone as an intermediary, Carnegie bought Lord Acton's library and allowed the historian to keep it during his lifetime; after Acton's death Carnegie gave the library to Cambridge University.

A ruthless conservative in America, Carnegie posed as a Chartist and radical in Britain, where by 1884 he owned or controlled seven daily newspapers and weeklies. In his writing, too, he tried to reconcile his radical Dunfermline past with his more plutocratic present. The same man who cut workers' wages and unsentimentally refused to loan money to help Thomas Scott when he had business problems later in his career, began after the 1880s to expound the virtues of the 'wise distribution' of his wealth. 'The man who dies thus rich, dies disgraced', declared Carnegie, a doctrine that received its fullest expression in his book *The Gospel of Wealth* (1900). In his view, plutocracy such as his could exist alongside democracy, but men who acquired great wealth must return it to the community to preserve individual initiative. Thus the wealthy were but a trustee and an agent for their poorer brethren, albeit of the better and aspiring sort. His 'scientific philanthropy' was to be carefully targeted according to a list of seven priorities. These were headed by his over-riding concerns—universities and free libraries—with churches in seventh place (an indication perhaps of his lukewarm interest in organized religion). His interest in libraries dated back to his early days as a messenger-boy in Pennsylvania, when each Saturday he borrowed a new book from a free library. He later declared that it was his own personal experience which led him to value a library beyond all other forms of beneficence.

Carnegie's giving had begun as early as 1873 when he had donated $25,000 to the Dunfermline swimming baths, but it gathered pace after the publication of his 'gospel'. Within five years he gave libraries to Allegheny and to Fairfield in Iowa, while several Scottish cities, such as Edinburgh and Aberdeen, were similarly endowed. In 'old smoky' Pittsburgh he founded a great civic educational centre—the Carnegie Institute. By 1900 his programme for founding libraries had become, from his house on East 91st Street in New York, as organized a business as that of churning out steel ingots. His acceptance of freedoms of cities and other civic honours also became routine. (At one stage he accepted six freedoms in six days, eventually reaching a record total of fifty-seven such awards by the end of his life.) Not surprisingly, his critics dismissed his philanthropy as mere publicity-seeking. However, not all his giving was well-publicized.

As well as free libraries, Carnegie's philanthropic vehicles included the Carnegie Teachers' Pension Fund, which targeted underpaid college personnel and pensionless professors with an endowment of $10 million. Yet despite his enthusiasm in the 1890s and early 1900s for philanthropy, he had made little impression on his great fortune (which was hardly surprising, in view of the fact that the interest on his capital was $15 million a year). He needed to disperse his fortune faster. After 1900 he began using trusts to administer his charitable gifts. After trying out the idea in Washington and Dunfermline, in 1911 he created the Carnegie Corporation of New York as his major vehicle for the 'advancement and diffusion of knowledge'. He transferred to it the bulk of his remaining fortune of $125 million. In 1913 he established, under a separate endowment, a British version of the New York trust. Bored with philanthropy, he had now given away 90 per cent of his fortune and was content to leave the direction of it to others. Eventually the trusts founded 2811 free public libraries, of which 1946 were in the USA and 660 in Britain.

The peacemaker Carnegie's other great enthusiasm after leaving steel making was his quest for world peace. Despite his early jingoism, he became a convinced pacifist after 1900. Between 1903 and 1914 he endowed four foundations and three imposing buildings ('temples of peace'), the largest of which was in The Hague. Also linked with his pacifism was the idea of a Simplified Spelling Board, which aimed to facilitate communication (it proved a total failure); and his Hero Fund, which rewarded peaceful (as opposed to warlike) individual acts of heroism. In 1910 he created the Carnegie Endowment for International Peace to hasten the abolition of war. An optimistic man, who had commanded whole industries and labour forces to do his bidding, Carnegie believed that peace could be organized on similarly rational lines. The businessman who had been a ruthless and machiavellian negotiator, and who had broken cartels and agreements to achieve his ends, now proved to have a naïve faith in international treaties and peace organizations. He proposed a league of peace, with the major superpowers—Great Britain, the USA, Germany, Russia, and France—acting as a kind of international peace force through a world court at The Hague. He also liked meddling in foreign affairs by writing to and meeting presidents, emperors, chancellors, and prime ministers. Much of his faith for the future was placed on Kaiser Wilhelm II and President Theodore Roosevelt. He counted the latter as a friend, even though their views rarely coincided, especially where naval rearmament was concerned. The First World War was therefore a considerable disillusionment to him and he did not long outlive it. He died at Lenox, Massachusetts, on 11 August 1919. By then his benefactions totalled over $350 million, leaving a fortune of a mere $30 million (two-thirds of which was left to the Carnegie Corporation). He was survived by his wife. Carnegie's *Autobiography* was published posthumously in 1920. His name is perpetuated in Britain by a number of trusts, notably the Carnegie United Kingdom, Dunfermline, and Hero trusts.

GEOFFREY TWEEDALE

Sources J. F. Wall, *Andrew Carnegie* (1970) · J. H. Bridge, *The inside history of the Carnegie Steel Trust: a romance of millions* (1903) · B. J. Hendrick, *The life of Andrew Carnegie*, 2 vols. (1932) · H. C. Livesay, *Andrew Carnegie and the rise of big business* (1975) · L. M. Hacker, *The world of Andrew Carnegie, 1865–1901* (1968) · D. Brody, *Steelworkers in America: the nonunion era* (1960) · *Autobiography of Andrew Carnegie*, ed. J. C. van Dyke (1920) · Gladstone, *Diaries* · DNB · K. Warren, *Triumphant capitalism: Henry Clay Frick and the industrial transformation of America* (1996)
Archives Andrew Carnegie Birthplace Museum, Dunfermline, personal and family corresp. and papers · L. Cong., corresp. and papers · NRA, priv. coll., corresp. · U. Aberdeen, corresp. and papers | BL, corresp. with W. E. Gladstone, Add. MSS 44490–44525, *passim* · BL OIOC, corresp. with Lord Morley, MS Eur. D 573 · Bodl. Oxf., letters to Lord Bryce · HLRO, corresp. with J. St L. Strachey · NL Scot., corresp. with Lord Haldane · NL Scot., corresp. incl. Lord Rosebery and Sir Patrick Geddes · U. Birm., corresp. relating to University of Birmingham | FILM BFI NFTVA, documentary footage; news footage
Likenesses E. Lanteri, bust, 1907 · B. J. Blommers, oils, *c*.1912, Palace of Peace, The Hague; study, Dundee City Art Gallery · E. A. Walton, oils, 1913, U. St Andr. · W. G. John, marble bust, 1914, Palace of Peace, The Hague · C. Ouless, oils (after W. W. Ouless), Scot. NPG · W. W. Ouless, portrait, repro. in *Royal Academy pictures* (1900) · Spy [L. Ward], chromolithograph caricature, NPG; repro. in *VF* (29 Oct 1903) · E. A. Walton, pencil drawing, Scot. NPG · photograph, NPG [*see illus.*]
Wealth at death $30,000,000: Wall, *Andrew Carnegie*

Carnegie, David, of Colluthie and Kinnaird (*d.* 1598), administrator, was the second son of Sir Robert *Carnegie (*d.* 1566) of Kinnaird, Forfarshire, lord of session, and his wife, Margaret Guthrie (*d.* 1571), and first appears in official records in 1555–6 as a debt manager. Given an estate by his father, at Panbride, Forfarshire, he also acquired through his first marriage, to Elizabeth (*d.* before 4 March 1567), daughter of Henry Ramsay of Colluthie, the latter's estate in Fife, which became his main base; the couple had two daughters. His second marriage, by contract dated 4 October 1568, was to Euphame (*d.* 1593), daughter of Sir John Wemyss of that ilk; they had four daughters and four sons, including David *Carnegie, later first earl of Southesk (1574/5–1658), and John *Carnegie, later first earl of Northesk (1578/9–1667). Carnegie had graduated MA, probably in law, but though he used his legal skills in his private business he only rarely used these officially (an exception being when he was named to the parliamentary commission on law reform in 1578) and he never practised as a professional lawyer.

From 1580 Carnegie was employed by the crown in ecclesiastical affairs and he was king's commissioner to the general assembly which met on 24 April 1583. But it was the experience gained from managing his estates that was particularly exploited by the crown. From 1586 Carnegie was a regular auditor of the exchequer and held other fiscal offices; a privy councillor from 1592, he was a member of more financial commissions than anyone except John Lindsay of Balcarres. Archbishop John Spottiswoode considered that Carnegie was 'a wise, peaceable and sober man, in good credit and estimation with the king, and taken into his Privy Council for his skill and knowledge in civil affairs' (Fraser, 1.59). He was no courtier and, following the death of his second wife on 16 November 1593, married by contract dated 26 April 1594 a woman of relatively humble origins, Janet Henrison (*d.* in or after 1599), possibly widow of Alexander Guthrie, town clerk of Edinburgh. Following the death of his elder brother, Sir John Carnegie, some time between 7 November 1595 and 13 May 1596, he inherited the family patrimony of Kinnaird.

On 9 January 1596 Carnegie was named as one of the commissioners of a new permanent exchequer with powers of oversight over royal revenues. The commissioners, consisting of six members of the queen's financial council together with John Skene of Curriehill and Carnegie, became known as the *Octavians, and for two years constituted an effective team. Carnegie's financial acumen was his particular contribution. He died on 19 April 1598 and was buried, as he had wished, at Kinnaird church.

VIVIENNE LARMINIE

Sources W. Fraser, *History of the Carnegies, earls of Southesk, and of their kindred*, 2 vols. (1867) · *Scots peerage* · R. Zulager, 'A study of the middle-rank administrators in the government of King James VI of Scotland, 1580–1603', PhD diss., U. Aberdeen, 1991 · J. Goodare, *Parliament and society in Scotland, 1560–1603* (1989)

Carnegie, David, first earl of Southesk (1574/5–1658), nobleman, was the eldest son of David *Carnegie of Colluthie and Kinnaird (*d.* 1598) and his second wife, Euphame (*d.* 1593), daughter of Sir John Wemyss of that ilk. John *Carnegie, first earl of Northesk (1578/9–1667), was his younger brother. He was married (contract dated 8 October 1595) to Margaret (*d.* 1614), daughter of Sir David Lindsay, laird of Edzell, and they went on to have four sons and six daughters. In 1598 he succeeded to the family estates of Kinnaird, and in 1600 he first appeared in parliament as a commissioner for the shire of Forfar.

In 1601 Carnegie obtained royal permission to travel abroad, but it seems unlikely that he actually took advantage of this licence. He was certainly at home at Kinnaird in 1602 when James VI visited for a hunting expedition, an event which was to be repeated in 1617 on James's only post-union visit to Scotland. In the summer of 1603 Carnegie travelled south with Queen Anne and the royal children, for which service he was knighted. In 1604 parliament appointed him as one of the commissioners to negotiate what turned out to be James VI's abortive attempts at closer Anglo-Scottish union. In subsequent years he was appointed to a number of parliamentary commissions on such matters as taxation, penal statutes, visitation of the University of St Andrews, and various other financial and ecclesiastical affairs. He was nominated by the king as a member of general assemblies in 1606 and 1608, and in February 1610 was appointed as a lay member of the new ecclesiastical court of high commission for the province of St Andrews. In December 1615, when the two courts of Glasgow and St Andrews were united, he remained on the new national body.

On 14 April 1616 Carnegie was raised to the peerage as Lord Carnegie of Kinnaird, and three months later he became an extraordinary lord of session. In January 1617 he joined the privy council. At the general assembly at Aberdeen in August 1616 he accompanied the king's commissioner, the earl of Montrose. In the following year he was one of the royal commissioners at St Andrews and so acted again at Perth in 1618, when the assembly was forced to approve the liturgical innovations known as the five articles. Three years later he was elected to the committee of articles for the parliament of 1621, which ratified the five articles of Perth, and voted to approve them as well as using three proxy votes to the same end.

After the death of James VI, Carnegie was one of nine privy councillors nominated to govern Scotland while the rest of the Scottish nobles and bishops travelled south to kiss the hand of the new king. In 1626 all privy councillors who were also lords of session were removed from the bench but not long thereafter Carnegie was restored to his former position. On 22 June 1633, at the time of the Scottish coronation of Charles I, he was made earl of Southesk, Lord Carnegie of Kinnaird and Leuchars. Later in that year his heir, David, Lord Carnegie, died at Edinburgh.

In 1634 Southesk was appointed to a new court of high commission and, uneasy at the unrest resulting from the imposition of a new prayer book in 1637, he attempted to mediate between a number of dissident ministers and the bishops, but failed. The king nominated him as one of the assessors to the marquess of Hamilton, royal commissioner to the general assembly at Glasgow in 1638. At that assembly Southesk's son was excluded, in spite of a commission from the presbytery of Brechin bearing many more names than that carried by the laird of Dun, who was admitted as the presbytery's commissioner. Southesk argued heatedly with the moderator, Alexander Henderson, his parish minister at Leuchars, to no avail. A few days later his signature was one of those on the privy council's order for the assembly to dissolve.

In February 1639 Southesk refused to sign the national covenant when the earl of Montrose, his son-in-law, went to Forfar gathering subscriptions. Later in that year he was appointed as one of the lords of the articles at parliament but, because of his opposition to the covenant, he was arrested in 1640 and briefly imprisoned. He soon acquiesced and was appointed to the privy council by parliament, which also elected him to commissions for financial and ecclesiastical affairs. Although not the most enthusiastic covenanter, he remained prominent in national politics, being appointed to the committee of estates in 1645, 1648, and 1651. He was appointed sheriff of Forfar on 14 October 1646, and served on the committee for war for Forfar and Kincardine in 1648. After the Cromwellian invasion of Scotland, Southesk retired from public life but, having remained loyal to the crown until its downfall, he was fined £3000 by Cromwell's regime in 1654. In the following year, however, he was appointed a commissioner for the assessment for Forfar. He died at Kinnaird on 27 February 1658, aged eighty-three, and was buried at Inverkeilor kirk, Forfarshire, on 11 March.

ALAN R. MACDONALD

Sources W. Fraser, *History of the Carnegies, earls of Southesk, and of their kindred*, 2 vols. (1867) · *Scots peerage* · *The historical works of Sir James Balfour*, ed. J. Haig, 4 vols. (1824–5) · J. Gordon, *History of Scots affairs from 1637–1641*, ed. J. Robertson and G. Grub, 3 vols., Spalding Club, 1, 3, 5 (1841) · D. Calderwood, *The history of the Kirk of Scotland*, ed. T. Thomson and D. Laing, 8 vols., Wodrow Society, 7 (1842–9) · *APS* · *The letters and journals of Robert Baillie*, ed. D. Laing, 3 vols. (1841–2)
Archives Kinnaird Castle, Brechin, Angus, corresp., estate papers, legal papers | priv. coll., corresp. incl. to Sir Robert Moray and Sir George Elphinstone
Likenesses G. Jamieson, oils, 1637, Kinnaird Castle, Brechin, Angus; repro. in Fraser, *History of the Carnegies*, facing p. 70

Carnegie, James, sixth earl of Southesk (1827–1905), poet and antiquary, was born at Edinburgh on 16 November 1827, the eldest son of the three sons and two daughters of Sir James Carnegie, fifth baronet of Pittarow (1799–1849), and his wife, Charlotte (1800–1848), daughter of Daniel *Lysons (1762–1834) of Hempstead Court, Gloucester. The father, who was fifth in descent from Alexander, fourth son of David *Carnegie, first earl of Southesk, laid claim without success to the family earldom which had been forfeited in 1715 on the attainder of James Carnegie, fifth earl, for his share in the Jacobite rising of that year.

Educated at Edinburgh Academy and at the Royal Military College, Sandhurst, James Carnegie was commissioned in the Gordon Highlanders in 1845, was transferred in 1846 to the Grenadier Guards, and retired on succeeding his father as sixth baronet in 1849. On 19 June of that year he married Lady Catherine Hamilton (d. 1855), second daughter of Charles Noel, first earl of Gainsborough. They had one son, Charles Noel, who was to succeed as seventh earl of Southesk, and three daughters. By 1854 Carnegie had restored the family residence, Kinnaird Castle at Brechin, and began collecting antique gems, books, old master paintings, and a large assortment of mid-eastern cylinders. He also disposed of much of the extensive family property, selling his estate of Glendye to Sir Thomas Gladstone of Fasque, baronet, brother of the prime minister. Renewing his father's claim to the earldom of Southesk in 1855, he obtained on 2 July an act of parliament reversing the attainder of 1715, and was confirmed in the title by the House of Lords on 24 July. In 1869, on Gladstone's recommendation, he was made a knight of the Thistle, and on 7 December of the same year a peer of the United Kingdom, with the title Baron Balinhard of Farnell.

Southesk's wife died in 1855, and in 1859, for health reasons, he went on a long hunting expedition in western

Canada. On his return in 1860 he married, on 29 November, Lady Susan Catherine Mary Murray, daughter of Alexander Edward, sixth earl of Dunmore, with whom he was to have three sons and four daughters. Also in 1860 he was made a fellow of the Royal Geographical Society, but the diary of his Canadian travels, *Saskatchewan and the Rocky Mountains*, was not published until 1875. The work records his travel and sporting adventures and has some interesting plates, maps, and illustrations.

However, Carnegie's chief writing interests were literary. He had published *Herminius, a Romance* in 1862 and an essay, 'Britain's art paradise' (on the Royal Academy exhibition of 1871). In 1875 he published anonymously *Jonas Fisher: a Poem in Brown and White*, which caused some controversy. In a hostile review in *The Examiner*, the book was incorrectly ascribed to Robert Buchanan, who successfully sued the editor of the journal, Peter A. Taylor, for libel. This title, and those which followed, were minor poetic works. Rhys described Carnegie as having a 'certain mystic tendency' (Rhys, 345) and this attraction to fantasy and the occult is reflected in the titles of some of his publications: *Lurida lumina* (1876), *Greenwood's Farewell* (1876), *The Meda Maiden* (1877), *The Burial of Isis* (1844), and *Suomira, a Fantasy*, which was printed privately in 1899.

In later years Carnegie's interest in the recondite found a more productive outlet in his antiquarian and archaeological research, particularly in Pictish stones and symbols. A distinguished member of the Society of Antiquaries of Scotland, he read several papers, some of which were later published: 'The Newton stone' (1884), 'The ogham inscriptions of Scotland' (1885), and 'The origins of Pictish symbolism' (1893).

Carnegie was made an honorary LLD of St Andrews in 1872, and of Aberdeen University in 1875. He died at Kinnaird Castle on 21 February 1905.

CATHERINE KERRIGAN

Sources Burke, *Peerage* · *Scots peerage* · *The Times* (22 Feb 1905) · J. Rhys, *The Athenaeum* (18 March 1905) · *DCB*, vol. 10 **Archives** NL Scot., letters to Alan Reid **Likenesses** R. J. Lane, lithograph, 1861 (after J. R. Swinton), NPG · J. R. Swinton, chalk, 1861, Kinnaird Castle · J. Watson-Gordon, oils, 1861, Kinnaird Castle · A. D. Wilson, oils, 1899, Kinnaird Castle **Wealth at death** £56,296 3s. 3d.: confirmation, 26 April 1905, *CCI*

Carnegie, John, first earl of Northesk (1578/9–1667), nobleman, was the second son of David *Carnegie of Colluthie and Kinnaird (d. 1598) and his second wife, Euphame Wemyss (d. 1593), daughter of Sir John Wemyss of that ilk. David *Carnegie, first earl of Southesk (1574/5–1658), was his elder brother. On 1 March 1595 he received a charter of the barony of Ethie from James VI, his father having resigned the lands into the king's hands, and this grant was confirmed by the king in 1604. In December 1609 he left Scotland to travel on the continent, visiting Marseilles and Paris where, according to his correspondence, he went to some lengths to buy a clock. He returned to Britain in the latter part of 1610 and was knighted. He acquired various lands in Forfarshire (Angus) and became its sheriff-principal in July 1620.

Carnegie was initially opposed to the national covenant of 1638, and in 1639 he and a number of others of like mind attempted to leave Scotland. Stayed at Dunbar by storms, however, they were arrested and briefly imprisoned. On 20 April of that year Charles I raised Carnegie to the peerage as Lord Lour. He must have subscribed the covenant, for he attended parliament quite regularly during the 1640s and was in 1641 appointed to the first committee of estates, and in 1644 was made a member of the committee of war for Angus and the Mearns. In November 1647 he was made earl of Ethie, Lord Lour and Eglismaldie, and in the following year was again appointed to the committee of estates. His first marriage, some time after March 1610, was to Magdalen, daughter of Sir James Haliburton of Pitcur and widow of John Erskine of Dun. They had three sons and five daughters. She died on 10 March 1650, and on 29 April 1652 he married Marjory, daughter of Andrew Maule of Guildie and widow of William Nairne. They had no children.

During the Cromwellian occupation of Scotland, Ethie was fined £6000 sterling under Cromwell's ordinance of pardon and grace in April 1654, although an appeal reduced this to only £2000. After the restoration of Charles II, he succeeded his younger brother Sir Robert Carnegie of Dunnichen as dempster of parliament and of the justice and circuit courts of Forfarshire. In 1663 he was appointed by parliament a justice of the peace for Forfarshire. By a patent dated 25 October 1666 Ethie obtained a change in his titles, becoming earl of Northesk, Lord Rosehill and Eglismauldie. He died at Ethie on 8 January 1667, aged eighty-eight, and was buried in the family burial place at Inverkeilor kirk. ALAN R. MACDONALD

Sources W. Fraser, *History of the Carnegies, earls of Southesk, and of their kindred*, 2 vols. (1867) · *Scots peerage* · *The historical works of Sir James Balfour*, ed. J. Haig, 2 (1824) · *APS* **Archives** Dundee Central Library, MSS, GD/N **Likenesses** G. Jamieson?, oils, 1637, priv. coll.

Carnegie, Sir Robert, of Kinnaird (d. 1566), diplomat and judge, was the son of John Carnegie of Kinnaird (d. 1513) and Jane Vaus. He inherited the family estates in Forfarshire on his father's death. He married Margaret Guthrie, the daughter of a north-east laird, and they had at least three sons. He also had an illegitimate son, John Carnegie of that ilk and of Ethie (d. 1604), 'a gifted administrator' (Bardgett, 58), who became prominent in local affairs.

In the 1540s Carnegie was one of a group of lairds in Angus and the Mearns who favoured the reformation of the church. In 1544 he supported Matthew Stewart, fourth earl of Lennox, in his opposition to the governor, James Hamilton, second earl of Arran, who had ceased his short-lived programme of protestant reform and was pursuing a more pro-French policy. Carnegie was with Lennox when he was besieged by the governor at Glasgow in April 1544; he later received a remission for his support of Lennox and for being absent in England without licence and collaborating with the English.

Thereafter, however, Carnegie remained on good terms with Arran, who made him a lord of session on 4 July 1547 and treasurer-clerk from 1551, and with whose administration he was associated. He was justice depute for the trial of the earl of Rothes following the assassination of Cardinal Beaton. In 1548 he was dispatched to England to negotiate the ransom of George Gordon, fourth earl of Huntly, who had been captured at the battle of Pinkie in 1547; he subsequently helped Huntly to escape. Having become keeper of the great seal, he enjoyed its profits while Huntly, who was chancellor, remained abroad. Carnegie then proceeded to France on Arran's behalf to thank Henri II for the assistance he had given the Scots. He also had connections with Mary of Guise and, according to John Lesley, was involved in the negotiations by which Arran acquired the duchy of Châtelherault, allegedly on the understanding that Mary of Guise would succeed him as regent. Carnegie was further employed in negotiations with England on several occasions: in 1551 he was in charge of the Scottish deputation to finalize the peace treaties, in 1553 and 1554 he was one of the Scottish commissioners appointed to resolve disputes on the border, and in 1557 Mary of Guise, who had become regent in 1554, appointed him as an ambassador to England and he was again a commissioner to resolve border disputes. Before his departure, on 1 April 1557 he made a will which omitted both traditional Catholic clauses involving the intercession of the saints and common protestant phraseology, but naming as his overseers John Hamilton, archbishop of St Andrews, and Robert Reid, bishop of Orkney, who were both at this date sympathetic to moderate reform. In 1558 Carnegie stood surety for Abbot Donald Campbell when the latter borrowed money to procure the bishopric of Brechin following his nomination by the regent.

Although his connections with the reformers dated back to the 1540s and he continued to have ties with such men as John Erskine, Lord Erskine of Dun, Carnegie's role during the Reformation crisis of 1559–60 was dictated more by his close links with both Châtelherault—he was later described as 'frende to the Duke' (*CSP Scot.*, 2.174)—and Mary of Guise. John Knox accused him of being one of those who in 1559 'for the fainting of the brethren's hearts, and drawing many to the Queen's faction against their native country, have declared themselves enemies to God, and traitors to their Commonwealth' (*Knox's History*, 2.219). According to Knox, Carnegie was used by the regent to solicit support for her cause, particularly with Châtelherault, and declared by her to be 'of good credit and reputation' (ibid., 2.237), yet it is probable that his loyalty was more to the crown than to the regent personally.

Carnegie's political career continued into the personal reign of Queen Mary. He remained loyal to the queen during the rebellion which followed her marriage to Henry Stewart, Lord Darnley, and was appointed as a member of the privy council in 1565, which he attended for the last time on 1 December 1565. He died on 5 July 1566, having made a second will at Leuchars, 'beinge in his bed deidly seik in bodie' (Bardgett, 156), in the presence of his three legitimate sons. The eldest, John (*d.* 1596), became Sir John

Carnegie of Kinnaird; David *Carnegie (*d.* 1598) was established at Colluthie; Robert had become minister of Kinnoull. Carnegie was possibly the author of the legal work *Lib. Carneg.*, the text of which has not survived, referred to by Sir James Balfour in his *Practicks*.   SHARON ADAMS

Sources J. Leslie, *The historie of Scotland*, ed. E. G. Cody and W. Murison, trans. J. Dalrymple, 2 vols. in 4 pts, STS, 5, 14, 19, 34 (1888–95) [1596 trans. of *De origine moribus, et rebus gestis Scotorum libri decem* (Rome, 1578)] • *John Knox's History of the Reformation in Scotland*, ed. W. C. Dickinson, 2 vols. (1949) • *CSP Scot.* • *Reg. PCS*, 1st ser. • F. D. Bardgett, *Scotland reformed: the Reformation in Angus and the Mearns* (1989)

Archives Kinnaird Castle, Brechin, Angus, Southesk private family muniments

Carnegie [*née* Scott], **Susan** (1743–1821), writer and benefactor, was born on 7 August 1743 in Edinburgh, the daughter of David Scott of Benholm (1700–1768), director and treasurer of the Bank of Scotland, and Mary Brown (1712–1794). She was tutored at home and gained a wide and deep knowledge of French and Italian literature and of philosophy, a proficiency in drawing (which she was taught by a relative Sir Alexander Ramsay of Balmain), and an interest in social and economic affairs. From her reading of Rousseau's *Émile* she learned to challenge the idea that women were intellectually less able than men, choosing instead to explain discrepancies in terms of women's educational opportunities and their general treatment in a patriarchal society. Certainly in her correspondence Susan was fearless in drawing attention to a lack of respect or of rudeness on the part of male writers. Prior to her marriage (contract signed on 17 March 1769) to George Carnegie of Pitarrow (1726–1799), the son of Sir John Carnegie and Mary Burnett, she acknowledged her future husband's right to command her, but hoped 'that he never will have [the] occasion or inclination to exercise it'.

As a young woman Carnegie published a number of poems under the pseudonym Juliette North, and took the name Arethusa in her correspondence with James Beattie, the Aberdeen poet and moral philosopher. Carnegie's own interest in moral philosophy led her to the belief that the most important motive for doing good was not to please God but the innate propriety of an action. It was this which proved the foundation of her philanthropic activities in which she was involved while bringing up a family of six sons and three daughters. Following her marriage she moved from the family home at Benholm Castle to Charleton House, Montrose, where she lived for the rest of her life.

In 1779 Carnegie began work with Provost Alexander Christie on the project for which she is now best known: the construction at Montrose of Scotland's first lunatic asylum. Prior to this date the mentally ill had been held at the town's prison with little or no chance of rehabilitation. Carnegie's desire to treat such people humanely and to provide them with the chance of reintegration within the community proved a principal motivation throughout the programme. Having secured the approval of the kirk session of the town council in March 1779, Carnegie engaged in fundraising through her numerous social connections and from revenue of the estates she received from her husband at their marriage. By March 1781 subscriptions had reached £679 18s. 9d.; building work now began and was completed in budget later that year. Within a decade Carnegie had established the asylum's place as a refuge for patients in and beyond Montrose which was staffed—in what was then a new innovation—by a resident medical superintendent. Carnegie's asylum became a model for similar institutions both in Scotland and in Göteborg in Sweden (the Sahlgranska sickhouse opened 1782), where her husband worked for the Swedish East India Company during the 1750s.

In addition to her work for the asylum Carnegie was also involved in raising funds for the kirk at Montrose, helped the kirk session to organize local poor relief (for which she wrote *An Appeal to the Inhabitants of the Town and Parish of Montrose* in 1803), and assisted many widows, orphans, and bankrupts in the parish. In 1814 she was praised by one local man for 'Mr Carnegie's little work on the poor of her parish. I say *Mr*, for it is *une production male*'. During the Napoleonic wars she made use of the friendly society and the savings bank in the general organization of poor relief, as well as founding a female friendly society in Montrose.

Carnegie's tolerance of all aspects of her local community was also evident in her religious faith. Originally from an episcopalian family (which converted to presbyterianism following the revolution of 1688) she prayed regularly with her husband, whose own enduring episcopalianism led him to support the Jacobite challenge at Culloden before spending his decade as a merchant in Sweden. Susan Carnegie died on 14 April 1821 at Charleton, and was buried in the family vault at Howff, Charleton. The asylum at Montrose, Carnegie's lasting achievement, was used for this purpose until 1966, when it was sold to the War Office.   NICK HERVEY

Sources U. Aberdeen, Susan Scott Carnegie (1744–1821) MSS · A. A. Cormack, *Susan Carnegie, 1744–1821: her life of service* (1966) · A. A. Cormack, 'First mental hospital in Scotland: Montrose asylum, 1781', *Aberdeen University Review*, 37 (1957–8), 69–79 · A. A. Cormack, *The Carnegie family in Gothenberg* (1947) · bap. reg. Scot.
Archives U. Aberdeen, corresp. and papers | U. Aberdeen, Cormack papers, MS 2937
Likenesses oils, 1815, repro. in Cormack, *Susan Carnegie*, frontispiece
Wealth at death see will, Cormack, *Susan Carnegie*

Carnegie, William, seventh earl of Northesk (1756–1831), naval officer, was born in Hampshire on 10 April 1756, the third son of George Carnegie, sixth earl of Northesk (d. 1792), admiral of the white, and Lady Anne Leslie, eldest daughter of Alexander, fifth earl of Leven. Carnegie entered the navy in 1771 on board the *Albion* with Captain Samuel Barrington and afterwards served with captains Macbride in the *Southampton* and Stair Douglas in the *Squirrel*.

On 7 December 1777 Carnegie was made lieutenant in the *Apollo*. He was afterwards with Sir John Lockhart Ross in the *Royal George* and then went to the West Indies in the *Sandwich* with Sir George Rodney, serving with him in the

battle with the French Admiral De Guichen on 17 April 1780. After the battle Rodney promoted him commander, though this was not confirmed until 10 September 1780. He continued in the West Indies as commander of the fireship *Blast* and then of the hired ship *St Eustatius*. In her Carnegie was present at the capture of the Dutch island of St Eustatius in February 1781. On 7 April 1782 he was made post and given command of the frigate *Enterprise* which he brought to England and paid off at the peace in 1783. In 1788, after the death of his elder brothers, he became Lord Rosehill, and on 9 December 1788 he married Mary, only daughter of William Henry Ricketts of Longwood, Hampshire, and niece of Lord St Vincent; the couple had four sons and five daughters. In 1790 he commanded the *Heroine* for a short period and then, on 22 January 1792, he succeeded to the earldom on the death of his father. In 1793 he briefly commanded the frigate *Beaulieu* and the *Andromeda*.

In 1796 Northesk became captain of the *Monmouth* (64 guns), one of the ships in the North Sea squadron which, in 1797, took part in the mutiny at the Nore. Having confined Northesk to his cabin for some time, the mutineers wished to use him as an emissary and he appeared before the committee of delegates on the *Sandwich*. They sent for him as 'one who was known to be the seaman's friend'. Richard Parker, the chairman of the delegates, presented him with the terms 'on which alone, without the smallest alteration, they would give up the ships' and ordered Carnegie to wait upon the king, present the resolutions of the committee, and return with an answer within fifty-four hours from 3.00 p.m. on 6 June (Marshall, 1, suppl. i.200).

Northesk carried the propositions of the mutineers to the Admiralty and was taken by the first lord, Lord Spencer, to the king. The demands were rejected and a message to that effect was sent to Parker and the delegates at the Nore. Northesk did not return and, shortly after the mutiny had been quelled, he resigned the command of the *Monmouth*. In 1800 he was appointed to the *Prince* (98 guns) in the Channel Fleet and remained with her until the peace of Amiens (1802). On renewal of the war in 1803 he was appointed to the *Britannia* (100 guns) in the fleet under Cornwallis engaged in the blockade of Brest. He continued in her, on the same station, after his promotion to flag-rank on 23 April 1804 as rear-admiral of the white. In August 1805 he was detached in the *Britannia* to reinforce the fleet with Sir Robert Calder off Cadiz.

Northesk was third in command to Lord Nelson in the battle of Trafalgar on 21 October 1805. *Britannia* was in the weather line led by Nelson, and was certainly early in action (accounts vary as to whether she was fourth or sixth in line), remained closely engaged to the end, and sustained a loss of fifty-two killed and wounded. Vice-Admiral Cuthbert Collingwood's dispatch following the battle praised all the commanders: 'all deserve that their high merits should stand recorded and never was high merit more conspicuous' (PRO, ADM 1/411, fol. 564). Northesk's services, both during the battle and in the subsequent task of rescuing crews from prizes ordered to be destroyed in the rising storm, were recognized by his being nominated a knight of the Bath, the investiture taking place on 5 June 1806. He became vice-admiral of the blue on 28 April 1808 and admiral of the blue on 4 June 1814, but had no further service during the war. On 19 July 1821 he was promoted admiral of the white and rear-admiral of Great Britain, and from 1827 to 1830 he was commander-in-chief at Plymouth.

In 1796 Northesk had been elected one of sixteen representatives of the peerage of Scotland in the parliament of Great Britain; he subsequently served in the parliaments of 1802, 1806, and 1830. He died after a short illness on 28 May 1831, and on 8 June he was buried in the crypt of St Paul's Cathedral, London, where a plain slab marks his grave near those of Nelson and Collingwood. Northesk's will, proved on 5 August 1831, initially left his various properties to his wife.   KENNETH BREEN

Sources admiral's dispatches, PRO, ADM 1/411, 124, 125 · lieutenant's passing certs., PRO, ADM 107/ · W. James, *The naval history of Great Britain, from the declaration of war by France, in February 1793, to the accession of George IV in January 1820*, 5 vols. (1822–4), vol. 3 · Burke, *Peerage* · *Debrett's Peerage* · J. Marshall, *Royal naval biography*, 4 vols. (1823–35) [with 4 suppls.] · J. Charnock, ed., *Biographia navalis*, 6 vols. (1794–8) · *GM*, 1st ser., 101/1 (1831) · Carnegie will, PRO, PROB 11/1789
Archives NRA, priv. coll., letters to his sister, Lady Betty Hope
Likenesses Ridley and Holl, stipple, pubd 1806, BM · H. Cook, stipple, 1831 (after H. Patterson), BM, NPG; repro. in W. Jerdan, *National Portrait Gallery* (1831) · J. Hibbert jun., etching and aquatint, BM
Wealth at death see will, PRO, PROB 11/1789

Carnell, Edward John (1912–1972), science fiction writer, journal editor, and literary agent, was born on 8 April 1912 in Plumstead, London, the only child of William John Carnell, a charge hand who worked at the Royal Arsenal in Woolwich, and his wife, Louisa Woollett.

Ted, as he was always known, became a printer, but joined the army at the outbreak of war in 1939, was promoted to sergeant, and served as a gunner in combined operations, when he was involved in more than one beachhead invasion. He was already devoted to the more peaceful microcosm of science fiction, and loved to tell the tale of how, patrolling the Mediterranean in a corvette, he had boarded a deserted ship; on the captain's desk lay a gold watch and a copy of *Astounding Science Fiction*. He took the latter.

Carnell attended Britain's first science fiction convention in 1937, together with other devotees who were later to succeed as writers, including Arthur C. Clarke and Eric Frank Russell. His administrative abilities soon came to the fore. He was made treasurer of a newly formed Science Fiction Association, and edited the journal of the British Interplanetary Society. After the war, with backing from dedicated followers, Carnell published *New Worlds*, Britain's most successful and long-lived science fiction magazine (200 issues between 1946 and 1970). As *New Worlds* achieved regular publication, Carnell added a sister magazine, *Science Fantasy* (eighty-one issues between 1950 and 1966). Later Carnell added a third magazine, the American-originated *Science Fiction Adventures*, which, through his intervention, survived when the parent

magazine died, to yield twenty-seven issues between 1958 and 1963.

These magazines were crucial to the development of British science fiction: they allowed native writers to find their own audience, instead of having to adopt an American idiom for the New York market. Writers who took advantage of this, and supported Carnell, included Arthur Sellings, J. G. Ballard, Brian Aldiss, and Michael Moorcock—the last taking over the editorship of *New Worlds* in 1964, when Carnell's health, and his publishers, were failing. Under Moorcock, *New Worlds* became as much a crusade as a magazine, while Carnell went on to lead a quieter life as editor of a regular series of anthologies, *New Writings in S-F*, which provided a forum for a generation of newer authors. Twenty-one numbers were published between 1964 and Carnell's death in 1972, whereupon H. Kenneth Bulmer—another British stalwart—took over the editorship.

Carnell also edited many anthologies: *No Place Like Earth* (1952), *Gateway to Tomorrow* (1954), *Gateway to the Stars* (1955), *The Best from New Worlds Science Fiction* (1955), *Lambda I and other Stories* (reprinted 1964), *Weird Shadows from Beyond* (1965), and *Best from New Writings in S-F 1–4* (1971).

Carnell was always steady, reliable, and honest, and thoroughly understood routine science fiction. As his magazines and his writers succeeded, he was practically forced to become a literary agent in order to market the fiction he had summoned into being. Thus the E. J. Carnell Literary Agency was founded. He knew none of the techniques, but learned fast, representing such writers, in whole or in part, as John Christopher, Theodore Sturgeon, Damon Knight, Frederik Pohl, Samuel Delaney, Harry Harrison, and the British authors already mentioned. Carnell never failed to be surprised when he managed to sell a book to a regular publisher such as Faber and Faber, or to get £30 from the Spanish. Then his high, nervous chuckle would come into play—not always echoed by the more ambitious of his authors.

The science fiction world provided Carnell with his few recreations. He was chairman of the first world convention to be held outside the United States (London, 1957). He was one of the four founders of the respected international fantasy award in 1951, which immediately recognized the merits of such works as George Stewart's *Earth Abides* (1949) and the trilogy by J. R. R. Tolkien. Very little science fiction appeared in hardcover before the 1950s. Carnell helped promote hardcovers, becoming a founder and member, with Kingsley Amis and Dr George Porter, of the selection board of the Science Fiction Book Club, on which he served for many years. He was English linkman for the Trieste science fiction film festivals (1961 onwards), the first such international events. Throughout all this activity, Carnell remained a Plumstead man, modest and pleasant, a good friend to his friends and authors. Indisputably, he did more for British science fiction on the administrative side than anyone else. His was an example of the way in which devotees valiantly supported the literature no one but they seemed to love; his pleasant nature and fondness for 'loony' jokes left their imprint on British science fiction.

In 1939 Carnell married Irene, daughter of William Henry Read Cloke, a caterer. They had a son and a daughter. Carnell died at St Nicholas Hospital, Plumstead, on 23 March 1972; his remains were cremated on 30 March at Falconwood cemetery, London.   BRIAN W. ALDISS

Sources W. Contento, ed., *Index to science fiction: anthologies and collections* (1978) · J. Clute, ed., *Encyclopaedia of science fiction* (1993) · B. Aldiss and H. Harrison, eds., *Hell's cartographers* (1975) · personal knowledge (2004)
Wealth at death £18,169: probate, 23 Aug 1972, *CGPLA Eng. & Wales*

Carnmoney Witch, the. *See* Butters, Mary (*fl.* 1807–1839).

Carnock. For this title name *see* Nicolson, Arthur, first Baron Carnock (1849–1928).

Carnwath. For this title name *see* Dalzell, Robert, first earl of Carnwath (*d.* 1654); Lockhart, Sir George, of Carnwath, Lord Carnwath (*c.*1630–1689); Dalzell, Robert, fifth earl of Carnwath (*c.*1687–1737).

Caroe, Sir Olaf Kirkpatrick Kruuse (1892–1981), administrator in India, was born in London on 15 November 1892, eldest of the three children of William Douglas *Caröe (1857–1938), architect and son of the Danish consul in Liverpool, and his wife, Grace Desborough (*d.* 1947), daughter of John Randall, barrister. From Winchester College, where his maternal uncle Monty Randall was headmaster, he won a demyship to read classics at Magdalen College, Oxford, entering in 1911. In 1914, on the outbreak of war, he enlisted in the Royal West Surrey regiment, rising to the rank of captain.

To his delight, Caroe spent the whole of the war in India. There, in addition to rather tedious military duties, he began to learn Urdu and Pashto and explored Indian architecture and landscape. India held for him a certain magic, a mixture of Edwardian duty and the thrill of the exotic preserved from childhood readings of Kipling and Flora Annie Steele. He was determined to return after the war. His regiment went home in November 1919 and two months later, on 10 January 1920, he married his pre-war girlfriend, Frances Marion (Kitty; *d.* 1969), eldest child of Atherton Gwillym Rawstorne, bishop of Whalley. Later the same year, having topped the post-war service examinations, he returned to India as a member of the Indian Civil Service. Kitty, to whom he was devoted, followed in 1921 with the first of their two sons.

In October 1923, after three years' service in the Punjab, Caroe managed to obtain a transfer to the Indian political service and was posted to the North-West Frontier Province (NWFP) as city magistrate of Peshawar. Postings in Mardan and Kohat followed, before, in 1929, he was appointed secretary to the NWFP chief commissioner. In April 1930 he was dispatched as acting deputy commissioner to Peshawar when the city was paralysed by crowds protesting against the arrest of the brothers Dr Khan Sahib and Abdul Ghaffar Khan, local leaders of the Indian National Congress. Caroe reoccupied the city peacefully on 5 May, but trouble flared again and in one incident he

ordered troops to fire on an unruly crowd, killing about a dozen people. Although the government saw no need to censure him (and indeed confirmed him as deputy commissioner and in 1932 appointed him CIE), the affair was subsequently invoked by the Congress as proof of his antipathy to Indians.

In 1933 Caroe was appointed chief secretary to the North-West Frontier Province government and then, in 1934, deputy secretary to the government of India's foreign (external affairs) department. In July 1939 he was promoted to foreign secretary. In this capacity he made official visits to Afghanistan and Nepal and focused attention on India's vulnerable north-eastern frontier, the beginning for him of an abiding interest in Tibetan autonomy. Appointed CSI in 1941, he was promoted to KCIE in 1944 and KCSI in 1945.

In March 1946 Caroe was appointed governor of the North-West Frontier Province. The province had a new Congress ministry headed by Dr Khan Sahib which, to Caroe's eyes, showed dangerous signs of interfering with the executive. The viceroy, Lord Wavell, was sympathetic, but privately he believed that Caroe had not adjusted to the idea of Britain leaving India. As Caroe tried to guide and discipline the new ministry, rumours spread that he favoured the Muslim League. This was not true (he had a particular dislike of Jinnah), but he felt constrained to warn Khan Sahib that, given his Pathan constituency, he ought not to appear to be taking instructions from plains-dwelling Hindus—advice which led to Nehru's charge that he was unfit to be governor. As popular opposition to the ministry swelled, Caroe pressured Khan Sahib to go to the polls, further antagonizing Nehru. No election could be fair, Nehru argued, while an anti-Congress governor held sway. Stung by the accusation of partiality, Caroe refused to offer his resignation, but he was tired and, as a slightly built, sensitive man, he appeared to his colleagues to be close to collapse. In June 1947 Mountbatten succeeded in persuading him to take two months' leave while a provincial referendum was held. Caroe understood this to be a temporary expedient, but afterwards, even though the province had voted to join Pakistan no offer came for him to return to duty. With hindsight Caroe was glad he went when he did. He thought partition a dreadful mistake, but consoled himself that he at least had retained friends on all sides, including the Khan brothers and eventually even Nehru. In old age he was proud to have been the only British ex-governor invited back as a state guest by both Pakistan and India.

In retirement in Sussex Caroe championed Tibetan independence and, after the Lhasa uprising of 1959, founded the Tibet Society of the United Kingdom, which assisted in the resettlement of Tibetan refugees. He was also a leading member of the Royal Central Asian Society and the Conservative Commonwealth Council. Among his friends he counted Harold Macmillan and Lionel Curtis, for the latter of whom he wrote extensively in the *Round Table*. He published several books, including *Soviet Empire* (1953), intended as a riposte to left-wingers who condemned only capitalist forms of imperialism; *The*

Pathans (1958), which gained him the degree of LLD from Oxford; and, with Sir Evelyn Howell, a translation from the work of the seventeenth-century Pashto poet Khushhal Khan (1963). A devout Anglican, he also chaired the Chichester diocesan pastoral reorganization committee.

In January 1969 Kitty died, plunging Caroe into loneliness. He continued to write on central Asian affairs, but increasingly concentrated on putting the record straight about his service in the North-West Frontier Province. He reworked numerous drafts of an autobiography and responded in point-by-point detail to memoirs and monographs published on the transfer of power era. Caroe died on 23 November 1981 in hospital, and was privately cremated on the 27th. He was survived by his two sons, Richard and Michael.   KATHERINE PRIOR

Sources O. Caroe, 'Plain tales of the raj', interview, 1974, BL OIOC · O. Caroe, 'Five autobiographical fragments', BL OIOC · G. Chowdhray-Best, 'Olaf Caroe: a memoir', *Central Asian Affiars*, 1 (1982) · P. Moon, ed., *Wavell: the viceroy's journal* (1973) · A. Lamb, *Tibet, China and India, 1914–1950* (1989) · *The Times* (25 Nov 1984) · *DNB*
Archives BL OIOC, autobiographical narratives, MS Eur. C 273 · BL OIOC, corresp. and papers, MS Eur. 203 | BL OIOC, Cunningham MSS; Howell MSS; Reid MSS · Bodl. Oxf., Round Table MSS · SOAS, Hodson MSS | SOUND BL NSA, current affairs recording · BL OIOC, 'Plain tales of the raj', BBC, 1972–4 · IWM SA, 'British officer in queen's regiment and civilian in Indian civil service', BBC, 1974, 4909
Likenesses J. G. Laithwaite, group photograph, 1936, BL OIOC · Kinsey Bros, group photograph, 1943, BL OIOC
Wealth at death £111,862: probate, 13 Jan 1982, *CGPLA Eng. & Wales*

Caröe, William Douglas (1857–1938), architect, was born on 1 September 1857 at Holmesdale, Blundellsands, near Liverpool, the younger son of Anders Kruuse Caröe (d. 1897), Danish consul at Liverpool and a naturalized British subject, and his wife, Jane Kirkpatrick Green (d. 1877). He was educated at Ruabon grammar school, Denbighshire, and Trinity College, Cambridge, where he was a senior optime in the mathematical tripos of 1879.

Caröe was articled first, in 1879, to Edmund Kirby, an architect of Liverpool, and after one year his articles were transferred to John Loughborough Pearson, with whom he remained on a gradually diminishing part-time basis while he built up his own practice. In 1891 he married Grace Desborough, *née* Randall (d. 1947), with whom he had one daughter and two sons, the elder of whom was Sir Olaf Kirkpatrick Kruuse *Caroe (1892–1981), Indian administrator. It was at this period that he was responsible under Pearson for a great deal of the detailing of Truro Cathedral. His own practice at that time included a large amount of work in Ireland—houses, farm buildings, and stables—and his church work in England grew rapidly. In 1885 he was appointed architect to the ecclesiastical commissioners and the Charity Commission, where Pearson's brother-in-law Ewan Christian was then senior architect, a post to which Caröe succeeded on Christian's death in 1895, and which he then held for the remainder of his life. From 1897 to 1903 Caröe was in partnership with Christian's nephew J. H. Christian, of Christian and Purday, who designed Mombasa Cathedral (1901–4). From

1903 he went into partnership with his assistant Herbert Passmore, who continued the work of the firm after Caröe's death, when the latter was succeeded by his son Alban Douglas Randall Caröe.

A vast amount of ecclesiastical work passed through Caröe's hands in these years. He acted as consulting architect to the diocesan boards of finance of Lichfield, Canterbury, Bath and Wells, and Newcastle upon Tyne. He was architect to the cathedrals of Canterbury, Durham, Southwell, St David's, Brecon, and Jerusalem, and to many churches, including Great Malvern Priory, Tewkesbury Abbey, Romsey Abbey, and St Peter's, Wolverhampton. He built or reconstructed the archbishop's palace at Canterbury, and the bishops' palaces at Abergwili, Southwell (1907–8), Bristol (1905; des.), St Albans, Llandaff, Rochester, and Wolvesey (Winchester). He also designed many substantial suburban churches, including that of St David, Exeter (1897–1900). He designed internal fittings for many hundreds of medieval churches, including woodwork in Winchester College chapel, and between the years 1887 and 1937 he was responsible for the structural restoration of many medieval buildings; in 1910 he carried out important restoration work on Tom Tower at Christ Church, Oxford, recorded in an etching by Muirhead Bone. He designed the monuments to Archbishop Temple in Canterbury Cathedral, to Bishop Owen in St David's Cathedral, to Bishop Satterlee and Bishop Harding in Washington Cathedral, USA, and to Bishop Ridding in Southwell Cathedral. He was a member of the first commission on St Paul's Cathedral in 1912, and acted as adviser to the Norwegian government on Trondheim Cathedral.

Caröe's secular work includes the University College of South Wales and Monmouthshire at Cardiff, the Teddington laboratories of the National Physical Laboratory, the offices of the ecclesiastical commissioners in Millbank (1903), flats in Knightsbridge (1901), Coleherne Court, Kensington (1901–3), 37–43 Park Street, Mayfair, boardinghouses at Wycombe Abbey School (1898–1910), and new buildings for Trinity and Pembroke colleges, Cambridge (1905–7).

Caröe received the order of St Olaf of Norway, and was elected a fellow of the Royal Institute of British Architects in 1890. He was president of the Architectural Association in 1895–6 and became a fellow of the Society of Antiquaries. His publications include *Sefton* (1893) and *King's Hostel, Trinity College, Cambridge* (1909); he also edited *'Tom Tower', Christ Church, Oxford: some Letters of Sir C. Wren to J. Fell* (1923).

Caröe was a man of forceful character and great energy and business capacity. A recent historian noted that, 'his early churches established him as the leading Arts and Crafts Gothic church architect outside the High Church party' (Bettley, 2.10). His metropolitan works in warm red brick were richly arrayed, and his remarkable offices for the church commissioners in Millbank gave architectural expression to the theme of 'a Church jubilant' (Gray, 135). In the same year as his Millbank project Caröe designed the working men's college in Crowndale Road, London, and he took an active interest in the work of the college.

From his home at Vann, Hambledon, Surrey, he gave his professional services gratis to community projects, and founded the Fold County Rural Preservation Society. One of the first building conservators, this aspect of his work has been continued by his grandson Martin Bragg Caroe FSA in the firm Caröe & Partners. Caröe's career extended to the design of furniture and metalwork, sculpture and embroidery. He maintained an interest in Scandinavia and was an authority on the vikings.

Towards the end of his life Caröe retired to Cyprus, where he took an active interest in preserving the antiquities of the island: his last published work was *The Importance of the Historical Buildings of Cyprus* (1931). He died on 25 February 1938 at Latomia, a house he had built in Kyrenia, Cyprus, and was buried in the old British cemetery in Kyrenia.　　　IAN MACALISTER, *rev.* ANNETTE PEACH

Turlough Carolan (1670–1738), by Francis Bindon

Sources J. M. Freeman, *W. D. Caröe, R St O, FSA: his architectural achievement* (1990) · *Dir. Brit. archs.* · A. S. Gray, *Edwardian architecture: a biographical dictionary* (1985) · J. Bettley and R. Raper, eds., *Catalogue of the drawings collection of the Royal Institute of British Architects: a cumulative index* (1989) · *The Builder*, 154 (1938), 435 · Graves, *RA exhibitors* · Venn, *Alum. Cant.* · *CGPLA Eng. & Wales* (1938)
Archives Croxteth Hall and Country Park, Liverpool, letters to Captain Sir Richard Molyneux relating to St Helen's Church, Sefton · Durham RO, corresp. and plan relating to alterations to St Hilda's, Hartlepool · LPL, corresp. and MSS concerning Old Palace at Canterbury · priv. coll., sketchbooks, corresp., card indexes, rolls of architectural drawings · RIBA, nomination papers · Royal Commission on the Historic Monuments of England, London, photographic collection
Likenesses crayon drawings, 3 Great College Street, Westminster · photographs, repro. in Freeman, *W. D. Caröe, R St O, FSA*
Wealth at death £52,909 19s. 10d.: probate, 5 Aug 1938, *CGPLA Eng. & Wales* · English probate sealed in Vancouver, 2 March 1939, *CGPLA Eng. & Wales*

Carolan, Turlough [Toirdhealbhach Ó Cearbhalláin] (1670–1738), harper and composer, was born near Nobber, co. Meath, where his father (identified variously as John and Brian) was probably a small farmer and perhaps also an ironworker. When the young Carolan was in his early teens the family moved to Carrick-on-Shannon, co. Leitrim, and then to nearby Ballyfarnon, co. Roscommon, where his father's employers were the MacDermott Roe family who were to play a crucial role in the life and career of the young Carolan. Struck by the boy's intelligence Mrs MacDermott Roe arranged for his education. When an attack of smallpox left him blind, she had him trained as a harper by a namesake of hers, MacDermott Roe. After three years' training she launched him—now twenty-one years old—on his career as an itinerant harper, providing him with the necessities of his profession, including a horse and a guide. The MacDermott Roes remained his special patrons all his life—for half a century. Their substantial house still stands at Alderford, beside Ballyfarnon.

In Gaelic Ireland the professional harper had enjoyed a high social status, accorded an honour price by the Brehon (native) law—legal acknowledgement (although below that of the bardic poet) of his position as the doyen of musicians in a society that took its music very seriously (with echoes of ancient belief in its supernatural dimensions). Not only was instrumental performance (solo or group) of the greatest importance in its own right, but the harp was also closely associated with the court performance of the learned bardic poetry, sung by the *reacaire* accompanied by the harper. Carolan arrived on the scene about the time of the watershed treaty of Limerick (1691), which symbolized the final completion of the English conquest, with the elimination or dispossession of the native Irish-speaking Catholic aristocracy—together with the institutions that flourished under their patronage—and their replacement by protestant English and Scottish planters. Music-making native style was among the cultural features that survived for a time, including the playing of the harp, which continued to be 'an aristocratic pastime or accomplishment rather than a popular one' (MacLysaght, 35). Carolan moved about the country from one 'big house' to another, welcomed as an honoured guest. In a rural society where music was an integral part of life—literally from the cradle to the grave—with a passion for song and for dancing, where even the educated read little in the evenings because of poor lighting, and where the live musician was the only source of the art, his visit would have been a major cultural contribution.

Carolan's forte was as a composer both of instrumental harp pieces (frequently dance music) and of songs in which he added simple verses to his own new tune. Although he enjoyed a fellowship and camaraderie with some of the Irish poets of the time, Carolan would not have been considered a poet by the *cognoscenti*. Nevertheless his songs—complete with amateurish verses—were greatly relished not only by his flattered hosts but also by a wider public for whom song (often extempore) was a normal means of giving heightened expression to emotions of all kinds. Hence many of his songs passed into the oral folk repertoire where they were still alive more than a century later. Carolan was an exuberant personality of cheerful temperament with a ready wit—satirical when called for—and a puckish sense of humour which delighted in tales of the ludicrous. Storytelling may well have been part of his professional repertory, following what seems to have been the medieval tradition of the harpers (Murphy, 191). Charles O'Conor of Belanagare—one of his greatest patrons, a protégé of his on the harp, as well as being a noted scholar and man of affairs—had a high regard for his innate intelligence: 'Very few I have ever known who had a more vigorous mind, but a mind undisciplined through the defect or rather absence of cultivation' (O'Sullivan, *Carolan*, 160). These characteristics, and the ethos of the time, are well presented in the musical drama (in Irish) *Carolan*, by Eoghan Ó Tuairisc, premièred in Dublin in 1979.

Professionally Carolan would have been in great demand at special occasions such as weddings and christenings, and some of the personalized epithalamia he composed have survived. At the other end of the emotional spectrum, the medieval Gaelic harper was a central figure in the obsequies following the death of the chieftain, both playing his specially composed instrumental lament (Irish *cumha*) and accompanying the singing (by the *reacaire*) of the learned elegy (*marbhna* or *tuireamh*) composed by the bardic poet for the commemorative ceremony. In the few surviving laments that can confidently be ascribed to him (O'Sullivan, *Carolan*, nos. 206 ff.), Carolan combined these various functions, apparently singing his own elegy to his instrumental lament.

Carolan acquired patrons all over Ireland. Remarkably these were drawn equally from both sides of the political and religious divide, including many of the new protestant planter families—Crofton, Drew and Jones—as well as the remnants of the old native Catholic aristocracy, for example the MacDermott Roe, O'Conor, and Maguire families. Carolan took the political situation as he found it and eschewed politics in his songs (in contrast with the Irish poets of his time). Nevertheless, as a devout Catholic, from a Gaelic background, it is clear that he was not without some partiality. Irish was still the vernacular language of most of rural Ireland, and Carolan did not learn English until he was 'advanced in years', and 'delivered himself but indifferently in that language' (O'Sullivan, *Carolan*, 1.157). With only one known exception all his songs were in Irish, even those for his English-speaking patrons who evidently understood them.

Among Carolan's important patrons there was at least one protestant clergyman, Charles Massey, afterwards dean of Limerick from 1740 to 1766, whose grandfather, typically, 'came into this kingdom with a principal command in the army sent to suppress the rebellion in the year 1641' (J. Lodge, *Peerage of Ireland*, 1754). It is to Massey that we are indebted for the commissioning, in the 1720s, of the portrait of Carolan now in the National Gallery of Ireland (reproduced in O'Sullivan, *Carolan*, 1, frontispiece, artist's name unknown).

In 1720 Dean Swift translated the words of a song by Carolan, 'Pléaráca na Ruarcach' ('O'Rourke's feast', published in 1735; the words were, exceptionally, not Carolan's), most likely assisted by his close friend, fellow clergyman, and remarkable Irish scholar Anthony Raymond, vicar of Trim. Swift may well have known Carolan—as claimed by folklore—but this cannot be proven.

Carolan married Mary Maguire (*d.* 1733) of co. Fermanagh. They had a loving marriage, living at Mohill, co. Leitrim, where a public sculpture in bronze by Oisín Kelly was erected in memory of the harper. They had six daughters and a son. The latter became a harper (of little distinction), and later went to London bringing his father's harp with him. An Irish harp on exhibition at the O'Conor-Nash house at Clonalis, co. Roscommon (formerly home of the O'Conor Don) is claimed to be that of Carolan. His wife predeceased him by five years in 1733, and poignant verses of his, lamenting her, have survived. The relevant harp music (which no doubt he composed) is not known.

Carolan died on 25 March 1738 at Alderford House, Ballyfarnon, the home of his lifelong patron Mrs MacDermott Roe. The vast and distinguished attendance at his funeral indicated the extent to which he had become a national figure. A modern monument, inscribed in Irish and in English, was erected to mark his grave in the medieval churchyard of Kilronan, co. Roscommon.

Some 200 of Carolan's tunes were edited by Donal O'Sullivan (1958)—the total that he succeeded in recovering from printed and manuscript sources. The Irish harping tradition had been handed on orally and aurally, unwritten. It was a new departure when in 1724 (during Carolan's lifetime) music publishers from outside that tradition John and William Neal printed *A Collection of the most Celebrated Irish Tunes Proper for the Violin German Flute or Hautboy*, including some of Carolan's tunes, their first printing. Other printings followed. Manuscript notation of his music was also commenced by collectors from outside the tradition, the earliest being Bunting, as late as 1792. Only the melody line of the tunes was recorded (O'Sullivan plausibly suggesting that 'it is probable that he would largely have recreated the accompaniment on every occasion that he played a particular tune' (*Carolan*, 1.150)). Carolan's own Irish verses for many of these tunes have survived separately in manuscript (never underlaid to the notation) and been edited (Ó Máille, O'Sullivan, 'Bunting collection'), but the relationship of these to the tunes is often problematical.

In Carolan's compositions the native style was frequently influenced by the continental music (including that of Vivaldi, Corelli, and Geminiani) popular in Ireland at the time and admired by Carolan himself. His music enjoyed a popular revival in Ireland in the late twentieth century (thanks especially to O'Sullivan's edition), but the most significant assessment of it must remain that of his own contemporaries who were in a position to evaluate it fully in context.   BREANDÁN Ó MADAGÁIN

Sources D. O'Sullivan, *Carolan, the life, times and music of an Irish harper*, 2 vols. (1958) · D. O'Sullivan, 'Bunting collection of Irish folk music and songs', *Journal of the Irish Folk Song Society*, 22–9 (1927–39) · T. Ó Máille, *Amhráin Chearbhalláin, the poems of Carolan* (1916) · J. Neal and W. Neal, *A collection of the most celebrated Irish tunes proper for the violin German flute or hautboy*, ed. N. Carolan, 1986, facsimile (1724) · N. Carpenter and A. Harrison, 'Swift's "O'Rourke's feast" and "Sheridan's letter": early transcripts by Anthony Raymond', *Proceedings of the First Münster Symposium on Jonathan Swift*, ed. H. J. Real and H. J. Vienkon (1985), 27–46 · L. Duignan, 'A checklist of the publications of John and William Neal', *Irish Booklore*, 2 (1972–6),

231–7 · J. Hardiman, ed., *Irish minstrelsy, or, Bardic remains of Ireland*, 2 vols. (1831) · F. Kelly, *A guide to early Irish law* (1988) · E. MacLysaght, *Irish life in the seventeenth century* (1939) · G. Murphy, ed. and trans., *Duanaire Finn*, 3, ITS, 43 (1953) · B. Ó Madagáin, 'Irish vocal music of lament and syllabic verse', *The Celtic consciousness*, ed. R. O'Driscoll (1981), 311–32 · J. Rimmer, 'Foreign elements in Irish 18th-century dance music', *Historical Dance*, 2/4 (1984–5), 28–35 · J. Rimmer, 'Patronage, style and structure in the music attributed to Turlough Carolan', *Early Music*, 15 (1987), 164–74 · J. Rimmer, 'Carole, rondeau and branle in Ireland 1300–1800', *Journal of the Society for Dance Research*, 7/1 (1989), 20–46, pt 1 · J. Rimmer, 'Carole, rondeau and branle in Ireland 1300–1800', *Journal of the Society for Dance Research*, 8/2 (1990), 27–43, pt 2 · J. Rimmer, 'Harp repertoire in eighteenth-century Ireland: perceptions, misconceptions and reworkings', *Proceedings of the International Historical Harps Symposium* (1995), 1–13

Likenesses oils, 1720, NG Ire. · F. Bindon, portrait, NG Ire. [*see illus.*] · mezzotint, NPG

Caroline [Princess Caroline of Brandenburg-Ansbach] (**1683–1737**), queen of Great Britain and Ireland, and electress of Hanover, consort of George II, was born on 1 March 1683 in the palace of Ansbach, south Germany. She was the elder of the two children of Johann Friedrich, margrave of Brandenburg-Ansbach (1654–1686), and his second wife, Eleanore Erdmuthe Louisa (1662–1696), daughter of Johann Georg I, duke of Saxe-Eisenach (1634–1686), and his wife, Johanette (1626–1701), daughter of Ernst von Sayn-Wittgenstein. She was baptized Wilhelmine Karoline (Wilhelmina Caroline).

Princess of Brandenburg-Ansbach and electoral princess of Hanover Following the death of Johann Friedrich in 1686, the margravine returned to Eisenach. In 1692 the family moved to Dresden, on the marriage of Eleanore to Johann Georg IV, elector of Saxony (1668–1694). This unhappy alliance was brought to an end in 1694 when the elector died from smallpox, caught while nursing his mistress. For the next two years the Electress Eleanore lived at Pretsch in Saxony with her children. There is little evidence that Caroline had received much formal education up to this time. Her handwriting remained poor and her spelling idiosyncratic all her life—even her husband observed that she wrote 'like a cat' (Royal Archives, Geo. Addl. 28, no. 52)—although in this respect she was no different from many aristocratic women. In 1696, however, Caroline's mother died. She returned briefly to Ansbach, but then went to Lützenburg, outside Berlin, to live with her guardians, the elector and electress of Brandenburg.

At Lützenburg the Electress (queen in Prussia from 1701) Sophia Charlotte presided over a liberal, cultivated court, where intellectual discussion was encouraged. In this setting Caroline was introduced to Gottfried Wilhelm Leibniz among others, and she clearly developed a close relationship with the queen, who, on one of Caroline's visits to Ansbach, declared that Berlin was 'a desert' without her (Wilkins, 18). As early as 1698 Caroline was being discussed at the court of Vienna as a possible wife for the Archduke Charles, subsequently (1711) Holy Roman Emperor Charles VI. Formal overtures do not appear to have been made, however, until the autumn of 1703. The match was encouraged by Frederick I of Prussia, and ini-

Caroline (1683–1737), by Jacopo Amigoni, 1735

tially Caroline indicated that she was prepared to convert to Catholicism, an essential prerequisite to the marriage. But she found her conversations with Father Orban—the Jesuit sent to show her the errors of Lutheranism—traumatic, frequently breaking down in tears. Finally, after much soul-searching, Caroline decided that she could not embrace Catholicism, and the impression was allowed to spread that she had turned down a formal offer of marriage. This was an episode of which she was inordinately proud. When in 1714 John Robinson, bishop of London, offered to explain to her anything about Anglicanism which she did not fully comprehend, she promptly dismissed him, remarking that 'he is very impertinent to suppose that I who refusd to be Empress for the sake of the Protestant Religion don't understand it' (diary of Mary, Countess Cowper, fol. 12v). Indeed, both before and after the Hanoverian succession, the image of Caroline as a protestant heroine was promoted in Britain. Her coronation medal in 1727 was used to emphasize her commitment to the protestant cause and many preachers commented on her refusal 'to buy a crown' (*Bishop Burnet's History*, 5.322) at the 'expence of a good conscience' (J. Evans, *The King and his Faithful Subjects Rejoycing in God; and the Mouths of Liars Stopped, a Sermon*, 1727, 21).

In June 1705, when the Habsburg court was still hoping

that the marriage negotiations might be revived, Caroline was visited at Triesdorf, where she was staying for the summer, by George Augustus (1683–1760) [*see* George II], the electoral prince of Hanover. He was immediately struck with her 'good character', the British envoy reporting that 'he would not think of anybody else after her' (Arkell, 19). Their marriage followed on 22 August / 2 September 1705 in the chapel of the palace of Hanover. George appears to have been a devoted husband, nursing his wife through smallpox and then pneumonia in 1707. Before Caroline fell ill, however, she gave birth to *Frederick Louis, later prince of Wales (*d.* 1751), on 20 January / 1 February 1707. Three further children soon followed: *Anne (1709–1759), who married William IV, prince of Orange, *Amelia (1711–1786), and Caroline Elizabeth (1713–1757).

At Hanover Caroline renewed her acquaintance with the Electress Sophia, heir to the British throne and mother of Queen Sophia Charlotte, whose death early in 1705 had caused Caroline much grief. The electress encouraged the intellectual and literary interests of her grandson's wife, who was able to continue her friendship with Leibniz, with whom she discussed religious, historical, and philosophical questions. Caroline also developed an interest in politics, sharing her husband's ambition for the British crown. She even became involved in the manoeuvrings in London and Hanover during the last years of Queen Anne's reign to safeguard the protestant succession, pressing her father-in-law, the Elector George Louis, to allow her husband to go to England, where he could take his seat in the House of Lords as duke of Cambridge and represent the interests of the dynasty. Leibniz showed his ability to play the courtier by comparing her to Queen Elizabeth, and there is little doubt that she was preparing herself for her future role. In 1713 she employed an Englishwoman to read to her, though, as she herself admitted towards the end of her life, she always 'found some difficulty in speaking' the language (*Egmont Diary*, 2.319). From 1710 she corresponded in French with some aristocratic Englishwomen, including Mary, Countess Cowper, the wife of the prominent whig lawyer. It was also during this period that a friendship developed between Caroline and Henrietta Howard, the future countess of Suffolk, who was living in Hanover with her husband. Cultivated and educated, Mrs Howard was soon appointed a *dame du palais* by Caroline and shortly after became the mistress of George Augustus.

On 8 / 19 June 1714 the Electress Sophia collapsed and died in the arms of Caroline while walking in the gardens at Herrenhausen. Her role as the princess's closest confidante seems to have been taken by Sophia's niece, Elisabeth Charlotte, duchess of Orléans, with whom Caroline maintained a regular correspondence over the next few years. A few weeks later, on 1 August, Queen Anne also died and the elector became king of Great Britain. The new king and his son departed for England the next month, followed in October by Caroline. However, at the insistence of George I, she had to leave her seven-year-old son behind in Hanover as the representative of the dynasty.

Princess of Wales In London, George I's preference was for a private and secluded court. The gap which this created in social and political life was partly filled by the new prince and princess of Wales. They were seen walking around the royal parks, frequently attended the theatre and opera and visited the City for lord mayor's day in October 1714. Through the winter of 1714–15 Caroline herself 'held an evening drawing-room twice a week, and also gave a series of balls at Somerset House and St James's' (Beattie, 262). While the prince of Wales acted as regent during the king's absence in Hanover in 1716, he and Caroline dined publicly every day in the princess's apartments. In the months after George I's accession, Caroline also helped to defuse controversy about the Lutheranism of the new dynasty which was being stirred up by high-churchmen. She was noted for her attendance at daily prayers, and her conduct in chapel was described as the 'devoutest in the world' (diary of Mary, Countess Cowper, fol. 12*v*).

From the very beginning of the reign, commentators noted the hostility between the king and the prince which had been observed by Caroline on her arrival in Hanover. As tensions grew in summer 1717, the prince and princess were kept more and more in the background and were not allowed to dine in public. The occasion for the decisive breach within the royal family was the baptism of Caroline's sixth child, George William, in November 1717—a fifth had been stillborn the previous year. When the prince of Wales was ordered to leave St James's, Caroline followed, rather to the surprise of George I and despite the fact that she had to leave behind her children, including the infant George William, who died in 1718. There was some public and international sympathy for the prince and princess, although the king did make some efforts to ease the position of the princess, conniving at her daily visits to the children, when she played with them, stayed while they had supper and then put them to bed. Even after the reconciliation between the king and the prince in 1720, however, the children continued to live apart from their parents at St James's. Their loss may have been compensated for to some extent by the birth of three more—*William Augustus, later duke of Cumberland (*d.* 1765), in 1723, *Mary in 1723, and Louisa in 1724. Mary (*d.* 1772) married Frederick, landgrave of Hesse-Cassel, and Louisa (*d.* 1751) married Frederick V, king of Denmark.

Caroline also played a significant political role in the early years of George I's reign. The appointment of William Wake as archbishop of Canterbury in December 1715 was widely attributed to her influence, and a year later she worked with Wake and Earl Cowper to secure the bishopric of Exeter for Lancelot Blackburne. Any influence that the princess exercised over crown patronage was curtailed after 1717, but George I was in no doubt that his daughter-in-law was a crucial figure in the dispute between him and the prince of Wales. As early as February 1717 the king and James Stanhope tried unsuccessfully to use her as an intermediary in negotiations with George Augustus. Caroline's own correspondence suggests that she and her husband were close political allies throughout the breach in the royal family—during the campaign against the Peerage Bill she noted that the 'Prince & I work like dogs' (Royal Archives, Geo. Addl. 28, no. 51). George I was so infuriated with her behaviour that he reputedly described her as 'Cette Diablesse Madame la Princesse' (*Reminiscences … Walpole*, 27). However, it was Caroline rather than the prince who played the crucial role in the reconciliation of 1720, negotiating with Robert Walpole, one of the leading figures in the Leicester House opposition, and the king's ministers for three months before either George or the prince was informed. The princess was in 'transports of Joy' at the 'Success of her Court Arts', though Lady Cowper was more sceptical, believing that she had been deceived and betrayed by Walpole, who 'had so possest her Mind there was no room for the least truth' (diary of Mary, Countess Cowper, fols. 104, 108). Little evidence about the activities of the prince and princess has survived for the latter part of George I's reign. But even after 1720 their court at Leicester House (rented in 1718) and Richmond Lodge (purchased as a summer residence in 1719) continued to provide a focus for disaffected whig politicians. Caroline's court in particular attracted a glittering array of young aristocratic ladies, some of whom were celebrated in Alexander Pope's 'Court Ballad' of 1717.

Queen consort The events surrounding the accession of George II in June 1727 have done much to influence perceptions of the role of Caroline as queen consort among both contemporaries and historians. The new king had come to believe that Walpole had betrayed him over the terms of the reconciliation in 1720 and freely denounced him as a 'rogue and rascal' (Hervey, 1.29). The old ministry expected to be turned out *en bloc*, with Walpole being replaced as prime minister by Sir Spencer Compton. Within days, however, it became clear that Walpole had triumphed over his rival. The accounts in Hervey and Coxe, on which historians have tended to rely, attribute Walpole's success in large part to the influence of the queen. Caroline was less concerned than her husband at the alleged betrayal of 1720, and had maintained cordial relations with Walpole during the last years of George I's reign. She was convinced of the superior abilities of Walpole, possibly influenced by his offer to obtain for her from parliament a jointure of £100,000 per annum, and persuaded the king to retain his services, a task facilitated by Compton's obvious incompetence. Hervey had no hesitation about calling him 'the Queen's minister' (Hervey, 1.39). Walpole, in his characteristically coarse way, is alleged to have attributed his success to the fact that Compton 'took the wrong sow by the ear … I the right' (Yorke, 6)—Compton had paid court to Henrietta Howard, whereas Walpole had recognized that George paid far more attention to his wife than to his mistress.

It is difficult to know how much credit to give to this version of events. It is likely that all the major accounts of Caroline's influence at the time of the accession derive originally from a single source, Walpole himself, and there were other reasons for George II to favour his father's leading minister. But 1727 was not the only occasion on which the queen's support was believed to have been important to Walpole. Caroline's dislike of Charles, second Viscount Townshend, helped Walpole to secure his predominance within the ministry and contributed to his rival's resignation in 1730; stories abound in the accounts of Hervey, Chesterfield, and Horace Walpole of the ways in which the two combined to manage the king. It is clear that, in a period when the position of the prime minister depended as much upon his standing at court as in parliament, Walpole enjoyed the confidence of the monarch to a remarkable degree. Only twice did this confidence appear briefly to falter—in 1733 during the excise crisis and in 1737 during the disputes between the king and queen and their son, Frederick, prince of Wales. It is also clear that Walpole attributed his position to his relationship with Caroline. He certainly feared the political consequences of her death in 1737, writing to his brother that he was oppressed not only with sorrow but also with 'dread' (Coxe, 1.554).

Walpole's assessment of the queen's political power was shared by other leading politicians and courtiers. When John Dalrymple, second earl of Stair, was seeking to undermine the prime minister's influence in 1733, he sought an interview with Caroline, not with George. Hervey was doubtless summing up the view of many when he recorded that her 'power was unrivalled and unbounded', and that she 'directed everything … either at home or abroad' (Hervey, 1.45). This was also the public perception, as revealed by the London mob and press. Despite the efforts of the royal family to make the dynasty more popular—as, for example, by reviving the custom of dining in public on Sundays—there was a considerable amount of popular anti-Hanoverianism, and it was often the queen who was the object of scandalous stories circulating around the capital. Revealingly, it was Caroline, not her husband, who was burned in effigy alongside Walpole at the height of the demonstrations against the Excise Bill. Many lampoons echoed the claim of the one recorded by Hervey:

> You may strut, dapper George, but 'twill all be in vain;
> We know 'tis Queen Caroline, not you, that reign.
> (ibid., 1.69)

These perceptions of Caroline's power, however widespread, should not be allowed to obscure the reality. George II was a conscientious and hard-working king. He kept military affairs and appointments firmly in his own hands. He also maintained a close interest in foreign affairs, on which he received regular reports from Hanover as well as from his English ministers. Recent research suggests that this is an area where Caroline's influence has been much exaggerated. In particular, the traditional interpretation, derived in large part from Hervey, that it was Walpole, assisted by Caroline, who deterred George from intervention in the War of the Polish Succession, has been shown to have ignored the king's concern to maintain the neutrality of Hanover (Black, 52).

But contemporaries were not altogether wrong in suggesting that Caroline exercised a remarkable degree of power. George II clearly discussed politics with his wife and trusted her judgement. During his four absences in Hanover in 1729, 1732, 1735, and 1736–7 he left her as regent entrusted with 'all domestic matters'. Foreign affairs were dealt with by the king and the secretaries of state, one of whom accompanied him to Germany, but other affairs were left 'entirely to the Queen with the advice of the Lords of the Council' (Arkell, 168). Consequently, she played an important role in the government's response to events like the Porteous riots in Edinburgh in the summer of 1736. Despite well-publicized visits to dine with the duke of Newcastle at Claremont and Walpole at Chelsea, the atmosphere of the court was retired during the regencies. Caroline thought it politic not to flaunt her power, preferring to reside at Kensington or Richmond, rather than St James's.

Moreover, even while he was in the country, George II was prepared to allow Caroline great influence in some areas of government. One of these was ecclesiastical affairs, in which the king took little interest until after his wife's death. Caroline exerted herself vigorously, playing a crucial role in the appointment of at least four, and possibly as many as eight of the thirteen bishops consecrated between 1727 and 1737. Few clergymen, however, owed more to her influence than Joseph Butler, plucked from the comfortable obscurity of a Durham parish in 1736 and moved back to London as her clerk of the closet. As she was unable to provide for him before her death in 1737, he was the only person whom she recommended 'particularly and by name' on her deathbed (Hervey, 3.908), and the following year he was created bishop of Bristol. Caroline was not always successful—failing, for example, to secure a bishopric for Samuel Clarke—but even as queen consort she exercised more influence over ecclesiastical patronage than any other Hanoverian monarch.

Caroline attracted criticism from some of the leading literary figures of the day, notably Jonathan Swift and John Gay, who thought the offer of the sinecure post of gentleman usher to Princess Louisa beneath him. However, she was by no means hostile to the arts. On the contrary, she was widely read, particularly in French romances, and offered her patronage to a number of minor writers, including Richard Savage and Stephen Duck. She was frequently ridiculed for what her husband dismissed as 'that lettered nonsense', but others, including Leibniz and John Perceval, first earl of Egmont, were impressed by her learning and intelligence. What interested her most were religious and philosophical debates. In a role more characteristic of continental than English court culture, she acted as patron and intermediary in the correspondence between Leibniz and Samuel Clarke about Newtonian doctrines and the nature of free will, which was published in 1717. As both princess of Wales and queen, she gathered around herself an eclectic circle of theologians and clergymen, embracing both impeccably orthodox figures, such as Wake, Butler, and Thomas Sherlock, and others suspected of heterodoxy, like Samuel Clarke and Benjamin Hoadly. In the 1730s Pierre le Courayer, the exiled French theologian who had defended the validity of Anglican

orders, was a regular visitor at court. Indeed, Caroline consciously projected an image of herself as a promoter of enlightened ideas. In an attempt to publicize the English contribution to science and natural religion, busts of Boyle, Locke, Newton, Clarke, and Wollaston were placed in the hermitage she erected at Richmond, and she gave her support to the practice of inoculation against smallpox. This latter action in particular attracted the attention of Voltaire, who praised her in his *Lettres philosophiques* (1734) as 'a delightful philosopher on the throne' (p. 55).

On coming to the throne Caroline also revealed great enthusiasm for gardening. At Kensington Charles Bridgeman was responsible for extending and landscaping the park, while the water-works, notably the creation of the 'Serpentine', were directed by Charles Withers. At Richmond, settled on Caroline as a potential dower house, the queen probably employed Bridgeman again to create the extensive gardens, consisting of 'three principal landscaped areas, charmingly interspersed with fields and parkland so as to create a great variety of scenery' and linked by a long 'forest walk' stretching from Richmond to Kew (Colvin and others, 221). She was a strong supporter of the new fashion for a more 'natural' style, her aim consisting, in her own words, 'in helping nature, not losing it in art' (*Egmont Diary*, 2.138). A variety of buildings were added to the landscape. The two which most attracted the notice of contemporaries were designed by William Kent: a hermitage, described by Egmont as 'very solitary and romantic' (ibid., 2.190), and Merlin's Cave, a thatched building containing waxworks of Merlin, Queen Elizabeth, Elizabeth of York, the wife of Henry VII, and other figures. Both were intended, through their architectural associations and the identity of the figures placed in them, to promote the English identity of the new Hanoverian dynasty. Rysbrack and Guelfi were commissioned to make the busts for the hermitage, and Caroline turned to Rysbrack again for a series of busts of former queens of England to decorate the library which she built on the west side of St James's Palace, overlooking the park, to house her extensive collection of books. Apart from these commissions there is little evidence that the queen was a great patron of artists, but she took 'great pleasure in collecting and preserving the dispersed remains of the collection belonging to the crown' (Walpole, *Corr.*, 16.322). At Kensington she brought together a collection of royal portraits, while in Richmond Lodge she hung the collection of Holbein sketches which she had rediscovered while rummaging through an old bureau.

In November 1734 Henrietta Howard, now countess of Suffolk, finding herself neglected by the king, retired from court. Her long presence there had, if anything, tended to highlight the closeness of the relationship between Caroline and her husband. It was widely rumoured that George discussed his affairs with his wife, and her complaisance was often seen as one of the keys to her influence over him. But there was genuine affection on both sides, the couple exchanging letters of between forty and sixty pages every week during George's absences in Hanover. There is some evidence that they became estranged in 1736 following the king's visit to Hanover, where he formed a new attachment, to Amalie Sophie Marianne von *Wallmoden. But Caroline was deeply distressed when it was feared that George had been drowned at sea in December 1736, and any problems between them had clearly been resolved by the time he returned to London in January 1737. By now, however, relations between Frederick, prince of Wales, and his parents were deteriorating rapidly. As in 1717 the roots of the quarrel in the royal family were political, with the prince chafing at his lack of influence and dabbling in opposition politics. However, Caroline bore the brunt of the dispute. Frederick tried to pick a number of quarrels with her during her regency in 1736, and his behaviour remained rude and offensive through 1737. In many ways Caroline offered a convenient proxy through whom he could attack and irritate the king. The effect, according to Hervey, was that she became bitterly alienated from her son. On one occasion, seeing him walking through St James's, she is reported to have said: 'Look, there he goes—that wretch!—that villain!—I wish the ground would open this moment and sink the monster to the lowest hole in hell!' (Hervey, 3.681). He was not admitted to see her on her deathbed, though accounts vary on whether that was the decision of the king or the queen.

Caroline suffered occasionally from gout and was seriously ill in 1734. When she complained of pains at St James's on 9 November 1737, it was initially thought that she was suffering from a recurrence of the colic that she had experienced earlier that summer. However, it soon emerged that the cause was a rupture, which she had concealed ever since the birth of Princess Louisa. Numerous operations proved ineffective and she lingered in considerable pain for over a week, finally dying on the evening of 20 November. Surrounded by members of her family, the last word she uttered was 'Pray' (Hervey, 3.915). Her death, characterized by 'patience, tranquillity, and resignation' (BL, Add. MS 9200, fol. 60), revealed more than a touch of protestant, enlightenment piety. Her last days were punctuated by periods of prayer with members of her family and her favourite clergymen, but ultimately she placed her trust in her own faith. She made no effort to receive the sacrament, explaining to Archbishop Potter that 'tho her body suffer'd she had a good conscience which spoke inexpressable comfort to her & supported her in the midst of all her torments' (Royal Archives, Geo. MS 52824).

George II, who had attended her throughout, often sleeping on the floor at the foot of her bed, was distraught. He ordered a new vault to be constructed in Henry VII's chapel in Westminster Abbey and that one side of her coffin should be removed, so that, on his burial, one side of his coffin could also be removed and their bones mingle in death. Caroline was buried on 17 December. According to contemporary accounts, her funeral was not perhaps the spectacle which George II would have wished. A new anthem, 'The Ways of Zion do Mourn', was commissioned for the occasion from Handel, the royal couple's favourite composer, but the performance did not match the composition, while the earl of Egmont recorded that the procession was 'very disorderly managed', with 'too little gravity … in almost every person who assisted' (*Egmont Diary*, 2.456). In the weeks after her death, she attracted all the usual panegyrics, though the many references to her extensive charity were much more than conventional pieties. The public reaction, however, was more mixed, as revealed by a squib found at the Royal Exchange:

O Death, where is thy sting,
To take the Queen and leave the King?
(*Egmont Diary*, 2.458)

Eighteenth-century memoirists, who did so much to form nineteenth-century views of their predecessors, presented conflicting portraits of Caroline. Against the almost hagiographical treatment of Lord Hervey must be set the more critical portraits of Lord Chesterfield and Lady Mary Wortley Montagu. Her twentieth-century biographers have tended to exaggerate her importance. To Wilkins she was 'Caroline the Illustrious', while for Arkell she was the person who 'ensured the dynasty's rooting itself in England' (Arkell, vii). Twentieth-century political historians, by contrast, have either minimized her influence or have simply ignored it. The court, however, was still an arena of considerable political as well as social importance, and it was also a place in which women could effectively seek and exercise power and influence. In this context, it is difficult to deny that Caroline was the most powerful queen consort of the Hanoverian period. Indeed, Leibniz's comparison was almost prophetic, since she probably exercised more influence over English government than any queen since Elizabeth I.

STEPHEN TAYLOR

Sources R. L. Arkell, *Caroline of Ansbach, George the Second's queen* (1939) • W. H. Wilkins, *Caroline the illustrious, queen-consort of George II and sometime queen regent: a study of her life and times*, new edn (1904) • *Manuscripts of the earl of Egmont: diary of Viscount Percival, afterwards first earl of Egmont*, 3 vols., HMC, 63 (1920–23) • John, Lord Hervey, *Some materials towards memoirs of the reign of King George II*, ed. R. Sedgwick, 3 vols. (1931) • J. Van der Kiste, *King George II and Queen Caroline* (1997) • S. Taylor, 'Queen Caroline and the Church of England', *Hanoverian Britain and empire: essays in memory of Philip Lawson*, ed. S. Taylor, R. Connors, and C. Jones (1998), 82–101 • *The Wentworth papers, 1705–1739*, ed. J. J. Cartwright (1883) • J. M. Beattie, *The English court in the reign of George I* (1967) • P. Yorke [second earl of Hardwicke], *Walpoliana* (1781) • *Reminiscences written by Mr Horace Walpole in 1788*, ed. P. Toynbee (1924) • Royal Arch., Geo. Addl. 28 • Mrs Selwyn, letter to Mrs Lowther (copy), 29 Nov 1737, Royal Arch., Geo. MS 52824 • M. Cowper, diary, 1714–16, 1720, Herts. ALS, Panshanger MS, D/EP F205 • J. Black, 'George II reconsidered: a consideration of George's influence in the conduct of foreign policy, in the first years of his reign', *Mitteilungen des Österreichischen Staatsarchivs*, 35 (1982), 35–56 • J. M. Kemble, ed., *State papers and correspondence illustrative of the social and political state of Europe from the revolution to the accession of the house of Hanover* (1857) • J. Colton, 'Kent's hermitage for Queen Caroline at Richmond', *Architectura*, 4 (1974), 181–91 • J. Colton, 'Merlin's cave and Queen Caroline: garden art as political propaganda', *Eighteenth-Century Studies*, 10 (1976–7), 1–20 • R. Hatton, *George I: elector and king* (1978) • H. M. Colvin and others, eds., *The history of the king's works*, 5 (1976) • Walpole, *Corr.* • Voltaire, *Letters on England*, ed. and trans. L. Tancock (1980) • P. D. Stanhope [earl of Chesterfield], *Characters* (1778, 1845), ed. A. T. McKenzie (1990) • *The letters and works of Lady Mary Wortley Montagu*, ed. Lord

Wharncliffe, 3rd edn, 2 vols. (1861) · collections of Revd H. Etough, BL, Add. MS 9200 · *Minor poems*, ed. N. Ault (1954), vol. 6 of *The Twickenham edition of the poems of Alexander Pope*, ed. J. Butt (1939–69); repr. (1964) · H. Walpole, *Memoirs of King George II*, ed. J. Brooke, 3 vols. (1985) · *Correspondance de Leibniz avec l'électrice Sophie de Brunswick-Lunebourg*, ed. O. Klopp, 3 vols. (1874) · D. B. Meli, 'Caroline, Leibniz, and Clarke', *Journal of the History of Ideas*, 60 (1999), 469–86 · A. T. Thomson, *Memoirs of Viscountess Sundon, mistress of the robes to Queen Caroline*, 2 vols. (1847) · *Letters to and from Henrietta countess of Suffolk*, ed. J. W. Croker, 2 vols. (1824) · L. Melville, *Lady Suffolk and her circle* (1924) · *GM*, 1st ser., 2 (1732), 925 · C. Hogwood, *Handel* (1984) · J. D. Hunt, *William Kent, landscape garden designer: an assessment and catalogue of his designs* (1987) · *Bishop Burnet's History* · E. B. Fryde and others, eds., *Handbook of British chronology*, 3rd edn, Royal Historical Society Guides and Handbooks, 2 (1986) · *Stammtafeln zur Geschichte der Europäischen Staaten* (1953), Band 1–2 · W. Coxe, *Memoirs of the life and administration of Sir Robert Walpole, earl of Orford*, 3 vols. (1798)

Archives BL, catalogue of her library, Add. MS 11511 | BL, corresp. with Horatio Walpole, Add. MSS 73770, 73774, 73902 · Herts. ALS, Panshanger MSS, letters to Lady Cowper, D/EP F201 · Koninklijk Bibliotheek, The Hague, letters to her daughter Anne, Anna van Hannover 430 · Royal Arch., letters to Mary Clayton, Geo. Addl. 28

Likenesses oils, *c*.1705, repro. in Arkell, *Caroline of Ansbach* · G. Kneller, oils, 1716, Royal Collection; copy, NPG · studio of C. Jervas, oils, *c*.1727, NPG · medal, 1727, BM · oils, *c*.1730, repro. in Wilkins, *Caroline the illustrious* · silver medallion, 1732, BM · J. Amigoni, oils, 1735, NPG [*see illus.*] · J. Highmore, oils, *c*.1735, Royal Collection · J. Vanderbank, oils, 1736, Goodwood House, West Sussex · D. Savile, drawing, 1737, Chatsworth Trustees; photograph, Courtauld Inst. · J. M. Rysbrack, terracotta bust, 1739, Royal Collection · J. Faber, engraving (after J. Vanderbank, 1736), repro. in Arkell, *Caroline of Ansbach* · W. Hogarth, group portrait, oils (*George II, king of England and his family*), NG Ire. · J. M. Rysbrack, bust, Wallace Collection, London · E. Seeman, oils, Hampton Court Palace

Wealth at death all possessions, incl. Richmond Lodge, left to king: Wilkins, *Caroline the illustrious*, 622

Caroline [Princess Caroline of Brunswick-Wolfenbüttel] (1768–1821), queen of the United Kingdom of Great Britain and Ireland, consort of George IV, was born on 17 May 1768 at Brunswick, the second daughter of Karl II, duke of Brunswick-Wolfenbüttel, and Princess Augusta, sister of George III. She was named Caroline Amelia Elizabeth and brought up in the informal atmosphere of the ducal court. At the age of fourteen she was described as 'a lively, pretty child with light-coloured hair hanging in curls on her neck, with rosebud lips … and always simply and modestly dressed' (Smith, 1). She always remained extrovert and frivolous in her manner, but she was kind-hearted, good-natured, fond of children, and enjoyed society. She was chosen as the intended bride of George, prince of Wales [*see* George IV] partly because her mother was a favourite sister of George III, partly through the favourable reports of her given by the dukes of York and Clarence when they visited Germany, and partly for lack of a suitable alternative German protestant princess. The king also hoped that 'domestic felicity' would settle the prince's life and take his mind off his importunate desire for a military command against the French. The prince, who had secretly married Maria Fitzherbert in 1785, was forced by his enormous debts to seek his father's financial assist-

Caroline (1768–1821), by Sir Thomas Lawrence, 1804

ance in 1794 and it was made a condition of his relief that he should marry legitimately, to produce an heir to the throne. He was willing to desert Mrs Fitzherbert, being currently involved with Lady Jersey, but he declared that he had no interest in the choice of a bride, being reported as saying 'One damned German frau is as good as another' (Smith, 2).

Marriage to the prince of Wales Lord Malmesbury, a friend of the prince, was sent to fetch Caroline from Brunswick but their departure for England was delayed. During the period of waiting Malmesbury became alarmed by what he thought were Caroline's loose conduct, indecent language, and lack of hygiene, though the first two at any rate were more probably simply youthful high spirits. His efforts to educate her in the more restrained and polite manners of the English court and the fastidious habits of her future husband were unavailing and she always found the etiquette of the court stifling. On his first meeting with his bride in April 1795 the prince, Malmesbury reported, turned aside and asked for brandy.

The marriage took place on 8 April 1795 in the Chapel Royal, St James's. The prince was reportedly the worse for alcohol and had to be supported to go through the ceremony. Caroline alleged that he spent most of the wedding night insensible on the floor. This inauspicious beginning heralded a series of quarrels between the royal couple. Caroline had been warned by anonymous letters of the prince's attachment to Lady Jersey and naturally objected when he nominated his mistress to meet his bride on her arrival in England, to be a member of her household, and to be the only female attendant to accompany her on her honeymoon. Caroline alleged that throughout the honeymoon the prince consorted with his drunken cronies and ignored her. On his part, the prince took offence at Caroline's accusation that Lady Jersey was his mistress, refused to change his social and domestic habits for her benefit, and demanded that she should submit to his authority, which she refused to do.

Separation The only child of this stormy marriage, Princess *Charlotte Augusta (1796–1817), was born on 7 January 1796. Three days after his wife's confinement, the prince wrote a will in which he declared that Mrs Fitzherbert was his only true wife, and that 'to her who is call'd the Princess of Wales' he left one shilling (*Correspondence of George, Prince of Wales*, 3.132–40). Caroline had attempted to live on amicable terms with him, but he neglected her and she became increasingly lonely, bored, and resentful. The inevitable separation took place in 1796. The prince had written to her that 'we have unfortunately been oblig'd to acknowledge to each other that we cannot find happiness in our union' (*Correspondence of George, Prince of Wales*, 3.170) and despite the efforts of George III to mediate, Caroline left Carlton House in 1797 and went to live in a rented house near Blackheath. The prince would have forbidden her access to her child, but the king, who always favoured Caroline, insisted that she should be allowed to visit Charlotte. He wrote in 1801 of 'the propriety of your conduct in a very difficult and unpleasant situation' (*Correspondence of George, Prince of Wales*, 4.240).

Caroline made no attempt to exploit her situation politically. She remained prominent in society and entertained frequently at Blackheath, often in an informal and high-spirited atmosphere. Her guests included the leading political men of the day from both parties, such as Pitt, Eldon, Charles Grey, and Spencer Perceval; and Sir Thomas Lawrence and George Canning, with both of whom she was believed to have had affairs. In 1800 she made the acquaintance of Admiral Sir Sidney Smith who was also accused of making her his mistress. Through him she met Sir John and Lady Douglas with whom she became intimate until they quarrelled in 1803, when Lady Douglas was accused in anonymous letters of spreading malicious gossip about Caroline's morals, including allegations that she had borne a child since her separation from the prince of Wales. Lady Douglas later affirmed that in 1802 the princess had told her that she was 'in the family way' (*Correspondence of George, Prince of Wales*, 5.389). This was certainly not the case, although suspicions were aroused by her habit of adopting stray children, one of whom, William Austin, possibly the son of a Deptford shipwright, was reputed to be her natural child.

These unsavoury rumours led to the setting up in 1806 of an official commission of inquiry known as the 'delicate investigation'. The report found that the rumours about a pregnancy were false, but censured Caroline's 'levity of conduct'. George III demanded the cabinet's advice: it recommended that he should warn the princess about her future conduct, but, to the prince's fury, advised that she should not be excluded from the court. Caroline continued to enjoy the king's support, although the queen, who had taken a dislike to her from the outset, always sided with her son. After the king's relapse into insanity in 1810 Caroline's position accordingly became weaker.

During the Regency Caroline was excluded from the court and only with difficulty could she obtain permission to see Charlotte, who was educated under the prince of Wales's supervision. The prince declared that Caroline's efforts to gain access to her daughter were merely intended 'to create discord or confusion in the Family'. Charlotte, however, resented this treatment of her mother and when in 1813 her father demanded that she should live at Carlton House she fled to join the princess of Wales. A crisis was averted when Lord Grey, leader of the parliamentary opposition, refused to become embroiled in the affair and Henry Brougham, who had become adviser to both Caroline and Charlotte, persuaded the latter to submit to the prince's paternal authority. Caroline thereupon decided to leave England, and set off on a series of travels, initially to Brunswick but shortly afterwards around the Mediterranean. She went at first with a suite of English companions but when, for various reasons, these friends returned home, she replaced them with mainly Italian followers of lower social status and reputation. Chief among them was Bartolomeo Bergami, or Pergami, a pretended Milanese baron, a man about thirty years old, tall, handsome, and of superb physique. He became successively her courier, bodyguard, groom of the bedchamber, and major-domo.

Caroline's movements throughout her travels were closely watched by paid spies, notably one Baron Ompteda who was recruited by the Regent's Hanoverian minister, Count Münster, in 1814 to gather evidence against her. Almost weekly reports came in of indiscreet and scandalous behaviour, improper entertainments in which she took part, and above all of suspected intimacy with Bergami. He was alleged to have slept in communicating rooms or even in the same bed, to have shared a bed with her on board a sailing vessel in the Bay of Naples, and to have been present when she bathed. Caroline seemed to have become infatuated and to be completely under his influence. She procured for him a Sicilian barony and a knighthood of Malta and instituted for him her own order of St Caroline. His sister, Countess Oldi, became a close companion and lady of honour and two of his brothers were also taken into her service.

Caroline's conduct became increasingly eccentric. When she embarked on a tour of the East, visiting Athens, Palermo, Constantinople, and Jerusalem, her extravagant and theatrical behaviour became a subject of scandal in the newspapers, providing further ammunition for her estranged husband in his efforts to divorce her before he became king. In 1816 legal advisers had warned him that divorce in the ecclesiastical courts would be a lengthy and difficult process, particularly since he would be obliged to confess his own adultery. Moreover, the evidence against Caroline was of doubtful quality, being drawn almost entirely from foreigners and servants who might be suspected of taking bribes. In 1818 the prince therefore appointed a commission of three persons, William

Cooke, a barrister, J. A. Powell, a solicitor, and Major J. H. Browne, who spoke some Italian, to go to Milan and gather further evidence prior to seeking a divorce by act of parliament. Depositions were taken from numerous witnesses but no further proceedings had been begun before the death of George III in January 1820 brought the prince to the throne. The evidence collected by the 'Milan commission' was to form the basis of the accusations in the 'Queen's trial' later that year.

The 'trial' of Queen Caroline As soon as George IV became king he took the first steps against his wife by ordering her exclusion from the prayers for the royal family in the Anglican liturgy. Incensed by this insult, Caroline set off for England to claim her position as queen. She was met at St Omer by Henry Brougham, whom she made her attorney-general, and by Lord Hutchinson on behalf of the cabinet who brought a proposal, reluctantly accepted by the king, to give her an annuity of £50,000 provided she would not cross the channel nor claim the title of queen. She peremptorily refused, despite Brougham's plea to her to negotiate a settlement. She was now being advised by Matthew Wood, an alderman and former lord mayor of London, who represented a group of metropolitan radicals who wanted to use her to stir up opposition to the king and the government. The queen's arrival became, as the government had feared, the occasion for widespread public rejoicings. She reached London on 6 June and went first to Alderman Wood's house in South Audley Street, later renting Brandenburg House at Hammersmith. Throughout the proceedings against her in the summer and autumn of 1820 she was the focus of many demonstrations, receiving over 350 addresses of support from all sections of the population, many from groups of women who saw her as a symbol of the oppression of their sex. She also had the support of *The Times* and many other opposition or radical newspapers. She herself had no interest in or sympathy with radicalism, but her cause was now overtly political as the nation divided into two camps.

The cabinet, spurred on by the vengeful king, unwillingly prepared a bill of pains and penalties to strip Caroline of her title and to end her marriage by act of parliament. The bill was introduced into the House of Lords on 17 August. It was one of the most spectacular and dramatic events of the century. The queen's progresses to and from Westminster to attend the 'trial', as it became known, were attended by cheering crowds; deputations by the dozen visited Brandenburg House to present addresses, the newspapers published verbatim accounts of the Lords' proceedings, and the caricaturists on both sides had a field day. So obscene were some of the prints against the king that over £2500 was spent in buying them up and suppressing their publication. Against this proof of public support for the queen the 'trial' was doomed to failure. The witnesses were clearly unreliable and were discredited by the cross-examination of her counsel, Henry Brougham and Thomas Denman. Many of the witnesses were believed to have been bribed or intimidated, and the

widespread knowledge that George himself had had several mistresses added to the belief that Caroline was a victim, if not an entirely innocent one, of royal and political persecution. In the end, though the circumstantial evidence against her was strong enough to convince many peers of her guilt, many also feared that her condemnation would spark off popular rioting or even revolution. Ministers realized that even if the Lords passed the bill the House of Commons would almost certainly reject it under intense pressure from their constituents. The bill passed its third reading in the Lords by only nine votes and Liverpool, the prime minister, announced on 10 November that it would proceed no further.

Caroline had not, strictly speaking, been acquitted of the charges against her, but the public verdict was in her favour as a wronged woman unjustly persecuted by a husband no better than she was. A great crowd turned out to witness her procession to a thanksgiving service organized by her supporters in St Paul's Cathedral on 29 November 1820, when the psalm ordered for the service was no. 140—'Deliver me, O Lord, from the evil man'. Nevertheless, attempts to exploit her victory were unsuccessful. The cabinet rejected her demand for a palace and the king refused to let her be crowned with him. He was supported by the privy council who declared that a queen had no inherent right to coronation, which was at her husband's discretion. When she tried to force her way into the abbey on coronation day, 20 July 1821, she was humiliated by being refused entry and she was jeered by the crowd that had so recently acclaimed her. The king spent most of his coronation service ogling Lady Conyngham, his current mistress. The honours for bad behaviour were fairly evenly divided between George and Caroline, but the coronation restored some of the king's popularity. The exhaustion of public interest in the queen's cause was summed up in the epigram quoted in November 1820:

> Most Gracious Queen, we thee implore
> To go away and sin no more;
> But, if that effort be too great,
> To go away, at any rate.
> (Smith, 147)

Settlement and death Caroline now accepted the government's offer of an allowance of £50,000 a year if she went to live abroad, but less than a fortnight after the coronation she was taken ill at the theatre, and after a short but painful illness she died, apparently of an intestinal obstruction, on 7 August 1821. She wished to be buried beside her father at Brunswick, and the British government was only too anxious to get her corpse out of the country. Her funeral procession was intended to pass round to the north of the city of London to avoid public demonstrations. The cortège was intercepted by a crowd at Hyde Park Corner and forced to go through the city after a battle with the Life Guards in which two men were killed by the soldiers. The coffin was eventually embarked from Harwich, her supporters placing on it as it left British waters the inscription 'Caroline, the injured Queen of England'. Her body was taken to Brunswick and laid in the ducal vault on 24 August. She named William Austin as her heir, but he had a tragic life, spent several years in a lunatic asylum and died in 1846.

Caroline was a woman of strong character who refused to be dominated by her surroundings or by her husband. She craved affection, which she could not find in her marriage, and lavished it indiscreetly on others. Tied to an unwilling husband for the propagation of the royal line, the death of Princess Charlotte in 1817 made the sorry history of Caroline's marriage a farce. The adoption of her cause by radical and whig politicians gave the private lives and morals of the royal family a public and political significance.   E. A. SMITH

Sources The correspondence of George, prince of Wales, 1770–1812, ed. A. Aspinall, 8 vols. (1963–71) · The letters of King George IV, 1812–1830, ed. A. Aspinall, 3 vols. (1938) · J. Richardson, The disastrous marriage: a study of George IV and Caroline of Brunswick (1960) · A. Plowden, Caroline and Charlotte: the regent's wife and daughter, 1795–1821 (1989) · E. A. Smith, A queen on trial: the affair of Queen Caroline (1993) · R. Huish, Memoirs of Caroline, queen of Great Britain, 2 vols. (1821) · J. Nightingale, Memoirs of her late majesty, Queen Caroline, Consort of King George IV, 3 vols. (1820–22) · The trial at large of her majesty Caroline Amelia Elizabeth, queen of Great Britain, in the House of Lords, on charges of adulterous intercourse, 2 vols. (1821) · R. Fulford, The trial of Queen Caroline (1967) · J. Stevenson, 'The Queen Caroline affair', London in the age of reform, ed. J. Stevenson (1977), 117–48 · E. Parry, Queen Caroline (1930) · Diaries and correspondence of James Harris, first earl of Malmesbury, ed. third earl of Malmesbury [J. H. Harris], 2nd edn, 3 (1845) · F. Fraser, The unruly queen: the life of Queen Caroline (1996) · Royal Arch.
Archives Beds. & Luton ARS, corresp. and papers relating to her defence · PRO, corresp. and papers relating to moral conduct, HO126 · Royal Arch. · U. Nott. L., letters and papers relating to her debts · W. Sussex RO, letters and papers relating to her claim to attend George IV's coronation | Beds. & Luton ARS, letters to Samuel Whitbread · BL, corresp. with Keppell Craven, Add. MS 63172 · BL, corresp. with Lord Holland, Add. MSS 51520–51521 · BL, corresp. with Lord Liverpool, loan 72 · CUL, corresp. with Spencer Perceval and other papers relating to her · NRA, priv. coll., letters to Lord Eldon · RA, corresp. with Sir Thomas Lawrence · Sheff. Arch., corresp. with Earl Fitzwilliam and memoranda · U. Nott. L., Portland MSS
Likenesses G. Dupont, oils, c.1795, Royal Collection · P. Jean, miniature, 1795, Royal Collection · R. Cosway, pencil and watercolour drawing, 1798, Royal Collection · T. Lawrence, oils, 1798, V&A · T. Lawrence, double portrait, oils, 1800–01 (with Princess Charlotte), Royal Collection · T. Lawrence, oils, 1804, NPG [see illus.] · J. Lonsdale, oils, 1820, Guildhall Art Gallery, London · British school, mezzotint, Museum of London · I. Cruikshank and G. Cruikshank, caricatures, BM · A. W. Devis, portrait · Gillray, caricatures, BM · W. Hamilton, group portrait, oils (The marriage of George, prince of Wales, 1795), Royal Collection · G. Hayter, group portrait, oils (The trial of Queen Caroline, 1820), NPG · G. Hayter, oil study (for The trial of Queen Caroline, 1820), NPG · G. Hayter, pencil studies (for The trial of Queen Caroline, 1820), BM, NPG · S. Lane, oils, Scot. NPG · H. Singleton, group portrait, oils (The marriage of George, prince of Wales, 1795), Royal Collection · Williams, caricatures, BM · caricatures, repro. in Smith, Queen on trial · caricatures, BM · group portrait (after J. Russell), BM · plaster medallion (after J. Henning), Scot. NPG; cast from a medallion in possession of Mrs D. Robertson, 1889 · watercolour, Scot. NPG
Wealth at death £22,840 11s. 5d.; net balance £352 7s. 3d.; plus jewels, etc. valued at £138 10s.: will, Queen Caroline papers, Royal Arch., box 8/2, envelopes 14–15

Caroline Elizabeth, Princess (1713–1757). *See under* Amelia, Princess (1711–1786).

Caroline Matilda, Princess (1751–1775), queen of Denmark and Norway, consort of Christian VII, was the ninth and youngest child of *Frederick Lewis (1707–1751) and *Augusta (1719–1772), prince and princess of Wales. She was born at Leicester House in London on 22 July 1751, a little more than four months after her father's unexpected death. Her childhood was spent within the defensive confines of the court of her mother. Caroline Matilda's education was no more than adequate, but her upbringing at Kew was happy, and she was close to her eldest brother, the future *George III, to whom she bore a marked facial resemblance, and to her delicate elder sister Louisa Anne, who died unmarried in 1768 aged nineteen.

The Danish marriage On 10 January 1765 George III's announcement in his speech from the throne that, 'as soon as their respective ages would permit', Princess Caroline Matilda would marry her Danish cousin the crown prince, Christian (1749–1808), was received by parliament with an approval pleasing to Copenhagen, where the proposal had originated the previous summer. Christian's father was Frederick V of Denmark (r. 1746–66) and his mother, Queen Louise, a daughter of George II who, having enjoyed much popularity in Denmark, had died in 1751. Hence there would be a renewal of a connection between the British and Danish royal houses, one wished for especially by Frederick V, who in June 1765 confided as much to the long-serving British representative at his court, Walter Titley. Frederick's wish to 'disadvantage the French through a new management' (PRO, SP 75/118, fol. 172, Titley to Sandwich, 4 June) gratified British ministers who both overestimated French influence at Copenhagen and did not realize that the Francophile sentiment of Johan Hartwig Ernst von Bernstorff, the leading Danish minister, was the product of a past association with France rather than a present political determinant. Their misapprehensions shaped the opinions of George III. Bernstorff, a Hanoverian expatriate who in 1749 might have taken service with Caroline Matilda's father, placed Danish interests as he conceived them first, and in 1764 was supportive of the nascent 'northern system' of Catherine II's head of foreign affairs, Nikita Ivanovich Panin: a combination of northern powers, to include Britain, to counter-balance Bourbon and Habsburg power. Despite this, the fifteen-year-old Caroline Matilda, in so far as she had been tutored at all for her role in Denmark beyond George III's moral admonitions, arrived in Denmark in the autumn of 1766 briefed that Bernstorff was 'false and certainly in his heart a Frenchman' (Royal Archives, GEO 15810, undated letter from George III). The crudity of the assessment, which the princess must have imbibed, was primarily symptomatic of British diplomatic perceptions at a time of national 'isolation' after the 1763 peace of Paris: in April 1766 Bernstorff had in fact been bluntly told by his friend Choiseul that France could no longer count on Denmark as an ally against Britain. An important component of Bernstorff's inclination towards Russia was Catherine II's preparedness to abrogate the forty-year

Princess Caroline Matilda (1751–1775), by Jens Juel, 1769

dynastic connection with the duchy of Holstein-Gottorp, so relieving Denmark of a perennial challenge to her possession of all Schleswig; but, as events proved, the tsarina's employment for this purpose of the hectoring and xenophobic Holsteiner Caspar Von Saldern, who reached Copenhagen from Russia shortly after Caroline Matilda, only added to the latter's experience of the 'thorns of her station' for which George III had tried to prepare her in his last letter before she left England (Royal Archives, GEO 15813–14, letter dated 2 October).

Frederick V had died on 14 January 1766; it was thus King Christian VII whom Caroline Matilda married by proxy on 1 October 1766 at St James's. Following her journey to Denmark she went through a second ceremony at Fredriksborg Palace, near Copenhagen, on 8 November. When in early December 1766 Caroline Matilda told George III that within a week of her arrival her husband did not want 'to be troubled' with her (Royal Archives, GEO 52293, letter of 9 December) on a projected visit to Holstein the following spring, she betrayed not only an understandable hurt but the superficiality of her preparation at home for her role. Christian VII's visit was in fact concerned with the implications of Russia's future abrogation of the Holstein-Gottorp rights, a Dano-Russian exchange of German territories for which Bernstorff had already worked with the tsarina; and shortly after his return Caroline Matilda conceived her first child (the future Frederick VI, born on 28 January 1768). Yet it was also symptomatic of the young queen's defencelessness as the consort of an absolutist king wielding untrammelled authority that she later imputed her exclusion from the Holstein journey to Conrad Holck, an apolitical adventurer whom Christian had whimsically appointed his impresario for all court diversions.

Following the indolent Frederick V's death Titley sedulously had reported home on Christian VII's application and commendable motivation, but Titley had served at Copenhagen since 1730 and was merely reflecting Danish state practice that the repute of Denmark-Norway's crown had at all costs to be protected and in no way exposed to criticism. Actually Christian was already suspected of mental derangement, but his frenetic liking for military parades and theatrical extravaganzas was as yet being given the benefit of the doubt. Also some 'balance' was afforded the royal house by two other courts, those of Frederick V's mother, Sofie Magdalene, from which was drawn Caroline Matilda's chief attendant, Louise von Plessen, whom she came implicitly to trust, and Frederick's widow, his unpopular second wife, Juliane Marie of Brunswick-Wolfenbüttel, with her son, Prince Frederick, five years the junior of his half-brother the king. But by the end of 1767 the king's unpredictable inclinations reached a climax through Holck's agency: Christian was consorting with a well-born and notorious prostitute, Katrine Benthagen (Stövlet Katrine), and the pair went on noisy nightly forays of dissipation through the capital. The furore was such that Katrine, who had certain refinements beyond her obvious trade and whose 'style' may have intrigued as well as it assuredly shocked Caroline Matilda, was banished from the realm through conciliar initiative in January 1768. That another boon companion of the king's, Sperling, a nephew of Christian's one-time governor Reventlow, was simultaneously banished was owing to the buttressing of Bernstorff's position by the intrusive Von Saldern, who at this time also applauded the dismissal by Holck of Louise von Plessen, saltily described by Von Saldern to a receptive Tsarina Catherine as Caroline Matilda's 'flea-catcher' (quoted by S. C. Bech, 'Oplysning og tolerance, 1721–1784', Danmarks Historie, bind 9, 1965, 423). He proceeded to ensure Louise von Plessen's withdrawal to Celle in George III's Hanoverian dominions.

Although Caroline Matilda was now virtually friendless, it was no longer possible within the court's confines to pretend that the king's condition was anything but pathological. His absence from Denmark in the second half of 1768 and from Caroline Matilda, during an eight-month visit to Britain and France, afforded Christian the stimulus of changing scenes and social milieus which could have neutralized his more manic bouts. At all events, he spared his accompanying entourage, which included Bernstorff, much feared embarrassments, while back in Denmark the queen could lead a quieter life with her infant son. Dividing her time between the courts of the queen dowagers, Sofie Magdalene and Juliane Marie (the latter, as a votary of her brother-in-law Frederick II of Prussia, no friend to Britain), Caroline Matilda became esteemed for her modesty and good temper. But this period would prove but a calm before three years of turmoil and scandal during which the queen would herself undermine what standing she had acquired in Denmark and, by the autumn of 1770, unregardingly jeopardize the British and Danish places in Panin's 'northern system'.

Struensee On his return to Copenhagen in January 1769 Christian's condition seemed improved. The credit for this might be ascribed to a freethinking physician from Altona, Johan Friedrich Struensee (1737–1772), who had first met Christian in Holstein in 1767. He had been introduced by Charles, count von Rantzau-Ascheberg, a fellow freethinker and a bitter opponent of Bernstorff's policy as regards Holstein and of the government of stratified privilege in which Bernstorff was so prominent. At this time Struensee had no evident political ambitions beyond a discipleship of the *philosophes*, but, invited by the king, he happily joined the royal retinue on the foreign tour of 1768. Intelligent and enquiring, his manner towards Christian, perhaps countering the pernicious influence of Holck, won him the royal confidence, and on returning to Copenhagen Struensee entered the court. Whatever his professional abilities Struensee was a self-confessed philanderer, and it is not surprising that Caroline Matilda did not initially distinguish him from the general run of her husband's intimates. She herself suffered some form of breakdown in the summer of 1769, and it was Struensee's genuine efforts to ameliorate the king and queen's relationship, and his successful vaccination of the infant crown prince against smallpox, which drew Caroline Matilda towards him. Struensee's most recent mistress had died during the queen's illness, and it may be inferred that it was Caroline Matilda, susceptible to Struensee's personal charm, who really advanced the relationship, evidently with the king's voyeuristic concurrence, to the point of sexual intercourse before 1769 was out. The physician's better judgement was insufficient to steer him off a perilous course, for Christian's incapacity was leaving a vacuum at the very centre of government in which the young queen was in dire need of counsel.

The extent of Struensee's influence within government may have been largely concealed for some eighteen months, for the fiction of the king's normal exercise of his authority was effectively maintained, and Struensee did not actually enter the royal council until May 1770. But a critical situation was compounded by the surfacing of Caroline Matilda's more headstrong qualities. During the court's spell in Holstein that summer, perhaps in imprudent emulation of Catherine II, Caroline Matilda cavorted as an equestrienne in military uniform, and this indelicacy laid her open to lampoons once press freedom was decreed by Struensee himself a year later. London saw as no less ominous the reappearance at court of Rantzau, for this boded ill for Bernstorff's future (he was actually dismissed in September 1770 to his shock and the tsarina's anger) and hence future relations with Russia. Such was the concern of the dowager princess of Wales at the reports reaching her that she made her way in August 1770 to Lüneburg, to confront Caroline Matilda and Struensee. It was an effort which availed nothing, and certainly brought no diminution in her daughter's passions. Caroline Matilda conceived a second child in October, the Princess Louisa Augusta, born on 7 July 1771. The birth was enthusiastically greeted by Christian, and Juliane Marie stood as godmother. All the same, Struensee's paternity was widely suspected at the time and afterwards. While that should not be certainly accepted, it could be significant that when on 28 June 1771 she congratulated George III and Queen Charlotte on the birth of a prince Caroline Matilda made no reference to her own imminent delivery.

Downfall The period which elapsed between Bernstorff's dismissal, in which Struensee himself had no hand, and his own arrest by reactionary elements with popular support on 17 January 1772, was without parallel in Europe, not so much owing to the objectives of his reform programme as to the instantaneousness of their implementation. Caroline Matilda could only welcome the replacement of Holck by an intimate of Struensee, and yet of a conciliar background, Envold Brandt; and Struensee's first formal government post in December 1770. But while on a personal level she could only deprecate the award of a pension to Stövlet Katrine, she may be presumed to have favoured the abolition of torture and the granting of rights for illegitimate children. In January 1771 she instituted, on Christian VII's twenty-second birthday, the order of Caroline Matilda, which was distributed among her supporters and may be regarded as her imprimatur of support for a programme long suppressed and now to be implemented. It is hard to tell what role in it, other than a crucially supportive one for Struensee, Caroline Matilda played. At his trial Struensee, in answer to the leading charge that he had severed the monarchy from its subjects by breaching the *Lex regia* of 1665, claimed that Christian knew of and acquiesced in the reforms. Given what is now known of the schizophrenic condition Struensee here may have been largely truthful, even though it was incontrovertible that the king's signature had been appended to ordinances without his direct participation. In fact, what counted hardly less against Struensee was his close association with Envold Brandt, who was to share in Struensee's barbaric execution by dismemberment on 24 April 1772: in his relations with the king Brandt occasionally resorted to a bullying which shocked interrogators who could not comprehend Christian ever being a compliant party. Struensee's association with the queen, for all the past publicity and the proximity in the palace of his quarters to hers, did not feature in the framed charges, but the central fact emerged under interrogation, and perhaps through the use of torture.

Caroline Matilda's immediate fate after Struensee's arrest was to be separated from her four-year-old son, though until the end of May she was permitted to keep the six-month-old princess. She was detained at the fortress of Kronborg, though it was intended she should end up in the more remote Aalborg. Christian VII was frustrated in his wish to see her, but secured for her the retention of her rank, protesting to the princess dowager on 17 January that it was not within his power to do otherwise than order her detention. She was barely permitted consultation with her able defence counsel, Peter Uldall, and on 9 March was outmanoeuvred by interrogators revealing to her that Struensee had already confessed to their relationship. The judicial commission's verdict of 8 April was that misconduct was proven, but *raison d'état* itself required a formal affirmation of Princess Louisa Augusta's legitimacy. On 20 May Christian forwarded protocols of divorce to George III and it is noteworthy that he himself repeated at the end of the letter the conventional sentiments of friendship which had already been penned by a secretary. The dowries provided for Caroline Matilda by Britain and Hanover in 1766 were to be returned by Denmark, which also accepted that the upbringing of the royal children would be at Denmark's exclusive charge.

George III appeared impassive at the turn events had taken in Copenhagen in January 1772. While shocked at the cruelty shown to his sister, his initial reactions were shaped by his impatience with her and perhaps a fear that her behaviour had hastened their mother's death on 8 February. English lawyers considered the evidence against Caroline Matilda 'presumptive and inconclusive'. Opinions expressed in the British press were sympathetic to Caroline Matilda's cause, her mistakes being blamed on Juliane Marie. As soon as a plan had been formulated, George III showed no hesitation in responding to her pleas for help. Through the shrewd diplomacy of the British envoy at Copenhagen, Robert Murray Keith, the Danes were forced to surrender her to the Royal Navy at Kronborg whence, on 30 May, Caroline Matilda sailed for her brother's Hanoverian dominions. She left behind her thirty-three-piece silver gilt toilet service by Hemmings of London, probably a wedding present from her mother, and a 7 inch long watch and chain covered in brilliants. Both remain in the Danish royal collection at Rosenborg Palace.

Caroline Matilda's final place of exile was Celle, and here she lived, in dignity, for the remaining three years of her life. She was financially sustained in part by £8000 inherited from her mother, and also by a quarterly allowance from the Hanoverian exchequer based upon her British and Hanoverian dowries. She kept in touch with her brothers and sisters, but was concerned for her husband and above all her children. Her death on 10 May 1775 after only five days of illness, may have been due to porphyria, but her symptoms: weariness, 'paralysis of vital centres', and a 'putrid spotted fever' (Macalpine and Hunter, 226–7), are also suggestive of scarlet fever; this in combination with a porphyriac metabolism might have been fatal. She was buried in the Stadtskirche, Celle.

Although during her years at Celle Caroline Matilda betrayed no ambition to assume regency powers in Denmark were she to return there in the wake of a successful coup against the regime of Juliane Marie, the latter welcomed the news of her death. Court mourning was indeed ordered, but not in respect of Caroline Matilda as queen consort, only as a foreign princess associated with the Danish crown. The regime of the queen mother and her son Frederick, by fifteen years the senior of the crown prince for whose future his mother Caroline Matilda had to fear, especially after the older prince's marriage in October 1774, was not unaware of its fragile popularity.

Even before the end of 1772 there was a growing network of disaffected Danes centred on Hamburg who enjoyed Hanoverian officialdom's connivance at their activities; and Hamburg was within easy reach of Celle and Caroline Matilda's relaxed and welcoming court. Their earlier approaches, however, to Caroline Matilda, who only wished to be reunited with her children, were without result, for she remained mindful of George III's words of April 1772: 'I certainly said (to the Danes) I would not assist in getting you back to that kingdom (unless) the king should recall you with that éclat and dignity which alone can make it desirable' (Royal Archives, GEO 16030, letter of 23 April). George III's attitude remained unchanged, and this explains why the indefatigable English traveller Nathaniel Wraxall, who was in touch with the Hamburg dissidents and, like others, was chivalrously stirred by Caroline Matilda's situation, needed to persuade her at a fourth interview in March 1775 to write to George III for his support. This the king would only give in the event of a coup's successful outcome, and Caroline Matilda's death meant the removal of the venture's mainspring.

D. D. ALDRIDGE

Sources Royal Arch., George III papers, 15810–16030; 52289–52411 [very variable value; Add. MSS 21/149 spurious] · S. C. Bech, *Oplysning og tolerance, 1721–1784*, vol. 9 of (1965) *Danmarks historie*, ed. J. Danstrap and H. Koch (Copenhagen, 1962–6), 404–90 · H. Jørgensen, *The unfortunate Caroline Matilda's last years, 1772–75* (Copenhagen, 1989) · M. Roberts, 'Great Britain, Denmark and Russia, 1763–1770', *Studies in diplomatic history*, ed. R. M. Hatton and M. S. Anderson (1970) · H. A. Barton, *Scandinavia in the revolutionary era, 1760–1815* (Minneapolis, 1986), chaps. 2–3 · PRO, SP Denmark, 75/117–19 · A. Friis, *Andreas Peter Bernstorff, og, Ove Høegh Guldberg* (Copenhagen, 1899), chaps. 1–2 · K. Willich, *Struensae* (Leipzig, 1879) · O. Brandt, *Caspar von Saldern und die nord-europäische Politik im Zeitalter Catherine II* (Erlangen/Kiel, 1932) · O. Brandt, *Historische Zeitschrift* (1929), 550–64 · W. F. Reddaway, 'Struensee and the fall of Bernstorff', *EngHR*, 27 (1912), 274–86 [see also article by Reddaway in vol. 31] · M. Roberts, 'Great Britain and the Swedish Revolution, 1772–73', *Essays in Swedish history* (1967) · K. R. Schmidt, 'Treaty between Great Britain and Russia, 1766', *Skandoslavica* (1954), 115–34 · M. Roberts, *British diplomacy and Swedish politics, 1758–1773* (1980), 332–5 · I. Macalpine and R. Hunter, *George III and the mad-business* (1969), 223–8

Archives Niedersächsisches Hauptstaatsarchiv Hannover, Hanover, König Georg MSS · Royal Arch., Georgian MSS

Likenesses R. Read, pastel drawing, c.1765, Royal Collection · F. Cotes, pastel drawing, 1766, Fredericksborg · F. Cotes, oils, 1767 (with Louisa Anne), Royal Collection · J. Juel, portrait, 1767 · C. G. Pilo, portrait, 1768–9, Fredericksborg · J. Juel, oils, 1769, Statens Museum for Kunst, Copenhagen [see illus.] · H. P. Sturz, portrait, 1771, Fredericksborg · C. D. Voigt, miniature, 1774, Celle · A. F. Oeser, sculpture, c.1790, French park, Celle · J. Juel, oils, Schloss Celle · Liotard, pastel drawing (aged three), Royal Collection; repro. in *Burlington Magazine*, 68 (1936), facing p. 118

Wealth at death inherited £8000 from mother; had quarterly allowance from Hanoverian exchequer: Jørgensen, *Unfortunate Caroline Matilda's last years*

Caron, Sir Noel de (*b.* before **1530**, *d.* **1624**), diplomat, was born in Flanders, probably the son of Jacques Caron van Schonewalle, who was from 1530 *magistraat* of the Brugge Vrije (the free region of Bruges). Through a convoluted family connection he was related to Simon Stevin, the sixteenth-century mathematician. After inheriting the lordship of Schonewalle Caron became magistraat and mayor of the Brugge Vrije in 1578 and served as a deputy at the states general for the Vrije between 1577 and 1586. He also served as a member of the state council.

Caron was an ardent supporter of the prince of Orange, dealing in the negotiations with the duke of Anjou and the talks leading to the treaty of Plessis les Tours in 1580. After the duke of Parma conquered Bruges in April 1584, Caron fled to Orange. Between June 1584 and 1585 he acted as a deputy in France before being sent to England as a member of the delegation which again offered Elizabeth the sovereignty of the Low Countries and which negotiated the treaty of Nonsuch. In May 1591 he returned to England to act as agent for the United Provinces. He remained in this post until the queen's death.

On the accession of James VI and I, Caron was one of only two representatives to retain their posts. He was promoted to the office of ordinary, traditionally in the gift of the province of Zeeland, in July 1609. Although he was given the title of ambassador and received at James's court as such, the Spanish refused to acknowledge Caron as their diplomatic equal or even as their colleague. However, he enjoyed a remarkable reputation among other residents at court, and with the king, who knighted him in 1607. A further demonstration of the king's favour was exhibited in 1612 when he conferred on Caron for life the office of keeper of Bagshot Park.

Caron was one of the few ambassadors to maintain their own property in London, having been granted by Elizabeth land at South Lambeth, on which he erected a large and impressive house, surrounded by a large deer-park which extended to Vauxhall and Kennington. It took ten years to build and consisted of two large wings connected by a hall, with a block of guest apartments. It became a meeting-place for Dutch merchants and immigrants resident in the City, but, although large and sumptuous, it was not used to accommodate the Dutch commissioners regularly arriving in London to treat with James and his ministers. These men were usually to be found lodged in Bread Street, their costs defrayed by the Dutch merchants. There were two fundamental reasons for this: first, South Lambeth was a considerable distance from the hub of social and diplomatic life at court; and second, Caron House was not in effect an embassy maintained by the states general but Sir Noel's private residence, owned and maintained by him personally. However, the ambassador regularly used his house for diplomatic purposes, entertaining the king and other ambassadors on many occasions.

It was through Caron that the young Constantine Huygens was first presented to the king when he made one of his many unceremonious descents on the Dutch ambassador. On these occasions the king arrived in a small procession of coaches and usually accompanied by Prince Charles, the younger privy councillors, or the royal favourites. The object of these visit was not, ostensibly, to discuss affairs of state but to sample the Dutch cherries

that Caron grew. The ambassador's extensive fruit gardens were well known and the king, renowned as something of a fruit addict, visited regularly to sample the different varieties. These frequent, rather private, and unofficial visits, which arose from a shared interest, allowed a certain degree of intimacy to develop between the king and Caron which gave the ambassador a distinct advantage over his rivals. At these impromptu meetings a cold collation, at which official matters could be discussed in a private way, and a stroll around Caron's well-stocked picture gallery invariably followed the fruit tastings. Finally, before departing, the king would allow his hand to be kissed by a number of foreign visitors presented by the ambassador.

Caron was regarded as a 'worthy and charitable' Anglophile, and was known for his good works among the local community. In 1607 he gave £10 towards the repairs of Lambeth church and £50 to the poor, while in 1615 he founded almshouses at Vauxhall, in what is now Fentiman Road, about a half a mile from his own house. Over the gate of the almshouses was a Latin inscription informing the visitor that it was founded in the thirty-second year of his embassy, 'as an insignificant monument of what he owed to the glory of God, in gratitude to the nation, and in munificence to the poor'. This building housed seven poor women, upwards of sixty years of age, all parishioners of Lambeth and all granted a pension of £4 annually. These pensions continued from his estate after Caron's death.

Caron remained unmarried and died, still in office, on 1 December 1624, naming the prince of Wales as his heir. He was buried at Lambeth on 25 January 1625 and his helmet, coat of mail, gauntlets and spurs, together with his arms, were placed in the sanctuary of St Mary, Lambeth. The memorial had been removed some time before 1826 and the ambassador's tomb did not survive the Victorian rebuilding programme.   ROBERTA ANDERSON

Sources O. Schutte, *Repertorium der Nederlandse Vertegenwoordigers, Residerende in het Buitenland, 1584–1810* (The Hague, 1976) · Nationaal Archief, The Hague, S. G. book of decrees II, 167 [31 March 1610] · Nationaal Archief, The Hague, S. G. instruction book, no. 107 [instructions to Caron, 12 July 1591] · Nationaal Archief, The Hague, S. G. no. 3797, p. 355 [James I and VI to States, 10 April 1610] · Nationaal Archief, The Hague, S. G. inv. no. 8298 · PRO, SP 14/43/71; 14/99/47 · will, PRO, PROB 11/154, sig. 74 · A. G. H. Bachrach, *Sir Constantine Huygens and Britain*, 2 vols. (Leiden, 1962), vol. 1, p. 125 · *VCH Surrey*, 4.50–53 · G. N. Clark and J. W. van Eysinga, *Bibliotheca Visseriana, Dissertationum Jus Internationale Illustrantium*, vol. 34, p. 18 · W. D. Cooper, ed., *Lists of foreign protestants and aliens resident in England, 1618–1688*, CS, 82 (1862) · *CSP dom.*, 1625

Archives National State Archives, Brussels, reports, corresp., instructions, etc

Wealth at death small bequests to nephew and others: will, PRO, PROB 11/154, sig. 74

Caron, Redmond (*c*.1605–1666), Franciscan friar and theologian, was known as a Meath man: he was born some 10 miles from Athlone in the present county of Westmeath. Having been taught the humanities at home he entered the Franciscan order probably in the Athlone friary when he was about sixteen. He was sent to the Drogheda friary to study philosophy, but had to go to Salzburg, where he also studied theology, and then spent two years in St Anthony's College, Louvain. He began to teach philosophy there about 1634, and theology from 1639 to the beginning of 1649. He was then sent to Ireland as visitator of the Franciscan friars and delegate of a commissary general of the order, Peter Marchant, who was influenced by the Ormondist group among the confederate Catholics at Kilkenny. Caron's credentials were questioned, and he was strongly opposed in his efforts to divide the Irish Franciscan province into two, a policy favoured by the Ormondists. He submitted to the minister provincial in 1650, was replaced, and his official acts were annulled.

Caron returned to the continent in 1651 and, based first at Ghent and Antwerp, began to write books reflecting his political and theological opinions, with a fair degree of repetition. He believed in the absolute supremacy of the king, as God's anointed deputy, in all temporal matters. In 1653 he published three works: *Roma triumphans septicollis*, a work of controversial theology, with a new comparative methodology, arguing the claim of the Roman church to be the true Christian church; *De libertate Gallicana*, written in defence of the king's rights even in church matters which had nothing to do with defined doctrine (later reprinted in his *Remonstrantia*); and *Apostolatus evangelicus missionariorum*, a pioneering work for priests sent 'on the mission', which was enlarged and republished in 1659, but was placed on the Index in 1661 until corrected. Efforts were made to have him banished from Spanish Flanders, where he was a military chaplain in 1654. He had taken charge of some Poor Clares who had fled from Ireland, and he eventually received permission to help them. He then went to the new Irish Franciscan residence in Paris, with other Ormondist friars, where he studied Gallican theology. His *Controversiae generales fidei*, against the arguments of 'all infidels', appeared in 1660, and the following year he went to London, where he showed the manuscript of his Gallican inspired *De sacerdotio et imperio* to his fellow Franciscan Peter Walsh.

Having settled in London with Walsh, Caron went to Wales for a few months, staying with a friend from his Paris days (probably William Herbert, later Lord Powis). He defended Walsh's remonstrance or 'loyal formulary', a pledge of Catholic obedience to Charles II, in his correspondence and in his next book, *Loyalty Asserted* (1662), which was dedicated to Charles II. It claimed many authors in favour of his point of view on the separate powers of church and state, and corrected Cardinal Jacques-Davy du Perron's criticism. In May 1662 he signed an approbation for Walsh's *The More Ample Accompt* of the remonstrance; all this got him into more trouble with his order and the Holy See. In September 1664, in the 'area' of Somerset House, Caron and Walsh faced a stern, undercover internuncio, Girolamo de' Vecchi. Nevertheless, in the following year Caron published *Remonstrantia Hibernorum* (dedicated to Charles II) in answer to the censure, at Louvain and elsewhere, of the 'Irish remonstrance' of 'indispensable obedience' to the king. After that, he left a plague-ridden London for his friend's house

in Montgomeryshire, and in September 1665 went (perhaps a sick man) to the Dublin friary. A meeting of the clergy of Ireland was due in the following summer, but Caron became ill in January and died at the friary about 22 May 1666. Peter Walsh was there and recorded Caron's regret for any intemperate words ever used in his defence of the remonstrance, which he urged Walsh to continue to uphold. Walsh preached at the obsequies, and a large crowd watched the funeral at St James's churchyard. A marble tombstone with a short inscription was later erected there by Anthony Gearnon OFM. In 1683 Walsh penned a tribute to Caron in the 'Additamentum' of his *Causa Valesiana*, adding the index from Caron's *Remonstrantia* of 1665 (most copies of which had been destroyed a year later in the great fire of London) which Walsh used also in the 'Appendix altera de Gregorio VII' of the *Causa Valesiana*. Besides the works mentioned above, Caron had printed in Louvain (1643–7) some theological theses and a short commentary on two letters of St Paul. A *Vindication of the Roman Catholics of England*, said to be his, was published in London in 1660. He left in manuscript 'De canone sacrae scripturae contra episcopum Dunelmensem', and possibly a catalogue of Franciscan saints.

IGNATIUS FENNESSY

Sources P. Marchant, *Relatio veridica et sincera status provinciae Hiberniae* (c.1651) · P. Irenaeus [J. MacCallaghan], *Vindiciarum Catholicorum Hibernicae … libro duo* (1650), 158–82 · P. Walsh, *The history and vindication of the loyal formulary, or Irish remonstrance* (1674) · P. Walsh, *Causa Valesiana epistolis ternis praelibata et in fine additamentum* (1684) · *The whole works of Sir James Ware concerning Ireland*, ed. and trans. W. Harris, rev. edn, 2 vols. in 3 (1764) · C. Giblin, ed., 'Catalogue of material of Irish interest in the collection *Nunziatura di Fiandra*, Vatican archives [pt 2]', *Collectanea Hibernica*, 3 (1960), 7–144 · B. Jennings, ed., 'Sint-Truiden: Irish Franciscan documents', *Archivium Hibernicum*, 24 (1961), 148–98; 25 (1962), 1–74; 26 (1963), 1–39 · B. Millett, *The Irish Franciscans, 1651–1665* (1964) · T. Sweeney, *Ireland and the printed word: a short descriptive catalogue of early books … relating to Ireland, printed, 1475–1700* (Dublin, 1997), no. 863–73, 5505 · R. L. Browne, ed., 'A history of the Franciscan order in Ireland', *The Franciscan Tertiary*, 8/11 (1898), 259f., 289f., 321f.

Archives Archivio Vaticano, Vatican City, Nunziatura di Fiandra, letters referring to him · Archivio Vaticano, Vatican City, Fondo di Vienna, letters by and about him · Belgian Franciscan Archives, Sint-Truiden, corresp., reports and documents concerning his actions in Ireland, his statements

Carpenter, Alexander (*fl. c.*1429), religious author, is of unknown origins. Almost nothing is known of the external facts of Carpenter's life, though a medieval note in a flyleaf associates him with Oxford. His one known surviving work, the *Destructorium viciorum*, constitutes his claim to fame and reveals something of his attitudes. It appears to have been completed in 1429. Carpenter is cited in a work completed in 1424 so there may have been an earlier version of the *Destructorium*; alternatively, the work cited might be the *Homiliae eruditae* attributed to him, which is not known to be extant. The incipit of the *Destructorium* is 'Omne peccatum, ut dicit beatus Augustinus contra Faustum, est dictum vel factum vel concupitum contra legem Dei, hoc est peccatum cordis, oris, vel operis' (Bloomfield, no. 3612). It is a work belonging to the genre of treatises on virtues and vices compiled with an eye to the needs of preachers.

This huge specimen owes a large debt to the most influential single work of the genre, the *Summa* of the mid-thirteenth-century Dominican homilist Guillaume Peyraut. Its approach is familiar: an analytical structure (built around the seven deadly sins, after an initial more general section); *exempla* and similitudes, notably from everyday life and the animal world; and plentiful citations of the church fathers, later theologians, and canon law. The sharp tone of reforming criticism is nothing new in the genre, but was perhaps somewhat radical in the context of the campaign against Lollardy that was proceeding at the time the work was completed. There is no evidence that Carpenter himself was a Wycliffite or Lollard, but there are remarks that suggest he considered the reaction against the dissidents to be too severe and indeed shared some of their feelings. The *Destructorium*, which survives in at least two manuscripts, is an excellent source for the history of mentalities, and notably for attitudes to witchcraft and magic. It appeared in eleven printed editions between 1480 and 1582; the colophon to the Nuremberg edition of 1496 assigns its compilation to the year 1429. In modern times the value and interest of the *Destructorium* have come to be appreciated largely through the work of G. R. Owst.   D. L. D'AVRAY

Sources G. R. Owst, *The 'Destructorium viciorum' of Alexander Carpenter: a fifteenth-century sequel to 'Literature and pulpit in medieval England', being an expansion of a lecture delivered in the University of Durham on 2 March 1951* (1952) · H. L. Spencer, *English preaching in the late middle ages* (1993), index · Emden, *Oxf.* · J.-T. Welter, *L'exemplum dans la littérature religieuse et didactique du moyen âge* (Paris, 1927), 425–7 · M. W. Bloomfield and others, *Incipits of Latin works on the virtues and vices, 1100–1500 A.D.* (1979)

Carpenter, Alfred Francis Blakeney (1881–1955), naval officer, was born at Barnes, Surrey, on 17 September 1881, the only son of Lieutenant (later Captain) Alfred Carpenter RN and his first wife, Henrietta, daughter of G. A. F. Shadwell. His father in 1876 received the Albert medal and the Royal Humane Society bronze medal for rescuing a man overboard while serving in the *Challenger*, and while in command of the marine survey of India, at the time of the Third Anglo-Burmese War, was among the first naval officers to be appointed to the DSO. His grandfather Commander Charles Carpenter in 1814 assisted in the capture after a long chase of the American privateer *Rattlesnake*. His uncle was the writer Edward Carpenter.

On leaving his preparatory school Carpenter entered the Royal Navy as a cadet in 1897. The following year as a midshipman he saw service in Crete during the massacres, and in 1900 he was with the naval brigade landed during the Boxer uprising in China. After promotion in 1903 to lieutenant he specialized in navigation, becoming a lieutenant-commander in 1911. In the year preceding the war he gained experience in staff duties on a war staff course and received the thanks of the Admiralty for various inventions of a specialized nature. In the same year he was awarded the silver medal of the Royal Humane Society for saving life at sea.

Alfred Francis Blakeney Carpenter (1881–1955), by Olive Edis, 1920s

The outbreak of war in 1914 found him in the *Iron Duke* on the staff of Sir John Jellicoe, but in November 1915, after his promotion to commander, he was appointed navigating commander in the *Emperor of India*. In 1917 Roger Keyes was appointed director of plans at the Admiralty and Carpenter, who had been Keyes's navigating lieutenant in the *Venus*, successfully begged to be taken on his staff. There he was engaged in the secret plans for attacking Zeebrugge and Ostend with the purpose of blocking the exits from the submarine and destroyer bases. Keyes in his *Naval Memoirs* wrote: 'Commander Carpenter's gift for going into the minutest details with the most meticulous care, greatly assisted me in preparing a detailed plan, and orders, which embodied the work of several officers' (2.215).

In selecting Carpenter for the command of the *Vindictive* Keyes knew he was choosing a man familiar with all the main phases of the operation. The whole conception of the attack on Zeebrugge and Ostend had the spirit and elements of the cut-and-thrust raids of Drake and Hawkins. The chance of favouring winds and currents coinciding with the eve of St George's day 1918 gave the expedition an additional romantic appeal. To Keyes's signal 'St George for England' Carpenter replied 'May we give the Dragon's tail a damned good twist' (Keyes, *Naval Memoirs*, 2.262).

Carpenter had been promoted to acting captain for the expedition but his duties were confined to the command of the ship and Acting Captain H. C. Halahan, who was senior to him, was in command of the landing force designed for attacking the Mole at Zeebrugge, partly to divert attention from the block ships and partly to destroy enemy armament. Carpenter's part in bringing the *Vindictive* alongside the Mole was vital to the success of the operation and his achievement in doing so is not to be underrated even though he brought her 340 yards beyond her planned position and thus out of reach of her primary object: the guns which commanded the approach to the harbour. It was characteristic that Carpenter freely admitted this error was entirely his, explaining that it was due to the great difficulty in recognizing the objects on the Mole amid the shell and smoke flare. Keyes, in his first dispatch, paid tribute to Carpenter's personal share in the attack, pointing out that, from all reports he had, Carpenter's

> calm composure when navigating mined waters and bringing his ship alongside the Mole in darkness, and his great bravery when the ship came under heavy fire, did much to encourage similar behaviour on the part of the crew, and thereby contributed greatly to the success of the operation. (*Ostend and Zeebrugge*, 164)

His skill in bringing his ship away after the action was also highly praiseworthy.

Carpenter, as the senior surviving officer, was asked by Keyes to make recommendations for conspicuous gallantry, but he replied that he felt it would be invidious to select individuals where everyone had acted so splendidly. Nor would he take part in the ballot which was then arranged for an officer and rating for the VC in accordance with rule 13. In this ballot, in which officers could only be elected by officers, Carpenter received one more vote than Commander Harold Campbell of the *Daffodil* and was thus awarded the cross. He was immediately confirmed in his promotion to captain and later received the Croix de Guerre with palm and was made a chevalier of the Légion d'honneur. His detailed account of *The Blocking of Zeebrugge* was published in 1921.

After Zeebrugge, Carpenter was sent on a lecture tour of Canada and the United States (1918–19) and on his return, after a brief time in the naval intelligence department, on 1 October 1919 he was given command of a war course at Cambridge for naval officers. In 1921 he took over the command of the light cruiser *Carysfort* and in October 1923 was given charge of the senior officers' technical course at Portsmouth. From February 1924 to September 1926 he held the triple post of captain of the dockyard, deputy superintendent, and king's harbour master at Chatham. After a period on special duty at the Admiralty he was given command of the *Benbow* in August 1927, transferring to the *Marlborough* the following May. He was promoted rear-admiral in August 1929, at a time when opportunities for employment in flag rank were limited, and placed on the retired list, on which he was promoted vice-admiral in 1934.

During his retirement Carpenter interested himself in the merchant navy, particularly in the training of its junior officers and cadets. He introduced the idea of a training ship, the *St Briavels*, in which they could have practical experience in handling, manoeuvring, and mooring ships, which was necessarily in the hands of senior officers on actual voyages. During the Second World War he commanded the 17th Gloucestershire battalion of the Home Guard from 1940 to 1944. He was appointed a deputy lieutenant for Gloucestershire in 1946.

He married in 1903 Maud (*d.* 1923), daughter of the Revd Stafford Tordiffe, rector of Staplegrove, Somerset, and they had a daughter. He married second, in 1927, Hilda Margaret Alison, daughter of Dr W. Chearnley Smith.

Lean and ascetic in appearance, Carpenter, brought up in the traditions of the navy, although somewhat conventional in his outlook, embodied many of the highest qualities of the best type of naval officer. Disciplined in mind, courageous and calm in action, energetic and inspiring as a leader and generous in his praise for subordinates, he also possessed an unusual gift for the mastery of detail and exactness in planning. He died at his home, Chantersluer, St Briavels, Gloucestershire, on 27 December 1955.

G. K. S. HAMILTON-EDWARDS, *rev.*

Sources *The Times* (28 Dec 1955) · *The Times* (4 Jan 1956) · A. F. B. Carpenter, *The blocking of Zeebrugge* (1921) · R. Keyes, *The naval memoirs of Admiral of the Fleet Sir Roger Keyes*, 2 (1935) · *Ostend and Zeebrugge, April 23 – May 10, 1918: the dispatches of Vice-Admiral Sir Roger Keyes … and other narratives of the operations*, ed. C. S. Terry (1919) · private information (1971) · *WWW* · H. J. Newbolt, *A naval history of the war, 1914–18* (1920) · *CGPLA Eng. & Wales* (1956)
Archives FILM BFI NFTVA, news footage · IWM FVA, documentary footage · IWM FVA, news footage
Likenesses A. Cope, oils, 1918, NPG · W. Stoneman, two photographs, 1918–29, NPG · O. Edis, photograph, 1920–29, NPG [see illus.]
Wealth at death £12,075 18s. 9d.: probate, 6 Feb 1956, *CGPLA Eng. & Wales*

Carpenter, Alfred John (1825–1892), physician and propagandist for the cause of sewage farming, the son of John William Carpenter, surgeon, of Rothwell, Northamptonshire, was born at Rothwell on 28 May 1825. He attended Moulton grammar school in Lincolnshire, before becoming a pupil of William Percival at the Northampton Infirmary about 1841 and later assisting John Syer Bristale. He entered St Thomas's Hospital, London, in 1847, taking the first scholarship, and went on to win the treasurer's gold medal. He was appointed house surgeon and resident accoucheur, and, after becoming a member of the Royal College of Surgeons and a licentiate of the Society of Apothecaries in 1851, he went into practice at Croydon in the next year. On 22 June 1853 Carpenter married Margaret Jane, eldest daughter of Evan Jones, marshal of the high court of Admiralty; they had three sons and a daughter.

Although spending the great bulk of his career in unfashionable Croydon, Carpenter moved effortlessly upwards through the metropolitan and national medical hierarchies, gaining an MD at London in 1859, returning to St Thomas's to lecture on public health between 1875 and 1884, and becoming a vice-president of the Social Science Association in 1881. He was also medical adviser to four successive archbishops of Canterbury and in 1885 (for Reigate) and 1886 (for North Bristol) stood for parliament unsuccessfully as a Gladstonian Liberal. Carpenter was not a teetotaller, but he campaigned vehemently against the dangers of excessive consumption of alcohol. Both as moralist and magistrate, he 'betrayed a remarkable belief in the ancient theory of "sparing the rod and then hating the juvenile offender". His invariable remedy for the [juvenile] class of offender was a "sound whipping"' (*Lancet*, 6 Feb 1892, 338).

Between 1859 and 1879 Carpenter was a leading light on the Croydon local board of health, and he was the founder manager of one of the earliest municipal sewage farms, at the village of Beddington. His views on the transmission of infection belonged neither to the miasmatic school, associated with the name of Edwin Chadwick, nor to that which was beginning to champion the specificity of disease. Committed to the centrality of fresh air and ventilation as preconditions for the maintenance of good health, Carpenter nevertheless believed that no significant danger attached to the controlled irrigation of sewage in the immediate vicinity of large centres of population. Undertaking epidemiological investigations to prove that Croydon and Beddington were characterized by lower rather than higher death rates in general, following the establishment of the farm, he insisted that there was no connection between the 'natural' treatment of sewage and an increase in infection among humans, or parasitic diseases among cattle.

To further counter disquiet Carpenter declared that the herds raised on the sweet ryegrass at Beddington produced beef of the highest quality, 'not fat, but exceedingly tender and juicy ... no epicure could wish for a better joint' (A. Carpenter, *Preventive Medicine in Relation to the Public Health*, 1877, 296). An enthusiastic supporter of the view that economic co-operation between town and country must be encouraged if dependence on foreign food, and repeated outbreaks of cattle plague, were to be eradicated, Carpenter calculated that the sewage of 20 million Britons could be used to sustain nearly half a million additional cattle. All this could be achieved with no more than an extra 1½d. on the rates.

Carpenter's position in relation to the processes underlying successful sewage irrigation was idiosyncratic. Drawing analogies between his own work and Darwin's research into *Drosera dionaea*, he argued that ryegrass was carnivorous:

> the rootlets of a young crop ... seize upon the organic elements which are contained in sewage, bring them into immediate contact with the extremities of the spongules of the plant [so that] an actual digestion of the animal matter takes place without any reduction to organic salts coming to pass. (A. Carpenter, *Preventive Medicine*, 1877, 211)

But this eccentric stance in no way compromised the validity of Carpenter's belief that sewage farming might offer viable and non-polluting solutions to pressing environmental problems.

During a period in which scientists and municipalities were becoming disenchanted with the costly and inefficient chemical deodorization of human waste enforced upon them by the court of chancery, the Beddington experiment attracted widespread attention. For Carpenter, however, and for many other mid- and late-Victorian sanitarians and medical practitioners, sewage farming held out the promise of a social order in which town waste could be returned to the countryside, thereby subsidizing and reviving the declining agricultural sector. Although he wrote extensively and with great clarity on many other medical and scientific subjects, to Carpenter this utopian vision represented nothing less than a creed and an obsession. Carpenter died at the Esplanade Hotel, Ventnor, Isle of Wight, on 27 January 1892. He was buried at Croydon.

BILL LUCKIN

Sources C. Hamlin, *What becomes of pollution? Adversary science and the controversy on the self-purification of rivers in Britain, 1850–1900* (1987) · H. Goddard, '"A mine of wealth": the Victorians and the agricultural value of sewage', *Journal of Historical Geography*, 22 (1996), 274–90 · J. Sheail, 'Town wastes, agricultural sustainability and Victorian sewage', *Urban History*, 23 (1996), 189–210 · *The Lancet* (6 Feb 1892), 338 · *DNB* · m. cert. · d. cert. · *CGPLA Eng. & Wales* (1892)

Archives Croydon Central Library | UCL, letters to Edwin Chadwick

Likenesses E. R. Mullins, bust, 1901, Croydon public hall

Wealth at death £23,019 18s. 7d.: probate, 19 March 1892, *CGPLA Eng. & Wales*

Carpenter, Lady Almeria (1752–1809). *See under* William Henry, Prince, first duke of Gloucester and Edinburgh (1743–1805).

Carpenter, Edward (1844–1929), campaigner for homosexual equality and socialist writer, was born on 29 August 1844 at 45 Brunswick Square, Brighton, Sussex, the third son of Charles Carpenter RN (1797–1882) and his wife, Sophia, the daughter of Thomas Wilson RN of Walthamstow. The Carpenters were a west-country family, and Edward's grandfather Admiral James *Carpenter (1760–1845) fought naval battles against revolutionary France in the West Indies. Edward's father, a lieutenant stationed at Trincomalee, retired early, became a barrister, and led the life of a respectable *rentier* in Brighton, occupying a large house and investing heavily in stocks and shares. Edward had three brothers and six sisters, and he was the seventh child. He attended Brighton College from 1854 to 1863. After his three brothers entered the colonial, army, and naval services respectively, he was left alone with his sisters, most of them unmarried. The Brighton household, in which his mother was a conventional matron, helped to shape his personality; he combined an unconscious revolt against Victorian standards of social ethics with frustration of his sexual desires, which he soon realized were for his own sex.

In 1864, after spending some months in Heidelberg, Carpenter entered Trinity Hall, Cambridge, with the intention of being ordained. He won a college prize in 1866 for his essay 'On the continuation of modern civilization', which showed him well on the road to advanced liberalism. He was tenth wrangler in the mathematical tripos of 1868, and was elected to the clerical fellowship at his college vacated by Leslie Stephen. In 1869 he won the Burney prize at Cambridge for his essay 'The religious influence of

Edward Carpenter (1844–1929), by Roger Fry, 1894

art'. After being ordained in 1870, he served as curate to Frederick Denison Maurice, the incumbent of St Edward's, Cambridge, of which the fellows of Trinity Hall were patrons. Maurice's liberal Anglicanism, however, was not broad enough for Carpenter, who read Mazzini with W. K. Clifford and attended the Republican Club at Cambridge, led by Henry Fawcett. He joined with thirty-three other clerics, most of them Oxford or Cambridge fellows, in a memorial presented to Gladstone in 1870 seeking the freedom to resign clerical orders. The Clerical Disabilities Relief Act was passed in 1870, and was followed by the University Tests Act of 1871. Carpenter's commitment to the cause of university reform coincided with his reading Walt Whitman's *Leaves of Grass* and *Democratic Vistas*, extolling 'manly love and friendship'. He also broadened his social vision by visiting Paris shortly after the suppression of the Paris commune. All this affected his sermons, which became Whitmanesque and even proto-socialist. In 1873 he took a long holiday in Italy, where the works of Greek sculpture at Paestum and elsewhere convinced him of the beauty and cleanness of the human body remote from commercialism and Christianity. Taking advantage of the Clerical Disabilities Relief

Act, he relinquished his orders in 1874, which meant resignation of his college fellowship. He was disappointed in his hope of being elected to a lay fellowship.

In October 1874 Carpenter started lecturing on astronomy at Leeds (where he lived) and other northern towns for the university extension scheme, a 'peripatetic' university for the people, which had been started in the previous year by James Stuart. In May 1877 he visited Whitman in Camden, New Jersey, and some of the New England celebrities: Ralph Waldo Emerson, Oliver Wendell Holmes, and John Burroughs. He wrote to Whitman on 'the squalor and raggedness' of manufacturing towns such as Sheffield and on the workmen, proud and poor. Strains due to overwork and also to continued sexual frustration led him to seek a more natural way of living—he became mainly a vegetarian and a teetotaller. He interested himself in John Ruskin's experiment at St George's Farm, and in May 1880 he took lodgings with Albert Fearnehough, a scythe maker, and his family at Totley, near Sheffield, and from March 1881 at Bradway in a cottage owned by a young farmer, Charles Fox. Fearnehough became his lover and the long-delayed fulfilment of his sexual needs was attained at last.

Carpenter's sexual liberation was accompanied by his conviction of spiritual freedom and equality gained through his study of the *Bhagavad Gita*, a gift from his Cambridge friend Ponnambalam Arunachalam (1853–1924). By the spring of 1881 he had given up lecturing altogether, and in a small wooden hut built in the gardens of the Bradway cottage he began to write poems, or a hymn of the soul, charting its 'slow disentanglement', in the style of Whitman. The result was a slender volume published anonymously in 1883 under the title *Towards Democracy*. About 400 copies out of 500 printed were sold in two years. It was saved from oblivion by a favourable review by George C. Moore Smith in the *Cambridge Review*.

The death of his father in 1882 brought Carpenter some £6000; he now set himself up as a market gardener, bought three fields of about 7 acres at Millthorpe, halfway between Sheffield and Chesterfield within walking distance of the moors, and built a substantial cottage, where he and the Fearnehoughs moved in October 1883. As well as cultivating an orchard and market garden, he also took up sandal making. About the same time he began to play a role in the nascent socialist movement. Relying on H. M. Hyndman's *England for All* (1881) for economic argument to explain the cause of alienation, he wrote an important tract, *Modern Money-Lending and the Meaning of Dividends* (1883), which presents a world of surplus value from which the moneyed class could extricate themselves by adopting a simple mode of living, and by starting co-operative production or disseminating ideas on the subject. He joined the Democratic Federation founded by Hyndman and contributed £300 to its organ *Justice*, started in January 1884. He was critical of those who split the federation in December 1884 and was attracted to the Fellowship of the New Life, the parent body of the Fabian Society; it was members of this circle, such as Edward Pease, Havelock Ellis, and Ellis's friend Olive

Schreiner, who really appreciated *Towards Democracy* when its second, enlarged, edition came out in 1885.

For the Sheffield Socialist Society that came into existence in March 1886 Carpenter prepared a programme asserting independence from the claims of the national socialist bodies. Their socialist work was assisted by Raymond Unwin of Chesterfield, later known as a promoter of garden cities, and by Robert Franklin Muirhead (1860–1941) of Glasgow, a Cambridge graduate and mathematician, who shared Carpenter's ideals of nature and manly love. Carpenter wrote *England Arise: a Socialist Marching Song* (1886) for the new movement. Millthorpe and Sheffield attracted some of the Cambridge élite—Charles Robert Ashbee, Goldsworthy Lowes Dickinson, and Roger Fry—and Carpenter for a while entertained the idea of reconciling culture and labour.

Carpenter's new year Fabian lecture of 1889 came out as a book, *Civilization: its Cause and Cure* (1889), in which he described civilization as a social and moral disease, and earned the nickname of the Noble Savage. One of the sores of civilization was 'smoke nuisance' or air pollution, against which he and Sheffield socialists conducted a well-organized campaign. He helped Kropotkin in his studies of small industries. In 1892, when the Walsall anarchists were tried for an attempt to manufacture bombs allegedly for the Russians, Carpenter as a witness defended them by dissociating anarchism from terrorism.

Carpenter's journey to Ceylon and India in the winter of 1890–91, described in his book *From Adam's Peak to Elephanta* (1892), was memorable for his visit to a guru and for reinvigoration of his faith in spiritual freedom and equality. Carpenter co-operated with his friends Henry and Kate Salt in their work for the Humanitarian League and joined in its campaigns against vivisection, for prison reform, for the abolition of cruel sports, and for other similar causes.

Carpenter indulged in a new comradeship of a serious and extremely tender nature in 1886–7 with George E. Hukin, a razor grinder. He was deeply wounded when Hukin decided to marry. His homosexual life, however, remained well protected from curiosity, though Henry Labouchere's amendment to the Criminal Law Amendment Act of 1885 made all male homosexual acts liable to legal prosecution. Carpenter's reticence on the subject ended in 1892, when he met John Addington Symonds, who was preparing a full-scale book on sexual inversion in collaboration with Havelock Ellis. Carpenter supplied notes on his and his friends' homosexual cases for this study. Symonds's sudden death in 1893 deprived Ellis's *Studies in the Psychology of Sex* (1897) of his contribution. Carpenter felt that he was destined to succeed him in defence of homosexuality.

In the course of 1894–5 the Labour Press, Manchester, published four of Carpenter's pamphlets on sex: *Sex-Love, and its Place in a Free Society*; *Woman, and her Place in a Free Society*; *Marriage in Free Society*; *Homogenic Love, and its Place in a Free Society*. The last of these was for private circulation only, and was reissued as *Love's Coming of Age* in 1896 (enlarged in 1906). Carpenter did not regard sexual inversion as environmental and abnormal but as congenital,

and called men and women with an innate homosexual bias 'urnings', a word which he derived from *uranos* ('heaven'). His *The Intermediate Sex* (1908) had a significant readership both in Britain and abroad. Among those who were influenced by his works were Siegfried Sassoon, Robert Graves, E. M. Forster, and D. H. Lawrence.

After the Fearnehoughs left Millthorpe in March 1893, George Merrill, the son of an engine driver and a product of the Sheffield slums, became Carpenter's sole companion. George Oates of Leeds, his Cambridge friend with whom he had maintained an intimate friendship, died (unmarried) in 1902 and left £3000 to Carpenter. The third edition of *Towards Democracy* (1892) included a new third part, entitled 'After civilisation'. Its fourth edition (1905) brought in another addition, a fourth part, overtly homosexual, which was originally published in 1902 under the title *Who shall Command the Heart?*

Carpenter was a pro-Boer in the Second South African War. His socialism was catholic enough to welcome both the Labour Party and its critics. His *Non-Governmental Society* (1911) contains his mature thought on syndicalism or guild socialism. For the suffragette movement he worked with Mrs Charlotte Despard and the Women's Freedom League. During the First World War he condemned the war as part and parcel of 'civilization' and advocated 'a United States of Europe' in *The Healing of Nations* (1915). His 'Never Again!' (1916) was a powerful anti-war poem. His autobiography, *My Days and Dreams*, also appeared in 1916. Fenner Brockway, the founder of the No Conscription Fellowship, remembered his appearance at this period: 'his head and features were of extraordinary beauty; his face a chiselled statue, clear-cut and of perfect outline; his eye bright and kindly' (Brockway).

The death in 1917, at the age of fifty-six, of George Hukin, who appeared prominently in part 4 of *Towards Democracy*, snapped Carpenter's emotional tie with the north. In 1922 he and Merrill moved south and settled at the new Millthorpe, Mountside Road, Guildford, Surrey, where George took to drink and died in January 1928 in his early sixties. Carpenter sold the house, and with Edward Inigan from Wigan, another 'personal friend', moved to a bungalow, Inglenook, in Joseph's Road, Guildford. He had a stroke and died on 28 June 1929 of uraemia and senility. He was buried in the same grave as Merrill at Guildford cemetery. Carpenter survived all his brothers and sisters, and his estate, estimated at £5214 gross (£4152 net), mostly went to his nephews and nieces, apart from £1000 left to Inigan in his will. He was sometimes called the English Tolstoy, and Tolstoy considered him 'a worthy heir of Carlyle and Ruskin'.   CHUSHICHI TSUZUKI

Sources E. Carpenter, *My days and dreams* (1916) · C. Tsuzuki, *Edward Carpenter, 1844–1929* (1980) · G. Beith, ed., *Edward Carpenter: in appreciation* (1931) · E. Delavenay, ed., *D. H. Lawrence and Edward Carpenter* (1971) · S. Rowbotham and J. Weeks, *Socialism and the new life: the personal and sexual politics of Edward Carpenter and Havelock Ellis* (1977) · K. Nield, 'Carpenter, Edward', *DLB*, vol. 2 · E. Lewis, *Edward Carpenter* (1915) · T. Swan, *Edward Carpenter* (1913) · F. Brockway, 'Edward Carpenter, an obituary', *New Leader* (5 July 1929) · b. cert. · d. cert.

Archives BL, corresp. and papers, Add. MSS 70536, 70556 · JRL, letters and papers, incl. autobiographical notes · Ransom HRC, literary papers · Sheff. Arch., corresp. and literary MSS | BLPES, corresp. with Independent Labour Party; corresp. with Edward Pease; letters to the Fabian Society · Honjo City Library, Japan, Kyokuzan collection · King's AC Cam., letters to C. R. Ashbee · King's AC Cam., corresp. with E. M. Forster · Nuffield Oxf., letters to the Fabian Society · Sheff. Arch., letters to George Clemas · U. Birm. L., letters to Granville Bantock · U. Lpool, Sydney Jones Library, letters to John and Katherine Glasier · U. Nott. L., letters to Constantin Sarantchoff · Worcester College, Oxford, letters to J. N. Dalton

Likenesses three photographs, 1887–1910, Sheffield City Library · R. Fry, oils, 1894, NPG [*see illus.*] · A. L. Coburn, photograph, 1905, NPG · H. Bishop, oils, 1907, NPG · Elliott & Fry, photogravure, NPG · F. Hollyer, photograph, V&A

Wealth at death £5214 5*s.* 8*d.*: probate, 9 Aug 1929, *CGPLA Eng. & Wales*

Carpenter, Edward Frederick (1910–1998), dean of Westminster and ecclesiastical historian, was born on 27 November 1910 at 17 New Haw Road, Addleston, Surrey, the younger son and younger child of Frederick James Carpenter (1880–1969), a master craftsman and builder, and his wife, Jessie Kate (1880–1960), daughter of Thomas and Ellen Arscott of Washfield, Devon. From the age of about five he attended St Paul's Boys' School, Addleston, and in 1922 he entered Strode's Secondary School for Boys, Egham, where despite poor eyesight from birth he displayed skill and courage at football and cricket and became a highly proficient tennis player. He also acquired a passion for the poetry of Shelley, and shone from the start as a scholar of history and divinity, despite his near illiterate background, his father having left school at the age of twelve. In 1928 he achieved a University of London higher school certificate in English, modern history, and French, and in 1929 he entered King's College, London, where he was awarded the Barry prize for divinity and the Gladstone memorial history prize. In 1932 he graduated with first-class honours in history.

In the following year Carpenter was admitted to the faculty of theology at King's College, London, where he graduated MA in history with distinction, and took another first, in the combined bachelor of divinity and associate of King's College courses. For his MA thesis he chose 'his worth for church and state' of an eighteenth-century bishop, Thomas Sherlock, whose biography became Carpenter's first published work in 1936, the year of his ordination to the priesthood. He had been ordained deacon and appointed assistant curate at Holy Trinity, Marylebone, the previous year. In 1941 he moved, again as assistant curate, to St Mary's, Harrow on the Hill. On 10 December that year he married Lilian Betsy Wright (*b.* 1917), the second daughter and third of the six children of Albert Wright, a cobbler in north London, and his wife, Alice. They had three sons, David (*b.* 1946), Michael (*b.* 1948), and Paul (*b.* 1953), and a daughter, Louise (*b.* 1960).

In 1943 Carpenter was awarded the London degree of PhD for a thesis on Thomas Tenison, a seventeenth-century archbishop of Canterbury, which was published in 1948 as *Thomas Tenison: his Life and Times*. Two years later he was inducted to the living of St John the Evangelist,

Great Stanmore, where it was fortunate for his future career that one of the parishioners happened to be Clement Attlee. In 1951 Attlee offered Carpenter a residentiary canonry at Westminster Abbey. Carpenter, who accepted, remained a member of the abbey chapter for the next thirty-four years.

While a canon of Westminster, where he served as *lector theologiae* (1958), treasurer (1959–74), and archdeacon (1963–74), Carpenter combined the traditional role of a residentiary canon—producing scholarly biographies and books on ethics and clerical life—with a prodigious capacity for pastoralia and work for a variety of causes. These included most notably animal welfare (he and his wife were vegetarians), the ecumenical movement, reform of clergy pay and deployment, the education of girls (he was chairman of the governors of the North London Collegiate School), and the Modern Churchmen's Union, of which he became president in 1966. He always regretted that in 1956 Dean Alan Don did not use his influence to have him appointed rector of St Margaret's, Westminster, but his most devastating disappointment was Harold Wilson's failure in 1967 to offer him the deanery of St Paul's, for which he yearned. It went instead to the less distinguished archdeacon of London, Martin Sullivan. Despite the blandishments of the archbishop of Canterbury, Michael Ramsey, Carpenter declined in 1968 an informal offer of the deanery of Guildford, believing that despite his lack of preferment his roots and his future should remain in London. On the resignation in 1974 of Eric Abbott, Wilson made amends by inviting Carpenter to succeed him as dean of Westminster, a rare appointment at the time for someone educated neither at a public school nor at Oxford or Cambridge.

In 1966, the 1000th anniversary of Westminster Abbey, Carpenter undertook to edit the abbey's official history. The most important of the ten books for which he was responsible while at Westminster was *Cantuar: the Archbishops in their Office* (1971), a *tour de force* of scholarship presented as a tapestry of English ecclesiastical history and easily accessible to the general reader. The book on which he spent most labour, but to less happy effect, was a major life of Geoffrey Fisher, archbishop of Canterbury from 1945 to 1961. Published in 1991 to mixed reviews, it was full of factual errors, badly proof-read, and too long, but by then Carpenter was eighty, plagued by poor eyesight, and ill-served by his publishers.

Carpenter was a man of great integrity and moral courage, a pacifist who was prepared to defy prime ministerial edicts, even refusing to read the bidding prayer at a memorial service for Sir Arthur 'Bomber' Harris. He was generally reckoned to have been a great dean, perhaps the last of a very Anglican breed of independent-minded, slightly eccentric deans, men of God for whom daily worship was infinitely more attractive than the chore of raising money. His informality and hospitality (the deanery was open to one and all) became legendary. His preferred mode of transport was by bicycle. He encouraged adventurous liturgical experiments, and transformed a national shrine into an intimate place of warmth and welcome.

Carpenter was appointed KCVO on his retirement in 1985, without, of course, using the title. He was not offered appointment as dean emeritus, for the statutes of the abbey made no such provision. He retired to Richmond in Surrey, where a decade later he was beset by Alzheimer's disease. He died at Twickenham on 26 August 1998, and his funeral service took place in Westminster Abbey on 4 September. A memorial stone to him was unveiled in the nave on 27 July 2000. He was survived by his wife and four children.   MICHAEL DE-LA-NOY

Sources M. De-la-Noy, *A liberal and godly dean: the life of Edward Carpenter* [forthcoming] · *The Times* (27 Aug 1998) · *The Guardian* (27 Aug 1998) · *Daily Telegraph* (27 Aug 1998) · *The Independent* (28 Aug 1998) · *WWW* · private information (2004) · personal knowledge (2004)
Archives LPL, working manuscript relating to biography of Archbishop Fisher
Likenesses photograph, 1977, repro. in *Daily Telegraph* · photograph, 1981, repro. in *The Independent* · C. Hildyard, oils, priv. coll. · J. Whittal, oils, Westminster Abbey · photograph, repro. in *The Times* · photograph, repro. in *The Guardian* · photograph, Hult. Arch.
Wealth at death £347,863: probate, 10 June 1999, *CGPLA Eng. & Wales*

Carpenter, Emily Ann (1834–1933), college head, was born at Newington, London, the daughter of Joseph Carpenter and his wife, Sarah. She was baptized on 28 October 1836 at Lady Huntingdon's Surrey Chapel, Blackfriars Road, Southwark. Nothing is known of her early life. In 1880 she raised money for the Education Society, of which she was a council member at the time of the society's amalgamation with the Teachers' Guild in 1887. In that year she was appointed from a field of eighty-three applicants to the post of lady principal at the University College of Wales, Aberystwyth. In 1885 a hall of residence had been opened for women students, who had been admitted to the college for the first time in the previous year. Financial problems forced its closure, but the authorities decided to reopen the hall in October 1887, under the watchful eye of Miss Carpenter. Residence in the hall was made compulsory for all women students unless they were living with their parents or guardians. At first the hall was located in houses on the seafront, but as the number of women students rose (there were eighty-four in 1892–3), Miss Carpenter pressed for a purpose-built hall of residence. After energetic fund-raising the new premises, Alexandra Hall, were opened on 26 June 1896 during a royal visit by the prince and princess of Wales and in the presence of the aged Gladstone.

As lady principal Miss Carpenter was entrusted with general disciplinary authority over women students. Strict regulations governed women students' conduct both in the hall and out in the town, and were particularly designed to keep male and female students apart. While encouraging women students to participate in debates, dramatics, clubs, and societies—she herself founded a Browning Society and a German reading society—she insisted on chaperonage. By the early twentieth century her continued enforcement of rules inspired by Victorian social and moral attitudes caused much irritation. Lady Stamp (*née* Olive Marsh), a student at Alexandra Hall during 1898–1900, while recalling the rich social life of concerts, operas, and literary and debating societies, nevertheless revelled in the freedom the students were able to enjoy during Miss Carpenter's occasional absences.

Emily Carpenter, who was a signatory to the declaration in favour of women's suffrage published in the *Fortnightly Review* in July 1889, was vice-principal in 1892 of the Women's Liberal Association at Aberystwyth and was on the council of the Union of Welsh Women's Liberal Associations. She chaired meetings of the Women Students' Total Abstinence Society. She retired as lady principal in 1905, when numbers of women students had reached a healthy enrolment of 205. In a farewell address she stated that, over her eighteen years at Aberystwyth, she 'had but one purpose, to strengthen the position of our women in their efforts after the higher education and personal freedom that were denied to all women in my young days'. Acknowledging the restiveness which students felt towards her disciplinary regime and her caution, she explained that 'if, at times, I have seemed obstructive it has only been because it was evident to me that too early an advance would lose them the whole field' (*The Dragon*, 27, 1905, 220–22). During a long retirement she lived at Leatherhead, Surrey, and Tunbridge Wells, Kent, where she taught English to Belgian refugees during the First World War. Emily Carpenter died at her home, Lilian House, 82 London Road, Tunbridge Wells, on 30 April 1933, in her ninety-ninth year. She was buried in Tunbridge Wells cemetery after a religious ceremony conducted by the Society of Friends, with whom she latterly worshipped. Alexandra Hall closed in 1986 but a second hall of residence for women, opened in 1919 and named Carpenter Hall, bears continuing witness to her contribution to women's higher education in Wales.

W. GARETH EVANS

Sources E. L. Ellis, *The University College of Wales, Aberystwyth, 1872–1972* (1972) · E. L. Ellis, *Alexandra Hall, 1896–1986* (1986) · Alexandra Hall—miscellaneous MSS, U. Wales, Aberystwyth · letters to Lady Stamp (Olive Marsh), 1898–1900, U. Wales, Aberystwyth · E. Morgan, ed., *The college by the sea* (1928) · *The Dragon*, 55/3 (1933), 58–9 · *Cambrian News* (1887–1905) [esp. suppl., 26/6/1896; tribute, 2/6/1905] · W. G. Evans, *Education and female emancipation: the Welsh experience, 1847–1914* (1990) · *Woman's Herald* (13 Aug 1892), 8 · *Transactions of the Teachers' Guild of Great Britain and Ireland* (1887) · Will, 29 June 1933 · *CGPLA Eng. & Wales* (1933) · census returns, 1891 · MSS, PRO, Nonconformist register, PRO RG4
Likenesses portrait, c.1884, NL Wales · portrait, 1905, U. Wales, Aberystwyth · portrait, repro. in Ellis, *Alexandra Hall*
Wealth at death £5405 9s. 1d.: probate, 29 June 1933, *CGPLA Eng. & Wales*

Carpenter, (Joseph) Estlin (1844–1927), Unitarian minister and college head, the second of the five sons of William Benjamin *Carpenter (1813–1885), a prominent naturalist, and Louisa Powell (1812–1887), was born on 5 October 1844, in Ripley, Surrey. He was the grandson of Lant *Carpenter and the nephew of Mary *Carpenter, both honoured names in the annals of Unitarianism; his uncles, Russell Carpenter and Philip Pearsall *Carpenter, were also Unitarian ministers. William Carpenter was, at

(Joseph) Estlin Carpenter (1844–1927), by Elliott & Fry, 1922

the time of his son's birth, tutor to the children of Lord Lovelace, but the family moved soon afterwards to London. Known throughout his life as Estlin, rather than Joseph, Carpenter grew up in a home where rational religious faith and puritan austerity (which included abstinence from alcohol) were balanced by scientific, literary, and musical enthusiasms. Among the family's treasured possessions were an organ (always whimsically known as 'Dagon') and a microscope. They were committed members of Rosslyn Hill Unitarian Chapel, Hampstead, and William Carpenter served for a time as organist and choirmaster.

Estlin was educated first at University College School, and then, in 1860, having decided to follow his uncles into the Unitarian ministry, he moved to University College, London, where he studied mental and moral philosophy. In 1863 he proceeded to Manchester New College, the noted inheritor of the tradition of the dissenting academies, which by that time had moved from Manchester to London. Here, his intellectual ability and personal charm made a great impression on his fellow students. One of them, Philip Henry Wicksteed, was destined to become his lifelong friend and comrade, and his equal in academic eminence. Somewhat unexpectedly, during his student days Carpenter experienced a brief period of spiritual aridity. But this was resolved by a mystical experience in north Wales, described some years later, in graphic terms, in a letter to a friend. He left Manchester New College in

June 1866 and spent the rest of the summer enjoying an extended holiday in Zürich. This enabled him to perfect his knowledge of the German language—an important factor in his later competence in critical scholarship. His stay in Switzerland also provided him with welcome opportunities for rowing and mountaineering, always his favourite recreations.

In the autumn of 1866 Carpenter was appointed minister of Oakfield Road Church, Bristol, and in 1869 he moved to Mill Hill Chapel, Leeds, where Joseph Priestley had once ministered. At both places he was much admired, not only for the spirituality of his preaching, sustained by a well-grounded intellectual faith, but also for his wide interests. At Leeds in particular, his Sunday services were supplemented by regular academic lectures on many different topics, and he also found time to translate and edit (from the original German) a large part of G. H. A. von Ewald's *History of Israel* (1871–8). But his career in the pastoral ministry was cut short by the onset of a curious speech defect, not finally eradicated until some nine years later, which seriously affected his preaching and lecturing.

In 1875 Carpenter accepted, not without some initial reluctance, an invitation to return to Manchester New College as professor in ecclesiastical history, comparative religion, and Hebrew. Though his initial qualifications for such an appointment were questionable, he threw himself into the work of ministerial training with great enthusiasm, devoting much time and energy to improving the range of his knowledge. He also showed, from the first, a special pastoral concern for the welfare of his students, offering them regularly the hospitality of his home in Hampstead, where he held frequent literary and musical evenings, and occasionally taking them on outings to cathedral cities and other places of interest. On 12 July 1878 he married Alice Mary (1854–1931), the daughter of George Buckton, a leading member of his former congregation at Leeds. Though no children were born to them, their union was to prove in every respect a 'marriage of true minds', and throughout the rest of his life Alice remained his beloved helpmate and companion.

Thanks to the zealous and methodical dedication to study which was to mark Carpenter's entire career, his fame soon spread beyond the college, and in the wider academic world he eventually became an acknowledged authority in two spheres in particular—biblical criticism and comparative religion. In the latter field he learned the Pali language with the assistance of Thomas Rhys Davis, the leading Buddhist scholar of the day, and in association with him he later undertook the onerous task of transliterating and editing some of the Pali Buddhist texts.

In 1885 James Martineau, always very highly esteemed by Carpenter, retired from the principalship of Manchester New College; he was succeeded by James Drummond, and Carpenter became vice-principal. Four years later, not without some controversy, the college moved to Oxford, subsequently dropping 'New' from its name, and Carpenter moved with it. For the rest of his life he was to remain closely linked with Oxford, and his reputation and personality probably did much to secure the successful establishment of the college in its new home. In 1899, under somewhat obscure circumstances, Carpenter resigned from the vice-principalship, retaining only the Case lectureship in comparative religion. But this probably merely reflected a desire on his part to devote himself more earnestly to academic pursuits, and in 1906 he resumed a full involvement in the work of the college upon his appointment as principal in succession to Drummond. He retired in 1915 on attaining the age of seventy, but he continued as principal-emeritus, and from 1920 to 1925 he held the honorary office of president of the college. From 1914 until 1924 he was the Wilde lecturer in comparative religion at Oxford University.

Carpenter lived an extraordinarily busy and well-filled life. His very considerable literary output, which included some major works in both biblical criticism and comparative religion, is listed in full in C. H. Herford's *Memoir*. In the field of biblical criticism perhaps his most famous work was what came to be known as *The Oxford Hexateuch* (1900). Though this was originally a composite production, edited by Carpenter and G. Harford Battersby, it was Carpenter who was most closely involved in the enterprise, and the one-volume second edition (1902) was almost entirely his responsibility. The work did much to secure a general acceptance of the Graf-Wellhausen hypothesis—the theory that the Pentateuch, and possibly other parts of the Old Testament, were an untidy combination of four separate sources, designated by the symbols J, E, D, and P. He also wrote some important books on the New Testament, such as *The First Three Gospels, their Origin and Relations* (1890), and in his eighty-third year he published *The Johannine Writings, a Study of the Apocalypse and the Fourth Gospel* (1927). In comparative religion perhaps his best works, apart from the editions of the Pali texts, were *Theism in Medieval India* (Hibbert lectures, 1921) and *Buddhism and Christianity, a Contrast and a Parallel* (Jowett lectures, 1923). His small comprehensive manual entitled *Comparative Religion*, a contribution to the Home University Library series, published in 1913, though much admired in some quarters, was probably one of his less successful efforts. He also wrote definitive biographies of his revered teacher James Martineau (1905) and his aunt Mary Carpenter (1879).

Carpenter was always an assiduous organizer of conferences and summer schools, especially during his time at Oxford. This brought him into contact with many of the leading academics of the day, both at home and abroad. It also led to new collaborations and friendships, notably with F. Max Müller, A. S. Peake, and L. R. Farnell. When Peake came to compile his famous one-volume *Commentary on the Bible*, he asked Carpenter to contribute an introductory article on the Pentateuch. His intellectual eminence earned him honorary degrees from several universities, including a DLitt and a DD from Oxford. Passages in the many letters which he received underline the extent to which his contemporaries acknowledged his competence and expertise. Max Müller once said to him, in a

brief note: 'Could you, without much trouble, tell me the latest date that can safely be assigned to Exodus 3.14?' A. J. Edmunds, another academic, wrote to him as follows: 'There are hundreds of scholars who know more about the New Testament than I do, and scores who know more about the Pali Texts; but I know of only one man on earth who is equally well acquainted with the two, and that man is Estlin Carpenter' (Carpenter MSS, Manchester College, Oxford).

But Carpenter was also from first to last a dedicated Unitarian. In spite of his multifarious academic activities, he seems nevertheless to have found time to involve himself, to quite a surprising degree, in the practical affairs of the Unitarian denomination. He devoted much energy, for example, to a personal campaign for the establishment of a pension fund for ministers. His abilities as lecturer and preacher were occasionally instrumental in the founding of new Unitarian causes—most notably at Cambridge, where a congregation, founded in 1908, was the eventual outcome of regular weekly services held during university term time, which had been inaugurated after a series of lectures by Carpenter in 1903. In addition, throughout his life—true to a family tradition—he showed an active concern for social service, and always retained a special interest in such causes as temperance, international peace, and the relief of poverty. In pursuit of the latter he was from 1880 to 1889 the secretary of the London Domestic Mission Society, a pioneer Unitarian organization with a practical concern for the problems of urban deprivation.

Always firmly committed to the Unitarian tradition in all its aspects, Carpenter was an untiring advocate of friendly relations with all the great world faiths, and especially with the religions of the East, of which he had an astonishingly detailed knowledge. He also fostered and encouraged close contacts with liberal churches in India and Japan. In his own personal life, as was always evident from his conduct of worship, he possessed a rich and emphatically Christian spirituality, characterized by a deep assurance of an all-embracing divine love. Here, perhaps, was the source of his unswerving belief in a universal revelation.

To those who did not know him well, Carpenter sometimes seemed a rather shy and austere figure. Someone is supposed to have said of him, rather unkindly, that 'he had no redeeming vices' (Herford and others, 102). But he was in reality an unusually friendly individual who always took a close personal interest in the lives of all his former students. The enterprising house parties at his country cottage in the Lake District, to which students and colleagues both past and present were regularly invited, were at one time quite legendary. With his full beard and handsome face Carpenter was an imposing figure, and for most of his life he was endowed with robust health and much given to vigorous exercise, especially rowing and hill walking. His final years, however, were marred by painful illness, and at an earlier period he had had to endure some tragic experiences, the details of which his biographer does not disclose. But nothing could shake the serenity of his personal faith. A month before his death, in a letter to a former student, he wrote: 'A recent attack has made me an old man, and my walking days are over. But from my windows I can still enjoy the glories of spring, and even in bed I can say "How beautiful it is to be alive!"' (*The Inquirer*, 25 June 1927).

Carpenter died at his home, 11 Marston Ferry Road, Oxford, on 2 June 1927, and was buried at Wolvercote cemetery on 7 June. The public orator at Oxford University, in sonorous Latin, mourned the passing of 'a learned, gentle, and most Christian soul' (Herford and others, 90). After his death the memory of Carpenter's saintly life eventually faded—even within his own denomination—and his academic reputation suffered a marked eclipse. In biblical scholarship, some at least of his conclusions have stood the test of time, and his books, especially those on the New Testament, can still be read with profit. But the world of comparative religion is no longer in tune with his essentially evolutionary approach, and his obvious Christian commitment, despite his wider sympathies, makes him suspect. But in both of the fields in which he excelled he undoubtedly deserves an honourable place as a remarkable pioneer in objective critical study, and the Carpenter Library of Comparative Religion, established at Manchester College (now incorporated into the university as Harris Manchester College) constitutes a unique and lasting memorial to his genius.   A. J. LONG

Sources C. H. Herford and others, *Joseph Estlin Carpenter: a memoir* (1929) • *DNB* • A. J. Long, 'The life and work of J. Estlin Carpenter', *Truth, liberty, religion: essays celebrating two hundred years of Manchester College*, ed. B. Smith (1986) • *The Inquirer* (11 June 1927) • J. Deacon, 'Joseph Estlin Carpenter: an intellectual biography', MA diss., Lancaster University, 1977 • Harris Man. Oxf., Carpenter papers • D. Vernon Marshall, 'The work of Estlin Carpenter in the field of comparative religion', MPhil diss., Open University, 2001
Archives Harris Man. Oxf., corresp. and notebooks | Bodl. Oxf., letters to Asquith • Bodl. Oxf., letters to Gilbert Murray • DWL, letters to J. M. Connell
Likenesses Elliott & Fry, photograph, 1922, repro. in Herford and others, *Carpenter* [*see illus.*] • H. Somerville, two portraits, Harris Man. Oxf. • M. Tayler, portrait, Essex Hall, London
Wealth at death £14,627 19s. 7d.: probate, 10 Aug 1927, *CGPLA Eng. & Wales*

Carpenter, George, first Baron Carpenter of Killaghy (1657–1732), army officer, was born on 10 February 1657 at Ocyle Pychard, Herefordshire, the youngest of seven children of Warncomb Carpenter and his wife, Eleanor, daughter of William Taylor of Herefordshire and widow of John Hill. The Carpenter family, established in the county for 400 years, owned extensive estates. Warncomb, himself one of at least six sons of Thomas Carpenter, had fought for the royalists in the civil war. Educated at a private grammar school, George started his career at the age of fourteen as a page to the earl of Montagu, ambassador to Paris. In 1672 he enlisted as a private soldier in the 3rd troop of guards and shortly afterwards joined the earl of Peterborough's regiment of horse as quartermaster. He remained with the regiment for many years, serving in the Irish campaign of 1690, and in Flanders, eventually becoming lieutenant-colonel. In 1693 he married Alice (c.1660–1731), daughter of William, Baron Cawfield (later Viscount Charlemount), and wealthy widow of James Margetson. In 1703 he bought the colonelcy of the Royal regiment of dragoons (later 3rd hussars) and the forfeited estates of Baramount and Killaghy in co. Kilkenny. He was MP for Newtonards in the Irish parliament from 1703 to 1705.

Appointed brigadier-general under Peterborough in 1705, Carpenter performed the dual roles of quartermaster-general and general of cavalry in Spain during the War of the Spanish Succession. At the disastrous battle of Almanza he led his brigade of dragoons in a final charge that covered the allied retreat and saved the English baggage train. He was promoted major-general in 1708 and lieutenant-general two years later. As Stanhope's deputy during his absence in England, he made himself unpopular in the ranks by threatening to hang deserting cavalrymen. During the unsuccessful defence of Briheuga in 1710, he was badly wounded by a musket ball that broke his jaw, displaced half of his teeth, and lodged in the base of his tongue. Until it was removed a year later, he was unable to eat solid food.

When he returned to England following captivity Carpenter identified himself strongly with the protestant succession and was nominated by Stanhope as George I's ambassador to Vienna. However, with the outbreak of the rising in 1715 he received command of all forces in northern England instead. He turned the Jacobite force from Newcastle and followed them to Preston. By the time he arrived there the Jacobites had already thrown back several attacks by General Wills's troops. Carpenter's reinforcement of Wills and particularly his blocking of an escape route that Wills had overlooked persuaded the Jacobites to capitulate. At Preston the two generals had agreed to put aside a long-standing animus between them. In London the following February, however, Carpenter challenged Wills, and it was only the intervention of the dukes of Montagu and Marlborough that prevented a duel. Appointed governor of Minorca and commander-in-chief in Scotland in 1716, he was MP for Whitchurch in 1715–22 and for the city of Westminster in 1722–7. He was created Baron Carpenter of Killaghy in the kingdom of Ireland in 1719. A fall soon afterwards loosened his remaining teeth, which stopped him eating properly. After a gradual decline he died on his seventy-fifth birthday, four months after his wife. He is buried at Owslebury, Hampshire. His son, also George (c.1695–1749), was MP for Morpeth in 1717–27 and for Weobley in 1741–7.

H. M. STEPHENS, *rev.* TIMOTHY HARRISON PLACE

Sources G. Carpenter, *The life of the late Right Honourable George Lord Carpenter* (1736) • A. Boyer, *The political state of Great Britain*, 10 (1715), 502–4; 11 (1716), 177–85 • A. Parnell, *The war of the succession in Spain during the reign of Queen Anne, 1702–1711* (1888); repr. (1905) • A. D. Francis, *The First Peninsular War, 1702–1713* (1975) • D. Whyte and K. A. Whyte, *On the trail of the Jacobites* (1990) • B. Lenman, *The Jacobite risings in Britain, 1689–1746* (1980) • P. H. Stanhope, *History of the war of the succession in Spain* (1832) • *HoP, Commons, 1715–54* • GEC, *Peerage* • N. B. Leslie, *The succession of colonels of the British army from 1660 to the present day* (1974)

Archives BL, corresp. | CKS, corresp. with James Stanhope · NA Scot., corresp. with duke of Montrose
Likenesses J. Faber junior, mezzotint, NPG
Wealth at death £1000 to son; £1000 to George Freeman; colonelcy and estates valued at £4400 in 1703: will, Carpenter, *The life*

Carpenter, George Alfred (1859–1910), physician and paediatrician, was born on 25 December 1859 at 176 Lambeth Road, London, the son of John William Carpenter MD and his wife, Mary, daughter of George Butler of New Shoreham, Sussex. Alfred John *Carpenter was his uncle.

After two years (1874–6) at Epsom College, a school then much favoured by doctors, Carpenter spent a year (1877) at King's College School, London, which had established an outstanding academic reputation and which educated many future distinguished members of the medical profession.

Carpenter trained first at St Thomas's Hospital, London, where he was a prizeman, qualifying MRCS and LSA in 1885. He graduated MB (London) in 1886 with first-class honours. Subsequently he studied at Guy's Hospital in 1889, qualifying MRCP in 1889 and MD (London) in 1890.

After a brief period as deputy medical superintendent at the Coppice Lunatic Hospital, Nottingham, Carpenter returned to London to practise at 12 Welbeck Street, Cavendish Square. His medical career, however, centred on his work with the young children of the poor. Between 1885 and 1903 he was on the staff of the Evelina Hospital for Sick Children, Southwark, where he was finally physician in charge of the extensive outpatients' department. In 1903 Carpenter was appointed assistant physician at the North Eastern Hospital for Sick Children, renamed the Queen's Hospital in 1908, which treated sick children of the poor under the age of twelve. At the time of his death Carpenter was full physician.

Carpenter's significant contributions to the study of paediatrics consisted not so much in any innovations he made in clinical treatment as in his assiduous compilation of case notes, his tireless efforts to encourage specialization in that branch of medicine, and in his meticulous editing and documentation of such work.

In 1900 Carpenter was joint founder and leading figure of the Society for the Study of Disease in Children of which provincial branches were rapidly established in England. He edited eight volumes of the society's reports between 1900 and 1908, after which it was incorporated as a section of the Royal Society of Medicine, of which Carpenter was vice-president at the time of his death.

In 1904 Carpenter founded the *British Journal of Disease in Children*, partly to fill the gap left when the American journal *Pediatrics* ceased publication. This was published jointly in New York and London, between 1896 and 1901. Carpenter was its English editor and a copious contributor to the eleven volumes. He was also a corresponding member of La Société Pédiatrie of Paris and a member of La Société Française d'Ophtalmologie, to both of which he contributed papers. He was also a regular contributor to *The Lancet* and the *British Medical Journal* and he read a number of papers to the Hunterian Society, the Royal Society of Medicine, and the Institute of Hygiene.

The time spent by Carpenter on his editorial and administrative tasks, besides his medical attention to sick children, may explain why he published only two books, both in 1901, *Syphilis in Children in Every-Day Practice* and *Golden Rules for Diseases of Infants and Children*. The former, one of the Medical Monograph series, draws heavily on Carpenter's comprehensive experience of the congenital complaints he had treated in infants of the poor. In reviewing the book *The Lancet* commented that though 'there is no new or original feature' yet 'nothing, except for certain matters of treatment, is omitted'.

Carpenter's Wightman lecture of 1909 is an account of the various congenital heart complaints that he had noted, mainly during his work at the two hospitals, together with references to the research of other specialists. The paper that he read to the Institute of Hygiene in 1907, 'The rearing of children', stresses the necessity of suitable food, clothing, and hygiene and moral guidance in the care of young children. One sentence in this paper voices the conviction brought home to him by his lifelong work among the poor: 'Many of life's failures are not so much hereditary as environmental'.

Carpenter married Hélène Jeanne, daughter of Henry, Baron d'Este, on 21 April 1908. He died of a cerebral haemorrhage at Cold Harbour, Waddon, Surrey, on 27 March 1910, and was buried in the old Sanderstead churchyard.

F. R. MILES

Sources *Medical Register* (1889–1909) · *King's College School alumni, 1866–1889*, 2 · *Men of the age* (1909) · *The Lancet* (9 April 1910) · *BMJ* (9 April 1910), 910 · *DNB*
Likenesses W. Nicholson, oils, priv. coll.
Wealth at death £4750 2s. 4d.: administration, 1 July 1910, CGPLA Eng. & Wales

Carpenter, Sir (Henry Cort) Harold (1875–1940), metallurgist, was born at Clifton, Bristol, on 6 February 1875, the second son of William Lant Carpenter, engineer, of Bristol, and his wife, Annie Grace Viret. He was a grandson of the naturalist William Benjamin *Carpenter and a great-great-grandson of Henry Cort, the inventor of the puddling process for iron. Owing to his father's early death, his ideas were much influenced by his uncle, the Unitarian minister (Joseph) Estlin *Carpenter (1844–1927). He was educated at St Paul's School, then at Eastbourne College for a year, and in 1893 entered Merton College, Oxford, as a postmaster. Having obtained a first-class degree in natural science in 1896, he studied organic chemistry at Leipzig and took his PhD at the end of two years. He then worked with W. H. Perkin at Owens College, Manchester, until 1901, when he was appointed to take charge of the new departments of chemistry and metallurgy at the National Physical Laboratory. His interest soon shifted from organic chemistry to metallurgy, and from 1905 he confined his work to that subject, his first original contribution, with B. F. E. Keeling, being a study of the alloys of iron and carbon, involving accurate measurements in the range of high temperatures. This difficult investigation, establishing the main features of the system, was followed by studies of the structure of other alloys, especially the complex alloys of copper with aluminium. In 1905 Carpenter married Ethel Mary, daughter of George Henry Lomas, of Brooklands, Cheshire; there were no children of the marriage.

The following year Carpenter accepted the new chair of metallurgy in the University of Manchester, where he built up a school of research, investigating tool steels and various complex alloys containing copper and aluminium. He left Manchester in December 1913 for the chair of metallurgy at the Royal School of Mines, South Kensington, but before taking up the duties he made a six months' tour of Canada and the United States of America in order to study metallurgical operations on a large scale. At the Royal School of Mines, however, he devoted himself mainly to the metallographic side of the subject. In a series of papers, mostly in collaboration with Constance Fligg Elam (later Mrs Tipper), he followed the process of recrystallization of metals which had been deformed, in the course of which means were devised for growing crystals of metals, especially aluminium, large enough to allow a study of their mechanical properties. This research laid the foundation of later work on single crystals. In collaboration with John Monteath Robertson he wrote numerous papers and a two-volume work, *Metals* (1939).

Carpenter was successively president of the three principal British metallurgical institutes—of Mining and Metallurgy (1934), of Metals (1918–20), and of Iron and Steel (1935–7). He had been instrumental in founding the Institute of Metals, and as chairman of a Treasury committee was responsible in 1929 for a report which resulted in improving the status of professional people in government service. He was elected FRS in 1918 and knighted in 1929. He received the honorary degree of DMet from the University of Sheffield and that of DSc from the University of Wales. He also received numerous gold medals, including the Japanese Honda medal (1940).

In the First World War Carpenter served on the Admiralty board of invention and research. On the outbreak of war in 1939 the metallurgical department of the Royal School of Mines was transferred to Swansea, and it was while on a country walk in Clyne valley wood, near Swansea, that he succumbed to heart failure, on 13 September 1940.   C. H. DESCH, *rev.* ANITA McCONNELL

Sources *The Times* (16 Sept 1940) · C. A. Edwards, *Obits. FRS*, 3 (1939–41), 611–25 · *Journal of the Iron and Steel Institute*, 142 (1940) · *Metallurgia* (Oct 1940) · personal knowledge (1949) · *WWW* · M. E. Day, ed., *The engineers' who's who* (1939) · *CGPLA Eng. & Wales* (1941)
Likenesses W. Stoneman, two photographs, 1936, NPG · portrait, repro. in Edwards, *Obits. FRS*
Wealth at death £28,050 6s. 11d.: resworn probate, 4 April 1941, *CGPLA Eng. & Wales*

Carpenter, James (1760–1845), naval officer, entered the navy in March 1776 on board the *Foudroyant*, commanded by Captain Jervis, later earl of St Vincent. He was sent in 1777 to North America in the frigate *Diamond*, then was transferred to the *Sultan*, in which he was present in the action off Grenada on 6 July 1779. In 1780 he was in the *Sandwich*, bearing Sir George Rodney's flag, then was appointed to the *Intrepid* as acting lieutenant, and was

present in the actions off Martinique on 30 April 1781 and off the capes of Virginia on 5 September 1781. He was not confirmed in his rank until 18 April 1782.

In 1793 Carpenter was appointed to the *Boyne*, flagship of Sir John Jervis in the West Indies, and was promoted by the admiral to command the *Nautilus* on 9 January 1794. He was then employed on shore at the capture of Martinique, and on 25 March 1794 was posted captain of the prize-frigate *Bienvenu*, from which he was moved in rapid succession to the *Veteran* (64 guns) and the *Alarm* (32 guns). He continued serving in the West Indies until 1795, when he returned to England. In 1799 he was appointed to the *Leviathan* (74 guns), bearing Sir John Duckworth's flag in the Mediterranean and afterwards in the West Indies, but was invalided out; then while travelling home in a merchant ship he was captured by a French warship and taken to Spain as a prisoner. He was shortly afterwards exchanged through the efforts of Lord St Vincent. For a short time he commanded the *San Josef*, then from 1803 to 1810 had charge of the Devonshire sea fencibles; in 1811 he went out to Newfoundland in the *Antelope*, again as flag captain to Duckworth. He remained there for only a year, for on 12 August 1812 he became a rear-admiral. He had no further service, but was advanced in course of seniority to vice-admiral on 12 August 1819 and admiral on 10 January 1837. He died in Cumberland Street, London, on 16 March 1845.

J. K. LAUGHTON, *rev.* ROGER MORRISS

Sources O'Byrne, *Naval biog. dict.* · J. Marshall, *Royal naval biography*, 1/2 (1823), 528–30 · *GM*, 2nd ser., 24 (1845), 79

Carpenter, John (d. 1442), common clerk of London, was the son of Richard Carpenter, possibly a London chandler, and his wife Christine. He became common clerk of the city of London on 17 April 1417, succeeding John Merchaunt whom he had served as a clerk while also appearing as an attorney in the city courts. He held this important post until October 1438, sometimes styled the *secretarius* of the city, and received a stipend of £10 per annum. Further rewards included a grant of an annual rent of £10 in 1430, and in 1431 the city leased to him and his wife, Katherine, land and shops in the parish of St Peter, Cornhill, for a nominal rent. While common clerk Carpenter was responsible for signing proclamations in the name of the mayor, aldermen, and commonalty, and was the author of a long letter of February 1432 describing the entry of Henry VI into London following his return from France. He represented the city of London in parliament in 1437 and 1439, and was a popular choice as a feoffee and as an arbitrator in disputes involving the city government. In December 1436, perhaps preparing for retirement, Carpenter secured exemptions from minor city offices and juries. By October 1438 he had resigned as common clerk, but continued to be consulted on questions of city custom, and in 1440 was voted 20 marks for his services. His most notable achievement as common clerk was the compilation of the *Liber albus*, an important collection of customs and ordinances relating to London, completed in November 1419. It was probably written with the encouragement of his friend Richard Whittington, who was mayor at the time. The work was undertaken to ensure that the customs of London did not fall into oblivion. The preface explained how, in the past, many of the most experienced of the city's elder statesmen had fallen victim to outbreaks of pestilence, and in consequence 'their successors have, at various times, been at a loss for written information and disputes have arisen as to what decisions should be taken' (Riley, 1.3).

As the chief executor of Richard Whittington's estate from 1423, Carpenter played an important role in the building up of an endowment to fund the almshouse and college for priests administered by the Mercers' Company following Carpenter's death. Though also funded out of Whittington's estate, the establishment of the 'fayre and large library' (Stow, 2.275) near the Guildhall may well have been Carpenter's own idea, and it is possible that it was he who administered the library from 1425. His interest in books and education also lay behind his own foundation of a choir school in the newly restored Guildhall chapel, which was probably intended to complement the library. The endowment provided for four boys born within the city, who were to be known as 'Carpenter's children', to receive 3s. between them each week, as well as food and accommodation. The choristers were to receive schooling at a convenient place. In 1417 the endowment, which had been in the hands of trustees, was settled on the city. In 1837 it was applied to the new City of London School, and eight Carpenter scholarships were set up in memory of its first benefactor.

Among Carpenter's other works, according to John Stow, was the commissioning of a painting of the *Danse macabre* which was to hang in the north aisle of St Paul's Cathedral. He drew up his surviving will on 8 March 1441, and made numerous bequests to friends and family, the latter including his two brothers, John and Robert, and their children. Among the friends mentioned were his namesake, the master of St Anthony's Hospital who later became bishop of Worcester, and Reginald Pecok, then master of Whittington's college. As well as numerous bequests of plate and clothing, Carpenter listed twenty-six books in his will which were to be left to a number of individuals. Along with works by Aristotle and Seneca these included a collection of city customs, perhaps a version of the *Liber albus*, which he left to one of his clerks, a book on architecture, given to him by the architect and chaplain, William Cleve, and a treatise written by Roger Dymmok against Lollardy. The residue of his personal collection was left to the Guildhall Library. The will, in which Carpenter had asked to be buried near the pulpit before the entrance to the chancel in the church of St Peter, Cornhill, was proved on 12 May 1442. There were no children surviving from his marriage to Katherine, who was his principal executor and who died in 1458.

MATTHEW DAVIES

Sources T. Brewer, ed., *Memoir of the life and times of John Carpenter, town clerk of London, in the reigns of Henry V and Henry VI* (1856) • W. Kellaway, 'John Carpenter's *Liber albus*', *Guildhall Studies in London History*, 3 (1977–9), 67–84 • CLRO • MS records, GL • J. Imray, *The charity of Richard Whittington: a history of the trust administered by the Mercers' Company, 1424–1966* (1968) • C. M. Barron, 'Richard Whittington: the man behind the myth', *Studies in London history presented to Philip Edmund Jones*, ed. A. E. J. Hollaender and W. Kellaway (1969), 197–248 • R. Smith, 'The library at Guildhall in the 15th and 16th centuries', *Guildhall Miscellany*, 1/1 (1952), 3–10 • H. T. Riley, ed., *Munimenta Gildhallae Londoniensis*, 1: *Liber albus, compiled AD 1419*, ed. J. Carpenter, Rolls Series, 12 (1858) • J. Stow, *A survay of London*, rev. edn (1603); repr. with introduction by C. L. Kingsford as *A survey of London*, 2 vols. (1908); repr. with addns (1971) • Copy of ordinances of Whittington's almshouse, 1442

Archives CLRO, 'Liber albus'

Likenesses S. Nixon, statue, 1844, City of London School • group portrait, copy of ordinances of Whittington's almshouse, 1442

Wealth at death substantial wealth, goods and chattels: will, GL, MS 9171/4, fols. 84v–86v

Carpenter, John (c.1402–1476), bishop of Worcester, like his friend William Canynges (d. 1474), may have been a member of a Bristol merchant family with London associations. A John and Roger Carpenter—conceivably related to him—were tenants of the manor of Stoke Bishop by Westbury about 1410. The bishop was almost certainly a relative of John Carpenter (d. 1442), who became town clerk of London. He was associated with him in the royal grant of Theobalds, Hertfordshire, to St Anthony's Hospital, and was named supervisor of his executors. A John Carpenter, mercer, was involved in the transfer of property in Worcester to the Carnary Chapel there.

John Carpenter, the future bishop, was fellow of Oriel College by 1417, dean in 1425, and provost between 1428 and 1435. After graduating MA he studied theology and was BTh by 1426 and DTh regent two years later. Chancellor of the university by February 1428, he resigned a year later. His fellowship provided title for his ordination in Lincoln diocese as subdeacon (1420), and as deacon and priest (1421), shortly after which he was collated to St Mildred's rectory, Oxford. Thereafter he accumulated various rectories and, less excusably, two vicarages, Romsey, Hampshire, in 1427 and Steeple Ashton, Wiltshire, in 1428—exchanged the following year. A papal indult permitted five-year enjoyment of the Romsey revenues on account of his regency in theology. He held only two cathedral prebends, in St David's and Lincoln, and exchanged the latter for another in St Stephen's, Westminster, in 1439.

As clerk and chaplain to Henry VI, he accompanied the king to France in May 1430, and in February 1431 was at Rouen for the trial of Jeanne d'Arc. At the convocation of 1437, summoned to grant a tenth, he delivered the Latin address. He was deputed in 1459 to lead an embassy to the abortive papal congress at Mantua. In 1433 Henry appointed him master of St Anthony's of Vienne, Threadneedle Street, London, formerly an 'alien' hospital, with the obligation to enter the Augustinian order. He secured dispensation from adopting the habit outside the precincts provided he wore an appropriate insignia. Under him St Anthony's acquired, besides Theobalds, the manor of Povyngton, Dorset, for the exhibition of five scholars in the arts course at Oxford. To avoid the penalties of the mortmain statute he petitioned the king in 1439 for confirmation to the hospital of the advowson of St Benet Fynk.

Eugenius IV provided Carpenter to the see of Worcester by bulls dated 20 December 1443. These reached him in London on 24 February and on the 26th he had livery of the temporalities at Sheen Palace. He was professed at Canterbury on 28 February and consecrated by Bishop Aiscough of Salisbury (*d.* 1450) in Eton College chapel on 22 March. The next day, from his house in the Strand, he commissioned a vicar-general. His enthronement was delayed until Christmas eve. His two-volume register of nearly 400 folios is the most rewarding of the fifteenth-century Worcester series. The bishop, unwilling to sever connections with his London interests and parliamentary affairs, made regular trips to his Hillingdon manor and to his house in the Strand, so that between 1444 and 1456 vicars-general were acting for him on at least twelve occasions. These were Oxford men, with either canon- or civil-law degrees. Theologians, surprisingly, are not much in evidence in his *familia*, with the notable exception of Thomas Balsall, a doctor of theology of Merton College.

Despite the length of his episcopate Carpenter is only known to have made two visitations, the first in 1461, the second in 1466, but to judge from the itineraries neither was particularly thorough. But in 1451 he did issue hard-hitting injunctions for the diocese, a rare example of late medieval legislation in the tradition of the thirteenth century. This provides an early mention of church wardens under that name, and suggests that the bishop was holding synods, rarely noted in Worcester records. He also left a good record with respect to ordinations. It was not until 1464 that a suffragan, Richard Wolsey, bishop of Down and Connor, acted for him, but from March 1465 Wolsey conducted all the ordinations. A bachelor of theology, he was to be the librarian at Worcester.

Carpenter's foundation of libraries in Worcester—attached to the Carnary Chapel next to the cathedral—and Bristol was indeed remarkable. In 1458 properties in Worcester were granted to the prior and chapter for the sacrist's use. The latter was to find a chaplain, preferably a bachelor of theology, who would act as librarian, lecture once or twice a week on the Old or New testament, and preach an annual sermon on Good Friday. The chaplain was to have upper and lower rooms in the library and a salary of £10—£8 if he took meals with the sacrist—and cloth for hood and gown. The library was to be open on week-days, two hours before and two hours after noon. The catalogue was to be in triplicate, and on Friday after the feast of the Relics (15 October) an inventory was to be taken. If books were missing through his carelessness the librarian was to be fined. The library's fate is unknown; none of its books has survived, but already in 1513 the sacrist was being summoned for neglect. Similar regulations were provided for a library of the 'priory' or college of four secular priests, called calendaries, in All Saints, Bristol. Carpenter's concern did not stop there; he granted five licences for graduates to preach in the diocese, and in one licence for non-residence he required the preaching of two formal sermons a year.

Carpenter bequeathed to Oriel College, Oxford, the Oxfordshire manors of Deane and Chalford for support of a Worcestershire-born fellow. Property in Barling, Dagenham, and Havering in Essex was leased to St Anthony's for the maintenance of scholars at the college, for which Carpenter also acquired Bedell Hall in Oxford and made other gifts and bequests. For his Hartlebury manor he built a gatehouse, but he is best remembered for his refoundation of Westbury-on-Trym College. His precise motives are unfathomable. It has been suggested that he wished to continue the efforts of Godfrey Giffard (*d.* 1302) to create a secular cathedral chapter to balance the monastic one at Worcester, styling himself, unofficially at least, bishop of Worcester and Westbury, or even that he sought to found a see of Bristol in anticipation of Henry VIII. Be that as it may, he drew up new statutes which received papal confirmation in 1455. Their purpose was to restrict the income of the prebends; to allow the dean, who was not bound to residence, limited subsistence when at the college; to provide a resident subdean and treasurer, and to leave the bulk of the income for the maintenance of the vicars-choral, clerks, boys, and other ministers. Attached to the college subsequently were a schoolmaster, almshouses, and a chantry to be served by six aged priests. An immense sum of money was spent on the buildings—only the gatehouse remains. The provost of Oriel, Henry Sampson, was collated to the deanery in 1459, and in 1464 Edward IV became a benefactor. William Canynges, the Bristol merchant who abandoned the secular life under the bishop's auspices, was rapidly advanced to the priesthood and became dean in 1469.

Carpenter died at his manor of Northwick, probably in June 1476 (his successor's bulls are dated 15 July), although his obit at Oriel was observed on 21 October. He was also remembered in the chantry he founded in St Mary's, Oxford. He was buried in the crypt under the high altar at Westbury, but his tomb, with his effigy above and cadaver beneath, has been desecrated.   ROY MARTIN HAINES

Sources J. Carpenter, bishop's register, Worcs. RO [2 vols.] • S. de Gigli, bishop's register, Worcs. RO • White Book, Worcs. RO, fols. 162r–163v • M. J. Morgan, 'John Carpenter, bishop of Worcester, 1444–1476', MA diss., U. Birm., 1960 • H. J. Wilkins, *Westbury College* (1917) • R. M. Haines, 'Aspects of the episcopate of John Carpenter, bishop of Worcester, 1444–1476', *Journal of Ecclesiastical History*, 19 (1968), 11–40 • R. M. Haines, 'Bishop Carpenter's injunctions to the diocese of Worcester in 1451', *BIHR*, 40 (1967), 203–7 • A. Hamilton Thompson, 'Notes on the ecclesiastical parish of Henbury', *Trans. B&G. Arch. Soc.*, 38 (1915), 99–186 • T. Brewer, ed., *Memoir of the life and times of John Carpenter, town clerk of London, in the reigns of Henry V and Henry VI* (1856) • C. L. Shadwell and H. E. Salter, *Oriel College records*, OHS, 85 (1926) • Dugdale, *Monasticon*, new edn • E. F. Jacob, ed., *The register of Henry Chichele, archbishop of Canterbury, 1414–1443*, 4 vols., CYS, 42, 45–7 (1937–47) [index to vol. 4 incl. John Carpenter] • R. M. Clay, *The mediaeval hospitals of England* (1966) • *Fasti Angl., 1300–1541*, [Lincoln; Mon. cath. (SP); Welsh dioceses; Introduction] • Emden, *Oxf.* • *The itinerary of John Leland in or about the years 1535–1543*, ed. L. Toulmin Smith, 11 pts in 5 vols. (1906–10)
Archives Worcs. RO, registers

Carpenter, John (*d.* 1621), Church of England clergyman and author, was born in Cornwall of unknown parents. He entered Exeter College, Oxford, about 1570, and studied there for about four years, but left without taking a degree. In 1587 he became rector of Northleigh, near

Honiton, Devon, where he remained for the rest of his life. By 1588 he had married; his son Nathanael *Carpenter was born in February 1589.

From the 1580s Carpenter published a number of conventional and patriotic works. *Time Complaining, Giveth a most Godly Admonition to England in this our Dangerous Time* (1588), a work partly in verse, was dedicated on 30 June as the Armada was awaited. In two sermons, delivered at Exeter Cathedral the same year and published as *Remember Lot's Wife* with a dedication to Mary Woolton, the bishop's wife, Carpenter warned against characteristic female sins, although he noted the existence of many virtuous women in both the Old and New testaments. *A Preparative to Contentation* (1597), which specifically identified the pope, rather than 'Mahomet', as 'the enemy of England', applauded the just punishment of traitorous papists, condemned those who censured those in authority or hatched their own opinions, and exhorted 'every man to keep within the bounds of his vocation'. In *The Song of the Beloved Concerning his Vineyard* (1599), dedicated to Sir John Stawell of Somerset, he returned to the theme of an England which, like Israel, had neglected the worship of God, and now faced condemnation unless she repented. A catechism, *Contemplations for the Institution of Children in the Christian Religion*, followed in 1601. *Schelomonocham, or, King Solomon his Solace* was presented to James I before being published in 1606 with an elaborate frontispiece displaying the royal arms and with a prefixed panegyric to the king. *The Plain Man's Spiritual Plough* (1607), dedicated to Bishop William Cotton of Exeter, was a detailed and biblically allusive 240-page treatment of the Christian's 'godly and spirituall husbandrie'. Carpenter died at Northleigh in March 1621, and was buried in the chancel of his church before 25 March.   VIVIENNE LARMINIE

Sources Foster, *Alum. Oxon.* · Wood, *Ath. Oxon.*, new edn, 2.287–8 · *STC, 1475–1640* · C. W. Boase, ed., *Registrum Collegii Exoniensis*, new edn, OHS, 27 (1894), xcvi

Carpenter, John [Seán Mac an tSaor] (1729–1786), Roman Catholic archbishop of Dublin, was born in Chancery Lane, Dublin, the son of a merchant tailor. He received his early schooling in Dublin and, between 1744 and 1747, was associated with the Gaelic language and cultural circle that had formed around Tadhg Ó Neachtain, scion of a Connaught bardic family who had settled in Dublin. It was probably under Ó Neachtain's influence that Carpenter compiled an Irish grammar, a miscellany of prose and poetry, and a book of devotion for his personal use that included part of the *Imitatio Christi* in Ulster Irish. In 1747 he sailed to Lisbon and entered the Irish College there, and in 1752 he was ordained priest. He took a doctorate in theology before returning to Dublin in 1754.

Carpenter's first years in the pastoral ministry were spent in St Mary's Chapel, Liffey Street. According to one account he was an elegant preacher and a zealous catechist who had three schools built for the poor and the orphaned and who managed to stay above diocesan party politics. He was not afraid, however, to challenge established, diocesan custom. In 1763, for instance, he put his name to a complaint that many parish priests were defrauding

their assistant priests. The following year, securely in favour with Archbishop Patrick Fitzsimons, he was admitted to the archdiocesan chapter as prebendary of Cullen. He quickly won the confidence of Fitzsimons's episcopal colleagues. When the Irish College at Lisbon fell into difficulty they appointed him their representative to the Portuguese court, to save the institution. About this time too he became involved in the Catholic Committee, formed in 1760 to represent Catholic interests. He began to work closely with John Curry and Charles O'Conor of Belanagare, both prominent members of the committee. He shared their view that the penal laws were not only unjustified but also economically damaging. With O'Conor he also shared a serious academic interest in Irish language and history. In late 1767 Archbishop Fitzsimons sent him to London to act as secretary to Nicholas Taaffe, sixth Viscount Taaffe, the prominent nobleman of Irish origin who had travelled from Vienna to support the Catholic delegation then negotiating, with the earl of Bristol, the wording of a test oath. It was hoped that this would be a preliminary to the passage of relief acts in the Irish parliament. Despite the importance of his mission Carpenter had to appeal twice to Fitzsimons to pay his expenses, explaining: 'Let only a reasonable estimate be made of a proper allowance of a plain honest man, who can go a-foot and drink porter' (Moran, 3.279). Carpenter impressed Taaffe, who recommended him for promotion.

Fitzsimons was already ill, being described in a letter from France in late 1769 as 'old, blind, *hors de combat* and perhaps already dead' (William Fitzharris Gifford to cardinal prefect, 15 Sept 1769, Rome, Vatican City, Archivio Segreto Vaticano, fondo missioni, pacco 58). Carpenter was appointed his successor on 16 April 1770. His consecration, on 3 June 1770 in a private house, hints at the limits of tolerance in Dublin at the time. He held the parish of St Nicholas as mensal, resided in a large house on Usher's Island, and said mass in Francis Street every Sunday at eight o'clock. The Dublin clergy gave him their firm support. His first act as archbishop was to ensure that collections taken up at the church door were properly divided between parish priests and assistants. An assiduous administrator, he visited his diocese regularly and his first publication was a set of provincial and synodal constitutions; this appeared in 1770. His pastoral priority was to improve standards of religious and moral practice among clergy and laity alike. In this context he was especially concerned about clerical drunkenness. His social concerns were part of a broader political vision, for he was convinced that the maintenance of moral and social order was the best way to persuade the government to relax anti-Catholic legislation. He enjoyed good relations with protestants. In 1773 he was admitted to the Royal Dublin Society, an event described by the antiquary Charles O'Conor as 'a revolution in our moral and civil affairs the more extraordinary, as in my own days such a man would only be spoken to through the medium of a warrant and constable' (Ó Catháin, 154). This was an indication not only of changing religious attitudes in the establishment but also of widespread esteem for Carpenter's character and learning.

To mark the jubilee year of 1776 Carpenter prepared a form of instruction, suitable for use before the Sunday parochial mass, which was published as his *Rituale*. Because he was aware of the importance of local traditions in the personal piety of the faithful he gave prominence to native saints in the *Missale* published in the same year. In 1777 he caused Butler's new catechism to be published anonymously in Dublin. Three year later, in 1780, he produced the second and fuller edition of Alban Butler's *Lives of the Saints*, in which, as in his *Missale*, he gave prominence to the Irish saints. The work included an appendix by the archbishop on the glories of the ancient Irish church; he probably had the assistance of Charles O'Conor in preparing this piece.

Carpenter's episcopate saw continuing progress in the provision of Catholic primary education. There was a slowing down in the rate of church building in the 1770s and 1780s—a reflection perhaps of lingering hesitation over the wisdom of leaving the existing, retiring chapel for more commodious, ostentatious accommodation. In rural areas, however, the construction of new chapels greatly improved access to the sacraments. His formal report to Rome of 1780 offers an account of his view of the state of the church in the city. It is especially interesting for what it reveals of his attitude towards the local regular clergy. Carpenter accuses them of failing to live the common life. He claims that they persist in maintaining the fiction of 'blind convents', in other words religious houses that existed only on paper or in memory. The regulars' tendency to appoint superiors to, and even accept novices into, these phantom establishments means, Carpenter continues, that the city is overrun with unemployed religious, some of whom turn 'couple beggar' and perform clandestine marriages or, worse still, protestant.

Carpenter was frequently consulted by *propaganda fide* regarding Irish domestic matters. His status permitted him to intervene personally in other dioceses on occasion, most notably in Dromore in 1772 and in Armagh in 1774-5. Rome also sought his advice regarding the affairs of the Irish colleges' network in Europe. In 1774, following the suppression of the Jesuits, he recommended the appointment of Irish rectors in Rome and Salamanca in order to prevent their falling into the hands of foreign nationals.

As the penal code gradually loosened between 1771 and 1782 Carpenter found new responsibilities falling on his shoulders. This was mainly because the relaxation of anti-Catholic legislation was made to depend on a test oath that had been devised by the protestant bishop of Derry, Frederick Hervey, earl of Bristol, to divide Catholic opinion. Crucially it included a denial of the pope's temporal power, a point that rendered it unacceptable to Rome and to Carpenter. He did not take the oath until 1778, when he was assured of the Holy See's formal approval. Though his hesitation annoyed many of his episcopal colleagues in Munster and not a few prominent Catholic laymen it preserved both the unity of the Irish church and the doctrinal link with Rome. His gradualist approach towards re-establishing links with the government did not betoken, however, any social radicalism. Carpenter was a firm defender of property and law. He denounced the 'combination' of Dublin workers and their oath-bound opposition to employers. For him industrial strife was unacceptable not only because it damaged the economy but, more significantly, because it gave the government a bad impression of Catholics.

After 1780 Carpenter was less active, probably due to bad health. Most of the lobbying at Dublin in connection with the Catholic Relief Act of 1782, for instance, was done by the bishop of Ossory, John Thomas Troy, who eventually succeeded him. He did write to Rome to complain that Bishop Hervey had exercised influence over the bishops of Cashel, Meath, and Waterford to accept a new, Gallican mode of electing bishops with little reference to Rome. Carpenter died in Dublin on 29 October 1786 and was buried in St Michan's graveyard in a grave owned by his brother-in-law Thomas Lee. The proceeds of the sale of his effects went to Teresa Mulally for the benefit of her school. His library of over 4000 books was dispersed.

Under Carpenter the Catholic church in Dublin continued its tentative emergence from the political and cultural ghetto of the penal laws. He proved a sensitive, cultured guide. However, he was perhaps the last archbishop of Dublin sufficiently rooted in the Anglo-Irish, Gaelic, and European elements of Irish Catholicism to recognize the importance of blending all three to face the political, cultural, and intellectual challenges of the time. Under his successors the re-integration of the Catholic church into the British state dominated the Dublin archiepiscopal agenda. To this overwhelming priority the cultural and intellectual dimensions of religious practice and belief took second place.   THOMAS O'CONNOR

Sources H. Fenning, 'The archbishops of Dublin', *History of the Catholic diocese of Dublin* (Dublin, 2000), 175–214 · T. Wall, 'Archishop John Carpenter and the Catholic revival', *Repertorium Novum*, 1 (1955), 173–82 · P. MacGiolla Phadraig, 'Dr John Carpenter, 1770–1786', *Dublin Historical Review*, 30 (1976), 2–17 · H. Fenning, ed., 'Irishmen ordained at Lisbon, 1740–1850', *Collectanea Hibernica*, 36–7 (1994–5), 140–58 · P. F. Moran, ed., *Spicilegium Ossoriense*, 3 vols. (1874–84) · D. Ó Catháin, 'Charles O'Conor of Belanagare: antiquary and Irish scholar', *Journal of the Royal Society of Antiquaries of Ireland*, 119 (1989), 136–63

Archives Archivio Vaticano, Vatican City, archives of propaganda fide, varia · Roman Catholic archdiocese, Dublin, corresp. and papers | NL Ire., MSS of early Gaelic work, MS 682 · Royal Irish Acad., MSS of early Gaelic work, MS 23 A8

Wealth at death library auctioned: *Freeman's Journal* (July 1787)

Carpenter, John Archibald Boyd-, Baron Boyd-Carpenter (1908–1998), politician, was born on 2 June 1908 at 22 Park Avenue, Harrogate, Yorkshire, the only son (there was one daughter) of Sir Archibald Boyd Boyd-Carpenter (1873–1937), politician, and his wife, Annie, second daughter of Thomas Dugdale, of Cross Hill, Blackburn, Lancashire. His father was Unionist MP for North Bradford (1918–23) and Coventry (1924–9), and was briefly financial secretary to the Treasury and then paymaster-general in the Conservative government of 1922–4. His grandfather was William Boyd *Carpenter, bishop of

John Archibald Boyd-Carpenter, Baron Boyd-Carpenter (1908–1998), by Walter Bird, 1961

Ripon and canon of Westminster, reputedly Queen Victoria's favourite bishop.

Boyd-Carpenter was educated at Stowe School and Balliol College, Oxford, where he graduated with a second-class degree in modern history in 1930, and a diploma in economic and political science in 1931. He was elected president of the Oxford Union in 1930 and then studied at the Middle Temple, where he was made Harmsworth law scholar in 1933 and won the Council of Legal Education prize for constitutional law the same year. He was called to the bar in 1934, and practised on the London and south-eastern circuit until the outbreak of the Second World War. In 1934 he engaged in his first political campaign when he stood as the Municipal Reform candidate for Limehouse in the London county council elections. On 25 June 1937 he married Margaret Mary Hall (b. 1909/10), daughter of Lieutenant-Colonel George Leslie Hall, officer in the Royal Engineers. They had one son and two daughters. During the Second World War he served in the Scots Guards and rose to the rank of major. His legal experience was deployed when he served from 1943 to 1945 with the allied military government in Italy, for whom he acted as a president of military courts.

Boyd-Carpenter entered parliament at the general election of 1945 as MP for the safe Conservative seat of Kingston upon Thames, a constituency which he represented until 1972. In opposition from 1945 to 1951 he established a reputation as an effective and pugnacious debater in the Commons and attracted the attention of the Conservative

leadership. When the Conservatives were returned to power in October 1951 he was appointed financial secretary to the Treasury, and in July 1954 he was promoted to the (non-cabinet) position of minister of transport and civil aviation. While holding the latter post he set in motion the building of Britain's first major length of motorway, the M1, which was completed under his successor Ernest Marples. In December 1955 he was moved to the (non-cabinet) position of minister of pensions and national insurance, which he occupied until July 1962. In this post he was responsible for the pensions legislation of 1959, which broke from Beveridge's principle of flat-rate contributions for flat-rate benefits as it introduced earnings-related pensions for earnings-related contributions, and gave individuals the opportunity to 'contract out' of the state pension scheme into private occupational pensions. From 1960 to 1962 he also made important contributions to the Conservative Party's internal policy committee on the future of the social services, which discussed in detail the structure and funding of the welfare state and examined the possibility of introducing radical reforms. When he was pensions minister he also oversaw the appointment of Margaret Thatcher to her first ministerial position, which was in his department. In July 1962 he entered the cabinet as chief secretary to the Treasury and paymaster-general, which at the time was only the second occasion on which cabinet rank had been granted to that position. At the Treasury he participated in the establishment of the National Economic Development Council and the National Incomes Commission, and he played an important role in approving funding for the Concorde project. In 1963 Harold Macmillan's successor as prime minister and leader of the Conservative Party, Sir Alec Douglas-Home, offered Boyd-Carpenter the position of chairman of the Conservative Party, but he declined.

After the Conservative defeat in October 1964 Boyd-Carpenter was made shadow cabinet spokesman on housing. In 1965 he was one of the few senior figures in the party who opposed the introduction of the new electoral procedure for choosing the Conservative leader. He was dropped from the shadow cabinet in 1966 by the first Conservative leader chosen under the new process, Edward Heath, and he remained a back-bencher until he left the Commons in 1972. He was an active back-bencher. He extended his reputation as an aggressive parliamentary debater, and he held the post of chairman of the House of Commons' public accounts committee from 1964 to 1970. He hoped in 1972 to become speaker of the House of Commons, but the Labour opposition supported the election of Selwyn Lloyd. Disappointed, Boyd-Carpenter resigned his seat to take up the position of chairman of the Civil Aviation Authority (CAA), and he was made a life peer, as Baron Boyd-Carpenter.

As chairman of the CAA Boyd-Carpenter was responsible for granting the certificate of airworthiness to Concorde, and he was a passenger on its first commercial flight to Bahrain in 1976. He left the CAA in 1977, having in 1976 taken the post of chairman of Rugby-Portland Cement, of which he had been a director since 1970. He held this position until 1984. He also held directorships of two financial institutions, the Orion insurance company from 1969 to 1972, and the CLRP investment trust from 1970 to 1972. Although business was his primary interest after he left the Commons, he remained politically active. From 1977 to 1980 he was president of the Wessex National Union of Conservative and Unionist Associations, from 1979 to 1986 he was chairman of the Carlton Club, and from 1985 to 1990 he was chairman, and then from 1991 to 1998 president, of the Association of Conservative Peers. His children's careers reinforced his continued political ties. His son Sir Thomas Boyd-Carpenter was chairman of Kensington, Chelsea, and Westminster Health Authority after a distinguished career in the army, and his younger daughter, Sarah, Baroness Hogg, was head of the prime minister's policy unit from 1990 to 1995.

Although he never reached the highest levels in politics, Boyd-Carpenter was a substantial political figure. He enjoyed a reputation as a tough Commons debater, a reputation which in part helped to explain why the Labour Party was not supportive of his claim to the speakership in 1972. As a minister his colleagues, both senior and junior, always found him competent, well informed, and thorough, and Thatcher referred to his 'grasp of detail, and capacity for lucid exposition of a complex case' (Thatcher, 119). Both his political longevity and his failure to advance to the front rank perhaps reflected the fact that he did not take up a strong ideological position and excited little in the way of strong praise or opprobrium from either side of politics. In the late 1940s he described *The Industrial Charter* as occupying 'a central position between Manchester and Moscow', and he seemed content to take a moderate, central position himself. In 1968 Arthur Seldon, writing in the *Swinton Journal*, saw Boyd-Carpenter as a supporter of state intervention, yet at the Ministry of Pensions he had greatly extended the scope of private pensions. In his memoirs, *Way of Life* (1980), he noted that 'When I was young I was a long distance runner—not fast but I could go on for ever' (p. 204), and used this as a metaphor for his career. As a description of a solid but unexciting political career it was very apt. He died at his home, Crux Easton House, Crux Easton, Highclere, near Newbury, Berkshire, on 11 July 1998, of cancer, and was survived by his wife and their three children. A memorial service was held at St Margaret by Westminster Abbey, on 3 November 1998, at which Lady Thatcher gave the address.

E. H. H. GREEN

Sources *The Times* (14 July 1998) · *Daily Telegraph* (14 July 1998) · *The Independent* (15 July 1998) · *WWW* · J. Boyd-Carpenter, *Way of life* (1980) · J. Ramsden, *The winds of change: Macmillan to Heath, 1957–1975* (1996) · M. Thatcher, *The path to power* (1995) · R. Lowe, 'The replanning of the welfare state, 1957–64', *The conservatives and British society, 1880–1990*, ed. M. Francis and I. Zweiniger-Bargielowska (1996) · *Balliol College Register* · b. cert. · m. cert. · d. cert.
Likenesses group portrait, photograph, 1955, repro. in *Daily Telegraph* · photograph, 1955, repro. in *The Independent* · W. Bird, photograph, 1961, NPG [*see illus.*] · photograph, 1974, repro. in *The Times*

Wealth at death £672,214: probate, 18 Sept 1998, *CGPLA Eng. & Wales*

Carpenter, Lant (1780–1840), Unitarian minister and schoolmaster, was born at Kidderminster on 2 September 1780, the third son of George Carpenter (1748/9–1839), carpet manufacturer, and his wife, Mary Hooke (1751/2–1835); Lant was the maiden name of George Carpenter's mother.

Education and early career George Carpenter's business failed and he left Kidderminster, but Lant remained there with his mother's guardian, Nicholas Pearsall, who adopted him, intending him to become a minister. A committed Unitarian, Pearsall sent his nephew to a school run by Benjamin Carpenter at Stourbridge (1783–5); he was then taught by the dissenting minister William Blake (1773–1821) at the school which Pearsall had himself founded in Kidderminster (1785–7). In 1797 Carpenter entered the dissenting academy at Northampton under John Horsey, and was placed in the second year of the five years' course. The Northampton academy was the immediate successor of the one at Daventry, from which Thomas Belsham had retired after his conversion to Unitarianism. Horsey was moderately orthodox; the classical tutor, however, was a polemical Calvinist from Scotland. Such diversity of opinion among the tutors apparently unsettled the minds of the students, and in 1798 the trustees abruptly closed the academy.

In October of that year Carpenter, with two fellow students, entered the University of Glasgow as exhibitioners under Dr Williams's trust. His studies there, interrupted initially by attacks of rheumatic fever and depression, lasted until 1801. He took the arts course, but did not graduate; he also studied chemistry and anatomy, and at one time considered combining the duties of a physician and a dissenting minister; indeed, he won the natural philosophy prize at Glasgow. Divinity he studied by himself, especially during the vacations. Circumstances prevented him from remaining at Glasgow to follow the divinity course. He now hoped to combine a career in teaching with the ministry, which he had already entered in 1801. In September of the same year he became assistant in the school of Revd John Corrie, to whom he was distantly related, at Birch's Green, near Birmingham. For a few months in 1802, seeking more opportunity for private study, he served as minister to the New Meeting, Birmingham, vacant after the resignation of John Edwards, but soon accepted the offer of a librarianship at the Liverpool Athenaeum. He held this office from the end of 1802 until March 1805, simultaneously running classes in divinity and philosophy for young people and occasionally preaching. He declined overtures from congregations at Ipswich, Bury St Edmunds, Ormskirk, and Dudley, and an invitation (in 1803) to become tutor in *belles-lettres* at Manchester College, York. This invitation, which was renewed in 1807 and again declined, strongly tempted Carpenter, but it would have involved a decline in his income from £200 per annum at Liverpool to £130.

At Exeter On 9 January 1805 Carpenter accepted a co-pastorate at George's Meeting, Exeter, as colleague with James Manning, and in succession to Timothy Kenrick. Manning, as an Arian, rejected the doctrine of the Trinity but accepted the pre-existence of Christ; Kenrick, by contrast, believed in the simple humanity of Christ, an opinion which Carpenter now shared. In philosophy he was a determinist, and an admirer of David Hartley (1705–1757); according to Harriet Martineau, he spoke of Hartley as a man who had 'the intellectual qualities of the seraphic order combined with the affections of the cherubic'. Shortly after his arrival at Exeter, Carpenter married (on 25 December 1805) Anna (d. 1856), daughter of James Penn of Kidderminster; they had three daughters and three sons. Their eldest child, Mary *Carpenter (1807–1877), became a noted philanthropist and campaigner for the education of poor children. Of their sons, the eldest, William Benjamin *Carpenter (1813–1885), achieved recognition as a naturalist; the second, Russell Lant, became his father's memoirist; and the youngest, Philip Pearsall *Carpenter (1819–1877), was a celebrated conchologist. The two younger sons were both Unitarian ministers. At Exeter, Carpenter undertook both an extensive pastorate and the responsibilities of a boarding-school; his constant enthusiasm and powers of organization were widely regarded as extraordinary in the light of his frail health and slight physique. In 1806 he published a popular manual of biblical topography entitled *An Introduction to the Geography of the New Testament*. On applying to Glasgow in 1806 for the degree of MA by special grace, he was made LLD. In August 1807 the temporary loss of his voice led him to send in his resignation; his congregation offered him a year's dispensation from preaching, and his colleague undertook his pulpit duties. Carpenter employed his leisure in founding and managing a public library. His return to the pulpit in 1808 was followed by a controversy over the validity of Unitarian doctrine in which his chief opponent was Daniel Veysie, vicar of Plymtree, Devon. In 1813 and again in 1823 Carpenter declined a pressing invitation to become colleague with John Yates at Paradise Street Chapel, Liverpool. He remained at Exeter until 1817, taking an increasing interest in national politics, especially the campaign for Catholic emancipation, a cause towards which he was sympathetic.

At Bristol With the approaching retirement of John Prior Estlin, Carpenter was invited (on 28 August 1816) to Lewin's Mead Chapel, Bristol, as colleague to John Rowe. The Exeter congregation made every effort to retain him, but in the summer of 1817 he moved to Bristol. Here the congregation was large and wealthy, but lacked cohesion: Carpenter claimed on his arrival that the congregation was hampered by a genteel aloofness on the part of many of its better-off members. His response to this problem included a vigorous philanthropic initiative on the lines of a domestic mission and the establishment of a school. On the resignation of Rowe in 1832, Carpenter briefly had as colleague Robert Brook Aspland; in 1837, the year following Aspland's departure, his place was filled by George Armstrong, a seceder from the Church of Ireland. One of the more unusual events of his ministry was the arrival in Bristol of the Indian religious reformer Rammohun Roy, in whose monotheistic movement Carpenter was strongly interested; Roy died during his visit and Carpenter preached his funeral sermon (afterwards published with a memoir).

As schoolmaster Carpenter's school proved to be very successful, educating some of the most prominent Unitarians of the period, including James and Harriet Martineau. Of Carpenter as a schoolmaster there are two sketches by James Martineau, who also served for a time as his locum-tenens; Martineau recorded 'the earnestness with which he insisted on the smallest things being done *well*' and his inculcation of 'reverence for great men among the living and the dead', but added that Carpenter possessed only 'a faint perception of beauty' and 'little appreciation of art, as such' (*Life and Letters*, 345, 348). Carpenter was popular among his pupils for his scholarship, enthusiasm, and sympathetic exercise of discipline; Sir John Bowring says: 'For many a year I deemed him the wisest and greatest of men, as he assuredly was one of the best' (Bowring, 43). Such was his didactic reputation that John Wilson, the journalist 'Christopher North', who had been his fellow student at Glasgow, when appointed in 1820 to the moral philosophy chair at Edinburgh, consulted him about the plan of his lectures and the literature of the subject. Even Harriet Martineau, who after her abandonment of Unitarianism caricatured him as 'superficial in his knowledge, scanty in ability, narrow in his conceptions and thoroughly priestly in his temper', had earlier acknowledged his abilities (*Harriet Martineau's Autobiography*, 1.73). Carpenter devoted much time to the encouragement of physical science, and was one of the chief organizers of the Bristol Literary and Philosophical Institution in 1822.

As minister and theologian Carpenter did much to widen the theological ethos of his denomination. With one exception, the earlier Unitarian tract and mission societies had adopted a Socinian-inspired preamble, branding Trinitarianism as 'idolatrous' and limiting the Unitarian name to the exclusion of Arians. As early as 1811 Carpenter endeavoured to expunge the preamble from the rules of the Western Unitarian Society, but it took him twenty years to effect this change. When in 1825 three older metropolitan societies were amalgamated into the British and Foreign Unitarian Association, Carpenter succeeded in removing from its constitution the restrictive preamble, which had previously had seriously divisive implications. His polemical publications in reply to the archbishop of Dublin, William Magee, particularly his *Examination of the Charges Made Against Unitarians and Unitarianism* (1820), and other similar works were commended for their mildness by orthodox critics; for that very reason, perhaps, although able works, few of them were much read.

During Carpenter's ministerial career Unitarianism was increasingly divided between those who sought to preserve the rigorously Socinian legacy of Joseph Priestley, with the materialistic determinism of its 'doctrine of necessity', and those (mainly of a younger generation) who reacted—partly intellectually, partly emotionally—against what they regarded as cold rationalism and sought to rediscover the more spiritual, mystical, and comforting dimensions of Christianity. Unitarianism suffered several secessions over this issue and some of Carpenter's own students subsequently joined the Church of England. Carpenter himself remained committed to the older forms of Unitarianism; in 1822–3 he served as visitor of Manchester College, York, of which his grandson Joseph Estlin Carpenter (1844–1927) was (after its move to Oxford) the principal. He retained a characteristically Unitarian belief in the ultimate benevolence of God and dismissed the idea of eternal punishment. Less typically, he rejected the rite of infant baptism as unscriptural and used a form of infant dedication in its place. It is true that he was in harmony with the newer theological developments to the extent of placing a greater stress than Priestley had done upon the person of Jesus as distinct from a sole emphasis upon God the Father. But this in no way made him an evangelical, a term which, with its association with justification by faith, cruci-centrism, and a personal conversion experience, cannot be applied to Carpenter or to his Unitarian contemporaries. Carpenter's contribution was thus limited to a broadening of Unitarianism which enabled it to include a wider variety of theological opinion while retaining a distinctive identity.

Politics and publications In politics Carpenter was a moderate whig, who deplored the 'Peterloo' events of 1819 and strongly supported the cause of parliamentary reform at Bristol, where two pro-reformers were elected to the House of Commons in 1831 and where, in that year, some of the most dangerous rioting of the reform era took place. He was also active in the anti-slavery movement in Bristol (his son William Benjamin had travelled in the West Indies), although he was not associated with the more radical abolitionists. It was characteristic of his moderation that he warmly commended the financial compensation paid to West Indian planters after the abolition of slavery in the British empire in 1834, and the *Christian Reformer* commented that 'we are not sure that his reverence for Whig Lords and Bishops was not a little too strong' (9, Jan–Dec 1842, 303). He published thirty-eight separate works, of which the most important from the denominational point of view were *Unitarianism the Doctrine of the Gospel* (1809; 3rd edn, 1823), *Errors Respecting Unitarianism Considered, and Motives and Means for the Dissemination of it Stated* (1808), both of which formed part of his controversy with Veysie, and *An Examination of the Charges Made Against Unitarians … by the Right Revd Dr Magee* (1820). His most significant educational publication was *Systematic Education* (2 vols., 1815; 3rd edn, 1822), written in conjunction with William Shepherd and Jeremiah Joyce; Carpenter's contribution included the sections dealing with mental and moral philosophy. He also published *Principles of Education* in 1820, and his *Sermons on Practical Subjects* was edited for publication by his son R. L. Carpenter in 1840; an abridged edition was produced by Mary Carpenter in 1875.

Death Carpenter gave up his school in 1829; by 1839 his constitution was completely exhausted under his unsparing labours. He left home on 22 July and was recommended by London doctors to travel. Accompanied by John Freeman, a medical adviser, he went to the continent, but his health did not revive. He was drowned on the night of 5–6 April 1840 while travelling by the French steamer *Sully* from Leghorn to Marseilles. According to his son's memoir he suffered from seasickness, went upon the deck in the darkness, and was washed overboard; he was not missed until the following morning. The statement by H. W. Schupf that he committed suicide by jumping overboard is not supported by any evidence, although Carpenter's depressed mental condition, the fate of similar sufferers, and the wish of the family to prevent any such speculation combine to forbid the absolute exclusion of that possibility. His body was washed ashore near Porto d'Anzio, about two months afterwards, and was buried with lime on the beach. A funeral service was conducted by the Revd Joseph Hutton at Lewin's Mead Chapel on 26 April, and funeral sermons were delivered from several other Unitarian pulpits. A memorial to Carpenter was erected in his chapel; its inscription was printed in the *Christian Reformer* of 1842.

ALEXANDER GORDON, *rev.* G. M. DITCHFIELD

Sources *Memoirs of the life of the Rev. Lant Carpenter, LLD, with selections from his correspondence*, ed. R. L. Carpenter (1842) • J. E. Carpenter, *The life and work of Mary Carpenter* (1879) • J. Manton, *Mary Carpenter and the children of the streets* (1976) • *Memoirs of the life and work of Philip Pearsall Carpenter*, ed. R. L. Carpenter (1880) • R. Waller, 'James Martineau: the development of his religious thought', *Truth, liberty, religion: essays celebrating two hundred years of Manchester College*, ed. B. Smith (1986) • D. C. Strange, *British Unitarians against American slavery, 1833–65* (1984) • *The life and letters of James Martineau*, ed. J. Drummond and C. B. Upton, 2 vols. (1902), 1.18–19, 44–9, 122 • H. W. Schupf, 'Single women and social reform in mid-nineteenth century England: the case of Mary Carpenter', *Victorian Studies*, 17 (1973–4), 301–17 • *Christian Reformer, or, Unitarian Magazine and Review*, 7 (1840), 352, 551–6, 650–51 • *Christian Reformer, or, Unitarian Magazine and Review*, 9 (1842), 296–305, 371 • *Harriet Martineau's autobiography*, ed. M. W. Chapman, 1 (1877), 73, 80 • J. Murch, *A history of the Presbyterian and General Baptist churches in the west of England* (1835), 117ff., 409, 564 • *Autobiographical recollections of Sir John Bowring*, ed. L. B. Bowring (1877), 42–3 • will of L. Carpenter, PRO, PROB 11/1929/401
Archives Harris Man. Oxf., corresp. | BL, Joseph Hunter MSS
Likenesses R. Woodman, stipple, pubd 1837 (after portrait by N. C. Branwhite), NPG; repro. in Carpenter, ed., *Memoirs of the life of the Rev. Lant Carpenter* • H. Wood, medallion on tablet, 1840, Lewin's Mead Chapel, Bristol • Bentley, bust, 1842, Lewin's Mead Chapel, Bristol • portrait, repro. in Manton, *Mary Carpenter*
Wealth at death several thousand pounds; also house, land, shares in Great Western Railway, and insurance policies: will, PRO, PROB 11/1929/401; Manton, *Mary Carpenter*, 61

Carpenter [*née* Geddes], **Margaret Sarah** (1793–1872), portrait and genre painter, was born on 1 February 1793 at Salisbury, Wiltshire, where she was baptized at St Thomas's Church on 7 June 1793, the second of six children of Alexander Geddes (1763–1843), retired army officer, and his wife, Harriet Easton (1762–1842).

Although largely self-taught, Margaret Geddes received some painting tuition from Thomas Guest in Salisbury

Margaret Sarah Carpenter (1793–1872), self-portrait, 1817

c.1805, and copied old masters in the earl of Radnor's collection at nearby Longford Castle. Lord Radnor helped her financially to move to London in 1813, where she won three major medals at the Society of Arts. Exhibiting regularly at the Royal Academy and British Institution from 1814, she was one of a circle of aspiring young painters, including William Collins (her future brother-in-law), Andrew Geddes (not related), David Wilkie, and James Stark. Almost certainly she was a pupil of Sir Thomas Lawrence c.1815 or earlier, and was seen later by many as his natural successor.

On 27 October 1817 Margaret Geddes married William Hookham *Carpenter (1792–1866), son of Old Bond Street bookseller James Carpenter. She had eight children, three dying in infancy, and three becoming painters: William (1818–1899), Percy (1820–1895), and Henrietta (1822–1895). Margaret was ambitious and determined to pursue her career, but bore a strong sense of duty towards her family responsibilities. For most of her career she earned more than her husband. From her 1817 self-portrait (British Museum, London), the 1846 portrait by her son William (exh. Royal Academy; National Portrait Gallery, London), and even a photograph taken c.1862 (National Portrait Gallery, London), she was an attractive woman who kept her youthful looks. Following her marriage, she lived in London for the rest of her life, principally in Marylebone, 1830–52, and at the British Museum, 1852–66, where her husband was keeper of prints and drawings. During the latter period Margaret's work reduced, but she continued to exhibit at the Royal Academy until 1866.

Margaret Carpenter's portraits—of men, women, and children—were mostly in oils, but many in chalks and, more rarely, watercolours. Some were engraved. She also painted genre subjects, including sixty-three exhibited at the British Institution. Although influenced by Reynolds and Lawrence, her style shows a more straightforward reality and energy, with a warmth of character. Her command of drawing is evident from her small 10 x 8 in. panels up to the largest whole-length canvasses 96 x 57 in.

Over more than fifty years Carpenter produced some 1100 pictures, 263 exhibited in her lifetime. Of those the 156 shown at the Royal Academy are more than for almost any other nineteenth-century woman artist, and her sitters' account book (a copy of which is in the National Portrait Gallery, London) of over 600 individuals reads like a who's who of early Victorian England. She sometimes stayed outside London to work on particular groups of clients, for example in Leeds, the Lake District, and north Wales. Among her more notable sitters were Byron's daughter Ada, countess of Lovelace (1836; Gov. Art Coll.), Archbishop Sumner (five versions, including one in the National Portrait Gallery, London), the painter Richard Bonington (1833), and the sculptor John Gibson (1857) (both National Portrait Gallery, London). Through her contacts with Eton College she painted over 100 commissions, mostly 'leaving portraits' of boys. Her work can be seen in several collections including the National Portrait Gallery, Victoria and Albert Museum, and British Museum, London, and Eton College, Berkshire, although much of it remains in the private collections of the families who commissioned her.

As the most successful English woman painter of her time, Margaret Carpenter received regular critical acclaim, especially for her portraits of women and children, and 'far surpassed in merit most of her contemporary portrait-painters' (Frith, 3.420). That she was able also to bring up a family is a tribute to her character and determination. Had she not been a woman, she would 'most assuredly' have gained election to the Royal Academy (Art Journal, 6). She died at her home at 22 Upper Gloucester Place, Marylebone, on 13 November 1872, aged seventy-nine, and was buried with her husband in Highgate cemetery.

RICHARD J. SMITH

Sources memoir of Harriet Collins, untitled MS, Ransom HRC · M. Carpenter, sitters account book (transcript), 1899, NPG, Heinz Archive and Library · Graves, RA exhibitors · NPG, Heinz Archive and Library · D. Gaze, ed., Dictionary of women artists, 1 (1997), 348–50 [incl. bibliography] · Engraved Brit. ports. · W. P. Frith, My autobiography and reminiscences, 3 (1888), 419–21 · Art Journal, 35 (1873), 6 · CGPLA Eng. & Wales (1872) · architectural drawings of the Carpenters' residence, BM · officers' reports, correspondence, and trustees' committee minutes relating to W. H. Carpenter and his family, BM · baptism register, St Thomas's Church, Salisbury, Wiltshire · d. cert. · Highgate cemetery records · parish register, London, St George, Hanover Square, 27 Oct 1817 [marriage]

Archives NPG, corresp. · NRA, priv. coll., corresp.

Likenesses M. Carpenter, self-portrait, watercolour, 1817, BM [see illus.] · S. P. Denning, miniature, 1835 · W. Carpenter jun., lithograph, 1840, BM · W. Carpenter jun., oils, exh. RA 1846; photograph NPG · W. Carpenter jun., etching, c.1858, NPG · J. Foley, marble medallion, c.1858–1866, South London Gallery, Camberwell ·

H. Webster, carte-de-visite, 1862, NPG · W. Carpenter, oils, Salisbury town hall · A. Geddes, oils

Wealth at death under £1500: resworn probate, Jan 1873, *CGPLA Eng. & Wales* (1872)

Carpenter, Mary (1807–1877), educationist and penal reformer, was born on 3 April 1807 at Exeter, the eldest of six children of the Unitarian minister Lant *Carpenter (1780–1840) and his wife, Anna Penn (1782?–1856), a supervisor of schools for girls. The Carpenters belonged to the intellectual aristocracy of English puritanism, a world largely set apart from the wider society. Piety, an exacting sense of obligation, and reforming principles marked the household. Though vowed to tolerance, the Carpenters found it difficult to countenance the world as they found it. In 1817 the family moved to Bristol. Mary Carpenter's liberal education, which included lessons in science, history, and Greek, centred on her father's school, where she eventually became an effective assistant. James Martineau, the Unitarian divine, who shared lessons with her, recalled that she was a self-possessed girl, plain and ungainly, who 'always talked like a book' (Manton, 29). Like her father, whose influence on her was lifelong and profound, Mary developed a compulsion to set the world to rights. Apart from watercolour painting, which expressed a sensitivity to the beauty of her surroundings, she had little interest in female accomplishments. A more typical girl of the period would have thought her a prig.

In 1827 Mary Carpenter left home to serve as a governess, first in the Isle of Wight, then at Odsey, near Royston. Two years later she returned to Bristol to help her mother set up a girls' school, to which a Sunday school was added. In 1833 she came under the influence of the Raja Rammohun Roy and the American philanthropist Joseph Tuckerman, who excited her interest in India and the ragged children of Bristol. Two years later she founded an association in the city which was named the Working and Visiting Society, based on Tuckerman's work in Boston. (Carpenter published *A Life of Joseph Tuckerman* in 1848.) Aided by John Bishop Estlin, a local surgeon, she opened the first ragged school in the Lewin's Mead section of Bristol in 1846; this soon moved to larger premises in an unsalubrious street called St James's Back. Her day-to-day experience in the slums turned her attention to government blue books and the law, and like other reformers of her generation she began to compile data on social conditions.

Many of Mary Carpenter's ragged charges were petty thieves and gang members, and over the next few years she developed a particular interest in the most hardened children—those who were likely to end up in the criminal courts. In the 1850s the law still required judges to try seven-year-olds for the theft of a penny tart. As a humanitarian Carpenter took exception to the harshness of the penalties applied to children. As a Unitarian she took a somewhat broader and more benign view of delinquency than evangelical reformers. In her opinion, unusual at the time, a child in trouble was still a child and must be treated as such. As a method of reform punishment was useless. Preferring rehabilitation to retribution, she emphasized the need to re-create a family environment in reformatories. In her influential book *Reformatory Schools for the Children of the Perishing and Dangerous Classes, and for Juvenile Offenders* (1851), she stated that love 'draws with … cords far stronger than chains of iron'. The practical application of such principles would require not only the establishment of special residential institutions for young offenders but a shift in official policies towards juvenile delinquency.

Mary Carpenter's writings and discussions with other reformers, most notably the jurist Matthew Davenport Hill, prepared the ground for a conference in Birmingham in December 1851. Reluctant to be seen as an advocate of women's rights, she did not speak at the gathering but was none the less one of its leading lights. The meeting's recommendations were in keeping with her view that there should be three different types of school—ragged, industrial, and reformatory—for different children. Ideally, all three types of school were to be conducted by voluntary agencies but subject to state inspection and public support. Though she was chary of state interference, she envisaged in the institutional model a partnership between charitable and public authorities which would provide government assistance and supervision without coercion.

The Birmingham conference raised the profile of juvenile delinquency as a public issue and prompted reformers to put their theories into practice. Mary Carpenter took the initiative in Bristol, where she founded a school at Kingswood in 1852, and a separate reformatory school for girls at the Red Lodge in Park Row in 1854. Meanwhile she gave evidence before a parliamentary inquiry on juvenile delinquency (1852) and wrote *Juvenile Delinquents, their Condition and Treatment* (1853). Her testimony, writings, and practical effort did much to bring pressure to bear on parliament to recognize a need for reform. The Youthful Offenders Act of 1854, 'the Magna Carta of the neglected child', owed much to her influence. It authorized the establishment of reformatory schools by voluntary bodies, certified by the state and partly funded by the Treasury. Though imperfectly enforced, the act represented a major change in penal policy and established a pattern of relations between statutory and voluntary bodies that would serve as a model for the future. Mary Carpenter's influence was also felt in the act of 1857, which applied similar procedures and support to industrial schools.

Despite recurring ill health—she suffered from a bout of rheumatic fever at the end of 1854—Mary Carpenter corresponded with a host of leading reformers, opened a certified industrial school in Bristol in 1859, and contributed regularly to the annual conferences of the National Association for the Promotion of Social Science. She continued to write extensively on ragged schools, reformatories, and pauper children. *The Claims of Ragged Schools to Pecuniary Educational Aid from the Annual Parliamentary Grant* appeared in 1859, and *On the Principles of Education* was published the following year. Whether writing or lecturing, Mary Carpenter's guiding principle was to make the individual child conscious of his or her own worth as a member of society. In turn she insisted that society had a responsibility to children, and, if it knowingly left them in a state of degradation, it owed them reparation. She continued to lobby on behalf of workhouse children and pressed the government to amend its legislation on industrial schools with some success. But her campaign to extend parliamentary grants to ragged schools, in which she found herself at odds with Lord Shaftesbury, failed.

Mary Carpenter was one of those Victorian social reformers who carried her philanthropic bags, full of improving schemes, across the globe. Visits to England by a series of exceptional young Indians, including Satyendranath Tagore, the brother of the poet Rabindranath Tagore, kindled her interest in the condition of female education on the subcontinent. She made her first visit to India in 1866 in the company of the Bengali barrister Monomohun Ghose. To her surprise she found herself being treated as a celebrity, which was remarkable in a society in which unmarried women were held in such low esteem. In Bombay, Madras, and Calcutta, officials sought her advice on female education and prison discipline. At the end of 1866 she summed up her general impressions of Indian female education in a memorandum to the viceroy, Sir John Lawrence, in which she asked, with characteristic boldness, why the British government was doing less for girls than boys. She wrote an account of her travels in *Six Months in India* (1868), a copy of which she sent to Queen Victoria.

Back home Mary Carpenter had discussions with India Office officials, and in March 1868 she had an interview with the queen, who took an interest in Indian education. Later that year she returned to India, but her attempt to set up a normal school at Bombay was unsuccessful, if only because the curriculum with its Western bias was unsuitable. She returned to England in poor health in April 1869. On a third visit to India during the winter of 1869–70, she set up girls' schools at Bombay and Ahmadabad at her own expense, but she returned convinced that more might be done for female education in India from England. Back in Bristol she inaugurated a National Indian Association under the presidency of Princess Alice, which promoted reform and provided information on English education for Indian visitors. On her final tour of India in 1875–6, she visited prisons and reformatories, and initiated branches of the National Indian Association in Bombay, Calcutta, and Dacca. She recorded details of her trip in a correspondence with Lord Salisbury, who was then secretary for India.

Although India took up much of her energy in her last years, Mary Carpenter found time to attend a congress on women's work at Darmstadt in 1872 as the guest of Princess Alice. The following year she toured the United States and Canada for three months, lecturing on prison reform and enquiring into the plight of Native Americans. Not a feminist by temperament, her views on the women's movement nevertheless changed over the years. Like so many reforming women of her generation she was appalled by the sexual double standard of the Contagious Diseases Acts, which the government passed in the 1860s

to reduce venereal disease in the armed forces. She became a vice-president of the Ladies' National Association for the Repeal of the Contagious Diseases Acts and, in an unusual departure, took the chair herself at a meeting. In keeping with her interest in female education she signed a memorial to the senate at the University of London, calling for degrees to be open to women. She did not wish her educational work to be side-tracked by the women's suffrage campaign, but she gradually came around to the view that women needed to organize politically to defend their interests. Only a month before her death she added her voice to the cause, speaking at a meeting of the Bristol and West of England Society for Women's Suffrage.

Mary Carpenter was the leading female advocate of deprived and delinquent children in mid-nineteenth-century England, and one of the first philanthropists to see the need to provide special facilities for their care. Her child-centred philosophy can be detected in remedial institutions and legislation from the 1850s onwards. As a writer she was maternal, though unsentimental. As an administrator she was systematic and persuasive. Despite social indifference and conflicts with officialdom, her record of achievement would have been the envy of many contemporary male reformers. Ironically it was her Indian experience, where her projects met with relatively little success, that brought her national recognition and turned her into a Victorian worthy. Her own institutions in Bristol were pioneering, but her distrust of state intervention put an enormous burden on their voluntary administration as the economic climate became more severe towards the end of the century. After her death Red Lodge was overtaken by rising standards of care and a change in social attitudes. Short of funds and out of date, it closed in 1919.

Stiff and unattractive, Mary Carpenter cut a somewhat alarming figure, which her sardonic humour did little to alleviate. But what she wanted in tact and grace she made up for in doggedness. As *The Spectator* noted at her death:

> The concentration of her purposes, and the tenacity of her just self-confidence, concealed from the eye of the world a depth of sentiment, which if it had been as visible as her social aims, would have given her perhaps a greater charm. (Quoted in Manton, 245)

Her friend Frances Power Cobbe compared her to a plough, driving obstacles relentlessly out of her path. She took great strength from her religion, which she had imbibed as a child. Unlike so many Victorians, she was never troubled by spiritual doubt. When Cobbe once pressed her about her religious views, she curtly replied that they could be found in her *Meditations and Prayers* (1845) and her father's writings. Active until the end, she died of rheumatic heart disease on the night of 14–15 June 1877 at Red Lodge, Bristol. She was buried later in the month in Arnos Vale cemetery in the city. There is a memorial to her in Bristol Cathedral, with an inscription composed by James Martineau: 'No human ill escaped her pity, or cast down her trust'.   FRANK PROCHASKA

Sources J. Manton, *Mary Carpenter and the children of the streets* (1976) · J. E. Carpenter, *The life and work of Mary Carpenter* (1879) · N. C. Sargant, *Mary Carpenter in India* (1987) · J. J. Tobias, *Crime and industrial society in the 19th century* (1967) · D. E. Owen, *English philanthropy, 1660–1960* (1964) · M. Carpenter, *Reformatory schools for the children of the perishing and dangerous classes* (1851) · H. W. Schupf, 'Single women and social reform in mid-nineteenth century England: the case of Mary Carpenter', *Victorian Studies*, 17 (1973–4), 301–17 · CGPLA Eng. & Wales (1877) · *DNB*
Archives Boston PL, corresp. and papers · Bristol RO, corresp. and papers · County House, Bristol, archives · Dorset RO, letters | BL, corresp. with Florence Nightingale, Add. MS 45789 · Harris Man. Oxf., letters to Theo Parker and others · Hunt. L., letters to Frances Cobbe
Likenesses C. H. Jeen, engraving, repro. in Carpenter, *Life and work* · engraving (after photograph by T. R. Williams, 1850), repro. in Manton, *Mary Carpenter* · wood-engraving (after photograph by C. Voss Bark), NPG; repro. in *ILN* (7 July 1877)
Wealth at death under £8000: probate, 27 July 1877, CGPLA Eng. & Wales

Carpenter, Nathanael

Carpenter, Nathanael (1589–1628), Church of England clergyman and philosopher, was born on 7 February 1589 at Northleigh, Devon, son of John *Carpenter (d. 1621), the rector there, who was a Cornishman. After matriculating at St Edmund Hall, Oxford, on 7 June 1605, he was elected fellow of Exeter College, on the recommendation of James I, on 30 June 1607. He graduated BA on 5 July 1610, and proceeded MA on 28 April 1613 and BD on 11 May 1620. Between 1619 and 1622 he was tutor to William Morice, later secretary of state to Charles II. Much admired as a 'philosopher, poet, mathematician, and geographer' (Wood, 1.516), Carpenter attracted the attention of prominent divines. Matthew Sutcliffe, dean of Exeter, named him one of the fellows of his abortive theological college at Chelsea, and Archbishop James Ussher made him his chaplain in 1626 and took him to Ireland, where he served as schoolmaster to the king's wards in Dublin.

Carpenter's earliest publication, *Philosophia libera* (Frankfurt, 1621; Oxford, 1622), repudiated Aristotelian orthodoxy. Against blind submission to ancient authorities and the fruitless speculations of schoolmen, he stressed the importance of suspended judgement and observation. His next treatise, *Geographie Delineated* (Oxford, 1625), with its emphasis on experiment, reveals still more clearly the influence of William Gilbert. Unable himself fully to accept the Copernican system, Carpenter presented his readers with a faithful account of it and encouraged them to weigh the evidence for themselves. That his philosophical works were reprinted at Laudian Oxford illuminates the considerable spirit of tolerance which prevailed there among men of science notwithstanding the increasingly embittered nature of Caroline theological contests.

Carpenter's preaching was as celebrated among his contemporaries as his pleas for scientific freedom. An avowed opponent of the Arminians, he preached three sermons at St Mary's, Oxford, published as *Achitophel, or, The Picture of a Wicked Politician* (1627), which established his reputation as a defender of the Calvinist heritage of the Church of England. His attack on 'our own mungrel divines' (*Achitophel*, 13), whom he repeatedly linked with the Jesuits, was so

obnoxious to the Laudian party that, according to William Prynne in *Canterburie's Doome* (1646), the first edition was recalled and its offensive passages purged. It became a best-seller none the less, with editions in 1628, 1629, 1633, 1638, 1640, and 1703. In 1633 Carpenter's sermons on Matthew 11: 21, entitled *Chorazin and Bethsaida's Woe*, were published posthumously. Like his patrons Ussher and Sutcliffe and his friends Matthias Styles and Thomas Winniffe, Carpenter was among those respectable Calvinist conformists who had constituted and defined the mainstream of the Jacobean church. His sermons reflect the discomfiture of such men during the reign of Charles I. He complained that his enemies had so 'abused many a sincere Christian' with 'the odious name of a Puritan', that 'a protestant must make a hard shift (either by popery or Arminianism) to save himself harmless' (ibid.). Despite his criticisms of Brownists, Carpenter was far more exercised by the threat of an Arminian takeover of the church. He denounced those great men and flattering courtier-divines who seemed determined to sacrifice English religion and liberties to their own ambition. Reminding protestants of their conscientious duty to resist magistrates whose commands violated the honour of God, he encouraged them to 'stake their lives in God's cause' (Carpenter, 24).

Carpenter also wrote a treatise on optics, which, according to Thomas Fuller, if printed would have been a masterpiece. It never appeared, either as Fuller says, because it was used to 'case Christmas pies in his printer's house' (Fuller, 138) or as the editor of *Chorazin* claimed, probably more reliably, because it was lost in the Irish Sea. Carpenter, who apparently never married, died at Dublin early in 1628 and was buried there. Robert Ussher, the archbishop's cousin, preached his funeral sermon. On his deathbed Carpenter reportedly 'did much repent … that "he had … so much courted the maid instead of the mistress", meaning that he had spent his chief time in philosophy and had neglected divinity' (Wood, 1.517).

JIM BENEDICT

Sources Wood, *Ath. Oxon.*, 2nd edn, 1.516–17 · J. Prince, *Danmonii orientales illustres, or, The worthies of Devon*, 2nd edn (1810), 173–5 · T. Fuller, *The worthies of England*, ed. J. Freeman, abridged edn (1952), 138 · C. W. Boase, ed., *Registrum Collegii Exoniensis*, new edn, OHS, 27 (1894), 92–3, 370 · N. Tyacke, 'Science and religion at Oxford before the civil war', *Puritans and revolutionaries: essays presented to Christopher Hill*, ed. K. Thomas and D. Pennington (1978), 79–82, 89 · M. Feingold, 'The mathematical sciences and new philosophies', *Hist. U. Oxf. 4: 17th-cent. Oxf.*, 359–448, esp. 388, 395, 443 · R. F. Jones, *Ancients and moderns: a study of the background of the 'Battle of the Books'* (1936), 65–71, 288–9 · N. Carpenter, *Chorazin and Bethsaida's woe*, ed. N. H. (1633), epistle · K. Sharpe, *The personal rule of Charles I* (1992), 295 · C. Webster, *The great instauration: science, medicine and reform, 1626–1660* (1975), 118 · Walker rev. · J. Davies, *The Caroline captivity of the church: Charles I and the remoulding of Anglicanism, 1625–1641* (1992) · *Fourth report*, HMC, 3 (1874), 590
Archives BL, Lansdowne MS, biographical notice, Dccccclxxxiv. 56 · CCC Oxf., biographical sketch, MS 308, fol. 66b · TCD, 'Encomia varia' *c.*1650, MS A. 6. 7. | Folger, extracts of Carpenter's *Achitophel* in the commonplace book of Joseph Hall, *c.*1650, MS V.a. 339

Carpenter, Philip Herbert (1852–1891), palaeontologist and zoologist, was born at 6 Regent's Park Terrace, London, on 6 February 1852, the fourth son of William Benjamin *Carpenter (1813–1885), physician and naturalist, and his wife, Louisa (née Powell). Among his brothers was (Joseph) Estlin *Carpenter, the Unitarian minister. He was educated at University College School, London, and from an early age was interested in natural science. In his seventeenth year he accompanied his father in the *Lightning* on a dredging and sounding cruise to the Faeroes; this was followed by two voyages in the *Porcupine* in 1869 and 1870, where he acted as a scientific assistant.

In 1871 Carpenter obtained a scholarship in natural science at Trinity College, Cambridge, where he studied geology and biology, obtaining a first class in the natural sciences tripos of 1874. He proceeded to the degree of MA in 1878, and of ScD in 1884.

In 1875 Carpenter made a voyage in the *Valorous* to Disko Bay for scientific purposes, after which he went to Würzburg and worked under Professor Semper. While there, as a result of a controversy which had arisen from his father's investigations into the structure of crinoids, he made his own study of the group, and soon became one of the leading authorities in the field.

In 1877 Carpenter was appointed an assistant master at Eton College in charge of biological teaching. Nevertheless, he managed to continue his own researches, and he eventually published about fifty papers, principally on echinoderms and crinoid morphology. His two chief works were reports on the crinoids collected by the *Challenger* expedition (1872–6); they were published in 1884 and 1888. Carpenter was also joint author (with R. Etheridge jun.) of the catalogue of the Blastoidea in the British Museum, and made important investigations into another fossil order, the Cystidea.

Carpenter believed in the value of studying both fossil specimens and their living representatives, to understand a group fully. He largely aided in the section dealing with the echinoderms in Nicholson and Lydekker's *Palaeontology* (1889), wrote a popular account of the same group in Cassell's *Natural History* (1883), and was ever ready to help fellow scientists.

Carpenter married Caroline Emma Hale, daughter of Edward Hale, an assistant master at Eton, on 19 April 1879. The couple had five sons. In the summer of 1891 Carpenter suffered from an unusually severe attack of influenza, possibly the result of many years' over-exertion. This illness, combined with domestic anxieties, resulted in a depression that led to his suicide at Eton College on 21 October 1891. The loss to science and to his family and friends was a heavy one. His wife and five sons survived him.

Carpenter was elected FLS in 1886, FRS on 4 June 1885, and in 1883 was awarded by the Geological Society part of the Lyell fund on the same day that his father received the medal. T. G. BONNEY, rev. V. M. QUIRKE

Sources A. M. M. C. [A. M. M. Carshall], *PRS*, 51 (1892), xxxvi–xxxviii, esp. xxxvi · *Proceedings of the Linnean Society of London* (1890–92), 263 · *Geological Magazine*, new ser., 3rd decade, 8 (1891), 573–5 · *Nature*, 64 (1901), 628 · W. T. Stearn, *The Natural History Museum at South Kensington: a history of the British Museum (Natural History), 1753–1980* (1981) · Venn, *Alum. Cant.* · personal knowledge (1901) · private information (1901) · b. cert. · m. cert. · d. cert.

Archives NHM, corresp. · U. Oxf., department of zoology, notes on T. H. Huxley's lectures

Wealth at death £10,252 16s. 7d.: resworn probate, Feb 1892, CGPLA Eng. & Wales (1891)

Carpenter, Philip Pearsall (1819–1877), social reformer and conchologist, youngest child of Lant *Carpenter (1780–1840), Unitarian divine and schoolmaster, and his wife, Anna (d. 1856), daughter of James Penn of Kidderminster, was born at Bristol on 4 November 1819. His sister Mary *Carpenter (1807–1877) was a social reformer and philanthropist, and his brother William Benjamin *Carpenter (1813–1885) was a naturalist and physiologist. Carpenter was educated in his father's school, at Bristol College (between 1833 and 1836), and at Manchester College, York (1836/7–40). He graduated BA from the University of London in 1841. In that year he became minister of a Presbyterian congregation at Stand, Lancashire, from where he moved in 1846 to a congregation at Warrington.

Carpenter did not confine his activity to preaching, but was concerned in endless philanthropic schemes, some rather eccentric. He established a printing press, and disseminated his opinions by frequent leaflets, letters, magazines, and other publications. He learned to swim in the canal, and instituted a swimming academy; he lectured on the necessity of proper drainage; he tried to alleviate unemployment; and he stood up for the preservation of ancient rights of way. He set an example of temperance in eating and abstinence from wine. He spoke of a public dinner to the officers of the militia as an expenditure for sensual gratification that could not be reconciled with Christian sobriety, and he refused to lend a copy of a song, 'Mynheer van Dunk', to a Christmas glee party because he would not encourage the singing of bacchanalian verses. He had always thought it a sin to drink wine and soon came to believe it foolish to eat meat. When his house was robbed, he published a handbill describing the candlesticks, silver spoons, and other stolen property. The notice informed the thieves that he had forgiven them, and that if they called he would converse with them, and if they did not, then they would have to meet him on the day of judgment.

Carpenter had been instructed in natural science as a boy; he had made a collection of shells, and always had a taste for natural history. In 1855, while walking down a street in Liverpool, he caught sight of some strange shells in a dealer's window. He went in, and found the specimens to be part of a vast collection made by Frederick Reigen, a Belgian naturalist, at Mazatlán in Mexico. The collector had died, leaving his fourteen tons of shells unsorted and unnamed. Carpenter bought them for £50.

The examination, description, naming, and classification of these shells was the chief work of the rest of Carpenter's life. By the comparison of hundreds of examples, 104 previous species were shown to be mere varieties, while 222 new species were added to the catalogue of the Mollusca. From this time onwards Carpenter devoted his time to the shells; even when he received or paid visits he would wash and pack up his shells during conversation. The monetary value of the shells, when named and arranged in series, was great, but Carpenter never tried to profit by them. His whole endeavour was to spread the knowledge of them and to supply as many public institutions as possible with complete collections of Mazatlán Mollusca. Details of the shells were provided in the *British Association Reports* for 1856 and 1863, and in the *Smithsonian Reports* for 1860.

Carpenter visited America in 1858, where he arranged Mazatlán shells at Albany and at the shell collection at the Smithsonian Institution, Washington. He travelled over 12,000 miles, meeting with temperance and anti-slavery groups. In 1860 he received the first PhD awarded by the University of the State of New York. In the same year he returned to Warrington, and on 1 October married Minna Meyer, originally from Hamburg. At the conclusion of the ceremony, in Manchester, the couple formally adopted a boy whom Carpenter had found in a refuge at Baltimore.

In 1865 Carpenter sailed with his wife and adopted son for America and settled in Montreal. There he continued to campaign for social reform and for the improvement of sanitation. He ceased to be a Presbyterian and became reconciled to the doctrines of the Anglican church. He took pupils, and his teaching was conducted in his own eccentric style: he used to imitate the movements of polyps, for example, with his arms and legs in a way that, though entertaining, diverted his pupils' attention from the subject of the lesson. He gave his large shell collection to McGill College, where it became known as the Carpenter collection. Shells continued to occupy much of his time, and he was working on the Chitonidae, of which he had formed a great collection, when he died of typhoid on 24 May 1877, in Montreal.

NORMAN MOORE, rev. YOLANDA FOOTE

Sources DCB, vol. 10 · *Memoirs of the life and work of Philip Pearsall Carpenter*, ed. R. L. Carpenter (1880) · personal knowledge (1886) Likenesses portrait, repro. in Carpenter, *Memoirs of the life and work of Philip Pearsall Carpenter*

Carpenter, Richard (*fl.* 1450?). *See under* Carpenter, Richard (1604/5–1670?).

Carpenter, Richard (1575–1627), Church of England clergyman, was born in Cornwall of unknown parents. He matriculated at Exeter College, Oxford, on 28 May 1592, and graduated BA on 19 February 1596. Elected to a fellowship on 30 June 1596, he retained it until 30 June 1606, during which time he studied theology under Thomas Holland, rector of Exeter, proceeded MA on 7 November 1598, and became a noted preacher.

At Oxford, Carpenter was also tutor to Christopher Trevelyan, the fourth son of John Trevelyan of Nettlecombe, Somerset, and his wife, Urith, sister of Sir Arthur Chichester, lord deputy of Ireland. Before September 1609 he married his pupil's youngest sister, Susanna. From the lord deputy's son Sir Robert Chichester he obtained on 24 July 1605 the rectory of Sherwell, near Barnstaple, Devon. Having proceeded BD on 25 June 1611, he was instituted to the adjoining living of Loxhore on 19 July. His relations with his patron seem to have been difficult, for he complained in his will that Chichester had 'notoriously wronged' him by detaining a portion of his tithes from the time of his induction (PRO, PROB 11/153, fol. 82). He occasionally lectured at Barnstaple, where he enjoyed the support of its mayor and MP, John Delbridge, whom the earl of Bath described as the 'factious and schismatical head' of north Devon puritans (*Salisbury MSS*, 11, 443). On 10 February 1617 Carpenter proceeded DD.

Carpenter published several sermons, including *The Soul's Sentinel* (1613), preached at the funeral of Sir Arthur Acland, and three assize sermons preached at the invitation of his father-in-law, then sheriff of Somerset; these were published as *The Conscionable Christian* (1623). Throughout his works he distanced himself from popery, profanity, and 'precise' nonconforming puritans. His apparent moderation, however, hardly concealed his godly sympathies. After denouncing all obstacles to further reformation, he lamented that 'zealous ministers' were now charged as movers of sedition, and maintainers of sects (*Conscionable Christian*, 2). In a visitation sermon Carpenter reproved Bishop William Cotton for his failure to root out popery, whoredom, and drunkenness. He urged the bishop to 'give a downright blow' to such evils 'that they may no more stalk by you, much less stare upon you uncontrolled' (*A Pastoral Charge*, 1616, 30). Further evidence of his godly credentials is offered by the books Carpenter eventually bequeathed to his children: the English works of Joseph Hall, William Perkins, John Downame's *Christian's Warfare*, and John Dod on the commandments.

In addition to his other livings Carpenter was probably rector of Cullompton, Devon, from 1602 until his resignation in 1626; if so he was the father of Henry Carpenter (*d.* 1662), who matriculated at Exeter College in 1624, and who subsequently became rector of St Dionis Backchurch, London, and, in 1661, chaplain to the House of Commons. Henry was the author of a discourse on conscience, *The Deputy Divinity* (1657), which bears a strong resemblance to Richard's work on the same topic.

In his will of 1625 Carpenter mentioned four sons and five daughters. His son John was a student at Exeter College, intended for the ministry. He named his wife executrix, to be assisted by his 'very loveinge and most trusty friendes' John Delbridge and George Hakewill (PRO, PROB 11/153, fol. 82). He died at Loxhore on 18 December 1627, and was buried in the chancel of Loxhore church.

JIM BENEDICT

Sources Wood, *Ath. Oxon.*, 2nd edn, 1.514–15 · W. C. Trevelyan and C. E. Trevelyan, eds., *Trevelyan papers*, pt 3, CS, 105 (1872), xxvi, 77, 84, 110–12, 138–40 · Carpenter's will, PRO, PROB 11/153, fols. 81–3 · C. W. Boase, ed., *Registrum Collegii Exoniensis*, new edn, OHS, 27 (1894), 52–3, 210, 370 · G. Oliver, *Ecclesiastical antiquities in Devon*, 1 (1840), 114 · K. Fincham and P. Lake, 'Popularity, prelacy and puritanism in the 1630s: Joseph Hall explains himself', *EngHR*, 111 (1996), 856–81, esp. 871 · K. Fincham, 'Episcopal government, 1603–40', *The early Stuart church, 1603–1642*, ed. K. Fincham (1993), 71–91, 73 · Foster, *Alum. Oxon.* · M. Stoyle, *Loyalty and locality: popular allegiance in Devon during the English civil war* (1994) · *Calendar of the manuscripts of the most hon. the marquis of Salisbury*, 11, HMC, 9 (1906),

443 • Boase & Courtney, *Bibl. Corn.*, 1.63; 3.1115 • *Remarks and collections of Thomas Hearne*, ed. C. E. Doble and others, 7, OHS, 48 (1906), 78 • I. Cassidy, 'The episcopate of William Cotton, bishop of Exeter, 1598–1621', BLitt diss., U. Oxf., 1963, 77

Archives BL, 'prologue on the philosopher's stone in verse', Sloane MS 1098, fol. 10 • BL, 'alchemical verses', Sloane MS 288, fol. 64 • Bodl. Oxf., letters to and from Degory Wheare, 3469 **Likenesses** two engravings, Bodl. Oxf., Rawlinson MS B 266, fol. 17b

Carpenter, Richard (1604/5–1670?), Roman Catholic priest and apostate, was the son of William Carpenter (*d.* 1611) of Denshanger, Passenham, Northamptonshire, and his wife, Anne, daughter of Thomas Piggot of Doddershall, Quainton, Buckinghamshire. Born at Doddershall, he had one brother and two sisters. Carpenter was educated at Eton College from 1617 to 1623, at Trinity College, Oxford (according to his own somewhat suspect claim), and at King's College, Cambridge, where he was admitted, aged eighteen, on 25 August 1623. On Christmas eve 1625, at King's, he announced himself a Roman Catholic. This aroused some concern on the part of the government, which tried unsuccessfully to intercept him before he left the country. Having been received into the Roman Catholic church by the Benedictine Peter Wilford in London, he left for Catholic education abroad, first arriving at St Omer. Carpenter entered the English College at Valladolid in 1627, leaving three years later to join the Benedictines at Douai in Flanders. (He may have also spent some time in the Franciscan order.) After a sojourn in Paris, he next turned up in Rome, where he claimed to have been sent by the provincial of the English Jesuits. He was entered at the English College on 13 December 1633, ordained priest on 24 March 1635, and then sent back to England. His aliases included Francis Carpenter, Francis Dacre, and Charles Vincent. In England he apostatized, making a recantation sermon at St Paul's Cathedral, London.

Carpenter became caught in the struggle between William Laud and the puritan faction in the Church of England. He complained that Laud's chaplain had urged him to praise the ceremonies in the Church of England in his recantation. He received a modest living at Poling in Sussex, only 4 miles from Arundel Castle, a major centre of English Catholicism, in 1638. Carpenter claimed to have been harassed by Catholics, particularly a priest named Franciscus à Santa Clara, at Poling, and bore a grudge against Laud. He submitted evidence against him to the parliamentary committee of religion in 1640; he also appeared before the committee that December to claim that Samuel Baker, licenser and chaplain to William Juxon, bishop of London, had forbidden his recantation sermon to appear in print on account of being too anti-Catholic.

Carpenter's first published work was *Experience, Historie and Divinitie* (1641), a mixture of spiritual autobiography, anti-Catholic satire, and devotion. It was reprinted in 1642. Both editions are identified on their title-pages as having been printed by order of the House of Commons, to whom the work is dedicated. With the addition of apocalyptic material identifying the pope as Antichrist, the book was printed twice more, in 1644 and 1647, with

Richard Carpenter (1604/5–1670?), by William Marshall, 1641

the new title *The Downfall of Antichrist*. Carpenter's movements in the civil war are obscure. He went to Paris and returned to Catholicism at one point. However, he returned to England and protestantism. He may have been the Richard Carpenter who resigned a living in Kent to the committee for plundered ministers in 1647. In 1648 some parishioners of St James's, Duke's Place, in the City of London chose Carpenter as a curate, but in November the city authorities ordered him to desist from preaching; the eighth London classis had issued a certificate against him, and there were 'some fowle things now informed against him' (*Walker rev.*, 43). By the end of the decade he was a travelling Independent preacher. During the interregnum Carpenter settled at Aylesbury in Buckinghamshire and married. Publications from his Independent period include *The Perfect Law of God, being a Sermon and No Sermon, Preached and yet not Preached* (1652) and *The Anabaptist Washt and Washt, and Shrunk in the Washing* (1653). The last, upholding the validity of infant baptism, originated in a debate with the Baptist preacher John Gibbs held at the church in Newport Pagnell, Buckinghamshire. He also published an anti-Catholic sermon, *The Jesuit and the Monk, or, The Serpent and the Dragon* (1656), and *Astrology Proved Useful, Harmless, Pious* (1657), which appeared with a Latin dedication to Elias Ashmole. His self-published book *The last and highest appeal, or, An appeal to God, against the new-religion makers, dresters, menders, or venders among us* (1656) survives in a single copy in the Thomason collection. He continued his anti-Catholic writings after the Restoration, with another Gunpowder Plot day sermon called *Rome in her Fruits* (1663), answering the pamphlet *Reasons why the Roman Catholics should not be Persecuted*, and a closet-drama, *The Pragmatical Jesuit New Leven'd* (1665), whose characters include Lucifer and a hero called Aristotle junior.

Carpenter was obsessed with his own image. Most of his works included portrait frontispieces, which show him as a round-faced man with a sloping forehead and prominent nose. The frontispiece to *The Anabaptist Washt* shows him engaging in a vomiting contest with the devil.

Carpenter's controversial works show some learning. Even at their most protestant they show traces of his Catholic education, as he makes more use of medieval and early modern scholastic philosophy than was common in protestant polemic. Although all Carpenter's published writings are from the protestant phases of his career, his break with the Roman Catholic church was never final. George Leyburn, the president of the English College at Douai, wrote of his repentance and desire to do penance in a letter of 1654, and there is an undated petition to the Congregation on the Propagation of the Faith asking for reconciliation and stating that he had converted his wife. Since Carpenter was ordained a Catholic priest and was also a monk, converting his wife meant convincing her their marriage was illegitimate. Anthony Wood, who stated that Carpenter was regarded as 'an impudent, fantastical man that changed his mind with his cloaths' and as a 'theological mountebank', heard from Carpenter's acquaintances that he died a Catholic (Wood, 2.420). Carpenter was still alive in 1670, but died later that year or shortly afterwards. Wood claims that he did not die in Aylesbury.

A **Richard Carpenter** (*fl.* 1450?) was the author of an English alchemical poem on the preparation of the philosopher's stone included in Elias Ashmole's *Theatrum chemicum Britannicum* (1651). Ashmole identified him as the brother or kinsman of a fifteenth-century bishop of Worcester, John *Carpenter.   WILLIAM E. BURNS

Sources DNB · G. Anstruther, *The seminary priests*, 2 (1975), 45–6 · A. Shell, 'Multiple conversion and Menippean self: the case of Richard Carpenter', *Catholicism and anti-Catholicism in early modern English texts*, ed. A. F. Marotti (1999), 154–97 · Wood, *Ath. Oxon.*, new edn, 2.419–20 · A. Kenny, ed., *The responsa scholarum of the English College, Rome*, 2, Catholic RS, 55 (1963), 439 · R. Carpenter, *Experience, historie and divinitie* (1641); repr. (1642) · *Walker rev.*, 43–4 · R. Carpenter, *The Anabaptist washt and washt, and shrunk in the washing* (1653) · Venn, *Alum. Cant.* · *CSP dom.*, 1625–6 · W. Sterry, ed., *The Eton College register, 1441–1698* (1943) · E. Ashmole, *Theatrum chemicum Britannicum* (1651)
Likenesses W. Marshall, line engraving, 1641, NPG [*see illus.*] · W. Faithorne, line engraving, pubd 1657, BM, NPG · T. Cross, line engraving, NPG · portrait, repro. in Carpenter, *Experience, historie and divinitie*, frontispiece

Carpenter, Richard Cromwell (1812–1855), architect, was born in Clerkenwell, London, on 21 October 1812, the elder of two sons of Richard Carpenter (1779–1849), cattleman and property developer, and his wife, Sophia, *née* Page (*b.* 1779). He was educated at Charterhouse School, and then from 1827 or 1828 apprenticed to John Blyth (1806–1878), who 'early discovered in the mind of his pupil a strong inclination towards the study of ecclesiastical architecture' (*The Builder*, 165). He married Amelia Dollman (1821–1891) at St Mark's Church in Myddleton Square, Clerkenwell, on 6 October 1840 and they had four children.

A design entitled *Transepts of a Cathedral*, which was exhibited at the Royal Academy in 1830, provides the first proven record of Carpenter as an architect. Other unexecuted designs—both secular and ecclesiastical—followed during the next three years, most being exhibited at the Royal Academy and the Royal Manchester Institute. The first executed commissions were provided through his father. These included designs for the development of Lonsdale Square in Islington (1838–42), the construction of Victoria Street linking Holborn Bridge with Clerkenwell Green (1840–48), and others with three aspiring railway companies.

Carpenter is best-known, however, as an ecclesiastical architect, and one connected with the Victorian high church. He was one of the favoured architects of the Cambridge Camden Society, to which he was introduced by Pugin, and provided several designs for its second edition of *Instrumenta ecclesiastica* (1856), including designs for a wooden church and a chapel school. He was also commissioned to design an iron church, but died before this could be completed. He designed twenty-eight churches, half of which were built. For rural parishes there was an idealized reproduction of a fourteenth-century country church, small and simple, with separate chancel and nave, and a western bell-cote. Examples in England include: St John the Baptist, Cookham Dean, Berkshire (1844–5); St James-the-Less, Stubbing, Berkshire (1849–50); and St John the Evangelist, Bovey Tracey, Devon (1852–3). These designs were exported to Australia and resulted in St John the Baptist, Buckland, Van Diemen's Land (1846–8), and Holy Innocents', Rossmore, near Sydney, New South Wales (1848–50).

For towns there was something more substantial; a hall church which was usually intended to be accompanied by a dominant spire. The most illustrious of these is St Mary Magdalene in Munster Square, London (1849–52), a church which was based upon the Austin Friars' church in the City of London, with details from Exeter Cathedral and Sherborne Abbey. Other notable town churches included: St Stephen's (1841–4; dem.) and St Andrew's (1844–6; dem.) in Birmingham, St Paul's (1845–8) and All Saints (1847–52; dem.) in Brighton, St Peter the Great in Chichester (1848–52), and Christ Church, at Milton, near Gravesend (1854–6).

Carpenter also produced designs for cathedrals in Colombo (1846–7), Kingston, Jamaica (*c.*1850), and Inverness (1853–6), which were not executed. He restored thirty-six churches, as well as St Patrick's Cathedral in Dublin, Chichester Cathedral, and Sherborne Abbey. He designed thirteen local schools, seven parsonages, and reordered two major houses: Campden House, Chipping Campden, Gloucestershire, for the earl of Gainsborough, in 1846, and Bedgebury Park, Kilndown, Kent, for A. J. Beresford Hope, in 1854–5. He was a friend of Nathaniel Woodard and designed the school which was intended for New Shoreham, as well as St John's College, Hurstpierpoint, and St Nicholas's, Lancing, all in Sussex.

According to A. J. Beresford Hope, Carpenter was 'superior even to Pugin,—safer and more equable'. More specifically, his 'eye for colour was exquisite' and his 'success lay in the perfect keeping of everything which he did,—the harmony of parts and general unity of proportion running through the entire building' (*The Ecclesiologist*, 138). He died at the age of forty-two from tuberculosis at his home, 40 Upper Bedford Place, London, on 27 March 1855. He was buried at Highgate cemetery on 2 April 1855.

JOHN ELLIOTT

Sources J. P. Elliott, 'The architectural works of Richard Cromwell Carpenter (1812–55), William Slater (1819–72) and Richard Herbert Carpenter (1841–93)', PhD diss., U. Lond., 1995 · *The Ecclesiologist*, 16 (1855), 138–42 · *The Builder*, 13 (1855), 165 · *GM*, 2nd ser., 43 (1855) · P. F. Anson, 'Richard Cromwell Carpenter', *Fashions in church furnishings, 1840–1940* (1965), 75–8 · Lancing College Archive, Woodard MSS · parish register (baptism), Clerkenwell, Pentonville Chapel · IGI · census returns · parish register (marriage), 6 Oct 1840, Clerkenwell, St Mark's, Myddleton Square · private information (2004) · d. cert.
Archives Lancing College, West Sussex, Woodard MSS
Wealth at death under £6000: will, PRO, PROB 11/2215, fol. 336; PRO, death duty registers, IR 26, 2060, fol. 676

Carpenter, Robert Pearson (1830–1901), cricketer, was born at 45 Mill Road, Cambridge, on 18 November 1830. Both of his brothers—George (1818–1849), a butcher, and William—played cricket for Cambridge town. Originally a boot-closer by trade, Robert soon became a professional cricketer with engagements at Godmanchester (1854), Ipswich (1855–7), Birkenhead (1858), and Marlborough College (1859–60). In Cambridge he became known as the 'Old Gardener', because of his custodianship of Parker's Piece (until 1881). It was there he played in 1856 for the town against the university.

Carpenter's first match at Lord's was in June 1858, when he scored 45 for the United All England eleven against the All England eleven. Throughout the 1860s he was the leading batsman in the United All England eleven; in the matches against the All England eleven, no batsman on either side surpassed his average of 24.44. He also appeared in nearly 150 matches against 'odds' of eighteen or twenty-two players. While loyal to the United All England eleven, as a professional he was ready to appear for the All England eleven when available and it was for this side that he made 174 against the Radcliffe-on-Trent XVIII in 1870 and 134—his highest score in first-class cricket—against Yorkshire in 1865. In the same decade he also played for Cambridgeshire, when his batting, together with that of Tom Hayward and the fast bowling of George Tarrant, gave the county pre-eminence for a few seasons. Against Surrey at the Oval in 1861 he made 100. He made

eighteen appearances (1859–73) for the Players in matches against the Gentlemen, scoring centuries in 1860 and 1861, both at the Oval. He went to America in 1859 with the first English overseas touring team, led by George Parr, and to Australia, under the same captain, in 1863–4.

Carpenter was an attacking batsman, especially off the back foot. After he retired, in 1876, he umpired, standing in two test matches (1886, 1888). He died on 14 July 1901 at his home, 45 Mill Road, Cambridge. He left a widow, Eliza. One of their sons, Harry Carpenter (1869–1933), played for Essex (1888–1920).   GERALD M. D. HOWAT

Sources A. Haygarth, *Arthur Haygarth's cricket scores and biographies*, 15 vols. (1862–1925) · W. A. Bettesworth, *Cricket* (18 July 1901) · *Wisden* (1902) · *The Times* (15 July 1901) · J. Pycroft, *Cricketana* (1865) · A. W. Spratt, *Short account of the career of Robert Carpenter* (1897) · W. Caffyn, *Seventy one not out* (1899) · R. Daft, *Kings of cricket* (1893) · G. D. West, *Twelve days of Grace* (1989)
Likenesses photograph, *c.*1870, Lord's, London
Wealth at death £398 12s.: probate, 20 Nov 1901, CGPLA Eng. & Wales

Carpenter, William (1797–1874), journalist and compiler of religious books, was probably born in St James's, Westminster, on 8 August 1797, the son of William and Mary Carpenter. It is firmly established that his father was a tradesman in St James's, and that Carpenter himself lived all his life in London. He had little or no formal education and, at an early age, was apprenticed to a bookbinder in Finsbury. He taught himself several ancient and modern languages. From his early years, he established a pattern of extreme industriousness and productivity which he maintained to the end of his life. Relatively little is known about his private life, although he married one Harriet in his twenties and they had at least three children, one of whom was a failed actor.

In the 1820s Carpenter met William Greenfield, a well-known editor of biblical and theological publications. The two men worked together for four years, producing *Critica biblica*, a monthly journal of religious literature (1824–7). Carpenter began to compile other theological works on his own, all in the service of a non-sectarian Christianity. He believed that the dissemination of knowledge, particularly on religion, was the key to personal improvement. Though lacking creative ability and not an original scholar, he became a formidable encyclopaedist. In 1825 he edited *Scientia biblica* in three volumes, a collection of parallel passages of scripture designed to encourage theological interpretation. The following year he edited *A Popular Introduction to the Study of the Holy Scriptures for the Use of English Readers*, which drew entirely upon the published work of other writers. As a result of this volume he was forced to defend himself against charges of having plagiarized the writings of the Revd Thomas Horne. He edited several other popular religious compilations during the decade and became a lecturer on biblical criticism and interpretation. He seems to have earned a solid income from his publications and lectures.

Carpenter's life began to change significantly in the late 1820s, when he took up the twin causes of political reform and freedom of the press. During 1828–9 he edited (and partly owned) the *Trades Weekly Press*, a newspaper inspired by Owenite ideas of co-operation which was published by the British Association for Promoting Co-operative Knowledge. After severing his ties with this organization, in part because of his own preference for a competitive economic system, he thrust himself into the campaign for an untaxed press. In October 1830, nine months before the first appearance of Henry Hetherington's *Poor Man's Guardian*, he began to issue a series of weekly tracts known as the *Political Letters and Pamphlets*. These 2d. epistolary 'newspapers' were intended to challenge the stamp duty, which required that every periodical published more than monthly on a regular basis pay a 4d. tax. The content of the *Political Letters and Pamphlets* was supportive of political and economic radicalism, though it rejected the more extreme views of Henry Hunt and others.

In May 1831 Carpenter was prosecuted in the court of exchequer for publishing an unstamped newspaper. He resorted to a technical defence which emphasized the discretionary nature of the law. The jury took only one minute to convict him. After refusing to pay a heavy fine of £120, he was sentenced to six months in the king's bench prison. In December 1831, shortly before his term was due to end, he was released, but unlike Hetherington and other participants in this 'war of the unstamped', he was not warmly acclaimed by reformers. This was because of his firm refusal to endorse further violations of the law. During the remainder of the decade Carpenter issued no other illegal publications, though he wrote and published a large amount of political literature. This included numerous tracts and journals such as *The Political Anecdotist and Popular Instructor* (1831), *The People's Book* (1831), which featured a borough-by-borough exposition of the iniquities of the unreformed electoral system, *Carpenter's Monthly Political Magazine* (1831–2), *A Slap at the Church* (1832), and the *Church Examiner and Ecclesiastical Record* (1832). None of these publications had an appreciable impact on the reform politics of the 1830s, but the latter two, written primarily by the more radical John Cleave, are notable for their pungent attacks upon the clergy. Also of interest is Carpenter's short biography of John Milton (1836), which aimed to make the working classes 'familiar with those unchanging principles of freedom on which [Milton] has demonstrated that the safety of states and the virtue and happiness of the people must ever be built' (p. iv).

During the 1830s Carpenter championed many reform causes. He enthusiastically endorsed the Reform Bill of 1832, which was rejected by some radicals because it failed to enfranchise the working class and bring about political democracy. He took up the cause of the Dorchester labourers, who were transported to New South Wales in 1834 after their abortive effort to form a trade union of agricultural labourers. He launched numerous attacks upon the hereditary peerage, an institution which he believed to be at the root of social and political corruption.

He fervently denounced church rates and called for the disestablishment of the Church of Ireland.

In 1839–40 Carpenter became a participant in the Chartist movement. He was elected to represent Bolton at the first Chartist convention of 1839, where he attacked Feargus O'Connor's extreme political rhetoric and opposed proposals for a general strike. He also edited two Chartist journals: *The Charter* (1839–40), which generated heavy financial losses for him, and the *Southern Star* (1840), which led to an estrangement from Bronterre O'Brien, the prominent Chartist leader. After 1840 Carpenter drifted away from radical politics. But he vociferously espoused chancery reform (he had qualified as a lawyer in 1832), reform of the corporation of London, and assisted emigration to the colonies for the poor and unemployed.

Carpenter's subsequent career as a paid journalist reflects his inordinate capacity for hard work. He was connected with many newspapers, primarily as a sub-editor, beginning with the radical *True Sun* and *Weekly True Sun* (1832–4). Occasionally he wrote leaders and did some reporting for the newspapers which employed him. But his chief talent lay in putting a newspaper together. He was primarily concerned with disseminating 'useful knowledge' (broadly defined) as distinct from specific political opinions, and in this he was in tune with popular trends in journalism, which increasingly veered away from the confrontational. It is difficult to trace Carpenter's journalistic meanderings over the course of several decades because his work was unsigned and attracted relatively little attention. However, it is known that he worked on the *Shipping Gazette* (1836), the *London Journal* (1836), *The Era* (1838), the *Railway Observer* (1843), the *Family Herald* (1843), *Lloyd's Weekly Newspaper* (1844–5), the *Court Journal* (1848), the *Sunday Times* (1854), the *Bedfordshire Independent* (1854), and the *Mining and Military Gazette*. Rarely did he leave traces of his presence behind, though he has been credited with introducing a legal section into *Lloyd's Weekly Newspaper* during his tenure there.

In the 1840s and 1850s Carpenter directed his attention once more to encyclopaedic works, of the kind he had laboured on several decades before. He expanded and updated a previously published book, *A Comprehensive Dictionary of English Synonymes*, which went through at least six editions. Affirming the need to make Christianity intelligible and attractive to those with comparatively little education, he brought out several editions of *An Introduction to the Reading and Study of the English Bible*, a substantial volume which he had compiled earlier. A year before his death he produced a curious book entitled *The Israelites Found in the Anglo-Saxons* (1872). In it he drew upon his budding interest in freemasonry, maintaining that the earliest 'civilizers' of England were descended from the ten lost tribes of Israel.

Carpenter's final years are obscure. Financially, his fortunes fluctuated during his lifetime. In the 1830s he was in substantial debt as a result of his prosecution and imprisonment. During the 1840s and 1850s he recovered his footing. Then, towards the end of his life, he was once more in considerable privation. From the 1860s on, he was nearly blind and in deteriorating health. He died virtually unnoticed at his home, 28 Colebrook Row, Islington, on 21 April 1874; he was survived by his wife.

JOEL H. WIENER

Sources J. H. Wiener, *The war of the unstamped* (1969) • P. Hollis, *The pauper press* (1970) • *Sunday Times* (3 May 1874) • *DNB* • Boase, *Mod. Eng. biog.* • *IGI* • I. J. Prothero, *Artisans and politics in early nineteenth-century London: John Gast and his times* (1979) • T. H. S. Escott, *Masters of English journalism* (1911)
Archives BL, Francis Place collection
Wealth at death under £100: probate, 3 June 1874, *CGPLA Eng. & Wales*

Carpenter, William Benjamin (1813–1885), biologist and university administrator, was born in Exeter on 29 October 1813, the fourth child and eldest son of Dr Lant *Carpenter (1780–1840) and his wife, Anna (*d.* 1856), daughter of James Penn, of Kidderminster. He was the brother of Mary *Carpenter (1807–1877) and Philip Pearsall *Carpenter (1819–1877). His father, a Unitarian minister intensely involved with reform questions, moved to Bristol when William was four, and established a school, connected to Lewin's Mead congregation, where the son was educated; it was well known for advanced teaching, in the sciences as well as the classics. Though William wanted to be an engineer, and retained a fascination with mechanical devices, he was apprenticed to the family friend and doctor John Bishop Estlin, with whom he travelled in the Caribbean in 1833. Carpenter studied initially at the Bristol medical school and then in London, and in 1835–7 and again in 1839 in Edinburgh, where he took the MD degree. During this time, he began the career teaching and reviewing and writing about science and medicine, rather than practising medicine, with which he made his name. He combined a penchant for wide generalizations with great thoroughness of exposition. Struggling to establish himself, Carpenter took on a heavy burden of writing, especially the several editions of *The Principles of General and Comparative Physiology* (1838), *The Principles of Human Physiology* (1842), and a *Popular Cyclopaedia of Natural Science* (3 vols., 1841–3). After appointment to the Fullerian professorship in physiology at the Royal Institution in 1844, when he also became FRS, he moved to London. Subsequently he gained appointments at University College, contributed extensively to the *British and Foreign Medico-Chirurgical Review*, and integrated himself into the dynamic scientific network in the city. From 1853 to 1859 he was principal of University Hall, a residence for students, and from 1856 to 1879 the registrar of University College, when, resigning his teaching, he became an unyieldingly thorough administrator during the creation of the modern University of London, contributing notably to the expansion of science degrees. On his resignation in 1879 he was created CB.

Carpenter's career in science was marked by a breadth of knowledge and thoroughness of exposition rather than analytic depth, but he significantly aided the creation of a public scientific culture. Carpenter also advanced specific views. Thomas Henry Huxley credited him with contributing 'in no small degree to the foundation of a rational, that

William Benjamin Carpenter (1813–1885), by Maull & Polyblank, 1855

is to say, a physiological psychology' (Carpenter, 67). His ideas on the nervous system, which brought together new experimental knowledge—especially on reflex action—and a stress on the moral will, mediated the spread of a physiological and psychological science of human nature in Britain. An influential article in 1846 sealed the status of phrenology as a pseudo-science, and his explanation of hypnotism and spiritualist experiences in terms of 'unconscious cerebration' or 'ideo-motor' action made familiar the role of unconscious activity in ordinary life. He systematically expounded this work in *The Principles of Mental Physiology* (1874). He made a bid to integrate the understanding of life itself with physical principles in a paper 'On the mutual relations of the vital and physical forces' (1850), and he wrote an early positive review of Darwin's theory of evolution. His credentials as an empirical researcher were established with his microscopical studies of the *Foraminifera*, minute shelled creatures found in surface waters and oceanic (and geological) deposits. This led him to become a leading popularizer of the microscope, and, in the late 1860s, to take a central part in the debate about the supposed discovery of 'dawn life', *Eozoon canadense*, in ancient Canadian rocks. When he began to spend summers on the Scottish island of Arran, he developed dredging and sampling techniques to extend studies of ancient crinoids, the sea fauna, currents and temperature gradients. He was directly influential in persuading the Admiralty to fund the *Challenger* expedition, led by his friend and colleague the Belfast zoologist

Wyville Thomson, which was regarded as the major pioneer scientific study of the deep oceans. Carpenter drew on the results in theories about the form of temperature gradients and the ocean circulation.

Carpenter had returned to Exeter to marry on 24 October 1840 Louisa Powell (1812–1887), the daughter of Joseph Powell, a local merchant and the granddaughter of Henry Cort, the iron puddler; they subsequently had five sons, including (Joseph) Estlin *Carpenter and Philip Herbert *Carpenter. Domestic life helped him to soften a sometimes cold and irritable manner, and it was the background for a devotional involvement with the Unitarian church in Hampstead over many decades. At home or at church playing hymns on the organ, Carpenter found expression for his feelings, and he published a handbook of psalmody (1858). His religious concern ran through all his commitments, and in the 1860s and 1870s he was a notable contributor to debates about science and religion; he was, for instance, a member of the élite dining and discussion group the Metaphysical Society. He accepted the process of evolution as the working of secondary causes in nature while retaining faith in the Creator as a designing first cause; similarly, he believed in the causal processes of the nervous system while arguing for the moral will as a real agent. He was very much a transitional figure in the development of a modern scientific culture in Christian terms.

In person, Carpenter was described as taller than average, quiet and somewhat formal in manner, spare, keen-eyed, and tenacious-looking. He was above all industrious and moral, characteristics evident in his work for social movements, notably temperance, and devotion to the institutional causes of science and to London University. As president of the British Association for the Advancement of Science in 1872, he gave an address, 'Man the interpreter of nature' (*Nature and Man*, 210), which expressed a deeply felt vision of 'the deep-seated instincts of humanity' to find in the order uncovered by science the power of God and the source of moral energy for intense activity.

He died at his home, 56 Regent's Park Road, London, on 10 November 1885 after collapsing with severe burns following an accident with a vapour bath. He was buried in Highgate cemetery.

A deeply earnest Victorian, Carpenter sought a secure place for the biological and medical sciences in a moral and Christian culture and thereby helped shape the modern life sciences in Britain. His textbooks on physiology, the microscope, and mental science had many readers, and he contributed throughout his life to contemporary periodicals and encyclopaedias on a huge range of topics. His scientific contribution was principally to popularize the idea of 'unconscious cerebration', to use shell form in research on the *Foraminifera*, and to initiate research on the biology and physical conditions of the oceans.

ROGER SMITH

Sources W. B. Carpenter, *Nature and man: essays scientific and philosophical* (1888) [incl. introductory memoir by J. E. Carpenter, and

appx, 'List of Dr Carpenter's writings'; repr. Westmead, Farnborough: Gregg International, 1970] · *DNB* · L. S. Hearnshaw, *A short history of British psychology, 1840–1940* (1964) · R. M. Young, *Mind, brain, and adaption: cerebral localization and its biological context from Gall to Ferrier* (1970) · R. Smith, 'The background of physiological psychology in natural philosophy', *History of Science*, 11 (1973), 75–123 · m. cert. · d. cert. · R. Smith, 'The human significance of biology: Carpenter, Darwin and the *vera causa*', *Nature and the Victorian imagination*, ed. U. C. Knoepflmacher and G. B. Tennyson (1977), 215–30 · K. Danziger, 'Mid-nineteenth century British psychophysiology: a neglected chapter in the history of psychology', *The problematic science: psychology in nineteenth-century thought*, ed. W. R. Woodward and M. G. Ash (1982), 119–46

Archives NHM, drawings and papers · RS | BL, geology lectures, Add. MS 31196 · Bodl. Oxf., corresp. with Lord and Lady Lovelace · CUL, letter to Charles Darwin · CUL, letters to Sir George Stokes · ICL, letters to Thomas Huxley · NHM, corresp. with Richard Owen and William Clift · NHM, corresp. with George Charles Wallich · RS, letters to Sir John Herschel · U. Edin. L., letters to Sir Charles Lyell · UCL, corresp. with G. C. Robertson · Wellcome L., letters to Henry Lee

Likenesses T. H. Maguire, lithograph, 1851, BM, NPG, Wellcome L.; repro. in T. H. Maguire, *Portraits of honorary members of the Ipswich Museum* (1852) · Maull & Polyblank, photograph, 1855, NPG [*see illus.*] · E. Edwards, photograph, 1864, NPG · E. Edwards, photograph, 1868, Wellcome L.; repro. in L. Reeve, ed., *Men of eminence*, 3 (1864) · J. Collier, oils, exh. RA 1880, U. Lond. · Lock & Whitfield, woodburytype, 1883, NPG, Wellcome L.; repro. in T. Cooper, *Men of mark, a gallery of contemporary portraits* (1883) · Annan and Swan, photogravure, Wellcome L. · Barraud, photograph, Wellcome L. · Maull & Co., photograph, NPG, Wellcome L. · H. G. Smith, photograph, Wellcome L. · photograph, repro. in Carpenter, *Nature and man*, frontispiece

Wealth at death £14,010 9s. 9d.: resworn probate, April 1886, *CGPLA Eng. & Wales* (1885)

Carpenter, William Boyd (1841–1918), bishop of Ripon, the second son of the Revd Henry Carpenter, incumbent of St Michael's, Liverpool, and his wife, Hester, daughter of Archibald Boyd, of Londonderry, was born at Liverpool on 26 March 1841. His mother's brother, Archibald *Boyd, was dean of Exeter. Educated at the Royal Institution, Liverpool, he won an open scholarship at St Catharine's College, Cambridge, and graduated BA (senior optime) in 1864. Ordained the same year, he served as curate at All Saints, Maidstone (1864–6), St Paul's, Clapham (1866–7), and Holy Trinity, Lee, Lewisham (1867–70). He rapidly gained a reputation as a preacher, his last vicar nicknaming him 'the extinguisher'. In 1870 he was appointed vicar of St James's, Holloway, London, and became known as a capable parish priest. In 1879 he passed to the fashionable parish of Christ Church, Lancaster Gate, London. Originally evangelical in inclination, he became a moderate liberal churchman, influenced in part by study of F. W. Robertson. He was much liked by Queen Victoria and was appointed a royal chaplain in 1879 and canon of Windsor in 1882. Later he was clerk of the closet to Edward VII (1903–10) and to George V (1911–18), by whom he was created a KCVO in 1912. In these offices he came into close contact with the German court and was a friend of the Empress Frederick and of Kaiser Wilhelm II, who made him a knight of the royal crown of Prussia.

In 1884 W. E. Gladstone selected Boyd Carpenter, despite reservations about the audibility of his sermons, for the see of Ripon. This he administered successfully for twenty-five years. He helped to create the see of Wake-field, and prepared the way for that of Bradford; he instituted the Queen Victoria Clergy Fund to provide pensions for poor clergy, and founded the Ripon Clergy College in 1897 to train graduates for holy orders. This foundation (renamed Ripon Hall) was moved to Oxford in 1919. He supported many forms of philanthropic endeavour, and keenly advocated the national league of physical training, the passing of the Children Act (1908), and the old-age pensions scheme. A lover of drama, he promoted the British Empire Shakespeare Society. He delivered the Hulsean lectures at Cambridge in 1878, the Bampton lectures at Oxford in 1887—presenting an important essay in comparative religion, published as *Permanent Elements of Religion* (1889)—the Noble lectures at Harvard in 1904 and 1913, the pastoral theology lectures on preaching at Cambridge in 1895, and the Liverpool lecture (translated into German) in 1913. In these utterances he showed himself a persuasive exponent of Victorian religious liberalism. He was a prolific writer; commentaries, reviews, religious poetry, books of devotion, and popular expositions of the poets, particularly Dante, flowed from his pen. His recreation was the collecting of works on Dante. His *Introduction to the Study of the Scriptures* (1902) is perhaps the best example of his popular religious teaching. In 1905 under the *nom de plume* Delaval Boyd he produced a tragedy, *Brian*; earlier, under the same name, he had written a 'shilling shocker', *The Last Man in London*. His reputation, however, rests mainly on his oratory. He spoke, without manuscript or notes, with extreme rapidity, and in a beautifully modulated voice; this caused him to be known as 'the silver-tongued bishop of Ripon'. His most notable sermon was that before the House of Commons at the queen's jubilee in 1887.

Boyd Carpenter was married twice: first, in 1864, to Harriet Charlotte, only daughter of the Revd J. W. Peers, of Chiselhampton, Oxfordshire; and secondly, in 1883, to Annie Maude (*d.* 1915), daughter of W. W. Gardner, publisher. He had five sons and six daughters.

On resigning his bishopric in 1911 Boyd Carpenter became canon, and was later subdean, of Westminster. He died, comfortably off, at his home, 6 Little Cloisters, Westminster, London, on 26 October 1918 and was buried in the cloisters at Westminster Abbey. There is a memorial window to him in Ripon Minster.

H. D. A. MAJOR, rev. H. C. G. MATTHEW

Sources H. D. A. Major, *Life and letters of William Boyd Carpenter* (1925) · W. B. Carpenter, *Some pages of my life* (1911) · W. B. Carpenter, *Further pages of my life* (1916) · L. E. Binns, *English thought, 1860–1900* (1956) · A. M. G. Stephenson, *The rise and decline of English modernism* (1984) · Gladstone, *Diaries* · CGPLA Eng. & Wales (1919)
Archives BL, corresp.; diaries; papers; sermons · Glamorgan RO, Cardiff, corresp. and papers | BL, letters to W. E. Gladstone, Add. MSS 44435–44517, *passim* · LPL, corresp. with Edward Benson
Likenesses Barraud, photograph, 1889, NPG; repro. in *Men and Women of the Day*, 2 (1889) · W. & D. Downey, woodburytype, 1891, NPG; repro. in W. Downey and D. Downey, *The cabinet portrait gallery*, 2 (1891) · Elliott & Fry, two cabinet photographs, NPG · Lafayette, postcard photograph, NPG · H. G. Riviere, oils, Ripon Hall, Oxford · Spy [L. Ward], chromolithograph, NPG; repro. in *VF* (8 March 1906)

Wealth at death £25,272 18s. 8d.: probate, 3 Jan 1919, *CGPLA Eng. & Wales*

Carpenter, William Hookham (1792–1866), museum keeper, was born on 2 March 1792 in Bruton Street, London, the only son of James Carpenter (*bap.* 1768, *d.* 1852), bookseller and print publisher, and his wife, Jennet Jane (*d.* 1795), daughter of Thomas Hookham, librarian and bookseller of Bond Street. He was trained in his father's business at 14 Old Bond Street, which specialized in art books and prints, and with his talent for drawing and interest in the techniques of printmaking, became acquainted with many artists and engravers. His father also collected and dealt in paintings, and through this William formed special friendships with both John Constable and Richard Parkes Bonington.

On 27 October 1817 Carpenter married Margaret Sarah Geddes [see Carpenter, Margaret Sarah (1793–1872)], born in Salisbury and a talented and successful painter of portraits and genre subjects. Over the next twelve years they had eight children, three of whom died in infancy; three became painters: William Carpenter (1818–1899), Percy (1820–1895), and Henrietta (1822–1895). At the time of the marriage Carpenter fell out with his father and set up in business on his own at 58 (now 23) Lower Brook Street. He published, among other books, Joseph Spence's *Anecdotes, Observations, and Characters, of Books and Men* (2 vols., 1820), and the first volume of John Burnet's *Practical Hints on Portrait Painting* (1822), but after five years with little business success—albeit helped by his wife's burgeoning career—he and his father were reconciled, and he returned to work with James.

The two men were of very different personalities. The elder Carpenter was a thrusting, wily, hard-headed businessman with a streak of meanness (he managed to alienate both the poet Thomas Moore and the painter John Constable), whereas William Carpenter's letters and handwriting suggest a gentle aesthete, academically inclined, meticulous but unassertive. In one sense he and his father complemented each other in business, but as time went on William became increasingly drawn to academic interests, and in 1844 wrote and published *Pictorial Notices*, a scholarly monograph on Van Dyck and his etchings.

In 1845 Carpenter was appointed keeper of prints and drawings at the British Museum. The family politics behind this move are intriguing: James gave up his business only in 1850, at the age of eighty-three, and even on his museum salary of £350 William was still earning considerably less than his wife, Margaret. He held his new post for twenty-one years until his death, and greatly increased the size, scope, and value of the collections under his care.

Among Carpenter's more important acquisitions for the museum were: the Coningham collection of early Italian engravings in 1845, a selection of Rembrandt's etchings from the collections of Lord Aylesford and Baron Verstolk, and some valuable Dutch drawings from the latter collection in 1847, various fine old master drawings which had belonged to Sir Thomas Lawrence, some drawings of

Michelangelo from the Buonarroti family, and a volume of drawings by Jacopo Bellini, purchased in 1855 at Venice. Carpenter also took a great interest in photography and collaborated with the pioneer Roger Fenton. In 1856 he proposed that drawings by Raphael in the museum's collection be photographed and copies sent to Prince Albert (Royal Library, Windsor Castle). In return, the prince consort gave thirty-two photographs of Raphael drawings in the Royal Collection to the museum in 1861. Carpenter was highly regarded by Prince Albert, and worked closely with the librarian at Windsor. In 1847 he was elected a member of the Koninklijke Academie van Beeldende Kunsten (the Academy of Fine Arts) at Amsterdam, and in 1852 a fellow of the Society of Antiquaries, on whose council he served in 1857–8. In 1856 he was appointed one of the founding trustees of the new National Portrait Gallery. He was a close friend of George Scharf (secretary and later director), and with his specialized knowledge of the subject was highly respected by the historians, peers, and government ministers who were his fellow trustees.

In 1852 Carpenter and his family moved from Marylebone, where they had lived since 1830, into one of the British Museum residences, and it was at the museum that he died on 12 July 1866 at the age of seventy-four. He was buried five days later in Highgate cemetery.

RICHARD J. SMITH

Sources archives, 1845–66, minutes of the trustees, committee meetings, officers' reports and corresp., BM · trustees' letters to G. Scharf, 1857–64 [incl. sixty-six from Carpenter]; secretary's journals, 1861–6, NPG, Heinz Archive and Library · *GM*, 4th ser., 2 (1866), 410–11 · *Men of the time* (1865) · *Proceedings of the Society of Antiquaries of London*, 2nd ser., 3 (1864–7), 480 · *John Constable's correspondence*, ed. R. B. Beckett, 4, Suffolk RS, 10 (1966) · *John Constable's correspondence*, ed. R. B. Beckett, 6, Suffolk RS, 12 (1968) · R. B. Beckett, *John Constable and the Fishers: the record of a friendship* (1952) · notes on Constable and 'dealers', Tate collection · P. Noon, *Richard Parkes Bonington: on the pleasure of painting* (1991) [exhibition catalogue, Yale U. CBA and the Petit Palais, Paris] · M. Pointon, *The Bonington circle: English watercolour and Anglo-French landscape, 1790–1855* (1985) · letter from R. P. Bonington to John Barnett, 21 Oct 1827, BL, 41178 · Morgan L., MA 4581 · M. Carpenter, sitters account book (transcript), 1899, NPG, Heinz Archive and Library · *The Athenaeum* (21 July 1866), 79 · *Art Journal*, 28 (1866), 286 · F. Madden, journal, 1866, Bodl. Oxf., MS Eng. hist. c. 179 · R. K. Engen, *Dictionary of Victorian engravers, print publishers and their works* (1979) · *DNB* · d. cert.

Archives BM, minutes, officers' reports, and corresp. · NPG, trustees' letters, secretary's journals

Likenesses M. Carpenter, oils, 1816, NPG · M. Carpenter, watercolour and pencil drawing, 1817, BM · W. Carpenter, charcoal drawing, c.1847 (after M. Carpenter), BM · W. Carpenter, etching, 1847, BM · J. Foley, marble medallion, c.1858–1866, BM · Caldesi, Blandford & Co., carte-de-visite, NPG

Wealth at death under £6000: probate, 11 Aug 1866, *CGPLA Eng. & Wales*

Carpentière, Andries [Andrew Carpenter] (c.**1677–1737**), sculptor, is thought to be of Flemish origin; by 1700 he had arrived in England, where he was known by his Anglicized name of Andrew Carpenter. He became principal assistant to John Van Nost the elder, the maker of lead figures for gardens, and his main claim to fame was in that sphere. By 1708 Carpentière had set up his own business in Portugal Row near Hyde Park, the centre for many lead

yards of the time. Because of his employment with Nost and his use of Nost's casts after the latter's death, it is sometimes difficult to distinguish between their respective work. A list of the figures which he offered for sale is in the Castle Howard archives, but several of the pieces are also to be found in Nost's catalogue. In some cases, however, Carpentière modified Nost's work. His output was considerable, and he had commissions to supply figures for Canons, Ditchley, Castle Howard, Powis Castle, Stowe, and Wrest Park. In addition, work attributed to him is to be seen at Studley Royal (the *Wrestlers*) and at Chatsworth (the *Cain and Abel* transferred from Chiswick); the *Blackamoor* at Dunham Massey may also be his. Carpentière's garden sculpture was not confined to figures or to lead: the stone vase finials at Wimpole are attributed to him. He carved twelve vases and twenty-four baskets there in 1719–20.

Carpentière's patrons included the duke of Chandos, with whom he fell out after building some houses and an inn with a statue for a sign too close to the entrance lodge at Canons. Another was Lord Carlisle: his *Farnese Hercules*, *Sitting Venus*, and *Faunus with Kid* survive at Castle Howard. At Wrest Park he was probably responsible for the statue of William III and the series of lead groups as well as the vases on the bowling green. His *Fame* at Powis Castle is signed, which makes it likely that he executed the other lead figures there. Carpentière's business was initially successful, but, according to George Vertue, 'he had much ado to hold up his head at last' as a result of being undersold and having to lower his prices (Vertue, *Note books*, 3.83). His price list, as submitted to Lord Carlisle, contained mostly classical figures but also a bagpiper and a pair of French peasants.

Apart from his garden practice, Carpentière worked in stone and marble in the field of monuments, where his work dates from after 1720. Sometimes he worked from designs by James Gibbs in his *Book of Architecture* (1728), and indeed Gibbs employed him at Ditchley and Amersham. His effigy of Sir John Thorneycroft (1725) is in the church at Bloxham, Oxfordshire; in the same year, at Amersham church, he executed a Gibbs design for the Montague Drake monument with two portrait medallions above a sarcophagus. A similar monument was created for Henry and Langham Booth at Bowdon, Cheshire (1727); in the same church is his greatest monument, to the first earl and countess of Warrington (1734), which closely follows the Gibbs-inspired tomb of Katherine Bovey in Westminster Abbey by Michael Rysbrack.

The final work that should be mentioned is the marble statue of Queen Anne (1712), now in the Leeds City Art Gallery. Carpentière had a high reputation in his day, and his work illustrates the transition from formal representation of figures to a freer and more naturalistic style in the rococo manner. He was one of several sculptors who, like Quellin and Nost, came to England from the Low Countries in the late seventeenth century, bringing with them both the techniques of casting in lead and a stylistic expressiveness that foreshadowed the work of Roubiliac and the Cheere brothers. As a garden sculptor Carpentière ranks high, perhaps just below John Cheere and the various Nosts, his compositional deftness making his work popular in the growing market for lead garden sculpture. As a creator of monuments and modeller in stone he was a fine craftsman, but lacked originality, being content in the main to follow the ideas of others. Vertue described him as 'a gross heavy man', who was brought to his end through age and cares which included his son John, 'an Idle fellow many years' (Vertue, *Note books*). Carpentière was married but nothing is known of his wife. He died in London in July 1737 and was buried in St George's, Hanover Square. MICHAEL SYMES

Sources M. Whinney, *Sculpture in Britain, 1530 to 1830*, rev. J. Physick, 2nd edn (1988) · J. Davis, *Antique garden ornament* (1991) · R. Gunnis, *Dictionary of British sculptors, 1660–1851* (1953); new edn (1968) · Vertue, *Note books*, vol. 3 · H. Walpole, *Anecdotes of painting in England: with some account of the principal artists*, ed. R. N. Wornum, new edn, 3 vols. (1888) · M. Baker, '"Squabby cupids and clumsy graces": garden sculpture and luxury in eighteenth-century England', *Oxford Art Journal*, 18/1 (1995), 3–13 · M. Symes, *Garden sculpture* (1996)
Archives Castle Howard, Yorkshire, archives · Wrest Park, Bedfordshire, archives

Carpentiers, Adrien (*fl.* **1739–1778**), portrait painter, whose name has also been spelt Carpentier or Charpentiere and who has mistakenly been stated to be the son of the sculptor Andries Carpentière, is believed to have been of Flemish descent. Having arrived in England in 1739, he lived in London from *c.*1760, and was one of the artists who signed the deed of the Free Society of Artists in 1763. He sent pictures to the exhibitions of that society and to those of the Society of Artists and the Royal Academy (fourteen works in all) from 1760 to 1774. His style displays an individuality, but is not very pronounced. Carpentiers was a competent itinerant portrait painter; in 1739 he is recorded as having worked in Kent, in 1743 Bath, in 1745 Oxford, and in 1751 East Anglia. A portrait by him of Zuccarelli is in the British Art Collection at Yale University, and another, of Roubiliac, is in the National Portrait Gallery, London; the latter was engraved by Chambers in line and by Martin in mezzotint. Two of his portraits, *The Quarm Family*, signed and dated 1767 (exh. Christies, 12 July 1940) and *A Member of the Twisden Family of Bradbourne* (1739?, formerly at Bradbourne, Derbyshire) are reproduced in Waterhouse, *18c Painters*, 70. His own portrait hung in Salters' Hall, London. Carpentiers died at Pimlico, London, in 1778. W. C. MONKHOUSE, *rev.* ASIA HAUT

Sources Waterhouse, *18c painters* · Bryan, *Painters* · Redgrave, *Artists* · E. Edwards, *Anecdotes of painters* (1808); facs. edn (1970)
Likenesses portrait, Salters' Hall, London

Carpue, Joseph Constantine (*bap.* **1764**, *d.* **1846**), surgeon and anatomist, was baptized on 4 May 1764 at the Sardinian embassy chapel, Lincoln's Inn Fields, London, the son of Henry Carpue (*d.* 1794), a Roman Catholic gentleman of Brook Green, and his wife, Catherine Lewis (*d.* 1797), sister of the bookseller William Lewis of Russell Street, whose son and daughter-in-law, Thomas and Dorothy Lewis, were Carpue's godparents. His sister Anne married Thomas Phillips of Somerstown. His grandfather Charles Carpue of Hammersmith (*d.* 1773) had made a fortune as a

shoemaker, having come to London from Little Missenden, Buckinghamshire, where his own father, also called Charles, had been a husbandman under the patronage of the Roman Catholic barons Dormer. The Carpues probably originated in the Spanish Netherlands, where the Dormers had strong connections. The other Carpues in London, who feature prominently in Roman Catholic records of the period, were all descended from other sons of the same husbandman. Carpue's paternal grandmother, Mary Elizabeth Smallwood, was related to the prominent London Roman Catholic priest Joseph Alexius Smallwood (1694–1756), sometime chaplain to the Dormers. Carpue's paternal grandfather's second wife, Frances Dean, founded 'The Ark', a refuge for Roman Catholic girls in Hammersmith. She was in turn related to the Mr Dean whose school was attended by William Lewis and Alexander Pope.

Carpue thus had impeccable Roman Catholic connections. Intended for the priesthood he was educated at the Jesuits' College at Douai but embarked for a continental tour in 1782, seeing much of Paris before and after the French Revolution. Being somewhat erratic, he thought of working for his uncle William Lewis, and then toyed with the bar and also the stage, being an enthusiastic student of Shakespeare. He settled on surgery, studying at St George's Hospital, London, and then serving for twelve years as a staff surgeon at the Duke of York's Hospital, Chelsea, resigning because he objected to serving abroad.

At Chiswick on 8 January 1799, when he was living in St Martin-in-the-Fields, Carpue married Elizabeth, daughter of Thomas Holland of Chiswick, sister of the actor Charles Holland (1768–1849) and niece of Charles Holland (1733–1769) who was also an actor. They had five children, all baptized at St Anne's, Soho: Elizabeth (*b.* 1802), Anne Augusta (*b.* 1806), Mary (*b.* 1807), Emma (*b.* 1809), and Sophia (*b.* 1812). From 1800 to 1832 Carpue became a freelance anatomy teacher, charging a regular 20 guineas, giving three courses of daily lectures at 50 Dean Street on anatomy, and twice weekly evening lectures on surgery. He made his pupils, in whom he took an affectionate interest, take a personal share in his demonstrations, teaching them by making them repeat what he had just said. His use of chalk drawings earned him the nickname 'the Chalk Lecturer'. Although for many years he had many pupils, his school is said to have foundered in the end for lack of them. Owing to his association with George Pearson at St George's Hospital, Carpue became a proponent of vaccination, visiting many military depots to promote the new idea, and, after leaving Chelsea, he joined Pearson as a surgeon at the National Vaccine Institution, a post he held until his death.

Early in his career Carpue carried out the wish of Benjamin West, Thomas Banks, and Richard Cosway, to ascertain how a recently killed corpse would hang on a cross by crucifying a recently executed murderer and making a cast once the corpse was cold (*The Lancet*, 166–8). His use of newly dead bodies associated him in the popular mind—and probably in truth—with body snatchers, and he was lampooned in Thomas Hood's poem *Mary's Ghost*, in which the recently exhumed Mary exclaims:

I can't tell where my head has gone,
But Dr Carpue can:
As for my trunk, it's all packed up,
To go by Pickford's van.

Carpue published a *Description of the Muscles of the Human Body* (1801); *Account of Two Successful Operations for Restoring a Lost Nose from the Integument of the Forehead* (1816); *History of the High Operation for the Stone, by Incision above the Pubis* (1819); and, having studied medical electricity through a plate (electrical) machine in his dining room, he also wrote *An Introduction to Electricity and Galvanism, with Cases Showing their Effects in the Cure of Disease* (1803).

Probably because of his background as a member of the formerly persecuted and still not fully emancipated Roman Catholic minority, Carpue was an uncompromising reformer, lending vociferous support to Francis Place's proposed Metropolitan Political Union (1831), which was intended 'to include all classes without distinction'. He opposed ardently the backward-looking Royal College of Surgeons, who consistently refused him a place on its council or an examinership. He did, however, become a fellow of the Royal Society (1817) and a consulting surgeon to the St Pancras Infirmary, and met and was much admired by George IV. In 1834 Carpue gave evidence to Henry Warburton's select committee on medical education and following the demise of his anatomy school he 'turned popular politician' and organized Joseph Hume's return as the radical MP for Middlesex (Desmond, 160).

In later life Carpue lived at 45 Charlotte Street, Fitzroy Square, although he also had a house at 21 Portland Place, Fulham. He suffered severe injuries in a crash on the new London–Brighton railway, in which two of his servants were killed. This led to dropsy, from which he died at his Charlotte Street address on 30 January 1846. His will, written in 1825, the main beneficiaries of which were his wife and daughters, was proved on 13 March 1846. His wife survived him. He ordered his funeral to be of the simplest kind possible.

Contemporaries recalled him variously: 'clever but very eccentric'; 'a tall, ungainly, good-tempered, grey-haired man, in an unfitted black dress, and his neck swathed in an enormous white kerchief, very nearly approximating to a jack-towel' (Feltoe, 102); 'a warm and faithful friend, abstemious and regular in habits, and a great admirer of simplicity in manners and appearance' (*DNB*); and a man who 'attained the highest character in his profession … leaving behind him the reputation of one of its most skilful members' (*ILN*, 93). ANTHONY R. J. S. ADOLPH

Sources DNB · chapel registers, Sardinian embassy, 1764, SS. Anselm and Cecilia, Kingsway, London · C. Lindsay, 'Catholic Registers of Lincoln's Inn Fields Chapel, London, 1731–1831', *Catholic Record Society*, 19 · *The Lancet* (7 Feb 1846), 166–8 · *Memorials of John Flint South*, ed. C. L. Feltoe (1884) · Spanish Embassy Chapel registers, 1761 · *ILN* (7 Feb 1846), 93 · A. Desmond, *The politics of evolution: morphology, medicine and reform in radical London* (1989) · *London radicalism, 1830–1843: a selection from the papers of Francis Place*, ed. D. J. Rowe, London RS, 5 (1970) · A. R. J. S. Adolph, 'The Carpue family of London', *Catholic Ancestor* (Feb 1992), 7–13 · will, proved, 13 March 1846, PRO, PROB 11/2032, sig. 176 · parish register (baptism), Soho, London, St Anne, 1802–12 · *London Directory* · *The record of the Royal Society of London*, 4th edn (1940) · *Laity's Directory* · parish register (marriage), 8 Jan 1799, Chiswick, London

Likenesses C. Turner, mezzotint, pubd 1822, BM, NPG · wood-engraving, 1846, NPG; repro. in *ILN* (7 Feb 1846) · W. Behnes, bust, 1847, St George's Hospital, London · stipple, Wellcome L.

Carr, Ann (1783–1841), Female Revivalist Society preacher, was born into humble circumstances at Market Rasen, Lincolnshire, on 4 March 1783, the youngest of the twelve children of Thomas and Rebecca Carr. Ann's mother died when she was five, and an aunt came to be housekeeper to the family. When Ann was eighteen the young man she had expected to marry died; she became ill and began to reflect on the transience of life. She was converted and joined the Wesleyan Methodists.

Carr felt compelled to tell other people 'what God had done for my soul', even though she faced considerable opposition. She became a class leader, spoke in prayer meetings, and gave exhortations. Before long she was receiving invitations to go further afield to speak, and felt that she could not refuse the call. She was attracted to Primitive Methodism, which was spreading into the east midlands, and in 1816 visited Nottingham where Sarah Kirkland, the first female Primitive Methodist travelling preacher, was working. While there she preached for the Primitive Methodists and led a mission to the colliers. Back in Market Rasen, Carr and the ranters (as the Primitive Methodists were known) were persecuted, so to keep the peace and avoid a division with the Wesleyans Carr moved to Hull, where she met Sarah Eland (or Healand) in 1818. Carr laid the foundation-stone of Mill Street Primitive Methodist Chapel on 12 April 1819. Carr and Eland returned to Lincolnshire and a revival broke out, particularly in the Market Rasen and Louth areas.

In June 1821 Carr, Eland, and Martha Williams were sent to Leeds, probably acting as revivalists, under the authority of the Primitive Methodist circuit. They were popular, but soon caused controversy because they would not accept circuit discipline; they seceded, and about 1822 started the Female Revivalist Society. Their first meeting-place was in Spitalfields on the Bank, Leeds, after which they met in a large room in George's Court, George Street, for three years. The chapel in the Leylands, Regent Street, was opened in 1825 and soon became noted for its social work in this notorious slum area. In the mid-1830s it was especially prominent in temperance work. Other premises were obtained to further their work—a chapel was built in Brewery Field, Holbeck, in 1826 and in 1837 a large schoolroom was built in Jack Lane, Hunslet. There were also societies in Stanningley and Morley.

The work of the Female Revivalists was supported by members of most of the nonconformist denominations, with the exception, unsurprisingly, of the Primitive Methodists. In 1837–8 Carr visited Hull and London, particularly promoting temperance ideas. During the summer of 1839 her health gave cause for concern and she went to Lincolnshire to recuperate. She did not really recover, and by 1840 she was obviously ill. Again a change of air was prescribed and she went to Hull, and then in October 1840 to Nottingham with Martha Williams. On her return to Leeds it was evident that she was failing, and she died from cancer at the Chapel House, Regent Street, on 18 January 1841. She was buried on 21 January at Woodhouse cemetery, Leeds.

Shortly before her death Carr made a will naming Martha Williams her executrix, to act with the trustees, in order to pay all the debts on the properties, but empowering them to sell some of the property if there were insufficient funds to cover the demands 'so that the Leylands Chapel should be carried on, and perpetuated for the purpose for which it was erected' (Williams, 76). Ann Carr was described as robust-looking, bold, courageous, and energetic, her preaching being characterized by zeal, correctness, and sincerity rather than by eloquence and culture. The meetings of the Female Revivalists sometimes became so emotional and fervent that the members were nicknamed jumpers. Welcomed for their novelty value in attracting crowds and promoting evangelism, Carr's Female Revivalists were an important example of a religious movement led and run exclusively by women.

E. DOROTHY GRAHAM

Sources M. Williams, *Memoirs of the life and character of Ann Carr* (1841) · D. C. Dews, 'Ann Carr (1783–1841) and the female revivalists of Leeds', in D. C. Dews, *From Mow Cop to Peake, 1807–1932: essays to commemorate the one hundred and seventy fifth anniversary of the beginnings of Primitive Methodism* (1982) · Z. Taft, *Biographical sketches of the lives … of various holy women*, 1 (1825) · d. cert. · will, proved 18 June 1841, W. Yorks. AS, Leeds

Archives Leeds City Archives

Likenesses portrait, repro. in Williams, *Memoirs*, frontispiece

Carr, Arthur (1855–1947), biscuit manufacturer, was born at Bowerbank, Barton, Westmorland, on 16 August 1855, the younger son of John Carr (1824–1912) and his wife, Harriet Ellis. John Carr's elder brother was Jonathan Dodgson Carr, who in 1831 founded the milling and biscuit making firm of Carr & Co. in Carlisle. After completing his apprenticeship, John Carr became a farmer and occasionally travelled for the firm. Having visited the rival biscuit manufacturing firm of Peek Frean & Co. (established in 1857 at Bermondsey), Carr joined that business in 1860 and subsequently moved with his family to London.

The Carrs being Quakers, Arthur probably attended a Friends' day school near his Clapham home. After he and his elder brother Ellis (1852–1930) had spent a year in Germany, in 1872 he became an apprentice in Peek Frean at £3 a week, initially employed to open each morning's post. He nevertheless made rapid progress and was made a partner in 1877, two years after his brother. On 2 June 1881 he married Marie Georgette Baumann (*b.* 1855/6); they had two sons. About this time he left the Quakers to join the Church of England.

In the 1880s and 1890s Peek Frean's progress was only slow: turnover fluctuated, while profits were inadequate. The Carrs had to cope with three unprogressive senior partners on the Peek side. Even so, after a visit to the United States, where he was impressed by their employment, Arthur Carr was able to recruit female clerks into the office. In 1901, with the disappearance of the obstructive partners, the Carrs registered Peek Frean & Co. Ltd as a limited company. Since John Carr was now elderly and the diffident Ellis immersed himself in production, Arthur Carr thereafter dominated the company. At first a joint managing director with his brother, in 1904 he became chairman and sole managing director. He used his organizing talents and energies not only to build the company up into an industry leader, but also to create contacts with the rest of the biscuit industry.

In particular, Carr launched important new varieties of biscuit, and backed them with innovative advertising and publicity schemes. These included the enduringly successful Pat-a-Cake of 1902, of the novel shortcake type. The first ever cream sandwich biscuit, the Bourbon, followed in 1910 and the Custard Cream in 1913. A range of the company's assortments also caught the public's fancy.

Realizing the importance of marketing, Carr spent freely on newspaper and display advertising, which featured catchy slogans such as 'For goodness sake, eat Pat-a-Cake'. Among his ingenious publicity stunts, he treated some 20,000 London grocers to a free outing at the Crystal Palace, and sent 200,000 picture postcards to housewives up and down the country, with alluring (and frequently misinterpreted) messages which turned out to be about gift schemes. A 33-minute film of the company's activities (1904) was one of the earliest of its kind to be made in Britain. Deplored by rivals, such wheezes helped to double the company's sales between 1900 and 1913 and almost quadrupled profits.

Carr tirelessly strove for closer co-operation with similar companies in spite of remaining outside the Association of Biscuit Manufacturers, set up in 1903 to counter the increasing power of grocers. He had more ambitious plans for the industry: to corral member firms into a huge biscuit combine, like those in soap and tobacco. His idea was both to end cut-throat competition and to improve the low wages in the industry. In 1912 Carr unavailingly wooed Huntley and Palmers, the potential leader in any combine; and he was no more successful in discussions with the Scottish and Irish firms manufacturing 'quality' biscuits.

The post-war problems of high income tax and death duties persuaded the directors of Huntley and Palmers in 1921 to merge with Peek Frean into the Associated Biscuit Manufacturers Ltd. Within this holding company both units maintained their own production and marketing strategies. Carr was first vice-chairman, becoming chairman in 1923. No other company joined them. Carr retired in 1927, when turnover of Peek Frean was nearly £2 million, with profits of £230,000: both greater than those of Huntley and Palmers. He nevertheless continued to go into the office, declaring that he 'would be seen as before' (*DBB*).

In appearance, his gold pince-nez and high collar stamped Carr as essentially Victorian in habit and outlook. As a youngster, he had ridden into work from Clapham on horseback; later he could be seen boarding a

London bus just like any ordinary commuter. He found the intrusions of the telephone and unheralded visitors distasteful. Like his father before him, he concerned himself with all aspects of his employees' lives. From 1889 the company had in-house medical facilities, justified by him as 'a business proposition'. In 1905 free dental and optician's services were added. He organized an evening school for the younger hands. A keen cricketer until well into the 1890s, he also established a sports club in 1905 and became chairman. In 1922 he and his brother jointly gave £10,000 to set up an employees' benevolent club. Seven years later they introduced a pensions scheme with donations totalling £130,000.

Carr kept free of public commitments, and therefore remained unknown to the wider world. His many outside benefactions were either anonymous or made unobtrusively. When he died at his home, 10 The Downs, Wimbledon, on 23 May 1947, neither the local nor national press seems to have noticed his passing.   T. A. B. CORLEY

Sources T. A. B. Corley, 'Carr, Arthur', *DBB* · F. C. Davis, 'Historical survey of Peek Frean & Co. Ltd, 1857–1957', typescript, 1957, U. Reading · 'Souvenir of Mr Arthur Carr's fifty years' association with Peek Frean & Co.', *Biscuit Box* (5 Dec 1922) · E. Carr, 'Reminiscences', *Biscuit Box*, 16–17 (1931–4) · T. A. B. Corley, *Quaker enterprise in biscuits: Huntley and Palmer of Reading, 1822–1972* (1972) · m. cert. · d. cert. · b. cert.

Archives U. Reading L., Peek Frean archives

Likenesses photograph, 1920, U. Reading L., Peek Frean Archives

Wealth at death £630,206 8s. 5d.: probate, 25 Oct 1947, *CGPLA Eng. & Wales*

Carr, Sir Arthur Strettell Comyns (1882–1965), barrister and politician, was born on 19 September 1882 at 19 Blandford Square, Marylebone, London, the son of Joseph William Comyns *Carr (1849–1916), a barrister and later a dramatist and art critic, and his wife, Alice Laura Vansittart, *née* Strettell (1850–1927), a novelist. The artistic and theatrical circles in which his family moved were described in his mother's memoirs, *Mrs J. Comyns Carr's Reminiscences* (1926). Carr, as he was then known (he later adopted the surname Comyns Carr), was educated at Winchester College and Trinity College, Oxford, where he took a second in classical moderations (1903) and a second in *literae humaniores* (1905). On 19 October 1907 he married Cicely Oriana Raikes Bromage (*d.* 10 Oct 1935), the daughter of Richard Raikes Bromage, clerk in holy orders; they had three sons.

In 1908 Comyns Carr was called to the bar at Gray's Inn of which he later became a bencher and treasurer. He acquired 'a good "rough and tumble" practice', both civil and criminal, and a reputation as a 'bold and persistent' cross-examiner who feared 'neither judges nor eminent opponents' (*The Times*, 21 April 1965). He came to notice in 1922 when, still a junior, he conducted the defence in the libel case brought by the financier and publicist Horatio Bottomley against his one-time associate Reuben Bigland. Comyns Carr handled his brief 'with considerable skill, keeping his temper despite Mr Bottomley's provocative

efforts' (Biron, 355). His cross-examination of a key witness exposed Bottomley's perjury and broke his case, leading to his eventual imprisonment on charges of fraudulent conversion.

Comyns Carr afterwards specialized in rating law and appeared in a number of important rating appeals. He acted as counsel to several government offices and became an expert in the subject of national insurance. He was co-author, with W. H. Stuart Garnett and J. H. Taylor, of *National Insurance* (1912), to which Lloyd George wrote a preface. He was a member of the Liberal land inquiry committee (1912), chaired by Arthur Acland, and of the land acquisition committee (1917). In 1924 he was appointed king's counsel.

Comyns Carr combined a versatile legal career with regular forays into politics. A lifelong Liberal and at one time president of the Liberal Candidates' Association he stood for parliament on no fewer than eleven occasions, winning only once, and losing to a Conservative at the other ten attempts. His first candidature was at St Pancras South West, for which he was adopted in June 1914. At the outbreak of war he joined the Royal Naval Volunteer Reserve and was later on the staff at the Ministry of Munitions, and an adviser to the Ministry of Reconstruction. In the last months of the war he joined the army as a private soldier and served with a home-based unit. Somewhat opportunistically, he described himself in his election literature in December 1918 as 'Private Comyns Carr'. This drew thinly veiled contempt from his Conservative opponent, Captain R. W. Barnett, who won the seat convincingly. Comyns Carr, however, polled respectably and contested the seat again in 1922. His sole victory came at Islington East in December 1923 when he won with a majority of 1632. He worked assiduously during his short time in parliament, but could make little real impact before losing the seat at the general election of 1924. In the polarized atmosphere of that poll Conservative and Labour candidates gained at Liberal expense throughout the country, and at Islington he came last, with less than a quarter of the votes cast. Undeterred, he contested Ilford at a by-election in 1928 and again at the general election in the following year.

In 1930 Comyns Carr attracted considerable attention with the publication of a pamphlet, *Escape from the Dole*, which questioned why the unemployment fund should not be used to create employment instead of simply maintaining those who were out of work. By subsidizing firms that employed a full workforce Comyns Carr hoped to regenerate the economy, and on the strength of his pamphlet he appeared as a witness before the royal commission on unemployment insurance on 26 February 1931. *The Times*, though, was less than satisfied that his plan would work, pointing out that a subsidy of production costs undercut one of the basic principles on which the economy functioned, and that the fund would inevitably soon be exhausted. At the general election in that year Comyns Carr stood against Winston Churchill at Epping, a near hopeless contest, and in 1935 he suffered his worst defeat when he polled less than 17 per cent of the vote at Nottingham East. He unsuccessfully contested Shrewsbury at the 1945 general election, the City of London at a by-election that October, and, finally, Berwick upon Tweed, Northumberland, in the general election of 1950.

After the Second World War, Comyns Carr was chief British prosecutor on the international military tribunal for the Far East, where he led the prosecution of Japanese war criminals. He was said to have been deeply affected by the experience but believed that such trials, by upholding international law in an international tribunal, were of 'the utmost importance, not so much in relation to the past as to the future' (*The Times*, 4 Aug 1948, 3b). In Hamburg in August 1949 he led the case against Field Marshal von Manstein, one of the last of the German generals to be tried, and that year he was knighted for his work as a prosecutor. Comyns Carr served as chairman of the Foreign Compensation Commission from 1950 to 1958 and was a president of the Institute of Industrial Administration and of the Association of Approved Societies. He was president of the Liberal Party in 1958–9, and in this capacity chaired the party conference at Torquay in 1958. He died on 20 April 1965 at 11a Maresfield Gardens, Hampstead, London.   MARK POTTLE

Sources *The Times* (7 Feb 1912), 7d · *The Times* (9 Dec 1918), ELS, 1e · *The Times* (10 Dec 1918), 10d · *The Times* (8 Dec 1923), ELS, 1c · *The Times* (5 Aug 1930), 6e · *The Times* (27 Feb 1931), 8d · *The Times* (27 March 1931) · *The Times* (14 Oct 1935), 20b · *The Times* (15 Jan 1948) · *The Times* (4 Aug 1948), 3b · *The Times* (12 May 1949) · *The Times* (9 June 1949), 5f · *The Times* (21 June 1949), 3c · *The Times* (16 July 1949) · *The Times* (17 Aug 1949) · *The Times* (26 Nov 1951) · *The Times* (19 Sept 1958) · *The Times* (21 April 1965) · R. Douglas, 'Sir Arthur Comyns Carr', *Dictionary of liberal biography*, ed. D. Brack and others (1998) · F. W. S. Craig, *British parliamentary election results, 1918–1949*, rev. edn (1977) · F. W. S. Craig, *British parliamentary election results, 1950–1970* (1971) · WWBMP, vol. 3 · C. Biron, *Without prejudice: impressions of life and law* (1936) · b. cert. · m. cert. · d. cert. · Burke, *Peerage* (1959)
Wealth at death £28,015: probate, 11 June 1965, CGPLA Eng. & Wales

Carr, Barbara Irene Veronica Comyns [*née* Barbara Irene Veronica Bayley; *pseud.* Barbara Comyns] **(1907–1992)**, writer, was born on 27 December 1907 at Bell Court, Bidford-on-Avon, Warwickshire, the fourth among the six children (five girls and one boy) of Albert Edward Bayley (*d.* 1922), a Birmingham brewer and industrialist, and his wife, Margaret Eva Mary, *née* Fenn. Her childhood was described in her first book, *Sisters by a River* (1947), a memoir that evokes both the enchantment and the darker dimensions of her early family life. Having married at seventeen a much older and ostensibly a more wealthy man, Margaret Bayley lost her hearing in the trauma of her final confinement and remained deaf for the rest of her life. She communicated with her children through sign language and strange little notes left around the house, which suggest that her handicap exaggerated her wayward thinking. The marriage was turbulent, her husband drank too much, and, like so many at the time, the family declined from bourgeois security through poverty into debt. The tragic vulnerability of women, especially to the cruelty of men, later became a major theme in Barbara Comyns's work.

The Bayley girls were ineffectually educated by a succession of governesses. After the death of her father when she was fifteen, Barbara, intending to be a painter, attended art school, first in Stratford upon Avon. She then won a scholarship to the Heatherley School of Fine Art in London, a college which, unusually for the time, employed live models for life drawing. She found work in an animation studio drawing cartoons, and, inspired by the literature she had read in public libraries, also began to write, although she found her early work too derivative and destroyed it all when she married.

On 30 May 1931 she married John Francis Pemberton (*b.* 1909/10), a painter not destined for success. Barbara lost her job when she told her boss she was expecting a baby. Their son, Julian, was born in 1932, followed by a daughter, Caroline, in 1935. The couple's struggles later became the basis of her first novel, *Our Spoons Came from Woolworths* (1950). Over the next few years Barbara lived in London and supported her family in many ways: renovating pianos, trading antiques, working as a cook, dealing in classic cars, breeding poodle puppies, converting flats, and—having considerable beauty—modelling for artists and photographers. For a while during the Second World War, her marriage having broken down, she lived with Arthur Price, a benevolent and mildly disreputable character who later became the basis of her last novel, *Mr Fox* (1987). When the blitz came and a flying bomb landed in her Hampstead garden, Barbara left London with her family and took a job as a cook in a country house. It was there, living in a tied cottage, that she began to write notes of her own childhood to amuse her children.

Divorced from John Pemberton, Barbara married on 29 August 1945 Richard Strettel Comyns Carr (*b.* 1908/9), a Foreign Office official and the grandson of a prominent QC and playwright. Thinking that her full married surname of Comyns Carr was too long to appear on a book jacket, she chose to use Barbara Comyns as a shorter, more convenient pen-name. On their honeymoon in a cottage in Wales she began another novel, eventually published as *The Vet's Daughter* (1959), but put it aside in favour of a biography of the painter Leigh Hunt, which never found a publisher.

Meanwhile, at the encouragement of a friend, Comyns collected the fragments of the memoir of her childhood, which she had put away in a suitcase containing old photographs, and sent them to publishers. The honesty, even relish, with which she related a pre-war middle-class household, complete with cruelty, violence, drunkenness, and attempted murder, did not accord with the post-war craving for normality, so at first the proposed book met with no success. *Lilliput* magazine eventually serialized extracts under the title 'The Novel Nobody will Publish'. These were read by the literary adviser to Eyre and Spottiswode, who subsequently published the whole text in 1947 under the title *Sisters by a River*. Although the family's descent from luxury to poverty provides a narrative thread, *Sisters by a River* is a collection of sketches rather than a novel. The mood meanders from pastoral beauty, nursery escapades, kittens, strawberries, new frocks, and childish treats to surreal terrors, macabre discoveries, violence, and cruelty. Fantasy interludes are given the weight of reality, as in a scene where a magic twig gives two five-year-olds the power of levitation. These random transitions, which occur often within a few sentences, convey vividly a world viewed with a child's understanding. Critics responded warmly to *Sisters by a River*, but Comyns was annoyed that, to enhance the childlike tone of the book, her publishers made a feature of her eccentric spelling. While her naïve vision remained part of the charm of her writing, Comyns later ensured that her husband edited her work.

The success of *Sisters by a River*, added to the happiness and security of the Comyns Carr marriage, encouraged a prolific period which first produced *Our Spoons Came from Woolworths*. This novel tells the tragic tale of Sophia and Charles, two young London bohemians whose marriage is too ephemeral to survive on love, art, and idealism alone. Although a more disciplined and mature work than Comyns's first book, it is as much autobiographical as fictional, with only a few wholly imaginary incidents, such as the Dickensian horror of the scene in which the rejected and feverish young wife collapses in a doorway with her child dying in her arms. Comyns found confidence to complete *The Vet's Daughter*, her most admired work of pure fiction. It was serialized by BBC Radio, adapted for the stage, and turned into a musical, *The Clapham Wonder*, by Sandy Wilson. London life in Edwardian Battersea, in a household losing its grip on middle-class values, is viewed through the eyes of the narrator, Alice. From childhood onwards her sadistic father and vulgar stepmother destroy her faint chances of happiness. In the final pages, impelled by sheer terror of her father, the young woman flies into the air above Clapham Common, drawing a large number of onlookers. When she falls to earth she and her malevolent stepmother are trampled to death in the crowd. Next Comyns wrote *Who was Changed and who was Dead* (1954), a novel inspired by newspaper reports of an epidemic of ergot poisoning in a French village. She relocated the story to the Warwickshire village of her childhood and imagined a macabre fantasy in which the river floods and the villagers are driven murderously insane.

Comyns had little time to enjoy the success of her work, however. Her husband's Whitehall superior, indeed the owner of their honeymoon cottage, was Kim Philby, now exposed as the mastermind of the Cambridge spy ring. Association with Philby ended Richard Comyns Carr's career and the family faced not only poverty but also scandal. They moved to Spain, where they lived for eighteen years, first in Barcelona and later in Andalucia. Their flight produced another memoir, *Out of the Red and into the Blue* (1960), which was followed by three more novels, *The Skin Chairs* (1962), *Birds in Tiny Cages* (1964), and *A Touch of Mistletoe* (1967), in which Barbara responded, perhaps unwisely,

to her publisher's request for something 'less macabre' (private information).

In the early 1980s, when the feminist imprint Virago republished Barbara's early work, the Comyns Carrs returned to England to live in the Richmond area, in homes where she always insisted on painting the ceiling of one room blue with white or gold stars. This move also inspired a renaissance in Comyns's writing, and she produced three more novels: *The Juniper Tree* (1985), *The House of Dolls* (1989), and finally *Mr Fox*.

After a short illness, Barbara Comyns died at 14 Stanton Cottages, Stanton upon Hine Heath, Shrewsbury, Shropshire, on 15 July 1992, and was buried at Stanton church. As a writer, her surreal imagination, elliptical style, and delicate lyricism foreshadowed the magic realist school and provide a record of bohemian life in London in the mid-twentieth century. In life, her unique charm, vivacity, and courage won her loyal friends but not the recognition of the literary establishment; she remains an unjustly neglected author.   CELIA BRAYFIELD

Sources private information (2004) [Caroline Urbano, daughter] · B. Comyns, *Sisters by a river* (2000) · B. Comyns, *Our spoons came from Woolworths* (2000) · K. Saunders, 'Mad Hatter's tea party', *Books and Bookmen* (June 1989) · C. Moorehead, 'Afloat, with a down-to-earth girl called Alice', *The Times* (28 Jan 1981) · b. cert. · m. certs. · d. cert.

Likenesses photograph, News Int. RO; repro. in Moorehead, 'Afloat, with a down-to-earth girl called Alice' · photograph, repro. in Saunders, 'Mad Hatter's tea party' · photographs, priv. coll.

Carr, Sir Cecil Thomas (1878–1966), lawyer, was born at Poolemeade, Twerton, near Bath, on 4 August 1878, the younger son in the family of two sons and two daughters of Thomas Carr, a cloth manufacturer of Twerton, and his wife, Susan Arnell Creed. Educated first at Bath College under T. W. Dunn, who made boys enjoy working to their limits and gained their lasting devotion, Carr kept alive an association of old boys more than fifty years after the school closed.

In 1897 Carr went to Trinity College, Cambridge, with an exhibition soon converted into a scholarship. He was placed in the second division of the first class of part one of the classical tripos in 1899—and the classics remained a resource throughout his life—and in the third class of part two of the law tripos in 1901. Called to the bar by the Inner Temple in 1902, he practised on the western circuit; and although his practice was still small when war broke out, private means had enabled him in 1911 to contract his happy marriage with Norah, daughter of the civil engineer Sir Alexander R. Binnie. There were no children of the marriage.

His early years as a barrister, with comparatively few briefs, allowed Carr time to write. He twice won the Cambridge Yorke prize (in 1902 and 1905) with books published as *The General Principles of the Law of Corporations* (1905) and *Collective Ownership* (1907); and F. W. Maitland entrusted him with a Selden Society volume, which appeared in 1913 as *Select Charters of Trading Companies*. More light-heartedly Carr regularly entered for literary

Sir Cecil Thomas Carr (1878–1966), by Walter Stoneman, 1947

competitions, developing the lugubrious wit characteristic of his letters and speeches. He was good enough at various games to be an occasional recruit for county sides, and organized a cricket team for west country tours which inspired a series in *Punch* by A. A. Milne, one of his regular players; a tall, awkward character seems to be based on Carr.

Carr joined the 2nd / 4th Wiltshire regiment in September 1914, and spent the war in staff appointments in India. A year before he proceeded to the degree of LLD, Cambridge, in 1919 he became assistant to the editor and in 1923 editor of the Revised Statutes and of the statutory rules and orders (later called Statutory Instruments). His appointment followed from the chance recollection of his qualities by a former member of his chambers; and his main quality was a determination to make something of whatever engaged him. His duties lay in the edition and consolidation of the growing mass of delegated legislation, and in the consolidation of the statute book; and without the staff which Carr was later instrumental in securing for his successors most men would have been proud just to keep up with the work. But not Carr: with delegated legislation he made it his business to understand each item, and caught many flaws which had passed departmental muster; and with the Revised Statutes he hunted down suspect enactments, verified that they were obsolete, and himself drafted statute law revision bills.

Ultimately more important than his official duties was Carr's work in focusing thought on the problems of delegated legislation. He was one of the founders of administrative law in England, and played some part in the United States. This originated with three lectures given in Cambridge in 1921, subsequently published as *Delegated Legislation* (1921). When a congressional committee was considering the systematic notification of administrative regulations in the United States, a travelling fellowship was arranged which took Carr in 1935 to Washington, where he advised on techniques for the *Federal Register*, first published in 1936. This journey took him also to universities in the east and mid-west, where talks enhanced his reputation and gained him many friendships. In 1940 he gave the Carpentier lectures at Columbia University, published on both sides of the Atlantic in 1941 as *Concerning English Administrative Law*. Paradoxically this book was influential in England precisely because it was not addressed to English lawyers. Its historical detachment showed them the point they had reached after Lord Hewart's *The New Despotism* (1929) and the *Report of the Committee on Ministers' Powers* (1932). Ignoring slogans for and against the inevitable, Carr addressed the actual problems. It is the spirit in which the subject has since grown; though one might wish that Carr's imagination and values could also have been perpetuated.

In 1943, at an age when most men retire, Carr became counsel to the speaker, an office largely concerned with private bills. In securing procedural improvements generally, and in the passage of individual bills, Carr's resourceful helpfulness was widely appreciated. It was also extensively used. From 1944 to 1947 he headed a committee considering the law about parliamentary and local elections. From 1943 to 1965 he served on the statute law committee, and helped initiate more radical consolidation of the statute book. And in 1944 his experience with delegated legislation was again enlisted: the 'watchdog' select committee then set up was granted the assistance of speaker's counsel, and Carr did much to settle the principles upon which it was to act.

Carr retired in 1955 at the age of seventy-seven. He was knighted in 1939 and became KCB in 1947. He became bencher of the Inner Temple in 1944 and KC in 1945. He received honorary degrees from Columbia in 1940, London in 1952, and the Queen's University of Belfast in 1954; and he became fellow of the British Academy in 1952, and honorary fellow of Trinity College, Cambridge, in 1963. From 1943 to 1956 he was election secretary, then chairman, of the Athenaeum. From 1958 to 1961 he was president of the Selden Society, editing for it after almost fifty years a second volume, *Pension Book of Clement's Inn* (1960), and travelling to Washington in 1960 to address American members. A year earlier he had captained a team sent to the United States by the Senior Golfers' Society, of which he later became president, to compete with their North American counterparts; and at the age of eighty-two he combined this with addresses to the American Philosophical Society and two law schools.

Carr played golf, on the course beside which he lived at Rock in Cornwall, almost to the end. No less energetic was his reading, also kept up to the end. As in his Westminster offices, everything was digested into untidy piles of clear notes which he could always find but rarely needed: what mattered remained in his head. He was offered an academic post when the First World War ended; and had he accepted, the problems of English public law might have been identified more clearly, more quickly, and much more quietly. But there is no saying what would have been lost without the practical authority exercised during a critical period by a shy man whose few words were always so compelling. Carr died on 12 May 1966 in the Nuffield Nursing Home, Wanford Road, Exeter. He was survived by his wife.   S. F. C. MILSOM, *rev.*

Sources H. A. Holland, 'Cecil Thomas Carr, 1878–1966', *PBA*, 52 (1966), 311–21 · *The Times* (14 May 1966) · *CGPLA Eng. & Wales* (1966) · Venn, *Alum. Cant.* · b. cert. · personal knowledge (2004)
Archives Bodl. Oxf., letters to A. L. Goodhart
Likenesses W. Stoneman, photograph, 1947, NPG [*see illus.*] · photograph, repro. in Holland, *PBA* · photographs, NPG
Wealth at death £162,336—save and except settled land: probate, 22 Aug 1966, *CGPLA Eng. & Wales* · £10—limited to settled land: probate, 14 Nov 1966, *CGPLA Eng. & Wales*

Carr, Edward Hallett (1892–1982), historian and diplomatist, was born at 62 Gladsmuir Road, Upper Holloway, London, on 28 June 1892, the first of three children, to Francis Parker Carr (*d.* 1945), who worked in the family business of Carr's Inks, and Elizabeth Jessie, *née* Hallett. A scholar at Merchant Taylors' School, London, from 1906, he won an entrance scholarship to Trinity College, Cambridge, and went up in October 1911 to read classics. After illness abruptly curtailed his studies, he none the less won the Porson prize and the Craven scholarship and took a first in both parts of the tripos (1915–16). The country had been at war since 1914. Because of previous illness Carr was judged unsuitable for the fighting services and instead was recruited as a temporary clerk at the Foreign Office, where he worked in the all-encompassing contraband department that organized the blockade against the central powers. His remit extended to Russia, where he worked to get goods in (while they fought the Germans) and later to keep goods out (once the Bolsheviks seized power). He served at the Paris peace conference and its succeeding conference of allied ambassadors (1919–22), being made CBE for his efforts in 1920.

Still only a third secretary but very much a specialist on central and east European affairs, Carr was transferred back to London in 1922. On the eve of his departure for Riga as second secretary in January 1925 he hastily married, on the 22nd, Anne Rowe, *née* Ward (*d.* 1961), the widow of Gilbert Rowe, a close acquaintance made during official tours of eastern Europe to review territorial problems still outstanding. Anne brought with her three children: Rachel (*b.* 1917), Philippa (*b.* 1919), and Martin (*b.* 1921). To these Carr added John (*b.* 1926). Riga was entirely uneventful except for Carr's mastery of Russian, which resulted in a memorable biography of Dostoevsky (1931), a

Edward Hallett Carr (1892–1982), by Elliott & Fry

delightful portrait of Herzen and his circle, *The Romantic Exiles* (1933), and a penetrating study of Bakunin (1937).

After returning to London in 1929, Carr also began reviewing and writing (under the *nom de plume* John Hallett) on both Russian industrialization, which caught his interest, and German affairs, which fell within his purview in the Foreign Office. It was Hitler's attempt to break out of the constraints created by the allies in 1919 (of which Carr strongly disapproved) that seized his attention and resulted in the first 'realist' monograph on international relations in the twentieth century: *The Twenty Years' Crisis* (1939). That treatise, still widely read worldwide and still somewhat shocking to untutored minds, was made possible only by leaving the Foreign Office and taking up the Woodrow Wilson chair in international politics at the University of Wales in Aberystwyth in 1936, which he held until 1947. Although rarely noted, Carr's speedily constructed text *International Relations since the Peace Treaties* (1937) is a model of clarity and compression, explaining the main events of those years from the unusual vantage point of access to Foreign Office records which were not declassified for another thirty years.

Once again war supervened, and after a false start at the Ministry of Information Carr joined *The Times* as a leader writer on foreign affairs in 1940, graduating to assistant editor when Barrington-Ward finally succeeded Dawson to the chair in the following year. It was here that Carr made his most dramatic impact on public opinion with the publication of 'The two scourges', about war and unemployment, in December 1940. Henceforth his advocacy of radical social reform matched the mood of the country and paved the way for the Beveridge report of 1942 and Labour's victory in 1945. His writing on foreign affairs was no less significant or controversial. Under Carr *The Times* became the platform for pressing on a reluctant prime minister (Churchill) the policy of accommodation with the Soviet Union in its desire for a protectorate over eastern Europe at the war's end. Much of the rationale for both this and social reform was also expressed in the best-selling *Conditions of Peace* (1942). Carr's prognostications on the importance of economic and social planning on a European scale, free of editorial constraint, appeared later, as he withdrew from *The Times*, in *Nationalism and after* (1945) and his Oxford lectures, *The Soviet Impact on the Western World* (1946). A sequel appeared with his BBC lectures in 1951 in the form of *The New Society* which was, however, subsequently more notable as the precursor to his iconoclastic polemic *What is History?* (1961), delivered as the Trevelyan lectures at Cambridge, where he had moved as senior research fellow at Trinity in 1955. From 1947 he had to live by his writing. With the exception of two years (1953–5) at Balliol College, Oxford, he was effectively something of an outcast, and even there not entirely viewed without suspicion, his views on the Soviet Union scarcely in tune with the severe deterioration in the political climate following the Berlin blockade (1948–9), which had been worsened still further by the outbreak of war in Korea (1950).

By then, however, the urge to dig more deeply into the Soviet experiment had enveloped Carr in full-time historical research and in writing what became a massively detailed fourteen-tome *History of Soviet Russia* (1950–78), researched and written with the help of several able hands including, latterly, R. W. Davies and Tamara, widow of the biographer Isaac Deutscher. The *History* was later crisply summarized as a textbook, *The Russian Revolution from Lenin to Stalin* (1979). The premiss for the work was that the Soviet Union was as legitimate a subject of study as England under Henry VIII; that the Soviet experience had something to teach mankind; and that the system in some form was here to stay. As time went on, the first assumption took hold and opened up a field of research to many scholars who had had no idea that such work was practicable; the second assumption gradually fell away or was subsumed under lessons for less developed countries which have now largely been discarded; and the final assumption collapsed with the downfall of the Soviet Union in August 1991. By then, however, Carr had died, leaving behind him a partially completed history of the Communist International—*Twilight of Comintern* (1982) and *The Comintern and the Spanish Civil War* (1984). The latter was pulled together for publication by Tamara Deutscher.

Carr's intellectual journey had been occasioned by an accident of fate through what he witnessed from afar at the Foreign Office in 1917. As a result his life became extraordinarily fruitful, packed with controversy at every step, and left a great deal to posterity; but a price was paid in terms of his private life. He left Anne at the end of the war, and cohabited with Joyce Marion Forde, *née* Stock (*b.* 1903), who was the jilted wife of the noted anthropologist (Cyril)

Daryll Forde, until January 1964. He then married (Catherine) Betty Abigail *Behrens (1904–1989), historian of France, on 10 December 1966, only to part with her in the summer before his death, which occurred at a nursing home in Queen Edith's Way, Cambridge, on 4 November 1982; he was cremated at Cambridge crematorium in Huntingdon Road.

Fervently individualist, ferociously intelligent, and scrupulously honest, Carr was by nature reserved and taciturn. Burdened by emotions with which he found it difficult to cope, he was always more relaxed in writing than in conversation. He none the less had a mordant wit and a certain charm when he chose to exercise it, delighting in gossip yet without ever entirely escaping a sense of guilt—doubtless stemming from a strict Victorian upbringing—at such reckless indulgence. No one ever claimed that he was boring.   JONATHAN HASLAM

Sources J. Haslam, *The vices of integrity: E. H. Carr, 1892–1982* (1999) · R. Davies, *PBA*, 69 (1983), 473–511 · J. Haslam, 'We need a faith', *History Today* (1983) · T. Deutscher, 'Remembering E. H. Carr', *New Left Review*, 137 (Jan–Feb 1983) · M. Cox, ed., *E. H. Carr: a critical appraisal* (2000) · *CGPLA Eng. & Wales* (1983)
Archives CAC Cam., corresp. and papers · U. Birm. L., papers and appointment diaries | Internationaal Instituut voor Sociale Geschiedenis, corresp. with Isaac Deutscher · News Int. RO, papers relating to his work on *The Times* newspaper
Likenesses Elliott & Fry, photograph, NPG [*see illus.*]
Wealth at death £153,058: probate, 25 Feb 1983, *CGPLA Eng. & Wales*

Carr, Sir (William) Emsley (1867–1941), newspaper proprietor and philanthropist, was born on 1 May 1867 at 9 Hunslet Road, Hunslet, Leeds, Yorkshire, the eldest son of Thomas Hay Carr, a cloth manufacturer, and his wife, Sarah Jane Emsley. Educated in his native city, he became a journalist when summoned to Cardiff by his uncle, Lascelles Carr, co-founder and first editor of the *Western Mail*. In 1891 a syndicate headed by Lascelles Carr purchased the *News of the World*, an ailing Sunday scandal sheet founded nearly half a century earlier. The new proprietor dispatched his nephew to London as editor. However, Carr's arrival in Fleet Street did not terminate his close connection with the *Western Mail* and its associate newspapers: he remained their chief political correspondent until well into the 1930s. Business and family links were consolidated when he married Lascelles's daughter, Jennifer Lascelles (Jenny) Carr, on 19 June 1895. Not long after this he became deputy chairman of the parent company, Western Mail and Echo Ltd.

The *Western Mail*'s legal representative in London, George *Riddell, became a major shareholder in the *News of the World*, working zealously to boost sales of the new enterprise. Riddell and Carr formed an effective partnership, yet were curiously reticent in acknowledging the scale of their enterprise. Although weekly sales were well over 1 million by the early 1900s, and quadrupled over the next four decades, the *News of the World* never publicly acknowledged the full extent of its commercial success. Before the First World War Sabbath-day publication was regularly denounced in the pulpit. Even after all but the

Sir (William) Emsley Carr (1867–1941), by unknown photographer

most fervent evangelist had acknowledged a seven-day hunger for news, the best-selling Sunday newspapers were still frowned upon within polite circles. Unlike Riddell, whose death in 1934 enabled the Carr family to consolidate their control of the publishing company, the editor and eventual chairman and managing director was always sensitive to middle-class opinion. Knighted in 1918 as reward for his wartime charity work supporting Welsh troops, particularly those captured by the enemy, Carr was a pillar of respectability, successfully distancing himself from even the sauciest front page story. In 1938 he was appointed high sheriff of Glamorgan. When in May 1941 he celebrated fifty years as an editor, Carr found himself enthusiastically toasted by the prime minister and warmly congratulated by the king.

One of the first provincial correspondents at Westminster to gain admittance to the lobby, Carr was a respected pioneer of modern parliamentary reporting, and in 1930–31 he became chairman of the press gallery. He also helped to found the Institute of Journalists, eventually becoming a fellow and in 1932–3 serving as president. Carr took special responsibility within the institute for ensuring that all journalists were adequately provided for in their retirement, and he undertook a similar role in chairing both the Newspaper Press Fund and the Printers Pension Corporation. He was a delegate at the Imperial Press Conference in Canada in 1925, and again five years later in Australia. As a leading figure in the Empire Press Union, Carr also travelled widely across the Indian subcontinent.

An inveterate traveller as well as a reporter, the editor vacated his chair to report on the stalemate in France, the surrender of the German fleet at Scapa Flow in 1919, and the subsequent peace conference in Paris.

As chairman of the Alfred Robbins Lodge, Carr raised large sums of money for the Royal Masonic Hospital Fund, fulfilling a similar role for the Royal Free Hospital, in acknowledgement of which he was made a life governor. His sponsorship of such annual athletics events as the Emsley Carr Mile is a lasting reminder that he loved sport almost as much as he loved newspapers. His involvement in athletics, and in particular middle-distance running, extended to the organization of the British games, and the selection and preparation of national teams to compete in both the empire games and the Olympic games.

From track to links was but a short stride: witness Carr's vice-presidency of the Professional Golfers' Association, one of several honorary posts awarded for his service to the sport. A member of St Andrew's Royal and Ancient, and chairman of Lloyd George's favourite club, Walton Heath, Carr used golf to bring politicians and the press together in convivial surroundings: he promoted the parliamentary golf tournament, and was president of the Newspapers and Advertisers Golfers Society. A scratch player, Carr was as successful on the greens as off them: his happiest tournament win was probably the press gallery's Arnott cup.

Carr lived only a short distance from the Walton Heath golf course, and he died at his Surrey country residence, Wonford, Walton on the Hill, on 31 July 1941. He was buried at St Dunstan-in-the-West, Fleet Street, London, on 5 August 1941. His wife, Jenny, survived him. Their family comprised two daughters and six sons, of whom the oldest had died in action during the First World War. Their third son, Harry, followed a similar career path to his father, but service in the RAF prevented an early return to the *News of the World*. Harry's death in August 1943 left the fourth son, Sir William Emsley *Carr (1912–1977), as the family's senior representative on the board of an unusually lucrative newspaper enterprise: his father's sensationalist Sunday broadsheet was to emerge from the Second World War with liquid assets of over £2 million, an unprecedented rate of profitability, and weekly sales of approximately 7.5 million. A man of many talents, Sir Emsley Carr had in the course of half a century quietly created the biggest-selling newspaper in the western world.

ADRIAN SMITH

Sources Viscount Camrose [W. E. Berry], *British newspapers and their controllers*, rev. edn (1948), 81–5 · *The Times* (1 Aug 1941) · *The Times* (2 Aug 1941) · *The Times* (6 Aug 1941) · *WWW, 1941–50* · M. Engel, *Tickle the public: one hundred years of the popular press* (1996), 212–29 · C. Bainbridge and R. Stockdill, *The News of the World story* (1993) · b. cert. · m. cert. · d. cert.
Likenesses photograph, NPG [*see illus.*]

Carr, Frances. *See* Howard, Frances (1590–1632).

Carr, Frank Osmond (1858–1916), composer, was born on 23 April 1858 in the school house, Kirkstall, Hunslet, Yorkshire, the second son of George Saxton Carr, a schoolmaster, and his wife, Margaret Durden Carr, *née* Painter. He matriculated at New College, Oxford, in 1877 and graduated BMus in 1884, having meanwhile been accepted at Downing College, Cambridge, in 1882 and gained a BA there in 1883. In 1885 he entered Trinity College, Cambridge, and gained an MA and BMus in 1886, before returning to Oxford, where he finally received his DMus in 1891. He made an initial foray into the London musical theatre in 1889 with the burlesque comic opera *Faddimir*, which he composed under the pseudonym Oscar Neville in collaboration with his fellow Cambridge graduate Arthur Reed Ropes (1859–1933), who was to become known as Adrian Ross, the lyricist. The work brought Carr to the attention of the impresario George Edwardes, and led to commissions for the scores of the burlesque *Joan of Arc, or, The Merry Maid of Orleans* (1891) and the musical farce *In Town* (1892). Part comic opera, part variety show, the latter had a score by Carr that was praised for its pretty ballads, tuneful songs, and sprightly dances. It ran for several months and came to be regarded as the first modern-dress 'musical comedy'. A successor, *Morocco Bound* (1893), ran for even longer and resulted in Carr being selected as the collaborator of W. S. Gilbert on the more ambitious comic opera *His Excellency* (1894). Inevitably Carr was judged no match for Sullivan, though the work achieved a fair international success. Thereafter Carr's star declined almost as rapidly as it had risen. He composed scores for several further musical shows, including *Lord Tom Noddy* (1896) for Little Tich, but these were either unsuccessful in London or confined to the provinces. His other published compositions included songs, instrumental pieces, and the score for the ballet *Sir Roger de Coverley*, produced at the Empire Theatre in 1907. In later years he sought in vain to revise his older successes for production in the currently popular revue style. In August 1916 he left London to spend some time in the country but died suddenly of a heart attack at the Chequers Hotel, Uxbridge, on 29 August.   ANDREW LAMB

Sources K. Gänzl, *The encyclopedia of the musical theatre*, 2nd edn, 3 vols. (2001) • J. Parker, ed., *Who's who in the theatre*, 3rd edn (1916) • Venn, *Alum. Cant.* • *The Stage* (31 Aug 1916) • b. cert. • d. cert.
Wealth at death £181 18s. 8d.: probate, 2 Nov 1916, CGPLA Eng. & Wales

Carr, John (1723–1807), architect, the eldest of the nine children of Robert Carr (1697–1760) and his wife, Rose Lascelles (1697–1774), was born on 28 April 1723 at Horbury, near Wakefield, and baptized there on 15 May 1723. He had some mastery of Latin, which suggests a grammar school education, presumably at Wakefield. His father, a mason–architect, probably trained him as a stonecutter before Carr joined the family business as a building contractor. He succeeded to his father's salaried post as a joint county surveyor for the West Riding, but resigned from it in 1772 to take up a similar post in the North Riding. Local government was in the hands of the county's magistrates, several of whom became Carr's patrons. On 31 August 1746 he married Sarah Hinchcliffe (1712–1787) and by 1752 he had moved to York.

Carr's first significant work was designing the rich internal decoration of Kirby Hall, Yorkshire (1747–c.1755),

the shell of which was devised by Richard Boyle, third earl of Burlington, Roger Morris, and its owner, Stephen Thompson. Many elements of Kirby, most obviously the bay windows with their apsidal or circular rooms within, remained part of Carr's repertory. Public success followed the building of the grandstand at York racecourse (1755–6), perhaps with the helpful influence of Charles Watson-Wentworth, second marquess of Rockingham, whose faithful political follower Carr was to remain. Indeed, Carr was patronized mainly by the whig establishment, and built up a network of clients through parliamentary, family, and social interconnections. Hence his prime concern was for domestic work in town or country. He seems to have designed only one commercial building, Somerset House, Halifax, for the Royds family, and avoided either speculative development or industrial building. His whig supporters also secured him commissions for public buildings, as well as becoming personal friends. In addition, Carr was a magistrate for the city of York (of which he was twice lord mayor), and for the West and North Ridings: he was thus exceptionally well placed to win those public or semi-public commissions put out to competition, such as Newark town hall, York County Lunatic Hospital, or Ferrybridge Bridge. He did not indulge in self-publicity, but volume 5 of *Vitruvius Britannicus* illustrates no fewer than five Carr designs (including Kirby Hall), and in its continuation of 1797 and 1802 there are a further five of Carr's schemes, in total the largest number of designs of any single architect. This contemporary validation was confirmed by an invitation to join the London Architects' Club in 1791. Carr is reputed to have been worth £150,000 at his death, a fortune only exceeded by that left by the sculptor–architect Sir Robert Taylor.

Carr's formative influences included the books of Sebastiano Serlio and Andrea Palladio, and the contemporary publications of Robert Morris, Sir William Chambers, and possibly Jean François de Neufforge. Carr subscribed to numerous architectural pattern books, including the works of his friend George Richardson. He paid meticulous personal attention to every aspect of construction and long-term maintenance, using damp-proof courses, ventilated roof trusses and water-closets, double glazing (at Middleton Lodge, Yorkshire, 1770–80), metal reinforcement and constructional members such as cast-iron window sills (at The Crescent, Buxton, Derbyshire), and an early form of roofing felt was proposed for a racecourse grandstand at Kelso, although the design was never executed.

Carr's first designs were conventionally Anglo-Palladian, until he recognized the new significance of the landscape garden. Thereafter he devised houses viewed from the diagonal externally, with rooms planned around a top-lit staircase, to take in the newly contrived panoramic prospects. Façades opposite the best landscapes could be austere, while those facing duller prospects were given the maximum enrichment, as at Constable Burton, Yorkshire (c.1762–8), built for Sir Marmaduke Wyvill, bt and illustrated in *Vitruvius Britannicus*. If a display was demanded, Carr employed a seven-part compositional massing in place of the five-part 'villa with wings' as at Tabley House, Cheshire (*c*.1760–67), for Sir Peter Leicester, Denton Park, Yorkshire (*c*.1770–81), for Sir James Ibbetson, or Basildon House, Berkshire (*c*.1776), for Sir Francis Sykes. His grasp of solid geometry is further exemplified by the monumental convex rear elevation of The Crescent, Buxton, built for the fifth duke of Devonshire between 1779 and 1789. Carr employed a simple theory of proportion to give consistency to plans and elevations, and his study of the architectural orders early led him into unorthodoxies such as two-part entablatures, the first of them for the stables at Harewood House, Yorkshire (1755–8). He used the dissonance of an unresolved duality to point up harmony, as in the wing designs for Tabley, and accepted asymmetry where this aided proper function, as in his designs for the flank elevations of Newark town hall, Nottinghamshire (1773–6), or the county lunatic asylum, York (1774–7; now Bootham Park Hospital). Carr's estate housing was solidly and generously built, most notably at Harewood for Edwin Lascelles from *c*.1760, and on the fourth Earl Fitzwilliam's estate at Wentworth Woodhouse, Yorkshire, during the 1780s and 1790s.

Vigorous rococo interiors can be seen at Arncliffe Hall, Yorkshire, built for Thomas Mauleverer, and Heath Hall near Wakefield, Yorkshire, for John Smyth (both 1750s), and at Somerset House, Halifax (dated 1766). Carr's Adamesque manner is clearly distinguishable, and is at its best at Denton (1770s), in the assembly rooms at Buxton (1780s), and at Farnley Hall, Yorkshire (1790), though not all of his interiors have comparable strength. Carr preferred the enrichments of Rome, Palmyra, or Baalbek to those of ancient Athens. The doorcases and chimneypieces at The Hall (now Lairgate Hall), Beverley, Yorkshire, and Wiganthorpe Hall, Yorkshire (*c*.1780; dem.), represent Carr's Palmyrene taste. His only known use of the Greek Doric order was for an intended garden building at Kilnwick Hall, Yorkshire, modelled on the so-called Temple of Rome and Augustus at Athens. This predilection for antiquity is also expressed in his early use of monoliths, for example those of the portico at Tabley erected in 1762, and in this he anticipated a similar usage by Thomas Harrison of Chester. In his bridge work he adapted the styles, building materials, and techniques of the localities concerned, observing economy of expression. Where elegance was sought, the side more in public view received the greater enrichment, as at Greta Bridge, near Rokeby, of 1773, or Blyth, Nottinghamshire, dated 1776, though in both cases these enrichments were privately financed. He ignored conventional wisdom when he placed bridge piers in the centres of rivers, for instance that over the Swale at Morton (1800–03).

Towards the end of his life Carr retired to Askham Richard, near York, where he had purchased an estate. He died on 22 February 1807 at his home, Askham Hall, and was buried at Horbury church. Carr was among the most prolific of eighteenth-century English architects, and it is a tribute to his manifest skills that the majority of his buildings survive.   IVAN HALL

Sources [W. Papworth], ed., *The dictionary of architecture*, 11 vols. (1853–92) · R. Davies, 'A memoir of John Carr, esq.', *Yorkshire Archaeological and Topographical Journal*, 4 (1875–6), 202–13 · *The works in architecture of John Carr*, York Georgian Society (1973) · Colvin, *Archs.* · S. D. Kitson, 'Carr of York', *RIBA Journal*, 17 (1909–10) · Browsholme Hall, Carr family papers · parish register, Horbury, 15 May 1723 [baptism]
Archives Chatsworth House, Derbyshire, accounts · Hospital of San Antonio, Oporto, Portugal, drawings, letters, and accounts (public buildings) · N. Yorks. CRO, survey book of bridges · Newark Museum, Nottinghamshire, drawings and accounts · The Crescent, Assembly Rooms, and Great Stables, Buxton, Derbyshire, accounts · W. Yorks. AS, Wakefield, survey book of bridges | Campsmount, near Doncaster, Cooke-Yarborough family papers · Castle Howard, Yorkshire, papers relating to Castle Howard · Chatsworth House, Derbyshire, papers relating to Buxton Crescent, Derbyshire, Buxton MSS, C38, C41, C43 · Ches. & Chester ALSS, Leicester-Warren Archive, papers relating to Tabley House, Cheshire · Cumbria AS, Curwen's General Ledgers, papers relating to Workington Hall, Cumberland · Durham RO, papers relating to Raby Castle · East Riding of Yorkshire Archives Service, Beverley, papers relating to Everingham Park, DDEV/70/21, DDEV/56/283 · East Riding of Yorkshire Archives Service, Beverley, corresp. and papers relating to Grimston Garth, Kilnwick, and other places · N. Yorks. CRO, papers relating to Middleton Lodge, Middleton Tyas, ZKU · NL Ire., papers relating to Coolattin Park, co. Wicklow, Ireland, MSS 6012–6025 · Northants. RO, Fitzwilliam papers, papers relating to Milton House, Northamptonshire · Sheff. Arch., Wentworth Woodhouse Muniments, papers relating to Wentworth Woodhouse · Sheff. Arch., letters to Bacon Frank · U. Nott. L., Manvers papers, papers relating to Thoresby House, Nottinghamshire · U. Nott. L., Portland Papers, papers relating to Welbeck Abbey, Nottinghamshire, PwF2, 540, etc. · W. Yorks. AS, Leeds, Yorkshire Archaeological Society, Farnley Hall archives, papers relating to Farnley Hall · W. Yorks. AS, Leeds, Yorkshire Archaeological Society, Ibbetson papers, papers relating to Denton Park · W. Yorks. AS, Leeds, papers relating to Harewood House, archives · W. Yorks. AS, Leeds, papers relating to Thorpe Arch Hall, Thorpe Arch estate papers box 21
Likenesses W. Beechey, oils, *c*.1786, priv. coll. · attrib. J. Russell, pastel drawing, *c*.1790–1795, York City Art Gallery · W. Beechey, oils, *c*.1791, NPG · C. H. Hodges, mezzotint, 1794 (after W. Beechey), priv. coll. · W. Daniell, etching, 1796 (after G. Dance), York City Art Gallery · J. Nollekens, marble bust, 1800, York City Art Gallery · W. Daniell, soft-ground etching, pubd 1814 (after G. Dance), BM, NPG
Wealth at death £150,000—value of personal effects: Davies, 'A memoir'

Carr, John (1732–1807), translator, was born at Muggleswick, Durham. His father was a farmer and small landowner. Carr was educated at the village school, and then privately by the curate of the parish, the Revd Daniel Watson. Subsequently he was sent to St Paul's School, London. He became an usher in Hertford grammar school under Dr Hurst, and succeeded him in the headmastership, which he held until about 1792. He is said to have been a candidate for the headmastership of St Paul's, but to have failed from the lack of a university degree. This seems to have been a sensitive issue for Carr, who explains in the preface to his translation of Lucian that 'no reckless intruder appears in the title page. The inclemency of reading has been known to spend itself there; and a name, unsheltered with academical honours, stands less exposed at the end of a Preface'. He published the first volume of his translations from Lucian in 1773; four further volumes appeared in subsequent years, the last in 1798. Carr apparently felt obliged to apologize for his choice of Lucian, and explained in the preface to the 1786 volume that he worked in the evening 'when I was not in a temper to face a graver author, and wished to forget every unwelcome occurrence of the day'. The favourable reception of these translations led to Carr being awarded the degree of LLD by the Marischal College of Aberdeen, on the advice of James Beattie.

Carr's whimsical humour emerges in the lively prefaces as well as the translation itself. At the end of his preface to the second edition of Lucian he writes: 'I return thanks to the voluntary subscribers. It was not my fault, that a gentleman's name was printed without his consent, nor that he does not "*understand* such odd stuff"'. The same qualities are apparent in *A Third Volume of Tristram Shandy* (1760), a convincing pastiche of Sterne's style. His other works include a mock-heroic poem, *Filial Piety* (1764), and *Epponina* (1765), a verse drama based on the life of Julius Sabinus's wife.

From 1805 until his death Carr was prebendary of Lincoln. He died on 6 June 1807, having been predeceased by his wife, and was buried in St John's Church, Hertford.

E. S. SHUCKBURGH, *rev.* SARAH ANNES BROWN

Sources BL cat. · J. Carr, preface, in *Dialogues of Lucian*, trans. J. Carr, 1 (1774) · J. Carr, preface, in *Dialogues of Lucian*, trans. J. Carr, 3 (1786) · ESTC · GM, 1st ser., 74 (1804), 1048 · GM, 1st ser., 82/2 (1812), 602 · M. McDonnell, ed., *The registers of St Paul's School, 1509–1748* (privately printed, London, 1977)

Carr, Sir John (1772–1832), travel writer, was born in London on 6 December 1772. Variously described as the youngest and the only son of a tradesman, possibly Benjamin Carr, he entered Rugby School in 1785 by which time his father was dead and he was the ward of William Hodges of Mayfair, Westminster. On leaving Rugby he was articled to a solicitor in Devon and, after practising briefly in London, he formed a partnership with another solicitor in Devon. He was called to the bar at the Middle Temple but gave up the law to travel for health reasons and published accounts illustrated by his own sketches of his journeys in various European countries. After the success of *The Stranger in Paris* (1803) he published *A Northern Summer* (1805) and *The Stranger in Ireland* (1806), soon after which he was knighted by the duke of Bedford, then viceroy of Ireland. *A Tour through Holland* followed in 1807. The rapidity with which he turned out his books and their superficiality began to attract comment and earned him the nickname 'the jaunting car'. In 1807 his Irish book was satirized by Edward Dubois in *My pocket-book, or, Hints for a 'ryghte merrie and conceitede' tour, in quarto, to be called, 'The stranger in Ireland'*. For this satire the publishers were prosecuted in 1809. Dubois had mocked not only the style of Carr's books but also their profitability to Carr and his publishers and the trial revealed that Carr had received £1900 for his four travel books. Carr lost his case. Undeterred by Dubois's satire, in 1808 he published *Caledonian Sketches* which in turn became the subject of a witty review by Sir Walter Scott in the *Quarterly Review*. His last travel book, *Descriptive Travels in … Spain*, appeared in 1811.

Lord Byron, who had met Carr in Cadiz, refers to him in some suppressed stanzas of canto 1 of *Childe Harolde* as 'Green Erin's knight and Europe's wandering star'. Carr also published two volumes of poetry and a play. In 1811 he married an heiress in Essex. He became depressed following her death and himself died, at his home, New Norfolk Street, London, on 17 July 1832. His books have little merit and, although they gained a wide circulation in his lifetime because of their light style and the fact that there was then little competition in the genre, they soon fell into well-deserved obscurity.

T. F. HENDERSON, *rev.* ELIZABETH BAIGENT

Sources GM, 1st ser., 102/2 (1832), 182–3 · D. E. Baker, *Biographia dramatica, or, A companion to the playhouse*, rev. I. Reed, new edn, rev. S. Jones, 3 vols. in 4 (1812) · *A new biographical dictionary of 3000 cotemporary* [sic] *public characters, British and foreign, of all ranks and professions*, 2nd edn, 3 vols. in 6 pts (1825) · [J. Watkins and F. Shoberl], *A biographical dictionary of the living authors of Great Britain and Ireland* (1816) · *Rugby School register, 1: From 1675 to 1849 inclusive* (1881) · J. Hutchinson, ed., *A catalogue of notable Middle Templars: with brief biographical notices* (1902) · *Byron's letters and journals*, ed. L. A. Marchand, 1 (1973)

Likenesses Freeman, stipple, pubd 1809 (after R. Westall), NPG · W. Brockedon, pencil, 1832, NPG · R. M. Meadows, stipple (after E. Smith), BM, NPG

Carr [Kerr], **Johnson** (1743–1765), landscape painter. Nothing is known of his family other than they were respectable and came from the north of England. He was a pupil of Richard Wilson between about 1757 and about 1763, and his drawing style is similar to that of his master, whom he also assisted. Joseph Farington, another pupil, records that in 1807 he went to see a painting by Wilson and that 'Segar had looked at it, & thought the edges of some trees were by Carr' (Constable, 137). Carr successfully entered a number of competitions at the Society of Arts. In 1759, at the age of sixteen, he entered a landscape drawing which Ozias Humphry witnessed as Carr's own work, and in 1762 and 1763 he won the prize for the best drawing of a landscape by a youth under nineteen. The 1763 drawing is probably that exhibited in 1948–9 (Birmingham and the Tate Gallery, London, no. 147), *Westminster Abbey from Pimlico* (priv. coll.), executed in black and white chalk on blue paper. This, and another prize drawing in the Royal Society of Arts, are the only two known extant works by Carr (Constable, 137). Carr died of consumption on 16 January 1765 in his twenty-second year.

W. C. MONKHOUSE, *rev.* DEBORAH GRAHAM-VERNON

Sources Redgrave, *Artists* · E. Edwards, *Anecdotes of painters* (1808); facs. edn (1970) · W. G. Constable, *Richard Wilson* (1953) · Waterhouse, *18c painters* · *Richard Wilson and his circle*, City Museum and Art Gallery, Birmingham (1949) [exhibition catalogue, Tate Gallery, London, Jan 1949]

Carr, Jonathan Dodgson (1806–1884), biscuit manufacturer, was born in Stricklandgate, Kendal, on 9 December 1806, the second in a family of four sons and five daughters of Jonathan Carr, a Quaker wholesale grocer and tea dealer of Yorkshire weaving stock, and his wife, Jane Dodgson, daughter of another Kendal grocer. He was apprenticed to a baker in Stockton from 1822 to 1828. Finding the commercial opportunities in his home town to be distinctly limited, in 1831 he tramped the 50 miles to the city of Carlisle, where he opened a bakery and mealman's shop. Two years later, he felt well enough established to marry Jane, daughter of Thomas and Mary Nicholson of Whitehaven. They were to have two daughters and four sons, three of whom later became partners in the family business.

For much of the 1830s Carr was energetically building up an integrated business which ranged from corn merchanting and flour milling to baking, biscuit manufacture, and retailing. He subsequently added a fleet of ships to transport his requirements of wheat. Biscuits soon became the leading product group and in 1841, with the help of his local MP, he was granted the royal warrant for them. In 1846 he produced 400 tons of biscuits, employing 90 staff. He installed steam-powered machines for mixing the ingredients, though the manually operated cutting machine, adapted by the Carlisle printer Hudson Scott, fell short of the continuously running biscuit machinery evolved in Reading by George Palmer. By 1860 Carr was offering seventy-two varieties of fancy biscuit. The steady expansion of the business led to three of his brothers joining the firm of Carr & Co.; the youngest, John, departed in 1860 to Peek Frean & Co., the London biscuit firm, to be succeeded there by his son Arthur.

Carr was a giant of a man, with a benevolent expression and a full white beard in his riper years. To demonstrate his strength, he once carried three sacks of flour, each weighing 280 lb (127 kg), the length of the mill and back. His treatment of the workforce was humane, the factory being clean and airy; he ensured personal cleanliness by providing a bath which was 14 feet square, with hot water from the steam engine. He had a schoolroom, library, and reading room close by, and he gave religious instruction in his house on Sunday afternoons. Annual outings took place to the Lake District, and once there was an excursion to Edinburgh; one of the Carrs attended the weekly employees' meeting, at which matters to do with conditions in the firm could be raised.

Although Carr never became a local councillor, he took a lively part in public affairs. As a secretary of the Carlisle Anti-Cornlaw Association, he placed in his shop window both a taxed and an untaxed (much larger) loaf. When the corn laws were repealed in 1846, he presented every inmate in Carlisle gaol with a fruit loaf, and had a silk waistcoat made, decorated with ears of corn marked 'FREE'. He helped to promote gas and water undertakings in the city; as a founder of the Cumberland Co-operative Benefit Building Society, he spoke on housing conditions at its meetings, and he actively supported the Cumberland Infirmary. He took the initiative in developing the docks and railway in Silloth, whither the firm later transferred its flour milling operations.

As a businessman Carr showed abundant energy and vision, and a rigid adherence to the Quaker principles of offering good-quality products at fair and fixed prices. However, his strong-minded individualism caused some friction in the Quaker community. Having become used to taking his Bible into meeting, he was censured on the grounds that reading any book during meeting weakened worshippers' dependence on the promptings of the Holy Spirit. After his two eldest sons were disowned, he and his wife resigned from the society, and soon afterwards they joined the Brethren Assembly in Carlisle and became prominent members. Carr died at his home, Coldale Hall in Carlisle, on 6 April 1884.   T. A. B. CORLEY

Sources M. Forster, *Rich desserts and captain's thin: a family and their times, 1831–1931* (1997) • S. I. Dench, 'Carr, Jonathan Dodgson', *DBB* • J. S. Adam, *A fell fine baker: the story of United Biscuits* (1974), 95–110 • *Chambers' Edinburgh Journal* (9 Sept 1848) • *Carlisle Journal* (8 April 1884) • 'Carrs' four freedoms', *Woman and Home* (Feb 1960) • 'Jonathan "printed" his biscuits', *Evening News* (26 March 1958), 11 • 'Carrs of Carlisle', *Grocery World* (2 March 1912) • Burke, *Gen. GB* • *CGPLA Eng. & Wales* (1884)

Archives Cumbria AS, Carlisle, Carr & Co. MSS

Likenesses photograph, repro. in Dench, 'Carr, Jonathan Dodgson'

Wealth at death £38,552 5s. 3d.: probate, 18 June 1884, *CGPLA Eng. & Wales*

Carr, Jonathan Thomas (1845–1915), property developer, was born in Dublin, the eldest son among the ten children of Jonathan Carr (d. 1881), a wholesale woollen draper of Cumbrian origin with a business in the West End of London, and his Irish wife. The family was liberal in outlook, art loving, and gregarious: one brother, Joseph William Comyns *Carr (1849–1916), became known as an art critic and minor dramatist; another, David Alexander Carr (1847–1920), and a sister, Kate (Hastings), both studied at the Slade School of Art and became painters.

Carr was brought up in Barnes and in Devonshire Street, St Marylebone, before going to Bruce Castle School, Tottenham, and then King's College, London. He attached himself to John Stuart Mill during his Westminster election campaign of 1865 as a 'political secretary'; he evidently harboured ambitions in radical politics, but for the time being joined his father's firm.

In 1873 Carr married Agnes Fulton (1849–1902), daughter of the civil engineer Hamilton Henry Fulton (1813–1886), who owned 24 acres close to the new railway station of Turnham Green in suburban west London. This from 1875 became the core of Bedford Park, Carr's first and most successful venture into enlightened property development. Observing that most Victorian estate development was authoritarian in management and gloomy in appearance, Carr harnessed the rising demand for middle-class homes in the suburbs with the fashion for the Queen Anne style in architecture and the aesthetic art-furnishing movement. Bedford Park's layout was not novel, but Carr employed some of the best domestic architects of the day, such as E. W. Godwin, Norman Shaw, and E. J. May, to design the pretty and well-planned houses that line the streets. As well as the customary church, an inn, stores, a club with a library, and even an art school were provided. Minor artists, actors, literati, and liberal emigrés from continental Europe flocked to Bedford Park, which was shrewdly puffed in the periodicals. It became admired and lampooned as an aesthetic community, and was satirized in the 'Ballad of Bedford Park', which appeared in the *St James's Gazette*. It proved a genuine social and architectural novelty, and the chief middle-class precursor of the later garden suburb. Carr built himself a handsome house to Norman Shaw's designs, Tower House (1878–9), in the centre of the development. He presided over Bedford Park as its sole promoter, though the Carr and Fulton families were much involved in its finances.

In 1881 Carr turned Bedford Park into a limited company and sought new fields of endeavour. The first was Kensington Court, begun in 1882, an effort to shake up London town-house development just as Bedford Park had improved the suburban estate. Special attention was paid to the services: hydraulic lifts were to replace back stairs, and every house was to be electrically lit. He again employed a fashionable architect, J. J. Stevenson, but Kensington Court was never finished to Carr's plans and its fortunes became involved with the larger scheme which caused his downfall. This was Whitehall Court, a huge block of apartments on a prime tract of crown-owned land overlooking the Thames. Carr agreed in November 1883 to take this site, sharing it with the newly founded National Liberal Club, with which he had connections, but the scale of the development was too big for his amateurish methods of finance. In January 1886, with the building hardly begun, Carr and his development company, Whitehall Court Ltd, were saved only by selling out to associates of Jabez Balfour.

Though Carr escaped bankruptcy his indebtedness was severe and his reputation did not recover. Bedford Park Ltd was wound up in 1886, and in the next year he and his fellow directors in Whitehall Court Ltd were found guilty of gross breach of trust for paying themselves salaries when the company had no dividend. He managed to stay on at Tower House until after his wife's death, according to Lucien Oldershaw 'with the bailiff as his butler. He and his equally impoverished brother would spend long hours playing cards together and getting highly excited when three shillings changed hands' (Ward, 25). Carr was called as a witness at the celebrated Jabez Balfour trial in 1895, when irregularities about the Whitehall Court rescue came out. In 1902 Carr tried to promote a fanciful scheme for a second Bedford Park, to be called Burlingwick, on Chiswick meadows, but this came to nothing. He died at 13 Queen Anne's Grove, Bedford Park, on 1 February 1915, following a bout of influenza.

Like many property developers, Carr had a sanguine, genial, and persuasive temperament. He had original ideas, imagination, and courage, but was not averse to cutting corners and attracted a reputation for less than complete probity. He may have intended his career in property as a prelude to one in radical politics. The one known photograph of Carr shows him in middle age, with a piercing eye and a full beard. He is said to have indulged in radical and aesthetic dress, notably red ties and velvet jackets. He had two sons, Horace Fulton Carr (d. 1900) and Jonathan Fulton Carr.   ANDREW SAINT

Sources A. Saint, 'Whatever happened to Jonathan Carr?', *London Journal*, 12 (1986), 65–79 • M. Ward, *Return to Chesterton* (1952), 52 • T. Affleck Greeves, *Bedford Park, the first garden suburb* (1975) • M. Girouard, *Sweetness and light: the Queen Anne movement, 1860–1900* (1977) • H. Hobhouse, ed., *Southern Kensington: Kensington Square to Earl's Court*, Survey of London, 42 (1986), 67–76 • *Chiswick Times* (18 April 1902) • *Chiswick Times* (25 April 1902) • *Chiswick Times* (5 Feb 1915) • *Building News*, 108 (1915), 154 • M. Jones Bosterli, *The early community at Bedford Park* (1977) • census returns, 1881

Likenesses bronze bas relief, c.1915, St Michael's Church, Bedford Park, London • photograph, priv. coll.

Carr, Joseph Lloyd (1912–1994), writer and publisher, was born on 20 May 1912 in the village of Carlton Miniott, near Thirsk in the North Riding of Yorkshire, the youngest among the four children of Joseph Carr, an employee of the local railway company, and his wife, Hannah Elizabeth, *née* Welbourn. Carr senior's alternative career as a Wesleyan lay preacher was an appreciable influence on his son's development, while the memories of his Yorkshire boyhood form the background to his best-known novel, *A Month in the Country* (1980).

Having twice failed his eleven-plus examination, Carr was sent by his parents, at their own expense, to Castleford secondary school; its alumni included the sculptor Henry Moore, and Carr himself became an accomplished amateur sculptor. Subsequently he spent three years at Dudley Teacher Training College before taking jobs as a schoolmaster in Yorkshire, Hampshire, and finally Birmingham. In 1938–9 he took advantage of an exchange scheme which allowed him to spend a year teaching in South Dakota. During the Second World War, Carr flew on reconnaissance missions for RAF Coastal Command. About this time he adopted the name Jim by which all his friends came to know him. On 14 March 1945 he married Hilda Gladys Sexton (1918/19–1981), known as Sally, a former children's nurse. They had one son, Robert (Bob) Duane. Grateful to the Birmingham authorities for continuing to pay his salary throughout the war, Carr made a point of remaining in the city for some time after demobilization.

Carr's teaching career culminated in an appointment in 1951 as headmaster of Highfield primary school, Kettering, Northamptonshire. He was a much-loved, if idiosyncratic, teacher, whose exploits included encouraging the 200 children in his charge to launch bottles containing their names and addresses onto the local river. He and his family spent another exchange year in South Dakota in the mid-1950s, and in 1956 he published an account of his return to the American state, *The Old-Timers of Beadly County*. By this stage in his life, however, his ambitions lay in a direction different from teaching. Carr had always wanted to write. The decisive stimulus apparently came from an exigent WEA course tutor ('Show us your written work' this lady would command her class), and he published his first novel, *A Day in Summer*, in 1963. A successor, *A Season in Sinji*, drawing on his wartime experiences in Sierra Leone and reflecting his lifelong passion for cricket, appeared four years later. By this time Carr, backed by Sally, had resigned his teaching post and had set up as a small publisher.

The Carrs began by publishing hand-drawn maps of the English counties, followed by pocket-sized editions of classic English poets such as Shakespeare, Blake, and John Clare. Precariously financed at first—the capital was down to £400 within eighteen months—the business eventually prospered. A breakthrough came with an original production, *Carr's Dictionary of Extraordinary English Cricketers* (1977), described in a leading article in *The Guardian* as 'one of the books of the Century'. Other successes included the *Dictionary of English queens, kings' wives, celebrated paramours, handfast spouses and royal changelings*.

Meanwhile, Carr's career as a novelist proceeded alongside. He wrote eight novels in all, each in some way reflecting the experiences of his life. *The Harpole Report* (1972), for example, is set in a village primary school, while *How Steeple Sinderby Wanderers Won the F.A. Cup* (1975) has its roots in the local football matches of his youth. (Bizarrely, towards the end of his life, Carr reissued it himself as a work of non-fiction, including supposed photographs of the Sinderby side.) Though wildly different in tone, setting, and structure, they constitute an English fictional world as distinctive in its way as those of Evelyn Waugh and Anthony Powell, riven with melancholy but always capable of irradiation by Carr's irrepressible high spirits. A good example of Carr's humour comes in *The Harpole Report*, where a female teacher to whom a mild rebuke is being administered informs the headmaster briskly that she has had twenty years' experience. No, he replies, she has had one year of experience, twenty times.

Though late in coming, Carr's success was triumphant. *A Month in the Country*, an elegiac account of an unconsummated rural love affair, set in the year after the First World War, won the *Guardian* fiction prize (1980) and was shortlisted for the Booker prize. The novel, adapted by Simon Gray, was filmed in 1987, with Colin Firth, Kenneth Branagh, Natasha Richardson, and Patrick Malahide. *A Day in Summer* was similarly adapted, this time for television, by Alan Plater in 1989.

The Battle of Pollocks Crossing (1985), which drew on Carr's American interludes in South Dakota, was also shortlisted for the Booker prize. But by now Carr despaired of the ability of commercial publishers to do a job properly, and his two subsequent novels—*What Hetty did* (1988) and *Harpole and Foxberrow, General Publishers* (1992)—were issued under his own Quince Tree Press imprint.

In appearance Carr was a shortish, quizzical-looking, neatly dressed man with faint dandyish tendencies. Although he retained a suspicion of London, London publishing, and London morals, he could occasionally be persuaded to visit. His wife, Sally, died in 1981, and he died of leukaemia, at 1 Cranleigh Road, Kettering, aged eighty-one, on 26 February 1994. He was buried in Kettering on 4 March. His memorials include the extraordinary *Northamptonshire Record*, seven gilt-bound volumes containing forty years' worth of his paintings of local antiquities, and the J. L. Carr collection held by Kettering Library, comprising his novels, pocket books, maps, drawings, and articles.   D. J. TAYLOR

Sources B. Rogers, *The life and times of J. L. Carr* (1996) · personal knowledge (2004) · *The Independent* (28 Feb 1994) · *The Times* (2 March 1994) · b. cert. · m. cert. · d. cert.

Archives Kettering Library
Wealth at death £266,955: *The Times* (5 Dec 1994)

Carr, Joseph William Comyns (1849–1916), author, gallery director, and theatre manager, was born on 2 March 1849 at 47 Devonshire Street, Marylebone, Middlesex, the seventh of the ten children of Jonathan Carr, a woollen draper, and his wife, Catherine Grace Comyns. His father was from Cumberland, and his mother was Irish. His sister, Kate Comyns Carr, was a portrait artist. From 1862 to 1865 he attended Bruce Castle School, Tottenham, Middlesex, in the dining room of which, he later recalled, he had his first encounter with the wallpaper designs of William Morris. He matriculated at London University in 1870 and was called to the bar at the Inner Temple, London, on 30 April 1872. His ambition, however, was for a literary career. He established his name as a journalist, especially in the fields of dramatic and art criticism, and his appointment as art critic to the *Pall Mall Gazette* in 1873 allowed him to retire from the law. On 15 December 1873 he married, in Dresden, Alice Laura Vansittart Strettell (1850–1927), daughter of the Revd Arthur B. Strettell, consular chaplain at Genoa. They had three children: Philip, Dorothy, and Arthur (later Sir Arthur Strettell Comyns *Carr (1882–1965), barrister and Liberal MP).

Carr was a passionate advocate of Pre-Raphaelite art and a vigorous critic of what he saw as the short-sightedness of the art establishment. A series of articles on contemporary artists in *The Globe* in 1873 attracted attention and resulted in a friendship with Dante Gabriel Rossetti. In 1875 he became English editor of the sumptuous and influential French journal *L'Art*; he founded and edited *Art and Letters* in 1881–3; and he was editor of the *English Illustrated Magazine* in 1883–6, where he launched the career of the illustrator Hugh Thomson. He published several books based on his journalism, including *Drawings of the Old Masters* (1877), *Examples of Contemporary Art* (1878), *Art in Provincial France* (1883), and *Papers on Art* (1885).

In 1877 Sir Coutts Lindsay invited Carr and the amateur artist Charles Hallé to become co-directors of the newly founded Grosvenor Gallery in Bond Street with the express intention of promoting Pre-Raphaelite painters and challenging 'the sleepy self-complacency of the dwellers in Burlington House [the Royal Academy]' (Carr, *Some Eminent Victorians*, 131). The successful opening exhibition, to which many important artists contributed, marked a turning point in the appreciation of the work of Sir Edward Burne-Jones. Carr also organized several innovative exhibitions of old master paintings and drawings. Private views at the Grosvenor Gallery quickly became fixtures in the London social calendar.

At the end of 1886 Carr and Hallé resigned from the Grosvenor Gallery after a dispute with Sir Coutts Lindsay, and in the remarkable space of barely four months they planned, built, and opened the New Gallery in Regent Street in time to compete with the spring exhibitions of the Royal Academy and the Grosvenor (which closed in 1890). Crucially, they took with them all the Grosvenor's major contributors, and the New Gallery was to remain the most important showcase for Pre-Raphaelite art until the death of Burne-Jones in 1898. Carr continued as co-director until 1908. He was chosen to write the introduction to the British section of the International Exhibition of Fine Arts at Rome in 1911 and was afterwards appointed English representative on the Art Congress.

His gallery work did not cause Carr to neglect his interest in drama. In the early 1880s he contributed several light comedies to the 'Entertainment' of Thomas German Reed and his wife, Priscilla, at St George's Hall. He also discovered a talent for adaptation: Hugh Conway's *Called back* in 1884 (in collaboration with the author) for the actor-manager Herbert Beerbohm Tree was a huge popular success. Many other adaptations and collaborations followed, including *Madame Sans-Gêne* by Victorien Sardou and Emile Moreau in 1897 for Sir Henry Irving; *The Beauty Stone* in 1898, a comic opera (in collaboration with Arthur Wing Pinero and with music by Sir Arthur Sullivan); and Goethe's *Faust* in 1908 (in collaboration with Stephen Phillips) for Tree. Of his original non-collaborative work for the theatre *King Arthur* (1895) for Irving is noteworthy for its production; Carr persuaded his old friend Burne-Jones to design the sets and costumes (the artist's only essay in this field) and enlisted Sullivan to compose the incidental music. The result was a *succès de spectacle* which ran for 100 performances and went on to tour the United States and Canada. Carr wrote two further pseudo-medieval dramas: *Tristram and Iseult* (1906) and *The Lonely Queen* (unpublished).

Carr was Tree's literary adviser and partner at the Haymarket Theatre (1887–93); leased his own theatre, the Comedy (1893–6); and managed the Lyceum (1899–1904) after Irving transferred its control to a company. He was artistic adviser at the Covent Garden Theatre (1913–14), where he staged the first English performance of Richard Wagner's *Parsifal* on 2 February 1914.

Carr's two volumes of memoirs, *Some Eminent Victorians* (1908) and *Coasting Bohemia* (1914), provide a fascinating record of his artistic and literary friendships. His last work, *The Ideals of Painting* (1917), was published posthumously. He died of cancer on 12 December 1916 at his home, 6 Canning Place, South Kensington, London, and was buried in Highgate cemetery.

Carr was, in his own words, 'an impenitent Victorian'. He was a man of many talents, of boundless energy, and of unflagging confidence. He had a flair for organization and promotion; he was a great conversationalist, a renowned after-dinner speaker, and an expert fly-fisherman; he was once even offered a seat in parliament in the home-rule interest by Charles Stewart Parnell.

ANTHONY ESPOSITO

Sources J. C. Carr, *Some eminent Victorians: personal recollections in the world of art and letters* (1908) · J. W. C. Carr, *Coasting Bohemia* (1914) · A. S. Carr, *J. Comyns Carr: stray memories* (1920) · A. S. Carr, *Reminiscences*, ed. E. Adam (1926) · b. cert. · d. cert.
Archives NRA, corresp. and literary papers | BL, corresp. with Macmillans, Add. MS 54990
Likenesses photograph, 1872, repro. in Carr, *Reminiscences* · J. S. Sargent, caricature, c.1890, repro. in Carr, *Reminiscences* · photograph, c.1899, repro. in Carr, *J. Comyns Carr* · Spy [L. Ward], cartoon, repro. in *VF*

Wealth at death £4266 5s. 9d.: probate, 10 May 1917, *CGPLA Eng. & Wales*

Carr, Michael [*real name* Maurice Alfred Cohen] (1905–1968), songwriter, was born at 85 Portland Crescent, Leeds, on 11 March 1905. He was the son of Morris Cohen, cabinet-maker and boxer, known as Cockney Cohen, and an Irish mother, Gertrude Jane, *née* Beresford. While he was still a young child he moved to Dublin, where his father had chosen to take up the trade of a restaurateur. As he grew up, he met many people in show business who dined at his father's restaurant, but it was without apparent impact at this period of his life.

When he reached the age of eighteen, Cohen ran away to sea and was able to visit a great deal of the world. He decided to settle in the USA, where he became a journalist for a time, and then began to find work as an actor playing short roles in Hollywood films, taking the name Michael Carr. Bebe Daniels, a singing film star, obtained some American film engagements for him about 1930. The prospect of developing a career in Hollywood was cut short, however, by news that his mother had been taken ill. On hearing of this, he returned to the family home.

Following his mother's death, Carr moved to London and in 1934 was offered a job as a staff arranger at the Peter Maurice Music Company. It was here that he met Jimmy Kennedy, another staff arranger for the same company, with whom he collaborated on a large number of hit songs. Kennedy was generally responsible for providing the lyrics. Together, they wrote songs for many of the *Crazy Gang shows at the Palladium in London before the outbreak of the Second World War. 'Home Town' was the hit number of the Crazy Gang film *O.K. for Sound* of 1937.

One of the features of the music to Carr's songs of the 1930s was its ability to conjure up effectively different geographical and cultural locations by means of an economic use of musical devices that held particular associations for listeners. Examples are 'On Linger Longer Island' with its Hawaiian guitar effects, 'Did your Mother Come from Ireland?' with its dotted rhythms (and solo fiddle in the arrangement for Billy Cotton's band), and the jog-trot 'cowboy' bass lines of 'South of the border' and 'Ole Faithful'. The latter, incidentally, became the supporters' song of Hull Rugby League Football Club (the Airlie Birds).

Carr's interest in exoticism, albeit of a restrained variety, continued after the war in some of the instrumental music he composed for the pop guitar group the Shadows, such as 'Man of Mystery' (1960) and 'Kon-Tiki' (1961). These were not his first purely instrumental successes; he wrote a very popular piece called 'Lonely Ballerina' for the light orchestra leader Mantovani in 1954. In the year of his death he demonstrated that he had still not lost his ability to find popular favour when he had a hit with 'White Horses' (written with Ben Nisbet); it was the theme song to a BBC television children's programme. He was found dead in bed at his flat at 110 Wellesley Court, Maida Vale, London, on 16 September 1968. He will undoubtedly be remembered best for the enormously popular songs he wrote with Jimmy Kennedy, and for 'We're Going to Hang out the Washing on the Siegfried Line' (1939), which was a favourite during the Second World War. Carr's music was typical of that of British and American dance bands of the inter-war years, dominated by foxtrot rhythms and 32 bar melodies. He had a great facility with melody, which accounts for his success, but was in no way an innovator.

DEREK B. SCOTT

Sources *The Times* (17 Sept 1968), 13 · B. Rust, 'The great British dance bands play the music of Jimmy Kennedy and Michael Carr', sleeve notes to World Records SH 340, 1979 · P. Gammond, 'Carr, Michael', *The Oxford companion to popular music* (1991); repr. with corrections (1993), 102 · b. cert. · d. cert.

Wealth at death £3255: probate, 2 Jan 1969, *CGPLA Eng. & Wales*

Carr, Nicholas (1522/3–1568), classical scholar, was born late in 1522 or in 1523, since he is recorded as being aged forty-five at the time of his death in the notice following the biography by Bartholomew Dodington attached to Carr's posthumously published *Demosthenis ... orationes* (1571). The notice and biography provide almost the only available information about Carr other than that from his published works. According to Dodington, Carr was born in Newcastle of a respectable family; the place of birth is confirmed by the title of Carr's *De scriptorum Britannicorum paucitate* (1576). He was sent to Christ's College, Cambridge, there to be taught by Cuthbert Scot. Carr later moved to Pembroke College, being taught by Nicholas Ridley and becoming a fellow, and then became one of the original fellows of Trinity College, Cambridge, when it was founded in 1546. Soon afterwards Carr substituted for John Cheke, the first regius professor of Greek at Cambridge, since Cheke had become tutor to Prince Edward in 1544. Carr himself succeeded to the regius professorship on 12 October 1551. Cheke's admiration for Carr as a Greek scholar is on record: he compared Carr with Theodorus Candius of Louvain, heard by Cheke in 1550.

Carr lectured on a wide range of authors: Aeschylus, Sophocles, Hippocrates, Plato, Demosthenes, Aeschines, Theocritus, and Galen, the choice of Aeschylus being particularly innovative. In 1551 Carr published his *Epistola de morte Buceri ad Johannem Checum*, a eulogy of Martin Bucer, a major protestant figure. The claim that Carr later testified against the doctrines of Bucer and Fagius appears to be without foundation. Nor does there appear to be any evidence for the claim that Carr 'seems always to have been attached to the ancient faith' (Cooper, *Ath. Cantab.*, 1.262). In the *De paucitate* he makes a clear reference to the felicity of England under Elizabeth. Furthermore, had Carr been a Catholic, it would be quite incomprehensible that his funeral sermon should have been preached by William Chaderton, two affectionate letters to whom by Carr survive, or that the posthumous publication of his translations from Demosthenes should have been furthered by Walter Mildmay, pillars respectively of the Elizabethan church and state.

Carr had married a few years after becoming the substitute for Cheke; he was then living at Bucer's house in Cambridge, where he still resided at the time of his death. The need to support his family led him to qualify as a medical doctor, which he did in 1558. He was allowed by the royal commissioners to combine the functions of medical practitioner and regius professor of Greek; Dodington sings the praises of his medical practice. In 1562 he appointed Hugh Blithe as his substitute for the teaching of Greek, then in 1564 Dodington. He died on 3 November 1568, leaving his wife and three daughters; his will in their favour was proved on 13 November. He was buried in St Michael's Church, Cambridge; a monument in St Giles's Church was erected in his memory and that of his middle daughter Catharine by her husband William James.

Although it appeared posthumously, Carr had before his death allowed the inclusion of his translation of book 4 of Eusebius in the edition of the Latin translation of the works of Eusebius by John Christopherson. Carr had also intended his translations from Demosthenes for publication, and had dedicated the manuscript to Mildmay for this end. The *De paucitate* was published only in 1576 (the occasion of its composition is unknown); in it Carr talks of a British disdain for teachers, even of law, and preference for foreign writers; he also records resentment at his praise for his teacher, perhaps Cuthbert Scot.

MICHAEL H. CRAWFORD

Sources T. Wilson, *Vita et obitus duorum fratrum Suffolciensium Henrici et Caroli Brandon* (1551), fol. 23*v* · N. Carr, *Epistola de morte Buceri ad Johannem Checum* (1551) · M. R. James, *A descriptive catalogue of the manuscripts in the library of Gonville and Caius College*, 1 (1907) · N. Carr, *Demosthenis, Graecorum oratorum principis* (1571) · N. Carr, *Nicolai Carri ... de scriptorum Britannicorum paucitate et studiorum impedimentis oratio* (1576) · Rymer, *Foedera*, 2nd edn, 106–10 · [J. Gibbons and J. Fenn], *Concertatio ecclesiae catholicae in Anglia adversus Calvinopapistas et puritanos*, 2nd edn (1588), fols. 408*r*, 416*r* · J. Lamb, ed., *A collection of letters, statutes and other documents ... illustrative of the history of the University of Cambridge during the Reformation* (1838), 172–6; 184–236 · F. Blomefield, *Collectanea Cantabrigiensia* (privately printed, Norwich, 1750), 64–5 · BL, Add. MS 5865, fol. 63*v* · Tanner, *Bibl. Brit.-Hib.*, 155 · E. Brydges, *Censura literaria: containing titles, abstracts, and opinions of old English books*, 2nd edn, 2 (1815), 258 · E. Brydges, *Censura literaria: containing titles, abstracts, and opinions of old English books*, 3 (1815), 420 · Cooper, *Ath. Cantab.*, 1.262–3, 555 · Cooper, *Ath. Cantab.*, 3.76 · H. C. Porter, *Reformation and reaction in Tudor Cambridge* (1958) · Gillow, *Lit. biog. hist.*

Archives CUL, Add. MS 49, fol. 188*v* · Gon. & Caius Cam., MS 197, pp. 462–4

Carr, R. (*fl.* 1668), printmaker, worked in the manner of Wenceslaus Hollar. His only known work is an etched map of England dated 1668.

W. C. MONKHOUSE, *rev.* ANNE PUETZ

Sources M. H. Grant, *A dictionary of British etchers* (1952) · Redgrave, *Artists* · Bryan, *Painters* (1886–9) · Bénézit, *Dict.*, 3rd edn · [K. H. von Heinecken], *Dictionnaire des artistes dont nous avons des estampes*, 4 vols. (Leipzig, 1778–90) · J. Strutt, *A biographical dictionary, containing an historical account of all the engravers, from the earliest period of the art of engraving to the present time*, 2 vols. (1785–6) · Thieme & Becker, *Allgemeines Lexikon*

Carr, Ralph (1711–1806), merchant and banker, was born on 22 September 1711, the eldest son of John Carr (1667–1739), of Whickham and Newcastle upon Tyne, and his wife, Sarah (1679–1733), daughter of William Wynne of Newcastle. Carr was apprenticed to a Newcastle merchant at the age of seventeen, serving out the last year of his time with one of his master's correspondents in Amsterdam, an experience which proved advantageous when he returned to Newcastle in 1738 to set up in business on his own account. He soon built up an extensive network of correspondents in coastal ports throughout Europe, dealing principally in grain, but gradually extending his interests to a wide range of other goods, from grindstones to groceries, and usually trading on his own behalf, but sometimes acting as shipping agent for other merchants. Trading networks of this kind depended on a complicated subsidiary trade in bills of exchange, and within a few years he had become convinced that opening a bank in Newcastle to handle this business would yield a handsome profit, a conviction that was strengthened during the 1745 rebellion when he became involved in transmitting funds as well as provisions to the army in Scotland. However, Carr was a deeply cautious man, unwilling to take even moderate risks, an attitude that prevented him from developing his potentially lucrative contacts with merchants in Boston and New York. The banking project therefore hung fire until 1755, when he entered into a partnership with three other Newcastle merchants, each of whom contributed £500 to the initial capital of the enterprise that became known as the Old Bank. The venture, which Carr described as his 'hobby horse', yielded its founder a handsome profit, not least because he channelled his own business through the bank free of charge. In 1786 he used some of the proceeds to purchase an estate at Hedgeley in Northumberland and shortly afterwards retired from active trade.

Like his father before him, Carr had prudently delayed marriage until he was well established in the world, and it was not until 29 November 1758 that he married Isabella (1727–1797), the daughter of Henry Byne, vicar of Ponteland, Northumberland. They had six children. He died on 7 May 1806 and was buried at Ponteland. He was succeeded by his eldest son, John Carr (1764–1817), who in 1802 had married the granddaughter and eventual heiress of William *Cotesworth (c.1668–1726) of Gateshead.

J. M. ELLIS

Sources The manuscripts of Shrewsbury and Coventry corporations, HMC, 47 (1899), 92–100 · M. Phillips, A history of banks, bankers and banking in Northumberland, Durham, and North Yorkshire (1894) · W. I. Roberts, 'Ralph Carr: a Newcastle merchant and the American colonial trade', Business History Review, 42 (1968), 271–87 · R. E. Carr and C. E. Carr, A history of the family of Carr of Dunston Hill, 3 vols. (1893–9) · M. Phillips, '"The old bank" (Bell, Cookson, Carr and Airey), Newcastle-upon-Tyne', Archaeologia Aeliena, 16 (1894), 452–70
Archives Northumbd RO, Carr–Ellison (Hedgeley) MSS
Likenesses portrait, Hedgeley Hall, Powburn, Northumberland

Carr, Richard (bap. 1651, d. 1706), physician, the son of Griffith and Mary Carr of Louth in Lincolnshire, was baptized there on 17 July 1651. He attended the local grammar school and entered Magdalene College, Cambridge, as a sizar on 31 May 1667. He graduated BA (1670) and MA (1674), and became master of Saffron Walden grammar school in 1676. In 1683 he went to Leiden to study medicine, and in 1686 proceeded MD at Cambridge. He was created a fellow of the Royal College of Physicians by James II's charter, and was admitted in 1687.

Carr is remembered for his Epistolae medicinales variis occasionibus conscriptae (1691), a collection of eighteen letters of advice to patients. The book is dedicated to the Royal College of Physicians, and received the imprimatur of the president and censors. It was later translated into English by John Quincy and published in 1714 under the title Dr. Carr's Medicinal Epistles upon Several Occasions, as a companion volume to his translation of the aphorisms of Sanctorius. The first epistle is on the use of snuff, the second on smoking tobacco, the third, fourth, seventh, fifteenth, and seventeenth on various points of dietetics. The most interesting is the third, on the drinks used in coffee houses: coffee, tea, twist (a mixture of coffee and tea), sage, and chocolate. The seventh compares the merits of mother's and nurse's milk, and the fifteenth is a refutation of the doctrine that it is beneficial to get drunk once a month. The eighth recommends a visit to Montpellier for consumption, while the fifth discusses the use of Tunbridge Wells waters in the treatment of kidney stones, and the sixth the benefits of the hot baths of Bath in promoting conception. The fourteenth is on the cure of scrofula by the royal touch, and in it Carr mentions that Charles II touched 92,107 persons between 1660 and 1682, concluding that, whether or not the royal touch was beneficial, it could certainly do no harm. Carr shows some acquaintance with the medical writings of his time, and speaks with admiration of Sir Thomas Browne's Religio medici. The impression left after reading his epistles is that he was a doctor of pleasant personality, not a profound physician, but one whose daily visit cheered the valetudinarian, and whose elaborate discussion of symptoms satisfied the hypochondriac.

Carr died in September 1706, and was buried in London on 29 September in St Faith's under St Paul's.

NORMAN MOORE, rev. JOHN SYMONS

Sources IGI · Venn, Alum. Cant. · Munk, Roll · R. W. Innes Smith, English-speaking students of medicine at the University of Leyden (1932)

Carr [Kerr], Robert, earl of Somerset (1585/6?–1645), favourite of James I, was born in Scotland, probably in 1585 or 1586, the youngest son of Thomas *Ker (d. 1586), laird of Ferniehirst, and his second wife, Jean (Janet) *Scott (b. c.1548, d. after 1593), daughter of William Scott of Buccleuch. Widely suspected of being a Catholic, Thomas Kerr was a staunch supporter of Mary, queen of Scots, a leading figure in the pro-Marian revolt of the early 1570s, and an exile for her cause from 1574 to 1580. Thanks to James VI's first great favourite, Esmé Stuart, later duke of Lennox, Ferniehirst returned to Scotland and, in 1581, received royal pardon and favour. Following Lennox's fall Ferniehirst was briefly exiled, but his court connections eventually brought him advancement, and in November 1584 he was appointed warden of the Middle March. But in July 1585, at a meeting with the English warden, Ferniehirst's men were involved in a brawl that left Lord

Robert Carr, earl of Somerset (1585/6?–1645), by John Hoskins, *c*.1620

Russell, son of the earl of Bedford, dead. The killing was probably unpremeditated, but the English blamed Ferniehirst and, under pressure, James had him arrested. Ferniehirst escaped from custody but died early in 1586.

The making of a favourite Thomas Kerr was succeeded as laird of Ferniehirst by Andrew, his eldest son from his first marriage. Young Robert, presumably helped by his late father's connections, came to court at some point after his father's death, was brought up in the royal household, and eventually became a page to George Home, later earl of Dunbar. On James VI's accession to the English throne in 1603 Kerr went south with Dunbar and, in 1604, probably on Dunbar's recommendation, he became a groom of the bedchamber, a post that brought frequent access to the royal person. At the accession day tilt in March 1607 Kerr (or, as the English spelt it, Carr) fell from his horse and broke his leg. The accident proved a turning point in his fortunes. The king decided to help nurse the injured groom and was soon captivated. By the end of 1607 Carr was widely recognized as a royal favourite, and in December he was knighted and created a gentleman of the bedchamber. The exact nature of his personal relationship with James remains difficult to assess. Carr enjoyed constant and unique access to the king's person, day and night, at Whitehall and at the hunt. The king, it was reported, would pinch Carr's cheek in public, smooth his clothes, and gaze at him adoringly, even while talking to others. Although historians disagree about whether the relationship was sexual the intensity of the king's love is evident in at least one of his few surviving letters to Carr.

Over the next eight years Carr steadily accumulated the material rewards of royal infatuation. Late in 1608 James gave him the manor of Sherborne, worth about £1000 a year, which had been confiscated from Sir Walter Ralegh. In 1611 Carr received the barony of Winwick and the custody of the Castle of Rochester. And in 1613 he obtained a significant block of lands in Westmorland and co. Durham. He also received a steady stream of cash and gifts from the king and from would-be clients seeking his assistance as a broker of royal favour.

Politics, 1610–1613 For his first three years as favourite Carr was content to translate James's affection into money, land, and prestige. At the end of 1610, however, he took his first steps towards more active political participation. If Sir Thomas Lake's report is reliable Carr's first intervention was an act of sabotage: in an attempt to damage the position of Robert Cecil, earl of Salisbury, Carr reportedly spread rumours that the Commons was intent on withholding supply until the king sent the Scots home. The rumour was calculated to turn James against the Commons, and thus scupper Salisbury's attempts to keep parliament in session long enough to get supply. The origin of this attempted sabotage is now impossible to uncover, though Carr may have been working with his old patron, Dunbar, a leading court critic of Salisbury's dealings with parliament. Whatever its origins the episode opened a new phase in Carr's career as favourite. With the king's encouragement Carr began to assume English dignities and to take on office and responsibility in the royal administration. In March 1611 James created him Viscount Rochester with the right to sit in the House of Lords. Two months later the new peer was installed, alongside the earl of Arundel, as a knight of the Garter. In June 1611 he was made keeper of Westminster Palace, and in April 1612 he was appointed to the English privy council. Shortly after Rochester's elevation to the council the Scotsman Viscount Fenton opined that the favourite was 'exceeding great with his Majesty, and if I should say truly, greater than any that ever I did see' (*Supplementary Mar and Kellie MSS*, 40–41).

Rochester also began to play a greater role in court factional politics and in the heated debates over domestic and foreign policy that were dividing the English élite. In these efforts he was encouraged not so much by the king as by an old friend, Sir Thomas Overbury. Late in Elizabeth's reign the two men had been introduced in Edinburgh, and their close friendship continued when Carr moved south. Beginning in 1610 or 1611, under Overbury's guidance, Carr began to forge a set of patronage and political connections at court, connections that moved him from a Scottish into an English orbit and landed him squarely in the middle of many of the bitterest political and factional disputes of the age.

Straitened royal finances remained the most pressing domestic problem, and the leading courtiers were divided over appropriate solutions. Some, like Henry Howard, earl of Northampton, and his nephew Thomas Howard, earl of Suffolk, advocated a series of money-raising projects that would obviate the need to work with parliament. Others, like the earls of Southampton and Pembroke, thought that a working relationship with parliament could be re-established and that an appropriately managed House of Commons would supply the king's fiscal wants. The court was also split over foreign policy, in particular the question of the prince of Wales's marriage. Northampton, Suffolk, and others, many of whom were crypto-Catholics, advocated a marriage alliance with Spain. Many Scots sought an alliance with France. And a third group, headed by Southampton, Pembroke, and Archbishop Abbot, favoured a protestant alliance as part of a generally pro-Dutch, anti-Spanish foreign policy.

Thomas Overbury helped broker a connection between Rochester and the Southampton–Pembroke group. The faction's initial political goal was to secure the appointments of Sir Henry Neville and Sir Ralph Winwood to the secretaries' offices vacated by Salisbury's death in May 1612. Neville offered a plan to manage parliament that, he claimed, would assure the crown significant financial assistance from the Commons. Winwood, an experienced diplomat, would, the faction hoped, be a powerful anti-Spanish voice in the formulation and administration of royal foreign policy. The plan was to use Rochester's position with the king to win Neville and Winwood a royal audience, and then to have the beloved favourite lobby James for the appointments. James, however, refused to fill the secretaries' offices. At the end of June 1612 he declared his intent to act as his own secretary, and by late July he had made Rochester his assistant. This *ad hoc* arrangement lasted for nearly two years. Some observers believed that Rochester had personally coveted the secretary's office and had therefore failed to lobby for Neville and Winwood, but the only real evidence for this view is Rochester's failure to secure the appointments. And for that failure, other more compelling explanations suggest themselves. Perhaps the most plausible is that Rochester realized that James was wary of appointing men too closely connected with the parliamentary trouble-makers who had stymied his ambitions during the 1604–10 sessions. Knowing the king's reluctance Rochester may have deliberately chosen to remain politically flexible. Although he worked with Neville and Winwood and got Neville an audience with James, Rochester clearly did not stake his all on the two men: for instance, he simultaneously developed a more than cordial relationship with Northampton, who openly backed alternative candidates for the offices. The campaign for Neville and Winwood was also hampered by Rochester's difficult relationship with Pembroke. During 1612 the favourite and the earl fell out over Rochester's securing of the reversion to the mastership of the horse. Stung by Pembroke's criticism Rochester circulated a defence of his conduct in which he claimed to be the virtuous courtier 'whose hands never took bribe' (Inner Temple Library, Petyt MS 538, vol. 36, fol. 81v).

The Essex annulment and the fall of Overbury Other forces were working to separate Rochester from Overbury and his allies. At some time probably in 1611 or 1612 Rochester had begun a secret romantic relationship with the earl of Suffolk's daughter, Frances *Howard (1590–1632), who was unhappily married to Robert Devereux, third earl of Essex. Initially Overbury had aided Rochester's romantic pursuit, penning love letters for the inarticulate Scot, but when the relationship deepened Overbury became understandably nervous. Rochester's romantic ties to the countess of Essex threatened to pull him into the political orbit of her father's family, and any ensuing quarrel with her husband would pit Rochester against Essex's closest allies at court, Southampton and Pembroke. But Overbury's heavy-handed attempts to end the relationship succeeded only in antagonizing Rochester and Frances Howard. At the same time James himself had become tired of Overbury's influence over Rochester—an element of jealousy was clearly at work—and had resolved to separate the two men. In April 1613 James offered Overbury an embassy abroad. Promised Rochester's protection Overbury refused the offer and a furious James ordered Overbury to be imprisoned in the Tower of London for contempt. A few weeks later the countess of Essex sued for a nullity of her marriage on the grounds of her husband's sexual impotence. Court observers, many of whom were shocked by the proceedings, soon learned that the nullity was to pave the way for the countess's remarriage to Rochester. With the open encouragement of the king, a narrow majority of a panel of ecclesiastical commissioners found in the countess's favour, ending her marriage to Essex on 25 September 1613. Ten days earlier, still imprisoned in the Tower of London, Sir Thomas Overbury had died. These two events transformed Rochester's career. They broke his old political alliances and decisively forged new ones, they brought him to the height of royal favour and reward, and they sowed the seeds of his ultimate destruction.

The true story of the events of 1613 is now almost impossible to distil from the versions presented during 1615 and 1616 when Rochester, his wife, and their alleged accomplices stood trial for Overbury's murder. Rochester, it was then charged, had cynically manipulated Overbury into refusing the offer of an embassy, had deliberately failed to work for his release, and had plotted with Frances to poison him. None of the evidence later used against Rochester conclusively proves his guilt, however. What little untainted evidence survives from the summer of 1613 is susceptible of an alternative reading that acquits Rochester of murder, although not of conspiracy and betrayal. A series of letters from Northampton to Rochester reveals that the favourite took part in a scheme to compel Overbury, as the price of his freedom, to forge an alliance with the Howard family. For much of the summer Overbury believed that Rochester was working for his release—indeed, Overbury's letters from the Tower show him trying to orchestrate the timing and manner of Rochester's approaches to the king. The two men also discussed using the white powders that Rochester had sent Overbury, which eventually became crucial evidence in the poisoning case, as emetics to sicken Overbury and thus work on the king's sympathy. Unbeknownst to Overbury, however, Rochester's chief goal was to make his former friend acknowledge the new facts of court life. Rochester and Northampton wanted to neutralize Overbury's threat to the nullity, the remarriage, and the consequent Rochester–Howard alliance by convincing Overbury to pledge himself in writing to the earl of Suffolk. With the new lieutenant of the Tower, Sir Gervase Elwes, acting as a go-between Overbury was badgered to commit himself. Late in August 1613 Overbury at last gave in and sent conciliatory letters to Suffolk—yet his release never came. Perhaps James himself refused the petition for Overbury's freedom; perhaps Rochester and the Howards were waiting for the nullity decision before letting Overbury go; or perhaps, least plausibly, the complicated effort to engineer Overbury's alliance with the Howards was a ruse concealing a murderous intent. Whatever the reason, early in September, Overbury became convinced that Rochester had been playing a double game. In an extraordinary letter from the Tower, Overbury bitterly accused his friend of ingratitude and betrayal and threatened to publicly expose his dishonour. A few days later Overbury was dead. Shortly afterwards, in a letter to Rochester, Northampton poured scorn upon the dead man, a sure sign that Northampton, at least, believed that Rochester would shed few tears at Overbury's passing. Indeed, his death occasioned little grief in court circles, and many believed the malicious rumour that he had died of syphilis. In all likelihood, however, Overbury had been murdered. While Rochester and Northampton worked to bend him to their will Frances Howard, stung by Overbury's bitter insults, had, after several botched attempts, successfully plotted to poison him.

Politics, 1613–1615 Overbury's death removed the last obstacle to Rochester's personal and political alliance with the Howards. It also seems to have encouraged the king to bestow further honours and responsibilities on his favourite. In October 1613 Rochester was appointed to the Scottish privy council, and in December he became lord treasurer of Scotland, a post he exercised by delegation. On 4 November 1613 he was created earl of Somerset and Baron Brancepeth, and on 26 December, in a lavish court wedding, he finally married Frances Howard. In the summer of 1614, following Northampton's death, Somerset was given the earl's offices of lord privy seal and warden of the Cinque Ports and succeeded his father-in-law, Suffolk (who had been appointed lord treasurer), as lord chamberlain.

Somerset had reached the pinnacle of power. He was a privy councillor in Scotland and England, the most dominant figure in the royal bedchamber, and ceremonial head of the court; his kinsmen occupied key administrative posts in both England and Scotland; and he was immensely wealthy, with a major landed base in the north of England—where he was to be appointed lieutenant of Durham in 1615—and a large suite of rooms in Whitehall, crammed with jewellery, gold and silver metalwork, rich clothing, paintings, and statues. During 1614 and 1615 he continued to intervene in the political life of the court and

nation, working for the most part in harness with his new Howard allies. Along with Suffolk and Northampton he reluctantly agreed that straitened royal finances required the calling of parliament early in 1614. Although he played a minor role in the Lords' sessions, he played a more significant part in preparing for the meeting. Some evidence suggests that he was party to at least some of Northampton's and Suffolk's duplicitous schemes to ensure the parliament's failure, though other evidence indicates that he may have kept his political options open—he personally intervened, for instance, to secure the selection of the contrarian Sir Edwin Sandys as MP for Rochester. After the parliament's dissolution, however, Somerset enthusiastically supported Suffolk's attempts to finance the government through non-parliamentary projects.

More important, perhaps, Somerset became the leading figure in attempts to secure a Spanish marriage for Prince Charles. His motives in this endeavour are unclear but were probably political and strategic rather than religious. He was probably not Catholic, but his wife and many in her family were, and there is no evidence that he shared the hatred and fear of popery that animated so many of his contemporaries. In January 1614, probably on Northampton's suggestion, he had opened informal dealings with the Spanish ambassador in London. During the summer of 1614, after James had been brought into the negotiations, Somerset was the chief intermediary exchanging offers and counter-offers with the Spanish. By the summer of 1615 the earl, working with his adviser Robert Cotton, had stepped up the pace of negotiations; he may even have begun making offers to the Spanish without the king's full knowledge and prior approval.

Somerset's high-risk negotiations with the Spanish in 1615 were probably a response to the crisis in his position at court. During the summer progress of 1614 the young George Villiers had caught the royal eye. A loose coalition of courtiers, some personally and some ideologically opposed to Somerset and the Howards, began working for Villiers's advancement as a way of displacing Somerset from royal favour. His response to this challenge was so heated that he risked permanently alienating the king's affections. He angered James by disrupting the royal repose with late night verbal tirades and threats, by bemoaning his mistreatment, and by refusing to continue sleeping in the royal chamber, despite the king's pleas. The spring and summer of 1615 were marked by struggles between Somerset's supporters and enemies over court appointments and privileges, and for months the balance of factional power tipped back and forth, to the confusion of observers. Early in the summer Somerset, fearing imminent defeat, requested a royal pardon covering offences that might later be alleged against him. James granted a pardon for minor crimes and agreed to sign a second concerning major ones, but late in July he was dissuaded from doing so by the opposition of Lord Chancellor Ellesmere. After the pardon was refused many observers gave Somerset up for lost, but a series of surprising victories in the late summer once more buoyed his hopes.

The Overbury scandal At this moment of apparent recovery the machinery of Somerset's final destruction was set in motion. In June 1615 Ralph Winwood, who had been appointed secretary shortly before the meeting of the 1614 parliament, and who was personally and ideologically inclined to the anti-Somerset faction, had acquired evidence raising significant doubts about the cause of Overbury's death. Sir Gervase Elwes had confessed to Winwood that early in his tenure as lieutenant of the Tower he had uncovered and, as he then believed, thwarted an attempt by Overbury's keeper, Richard Weston, to poison his prisoner. As the factional struggle raged through the summer of 1615 Winwood sat on this potentially damaging information. Early in September, however, when Somerset's position seemed to have stabilized, Winwood presented Elwes's evidence to James. The king ordered Elwes to put his statement in writing, and this time the lieutenant revealed that Weston had recently confessed that Overbury had, in fact, been murdered with a poisoned enema. Elwes's testimony implicated not only Weston but also the courtier Sir Thomas Monson, a Howard client, and Anne Turner, a close confidante of the countess of Somerset. By the end of September 1615 a full-scale murder investigation had begun. Early in October, over Somerset's heated objections, James appointed Lord Chief Justice Sir Edward Coke to lead a special investigatory commission. Evidence against the Somersets mounted, and on 17 October the earl and his pregnant wife were put under arrest. On 9 December, still imprisoned, the countess of Somerset gave birth to their daughter, Anne.

During the autumn and early winter of 1615 several of the Somersets' alleged accomplices were tried and executed for Overbury's murder, and many of the trials featured damning evidence against the earl and countess. The affair caused much comment and speculation. Rumours spread that the Overbury murder had been part of an international Catholic conspiracy to destroy the royal family and install Somerset as king. Poets and other writers offered the public various understandings of the earl's crime. Some presented him as a weak man seduced into murder by his wife's sexual wiles. Others dwelt at length on Somerset's hideous betrayal of his virtuous friend, Overbury. The predominant theme, however, was an indictment of Somerset as the quintessential man of ambition who had risen from social obscurity to great power not because of birth or virtue but because of his physical beauty. His ambition, it was argued, had almost inevitably led him on to other, more serious, crimes.

The Somersets were indicted for murder in January 1616, but throughout the spring their trials were repeatedly postponed—delayed, in part, by attempts to build a treason case against the earl for his dealings with the Spanish. By the end of April, however, the treason investigation had stalled, and prosecutors, now led by Sir Francis Bacon, returned to the murder case. By the time the Somersets stood trial, on 24–5 May 1616, the king, with Bacon's guidance, had already decided to spare them. The countess cleared the way by confessing to the murder

before her trial and then pleading guilty in court. The earl, however, adamantly maintained his innocence. Before his trial Somerset received messages from the king urging him to confess, but he stood his ground. He pleaded not guilty to the charge, but after twelve hours in court he was convicted and sentenced to die.

In the days following the convictions most observers thought the pair would hang, but as the weeks passed it became clear to all that the king would not carry out the sentences. In July the countess was granted a pardon, though she remained imprisoned in the Tower. The same month observers began to note signs of improvement in Somerset's fortunes. His arms were not torn down during the Garter ceremonies at Windsor, and he successfully negotiated full liberty of the Tower, where he was seen walking with the Garter medallion around his neck. By December 1616 it was falsely rumoured that the countess was pregnant again and somewhat more reliably reported that Somerset was to be granted a £4000 annual pension. In the summer of 1617 during the king's progress to Scotland Somerset's sisters, their husbands, and several prominent Scots nobles petitioned unsuccessfully for his freedom. Through 1618 the rumours continued—of money grants made to the earl, of quarrels between the earl and the countess—but no word of their release ever came.

In January 1622 the Somersets were finally freed from the Tower. They retreated to Lord Wallingford's house in Oxfordshire, with orders from the council to remain there. Late in 1623 they were living in Aldenham, Hertfordshire, but were now eager to move to Surrey. During the summer of 1624 Somerset at last petitioned James for a pardon, and in October the document was drawn up 'in as ample a manner as could be devised' (*Letters of John Chamberlain*, 2.582). Fully pardoned, Somerset moved to a house in Chiswick, but he was required to promise he would attend neither court nor parliament. The earl and countess were still living in Chiswick when the countess died, on 23 August 1632.

Later years During the 1620s and 1630s much of Somerset's time was devoted to his complicated financial affairs. He had lost his jewels and lands upon his conviction, but, as the newsmongers had reported late in 1616 and early in 1617, the king had agreed to a financial arrangement that granted him £4000 a year and restored the barony of Winwick, worth about £900 annually in rents. In the summer of 1623 Somerset approached Lord Treasurer Middlesex concerning some £7000 still owed him from a 1615 land transaction. Middlesex, who now owned the lands in question, settled the account by paying off £7000 worth of Somerset's debts; the remainder of his debts seems to have been cleared with moneys raised by the crown from other lands he had once owned. Loose ends remained. Early in the 1630s Charles I tried to retrieve a jewel still in Somerset's possession and was angered when the earl at first refused to surrender it. In 1635 the council investigated the whereabouts of £60,000 from the French debt allegedly paid into Somerset's hands long ago. In the same year Somerset petitioned the king for a grant of the full amount that he had been promised in 1617, claiming that he had received only £3000 a year of the £4000 granted by James. In 1637 Somerset's financial resources were again strained when his only child, Anne, married William, Lord Russell, son of the fourth earl of Bedford. The groom's father, no doubt worried by Somerset's problematic past—and perhaps even aware that the earl's father had been involved in the death of a Russell fifty years earlier—drove a hard financial bargain before approving the match. Somerset eventually agreed to pay a dowry of £12,000.

Although forbidden to attend court or parliament Somerset continued to play a minor part in the politics of the age. He initially refused to pay the controversial forced loan of 1626, and in 1630 he was among a group of Robert Cotton's friends arrested for circulating a treatise on arbitrary rule that was taken to be a critique of Charles I's political ambitions. The treatise was in fact a document sent to Somerset many years before, during his days as favourite, which had ended up in Cotton's collection. The authorities eventually dropped the investigation. There is little evidence of Somerset's response to the political crisis of the late 1630s and early 1640s. He did not, however, side with the king during the civil war, and appears to have remained instead in the parliamentarian stronghold of London. Somerset died in July 1645 and was buried on 17 July in St Paul's, Covent Garden.

Although his efforts never equalled those of some of his contemporaries Somerset was a significant collector of art and patron of writers. Among his literary clients was the poet George Chapman, who continued to celebrate Somerset's virtues in the years following his disgrace. Somerset's art collection, begun when he was favourite, mostly dispersed at his fall, and rebuilt after his release, included many Netherlandish and Italian paintings, which reveal him to have been on the cutting edge of aristocratic taste. The collection seems, however, to have been dispersed for good in 1637, when the earl sold much of it off to raise money for his daughter's dowry.

Somerset himself was painted several times. Two miniatures in the National Portrait Gallery—one from his days as favourite, one from c.1620—neatly encapsulate the remarkable story of his rise and fall. In the earlier portrait, a court miniature from the Hilliard school, he is depicted in the rich, flamboyant, and colourful clothing of the mid-Jacobean court, whose fashions were shaped by a king who liked his male courtiers to indulge in sartorial display. The later portrait, by John Hoskins, shows the fallen favourite in sober black, the antithesis of his gaudy earlier self. A decade after his fortunes had been dashed by the most spectacular and notorious court scandal of the age, Robert Carr chose to present himself as a man of distinctly non-courtly virtue.   ALASTAIR BELLANY

Sources Letters of James VI and I, ed. G. P. V. Akrigg (1984), 335–40 · T. Birch, ed., The court and times of James the First, 2 vols. (1848), vol. 1 · CSP dom., 1603–18; 1633–4, 58, 66; 1635, 45, 244; 1635–6, 78–9; 1636–7, 297 · CSP Scot., 1563–71; 1574–86 · GEC, Peerage, new edn, 2.79–80; 12/1.66–8 · E. R. Foster, ed., Proceedings in parliament, 1610, 2 (1966), 346 n. · W. Fraser, The Scotts of Buccleuch, 2 vols. (1878), vol. 1, p. 133 · F. Francisco de Jesus, El hecho de los tratados del matrimonio pretendido por el principe de Gales con la serenissima infante de España, María / Narrative of the Spanish marriage treaty, ed. and trans. S. R. Gardiner, CS, 101 (1869) · The manuscripts of his grace the duke of Buccleuch and Queensberry … preserved at Drumlanrig Castle, 2 vols., HMC, 44 (1897–1903), vol. 1 · Report on the manuscripts of the marquis of Downshire, 6 vols. in 7, HMC, 75 (1924–95), vols. 3–6 · H. Paton, ed., Supplementary report on the manuscripts of the earl of Mar and Kellie, HMC, 60 (1930) · State trials, vol. 2, pp. 785–850, 911–1034 · Correspondence of Sir Robert Kerr, first earl of Ancram, and his son William, third earl of Lothian, ed. D. Laing, 2 vols., Roxburghe Club, 100 (1875), vol. 1, pp. 5–6 · The letters of John Chamberlain, ed. N. E. McClure, 2 vols. (1939) · The letters and epigrams of Sir John Harington, ed. N. E. McClure (1930), 32–4 · Letters of John Holles, 1587–1637, ed. P. R. Seddon, 1, Thoroton Society Record Series, 31 (1975) · R. Surtees, The history and antiquities of the county palatine of Durham, 4 vols. (1816–40), vol. 4, pp. 67–8, 165 · Memorials of affairs of state in the reigns of Q. Elizabeth and K. James I, collected (chiefly) from the original papers of … Sir Ralph Winwood, ed. E. Sawyer, 3 vols. (1725), vol. 3, pp. 478–9 · 'Sir Gervase Ellowis, Lieutenant of the Tower, his Apologie, touching his knowledge of the Death of Sir Thomas Overbury', 1615, Bodl. Oxf., MS Tanner 299, fols. 194r–196r · recollections of Nicholas Overbury, BL, Add. MS 15476, fol. 92v · Thomas Overbury's letters to Carr, summer 1613, BL, Harley MS 7002, fols. 281r–288r, 290–91 · Carr's installation as earl of Somerset, BL, Lansdowne MS 261, fol. 134 · correspondence of Sir Thomas Edmondes, BL, Stowe MS 175 · Earl of Northampton, letters to R. Carr, summer 1613, CUL, MS Dd.3.63 · Winwood's account of Elwes's testimony, Hunt. L., Huntington MS 41952, fols. 104v–105r · copy of Carr's self-defence, 1612, Inner Temple Library, London, Petyt MS 538, vol. 36, fol. 81v · Somerset's financial dealings with Middlesex, CKS, Cranfield MSS U269/1 E64, and U269/1 OE888 · state papers, James I, PRO, 14/81/86; 14/82/59, 60; 14/172/2 · Garrard newsletters on Anne Carr's marriage, City of Sheffield Libraries, Strafford papers, WWM Str P 16 (3); Str P 17 (137) · letters, Staffs. RO, MS D593S/4/60/11, 13 [on the selection of Sir Edwin Sandys as MP for Rochester, 1614] · S. L. Adams, 'The protestant cause: religious alliance with the west European Calvinist communities as a political issue in England, 1585–1630', DPhil diss., U. Oxf., 1973 · A. Bellany, The politics of court scandal in early modern England: news culture and the Overbury affair, 1603–1660 (2002), esp. chaps. 1, 3–5 · A. R. Braunmuller, 'Robert Carr, earl of Somerset, as collector and patron', The mental world of the Jacobean court, ed. L. L. Peck (1991), 230–50 · R. P. Cust, The forced loan and English politics, 1626–1628 (1987), 102 n. 13, 231 · A. M. Hind, Engraving in England in the sixteenth and seventeenth centuries, 2 (1955), 191, 268–9 · M. Lee, jun., John Maitland of Thirlestane and the foundation of the Stewart despotism in Scotland (1959), 71–5 · T. L. Moir, The Addled Parliament of 1614 (1958) · M. Prestwich, Cranfield: politics and profits under the early Stuarts (1966) · R. Strong, Tudor and Jacobean portraits, 2 vols. (1969), vol. 1, pp. 295–7; vol. 2, pl. 579–83

Archives BL, letters to William Trumbull

Likenesses Hilliard school, watercolour miniature, c.1611, NPG · R. Elstrack, double portrait, line engraving, c.1613–1615 (with countess), BM, NPG, V&A; repro. in Truth brought to light (1651) · S. Passe, line engraving, c.1613–1616, BM; repro. in Hind, Engraving in England · J. Hoskins, miniature, c.1620, Royal Collection [see illus.] · J. Hoskins, miniature, second version, Buccleuch estates, Selkirk · oils (after miniature by J. Hoskins, c.1620–1630), NPG · portrait, repro. in R. Strong, Tudor & Jacobean portraits

Carr, Robert James (1774–1841), bishop of Worcester, the son of the Revd Colston Carr, a schoolmaster at Twickenham and later vicar of Ealing, was born at Twickenham, received his primary education in his father's school, and afterwards went to Worcester College, Oxford, where he matriculated in 1792, graduating BA in 1796 and MA in 1806. In 1797 he married Nancy (d. 1826), daughter of John Wilkinson of Roehampton, with whom he had a numerous family, of which only four children survived him. In

1798 he was ordained by the bishop of Salisbury, and, after holding some unimportant preferments for a short time, he was presented to the vicarage of Brighton in 1804. During this appointment he began a lasting friendship with the prince regent, who acted as his patron. He was prebendary of Salisbury 1819–24, of Chichester 1821–4, and of Hereford 1822–4; in 1820 he was appointed dean of Hereford, and graduated BD and DD.

In 1824 Carr's patron, now George IV, who regarded him as 'an excellent and exemplary man' (*Correspondence*, 8.444), planned for him to become bishop of Chichester. This he became in 1824, and with his bishopric held a canonry in St Paul's Cathedral. His visit to Chichester Cathedral was the first by a bishop since 1755. Despite his friendship with George IV, he failed to persuade the king in 1824 to allow bishops not to wear wigs. He was also appointed clerk to the closet, an honorary position which he held until the accession of Queen Victoria, when he was dismissed for his conservatism. In 1831 he was translated to the bishopric of Worcester, in fulfilment, as it was understood at the time, of a promise made by his late patron (Carr was the bishop who attended George IV during his last illness).

Carr devoted himself almost entirely to his episcopal duties, and, although constant in his attendance at the House of Lords, took little interest in politics. He was one of the bishops who voted against the Roman Catholic Relief Bill and, if he did not speak against the measure, allowed his opinions to be seen by the number of petitions against it which he presented. He abstained on the Reform Bill in 1832, having been translated by the whig government which sponsored it. Although strict in the enforcement of religious observances, he had a decided leaning towards evangelicalism. He died on 24 April 1841, at Hartlebury Palace, near Worcester, from paralysis, and was buried on 3 May in the churchyard of Hartlebury parish. His only published works were sermons preached for charitable objects.

A. C. BICKLEY, *rev.* H. C. G. MATTHEW

Sources *Annual Register* (1841) · *GM*, 2nd ser., 15 (1841), 650 · O. Chadwick, *The Victorian church*, 2 vols. (1966–70) · P. Barrett, *Barchester: English cathedral life in the nineteenth century* (1993) · *The correspondence of George, prince of Wales, 1770–1812*, ed. A. Aspinall, 8: 1811–1812 (1971)
Archives Kirkoswald College, Kirkoswald, Cumbria, corresp.
Likenesses S. W. Reynolds, mezzotint, pubd 1828 (after G. Hayter), BM, NPG · G. Hayter, oils

Carr, Sir (Charles) Roderick (1891–1971), air force officer, was born in Fielding, New Zealand, on 31 August 1891, the eldest son in the family of four sons and one daughter of Charles Carr, a landowner, and his wife, Margaret Douglas, *née* Liddell. Both parents had emigrated from England. Educated at Fielding public school and Wellington College, New Zealand (1906–8), Carr then farmed at Manawatu before enlisting, in 1914, as a trooper with the 6th Manawatu mounted rifles in Egypt. In July 1915 he was commissioned as a temporary flight sub-lieutenant into the Royal Naval Air Service (RNAS) initially in no. 6 kite balloon section, spotting for the artillery at the battle of

Loos. In March 1916 he graduated as a pilot from the Grahame-White Flying School at Hendon, after which he qualified on both aeroplanes and seaplanes with the RNAS. He subsequently served at RNAS Eastbourne then, for a year, as 'an excellent instructor' (PRO, ADM 273) on Caudron G3 aircraft at the Vendôme naval air station, at Tours in France, where he was promoted flight commander.

On 1 April 1918, when the Royal Air Force was established, Carr transferred to that service with the rank of lieutenant (temporary major), again qualified on both aeroplanes and seaplanes. In May 1919 he joined General Ironside's short-lived north Russian expedition supporting the White Russian (anti-Bolshevik) forces centred on Archangel and Murmansk. Carr commanded the locally designated 2 squadron flying DH9, DH9a, and Sopwith Snipe aircraft and based at Troitsa on the Dwina river front. Ironside later wrote that the task of supporting the White Russians required 'indefatigable energy and daring, under conditions which were always hazardous and sometimes attended by almost insurmountable difficulties' (PRO, WO106/1179). He recalled visiting Troitsa, where he met 'the Officer Commanding the fighters, Major Carr, [who] carried out a feat of chasing an enemy plane back to its aerodrome, landing after it and shooting up the other planes before coming back' (Ironside, 157). Carr was awarded the DFC, and the (White) Russian government made him a commander of the orders of St Stanislav and of St Anne—both with crossed swords. In October 1919 he was placed on the long list of unemployed officers in the *Air Force List*, but he was then appointed as chief of the aviation staff of the newly independent state of Lithuania. His programme for the expansion of the new force was not accepted, and he resigned in March 1920, although he remained in Lithuania with a trading company which he and others (including the New Zealander Frank Worsley) had formed. In the following year Carr joined Sir Ernest Shackleton's final Antarctic expedition to pilot the tiny Avro 554 *Antarctic Baby* aircraft, which was shipped stowed between decks on the expedition's ship *Quest*. Shackleton had also been in north Russia as Ironside's cold-weather equipment adviser. The expedition was curtailed before reaching Antarctica as a result of Shackleton's death in January 1922.

Back in Britain, Carr took part in the king's cup air race of 1922 and returned to air staff duties in the RAF with the rank of flying officer in February 1923. In 1927 he was chosen to make an attempt on the world long-distance flight record by flying non-stop from the United Kingdom to Karachi in a standard RAF Hawker Horsley bomber fitted with extra fuel tanks. His first attempt, on 20 May 1927, ended after flying 3420 miles from RAF Cranwell in 34½ hours, when Carr and his navigator (L. E. M. Gillman) had to ditch their aircraft in the Persian Gulf. Their new world record stood for only a short time as, two hours later, Charles Lindbergh landed near Paris on the evening of 21 May, having flown 180 miles further. Carr subsequently made two further, and less successful, attempts at the record. He was awarded the AFC and promoted squadron leader in 1928.

In December 1928 Carr joined 9 (bomber) squadron at Manston and a year later was appointed chief instructor of 4 flying training school at RAF Abu Sueir in Egypt. On 31 January 1931, at the Savoy Chapel, he married Phyllis Isabel (c.1899–1969), the daughter of Charles Stephen Elkington, a merchant of Amersham, Buckinghamshire. They had one son. In late 1932 Carr was made adjutant of the RAF depot in Aboukir, Egypt, and in August 1934 he was posted home to RAF Gosport to work up Fleet Air Arm squadrons of Swordfish aircraft. Promoted wing commander in July 1935, he joined the royal naval aircraft-carrier HMS *Eagle* in January 1937 as senior air force officer in charge of flying, the carrier's two Swordfish 'torpedo spotter reconnaissance' squadrons (nos. 813 and 824) being manned by both Fleet Air Arm and RAF personnel. In November 1938, towards the end of his two year tour in *Eagle* on the China station, he was promoted group captain.

In May 1939 Carr commanded a flying training school at Brize Norton, then, when the Second World War broke out, he moved to a base of the advanced air striking force in France, behind the Maginot line. Following the withdrawal of allied forces from the continent in June 1940, he spent twelve months as air officer commanding Northern Ireland and was awarded the CBE. After a short period at Bomber Command headquarters, in July 1941 he started a three and a half year tour as air officer commanding 4 group in Bomber Command. From his headquarters at Heslington Hall, near York, and now promoted air vice-marshal, he had command of thirteen bomber squadrons (including two manned by French personnel), equipped by 1944 with Halifax aircraft, which operated from fourteen airfields in north Yorkshire. He was appointed CB in 1943 and mentioned in dispatches, then awarded the Croix de Guerre and Légion d'honneur by the French government. In June 1945, promoted acting air marshal, he was made deputy chief of staff (air) to the Supreme Headquarters of the Allied Expeditionary Force on the continent.

Appointed KBE in July 1945, Carr was made air officer commanding headquarters base air forces, south-east Asia, in August 1945, then in January 1946 became air officer commanding-in-chief India (commanding air forces in south-east Asia) before he returned to the UK in October 1946. On his retirement from the RAF in February 1947 he joined the Ministry of Civil Aviation as controller of airfields for the London area and south-east England, a position which he held until January 1950. He then spent a period as a market gardener. From 1947 to 1968 he was king-of-arms of the Order of the British Empire. Having lived in retirement at Bampton, Oxfordshire, he died of prostate cancer and bronchopneumonia at the RAF Hospital, Uxbridge, on 15 December 1971.

ROBIN WOOLVEN

Sources *The Times* (18 Dec 1971) · *Daily Telegraph* (18 Dec 1971) · *WW* · Burke, *Peerage* (1967) · C. Bowyer, *RAF operations, 1918–1938* (1988) · O. Tapper, *The world's great pioneer flights* (1975) · C. Dobson and J. Miller, *The day we almost bombed Moscow: the allied war in Russia, 1918–20* (1986) · Lord Ironside, *Archangel* (1953) · memo for the general staff by General Ironside on the evacuation of north Russia, 15 July 1919, PRO, WO106/1179 · PRO, AIR27/125, AIR28/313 · J. W. Best, 'Sir Roderick Carr', *Journal of the Aviation History Society of New Zealand*, 41/2 (1998); 42/1–2 (1999) · royal naval air service personal records, PRO, ADM 273 · m. cert.

Likenesses photographs, repro. in Best, 'Sir Roderick Carr'

Wealth at death £13,363: probate, 23 May 1972, *CGPLA Eng. & Wales*

Carr, Roger (1543?–1611/12), Church of England clergyman, was born in Yorkshire, of unknown parentage. He matriculated sizar from Pembroke College, Cambridge, at Michaelmas 1566 and graduated BA in early 1570. On 23 January 1573 he was instituted to the Essex rectory of Rayne near Braintree, on the presentation of Henry Capell of Rayne Hall. He was ordained priest by Edwin Sandys, bishop of London, on 6 January 1574, when the registrar recorded his age as thirty and his birthplace as 'Runthmell' in the diocese of York—presumably Rothwell, in the West Riding. Three published works by R. C. were formerly assigned tentatively to Carr, but the first, *The Defence of the Soul Against the Strongest Assaults of Satan* (1578), is no longer extant.

Granted a diocesan preaching licence on 28 November 1581, Carr became a member of the nonconformist clerical conference known as the Braintree classis, probably at its inception a few months later. He was thus a close associate of George Gifford, Richard Rogers, and Ezekiel Culverwell. *A Godly Learned and Fruitfull Sermon*, on the fourteenth chapter of St John, appeared under the initials R. C. in 1584. It was dedicated to Sir William Pelham by one John Jorden, who claimed to have no personal knowledge of the author. The copy which survives in Lambeth Palace Library has a manuscript attribution to 'D. Squire'—presumably Dr Adam Squire, archdeacon of Middlesex, who is not otherwise known to have published anything.

Early in 1584 Carr was one of twenty-seven Essex ministers who petitioned against Archbishop Whitgift's drive for conformity by means of subscription to his three articles. Many of these men, Carr included, were suspended for nonconformist practices as a result of John Aylmer's diocesan visitation of London in July 1586. In March 1587, with five other members of the Braintree meeting, including Gifford and John Huckle, he petitioned parliament for restoration. Perhaps as a direct result of this initiative William Tunstall of Great Totham and Giles Whiting of Panfield, the only other beneficed petitioners, were deprived by the high commission in May 1587.

Carr, however, survived, remaining a member at Braintree probably until it ceased to meet in 1589 or 1590. He was admonished to wear the surplice at the 1589 episcopal visitation and again told to certify that he was using it in that of 1592. Yet after 1604, when James I insisted on the reintroduction of Whitgift's three articles as his yardstick of conformity within the church, Carr was never again cited at an episcopal visitation for failure to observe the ceremonies and must be accounted one of the many former radicals who reluctantly conformed. He probably died at Rayne late in 1611, since his successor there was instituted by 20 January 1612.

Carr left no will but in December 1590 a parishioner, Thomas Binckes, appointed Carr his joint executor, leaving bequests to his (unnamed) wife and six children: Katherine, Arthur, Gamaliel, Margaret, Mary, and Elizabeth. The third book by R. C. attributed to Carr, *A Godlie Form of Household Gouernment* (1598), is now known to have been by Robert Cleaver. BRETT USHER

Sources Venn, *Alum. Cant.*, 1/1.296 · GL, MSS 9531/13, fol. 169v; 9535/1, fol. 152r; 9537/3–10 · A. Peel, ed., *The seconde parte of a register*, 2 vols. (1915) · R. G. Usher, ed., *The presbyterian movement in the reign of Queen Elizabeth, as illustrated by the minute book of the Dedham classis, 1582–1589*, CS, 3rd ser., 8 (1905) · F. G. Emmison, ed., *Essex wills*, 5: *The archdeaconry courts, 1583–1592* (1989), no. 1026 [will of T. Binckes]

Carr, William (1921–1991), historian, was born on 1 April 1921 in Workington, Cumberland, the only child of William Carr (1876–1933), a colliery cashier, and his wife, Eleanor Stewart (1880–1933). He was educated at Workington County Technical School. Bill (as he was known to his family and his many friends) was among the finest historians of Germany of his generation. His interest in Germany had been shaped by personal experience of war and subsequent service in the occupation forces. He had fought in France as part of the signals corps and the Royal Artillery before working from July 1945 as part of the team interrogating suspected Nazi war criminals. His deployment in the following months with the field security police at Husum in Schleswig stirred the interest in that region that was to culminate in his first book, *Schleswig-Holstein 1815–1848: a Study in National Conflict* (1963). The book emanated from the thesis he had submitted for his PhD, awarded in 1955 at the University of Birmingham, where he had graduated with first-class honours in 1948; he had recommenced in 1947 the studies he had begun in 1939, which were interrupted in 1941 through service with the armed forces.

In fact, Carr's interest in the Schleswig-Holstein question had already borne its first fruits in his undergraduate dissertation, which drew the particular commendation of his tutors. They commented that 'Mr. Carr possesses a distinct flair for research and is capable of going on to produce valuable and original work'. The remarks accompanied the successful application that Bill made in 1949 for an assistant lectureship at the University of Sheffield. With his new post, Bill began the career at Sheffield that would eventually lead to a personal chair in 1979, and commenced the loyalty to Sheffield University that lasted until his retirement.

Bill was a popular and effective university teacher, and was in great demand as a speaker at other universities and to audiences of sixth-form pupils, not least because of his extensively used *History of Germany, 1815–1945* (1969), which went into a fourth edition months after his death in 1991. Excellent teacher though he was, Bill insisted that the essence of the historian's work was in research and writing, and his own publications form the base of his lasting reputation as a historian. His main interests—in

issues of foreign policy and war—found expression in a brief but incisive study of Nazi foreign policy, *Arms, Autarky, and Aggression* (1970), an excellent account of the interwoven strategies of Germany, the USA, and Japan in *Poland to Pearl Harbour* (1985), and *The Origins of the Wars of German Unification* (1991). In tackling such major issues he looked at them afresh, with an independent and original mind. He was open to new approaches and flexible in interpretation. His clarity of thought owed much to the heavy dose of common sense that characterized all his work. His way was invariably to question the obvious or orthodox, to read sources 'against the grain', to reject any notion of outcomes predetermined by impersonal forces, while at the same time to emphasize the structural agencies which influenced individual actions in history. These qualities were especially well reflected in his *Hitler: a Study in Personality and Politics* (1978), a work described as 'a remarkable synthesis' (J. Lukacs, *The Hitler of History*, 1998, 32). For all its brevity, it remains an outstanding analysis, less a biography than a blend of thematic reflections, full of originality and penetrating insight.

Outside his scholarly career, Bill was actively engaged in public service in his adopted city of Sheffield. He was a member of the national health executive in Sheffield between 1966 and 1971, a member of the city's education committee from 1968 to the early 1980s, chairman of the governors of the city college of education from 1971 to 1976, and chairman of the finance and general purposes committee of Sheffield City Polytechnic from 1976 to 1989. In addition, he was a JP in Sheffield from 1969 until his death, and a member (subsequently vice-chairman and chairman) of the board of visitors at Wakefield prison from 1967 until 1991. He was also a committed trade unionist and a lifelong active supporter of the Labour Party: he served as chairman of the Hallam divisional Labour Party between 1959 and 1966. More surprising to those who did not know him well was that, following his conversion to Roman Catholicism at the age of seventeen, he continued to hold strong religious beliefs.

Not least, Bill was a devoted family man. He had met Kathleen Mary (Kate) Williams (*b.* 1926), then a fellow student (subsequently a teacher), while at Birmingham University. They married on 28 December 1950, and their daughter Mary Louise was born two years later. Bill drew great strength from his family, and rejoiced in the birth of his granddaughter, Eleanor, in 1990. Bill and Kate, an inseparable couple, were generous hosts with an extensive circle of friends, arising in part from his public service and work for Sheffield Labour Party as well as from academic contacts in Britain, America, and Germany. Bill was a cultured man, with interests in art, music, literature, and foreign travel. He was a warm, kind person, full of good humour and good sense, sharp in intellect, generous in feelings, unstinting in support for younger colleagues, loyal in friendship. His northern working-class roots left a lasting mark on his personality and values, as well as on his approach to the past. When given a professorial room—a 'Führerzimmer', as he dubbed it—in the history department at Sheffield, one of his first acts was to remove the picture of Charles I on the wall and replace it with a more ideologically conducive one of his political hero, Aneurin Bevan. He regarded a career in a university lecturing and writing on German history as a privilege and was wont to comment—reminding himself of the privations of his parents' generation—that, whatever its less appealing sides, it was certainly 'better than working'.

Bill's growing distinction led inevitably to his promotion to a chair in Sheffield and offers to take up visiting professorships in the USA, which he accepted at Lincoln, Nebraska (1970), the University of Pennsylvania (1972), Salt Lake City, Utah (1983), and New Mexico (1986). He retired from his post at Sheffield University in 1986. Only days before he died Bill heard the news that he had been awarded, for services to German history, the Bundesverdienstkreuz by the president of the Federal Republic of Germany, a fitting tribute to a fine scholar. William Carr died of a coronary thrombosis on 20 June 1991 at his home, 39 Tapton Crescent Road, Sheffield, and was buried on 28 June in Sheffield.   IAN KERSHAW

Sources private information (2004) [Kate Carr] · Sheffield University, Carr MSS · *German History*, 9/3 (1991), 327–9 · *CGPLA Eng. & Wales* (1992)
Likenesses photograph, priv. coll.
Wealth at death under £125,000: probate, 19 Feb 1992, *CGPLA Eng. & Wales*

Carr, Sir **William Emsley** (1912–1977),

newspaper proprietor, was born on 30 May 1912 at 9 Pembridge Square, Kensington, London, the fourth son of Sir (William) Emsley *Carr (1867–1941), editor and chairman and managing director of the *News of the World*, and his wife and cousin, Jennifer Lascelles (Jenny), the daughter of Lascelles Carr, co-founder and first editor of the *Western Mail*. Educated at Clifton College and Trinity College, Cambridge, Carr joined the *News of the World* in 1937. His father was still at the editorial helm, with William's elder brother Harry his trusty lieutenant and obvious heir. Harry Carr had inherited Sir Emsley's business acumen and eye for a good headline. He also shared his father's sporting prowess, his standing in polite society, and above all his remarkable capacity to remain a model of rectitude while at the same time enlivening Sunday mornings across the nation: news of lurid court cases and exposés of sexual nonconformity, reluctantly conveyed to open-mouthed readers by shocked but dutiful reporters, provided the *News of the World* with a sensationalist recipe for success, its sales peaking around 8 million in the early 1950s. On 22 September 1938 William Carr married Jean Mary (b. 1911/12), daughter of Neil Forsyth, a managing director. They had a son and a daughter.

In July 1941 Sir Emsley Carr died. Two years later, Harry Carr was killed while serving as a pilot in the RAF. William Carr, familiarly known as Bill, was now entrusted with protecting the family stakehold in a business focused on a single purpose: publication every Sunday of a newspaper purchased by half the households in Britain. The formula

was simple and successful, the overheads low, and the staff loyal. With a board reluctant to risk change, the price was complacency. Nevertheless, the late 1950s did see the *News of the World* pioneer a fresh mix of sexual revelation and criminal investigation, culminating in its coverage of the 1963 Profumo scandal.

Carr did not actually become chairman of News of the World Ltd until 1952. He had already assumed several of his father's honorary appointments in both golf and athletics, not least club chairman at Walton Heath. However, despite his membership of the general council of the press, Carr refused to adopt a similar high profile within the newspaper industry. He eschewed any wider responsibility for the well-being of Fleet Street, or of the provincial press, despite acquiring Berrow's Ltd, a group of newspapers concentrated on Hereford and Worcester. Carr was only interested in the *News of the World* and its workforce. Knighted in 1957, Sir William entertained lavishly. His largesse was legendary, and he indulged his editorial staff, who were always invited to Lady Carr's annual garden party at Bentley Wood, the family's country home in Sussex. The chairman would also foot the bill, including the green fees and the bar tab, at Walton Heath, where staff had the freedom of the course every Monday.

Not surprisingly, by 1960 Carr and his board were poorly regarded in the City. The *News of the World* failed to acquire the Newnes publishing group. There were rumours in 1961 of a bid for the ailing Odhams conglomerate; but Carr could see that reversing the fortunes of the *Daily Herald* would prove a hopeless task. Nevertheless, Carr was a director of Reuters from 1960 to 1967, and he was able to identify investment opportunities outside publishing: a new holding company invested substantially in TWW, the Welsh commercial television station, and acquired a 38 per cent stake in the French production company Tele-Europe Société Anonyme. Neither of these initiatives was likely to prove a major revenue earner, at a time when sales of the *News of the World* were beginning to slip. The company was ripe for a take-over, being highly profitable but poorly led, and heavily dependent upon a single product.

In 1969 Robert Maxwell seized on City rumours that Carr might lose his controlling interest: a cousin's substantial shareholding was for sale, and Carr could not afford to buy him out. Maxwell launched a hostile bid, and Carr looked to the then little-known Australian media magnate Rupert Murdoch as his company's saviour. A complicated share deal gave News International its first British title. Carr served as chairman of the new company for three months, with Murdoch as chief executive. But then Murdoch assumed full control. Sir William was left with the honorary titles of life president and consultant to the board.

A generous and convivial man, Sir William Carr lacked the business skills to survive the ruthless approach a new generation brought to boardroom politics in the late 1960s. During his final years, although never short of loyal golfing and drinking partners such as Sir Douglas Bader, he had to cope with serious illness. Carr died on 14 November 1977 at his home, Bentley Wood, Framfield, Uckfield, Sussex. He was survived by his wife.   ADRIAN SMITH

Sources M. Engel, *Tickle the public: one hundred years of the popular press* (1996), 230–42 · *The Times* (15 Nov 1977) · *The Times* (25 Nov 1977) · *WWW, 1971–80* · Viscount Camrose [W. E. Berry], *British newspapers and their controllers*, rev. edn (1948), 81–5 · C. Bainbridge and R. Stockdill, *The 'News of the World' story* (1993) · b. cert. · m. cert. · d. cert. · *CGPLA Eng. & Wales* (1978) · *The Times* (2 Aug 1941)
Wealth at death £1,125,835: probate, 17 Feb 1978, *CGPLA Eng. & Wales*

Carr, William Holwell (1758–1830), benefactor to the National Gallery, was born in Exeter (and baptized there on 4 April 1759), the son of Edward Holwell (*d.* 1793), apothecary, and his wife, Isabella Newte. Named after his uncle, the Revd William *Holwell, he was himself known as William Holwell until 1798, when he acquired the additional surname Carr. He went up to Exeter College, Oxford, in 1776, and continued as a fellow of the college until 1793; but in 1781, aged twenty-three, he was 'allowed to travel' and went to Italy, where he studied art and began the picture buying which was to become his obsession.

An opportunity to acquire effortless income presented itself in 1791, when the rich benefice of Menheniot in Cornwall fell vacant. The living was in the gift of Exeter College; only its fellows were eligible. Hastily, Holwell acquired a degree in divinity. On 17 November 1791 the dean of the college presented him with the living, worth £1134 per annum. Holwell (later Carr) never resided at Menheniot, but drew its income for life, employing a curate at £100 per annum to undertake his duties, in due course defending his absenteeism to the church commissioners on the grounds that the climate was 'very inimical to my health' (Cook, 54). He might almost have been Trollope's model for 'The College Fellow who has Taken Orders' (essay in *Clergymen of the Church of England*, 1866).

Holwell's fortunes were further improved by his marriage on 18 May 1797 to Lady Charlotte Hay (1761/2–1801), the 35-year-old eldest daughter of James Hay, fifteenth earl of Erroll, and his wife, Isabella Carr, and heir to large Carr estates in Northumberland. Those estates devolved upon Lady Charlotte the following year; in order to claim them, both she and her husband took the additional name of Carr (by royal authority, 20 November 1798). Holwell Carr's wife died in 1801, after giving birth to their only child, a son who died at the age of five; on his death the Carr estates reverted to his mother's family.

How far four years of marriage to Lady Charlotte Hay had increased Holwell Carr's purchasing power can only be guessed at. Certainly it appears that he acquired his most important pictures after his marriage. He did not marry again, devoting his energies single-mindedly to improving his collection, haunting the salerooms and the dealers, continually trading upwards. For just over a year from March 1805 he owned a one-sixth share in the dealer William Buchanan's highly speculative trade in importing old masters from war-torn Europe. This gave him the right to select newly arrived pictures for himself, on special terms; in this way he acquired, for instance, Federico

Barocci's *Madonna and Child* and Rubens's oil sketch *S. Bavo about to Receive the Monastic Habit at Ghent*. Farington notes some sharp practice on Carr's part, and his relationship with Buchanan soon soured. Carr withdrew his stake in the business—to the relief of Buchanan, who pronounced Carr 'a perfect Grumbler' and 'a damned bore' (Brigstocke, 424, 431).

Holwell Carr acquired more respectable status by joining such distinguished collectors as Sir George Beaumont, John Julius Angerstein, and Sir Abraham Hume in 1805 as a founding subscriber and director of the British Institution. He was elected FRS in 1806, and as an honorary (that is, amateur) exhibitor he showed twelve landscapes (all now untraced) at the Royal Academy between 1804 and 1821; he was also not above 'touching up' old pictures. In the bitterly satirical anonymous *Catalogue Raisonné* of 1816, attacking directors of the British Institution, Carr was described as 'Priest patcher and picture dealer ... He with these qualifications has wriggled himself into a dependent acquaintanceship with the other members of the Society, who despise him while they use him'.

An assertive man, obsessed with prices and provenance, Holwell Carr had no small talk. Farington relates instances of his habit of publicly disputing, 'arms *akimbo*', the authenticity of other collectors' pictures. Carr himself was not infallible, but did not live long enough to read Dr Waagen's scornful verdict (Waagen, 1.187) on what was generally considered the 'crown of his collection'—Carr's 'Leonardo' (*Christ Disputing with the Doctors*, promptly reattributed by the National Gallery to Bernadino Luini).

Between 1800 and 1825 Carr added to his collection such works as Titian's *Holy Family and a Shepherd*, Claude's *Landscape: David at the Cave of Adullam*, Tintoretto's *St George and the Dragon*, Guercino's *Angels Weeping over the Dead Christ*, and Garofalo's *St Augustine with the Holy Family* (all works mentioned here are in the collection of the National Gallery, London). Most of the paintings he bought were by Italian (and some French) masters, but, arguably, the finest of all was Rembrandt's *Woman Bathing in a Stream*, bought for £165 at Lord Gwydir's sale in 1829, when Carr was seventy-one. It was his last purchase, and in many ways the most courageous he ever made.

Holwell Carr led a mostly solitary life, devoting himself to his collection, his socializing limited to the Athenaeum and the Roxburghe Club, of each of which he was a founder member. He lived in Devonshire Place, where his collection hung 'in two drawing rooms'. Prince Pückler-Muskau, to whom Carr showed it in 1828, records that it 'has cost him twenty thousand pounds' (Pückler-Muskau, 308–10).

Carr's will, made in 1828, was very short. It bequeathed 'the whole of my collection of Ancient Pictures' to the nation, but (following Sir George Beaumont's example) in trust to the British Museum until a purpose-built national gallery could accommodate them. A portrait of himself, painted by John Jackson (*c*.1828), was to be placed beside his pictures. Carr did not entirely forget the parish of Menheniot, where his benefice over forty years is likely to have yielded him about £20,000, or roughly the estimated cost of his collection. To the poor of Menheniot he left £500. Holwell Carr died in Devonshire Place on 24 December 1830. He was buried at Withycombe Raleigh, near Exmouth. Six months after his death his collection of thirty-five paintings was delivered to the National Gallery, London. JUDY EGERTON

Sources J. Egerton, 'Revd. William Holwell Carr', *National Gallery catalogues: the British paintings* (1998), 399–405 · C. W. Boase, *Register of the … members on the foundation of Exeter College, Oxford* (1879), 111–12 · M. Cook, ed., *The diocese of Exeter in 1821, vol. 1: Cornwall* (1958), 54 · *A complete parochial history of the county of Cornwall*, 3 [n.d.], 311 · Farington, *Diary*, 8.3033; 13.4480, 4514–15, 4643; 15.4928–9 · H. Brigstocke, ed., *William Buchanan and the 19th century art trade* (privately printed by the Paul Mellon Centre for Studies in British Art, 1982), 17, 464; letters 90, 95–8 · *A catalogue raisonné of the pictures now exhibiting in Pall Mall* (1816) [exhibition catalogue, Pall Mall, London] · G. F. Waagen, *Works of art and artists in England*, 1 (1838) · H. L. H. Pückler-Muskau, *Tour in Germany, Holland and England in the years 1826, 1827, and 1828*, 4 (1832)
Likenesses L. Vaslet, pastel drawing, *c*.1790, Exeter College, Oxford · J. Jackson, oils, *c*.1828, NPG · J. Jackson, oils, National Gallery, London · P. C. Wonder, group portrait, oils study (patrons and lovers of art), NPG

Carre, Thomas. *See* Pinkney, Miles (*bap.* 1599, *d.* 1674).

Carre, Walter Riddell- [*formerly* Walter Riddell] (1807–1874), topographer, the second son of Thomas Riddell of Camieston (*d.* 1824) and his wife, Jane (*d.* 1833), daughter of Captain Walter Ferrier of Somerford, was born in Edinburgh on 4 August 1807. He was descended from the family of Riddell of Riddell in Roxburghshire (which appeared in Sir Walter Scott's *Lay of the Last Minstrel* as 'ancient Riddell's fair domains'). After completing his education at the high school in Edinburgh, he joined the firm of Messrs Fletcher, Alexander & Co. in London. On 30 November 1830, in Edinburgh, he married Elizabeth Riddell (*d.* 1869), the daughter of Lieutenant-Colonel Lachlan Maclauchlan of the 10th regiment; she may have been related to him. He retired from the firm in 1848 and moved to Hertfordshire.

In 1860 Riddell succeeded by the will of his uncle Admiral Robert Riddell-Carre to the estate of Cavers Carre in Bowden, Roxburghshire; he assumed the additional surname and arms of Carre. From this time he devoted himself to extensive research into family and county records, and the biography of border worthies. He gave occasional lectures on these subjects, and contributed to newspapers and to *Notes and Queries*. Only one book resulted from his research: *Border Memories, or, Sketches of Prominent Men and Women of the Border*, which contained the genealogical history not only of his own family, the Riddells, but also of the Elliots, Scotts, Douglases, and other ancient border families. The book was published posthumously in 1876, with a biographical sketch by James Tait. Riddell-Carre also took an active interest in various border societies, and he was a justice of the peace and a commissioner of supply for the county of Roxburghshire. On 15 September 1871 he married for the second time; his second wife was Mary Falconer (*d.* 1878), the daughter of William Currie of Linthill. She survived Riddell-Carre when he died on 1 December 1874 at Cavers

Carre. He was interred at Bowden on 7 December 1874. His only son (from his first marriage), Captain Thomas Alexander Riddell-Carre, succeeded to his estate.

T. F. HENDERSON, *rev.* NILANJANA BANERJI

Sources J. Tait, 'memoir', in W. Riddell-Carre, *Border memories, or, Sketches of prominent men and women of the border*, ed. J. Tait (1876) · Burke, *Gen. GB*
Wealth at death £12,168 3*s.* 1*d.*: additional estate, 13 Jan 1876, NA Scot., SC 62/44/59

Carreras, Sir James Enrique (1909–1990), film executive, was born on 30 January 1909 at 9 Chiswick Lane, Chiswick, as Jaime Enrique Carreras, the only child of Enrique Carreras, commission merchant, and his wife, Dolores Montousse. He was educated privately. In 1913 his father, who came from the Carreras tobacco family of Spain, became a film exhibitor and built the first of a small chain of cinemas in London, the Blue Halls. James joined the business as a youth and worked his way up from usher to assistant manager. In 1927, when he was very young, he married Vera St John (*d.* 1986); they had one son, Michael [*see below*]. In 1935 his father and William Hinds, known professionally as Will Hammer, founded Exclusive Films. James worked for this firm also. It distributed imported second features and a few films made by Hammer himself for Hammer Productions, a small company which he had registered in 1934. This was moribund by 1937. During the Second World War James rose from private to lieutenant-colonel in the Honourable Artillery Company, but he rejoined the firm after the war.

Will Hammer now wished to return to production and revive the name of Hammer. He was associated with a few films made at Marylebone Studios in 1947. In 1948 he joined with Enrique and James Carreras to form a new company, Hammer Film Productions, as the production arm of Exclusive Films. Production proper began in 1948 at a mansion studio at Bray, near Windsor. The company was registered in February 1949 and James Carreras, who was to dominate the company, became chairman. They made routine second features, a number of them based on BBC radio serials, using the large house and nearby locations as inexpensive settings. Output was large, and films were quickly and cheaply made by a small permanent team. Much of the writing and direction was by James's son Michael and Will Hammer's son Anthony Hinds, and there was an informal and family atmosphere in the unit.

In 1955 they made a science fiction thriller, *The Quatermass Experiment*, in which the survivor of a space journey is gradually consumed by a mysterious fungus. This had been a popular BBC television serial, and its enormous success as a film encouraged Carreras to introduce a second seeping mass of something horrible in *X the Unknown* the next year. A third successful film, shown in 1957, was *Quatermass II*, which portrayed people taken over by menacing space organisms. The Gothic horror tale was out of fashion at the time, but Carreras now took a well-considered gamble, and with *The Curse of Frankenstein* later that year found his niche. Christopher Lee and Peter Cushing first appeared as Hammer's favourite bogeymen in this lurid and profitable colour remake of the 1931 film

Frankenstein. From now on an important part of Hammer Films' output featured vampires, werewolves, resurrected mummies, blood, and gore, and there were repeated appearances of Frankenstein and Dracula, producing delicious dread in the audience. Most other film-makers and the critics scorned these films, made in six to eight weeks and promoted with lurid posters and stunts. But they had a large and enthusiastic public in Britain and abroad, especially in America, where they had a huge cult following among teenagers. Ironically, it was Carreras who achieved the assured distribution in America which had so long eluded more serious British producers. His was the most consistently profitable film company in Britain, earning £1.5 million in foreign exchange one year. The company received the queen's award for industry in 1968. Carreras took no part in the creative side of film-making.

However, times changed. The studio was sold in 1968, and although production continued elsewhere the verve had gone. In 1972 Carreras sold his holding to Michael and resigned as chief executive, though he remained chairman. He moved to the EMI group of companies, where he acted as special adviser for some years. With the appearance in 1973 from America of *The Exorcist*, an exceptionally frightening film, the writing was on the wall for the escapist Hammer brand of horror. The last Hammer film was made in 1978, and the company was in the hands of the receivers by 1979. Carreras then had a remarkable idea: to sell the Hammer House of Horror series to television in the early 1980s. This was then repackaged as video cassettes in the late 1980s for yet another set of youngsters going through the monsters stage.

In appearance and character Carreras, a good-looking, mild-mannered, soberly dressed businessman, who was a strong family man and devout Christian, was a surprising person to have brought about the phrase 'Hammer horror'. But the essential innocence of the genre, with its saving grace of absurdity, was very different from the sadistic and violent films produced by other companies in later years.

Carreras was a prominent member of the Variety Club, the show-business charity, being its chief barker in 1954-5. He was chairman of the board of Variety Clubs International for eleven years and president from 1961 to 1963. In 1970 he was knighted for his extensive charity work over many years, especially in the cause of young people—he was president of the London Federation of Boys' Clubs for five years. He had been appointed MBE in 1944, possibly for secret operations in Spain during the war. He became KCVO in 1980 and also received honours from Spain and Liberia. Carreras died of a heart attack on 9 June 1990 at his home, Queen Anne Cottage, Friday Street, Henley-on-Thames.

Carreras's only son, **Michael Henry Carreras** (1927–1994), film producer and director, was born on 21 December 1927 in London and educated at Frays College, Uxbridge, and Reading School. He had early ambitions to be a jazz trumpeter, and remained a jazz enthusiast. At sixteen (being too young for military service) he joined Exclusive Films, initially in the publicity department. Following national service in the Grenadier Guards, he rejoined the company. His first film as producer was Vernon Sewell's *The Dark Light* (1951), and he went on to produce many of Hammer's most successful films of the 1950s, including its first science-fiction film, *Four-sided Triangle* (1952). He won critical acclaim for *Yesterday's Enemy* (1959) and *Hell is a City* (1960). However, there was friction between Carreras and his father, and in 1961 he established his own company, Capricorn Productions, though he continued to work for Hammer. His most profitable Hammer film was *One Million Years BC* (1966), starring Raquel Welch. He rejoined Hammer as head of production in 1971, and in 1972 bought out his father, becoming managing director. Seven years and only a handful of films later Hammer was bankrupt and Carreras was forced to resign. After unsuccessful attempts to revive his film career he died of cancer on 19 April 1994 in London, survived by his wife, Jo, and three sons. RACHAEL LOW, rev.

Sources *The Times* (12 June 1990) · *Daily Telegraph* (20 June 1990) · *The Independent* (18 June 1990) · D. Pirie, *A heritage of horror* (1973) · D. Gifford, *The British film catalogue, 1895–1970: a guide to entertainment films* (1973) · *CGPLA Eng. & Wales* (1990) · b. cert. · d. cert. · *The Times* (21 April 1994) · *The Independent* (22 April 1994) · *The Guardian* (27 April 1994) · *Daily Telegraph* (7 May 1994) · *CGPLA Eng. & Wales* (1995) [Michael Henry Carreras]
Archives FILM BFI NFTVA
Wealth at death £518,985: probate, 5 Sept 1990, *CGPLA Eng. & Wales* · £21,267—Michael Henry Carreras: probate, 19 April 1995, *CGPLA Eng. & Wales* (1995)

Carreras, Michael Henry (1927–1994). *See under* Carreras, Sir James Enrique (1909–1990).

Carrick. For this title name *see* Brus, Robert (VI) de, earl of Carrick and lord of Annandale (1243–1304); Butler, Edmund, earl of Carrick (*d.* 1321); Bruce, Edward, earl of Carrick (*c.*1280–1318); Bruce, Alexander, earl of Carrick (*d.* 1333) [*see under* Bruce, Edward, earl of Carrick (*c.*1280–1318)].

Carrick, Edward. *See* Craig, Edward Anthony (1905–1998).

Carrick, James [*alias* Valentine Carrick] (*c.*1695–1722), highwayman, was born in Dublin, the third son of a jeweller (*d. c.*1714) who had 'left off Trade and liv'd upon his Estate' after 'having acquired a considerable Fortune' (*Select Trials*, 1.200). The elder Carrick was supposed to have purchased an ensigncy for his youngest (and allegedly, favourite) child when the latter was still 'a perfect Boy'—probably about 1710 (*Lives of the most Remarkable Criminals*, 1.163). James Carrick was stationed in Spain for several years, where he was said to have 'signalized himself' less by his martial valour than his numerous 'Engagements with the Spanish Ladies of Pleasure' (*Select Trials*, 1.200). About 1714, after peace was concluded, Carrick made his way to London, where he 'squander'd away his Time and his Money in Dressing, Gaming, Drinking and Whoring' (ibid., 1.201). And, while accounts characterizing Carrick as an inveterate fop, coxcomb, and rake conform all too conveniently to the contemporary profile of the gentleman highwayman, this was a stereotype not only borne out by subsequent events, but also one to which Carrick himself appears to have in large measure subscribed.

Needless to say, Carrick was 'quickly reduced to very low Circumstances', and, after subsisting for a time as the 'Pensioner' of various 'Women of the Town', some time in 1719 he and another Irishman, named Smith, resolved to 'take a Purse on the High-way' (*Select Trials*, 1.201; *Lives of the most Remarkable Criminals*, 1.169; *Ordinary's Account*, 18 July 1722, 5). The two soon fell in with a more experienced highwayman, one Thomas Butler, and committed 'a very great Number of Robberies' in Kent and Essex (*Ordinary's Account*, 8 Feb 1721, 6). From 1719 to 1720 Carrick lodged in London with Butler, who styled himself esquire and passed for 'a Person of Fashion', while 'his Man Jack … went for his Footman' (ibid.; *Select Trials*, 1.12). In September 1720 Carrick was tried at the Old Bailey for stealing a sword and sentenced to be transported; however, his judgment being commuted, he was branded on the thumb and released the following May. It seems likely that Carrick owed this reprieve to the fact that while imprisoned in Newgate he turned evidence against Butler: the latter was tried and convicted in January 1721 for a robbery that he, Smith, and Carrick had committed the previous year, and was hanged the following month at Tyburn.

Upon learning of these developments Carrick's relatives 'entreated him to return Home [to Dublin]', where his brother promised to procure him a respectable place; James, however, soon resumed 'his former Courses'—in the spring and summer of 1721 committing 'a Multitude' of highway robberies in the neighbourhood of London, and in 1722 becoming chief of 'the most Villanous Set' of (largely Irish) street robbers in the metropolis (*Ordinary's Account*, 18 July 1722, 5; *Lives of the most Remarkable Criminals*, 1.170; *Daily Journal*, 4 July 1722; *Select Trials*, 1.204). In the small hours of 1 July 1722 Carrick and two of his countrymen, John Molony and Daniel Carrol, robbed two gentlemen returning in a chair from a tavern (*Lives of the most Remarkable Criminals*, 1.170). Carrick, while issuing threats at gunpoint, demanded their money civilly enough, but at first receiving only silver—much of which, 'his Hand trembling', he dropped—became enraged, 'sw[earing] G[od] d[am]n ye Sir, do you trifle?' (*Proceedings*, 4–7 July 1722). Carrick and Carrol then made off with a quantity of gold and other valuables; Molony, however, was pursued by the chairmen, and, after narrowly escaping a watchman, was seized by the latter's dog. Carrick was apprehended with the stolen items on his person a few days later, when he was recognized while buying a suit of clothes.

On 5 July Molony and Carrick were tried at the Old Bailey, where they made a 'very frivolous defence'; their cross-questioning of witnesses served only to confirm their guilt, and seems to have been calculated 'to make the People smile at their Premeditated Bulls' (*Proceedings*, 4–7 July 1722; *Lives of the most Remarkable Criminals*, 1.176). At one point Carrick archly informed the prosecutor that at the time of the robbery he had been holding not one pistol, as he had testified, but two. Both men were found guilty and condemned to death. While awaiting sentence in Newgate, Carrick's behaviour continued 'equally singular and Indecent': he cavorted with 'loose Women', and regaled the throngs of curious visitors who paid admission to see him with witticisms and 'the Adventures of his Life' (*Lives of the most Remarkable Criminals*, 1.172). Carrick, a Catholic, scornfully rejected the ministrations of the ordinary of Newgate and, in the picaresque and largely impenitent account of his life he supposedly dictated himself, complained bitterly of the latter's 'Importunities' in attempting to extract his confession (*Compleat and True Account*, 1).

Carrick, also known as Valentine Carrick, was 'a brisk young Fellow' with fair hair and a pale complexion, who, although described as 'a little Man', made up for his lack of stature with a 'genteel … Appearance' and an engaging 'Person', not to mention 'the Gaiety of his Temper' (*Select Trials*, 1.201; *Proceedings*, 4–7 July 1722; *Lives of the most Remarkable Criminals*, 1.163; *Ordinary's Account*, 18 July 1722, 5). Indeed, more so even than Jack Sheppard, it may well have been Carrick—the favourite of both 'the Ladies' and 'the Mob'—who served as the model for John Gay's Macheath in *The Beggar's Opera* (1728) (*Lives of the most Remarkable Criminals*, 1.169; *Select Trials*, 1.205). Even on his way to Tyburn, on 18 July 1722, aged about twenty-seven, Carrick 'failed not in the least' in his 'Resolution' to cut a bold and dashing figure, spending his last moments 'Giggling, taking Snuff' and 'making apish Motions to divert himself and the Mob' (*Lives of the most Remarkable Criminals*, 1.172; *Select Trials*, 1.205). At the place of execution Carrick 'laughed and smiled upon all whom he there knew', and shortly before being turned off 'gave himself genteel Airs in fixing the Rope aright about his Neck' (*Ordinary's Account*, 18 July 1722, 6). Thus Carrick, the quintessential 'game' highwayman, died as he had lived.

ANDREA McKENZIE

Sources *A compleat and true account of all the robberies committed by James Carrick, John Malhoni, and their accomplices* (1722) · *The lives of the most remarkable criminals*, 3 vols. (1735) · T. Purney, *The ordinary of Newgate: his account of the behaviour, confessions, and last dying words of the malefactors that were executed at Tyburn on Wednesday the 18th of July, 1722* (1722) · *The proceedings on the king's commission of the peace* (1721–2) [Old Bailey sessions papers, 4–7 July 1722] · *Select trials at the sessions house in the Old Bailey*, 4 vols. (1742) · *Daily Journal* (4 July 1722) · *Daily Journal* (19 July 1722) · *Daily Post* [London] (4 July 1722) · *St James's Journal* (5 July 1722) · *Weekly Journal, or, British Gazetteer* (7 July 1722) · *Weekly Journal, or, Saturday's Post* (28 July 1722)

Carrick, John (d. 1380/81), chancellor of Scotland, is of unknown origins, but his surname and strong links throughout his career with the diocese of Glasgow may suggest descent from the kindred of the ancient earls of Carrick. He is described as 'skilled in decrees' in a papal grace of 10 April 1374 (Rome, Vatican City, Archivio Segreto Vaticano, registra Avinionensia, vol. 193, fol. 345v), and therefore presumably studied canon law at a European university; although sometimes styled 'master' in contemporary sources, it does not appear that he was in fact a graduate. Probably before 1360 he had become chancellor in the diocese of Glasgow under Bishop William

Raa, but it is not clear how long he held this office. In 1362 he acted as proctor for the Glasgow chapter in a dispute with Bishop Raa, an appointment which hints at the forensic skills of the canon lawyer; these may also have been exercised when he was one of the arbiters in a dispute between Sempringham and Paisley abbeys in April 1373. Carrick acquired the prebend of Moffat, Dumfriesshire, and at some time before 1374 also came to hold the church of Bothwell in Lanarkshire, both charges being in the diocese of Glasgow.

By 1361 Carrick was a papal sub-collector in Scotland under William Grenlaw and had also entered royal service as clerk of the wardrobe, perhaps helped by the patronage of Archibald Douglas, later third earl of Douglas (d. 1400), himself prominent in the king's service. During the 1360s he was successively audit clerk of the king's household and king's secretary or keeper of the privy seal. Carrick resigned the latter to become royal chancellor in March or April 1370, being in charge of the king's writing office or chapel and the great seal. He held this post until February or March 1377, and it is noteworthy that, although appointed by David II, he continued in office when Robert II succeeded as king in 1371. His period in charge of the royal seals was one of significant development in their use.

Carrick was a regular envoy to England under David II, an exchequer auditor every year from 1364 to 1377 except 1365, and a participant in the general and judicial business of parliament during the same period. He was the king's choice to fill the bishopric of Dunkeld when it fell vacant in 1369, but failed to secure the appointment at the papal court. Apart from his links with Archibald Douglas and the diocese of Glasgow, Carrick's later career seems to have been almost entirely confined to the service of the king. He was the recipient of many payments from royal revenues, and after his retirement from the chancellorship he continued to draw a pension from the burgh ferme of Lanark. It was reported to the exchequer audit of February 1379/80 that he had collected this pension, but in March 1380/81 it was said to have been paid to his executors. His death therefore took place between these dates. Carrick's career is an excellent example of how in the later middle ages clerics possessed of legal, financial, and administrative skills could come to play an important role at the highest levels of lay administration and government. HECTOR L. MACQUEEN

Sources D. E. R. Watt, A biographical dictionary of Scottish graduates to AD 1410 (1977), 89–91 · G. Burnett and others, eds., The exchequer rolls of Scotland, 2–3 (1878–80) · C. Innes, ed., Registrum episcopatus Glasguensis, 2 vols., Bannatyne Club, 75 (1843); also pubd as 2 vols., Maitland Club, 61 (1843) · RotS · CDS, vol. 4

Carrick, John Donald (1788–1837), songwriter and journalist, was born on 22 April 1788 at Glasgow, the son of Elizabeth Donald and William Carrick, a porter. His father was originally from Buchlyvie, Stirlingshire. He was put to work early in the office of a Glasgow architect, and around 1805 he became a counting-house clerk. In 1807 he abandoned the post and walked to London, where a Scottish tradesman gave him a trial as a shop-boy. In 1809 he gained employment with a London branch of the Staffordshire potters Spodes & Co. He acquired sufficient knowledge of china to return to Glasgow in 1811, and set up business in Hutcheson Street.

At this time Carrick took up writing, producing several humorous Scottish songs, and a Life of Wallace for young people; but in 1825 a prolonged litigation led to his insolvency. As a manufacturer's agent he subsequently visited the highlands, and learned Gaelic. On returning to Glasgow in 1828 he was engaged as sub-editor on the Scots Times, and contributed articles to The Day, a short-lived Glasgow daily paper.

In 1830 Carrick produced a two-volume Life of Sir William Wallace of Elderslie, which was generally well received. In 1832 he edited and partly wrote Whistle-Binkie, or, The Piper of the Party, a collection of humorous songs. A year later he accepted the full editorship of the Perth Advertiser, but quarrelled with the managing committee; in February 1834 he started the Kilmarnock Journal, but once again fell out with the proprietors. Around this time he was attacked by a paralysis of the mouth, and in 1835 he returned to Glasgow, his health completely shattered.

Carrick edited and contributed to The Laird of Logan (1835), a collection of Scottish tales and witticisms, and contributed articles to the Scottish Monthly Magazine. He died in Glasgow on 17 August 1837, and was buried in High Church graveyard, Glasgow. A new edition of The Laird of Logan appeared in 1841, and numerous editions of Whistle-Binkie were published over the half-century following his death. JENNETT HUMPHREYS, rev. DOUGLAS BROWN

Sources Anderson, Scot. nat. · Irving, Scots. · J. D. Carrick, ed., The laird of Logan, or, Wit of the west, 2nd ser. (1841) · old parochial register, Glasgow

Carrick, Thomas Heathfield (1802–1875), miniature painter, was born on 4 July 1802 at Upperby, near Carlisle in Cumberland, and was baptized at St Cuthbert's, Carlisle, on 4 November 1802, the second child of John Carrick, a glass and china merchant and cotton-mill owner of Castle Street, Carlisle, and his wife, Mary Anderson. He was educated at Carlisle grammar school and by his uncle, the Revd John Topping. As an artist he was entirely self-taught; his skill in portraiture was evident at an extraordinarily early age. Having quarrelled with one of the members of his family, he suddenly left home and went to work for a chemist in Carlisle named Brunel, who soon began to take an interest in his advancement. Carrick himself eventually became a chemist in Carlisle, but his attention was so entirely focused on painting that he neglected his business. He began to paint miniatures on ivory of well-known northern sitters and, from 1827, to exhibit them at the Carlisle Academy.

In 1829 Carrick married Mary Mulcaster, with whom he had five children. Having by then established a high reputation as a miniaturist in Carlisle, he soon gave up his business and in 1836 moved to Newcastle upon Tyne and then, in November 1839, to London. Two years later he began to exhibit miniatures, from an address at 44 Berners Street, London, at the Royal Academy, and he continued to show miniatures there until 1866. Among his most remarkable sitters were Sir Robert Peel and Lord John Russell, the poets Samuel Rogers (exh. RA, 1848; Weston Park, Shropshire), William Wordsworth (priv. coll.), Caroline Norton, Eliza Cook, and Henry Wadsworth Longfellow; and, from the stage, William Farren (Garrick Club, London), William Macready, and Luigi Lablache. Carrick's vivacity as a conversationalist, and his store of anecdotes, enabled him to awaken the interest of his sitters and seize a lively likeness. His miniature of Thomas Carlyle was notable as one of his most brilliant successes; yet while it was in progress Mrs Carlyle more than once exclaimed that she was sure it would never be a convincing likeness, as she had never seen her husband so animated as when he was sitting to Carrick. Carrick was straightforward and unambitious; although more than once offered an associateship in the Royal Academy, he invariably declined it.

Carrick was one of the first miniaturists to paint miniatures on marble, a technique which he developed about 1830 and which later earned him the Silver Isis medal at the Society of Artists (1838) and a medal from Prince Albert, the prince consort (1845). Towards the end of his career, with the demise of the miniature in sight, he also turned his hand to the new science of photography. He moved to Scarborough to work for a photographer called Sarony, making miniature copies after photographs and colouring miniatures over a photographic base, and he later set up his own photography business in Regent Circus, London. When this failed, in 1868 he abandoned his profession and retired to Newcastle upon Tyne on the Turner annuity awarded to him by the Royal Academy. There, seven years later, he died on 31 July 1875. Carrick's *Self-Portrait* on marble (c.1830) is in the Tullie House Museum, Carlisle, and several examples of his miniatures on ivory and marble are in the Victoria and Albert Museum, London.

CHARLES KENT, *rev.* V. REMINGTON

Sources *Cumberland artists, 1700–1900* (1971), 28–9 [exhibition catalogue, Carlisle City Art Gallery, 1971] · D. Foskett, *Miniatures: dictionary and guide* (1987), 282–3, 506 · B. S. Long, *British miniaturists* (1929), 62–3 · L. R. Schidlof, *The miniature in Europe in the 16th, 17th, 18th, and 19th centuries*, 1 (1964), 129 · B. Stewart and M. Cutten, *The dictionary of portrait painters in Britain up to 1920* (1997) · Graves, *RA exhibitors* · private information (1886) [I. Allom] · G. Ashton, *Pictures in the Garrick Club*, ed. K. A. Burnim and A. Wilton (1997), no. 212 · personal knowledge (1886)
Likenesses T. H. Carrick, self-portrait, watercolour on marble, c.1830, Tullie House Museum, Carlisle

Carrie, Isabella Scrimgeour (1878–1981), suffragette and schoolteacher, was born on 3 May 1878 at 26 Wardmill Road in the parish of St Vigeans, Arbroath, the daughter of Richard Carrie (c.1836–1912), bleachfield worker, and his wife, Ann Robertson Harris (c.1842–1903). Isabella was one of only three children who survived beyond infancy and the only one to survive into adulthood.

Carrie spent her early years in Arbroath, where she

attended Inverbrothock public school and then Arbroath high school. She left school at fourteen to become a pupil teacher at the Abbey School. The pupil-teacher system was common in Scotland at this time, especially for women, providing a four-year apprenticeship of teaching by day and studying at night. She then sat an examination for a queen's scholarship which enabled her to study further at the Church of Scotland Training College in Edinburgh, one of three such denominational teacher training colleges. She recalled being unimpressed by the college because the lecturers were 'old and dull and I got nothing new or interesting' ('Memories', fol. 9). She also noted that the men and women students were allowed to meet only once a year.

Once qualified Carrie worked in the mining village of Kelty, Fife, and then was an infant teacher at Parkhouse, Arbroath, from 1904 until 1908. Unfortunately she began to suffer ill health caused by the ventilation system in Parkhouse; this prompted a brief move to another school and then on to Wallacetown School, Dundee, in September 1908. She later became infant mistress at Tay Street School in the early 1930s. Throughout her teaching career she witnessed the impact of poor social conditions on her pupils and her main priority was to ease their poverty, which she did through many quiet voluntary and philanthropic actions.

Within the story of the 'votes for women' campaign, Isabella Carrie can be said to represent the countless unknown women campaigners who never received recognition, and she is probably typical of many who were recruited to the cause because of their sense of outrage and indignation at the treatment of women. She always had an interest in politics. Her father had been an ardent tory, and she sometimes attended local political meetings. One of her earliest recollections was of seeing William Ewart Gladstone when he visited Forfar. Carrie's interest in women's issues may well have been sparked off by teasing from her brother. He used to tell her that 'lassies dinna hae brains' but, she recalled, she had 'a feeling that my brain was as good as his' (interview, 14 Nov 1976). This conviction had a major impact on her outlook and subsequent involvement in the women's movement in Dundee.

Carrie's arrival in Dundee in 1908 coincided with the rise of the suffrage movement in the city, which was a particular target of both suffragists and militant suffragettes: earlier in the year Winston Churchill had won the Dundee by-election and he did not support women's suffrage. Carrie liked to hear good women speakers and often attended public meetings. The significant moment for her was when she was given a ticket to hear Churchill speak at a ladies' meeting in the Gilfillan Hall, Dundee, about 1913. She was incensed at the rough tactics of the stewards towards some women and even more so at Churchill's attitude to women, so much so that she stood up and protested. She too was evicted rather roughly from the hall. Her actions caught the attention of the leaders of the Women's Social and Political Union (WSPU), who thought it had been a planned interruption. Carrie was asked to join the WSPU but was not prepared to be militant, and she kept in the background, introducing speakers and helping in the library and office.

Although Isabella Carrie was never a leading figure, her role in the local WSPU was none the less significant. Despite her aversion to militancy she took on a task which was fraught with danger and surrounded by secrecy. By this time, living on her own after the death of her father in 1912, she began to give hospitality to visiting activists in the WSPU. Her quiet, respectable neighbourhood and her regular stream of visitors were a good cover for her secret visitors. She never knew the identity of those who stayed, rarely spoke to them, and never questioned them or gave information away. The need for secrecy remained with her until her nineties, when she still would not reveal the names of the WSPU leaders in Dundee.

On one notable occasion in 1914 Carrie was asked if she would shelter Mrs Pankhurst, a request which she viewed as both an honour and a risk. She agreed and decided she would stay up late to speak to her, but unfortunately Mrs Pankhurst was arrested in Glasgow. Like many women campaigners Carrie continued her interest in women's issues after the First World War; she was a founding member of the Women Citizens' Association in Dundee and of the Scrimgeour Clan Society founded in the early 1970s.

Carrie's retirement in 1938 was prompted by the fear that she would not live long because of ill health. She decided to spend her annuity on a year-long trip around the world. However, she was in New York in 1939 when war broke out, and returned home. She thought about going back into teaching but decided to continue her voluntary work, including giving hospitality to evacuees. In old age she remained a great letter-writer, and she maintained a lively interest in others and also wrote down her memories. She had a much longer life than she had anticipated, and died, unmarried, aged 103 on 29 November 1981 at the Duneaves Eventide Nursing Home, Broughty Ferry, Scotland. The policeman who caught her as she was thrown out of the Churchill meeting claimed she was the gentlest suffragette he had ever seen—a suitable epitaph.

SHEILA HAMILTON

Sources 'Memories of I. Carrie' [unpublished typescript held by S. Hamilton] · I. Carrie and S. Hamilton interview, 14 Nov 1976; 20 Feb 1977 · Arbroath Herald (4 Dec 1981) · Dundee Courier and Advertiser (1 Dec 1981) · Dundee Evening Telegraph (26 April 1978); (1 May 1978); (3 May 1978) · L. Leneman, 'Dundee and the women's suffrage movement, 1907–1914', The remaking of Juteopolis: Dundee, c.1891–1991, ed. C. Whatley (1992), 80–95 · L. Leneman, A guid cause: the women's suffrage movement in Scotland (1991) · M. Cruickshank, A history of the training of teachers in Scotland (1970) · C. Whatley, D. B. Swinfen, and A. M. Smith, The life and times of Dundee (1993) · N. Watson, Daughters of Dundee (1997) · E. King, The Scottish women's suffrage movement (1978) [exhibition pamphlet, People's Palace Museum, Glasgow, 9 Sept–7 Oct 1978] · L. Leneman, The Scottish suffragettes (2000) · b. cert. · d. cert. · www.scotsorigins.com, March 2002
Archives Dundee city archives, compilation of memories, GD/X53 · priv. coll., compilation of memories and diaries | SOUND taped interview with subj (and transcript), 14 Nov 1976 and 20 Feb 1977

Likenesses I. S. Carrie, photograph, 1973, priv. coll. · group portrait, photographs, priv. coll. · photograph, priv. coll.
Wealth at death £2367.01: confirmation, 16 Nov 1982, CCI

Carrier, Martha (d. 1692). See under Salem witches and their accusers (act. 1692).

Carrington. For this title name see Primrose, Sir Archibald, first baronet, Lord Carrington (1616–1679); Smith, Robert, first Baron Carrington (1752–1838).

Carrington, Charles Robert Wynn-, marquess of Lincolnshire (1843–1928), politician and landowner, was born in Whitehall, London, on 16 May 1843, the elder son of Robert John Carrington (formerly Smith), second Baron Carrington, and his second wife, Charlotte, younger daughter of Peter Robert, twenty-first Baron Willoughby de Eresby. Educated at Eton College and, from 1861, at Trinity College, Cambridge, where he graduated BA in 1863, Carrington entered the Royal Horse Guards (captain 1869, retired 1878). His careers were those of great landowner and Liberal politician, and he combined the two with unwavering conviction over half a century of radical social and political change that drew almost the entire aristocracy into the Conservative Party and saw its power rapidly wane. In 1865, at the age of twenty-two, Carrington was returned to the House of Commons unopposed for his home town of High Wycombe, taking the Liberal whip. On the death of his father three years later he succeeded to the peerage as third Baron Carrington and to an estate of 26,000 acres, predominantly in Buckinghamshire and Lincolnshire, the maintenance and improvement of which were lifelong preoccupations. In 1878 he married the Hon. Cecilia Margaret Harbord (1856–1934), daughter of Charles, fifth Baron Suffield; they had one son and five daughters.

For the next sixty years after succeeding to his title Carrington held a succession of posts spanning the political, royal, and imperial spheres. In 1875–6 he accompanied the prince of Wales (later Edward VII) on his Indian tour as aide-de-camp. He was a government whip and a court official—as captain of the gentlemen-at-arms—in the last four years (1881–5) of Gladstone's second ministry. From 1885 to 1890 he was governor of New South Wales, establishing a pattern of aristocratic 'constitutional monarchy' in the self-governing white colonies that was to endure until the inter-war years of the next century. On his return to England he was elected a Progressive (Liberal) member of the newly established London county council for the working-class ward of West St Pancras, taking an active part in LCC business and retaining his seat until 1907. Between 1892 and 1895 he again held court office, as lord chamberlain, in Gladstone's final ministry and in that of Rosebery, his cousin. At Gladstone's request he also chaired a controversial royal commission on Welsh land tenure, which reported in 1895, deftly deflating radical land agitation in the principality while encouraging landowners to meet moderate demands for allotments, small-holdings, improved rural housing, and rent abatements. In 1895 he was created Earl Carrington.

Carrington continued to advance the cause of land

reform until the First World War, pioneering small-holding and cottage-building schemes on his own estates. By 1914 a quarter of the total estate was let as allotments or small-holdings. Rural regeneration was Carrington's principal goal. His policies were the stock-in-trade of late Victorian and Edwardian new Liberal reformers. In a wider view, they were but one incarnation of a 'back-to-the-land' movement persisting from the industrial revolution to the present day. However, behind them lay a concern to modernize and popularize the great estates—and so underpin their survival in the democratic age. Like Gladstone, his mentor, he saw progressive reform as the friend, not the foe, of the aristocracy and traditional social forces if carried through with confidence by the élite itself.

Campbell-Bannerman appointed Carrington president of the Board of Agriculture and Fisheries in his Liberal ministry of 1905, a post he continued to hold under Asquith until 1911. Carrington was responsible for two allotments and small-holdings statutes in 1908, which extended rights to tenants and labourers. Neither measure was seriously injurious to landowners, but both bitterly antagonized the tory peers, who saw them as the thin end of a socialistic wedge leading to expropriation. As such they were part of the backdrop to Lloyd George's 'people's budget' of 1909, which Carrington supported as a moderate measure necessitated by a projected budget deficit, but which the House of Lords rejected as an act of immoral confiscation. The rejection led to the constitutional crisis of 1909–10, in which Carrington's close links with the royal family were an asset to Asquith. He supported the proposed creation of peers to force the House of Lords to accept the Parliament Bill. On the accession of George V in 1910, he exercised the office of lord great chamberlain, fighting with characteristic vigour to sustain his claim to the largely honorific office (which came through his mother) against other aristocratic claimants to the post.

In 1911 Carrington moved to the non-departmental post of lord privy seal, retiring from the government a year later as marquess of Lincolnshire. His later years brought a succession of disappointments: the death of his only son in war in 1915; the ravages suffered by the great estates, which led him to dispose of some three-quarters of his estates between 1919 and 1924; and the decline of the Liberal Party which, by his death, had become a marginal political force. His retreat from land was but one act in an aristocratic stampede; however, in common with most of his fellow peers, his personal income rose as he moved into stocks. Lincolnshire's dedication to Liberalism and the cause of rural development remained undiminished to the end, and as lord lieutenant of Buckinghamshire from 1915 to 1923 he found a new outlet for his energies. His reaction to the general strike of 1926 typified a whig political outlook formed in the early Victorian era. He condemned the strike in public, but subscribed £50 to the Miners' Women and Children Relief Fund, and dismissed more extreme forebodings with his recollection of the

Chartists' 1848 demonstrations in London, 'when gamekeepers sat in the Hall with loaded guns between their knees … but the Charter is now practically the law of the land'. He left three unpublished works, based on his extensive diaries, a life of Edward VII in three volumes, a life of Lord Rosebery in two volumes, and a volume of recollections.

Having earlier sold his ancestral home, Wycombe Abbey (which became a private girls' boarding-school), Lincolnshire died at his home, Daws Hill House, High Wycombe, on 13 June 1928. The barony (but not his other titles) passed to his younger brother, Rupert Clement George (b. 1852).

Carrington's political role was greater than his tenure of second-rank cabinet offices in the Campbell-Bannerman and Asquith governments might suggest. As a lifelong friend of Edward VII, as a close associate of successive Liberal leaders, as a colonial governor, as one of the few great landowners to remain loyal to Gladstone after the home-rule split of 1886, and as an indefatigable activist among the small band of Liberal peers thereafter, he had an abiding influence on the policy and tone of the late Victorian and Edwardian Liberal Party. He also helped to keep it respectable in royal quarters as, in government before the First World War, it engaged in increasingly fierce conflicts with the Conservative Party and the House of Lords—conflicts in which Edward VII and George V were forced to take a decisive role, and did so in a spirit of strict neutrality.

ANDREW ADONIS

Sources A. Adonis, 'Aristocracy, agriculture and liberalism: the politics, finances and estates of the third Lord Carrington', *HJ*, 31 (1988), 871–97 · *The Times* (14 June 1928) · GEC, *Peerage* · Gladstone, *Diaries* · *CGPLA Eng. & Wales* (1928)
Archives Bodl. Oxf. · NL Aus. | BL, Campbell-Bannerman MSS · Bodl. Oxf., Asquith MSS · HLRO, Lloyd George MSS · Mitchell L., NSW
Likenesses H. Speed, chalk, 1910, NPG · Ape [C. Pellegrini], chromolithograph, NPG; repro. in *VF* (7 Feb 1874) · Spy [L. Ward], cartoon, NPG; repro. in *VF* (11 Sept 1907) · mezzotint (after D. A. Wehrschmidt, 1901), NPG
Wealth at death £77,486 3s.: probate, 21 Sept 1928, *CGPLA Eng. & Wales* · £266,603: further grant, 9 Oct 1928, *CGPLA Eng. & Wales*

Carrington, Sir Codrington Edmund (1769–1849),

judge in Ceylon, was born on 22 October 1769 at Longwood, Hampshire, the son of the Revd Codrington Carrington (b. 1749) of Llangattock, Monmouthshire, and formerly of Barbados, and his wife, Martha, eldest daughter of Edmund Morris, rector of Nutshalling, the friend of Lady Hervey. He was descended from an old Norman family, one of whom, Sir Michel de Carrington, was standard-bearer to Richard I. The family at an early period settled at Carrington in Cheshire, and a branch later emigrated to Barbados. Carrington was educated at Winchester College and called to the bar at the Middle Temple on 10 February 1792 (bencher, 1 June 1832; reader, autumn 1836).

In 1792 Carrington went to India, where he was admitted an advocate of the supreme court of judicature and for some time acted at Calcutta as junior counsel to the East India Company, making the acquaintance of Sir William

Sir Codrington Edmund Carrington (1769–1849), by Sir Thomas Lawrence, *c.*1800

Jones, the oriental scholar. Ill health caused him to resign to return to England in 1799. In Ceylon that year he was employed by Frederick North (governor, 1798–1805) to draw up a legal code and advise on judicature reorganization. In 1800, while in England, he prepared further judicial change for Ceylon (embodied in a royal charter of 18 April 1801), and on 19 March 1801 was appointed the first chief justice of the supreme court of judicature thereby created. He was knighted on 24 June 1801 before sailing to Ceylon where he arrived in January 1802. He and North reformed lower court procedure. Carrington was involved in the dispute of General David Wemyss, commanding the troops, with the judiciary and in June 1805 was insulted by him, following which Wemyss was recalled. In October 1805 Carrington resigned from ill health and for the same reason declined other important colonial appointments.

Having purchased Chalfont House and its estate in Buckinghamshire, Carrington became a magistrate and deputy lieutenant and was many years chairman of quarter sessions. He was made an Oxford DCL (5 July 1810) and elected FRS (18 December 1800), FSA, and honorary member of the Société Française Statistique Universelle. On the occasion of the Manchester disturbances he published in 1819 an *Inquiry into the Law Relative to Public Assemblies of the People*, and he also published a *Letter to the Marquis of Buckingham on the Condition of Prisons* (1819) and other smaller pamphlets. In June 1826 he was elected a tory MP for the duke of Buckingham's 'rotten borough' of St Mawes, Cornwall, which he represented until 1831 (St Mawes was disfranchised by the 1832 Reform Act). After

1831 he resided chiefly at St Helier's, Jersey. He was twice married and had children. His first wife was Paulina, daughter of Charles Belli of Southampton; his second, whom he married in 1830, was Mary Ann, only daughter of John Capel of Russell Square, London, MP for Queenborough. Carrington died at Exmouth, Devon, on 28 November 1849 and was survived by his second wife.

T. F. HENDERSON, *rev.* ROGER T. STEARN

Sources *Annual Register* (1850) · *GM*, 2nd ser., 34 (1850), 92–3 · private information (1886) [family] · Venn, *Alum. Cant.* · H. A. C. Sturgess, ed., *Register of admissions to the Honourable Society of the Middle Temple, from the fifteenth century to the year 1944*, 3 vols. (1949) · J. Hutchinson, ed., *A catalogue of notable Middle Templars: with brief biographical notices* (1902) · C. R. De Silva, *Ceylon under the British occupation, 1795–1833*, 1 (1941) · L. A. Mills, *Ceylon under British rule, 1795–1932* (1933) · *Parliamentary Pocket Companion* (1858–78) · Walford, *County families* (1860)
Archives JRL, letters and papers
Likenesses T. Lawrence, oils, *c.*1800, V&A [*see illus.*] · W. Drummond, lithograph, pubd 1836, BM; repro. in *Athenaeum portraits*, 12 (1836)

Carrington, Dora de Houghton (1893–1932), painter, was born in Hereford on 29 March 1893, the second of the two daughters and fourth of the five children of Samuel Carrington, railway engineer, and his wife, Charlotte Houghton. When the family settled in Bedford, Dora went to Bedford high school, whose records show that her skill in drawing was soon noticed. 'I had an awful childhood', she wrote later, probably because she 'hated' her strict, fussy mother, a former governess. However, she was devoted to her more unconventional father, who agreed that she should go to art school, and in 1910 she became a student under Henry Tonks at the Slade School of Fine Art. This new and fertile soil rapidly developed her character and painting style. Among her fellow students were John and Paul Nash, C. R. W. Nevinson, Dorothy Brett, and, most important of all, the gifted young Mark *Gertler, who fell deeply in love with her. She was an attractive and popular figure with her large blue eyes and her shock of thick hair bobbed in the fashion she had set—she also set that of using her surname alone. Lady Ottoline Morrell described her as 'a wild moorland pony'. Moreover, her individual sense of fun and fantasy made her an enchanting companion, though a neurotic strain was also apparent. Carrington worked hard, and with dedication, winning a scholarship. Her oil paintings were much influenced by Gertler in their careful, smooth technique, three-dimensional effect, and dense, rich colour. Her skill as a draughtsman appears in innumerable witty pen-and-ink illustrations to her letters. However, her lack of confidence was shown in her reluctance to exhibit or even sign the work she sent to the London Group, where it was seen and admired by André Derain. When she left the Slade in 1914 she had many new friends. Virginia and Leonard Woolf commissioned her woodcuts; Roger Fry sought her help in restoring a Mantegna for Hampton Court; Aldous Huxley put her in a novel (as Mary Bracegirdle in *Crome Yellow*).

Dora de Houghton Carrington (1893–1932), by Mark Gertler, c.1912

Carrington's fateful meeting with the essayist and biographer (Giles) Lytton *Strachey (1880–1932) caused a *coup de foudre* which grew into lifelong love for him, despite his homosexuality. The pair set up house at Tidmarsh Mill, Pangbourne, Berkshire, and their relationship developed regardless of love affairs on both sides and Carrington's marriage in 1921 to Reginald Sherring Partridge (always called Ralph from 1919 onwards), who joined the ménage. He was the son of Reginald Partridge, of the Indian Civil Service. In 1924 Ralph Partridge and Strachey bought Ham Spray House in Wiltshire, where a studio was made for Carrington and a library for Strachey. This peaceful working life ended in 1931 when Strachey became ill. He died of cancer in January 1932, leaving his companions grief-stricken. Carrington never wavered from her suicidal intentions, and despite all efforts to deter her, shot herself at Ham Spray House on 11 March 1932.

Carrington left striking portraits of Lytton Strachey (1916, priv. coll.), E. M. Forster (1920, National Portrait Gallery, London), Gerald *Brenan (c.1921, National Portrait Gallery, London), and others; and landscapes, still lifes, and glass pictures, as well as a large number of brilliant and amusing letters. First brought to the attention of the public through Michael Holroyd's two-volume biography of Lytton Strachey in 1967, interest in her work grew with the publication in 1970 of her letters edited by David Garnett, and the biography of her by Gretchen Gerzina in 1989. Her work became much sought after. In 1995 the film *Carrington*, written and directed by Christopher Hampton and starring Emma Thompson as Dora

Carrington, won the special jury prize and Jonathan Pryce (as Lytton Strachey) the best actor award at the Cannes film festival. In the same year 'Carrington: the exhibition' was held at the Barbican Art Gallery, London.

FRANCES PARTRIDGE

Sources M. Holroyd, *Lytton Strachey: a critical biography*, 2 vols. (1967–8) · *Carrington: letters and extracts from her diaries*, ed. D. Garnett (1970) · N. Carrington, *Carrington: paintings, drawings and decorations* (1978) · G. Gerzina, *Carrington: a life of Dora Carrington, 1893–1932* (1989) · *CGPLA Eng. & Wales* (1932) · personal knowledge (2004)

Archives BL, diary and commonplace book, Add. MS 65159 · Tate collection, corresp. and papers [photocopies] | BL, letters to Poppet John, Egerton MS 3867 · BL, letters to James Strachey and Alix Strachey, Add. MS 65158 · BL, corresp. with Lytton Strachey, Add. MSS 62888–62897 · King's AC Cam., letters and postcards to G. H. W. Rylands · King's Cam., letters to W. J. H. Sprott · Tate collection, letters to Christine Nash · Tate collection, letters to John Nash · Tate collection, letters to Margaret Waley and Hubert Waley · U. Sussex Library, letters to Virginia Woolf

Likenesses E. McNaught, pastel drawing, c.1911, Slade School of Fine Art, London · M. Gertler, portrait, c.1912, priv. coll. [*see illus.*] · photograph, c.1920, Hult. Arch. · L. Strachey, photographs, c.1920–1929, Hult. Arch. · F. Partridge, photographs, 1927–30, Hult. Arch. · photographs, NPG

Wealth at death £9510 18s. 11d.: probate, 1932, *CGPLA Eng. & Wales*

Carrington, Sir Frederick (1844–1913), army officer, was born at Cheltenham on 23 August 1844, the second son of Edmund Carrington JP, and his wife, Louisa Sarah Henney. After education at Cheltenham College, he entered the 24th foot (South Wales Borderers) in 1864. He quickly made himself expert in musketry, and became instructor to his regiment in 1870; in 1875 a rebellion in Griqualand West, northern Cape Colony, collapsed before a small force commanded by Lieutenant Carrington, who had been selected for the duty on the strength of this special qualification. For the Transkei War (1877–8) he raised and commanded the frontier light horse, which he led with great success.

Early in 1878 Carrington was promoted captain, and in the same year commanded the Transvaal volunteer force against Sekukuni in the Transvaal. For his services he was gazetted brevet major, and later (1880) given a step in brevet rank and the CMG. He commanded the African levies against the Zulu. In the Basuto War, while in command of the colonial forces, he was surrounded at Mafeteng for nearly a month (September–October 1880) by 5000 Sotho. Though rations were so reduced that horse-flesh had to be eaten, he and his little force held out until relieved by Brigadier-General Charles Mansfield Clarke.

Carrington was promoted colonel in 1884, and in the following year accompanied Sir Charles Warren's expedition to Bechuanaland in command of the 2nd mounted infantry, known as Carrington's Horse. Subsequently he raised and commanded the Bechuanaland border police (1885–93). He was created KCMG in 1887, and, in the Matabele (Ndebele) campaign of 1893 was military adviser to the high commissioner.

In 1895, on promotion to major-general, Carrington took command of the infantry at Gibraltar, then was again sent to southern Africa, where he played an important part in quelling the Matabele uprising (1896), for which he was created KCB (1897). On the outbreak of the Second South African War his unique experience of irregular warfare in southern Africa made his appointment to a high command natural; with the temporary rank of lieutenant-general, he was selected to organize and lead an expedition which, starting from the east coast and marching through Rhodesia, entered the Transvaal soon after Roberts had captured Pretoria (5 June 1900).

In 1904 Carrington retired from the army, and pursued his favourite recreations—hunting, shooting, and fishing. He had married in 1897 Susan Margaret, only daughter of Henry John *Elwes of Colesborne, Cheltenham, with whom he had two daughters. He died of pneumonia at Colesborne Park, Cheltenham, on 22 March 1913, and was buried at Cheltenham cemetery.

C. V. OWEN, *rev.* JAMES LUNT

Sources C. T. Atkinson, *The south Wales borderers, 24th foot, 1689–1937* (1937) · G. Powell, *Plumer* (1990) · *The Times* (24 March 1913) · *The Times* (27 March 1913) · J. F. Maurice and M. H. Grant, eds., *History of the war in South Africa, 1899–1902*, 4 vols. (1906–10) · A. G. Leonard, *How we made Rhodesia* (1896) · F. Carrington, *Operations in Rhodesia* (1897), WO 32/7840 · D. T. Laing, *The Matabele rebellion, 1896* (1897) · R. S. S. Baden-Powell, *The Matabele campaign, 1896* (1897) · *WWW*
Archives National Archives of South Africa, Pretoria, Transvaal archives depot
Likenesses P. May, double portrait, pen-and-ink sketch, 1897 (with C. Rhodes), Africana Museum, Johannesburg, South Africa
Wealth at death £60,049 13s. 1d.: probate, 1 May 1913, CGPLA Eng. & Wales

Carrington, Frederick George (1816–1864), journalist, was the third son of Nicolas Toms *Carrington (1777–1830), and was only fourteen years old when his father died. He was placed under the protection of his eldest brother, Henry E. Carrington, proprietor of the *Bath Chronicle*, and devoted the literary talent of which he showed early promise to journalism. He mainly contributed to west of England papers, largely 'on Conservative and Church principles' (*GM*), including the *Bath Chronicle*, *Felix Farley's Bristol Journal*, the *Cornwall Gazette*, the *West of England Conservative*, the *Bristol Mirror*, the *Gloucester Journal*, and the *Gloucestershire Chronicle*. Of the last he was for several years editor and proprietor. He also contributed to various magazines, and wrote treatises, 'Architecture' and 'Painting', for the Society for the Diffusion of Useful Knowledge. To the eighth edition of *Encyclopaedia Britannica* he supplied the topographical descriptions of Gloucestershire and other counties. He died at his home in Park Road, Gloucester, on 2 February 1864, and was buried in the cemetery there. He left a widow, Louisa Maria, and six children.

L. H. CUST, *rev.* ROGER T. STEARN

Sources *GM*, 3rd ser., 16 (1864), 535 · *Gloucestershire Chronicle* (6 Feb 1864) · CGPLA Eng. & Wales (1864)
Wealth at death under £5000: probate, 1 Aug 1864, CGPLA Eng. & Wales

Carrington, Nicholas Toms [Noel Thomas] (1777–1830), poet, was born in Plymouth and baptized there on 11 August 1777, the son of Henry Carrington, a retail grocer, and his wife, Rosamund, *née* Verant. Shortly after his birth

his parents moved to Plymouth Dock. For some time Carrington was employed as a clerk in the Plymouth dockyard, but he disliked this work and consequently became a seaman on board a man-of-war. In this capacity he was present at the defeat of the Spanish fleet off Cape St Vincent by Sir John Jervis on 14 July 1797. After his term of service expired he settled at Maidstone, Kent, where for five years he was a schoolteacher. In 1809, at the suggestion of several friends, he established a private academy at Plymouth Dock which he ran without intermission until six months before his death.

At an early period of his life Carrington began to contribute occasional pieces in verse to the London and provincial papers. His poems are chiefly descriptive of the scenery and traditions of his native county and possess literary grace, but lack any striking individuality in matter or manner. He published separately '*The Banks of the Tamar*', *a Poem with other Pieces* in 1820 and *Dartmoor* in 1826. He died on 2 September 1830 at the home of his eldest son, Henry Edmund Carrington, in St James's Street, Bath, and was buried at Comisnay village churchyard near Bath. His widow and six younger children, including Frederick George *Carrington, journalist, were left in the care of his son, who also edited Carrington's collected poems, published in two volumes in 1834.

T. F. HENDERSON, *rev.* M. CLARE LOUGHLIN-CHOW

Sources H. E. Carrington, 'Memoir', in *The collected poems of the late N. T. Carrington*, ed. H. E. Carrington, 2 vols. (1834) · *GM*, 1st ser., 101/1 (1831), 276–9 · Allibone, *Dict.* · *IGI* · *DNB*
Likenesses drawing, pencil, *c.*1807, NPG

Carrington, Richard Christopher (1826–1875), astronomer, was born in Chelsea, London, on 26 May 1826, the elder of the two sons of Richard Carrington (1796–1858) and his wife, Esther Clarke (1796–1877). His father was then the joint owner of a large brewery and distillery at Pimlico. Carrington was intended for the church, and was privately educated. However, his aptitude for science and mathematics was apparent by the time he entered Trinity College, Cambridge, in 1844, and his father allowed him to abandon theology and concentrate on the mathematical tripos. He graduated in 1848, having been especially intrigued by the astronomy lectures of Professor Challis, and decided to make that subject his life's work.

Astronomy at Durham Carrington was appointed observer at the University of Durham. The observatory, built in 1841, was supervised by Professor Temple Chevallier, who arranged with the astronomer royal, George B. Airy, for Carrington to train at the Royal Greenwich Observatory. The second-hand equipment at Durham fell far short of the Greenwich standards, according to Carrington. A letter to J. C. Adams at Cambridge shows that Carrington felt that his offer to provide a first-rate instrument, conditional on his being made director, was dealt with neither promptly nor courteously by the university, which was influenced by Chevallier. While admitting that Chevallier's supervision had not been excessive, Carrington was determined, and could afford, to be his own master. He tendered his resignation in December 1851 and left three months later.

Carrington's time at Durham had not been wasted. He carried out a meticulous measurement of the difference in longitude between Greenwich and Durham, involving the careful and laborious transport of three chronometers between the two observatories, and his name had begun to appear in astronomical journals, where he recorded sightings of minor planets, comets, and asteroids. In 1851 he financed his own expedition to Sweden to witness a total eclipse of the sun, and published a detailed account with illustrations of the red flares visible at totality. He familiarized himself with astronomical literature, and planned a catalogue of circumpolar stars which would complement the work of Bessell and Argelander. In 1851 he was elected fellow of the Royal Astronomical Society (RAS).

Redhill observatory On leaving Durham, Carrington found a site on Furze Hill, Redhill, near Reigate, where, with the aid of £5000 borrowed from his father, he built a substantial house with an observatory which became the last amateur observatory in England to publish meridian observations. He moved there in July 1853. His principal instruments, both by Troughton and Simms, were a transit circle of 5½ foot focus, reduced in scale from the Greenwich version, and an equatorial of 4½ inch aperture. The catalogues of Bessell and Argelander had included stars down to the ninth magnitude as far as 81° declination. Carrington saw the opportunity to extend that work by recording all remaining circumpolar stars down to the tenth magnitude. For three years he and his former Durham assistant and friend George Hervey Simmons concentrated on those stars in the zone from 81° to the zenith—a tedious and protracted programme, involving multiple observations of 3735 stars. In 1857, with the reluctant support of the Admiralty, Carrington published the volume of results known as *The Redhill Catalogue*, with an appendix comprising an 'elaborate and instructive dissertation on the whole theory of precession, nutation and aberration', according to the Revd Robert Main, then president of the Royal Astronomical Society, when awarding the society's gold medal to Carrington in 1859. One reason for the Admiralty's hesitation may have been that the astronomer royal, in a confidential assessment of Carrington's achievement, was distinctly lukewarm. Airy pointed out that, great though the labour of observation and computation had been, there was in his view little of real originality in the catalogue. Nevertheless he was one of a distinguished group of scientists, including Rosse, John Herschel, Adams, Challis, and Smyth, who sponsored Carrington on his election to the fellowship of the Royal Society in June 1860.

It was the Royal Society which in 1863 sponsored the publication of Carrington's second and far more significant book, *Observations of the spots on the sun, from November 9, 1853, to March 24, 1861, made at Redhill*. That research secured Carrington's place in the history of astronomy. While awaiting the completion of his observatory at Redhill in 1853 he studied the RAS's archive collection of drawings of the sun's disc made by different observers

during the previous century. He was struck by the capricious way in which the subject had been taken up and then laid aside, by the official neglect of the subject, and by the defects in the manner of observing and in the recording of the sun's appearance. In particular he noticed the wide discrepancies in respect of the position of the sun's pole and period of rotation. Without this information, all that had been achieved were simple, uncalibrated drawings of the disc.

Carrington was not interested in producing astronomical picture books. In the preface to his 1863 volume he wrote: 'That the Solar phenomena, amid the universal subjection to order, should alone be subject to caprice could never gravely be entertained by any mind of philosophic training.' Under the influence of the Newtonian system of mechanics, and in the knowledge of the work of the French mathematicians of the eighteenth century, he believed that the whole natural world was constructed on logical principles which could be expressed by mathematical laws, the discovery of which was the main task of science. He had taken up the subject of solar eclipses during his term at Durham, and he returned to the subject in 1858 in a pamphlet addressed to those who would be witnessing the total eclipse of September that year in South America. Like many others, Carrington had been impressed by Schwabe's remarkable series of 9000 observations of some 4700 groups of spots on the sun during the years 1826 to 1843, which had revealed a regular variation in the number of spots on a cycle of ten or eleven years. Carrington determined that, alongside nocturnal observations of the circumpolar stars, he would observe the sun by day, a task which offered more variety and interest. He and Simmons commenced this arduous double schedule in November 1853, planning to include the complete sunspot cycle, which would commence with the minimum which was expected in 1855.

Carrington realized that the accurate measurement of the position of spots was crucial for his work, and for his refractor he devised a method of measuring the co-ordinates of the spots on the sun's disc by timing the moment that the projected images of the spots and of the sun's limb coincided with the image of the cross-wires placed at the focus of the telescope. Repeat observations were possible by simply swinging the telescope. The observations were simple, being time intervals measured to within one-tenth of a second by reference to the ticking of a chronometer, but the subsequent computations were laborious. Carrington knew that photography would eventually become the standard method of sunspot observation, but he did not wish to wait for its development, and he thought he saw an opportunity to make this work his own for the next eleven-year period. In fact Warren De La Rue (1815–1889) and other contemporaries had established solar photography by the time he published his results.

Royal Astronomical Society politics In spite of his heavy programme at Redhill, Carrington was elected to the RAS council in 1854. He proposed Schwabe for the society's gold medal in 1855, and urged the council to meet more often and to adopt a more proactive role by monitoring what was going on in observatories in all parts of the world. Airy and others were not inclined to follow his energetic lead, even when he was elected one of the two secretaries of the society in 1857. He discharged his duties diligently until 1862, although the sudden death of his father in 1858 threatened his scientific life.

In 1857 Simmons had resigned on completion of *The Redhill Catalogue*, leaving Carrington dependent on temporary assistants. When his father died in July 1858 he was drawn into the running of the large Royal Brewery at Brentford, of which his father had become joint owner in 1851. He kept up his daily sunspot observations as best he could, but commitments at Brentford jeopardized his projected eleven-year programme. His unlikely solution was to mobilize support for applications he made for the observerships which became vacant at Oxford in 1860 and Cambridge in 1861. He was confident of his ability to fill either post but, perhaps in consequence of having antagonized influential members of the RAS, he was successful in neither—Main going to Oxford and Adams taking over at Cambridge. Within weeks of his rejection at Cambridge in 1861 Carrington abandoned the observations of sunspots, sold the Redhill house and observatory, and moved to Isleworth to facilitate his daily management of the brewery. His observations had lasted seven and a half years, instead of eleven, but produced enough results for him to draw conclusions and prepare results.

Solar results   First, Carrington's observations of 5290 spots had established that during a sunspot cycle there was a steady drift in the locations at which spots erupted from higher solar latitudes early in a cycle to equatorial latitudes towards the end of a cycle; he confirmed earlier indications that spots which appeared near to the sun's equator reappeared more rapidly than spots at higher latitudes in either hemisphere, and he deduced a somewhat cumbersome formula relating the speed of rotation of spots round the sun to their latitude. In fact, the establishment of this numerical 'law', the main object of his labours, did nothing to support physical explanations either of the occurrence of sunspots or of their positions. His graphical representation of the phenomenon of drift was later developed and extended by E. W. Maunder (1851–1928). Second, in a separate study he carefully selected 86 spots which remained well-defined during more than one rotation of the sun. Based on these he derived a period of rotation of 25.38 days for the bands lying at latitudes of 14° on either side of the equator. He also derived the inclination of the sun's pole with respect to the plane of the ecliptic. He put forward his values with some confidence, as he had measured the positions of far more spots than any other observer, and prophesied that they would stand until someone could observe regularly for more than eight years, with clear skies, and perhaps using photography. In fact his values are close to modern results.

Carrington left two other astronomical legacies. In November 1853 he commenced the sequential numbering of complete rotations of the sun; he reached rotation 99, but his series was continued, and rotation 2000 was passed in 1995. The Carrington rotation numbers are given in each annual edition of astronomical almanacs. Carrington is also remembered as the first person to record a solar flare. On 1 September 1859 he saw a spectacular flare: later in the same day the magnetic instruments at Kew observatory were disturbed, a great magnetic storm disrupted telegraphic communication, some telegraph offices were set on fire, and aurorae appeared. There had been speculation for some time on the apparent coincidence of the sunspot cycle with the periodic variation of the earth's magnetic field, but Carrington was reluctant to indulge in speculation of any kind.

Although Carrington remained on the RAS council until 1866, his attendances became spasmodic and his contributions increasingly controversial. He was listed for a second gold medal for sunspot work, but withdrew his name. He conducted a long, acrimonious, and very public campaign against the traditional way in which the society's accounts were presented at the annual meetings, and attacked Airy and Charles Pritchard. He did not allege dishonesty on the part of the treasurer, but criticized the mode of presenting accounts which he, Carrington, considered old-fashioned and incomplete. The senior members of the society were not amused. In 1860 Airy said he would retire to private life rather than serve under Carrington's presidency, and in 1865 Airy told Pritchard, 'I believe him to be truly insane' (letter, 13 Nov 1865, CUL, RGO 6/240, 468). The mutual antagonism reflects both Carrington's zeal and lack of elementary tact, and Airy's almost pathological resentment of any questioning of his authority. Carrington was accepted normally as a regular attender of the exclusive RAS dining club. His campaign had failed before he suffered a serious illness in 1866; the exact nature of his breakdown in health is not known, but he disposed of the brewery and withdrew from the activities of the society.

Carrington bought a property in Churt, near Farnham, Surrey, on which he established another observatory, constructed on a small hill known as Middle Devil's Jump. Tunnels were bored horizontally and vertically, and Carrington established his altazimuth instrument inside the vertical tunnel, obviating any need for a dome. Although he described elaborate instruments in papers to the RAS, he apparently did little scientific work, and led the life of a recluse.

Domestic disasters   The last nine years of Carrington's life were marked by bizarre personal events. On 16 August 1869 he married, apparently rather precipitately, Rosa Helen Jeffries, a beautiful but illiterate young woman aged about twenty-four, who had for some time been living as the common-law wife of a former dragoon called Rodway. Carrington set her up in a house, intending that she should be educated and join him thereafter, but Rodway continued to live with her. Rosa went to live with Carrington at Churt in July 1871, but Rodway followed, and one month later Rodway stabbed Rosa and then injured himself. Rosa's injuries were so severe that Rodway's trial was delayed until March 1872, when he was found guilty of assault and sentenced to twenty years' imprisonment.

Rosa recovered from the attack but began to suffer from epilepsy and went several times into a nursing home. In spite of her revealing evidence at Rodway's trial, Carrington bore her no grudge, and made her his principal beneficiary in the will which he drew up in 1873. On 17 November 1875 Rosa died in her sleep, apparently of suffocation attributed to her dependence upon chloral as a sedative. At the inquest Carrington was criticized for failing to provide adequate nursing care. He thereupon closed the house, dismissed the servants, and went to visit his mother in Brighton. On 27 November 1875 he returned alone to the empty house at Churt, and there, two days later, he was found dead. An autopsy suggested a brain haemorrhage and fit. The report in *The Times* of Rosa's death 'from suffocation; how produced the doctor could not say' (*The Times*, 22 Nov 1875), followed by that after Carrington's, when 'four empty chloral bottles [were] found in the dining room' (*The Times*, 7 Dec 1875), led to speculation. There is no other evidence for J. A. Eggar's assertion, in 1924, that Carrington murdered his wife and then committed suicide. The matter was never resolved.

Carrington's will shows evidence of his idiosyncrasies; he requested that, if he died in England, he should be buried at a depth of between 10 and 12 feet in the ground surrounding his house at Churt, at an expense not exceeding £5, and without any service being read over his grave or any memorial being erected to his memory, and that after his death his chin should not be shaved or his shirt be changed. There is no record that his wishes were carried out. He also forgave his younger brother David any debts. He had for some years been supporting David, who when he died in 1902 had spent the last thirty years of his life in mental institutions. The will made two specific bequests of money, £2000 to the RAS and the same to the Royal Society. In 1887, twelve years after Carrington's death, a cousin who was then caring for David applied to the Royal Society for assistance towards his upkeep, referring to this bequest. The application was granted and the Royal Society contributed £30 per year until David's death. Carrington's name appears on a family gravestone in Norwood cemetery, together with those of his father, mother, brother, sister, and wife.   NORMAN LINDOP

Sources R. C. Carrington, *Observations of the spots on the sun from November 9, 1853, to March 24, 1861, made at Redhill* (1863) · CUL, Royal Greenwich Observatory papers, G. B. Airy collection · R. C. Carrington, *A catalogue of 3735 circumpolar stars observed at Redhill in the years 1854, 1855, and 1856, and reduced to mean positions for 1855.0* (1857) · RS, Herschel papers · *Surrey Advertiser & County Times* (30 March 1872) · records of council meetings, 1851–65, RAS · N. Lindop, 'Richard Christopher Carrington (1826–1875)', *Astronomy Now* (May 1997), 41–4 · *The Times* (22 Nov 1875) · *The Times* (7 Dec 1875) · J. A. Eggar, *Remembrances of life and customs in Gilbert White's, Cobbett's, and Charles Kingsley's country* [1924], 46 · parish records (baptism), St Luke's, Chelsea · d. cert.
Archives RAS, observations · Royal Observatory, Edinburgh, papers · RS, papers | CUL, corresp. with Sir George Airy · CUL, Royal Greenwich Observatory papers · CUL, letters to Sir George Stokes · RAS, letters to Royal Astronomical Society · RS, corresp. with Sir John Herschel · St John Cam., corresp. with J. C. Adams

Wealth at death under £20,000: administration with will, 6 Jan 1876, *CGPLA Eng. & Wales* · under £50—goods unadministered at death of first executor: administration, June 1878, *CGPLA Eng. & Wales*

Carritt, (Hugh) David Graham (1927–1982), art historian and picture dealer, was born at 2 Royal Avenue, Chelsea, London on 15 April 1927, the only son of Reginald Graham Carritt, a lecturer in music, and his wife, Christian Norah Begg. He had two sisters, one older, the other his twin. Arriving at preparatory school, he was told he might have one magazine subscription. He asked for *Country Life*, which he had been enjoying in bound volumes since he was five or six, in his grandfather's library. He was sent to Rugby School when twelve. Starved of beautiful things to look at, he wrote to owners of collections within bicycle range, asking if he might visit.

Carritt won an open scholarship to Christ Church, Oxford, where he took a third-class degree in modern history (1948). While at Oxford he caught the attention of Benedict Nicolson, editor of the *Burlington Magazine*. Nicolson took his protégé to visit the art historian Bernard Berenson in Florence—'The finest eye of his generation', was Berenson's considered judgement.

Always a Londoner, Carritt settled first in a flat over a dairy in Mayfair, working as a private dealer and writing not only for the *Burlington Magazine*, but also for the *Evening Standard* and *The Spectator*. In 1964 he joined Christies' old master paintings department, where he played a large part in reviving the fortunes of the firm; and in 1970 he set up David Carritt Ltd, owned by the international art-investment company of Artemis. Here, in his later years, he mounted a number of small and very personal exhibitions.

For a quarter of a century, between 1952 when he discovered a Caravaggio (*The Concert*, Metropolitan Museum of Art, New York) in a retired naval officer's house, and 1977 when he saw that a picture (*Psyche Showing her Sisters her Gifts from Cupid*, National Gallery, London) catalogued as by Carle van Loo in Lord Rosebery's Mentmore collection sale was in fact an early J. H. Fragonard, Carritt dazzled the art world and intrigued the general public with a series of detective feats remarkable for their number, variety, and importance. 'Connoisseurs agree', stated the *New York Times*, 'that he had no peer, and has no successor'.

Carritt himself took most pleasure in his discovery of a painting by Rogier van der Weyden (*St Ivo*[?], National Gallery, London) at the cottage of Joan, Lady Baird. This beautiful picture was not just lost; it was unrecorded. Its attribution to van der Weyden entailed much pacing round the Flemish rooms of the National Gallery. He also attributed the Tiepolo allegory fixed to a ceiling of the Egyptian embassy in London, scanned by countless pairs of eyes before his comprehended it. There was a fictional flavour to his discovery of five large and very dirty Francesco Guardi canvases rolled up like linoleum in a Dublin shed. In 1956, when he was still in his twenties, a photograph in the Courtauld Library recalled to Carritt a drawing in Hamburg, on the basis of which he attributed to Dürer a painting held to be by a minor Veronese master.

Carritt published little, but devoted much effort to other men's causes. Pierre Rosenberg, for example, in the catalogue of the Paris Chardin exhibition of 1979, acknowledged his very significant contribution to that great enterprise.

In the earlier days, when he practised regularly, Carritt was an excellent pianist, and his knowledge of the baroque and Viennese classics was thorough. He was a witty and indiscreet talker. Friends relished his cooking. Colleagues agreed that he was no businessman. Friends and colleagues united in admiration of his courage when in the grip of cancer. He died on 3 August 1982 at his flat at 120 Mount Street, London. He never married.

H. J. F. JONES, rev.

Sources The Times (4 Aug 1982) · The Times (9 Aug 1982) · New York Times (5 Aug 1982) · Art and Auction (Oct 1982) · Christie's House Magazine (Dec 1982) · personal knowledge (1990) · private information (1990) · CGPLA Eng. & Wales (1982) · b. cert.
Archives Harvard University, near Florence, Italy, Center for Italian Renaissance Studies, letters to Bernard Berenson
Wealth at death £94,641: probate, 27 Sept 1982, CGPLA Eng. & Wales

Carrodus, John Tiplady (1836–1895), violinist, was born on 20 January 1836 at Braithwaite, near Keighley, Yorkshire, the son of Tom Carrodus, a barber and music-seller. He had his first lessons on the violin from his father, a proficient musician, and gave a concert at Keighley in January 1845. After tuition with a professor in Bradford named Baker he studied from 1848 under Bernhard Molique in London and in Stuttgart (where he joined the court orchestra, of which Molique was leader). He made a brilliant London début at the Hanover Square Rooms on 1 June 1849, playing the Fantasie-caprice of Vieuxtemps.

Carrodus's playing and musicianship impressed Louis Spohr and especially Michael Costa, and, after appearances as a soloist and in the orchestra at the Bradford Festival (31 August 1853; 1856; 1859), in the orchestra at the Three Choirs Festival (1854), and as a member of the band at the first Glasgow Festival (January 1860), he joined the orchestra of the Royal Italian Opera at Covent Garden c.1861. He performed Molique's B minor concerto at the London Musical Society on 22 April 1863 and was employed in Arditi's orchestra at Her Majesty's Theatre before that building was destroyed in 1867, after which he returned to Covent Garden. When Costa and Sainton resigned in 1869, he was appointed leader, a post which he retained until his death. Ultimately he became principal violinist in the Philharmonic and several other leading orchestras. In addition to appearing in London concerts and performing chamber music (for example, at Molique's concerts in 1850), Carrodus continued to perform at various provincial festivals (in particular the Three Choirs), mainly as leader and soloist.

In 1876 Carrodus was appointed professor of the violin at the newly opened National Training School for Music (the precursor of the Royal School of Music) and he also taught, with Samuel Coleridge-Taylor, at the Croydon conservatory (established in 1883). For some time he was a professor at the Guildhall School of Music and at Trinity College, London. A performance at St James's Hall in 1881 is claimed by Carrodus as 'the first violin Recital which had ever been given. I was the sole performer, being assisted only by an accompanist' (J. T. Carrodus, 49). He is also said to have undertaken extensive tours during his professional life sometimes accompanied by one of his sons. Carrodus was twice married and had five sons, all of whom were musical and entered the profession. Bernhard Molique Carrodus, a prominent and highly capable musician in his own right, and R. Carrodus were violinists, Ernest Alexander Carrodus was a double bass player, J. Carrodus a cellist and organist, and W. O. Carrodus a flautist. Unusually, they all played in the orchestra at the Hereford Festival in 1894 with their father leading. Shortly afterwards, in January 1895, the freedom of Keighley was presented to John Carrodus in commemoration of the fiftieth anniversary of his first public appearance there.

As an acclaimed teacher, a conscientious and resourceful leader in orchestras and chamber music, and a powerful and skilful soloist (particularly in the concertos of Beethoven, Spohr, and Molique), Carrodus was one of the leading English violinists of his time. Besides editions of the violin treatises of J. D. Loder (1884) and Spohr (1896), his published works include a romance for violin and piano (1881); several fantasias (1865, 1876, 1893); a collection of celebrated violin duets edited for Pitman's Sixpenny Musical Library in eight books (1880); and some violin excerpts from 'the principal overtures of the Great Masters' (1884). He wrote a good deal on his art in musical and other journals and his 'Chats to violin students on how to study the violin', originally published in The Strad, were issued in book form following his death in 1895. A portrait contained in this work shows Carrodus to have had a long, thin face, with a beard and moustache. His contemporaries described him as a man of exceeding modesty and of a retiring disposition. He died suddenly at his home, 199 Camden Road, London, from a rupture of the oesophagus, on 13 July 1895.

J. C. HADDEN, rev. DAVID J. GOLBY

Sources J. T. Carrodus, Chats to violin students on how to study the violin (1895) · A. Carrodus, J. T. Carrodus, violinist: a life story, 1838–1895 (1897) · MT, 36 (1895), 549 · C. Ehrlich, The music profession in Britain since the eighteenth century: a social history (1985), 106–7 · B. W. Harvey, The violin family and its makers in the British Isles: an illustrated history and directory (1995)
Likenesses portrait, repro. in Carrodus, Chats to violin students · wood-engraving (after photograph by Russell & Sons), NPG; repro. in ILN (20 July 1895)
Wealth at death £5433 14s. 9d.: probate, 11 Sept 1895, CGPLA Eng. & Wales

Carroll, Anthony (1722–1794), Jesuit, born in Ireland on 16 September 1722, was the son of Daniel Carroll. He entered the Society of Jesus at Watten, near St Omer, in 1744, and was professed of the four vows in 1762. Ordained priest at Liège in 1754, he was sent to the English mission about 1754 and for some time was stationed at Lincoln. After the suppression of the order in 1773 he accompanied his cousin, Father John Carroll (afterwards the first archbishop of Baltimore), to Maryland. Having returned to

England in 1775, he served the missions of Liverpool, Shepton Mallet, Exeter, and Worcester. On 5 September 1794 he was knocked down and robbed in Red Lion Court, Fleet Street, London, and carried speechless to St Bartholomew's Hospital, where he died at one o'clock the following morning. He translated some of L. Bourdaloue's sermons under the title of *Practical Divinity* (4 vols., 1776).

THOMPSON COOPER, rev. ROBERT BROWN

Sources Gillow, *Lit. biog. hist.* · H. Foley, ed., *Records of the English province of the Society of Jesus*, 7 vols. in 8 (1875–83) · *GM*, 1st ser., 64 (1794), 1055 · G. Holt, *The English Jesuits, 1650–1829: a biographical dictionary*, Catholic RS, 70 (1984)
Wealth at death left £500 to two nieces in Ireland: *GM*

Carroll, Charles [*known as* Charles Carroll the Settler] (1661–1720), planter and lawyer in America, was born in Ireland, the second son of Daniel Carroll of Aghagurty (*b.* in or before 1642, *d.* in or before 1688), tenant farmer. Historians use the appellation 'the Settler' to distinguish him from other Charles Carrolls, most notably his son Charles *Carroll of Annapolis (1702–1782) and grandson Charles *Carroll of Carrollton (1737–1832). Carroll was a staunch Roman Catholic with an identity rooted in the Gaelic Irish past. His defiant adherence to his cultural and religious heritage shaped the course of his life.

Carroll's forebears once held considerable land in their clan's ancestral territory, Ely O'Carroll, in the Irish midlands. Although English policies in the aftermath of the 1641 rising severely reduced his family's holdings, Carroll received a fine education at universities in Lille and Douai, Jesuit institutions in Europe, probably with help from his cousin Richard Grace, a man with important ties to the Stuarts. In 1685 Carroll was admitted to London's Inner Temple to study law, but he saw little prospect of advancing himself in either England or Ireland. On obtaining a commission as attorney-general of Maryland from the colony's Roman Catholic proprietor, Charles Calvert, third Lord Baltimore, Carroll left England in the summer of 1688.

Within a year of Carroll's arrival in Maryland, the strong anti-Catholic sentiments unleashed there by the revolution of 1688 and the accession of William and Mary provoked protestant colonists to seize the provincial government for the crown. During the period of royal rule, 1690–1715, Lord Baltimore's power in the colony was restricted to the collection of revenues and granting of land through his private proprietary establishment. Carroll and all other Catholics who held public office lost their positions and could not regain them without swearing oaths inimical to their religion. Laws enacted by the Maryland legislature further deprived Catholics by denying them the right to maintain religious schools, worship publicly, and practise law in most courts. Soon after going to the Chesapeake Carroll married, in November 1689, Martha, the widow of Anthony Underwood; she died in childbirth in November 1690. In February 1694 he wed his second wife, Mary (1678–1742), a daughter of Colonel Henry Darnall, the Calvert family's principal representative in Maryland and the colony's most powerful Catholic. As Darnall's protégé, Carroll rose rapidly in the proprietary organization,

and upon the colonel's death in 1711 he succeeded to his father-in-law's most important position as Lord Baltimore's agent and receiver-general.

From the time of his marriage to Darnall's daughter, Carroll acquired land and slaves, built a lucrative mercantile business, practised law in the courts still open to Catholics, and lent money at interest, becoming the colony's principal banker. He and his wife moved from St Mary's City in southern Maryland to the new capital, Annapolis, about 1696. Of their ten children, five died in infancy. The conversion of the third Lord Baltimore's heir, Benedict Leonard Calvert, to the Anglican faith in 1714, led the crown to return the power to govern Maryland to his son, Charles Calvert, fifth Lord Baltimore, in 1715. Confident that his many years of service to the Calverts merited a significant reward, Carroll went to England in 1716 to persuade the proprietor and his advisers to restore to Catholics the civil rights denied them under crown rule. Paramount among these was the ability to hold public office without swearing oaths that denied Catholicism's basic tenets.

Carroll gained his objective and returned to Maryland confirmed in his position as Lord Baltimore's agent and receiver-general and with measurably increased powers relative to those of the colonial governor. Objecting fiercely to this diminution of his prerogatives, the governor, a protestant Irishman named John Hart, took his case to the legislature and then to Lord Baltimore. The contest raged bitterly until 1717, when the proprietor, fearful of having the efficacy of his Anglican conversion questioned, sided with the governor and stripped Carroll of all his posts. The following year the legislature passed a law depriving Catholics of the right to vote. They did not regain the franchise until the American revolution.

Charles Carroll the Settler died at his home in Duke of Gloucester Street, Annapolis, on 1 July 1720, possessed of the most substantial estate ever probated in Maryland to that time. It included more than 45,000 acres of land, 112 slaves, and personal property valued at £7535. He was buried in the family graveyard at Annapolis quarter. He was survived by his wife, two sons, Charles and Daniel, and two daughters, Mary and Eleanor.

RONALD HOFFMAN

Sources R. Hoffman and E. S. Darcy, eds., *Microfilm edition of the Charles Carroll of Carrollton family papers located at the Maryland Historical Society, Baltimore* (1986) · R. Hoffman, *Princes of Ireland, planters of Maryland: a Carroll saga, 1500–1782* (2000) · *Dear papa, Dear Charley: the peregrinations of a revolutionary aristocrat, as told by Charles Carroll of Carrollton and his father, Charles Carroll of Annapolis*, ed. R. Hoffman and others, 3 vols. [forthcoming] · research files, Maryland Historical Society, Baltimore, Maryland, USA [the Charles Carroll of Carrollton papers editorial project]
Likenesses J. E. Kuhn, oils, *c.*1700–1720, Maryland Historical Society, Baltimore
Wealth at death more than 45,000 acres of land; 112 slaves; personal property valued at £7535: inventories, ledger X, 1721–1726, Carroll–Mactavish MSS, MS 220, Maryland Historical Society, Baltimore; analysis of inventories prepared for Charles Carroll of Carrollton MSS

Carroll, Charles [*known as* Charles Carroll of Annapolis] (1702–1782), planter and ironmaster in America, was born on 2 April 1702, in Annapolis, Maryland, the second surviving son of Charles *Carroll the Settler (1661–1720), proprietary agent, merchant, planter, moneylender, and lawyer, and Mary, *née* Darnall (1678–1742). An unbending Roman Catholic like his father, Charles is distinguished from other Charles Carrolls by the appellation 'of Annapolis'. Educated at the English College of the Jesuits at St Omer, in Flanders, and at the Scots College at Douai, he planned to study law at the inns of court but was called home by his father's death on 1 July 1720. His elder brother, Henry (1698–1719), having died the previous year, Charles became responsible for the administration of the Settler's estate.

Denied by law the right to participate in Maryland's civic life through office-holding and voting and lacking the connections to Lord Baltimore that his father once enjoyed, Charles Carroll of Annapolis concentrated on expanding the family's wealth into one of the great colonial fortunes. Adroitly managing the assets he controlled as his father's executor, he consolidated his portion of the landed estate into a 12,500 acre dwelling plantation, Doohoragen Manor, at Elk Ridge, about 30 miles west of Annapolis, and two smaller operations on a quarter near his residence in the capital and on Poplar Island in the Chesapeake Bay. On this acreage slaves cultivated tobacco, corn, and wheat and tended livestock. In the 1730s he began recruiting tenants for his 10,000 acre tract, Carrollton Manor, in Frederick county, and within thirty years his annual rental income was at least £250 sterling. With four other investors, including his younger brother Daniel (1707–1734) and his kinsman Dr Charles Carroll (1691–1755), Charles Carroll of Annapolis founded an ironworks, the Baltimore Company, in 1731; by the 1760s it was yielding him £400 sterling a year. An even greater portion of his income derived from the money he lent at interest, a sum totalling £24,230 by the mid-1760s. In 1764 he estimated his net worth at £88,380 sterling and his yearly income at £1800.

Determined to bequeath this legacy only to an heir who had proved himself competent to protect and enhance it, Charles Carroll of Annapolis developed rigorous educational and moral requirements for his only child, Charles *Carroll (later of Carrollton; 1737–1832). His principal strategy for assuring his son's obedience was to keep the boy illegitimate for nearly twenty years. He did not marry his son's mother, Elizabeth Brooke (1709–1761), until 15 February 1757, although their child was born on 19 September 1737. A Roman Catholic and a cousin of her child's father, Elizabeth was a daughter of Clement and Jane, *née* Sewall, of Prince George's county, Maryland. She and Charles were a devoted couple and maintained a home together both before and after their marriage. He did not remarry after her death.

Angered by the injustice of the double tax imposed on Roman Catholic landowners in 1756, Charles Carroll of Annapolis tried to liquidate his Maryland holdings and move to French—and Catholic—Louisiana. When his negotiations with French officials in Paris, in 1757, failed to produce the financial incentives he desired, he gave up his plan. Upon his son's return to Maryland in 1765, after sixteen years of study abroad, Charles Carroll of Annapolis relinquished to him the daily management of most of the family enterprises. After the younger Carroll's marriage in 1768, the elder retired to Doohoragen Manor, where he immersed himself in his favourite occupation, agriculture.

Charles Carroll of Annapolis died on 30 May 1782 at his home in Annapolis, of injuries sustained in a fall, and was buried in the family graveyard at Annapolis quarter. He left his entire estate to his son and requested that no accounting of his property be made. However, according to the tax assessment for 1783 Carroll's holdings included personal property (434 slaves and 362 ounces of plate) worth £12,864, twenty-eight lots in Annapolis, and nearly 30,000 acres of land.   RONALD HOFFMAN

Sources R. Hoffman and E. S. Darcy, eds., *Microfilm edition of the Charles Carroll of Carrollton family papers located at the Maryland Historical Society, Baltimore* (1986) • R. Hoffman, *Princes of Ireland, planters of Maryland: a Carroll saga, 1500–1782* (2000) • *Dear papa, Dear Charley: the peregrinations of a revolutionary aristocrat, as told by Charles Carroll of Carrollton and his father, Charles Carroll of Annapolis*, ed. R. Hoffman and others, 3 vols. [forthcoming] • E. C. Papenfuse and others, eds., *A biographical dictionary of the Maryland legislature, 1635–1789*, 2 vols. (1979–85) • research files, Maryland Historical Society, Baltimore, Maryland, USA [the Charles Carroll of Carrollton papers editorial project]
Archives L. Cong., family MSS • Maryland Historical Society, Baltimore, MS 206 | L. Cong., Daniel Carroll of Duddington MSS • Maryland Historical Society, Baltimore, Carroll–McTavish MSS
Likenesses J. Wollaston, two portraits, c.1753–1754, priv. coll.
Wealth at death ordered that no inventory be made of estate: will and testament, 19 June 1780, Maryland Historical Society, Baltimore, Carroll–McTavish MSS

Carroll, Charles [*called* the Barrister] (**1723–1783**), planter and revolutionary politician in America, was born on 22 March 1723, at King George Street, Annapolis, Maryland, the eldest of three children of Charles Carroll (1691–1755), physician and ironmaster, and his first wife, Dorothy Blake of Talbot county, Maryland. His siblings were a younger brother, John Henry Carroll (1732–1754), and a sister, Mary Clare, who married Nicholas Maccubbin in 1747. Carroll's father, an emigrant from his native Ireland to Maryland about 1715, was raised a Roman Catholic, and was thus subject to the colony's statutes that denied adherents of that faith crucial civil privileges, among them the right to vote and to hold public office. By 1738 had converted to Anglicanism and gained election to the lower house of the colonial assembly, where he became a vigorous opponent of his former co-religionists, especially his kinsman Charles Carroll of Annapolis. A member and officer of St Anne's, Annapolis's Anglican church, he brought his children up in that communion. The younger Charles Carroll did not share his father's religious prejudices. He belonged to St Anne's until joining St Paul's in Baltimore in 1769, and served on the vestry in both churches.

Carroll received his education at the English school at Bairro Alto, Lisbon, at Eton College, and at Clare College,

Cambridge. Having trained as a lawyer at London's Middle Temple, to which he gained admission in 1751, he did not practise law after his return to Maryland in 1755, but he chose the appellation 'barrister' to distinguish himself from other Charles Carrolls. On 23 June 1763 he married Margaret (1742–1817), a daughter of the Maryland planter and politician Matthew Tilghman and Anne, *née* Lloyd, of Queen Anne's county, Maryland. Their only children, twins, died in infancy. Lacking heirs, the Barrister would leave his estate to his nephews James Maccubbin (1761–1832) and Nicholas Maccubbin (1751–1812), with the stipulation that they assume the surname Carroll. They did so by an act of the legislature in 1783.

The Barrister's political career began in 1756, with his election to the lower house of the Maryland assembly as a representative of Anne Arundel county. He remained in the lower house until 1761, and did not hold public office again until the American War of Independence. An active participant in the coalition of ambitious young men who brought Maryland through the revolution's turmoil, and then established a state government weighted in favour of propertied interests, the Barrister served in all nine of the provincial conventions that constituted the provisional government from 1774 to 1776. He was president of the seventh convention and a member of the first four councils of safety (1775–6). A principal author of Maryland's first state constitution, he resigned from the ninth convention on 27 August 1776 because he could not support the radically democratic views which his constituents demanded be incorporated in that document. Having been elected to the Maryland senate in 1777, he retained a seat in that body until his death. In November 1776 the ninth convention chose him as a delegate to the continental congress, where he served until 1777. Although he did not sign the Declaration of Independence, he played a major role in drafting Maryland's declaration of independence, which the eighth convention adopted on 3 July 1776.

From his father, the Barrister received a handsome inheritance that included a substantial landed estate, slaves, livestock, and a one-fifth share in the Baltimore Company, an ironworks of which Dr Carroll had been a founder. By 1764 his ironworks stock alone was producing an annual income of £400 sterling. The Barrister speculated in land, and at his death possessed some 15,000 acres in four Maryland counties and seven lots in Annapolis. He was an erudite man of many interests who regularly ordered books and periodicals from England for his library, and provided money and letters of introduction to assist artist Charles Willson Peale's studies in London. In addition to his residence in the capital, the Barrister built a country estate, Mount Clare, on the Patapsco River, near Baltimore, where he developed an ornamental garden and orangery that displayed his interest in horticulture and agronomy. He died at Mount Clare on 23 March 1783, and was buried at the family vault in St Anne's Church, Annapolis. As he requested, no inventory of his estate was made.   RONALD HOFFMAN

Sources E. C. Papenfuse and others, eds., *A biographical dictionary of the Maryland legislature, 1635–1789*, 2 vols. (1979–85) · private information (2004) [Charles Carroll of Carrollton papers editorial project] · M. F. Trostel, 'Carroll, Charles', *ANB*
Archives Maryland Historical Society, Baltimore, family papers, MS 1873 · Maryland Historical Society, Baltimore, letter-books, MS 208.1
Likenesses C. Willson Peale, oils, 1770–71, Mount Clare Museum, National Society of the Colonial Dames of America in the State of Maryland
Wealth at death requested that no inventory of estate be made and no accounts filed: Papenfuse and others, eds., *Biographical dictionary of the Maryland legislature*, 1.197

Carroll, Charles [*known as* Charles Carroll of Carrollton] (**1737–1832**), planter and politician in the United States of America, was born on Duke of Gloucester Street, Annapolis, Maryland, on 19 September 1737, the only child of Charles *Carroll of Annapolis (1702–1782) and his common-law wife, Elizabeth Brooke (1709–1761). His parents married in 1757. In 1765 he chose the appellation 'of Carrollton', from the family's tenanted manor in Frederick county, Maryland, to distinguish himself from other Charles Carrolls.

Kept illegitimate by his father until he had proved himself, Carroll was sent to Europe at the age of ten to begin the educational odyssey designed to mould him into an acceptable heir. Raised as a Roman Catholic, he spent six years at the Jesuit English College at St Omer (1748–54). He later studied classical literature at Rheims (1754–5), completed a thesis in philosophy at the Collège Louis-le-Grand in Paris (1755–7), and read civil law at Bourges and in Paris (1757–9). He moved to London in September 1759, to study at the inns of court. His father regarded mastery of the common law as the crowning achievement of his son's education, but the younger Carroll's antipathy for the subject became so intense that he ultimately defied the older man's intention. More palatable was his father's insistence that he acquire the social graces which defined a gentleman, and he became adept at dancing, drawing, and fencing and at more practical skills such as Italian bookkeeping and surveying. His willingness to follow his father's dictates faltered for a time in 1761, when he learned that his mother, whom he had last seen as a boy of ten, had died.

Carroll returned to Annapolis in 1765 and began, under his father's tutelage, to administer the family's wide-ranging business interests: the growing and marketing of tobacco; the management of their 12,500 acre dwelling plantation at Elk Ridge, Doohoragen Manor, with its workforce of nearly 300 slaves; the supervision of tenants on Carrollton Manor; the lending of money on bonds and mortgages; and the Baltimore Company ironworks. On 5 June 1768 he married Mary (Molly) Darnall (1749–1782), his nineteen-year-old first cousin once removed and the only child of Henry (IV) Darnall of Prince George's county and Rachel Brooke Darnall. The couple lived in the family's Annapolis house, while the elder Carroll retired to Doohoragen Manor. In the fourteen years of their marriage the Carrolls had seven children. Three survived to adulthood: Mary (1770–1846) married Richard Caton in 1787;

Charles Carroll [of Carrollton] (1737–1832), by Thomas Sully, 1826

Charles Carroll of Homewood (1775–1825) married Harriet Chew of Philadelphia in 1800; and Catharine (Kitty; 1778–1861) married Robert Goodloe Harper in 1801.

Like his father and grandfather Carroll was prevented by Maryland's anti-Catholic statutes from voting and holding public office. Early in 1773, however, a heated controversy over Governor Robert Eden's unilateral raising of the fees public officials charged for their services brought Carroll to public attention. Using the pseudonym First Citizen, he published in the *Maryland Gazette* a series of letters that attacked the higher rates and criticized the principal supporter of the governor's action, the provincial secretary Daniel Dulany. The newspaper contest between First Citizen and Antilon, the pseudonym Dulany used to argue his case, led to the formation of a new political coalition composed of ambitious young men centred around Carroll. In the May 1773 elections candidates who supported First Citizen's position gained a majority in the general assembly's lower house.

Although Carroll was still barred from voting and holding office, the events of 1773 marked the beginning of his political career. As the imperial crisis superseded provincial disputes, he became an advocate of separation from Great Britain. Beginning in November 1774 he served in most of the provincial conventions that formed Maryland's provisional government and played a major role in drafting the state's declaration of rights and highly conservative constitution. In March 1776 the second continental congress sent Carroll, his cousin Father John Carroll, Samuel Chase, and Benjamin Franklin to Montreal in

a vain attempt to persuade the Canadians to join the American cause. Chosen a delegate to congress early in July 1776, he signed the Declaration of Independence on 2 August, the only Roman Catholic to do so.

As civil disorder unleashed by the revolution threatened to plunge Maryland into anarchy, Carroll feared that chaos could be avoided only through reunion with Great Britain. By the autumn of 1776 he had acknowledged the impossibility of that solution and begun working to save both the revolutionary cause and the political and economic power of the élite leadership group to which he now belonged. After drafting a state constitution that guaranteed governing authority to men of property, he and his allies popularized the revolution through fiscal policies that shifted the tax burden from polls to land and slaves and made paper currency legal tender for the payment of sterling debts. Because the legal tender law endangered the third of the Carroll fortune lent at interest, Carroll's support for the measure as a revolutionary necessity brought him into sharp conflict with his father.

Carroll's father and wife died within two weeks of each other in May and June 1782, leaving him a widower with four children, of whom the youngest survived only another year. He never remarried. A delegate to congress between 1776 and 1778, he remained in public life until 1800, serving continuously in the Maryland senate, to which he was first elected in 1777, and as a United States senator (1789–92). He declined election to the 1787 Philadelphia convention but strongly supported the constitution as the supreme guarantor of the rights of men of property. Embracing opportunities for making money in the new republic, he invested in banks, insurance, railroads, and turnpike and canal companies. Personally, Carroll greatly enjoyed the international success garnered by three of his Caton granddaughters—Mary Ann, Louisa, and Elizabeth. Dazzling British society upon their arrival in London in 1816, these women eventually contracted marriages with members of the aristocracy, thereby wedding their grandfather's New World money to Old World titles.

With the deaths of John Adams and Thomas Jefferson on 4 July 1826, Carroll became the last living signer of the Declaration of Independence. He died at Lombard Street, Baltimore, on 14 November 1832, at the age of ninety-five, and was buried on 17 November in the chapel of Doohoragen Manor. President Andrew Jackson ordered the federal government closed to mark his passing, an honour previously accorded only to George Washington. The total value of Carroll's estate, which included at least 30,000 acres of land in Maryland, 45,000 acres in Pennsylvania and New York, and $750,000 of personal property, was approximately $1,600,000.   RONALD HOFFMAN

Sources R. Hoffman and E. S. Darcy, eds., *Microfilm edition of the Charles Carroll of Carrollton family papers located at the Maryland Historical Society, Baltimore* (1986) • R. Hoffman, *Princes of Ireland, planters of Maryland: a Carroll saga, 1500–1782* (2000) • R. Hoffman, *A spirit of dissension: economics, politics, and the revolution in Maryland* (1973) • *Dear papa, Dear Charley: the peregrinations of a revolutionary aristocrat, as told by Charles Carroll of Carrollton and his father, Charles Carroll of Annapolis*, ed. R. Hoffman and others, 3 vols. [forthcoming] • S. D.

Mason, 'Charles Carroll of Carrollton and his family, 1688–1832', *'Anywhere so long as there be freedom': Charles Carroll of Carrollton, his family, and his Maryland*, ed. A. C. Van Devanter (1975), 9–33 • E. C. Papenfuse, 'English aristocrat in an American setting', *'Anywhere so long as there be freedom': Charles Carroll of Carrollton, his family, and his Maryland*, ed. A. C. Van Devanter (1975), 43–57 • E. C. Papenfuse and others, eds., *A biographical dictionary of the Maryland legislature, 1635–1789*, 2 vols. (1979–85) • research files, Maryland Historical Society, Baltimore, Maryland, USA [the Charles Carroll of Carrollton papers editorial project]

Archives Archives of the Archdiocese of Baltimore, Baltimore, Maryland • Georgetown University, Washington, DC • L. Cong., family MSS • Maryland State Archives, Annapolis, Maryland • University of San Francisco | Hist. Soc. Penn., Chew family MSS • L. Cong., Daniel Carroll of Duddington MSS [microfilm, 8 reels] • NYPL, Arents collection

Likenesses J. Reynolds, oils, 1763, Yale U. • C. B. Févret de Saint-Memin, charcoal and white chalk drawing, 1804, Maryland Historical Society, Baltimore • R. Peale, oils, *c.*1816–1819, Baltimore Museum of Art • T. Sully, oils, 1826, Maryland State House, Annapolis [*see illus.*]

Wealth at death approx. \$1,600,000: Papenfuse, 'English aristocrat', 57

Carroll, Lewis. *See* Dodgson, Charles Lutwidge (1832–1898).

Carroll, Madeleine [*real name* Marie-Madeleine Bernadette O'Carroll] (**1906–1987**), actress, was born on 26 February 1906 in West Bromwich, Warwickshire, one of at least two daughters of John O'Carroll, an Irish professor of philology, and his French wife, Hélène de Rosière Tuaillon. Brought up in France until she was eleven, she followed her father to the University of Birmingham, where she began acting in a dramatic society production of *Selma*. Defying her father's wishes she abandoned her MA course in Paris and, having briefly taught French at a Hove girls' school, made her stage début in Cyril Campion's *The Lash* at the Winter Gardens, New Brighton, in 1927.

Carroll's success in Sir Seymour Hicks's West End hit *Mr What's His Name* (1927) began a run of ten plays in four years, including Margaret Kennedy's and Basil Dean's *The Constant Nymph* (1928), Reginald Berkeley's *French Leave* (1930), and John Van Druten's *After All* (1931). Her screen career also blossomed from its unprepossessing start in *The Guns of Loos* (1928). She made *L'Instinct* (1928) for Franco Films in Nice before making her talkie bow in *The American Prisoner* and finding fame in *Young Woodley* (both 1930).

On her marriage to guards officer Philip Astley in 1931 Carroll announced her retirement. However, she was lured back to films by Gaumont with a reported £650-a-week contract and showy leads in *Sleeping Car* and *I was a Spy* (both 1933). She even ventured to Hollywood to make *The World Moves On* (1934) for John Ford. Such was her celebrity that she inspired a character in A. G. Macdonnell's novel, *England, their England* (1933):

> the loveliness of Esmeralda d'Avenant was an inspiration to millions. Theatre-goers adored her at Daly's, the Winter Garden, Drury Lane. Film fans worshipped her from Pole to Pole. She had the most famous smile and the best publicity man in the English-speaking world, and her legs, which, though excellently shaped, were not more noticeably alluring than the legs of many a humble shopgirl or typist, were always insured for ten per cent more than

> Mistinguett's. (A. G. Macdonnell, *England, their England*, Penguin edn, 1933, 56)

It was Carroll's association with Alfred Hitchcock that transformed her fortunes. Ironically, she landed a leading part in *The Thirty-Nine Steps* (1935) only because Jane Baxter withdrew, but Hitchcock was sufficiently impressed to build up her role, having her famously remove her wet stockings while handcuffed to the fugitive Robert Donat. She was 'precisely the type of cool, prim blonde whom Alfred Hitchcock enjoyed humiliating on screen' (*The Independent*). Consequently he cast her opposite John Gielgud in *Secret Agent* (1936). But it proved to be her last British assignment before Walter Wanger signed her to Twentieth Century Fox. 'Mr Wanger does not visualise a future for me as a second Dietrich; another Garbo or Hepburn; or a star in the Colbert class', she confessed in an interview before her departure. 'I am grateful to him for that, because I have always abhorred imitation' (*Film Weekly*, 30 May 1936). However, cutting an original figure proved difficult to achieve.

Carroll was billed as 'the most beautiful woman in the world' for *The Case Against Mrs Ames* (1936), but she was soon being contracted out to co-star with Ronald Colman in *The Prisoner of Zenda* and Gary Cooper in *The General Died at Dawn* (both 1937). In the following year, she was voted 'The girl most liked to be cast on a desert island with' in a student poll—to which she responded, 'I'm very flattered, but if I'm ever cast away, I hope the man is a good obstetrician' (Rode). But despite her status among Hollywood's top female earners, the critics had begun to turn. Graham Greene was particularly vitriolic in his review of *On the Avenue* (1937):

> she has what must be, to all but the most blindly devoted keepers, the less endearing traits of a young elephant. We expect to see the sets rock a little beneath her stupendous coquettery … Handsome in a big way, given to intense proboscine whistling, she lends an impression of weight to every action, of awful fidelities to the lightest love. (*Night and Day*, 29 July 1937)

Carroll moved to Paramount in mid-1938, hoping to make 'important films, promoting world peace' (Rode). But she was increasingly relegated to minor works, enduring six assignments with journeyman director Edward H. Griffith. In two of these the co-star was Sterling Hayden (1916–1986), who became her second husband in 1942 (she and Astley had divorced in 1939). Following *My Son, My Son* (1940) and *My Favourite Blonde* (1942), Carroll began to devote her energies to war work. Her sister, Marguerite, had been killed in the blitz in 1943 and Carroll, now an American citizen, went to France under the name of Hamilton to serve with the Allied Relief Fund and the American Red Cross. In addition to entertaining the troops, she also cared for 150 orphans in a château near Paris. She received the US medal of freedom and was appointed to the French Légion d'honneur for her efforts.

In 1945 Carroll was again divorced, and the next year she married her third husband, former French resistance leader Henri Lavorel. That marriage, too, ended in divorce, in 1949. She struggled to relaunch her career, before finally retiring from films after *Lady Windermere's*

Fan (1949). She made occasional television appearances in the 1950s, and attempted a stage comeback in *Beekman Place* (1964). A fourth marriage in 1950, to *Life Magazine* publisher Andrew Heiskell, survived until dissolution in 1965. Thereafter, Carroll concentrated on running her French fruit farm and her charitable activities. However, the death of her only child, Anne-Madeleine, in 1984, drove her into seclusion in Marbella, Spain, where she died on 3 October 1987.   DAVID PARKINSON

Sources J. Vinson, ed., *The international directory of films and filmmakers* (1986) · D. Rode, *Film Fan Monthly* (Sept 1974) · *The Independent* (5 Oct 1987) · *Daily Telegraph* (5 Oct 1987) · *The Times* (6 Oct 1987) · *New York Times* (31 Oct 1987) · *Film Dope* (Oct 1974) · *Film Weekly* (12 April 1930) · *Film Weekly* (23 May 1936) · *Film Weekly* (30 May 1936) · *The Guardian* (5 Oct 1987) · *Sunday Express* (10 June 1984) · *Films and Filming* (Oct 1971) · D. Parkinson, ed., *Mornings in the dark: the Graham Greene film reader* (1993)
Likenesses photographs, Ronald Grant Archive, London · photographs, Kobal collection, London · photographs, Huntley Archive, London

Carroll, Susanna. *See* Centlivre, Susanna (*bap.* 1669?, *d.* 1723).

Carroll, Walter (1869–1955), music educationist and composer, was born on 4 July 1869 at 156 Bury New Road, Manchester, the only son and last of the five children of Robert Carroll (*bap.* 1829), a commercial traveller, and his wife, Fanny Wormald, *née* Flinn (*b. c.*1832). The Carroll family had no privileges of birth, money, or schooling nor any special musical interest. After leaving Longsight high school at fourteen Carroll started work as a textile warehouse clerk. At the same time he attended evening classes in piano, organ, and music theory, and joined the choir of St Chrysostom's Anglican church, Victoria Park, Manchester. The development of pericarditis at seventeen left him with a permanently damaged heart but also with a determination to succeed in his musical training.

In 1891 Carroll was among the first to graduate with the external MusB degree from the University of Durham and was appointed singing master to the Manchester Day Training College. On 3 October 1893 he gave the inaugural lecture at a new conservatory, the Royal Manchester College of Music. He took up a lectureship there in harmony and composition at the invitation of Charles Hallé, the first principal. In 1894 he was awarded the degree of MusB by the University of Manchester, and in 1900 he was the first to gain its degree of MusD by examination. He was appointed lecturer in music at the same university in 1904, and served as dean of the faculty of music in 1909–11 and 1917–19.

On 12 August 1896 Carroll married Gertrude Southam (*b.* 1868). They had two daughters, Elsa and Ida (1906–1995). The latter, like her father, pursued a musical career; she became principal of the Northern School of Music, Manchester, in 1956, and was elected president of the Incorporated Society of Musicians in 1976.

In 1906 Carroll established lectures in the teaching of music at the Royal Manchester College of Music. A year later he founded a training class for music teachers in Manchester, which ran until 1919. Hundreds of teachers benefited from lectures and demonstrations. He lectured throughout England, Scotland, and Wales at the invitation of education authorities and professional associations. Prominent among these was the Incorporated Society of Musicians, of which he was a member from 1896 to 1911, holding the highest regional and national offices.

In 1909 Carroll was appointed as the first professor in a new department—the art and practice of teaching—at the Royal Manchester College of Music. His overriding aim was stated in 1910: 'Gradually to substitute the trained teacher for the untrained is a work full of glorious possibilities for the art of music' (*Manchester City News*, 2 April 1910, 8). In 1918 he renounced his academic posts serving the musically talented to devote himself to underprivileged elementary schoolchildren, on his appointment as the first music adviser to Manchester education committee. When his post was made permanent in 1920 he was the first full-time music adviser in Britain.

Carroll's pioneering work in schools, which included lectures and practical sessions with children and teachers, was inspirational. In 1919 an innovatory scheme of teaching music appreciation was established. He organized concerts for children and founded both a children's orchestra and the Manchester Elementary Schools' Choir. The culmination of his efforts came on 4 June 1929 when 250 schoolchildren made a gramophone recording with the Hallé Orchestra conducted by Hamilton Harty in the Free Trade Hall, Manchester. This Columbia recording—a unique event in British music education—of Purcell's *Nymphs and Shepherds* and the dance duet from Humperdinck's *Hansel and Gretel* has no parallel and remains a permanent legacy.

By the time of his retirement in 1934 Carroll had given some 1200 specimen lessons in Manchester schools, and 11,187 schoolteachers had attended his courses of lectures. In 1934 alone 12,000 children were taught music appreciation. When his career began the concept of education was limited. Little time was allotted to the teaching of music or to the training of teachers. Forty years later his pioneering work had brought about a change of emphasis. The importance of music within the curriculum had been recognized. Education authorities and advisory staff, at home and abroad, as well as thousands of teachers and several generations of schoolchildren, came under his influence.

Carroll was director of music at St James's Church, Rusholme, Manchester, from 1916 until 1938. His choral music is rarely performed. He lives on in his piano music for children. From 1912 to 1953 he composed a series of descriptive and imaginative piano works, integrating music, poetry, and design, commencing with *Scenes at a Farm*. For later volumes such as *Forest Fantasies* (1916) and *River and Rainbow* (1933) Carroll employed the foremost illustrators of the day, including Arthur Rackham and William Heath Robinson. Leading a new era in the education of child pianists Carroll ranks among the finest twentieth-century composers for children.

In his retirement Carroll continued composing for

children, producing essays and booklets on music education and lecturing throughout the country. He died at his home, Glenluce, Lapwing Lane, Didsbury, Manchester, on 9 October 1955.   ANTHONY C. WALKER

Sources A. C. Walker, 'The contribution of Walter Carroll (1869–1955) to music education', MEd diss., University of Manchester, 1983 · A. Walker, *Walter Carroll: the children's composer* (1989) · J. Robert-Blunn, *Northern accent: the life story of the Northern School of Music* (1972) · M. Kennedy, *The history of the Royal Manchester College of Music, 1893–1972* (1971) · b. cert. · private information (2004) [family] · parish register, Chorlton-on-Medlock, St Saviour, 9 Jan 1868 [marriage] · diaries and notebooks, Royal Northern College of Music, Walter Carroll collection
Archives Royal Northern College of Music, Manchester, papers
Likenesses portrait, repro. in Walker, *Walter Carroll*, frontispiece · portrait, repro. in Walker, 'The contribution of Walter Carroll (1869–1955) to music education', frontispiece
Wealth at death £35,206 15s. 10d.: probate, 12 Dec 1955, *CGPLA Eng. & Wales*

Carron, William John, Baron Carron (1902–1969), trade unionist, was born on 19 November 1902 at 63 Williamson Street, Hull, the younger of two sons of John Carron and his wife, Frances Ann Richardson. His father, a corporation clerk who later became a carting contractor, was Irish and his mother came from Yorkshire. He attended St Mary's Roman Catholic Primary School, which was run by the Sisters of Mercy, and then Hull Technical College. He left the technical college prematurely on his father's death, and was apprenticed in September 1918 as a turner to Messrs Rose, Downs, and Thompson Ltd in Hull. He completed his apprenticeship in November 1923 and was kept on as a journeyman. On 5 August 1931 he married at St Mary's Catholic Church, Wilton Street, Hull, Mary Emma McGuire (1904–1984), the daughter of John McGuire, a bricklayer, and his wife, Harriet.

Carron followed the course expected of a time-served craftsman in a specialist engineering firm in the north of England. On finishing his apprenticeship he joined the Hull no. 4 branch of the Amalgamated Engineering Union (AEU) as a section one member. He had no special interest in union affairs, attending branch meetings from time to time.

Carron was drawn into participation in union life by chance at the age of twenty-nine. He was confined to bed with a rash from eating strawberries. A veteran branch official called round with the sick pay to which he was entitled as a section one member, but he also had another aim. He wanted to persuade Carron to accept nomination for branch secretary, evidently judging him to be capable of the serious commitment considered essential to discharge branch office in this highly democratic union. Carron was initially highly resistant, but eventually agreed. He was duly elected.

Carron found union branch office satisfying, and his interest in the union deepened. In 1935 he changed jobs, moving to the maintenance department of the large food and household goods manufacturing works of Reckitt and Coleman in Hull. He became a shop steward and in 1941 became the union side's chairman of the works committee. In that year he was also elected to the prestigious

William John Carron, Baron Carron (1902–1969), by Walter Bird, 1963

office of district president. When the post of divisional organizer for his division became vacant in 1945, Carron stood and won the election comfortably. He was a conscientious full-time officer, both respected and popular with the lay officials he served.

Carron's subsequent advancement through the AEU hierarchy to executive councillor in 1950 and president in 1956 was not primarily motivated by personal ambition. During the war left-wing candidates, notably communists, had won many AEU offices. His decision to stand for high union office was grounded in his Roman Catholicism and support for social democracy. The cold war affected him profoundly. He felt called to ensure his union's future and to propagate his views on social partnership and mutual trust between employers and unions.

After his election to the executive, Carron moved to suburban south-east London near the AEU head office with his wife and two daughters, Hilary (born in 1933) and Patricia (born in 1945). He became involved in the social democratic wing of the Labour Party, developing personal bonds with Gaitskell and other MPs in the Campaign for Democratic Socialism. He joined the TUC general council in 1954, and remained a pivotal figure until stepping down in September 1968.

Carron's election as president in 1956 was highly contentious. His principal opponent, the well-known north London communist Reg Birch, won a small majority of votes over Carron on the first ballot. Carron feared defeat on the second ballot, and approached his friend Woodrow

Wyatt for assistance. Having cleared the project with the BBC director-general, Wyatt covered the election and the possibility of a communist victory on his popular current affairs programme *Panorama*. The attendant publicity produced a record turn-out, and Carron won by an unprecedented majority.

Carron proved a shrewd, even Machiavellian president. He worked closely with executive councillor John Boyd to stymie the left wing's domination of the executive. Faced with apparently endless and intractable internal conflicts, he had recourse to prayer and meditation. He found going on retreat before critical AEU, TUC, and Labour Party meetings particularly helpful. His strong personal commitment to social democratic policies and his friendship with Hugh Gaitskell provided a strong motivation for his open and unabashed manipulation of the AEU's important block vote at the annual TUC conference and Labour Party conference. As president, Carron enjoyed personal possession of the all-important card. He routinely cast the union's approximately 700,000 votes with the right wing on contentious issues such as incomes policy, unilateral disarmament, and nuclear testing, even though the union's policy-making body (the national committee) had passed left-wing motions to the contrary.

Many of the AEU's rank-and-file delegates concerted elaborate manoeuvres to counter Carron's increasingly self-confident legerdemain. Carron, however, was usually able to quash their stratagems with his own offensives, carefully prepared with the other members of the union's right-wing faction. '[Carron] was shrewd, he learnt fast how to react to and control a situation. ... he had the advantage of a bland effrontery which stopped strong men speechless in their tracks, and a quiet calculated ruthlessness' (Minkin, 179). His ability to control the AEU's rebellious delegations became legendary, and was aptly described as Carron's Law. Of uncertain provenance, the expression was used universally by detractors and supporters in appreciation of his tactical virtuosity and strong will to have his own way.

Though he never realized his ambition of eradicating communist and left-wing influence in the union, Carron's achievement in providing a counterbalance to the left wing was recognized by the Roman Catholic hierarchy and British governments. He was appointed knight of the order of chivalry of St Gregory the Great in October 1959. He received a knighthood in 1963, and was made a life peer in 1967. He was appointed a director of the Bank of England in 1963.

Carron retired from the AEU presidency on 19 November 1967. He had a quiet retirement, cut short by his sudden death from heart failure at his home, 174 Grierson Road, Honor Oak Park, Forest Hill, London, on 3 December 1969.   NINA FISHMAN

Sources CAC Cam., Carron MSS, curriculum vitae and file 8/1 · *AEU Journal* (April 1965) · *The Times* (5 Dec 1969) · *Financial Times* (5 Dec 1969) · b. cert. · m. cert. · d. cert. · 'A man with a million', *The Director* (June 1961), 486–8 · transcript of interview with Lord Gladwin of Clee, 12 July 1998, priv. coll. · transcript of interview with Geoffrey Goodman, 13 July 1998, priv. coll. · *AEU Journal* (April 1956) · *AEU Journal* (Aug 1956) · *AEU Journal* (Sept 1945) · transcript of interview with Les Ambrose, 28 June 1998, priv. coll. · TUC biography, London Metropolitan University, Trade Union Congress collection · W. Wyatt, *Confessions of an optimist* (1985), 249–52 · private information (2004) [Hilary Weidemann, née Carron] · L. Minkin, *The labour party conference: a study in the politics of intraparty democracy* (1978); repr. (1980), chap. 7

Archives CAC Cam., corresp. and papers, mainly as executive councillor and president of the Amalgamated Engineering Union | FILM BFI NFTVA, party political footage

Likenesses W. Bird, photograph, 1963, NPG [*see illus.*]

Wealth at death £29,825: probate, 15 April 1970, *CGPLA Eng. & Wales*

Carruthers, Andrew (1770–1852), Roman Catholic bishop and vicar apostolic of the eastern district of Scotland, was born on 7 February 1770 at Drumillan near New Abbey in the stewartry of Kirkcudbright, and was baptized the following day. He was the son of Andrew Carruthers and his wife, Lucy Rigg, both of old Catholic families. He was educated in the local school and often spent hours in the nearby romantic ruins of Sweetheart Abbey. At sixteen he entered the Scots College at Douai in France, where he studied for the next six years. Forced out by the French Revolution in 1792 he was temporarily in charge of the seminary at Scalan. Genial if stern, he impressed the duke of Gordon, but demands on his time for the supervision of studies, examinations, and devotions proved stressful, and some found him insensitive and authoritarian. He also acted as surgeon, amanuensis, and valet to his ailing superior, Bishop Andrew Geddes. Too young for ordination, he became the uncomfortable overseer of the Scalan house farm. He found fault with some missionary priests, indifferent local families, and the assertive seminary maids. He antagonized the farm manager, John Williamson, and the housekeeper, Annie Gerard; both they and some of the students wanted to leave. Carruthers found the philosophy and theology studies unsatisfactory. Replaced in 1793 by a fellow student, Andrew Scott, later bishop of Glasgow, he completed his theological studies in Aberdeen under the Revd John Farquharson, formerly principal of Douai.

After ordination on 25 March 1795 Carruthers served until 1797 as missionary near Drummond Castle, Balloch, to the scattered Catholics of Crieff and Perthshire. He then moved to the ancient Catholic family of Traquair House, Peeblesshire. Three years later he went to serve the Maxwell family at Munshes, Kirkcudbright. In 1814, when protestants inherited the house, he moved to nearby Dalbeattie, where he established a chapel and built himself a house with funds left for that purpose by Miss Maxwell, the last Catholic proprietor of the family house. His botanic garden there became something of a tourist attraction. Carruthers worked for thirty-two years in an area covering Dumfries to Stranraer, establishing many new missions within a 40 mile radius of his home, including those at Kirkcudbright, Gatehouse of Fleet, Parton, and Newton Stewart.

Unknown to most Scottish clergy on account of his remote situation, he made an impression at the first clerical gathering he attended, in Huntly in 1827. That year

Andrew Carruthers (1770–1852), by unknown engraver

coadjutor, and from 1838 to 1844 he settled at Blairs College in Aberdeenshire. But Gillis's frequent absences in Europe on Scottish business forced him back to Edinburgh, until he retired to Dundee in 1849. He died there on 24 May 1852, eleven days after contracting typhoid. Bishop Gillis, assisted by Bishops Murdoch and Smith of the western district of Scotland, conducted his funeral service. He was buried in St Mary's, Edinburgh, on 28 May 1852.

The typical enlightened Catholic gentleman, Carruthers was a delightful conversationalist, well-read, and proficient in French; he passed on his enthusiasm for experimental philosophy and chemistry to the students at Blairs College. One of the last of the old Catholic school, he laid the foundations for the eastern Scottish Catholic revival.   BERNARD ASPINWALL

Sources J. F. S. Gordon, *Scotichronicon*, 2 vols. (1867), 348–61 [appx] · *Catholic Directory for Scotland* (1853), 127–33 · J. Darragh, *The Catholic hierarchy of Scotland: a biographical list, 1653–1985* (1986) · W. M. Brady, *Annals of the Catholic hierarchy in England and Scotland* (1877) · C. Johnson, 'The secular clergy of the Lowland district', *Innes Review*, 34 (1983), 66–87 · Archives of Propaganda, Rome · Archives of the Scots College, Rome · Scottish Catholic Archives, Edinburgh · NA Scot.

Archives Archivio Vaticano, Vatican City · NA Scot. · Scots College, Rome, archives · Scottish Catholic Archives, Edinburgh, corresp. and papers

Likenesses line engraving, repro. in J. F. S. Gordon, *Ecclesiastical chronicle for Scotland*, 4 vols. (1867), vol. 4, p. 474 [see illus.] · portrait, archbishop's house, St Benet's, Edinburgh; repro. in Gordon, *Scotichronicon*, 2 vols. (1867)

the Scottish Catholic church was divided from two into three districts. The death of Bishop Alexander Paterson in 1831 gave rise to a debate over a successor. In a trusteeism controversy, the lay Edinburgh élite, including a founder of the publishing firm Burns and Oates and the father of a later archbishop of Edinburgh, had strongly—and publicly—opposed Paterson. His 'alien' authoritarian style, his control of temporalities, and his sympathy for Jesuits created difficulties. A safe 'Scottish' appointment was needed. Carruthers wrote to *Propaganda* on 21 November 1831 to oppose the appointment of the exuberant and inexperienced Revd James Gillis, the Canadian-Scots protégé of John Menzies of Pitfodels, who had given his magnificent Blairs estate for a national seminary. Ironically Carruthers was appointed in his stead. Nominated bishop of Ceramis *in partibus infidelium* in November 1832, he was consecrated on 13 January 1833 in Edinburgh by Bishop Penswick of the northern district of England, assisted by bishops Andrew Scott and James Kyle.

Despite limited funds Carruthers oversaw a rapid expansion of Catholic numbers, clergy, missions, and institutions. Thanks to Menzies' generosity, he established St Patrick's Church in Edinburgh in 1834. Other churches followed: two in Dundee, in 1836 and 1851, and others in Falkirk, Hawick, Portobello, Annan, Arbroath, Campsie, Forfar, and Leith. Carruthers warmly supported the Society of St Andrew in its work to establish missions for poorer Catholics. He encouraged the founding of Wellburn Academy, Dundee, and was active in the United Industrial Schools, Edinburgh, for the Catholic poor. In 1837, as his burdens increased, he secured Gillis as his

Carruthers, (Alexander) Douglas Mitchell (1882–1962),

explorer and naturalist, was born in London on 4 October 1882, the eldest son of William Mitchell-Carruthers (1853–1931), who took orders in 1886, and his wife, Antonia, daughter of Atkinson Alexander Holden, who had been rector of Hawton, Newark-on-Trent. Educated at Haileybury College and Trinity College, Cambridge, he started in quite a humble way as secretary to various people who were working at the Royal Geographical Society, and underwent training in land survey work. He also learned how to skin animals and became an expert taxidermist. This enabled him to take part in expeditions which advanced his career. On the British Museum expedition to Ruwenzori and the Congo (1905–6) he sent home remarkable specimens of birds and mammals. In 1907–8 a German businessman and natural historian enabled Carruthers to travel in Russian Turkestan and the borders of Afghanistan. There he did research work on the various kinds of wild sheep in the Tien Shan (Tianshan) range of mountains. He established the territories inhabited by the *Ovis ammon* and *Ovis poli* and found another specimen of sheep, new to natural history, and later named *Ovis karolini*. He supplied many museums in Europe and America with specimens of these sheep at a time when very little was known about them. He then explored by himself the countries south-east of Syria and shot certain rare deer, among them the Arabian oryx, one species of which was hitherto unknown. He also made a collection of marmots, one of which was new.

Carruthers's next most important work was undertaken in collaboration with the big-game hunter John H. Miller and Morgan Philips Price. In 1910 they decided to explore the stony desert of Outer Mongolia, then part of the old Chinese empire, during the last years of the Manchu dynasty. The expedition took eleven months, crossed Siberia, and went up the Yenesei River to the source. The explorers had some difficulty in crossing the Sayansk Mountains on the Russo-Chinese frontier as they entered Outer Mongolia, but Carruthers was expert in dealing with obstructive officials. The country of the upper Yenesei basin was largely unknown. Only two Russian explorers had been there before and virtually no mapping had been done. Carruthers did some surveying and made some maps of the country watered by the Japsa River, which flows into the upper Yenesei north of the Tannu-ola Mountains. This was difficult forested and mountainous country which had never been worked at before. Carruthers and his colleagues were real pioneers, and the expedition owed much to his capacity for organization and leadership and his knowledge of human nature. His two volumes on *Unknown Mongolia* were published in 1913 and in the meantime he had been awarded the Gill memorial (1910) and the patron's gold medal (1912) of the Royal Geographical Society, which he was to serve as honorary secretary in 1916–21.

During the First World War Carruthers was employed mainly at the War Office compiling maps of the Middle East. He ceased active exploration following his marriage, on 9 October 1915, to Mary (1878–1962), the divorced wife of Major James Archibald Morrison MP and the daughter of Arthur Edwin Hill-Trevor, the first Lord Trevor. He settled in the countryside of East Anglia and his later career consisted largely in working at map making and with explorers and travellers. He published some articles and memoranda on various aspects of geography. His later books included *Arabian Adventure* (1935) and *Beyond the Caspian: a Naturalist in Central Asia* (1949). His work showed alertness to the impact of climatic and physical variations on all forms of life: a thought which ran through most of his lecturing and writing. He did some work on climatic conditions in central Asia, and continued some of the work started by Ellsworth Huntington and other geographers and explorers. He was interested in the idea that in the course of centuries a process of desiccation had been going on in the centre of the continent. This induced him to work in getting information about the old civilizations which had arisen and disappeared in central Asia, thereby adding to what had been done by Sven Hedin, Aurel Stein, and others. He was awarded the Sykes medal of the Royal Central Asian Society in 1956.

Carruthers's first marriage was dissolved in 1948 and in that year he married Rosemary Arden, daughter of Lieutenant-Colonel Ernest Charles Clay. He died in the Royal Free Hospital, Islington, on 23 May 1962.

M. PHILIPS PRICE, *rev.*

Sources personal knowledge (1981) · *The Times* (26 May 1962) · *The Times* (30 May 1962) · Venn, *Alum. Cant.* · *WWW* · Burke, *Peerage* (1939) · d. cert. · *CGPLA Eng. & Wales* (1962)

Archives RGS, corresp. and papers | St Ant. Oxf., Middle East Centre, letters to H. St J. B. Philby | SOUND BL NSA, recorded lecture
Likenesses M. Carruthers, bronze bust, 1936, RGS
Wealth at death £5838 15s. 9d.: probate, 19 Sept 1962, *CGPLA Eng. & Wales*

Carruthers, James (1759–1832), historian and Roman Catholic priest, was born at New Abbey, Kirkcudbrightshire, the son of Andrew Carruthers and Lucy Rigg. His brother was Andrew *Carruthers, vicar apostolic of the eastern district. He was educated for six years at the Scots College at Douai and on his return to Scotland in 1785 he was ordained priest and appointed to the extensive charge of Glenlivet. He was stationed at Buchan in Aberdeenshire from 1794, at Preshome in Banffshire from 1803, at Dumfries from 1815, and at New Abbey from 1826.

During his last years Carruthers published two works on Scottish history. The *History of Scotland from the earliest period of the Scottish monarchy to the accession of the Stewart family* (1826) was a curious narrative which combined superficial acknowledgement of the fashionable interest in the history of literature and ideas with a resolute rejection of 'the pretended discoveries of modern and discordant antiquaries' (p. iv). The result was a work strongly indebted to the traditional chronology of Scottish kingship which had been widely discredited during the previous century. Carruthers's *History of Scotland during the Reign of Queen Mary* (1831) attempted to refute the 'speculative tenets' of the Reformation (p. 22) and to exculpate 'the illustrious and unfortunate Mary' (ibid., v). Neither work was well received. Carruthers died at New Abbey on 14 February 1832. THOMPSON COOPER, *rev.* DAVID ALLAN

Sources J. Darragh, *The Catholic hierarchy of Scotland: a biographical list, 1653–1985* (1986), 18 · J. F. S. Gordon, ed., *The Catholic church in Scotland* (1874), 533 · *Catholic Magazine and Review*, 2 (1832), 329 · *Edinburgh Catholic Magazine*, 1 (1832), 24

Carruthers, Robert (1799–1878), newspaper editor and writer, was born on 5 November 1799 in Dumfries, Scotland, the son of Walter Carruthers, farmer, and Isabella Roddick. He received a little formal education before being apprenticed to a Dumfries bookseller. He also learned bookbinding. On completing his apprenticeship Carruthers moved to Huntingdon to serve as master of its national school, which operated on the Bell instructional system. There he began his writing career with the *History of Huntingdon* (1824), based on the corporation's records, and the *Poetry of Milton's Prose* (1827). He also contributed to the *Dumfries Magazine*, published by John M'Diarmid, editor of the weekly *Dumfries and Galloway Courier*. About this time he married Janet Roberts.

In April 1828, on M'Diarmid's recommendation, Carruthers was named editor of the *Inverness Courier*, then just ten years old. He became its proprietor in 1831, determined that it should contribute to the literary and general improvement of highland readers. During his fifty years' direction it became the most popular newspaper in the north of Scotland. It addressed the conditions of the highlands and changes occurring in the region as well as its history. He encouraged local writers, most notably Hugh

Miller, whose poetry and essays on Cromarty herring fishing, later published as *Letters on the Herring Fishery* (1839), appeared in the *Courier*. Carruthers also published writers from outside the area, including Wordsworth's son-in-law Edward Quillinan. The *Inverness and Northern Agriculturalist* (1845–6), a monthly periodical, was another of his publications. Carruthers's own contributions to the *Courier* were collected in the *Highland Note-Book, or, Sketches and Anecdotes* (1843).

During the 1840s Carruthers also began a long association with W. and R. Chambers, the Edinburgh publishers. He assisted Robert Chambers with *Chambers's Cyclopaedia of English Literature* (1843–4), by providing biographies of writers of the day with extracts from and commentary on their works, in addition to those from earlier centuries. Besides his extensive contributions to the first edition, Carruthers oversaw revisions and additions to the *Cyclopaedia's* second (1856) and third (1876) editions.

Carruthers produced the works for which he has been best-known in the 1850s. After editing Boswell's *Journal of a Tour in the Hebrides* (1851) for the National Illustrated Library, he prepared for the same series the four-volume *Poetical Works of Alexander Pope* (1853). The first volume included a memoir of Pope. Carruthers used Pope's papers and correspondence with Teresa and Martha Blount which he discovered at Mapledurham where the Blount family had preserved them. He made his own additions to the notes and included previously unpublished ones by George Steevens and John Wilkes. Although the memoir was more detailed and accurate than any previous Pope biography, it was questioned and corrected almost at once by C. W. Dilke. Carruthers responded to these criticisms by making corrections and adding more selections from Pope's correspondence to a second, revised edition of the *Life of Pope* (1857).

Carruthers engaged in biographical writing on other literary and historical figures. For the eighth edition of the *Encyclopaedia Britannica* he supplied articles on, among others, Queen Elizabeth, William Penn, Francis Jeffrey, and James Hogg, the Ettrick shepherd. For *Chambers's Encyclopaedia* (1860–68) he wrote the entries on William Wycherley, Samuel Pepys, and William Makepeace Thackeray. He wrote memoirs for William Falconer's *The Shipwreck* (1858, 1868), and for collections of James Montgomery's and Thomas Gray's poetry. For the Chambers firm, he edited their bowdlerized *Household Edition of Shakespeare* (1861–3) and added the Abbotsford *notanda* to the third edition of Robert Chambers's *Life of Scott* (1871). He wrote 'Jeffrey and criticism' for *Chambers's Papers for the People* (1853) and contributed to *Chambers's Journal*, the *Gentleman's Magazine*, and the *North British Review*.

Besides Hugh Miller and Robert Chambers, Carruthers knew and worked with a wide range of nineteenth-century literary figures, among them Allan Cunningham, Thomas Babington Macaulay, Douglas Jerrold, Thomas Carlyle, John Hill Burton, Joseph Robertson, and Alexander Russel. His friendship with Thackeray is most memorable because of their marked physical resemblance, amusing both to them and their associates. Carruthers's writing was highly regarded by his contemporaries for its vigorous style and for its accuracy and attention to detail. Carruthers delivered a series of lectures to the Edinburgh Philosophical Institution. He received an LLD from Edinburgh University in 1871 and was honoured in the same year by a public dinner in Inverness at which he was presented with a bust and portrait of himself. He was married for more than fifty years. At the celebration of their fiftieth wedding anniversary, he and his wife counted more than thirty descendants, children and grandchildren. Carruthers's sons Walter and Robert were both associated with the *Courier*, Walter succeeding his father as editor. His daughters Mary and Robina married the sculptors Alexander Munro and Patric Park respectively. Another married the watercolourist Samuel Reed. Following Carruthers's death in Inverness on 26 May 1878 from 'organic disease of the stomach', the city of Inverness conducted a public funeral for him.

SONDRA MILEY COONEY

Sources *DNB* · *Inverness Courier* (30 May 1878) · *Scotsman* (28 May 1878) · R. Carruthers, *The life of Alexander Pope, including extracts from his correspondence*, 2nd edn, 4 vols. (1857) · J. Hedderwick, *Backward glances* (1891) · NL Scot., W. and R. Chambers MS deposit 341 · *GM*, 257 (1884), 444–58 · d. cert.
Archives NL Scot., letter-book and editorial corresp. | U. Edin. L., letters to David Laing
Likenesses D. O. Hill, calotype, *c*.1840, Scot. NPG · bust (presented to Carruthers in Nov 1871) · portrait (presented to Carruthers in Nov 1871) · wood-engraving, NPG; repro. in *ILN*, 357 (1878), lxii

Carryl, Mary (*d.* 1809), servant and friend of the Ladies of Llangollen, was one of at least three children of humble parents from Ross, co. Wexford. Little is known of her background or upbringing, but her forceful personality was apparent at an early age; it was reported that as a young woman 'she went by the name of Molly the Bruiser' because of her quarrelsome nature (Bell, 42).

While employed as a housemaid by Sir William and Lady Betty Fownes at Woodstock, Inistiogue, co. Kilkenny, Mary became deeply involved in the events leading up to the elopement of Sarah Ponsonby (1755–1831), Lady Betty's cousin and charge, and Lady Eleanor Butler (1739–1829) [see Butler, Lady (Charlotte) Eleanor]. In April 1778 the Butler family's opposition to the friendship prompted Lady Eleanor to run away from her relatives and to take refuge with Sarah at Woodstock. Mary's name first appears in connection with the story on 23 April 1778, when Lady Betty reported to a family friend that 'Miss Ponsonby had kept her friend concealed in a closet inside her room and the housemaid Mary Carryl … had brought her food' (Bell, 36). On 4 May 1778 Sarah Ponsonby and Lady Eleanor left Woodstock, with their families' grudging consent. From Ireland they travelled to Wales, and in early 1780 set up home in a cottage, Plas Newydd, in the village of Llangollen in north Wales. From there they sent for Mary, who had meanwhile been dismissed from Woodstock for severely wounding a fellow servant by throwing a candlestick at him (ibid., 42).

Mary remained in the service of the Ladies of Llangollen, as they came to be called, for the rest of her life.

Initially, according to a family source, 'her masculine qualities afforded them protection till they were well known and established in a village not remarkable for sobriety' (Bell, 42), but she quickly became the acknowledged mainstay of their household. Vociferous and assertive, her quarrels, prejudices, and eccentricities are affectionately recorded in Lady Eleanor's journal and in the Ladies' voluminous correspondence. On 21 October 1784, for instance, Lady Eleanor reported a 'loud and violent altercation between Mary and the fisherman. Mary triumphant' (ibid., 59), and later, 'Mary in her Glory, purchasing Beef for hanging and exerting all her powers of Eloquence in bargaining with the Butchers' (ibid., 64). On 5 November 1806 Sarah described her contributing 'about a soup ladlefull of Coals' to the village bonfire, and expecting the children 'to shout applauses of her generosity' (Blackburne, 137). Mary repaid the Ladies' confidence with intense loyalty as well as with presents, such as the seal which she gave Sarah in 1787, upon which was cut 'the most Deformed Hope that any mortal ever laid hold upon' (Mavor, 150).

Through correspondence and visits from relatives and acquaintants, the Plas Newydd household was kept fully informed of events in Ireland. In 1798 its members' consternation at news of the rebellion there was intensified by concern about the safety of family members, including that of Mary Carryl's mother, who lived in Enniscorthy, a rebel stronghold. In June it was reported that she had been murdered, and Sarah Tighe, Sarah Ponsonby's cousin, attempted to get a list 'of the Protestants killed at Enniscorthy … on Mary's account' (Blackburne, 314). However, this rumour appears to have been false, since Mary's will, made in 1808, includes a reference to her mother (Mavor, 128).

Mary Carryl died at Plas Newydd on 22 November 1809 after a long illness, during which she had been nursed by the Ladies. In a letter to Mrs Tighe, Sarah Ponsonby described the visions which Mary had allegedly seen on her deathbed, and a year later continued to regret 'the dreadful vacancy made in our family and our comfort' by her death (Mavor, 173). In a final act of friendship, Mary bequeathed to Sarah Ponsonby a field which she had bought with her life savings, while to her brother and sister in Ireland she left just 1s. each. At the Ladies' request, the local physician, Dr Dealtry, composed an inscription for Mary's grave, which extolled her virtues and exemplary death. Eleanor Butler died in 1829 and Sarah Ponsonby in 1831. They were buried together, beside Mary Carryl, in Llangollen churchyard.

ROSEMARY RAUGHTER

Sources G. H. Bell, ed., *The Hamwood papers of the Ladies of Llangollen and Caroline Hamilton* (1930) · E. Mavor, *The Ladies of Llangollen* (1971) · E. Blackburne, *Illustrious Irishwomen* (1877)
Archives NL Ire., memoirs of Mrs Caroline Hamilton
Wealth at death see will, Mavor, *Ladies of Llangollen*, 139

Carse. For this title name *see* Lyon, Sir Patrick, of Carse, Lord Carse (1637–1694).

Carse, Alexander (*bap.* 1770, *d.* 1843), genre painter, was born in Innerwick, Haddingtonshire, and was baptized in that parish on 25 March 1770, which was possibly also the day of his birth, the son of William Carse, a tailor in Thorntounloch, and his wife, Catherine, *née* Denholm. He was a pupil of David Allan the renowned Scottish genre painter, whose influence can clearly be seen in Carse's early works (for example, *Oldhamstocks Fair*, watercolour, *c.*1796; Glasgow Art Gallery and Museum). He attended the Trustees' Academy in Edinburgh as a student from December 1801 (although Carse himself applied for admission to the Trustees' Academy in 1806), where he would have received an education in drawing and compositional painting classes.

Carse's first known oil paintings date from 1803. In 1808 David Steuart, eleventh earl of Buchan, described Carse as the best Scottish painter of village scenery. From that date he was a regular exhibitor with the Associated Artists in Edinburgh, where he displayed many small genre scenes. In 1812 he exhibited *The Country Relations* (oils, *c.*1812; priv. coll.), now regarded as his masterpiece. The painting is full of detail and wittily records the costume and manners of the early nineteenth century, as does Carse's painting *Grace before Meat* (n.d., priv. coll., oils). Carse's paintings illustrate life and customs in rural Scotland, for example, *The Doonies versus the Croonies on New Years Day* (*c.*1810; priv. coll.). This painting depicts a football game traditionally played between the inhabitants of the upper end of a town against those of the lower end.

Carse spent the years 1812–20 in London, exhibiting at the Royal Academy and at the British Institution. During this time he was competing with and influenced by his fellow Scot David Wilkie, also resident in London. Carse painted his *Penny Wedding* in 1819 (priv. coll.), a subject Wilkie also painted between 1817 and 1819. Both artists' depictions are indebted to Allan's *Penny Wedding* of 1795 (watercolour; NG Scot.). Carse's *Penny Wedding* is full of activity as the dancers occupy the centre floor; Wilkie's representation is far less frenetic (oils, 1818; the Royal Collection). Wilkie's representation was bought by the prince regent, financial and artistic patronage Carse did not enjoy. Financially impoverished, Carse ceased to exhibit in London and returned to Edinburgh, where he exhibited at the Royal Institution for the Encouragement of the Fine Arts (1821–30) and then, from 1827 until 1836, at the newly created Royal Scottish Academy. He had, however, to apply for financial assistance to the Royal Institution's trustees of the Spalding fund for the relief of decayed and superannuated artists, and received assistance from them in 1843.

In 1822 Carse painted *George IV Landing at Leith* (City of Edinburgh Museums and Art Galleries). This large painting, 5 feet high and 11 feet long, contains several hundred figures—many of them portraits—a variety of military uniforms, ships, and a representation of the harbour and waterfront at Leith. His earlier topographical views of country houses drawn in the mid-1790s stood the artist in good stead for the depiction of the Leith waterfront. He wrote an unpublished poem, 'The Witches' Late Wake'

Alexander Carse (*bap.* 1770, *d.* 1843), self-portrait, 1811

(MS, NG Scot.), and illustrated the poetry of Robert Burns, including a drawing of Tam O'Shanter watching the witches dance (NG Scot.). He supplied illustrations to Robert Brown of Newhall for *The Gentle Shepherd, with Illustrations of the Scenery* (1808), an edition of Allan Ramsay's poem.

Carse's self-portrait (oil on steel, 1811; Scot. NPG) is typical of the artist's work. The painting, only 22.9 cm x 20.4 cm (9 inches x 8 inches) shows a very unassuming artist almost hiding behind his easel. The painting believed to depict Alexander Carse with his mother and sister (Scot. NPG) portrays the siblings listening to their mother reading from the family Bible. Carse's ability to represent seduction can be seen in *The Return from the Hunt* (priv. coll.), where the hunter proffers to his sweetheart his prize kill, a pheasant. These two interior scenes are painted with great restraint; each object, faithfully depicted in its own space, lends an air of still life to these paintings. The people in his genre scenes are painted with touches of comic character but his honest realism avoided caricature. His early opportunity while a student at the Trustees' Academy to study prints after Dutch still lifes is evident in his interiors.

Carse died between 21 and 28 February 1843. He is perceived as the Scottish genre painter of the early nineteenth century who provides continuity between David Allan's first naïve attempts and David Wilkie's more vibrant and lively depictions of ordinary life.

LUCY DIXON

Sources L. Errington, *Alexander Carse, c.1770–1843* (1989) · D. Macmillan, *Painting in Scotland: the golden age* (1986) [exhibition catalogue, U. Edin., Talbot Rice Gallery, and Tate Gallery, London, 1986] · K. Andrews and J. R. Brotchie, *Catalogue of Scottish drawings* (1960) · H. Smailes, *The concise catalogue of the Scottish National Portrait Gallery* (1990) · [J. Lloyd Williams], *National Gallery of Scotland: concise catalogue of paintings* (1997) · D. Irwin and F. Irwin, *Scottish painters at home and abroad, 1700–1900* (1975) · M. Campbell, *The line of tradition: watercolours, drawings and prints by Scottish artists* (1993) [exhibition catalogue, Royal Scot. Acad., 4 Aug – 12 Sept 1993] · Graves, *RA exhibitors* · Graves, *Brit. Inst.* · [E. Cumming], *Catalogue of the city of Edinburgh art collection*, 1 (1979) · J. Halsby and P. Harris, *The dictionary of Scottish painters, 1600–1960* (1990) · P. J. M. McEwan, *Dictionary of Scottish art and architecture* (1994) · J. Caw, *Scottish painting past and present, 1620–1908* (1908); repr. (1990) · earl of Buchan to Caleb Waiteford, 19 Jan 1808, BM, department of prints and drawings, Whitley papers · bap. reg. Scot.

Archives NA Scot., letters to Royal Institution for the Encouragement of the Fine Arts Edinburgh, NG 1/59/13, NG 1/59/116 · NA Scot., Trustees' Academy minute book, NG 1/1/32

Likenesses A. Carse, self-portrait, oil on steel, 1811, Scot. NPG [see illus.] · A. Carse, self-portrait, pencil drawing, 1830, Scot. NPG · A. Carse, group portrait, panel (of Carse? with his mother and sister), Scot. NPG

Carse, William (*b.* 1800, *d.* in or after 1845), landscape painter, was born on 29 August 1800 in the parish of Liberton, near Edinburgh, the son of Alexander Carse and his wife, Jean Falconer. His father may have been the landscape and genre painter Alexander *Carse (*bap.* 1770, *d.* 1843). In 1818 he was a student at the British Institution, London, and lived with Alexander Carse at Grenville Street, Somers Town. His first pictures were of cattle, in the style of the seventeenth-century Dutch painter Paulus Potter, but later he devoted himself to landscapes and genre paintings, mainly scenes from rural Scottish life. Samuel Redgrave commented that his pictures showed 'much humour, but they were coarse and ill drawn'. Between 1820 and 1829 Carse exhibited pictures at the Royal Academy, the British Institution, and the Society (later Royal Society) of British Artists in Suffolk Street. During the latter part of his residence in London he lived in Southampton Crescent, Euston Square. About 1830 he returned to Edinburgh and exhibited pictures in the Royal Scottish Academy up to 1845, after which date he cannot be traced. The painter John Howe Carse (*c.*1819–1900), who worked in Scotland and exhibited in London in 1860–62 before emigrating to Australia, is believed to be his son.

L. H. CUST, *rev.* EMILY M. WEEKS

Sources M. H. Grant, *A chronological history of the old English landscape painters*, rev. edn, 7 (1960) · Graves, *RA exhibitors* · J. Johnson, ed., *Works exhibited at the Royal Society of British Artists, 1824–1893, and the New English Art Club, 1888–1917*, 2 vols. (1975) · J. Halsby and P. Harris, *The dictionary of Scottish painters, 1600–1960* (1990) · Redgrave, *Artists* · private information (1886) · register of births and baptisms, 1800, General Register Office for Scotland, Edinburgh

Carslaw, Horatio Scott (1870–1954), mathematician, was born on 12 February 1870 at Helensburgh, Dunbartonshire, Scotland, the fifth son of William Henderson Carslaw, a Free Church minister, and his wife, Elizabeth, *née* Lockhead. After an early education at Glasgow Academy he attended Glasgow University where he studied under Professor William Jack, gaining his MA in 1891. He went on to study mathematics at Emmanuel College, Cambridge, and was fourth wrangler in 1894. His first academic appointment was as assistant to Jack at Glasgow in 1896. In 1897 he made study visits to Rome, Palermo, and

Göttingen. He was made a Cambridge MA in 1898 and subsequently took doctorates at both Glasgow (1899) and Cambridge (1905).

Carslaw's visit to Göttingen was the principal influence shaping his future research. During his stay the theoretical physicist Arnold Sommerfield introduced him to continental advances, then poorly known in the English-speaking world, and to modern notions of mathematical exactitude, especially the rigorous attention to detail in the application of mathematics. Carslaw worked intensively to apply advanced complex variable analysis to problems of heat and diffraction. In 1903 he took up an appointment to the chair of pure and applied mathematics at the University of Sydney. Aquiline, keen-eyed, bespectacled, already balding, he was by office the leading mathematician in New South Wales, indeed in Australia as a whole. This context drew his attention to matters of mathematical education. He once described himself as a teacher who enjoyed teaching; others saw him as something of a showman in the lecture room. He was active in both the administrative and the expository aspects of school and undergraduate mathematics, and wrote texts on calculus, trigonometry, and non-Euclidean geometry. His many students included E. M. Wellish (later his deputy) and J. C. Jaeger, his subsequent collaborator.

More than a textbook, and incorporating then recent results, was Carslaw's *Introduction to the theory of Fourier's series and integrals and the mathematical theory of the conduction of heat* (1906). Work on Fourier (trigonometric) series and their applications was a lifelong preoccupation, and this text was several times revised and reissued.

Carslaw married a widow, Ethel Maude Cruickshank, *née* Clarke, on 12 February 1907. She died on 3 June of the same year, and he never remarried. Not surprisingly, these events correspond to a hiatus in Carslaw's mathematical output; he published nothing during 1907–8. However his research work in time resumed and he contributed many papers, both innovative and expository, some seventy in all. Honours came to him, including doctorates of science (Adelaide, 1926) and laws (Glasgow, 1928). He was a fellow of the royal societies of Edinburgh and of New South Wales. He retired in 1935.

Carslaw's most enduring mathematical legacy, *Operational Methods in Applied Mathematics* (1941; 2nd edn, 1948; co-authored with Jaeger), is a product of his retirement. This book introduced into undergraduate curricula the 'Laplace transform', a front-line research topic which became in record time standard fare, displacing the earlier, unsatisfactory 'operational calculus'.

Carslaw continued to work after his retirement, despite failing eyesight. Ever humanely left-leaning, he devoted his later years to another long-standing interest, the pursuit of equitable income tax schemes. He died at his home, Thule, Osborne Road, Burradoo, New South Wales, Australia, on 11 November 1954 and was buried the next day in the Anglican section of Bowral cemetery.

MICHAEL A. B. DEAKIN

Sources *Journal of the London Mathematical Society*, 31 (1956), 494–501 · *AusDB*, 7.578–9 · J. C. Jaeger, 'Horatio Scott Carslaw, 1870–1954: a centennial oration', *Gazette* [Australian Mathematical Society], 8 (1981), 1–18 · *The Australian Mathematics Teacher*, 11/3 (Nov 1955) · I. S. Turner, 'The first hundred years of mathematics at the University of Sydney', *The Australian Mathematics Teacher*, 9 (1953), 12–17, 26–34 · M. A. B. Deakin, 'The ascendancy of the Laplace transform and how it came about', *Archive for History of Exact Sciences*, 44 (1992), 265–86 · *Sydney Morning Herald* (12 Nov 1954), 3, 10 · *The Times* (26 Nov 1954), 10 · *Journal and Proceedings of the Royal Society of New South Wales*, 89 (1956), xxvii · M. S. Paterson, *Memoirs FRS*, 28 (1982), 162–203 [obit. of J. C. Jaeger] · M. S. Paterson, 'John Conrad Jaeger, 1907–79', *Historical Records of Australian Science*, 5/3 (1982), 64–88 · *Sydney Morning Herald* (16 Feb 1907), 12 · *Sydney Morning Herald* (5 June 1907), 8 · H. O. Lancaster, 'The departments of mathematics at the University of Sydney', *Gazette of the Australian Mathematical Society*, 13/2 (1986), 29–38

Archives Basser Library, Canberra

Likenesses three photographs, 1903–39, repro. in *Australian Mathematics Teacher*

Wealth at death A$55,579: *AusDB*

Carson, Aglionby Ross (1780–1850), headmaster, was born at Holywood, Dumfriesshire. He was educated at Wallace Hall endowed school, in the parish of Closeburn, and at the University of Edinburgh, which he entered in 1797. In 1801 he was elected rector of the grammar school at Dumfries, and in 1806 was appointed a classical master at Edinburgh high school, of which he became rector in 1820. In 1826 he received the degree of LLD from the University of St Andrews. On account of failing health he resigned the rectorship of the high school on 9 October 1845, and he died at Edinburgh on 4 November 1850. He published several classical school books and was also a contributor to the *Classical Journal*, the *Scottish Review*, and the *Encyclopaedia Britannica*.

T. F. HENDERSON, rev. M. C. CURTHOYS

Sources Anderson, *Scot. nat.* · W. Steven, *The history of the high school of Edinburgh* (1849)

Archives NRA Scotland, letters to subject [1824–45]

Likenesses W. Gordon, portrait, 1833, Edinburgh high school

Carson, Alexander (1776–1844), Baptist minister, was born at Annahone, near Stewartstown, co. Tyrone, the eldest son of William Carson, a Scottish Presbyterian who had settled in Ireland. As preparation for the Presbyterian ministry he was educated in a classical school taught by a Mr Peebles in the village of Tullyhogue, near Cookstown. He subsequently entered Glasgow University where he proceeded BA and MA; under Professor Young he became a good Greek scholar with a special interest in philology. He was licensed by the Tyrone presbytery and ordained pastor of the congregation at Tobermore, co. Londonderry, in December 1798. In appearance he was about 5 feet 9 inches in height, fairly well built, with brown hair and fresh complexion. He married about 1799 Margaret (1781–1844), fourth child of George Ledlie, a prosperous linen-bleacher of Ballygoneymore, near Coagh, co. Tyrone; they had thirteen children, one of whom, James Crawford Ledlie Carson, was to practise as a surgeon in Coleraine, and another, Robert Haldane Carson, was to succeed his father in the pastorate of the Tobermore Baptist Church.

Carson's evangelical Calvinism brought him into conflict with the Arianism favoured by many Presbyterian ministers of the day. This, combined with his objections to laxity in ministerial morals, 'indiscriminate ordination', and 'promiscuous communion', led to his rejection of the presbyterian form of church government in favour of Independency. He severed his connection with the Presbyterian church in May 1805, setting out his position in *Reasons for Separating from the Synod of Ulster*. His secession involved the forfeiture of a secure income from church and state and from a comfortable farm: 'The day that I gave up my connection with the General Synod ... I sacrificed not only my prospects in life, and my respectability in the world, but every settled way of support.' Although the presbytery had declared the congregation vacant, he continued to preach in the Presbyterian meeting-house in Tobermore until a long and expensive lawsuit before the synod established ownership in favour of the presbytery. The next minister, William Brown, was not installed until November 1810. Subsequently Carson appears to have preached in whatever accommodation his supporters could provide, until in 1814 the Independent church which he had formed erected its own meeting-house.

Carson's views on baptism changed after an attempt to defend infant baptism against the arguments in James Haldane's *Reasons for a Change of Sentiment on the Subject of Baptism* (1808–9). He had met Haldane in Coleraine in 1801. Carson followed the route taken earlier by James and Robert Haldane, from Presbyterianism to Independency and then to the Baptist position. His ideal was to have a 'pure communion', that is, a regenerate membership, but at no time did he insist on believer's baptism as a prerequisite of church membership. The church grew to over 500 members, though it was subject to strict discipline. Carson's contribution to the baptismal controversy, *Baptism in its Mode and Subjects*, was published in 1831 and gained him international recognition: Bacon College, Kentucky, and Jackson University, Louisiana, both conferred honorary degrees on him in 1841. An enlarged edition, appearing in 1844, was soon followed by a second impression of 10,000 copies. The work was reprinted in the United States in 1965. Carson's collected works were published by subscription in five volumes between 1847 and 1863. They are wide-ranging and often controversial, and deal with the burning issues of his day, including Arianism, Roman Catholicism, the inspiration and interpretation of the scriptures, the atonement, divine providence, civil obedience, the Irish education debate of the 1820s, and the quarrel between the Baptist Missionary Society and the British and Foreign Bible Society over corrections to translations of the scriptures. His writings are marked by independence of thought, sound logic, and a lucid style.

After the publication of *Baptism in its Mode and Subjects*, Carson was invited, but declined, to visit the USA, although he responded positively to frequent invitations to speak throughout Great Britain on behalf of the Baptist Missionary Society. He was one of four eminent preachers at a meeting in Surrey Chapel, London, in October 1842 marking the fiftieth anniversary of William Carey's missionary enterprise. On 16 August 1844, returning from a tour of English and Welsh churches and about to board ship in Liverpool, he fell off the dockside into the water and dislocated a shoulder. After attention he continued his journey to Belfast where he arrived the next day in a feverish condition and died on 24 August 1844. The funeral procession went from his residence, Solitude, not far from the scene of his labours at Tobermore, to the parish churchyard of Dromore near Desertmartin, where he was buried alongside his wife who had died seven months earlier. JOSHUA THOMPSON

Sources G. C. Moore, *The life of Alexander Carson, LLD* (1851) · T. Witherow, *Three prophets of our own* (1855) · R. A. Boggs, *Alexander Carson of Tobermore* (1969) · J. Douglas, *Biographical sketch of the late Dr. Alexander Carson* (1884) · *A history of congregations in the Presbyterian Church in Ireland, 1610–1982*, Presbyterian Church in Ireland (1982) · *Coleraine Chronicle* (24 Aug 1844) · *Coleraine Chronicle* (31 Aug 1844)
Archives Irish Baptist College, Belfast · Irish Baptist Historical Society Archive, Belfast · Regent's Park College, Oxford, Angus Library
Likenesses portrait, 1840?, Baptist Union of Ireland, Belfast

Carson, Mrs Charles L. *See* Dutton, Emily Courtier- (1862?–1919).

Carson, Edward Henry, Baron Carson (1854–1935), politician and lawyer, was born in Harcourt Street, Dublin, on 9 February 1854, the second son of Edward Henry Carson, architect and civil engineer, and Isabella Lambert of Castle Ellen, Athenry, co. Galway. His family was typical of the Irish protestant, or 'Anglo-Irish' people, with its mixture of professional and landed backgrounds.

Education and early legal career Carson was educated at Arlington House, a boarding-school in Portarlington, Queen's county. In 1871 he took the entrance examination to read classics in Trinity College, Dublin, where he joined the celebrated debating society. In that society he displayed traits of his Liberal Unionist disposition, supporting radical causes such as the disestablishment of the Church of Ireland but in the broader context of maintaining the union with Britain. After taking only a pass degree in 1876 he studied at the King's Inns, Dublin, and was called to the Irish bar in the Easter term of 1877.

Carson soon built up a reputation as a junior counsel, making the acquaintance of Edward Gibson (afterwards Lord Ashbourne), then Disraeli's attorney-general for Ireland, and Gerald FitzGibbon, solicitor-general. Like many of his contemporaries, he was lucky in that, at a crucial time in his career, he was soon involved in the increase of litigation resulting from Gladstone's Land Act of 1881, and by 1886 he had acquired a leading reputation at the Irish bar. By then he had left any active political interests behind, but in 1886 John Gibson, recently appointed Irish attorney-general by the new Conservative administration, nominated him to be his crown counsel. Carson was only thirty-two years old, and the position carried with it some personal risk. He was soon embroiled in cases arising from the Plan of Campaign launched by members of the Irish Parliamentary Party to reduce rents in selected

Edward Henry Carson, Baron Carson (1854–1935), by George Charles Beresford, 1903

estates through direct and concerted action by the tenants. Carson was retained in his post by Peter O'Brien, Gibson's successor, and he caught the eye of Arthur James Balfour, chief secretary for Ireland, who was impressed by his legal skills and dogged courage.

Carson's role in prosecuting cases during the Plan of Campaign earned him the nickname of Coercion Carson, and the accusation that he had sold out on his earlier principles (when he had acted for tenants under the Land Act of 1881) in the hope of a government job. But it was characteristic of Carson to ignore criticism, however savage, if he thought that what he was doing was right: and Carson, always an admirer of the landlords of Ireland, believed that the Plan of Campaign must be faced down. He showed his mettle in the celebrated Mitchelstown affair on 9 September 1887, when the Royal Irish Constabulary fired on demonstrators, inflicting two fatalities. Carson deplored the mishandling of the episode which had led to the confrontation, but declared 'I think that as far as the people are concerned, the firing would have a satisfactory result' (Hyde, 71).

Carson's rise to the top of his profession was now rapid. In 1889 he was appointed a QC, and in June 1892 he became solicitor-general for Ireland. In 1892 he entered politics as one of the Unionist members for Dublin University, though he never lost his liberal disposition, and indeed preferred to describe himself as a 'liberal unionist'. But his overwhelming interest still lay in the legal profession. He was called to the English bar by the Middle Temple in 1893, and became a QC in 1894. It was now that he made his name in some famous cases, notably the libel action brought by Oscar Wilde against the marquess of Queensberry in 1895. Carson acted for Queensberry, revealing his formidable powers of cross-examination in destroying Wilde in a celebrated encounter. By 1900 he was earning some £20,000 a year in fees, and was reckoned one of the great advocates in an age when advocates had a following among the public. In 1900 he was appointed solicitor-general for England, a ministerial post which carried a knighthood, and he went on to take further high

profile cases. In 1910 he acted for the Archer-Shee family in their action following their son's expulsion from the Royal Naval College at Osborne for allegedly stealing a postal order. This case, which Carson won, showed him at his best: emotional, yet professional, and determined to gain justice for the smallest in the land against the greatest.

Entering unionist politics Carson entered his most active political phase only belatedly. But, in a real sense, his Irish experience at the bar had already helped him formulate his political ideas. His early career had been marked by his appearing for tenants under Gladstone's Land Act; but his experience during the Plan of Campaign, and his concern to defend the landlord system, made him a stern advocate of the landlord class. In 1892 he represented one of the most unpopular landlords, Lord Clanricarde, during the hearings of John Morley's evicted tenants commission. He condemned the Irish Land Bill of 1895, and led a revolt against the Land Act of 1896, which extended the right of tenants to purchase their farms. Carson was no passive spectator of Irish policy, as his revolt showed. He castigated British ministers for their occasional asides against the Irish members, denouncing A. J. Balfour for his remark that the Irish members 'will invariably come down to the House and press for money when they think it can be squeezed out of the Treasury' (Boyce, 150). He warned British ministers against their 'everlasting attempt to make peace in Ireland by giving sops to one party at the expense of the other' (Beckett, 163). When he told Balfour in 1900 that it was 'only for Ireland that I'm in politics' he spoke the plain truth. But his coming to the forefront of Irish, and British, politics was delayed until 1910, when Carson was fifty-six years old and (as always) obsessed with what he regarded as his poor health. This, the apogee of his political career, revealed Carson's strengths and weaknesses as a political leader and as a man. And it seemed at variance with his career in the law that had been the mainstay of his rise to fame and fortune.

In February 1910 Carson became leader of the Irish Unionist MPs at Westminster. These members, about twenty in number, were drawn almost entirely from the unionist constituencies of the north, and Carson assumed the leadership at a time when the political outlook for unionist Ireland seemed dangerous. The general election of January 1910 left Asquith's Liberal government dependent for its Commons majority on John Redmond and the Irish nationalists. A second election in December left the position virtually unchanged, and now the Liberals set about removing the House of Lords' veto over Commons' legislation. Once this was done, the last constitutional barrier against Irish home rule would be dismantled. A man of Carson's temperament would have disliked the Liberals' attack on the Lords anyway, for it showed the exercise of government power at its most ruthless. But the price of nationalist support for the attack on the Lords was a new Home Rule Bill, which Asquith introduced in April

1912. Carson now prepared himself for the last great struggle of his career, to preserve the union, which he described as the guiding star of his political life.

The home-rule crisis, 1912–1914 This brought Carson to confront the nature of his political beliefs, and test them against the harsh realities of power; to struggle between his passionate, emotional temperament and the need to act as a pragmatic leader of a volatile Ulster unionist rebellion against home rule; and to reconcile this leadership with a lifetime spent in the law. Carson had shown Balfour in 1896 that he would not spare unionist politicians if he thought they were betraying Ireland; it was unlikely that Liberal politicians would fare any better. But his struggle against home rule proved to be more protracted than anyone could have imagined, and lasted until after the First World War. And the changing backdrop against which it took place called upon Carson to weigh up his love of unionist Ireland against his equally deeply held belief in the British empire. It was indeed only for Ireland that Carson was in politics; but politics soon made other demands on his loyalties, demands which could not be set aside. Small wonder, then, that the years between the Home Rule Bill of 1912 and the partition of Ireland in 1921 were to prove the most dramatic and testing of Carson's long and distinguished life.

His life rather than his career; for there was little to be gained by Carson in terms of career politics from his special connection with Ulster Unionism. His purpose was to defeat home rule for the whole of Ireland; his means were the special case that he could make for Ulster opposition to home rule which, he believed, would force the government to abandon its bill. If Ulster could not be coerced, then home rule was dead. This course of action must involve him in some dangerous circumstances; and, while Carson never feared danger, he went into the Ulster camp in what was a risky venture. At a great demonstration on 23 September 1911 held at Craigavon, the home of the Ulster Unionist MP for East Down, Sir James Craig, Carson was welcomed as the leader of Ulster's stand for union. Carson pledged himself to join with the Ulster unionists to defeat 'the most nefarious conspiracy that has ever been hatched against a free people' (Hyde, 291). There is no doubt that Carson's bond with Ulster unionists was sincere; no doubt, too, that he was loved as much by them as he was hated by nationalists. But, while in public their unity was proclaimed, this concealed deep differences not only of tactics but of strategy as well. Carson came from the outside; and he struggled to control the Ulster unionists, and to keep them to peaceful processes. Thus he joined enthusiastically in the brilliant propaganda coup of 'Ulster's solemn league and covenant' in September 1912, in which Ulster unionists pledged themselves to resist home rule, which was as much an attempt to control passions as to express defiance. He accepted the raising of the Ulster Volunteer Force (UVF) in 1912 to resist home rule, and acquiesced in its arming in 1914. But he was no proto-fascist, leading armed men against lawful authority. And, despite his grand strategic design of defeating home rule for the whole of Ireland, he knew

that his duty lay in making whatever reasonable settlement could be achieved. On 23 September 1913 he wrote to the Conservative and Unionist Party leader, Andrew Bonar Law, that he was 'fully conscious of the duty there is to try and come to some terms' (ibid., 339–40). This would entail getting the best terms that he could for the Ulster unionists, should his more ambitious plan to save all Ireland for the union come to nothing. These would take the form of some form of exclusion of unionist Ulster from the operation of the Home Rule Act, be it county option, or a six-county 'clean cut'. In March 1914 fifty-eight officers of the British army, stationed at the Curragh camp, co. Kildare, declared that they would accept dismissal from the service rather than attack Ulster unionists. Carson used the government's loss of face to press, not for the abandonment of the Home Rule Bill, but for the exclusion of six counties of Ulster. He accepted the Ulster unionist plan of a gun-running expedition when he became convinced that not to proceed would weaken the Ulster Volunteers and thus undermine the whole Ulster unionist position. 'I rely on you to keep your arms with a view to keeping the peace', he warned one UVF regiment (ibid., 368). Carson now appeared to have become the servant of events rather than their master: by May 1914 the Home Rule Bill had proceeded through all the formalities, and only required the royal assent. Carson's mood, seldom optimistic, now darkened, and he awaited with despair the final crisis, one that seemed inevitable when a conference held at Buckingham Palace at the end of July to try to resolve the deadlock ended in failure on the issue of which Ulster counties would be excluded temporarily from the jurisdiction of the Home Rule Act.

Carson warned that the great crisis of 'our country' and 'our fate' was imminent 'unless something happens'. That something turned out to be the involvement of the United Kingdom in the European war in August 1914. As the new crisis approached, Carson and Bonar Law met Asquith on 30 July and agreed that, subject to the cabinet and John Redmond's approval, an amending bill which the government had offered dealing with the Ulster question should be postponed. Asquith's decision, announced on 15 September, to place the Home Rule Bill on the statute book, but postpone its operation until the war ended, was naturally regarded by unionists as a betrayal. But Carson showed that he was a loyal servant of the state. He swallowed the government's 'betrayal' and promised the Ulster Volunteer Force for overseas service without qualification.

Carson and the First World War But it was from now on that Carson's political guiding star—the defence of the union—found itself influenced by other, and at times much more pressing, issues. Carson, the unionist backbencher, now proved himself a formidable scourge of the government's mishandling of the war. When Asquith reconstructed his administration in May 1915 to include members of the opposition, Carson entered the cabinet as attorney-general, but resigned in October because of the series of military and strategic blunders that began with the disaster of the Gallipoli landings, and ended with the collapse of Serbia. Carson's stock in the Unionist Party now rose to new heights. He led the unionist war committee, a 'ginger group' formed in June 1916 and dedicated to a more vigorous prosecution of the war. He played a significant role in the fall of Asquith and his replacement by Lloyd George in December 1916. Carson now became first lord of the Admiralty, but he proved a surprisingly ineffective minister. Lloyd George ascribed this to Carson's Irishness, asserting that an Irishman was naturally opposed to every government, even one supported by his own party. This trite remark contained a germ of truth: Carson's real power lay, as it did in his legal career, in his strength of critical attack. He had not the temperament to hustle civil servants, and his admiration for the navy lowered his guard against the prejudices and conservatism of the service. In July 1917 he moved to the war cabinet as minister without portfolio.

But Carson's involvement in, and sincere commitment to, the British war effort modified his deep-seated love of the union. Following the Easter rising in April 1916 Asquith gave Lloyd George the task of making a quick settlement between nationalists and unionists so that the kingdom would not be weakened by a renewal of the Irish crisis. Carson accepted Lloyd George's suggestion for a settlement based on the exclusion of six Ulster counties (Antrim, Armagh, Down, Fermanagh, Londonderry, and Tyrone) from a Dublin parliament, which would now be introduced at once. Carson yielded to the loss of most of Ireland from the union because, as he exclaimed when Lloyd George warned him that not to settle might lose the war, 'if the war is lost, we are all lost'. It was a measure of his distance from his fellow southern unionists that his support of partition was accepted by the Ulster Unionist Council in June 1916, but rejected by leading southern unionists such as Lord Lansdowne and Lord Middleton. Carson was deeply disappointed at the failure of the Lloyd George mission; but Ireland returned to the agenda in March 1917, when the government was anxious that the Irish question should not hinder its efforts to induce the United States of America to enter the war on the allied side. Carson consented to the setting up of a convention of representative Irishmen under the chairmanship of Sir Horace Plunkett to find a basis for agreement. Carson did not participate in the convention. And it was a sign of his growing remoteness, not only from southern but also from Ulster unionists, when he moved towards the idea of a federal settlement of the Irish question (which he had considered in 1914), only to see this now firmly rejected by the Ulster unionists in the convention. In January 1918, thoroughly unhappy in office, Carson resigned from the government, on the grounds that he wanted to be 'unfettered' in considering any Irish settlement proposal that Lloyd George might derive from the convention's report.

Carson and the Irish settlement Carson now seemed to have lost all his political bearings. He supported conscription for Ireland, but warned that the inclusion of Ulster in a home rule bill as the price of conscription was impossible. 'Nothing', he exclaimed in a remarkable outburst in the House of Commons in April 1918, 'Ireland—north, south, east and west—has suffered so much in its history as from the broken pledges of British statesmen' (Colvin, 3.343). When the Lloyd George coalition published its manifesto for the general election of December 1918, Carson supported its promise that Ulster would not be coerced into any home-rule settlement. In that election Carson finally abandoned his southern Irish constituency and successfully contested the Duncairn division in Belfast; but he pressed for the government to introduce better services of health, housing, and education into the whole of Ireland. When the government introduced its Irish legislation, in the form of double-barrelled home rule, with parliaments for northern and southern Ireland, Carson advised the southern unionists to accept the inevitable, or take refuge in Ulster, but although he chaired the meeting of the Ulster Unionist Council held in March 1920 to decide its response to the bill, Carson took no part in the debates. This meant that Ulster would accept home rule, and although Carson approved of the decision, he then went on to say in Westminster that home rule was fraught with disaster: 'As regards my own country, it will be cut off from the greatest Kingdom that has ever existed.' His political impotence was clear to all when he confessed that he would 'not vote for home rule. At the same time I shall do nothing to prevent this Bill from becoming law' (Hyde, 447).

Carson formally resigned the Ulster Unionist leadership in February 1921, a few days before his sixty-seventh birthday, urging the Ulster unionists 'from the outset' to see that 'the Catholic minority have nothing to fear from the Protestant majority' (Hyde, 449). In May 1921 he was appointed lord of appeal and was created Baron Carson of Duncairn. But his last, and in many ways his greatest, speech was made on 14 December 1921 during the debates in the Lords on the Anglo-Irish treaty which Lloyd George had signed with Sinn Féin on 6 December. Carson was now fully liberated from the need to put loyalty to Britain before loyalty to Ireland, and he attacked the treaty in a superb display of invective. But his speech was a commentary on his own failure to defend the union as much as it was an attack on the treaty. 'Loyalty', he declared, 'is a strange thing. It is something you cannot get by sitting round a table and trying to find a formula for an Oath of Allegiance which means nothing. It is something born and bred in you.' It was Carson's tragedy that his loyalty could not remain all of a piece, but was divided between his southern upbringing, his Ulster affiliations, and his wider British and imperial patriotism. His bitter attack on the Conservative and Unionist Party, in particular, was an expression of his frustration, as negative as it was brilliant.

Carson may have damaged the coalition government by his attack, though it is doubtful if it made a substantial difference to what was an already uneasy political arrangement. Carson continued as a law lord, between 1921 and 1929, defending the interests of southern unionists in the new Irish Free State. He was regarded by his contemporaries as a competent rather than a great judge, but he remained, as always, well disposed towards even the most junior barrister. He revisited Ulster only three times: to receive an honorary LLD from Queen's University, Belfast, in 1926, to attend the opening of the new Northern Ireland parliament buildings at Stormont in 1932, and on the occasion of the unveiling of his own statue in front of those buildings in July 1933.

Character, marriages, and death Carson was a man of powerful and brooding presence. His features were usually set in a scowl, and his political speeches were marked by a menacing, and yet homely, style. However, he could look jaunty and dashing, and he possessed great charm. His outward appearance hid a lack of confidence and an emotional nature which placed him under great strain. He occasionally took to his bed, complaining of bad health but, considering the demands he made on himself in the course of his career, and especially between 1911 and 1921, his constitution was clearly sound. Carson was married twice: first, on 19 December 1879, to Sarah Annette Foster (d. 1913), the adopted daughter of Henry Persse Kirwan of Triston Lodge, co. Galway, and second, on 17 September 1914, to Ruby (1881–1966), elder daughter of Lieutenant-Colonel Stephen Frewen of Charlton Musgrove, Somerset. His friendships with women—with whom he was more at ease than with men—caused strained relations with his first wife. His second wife was younger than Carson by some thirty years, and this provoked ribald jokes from his contemporaries about the reasons for his fatigue during the day. His children (two daughters and two sons from his first marriage, and a son from his second) caused him concern, and he once described them as a 'rum lot'. His elder son and younger daughter by his first marriage predeceased him; Edward Carson, his son by his second marriage, was elected Conservative member of parliament for the Isle of Thanet in July 1945.

Carson died at home at Cleve Court, Isle of Thanet, on 22 October 1935 and was buried in St Anne's Cathedral, Belfast. He belonged to the Anglo-Irish tradition which held fast to the belief that the union between Great Britain and Ireland was axiomatic. This earned Carson the jibe from one opponent that 'he has no country—he has a caste'. Certainly he and his people depended on England's support, and it was a measure of the essential fragility of their position that Carson found himself on the losing side in 1921. But he believed in the greatness of the British empire, and in this sense he possessed a broader patriotism that he always hoped would be compatible with his Irish patriotism. Perhaps a better judgement was that of T. M. Healy, who remarked of Carson that 'although a Unionist, he never was un-Irish'. Carson saw no conflict between being Irish and being a unionist. This is why, in both parts of the partitioned island, he felt, like Garibaldi, that he had been made a stranger in the land of his birth.

D. GEORGE BOYCE

Sources E. Marjoribanks, *The life of Lord Carson*, 1 (1932) · I. Colvin, *The life of Lord Carson*, 2–3 (1934–6) · H. M. Hyde, *Carson: the life of Sir Edward Carson, Lord Carson of Duncairn* (1953) · A. T. Q. Stewart, *Edward Carson* (1981) · A. Jackson, *Sir Edward Carson* (1993) · R. B. McDowell, 'Sir Edward Carson', *The shaping of modern Ireland*, ed. C. C. O'Brien (1960), 85–97 · J. C. Beckett, 'Carson: unionist and rebel', *Confrontations: studies in Irish history* (1972), 160–70 · D. G. Boyce, 'Edward Carson and Irish unionism', *Worsted in the game: losers in Irish history*, ed. C. Brady (1989), 145–57

Archives CAC Cam., cabinet papers [copies] · PRO NIre., corresp. and papers | BL, corresp. with Arthur James Balfour, Add. MS 49709, *passim* · BL, corresp. with Lord Northcliffe, Add. MS 62158 · Bodl. Oxf., corresp. with Herbert Asquith · Bodl. Oxf., corresp. with H. A. Gwynne · Bodl. Oxf., corresp. with Lord Selborne · HLRO, letters to R. D. Blumenfield · HLRO, corresp. with Andrew Bonar Law · HLRO, letters to David Lloyd George · HLRO, corresp. with Herbert Samuel · HLRO, corresp. with John St Loe Strachey · Linen Hall Library, Belfast, Ulster day scrapbook · Lpool RO, corresp. with seventeenth earl of Derby · NL Scot., letters to F. S. Oliver · PRO NIre., corresp. with H. de Fellenburgh Montgomery · PRO NIre., letters to Lady Londonderry |FILM BFI NFTVA, 'The sportsmen battalion', Warwick Bioscope Chronicle, 1912; 'Scenes and incidents in connection with "Ulster day"', 28 Sept 1912; 'The Belfast unionist demonstration held at Balmoral Belfast', 1913; 'The Ulster covenant', 1962

Likenesses R. P. Staples, chalk, 1898, NPG · B. Stone, photograph, 1898, NPG · G. C. Beresford, two negatives and photograph, 1903, NPG [*see illus.*] · M. Beerbohm, watercolour caricature, 1913, NPG · J. G. Day, etching and drypoint, 1914, NPG · J. Lavery, oils, 1921, Ulster Museum, Belfast · G. C. Beresford, negative, 1923, NPG · G. C. Beresford, photograph, 1923?, NPG · L. S. Merrifield, statue, c.1933, Stormont, Belfast · H. Furniss, pen-and-ink sketch, NPG · W. Hester, caricature, Hentschel-colourtype, NPG; repro. in *VF* (8 Feb 1911) · P. de Laszlo, oils, Middle Temple, London · Lib [L. Prosperi], cartoon, NPG; repro. in *VF* (9 Nov 1893) · L. S. Merrifield, marble bust, Belfast corporation · B. Partridge, pen-and-ink sketch, NPG; repro. in *Punch* (26 Nov 1913) · A. P. F. Ritchie, cigarette card, NPG · W. H., chromolithograph caricature, NPG; repro. in *VF* (17 Jan 1912)

Wealth at death £150,295 18s. 5d.: probate, 19 Dec 1935, *CGPLA Eng. & Wales* · £398 14s. 5d.: probate, 29 May 1936, *CGPLA Éire*

Carson, James (1772–1843), physician, of Scottish origin, was educated for the ministry but switched to medicine. He attended medical classes at Edinburgh and graduated MD in 1799 with a thesis on the circulation of the blood, which he expanded and published as *An Enquiry into the Causes of the Motion of the Blood* (1815). He enlarged it further in *An Enquiry into the Causes of Respiration* (1833). Carson married in 1802 Ann McNeight of Ayr, with whom he had several children. He established himself at Liverpool, where at first he attended the prisoners of war as a surgeon. He later built up a flourishing practice and served as physician to the Workhouse Fever Hospital and the Asylum for Pauper Lunatics; and he was in charge of the Military Hospital.

In 1808 Carson achieved notoriety for his part in the trial of Charles Angus, a former chemist. Angus's wife had died and his sister-in-law had moved in to care for his children. When she was found dead, allegedly poisoned, there was no trace of the child who neighbours thought she was carrying. Angus was charged with administering a corrosive mercury compound. At Lancaster assizes Carson testified on Angus's behalf against four expert witnesses for the prosecution, declaring that the perforation in the stomach of the dead woman had occurred after death and that the dilated uterus was not the result of a miscarriage but due to the passage of dropsical hydatids. Forensic medicine was then a primitive science; neither judge nor jury was competent to assess the medical evidence, and a verdict of not guilty was returned. Angry pamphleteering ensued, and Carson defended himself in *Remarks on a late publication entitled 'A vindication of the opinions delivered in evidence by the medical witnesses for the crown on a late trial at Lancaster'* (1808).

Carson's most notable work, 'On the elasticity of the lungs', was read before the Liverpool Literary and Philosophical Society and submitted for publication to the Royal Society, where it appeared in *Philosophical Transactions* (vol. 110, 1820, pp. 29–44). In his paper 'On lesions of the lung', delivered in Liverpool in 1821, Carson suggested that lesions were prevented from healing because the lung was continually stretching, and that if it were collapsed and resting a cure might be effected. Carson had experimented successfully on rabbits; he was able to proceed to clinical trials when two Liverpool merchants, both with advanced tuberculosis and close to death, implored him to try a cure by this means. The attendant surgeon made incisions between the sixth and seventh ribs, but in both cases widespread pleural adhesions prevented the lung from collapsing. The disease took its course, and both men died shortly afterwards.

Feeling somewhat isolated in Liverpool from the main centres of learning, Carson applied for the Edinburgh chair vacated by the death of James Gregory in 1821, and for the Glasgow chair vacated by Robert Freer, but failed in both attempts. He was, however, elected fellow of the Royal Society in 1837. In 1839 he issued a pamphlet, *A New Method of Slaughtering Animals for Human Food*, advocating induced collapse of the lungs as the ideal method. His attempt to cure tuberculosis by surgery was original, but his work was not fully understood at the time and his pioneering role was overlooked until the twentieth century. Carson died of diabetes, at Sutton, St Helens, Lancashire, on 12 August 1843.

GORDON GOODWIN, *rev.* ANITA MCCONNELL

Sources T. R. Forbes, *Surgeons at the Bailey: English forensic medicine to 1878* (1985), 139–40 · T. R. Forbes, 'Early forensic medicine in England: the Angus murder trial', *Journal of the History of Medicine and Allied Sciences*, 36 (1981), 296–309 · R. Y. Keers, 'Two forgotten pioneers—James Carson and George Bodington', *Thorax*, 35 (1980), 483–9 · J. Carson, *An enquiry into the causes of respiration* (1833), ix, vi-viii, 53–4, 57–8 · R. Y. Keers, *Pulmonary tuberculosis* (1978), 104–9 · *DNB*
Archives Lpool RO, MSS relating to French prisoners of war

Carson, Violet Helen (1898–1983), actress, was born on 1 September 1898 at 1 Corporation Terrace, in the Ancoats district of Manchester, one of at least two daughters of William Brown Carson, a Scottish flour miller, and his wife, Mary Clarke Tordoff, an amateur singer. Violet Carson learned the piano from the age of two and her sister Nellie played the violin. As the Carson Sisters they sang at church functions and wedding receptions.

At the age of fifteen Violet Carson became a pianist accompanying silent films, for £2 5s. a week, with the cinema orchestra at Manchester's Market Street Cinema, where Nellie was employed as a violinist. The two sisters then formed their own orchestra and moved to the Devonshire Cinema, before Nellie left to join the English Singers

Violet Helen Carson (1898–1983), by John Madden, 1970 [as Ena Sharples in *Coronation Street*]

and Violet moved to the Scala Cinema in Withington. On 1 September 1926, at the age of twenty-eight, Violet married the road contractor George Frederick Peploe in Manchester Cathedral, but two years later he died. She returned to work, which she had given up during her marriage, and played the piano at the Ambassador Cinema, in Pendleton, Manchester, for six years until 'talkies' replaced silent films.

In 1935 Violet Carson joined BBC radio in Manchester, singing everything from Stanley Holloway-style comic songs to operatic arias. She began in a show called *Songs at the Piano* and eventually became known as the voice of Auntie Vi in *Children's Hour*. She worked with the Council for the Encouragement of Music and the Arts during the Second World War, then spent six years as the pianist in the Wilfred and Mabel Pickles radio quiz show *Have a Go!* She was also a presenter and interviewer on *Woman's Hour* for five years and acted in many radio dramas. On stage she played the duchess of York in *Richard III*. But her greatest fame was to come on television, as Ena Sharples, the hairnetted harridan of *Coronation Street*. She appeared in its first episode, on 9 December 1960, and stayed with the programme for twenty years. When the characters were being cast, the programme's creator, Tony Warren, had remembered the fearsome Auntie Vi with whom he worked as a child actor on radio in *Children's Hour*. When he told her about the part, Carson commented that it amounted 'to nothing more than a back-street bitch'. Warren suggested that maybe she thought the role was too difficult, but she retorted, 'Don't be ridiculous! I have lived with this woman all my life. There is one in every street in the North of England' (Kay, 12).

The part was hers and Ena Sharples, the God-fearing battleaxe with a razor-sharp tongue, was an immediate hit with viewers. She was often seen sitting drinking milk stout in the Rovers Return snug with Minnie Caldwell and Martha Longhurst, setting the world to rights. Ena was the matriarchal figure who epitomized the programme's tough, gritty, northern character, and Carson became the serial's biggest star. Her piano-playing talents were often used in Rovers Return singalongs and street shows.

By the end of the programme's first year Ena was introduced at Tussaud's Blackpool waxworks. In 1965 Carson was appointed OBE in the queen's birthday honours and, eight years later, made an honorary MA by Manchester University. Her only regret about this success was that it did not allow her enough time to do other work, especially acting in the classics on stage. But she became a frequent guest on the popular religious programme *Stars on Sunday*, giving viewers a chance to hear her fine singing voice. Somewhat sadly, she once said, 'I don't want to be Sharples—that old bag—all my life. I want people to remember I'm Violet Carson' (*United Press International*, 28 Dec 1993).

Carson took time off from *Coronation Street* in 1973 after suffering a nervous breakdown and left through ill health seven years later, having completed 1148 episodes. She was last seen in the serial in February 1980, with the character of Ena leaving for Lytham St Anne's to look after an elderly friend of her late husband. Carson died in her sleep at her home at 18 Fleetwood Road in Blackpool on Boxing day 1983, aged eighty-five, having suffered pernicious anaemia during her last years. The pleasure she had brought to millions was rewarded with a memorial service at Manchester Cathedral.   ANTHONY HAYWARD

Sources A. Hayward and D. Hayward, *TV unforgettables* (1993) · G. Kay, *Coronation Street: celebrating 30 years* (1990) · *The Times* (28 Dec 1983) · *CGPLA Eng. & Wales* (1984) · b. cert. · m. cert. · d. cert.
Archives FILM BFI NFTVA, performance footage | SOUND BL NSA, 'Violet Carson', BBC Radio 4, 3 June 1981, NP7577W TR1 · BL NSA, 'A portrait of the actress and singer Violet Carson', T3825W · BL NSA, performance recording
Likenesses photographs, *c*.1962–1963, Hult. Arch. · Wood, photograph, 1968, Hult. Arch. · J. Madden, photograph, 1970, Hult. Arch. [*see illus.*] · J. Jackson, photograph, 1971, Hult. Arch. · R. Jackson, photograph, 1971, Hult. Arch.
Wealth at death £194,602: probate, 13 March 1984, *CGPLA Eng. & Wales*

Carstairs, George Morrison [Morris] (1916–1991), psychiatrist, was born on 18 June 1916, the son of the Revd Dr George Carstairs, a distinguished, dedicated Church of Scotland missionary stationed in Mussooree, India, and his wife, Elizabeth Huntley Young. Son and father shared a passion for their adopted country, and from childhood onwards Morris (as the son was known) became fluent in both English and Hindi. Perhaps deliberately, he never lost that trace of Hindi which flavoured his soft Edinburgh English.

At the age of ten Carstairs returned to his ancestral city, Edinburgh, to be schooled at George Watson College and, later, to study medicine at Edinburgh University, from which he graduated MB and ChB in 1941. His career thereafter was somewhat unusual. His upbringing in India had exposed him to the widespread suffering of the underprivileged, which had in turn engendered compassion for the underdog. He became acutely aware of the inadequacies of his traditional medical education: it had given him only the vaguest insight into the causes of, and even less on how to mitigate, the social problems that plagued his conscience. His ignorance prompted him to take a course in anthropology at Cambridge and later in New York, where he worked for a time with the world-famous anthropologist Margaret Mead. He was an apt student, and his early book *The Twice Born* (1957), a study of the Brahmans, won praise from Mead herself. On 14 December 1950 Carstairs married Vera Dorris Lilian Hunt (*b*. 1924/5), an anthropologist, and he and his young wife began a study of an Indian village, Sujarupa, where they lived and shared the primitive life of the inhabitants. The study assumed marathon proportions and was completed only after twelve separate visits to India; it was finally published thirty-two years after it had begun, under the title *The Death of a Witch* (1983).

So launched, Carstairs was firmly committed to combining the profession of anthropology (with allied interests) with that of medicine and psychiatry. After graduating in medicine he worked as an assistant physician at the Royal Edinburgh Hospital, then from 1942 to 1946 served in the RAF as a medical officer. After demobilization he was elected a Commonwealth fellow to work in the USA from 1948 to 1949, then spent a further year there as a Rockefeller research fellow (1950–51). Having returned to the UK, he was appointed in 1953 a senior registrar at the Maudsley Hospital, London, the Mecca of British psychiatry. Here he worked under Professor Sir Aubrey Lewis. The relationship between master and pupil was not entirely harmonious, although each respected the other's talents. Nevertheless, Lewis, being aware of Carstairs's particular interest and expertise, gave him the opportunity to study a quite different disadvantaged population much nearer to home than India—namely, those suffering chronic psychoses, in the main, chronic schizophrenia.

In 1960 Carstairs was given his own Medical Research Council unit at University College, London, designated for the study of psychiatric epidemiology. In the following year, 1961, he was elected to the chair of psychological medicine (psychiatry) in the University of Edinburgh, with the proviso that he take his unit with him. This was agreed.

Of all the many achievements Carstairs crammed into his life, the tenure of the chair in Edinburgh was without doubt his most successful. He collected around him distinguished colleagues, both academics and clinicians working in neighbouring National Health Service hospitals. With this spread of talents, Carstairs built his department into a centre of excellence for research and for teaching graduate and undergraduate students. But above all he continued to focus on his primary interest: the psychiatric concomitants of anthropology and sociology.

To add to his insatiable appetite for hard work, Carstairs travelled widely, particularly in India, on behalf of the plans of the World Health Organization for the development of psychiatric facilities in under-developed countries. About the same time (1967–71) he presided over the World Mental Health Organization. At a different level he achieved fame, or infamy, as the result of his highly controversial Reith lectures of 1962, 'This island now', where he argued that chastity was not the supreme moral virtue. The views he put forward were, in certain quarters, deemed the more outrageous because they were held by the son of a distinguished Scots cleric.

Carstairs's exemplary success in Edinburgh, coupled with his prominent role on the royal commission on medical education, prompted an invitation in 1973 to accept the vice-chancellorship of York University. He agreed; but what should have been a triumph turned out to be something akin to disaster. The time and place were wrong, and he missed the ambience of the medical school and the company of medical colleagues. Additionally, he found himself having to cope with the unpleasantness of the student protest movement, rampant at that time, and with the anti-authority atmosphere it created, which was incompatible with the role of the guru to which he had become accustomed.

After five years Carstairs shed the trappings of a vice-chancellor and returned to what was to him by far the more congenial work in India, where he completed a major report for the World Health Organization together with an update of earlier psychiatric and anthropological studies. The final touches of this work were completed during a year as fellow of the Smithsonian Institution in Washington. Carstairs then returned to London and finally to his last resting place, Edinburgh.

Carstairs was self-evidently a complex man, yet his personal tastes were simple, verging on the ascetic: he preferred the shabby but culturally rich International Centre in Delhi to the grandeur of the vice-chancellor's house in York. He was not, by the same token, an establishment man: in 1971 he declined the invitation to stand for election as president of the newly established Royal College of Psychiatrists, a post which he might well have won. A man of absolute integrity, Carstairs refused to be intimidated no matter what. For example, he must have known how much outrage the forthright opinions he expressed in his Reith lectures of 1962 would generate. Similarly, he knew full well that he was swimming against the tide when he fearlessly attacked R. D. Laing and his cohorts, the leaders of the zany anti-psychiatrists, when they were at the peak of their popularity in the 1970s. Towards the end of his life Carstairs, who was divorced from his first wife, contracted a brief second marriage to Nancy Shields Hardin.

Carstairs was a great human being, an exemplary teacher, a born leader, and an outstanding doctor, all attributes that serve to highlight the tragedy of his decline into senile dementia. He died at his home, 12 Hermitage Gardens, Edinburgh, on 17 April 1991, supported to the end by his former wife, Vera, and their three children. HENRY R. ROLLIN

Sources WWW · Medical directory (1984) · private information (2004) · The Times (2 May 1991) · The Independent (23 April 1991) · BMJ (18 May 1991) · The Guardian (25 April 1991) · Bulletin of the Royal College of Psychiatrists (Aug 1991) · The Times (10 Oct 1950), 6b [on Rockefeller grant] · The Times (1974–82) [correspondence on Carstairs's position in the University of York] · m. cert. [Vera Hunt] · d. cert. Archives U. Lond., Institute of Education, corresp. with World Education Fellowship | FILM Reith lectures, BBC, 1962

Carstairs, Joe [*formerly* Marion Barbara] (1900–1993), heiress and motor-boat racing driver, was born on 1 February 1900 at 115 Park Street, Mayfair, London, the daughter of Albert Joseph Carstairs, a captain in the Royal Irish Rifles, and his wife, (Frances) Evelyn (1872–1921), the daughter of Jabez and Helen Celia Bostwick, of New York. Evelyn Bostwick was heir to the fortune amassed by her father, a founder of the Standard Oil Company. She met her husband on a visit to Europe and they married on her twentieth birthday. They divorced eight years later, soon after the birth of a daughter, Marion Barbara. Albert Carstairs played no part in the girl's upbringing and there has been speculation that he was not her father. Marion Carstairs later reinvented her early life, rejecting the names given to her at birth and the gender that they implied: 'I was never a little girl,' she said, 'I came out of the womb queer' (Summerscale, 18). She took on a male persona instead, and the name Joe Carstairs.

In 1903 Carstairs's mother married Francis Francis, a captain in the British army, with whom she had a son and a second daughter. Carstairs was not close to her stepfamily and was neglected by her mother, whose 'vaulting moods were fed by alcohol and heroin' and whom she regarded with a mixture of love and loathing (Summerscale, 19). In 1911 she was sent to Low Heywood, a girls' boarding-school in Stamford, Connecticut. An unacademic tomboy, she revelled in freedom from the oppressive atmosphere of home. In 1915 her mother divorced and married a French army officer: she spent most of the remainder of her life in Paris, and divorced and remarried for a fourth time. In 1916 Carstairs, with her grandmother's support, was sent to France as an ambulance driver with the American Red Cross. It entailed her seventeenth crossing of the Atlantic: she always felt at home at sea and from an early age loved sailing.

Carstairs arrived in Paris 'a stocky, gauche American girl, steeped in new money and unschooled in art or literature' (Summerscale, 28). She shared an apartment in Montparnasse with four other ambulance drivers and was drawn to the periphery of the lesbian literary world that centred on Natalie Barney. In this Bohemian milieu she remained a straightforwardly physical and athletic character. Her first sexual encounter was with another woman in a Paris hotel room, and she later had an affair with Dolly Wilde, the niece of Oscar Wilde. When her mother heard of her daughter's lesbianism she threatened to disinherit her. To avert this Carstairs married her childhood friend,

Joe Carstairs (1900–1993), by Brooke, 1925

Count Jacques de Pret, in 1918. The marriage, which was never consummated, was annulled in 1921, the year of Evelyn Bostwick's death. That year Carstairs's annual income rose to nearly $145,000.

After the armistice Carstairs worked as a driver for the British army in Dublin and later northern France. Following her demobilization in April 1920 she opened, with some driver friends, an all-woman chauffeur service, the 'X Garage', in Kensington. It closed in 1928. Carstairs was wealthy enough never to have to work, but she gained satisfaction from utilizing her skill as a mechanic and driver. She also enjoyed subverting gender roles and developed a lean, muscular build, dressing like a man, with daringly short hair. She shared a London home, 5 Mulberry Walk, Chelsea, with her lover and secretary, Ruth Baldwin (d. 1937). They both indulged in 'the decadence of the metropolitan scene' and Carstairs had affairs with the actresses Gwen Farrer and Tallulah Bankhead (Summerscale, 91). But she also enjoyed a quiet country life at a secluded Hampshire estate, where she went horse-riding and sailing.

Though Carstairs strove for manliness the effect fell somewhat short in the eyes of some. The yachtsman Anthony Heckstall-Smith remembered her as a 'neat, trim little girl who … was like an exuberant schoolboy with her zest for speed and adventure' (Heckstall-Smith, 163). She was also, he noted, a 'first-class helmswoman', her yacht *Sonia* winning almost every race in its class at East Cowes in the 1920s. In 1924 she became substantially richer with the settlement of her mother's will and that of her grandmother. This enabled her to break in to the male-dominated world of motor-boat racing. Her performances in a series of specially commissioned hydroplanes were watched by Ruth Baldwin, 'cheerleading an ever-changing bevy of attractive girl supporters' (Summerscale, 71). At Christmas 1925 Baldwin gave her a stuffed leather man-doll, which Carstairs christened Lord Tod Wadley. Wadley became her alter ego and accompanied her everywhere, the centre of an elaborate and often absurd game of make-believe: a playboy adventurer, he had his own miniature wardrobe made at Savile Row.

Carstairs believed that Wadley brought her luck and her crowning achievement in motor-boat racing came in 1926, with victory in the duke of York trophy race. She won ahead of a strong international field and briefly became a national celebrity, 'Miss Betty Carstairs'. She afterwards made three valiant attempts to win the sport's premier event, the Harmsworth British international trophy, in America. In the race at Detroit in 1928 she escaped serious injury when her hydroplane *Estelle II* flipped over. Undeterred, she entered again in 1929, without success. After a mechanical failure in 1930 she told reporters: 'Well, you'd better get a good look at me, because I am not coming over again. It's too frightfully expensive' (Summerscale, 115). That year she gave generous financial backing to her friend Malcolm Campbell in his attempt on the world land-speed record. She affected nonchalance on hearing of his success in February 1931: 'usually he drives like an old woman' (ibid., 118). By then she sensed the press turning against her. In a less permissive atmosphere greater attention was given to her ostentatious masculinity: her tattooed arms, cigars, swearing, spitting, and gum chewing. She left England on a world tour and afterwards lived mostly on her schooner *Sonia II* and mini-liner *Berania*. Her self-imposed exile became permanent when, in 1934, she bought an island in the Bahamas, announcing: 'I am going to live surrounded only by coloured people … I cannot say if I will ever return' (ibid., 122). She claimed that punitive taxation in Britain had driven her away.

Whale Cay, a tiny island some 30 miles north-west of Nassau, was undeveloped when Carstairs arrived. She spent $40,000 on its purchase and another $250,000 creating an infrastructure. The growing economy, centred on farming, attracted workers from surrounding islands, and by March 1941 the population was 500. She governed her dominion like a latter-day plantation owner, effectively given free rein by the authorities in Nassau. She believed that the islanders held Wadley in voodoo-inspired awe and her approach to them was a 'jumble of idealism and prejudice' (Summerscale, 178). Job segregation in Nassau appalled her, yet her workers kept to their own beach: 'We couldn't have them all over the place' (ibid., 136). She disapproved of sex outside marriage and punished adultery severely, but was less hard on wife beating. Alcohol was forbidden. Her seigneurial rights included the naming of all children born on the island. She gave to several girls the names she had rejected, Marion Barbara, confessing: 'God knows why' (ibid., 168).

At Carstairs's Spanish-style villa, the Great House, different laws prevailed. Sex, alcohol, and drugs were freely indulged in by a stream of visitors from Britain and America, on whom she sometimes played cruel practical jokes. On one occasion islanders staged a mock rebellion, which she subdued with a few gunshots while her frightened guests cowered inside. 'The blacks are going to kill us all,' she warned: 'Pansies first, women last' (Summerscale, 141). She had black girlfriends, but none were islanders: she favoured instead the company of society women whom she met on her annual holidays in New York, Miami, or the Riviera. On one such excursion, in 1938, she began a brief affair with Marlene Dietrich. She had lengthy relationships with a number of women besides Ruth Baldwin, who refused to live on Whale Cay. Carstairs was deeply affected by Baldwin's death from a suspected drug overdose in London in August 1937.

Carstairs's success on Whale Cay convinced her that she could effect the economic regeneration of the British West Indies. In the late 1930s she briefly clashed with the white establishment in Nassau, where some regarded her as a liberal defender of black rights. The reality was more complex and her outlook essentially colonial: her plans for reform came to nothing. In January 1941 the duke and duchess of Windsor made an official visit to Whale Cay and were received with great ceremony. The duke praised the roads while the duchess charmed Carstairs by asking, on spotting Wadley, 'Who is that?' Carstairs answered: 'That's my boy, that's Wadley'. 'My God,' said the duchess, 'he's just like my husband' (Summerscale, 169). During the war Carstairs's various offers to assist the war effort were declined. Disappointed by this she set up the North Caribbean Transport Company in 1943 to carry goods to Miami, remarking 'It's a sort of war work' (ibid., 203).

From the late 1950s Carstairs's health deteriorated and she spent less time on Whale Cay, where her authority declined as Bahamian nationalism rose. In 1975 she sold the island for just under a million dollars. On leaving she cried, something that she almost never did. As she predicted, Whale Cay reverted to its former state without her. She spent the remainder of her life in Florida and Long Island, surrounded by Whale Cay memorabilia. On a glass-topped table she displayed the photographs of some 120 girlfriends. She had always tried to insulate herself from emotional hurt, but allowed that there were 'one or two' that she liked 'apart from sex' (Summerscale, 218). She was led to believe that she was a good lover and her girlfriends remembered a romantic nature. But it was also said that she 'had a cheque-book where her heart ought to be', and her friends were bound by 'ropes of money as well as affection' (ibid., 220). Wadley was the only one whose friendship she never had to question.

From 1978 until her death Carstairs lived with Hugh Harrison, a friend and paid companion whom she met in Long Island. A handsome man nearly twenty years her junior, he was homosexual, something she used against him. 'I like men', she once said: 'Most of my friends are ordinary men. I've never been frightfully fond of pansies, but manly men' (Summerscale, 161). Throughout her life she was a generous provider to her friends and personal employees, and in death she divided the bulk of her $33 million fortune among them. Joe Carstairs died, probably in Florida, on 18 December 1993. She and Wadley were cremated together and their ashes, with those of Ruth Baldwin, were taken to Long Island and placed in a tomb near the sea.   MARK POTTLE

Sources K. Summerscale, *The queen of Whale Cay* (1997) · *The Times* (13 July 1926), 4d · *The Times* (3 Sept 1928), 4d · A. Heckstall-Smith, *Sacred Cowes* (1965) · J. Wentworth Day, *Speed: the authentic life of Sir Malcolm Campbell* (1931) · L. Villa and T. Gray, *The record breakers: Sir Malcolm and Donald Campbell — land and water speed kings of the twentieth century* (1969) · *London Review of Books*, 20/5 (5 March 1998)
Likenesses Brooke, photograph, 1925, Hult. Arch. [*see illus.*] · photographs, *c.*1930, Hult. Arch. · photographs, repro. in Summerscale, *Queen of Whale Cay*

Carstairs, John Paddy [*formerly* Nelson John Keys] (1910–1970), film-maker and writer, was born at 1 St Stephen's Mansions, Smith Square, London, on 11 May 1910, the eldest of four sons of Nelson Waite (Bunch) Keys (1887–1939), actor and comedian, and his wife, Hazel Eileen Saqui, actress, of Dublin. After Alleyn Court preparatory school, Westcliff-on-Sea, Essex, he went to Repton School in 1924. Self-confessedly a genial exhibitionist, he became a proficient lightweight boxer. His headmaster, the Revd Geoffrey Fisher, later archbishop of Canterbury, supported his formation in 1927 of a cinema club, with its own tie and magazine; he produced a full-length melodrama of public-school life, *The Hero of St Jim's*, and news of its success reached Fleet Street. To the initial annoyance of his father, he abandoned any idea of proceeding to Cambridge, becoming instead an apprentice to his father's old friend Herbert Wilcox, the film producer and director.

Henceforth Carstairs was irretrievably wedded to the film industry. Having changed his name so as not to cash in on his father's success, he profited from Wilcox's sponsorship and from him learned the spadework of the film business: editing, camera work, and scenario writing. This proved invaluable in his later career as a director. At the age of nineteen, after a year in Hollywood, he went on to spend two years as assistant director to Basil Dean, who disliked his loud clothes and the American accent he had acquired in his time there. At this time Carstairs also collaborated on scripts with A. P. Herbert, Miles Malleson, and Evelyn Waugh, and wrote a series of articles on Hollywood for the *Evening News*. A trip around the world was followed by script writing for Gaumont-British and an unsuccessful directorial début with *Paris Plane* (1933). In 1934 he secured a six-month contract in Hollywood with MGM as a scenario writer and collaborated on *A Yank at Oxford* (1937). Back in England, he survived a serious car accident; directed *Night Ride* (1937); wrote and directed *Incident in Shanghai* (1938), set during the Sino-Japanese War; and directed *Lassie from Lancashire* (1938) and, with George Sanders in the title role, *The Saint in London* (1939).

On the outbreak of war Carstairs made three short films for the Ministry of Information on 'careless talk' and directed George Formby in *Spare a Copper* (1940), a comedy set in Merseyside which netted £130,000. For much of the war he worked in the Royal Navy's air photography section. When he resumed his film career in 1945, his speed and efficiency as a director and his flair for comedy ensured his constant employment. In all, Carstairs directed forty-five feature films, including the comedies *The Chiltern Hundreds* (1949), *Made in Heaven* (1952), *Sands of the Desert* (1960), and *A Weekend with Lulu* (1961). Despite some clash of personalities, he directed Norman Wisdom's earliest films, including *Trouble in Store* (1953) and *The Square Peg* (1958). He directed Tommy Steele in the musical *Tommy the Toreador* (1959).

John Paddy Carstairs (1910–1970), by Fred Daniels

Carstairs was also a prolific author, producing more than thirty books. A light novel, *Vinegar and Brown Paper* (1939), sold 144,000 copies. *Movie Merry-Go-Round* (1937) was a technical analysis of film-making. The war years saw him publish *Bunch* (1941), a biography of his father, and two volumes of autobiography, *Honest Injun!* (1942) and *Hadn't we the Gaiety?* (1945). He also wrote eight popular novels and romances, including *Gremlins in the Cabbage Patch* (1944) and *No Music in the Nightingale* (1945). Post-war works included the satirical *Sunshine and Champagne* (1955); a book of short stories, *My Fancy has Wings* (1948); a third autobiographical work, *Kaleidoscope and a Jaundiced Eye* (1946); and a book for children, *Lollipop Wood* (1946). In addition to eight other novels, he published seven detective novels from 1958 to 1967 featuring his sleuth Garway Trenton.

Carstairs was also a painter of figures and townscapes in watercolours, oils, tempera, and gouache. He studied under Sir William Coldstream at London University and attended life classes at the Slade. His initial London exhibition was in 1949, and he later exhibited at the Paris Salon, and the John Whibley, Redfern, and Leger galleries. Between 1957 and 1968 he showed a dozen paintings at the Royal Academy and his work is represented in public collections. He painted in the manner of the Impressionists, and he was much influenced by great colourists like Derain, Matisse, Dufy, and Picasso. He favoured harbour scenes, crowded streets, and seascapes, many set in the south of France. Works such as *Venice, 1970* have a naïve quality. In 1958 he published an artists' handbook, *Watercolour is Fun*. He died of heart failure on 12 December 1970

at Kingston Hospital, Kingston upon Thames, and was cremated at the Kingston crematorium. He was survived by his wife, Molly. BASIL MORGAN

Sources J. P. Carstairs, *Honest injun!* (1942) · D. Gifford, *The British film catalogue, 1895–1985: a reference guide*, [2nd edn] (1986) · A. Windsor, ed., *Handbook of modern British painting, 1900–1980* (1992) · J. P. Carstairs, 'Bunch' (1941) · *The Times* (14 Dec 1970) · A. Jarman and others, eds., *Royal Academy exhibitors, 1905–1970: a dictionary of artists and their work in the summer exhibitions of the Royal Academy of Arts*, 1 (1973); repr. (1985) · J. P. Carstairs, *Hadn't we the Gaiety?* [1945] · S. Irving, 'John Paddy Carstairs', *Film and Television Technician* (Jan 1971) · b. cert. · d. cert.

Likenesses F. Daniels, photograph, NPG [see illus.] · photographs

Wealth at death £7123: probate, 12 Feb 1971, *CGPLA Eng. & Wales*

Carstares [Carstairs], **William** (1649–1715), Church of Scotland minister and political adviser, was born on 11 February 1649 at Cathcart, near Glasgow, the eldest child of John Carstairs (1623–1686), the parish minister, and his wife, Janet (1625–1685), daughter of William Mure of Glanderston.

Early life, 1649–1672 Carstares's childhood was spent in Glasgow, where his father was minister of the Outer High Church from 1650, and with his numerous relations in Renfrewshire and Ayrshire. By 1662 he was being schooled by his father's friend John Sinclair, minister of Ormiston, Haddingtonshire, from whose insistence on Latin conversation in the manse as well as the schoolroom he gained his fluency in Latin. In October 1663 he matriculated at the University of Edinburgh, graduating in July 1667. At some time during the next two years he went to the Netherlands to complete his studies, like many other Scottish presbyterians whose principles debarred them from prospects under the re-established episcopate. His political and religious sensibilities were being shaped by the harsh early attempts of the Restoration government to crush presbyterian dissent. Just as important, his father was an outlaw. A convinced presbyterian of the protester party John Carstairs had been deprived in May 1662 for refusing to conform to the new regime or take the oath of allegiance. A marked man, he fled to Ireland in 1664. After a period hiding there and in Scotland, Carstairs was reluctantly drawn, with his wife's kinsman Mure of Caldwell, into the failed rebellion of 1666, which ended at Rullion Green. Despite being forfeited Carstairs remained at large, and probably went to the Netherlands about the same time as his son. William's first biographer, McCormick, recorded that his 'active, bold, and enterprising spirit' disposed him to assist in redressing grievances and to act 'in defence of the civil and religious liberties of his country' (McCormick, 4).

Fearing a rash move John Carstairs arranged for William to pursue his studies abroad. In 1669 he was designated 'Scoto-Britanus' (Dunlop, 36) in the enrolment register of Utrecht University. Although nothing is known of his studies there the university was a more traditional and conservative setting than Leiden for his divinity studies. It is probable that by 1672 the young student was ordained as a presbyterian minister by a classis of the Dutch church, for in 1681 he received a testimonial of his lawful ordination. While in the Netherlands he was assisted by

William Carstares (1649–1715), by William Aikman, *c.*1712

Andrew Russell, the leading Scottish merchant in Rotterdam.

Agent for the house of Orange, 1672–1682 Besides the intellectual broadening of his foreign study Carstares was drawn away from a pastoral career. The 'foundation of his future fortunes in life' (McCormick, 5) arose from an introduction by a medical friend of his father in London to Dr Rumpf, physician to William, prince of Orange. Rumpf soon introduced Carstares to Caspar Fagel, pensionary of Holland, through whom he had an interview with the prince, who seems to have discerned that his personal abilities, political sympathies, and exceptional grasp of public affairs could be useful. The Hague required news and contacts with the politically disaffected in England because of the difficulties caused by Charles II's support for the French. Exactly when Carstares began to act as an agent is unclear, but he dated his first known letter using the pseudonym Williams at London on 10 December 1672, having escaped arrest when his ship from Rotterdam was seized. Five extant letters concerning political intelligence, which he sent as William Williams to Pierre du Moulin (*d.* 1676), Prince William's spymaster, date from 12 December 1673 until April 1674, by which time he had twice returned to the Netherlands with letters or to receive further instructions. In January 1674 he again avoided arrest when other agents were under surveillance on a London bound ship. While his reports on English affairs were not unique, and he misjudged Charles's willingness to sign the 1674 peace treaty with the Dutch, his Scottish intelligence was more useful, for example reporting the attempt to oust the duke of Lauderdale in 1673, and the latter's clashes with the duke of Hamilton.

Indeed, a set of instructions dated 25 May 1674 suggests that Carstares was instrumental in clandestine contacts between Hamilton and The Hague. In a letter of 17 April to his sister he expressed his hopes of having the opportunity of being 'in a capacity to do some little service in my generation, and not always be insignificant in my station' (Dunlop, 37).

While Carstares was back in the Netherlands from July the discovery of treasonable contacts led on 7 August to a warrant for the arrest of 'Williams', which happened on 19 September 1674 on his return to England. Despite his denial that the secret instructions he carried were prejudicial to the king it was clear there was a hostile design. Lauderdale got him to admit his responsibility for printing in the Netherlands the recent pamphlet attack on his ministry, *The Accompt of Scotland's Grievances* (1674). Its suspected author, James *Stewart, had escaped arrest. Carstares's refusal to answer most other questions led his exasperated captors to threaten him that he would be taken to Scotland and subjected to the torture of the boots. Although he was transferred to Edinburgh Castle on a warrant dated 26 February 1675 Carstares was not tortured, nor is there evidence of a trial being held. Instead, the government saved itself the trouble of proving treason by holding him as a close prisoner, which he remained until 1679.

There Carstares befriended the twelve-year-old son of the castle governor, who told stories to console him, covertly brought him pen, ink, and paper, and delivered letters for him. On parting tears flowed on both sides. Reading Jacques-Auguste de Thou's *Historia sui tempis* three times, Carstares taught himself to think in Latin. As part of the policy of leniency following Bothwell Brig, an order for the prisoner's release was signed on 29 July 1679. Although his father was now back in Scotland, after a few months William evidently saw no point in remaining in his homeland, where he could not be politically active without further imprisonment, act as a minister without compromising his principles, or join with the covenanting extremists.

Carstares therefore travelled to Ireland to visit relatives about February 1680. By September he was in London, where he settled among nonconformists. By June 1681 he had taken up his first pastoral charge, a presbyterian congregation at Theobalds, Hertfordshire. On 6 June 1682, at Raynham parish church, Essex, he married Elizabeth Kekewich (*d.* 1724), daughter of Peter Kekewich of Trehawk, head of a respectable Cornish gentry family. Carstares's correspondence provides evidence of their happy marriage, despite long periods of separation; they seem not to have had any children.

Plots against the crown, 1681–1685 Carstares's name occurs in secret Dutch correspondence during 1681, and soon after his marriage he returned to Utrecht. Plotting against Charles II had begun in earnest after the exclusion crisis, and Carstares helped in negotiations between the earl of Argyll in the Netherlands and the plotters in England, the duke of Monmouth, Lord Russell, and their associates, and the Scots George Baillie of Jerviswood and Andrew

Fletcher of Saltoun. Correspondence between the Scottish conspirators was conducted under the pretext of arrangements for the colony in Carolina then being planned by a group including Carstares's brother-in-law, William Dunlop. He returned to England in November 1682 with a request from James Stewart, Argyll's agent in the Netherlands, for funds for a Scottish rising, but frustrated with the plotters' dissensions he was back in Utrecht by early 1683. After Shaftesbury's desertion a second mission of negotiations with Algernon Sidney ended with the Scots' decision to postpone everything until English action was guaranteed. Then the government discovered the plot.

Besides the design for armed insurrection some plotted the king's death. Carstares held that assassination was not only unchristian and dishonourable, but contrary to the essentially constitutional purpose of the armed rising, which was justified in order to secure a free parliament, redress of public grievances, and the exclusion of the duke of York from the succession. He claimed he indignantly repudiated hints by Robert Ferguson 'the Plotter' about killing the king and duke of York, so although he was aware of such ideas he was probably ignorant of the Rye House plot itself. From 12 June 1683 details of the plots began to reach the authorities, who quickly arrested several of Carstares's associates. Privy councillor John Drummond recognized a cipher key in the agent's hand, and two days after Russell's execution on 21 July Carstares was taken at Tenterden, Kent, hiding under the name of Mure.

Carstares denied being concerned in any plot against king and government, but on 17 August he was committed close prisoner in London for conspiring the death of the king and levying war. There the lord advocate, Sir George Mackenzie, threatened him with torture. His wife petitioned the council unsuccessfully, and applied for his trial or bail under habeas corpus, but on 1 November he was transferred by sea to Edinburgh, along with other Scottish dissidents. From 14 November he was a close prisoner in Edinburgh tolbooth for twenty-two weeks. In April 1684, now in poor health, he was allowed open confinement. In July the privy council tortured William Spence, Argyll's servant, who agreed to decipher some intercepted letters, in one of which Carstares went under the name Mr Red. Carstares declined to swear that he knew nothing, and determined to 'adventure upon the torture' (Story, 89), believing that the council would not carry it beyond the point of endurance, or that he would die if they did. On 8 August he was put in irons, and on 27 August his wife was allowed to join him in his close cell.

Carstares's interrogation began on 5 September with his refusal to answer either spoken or written questions. The council ordered torture by the thumbikins, which proved too disgusting for the dukes of Hamilton and Queensberry, who left the chamber. The earl of Perth watched impassively as Carstares bravely endured for at least an hour. Next came the application of the iron boots to his legs, which, fortunately for Carstares, the novice executioner botched. Before the torture resumed next day

he accepted John Drummond's assurances that his deposition would not be used against any other accused person in any court. He later declared that he 'absolutely refused' to speak (Dunlop, 47) without guarantees from the council. After medical treatment he answered the council's questions, and signed a deposition, despite some reservations, confirming it before the council on 18 September. A pro-government version of his deposition, *Mr Carstares' Confession*, was quickly printed for sale.

After receiving a remission for all his crimes on 27 September 1684 Carstares was transferred to open prison at Stirling Castle. On 22 December Robert Baillie of Jerviswood, whom Carstares had named in his confession, was tried for plotting. Since he refused to testify in court the lord advocate used Carstares's deposition as a form of indirect proof instead. The sick old man was found guilty and hanged, drawn, and quartered. Carstares protested bitterly, and was freed, but refused the offer of his expenses while in prison. He wanted nothing more to do with Scotland until 'things go there in another channel' (Dunlop, 50). He had maintained silence about Prince William's contacts with the disaffected, and later admitted that his greatest anxiety was the discovery of his correspondence with Fagel and William Bentinck. Some councillors perhaps guessed at this, and sought to make credit with The Hague by releasing Carstares despite extracting so little from him, while others judged he would be discredited by having divulged secrets. The prince himself showed his gratitude by placing entire and lifelong confidence in him.

After Carstares's release his father refused to see him for a period, so strongly did he disapprove of his political activity, but they were reconciled before Carstares sailed with his wife to London after 26 February 1685. His embarkation from London on 9 May was probably owing to knowledge of the sailing of Argyll's expedition from Amsterdam on 2 May. While Argyll and Monmouth set out on their ill-fated expeditions, for the like of which Carstares had courageously acted and suffered torture, he now set off on a leisurely tour through Flanders, parts of Germany, and the United Provinces. His demonstrative rejection of armed insurrection and espionage seems to mark a turning inward and reflection on his role as the unwitting instrument of Jerviswood's death. During the next four years, as he resumed his ministerial vocation, his political involvement developed into personal service to William of Orange, but as adviser not agent.

Chaplain and adviser, 1685–1688 Carstares's travel journal reveals an open and inquisitive mind, alert to the views of the diversity of Catholics and protestants whom he encountered. After six weeks he came to his cousin's in Rotterdam, and on 6 July visited The Hague. News of his mother's death came as he awaited his wife's arrival. In August he and Elizabeth took a house in Cleves, hoping that his father could join them in their pleasant retreat, where he enjoyed the duke of Brandenburg's protection. Among the rules of conduct he devised in January 1686 were resolutions to moderate his passion, and to spend part of his recuperation in writing 'a just vindication of myself, principles and friends' (Dunlop, 52–3). If written, it appears to have been lost. After his father died on 5 February, he wrote tenderly to invite his sisters to live in Cleves, begging Sarah, who intended to follow her husband to Carolina, to leave behind one of her sons to treat as his own. In the event she and her children remained in Edinburgh.

In autumn 1686 Carstares moved to Leiden. Prince William appointed him his chaplain and received him into his family, a mark of his great esteem. Carstares was drawn into his counsels, and briefed him about events and personalities, including the political exiles who arrived in increasing numbers at this period. His biographer Joseph McCormick credits him with the ability to 'prognosticate the still greater calamities' to which James's catholicizing government would expose Scotland and England (McCormick, 25). Certainly his experience and political sense were of enormous benefit, while his discretion made him a safer confidant than Gilbert Burnet. William found in him 'a man as secretive as himself and as committed to the Calvinist faith' (Dunlop, 58).

After the second indulgence of James VII in July 1687 Carstares declined an invitation to serve a presbyterian congregation in Glasgow, but hoped to visit his family if an indemnity was enacted. Between July 1687 and April 1688 James Stewart wrote to Carstares, arguing that the king's policy of religious toleration was the only way to avoid further repression of protestant dissent by the established churches. William and Mary were unconvinced, and Stewart chided Carstares for his cold, slow, and cautious replies. Carstares and Burnet were consulted on Fagel's famous letter, which officially set out the prince's objections to the removal of the tests and the admission of Roman Catholics to office. During 1688 Stewart was discredited as a result of the letter's publication and the ensuing pamphlet war, and blamed his friend Carstares for failing to suppress their correspondence. Carstares's life as an exiled minister continued. Early in 1688 he accepted an appointment to be second minister of the Scottish church in Leiden. However, the issue of the protestant succession remained to the fore with the possibility of a male heir for James, and Carstares was closely involved in intelligence reports from friends in Scotland as William's plans developed for an expedition to secure protestantism.

Revolution, 1688–1690 When the Dutch expedition finally set out Carstares sailed on William's ship, and on 5 November 1688 led a service of thanksgiving for the expeditionary forces on the beach at Torbay. Thereafter he constantly attended the prince during his advance on London and the events that led to the offers of the English and Scottish crowns to William and Mary in early 1689. When the success of William's enterprise became clear, Carstares resigned his charge at Leiden, expressing thanks to the burgomeisters. William consulted and employed him in negotiations and entrusted him alone with certain disbursements, to the extent that he became a confidential adviser and secretary for Scottish business, despite only holding the formal position of royal chaplain. On his appointment the king required his constant attendance, and granted him palace apartments. Of all the Scottish exiles who accompanied William to England, Carstares was thus best placed to compensate for William's and his adviser Bentinck's limited knowledge of Scottish politics, and of the inevitable place-seekers who crowded the court in the winter of 1688–9.

Carstares influenced William's initial policy of removing episcopacy in Scotland, on the grounds that it did not command popular support, and replacing it with a presbyterian system. When William realized that support for episcopacy was greater than supposed, especially among the nobility and gentry, he was amenable to maintaining it for uniformity of church government in his kingdoms. The Scottish bishops' Jacobitism frustrated William's aim during 1689, and proved the reliability of Carstares's judgement. He arranged for the presbyterian ministers to send delegates to congratulate William, and he introduced them personally. Nevertheless, having consented to the abolition of the bishops in July 1689, the king now aimed at a comprehensive church embracing episcopalians and presbyterians, in order to achieve stability and forbearance, if not tolerance.

Carstares tried to persuade William that since almost all the episcopal clergy were Jacobites, nothing short of a presbyterian establishment would settle the Scottish church, preferably with provision for complying episcopalians to continue in their parishes. He knew well that some presbyterian brethren would be tempted to express their strong opposition to this form of indulgence, and their personal grievances, in ways counter to the king's interest. Therefore he counselled William to hear just complaints by episcopalian clergy, but to allow no party to think they monopolized his favour. He and Secretary of State for Scotland George Melville (from 1690 earl of Melville) busily counteracted complaints raised in England about the privy council's purge of episcopalians conducted by the zealous earl of Crawford in summer and autumn 1689, but little was done to rectify grievances.

Carstares's next challenge was to ensure the settlement of moderate presbyterian government, and during spring 1690 he went over the draft act clause by clause with the king. The amendments reflect Carstares's knowledge, and both his and William's moderating intentions. Rather than be held to have ratified presbytery as 'the only government of Christ's Church in this Kingdom', the king desired it to be expressed as 'the government of the church in this kingdom established by law' (Dunlop, 71). William wished to avoid obstructions to a future church union, but the act was passed on 7 June with the exclusive description in place, and without the king's intended provision for episcopal clergy to be allowed an indulgence, like English dissenters, on giving security to live peaceably. The kirk's sweeping powers to purge them were to cause trouble for many years. Next came the abolition of patronages, to which Carstares was opposed, believing it was prudent to retain them, as they were a private right distinct from the essence of presbyterian church government, and congregations might exercise their rights unwisely. Melville yielded to his presbyterian clerical supporters, who favoured a system of popular choice, and gave the royal consent to the abolition. If the public acts of the 1690 session frustrated Carstares's instincts as an ecclesiastical adviser the parliament gratified him personally by acknowledging the injury done to him in 1683.

Consolidating the church settlement, 1690–1694 That autumn the first general assembly of the church since 1653 was held. The king's instructions enjoining moderation were probably drafted by Carstares; he attended throughout, although not a member, and he insisted on his brethren reporting its deliberations at court. In January 1691 he accompanied the king to the Netherlands, where he advised him about episcopalian complaints against the harsh proceedings by the assembly's commission, but was unable to secure the presbyterian delegation more than one interview, or any favour. The king ordered a stop to proceedings, and Melville and Carstares rebuked their presbyterian allies for their excesses. Worse came in January 1692, when the general assembly frustrated the king's scheme for the reception into the church of loyal episcopalians. Even Carstares's powers to persuade his high-flying brethren failed him.

The royal prerogative of calling the assembly was threatened by the moderator's setting of a date for the next assembly, but a crisis was deferred by a postponement until March 1694. Meanwhile Carstares was not kept informed of all the assembly commission's plans. He knew that his policy of restoring the duke of Hamilton to government in 1693 appeared to some as lukewarmness to the church. Before the assembly of 1694 the king was advised to order the taking of the oaths of allegiance and assurance by the clergy as conditions of sitting. McCormick records how Carstares dramatically prevented the order from being sent, and in his nightshirt begged the king's forgiveness, securing an order dispensing with the oaths. Whatever the truth of the story Carstares earned credit with his brethren, most of whom were against taking oaths imposed by civil authority, and with the king, for preventing a breach between crown and church. In order to strengthen the church settlement he strongly advised the postponement of the assembly in summer 1695, risking the odium of his high-flying brethren, who regarded him as overmuch the courtier.

Personal attendance and political affairs, 1688–1702 Carstares's life was indeed that of the courtier, constantly attending the king at court and on campaign, which afforded him close observation of his courage and determination. William delegated Scottish affairs to Bentinck, now the earl of Portland, and as most communications went through Carstares he thus wielded great influence, earning him the nickname Cardinal. He sought to maintain the royal prerogative, to achieve a balance of interests among the office-holders, and at all costs to preserve presbyterian government as the core of the church settlement. In Melville he saw an assured Williamite and the

presbyterian party's champion, and so loyally served him, even after his dismissal. The support which he and Portland showed, long after Melville's enemies had isolated him and the magnates sought dominance, amounted to 'blind loyalty, ignorance and gross miscalculation' (Riley, 70).

With James Johnston, Melville's replacement as joint secretary, Carstares was at first a cordial ally, approving his attempts to settle the church and isolate the Jacobite episcopalians. However from autumn 1694 he successfully thwarted the arguments for a ministerial change before the next parliament, which were being promoted by Johnston and his presbyterian allies. In January 1695 his assurances concerning the church even dissuaded a presbyterian delegation including William Dunlop from pressing their claims. His opposition to Johnston may even have driven him to temporary alliance with the episcopalian interest, and he opposed Lord Annandale's appointment as commissioner to parliament. On a mission to gauge political opinion in Edinburgh in 1695 Carstares was intercepting Johnston's mail, which helped cause the collapse of the Tweeddale–Johnston ministry that year.

Despite their estrangement, when Johnston was dismissed in January 1696, Carstares conscientiously wished to see him provided for. He was closely involved with the ministerial changes of early 1696, but in pursuing the goal of religious balance in the ministry failed to recognize the magnates' overwhelming desire for direct personal influence. A further instance of his fallible political judgement, although not of his personal loyalty, was his support for the discredited Melville in winter 1695–6, when his suggestion that the earl replace Tweeddale as chancellor caused mirth at court.

Next Carstares was embroiled in the struggles between Queensberry, whom he supported, and the secretary, the earl of Tullibardine, who blamed the influence of Carstares and Portland in frustrating an appointment to the lord presidency of the court of session. Carstares was indeed Tullibardine's 'unscrupulous enemy' (Hopkins, 437), thereby disrupting the reconstructed court interest of 1696. After Tullibardine's dismissal in March 1698 Queensberry rose to a dominant position by 1700–01, continually using his persuasive powers on his intermediaries, Carstares and Portland, and thus weakening the secretaries. When Portland's political involvement decreased Carstares maintained his advisory and quasi-secretarial roles, and continued to undertake special managerial tasks, as in February 1698, when he visited Edinburgh to 'feel pulses' before the parliament (*Hope Johnstone MSS*, 104). In 1699 on Argyll's behalf he sought a pardon for Simon Fraser's treason. Increasingly he was at Queensberry's disposal, and in 1700 became almost his personal agent at court, but after the uproar of the adjournment in February 1701, which revealed splits between Queensberry and his resentful court allies, Carstares became more circumspect in what he promised.

For over twelve years Carstares acted for William's service and the security of the church, playing the political game and accepting the inevitable personal attacks. In 1696 Adam Cockburn of Ormiston remarked that he would be dangerous until he was placed in a Scottish parish, a view echoed in 1698 by Tullibardine, against whom Carstares's personal dislike was clearest. In 1701 Carstares warned the marquess of Annandale that Tullibardine would try to thwart him in his role as commissioner to the general assembly. His correspondence shows the extent to which he was consulted on appointments and importuned by place-seekers and their patrons, but his favour tended to be accorded by the criterion of public good, and he himself seems not to have pursued material gain. There was integrity in his manipulations, but above all he displayed single-mindedness and stamina. King William said of him, 'I have known him long, and I know him thoroughly, and I know him to be a truly honest man' (Story, 270).

Principal and moderator, 1702–1715 After William's death in 1702 Carstares's role at the heart of government ended, although the duke of Hamilton believed, perhaps cynically, he would serve the court in anything to retain his 'bishoprick' (NL Scot., MS 7104, fol. 60). Early in 1703 he returned to Edinburgh on a mission to ensure calm in the ensuing assembly, and when some clergy moved for an assertion of the church's intrinsic rights he typically counselled against risking the church settlement. While there he succeeded Gilbert Rule as principal of the University of Edinburgh on 12 May. He had long been active in support of the Scottish universities. In 1690 an act of benign nepotism had placed his brother-in-law, William Dunlop, as principal of the University of Glasgow, and in 1693 as historiographer royal. In 1692 Carstares had sought funding for the universities, and next year succeeded in securing an annual grant of £1200 from the bishops' rents, to be shared by the four universities. Helped by Queensberry his lobbying during winter 1703–4 secured the continuance of the grant. With his learned inaugural address in fluent Latin, admired even by Dr Archibald Pitcairn, Carstares set the tone for his innovative tenure of office. First he diplomatically reformed the college's relationship with the town council, which had been soured by patronage disputes.

In September 1704 the council rewarded Carstares with the charge of Greyfriars Kirk, and a higher salary of 2200 merks. Even after fifteen years' absence from the pulpit Carstares capably combined his parochial duties with his weekly divinity lectures and his administrative responsibilities. He tackled the student rowdiness which had persisted under his predecessor, and the university began to attract more students. With the English dissenter Edmund Calamy, Carstares planned a residential hall for dissenters, but it caused a competitive squabble with Glasgow University, and failed for lack of support. His outstanding achievement was the abolition in 1708 of the ancient system of regenting. Instead of teaching by regents, who took their class through the entire arts curriculum of Greek and the branches of philosophy, from 1709 specialist teaching by professors was introduced on

the Dutch model. A chair of anatomy had been established in 1705, and chemistry followed in 1713. The changes allowed the necessary specializations to develop within a nascent faculty structure, for example the pioneering teaching of natural philosophy on Baconian and Newtonian lines. These reforms, which continued after their author's death, laid the foundations of the university of the Enlightenment, and a pattern for the other Scottish universities to follow.

Carstares was naturally drawn into ecclesiastical affairs. In 1704 he attended his first general assembly as a representative, on behalf of the university, contributing to the form of process for disciplining errant ministers, which proved a robust and long-lived tool. He was elected moderator in 1705 and his role as a 'calm and judicious Churchman' (Story, 276) proved decisive in persuading his brethren of the benefits of the proposed parliamentary union, thereby heading off a potential threat to its passage from their pulpits. In constant contact with his political patrons Carstares displayed his adroitness in discreet negotiations. He influenced the defeat of a proposal in the 1706 assembly for a fast in connection with the union, and managed the assembly commission's petition for protection under the union. Robert Harley's agent, Daniel Defoe, judged that Carstares 'Merits Great Consideration' for his work for the union (Backscheider, 571). The act of security of the established church, which was enacted as part of the treaty, assured the majority of Scottish presbyterians that the kirk was safeguarded.

The kirk in danger, 1711–1714 The kirk's position was nevertheless undermined by the decision of the House of Lords in the Greenshields case in 1711. During the preceding years Carstares had attempted to use his friendship with Robert Harley, earl of Oxford, to counteract the episcopalians' increasing clamour for freedom to worship. Afterwards in the 1711 assembly, despite his surprise at the judgment, he successfully urged caution on his brethren, whose outrage the episcopalians and their Anglican allies were ready to exploit. In August he went to London to complain about episcopalian intrusions and other grievances. Receiving assurances of royal support for the establishment, he was said to have secured the replacement of Sir David Dalrymple as lord advocate by his old friend Sir James Stewart, thereby reinvigorating proceedings against the nonjurors. During winter 1711–12 he and the kirk's delegation found themselves fighting to preserve the national church against a strong episcopalian alliance lobbying for toleration. In one of his few known publications, *The Case of the Church of Scotland with Relation to the Bill for a Toleration* (1712), Carstares argued pithily that complying episcopal clergy enjoyed sufficient indulgence, and would not countenance toleration of a Jacobite faction which threatened the worship, discipline, and uniformity of the kirk. He helped to ensure that a modified form of abjuration oath would mitigate the damage to their establishment, but the kirkmen could stop neither toleration nor its sequel, the restoration of patronages, which Carstares also opposed, despite having opposed the abolition in 1690. The reassurances of no further changes, which he carried back to Edinburgh, were insufficient to stem bitter criticisms of the legal encroachments on the kirk. The refusal of many parish clergy to take the abjuration oath in terms of the Toleration Act forced the authorities to allow more time, during which Carstares devised a persuasive statement qualifying the sense in which they took the oath. He prevented a split during the 1712 assembly.

Final years, 1714–1715　Carstares's parochial and university work continued, with some ill health, which in 1710 and 1713 took him to Scarborough, Yorkshire. In 1714 he was in the kirk's delegation to congratulate King George on his accession, but attracted criticism for insufficiently representing their grievances. In 1715, moderating the general assembly for the fourth time, he, with his usual skill, quashed moves by the hotheads to make the assembly address the king directly over its grievances. His final letters in the spring and summer reveal an assured, skilful churchman, vigilant against Jacobitism in church and state, seeking to reconcile his nonjuring brethren to the abjuration oath, arranging benefits for his own university and Marischal College, Aberdeen, pressing for increased stipends, assisting needy colleagues, friends, and relations, and arranging the renewal of his modest grant as royal chaplain.

Such tireless work ranked among Carstares's greatest achievements, for which he sometimes paid the price of ingratitude from the rising generation of ministers, who could forget that without his courtliness the revolution settlement might have unfolded less to their advantage. Whatever the limits to his political acumen revealed by his role amid the intricacies of secular politics in the 1690s, he seems always to have acted in the interest of the crown and of the kirk. An orthodox but broad-minded minister, warm in his piety and sermons, he sought a broader base for the church than the covenants offered, acknowledging its boundaries in relation to the secular power. He came to be regarded as a forefather of the later moderate tendency in the church, and R. H. Story portrayed him as a liberal before his time. His courage and his influence as an ecclesiastical statesman commanded the respect of contemporaries, one of whom summed him up in 1711 as 'a Composition of Gravity Superior Sense and Moderation with Experience and Dextrous Address' (NL Scot., MS 9251, fol. 253).

Carstares was generous to his family and friends, and despite his sterling defence of presbyterian interests, to his antagonists, secretly supporting some episcopal ministers and their families. Once he had a new suit of clothes made for the impoverished episcopalian polemicist, Robert Calder, and tricked him into accepting them by pretending they had been badly tailored for himself. In the second half of August 1715 Carstares suffered an apoplectic attack, partially recovered, but died in Edinburgh on 28 December, and was buried there on 2 January 1716 in Greyfriars churchyard.　　　TRISTRAM CLARKE

Sources　R. H. Story, *William Carstares: a character and career of the revolutionary epoch (1649–1715)* (1874) • A. I. Dunlop, *William Carstares and the kirk by law established* (1967) • *State papers and letters addressed to William Carstares*, ed. J. M'Cormick (1774) • G. Gardner, 'The Scottish exile community in the United Provinces, 1660–1690', DPhil diss., U. Oxf., 1998 • P. W. J. Riley, *King William and the Scottish politicians* (1979) • P. Hopkins, *Glencoe and the end of the highland war* (1986) • *Letters and correspondence of the Rev. John Carstaires*, ed. W. Ferrie (1846) • K. H. D. Haley, *William of Orange and the English opposition* (1953) • J. Scott, *Algernon Sidney and the restoration crisis, 1677–1683* (1991) • A. C. Cheyne, *Studies in Scottish church history* (1999) • P. Backscheider, *Daniel Defoe: his life* (1989) • 'Letters from Professor Blackwell, and others, to John Ross of Arnage … MDCCXI–MDCCXVII', *The miscellany of the Spalding Club*, ed. J. Stuart, 1, Spalding Club, 3 (1841) • G. Grub, *An ecclesiastical history of Scotland*, 4 vols. (1861); vol. 3 • W. L. Mathieson, *Politics and religion: a study in Scottish history from the Reformation to the revolution*, 2 (1902) • *The manuscripts of J. J. Hope Johnstone*, HMC, 46 (1897) • letters of 'Williams' to A. Russell, 1673, NA Scot., RH15/106/163 • letter-book of James Johnston, 1692–4, NA Scot., SP3/1 • letters of W. Carstares to duke of Montrose, 1715, NA Scot., GD220/5/545 • letter to W. Dunlop, 11 June 1711, NL Scot., MS 9251, fol. 253 • Duke of Hamilton, letter to marquess of Tweeddale, 1703, NL Scot., MS 7104, fol. 60 • will, NA Scot., CC8/8/86, fols. 196–8

Archives　Mount Stuart Trust, Rothesay, Isle of Bute, corresp. • NA Scot., letters • U. Edin., sermon • U. Edin. L., corresp. and papers | NA Scot., letters to Lord Leven and Lord Melville • NA Scot., Mar and Kellie papers • NA Scot., Marchmont papers • NA Scot., letters to duke of Montrose • NA Scot., Andrew Russell's papers • Nationaal Archief, The Hague, Fagel family papers • NL Scot., letters to William Dunlop • NL Scot., corresp. with first marquess of Tweeddale and second marquess of Tweeddale • NL Scot., Wodrow papers • NRA Scotland, priv. coll., Bute papers • NRA Scotland, priv. coll., Annandale papers • priv. coll. • priv. coll. • U. Glas., Stirling papers, MSS Gen 204, 206

Likenesses　W. Aikman, oils, *c*.1712, U. Edin. [*see illus.*] • engraving, 1873, repro. in Story, *William Carstares*, frontispiece • engraving, repro. in R. Wodrow, *The history of the sufferings of the Church of Scotland* (1721–2), vol. 2, p. 294 • oils, Scot. NPG

Wealth at death　£12,222 13s. Scots: inventory, registers of commissary court of Edinburgh, 13 Aug 1716 • was owed debts plus arrears of salaries and incomes; all to wife; arrears of teinds of chapel royal 1689–1715, owing to widow in 1724, value £44,822 18s. 6d.: will, 3 May 1700, NA Scot., CC 8/8/86, fols. 196–8

Carsuel, Séon. *See* Carswell, John (*c*.1522–1572).

Carswell [*née* Macfarlane], **Catherine Roxburgh** (1879–1946), novelist and book reviewer, was born on 27 March 1879 at 101 Hill Street, Garnethill, Glasgow, the second of the four children of George Gray Macfarlane (*d*. 1899), and his wife, Mary Anne Elizabeth (*d*. 1912), the daughter of George Lewis and his wife, Mary Anne. George Macfarlane was a commission agent who negotiated the shipping and sale of textiles. His erratic business career provided a middle-class lifestyle which was deeply religious. Both Catherine Macfarlane's grandfathers were ministers who left the Church of Scotland at the Disruption of 1843, and her parents were devout evangelicals, active in charitable works and mission: Mrs Macfarlane was especially linked with Jewish missions. This thoughtful life co-existed with Catherine's daring. Around her homes in 101 Hill Street and 172 Renfrew Street she played freely, and during family holidays at Mount Quharrie, near Abernethy, Perthshire, she swapped hanging onto the back rails of horse trams for climbing treetops.

Catherine Macfarlane was educated at Park School, Glasgow, and recalled becoming 'at fourteen a life long socialist (through reading Robert Blatchford)' (*Lying*

Awake, 16). She rejected her father's Liberalism and his Christianity without dismissing the integrity of her parents' faith. Interests in music and painting were encouraged and she recorded her delight in seeing the first impressionist exhibition in Scotland. She was able to visit relatives in Italy before spending two years at the Schumann Conservatorium, Frankfurt am Main, Germany, studying the piano. She returned in 1901 to Glasgow, where she attended the Glasgow School of Art and met Maurice *Greiffenhagen (1862–1931), a painter. She took classes in English literature at Glasgow University, although she could not be formally enrolled there, as the university did not then admit women students. There she met Walter Raleigh, professor of English literature, and Donald Carswell, a student contemporary, with whom she collaborated on the *Glasgow University Magazine*. From 1907 to 1915 she reviewed fiction and drama for the *Glasgow Herald*.

Catherine Macfarlane was introduced to Herbert Parry Malpas Jackson (*b*. 1867/8), Raleigh's brother-in-law, and after a brief courtship the couple married, on 8 October 1904. It soon became apparent that Jackson was mentally unstable, groundlessly accusing his wife of infidelities. Later, when she became pregnant, Jackson became convinced the baby was not his, and after a struggle, during which he had to be deprived of a pistol, he was admitted to a mental hospital suffering from progressive paranoia. A daughter, Diana, was born in October 1905. She died of pneumonia in 1913, aged eight.

Catherine Jackson and her daughter returned to Mrs Macfarlane. In Glasgow she embarked on an affair with Maurice Greiffenhagen. She loved him passionately but he would not leave his wife, and eventually the affair ended. At this time she raised a court action for an annulment of her marriage, on the grounds that Jackson could not have fully understood the marriage contract. In the face of opposition from Jackson's family, and in spite of the fact that the annulment would make Diana illegitimate, she won, and *Jackson v. Jackson* (1908) was a leading case in matrimonial law until the reforms of the 1930s.

In 1911 Catherine Jackson reviewed D. H. Lawrence's *The White Peacock*, recognizing early his significant talent. By 1912 she was in London. Her favourable review of Lawrence's *The Rainbow* in 1915 cost her her position with the *Glasgow Herald*, but she quickly became assistant theatre critic to St John Ervine at *The Observer*. On 9 January 1915 she married Donald *Carswell (1882–1940), who had come to London to work on *The Times*. Their marriage lasted until Donald's death in a car accident in the early days of the blackout in 1940. Donald held a variety of jobs and also wrote biography, but he never became the regular provider Catherine Carswell had hoped for—their finances were always precarious. She valued their 'real and rich' marriage, particularly their interest in each other's writing. Their son, John Patrick Carswell (*b*. 1918) remembers his mother as 'tall and well-made with brown hair and strong features' (introduction to *The Savage Pilgrimage*, 6).

Carswell first met D. H. Lawrence in 1914. The friendship, initiated by Ivy Low, soon became strong and lasting,

and in 1916 they swapped manuscripts of *Open the Door!* and *Women in Love*. *Open the Door!*, a novel with autobiographical elements, follows the growth to maturity of its Glasgow heroine Joanna Bannerman; it is modernist in conception, values, and technique. An epistolary novel, *The Camomile*, followed in 1922. In order to write, it was Carswell's habit to hire a room of her own. She took rooms at 17 Keats Grove, Hampstead, eventually moving her family to this building; thereafter she took a room in Windmill Street. The Keats Grove house was given up for one at 35 Gloucester Crescent. She moved repeatedly within London, while also leasing a string of cottages in the home counties, maintaining the pattern of city and country homes that was a successful feature of her childhood.

Carswell achieved literary recognition through *The Life of Robert Burns* (1930). Offended by the sentimental mythologizing which surrounded Burns, she aimed to present him candidly and fairly. The work caused much offence to sentimental Burnsians: it was preached against in Glasgow Cathedral and Carswell once received a bullet by post. Owing to the biography's success she made contact with the Scots modernists and identified with their literary projects. She corresponded with Florence MacNeill, Helen Cruickshank, Edwin and Willa Muir, Hugh MacDiarmid, and Neil Gunn. After Lawrence's death in 1930 Carswell was sufficiently angered by Middleton Murry's biography of him, *Son of Woman* (1931), to write *The Savage Pilgrimage* (1932), an affectionate first-hand portrait. Murry issued a libel writ and the book was reissued in a modified form in 1933. As a result of this row Carswell began corresponding with Vita Sackville-West, though she was not otherwise close to the Bloomsbury group.

In later years Carswell continued to produce anthologies, biography, and theatre history. She became friendly with John Buchan and after his death helped his widow to edit his papers, *John Buchan by his Wife and Friends* (1947), which included her own striking memoir. Her last projects were an informal autobiography, *Lying Awake* (1950) and preliminary studies for a biography of John Calvin. After bouts of pneumonia and pleurisy in the winter of 1945–6 Catherine Carswell died at the Radcliffe Infirmary, Oxford, on 18 February 1946. *The Savage Pilgrimage* was reprinted in 1981, and *Open the Door* in 1986, both with introductions by her son.   B. DICKSON

Sources C. Carswell, *Lying awake* (1950) · J. Carswell, introduction, in C. Carswell, *Open the door!* (1986) · J. Carswell, 'introduction', in C. Carswell, *The savage pilgrimage* (1981) · I. Carswell, introduction, in C. Carswell, *The camomile* (1987) · T. Crawford, 'Introduction', in C. Carswell, *The life of Robert Burns* (1990) · *Glasgow Herald* (23 Feb 1946) · *The Times* (22 Feb 1946) · J. Pilditch, 'Carswell', *Glasgow Herald* (15 Feb 1997) · C. Carswell, letter to F. M. MacNeill, 1940, NL Scot., MS 26195, fol. 139 · D. Macmillan, *Scottish art, 1460–1990* (1990) · b. cert.

Archives U. Nott. L., corresp. and papers | BL, letters to S. S. Koteliansky, Add. MS 48975 · Mitchell L., Glas., letters to John de Lancey Ferguson · NL Scot., letters to F. M. MacNeill · Queen's University, Kingston, Ontario, corresp. of her and her husband with John Buchan · TCD, corresp. with Thomas McGreevy

Likenesses E. Coia, portrait, NL Scot. · photographs, repro. in Carswell, *Lying awake*

Wealth at death £229 10s. 1d.: probate, 29 May 1946, *CGPLA Eng. & Wales*

Carswell, Donald (1882–1940), journalist and author, was born at 5 Windsor Street, Glasgow, on 11 February 1882, son of John Carswell (*b.* 1856), a physician and surgeon who became a leading psychiatrist and commissioner of the General Board of Control for Scotland, and his wife, Flora Macdougall. He was educated at Glasgow Academy and the University of Glasgow, graduating MA in 1904. He began his career as a journalist, and devoted most of his life to writing. He worked on the editorial staff of the *Glasgow Herald* from 1904 to 1912, and then on *The Times* from 1912 to 1917. According to his obituary in *The Times*, it was at this point that 'a keen literary sense showed itself in all its work'.

On 9 January 1915 Carswell married Catherine Roxburgh Jackson (1879–1946), *née* Macfarlane [*see* Carswell, Catherine Roxburgh], whom he had first met at Glasgow University. They came into close contact again when they were both working on the *Glasgow Herald*. Despite their long association, it was in some ways an odd affair. She was athletic, impulsive, and practical. He was studied, had a loathing for competitive sports matched only by his incapacity to perform them, and was more at home in scholarly than in worldly pursuits. He was pressed into riding by his military masters while serving in the Royal Horse Artillery in 1917. A sensitive man, he was shocked by their brutality, and later in life he spoke frequently to his son about their cruelty.

Carswell's position at *The Times* was prestigious and secure, but one that offered little advancement. With an eye to improving his new family's lot, he opted to train as a barrister, hoping it would serve as a ladder to a career in the Liberal Party. In 1916 he was called to the bar at the Middle Temple, but his legal career was undistinguished, and his political career non-existent. Character and contingency conspired against him. The Liberal Party began its decline. The bar was saturated, and more importantly he lacked the aggressiveness and mental agility necessary for success in it. After several years he had managed to obtain only a modest, fixed-term part-time post. In 1923, with a child of five, he was forced to give up his house in Hampstead and retired to a small cottage in Buckinghamshire: Hawthorne Cottage, in a village between Great Missenden and High Wycombe.

By the mid-1920s the Carswells' marriage was feeling the strain, with financial pressure bearing down on them and the figure of D. H. Lawrence slipping into and out of their lives, but the couple achieved a reconciliation. The family moved into a large studio in London, all three sharing one room with many books. Out of this bohemian existence emerged more happiness, and much literary productivity. In 1925 Carswell published *The Trial of Ronald True*, in a series on Notable British Trials. This was followed by *Brother Scots* (1927), *Sir Walter: a Four-Part Study in Biography* (1930), *Trial of Guy Fawkes and Others* (1934), also in the series on notable British trials, and, with Catherine Carswell, *The Scots Week-End and Caledonian Vade-Mecum for Host, Guest and Wayfarer* (1936). He was best-known for a

one-act play entitled *Count Albany*—a study of Charles Edward Stuart during his later days at Rome.

From the late 1910s Carswell maintained an association with the Home Office, and from 1919 he was secretary to the certificates of naturalization (revocation) committee. The committee, which stripped people of their British subjecthood, had a light load in times of peace, a heavier one in war. On 2 January 1940, leaving the Home Office in the middle of a blackout, he was struck by an oncoming vehicle as he crossed the road, and died shortly afterwards on the way to New Westminster Hospital, Westminster, London.   RANDALL HANSEN

Sources *The Times* (3 Jan 1940) · *WWW* · b. cert. · memoir by his son, John Carswell, priv. coll. · d. cert.
Wealth at death £20: administration, 8 June 1940, *CGPLA Eng. & Wales*

Carswell, John [Séon Carsuel] (*c.*1522–1572), bishop of the Isles, known in tradition as 'Carsualach Mór Chàrn-Àsaraidh' ('Big Carswell of Carnassarie'), was probably born at Kilmartin in Argyll. His ancestors may well have been recently brought over from Corsewall in Wigtownshire, an estate then under Campbell ownership. John Carswell, *nationis Britanniae* (from the west coast of Scotland) and *pauper*, matriculated at St Salvator's College, St Andrews, in November 1540, presumably in his late teens, and graduated MA in either 1544 or 1545. Two documents dating from the latter year strongly suggest that he joined the rising of Donald Dubh MacDonald, claimant of the lordship of the Isles. If so, it was a youthful aberration, and Carswell soon became a staunch supporter of Gilleasbaig or Archibald Campbell, fifth earl of Argyll. By September 1550 he was treasurer of Lismore, and three years later he was in possession of the highly important parsonage of his native Kilmartin. Carswell's support of the reforming ecclesiastical policies of his patron—he is recorded as Argyll's personal chaplain—led to his being granted the custody of the strategic Carnassarie Castle (which he later rebuilt) in February 1559, followed by Craignish Castle a year later, both being endowed with grants of land and produce. He also received benefices in Bute, which involved him in a series of lawsuits over the next decade. Subsequent acquisitions of land in Argyll, Cowal, and Lochgoilhead suggest that Carswell's reputation for ruthless avarice was well founded (a traditional quatrain accuses him of having a 'sgròban lom gionach farsaing'—'an empty greedy capacious maw'; Ó Baoill and MacAulay, 5). Carswell's own words, in a letter of May 1564 to Robert Campbell of Kinyeancleuch concerning accusations about his collecting teinds and other revenues, are worth quoting: 'latt thame say quhat thai list, my conscience will nocht lat me use rigour bot aganis the stubburne' (Laing, 285).

Carswell's most spectacular coup was his leasing of the bishopric of Argyll and the abbacy of Saddell in 1563, followed in January 1565 by his accepting from Queen Mary the gift of the bishopric of the Isles and the abbacy of Iona, to which he was formally presented in March 1567. The latter bishopric was acquired through the removal of the bishop-elect, Mr Patrick Maclean, a man whose kindred was at the time increasingly estranged from the Campbells. Carswell had already been nominated as superintendent of Argyll on 19 July 1560. Such powerful ecclesiastical and indeed financial positions could hardly have been obtained without the full support of the earl of Argyll, whose policies Carswell followed in political as well as religious matters. Elected to the committee of articles in April 1567, he, like his patron, was actively of the queen's party. On 6 February 1559 he became chancellor of the Chapel Royal, a position he held until his death.

The most tangible proof of Carswell's reforming zeal, indeed his monument, is his *Foirm na n-urrnuidheadh* ('The form of the prayers'), a Gaelic translation of the Book of Common Order, whose printing was completed by Robert Lekprevik in Edinburgh on 24 April 1567. It has been described as 'a work of major literary and liturgical significance' (Kirk, 298) and as 'an astonishing achievement' (Meek, 55). Equipped with a dedicatory epistle to its patron, the earl of Argyll, an epistle for the reader emphasizing the importance of the new technology of print and apologizing for any shortcomings in the translation, as well as a poem by Carswell himself wishing his volume well, *Foirm na n-urrnuidheadh* was the first printed book in Gaelic. Despite nods towards the Geneva original, it was based primarily upon the 1564 Scottish edition of the Book of Common Order. *Foirm na n-urrnuidheadh*, however, is far from being a literal translation: in his exuberant, highly decorated classical common Gaelic, Carswell takes care to stress fundamental principles of the reformed faith, albeit with an emphasis on obedience to civil magistrates and a concomitant disregard for the function of elders and congregation which were probably tailored to the particular problems then facing the church, and the earl of Argyll, in the western Gàidhealtachd.

Although Carswell evidently intended *Foirm na n-urrnuidheadh* as the first of a series of religious publications aimed at Gaels in Ireland as much as in Scotland, doubtless culminating in a Gaelic Bible, he was unable to carry his project through. Reported as very sick in December 1570, he died some time between 10 July and 4 September 1572. The violent storm which accompanied his burial, in a stone coffin outside what is now a kitchen fireplace in Ardchattan Priory, Argyll, was long remembered in tradition, though this funeral may well have been confused with that of his son Archibald, of whom 'the traditionary reports preserved … are equally unfavourable with those respecting his father' (Wodrow, 474). Carswell was apparently married first to a daughter of Hamilton of Halcraig, with whom he had his heir Gilleasbaig or Archibald. His daughter Christian may have been born to his second wife, Margaret Campbell, the sister of the laird of Ardkinglas, who outlived him.

Carswell, a giant physically as well as intellectually—his skeleton, unearthed towards the end of the nineteenth century, measured a full seven feet—possessed a fascinating scholarship mixing traditional Gaelic learning and contemporary Renaissance humanism. Although his farsighted vision of religious printing transforming the Gaelic world was at least two centuries ahead of its time,

he nevertheless created within five years an entirely new and durable lexicon for the worship and ministry of the protestant church. Carswell translated 'not just the *Book of Common Order*, but also the Reformation itself, into Gaelic terms' (Meek, 41).   DOMHNALL UILLEAM STIÙBHART

Sources J. Kirk, *Patterns of reform: continuity and change in the Reformation kirk* (1989), 280–304, 331–2, 469–70, 472–3 · D. E. Meek, 'The Reformation and Gaelic culture: perspectives on patronage, language and literature in John Carswell's translation of "The Book of Common Order"', *The church in the Highlands*, ed. J. Kirk (1998), 37–62 · R. L. Thomson, ed., *Foirm na n-urrnuidheadh* (1988) · A. Matheson, 'Bishop Carswell', *Transactions of the Gaelic Society of Inverness*, 42 (1953–9), 182–205 · R. Wodrow, *Collections upon the lives of the reformers and most eminent ministers of the Church of Scotland*, ed. W. J. Duncan, 1, Maitland Club, 32 (1834), 133–7, 471–4 · *Fasti Scot.*, new edn, 7.348 · C. Ó Baoill and D. MacAulay, *Scottish Gaelic vernacular verse to 1730: a checklist* (2001), 5 · *Argyll: an inventory of the ancient monuments*, Royal Commission on the Ancient and Historical Monuments of Scotland, 7: *Mid-Argyll and Cowal: medieval and later monuments* (1992), 214–26 · J. M. Anderson, ed., *Early records of the University of St Andrews*, Scottish History Society, 3rd ser., 8 (1926) · A. I. Dunlop, ed., *Acta facultatis artium universitatis Sanctiandree, 1413–1588*, 2 vols., Scottish History Society, 3rd ser., 54–5 (1964), 135–6 · J. E. A. Dawson, ed., *Campbell letters, 1559–1583*, Scottish History Society, 5th ser., 10 (1997) · D. E. R. Watt, ed., *Fasti ecclesiae Scoticanae medii aevi ad annum 1638*, [2nd edn], Scottish RS, new ser., 1 (1969), 206, 338 · D. Laing, ed., *The miscellany of the Wodrow Society*, Wodrow Society, [9] (1844) · M. Livingstone, D. Hay Fleming, and others, eds., *Registrum secreti sigilli regum Scotorum / The register of the privy seal of Scotland*, 6 (1963), vol. 6 · G. Donaldson, *The Scottish Reformation* (1960) · J. E. A. Dawson, *The politics of religion in the age of Mary, queen of Scots: the earl of Argyll and the struggle for Britain and Ireland* (2002)

Carswell, Sir Robert (1793–1857), physician and pathological anatomist, was born on 3 February 1793 in Paisley, the son of Robert Carswell, a print cutter of Thornliebank, and his wife, Bethia Foulds. He studied medicine at the University of Glasgow, and probably took an anatomy course at the University of Edinburgh. He was described by a contemporary colleague as 'a man of singularly unobtrusive and retiring disposition with a soft voice [and] a melancholy expression of countenance' (Clarke). While still a student he became a protégé of John Thomson, then professor of military surgery in the University of Edinburgh. Thomson engaged him to go to France to collect and draw illustrations for a new course exclusively on morbid anatomy that Thomson was planning. Carswell probably spent more time in France than any of the many British medical practitioners who flocked there after the end of the Napoleonic wars. All sought direct experience in the large French hospitals of the new clinicopathological approach to disease, of new techniques like auscultation (especially with the stethoscope), and greater access to cadavers for dissection. In 1821–2 Carswell was in Paris attending and performing dissections at nearly all of the major teaching hospitals and preparing coloured representations of disease. During 1823–4 Carswell (with William Thomson, one of John Thomson's sons) worked with and observed clinicians (mostly surgeons) in the wards, and pathologists at dissections, at the Hôtel-Dieu in Lyons. In 1824 Carswell published, with

William Cullen, an article, 'On melanosis' (*Transactions of the Medico-Chirurgical Society of Edinburgh*, 2, 264). He later (1830) published on the digestive capacities of the stomach post mortem. Carswell returned to Scotland and took his degree of MD at Marischal College, Aberdeen, in 1826. Also in 1826, after his return to France to continue his study and drawing, he married Mlle Marguerite (or Margaretha) Chardenot. The marriage was childless. Carswell worked mainly with Pierre Louis, but also with René T. H. Laennec. He continued to prepare and send back pictures for Thomson. Many of these reflected a localized conception of disease, but the corresponding case notes revealed a more holistic view, influenced by the contemporary tissue pathology of Xavier Bichat which Carswell had absorbed in France, along with an ability to correlate clinical (diagnostic) observations on the wards with pathological observations at post-mortem.

In 1828 Carswell obtained the chair of pathological anatomy and curatorship of the medical museum at the new London University. He also obtained leave to stay in Paris for two further years to continue to amass case histories with pictures, and diseased organs in spirits. Influenced by Thomson's perception of medical illustrations as exact captures of disease, he now began to collect case histories and create pictures to use as an up-to-date pedagogic tool to attract students to his own future courses, which would form the basis of a later textbook. Carswell wished to promote both his own career, and also the emerging medical speciality of pathological anatomy (later pathology) as an essential but discrete part of medical education. In 1831 Carswell was appointed physician to the dispensary of what was later the North London Hospital. Charles Williams, in his *Pathology and Diagnosis of Diseases of the Chest* of 1835, credits him with elucidating the cause of the second heart sound during a lecture to the Paris Academy of Medicine in July 1831. Carswell began lecturing at London University in the winter term of 1832–3. The London chair was the first in England, but Carswell soon found his fledgeling discipline squeezed within the university by the more traditional subjects of normal and practical anatomy, and the practice of medicine. Resources were tight after an increase in student numbers, and the new course was not required for the examinations of the Royal College of Surgeons of London, or of the Society of Apothecaries, which then licensed practitioners, so it attracted a dwindling number of enrolments. In order to earn a living Carswell was forced to divide his time between lecturing in the university and working in the pathological museum, in the hospital, and in an unsuccessful private practice. He was thus unable to focus on building up his emerging discipline within the university. In 1837 he published *Pathological Anatomy: Illustrations of the Elementary Forms of Disease*, which contained illustrations from his French excursions.

Carswell was a transitional figure in the development of pathological anatomy as a separate medical discipline. He attempted to establish means of intellectual and financial support for himself and pathological anatomy, including a research programme separate from the concerns of clinical medicine, but was frustrated by the continuing dominance of traditional, broad subject divisions whose professors were keen to keep their interconnected existing intellectual domains and social positions intact. His health failing, Carswell retired from his professorship in 1840, having secured, by the intercession of his friend Sir James Clarke, the post of personal physician to the king of the Belgians. Carswell was knighted at St James's Palace by Queen Victoria on 3 July 1850 for his services to the king while he was in England. Carswell remained at Laeken near Brussels until his death there on 15 June 1857 after a lingering illness caused by chronic lung disease. He was survived by his wife.   ANDREW HULL

Sources R. C. Maulitz, *Morbid appearances: the anatomy of pathology in the early nineteenth century* (1987), 214–23 · L. S. Jacyna, *Philosophic whigs: medicine, science and citizenship in Edinburgh, 1789–1848* (1994) · S. Jacyna, 'Robert Carswell and William Thomson at the Hôtel-Dieu of Lyons: Scottish views of French medicine', *British medicine in an age of reform* [London 1987], ed. R. French and A. Wear (1991), 110–35 · P. Huard and M. D. Grmek, 'Les élèves étrangers de Laennec', *Revue d'Histoire des Sciences*, 26 (1973), 315–37 · *IGI* · bap. reg. Scot. · J. F. Clarke, *Autobiographical recollections of the medical profession* (1874) · Boase, *Mod. Eng. biog.* · *DNB*
Archives U. Edin. L., case notes · UCL, anatomical drawings and notes; letters to university council, MS 304 · UCL, D. M. S. Watson library, corresp., MSS 673–674
Likenesses portrait, RCS Eng.

Carte, Dame **Bridget Cicely D'Oyly** (1908–1985), theatre manager, was born on 25 March 1908 at Suffolk Street, Pall Mall, London, the elder child of Rupert D'Oyly Carte (1876–1948), chairman of the Savoy group of companies and proprietor of the D'Oyly Carte Opera Company, and his wife, Dorothy Milner (1889–1977), third daughter of John Stewart Gathorne-Hardy, second earl of Cranbrook. Her paternal grandfather was Richard D'Oyly *Carte (1844–1901), theatre impresario. She disliked her second forename, Cicely, and later renounced it by deed poll. She was educated privately in England and abroad. Under some pressure from her mother, she married on 7 October 1926 her first cousin, John David Gathorne-Hardy, fourth earl of Cranbrook (1900–1978), an enthusiastic explorer and naturalist. The marriage, which was childless, broke down within five years and she resumed her maiden name in 1932. Between 1931 and 1933 she studied at Dartington Hall, Devon, taking courses in dance and teacher training, including art and design. Here she gained a small circle of lifelong friends; in a dance-drama group she met Peter Goffin, who from 1940, when at her instigation he created the set for *The Yeomen of the Guard*, designed for a number of new productions of the D'Oyly Carte Company's operas.

The death of her brother, Michael, in a motoring accident in Switzerland in 1932 changed Bridget D'Oyly Carte's life radically, making her the heir to her father's hotel and theatre interests. In 1933 she joined the hotel business, taking responsibility for furnishing and interior decoration, for which she had a flair. During the Second World War she worked in child welfare, dealing with the evacuation of nursery schoolchildren, at Nethway House,

Dame Bridget Cicely D'Oyly Carte (1908–1985), by Jane Bown, 1982

Kingswear, Devon, and then in the childcare office in Bermondsey, where she remained until her father's death in 1948. This was, she was later to own, a 'grave and serious moment' for her, since she inherited control of the D'Oyly Carte Opera Company, which was dedicated to the performance of works by W. S. Gilbert and Arthur Sullivan. She 'did not feel qualified to sustain the responsibility' facing her (Mander and Mitchenson, 'Foreword'). None the less she proved a woman 'dedicated to her inheritance' (F. Lloyd, 'The D'Oyly Carte Opera Company—how it works', *Gilbert and Sullivan Journal*, 8/14, May 1964, 220–21). She was also now a director of the Savoy group in which she was a major shareholder, but she remained conscious of being a woman in what was then a man's world. She moved reluctantly into a suite in the Savoy Hotel for which she insisted on paying rent, and took control of the furnishing and decoration departments. When the group acquired them she had a particular interest in the soft-furnishing company, James Edwards, and was chairman of the royal florists, Edward Goodyear Ltd. She was influential in 1969–72 in ensuring that the marble mantelpieces and Lutyens panelling were brought to the new Berkeley Hotel from the original premises. She became vice-chairman of the group in 1971 and was its president at the time of her death.

Bridget D'Oyly Carte oversaw all new productions of the opera company with a keen eye for detail, especially in terms of their design. She claimed that the most important function of the operas, which in later years she advertised rather as musicals, was 'to bridge the generation gap and link serious music to pop' (*Sunday Times*, 1 March 1981). Among the innovations and highlights of her years at the helm were televised and colour-film productions of some of the operas, the Festival of Britain season in 1951 at its original home, the Savoy Theatre, London, with Sir Malcolm Sargent conducting some of the performances, and an increasing number of tours of the United States, including one marking the seventy-fifth anniversary of the company's first visit, and a festival season at Central City, Colorado. The 1954 revival of *Princess Ida* at the Savoy Theatre was based on a Victorian gothic conception.

Another innovation was the design by Peter Goffin in 1957 of the 'unit' set, which had become necessary to counter the heavy financial cost and physical difficulties of touring. In 1960 the company's own touring orchestra was formed as a change from the *ad hoc* recruitment of players at each venue. In 1975 the company enjoyed a centenary season back at the Savoy Theatre; in 1977 it gave a royal command performance at Windsor Castle, and in 1979, for the first time, it toured Australia and New Zealand.

The D'Oyly Carte monopoly of the Gilbert and Sullivan operas ceased in 1961 when the copyright on Gilbert's work ended. Bridget D'Oyly Carte dissociated herself firmly from a petition, which originated in 1955 and was presented, unsuccessfully, to parliament by Lawrence Turner in March 1959, asking for steps to be taken to maintain the copyright in perpetuity. Instead, in 1960, she prompted a fundamental reorganization of the company: she established the D'Oyly Carte Opera Trust, to which she donated the company's rights and properties, stage sets, costumes, band parts, contracts, and recording, film, and television rights, altogether said to have been worth at least £150,000, and a further £30,000 in cash; at the same time Bridget D'Oyly Carte Ltd was formed, with herself as chairman and managing director, to present the operas. The feared threat from rival productions proved minimal but touring became increasingly uneconomic. Her great achievement was to ensure the survival of the D'Oyly Carte Opera Company until 1982, when mounting losses (some £5000 a week) and the refusal of the Arts Council to provide a grant brought the operation to an end.

Bridget D'Oyly Carte's wide-ranging interests included art and architecture. Shortly after her father's death she sold the family's country house, Coleton Fishacre, Devon, which had been built for her parents in 1925, and in 1949 she bought Shrubs Wood, Chalfont St Giles, Buckinghamshire, the work of the art deco architect Serge Chermayeff. Here she was able to pursue her love of gardening, and in the summer gave parties for disadvantaged or disabled children. In the 1970s she became the tenant of the semi-ruined Barscobe Castle, Balmaclellan, a small seventeenth-century fortified house in south-west Scotland, which she restored.

Bridget D'Oyly Carte was shy and retiring, shunning parties and publicity, with a fear of having to appear prominently at formal events. She was almost too unnerved to go to Buckingham Palace when she was appointed DBE in 1975, an award marking international women's year. In politics she was a supporter of the Labour Party. She could be very firm and quite immovable once she had made up her mind, but she inspired loyalty. She smoked as many as eighty du Maurier cigarettes in a day. Although in her professional sphere she used old-fashioned, formal modes of address rather than forenames, she did not like people to 'kow-tow' to her and appreciated plain speaking. Her sense of humour was wicked, sometimes childish. She dressed simply, but elegantly, in colour co-ordinated clothing, often in a two-piece suit with a silk blouse, and frequently had a scarf round her neck, through a buttonhole, or round her handbag. This she used as a plaything, twisting it when nervous. She shunned expensive jewellery, instead wearing quiet costume jewellery to good effect. She was to be found still smartly dressed even in the late evenings in her Savoy apartment, and when gardening she still wore formal, if old, clothes.

Bridget D'Oyly Carte died at Shrubs Wood on 2 May 1985, of lung cancer, and was cremated at Amersham on 10 May. A legacy from her own private fortune enabled a new D'Oyly Carte Opera Company to be set up. It began in 1988 with two productions and continued on an *ad hoc* basis.   C. M. P. TAYLOR

Sources DNB · T. Joseph, *The D'Oyly Carte Opera Company, 1875–1982* (1994) · R. Mander and J. Mitchenson, *A picture history of Gilbert and Sullivan* (1962) · *D'Oyly Carte centenary, 1875–1975* (1975) · *W. S. Gilbert Society Journal*, 1/2 (autumn 1985), 42–4 · *The Times* (3 May 1985) · *Savoy Standard* (21 June 1985) · M. Green, *Here's a how-de-do: travelling with Gilbert and Sullivan* (1952) · C. Rollins and R. J. Witts, eds., *The D'Oyly Carte Company in Gilbert and Sullivan operas* (1962) · A. Jacobs, *Arthur Sullivan: a Victorian musician*, 2nd edn (1992) · *Gilbert and Sullivan Journal* · B. Jones, 'Albert Truelove: in London and on tour', *The Savoyard* · V. Bonham-Carter, Dartington Hall, 1925–56 [privately circulated MS] · *Daily Telegraph* (10 Aug 1955) [letter from Bridget D'Oyly Carte] · private information (2004) [family, friends] · Burke, *Peerage*
Archives Savoy Group archives, London | SOUND BL NSA, performance recording
Likenesses J. Bown, photograph, 1982, priv. coll. [*see illus.*] · photograph, repro. in Mander and Mitchenson, *Picture history*, 94 · photograph, repro. in Rollins and Witts, *D'Oyly Carte Company*, facing p. 116 · photograph, repro. in *Daily Telegraph* (8 April 1972)
Wealth at death £5,479,888: probate, 26 March 1986, CGPLA Eng. & Wales

Carte, Helen [*née* Susan Helen Couper Black] (1852–1913), businesswoman and theatre manager, was born on 12 May 1852, at Wigtown, Scotland, the second daughter of George Couper (or Cowper) Black (1820–c.1874), procurator fiscal, and his wife, Ellen Barham (1823–1875?). Originally christened Susan Helen, she early reversed her names and later changed 'Black' to 'Lenoir', the original surname of the Black family in seventeenth-century France.

Between 1871 and 1874 Helen Black passed with honours the examinations in mathematics, logic, and moral philosophy at the University of London, for which she was privately tutored since the university did not admit women to courses or degrees. When, around this time, her widowed mother emigrated to Australia, Helen stayed behind, first briefly as a teacher, then as an actress—a strange choice for a woman as essentially shy and private as she. Nevertheless by 1877 as Helen Lenoir she had appeared at Dublin and Glasgow in *The Great Divorce Case*, and had been engaged to play in India. This engagement, however, was formally broken so that she could join Richard D'Oyly *Carte's theatrical organization at the Opera Comique.

As Carte's secretary, Helen soon proved indispensable. She was a 'workaholic', enjoying minutiae, even drudgery, as well as larger details of successively mounting operas by W. S. Gilbert and Arthur Sullivan, of building

the Savoy Theatre and the Savoy Hotel, into which she introduced the new hydraulic passenger lifts. She also assisted Carte in arranging American lecture tours for Oscar Wilde, Matthew Arnold (who called her Carte's 'American brain'), and others. As Carte's business associate, she frequently crossed the Atlantic to superintend American productions and tours of what became known as Gilbert and Sullivan's Savoy Operas. In 1886 Carte raised Helen's salary to £1000 a year with an additional 10 per cent on net profits. When she demurred, he wrote, 'You know very well, and so do all those who know anything about my affairs, that I could not have done the business at all, at any rate on nothing like the same scale, without you' (D'Oyly Carte MSS). Eighteen months later on 12 April 1888 she became his second wife, Sir Arthur Sullivan acting as his best man.

As the editor of *The Era* wrote in Helen Carte's obituary, 'She never took advantage of anybody; but I never heard of her letting anybody take advantage of her' (*The Era*). Yet she was very tactful, maintaining a more or less even balance among the often conflicting temperaments of Gilbert, Sullivan, and Carte; dealing sympathetically with problems, personal and professional, of the D'Oyly Carte London and touring companies; always emending her typewritten letters by hand to show she had read them herself.

In person Mrs Carte was small and slim, but very energetic. A dog lover, she was also so generous to humans that King George V conferred on her the order of the League of Mercy in 1912. James McNeill Whistler, one of her friends, did an etching of her and told her she was delightful. He himself mixed the paint for the Cartes' Adelphi Terrace flat, including his favourite yellow.

During Carte's last, invalid years, Helen Carte oversaw every detail of their far-flung organization. Lonely after his death in 1901, she married Stanley Carr Boulter, a barrister, in 1902, but continued to use the name Carte for all her business dealings. Contemporary newspapers describe her on opening night of the 1906 revival of *The Yeomen of the Guard*, when she and Gilbert took three curtain calls: dressed in white, carrying white flowers, she peeped out shyly and trembled visibly at a 'hurricane' of applause. Illness prevented her from attending the last night of the 1909 Gilbert and Sullivan revivals, and she then gave up the management of the Savoy Theatre.

After another illness lasting several months, Helen Carte died in London on 5 May 1913 of cerebral haemorrhage complicated by acute bronchitis. At her wish, her funeral at Golders Green crematorium on 7 May was private. She was perhaps the foremost businesswoman of her era.   JANE W. STEDMAN

Sources Theatre Museum, London, D'Oyly Carte MSS [unreferenced MSS] · P. Seeley, 'Who was Helen Lenoir?', *Savoyard*, 21 (Sept 1982), 16–18 · *The Era* (10 May 1913) · *Evening News* (6 May 1913) · *The Star* (6 May 1913) · *Daily Mail* (6 May 1913) · *The Times* (6 May 1913) · *Westminster Gazette* (6 May 1913) · [C. Prestige], 'Ourselves and the operas', *Gilbert and Sullivan Journal*, 8 (May 1963), 159 · B. Jones, 'Patrick W. Halton', *W. S. Gilbert Society Journal*, 1 (1993), 208–20 · T. Joseph, *The D'Oyly Carte Opera Company, 1875–1982* (1994) · F. Cellier and C. Bridgeman, *Gilbert, Sullivan, and D'Oyly Carte*

(1914) · H. Pearson, *Gilbert: his life and strife* (1957), 229–37, 249–50, 255 · *CGPLA Eng. & Wales* (1913)
Archives BL, W. S. Gilbert MSS · Morgan L., Gilbert and Sullivan collection · Theatre Museum, London, D'Oyly Carte MSS
Likenesses W. Sickert, etching, 1884, repro. in W. R. Sickert, *Sickert paintings*, ed. W. Baron and R. Shone (1992), 62 · W. Sickert, oils, 1885–6, repro. in W. R. Sickert, *Sickert paintings*, ed. W. Baron and R. Shone (1992), 63 · photograph, 1909, repro. in *Daily Graphic* (6 May 1913) · R. Barrington, photograph, repro. in R. Barrington, *More Rutland Barrington by himself* (1911), facing p. 60 · J. M. Whistler, etching · photograph, repro. in R. Mander and J. Mitchenson, *A picture history of Gilbert and Sullivan* (1962), 93 · photograph, repro. in R. Wilson and F. Lloyd, *Gilbert & Sullivan: the official D'Oyly Carte picture history* (1984), 9 · photograph, repro. in *The Era*
Wealth at death £117,670 5s. 1d.: probate, 23 May 1913, *CGPLA Eng. & Wales*

Richard D'Oyly Carte (1844–1901), by Ellis & Walery

Carte, Richard D'Oyly (1844–1901), theatre impresario, was born on 3 May 1844 in Greek Street, Soho, London, the son of Richard Carte (*d.* 1891) (originally Cart; he frenchified the surname) and his wife, Eliza, *née* Jones. The name D'Oyly, arising from his mother's side, was a forename (not part of a double surname), by which he was addressed. He matriculated at University College, London, in 1861 but left his studies to join his father's firm of Rudall, Carte & Co., well-known makers of woodwind instruments. From within his father's firm, then from an adjacent address in Craig's Court, Charing Cross, he set up a management agency for musical performers: some two hundred instrumentalists and singers (including those of such distinction as Adelina Patti and Clara Schumann, the widow of the composer) appear on his prospectus of the late 1870s.

A dilettante composer, Carte published a few songs and other pieces. Three light operas composed by him were produced in London: *Dr Ambrosias: his Secret* (1868), *Marie* (1871), and *Happy Hampstead* (1877, preceded by provincial tour). His commanding role, however, was to be in theatrical promotion. As lessee and manager of London's Opera Comique between June and October 1874, he presented a Brussels company in *Giroflé-Giroflà* (its first staging in Britain) by one of the most popular composers of French operetta, Lecocq. An English adaptation of Gaston Serpette's *La branche cassée* followed, and Carte announced his ambition 'to establish in London a permanent abode for light opera'. Not French but British works were, however, to provide his route.

In 1875 Selina Dolaro, a musical actress who headed her own company, installed him as manager of the Royalty Theatre for a run of Offenbach's operetta *La Périchole*. To fill out the evening Carte suggested that Arthur *Sullivan should set W. S. *Gilbert's *Trial by Jury*, a libretto originally intended for Carl Rosa. While it was in gestation other works plugged the gap, but these were eclipsed by the brilliant success of *Trial by Jury* on its first performance on 25 March 1875. Carte needed no further prompting to pursue the long-term promotion of Gilbert and Sullivan's works (and others compatible with them). He organized a syndicate, the Comedy Opera Company, which financed *The Sorcerer* in 1877 and *HMS Pinafore* in 1878. In 1879 he obtained sole control, and 'Mr R. D'Oyly Carte's Opera Company' (as it was thenceforward known) presented all the subsequent joint theatrical works of the pair.

To counter a wave of unauthorized (pirated) American productions of *HMS Pinafore*, Carte went to New York with Gilbert and Sullivan and presented his own production there in 1879, followed by its successor *The Pirates of Penzance* (prior to its London production). The financial rewards of the operettas enabled Carte to construct a new London theatre, the Savoy, which opened on 10 October 1881 with a transfer from the Opera Comique of the newest Gilbert and Sullivan operetta, *Patience*. The most up-to-date and comfortable of all London theatres, the Savoy was claimed as the world's first public building to be lit entirely by electric light.

The label of 'Savoy Operas' was thenceforward most commonly used to identify Gilbert and Sullivan's works, though it was also applied by Carte to other operettas he later presented at that theatre. His contractual arrangement with his two colleagues (from 1883) was as follows. For an annual rent, Carte formally let the theatre to a partnership of himself, Sullivan, and Gilbert; once the expenses of mounting the productions had been deducted, each was entitled to one-third of the profits. For his part, Carte had the right to demand a new work from his creative partners at six months' notice.

Continuity of style was assured by the maintenance of what was, in effect, a permanent company of soloists and chorus; such soloists as Jessie Bond, George Grossmith, and Rutland Barrington won their own following. Long runs became an expectation: *The Mikado* (14 March 1885) set a London theatrical record with 672 performances.

Carte's meticulous standards of staging and dresses were extended to the supporting companies which he sent to tour the repertory in the provinces. Thus his monopoly of the works was reaffirmed while a national taste was formed for them.

Carte also took a company from London to give the first New York performance of *The Mikado* on 19 August 1885 and then accompanied almost the same set of artists to Berlin and other continental cities. Vienna's leading critic, Eduard Hanslick, reviewing *The Mikado* in September 1886, specifically noted that its 'unparalleled success' was owing not merely to the libretto or the music or both together but also to 'the wholly original stage performance, unique of its kind, by Mr D'Oyly Carte's artists ... riveting the eye and ear with its exotic allurement'. There was a further continental tour in 1887.

As up-to-date as his London theatre was the new, luxurious Savoy Hotel built by Carte: it opened in 1889, the year of Gilbert and Sullivan's *The Gondoliers*. The creative partnership was by then under strain, Sullivan wishing to move away from operetta towards grand opera; Carte, with every confidence, resolved to build a new theatre to launch that enterprise. In the meantime Gilbert had precipitately accused Carte of cheating on the accounts, provoking the so-called 'carpet quarrel', the issue being whether a front-of-house carpet could be included in production expenses. An astonished public beheld the partnership in tatters, Gilbert challenging Carte in a legal action spanning from July to September 1890, with Sullivan on Carte's side. The legal result was inconclusive, the artistic consequences lamentable.

Estranged from Gilbert, Sullivan conducted his grand opera, *Ivanhoe*, at the opening of Carte's new theatre, the Royal English Opera House (now the Palace Theatre, Cambridge Circus), on 31 January 1891. Defying grand opera custom, Carte presented *Ivanhoe* not in repertory with other works but in a continuous run, with multiple casting of leading roles. It was the sole major failure of his career: the total of 160 performances exceeded any precedent for such a work but the run was insufficient to cover the financial costs. He had no other opera to replace *Ivanhoe* immediately, and its eventual successor, Messager's *La Basoche*, likewise failed (though much praised by Bernard Shaw). Late in 1892 Carte sold the theatre to Sir Augustus Harris, his only rival in vigour of theatrical promotion.

On 24 August 1870 Carte married Blanche Julia Prowse, who died in 1885; on 12 April 1888, at the Chapel of the Savoy, he married his professional assistant, known as Helen Lenoir (really Susan Helen Couper Black) [*see* Carte, Helen (1852–1913)], whose work both before and after her marriage to Carte identifies her as one of the most remarkable of Victorian businesswomen. Her decisive managerial role in relation to both Sullivan and Gilbert is evident from the time of the carpet quarrel; the subsequent reconciliation of composer and librettist and the mounting of their two final collaborations (*Utopia Limited* and *The Grand Duke*) devolved largely on her as Carte became increasingly ill.

Neither of these operettas renewed the spell which Gilbert and Sullivan had once exerted on the public. No longer able to depend on their joint output to fill the Savoy, Carte produced new operettas by Sullivan with other librettists (*Haddon Hall*, 1892; *The Chieftain*, 1894; *The Beauty Stone*, 1897; *The Rose of Persia*, 1899) and extended the repertory to other composers, including Messager (*Mirette*, 1894) and Alexander Mackenzie (*His Majesty*, 1897). None of these had much success.

From the time of his second marriage Carte lived at 4 Adelphi Terrace, in the area of the Savoy, with a handsome summer residence on an island in the Thames at Weybridge, Surrey. He died at his London home from dropsy and heart disease on 3 April 1901. At the same time as he was buried, on 6 April at Fairlight church, Hastings, a memorial service for him was held at the Chapel Royal of the Savoy. Despite the disastrous enterprise of his Royal English Opera, he left some £250,000, twice the amount of Gilbert's legacy and more than four times Sullivan's.

After Helen Carte's death in 1913, control of the D'Oyly Carte Opera Company, as it was later styled, passed to Rupert D'Oyly Carte (1876–1948), a son of Carte's first marriage, and then to Rupert's daughter Bridget D'Oyly *Carte (1908–1985). The company continued under the family's management, but with a final change of name to the D'Oyly Carte Trust, until 1982.   ARTHUR JACOBS

Sources New Grove · K. Gänzl, *The British musical theatre*, 2 vols. (1986) · A. Jacobs, *Arthur Sullivan: a Victorian musician*, 2nd edn (1992) · *The Stage* (4 April 1901) · *The Stage* (11 April 1901) · A. Goodman, *Gilbert and Sullivan's London* (1988) · R. Mander and J. Mitchenson, *The lost theatres of London* (1968) · T. Joseph, *The D'Oyly Carte Opera Company, 1875–1982* (1994) · P. Seeley, 'Who was Helen Lenoir?', *The Savoyard*, 21/2 (1982) · MSS, Theatre Museum, London, files of D'Oyly Carte and of Opera Comique and Royalty Theatres · private information (2004)

Archives Morgan L., Gilbert and Sullivan collection · Theatre Museum, London

Likenesses photograph, *c*.1880, repro. in Joseph, *D'Oyly Carte Opera Company* · Ellis & Walery, photograph, Theatre Museum, London [*see illus.*] · Faustin, cartoon, Theatre Museum, London; repro. in *Figaro* (1783–7) · Spy [L. Ward], cartoon, NPG; repro. in *VF* (14 Feb 1891) · drawings, repro. in L. Baily, *The Gilbert and Sullivan book* (1952) · drawings, Morgan L.

Wealth at death £253,846 17*s*. 7*d*.: resworn probate, Aug 1901, *CGPLA Eng. & Wales*

Carte, Samuel (1652–1740), antiquary and Church of England clergyman, was born on 21 October 1652 at Coventry, Warwickshire, the son of Thomas Carte, clothier. He was educated at the free school in Coventry before attending Magdalen College, Oxford, where he graduated BA in 1673 and MA in 1675. He was ordained deacon in 1673 and priest in 1677. His wife, Anne, with whom he had thirteen children between 1686 and 1704, predeceased him.

Carte was vicar of Clifton upon Dunsmore, Warwickshire, from 1684 until 1691 when he returned to Coventry as master of the free school. In 1700 he took the living of St Martin's, Leicester, where he served until his death. He was a keen advocate of baptism by immersion and of the doctrine of the Trinity; in the 1720s he engaged in protracted arguments with John Jackson, a cleric of unitarian persuasion who held a lectureship at St Martin's. Two of

Carte's sermons were published, *A Dissuasive from Murmuring*, 1694, and *The Cure of Self-Conceit*, 1705.

Carte's chief work was antiquarian, including the compilation of lists relating to parliamentary elections and the descent of bishoprics, the latter leading to the publication of his *Tabula chronologica archiepiscopatum et episcopatum in Anglia et Wallia* (1714). He collected material for a history of the town of Leicester, about which he was consulted by fellow antiquaries Browne Willis and John Throsby. John Nichols later drew extensively on Carte's research in his *History of Leicestershire*.

Carte died at Leicester on 16 April 1740, and was buried in the church of St Martin beside his wife, where an epitaph recorded his 'great learning', 'piety', and 'orthodox principles'. His will, dated 19 January 1736, requested that the 'writings which I had from Sir William Boughton' be restored. The bulk of his estate passed to his eldest son, Thomas *Carte (*bap*. 1686, *d*. 1754), the historian, among whose papers in the Bodleian Library some of the elder Carte's work can be found.   PETER SHERLOCK

Sources J. Nichols, *The history and antiquities of the county of Leicester*, 1/2 (1815) • Foster, *Alum. Oxon.* • *Letters of Samuel Johnson*, ed. G. B. Hill, 2 (1892), 281 • Nichols, *Illustrations*, 2.271, 726 • gravestone
Archives Bodl. Oxf., antiquarian collections and papers | Bodl. Oxf., Willis MS 85
Wealth at death see will, 19 Jan 1736, PRO, PROB 11/703, sig. 195

Carte, Thomas (*bap*. 1686, *d*. 1754), historian, was born in Clifton upon Dunsmore, Warwickshire, and baptized there on 23 April 1686, the son of the Revd Samuel *Carte (1652–1740), the vicar of Clifton upon Dunsmore. The identity of his mother is unclear, although Samuel Carte and his wife, Anne, had several children baptized in the early eighteenth century.

Education, ordination, and early controversy Carte attended Rugby School in 1695 and matriculated on 8 July 1698 from University College, Oxford. He obtained a BA degree from Brasenose College, Oxford, in 1702 and was ordained a deacon at Peterborough on 24 September 1704. He was incorporated at Cambridge in 1706, proceeding MA from King's College that same year. In 1707 he was appointed reader at Bath Abbey church, and on 3 June 1710 he was ordained priest. On 30 January 1714 he preached a sermon at Bath in which he defended Charles I from the charge that he had secretly instigated the Irish rising and massacre of 1641. This provoked an attack from Henry Chandler, a dissenting minister from Bath, to which Carte responded in print in May 1714 with *The Irish massacre set in a clear light*. This enjoyed a high reputation with tories, Thomas Hearne remarking in November 1714: 'I have a very great honour and respect for him [Carte], particularly for his late excellent vindication of the blessed Saint and Martyr King Charles' (*Remarks*, 4.434–4).

Carte refused to take the oaths to George I and became a nonjuror, although he rarely wore clerical garb. In June 1715 a correspondent of the nonjuror Thomas Brett wrote: 'we have lately had an accession of another valuable clergyman to our communion, Mr Carte of Bath' (Broxap, 310). During the Jacobite rising of that year Carte was suspected of disloyalty by the government, but appears to have lain low (possibly at the house of a Mr Badger, the curate of Coleshill, Warwickshire, which was the parish where William, Lord Digby, a noted nonjuror, resided).

The Atterbury plot and exile Carte seems to have been an acquaintance and possible agent for Francis Atterbury, bishop of Rochester. Atterbury was able to use his position as dean of Westminster to secure for Carte's brother John a living in the gift of the Westminster chapter. Carte was able to use his antiquarian researches as a cover for extensive travelling on behalf of Atterbury and the exiled Jacobite court. When Philip Neynoe informed upon Carte, on 13 August 1722 a proclamation offering a reward of £1000 for his arrest was issued and later published in the *London Gazette* on the 15th, describing him as 'of a middle stature, a raw-boned man, goes a little stooping, a sallow complexion, with a full grey or blue eye, his eyelids fair, inclining to red, and commonly wears a light-coloured peruke' (*DNB*). Sought for high treason, Carte took refuge with Sir Coplestone Bampfylde, third baronet, of Poltimore, near Exeter, and escaped to France. In his speech to the House of Lords on 22 March 1723 Atterbury denied that he had directed the correspondence held by Carte and George Kelly with the Jacobite court, and was even prepared to deny an intimate acquaintance with Carte. The *Freeholder's Journal*, which Carte helped to edit, was closed down in 1723 following the forfeiture of sureties for good behaviour.

In exile in France, Carte was excluded from the inner circles of Atterbury on account of being 'a very great talker, and so imprudent that way as not to distinguish friend from foe' (*Remarks*, 10.100). Lord Egmont thought that he was 'Lord Granville's' chaplain, presumably meaning George Granville, Lord Lansdowne. Consequently Carte spent much of his time in antiquarian research, particularly in collecting materials for illustrating a translation of his *History of Thuanus*. In November 1729 Swift referred to this as a 'monstrous unreasonable edition' (*Correspondence of Jonathan Swift*, 3.361). Carte as editor sent it to the printers in June 1730 and it was eventually published in seven volumes in 1733. Carte was allowed to return from exile in 1728 following the intervention of Dr Mead and the king's printer, Samuel Buckley, and Queen Caroline. He immediately tried to pick up his scholarly interests, including work on Archbishop Sancroft, and he was busy writing from Westminster in November 1728.

Historical research In May 1731 Lord Egmont recorded that Carte had visited him to look at his papers, preparatory to writing a 'Life' of the first duke of Ormond, and added in February 1732 that Carte was 'amassing vast materials' for this purpose. This work also entailed several extensive research trips to Ireland, Carte being in Dublin in August 1732 and again in March 1733. In June 1734 it was reported that Carte's work had been delayed by 'his infirmities, having been much disabled of late by a rheumatism' (*Remarks*, 9.348). February 1735 saw him at Enfield working on this project. Finally, in 1736, 'after a long anticipation and in the midst of sharp rheumatic pains' (*Correspondence of Jonathan Swift*, 4.523–4), Carte finished his *Life of James,* *duke of Ormond* (2 vols., 1736). In sending a copy to Jonathan Swift, Carte alerted him to his next project, a history of England 'upon authentic and proper materials', in order to remedy the existing works, such as Rapin, which were inadequate 'for want of a proper knowledge of the antiquities, usages, laws and constitutions of this nation' (*Correspondence of Jonathan Swift*, 4.523–4). The next few months, however, were spent in trying to suppress a pirate edition of his work on Ormond, which some Dublin booksellers were promoting. Eventually Carte had recourse to publicizing an order of the British House of Lords of 1721 that ruled it a breach of privilege for anyone to print the 'life, letters or other works of any deceased peer, without the consent of his heirs and executors' (*Eglinton MSS*, 485). Not surprisingly Carte then went into print with *Further reasons addressed to parliament for rendering more effectual an act of Queen Anne relating to vesting in authors the rights of copies, for the encouragement of learning*, in support of the bill before parliament in 1737.

In April 1738 Carte printed his proposals for his history, *A general account of the necessary material for a history of England, the society and subscriptions proposed for the expenses thereof, and the method wherein Mr Carte intends to proceed in carrying on the said work*. He then proceeded to Cambridge for a trawl of materials, staying with Sir John Hynde Cotton, third baronet, of Madingley Hall, and reorganizing his extensive collection of civil war pamphlets.

Jacobite and tory Carte's lack of political guile became apparent in the late 1730s when he became convinced that Sir Robert Walpole favoured James Stuart, the Pretender, and in conversation discussed Jacobitism extensively with the minister. This led to his being excluded from important business by the Pretender, although he still provided the exiled court with information provided by MPs such as Hynde Cotton and Sir John St Aubyn, third baronet, and City figures such as Sir John Barber and Humphrey Parsons. However, Carte was no longer a roving Jacobite agent, noting in 1739 that he made a single journey to visit his father each year, 'industriously avoiding all other parts of the kingdom, that I might not give any umbrage to the state' (Greaves, 67).

The poor reputation of Stuart government prompted Carte to engage in a pamphlet controversy. In 1741–2 he wrote *A full answer to a letter of a bystander, wherein his false calculations and misrepresentations of facts in the time of Charles II are refuted*. This may have led to a public disputation in a London coffee house, and a further pamphlet from Carte entitled *A full and clear vindication of 'A full answer to a letter from a bystander'*.

Carte was keen to fuel the anti-Hanoverianism of the early 1740s, suggesting to the exiled court in May 1743 that a newspaper be set up so that articles 'proper to be drawn up and published for your Majesty's service; the despair of getting such writings inserted hindering their being drawn on several very proper occasions that have been offered' (M. Harris, 131). Another of Carte's schemes dating from the early 1740s concerned the setting up of a more effective tory election machine, which would comprise a central co-ordinating committee of MPs and peers, possibly chaired by the duke of Beaufort, to supervise election strategy, and the setting up of clubs of local electors. However, no such directive central organization emerged to co-ordinate local efforts.

The death of Carte's father in 1740 led to a dispute between Thomas on the one hand and his siblings Samuel and Sarah on the other, over some wording in the will relating to Thomas's executorship which in certain circumstances was to fall to his siblings. In March 1744 the case came to court and Carte duly won his case. However, the dispute rumbled on, with Samuel Carte writing in his will of May 1752 of 'certain disputes depending between me and my brother Thomas Carte in respect to the legacies given and bequeathed to me by the will of my late father' (PRO, PROB 11/844, fol. 294). Samuel Carte senior's concerns about the repercussions of his son's penchant for Jacobite intrigue were seemingly vindicated when Carte was arrested in 1744 under suspicion of involvement in plans for a Jacobite rising, following a French invasion. However, Carte was released in May, claiming he had been imprisoned 'for he knew not what, and released he knew not why' (*DNB*).

In February 1744 Carte's project for a history of England had finally been launched and began to attract a significant number of subscribers, including the corporation of London, which on 18 July 1744 voted him £50 per annum for seven years, and several city companies (the Vintners, Goldsmiths, and Grocers), Oxford colleges, and prominent peers. However, several whigs who had been solicited in the past for support now declined. Lord Egmont, when approached for such a subscription first promised about 1740, wrote: 'there is reason to believe that his history will be wrote to support the doctrine of indefeasible hereditary right, in order [to] serve the Pretender' (*Egmont Diary*, 3.312). Meanwhile Carte was reputedly the author of *The case fairly stated in a letter from a member of parliament in the country interest to one of his constituents* (1745), a defence of tory participation in the 'broad-bottom' ministry, whose members included Sir John Hynde Cotton.

Marriage, death, and significance On 14 February 1747 Carte, then of Ealing, Middlesex, married at St Mildred's, Bread Street, Sarah (*d*. 1770?), daughter of Arthur Brett of Yattenden, Berkshire, who was then residing in the parish of St George the Martyr, Middlesex. They had no children. He was probably the Thomas Carte who performed the marriage ceremony of Elizabeth Brett at the same church in May 1747. Also in 1747 Carte published the first volume of his *History of England* (4 vols., 1747–55), and was immediately engulfed in a controversy over touching for the king's evil. Carte had used a story concerning a Bristol labourer, Christopher Lovell, who had been sent to France and been cured of scrofula by the Old Pretender. The fact that the disease had later returned was reported by Josiah Tucker in the *London Evening-Post* and repeated in such publications as the *Gentleman's Magazine*. Politically Carte's support for this manifestation of divine hereditary right was to lose him some financial support for his history, including that of the corporation of London, which withdrew support in a resolution of April 1748. The withdrawal of some financial support may explain why the other volumes of the *History* appeared in 1750, 1752, and 1755 (the last posthumously). However, this controversy did not deter Carte from continuing to espouse the Jacobite cause, as there is evidence of his involvement in the Elibank plot in 1752 as an intermediary between Prussia and the Jacobite court.

Carte died of diabetes on 2 April 1754 at Caldecott House, Sutton Courtenay, near Abingdon, Berkshire. In accordance with his will of July 1752 he was buried at Yattenden on 11 April. He left his estate to his wife, including any profits from the French translation of his *History*. In both 1753 and 1754 Carte had deposited part of his extensive collections (fifty-six volumes) in the Bodleian Library. In 1757 his executors handed over a further deposit relating to the *History of England*. Finally in 1778 the university purchased the life interest of the second husband of Carte's widow, Nicholas Jernegan, in the remainder of the collection.

Carte published many minor works of history, and his major works were massive in scope. His *History of Thuanus* was seven volumes, and the *History of England* four volumes. Mary Delany, after hearing Carte's *Life of Ormond* read out aloud in company, wrote that 'there is a repetition of facts that might have been avoided; it is upon the whole rather tedious, but the subject is so interesting that it carries one along' (*Autobiography … Mrs Delany*, 2.633). Historians have disagreed on Carte's importance as a source for Jacobite politics in England. His usefulness to the Pretender was limited by his tendency to indiscretion, which may have been an attempt to inflate his own importance in the eyes of other people.

STUART HANDLEY

Sources Foster, *Alum. Oxon.* · Venn, *Alum. Cant.* · G. A. Solly, *Rugby School register*, 1: 1675–1857 (1933), 20 · *Remarks and collections of Thomas Hearne*, ed. C. E. Doble and others, 11 vols., OHS, 2, 7, 13, 34, 42–3, 48, 50, 65, 67, 72 (1885–1921), vols. 4, 7, 10–11 · Nichols, *Illustrations* · Nichols, *Lit. anecdotes* · F. Madan, *A summary catalogue of Western manuscripts in the Bodleian Library at Oxford*, 3 (1895), 113–15 · *The registers of St Mildred, Bread Street*, ed. W. B. Bannerman, Harleian Society, 42 (1952), p. 42 · C. W. Russell and J. P. Prendergast, *The Carte manuscripts in the Bodleian Library, Oxford* (1871) · *Reports on the manuscripts of the earl of Eglinton*, HMC, 10 (1885) · *Manuscripts of the earl of Egmont: diary of Viscount Percival, afterwards first earl of Egmont*, 3 vols., HMC, 63 (1920–23) · *The correspondence of Jonathan Swift*, ed. H. Williams, 5 vols. (1963–5), vols. 3–4 · E. Cruickshanks, *Political untouchables: the tories and the '45* (1979) · L. Colley, *In defiance of oligarchy: the tory party, 1714–60* (1982) · P. K. Monod, *Jacobitism and the English people, 1688–1788* (1989) · will, PRO, PROB 11/811/295, fol. 333r–v · PRO, PROB 11/703, fols. 279–80 [will of Samuel Carte, father] · PRO, PROB 11/844, fol. 294 [will of Samuel Carte, brother] · R. Harris, *A patriot press: national politics and the London press in the 1740s* (1993) · J. C. D. Clark, *English society, 1688–1832: ideology, social structure and political practice during the ancien régime* (1985) · M. Harris, *London newspapers in the age of Walpole: a study in the the origins of the modern English press* (1987) · R. W. Greaves, 'Fathers and heretics in eighteenth-century Leicester', *Essays in eighteenth-century history presented to Dame Lucy Sutherland*, ed. A. Whiteman, J. S. Bromley, and P. G. M. Dickson (1973), 65–80 · J. T. Atkyns, *Reports of cases argued and determined in the high court of chancery in the times of Lord Chancellor Hardwicke*, 3 vols. (1781), 3.154–9 · C. Petrie, 'The Elibank plot, 1752–53', *TRHS*, 4th ser., 14 (1931), 175–

96 · H. Broxap, *The later non-jurors* (1924) · *The epistolary correspondence, visitation charges, speeches, and miscellanies of Francis Atterbury*, ed. J. Nichols, 5 vols. (1783–90), vol. 2 · *The autobiography and correspondence of Mary Granville, Mrs Delany*, ed. Lady Llanover, 1st ser., 3 vols. (1861), vol. 2 · *DNB*
Archives Birm. CA, antiquarian collections · BL, letters, Add. MS 21500 · Bodl. Oxf., MSS | Som. ARS, letters to Thomas Carew

Carter [*née* Stalker], **Angela Olive** (1940–1992), writer, was born on 7 May 1940 at 12 Hyde Gardens, Eastbourne, Sussex, the second child and only daughter of Hugh Alexander Stalker, a journalist, and (Sophia) Olive, *née* Farthing, who had been a cashier at Selfridge's store in Oxford Street. She spent much of her childhood in Yorkshire, near Rotherham, where she went to stay with her maternal grandmother to escape wartime bombing. She always remembered these years with affection. One uncle was a miner and she retained a sympathy with working people all her life. She said that, as a child, she grew up thinking that all sheep were black, so dense was the industrial pollution. Her grandmother's house contained three copies of Foxe's *Book of Martyrs*. Its horrific accounts of martyrdoms, and the even more horrific illustrations, may have influenced her fiction, through which violence ran like a thread.

After the war Angela Stalker was educated at Balham direct-grant school in south London. She made many cinema excursions with her father, especially to the vividly decorated Granada Cinema at Tooting. The love affair with films and film-going lasted the rest of her life, and features strongly in her fiction and essays. When she left school, her father got her a job as reporter on a local paper, the *Croydon Advertiser*; but the direct reporting of events was not her forte. She met an industrial chemist, Paul Malcolm Carter (*b*. 1931/2), and on 10 September 1960 married him, following him to Bristol when he started teaching in a technical college there. From 1962 to 1965 she read English at Bristol University, specializing in medieval literature, because she disliked the prevailing critical fashion for 'relevance' and 'social content', as advocated by F. R. Leavis and his many acolytes. She derided this as the 'eat up your broccoli' school of fiction and plunged wholeheartedly into reading legends and romances.

Angela Carter, who began to write at university, became, thereafter, one of the most startling writers of her time. Her short stories and novels were in the line of descent from Gothic fantasy, but with the strand of sexual menace made more explicit. She wrote wide-ranging essays on both literary and social subjects, notable for their sardonic wit. She delighted in paradox: thus, she was a feminist, but she detested the puritanical aspect of such beliefs; she had a soft spot for the marquis de Sade, but she deplored the concept of woman as victim. Her best writing had many of the qualities of an unexpurgated fairy story by the Brothers Grimm. Thinking back to the libertarian 1960s, she compared that period's would-be overthrow of existing moralities to the French Revolution: 'Truly, it felt like Year One' (M. Wandor, ed., *Gender and Writing*, 1983). She admired the surrealists, and one critic

Angela Olive Carter (1940–1992), by Sally Soames, 1981

called her 'the Salvador Dali of English letters' (*Daily Telegraph*, 17 Feb 1992).

Her first novel, *Shadow Dance* (sometimes reprinted as *Honeybuzzard*), was written during her second summer vacation at university and published in 1966. Two more novels followed at precocious speed: *The Magic Toyshop* (1967), one of her best and most widely read fictional works, and *Several Perceptions* (1968). With the latter she won the Somerset Maugham award, which specifies that the prize money is for foreign travel. She used it to leave her husband (they were divorced in 1972) and go to Japan; she liked to think that Maugham would have approved.

Sometimes *Shadow Dance*, *Several Perceptions*, and *Love* (1971) are referred to as the Bristol trilogy. They can all be read as grotesque fantasies, in parallel with *The Magic Toyshop*, which features a Gothic wicked uncle and a heroine under sexual and physical threat. But their settings also reflect the world in which Carter moved after she first left home, the provincial bohemia of Bristol and Bath. Here, she tried to live as much like a French left bank *habituée* as she could. She dressed in black like the singer Juliette Greco and thought the films of Jean-Luc Godard were 'some sort of touchstone'. Her most admired film actress, however, was Louise Brooks, as much for her free-living life and her stylishness as for her films, of which Pabst's version of Frank Wedekind's expressionist drama *Lulu* is the most famous. In 1988, Carter wrote her own version for the National Theatre, which remained unperformed.

In 1967 Carter had begun to publish essays in the London-based weekly *New Society*, and for the next twenty

years was one of its characteristic voices. Her time in Japan (1969–72) created a hiatus in the public appreciation that she had begun to receive for her fiction. Thereafter, for several years, many readers first encountered her through her pungent, highly original essays. (She published a first selection in book form as *Nothing Sacred* in 1982. The complete essays were published posthumously with other journalism in 1997 as *Shaking a Leg*.) One much-quoted essay, 'Lorenzo the closet-queen', attacked D. H. Lawrence's view of women. But some of her most powerful essays sprang from her experiences in Japan, including 'Once more into the mangle', a ferocious account of Japanese sado-masochistic comic books, in which she propounded a thesis she later developed at book length in *The Sadeian Woman* (1979). The women in these comics are raped, tortured, and often murdered in horrible and ingenious ways. 'But, whichever way the women go,' she wrote, 'they all go through the mangle—unless they are very wicked indeed; when they obey the Sadeian law and live happily ever after.' Carter was a child of the post-1945 welfare state, she said—'all that free milk and orange juice and cod liver oil' (S. Maitland, ed., *Very Heaven: Looking Back at the 1960s*, 1988)—and she always claimed allegiance to the protestant work ethic, but this sometimes took an eccentric form; pornography, she argued, was art with a job to do.

She had gone to Japan to join a lover; he told her he would never forget her, which she noted 'is not the kind of thing one says to a person with whom one proposes to spend the rest of one's life' (A. Carter, 'The Quilt-Maker', *Burning your Boats*, 1995). After a short-lived job with the NHK Broadcasting Company in Tokyo, she lived penuriously. She worked for a time as a bar hostess in the Ginza entertainment district, where, she said, 'I could hardly call my breasts my own' (*Independent on Sunday*). She wrote about the experience not only in a collection of semi-autobiographical short stories, *Fireworks* (1974), but also in a gleefully ironic essay, 'Poor butterfly', in which she noted the attraction of western hostesses for Japanese businessmen and described her role and that of her colleagues as 'a masturbatory device for gentlemen'.

Carter found in Japan an exoticism and an obsession with violence and style which continued to mark her own writing. She wrote often, and brilliantly, about the importance of apparently trivial details of fashion, frequently emphasizing its fetishistic aspects. Style, she thought, had 'heartless innocence'. Dandies are usually thought of as male, but Carter wrote with a dandy's wild grace. Among the authors she admired was the aesthete Ronald Firbank, about whom she wrote a radio play, *A Self-Made Man* (1984).

Her novels moved, for a period, into a macabre version of science fiction, starting with *Heroes and Villains* (1969) and followed by *The Infernal Desire Machines of Dr Hoffman* (1972) and *The Passion of New Eve* (1977). These began to seem strained, with their obsessive breaking of taboos. Harking back to her studies of medieval literature, they were also allegories, a form of writing later authors have found it hard to tackle successfully. These novels were often seized on by academic analysts of her work, because they lent themselves to thematic dissection.

One of Carter's most successful books came next, a retelling of traditional fairy stories, whose overall title *The Bloody Chamber* (1979) evoked the legend of Bluebeard's castle; she later wove some of these violent and erotic tales into the script of an intellectual horror film, *The Company of Wolves* (1984), directed by her fellow novelist and short-story writer Neil Jordan. One of Carter's most provocative books, *The Sadeian Woman*, also appeared in 1979. This was the first non-fiction title commissioned by the feminist publishing house Virago, with which she had been closely associated from its launch in 1972. With its defence of de Sade, and its teasing interpretation of his most notorious works as psychological insights into the freedom that non-procreative sex could bring for women, it created an outcry among feminists. She suggested to Virago that it should be followed by a republication of de Sade's novel *Juliette*, a tale of wickedness rewarded, but Virago declined.

After her return from Japan Carter lived in Bath again, but then settled in south London with Mark William Pearce, a potter. From the late 1970s she increasingly depended on university teaching for a regular income, holding temporary posts at, for example, the universities of Sheffield and East Anglia in England, Brown in the United States, and Adelaide in Australia. Her teaching helped to strengthen her following among students, but her campus life meant that some of the direct observation of a wider world that gave such force to her essays and fiction began to fade. Her novel *Nights at the Circus* (1984) marked a change of approach. Her previous novels and short stories had been bejewelled miniatures (one East European translator of her densely written, sparkling prose described it as 'embroidery'); but this was much longer than any previous book. The story of Fevvers, a Cockney trapeze artist who grows wings, it was laden with symbolism, and it took her into the mainstream of the 'magic realism' school of writing, whose founding father is usually said to be the South American novelist Gabriel Garcia Marquez and whose best-known practitioner in Britain at the time was Carter's friend Salman Rushdie.

Unfortunately, *Nights at the Circus* had a mixed reception, and Carter wrote only one more novel: *Wise Children* (1991). This too was more diffuse than her earlier work, but it had an attractively light touch. Set in south London, the fantastical life story of Dora and Nora Hazard evokes music-hall and cinema history, with strong undertones of the transformations and sexual confusions of *A Midsummer Night's Dream* and *As You Like It*.

There had been a crammed toy-box in the Carter–Pearce household long before there was a child. In 1983 Carter had a late and much loved son, Alexander, with Mark Pearce, whom she married on 2 May 1991. She told one fellow writer, 'Sometimes, when I read my back pages, I'm quite appalled at the violence of my imagination. Before I had a family and so on' (*Vogue*, August 1985). She was a good judge of her own writing; probably her best work

was done before she was forty. At that age, also, she suddenly changed her appearance, from her previous sprite-like look to that of a wise witch from a fairy tale. She stopped hennaing her hair and pursuing fashion. She was much older than Pearce, and the change emphasized this. The two of them went around London by narrow boat, exploring the hidden backwaters of canals. They sometimes wore identical greatcoats.

Carter spoke with a slight stutter, and her conversation was ribald, allusive, and often caustic; none of this helped to make her a well-known public figure. She depended on readers falling in love with her baroque prose, aflame with artifice; and for many of those initial readers she was an almost private passion. Early in spring 1991 she was diagnosed with lung cancer. She died in London on 16 February 1992 and was cremated at Putney Vale crematorium. The obituaries were longer and more generous than most of the reviews she received in her lifetime. In the days after her death there was a sudden upsurge in sales of her books, and many sold out: 'There is a popular necrophilia,' said one friend, the cultural historian Marina Warner. Carter became one of the most widely taught novelists in British universities. Soon three posthumous collections were published: *Burning your Boats* (1995), containing all her short stories; *The Curious Room* (1996), containing her forays into drama, most notably her radio plays; and *Shaking a Leg*. Her memorial celebration was held at the Ritzy Cinema in Brixton, south London, her beloved Granada, Tooting, having been converted into a bingo hall.

PAUL BARKER

Sources A. Carter, *Nothing sacred* (1982) · L. Sage, *Angela Carter* (1994) · P. Barker, 'The magic story-teller', *Independent on Sunday* (8 Jan 1995) · personal knowledge (2004) · b. cert. · m. cert. [Paul Malcolm Carter] · m. cert. [Mark William Pearce] · S. Clapp, 'Diary', *London Review of Books* (12 March 1992)
Archives UCL, corresp.
Likenesses F. Godwin, photograph, 1976, repro. in F. Godwin, *Landmarks* (2001) · S. Soames, photograph, 1981, NPG [*see illus.*] · photograph, repro. in Sage, *Angela Carter* · photographs, repro. in Carter, *Nothing sacred* · photographs, repro. in Barker, 'The magic story-teller'

Carter [*formerly* Barrington]**, Ann** (*d.* 1629), protester, of Maldon in Essex, was twice leader of protests over food in 1629, actions which brought her brief public notice and execution in the same year. Details of her parentage and birth, or whether she married more than once, are unknown.

Ann Barrington married John Carter, a Maldon butcher, on 6 December 1620. What little is known of her personal life after marriage suggests that the couple struggled to maintain a living. Rather more is on record about her public relationship with the authorities. By 1629 she had had a number of clashes with the town's rulers which reflected a willingness by her to defy authority. Questioned in 1623 as to why she was not at church, she told one of the town's rulers, 'yf he woold provide one to do hir worke shee would goe', adding that 'she searved god as well as he' (Essex RO, D/B3/3/1/19, fol. 154). A year later she prevented the arrest of her husband, cudgelling the town's serjeant-at-arms in the process.

In March 1629 Ann Carter was part of a large crowd of women who protested over the export of grain. Defying attempts by Maldon's authorities to stop them, the women marched to where foreign ships were loading and made the sailors pour grain into their bonnets and aprons. The women's actions reflected a belief that to allow grain to be exported when local populations faced dearth and possibly famine was both against the moral economy and government policy. As one of the women replied when asked who had prompted her to riot: 'the crie of the country and her own want' (Essex RO, D/B3/3/208). Maldon's authorities suspected Ann Carter of being the women's leader. Her previous history as well as her behaviour at examination (where the surviving document with its many crossings-out suggests a confidence to challenge any description of her action as either violent or illegal), certainly qualified her for the role. That she had found herself in the same month presented to the court for a minor infringement of market regulations while the town's authorities failed to stop the larger activities of foreign merchants probably increased her sense of outrage.

To this point, the episode reflected the protocols of early modern protest—crowd restraint was matched by reform by authority—and Ann Carter's actions were no different from those of other women who often predominated in crowd actions over food, exploiting the licence given them by their marginal political and legal positions and responsibility for feeding their families. But two months later Ann led a second crowd of several hundred unemployed clothworkers. This time there was no doubt about her role. She had ridden through the region, and had a local baker write letters, to summon support. Giving herself the title of Captain, she was reported to have said, 'Come my brave lads of Maulden, I will be your Leader, for we will not starve' (BL, Harleian MS 7000, fol. 259). Two protests in as many months challenged the convention whereby crowds expressed contrition in exchange for conciliation by the authorities. The changed context of intensifying depression in the cloth industry and the changed nature of the crowd's behaviour—the protesters broke into a grain store and took away a large quantity of grain—alarmed the central government which moved swiftly to punish the attack. Only a week after the riot a special judicial commission sat to execute justice. Ann Carter was found guilty and hanged the next day, 30 May 1629. This exceptional punishment—she was the only woman hanged in the period for a food riot—owed less to the nature of her crime than to the political instability of Charles I's government. Her husband survived her, but his frequent appearances before the town's courts confirm the family's slide into poverty and, perhaps, suggest anger at the authorities' treatment of his wife.

JOHN WALTER

Sources J. Walter, 'Grain riots and popular attitudes to the law: Maldon and the crisis of 1629', *An ungovernable people: the English and their law in the 17th and 18th centuries*, ed. J. Brewer and J. Styles (1980), 47–84 • borough records, Maldon, Essex, Essex RO, D/B3/3 • Bodl. Oxf., MS Firth c. 4 • BL, Harleian MS 7000, fol. 259 • Privy council register, PRO, PC2/39, 1628–1630 • State papers domestic, April– May 1629, PRO, SP16/141–142 • N. Z. Davis, 'Women on top', *Society and culture in early modern France* (1978), 148 • parish register, Maldon, St Peter's, Essex RO, T/R 149/3 [marriage]

Carter, Charles (1707–1764), planter and politician in America, was born at Corotoman, Lancaster county, Virginia, the seventh of twelve children of Robert 'King' *Carter (1663–1732), Virginia planter, merchant, and politician, and the third with his second wife, the widow Elizabeth Willis, née Landon (1683–1719). As one of the wealthiest and most influential men of early eighteenth-century Virginia, King Carter owned 45 plantations in nine counties, over 1000 slaves, and more than 200,000 unsettled back-country acres; he also served as speaker of the Virginia house of burgesses, speaker of the council of Virginia, and acting governor of the colony. Although less well known than his father or his brother the diarist Landon *Carter (1710–1778), Charles took full advantage of King Carter's remarkable economic and political legacy, and became one of the most powerful political figures in mid-eighteenth-century Virginia.

At the age of twelve Charles Carter was sent with his brothers Robert and Landon to receive a classical education at Solomon Low's private school in London. After four years of satisfactory, but not exceptional, progress, he returned to Virginia and began a more practical schooling in estate management and public service. His father had already begun shifting substantial acres on the upper Rappahannock River into his name, and this accelerated after his return to Virginia in 1724. King Carter's death in August 1732 brought Charles additional lands in four counties, as well as the slaves and equipment to build productive plantations. That year Charles moved to Stanstead, which he used as his principal seat for the next two decades; about 1750 he built Cleve in King George county, and lived there until his death. Although always a major producer of tobacco, he diversified earlier than many planters into wheat, copper mining, winemaking, milling, and baking. Even in death his will instructed his survivors to follow an elaborate set of plans to diversify and improve production at Cleve. Like most élite Virginians of his era, he maintained elaborate credit accounts with British merchants and shippers.

Carter's public career paralleled his economic achievements. Upon reaching the age of twenty-one he immediately assumed public duties, first as a director of the new town of Fallmouth (1728), then as naval officer for the Rappahannock (1729), and next as a justice of the peace for King George county (1734). In 1736 Charles was one of three commissioners appointed by Lord Fairfax to supervise the surveying of the extensive Northern Neck proprietorship. He was styled 'colonel' by the late 1730s, and did become lieutenant of King George county in 1752. Although he lost his first house of burgesses election in 1734, he won the following year and in six subsequent contests, serving continuously in the colonial assembly until his death.

By the 1740s Carter had assumed major leadership roles

in the house, chairing important committees, speaking forcefully on legislation, and working out compromises with the upper chamber. Although he sought but never attained the coveted speaker's chair, by the 1750s he was one of the most powerful men in the assembly, working tirelessly on numerous issues and problems. In 1759 he sponsored legislation to study alternatives to a tobacco economy that was placing many of his fellow planters heavily in debt to British merchants. Using his own economic diversification as a model, he corresponded with the Royal Society of Arts and proposed that it help Virginians to experiment with hemp, iron, tar, pitch, turpentine, saltpetre, salt, fishing, potash, wine, and silk production. Carter's activities may have helped turn some planters slowly toward wheat and other crops over the next decade.

Carter's familial activities were equally busy and prolific. He was married three times: in 1728 to Mary Walker (d. 1742); in December 1742 to Anne (1725–1757), daughter of William Byrd (II); and in 1763 to Lucy Taliaferro, who survived him. These unions produced thirteen children, three sons and ten daughters. Carter died of 'confirmed dropsy through use of Opiates' on 26 April 1764, at Cleve, where he was buried (Diary of Colonel Landon Carter, 898). His will distributed over 300 slaves, a dozen plantations, and more than £12,000 among his large family.

JOHN G. KOLP

Sources F. Harrison, ed., 'The will of Charles Carter of Cleve', Virginia Magazine of History and Biography, 31 (1923), 39–69 • The diary of Colonel Landon Carter of Sabine Hall, 1752–1778, ed. J. P. Greene, 2 vols. (1965); repr. (1987) • R. L. Hilldrup, 'A campaign to promote the prosperity of colonial Virginia', Virginia Magazine of History and Biography, 67 (1959), 410–28 • P. P. Hoffman, ed., Guide to the microfilm edition of the Carter family papers, 1659–1797, in the Sabine Hall collection (Charlottesville, Va., 1967) • F. C. Baldwin, 'Early architecture of the Rappahannock valley, 2: Cleve Manor', Journal of the American Institute of Architects, 3 (1915), 234–40 • University of Virginia, Charlottesville, Virginia, Carter family MSS [microfilm] • The papers of George Washington, ed. W. W. Abbot and others, [10 vols.] (1983–) • H. R. McIlwaine and J. P. Kennedy, eds., Journals of the house of burgesses of Virginia, 1619–1776, 13 vols. (1905–15) • Executive journals of the council of colonial Virginia, 4, ed. H. R. McIlwaine (1930) • King George county deed books, Library of Virginia, Richmond, Virginia • Letters of Robert Carter, 1720–1727, ed. L. B. Wright (1940) • Robert 'King' Carter: builder of Christ Church (1986)

Archives University of Virginia, Charlottesville • Virginia Historical Society, Richmond | L. Cong., George Washington MSS • RSA, guard books

Likenesses J. Hesselius, portrait, c.1730–1739, repro. in Harrison, ed., 'The will of Charles Carter of Cleve' • C. Bridges, portrait, c.1735–1740, repro. in L. M. Watson, 'The colonel and his lady come home', Antiques, 74 (1958), 436–8

Wealth at death over £12,000; more than 300 slaves; tens of thousands of acres of land: Harrison, ed., 'The will of Charles Carter of Cleve'

Carter, Sir Charles Bonham- (1876–1955), colonial governor and army officer, was born on 25 February 1876 at 91 Gloucester Terrace, Kensington, London, the ninth son of Henry Bonham *Carter (1827–1921), barrister and company director, and his wife, Sibella Charlotte (1836/7–1916), daughter of George Warde *Norman (1793–1882),

merchant and director of the Bank of England. He was educated at Clifton College in 1889–94 and at the Royal Military College, Sandhurst, where he was awarded the sword of honour. It was while at Sandhurst that he realized the lack of general education in the army, and a determination to rectify this took root. In February 1896 he was commissioned 2nd lieutenant, 2nd battalion Queen's Own Royal West Kent regiment, spending a leave in London where he studied singing. He could have sung professionally, but instead remained a gifted amateur.

A late developer, who never shone scholastically, Bonham-Carter found his niche in the army. When the Second South African War broke out he was in Egypt, but in 1899 he returned home to raise a mounted infantry unit to serve in South Africa. He served for nineteen months, including a short spell as adjutant, but he was invalided home in November 1901 with enteric fever, an illness which was to have later repercussions. He was awarded the queen's medal with four clasps.

On 22 February 1902 Bonham-Carter married Gladys Beryl, daughter of Lieutenant-Colonel Arthur Blayney Coddington RE; they had two sons. That marriage having ended in 1909, he married on 3 January 1911 Gabrielle Madge Jeanette (b. 1886/7), daughter of Captain Ernest Fisher. This was a marriage of great happiness and companionship, and they had a son. In 1902–4 Bonham-Carter attended the Staff College, Camberley (p.s.c.). In 1904–6 he was an instructor at Sandhurst, where he was able to develop his views on broadening the role of education in the army. For eight years from 1906 he held staff appointments; first as brigade major at Gibraltar, followed by a spell with the coast defences of southern command at Portsmouth. In 1910 he was appointed company commander in the 2nd battalion Royal West Kent regiment, stationed on the north-west frontier, India. Two years later he was posted back to Britain.

In July 1914 Bonham-Carter was ordered to Scotland as GSO2 to help organize the Cromarty Firth as a defended port. This probably saved his life, for his unit, the 1st battalion of the Royal West Kent regiment, was almost wiped out at the onset of war. Bonham-Carter rejoined his regiment in France on 14 November, when he immediately took a draft up to the front line. On 1 January 1915 he was transferred to First Army headquarters as liaison officer to Sir Douglas Haig. A year later he was promoted brevet lieutenant-colonel and appointed GSO1 to the 7th division. He fought in the battle of the Somme, and his outstanding qualities were recognized as those of a skilled and visionary planner, who was respected and liked by both superiors and subordinates. As a result he was posted as GSO1 to the senior of two staff schools at Hesdin, where his passion for training and education in the widest sense was given full rein.

Between April and October 1917 Bonham-Carter acted as chief of staff to General Pulteney, commander of 111 corps. In October 1917 he was posted to general headquarters to take charge of the training of the whole of the British army in France. In that year Bonham-Carter was made a DSO, being appointed CMG in 1919. After the war he received command of the 2nd battalion of the Royal Dublin Fusiliers, with whom he served in Constantinople and in India in 1919–20. On his return to England he took command of the 129th South Wessex infantry brigade, Territorial Army. Though this was only a part-time post he was typically enthusiastic, and bought a house near Bath. In 1924 the result of his enteric fever in the Second South African War manifested itself, and he had four major operations in two and a half years. He was appointed to the rank of major-general in 1926, and from 1927 to 1931 was director of staff duties at the War Office. He was commander of the 4th division in 1931–3, gaining the rank of lieutenant-general in 1933. From 1933 to 1936 he was director-general of the Territorial Army. During these appointments he played an important role in educational affairs within the army. He was knighted in 1935.

In February 1936, at the age of sixty, Bonham-Carter was appointed governor and commander-in-chief of Malta. He arrived at a vital time when all was not well in the island: the constitution had been suspended for three years and the political situation was confused, with fascist Italy posing a real threat. Aware of the anti-British feeling, and appalled by the exclusiveness of the British population on the island, it was Bonham-Carter's training as a commander and staff officer that now stood him in good stead. He began by making it his business to meet the most influential people on the island, the parish priests; he also attended every village club in Malta and Gozo, where the islanders foregathered. He formed a close working relationship with Malcolm Macdonald, who in 1938 had become secretary of state for the colonies, and between them they devised the 1939 Macdonald constitution, a step towards self-government for Malta. When war broke out in 1939 Bonham-Carter remained in overall command of the island, his main task being to oversee the defence of Malta.

In April 1940, with one year of his term as governor to run, Bonham-Carter had a major heart attack. He was forced to retire, but his contribution towards gaining the loyalty of the Maltese people during the war was acknowledged to be very great. He was appointed GCB in 1941. Charming, cultivated, a born teacher, a thinker, and a man of vision, with the common touch, he contributed much to each post throughout his life, not least to the benefit of the army. In retirement he chaired the board of governors of two schools connected with the army. He was aide-de-camp general to the king in 1938–41. Bonham-Carter died on 21 October 1955, aged seventy-nine, at his home, Durford Height, Petersfield, Hampshire. His body was cremated at Petersfield and the ashes scattered in the crematorium garden.   JOAN CARNWATH

Sources V. Bonham-Carter, *In a liberal tradition* (1960) · H. Smith and A. Koster, *Lord Strickland, servant of the crown*, 2 (1984) · J. Alexander, *Mabel Strickland* (1996) · *WWW* · *The Times* (22 Oct 1955) · b. cert. · m. cert. [G. Fisher] · d. cert. · Burke, *Peerage* (1939)
Archives CAC Cam., corresp., journal, and papers | King's Lond., Liddell Hart C., corresp. with Sir B. H. Liddell Hart

Wealth at death £10,691 18s. 9d.: probate, 1955, *CGPLA Eng. & Wales*

Carter, Sir Edgar Bonham- (1870–1956), jurist and legal administrator, was born in London on 2 April 1870, the fifth of the eleven sons of Henry Bonham *Carter (1827–1921), barrister and managing director of the Guardian Assurance Company, and his wife, Sibella Charlotte (1836/7–1916), daughter of George Warde *Norman (1793–1882), a director of the Bank of England. Florence Nightingale was a relative, and took great interest in his early career. General Sir Charles Bonham-*Carter and Sir Maurice Bonham Carter were among his brothers. He was educated at Clifton College, to which his loyalty was lifelong: he was vice-chairman of its council from 1934 to 1946. At New College, Oxford, he obtained second-class honours in jurisprudence in 1892, and played rugby football as a forward for the university and for England. He read law with Edward Beaumont, and was called to the bar by Lincoln's Inn in 1895.

In 1899, after the conquest of Sudan, Bonham-Carter was chosen by Lord Cromer at the age of twenty-nine to devise and set on foot a complete system of civil and criminal law in Sudan, where no legal system existed. He became judicial adviser, later legal secretary and a member of the governor-general's council, the only senior civilian member of a military administration. His success was immediate and brilliant. In the year of his appointment he introduced a simplified version of the Indian penal and criminal procedure codes; his modification of the Indian law of murder and homicide was considered by most Sudan judges to be an improvement on the original. In 1900 there followed a simple code of civil procedure, derived from the Indian, substantive law being based on the English common law, Sudan statute, and (particularly as to land) local customary law. He rescued Islamic law courts from decay, and gave them a solid organization under an ordinance promulgated in 1902. These codes established a complete system of courts with appropriate jurisdiction, and he followed up his acts as a lawgiver by years of guidance, firm but courteous and patient, of the British, Egyptian, and Sudanese officers and magistrates who then staffed the courts. The law so declared and administered was understood by the people, by the early amateur magistracy, and later by the professional judges; to the ordinary Sudanese his work seemed the embodiment of justice; the structure was maintained after the independence of Sudan.

In 1917 Bonham-Carter became senior judicial officer in Baghdad and in 1919 judicial adviser in Mesopotamia, then freed from Turkish rule. There his task was different, for the Ottoman law existed in the vilayets; he laid no foundations, but built up and modernized what he found, and established a system of courts under judges with professional qualifications, and a competent clerical staff. He founded a school of law; established the machinery of justice; and drafted a great deal of the necessary legislation himself. In the face of the political ferment engendered by an ardent nationalism which accompanied the transition from subjection to freedom, by the sympathy and trust which he inspired he set up a soundly based Iraqi judicial system under Iraqi judges which survived the transition from mandate to treaty, and finally to complete independence. Nuri Said called him the father and founder of the legal system in the country; Gertrude Bell wrote of him as the wisest of men.

In 1921 Bonham-Carter left the Middle East to begin a new phase of public work at home, which continued until his death, in spite of increasing lameness in his later years. From 1922 to 1925 he represented North-East Bethnal Green as a Liberal member of the London county council, and became the council's representative on the governing body of the School of Oriental and African Studies, to which he was regularly reappointed until his resignation in 1945. In 1926 he married Charlotte Helen, daughter of Colonel William Lewis Kinloch Ogilvy, 60th rifles; they had no children.

With the decline in Liberal fortunes, he did not sit again as a councillor, but an interest in housing and planning remained with him. He was chairman of the National Housing and Town Planning Council from 1940 until 1942; and remained a member of the council of the Town and Country Planning Association until his death. From 1927 to 1950 he was a member of the executive committee of the National Trust, and also of its finance and general purposes committee; and he gave long service to the Commons, Open Spaces and Footpaths Preservation Society. From the 1920s he had been interested in the work of First Garden City Ltd in developing the garden city at Letchworth, and from 1929 to 1939 he was a chairman in whom there was complete confidence. His vision and understanding of educational matters as a governor of Letchworth grammar school won the admiration of his colleagues. At his death he was the last surviving founder member of the Gordon Memorial Trust and the Kitchener School Trust.

From the 1930s he was closely associated with the British School of Archaeology in Iraq, towards the foundation of which Gertrude Bell had left a legacy. The friendship and respect which had grown up between Gertrude Bell and Bonham-Carter during his years in Iraq impelled him, with his wife, to throw himself into the task of raising by public subscription a sufficient fund to realize the project. In 1932 the school was launched with adequate finances, and with Bonham-Carter as the first chairman of the executive committee, an office which he held until 1950, when he yielded to eighty years and impaired health, but remained a member until his death. From 1953 he was president of the North-East Hampshire Agricultural Association.

Bonham-Carter was distinguished in appearance, and was remarkable for his courtesy. Although not a fluent speaker, he impressed all who knew him with the great range of his knowledge, his gentle wisdom, his solicitude for those with or for whom he worked, and his moral strength, touched with a delicate humour.

In 1916 Bonham-Carter was awarded the order of the Nile, first class; he was appointed CMG in 1909, CIE in

1919, and KCMG in 1920. He died at his wife's estate, Binsted Wyck, near Alton, Hampshire, on 24 April 1956. He was survived by his wife.   K. O'C. HAYES, *rev.*

Sources *The Times* (25 April 1956) · *WWW* · private information (1971) · personal knowledge (1971) · H. V. F. Winstone, *Gertrude Bell* (1978) · *CGPLA Eng. & Wales* (1956)
Archives Hants. RO, corresp. and papers; letters to his family | U. Durham L., corresp. with Sir Reginald Wingate
Likenesses W. Stoneman, photograph, 1931, NPG
Wealth at death £45,287 7s. 11d.: probate, 24 July 1956, *CGPLA Eng. & Wales*

Carter, Edmund (d. in or before **1788**), topographer, is known to have mapped the estate of the Revd Mr Smith at Weston Longueville, Norfolk, in 1731. Five years later he had an address near St Giles's Church, Norwich, from where he advertised as a tutor in mathematics, an estate surveyor, and a seller of black ink, and announced a calendar he had compiled for fifty-six years in advance. His *Perpetual and Universal Table, Readily Shewing the Day of the Month and of the Week* was published in 1743, by which time he had moved to Cambridge. There he kept a school near St Botolph's Church and compiled histories of the county and university of Cambridge. He asked the antiquary William Cole for help in this task. According to Cole's notes on his copy of Carter's history of the university (Bodl. Oxf., Gough Camb. 39), Cole refused as he had a low opinion of the author and did not want to be associated with him. Others were more forthcoming: the Revd Robert Smyth, rector of Woodstone, near Peterborough, provided much material (though mainly from standard printed sources); Dr John Newcome, master of St John's College, communicated some of Baker's manuscripts; and the Revd Robert Masters of Corpus Christi College read Carter's correspondence.

Cole described Carter as 'a cripple in both his legs' and as 'having a small family and a bad wife' (Bodl. Oxf., Gough Camb. 39), and used these facts to explain that during the compilation of his histories he had been forced to move to Ware in Hertfordshire, where again he kept a school. By the time *The History of the County of Cambridge* and *The History of the University of Cambridge* were published in 1753, he was a schoolmaster in Chelsea, Middlesex.

Carter's history of Cambridgeshire, the first printed work to call itself a history of the county, describes the towns of Cambridge and Ely, their parishes, and the diocese. This is followed by a county gazetteer, which includes information about each parish and lists freeholders in 1722. The volume ends with lists of notable figures: gentry in 1433, nobility in 1673, martyrs, prelates, statesmen, learned writers, kings of the East Angles, members of parliament from 1660, sheriffs from 1509, and archdeacons of Sudbury. His history of the university incorporates material from earlier published histories and starts with a description of the institution, its degrees, officers, and public buildings. After a list of inns and halls, Carter describes the history of each college, its foundation, founders and benefactors, bishops, masters and fellows, distinguished members including bishops and learned writers, livings, buildings, and arms. He ends with lists of chancellors, vice-chancellors, proctors, taxors, professors, public orators, members of parliament, printers, and the current officers of the university. Both works contain contemporary information and also describe the destruction of ecclesiastical decorations and ejections from college fellowships during the 1640s. Despite being badly arranged and full of errors, the history of Cambridgeshire was of sufficient interest to be reprinted and updated in 1819. William Cole was not complimentary about the history of the university and Richard Gough described it as a 'flimsey account' (Gough, 218). Although Carter compiled notes for a second edition, this was not published. Carter's later career is not known; his widow died in Enfield workhouse on 15 September 1788.   SARAH BENDALL

Sources E. Carter, *The history of the University of Cambridge* (1753) [annotated copy with MS notes by William Cole, Bodl. Oxf., Gough Camb. 39–40 ; see also annotated copy with notes by Richard Farmer, BL, MS 731.i.11, and annotated copy with corrections by author, BL, MS 731.i.14] · F. W. Steer and others, *Dictionary of land surveyors and local map-makers of Great Britain and Ireland, 1530–1850*, ed. P. Eden, 2nd edn, ed. S. Bendall, 2 vols. (1997) · R. V. Wallis and P. J. Wallis, *Biobibliography of British mathematics and its applications: part II, 1701–1760* (1992) · A. Taigel and T. Williamson, 'Some early geometric gardens in Norfolk', *Journal of Garden History*, 11 (1991), 1–111 · R. G. [R. Gough], *British topography*, [new edn], 1 (1780) · A. P. M. Wright, 'Cambridgeshire', *English county histories: a guide*, ed. C. R. J. Currie and C. P. Lewis (1994), 62–70 · Nichols, *Lit. anecdotes*, 2.694; 5.47; 6.112, 201 · *GM*, 1st ser., 58 (1788), 841 · *DNB*

Archives BL, copy of *History of University of Cambridge* with his MS notes and additions · Bodl. Oxf., collections relating to statutes of Cambridge University, MSS Gough Camb. 44–45

Wealth at death widow died in workhouse: Carter, *The history*

Carter, Elizabeth

Carter, Elizabeth (1717–1806), poet, translator, and writer, was born on 16 December 1717 at Deal in Kent, the first child and eldest daughter of the Revd Nicolas Carter (1688–1774), perpetual curate of Deal Chapel, and one of the six preachers at Canterbury Cathedral, and his first wife, Margaret (*d. c.*1728), only daughter and heir of Richard Swayne of Bere Regis, Dorset. Margaret, who married with a fortune of £15,000, died when Carter was about ten. Montagu Pennington, Carter's nephew and biographer, says Margaret's death was hastened by the loss of her fortune in the South Sea Bubble, but if so, as the Bubble burst in 1720, it seems a delayed reaction. In the seventeenth century members of the Carter family were active in the parliamentary cause in the civil war; in the eighteenth they were loyal supporters of the monarchy.

Education and early career Nicolas Carter, an accomplished linguist who published several pamphlets and sermons, educated all his children, both boys and girls, to a high standard. Elizabeth, however, was at first such a slow learner that he advised her to give up classical languages. Yet by dint of application she became so expert at Greek that, as she used to relate, 'Samuel Johnson had said, speaking of some celebrated scholar, that he understood Greek better than any one whom he had ever known, except Elizabeth Carter' (Pennington, 1.13). She also prepared her half-brother, Henry (son of her father's second marriage, to Mary Bean), for Cambridge in 1756, much to the consternation of the fellows of Corpus Christi College.

Elizabeth Carter (1717–1806), by Katharine Read, *c.*1765

In order to persevere with her studies she resorted to various extreme measures. She used to employ a sexton to wake her between 4 and 5 a.m. by pulling a string attached to a bell hanging at the head of her bed. To keep herself awake late at night she used to wrap wet towels about her head, chew green tea, and take snuff, until she was both addicted to snuff and painfully vulnerable to debilitating headaches for the rest of her life. By these means she first learned Latin and Greek, then Hebrew, French, Italian, and Spanish. Later in life she also taught herself Portuguese and Arabic. When she was about twenty she studied German on the recommendation of her father and his friends who wanted her to seek a place at court. Although she decided that court life was not for her, she liked the language and towards the end of her life enjoyed conversations about German literature with Queen Charlotte, who lent her German books. To a less advanced level she studied astronomy, mathematics, and Greek history and geography under the antiquarian and natural philosopher Thomas Wright, to whom she alludes in her poem 'While clear the night, and ev'ry thought serene'. Through him she met one of her most important friends, Catherine Talbot, who lived in the household of Thomas Secker (then bishop of Oxford, later dean of St Paul's, and afterwards archbishop of Canterbury). In order to learn more 'feminine' accomplishments, she boarded for a year in Canterbury at the house of a refugee French minister, M. Le Suer, and learned needlework, which she busied herself with throughout her life, as well as drawing and music which she claimed were not her forte. While her scholarship was outstanding by any standards, and certainly prodigious for a woman of her time, her proficiency in domestic skills to a large degree saved her from the general censure directed against learned ladies. Samuel Johnson's remark upon hearing a lady commended for her learning crystallizes contemporary attitudes:

> A man is in general better pleased when he has a good dinner upon his table, than when his wife talks Greek. My old friend, Mrs. Carter, could make a pudding as well as translate Epictetus from the Greek, and work a handkerchief as well as compose a poem. (*Works of Samuel Johnson*, ed. J. Hawkins, 1787, 11.205)

It is by this 'intended compliment', as Roger Lonsdale says, that she is 'perhaps doomed to be best remembered' (R. Lonsdale, ed., *Eighteenth-Century Women Poets*, 1989, 167). The study of religion was one of Carter's chief concerns throughout her life, and her piety no less than her domestic science helped her gain a wider acceptance than most women writers in her day.

Carter first came to notice as a writer in the poetry pages of the *Gentleman's Magazine*, whose proprietor, Edward Cave, was a friend of her father's. Her first published poem, a riddle on fire (*GM*, 1st ser., 4, 4 November 1734), printed above the name Eliza, prompted a reply from Sylvius (*GM*, 5 June 1735). Her youth, talent, and sex made her something of a sensation; various epigrams, riddles, and verses celebrated her as a prodigy. With her father's encouragement she went to London to establish a literary career, spending some part of each winter from 1735 to 1739 in the city, mostly staying with her merchant uncle in Bishopsgate, or her friend Mrs Rooke. She joined Cave's circle of (mostly minor) writers, and through him she got to know Thomas Birch, Jane Brereton, Moses Browne, Mary Masters, Richard Savage, and the as yet little-known Samuel Johnson. Johnson, who remained her friend until his death in 1784, celebrated her in Greek and Latin epigrams, and together with Cave and Birch fostered her talents, suggesting projects and promoting her publications. In 1738 Cave printed a slim quarto pamphlet of her poems, *Poems on Particular Occasions*. The following year he printed her translations, *An Examination of Mr. Pope's Essay on Man, from the French of M. Crousaz* and *Sir Isaac Newton's Philosophy Explain'd for the Use of the Ladies*, from the Italian of Francesco Algarotti. All three works appeared anonymously and were not prized by Carter when she later became famous for her Greek scholarship. Birch's attentions were assiduous. After encouraging Carter to translate Algarotti, he unsuccessfully tried to secure for her the patronage of Frances, countess of Hertford, through the agency of her secretary, John Dalton, and then gave the translation a glowing review in the *History of the Works of the Learned* (1 June 1739). (Although the countess declined to accept a dedication, she began a correspondence with Carter. Dalton ten years later became Carter's suitor, but she rejected him for some real or imagined impropriety in his behaviour.) Birch's persistence suggests an amorous as well as intellectual interest and it may have been an unwanted proposal of marriage from him which led to Carter's abrupt departure from London in June 1739.

It is commonly supposed that Carter spent the next decade in Deal in retreat from marriage and from writing. She certainly devoted much time to her female friends in Kent during the 1740s, but not only does she record in her letters frequent and flirtatious attendance at balls and parties, she was also still writing poetry. When Cave wrote to her in 1746 complaining that he had not received any poems from her for a couple of years, she had already contributed over twenty poems to his magazine. She published riddles, odes, epigrams, and poems in the Augustan mode. Some of her poems were circulating in manuscript, which is how Samuel Richardson came across her 'Ode to Wisdom'. He inserted it in his novel *Clarissa* (vol. 2, 1747), attributing it to a lady, not knowing its author. This piracy caused Carter some distress, which was alleviated by the authorized publication of the corrected poem in the *Gentleman's Magazine* (17 December 1747; actually appeared January 1748), and by a public apology from and private reconciliation with Richardson. She joined his circle of readers and advisers but was never as admiring of him as his other female friends. To her annoyance some of her poems also appeared without her permission in anthologies such as Robert Dodsley's *Collection of Poems by Several Hands* (1748, 1755–8).

In the 1750s Carter published several short works arising out of personal relationships. Her friendship with Johnson led her to try to keep his *Rambler* going by recruiting both readers and contributors. She encouraged Hester Mulso Chapone and Talbot to write for it and herself contributed two papers which were both imaginatively lively and morally improving (*Rambler*, 44, 1750, and 100, 1751). Another short anonymous publication is also attributed to her in some library catalogues and evidences less happy circumstances: *Remarks on the Athanasian Creed* 'by a Lady' (probably 1753). It is an intervention in an acrimonious dispute between Nicolas Carter on the one hand, and the Revd Mr Randolph and the mayor and corporation of Deal on the other. The dispute concerning the extent of Nicolas Carter's powers and privileges arose over his refusal to read the Athanasian creed because he disagreed with the doctrine of the divinity of Christ. The matter was finally settled by a donation from his brother which enabled him to hire a clerk to read the creed in his place. The tone of the *Remarks* is much more contentious than the sober reasonableness of Carter's other religious writings—marginalia, prayers, letters, and 'Answers to objections concerning the Christian religion'—first collected in Pennington's *Memoirs*.

Translating Epictetus In 1749 Carter was encouraged by friends to undertake two translations. William Duncombe sought her involvement in his translation of the complete *Odes* of Horace. She declined to be a major contributor, but in 1751 completed a translation of book 1, ode 15, which was published in Duncombe's *The Works of Horace in Several Hands* (1757). More importantly Talbot encouraged her to translate the works of the Greek Stoic philosopher Epictetus. It is this work which brought her fame and lasting respect. She worked on the translation under the supervision of Secker and Talbot from 1749 to 1756, but always interrupted her work when domestic responsibilities such as the education of her stepbrother made a stronger claim on her sense of duty. In 1755 she complained: 'Whoever that somebody or other is, who is to write the life of Epictetus, seeing I have *a dozen shirts to make*, I do opine, dear Miss Talbot, that it cannot be I' (Pennington, 1.186). Secker advised her principally on matters of style and Talbot on issues of interpretation. Talbot was chiefly concerned about conflicts between Stoic philosophy and Christian teaching and, when it was decided that the work should be published, insisted that Carter warn her readers against the potentially dangerous influence of Epictetus's doctrines, especially his lack of belief in an afterlife, and apparent recommendation of suicide. Carter followed her friend's advice and added an introduction and footnotes stressing the superiority of Christianity, even though she believed that, while deists found support for their beliefs in Epictetus, most readers would be intelligent enough not to be led astray by his teaching. She herself did not agree with the Stoics' suppression of all feeling.

In 1758 *All the Works of Epictetus which are now Extant* was published by subscription by Andrew Millar, John Rivington, and Robert and James Dodsley in a handsome quarto volume, priced at 1 guinea. It was prefaced by an ode to Carter by Hester Mulso Chapone, and was the first of Carter's works in which her name appeared on the title-page. Although 1018 copies were printed by Samuel Richardson, this was not sufficient for her subscribers and another 250 copies were printed. A Dublin edition appeared in the following year and there were further London editions in 1766 and 1768. Pennington prepared a posthumous edition in 1807, incorporating a few additions and corrections made by his aunt in her own copy. Selections were included in various works and the text was the basis of several popular editions in the nineteenth and twentieth centuries. The translator of the Loeb Classical Library edition of Epictetus, W. A. Oldfather, acknowledges his debt to Carter's 'vigorous and idiomatic reproduction' (Epictetus, *The Discourses as Reported by Arrian, the Manual, and Fragments*, trans. W. A. Oldfather, vol. 1, 1926, xxxvii). The significance of Carter's achievement should not be underestimated. While several translations of the *Enchiridion* or *Manual* existed, and, as she acknowledged, she benefited from a French translation of the works and John Upton's parallel Latin/Greek text (1739), Carter was the first to translate the complete works of Epictetus into English. Oldfather considered it 'a very respectable performance under any conditions, but for her sex and period truly remarkable' (*Contributions toward a Bibliography of Epictetus*, 1927, 15). Her contemporaries were both lavish and patronizing in their praise. The *Monthly Review* proclaimed that Carter proved that 'France can no longer boast of her *Dacier*, but must be compelled to own that our women excel theirs in Sense and Genius, as far as they surpass them in Modesty and Beauty' (*Monthly Review*, 18, 1758, 588).

Epictetus made a material difference to Carter's life. Pennington estimates that she made a profit of 1000 guineas. She became less dependent financially on her father and was able most years to winter in London, taking lodgings at 20 Clarges Street, always dining out with friends, and often attending gatherings of what became known as the bluestocking circle. Later she leased a group of houses in South Street, Deal, which in 1763 she had refurbished so that she and her father could live independently but together—Nicolas Carter actually renting his accommodation from her. The leases were held by Secker but he would take no money for them (he also made her gifts totalling £200).

Epictetus was also the means of introducing Carter to Elizabeth Montagu, 'the queen of the bluestockings', and thus increasing her horizons in other ways. Through Montagu she met William Pulteney, Lord Bath, and together they made a leisurely excursion to Spa, Germany, in 1763. Excerpts from the many letters Carter wrote home are printed in Pennington's *Memoirs*. When Bath failed to leave her anything at his death in 1764, though Carter insisted that she had not expected anything because of Bath's generosity when alive, his descendants William and Francis Pulteney settled on her an annuity of £100, later raised to £150. In 1782, though feeling the effects of age, she accompanied Miss Henrietta Pulteney, later countess of Bath, to Paris where Miss Pulteney was to spend some time in a convent.

On a visit to Tunbridge Wells in 1761 Montagu and Bath persuaded Carter to publish a volume of poems which, with a dedication to Bath (penned by Bath himself), and congratulatory verses by George, Lord Lyttelton, was published as *Poems on Several Occasions* in 1762. It included her *Rambler* papers but only reprinted two items from *Poems on Particular Occasions*. 1000 copies of the first edition were printed; it ran to five lifetime editions with six new poems and an inscription added to the third edition in 1776. Most of the poems in this collection are stanzaic in form and more lyrical or sentimental in tone than her earlier verse. Most of them are addressed to women, either her Kentish friends or her bluestocking associates. Also included is 'On the Death of Mrs. Rowe', a tribute to a poet she much admired (earlier versions of this poem appeared in the *Gentleman's Magazine* 7 (1737) and 9 (1739), and in a memorial edition of Rowe's works (1739)).

Personal relationships Although Carter continued to write poetry from time to time, this collection is her last original publication in her lifetime. Because of her dislike of public exposure and fear of censure, it took the insistence of friends to persuade her into print. However, her cultural significance did not cease with her last publication. She was indefatigably active as a correspondent, conversationalist, and supporter of her friends' literary endeavours. In the 1760s she encouraged and assisted Montagu in writing her *Essay on … Shakespear* (1769), and in 1772 published a posthumous edition of the works of Catherine Talbot at her own expense. Because she never married, she had more liberty to develop both her friendships and her mind. The bluestocking circle—never a club with rules, but a network of like-minded people—allowed her to foster both. In her conversation and her voluminous correspondence she promoted women's education and participation in the world of letters, consciously creating a sense of female community, both high-minded and intimate. Pennington edited two volumes of her letters to Talbot and Elizabeth Vesey (1808), and another three volumes of letters to Montagu (1817), as well as including countless excerpts from letters to a wide range of correspondents in the *Memoirs*. They are for modern readers among her most satisfying productions, at once informal and literary. Witty gossip jostles with sublime philosophy, Christian piety is tempered by ironic insights, and weighty learning is accompanied by a delightful flirtatiousness which comes as a surprise to those only familiar with her *Epictetus*.

Carter's most significant relationships were with family and friends, although she was not without admirers. Thomas Birch, John Dalton, and Dr John Burton probably proposed marriage, and her letters in 1740, 1747, 1749, and 1758 allude to other suitors who were not seriously entertained. Rumours circulated that bishops Secker and Hayter were rivals for her affections. At some point, perhaps as early as 1743, Carter probably made a conscious decision not to marry in order to preserve her independence and her freedom to study and to write as she wished. Her literary fame and personal qualities brought her a wide circle of friends and acquaintances including, aside from those already mentioned, the Highmores and Chapones, William and John Duncombe, James Beattie, James Boswell, Edmund Burke, Eva Maria Garrick, the countess of Hertford, the countess of Holdernesse, Catharine Macaulay, Lord Monboddo, Hannah More, Sir George Oxenden, Hester Thrale Piozzi, Bishop Porteus, Joshua Reynolds, Elizabeth Vesey, and Horace Walpole. As her years increased and she lost loved ones (her father in 1774, Talbot four years earlier, Montagu and Chapone in 1800 and 1801), she continued as far as possible to live an active social life and to make the acquaintance of a younger generation of writers such as Fanny Burney and Jane West. In December 1805 she was determined to see her friends in London, probably knowing it would be her last opportunity. She had never fully recovered from an attack of what was probably St Anthony's fire (erysipelas) in 1797, and four years later she suffered another attack, which left her too weak to study or read for long periods. She died peacefully in lodgings in 21 Clarges Street, London, on 19 February 1806. She was interred in the burial-ground of Grosvenor Chapel, an appendage to St George's, Hanover Square, having requested in her will that she should be buried where she died and with as little expense as possible. A mural monument was erected to her memory in Deal. Her will divided her fortune among her relatives; she left £40 to each of her maidservants and various tokens to numerous friends (listed in *Memoirs*, 1.499–500). Her house in Deal she left to Pennington, who had lived there with her for the last twenty years of her life.

Fanny Burney in 1780 thought her 'a really noble-looking woman; I never saw age so graceful in the female sex yet; her whole face seems to beam with goodness, piety, and philanthropy' (Boswell, *Life*, 4.275), but Betsy Sheridan described her in 1785 as 'rather fat and not very striking in appearance' (*Betsy Sheridan's Journal*, ed. W. LeFanu, 1986, 40). Most of the known portraits were made after *Epictetus* had brought her fame and do indeed depict her as 'rather fat' (despite a lifetime of energetic walking), but beaming with the goodness and nobility appropriate to a translator of Greek philosophy.

Because of her remarkable talents countryfolk in Kent, Carter reported, thought her 'more than half a witch'. Yet she was widely viewed with respect as well as awe and celebrated for her modesty and genius in, for example, John Duncombe's *Feminead* (1757). She was also immediately seen as a pioneer; J. Swan stated that her translation of Algarotti taught women to 'boldly tread where none had reach'd before' (*GM*, 9, 1739, 322). In the early nineteenth century Pennington portrayed her as a rather pious old maid. More recently feminist critics have appreciated her strong-mindedness and independent spirit, and, reassessing the cultural significance of the bluestockings, have stressed how, although not fully professional herself, she helped make writing a respectable occupation for women. JUDITH HAWLEY

Sources J. Hawley, ed., *Elizabeth Carter* (1999), vol. 2 of *Bluestocking feminism: writings of the bluestocking circle, 1738–1785*, ed. G. Kelly [incl. bibliography of Carter's works] · M. Pennington, *Memoirs of the life of Mrs Elizabeth Carter, with a new edition of her poems … to which are added, some miscellaneous essays in prose, together with her notes on the Bible, and answers to objections concerning the Christian religion*, 3rd edn (1816) [with MS annotations by H. Carter Smith] · S. Harcstark Myers, *The bluestocking circle: women, friendship, and the life of the mind in eighteenth-century England* (1990) · *All the works of Epictetus that are now extant. Translated from the original Greek by Elizabeth Carter. With an introduction and notes by the translator* (1758) · *A series of letters between Mrs. Elizabeth Carter and Miss Catherine Talbot … to which are added, letters from Mrs. Elizabeth Carter to Mrs. Vesey*, ed. M. Pennington, 2 vols. (1808) · *Letters from Mrs. Elizabeth Carter, to Mrs. Montagu, between the years 1755 and 1800*, 3 vols. (1817) · [E. Carter], 'Religion and superstition, a vision', *The Rambler*, 44 (18 Aug 1750) · E. Ruhe, 'Thomas Birch, Samuel Johnson, and Elizabeth Carter', *Publications of the Modern Language Association of America*, 73 (1958), 491–500 · Boswell, *Life*, 1.122, 138–40, 203, 208, 242, 546; 3.43, 168; 4.246, 275, 494–5, 526 · C. Thomas, '"Th'instructive moral, and important thought": Elizabeth Carter reads Pope, Johnson and Epictetus', *Age of Johnson*, 4 (1991), 137–69 · C. D. Williams, 'Poetry, pudding and Epictetus: the consistency of Elizabeth Carter', *Tradition in transition: women writers, marginal texts and the eighteenth-century canon*, ed. A. Ribeira and J. G. Basker (1996), 3–24 · *GM*, 1st ser., 4–5 (1734–5) · *GM*, 1st ser., 7–9 (1737–9) · *GM*, 1st ser., 11 (1741) · *GM*, 1st ser., 14 (1744) · *GM*, 1st ser., 17 (1747) · L. H. Ewert, 'Elizabeth Montagu to Elizabeth Carter: literary gossip and critical opinions from the pen of the queen of the blues', PhD diss., Claremont College, California, 1967 · *DNB* · A. C. C. Gaussen, *A woman of wit and wisdom: a memoir of Elizabeth Carter* (1906) · W. A. Oldfather, *Contributions toward a bibliography of Epictetus* (1927) · *Epictetus; the discourses as reported by Arrian, the manual, and fragments*, trans. W. A. Oldfather, 2 vols. (1926) · *Correspondence between Frances, countess of Hartford (afterwards duchess of Somerset) and Henrietta Louisa, countess of Pomfret, between the years 1738 and 1741*, ed. W. Bingley, 3 vols. (1805) · W. P. D. Stebbing, typescript of, and notes for, various lectures given in

Deal, and transcribed extracts from letters by E. Carter and from N. Carter to E. Carter, Deal County Library, Stebbing Collection **Archives** BL, letters, Add. MSS 4302, fols. 69–79; 4297, fols. 60–60b; 4457, fol. 112 |copies| · BL, letters and papers · BL, papers and copies of poems and epigrams, Add. MSS 4456, fols. 57–58b, 60; 4457, fols. 41–42b, 73,115, 123b; 48252, fol. 3 · Bodl. Oxf., corresp. and papers [incl. facsimiles] · Mitchell L., Glas., prayer from her pocket book · Wordsworth Trust, Dove Cottage, Grasmere, fragment of letter with engraved portrait and related items | BL, letters to Mrs Berkeley, Add. MS 39312, fols. 53, 183 · BL, letters in Latin to Thomas Birch, Add. MSS 4456, fols. 57–58b, 60; 4302, fols. 69–79 · BL, letters and copies of letters to Edward Cave, Stowe MSS 748, fols. 169, 171–77; Add. MS 4297, fols. 49–50b, 57–59, 61; Add. MS 4456, fol. 59 · BL, letters to Countess Spencer · Hunt. L., letters to Henrietta Pulteney, [Edward Jernyngham], Matthew Montagu, Dorothea Alison, HM 17023, 17024, JE 184, MO 703, HM 17025 · Trinity Cam., letters to Isaac Hawkins Browne, and notes on 'De animi immortalitate' · U. Aberdeen L., letters to Elizabeth Montagu, MS 30/29 **Likenesses** attrib. J. Fayram, oils, 1738, priv. coll.; formerly in the possession of Mrs G. I. Barrett, Deal, in 1978 · attrib. J. Highmore, oils, c.1738, Deal town hall, Kent · J. Highmore, oils, c.1745, Dover Museum, Kent · K. Read, oils, c.1765, Dr Johnson's House, London [*see illus.*] · R. Samuel, group portrait, oils, c.1779 (*The nine living muses of Great Britain*), NPG · J. H. Hurter, oils, miniature, 1781; Sothebys, 1956 · J. R. Smith, mezzotint, pubd c.1781 (after J. Kitchingman), BM · T. Lawrence, pastel on vellum, exh. 1790, NPG · C. Watson, engraving, 1806 (after T. Lawrence), BM · Mackenzie, stipple, pubd 1807 (after cameo by J. Smith), BM, NPG · oil on enamel, 1860–99, Dr Johnson's House, London · C. Geertz, ivory miniature relief (after T. Lawrence); formerly in Deal town hall, Kent · J. Tassie, miniature relief (after cameo), repro. in Gaussen, *Woman of wit* · E. Walker, engraving (after T. Lawrence), repro. in Gaussen, *Woman of wit*

Carter [*née* Vavasour], **Ellen** (*bap.* 1762, *d.* 1815), artist and book illustrator, was baptized at St Olave's Church, York, on 16 May 1762. She was the daughter of Walter Vavasour, a country gentleman whose estate was in Weston, Yorkshire, and Ellen, his wife, daughter of Edward Elmsall of Thornhill in the same county. At an early age, though a protestant, she was educated at the convent of the Poor Clares at Rouen, with which the Vavasour family had been connected for some generations. Though strongly influenced by Roman Catholicism during this period, she remained a member of the Church of England. She was noted for her charitable, sincere, and pious nature. On 24 November 1787 she married at Thornhill the Revd John Carter of Trinity College, Cambridge, then curate of Thornhill, afterwards headmaster of Lincoln grammar school, and incumbent of St Swithin's, Lincoln. While at the convent Ellen Carter received a sound artistic training and went on to excel at drawing the human figure. She also copied subjects of antiquity and drew illustrations for *Archaeologia*, the *Gentleman's Magazine*, and other similar works. A print from her drawing entitled *The Gardener's Girl* was intended as a companion to Thomas Barker's *Woodboy*. Many of her drawings entered private collections. She suffered for six years from a lung condition and was in very weak health in the winter of 1814. The death of her eldest son, Ensign John Vavasour Carter of the 30th regiment of foot, from exposure and sunstroke at Ciudad Rodrigo in the Peninsular War in July 1812, was a shock

from which she never recovered. She died on 22 September 1815, and was buried in the churchyard of St Peter's in the East Gate, Lincoln. She was survived by her husband and a son and a daughter.

L. H. Cust, *rev.* Heather M. MacLennan

Sources *GM*, 1st ser., 82/2 (1812), 399 · *GM*, 1st ser., 85/2 (1815), 374–5 · Redgrave, *Artists* · Bénézit, *Dict.* · Mallalieu, *Watercolour artists* · IGI

Carter [*née* Fantl], **Ernestine Marie** (1906–1983), museum curator and writer on fashion, was born on 10 October 1906 in Savannah, Georgia, USA, the daughter of Siegfried Fantl. Carter was brought up in Savannah. She graduated from Wellesley College, Massachusetts, in 1927, where, remarkably for the time, she studied modern and contemporary art and design under the tutelage of Alfred Barr. She worked as a curatorial assistant at New York's newly formed Museum of Modern Art and from 1933 to 1937 she was its curator of architecture and industrial art. In 1936 she married the British antiquarian book dealer and bibliographer, John Waynflete *Carter (1905–1975), and later took up permanent residence in London.

During the Second World War she worked on exhibitions for the Ministry of Information, and edited a propaganda book of photographs, some specially commissioned from Lee Miller, *Grim Glory: Pictures of Britain under Fire* (1941). It was popular enough to go into five printings. Later in the war she worked for the American office of war information in London, 'explaining America to England' (Carter, 62). She worked on the fashion component of the important design exhibition 'Britain can make it', organized by the Council for Industrial Design and held at the Victoria and Albert Museum in London in 1946. From 1946 to 1949 she was fashion editor for *Harper's Bazaar*. Her first trip to Paris for the magazine was to report on Christian Dior's exhilarating first *haute couture* fashion show in 1947. Carter's newspaper writing began with a cookery column for *The Observer* from 1952 to 1954, during which time her lively cookbook *Flash in the Pan* (1953) was published. In 1955 she began editing the woman's page of the *Sunday Times*, becoming associate editor of the paper in 1968. She was appointed OBE in 1964. She retired in 1972 and wrote discerning, well-illustrated books on fashion history: *20th Century Fashion: a Scrapbook* (1975), *The Changing World of Fashion* (1977), and *Magic Names of Fashion* (1980). Her vivid autobiography, *With Tongue in Chic* (1974), includes much of interest to fashion history. Ernestine Carter died at her home, 113 Dovehouse Street, Chelsea, London, on 1 August 1983.

Carter wrote lucidly about fashion in its widest sense. 'To me fashion is essentially people … I wrote about them all' (Carter, 179). She communicated the excitement and importance of fashion as it developed through the 1940s and 1950s. Looking back on the late 1940s as 'halcyon years' for couture, she judged the 'unforgettable' and 'voluptuous' new look to be unsurpassed as the most universally becoming and enduring fashion ever devised (ibid., 75–8). It is hard to imagine a more auspicious moment for her to start her career in fashion journalism.

She took fashion seriously, a rare approach in post-war Britain, and was irritated by intellectually snobbish dismissal of fashion as frivolous, declaring it was 'surely no more frivolous than architecture, to which it is closely related' (ibid., 181). She interpreted developments in Paris fashion to her British readers, then later played a crucial role in nurturing British designer talent. Carter used her opportunities on the *Sunday Times* to help modernize a then Conservative newspaper and forcefully to encourage the emergence of London as a major fashion centre in the 1960s. Her insight was to recognize that this new order was symptomatic of major social shifts. Her education and curatorial experience gave her a trained eye; this combined with pithy, intelligent prose, great energy, and uncompromising standards. On the *Sunday Times* she became an authoritative figure in the fashion world.

The Museum of Costume at Bath benefits from her foresight, which led to the donation of 2000 fashion photographs from her newspaper, dating from 1958 to 1972, known as the *Sunday Times* fashion archive. Not surprisingly, Carter enjoyed fine clothes herself. Some are in the museum. Her personal style was distinctively neat and tailored, avoiding extremes of fashion.

BARBARA BURMAN

Sources E. Carter, *With tongue in chic* (1974) · D. Griffiths, ed., *The encyclopedia of the British press, 1422–1992* (1992) · *The Times* (3 Aug 1983) · B. Keenan, 'The importance of being Ernestine', *Sunday Times* (7 Aug 1983) · private information (2004) [E. W. Playfair] · d. cert.
Wealth at death £351,826: probate, 21 Nov 1983, CGPLA Eng. & Wales

Carter, Francis (1741?–1783), traveller and collector of coins, is reported in the *Dictionary of British Portraiture* (vol. 2) to have been born in 1741. He spent most of his life (except five years in France) in Andalusia and in the kingdom of Granada. Nothing is known of his family nor of his early years, but that he had known Spain since his childhood which he dates to 1753. He travelled through Moorish Spain in 1772. The outcome of this experience was his two-volume *A Journey from Gibraltar to Malaga*, published in 1777, which explored the Roman and Moorish antiquities in the kingdom of Granada. Richard Gough, in a letter dated 6 March 1776 to the Revd Michael Tyson, wrote that the 'curious' book 'is printing with all speed, and correcting by Arabic Jones [Sir William Jones]. Much is expected from it' (Nichols, 8.618). The work included thirteen engraved plates, selected from Carter's drawings of the different towns and places he passed through. The first volume of the 1777 edition included two plates of medals, most of which were engraved from the originals in Carter's cabinet. The thirteen plates were sold in a separate volume the publication of which was heavily subsidized by Carter himself in order to illustrate the text, which, he claimed, 'cost me so many years of labour', with 'every possible embellishment' (Carter, vi). The work was reissued in 1778 in two volumes, with the plates inserted. Carter collected gold and silver Spanish and Carthaginian

coins and Spanish books, including the Spanish chronicles which formed, he claimed, the 'most valuable part of my library' (*GM*, 843). Carter proudly stated that his collection of Spanish coins was the most complete in England, following the addition of the collection of Don Thomas Joseph Calbelo, canon of the metropolitan church in Granada. Carter's coin collection also included Flores's cabinet, which Carter purchased on his death.

Carter was elected a fellow of the Society of Antiquaries on 1 May 1777, and soon afterwards began working on 'An historical and critical account of early printed Spanish books', a study embracing the development of Spanish literature from the reign of John II, king of Castile, to the eighteenth century. Carter claimed that 'the pure Latin tongue was that of the Spaniards till the arrival of the Goths in the fifth century' (*GM*, 843). His own collection of Spanish literature was extensive.

Carter completed the work in manuscript, and printed the first sheet, but died immediately afterwards at Woodbridge, Suffolk, on 1 August 1783. He was buried at St Mary in Woodbridge on 5 August 1783. He left a widow, Sarah, of whom no more is known. A friend, 'Eugenio', contributed to the *Gentleman's Magazine* for October of the same year (pp. 843–5) a specimen of Carter's 'curious' observations, with the promise of a continuation, which was never fulfilled. A letter from Carter dated 28 November 1780 and written from Woodbridge, giving anecdotes of Dr William Battie, is printed in Nichols's *Literary Anecdotes* (4.607).

SILVIA LAUZZANA

Sources F. Carter, *A journey from Gibraltar to Malaga* (1777) · *GM*, 1st ser., 53 (1783), 716, 843–5 · Nichols, *Lit. anecdotes*, 3.237–8; 4.607; 8.618 · administration, 23 Aug 1783, PRO, PROB 6/159, fol. 371 · E. Kilmurray, *Dictionary of British portraiture*, 2 (1979) · papers, S. Antiquaries, Lond. · archives, Suffolk CRO
Likenesses J. Basire, line engraving, 1777 (after S. Howitt), BM, NPG; repro. in Carter, *Journey*

Carter, George (*bap.* 1737, *d.* 1794), painter, was baptized on 10 April 1737 at St James's Church, Colchester, the son of George and Elizabeth Carter. Educated at the local free school, he went to London as a servant before working as a shop assistant to a mercer. He set up in partnership as a mercer, in Chandos Street, Covent Garden, but the business failed and he turned to painting. He entered the Royal Academy Schools in 1770, a year after first exhibiting at the Society of Artists, where he continued to exhibit rustic genre scenes until 1774. On 20 August 1774 he set out for Rome with John Singleton Copley, and kept a diary of his tour. A mutual dislike arose between the artists and they parted at Rome; Copley described Carter as 'a sort of snail which crawled over a man in his sleep, and left its slime and no more' (Ingamells, 187). Carter sent from Rome *A Wounded Hussar on the Field of Battle*, which was exhibited at the Royal Academy in 1775 and engraved by Valentine Green.

Carter had returned to England by 1776 and exhibited history paintings at the Royal Academy in 1776, 1777, 1779, and 1784. He presented *Adoration of the Shepherds*, exhibited in 1777, to the church of St James in Colchester. He did not exhibit between 1779 and 1784, and it is likely that it was at this time that he made visits to Gibraltar and St Petersburg. In 1785 he opened an exhibition in Pall Mall, London, of a collection of his own pictures. The catalogue, which caused much hostility and derision, stated that 'these pictures were all painted without commission, the motive, to celebrate good men and brave actions. They are now at the disposal of any nobleman or gentleman who may wish to possess either the whole or a part of them' (Redgrave, 72). Carter had some success with engravings after the pictures, despite the failure of the exhibition. In December 1785 he sailed for India, arriving in Calcutta by June 1786. He took a large stock of pictures with him and held a lottery, and then an auction, of pictures at his house in Council House Street, between November 1786 and January 1787. He left India about a year later, but his contacts continued after he returned to England, and two further auctions of his pictures took place in Calcutta in 1793 and 1794. In 1791 Carter published a written account of the wreck of the *Grosvenor* off the coast of Africa in 1782, which he illustrated with four engravings.

Waterhouse noted that Carter 'was always a feeble executant' (Waterhouse, 72). He died in 1794 and was buried on 19 September at Hendon, London.

DEBORAH GRAHAM-VERNON

Sources Redgrave, *Artists* · E. Edwards, *Anecdotes of painters* (1808); facs. edn (1970) · *DNB* · P. Morant, *The history and antiquities of the most ancient town and borough of Colchester in the county of Essex* (1748) · register of St James's Church, Colchester · register of Hendon Church · M. Archer, *India and British portraiture, 1770–1825* (1979) · J. Ingamells, ed., *A dictionary of British and Irish travellers in Italy, 1701–1800* (1997) · Waterhouse, *18c painters* · Graves, *Soc. Artists* · Thieme & Becker, *Allgemeines Lexikon* · A. Cunningham, *The lives of the most eminent British painters*, rev. Mrs C. Heaton, 2 (1879)
Likenesses W. Sharp, line engraving, BM

Carter, Harry William (1787–1863), physician, was born at Canterbury, Kent, on 7 September 1787, the son of William Carter (1757?–1822), a physician at Canterbury and formerly fellow of Oriel College, Oxford, and his wife, Mary, daughter of Lancelot Lee, of Shropshire. He was educated at King's School, Canterbury, and on 10 October 1803 matriculated at Oriel College, Oxford, where he graduated BA (1807), MA (1810), BM (1811), and DM (1819). In 1812 he was elected a Radcliffe travelling fellow, and he spent several years afterwards on the continent. In 1821 he published *A short account of some of the principal hospitals of France, Italy, Switzerland, and the Netherlands, with remarks on the climate and diseases of these countries*, based on his travels. He had earlier written a pamphlet defending Church of England doctrine against Unitarian criticism, and he also contributed some essays to the *Cyclopaedia of Practical Medicine*. He became a fellow of the Royal College of Physicians in 1825.

Carter settled in practice at Canterbury. He was appointed in 1819 honorary physician to the Kent and Canterbury Hospital, which his father had helped to found. He retired from the post in 1835 but remained consultant physician until 1857. He was for some time a justice of the peace and deputy lieutenant of Kent. After 1835 he lived at Kennington Place, near Ashford, Kent, and he died there on 16 July 1863.   G. T. BETTANY, *rev.* PATRICK WALLIS

Sources Munk, *Roll* · Foster, *Alum. Oxon.* · *GM*, 3rd ser., 15 (1863), 250 · F. M. Hall, *The Kent and Canterbury Hospital, 1790–1987* (1987) · *CGPLA Eng. & Wales* (1863) · H. W. Carter, *Remarks upon a late publication by Mr. Belsham* (1819)
Wealth at death under £25,000: resworn probate, May 1866, *CGPLA Eng. & Wales*

Carter, Henry [Harry] (1749–1829), smuggler and Methodist preacher, was born early in 1749 at Pengersick, Germoe parish, near Breage, Cornwall, the seventh of ten children of Francis Carter (*bap.* 1712, *d.* 1774), smallholder and miner, and Annice Williams (1714–1784). Henry (always known as Harry) grew up in decent poverty with scarcely any education, working in a tin mine from the age of nine or ten. John Wesley was at that time frequently preaching in Cornwall, and Harry and his elder brother Francis encountered Methodist teaching in childhood which influenced their later lives.

The second son, John (nicknamed King of Prussia in childhood) initiated the Carters' smuggling empire. He leased a coastal smallholding (later known as Prussia Cove), choosing a secluded inlet as the centre of operations, cutting a harbour and roadways, adapting caves and tunnels for storage, and mounting guns for protection. Harry joined his brothers fishing and smuggling when nineteen, having already taught himself to write and keep accounts. His abilities ensured spectacular advancement, from owning a small boat to becoming, when only twenty-eight, captain of the *Swallow*, owned by John, one of the largest cutters afloat with a crew of sixty. Seven family members were involved, normally bringing in spirits or tea from Guernsey. Their successes were great and expectations high. With a reputation for prompt and honest service, the Carters enjoyed popular support and protection from powerful patrons. During the American War of Independence they successfully commissioned five vessels as privateers to attack enemy shipping, but the dangers were considerable. Upon his taking the *Swallow* into St Malo for repairs in 1777 Harry was gaoled on suspicion of piracy and the cutter confiscated. John brought over appropriate papers but was also imprisoned. After two years both were freed in exchange for two Frenchmen, thanks to Admiralty intervention.

The family fortunes revived; by 1780 Harry Carter commanded and part-owned the *Shaftesbury* with a crew of eighty. In April 1786 he married Elizabeth Flindel, and their daughter was born in 1787. Disaster struck in January 1788 as Harry landed goods at Costan (Cawsand) near Plymouth. Two boats appeared from the Royal Navy ship *Druid*, and in the fighting which followed a naval seaman was killed. Carter was savagely injured and left for dead. Incredibly he escaped ashore, and with help got back to Prussia Cove. When £300 was offered for his capture he hid locally for three months, but then fled to New York, where he contacted a Wesleyan Methodist group and sought by prayer and self-denial to atone for his sins. Poverty forced him into casual farmwork alongside African slaves.

Carter returned briefly to his family in 1790 (his wife had died of tuberculosis between October 1788 and August 1789), but then went as a buyer among smugglers' merchants in Roscoff, continuing his prayerful life and acting as a lay preacher. In 1793, when war with France broke out, he was again imprisoned, this time alongside victims of the terror, and he experienced great privations in the shadow of the guillotine. In happier moments he was joined by family members, was befriended by James Macculloch (an important merchant), and struggled to speak French with imprisoned Carmelite nuns.

Finally freed in January 1795, Carter returned to his daughter and family. Thereafter he settled quietly on a smallholding at Rinsey (near Breage), but continued preaching locally. In 1809, while his brothers still smuggled, Harry wrote his autobiography, essentially as an act of expiation. The writing is neat and purposeful, the spelling phonetic: as a record of the triumphs and disasters of a very able and religious man it is unique. Harry Carter died, aged eighty, in debt to James Macculloch, and was buried at Breage on 19 April 1829.   MARY WAUGH

Sources *The autobiography of a Cornish smuggler: Captain Harry Carter of Prussia Cove*, ed. J. B. Cornish, 2nd edn (1900) · E. Pollard, 'Smuggler: Captain Harry Carter', *Journal of the Royal Institution of Cornwall*, new ser., 5 (1965–8), 324–81 · M. Waugh, 'The iniquities of Mount's Bay and the Carters of Prussia Cove', *Smuggling in Devon and Cornwall, 1700–1850* (1999), 127–46 · C. Noall, 'The famous smugglers of Mount's Bay', *Smuggling in Cornwall* (1971), 37–48 · E. M. Cunnack, 'The Carters of Rinsey. Their forebears and descendants', [n.d.], Cornwall RO, X635 [unpubd typescript deposited 1981] · will, 13 July 1826, Cornwall RO, X634/67A 1, 2 · bond to repay £326 19s. 8d. to James Macculloch on or before 18 April 1800, 18 April 1799, Cornwall RO, X634/62 · F. Truscott, 'Memoir of Mr Henry Carter', *Wesleyan Methodist Magazine*, 54 (1831), 657–66
Wealth at death see will, Cornwall RO, X 634/67A 1, 2

Carter, Henry. *See* Leslie, Frank (1821–1880).

Carter, Henry (1874–1951), temperance campaigner and pacifist, was born on 3 November 1874 at 17 Cornwall Street, Plymouth, the son of George Henry Richards Carter, a basket-maker, and his wife, Lavinia Johns Kingdon. His father died when Henry Carter was young, so he was brought up by his mother, a devout Methodist and committed teetotaller. At the age of fourteen Carter left school and moved to Cardiff, where he first was apprenticed in an ironmongers' firm and later worked for various wholesale provision merchants, eventually selling on the road. In 1898–1901 he studied at Handsworth College, Birmingham, a Wesleyan Methodist divinity school, and in 1905 he was ordained as a minister. On 5 August 1905 he married Sarah Elizabeth (*b.* 1869/70), daughter of John Rumbelow a machinist. They had a daughter.

Carter found his life work in 1911 when he was appointed secretary of the temperance committee of the Wesleyan Methodist church. In 1918 this office was expanded to include social welfare. After the merger of the Methodist churches in Britain in 1932 he continued as secretary of the temperance and social welfare committee for the unified Methodist church until his retirement in 1942. As a temperance reformer his watchwords were 'Elevate! Educate! Legislate!' In 1912 he founded the Wesleyan Methodist League of Abstainers. In 1915 he became honorary secretary of the new Temperance Council of the Christian Churches of England and Wales, and in 1916–21 he served as a member of the central control board (liquor traffic). Carter published a respected history of the board's experiment in state management, *The Control of the Drink Trade: a Contribution to National Efficiency* (1918; 2nd edn, 1919). His conversion to state purchase of the alcoholic drink trade offended many prohibitionists, however, as did his support for the compromise licensing act of 1921 which sharply reduced the hours of sale from those which had existed before the war.

In 1919, during a visit to the United States to study national prohibition, Carter became a member of the general council of the new World League against Alcoholism. In 1929–31 he served on the royal commission on liquor licensing laws: he signed the majority report, but with reservations. In its support he published a booklet, *The Nation Surveys the Drink Problem* (1932) and also signed what was called the nine-point programme, published in the *Christian World* (11 February 1932). In the same year, frustrated with what he considered the impractical rigidity of the prohibitionist United Kingdom Alliance, he published the first, nineteenth-century volume of *The English Temperance Movement: a Study in Objectives*. Prohibitionists were furious, and, having made his point in defence of moral suasion, Carter decided that it was unnecessarily provocative to write the second volume, on the twentieth century. In 1933, after the unification of the Wesleyan Methodists with the other Methodist churches, some of them committed to prohibition, Carter signed a conciliatory 'agreed temperance programme', along with representatives of the United Kingdom Alliance. He was opposed to gambling as well as to drinking, and wrote *Facts about Greyhound Racing* (1928) in support of the National Emergency Committee of Christian Citizens, which advocated a local option for the opening of dog tracks.

Carter's concern for world peace and justice led him to pacifism and to work on behalf of refugees: he announced his commitment to Christian pacifism in an article in the *Methodist Recorder* (23 March 1933). Carter later helped found the Methodist Peace Fellowship and chaired the National Peace Council. He also was a vigorous opponent of antisemitism. Shortly after the creation in 1938 of the Christian Council for Refugees he became chairman of the board of management. From 1948 until his death he served as chairman of the council. In 1945 he was chosen as chairman too of the Ecumenical Refugee Commission under the auspices of what became the World Council of Churches. Carter later helped form the European Refugee Commission and the Methodist Refugee Fund. He also chaired the executive of the Council of Christians and Jews. In 1950 he published *The Refugee Problem in Europe and the Middle East*.

Carter's humanitarian passions were rooted in his evangelical religiosity. His busy schedule did not intrude upon his 'regular, systematic and intense habit of private devotion' (Urwin, 125). His books on Methodism, beginning with *The Church and the New Age* (1911) and ending with *The Methodist Heritage* (1951), extended across virtually his entire life as an ordained minister.

Much of what is known about Carter the man comes from a memoir published by Evelyn Clifford Urwin in 1955. Urwin had access to Carter's diaries and correspondence, interviewed friends, relatives, and staff members, and himself had worked with Carter from 1933. Urwin admiringly recalled Carter's energy, his organizational ability, his gift for winning the loyalty of his staff, and 'his almost boyish boisterous laugh' (Urwin, 120). Although Carter was a prolific writer, 'writing did not come easily to him' (ibid., 103). He spoke little about himself and kept his family life intensely private. His wife's health was fragile and their daughter predeceased them. He irritated critics with what they derided as 'Henry Carter's stunts' (ibid., 122) and suffered from 'a tiny streak of vanity and pleasure in success and esteem' (ibid., 126). He won the admiration of many people prominent in public life. In recognition of his public services he was made CBE in 1934. Carter died from heart failure on 19 June 1951 at the Hospital of St John and St Elizabeth, Marylebone, London, and was buried in Cardiff. His wife survived him.

DAVID M. FAHEY

Sources E. C. Urwin, *Henry Carter, C. B. E.: a memoir* (1955) · G. P. Williams and G. T. Brake, *Drink in Great Britain, 1900–1979* (1980) · 'Death of great Methodist temperance leader: Rev. Henry Carter's work for Christian citizenship', *Methodist Recorder* (27 June 1951) [tributes by E. C. Urwin, W. F. Lofthouse, and others] · *Minutes of Conference* (1951), 150–51 · G. I. T. Machin, *Churches and social issues in twentieth-century Britain* (1998) · WWW · CGPLA Eng. & Wales (1951) · b. cert. · m. cert. · d. cert.
Archives PRO, Home Office, central control board MSS
Likenesses photographs, repro. in Urwin, *Henry Carter*
Wealth at death £11,696 19s. 7d.: probate, 8 Sept 1951, CGPLA Eng. & Wales

Carter, Henry [Harry] **Bonham** (1827–1921), barrister and company director, was born on 15 February 1827 in London, the third son of John Bonham Carter (1788–1838) and his wife, Joanna Maria (d. 1884), daughter of William Smith of Parndon Hall, Essex, MP for Norwich, and sister of Florence Nightingale's mother, Frances.

The Carters were a Portsmouth burgess family, in the eighteenth and early nineteenth centuries Unitarian, whig, and dominant in local politics: there were thirty-two Carter mayors of Portsmouth between 1747 and 1835. John Carter (1741–1808), a brewer, was mayor nine times and was knighted by George III in 1773. His son John, the father of Henry, was whig MP for Portsmouth (1816–38). On inheriting the estate of his cousin Thomas Bonham of Petersfield, Hampshire, in March 1827, John Carter assumed the additional name Bonham (subsequently some members of the family hyphenated the names Bonham and Carter).

Henry Bonham Carter was educated at Dr Malleson's boarding-school, Hove, Sussex, in Lausanne and Berlin,

and at Trinity College, Cambridge (matriculated 1845) where he read mathematics (senior optime 1849), but as a Unitarian he refused to 'conform' and so did not take his degree. He was admitted to Lincoln's Inn in June 1846, was called to the bar in January 1853, and practised on the western circuit. On 10 June 1862 he married at Bromley Common church Sibella Charlotte (1836/7–1916), elder daughter of George Warde *Norman (1793–1882) of The Rookery, Bromley Common, Kent, a director of the Bank of England. They lived in London and from 1863 to 1880 had eleven sons and one daughter. Through the Normans' influence Bonham Carter was managing director of the Guardian Fire and Life Assurance Company from 1861 to 1899, and he also profited much from fortunate investment in a Welsh coalmine. His wife was Anglican and he, though apparently retaining Unitarian beliefs, attended Anglican services. His cousin Florence Nightingale wrote that 'Harry B.C.' was 'not Church-y' (Cook, 2.392). He helped her in her public and private affairs, was secretary of the Nightingale Fund (1861–1914), and assisted in the organization of the Nightingale Training School. In the nurse registration controversy during the 1880s he actively supported her 'anti-registrationist' campaign, and published *Is a General Register for Nurses Desirable?* (1888). She appointed him one of her executors and left him her papers. During the Franco-Prussian War he went, under the auspices of the National Society for Aid to the Sick and Wounded (later the British Red Cross Society), to distribute grants to German military hospitals. In 1874 he was a founder of the Metropolitan Nursing Association, and in 1877 he assisted in founding the Queen Victoria's Institute for District Nurses. Probably persuaded by A. V. Dicey, husband of his youngest sister Elinor Mary, he broke with the Gladstonians over home rule in 1886 and became a Liberal Unionist. He died on 22 March 1921 at his home, 5 Hyde Park Square, London, and was buried at Buriton, near Petersfield, Hampshire.

The Bonham Carter family were an example of the Victorian incorporation of prosperous provincial dissenting bourgeoisie into the establishment. Henry Bonham Carter's sons were brought up as Anglicans, attended public schools (four of them went on to Oxford), entered the armed services and professions and, except Maurice, were unionists. His fifth son was Sir Edgar Bonham-*Carter (1870–1956), a barrister and official in Sudan and Iraq. His ninth son was General Sir Charles Bonham-*Carter (1876–1955), an army officer and governor of Malta (1936–40). His youngest son was Sir Maurice ('Bongie') Bonham Carter (1880–1960), educated at Balliol College, a barrister and private secretary to Asquith (1910–16) who married Asquith's daughter Helen Violet (Lady Violet Bonham *Carter, Baroness Asquith of Yarnbury (1887–1969)): the actress Helena Bonham Carter (b. 1966) is the daughter of their son Raymond Henry Bonham Carter.

Henry Bonham Carter's fourth son, **Norman Bonham-Carter** (1867–1917), administrator in India and army officer, was born at 91 Gloucester Terrace, Paddington, London, on 29 December 1867, was educated at Rugby

School (January 1881 to December 1885), where he was a scholar (1882), head of his house, and in the VI and XXII. After cramming at Scoones' in 1886 he passed the Indian Civil Service (ICS) entrance examination and went to Balliol College, Oxford (1886–8), on the two-year ICS probationer course: under Jowett, Balliol especially welcomed ICS men, and from 1879 more than half went there. Bonham-Carter played cricket for the Balliol eleven and was a member of the Dervorguilla Society. In 1888 he went to India, where he had a varied career and was often selected for difficult posts. From 1893 to 1896 he was under-secretary to the governor of Bengal, and in 1898 under-secretary in the home department of the government of India at Simla. As collector at Mymensingh (1900–02) he dealt with much unrest and, reportedly, was respected for his fairness. In 1905, after Curzon's partition of Bengal, Bonham-Carter became the first inspector-general of police in the new province of Eastern Bengal and Assam, and organized the police department. He married on 10 December 1910 Eileen Beatrice (*b.* 1870/71), widow of A. E. Silk of the Indian public works department, and daughter of Lieutenant-Colonel Robert George Mathew, of the Indian medical service (IMS); they had no children. In 1911 he became commissioner of Dacca, the capital of the new province.

Bonham-Carter was on home leave in 1914 when the First World War began. He wanted to join the army, but was recalled to India and made commissioner of Jelpaiguri in northern Bengal. By 1915 he had completed twenty-five years' service and, although he was offered an important financial post, he resigned and returned home in May. In status-obsessed, precedence-defined Anglo-India an ICS commissioner ranked with a brigadier-general. He was one of many middle-aged men and teen-aged boys whose age could have exempted them, but who chose to serve. In May 1915, aged forty-seven, he was commissioned second lieutenant in the 2nd/1st West Kent yeomanry. Dissatisfied with home service, he obtained an exchange to the reserve Household battalion (a wartime reserve regiment of cavalry, which fought as infantry) in December 1916. His unit was part of the 4th division. He acted as town major, then refused 'safe billets' and went to the front. Early in 1917 his younger brother Charles, a regular army staff officer, met him in France. Charles later wrote that Norman was '49, the most magnificent physical specimen, and appeared much younger … I had tried to get him transferred to the Provost Marshal's department, but he said he wished to take his platoon into action twice before leaving the battalion' (Bonham-Carter, 165). On 3 May 1917 Second Lieutenant Norman Bonham-Carter was killed while leading his men at Roeux on the Scarpe in the battle of Arras. He was buried in Crump Trench British Cemetery, Fampoux, Pas de Calais, France, and is commemorated on the Balliol College war memorial.

ROGER T. STEARN

Sources V. Bonham-Carter, *In a liberal tradition: a social biography, 1700–1950* (1960) · Burke, *Gen. GB* · HoP, *Commons, 1790–1820*, vol. 3 · W. P. Baildon, ed., *The records of the Honorable Society of Lincoln's Inn: admissions*, 2 (1896) · E. Cook, *The life of Florence Nightingale*, 1, 2 (1913) · *Balliol College war memorial book, 1914–1919*, 1 (1924) · F. J. Salt and F. T. Dallin, eds., *Rugby School register, 1858–1891*, rev. edn (1952) · I. Elliott, ed., *The Balliol College register, 1833–1933*, 2nd edn (privately printed, Oxford, 1934) · Venn, *Alum. Cant.* · E. S. Craig, *Oxford University roll of service* (1920) · J. Foster, *Men-at-the-bar: a biographical hand-list of the members of the various inns of court*, 2nd edn (1885) · *WWW*, 1951–60 · *Monthly army list* (Oct 1915) · *Monthly army list* (Jan 1917) · R. Symonds, *Oxford and empire: the last lost cause?* (1991) · P. Woodruff, *The men who ruled India*, 2: *The guardians* (1963) · P. Spear, *The Oxford history of modern India, 1740–1947* (1965) · R. Jenkins, *Asquith* (1964) · b. cert. [Norman Bonham-Carter] · m. cert. [Norman Bonham-Carter]

Archives LMA, corresp. and papers as secretary of Nightingale Fund Council | BL, corresp. with Florence Nightingale and related papers, Add. MSS 45755–45815, *passim* · Hants. RO, corresp. with Edgar Bonham-Carter

Likenesses photograph, *c.*1914, repro. in *Balliol College war memorial book*, 1, facing p. 43

Wealth at death £91,951 17*s.* 6*d.*: probate, 25 May 1921, *CGPLA Eng. & Wales* · £15,958 4*s.* 10*d.*—Norman Bonham-Carter: probate, 14 July 1917, *CGPLA Eng. & Wales*

Carter, Henry Vandyke (1831–1897), epidemiologist, was born on 22 May 1831 in Hull, the son of Henry Barlow Carter (1803–1867), a well-known artist; nothing is known of his mother. His brother, Joseph Newington Carter (1835–1871), was also an artist, and Henry showed some talent in this area himself but was inclined from an early age towards the study of science. After leaving Hull grammar school, where he was instructed in science by his uncle John Sollitt, Carter studied at St George's Hospital, London, and shortly afterwards, in 1852, he was admitted a member of the Royal College of Surgeons and a licentiate of the Society of Apothecaries. Four years later he graduated MD at the University of London, and in 1858 he joined the Indian Medical Service as an assistant surgeon.

Carter joined the Bombay establishment and spent most of his career in the city and its environs. His scientific interests marked him out from most of his colleagues, and he was soon appointed professor of anatomy and physiology at Grant Medical College; he was later to become its principal. During his time in Bombay he devoted himself to a number of schemes for medical reform, including one which aimed at appointing honorary physicians and surgeons to the Jamsetji Jijibhai Hospital—a charitable institution founded by the Parsi philanthropist of that name. Carter was also instrumental in establishing, in 1884, a course for women doctors at Grant Medical College and in endowing a lectureship in physiology on the occasion of his retirement.

The scientific work for which Carter is chiefly remembered is his research on leprosy and 'spirillum fever'. Research into the latter began during the famine years of 1876–80, when large numbers of starving people flooded into Bombay from the surrounding countryside in search of food and work. A disease broke out among them which Carter identified as a form of relapsing fever. His research was published in 1882 under the title of *Spirillum Fever—Synonyms, Famine, or Relapsing Fever—as Seen in Western India*, winning him the British Medical Association's Stewart pathological prize.

Carter's work on leprosy did not involve laboratory or clinical research but rather a comparison of leprosy in a number of different contexts. His first publication on the subject came in 1874, with his *Report on Leprosy and Leper Asylums in Norway, with Reference to India*. This followed a visit to Norway—paid for by the government of India—in which Carter attempted to ascertain whether the leprosy identified in Norway was the same disease as that found in India, and what measures might be useful in the treatment and prevention of the disease. Carter concluded that the leprosies of Norway and India were the same disease and that leper asylums like those in Norway should be established in India. As he made clear in his book *On Leprosy and Elephantiasis* (1874), he thought that leprosy was primarily a hereditary disease and that it might be eradicated if lepers were prevented from having children. He therefore recommended that, if asylums were to be established, a policy of sexual segregation should be enforced.

By the 1880s, however, Carter had changed his mind about the way in which leprosy was spread. The gradual acceptance of G. H. A. Hansen's claim to have discovered the bacillus causing leprosy in 1874, together with the discovery of the micro-organisms causing other diseases, led Carter to place more emphasis on contagion than on heredity, believing that the disease might be spread in a similar manner to tuberculosis. In his earlier work he had been prepared to acknowledge that contagion might play some role in the spread of the disease but had stated that there was no conclusive evidence for this. Carter's conversion to the contagion theory served only to strengthen his advocacy of leper asylums. Working with other Europeans, who were concerned about the number of vagrant lepers congregating in the centre of Bombay, and with a number of Parsi philanthropists, Carter persuaded the government to establish a number of leper asylums in the region and, in 1882, to permit the passage of by-laws pronouncing the congregation of lepers to be a sanitary threat.

The prominent part played by Carter in the campaign for leper asylums in Bombay, and his other philanthropic and scientific achievements, led to his being promoted to the rank of deputy surgeon-general in the Indian Medical Service. He also became an honorary surgeon to Queen Victoria. After leaving India, Carter retired to his native East Riding of Yorkshire. He died at his address, 2 Belgrave Crescent, Scarborough, on 4 May 1897.

MARK HARRISON

Sources *The Lancet* (15 May 1897) · *BMJ* (15 May 1897), 1256–7 · S. Kakar, 'Leprosy in British India, 1860–1940: colonial politics and missionary medicine', *Medical History*, 40 (1996), 215–30 · M. Harrison, *Public health in British India: Anglo-Indian preventive medicine, 1859–1914* (1994) · *CGPLA Eng. & Wales* (1897)
Archives BL OIOC, V/11/2232 · Wellcome L., corresp. and papers
Wealth at death £21,561 5s. 0d.: probate, 9 Sept 1897, *CGPLA Eng. & Wales*

Carter, Horatio Stratton [Raich] (1913–1994), footballer, was born on 21 December 1913 at the Ocean Queen public house, 1 Tower Street, Hendon, Sunderland, co. Durham, the son of Robert ('Toddler') Carter (*d. c.*1927), licensed victualler, and his wife, Clara Augusta, *née* Stratton. His father had formerly been a professional footballer, playing for Burslem (Port Vale), Fulham, and Southampton, while his maternal grandfather, Horatio Stratton, had been much involved in local cricket. Educated at Hendon School, Raich, as he was known, played for the elementary side at the age of ten. His talents led to representative honours for Sunderland schools and co. Durham schoolboys and, eventually, to a place in the England schoolboy squad in 1927 and 1928. Leicester City gave him a trial in 1930 but he was rejected as too small (at the height of his powers he stood 5 feet 7 inches and weighed 10 stone).

In 1931 Carter abandoned an engineering apprenticeship to sign up for his home team, Sunderland. He remained on their books until 1945. Although his early play showed inconsistency, he soon settled into the first team, and by the age of twenty-three had achieved all the honours then possible in English football. In 1934 he made his début for England against Scotland at Wembley; he played thirteen times for his country between 1934 and 1947. In 1936 he was part of the championship-winning Sunderland team. In 1937 he captained the side to victory in the FA cup. He was then the youngest captain to lift the trophy, and also scored a goal in the final as Sunderland overcame Preston North End 3–1. On 26 April 1937, the week before the final, he married (Gertrude) Rose Marsh, typist, the daughter of Edgar Marsh, engineer.

Carter was in his mid-twenties when the Second World War broke out. During the war he was based in the midlands, helping to rehabilitate injured RAF personnel at Loughborough. He played in fourteen wartime internationals as well as appearing as a guest for a local side, Derby County. In 1945 he joined Derby on a permanent basis and featured in their victory in the 1946 cup final. In 1948, soon after joining third division north side Hull City, he undertook a new role as player-manager. Success followed, with promotion gained in front of home crowds in excess of 30,000. In 1951 he resigned as manager after a policy dispute, but he continued as a Hull player until 1952. He then moved to an Irish side, Cork Athletic, where he finished his career as a player as part of an Irish cup-winning team. His silver-grey hair in later playing days induced former England colleague Billy Wright to describe his presence on the pitch as 'rather like Charlie Chaplin without makeup' (Wright, 89).

After his playing days, Carter turned to full-time football management, with mixed results. He was in charge at Leeds from 1953 to 1958, leading them to promotion to the first division in 1956. From 1960 to 1963 he managed Mansfield, helping them to gain promotion from the recently formed fourth division. He was then at Middlesbrough from 1963 until his dismissal in 1966. Contemporaries noted that success did not lead to a managerial appointment at one of the top English clubs. This they put down to the very characteristics that made him a great footballer. He was considered a 'rough master' (*The Times*, 11 Oct 1994), making huge demands of others as of himself.

As a player Carter had supreme confidence in his abilities, and at times appeared arrogant. In contrast, his massive sense of duty to supporters endeared him to those who watched him week in, week out. He was immensely popular in his native Sunderland and was acknowledged as one of the greatest inside-forwards produced by English football. The classic inside-forward could tackle, score goals, and make them. Carter's ability to do all three was universally recognized by other great players who played with him. Nor were his talents confined to football. He was a capable cricketer, drawing large crowds to league games in Sunderland. In 1934 he played for Durham against Australia; later, three appearances for Derbyshire gained him an entry in the *Who's Who of Cricketers*. He was equally at home as a batsman or bowler.

Carter's first marriage was ended by the death of his wife, and on 3 January 1955 he married Eileen Patricia (Pat) Dixon (*b*. 1929/30), daughter of Harold Dixon, a railway goods guard. In his later years he was involved in the sports department of a Hull store and ran his own small business. Ultimately he settled down to a quiet life at Willerby, close to Hull. He suffered a stroke in 1993 and died at his home, 7 Ash Grove, Willerby, on 9 October 1994. He was survived by his wife, Pat, two daughters, and a son. His reputation as Hendon's local hero is guaranteed. In 2001 the Raich Carter Sports Centre was opened a corner-kick away from his birthplace, and his memory is enshrined in Sunderland's modernized Museum and Winter Gardens as one of six Sunderland all-time 'greats'.

KEITH GREGSON

Sources R. Carter, *Footballer's progress* (1950) · *The Independent* (11 Oct 1994) · *The Times* (11 Oct 1994) · *The Guardian* (11 Oct 1994) · *The Independent* (24 Oct 1994) · *The Independent* (13 Oct 1994) · B. Wright, *The world's my football pitch* (1953) · C. Harvey, ed., *Encyclopaedia of sport* (1959) · D. Thompson, *The Sunderland story* [n.d., *c*.1989] · P. Bailey, P. Thorn, and P. Wynne-Thomas, *Who's who of cricketers* (1984) · *East Wise* [Hendon & East End magazine] (Oct 2001) · J. Gibson, *Soccer's golden nursery* (1970) · www.mightyleeds.co.uk, Nov 2001 · b. cert. · m. cert. [Eileen Patricia Dixon] · m. cert. [Gertrude Rose Marsh] · d. cert.

Archives Sunderland Museum & Winter Gardens, Mowbray Gardens, Burdon Road, Sunderland, caps and medals | FILM BBC Sports Library, London

Likenesses photographs, repro. in Carter, *Footballer's progress* · photographs, Hult. Arch. · portrait, repro. in *The Independent* · portrait, repro. in *The Times* · portrait, repro. in *The Guardian*

Carter, Howard (1874–1939), artist and archaeologist, was born on 9 May 1874 at 10 Rich Terrace, Brompton, Kensington, London, youngest child of Samuel John Carter (1835–1892), artist and illustrator, of Kensington and Swaffham, Norfolk, and his wife, Martha Joyce (1837?–1920), daughter of Mr Sands, a builder of Swaffham. Carter's childhood was passed mostly in Swaffham, where he was cared for, and probably educated, by maiden aunts in the Carters' 'country house', a cottage in Sporle Road. He was not a strong child, and was never exposed to the rough-and-tumble of conventional schools. He was, however, carefully trained in drawing and watercolour by his father, who was an accomplished artist, exhibiting regularly at the Royal Academy Summer Exhibition (1855–90), and serving as a staff illustrator on the *Illustrated London News* (1867–89).

Like most of Samuel Carter's children, Howard was brought up to be an artist, and it was as an artist that he

Howard Carter (1874–1939), by William Carter, 1924

was first sent to Egypt, on the recommendation of the Amherst family of Didlington Hall, not far from Swaffham. William Amhurst Tyssen-Amherst was a collector of Egyptian antiquities and an influential member of the committee of the Egypt Exploration Fund. Through him the young Howard Carter went to Egypt in late 1891 to work as a 'tracer' of tomb scenes at Beni Hasan. After a few weeks he was sent to join W. M. Flinders Petrie who was excavating at Tell al-Amarna. Four months with Petrie, an obsessive but outstanding fieldworker, inspired Carter with a desire to excavate. He was still just seventeen.

From 1893 to 1899 Carter was responsible for the drawing of the painted reliefs in the temple of Queen Hatshepsut at Deir al-Bahri, Thebes. The results, published in six large folio volumes, *The Temple of Deir el Bahari* (1894–1908), are considered among the finest records of Egyptian inscribed monuments. His experience in archaeological management during this time led to his being appointed in 1899 the first chief inspector of antiquities in Upper Egypt by Gaston Maspero, director-general of the antiquities service of Egypt.

Carter's appointment at the age of twenty-six, with limited archaeological experience and no formal qualifications, surprised the archaeological community in Egypt, but he justified Maspero's trust by pursuing active campaigns against tomb-robbers, and by protecting and restoring monuments at Thebes and elsewhere. He also directed excavations for the antiquities service at the tomb of King Mentuhotpe II, and initiated with the American Theodore Davis explorations in the Valley of the Kings. For Davis, Carter discovered the tomb of King Tuthmosis IV.

In the autumn of 1904 Carter was transferred to the lower Egyptian inspectorate in Cairo. Shortly afterwards, at Saqqara in January 1905, foreign visitors were involved in a skirmish with Egyptian antiquities guards. Carter was held to be responsible. He refused to offer an apology, and was reprimanded and transferred to Tanta in the Nile delta. A stubborn, unbending attitude, especially towards official interference, would on more than one subsequent occasion bring him to the brink of calamity. In 1905, dissatisfied with the apparent lack of support for his position, he resigned from the antiquities service. For three years he scraped a living by painting watercolours, and by conducting rich foreign tourists around the ancient sites of Egypt.

Carter's rehabilitation came in early 1909 when, on the recommendation of Maspero, he began his association with George *Herbert, fifth earl of Carnarvon. Until the First World War they excavated in the Theban necropolis, making important, but unspectacular, discoveries, partly published in *Five Years' Explorations at Thebes: a Record of Work Done, 1907–1911* (1912). Additional, but short-term, exploratory excavations were also carried out on two delta sites, Sakha (1912) and Balamun (1913). Carnarvon was then encouraged by Carter to apply for the concession for the Valley of the Kings, surrendered finally by Davis in 1914. The time was not right, and the prognostications for discovery were not favourable. Davis, Maspero, and others believed that there was nothing of importance left in the valley to be discovered. Carter thought otherwise.

A short campaign by Carter in the tomb of King Amenophis III in 1915 produced trifling results, and for the rest of the war until 1917 he was employed as a civilian by the intelligence department of the War Office in Cairo. His duties were not onerous, and he was able to spend much time at Thebes, even carrying out some epigraphic work for Alan Gardiner, a leading British Egyptologist. In 1917 he was at last free to return to working for Carnarvon, and until 1922 he conducted annual campaigns in the Valley of the Kings; but few positive results were achieved.

In the summer of 1922 Carter persuaded Carnarvon to allow him to conduct one more campaign in the valley. Starting work earlier than usual Howard Carter opened up the stairway to the tomb of Tutankhamun on 4 November 1922. Carnarvon hurried to Luxor and the tomb was entered on 26 November. The discovery astounded the world: a royal tomb, mostly undisturbed, full of spectacular objects. Carter recruited a team of expert assistants to help him in the clearance of the tomb, and the conservation and recording of its remarkable contents. On 16 February 1923 the blocking to the burial chamber was removed, to reveal the unplundered body and funerary equipment of the dead king. Unhappily, the death of Lord Carnarvon on 5 April seriously affected the subsequent progress of Carter's work.

In spite of considerable and repeated bureaucratic interference, not easily managed by the short-tempered excavator, work on the clearance of the tomb proceeded slowly,

but was not completed until 1932. Carter handled the technical processes of clearance, conservation, and recording with exemplary skill and care. A popular account of the work was published in three volumes, *The Tomb of Tut·ankh·Amen* (1923–33), the first of which was substantially written by his principal assistant, Arthur C. Mace.

No archaeological discovery had met with such sustained public interest, yet Carter received no formal honours from his own country. In 1926, however, he did receive a decoration from the king of Egypt, and he was made a *commandeur* of the order of Léopold II by the king of the Belgians in 1932. He was awarded an honorary doctorate by Yale University in 1924, and was made a corresponding member of the Real Academia de la Historia, Madrid, in the same year.

The last years of Carter's life were plagued by illness, and he found himself incapable of preparing the full scientific publication of his remarkable discovery. Disillusioned, largely neglected by his few Egyptological friends, and suffering painfully from Hodgkin's disease, he eventually died on 2 March 1939 at his London home, 49 Albert Court, Kensington, Gore, and was buried on 6 March at Putney Vale cemetery. He was unmarried.

T. G. H. JAMES

Sources autobiographical essays, AM Oxf., Carter MSS · autobiographical essays, Metropolitan Museum of Art, New York, department of Egyptian art · private information (2004) [J. Carter] · T. G. H. James, *Howard Carter: the path to Tutankhamun* (1992) · N. Reeves and J. H. Taylor, *Howard Carter before Tutankhamun* (1992) · b. cert. · d. cert. · *The Times* (7 March 1939)

Archives Egypt Exploration Society, London, MSS · Metropolitan Museum of Art, New York, department of Egyptian art, corresp. · priv. coll., family MSS · U. Oxf., Griffith Institute, archaeological papers, notebooks, and indexes, incl. complete record of objects found in tomb of Tutankhamun · U. Oxf., Griffith Institute, Egyptological drawings | FILM Metropolitan Museum of Art, New York | SOUND BBC WAC · BL NSA, documentary recording

Likenesses W. Carter, pencil or crayon drawing, *c*.1882, priv. coll. · W. Carter, oils, 1924, U. Oxf., Griffith Institute [*see illus.*] · photographs, U. Oxf., Griffith Institute · photographs, priv. coll.

Wealth at death £2002 19*s*. 8*d*.: probate, 5 July 1939, *CGPLA Eng. & Wales* · English probate sealed in Cairo, 1 Sept 1939, *CGPLA Eng. & Wales*

Carter, Hugh (1837–1903), painter, was born in Birmingham on 4 March 1837, the son of Samuel *Carter (1805–1878), solicitor to the London and North Western and Midland railway companies and one-time MP for Coventry. After moving to London, he studied for a short time at Heatherley's Art School. He then trained with J. W. Bottomley, whose daughter, Maria Concordia, he married on 7 July 1866. They had four daughters and two sons, one of whom, Frank W. Carter, also became a painter. Carter also studied with Alexander Johnson, F. W. Topham, and John Phillip, as well as K. F. von Gebhardt in Düsseldorf.

From 1859 to 1902 Carter exhibited twenty-four pictures at the Royal Academy, domestic genre paintings as well as portraits of Alexander Blair (exh. 1873 and 1898), the antiquary Sir Joshua Staples (exh. 1887), and Mrs Worsley Taylor (exh. 1890). Two of his most successful exhibits at the academy were *Music hath Charms* (exh. 1872) and *Card Players* (exh. 1873), both representing scenes from Westphalian peasant life. Much of his best work was done in watercolour and pastel, and in those media he painted a number of landscapes which displayed a fine sense of colour and atmospheric effect. As a watercolour painter he was a frequent exhibitor at the Royal Institute of Painters in Water Colours, of which he became an associate in 1871 and a member in 1875. He was also a member of the Institute of Painters in Oil Colours from its foundation in 1883, and later of the New English Art Club. *The Last Ray*, an oil painting in the Tate collection, was donated by his wife in 1905. The Guildhall Art Gallery in London has his work *Hard Times*; and the Victoria and Albert Museum in London owns two watercolours, *Buildings and Gondolas at Venice* and *Interior of the Capuchin Convent at Albano*. His portrait of his uncle, Sir Francis Ronalds (1788–1873), the inventor of the first working electric telegraph, is in the National Portrait Gallery in London. Hugh Carter died on 27 September 1903 at his home, 12 Clarendon Road, Notting Hill, London; he was buried at Kensal Green cemetery. A memorial exhibition of his works was held at Leighton House, London, in October 1904.

MARTIN HARDIE, rev. SUZANNE FAGENCE COOPER

Sources Wood, *Vic. painters*, 3rd edn • Mallalieu, *Watercolour artists* • Graves, *RA exhibitors* • R. F. S. [R. F. Sketchley], ed., *A catalogue of the National Gallery of British Art at South Kensington*, rev. edn, 2 vols. (1893) • O. Sickert, 'The twenty-seventh exhibition of the New English Art Club', *The Studio*, 24 (1901–2), 263–8, esp. 267 • K. K. Yung, *National Portrait Gallery: complete illustrated catalogue, 1856–1979*, ed. M. Pettman (1981) • *The Tate Gallery collections: British painting, modern painting and sculpture*, Tate Gallery, 7th edn (1980) • private information (1912) • d. cert. • *CGPLA Eng. & Wales* (1903)
Wealth at death £10,353 14s. 3d.: probate, 30 Oct 1903, *CGPLA Eng. & Wales*

Carter, Isaac (d. 1741), printer, is a figure whose origins and early life are obscure, but he may have been a native of Carmarthenshire. He is credited with being the first legal and overt printer in Wales. On 11 January 1721 Carter married Ann Lewis at Cenarth.

Carter set up his printing press in Trerhedyn on the Cardiganshire side of the River Teifi at Newcastle Emlyn, where the first of his publications are dated 1718. This area in south Cardiganshire and north Carmarthenshire, around the Teifi valley, was, in the late seventeenth and eighteenth centuries, a notable centre for a great deal of literary activity, both religious and antiquarian. It was almost inevitable that a press should be established in the area, more for religious and educational reasons, perhaps, than strictly commercial ones. Carter is said to have been encouraged in his venture by the Carmarthen printer Nicholas Thomas, and at Trerhedyn he printed at least five (possibly six) titles. The earliest are two moralizing ballads, one against smoking and the other an appeal to heed the voice of conscience: *Cân o senn iw hên feistr tobacco*, by Alban Thomas, appeared in 1718, followed by *Can ar fesur triban ynghylch cydwybod a'i chynheddfau* (1718). Carter then printed a translation of Thomas Vincent's *Explicatory Catechism: Eglurhaad o gatechism byrraf y gymanfa* (1719; trans. J. P. and T. J.), and other devotional and instructional

works. These included *Dwysfawr rym buchedd grefyddol* (1722), a translation by Alban Thomas of William Melmoth's *The Great Importance of a Religious Life Considered*; *Y Christion cyffredin* (1724), a translation of Edward Wells's catechism *The Common Christian Rightly and Plainly Instructed*; and perhaps a parochial charge, *Annogaeth difrifol gweinidog iw blwyfolion* (c.1722).

In 1725 Carter moved his press to the flourishing market town of Carmarthen, where he was active at least until 1733. There was, however, no change in the nature of his output, and most of his titles reflect the concern of local clergy (Anglicans and dissenters) and of the gentry, who frequently commissioned or were patrons of both the translating and publishing of these works, for the spiritual life of the community. Some are translations of popular English books of devotion and instruction: *Maddeuant i'r edifairiol* (1725) was a translation by William Lewis and Evan Pryce of John Goodman's *The Penitent Pardoned*; another was *Llythr bugailiaidd oddiwrth Weinidog at ei blwyfolion* (1729), Alban Thomas's translation of William Assheton's *A Pastoral Letter from a Minister to his Parishoners*. Other titles were sermons or selections of writings from other published works.

Carter died early in 1741 and was buried at St Peter's Church, Carmarthen, on 4 May 1741.

BRYNLEY F. ROBERTS

Sources I. Jones, *A history of printing and printers in Wales to 1810* (1925), 34–5, 38–42 • E. Rees, ed., *Libri Walliae: a catalogue of Welsh books and books printed in Wales, 1546–1820*, 2 vols. (1987) • J. H. Davies, ed., *A bibliography of Welsh ballads printed in the 18th century* (1911), 167–8 [1908–11] • D. Jenkins, 'Braslun o hanes Argraffu yn Sir Aberteifi', *Journal of the Welsh Bibliographical Society*, 7 (1950–53), 174–91 • B. Williams, 'Early printers in Wales', *Archaeologia Cambrensis*, 4th ser., 7 (1876), 238 • parish records (burial), 4 May 1741, Carmarthen, St Peter's

Carter, James (bap. 1798, d. 1855), engraver, the son of William Carter, a comb maker, and his wife, Sarah, was baptized on 14 January 1798 in the parish of Shoreditch, London. He gained the silver medal of the Society of Arts for drawing in 1819 and was articled to J. Tyrrel, an architectural engraver. Carter found employment with John Weale, the fine art publisher and bookseller, and worked on numerous architectural and engineering works, including J. Stuart and N. Revett's *Antiquities of Athens* (2nd edn, 1841) and Sir William Chambers's *A Treatise on the Decorative Part of Civil Architecture* (rev. edn, 1862). However, he abandoned this class of engraving for landscapes and figures and attained great proficiency, although he does not appear to have had any further instruction. He worked on both copper and steel, and produced line and mezzotint engravings. Throughout the 1830s and much of the 1840s he was employed largely on engravings for the annuals, especially *Heath's Picturesque Annual* and *Jennings's Landscape Annual*, for which he executed several plates after Samuel Prout, David Roberts, and James Holland, and he also reproduced many of William Henry Bartlett's middle-eastern subjects.

Much of the remainder of Carter's life was spent engraving works for *The Vernon Gallery of British Art* (ed. S. C. Hall, 3 vols., 1854), which also appeared in the *Art Journal*. These included Frederick Goodall's *The Village Festival* and *Hadrian's Villa* (both 1850), painted by Richard Wilson. He also engraved a plate from his own design of *Cromwell Dictating to Milton the Despatch on Behalf of the Waldenses* and a number of portraits including that of Sir Marc Isambard Brunel, after Samuel Drummond. Edward Ward was so impressed with Carter's work that he specially requested that he should be employed to engrave his picture of *The South Sea Bubble*, and in 1849 employed him on his own behalf to engrave his picture of *Benjamin West's First Essay in Art*. He completed this plate a short time before his death, which occurred on 23 August 1855. Like many engravers Carter found his work to be very unremunerative, and was unable to make provision for his six children and widow, Sarah.

The *Dictionary of National Biography* article on a 'James Carlse' was an erroneous entry, apparently based on information about Carter mistakenly entered under the name of Carlse in Redgrave, *Artists*. No such James Carlse existed. L. H. Cust, rev. Greg Smith

Sources *Art Journal*, 17 (1855), 283–4 · Redgrave, *Artists* · R. K. Engen, *Dictionary of Victorian engravers, print publishers and their works* (1979) · B. Hunnisett, *A dictionary of British steel engravers* (1980) · B. Hunnisett, *An illustrated dictionary of British steel engravers*, new edn (1989) · *IGI*
Archives BM, department of prints and drawings · V&A, department of prints and drawings
Likenesses engraving, repro. in Hunnisett, *Illustrated dictionary*
Wealth at death left his family unprovided for: *DNB*

Carter, John (1554–1635), Church of England clergyman, born at Wickham, Kent, was educated at King's School, Canterbury, and then, through the generosity of a Mr Rose of Canterbury, at Clare College, Cambridge, under Thomas Byng. After Carter had taken his degree Byng offered him rooms in his own house to enable him to continue his studies, and it was at this time that he attended weekly meetings, applying logical, etymological, grammatical, and doctrinal interpretations to scripture with Laurence Chaderton, Lancelot Andrewes, and Ezekiel Culverwell.

Carter's links with Canterbury were maintained when in 1583 he became vicar of Bramford, Suffolk, a living under the patronage of the dean and chapter of Christ Church in Canterbury. The parish was a large one, with 340 communicants in 1603, and Carter performed his pastoral duties with great zeal. His avowal of puritanism led to conflict in his parish. The churchwardens of Bramford informed the episcopal visitation of 1597 that Carter 'hath not worne the surples these xij yeres at service or sacraments, and he never useth the signe of the crosse in baptisme' (Williams, 146), and after many disputes with his bishop he moved, with initial reluctance, to the smaller but better paid rectory of Belstead (fifty-six communicants in 1603), also in Suffolk, in 1617, where he was permitted to serve without subscription or using ceremonies which offended his conscience. In both Bramford and Belstead he drew hearers from Ipswich to his weekly lectures. He was the author of a commentary upon the sermon on the mount, of two catechisms for 'young novices in religion' (one of which is now lost), and of an unpublished petition to James I for the removal of burdensome ceremonies.

Carter died soon after 22 February 1635, presumably at Belstead, and Samuel Carter of Ipswich preached a commemorative sermon. His son, also John *Carter, drew up an anecdotal life of his father, which attests his piety, good humour, and wit. It was first published in 1653 under the title *The Tomb-Stone, and a Rare Sight … a Broken and Imperfect Monument, of that Worthy Man … Mr. John Carter*. It was republished in Samuel Clarke's *Collection of the Lives of Ten Eminent Divines* in 1662.

  Sidney Lee, rev. Jason Yiannikkou

Sources J. Carter, *The tomb-stone, and A rare sight* (1653) · 'The condition of the archdeaconries of Suffolk and Sudbury in the year 1603', *Proceedings of the Suffolk Institute of Archaeology and Natural History*, 6 (1885–8), 389, 394 · R. Freeman Bullen, 'Catalogue of beneficed clergy in Suffolk, 1551–1631', *Proceedings of the Suffolk Institute of Archaeology and Natural History*, 22 (1934–6), 294–333, esp. 298–9 · J. F. Williams, ed., *Diocese of Norwich, Bishop Redman's visitation, 1597*, Norfolk RS, 18 (1946), 146, 151 · BL, Add. MS 19165 · J. Carter, *Winterevenings communication with young novices in religion* (1628) · S. Clarke, *A collection of the lives of ten eminent divines* (1662) · Venn, *Alum. Cant.*, 1/1.299
Likenesses J. Dunstall, etching, BM, NPG; repro. in S. Clarke, *Collection of the lives* (1683) · engraving (after R. Vaughan), repro. in Carter, *Tomb-stone*

Carter, John (1594/5?–1655), Church of England clergyman, was born at Bramford, Suffolk, the youngest of nine children of John *Carter (1554–1635), the vicar there; according to his own account in *The Tomb-Stone, and a Rare Sight* (1653), he was born when his father was forty. Like his father he was educated at Clare College, Cambridge, where he probably matriculated in Michaelmas term 1610, graduated BA in 1614, and proceeded MA in 1617. He was ordained deacon in March 1618 and priest on 21 February 1619 in the diocese of Lincoln. Nothing is known of his activities in the 1620s.

About 1630 Carter married Anne. In 1631 the parishioners elected him curate of St Peter Mancroft, Norwich, and two years later the city appointed him one of the four lecturers at the church. By late 1634 he had acquired a reputation as a visiting preacher, for instance at Wethersfield in the Stour valley, but his preaching licence was suspended on 26 March 1636 following a drive for stricter conformity by the new bishop of Norwich, Matthew Wren, and his chancellor, Clement Corbet. Anxious to win back his licence, Carter reluctantly read the whole of the prayer book service in his church, though he made a point of officiating partly from the reading desk and not wholly, as instructed, from the chancel, telling his congregation that he obeyed only 'as I must do it or leave my ministry' (Webster, 212). Corbet complained to Wren that Carter had 'played fast and loose and peepbo with you' (Ketton-Cremer, 80), and in June the suspension was still in force. In October it was reported that Carter had been deputed to present to the king a petition devised by some members of the assembly of Norwich on behalf of suspended ministers, but by 20 December he seems to have given up his living.

Carter's whereabouts and status at this period are uncertain. While one report had it that he and his wife had fled the diocese 'for two years together … going where they had no maintenance assured' (*An Hue and Cry*, 26), John Collinge, minister of St Stephen, Norwich, later recalled that Carter acted as minister at Newport, Essex, although this cannot be corroborated. Carter himself remembered bitterly the failure of the city fathers to act in his defence during the 'prelatical persecution': 'you let in all the popish trash, and tucked away your most faithful ministers' (ibid., 129). However, he regained his preaching licence, for in 1638 he was elected chaplain or chief minister of St Peter Mancroft. He retained the post when, in the following year in a *cause célèbre*, his parishioners defeated at law a challenge from one Hugh Roberts to their right of presentation, although his licence was suspended again by Wren's successor, Richard Mountague, possibly in retaliation for parishioners' resistance to Mountague's imposition of altar rails on the church. Yet Thomas Knyvett noted that in January 1641 Carter was an active preacher, one of only two left in Norwich. Following a petition of support from his parishioners, on 23 February the House of Commons voided the suspension as illegal, formulated the general principle that every properly instituted minister could preach freely in his own parish, and voted to deprive the bishop of Norwich.

In a sermon at the Greenyard, Norwich, on 17 June 1644, later published with a narrative of subsequent events in *The Nail and the Wheel* (1647), Carter expressed support for parliament and for religious reform, but he was becoming increasingly anxious at the toleration of religious and civil indiscipline from vagrants, 'profane persons', 'malignants', and sectarians, while 'the orthodox party are slighted' (pp. 21–2, 27). In 1646 he was one of seven ministers who urged the city assembly to endorse demands for the immediate implementation of presbyterianism, unwisely provoking local Independents by boasting of support from unnamed 'great persons above' in London. Following encouragement from the speaker of the Commons, in June 1647 the city governors planned a presbyterian classis and considered eldership nominations, but although Carter had firm allies in Norwich, most notably the dedicatee of *The Nail and the Wheel*, Lady Frances Hobart, no further progress was made. He also experienced increasing disrespect from his parishioners—not just from lower-class sectaries, but also among the wealthier, because of growing royalist sympathies. Disenchanted with life in the city Carter looked elsewhere and in August 1647 he was instituted as minister of Barnham Broom, Suffolk.

However, perhaps, as his friends hoped, through Lady Frances's persuasion, Carter remained in Norwich. In a sermon on 18 June 1647 at the inauguration as mayor of his friend the conservative John Utting, he attacked violently those city governors whom he saw as having self-interestedly turned from conniving at Laudian innovations to hastening towards separatism. Utting, 'who lives under my charge' at St Peter, was expected to break with the past and 'with all your weight, turn over idolators, hereticks, schismacks [and] sabbath-breakers' (Carter, *The Nail and the Wheel*, 98). Utting's efforts in this direction proved counterproductive. Utting allowed deprived clergy in the city to preach openly in favour of the prayer book and on 24 April 1648 openly supported a royalist riot. Carter does not seem ever to have called publicly for the restoration of the king, and he accepted an invitation to preach a thanksgiving sermon at the cathedral on 26 April following Charles Fleetwood's defeat of the insurrection. His relations with the city magistracy continued to deteriorate. Although a tirade against well-intentioned but spineless magistrates in a sermon of 18 June 1650 temporarily relieved his frustrations and was followed by a partial reconciliation, in 1653 he was sufficiently angry with them again to publish the sermon in *The Tomb-Stone*.

In 1654 Carter moved from St Peter, having been elected rector of another city parish, St Laurence. In his will, begun on 17 September 1655, he initially intended to leave books to Norwich Library, but finding that 'the library is locked up, the ministers locked out of it, and that it is never like to be of publique use againe, but that the books are devoted to the wormes, dust and rottenness' (Blomefield, 262) he withdrew the grant, providing instead for the purchase of coal for the poor. He died on 10 December and was buried two days later at St Laurence, following a service led by John Collinge, who in compliance with Carter's wishes did not preach a funeral sermon. His new parishioners 'had such a value for him, that they repaired his house, and laid a tombstone over him at their expense' (ibid., 263).   STEPHEN WRIGHT

Sources J. Evans, *Seventeenth century Norwich* (1979) • F. Blomefield and C. Parkin, *An essay towards a topographical history of the county of Norfolk*, [2nd edn], 11 vols. (1805–10), vol. 4 • J. Carter, *The nail and the wheel* (1647) [E411/6] • J. Carter, *The tomb-stone, and A rare sight* (1653) • *Report on the manuscripts of the family of Gawdy, formerly of Norfolk*, HMC, 11 (1885) • R. W. Ketton-Cremer, *Norfolk in the civil war: a portrait of a society in conflict* (1969) • Venn, *Alum. Cant.* • T. Webster, *Godly clergy in early Stuart England: the Caroline puritan movement, c.1620–1643* (1997) • *The journal of Sir Simonds D'Ewes from the beginning of the Long Parliament to the opening of the trial of the earl of Strafford*, ed. W. Notestein (1923) • J. Collinge, *Elisha's lamentation for Elijah* (1657) • *An hue and cry after vox populi, or, An answer to vox diaboli* (1646) [E355/13; Thomason tract E 355(13)] • *Vox Norwici, or, The city of Norwich vindicated* [E358/4] • B. Schofield, ed., *The Knyvett letters, 1620–1644*, Norfolk RS, 20 (1949)

Carter, John (1748–1817), draughtsman and antiquary, the son of Benjamin Carter, a marble-carver and sculptor, and his wife (whose maiden name was Jameson), was born on 22 June 1748 in Piccadilly, London, 'two doors down from the south end of White Horse Street', where his family had been sculptors and carvers since the sixteenth century (*GM*, 1st ser., 86/1, 229). After being sent at an early age to a boarding-school in Battersea, and afterwards to one in Kennington Lane, he returned when about twelve years old to Carter's Statuary; there he trained as a sculptor and draughtsman, making drawings for the workmen. When his father died young in 1766, Carter was apprenticed to Joseph Dixon, surveyor and builder, who with his brother Richard became a developer in London's West End. Before they went bankrupt in 1778 the Dixon brothers had built a number of houses in Pall Mall. In this operation the young Henry Holland was involved, and thus Carter found himself working, from 1768 onwards, probably as a draughtsman and improver, for the future architect of Carlton House. Whether about this time he also drew for his future arch-enemy James Wyatt remains a matter for speculation.

It was in the pages of the *Builder's Magazine* (1774–8), as a draughtsman and writer, that Carter first established himself as a zealous admirer of Gothic. But it was as one of the draughtsmen for the Society of Antiquaries' series *Vetusta monumenta* that Carter first emerged as a notable figure: his drawings, published in 1789 and 1796, set new standards in recording Gothic detail. Soon afterwards he became involved in a programme which established for the first time the archaeological status of Gothic as fully comparable to the Antique: the Cathedrals Series published by the Society of Antiquaries. Carter was responsible in particular for the measured plans, elevations, sections, and details of St Stephen's Chapel, Westminster (1795), Exeter Cathedral (1797), Bath Abbey (1798), Durham Cathedral (1801), Gloucester Cathedral (1809), and St Albans Abbey (1813). Unique in their time for precision and scholarship, these volumes were designed 'not alone to please the eye … but to give information and instruction to the rising generation of Antiquaries and Architectural Professors' (*GM*, 1st ser., 73/1, 1803, 106–7). For that pioneering aim, at least, the series deserves to stand as Carter's monument.

It was Carter's work as draughtsman to the Society of Antiquaries—unofficially from 1780, semi-officially from 1784, and officially from 1792—which brought him into conflict with James Wyatt. In 1795 Wyatt's 'restorations' at Durham Cathedral—and his alterations at Westminster—were condemned by Carter as desecration. That was the year in which Carter himself was elected to the society. Now, with help from the antiquary Richard Gough, the Catholic vicar apostolic of the midland district, John Milner, and the scientist-cum-antiquary Sir Henry Englefield, he set out to prevent Wyatt's election. In this he was temporarily successful: the king's surveyor-general was blackballed on 29 June 1797, but later elected thanks to royal influence. After that Carter's role in antiquarian circles was reduced to that of a *franc-tireur*. Gough, however, stayed loyal to his protégé; he had already employed him as a draughtsman in preparing the *History of Croyland Abbey* (1783) and *Sepulchral Monuments* (1786); he also contributed to the cost of Carter's *Specimens of Ancient Sculpture and Painting* (2 vols., 1780–94; new edn, 1838; repr. 1887). While *Specimens* was in progress, Carter also published, in six miniature volumes, *Views of Ancient Buildings in England* (1786–93; republished in 4 vols. as *Specimens of Gothic Architecture, and Ancient Buildings in England*, 1824): all the plates for these volumes were drawn and etched by the author himself. In 1795 Carter began what was to have

been his most ambitious work, a synoptic history of medieval architecture arranged systematically on the basis of measured examples and entitled *The Ancient Architecture of England* (2 pts, 1795–1814; ed. J. Britton, 1845). This was a pioneering effort, but it was methodologically unsatisfactory: its terminology was confused, its chronology wilful, and its whole approach chauvinistic. The project was never completed.

It was Carter's journalism in the *Gentleman's Magazine* which eventually earned him his permanent niche in the history of the Gothic revival. Between 1797 and 1817, in a mammoth series of articles—signed, anonymous, and pseudonymous, amounting to some 380 in twenty years—he displayed a formidable, if eccentric, mastery of the polemical arts. Travelling the country in search of medieval antiquities—and hunting down modern 'architectural innovation'—he established himself as England's first architectural journalist. His ideal was a Gothic myth, a dream of fourteenth-century England; his enemies—apart from neo-classicists and Frenchmen—were all those secularists, progressives, and improvers whom he blamed for the decline of English architecture.

Carter practised little as an architect. Midford Castle, Bath (*c*.1775), a triangular folly, is probably from his hand: part rococo, part picturesque, and wholly charming. The Chiswell monument (1797) at St Mary, Debden, Essex, also his work, displays a precocious knowledge of Gothic forms. And at St Peter's Roman Catholic Chapel, Winchester (1792; partly rebuilt, 1888), he designed a place of worship for Bishop Milner which anticipated the historical approach of later ecclesiology. Although often assumed to be Irish and Roman Catholic—his maternal grandfather, John Jameson of Lancaster, may well have been both—Carter went out of his way to deny both assumptions in the *Gentleman's Magazine* in 1799. Architecturally at least, he was neither Catholic nor protestant: in his own words, he stood 'between the altar and communion table' (*GM*, 1st ser., 78/2, 1808, 1166n.), an ambivalence perhaps reflected in his church designs. But in any case Carter's forte was not design but propaganda. His contribution to the Gothic revival was neither academic nor strictly archaeological, nor even antiquarian: it was essentially inspirational. A. W. Pugin and William Burges, for example, both acknowledged his leadership. In Mitford's phrase, Carter turned out to be 'the Wyclif of our architectural reformation' (*GM*, 2nd ser., 16, 1841, 527).

Apart from a love of medieval Gothic architecture, Carter's great passion was the music of Purcell and Handel: 'I am a man lost in two extremes', he wrote, 'one for the Antiquities of England, and the other for the Divine Melodies of the immortal Handel' (*GM*, 1st ser., 75/2, 1805, 726). His own compositions—songs, operas, comic opera—have not survived as musical scores and only their titles are known, such as 'The white rose, a dramatick romance, founded on historic facts of the fifteenth century, written and set to music for the harpsichord, with an accompaniment for the violin, by John Carter … [with] eleven highly finished drawings for scenery' (Bodl. Oxf., MS Douce cc284). Carter died of dropsy in Upper Eaton

Street, Pimlico, where he was living, on 8 September 1817 and he was buried at Hampstead parish church. An inscribed stone to his memory was placed on the south side of the church. His collection of drawings, antiquities, and other items was sold by auction at Sothebys on 23–5 February 1818, and raised £1527 3s. 6d. It included a series of sketches relating to the antiquities of England and south Wales, from the years 1764 to 1816, in twenty-six volumes, the product of his summer travels over more than half a century; many are now in the British Library.

In his writings Carter displayed both the qualities and the defects of an autodidact. In person he was lean and lanky; in manner nervous, obstinate, and irascible. Although a lifelong bachelor, he published an account of an early love affair, with an engraving of his inamorata in the nude (*The Scotch Parents, or, The Remarkable Case of John Ramble*, 1773); in later years he travelled with a young female servant dressed in boy's clothes. 'In his habits', wrote J. C. Buckler,

> he was frugal, even to parsimony, and very temperate; and his make, which was tall and thin, rendered him capable of enduring privation and hardship … His principles were certainly sound; his integrity incorruptible; but no man created more adversaries, if not enemies, by his opinions and writings … [Even so, he was] Antiquity's most resolute friend. (*GM*, 1st ser., 87/2, 367–8)

J. MORDAUNT CROOK

Sources J. M. Crook, *John Carter and the mind of the Gothic revival*, Society of Antiquaries of London Occasional Papers, 17 (1995) · Colvin, *Archs.* · J. C. Buckler, *GM*, 1st ser., 87/2 (1817), 363–8 · J. C. Buckler, *GM*, 1st ser., 88/1 (1818), 273–6, 382 · J. C. Buckler, *GM*, 1st ser., 92/1 (1822), 102–3 · *GM*, 1st ser., 75 (1805), 630, 726 · *GM*, 1st ser., 86/1 (1816), 229 · J. Britton, 'Memoir', *The Builder*, 8 (1850), 302–4 · M. E. Roberts, 'John Carter and St Stephen's Chapel', in W. M. Ormrod, *England in the fourteenth century* [Harlaxton 1985] (1986), 202–12 · will, PRO, PROB 11/1596, sig. 472
Archives BL, corresp. and papers, Add. MSS 29925–29944, 31113, 31153 · Bodl. Oxf., papers · King's Lond., personal papers incl. autobiography and drawings | Lincoln Cathedral, accounts by John Carter and Richard Gough of architectural discoveries at Lincoln
Likenesses S. Harding, pencil, 1817, BM; repro. in Crook, *John Carter*
Wealth at death see will, PRO, PROB 11/1596, sig. 472

Carter, John (1815–1850), silk weaver and draughtsman, was born in Coggeshall, Essex, on 31 July 1815, the son of a labourer. After attending the local school he went to a charity school for two years, from 1828. Although he showed signs of artistic talent, his social circumstances prevented him from developing his gifts. He was subsequently apprenticed to Charles Beckwith, a silk weaver, and set up independently after his marriage in 1835 to a woman named Lucy (d. 1841).

In May 1836, while climbing a tree in search of birds, Carter fell 40 feet to the ground, receiving a severe injury to his spine which virtually paralysed him from the neck down. On hearing of a young woman who had learned to draw with her mouth after losing the use of her hands, he resolved to follow her example, and by dogged perseverance and without any personal instruction he acquired an extraordinary proficiency. He concentrated mainly on line drawing and, by holding the pencil or brush between his teeth, was able to produce accurate and delicate strokes which made his drawings resemble engravings.

Carter died on 2 June 1850 in Church Street, Coggeshall, of injuries received in a carriage accident on 21 May. The Revd W. J. Dampier, vicar of Coggeshall, published a memoir in 1850, which also appeared in a revised edition in 1875. It lists eighty-three of Carter's drawings, including copies of works by Dürer, Raphael, Rembrandt, Van Dyck, and Edwin Landseer, with the names of their owners.

T. F. HENDERSON, rev. DELIA GAZE

Sources W. J. Dampier, *A memoir of John Carter*, 1850; rev. edn (1875) · F. J. Mills, *The life of John Carter* (1868) · d. cert.

Carter, John Waynflete (1905–1975), bibliographer and antiquarian bookseller, was born at 6 High Street, Eton, on 10 May 1905, the eldest of two sons and two daughters of Thomas Buchanan Carter, an architect but later an Eton master and in Anglican orders, and his wife, Margaret Teresa Stone. Strong family connections on both sides prompted his lifelong devotion to Eton College, where he was a king's scholar (and eventually became a fellow in 1967). He was subsequently, from 1924, a scholar of King's College, Cambridge, where he took first classes in both parts of the classical tripos. In his last year at Cambridge he attended A. E. Housman's lectures, which he found highly sympathetic. Housman's account of the Renaissance editors of Catullus encouraged Carter's collection of the works of a poet whom he long cherished intentions of editing (the books are now at the University of Texas). Carter repaid his debt to Housman by editing his *Collected Poems* (editions from 1939 onwards, anonymously) and *Selected Prose* (1961); and with John Sparrow he compiled a bibliography first published in 1941 and revised in 1952. His enthusiasm for old books was thus sharpened by the critical spirit and a systematic approach that marked all his bibliographical work. His wife, Ernestine Marie Fantl (1906–1983) [see Carter, Ernestine Marie], daughter of Siegfried Fantl of Savannah, Georgia, whom he married in 1936, shared his tastes and discrimination; she became a leading fashion writer and an associate editor of the *Sunday Times*.

On leaving Cambridge Carter joined the London branch of the New York publishers and booksellers Charles Scribner's Sons, for whom he worked as European agent from 1927 to 1939, returning after war service as managing director from 1946 to 1953. The antiquarian book business Carter built up rapidly gained a high reputation in the trade. He came into contact with the book collector Michael Sadleir, who as a director of Constable's published his first book, *Binding Variants in English Publishing, 1820–1900* (1932).

It was Sadleir, too, who had the courage to publish *An Enquiry into the Nature of Certain Nineteenth Century Pamphlets* (1934), in which Carter had collaborated with Graham Pollard. The young co-authors had come to suspect as creative forgeries some fifty early 'editions' of the lesser works of prominent Victorian authors (for example, the so-called 'Reading' edition of Elizabeth Barrett Browning's *Sonnets from the Portuguese*) which all antedated the known first editions and were therefore of special interest to collectors. The *Enquiry* combined textual criticism with the chemical analysis of papers and intensive scrutiny of the typographical anachronisms these expensive pamphlets shared. It made a fine detective story in a great age of detective stories, and its final, carefully unstated indictment of the then most eminent and respected of living British book collectors, Thomas James Wise, created a sensation. The bibliographical establishment was strongly defensive of its pundit, but Carter (as the better-known of the two authors) did not weaken; neither did Pollard and Sadleir. Beyond initial general denial, Wise could offer no defence; he died in 1937. Carter and Pollard continued to gather additional evidence for a second edition of the *Enquiry*, which eventually came out posthumously (much augmented in a *Sequel*, by Nicolas Barker and John Collins) in 1983.

Carter's bibliographical interests extended far beyond scrutinizing suspect Victorian pamphlets. He had excellent taste in fine printing, particularly of the sixteenth century, and his own fine italic hand was modelled on the calligraphy of the same period. His enthusiasms for the prose of Sir Thomas Browne and the illustrative work of Paul Nash were happily combined in the Curwen Press edition of *Urne-Buriall* (1932), a masterpiece of inter-war British book production. With his bookseller friends Percy Muir and David Randall he made a speciality of music manuscripts and first editions. His serendipity as a book hunter once discovered a set of Audubon's signed drawings of 1827 for *Birds of America*. Carter discerned the potential of detective fiction as a collecting genre, on which he contributed a pioneering essay to *New Paths in Book Collecting*, which he edited in 1934. He was a pioneer, too, in the history of science, preparing in 1938 a Scribner catalogue of *Science and Thought in the 19th Century*. His interest continued as the fashion and the academic discipline developed, with the great *Printing and the Mind of Man* exhibition of 1963, and its authoritative catalogue; Carter was one of the principal organizers.

In 1939 Carter joined the Ministry of Information, first in censorship duties and from 1944 in New York, where his work for British information services included *Victory in Burma* (1945), to tell America of the British share in the burden of war in the Far East. He returned to Scribner's in 1946, until the London branch closed in 1953. In 1951 his career as a bookseller had culminated in his tracing and purchasing the Shuckburgh copy of the Gutenberg Bible, which as a great novelty he arranged to be flown across the Atlantic to its new owner. Carter briefly resumed his career in the public service as personal assistant to Sir Roger Makins, then ambassador in Washington, from 1953 to 1955; he was appointed CBE for his services in 1956. He then joined Sothebys as an associate director (1956–72) and was much involved in the rapid expansion of the firm, using his transatlantic connections to great advantage.

In 1947 Carter was Sandars reader at Cambridge University; the lectures were published as *Taste and Technique in Book-Collecting* (1948), and were followed by *Books and Book-*

Collectors (1956), a gathering of his elegant occasional writings. His *ABC for Book Collectors* (1952, and frequently revised) was immediately recognized as authoritative; it is still valued, not least for its pungent commentary. Carter was a regular contributor to the *Times Literary Supplement*, and to the *Book Collector*, edited by his friend John Hayward. Although he never produced the major work of scholarship his friends hoped for, having too modest an estimate of his own capacity, he was a fine ambassador for the whole world of antiquarian books. Some members of the trade, thinking him condescending, disliked him, but he was unfailingly kind, and generous with his time, particularly to beginners. The award of the gold medal of the Bibliographical Society in 1974 (by which time illness forbade a formal presentation) showed that the world of books knew him what it owed him.

Carter's standards were high, in scholarship and deportment alike. Tall and handsome in appearance, elegant in dress, with an eyeglass 'before which' (his *Times* obituarist, A. N. L. Munby, claimed) 'head waiters quailed', he took his transatlantic cultural responsibilities seriously enough to compose a short treatise on the correct mixing of a dry Martini. Carter died at St George's Nursing Home, 61 St George's Square, Westminster, on 18 March 1975.

ALAN BELL

Sources N. Barker, *The Book Collector*, 24 (1975), 202–16 · A. N. L. Munby, *The Times* (19 March 1975) · *DNB* · *WWW* · *CGPLA Eng. & Wales* (1975) · b. cert. · d. cert.
Archives King's Cam., papers | BL, corresp. with S. Cockerell, Add. MS 52709 · Bodl. Oxf., corresp. with W. Clark · Bodl. Oxf., corresp. with G. Pollard · King's AC Cam., corresp. with A. N. L. Munby
Wealth at death £32,238: probate, 30 May 1975, *CGPLA Eng. & Wales*

Carter, Landon (1710–1778), diarist and planter in America, was born on 18 August 1710 at Corotoman, his family's country seat in Lancaster county, Virginia, the son of a very wealthy first-generation Virginian, Robert (King) *Carter (1663–1732), a planter–merchant member of the king's council in Virginia, and his second wife, Elizabeth Willis, *née* Landon (1683–1719), an English-born widow. From his father's first marriage had come a son and three daughters, and from the second came four daughters and four sons, of whom Carter was the third. One of his brothers was the planter and politician Charles *Carter (1707–1764). He was educated at the school of Solomon Low in London (1720–26), and briefly (1727–8) at the College of William and Mary in Williamsburg, Virginia; his surviving, annotated library indicates lifelong self-education. In 1732 he married Elizabeth Wormeley (1712–1740), with whom he had four children, three sons and a daughter.

Carter followed the career of a high-born Virginia gentleman. Settled in Richmond county from about 1734 he soon became a JP, a colonel of militia, and a vestryman of his parish of the established Church of England. After Elizabeth's death in January 1740, he married in 1742 Maria Byrd (1727–1744), with whom he had a further daughter. In 1746 he married his third wife, Elizabeth

Beale (d. c.1752), with whom he had three more daughters.

Carter was elected burgess for his county from 1752 to 1768, and in 1774 was chosen to chair the resistance committee. He was a fierce American patriot who contributed a stream of pamphlets and newspaper polemics resisting encroachments on the traditional English liberties to which (as he saw it) American colonists were entitled. He continued to be active in patriot mobilization to the end of his life.

Carter is now most famous for his diary, extensive portions of which survive for 1752 to 1778. Published in full in 1965, the assemblage makes striking contributions to eighteenth-century science and letters. Carter was well read in current medical literature; he wrote many detailed clinical reports of cases among his nearly two hundred enslaved workers. In agricultural improvement, his diary observations and experiments cumulate as the most detailed such English-language record surviving from his time. The literary qualities of many of his descriptions make this a fine Enlightenment georgic, though in unpolished first draft. But it is the stories of estate-household conflicts that are unmatched. The narrative outpourings often blend the sentimental modes of the mid-eighteenth century with ancient English folkloric traditions. There are stories of heirs who wait to step into a dead man's shoes, and there are numerous stories pondering whether the servants are drunken knaves or drunken fools. (These 'servants' are nearly all enslaved African Americans, but that does not preclude great continuities between Carter's narratives and English traditions that were part of an estate-house lore as old as the division between landlord and peasant.)

So Carter's historical significance now derives overwhelmingly from an extraordinary scientific gentleman's diary studded with dramatic accounts of life in a colonial plantation house. The diarist's patriarchal angst was evidently induced by the king-defying revolution in which he and so many of his peers were involved. Attached to monarchical patriarchalism to the end, he resisted republican Virginia's abolition of entails, and was proud to have endowed all his offspring with substantial inheritances. His health having declined, he died of a dropsy on 22 December 1778 at his own country seat, Sabine Hall, and was buried nearby in the now-vanished graveyard of the Lunenburg parish church in present-day Warsaw, Richmond county, Virginia.

RHYS ISAAC

Sources *The diary of Colonel Landon Carter of Sabine Hall, 1752–1778*, ed. J. P. Greene, 2 vols. (1965) · W. R. Wineman, *The Landon Carter papers in the University of Virginia Library: a calendar and biographical sketch*, ed. J. A. Garraty and M. C. Carnes, 3 (1962), 491–2 · P. P. Hoffman, ed., 'The Carter family papers, 1659–1797, in the Sabine Hall collection', 1967, University of Virginia, Charlottesville [microfilm, 4 reels] · R. Isaac, 'Carter, Landon', *ANB* · R. Isaac, 'Stories and constructions of identity: folk telling and diary inscriptions in revolutionary Virginia', *Through a glass darkly: reflections on personal identity in early America*, ed. R. Hoffman, M. Sobel, and F. J. Tente (1997), 206–37 · private information (2004) [Beverley Wellford, descendant] · R. Isaac, *The transformation of Virginia, 1740–1790* (1982) · *Parks's Virginia Gazette* (12 Dec 1745)

Archives College of William and Mary, Williamsburg, Virginia, family papers | University of Virginia, Charlottesville, Sabine Hall Collection
Likenesses attrib. C. Bridges, oils, c.1750, Sabine Hall, Warsaw, Richmond county, Virginia; repro. in Greene, ed., *Diary*
Wealth at death thousands of acres (uninventoried) in several counties; about 400 slaves; sterling value of all this property was c.£40,000: Wineman, *Landon Carter papers*, 46

Carter, Sir Lawrence (*bap.* 1668, *d.* 1745), judge, was baptized at St Mary de Castro, Leicester, on 30 September 1668. He was the first son of Lawrence Carter (c.1641–1710), politician, of the Newarke, Leicester, and his first wife, Elizabeth (d. 1671), daughter of Thomas Wadland of the Newarke, a solicitor. After being articled to his wife's father, Carter senior served as MP for the town in several parliaments of William III, of whom he was a firm supporter, and in 1685 projected and carried out a system of water supply for Leicester.

The younger Lawrence Carter matriculated at Trinity College, Oxford, on 30 May 1688. He was called to the bar at the Inner Temple in 1694, and at Lincoln's Inn, *ad eundem*, in 1702. On 1 September 1697 he was unanimously elected recorder of Leicester in succession to Sir Nathan Wright, an office he held until 1729. He represented Leicester in parliament from 1698 to 1702; and then sat for Bere Alston, Devon (1710–22), under the aegis of Lord Stamford, leader of the Leicestershire whigs. He sided with the government in every documented division from the accession of George I. From 30 May 1717 he chaired the Commons committee considering the impeachment of Lord Oxford. Carter spoke in favour of the Occasional Conformity and Schism Acts. After Lord Stamford's death, he again represented Leicester, from 1722 to 1726.

In 1715 Carter was counsel for the crown against several of the prisoners taken during the Jacobite rising of 1715, first at Liverpool with Sir Francis Page, king's serjeant, and then at Carlisle on a special commission with Baron Fortescue. In December 1715 he became solicitor-general to the prince of Wales, afterwards George II. Appointed serjeant-at-law in 1724, he was made king's serjeant on 30 April, and knighted on 4 May in the same year. On 16 October 1726 he was raised to the bench of the court of exchequer in succession to Baron Price, and continued in the office until his death. He lived in Redcross Street, the Newarke, Leicester, in a house built on the site of the collegiate church, which was destroyed during the Reformation. He was highly esteemed in the town, and with his half-brother Thomas was a trustee of the Holbech charity. He died on 14 March 1745, and was buried in the church of St Mary de Castro. He was never married, and his estates passed to his half-brother.

J. A. HAMILTON, *rev.* ROBERT BROWN

Sources HoP, *Commons* · E. Foss, *Biographia juridica: a biographical dictionary of the judges of England … 1066–1870* (1870) · J. Nichols, *The history and antiquities of the county of Leicester*, 4 vols. (1795–1815) · N. Luttrell, *A brief historical relation of state affairs from September 1678 to April 1714*, 6 vols. (1857) · *GM*, 1st ser., 15 (1745), 164 · W. P. Baildon, ed., *The records of the Honorable Society of Lincoln's Inn: admissions*, 2 vols. (1896)
Likenesses G. Vertue, line engraving (after J. Richardson), BM, NPG

Carter, Mark Raymond Bonham, Baron Bonham-Carter (1922–1994), public servant and politician, was born in London on 11 February 1922, the elder son and the third of four children of Sir Maurice Bonham Carter (1880–1960), private secretary to the prime minister from 1910 to 1916, and his wife, (Helen) Violet Bonham *Carter, later Baroness Asquith of Yarnbury (1887–1969), the only daughter of Herbert Henry *Asquith, prime minister (1908–16), and later first earl of Oxford and Asquith, and his first wife, Helen Kelsall, *née* Melland. Bonham Carter was educated at Winchester College, Balliol College, Oxford (where he obtained a second-class degree in politics, philosophy, and economics in 1946), and (as a Commonwealth Fund fellow) the University of Chicago. He was born and educated into the Liberal purple, but at a time when purple, at any rate Liberal purple, was a less fashionable colour than it had been. As a result those great opportunities which his grandfather had so effortlessly seized were not as open to him, and he was never able to test his quality in government. Yet although his talents exceeded his opportunities, it would be a mistake—and one to which, with his continuing zest, he never succumbed—to see his life as one of frustrated promise. To make a natural but testing comparison, his actual achievements far exceeded those of his legendary uncle, Raymond *Asquith, to whom he bore many resemblances of wit and verve, and this was not only because his life lasted nearly twice as long.

Before he could engage with these achievements or frustrations Bonham Carter had to go through a peculiarly testing war. As a Grenadier Guards subaltern in March 1943, he took part in a particularly murderous battle in Tunisia. His battalion lost fourteen officers killed, five wounded, and five taken prisoner (with the casualties among other ranks 255). As the total officer strength of a battalion was under forty this was an appalling rate of loss. Bonham Carter was lucky to be among the five taken prisoner. He was transported to a camp in the north of Italy, from where he escaped six months later. He and another officer then proceeded in night marches and thirty days to cover 400 miles before they reached British lines near Bari.

Returned after rehabilitation and amid some publicity to the guards depot at Windsor, Bonham Carter became a frequent guest at the royal castle and found lifetime friendships with all four members of the close-knit family there. Roy Jenkins heard direct from the highest authority how, in the fifth year of the war, 'life had become rather dull here until Mark arrived, made a lot of jokes and cheered us all up.' He was then a frequent guest at Balmoral during the post-war summers and was considered very much a member of the 'Princess Margaret set', as long as that coterie persisted. In the meantime he had both seen another period of military action in north-west Europe and been Liberal candidate for the Barnstaple division of Devon at the 1945 general election. There he had not won, but at the age of twenty-three he had performed very respectably, running a strong second. This west country connection led to his fighting and winning a by-election in the adjacent Torrington division in March 1958, and thus securing his only period as an MP. He was narrowly defeated at the general election of October 1959. This brief experience, however, had two strong effects on his future political orientation. First, coming as it did quickly on top of his bitter opposition to Anthony Eden's Suez venture, it turned him in a strongly anti-Conservative direction. Regarding him as a usurper in one of their traditional seats and an upper-class traitor, they were beastly to him in the House of Commons. Thereafter he was also very much a radical Liberal, better disposed to moderate Labour than to the Conservative Party. Second, his membership of the British delegation to the Council of Europe reinforced his natural Europeanism, and made this one of his persistent causes.

After his return from the University of Chicago Bonham Carter became a publisher. He joined William Collins & Sons, then still very much a family firm, although they exceptionally welcomed him as an outsider in through the gentlemen's entrance. The firm was erecting a major contemporary metropolitan list upon the solid but unexciting foundation of a Glasgow printing works concentrated upon bibles and dictionaries. He retained a fluctuating connection there until almost the end of his life. His major early coup for Collins was *Dr Zhivago* in 1956, and this led to his being latterly primarily concerned with what became the separate imprint of Harvill, which, well before the separation, had been becoming an intellectually upmarket branch of Collins. He was on the board of the Royal Opera House from 1958 to 1982, an almost unprecedented length of service, which stemmed partly from the fact that he was almost the only member of the board who was primarily interested in ballet.

In 1966 the direction of Bonham Carter's life was changed when he became the first chairman of the Race Relations Board, appointed by the home secretary, Roy Jenkins. It was a classic example of the virtue of appointing friends—provided they are good enough. He had all the high Liberal confidence necessary for that formative phase of the job, and he had in addition the paradoxical virtue that, as a loyal Asquithian not forgetting Lloyd George's lethal blow, he worked off any subconscious racialism in relatively harmless prejudice against the Welsh. Everyone else he regarded with an even and tolerant light. After four years there he succeeded Frank Cousins as chairman of the Community Relations Commission, retiring in 1977 shortly before that body was merged with the Race Relations Board to form the Commission for Racial Equality. In 1975 he had become vice-chairman of the BBC, under Sir Michael Swann, and held that position until 1981 when, under a different regime, he was replaced by William Rees-Mogg. After that, with his race relations appointments also over, his career, although not his interests, hung fire for a time. It was revived by his nomination as a Liberal life peer in 1986. For the remaining eight and a half years of his life he made an exceptional one-man contribution to the Liberal iconoclastic side (which was quite strong under Thatcherism) of the reputation of the House of Lords. For much of the period he was Liberal Democrat foreign affairs spokesman.

On 30 June 1955 Bonham Carter had married Leslie Grenfell, the almost wholly Anglicized daughter of Condé Nast, the founder of *Vogue* and of other New York magazines. They had three daughters, Jane Mary (b. 1957), Virginia Leslie (b. 1959), and Elizabeth Cressida (b. 1961). There was also a stepdaughter—Laura Claire (b. 1950), later the wife of Sir Hayden Phillips, permanent secretary of the Lord Chancellor's Department—from Leslie Bonham Carter's brief marriage to Peter George Grenfell, second Baron St Just. Bonham Carter was almost equally close to all four of the daughters, for he was intensely *familiale*, although not at all in an enclosed way, as he was also highly gregarious. He saw his family as a core for wider friendships and not as a shuttered fortress against the surrounding countryside. It was exactly in that context that he died suddenly on 4 September 1994 in Bussento, a hilltop village in the south of Italy, during a brief Sunday evening excursion from the fine house near Policrastro which his mother-in-law had built. He was survived by his wife.   ROY JENKINS

Sources WWW, 1991–5 · D. Brack and M. Baines, eds., *Dictionary of liberal biography* (1998) · *The Times* (6 Sept 1994) · *The Independent* (7 Sept 1994) · *The Independent* (12 Sept 1994) · personal knowledge (2004) · private information (2004)
Archives Bodl. Oxf., corresp. with Margot Asquith · Bodl. RH, corresp. with Margery Perham · CUL, corresp. with Sir Samuel Hoare · U. Edin., corresp. with Michael Meredith Swann, Baron Swann · U. Glas., Archives and Business Records Centre, corresp. and papers as editor for William Collins & Co. | SOUND BL NSA, Bow dialogues, 18 July 1967, L812/17 C9 · BL NSA, party political recording
Likenesses photograph, 1986, Hult. Arch. · photograph, repro. in *The Times* · photograph, repro. in *The Independent* (7 Sept 1994)

Carter, Martin Wylde (1927–1997), poet, was born in Georgetown, British Guiana (now Guyana), on 7 June 1927, the third son of Victor Immanuel Carter (d. 1948), a civil servant, and Violet Eugene, *née* Wylde. Both were of principally African descent; Victor Immanuel's family came from Barbados, that of Violet Eugene, who also had some Amerindian blood, from Grenada. A member of a large, intellectually lively family, with five brothers and one sister, Martin was educated at Queen's College, Georgetown, from 1938 to 1947. He left after taking his school certificate, and worked briefly in an iron foundry, before entering the civil service. He worked first in the post office and later rose to become secretary to the superintendent of prisons. But he had already discovered his real vocation, poetry. His long poem *To a Dead Slave* was privately printed in May 1951, followed by the slim collection, *The Hill of Fire Glows Red* (1951). Both revealed Carter's passionate radical concerns and meticulous poetic craft. *The Kind Eagle* and *The Hidden Man* appeared in 1952, and *Returning* in 1953. Carter also contributed to *Kyk-over-al*, a magazine seminal in the creation of a local and West Indian culture.

In 1953 Martin Carter married Phyllis Howard, henceforth his constant support, and the mother of their four children, Keith, Sonia, Howard, and Michele. But their marriage was tested by turbulent times as British Guiana moved towards independence. In 1953 Carter left the civil service, having become increasingly involved in Cheddi Jagan's People's Progressive Party (PPP). He became a secret member of the party's executive, and in the colony's first elections, held in 1953, he stood as the PPP candidate for New Amsterdam. Although Carter lost to a local candidate, Jagan's party won by a massive majority. Fearing a communist coup, the British government summarily suspended the constitution. On returning from a political conference in Romania, Carter was arrested and interned without charge for three months at Atkinson's Field, now Timehri airport.

Outraged, Carter wrote some of his finest work, which was included in *Poems of Resistance* (1954), published in London. Its stark lyricism and passionate vision made this work much more than simply protest poetry, and the volume became a classic of Caribbean literature; its poems contributed directly to the national struggle, selections being printed secretly in Guyana and recited at political meetings. From 1953 to 1955 Carter also contributed trenchant prose to the local radical journal *Thunder*. He was placed under house arrest, harassed by the authorities, and in 1954 imprisoned for disobeying emergency regulations.

In 1956, however, Carter left the PPP, disillusioned with his country's politics, which were becoming increasingly split between African and Indian factions, though he never lost his faith in individual humanity. His poetry and political stance had attracted support within the colony's administration, and after his release from detention he worked for the British Council. In 1957 he joined the Guyana office of the multinational trading firm Booker as information officer and editor of the house journal *Booker News*. He assisted in the company's reorganization, preparing for the post-colonial era. He was also edging back into politics. In 1966 he attended the conference at Marlborough House, London, that drafted a constitution for Guyana's independence in 1967. Carter now left Booker to serve as a Guyanese delegate to the United Nations, New York (1966–7), and then, from 1967, as minister of public information and broadcasting in Forbes Burnham's government.

The sequence of five poems, 'Jail me Quickly', published in *New World* in February 1967, revealed Carter's despair as his country declined into political despotism, economic failure, and racial violence verging on civil war, demoralized by the after-effects of slavery and colonialism. He wrote of being 'muzzled' by Burnham's administration, in whose cabinet he briefly served. Poetry was his consolation. He used his ministerial position to encourage the country's young writers. In 1965 he attended the Cardiff Commonwealth poetry conference. In 1970, when Guyana became a republic, he organized a landmark conference that gathered émigré West Indian artists and intellectuals back onto home soil, and opened the way for the major pan-Caribbean cultural event, Carifesta, held in Guyana in 1975. In 1971, however, Carter resigned from the government, and in 1978 he was beaten by government thugs for opposing the legislation that was to establish Burnham perpetually in office.

In 1977 Carter published a major volume of poetry, *Poems of Succession*, followed in 1980 by *Poems of Affinity, 1978–1980*. His verse, though never losing its social concerns, was becoming more cerebral and inward-looking. Carter was increasingly drawn to the work of Spanish-speaking South American poets, including Pablo Neruda, Octavio Paz, and Cesar Vallejo. Like his poetry, Carter's personality combined intense feelings with hard-won control. He was a man with strong passions, which, when he was drinking, could erupt in moments of violence. But this was his private self. To meet, Carter was a tall, slim, elegant figure with thick spectacles, quietly spoken and radiating an impressive calm. He was poet in residence at the University of Essex in 1975–6, and in 1992 he toured Britain reading for the Arts Council. But he remained based in the Caribbean, becoming poet in residence at the University of Guyana from 1977 to 1981, and senior research fellow there from 1991. He was awarded the Cacique crown of honour and the order of Roraima (Guyana), 1994, and the Gabriel Mistral award (Chile), 1995.

Martin Carter died of a heart attack at his home, 22 Lamaha Street, Queenstown, Guyana, on 13 December 1997. He was given a state funeral and was buried in the national cemetery plot in the Botanic Gardens, Georgetown.

The quality of *Poems of Resistance* (1954) made Carter a pioneer of the post-war Caribbean literary renaissance. Though his highly independent voice, and his local commitment to Guyana, denied him the exposure that brought international fame to West Indian writers such as Derek Walcott, Carter was a strong creative influence on his contemporaries. The power of his terse, visionary verse gives it a poetic authority that places it among the major writing of the twentieth century.

LOUIS JAMES

Sources I. McDonald, foreword, in M. Carter, *Selected poems* (1989) · S. Brown, ed., *All are involved: the art of Martin Carter* (2000) · B. Lindfors and R. Sander, eds., *Twentieth-century Caribbean and black African writers* (1992) · G. Robinson, 'Martin Carter and Guyanese literary culture', PhD diss., U. Cam. [in preparation] · L. W. Brown, 'Martin Wylde Carter', *Fifty Caribbean writers*, ed. D. C. Dance (1986) · P. Trevis, 'Interview with Martin Carter', *Hinterland*, ed. E. A. Markham (1989) · I. McDonald and V. Rodzik, eds., 'Tribute to Martin Carter', *Kyk-over-al* [special issue], 49/50 (2000)

Carter, Matthew (*fl.* 1648–1650), royalist army officer, was the scion of a long-established but minor Kentish gentry family of Great Winchcombe in the remote parish of Crundale near Wye. He played a notable part in the second civil war in Kent and Essex in 1648, first appearing in mid-May, when a party of dissidents marching on Sandwich chose him to summon the mayor to surrender that town, whose magazine furnished valuable military resources to the insurgents. While in Sandwich he was also involved in an interview with and attempted arrest of an impostor whose bogus claim to be the prince of Wales had deceived many of the inhabitants.

Later in May Carter was appointed quartermaster-general of the Kentish insurgent forces, though what particular qualifications he had for this post is something of a mystery. At a rendezvous at Rochester at the end of the month he organized the mustering and quartering of some 7000 infantry and an unspecified number of cavalry. Following the royalist defeat at Maidstone at the beginning of June he threw in his lot with those Kentish insurgents who decided to follow their commander, the earl of Norwich, into Essex. Ignoring the protests of the local constable, Carter quartered his men at Stratford between 4 and 7 June, and on 10 June, *en route* from Chelmsford, took possession of the earl of Warwick's fortified house at Great Leighs. The members of the garrison, who had sworn to die rather than surrender the house, were persuaded otherwise by Carter's assurances of fair treatment. On 12 June he entered Colchester with the combined insurgent force, and until its surrender to Fairfax on 27 August was chiefly engaged, under Lord Loughborough, in the supplying and quartering of the beleaguered town. Of these matters, along with a description of fruitless royalist sorties against the besiegers, Carter gives a graphic account in *A … True … Relation of that as Honourable as Unfortunate Expedition of Kent, Essex, and Colchester*, produced in 1650 in prison, where he had been since the fall of Colchester. Although naturally not unbiased, this is valuable for the abundance of detail it provides and, not least, for its appraisal of the royalist leadership in Kent and Essex, including a vigorous repudiation of allegations that responsibility for the disaster at Maidstone lay with the earl of Norwich. Another product of Carter's imprisonment was a treatise on heraldry, *Honor redivivus*, which appeared in 1655 and went into two editions after the Restoration. He is a somewhat shadowy figure and returned to the obscurity from which he had so fleetingly emerged during the summer of 1648.

ROBERT ASHTON

Sources M. C. [M. Carter], *A … true … relation of that as honourable as unfortunate expedition of Kent, Essex, and Colchester* (1650); 2nd edn (1789) · *The manuscripts of the duke of Beaufort … the earl of Donoughmore*, HMC, 27 (1891), 19–31, pt 4 · *The manuscripts of the earl of Buckinghamshire, the earl of Lindsey … and James Round*, HMC, 38 (1895), 281–90 · R. L' Estrange, *L'Estrange: his vindication to Kent, and the justification of Kent to the world* (1649) · *A true and perfect relation of the condition of those noblemen and gentlemen in Colchester* (1648) [Thomason tract E 462(16)] · *A letter from Sandwich*, 1648, BL, E443/26 · *A letter from a gentleman in Kent*, 1648, BL, E448/34 · *Sad newes out of Kent*, 1648, BL, E443/41 · *Colchester's teares*, 1648, BL, E455/16 · T. Cromwell, *History and description of the ancient town and borough of Colchester*, 2 vols. (1825), vol. 1, chap. 4 · A. Everitt, *The community of Kent and the great rebellion, 1640–60* (1966) · *DNB*

Carter, Norman Bonham- (1867–1917). *See under* Carter, Henry Bonham (1827–1921).

Carter, Oliver (*d.* 1605), Church of England clergyman, is said to have been a native of Richmondshire. Nothing is known of his background, or of his early years, before he entered St John's College, Cambridge, in 1555. He graduated BA in 1560, MA in 1563, and BTh in 1569; he was elected fellow in 1563, senior fellow in 1564, and one of the college preachers in 1565. In 1565 he became vicar of

Histon and Croydon, in Cambridgeshire, and in 1567 a university preacher. Some time between July 1571 and October 1573 he was appointed to the staff of the collegiate church in Manchester, where he was employed until his death. But Carter's career in Manchester was bedevilled by the financial problems of the college, caused by long leases, low rents, and uncertain title to property. Quarrels with tenants provoked much bitterness, and in March 1574, when riding off to preach at an outlying chapel, Carter was attacked and stabbed, but saved when his horse bolted. In 1575–6 he was forced to borrow money, and in 1576 he sued the warden of the college for his unpaid stipend. Through Alexander Nowell, the Lancashire-born dean of St Paul's, Carter secured support from Lord Treasurer Burghley and Secretary Walsingham, who tried to arrange for increases in rents.

The college was refounded in 1578 in an attempt to sort out its difficulties, with Carter the only one of the fellows to be reappointed, but problems continued. Carter tried to improve his own finances by drawing up wills, leasing college tithes, and by refusing to pay his own tithes and fees to another lessee: he became involved in extensive litigation, and it was reported at the metropolitan visitation in 1590 that 'he liveth not according to his calling, he is a common solicitor in temporal causes, by reason whereof he is often absent' (Borth. Inst., V.1590/CB1, fol. 79v). Although he was again presented for absence in 1601, Carter was an active preacher and anti-Catholic propagandist. In 1579 he published *An answere, made by Oliver Carter, bacheler of divinitie, unto certaine popish questions and demaundes*, a response to Catholic claims for the antiquity of their church and the novelty of protestantism. The book was dedicated by Carter to 'his very good lord Henry, earl of Derby', and Carter preached before the earl and his household three times in 1588–9. From 1582 he was one of the four moderators of the Lancashire ministers' exercise held three times a year at Preston, and when in 1585 Bishop Chadderton extended the system he appointed Carter to be a moderator of the monthly Bury exercise.

Like many protestant ministers in a heavily Catholic county, Carter was a liturgical nonconformist: in 1590 he signed a letter of protest against the archbishop of York's efforts to enforce conformity, and he was presented for not wearing the surplice in 1592 and 1604. His last years at Manchester were disrupted by disputes with Dr John Dee, appointed warden in 1595, over finance and such issues as the use of an organ in the church. Oliver Carter married twice. He had at least seven children with his first wife, Emma, who died in 1590, and he then married Alice, who survived him. He was taken ill early in 1605 while preaching in Manchester on Matthew 9: 38 ('Pray ye therefore the Lord of the harvest, that he will send forth labourers into his harvest'): his colleague William Bourne famously continued the sermon, 'a visible and present proof of Mr. Carter's doctrine' (Hollingworth, 87). Carter made his will on 22 February 1605, leaving his tithe leases, cattle, farming equipment, and a little money to his wife and four surviving children, Dorothy, Abraham, John, and Mary. He asked to be buried in the chancel of Manchester church, and was

interred on 20 March; the will was proved at Chester on 4 April 1605.

Although Oliver Carter was not a major figure, he is a good example of the difficulties clergy of the Church of England faced in north-west England: a rival Catholicism was widespread and energetic, but preachers were distracted from effective evangelism by financial and organizational weaknesses. CHRISTOPHER HAIGH

Sources O. Carter, *An answere, made by Oliver Carter, bacheler of divinitie, unto certaine popish questions and demaundes* (1579) · F. R. Raines, *The fellows of the collegiate church of Manchester*, ed. F. Renaud, 1, Chetham Society, new ser., 21 (1891) · W. Ffarington, *The Derby household books*, ed. F. R. Raines, Chetham Society, 31 (1853) · R. Hollingworth, *Mancuniensis*, ed. W. Willis (1839) · S. Hibbert and W. R. Whatton, *History of the foundations in Manchester of Christ's College, Chetham's Hospital and the free grammar school*, 4 vols. (1828–48) · J. Strype, *Annals of the Reformation and establishment of religion … during Queen Elizabeth's happy reign*, new edn, 4 vols. (1824) · F. R. Raines, ed., 'A visitation of the diocese of Chester, by John, archbishop of York', *Chetham miscellanies*, 5, Chetham Society, 96 (1875) · T. Baker, *History of the college of St John the Evangelist, Cambridge*, ed. J. E. B. Mayor, 2 vols. (1869) · Gon. & Caius Cam., MS 197 · Borth. Inst., V.1590/CB1 · Ches. & Chester ALSS, EDV1/10; EDV1/1/12b; EDV1/13 · A. B. Grosart, ed., *The spending of the money of Robert Nowell* (1877) · parish register, Manchester parish church, 20 March 1605 [burial]

Carter, Owen Browne (1805/6–1859), architect and draughtsman, was born in London. Nothing is known of his parentage or early life. He spent most of his life in Winchester, where he was articled to William Garbett, a noted exponent of the Gothic style. In 1829–30 he travelled to Cairo as part of Robert Hay's archaeological expedition to the Nile valley; an album of some fifty of Carter's drawings is in the department of prints and drawings of the British Museum, and some of these were later lithographed and published, as well as featuring in the Egyptian court when the Great Exhibition reopened at Sydenham in 1854. In 1830 Carter published lithographs in *Picturesque Memorials of Winchester*.

After Garbett's death in 1834 Carter completed the construction of the neo-Tudor St John's Hospital South and sought to succeed his master as architect of Winchester Cathedral, in competition with the latter's son Edward and George Forder. Although he was not appointed, he was responsible for the canopy and steps to the choir pulpit (1848), as well as the stained-glass designs for the restoration of the east window (1852), more usually credited to David Evans. When Prince Albert visited the cathedral in August 1849, it was Carter, and not the man appointed to the post, Forder, who accompanied him. In 1835 Carter won the competition for the Winchester corn exchange. Vitruvian Italianate in style, with a Tuscan portico modelled on that of Inigo Jones's St Paul's Church, Covent Garden, it was his most effective design. Carter worked freely in a wide range of architectural styles: Norman at St Peter's Church, Southampton (1845–6), and in designs for a well-house (probably not built); Tudor Gothic in the Grand Jury Chamber (1845) and the West Hill cemetery buildings (1840) in Winchester and at Wallop House rectory, Nether Wallop (1838); and classical in several terraces and individual houses in Winchester. He built two Gothic churches for the Oxford Tractarian and vicar of Hursley, John Keble, at Otterbourne and Ampfield (1837–9). At St Mark's Church, Ampfield, Carter's 'second pointed' window tracery—copied from Beverley Minster and Lincoln Cathedral—is a very early example of the revival of this phase of Gothic. Church restorations carried out by Carter in Hampshire include those at Oakley (1839), Colemore (1845), Nutley (1846), and Grateley (1851); he also added a vestry at St Matthew's Church at Weeke, near Winchester (1850).

Carter married Anne Goldsmith (b. 1809) on 3 March 1832, and they had at least eight children. In 1841 he took on as articled pupil a distant relative of his wife, the future principal exponent of high Victorian architecture, George Edmund Street, to whom is attributed a drawing for a new Gothic doorway on the north side of Winchester Castle great hall, where Carter replaced some unfortunate eighteenth-century timber sashes with replicas of the original full-height thirteenth-century windows. In 1845 Carter acted as one of the secretaries at the meeting of the Archaeological Institute in Winchester; he gave a paper on the church at East Meon and provided drawings to illustrate papers by other contributors.

Later in his career Carter's architectural work seems largely to have been supplanted by his increased output of drawings for publication as lithographs. *Illustrations of the Churches of Wiltshire* was an ambitious project which resulted in four published volumes and a portfolio of sixty-eight measured drawings of unpublished subjects (for the six additional volumes projected but never completed), now in the library of the Wiltshire Archaeological and Natural History Society in Devizes. He also contributed topics of local interest to five issues of *Weale's Quarterly Papers on Architecture* in 1844–5. He exhibited on several occasions at the Royal Academy, and his 1849 *Design for Restoration of the Poultry Cross at Salisbury* led to the execution of these proposals under his supervision in 1852–4.

Carter produced at least twelve large-format lithographs in the Cathedrals of England series between 1851 and 1855, but this venture came to an abrupt halt in February 1856, when he was arrested after his London partner accused him of forging a cheque for £400 for payment due to him for his drawings. His reputation as a 'man given to drink' (Stopher) is perhaps supported by his inability to attend a court hearing after his arrest because of rheumatic gout. Carter was finally acquitted at Hampshire Lent assizes in March 1856, but not before his household furniture and effects had been put up for sale on the instructions of the county sheriff. The decline in his career as an architect and artist is underlined by his advertising his services as a drawing teacher in Winchester in January 1858, and his financial difficulties were confirmed by a reference to 'very straitened circumstances brought on by his eccentricities' in a newspaper report of his death, on 25 March 1859, in the Salisbury Fever Hospital, at Bugmore, 'from exhaustion, the result of sloughing bed sores' (*Hampshire Advertiser*, 2 April 1859, 4). He was probably survived by his wife.　　　　　　　　　　ROBIN FREEMAN

Sources R. Freeman, *The art and architecture of Owen Browne Carter* (1991) · *Hampshire Chronicle* (1833–59) · *Hampshire Advertiser* (2 April 1859), 4 · T. Stopher, 'The history of Winchester streets (1895–1926)', Winchester county library, local studies collection · [P. Hall], *Picturesque memorials of Winchester* [1830] [incl. lithographs by O. B. Carter] · A. E. Street, *Memoir of George Edmund Street* (1888) · L. Binyon, *Catalogue of drawings by British artists and artists of foreign origin working in Great Britain*, 4 vols. (1898–1907), vol. 1, pp. 199–201 · R. H. Harper, *Victorian architectural competitions: an index to British and Irish architectural competitions in The Builder, 1843–1900* (1983) · J. F. Moor, *The birthplace, home, churches etc ... of the author of the Christian year (John Keble)*, 2nd edn (1867) · C. M. Yonge, *Musings over the Christian year etc ... recollections of the Revd John Keble* (1872) · C. M. Yonge, *Old times at Otterbourne* (1891) · C. M. Yonge, *John Keble's parishes* (1898) · R. Hay, *Illustrations of Cairo* (1840) · S. Tillett, *Egypt itself: the career of Robert Hay* (1984) · d. cert.
Wealth at death practically a pauper: Stopher, 'History of Winchester streets'; *Hampshire Advertiser*

Carter, Peter (1530?–1590), logician, was born in Lancashire. He attended St John's College, Cambridge, and though he had not met all the formal requirements for either degree, he graduated BA in 1553/4, and proceeded MA in 1557. He had already become a fellow of the college in 1555, thanks to money bequeathed by Hugh Ashton for the support of students from the northern counties. In 1571 his name appeared in a decree of the exchequer which revived a lapsed stipend paid to the master of the grammar school in Whalley, Lancashire. When he died in 1590 he was master of the grammar school in Preston, Lancashire. He was buried in Preston on 8 September, and his tombstone recorded that he was 'author of annotations on John Seton's Logic and died nearly 60 years old'. John Seton, also a fellow of St John's College, had published a short logic text in 1545 which was an epitome of the new humanist-oriented Aristotelianism, though it also contained some remnants of medieval logic, notably supposition theory. The book was divided into sections, each consisting of a series of short statements followed by a densely printed prose exposition. Carter's contribution was to organize the material for teaching purposes. Following each section, he added a list of headings, definitions, and rules, supplemented with schematic lists and tables. Seton's logic with Carter's annotations, described in the Stationers' register for 1562/3 as 'a boke in laten perused by my lorde of London', was first printed in 1563, and from 1563 to 1639 it received no fewer than seventeen editions. Its popularity in late sixteenth-century Cambridge is attested by the number of times it appears in students' and booksellers' inventories of books.

E. J. ASHWORTH

Sources *Dialectica Joannis Setoni Cantabrigiensis, annotationibus Petri Carteri, ut clarissimia, ita brevissimis, explicata* (1572) · STC, 1475–1640 · Venn, *Alum. Cant.* · A. F. Leach, 'Preston grammar school', *VCH Lancashire*, 2.569–74 · H. J. Chaytor, 'Whalley grammar school', *VCH Lancashire*, 2.604 · J. Venn, ed., *Grace book Δ* (1910) · L. Jardine, 'The place of dialectic teaching in sixteenth-century Cambridge', *Studies in the Renaissance*, 21 (1974), 31–62 · E. J. Ashworth, editor's introduction, in R. Sanderson, *Logicae artis compendium* (1985) · Arber, *Regs. Stationers*, 1.1875 (22 July 1562–22 July 1563, 88v) · Cooper, *Ath. Cantab.*, vol. 3 · J. B. Mullinger, *St John's College* (1901) · E. Miller, *Portrait of a college: a history of the College of Saint John the Evangelist, Cambridge* (1961)

Carter, Richard (d. 1692), naval officer, was a servant of Sir Frescheville Holles and was commissioned first lieutenant of the *Cambridge*, commanded by Holles, on 8 January 1672. He remained lieutenant after Holles's death at the battle of Solebay on 28 May 1672 and was left £500 in Holles's will. Prince Rupert promoted him to captain of the *Success* on 6 February 1673. From 5 June 1673 he was captain of the *Crown* (42 guns) but was discharged on 10 October 1674. He was heavily fined for undertaking 'good voyages', that is, private trading using naval vessels. It is possible that he was an Ormond client in the mid-1670s.

In April 1675 Carter was appointed to the *Swan* and in 1677 was commended for performing his duties well. He took command of the *Centurion* on 11 January 1678 and was employed in the Mediterranean against the Barbary corsairs. The ship was paid off on 24 October 1681. On 26 February 1682 Carter was appointed deputy governor of Southsea Castle and captain of an independent army company there. When George Byng, the future admiral, threatened to leave the navy because he had not been made a captain Carter was sent to dissuade him from doing so. In August 1688 he was appointed to the *Plymouth*, part of the fleet of George, earl of Dartmouth, in November 1688. Carter took part in the battle of Bantry Bay on 1 May 1689, and on 30 June 1690 his *Plymouth* was the lead ship of the Red squadron at the battle of Beachy Head. He was highly critical of the behaviour of the allied Dutch during the battle but did not give evidence at the court martial of Arthur Herbert, earl of Torrington, for his part in the defeat, alleging that he had fallen off his horse at Sheerness and was too badly bruised to attend. On 21 January 1691 he was turned over from the *Plymouth* to the *Vanguard* and on 29 January 1692 was promoted to the post of rear-admiral of the Blue. With a few ships, he cruised off the Channel Islands and surveyed La Hague on the French coast before rejoining the fleet.

Then and later allegations of Jacobite leanings were to be made against Carter, and it was claimed that he had received £10,000 to make his division over to the French. It was reported that an attempt in June 1690 had been foiled by his crew, and Edward Russell remarked of him in November 1691 that he was 'a good man if true to the present government' (Folger Shakespeare Library, Rich MS xd 451 (98)). Against this, he is known to have signed the fleet's 'loyal address' to William and Mary on 15 May 1692. At the start of the battle of Barfleur, on 19 May, his Blue squadron had tacked but a light wind meant that the manoeuvre could not be finished and the squadron was left far away from the rest of the fleet. However, a shift in the wind meant that by about six o'clock Carter in the *Duke* and the rest of his ships were heavily engaged as the tide took them among the French. He lost a leg in the fighting and later, at 10 p.m., died from his injuries, having given dying instructions to his crew to fight the ship as long as she would swim. He was buried at Portsmouth on 3 June 1692; the ships of his division fired twenty-two gun salutes as his remains were rowed ashore. His widow, Mary, was granted a yearly pension of £200.

J. K. LAUGHTON, *rev.* PETER LE FEVRE

Sources report on petition, 22 March 1674, PRO, SP 29/360, fol. 388 · will of Sir Frescheville Holles, PRO, PROB 11/342, fol. 208 · will of Richard Carter, PRO, PROB 11/410, fols. 232r–232v · J. R. Tanner, ed., *A descriptive catalogue of the naval manuscripts in the Pepysian Library at Magdalene College, Cambridge*, 4, Navy RS, 57 (1923) · *Calendar of the manuscripts of the marquess of Ormonde*, new ser., 8 vols., HMC, 36 (1902–20), vol. 4 · C. Dalton, ed., *English army lists and commission registers, 1661–1714*, 1 (1892) · *Memoirs relating to the Lord Torrington*, ed. J. K. Laughton, CS, new ser., 46 (1889) · reports on the battle of Beachy Head, NMM, MS HIS 3 · *Report on the manuscripts of Allan George Finch*, 5 vols., HMC, 71 (1913–2003), vol. 2 · *LondG* (16–19 May 1692) · E. Russell, 'Characters of captains, Nov. 1691', Folger, Rich MS xd 451 (98) · *CSP dom., 1691–2*, 295, 370, 503 · 'Jacobite relation', BL, Add. MS 72569 · journal and captain's log, *Hope*, 3 June 1692, PRO, ADM 51/4220 · journal and captain's log, *Victory*, 3 June 1692, PRO, ADM 51/4384 · 4th lieutenant's log, *Duke*, 19 May and 3 June 1692, NMM, MS ADM/L/D260

Wealth at death see will, PRO, PROB 11/410, fols. 232r–232v

Carter, Robert [*called* King Carter] (1663–1732), planter and politician in America, was born in Lancaster county in the Northern Neck of colonial Virginia. He was the son of Colonel John Carter (d. 1669), 'the emigrant', a prosperous planter, and his fourth wife, Sarah (d. 1668), daughter of Gabriel Ludlow of Middlesex county. His mother died when he was five. When his father died a year later he left detailed instructions that Robert should be educated 'for the use of his estate' (Dowdey, 95) and that an indentured servant be purchased to tutor him in Latin or English. About 1672 he was sent by his elder half-brother John to England where he spent six years at a London grammar school under the supervision of a merchant, Arthur Bailey. As a younger son, Robert inherited a relatively modest estate of 1000 acres and one-third of his father's personal property; on John's death in 1690, however, followed shortly afterwards by those of John's daughter and widow, he acquired a substantial proportion of his half-brother's estate of 9000 acres and 115 slaves.

Robert Carter followed the usual path taken by young gentlemen who aspired to political power in colonial Virginia. He became a member of the parish vestry and a justice on the county bench and, in 1691, like his father and brother before him, was returned to the house of burgesses as one of two representatives for Lancaster county. On entering the lower house of assembly he was immediately appointed to the all-important committee of propositions and grievances. He served two terms in the house before being elected speaker in 1696. He was again appointed to this position in 1699, the same year in which he also became treasurer. In December 1699 he was elevated to the upper house of the Virginia assembly, the council, membership of which was in the gift of the crown and comprised members of the colony's wealthiest and most prestigious families. Whereas in 1690 the Carters were merely one of three prominent 'long tailed families' in Lancaster county (Kolp, 125), within ten years Robert had attained that position in Virginia politics which, combined with his drive and ambition, would make him in succeeding decades arguably the most powerful Virginian of his generation and certainly the wealthiest. By 1705 he was already known as King Carter.

Carter sat on the council for the three decades during

Robert Carter (1663–1732), by unknown artist, c.1720

which it reached the height of its power and influence in Virginia affairs. It was a thorn in the side of colonial governors, and a focus of factionalism within the ruling oligarchy. Part of an inner group on the council, Carter made an enemy of Lieutenant-Governor Francis Nicholson who commented disdainfully on the Virginian's hauteur, vanity, and covetousness, and, though he sided with the general opposition of the council to Lieutenant-Governor Alexander Spotswood, he was not among Spotswood's inveterate enemies. He made a friend of the colourful William Byrd II on the latter's return from England, and was a rival of Edmund Jennings whom he succeeded as president of the council in the 1720s and helped ruin financially. On the sudden death in 1726 of Spotswood's replacement, Carter served as acting governor of Virginia until the arrival of his successor, Major William Gooch, in 1727. He was also a member of the board of visitors of the College of William and Mary, as well as a trustee and rector.

Though foremost a planter who prided himself on the quality of his tobacco, Carter's economic activities were varied. He traded with merchants in London, Bristol, and Glasgow, lent out money, collected debts, dealt in slaves (acting as a middleman between traders and planters), ventured into copper mining (one of his rare failures), and lost money in the South Sea Bubble. Through the influence of his mercantile contacts Perry and Lane, Carter became agent in 1703 for the Fairfax family, proprietors of the Northern Neck of Virginia, and opened a land office at Corotoman, his home plantation in Christ Church parish. He lost the agency to Edmund Jennings in 1712, but following the latter's failures was reappointed on favourable

terms in 1721. Despite public criticism, Carter extended the bounds of the proprietary threefold, opening up new land to settlement and, during the 1720s especially, enriching himself and his extensive family. In the process he pushed back the Virginia frontier.

In 1688 Carter married Judith (1665–1699), daughter of John Armistead. His second marriage, to seventeen-year-old Elizabeth, née Landon (1683–1719), widow of Richard Willis, took place in 1701. Ten of his offspring lived to maturity and all five of his sons were educated in England. Through his own marriages and the intermarriage of his children Carter was linked to many gentry families in 'one great tangled cousinry' (Bailyn, 111). Out of his vast landholdings he created estates for each of his sons and some of his grandsons. His son John, a barrister of the Middle Temple, secured the lucrative post of secretary of Virginia and, despite opposition, joined his father and brother-in-law, Mann Page, on the council. Another son, Robert, was naval officer of the Rappahannock River while Landon *Carter and Charles *Carter achieved prominence in colonial politics. George remained in England.

Carter died at Corotoman on 4 August 1732 and was buried in the grounds of Christ Church, Lancaster county. At his death he owned about one-eightieth of the land in present-day Virginia, virtually all of which he left locked in entail, the land under cultivation being divided into forty-five separate units and spread across many counties. Carter's celebrity was such that notice of his death appeared in the Gentleman's Magazine in November 1732 where it was claimed that he had left over 300,000 acres, 1000 slaves, and £10,000.　　　　　　GWENDA MORGAN

Sources L. Morton, *Robert Carter of Nomini Hall: a Virginia tobacco planter in the eighteenth century* (1941) • C. Dowdey, *The Virginia dynasties: the emergence of 'King' Carter and the golden age* (Boston, Massachusetts, 1969) • R. L. Morton, *Colonial Virginia*, 2: *Westward expansion and prelude to revolution* (1960) • *Letters of Robert Carter, 1720–1727: the commercial interests of a Virginia gentleman*, ed. L. B. Wright (San Marino, California, 1940) • W. M. Billings, J. E. Selby, and T. W. Tate, *Colonial Virginia: a history* (1986) • J. G. Kolp, *Gentlemen and freeholders: electoral politics in colonial Virginia* (1998) • H. Brewer, 'Entailing aristocracy in colonial Virginia: "antient feudal restraints" and revolutionary reform', *William and Mary Quarterly*, 54 (1997), 307–46 • L. B. Wright, *The first gentlemen of Virginia: intellectual qualities of the early colonial ruling class* (Charlottesville, Virginia, 1940) • T. H. Breen, *Tobacco culture: the mentality of the great tidewater planters on the eve of revolution* (Princeton, New Jersey, 1985) • C. S. Sydnor, *Gentlemen's freeholders: political practices in Washington's Virginia* (Chapel Hill, North Carolina, 1952) • *GM*, 1st ser., 2 (1732), 1082 • H. R. McIlwaine and J. P. Kennedy, eds., *Journals of the house of burgesses of Virginia, 1619–1776*, 13 vols. (1905–15) • H. R. McIlwaine, ed., *Legislative journals of the council of colonial Virginia*, 2nd edn (Richmond, Virginia, 1979) • H. R. McIlwaine and others, eds., *Executive journals of the council of colonial Virginia*, 6 vols. (1925–66) • S. H. Godson and others, *The College of William and Mary: a history* (1993) • B. Bailyn, 'Politics and social structure in Virginia', *Seventeenth-century Virginia*, ed. J. M. Smith (Chapel Hill, North Carolina, 1959), 111

Archives University of Virginia, Charlottesville, letter-books and diary • Virginia Historical Society, Richmond, MSS

Likenesses portrait, c.1720, Smithsonian Institution, Washington, DC, National Portrait Gallery [see illus.] • M. M. Andrews, oils (after portrait formerly at Oatlands, Landown county, Virginia), Virginia Historical Society, Richmond, Virginia • portrait, repro. in Morton, *Colonial Virginia*, vol. 2, facing p. 478

Wealth at death approx. £10,000, incl. approx. 300,000 acres of land and approx. 700 slaves: will and inventory, *Virginia Magazine* vols. 5 and 6 (1898–9), vol. 5, pp. 408–28, 145–52; vol. 6, pp. 1–21, 260–68, 365–70; repr. in Dowdey, *Virginia dynasties*, 389–409

Carter, Sampson (*d. c.*1814?). *See under* Carter, (Charles) Thomas (*c.*1735–1804).

Carter, Samuel (*bap.* 1641, *d.* 1713), law reporter and legal writer, was baptized at St Martin's, Birmingham, on 5 August 1641, the son of Thomas Carter and Margaret Ailesbury. He was admitted to Pembroke College, Cambridge, on 26 May 1657, graduating BA in 1660–61. He was admitted to the Inner Temple in 1665 and called to the bar on 23 November 1673.

Carter's main activity appears to have been the research and publication of legal texts. In 1688 he published some law reports relating to the reign of Charles II. His next work appears to have been published in 1701: *Lex custumaria, or, A Treatise of Copy-Hold Estates*. In keeping with this kind of work, in 1706 he published *The Law of Executions*.

No doubt Carter's legal researches were facilitated by his appointment on 4 June 1709 as 'library keeper' at the Inner Temple at a salary of £20 p.a., his son, Thomas, providing the surety. In 1710 he published *Legal Provisions for the Poor, or, A Treatise of Common and Statute Laws Concerning the Poor*, which proved sufficiently popular to run to a fifth edition in 1725. Finally, he published *Lex vadiorum: the Law of Mortgages*, a second edition of which appeared in 1728.

Carter was buried on 8 March 1713 in the Temple Church. His will appears to have been proved by his sister Mary Lostin in October 1713.   STUART HANDLEY

Sources F. A. Inderwick and R. A. Roberts, eds., *A calendar of the Inner Temple records*, 3 (1901), 94, 416, 423, 462 • Venn, *Alum. Cant.* • IGI • J. W. Wallace, *The reporters*, 4th edn (1882), 328–34 • will, PRO, PROB 6/89, fol. 222v

Carter, Samuel (1805–1878), lawyer, was born on 15 May 1805 in Coventry, where his father, Samuel Carter, lived and his grandfather was mayor in 1786 and 1799. He was educated in West Bromwich at the school run by his uncle the Revd John Corrie. At the age of sixteen or seventeen he became an articled clerk in the office of another uncle, Josiah Corrie, a leading Birmingham solicitor. The choice of law as a career was not surprising given that another uncle, John Carter, was an attorney and town clerk of Coventry from 1812 to 1836.

On admission, Carter joined Corrie in partnership and commenced practice in Birmingham. Shortly afterwards began his connection with railways. In 1831 Corrie and Carter were appointed solicitors to the newly formed London and Birmingham Railway, which later became the London and North Western Railway Company. When the Birmingham and Derby Railway Company was constituted in 1835, Carter was again appointed solicitor. This company later developed into the Midland Railway. For the next twenty-five years railway work was to dominate Carter's life to the exclusion of other professional and public interests. It was said that in one parliamentary session he had control of forty bills relating to these two companies. Carter developed an unrivalled expertise in parliamentary business and railway policy, being noted in particular for his sound judgement, ability in delicate negotiations, and a combination of shrewdness, intellect, and a strict sense of integrity.

After Corrie's death about 1840, Carter continued to practise in Birmingham until 1850. He then moved to London and carried on the railway work. In 1860 he resigned his position as solicitor to the London and North Western and eight years later he retired from practice, having ended his connection with the Midland. By this time Carter had become a landowner, having purchased an estate at Battle, Sussex, in the late 1850s. This was sold about 1875, though he did retain a small estate in Kenilworth, which had been inherited from his mother's family.

In 1868 Carter returned to Coventry. Up until this time he had shown little interest in public life, but he was persuaded to stand as a Liberal candidate at a by-election in Coventry in March 1868 and was elected. However, it was to be a short parliamentary career; he was defeated at the general election in November 1868. Nevertheless, he had during that time addressed the house on the Irish Church question and the general carriers acts. Carter stood again unsuccessfully at the general election of 1874.

Shortly before his death Carter published two pamphlets on the subject of the jurisdiction of the railway commissioners and the question of debenture holders. Despite his former connection with the industry these pamphlets were not well received by the trade press. Carter's interests were not confined exclusively to his profession and railway business, but also ranged over art, literature, and science. Carter died at his London home, 3 Clifton Place, on 31 January 1878, and was buried in the family vault at Kenilworth. He was survived by his wife, three sons, including the painter Hugh *Carter, and one daughter.   ANDREW ROWLEY

Sources *Coventry Herald* (8 Feb 1878) • *Solicitors' Journal*, 22 (1877–8), 302 • Boase, *Mod. Eng. biog.* • *Herpath's Railway and Commercial Journal*, 40 (1878), 190 • *Hansard 3* (1868), vols. 191–2 • *CGPLA Eng. & Wales* (1878)

Carter, Thomas (1690–1763), politician, was born at Hollybrook, co. Dublin. He was the only surviving son of Thomas Carter (*c.*1650–1726), a lawyer and MP, and his wife, Margaret, *née* Houghton (*c.*1660–1696), and descended from Thomas Carter, armiger, born in the reign of Edward IV. Following his early education at Mr Wall's school in Dublin he matriculated at Trinity College, Dublin, in 1707 and graduated BA in 1710. He entered the Middle Temple, London, in 1708. He became an attorney of the court of king's bench, Dublin, and clerk of the crown and protonotary in the same court following his father's purchase of that office in 1717 for the sum of £4000 (it remained in the family until 1790). In 1718 he was admitted a bencher of King's Inn, and from 1737 to 1741 served as treasurer there.

Carter married in 1719 Mary (*c.*1700–1780), the daughter and coheir of Thomas Claxton, armiger, of Dublin, and his wife, Mary Pearce, the sister of Lieutenant-General Thomas Pearce, military governor of Limerick; she brought Carter a dowry of £3000. The couple had two sons, Thomas Carter (*bap.* 12 July 1720), MP for Old Leighlin, and Henry Boyle Carter (*bap.* 21 Nov 1726), and three daughters, one of whom, Frances, married Philip Twysden, bishop of Raphoe.

Carter was MP for Trim, Meath, from 1719 to 1727, and was returned as a member for Hillsborough, Dungarvan, and Lismore in 1727; he elected to sit for Hillsborough, and held the seat until 1761. In 1723 he obtained the reversion of the office of second serjeant-at-arms from his father (the office was in the Carter family from 1692 to 1753). In April 1725 William, Lord Berkeley, master of the rolls, appointed Carter his deputy and obtained permission to sell him the reversion of that office, much to the disapproval of Hugh Boulter, Anglican primate of Ireland, who was promoting the English interest, that such an important office could be purchased by an Irishman.

Carter was a protégé of Lord Chancellor Midleton. By September 1725 he had allied himself with Midleton's son St John Brodrick, who headed an influential party in the Commons. They proposed to the viceroy, Lord Carteret, to undertake the king's business in parliament, but as he rejected their plan they opposed practically everything his parliamentary managers initiated.

On 6 May 1727 Carter was appointed second examiner in chancery. In 1729 he acquired Castle Martin, co. Kildare, as his family seat, and from 1730 to 1752 he was judge and ranger of the curragh of Kildare.

By the end of the 1720s Carter had been won over to the Dublin Castle party, and he was approached by the duke of Dorset, appointed viceroy in June 1730, to secure his support. Dorset assisted him in his purchase of the mastership of the rolls in 1731—for which Carter paid in excess of £11,000—made him his chief parliamentary manager, and entrusted him with the care of his son, Lord George Sackville, in his absence. Dorset recognized that Carter was due further reward for the considerable expense in purchasing this office, and the following May the king granted him an additional £500 per annum to his office of clerk of the crown and protonotary. It was in 1731 that Carter commissioned Sir Edward Pearce, his wife's cousin, to build him a magnificent house, with the finest staircase hall in Dublin, opposite Archbishop Boulter's residence in Henrietta Street, where much government business was conducted.

In 1732 Carter was raised to the privy council, and when Speaker Gore died in February 1733 he was among the candidates most acceptable to Dublin Castle; however, the position went to Henry Boyle, a close friend and godfather to his younger son. When Walpole sent instructions to Dorset to attempt the repeal of the Sacramental Test Act of 1704 (which prevented protestant dissenters from holding public office, from receiving a military commission, and from enjoying full civil rights), Carter and Boyle were against it, and Dorset soon realized this proposal would fail.

Carter now had a substantial income. He had inherited about 4000 acres in co. Meath from his father, following the latter's death in 1726. In addition to this he inherited the extensive Roscommon estates in and around Trim which his father had acquired in 1702 when he married Isabella, the widow of the celebrated Wentworth, fourth earl of Roscommon. Carter's estates realized £4000 per annum and his combined offices a further £7500 per annum.

Carter was still at the height of his political career when in 1745 Lord Chesterfield, as viceroy, described him as 'the leading person in the [Irish] Parliament' (*Letters*, 3.638). However, in 1748 he was seriously ill and wished his eldest son to be granted the reversion of the office of master of the rolls. He approached Lord Harrington and then George Stone, primate of Ireland, but the latter, who wanted his nominee to occupy the post, refused to countenance the suggestion. Carter, who believed he had a right to determine the reversion because of his purchase, was resentful, and this drove him into opposition and led to his co-ordinating an intensive campaign against Stone.

For many years Carter had been in charge of financial business in the Commons, as chairman of the committees of supply and ways and means. In 1753 he opposed the claim of the crown to dispose of unappropriated revenue in the Irish exchequer and engineered the defeat of this money bill. This incurred the king's displeasure, and as a result Carter was dismissed from his office as master of the rolls in 1754. Although a settlement followed the next year when Carter was appointed principal secretary of state, keeper of the privy seal, with an additional salary of £1200 per annum (which office he held until his death), he remained dissatisfied and was regarded by Dublin Castle as one who was most against English interests in Ireland.

The earl of Shelburne described Carter as 'a man of a very original character, whose uncommon sagacity and shrewdness as well as depth of understanding, would have distinguished and advanced him in any country' (Fitzmaurice, 1.239). His shrewd judgement of character is well illustrated by his advice to the duke of Dorset: 'whatever he did with his son never to put him into the army' (ibid.). Lord George Sackville was later to face a court martial and was found 'unfit to serve his Majesty in any military capacity whatsoever' (A. C. Valentine, *Lord George Germain*, 1962, 68). Speaker Pery attributed to Carter the ingenious invention of conveying libels in toasts which afterwards gained circulation through the newspapers, while Walpole characterized him as 'an able, intriguing man, of slender reputation for integrity' (Walpole, 1.192). Plowden's *Historical Review* refers to Carter's talent for 'keeping the table in a roar of laughter by his archness, vivacity and wit' (Plowden, 1.310).

Carter also made significant contributions to farming and country pursuits, not sparing any expense to bring them to perfection. He imported the best breed of cattle and built several mills for grinding corn. He died while staying with his son at Rathnally House, near Trim, on 3 September 1763 and was buried at St Patrick's Cathedral at Trim.

PETER ARONSSON

Sources The manuscripts of the earl of Buckinghamshire, the earl of Lindsey ... and James Round, HMC, 38 (1895) • R. E. Burns, Irish parliamentary politics in the eighteenth century, 2 vols. (1989–90) • Dublin Journal (3–6 Sept 1763) • priv. coll., T. Carter MSS • Burtchaell & Sadleir, Alum. Dubl. • F. E. Ball, The judges in Ireland, 1221–1921, 2 vols. (New York, 1927) • F. G. James, Ireland in the empire, 1688–1770 (1973) • D. O. Donovan, 'The money bill dispute', Penal era and golden age: essays in Irish history, 1690–1800, ed. T. Bartlett and D. W. Hayton (1979), 55–87 • F. E. Ball, 'Some notes on the judges of Ireland in the year 1739', Journal of the Royal Society of Antiquaries of Ireland, 5th ser., 14 (1904), 1–19 • Life of William, earl of Shelburne ... with extracts from his papers and correspondence, ed. E. G. P. Fitzmaurice, 3 vols. (1875–6) • C. L. Falkiner, Essays relating to Ireland, biographical, historical and topographical, ed. F. E. Ball (1909) • F. Plowden, An historical review of the state of Ireland, 2 vols. (1803) • The letters of Philip Dormer Stanhope, fourth earl of Chesterfield, ed. B. Dobrée, 6 vols. (1932) • H. Walpole, Memoirs of King George II, ed. J. Brooke, 3 vols. (1985) • parish register (baptism)
Archives priv. coll. | PRO NIre., letters to Lord Shannon
Likenesses C. Jervas, oils, 1734 • J. Brooks, mezzotint (after C. Jervas), NG Ire.; version, BM, NPG
Wealth at death town house in Henrietta Street, Dublin; family seat at Castle Martin, co. Kildare; estates in counties Meath, King's, and Kildare: Carter MSS, priv. coll.

Carter, Thomas (d. 1756), sculptor, was the elder son of Thomas Carter, a yeoman farmer of Datchet, Buckinghamshire. He began to work as a sculptor in modest circumstances in a small workshop in Shepherd's Market, London, and in 1729 his talent and industry were spotted by the painter Charles Jervas, who loaned him £100 to expand his business. By the early 1730s he had set up shop near Hyde Park Corner, where he took on prestigious commissions for figurative sculpture. From about 1732 to 1736 he seems to have concentrated on funerary monuments. His statuary work of this period is impressive; good examples include the figures of Arthur Moore at Great Bookham, Surrey, and Speaker Conolly and his consort at Celbridge, co. Kildare. It is possible that Louis François Roubiliac was employed by him about the same time. About 1736 Carter turned to the production of decorative sculpture and marble architectural features. From this point onwards, over an uncertain number of generations, Carter and his family specialized in the making of fine marble chimney-pieces. Of the occasional funerary sculpture he continued to produce, a fine example is the monument to General Townsend (1759) in Westminster Abbey, signed by Thomas and his brother, Benjamin Carter (d. 1766), in conjunction with their assistant, John Eckstein (1735–1819).

Thomas Carter was the first in a family of marble sculptors who were based in the parish of St George's, Hanover Square, London. After his death the business was carried on by his brother, Benjamin, who bequeathed it to a nephew, Thomas Carter, who relocated the firm to St James's, Piccadilly, in 1766. The family business served an élite market: Carter numbered among his patrons the earl of Radnor, Earl Fitzwilliam, and the duke of Portland. Following his death in 1756 the firm continued to receive aristocratic patronage, and in the last forty years of the century it provided marble fittings for many of London's premier architects, notably Robert Adam, James Stuart, Henry Holland, and Sir John Soane. The Carters were not innovative but supplied high quality products that fulfilled the needs of architects and embellished decorative schemes commissioned by their patrons. From the 1730s to the 1790s the family shops adapted to the demands of fashion and remained at the apex of the market of their choice. A fine marble wine cooler at Blair Atholl, Perthshire, commissioned in 1751 by the second duke of Atholl, is an example of the quality of work produced in Thomas Carter's shop. Magnificent fireplaces at Saltram House, Devon, indicate that this quality of workmanship was maintained by his successors in the 1760s. It is probable, though not certain, that the Thomas Carter who auctioned the entire stock of a yard at Hyde Park Corner on 19 December 1777 was Carter's nephew. He is probably identical with Thomas Carter the younger who died in 1795.

The Carters were one of the great sculpture families in England and take their place alongside the Stantons, Bacons, and Westmacotts. Despite their wealth and renown there is no known surviving record of the appearance of any of them. A bust of Thomas Carter by Roubiliac was recorded in the latter's posthumous sale, but its whereabouts is unknown. It is possible that a portrait by Francis Hayman of a sculptor working on a model of a fireplace with caryatids is an image of Benjamin Carter, rather than Joseph Williams. The model in the portrait is for a marble fireplace erected in Northumberland House and now in the Victoria and Albert Museum, London, where it is exhibited as the work of Benjamin Carter. A fine relief bust of Thomas Carter, yeoman farmer, survives upon his funerary monument at Datchet. This was almost certainly the work of his son Thomas, who was buried in a vault below. MATTHEW CRASKE

Sources R. Gunnis, Dictionary of British sculptors, 1660–1851 (1953); new edn (1968) • European Magazine, 2 (1803), 178 • R. Beatniffe, The Norfolk tour (1772) • collection of auction catalogues for sculptors' yards, compiled by R. Hayward, BM, a.5.9.sc [formerly in the Finberg Collection] • DNB • will, PRO, PROB 11/1257/153, fols. 157v–159r [Thomas Carter (c.1795)]

Carter, (Charles) Thomas (c.1735–1804), musician and composer, was born in Dublin. He was the elder son of Timothy Carter, who became a member of the choir of Christ Church, Dublin, in March 1740. Carter received his musical education probably from his father and as a chorister at Christ Church Cathedral. In 1751 he was appointed organist of St Werburgh's Church. Following destruction of the organ by fire in 1754 he moved to St Peter's (1757–63). He returned to St Werburgh's 'as soon as the organ had been rebuilt in 1767' (Fiske, 'Carter, (Charles) Thomas') and married Margaret May there in 1769. Unfortunately, C. T. Carter has long been confused with two younger individuals of the same name and also of Irish birth. He left for London in 1769 to further his career in the theatre. A highly competent overture that he had composed for Giusto Ferdinando Tenducci's staging of Amintas in Dublin in 1765 was performed at Covent Garden in December 1769. It was probably this Carter who performed a new organ concerto by François Hippolyte Barthélémon on 21 August 1770 at Marylebone Gardens. He then wrote music for Henry Bate Dudley's comic opera The

Rival Candidates, which was first performed at Drury Lane on 1 February 1775. The music enjoyed some critical and popular success, and Carter received a fee of £42 the next month. This was followed on 20 March 1777 at the same theatre by *The Milesian*, a two-act comic opera written by Isaac Jackman. The song 'Stand to your guns, my hearts of oak' from the opera was very popular for many years and was performed by Charles Bannister among others. The songs Carter composed for Vauxhall around this time also enjoyed a great deal of success. At various times (mainly during the 1770s and 1780s) Carter published several collections of glees, anthems, catches, and songs, in one of which (*Songs Sung at Vauxhall*, 1773) appeared the extremely popular and his best-known composition, 'O Nanny, wilt thou gang [or 'fly'] with [or 'from'] me' (to words from Percy's *Reliques*). It was subsequently reprinted in numerous editions and arrangements well into the nineteenth century. In 1847 a claim was made by a grandson of Joseph Baildon that his grandfather was the composer of 'O Nanny' (the affair is covered in *GM*, new ser., 27/1, 1847, 377, 481, 604); but this appears to have been dismissed (see *MT*). In 1782 Carter wrote impressive new music for F. Pilon's *The Fair American*, which was played at Drury Lane on 18 May. However, Carter received no payment and sued his librettist, but Pilon absconded to avoid the consequences. In 1783 he contributed an epilogue song ('When I was a little baby') to Mrs Cowley's *A Bold Stroke for a Husband*, and he produced the song collection *The Days of Love* the following year, but his bad luck continued. His application for the post of organist at St George's, Windsor, in 1785 was unsuccessful, although the idiosyncratic mixture of styles in the anthem he submitted appears to have been largely responsible for his failure. For John Palmer's new but short-lived Royalty Theatre, in Wellclose Square, near the Tower of London, Carter, as musical director, wrote music for an incidental pastoral, *The Birthday, or, Arcadian Contest* (1787); *True Blue* (1787), a new setting of Henry Carey's *Nancy*; and *The Constant Maid, or, Poll of Plympton* (1788), besides several songs and glees. His last operatic work was *Just in Time*, to poetry by Thomas Hurlstone (Carter contributed some verses for a song in the last act). This work was produced unsuccessfully at Covent Garden for Joseph Munden's benefit on 10 May 1792, with Charles Incledon in the lead role. Unfortunately Elizabeth Billington had turned down the part of Augusta at the last moment. Carter continued to compose as director of music for the private theatre of Richard Bary, seventh earl of Barrymore, at Wargrave from about 1790, including a song, 'When we're married', which was introduced by Maria Theresa Bland in *The Surrender of Calais* (1791). Carter's songs remained in the repertory, including performances by Delpini at Covent Garden in 1797. Resident at 51 Edgware Road in 1794, Carter died in London on Friday 12 October 1804. He was undoubtedly a talented musician, who was often bold and innovative in his compositional style, particularly in the case of his overtures. However, it seems that his improvidence and carelessness left him in poverty and debt at the end of his life, although the oft-cited story, originating from the

Gentleman's Magazine (1804), that he forged a Handel manuscript and sold it for 20 guineas is perhaps apocryphal. An excellent performer on the harpsichord as well as the organ, he produced numerous keyboard (piano and harpsichord) works, including lessons, sonatas, sonatinas, variations, and arrangements. In addition to his stage and vocal works, there is evidence to suggest that he also composed concertos for clarinet, bassoon, and violin with orchestra, although these have not been located.

As mentioned above, Carter's details after 1769 have often been muddled with those of **Thomas Carter** (1769–1800). This Carter, also from Ireland, born in May 1769, studied music in Naples from about 1788; his studies were paid for by Murrough O'Brien, fifth earl of Inchiquin, and he was also encouraged by Sir William Hamilton. Following a period as musical director of the theatre in Calcutta, he returned to England and married a Miss Wells of Cookham, Berkshire, in 1793. He was more financially successful than his namesake and was able to publish some of his works before he died 'of the fatal ravages of the liver complaint' (*GM*, 1st ser., 70/2, 1800, 1117) on 8 November 1800 in Thornhaugh Street, London: the *Gentleman's Magazine* wrote that 'the Harmonists, and various musical societies, have lost the "choicest feather of their wing"' (ibid.). He was survived by his wife.

A third Thomas Carter, also a musician, was living in Dublin at the beginning of the nineteenth century and can be traced as a member of the Irish Musical Fund, from 1803 to 1809. He may have been related to the subject of this article, whose brother (sources differ as to whether he was younger or older) **Sampson Carter** (*d.* c.1814?) joined the Irish Musical Fund on 1 June 1788 and remained a member, including a period as president, until 1809. Sampson was a chorister in St Patrick's Cathedral, Dublin, until 1766. He subsequently settled in Dublin as a music teacher and composer, took the degree of MusD at Dublin University in 1771, and in 1797 was appointed a vicarchoral of St Patrick's. He probably died about 1814.

W. B. SQUIRE, rev. DAVID J. GOLBY

Sources R. Fiske, 'Carter, (Charles) Thomas', *New Grove*, 2nd edn · Highfill, Burnim & Langhans, *BDA* · *GM*, 1st ser., 74 (1804), 986, 1165 · *GM*, 2nd ser., 27 (1847), 377, 481, 604 · *MT*, 19 (1878), 502–3 · R. Fiske, 'Carter, Thomas (ii)', *New Grove* · *GM*, 1st ser., 70 (1800), 1117

Carter, Thomas (1769–1800). *See under* Carter, (Charles) Thomas (c.1735–1804).

Carter, Thomas (*d.* 1867), military writer, entered in April 1839 as a temporary clerk at the Horse Guards, Whitehall, London, and subsequently rose to the position of firstclass clerk in the adjutant-general's office, a post he held until his death. He assisted Richard Cannon in the preparation of the historical records of the army, and after Cannon's retirement edited the published records of the 26th regiment (the Cameronians) and 44th (Essex) regiment, and a new edition of the records of the 13th light infantry. These works, however, were not treated as official publications. He also published *Curiosities of War* (1860) and *Medals of the British Army* (1861–2), and frequently contributed to

Notes and Queries. He died at his residence, 11 Lorrimore Square, Walworth, London, on 9 August 1867, and was survived by his widow, Elizabeth.

H. M. CHICHESTER, rev. JAMES LUNT

Sources Boase, *Mod. Eng. biog.* · *War office lists* · *CGPLA Eng. & Wales* (1867)

Wealth at death under £1500: probate; administration with will, 17 Oct 1867, *CGPLA Eng. & Wales*

Carter, Thomas Thellusson (1808–1901), Church of England clergyman, was born at Keate's Lane, Eton, on 19 March 1808, the younger son of the Revd Thomas Carter, lower master and afterwards vice-provost of Eton College, and his wife, Mary, daughter of Henry Proctor of Clewer. He had a brother and five sisters. He entered Eton College aged six and spent twelve years there, leaving as captain of the oppidans. After matriculating at Christ Church, Oxford, on 8 December 1825, he went into residence in 1827. There he met Edward Bouverie Pusey, one of his father's former pupils, who in 1828 became regius professor of Hebrew; W. E. Gladstone was Carter's junior by a year. Carter graduated with a first class in classics in 1831 and sat unsuccessfully for an Oriel fellowship, but left Oxford before the Tractarian movement developed, following Keble's assize sermon in July 1833.

On 21 October 1832 Carter was ordained deacon by Bishop Burgess of Salisbury and was licensed to St Mary's, Reading, of which Henry Hart Milman (1791–1868) was vicar. Following his ordination to the priesthood by the bishop of Lincoln on 22 December 1833, he went to Burnham, Buckinghamshire, as his father's curate. While there he was greatly influenced by the Tracts for the Times, which were then being published. On 26 November 1835 Carter married Mary Anne Gould (d. 1869), daughter of John Gould of Amberd, near Taunton, and they had a son and two daughters. She had been a childhood friend of Richard Hurrell Froude (1803–1836), and it was through the Goulds that Carter met Tractarian sympathizers. In 1838 he became rector of Piddlehinton, near Dorchester, in Dorset, an unhappy appointment during which his health suffered. From 1842 to 1844 he took leave of absence and returned to Burnham; in 1844 he was appointed rector of Clewer, near Windsor. Clewer found in Carter a zealous incumbent bent on social as well as ecclesiological reform. Aided by his friend the architect Henry Woodyer (1816–1896), he restored the fabric of Clewer church, established two mission churches within the parish, and brought order and dignity into the worship, steadily developing the ritual used and the doctrine taught. A benefit society was established to aid the poor; part of the glebe was given for allotments and, in an attempt to stem the drink problem, a temperance society was started.

Clewer parish was large and included a slum district known as Clewer Fields. Two army barracks and a large number of itinerant railway navvies compounded the social problems of drink, poverty, and prostitution. In December 1848 Mariquita Tennant (1811–1860), a widow living in Clewer, rescued a young woman from a life of poverty and abuse in Clewer Fields; she soon had over a

Thomas Thellusson Carter (1808–1901), by Frank Holl, exh. RA 1882

dozen women under her roof in what became the Clewer House of Mercy. Carter, who had been influenced by the writings of the Revd John Armstrong (1813–1856), later bishop of Grahamstown, Cape Colony, on the need for church rescue work, supported her efforts to found a religious community, but ill health forced her to withdraw in 1851. Carter was fortunate in Mrs Tennant's successor, the recently widowed Harriet Monsell (1811–1883), who was installed as mother superior of the newly founded Community of St John Baptist, Clewer, on 30 November 1852.

The work of the community was conducted on clearly defined lines and led to over forty branch houses, besides extensive work in the United States and India. The development of sisterhoods was viewed by many with alarm, provoked controversy, and caused Samuel Wilberforce, bishop of Oxford, much anxiety, although he remained the visitor until his translation to Winchester in 1869. Owing to the nature of Carter's pastoral work and his role in the revival of the religious life, requests for spiritual direction came to him from all sides, and he discharged the task with growing conviction and sympathy. Perhaps the most widely used of his books was *The Treasury of Devotion* (1869). He also pioneered the retreat movement and led some of the earliest recorded retreats in the Church of England.

In the midst of the controversies surrounding ritualism within the church, Carter found a role both as leader and conciliator. He was an early member and vice-president of the English Church Union, founded in 1859, and in 1875 suggested the so-called 'six points' as a guideline for ritual practice. His role of warden at the Clewer House of Mercy had deepened his awareness of the importance of sacramental confession, leading to one of his major works, *The*

Doctrine of Confession in the Church of England (1865). When, in 1873, amid great controversy, a petition signed by 483 clergymen requesting the education, selection, and licensing of duly qualified confessors was read in the Canterbury convocation, Carter and others drew up a *Declaration on Confession and Absolution, as Set Forth by the Church of England* as a defence of the practice. In 1878 he became the master of the influential Society of the Holy Cross during the controversy surrounding a manual for confessors entitled *The Priest in Absolution*.

His allegiance to the Tractarian movement led Carter to hold a high view of the sacraments and the ordained ministry. In 1856 he signed the protest against the Bath judgment in the case of Archdeacon George Denison, which was a considered statement on the doctrine of the real presence in the eucharist. A year later he published the *Doctrine of the Priesthood in the Church of England*, which was followed in 1870 by *The Holy Eucharist*. In 1862 he had been instrumental in the founding of the Confraternity of the Blessed Sacrament and remained superior-general until 1897. In common with many of his contemporaries Carter was dismayed by biblical criticism, and in 1870 he sent to Archibald Campbell Tait, archbishop of Canterbury, the memorial of 1529 clergy against the admission to holy communion in Westminster Abbey of the interdenominational committee appointed by convocation to revise the New Testament. In 1870 Bishop John Mackarness of Oxford acknowledged his pastoral work by making him an honorary canon of Christ Church. Though his zeal and personal charm had won over most of his parishioners, his ritual changes provoked some opposition, which in time produced appeals to the law.

Three times between 1871 and 1878 the law was set in motion against Carter on the charge of ritualism, and each time the bishop of Oxford vetoed proceedings. On the third occasion Dr Julius, an absentee parishioner, obtained from the queen's bench a writ of mandamus against the bishop. In March 1879 the judges found in Julius's favour; the bishop won an appeal, but Julius took the case to the House of Lords, which upheld the Court of Appeal, thus vindicating the bishop's power of veto. Carter knew, however, that the bishop disapproved of ritualism, and when the House of Lords delivered its judgment on 22 March 1880 he resigned the rectory of Clewer.

Carter retired to St John's Lodge, built for him by public subscription: situated opposite the Clewer House of Mercy, it enabled him to continue as warden of the house and community. He maintained a close interest in the wider church and continued to be a respected authority; following the publication of *Lux mundi* (1889) he was a signatory to a *Declaration on the Inspiration of Holy Scripture* in December 1891. In 1893 he spoke at the Birmingham church congress, and as late as 1898 addressed a meeting of priests in London on the limits of ritual.

Thomas Thellusson Carter died at St John's Lodge on 28 October 1901 after a short illness. Following a service in the chapel of the House of Mercy he was buried on 31 October in Clewer churchyard alongside his wife, who had died in 1869. He was survived by his two daughters, Jane,

who wrote his biography, and Mary; his son, John, had died in 1899. While his detractors counted him among the ritualists, Carter was a Tractarian at heart, firmly grounded in scripture, the church fathers, and the Anglican divines. His obituarists praised his quiet dignity and his deep spirituality: the protestant journal *Truth* described him as 'a saintly man' and the *Daily Telegraph* declared him 'one of the most venerated and the last of the Tractarians'. Carter was one of the most influential men of his day, but, for all his wider associations, he was essentially a parish priest ministering to the people of Clewer and to the House of Mercy.   VALERIE BONHAM

Sources *Life and letters of Thomas Thellusson Carter*, ed. W. H. Hutchings (1904) · J. F. M. Carter, *Life and letters of the Rev. T. T. Carter* (1911) · P. M. Rampton, 'Thought and work of Thomas Thellusson Carter of Clewer', PhD diss., King's Lond., 1984 · V. Bonham, *In the midst of the people* (1983) · V. Bonham, *A place in life: the Clewer House of Mercy, 1849–83* (1992) · V. Bonham, *A joyous service: the Clewer sisters and their work* (1989) · V. Bonham, 'A complication of circumstances: Canon Carter and the "Clewer Case"', *Windlesora*, 8 (1989), 15–24 · *Morning Post* (29 Oct 1901) · *The Sketch* · *The Times* (29 Oct 1901) · *Daily News* (29 Oct 1901) · *Daily Telegraph* (29 Oct 1901) · *Truth* (29 Oct 1901) · *Church Times* (29 Oct 1901) · *Windsor and Eton Express* (29 Oct 1901) · H. P. Liddon, *The life of Edward Bouverie Pusey*, ed. J. O. Johnston and others, 4 vols. (1893–7) · W. Benham and R. T. Davidson, *Life of Archibald Campbell Tait*, 2 vols. (1891)

Archives Community of St John Baptist, Clewer · NRA, corresp. and notes | Bodl. Oxf., letters to S. Wilberforce · Borth Inst., corresp. with second Viscount Halifax · CKS, Society of Holy Cross MSS · LPL, corresp. with Archbishop Benson relating to sisterhoods · LPL, Church Union MSS · LPL, corresp. with A. C. Tait · Pusey Oxf., letters to Pusey

Likenesses M. Carpenter, oils, 1825–6 (*Mr Carter on leaving Eton*), Eton · F. Holl, oils, exh. RA 1882, Community of St John Baptist, Clewer [*see illus.*] · G. F. Bodley, marble effigy, 1903, Community of St John Baptist, Clewer · Hills & Saunders of Eton, sepia photograph, priv. coll. · Mrs Newton, chalk drawing · bronze mural tablet, St Andrew's Church, Clewer · marble or alabaster bas-relief (in middle age), Community of St John Baptist, Clewer · oils, Community of St John Baptist, Clewer · photographs (most in old age), Community of St John Baptist, Clewer · stained-glass window, Community of St John Baptist, Clewer

Carter, (Helen) Violet Bonham [*née* (Helen) Violet Asquith], **Baroness Asquith of Yarnbury (1887–1969)**, politician, was born on 15 April 1887 at Eton House in John Street, Hampstead, London, the only daughter and the fourth of the five children of Herbert Henry *Asquith, later first earl of Oxford and Asquith (1852–1928), and his wife, Helen Kelsall, *née* Melland (1854–1891). The youngest child, Cyril *Asquith, became Lord Asquith of Bishopstone. In 1891, when Violet was four, her mother died of typhoid fever. Three years later her father married Margaret Emma Alice (Margot) Tennant [*see* Asquith, Margaret Emma Alice]; of their two surviving children, the youngest, Anthony *Asquith, became a noted film director.

Edwardian society and politics The early death of Violet's mother drew her closer to her father, who in 1892 became home secretary in Gladstone's last administration. Asquith spoke to his young daughter, who had a precocious intellect, 'on even terms, as though to a contemporary' (V. Bonham Carter, memoir, Bonham Carter MSS). Irish home rule and prison reform, she later recalled, became 'inextricably entangled with visions of my father

(Helen) Violet Bonham Carter, Baroness Asquith of Yarnbury (1887–1969), by Howard Coster, 1937

shaving while he expounded them to me' (ibid.). It was the beginning of an extraordinarily close filial relationship, which had politics at its core.

Asquith's decision to remarry brought a spirited stepmother into the life of his young family. Margot Asquith was an important influence on Violet in particular. She ensured that her stepdaughter's informal education was of a high standard, employing good governesses and overseeing her 'finishing' in Dresden and in Paris. And she fostered the sense of style and ready turn of phrase that carried Violet triumphantly through the 'whirling social vortex' of her first season in 1905. Relations between the two women, though, were constantly strained. In 1909, the year after he became premier, Asquith lamented that they should be 'on terms of chronic misunderstanding' (H. H. Asquith to M. Asquith, Dec 1909, Brock and Brock, 10).

After 'coming out' Violet's life was one of great privilege and excitement. Her taste for adventure led to an early flight in a biplane. 'I only live to do it again', she wrote to a friend, 'and feel I must marry an air-man' (V. Asquith to V. Stanley, 22 Aug 1912, *Lantern Slides*, 327). She had a vibrant personality and came to know virtually everyone who crossed the threshold of 10 Downing Street. Henry James congratulated her: 'Happy child! You are seeing life from the stage box' (Bonham Carter MSS). A memorable early meeting was with the young Winston Churchill at a dinner party. She later told her father that she had been in the presence of genius. 'Well', he responded, 'Winston would certainly agree with you there', observing that not

many others might (Bonham Carter, *Churchill*, 18). Her close friendship with Churchill proved to be lifelong, though punctuated by sharp political differences.

The gaiety of Violet's youth was interrupted by the death in December 1909 of her close friend Archie Gordon, son of the earl of Aberdeen, following a motor car accident. They became engaged in Winchester Hospital as Archie lay dying. A visit to the Sudan in 1910 helped Violet recover from this loss, and the tempo of her life quickened again. It was abruptly halted by the First World War, in which innumerable friends, and her eldest brother, were killed. The conflict also brought to an end her father's premiership. In December 1916 he was succeeded by Lloyd George, and a schism in the Liberal Party ensued. Defeat at the 1918 election added to Asquith's humiliation. Violet once said of Lloyd George, 'having no fidelities he also has no rancours' (diary, November–December 1923, *Champion Redoubtable*, 156). Exactly the opposite was true of her, and she never forgave him his role in her father's downfall. She made a lifelong mission of defending her father's reputation and in later years responded fiercely, and not always to good effect, to the inevitable criticism of historians.

Inter-war Liberalism, marriage, and the BBC When Asquith attempted a political comeback, standing for election at Paisley in Glasgow in January 1920, Violet campaigned for him. Despite his pre-war anti-suffragism, which she had echoed, she successfully appealed for the women's vote. It contributed to a famous victory. Churchill later hailed her as 'a champion redoubtable even in the first rank of Party orators' (Churchill, 99). She helped her father hold Paisley in 1922 and 1923, before his final defeat in 1924. After the 1920 triumph she was invited to stand herself. Her decision was complicated by the fact that she now had young children. Her friend Lord Kilbracken advised her to accept. If women in her advantageous position did not, he reasoned, 'an unwritten law' would be established that would deprive her sex 'of a very large number of its best potential representatives' (Kilbracken to V. Bonham Carter, 11 March 1920, *Champion Redoubtable*, 115–16). While she accepted this argument she felt that her paramount duty was to her young family, a consideration which, as she later indicated, weighed with many women who contemplated entering politics (see her article 'The political future of women', *Good Housekeeping*, October 1922, 11–12, 110).

Violet had married in 1915 Maurice Bonham Carter (1880–1960), her father's principal private secretary, and they had two daughters, Cressida and Laura—the latter married Jo Grimond, later a leader of the Liberal Party—and two sons, Mark, later Lord Bonham-*Carter, himself a prominent Liberal, and Raymond. Violet served as president of the Women's Liberal Federation, 1923–5, but grew disillusioned with politics after her father ceded the party leadership to Lloyd George in 1926. Much time was now spent with her family in Wiltshire, from which county the 'Yarnbury' in her title is taken. By then she had become emotionally involved with O. T. Falk, a city figure who was her husband's business partner. The relationship lasted several years, but was long outlived by a happy and successful marriage.

Violet's withdrawal from politics became marked in 1929, the year after her father's death, when she described herself as 'a political trappist' (V. Bonham Carter to H. Currie, 15 Nov 1929, *Champion Redoubtable*, 178). She broke her silence in 1931, in support of the National Government, and abandoned it completely two years later in protest against the rise of fascism in Germany. As a young woman Violet had reflected the antisemitism of her social background, but the Nazi persecution of Jews fired her indignation. At Liberal meetings and on election hustings she publicly denounced 'Hitlerism, that monstrous portent' (speech at Liberal meeting, Scarborough, 18 May 1933, Bonham Carter MSS), and derided 'appeasement' as the policy of 'peace at any price that others can be forced to pay' (ibid., speech at Caxton Hall, London, 20 Oct 1938). Peace with honour, she argued, could come only through the 'collective security' of the League of Nations. Churchill recognized her important contribution to the debate when, in 1936, he gave her a central role in his anti-fascist Freedom Focus. This cross-party pressure group acted under the auspices of the League of Nations Union, of which Violet remained a patron until 1941. Although the Freedom Focus did little to change public opinion, she took comfort that it strengthened Churchill's claims to be included in the government at the outbreak of war.

After becoming premier Churchill repaid her loyalty by including her, in 1941, in a revitalized board of governors of the BBC. With Harold Nicolson and J. J. Mallon she fought to free the corporation from close political control and to make of public broadcasting a means of popular education, as well as entertainment. Despite some success she felt frustrated when, in April 1946, the Labour government did not renew her term of office.

Liberal decline, public activities, Suez A woman of exceptional public spirit, Violet Bonham Carter combined duties as an air-raid warden with a second term as president of the Women's Liberal Federation during 1939–45. In 1944 she became president-elect of the Liberal Party Organization. She was confirmed at the 1945 party assembly as its first ever woman president, and held the post until 1947. All her influence was used to identify the party with social reform. She championed Sir William Beveridge's seminal 1942 report and helped recruit him as a Liberal in 1944. At the 1945 election, however, the Liberals managed only a dozen seats, while Violet herself came bottom of the poll at Wells. It was a crushing disappointment, and for some time afterwards she feared the party's extinction. Although Churchill reassured her that he wanted its survival, he could not persuade Conservatives to throw Liberals the lifeline of electoral reform. And at the 1951 election he could not even guarantee Violet the undivided support of local Conservatives when she stood at Colne Valley. Though they withdrew their candidate in her favour, many abstained from voting. The election was narrowly lost to Labour.

To add insult to injury fellow Liberals attacked her for openly accepting Churchill's support. She regarded their lack of pragmatism as symptomatic of the Liberal decline. In the ebb and flow of the electoral tide the party survived only by clinging, barnacle-like, to a half-dozen seats. The charismatic leadership of her son-in-law, Jo Grimond, lightened her gloom. She hoped that a revival would follow each Liberal by-election victory. It never did. Just three Liberal MPs cheered her son, Mark, on his introduction to the Commons after victory at Torrington in 1958: 'I remembered my father's introduction when he took his seat after Paisley & how faint the cheers of the survivors of the Liberal Party then sounded to me. But they at least were 27' (diary, 1 April 1958, Bonham Carter MSS).

Great energy, and a range of interests to match, made Violet a recognizable figure in post-war Britain. She made frequent appearances on radio and television, and contributed articles and innumerable letters to the newspapers. In 1945 she became a governor of the Old Vic theatre, and served on the royal commission on the press during 1947–9. At Churchill's instigation she was honoured with a DBE in 1953. Two years later she became a trustee of the Glyndebourne Arts Trust. Her lifelong involvement in the arts was recognized when, in April 1967, she became the first woman to address the Royal Academy dinner. She combined a passion for travel with an abiding interest in foreign affairs, serving as a British delegate at the Commonwealth Relations Conference in Canada in 1949. She met Ben Gurion in Israel in 1957, Chiang Kai-shek in Taiwan (Formosa) in 1958, and President Kennedy in Washington in 1963. She was a patron of the United Nations Association, and in 1964 became president of the Royal Institute of International Affairs. The cause of European unity had her wholehearted support, and in 1947 she became a vice-chair of the United Europe Movement. From 1952 onwards she was a stalwart of the annual Königswinter conferences for Anglo-German friendship.

Besides her advocacy of Britain's entry into the Common Market, Violet probably made her greatest political impact after the war by condemning the British invasion of Suez in 1956. In a letter to *The Times*, published on 6 November 1956, and quoted that day in the House of Commons by Hugh Gaitskell, she argued that the invasion rendered Britain morally impotent at a time when it needed all of its authority to challenge the Soviet repression of Hungary (*Hansard 5*, 560, 1956, 37–8). The issue was as clear-cut to her as appeasement had been. Friends and acquaintances were privately marked as 'sound' or 'unsound' according to their views. She believed that Suez opened an unbridgeable gulf between Liberals and Conservatives. It undeniably led to a personal breach with Harold Macmillan, an old friend. Many believed that this was why she was not given a life peerage until December 1964, as Baroness Asquith of Yarnbury, after Labour had taken office.

The 1960s: the House of Lords The years prior to this were overshadowed by the death of Violet's husband, in June 1960, and by her own ill health. Her political activities were curtailed, but not stopped. She was in the vanguard of the anti-apartheid movement, and in January 1960 defended a boycott of South African goods on the BBC's

Matters of Moment radio programme. In June 1963 she became the first woman to give the Romanes lecture at Oxford, and later that month was made an honorary LLD by the University of Sussex. Admission to the House of Lords further rejuvenated her. In spite of failing health she regularly attended debates and helped to galvanize the small band of Liberal peers into co-ordinated action. She voted in favour of more liberal laws on abortion and homosexuality in 1966–7. In February 1968 she opposed, as too restrictive, the government's Immigration Bill. In August 1968 she spoke passionately about the humanitarian crisis in Biafra, which the 'miracle of television' made apparent to all: 'We have no alibi. We see these things happening'. She called for an immediate end to the sale of British arms to the Nigerian government, 'the most inhuman deed that I can recall in the history of our country' (*Hansard 5*, 296, 1968, 700–02). Her last speech, in November 1968, was on the need for reform of the House of Lords. She wryly observed that it was a matter that a half-century earlier had been deemed urgent.

When favourably reviewing her biography, *Winston Churchill as I Knew Him* (1965), Lord Attlee lamented that she had not written more. Asked why she had not, he is reputed to have said: 'Too busy talking' (K. Harris, *Attlee*, 1982, 560). Violet loved company and revelled especially in political talk. Her earnestness and high moral tone attracted ridicule in some quarters, and probably cost her friends. She was, by her own admission, 'red in tooth & claw' (V. Bonham Carter to W. S. Churchill, 24 July 1941, *Champion Redoubtable*, 232). Though slightly-built she had a formidable presence, with a strong face and an interrogative look. The wit and brilliance of her oratory, honed by observation of the great speakers of the Edwardian age, was her passport to a career in public life. She knew how to use her patrician tones to devastating effect, whether on a public platform or in conversation. She was exceptionally well read and well informed, and expected others to hold opinions as clearly formed as her own and to be prepared to defend them as vigorously. As a result she was quick to judge, and saw in her acquaintances 'swans' and 'geese'. Some of her assessments were neither favourable nor fair. But if her judgement could be faulty, her instinctive loyalty and readiness to fight injustice were undoubted. Tony Benn wrote admiringly of her in 1962, when she supported his successful campaign to allow peers to renounce their titles, that she belonged 'to the "couldn't care more" brigade' (T. Benn, *Years of Hope: Diaries, Letters and Papers, 1940–62*, 1995, 256).

The position of working women was always a special concern. She hailed housewives as the true 'unknown warriors' of the Second World War (16 Jan 1942, speech to 'Women's Parliament', Bonham Carter MSS). As early as 1925 she called for family allowances, which she maintained should be paid directly to the mother if they were to be effective (meeting of the WNLF council, Southport, 5 May 1925, Bonham Carter MSS). Later on she campaigned for equal pay for women, debating the measure on the BBC radio programme *Taking Stock* in January 1952. Her own experience as a wife and mother was central to her outlook, but she believed that no woman should be expected to confine her involvement in politics 'to strictly domestic questions' (*Good Housekeeping*, October 1922, 11–12, 110). In her eyes there was no conflict between her advocacy of women's causes and her strong dislike of feminism. In fact she enjoyed the irony. After becoming the first woman to address the Reform Club, in May 1968, she reflected on how many times she, 'an anti-feminist', had been 'the first to break virgin soil' (diary, 23 May 1968, Bonham Carter MSS). In so doing she undoubtedly paved the way for others, successfully combining femininity with great strength of character and executive ability.

Violet Bonham Carter witnessed the decline of Britain as a great power, and the parallel decline of the Liberal Party as a political force, but she lost faith in neither her country nor her creed. She believed that Britain still had a significant world role, through the Common Market, Commonwealth, and United Nations, and that Liberalism offered the sensible path between the extremes of socialism and unfettered capitalism. Churchill once remarked to her that post-1945 Conservatism was little different to pre-1914 Liberalism. She replied: 'Yes—but that was 40 years ago. Time moves on. One can't afford to follow events with a time-lag of 40 years' (diary, 6 Aug 1953, Bonham Carter MSS). And she did not. She never ceased trying to interpret to modern times the Liberal ideals that she had learned from her father in childhood. She died in London on 19 February 1969 and was buried three days later at Mells in Somerset. MARK POTTLE

Sources Bodl. Oxf., MSS Bonham Carter · *Lantern slides: the diaries and letters of Violet Bonham Carter, 1904–1914*, ed. M. Bonham Carter and M. Pottle (1996); another edn (1997) · *Champion redoubtable: the diaries and letters of Violet Bonham Carter, 1914–1945*, ed. M. Pottle (1998) · V. Bonham Carter, *Winston Churchill as I knew him* (1965) · M. Asquith, *The autobiography of Margot Asquith*, 2 vols. (1920–22); repr. in 1 vol. with introduction by M. Bonham Carter (1962) · *H. H. Asquith: letters to Venetia Stanley*, ed. M. Brock and E. Brock (1982) · W. S. Churchill, *Great contemporaries* (1937) · J. A. Spender and C. Asquith, *Life of Herbert Henry Asquith, Lord Oxford and Asquith*, 2 vols. [1932]

Archives Bodl. Oxf., corresp. and papers | BL, corresp. with Society of Authors, Add. MS 63214 · Bodl. Oxf., corresp. relating to Society for the Protection of Science and Learning · Bodl. Oxf., letters to Margot Asquith · CAC Cam., letters to Lady Diana Cooper · CAC Cam., corresp. with Sir W. J. Haley · CAC Cam., letters to Lady Spencer-Churchill · Herts. ALS, letters to Lady Desborough · JRL, letters to *Manchester Guardian* · King's AC Cam., letters to Sir George Barnes and Lady Barnes · King's Cam., letters to G. H. W. Rylands · King's Lond., Liddell Hart C., corresp. with Sir B. H. Liddell Hart · NL Wales, corresp. with Clement Davies · Som. ARS, corresp. with Aubrey Herbert · Tate collection, corresp. with Lord Clark | FILM BBC WAC | SOUND BBC WAC · BL NSA, 'Evening with Lady Asquith', 1969, P344W TR1 · BL NSA, 'Lady Violet remembers', 1969, BD1 · BL NSA, oral history interview · BL NSA, performance recordings

Likenesses G. C. Beresford, photograph, 1907, NPG · E. Barnard, watercolour, 1910, priv. coll. · photograph, 1912, Hult. Arch. · W. Orpen, portrait, 1915, priv. coll. · H. Coster, photograph, 1937, NPG [*see illus.*] · B. Brandt, bromide photograph, before 1945, NPG · K. Hulton, photograph, 1948, Hult. Arch. · S. Samuels, photograph, 1951, NPG · photograph, 1956, Hult. Arch. · O. Nemon, bronze bust, 1960–69, NPG · C. Beaton, photograph, NPG · H. Coster, photographs, NPG

Wealth at death £49,472: probate, 16 June 1969, *CGPLA Eng. & Wales*

Carter, William (*b*. in or before **1549**, *d*. **1584**), printer, son of Robert Carter, a draper of London, and his wife, Agnes, was bound as an apprentice to the queen's printer John Cawood for ten years from February 1563. From 1573 Carter acted as a secretary to Nicholas Harpsfield, then under house arrest. When Harpsfield died in 1575 he left his manuscripts, including his life of Thomas More and his account of Thomas Cranmer's last days, to Carter. It was in this year that Carter was recruited, along with another former Cawood apprentice, John Lyon, by George Gilbert and Stephen Brinkley to set up a clandestine Catholic press in London. According to T. A. Birrell, Carter and Lyon printed seven books before the latter retired to the continent in 1577, with Carter then printing a further nine Catholic works over the next two years, including John Fisher's *A Spiritual Consolation*. Birrell also associates him with six items issued by the Green Street clandestine press between 1579 and 1581.

A month-long imprisonment in the Poultry in September 1578, for an unknown offence, was followed by a longer incarceration in the Gatehouse begun in December 1579; in that month, John Aylmer, bishop of London, wrote to Lord Burghley that he had:

> founde out a presse of pryntynge wth one Carter, a very Lewed fellowe, who hath byne dyvers tymes before in prison for printinge of Lewde pampheletes. But nowe in searche of his Howse amongest other nawghtye papystycall Bookes, wee have founde one wrytten in *Frenche* inty[t]led the *innosency of the Scotyshe Quene*, a very Dangerous Book. Wherin he calleth her *the heire apparant of this Crowne*. [H]e enveyeth agaynst the Execucion of the Duck [*sic*] of *Norfolke*, Defendeth the rebellion in the north, and Dyscourseth agaynst yo^w, and the Late L[ord] *keper*. (BL, Lansdowne MS 28, fol. 177)

As part of a wider policy concerning recusants Carter was freed in June 1581, on condition that he remained within 3 miles of his house in Hart Street, London (an almshouse belonging to the Drapers' Company), until he 'shall have conformed and yelded himself unto the Orders for Religion' (*APC*, 13.41).

In July 1582 Carter's house was searched for illegal books, and Carter himself was examined and sent to the Tower; in a letter dated 19 July the spy P. H. W., who claimed to have known Carter for twenty years, reported to Sir Francis Walsingham that Carter's wife, Jane, was seeking the intercession of Lord Lumley, a near neighbour of the Carters in London and a probable patron of the printer, to help her husband. P. H. W. claimed that 'there is ne[i]ther Jesuete, prieste, nor papyste of anye acompt^e w^t in england but he [Carter] knowthe them', suggesting that Carter's knowledge might prove very helpful 'if this be Rypte to th^e bottom' (PRO, SP 12/154/62, fol. 107r). Four months later a fellow prisoner reported that Carter had been 'nearly killed on the rack, but nothing could be drawn from [him] but the name of Jesus' (*Miscellanea IV*, 74; translated in Pollen, 30). At some point during his imprisonment, probably in mid-1583, Carter's widowed mother,

Agnes, petitioned Walsingham: she acknowledged an earlier petition by Jane, who was now dead, and beseeched Walsingham to 'graunt unto me … his [Carter's] said goodes for my satisfaction and his relief in his extreme distress, as also that he may be removed to the prison of the Gatehouse' (PRO, SP 12/206/92, fol. 184r).

Early in 1584 Carter was moved to Newgate and on 10 January was presented for trial at the Old Bailey, charged with printing a book containing a passage inciting the women at court to assassinate Queen Elizabeth. This book has since been identified as Gregory Martin's *A Treatise of Schisme* (1578), issued by Carter under a false imprint (*Short-Title Catalogue*, no. 17508); the offending passage read: 'Judith foloweth, whose godlye and constant wisedome if our Catholike gentlewomen woulde folowe, they might destroye Holofernes, the master heretike, and amase al[l] his retinew, and never defile their religion by communicating with them in anye smal[l] poynt' (Martin, sig. D2r). Although Carter confessed to having been involved in the production of this book (an admission he claimed that he first made during his 1579–81 imprisonment), he disputed the judges' interpretation of the offending passage. Later scholars have upheld Carter's defence: A. C. Southern declared the charge 'bogus' when the passage was considered as a whole (Southern, 350–53). Nevertheless, Carter was found guilty, and the following morning he was 'drawne from Newgate to Tyborne, and there hanged, bowelled, and quartered' (Stow, sig. 2M6v).

Carter was catalogued in Roman Catholic martyrologies from 1585 onwards. He was one of the 255 martyrs declared venerable by Pope Leo XIII in 1886, and one of 85 beatified by Pope John Paul II in 1987.   I. GADD

Sources E. H. Burton and J. H. Pollen, eds., *Lives of the English martyrs: the martyrs declared venerable, 1583–88*, 2nd ser., 1 (1914), 22–33 · J. H. Pollen, ed., *Unpublished documents relating to the English martyrs*, 1, Catholic RS, 5 (1908), 8–9, 30–31, 39 · [J. Gibbons and J. Fenn], *Concertatio ecclesiae catholicae in Anglia adversus Calvinopapistas et puritanos*, 2nd edn (1588); repr. (1970), sigs. 2I3r–2L1r, fols. 127r–133r [facs. repr., 1970] · *STC, 1475–1640* · private information (2004) [T. A. Birrell] · Arber, *Regs. Stationers*, 1.196; 2.749–50 · BL, Lansdowne MS 28, fol. 177 [transcribed, with some minor errors, in Arber, *Regs. Stationers*, 2.749–50] · PRO, SP 12/154/62, fol. 107r [calendared in *CSP domestic, 1581–90*, 63; transcribed in Pollen, *Unpublished documents*, 30–31] · PRO, SP 12/206/92, fol. 184r [calendared in *CSP domestic, 1581–90*, 450; transcribed in Pollen, *Unpublished documents*, 39] · *APC, 1581–2*, 41, 76 · *Miscellanea, I–IV*, Catholic RS, 1–4 (1905–7) · G. Martin, *A treatise of schisme* (1578) · R. Connelly, *The eighty-five martyrs* (1987), 9–16 · 'Litterae Apostolicae', *Acta Apostolicae Sedis*, 83/10 (1991), 870–76, esp. 873 · J. Stow and E. Howes, *The annales, or, Generall chronicle of England … unto the ende of the present yeere, 1614* (1615), sig. 2M6v · A. C. Southern, *Elizabethan recusant prose, 1559–1582* (1950) · A. F. Allison and D. M. Rogers, eds., *A catalogue of Catholic books in English printed abroad or secretly in England, 1558–1640*, 2 vols. (1956); repr. 2 vols. in 1 (1968) · T. Cooper, 'Gregory Martin's *Treatise of schism*', *N&Q*, 6th ser., 12 (1885), 345

Carter, William (**1605–1658**), Independent minister, was educated at Cambridge, according to Benjamin Brook; he was probably the William Carter who matriculated as a sizar from Trinity College at Easter 1624, became a scholar in 1627, graduated BA in 1629, and proceeded his MA in 1632. In 1640 Carter was reported to be lecturing at St Mary-le-Bow in London, where he was listed among those suspected by the ecclesiastical authorities of being 'not very conformable', as omitting to bow at the name of Jesus or to wear the surplice and to administering the sacrament to those sitting (PRO, SP 16/474/67), and he may have been briefly deprived, for Nehemiah Wallington reported that he had been restored to his lectureship in February 1641. By 1642 Carter was sufficiently popular and respected to be invited to preach a fast sermon before the House of Commons on 31 August. Subsequently published as *Israels Peace with God, Benjamines Overthrow* (1642), it claimed that Israel 'held themselves obliged to see [Benjamin] punished' but although the war was justified, because their call was from God, 'yet the success was ill' because the Israelites 'had their idols and false worships, still among them unrepented of' (*Israels Peace with God*, 2–3)—a warning to parliament that military success would depend on ecclesiastical reform.

Given that outspoken call for further reform, it is not surprising that during the following year Carter was appointed one of the licensers of the press and a member of the Westminster assembly of divines. Although an Independent and active with the Dissenting Brethren, Carter was among those Independents whom the Scottish presbyterian, Robert Baillie, conceded were 'very able men' (*Letters and Journals of Robert Baillie*, 2.110). In 1645 he was active in the debate on the proposition that 'there is no judicial power to which appeals may lie from a presbytery … that Assembly which is the body of Christ hath no judicial ecclesiastical power above it', the central tenet of the Independents, and in 1646 was a prominent dissenter from the clause limiting Christian liberty and liberty of conscience (Mitchell and Struthers, 58, 293). Like many Independents, Carter was dissatisfied with the system of parochial discipline and as a consequence refused to accept a parochial living, instead lecturing at St Michael, Crooked Lane, from 1651 until his death, and apparently also at St Giles Cripplegate, where he was living when he died. In 1652 he was among the twelve Independents who were signatories urging parliament to support the evangelization of the American Indians, and in 1654 he joined others as a signatory to a letter addressed to the evangelical churches of Europe urging support for John Dury's efforts to achieve protestant unity, a cause he had also supported financially. In 1654 Carter was appointed one of the triers of public preachers. Despite his own reputation as a popular preacher, only three of his works were published: his fast day sermon in 1642, a second sermon entitled *Light in Darkness* (1648), and a substantial treatise, *The Covenant of God with Abraham Opened* (1654), in which he defended infant baptism and the crucial role of the preacher. 'The ministry is that ordinance of God whereby the truth of God is by degrees to be discovered to be his truth, should come upon the soul in the same authority and power, as if God himself did speak it to us' (*Covenant of God*, 172).

Carter apparently did not marry until 25 June 1650, when, according to his will, he married Martha; her other name is unknown but may have been Potter or Middleton since the will also mentions his 'loving brother, Master John Potter', who served as executor, and a 'brother-in-law' Thomas Middleton. William and Martha had four children living when Carter made his will on 1 September 1657: Martha, William, Mary, and Elizabeth. He left substantial properties in Blackburn, Lancashire, and elsewhere in the north, the bulk of which was to pass to his son, should he reach his majority, but which was in the meantime to provide an allowance of £150 per annum for life in addition to the jointure promised his wife at the time of their marriage, as well as portions for his daughters, specifying that a minimum of £400 was to go to Martha on her marriage or on reaching twenty-one. William Greenhill, a fellow Independent minister, and Moses Wall were named trustees. Carter died in the parish of St Giles Cripplegate on 21 March 1658 and on 6 May Potter brought the will before the prerogative court for probate.

P. S. SEAVER

Sources B. Brook, *The lives of the puritans*, 3 vols. (1813) · A. F. Mitchell and J. Struthers, eds., *Minutes of the sessions of the Westminster assembly of divines* (1874) · W. M. Hetherington, *History of the Westminster Assembly of Divines* (1843) · *The letters and journals of Robert Baillie*, ed. D. Laing, 3 vols. (1841–2) · *The correspondence of John Owen (1616–1683)*, ed. P. Toon (1970) · N. Wallington, *Historical notices of events occurring chiefly in the reign of Charles I*, ed. R. Webb, 2 vols. (1869) · T. Webster, *Godly clergy in early Stuart England: the Caroline puritan movement, c.1620–1643* (1997) · Venn, *Alum. Cant.* · J. J. Baddeley, *An account of the church and parish of St Giles, without Cripplegate* (1888) · *The obituary of Richard Smyth … being a catalogue of all such persons as he knew in their life*, ed. H. Ellis, CS, 44 (1849) · churchwardens' accounts, St Michael, Crooked Lane, 1617–93, GL, MS 1188/1 · PRO, PROB 11/276, fol. 246

Wealth at death approx. £3000 or more: will, PRO, PROB 11/276, fol. 246

Carteret, Sir George, first baronet (1610?–1680), naval officer and administrator, was the eldest son of Elie de Carteret (*c*.1585–1640), and his wife, Elizabeth Dumaresq (*d.* 1640). This cadet line of the Carterets had for generations held the manor of St Ouen, Jersey. George was born (as he subsequently celebrated) on 6 May, probably in 1610, in Broad Street, St Helier. He doubtless had some rudimentary schooling in the parish of St Peter's, where his father bought a farm in 1619. His defective education and provincial accent would later be mocked. He was 'bred a sea-boy' (*Memoirs of Lady Fanshawe*, 61), becoming lieutenant of the *Garland* in 1629 and of the *Convertine* in 1632. On 18 March 1633 he was appointed captain of the small *Eighth Lion's Whelp* but swiftly rose to command much larger and more powerful ships such as the *Mary Rose*. In 1637 he was vice-admiral to William Rainborowe in the expedition which rescued captives from Salé. He returned there with the *Convertine* in 1638, as recorded in his journal. On 6 May 1640 he married his first cousin Elizabeth de Carteret (*d.* 1697).

In 1641 Carteret bought the office of comptroller of the navy and in 1642 he was designated by parliament vice-admiral to the earl of Warwick, but the king prevented his acceptance. When the civil war began, he at first attempted to raise a troop of horse for the king in Cornwall, but was induced instead to undertake the supply of western royalists with arms and ammunition. He established himself at St Malo and used his own credit and great local influence to supply both the western gentry and the fortresses of the Channel Islands. On the death in August 1643 of his uncle Sir Philip de Carteret, he succeeded as bailiff of Jersey, the reversion having been granted to him by patent in 1639. From the king he received also appointment as lieutenant-governor of the island under Sir Thomas Jermyn. Landing there in November 1643, he reconquered it and expelled Major Lydcott, the parliamentary governor, before the end of the month. From Jersey he carried on a vigorous privateering war against English trade, by virtue of the king's commission as vice-admiral, which he received on 13 December 1644. He was knighted on 21 January 1645 and created baronet on 9 May following. Parliament excluded him ('a great Fomenter of these present Distractions') from amnesty in subsequent treaties with the king, and declared void all commissions granted by him (Firth and Rait, 1.772–4). Carteret governed with great severity, imprisoning the persons and confiscating the estates of parliamentarians, but developing with great skill all the resources of the island. These were strained to the utmost when in 1646 the island became the refuge of royalist fugitives, and the cessation of the war enabled the parliamentarians to turn their forces against it. In spring 1646 Prince Charles landed in Jersey and invested Carteret with his honours. Edward Hyde, who was two years on the island as Carteret's guest, wrote of him:

> He was truly a worthy and most excellent person, of extraordinary merit towards the crown and nation of England; the most generous man in kindness, and the most dexterous man in business ever known; and a most prudent and skilful lieutenant-governor, who reduced Jersey not with greater skill and discretion than he kept it. And besides his other great parts of honesty and courage, undoubtedly as good, if not the best seaman of England … deserving as much from his Majesty and the crown of England for his fidelity as an honest man can do.   (Hoskins, 1.179)

Carteret joined Arthur, Lord Capel, and Hyde in the articles of association for the preservation of Jersey, drawn up when Henry Jermyn (who had succeeded his father as governor) was suspected of designing to sell the island to the French. On the second visit of Charles II to Jersey, from 17 September 1649 to 13 February 1650, Carteret was again his host. Among other rewards he was granted Smith's Island at the mouth of Chesapeake Bay, Virginia (briefly known as New Jersey), but a ship sent by Carteret to establish the new colony was captured.

The growing naval strength of the Commonwealth rendered Carteret's position on Jersey more difficult each month; an attack threatened in May 1647 proved abortive, but a second was successful and Carteret surrendered on 12 December 1651, having secured very advantageous terms. He joined the exiles in France, and became vice-admiral under the duke of Vendôme. In August 1657 he was imprisoned in the Bastille on the complaint of Sir William Lockhart, the English ambassador, in consequence of an attempt to seduce the English forces then acting as auxiliaries of France in the Low Countries, or perhaps for giving secret intelligence to the Spaniards. He was released in December 1657, but banished from France, and went to

Venice intending to serve the republic. Nevertheless he was back in France soon after Cromwell's death (September 1658). He kept in touch with the royalist court, adopting the pseudonym Milton.

At the Restoration Carteret moved to the centre stage. He had notionally been vice-chamberlain of the household since 1647; on 30 May 1660 this appointment was confirmed and the practical arrangements for the return of the king and court to Whitehall were his immediate concern. In July he was sworn of the privy council and made treasurer of the navy. At the coronation, on 23 April 1661, he served as almoner. In 1661 he was also elected MP for Portsmouth. The navy treasurership, which he secured against competition from Sir Robert Slingsby, was his most important work. His new colleagues found him amiable, but increasingly disposed to delegate responsibility. Pepys admired his devotion to his family but called him 'the most passionate man in the world' (Pepys, *Diary*, 6.175) and deplored his 'perverse ignorance' of business affairs (ibid., 4.192). The complexities of naval accounting were, in fact, beyond him. He had been assigned a salary of £2000, but soon reverted to the previous custom of taking 3*d.* in the pound on all payments, of which most were to the victualler. This led to a long struggle with Sir William Coventry, then secretary to the lord high admiral and a navy commissioner, which lasted until Carteret's resignation. Yet Coventry:

> did not deny Sir G. Carteret his due, in saying that he is a man that doth take the most pains and gives himself the most to do business of any man about the Court, without any desire of pleasure or divertisements.   (ibid., 3.243)

During the Second Anglo-Dutch War, Carteret's personal credit with the bankers was of the greatest service; he borrowed £280,000 and thus kept the fleet at sea.

The fall of his friend Clarendon and the miscarriage of the war undermined Carteret's position. In June 1667 he exchanged his office with Lord Anglesey for the place of vice-treasurer of Ireland. 'The King', Carteret told Pepys, 'at his earnest entreaty, did with much unwillingness, but with owning of great obligations to him for his faithful and long service to him and his father … grant his desire' (Pepys, *Diary*, 8.301). Carteret could nevertheless not escape the censure of parliament. In October 1669 the commissioners for public accounts, sitting at Brooke House, presented their report which alleged gross mismanagement in the navy during the war, with ten 'observations' directed at Carteret's keeping of the accounts. Both houses appointed committees, before which Carteret declined to appear in person. The Lords committee, so far as it went, exonerated him. But in the Commons he was voted guilty on all but one of the ten counts, and on 10 December was suspended from the house by 100 votes to 97. His impeachment was averted only when the king prorogued the session. During the recess the issues were debated in meetings between the Brooke House commissioners and the privy council. The king, who chaired these proceedings, flatly announced that he had found nothing wrong with Carteret's accounts, repeating his assurances when parliament met again on 14 February. Carteret, meanwhile, had sold his vice-treasurership of Ireland (for £11,000) and would never again hold a major office. He was, however, appointed a commissioner of the Admiralty on 9 July 1673, serving until 14 May 1679. Among many other involvements he was a member of the councils of trade and of the plantations, and of successor bodies which directed these concerns, between 1660 and 1674. He was a member of the Tangier committee from 1662, and a prize commissioner in 1665–7. He was master of Trinity House in 1664–5, and sat on the bench and other local commissions in several English counties.

Outside the navy, colonial affairs chiefly occupied Carteret's attention. He was a founder member of the Guinea Company of 1660, being paid £300 as consultant on the strength of his previous experience of the African continent. But it was in America, which he never visited, that he was most involved. On 24 March 1663 he was named by patent one of the original proprietors of Carolina, where Carteret county preserves his name. In 1665 Cape Romano was also renamed after him. In 1669 he became the colony's first admiral. Meanwhile in 1664, following annexation of former Dutch possessions to the north, he was granted the whole land between the Hudson and the Delaware for the rent of a peppercorn. He re-employed the name first given to his abortive venture in Virginia, and so the state of New Jersey had its foundation. In 1670 he also acquired a share in the islands of the Bahamas. In England he bought in May 1667 a country estate of 800 acres at Hawnes in Bedfordshire. He also had a London house on the south side of Pall Mall, and official residences in Whitehall Palace (as vice-chamberlain), at Cranbourne Lodge in Windsor Great Park, and, while he was navy treasurer, at Deptford.

By the government of Jersey, by successful privateering, and by the various offices he had held since the Restoration, Carteret became, as Marvell termed him, 'Carteret the rich' ('Last instructions to a painter', *Poems and Letters of Andrew Marvell*, 1.152). He told Pepys in 1667 that he was worth £50,000 when the king came in, and was £15,000 better since then. 'I do take the Vice chamberlain for a most honest man', added the diarist (Pepys, *Diary*, 8.165). He was also a bold man, recommending to the king 'the necessity of having at least a show of religion in the government, and sobriety' (ibid., 8.355). Marvell sneered at his 'ill English' ('Last instructions', *Poems and Letters of Andrew Marvell*, 1.152) and Pepys thought his ignorance of the device SPQR 'not to be borne in a Privy-Counsellor … that a schoolboy should be whipt for not knowing' (Pepys, *Diary*, 4.217).

Carteret died on the afternoon of 14 January 1680, in his chamber at Whitehall, and was buried on 12 February in Hawnes church. His will, made on 5 December 1678, was proved on 14 February 1680. At the time of his death the king was about to raise him to the peerage, and consequently granted his widow, by warrant dated 11 February 1680, precedence as if the creation had taken place. There were three sons and five daughters of the marriage. The eldest son, Philip, whose wedding to Lady Jemima Montagu, daughter of the first earl of Sandwich, on 31 July

1665 was amusingly described by Pepys, had been killed with his father-in-law in the battle of Solebay in 1672. Philip's son George was elevated to the peerage on 19 October 1681 as Baron Carteret of Hawnes.

C. H. FIRTH, *rev.* C. S. KNIGHTON

Sources G. R. Balleine, *All for the king: the life story of Sir George Carteret* (1976) · P. Watson, 'Carteret, Sir George', HoP, *Commons, 1660–90* · Pepys, *Diary* · S. E. Hoskins, *Charles the Second in the Channel Islands*, 2 vols. (1854) · Clarendon, *Hist. rebellion*, 2.22–3, 224–5, 458–9; 5.64, 261–2 · C. H. Firth and R. S. Rait, eds., *Acts and ordinances of the interregnum, 1642–1660*, 1 (1911), 772–4 · *Memoirs of Lady Fanshawe, wife of the Right Hon. Sir Richard Fanshawe, bart. written by herself* (1829), 60–1 · *The poems and letters of Andrew Marvell*, ed. H. Margoliouth, rev. P. Legouis, 3rd edn, 2 vols. (1971), vol. 1, pp.152, 357n.; vol. 2, pp. 88, 92, 94, 96, 325 · CSP dom., 1637–81 · CSP col., 1661–80 · GEC, *Peerage*, new edn · *Mercurius Politicus* (25 Dec 1651–1 Jan 1652), 1036 · *Mercurius Politicus* (21–8 Oct 1652) · *LondG* (12–15 Jan 1680) · *First report*, HMC, 1/1 (1870); repr. (1874), 34 · *Eighth report*, 3 vols. in 5, HMC, 7 (1881–1910) · *Samuel Pepys and the Second Dutch War: Pepys's navy white book and Brooke House papers*, ed. R. Latham, Navy RS, 133 (1995) [transcribed by W. Matthews and C. Knighton] · Thurloe, *State papers*, 6.421, 682 · B. Whitelocke, *Memorials of English affairs*, new edn, 4 vols. (1853), vol. 3, p. 191 · W. Kennett, *A register and chronicle ecclesiastical and civil* (1728), 167 · *Calendar of the Clarendon state papers preserved in the Bodleian Library*, 1: *To Jan 1649*, ed. O. Ogle and W. H. Bliss (1872), 338; 2: *1649–1654*, ed. W. D. Macray (1869), 275 · E. McCrady, *The history of South Carolina under the proprietary government, 1670–1719* (1897), 56, 63, 92, 110 · K. R. Andrews, *Ships, money, and politics: seafaring and naval enterprise in the reign of Charles I* (1991) · PRO, PROB 11/362, fols. 129–32

Archives Société Jersiaise, Jersey, MSS · St Ouen's Manor, Jersey, MSS

Likenesses P. Lely, oils, St Ouen's Manor, Jersey; repro. in Latham and Mathews, eds., *The diary of Samuel Pepys*, vol. 6, facing p. 168

Wealth at death property in Jersey; whole island of Alderney; many manors in UK; property in North America: will, PRO, PROB 11/362, fols. 129–32

Carteret [*formerly* Thynne], **Henry Frederick, first Baron Carteret of Hawnes** (1735–1826), politician, was born in London on 17 November 1735, younger of two sons of Thomas Thynne, second Viscount Weymouth (1710–1751), landowner, and his second wife, Louisa (*c.*1712–1736), daughter of John Carteret, second Earl Granville. Educated at Market Street School, Markyate, Hertfordshire, he entered St John's College, Cambridge, in 1752, and proceeded MA in 1753 and DCL in 1769. In 1756 he was a possible parliamentary candidate for Wiltshire, where his family resided, but instead came in for Staffordshire on a vacancy on 4 January 1757, backed by a family friend, Lord Gower. In 1761 he was returned on his family interest for Weobley. His elder brother, Thomas *Thynne, third Viscount Weymouth, sought office for him, and after refusing the post of groom of the bedchamber, he accepted, in December 1762, the clerk comptrollership of the green cloth, worth £1000 a year. He lost this when the Grenville ministry fell in July 1765, and acted with the opposition. Weymouth joined the duke of Bedford's 'gang', and Thynne regained office, as master of the household, worth £518 a year, in 1768 when Bedford entered Chatham's administration. Weymouth was now a secretary of state, and Thynne was promised the Madrid embassy, but when this failed to materialize, he was awarded a pension of £1000 a year. He was denied the joint vice-treasurership of Ireland in April 1770, apparently because the king was informed that he was inactive in debate. When Weymouth resigned office in December 1770, Thynne obtained the joint postmastership-general, whereupon he vacated his parliamentary seat; this appointment brought him £3000 a year. He was sworn of the privy council on 19 December 1770.

At the Post Office, Thynne relied on the secretary, Anthony Todd, to handle his paperwork, and also turned to him for loans. In 1776 he changed his surname to Carteret on succeeding his uncle, Robert Carteret, third Earl Granville, to Hawnes Park, Bedfordshire. He was appointed high bailiff of Jersey for life. On 29 January 1784 he was created Baron Carteret of Hawnes. He gave up the Post Office in September 1789, after his brother's elevation to a marquessate. On 9 July 1810 Carteret married Eleanor Smart (1741/2–1817), a spinster from Hawnes, who had been his mistress for forty-three years. They had no children, and when Carteret died at Hawnes on 17 June 1826 he was succeeded in turn by his two nephews, George and John Thynne. As both died without heirs, the barony became extinct. ROLAND THORNE

Sources J. Brooke, 'Thynne, Hon. Henry Frederick', HoP, *Commons, 1754–90* · *GM*, 1st ser., 96/2 (1826), 174 · *The Grenville papers: being the correspondence of Richard Grenville … and … George Grenville*, ed. W. J. Smith, 4 (1853), 484 · Walpole, *Corr.*, 15.139, 155; 36.223 · R. F. Scott, ed., *Admissions to the College of St John the Evangelist in the University of Cambridge*, 3: *July 1715 – November 1767* (1903), 612 · GEC, *Peerage* · K. Ellis, *The Post Office in the eighteenth century: a study in administrative history* (1958), 92
Wealth at death under £7000: will, PRO, PROB 11/1721, sig. 75, 1827

Carteret, John, second Earl Granville (1690–1763), politician, was born on 22 April 1690, the eldest son of George Carteret, first Baron Carteret (1667–1695), and Lady Grace (*c*.1667–1744), daughter of John Granville, first earl of Bath. His family connections were royalist and tory. The Granvilles and Carterets, who for centuries held property in Cornwall and in Jersey, suffered for the king during the civil wars. Sir Bevil Grenville, Carteret's great-grandfather, was killed at Lansdowne in 1643, leading his Cornishmen; his son John was created earl of Bath in 1661. One grandson, John, was created Baron Granville in 1703; another grandson, George, first Lord Lansdowne, was one of the dozen tory peers created in 1712 to carry the treaty of Utrecht. On his father's side Sir George Carteret, royalist governor of Jersey, made a fortune after the Restoration but died in 1680 while his peerage was being granted; his grandson, George (John's father), was created Lord Carteret of Hawnes in 1681.

Carteret inherited the barony at the age of five, his father having died on 22 September 1695. He was educated at Westminster School before going to Christ Church, Oxford, in 1706, where Edward Harley, son of the tory first minister, was a friend. Oxford confirmed Carteret's deep love of the classics; he carried away from university, as Jonathan Swift put it, 'more Greek, Latin and Philosophy than properly became a person of his rank'. He added a

John Carteret, second Earl Granville (1690–1763), by Peter Pelham (after Sir Godfrey Kneller, *c*.1720)

remarkable command of modern languages and was credited with a knowledge of French, German, Spanish, Italian, Swedish, and Portuguese. He took his seat in the House of Lords in May 1711 at the earliest opportunity. He married (on 17 October 1710) Frances (1694–1743), daughter of Sir Robert Worsley of the Isle of Wight and described by Abigail Harley as 'a very pretty lady and £12,000' (Swift, *Vindication*; *Portland MSS*, 4.537).

The tories held a large majority in the lower house in 1711, and Carteret's family connections and friendship with the Harleys propelled him in that direction. He flung himself into the business of the House of Lords with relish, scarcely missing a day's attendance. In February 1712, when the initial enthusiasm might have worn off, he attended on every one of the seventeen days on which the house met and was appointed to five of the seven committees set up. Nor were these purely ceremonial courtesies, for in February and March he chaired two committees, and in February and May he acted as teller in divisions. He also gained much experience while administering the affairs of the Carolinas, where, together with seven other lords proprietor, he exercised palatinate powers. He gravitated towards the Hanoverian tories, joining Nottingham in December 1711 to vote an amendment to the queen's speech demanding 'No peace without Spain'. Yet in June 1714, a month before the queen died, he voted for the Schism Bill, intended as a blow to the protestant dissenters.

Diplomatic apprenticeship The death of Anne changed everything. Carteret supported the Hanoverians and reaped speedy rewards. He was appointed a lord of the bedchamber and made bailiff of Jersey. In January 1715 his mother, sister of Baron Granville, was not only given a peerage in her own right but was raised to the rank of Countess Granville. When the Jacobite rising broke out in 1715 Carteret was sent down to Cornwall to root out potential traitors, one of whom was his cousin Lord Lansdowne, who spent time in the Tower. In 1716 Carteret was made lord lieutenant of Devon.

Carteret's first reported speech revealed him as a committed Hanoverian, acting with the whigs. He defended the Septennial Act in April 1716, which the tories regarded as a shabby whig manoeuvre. Frequent meetings of parliament, he argued, were more important than frequent elections, and he struck off one nice phrase: most uprisings had been for liberty, the 'Fifteen was for slavery (Cobbett, *Parl. hist.*, 7.298–9). When the whigs split in 1717 Carteret remained with Earl Stanhope and the earl of Sunderland, while Robert Walpole and Viscount Townshend went into opposition. In the short term this assisted his advance. In October 1718 Montagu Bacon reported a rumour that Carteret was to be secretary of state (Paston, 289). That did not materialize but on 11 November 1718 Carteret moved the address to the king's speech, defending Stanhope's foreign policy and praising Sir George Byng for defeating a large Spanish fleet off Cape Passaro. In January 1719 he was appointed ambassador-extraordinary to Sweden, a post of critical importance since George I, as elector of Hanover, was keenly interested in the outcome of the northern war. Britain's main objective was to rescue the Swedes, facing disaster after the death of Charles XII, lest Peter the Great of Russia should obtain total domination. Carteret, his diplomacy backed by Sir John Norris's fleet, carried the day for the group in Stockholm determined to defy the Russians, though they were at the door. 'Our success', Carteret reported laconically, 'is chiefly owing to the Czar'. The endgame proved protracted and tedious, and Carteret did not return home until December 1720. His mission to Stockholm had been a triumph and it gave him a taste for diplomatic work.

In Carteret's absence the whigs had made up their quarrel but the country had been shattered by the bursting of the South Sea Bubble. The fallout was dramatic. Stanhope, after walking to the House of Lords with Carteret on 4 February 1721, suffered a stroke in debate. Townshend took his place. But when, twelve days later, the younger James Craggs, secretary for the south, died of smallpox, Carteret succeeded him. He was thirty, an age when, as Swift observed ironically, 'according to custom, he ought to have been busied in losing his money in a chocolate-house' (Swift, *Vindication*). He remained secretary for three years. His colleague in the northern department, Viscount Townshend, older and masterful, was supported by Walpole, his brother-in-law, who had succeeded Sunderland as first lord of the Treasury. Sunderland was Carteret's chief ally but he died in April 1722. The ministers were agreed on the importance of maintaining the rapprochement with France and of upholding the Quadruple Alliance (Britain, France, the Netherlands, the emperor) as a

means of curbing Jacobite intrigues. But by the summer of 1723 there were rumours of cabinet disunity and Walpole and Carteret were said to have met to try to reconcile differences (*Polwarth MSS*, 3.282). On his visit to Hanover in 1723 the king was accompanied by both secretaries, who watched each other carefully. Townshend's best coup was to persuade George I to send Horace Walpole, Sir Robert's brother, to Paris to check on Sir Luke Schaub, Carteret's representative; this move, Townshend reported to Walpole, 'will be a publication to the world of the superiority of our credit' (Coxe, *Lord Walpole*, 1.62). Carteret remained confident of his standing with the king, with whom he conversed in German, but it was an unequal contest. He had scarcely any personal following, no electoral interest, and little influence in either house. When Schaub was recalled from Paris in the spring of 1724 Carteret resigned.

Ireland Carteret's defeat was cushioned by transfer to the lord lieutenancy of Ireland. Walpole had no wish to alienate the king but there was no doubt that Carteret had been sidelined. To the duke of Newcastle Walpole wrote, 'I should not be for sending him over now, if I did not think it would end in totally recalling him. We shall at least get rid of him here' (BL, Add. MS 32687, fol. 54). Carteret's viceroyalty is usually seen through the admiring eyes of Jonathan Swift, who had known him from the days of Queen Anne, but there is little doubt that it was highly successful. It lasted six years, giving a degree of continuity to a country that had not always experienced it. Carteret inherited the problem of Wood's halfpence, with the Irish in revolt against what they deemed debased coinage. He had already expressed doubts about the wisdom of Wood's patent in a letter that Walpole had intercepted, and it gave Walpole sardonic pleasure to reflect that Carteret would have to face the storm he had helped to raise (J. Plumb, *Sir Robert Walpole*, 1956–60, 2.68–9; Coxe, *Sir Robert Walpole*, 1st edn, 2.276). Carteret handled the problem neatly, going through the motions of searching for the author of the inflammatory *Drapier's Letters* (Swift) before warning the Walpole ministry that the patent must be withdrawn and Wood compensated privately. He followed it up with a drive to root out financial corruption and negligence.

Carteret was unable to do much to modify the mercantilist system which bore heavily on Ireland's trade, and he was handicapped by a continuing famine. The government responded with a bill to promote the drainage of bogs but, even if pursued, that could be at most a long-term remedy. Much of the excitement of Dublin politics concerned patronage. Carteret was accused of promoting tories and of cultivating the Irish interest. He was defended with wit and irony by Swift in his *Vindication of John, Lord Carteret* and received enthusiastic addresses from the Irish parliament commending his 'unwearied application ... and the affectionate concern you have shown for the welfare of this nation' (RO Ireland, 63, fols. 384, 387).

Half-way through Carteret's six years as viceroy, in 1727, George I died, and momentarily Walpole's power rocked.

But Sir Spencer Compton, a friend of Carteret, fumbled his chance and, though Carteret was sent back to Dublin, his powers of patronage in ecclesiastical matters were curtailed. In prestige he had risen enormously but his success aroused considerable envy and much suspicion; observers doubted whether his genial and expansive manner could be trusted. In June 1728 Lord Hervey, a Walpole man, found Carteret 'marvellous … in spirit and in words' but 'a man that almost every body commends and no body is a friend to'. Lord Egmont, more disinterested, was amazed in October 1730 at Carteret's knowledge and grace of manner, which 'makes him shine beyond any nobleman or gentleman perhaps now living', but added, 'what pity 'tis he is not sincere' (Ilchester, *Lord Hervey*, 30; *Egmont Diary*, 1.106). When Townshend quarrelled with Walpole in 1730 and resigned office Carteret also left the government, though it was rumoured that he had been offered the lord presidency or the lord stewardship.

Opposition to Walpole On 21 January 1731 Carteret signalled his intention to go into opposition by moving an amendment to the address in reply to the king's speech, begging the king to prevent war in Flanders or in Germany. It had been agreed with other leaders of opposition, Sir William Wyndham and William Pulteney, who moved the same motion in the Commons, and was presumably a reminder to the king that there were alternative lines of foreign policy. The amendment was brushed aside by eighty-four votes to twenty-three. Carteret was a valuable addition to an opposition that, until then, had few outstanding speakers in the Lords. The opposition suffered from several disadvantages. Co-operation between tories and dissident whigs was awkward, while few people trusted Viscount Bolingbroke, who since 1727 had been conducting *The Craftsman* with a view to driving out Walpole. Carteret's next reported intervention, on 21 February 1731, was on a more popular topic, giving support to a bill to remove pensioners from parliament. In May he spoke again, on a motion to dismiss the Hessian troops in British pay, but lost by 73 to 22. In February 1732 the Pensions Bill, which Carteret supported at length, was lost by 95 votes to 10, and the following month he made a major speech against Walpole's proposal to reintroduce the salt duty, arguing that it must bear heavily upon the poor. Though he lost by 79 to 26, he carried on his own rearguard action, joining in several protests and denouncing it as 'the worst bill that had ever been brought before that House' (Cobbett, *Parl. hist.*, 8.1040–48, 1061).

From this unpromising routine, opposition was saved in 1733 by Walpole's misjudgement in bringing forward his excise scheme. The public outcry was resounding and the ministry in danger. Since Walpole read the warning signs and withdrew the measure before it reached the Lords, Carteret had no opportunity to speak on it but in March 1733 he devoted a long speech to urging a reduction in the land forces. In the summer of 1733 Newcastle's control of the House of Lords wobbled. In early May Carteret helped to defeat ministers 35 to 31 on the administration of the forfeited South Sea Bubble estates, and three weeks later, on the same subject, divided 75–75—a technical defeat for

government. Walpole's response was to dismiss the earl of Chesterfield, and Lord Clinton and several other deserters as a warning to others, and to strengthen his debating team in the Lords by promoting Hardwicke, Hervey, and Talbot. When the opposition counter-attacked in February 1734, with a motion deploring the disciplining of members, Carteret and his allies lost by 100 to 62. Walpole held his own in the general election of 1734 and when Carteret moved an amendment to the address in the new parliament he was defeated by 89 to 37 while Wyndham, in the lower house, went down by 265 votes to 185. Faced with the possibility of another seven years in the political wilderness Bolingbroke abandoned the struggle and went to France, a defection not necessarily to the disadvantage of his erstwhile allies.

Carteret, now sharing the lead in the Lords with Chesterfield, settled down again to regular opposition. Two events in the royal family offered modest encouragement. In November 1737 Queen Caroline, one of Walpole's staunchest supporters, died. A second development was the decision of Frederick, prince of Wales, to form his own political group. Carteret was soon a prominent figure at the prince's headquarters at Leicester House, and once more he achieved the remarkable feat of winning the prince's favour without alienating the king. His connection with Frederick gave Carteret some awkward questions to push. In February 1737 he moved for an increase in the prince's allowance from £50,000 to £100,000. Motions of this kind were rarely popular. The tories did not like so direct a challenge to the royal prerogative; forty-five of them absented themselves and no tory spoke in the debate. Pulteney, in the lower house, lost by 234 to 204. In the Lords Carteret lost by 103 to 40, after a speech that bordered on the ludicrous, with an elaborate comparison between Frederick and the Black Prince. Hervey noted that Carteret seemed determined 'to give as little offence as was possible on the king's side' (Hervey, *Some Materials*, 3.696; *The Diary of George Bubb Dodington*, 1809 edn, 391–423). He continued to pursue routine opposition issues, urging a reduction in army numbers and complaining that ministers were feeble in the face of Spanish provocation at sea (Cobbett, *Parl. hist.*, 10.479–561, 729–87, 917–29).

As the repeated clashes with Spain moved towards war, opposition prospects brightened. In a desperate attempt to head off conflict Walpole negotiated the convention of Pardo with Spain in January 1739. Carteret and his allies, as a matter of course, denounced it as a humiliating surrender, 'destructive and dishonourable to this kingdom'. The prince of Wales voted with opposition and the government survived with a reduced majority of 95 votes to 74. The convention failed to prevent war, which was declared in October 1739.

Carteret was in the forefront of the renewed onslaught on Walpole. In November 1740 he ridiculed the address of thanks, which had commended the 'vigorous and effective' conduct of the war, demanding to know 'where are the victories, where are the trophies our present minister has to boast of?' (Cobbett, *Parl. hist.*, 11.610–94). But the opposition's lack of unity could still expose them to mortifying defeats. After much discussion they resolved on a bold stroke before the general election. Samuel Sandys in the Commons and Carteret in the Lords moved an address requesting the king to remove Walpole from his presence and counsels for ever. Again the tories bridled at this attack upon the prerogative. In the Lords, Carteret achieved a respectable showing, dividing 59 against 108, but in the Commons a number of tories voted with the ministers and nearly forty others withdrew. Walpole triumphed by 290 votes against 106.

Secretary of state It was Walpole's last great victory. The general election in May 1741 went badly and in February 1742 he resigned. But the result was not a clean sweep of the ministers. Few of the tories were of the calibre to serve, although the appointment of Lord Gower as lord privy seal kept the door open. Pulteney had tied his own hands by a pledge that he would not take office and contented himself with the earldom of Bath and a seat in the cabinet. Carteret would have liked the Treasury but the post went to Compton (now earl of Wilmington), a placid and dignified nonentity. Chesterfield and Dodington were passed over, and William Pitt had made himself so offensive to the king that he was vetoed. Carteret himself became secretary of state for the north, with Newcastle as his colleague. Henry Pelham continued as paymaster but the promotion of Sandys and Pulteney to the Lords left him as chief government spokesman in the Commons and heir apparent. With Harrington as lord president and Hardwicke as lord chancellor the old corps whigs were well dug in, though a notable casualty was Lord Hervey, who was deprived of his post of lord privy seal after a struggle. The new ministry was therefore divided from the outset and many of the opposition to Walpole were bitter at what they deemed betrayal by their leaders.

Carteret's concept of foreign affairs involved a much greater exertion of British power. In one of his first dispatches, in March 1742, he wrote that every help would be given to the Austrians and that any threat to Hanover would be met by 'all the weight and power of these kingdoms in defence of them' (Williams, 125). Though Britain was still not officially at war with France her subsidies supported on the continent the army of British, Hessians, Hanoverians, and Dutch to collaborate with the Austrians, and it was at the head of this army that George II distinguished himself at Dettingen in June 1743.

At home there were sufficient tories and disappointed whigs to guarantee a sizeable opposition and, in the Lords, Chesterfield and Hervey made the running at first. The opposition sent up a place bill, always a popular measure, in April 1742; though Chesterfield asked what the nation would think if it was thrown out, it failed by 81 votes to 52. The following month the opposition proposed to indemnify witnesses giving evidence in the investigation of Walpole; Carteret replied that the bill would be an invitation to perjury and it was rejected by 109 to 57. In the debate on the address in November 1742 Chesterfield and Carteret once more crossed swords, the former complaining of the

'style of servility' with which the king was treated, the latter claiming a vast improvement in the position in Europe of Britain and her ally Austria. Opposition neither divided nor protested.

In July 1743 the death of Wilmington necessitated a reshuffle. The new earl of Bath, realizing the mistake he had made in 1742, asked Carteret, who was with the king in Hanover, to intercede for him. George II had no liking for Bath and the post went to Henry Pelham. Though Carteret explained his position to Newcastle in a 'manly' letter and promised to work well together, the episode soured relations with Pelham (Yorke, 1.337; Owen, 165–9; Ilchester, 1.97–8; Coxe, *Pelham*, 1.85–91). At the same time opposition found a stronger stick with which to beat the new ministry in the accusation that it pandered to Hanoverian interests; George II was said to have shown marked favour to his Hanoverian troops at Dettingen. There was a curious exchange in the debate of 1 December 1743 on the address. Chesterfield, anxious to be slyly offensive, wished to know what victories the king was being congratulated on and drew a distinction between the king's behaviour, which deserved praise, and his conduct, which might incur censure. Carteret retorted that the distinction was meaningless: 'His Majesty's behaviour in the field was intrepid, and his conduct in general wise'. Philip Yorke, who attended the debate, thought that Carteret had got the better of the exchanges (Cobbett, *Parl. hist.*, 13.102–35). In the lower house Pitt attacked Carteret more bluntly as 'an execrable, a sole minister, who had renounced the British nation, and seemed to have drunk of the potion … which made men forget their country' (ibid., 136). But Carteret's cabinet colleagues were becoming alarmed at the cost of his subsidy policy; Lord Egmont, reporting coffee-house gossip in January 1744, wrote that the ministers were at open breach and that Carteret had said that Henry Pelham 'was only a chief clerk to Sir Robert Walpole, and why he should expect to be more under me, I can't imagine: he did his drudgery and he shall do mine' (*Egmont Diary*, 3.281). The words may have been touched up for effect but they were not out of character. There was a good deal of arrogance in Carteret, assisted sometimes by heavy drinking, which caused him to rant, and tolerable to colleagues only if he could produce the kind of victories that Pitt would later achieve in the Seven Years' War. Carteret's success was not on that scale. In the Lords his performances remained impressive but in Europe his majestic schemes faltered. Frederick of Prussia, whom he had helped to persuade to call off his attack upon the Austrians in June 1742, became concerned at their recovery and re-animated his assault in August 1744. It was easier to get the Dutch to promise than to perform, even though Carteret paid visits to The Hague to stir them up. Carteret's triumphant treaty of Worms in September 1743, which brought Sardinia to the assistance of the Austrians, was cancelled by France's success in October in gaining full Spanish support, thus opening up the possibility of an invasion of Britain and the probability of a Jacobite enterprise.

Under these strains the fragile ministry disintegrated.

In February 1744 Sir Robert's brother, Horace Walpole, advised Robert Trevor, envoy at The Hague, not to offer too much praise for Carteret, since he and the Pelhams were 'notwithstanding the common danger, if possible more enemies than ever'. Trevor, in turn, warned Pelham that the 'want of harmony' at home made it hard to conduct diplomacy. Pelham, in reply, complained that every foreign ally was 'every day calling upon us for more' (*Buckinghamshire MSS*, 93, 96, 98). In June Carteret told Newcastle that 'things could not remain as they were … he would not be brought down to be overruled and out-voted upon every point, by four to one' (Coxe, *Lord Walpole*, 2.85–7). On 31 October the Pelhams delivered what was in effect an ultimatum to the king, and Carteret resigned on 24 November, three days before parliament met, to be replaced by Harrington. In the reorganization that brought about the 'broad bottom administration' Chesterfield was made lord lieutenant of Ireland.

Last years The king's speech for the session admitted ruefully that 'our success has not been answerable to our wishes' (Cobbett, *Parl. hist.*, 13.978–9). Carteret did not take the field and had much to occupy him in private life. His first wife had died in June 1743 and, to the excitement of the coffee houses, he was soon reported to be looking for a new spouse, perhaps because his only son was showing disturbing signs of eccentricity. On 14 April 1744 Carteret married a twenty-two-year-old beauty, Lady Sophia Fermor (1721–1745), daughter of the first earl of Pomfret. The opportunity was too good for the wits to miss. Less caustically than usual, young Horace Walpole reported that the bride had scarlet fever and the groom gout but that Carteret 'heroically sent her word, that if she was well, he *would* be so'. At a ball in June he saw them 'all fondness, walk together, and stop every five steps to kiss' (Walpole, *Corr.*, 18.431, 464). Their only daughter, Sophia, who married Lord Shelburne, was born in August 1745; her mother died in the following October. In October 1744, just before his resignation, Carteret's mother had died, whereupon he became Earl Granville.

George II was extremely upset at losing his favourite; the obligatory audience with newly-appointed Chesterfield, whom he detested, was said to have lasted forty-five seconds (Walpole, *Corr.*, 18.564–5). Pitt he refused to have in office. Though the Jacobites were in possession of Scotland, Newcastle confided to Richmond that the king 'will hardly vouchsafe to say one word about his own business' and followed it by 'the Closet grows worse than ever. We are now come to bad language … *Incapacity* to my brother … and yesterday *Pitifull Fellows*' (*First Report*, HMC, appx, 115). In February 1746, with the Jacobites in retreat but before Culloden, Newcastle and his allies resolved on a mass resignation. The king sent for Bath and Granville and for two days they endeavoured to form a ministry. There was no one adequate to lead the Commons and the City made it clear that without Pelham there would be no loans. Wags reported that old gentlemen were nervous to leave their houses lest they be drafted into the new cabinet. The king was forced to surrender, and the Pelhams' terms included the admission of Pitt and the exclusion of

Bath from the cabinet. Granville's own account was light-hearted: 'upon my soul, I knew nothing about it. I was sitting quietly by my fireside, reading in my study; the king sends to me to take the seals; I saw 'twould not do and was amazed at it. But like a dutiful subject of the crown, I obeyed'. He condemned the Pelhams for exploiting the national crisis but added, 'I will go home, into the country, to my books, to my fireside. For I love my fireside'. Horace Walpole, commenting on this 'rebellion within a rebellion', concluded: 'it is impossible to hate a politician of such jovial good humour' (Yorke, 1.507; *Memoirs*, 1.113–16; Walpole, *Corr.*, 19.210–13; *Private Correspondence of Chesterfield and Newcastle*, 68, 71, 84, 100, 105–19).

Granville's great days were over but he slid easily into the role of elder statesman. In 1749 he was given the Garter. Newcastle's friendship with Chesterfield did not last and Chesterfield resigned in 1748. His successor, the duke of Bedford, was eased out in 1751, by which time Newcastle was reflecting more kindly on Granville's talents. 'My Lord Granville', he wrote to his brother, 'is no longer the terrible man' (Coxe, *Pelham*, 2.388). He persuaded Pelham to bring Granville back as lord president and wrote in June to express his delight that friendship had been 'so happily and cordially restored between us' (BL, Add. MS 32724, fols. 175, 362, 372–4). The administrative demands of Granville's new post were not heavy but the prestige was great and it carried a seat at the cabinet table. When Newcastle in 1756 suggested that he might take the Treasury Granville replied that 'whatever might have been his object ten years ago, Experience had made him wiser, and that he was perfectly contented with the ease and dignity of his present situation' (J. Waldegrave, *The Memoirs and Speeches of James, 2nd Earl Waldegrave, 1742–1763*, ed. J. C. D. Clark, 1988, 185). He remained a very useful debater. In January 1752 Bedford made an attack upon his former colleagues, denouncing the subsidy treaties as expensive and useless. Newcastle's reply, according to Horace Walpole, was lengthy, incoherent, and incomprehensible. Granville's speech, by Newcastle's own account, was short 'and with his usual vivacity, set the House a-laughing' (Cobbett, *Parl. hist.*, 14.1175–97; *Memoirs*, 1.167–73; *Stopford-Sackville MSS*, 1.180–81).

Granville retained the presidency for twelve years and died in office. Though he had abandoned his own ambitions he was a valued intermediary and acted as patron to Henry Fox. Fox was not of Granville's calibre and, in 1756, when he opted to remain in the snug post of paymaster, Granville retorted:

> Fox, I don't love to have you say things that will not be believed. If you was of my age, very well. I have put on my nightcap; there is no more daylight for me; but you *should* be ambitious. I want to instil a noble ambition into you, to make you knock the heads of the kings of Europe together, and jumble something out of it that may be of service to this country. (*Memoirs of Horatio, Lord Walpole*, 2.178)

But Granville had chosen the wrong man to fulfil his own dreams.

Reputation Granville's health deteriorated gradually, though he remained alert; he died in Bath on 2 January

1763. He was buried in Westminster Abbey on 11 January. His contemporaries rated him very highly. Horace Walpole placed him first of the five great men he had known and Chesterfield, in December 1762, wrote that 'when he dies, the ablest head in England dies too, take it for all in all'. Chesterfield's considered judgement was balanced but not unkind: Granville had 'great parts and a most uncommon share of learning for a man of quality … In business, he was bold, enterprising and overbearing … he was neither ill-natured nor vindictive, and had a great contempt for money' (*Memoirs*, 3.1–3; Chesterfield to P. Stanhope, 13 Dec 1762, *Letters of … Chesterfield*, 6.2459; Chesterfield, *Characters*).

The conventional judgement that Granville was a 'brilliant failure' (Pemberton) is a rather brittle paradox (the phrase is repeated in Williams, *Carteret and Newcastle*, 228). It may overrate his brilliance, save as an orator and debater. His early success in the Baltic, where British naval power could be brought to bear, may have led him to exaggerate the extent to which one man, however gifted and industrious, could manipulate the affairs of Europe, and his downfall in 1744 was to a considerable extent the consequence of the collapse of his diplomacy. It certainly overrates his failure. A man of wealth, under no obligation to stir himself, he spent more than half his life in office, with great distinction. His viceroyalty was one of the most successful of the eighteenth century. His remarkable command of the House of Lords was supported by hard work, to which his opponents testified, although it is possible that his love of the classics, his warm home life, and, it must be admitted, his addiction to good wine may have robbed him of the drive of a Pitt or the perseverance of a Newcastle. Speaker Onslow, who presided over debates in the Commons for thirty-four years, may have had few opportunities to see him at his best, but offered a shrewd assessment:

> he thought consulting the interior interests and disposition of the people, the conduct of business in parliament, and the methods of raising money for the execution even of his own designs was a work below his applications, and to be left as underparts of government to the care of inferior and subordinate understandings.

Thomas Winnington, whose refusal to lead the Commons doomed Granville's enterprise of 1746, put the point more succinctly: 'had he studied Parliament more and Demosthenes less, he would have been a more successful minister' (Coxe, *Sir Robert Walpole*, 1816 edn, 1.347; Owen, 238).

JOHN CANNON

Sources B. Williams, *Carteret and Newcastle: a contrast in contemporaries* (1943) • *Memoirs of Horatio, Lord Walpole*, ed. W. Coxe, 2nd edn, 2 vols. (1808) • W. Coxe, *Memoirs of the life and administration of Sir Robert Walpole, earl of Orford*, 3 vols. (1798) • W. Coxe, *Memoirs of the life and administration of Sir Robert Walpole, earl of Orford*, new edn, 4 vols. (1816) • W. Coxe, *Memoirs of the administration of the Right Honourable Henry Pelham*, 2 vols. (1829) • Cobbett, *Parl. hist.*, 7.298–9, 560–62; 8.832, 848, 860, 1040–8, 1061; 9.100–06, 327–48, 642–8, 671–90; 10.479–561, 729–87, 917–29, 1091–246; 11.610–94, 1047–388; 12.592–610, 643–714, 833–53; 13.102–36, 975–83; 14.1175–97 • H. Walpole, *Memoirs of King George II*, ed. J. Brooke, 3 vols. (1985) • Walpole,

Corr. • J. Swift, *A vindication of John, Lord Carteret, The prose works of Jonathan Swift*, 12: *Irish tracts, 1728–1733*, ed. H. Davis (1955), 149–69 • J. B. Owen, *The rise of the Pelhams* (1971) • P. C. Yorke, *The life and correspondence of Philip Yorke, earl of Hardwicke*, 3 vols. (1913) • *The letters of Philip Dormer Stanhope, fourth earl of Chesterfield*, ed. B. Dobrée, 6 vols. (1932) • P. D. S. Chesterfield, *Characters* (1778) • A. Ballantyne, *Lord Carteret, a political biography* (1887) • W. B. Pemberton, *Carteret, the brilliant failure of the eighteenth century* (1936) • *The manuscripts of his grace the duke of Portland*, 10 vols., HMC, 29 (1891–1931), vols. 5–10 • *The manuscripts of the earl of Carlisle*, HMC, 42 (1897) • *Report on the manuscripts of Lord Polwarth*, 5 vols., HMC, 67 (1911–61) • *Manuscripts of the earl of Egmont: diary of Viscount Percival, afterwards first earl of Egmont*, 3 vols., HMC, 63 (1920–23) • *The manuscripts of the Marquess Townshend*, HMC, 19 (1887) • *First report*, HMC, 1/1 (1870); repr. (1874) • *The manuscripts of the earl of Buckinghamshire, the earl of Lindsey … and James Round*, HMC, 38 (1895) • *Report on the manuscripts of Mrs Stopford-Sackville*, 1, HMC, 49 (1904) • *JHL*, 19 (1709–14) • *JHL*, 23 (1726–31) • *Journal of the commissioners for trade and plantations*, [vol. 3]: *From March 1715/14 to October 1718* (1924) • B. Williams, *Stanhope: a study in eighteenth-century war and diplomacy* (1932) • J. Black, *Britain in the age of Walpole* (1984) • C. Franklin, *Lord Chesterfield: his character and 'Characters'* (1993) • L. Colley, *In defiance of oligarchy: the tory party, 1714–60* (1982) • W. Nicolson, *Letters on various subjects*, 2 vols. (1809) • *The autobiography and correspondence of Mary Granville, Mrs Delany*, ed. Lady Llanover, 1st ser., 3 vols. (1861); 2nd ser., 3 vols. (1862) • *Private correspondence of Chesterfield and Newcastle, 1744–6*, ed. R. Lodge (1930) • F. G. James, *Ireland in the empire, 1688–1770* (1973) • C. B. Realey, *The early opposition to Sir Robert Walpole, 1720–27* (1931) • *Life of William, earl of Shelburne … with extracts from his papers and correspondence*, ed. E. G. P. Fitzmaurice, 3 vols. (1875–6) • J. C. Sainty and D. Dewar, eds., *Divisions in the House of Lords: an analytical list, 1685–1857* (1976) • John, Lord Hervey, *Some materials towards memoirs of the reign of King George II*, ed. R. Sedgwick, 3 vols. (1931) • Earl of Ilchester [G. S. Holland Fox-Strangways], *Henry Fox, first Lord Holland, his family and relations*, 2 vols. (1920) • G. Paston [E. M. Symonds], *Lady Mary Wortley Montagu and her times* (1907) • *Lord Hervey and his friends, 1726–38*, ed. earl of Ilchester [G. S. Holland Fox-Strangways] (1950) • *The correspondence of Jonathan Swift*, ed. H. Williams, 5 vols. (1963–5) • countess of Cork and Orrery [E. C. Boyle], ed., *The Orrery papers*, 2 vols. (1903) • A. Goodwin, 'Wood's halfpence', *EngHR*, 51 (1936), 647–74 • G. S. Holmes, *British politics in the age of Anne* (1967) • [H. Boulter], *Letters written by … Hugh Boulter … to several ministers of state*, ed. [A. Philips and G. Faulkner], 2 vols. (1769–70) • G. H. Rose, *A selection from the papers of the earls of Marchmont*, 3 vols. (1831) • GEC, *Peerage*

Archives BL, corresp., Ireland, Add. MSS 24137–24138 • BL, corresp., Sweden, Add. MSS 22511–22514 • BL, corresp., secretary of state, Add. MSS 22511–22519; 22542–22544 • BL, corresp. and papers, Add. MSS 22511–22545 • Bodl. Oxf., family corresp. • NYPL, diplomatic corresp. • U. Mich., Clements L., papers • Yale U., Beinecke L., letter-book | BL, corresp. with Lord Hardwicke, etc., Add. MSS 35407–35838, *passim* • BL, corresp. with the duke of Newcastle, Add. MSS 32686–32934 • BL, letters to Sir Thomas Robinson, Add. MSS 22529, 23807–23822 • BL, letters to Edward Southwell, Add. MS 38016 • BL, corresp. with Walter Titley, Egerton MSS 2689–2693 • BL, letters to Lord Tyrawley, Add. MSS 23630–23631 • BL, corresp. with Charles Whitworth, Add. MSS 37375–37394 • Hants. RO, letters to Prince William of Hesse [copies] • NA Scot., corresp. with Lord Polwarth • NL Ire., corresp. with Lord Molesworth

Likenesses probably T. Hudson, oils, 1740–49, Althorp, Northamptonshire • J. Robinson, portrait, *c.*1744, probably Althorp, Northamptonshire • studio of W. Hoare, oils, *c.*1750–1752, NPG • D. van der Suissen, oils, 1757, Longleat, Wiltshire • probably C. Boit, miniature, Althorp, Northamptonshire • J. A. Dassier, copper medal, BM • Dassier, medallion, BM • I. Gosset, wax medal, Ham House, Richmond-upon-Thames, London • P. Pelham, mezzotint (after G. Kneller, *c.*1720), BM, NPG [*see illus.*] • probably C. F. Zincke, miniature, Althorp, Northamptonshire

Wealth at death wealthy, plus inheritance and marriages, but allegedly careless, extravagant, and died in difficulties: *DNB*

Carteret, Philip (1733–1796), explorer, was born on 22 January 1733 at Trinity Manor, Jersey, the younger son of Charles de Carteret, seigneur of Trinity, and his wife, Françoise Marie St Paul. He had also a sister. In 1747 he left Jersey to begin his naval career, serving first as an officer's servant and from 1751 following John Byron from the *St Albans* (1751–2) to the *Augusta* (1753) and then the *Vanguard* (1753–7). In 1755 he passed his officer's examination. In 1761 he inherited Trinity Manor after the death of his elder brother, François, but he did not abandon his naval career. Between 1764 and 1766 he was lieutenant of the frigate *Dolphin* (24 guns), captain John Byron, for his circumnavigation via the Falkland Islands and through the Pacific. Carteret was appointed commander on his return in May 1766. A second expedition was dispatched soon after Byron's return to search for the great southern continent in whose existence Byron now firmly believed. The expedition consisted of the *Dolphin*, captain Samuel Wallis, and the *Swallow*, a sixth rate sloop of fourteen guns, commanded by Carteret. Carteret knew that *Swallow* was old, decrepit, poorly fitted out, and incompletely manned, and lost no opportunity of telling the Admiralty so. His complaints brought a few improvements, but probably damaged his subsequent career by souring his memory at the Admiralty.

The ships set sail, but *Swallow* became separated from the much faster *Dolphin* after the two had struggled for nearly four months to clear the Strait of Magellan. Carteret's suspicions that he had been deliberately abandoned were probably unfounded, but did nothing to mitigate his sense of grievance. His resolve and courage were shown by his decision to press on, and this decision in turn allowed his skill and good sense as an explorer to show themselves. Sailing north he discovered Pitcairn Island (later made famous by the *Bounty* mutineers) and then the Duke of Gloucester's Islands in the Tuamotu archipelago, and Queen Charlotte's Islands (later the Santa Cruz Islands): Carteret named one island in the latter group Egmont Island, not realizing that it was Santa Cruz, discovered in 1595. Having aroused the enmity of the islanders he failed to secure supplies there and was forced to sail on with a crew weakened by hunger, thirst, and especially scurvy. He sailed for New Britain, discovering *en route* Gower's Island (later Ndai, Solomon Islands), named after his old friend Erasmus Gower, Simpson's Island (later Manaobo, Solomon Islands), named after Alexander Simpson, master on *Swallow*, Carteret's Island (later Kilinailau), Wallis's Island (later Lambou Island, New Britain), named after Samuel Wallis, and Leigh's Island (Ningin Island), named after Edward Leigh, purser of *Swallow*. He spent no time in exploring the islands, not realizing that many were part of the Solomon Islands, discovered in 1568, and thus lost an opportunity to correct or confirm existing charts and accounts. By this time he had, however, realized that he was too far north to find the great southern continent. Arriving at New Britain, where

he hoped to secure supplies, he discovered a second island, which he named New Ireland, separated from New Britain by a channel which he named St George's. This was probably his most important discovery and opened up a useful new route for merchant shipping. He sailed on discovering and naming further islands until he reached Mindanao, the most southerly of the Philippines, where his observations enabled him to check some errors in William Dampier's survey. On 12 December 1767 he reached Macassar in the Celebes, desperate for supplies, but was greeted with suspicion by the Dutch authorities, and after a stand-off which nearly ended in violence he sailed for Batavia, reaching it in June 1768. He met the French explorer Bourgainville on his journey home round the Cape of Good Hope, and arrived at Spithead on 20 March 1769.

In 1770 Carteret returned to Jersey, where as the seigneur of Trinity he entered local politics, joining the rebels against the Lemprière family's hold over the island. In March 1772 he married in London Marie Rachel (*d.* in or after 1797), daughter of Sir Jean Baptiste Silvestre (or John Baptist Silvester; *d.* 1789), doctor of medicine, and Alathea Catherine D'Aulnis. They had one child who died and four surviving children, of whom the second son, Philip Carteret *Silvester, followed his father into the navy and later inherited a baronetcy from Sir John *Silvester, recorder of London, his mother's brother.

Carteret was left with his health ruined and with scant reward from the Admiralty, in marked contrast to their treatment of Byron and his crew. Lacking effective patronage and having turned the Admiralty against him by his complaints about *Swallow* and by importuning them on his return for a new ship, he was left on half pay. He organized a petition to get half pay increased: it was to help some officers but not himself. His journal of the voyage was given to John Hawkesworth and published as part of *An Account of the Voyages undertaken by Byron, Wallis, Carteret and Cook* (1773). Carteret was so angered by Hawkesworth's many ill-judged changes that he prepared his own version, though this had to wait for publication until Helen Wallis's edition of 1965 for the Hakluyt Society. On 1 August 1779 he was at last given a new ship, the *Endymion* (44 guns); earlier reports that he secured the command of *Druid*, repeated in the *Dictionary of National Biography*, stemmed from his being mistaken for a Captain Peter Carteret. After some misadventures in the English Channel and off Senegal he sailed for the West Indies, where he was nearly killed in a hurricane off the Leeward Islands in 1780. He shared four prize ships, but to his astonishment and mortification he was then paid off and the ship was given to someone else. These misfortunes and his unsuccessful petitions for a new ship increased his bitterness. He had a stroke in 1792 and retired in 1794 with the rank of rear-admiral. On 21 July 1796 he died at his home in Southampton, where he had lived since 1780. He was buried in the catacombs of All Saints' Church, Southampton.

Carteret was unquestionably dogged by ill fortune, though Wallis suggests that he was not helped by his inflexibility and his harbouring of resentments. His subsequent reputation was marred by the fact that Hawkesworth's mangled version of his journal was the only account available, and particularly by the fact that his achievements were so soon eclipsed by the triumphs of Cook. Though he died disappointed and embittered, his contributions to Pacific geography were notable and a fitting testimony to his powers of observation and his courage. ELIZABETH BAIGENT

Sources Carteret's voyage around the world, 1766–1769, ed. H. Wallis, 2 vols., Hakluyt Society, 2nd ser., 124–5 (1965) · GM, 1st ser., 66 (1796), 622 · G. Williams, The great South Sea: English voyages and encounters, 1570–1750 (1997)
Archives Boston PL, journal, incl. battle of Cape Lagos · NMM, journals, letter-book, and logbooks · State Library of New South Wales, Sydney, Dixson Wing, MSS incl. journal
Likenesses silhouette, NL NZ, Turnbull L.; repro. in Wallis, ed., Carteret's voyage around the world, pl. xx · watercolour, Société Jersiaise; repro. in Wallis, ed., Carteret's voyage around the world, pl. 1

Carteret, Sir Philippe [Philip] **de** (1584–1643), landowner and office-holder, was born in Sark on 18 February 1584, the eldest son of Sir Philippe de Carteret (d. 1594) and his wife, Rachel, daughter of George Poulet, lieutenant-governor and bailiff of Jersey. His grandfather, Helier de Carteret, had colonized the island of Sark in 1565. The fief of St Ouen's, the leading fief in Jersey, had belonged to the de Carteret family since time immemorial, but the fief of Rozel was added to the family estate when Philippe de Carteret bought it in 1625. Besides being the eldest son of the leading family in Jersey, de Carteret had the advantage, through his mother's side, of connection to the Poulets, the English noble family of Hinton St George. He was educated at Oxford University and returned to Jersey after graduating BA in 1601. His father having died in 1594, the nine children had been under the wardship of their maternal grandfather, who had purchased it from the governor, Sir Anthony Poulet. Before 1605 de Carteret married Anne (d. in or after 1643), daughter of Sir Francis Dowse of Nether Wallop, Hampshire.

De Carteret was frequently deputed to represent the island in England, including in the negotiations with the privy council for the establishment of a set of canons to bring the island to conformity with the Church of England. On attaining his majority in 1605 he was elected a jurat of the royal court. In 1626 he was appointed judge-delegate and at the beginning of the following year bailiff of the island. He was appointed lieutenant-governor under the governor Sir John Peyton in 1624 and nominated his brother Elie as his substitute in this office when he went to England the following year. Reappointed lieutenant-governor by the governor Sir Thomas Jermyn in 1634, he again had his brother sworn to act in his absence. He retained both the office of lieutenant-governor and that of bailiff until his death. As governor, he lived with his family in Mont Orgueil, and treated William Prynne, who spent three years in close confinement there, with kindness, inviting him to dinner and allowing him considerable freedom within the castle.

At the period of the civil war the island was a prey to internal dissensions among the principal inhabitants, and de Carteret was far from being generally popular, with a particular grievance against him being his combining of the offices of bailiff and lieutenant-governor and his penchant for preferring members of his own family to all manner of public offices. In 1642, while de Carteret was in London, twenty-two articles signed by some of the principal inhabitants were presented against him, and he was summoned to answer them before the House of Lords. On the ground, however, that Jersey was in danger from a French invasion, he was permitted to return home. De Carteret made a proclamation soon after his return of his adherence to the royal cause. Prynne devoted a substantial section of The Lyar Confounded (1645) to rebutting the charge that he had shown royalist sympathies by associating with de Carteret, and he argued that de Carteret was not really a royalist at all, for the position he had taken earlier was to look upon the king and parliament as undivided, and had he lived longer he would, once he had understood his earlier position to be no longer tenable, have sided with the parliament. Prynne alleged that the parliamentarians in Jersey were motivated entirely by local grievances and a desire to grasp power themselves. It is true that de Carteret and the states of Jersey did express a wish to look upon the king and parliament as undivided, hoping to keep out of a quarrel which they believed did not concern them as they had no connection with the parliament of England, but the claim that de Carteret was really a crypto-parliamentarian is far-fetched, and Prynne's charge that his opponents were motivated entirely by their self-interest also exaggerated. From Jean Chevalier's contemporary account of this period in Jersey, it is clear that he saw the issues in royalist–parliamentarian terms at the time when Prynne claims that de Carteret still did not, which tells against Prynne's claim in this respect.

De Carteret held out for Charles with a resolution that nothing could shake. While he retired to Elizabeth Castle, his wife and eldest son, Philip, took charge of the defence of Mont Orgueil. All his appeals to those in authority for the parliament in the island were rejected and it was not until a short time before he died that some members of his immediate family were allowed to visit him. He died at Elizabeth Castle on 23 August 1643. He had given orders on his deathbed that his body should not be buried until the king had overcome all his enemies, so his wife sent to St Malo for a surgeon to embalm the body. The heart and viscera were buried in the old abbey church in Elizabeth Castle, and the embalmed body kept there in a lead coffin until 20 June 1644, when, after the island had been conquered by the royalists, it was carried in state to St Ouen's Church, where a funeral sermon was preached in English, and then de Carteret buried in the church. In 1869 the coffin was found and opened, and was found to contain the skeleton of a man over 6 feet tall. De Carteret had seven sons and four daughters, one of whom, Elizabeth, married her cousin Captain George Carteret.

HELEN M. E. EVANS

Sources *Journal de Jean Chevalier*, ed. J. A. Messervy, 9 parts (1906–14) · W. Prynne, *The lyar confounded* (1645) · G. R. Balleine, *A biographical dictionary of Jersey*, [1] [1948] · J. A. Messervy, 'Liste des baillis, lieut.-baillis et juges-délégués de l'île de Jersey', *Annual Bulletin* [Société Jersiaise], 4 (1897–1901), 92–116 · J. A. Messervy, 'Liste des gouverneurs, lieut.-gouverneurs et députés gouverneurs de l'Île de Jersey', *Annual Bulletin* [Société Jersiaise], 4 (1897–1901), 373–94 · J. A. Messervy, ed., *Actes des états de l'Île de Jersey, 1524–1675* (1897–1900)
Archives PRO, state papers, domestic, James I, corresp.

Carthach mac Fianáin [Carthach the elder] (*fl.* **late 6th cent.**). *See under* Munster, saints of (*act. c.*450–*c.*700).

Carthew, George Alfred (1807–1882), antiquary and genealogist, was born at Harleston, Norfolk, on 20 June 1807 and baptized privately at Redenhall church the same day. He was the eldest of three sons of George Carthew (*bap.* 1777, *d.* 1861), solicitor, of Harleston, and his wife, Elizabeth (1785–1858), daughter of Peter Isaack, gentleman, of Wighton, also in Norfolk. His forebears were of St Issey in Cornwall from Tudor times until his great-grandfather Thomas inherited Benacre Manor in Suffolk and built the hall there in the 1720s. Carthew's father, a fifth son, could not afford to give him much schooling, but put him through articles in his own office and gave him access to many original documents in his keeping, including a large collection of charters of Mendham Priory, Suffolk. These the young man taught himself to transcribe and analyse, and mastered their contents. He did so most effectively, as appears from his reply to a letter by John Adey Repton in the *Gentleman's Magazine* for May 1837 correcting several persistent errors.

After qualifying as a solicitor in 1830, Carthew became his father's partner, but practised in Framlingham for nine years before accepting a partnership in East Dereham, where he spent the rest of his life. It took him forty years to compile an exemplary history of the neighbouring hundred of Launditch, which he published in three parts between 1877 and 1879. Walter Rye, calling it 'the amplest and best history of any [Norfolk] hundred' (Rye, xxii), estimated that it gave ten times more information than the existing county history by Francis Blomefield. Bouts of poor health hindered the progress of Carthew's topographical projects and, owing to their small circulation, his publications proved costly to him. He and his father joined the Norfolk and Norwich Archaeological Society on its foundation in 1845. At the first general meeting he gave a paper on East Dereham church and became one of the first local secretaries. A manuscript diary of Peter Le Neve, Norroy king of arms, had been given by Thomas Martin (who married Le Neve's widow) to Carthew's grandfather the Revd Thomas Carthew FSA, of Woodbridge Abbey, Suffolk. It eventually passed to Carthew himself, who published extracts referring to Norfolk, with full pedigrees of Le Neve, in the second volume of *Norfolk Archaeology*, to which he was a frequent contributor.

Carthew was elected a fellow of the Society of Antiquaries in 1854. Two years later, on 9 July 1856, at Sherborne in Dorset, he married his first cousin Anna (*bap.* 1806, *d.* 1877), the daughter of Morden Carthew, vicar of Mattishall, Norfolk. She first married her eldest brother, Morden's, fellow officer Captain George Gray of the 21st regiment native infantry, Madras, at Ellore, East Indies, in 1830. When George Henry Dashwood died in 1869, Carthew was one of those who helped to complete the first volume of William Hervy's 1563 *Visitation of Norfolk*, which appeared nine years later. After his wife died (she was buried on 4 September 1877) Carthew was left ailing and making very slow progress with his work. He died in his sleep in his chair at his home, Millfield House, Quebec Road, East Dereham, on 21 October 1882, and was buried with his wife and parents in the family vault at Redenhall church four days later. The burial service was conducted by the Revd Benjamin Armstrong, the Tractarian vicar of Dereham, whom Carthew had served as churchwarden for twenty-five years. Armstrong pays tribute in his (published) diary to the constant support of 'the only intelligent churchman in the place' when he arrived as vicar in 1850, calling him 'a great archaeologist and a man of considerable taste'. Even so, he had described Carthew's public lectures as 'very prosy and dull' (*Norfolk Diary*, 85). Carthew left an unfinished history of East and West Bradenham parishes with Necton and Holme Hale, and a treatise on the origins of family or 'sur-names' drawing on Dereham examples, both of which were seen through the press by his friend Augustus Jessopp in 1883.

J. M. BLATCHLY

Sources *DNB* · *IGI* · *A Norfolk diary: passages from the diary of the Rev. Benjamin John Armstrong*, ed. H. B. Armstrong [1949] · W. Rye, *Index to Norfolk topography*, Index Society (1881) · Burke, *Gen. GB* · *The Athenaeum* (4 Nov 1882), 598 · census returns for East Dereham, 1851, 1861, 1871, 1881 · parish register, Norfolk, Redenhall cum Harleston [baptism] · parish register, Norfolk, Redenhall cum Harleston [burials] · parish register, Dorset, Sherborne Abbey [marriage] · parish register, Frettenham [baptism] · D. E. Davy's Suffolk pedigrees, BL, Add MS 19122
Archives Norfolk RO, collections, corresp., and notes relating to East Dereham and Harleston · Norfolk RO, notes for pedigrees; notes relating to various hundreds and genealogical papers; transcripts of Norfolk deeds · priv. coll. (NRA), notes and papers written by or belonging to Carthew, chiefly relating to hundred of Launditch
Wealth at death £6180 11s. 2d.: probate, 21 March 1883, *CGPLA Eng. & Wales*

Carthew, Thomas (1657–1704), lawyer, was born in Cannaliggy, St Issey, Cornwall, on 4 April 1657, and baptized on 4 June 1657 at St Issey, the eldest son of Thomas Carthew (1636–1708) of Cannaliggy and Mary Baker (*b.* 1634) of Bodmin. If the authority of William Hals, the Cornish historian, can be trusted, he was for some time 'in the inferior practice of the law under Mr. Trevenna, without being a perfect Latin grammarian, always using the English words for matters and things in his declarations where he understood not the Latin' (*DNB*). Carthew became a student at the Middle Temple on 21 May 1683, and on 14 June 1686 was called to the bar. According to Hals he gained this early advancement 'by a mandamus from the lord keeper North', a relative of his wife. In April 1685 Carthew married Mary (*d.* 1726), daughter of John Colby of Banham, Norfolk, whose widow married Edward

North of Benacre, Suffolk, who died in 1701. Mary Colby's sister married Edward North's son Edward (*d*. 1708), and Carthew's son eventually inherited Benacre. On 23 November 1698 Carthew was called to the bar of the Inner Temple and on 7 November 1700 became a serjeant-at-law, his sponsors being Bishop Trelawny of Exeter and the Cornish MP John Speccot.

Hals prophesied Carthew's growth 'into such great fame and reputation, that he is likely to make a considerable addition to his paternal estate' (*DNB*), but on 4 July 1704 Narcissus Luttrell recorded that he was dead. He had made his will on 28 June, appointing Edward North his executor until his sons reached their majority, and leaving Anne North (*née* Colby) his chariot. He was buried in the Temple Church on 12 July, predeceasing his father by four years. His widow died on 15 June 1726. His son Thomas published his father's *Reports of Cases Adjudged in the Court of King's Bench from 3 Jac. II to 12 Will. III* in 1728, with a second corrected edition appearing in 1741.

STUART HANDLEY

Sources Boase & Courtney, *Bibl. Corn.*, 1.64, 1116 • Baker, *Serjeants* • J. Polsue, *A complete parochial history of the county of Cornwall*, 2 (1868), 241, 237 • H. W. Woolrych, *Lives of eminent serjeants-at-law of the English bar*, 2 vols. (1869) • *IGI* • will, PRO, PROB 11/477, sig. 144 • N. Luttrell, *A brief historical relation of state affairs from September 1678 to April 1714*, 5 (1857), 142 • A. I. Suckling, *The history and antiquities of the county of Suffolk*, 2 (1848), 123–4 • H. A. C. Sturgess, ed., *Register of admissions to the Honourable Society of the Middle Temple, from the fifteenth century to the year 1944*, 1 (1949), 210 • *DNB*

Archives priv. coll., MSS • Yale U., MSS

Likenesses portrait; said to be at Woodbridge Abbey, Suffolk, in 1886

Sir George-Étienne Cartier, baronet (1814–1873), by unknown engraver, pubd 1864

Cartier, Sir George-Étienne, baronet (1814–1873), lawyer and politician in Canada, was born on 6 September 1814 at Seven Chimneys, St Antoine-sur-Richelieu, Lower Canada, the seventh of the eight children of Jacques Cartier (1774–1841), a merchant, and his wife, Marguerite (1779–1848), the daughter of Joseph Paradis, a merchant. The Cartiers had been established in British North America since 1738, and as grain merchants at St Antoine since 1772. George-Étienne entered the Sulpician college at Montreal in 1824 and completed the classical programme with brilliance. After graduating in 1831 he was articled at the Montreal law office of E. E. Rodier, and was admitted to the bar in 1835.

Drawn by Rodier into the *patriote* movement, which advocated liberal reforms and the advancement of French-Canadian nationality, Cartier attracted attention by his patriotic songs and verses, one of which, 'O Canada, mon pays, mes amours', remained well known through his lifetime. In 1837 he participated in the *patriote*-led Lower Canadian uprising, and escaped to the United States when it was crushed.

In October 1838 Cartier was allowed to return to Montreal, where he began to practise law. His clients were chiefly businessmen and landholders. In the 1850s he came to represent the Seminary of St Sulpice (the religious corporation that had once held all Montreal in fief and was still its largest landholder) and Canada's principal railway company, the Grand Trunk Railway Company. He became a director of the Grand Trunk and other corporations, and also invested in commercial real estate, which provided a significant part of his income.

In politics Cartier supported Louis-Hyppolyte LaFontaine, who repudiated *patriote* radicalism and accepted the legislative union of Upper and Lower Canada, which the imperial government had imposed in 1840. LaFontaine achieved power by co-operating with Upper Canadian Reformers, the Roman Catholic church, and Lower Canada's largely English-speaking business class. It was as a follower of LaFontaine that Cartier was elected to the legislature in 1848. In the assembly he urged government support for railway construction, and worked to make Montreal the pivot of a great transportation system carrying Upper Canadian grain to Europe and both imported and Montreal-made goods to consumers in Upper Canada. In 1852 Cartier became chairman of the assembly's railway committee, in 1855 provincial secretary, and in 1856 attorney-general for Canada East (Lower Canada) in the Liberal–Conservative government of Étienne-Pascal Taché and John A. Macdonald. He soon replaced Taché as Lower Canadian leader, and in 1858 he assumed the premiership in a reorganized Cartier–Macdonald government.

Cartier championed the 1854 Commutation Act which abolished feudal tenure in Lower Canada, but in separate negotiations with the Sulpicians (his former teachers and now clients of his law firm) he secured them an exceptionally advantageous commutation for their property. In 1857 he introduced legislation to provide for the codification of Lower Canada's civil law and appointed a commission to carry out the work. The finished code, adopted in 1865, brought order to the civil law system, while facilitating the buying and selling of land, raising of capital, and securing of contracts. Cartier was thus important in ending Lower Canada's old regime institutions and bringing in an order friendly to business and economic development.

Cartier's family life was less successful. His wife, Hortense (1828–1898), the daughter of the wealthy merchant Edouard-Raymond Fabre, whom he married on 16 June 1846, was an austere and pious woman, while he was outgoing, lively, and a bon vivant. They had three daughters, but the youngest (born in 1853) died within a year. After that Cartier and his wife appeared together in public. In the late 1860s he began to be seen in company with Luce Cuvillier (1817–1900), the sister of his personal investment adviser, and his intimate friendship with her lasted for the rest of his life.

In 1862 Cartier's government was defeated, but it was hard to find a durable successor. The Canadian union was in difficulty, as the two sections clashed on important issues, while the system of equal parliamentary representation prevented either from gaining the upper hand. Fundamental change seemed necessary, so in June 1864 Cartier and Macdonald joined the Upper Canadian Liberal George Brown in a coalition to try to obtain a federal constitution for the Canadas, including other British provinces if possible.

As leader of the largest party in the Canadian legislature (the Lower Canadian *bleus* or Conservatives), Cartier had a strong voice in the making of confederation. His connection with the Montreal business community made him sensible of the need for a central government with sufficient power and fiscal authority to extend Canada's railway and commercial empire throughout British North America. A central government must also be able to organize military defences, particularly against the United States, of which Cartier had a morbid fear. But at the same time, as the leading French-Canadian political spokesman, he was conscious of the need for strong provincial government to foster French-Canadian nationality. Confederation would break up the union of the Canadas, creating separate provinces of Ontario and Quebec and giving French Canadians a government of their own. In that way, proclaimed *La Minerve*, the Montreal newspaper considered to be Cartier's organ, confederation acknowledged the French Canadians 'as a distinct and separate nationality' with 'the formal recognition of our national independence' (1 July 1867).

After confederation, Cartier influenced Quebec politics at both the federal and the provincial level. Elected to the Quebec assembly in 1867, he controlled the selection of the province's first premier. At the same time he was elected to the federal parliament and took the militia and defence portfolio in the government led by Sir John A. Macdonald.

Cartier's public accomplishments were rewarded in 1868, when he was made a baronet; but his career was not ended. That winter, accompanied by his cabinet colleague William McDougall, he went to London to arrange for the annexation to Canada of the Hudson's Bay Company's territories in the north-western prairies. Unfortunately, the transfer was interrupted by an uprising of north-western inhabitants, led by Louis Riel. The difficulty was resolved in the spring of 1870, when delegates from the north-west met Cartier at Ottawa to receive assurances for their property and other rights. Parliament ratified their agreement in the Manitoba Act, which created the first western province of Canada. Later that year Cartier negotiated British Columbia's entry into confederation, expanding Canada (and the railway) to the Pacific.

Notwithstanding these achievements, Cartier was defeated in the 1872 elections, returning to the commons only after Riel declined a Manitoba nomination in his favour. The 1872 session was his last; he left for England soon after, seeking treatment for his chronic nephritis, and died of the disease at his London home, 47 Welbeck Street, Cavendish Square, on 20 May 1873. A few weeks before, he and Macdonald had been accused of accepting money from a Montreal businessman, Sir Hugh Allan, in return for granting Allan's company the charter to build the Pacific Railroad. The scandal toppled Macdonald's government that autumn, but by then Cartier had been buried at Montreal's Côte-des-Neiges cemetery, after a spectacular public funeral (13 June) arranged by his former teachers and clients, the Sulpicians. The mass was conducted by his wife's brother, Montreal's coadjutor bishop, E.-C. Fabre.

Formerly highly regarded as a father of his country, Cartier has suffered towards the end of the twentieth century as Quebec nationalism has repudiated his work of confederation and as Marxist historians have emphasized the business motives in his career. But whether admired or not, Cartier must be recognized as one of the principal shapers of nineteenth-century Canada.   A. I. SILVER

Sources J. C. Bonenfant, 'Cartier, Sir George-Étienne', *DCB*, vol. 10 • B. Young, *George-Etienne Cartier: Montreal bourgeois* (1981) • M. Hamelin, *Les premières années du parlementarisme québécois, 1867–1878* (Quebec, 1974) • A. I. Silver, *The French-Canadian idea of confederation, 1864–1900* (1982) • B. Young, *The politics of codification: the Lower Canadian civil code of 1866* (1944) • G. P. Browne, ed., *Documents on the confederation of British North America* (1969) • J. Tassé, ed., *Discours de Sir Georges Cartier* (1893) • B. Young, *In its corporate capacity: the seminary of Montreal as a business institution* (1986)
Archives McGill University, Montreal, McCord Museum • NA Canada | Archives Nationales du Québec, Chapais, Langevin MSS • NA Canada, MacDonald MSS
Likenesses W. Notman, photograph, NA Canada, MacDonald collection • engraving, NPG; repro. in *ILN* (12 Nov 1864) [*see illus.*] • monument, Mount Royal Park, Montreal, Canada • photograph, NA Canada, Canadian library of parliament collection • photographs, NA Canada • portraits, McGill University, Montreal, Canada, McCord Museum • ten photographs, NA Canada, Canadian high commission (Great Britain) collection
Wealth at death C$83,353: Young, *George-Etienne Cartier*

Cartimandua [Claudia Cartimandua, Julia Cartimandua] (*d.* after AD 69), queen of the Brigantes, a large tribal grouping in northern Britain, was married to *Venutius, with whom she quarrelled and whom she replaced after *c.*AD 57 with Vellocatus, his armour bearer; no offspring are known. She died after AD 69, when she lost her throne to Venutius and took refuge with the Romans.

Under Cartimandua, the Brigantes seem to have been the largest of the British tribes of the first century AD, occupying the greater part of the north of the province. They are probably best seen as an agglomeration of tribes, from one of which Cartimandua emerged as queen, perhaps by succession, for she was queen in her own right and there is mention of her illustrious birth. Given the size and diversity of the Brigantes, it is probable that she found it difficult to exercise complete and steady control throughout her realm.

Knowledge of Cartimandua is derived almost entirely from the writings of the Roman historian Tacitus, composed half a century after her floruit. She was one of the several female rulers of Britain and Germany who fascinated the Roman male author. In any case she could only be of prime concern to Tacitus in view of the scope of her realm and the importance of its location on the northern frontier of the expanding Roman province in Britain. Her capital has been located variously (for example, at York and at Aldborough): if she had a single centre (which cannot be assumed), then archaeology suggests that Stanwick (near Scotch Corner, north Yorkshire) is its most likely location. Everything that is known about Cartimandua indicates her allegiance to Rome, which seems to have been a constant feature of her rule. Indeed, the Roman source tends to suggest that she depended upon Roman support for the retention of her throne.

Cartimandua enters history in the pages of Tacitus in the year AD 51, when she handed in chains to the Romans the British leader Caratacus, a thorn in their side for almost a decade. It is related that Caratacus came to her in search of refuge from his Roman enemies and that he was passed to the Romans against his will. If that is the whole story, Cartimandua could be accused of treachery, even allowing for the inter-tribal hostilities that characterized ancient Britain. However, Cartimandua's closeness to Rome (subsequently, at any rate) made her an odd choice by Caratacus as a protectress against Rome. It may be that Caratacus came to Cartimandua not simply in search of refuge but also to engage her services as a mediator to negotiate his surrender: he certainly suffered no great punishment at Roman hands, thanks perhaps to Cartimandua's negotiating skills. In any event, she gained great credit at Rome for providing the emperor Claudius with Caratacus, who became the centrepiece of his celebration of victory in Britain.

Cartimandua's accession cannot be dated. She may have been on the throne for decades before AD 51, even before Claudius's invasion of Britain in 43. As a royal ally of Rome under the principate, she would have been awarded Roman citizenship, if she had not inherited it. If granted her citizenship by the emperor Claudius (*r.* AD 41–54), she

had the right to call herself Claudia Cartimandua. If her citizenship derived (directly or indirectly) from a grant of an earlier emperor, she was Julia Cartimandua. Neither name is attested, but one was certainly hers.

Evidence for the rest of Cartimandua's reign comes from two passages in Tacitus, one in his *Histories* (iii.45), completed about 110, and the other in his *Annals* (xii.40), completed about 116. Over the last century there has been recurrent and polarized scholarly debate on the relationship of these two passages. On the face of it, *Annals*, xii.40, describes Cartimandua's activities about AD 57, while *Histories*, iii.45, treats events of AD 69. Yet, given some broad similarities between the two passages, it has been argued that they are in fact doublets and that *Annals*, xii.40, is somehow a Tacitean error, the events described in the two passages having actually occurred together in AD 69. However, such similarities as exist between the two passages are quite inadequate to support so large an inference: most of them derive from the fact that the *Histories* passage briefly reprises earlier events (subsequently recorded at *Annals*, xii.40) as background to the events of AD 69, with which it is primarily concerned. Despite persistent controversy, there can be no real doubt that the two passages present two different events, as they claim to do, and with two very different outcomes: after the events of *c.*AD 57 Cartimandua retained power, but in AD 69 she was deprived of her throne.

Cartimandua had taken a consort from among the Brigantes, named Venutius; he probably came from a powerful sub-group within the large Brigantian realm. In AD 57, like Cartimandua, Venutius had a long record of fidelity to Rome; together they had prospered in alliance with Rome. But about AD 57 they fell out; Tacitus, disposed to moralizing, blamed the damaging effects of growing prosperity in the wake of the Caratacus affair. Their quarrel became a wider internal conflict, doubtless always a threat within the large and disjointed kingdom. Cartimandua remained close to Rome, but Venutius now became hostile, not only to the queen but also to her Roman supporters. It may be significant that he is not mentioned in the Caratacus affair: it seems that Cartimandua had taken all the responsibility in that affair and had received all the credit.

Cartimandua captured the brother and kinsfolk of Venutius by trickery, precipitating a major civil war among the Brigantes. It seems that Venutius's forces could be imagined as invaders from outside Cartimandua's realm, supporting the probability that he represented a regional grouping. Tacitus prefers to focus upon the supposed objections of the Brigantes to being ruled by a woman, which were very much his own. However, Cartimandua's Roman allies had foreseen the invasion of Venutius's forces and after fierce fighting repelled it; thanks to the Romans, the queen retained her throne, while Venutius was left hostile to her and to Rome.

In Venutius's place, Cartimandua took Vellocatus, his erstwhile armour bearer. Perhaps Vellocatus represented some of the interests which had brought Venutius to prominence; again, Tacitus prefers to moralize. In AD 69 Venutius attacked again, taking advantage of an uprising against Cartimandua among the Brigantes. This time Cartimandua's Roman allies had not anticipated his attack, doubtless more concerned with the tumultuous civil wars of their own in that year. Some Roman auxiliary infantry and cavalry arrived in time to save the queen's life, but not her throne. From AD 69 Venutius was king of the Brigantes.

Cartimandua's fate thereafter is unknown. A fragmentary inscription from Chester, which may mention a woman, has been taken to refer to her; it has been suggested that she lived out her days there. It is very likely that Cartimandua enjoyed a privileged retirement, as did other client rulers with similar histories, but there is nothing to connect her with Chester. It is just as likely that she retired to Italy, even Rome. Since she was well established as queen by AD 51, she was probably dead by 100.

Cartimandua had done Rome a great service through the middle of the first century AD. The Brigantes were not an easy people to rule: they were diverse and apparently prone to unrest. Cartimandua's difficulties with Venutius, which Tacitus couches in personal and moralistic terms, seem to have been symptomatic of a broader instability among the Brigantes.   DAVID BRAUND

Sources D. Braund, 'Observations on Cartimandua', *Britannia*, 15 (1984), 1–6 · W. S. Hanson and D. B. Campbell, 'The Brigantes: from clientage to conquest', *Britannia*, 17 (1986), 73–89 · B. Hartley and L. Fitts, *The Brigantes* (1988) · K. Branigan, ed., *Rome and the Brigantes* (1980) · C. Tacitus, *The histories [and] the annals*, ed. and trans. C. H. Moore and J. Jackson, 4 vols. (1925–37)

Dame (Mary) Barbara Hamilton Cartland (1901–2000), by Dorothy Wilding

Cartland [*married name* McCorquodale], **Dame (Mary) Barbara Hamilton** (1901–2000), novelist, was born on 9 July 1901 at Vectis Lodge, 37 Augustus Road, Edgbaston, near Birmingham, the eldest of the three children of Captain (James) Bertram Falkner Cartland (1874/5–1917), son of James Cartland, a financier and inheritor of brass foundry wealth, and his wife, Mary Hamilton (Polly) Scobell (1877–1976), whose father, a retired colonel in a Worcestershire landed family, felt that his daughter had married beneath her. His failure to agree to a financial settlement on the couple had severe consequences on their life.

Two years after Barbara's birth James Cartland overextended himself with an investment in the London–Fishguard railway, was declared bankrupt, and killed himself. His son's family, shorn of money allowances, had to move from a house with twelve servants to a rented farmhouse with two. Polly Cartland, however, maintained, 'Poor I may be, common I am not' (Heald, 38). Her cheerful, strong-willed character was the predominant influence on Barbara, who she still hoped would marry an earl. While her husband tried to maintain his old pursuits of hunting and gambling, the mother's spirit of dignified make-do-and-mend enabled the family to retain some social cachet. When Bertram Cartland, by then a major, was killed in May 1917 at the age of forty-two during the last German counter-offensive of the First World War, they had to dye everyday clothes black because they could not afford mourning wear.

Barbara was educated at Worcester high school, at Malvern Girls' College, and at a finishing school at Netley Abbey, Hampshire. In youth she was forbidden to read newspapers at home; lending-library romances were her only texts, she said. In 1919 Polly Cartland moved the family to South Kensington, London, and opened a woollens shop. She managed to afford a modest social season for Barbara, who earned money by drawing menu cards for parties, and persuaded an art student, Norman Hartnell, later couturier to Queen Elizabeth, to make her ball gowns free of charge. Through selling society-gossip paragraphs to the *Daily Express*, she was befriended by Lord Beaverbrook, who found the young woman, with her gaiety and 'rather large surprised eyes' (her own words), congenial enough to introduce to Winston Churchill, F. E. Smith, and other eminences as a lunch guest (Cartland, 14). The very short paragraphs of most of her 723 books, each named by her own insistence in her *Who's Who* entry, are Beaverbrook's literary legacy to her. In romantic fiction her declared model was the author Ethel M. Dell. Her first published romance, *Jigsaw* (1923), earned her £200. Her observant, down-to-earth memoir of the first war and 1920s, *We Danced All Night* (1970), is an unusually valuable resource for those who wish to understand the material circumstances and spirit of the period.

On 23 April 1927 Cartland married Alexander George (Sachie) McCorquodale (*b.* 1897/8), of Cound Hall, Shropshire, holder of a government licence to print postal orders. In 1929 they had a daughter, Raine, who became through marriage countess of Dartmouth in 1948 and Countess Spencer in 1976. In 1933 Cartland divorced McCorquodale for adultery. He counter-sued, alleging in a highly publicized but unsuccessful action that his cousin Hugh McCorquodale (1897/8–1963) had visited her bedroom by day. Barbara responded in court that this was because she wrote in bed. On 28 December 1936 she married Hugh. By then she had published seventeen novels. The couple had two sons, Ian, later her literary agent, and Glen, a stockbroker. Early in the Second World War she went to Canada with her sons, but returned after her brothers, Ronald (a Conservative MP) and Tony, were killed within one day of each other during the retreat to Dunkirk. She became lastingly active in voluntary work, particularly with the Auxiliary Territorial Service and the St John Ambulance Brigade.

Hugh McCorquodale died in 1963, of complications from wounds received in the First World War. Widowhood brought Cartland into full flower as prolific novelist and self-publicist. A streak of sexual bawdy in her private conversation (more than one interviewer was surprised by her interest in the rumoured penis size of the duke of Windsor) never reached her prose: this was virtually all about virgins, landed wealth, and moodily passionate men. 'Every woman wants instinctively to tame a devil through the purity of her love', she wrote (Cartland, 16). In her 510th—and not unrepresentative—story, *Love Flies In* (1991), the heroine, Novella Wentworth, a lonely gentlewoman whose father is at the Napoleonic wars, gives sanctuary to a handsome young fugitive from the debauched, powerful Lord Grimstone, whose sexual advances she rebuffs. The fugitive turns out to be Vale Chester, a secret agent who finally exposes Grimstone as an accomplice of the French. As a reward, Chester is instantly appointed minister of state for war. He proposes marriage to Novella. The story ends:

> Then he was kissing her again.
> Then they were both aware of a light that surrounded them which was not of this world.
> It was the love which came from God and which goes on to Eternity.

Her heroines were almost always exotically named. In addition to Novella there were Mistral (*Ghost in Monte Carlo*), Fyna MacSteel (*The Loveless Marriage*), and Udela (*Love for Sale*). She was particularly inventive with names of Scottish male nobility: the duke of Arkrae, chief of clan Macraggan (*The Little Pretender*), Torquil McCarron (*The Head of the Clan*), and 'the masterful Earl of Barradale' (*The Loveless Marriage*).

Cartland's books, copiously serialized in women's magazines until the 1970s, were capable of having an intense private appeal to their readers in their youth. At the 2001 Whitbread book awards dinner, nine months after the author's death, a woman guest of high intellectual accomplishment reminisced about how avidly she had tried as a teenager to discover the secret of how Cartland's heroines always let their hair down in a single elegant shake at bedtime. However, her books were largely unreviewed and ignored by the literary world, which sometimes doubted her claims about her readership. In January 2001 Ian McCorquodale said that she had been translated into thirty-six languages and still sold more than 1 million copies a year in France. Where claims about her can be independently tested, they have considerable substance. From 1988 to 1994 between 500,000 and 1 million copies of her work were recorded as borrowed each year from British public libraries. From 1994 to 1996 the figure was 300,000–500,000 copies. From 1996 to 2000 it was below 400,000. In 1995 Essex county libraries, which vigorously discard little-read books, had more than 300 of her titles in stock, compared with 208 for her romantic novelist contemporary Ursula Bloom and 27 for Ethel M. Dell. In 2001 a total of 177 of her titles were listed as still in print in the book-trade market area covering the UK, USA, and Canada. Three further titles were listed as forthcoming; she continued to write until six months before her death. In the USA alone, fifty-four titles were still in print. Discussion groups about her books continue on the internet, and an electronic auction market exists for copies of her earlier titles.

In the mansion of her later years, Camfield Place, Hertfordshire, formerly the home of Beatrix Potter, Cartland continued to live and speak like a celebrity novelist long after others had ceased doing so. When interviewed, she talked as though she was automatically a public figure and, like Norma Desmond, the veteran Hollywood goddess in the film *Sunset Boulevard*, was always conscious of the need to be ready for her close-up. She was friendly to journalists, to whom she sent an advance, self-composed obituary, tied with pink ribbon, entitled 'How I wish to be remembered'. She was especially in demand from them after her daughter's stepdaughter Diana became princess of Wales in 1981. She was made a dame commander in the Order of the British Empire in 1991.

Barbara Cartland died on 21 May 2000 after a short illness, and was buried in the grounds of Camfield Place. After her death she was disparaged in some quarters as a superannuated caricature of a *monstre sacré*, ridiculed for her taste in heavy make-up and in pink clothes and accessories. Even her Pekinese were rose-tinted. She was, however, a professional of consummate stamina, immensely strong in her will to make the best of things, the most hard-headed of realists as well as a dreamer and hoper, with the slight air of pathos often found in people who have this mixture of qualities. Aptly and with her underlying realism, she said in an interview when she was asked about reincarnation, 'Most people tell you they were Cleopatra or some Queen. I was Scheherazade in the bazaar, telling a story every few minutes.' JOHN EZARD

Sources T. Heald, *A life of love* (1994) · B. Cartland, *We danced all night* (1970) · personal knowledge (2004) · private information (2004) [Commonwealth War Graves Commission; Public Lending Right Office; Global Books in Print; Bowker's Books in Print] · b. cert. · m. certs.

Archives BBC WAC, corresp. and literary MSS · priv. coll., letters and MSS

Likenesses photographs, c.1930–1981, Hult. Arch. · D. Wilding, photograph, NPG [*see illus.*]

Carton, Claude [*real name* Richard Claude Critchett] (1856–1928), actor and playwright, was born at 46 Finsbury Square, London, on 10 May 1856. He was the younger son of George *Critchett (1817–1882), ophthalmic surgeon, and his wife, Martha Wilson, daughter of Captain Nathanael Brooker RN, of Bosham, Sussex; his brother was Sir George Anderson Critchett (1845–1925), also an eye specialist. In 1875, adopting the surname Carton, he took to the stage at Bristol (29 March) in T. W. Robertson's *Sea of Ice*, and made his London début (19 June) as Osric in *Hamlet* at Henry Irving's Lyceum Theatre, where he later created Courtenay in Tennyson's *Queen Mary* (1876). His early career, interspersed with several out-of-town engagements (especially Liverpool), involved in the autumn of 1876 a provincial tour with Irving, in whose acting company Carton began his lifelong friendship with Arthur Wing Pinero. At the Folly Theatre, London, which he managed briefly, Carton produced and performed in Pinero's early comedy *Imprudence* (1881), winning qualified approval for his 'cynical, cool', but 'crude' style (Pascoe, 43) as the adventurer Baines Durant.

Carton never really liked acting: his unremarkable career ended when the success of the boulevard-type farce *The Great Pink Pearl* (1885), the first of three collaborations with Cecil Raleigh, established him as a professional playwright. His first solo drama, the sentimental comedy *Sunlight and Shadow* (1890), starred George Alexander and Marion Terry. *Liberty Hall* (1892) was written during a period of severe ill health and uneasily slotted between *Lady Windermere's Fan* and *The Second Mrs Tanqueray* at the St James's Theatre. It was Carton's first major artistic and financial success, running to 182 performances. Set mainly in a Bloomsbury bookshop, it combines sentiment with humour in the manner of the early Dickens, Carton's professed model.

Carton's writing, especially from the late 1890s onwards, was largely shaped by the comic acting strengths of his wife, Katherine Julia Mackenzie (1853–1928)—stage name Miss Compton—the younger daughter of the actor Henry *Compton (1805–1877). She and Carton acted together in the late 1870s and the early 1880s, in plays that included some early ones by Pinero. In 1885 she appeared in her husband's first play as a haughty Russian countess, foreshadowing the *grande dame* character which, in middle age, became her speciality in such notably successful roles as Lady Algernon Chetland in *Lord and Lady Algy* (1898)—with Charles Hawtrey as hero—and Joanna, duchess of Rushmere, in *Mr Preedy and the Countess* (1909). Carton's writing was perfectly attuned to her 'deep-toned drawl', 'deceptively vacant smile', 'stately deliberation', and 'consummate knowledge of how to make the points' (*The Times*, 17 May 1928).

After Pinero, Henry Arthur Jones, and Sydney Grundy, Carton was the most performed playwright of the 1890s. Shaw remarked that Carton's plays might lack originality but were 'so extremely goodnatured that they disarm criticism' (Shaw, 3.232). Carton had some gift for humour and for witty, if occasionally overly metaphoric, dialogue. His success continued with sometimes morally tendentious society comedies, often bordering on farce, such as *Lady Huntworth's Experiment* (1900), *The Rich Mrs Repton* (1904), *Mr Hopkinson* (1905), *Eccentric Lord Comberdene* (1910),

and *The Bear Leaders* (1912). Carton's last substantial success (in collaboration with Justin McCarthy) was *Nurse Benson* (1918), a topical wartime farce, featuring Marie Löhr as a nurse in love with a wounded patient. Carton's work has not been printed or reprinted since 1925. *Liberty Hall* was last revived in London, briefly, in 1930.

A bookish and to some extent retiring—even reclusive—individual, Carton never attended his first nights; yet he insisted on conducting his own rehearsals, believing that authors were best fitted to help actors to develop their parts. Although he had no time for the bohemian side of the theatre, he actively promoted fellow playwrights' professional interests as founder member in 1909 of the dramatic subcommittee of the Society of Authors, and of the Dramatists' Club. Carton died at his home, Red Lodge, Springfield Park, Acton, Middlesex, on 1 April 1928; his wife died at the same address the following month. Both were buried in Acton cemetery. They had one daughter, named Lenore.   JOHN RUSSELL STEPHENS

Sources *The Times* (2 April 1928), 19 · *The Times* (5 April 1928), 15 · *The Times* (28 May 1928), 13 · *The Times* (17 May 1928), 18 · 'Mr R. C. Carton at home', *The Era* (4 Feb 1893), 11 · *Era Almanack and Annual* (1897), 35–6 · C. Pascoe, *Dramatic notes: a chronicle of the London stage, 1879–1882* (1883), 43 · A. E. W. Mason, *Sir George Alexander and the St James's theatre* (1935) · G. B. Shaw, *Our theatres in the nineties*, rev. edn, 3 vols. (1932) · W. Archer, *The theatrical 'World' for 1893* (1894) · C. Scott, *The drama of yesterday and today*, 2 vols. (1899) · A. Nicoll, *Late nineteenth century drama, 1850–1900*, 2nd edn (1959), vol. 5 of *A history of English drama, 1660–1900* (1952–9), 305 [performance data] · A. Nicoll, *English drama, 1900–1930* (1973), 552 [performance data] · J. P. Wearing, *The London stage, 1890–1899: a calendar of plays and players*, 2 vols. (1976) [performance data] · J. P. Wearing, *The London stage, 1900–1909: a calendar of plays and players*, 2 vols. (1981) [performance data] · J. P. Wearing, *The London stage, 1910–1919: a calendar of plays and players*, 2 vols. (1982) [performance data] · J. P. Wearing, *The London stage, 1920–1929: a calendar of plays and players*, 3 vols. (1984) [performance data] · DNB · IGI

Wealth at death £5918 10s. 10d.: probate, 19 May 1928, CGPLA Eng. & Wales

Carton de Wiart, Sir Adrian (1880–1963), army officer, was born in Brussels on 5 May 1880, the eldest son of Léon Constant Ghislain Carton de Wiart (1854–1915), barrister, who later moved to Cairo, and his first wife, M. I. James, who died when the boy was six. He was educated at the Oratory School, Edgbaston, from 1891, and went to Balliol College, Oxford, in January 1899. His college career was marked by a conspicuous lack of success in examinations, and he ran away later that year and enlisted (under a false name and age) in Paget's horse, a newly raised, independent regiment. 'Trooper Carton' was severely wounded fighting the Boers and, his real identity revealed, he returned to Balliol in 1900, but he did not complete his studies there. He went back to South Africa with the Imperial light horse, and in 1901 obtained a regular commission in the 4th dragoon guards. After service in India (1902–4), he became aide-de-camp to Sir Henry Hildyard, commander-in-chief, South Africa (1904–8). At Vienna in 1908 he married Countess Frederica, eldest daughter of Prince Fugger-Babenhausen of Klagenfurt and his wife, Nora, Princess Hohenlohe; they had two daughters. From 1910 to 1914 he was adjutant of a yeomanry unit, the Royal

Sir Adrian Carton de Wiart (1880–1963), by Sir William Orpen, 1919

Gloucestershire hussars. In the summer of 1914 he was attached to the camel corps in Somaliland, in operations against Mohammed bin Abdullah. In November he was wounded in an eye, which had to be removed; his black eye-patch was thereafter a distinguishing feature. He was appointed to the DSO, and joined the 4th dragoon guards in the trenches near Ypres.

Carton de Wiart's career in the First World War was legendary. Severely wounded eight times, he lost his left hand, and was awarded the Victoria Cross for an action on the Somme in which he assumed command of 57 brigade of 19th division during the capture and defence of La Boiselle (3–4 July 1916). He subsequently commanded in succession the 12th, 105th, and 113th infantry brigades. He ended the war a brigadier-general. After the armistice he was appointed second-in-command of the British military mission to Poland, succeeding to the command on the death of General Louis Botha in 1919. He was involved in the widespread fighting, including the battle of Warsaw against the Bolsheviks, but had little influence over the course of the Polish–Soviet war. Indeed, Carton de Wiart was embarrassed by the Lloyd George government's off-hand attitude towards the Poles. In 1924 he resigned his commission, and spent the rest of the interwar years happily shooting duck in the Pripet marshes in Poland, from a house there lent to him by Prince Charles Radziwill, his last Polish aide-de-camp. He was summoned back to England in July 1939, and was asked to resume his old mission

to Poland. Unhappily for him, Carton de Wiart found himself reprising his role of the early 1920s, acting as the representative of a state friendly towards Poland but unwilling or unable to offer any immediate military aid. He had strong disagreements with the Polish commander-in-chief, Marshal Smigly-Rydz. With the Polish forces defeated by the invading Germans, Carton de Wiart returned to England by way of Romania and was given command of the 61st (territorial) division. In April 1940 he was appointed to command, as lieutenant-general, the central Norwegian expeditionary force. He failed to capture Namsos, but skilfully extracted his force, emerging from the disastrous campaign with his stock high with Churchill.

In April 1941 Carton de Wiart was dispatched to form a British military mission in Yugoslavia, but his aircraft was shot and came down in the sea, and he became a prisoner of the Italians. Held with other senior officers at Sulmona and the Castello di Vincigliati at Fiesole, he was at once busy with attempts to escape. With Lieutenant-General Richard O'Connor, on one occasion he eluded recapture for eight days, no small achievement given Carton de Wiart's distinctive appearance. In August 1943 the Italians dispatched Carton de Wiart to Lisbon to act as an intermediary in the negotiations which led to Italy's withdrawal from the war in the following month.

In October 1943 Churchill sent Carton de Wiart, as a lieutenant-general, as his personal representative to Chiang Kai-shek in China. The rest of the war he spent in Chungking (Chongqing), where he could do little to resist the erosion of British power in the face of increasing American power in the region. He attended the Cairo conference in November–December 1943, and in December 1944 made a personal report to the cabinet on the situation in the Far East. His dismissive view of Mao Zedong and the Chinese communists revealed the shallowness of his grasp of Chinese politics. He eventually retired to England in 1946, having broken his back in Rangoon en route. He was appointed KBE in 1945, was elected an honorary fellow of Balliol in 1957, and held an honorary doctorate from the University of Aberdeen, as well as many foreign decorations.

Carton de Wiart's wife died in 1949, and on 18 July 1951 he married (Ruth Myrtle Muriel) Joan (b. 1903/4), daughter of George McKechnie and divorced wife of Arthur Henry Carr Sutherland. They settled at Aghinagh House, Killinardrish, co. Cork, where he continued his tireless pursuit of snipe and salmon. He died there on 5 June 1963.

With his black eye-patch and empty sleeve, Carton de Wiart looked like an elegant pirate, and became a figure of legend. In 1916 Cynthia Asquith called him 'the hero of the war' (Diaries, 244), and Evelyn Waugh based the figure of Ritchie-Hook in his Sword of Honour trilogy on Carton de Wiart. His autobiography, Happy Odyssey (1950), gives something of the flavour of the man. He was quick-tempered and modest, omitting any mention of his decorations from his autobiography, and he loathed humbug and meanness. Carton de Wiart was a battlefield leader in the most literal sense, rather than a commander or a diplomat. It was ironic that much of his post-1918 career was concerned with quasi-diplomatic roles for which he was neither well-suited nor well-qualified, and in which he was not particularly successful. In the view of one historian, he was 'almost as politically naive as he was brave' (Thorne, 560).   E. T. WILLIAMS, *rev.* G. D. SHEFFIELD

Sources G. D. Sheffield, 'Carton de Wiart and Spears', *Churchill's generals*, ed. J. Keegan (1991), 323–49 · A. Carton de Wiart, *Happy odyssey* (1950) · *The Times* (6 June 1963) · *Balliol Record* (July 1964) · E. Wyrall, *The history of the 19th division, 1914–18* [1932] · *The memoirs of Lord Ismay* (1960) · N. Davies, *White eagle, red star: the Polish–Soviet war, 1919–20* (1972) · C. Thorne, *Allies of a kind: the US, Britain, and the war against Japan, 1941–5* (1978) · *Lady Cynthia Asquith: diaries, 1915–1918* (1968) · *WWW* · m. cert. · *CGPLA Éire* (1964) · *CGPLA Eng. & Wales* (1964)
Archives U. Reading L., Jonathan Cape Archives, material relating to an unfinished biography, Peter Fleming MSS | FILM IWM FVA, news footage | SOUND IWM SA, oral history interview
Likenesses W. Orpen, oils, 1919, NPG [*see illus.*] · S. Elwes, oils, exh. RA 1972 · photograph, repro. in Carton de Wiart, *Happy odyssey*, frontispiece
Wealth at death £4158: probate, 1964, *CGPLA Éire* · £3496—in England: probate, 24 April 1964, *CGPLA Eng. & Wales*

Cartwright, Christopher (*bap.* 1602, *d.* 1658), Church of England clergyman and religious controversialist, was baptized at St Michael-le-Belfrey, York, on 1 October 1602, probably the son of Guye Cartwright and Ellen Calley, who had married there on 28 June 1590; the 'very loveing mother Mrs Ursula Cartwright widdowe', mentioned in Christopher's will, was most likely his stepmother (PRO, PROB 11/276, fol. 223). On 29 June 1617, aged fifteen, Cartwright matriculated as a pensioner from Peterhouse, Cambridge. He graduated BA in 1620, proceeded MA in 1624, and became a fellow in 1625.

Within a few years, for reasons that are unclear, Cartwright left Cambridge. Richard Baxter reports that he succeeded William Fenner, minister of Sedgely, in the 'Stafford-shire Lecture against Poperie' (Baxter, *Treatise of Justifying Righteousness*, sig. A3), following Fenner's forced departure in 1626–7 because of his puritan sympathies. Though it is unclear whether Cartwright was also minister in Sedgely or in another Staffordshire parish, Baxter reports that Cartwright was one of the local ministers attending a lecture day in 1640 when Baxter was a young curate at Bridgnorth. With the major agenda item a formal debate of the recently issued 'et cetera' oath Baxter recalls that 'at the meeting it fell to my lot to be the Objector, or Opponent, against Mr. *Christopher Cartwright*' (Baxter, *Treatise of Episcopacy*, sig. A2v). Cartwright impressed Baxter as being 'a very Learned, Peaceable, Godly Man' (Baxter, *Treatise of Justifying Righteousness*, sig. A3).

It is unclear how much longer Cartwright remained in Staffordshire. In 1647 he published as minister of St Martin and Gregorie in Micklegate, York, *The Magistrates Authority … and the Souls Immortality Vindicated*, two sermons 'preach'd at York'. This was his response to 'some which had relation to the Army' who maintained that 'the Magistrate hath no power to punish or restrain any that shal vent never so false doctrines & heretical opinions'

(Edward Leigh's 'To the Christian Reader', in C. Cartwright, *The Magistrates Authority*, 1647, sig. A2). Cartwright also published a series of rabbinical commentaries that secured his reputation as a meticulous Hebraist, *Electa Thargumico-rabbinica, sive, Annotationes in Genesin* (1648), *Electa Thargumico-rabbinica, sive, Annotationes in Exodum* (1653), and *Mellificium Hebraicum, seu, Observationes diversmodae ex Hebraeorum* (published posthumously in 1660 and 1698), and several sermon series intended as pastoral helps to Christian maturity, *A Brief and Plain Exposition of the Creed* (1649), *The Doctrine of Faith* (1649), and *A Practical and Polemical Commentary … on the Whole Fifteenth Psalm* (1658). During his lifetime he was probably most noted as the author of *Certamen religiosum, or, A Conference between the Late King of England and Late Marquesse of Worcester, Concerning Religion* (1651), in which Charles I's role as a defender of the protestant cause was recounted. But it was his literary relationship with Richard Baxter that has sustained subsequent interest in his work.

Cartwright was one of the 'learned, judicious and friendly' reviewers who responded to the published request for animadversions contained in Baxter's controversial *Aphorisms of Justification* (1649) (Baxter, *Treatise of Justifying Righteousness*, sig. A2). After an extensive exchange over 'the little Matters that we differed in', 'none of [which was] intended for Publick view', Baxter records that Cartwright asked that his papers be returned to him, as he 'was not willing, that so large Pains, as he had taken, should be so buried'. But Baxter could not comply with Cartwright's request because 'they were lost, (and I had no mind to be very inquisitive after them, in order to a Publick view)' (ibid., sig. A2v). After Cartwright's death Baxter reports that Cartwright's papers were located. Not wishing to 'wrong the dead by suppressing so learned and elaborate a treatise, which I think he desired should not be suppressed', Baxter published an account of Cartwright's original animadversions along with Cartwright's later *Exceptions Against a Writing of Mr. Baxters*, together with his own response, *The Substance of Mr Cartwright's Exceptions Considered* (ibid., sig. A3). These were all contained in Baxter's 1676 *A Treatise of Justifying Righteousness*. Baxter's claim that Cartwright's concerns with his *Aphorisms* were rather 'about the *Aptness of Notions*, than the *Truth of the Matter*' reflect a curious inability to acknowledge the reality and severity of the differences that set his view of justification apart from the Calvinistic orthodoxy of most of his colleagues (ibid., sig. A2v). It was a point Baxter continued to contest for the rest of his life. By understanding justification by means of a political metaphor following a line of interpretation developed by Hugo Grotius, Baxter hoped to chart a middle way between what he perceived were the excesses of antinomianism on the one hand, and Arminianism on the other. Cartwright's exceptions to Baxter's doctrine may have been friendly, but they were of the same piece of cloth that characterized the more strident responses generated by his unusual understanding of justification. What Cartwright found troubling was Baxter's emphasis on a believer's two-fold righteousness—the legal righteousness provided by Christ and the individual's personal evangelical righteousness provided by faith.

Cartwright signed his will on 1 March 1658. His bequests revisit the significant communities where he lived and ministered, with gifts to the poor in York and Staffordshire and books to friends in Staffordshire and to the library of Peterhouse in Cambridge. Five pounds went to Ursula Cartwright and a sum to his aunt Jane Caley; it appears that he was unmarried. He died within a few weeks and was buried on 1 April 1658 in the chancel to the north of the communion table in the now redundant church of St Martin-cum-Gregory in York.

J. WILLIAM BLACK

Sources R. Baxter, *A treatise of justifying righteousness* (1676) · R. Baxter, *A treatise of episcopacy* (1681) · will, PRO, PROB 11/276, fol. 223 · parish register, St Michael-le-Belfrey, Borth. Inst. · Venn, *Alum. Cant.* · T. A. Walker, ed., *Admissions to Peterhouse or St Peter's College in the University of Cambridge* (1912) · *DNB* · *Reliquiae Baxterianae, or, Mr Richard Baxter's narrative of the most memorable passages of his life and times*, ed. M. Sylvester, 1 vol. in 3 pts (1696) · F. Collins, *The registers of St Michael-le-Belfrey, York (part 1, 1565–1653)*, Yorkshire Parish Register Society (1899) · J. I. Packer, 'The redemption and restoration of man in the thought of Richard Baxter', DPhil diss., U. Oxf., 1954 · J. Boersma, *A hot peppercorn: Richard Baxter's doctrine of justification in its seventeenth-century context of controversy* (Zoetermeer, 1995), 1–25

Archives BL, sermons, notes, and MSS, Add. MS 4927

Wealth at death bequests totalling £156; additional bequests totalling £13 4*s.*; also books; two houses to sister: will, PRO, PROB 11/276, fol. 223

Cartwright, Edmund (1743–1823), Church of England clergyman and inventor of a power loom, was born on 24 April 1743 at Marnham in Nottinghamshire, the fourth of five sons of William Cartwright (*d.* 1781) and his wife, Anne (*d.* 1787), daughter of George Cartwright. The family had long been an influential one in Nottinghamshire. Three brothers had military careers but Edmund was destined for the church. His wealthy background, good family connections, and breadth of interests distinguish him from his fellow 'inventors' of the period, notably James Hargreaves, Richard Arkwright, and Samuel Crompton, with whom his 'invention' of the power loom has frequently associated him. Educated at Wakefield grammar school, he was a first-rate scholar and entered University College, Oxford, in 1757. He was allowed to take his degree early and became a fellow of Magdalen in 1764. Under the tuition of Dr Langhorn, editor of *Plutarch's Lives*, he developed a fine literary style and emerged as a minor poet of the period, although commentators have regretted that he was not directed into the sciences. In 1770 he published *Armine and Elvira—a Legendary Poem*, which rapidly went through a series of editions, and was later thought highly of by Sir Walter Scott. His most important work, *Prince of Peace*, published in 1779, deplored the war in America. A new edition of his poems appeared in 1786, and a volume of letters and sonnets was published in 1806. In old age Cartwright could style himself 'Father of the living poets', though his writing subsequently fell out of favour.

A young clergyman with literary aspirations, Cartwright married, on 15 December 1772, Alice Whitaker (*d.*

Edmund Cartwright (1743–1823), by Thomas Oldham Barlow, pubd 1862 (after Robert Fulton)

1785), daughter and coheir of Richard Whitaker, of Doncaster, and was presented to the perpetual curacy of Brampton near Wakefield. An outbreak of fever in his parish led him into a successful study of medicines, bringing his name into the medical literature of the day. In 1779 he became rector of Goadby Marwood, Leicestershire, an office he seems to have held until 1808, and he was prebendary of Lincoln from 1786 until his death. The early years at Goadby Marwood he later described as the happiest of his life. He was able to farm his glebe, contributed to the *Monthly Review*, and became a close friend of George Crabbe, who was his neighbour at Belvoir. His political and social opinions seem to have been in accord with those of his brother Major John *Cartwright (1740–1824). In 1806 he took the degree of DD, and became chaplain to the duke of Bedford, despite his censure for preaching a funeral sermon for the ninth duke, deemed improper from a clergyman.

In 1784 a holiday visit to Matlock pushed Cartwright's life into an altogether different direction. During a casual mealtime conversation with 'some gentlemen from Manchester', Cartwright proposed the mechanization of weaving as a counterbalance to that of spinning, as a means of restricting the export of cheap British yarn to foreign competitors. Returning home he set to work to produce such a machine. Despite his avowed ignorance of machinery the 42-year-old clergyman in April 1785 obtained a patent for his 'New invented machine for weaving' (patent no. 1470). Though an extremely primitive affair requiring the strength of two strong men to operate it, the machine established the feasibility of power-loom weaving, and the underlying principle remained little changed until the development of the Sulzer loom in the twentieth century.

Cartwright's status as sole inventor of the power loom is less secure, for the development of an efficient system owed much to the subsequent work of Radcliffe, Horrocks, and Marsland. In Scotland Jeffrey was developing a power loom at Paisley, Bell of Glasgow was conducting important experiments by 1794, and John Menteith's mill at Pollokshaws, Glasgow, was running 200 looms as early as 1801. In 1785 Alice Cartwright died, and the family inherited property at Doncaster. Working with skilled mechanics helped Cartwright to overcome many of the early problems, and the Doncaster loom was developed, leading to further patents registered in 1786, 1787, and 1790. Cartwright now had the funds to take advantage of his discovery, and a power-loom mill was established in the town with his brothers John and Charles. A lesser-known enterprise was established at Retford in Nottinghamshire. At the former twenty looms were set to work powered by the efforts of a bull, this animal being replaced by a steam engine in 1788–9. Though successful in promoting the principle, the concern was not a success. The rural clergyman, regarded by some as a deserter of his caste, faced powerful opposition from competitors, and his patents were infringed.

In 1790 Grimshaws of Knott Mills, Gorton, Manchester, contracted with him to run up to 400 of his looms. Two dozen were deployed at a 50 per cent saving on hand weavers' wages, when the premises were mysteriously destroyed by fire. This was a mortal blow to Cartwright's schemes, disaster coming at a point when success may have been close at hand. Since no other manufacturer could be induced to take the loom, he rapidly began to run out of money. In 1793, facing losses in excess of £30,000, he assigned his patents to his brothers to pursue in the courts, and gave up the Doncaster works. At Doncaster he had invented a rope-making machine, and a very successful wool-combing machine. Known as Cartwright's comb, or Big Ben (after the contemporary pugilist), this was a truly visionary development, patents being granted in 1789, 1790 (two), and 1792. Cartwright estimated that savings of £40,000 per year were being made from it, and predicted, rather wildly, that these would soon rise to over £1 million. 50,000 wool combers petitioned parliament unsuccessfully for its suppression. The failure of this aspect of the Doncaster concern was thus perhaps a greater loss to Cartwright than the failure of the 'Patent' loom with which he has been more closely associated.

Infringement of the patents was a constant and costly problem, pursued in the courts by Cartwright's brothers on his behalf with indifferent success. In 1800 he successfully petitioned parliament for the extension of the patent on the wool-combing machine (1801), but gained little by it, and the power loom patent expired in 1804. In contrast to that of spinning, the mechanization of weaving was a much longer drawn-out process. Cartwright had given insufficient attention to the preparatory stages necessary to make his machine truly labour saving. A key stage was William Radcliffe's dressing machine, introduced in 1803, and William Horrocks's improved method for winding cloth onto the beam as it was woven. The cheapness and over-supply of labour also acted as a disincentive to mechanization and, notwithstanding the fears of the hand-loom weavers, fewer than 2500 power looms were operating as late as 1813. The wider introduction of the new technology was deferred until the investment booms of the early 1820s and 1830s, but by 1833 more than 100,000 were in operation.

In 1806 Cartwright discovered that his loom had come into widespread use around Manchester. His debts had continued to rise after 1793, and friends in Manchester presented a petition to parliament on his behalf in 1807, signed by fifty of the largest firms. It was claimed that his loom had benefited Britain to the amount of £1.5 million, which accordingly had been successful in keeping the textile trade. Parliament recognized his contribution, and in 1809 voted him a grant of £10,000—twice the sum that Crompton had received for his 'mule'.

After the failure at Doncaster, in 1793 Cartwright moved to London to enable him to pursue his scientific interests. With his wider interests, however, his energies became dissipated over a range of schemes and he lacked the focus of his Doncaster years. In 1795 he patented his geometric bricks, and in 1797 he obtained a patent for fireproof tiling. Given his extreme modesty and openness, his home became a meeting place for inventors. With Robert Fulton he explored the application of power to the propulsion of boats, and he obtained patents for an alcohol steam engine in 1797 and 1801. During these years Cartwright's reputation grew markedly. In 1798 he became a member of the Society of Arts and in 1804 an honorary member of the board of agriculture. Sir Humphry Davy was proud to assist his researches.

Cartwright became superintendent of the duke of Bedford's model farm at Woburn in 1801. Agriculture was an abiding interest. His reaping machine of 1793 was followed by a three-furrow plough, and he conducted important work on manures and the culture of potatoes. The remarkable breadth of Cartwright's intellect—a feature which sets him apart from his fellow textile pioneers—is illustrated by the fact that this work also coincided with the taking of his DD degree, the publication of a volume of his writings, and the successful campaign for compensation from parliament for his mechanical innovations. With his award Cartwright purchased a small farm at Hollanden in Kent, where he continued to work. His last patent, for roller print presses, was granted the year after his death. Perhaps his most remarkable achievement was his invention in 1820 of a carriage 'to go without horses'. Used to collect groceries, this 'Centaur Carriage' was powered by two men working cranks, and was claimed to be able to travel 27 miles with ease in a single day, hills notwithstanding (Strickland, 277).

Edmund Cartwright died at Hastings on 30 October 1823, and was buried at Battle, Sussex. He attributed his long life to early rising and temperate habits. He had married, on 5 June 1790, Susannah Kearney, daughter of the

Revd Dr John Kearney; she nursed him in his old age. He was survived by four children from his first marriage, Edmund, Mary (his biographer), Elizabeth *Penrose, and Frances Dorothy *Cartwright.   DAVID HUNT

Sources M. S. [M. Strickland], *A memoir of the life, writings, and mechanical inventions of Edmund Cartwright* (1843); repr. with introduction by K. G. Ponting (1971) · *Encyclopaedia Britannica*, 11th edn (1910–11), vol. 5, p. 435 · *Chambers's encyclopedia: a dictionary of universal knowledge*, 2 (1926), 814 · G. Timmins, *The last shift: the decline of handloom weaving in nineteenth-century Lancashire* (1993), 19–20 · W. English, *The textile industry* (1969), 102–3 · E. Baines, *History of the cotton manufacture in Great Britain* (1835); repr. (1966) · S. D. Chapman, *The cotton industry in the industrial revolution* (1977), 23 · G. Unwin and others, *Samuel Oldknow and the Arkwrights*, 2nd edn (1968), 98 · T. S. Ashton, *The industrial revolution, 1760–1830* (1948) · J. de L. Mann, 'The textile industry: machinery for cotton, flax, wool, 1760–1850', *A history of technology*, ed. C. Singer and others, 4: *The industrial revolution, c. 1750 to c. 1850* (1958), 277–307 · R. Marsden, *Cotton weaving: its development, principles and practice* (1895) · B. Woodcroft, *Brief biographies of inventors of machines for the manufacture of textile fabrics* (1863), 20–26 **Archives** Glos. RO, corresp. and papers **Likenesses** T. O. Barlow, mezzotint (after R. Fulton), BM, NPG; repro. in *Portraits of inventors* (1862) [*see illus.*] · H. Fehr, marble statue (posthumous), City of Bradford Museum and Art Gallery · J. F. Skill, J. Gilbert, W. Walker, and E. Walker, group portrait, pencil and wash (*Men of science living in 1807–08*), NPG · J. Thomson, stipple, NPG

Cartwright, Frances Dorothy (1780–1863), biographer, was born on 28 October 1780 at Marnham, Nottinghamshire, or Goadby Marwood, Leicestershire, the youngest child of Edmund *Cartwright (1743–1823), who was rector there, and his first wife, Alice (d. 1785), the youngest daughter and coheir of Richard Whitaker, of Doncaster. Frances Cartwright came from an energetic and intelligent family: her father was the inventor of textile machinery, and her uncle, Major John *Cartwright (1740–1824), was a radical reformer. Her sister Elizabeth *Penrose (c.1779–1837), was later the writer of a well-known textbook, *A History of England* (1823), under the pseudonym of Mrs Markham; another sister, Mary Strickland, wrote a biography of their father (1843). After her mother's death Frances was adopted by her uncle and his wife, to whom she became devoted; she was educated at a school at Richmond.

In 1802 Frances Cartwright began to write poetry; many years later, in 1835, she published anonymously *Poems, Chiefly Devotional*. After the death of her uncle, in 1824, she moved to Worthing with his widow; in 1826 she published her principal work, *The Life and Correspondence of Major Cartwright*, which remained the standard and only account of his life until 1972. In this laudatory biography she presented her uncle as the beneficent and Olympian sponsor of radical reform politics, playing down his political ambitions in order to emphasize his idealism; she also passed lightly over his later involvements with radical politicians and causes of which she disapproved, such as his association with Thomas Wooler of the *Black Dwarf* and his advocacy of Queen Caroline. John Cartwright's twentieth-century biographer comments that 'seldom can anyone have had a less critical and more devoted admirer narrate the course of a career which was, more often than not, bound in shallows' (Osborne, 37).

At her uncle's home in the early 1820s, Frances Cartwright had met Spanish activists who had been involved in the 1820 revolt against the despotic King Ferdinand VII, led by Rafael del Riego y Nunez (1784–1823). She learned Spanish and translated some of Riego's poems into English; in 1844, these translations appeared, with her initials, in *Obras póstumas poéticas*, a volume of translations from several works by the Riego family published by Sir John Bowring and W. Reid. She seems to have moved from Worthing to Langton, near Wragby in Lincolnshire, possibly to be nearer her sister Elizabeth and her family; she died at 21 Medina Villas, Cliftonville, Hove, Brighton, on 12 January 1863.   ROSEMARY MITCHELL

Sources *The life and correspondence of Major Cartwright*, ed. F. D. Cartwright, 1 (1826), 163, 408–12; 2 (1826), 243 · Boase, *Mod. Eng. biog.* · *Brighton Examiner* (20 Jan 1863) · J. W. Osborne, *John Cartwright* (1972) · Allibone, *Dict.* · *CGPLA Eng. & Wales* (1863) · IGI **Wealth at death** under £4000: probate, 10 April 1863, *CGPLA Eng. & Wales*

Cartwright, George (*fl.* 1661), playwright, whose home was possibly in Fulham, Middlesex, wrote *The Heroick Lover, or, The Infanta of Spain*, a comedy in verse, published in London in 1661 by R. W. for John Symmes. Dedicated to Charles II, it depicted the concerns of Princess Flora, the infanta, Bellarius, a young lord, and Symphrani, a beautiful lady, mistress of Bellarius, who becomes a nun when she thinks he is dead. All is resolved happily. Added to the publication were some miscellaneous royalist poems.
          F. D. A. BURNS

Sources DNB · Genest, *Eng. stage* · [C. Gildon], *The lives and characters of the English dramatick poets … first begun by Mr Langbain* [1699]

Cartwright, John (1740–1824), political reformer, was born on 17 September 1740 at Marnham, Nottinghamshire, the third son of William Cartwright (d. 1781) of Marnham, and Anne (d. 1787), daughter of George Cartwright of Ossington, also in Nottinghamshire. The family had risen to prominence in the sixteenth century owing to the fortuitous marriage of Edward Cartwright to a daughter of Thomas Cranmer, archbishop of Canterbury. The marriage brought the Cartwrights estates in three counties, and if, at the time of John Cartwright's birth, the family had been reduced to modest fortune, it remained well connected. Cartwright's aunt had married John Brownlow, Viscount Tyrconnel, who stood as Cartwright's godfather at his birth. Little is known of Cartwright's five sisters, but his brothers would benefit from the family's connections; while John Cartwright and two brothers were commissioned in the armed services, the eldest brother was found a position in the Treasury. Another brother, Edmund *Cartwright, was ordained a clergyman, married a woman of fortune, and became famous as the inventor of the power loom. In 1780 John Cartwright married Anne Dashwood (d. 1834), the daughter of a Lincolnshire gentleman; although their union was happy it produced no children. In 1786 they adopted their niece Frances *Cartwright (1780–1863), who wrote the first, if largely uncritical, biography of her uncle.

John Cartwright (1740–1824), by Adam Buck

Early years, 1740–1775 Educated at the grammar school in Newark and at Heath Academy, Yorkshire, Cartwright was commissioned in the navy in 1758 and proved to be an able officer. Serving under Richard, Lord Howe, he took part in the capture of Cherbourg in 1759. He also served under Sir Edward Hawke at the notable British victory at Quiberon Bay in the following year. Cartwright rose rapidly in the service. In 1762 he served in the Bay of Biscay as a lieutenant in the *Wasp*, commanded the *Spy* (1763–6), and devised certain improvements in naval gun exercises, afterwards incorporated in William Falconer's *Marine Dictionary*. Promoted first-lieutenant in May 1766, Cartwright was sent to the Newfoundland station to serve in the *Guernsey*, and in 1767 was appointed deputy commissary to the vice-admiralty court there. The next year he led a short expedition to discover the source of the River Exploits, but service in the *Antelope* in 1769 seriously damaged his health. In 1770 he returned to England to convalesce and, without active command, turned his attention to improving the supply of oak for the navy. In the years before the outbreak of the American War of Independence Cartwright also undertook to improve his poor education by becoming a voracious reader. In these years he laid the basis for his maturing political outlook, which later justifiably earned him the title Father of Reform and led him to publish over eighty works between 1774 and 1824.

Concerned with the growing imperial crisis between Britain and her American colonies, Cartwright published in 1774 *American Independence: the Glory and Interest of Great Britain*, a work advanced in its political outlook. Rejecting the British notion of virtual representation, Cartwright advocated the conciliation of the colonies, believing they had the right to choose their own rulers and to tax themselves. Believing that Britain and the American colonies should have separate legislatures, he looked forward to a political union based upon a commonwealth of interest. Concerned that his advanced views might jeopardize his naval career, he none the less republished the pamphlet in 1775 and followed it with another call for conciliation, *A Letter to Edmund Burke, Esq.*, which correctly prophesied that Anglo-American trade would eventually transcend major political change. It was this developing political outlook which led him to refuse a commission to serve in American waters under Lord Howe in 1775, a decision which effectively ended his naval career. He did accept, however, an appointment as major in the Nottinghamshire militia, which led to his being called Major Cartwright for the rest of his life.

Gentleman reformer, 1776–1823 The American War of Independence convinced Cartwright that the British parliament itself was corrupt and was in need of political reform. He outlined his own reform programme in his most famous work, first published in 1776, *Take Your Choice!* Cartwright's massive literary output would remain something of a reiteration of his earlier views in *Take Your Choice!*, a work which was one of the first to advocate universal manhood suffrage. His programme, later revised in a fuller edition of the work published in 1780, *The Legislative Rights of the Commonalty Vindicated, or, Take Your Choice!*, and his *The People's Barrier Against Undue Influence and Corruption*, the finest of his pre-French Revolution works, revolved around six points. Continuing to advocate universal manhood suffrage, Cartwright also supported annual parliamentary elections, equal electoral districts, a secret ballot, the abolition of property qualifications for parliamentary candidates, and (to lessen political bribery) the payment of members of parliament. If radical, these views were hardly original in content and reflected notions that English liberties, once clearly evident in the pre-Norman conquest Anglo-Saxon constitution, had been usurped by the crown. Never a social leveller, Cartwright at this period continued to believe that politics were a gentlemanly preserve, and his outlook remained rooted in the eighteenth-century belief in a lost Anglo-Saxon Arcadia, rather than forward to a new modern political alignment. If the validity of Cartwright's constitutional ideas is questionable, there can be no doubt that his dedication to the cause of reform was crucial in the continuation of an English reform movement, a movement which would come to include working-class participation in the nineteenth century.

Throughout the years of the American War of Independence and the 1780s, Cartwright attempted to create a united reform movement among very divergent groups. He co-operated with the Westminster Committee under the whig Charles James Fox and the moderate association movement headed by the Revd Christopher Wyvill. In April 1780 he helped found the Society for Constitutional Information, an organization of like-minded reformers, many of whom were drawn from the rational dissenting community, dedicated to publishing political tracts aimed at educating fellow citizens on their lost ancient liberties. Cartwright also attempted to further reform by gaining election to the House of Commons in 1780 for Nottinghamshire. Unsuccessful, he later contested Boston, Lincolnshire, in 1806 and 1807, where he attracted only fifty-four votes, on account, it was thought, of his weakness as a speaker.

The Gordon riots in London in June 1780 frightened men of property and weakened even demands for moderate reform. However, Cartwright continued to labour in the cause. Following the disastrous military defeat in America the Rockingham whigs came to power, yet Cartwright lambasted their continued opposition to even moderate reform in *Give us our Rights* (1782). As the French Revolution further weakened domestic support for political change, he remained constant in his opinions. He continued to praise American republican government and advocated a policy of conciliation towards France, at war with Britain since 1793, in *The Commonwealth in Danger* (1795). His activities finally cost him promotion in the Nottinghamshire militia and eventually, owing to the hostility of the duke of Newcastle, his commission. Annoyed at this loss of his local county standing he wrote in 1792 one of his few angry works, *A Letter to the Duke of Newcastle*. In view of the government's growing paranoia over radical political activities, Cartwright was lucky to escape prosecution in 1794, but continued to seek reform through the rather exclusive Society of Friends of the People.

Never in robust health following his service in Canada, Cartwright maintained a busy personal schedule which would have taxed a much fitter man. After rising at 6 a.m. every morning he worked for over eleven hours a day. This regime was increased when he purchased, at public auction in 1781, the family estate at Marnham. His attempt to restore its productivity was seriously hampered by unwise investments. In 1788 he bought the Brothertoft estate in Lincolnshire, where his successful experiments in cultivating woad for dyeing helped restore his finances. Other campaigns attracted his attention. Between 1799 and 1809 he championed his brother Edmund's claim for parliamentary compensation for his invention of the power loom; a campaign which resulted in Edmund Cartwright being awarded £10,000 in 1809. Cheerful and open-handed, he devoted himself to an increasing number of causes. These included a national campaign in 1800 to build a monument to the exploits of the Royal Navy; he published in 1802 his own design for the monument in *The Trident*. Ever the patriot, when Britain was facing possible French invasion he took up a passionate advocacy of the utility of the pike and the creation of an Anglo-Saxon-type militia in his two-volume work of 1804–5, *England's aegis, or, The Military Energies of the Constitution*. Concerned with the liberty of oppressed people outside Britain, he published works supporting the Spanish opposition to Napoleon in 1808, opposing the international slave trade in 1812, and advocating the independence of Greece in 1821. All his campaigns, however, led him back to his lifelong passion, the reform of the British parliament. It was the continuing failure of the movement to achieve lasting results that promoted a more radical approach in Cartwright's tactics, an outlook which increasingly identified

him with metropolitan London politics and, later, growing working-class discontent in the north of England.

In 1800 Cartwright was sixty years old, and although he often complained of exhaustion, he launched himself into an even more active career. When Christopher Wyvill broke with him in 1801 over manhood suffrage, Cartwright allied himself with the wealthy whig Sir Francis Burdett. To support Burdett's election to parliament Cartwright helped create the Middlesex Freeholders Club in 1804. His closer interest in London politics prompted him to leave Lincolnshire for Enfield, Middlesex, and finally in 1819 to move to 37 Burton Crescent, London. His renewed campaign led to an association with Francis Place; with William Cobbett, whose *Political Register* often published Cartwright's letters; and with the printer Thomas Wooler, whose own journal *Black Dwarf* Cartwright helped to subsidize. In April 1812 he helped create the most successful of his organizations, the first Hampden Club in London, a broad-based united reform club; the movement itself became increasingly radical and had approximately 150 active clubs in the midlands and the north by 1817. Since 1783 Cartwright had become something of a political missionary, and after 1812 began a series of tours of the country to organize petitions in support of parliamentary reform. He claimed that his tour of 1813 alone produced 130,000 signatures from people demanding a tax-paying franchise and annual parliaments.

As a successful political agitator, Cartwright inevitably attracted the attention of the British government. First arrested in Huddersfield in January 1813, he escaped prosecution, yet it was clear to friends that his family connections would no longer automatically protect him. In an atmosphere of increasing political repression, however, Cartwright continued his crusade and, having finally realized that limited reform through parliamentary action alone would never come, returned to his old demands of full manhood suffrage first outlined in 1776. If he detached himself from the rising political violence which accompanied demands for reform following the Napoleonic wars, he was not averse to supporting extra-parliamentary activities as a means to achieve reform. Despite declining an invitation from John Knight, the founder of the first Hampden Club in Lancashire, to address a meeting at St Peter's Fields, Manchester, Cartwright did accept the crowd's thanks, at a monster open-air meeting of the Birmingham Union in 1819, an action which led to his indictment, together with Thomas Wooler and three others, for sedition. Cartwright again attracted attention on 16 August 1819 when, after escaping the carnage of the yeomanry charge at 'Peterloo', he was called to answer his charges. Finally, in Warwick on 29 May 1821, he was convicted of sedition at the age of eighty-one, and when Mr Justice Bayley refused his request for imprisonment, Cartwright paid his fine of £100, happily noting each gold coin was a good sovereign.

Last years, 1823–1824 Free to continue his activities, Cartwright completed a massive 400-page summary of his political legacy, *The English Constitution Produced and Illustrated*

(1823). If yet another restatement of lost Anglo-Saxon liberties, it praised the political equality of man as well as recognizing the continued success of the American republican experiment. In July 1824 the former president of the United States Thomas Jefferson wrote to Cartwright congratulating him on the work, and in a touching note suggested that, given both their advanced years, they would soon have an eternity to discuss good government. In ill health, Cartwright published his last work, *A Problem*, which used the United States as an example for a union of all nations.

John Cartwright died on 23 September 1824 at his house on Burton Crescent, later renamed Cartwright Gardens in his honour. He was buried in Finchley parish church on 30 September. Many London journals, such as the *Annual Register*, noted his death, and the October edition of *Black Dwarf* in 1824 devoted itself to his career. At a reformist meeting held in the Crown and Anchor tavern in June 1825, those present decided to raise a bronze statue to Cartwright. On 29 July 1831, with the whigs under Earl Grey finally back in power and their Great Reform Act winding its difficult and tortuous path through parliament, the statue to Major Cartwright was finally erected outside his London house. On 24 December 1834 Cartwright's wife, Anne, died and was buried next to her husband in Finchley. A full bibliography of John Cartwright's published works is given in Frances Cartwright's biography.

Cartwright's importance rests in his creation of a domestic reformist tradition which, owing little to European inspiration, rejected political violence and attempted to achieve change within the system itself. If his constant and repetitive discussions upon the restorative value of Anglo-Saxon liberties lost more supporters than they made converts, it should be remembered that Cartwright remained tolerant and humane throughout his life. If sometimes troublesome, Cartwright never generated hatred and fear among his contemporaries, and his organizational abilities were crucial in maintaining even a movement for reform. It should be remembered that during the 1817 march of the blanketeers his 'Hold fast by the laws' was adopted as their motto. Similarly when the working-class political reform movement of the Chartists demanded an extension of the franchise, it did so along the lines first suggested 'by the late Major John Cartwright'. A landed eighteenth-century gentleman, Cartwright transcended his background in the early decades of the nineteenth century and helped lay the foundation for the modern notion of political inclusion.

RORY T. CORNISH

Sources *DNB* · *The life and correspondence of Major Cartwright*, ed. F. D. Cartwright, 2 vols. (1826); repr. (1969) · J. Osborne, *John Cartwright* (1972) · R. E. Toohey, *Liberty and empire: British radical solutions to the American problem, 1774–1776* (1978) · G. S. Veitch, *The genesis of parliamentary reform*, new edn (1965) · I. R. Christie, *Wilkes, Wyvill and reform: the parliamentary reform movement in British politics, 1760–1785* (1962) · C. B. Cone, *The English Jacobins: reformers in late eighteenth-century England* (1968) · *The Times* (25 Sept 1824) · *Monthly Chronicle* (24 Sept 1824) · *Black Dwarf* (1 Oct 1824) · *Annual Register* (1824), 233 · N. C. Miller, 'John Cartwright and radical parliamentary reform, 1808–1819', *EngHR*, 83 (1968), 705–28 · N. C. Miller, 'Major John Cartwright and the forming of the Hampden Club', *HJ*, 17 (1974), 615–19 · C. Bonwick, *English radicals and the American Revolution* (1977)

Archives Duke U., Perkins L., letters · Harvard U., MSS | Beds. & Luton ARS, letters to Samuel Whitbread · BL, corresp. with J. C. Hobhouse, Add. MSS 36457–36458, 36460, *passim* · Bodl. Oxf., corresp. with William Wilberforce · Glos. RO, testamentary papers · Hants. RO, corresp. with Thomas Holt White · N. Yorks. CRO, corresp. with Christopher Wyvill · NRA, priv. coll., corresp. with fifth duke of Roxburghe · U. Durham L., corresp. with second Earl Grey

Likenesses stipple, pubd 1820, NPG · H. Meyer, stipple, pubd 1821 (aged eighty), NPG; version, pubd 1831, BM · G. Clarke, bronze statue, c.1831, Cartwright Gardens, London · A. Buck, engraving, NPG [*see illus.*] · G. S. Facing, stipple (aged forty-nine; after J. Hoppner), BM, NPG · print, BM; repro. in G. Smeeton, *The unique* (1823)

Wealth at death see will, 1824, Cartwright, *Life and correspondence*, 2.288

Cartwright, John (*d.* 1811), painter, of whose parents nothing is known, was one of the fifty members of the Free Society of Artists who in 1763 signed the deed of enrolment of that society in the court of king's bench, although he exhibited only in 1767 while lodging at Clare Market, London. About 1770 he went to Rome to pursue his artistic studies, where he was encouraged and patronized by the third duke of Dorset, who commissioned two 'views' from him about 1774. However, Father John Thorpe considered that Cartwright showed 'more inclination than genius' and feared he would 'fall down into a Landscape painter' (Ingamells, 188). While in Rome Cartwright became acquainted with Henry Fuseli, who corrected his drawings. The Kunsthaus Zürich owns a sketchbook (the 'Roman sketchbook') that once belonged to Cartwright but was retained and used by Fuseli. About forty of the one hundred plus drawings it contains are by Cartwright, of which about half are copies after antique vase paintings and pots illustrated in d'Hancarville's *Antiquités étrusques, grecques et romaines* (1766). A number of these sketches have been marked up by Fuseli with appended studies of arms and legs and so on, as hints to Cartwright. By 1779 Cartwright was back in England and settled at 100 St Martin's Lane, London, where he remained until about 1793. When Fuseli returned to London in 1779 he shared rooms with Cartwright until the end of June 1788. Between 1778 and 1808 Cartwright exhibited twenty-one paintings at the Royal Academy: eleven portraits, seven landscapes, and three history paintings. One of Cartwright's paintings, *Match-Girls*, was engraved, but none of his exhibited works has been traced. According to Lionel Cust, Cartwright's historical pictures strongly show Fuseli's influence, which was, however, unsuited to an artist of Cartwright's calibre. Cartwright died on 20 February 1811 after a short illness. His will gives his last residence as Christopher Street, Hatton Garden, London. He was survived by his wife, Anne, and his brother Charles. Cartwright left a large estate of £23,000.

D. H. WEINGLASS

Sources J. Ingamells, ed., *A dictionary of British and Irish travellers in Italy, 1701–1800* (1997), 188 · M. Fischer, *Das römische Skizzenbuch von Johann Heinrich Füssli, 1741–1825* (1942) · G. Schiff, *Johann Heinrich*

Füssli, 1741–1825, 2 vols. (1973), 1.657–8n. • *The collected English letters of Henry Fuseli*, ed. D. H. Weinglass (1982) • J. Knowles, *The life and writings of Henry Fuseli*, 1 (1831), 57–8 • J. Pye, *Patronage of British art: an historical sketch* (1845), 285–6 • Graves, *RA exhibitors*, 2 (1905), 9 • Graves, *Soc. Artists* • *GM*, 1st ser., 81/1 (1811), 296 • *The Times* (21 Feb 1811), 3 • *Art Prices Current* (1908–9), 64, no. 115 • Thieme & Becker, *Allgemeines Lexikon* • G. Meissner, ed., *Allgemeines Künstlerlexikon: die bildenden Künstler aller Zeiten und Völker*, [new edn, 34 vols.] (Leipzig and Munich, 1983–) • M. H. Grant, *A dictionary of British landscape painters, from the 16th century to the early 20th century* (1952) • will, PRO, PROB 6/187, fol. 369

Wealth at death £23,000: will, PRO, PROB 6/187, fol. 369

Cartwright, Joseph (*c*.1789–1829), marine painter, whose early life is obscure, is first recorded while working for the British services in an administrative capacity. After the Ionian Islands had come under British protection in 1815, he served in Corfu as paymaster-general to the British forces in the region. While there he produced watercolours of local landscapes and maritime scenes, some of which formed the basis for the twelve coloured aquatint plates in his *Views in the Ionian Islands*, published in 1821. He had returned to England by the early 1820s and thenceforward pursued a career as an artist, exhibiting maritime scenes and pictures of naval engagements at the Royal Academy, the British Institution, and the Society of British Artists' galleries in Suffolk Street from 1823 to 1829. Scenes with Italian titles exhibited in 1827 and 1828 may indicate a visit to Italy at that time. He was elected a member of the Society of British Artists in 1826 and in 1828, the year before his death, was appointed marine painter in ordinary to the duke of Clarence, later William IV.

A number of Cartwright's watercolours and pencil sketches survive in the collections of the British Museum, the Victoria and Albert Museum, and the Peabody Essex Museum, Salem, Massachusetts. A large canvas showing the burning of the French flagship *L'Orient* at the Battle of the Nile, exhibited with the Society of British Artists in 1826, Cartwright's election year, is in the Royal Collection. A pair of smaller paintings, entitled *The Battle of Trafalgar* and *The Battle of the Nile*, were exhibited at the British Institution in 1825. Cartwright died unmarried at his home, 39 Charing Cross, St Martin-in-the-Fields, London, on 16 January 1829. His estate, amounting to £300, was left to his brother William, then residing in the Ionian Islands.

PAUL A. COX

Sources Redgrave, *Artists* • *Annual Register* (1830) • J. Cartwright, *Views in the Ionian Islands* (1821) • Graves, *RA exhibitors* • Graves, *Brit. Inst.* • J. Johnson, ed., *Works exhibited at the Royal Society of British Artists, 1824–1893, and the New English Art Club, 1888–1917*, 2 vols. (1975) • O. Millar, *The later Georgian pictures in the collection of her majesty the queen*, 2 vols. (1969) • will, PRO, PROB 6/205, fol. 192*r*

Wealth at death £300: will, PRO, PROB 6/205, fol. 192*r*

Cartwright [*married name* Ady], **Julia Mary** (1851–1924), art historian and biographer, was born at the family home, Edgcote House, Edgcote, Northamptonshire, on 7 November 1851, one of the ten children of Richard Aubrey Cartwright and his wife, Mary Fremantle (*d*. 1885). She was educated privately at home; the Cartwright family were

Julia Mary Cartwright (1851–1924), by James Russell & Sons, pubd 1902

highly cultured and learned languages, music, and dancing as well as attending concerts and lectures in London, Oxford, and Leamington Spa. Julia had nine siblings but was closest to her younger brother Chauncy, who later joined the Foreign Office and helped her career through his diplomatic contacts. Her uncle William Cornwallis Cartwright was an art collector and a fervent supporter of the Italian *Risorgimento*: both his passions influenced his niece, who had the run of his library and gallery at Aynhoe. In 1868 the family toured France, Austria, and Italy: Julia kept a journal of the voyage. Soon after, she 'came out', by which time her literary ambitions were alarming her parents.

In 1871 Julia Cartwright published a piece in *Aunt Judy's Magazine*; shortly afterwards she became a regular contributor to C. M. Yonge's *Monthly Packet*, another publication for young people, to which she was invited to contribute a series, 'The lives of the saints'. To the concern of her mother, who felt that literary pursuits distracted her from looking for a husband, Julia Cartwright became increasingly interested in Renaissance Italy and its culture, reading the works of Anna Jameson, John Ruskin, Charles Eastlake, Walter Pater, J. A. Crowe, and Giovanni Battista Cavalcaselle, as well as the poetry of Robert Browning. In 1873 she submitted an article on Giotto to *Macmillan's Magazine*: it was her first fully referenced and researched piece of work. It was rejected, but eventually appeared in the *New Quarterly* in 1877. She retained an interest in many other fields, including contemporary art: an early fondness for Maclise, Turner, and Landseer gave way to an appreciation of Whistler.

In the 1870s Julia Cartwright also wrote novels for the SPCK—the first of which was *Madelaine* (1872)—and visited Italy three times, becoming increasingly interested in matters of patronage and the life of the religious reformer Savonarola. In 1877 she sent a review of Margaret Oliphant's *Makers of Florence* (1876) to *The Academy*, an arts journal edited by Charles Appleton, who became a supportive critic of her work. In the late 1870s and early 1880s she became involved in artistic and literary circles in London; she met Oscar Browning and the architect T. P. Jackson and became a good friend of Lady Knightley, with whom she visited the British Museum print room to view drawings by Botticelli. She visited the studios of leading artists such as Watts and Burne-Jones, and attended exhibitions at the Grosvenor Gallery.

Despite her growing commitments, by the late 1870s Julia Cartwright was becoming lonely, as many of her female friends married. In 1878, however, (William) Henry Ady (d. 1915), the son of William Ady, the rector of Little Baddow in Essex, became rector of Edgcote: he had high-church sympathies, like Julia herself, and had been a friend of her beloved uncle Stephen Fremantle (d. 1874). Julia married him on 24 August 1880 at Edgcote, and he proved to be a supportive husband who encouraged her to continue her work. Their only daughter, Cecilia Mary *Ady, was born in November 1881. Julia successfully funded her daughter's education through her literary earnings and Cecilia later became a tutor in Renaissance history at St Hugh's College, Oxford. In 1881 Julia Ady published her first art book, *Mantegna and Francia*; it was the first of a series of publications on Mantegna in the later nineteenth century. She was becoming a significant figure in the expanding world of art criticism, writing for journals such as *Portfolio*, the *Magazine of Art*, and (later) the *Art Journal*. In 1882 her earnings from her publications totalled £139.

In the 1880s and 1890s Julia Ady combined her duties as a vicar's wife (first at Edgcote and later at Charing, Kent) with visits to London and her writing career, producing a wide range of articles on the Renaissance art world. She also became increasingly interested in modern art, particularly the work of landscapists and aesthetic and symbolist painters. She was impressed with the work of Rossetti, Burne-Jones (the subject of a full-length monograph in 1894), and Watts (on whose work she published a monograph in 1896). She was also interested in the work of the Italian landscapist Giovanni Costa (on whom she wrote an article for the *Magazine of Art*), and French artists including Millet, Bastien-Lepage, and Puvis de Chavannes (on all of whom she eventually wrote in the 1890s).

During the 1880s and 1890s Julia Ady read most of the major new works of art criticism, ranging from Pater's impressionistic essays on the Renaissance to the more scholarly publications of Giovanni Morelli. She became firm friends with Vernon Lee, an expert on eighteenth-century Italian culture, and in 1894 she met the critic Bernard Berenson. Both became friendly critics of her work as she developed from an amateur writer into a professional art historian. The impact of new art-critical methods was apparent in three works published on Raphael in 1905. Similarly, her monograph on Sandro Botticelli (1903; rev. edn. 1904) showed a full awareness of both Berenson's and Herbert Horne's work on this artist.

In 1893 Julia Cartwright published *Sacharissa*, a biography of Dorothy Sidney, Edmund Waller's muse; it was followed in 1894 by *Madame*, a biography of Charles II's sister Henriette, duchess of Orléans. Both were based on extensive archival research, and represented an important new direction in her work: biographies of women who had played a role in the cultural politics of their age. In 1899 she published *Beatrice D'Este*, an appetizer for her comprehensive biography *Isabella D'Este* (1903), on the Renaissance art patron. This was an extensively researched work, for which she had been preparing for some fifteen years. While presenting a sanitized portrait of Isabella as an ideal Victorian domestic heroine, it also revealed her extensive cultural activities and (more tangentially) her significant role in Renaissance politics. Unfortunately, *Isabella* led to a publishing controversy: two Italian scholars, Alessandro Luzio and Rodolpho Renier, who had long been working on the life of the marchioness and had published groups of her letters upon which Julia Cartwright had drawn (with acknowledgement) charged her with a copyright violation. A settlement was reached, but not without considerable distress to Cartwright.

Working on the Este sisters provided Julia Cartwright with much of the material for her next publication, a biography of Baldassare Castiglione, published in 1908. Extensively researched (she spent long hours in the British Museum and visited Italian libraries in 1904 and 1906), it remains the best biography in English of *The Courtier*'s author, despite her idealization of the poet-courtier: Cartwright was determined to redress the British perception of the Italian Renaissance as an age of treachery, Machiavellian politics, and debauchery.

Castiglione was Cartwright's last major work. In 1914 she published *The Italian Gardens of the Renaissance and other Studies*, a compilation of articles which had been previously published in *Nineteenth Century*. She also edited the journals of Lady Knightley (1915) and wrote a biography of Christina of Denmark (1913), the subject of a full-length portrait by Holbein. It was not a success: hagiographical biographies were losing their appeal even before Lytton Strachey's reinvention of the genre. She travelled with her daughter (who, to her horror, declared her intention of remaining single) and met Cecilia's Oxford friends, including the art historian Joan Evans. This exposure to independently minded women of learning—as well as her admiration for Renaissance women such as Isabella—may well have influenced her changing view on women's suffrage, as she now became a cautious supporter of votes for women.

In 1915, when her husband died, Julia Cartwright moved

to Oxford to be closer to her daughter. During the First World War she became involved in the foundation of the Italian League, which was intended to further Anglo-Italian understanding. Her ability to appreciate modern art was by now declining: she had been horrified by the post-impressionist exhibition of 1912. In 1919 she ceased to keep a diary, and little is known of her last years. She died at her Oxford home, 40 St Margaret's Road, on 28 April 1924. Her daughter, Cecilia, was the sole beneficiary of her will.

Julia Cartwright's career reflects the transition of the historical disciplines from the amateur and antiquarian enthusiasms of the nineteenth century to the more academic and professional approaches of the early twentieth century. As a historian of women she helped to rediscover figures such as Isabella D'Este, who had played significant roles as the inspiration, patrons, and mediators of cultural production. As a cultural historian she contributed to developing modern Renaissance studies through her research into the works, lives, and interactions of leading figures. As John Hale memorably put it, 'she stands for that pre-academic relish for Renaissance Italy which placed, as it were, an archival filling within the truffles of near-adoration' (*Bright Remembrance*, x). But although she was essentially a late Victorian in her perspective on culture and cultural history, she responded to new art-critical methods and new research in her field, a field in which her own professionally trained daughter was to succeed her.   ROSEMARY MITCHELL

Sources A. Emanuel, 'Julia Cartwright 1851–1924: art critic and historian of Renaissance Italy', PhD diss., UCL, 1985 · *A bright remembrance: the diaries of Julia Cartwright*, ed. A. Emanuel (1989) · H. Fraser, 'Victorian women on Renaissance women', unpublished article, 2000 · R. A. Mitchell, '"Absolutely without knowledge and instinct of painting": women art historians and the gendering of Victorian art historians', unpublished paper, 2000–01 · will · *WWW* · b. cert. · d. cert.
Archives John Murray, London, archives, letters · Northants. RO, diaries
Likenesses J. Russell & Sons, photograph, NPG; repro. in L. Wilson, *The imperial gallery of portraiture* (1902), 176 [*see illus.*]
Wealth at death £21,612 10*s*. 7*d*.: probate, 16 June 1924, *CGPLA Eng. & Wales*

Cartwright, Dame Mary Lucy (1900–1998), mathematician, was born on 17 December 1900 at Church Cottage, Aynho, Northamptonshire, third child of William Digby Cartwright and his wife, Lucy Harriette Maud, *née* Bury. Her father acted as curate of Aynho for his incapacitated uncle, becoming rector in 1906. Her two older brothers were killed in the First World War leaving a younger sister, Jane, and brother, William Frederick Cartwright. It was out of the question for the rector's daughter to attend the village school, so at eleven Mary was sent first to Leamington high school and later to the Godolphin School, Salisbury. She thought of history as her best subject, but in her last year a gifted self-taught teacher, Miss Hancock, encouraged her into mathematics. She went up to St Hugh's College, Oxford, in 1919, at which time there were only some five women studying mathematics in the whole university. Her patchy schooling and the difficulty

Dame Mary Lucy Cartwright (1900–1998), by Sir Stanley Spencer, 1958

of getting into post-war lectures led to a second class in honour moderations. However, inspired by G. H. Hardy's famous extra-curricular classes, she became the first woman to last the course, being awarded a first-class degree in 1923.

Not wanting to impose further on her family for finance, Cartwright taught first at the Alice Ottley School, Worcester (1923–4), and then at Wycombe Abbey School, Buckinghamshire (1924–7). Dissatisfied with her prospects, she returned to Oxford in 1928 to read for a DPhil under Hardy, receiving her doctorate for a thesis on zeros of integral functions of special types in 1930; here she first met J. E. Littlewood, who was her external DPhil examiner.

Following Hardy's move to Cambridge, in 1930 Cartwright went to Girton as a Yarrow research fellow, rapidly becoming fellow and director of studies in mathematics in 1934; she held these positions until 1949. She became a university lecturer in 1935 and then reader in the theory of functions from 1959 until her retirement in 1968. The move to Cambridge heralded a period of great mathematical activity. Her work came strongly under the influence of Littlewood, who with Hardy dominated British pure mathematics of the period. Her first important result, in complex function theory, was a sharp estimate for the maximum modulus of analytic functions p-valent in the unit disc, a result still applied in signal processing. In a long series of papers over the next ten years, Cartwright continued to explore the subtleties of the theory of complex (especially integral or entire) functions; particularly their asymptotic behaviour. The essence of this work was contained in her one book, *Integral Functions* (1956).

In 1938 the Radio Research Board of the Department of Scientific and Industrial Research appealed to the London Mathematical Society for help with certain equations occurring in radio work. Cartwright drew the memorandum to Littlewood's attention. Together they began a detailed investigation of a deceptively simple-looking non-linear second order differential equation introduced by the Dutch physicist Van der Pol in 1920 to describe the oscillation of radio waves, now a textbook example. Despite their lack of expertise on this subject, Cartwright and Littlewood soon found a rich variety of behaviour, some of it very bizarre. They found ranges of the parameter values with an infinite number of unstable periodic solutions and a highly complicated but stable region of non-periodic behaviour. Fifteen years later, this work inspired S. Smale to develop the horseshoe map, the driving mechanism of the mathematical theory of chaos, of which Cartwright and Littlewood's fine structures were in fact typical manifestations.

Cartwright continued her work on differential equations and in 1949 held consultancies on US Navy mathematical research projects at Stanford and Princeton. In 1950 she resumed a collaboration with Sir Edward Collingwood, begun before the war, and culminating in the Collingwood–Cartwright theory of cluster sets.

Meanwhile Cartwright was becoming more deeply involved in college life. From 1940 to 1944 she was commandant, Girton College Red Cross detachment, and she took on an increasing load of teaching. In 1948 she was pre-elected mistress of Girton, which office she held from 1949 until 1968, the longest tenure in the college's history. Here began a second distinguished career. Women had been admitted to full membership of the university in 1948 and Cartwright provided clear-headed yet unassuming leadership at a time of rapid change, skilfully steering the college to assume quietly its proper role in the routine running of the university. Shrewd and immensely hard-working, she gave long service on many committees including the Cambridge University women's appointments board and the education syndicate. From 1961 she was on the council of senate. She was president of the Cambridge Association of University Women from 1957 to 1960. Despite this heavy load she continued her lecturing and research, seemingly never harassed, always finding time for students' problems, and ably supervising a number of doctoral students.

In all, Cartwright wrote over ninety articles published in mathematical journals, making important contributions to the theory of functions and differential equations. Her work with Littlewood was among the first to recognize the potential power of combining topological and analytical methods to study differential equations. Despite the technicality of most of her mathematical writing, she was also able to inspire a general audience, as demonstrated in her short monograph *The Mathematical Mind* (1955).

Cartwright inspired generations of young women. Her somewhat timid yet forbidding appearance, combined with her very considerable intellectual reputation, belied the warmth and sympathy beneath. In human affairs as in mathematics she had a gift for going straight to the heart of the matter. She was exceptionally well-informed on many subjects, among them painting and music. She had a wry sense of humour.

Cartwright was elected to the Royal Society in 1947, the first woman mathematician to be accorded this honour, and was later the first woman to serve on its council. She was awarded a Cambridge ScD in 1949. She felt strongly about mathematical education, taking a keen interest in the Mathematical Association and serving as its president from 1951 to 1952. In 1956 she was a member of a Royal Society delegation that visited the Soviet Union as guests of the Academy of Sciences. A member of the London Mathematical Society from 1928, she held office at various times and was president from 1961 to 1963. She received awards, medals, and honorary degrees from universities and learned societies in Britain and several foreign countries. Her contributions led to the award of the Royal Society's Sylvester medal in 1964, the London Mathematical Society's De Morgan medal in 1968, and she was created DBE in 1969.

Cartwright was resident in Girton from 1930 to 1968, retiring to live in a modest flat nearby. She was life fellow and emeritus reader at Girton from 1968 until her death. She enjoyed travelling and was visiting professor at Brown University (1968–9), then at Claremont Graduate School, California (1969–70); she also visited Case Western Reserve, the Polish Academy of Sciences, and the University of Wales (1970–71). She continued writing research papers until well after her retirement and was among the editors of Hardy's collected papers. In her last years she moved to Midfield Lodge Nursing Home, Cambridge Road, Oakington, where she died peacefully on 3 April 1998. She never married.   C. M. SERIES

Sources R. Williams, biographical notes and bibliography, 1994, Girton Cam. · *The Times* (7 April 1998) · *The Independent* (9 April 1998) · *The Guardian* (9 April 1998) · S. L. McMurran and J. J. Tattersall, 'The mathematical collaboration of M. L. Cartwright and J. E. Littlewood', *The American Mathematical Monthly*, 103/10 (1996), 833–45 · M. L. Cartwright, 'Non-linear vibrations: a chapter in mathematical history', *The Mathematical Gazette*, 36 (1952), 81–8 · private information (2004) · M. Cartwright, 'Moments in a girl's life', *Institute of Mathematics and its Applications*, 25 (1989) · *WWW* · b. cert. · d. cert.

Archives Girton Cam. | FILM 'Our Brilliant Careers', ZKK production for Channel 4 (19 Aug 1996), television documentary | SOUND Girton Cam., taped interview (27 Feb 1989)

Likenesses photographs, 1950–70, Girton Cam. · S. Spencer, oils, 1958, Girton Cam. [*see illus.*]

Wealth at death £594,321: probate, 15 Sept 1998, *CGPLA Eng. & Wales*

Cartwright, Sir Richard (1835–1912), businessman and politician in Canada, born in Kingston, Upper Canada, on 4 December 1835, was the son of the Revd Robert David Cartwright (*d.* 1843) and his wife, Harriet Dobbs (1808–1887). His paternal grandfather, Richard Cartwright (1759–1815), the founder of the Canadian family, was a very wealthy man and one of the Conservative leaders of early Upper Canada.

Cartwright received his secondary education in Kingston. From 1851 to 1856 he attended Trinity College, Dublin, but took no degree. A lifelong Anglican, he was married in 1859 to Frances, the daughter of Colonel Alexander Lawe of Cork. After his return to Canada he studied law, but he was never admitted to the bar. Instead of following a legal career Cartwright became a businessman and an investor with numerous interests. He was able to use the ample fortune that he inherited to acquire a lot of property in the town of Napanee to the west of Kingston and throughout Lennox and Addington county, including the valuable water rights on the Napanee River. He also served as president of the Commercial Bank, which folded in 1867: Cartwright's biographer W. R. Graham largely exonerates him from personal blame. He was active in lumbering, working on behalf of various firms.

A director of the Bedford Navigation Company, Cartwright was instrumental in the formation of a company to mine iron and plumbago. He was also a shareholder of the Kingston and Sherbrooke Gold Mining Company (Nova Scotia) and president of the Canada Gold Mining Company. He held an interest in the Ontario Concentrated Tannin Company, he was a director of the Canada Life Assurance Company and president of the Frontenac Loan and Investment Society, and he was involved with the Trusts Corporation of Ontario, the Bank of Montreal, and the Equitable Life Insurance Company. Like many members of Kingston's élite he was active in the promotion of the Kingston and Pembroke Railway, of which he was a director. And his routine business activities in Kingston went on: overseeing office rentals, purchasing land, selling land, dealing with mortgages, trading shares, serving on boards of directors, and managing his substantial properties. During the 1880s he acquired much land in Manitoba, where as a result a township was renamed Cartwright. Between 1867 and 1873 his traceable investments totalled C$41,000, a substantial sum during the confederation era.

Without the benefit of a career in municipal politics, Cartwright contested and won the parliamentary seat of Lennox and Addington riding in 1863. While he did not live in the riding, he owned much of the land and had numerous business connections there; he spent a minimum of C$5596.08 to secure his return. Cartwright held Lennox (Addington was turned into a separate seat in 1867) until he was defeated in 1878. He was then elected for Centre Huron, which he lost in 1882. South Huron provided an opening for him in 1883, and in 1887 he won South Oxford, which he held until his appointment to the senate in 1904. He remained in the senate until his death in 1912.

Sir Richard Cartwright (1835–1912), by unknown photographer, 1881

Initially Cartwright sat as a Conservative and was on cordial terms with the prime minister, Sir John A. Macdonald. That changed in 1869 because of Cartwright's strong opposition to the appointment of Sir Francis Hincks as minister of finance. Thereafter he adopted a neutral stance for a while: what precipitated his complete break with the Conservative Party was the Pacific scandal of 1872–3, which ultimately brought down Macdonald's government. During 1873 Cartwright emerged as a key opposition figure, and when the Liberal Party formed a government late that year he became minister of finance. He held the portfolio until the government fell in 1878, and was a competent if not a distinguished minister. As an ardent advocate of free trade between Canada and the United States he was not able to counter the Conservatives' increasingly popular policy of higher tariffs, known as the national policy. The Conservatives used that policy to win the election of 1878, and Cartwright was forced into opposition.

During the 1880s Cartwright was prominent in opposition and emerged as the leader of the Ontario wing of the federal Liberal Party. He continued to espouse a form of free trade between Canada and the United States, which became the main plank in the Liberals' platform at the general election of 1891. They lost, and, within the Liberal Party, Cartwright's star was on the wane. None the less, when the Liberals won the general election of 1896 the prime minister, Sir Wilfrid Laurier, found a cabinet place for him. He was made minister of commerce, a portfolio he held until 1911, though this was a relatively unimportant post and his tenure was uneventful.

In 1909 Cartwright became government leader in the senate. He was made a KCMG in 1879 and a GCMG in 1897. He died on 24 September 1912 at his home, 191 King Street East, Kingston, Ontario, and was buried at Cataraqui cemetery, near Kingston.   DONALD SWAINSON

Sources W. R. Graham, 'Sir Richard Cartwright and the liberal party, 1863–1896', PhD diss., University of Toronto, 1950 · J. A. Eadie, 'Politics in Lennox and Addington county, 1854–1867', MA diss., Queen's University, 1967 · R. Cartwright, *Reminiscences* (1912) · D. Swainson, 'Richard Cartwright joins the liberal party', *Queen's Quarterly* (1968) · House of Commons, *Debates*: Canada · *Men* *and women of the time* (1899) • H. J. Morgan, ed., *The Canadian parliamentary companion*, 11 vols. (1862–76) • J. Pope, *Sir John A. Macdonald vindicated* (1912) • J. Pope, *Memoirs of the Right Honourable Sir John Alexander Macdonald*, 2 vols. (1912) • M. K. Christie, 'Sir Alexander Campbell', MA diss., University of Toronto, 1950 • D. G. Creighton, *John A. Macdonald*, 2 vols. (Toronto, 1952–5) • P. G. Cornell, *The alignment of political groups in Canada, 1841–1867* (Toronto, 1962) • D. C. Macdonald, *Honourable Richard Cartwright, 1759–1815* (1961) • W. A. McKay and W. S. Wallace, eds., *The Macmillan dictionary of Canadian biography*, 4th edn (1978) • *DCB*, vol. 14

Archives Public Archives of Ontario, Toronto • Queen's University, Kingston, Ontario | NA Canada, Brown MSS • NA Canada, Macdonald MSS • Public Archives of Ontario, Toronto, Blake MSS • Public Archives of Ontario, Toronto, Campbell MSS

Likenesses photograph, 1881, NA Canada [*see illus.*] • photograph, repro. in Cartwright, *Reminiscences*

Cartwright, Samuel (1789–1864), dentist, was born at Northampton and originally trained there as an ivory turner. He went to London at an early age, wholly dependent upon himself for support, and became employed as a mechanical assistant to Charles Dumergue of Piccadilly, dentist to George IV, where he quickly demonstrated the worth of his skills as an ivory turner in the construction of dentures. During this period of service he found time regularly to attend anatomical and surgical lectures.

In 1811 Cartwright started in practice on his own account at 32 Old Burlington Street, London, and he soon acquired an excellent reputation and an extensive practice. He was as remarkable for the accuracy and speed of his judgement as he was for his marvellous dexterity in all operations. During the greater part of his career he saw forty to fifty patients every day, for months on end, working constantly from seven o'clock in the morning until the same hour in the evening, and yet treating every case without the slightest appearance of hurry or fatigue. He did much to improve and elevate his profession, and is said to have had an income of more than £10,000 for some years. He was the obvious choice to become the first president of the Odontological Society, and he also became dentist-in-ordinary to George IV.

Cartwright became a member of the Royal College of Surgeons and was one of the signatories of a letter to the college in 1843 which requested that no one should be allowed to practise dentistry without having undergone examination by the college. He also called for the establishment of a dental fellowship of the college; there is no record of the college's reply. Cartwright became a fellow of the Linnean Society on 19 November 1833, FRS on 11 February 1841, and a fellow of the Geological Society; but he never found time to make any contributions to the *Proceedings* of these institutions. His pleasing manners, liberal hospitality, and professional fame won him the friendship of many of those distinguished in science, literature, and art in his day. He continued in practice at Old Burlington Street until 1857, when he retired. In the following year he suffered an apoplectic seizure which resulted in palsy, from which he suffered for the rest of his life. He died at his residence, Nizell's House, near Tonbridge, Kent, on 11 June 1864.

G. C. BOASE, *rev.* PATRICK WALLIS

Sources *GM*, 3rd ser., 17 (1864) • *British Journal of Dental Science*, 7 (1864), 287 • L. Lindsay, 'Personalities of the past: IX', *British Dental Journal*, 98 (1955), 259 • d. cert. • Boase, *Mod. Eng. biog.* • *The record of the Royal Society of London*, 4th edn (1940) • *London Medical Directory* (1845) • Z. Cope, *The Royal College of Surgeons of England: a history* (1959)

Likenesses B. Pistrucci, marble bust, NPG • oils, British Medical Association, London

Wealth at death under £30,000: probate, 18 Aug 1864, *CGPLA Eng. & Wales*

Cartwright, Thomas (1534/5–1603), theologian and religious controversialist, was probably born at Royston in Hertfordshire. His parents may have been John and Agnes Cartwright. He later inherited a farm at Whaddon, over the Cambridgeshire border, which he sold, using the proceeds to purchase a manor at Saxmundham in Suffolk.

Career and controversy at Cambridge At the tender age of twelve Cartwright matriculated as a sizar at Clare College, Cambridge, in 1547. In 1550 he became a scholar of St John's College, a crucible of 'good letters' and advanced protestantism. It was once thought that Cartwright left Cambridge soon after Mary's accession, but in fact he proceeded BA in 1554, in the same batch of graduands as his future antagonist John Whitgift. It was probably no earlier than 1556 that Cartwright left the Marian university to earn his living as clerk to a counsellor-at-law, an episode undocumented and reported only by his seventeenth-century biographer, Samuel Clarke. The implication is that at this point this future arch-Calvinist belonged to the ranks of those trimmers whom Calvin called Nicodemites. In 1559 Cartwright returned to St John's and in April 1560 was admitted to a fellowship. In June he commenced MA, and in 1562 became a fellow of Trinity.

The royal visit to Cambridge in 1564 gave rise to a somewhat mythical account of what it was that made Cartwright a disaffected and radical critic of the ecclesiastical *status quo*. Queen Elizabeth was said to have been displeased by Cartwright's performance in a public disputation, a rebuff that left him embittered. It is true that Cartwright did take the lead in the philosophy act, confuting the thesis that 'Monarchia est optimus status Reipublicae' ('Monarchy is the best form of body politic'). It is of some interest that the future advocate of presbyterianism, an ecclesiastical form of republicanism, should have presented Aristotelian arguments against government by a single person in the presence of the queen, but this was role-playing in a formal academic exercise, and there is no evidence that Elizabeth disapproved or that the affair damaged Cartwright's career prospects.

In the following year Cambridge began to be racked with controversy over 'apparel', the surplice, square cap, and other ceremonial symbols of conformity to the religion of the established church. There were disturbances in St John's College, where the majority of fellows and scholars appeared in chapel without surplices. But before these early manifestations of what would soon be called puritanism spread to Trinity, Cartwright had again withdrawn from Cambridge, to become domestic chaplain to Adam Loftus, archbishop of Armagh. In spite of the war in the north against Shane O'Neill (in the course of which

Loftus's cathedral was burnt to the ground), Ireland was a more friendly environment for a puritan than England. Some years later Loftus wrote, disingenuously, 'I am utterly ignorant what the terme and accusation of a puritane meaneth' (Scott Pearson, 20). By 1567 Cartwright had returned to Cambridge, where he took the degree of BTh on 31 May. Loftus had been appointed to Dublin, and he wrote to Cecil urging that Cartwright be made his successor in Armagh. But even in Tudor Ireland archbishops were not often appointed at the age of thirty-two, and Cartwright stayed in Cambridge.

It was now that Cartwright began to earn his formidable reputation as a preacher. His early biographer Clarke tells of a return visit to Cambridge in the 1580s, when 'grave men ran like boys in the streets to get places in the Church' (Scott Pearson, 23–4). In 1570 his skills were deployed to devastating effect from the dignity of the Lady Margaret chair, to which Cartwright was elected in the reshuffle that followed Whitgift's resignation of the regius chair. Cartwright's inaugural lectures were on the early chapters of the Acts of the Apostles, an exegesis of the constitution of the primitive church which he declared to be normative for all time, and by which the hierarchical, episcopal Church of England stood utterly condemned. This was presbyterianism *avant la lettre*. Cartwright's novel doctrines rapidly attracted a large following in the university, especially among the younger scholars who, under the existing statutes, were in charge of its affairs as regent masters.

The first necessity in the perception of some of the seniors was to change the statutes, and then to use the reformed statutes to get rid of Cartwright, who at this very moment was a candidate for the degree of DTh. The statutes of 1570, which were to remain in force until 1853, were devised by Whitgift, master of Trinity, and his older patron, Andrew Perne, master of Peterhouse, and they converted the university into a kind of Venetian oligarchy, with power vested in the heads of houses. Statute 45 legislated against public criticism of the established religion, and its first use was to deprive Cartwright of his chair. Opposition to the statutes was now inextricably confused with support for the martyred Cartwright. In May 1572 the 164 protesters included, surprisingly, the future Archbishop Richard Bancroft. But the conservative reformers stood their ground, backed by Lord Burghley, the chancellor, and Cartwright had no friends among the older, more responsible generation. Even the profoundly evangelical and moderate Archbishop Edmund Grindal denounced him as a hothead who should never again be allowed to lecture in the university.

The Admonition controversy Cartwright remained a fellow of Trinity, but no later than June 1571 he was at Geneva, teaching in the academy as the colleague of Calvin's successor, Theodore Beza. In the spring of 1572 Cartwright responded to a clamour for his return by coming back yet again to Cambridge, after a brief sojourn in Rouen. In September Whitgift deprived him of his fellowship on the technicality that he was in breach of the college statutes

by not proceeding to the priesthood. For the next year Cartwright moved from one private house to another, earning his keep by teaching the children of these no doubt great and good families, who included two prosperous householders in Cheapside, Richard Martin the goldsmith, and, a lifelong friend, Michael Hicks, secretary to the Cecils.

In June 1572 Cartwright's presbyterianism acquired populist associations with the publication by the young London preachers John Field and Thomas Wilcox of *An Admonition to the Parliament*, an attack on the very foundations of the Elizabethan church so extreme as to make it a seditious libel; the work was presently denounced by royal proclamation and its authors imprisoned in Newgate. The first generation of Elizabethan puritanism on the whole disapproved of the *Admonition*. That staunch protestant the London lawyer and 'parliament man' Thomas Norton called the book fond, unreasonable, and unseasonable, and in a letter to Whitgift begged him not to prolong a nine-day wonder by responding to it.

But respond Whitgift did, in his *Answere to a Certan Libel Intituled, 'An Admonition'* (1572), to which Cartwright published, from a secret press, a *Replye* (April 1573). The same press had already produced the *Second Admonition*, prescribing in more detail than the first the essentials of presbyterianism, a book often misattributed to Cartwright. By the time Whitgift had published *The Defense of the Aunswere to the 'Admonition', Against the 'Replie'* (1574), and Cartwright *The Second Replie* (1575), and even *The Rest of the Second Replie* (1577), the *Admonition* controversy had generated many hundreds of pages in which the fatal fault-line in the English church was explored in exhaustive detail. The nub of the controversy was the question of scripture, whether in all circumstances and conditions it was binding, a matter later handled on broader, more philosophical grounds in Richard Hooker's *Of the Lawes of Ecclesiasticall Politie*.

Heidelberg and Antwerp Cartwright's later salvoes against Whitgift were printed overseas, for in late 1573 the high commission had issued a warrant for his arrest and he had gone back into exile, choosing to settle in the Rhenish palatinate, under the elector Frederick III a Calvinist principality. On 25 January 1574 he matriculated as a student at the University of Heidelberg, which counted among its luminaries the leading reformers of the second and third generations, those authors of confessionalization Olevian, Tremellius, Zanchius, Ursinus, and Junius. It was in Heidelberg that he published *The Second Replie*, and on 2 February 1574 dated a preface to a learned presbyterian manifesto, *Ecclesiasticae disciplinae ... explicatio*, composed by another Trinity man, later destined to cross swords with Richard Hooker, Walter Travers. The English translation of Travers's book, *A Full and Plaine Declaration of Ecclesiastical Discipline* (not to be confused, as it often is, with the Book of Discipline, or its title when printed in 1644, *A Directory of Church-Government*) is also thought to have been Cartwright's work. Cartwright was now a distinguished member of the Calvinist international. When in 1576

Friedrich was succeeded as elector by the Lutheran Ludwig VI, he joined in the general exodus from the Palatinate, settling in Basel, where he entered the local university and published his *The Rest of the Second Replie*.

One sequel of *The Rest* was that Cartwright now took issue with and parted company from the most radical English puritans, including the authors of the *Admonition*. Under the influence of the Heidelberg divines, he now taught it to be wrong to forfeit a pastoral vocation and the opportunity to preach on account of conscientious scruples in respect of ceremonies which were of themselves indifferent. The radical ultras begged to differ, claiming that in what he had now written Cartwright had set himself against himself, 'and against the Church and brethren' (Peel, 1.138). In the complexity of the Elizabethan church there was no single middle way but many middle ways. Soon Cartwright would be contending with the first separatists (who included his own sister-in-law) for the legitimacy and integrity of the established church.

By 1577 the peripatetic Cartwright was on the move again, not, as the seventeenth-century polemical historian Peter Heylyn supposed, to the Channel Islands, but to Antwerp, where he found employment as a factor in the headquarters of the Merchant Adventurers. It was perhaps on the strength of this position that in 1578 he married Alice Stubbs (*d. c.*1617), sister of John Stubbs, the close friend of Michael Hicks. There was now a benign conspiracy involving English merchants and diplomats to establish a thoroughly reformed English church in Antwerp, no doubt intended for an ecclesiological role model. In April 1578 Walter Travers arrived to become its minister, and on 8 May the congregation was established and Travers received a form of non-episcopal ordination from the reformed ministers of Antwerp, headed by Pierre Loiseleur de Villiers, friend of the English great and godly.

When Travers returned to England on indefinite leave in July 1580, Cartwright took his place, insisting in later years that in his case this had not involved a presbyterian calling, but that he stood upon his original episcopal ordination: if only to the diaconate, which, as Travers pointed out, entitled him to preach. But Cartwright's position remained irregular, in the opinion of many of the leading English merchants, and, since he was the brother-in-law of the author of *The Gaping Gulfe*, an embarrassment in other respects. But when Travers resigned, he recommended Cartwright as his successor, and Cartwright continued to minister to the congregation until the spring of 1585, by which time (October 1582) the Merchant Adventurers had moved their operations to Middelburg. To his own satisfaction, Cartwright had for these five years exercised a legitimate ministry within the Church of England. In 1580 he was headhunted for chairs in the universities of both Leiden and St Andrews. According to Cartwright's own expostulations, at the time and later, it was his obligations to the Antwerp church that compelled him to refuse these offers.

But the queen knew of Cartwright's presence in Antwerp, and resented it, and something had to be done. In July 1582 Sir Francis Walsingham dangled a bait intended to convert Cartwright into a moderate and safe puritan, expending his scholarly energies in anti-Catholic polemics. It was suggested that he should compose a confutation of the Catholic version of the New Testament, recently published at Rheims. This major undertaking occupied Cartwright for some time to come, and the *Confutation* was published only posthumously, at Leiden, in 1618. It had proved impossible to render Cartwright altogether safe. Archbishop Whitgift did all he could to stop the project in its tracks, believing, not without reason, that it would prove a presbyterian Trojan horse, while Cartwright was spurred on by puritan cells, like the conference of ministers meeting in and around Dedham in Essex.

Reformist champion In England, where Whitgift was now in charge, the year 1584 faced the puritans with the critical choice whether to subscribe or not subscribe to his new code of conformity, and Cartwright's presence was badly needed, not least to hold together radical and moderate elements which were likely to tear each other apart. Edmund Chapman, a moderate, wrote from Dedham about 'the miserable distraction that is betwene the preachers and professors of our english church for matters of ecclesiasticall governemente', confessing in himself 'some dislike of both parties for their hotte and violent manner of proceedinge, either seekinge by all meanes to conquer and deface thother' (Usher, 81). And Middelburg was not good for Cartwright's health. But was it safe to return? Elizabeth refused him leave, whereupon Cartwright returned without it, to be committed to the Fleet by Bishop John Aylmer of London. But his friends did not allow him to stay there for long, and they included the earl of Leicester, who negotiated with Whitgift for a preaching licence (unsuccessfully). Soon Cartwright was back in the Netherlands, as part of the preparations for Leicester's military expedition. But early in 1586 Leicester found him a safe berth as master of his hospital in Warwick, and he remained in possession of this valuable sinecure (worth £50 a year, which Leicester topped up with another £50) for the rest of his life, his only formal duties being the care of twelve old men.

Not that Cartwright's new life settled into some Trollopeian idyll. He took an active and controversial role in Warwick's parochial ministry, added to his reputation as a preacher (probably unlicensed), and indeed was busy far beyond Warwick. He was a natural ally of the puritan politician Job Throckmorton of Haseley, who twice accompanied Cartwright when he preached at Stratford upon Avon. And in a roundabout way it may have been Throckmorton who proved his undoing. It appears likely that Throckmorton was the author of the seditious anti-episcopal libels printed between the autumn of 1588 and the summer of 1589 over the name of 'Martin Marprelate'. Marprelate made himself the champion of Cartwright. No other puritan minister was mentioned so often, or with more approval. But the admiration was not reciprocated, and Cartwright expressed his distaste and distanced himself from the tracts, Chapman of Dedham confirming that he had had no affinity 'with that marre matter marten …

what small pleasure you ever tooke in such inventions' (Usher, 77).

But it was the trail laid by Marprelate that led the future Archbishop Richard Bancroft and other ecclesiastical sleuths to incriminating evidence of the quasi-presbyterian conferences and synods in which Cartwright and other puritan preachers had been active, meetings that had been reviewing drafts of a Book of Discipline, a blueprint for a presbyterian English church. Cartwright's involvement in this movement is not as well documented as that of the ministers meeting around Dedham, or in Northamptonshire, but he and Humfrey Fen of Coventry were its leaders in Warwickshire, and both represented the county at a general meeting held in Cambridge at Stourbridge fair time in September 1587. Cartwright was in Cambridge again in September 1589 for another synod, held in St John's College, when the Book of Discipline was allegedly subjected to its final revisions. And there was inconclusive debate about the question of the hour in these circles: were non-preaching ministers true ministers, and the sacraments they administered valid sacraments?

On trial In the course of the winter that followed, Bancroft's special branch picked out eight ministers to stand exemplary trial in the court of high commission, all but one summoned from the hot spots of Northamptonshire and Warwickshire. The high commission case was stymied when the defendants refused on legal and conscientious grounds to take the oath *ex officio mero*. But the commission had the power to imprison them, and did. Only belatedly was Cartwright added to their number and it was not until October that he too confronted the high commission, charged under thirty-one articles which related in part to his activities in the Netherlands, including his supposed presbyterian ordination, his ministry in Warwick, and the alleged connection with Martin Marprelate. Only the last seven charges concerned the Book of Discipline and the conference movement. Cartwright had been and continued to be protected by his powerful friends, for although Leicester was now dead Whitgift was advised by none other than Lord Burghley: 'I see not that diligence or care taken to win these kind of men that are precise, either by learning or courtesy, as I imagine might reclaim them' (Collinson, 411). But Burghley was unable to prevent Cartwright's imprisonment in the Fleet (where he was allowed visits only from his wife and those who had necessary business with him), or to do much about the extreme displeasure of the queen herself. Some of the ministers still at liberty met in London to discuss whether Cartwright, as their acknowledged leader, should make a clean breast of what they had been up to in their allegedly illegal assemblies.

But it was decided to stand shoulder to shoulder in refusing to plead. Things dragged on until July 1590, when the high commission, reinforced by the judges and principal legal officers of the crown, stripped the defendants of their ecclesiastical offices and orders and declared them incapable of holding any future title or dignity in the church. Only Cartwright retained a position, his sinecure

at Warwick. However, this was not enough for Whitgift and Bancroft. It was necessary to prove a seditious conspiracy, the intention to put the Book of Discipline into practice, and for this purpose the case was transferred to the court of Star Chamber, where the ministers made their first appearance on 13 May 1591. The ground had been prepared by a further, and unproductive, interrogation of Cartwright. Was he the author of the Book of Discipline, or if not who was? The stonewalling continued. Brought back to the high commission, Cartwright again refused the oath.

The highest legal opinion had advised that the 'enormities' of which the ministers stood accused, aggravated by their 'intolerable disobedience' in refusing the oath, constituted an offence 'of as great and dangerous consequence to the Commonwealth as any that of long time hath happened', meriting a severe punishment 'to the terror of others', most probably perpetual banishment (Collinson, 418). But in the event, and after lengthy proceedings—which were enlivened in July 1591 by action off stage in the mad enterprise of Edmund Copinger and Henry Arthington to proclaim 'frantic' William Hacket a new Messiah, which Bancroft and others exploited against Cartwright for all the story was worth—the matter proved impossible to prove. The ministers had excellent lawyers, especially Nicholas Fuller, and they were further advised by the ineffably learned Robert Beale. So sentence was never passed, and by January 1592 there was stalemate. There were reports that the death on 20 November 1591 of the lord chancellor Sir Christopher Hatton, who had headed the forces of prosecution, enabled the judges to recommend that the case should go no farther.

Gradually conditions for the prisoners improved, and even Cartwright was allowed to leave prison to go to church and for other necessary business. The path to liberty was still tortuous, since although the ministers were willing to regret that their meetings had caused offence, and even to undertake not to continue them in future, they were still unable to make the kind of submission that was required. But by 21 May 1592 Cartwright was released to house arrest in Hackney, although bound for years to come to return to custody on twenty days' warning. Soon he was able to return to Warwick.

Last years, death, and influence The ministers, and especially Cartwright, were now subjected to literary assassination: Richard Cosin's book about Copinger and Hacket, *Conspiracie for Pretended Reformation* (1592), two sensational books by Bancroft, *Daungerous Positions and Proceedings* and *A Survay of the Pretended Holy Discipline* (both 1593), and Matthew Sutcliffe's highly personalized *The Examination and Confutation of M. Thomas Cartwright's Late Apologie* (1596), a retort to *A Brief Apologie of Thomas Cartwright* (Middelburg, 1596), which in its turn had been a response to earlier attacks by Sutcliffe. In 1593 appeared the first four books of Hooker's more suave and magisterial *Laws*.

By the time of Sutcliffe's counter-attack Cartwright was in Guernsey, appointed chaplain to the governor, Leicester's old protégé Sir Thomas Leighton (soon succeeded by Edward, Lord Zouche), and minister of Castle Cornet where he remained until 1601, presiding over the regularization of a presbyterian polity for the churches of the Channel Islands, which required the healing of a breach between the presbyteries of Guernsey and Jersey, where another of the Star Chamber nine, the Northamptonshire minister Edmund Snape, was now installed.

Cartwright's last and declining years were spent back in Warwick. Following the accession of James I he was at once involved in the renewed puritan campaign for further reformation. On 12 November 1603 he wrote to Sir Christopher Yelverton, asking him to organize a petition to the king from the gentlemen of Northamptonshire—a petition which in the event badly backfired—and he was on the original list for the Hampton Court conference which met in January 1604. But on 27 December 1603 Cartwright died and was buried at Warwick. He was survived by his wife, Alice, his son Samuel, still a minor, and three daughters, Mary and Anne, who were already married, and Martha.

Cartwright had spent twenty of his sixty-eight years outside England, in one kind of exile or another—more than any other English protestant (and three years in prison). Was his life a tragic waste? It might be considered so, and Edmund Chapman of Dedham even wrote (about 1589 or 1590) that 'if the worke were to begyne againe yow would mend some peece of the matter or manner of yt'. But Chapman also observed:

What know yow or me whether all the fruites of your labors be yet risen or sprunge up, or lie still closse and hidden under the grounde, bicause of the stormy and sharpe seasons and winterlike wether … You have no cause to repente that ever you tooke yt in hande.   (Usher, 78)

These fruits would indeed spring up, in the 1640s, and even in later centuries, for Cartwright was the true progenitor of English presbyterianism.

PATRICK COLLINSON

Sources A. F. Scott Pearson, *Thomas Cartwright and Elizabethan puritanism, 1553–1603* (Cambridge, 1925); (Gloucester, MA, 1966) • P. Collinson, *The Elizabethan puritan movement* (1967); pbk edn (1990) • *A parte of a register* (Middelburg, 1593) • A. Peel, ed., *The seconde parte of a register*, 2 vols. (1915) • *The works of John Whitgift*, ed. J. Ayre, 3 vols., Parken Society (1851–3) • T. Cartwright, *The second replie* (Heidelberg, 1575) • T. Cartwright, *The rest of the second replie* (Basel, 1577) • A. Peel and L. H. Carlson, eds., *Cartwrightiana* (1951) • P. Lake, *Anglicans and puritans? Presbyterianism and English conformist thought from Whitgift to Hooker* (1988) • R. G. Usher, ed., *The presbyterian movement in the reign of Queen Elizabeth, as illustrated by the minute book of the Dedham classis, 1582–1589*, CS, 3rd ser., 8 (1905) • [R. Bancroft], *Daungerous positions and proceedings* (1593) • R. Bancroft, *A survay of the pretended holy discipline* (1593) • J. Heywood and T. Wright, eds., *Cambridge University transactions during the puritan controversies of the 16th and 17th centuries* (1854), vol. 1 • Folger, MS V.a.176, fols. 69–77 [the source of John Nichols's account of the royal visit to Cambridge in 1564 in *The progression and public procession of Queen Elizabeth* (1823), vol. 1, pp. 151–89] • S. Clarke, *A generall martyrologie … whereunto are added, The lives of sundry modern divines* (1651) • P. Heylyn, *Aerius redivivus, or, The history of the presbyterians* (1670)

Likenesses line engraving, BM, NPG; repro. in Scott Pearson, *Thomas Cartwright*, frontispiece

Cartwright, Thomas (1634–1689), bishop of Chester, was born in Northampton on 1 September 1634, the son of Thomas Cartwright, formerly a schoolmaster in Brentwood, Essex, and son of the renowned Elizabethan puritan Thomas *Cartwright (1534/5–1603). Both his parents were puritan-inclined. Cartwright was educated at Northampton grammar school, whence he proceeded to Magdalen College, Oxford, where he studied logic. He was intruded by parliamentarian visitors into Queen's College in 1649, matriculated from the college on 18 November 1650, and graduated BA on 17 February 1653. Despite his puritan antecedents he chose to be episcopally ordained, served as chaplain of Queen's, proceeded MA on 21 June 1655, and was appointed vicar of Brentwood in 1657. In 1659 he served as chaplain to John Robinson, the London royalist alderman and MP, and published the first of a series of his sermons in print, *God's Arraignment of Adam*; about this time he became preacher at St Mary Magdalen, Milk Street, London.

With the Restoration and his adoption of a firm royalist profile—he acted as chaplain to Henry, duke of Gloucester (1639–1660)—Cartwright's career blossomed as he applied himself to the systematic collection of benefices: canon-prebendary of Shalford in Wells Cathedral in 1660 and vicar of Barking in Essex in the same year. Like his later dean at Chester, James Arderne, Cartwright was one of a number of post-Restoration royalists with parliamentarian and puritan antecedents. He took his Oxford DD degree on 12 September 1661 and, already a widower, married Sarah, daughter of Henry Wight of Barking, probably in May 1662. Cartwright became canon-prebendary of Twyford in St Paul's Cathedral in 1665 and rector of St Thomas the Apostle, Queen Street, London, in the same year, and acquired a further cathedral canonry, in Durham, in 1672, when he also became chaplain to the king. In 1676 he became dean of Ripon and at some point in the 1670s, ambitious but still a relatively young man, apparently made a thwarted attempt to put his foot on the first rung of the episcopal ladder by attempting to lay claim to the bishopric of St David's. A sermon he published in 1676 on Jude 22: 23 was delivered before Charles II, evidence of the links with the crown that were the key to Cartwright's career success, most markedly in the next reign. In 1676 he published another sermon, delivered in York Minster to the assize judges and on the verse in the book of Judges (17: 6) concerning the chaos that arises in the absence of kingship. Yet another published sermon was delivered before the duke of York's daughter, Princess Anne, at Holyroodhouse in Edinburgh on 30 January 1682 on the verse in Acts (7: 60) describing the death of the first Christian martyr, St Stephen. This occasion of the commemoration of the death of the royal martyr, Charles I, brought Cartwright into association with the York family, still in exile in Scotland before the royalist recovery accelerated in 1682. A further published sermon in 1684 expatiated again on a politically charged text of scripture, Proverbs 24: 21, 22: 'fear thou the LORD and the king: *and* meddle not with those that are given to change'. Owing to his

Thomas Cartwright (1634–1689), after unknown artist, c.1686–9

ultra-absolutist views, Cartwright's career was stalled during the tory reaction through the influence of archbishops Sancroft (1617–1693) and Dolben (1625–1686), both royalist churchmen who accepted the need for some restraint on the crown's authority, especially over the Church of England. However, preaching in Ripon in February 1686, on the first anniversary of 'the happy Inauguration of … King James II' (BL cat., 34.756), on the text from 1 Kings 8: 66 ('and they blessed the king'), Cartwright, as in 1681, found in the Bible a warrant for affirming his Stuart allegiance, and his personal commitment to James. On 11 August 1686 he commenced the diary that he now began to keep, with the memorandum, 'King James the Second, my most gracious master, called me aside in his bedchamber at Windsor this morning, and promised me the Bishoprick of Chester' (Diary, 1). He was consecrated on 17 October of that year, Sancroft having to be coerced into ordaining him: Cartwright was allowed to keep his vicarage of Barking and, as was customary with Chester's meagrely remunerated bishops, held the living of Wigan.

This choice on James's part may be regarded as politically strategic. Cheshire in the early 1680s had been a hotbed of Monmouthite whiggery, where the duke had ventured a claim to the throne in 1682. However, in that year James Arderne (1636–1691), an extreme pro-absolutist, was appointed dean of Chester and set about establishing the cathedral as a high tory base. From the time of Cartwright's appointment, he and Arderne saw in one another kindred spirits and allies: the ceremony of episcopal induction of 1 December 1686, when, Cartwright recorded, 'I was sung into the Cathedral by the choir and enthroned by Mr. Dean' (Diary, 15) may be read as a ritual

confirmation of the alliance of these men, for they saw eye to eye not just over the territory of high tory politics but also over ecclesiastical issues, and were churchmen who insisted on exacting standards of neo-Laudian propriety in the conduct of the cathedral's worship. Thus Cartwright recorded: 'I admonished Mr Ottway, the precentor, … of his neglecting services and anthems, and his teaching of the quire … I rebuked, as they deserved, Mrs Brown, Mrs Crutchley, Mrs Eaton, and her sister, for talking and laughing in the church' (Burne, 154). This programme of restoring seemliness in the cathedral services was accompanied by insistence on the inculcation of strong monarchist views in the prayers and sermons delivered there, and especially in censoring all adverse reflections on King James and his Catholic religion: 'Mr. Morrey preached in the cathedral, and I admonished him to mend his prayer, in which he gave not the King his titles, and to be wary of reflecting so imprudently as he did upon the King's religion' (Diary, 30).

From 7 April 1687 Cartwright was in London, where he tried to obtain Anglican clerical backing for James's policies of toleration; in June he submitted the address of the corporation of Wigan in support of the king's measures, and in May and July showed his complicity with James's plans to advance Catholicism by attending ceremonies to honour the papal nuncio Count d'Adda. Returning to Chester, Cartwright had the month between 27 July and 27 August to prepare for James's own arrival at the cathedral, where, prior to touching for the king's evil, the king expressed displeasure at the poor state of the cloisters: Dean Arderne's responsibility for the upkeep of the premises may have been the cause of a temporary falling out between him and the bishop in the autumn of 1687. Having concluded a visitation of his cathedral on 6 October, on the thirteenth Cartwright, once more in London, heard from James of his appointment as one of the 'High Commissioners for Ecclesiastical Affairs', with a brief to bring Magdalen College into submission to the king's plan to give the institution a Catholic head. He accused the fellows of quarrelsomeness, sexual immorality, and seeking to be 'popular' (Western, 202). He fully supported repeal of the Test Acts, endorsed the reading by clergy of the Church of England of James's second declaration of indulgence, of April 1688, and during that year was kept out of the plans and discussions of the majority of the episcopate who were hostile to the royal programme.

Fatally compromised by his unhesitating complicity with James's plans and by his intimacy with leading Catholic clergy, Cartwright had hardly any option but to leave England as William of Orange approached, and quit London a few days before James in December 1688. When he was reunited with his master at St Germain, he provided the liturgy of the Church of England for the protestants among the Jacobite exiles—testimony to his adherence to the religion he professed. James went through the motions of appointing him to the vacant bishopric of Salisbury. As for his allegiance to the king, this was displayed when he went with him to Ireland early in 1689. They landed at Kinsale on 12 March and proceeded by way of Cork and Kilkenny to Dublin where, amid talk of his promotion in the Irish church, Cartwright caught a fatal infection of dysentery, from which he died on 15 April 1689. His last hours, when he went through the full sacramental and liturgical order of the Church of England and withstood Roman Catholic attempts to make a convert of him, further attested the firmness of his loyalty to the Church of England and rebutted the rumour that he had apostatized to Rome. He was buried at Christ Church, Dublin.

Cartwright has been the subject of intense vilification, seen as the primary clerical quisling of the Church of England under James II, with generalized allegations of immorality thrown in—'much scandal of the worst sort', in Wood's words (Wood, *Ath. Oxon.*, 3rd edn, 4.256). He was, though, a conscientious diocesan and, throughout his career, a regular and published preacher. His political authoritarianism was undoubtedly extreme, but the charge that he was a mere time-server may be disproved by his adhesion to James II during and after the revolution.　　　　　　　　　　　　MICHAEL MULLETT

Sources *The diary of Thomas Cartwright, bishop of Chester*, ed. J. Hunter, CS, 22 (1843) · R. A. Beddard, 'Bishop Cartwright's deathbed', *Bodleian Library Record*, 11 (1982–5), 220–30 · Foster, *Alum. Oxon.* · Wood, *Ath. Oxon.*, new edn, 4.452 · R. V. H. Burne, *Chester Cathedral: from its founding by Henry VIII to the accession of Queen Victoria* (1958) · J. Spurr, *The Restoration Church of England, 1646–1689* (1991) · F. C. Turner, *James II* (1950) · J. R. Western, *Monarchy and revolution: the English state in the 1680s* (1972) · *BL cat.*, vol. 34

Archives BL, diary, Add. MS 24357

Likenesses oils, c.1680 (after G. Soest), NPG; version, Queen's College, Oxford · oils, copy, c.1686–1689, NPG [*see illus.*] · oils, second version, Queen's College, Oxford

Cartwright, Sir Thomas (1795–1850), diplomatist, eldest son of William Ralph Cartwright (1771–1847), MP, of Aynho, Northamptonshire, and Emma Maude (d. 1808), daughter of Cornwallis, first Viscount Hawarden, was born on 18 January 1795. He was educated at Christ Church, Oxford, and entered the diplomatic service. He was secretary of legation at Munich (1821–8) and at The Hague (1828–30), then minister-plenipotentiary at Frankfurt until 1838 and at Stockholm from 1838 until his death. He was a supporter and friend of Lord Palmerston. He was knighted in 1834. Cartwright married, in 1825, Maria Elizabeth Augusta, known as Lili (1805–1902), daughter of Count von Sandizell of Bavaria. They had two sons, the younger of whom was William Cornwallis *Cartwright (1825–1915). Cartwright's later years were complicated by the debts he inherited from his father. He died at Stockholm on 17 April 1850. His wife died on 13 April 1902.

　　　　　　　T. F. HENDERSON, *rev.* H. C. G. MATTHEW

Sources *GM*, 2nd ser., 34 (1850), 91 · Burke, *Gen. GB* · d. cert.

Archives Northants. RO, corresp. and papers | BL, corresp. with Lord Aberdeen, Add. MSS 43087, 43151 · NL Scot., letters to second earl of Minto · U. Southampton L., corresp. with Lord Palmerston · Woburn Abbey, Bedfordshire, letters to Lord George William Russell

Wealth at death heavily indebted

Cartwright, William (1606–1686), actor and art collector, was born at the end of December 1606, the son of William

William Cartwright (1606–1686), by John Greenhill, mid-1660s

Cartwright, actor, and was baptized at St Mary Magdalen, Old Fish Street, London, on 1 January 1607. The elder Cartwright was playing for the Lord Admiral's Company in 1598 and in 1606 with Prince Henry's Company at the Fortune Theatre. His name appears in the patent list for Prince Henry's (now Lord Palsgrave's) in 1613, along with Richard Gunnell, who was to become the company's impresario. The elder Cartwright became a senior figure in the Palsgrave's. He remained with its successor company, the King and Queen of Bohemia's Men, under Charles I, playing first at the open-air Fortune and later at a new hall playhouse, the Salisbury Court, built by Gunnell. 'Ould Cartwright' is last certainly sighted in theatrical records in May 1636 (Bentley, 2.404). However, the records of St Giles Cripplegate record the burials of three women each recorded in the register as 'wife of Wm Cartwright Player' (and not widow) in July 1637 (a mere five months after marriage), May 1642, and March 1651 respectively. The elder William lived in the parish, and it has been generally assumed that they were his wives rather than those of his son, if so implying three marriages at an advanced age; the dating of the costume in a portrait of him aged fifty-nine suggests he may have been born as early as the late 1550s; at the least, the first of these marriages took place thirty years after the birth of his son.

The younger Cartwright probably joined his father's company, the King and Queen of Bohemia's Men, when they were playing at the new Salisbury Court from 1629. He went on to play for Queen Henrietta's Men, with whom he may have been linked from their Salisbury Court days, but his major days as player and businessman came much later.

Cartwright seems, like his father, to have been a thoroughly married man. His inventory of paintings, drawn up in the 1680s, lists 'my first wifes pictur Like a Sheppardess' and 'my Last wifes pictur, with a black vaile on her head' (*Mr. Cartwright's Pictures*, 78). The last wife can be confidently identified as Jane Hodgson (who appears to have died in or before 1669), whom he married on 19 November 1654 at St Giles-in-the-Fields, where he was then living. Beyond that, the Cartwrights' marriage records are confused, as the doubt over the women buried in St Giles Cripplegate suggests, and, given that the name is a common one, near impossible to disentangle. Jane's predecessor is generally taken to be Andria Robins (*d*. 1652), whom a William Cartwright married on 28 April 1636 and who was buried at St Giles-in-the-Fields on 12 May 1652. The younger Cartwright's first wife may have been Elizabeth Cooke, married on 1 May 1633 in St Giles-in-the-Fields, though this has been challenged on the grounds that she is probably the Elizabeth Cartwright who died in 1665.

With the closure of the theatres in 1642 Cartwright's business activities had to diversify. He was actively involved in a company playing for the prince of Wales in Paris, then possibly at The Hague, and also in various illegal efforts to stage plays in London in 1648. His main business, however, seems to have been bookselling from his house in Great Turnstile, off Holborn. In 1658 Cartwright issued an updated version of Thomas Heywood's *An Apology for Actors* (originally published in 1612), with a new title that showed the author's readiness to revive the then still-banned pastime. Retitled *The Actor's Vindication, Containing Three Brief Treatises, viz. I, Their Antiquity, II, Their Antient Dignity, III, The True Use of their Quality, Written by Thomas Heywood*, it appeared under Cartwright's own name, prefaced by a letter signed 'W. C.' justifying the republication and its additions. The main additions are notes on the qualities of his father's friend Edward Alleyn as actor and benefactor. This was among the books he gave to Dulwich College.

At the Restoration, Cartwright was in London, first at the Cockpit Theatre, then joining Thomas Killigrew's new King's Company, in which he became a sharer, in 1660. The company started at the old Red Bull Theatre in Clerkenwell, moving to the new Theatre Royal in Drury Lane in 1663. He was cast to play the Abbot in John Ford's *Love's Sacrifice* at this time. Samuel Pepys saw him play Falstaff on 2 November 1667: 'after dinner my wife and Willett and I to the King's House and there saw *Henry the Fourth*; and contrary to expectation, was pleased in nothing more than in Cartwright's speaking of Falstaff's speech about *What is Honour?*' (Pepys, 7.516). The duke of Buckingham in *The Rehearsal* (first performed in 1671) satirized Cartwright's acting style. When Thunder (presumably played by Cartwright himself) makes his entrance and announces himself as 'Bold Thunder', the author Bayes in directorial mode urges him 'Mr Cartwright, pr'ythee speak a little louder, and with a hoarser voice. I am the bold Thunder? Pshaw speak it me in a voice that thunders

it out indeed: I am the bold Thunder' ([G. Villiers, duke of Buckingham], *The Rehearsal*, 1672, 10).

In his heyday, as a veteran of his earlier playing years, Cartwright played three major Jonson parts (Mammon in *The Alchemist*, Morose in *Epicene*, and Corbaccio in *Volpone*) and was in six of John Dryden's and two of William Wycherley's plays. In 1685, when he was seventy-eight, he played one of the leads in John Fletcher's *Rollo*. Cartwright's career in the Restoration was distinctly prosperous. He owned several properties, including two thirty-sixths of the King's Company's playhouse. An elder statesman of the London theatre by the 1670s, he became entangled in several managerial disputes with the Killigrews over the King's Company's business and property enterprises. By 1681 illness was gradually forcing his withdrawal from company affairs and from the stage.

Cartwright's last days were clouded by the determination of his servants, who had been running his household for the last seventeen years, to thwart his intention to leave to Dulwich College £400 for an endowment, his collection of 'pictures of Storyes and Landskips', and his books (*Mr. Cartwright's Pictures*, 87). Their prevarications brought on a stroke on 9 December 1686. He never regained consciousness and died at his house in Great Turnstile on 17 December. Dulwich never saw the money, nor many of the books and some of the pictures: Cartwright's own inventory listed 239 paintings in all, of which it received all but forty-six. Seventy-seven are now in the Dulwich Picture Gallery. The collection covered a broad span of genres, including landscapes and seascapes, still lifes and religious paintings, and seventy-six portraits. It has been taken as an interesting illustration of 'the range of work available to a collector of moderate means in Restoration London' (ibid., 9). Cartwright's collecting showed a very strong tendency towards contemporary British and continental painters, including drawings and six portraits by John Greenhill, who painted one of the two portraits of Cartwright himself in the collection. The famous paintings of the actors Richard Burbage, Nathan Field, and Richard Perkins, and the poet Richard Lovelace, were all Cartwright's. Cartwright had asked to be buried in Dulwich College chapel but the request caused the college difficulty, and he was buried in St Paul's, Covent Garden, the day after his death.

ANDREW GURR

Sources G. E. Bentley, *The Jacobean and Caroline stage*, 7 vols. (1941–68), vol. 2, pp. 402–5 · E. Boswell, 'Young Mr. Cartwright', *Modern Language Review*, 24 (1929), 125–42 · E. A. J. Honigmann and S. Brock, eds., *Playhouse wills, 1558–1642: an edition of wills by Shakespeare and his contemporaries in the London theatre* (1993), 225–6, 238–44 · Pepys, *Diary*, 7.516 · *Mr Cartwright's pictures: a seventeenth century collection* [1987] [exhibition catalogue, Dulwich Picture Gallery, London, 25 Nov 1987–28 Feb 1988] · Highfill, Burnim & Langhans, *BDA*, 3.89–93 · H. J. Oliver, 'The building of the Theatre Royal in Bridges St.: some details of finance', *N&Q*, 217 (1972), 464–6

Likenesses J. Greenhill, oils, 1663–7, Dulwich Picture Gallery, London [*see illus.*]

Cartwright, William (1611–1643), poet, playwright, and Church of England clergyman, was born in December 1611 at Northway, Gloucestershire, and baptized there on 26

William Cartwright (1611–1643), by unknown artist

December, the first of two children of William Cartwright and his first wife, Dorothy (d. 1620), daughter of Rowland Coles of Northway. The family moved across the county to Cirencester, where they tried for a time to keep an inn; Cartwright was first educated at the free school in Cirencester, under the tutelage of one Henry Topp. About 1623 he became a king's scholar at Westminster School, where he studied under Lambert Osbaldeston. He was elected a student at Christ Church, Oxford, in 1628. In the next year he joined other students to contest abolition of privileges traditionally enjoyed by Westminster scholars at Christ Church, the so-called 'Westminster suppers' (Evans, 11). He matriculated on 24 February 1632, graduated BA the following 5 June, and proceeded MA on 15 April 1635.

Beginning in 1630 Cartwright published both English and Latin poems in collections of commemorative verse on various occasions in the lives of the royal family and other noble persons which were compiled by Brian Duppa, dean of Christ Church. He also contributed a commendatory poem in memory of Ben Jonson to *Jonsonus virbius* (1638). Except for a few poems published as song lyrics, most of his nearly 100 poems remained unpublished until after his death, among them a number of love poems resembling those of John Donne and Jonson, further commemorative and commendatory verse, including two poems on the dramatist John Fletcher, and several translations, including poems by Martial and Horace.

At Oxford Cartwright began also to write plays. His tragicomedy *The Lady-Errant* (unusually featuring both male and female actors) and his comedy *The Ordinary* were performed before both aristocratic and academic audiences by 1635. The first of these was Cartwright's response to Walter Montague's *The Shepherd's Paradise* (1633), which inaugurated a vogue of so-called Platonic drama stemming from the tradition of ancient Greek romance.

Queen Henrietta and her ladies-in-waiting had themselves performed Montague's play at court; Cartwright appears to have written his *Lady-Errant* for a related interest. *The Ordinary*, on the other hand, is straight Jonsonian comedy, perhaps a main cause for Jonson's reported acknowledgement of 'My Son Cartwright [who] writes all like a man' (*Comedies*, sig. A5).

Cartwright's third and most successful play was *The Royal Slave*, with music by Henry Lawes and elaborate sets and costumes by Inigo Jones. Another Platonic tragicomedy, this was produced in the great hall of Christ Church on 30 August 1636 as the main entertainment celebrating the progress of the king and queen to Oxford. In the play a Greek slave is made king of Persia for three days preceding his ritual execution. At the play's climax the slave soliloquizes profoundly on the dangers and responsibilities of monarchy and is overheard by the eavesdropping Persian queen. His obvious virtue (under difficult circumstances) impresses the queen, who persuades her husband to spare the slave's life. King Charles is said to have commended this play as 'the best that ever was acted' (Evelyn, 1.662). Queen Henrietta commanded another performance at Hampton Court on 12 January 1637, a production in which Cartwright directed the king's own players, earning himself an honorarium of £40. *The Royal Slave* was subsequently published at Oxford in editions of 1639 and 1640. A fourth play by Cartwright, *The Siege*, does not seem to have been performed.

In 1637 Archbishop William Laud, as chancellor of the university, had acknowledged Cartwright's literary and linguistic skills in a letter considering his application to supervise the editing of scholarly publications by the press at Oxford. This appointment was never made, but in the following year Cartwright was ordained. Although he preached for only five years before his death, Cartwright subsequently gained a reputation as 'the most florid and seraphical preacher in the university' (Wood, *Ath. Oxon.*, 3.69). By 1656 his preaching was recalled among the work of the '*Prime Masters*' of this Nation' (Wright, sig. A2v); yet only one of his sermons is extant, a sermon on the passion of Christ, posthumously published in 1652 as *An off-Spring of Mercy, Issuing out of the Womb of Cruelty*.

His ecclesiastical and academic careers were in full flight when, in 1642, Cartwright was appointed to the university readership in metaphysics. However, the outbreak of civil war interrupted his professional commitments. The king declared martial law at the university and early in September 1642 appointed Cartwright to serve on the Oxford council of war, with responsibility for the billeting and arming of troops. Moreover, Cartwright himself turned soldier, training with other scholars and divines. When parliamentary forces briefly took control of Oxford later in the month, Cartwright was arrested and imprisoned. Payment of £200 in bail money gained his release, but he and other scholarly prisoners were exiled from Oxford. At about this time Brian Duppa, having been appointed bishop of Salisbury, conferred on Cartwright the position of choral director, or succentor, at that cathedral (Wood, *Ath. Oxon.*, 3.70). However, he returned to

Oxford when the king's forces retook the town on 28 October following the battle of Edgehill. The king, at the head of the royalist army, commanded Cartwright to preach a victory sermon.

After resuming his offices at the university Cartwright was further appointed junior proctor in April 1643; but within eight months he had contracted a fever, the 'camp disease' (Wood, *Ath. Oxon.*, 3.70), an epidemic apparently resulting from conditions caused by the billeting of soldiers at Oxford. Cartwright died at Christ Church on 29 November 1643, and was buried on 1 December, 'the most eminent poet, orator and philosopher of his time' (ibid., 3.69), in the south aisle just near the choir of Christ Church Cathedral, without any grave marker.

DENNIS FLYNN

Sources G. B. Evans, *The plays and poems of William Cartwright* (1951) · Wood, *Ath. Oxon.*, new edn, vol. 3 · *Comedies, tragi-comedies, with other poems, by Mr William Cartwright*, ed. H. Moseley (1651) · Foster, *Alum. Oxon.* · G. Langbaine, *An account of the English dramatick poets* (1691) · *The works of the most reverend father in God, William Laud*, 5, ed. J. Bliss (1853) · *The life and poems of William Cartwright*, ed. R. C. Goffin (1918) · J. Evelyn, *Memoirs* (1819) · A. Wright, *Five sermons* (1656)

Archives Folger | BL, Add. MSS · BL, Egerton MSS · BL, Harley MSS · Bodl. Oxf., MSS Arch. Seld. · Bodl. Oxf., Bodley MSS · Bodl. Oxf., MSS Malone · Bodl. Oxf., MSS Rawl. D · Harvard U., Houghton L., Bedford MSS · NYPL, Drexel MSS

Likenesses W. Lombart, engraving, repro. in Moseley, ed., *Comedies*, frontispiece · portrait, LUL, Sterling Library [*see illus.*]

Cartwright, William Cornwallis (1825–1915), politician and journalist, was born on 30 November 1825 in Munich, the first of the two children of Sir Thomas *Cartwright (1795–1850), a British diplomatist, and his Bavarian wife, Maria Elizabeth Augusta (Lili; 1805–1902), daughter of Cajetan Peter Max, Graf von und zu Sandizell. He had one brother, Thomas (1830–1921). William was educated chiefly by private tutors, and grew up in the cosmopolitan milieu of diplomatic circles, becoming fluent in four languages. His indifferent health meant that studying at Balliol College, Oxford, was rejected in favour of the warmer climates involved in a grand tour. During the 1840s his visits included trips to Switzerland, Austria, Hungary, Malta, the Balkans, and Turkey, and in Egypt he made a trip down the Nile. But his favourite place was always Italy, to which he returned again and again. These travels provided the background knowledge for much of his later expertise in foreign affairs, shown in both his journalism and his political career.

In 1847 Cartwright's grandfather died, leaving his father the Aynho estates in Northamptonshire and a large burden of debt. There was insufficient money for William to stand for parliament, as had been planned, so he went back to travelling, and witnessed some of the revolutionary events of 1848 in Europe. This formed his political outlook as a Liberal, and he believed that the extension of the suffrage and education would be a bulwark against the dangers of revolution. He also espoused the cause of Italian unification. In 1850 his life was changed by the early death of his father, then Britain's diplomatic representative in Sweden. William inherited his enormous debts

(paid off only in 1881, when he was left money and property by a relative) and, with no profession to follow, he could live as a gentleman only by renting out Aynho and living cheaply abroad. His position in society was weakened further by his marrying his mistress, (Caroline Charlotte) Clementine Gaul (1821–1890), an uneducated Polish–German woman. They had five children, including Fairfax Leighton Cartwright (1857–1928), who was to serve as Britain's ambassador to Vienna in 1908–13. Living mainly in Rome, Cartwright knew most of the city's resident artists and writers; his friends included Frederic Leighton and Robert and Elizabeth Browning. But he was drawn more to Italian politics, especially the 'Roman question' (concerning the status of Rome and the Vatican). He was a close friend of Lord Odo Russell, Britain's political agent in Rome (1858–70). Cartwright's contacts among the Roman clergy and political liberals were a conduit of information for Russell, and he became almost an unpaid diplomatic agent himself. In 1866 he met both Gladstone and Clarendon, and accompanied the former during most of his trip to Italy that winter. The two men, from 1868 British prime minister and foreign secretary, sought Cartwright's opinions on Italian matters in subsequent years.

Cartwright began writing for reviews and periodicals in 1858. Some of his articles were eventually turned into his three books: *Papal Conclaves* (1867), *Gustave Bergenroth* (1870), and *The Jesuits* (1876). He also wrote for *The Spectator*, the *Pall Mall Gazette*, and *The Times*. Much of his writing derived from two propositions: that Italian unification was the main issue facing Europe and that the Roman Catholic church contained reformers as well as reactionaries, making reconciliation between Roman Catholicism and liberalism possible. Cartwright's greatest journalistic success was as an occasional correspondent for *The Times* during the early part of the First Vatican Council (1869–70). In contrast to the regular correspondents, his column provided the only reliable information in the British press on what was happening during the council's private sessions. He also fed information to Lord Acton (in Rome to help the anti-infallibility bishops), who was behind the famous Quirinus articles in the German press. Cartwright returned to England in February 1870 hoping to persuade the British government to intervene diplomatically to dissuade the council from defining papal infallibility. But his influence on Gladstone was thwarted by Lord Odo Russell's plea for non-interference and Lord Acton's view that only the French government could pressurize the Vatican.

Cartwright had entered parliament as Liberal MP for Oxfordshire in 1868, and his parliamentary life centred on foreign affairs. In 1880 he hoped for a ministerial position, but was overlooked by Gladstone in his need to balance the government between different groupings. Subsequently he parted from Gladstone over Irish policy, quarrelled with his constituency party, and did not stand in 1885. In 1886 he unsuccessfully stood as a Liberal Unionist for Mid-Northamptonshire. He retired to Aynho, but still travelled regularly. He died on 8 November 1915 at Aynho Park, near Brackley, Northamptonshire, and was buried there. PETÀ DUNSTAN

Sources Northants. RO, Cartwright papers · priv. coll., Cartwright MSS · P. Dunstan, 'William Cornwallis Cartwright: a foreign correspondent in Rome in the 1860s', PhD diss., U. Cam., 1985 · Gladstone, *Diaries* · *Wellesley index*
Archives Northants. RO, corresp. and papers · priv. coll. | Balliol Oxf., corresp. with Sir Robert Morier · BL, Gladstone MSS · CUL, letters to Lord Acton · PRO, letters to Odo Russell, FO 918
Likenesses F. Leighton, portrait, *c*.1855–1865, priv. coll. · photographs, Northants. RO
Wealth at death £77,952 17*s*. 11*d*.: probate, 5 Oct 1916, *CGPLA Eng. & Wales*

Carus, Thomas (*c*.1510–1571), judge, was the son of William Carus of Asthwaite, Westmorland, and Isabel, daughter of Thomas Leyburn of Cunswick in the same county. He became a member of the Middle Temple about 1530, a period for which the inn records are lost. Although he inherited and acquired land in Westmorland, he seems to have settled at Halton in Lancashire, and already by 1538 was a justice of the peace for the latter county. He was elected member of parliament for Wigan in 1547, in which year he became vice-chancellor of the county palatine of Lancaster, and represented Lancaster in 1553 and 1555. His professional progress was marked by his election as a bencher of the Middle Temple in 1548, when he read on voucher to warranty, and he gave a second reading in 1556 on dower; both readings are preserved at Harvard.

With his wife, Katherine, daughter of Thomas Preston of Preston Patrick, Westmorland, Carus had three sons and three daughters. He was created serjeant-at-law at the general call of April 1559, and appointed one of the queen's serjeants on 16 October. On 31 May 1567 he was appointed a puisne justice of the queen's bench, and served until his death on 5 July 1571. He was buried at St Dunstan-in-the-West, London, opposite the Temple, on 7 July; and his arms as displayed there were sketched by Nicholas Charles early in the next century. The burial register and inquisition post mortem both name him as 'esquire'; he was never knighted. The judge himself had ostensibly fallen in with the Elizabethan church settlement, but he bequeathed his soul to the Trinity, the Virgin Mary, and the saints, and his sons and their descendants were Roman Catholics until the eighteenth century. J. H. BAKER

Sources HoP, *Commons, 1509–58*, 1.589–90 · R. Somerville, *History of the duchy of Lancaster, 1265–1603* (1953), 480–81 · Sainty, *King's counsel*, 16 · Sainty, *Judges*, 30 · Baker, *Serjeants*, 171, 503 · *Collectanea Topographica et Genealogica*, 4 (1837), 101 · BL, Lansdowne MS 874, fol. 94*v*

Carvajal, Antonio Fernandez (*d.* 1659), merchant, was probably born in Portugal, for in his youth he seems to have lived in Fundão. He may have fled to Spain at some time, and apparently owned land in the Canary Islands. By the early 1630s he was in London, masquerading as a Roman Catholic in order to evade the prohibition of Jewish settlement in England.

Although no evidence of his activities before 1643 survives, by then he had married, had established a house and warehouse at Leadenhall Street, and had brought over many of his relatives to work for him in England. On 14 March 1643 he petitioned the House of Lords for payment for 300 barrels of gunpowder which he had shipped from Amsterdam, but which had been confiscated by Robert Rich, second earl of Warwick, for use by the parliamentary armies.

Carvajal was also very active in the bullion trade by that time, importing as much as £100,000 per annum during the early 1650s, and thus made himself so indispensable to the parliamentary side that, when he was denounced as a recusant in 1645, a number of City merchants petitioned parliament to have the charge dropped, and the House of Lords soon put an end to the prosecution. Like many other very wealthy Jews during the early modern period Carvajal became an army purveyor, and in 1649 was one of the City merchants who were given the corn contract for the parliamentary forces. His reward came in July 1655 when Carvajal and his two sons were endenizened, thus making him the first English Jew since the expulsion in 1290. His becoming a British subject put his Spanish goods at risk, and Oliver Cromwell himself took extraordinary precautions to ensure that they could be spirited out of the country and sent to England.

Like other Marranos in London, Carvajal prayed at the Catholic chapel of the Spanish ambassador, while simultaneously playing a leading role in the secret Jewish community, which met at the clandestine synagogue at Creechurch Lane. Although he sat on the fence with the rest of London's Jews during the noisy campaign of Rabbi Manasseh ben Israel of Amsterdam to secure a public readmission of the Jews to England, eventually he was forced to show his hand. Spain's war with England in February 1656 put the Spanish subjects in the Jewish community at risk, and when the goods and ships of a fellow Marrano, Antonio Rodrigues Robles, were seized as belonging to an enemy alien Carvajal finally joined with Manasseh ben Israel and five others on 24 March 1656 in petitioning the protector for a formal statement permitting Jewish residence. In doing this, Carvajal and his colleagues finally threw off the disguise of Roman Catholicism, which by then must have worn very thin. The following February, Carvajal and Simon de Caceres successfully petitioned Cromwell to allow the Jews to lease a bit of land at Mile End for use as a cemetery.

Carvajal's character may perhaps be gauged from his actions in the summer of 1658 when £15,000 worth of his logwood was seized by English customs off a Dutch vessel docked in London. Carvajal and his associates raided the warehouse, kidnapped the customs official, and liberated the logwood. The council of state was still examining the incident when Carvajal died in November 1659, according to Samuel Pepys after having been 'lately cutt (by the same hand with my selfe) of the Stone'. He was buried in the new Jewish cemetery at Mile End, and the great bell of St Katharine Cree was rung in his honour. Carvajal was survived by his wife, Maria, and two sons: one of them became a broker on the exchange, but neither of them seems to have married. DAVID S. KATZ, *rev.*

Sources L. Wolf, 'The first English Jew', *Transactions of the Jewish Historical Society of England*, 2 (1894–5), 14–46 • L. Wolf, 'Crypto-Jews under the Commonwealth', *Transactions of the Jewish Historical Society of England*, 1 (1893–4), 55–88 • W. S. Samuel, 'Carvajal and Pepys', *Miscellanies of the Jewish Historical Society of England*, 2 (1935), 24–9 • D. S. Katz, *Philo-Semitism and the re-admission of the Jews to England, 1603–1655* (1982)

Carvajal y Mendoza, Antonia Luisa de (1566–1614), Catholic missionary, was born in Jaraicejo, Extremadura, Spain, on 2 January 1566, the sixth child of Francisco de Carvajal y Vargas (*d.* 1572), a nobleman commissioned by the king to high regional posts, and María de Mendoza y Pacheco (*d.* 1572), also of the high nobility. She was baptized there on 15 January. Unsubstantiated seventeenth-century texts refer to Carvajal as the niece of Ignatius of Loyola, which would have facilitated her later intimacy with the Society of Jesus.

Following a move to León in 1571 both of Carvajal's parents died of a contagious disease a year later and she was moved to the royal palace in Madrid under the guardianship of her maternal grandmother's sister, María Chacón, governess of the crown prince. Carvajal's great-aunt died suddenly in 1576, thrusting the young girl into yet another dramatic change. Her maternal uncle, Francisco Hurtado de Mendoza, had unsuccessfully vied for her guardianship in 1572 and aggressively made her his ward at Almazán. A prominent figure in Spanish imperial politics, Mendoza also had close ties to the Jesuits. Under the tutelage of Mendoza's wife, the Marquesa María de Cárdenas, Carvajal learned Latin, accounting, estate management, and the exercise of charity—all standard fare for noblewomen of her day. Her uncle, on the other hand, exercised her in perverse rituals of mortification in which she was forced to disrobe and was whipped and disparaged by two servants appointed to carry out such 'exercises'. Similarly, he denied her the exercise of normal bodily functions and arranged other circumstances of deprivation, presumably to teach her to 'conquer herself'. Carvajal describes these unseemly activities in her spiritual life story.

In 1586 the family moved to Madrid, where Carvajal's guardians died in 1592. Carvajal took up the life of an urban holy woman, residing with a small community of women in a house close to the Jesuit college. In the 1590s she vowed poverty, obedience to her spiritual superior (whom she chose herself), and the pursuit of perfection. She was still unsatisfied. In 1598 she manifested her anxious desire for God by vowing to seek out martyrdom, a singular promise indeed. By this time Carvajal had designs on an English mission and these vows proved her solidarity with Jesuit politics and faith. She also wrote poetry, most of which dates from this period.

Carvajal's public display of her self-inflicted poverty scandalized her important relatives, and they sued for her inheritance. However, she managed to retain most of her sizeable estate, at the cost of nine years in court and a move to Valladolid in 1601. On 6 January 1605 she willed 12,000 ducats to the Jesuits for the foundation of an English college, leaving 5000 as settlement with her brother.

She probably wrote her spiritual life story during her years in Valladolid.

The exile of Catholic priests from England in 1604 moved Carvajal to seek permission officially, if secretly, to go to London, where she would be able to circulate openly in public, which a priest could not do. In spite of an illness related to a heart condition she left Valladolid on 26 January 1605, probably with her confessor, Jesuit Michael Walpole, in disguise as her servant. Five months later she reached Dover and was installed in the house of Henry Garnett, superior of the Jesuit English mission, only to be left to fend for herself when the group suddenly scattered upon threats of a raid. Late in 1605 the Spanish ambassador, Pedro de Zúñiga, installed her at his insistence in his residence in London. The Gunpowder Plot of 5 November 1605, which led to Garnett's execution, endangered Carvajal as a Catholic with close connections to the Jesuits. Insisting that she had not come to England to live with Spaniards, she firmly pursued independence.

By January 1607 Carvajal had rented a house next to the Spanish embassy, where she lived with select English companions, refining her English and beginning her mission in earnest. She visited imprisoned Catholics, particularly priests, to fortify them in the face of execution, recruited funds for Catholic vocations, catechized, hid priests in her house, and supervised the collection and care of the drawn and quartered body parts of executed Catholics. She also arranged baptisms, recruited prostitutes for conversion, and cared for the poor and infirm. Carvajal's Society of the Sovereign Virgin, modelled on the Jesuits, was founded during this period and included the six women who lived with her.

During the last week of June 1608 Carvajal was arrested for public proselytizing in a Cheapside shop, and spent four days in prison. Zúñiga refused to have her released, making it clear that her imprudence was becoming a national liability for Spain. Her letters, however, describe her own exaltation over the experience, which evidently only intensified her zeal.

George Abbott's succession as archbishop of Canterbury on 9 April 1610 assured Carvajal's downfall. Abbott had long been enraged by her freedom of movement and effectiveness, and ordered her arrest at any prison where she appeared. Deteriorating health led Carvajal to move to Spitalfields, where she lived enclosed with her companions because of illness. Such enclosure only fuelled Abbott's rage for its semblance to monastic retirement, and on 28 October 1613 one of the sheriffs of London broke into Carvajal's house and arrested her. However, the diplomatic crisis this provoked was resolved by the able Spanish ambassador, Diego de Sarmiento, who successfully bargained with King James for her release. Three days later Carvajal was removed to the Spanish embassy, where she died, probably resulting from her heart condition, quietly in her bed on 2 January 1614, her forty-eighth birthday.

In her will Carvajal had asked that her body be buried at the Jesuit college in Louvain that her money had founded. The society took her ducats but did not claim her corpse, which was instead welcomed into the reliquary collection of the Real Monasterio de la Encarnación in Madrid in 1615 by her dear friend, Prioress Mariana de San José. The members of Carvajal's company were reported to be continuing their work in the London Catholic underground several months after her death.   ELIZABETH RHODES

Sources 'Libro de la vida y virtudes de la venerable virgen Doña Luisa de Carvajal y Mendoza', Biblioteca Nacional de Madrid, MS 1881, fols. 198v–206r · *A Spanish heroine in England* [1905] · C. M. Abad, *Una misionera española en la Inglaterra del siglo XVII: Doña Luisa de Carvajal y Mendoza (1566–1614)* (Comillas, 1966) · L. de Carvajal y Mendoza, *Epistolario y poesías*, ed. C. M. Abad (Madrid, 1965) · L. de Carvajal y Mendoza, *Escritos autobiográficos*, ed. C. M. Abad (Barcelona, 1966) · Real Monasterio de la Encarnación, Madrid, L. de Carvajal y Mendoza papers · L. de Carvajal y Mendoza, *Poesías completas*, ed. M. L. García-Nieto Onrubia (Badajoz, 1990) · F. Edwards, *The Jesuits in England: from 1580 to the present day* (1985) · G. Fullerton, *The life of Luisa de Carvajal* (1904) · L. Muñoz, *Vida y virtudes de la venerable virgen Doña Luisa de Carvajal y Mendoza* (Madrid, 1897) [repr. Madrid, 1632] · E. Rhodes, *This tight embrace: Luisa de Carvajal y Mendoza (1566–1614)* (Milwaukee, 2000) · A. R. Moñino and M. B. Moñino, *Luisa de Carvajal (poetisa y mártir): apuntes biobibliográficos, seguidos de tres cartas inéditas de la venerable madre* (Madrid, 1933) · C. F. Senning, 'The Carvajal affair: Gondomar and James I', *Catholic Historical Review*, 56 (1970), 42–66 · M. Walpole, 'La vida de la venerable Doña Luisa de Carvajal y Mendoza', Real Monasterio de la Encarnación, Madrid, Carvajal papers
Archives Real Monasterio de la Encarnación, Madrid, papers
Likenesses I. de la Asunción, portrait, Real Monasterio de la Encarnación; repro. in documents for cause of beatification (np), Real Monasterio de la Encarnación, Madrid · oils, Real Monasterio de la Encarnación, Madrid · oils, Colegio Inglés (Jesuits), Valladolid · stained glass (washing the feet of Benedictine John Roberts), Tyburn Convent, London

Carvell, Nicholas. *See* Kervile, Nicholas (1527/8–1566).

Carver, Alfred James (1826–1909), headmaster, was born at King's Lynn on 22 March 1826, the only son of James Carver (1790–1866) and his wife, Anne Spurling. His father was an evangelical clergyman of an old Norfolk family, who, after graduating at Corpus Christi College, Cambridge, devoted himself in London to the spiritual welfare of prisoners for crime or debt in Newgate and other prisons. Carver was admitted to St Paul's School, London, on 20 February 1836, proceeding from there to Trinity College, Cambridge, as a scholar in 1845. At Cambridge he was elected Bell university scholar in 1846, and he won the Burney university prize essay in 1849. He graduated BA with a first class in classics and as a senior optime in 1849. Next year he became classical lecturer and fellow of Queens' College, Cambridge. His fellowship lapsed on his marriage in 1853 to Eliza (d. 1907), youngest daughter of William Peek, of Peek, Winch & Co., tea merchants. His active connection with his university ceased after he served as examiner in the classical tripos in 1857–8.

Meanwhile, in 1852, Carver became surmaster of St Paul's, his old school, and was ordained in the following year. In 1858 he was appointed master of Alleyn's College of God's Gift at Dulwich. A new scheme for the development of Alleyn's educational foundation had just been sanctioned by a private act of parliament. Although Alleyn had intended, by statutes drawn up in 1626, to found a public school of the high grade, his educational endowment was until 1858 applied solely to the instruction of 'twelve poor scholars'. The new act, which Carver was first to administer, created two schools of different types. The upper school, providing a public-school education for boys up to the age of eighteen, was soon known as Dulwich College, and the lower school, offering what was described as middle-class secondary education, mainly for boys intended for commerce, was named Alleyn's School. Both schools were under Carver's control and prospered greatly. The upper school or Dulwich College moved in 1870 to a building designed by Sir Charles Barry.

Carver's energy created Dulwich College, and made it one of the leading public schools, though not without a long period of controversy involving the chairman of the board of governors, William Rogers, who believed that Alleyn's legacy should be used to educate a larger number and wider social range of London children. Carver finally carried his point in 1882 when, under a new act, Dulwich College and Alleyn's School, which also moved into new buildings under his guidance, became two distinct schools under separate masters. He felt able to retire in the following year with a pension after twenty-five years' service.

During his headmastership Carver carried into practice broad-minded views on education. He saw that every subject could be of educational value, pioneered the teaching of science and modern languages, and promoted the study of art. His object was to develop a boy's faculties on lines most congenial to his natural aptitude, at the same time opposing rigid specialization. He was the first headmaster to pass boys direct from school into the Indian Civil Service; an old boys' club, the Alleyn Club, founded at his instigation in 1873, was one of the first of its kind.

In 1861 Carver was made DD of Lambeth by the archbishop of Canterbury, and in 1882 he was appointed an honorary canon of Rochester. In later life he was chairman of the governors of James Allen's Girls' Schools at Dulwich, and vice-president and member of the council of the Royal Naval School, Eltham (closed in 1909). Carver, who had three sons and five daughters, died at his home, Lynnhurst, Streatham Common, on 25 July 1909, and was buried in Norwood cemetery, the first part of the funeral service being held in the college chapel.

W. R. M. LEAKE, rev. M. C. CURTHOYS

Sources *The Times* (26 July 1909) · personal knowledge (1912) · S. Hodges, *God's gift: a living history of Dulwich College* (1981) · Venn, *Alum. Cant.* · R. B. Gardiner, ed., *The admission registers of St Paul's School, from 1748 to 1876* (1884)
Likenesses E. U. Eddis, portrait, presented in 1867; formerly in the possession of Arthur Wellington Carter, Wragby, 1912 · S. M. Fisher, portrait, exh. 1882, Dulwich College Picture Gallery, London · E. Hastain, portrait, Dulwich College Picture Gallery, London
Wealth at death £38,807 17s. 5d.: resworn probate, 24 Sept 1909, *CGPLA Eng. & Wales*

Carver, Catharine DeFrance (1921–1997), publisher's editor, was born on 17 September 1921 at 823 Oakland Boulevard, Cambridge, Ohio, USA, the only daughter and first of the two children of Don Carver (b. 1890/91), paymaster, and his wife, Harriett, *née* Aududdle (*b.* 1893/4). She completed a BA at Muskingum College, New Concord, Ohio, in May 1943, and briefly attended the University of Chicago, but by 1945 she was in New York as an editor with the firm of Reynal and Hitchcock. Hired by Robert Giroux at Harcourt Brace in 1950, and later by other American publishers, including Viking and the Philadelphia house of J. B. Lippincott, she worked with such authors as Saul Bellow, Flannery O'Connor, Elizabeth Bishop, Katharine Anne Porter, Lionel Trilling, Bernard Malamud, Leslie Fiedler, Hannah Arendt, Ralph Manheim, and John Berryman (who invoked her by name in 'Dream Song 318'). She edited four of the five volumes of Leon Edel's biography of Henry James, became assistant editor of *Partisan Review*, and early on published a few short stories of her own.

Carver had a turbulent emotional life at this time, and in the mid-1960s it was evidently the failure of an important love affair in combination with a romantic overvaluation of Europe that precipitated the decision to dispose of her possessions, burn her correspondence, and leave the United States deliberately and for ever. Arrived in Britain (of which she later became a citizen), she obtained editorial positions at Chatto and Windus and subsequently—and for a longer period—at Oxford University Press in London. But when the press moved all its operations to Oxford in 1976, Carver resigned, preferring to remain in London and find other employment there, first with Victor Gollancz and then as a freelance for Yale University Press and other publishers. The authors with whom she worked in England included Iris Murdoch, Christopher Fry, Salman Rushdie, Leonard Woolf, Richard Hoggart, Richard Holmes, Jon Stallworthy, and Sir Geoffrey Keynes.

In 1983, when in her early sixties, Carver made another of her absolute renunciatory gestures, giving up her Edith Grove flat and its pictures and books, and engaging in a second destruction of her letters. She then set off for Italy in a search for an ideal existence that deteriorated all too rapidly into a desultory succession of visits, sub-lets, and house sits in several countries. She continued to assist old friends—helping the dying Richard Ellmann complete his biography of Oscar Wilde, brilliantly condensing Edel's biography of James, participating in Paris in the final operations of the Trianon Press—and returned repeatedly to London and the round reading-room of the British Library, her 'Great Good Place'. But she generally refused payment for such work, her mode of living became ever more meagre, her health deteriorated, and a minor collapse in 1989 was succeeded two years later, in Paris, by a disabling stroke which disastrously restricted her ability to read, write, or effectively communicate. Back permanently in London with friends or in sheltered housing, she lived for six more melancholy but courageous years, her chief sources of solace being music, visitors, and occasional dinners with friends in restaurants. Finally, on 14 September 1997, she suffered a massive stroke and was taken to the Chelsea and Westminster Hospital; she died there on 11 November 1997 and was cremated at Mortlake crematorium on 18 November.

Catharine Carver (Katy to her American friends) was strikingly attractive as a young woman, short, slim, and dark-haired, with something quizzical and even stern in her glance that was emphasized by the spectacles she then wore. In later years she seemed to shrink a little and become more compacted, her hair lightened and whitened, the spectacles disappeared, and her face became at once plumper and more benign. She remained throughout her life an intensely private person who never married, kept her many friends in separate compartments, and spoke rarely of her past. Omnivorously interested—in painting, music, food, European literatures, and even in cricket—she combined a rich life of the mind with an outward style of self-effacement and proud self-sufficiency. Finding it impracticable to refuse a substantial PEN award orchestrated by her American friends in 1982, she kept the money unspent and bequeathed it back to PEN in her will.

As an editor Carver had a fine eye for detail which co-existed with an extraordinary gift for conceptualizing sequence and structure, and while she loved the creative challenge of what she called professional risk publishing she was no less devoted to the values and disciplines of scholarship. Her procedure was to familiarize herself thoroughly with the subject of each manuscript—reading all of Keats, for example, before undertaking Aileen Ward's biography—and transform its author or editor into a friend to be assisted, encouraged, praised, and, when necessary, scolded. She checked quotations and references as rigorously as punctuation and word usage, and the copy she returned would typically be decorated with her standard marginal signs of approval, disapproval, or interrogation, and accompanied by pages of questions and suggestions. She could be stern in her demands for corrections, rewritings, and reorganizations, and not all her friendships survived, but the able, the serious, and the responsive found her always ready with praise, sympathetic to difficulties, and imaginative to the point of inspiration in offering solutions. Small wonder that Flannery O'Connor should write Carver's editorial availability into her contracts with Harcourt Brace, or that Leslie Fiedler and Lionel Trilling should agree—along with so many others—in judging her the finest editor of her time.

MICHAEL MILLGATE

Sources *The Guardian* (13 Nov 1997) · *The Times* (27 Nov 1997) · *The Independent* (14 Nov 1997) · *New York Times* (16 Nov 1997) · personal knowledge (2004) · private information (2004) · F. O'Connor, *The habit of being: letters*, ed. S. Fitzgerald (1979), 76–7, 86–7, 319, 327–8 · b. cert. · d. cert.
Archives U. Texas, Bernard Malamud papers · University of Maryland, College Park, Katherine Anne Porter papers · University of Sheffield, Richard Hoggart MSS, corresp. and other papers · University of Tulsa, Oklahoma, Richard Ellmann papers
Likenesses photograph, repro. in *The Independent* · three photographs, University of Sheffield, Richard Hoggart MSS · two photographs, priv. coll.

Carver, John (*d.* 1621), colonial governor, is of uncertain parents and background. Several suggestions have been made as to his ancestry; in particular he has been identified with the son of Robert Carver who was baptized at Doncaster, Yorkshire, on 9 September 1565, but this remains unverified. By 1609 John Carver had married the widow Catherine Leggatt, *née* White (*d.* 1621), and was residing at Leiden in Holland. The couple had at least two children; one was buried in Leiden in 1609, a second was buried there in 1617. Carver's wife was probably the sister of the wife of John Robinson, minister to the English church at Leiden.

In 1617 some members of the Leiden congregation began planning to move to the New World, and sent 'our agent and a deacon of our church, John Carver' (Bradford, 32), along with Robert Cushman, to negotiate with the Virginia Company for a place to settle. In the following year Carver and Cushman shifted their attentions from the Virginia Company to a group of London merchants headed by Thomas Weston. As the plans for migration matured, Carver left Cushman to attend to affairs in London, while he went ahead to Southampton to prepare for the sailing from that port. This led to some dissension, as Cushman made an alteration in the articles of agreement, contrary to his instructions that only Carver could negotiate. But the pilgrims were dealing from a position of weakness and had to accept the demands of the London merchants, a fact which prejudiced the economic health of New Plymouth for many years.

On 11 November 1620, the day the *Mayflower* arrived in Provincetown harbour, Carver was one of those who signed the *Mayflower* compact. 'After this they chose, or rather confirmed, Mr. John Carver (a man godly and well approved amongst them) their Governor for that year' (Bradford, 76). On 6 December 1620 he was one of the party of ten who went out to explore Cape Cod. Carver survived the winter of 1620–21, during which nearly half of the *Mayflower* passengers died, but 'In this month of April, whilst they were busy about their seed, their Governor (Mr. John Carver) came out of the field very sick, it being a hot day. He complained greatly of his head and lay down, and within a few hours his senses failed, so as he never spake more till he died, which was within a few days after' (ibid., 86), in Plymouth, New England. His wife died a few weeks later. Carver lived less than half a year in New England. His great contributions to the success of the plantation at Plymouth were in his negotiations and preparations in London and Southampton on behalf of the Leiden congregation before their departure in 1620.

ROBERT CHARLES ANDERSON

Sources H. M. Dexter and M. Dexter, *The England and Holland of the pilgrims* (1906) · W. Bradford, *Of Plymouth Plantation, 1620–1647*, ed. S. E. Morison (1952) · R. C. Anderson, *The great migration begins: immigrants to New England, 1620–1633*, vol. 1 (1995) · D. B. Heath, *Mourt's relation* (1963) · Y. Kawashima, 'Carver, John', *ANB*

Carver, Jonathan (1710–1780), explorer and writer, was born at Weymouth, Massachusetts, on 13 April 1710, the son of David Carver (*d. c.*1727), town official, and Hannah Dyer. The family moved to Canterbury, Connecticut, when Jonathan was a boy. He remained in Canterbury after his father's death and may have been apprenticed as a shoemaker or studied medicine, but there is no evidence he pursued either career. On 20 October 1746 he married Abigail Robins (*d.* 1802), with whom he had five children.

About 1748 he took the family to the frontier settlement of Montague, Massachusetts, where he served as a selectman. When war erupted with France and its Amerindian allies in 1755, Carver enrolled in the Massachusetts militia and rose to the rank of captain. He participated in numerous engagements and was present at the infamous Amerindian 'massacre' of surrendered British troops at Fort William Henry in 1757, which was immortalized in James Fenimore Cooper's *Last of the Mohicans*. Carver's interpretation of events in his travel account was to contribute greatly to the historical misrepresentation of the massacre.

At the conclusion of the war Carver soon became involved with Major Robert Rogers's ill-fated endeavour to discover the elusive north-west passage, a west-flowing river that emptied into the Pacific Ocean. The mission, which began in August 1766, ended in the spring of the following year when Rogers was arrested on suspicion of treason and embezzlement. Carver's appeals for payment for his services were denied on the grounds that Rogers had not been authorized to send the expedition. The British commander-in-chief in America, Thomas Gage, was sympathetic to Carver, however, and was prepared to declare that Carver had carried out his services in good faith. In February 1769 Carver travelled to London to put his case before the Board of Trade. He received reimbursement of £1371 13*s*. 8*d*., which was far less than he had hoped, in exchange for his charts and journals. He subsisted in London on his combined work as a cartographer and rare successes from continued letters to officials begging for posts or compensation. Carver's desperate financial situation is most evident in his willingness to attach himself to yet another fruitless scheme of Rogers, though this came to nothing. By the mid-1770s Carver, still living in London, had made a second marriage, probably in 1774, this time to Mary Harris, a widow, though his first wife was still living; the couple had two children.

Carver's travels in search of the north-west passage gained the interest of Benjamin Franklin and Joseph Banks. During the winter of 1766–7 Carver had been separated from the rest of the expedition and resided with the Dakota Sioux Amerindians. He closely recorded their customs and culture in great detail in his journals, which he revised during the winter of 1767–8 and later in London in constant hope of its publication. With the assistance of Banks, then president of the Royal Society, his journals were first published in London as *Travels through America in the Years 1766, 1767, and 1768* (1778). His account was a vivid, well-illustrated, and insightful description of peoples who were known in the English-speaking world through the decades-old translated works of French Jesuits. The work was the most popular substantial account of any Amerindians originally written in English, and it enjoyed sixteen editions by the end of the century and translations into Dutch, German, and French. The authenticity of his travel account came into question immediately after publication, and in the second edition (1779) Carver added a preface defending its genuineness. Nevertheless, disbelief of various anecdotes and even Carver's authorship persisted, dogging the work throughout the next century. Carver's journals, bequeathed by Banks to the British Museum, demonstrate his authorship, but also that much had been altered for publication. Alexander Bicknell later claimed to be the editor of the account in the advertisement of his own *Doncaster Races*, but the extent and true orchestrator of the embellishments remain uncertain. Carver's clearest dishonesty was in the description of his own life story, which John Coakley Lettsom wrote up as a preface to the third edition (1781). Lettsom was not well acquainted with Carver and had no reason to lie about Carver's past, and thus the gross inaccuracies of his family's origins, his age, and his achievements were almost certainly Carver's handiwork; they remained uncorrected until the twentieth-century works of John Thomas Lee and John Parker. Their efforts, combined with the labours of other historians, have sifted much of the fact from fiction and redeemed Carver's account as a useful, credible description of a unique culture that was on the eve of extinction.

Although his travel account eventually won Carver fame and admiration, it did not save him from poverty. Carver died in London on 31 January 1780, 'absolutely and strictly starved' (*GM*, 49.183). He was buried at Holywell Mount. Both his wives outlived him.

TROY O. BICKHAM

Sources *The journals of Jonathan Carver and related documents, 1766–1770*, ed. J. Parker (1976) · J. T. Lee, 'A bibliography of Carver's travels', *State Historical Society of Wisconsin: Proceedings* (1909), 143–83 · J. Parker, 'Carver, Jonathan', *ANB* · D. S. Wilson, *In the presence of nature* (1978) · N. Gelb, 'Introduction', in *Jonathan Carver's travels through America, 1766–1768: an eighteenth-century explorer's account of uncharted America* (1993) · J. Parker, 'New light on Jonathan Carver', *American Magazine and Historical Chronicle*, 2 (1986), 4–17 · G. Williams, *The British search for the northwest passage in the eighteenth century* (1962) · *GM*, 1st ser., 50 (1780), 183 · *DNB*
Archives BL, journals, maps, and drawings during travels among the Sioux Indians, Add. MSS 8949–8950 | U. Mich., Clements L., corresp. with R. Rogers
Likenesses portrait, repro. in J. Carver, *Travels through the interior parts of North America, in the years 1766, 1767, 1768*, 3rd edn (1781), facing title-page
Wealth at death known to be impoverished: *GM*

Carver [Carvor], **Robert** [*pseud.* Robert Arnot] (*b.* 1487/8, *d.* in or after 1568), composer, was born between 25 March 1487 and 24 March 1488, possibly in Aberdeen. He is of uncertain parentage and upbringing, but a maternal uncle, Andrew Gray, was a chantry chaplain of St Nicholas's Church, Aberdeen; Andrew's parents, Robert and Ellen Gray, were thus the composer's maternal grandparents, and he may have been the son of a Robert Carver and Marjorie Gray of Aberdeen. Ample opportunity for a musical education was available in this city, through a choristership at the cathedral church, the chapel of St Mary's College, or the parish church of St Nicholas.

At about the age of fourteen Carver entered the noviciate at the Augustinian abbey of Scone, and he took his vows as a canon of the house in his sixteenth year. The key to understanding the next stage of his career is provided by the manner in which he chose to use in musical contexts the pseudonym Arnot. It appears that he took this name in recognition of patronage conferred by David Arnot, a trusted servant of James IV, who for some years after 1501 acted with the abbot of Scone to endow and found the royal collegiate church (sometimes called Chapel Royal) of St Mary and St Michael located within Stirling Castle. Established by 1503 for a dean and six dignitaries, and for ten other canons, ten minor canons, and six boy choristers all to be skilled in music and to form the choir, this immediately became the foremost institution in Scotland for the performance of divine service enhanced with elaborate polyphonic music. In 1508 Arnot was appointed its dean, and it seems likely that his particular service to Carver consisted of his persuading his colleague the abbot of Scone (an institution offering the composer no local scope for the exercise of his talents) to permit the young musician to accept appointment as a member of the Stirling choir. No documentation yet discovered fully substantiates this hypothesis; nevertheless, perhaps no choir in the kingdom other than that at Stirling could have tackled the monumental demands made by some of Carver's music, and such an act of patronage amply explains Carver's adopting the name of Arnot in gratitude.

Probably the composer is to be identified with the Robert Arnat who on 15 July 1543 was collated to a full canonry and prebend of the Stirling chapel; it seems likely that this promotion was conferred as due recognition for some thirty-five years' work at the college, and also as a sinecure source of income serving as a pension in his retirement. He returned to Scone Abbey, where he was at perfect liberty to continue composing and where his signature occurs frequently on a series of documents beginning in 1544. The community persisted even after the destruction of the abbey buildings in 1559, and Carver may well have remained in a form of religious life until his decease.

A single manuscript apparently originating at the Stirling royal chapel now serves as the sole surviving repository of Carver's attributed works, which extend to five masses (two dated) and two votive antiphons. The mass *Dum sacrum mysterium* (1508–13), for ten voices, was conceived on a gigantic scale; its cantus firmus honours St Michael, and probably it was begun when Carver (putatively) joined the Stirling chapel, dedicated to this saint, in 1508. Later works include the only extant mass composed by a Briton on the continental cantus firmus *L'homme armé*, a votive antiphon, *O bone Jesu*, for the remarkable number of nineteen voices, masses for six and five voices, and finally—dated 1546—a mass, *Pater creator omnium*. Between the earliest and latest works Carver travelled from a somewhat overblown engagement of the English late fifteenth-century style of ornamental, rhapsodic, and non-imitative polyphony to more concentrated forms of contrapuntal writing, admitting imitation and other points of structural integration, and examples of chordal orientation. He was capable of creating passages of considerable sonic beauty, and his vocal lines are never less than finely spun. His early achievement was commonly beset by a tendency to overwrite and by a somewhat stunted sense of harmonic structure and progression capable of generating rather graceless periods of static monotony. His finest compositions, especially the five-voice mass, overcame these debilities to yield work of high accomplishment. Advanced in years, Carver is presumed to have died soon after his latest documented appearance in 1568.   ROGER BOWERS

Sources R. Bowers, 'Robert Carver (1487/8–c.1568) at Scone and Stirling', *Early Music Review*, 48 (March 1999), 8–10 · D. J. Ross, 'New roots for a Renaissance Scottish master?', *Early Music Review*, 46 (Dec 1998), 8–10 · I. Woods, 'Towards a biography of Robert Carvor', *Music Review*, 49 (1988), 83–101 · K. Elliott, 'The Carver choirbook', *Music and Letters*, 41 (1960), 349–57 · D. J. Ross, *Musick fyne: Robert Carver and the art of music in sixteenth-century Scotland* (1993) · *The complete works of Robert Carver, and two anonymous masses*, ed. K. Elliott (1996) · C. Rogers, *History of the Chapel Royal in Scotland* (1882)

Archives NL Scot., MS Adv. 5. 1. 15

Carver, Robert (*d.* 1791), landscape and scene-painter, was born in Dublin, the son of Richard Carver (*d.* 1754), a history and landscape painter of some merit. Robert Carver studied under his father and also under Robert West at the Dublin Society Schools. His early career was based in Dublin, where he exhibited, with some success, landscapes in watercolour at the Dublin Society of Arts in 1765–8, and at the Free Society of Artists in London in 1765. His main occupation was that of a scene-painter for the theatre: in 1754 he began at the Smock Alley Theatre, Dublin, and in February 1760 at the rival Crow Street Theatre under Spranger Barry; this latter association continued with great success until Carver went to work for David Garrick in London. A press report of a 1766 production of *King Arthur* praises the scenery and emphasizes its importance for the production; 'the sudden Changes of the beautiful Variety of Scenery, seemed to surprise and alarm the Audience, as the effect of real magic … and not as the invention Theatrical Art' (Rosenfield and Croft-Murray, 15).

Barry recommended Carver to Garrick, who commissioned a scene for Drury Lane before inviting him to take up a permanent position there. Carver was employed at Drury Lane from 1770 to 1774 as one of a number of scene-painters including P. J. de Loutherbourgh. In the 1774–5 season, following his friend and countryman Barry, who had quarrelled with Garrick, Carver transferred to the rival Covent Garden Theatre, where he continued to paint scenes in conjunction with John Inigo Jones and other artists until his death. According to the painter Edward Dayes, Carver's first scene for Drury Lane, known as the Dublin Drop:

> was a representation of a storm on a coast, with a fine piece of water dashing against some rocks, and forming a sheet of foam truly terrific; this with the barren appearance of the surrounding country, and an old leafless tree or two, were the materials that composed a picture which would have done honour to the first artist, and will be remembered as the finest painting that ever decorated a theatre. (cited in Strickland, 161)

With his Irish pupil, Henry Hodgins, he painted the scenery for *The Touchstone* in 1779; his scenery for *The Castle of*

Andalusia in 1781 was noted to have been one of his greatest successes. Carver was also a successful landscape painter in oils and watercolours, exhibiting at the Incorporated Society of Artists from 1770 to 1780, and at the Royal Academy in 1789–90. A director of the Incorporated Society of Artists in 1772, Carver was also closely connected to the Free Society of Artists, elected a director in 1773, vice-president in 1776, and president in 1777. His landscapes, signed R. C. and painted in the style of Poussin, were well received, newspaper critics describing him as the 'ingenious and celebrated Mr Carver', and the atmospheric effects, such as those of early dawn, in which he excelled, are typical not only of his landscape paintings, but also his scene painting. *An Ideal Landscape* (n.d.) by Carver is reproduced in Waterhouse, *18c Painters*, p. 73. Reported to be of a sociable and generous temperament, Carver suffered from gout, and died in London at his home in Bow Street, Covent Garden, in November 1791. He was married, but nothing is known of his wife.

L. H. CUST, *rev.* DEBORAH GRAHAM-VERNON

Sources Redgrave, *Artists* · W. G. Strickland, *A dictionary of Irish artists*, 1 (1913); repr. with introduction by T. J. Snoddy (1989) · A. Crookshank and the Knight of Glin [D. Fitzgerald], *The painters of Ireland, c.1660–1920* (1978) · S. Rosenfeld and E. Croft-Murray, 'A checklist of scene painters working in Great Britain and Ireland in the 18th century [pt 1]', *Theatre Notebook*, 19 (1964–5), 6–20 · S. Rosenfeld, 'Scene painters at the London theatres in the 18th century', *Theatre Notebook*, 20 (1965–6), 113–18 · Graves, *Soc. Artists* · Waterhouse, *18c painters* · *The works of the late Edward Dayes*, ed. E. W. Brayley (privately printed, London, 1805) · E. Edwards, *Anecdotes of painters* (1808); facs. edn (1970)

Carvosso, Benjamin (1789–1854), Wesleyan Methodist minister, the son of William Carvosso, was born in Gluvian parish, Cornwall, on 29 September 1789. His father was born near Mousehole, in Mount's Bay, Cornwall, on 11 March 1750, and became first a fisherman and then a farmer; he was also for sixty years a most active class leader and local preacher in the Wesleyan Methodist Connexion, and he died at Dowstal, in the parish of Mylor, on 13 October 1834. Benjamin, though brought up by very pious parents, was not converted until his twenty-second year. He was admitted as a probationer by the Wesleyan conference in 1814, and, after working for five years as a minister in England, offered himself as a missionary.

On 5 October 1819 Carvosso married Deborah Banks. They arrived in Van Diemen's Land in 1820, Carvosso being the second minister of the Wesleyan denomination sent to the Australian colonies, and on 18 August he introduced Methodism to the island by the first Wesleyan public service in Hobart Town. In the same year he went to New South Wales, where, in the towns of Windsor, Sydney, and Paramatta, he passed the next five years of his ministry. He had a high sense of the importance of the press as a means of promoting religion, and with his brethren began in 1820 the publication of the *Australian Magazine*, the first of its type seen in the colony. Carvosso quarrelled with the Anglican clergy on theology and administration and in 1825 he returned to Hobart Town, where he conducted an active ministry.

After returning to Britain in 1830 Carvosso continued in the full discharge of his ministerial duties, and he lived in various parts of England for the remainder of his life. He wrote pietistic lives of members of his family, popular in their day, and temperance propaganda. He died at Tuckingmill, Cornwall, on 2 October 1854.

G. C. BOASE, *rev.* H. C. G. MATTHEW

Sources *Wesleyan Methodist Magazine*, 78 (1855), 382, 850–51 · G. Blencowe, *The faithful pastor: a memoir of B. Carvosso* (1857) · D. C. Colgrave, 'Carvosso, Benjamin', *AusDB*, vol. 1
Archives Mitchell L., NSW, Bonwick MSS

Carwardine [*married name* Butler], **Penelope** (1729–*c.*1801), miniature painter, was born at Withington, Herefordshire, on 29 April 1729, the eldest of the six daughters of John Carwardine of Thinghills Court, Withington, Herefordshire, and his wife, Anne Bullock of Preston Wynn, who was also a miniature painter. Her father having ruined the family estates Penelope took up miniature painting to earn a living and was established by 1754. She was probably the Mrs Carwardine (or Cawadine) exhibiting at the Incorporated Society of Artists in 1761, 1762, 1771, and 1772; in 1763 a Mrs Carwardine is listed as an artist in Thomas Mortimer's *Universal Director*. On 26 May of that year she married James Butler, organist, at St James's, Piccadilly.

No miniatures have yet come to light fully signed by Penelope Carwardine and much dispute has arisen from those miniatures signed with the initials PC (in his *English Portrait Miniatures*, 1952, Graham Reynolds discusses this problem of attribution). A discovery of drawings signed 'Carwardine' (shown at an exhibition at the Fry Gallery, Jermyn Street, London, October 1977) has helped to establish her qualities as an artist. While Ozias Humphry did paint a portrait of her in 1767, Reynolds notes:

> she may well at this time, or earlier, have sought to improve her style from him ... he did not guide her earliest work ... [this] shows the formality of the Lens manner mingling with the greater interest in character and humanity of the newer fashion. (Reynolds, 112)

A miniature of Maria Gunning, afterwards countess of Coventry, signed and dated 'P. C./1757', is in the Wallace Collection, London.

Penelope Carwardine was a close friend of Sir Joshua Reynolds and his sister Frances, and among Sir Joshua's works is a portrait of one of her sisters, painted by him as a present for her. She died, a childless widow, about 1801.

JENNETT HUMPHREYS, *rev.* EMMA RUTHERFORD

Sources B. S. Long, *British miniaturists* (1929) · D. Foskett, *A dictionary of British miniature painters*, 2 vols. (1972) · L. R. Schidlof, *The miniature in Europe in the 16th, 17th, 18th, and 19th centuries*, 4 vols. (1964) · H. Blättel, *International dictionary miniature painters / Internationales Lexikon Miniatur-Maler* (1992) · E. Lemberger, *Meisterminiaturen aus fünf Jahrhunderten* (1911) · D. Foskett, *Collecting miniatures* (1979) · G. Reynolds, *English portrait miniatures* (1952); rev. edn (1988) · C. Petteys, *Dictionary of women artists* (1985) · IGI
Likenesses O. Humphry, miniature, 1767, Fondation Custodia, Paris; repro. in Reynolds, *English portrait miniatures*, pl. 87 · T. Bardwell, portrait, priv. coll. [*see illus.*] · G. Romney, oils, repro. in *The art*

Penelope Carwardine (1729–*c.*1801), by Thomas Bardwell

collection of the late Lord Leverhulme (1926), 179 [sale catalogue, Anderson Galleries, New York, Feb 1926]

Carwell, Thomas. *See* Thorold, Thomas (*c.*1600–1664).

Cary, Archibald (1721–1787), revolutionary politician in America, was born in Williamsburg, Virginia, the son of Henry Cary (1675?–1749) and his second wife, Anne Edwards of Surry county (*d.* in or before 1741). The Virginia Carys were relatives of the merchant Carys of Bristol and London, who remained the Virginians' business correspondents. The immigrants settled in Warwick county, where several branches operated thriving plantations during the revolution of 1688. Archibald's grandfather and father relocated to Williamsburg, where they constructed most of the buildings of the College of William and Mary, which Archibald likely attended. In 1731 his father erected a new home, Ampthill, in Chesterfield county, 6 miles below Richmond on the James River (the house has been moved to Cary Street, Richmond). Archibald's father presented him with a 4000 acre plantation, Buckingham, in Goochland county, on his twenty-first birthday. In 1744 he married Mary Randolph (1727–1781), daughter of Richard Randolph of the Curles and Jane Bolling; they had five surviving daughters.

In 1746 Cary became a member of the Goochland county committee, and he served in the house of burgesses for Goochland (1748–9) and for Chesterfield (1756–76). He inherited Ampthill and a flour mill in nearby Warwick village in 1749. Cary expanded the family's manufacturing interests, with an iron mine in Buckingham and a foundry at Falling Creek, near Warwick, which remained active in 1779. As an agriculturist he imported British cattle to improve his herd.

By his own acknowledgement Cary was not a good speaker or writer in the legislature, but he gained the reputation of a dogged worker. He was one of only seven delegates who together chaired all the standing committees and two-thirds of the special committees in the house of burgesses between 1760 and independence. He served on the committee that framed the burgesses' temperate protest against the Stamp Act in December 1764 and, with most of the leadership, he opposed Patrick Henry's more forceful resolves in the following spring. Cary signed the associations against British imports in 1769, 1770, and 1774, protesting against the Townshend duties, the tea tax, and the punitive measures directed at Boston. He was on the first committee of correspondence in 1773, and attended each of Virginia's five extralegal conventions (1774–6). He chaired the committee to answer Governor Dunmore's emancipation proclamation in November 1775, the committee of the whole that proposed independence in May 1776, and the committee that drafted the declaration of rights and the state constitution. Having been elected to the republican senate in the autumn of 1776, he served as speaker until 1787.

During the early part of the war Cary and his partners operated several saltpetre plants on the James and Appomattox rivers, and in 1777 founded the Chatham Rope Yard Company of Richmond. In 1781 the British freed most of the rope-yard's slaves and burned the Warwick flour mill, until then a major supplier of the state's military. In June 1781, with Governor Thomas Jefferson at Monticello, Cary barely escaped capture by the British cavalry. In 1782 Jefferson and his daughters stayed at Ampthill while mourning Martha Jefferson. Three years later Cary participated in the state convention of the protestant Episcopal church of America, which elected Virginia's first bishop.

Although his estate included over 14,000 acres and 266 slaves, Cary struggled with debt throughout his life. In the scandal of 1766 Speaker John Robinson's loan to Cary of £3900 in public funds was among the largest. Two years later Cary mortgaged 11,000 acres for a British debt, and during the war he paid off £68,000 more in depreciated currency. At his death in late February 1787, at Ampthill, he was said still to owe £60,000, some of which remained outstanding in 1792. His burial place is unknown.

JOHN E. SELBY

Sources R. K. Brock, *Archibald Cary of Ampthill: wheelhorse of the revolution* (1937) · F. Harrison, *The Virginia Carys: an essay in genealogy* (1919) · J. Daniels, *The Randolphs of Virginia* (1972)
Likenesses portrait, priv. coll.; repro. in Harrison, *The Virginia Carys*, frontispiece
Wealth at death 14,108 acres and 266 slaves; £60,000 in debt: Brock, *Archibald Cary of Ampthill*; Harrison, *The Virginia Carys*, 91–2

Cary, Edward (d. 1711), Roman Catholic priest, was born at Melford, Suffolk, the third son of John Cary (d. 1639?) and Lucy Cary of Long Melford, Suffolk, minor gentry, but in reduced circumstances because of their recusancy. Cary was raised first in Suffolk, and then in Devon with his uncle Sir Edward Cary, probably after the death of his father in 1639. He entered the English Jesuit college at St Omer in 1635 but he returned to England in 1640 to enlist

in the royalist army. In August 1646 he went abroad to pursue a military career in the army of 'a Christian Prince' (Kenny, 501) but he abandoned it and was admitted into the English College, Rome, on 8 December to train for the priesthood. He said that he suffered from scruples which came and went suddenly. He was ordained on 25 March 1651 and left for England on 18 April 1653 to work on the Devon mission, probably as chaplain to his relatives. He appeared in Paris in June 1675 when he signed an attestation in support of the priest and controversialist John Sergeant; again in June 1679 in company with English Catholic exiles after the Popish Plot; and in May 1681 when he was made a canon. Using the pseudonym Adolphus Brontius he published *The Catechist Catechized* (1681), a defence of the oath of allegiance of 1606 which had been approved by the theologians of the Sorbonne and which most English Catholics accepted, but which was rejected by the Jesuits and condemned by Pope Innocent XI. It was a reply to the Jesuit John Huddlestone's *A Brief Instruction Touching the Oath of Allegiance*. Before the end of 1681 Cary was chaplain at Torre Abbey, Torquay (a property bought in 1662 by Sir George Cary, Sir Edward's son), and he was still there in 1684 when he was made vicar-general of Cornwall. He was appointed 'Chaplain-General to his Majesty's Catholic forces' (Gillow, *Lit. biog. hist.*, 1.418) by James II and in 1687–8 his own salary and those of two other army chaplains were paid from secret service funds; he maintained a chapel on Hounslow Heath for the soldiers. He fled the country at the revolution and is little heard of again. He served as second chaplain, or 'Extraordinary confessor', to the English Poor Clares at Rouen (1693–1703) and in 1693 he acted as a Jacobite courier into England. He died in France in 1711.

LEO GOOCH

Sources A. Kenny, ed., *The responsa scholarum of the English College, Rome*, 2, Catholic RS, 55 (1963), 500–01 · W. Kelly, ed., *Liber ruber venerabilis collegii Anglorum de urbe*, 2, Catholic RS, 40 (1943), 38 · Gillow, *Lit. biog. hist.*, 1.41 · G. Anstruther, *The seminary priests*, 2 (1975), 47 · E. Grew and M. S. Grew, *English court in exile: James II at St Germain* (1911) · G. Holt, *St Omers and Bruges colleges, 1593–1773: a biographical dictionary*, Catholic RS, 69 (1979), 57 · A. M. C. Forster, 'The chronicles of the English Poor Clares of Rouen [pts 1–2]', *Recusant History*, 18 (1986–7), 59–102, 149–91 · J. Y. Akerman, ed., *Moneys received and paid for secret services of Charles II and James II from 30th March 1679 to 25th December 1688*, CS, 52 (1851)

Cary [née Tanfield], **Elizabeth**, Viscountess Falkland (1585–1639), writer and translator, was born at Burford Priory, Oxfordshire, the only child of Lawrence *Tanfield (c.1551–1625), lawyer, and his wife, Elizabeth (d. 1629), daughter of Giles Symonds and Catherine, née Lee. Much of what is known of her derives from a manuscript life written about 1650 by one of her daughters, then a nun at Cambrai. She was educated at home, proving adept at foreign languages. It is possible that she was taught by both Michael Drayton and John Davies (1565?–1618). Her fluency in French and Italian was praised by Drayton when he dedicated to her two of his *Englands Heroicall Epistles* (1597); the fact that he addresses her as 'my honoured Mistres' suggests that he may have been employed in her father's household. Davies referred with pride to his 'pupill' when he made her a joint dedicatee of his *The*

Elizabeth Cary, Viscountess Falkland (1585–1639), by Paul van Somer, c.1620

twenty years of constant pregnancy and nursing, short stature, and a tendency to obesity, coupled with a possible rheumatic condition, were hardly conducive to performance in courtly theatricals.

In the first few years after their marriage Sir Henry pursued his career at court and as a soldier in the Low Countries, and the couple did not set up home together until 1606. Lady Cary first became pregnant in 1608, giving birth to a daughter, Catherine, in 1609. Ten more children followed: Lucius *Cary (1609/10–1643), Lorenzo (b. 1613), Anne (b. 1614), Edward (b. 1616), Elizabeth (b. 1617), Lucy (b. 1619), Vittoria (b. 1620), Mary (b. 1622), and Henry and Patrick *Cary (c.1624–1657).

Throughout Lady Cary sustained her literary activities. The first female author to write original drama in English, her first play, a tragedy set in Syracuse and dedicated to her husband, was probably written about 1604, although the manuscript has not been recovered. Her second play, *The Tragedy of Mariam*, probably composed between 1604 and 1608, was published in 1613, possibly as a result of John Davies's very public encouragement. It was not offered for performance in the public playhouses and is linked generically with the body of drama produced within the group of writers associated with Mary Herbert, countess of Pembroke. However, it is striking for its well-rounded characters and energetic dialogue, both of which render it entirely suitable for representation on stage. The plot is based upon stories surrounding the death of Mariam, the last of the Hasmoneans, the Jewish royal dynasty, as related in Thomas Lodge's 1602 translation of the works of the Jewish historian Josephus. Additionally Elizabeth's biography bears witness to a variety of manuscript works as yet unrecovered, including a verse life of Tamburlaine, verses to the Virgin Mary, the lives of St Agnes, St Elizabeth of Portugal, and St Mary Magdalene, and translations of Seneca and Blosius. Elizabeth was also the first female to attempt a literary narrative of events in English history: hers is the hand behind 'Edwarde the Seconde: his raigne and deathe' (Northants. RO, Finch-Hatton papers FH1), dated 1626 and published in 1680 as *The History of the Life, Reign and Death of Edward II* and *The History of the most Unfortunate Prince, King Edward II*, previously attributed to her husband. Like *The Tragedy of Mariam* it contains strikingly sympathetic portrayals of transgressive women. That her literary and linguistic skills were none the less widely recognized is evident from others' dedication of their works to her—for instance *Englands Helicon, or, The Muses Harmony* (1614), *A Sixthe Booke to the Countess of Pembroke's Arcadia* (1624), and *The Workes of Mr John Marston* (1633).

On 14 November 1620 Cary was created Viscount Falkland in the Scottish peerage. Lady Falkland went to Ireland following her husband's appointment in 1622 to the post of lord deputy, and her two youngest children were born there. When part of her jointure was mortgaged to meet expenses incurred in taking up the deputyship her father was so displeased that he disinherited her in favour of her eldest son, Lucius. From this point the Falklands

Muses Sacrifice (1612). Her precocious talent is revealed in her earliest extant work, which predates her marriage, 'The mirror of the world', a translation of Abraham Ortelius's *Le mirroir du monde* (1598), dedicated to her great-uncle Sir Henry Lee, champion of Elizabeth I.

In October 1602 Elizabeth married Sir Henry *Cary (c.1575–1633), son of Sir Edward Cary and his wife, Catherine Knyvett. According to John Chamberlain, Cary was to receive £2000 upon marriage, £2000 after two years, and either £3000 on Lawrence Tanfield's death (should Tanfield have other children in the meantime) or his entire estate as heir. The biography of Elizabeth suggests that this handsome financial package was the primary attraction of the marriage for Cary, an ambitious but impoverished courtier: 'he married her only for being an heir, for he had no acquaintance with her (she scarce ever having spoken to him) and she was nothing handsome, though then very fair' (Weller and Ferguson, 188). The fact that there are no known records of her taking part in court masques, even though she had a great interest in them, suggests that she did not fulfil the requisite aesthetic criteria. She was not particularly interested in her own physical adornment, although she allowed herself to be dressed finely to please her husband; besides, nearly were constantly in financial difficulties. Elizabeth tried to establish various schemes in Ireland, which failed owing to her lack of acumen. She returned to England in 1625 and set about trying to settle her husband's financial affairs, efforts that were a source of embarrassment to him. In the following year she embarked upon another course of action, which was to cause even more embarrassment to her staunchly protestant husband: she converted publicly to Catholicism, taking the additional name Maria.

Elizabeth's conversion incurred the displeasure of Charles I also, who placed her under house arrest. His anger seems to have been short-lived because when she requested her liberty, after a period of six weeks, he seemed to have quite forgotten about her and granted her freedom with a comment that he had not meant her to be incarcerated for so long. Falkland was less forgiving; he wrote to the king demanding a separation *a mensa et thoro*; furthermore he refused to give his wife any financial support and demanded that she rejoin her mother's household, but Lady Tanfield was extremely unwilling to receive her recusant daughter. Lady Falkland lived alone and in dire poverty for some time, while her husband was bent upon a course of virtually starving her into recanting her faith. She petitioned the king with her desperate circumstances and on 4 October 1627 the privy council ordered Falkland to pay her £500 a year in maintenance. He never fulfilled this obligation despite further orders, in 1628 and 1630, to do so. It is possible that relations between the couple gradually became more cordial after his recall from Ireland in 1629, although the two were never reconciled as husband and wife. Lady Falkland's high-profile religious stance remained a barrier. Her *Reply of the most Illustrious Cardinal of Perron* (1630) proved to be her most controversial work; an overt piece of Catholic propaganda, it was dedicated—publicly via the printed text, and privately via presentation volumes inscribed with an autograph verse—to Queen Henrietta Maria, identifying her as an ambassador for the Catholic faith in England. The book was printed at Douai and is reputed to have been burnt upon arrival in England; several copies have survived, however, including three inscribed presentation volumes.

Lady Falkland's poverty and marital troubles necessarily rendered her peripheral to court society. Nevertheless she forged links with some of the most influential women of the age, notably fellow Roman Catholic converts Mary, countess of Buckingham; Susan, countess of Denbigh; and Katherine, duchess of Buckingham—the mother, sister, and wife, respectively, of the king's favourite, George Villiers, duke of Buckingham. The duchess of Buckingham, for instance, tried to intercede on Elizabeth's behalf in the ongoing dispute between the Falklands. Furthermore the queen herself lent her support to her efforts to gain a place for her daughter Anne at the Spanish court, although this plan did not come to fruition.

In the aftermath of a leg injury sustained at Theobalds, Falkland suffered gangrene and died in September 1633,

his wife at his bedside. Lady Falkland thereupon determined that six of her children (Anne, Lucy, Mary, Elizabeth, Patrick, and Henry) be sent to the continent to be received into the Catholic faith. The children had been living with their eldest brother, Lucius, now second Viscount Falkland, partly owing to their mother's impecunious state, partly as a result of the fear of her influence upon their religious leanings. While Lady Falkland regained possession of her daughters with relative ease, and ensured their conversion to Catholicism and reception into a convent at Cambrai before her death, access to her sons was more difficult. In 1636 she daringly arranged for them to be kidnapped from their brother's house, and then kept them moving around London to avoid detection. She was called to account for her actions, undergoing examination first by Lord Chief Justice Sir John Bramston and second in the Star Chamber. Her questioners assumed that the boys were already abroad, and she was content to let them think so since this would facilitate their subsequent escape to the continent; she therefore gave elusive and unhelpful answers to her questioners, which resulted in a threat of imprisonment in the Tower, although there is no evidence that this threat was carried out.

Elizabeth Cary died in London in October 1639 and was buried in Henrietta Maria's chapel in Somerset House. Until comparatively recently she was viewed principally as the mother of the poet and royalist hero Lucius Cary, although it was her recusant activity that rendered her of interest to Catholic historians in the nineteenth and early twentieth centuries; no less than three biographical works appeared between 1861 and 1939. These works were largely based upon her daughter's biography, which, though rather hagiographical in tone, testifies to her remarkable steadfastness and integrity in the face of poverty and persecution; her personal motto was 'Be and seem'. However, the growth in feminist literary scholarship has demonstrated her significance within her cultural milieu.   STEPHANIE HODGSON-WRIGHT

Sources *CSP dom.*, 1602–40 · *CSP Ire.*, 1625–32 · biography of Lady Falkland, Archives Departementales du Nord, Lille, MS xx (c.1650) · G. Fullerton, *The life of Elisabeth Lady Falkland* (1883) · *Dudley Carleton to John Chamberlain, 1603–1624: Jacobean letters*, ed. M. Lee (1972) · *The letters of John Chamberlain*, ed. N. E. McClure, 2 vols. (1939) · K. B. Murdock, *The sun at noon* (1939) · B. Newdigate, *Michael Drayton and his circle* (1941) · R. B. Simpson, *The Lady Falkland: her life* (1861) · B. Weller and M. W. Ferguson, eds., *The tragedy of Mariam, the fair queen of Jewry, with The Lady Falkland: her life, by one of her daughters* (1994)
Likenesses P. van Somer, oils, c.1620, Sarah Campbell Blaffer Foundation, Houston, Texas [*see illus.*] · T. Athow, engraving (after P. Van Somer, c.1621), AM Oxf., Sutherland collection · T. Athow, wash drawing, AM Oxf. · marble tomb effigy (on Sir Lawrence and Lady Tanfield's tomb), Burford church, Oxfordshire

Cary, Francis Stephen (1808–1880), painter and art teacher, was born at Kingsbury, Warwickshire, on 10 May 1808, the son of the Revd Henry Francis *Cary (1772–1844), translator of Dante, and his wife, Jane (1777–1832), daughter of James Ormsby of Sandymount, near Dublin. In 1810 he moved with his family to London. A fragile child who

Francis Stephen Cary (1808–1880), by James Hayllar, 1851

was taken for his health to the seashore at Ramsgate and Littlehampton, he was educated at home, mostly by his father, and enjoyed the society of the latter's literary friends, including Samuel Taylor Coleridge and Charles and Mary Lamb, whose double portrait Francis later painted (1834; NPG). At the age of eighteen he began to study at Henry Sass's Art School in Streatham Street, Bloomsbury, later progressing to become a student at the Royal Academy Schools. For a brief period he painted in the studio of Sir Thomas Lawrence (1769–1830) with the intention of becoming his pupil, but Lawrence died before this expectation could be fulfilled. In 1829 he studied in Paris, and later in Italy and Munich. In 1833, 1834, and 1835 he accompanied his newly widowed father, to whom he was devoted, on extensive tours of Italy, France, and Germany, visiting many major picture galleries.

Cary exhibited at the Society of Artists and other London venues, making his début at the Royal Academy in 1837 and exhibiting there nearly every year thereafter until his death. The titles of the works he exhibited at the Royal Academy demonstrate his range: characters from Shakespeare (*Bianca, from the Taming of the Shrew*, 1856) and Cervantes (*Sancho at his First Meeting with the Duchess*, 1845), biblical subjects (*The Angel of the Lord*, 1850), rural genre, and a portrayal of *John Evelyn's First Meeting with Grinling Gibbons* (1855). On 9 August 1841 he married Louisa Octavia, daughter of Charles Allen Philipps of St Bride's Hill, Pembrokeshire, and in 1842 he assumed management of Henry Sass's school in Bloomsbury, London. He is best known as head of this school, where under the direction of Sass and Cary many later Victorian painters and sculptors trained, including Charles West Cope, John Everett

Millais, Dante Gabriel Rossetti, and Henry Hugh Armstead. In 1844 and 1847 Cary entered designs in the Westminster Hall competitions for the decoration of the new houses of parliament. He retired in 1874 to Abinger Wotton, Surrey, where he died at his home, Pasture Wood House, childless, on 5 January 1880; his wife survived him.   LUCY OAKLEY

Sources DNB · H. Cary, *Memoir of the Rev. Henry Francis Cary*, 2 vols. (1847) · *The exhibition of the Royal Academy* (1837); (1840–42); (1844–7); (1849–59); (1861–2); (1866–7); (1869); (1871); (1873); (1875–6) [exhibition catalogues] · *The Times* (9 Jan 1880) · *The Athenaeum* (17 Jan 1880) · *Art Journal*, 42 (1880), 108 · *The Builder*, 38 (1880), 81 · Bryan, *Painters* · Wood, *Vic. painters*, 3rd edn · m. cert. · CGPLA Eng. & Wales (1880)

Likenesses J. Hayllar, pencil and chalk drawing, 1851, NPG [*see illus.*]

Wealth at death under £10,000: probate, 24 March 1880, CGPLA Eng. & Wales

Cary, Henry, first Viscount Falkland (*c*.1575–1633), lord deputy of Ireland, said to have been born at Aldenham, was the son of Sir Edward Cary (*d*. 1618) of Berkhamsted and Aldenham, Hertfordshire, master of the jewel house, and his wife, Catherine (*d*. 1622), daughter of Sir Henry Knevet or Knyvett and widow of Henry, Lord Paget. He was entered at Gray's Inn on 2 August 1590. The date of his matriculation from Exeter College, Oxford, is unknown, although he is said to have been aged sixteen. Exhaustive investigation of the knighthoods bestowed on various Henry Carys, Careys, and Caryes in the late Elizabethan and early Jacobean period has decisively concluded that the future first viscount was knighted at Dublin on 12 July 1599. In October 1602 Cary married Elizabeth (1585–1639) [*see* Cary, Elizabeth], daughter of Sir Lawrence Tanfield, lord chief baron of the exchequer, a woman whose passionate engagement with the theological controversy of the early Stuart period led her ultimately to Roman Catholicism. They had eleven children, including Lucius *Cary and Patrick *Cary.

Cary left his wife and home in 1604 to undertake a period of military service on the continent, during which he evinced a valour recorded in the lines of an epigram by Ben Jonson. Taken prisoner by the Spanish at the siege of Ostend, his return cost his family a ransom which supposedly marked the beginning of enduring financial difficulties. Cary was then introduced at court, and became one of the gentlemen of the bedchamber. In 1617 he reputedly paid £5000 for his appointment as comptroller of the household, an office which also made him a member of the privy council. On 14 November 1620 he was created first Viscount Falkland and Lord Carye in the Scottish peerage. The title and its descent, to heirs male bearing the name of Carye, was confirmed by a patent of naturalization dated 18 September 1627, as if he and they had been natives of Scotland. Falkland was MP for Hertfordshire in the parliament which met in 1621.

Through the influence of the marquess of Buckingham, Falkland was appointed to succeed Viscount Grandison as lord deputy of Ireland. Rumours of his impending appointment began in the middle of 1621, but his patent was only sealed in March 1622, and he was not sworn at

Henry Cary, first Viscount Falkland (*c.*1575–1633), by Paul van Somer

Dublin until September. The delay has been accounted for partly by the need to engineer as graceful a recall as possible for Grandison, widely suspected of corruption, but mainly by the precariousness of the Falklands' own financial position, a solution to which was not found until his wife was persuaded to mortgage her jointure, whereupon she was disinherited by her outraged father. '[D]riven by his twin demons of pride and poverty', Falkland's efforts to exploit opportunities in Ireland to improve his own financial standing did not always accord well with those of his principal patron (Treadwell, 194). Appropriation of admiralty prize and customs revenues were not infrequent sources of tension between the two. However, there can be little doubt about who benefited most from the numerous plantation schemes over which Falkland presided. Having inveigled lands out of their owners and connived at and forced the establishment of major new estates, such as the manor of Villiers which sprawled across 11,000 acres of the most profitable land in the Ormond lordship of Ossory, the lord deputy was left feeling short-changed, while it was his handling of one of the more outrageous expropriations, concerning the lands of the O'Byrne lordship of Ranelagh in co. Wicklow, which provided the occasion of his own downfall. The cause, however, was more complicated. Falkland's appointment as lord deputy had been welcomed by those in Ireland who chafed at the restrictions placed on the inefficient and ineffective policy of plantation by the officious and reformist lord treasurer, the earl of Middlesex. Enjoying the support of Buckingham, the new lord deputy had far greater freedom to prosecute colonial rapine, and although Middlesex admonished him to put Irish finances

in order, Falkland did not disappoint New English expectations. Lobbied by Sir William Parsons and other proponents of vigorous plantation, Falkland formed the opinion that those Irish lords who transgressed against the king's rights were 'like nettles that sting being gently handled, but sting not being crushed' (Canny, 261).

The new lord deputy brought the same aspiration to the intractable question of recusancy and, at least until the dictates of Stuart foreign policy demanded otherwise, Falkland was enthusiastic in his application of the laws for the persecution of Catholic priests, whom he expelled by proclamation in January 1623, and the punishment of Catholic laity. However, it shortly became clear that, where profit was involved, Falkland and his leading backers at court in England did not differentiate on grounds of religion. The lord deputy managed to alienate significant sections of the protestant interest in Ireland. His determination to prosecute the interests of the crown brought him into conflict with the lord chancellor of Ireland, Adam Loftus, first Viscount Loftus of Ely, and Sir Francis Annesley, the future Viscount Mountnorris, another member of the Villiers affinity. Falkland also permitted an investigation of the Ulster plantations undertaken by the London companies which discovered grave abuses committed in breach of the original contracts. Just as the process of calling the companies to account gathered momentum, Falkland found himself presiding over a dramatic reversal in official attitudes towards Catholic Ireland. In 1626, with a war against Spain looming, in return for the promise of sizeable financial subventions the English crown indicated a willingness to concede proprietary rights and religious freedom to the Old English gentry, the so-called 'graces'. Not only did this forestall further progress in the expropriation of Catholic lands, it also held out the prospect of an official toleration for Catholicism, a prospect which scandalized planter society.

Finding his public authority undermined yet further by personal circumstances in which his own wife chose this less than auspicious moment finally to convert to Catholicism, Falkland's personal misgivings about the new direction of policy became stronger. Much doubting the loyalty of the Old English, he was probably relieved when negotiations for 'the matters of grace and bounty' were transferred from Dublin to Whitehall, where they were concluded in May 1628. 'More likely through ignorance rather than design' (Canny, 268). Falkland, falling foul of Poynings' law, which restricted the rights of the Irish parliament to introduce legislation, then managed to prevent the 'graces' from being put into effect by bungling the preparations for the parliament which was required to give them statutory authority. The concessions, which arguably the English government had never sincerely intended to implement anyway, remained in a discretionary limbo, largely unenforced and wholly unenforceable, until a future lord deputy, Thomas Wentworth, gave them the *coup de grâce*.

In the meantime, Falkland was free to resume his persecution of Catholic regulars, issuing a proclamation in

April 1629 forbidding the exercise of ecclesiastical jurisdiction derived from Rome, and ordering the dissolution of Catholic religious orders. Somewhat fancifully, the lord deputy claimed within a month that the houses of the religious orders had been generally abandoned. In reality, the regular clergy had simply resumed their habitual discretion. By then, Falkland's patron had been dead nearly a year, and moves towards peace with both France and Spain dramatically altered the complexion of affairs in England and in Ireland, leaving the lord deputy gravely exposed. When the Irish privy council investigated the complaints of the O'Brynes of Wicklow and found they had been the victims of false testimony made with official sanction, Falkland was powerless to resist recall to London in 1629. He still entertained hopes of retaining his post, mounting a counter-attack in Star Chamber against Mountnorris and others whom he claimed had slandered him, while his principal supporters in Ireland, Richard Boyle, earl of Cork, Sir William Parsons, and Roger Jones, Viscount Ranelagh, all desperately sought to stave off the ascendancy of their principal rivals, Loftus, Mountnorris, and Charles, Viscount Wilmot. In the event the outcome was very close-run, and the decision to replace Falkland was not made until March 1631.

Falkland broke his leg at Theobalds Park, Hertfordshire, in 1633. Amputation proved insufficient to prevent the spread of a fatal gangrene, and he died shortly afterwards. He was buried at Aldenham on 25 September 1633 and was succeeded by his eldest son, Lucius. Falkland has enjoyed a modest reputation as a man of letters, although a strong case has been made that the history of the reign of Edward II, not published until late 1679 or early 1680 but commonly attributed to him, was written by his wife. However, it has also been claimed that the book was in fact a product of the political crisis surrounding the supposititious Popish Plot of 1679.   SEAN KELSEY

Sources DNB · Wood, *Ath. Oxon.* · *Poems of Patrick Cary*, ed. V. Delany (1978) · J. A. R. Marriott, *The life and times of Lucius Cary* (1908) · A. Clarke, *The Old English in Ireland, 1625–1642* (1966) · J. C. Beckett, *The making of modern Ireland* (1966) · T. W. Moody and others, eds., *A new history of Ireland, 3: Early modern Ireland, 1534–1691* (1976) · GEC, *Peerage*, 5.239–40 · S. R. Gardiner, *Reports of cases in the courts of star chamber and high commission*, CS, 39 (1886), 1 ff. · A. Clarke, 'The army and politics in Ireland, 1625–30', *Studia Hibernica*, 4 (1964), 28–53 · D. R. Woolf, 'The true date and authorship of Henry, Viscount Falkland's *History of the life, reign and death of King Edward II'*, *Bodleian Library Record*, 12 (1985–8), 440–52 · N. Canny, *Making Ireland British, 1580–1650* (2001) · V. Treadwell, *Buckingham and Ireland* (1998) · I. Grundy, 'Falkland's *History of King Edward II'*, *Bodleian Library Record*, 13 (1988–91), 82–3

Archives BL, corresp. and papers, Add. MSS 11033, 18824; Sloane MS 3827 · PRO NIre., letter-book | Chatsworth House, Derbyshire, corresp. with first earl of Cork · CKS, corresp. with Lionel Cranfield

Likenesses J. Brown, oils, c.1620, Helmingham Hall, Suffolk · J. Brown, line engraving, pubd 1847 (after G. P. Harding), BM, NPG · J. Barra, line engraving (after P. van Somer), BM · J. Brown, line engraving and stipple (after P. van Somer), BM, NPG; repro. in Harding, *Ancient historical pictures* (1844) · P. Van Somer, portrait, priv. coll. [see illus.]

Cary, Henry Francis (1772–1844), translator, was born on 6 December 1772 at Gibraltar, the son of William Cary

(1745/6–1834), then serving as a captain in the 1st regiment of foot (the Royal Scots) there, and his first wife, Henrietta (d. c.1778), daughter of Theophilus Brocas, dean of Killala. His great-grandfather was Mordecai Cary (1687–1751), bishop of Clonfert (1732–5) and of Killala (1735–51). About 1778 his father left the army and settled in Staffordshire.

Henry Cary was educated at a school in Uxbridge, at Rugby School, at Sutton Coldfield grammar school, and, from 1787, at King Edward VI Grammar School in Birmingham. He contributed verse to the *Gentleman's Magazine*, some of which was reprinted in his *Sonnets and Odes* (1788). In that year he began to study Italian, being already proficient in Greek, Latin, and French. Before going up to Oxford as a commoner at Christ Church in April 1790, he made the acquaintance of Anna Seward (1747–1809), and they corresponded until her death. He took his BA degree in January 1794 and proceeded MA in 1796, but was disappointed at not obtaining a fellowship at Oxford. Although he would have liked to join the army, he acceded to the wish of his father (who was then living at Cannock) and was ordained in 1796. He was presented by his father's friend the earl of Uxbridge to the vicarage of Abbot's Bromley, Staffordshire. In August or September of 1796 he was married to Jane (1777–1832), daughter of James Ormsby, of Sandymount, Donnybrook, Dublin, whose wife was a friend of Cary's mother. The couple's first son was born in 1797; there were five more sons, born between 1802 and 1817, including Francis Stephen *Cary, painter and art teacher, and two daughters, born in 1799 and 1801.

In January 1797 Cary began his translation of Dante's *Divina commedia* into blank verse. He started with the *Purgatorio* in 1797–8, but in 1800 he turned his attention to the *Inferno*, and it was this part which was published first, in 1805–6, accompanied by the Italian text. Sales were small, but Cary continued, and his translation was completed in 1812. As he could not find a publisher he published the work at his own expense (which he could ill afford) in 1814. It was entitled *The Vision, or, Hell, Purgatory, and Paradise, of Dante Alighieri*, and was printed in three sextodecimo volumes in such small type that it was almost unreadable. Cary was not adept at self-promotion, and his translation initially attracted little attention.

While he was working on Dante, Cary's private life had undergone various vicissitudes. He had benefited in 1800 from his presentation by the lord chancellor (on the recommendation of the earl of Uxbridge) to the vicarage of Kingsbury, Warwickshire. Although the emoluments were not large, the house was bigger than the one at Abbot's Bromley, so he moved there and employed a curate to look after Abbot's Bromley. He suffered from ill health in the early 1800s, but worse was to follow in 1807 when his family was afflicted by typhus, and his younger daughter, Harriet, died of the disease, aged six. Cary was consequently afflicted with a mental illness which recurred in future years. Partly to escape from the scene of his grief he moved to London and installed a curate at Kingsbury. From 1810 to 1813 he held a readership at the Berkeley Chapel (near Berkeley Square), and then accepted the offer of a curacy and lecturership at Chiswick, where he lived in the house which was formerly the residence of Hogarth.

In 1816 Cary's elder daughter, Jane (of whom he had high hopes), died of consumption, aged seventeen. Cary had planned to take her to a warmer climate, and so had resigned his curacy at Chiswick. For financial reasons he had to seek new clerical employment and so he became curate of the Savoy Chapel. Then in October 1817 he made the acquaintance by chance of Coleridge at Littlehampton, and the praise which Coleridge gave to Cary's Dante in a lecture early in 1818 (reinforced by a favourable article by Ugo Foscolo in the *Edinburgh Review*) led to the sale of 1000 copies in less than three months, and the publication of a second edition in 1819.

In the early 1820s, in order to raise money for the education of his sons, Cary wrote numerous articles for periodicals, especially for the *London Magazine*. As a result he became acquainted with many writers including Charles Lamb, William Hazlitt, Thomas De Quincey, Thomas Carlyle, John Clare, Thomas Hood, and Gabriele Rossetti. He abandoned his journalistic work in 1825 and applied for the post of under-librarian (keeper) of antiquities of the British Museum. He failed to obtain this, but in June 1826 he became assistant keeper of the department of printed books. Cary began by working on the literature section of the classified catalogue of the department, which had been begun in 1824, but in the early 1830s the trustees of the British Museum decided that priority should be given to a new edition of the author catalogue. By this time Cary was engaged in the other routine duties of librarianship. Like the other officers of the museum he had a residence in the building (which he complained was too small for his family), and was visited there by many of his literary friends, particularly Charles Lamb.

In November 1832 Cary's wife died, and this precipitated another attack of mental illness. The trustees granted him six months' sick leave, during which he travelled to Italy with his fifth son, Francis. These recurrent nervous breakdowns led the principal trustees to pass over Cary in favour of Antonio Panizzi for the post of keeper of printed books when H. H. Baber retired in June 1837. The forceful Panizzi was the better choice, as Cary was not suited to administrative responsibilities, but he was bitterly hurt by his rejection, and he sent to *The Times* the letter of protest which he had addressed to the lord chancellor (one of the principal trustees). Cary resigned his post in October 1837 and left the museum in December. The remaining eight years of his life were devoted to literary work, including the preparation of a new edition of his translation of the *Divina commedia* which was published in 1844, just before his death. This work is his chief claim to fame, and it remained a standard text well into the twentieth century, despite the fact that the number of translators of the work between 1782 and 1966 amounted to eighty-four. Cary's version was admired by Wordsworth, Keats, Lamb, Coleridge, Macaulay, and Ruskin, and in 1966 the author of a work on translations of the *Divina commedia* wrote 'Cary's version still holds its place as a minor classic,

thanks to the fact that its author was a competent versifier with some poetic perception' (Cunningham, 2.274–5). His other writings included his translations of Aristophanes' *The Birds* (1824), and of Pindar (1833), and a work entitled *The Early French Poets* (1846) which was based on his articles in the *London Magazine*.

As a result of representations by the trustees of the British Museum and Samuel Rogers, Cary was in 1841 awarded a civil-list pension of £200 per annum. By this time he was financially comfortable because he had received a considerable legacy on the death of his father in 1834. Cary himself died on 14 August 1844 at his home, 6 Charlotte Street, Bloomsbury, where his son Francis conducted a school of art, and was buried in Poets' Corner, Westminster Abbey, on 21 August.   P. R. HARRIS

Sources R. W. King, *The translator of Dante: the life of Henry Francis Cary* (1925) · H. Cary, *Memoir of the Rev. Henry Francis Cary*, 2 vols. (1847) · G. F. Cunningham, *The 'Divine comedy' in English: a critical bibliography*, 2 vols. (1965–6) · P. Toynbee, *Dante in English literature*, 2 vols. (1909) · P. R. Harris, *A history of the British Museum Library, 1753–1973* (1998) · BM · H. F. Cary, letter, *The Times* (18 July 1837) · *GM*, 2nd ser., 3 (1835), 558, 562 · J. L. Chester, ed., *The marriage, baptismal, and burial registers of the collegiate church or abbey of St Peter, Westminster*, Harleian Society, 10 (1876) · will of William Cary, proved 10 Sept 1834, PRO, PROB 11/1836, quire 502 · will of Henry Francis Cary, proved 26 Aug 1844, PRO, PROB 11/2003, quire 620 · St George's, Bloomsbury, searchers' reports, death of Jane Cary, 24 Nov 1832, LMA, P82/GEO1/63 · d. cert.

Archives BM | BL, letters to John Clare, Egerton MSS 2246, 2248–2249 · CUL, letters to Messrs Taylor and Hessey · FM Cam., letters to James Bailey · Harvard U., Houghton L., letters to Anna Seward · U. Durham L., corresp. with Darley

Likenesses H. Robinson, stipple, 1847 (after F. S. Cary), BM, NPG; repro. in Cary, *Memoir*, frontispiece · F. S. Cary, portrait, exh. 1868, repro. in King, *Translator of Dante*, 150 · T. Richmond, miniature (in youth), repro. in King, *Translator of Dante*, 66 · bust, BM; repro. in King, *Translator of Dante*, frontispiece

Wealth at death under £12,000; plus £599 8s. 11d. for leaseholds and rents due: PRO, death duty registers, IR 26/1670, fol. 682

Cary, Sir John (d. 1395), justice, was the son and heir of Robert Cary of Torrington and Cockington, Devon, and his wife, Joan, daughter of Guy, Lord Brian. He himself married Margaret, daughter of Robert Holway of Holway, Devon. He entered the service of Edward, prince of Wales, and in 1365 was holding, by the prince's grant, the wardenship of the stannary in Devon. His appointment as a justice of the peace for Devon in 1369 was the first of many judicial appointments in the west country. In the 1370s he also held property to the use of Edward III's mistress, Alice Perrers. The Black Prince died in 1376, but Cary kept the favour of the prince's widow, Joan: on 7 November 1384, at her supplication, he was once more granted the keeping of the stannary in Devon, and of lordships in the shire that the prince had granted him, and in the following year a rival suitor for the stannary failed to dislodge him. On 26 November 1382 Cary had been ordered to assume the rank of a serjeant-at-law. He never did so, but did not lose royal favour as a result, for in June 1386, with two other royal servants, he received the keeping of the temporalities of the bishopric of Bath and Wells, and by 21 September he had been knighted.

On 5 November 1386, during a parliament in which the

king considered his authority to have been fundamentally challenged, Richard II appointed Cary chief baron of the exchequer. In the following August he was among the justices who, in response to Richard's questioning, pronounced that the recent proceedings in parliament had been detrimental to the king's prerogative, and those responsible for them traitors. Not surprisingly, in January 1388 Cary was one of the justices deprived of office at the instigation of the lords appellant, and on 2 March he was among the six brought before parliament to be impeached by the Commons for the opinions to which they had subscribed in 1387. Like his colleagues, he pleaded in mitigation that he had been coerced by Archbishop Alexander Neville, Robert de Vere, duke of Ireland, and Michael de la Pole, earl of Suffolk. The Lords, after a hard debate, found them guilty of treason; on 6 March they were sentenced to hanging and forfeiture, but the death sentences were immediately commuted, at the pressing instance of the bishops. Parliament eventually decided that life exile in Ireland was an appropriate substitute for death. Cary was condemned to reside in Waterford or its environs, with an annuity of £20 from his forfeited possessions. These included, besides property in Launceston, Cornwall, the manors of Forwode and Holway, Devon, held in right of his wife. He also had large cash reserves, in the hands of his family and in ecclesiastical strongboxes, amounting to £1464 6s. 8d.

The Cary family apparently had influence with the lords appellant. On 12 July 1388, less than six weeks after the dissolution of parliament, Cary's sons Robert and Thomas were granted by the royal council a ten-year lease on the forfeited properties, apart from Torrington and Cockington, both of which were granted to the king's half-brother John Holland, earl of Huntingdon, as part of the endowment for his new earldom. John Cary was never able to return to England, but died at Waterford in May 1395. But Robert Cary was able to position himself well for attempts to recover his father's estate. He was a king's esquire by August 1391, and the earl of Huntingdon's in February 1392. These connections probably facilitated the grant to him for life of much of his inheritance in September 1392, and the restitution of jointure to his mother in 1396. In May 1398, as a result of the reversion of his father's sentence in the parliament held in January that year, the inheritance was restored to him. However, the reaffirmation of the sentences against the justices in Henry IV's first parliament (1399) confronted him with the arduous task of recovering his father's lands all over again.

ANTHONY GOODMAN

Sources Chancery records · M. McKisack, ed., 'Historia, sive, Narracio de modo et forma Mirabilis Parliamenti apud Westmonasterium', Camden miscellany, XIV, CS, 3rd ser., 37 (1926) · L. C. Hector and B. F. Harvey, eds. and trans., The Westminster chronicle, 1381–1394, OMT (1982) · Knighton's chronicle, 1337–1396, ed. and trans. G. H. Martin, OMT (1995) [Lat. orig., Chronica de eventibus Angliae a tempore regis Edgari usque mortem regis Ricardi Secundi, with parallel Eng. text] · HoP, Commons, 1386–1421, 2.495–7 · John of Gaunt's register, ed. S. Armitage-Smith, 2 vols., CS, 3rd ser., 20–21 (1911) · RotP, vol. 3 · Tout, Admin. hist., vol. 3 · Baker, Serjeants
Wealth at death £20 p.a.: HoP, Commons, 1386–1421

Cary, John (1649–1719x22), merchant and writer, was born in March 1649 at Bristol, the eldest of the three sons of Shershaw Cary (1615–1681), a merchant and sugar refiner, and his first wife, Mary Scrope (d. 1650). (The Dictionary of National Biography erroneously states that he was the son of the Revd Thomas Cary of St Philip and St Jacob, Bristol; in fact, these two were brothers.) Shershaw Cary traded with the Iberian peninsula and the West Indies, and was master of Bristol's prestigious Society of Merchant Venturers in 1671. John Cary was apprenticed to Walter Stephens, a linen draper, and became a freeman of the city of Bristol in 1672. He married Mehitabel Warren (1652–1703) probably in 1671; they had seven sons and three daughters. Cary's second wife, whom he married in February 1704, was the daughter of Colonel Moor of Dublin; she died in 1712. An active Anglican, Cary was a churchwarden for St John's parish, Bristol, in 1679 and 1680, and in 1685 served as churchwarden in St Philip and St Jacob parish, where his brother Thomas held a benefice.

Commerce and politics According to Bristol's apprenticeship lists, Cary followed the trade of linen draper until 1679. Though little is known of his early professional life, he was already importing West Indian sugar in the 1670s and also traded in molasses in the 1680s. He became a member of the Society of Merchant Venturers in 1677 and then pursued a career as a merchant in Bristol. He was a warden of the Merchant Venturers in 1683, and was appointed to the common council of Bristol in 1688. He became involved in the political aspects of commercial affairs, being chosen by the Merchant Venturers to represent their interests in London. In 1688 he was the last burgess given the freedom of the staple in Bristol. A radical whig who was opposed to the high-church party in the revolution of 1688, Cary penned a proposal in 1691 for a new method of electing officers in Bristol whereby the aldermen elected by their constituents would be required to set a rate proportional to each parish's wealth. This plan was not implemented, but it illustrates Cary's interest in local politics, civic democracy, and social affairs. He stood as a candidate to represent Bristol at the general election of 1698, and expected to become an MP; but he came bottom of the poll, well behind the other whig candidates. Cary is best known today, however, not for his mercantile career or political views, but as a prolific pamphleteer on mercantilist topics and the poor law. He lived in Bristol for most of his life, paying rent on houses and gardens in Temple Street until 1720.

Pamphleteer In the 1690s Cary began to write on a variety of subjects, including currency reform, since he was particularly concerned with the clipping and debasement of coinage; he also wrote about cases in commercial and constitutional law, shipping, and the collection of customs. He made his national reputation through his Essay on the State of England in Relation to its Trade, its Poor and its Taxes, for Carrying on the Present War Against France (1695). This was the first work produced by William Bonny at his printing press in Bristol. It had an extensive circulation, and was reprinted either in its entirety or in fragments on numerous occasions down to 1745, when it was published as *A Discourse on Trade and other Matters Relating to it*; a translation into French with additions appeared in 1755, and the work was translated from French into Italian in 1764.

Cary's tract was a classic, rather conventional mercantilist text that argued for manipulating the volume of English foreign trade to secure an inflowing stream of bullion. It advocated two lines of policy: the promotion of trade with the plantations in North America and the West Indies to increase revenue; and the encouragement of England as a major market for wool. The latter could be achieved by cutting back the exportation of woollen goods and the importation of manufactured commodities, and by putting restrictions on Irish woollen manufacture. Cary assessed the value of the colonies to England's wealth and was particularly enthusiastic about the slave trade with Africa, referring to this as 'a trade of the most advantage of any we drive' (J. Cary, *Discourse on Trade*, 54). He also regarded manufacturing as an important source of England's economic development, and his *Essay on the State of England* dwells on improvements made to industrial organization and management in the production of iron, brass, and glassware. Cary wanted manufacturers freed from burdensome excises; he advocated simplifying customs duties; he criticized the loss of revenue to the nation's coffers from illicit trade; and he wanted the rate of interest on loans reduced. These proposals were intended to stimulate legitimate trade and, hence, the nation's wealth. Cary was a protectionist who had no truck with free trade proposals by tories.

The first edition of the *Essay on the State of England* also included a section on currency reform that may have been influential in the recoinage of 1696. In the third edition some of the above proposals were no longer applicable, and so the section on currency reform was replaced by a discussion of the Bank of England, the need to extend banking facilities, and the desirability of increasing the silver coin of the kingdom. In *An Essay on the Coyn and Credit of England as they Stand with Respect to its Trade* (1696) Cary added to this theme by addressing the problem of the scarcity of coin after the great recoinage. He advocated a national system of credit to prevent gambling in currency; such a system would fulfil the needs of government and traders.

Cary's *Essay on the State of England* argued vigorously against the monopolies of the great trading companies. It criticized the export of bullion by the East India Company as not being particularly beneficial to England, and suggested that the silks, muslins, and calicoes of the East India Company hindered the consumption of English manufactures in Europe. In putting forward these views, Cary opposed the influential arguments of Sir Josiah Child, Sir Thomas Mun, and Charles Davenant. He vigorously attacked the position of the Royal African Company, noting that there had been more ships, slaves, and commodities taken in the slave trade since the company's monopoly ended in 1698 than had been the case before. Cary's *Essay* devoted much space to trade and brought him

into correspondence with John Locke, who pronounced it 'the best discourse I have ever read on that subject', not just for its clarity and disinterested reasoning, but because it promoted the public good (Locke to Cary, 2 May 1696; de Beer, 5.625).

Relief of poverty Cary's economic thought stimulated his approach to poverty; he appeared before the Board of Trade and wrote pamphlets on political economy. Believing that unemployment decreased the wealth of the nation and diminished its moral worth, he devoted much attention to providing employment for the poor and their children. In his *Essay on the State of England* he argued that pauperism, based on human depravity, had worsened from the abuse of the old poor law; that large cities were not dealing adequately with parish-based poor relief; and that a solution could be found by erecting urban workhouses to prevent the poor being sent from parish to parish under the settlement laws and provided for nowhere. Cary wanted to cut down on idleness, which he regarded as a vice, but also wished to make the administration of the poor law more effective. He warmly appreciated the setting up of almshouses and schemes to aid pauper children, commending the efforts along these lines of the philanthropist Edward Colston in Bristol.

Cary had the opportunity to put his ideas into action in Bristol, where he was the chief instigator of the Bristol Corporation of the Poor and the main impetus behind establishing the city workhouse, opened in 1696. Aiming to make multitudes of people serviceable who were then useless to the nation, the workhouse was intended to have an educational and disciplinary basis rather than a purely financial one. Housed in a former mint, the pauper manufactory originally had 100 boys and 100 girls, plus the elderly and infirm. It was also a house of correction for vagabonds, beggars, and ballad-sellers. It provided compulsory employment and central control of parish relief. Presided over by the mayor and aldermen of Bristol, and by forty-eight guardians of the workhouse, who were elected for short terms by all ratepayers without religious discrimination, the Bristol scheme consolidated the seventeen city parishes and the castle precincts into one, with one set of officers and a common fund. Cary's scheme illustrated his dislike of the tory corporation, which had regained power in Bristol in 1689, and his distaste for the parish élites who favoured the tory party. Cary was supported in his workhouse scheme by the chairman and most of the active whig members among the officers of the Corporation of the Poor. His workhouse was established at virtually the same time as a similar Quaker establishment in Bristol.

By 1700 Cary was pleased with the success of the Bristol workhouse. The problem of beggars in the city had been dealt with; the elderly were provided for; children were educated to sobriety and taught the virtues of work; young children were looked after. In particular, Cary was satisfied that the workhouse had reformed the morals of its inhabitants; cursing, swearing and profane language were banished from it. Accordingly, he wrote *An account of the proceedings of the corporation of Bristol in execution of the act of parliament for the better employing and maintaining the poor of that city* (1700), in which he recommended the Bristol workhouse as a model for the nation as a whole. The Bristol scheme was followed up by the construction of workhouses in Colchester, Crediton, Exeter, Hereford, Hull, Shaftesbury, and Tiverton, but at the time, mainly for reasons of cost, workhouses did not replace the favoured branch of the poor laws, which was outdoor relief.

Affairs in Ireland Cary's publications gained him a reputation that led to his employment in public business. He spent most of 1700 and 1701 in Ireland as a commissioner elected by parliament to handle the sale of forfeited estates under the Resumption Act. In 1704, at the request of the government, he reported on a proposal to subsidize the linen industry in Ireland, publishing a pamphlet on the subject entitled *Some Considerations Relating to the Carrying on the Linnen Manufactures of Ireland* (1704), which was reprinted along with the second and third editions of the *Essay on the State of England*. Around this time Cary seems to have left Bristol to take up permanent residence in Dublin. Information about his final years is not easily come by, but he seems to have been involved, unsuccessfully, in a number of Irish chancery suits. His exact death date is unknown, but it appears to have been some time between 1719 and 1722. The administration of his estate in Dublin is recorded among the records for 1730 of the prerogative court of Canterbury. KENNETH MORGAN

Sources BL, John Cary MSS, Add. MS 5540 · BL, Stowe MSS, vol. 670 · H. J. Lane, 'The life and writings of John Cary', MA diss., University of Bristol, 1932 · F. Harrison, *The Devon Carys*, 2 (1920) · E. E. Butcher, ed., *Bristol Corporation of the Poor: selected records, 1696–1834*, Bristol RS, 3 (1932) · J. Cary, *An essay on the state of England in relation to its trade, its poor and its taxes, for carrying on the present war against France* (1695) · J. Cary, *An account of the proceedings of the corporation of Bristol in execution of the act of parliament for the better employing and maintaining the poor of that city* (1700) · J. Cary, *An essay on the coyn and credit of England as they stand with respect to its trade* (1696) · *The correspondence of John Locke*, ed. E. S. De Beer, 5 (1980) · I. V. Hall, 'John Knight, junior, sugar refiner at the great house on St. Augustine's Back, 1654–1679: Bristol's second sugar house', *Transactions of the Bristol and Gloucestershire Archaeological Society*, 68 (1949), 110–64, facing p. 110 [pedigree of the Cary family] · E. E. Butcher, *Bristol Corporation of the Poor, 1696–1898* (1972) · M. M. Tompkins, 'The two workhouses of Bristol, 1696–1735', MA diss., U. Nott., 1962 · P. McGrath, ed., *Merchants and merchandise in seventeenth-century Bristol*, Bristol RS, 19 (1955)

Archives BL, Add. MS 5540

Cary, John (1755–1835), cartographer, was born on 23 February 1755 in Corsley, Wiltshire, the second of the four sons and one of possibly five or more children of George Cary, maltster, and his wife, Mary (*d.* 1799). In 1770 he entered a seven-year engraving apprenticeship under William Palmer of New Street, London.

Cary set himself up in business as an engraver before 1782 at Johnson's Court, Fleet Street, London. By about 1783 he was at 188 Strand and about 1791 moved to 181 Strand, which he occupied until January 1820 when fire destroyed his workshop and his brother William *Cary's adjacent premises, bringing forward a planned move to 86 St James's Street. The Cary business continued to operate here until after John's death. Although he generally worked independently, Cary did collaborate, notably with John Wallis, who seems to have inspired his diversification into publishing about 1783 or 1784, with his brother William in globe production and his brother Francis (*c.*1756–1836) in engraving, and, most significantly, with the geologist William Smith and others in the development and publication of geological maps, including Smith's great map of 1815 and a county series, begun in 1819 but not completed.

Cary's first known engraved plan is dated 1779. Henceforth, the quality of his engraving established new standards and a new style, with his effective, starkly beautiful, plain design being widely adopted. His firm's cartographic output was prolific and diverse, ranging through maps, plans, atlases, astronomical and educational works, road-books (including works based on surveys by Aaron Arrowsmith the elder, who probably trained him), guides, and globes. Particularly noteworthy are the immensely popular *New and Correct English Atlas* (editions from 1787), which became the standard county atlas of the period, and the *Traveller's Companion* (from 1790), the printing plates of both of which had to be replaced having become worn in the effort to meet the huge demand, and the particularly fine *New English Atlas* (from 1801) and *New Universal Atlas* (from 1808).

Despite the high quality of his maps, Cary's only public recognition was the award of the Society of Arts gold medal (1804) for publishing Singer's Cardiganshire survey (1803). Cary's appointment as surveyor of the roads to the General Post Office (1794) led to his publication of authoritative road measurements (measured by perambulator) in his influential *New Itinerary* (numerous editions from 1798).

Cary probably married Ann Jackson (*c.*1752–1824) of Clerkenwell on 21 June 1779. They had three sons and one daughter. The Elizabeth Jackson of Clerkenwell who later married his brother William may have been his sister-in-law. In 1820 he was joined in business by his eldest son, George, who served his engraving apprenticeship under his father from 1802 and took over the business about 1821 in partnership with his brother John, although their father probably remained a partner until his death. The newly styled firm of G. and J. Cary continued at 86 St James's Street until 1850, although map production apparently ceased about 1846. It carried on William Cary's scientific instrument and terrestrial and celestial globe making business after his death (1825) until about 1853. The firm's cartographic materials were subsequently acquired by George Frederick *Cruchley and later Gall and Inglis, with both publishing adaptations of original stock and plates.

Cary died in Mortlake, Surrey, on 16 August 1835 and was buried in Kensington, London, on 22 August. He and the firm he created dominated British map production for a generation at least, being the most influential private-sector map maker of the age. His contemporary reputation is confirmed by the extended life of much of his output and by the widespread plagiarism of his productions.

DAVID SMITH, *rev.*

Sources H. G. Fordham, *John Cary: engraver, map, chart and print-seller and globe-maker, 1754 to 1835* (1925) · D. Smith, 'The Cary family', *Map Collector*, 43 (1988), 40–47 · D. Smith, 'George Frederick Cruchley, 1796–1880', *Map Collector*, 49 (1989), 16–22 · D. Smith, *Antique maps of the British Isles* (1982) · D. Smith, *Victorian maps of the British Isles* (1985) · G. Clifton, *Directory of British scientific instrument makers, 1550–1851*, ed. G. L'E. Turner (1995) · D. Smith, 'Gall & Inglis, c.1810–c.1910', *International Map Collectors' Society Journal*, 73 (1998)

Cary, (Arthur) Joyce Lunel (1888–1957), writer, was born on 7 December 1888 at the Belfast Bank, Londonderry, the elder son of Arthur Pitt Chambers Cary (1864?–1937), engineer, and his first wife, Charlotte Louisa (1861?–1898), elder daughter of James John Joyce, manager of the Belfast Bank, Londonderry. Joyce Cary, as he was immediately called to avoid confusion with his father, noted later that he had inherited conflicting qualities from 'Dad the sportsman, the practical man—and my dear Mother who had the Joyce dreaminess, and reflectiveness' (letter to his wife, 5 Nov 1919). This inward tension was mirrored in a life broadly divided between action and artistic creation. To his diverse parental inheritance were added complicating influences. He was Anglo-Irish. The Carys were an ascendancy family, with roots in the English west country, who had settled in the Inishowen peninsula, north of Londonderry, in the sixteenth century. Locally powerful, moderately wealthy, and respected as magistrates and benevolent landlords through the seventeenth and eighteenth centuries, the family then declined slowly, partly as a result of profligacy, and was finally ruined by the Land Act of 1881, a measure intended to alleviate abuses feeding nationalist agitation. Within two years the remnant of the family's once-extensive holdings, and even Castle Cary itself (the last of their three big houses and the one in which Cary's father was born) had been sold. Growing up in the shadow of these losses, Cary was aware from an early age of 'the tragedy of social conflict in which personal quality counts for nothing; where a man is ruined not because he has done any wrong, but because he represents a class or race' (J. Cary, 'Speaking for myself', *New York Herald Tribune Book Review*, 8 Oct 1950, 10). Injustice, and responses to it, were thus early established as a dominant theme in his thought.

The loss of Castle Cary precipitated a dispersal of the family's younger generation, even before Cary's grandfather, Arthur Lunel Cary, died in 1885. Cary's father, the second son in the family, moved to London in 1884 and trained as an engineer. He had met Charlotte Joyce the year before he left Inishowen, and they married in August 1887, setting up house in south London. Charlotte returned to Londonderry for the birth of their first child, in her parents' home above the Belfast Bank, in the following year. A second son, John (always called Jack), was born on 28 January 1892, but their mother died suddenly of pneumonia on 1 October 1898, when Joyce Cary was nine years old.

Cary's childhood was divided between Ireland and England: grey London streets and, every summer, the cherishing homes of his Irish grandmothers, Lough Foyle, green fields, and a horde of ebullient boys—his novel *A House of*

(Arthur) Joyce Lunel Cary (1888–1957), by Katerina Wilczynski, 1954

Children (1941) superbly memorializes that joyful, knockabout, evanescent life. Remarried, Cary's father sent him to Hurstleigh, a preparatory school in Tunbridge Wells; and then to Clifton College. In his first year there his beloved stepmother died, and the boy's renewed distress was clear when he ran away briefly. These early experiences of sharply contrasting lives and values, of painful loss, of removal from his family, and of the requirement to maintain rigorous self-control, prepared him for his adventurous early manhood and also helped to shape the patterns and themes of his fiction.

Cary set out to become an artist by living in Paris (an elderly painter he knew there, Charles Mackie, was later a model for Cary's most famous character, Gulley Jimson in *The Horse's Mouth*), and then trained at the Edinburgh College of Art from 1907 to 1909. But he recognized that his artistic talent was limited, and shifted his attention to literature, privately publishing a volume of poems, *Verse*, in 1908. He was persuaded by his father, however, to read law at Trinity College, Oxford. There his restlessness continued, and minimal academic effort resulted in the fairly rare achievement of a fourth-class degree in 1912. He had preferred to live a sociable life. Two of his many friends became influential on his later life: John Middleton Murry, with whom he shared digs, roistered in Paris and cultivated a bohemian literary life; and Heneage Ogilvie, a medical student, whose sister Gertrude he wanted to marry.

In October 1912 Cary rushed off to Montenegro, where

the First Balkan War had broken out: as a Red Cross orderly he observed some fierce fighting between Turks and Montenegrins. On his return to England he briefly set himself up as a writer in London, and wrote a vivid account of his war experiences (*Memoir of the Bobotes*, published posthumously, 1964). He knew now that if he was to be permitted to marry Gertrude Ogilvie he needed a paying job. Love and knowledge of Ireland pointed him to Sir Horace Plunkett's co-operative movement; but when, after several months, it was made clear that he would not be offered a permanent position, he fell back on his alternative plan to apply for a post in the Northern Nigerian political service, the élite colonial administration of Britain's African territories. He was accepted, and in May 1914 began work as an assistant district officer in a large province, Bauchi. There are traces of his two contrasting superiors, H. S. W. Edwardes and J. F. J. Fitzpatrick, in Gulley Jimson and in Jim Latter of *Not Honour More* respectively, and they both influenced his characterization of Cock Jarvis.

When the First World War broke out, the Nigerian administration was soon involved in conflict with the neighbouring German colony of Cameroons. Cary was seconded to lead Nigerian troops in an attack on the German redoubt of Mora Mountain. Some of his finest short stories vividly re-create experiences which culminated in his being shot through the ear on 3 September 1915, and being invalided back to England in very poor health. On 1 June 1916 he married Gertrude Margaret Ogilvie (1891–1949), and on 9 August he returned to his duties in northern Nigeria, leaving her pregnant. He was sent to govern a very remote district, Borgu, which had two competing emirs and a recent history of bloody rebellion. There, for two years, Cary put into successful practice his administrative and military experience, his own liberal principles, and those of indirect rule (the general governing policy formulated by the governor, later Lord Lugard). He presided over the building of roads, bridges, and *zungos* (inns for travellers), so increasing trade and the general standard of life in the district—at the cost of some local unrest, and tension with the emirs. In his *The Case for African Freedom* (1941) and *Britain and West Africa* (1946), Cary defended the British empire as largely benevolent in its effects, although he fully acknowledged the concomitant strains and injustices that he had observed critically.

During his often lonely years in Borgu Cary had continued to write fiction, completing one important short novel, 'Daventry', and some pot-boiling short stories which, accepted for publication by the *Saturday Evening Post*, supported his decision to resign from the colonial service and become a professional writer in England. He was now the father of two sons, Michael [see Cary, Sir (Arthur Lucius) Michael (1917–1976)] and Peter, and his wife had written forcefully of her increasing distress at his long absences. In 1920 they bought a house at 12 Parks Road, Oxford, which was Cary's home for the rest of his life, and where he began his long struggle to establish himself as a novelist. By the time he published his first novel, *Aissa Saved* (1932), the psychological and financial strain was extreme. Two more sons, Tristram and George, had been born—Cary was now avowedly a 'family man'.

Cary wrote strenuously through the 1920s, developing his 'philosophy of life': that creativity is fundamental for a fulfilled life, and the only foil to the pervasive change and injustice which are the price of human freedom. But a particular barrier was the chaotic method of writing he had developed in his unsettled Nigerian days, when, frequently travelling rough in Borgu, he would necessarily work randomly rather than consecutively on a novel, often writing several versions, and even several novels, side by side. What should have been his first published novel, *Cock Jarvis* (edited and published posthumously), with a seminal protagonist and theme, collapsed in confusion after years of hard work.

But Cary prevailed; his energy and ambition resulted in *An American Visitor* (1933) and *The African Witch* (1936), which drew mainly on his Nigerian memories, while *Castle Corner* (1938), intended as the first of a series, connected these with his family's history in Ireland. His intense experiences and relationships in Borgu were especially fruitful in his fiction, most strikingly as the heart of one of his finest novels, *Mister Johnson* (1939), about a young Nigerian clerk who works in a British colonial office, loves England, and who, as Cary explains in his preface, 'turns his life into a romance'. Thereafter—apart from *A House of Children*, which won the James Tait Black memorial prize in 1941—setting and characters were predominantly English. His most popular, admired, and lucrative novel was *The Horse's Mouth* (1944), the third of his first trilogy, which also included *Herself Surprised* (1941) and *To be a Pilgrim* (1942). This trilogy has a basic pattern of conflicting viewpoints—of the family-centred woman, the tradition-bound man, and the creative, innovative man—which was again fundamental in Cary's darker and more complex second trilogy: *Prisoner of Grace* (1952), *Except the Lord* (1953), and *Not Honour More* (1955).

During and after the Second World War Cary also published political treatises, *Power in Men* (1939) and *Process of Real Freedom* (1943); two idiosyncratic long poems, *Marching Soldier* (1945) and *The Drunken Sailor* (1947); and three novels reflecting his substantive themes of creativity, change, and injustice, in relation, especially, to children and women: *Charley is my Darling* (1940), *The Moonlight* (1946), and *A Fearful Joy* (1949). He also endured tragedy in his family life, with the death of his wife in 1949, and the early death of his fourth son, George, in 1953. He was given strong support by his family and by close friends in Oxford such as Lord David Cecil, Enid Starkie, and Helen Gardner, and by American friends such as Edith Haggard, his New York agent, who had placed many of his short stories in American journals.

By the mid-1950s Cary was famous and regarded around the world (and especially in the USA) as one of Britain's most eminent novelists. He had always enjoyed travel: during the Second World War, while writing *The Horse's Mouth*, he had gone on a risky expedition to Africa with Thorold Dickinson, director of *Men of Two Worlds* (for which Cary had written the film script). After the war he travelled extensively in India, on a similar but abortive project; then he had made a series of demanding lecture tours in Europe and the United States. At the height of his success he fell seriously ill with what was diagnosed early in 1955 as motor neurone disease. He was hospitalized for treatment, but this failed to halt the progressive atrophy of his muscles. By mid-1956 he was confined to bed, but was enabled (by an ingenious invention of his own to support his wasting right arm) to continue his prolific writing: short stories, the Clark lectures (published posthumously as *Art and Reality* and delivered at Cambridge by a nephew, Robert Ogilvie), and finally a novel, *The Captive and the Free*. For this, in his final months, he needed the devoted help of his friend Winifred Davin who acted as his amanuensis. To the end Cary was uncomplaining, sociable, and unremittingly creative. He died at his home on 29 March 1957. Davin, now acting as Cary's literary executor, edited *The Captive and the Free* for posthumous publication in 1959, and also a selection of his fine short stories, *Spring Song and other Stories* (1960).

A prolific, independent, wide-ranging writer with a place in three literatures (English, Irish, Nigerian), difficult to categorize because his writing integrates the traditional and experimental, Cary left behind a mass of unpublished material now held in the Bodleian Library. His reputation as a novelist, so high at the time of his death, has since dwindled. A varied, active life fed into his writings, giving even the most imaginative a strong basis in personal experience. His philosophical, historical, and political conclusions, sometimes criticized as simplistic, convey a profoundly moral, thoughtful, and generous response to human existence.　　　　ALAN BISHOP

Sources A. Bishop, *Gentleman rider: a life of Joyce Cary* (1988) · b. cert. · m. cert. · d. cert. · *CGPLA Eng. & Wales* (1957) · F. W. O. [F. Ogilvie], *Ogilvies and others* (1931) · *DNB*

Archives BBC WAC, corresp. and papers · Bodl. Oxf., corresp. and papers | BL, corresp. with Society of Authors, Add. MS 56680 · NL Scot., letters to John Dover Wilson

Likenesses photograph, 1916, Hult. Arch. · M. Gerson, photograph, 1953, NPG · K. Wilczynski, pen-and-ink drawing, 1954, NPG [*see illus.*] · J. Cary, self-portrait, lithograph, 1956, NPG · E. Kennington, oils, priv. coll.

Wealth at death £18,658 5s. 3d.: probate, 1 July 1957, *CGPLA Eng. & Wales*

Cary [*née* Morison], **Lettice, Viscountess Falkland** (*c.*1612–1647), noblewoman and benefactor, was the daughter of Sir Richard *Moryson (*c.*1571–1628) [*see under* Moryson, Fynes], vice-president of Munster, and Mary (*d.* 1654), daughter of Sir Henry Harington, sometime resident of Dublin; she had one known brother, Henry. Her father bought Tooley Park, near Leicester, where she spent some of her childhood. She learned to love reading and became a fluent Latin scholar. According to her later chaplain and biographer, at the age of thirteen she underwent a spiritual crisis when she was tempted to despair of God's mercy, but was finally assured of his grace.

In the spring of 1630 Lettice married secretly at Leire or Peckleton, Leicestershire, her brother's friend Sir Lucius *Cary (1609/10–1643), son of Henry *Cary, first Viscount Falkland (*c.*1575–1633), and Elizabeth *Cary (1585–1639).

Lettice Cary, Viscountess Falkland (*c.*1612–1647), by William Marshall, pubd 1648

In 1629 Sir Lucius had inherited Burford Priory and Great Tew Manor, Oxfordshire, from his maternal grandmother, Lady Tanfield, but as Lettice was not well-dowered his father was irreconcilably angry. The young Carys migrated to The Hague, but soon returned to England, where their four sons were born between 1632 and 1639. Dearly loved by their mother, they were brought up piously and had their own oratory in the nursery.

Following his father's sudden death in 1633 Lucius became second Viscount Falkland. At Great Tew, Lady Falkland became hostess to the circle of largely Arminian thinkers who visited her husband and whose conversation stimulated and developed her mind. Edward Hyde, a frequent visitor, described her as a lady of most extraordinary intelligence and judgement, and by that time she had acquired considerable theological knowledge. When Falkland followed Charles I to war in 1642 the separation was grievous to her, since according to her biographer she loved her husband more than anything else in the world. His death at the battle of Newbury in 1643 devastated her, as did that of their third son, Lorenzo, in 1645; both bereavements led to self-examination, repentance, and resolution towards greater piety.

At some time in the early 1640s the ejected Essex clergyman John Duncon was welcomed into Lady Falkland's household as her chaplain and spiritual director. As the brother of Nicholas Ferrar's friend Edmund Duncon he probably brought with him the Little Gidding pattern of an extended family living as a praying community. According to Duncon, in a household that included her mother and perhaps her aunt Ruth Harington, Lady Falkland daily catechized and prayed with her maids. Regular attendance at morning and evening prayer was encouraged, holy days celebrated, and communion carefully prepared for; the whole household kept a monthly fast.

Lady Falkland herself spent several hours daily in private devotions and meditations. Under Duncon's direction she used spiritual exercises: 'my heart is ravished with spiritual joy', she wrote (Duncon, *Returns of Spiritual Comfort*, 57). Having abandoned elaborate clothes and lavish living after her husband's death she used her medicinal skills to treat the sick, and her money in the service of God, the poor, and others in need. She built a school at Great Tew, where children learned reading and vocational skills. She also envisaged Burford Priory as a place for the propagation of religion and learning among young gentlewomen and widows, although this could not be implemented because of the war. Anonymously she sent relief to prisoners in Oxford and London, including parliamentarians. On being told that people would doubt her loyalty to the king, she retorted, 'I would rather be so misunderstood … then that any of mine enemies should perish' (Duncon, *The Holy Life*, 13).

Lady Falkland remained staunchly royalist, preferring to have a flock of sheep seized than to contribute to the parliamentary army, and staunchly Anglican, refusing to abandon the Book of Common Prayer when it became illegal. She had both Roman Catholic and Presbyterian friends, and persuaded some of each to adopt her views. She died, of tuberculosis, at Great Tew Manor on 24 February 1647, aged about thirty-five; she was buried in Great Tew church three days later.   ELIZABETH ALLEN

Lucius Cary, second Viscount Falkland (1609/10–1643), attrib. John Hoskins, 1630s

Sources J. Duncon, *The holy life and death of the Lady Letice Vi-Countess Falkland* (1653), A3–A3v, 1–10, 13–14, 18–27, 30–31, 42–4, 47, 50, 52, 54, 56–8, 60 [p. nos. from 47 misprinted, so 20 has been added to each] · J. Duncon, *Returns of spirtual comfort and grief* (1653) · K. Weber, *Lucius Carey, second Viscount Falkland* (New York, 1940), 4, 29, 54–5, 75 · A. L. Maycock, *Nicholas Ferrar of Little Gidding* (1938), 129–31, 157–80, 197–218 · M. F. Howard, ed., *Lady Letice Vi-Countess Falkland* (1908), 27–8, 47 · GEC, *Peerage*, new edn, vol. 5 · *CSP dom.*, 1611–18, 132, 167, 456; 1623–5, 39, 172 · BL, MS 7019, fol. 63 · *The life of Edward, earl of Clarendon … written by himself*, 3 vols. (1759), vol. 1, pp. 39–40 · transcript of will, Bodl. Oxf., Add. MS C. 303 · *Scots peerage* · Venn, *Alum. Cant.* · *CSP Ire.*, 1600, 462 · W. A. Shaw, *The knights of England*, 2 (1906), 78 · Oxfordshire Archives, MS DD Par Great Tew d 2 [no fol.]
Likenesses C. Janssen, oils, 1634; formerly in possession of the Falkland family, 1922 · attrib. G. Jameson, oils, *c.*1642 (aged thirty) · W. Marshall, engraving, pubd 1648, NPG [*see illus.*] · C. Dietrich, engraving (after attrib. G. Jameson, *c.*1642)
Wealth at death substantial: transcript of will, Bodl. Oxf., Add. MS C. 303

Cary, Lucius, second Viscount Falkland (1609/10–1643), politician and author, was born at Burford Priory in Oxfordshire, the son of Henry *Cary, first Viscount Falkland (*c.*1575–1633), and Elizabeth *Cary (*née* Tanfield) (1585–1639). The poet Patrick *Cary (*c.*1624–1657) was one of his younger brothers.

Early years Lucius was admitted to St John's College, Cambridge, in 1621. In 1622, when Lucius was twelve, his father was appointed lord deputy of Ireland and in the same year Lucius was transferred to Trinity College, Dublin, graduating BA in July 1625. That year his maternal grandfather, Sir Lawrence Tanfield, died, having entailed estates in Oxfordshire at Great Tew and Burford upon Lucius and his offspring. He took possession of this inheritance on the family's return from Ireland in November 1629. However, his father left Ireland following a violent quarrel with many of the Irish privy council and lords justices over the command of a company of 500 or 600 men, and this prompted Lucius to challenge Sir Francis Willoughby, to whom the commission was granted, to a duel. He was briefly imprisoned in the Fleet in January 1630, and it is possible that disillusionment with Irish politics may help to explain his subsequent hostility towards the earl of Strafford.

In 1630 Lucius married Lettice Morison (*c.*1612–1647) [*see* Cary, Lettice]. His father fiercely opposed the marriage, possibly because Lettice was from a poor family, and possibly because of his own exclusion from the Tanfield inheritance. Lucius offered to surrender the estate to his father, but the offer was rejected. Deeply upset by this quarrel, Lucius went to the Dutch republic seeking military service, but when he failed to find a suitable post he returned to England and settled at Great Tew about 1632. On his father's death in September the following year, he became the second Viscount Falkland. His father left him estates valued at nearly £57,000, with an annual income of £2700 but encumbered with debts said to be over £3000 a year. Falkland claimed in December 1636 that what he had to pay to and for his mother 'was neere as much yearely as (my debts considered) I had to maintaine my selfe, my wife, my children and my family' (PRO, SP 16/337/40, Falkland to the privy council, 16 Dec 1636). At Great Tew he lived a secluded life: he apparently played no part in local government and was not even a JP in Oxfordshire. He refused to pay ship money for his lands at Aldenham, Hertfordshire, and 'the bayleiffe durst not distraine for feare of being sued' (PRO, SP 16/376/106, ship money arrears in Hertfordshire, 1636). However, heavy debts were owed on these Aldenham lands and the fact that Falkland did pay ship money in Oxfordshire suggests that this was a dispute over rating rather than a refusal to pay on principle. Falkland was also admitted, on William Lenthall's recommendation, to Lincoln's Inn on 18 January 1638.

Falkland and the Great Tew circle For most of the 1630s Falkland lived quietly at Great Tew. There he assembled an extensive library and read voraciously. He learned Greek and studied the works of Greek historians and the fathers; he also wrote verse, mainly in the form of eclogues, elegies, and short dedicatory poems. But the most remarkable feature of this period of his life was the coterie of friends whom he invited to Great Tew at regular intervals from about 1634 onwards and who became known as the Great Tew circle. Falkland was a host of singular courtesy and urbanity, and at the heart of the circle were his closest friend Edward Hyde, his chaplain Charles Gataker, and the philosopher William Chillingworth. Other frequent visitors included divines such as Gilbert Sheldon, George Morley, Henry Hammond, and John Earle, poets like Sidney Godolphin, Sir John Suckling, and Edmund Waller, the playwright Ben Jonson, and the political philosopher Thomas Hobbes. Many of these subsequently testified to the intellectual stimulus that they found at Falkland's house, as well as to his generous hospitality and great capacity for friendship. Hyde later wrote that Great Tew, 'being within ten or twelve miles of the University [of Oxford], looked like the University itself, by the company that was always found there' (*Life of … Clarendon*, 1.41).

Falkland's talent as the host of this circle lay above all in his gentle tolerance and his respect for the intellectual differences among his guests. If he was the genial spirit presiding over the circle, Chillingworth has been described as its 'intellectual motor' and as Falkland's 'closest intellectual friend' (Trevor-Roper, 169, 170). Chillingworth's book *The Religion of Protestants* (1638) was written at Great Tew and was a direct product of the discussions which took place there. Although there was no single outlook associated with the members of the circle, the group nevertheless possessed some intellectual cohesion and certain common attitudes and values were evident. These included a characteristic blend of tolerance and scepticism which cast doubt on the possibility of any infallible authority in religion. Falkland himself wrote a tract entitled *Of the Infallibilitie of the Church of Rome* (1645), in which he argued that he could not see why someone:

> should be saved, because, by reason of his parents' beleife, or the religion of the countrey, or some such accident, the truth was offered to his understanding, when had the contrary been offered he would have received that; and the other

> damned that beleeves falshood, upon as good ground as the other doth truth. (p. 12)

Falkland certainly followed this maxim in his own life, and Hyde wrote that he 'never thought the worse, or in any degree declined the familiarity, of those who were of another mind' (*Life of … Clarendon*, 1.49). This tolerant acceptance of others' beliefs, and sceptical attitude towards religious authority, may in part have stemmed from Falkland's own experience of resisting his mother's attempts to convert him to Catholicism following her conversion about 1626.

Falkland and other members of the circle were also drawn towards the application of reason to religious mysteries, and as a result were sometimes accused of Socinianism. They were not Socinians in the strict sense of denying the doctrine of the Trinity, but rather in the more general sense of applying rational approaches to religious issues. They found Socinian writings attractive and Falkland amassed a large collection of them. This 'Socinianism' was closely linked to a strongly ecumenical outlook: committed to religious peace, the members of the Great Tew circle drew much inspiration from Erasmus, Philippe du Plessis Mornay, Richard Hooker, and above all Grotius, to whom Falkland dedicated one of his poems. Falkland and his friends were steeped in this Erasmian tradition, and profoundly disliked the narrow dogmatism associated on the one hand with Laudianism and on the other with radical Calvinism. Instead they sought the reunion of Christendom and admired Hooker's ideal of a *via media* between Catholicism and protestantism. They embraced tolerance, especially in matters 'indifferent', and abhorred violent or revolutionary change. These attitudes may help to explain why in 1639 Falkland served under Essex in the first bishops' war against the Scottish covenanters, and equally why in 1641 he attacked Laudianism while defending the institution of episcopacy.

Member of parliament, 1640–1641 In 1640 Falkland was returned as member for Newport in the Isle of Wight to both the Short and Long Parliaments. He apparently had no previous connection with Newport or the Isle of Wight, and he may have been returned through the patronage of Jerome Weston, second earl of Portland, who as governor of the island exercised considerable electoral influence over the borough. Although he does not appear to have been particularly close to Portland, his link with him may have dated back to the later 1620s when Falkland's father briefly hoped that he might marry Portland's sister, and Falkland later opposed John Pym's bid to oust Portland from the governorship on the grounds that he was a papist by arguing that he regularly went to church. In the Commons, Falkland soon emerged into national prominence as an eloquent critic of the policies of Thorough. When the Commons debated the Laudian altar policy on 29 April 1640 Falkland advised members 'to read the rubrick and then resolve' (*Diary of Sir Thomas Aston*, 88). This view reflected the fervent desire to defend the rule of law which became a consistent theme of Falkland's many documented speeches. In the opening weeks of the Long Parliament he played a particularly prominent role in the attack on ship money and the judges who had upheld it. In a speech on 7 December 1640 he reportedly asserted that 'the constitution of this commonwealth hath established, or rather endeavoured to establish to us the security of our goods, and the security of those laws which would secure us and our goods' (Rushworth, 4.86). The judges who had defended ship money, 'who should have been as dogs to defend the sheep, have been as wolves to worry them' (ibid.). He argued that their judgment was contrary to statute, and also to 'apparent evidences', for they had supposed 'mighty and eminent dangers, in the most serene, quiet, and halcion days that could possibly be imagined' (ibid.). He believed that the fundamental cause of England's troubles lay in breaches of the rule of law committed by a badly advised monarch:

> the cause of all the miseries we have suffered, and the cause of all our jealousies we have had, that we should yet suffer, is, that a most excellent prince hath been infinitely abused by his judges, telling him that by policy he might do what he pleased. (ibid., 87)

Other future royalists, including his friend Hyde, supported Falkland's denunciation and the Commons then established a committee, chaired by Falkland, to investigate how the judges were 'solicited or threatened, and in what manner, and by whom' to give their opinions (*JHC*, 2, 1640–42, 46). In the light of the committee's findings impeachment articles were drawn up against Lord Keeper Finch, and when these were read on 14 January 1641 Falkland made another powerful speech in which he described Finch's life as 'a perpetual warfare (by mines, and by battery, by battel, and by strategem) against our fundamental laws ... against the excellent constitution of this kingdom' (Rushworth, 4.139). Once again Falkland's preoccupation with the rule of law was very evident: he argued that Finch had coerced the judges into signing 'opinions contrary to law', and had thus committed 'a treason as well against the king as against the kingdom; for whatsoever is against the whole, is undoubtedly against the head, which takes from His Majesty the ground of his rule, the laws' (ibid., 140). At the end of the debate Falkland was one of four members to whom the Commons expressed its special thanks 'for the great service they have performed, to the honour of this House, and good of the Commonwealth, in ... the Business of the Ship-Money' (*JHC*, 2, 1640–42, 68); the others were Hyde and the future parliamentarians Bulstrode Whitelocke and Oliver St John.

Falkland's commitment to the rule of law was closely connected to a desire to preserve the institutional structures of the Church of England, including episcopacy, once the influence of the Laudians had been curtailed. When on 8–9 February 1641 the Commons debated whether or not to refer the London root-and-branch petition to a committee, Falkland declared that he found the Laudians 'to have been the destruction of unity, under pretence of uniformity; to have brought in superstition and scandal under the titles of reverence and decency; [and] to have defiled our Church by adorning our churches' (Rushworth, 4.184). He declared himself 'content to take away all those things from them, which to any considerable degree of probability may again beget the like mischiefs, if they be not taken away' (ibid., 186). While he felt that 'neither their lordships, their judging of tythes, wills and marriages, no nor their voices in Parliaments are *jure divino*', equally they were not '*injuria humana*' (ibid., 186, 187). Falkland therefore did not 'think it fair to abolish, upon a few days debate, an order which hath lasted ... in most churches these sixteen hundred years' (ibid., 187). He concluded that:

> we should not root up this ancient tree, as dead as it appears, till we have tryed whether by this, or the like lopping of the branches, the sap which was unable to feed the whole, may not serve to make what is left both grow and flourish. (ibid.)

This wish to reform rather than abolish episcopacy was highly characteristic of those who subsequently rallied to Charles, and the speakers who opposed root-and-branch reform in February 1641 almost without exception became royalists the following year.

The moderate constitutionalism of Falkland's attitudes towards both church and state went along with a hostility towards the policies associated with Thorough. He supported the attainder of Strafford, and on 15 April 1641 advocated the doctrine of cumulative treason:

> how many haires breadths makes a tall man, and how many makes a little man, noe man can well say, yet wee know a tall man when wee see him from a low man, soe 'tis in this, how many illegal acts makes a treason is not certainly well [known], but wee well know it when we see [it]. (Bruce, 49)

Four days later he argued forthrightly that 'in equity lord Straford deserves to dye' (ibid., 53).

Following Strafford's execution on 12 May 1641 the Commons returned to the issue of the future of the church, and Falkland again emerged as a prominent defender of episcopacy. He argued that 'we have lived long happily and gloriously under this forme of government, it hath very well agreed with the constitution of our lawes, with the disposition of our people' and he believed that the abolition of bishops would 'be the destruction of many estates, in which many, who may be very innocent persons, are legally vested' (Cary, *A Draught*, 3, 4). On the whole, however, the supporters of episcopacy failed to co-ordinate their efforts and apply concerted pressure. This prompted Falkland's savage comment that 'they who hated bishops hated them worse than the devil, and that they who loved them did not love them so well as their dinner' (Clarendon, *Hist. rebellion*, 1.363).

Falkland's hostility towards presbyterianism was associated with a dislike of the Scottish covenanters and a belief that the English parliament should not become involved in Scottish affairs. Thus, when news of the Scottish 'incident' arrived, Falkland (together with Hyde) 'mooved that wee should leave the busines of Scotland to the Parliament there and not to take upp feares and suspicions without very certaine and undoubted grounds' (*Journal*, ed. Coates, 15).

By the autumn of 1641 the demands of Charles's more radical critics increasingly convinced Falkland that the king represented the lesser of two evils. Thus, when William Strode demanded on 28 October that parliament should have a negative voice over the appointment of officers of state and privy councillors, Falkland was among those who 'stood as champions in maynten[a]nce of [the king's] prerogative, and shewed for it unaunswerable reason and undenyable p[r]esedents' (*The Diary of John Evelyn from 1641 to 1705–6*, ed. W. Bray, 4 vols., 1850–52, 4.116, Nicholas to Charles I, 29 Oct 1641). That month Falkland also opposed the second Bishops Exclusion Bill, and on 22 November he spoke against the grand remonstrance.

The approach of war Falkland's conduct in the closing months of 1641 helps to explain why, according to Hyde, at the beginning of December the crowds outside the Palace of Westminster read a list of 'persons disaffected to the kingdom' which included Falkland (Clarendon, *Hist. rebellion*, 1.464). By the same token the king was increasingly grateful for Falkland's support and on 1 January 1642 he was sworn a privy councillor and then, on 8 January, appointed secretary of state. Falkland's elevation, like that of John Colepeper, who became chancellor of the exchequer at the same time, probably owed much to Hyde's influence, and these appointments greatly strengthened the influence of moderates within the king's counsels: towards the end of January 1642 John Coke the younger reported that 'Hertford, Seymour, Southampton, Falkeland and Culpeper are the chiefe councelors' (BL, Add. MS 64922, fol. 88*r*, John Coke the younger to Sir John Coke, 27 Jan 1642). Over the months that followed Falkland, Colepeper, and Hyde emerged as the king's leading propagandists and were, as Hyde later wrote, 'often of one opinion' (*Life of … Clarendon*, 1.104).

Falkland only accepted appointment as secretary very reluctantly, after lengthy persuasion by Hyde, and his preferment placed him in a difficult position. Like many other moderate royalists he was embarrassed by the king's attempted arrest of the five members, and Hyde recorded the 'grief and anger' which Falkland, Colepeper, and he felt that 'the violent party had by these late unskilful actions of the Court gotten great advantage and recovered new spirits'. Thereafter, they 'could not avoid being looked upon as the authors of those counsels to which they were so absolute strangers, and which they so perfectly detested' (Clarendon, *Hist. rebellion*, 1.487). Falkland's official status made him immediately suspect in the eyes of some members of the Commons, and on 11 January he and Colepeper were required to defend themselves against the charge of popery. On 25 January Falkland received 1150 copies of the king's official messages relating to the five members; it is probable that the distribution of this material formed part of the 'secrett service' for which he at this time received £700 a year (PRO, SO 3/12, signet office docket book, fol. 183*r*). But when the Commons discovered that these messages were being distributed it investigated whether Falkland had 'offended in breach of privilege of parliament' (Coates, Young, and Snow, 1.323). By this stage loyalties to the crown and to the houses were becoming increasingly difficult to reconcile.

As the civil war approached Falkland joined the king's headquarters at York, probably towards the end of May 1642. Perhaps his greatest contribution to the royalist cause was his co-authorship, with Colepeper, of the king's *Answer to the Nineteen Propositions* the following month. This was not only a classic work of royalist propaganda, but also an eloquent statement of the moderate constitutional and ecclesiastical attitudes so characteristic of Falkland. The *Answer* condemned the houses for seeking to 'remove a troublesome rub in their way, the law', and defended laws as 'the birth-right of every subject in this kingdom' (Rushworth, 4.725). The houses' terms posed a direct threat to 'the antient, equal, happy, well-poised, and never enough commended constitution of the government of this kingdom', and to the 'regulated monarchy' which was vital to 'preserve the laws in their force, and the subjects in their liberties and properties' (ibid., 731). The *Answer* also picked up Falkland's earlier defences of the established church, and asserted its unique advantages against religious extremes:

> No Church could be found upon the earth, that professeth the true religion with more purity of doctrine than the Church of England doth, nor where the government and discipline are jointly more beautified, and free from superstition, than as they are here established by law; which (by the grace of God) we will with constancy maintain (while we live) in their purity and glory, not only against all invasions of popery, but also from the irreverence of those many schismaticks and separatists wherewith of late this kingdom and our City of London abounds.   (ibid., 734)

All in all the *Answer* portrayed the nineteen propositions as terms which the king could not 'in honour, or regard to … regal authority … receive without just indignation' (ibid., 725). Instead, it defended the crown's rightful powers and the rule of law as the true guardians of the people's liberties and property.

The *Answer* was published on 18 June 1642. Three days earlier Falkland was among those peers and commoners assembled at York who signed an engagement that the king intended to preserve 'the true Protestant religion, the just privileges of Parliament, the liberty of the subject, the law, peace, and prosperity of this kingdom' (Clarendon, *Hist. rebellion*, 2.185). On 16 June, Falkland and Colepeper were recorded as absent from the Commons without leave, and they both engaged to provide horse for the king on 22 June.

Civil war, 1642–1643 Falkland deeply lamented the outbreak of the civil war in August 1642, and hoped that a settlement might be reached as soon as possible. On 5 September the king sent him to Westminster with a declaration insisting that he had never intended to declare the houses traitors or to raise his standard against them. This was the second such royal message sent since the beginning of the war, and the houses reiterated their refusal to negotiate until the offending proclamations were withdrawn and the standard taken down. Despite the failure of this initiative, Falkland nevertheless hoped that the conflict would be over quickly. In a letter written on 27 September, shortly after the skirmish at Powick Bridge, he wrote that the parliamentarian forces were unequal to the royalists, for 'most of them were men of meane quality, and … raw souldiers … some said, they were taylors, some embroyderers, and the like' (Cary, *A Letter*, sig. A3v). In this letter Falkland also reiterated that the king had 'no other ambition, but the advancement of the Protestant Religion, and establishment of the fundamental lawes of this kingdome' (ibid.).

Clarendon later wrote that 'when there was any overture or hope of peace [Falkland] would be more erect and vigorous, and exceedingly solicitous to press any thing which he thought might promote it' (Clarendon, *Hist. rebellion*, 3.189). Falkland remained deeply committed to a constitutional royalist ideal of a symbiosis between royal powers and the rule of law. In February–April 1643 he played an active part in the treaty of Oxford, and his interventions revealed his characteristic attitudes. He defended the king's right to command the armed forces and to appoint senior military officers without needing to seek parliamentary approval:

> the nomination and free election is a right belonging to, and inherent in His Majesty, and having been enjoyed by all his royal progenitors, His Majesty will not believe that his well-affected subjects will desire to limit him in that right. (Rushworth, 5.201)

He argued that the king could not 'devest himself of those trusts which the law of the land hath settled in the Crown alone, to preserve the power and dignity of the Prince, for the better protection of the subject and of the law' (ibid., 203). Once again, for Falkland as for many other moderate royalists, the rule of law served to ensure an equilibrium between royal powers and the public interest: as he put it, 'the laws and statutes of the kingdom … will be always the most impartial judge between [the King] and his people' (ibid., 201).

Falkland expressed similar views in a tract entitled *An Answer to a Printed Book*, on which he collaborated with Dudley Digges and his old friend William Chillingworth. This presented a sustained rebuttal of Henry Parker's arguments. It argued that England was a legally limited monarchy in which the king was 'bound to maintain the rights and liberty of the subject'; but it was emphatically not a contractual monarchy, for the king's authority was not 'capable of forfeiture upon a not exact performance of covenant' ([D. Digges, W. Chillingworth, and L. Cary, second Viscount Falkland], *An Answer to a Printed Book, Intituled Observations upon some of His Majesties Late Answers and Expresses*, 1642, 11). The king was 'a part of the State', and therefore 'the other part hath not any power warranted by law to doe what they thinke fit to his prejudice, upon pretence of publique extremity' (ibid., 43). Likewise, the two houses alone were 'not the Parliament', and 'the subject of such power is the entire body, which consists of three estates' of king, Lords, and Commons (ibid., 51).

Such moderate views were sometimes at odds with those of more hard-line royalists. For example, Falkland urged Charles to suppress Griffith Williams's *Discoverie of Mysteries* (1643), a tract which bitterly condemned 'the plots and practices of a prevalent faction in this present Parliament', and warned that 'we must not idolize the Parliament as if it were a kinde of omnipotent creature' (title-page, p. 107). Falkland feared that such strong language would only impede the search for a settlement; however, it seems that Charles liked this work and ignored Falkland's advice.

In April 1643 Falkland was appointed lord privy seal, while also continuing to serve as secretary. That summer he began to suffer materially for his royalist allegiance when, on 10 July, the committee for the advance of money assessed him at £300. Far more dangerous, however, was the marked deterioration in Falkland's state of mind as a result of the miseries of war. According to Hyde, by the summer of 1643, Falkland would sit with his friends and:

> often, after a deep silence and frequent sighs, would, with a shrill and sad accent, ingeminate the word *Peace, Peace*, and would passionately profess that the very agony of the war, and the view of the calamities and desolation the kingdom did and must endure, took his sleep from him, and would shortly break his heart. (Clarendon, *Hist. rebellion*, 3.189)

He fell into a deep depression, and Hyde described how 'his natural cheerfulness and vivacity grew clouded, and a kind of sadness and dejection of spirit stole upon him which he had never been used to' (ibid., 187).

By the autumn of 1643 Falkland could see no prospect of peace, and wished no longer to witness his country's agonized conflict. At the siege of Gloucester, although he deliberately exposed himself to danger, he emerged unscathed. But at the first battle of Newbury on 20 September he found his opportunity. Telling his friends that 'he was weary of the times, and foresaw much misery to his own country, and did believe he should be out of it ere night' (B. Whitelocke, *Memorials of the English Affairs*, 1732, 73–4), he placed himself as a volunteer in the first rank of Lord Byron's regiment. He identified a gap in a hedge which was lined on both sides with parliamentarian musketeers, and through which their bullets were pouring. He deliberately rode straight at the gap and in an instant suffered a fatal bullet wound to the lower abdomen. His death was tantamount to suicide, and he was buried at Great Tew.

Assessment The most celebrated assessment of Falkland's life and character is that left by his close friend Hyde. In this moving eulogy, Hyde describes Falkland as:

> a person of such prodigious parts of learning and knowledge, of that inimitable sweetness and delight in conversation, of so flowing and obliging a humanity and goodness to mankind, and of that primitive simplicity and integrity of life, that if there were no other brand upon this odious and accursed civil war than that single loss, it must be most infamous and execrable to all posterity … He was superior to all those passions and affections which attend vulgar minds, and was guilty of no other ambition than of knowledge, and to be reputed a lover of all good men. (Clarendon, *Hist. rebellion*, 3.178–9, 181)

Leaving aside the particular loyalty that Hyde felt to a close friend, the essential moderation of Falkland's character and attitudes is evident from his surviving speeches and other writings. Throughout, his temperate views on religious and constitutional issues, and his innate dislike of dogma or tyranny on whichever side they were found, were expressed in language of unusual elegance and beauty. In his later years, when he found himself somewhat reluctantly elevated onto the national political stage, it became apparent that he was not a natural man of affairs or administrator. This owed less to a lack of ability or energy than to the fact that his personality was essentially too gentle and contemplative for him to be very effective politically. It was his tragedy to have lived in a period when England descended into the kind of violence, conflict, and partisanship that he abhorred. He displayed both wisdom and innocence, while his speeches and other writings reveal a kind of precocious maturity. The last word can fittingly be left to Hyde, who wrote that Falkland:

> so much despatched the business of life that the oldest rarely attain to that immense knowledge, and the youngest enter not into the world with more innocence; and whoever leads such a life need not care upon how short warning it be taken from him. (Clarendon, *Hist. rebellion*, 3.190)

DAVID L. SMITH

Sources State papers domestic, Charles I, PRO, SP 16 · K. Weber, *Lucius Cary, second viscount Falkland* (New York, 1940) · H. Trevor-Roper, *Catholics, Anglicans and puritans* (1987), 166–230 · J. Rushworth, *Historical collections*, 5 pts in 8 vols. (1659–1701) · JHC, 2–3 (1640–44) · L. Cary, second Viscount Falkland, *The lord Faulkland his learned speech in parliament, in the House of Commons, touching the judges and the late lord keeper* (1641) · L. Cary, second Viscount Falkland, *Of the infallibilitie of the Church of Rome: a discourse written by the Lord Viscount Falkland* (1645) · L. Cary, second Viscount Falkland, *A speech made to the House of Commons concerning episcopacy, by the Lord Viscount Faulkeland* (1641) · L. Cary, second Viscount Falkland, *A letter sent from the Lord Falkland, principal secretarie to his majestie, unto the Right Honourable, Henry earle of Cumberland, at York, Sept. 30, 1642* (1642) · L. Cary, second Viscount Falkland, *A draught of a speech concerning episcopacy, by the Lord Viscount Falkland* (1644) · *The poems of Lucius Carey, Viscount Falkland*, ed. A. B. Grosart (1871) · J. Bruce, ed., *Verney papers: notes of proceedings in the Long Parliament*, CS, 31 (1845) · Clarendon, *Hist. rebellion* · *The life of Edward, earl of Clarendon … written by himself*, new edn, 3 vols. (1827) · *The Short Parliament (1640) diary of Sir Thomas Aston*, ed. J. D. Maltby, CS, 4th ser., 35 (1988) · D. L. Smith, *Constitutional royalism and the search for settlement, c.1640–1649* (1994) · J. C. Hayward, 'New directions in studies of the Falkland circle', *Seventeenth Century*, 2 (1987), 19–48 · J. Tanner, *Lucius Cary, Viscount Falkland: cavalier and catalyst*, Royal Stuart Papers, 5 (1974) · M. A. E. Green, ed., *Calendar of the proceedings of the committee for compounding … 1643–1660*, 5 vols., PRO (1889–92) · Keeler, *Long Parliament* · *The journal of Sir Simonds D'Ewes from the first recess of the Long Parliament to the withdrawal of King Charles from London*, ed. W. H. Coates (1942); repr. (1970) · W. H. Coates, A. Steele Young, and V. F. Snow, eds., *The private journals of the Long Parliament*, 3 vols. (1982–92) · DNB · GEC, *Peerage* · *Scots peerage*, 3.609–10 · Pitt correspondence, BL, Add. MS 29974
Likenesses attrib. J. Hoskins, miniature, 1630–39, NPG [*see illus.*] · attrib. A. Van Dyck, oils, *c.*1638, Chatsworth House, Derbyshire, Devonshire collection; version, Holkham Hall, Norfolk; version, Longleat House, Wiltshire · C. Turner, mezzotint, pubd 1811 (after C. Johnson), BM, NPG
Wealth at death lands valued at £57,000 in 1633, which generated an annual income of £2700: Pitt corresp., BL, Add. MS 29974, fols. 144r–148r

Cary, Mary (*b.* **1620/21**), millenarian, is known only through her publications, which reveal little of her background. At first she identified herself by initials alone, styling herself a 'minister or servant of the Gospel' (*The*

Resurrection of the Witnesses, 1648), and she did not indicate her gender or give her full name until 1651. She explained then that her surname had changed to Rande, presumably by marriage, but she continued to write under her maiden name. Her husband has not been identified. Christopher Feake described her as a gentlewoman, and her fluent and confident style points in the same direction. She tells us that she had studied scripture from childhood, and had been drawn to the prophecies of Daniel and Revelation at the age of fifteen, in 1636. Dedications in an early work to the puritan MPs Francis Rous and Thomas Boon may indicate a west-country origin, though she was living in London during her years as a writer.

In her first published work, in 1645, Cary defended free grace while condemning the 'licentious' antinomianism with which it was often associated (Cohen, 5). In *A Word in Season* (1647) she championed lay preaching, and urged that godliness was to be found in many forms. She always condemned the use of force against religious nonconformists, and prayed that the presbyterians and Independents would never be in a position to impose their own brands of orthodoxy.

Cary's major interest was in the establishment of Christ's kingdom on earth. Her prophetic framework was based largely on the writings of Thomas Brightman and John Archer; she expected the conversion and restoration of the Jews in 1656, and the full establishment of Christ's kingdom by 1701. Her own contribution lay in revealing the apocalyptic significance of the English civil war. In *The Resurrection of the Witnesses* (1648) she interpreted the outbreak of the Irish rising in 1641 as the killing of the two witnesses (Revelation 11), and the creation of the New Model Army in April 1645 as their resurrection. *The Little Horns Doom & Downfall* (first drafted in 1644, published in 1651) interpreted Daniel's prophecies in a similar manner, identifying Charles I as the little horn of the beast. It was dedicated to Oliver Cromwell's wife and his daughter Bridget, and appeared with testimonials from three leading radical preachers, Hugh Peter, Henry Jessey, and Christopher Feake. In a sketch of the New Jerusalem, Cary insisted that Christ would appear to reign in person. She spoke mostly of the spiritual blessings to come, but she promised material joys too, predicting that infant mortality would cease and that poor men would no longer work 'to maintain others that live vitiously, in idleness' (Cary, *Little Horns Doom*, 308).

Like many radicals Cary became disillusioned with the Rump Parliament and welcomed its fall. In July 1653 she published a set of reform proposals addressed to Barebone's Parliament. Many were concerned with the propagation of the gospel and with ways of maintaining the clergy by means other than tithes. She wanted university endowments to be used to fund poor preachers and scholars from humble backgrounds. She also suggested raising a fund to relieve the poor and unemployed by a levy on all letters or contracts, and called for drastic simplification of the laws and the establishment of local courts.

Cary's final work, an enlarged edition of *The Resurrection*

(1653), was addressed to the saints' meeting at Blackfriars and Christ Church, showing that she was now closely associated with the Fifth Monarchists. Within a few years, she predicted, Christ's kingdom would spread through Europe, and she warned the Dutch and Danes that in fighting England (in the First Anglo-Dutch War) they were fighting God. Readers were told to beat their ploughshares into swords.

Cary then disappears from view. Whether she had died or lapsed into silence as the millennial dream faded is not known.   BERNARD CAPP, *rev.*

Sources C. Hill, *The world turned upside down: radical ideas during the English revolution* (1972) · B. S. Capp, *The Fifth Monarchy Men: a study in seventeenth-century English millenarianism* (1972) · A. Cohen, 'Mary Cary's *The glorious excellencie discovered*', *British Studies Monitor*, 10/1–2 (1980), 4–7

Cary [*née* Shadd], **Mary Ann Camberton** (1823–1893), schoolmistress, newspaper editor, and political activist, was born on 9 October 1823 in Wilmington, Delaware, eldest of thirteen children of Abraham Doras Shadd (1801–1882), a shoemaker, and his wife, Harriet Parnell (1806–1880). Free African Americans in a slave state, prominent in the anti-slavery and negro convention movements, her family moved to West Chester, Pennsylvania, in 1833, where she attended a Quaker school. In 1839 she returned to Wilmington to open a school for free black children, and later taught in Pennsylvania and New York. In 1849 she published *Hints for the Colored People of the North*, urging African Americans toward self-reliance and integration. In 1851, with her brother Isaac, she moved to Upper Canada to investigate prospects for African Americans who might seek refuge there. Her report, *A Plea for Emigration, or, Notes of Canada West* (1852), praised the land, climate, and economy of the province, where legal equality prevailed and separate institutions were not imposed upon black citizens. She castigated self-segregated communities, such as the Refugee Home Society, which hindered complete integration.

In September 1851 Shadd organized a school in Windsor, Upper Canada. Conflict soon developed with Henry Bibb, editor of the *Voice of the Fugitive* newspaper and leader of the Refugee Home Society, and his schoolteacher wife, Mary Miles Bibb. Shadd continually attacked the Refugee Home as an enemy to black interests; Bibb argued that impoverished fugitives required special assistance in Canada. The dispute was aired at public meetings and in the American abolitionist press. In March 1853, seeking a more permanent vehicle for her integrationist views, Shadd joined Samuel Ringgold Ward to launch a newspaper, the *Provincial Freeman*. Ward, a leading black abolitionist, was the titular editor, but actual editing was done by Shadd, who was officially the publishing agent. Ward soon left for England, and Shadd spent a year arranging financing before the *Freeman* appeared again in March 1854, published from Toronto. Under the motto 'Self-reliance is the true road to independence', the paper opposed separatism and special treatment, encouraged emigration to Canada, and promoted black engagement in Canadian politics. One constant theme was that slavery

Mary Ann Camberton Cary (1823–1893), by unknown photographer, *c.*1845–55

in America could best be overthrown through the example of black achievement in Canada. Shadd also called for more opportunities for women, and hoped that her example would inspire others to join in public affairs. Until 1856, however, she disguised her control of the paper behind nominal male editors and signed her editorials only with her initials. In July 1855 Shadd and her paper moved to Chatham, close to the largest concentration of fugitives and to Buxton where her parents were settled. On 3 January 1856 she married Thomas F. Cary, a barber and anti-slavery activist from Toronto. A daughter, Sarah Elizabeth, was born in 1857, and a son, Linton, in 1861, but Thomas had died in November 1860.

Throughout the 1850s Mrs Cary was involved in the underground railroad and the Chatham Vigilance Committee assisting runaway slaves. She made frequent tours in Canada and the United States, recruiting subscribers and lecturing on abolition and emigration to Canada. When John Brown visited Chatham in May 1858 she attended his meetings, at least one of which was held at her newspaper office. Her employee Osborne P. Anderson participated in the raid on Harpers Ferry, and Mary Ann Cary helped him write *A Voice from Harpers Ferry* (1861). By 1858 her paper was in serious financial difficulty. Publication became irregular, and ceased completely in 1859 or 1860. She returned to teaching and continued to write for American abolitionist journals. In 1864 she became a recruiting agent for black regiments in the Union army, the only black woman to serve officially in this capacity. She returned to Chatham after the war, receiving a British passport in 1865 (she had become naturalized in 1862), but by 1869 she had moved to Washington, DC, where she became a teacher and later principal in the black public school system. Convinced that law was an essential instrument for equality, she studied law in Howard University's evening school and received her LLB in 1883. She wrote for several African American newspapers and agitated for civil rights for emancipated slaves and for women's suffrage. In 1878 she founded the Colored Women's Progressive Franchise Association, and in 1881 visited Canada to organize a suffragist rally. She practised law in Washington from 1884 until 1893, when she died of stomach cancer on 5 June at 1421 West Street NW. She was buried in Harmony cemetery, in Washington.

Mary Ann Shadd is generally regarded as the first female editor in Canada, and the first black female editor anywhere in America. Her newspaper is an important source for African Canadian history, providing unique insight into ideologies and politics within the black community. In recent years she has emerged as an example of black and female achievement. A school has been named after her in metropolitan Toronto, a popular song celebrates her memory, and she is firmly located on the curriculum of black studies and women's studies in Canada.

JAMES W. ST G. WALKER

Sources J. Bearden and L. J. Butler, *Shadd: the life and times of Mary Shadd Cary* (1977) · J. Rhodes, 'Breaking the editorial ice: Mary Shadd Cary and the *Provincial Freeman*', PhD diss., University of North Carolina, 1992 · H. B. Hancock, 'Mary Ann Shadd: negro editor, educator, and lawyer', *Delaware History*, 15 (1973), 187–94 · S. C. Evans, 'Mrs Mary Ann Shadd Cary, 1823–1893', *Homespun heroines and other women of distinction*, ed. H. Q. Brown (1971), 92–6 · J. H. Silverman, 'Mary Ann Shadd and the search for equality', *Black leaders of the nineteenth century*, ed. L. Litwack and A. Meier (1988), 87–100 · C. P. Ripley, ed., *The black abolitionist papers*, 2: *Canada, 1830–1865* (1986) · *Provincial Freeman* (24 March 1853–15 Sept 1857) · Howard University, Washington DC, Moorland-Spingarn Research Center, Mary Ann Shadd Cary MSS · Tulane University, New Orleans, Amistad Research Center, American Missionary Association Archives, Mary Shadd Cary MSS · NA Canada, Mary Ann Shadd Cary MSS · Raleigh Township Centennial Museum, North Buxton, Ontario, Shadd family MSS · d. cert.
Archives Howard University, Washington, DC, Moorland-Spingarn Research Center · NA Canada · Raleigh Township Centennial Museum, North Buxton, Ontario · Tulane University, New Orleans, Amistad Research Center, American Missionary Association Archives
Likenesses photograph, c.1845–1855, NA Canada [*see illus.*]
Wealth at death $150: Bearden and Butler, *Shadd*, 232

Cary, Sir (Arthur Lucius) Michael (1917–1976), civil servant, was born in Harrow, Middlesex, on 3 April 1917, the eldest of four sons of (Arthur) Joyce Lunel *Cary (1888–1957), author, and his wife, Gertrude Margaret Ogilvie (1891–1949). He went to Eton College as a scholar from 1931 to 1935, and won the king's prize for German. He won a major classical scholarship to Trinity College, Oxford, where he took first classes in classical honour moderations and *literae humaniores* (1937 and 1939). He was prominent in college life and gained a half-blue at lacrosse. He passed the home civil service examination and joined the Air Ministry in 1939. He spent little more than a year there before joining the Royal Navy in December 1940.

During the Second World War Cary, who had shown an interest in electronics at Eton, served as a radar instructor, then as radar officer on the aircraft-carrier *Illustrious* before joining the staff of the director of radar equipment in the Admiralty. Early in 1945 he left the navy and returned to the Air Ministry, where he became private secretary to the parliamentary under-secretary of state for air, John Strachey. Finding him deluged with vast numbers of letters about demobilization, Cary asked for a team of bright young people to draft less formal replies and speed up the process. This was an early example of his positive method of work—to size up a problem, find the solution, and persuade colleagues to take action.

Cary soon became private secretary to the secretary of state for air. He was promoted to assistant secretary in 1951. After a spell as head of the air staff secretariat he went to Paris as counsellor in the United Kingdom delegation to NATO. He was admirably suited for the post, not least because of his fluency in French and German. He became a well-known figure in NATO, and in wider circles in Paris.

On his return to the Air Ministry in 1958 Cary became assistant under-secretary of state (personnel). This post primarily concerned RAF personnel, and involved many visits to talk directly with service personnel about their problems. In 1961 he then became deputy secretary of the cabinet, initially under Sir Norman Brook and subsequently under Sir Burke Trend. He was much involved in the 1962 Cuban missile crisis, when he was acting cabinet secretary because of his chief's illness.

In 1964 Cary became second permanent secretary in the Admiralty in the newly reorganized and unified Ministry of Defence. The next four years were difficult. There was much inter-service bickering over policy and roles. Resources were cut, which led in 1966 to the resignation of his minister, Christopher Mayhew, and the chief of the naval staff. The hard grind of these years required all his skills. He suffered a near-fatal heart attack and went on a recuperative voyage. He fell ill again and was flown off to hospital in Malta.

Cary was the last secretary of the Admiralty (Samuel Pepys had been the third). The first sea lord had seen to it that on Cary's arrival he was immediately measured for his 'board rig', invented by Winston Churchill for civilian board members to wear while on Royal Navy ships. Cary was the last person entitled to wear it. He questioned whether it was appropriate for him to appear on the Admiralty's letters patent as 'A.L.M. Cary Esq. C.B., late Lieutenant R.N.V.R.' after a row of senior admirals. He was told that records showed that no other secretary had held commissioned rank in the Royal Navy.

Cary next became permanent secretary of the Ministry of Public Building and Works, where from 1968 to 1970 he worked hard at modernizing the ministry, welding professional and administrative staff into single teams as recommended in the 1968 Fulton report, and paying many visits overseas to find out how the ministry managed its stewardship of government buildings. Once he stayed overnight at an RAF airfield in the Persian Gulf manned totally by males unaccompanied by wives. Cary inquired about accommodation for his female private secretary—then a relative rarity—and was told she would be safe in the sick bay under armed guard.

The year 1970 saw the advent of very large Whitehall departments. The Ministry of Public Building and Works was abolished and its functions included in the new Department of the Environment, in which Cary became the secretary, housing and construction. He was caught again by changes in the machinery of government in 1971, when he was sent as secretary to the newly established procurement executive, a free-standing part of the Ministry of Defence. He became its chief executive in 1972. He was permanent under-secretary of state for defence from 1974 until his death.

In all these posts—five in six years—there was a heavy, time-consuming and sometimes acrimonious problem of reorganization, restructuring, reducing, and redeploying of staff. Cary was heavily involved in the Labour government's defence review, which started in December 1974. Its aim was to cut defence expenditure from 5.5 per cent to 4.4 per cent of gross national product by 1985. In policy terms the outcome was to concentrate primarily on NATO and Europe. Service manpower was cut back and substantial equipment savings achieved by re-phasing or delaying deliveries. Cary was chairman, until he died, of yet another committee tasked with reviewing defence organization.

Cary was an extraordinary man by any standards. Possessed of outstanding intellectual ability, he used it not only in his career but over a wide range of other interests. He excelled in making harpsichords and clavichords in the well-equipped workshop in his house at Blackheath, to which he moved in 1947. He had a deep commitment to the highest standards of workmanship. He chose the wood and other materials with the utmost care, made the plans with meticulous concentration, and cut every piece with exactitude. The completed instrument was proudly endorsed with the letters A.L.M.C. He also had a penchant for old Rolls Royce motor-cars—rather battered—starting in the 1950s with a 1926 model. Into these he crammed his family and careered in style around the streets of Paris when he worked there. He was twice married: In 1942 he married Betty Yingcheng, daughter of Sao-Ke Alfred Sze, a Chinese diplomat, whom he divorced in 1946. In the same year he married Isabel Margaret (d. 1998), daughter of Charles Duff Leslie, mining engineer; they had four sons (one adopted) and a daughter.

Cary had enormous self-confidence. He was immensely good with people. He was relaxed and informal. His habit of talking to everyone on visits frequently upset minutely timed programmes. He was an outstanding conversationalist, enjoying his own talk as well as that of others. He was a complex character. He had much talent and so many interests that he did not always find it easy to decide on which to concentrate. He believed that there was more to life than work. He was a quick worker and a natural delegator, but as a craftsman his attention to detail was total.

Cary enjoyed to the full a wide and active social life. Growing up in the Joyce Cary family meant much to him. His own family life was important to him; family gatherings, rituals, and celebrations mattered. This zest for living a full life, and a range of abilities that few possessed, prevented him attaining the Whitehall heights that in early days had seemed within his reach. This was his choice.

Cary was appointed CB in 1964, KCB in 1965 and GCB in 1976. In 1967 Cary was elected a fellow of Eton; in 1971 he

became commodore of the Civil Service Sailing Association; in 1972 president of the Institution of General Technician Engineers; and in 1973 he was elected to an honorary fellowship of Trinity College, Oxford, and to a fellowship of the Royal College of Art. He died suddenly of a coronary thrombosis at his home, Huntswood House, Harpsden, Henley-on-Thames, Oxfordshire, on 6 March 1976.   FRANK COOPER

Sources DNB · The Times (9 March 1976) · WWW · ministry of defence records (limited access) · personal knowledge (2004) · private information (2004) [Michael Bell; Lady Wood; P. J. Hudson; T. C. G. James] · b. cert. [Gertrude Margaret Ogilvie]
Archives U. Birm. L., corresp. with Lord Avon
Likenesses photographs
Wealth at death £55,842: probate, 2 June 1976, CGPLA Eng. & Wales

Cary, Patrick (c.1624–1657), poet, was the eighth of nine children of Henry *Cary (c.1575–1633) created Viscount Falkland in 1602 by James I, and Elizabeth *Cary (1585–1639) daughter of Sir Lawrence *Tanfield, judge. He was born in Ireland but in 1625 settled with his mother, and three other siblings, in England where his mother became a Catholic in 1626. His early life was spent in penury. Henry Cary died in debt after a series of career failures and Patrick's mother, disinherited by her father, had to rely on others for assistance. Patrick and his younger brother Henry were sent to their eldest brother, Lucius *Cary, second viscount, at Great Tew, Oxfordshire. Clarendon lauds Lucius Cary's scholarly disposition and the Great Tew circle included figures such as Suckling, Carew, and Hobbes. Fearful of her sons' religious upbringing Elizabeth Cary managed their removal from Great Tew to London and thence to France, where they were educated in the monastic school of St Edmund's, Paris, Henry being admitted as novice with the name of Brother Placid.

Cary journeyed to Rome, where he arrived in 1638 at the English College and for twelve years was supported by Father John Wilfred, procurator of the English Benedictines. He was also sustained by Cardinal Francesco Barberini, from whom he received a pension, though his fortunes fell on the election of a new pope, the reformist Innocent X, anxious to disembroil the Barberinis' legacy of patronage. Unable to find similar support Cary attempted the life of a Benedictine novice but gave up unable to cope with the physical privations. Several years of wandering followed in Italy and France until his return to England in 1650 and his welcome by his sister Victoria and her husband Sir William Uvedale at Wickham, Hampshire. By the following year he had renounced Catholicism and later married Susan Uvedale, daughter of Francis Uvedale; their son John (who died in infancy) was born at Great Tew in 1654. After a period of training at Lincoln's Inn, Cary followed a successful career in Ireland with a series of civil appointments, finally becoming justice of the peace for co. Meath. He died in Ireland and was buried on 15 March 1657.

Cary's thirty-seven poems are divided between 'triviall ballades' and divine poems. All show his conscientiousness in terms of poetic form and structure. They are steeped in the culture of the period, the ballads displaying the conventions of courtship and the divine poems the author's idealized attitudes to the life of abstinence. All the twenty-three secular poems were composed to tunes of the day, and it is necessary to see Cary following a pattern of composition stretching back to the musical parody of Elizabethan court poets and earlier. The poems are, therefore, overtly courtly, and those that are not were probably composed as a means of aiding religious reflection during Cary's brief, though harsh, period as a Benedictine novice.

Two manuscript sources are extant though only one contains all thirty-seven of Cary's poems which were written between 1650 and 1652. This is the manuscript in the library at Abbotsford which belonged to Sir Walter Scott, and which he published in 1820. This is decorated with emblem designs and titles of the verses carry references to the tunes to which Cary wrote them. The other, an autograph manuscript in the Brotherton collection at the University of Leeds, contains only thirteen of the poems but is much more elaborately decorated with hand-drawn illustrations which mirror the themes of the verse and illustrate a cultured awareness of the art of the Renaissance. Though each aspect of Cary's life may only be known through fragments and the poetry composed for private pleasure, taken as a whole the life has a symbolic quality emphasized by Cary's reliance on the ethical, religious, poetic, and artistic models provided by his culture.

NICHOLAS JAGGER

Sources V. Delany, 'Biographical and critical introduction', in *The poems of Patrick Cary* (1978) · 'Ballades dedicated to Lady Victoria Uvedale', U. Leeds, Brotherton L. [autograph manuscript 1652/1653]

Cary, Robert (*bap.* **1615**, *d.* **1688**), antiquary, was the second child of the eight sons and three daughters of George Cary esquire (*d.* 1643) of Cockington and Elizabeth, daughter of Sir Edward Seymour, bt, of Berry Pomeroy, Devon, where he was baptized on 2 April 1615. He matriculated at Exeter College, Oxford, in 1631 and became a scholar of Corpus Christi College in 1634, and graduated BA in 1635, and MA in 1639. In 1644 his kinship to Oxford's chancellor, the marquess of Hertford, secured him the degree of LLD.

Earlier accounts of Cary's career depend largely on Prince's *Worthies of Devon*, yet original sources throw some doubt on Prince's account. He stated that Cary travelled abroad after he received his LLD in 1644 and on his return was appointed to the living of East Portlemouth. In fact Cary lived at Cockington from 1643 where seven of the children born to him and his wife, Anne, were baptized, and he did not move to East Portlemouth until after his brother Sir Henry had sold the family estate of Cockington late in 1654. Three more children were baptized at East Portlemouth, where his wife died in 1660. Prince is correct in saying that Cary 'was not drawn to the presbyterians' as he was not one of the 131 ministers who signed the articles of association of the Exeter assembly of Devon ministers in 1655, yet he was evidently persuaded to act as moderator for the Kingsbridge division in 1657.

Prince stated that Robert Cary was among the first to welcome Charles II on his return and so gained the king's favour for his appointment as archdeacon of Exeter from 1662 to 1664. It seems much more likely that the one concerned in welcoming the king was Robert Cary of Clovelly, who had been sequestered for his support of Charles I. He became a gentleman of the chamber and was knighted in August 1660. It may also have been Robert Cary of Clovelly who was the one travelling abroad as he was accused by the compounding committee in 1653 of having gone overseas after serving the king.

Cary preferred a retired life of study and may well have been glad to resign the task of archdeacon. His major work, *Palaeologia chronica*, was printed in 1678. His dedication to the king describes his work as 'under the Hammer and the File for many Years'. It first describes the varied methods of measuring time, then deduces the intervals of time from secular writers and finally from the Bible. An appendix charts events from the creation of Adam and Eve in 5708 BC and includes Hebrew, Chinese, Egyptian, Greek, and Latin dates. Prince noted a lengthy review of the *Palaeologica chronica* in the *Philosophical Transactions* of the Royal Society. In his younger days Cary is said to have been a skilled poet but his only other publication was some translations of hymns into Latin verse. Prince described him as 'of middle stature, sanguine of complexion, and in elder years somewhat corpulent'. He served East Portlemouth as rector until his death, and was buried there on 19 September 1688. MARY WOLFFE

Sources parish registers of Berry Pomeroy, Cockington, and East Portlemouth, Devon · Foster, *Alum. Oxon.* · J. Prince, *Danmonii orientales illustres, or, The worthies of Devon* (1701) · Wood, *Ath. Oxon.*, new edn · A. Kippis and others, eds., *Biographia Britannica, or, The lives of the most eminent persons who have flourished in Great Britain and Ireland*, 2nd edn, 3 (1784), 300 · J. L. Vivian, ed., *The visitations of the county of Devon, comprising the herald's visitations of 1531, 1564, and 1620* (privately printed, Exeter, [1895]) · R. N. Worth, 'Puritanism in Devon and the Exeter assembly', *Report and Transactions of the Devonshire Association*, 9 (1877), 250–91 · archdeacon of Exeter visitations, Devon RO, AE/V/9 · W. Kennet, ed., *Register* (1728), 744 · M. A. E. Green, ed., *Calendar of the proceedings of the committee for compounding … 1643–1660*, 5 vols., PRO (1889–92), vols 1, 3 · DNB

Wealth at death all family estates at Cockington sold by elder brother in 1654 for £10,500; subject not known to have received any of the proceeds of this sale: Devon RO 48/13/1/1/13

Cary, Thomas (*d.* *c.*1720), colonial governor, was probably born in Chipping Wycombe, Buckinghamshire, the son of Walter Cary (*d.* in or before 1673) and his wife, Ann Dobson. Details of Cary's early life are uncertain, but in 1673, after the death of his father, Cary's mother married John Archdale, a leading Quaker and proprietor and governor of Carolina. By 1695 Cary had settled in Charles Town, Carolina, where, undoubtedly through the influence of his stepfather, he was appointed as the secretary of the governor's council. He later served as provincial treasurer (1687–8) and register of the Admiralty court (1698). He also succeeded as a merchant and shipowner, amassing such wealth that in 1702 he posted a £2000 bond required by the proprietors of the colony for Sir Nathaniel Johnson to become governor as well as a bond of equal amount for the new governor of the Bahamas. At some point Cary appears to have married, but nothing is known about his wife.

Cary's bond investments paid off when in March 1705 Johnson appointed him deputy governor to the northern district of Carolina (later North Carolina). Although part of Carolina, the northern settlements, dominated by Albemarle county, enjoyed a substantial degree of autonomy from the colony's executive, based in Charles Town. Cary found the region to be rife with tensions, in part centred on the challenge by Bath county to the political hegemony of Albemarle county. A greater problem was posed by the growing rivalry between members of the Church of England and the substantial dissenting population, which had been drawn to the colony by the promises of toleration in the colony's charter. The Quakers, the most powerful dissenting group, dominated the early assembly and had even built Albemarle's first church, but in 1703 the Anglicans had managed to establish the Church of England. The vestry act that established the church also included the standard practice of requiring oaths of allegiance to the crown in order to hold public office. The Quakers, whose beliefs prohibited the taking of such oaths, were thus excluded from politics.

Any hopes that Cary's association with his stepfather would lead him to suspend the act were short-lived. Cary, who was probably a member of the Church of England, answered not to Archdale but to Governor Johnson, a staunch Anglican. He quickly allied himself with the Anglicans in Albemarle and enforced the statute requiring oaths of allegiance. The dissenters responded by sending the Quaker leader John Porter to England to plead with the proprietors to dismiss Cary from office. Porter's request was granted and in October 1707 Cary was removed and replaced with William Glover, who was elected president of the region's council (making him acting governor). Furthermore, Johnson's mandate over the region was suspended. Glover, however, followed in his predecessor's footsteps and aligned himself with the Albemarle Anglicans. Cary, who had settled in Bath county, began to draw supporters against Glover from the population of that county and the dissenters, and in October 1708 Cary and his armed supporters forced the acting governor to flee. Cary was duly elected council president with the support of his old rival John Porter, and in return nullified test oaths and returned dissenters to key offices.

Cary remained in power until the arrival in January 1711 of Edward Hyde, who succeeded Cary as president of the council and as deputy governor. Cary retired peacefully to his home in Bath county, but his enemies persuaded Hyde to arrest the former deputy governor. Hyde's alliances with the Albemarle Anglicans and calls for new legislation against dissenters rallied opponents of the incumbent deputy governor around Cary. In May Hyde went into Bath county with an armed force, prompting what has become known as 'Cary's rebellion'. After a short skirmish, Hyde's force was repelled at Cary's fortified plantation. Cary went on the offensive, fitting out a brigantine and sailing for Albemarle Sound in mid-June. After a series of indecisive engagements Hyde gained the upper hand in July when he received reinforcements from Governor Alexander Spotswood of Virginia. The enlarged force went into Bath county, where Cary and his supporters were defeated. Cary escaped to Virginia, but was captured by Spotswood's men and sent to London for trial. Cary and four of his lieutenants first appeared before Carolina's lords proprietor on 20 November 1711 in a trial that would last nearly a year. Cary and his co-defendants were released for lack of evidence, because Hyde, whose colony was in the throes of a desperate war with the Tuscarora Indians, had not sent a representative to London. Cary returned in the spring of 1713, settling once again in Bath county. The proprietors ordered that no local charges be brought against him until a full investigation had been made, but by this time Hyde was dead and the colony was enjoying peace. Cary spent his remaining days at his Bath county plantation; he died about 1720, and was survived by a son.　　　　　　　　　　　　　TROY O. BICKHAM

Sources W. S. Price, 'Cary, Thomas', *Dictionary of North Carolina biography*, ed. W. S. Powell, 1 (1979) · L. S. Butler, 'Cary, Thomas', *ANB* · W. L. Saunders and W. Clark, eds., *The colonial records of North Carolina*, 30 vols. (1886–1907), vols. 1–2 · W. S. Price, ed., *North Carolina higher-court records: the colonial records of North Carolina*, 2nd ser., 4–5 (1974)

Wealth at death substantial landholdings; one of wealthiest men in the Carolinas

Cary, Valentine. *See* Carey, Valentine (d. 1626).

Cary, William (1759–1825), maker of scientific instruments, was born on 6 June 1759, the fourth and youngest son of George Cary, maltster, of Corsley, Wiltshire, and his wife, Mary (d. 1799). He was apprenticed to the noted instrument maker Jesse Ramsden, probably from 1773 until 1780, though no record of this has been traced. He married Elizabeth Jackson, of Clerkenwell, London, on 27 December 1785 at St Clement Danes Church in the Strand. By 1789 he had established himself in business at 272 Strand, in Westminster, where he soon gained a reputation for excellent workmanship.

About 1790 a circle with telescope of 4 inches aperture was ordered from Cary by the astronomer Johan Feer for his observatory at Zürich. In 1791 Cary constructed for Dr Francis Wollaston (1731–1815) the first astronomical transit circle made in England, a fine instrument with a circle of 2 feet in diameter and provided with reading microscopes. He was, besides, the maker of the 2½ foot altitude and azimuth instrument with which Friedrich Wilhelm Bessel, first director of the Königsberg observatory, began his observations there, and of numerous excellent sextants, microscopes, and reflecting and refracting telescopes. In 1794 Cary moved to 182 Strand, from where he issued a catalogue of instruments sold by him. From 1797 until his death he provided instruments for Christ's Hospital mathematical school. In 1805 he sent to Moscow a transit instrument described and illustrated in Pearson's *Introduction to Practical Astronomy* (2.362–5; pl. xv), the safety of which was provided for by an order from Bonaparte in 1812.

At the same time as conducting his own business, Cary

produced a series of terrestrial and celestial globes in association with his brother John *Cary, who traded as a cartographer from the shop next door. When John Cary's premises at 181 Strand were destroyed by fire in 1820, William rebuilt them and took them over. He supplied a 3 foot theodolite for the great trigonometrical survey of India under George Everest. A particular type of pocket microscope invented in the 1820s became known as a 'Cary-type microscope', but this instrument was actually designed by William Cary's shopman, Charles Gould (Turner, 75).

In February 1820 Cary became a member of the newly formed Astronomical Society of London, later the Royal Astronomical Society. He contributed for several years the 'Meteorological diary' to the *Gentleman's Magazine*. Cary died on 16 November 1825, probably at his house at 181 Strand, and was buried on 25 November in the parish of St Mary Abbots, Kensington. It appears that there were no children of his marriage. After his death the business was continued under the name of William Cary by his nephews George and John, sons of his brother John.

GLORIA CLIFTON

Sources R. Wolf, *Geschichte der Astronomie* (Munich, 1877), 562–3, 578 · W. Pearson, *An introduction to practical astronomy*, 2 (1829), 362–5, 402, pl. 15 and 17 · *Memoirs of the Astronomical Society of London*, 2 (1826), 532 · *GM*, 1st ser., 95/2 (1825), 475–6 · F. Wollaston, 'Description of a transit circle', *PTRS*, 83 (1793), 133–4, 136–40 · G. L'E. Turner, *The great age of the microscope: the collection of the Royal Microscopical Society through 150 years* (1989), 75–7, 239–40 · J. T. Stock, 'Henry Barrow, instrument maker', *Bulletin of the Scientific Instrument Society*, 9 (1986), 11–12, esp. 11 · E. Dekker and P. van der Krogt, *Globes from the western world* (1993), 116, 118 · Christ's Hospital ledgers, GL, MS 12823/8, 347–51 · Christ's Hospital ledgers, GL, MS 12823/9, 699–703 · death duty registers, PRO, IR 26/1077, no. 15 · transcripts of burials in the parish of Kensington, Diocese of London, LMA, DL/T/47/27, no. 896 · Transcripts of parish registers of Corsley Magna, Wiltshire, GS Lond.

Archives BM, Heal collection, trade bill 105/18 · RAS, membership papers

Wealth at death £15,373 19s. 1d.: PRO, death duty registers, IR 26/1077, no. 15

Caryl, Joseph (1602–1673), clergyman and ejected minister, was born in London in November 1602 'of genteel parents', was attending Merchant Taylors' School in 1620, and matriculated in 1621 as a commoner from Exeter College, Oxford, where 'he became in a short time a noted disputant' (Wood, *Ath. Oxon.*, 3.979). He graduated BA in 1625 and proceeded MA in 1627. He was briefly curate of Battersea, Surrey. On 8 June 1632 the benchers of Lincoln's Inn elected Caryl divinity reader to preach twice on Sundays for a salary of £80 per annum, a lectureship which Anthony Wood claimed he owed to his being 'puritanically affected', and which he continued to preach until 1648 'with good liking and applause' (ibid.). The scope and frequency of his preaching is evident in his thirty-four publications, among which the most noted was *An Exposition with Practical Observations upon ... the Chapters of ... Job* (1643–66), which was based on a long series of sermons.

Caryl preached the first of a number of fast day sermons before parliament on 27 April 1642, calling for ecclesiastical reform, and was, after Stephen Marshall, the minister most frequently called on to preach before the house.

Joseph Caryl (1602–1673), by unknown artist

As a consequence, he was among those ordered by the House of Commons in October 1643 to preach in favour of the solemn league and covenant, a sermon subsequently published as *The Nature, Solemnity, Grounds, Property, and Benefits, of a Sacred Covenant* (1643), in which Caryl announced that 'as God's Covenant-people are his Chosen people, so must ours [be]'. Nevertheless, despite supporting the solemn league and covenant, he was, as one of the London representatives to the assembly of divines, soon identified as an Independent, albeit of a moderate cast, Edmund Calamy characterizing him later as 'a moderate Independent, a man of great piety, learning and modesty' (*Nonconformist's Memorial*, 1.146). Although he did not sign *An Apologeticall Narration*, in 1644 Caryl was among the Independent minority who opposed a presbyterial ordination, and in 1646 he voted in favour of the proposition 'that Jesus Christ as King and Head of His Church hath Himself appointed a Church government distinct from the Civil' and that 'this Church Government stands not in any power of external coercions' (Mitchell and Struthers, 252). On the other hand, while he preached in favour of liberal treatment of tender consciences, he willingly served as a licenser of religious works when appointed in 1643 and, despite his opposition to a presbyterial ecclesiastical order, served as one of the triers of elders for the fourth London classis when appointed in 1645, and attended fifteen of its meetings. Furthermore, having supported Dury's and Samuel Hartlib's ecumenical efforts since the 1630s, he also endorsed John Dury's call for a presbyterian–Independent accommodation in 1647.

In 1645 Caryl accepted the rectory of St Magnus the Martyr, London, where he preached twice on Sunday for the next seventeen years, in spite of a busy life outside the parish. He and Stephen Marshall were appointed to attend King Charles at Holmby House in 1647 and again to attend the commissioners at Newport in 1648, and Caryl was dispatched by the House of Commons to serve as a chaplain to the commissioners to Scotland in 1648 and 1651. With Marshall and Hugh Peter, fellow Independents, he was one of the preachers at a special fast on 8 December 1648, called on the day after Pride's Purge; on the other hand, after the king's death in 1649 he, Philip Nye, and others sought to persuade some of the members excluded in the purge to return to the house. The same year Caryl became one of the preachers at Westminster Abbey and remained so until 1660. In March 1651 he refused the deanery of Christ's Church, Oxford, a post that went to John Owen, but in June he accepted appointment as one of the Whitehall preachers. In 1654 he was appointed to the commissioners for the approbation of ministers, and, as a supporter of the lord protector, he conferred with Major Harrison and the Fifth Monarchists in 1655, advocated the readmission of the Jews late in that year, saw the Quaker James Nayler on behalf of the government in 1656, and advised on the settlement of the Scottish church in 1657. He was active in the assembly of Independents at the Savoy in 1658 and was one of the delegates sent to deliver a letter from the congregational churches urging General Monk to use his powers to protect liberty of conscience and the godly in 1659. A noted Greek scholar, Caryl also found time to publish a grammar in 1658, and was the principal author of an English–Greek lexicon published in 1661.

In 1662 Caryl was ejected from his rectory of St Magnus. His farewell sermon was noted by his contemporaries as a moving tribute to the reformed faith; in it he concluded that 'if I shall have no more opportunities among you, as you have been stirred up to get this [white robe] of grace, you and I may meet in glory, where we shall never part' (*Nonconformist's Memorial*, 1.148). Soon after, Caryl was arrested, while preaching to a congregation in Southwark. In 1663 he was reportedly living near London Bridge and preaching to an Independent congregation that met at various places in the City, but he apparently moved to a house on Bury Street in Duke's Place. He was licensed on 15 April 1672 to preach to a congregation numbering 136 communicants in Leadenhall Street.

Virtually nothing is known about Caryl's family. His will, dated 29 January 1672, mentions his wife, Anne, to whom he left during her life the bulk of his estate, principally land in Furneaux Pelham, Hertfordshire, which was then to pass to their son, Joseph. A daughter, Elizabeth, was to have a portion of £800 plus an additional £200 if she married by the advice of her mother. A sum of £10 was left to be distributed to deprived ministers or their widows. Caryl died at his Bury Street home on 25 February 1673 and was buried at College Hill.   P. S. SEAVER

Sources The nonconformist's memorial … originally written by … Edmund Calamy, ed. S. Palmer, [3rd edn], 3 vols. (1802–3) · Wood, *Ath. Oxon.*, new edn · *The letters and journals of Robert Baillie*, ed. D. Laing, 3 vols. (1841–2) · A. F. Mitchell and J. Struthers, eds., *Minutes of the sessions of the Westminster assembly of divines* (1874) · *Calamy rev.* · Greaves & Zaller, *BDBR* · W. P. Baildon, ed., *The records of the Honorable Society of Lincoln's Inn: the black books*, 1–4 (1897–1902) · Foster, *Alum. Oxon.* · C. E. Surman, ed., *The register-booke of the fourth classis in the province of London, 1646–59*, 2 vols. in 1, Harleian Society, 82–3 (1953) · W. A. Shaw, *A history of the English church during the civil wars and under the Commonwealth, 1640–1660*, 2 vols. (1900) · T. Webster, *Godly clergy in early Stuart England: the Caroline puritan movement, c.1620–1643* (1997) · churchwardens' accounts, St Magnus the Martyr, 1638–1734, GL, MS 1179/1 · PRO, PROB 11/341/33 · Mrs E. P. Hart, ed., *Merchant Taylors' School register, 1561–1934*, 2 vols. (1936)
Likenesses R. White, line engraving, BM, NPG; repro. in J. Caryl, *Commentary on Job* (1676) · oils, DWL [*see illus.*]

Caryll, Ivan [*real name* Félix Tilkin] (1861–1921), composer and music director, was born on 12 May 1861 in Liège, Belgium, the son of Henry Tilkin, an engineer. He was educated at the Paris Conservatoire and settled in Britain in the mid-1880s. His earliest days in London were spent largely in musical hack work and teaching, and although he had a comic opera, *The Lily of Léoville*, produced in London as early as 1886, it was as a conductor that he made his first noticeable mark in the musical theatre. When Henry J. Leslie bought the Gaiety Theatre production of *Dorothy* and transferred it to the Prince of Wales, the Gaiety's music director, Meyer Lutz, remained at his own theatre, and Caryll was appointed conductor for the revamped show which was to become the musical-theatre hit of the era. He remained Leslie's music director through the four years and three shows of the producer's dramatic career, shifting with him to his new Lyric Theatre on Shaftesbury Avenue, where *Doris* and *The Red Hussar* were produced, and staying there, when Leslie's operation went under, as music director for the theatre's new manager, Horace Sedger.

Caryll subsequently supplied part-scores for local adaptations of several French musicals and completed the score for the late Alfred Cellier's *The Mountebanks*, before he got the opportunity to write the complete music for the latter-day burlesque *Little Christopher Columbus*, built around the under-voiced American starlet May Yohé and backed by her lordly lover, Francis Hope. It featured two songs—the 'coon' song 'Oh Honey, my Honey' and the ballad 'Lazily, Drowsily'—which took Caryll straight to the fore of the musical-theatre profession.

The young musician was soon snapped up by the watchful George Edwardes for the Gaiety Theatre, where he remained as music director for fifteen years, supplying the music for all the great hits of that theatre's most prosperous period, from *The Shop Girl* (1894) through to *Our Miss Gibbs* (1909). Under Edwardes's aegis a writing partnership between Caryll and Lionel *Monckton (1861–1924) evolved, beginning with Monckton as the subsidiary 'additional songs' member, but later on equal terms, with both turning out much of the best of the light theatre music on the London stage in its most successful Victorian and Edwardian years.

Caryll did not confine himself in those years to writing for the Gaiety. In the early years of the new century he turned out a bevy of scores, both in the musical-comedy style, notably the charming *The Girl from Kay's* (1902), and in the light opera vein, with *The Duchess of Dantzic*, a score which echoed the most attractive tones of French *opéra comique*. *The Earl and the Girl*, written with Seymour Hicks and staged with the remnants of the D'Oyly Carte Opera Company, was another of Caryll's notable successes in this period. At Christmas 1903 he had the then unparalleled distinction of having five musicals running at the same time in the West End of London.

In 1910, with *Our Miss Gibbs* still giving him one of the greatest successes of his career, Caryll left Britain for America, where he combined with the American librettist C. M. S. McLellan on a series of musicals based, like *The Girl from Kay's*, on French plays. Their second Broadway venture, *The Pink Lady*, in particular, proved as great a success as his English shows, and while, in the wake of *The Merry Widow*, everything that was singable in Vienna was making its way to America, *The Pink Lady* unusually made the reverse trip, to play London, Paris, and Budapest. This series of shows based on French farces, of which *Oh! Oh! Delphine* and *The Girl behind the Gun* (known in Britain as *Kissing Time*) were the other prime examples, helped largely to set the fashion for modern 'musical comedy' on the American stage.

Throughout his career Caryll maintained close links with the European theatre. A considerable number of his musicals got showings in Paris, Vienna, and Budapest at a time when the product of the English-language stage was largely ignored on the continent, and he composed original scores both for Paris (*S.A.R.*, or *Son altesse royale*, 1908) and for Vienna (*Die Reise nach Cuba*, 1901).

Caryll's career encompassed three eras of the musical theatre, and he seemed to be equally happy in each of them. If his first great successes were made in the light musical-comedy area, epitomized by the Gaiety Theatre shows, he proved with scores as divergent as the operettic *The Duchess of Dantzic* and *S.A.R.*, on the one hand, and the post-war *The Girl behind the Gun*, with its modern fox-trot and one-step rhythms, on the other, that he was a theatre composer who (unlike his contemporaries Lionel Monckton and Sidney Jones) could and would move with times and musical styles. His scores for *The Pink Lady* and *Oh! Oh! Delphine* contain numbers which equal the best that both the Viennese waltz masters and the new wave of American dance- and songwriters were producing in the years around the First World War. Unlike so many of those who followed him, he was as capable of turning out a complicated finale or concerted number as a catchy point number or comedy song but, largely because so much of his work was written for a kind of show which was by its nature ephemeral, few of his songs have survived as standards. Caryll was married for a period to the American singer (Annie) Geraldine Ulmar (1862–1932) and later to another musical-comedy performer, Maud Hill. He died in the Ambassador's Hotel, New York, on 29 November 1921.　　　　　　　　　　　　　　　　　　KURT GÄNZL

Sources K. Gänzl, *The encyclopedia of the musical theatre*, 2 vols. (1994) • K. Gänzl, *The British musical theatre*, 2 vols. (1986) • *CGPLA*

Eng. & Wales (1922) • J. Parker, ed., *Who's who in the theatre*, 6th edn (1930)
Archives Harvard TC, musical scores by Ivan Caryll
Likenesses photograph, repro. in *Play Pictorial*, 14/71 (1912)
Wealth at death £7873 9s. 2d.: probate, 28 April 1922, *CGPLA Eng. & Wales*

Caryll, John (1460s–1523), law reporter, was born into an obscure Sussex family in the 1460s. As a young man, he occasionally spelt his name Caarle, which may import a peasant origin. By March 1485 he was studying law in the Inner Temple, and it is likely that he entered the inn as a protégé of John Baker, a bencher of the inn who also came from Sussex. He was a justice of the peace for Sussex from 18 February 1496 until his death. In 1493 he obtained the third protonotaryship of the court of common pleas in succession to Humphrey Coningsby under an agreement that he would pass the office on in due course to Coningsby's son. Caryll held the office until he became a serjeant-at-law in 1510, when it passed to William Coningsby. During this period as a protonotary, Caryll also practised privately, both as attorney and counsel, and from 1495 he was clerk of assize on the western circuit.

Caryll served as treasurer of the Inner Temple in 1507–8, and in 1510 as serjeant-elect delivered a second or third reading, the text being part of the Statute of Marlborough. Four years later, on 1 June 1514, he was taken into the royal service as a king's serjeant. His will mentions three wives, the last of whom survived him. The first was Griselda, or Gresild (d. 1498), daughter of Henry Belknap (d. 1488) of Sussex; her sister Alice was the wife of William *Shelley, the future judge, who was another member of this Sussex circle belonging to the Inner Temple. Griselda died in 1498, and Caryll married as his second wife Margaret, sister of Thomas Ellenbridge of Merstham, Surrey, with whom he had two sons. As his third wife, Caryll married Jane, daughter of Chief Justice Sir Robert *Rede, with whom he is said to have had four more sons.

Caryll is one of the first identifiable English law reporters. His reports were well known by their author's name until the beginning of the seventeenth century. In 1602 about half of them, beginning in 1496, were printed by John Croke from a manuscript formerly belonging to Robert *Keilwey. This edition, which has always been cited as *Keilwey*, was reprinted in 1633 and 1688. Although Croke did not mention Caryll as the reporter, it is obvious that the reports cannot have been written by Keilwey himself, who did not become a member of the Inner Temple until the 1530s, and indeed no such claim is made anywhere in the printed book. Whether Keilwey's manuscript was even the autograph is doubtful, since the latter is known to have passed to Caryll's eldest son, John (d. 1566), and there is no reason why he should have parted with it during his lifetime. Keilwey was a close friend of the son, who was about ten years his senior in the Inner Temple, and was presumably given an opportunity to copy from his manuscripts. Other copies were certainly made, and the reports were known later in the century both to Dyer and Coke. Coke, indeed, once referred to 'the written report of the famous Caryll of the Inner Temple' (translated from BL, Add. MS 16169, fol. 192).

The Keilwey text did not, however, represent the whole of Caryll's reports, which began about 1486 or 1487. The earliest notes attributable to him are in BL, Harley MS 5158, a collection of year-books which contains the names of Baker and Caryll in the *explicits*, and the name Johannes Caryll on the original vellum cover. Among the glosses and insertions are cases written in the second half of the 1480s, together with a number of disputations from the Inner Temple. The whole manuscript is full of marginal notes and cross-references, some of them attributable to the younger John Caryll, who refers in several places to Caryll's reports by name and in two places more explicitly cites 'the reports of my father' and 'the abridgment of my father'. A number of other manuscript texts can be attributed to Caryll, and these in turn enable the identification of the wrongly dated vulgate year-books of Easter and Trinity terms 13 Hen. VII (fols. 18–29) and the whole of 16 Hen. VII, first printed by Tottell in 1555, as being from the same source. From all these texts an edition has been published by the Selden Society.

By and large the reports are in the same anonymous style as the year-books, with a preponderance of common pleas cases, though there is some internal corroboration of authorship in the mention of five or six cases from the western circuit in 1503–5 when Caryll was clerk of assize there. There are more numerous personal touches after 1514, when Caryll became king's serjeant; there is then a heavy emphasis on crown business, including notes of the duke of Buckingham's claims of that year, the Hunne affair of 1516, the May day riots of 1517, the earl of Derby's case, the important cases of 1515 and 1519 on benefit of clergy and sanctuary—in which Henry VIII himself is reported as threatening to 'have that reformed which is encroached by abuse' (Croke, 191)—and numerous references to revenue practice. With the exception of a brief note, the reports end in 1519, four years before Caryll died. It is a notable coincidence that the printed year-books of Henry VIII begin the next year and continue in series until Easter term 1523, the very term before the serjeant's death. Yet there is a difference of style and content between the two series, not to mention a complete absence of reports after 11 Hen. VIII in any of the manuscript texts of Caryll, and so the reports of 1520–23 cannot convincingly be attributed to the same hand. Unlike John Port and John Spelman, Caryll generally kept his disputations completely separate from his reports of cases in the courts, which are written as a chronological register in the year-book tradition. Learning exercises from the Inner Temple are nevertheless found in several of the Caryll manuscripts that contain reports; and a substantial series from the 1480s was printed in *Keilwey* (fols. 102v–137) as *Casus incerti temporis*.

Caryll died on 17 June 1523, and was buried in London, at St Dunstan-in-the-West, Fleet Street, in the aisle where the judges and serjeants sat. Little is known of his estate at death, though his principal property transactions were evidently in the vicinity of his seat at Warnham in Sussex.

The serjeant directed in his will that his eldest son, John, was to be:

> sett to the lernyng of the lawes of the land, and he to have yerely for his exhibition in the Temple x s. at the lest, which I knowe will suffise for his exhibition yf he lyve and use himself well and honestly and wysely like a lerner and student.

John was already a member of the Inner Temple, and before he became a bencher in 1537 had followed in his father's footsteps as a reporter of cases and of Inner Temple moots. In 1540 he was offered the coif, which he declined, taking instead the office of attorney-general of the first-fruits and tenths, whence he was promoted in 1544 to the lucrative office of attorney of the duchy. He held the duchy office until his death on 10 March 1566, turning down the coif twice more, and continued reporting cases until at least 1560, though his reports (which have still to be edited) are not so full or as authoritative as those of his father.
J. H. BAKER

Sources *Reports of cases by John Caryll*, ed. J. H. Baker, 2 vols., SeldS, 115–16 (1999–2000) · L. W. Abbott, *Law reporting in England, 1485–1585* (1973), 38–49 · A. W. B. Simpson, 'Caryll's reports', *Law Quarterly Review*, 73 (1957), 89–105 · J. Croke, ed., *Relationes quorundam casuum* (1602) [known as *Keilwey*] · BL, Add. MS 16169, fol. 192 · BL, Harley MS 5158 · GL, MS 2968/1, fol. 34v
Archives BL, Harley MS 5158

Caryll, John, Jacobite first Baron Caryll of Durford (*bap.* 1626, *d.* 1711), poet and politician, was probably born at West Harting, Sussex, and was baptized on 2 November 1626, the son of John Caryll (1603–1681), head of an old Roman Catholic family settled in west Sussex, and Catherine (*d.* 1682), daughter of Lord Petre. His father compromised his religion and his politics during the civil war period but reverted to royalist Catholicism at the Restoration. Partly educated at St Omer, Caryll seems to have proceeded to the court of Parma where he served the duke, perhaps as a page or gentleman usher (BL, Add. MS 28226, fol. 2). He married Margaret Drummond, daughter of Sir Maurice Drummond; she died in 1656. At the Restoration he went to London and was for a time 'a man of Fortune and fashion' (Macaulay). He wrote two successful plays, *The English Princess* (1666) and *Sir Salomon Single* (1671), the first a legitimist political drama seeming to prophesy (from the fictionalized reign of Richard III) the reign of Charles II, the second an imitation of Molière's *L'école des femmes*. Behind the mask of the gentleman who wrote with ease Caryll was concerned with the situation of English Catholics, and his treatise, 'Not guilty, or, The plea of the Roman Catholick in England' (BL, Add. MS 28252, fols. 140–48), was probably written early in the Restoration before Charles II's religious policy was settled. At the same time Caryll's sister Mary founded from Ghent the new Benedictine convent of the Immaculate Conception at Dunkirk, with financial help from the king and encouragement and gifts from Anne, duchess of York. Dame Mary Caryll, elected abbess at Dunkirk in 1663, was an important figure in her own right, and her correspondence with her brother on family, religious, and political matters (BL, Add. MS 28226) is of lasting interest.

Religious and political issues, the Popish Plot, and the exclusion crisis prompted Caryll to write his lampoon, 'The Hypocrite', on the first earl of Shaftesbury who in 1678–80 was exploiting anti-Catholic fears to bar the Catholic duke of York from succession to the throne. Five popish lords were arrested and committed to the Tower on 28 October 1678. On 3 December the Middlesex grand jury found them guilty of treason. This prompted Caryll to write his best-known poem, *Naboth's vineyard, or, The innocent traytor: copied from the original in holy scripture, in heroick verse* (1679). It is a political poem of protest and (as its title suggests) the obvious precedent for Caryll's friend Dryden when he judged the same crisis in his *Absalom and Achitophel* (1681). Caryll himself was in the Tower for four months but released on 22 May 1680.

On the accession of James II, Caryll was sent to Rome as envoy to the papal court. He was to beg a bishopric *in partibus* for England for John Leyburn, and a cardinal's hat for Rinaldo d'Este, the queen's uncle. This last was difficult since Rinaldo favoured the French interest, unpopular at Rome. 'Mr. Caryll', however,

> finding where the shoo pinched, made a conditional proposal, not doubting but what it would be approved of by the King his master, Whether upon the Prince d'Este's engagement, not to concern himself with any interest but that of England, the Pope would agree to it, which his Holyness … promised he would. (*Life of James II*, ed. J. C. Clark, 1816, 2.75–6)

On his replacement as envoy by Lord Castlemaine, Caryll became secretary to the queen and was also, by 1688, a privy councillor. The birth of the prince of Wales now precipitated the planned invasion of England by the prince of Orange. When the king decided on flight, Caryll seems to have arranged the queen's departure for France with the infant prince. A copy of James II's incomplete declaration, prior to his own departure, that he withdrew only to fight back, and did not thus abdicate, is found among the Caryll family papers (BL, Add. MS 28252, fol. 55) and may suggest that Caryll followed rather than accompanied the royal family. He was at the court of St Germain-en-Laye in 1689 and was soon after acting as under-secretary of state to King James. He became full secretary of state in 1694, on the dismissal of the earl of Melfort.

From this date to his death Caryll was in the thick of Jacobite diplomacy. Highly esteemed by James and Mary, he was ennobled in 1698, becoming Baron Caryll of Durford, the name of the dissolved monastery on his Sussex estates. A letter to his sister, 15 July, 1695?, shows that he hesitated to accept this peerage, lest his nephew and heir should lack money to support it, 'nothing is so wretched as beggarly honour'. He therefore left his heir £2000 a year rents in the Hôtel de Ville, 'the best security for English Catholics' (BL, Add. MS 28226, fols. 103, 130).

Designated a compounder, or moderate Catholic, in contrast to the hardliner Melfort, Caryll did not hold a brief for all the measures of James II during his short reign in England or thereafter, but it is clear from his later letters and policy papers that he was increasingly sceptical of the prospects of a peaceful restoration as in 1660. Critical of the policy of the empire, Spain, and the papacy, he saw no security for France without the alliance of a Stuart Britain, and no stability for England (nor security for English Catholics) without alliance with France. This was his advice to the young James III (James Francis Edward Stuart), as it had latterly been to James II.

On his first going into exile Caryll was, at James II's request, allowed by William III to keep the revenues of his Sussex estates. In the 1696 invasion attempt, however, Caryll was charged, in England, with complicity in an attempt to assassinate William III. No convincing evidence for or against the charge has so far emerged, but Caryll was now attainted, and his estates granted by the crown to Lord Cutts, a general of William III, and thus seized from John *Caryll (1667–1736), Lord Caryll's heir. Owing to the entail of 1652 of the estates on the Caryll family it proved possible for them to buy back Lord Cutts's life interest, and thus resume their property.

Meanwhile Caryll's literary activities were not neglected. He was one of the best letter-writers of the exiled court (his family letters and his correspondence with the earl of Perth at Rome being exceptionally notable). Much of his writing, including his 'Summary of revealed religion' (probably composed in 1690), lies still in manuscript awaiting scholarly attention, but his new translation of the Psalms from the Vulgate, evidently done for James, prince of Wales, was published anonymously at Paris in 1700. Caryll's strong political satire on the England of Queen Anne, *The Duumvirate* (1705–6), was printed in France for circulation in England (Bodl. Oxf., MS Carte 208, item 62, fols. 397r–398v; the diary of Sir David Nairne, NL Scot., MS 689, under 18 December 1705 to 29 December 1706, establishes Caryll's authorship of the poem). It particularly attacks Marlborough and Godolphin, each of whom Caryll probably knew before going into exile. Finally, Caryll is evidently at work, in 1701, on the manuscript of King James's life of himself, a task at which later devoted hands laboured before its eventual publication in 1816.

Lord Caryll died on 4 September 1711; his sister Abbess Mary Caryll died on 8 August 1712. On 6 September he was buried at the church of the English Dominicans in Paris. His Sussex estates remained intact (though burdened with debt) for his nephew John Caryll to inherit. The Stuart cause, in which, perhaps, Caryll had once hoped to be a Catholic Clarendon, had still a vigorous and tragic future ahead. Taking his life as a whole, the epitaph written originally on him by the young Alexander Pope, friend of his nephew and heir, is a good assessment:

> A manly Form; a bold, yet modest mind;
> Sincere, tho' prudent; constant, yet resign'd;
> Honour unchang'd, a Principle profest;
> Fix'd to one side, but mod'rate to the rest:
> An honest Courtier, and a Patriot too;
> Just to his Prince, and to his Country true …
> (T. E. VI. 81)

HOWARD ERSKINE-HILL

Sources BL, Add. MSS 28224, 28226–28231, 28237, 28240–28241, 28244, 28250–28253, 28618, 34635, 36125 · Bodl. Oxf., MSS Carte 181, 208 [and elsewhere in this collection] · Westm. DA, Old

Brotherhood papers, AWW, iii [and elsewhere in this collection] · D. Nairne, diary, NL Scot., MS 689 · H. Erskine-Hill, *The social milieu of Alexander Pope: lives, example, and the poetic response* (1975), chaps. 2–3 · 'John, first Lord Caryll of Durford, and the Caryll papers', *The Stuart grant in exile and the Jacobites*, ed. E. Cruickshanks and E. Corp (1995), chap. 5 · M. de Trenqualéon, *West-Grinstead et les Caryll* (1893) · H. D. Gordon, *The history of Harting ...* (1877) · T. J. McCann, 'West Grinstead: a centre of Catholicism in Sussex, 1671–1814', *Sussex Archaeological Collections*, 124 (1986), 193–212 · *Imitations of Horace*, ed. J. Butt (1939), vol. 4 of *The Twickenham edition of the poems of Alexander Pope*, ed. J. Butt (1939–69)

Archives BL, corresp. and papers, Add. MSS 20297, 28224, 28226–28231, 28237, 28240–28241, 28244, 28247, 28250–28253, 28618, 34635, 36125, 46493–46494 · Royal Arch., corresp. and related material | BL, letters to Cardinal Caprara, Add. MS 31245 · Bodl. Oxf., Carte MSS 181, 208 · St Mary's Convent, Buckfast Road, Buckfastleigh, Devon, St Scholasticus archives · Westm. DA, AWW · Westm. DA, Old Brotherhood papers

Likenesses portrait, repro. in de Trenqualéon, *West-Grinstead*

Caryll, John, Jacobite second Baron Caryll of Durford (1667–1736), friend of Alexander Pope, was the son of Richard Caryll (1635–1701), of West Grinstead, Sussex, and Frances (*c*.1644–1704), daughter of Sir Henry Bedingfield, and nephew and heir of John *Caryll, Jacobite first Baron Caryll. He was probably educated at the Catholic college at Douai in France. He married Elizabeth Harrington, of Ore Place, near Hastings, Sussex, on 2 January 1686, and from 1690 managed his uncle's estate, Ladyholt, at West Harting. When in 1696 Lord Caryll was charged with complicity in a plot to assassinate William III, this estate was granted by the crown to Lord Cutts, one of William's generals. Outlawed with his uncle, Caryll was twice imprisoned in this year but, blameless in the plot, was finally released. Since the estate had been entailed on the Carylls in 1652 he was able to negotiate with Lord Cutts and eventually bought back the life interest of the estate (which was worth £2155 11*s*. 2*d*. in annual rentals) for £6060 on 13 May 1697 (BL, Add. MS 28250, fols. 149, 154). Still formally an outlaw, Caryll was free and back in charge of the family estates.

From young manhood Caryll shared his uncle's interest in literature. He inherited his uncle's literary friends, knew Dryden, Wycherley, and L'Estrange, and was interested in the Franciscan philosopher Antoine Le Grand. While the first surviving letter of Pope to Caryll is dated 31 July 1710, juvenile poems by Pope dated 1703 in the Caryll papers seem to suggest (though not prove) much earlier acquaintance, a conclusion supported by Pope's letter to Caryll of 2 June 1733. There can be no doubt of Pope's early admiration for and gratitude to Caryll who encouraged his poetic designs. Macaulay's tribute 'Half a line in "The Rape of the Lock" has made his name immortal' must be qualified by the fact that, in all the important editions of the poem in Pope's lifetime the line ran 'This Verse to C— [or "C—l"]—Muse! is due' (1.3). Whether this came from Pope's caution to acknowledge a member of a known Jacobite family, or from Caryll's aristocratic propriety, or personal modesty, is hard to know: but, for Pope, the plain words 'is due' acknowledge a lot. In so far as the quarrelling figures in *The Rape of the Lock* allude to real persons,

Caryll knew them all. He encouraged Pope in his composition of this poem, of the *Messiah* (1712), raised subscriptions for the *Iliad* translation, was an independent critic of *An Essay on Man*, and a close reader of the epistle *To a Lady* which suggested to him that Pope and Martha Blount might be planning to marry.

The later years of Caryll's friendship with Pope were not untroubled. Having early encouraged him, Caryll was mortified when the poet seemed to neglect him for later (and protestant) friends. Matters were made worse by Pope's repeated request that Caryll return his letters—though the motives behind the request changed, and Pope asked other friends, such as Swift, to do the same. Caryll eventually agreed and Pope almost entirely expunged from his printed *Letters* the friend with whom he had conducted his longest correspondence. Caryll, however, had had transcripts made of the letters. Pope last visited Caryll in 1734, before this correspondence was published. It is not known whether Pope then owned that he had redesignated letters originally to Caryll to other correspondents, nor whether Caryll told Pope about the transcripts which, on their discovery by C. W. Dilke in the next century, greatly altered the picture of Pope.

Choosing to live and raise a family on his estates, despite the penal laws against Catholics, Caryll represents a submissive period in the history of his family, between his uncle who had been secretary of state to the exiled James II and his grandson who between 1769 and 1777 held the same office under Charles Edward Stuart (Charles III to Jacobites). He had reason to feel some disappointment at his lot. He had married his eldest son to Lady Mary Mackenzie, sister of the Jacobite marquess of Seaforth, a great if not pecunious match. But this son, the young huntsman with whom Pope may have had more intimate confidence than with the father, died of smallpox on 6 April 1718. Then the French investments of the family, involved in the collapse of John Law's economic scheme, lost most of their value. He played the squire, not the lord, and when in 1725, exceptionally, he used his French connections to be presented to the young Louis XV, Pope ironically rebuked him for running about 'with a king of sixteen' (*Correspondence of Alexander Pope*, 2.341). Caryll expressed his view of his own condition in a poem found in the family accounts (and with accounts on the verso):

1724
A Serious Thought of my own Concern, in Rhyme,
Born in an Isle (so hard has been my Fate!)
Where Rich I never dar'd to be nor Great
Yett Sixty years of Life I have neerly run
Submitting still to see my self Undon!

He counts his blessings, however, and acknowledges that God has given him 'Joys more refin'd & of Sublimer Taste' (BL, Add. MS 28240, fol. 218r). He died at Ladyholt in April 1736.

The religious orientation of Caryll's poem underlines one final feature of his life, and of his whole family, kept discreet in the eighteenth century, but revealed in recent research. Since Tudor times until almost the end of the penal period the Carylls kept up their seigneurial patronage of Catholicism in west Sussex and maintained their covert mission house in the thinly populated area of West Grinstead. When Caryll's grandson John Baptist Caryll had by 1769 to sell the last and best of the family estates, and retired abroad to serve Charles Edward Stuart in Italy, Edward Caryll of Highden, a younger son of the second Lord Caryll, quietly took over this responsibility, as an indirect result of which there is a large Roman Catholic church in the small village of West Grinstead at the present time.　　　　　HOWARD ERSKINE-HILL

Sources BL, Caryll papers, Add. MSS 28224–28254, 28618, 34635, 36125 · *The correspondence of Alexander Pope*, ed. G. Sherburn, 5 vols. (1956) · M. de Trenqualéon, *West-Grinstead et les Caryll*, 2 vols. (1893) · H. Erskine-Hill, *The social milieu of Alexander Pope: lives, example, and the poetic response* (1975) · *The Twickenham edition of the poems of Alexander Pope*, ed. J. Butt and others, 11 vols. in 12 (1939–69), vol. 2 · A. Pope, *Selected letters*, ed. H. Erskine-Hill (2000) · H. D. Gordon, *The history of Harting* (1877) · A. Parry, *The Carylls of Harting: a study in loyalty* (1976) · M. M. Stewart, 'The account books of John Caryll', *N&Q*, 215 (1970), 288–93 · T. J. McCann, 'West Grinstead: a centre of Catholicism in Sussex, 1671–1814', *Sussex Archaeological Collections*, 124 (1986), 193–212 · T. J. McCann, 'Henry Hoghton … chaplain to the Caryll family at West Grinstead, Sussex, 1736–1750', *Opening the scrolls: essays in Catholic history in honour of Godfrey Anstruther*, ed. D. A. Bellenger (1987), 100–14 · *IGI*
Archives BL, papers relating to financial transactions with Pope, Add. MSS 28224–28254
Wealth at death estates, incl. West Harting

Carysfort. For this title name *see* Proby, John, first Baron Carysfort (1720–1772); Proby, John Joshua, first earl of Carysfort (1751–1828); Proby, Granville Leveson, third earl of Carysfort (1781–1868).

Casali, Andrea (1705–1784), painter, was born on 17 November 1705 in Rome, where he studied under Francesco Trevisani and Sebastiano Conca. Between 1728 and 1738 he worked primarily as a decorative painter in Roman churches, in 1729 being made a knight of the Golden Spur for his part in the decoration of the church of Santo Sisto Vecchio. In 1735–6 he worked in Madrid on the decoration of the palace of La Granja de San Ildefonso (province of Segovia). Casali's contact with British patrons began in Rome, where in 1738 he painted portraits of Charles Frederick (Ashmolean Museum, Oxford) and Mrs Smart Lethieullier (Passmore Edwards Museum, London). Both Frederick and the fourth earl of Carlisle (who was also in Italy in 1738–9), strongly encouraged him to come to England and, following the death of his wife, Casali arrived in 1741, after spending some eight months in Paris.

In England, Casali (sometimes recorded as Andrew Cassali) achieved some success over a period of twenty-five years. In 1743 he was working at Wanstead House, Essex, where Lord Castlemaine commissioned a set of six history pictures, of which *Coriolanus* is now at the Burton Constable Foundation Museum, Yorkshire. A set of four whole-length portraits, probably from the mid-1740s, of the second duke of Ancaster's children and son-in-law, Francis Beckford, are at Grimsthorpe Castle, Lincolnshire.

In 1748 he visited Prussia and Holland but returned to London in the same year to collaborate on the display of royal fireworks in Green Park, London, a celebration of the treaty of Aix-la-Chapelle. In 1750 he presented to the Foundling Hospital *The Adoration of the Magi* as an altarpiece for the chapel; it received some criticism for being 'not strong enough' and having 'pale weakly colouring' (Vertue, 3.157) and was eventually replaced in the chapel by Benjamin West's *Christ with a Little Child*.

Casali continued to find favour elsewhere, however. He exhibited regularly at the Free Society (1761–8) and once at the Society of Artists (1760), and undertook a number of decorative commissions. His most substantial patrons were Thomas Coke, earl of Leicester (1697–1759), and Alderman William Beckford (father of the aforementioned Francis Beckford). At Holkham, Norfolk, in the mid-1750s Casali created a series of imaginary portraits illustrating the descent of the earl of Leicester, who in 1720 had sat to Casali's master, Trevisani, in Rome. For Alderman Beckford, Casali painted ceilings and staircases at Fonthill, Wiltshire, (built 1755–70; des. 1807), besides a number of easel pictures (dispersed in the Fonthill sales of 1801 and 1807). Five of the decorative panels are now at Dyrham Park, Gloucestershire, while two of the easel paintings are at the Burton Constable Foundation Museum: *The Story of Gunhilda*, exhibited at the Society of Artists in 1760 (when it was awarded the society's second prize of 50 guineas), and *An Historical Picture of Edward the Martyr* (exhibited at the Free Society in 1761). Both appeared in Casali's sale at Prestage and Hobbs, on 23 and 24 March 1762, and in his second sale at Prestage, on 18 April 1766, held after he had announced his intention of returning to Italy. From Rome, Casali continued to exhibit in London at the Society of Artists between 1775 and 1778 and at the Free Society between 1769 and 1783. He died in Rome on 7 September 1784.

Casali was described as an 'ingenious well behaved man' (Vertue, 3.112) and Lady Pomfret said he passed 'for the most complete fine gentleman in the world', wearing 'fine suits of clothes' and an order 'set in diamonds' (Whitley, 1.120–21) which he said was given him by the king of Prussia. Although Casali's English portraits have a somewhat forced elegance, the flowing compositions and delicate colouring of his history pieces provide an interesting chapter in the history of eighteenth-century British taste.　　　　　JOHN INGAMELLS

Sources O. Michel, 'Casali, Andrea, Cavaliere', *The dictionary of art*, ed. J. Turner (1996) · Vertue, *Note books*, 3.107–8, 111–12, 141, 157 · E. Croft-Murray, *Decorative painting in England, 1537–1837*, 2 (1970), 181–3 · E. Edwards, *Anecdotes of painters* (1808); facs. edn (1970), 23–4 · W. T. Whitley, *Artists and their friends in England, 1700–1799*, 2 vols. (1928) · B. Nicolson, *The treasures of the Foundling Hospital* (1972), 42–3, 63–4

Casanova, Francesco (*bap.* 1727, *d.* 1803), battle and equestrian painter, was born in London, where he was baptized on 7 June 1727, one of six sons of the travelling Venetian actors Gaetano Giuseppe Casanova (*d.* 1733) and Giovanna Zanetta Farussi. His brothers included the infamous adventurer Giovanni Giacomo Casanova (1725–1798), better known as Casanova de Seingalt, and Giovanni Battista Casanova (1728/1730–1795), a draughtsman, painter, and forger who studied under Mengs. At an early age Casanova returned with his family to Venice, and after his father's premature death was placed, with his brothers, in the care of the Grimani family. According to G. G. Casanova's memoirs, Casanova began his artistic training About 1739, studying under Guardi, a relationship which continued for approximately ten years. During this time he also made copies after the battle painter Francesco Simonini, before studying with him in Florence from about 1749 to 1751. The works of Jacques Courtois were also influential. In the spring of 1751 Casanova moved to Paris and in 1752 to Dresden, where he encountered the works of Charles Parrocel and Philips Wouwerman.

Having returned to Paris in 1757, Casanova quickly gained a reputation as a first-rate battle painter, exhibiting at the Salon between 1761 and 1771 to critical acclaim. By the time of his first marriage in 1762, Casanova was *peintre du roi*, a position he retained until 1783. A battle piece exhibited in 1763 was purchased for the Louvre, and he was elected a member of the Académie Royale de Peinture et de Sculpture. Casanova exhibited *Hannibal Crossing the Alps* at the Free Society of Artists, London, in 1767, his use of light and shade causing a sensation. In Paris, Casanova's battle, hunting, and equestrian paintings achieved high prices and he was patronized by the nobility and royalty, designing tapestry cartoons for the royal factories by 1772. These included the fragment *Kneeling Man* (c.1772, Louvre, Paris) and the study *Fishing Scene* (early 1770s, Hermitage, St Petersburg). His pupils in Paris included Philippe Jacques De Loutherbourg. Despite artistic success, his reputed luxurious tastes and extravagant habits are said to have kept him in debt. He is depicted in one of his own etchings, *Le dîner du peintre*, alighting from a carriage to barter a picture for sausages.

Casanova left Paris in 1783 and settled in Vienna, where he continued to enjoy royal patronage. During the 1790s the empress Catherine of Russia probably commissioned a cycle of paintings representing the victories of the Russians over the Turks for the royal palace at St Petersburg. He travelled with Prince Nicholas Esterházy to Hungary in 1795, where he was said to have made numerous equestrian sketches, and two years later completed paintings for the king of Naples, Ferdinand IV. He died in Brühl, near Vienna, in 1803.

L. H. Cust, rev. Deborah Graham-Vernon

Sources J. Turner, ed., *The dictionary of art*, 34 vols. (1996) · Bénézit, *Dict.*, new edn · Thieme & Becker, *Allgemeines Lexikon*
Likenesses F. Casanova, self-portrait, etching

Casartelli, Joseph Louis [*formerly* Giuseppe Luigi] (1822–1900), maker of scientific instruments, was born in Tavernerio near Lake Como, northern Italy, on 9 September 1822, the eldest of the twelve children of Giovanni Battista Francesco Stefano Casartelli (1798–1872), farmer, and his second wife, Florinda Gerosa (b. 1803). The family emigrated to Liverpool when Joseph was eleven. A relative,

Luigi Antonio (Louis) Casartelli, had already set up in business at 20 Duke Street, Liverpool, as a barometer and thermometer maker and the young Casartelli may have served his apprenticeship with him. By 1845, Joseph and his uncle, Antonio Giovanni (Anthony), had taken over Louis' business. The two continued in partnership as barometer and thermometer makers and glass-blowers for the next six years.

In 1851 Joseph married Jane Henrietta Ronchetti and purchased the Ronchetti instrument making business at 43 Market Street, Manchester. Charles Joshua Ronchetti's father and grandfather also came from Tavernerio and had worked with the Casartelli family in both Manchester and Liverpool. The couple lived at 2 Clarence Street, Cheetham, in Manchester, and had six children including Louis Charles (who became the Catholic bishop of Salford) and Joseph Henry, who worked initially in a tailoring warehouse but later joined the family business. The family moved to 5 Egerton Terrace, Ardwick, Manchester, about 1853 (the house was later renumbered 22, and the address changed to Chorlton upon Medlock), and then again to a house at 5 Mayfield Road in the attractive suburb of Whalley Range by 1890. Casartelli expanded the business to produce all kinds of high-quality optical, surveying, textile, and engineering instruments. He also took over the Ronchetti family's chemical business in Clayton, Manchester, in the late 1850s and ran it until about 1868 when it was taken over by Hamor Lockwood. Casartelli continued Joshua Ronchetti's work of sending rainfall summaries to the local press, in 1853 moving the rain gauge to his home in Ardwick where he took measurements until 1888. He also supplied pyrometers and surveying instruments for the government Department of Science and Art in the 1870s.

Casartelli had a special interest in steam engines and boilers and took out seven patents for apparatus such as engine indicators which he developed with William Potter, the works manager. He also developed apparatus for testing the lubricating qualities of oils and a steam trap, with Edwin Travis, an engineer in Oldham. Another of Casartelli's patents was for an improvement to the surveying instrument known as the miner's dial in which a graduated arc was fitted above the compass.

By this time Casartelli's Market Street premises consisted of a saleroom, offices, and a warehouse. Customers could have their eyes tested free of charge and buy spectacles there. Instruments made in the works, on Clarence Street, included surveying instruments such as theodolites; textile testing instruments such as pick counters and yarn balances; meteorological instruments; and engineering instruments such as the engine indicators. Potter designed specialist machinery when necessary for use in the manufacture of the various instruments. The works also had adjoining warehouses and drying rooms for drying and storing the timber used for the manufacture of cabinets and cases.

Casartelli was one of Manchester's most important scientific instrument makers. His company had trading connections throughout the mining and manufacturing districts of northern England and south Wales and maintained a large export trade to all parts of the world. He was a devout Catholic all his life and a great believer in probity. He was elected a member of the Manchester Literary and Philosophical Society in January 1858 and published a pamphlet on the anatomy of the eye and several catalogues of his company's products.

Casartelli brought Joseph Henry into partnership in 1896 and the business became known as Joseph Casartelli & Son. Casartelli died at his home, 5 Mayfield Road, Whalley Range, Withington, on 20 March 1900 and was buried at Moston cemetery, Manchester, two days later. The business was carried on by Joseph Henry Casartelli and his sons but did not survive the great depression and went into liquidation in 1933. JENNY WETTON

Sources J. D. Casartelli, 'Brief history of the firm of Joseph Casartelli & Son', 1915, priv. coll. · J. Wetton, 'Scientific instrument making in Manchester, 1790–1870', *Manchester Memoirs*, 130 (1990–91) · Manchester street directories · census returns · company catalogues, known for 1868, c.1905–1922, c.1933–1940, Joseph Casartelli & Son, Manchester · patents, 1855–74 · d. cert.
Archives Museum of Science and Industry, Manchester, instruments
Wealth at death £8365 19s. 4d.: probate, 27 July 1900, *CGPLA Eng. & Wales*

Casaubon, Isaac (1559–1614), classical scholar and ecclesiastical historian, was born in Geneva on 18 February 1559 NS and baptized two days later, one of the nine children of Arnaud Casaubon (1525–1586), pastor in the Reformed church, and his wife, Jeanne, or Mengine, *née* Rousseau (d. 1607). Both his parents were Huguenots, from Gascony and Dauphiné respectively.

Early education and the University of Geneva Isaac Casaubon received his early education in Latin and Greek from his father, while the family lived in Crest, a small town in Dauphiné, but this was interrupted by Arnaud's pastoral duties and by religious persecution, so that Isaac was subsequently to describe himself as having been self-taught after coming unusually late to learning, adding that 'I have the consolation of having lost my best years through persecutions for the sake of the truth' (*Epistolae*, 1709, no. 453). He attended the University of Geneva, where he showed such unusual promise that the incumbent professor of Greek, who was near death, recommended him as his successor. In 1582 Casaubon was therefore appointed as 'professeur de la langue grecque'. On 24 August 1583 he married Marie Prolyot, whose parents had, like his own, come to Geneva as refugees from religious persecution. She died on 27 May 1585, within six months of giving birth to a daughter, who appears not to have survived to adulthood. A year later Arnaud Casaubon died in Dauphiné; Isaac was, to his sorrow, unable to visit his deathbed or attend his funeral. During this period of personal unhappiness he produced his first published works, a small volume of notes on Diogenes Laertius, and some notes published in a pocket edition of Theocritus. On 24 April 1586 he married Florence (d. 1636), daughter of the philologist, lexicographer, and printer Henri Estienne the second (Henricus Stephanus). Their relationship was, as they

Isaac Casaubon (1559–1614), by unknown artist

were both to testify in writing, an affectionate one. Shared religious faith played a part in it: Casaubon refers in a moving diary entry of 1608 to their practice of singing the Psalms together as they travelled by boat to the nearest protestant service. The relationship with Florence was also one on which Casaubon was to depend for practical support: for the rest of his life, despite frequent illness, to which the bearing of seventeen children (at least eight of whom died in infancy) must have contributed, she looked after his household, giving him the freedom to devote himself to scholarship. Her direct contributions to his academic work do not appear to have extended beyond the ability to find missing books, and she could not read Latin.

The first of Casaubon's major contributions to scholarship was made in 1587, with an edition of and commentary on the Greek geographer Strabo. Here, and in his publications of the next twenty-three years, Casaubon's scholarship is distinctive. He was a philologist: in other words, he was concerned with the fullest possible understanding of the cultures of the ancient world. This concern was the product of a widely enquiring mind, which led him to write on subjects as diverse as the various ways of mixing wine with water and the surprisingly numerous ancient names for the noises made by different animals and birds. The texts which he addressed were those which would provide as much information as possible about ancient Greek—and, to a somewhat lesser extent, Roman—civilization. He brought an exceptionally wide range of other texts to bear on them, and the notes he made as he read have begun to be valued as unusually full and interesting evidence for early modern practices of reading, although his difficult handwriting makes their study demanding. They are extant in the margins of many of his printed books, of which the largest collection is in the British Library, and on a series of loose leaves, now bound as part of the sixty-one Casaubon manuscripts in the Bodleian Library. The breadth of his intellectual interests led him to make his most sustained contributions to learning in the form of commentary rather than textual editing, although his work on the text of Aeschylus has been highly praised. His scholarship was thorough and accurate, and it has lasted: as Ulrich von Wilamowitz said in 1921, 'we are all still living on the capital accumulated by the industry of Casaubon and Stephanus' (von Wilamowitz-Moellendorff, 54). His Latin style was admired, although some readers found his very frequent use of Greek words and phrases unhelpful. In his maturity he was one of the three most eminent scholars in Europe, the others being his father-in-law Henri Estienne, and Joseph Justus Scaliger, both of whom he survived. Scaliger, indeed, described him as the greatest living expert in ancient Greek, and as the most learned man alive.

In 1589 Casaubon published the *editio princeps* of the Greek military writer Polyaenus, and in 1592 an edition and Latin translation of, and commentary on, the twenty-three *Characters* of Theophrastus then known to be extant. Since this is a very short text, he was able to make the commentary relatively exhaustive. The influence of Casaubon's edition of the *Characters* on English literature has been overestimated, but it was very widely used by undergraduates studying Greek in England and continental Europe in the seventeenth and eighteenth centuries (thirty-three editions appeared before 1800), and Scaliger singled it out for praise. In 1595 he edited Suetonius. By this time he had also produced a number of less substantial publications. One of these, a derivative edition of Aristotle (1590), was itself the basis for a number of seventeenth-century editions; another, some notes on the New Testament published with an edition of 1587, adumbrated the major undertaking of his last years.

Casaubon's work at Geneva was achieved in the face of four serious obstacles. The first of these was a personal one: he had a strong sense that he would be better employed in theological studies, and was to state explicitly that he had become a classicist very much by chance, and that he regretted having done so. The second was a very heavy load of teaching, to which, rather than to research, he was expected to devote his time. The third was an inconveniently limited access to books: the public library in Geneva was too small to be adequate for his purposes, and although he began to build up his library during the 1580s, he was away from the major centres of the book trade. The fourth was financial insecurity. He was poorly paid, and although he, or at least Mme Casaubon, supplemented his income by taking in lodgers, these could add to his problems, as did Henry Wotton, who left Geneva without paying Casaubon, who had moreover become surety for some of Wotton's considerable local debts (Wotton paid at last, and he and Casaubon continued to correspond). Although his stipend was raised twice in the 1590s he moved to the University of Montpellier as 'professeur stipendié aux langues et bonnes lettres' in 1596.

The University of Montpellier, 1596–1600 At Montpellier, Casaubon and his family lived in some discomfort, though on a more satisfactory income. He lectured, acted briefly as rector of the university, and began his *Ephemerides*, a daily private journal which is one of the most extensive of all early modern diaries. He also prepared, among other works, an edition of the *Deipnosophistae* of Athenaeus, a particularly rich source for ancient Greek fragments relating to eating and drinking. It was followed by a very extensive series of *Animadversiones* on Athenaeus's book (Casaubon did not regard them as a proper commentary). This is one of Casaubon's longest works, and shows the breadth of his learning to good and sustained advantage. He also revised his edition of Theophrastus, adding to it the *editio princeps* of five newly discovered *Characters*. By now he had, partly through the intermediation of the biblical scholar Richard Thomson, become a correspondent of Joseph Justus Scaliger, whose praise of his work was warm, sincere, and authoritative. It helped to establish his international reputation as a scholar of the highest distinction. In 1598 he was introduced to the king of France, Henri IV, who invited him to Paris 'pour la profession des bonnes Lettres'. He accepted the invitation, and moved to Paris in 1600, actuated in part by the prospect of access, at last, to great libraries.

Paris, 1600–1610 In Paris, Casaubon was drawn into formal religious debate as he had not been at the protestant universities of Geneva and Montpellier. He took part in the conference of Fontainebleau in 1600, at which the accuracy of Philippe de Mornay's protestant treatise on the eucharist was called into question. The conference was generally considered to have been a triumph for de Mornay's Catholic attackers, and Casaubon was felt by many Catholics and protestants to have taken the Catholic side. He was then rumoured to have become a Catholic. This story was false, and distressed him. His initial formal position in Paris was, however, academic rather than theological, that of 'lecteur du roi'. This was not a university post, so he was not called upon to teach. This did not guarantee him free time: he was variously inconvenienced while at Paris by the need to move house—which meant moving his expanding personal library—seven times, and by court business, personal visits, and visits from persons interested in meeting a celebrity. One of these was Thomas Coryate, who wrote that he had enjoyed:

> the sight and company of that rare ornament of learning *Isaac Casaubonus*, with whom I had much familiar conversation at his house … I found him very affable and courteous, and learned in his discourses, and by so much the more willing to give me entertainment, by how much the more I made relation to him of his learned workes, whereof some I have read. (Coryate, 31–2)

Coryate also recorded Casaubon's interesting suggestion that a biography of Elizabeth I written by 'some learned man' was to be desired.

Casaubon continued to have lodgers in his house, one of whom was Edward Herbert, later Lord Herbert of Cherbury. In 1601 he was promised the reversion of the keepership of the royal library, and in 1605 he succeeded to the post. In Paris he worked on pagan and Christian texts, editing an unpublished letter of St Gregory of Nyssa, the *Historiae Augustae scriptores*, and the very difficult Latin poet Persius: Scaliger said of the latter text and Casaubon's commentary on it that 'the sauce is better than the fish' (Scaliger, 64). He prepared an edition of the historian Polybius, with the *princeps* of the military writer Aeneas Tacticus, a translation into Latin, and an introduction which Joseph Warton described as one of the three finest of all prefaces (Dryden's 'Character of Polybius' of 1693 is based upon it); labouring on this edition helped him to endure his grief at the death of his daughter Philippa in 1608. His commentary on Polybius, which would have accompanied the edition, was never to be completed. He also published a pioneering monograph on satire, *De satyrica Graecorum poesi et Romanorum satira libri duo* (1605). Latin satire had previously been thought to be connected, etymologically and historically, with the satyrs of Greek satyr-plays, and early modern satirists often made explicit connections between the character of their work and that of satyrs. Casaubon's book disentangled the confusion definitively, and all subsequent accounts of the history of satire were to be indebted to him. Finally, he began, but was prevented from finishing, a monograph on papal authority, *De libertate ecclesiastica* (1607). Printed sheets of this text reached James I of England, who was impressed by their erudition and their resemblance to his own views on the relationship between papal and royal authority, which had recently found expression in the oath of allegiance of 1606; Donne refers to it in his treatise on the compatibility of that oath with the religious obligations of Roman Catholics in England, *Pseudomartyr*.

Casaubon's position as a protestant at the court of the Catholic convert Henri IV continued to be uncomfortable for the ten years following the conference of Fontainebleau. He was greatly distressed when his son John became a Catholic in 1610. He expressed his astonishment that he himself should be thought capable of doing likewise, but he did also express personal scruples about several aspects of reformed, and in particular of Calvinist, doctrine and discipline. These scruples were founded on the extensive and careful reading in the church fathers which had enabled him to work on *De libertate ecclesiastica*. They may have made him seem like a possible convert, and he remarked in 1610 that for years past 'I have scarcely had a day free from contests with persons of a different opinion in religion' (*Epistolae*, 1709, no. 1043). He knew that once Henri died he might be in real danger rather than merely under this pressure, and that he might need to emigrate. One possible destination was England. He had been in correspondence with English and Scottish men of letters since his dealings with Thomson in the early 1590s. John Spottiswood (later archbishop of Glasgow) and Andrew Lamb met him in Paris in 1601, and Spottiswood encouraged him to write to James VI, who replied

cordially. (Another Scot, Adam Abernethy, tried to persuade him to take up a position at the University of Nîmes in 1605.) The English ambassador to Paris and his wife, Sir George and Lady Carew, were personal friends, and it was in their household that Philippa Casaubon had died. An unofficial invitation to come to England was conveyed to Casaubon by Carew in March 1610, and he replied positively in April. After Henri's murder in May 1610 Casaubon felt that a massacre of protestants like that of 1572 might be imminent. An official invitation to England, sent by Richard Bancroft, archbishop of Canterbury, reached him on 20 July, and he travelled to England in October, nominally for a short visit, but in fact for the remaining years of his life.

England, 1610–1614 Casaubon was hospitably received in England. Successive archbishops of Canterbury, Bancroft and Abbot, were kind to him (Abbot was the godfather of his youngest child, James). John Overall had him and then his family to stay at the deanery of St Paul's for twelve months, after which Lady Killigrew, the sister-in-law of Alberico Gentili, gave them accommodation. He became a friend of Lancelot Andrewes and John Prideaux, and renewed his friendship with Richard Thomson. King James enjoyed his conversation; a visitor remembered Casaubon standing in attendance on him, talking in French and Latin about a document he had written against Cardinal Bellarmine, while the monarch sat and dined. He was made a prebendary of Canterbury, and given a royal pension of £300 a year. The Church of England was, he believed, in closer doctrinal accordance than any other with the Christian church of the first centuries, and he attended Church of England services, although appears to have regarded himself a member of the 'French church' on his deathbed. His son Meric *Casaubon was given patronage for his sake. There were difficulties in his new home as well. There were obstacles to sending his books from France. He never learned English, and had some unpleasant experiences in London, being attacked in the street and having his house burgled. Mme Casaubon was unhappy in England. Despite the royal pension the Casaubons found their outgoings heavy. A different sort of difficulty was that Casaubon did not have the opportunity to continue with his work on ancient civilizations. He would die with the commentary on Polybius unfinished. After a year's residence in England, he wrote that 'all my former studies have entirely perished' (*Epistolae*, 1709, no. 753). What took their place was theology and controversy.

The oath of allegiance of 1606 had occasioned a vigorous exchange of texts between supporters of the English and papal positions; the question being debated was one of European importance, and the participants were scattered across Europe. One reason why Casaubon had been so welcome in England was that he was a scholar with a high international reputation whose views were known, not least from *De libertate ecclesiastica*, to be close to the English position. Soon after his arrival in England, he was called on to read and comment on Lancelot Andrewes's latest polemic, the *Responsio ad apologiam Cardinalis*

Bellarmini (1610), before its publication. In 1611 Casaubon wrote a contribution to the debate under his own name, the *Epistola ad Frontonem Ducaeum*, addressed to the French Jesuit Fronton du Duc, seen before publication by James, and handsomely printed by John Norton as king's printer. This was a moderate defence of James (touching at some length on the execution of Henry Garnett), and of the oath of allegiance. It claimed from the outset to be written reluctantly and in an eirenic spirit, and both claims were probably true. At least three hostile replies to it appeared in 1612. Of these, the *Responsio ad epistolam Isaaci Casauboni* of the Jesuit controversialist known as Andreas Eudaemon-Joannes attacked Casaubon personally, suggesting that his support of King James was actuated by unprincipled greed for money.

Later in 1611 Casaubon wrote another controversial epistle, the *Responsio ad epistolam Cardinalis Perronii* (published by Norton in 1612), explaining why James's variety of Anglicanism could properly be described as Catholic even though he was not in communion with the papacy. In this he stated openly that the views he expressed were the king's, and that he was acting more as secretary than as author: something of a sad position for a man of Casaubon's stature. His dedication advocated strict state censorship of all religious polemics. More personal was an epistle, published in Paris in 1612, against Caspar Schoppe, who had written a malevolent and intemperate assault on the memory of Casaubon's old friend Scaliger, and had derided Casaubon's participation in the conference of Fontainebleau. Schoppe replied with a volume of sustained abuse, the *Responsio ad epist. I. Cazoboni*, printed in 1615 but circulated in several manuscript copies, one of which Casaubon saw, before the end of April 1614. Here Schoppe accused his target of a series of lurid fictitious crimes: inflamed by the story of the lovemaking of Venus and Anchises as he sat reading by the kitchen fire, he had leapt upon a passing serving-woman and tried to rape her; he had been caught burgling a nobleman's lodgings in order to steal money to buy a copy of Eustathius, and had been pitifully beaten; he had employed one of his servants as a prostitute for Henry Wotton when the latter lodged with him. These stories were doubtless not intended to be plausible, but rather to upset and embarrass Casaubon and his allies, and to entertain his enemies. After 1612 Casaubon wrote no more controversial epistles: the exercise had not made the most effective possible use of his learning, and had exposed him to unseemly insult.

Casaubon turned, instead, to his last project, an extended criticism of the vast Roman Catholic world history of Cardinal Cesare Baronio, the *Annales ecclesiastici*, which was to be published as the *De rebus sacris et ecclesiasticis exercitationes xvi ad Baronii annales*. This brought a number of his abilities together. His critical reading in the Bible and the fathers and his experience of protestant apologetics made him familiar with Baronio's subject matter; his expertise in Greek and his knowledge of Hebrew and Arabic gave him a better command of many of the primary sources than Baronio's own; commentary on

very long texts was something to which he was accustomed. His intention was to produce twelve volumes, to match the twelve of the *Annales*, following the chronological order of the earlier work. He therefore began with Baronio's treatment of the events of the New Testament, and remarked before long in a letter to Grotius that the work of confutation was not laborious, but that the formally ancillary task of marshalling the authentic evidence was more demanding. A reference of Baronio's to the corpus of writings attributed to the legendary Hermes Trismegistus occasioned Casaubon's demonstration that, rather than being works of stupendous antiquity, the Hermetic writings were demonstrably products of the Hellenistic age: here, as in the treatise on satyrs and satire, Casaubon was subjecting a long-established myth to precise, destructive criticism.

A first volume of the *Exercitationes* was in a penultimate draft by May 1613, and printing began the next month, ending in February 1614. By the time the book had been published Casaubon had been ill for some time, with what appeared from the symptoms to be a urological complaint. In June 1614 he was persuaded to make an excursion by coach to Greenwich for the day. Shortly after his return to London, he became critically ill, and joked that he was dying, as Theophrastus had done, from the exertion of taking a holiday. He died on 1 July, in the 'new rents', Drury Lane, London. The cause of death was a deformity of the bladder, taking the shape of a very large sac, which had become infected, opening off the main bladder. A drawing of the deformed organ was made during the dissection of Casaubon's body, circulated in manuscript, and was printed as the only illustration in the text of the 1709 edition of his letters. Casaubon was buried on 8 July in Westminster Abbey; six bishops were present at the funeral.

Most or all of the accounts of Casaubon's appearance date from the latter part of his life, and some of them from his last years. He was an unusually small man, whose physician commented more than once on the disproportion between his feeble body and his powerful intellect. His portraits, which are all of the same type, show him as plainly dressed, with a long, pointed beard, dark hair receding from a high forehead, and sunken cheeks. His eyes are dark and deeply set, and he appears to be frowning in concentration.

Posthumous reputation and place in creative writing In the years immediately after his death, Casaubon's reputation was a matter for confessional polemic. John Prideaux, for instance, wrote a refutation of Eudaemon-Joannes's personal libels (1614). Schoppe's *Responsio* was followed by the *Elixir Calvinisticum* of François Garasse (1615), in which Casaubon is dismissed from the gates of heaven by St Peter and sent, accompanied by the deity Hernia (an allusion to the cause of his death), to the underworld, there to be transformed into a Cyclops and set to work at an alchemical furnace, trying hopelessly to distil a purified protestantism from the attributes of the Roman Catholic church. The *Corona regia*, a mock-panegyric of James I which compared him in tones of reverence to the mad transvestite emperor Heliogabalus, was published in 1615 as an unfinished work of Casaubon's (its real author is uncertain). A protestant world history was published under the title *Casaubonus redivivus* in 1617. The false ascription of a tract called *The Originall of Idolatries* to him in 1624 called forth a rebuttal from Meric Casaubon in the same year. The last and most valuable edition of his letters, which appeared in Rotterdam in 1709, was the culmination of the first phase of interest in him.

Casaubon became an important symbolic figure again in the nineteenth century. In 1850 the *Ephemerides* were published in two volumes, edited by John Russell, canon of Canterbury, and in 1852, a joint biography of Lipsius, Joseph Scaliger, and Casaubon was published in France. Both these publications were reviewed by Mark Pattison in an essay in the *Quarterly Review* in 1853. Pattison was, at the time, depressed by his failure to be elected rector of his college, and his essay projects some of his gloom and self-doubt onto Casaubon, remarking that his wife's 'domestic distresses were not sparingly inflicted on her good-man, who perhaps on his part tried her patience by a scholar's indifference to household difficulties' (Pattison, 'Diary of Casaubon', 470), referring to his 'long, correct, but dull, sentences ... his profusion of learned illustration and quotation, which overloaded his subject' (ibid., 475), and calling the edition of Athenaeus 'utterly inadequate as an edition' (ibid., 480) and the *Exercitationes* 'a failure' (ibid., 499). The character Edward Casaubon in George Eliot's *Middlemarch* (1871–2), an ageing pedant who enters into a disastrous marriage with the heroine, and dies after a lifetime's futile study, has been associated with Pattison, whose wife, Emilia Francis, was a friend of Eliot's. Although it would be simplistic to see Edward Casaubon as a portrait of Pattison, there are certainly resemblances, both specific, such as the point that each married a woman twenty-seven years his junior, and general. Emilia Francis Pattison's second husband, Sir Charles Dilke, wrote that Eliot had given Edward Casaubon 'a name which could only show that she both meant Pattison and meant to be known to mean him' (Askwith, 11). Eliot can be shown to have read the review printed immediately after Pattison's essay in the *Quarterly* of 1853 (and indeed to have read another of Pattison's contributions to the history of scholarship, a piece on F. A. Wolf), and there appear to be echoes of the essay itself in *Middlemarch*. It is highly plausible that one element in the fictional character is Pattison's melancholy conception of Isaac Casaubon in the 1853 essay, with its autobiographical features, and that Pattison's own character, as far as it was known to her from personal acquaintance and from her friendship with his wife, was therefore at least at the back of Eliot's mind as she was writing.

Pattison published what is still the standard biography of Casaubon in 1875. This account, like the essay of 1853, is characterized by the author's high degree of identification with his subject, making it a vivid but untrustworthy account of Casaubon's personality. There are points, indeed, where Pattison comes close to explicit autobiography: for instance, his chapter on the *Exercitationes* ends,

'How sad must have appeared to himself the contrast between the promise and the performance eighteen years later! ... Compared with the vast designs we frame in youth, all production seems a petty and abortive effort!' (Pattison, *Isaac Casaubon*, 340–41). Other Victorians used Casaubon for their own purposes: in 1875, for instance, the epistle to Cardinal Du Perron was reprinted by the Anglo-Continental Society, edited by Frederick Meyrick and with a preface by Christopher Wordsworth, as a monument of early Anglican thought (the 1612 translation of the same epistle was reprinted in the United States in the same year, with the title *Anglican Catholicity Vindicated*). The twentieth century has tended to see interest in Casaubon divided between specialists, and therefore impoverished: historians of classical scholarship, for instance, have sometimes seen the *Exercitationes* as a regrettable diversion of his talents rather than as the culmination of a lifetime's concern with philology and religious reformation.

Casaubon's writings are so intimately a product of his intellectual and spiritual life that he can best be described by describing them, as here, in Eduard Fraenkel's discussion of his work on Aeschylus:

> We see here the endeavour of a great and good man to blend the kind of instruction that would be welcomed by an all but Greekless reader with the communication of the highest technical knowledge, to combine the discussion of choice grammatical and antiquarian problems with moral and religious edification, and above all to do full justice to the dominating ideas and the artistic qualities of the *Agamemnon* ... and at the same time not to shirk the minutest detail, however thorny. (Fraenkel, 38)

JOHN CONSIDINE

Sources M. Pattison, *Isaac Casaubon, 1559–1614*, ed. [H. Nettleship], 2nd edn (1892) · T. Janson ab Almeloveen, 'Vita Casauboni', in *Isaaci Casauboni epistolae*, ed. T. Janson ab Almeloveen, 2 vols. in 1 (Rotterdam, 1709), 1–76 · E. Fraenkel, introduction, *Aeschylus: Agamemnon*, ed. E. Fraenkel, 1 (1950) · J. P. Considine, 'Philology and autobiography in Isaac Casaubon, *Animadversionum in Athenaei Deipnosophistas libri xv* (1600)', *Acta conventus neo-Latini Cantabrigiensis: Eleventh international congress of neo-Latin studies* [Cambridge 2000] (Tempe, Arizona, [forthcoming]) · W. B. Patterson, *King James VI and I and the reunion of Christendom* (1997) · A. T. Grafton, 'Protestant versus prophet: Isaac Casaubon on Hermes Trismegistus', *Defenders of the text* (Cambridge, Massachusetts, 1991), 145–61 · M. Simon, 'Isaac Casaubon, Fra Paolo Sarpi, et l'Église d'Angleterre', *Aspects de l'Anglicanisme* [Strasbourg 1972], ed. M. Simon (Paris, 1974), 39–66 · D. B. Nimmo, 'Mark Pattison, Edward Casaubon, Isaac Casaubon, and George Eliot', *Proceedings of the Leeds Philosophical and Literary Society, Literary and Historical Section*, 17 (1979), 79–100 · M. Pattison, 'Diary of Casaubon', *QR*, 93 (1853), 462–500 · T. A. Birrell, 'Reconstructing Casaubon's library', *Hellinga Festschrift*, ed. A. R. A. Croiset van Uchelen (1980), 59–68 · J. J. Scaliger, *Scaligeriana, sive, Excerpta ex ore Josephi Scaligeri*, 2nd edn (1669) · T. Coryate, *Coryats crudities* (1613) · J. W. Neumayr von Ramssla, *Des durchlauchtigen hochgebornen Fürsten und Herrn/Herrn Johann Ernsten des jüngern/Hertzogen zu Sachsen/Jülich/Cleve und Berg … Reise in Frankreich/Engelland und Niederland* (1620) · B. Askwith, *Lady Dilke: a biography* (1969) · C. Nisard, *Les gladiateurs de la république des lettres aux xve, xvie, et xviie siècles* (1860) · A. Blair, *The theater of nature: Jean Bodin and Renaissance science* (1997) · W. H. Sherman, *John Dee: the politics of reading and writing in the English Renaissance* (1995) · F. Schriver, 'Liberal Catholicism: James I, Isaac Casaubon, Bishop

Whittingham of Maryland, and Mark Pattison', *Anglican and Episcopal History*, 56 (1987), 303–17 · M. Bull, 'Edward Casaubon and Isaac Casaubon', *N&Q*, 243 (1998), 218–19 · C. Vivanti, *Lotta politica e pace religiosa in Francia fra cinque e seicento* (1963) · U. von Wilamowitz-Moellendorff, *History of classical scholarship*, trans. A. Harris (1982) · J. Glucker, 'Casaubon's Aristotle', *Classica et Mediaevalia*, 25 (1964), 274–96

Archives BL, annotated printed books · Bodl. Oxf., MSS · Canterbury Cathedral, diary, archives · CUL, MS notes on the Apostolic Canons; MS notes, mostly on classical subjects | BL, Royal MSS, notes, and abstracts · Bodl. Oxf., corresp. with Petrus Bertius; corresp. with Peter Young

Likenesses oils, 17th cent., Bodl. Oxf. · R. van Gunst, line engraving, pubd 1709 (after copy by P. van der Werff), BM; repro. in I. Casaubon, *Epistolae* (1709), frontispiece · oil on panel, National Gallery, London · oils, NPG [*see illus.*]

Wealth at death over 1600 French crowns; 200 French crowns to each of his daughters: will, June 1614, Pattison, *Isaac Casaubon*, 467 ff.

Casaubon, (Florence Estienne) Meric (1599–1671), scholar and divine, was born on 14 August 1599 in Geneva, the tenth of the seventeen children of Isaac *Casaubon (1559–1614), classical scholar and church historian, and his second wife, Florence (1568?–1636), daughter of Henri Estienne. Meric was the most scholarly of Isaac's children, and his patrimony weighed heavily upon him: he signs the title-pages of his learned works 'Is.[aaci] F.[ilius]'. Isaac was invited to England by James I in 1610 and a year later Meric left school in Sedan to join him. Meric was the first Casaubon child to be confirmed into the Church of England, to which he adhered steadfastly all his life.

When Isaac died on 1 July 1614, the king's physician, Raphael Thorius, became the guardian of his children. Meric was tutored by James Wedderburn, and also spent time as a scholar at Eton College. Isaac had wanted Meric to study abroad in Leiden with Daniel Heinsius (he never did), but acquiesced in James I's desire that he spend time at Oxford first. Hence on 13 April 1614 James I wrote to the dean and chapter of Christ Church, Oxford, requiring them 'to admitt a sonne of Isaak Casaubon into the rome of a scholler' (Pattison, 469–70), and on 5 August 1614 'Meric Causabon. Gallus' was admitted to a studentship at Christ Church (dean's register, fol. 144). James I's concern for the Casaubon family, however, did not extend as far as keeping his promise of a pension of £300 per annum for Isaac's widow and longest lived child. Meric's tutor at Christ Church was Edward Meetkerke, the future professor of Hebrew. Casaubon matriculated in 1617; proceeded BA on 18 May 1618; and MA on 14 June 1621. He retained his studentship until 1626. In 1621 he published the first of many books: the *Pietas*, a defence of his father against what he later described as 'the railings & calumnies of some Papist'; this book attracted the renewed attention of James I, 'who ever afterwards had a good opinion of me' (Bodl. Oxf., MS Wood F.40, fol. 350). It also attracted an offer of advancement in France from Casaubon's godfather and his father's patron, Meric de Vic.

Casaubon decided to remain in England. In 1624 he published a second defence of Isaac (the *Vindicatio patris*) against a puritan work that had been falsely put out under his father's name; it was published in Latin, English, and

(Florence Estienne) **Meric Casaubon** (1599–1671), by Pieter Stevens van Gunst, pubd 1709 (after Adriaen van der Werff)

French by the king's printer, Robert Barker. In the 1620s Casaubon was associated with the advanced theological circle around Bishop Richard Neile known as the Durham House group, and later with Bishop Thomas Morton. At a young age Casaubon began to consider the project of continuing his father's *Exercitationes* (1614) against the *Annales ecclesiastici* of Cardinal Caesar Baronius. It was the promise of this that brought Meric Casaubon his early advancement. Lancelot Andrewes had followed Casaubon's career, and in 1626 collated him to his first living, at Bledon in Somerset; Casaubon acknowledged the debt with the prefatory epistle he wrote for Andrewes's *Opuscula* (1629). Among Casaubon's scholarly acquaintances at this time were William Bedwell, Thomas Erpenius (who changed the dedication of the second edition of his *Arabic Proverbs* from Isaac to Meric), and Samuel Bochart. Through Augustine Lindsell, Casaubon attracted the attention of William Laud, who on 19 June 1628 preferred him to a prebendal stall at Christ Church, Canterbury, a position Isaac had also held. Here Casaubon was a colleague of the nonresident Dutch scholar Gerard Vossius, with whom he corresponded extensively throughout the 1630s. In the same year Casaubon married Frances Harrison (d. 1652) of Hampshire. His first scholarly edition, Optatus of Milevis's (*fl.* 370) treatise *On the Donatist Schism*, came out in 1631. Casaubon followed this with an English translation of the *Meditations* of Marcus Aurelius (1634) that remained in print into the twentieth century, and subsequently published an edition of the Greek text with his own Latin translation (1643). He never ceased to praise Marcus Aurelius, and was bitterly stung by what he saw as Thomas Gataker's shabby treatment of his labours in the latter's 1652 edition of the same work. In 1634 Casaubon received the livings of Minster in Thanet and Monkton-cum-Birchington Chapel in Kent. In August 1636 he was made doctor of divinity at Oxford by Charles I. In 1638 he published *A Treatise of Use and Custom*; an appendix to this contains the first exposure in print of the Etruscan forgeries of Curzio Inghirami.

In January 1641 Casaubon's parishioners in both Minster and Monkton accused him of ecclesiological innovation, popery, and pluralism, and petitioned for his replacement by two more 'godly-minded' (and non-pluralist) ministers (Larking, 105). Casaubon defended himself against the charges, and trouble simmered until 1643, when parliament ordered that he resign Monkton; he was deprived of his prebendal stall, briefly imprisoned, and heavily fined. In 1644 he finally lost his living of Minster. His wife, however, was granted a fifth of the tithe income from Minster and firewood and a fifth portion of his prebendal stipend to support the family. It was about this time that Casaubon sought and received help to continue his studies from John Selden. Casaubon had retained part of his father's scholarly library, and added his own books to it, but about this time was forced to sell a number of the more valuable ones, which he never ceased to regret. In these years he lived a '*vitam desultoriam*' (Casaubon, *Generall Learning*, 86), initially in London, and latterly in West Ashling in Sussex under the protection of his wife's kinsman, the regicide William Cawley. Casaubon's wife, Frances, whom he loved dearly, died on 24 February 1652. (The commonly found statement that he married twice is mistaken.) There were two surviving children, John (1636–1692), a doctor in Canterbury who left a revealing medical diary; and Anne (1649–1685), who in 1668 married John Dawling, later Casaubon's executor.

Casaubon's deprivations did not prevent him from writing and publishing a good number of books, although they did eventually destroy his ambition of refuting Baronius. In 1645 he published *The Origin of Temporal Evils*, a study of pagan ideas of theodicy, and wrote a lost manuscript, *De origine idololatoria*. A *Discourse Concerning Christ his Incarnation, and Exinanition* (1646) offered a polemical course in the principles of Christianity against contemporary assaults on the established church. *De verborum usu* (1647) is a little treatise on the right use of words which takes the occasion to defend the posthumous protestant reputation of Hugo Grotius, who had earlier tried to find favour with Laud through Casaubon. *De quatuor linguis commentationis* (1650) argues that English is related to Greek. The book manifests Casaubon's interest in Anglo-

Saxon, which he shared with his lifelong 'trustie frend' William Somner (CKS, PRC 31/140); Casaubon's interest in antiquities more generally also emerges from his association with William Dugdale. Besides these men he was also acquainted at this time with the scholars Patrick Junius, Christopher Arnold, and Sir John Marsham.

The middle years of the seventeenth century brought two notable offers of advancement. In 1649 Queen Kristina's ambassador in Paris, 'having, it seemes, à better opinion of mee … then I have of my selfe' proposed that Casaubon move to Sweden, perhaps to take up an academic position; it was presumably not Descartes's presence there that caused him to decide not to go (BL, Evelyn MS UP 6, fol. 70). Casaubon was a committed loyalist to church and king, and often lamented the harm the 'Troubles' had done to his scholarly ambitions and his adopted country. Despite this he was approached in 1652 with a commission from Lord General Cromwell to write a history of the recent civil wars; the reward was to be £500 and the return of his father's books from the royal library. Casaubon declined the offer as being 'quit[e] against his conscience' (Bodl. Oxf., MS Wood F.40, fol. 352r).

In 1655 Casaubon published what is now perhaps his most widely read book: *A Treatise Concerning Enthusiasm* (revised 2nd edn, 1656). This work, characteristically, tackles a topical issue through discussion of ancient and scholarly sources in philosophy, theology, medicine, rhetoric, and poetics. In the later 1650s Casaubon lived for some time in Cotton House in Westminster as the guest of John Cotton, grandson of Sir Robert Cotton, and had the use of the Cotton Library. This bore fruit in the famous edition Casaubon published—somewhat unwillingly, but out of a sense of obligation to his host and Archbishop Ussher—of John Dee's *Conversations with Spirits* (1659). In the lengthy preface Casaubon argued that Dee's visitors were demonic, and his later publications, too, defended the existence of demons and witches against those who denied their existence.

After the Restoration, Casaubon recovered his prebendal stall at Canterbury, and his living at Minster from Richard Culmer, although not before he had written a begging letter to Gilbert Sheldon asking for 'some dignitie in some cathedrall of the old foundation that may be profitable and require noe great attendance, or some good donative, if it may be had' (Bodl. Oxf., MS Tanner 49, fol. 144). He exchanged Minster for Ickham in 1662, and divided his time between there, Canterbury, London, and Cambridge. In these years he published defences of the protestant churches against the Roman Catholic charge of schism (1664) and of himself and the historical claims of the Church of England against the Catholic controversialist John Sergeant (1665); and also a treatise, polemical in intent, *The Question, to whom it Belonged Anciently to Preach* (1663)—a rather slender return on his lifelong study of the early church. In 1668 he wrote a long epistolary treatise to Francis Turner on the subject of 'generall learning', and in 1669 printed an analogous letter to his colleague Peter du Moulin against some of the claims of Joseph Glanvill and

Thomas Sprat of the Royal Society for experimental natural philosophy; du Moulin subsequently dedicated his *Parerga* (1670) to Casaubon. In 1668 and 1670 Casaubon published the first two and the last parts respectively of *Of Credulity and Incredulity, in Things Natural, Civil, and Divine*. This work attempts to adjudicate between the extremes of 'unadvised belief, or unbelief' (p. 1) by means of general rules applied to historical examples; the first two parts were reprinted posthumously in 1672 as a defence of the existence of witchcraft.

In his popular vernacular writings Casaubon took it upon himself to examine the present through the lens of antiquity; he was also often autobiographical. His intellectual interests were broad. He had a strong fascination with the natural world: as a young man he attempted some of the experiments described in Francis Bacon's *Sylva sylvarum*. It is this interest in nature that explains his concern, which has interested modern historians, with the claims of the new experimental natural philosophy. Many of Casaubon's books evince an informed interest in the theory of rhetoric, although both his Latin and English writings are rather digressive, if ultimately structurally well organized. Casaubon was also a well-read medical amateur, and encouraged his son John in that profession. These interests led to him becoming an early, albeit hostile, English reader of Descartes, and a somewhat less hostile reader of Gassendi, whose Epicureanism he deeply mistrusted. His scholarship is unified by a syncretic search for connections between the writings of Greek and Roman antiquity and the Hebrew Old Testament, although his only sustained contribution to biblical criticism is his commentary on the Psalms in the Westminster *Annotations* (1645).

Aside from his editions of Optatus, Marcus Aurelius, and Dee, Casaubon's editorial endeavours consisted in revising his father's edition of Persius (1647), and in revising and finishing Thomas Farnaby's edition of Terence (1651). He also contributed notes on a number of other authors to editions of their works: Hierocles (1655); Edmund Bolton's English translation of Florus (1658); Epictetus and Cebes (1659); Diogenes Laertius (1664); and Polybius (1670). Anthony Wood suggests that he profited in his criticisms from his father's notes; he certainly imparted their contents freely to inquirers, including, in 1670, John Evelyn.

Anthony Wood praises Casaubon's charity, and Casaubon's son John gives this account of his character: 'full of Virtue, and a great lover of temperance, even to Morosenes … one of the most Hypochondricall Melancholy men living in his tyme' (Hunter and Macalpine, 52–3). From middle age he suffered much from the stone, and had near-fatal illnesses in childhood and in 1666. He died in Canterbury on 14 July 1671 at the age of seventy-one, after a period of paralysis, and was buried in Canterbury Cathedral. For a grievous but unspecified fault he cut his son John out of the greater part of his will. Edward Stillingfleet, whom Casaubon admired, bought many of his books, which are now in Archbishop Marsh's Library, Dublin.   R. W. SERJEANTSON

Sources memorial plaque, Christ Church Cathedral, Canterbury · M. Casaubon, 'What has been sett out by me Meric Casaubon to satisfie some friends', *c*.1688, Bodl. Oxf., MS Wood F.40, fol. 350 · Wood, *Ath. Oxon.*, new edn, 3.934–40 · will and probate inventory, CKS, PRC 31/140; PRC 27/23/16 · J. Casaubon, account of his father's life, Bodl. Oxf., MS Wood F.40, fols. 352–3 · R. Hunter and I. Macalpine, 'The diary of John Casaubon', *Proceedings of the Huguenot Society*, 21 (1965–70), 31–55 · BL, M. Casaubon papers, Burney MSS 368–369 · M. Pattison, *Isaac Casaubon, 1559–1614*, ed. [H. Nettleship], 2nd edn (1892) · *Isaaci Casauboni epistolae*, ed. T. Janson ab Almeloveen, 2 vols. in 1 (Rotterdam, 1709) · Casaubon–G. J. Vossius correspondence, Bodl. Oxf., MS Rawl. letters 83–4 · T. A. Birrell, 'The reconstruction of the library of Isaac Casaubon', *Hellinga Festschrift* (1980), 59–68 · L. B. Larking, ed., *Proceedings principally in the county of Kent in connection with the parliaments called in 1640, and especially with the committee of religion appointed in that year*, CS, old ser., 80 (1862) · 'Remarques concerning Dr Meric Casaubon', Bodl. Oxf., MS Ballard 46, fol. 82 · M. Casaubon, *Generall learning*, ed. R. Serjeantson (1999)

Archives BL, papers, Burney MSS 368–369

Likenesses P. S. van Gunst, line engraving (after A. van der Werff), BM, NPG; repro. in *Isaaci Casauboni epistolae* [see illus.] · oils, Canterbury Cathedral, chapter library · oils, Bodl. Oxf.

Wealth at death £1326 16s. 1d.: probate inventory, CKS, PRC 27/23/16

Case, Janet Elizabeth (1863–1937), classics teacher and journalist, was born on 28 July 1863 at 117 Adelaide Road, Hampstead, London, the youngest of the six daughters of William Arthur Case (1818–1872), schoolmaster and fellow of University College, London, and his wife, Sarah Wolridge Stansfeld, sister of Sir James Stansfeld, the radical politician. She was educated at her parents' co-educational school, Heath Brow, Hampstead, which her mother continued after William Case's death. When she entered Girton College to read classics in 1881 she had more grounding in the subject than was usual for girls at that time. She went on to obtain a first in part two of the tripos (philosophy) in 1885. This she was able to convert to an MA in 1907 when Trinity College, Dublin, offered suitably qualified Oxbridge women *quasi ad eundem* degrees. While she was at Girton she co-founded the college classical club in 1884 and was a member of Cambridge University Music Society, one of the few university societies open to women. She was remembered for her performances in Greek plays, taking the part of Electra in the college performance of 1883 and of Athena in Aeschylus' *Eumenides*, performed by the university in 1885.

On leaving Cambridge, Janet Case returned to live at home and teach classics. From 1887 to 1896 she was visiting classical mistress at Maida Vale high school. In addition she gave private tuition. One of her pupils, the artist Henry Holliday, said that he would 'learn Greek if he could find a lady like "Athena or Electra" and … was much surprised to find that she lived on the Heath, close by' (Margaret Llewelyn Davies to Helen McMorran, 23 July 1937, Girton College archives). Other pupils included Katherine Asquith, the widow of the Liberal prime minister's eldest son, Raymond, Lady Diana Cooper, and Virginia Woolf. Many pupils became lifelong friends, notably Virginia Woolf who, after an initial aversion to 'Case', came to regard her as not only an excellent teacher but also a valued critic, confidante, and support. She wrote Case's obituary notice in *The Times*.

Janet Case was a member of the Hellenic Society, and in 1905 published an edition, with notes, of Aeschylus' *Prometheus Bound*. However, as Virginia Woolf recorded, her Greek was 'connected with many things', most of which concerned humanitarian reform. She was an active suffragist and was involved with the newly founded Women's Co-operative Guild (WCG), of which her friend and Girton contemporary, Margaret Llewelyn Davies, was general secretary. She lectured for the guild on moral hygiene and on improved maternity care, and instructed WCG speakers on divorce law reform. She published a pamphlet which summarized the recommendations of the royal commission on divorce in 1912 and advocated the radical WCG proposal of appointing women assessors to the divorce court. As she grew older her political sympathies moved steadily to the left. In addition to her work for the WCG she became an active supporter of home rule for Ireland, and was a member of the Peace Pledge Union, and a Labour voter in a staunchly Conservative constituency.

In 1915, at the age of fifty-two, Janet Case's health broke down and she was forced to give up teaching and her active involvement in campaigning. During bouts of ill health she was cared for by her sister, with whom she shared a house in Hampstead. They were increasingly short of money, and Virginia and Leonard Woolf assisted them, the latter trying to find employment for Janet as a newspaper correspondent; however, her pacifist views found little sympathy in the post-war climate. In 1920 ill health and financial constraint forced the sisters to move to Surrey. Two years later an inheritance enabled them to build a small house at Lyndhurst in the New Forest. Here Janet Case lived very simply, devoting herself to her garden and the forest countryside. Her rural observations were published as weekly 'Country diaries', which she contributed to the *Manchester Guardian* for the last twelve years of her life.

Janet Case was described by contemporaries as tall, dignified, and classical looking, with an air of breeding and self-possession. Her friends valued her counsel as well as her lively sense of humour. Her scholarship was impeccable, but she was one of a group of Girtonians in the early 1880s for whom scholarship was not sufficient as an end in itself, and who went on to form a network of women closely involved in social reform. Janet Case died of cancer at her home, Hewers' Orchard, Minstead, Hampshire, on 15 July 1937. She did not adhere to any religious doctrine; Virginia Woolf described her as being too well educated to be a Christian, but she had devised her own funeral service with a text on gentleness and faith. She was instead, as her obituarist in the *Girton Review* described her, 'a rare humanist'.   KATE PERRY

Sources *The diary of Virginia Woolf*, ed. A. O. Bell and A. McNeillie, 5 vols. (1977–84) · *The letters of Virginia Woolf*, ed. N. Nicolson, 6 vols. (1975–80) · K. T. Butler and H. I. McMorran, eds., *Girton College register, 1869–1946* (1948) · *Girton Review* (1937) · *The Times* (22 July 1937) · *Manchester Guardian* (17 July 1937) · M. L. Davies, R. Nash, H. M. Swanwick, and B. Stephen, letters to the editor of the *Girton Review*, July 1937, Girton Cam. · J. Case, *The divorce law reform union* (c.1912)

[Fawcett Library pamphlet 347.647.2] · J. Case, letters to Leonard Woolf, 1913–19, U. Sussex, Leonard Woolf MSS 13, III; 18, II · J. Case, letters to Virginia Woolf, 1916–28, U. Sussex, Monks House MS 18, III · M. A. Leaska, ed., *A passionate apprentice: the early journals, 1897–1909* (1990) · Q. Bell, *Virginia Woolf: a biography*, 1 (1972) · b. cert. · d. cert.

Archives CUL, Greek play committee album for 1885 · U. Sussex, Monks House MSS · U. Sussex, Leonard Woolf MSS
Likenesses T. H. Lord, photograph, 1883, Girton Cam. · T. H. Lord, photograph, 1885, CUL · D. Day, photograph, c.1915, Girton Cam. · group portrait, photograph, repro. in G. Spater and I. Parsons, *A marriage of true minds: an intimate portrait of Leonard and Virginia Woolf* (1977)
Wealth at death £4037 5s. 9d.: probate, 9 Sept 1937, CGPLA Eng. & Wales

Case, John (1539/40?–1599), philosopher and physician, was born at Woodstock, Oxfordshire. He may have received his grammar-school education in Woodstock, where there was certainly a school before 1571. After spending some time as a chorister at New College and Christ Church, he transferred to St John's College, Oxford, as a scholar in 1564. He completed the requirements for the BA in 1568 and became a fellow of St John's in the same year. By 1572 he had completed the requirements for the MA. Case had apparently been frequenting the house of 'the widow of one [John] Dobson the keeper of Bocardo prison' (Wood, *Ath. Oxon.*, 1.687). A visitation of the college in August 1572 resulted in Case's being ordered to marry the widow or stop seeing her. Case married Elizabeth Dobson (d. 1611/12?) on 30 December 1574 and resigned his fellowship, but continued to teach logic and other subjects in his wife's house.

Wood alleges that Case lost his fellowship because he was 'Popishly affected' and that his students were 'mostly of the R. C. religion' (Wood, *Ath. Oxon.*, 1.685), but there is little evidence to support this. Case is mentioned by two of his former students in the *responsa scholarum* for admission to the English College at Rome, but not in connection with their conversions or flights from England. During his embassy to France (1579–83) Sir Henry Cobham wrote to Sir Francis Walsingham at least twice to report that Case's house was being used as a refuge for Catholics, but no apparent action was taken against Case. In 1583, when the university tried to eliminate Catholic elements by insisting that tutors should not receive students into their houses, Case was granted an exemption because of his teaching effectiveness and poor health.

In the 1580s and 1590s Case belonged to an intellectual circle that may have included Laurence Humphrey, Thomas Holland, William Gwinne, Griffin Powel, Richard Eedes, and John Lyly, all of whom contributed liminary verses to his publications. Case in turn contributed liminary verses or letters to works by Nicholas Breton, Richard Haydocke, John Rider, William Thorne, and William Gager. He also contributed verses to Oxford University publications commemorating the deaths of Christopher Hatton (1592) and Henry Unton (1596).

Case's first book, *Summa veterum interpretum in universam dialecticam Aristotelis* (1584), is a textbook in Aristotelian logic. Not only does Case criticize Peter Ramus for being

John Case (1539/40?–1599), by unknown artist

arrogant, but he recommends Duns Scotus and Walter Burleigh. His second book, *Speculum moralium quaestionum in universam ethicen Aristotelis* (1585), a commentary on Aristotle's *Nicomachean Ethics*, has the distinction of being the first major publication of the new Oxford University Press. Appended to a second edition, printed in 1596, were *Reflexus speculi moralis* (a commentary on Aristotle's *Magna moralia*) and *ABCedarium moralis philosophiae*. Case's lengthy *Sphaera civitatis* (1588), a commentary on Aristotle's *Politics*, discusses such modern-sounding topics as abortion, immigration, capital punishment, inflation, communism, and women in combat. It has been described as 'the most rigorous discussion of political theory and practice to survive from sixteenth-century England' (Binns, 368). His *Apologia musices* (1588), a treatise on music, has often been confused with *The Praise of Musicke* (1586), first attributed to Case by Thomas Watson in the 1580s; however, the two books are quite different and Case is probably not the author of the English work.

In a poem that prefaces *Sphaera civitatis*, William Gager implies that Case was childless, but he did have a stepdaughter, Anne Dobson, who married the Oxford physician Bartholomew Warner in 1583. In 1589, when Case was installed as prebendary of North Alton, Warner stood in for him at the ceremony. Though he may have been attending medical lectures as early as 1564, and seems to have begun practising medicine in 1574, Case did not supplicate for a medical degree until 1588. He completed the requirements for the MD in 1590. He may have served as personal physician to the historian William Camden and

the antiquarian Robert Cotton. He was probably the 'Doctor Case' summoned from Chester to attend Ferdinando Stanley, earl of Derby, on his deathbed in 1594. Though we cannot confirm that Case was ever in Chester, two certificates of residence indicate that he and his family were mobile at about this time. His treatment of Stanley apparently called for 'one dragme of rubarbe, and half an ounce of manna, in a draught of checkin brothe' (Lodge, 3.47). A student notebook in the British Library (Sloane MS 249) also contains medical recipes ascribed to Case.

Case's works, all written in Latin, were reprinted more often on the continent than in England. So frustrated was the Oxford printer Joseph Barnes by pirated editions that he refused to print Case's works for nearly eight years after *Sphaera civitatis*. Case's *Apologia academiarum* (1596), a defence of education, remains unpublished. His next publication after the 1596 reprint of the *Speculum moralium quaestionum* was *Thesaurus oeconomiae* (1597), a commentary on the pseudo-Aristotelian *Economics*, focusing on family and household matters. It has been called 'the most complex analysis of marriage that any early modern English writer produced' (Knapp, 415). His final two works may have been printed posthumously: *Lapis philosophicus* (undated), a lengthy commentary on Aristotle's *Physics*, and its companion *Ancilla philosophiae* (1599). In the former work Case covers many of Aristotle's topics in the *Physics*, but also takes a stand on such Renaissance controversies as the efficacy of alchemy and the Paracelsian doctrine of the *homunculus*. Case despised Paracelsus almost as much as Machiavelli, another recurring villain in his works.

According to the inscription on his monument in the chapel of St John's College, Oxford, Case died on 23 January 1599 at the age of nearly sixty. The Catholic biographer John Pits alleged that a Roman Catholic priest was present at Case's death. An inventory of his property, taken shortly after his death and now in the archives of Oxford University, indicates that Case was a man of some wealth. Though principally an author of commentaries on Aristotle's works, Case nevertheless made original contributions to Renaissance political theory and natural philosophy. He should be regarded as an important Elizabethan intellectual who played a key role in the English revival of Aristotelian philosophy at the end of the sixteenth century.

EDWARD A. MALONE

Sources C. Schmitt, *John Case and Aristotelianism in Renaissance England* (1983) · J. W. Binns, *Intellectual culture in Elizabethan and Jacobean England: the Latin writings of the age* (1990) · W. H. Stevenson and H. E. Salter, *The early history of St John's College, Oxford*, OHS, new ser., 1 (1939) · Wood, *Ath. Oxon.*, new edn · *Reg. Oxf.*, vols. 1–2 · PRO, E 115/74/86 and E 115/109/109 · PRO, SP 78/7/23–24 · inventory, 23 Feb 1599, Oxf. UA, hyp. B/11 · R. Knapp, '"Is it appropriate for a man to fear his wife?": John Case on marriage', *English Literary Renaissance*, 28 (1998), 387–415 · E. Lodge, *Illustrations of British history, biography, and manners*, 3 vols. (1791) · J. Pits, *Relationum historicarum de rebus Anglicis*, ed. [W. Bishop] (Paris, 1619); repr. (1969) · J. K. McConica, 'Humanism and Aristotle in Tudor Oxford', *EngHR*, 94 (1979), 291–317 · *Hist. U. Oxf.* 3: *Colleg. univ.* · *VCH Oxfordshire*, vol. 12 · A. Kenny, ed., *The responsa scholarum of the English College, Rome*, 1, Catholic RS, 54 (1962) · *Fasti Angl., 1541–1857*, [Salisbury] · E. Knight, 'The praise of musicke: John Case, Thomas Watson, and William Byrd', *Current Musicology*, 30 (1980), 37–51 · B. P. Copenhaver and C. B.

Schmitt, *A history of western philosophy* (1992), 3: *Renaissance philosophy* · H. Barnett, 'John Case—an Elizabethan music scholar', *Music and Letters*, 50 (1969), 252–66 · private information (2004) [M. Feingold, S. Hutton] · A. Wood, *The history and antiquities of the colleges and halls in the University of Oxford*, ed. J. Gutch (1786), pt 4, p. 561

Archives BL, Add. MS 4160, fols. 183–4, 194–5 · BL, Cotton MSS Julius C. III, fol. 81; V, fol. 50 · BL, Harley MS 6995, fols. 60–61 · Bodl. Oxf., Corpus Christi MS C321, fols. 1–21 · Oxf. UA, chancellor's court, register GG, fols. 180r–181v

Likenesses effigy on monument, St John's College, Oxford · oils, St John's College, Oxford [*see illus.*]

Wealth at death wealthy: inventory, 23 Feb 1599, Oxf. UA, hyp. B/11

Case, John (*c.*1660–1700), astrologer and quack, was born at Lyme, Dorset, about 1660, judging from the statement in his book, *The wards of the key to Helmont proved unfit for the lock, or, The principles of Mr Wm Bacon examined and refuted* (1682), that he has just attained his majority. At this date he was living in Lambeth. The work, prefixed by a letter of recommendation by Case's friend, the astrologer John Partridge, is a protest against Bacon's theory, expressed in his *Key to Helmont*, that water was the principle of all bodies. Case's *Prophecy of the Conjunction of Saturn and Jupiter* (1682) predicted a sabbatical era to last until the next revolution of those planets, bringing with it the end of the world, eight hundred years from the date the work was published.

The *Compendium anatomicum nova methodo institutum* (1695) was Case's best work and brought him to general notice, being republished in the following year at Amsterdam. It consisted of a masterly defence of the opinion of Harvey and De Graaf on the generation of animals from the egg, in the same manner as birds, and was in fact so superior to Case's other books that some doubted his authorship. It was followed by his *Ars anatomica breviter elucidata* (1695), then by *Flos aevi, or, Coelestial Observations* (1696). By this time Case was styling himself MD, and living near Ludgate, in the City of London. He took over the business of the physician Thomas Saffold (1620–1691), who had himself succeeded William Lilly. By this means he acquired all the magical apparatus of these noted astrologers, and he was particularly pleased to possess (and to ridicule to his own friends) the darkened room and illusionist apparatus by which Lilly showed people visions of their departed friends. He replaced the black ball which advertised Saffold's shop with a golden one, and put up his own verse in place of the previous sign: 'Within this place—lives Doctor Case' (*Tatler*, 3.234).

Case advertised profusely over decades; this, and the elevated price of some of his nostrums and elixirs, hints at a steady and affluent clientele, many of whom were seeking a cure for the clap. But he also advertised that the sick could have advice for nothing, and 'good medicine cheap', inscribing his pillboxes:

here's fourteen pills for thirteen pence—
enough in any man's own conscience.

(Porter, 99)

In 1697 Case published *The Angelical Guide, Showing Men and Women their Lott or Chance in this Elementary Life*, in four books, and dedicated to his friend Thomas Tryon. The bibliographer James Granger considered it to be 'one of the most profound astrological pieces that the world ever saw; the diagrams would probably have puzzled Euclid, though he had studied astrology' (Granger, 6.138). Case's last serious work was *The Medical Expositor in an Alphabetical Order in Latine, Greek, and English* (1698).

Case was the original of the story concerning a Dr Maundy, formerly of Canterbury, who on his travels abroad met an eminent physician who had been in England, who gave Maundy a token to spend on his return with Dr Radcliffe and Dr Case. Maundy, Radcliffe, and Case met together one evening and were very merry, when Radcliffe proposed a toast: 'Here, brother Case, to all the fools, your patients'. 'I thank you, good brother', replied Case; 'let me have all the fools and you are heartily welcome to the rest of the practice' (Granger, 6.139). Case died at the beginning of November 1700 and was buried at St Martin Ludgate, on 7 November.

EDWARD HERON-ALLEN, *rev.* ANITA MCCONNELL

Sources F. Leigh Gardner, *Bibliotheca astrologica* (1977) · J. Granger, *A biographical history of England from Egbert the Great to the revolution*, 5th edn, 6 vols. (1824), vol. 6, pp. 138–9 · D. F. Bond, ed., *The Tatler*, 3 vols. (1987), vol. 1, p. 159; vol. 3, p. 234 · R. Porter, *Health for sale: quackery in England, 1660–1850* (1989) · parish register (burial), London, St Martin Ludgate, 7 Nov 1700

Likenesses portrait, repro. in J. Case, *The angelical guide, showing men and women their lott or chance in this elementary life* (1697)

Case, Thomas (*bap.* 1598, *d.* 1682), clergyman and ejected minister, was born in Boxley in Kent, the son of George Case, vicar of Boxley, and baptized there on 20 August 1598. Having attended school in Canterbury and then at Merchant Taylors', he entered Christ Church, Oxford, on the recommendation of Archbishop Tobie Matthew of York, graduating BA in June 1620 and proceeding MA in June 1623. After returning to Kent he preached there before being ordained in Norwich on 24 September 1626. He then took up a curacy with Richard Heyrick in North Repps, Norfolk, and became rector of Erpingham, Norfolk, on 4 January 1629. In 1631 he married Ann Pots at Itteringham in the same county. Despite being licensed as a preacher as late as 9 April 1635, he fell victim to the anti-puritan drive urged by Canterbury on Norwich's Bishop Matthew Wren and was cited into the Norwich consistory court on 14 November 1637.

With Heyrick, Case now moved to the Manchester area, where the protection of such families as the Booths and Mosleys sheltered the puritan tradition that had become entrenched in the area since Elizabeth's reign. His second marriage, on 8 August 1637, in Stockport, Cheshire, to Ann (*d.* 1696), daughter of Oswald Mosley of Manchester, and widow of Robert Booth of Salford, brought him into the heart of the lay leadership of puritanism in the northwest. Case had already developed his puritan views before or during the period of the Laudian ascendancy, but it may be that his treatment at the hands of Wren intensified and embittered his anti-Laudian animus. By 1641 he was calling for 'root-and-branch' abolition of episcopacy and, indeed, in apocalyptic vein, for a total renewal of English society. A preacher to the Long Parliament, on 15 February

Thomas Case (*bap.* 1598, *d.* 1682), by unknown artist

1642 Case also became lecturer in St Martin-in-the-Fields, a position providing a platform for what Wood saw as his quest for political popularity in the world of the capital's parliamentarian puritanism, in which he became associated, as chaplain, with London's anti-royalist MP and mayor from August 1642, Isaac Penington. Case was probably 'T. C. one of the chaplains in the army', the author of the 1642 *A More True and Exact Relation of the Battaile of Keynton*—a report on Edgehill.

Despite a secondary interest in the north-west—he became rector of Stockport, Cheshire, on 31 July 1645—Case's ministerial career was thereafter heavily focused on London, where he was made rector of St Mary Magdalen, Milk Street. He was 'laborious and faithful' in that ministry (*Nonconformist's Memorial*, 1.154), introducing the successful 'Morning Exercise' series of lectures, and in 1643 urging the enthusiastic adoption of the presbyterian solemn league and covenant. However, Case's proximity to the centre of parliamentarian power probably intensified the deeply politicized cast of his godliness. He preached against mercy for royalists and became notorious for inviting to communion congregants 'that have freely and liberally contributed to the Parliament for the defence of God's cause and the gospel' (Pearl, 232). It was hardly surprising that he was in 1643 appointed to the Westminster assembly of divines.

By 1645, however, Case, his earlier millenarianism dulled, felt that the revolution should be halted, although he still offered thanksgiving for the surrender of Chester to parliament in his fast sermon of February 1646 before the house, *A Model of True Spiritual Thankfulnesse*. He was convinced of the validity of the presbyterian covenant and his political alignment, manifest in his signature of

the testimony of the London presbyterian ministers of 1647, was firmly with the presbyterians and opposed to the army and the Independents. Deeply suspicious of the proceedings of 1648 leading to Charles I's trial, in 1649 he signed the vindication, a similar manifesto. By this time the Independents were in the ascendant and Case was removed from St Mary Magdalen in 1650 for refusing the republican engagement. More actively, Case, with others including Heyrick, became involved in Christopher Love's presbyterian royalist plot against the regicide regime. Case was imprisoned in the Tower from 19 May to 15 October 1651, 'detained touching the late treason and conspiracy' (*CSP dom.*, *1651*, 457). Here he faced the most perilous passage of his entire career; his prison meditations were published as *Correction, Instruction* in 1652. By 9 August 1651, however, the council of state had considered a petition from him, probably that described by Anthony Wood as 'a petition to Oliver by way of acknowledgement and submission' (Wood, *Ath. Oxon.*, 4.46), and his release was finally secured.

On 1 November 1654 Case was made rector of the London church of St Giles-in-the-Fields but a fuller, albeit temporary, revival of his fortunes came only with the restoration of the presbyterian cause around the time of the demise of the Commonwealth. In March 1660, under Monck's transitional regime, he was appointed by parliament a commissioner for the approbation of ministers. Case was now able to return to the presbyterian royalism he had espoused between 1648 and 1650 and he became an active proponent of a royal restoration. In 1660 he was at Scheveningen, on the Dutch coast, as one of the representatives of the London clergy to attend on Charles II; unfortunately, he fell in the sea, or, as Pepys put it, was 'sadly dipped' (Pepys, 1.140).

In the new circumstances of the 1660s, however, Case faced new humiliation. Pepys, who had been used to hear Case preach in London, recorded how much his earnest style of discourse had dated, rendering him a target for the newly fashionable mockery of the puritan style of preaching: 'a dull fellow in his talk, and all in the presbyterian manner, a great deal of noise and a kind of religious tone, but very dull' (Pepys, 9.190). As a commissioner at the Savoy talks aimed at hammering out a post-Restoration settlement of religion to accommodate the heirs of the puritan tradition, Case believed that his party had more bargaining strength with the restored monarchy than it actually possessed, and when he intruded himself into Charles II's presence and told the king that he 'had a word of advice' (*Memoirs of Edmund Ludlow*, 2.283) about looking after the presbyterian interest, the monarch sardonically replied that he had no recollection of appointing Case to his council. Perhaps it was the anti-nonconformist drift in the capital in 1661 that induced Case to put out feelers to the northern presbyterian magnate, Lord Wharton, about a move to Lancashire.

None the less, the final stage in Case's career, that of a declared nonconformist, unfolded in London. The previous episcopalian minister at St Giles-in-the-Fields was reinstated after the Restoration and the ejected Case preached his farewell sermon in the parish on 17 August 1662 but he was not silenced. Always a preacher, he was reported in that role in London in 1663, and on 30 April 1672, described as 'Thomas Case, of Chiswick' (Bate, xl) and a presbyterian, he was issued a licence under the declaration of indulgence; in 1676 he was ministering in Holborn. He published the popular *Mount Pisgah, or, A Prospect of Heaven* (1670).

The last surviving dissenting member of the Westminster assembly, Case died on 30 May 1682, aged eighty-four, leaving £1200 to his wife, relations, and 'poor godly men and women'. He was buried at Christ Church Greyfriars, on 3 June. In his funeral address Thomas Jacomb caught the combination, or contradiction, in Thomas Case between the passionate partisan—'a quick and warm spirit'—and the minister of the word—'a scriptural preacher; a great man in prayer, and one who brought home many souls to God' (*Nonconformist's Memorial*, 1.154).

MICHAEL MULLETT

Sources *The nonconformist's memorial … originally written by … Edmund Calamy*, ed. S. Palmer, [3rd edn], 1 (1802) • *Calamy rev.* • V. Pearl, *London and the outbreak of the puritan revolution: city government and national politics, 1625–1643* (1961) • *CSP dom.*, 1651 • Foster, *Alum. Oxon.* • Wood, *Ath. Oxon.*, new edn, 4.45–8 • *The memoirs of Edmund Ludlow*, ed. C. H. Firth, 2 vols. (1894), vol. 2 • F. Bate, *The declaration of indulgence, 1672* (1908) • Pepys, *Diary*, vols. 1, 4, 9
Likenesses R. Cooper, stipple, NPG • oils, DWL [*see illus.*]
Wealth at death £1200: *Calamy rev.*

Case, Thomas (1844–1925), philosopher and college head, was born in Liverpool on 14 July 1844, the second son of Robert Case, a stockbroker there and later in London, and his wife, Esther, daughter of Alexander MacMillan. From Rugby School, where he earned a reputation for his intellectual, cricketing, and footballing skills, he entered in 1863 Balliol College, Oxford, where he obtained first classes in classical moderations (1865) and *literae humaniores* (1867). He was elected in 1869 fellow of Brasenose College. Pressed by his father, he joined the stock exchange for a year, but, claiming that Aristotle had spoiled his nerve for money-making, he returned to Oxford in 1870. In that year he married Elizabeth Donn Bennett (*b.* 1848), daughter of the composer Sir William Sterndale *Bennett; they had two sons and one daughter.

Invited by Jowett, who had just been elected master, Case joined the staff of Balliol College and lectured on Aristotle's *Ethics*, ancient history, and logic. Later he became lecturer at Corpus Christi College and in 1876, although Jowett wished to retain him, was persuaded to become a tutor of that college, adding Plato, English moral philosophy, Bacon, and Mill to his repertory. From 1883 to 1889 he also taught at Christ Church. In 1889, on the death of Henry William Chandler, Case was elected Waynflete professor of moral and metaphysical philosophy and fellow of Magdalen College. In 1904 he succeeded Thomas Fowler as president of Corpus Christi College; he held the two posts until 1910, when he resigned the professorship. He was elected an honorary fellow of Magdalen in 1914. In 1924, resigning the presidency, he retired to Falmouth.

Case was a realist philosopher at a time when the idealist school dominated British thought. As an undergraduate at Balliol College, surrounded by idealist influences, Case was initially drawn to idealism. The prominent idealist T. H. Green was a tutor at Balliol; the college also attracted students who were especially interested in speculative philosophy. But he began to move away from idealism; Aristotle, Bacon, and Newton engaged his attention much more than Plato, Kant, or Hegel. He decided to take up a position at Corpus Christi College primarily because he wished to develop an independent philosophy and he felt that the Balliol milieu was not conducive to this ambition. By 1877, when he published *Realism in Morals*, Case had parted company with the idealists, maintaining that they failed to understand the dualism of human nature and underestimated the power of physiological instincts to shape mind and spirit. Describing the position developed in this essay as 'realism without materialism', Case defined realism as 'the theory that things really exist whether we know them or not' (*Realism in Morals*, 1877, 5). He sought to disentangle realism from materialism by arguing that realism was consistent with Christian theology. In this he was much influenced by Aristotelian natural theology. The moral act was not produced solely by strong desires or instincts, Case stated, but also by a consideration of what is good; human will, therefore, moderated human desires. Although this seems similar to a utilitarian explanation of moral conduct, Case rejected utilitarianism and instead believed that Christianity and its creed of duty were the most binding moral force in society.

This position was developed much more fully in *Physical Realism*, published in 1888. In this book Case explored the implications of recent physiological research for theories of knowledge and moral philosophy. He argued here that metaphysics ought to begin with the objects of scientific knowledge; the sense data provided by science enabled the philosopher to infer the nature of an insensible and imperceptible world. He was very much opposed to what he called the 'Kantian fashion' of doubting the possibility of a complete knowledge of things: 'But truth is not in this parlous condition; it only requires us to compare our judgements with things known—a condition practical enough' ('Scientific method as mental operation', *Lectures on the Method of Science*, ed. T. B. Strong, 1906, 24).

Case intended to write a second volume of *Physical Realism* which would have applied physics and physiology to knowledge of time and space, motion, and causation, but this project was never realized. He wrote articles on 'Metaphysics', 'Aristotle', and 'Logic' for the eleventh edition of the *Encyclopaedia Britannica*, but most of his energies were expended on the duties of teaching, college and university administration, and on his many and varied interests.

A 'laughing philosopher' of genial and at times even rollicking temper, who understood young men, and was keen for their advancement, Case was an excellent tutor. He taught H. H. Asquith, Charles Gore, Alfred Milner, L. T. Hobhouse, and J. Cook Wilson, later Wykeham professor of logic. Students recalled in particular his lectures on Aristotle and Bacon. He was an authoritarian and forceful president, prompting college tutors to unite against what they regarded as an invasion of their own affairs.

'I am not a tory, I am what I always was, a Palmerstonian liberal', Case said in his seventieth year. As such he opposed alike Liberal changes and tory concessions in church, state, and university. Believing in 'never doing anything by law if it could be done by voluntary means', he opposed such forms of state 'interference' as state funding for the university and industrial legislation (Case, 1927, 24). He was also opposed to trade unionism. His notable letters to The Times punctuated his campaigns, especially those against the admission of women to Oxford and against the abolition of compulsory Greek. Both were 'thirty years wars', finally determined against him in 1920. His supporters, in 1911, after a signal success in the Greek question, presented him with two silver-gilt Homeric cups. Of the proposal to admit women to certain examinations for the bachelor's degree, Case wrote in 1884:

> Finding that women cannot come up to the standard of men, the University will gradually have to reduce the standard of men to that which can be attained by women ... Still more disastrous will be the effect on the life of Oxford, which is not only a place of learning, but a school of manliness. (Case, Letters, 33)

Young men would learn to like what young women like, 'light literature and the art of conversation at tea-parties' (ibid., 34). He was also distressed by plans in 1890 to admit women to examinations for the degree of bachelor of medicine, on the grounds that if women were to investigate 'those delicate matters which are of the very essence of medicine' in the company of young men, the moral well-being of the university would be compromised (Case, 'Objections', 5). Case's last letters to The Times (1919–22) criticized Einstein's theory of relativity.

Case's skill in architecture was shown in the restoration of the hall roof at Magdalen, where he materially assisted G. F. Bodley, in that of the spire and pinnacles of St Mary's, where he strove to control Thomas Graham Jackson, and in the new lodgings at Corpus Christi. A good pianist, his knowledge and taste in music were full and keen down to about the period of Mendelssohn. He loved the old English anthems and glees, and himself published two volumes of songs. His acquaintance with Shakespeare was exhaustive, and he was an ardent admirer of Nelson and a collector of Nelsoniana. He was a distinguished cricketer and played in the Oxford eleven from 1864 to 1867 as well as excelling in other games.

Beside playing, and writing on, cricket, Case persuaded the university, in the teeth of opposition, to admit that and other games into the university park, and was a most popular and efficient treasurer of the university cricket club.

As well as being a benefactor himself—he restored the east window of the hall at Magdalen and rebuilt the lodgings at Corpus—Case showed an astonishing power of attracting to his college large gifts from others. While some believed that Case's opposition to idealism was vindicated by the new realists of the early twentieth century, the realism that Case expounded, which looked back to the natural philosophy of the eighteenth century and was characterized by a rapidly outdated understanding of the connection between physiology and the mind, failed to engage the attention of contemporary realists (The Times, 2 Nov 1925).

Case died of heart failure at his home, Tredourva, Falmouth, on 31 October 1925, at the age of eighty-one. His funeral was held at Corpus Christi, the college to which he had been so closely affiliated for almost fifty years, and he was buried on 4 November in Wolvercote cemetery, near Oxford.   S. M. DEN OTTER

Sources DNB · T. Case, Letters to The Times, 1884–1922, ed. R. B. Mowat (privately printed, Oxford, 1927) · The Times (2 Nov 1925) · The Times (5 Nov 1925) · T. Case, 'Objections to the proposed statute for admitting women to examinations for the degree of bachelor of medicine', 1890, Bodl. Oxf., GA Oxon. 8°455 (6) · T. Case, 'To the electors of the Waynflete professorship of moral and metaphysical philosophy: an application', 1898, Bodl. Oxf., GA Oxon 4°430 · Hist. U. Oxf. 8: 20th cent. · CGPLA Eng. & Wales (1925)

Archives Magd. Oxf., letters and sketches

Likenesses E. Walker, photograph, 1910, repro. in Mowat, ed., Letters to The Times

Wealth at death £45,235 16s. 2d.: probate, 2 Dec 1925, CGPLA Eng. & Wales

Casella, Charles Frederick (1852–1916). See under Casella, Louis Pascal (1812–1897).

Casella, Louis Marino (1842–1923). See under Casella, Louis Pascal (1812–1897).

Casella, Louis Pascal [formerly Luigi Pasquale] (1812–1897), maker of scientific instruments, was born Luigi Pasquale Casella on 29 February 1812 in Edinburgh, the son of Pasquale Casella, teacher of painting, and his wife, who was a daughter of General Ramsay of Edinburgh. He was brought up and educated in Edinburgh, although nothing further seems to be known about his early life. About 1835 he moved to London, where he was employed by the instrument maker Caesar Tagliabue who, like Casella's father, had emigrated to Britain from near Como. On 5 November 1838 Casella married Caesar's daughter, Maria Louisa Tagliabue, who worked for the family firm in the office. In the same year Tagliabue took his son-in-law into partnership, changing the company's name to Tagliabue and Casella. In 1844, following Tagliabue's death, Casella took over the running of the firm, buying out the interests of his sister-in-law, Antonia Marina Tagliabue, in 1845.

At the time of Tagliabue's death, the firm was at Hatton Garden in the heart of London's scientific instrument making community. It was making and selling a variety of philosophical or scientific instruments, including thermometers, which became one of the main concerns of the firm under Casella's guidance. Its activities expanded considerably, and in 1848 Tagliabue was dropped from the company name. By the 1860s Casella & Co. sold thermometers, hydrometers, and drawing and surveying instruments, as well as meteorological instruments and accessories for photography. Many of the devices were made in the Casella workshop, but some were made—and engraved with Casella's name—under contract by others, including the light engineers R. W. Munro of London and Thomas Cooke of York. Among the company's customers were the British and overseas governments, universities, and other scientific institutions. In 1872 Casella moved the firm, which had been in Hatton Garden for forty-four years, to Holborn Bars, where it stayed until after his death. By the time of the move, his two sons, Louis Marino and Charles Frederick, were working for the company.

As well as, or possibly as part of, pursuing his business interests, Casella maintained his contact with the scientific community through membership of learned societies. He was elected a member of the Meteorological Society of London in 1841 and became a fellow of the Royal Meteorological Society in 1862, by which time he had also joined the Royal Astronomical Society. One of his principal scientific interests was in meteorology and he received wide acclaim for his development and production of first-class meteorological instruments. He was also a fellow of the Royal Geographical Society. The instruments for which Casella was most renowned were thermometers, and his name is associated with several designs, including a clinical thermometer based on the principle of the maximum thermometer, and the adaptation of a pressure gauge for the verification of thermometers to be used for determining deep-sea temperatures.

For most of his life Casella's company was profitable, and his family lived comfortably. In the mid-1870s a new family home, The Lawns, was built in Highgate, Middlesex, and in 1879 Casella bought a house for his daughter in neighbouring Finchley. However, during the 1890s the company went through some lean years, perhaps partly because of Casella's reluctance to loosen the reigns of control, despite his advancing years. On 29 February 1896 he celebrated his official twenty-first birthday, and a year later, on 23 April, he died from bronchitis at his home in Highgate. The firm, with its continuing problems, was left in the hands of his son, Charles Frederick.

Charles Frederick Casella (1852–1916), manufacturer of scientific instruments, was the younger son of Louis Pascal Casella and Maria Louisa Tagliabue. He was born in London on 25 February 1852. He was educated at Ushaw College, Durham, after which he spent time in Paris and at the university in Bonn. He was a fellow of the Royal Meteorological Society and a member of the Society of Engineers and of the Physical Society.

On his father's death in 1897 Charles Frederick was left in charge of the family business. Unfortunately, despite an interest in the instruments themselves, he lacked business acumen; he had inherited a company which was struggling and he was, for some years, unable to improve its situation. For a time there was confusion over the company name: formally it was changed to C. F. Casella, but leaflets, catalogues, and finished instruments continued to be issued under the name of L. P. Casella. By 1905, when the lease on the company's Holborn premises expired, affairs were in a poor state. The firm moved to cheaper but less convenient rooms in Westminster.

Having presided over the company's decline, Casella also oversaw its recovery, through two important appointments: Rowland Miall, an accomplished business manager, and Robert Abraham, who brought skills in engineering and some much needed capital. The three brought about a transformation; they formed a limited liability company in 1910, moved to new premises in south London in 1912, and launched a successful range of instruments. By the time of Charles's death from tuberculosis at his home, Kirkdale, 15 Spencer Road, Bournemouth, on 24 February 1916, Casellas was once more an instrument making company of renown.

Louis Marino Casella (1842–1923), manufacturer of scientific instruments, was born in London in 1842, the first son of Louis Pascal Casella and Maria Louisa Tagliabue. As a young man, Louis Marino joined his father's firm where he worked on the design of instruments, registering his first patent, for a mercurial minimum thermometer, in 1861. Louis maintained an interest in the firm throughout his father's lifetime and beyond but, following his father's death, his involvement was at arm's length. He kept his position as company director, but his own business interests took him in a different direction in manufacturing.

By the middle of the First World War, Louis Marino was chairman of D. Gilson & Co., a firm making screws and turned parts. During the war the firms of Gilson and C. F. Casella crossed paths as the latter set up a new factory alongside Gilson in Walthamstow. In 1918, the Casella company fared better than its neighbour in reverting to peacetime production, and absorbed some of the production capacity abandoned by Louis Marino's organization. This led to a partial amalgamation of the two companies, a situation which prevailed when Louis Marino died, at his home, 47 Fitzjohn's Avenue, Hampstead, on 28 July 1923, the last Casella to have direct involvement in the company.   MARI E. W. WILLIAMS

Sources '1810–1960: C. F. Casella & Company Limited', c.1960 [pamphlet in company archives] · *Quarterly Journal of the Royal Meteorological Society*, 24 (1898), 99–100 · *Monthly Notices of the Royal Astronomical Society*, 58 (1897–8), 133 · *The Times* (27 April 1897), 10f · *Quarterly Journal of the Royal Meteorological Society*, 42 (1916), 191–2 · d. cert. · m. cert. · b. cert. [Charles Frederick Casella] · d. cert. [Charles Frederick Casella] · d. cert. [Louis Marino Casella]
Archives C. F. Casella & Co. Ltd · Hackney Archives, London
Wealth at death £4693 12s. 6d.—Charles Frederick Casella: probate, 6 May 1916, CGPLA Eng. & Wales · £60,050 0s. 7d.—Louis Marino Casella: probate, 5 Oct 1923, CGPLA Eng. & Wales

Casement, Roger David (1864–1916), diplomatist and Irish rebel, was born on 1 September 1864 at Doyle's Cottage, Lawson Terrace, Sandymount, near Dublin, the youngest son of Captain Roger Casement (1819–1877) of the 3rd dragoon guards. His father was of Ulster protestant stock and his mother, Anne Jephson (1834–1873), was of a Roman Catholic branch of a protestant family from Mallow, co. Cork. The children were brought up as protestants, though his mother had Roger secretly baptized a Roman Catholic in Rhyl, north Wales, in August 1868. The Casements moved about frequently, living in France, Italy, and St Helier, Jersey. Casement's mother died in

Roger David Casement (1864–1916), by Sarah Purser

childbirth in 1873, and his father in 1877. The children became wards in chancery, and were dependent on their relatives, especially their uncle, John Casement, of Magherintemple, near Ballycastle, co. Antrim.

Casement lived with his uncle and was sent as a boarder to the diocesan school, Ballymena, in 1873. He left school in 1880 and there followed twelve years of peripatetic living. Casement went to Liverpool to live with Grace Bannister, his mother's sister, and her family. He was found a position as clerk in the Elder Dempster shipping line company, which was active in west Africa. But he found office work tedious and when only nineteen he became purser on the *Bonny*, an Elder Dempster ship bound for the Congo.

British consul: Africa and South America In 1884 Casement returned to Africa and stayed, with only brief intervals, for nearly twenty years. Between 1884 and 1889 he worked in various employments, travelling and acting as 'surveyor' on behalf of the commercial interests of several countries working under King Leopold of the Belgians' Congo International Association. Between December 1889 and March 1890 he was companion to Herbert Ward on a lecturing tour in the United States of America. In 1892 he returned to Ireland and in the same year he accepted his first British official post on the Gulf of Guinea, functioning as 'travelling commissioner and in other capacities for the government'. By October 1892 he was signing himself 'Acting Director-general of Customs' (Reid, 17). His first consular appointment came in 1895 at Delagoa

Bay on Delagoa Bay in Portuguese East Africa, and in July 1898 he was given a new appointment as consul for the Portuguese possessions in west Africa south of the Gulf of Guinea, to reside at Luanda. He was given further consular responsibility for the Congo state and Gabon. At this point in his career he was stridently pro-British, fulminating against the Boers and Kruger, and was awarded the queen's South Africa medal, but he showed signs of his later involvement in Ireland when he tried, unsuccessfully, to have a collection of poems, 'The Dream of the Celt' published by T. Fisher Unwin in 1901. His interest in Africa was still paramount, and he hoped that the Congo, if it were to be governed by Belgium, would be subject to a 'European authority responsible to public opinion, and not to the unquestioned rule of an autocrat whose chief preoccupation is that autocracy should be profitable' (ibid., 32).

In the spring of 1902 Casement persuaded the Foreign Office to move him to Boma, near the Congo mouth. It was at this stage that his homosexual relationships were first entered in his diaries. In June 1902 the Foreign Office authorized him to go into the interior and send reports on the misgovernment of the Congo. He amassed evidence of cruelty and even mutilation of the natives. In November 1903 he was recalled to London to write up his report, which condemned the Congo administration as a ruthless enterprise. His report had less impact that he had hoped, and he was disappointed that the British government did not set up consular courts to protect its own subjects in the Congo. But he was rewarded for his work with a CMG in 1905, which he accepted, though with some misgivings, for he was now more involved in Irish nationalism, particularly the Gaelic League, founded by Douglas Hyde and others in 1892 to further Irish culture and language.

In May 1904 Casement walked the Glens of Antrim and was busy learning Irish, a 'delightful study' (Reid, 61). He hoped to work out a future for himself in Ireland as one of those 'men of leisure, who would love her [Ireland] for herself' (ibid., 73) and give to Ireland what the English aristocracy gave to English public life, but he was poor, and he had to find more remunerative employment. He informed London in September 1905 that he was seeking a position, but his brief stay in one of the best consular posts, Lisbon, and his refusal of Bilbao, annoyed the Foreign Office and he was obliged to wait. In July 1906 he received overtures from the Foreign Office, and in August he was offered the consular post at Santos, Brazil. 'I am a queer sort of British consul' he mused, one who 'ought really to be in jail instead of under the Lion & Unicorn' (ibid., 79). He hated Santos, and a visit to Ireland in 1907 reinforced his rather incoherent, but increasingly fervent, desire to do something for Ireland. In November he left Santos for Pará, which he disliked even more, showing an aversion to the Brazilians because of their mixed race—a 'human compost' (ibid., 86), as he called them, but his improved financial position enabled him to donate money to Irish causes.

In 1908 Casement went to Rio as consul-general, and in the following year began to show a revived interest in his work, through investigating atrocities in the Putumayo basin in Peru. The Foreign Office decided that an investigation into abuses there was needed and Casement was the obvious choice, in view of his Congo experience and the high regard in which humanitarian societies in England held him. On 13 July 1910 his appointment was confirmed and he showed his great competence through a careful study of the papers, his thoroughness in investigation, and the indignation with which he described human rights abuses. He wrote up his report in 1911 and it was subsequently published as a blue book. Casement was rewarded with a knighthood (1911), which, like his CMG, occasioned some self-reflection. He naturally wished to accept the honour, but he worried about its reception in Irish nationalist circles. His response was open to criticism. He accepted, writing in fulsome terms to the foreign secretary, Sir Edward Grey, while confessing to Alice Stopford Green (another protestant nationalist), 'How I should have rejoiced if I could have said to the King what is really in my heart instead of the perfunctory words of thanks (cold and formal enough)' (Inglis, 188).

Irish rebel Casement was now at the height of his British official career; but there remained a void in his life, which was soon filled by Ireland. In 1912 two decisions reflected this mood. He became patron of the Irish summer school on Tawin island, co. Galway; and he wrote in reply to a request from the headmaster of his old school in Ballymena for a subscription to a school extension fund that 'I should be glad to help … were I sure it was not to help an institution that was doing its share to denationalise my fellow-countrymen' (Parmiter, 95). In that same year Irish politics entered a new and dangerous phase, when the Ulster unionists pledged themselves to resist the imposition of home rule, by force if necessary. Casement, like many nationalists, was radicalized by the crisis. In 1913 he became a member of the provisional committee set up to act as the governing body of the Irish Volunteer Force (IVF), created to emulate the Ulster Volunteer Force, but to defend the cause of home rule. His belief in Germany as the obstacle to the machinations of the British empire now found vocal expression: 'Oh! How I sometimes in my heart long for the thud of the German boot keeping guard outside the Mother of Parliaments', he wrote to Mrs Green in November 1913 (Reid, 184). He helped organize local IVF units, and in May 1914 he declared that 'It is quite clear to every Irishman that the only rule John Bull respects is the rifle', hoping that he could make the solution of the 'English Question' the 'chief case of Europe' (Sawyer, *Casement*, 114).

Germany and the rising in Ireland On 2 July 1914 Casement set off for the United States to raise support for the IVF. When the First World War broke out in August he resolved to travel to Germany via Norway in order to urge on the Germans the 'grand idea' of forming an 'Irish brigade' consisting of Irish prisoners of war to fight for Ireland and for Germany (Sawyer, *Casement*, 115), since Germany was 'fighting the battle of European civilization' (Reid, 203). By now British intelligence was on Casement's

trail, and was becoming aware of his homosexual proclivities. Casement arrived in Berlin on 31 October and negotiated what he called a treaty, of ten articles, one of which stated that in no circumstances would the Irish brigade fight directly for Germany, thus avoiding a charge of treason. But Casement's German experience was an unhappy one. He felt slighted that a man of his stature should not be received by the chancellor, von Bethmann-Hollweg, and his attempts to persuade Irish prisoners to enlist in his brigade met with a poor response. His arrogance surfaced in his description of the Irish soldiers as having 'retaliated in a manner characteristic of their class' (Sawyer, *Casement*, 118), and in his anger at being mistaken for an Englishman; he dismissed them as 'Englishmen, pure and simple' (ibid., 122). Ireland became more of an abstraction to him, the 'poor old woman' whose 'four Green fields' (ibid., 119) must be redeemed. His homosexual activity became more overt, troubling his hosts. He returned the insignia of his decorations to the British, but he confessed that he was 'very lonely often' and wished that he had a father and a mother 'to go to now' (Reid, 241); a young Irishman who had been interned and then released by the Germans described him as 'unhinged' (ibid., 291).

The contacts between Irish separatists who were planning a rising and Germany came to Casement's attention only through Robert Monteith, who had served in the British army in the Second South African War, and was now in Germany to enlist in the Irish brigade. Monteith was informed of the plan on 4 or 5 March 1916, and told Casement that a 'move' was on, asking him to come to Berlin to discuss the details (Reid, 329). Casement's old energy and animation revived, but he was shocked to learn that the Germans had, as their foreign office representative Nodalny remarked to Casement, 'no idealistic interest in Ireland … if it were not that we hope for a diversion there, we should not give the rifles' (McHugh, 182). There would be no German soldiers, no officers sent to Ireland, yet Casement was told that the rising was seen in terms of compelling England 'to surrender to us!!' (Reid, 330). Casement now resolved on the contradictory objects of making sure that Germany supplied rifles to the separatists; but also of preventing the rising taking place at all. He decided to go to Ireland, but the Irish-American nationalist John Devoy, who always had his doubts about Casement, tried to ensure that he stayed in Germany.

On 4 April 1916 Casement was told that he could go, but final arrangements were delayed until 6.30 p.m. on 7 April, when he was informed that a submarine would be provided to take him to the west coast of Ireland, where he would rendezvous with a ship carrying arms. Casement was overjoyed. The *Aud*, carrying the weapons, set out from Lübeck on 9 April with instructions to land the arms at Tralee Bay between 20 and 23 April. On 12 April Casement set out in a submarine which broke down, and he was transferred to another U-boat. The *Aud* was at its rendezvous on 21 April but the two vessels failed to meet because of an error in navigation. The U-boat waited, but then Casement and two companions, Monteith and David

Julian Bailey, embarked in a dinghy and landed, exhausted, on Banna strand in the small hours of 21 April. Monteith described them as 'three men in a boat—the smallest invading party known to history' (Reid, 351). The fugitives—for that is what they were—were arrested by the police and Casement was held in Tralee police barracks, where he called for a priest and urged him to carry a message to Dublin emphasizing the futility of a rising. He was taken to Dublin and then London, where he was lodged in the Tower in room 2A. He was given a preliminary examination by magistrates at Bow Street on 15 May, transferred to Brixton prison, and then committed for trial.

Trial and execution Casement surmised that the British, while finding him guilty of treason, would not dare hang him, following the adverse reaction to their executions of ringleaders of the rising. The trial began on 26 June with F. E. Smith leading for the crown. But the most controversial aspect of the trial took place outside the courts. Casement's diaries, detailing his homosexual activities, were now in the hands of the British police and intelligence officers shortly after Casement's interrogation at Scotland Yard on 23 April. There are several versions about precisely when and how the diaries were discovered, but they seem to have come to light when Casement's London lodgings were searched following his arrest. By the first weeks of May they were beginning to be used surreptitiously against him. They were shown to British and American press representatives on about 3 May and excerpts were soon widely circulated in London clubs and the House of Commons. This could not have been done without at least an expectation that those higher up would approve, though Smith opposed any use of the diaries to discredit Casement's reputation, as did Sir Edward Grey. The cabinet however made no attempt to stop these activities, the purpose of which was not to ensure that Casement would be hanged—that was inevitable—but that he should be hanged in disgrace, both political and moral.

On 29 June 1916 Casement was found guilty of high treason. He made a speech from the dock, which was unremarkable except for its significance in showing how he had accepted the mantle of Irish nationalist martyrdom. He was removed to Pentonville prison to await execution. On 30 June he was stripped of his knighthood and on 24 July an appeal was rejected. A campaign for a reprieve was supported by leading political and literary figures, including W. B. Yeats, George Bernard Shaw, John Galsworthy, and Arthur Conan Doyle, but not only the British, but the Irish public remained unmoved. Mrs Green admitted on 19 July that it was indeed true that 'Ireland does not care about this case' (Reid, 413). America also was unconcerned.

The Casement diaries Before his execution at Pentonville prison on 3 August, Casement was received into the Roman Catholic church, having declared himself ready to die 'a glorious death, for Ireland's sake' (Inglis, 370). But the contents of his diaries were more controversial than

his martyrdom. The British continued to use them to discredit Casement after his death; Alfred Noyes, on a visit to the United States in the winter of 1916, referred to Casement as having touched 'the lowest depths that human degradation has ever touched' (ibid., 377). Irish nationalists, for their part, denied that the diaries were genuine, thus implying that no real Irish patriot could be a homosexual. The diaries were opened to public inspection by R. A. Butler in 1959.

The controversy over the authenticity of the Casement diaries continues. Recently Angus Mitchell has made strenuous efforts to discredit them, claiming that they 'were manufactured in an age when acts of homosexuality were considered sexually degenerate', and that 'painstaking analysis', including the use of computerized analysis of key words and expressions, proves that the diaries were forged (Mitchell, 9). But Mitchell undermines his case by claiming that they were forged, not only to discredit Casement because of his treason, but also because of his Putumayo report. Thus the diaries, Mitchell alleges, enabled the British to divert attention from the inquiry, which they found damaging because of their own involvement in South America. But since the inquiry report was published in 1912, it seems unlikely that the forgers would wait until 1916 to publish their work. Roger Sawyer's explanation is more convincing. The problem with accepting the diaries' authenticity is, he points out, compounded by the fact that Sir Basil Thomson, in British intelligence, offered two different accounts of when the diaries were first discovered. The first was that they were found in the Easter weekend of 1916; the second, that they were found 'some months earlier, when we first had evidence of Casement's treachery' (Sawyer, *Diaries*, 9). Sawyer concludes that Thomson's contradictory statements are characteristic of history written from memory, and concludes that the diaries are genuine. Certainly the British authorities had enough evidence, gathered from decoders in Room 40 of the Admiralty old building, to convict Casement of treason; they hardly needed to begin work on a forgery as early as 1914. The motivation for publishing the diaries, Sawyer argues, was because the British realized that, having executed the leaders of the Easter rising, they must prevent Casement from achieving martyr status. And of course the diaries could hardly have been forged in the short time available during Casement's trial and execution. Discrepancies in the handwriting can be attributed to Casement's returning to the diaries to revisit his sexual encounters. Moreover, he may have fantasized about some of the incidents recorded in the diaries. As Sawyer points out, it is hardly likely that a forger would have included a reference to homosexuality as a 'terrible disease'; and, in any case, if the diaries were indeed forgeries, it would have made more sense for the British to destroy them once they had accomplished their purpose. Sawyer's conclusion, that the 'complexity of insider detail' (ibid., 25) bears out their authenticity, is hard to refute. A reading of the published 1910 diary is convincing evidence that it is genuine; the nature of the text, the jottings, the sense of a man writing about what came from his nature, attest to the diary's authenticity. Forensic tests carried out in 2002 by the Giles document laboratory, commissioned by Professor Bill McCormack of Goldsmiths' College, University of London, provided further—and surely final—proof that the diaries are genuine.

Posthumous reputation It is all too easy to make connections between Casement's homosexuality and his treason, citing the apparently parallel cases of the Cambridge Apostles and the like. But Casement made little secret of his growing disenchantment with the British empire, and because he was, as Joseph Conrad remarked, 'all emotion' (Reid, 15), his hatred of England soon dominated his life, as did his rather abstract love of Ireland. The key to his personality lies not in his sexual choices, but in his Anglo-Irish background, and his behaviour is more readily understood in the context of the Anglo-Irishman in revolt against the English part of his inheritance. His forebears are Robert Emmet and William Smith O'Brien, rebels against the English part of their Anglo-Irish nature, for Casement's outlook was essentially that of an Irish protestant, despite his brief encounters with Catholicism.

Casement's remains were returned to Ireland on 23 February 1965 and on 1 March reinterred in Glasnevin cemetery, Dublin, with full nationalist ceremony; his nearest relatives in Ireland ignored the rites. Casement met a last, equally significant fate at the hands of the country he once served. His *Who's Who* entry was not transferred into the *Who Was Who* volume after his death. He became in this sense a non-person, which was a measure of the hatred that he inspired in the British establishment. And yet Stephen Gwynn's *Dictionary of National Biography* entry of 1927 concluded that 'those who knew Roger Casement knew him to be honourable and chivalrous as well as able far beyond the ordinary measure of men'. It is this difference in perception between contemporaries who saw him as a fighter for human rights on the one hand, and a traitor to the country that honoured him with a knighthood, only to see that betrayed, on the other, that ensures that not only Casement, but his diaries, will remain a matter of the most profound controversy.   D. GEORGE BOYCE

Sources B. L. Reid, *The lives of Roger Casement* (1976) · B. Inglis, *Roger Casement* (1973) · R. Sawyer, *Casement: the flawed hero* (1984) · R. Mac-Coll, *Roger Casement: a new judgment* (1956) · H. O. Mackey, *The life and times of Roger Casement* (1954) · D. Gwynn, *The life and death of Roger Casement* (1936) · G. de C. Parmiter, *Roger Casement* (1936) · R. McHugh, 'Casement and German help', *Leaders and men of the Easter rising*, ed. F. X. Martin (1966), 177–87 · *Roger Casement's diaries, 1910: the black and the white*, ed. R. Sawyer (1997) · A. Mitchell, *The Amazon journal of Roger Casement* (1997) · *DNB*
Archives NL Ire., corresp. and papers, MSS 1689–1690, 12114–12118, 13073–13092 · PRO, HO. 161 · PRO NIre., letters [transcripts] | BL, Morel MSS · BLPES, corresp. with E. D. Morel · Bodl. RH, letters to Anti-Slavery Society · JRL, letters to *Manchester Guardian* · NL Ire., letters to John L. Burke, Francis H. Cowper, Richard Morten, and Alice Stopford Green · NYPL, letters to W. B. Cockran · PRO, diaries and notebooks · PRO, Foreign Office corresp., FO 369 and 371 · TCD, letters to Fritz Pincus | FILM BFI NFTVA, *Timewatch*, BBC2, 28 Oct 1992 · BFI NFTVA, current affairs footage · BFI NFTVA, news footage
Likenesses W. Rothenstein, two pencil drawings, 1911, NPG · A. Weckbecker, plaster bust, 1915, NG Ire.; copy, plaster cast, D. Ó

Murchadha · L. Fanto, chalk drawing, 1916, BM · J. Lavery, group portrait, oils (*Trial of Roger Casement, 1915*), Society of King's Inn, Dublin, Ireland; on loan · S. Purser, oils, NG Ire. · S. Purser, oils (study), NG Ire. [*see illus.*] · W. Weckbecker, bronze bust (after copy of plaster bust, 1915), NG Ire. · photographs, repro. in Inglis, *Roger Casement* · photographs, repro. in Reid, *Lives of Roger Casement*
Wealth at death £135 0s. 10d.: probate, 21 Feb 1917, CGPLA Eng. & Wales

Casey, John (1820–1891), mathematician, was born at Kilkenny, in May 1820, the son of William Casey. Educated at first in a small school in his native village, and afterwards at Mitchelstown, he became a teacher under the board of national education in various schools, and ultimately headmaster of the central model schools, Kilkenny. After he succeeded in solving Poncelet's theorem geometrically, he entered into correspondence with George Salmon (fellow of Trinity College, Dublin) and Richard Townsend (1821–1884). At Townsend's suggestion he entered Trinity College, Dublin, in 1858, obtaining a sizarship in 1859 and a scholarship in 1861, and graduating BA in 1862. From 1862 until 1873 he was mathematics master in Kingstown School. On 14 May 1866 he was elected a member of the Royal Irish Academy, and in March 1880 became a member of its council. In 1869 he received from Dublin University the honorary degree of LLD. In 1873 he was offered a professorship of mathematics at Trinity College, but he chose instead to accept the professorship of higher mathematics and mathematical physics in the Catholic University at St Stephen's Green, Dublin. He was elected a member of the London Mathematical Society on 12 November 1874, a fellow of the Royal Society of London on 3 June 1875, a member of the Société Scientifique de Bruxelles in 1878 and of the Société Mathématique de France in 1884, and received the honorary degree of LLD from the Royal University of Ireland in 1885.

In 1881 Casey relinquished his post in the (then partially defunct) Catholic University, and was elected to a fellowship in the new Royal University of Ireland and to a lectureship in mathematics in what was now the University College, St Stephen's Green, which he retained until his death. In the same year he began a series of mathematical textbooks, which had a high reputation. His own research was chiefly confined to two-dimensional geometry, a subject in which he showed great ability. The Italian geometer Cremona spoke with admiration of the elegance and mastery with which he handled difficult and intricate questions. He was largely self-taught, but widened his knowledge by an extensive correspondence with mathematicians in various parts of Europe. His eighteen published papers, almost all dealing with geometry, appeared between 1861 and 1880. From 1862 to 1868 he was one of the editors of the *Oxford, Cambridge, and Dublin Messenger of Mathematics*, and for several years was Dublin correspondent of the *Jahrbuch über die Fortschritte der Mathematik*. He died at home at 86 Iona Terrace, South Circular Road, Dublin, on 3 January 1891.

E. I. CARLYLE, *rev.* JULIA TOMPSON

Sources PRS, 49 (1890–91), xxiv–xxv · private information (1901) · CGPLA Ire. (1891)
Wealth at death £8037 10s.: probate, 6 Feb 1891, CGPLA Ire.

Casey, Richard Gavin Gardiner, Baron Casey (1890–1976), politician in Australia and diplomatist, was born on 29 August 1890 in George Street, Brisbane, Queensland, the elder son (there were no daughters) of Richard Gardiner Casey (1846–1919), a pastoralist with mining interests, of Brisbane, and his wife, Evelyn Jane (1866–1943), younger daughter of George Harris, merchant, of Brisbane. He was educated at Melbourne Church of England grammar school, Melbourne University, and Trinity College, Cambridge, from where he graduated with a second class in mechanical sciences in 1913. Casey returned to Australia via the United States and had barely begun an engineering career when he joined the Australian Imperial Force in October 1914. He served in Egypt, Gallipoli, and France, rising to the rank of general staff officer. He was awarded the MC in 1917 and appointed to the DSO in the following year.

When his father died in 1919, Casey returned to Australia to assume his father's directorships. However, he craved travel and public service, and on 1 October 1924 the Australian prime minister, S. M. Bruce, appointed him Australia's first liaison officer attached to the cabinet secretariat in Whitehall. Casey's task was to keep Bruce *au courant* with day-to-day imperial problems, and occasionally to act for the Australian government in relations with the City and at the League of Nations in Geneva. While in London, Casey married Ethel Marian Sumner (Maie; 1891–1983), writer and artist, and daughter of Major-General Sir Charles Snodgrass Ryan, surgeon, of Melbourne, on 24 June 1926. They were to have a daughter and a son.

In 1931 Casey joined the newly formed United Australia Party and entered the Australian federal parliament as member for Corio (Victoria). His rise was rapid, and he served as assistant treasurer from 1933 to 1935 and as treasurer from 1935 to 1939. His financial management was orthodox, though he had a social conscience which in 1938 led to Australia's first National Health Insurance Bill. Unfortunately R. G. Menzies chose the issue to split the cabinet in a challenge to the leadership of the prime minister, Joseph Lyons, and the bill was shelved. In April 1939 Lyons died, and Casey, Lyons's favourite for successor, chose to stand aside for Bruce. It was a bad miscalculation: Bruce reneged, Casey's rival Menzies assumed the mantle, and Casey lost the treasury.

Menzies appointed Casey minister for supply and development to organize the economy for the impending war. In October 1939 Casey visited London (where he was sworn a privy councillor) for supply talks and to help decide Australian military commitment to Europe. With Casey safely out of the country, Menzies won over the Country Party, who still had wanted Casey as prime minister. Consequently Casey resigned his seat to become Australia's first minister to the United States in March 1940. There he worked hard, usually in harness with the British ambassador, to bring the Americans into the war against Hitler and to secure a guarantee of aid against potential Japanese attacks on British possessions in the Pacific. Both objectives were achieved by late 1941.

Casey's work impressed Winston Churchill, who, in

Richard Gavin Gardiner Casey, Baron Casey (1890–1976), by Walter Stoneman, 1943

early 1942, appointed him British minister resident in the Middle East with a seat in the war cabinet. Among his most ticklish jobs was negotiating the replacing of Sir Claude Auchinleck as commander by Alexander and Montgomery in August 1942. After El Alamein, Casey concentrated upon civil administration. He employed characteristically simple and direct methods. Cabinet was persuaded to 'mop up' inflation in the Middle East, including Iran, by buying up £22¼ million of local currencies with gold between 1943 and 1945. Wheat shortages were solved by massive procurement campaigns. A Lebanese political crisis was averted when a Casey bluff induced the French to release the local cabinet from gaol.

So successful was Casey's trouble-shooting that, in early 1944, Churchill made him governor of Bengal to secure the base for the drive by Mountbatten against the Japanese in Burma. Here too his new broom was effective. He reorganized the embattled administration, inoculated virtually the whole population (54 of 65 million) against smallpox, and set about a gigantic food procurement programme to offset the likelihood of another famine of 1943 proportions, when over a million had died. Casey's methods impressed the government of India, which gave him an extra £10 million subvention in his first year, but upset local politicians, and in his last year in Bengal he ruled by decree. In March 1946 he returned to Australia and in the next year became federal president of the Liberal Party.

Only in December 1949 did Casey manage to re-enter Australian politics and the ministry. From 1951 to 1960, as minister for external affairs, he encouraged closer relations with Asia and the United States via the Colombo plan and ANZUS and SEATO pacts. A notable achievement was the Antarctic treaty of 1959 which secured the continent for peaceful scientific research. In 1956 he privately opposed the use of force over Suez, an issue which helped lose him a ballot for the deputy leadership of the Liberal Party. He retired in 1960 and was created a life peer, as Baron Casey of Berwick and the City of Westminster. From 1965 to 1969 he was governor-general of Australia. In the latter year he was created KG, the first Australian to receive the honour. Always happiest as a lieutenant to the great, Casey had a pleasant, direct manner, innate decency, and a capacity for sustained work which made him one of Australia's and the Commonwealth's outstanding diplomatists and administrators. Nevertheless, he lacked the mental agility, political sense, and sheer ruthlessness necessary to achieve the Australian prime ministership, to which he long aspired. He died of pneumonia in St Vincent's Hospital, Melbourne, on 17 June 1976, and was buried on 22 June in Macedon cemetery.

CARL BRIDGE

Sources NL Aus., Casey MSS · W. J. Hudson, *Casey* (1986) · W. J. Hudson and J. North, eds., *My dear P.M.: R. G. Casey's letters to S. M. Bruce, 1924–1929* (1980) · D. Langmore, *Glittering surfaces: a life of Maie Casey* (1997) · *Australian foreign minister: the diaries of R. G. Casey, 1951–60*, ed. T. B. Millar (1972) · *AusDB* · C. Bridge, 'Casey, Menzies and the politics of Australia's participation in the European war, 1939–40', *Flinders Journal of History and Politics* (1985), 70–80 · C. Bridge, 'R. G. Casey, Australia's first Washington legation and the origins of the Pacific War, 1940–42', *Australian Journal of Politics and History*, 28 (1982), 181–9 · *CGPLA Eng. & Wales* (1977)
Archives BL OIOC, Indian diaries, Photo Eur. 48 [copies] · National Archives of Australia, Melbourne · NL Aus. | CAC Cam., speeches, corresp. with Sir E. L. Spears · National Archives of Australia, Canberra, S. M. Bruce MSS · NL Aus., Maie Casey MSS · NL Aus., R. G. Menzies MSS | FILM BFI NFTVA, news footage · IWM FVA, news footage · National Sound and Film Archive, Canberra, Australia | SOUND National Sound and Film Archive, Canberra, Australia
Likenesses group portrait, photograph, *c.*1935, NL Aus. · photograph, 1942, Hult. Arch. · W. Stoneman, photograph, 1943, NPG [*see illus.*] · W. Dargie, oils, 1968, Parliament House, Canberra, Australia · J. P. Quinn, oils, NL Aus.
Wealth at death £65,800—in England and Wales: probate, 25 March 1977, *CGPLA Eng. & Wales* · A\$621,560—in Australia: *AusDB*

Casey, William Francis (1884–1957), newspaper editor, was born in Cape Town on 2 May 1884, the son of Patrick Joseph Casey, theatre proprietor, of Glenageary, co. Dublin. He was educated in Ireland at Castleknock College and Trinity College, Dublin, of which in later life he was made an honorary LLD. He spent two years reading medicine before changing his mind and turning to law. He was called to the Irish bar in 1909. But again he was undecided on his career. He described his period in the law as 'one year, one brief, one guinea' (*History of The Times*, 5.165). His thoughts had been drawn instead towards the theatre and, while reading for the bar, he became interested in the work of the Abbey Theatre when the directors included W. B. Yeats and Lady Gregory. He worked for a time on the business side, and then in 1908 two of his plays, *The Suburban Groove* and *The Man who Missed the Tide*, were produced

at the Abbey and with their success he decided to try his luck in London. He took with him a letter to Bruce Richmond, editor of the *Times Literary Supplement*. Richmond saw the young writer's promise and it was agreed that Casey should review for the supplement. In 1914 he married Amy Gertrude Pearson-Gee, a widow, daughter of Henry Wilmott. They had no children.

Shortly before the outbreak of the First World War, Casey was offered a post as a sub-editor in the sporting department of *The Times* and from then until his retirement he was a permanent member of that paper's staff. He then served as a foreign sub-editor, with his interest and skill leading to a posting to Washington in 1919, then to Paris in the following year. He returned to London in 1923 as chief foreign sub-editor, regarded as one of the most arduous and anxious positions on the paper. He held this post until 1928. He was part of the group of proprietors and editorial staff who attempted to produce the paper during the general strike of 1926. Afterwards a souvenir volume, *Strike Nights in Printing House Square*, was printed for private record. One of its pictures bore the caption 'Amateurs in the foundry' and showed Casey and Captain Shaw, the chairman's secretary, hard at work on a mechanical process, as 'the champion pair of matrix moulders'.

In 1928 Casey was promoted to the foreign leader-writing staff. He attended many of the Geneva sessions of the League of Nations. In the 1930s his concern grew as to German aspirations in Europe. He was known within the senior ranks as a francophile, but within *The Times* of that period he 'knew that his judgement on foreign matters carried little weight' (*History of The Times*, 4.929). He was part of the group of senior journalists who gathered in 1936 in the office of the paper's deputy editor, R. M. Barrington-Ward—a strong supporter of appeasement with Hitler, as was the editor, Geoffrey Dawson—to demand the paper take a stronger line to 'stand up to Hitler' (Heren, 36). They were ignored. But on the retirement of Dawson in 1941, the new editor, Barrington-Ward, appointed Casey his deputy; the selection was welcomed by the staff, partly because of his greatly more relaxed style. He was a member of many clubs and he would declare that, if he could squeeze in a game of billiards in his dinner break, work went much more easily on his return. Iverach McDonald described him as 'never over-eager to work' (*History of The Times*, 5.164).

Barrington-Ward's health was deteriorating and his death in 1948 threw the burden of the editorship on to Casey's shoulders sooner than he had expected: he himself had never wished to be editor. Only a few months before he had agreed with Barrington-Ward that he 'should very soon retire' (*History of The Times*, 5.164). Stephen Koss says it was 'clearly a stopgap appointment' (Koss, 643). John Pringle, on *The Times* staff, said of Casey's editorship that 'as time went on, he found it harder to face the detailed administrative work and constant decisions … [his deputy, Donald] Tyerman … often had to get the paper out for days on end without much guidance from the editor' (*History of The Times*, 5.199). Yet his willingness to listen to staff and the fact that, unusually for an editor, he 'seemed to have all the time in the world' (Heren, 90), made him a popular figure among the journalists under him. He retired as editor in 1952 and died in a nursing home at 10 Porchester Terrace, Paddington, London, on 20 April 1957. He was cremated at Golders Green on 26 April.   A. P. ROBBINS, *rev.* MARC BRODIE

Sources *The Times* (22 April 1957) · *The Times* (24 April 1957) · [S. Morison and others], *The history of The Times*, 4 (1952) · I. McDonald, *The history of The Times*, 5 (1984) · personal knowledge (1971) · S. E. Koss, *The rise and fall of the political press in Britain*, 2 (1984) · L. Heren, *Memories of 'Times' past* (1988) · *WWW · CGPLA Eng. & Wales* (1957)
Archives News Int. RO, papers
Likenesses C. Orde, chalk drawing, 1951, Times Newspapers Ltd, London
Wealth at death £2692 5s. 9d.: probate, 19 July 1957, *CGPLA Eng. & Wales*

Cash, John (1822–1880), ribbon manufacturer, was born on 16 February 1822 at Sherbourne House, Coventry, the eldest son of Joseph Cash, a Quaker stuff merchant and leading businessman. John's younger brother **Joseph Cash** (1826–1880), ribbon manufacturer, was born on 28 October 1826 at the same address. After serving seven-year apprenticeships with stuff merchants and so becoming entitled to become freemen of the city, the brothers operated a silk ribbon-making business from a warehouse in Hertford Street, Coventry, in the early 1840s.

In 1846 John and Joseph Cash built a factory at West Orchard, Coventry, equipping it mainly with steam-powered Jacquard looms and taking on French designers to create their ribbons. In 1852 John Cash married Mary Sibree, the daughter of an Independent minister. Joseph married Sarah Iliffe in 1851, and, like his brother, raised a large family. By 1856, they employed 200 weavers in the factory, and expressed their Quaker ideals by operating a sickness benefit club and organizing outings for their employees' holidays. The brothers paid some of the highest wages in the local ribbon trade until 1857, when they were obliged to adopt the lower wage standard imposed by Coventry masters.

Following wage disputes among the outworkers, however, and under the guidance of their philosopher friend Charles Bray, as well as being prompted by their Quaker principles, the Cash brothers drew up plans to build a factory which combined the old outwork method of weaving with modern factory organization. They bought a 7 acre field a mile from the city centre and planned to build 100 'top shops', or cottage factories, arranged round a square. Capital for their project came mainly from relatives and fellow Quaker businessmen. In the event, only forty-eight houses were built at Kingfield, starting in 1857. Even so, the Cashes set up a dramatic society, sports clubs, and evening classes for their workers.

In 1860 the Anglo-French trade treaty brought an influx of high-quality, low-priced ribbons, and many Coventry firms collapsed, unable to compete. J. and J. Cash, as it now was, suffered severe losses, and the brothers were obliged radically to restructure their partnership. They reorganized the top shops on factory lines and set up a departmental structure to embark on diversification. Their first new line was narrow frillings, for which they took out a patent in September 1860. Thanks to the Cash brothers' prudent management, as well as the guarantee of capital from relatively safe sources, the business survived, with diversification into other fabric lines an important factor in its continuing viability.

The brothers preserved their reputation as benevolent employers, and during a strike in 1860 refused to lock out their employees. By 1862, however, the general collapse of trade appears to have made them somewhat more exacting and harsher.

John and Joseph Cash were known throughout Coventry for their philanthropy, and Joseph founded St Thomas's infant school. Both brothers made handsome contributions to local charities. Additionally, John served as a Liberal on Coventry city council, 1868–76. John Cash became increasingly drawn to the Independent nonconformists, and established an Independent chapel in Vicar Lane. His work for the Independents caused him to be disowned by the Quakers in 1844.

John Cash was in poor health for the last two years of his life, but kept up his daily routine and his regular visits to business acquaintances. On one occasion he injured his leg at Cheltenham railway station, but was determined to fulfil his day's engagement. On returning home, he had to have the boot cut off the swollen limb, which was found to be broken.

John Cash was reserved in character, but inclined to be abrupt in manner in business discussions, as a result of which he was sometimes misunderstood. Although keen to support local causes dear to his heart, such as education, he was never one to court popularity. In private life, among family and friends, he was generally frank and genial, and eager to hear the views of others as well as (sometimes forcibly) express his own.

Both brothers died in 1880, John on 9 September at Rosehill, his Coventry residence, leaving a personal estate of less than £60,000, and Joseph on 14 October at his home, Bird Grove, Coventry, leaving an estate of under £45,000. John was buried at Coventry cemetery on 14 September; the chief mourners included his five sons and three nephews. The partnership was taken over by John's eldest son, Sidney (1856–1931), and his cousin Joseph (1853–1927). The well-known Cash's name-tapes were introduced only in the early twentieth century, originally as labels for manufacturers who wished to identify their products.

ADRIAN ROOM

Sources S. A. Vertigan, 'J. & J. Cash Limited: a business history, 1846–1928', BA diss., U. Nott., 1982 · S. A. Vertigan, 'Cash, John, and Cash, Joseph', *DBB* · *Coventry Herald* (17 Sept 1880) · *Coventry Standard* (17 Sept 1880) · *Coventry Standard* (22 Oct 1880) · *CGPLA Eng. & Wales* (1881)
Archives Coventry City RO
Wealth at death under £60,000: probate, 6 Jan 1881, *CGPLA Eng. & Wales* · under £45,000—Joseph Cash: probate, 18 Nov 1880, *CGPLA Eng. & Wales*

Cash, John Theodore (1854–1936), physician and pharmacologist, was born at Manchester on 16 December 1854, the younger son of John Walker Cash, who retired from business and took up farming near Leeds, and his wife, Martha Midgley. He was educated at Bootham School, York, and the Edinburgh collegiate school, and studied medicine at the University of Edinburgh, where he qualified MB, CM, and MRCS (Eng.) in 1876, and gained a gold medal for his MD thesis in 1879. In 1881 he married (Margaret) Sophia (d. 1924), daughter of the statesman John *Bright; the couple had two sons and two daughters. Sophia Cash was an accomplished artist and painted the beautiful watercolours used to illustrate her husband's lectures on materia medica.

After graduation Cash studied the methods of pharmacological research in Berlin, Vienna, and Paris. He was then house physician at the Edinburgh Royal Infirmary, but returned to Berlin and afterwards moved to Leipzig, where he worked with the celebrated physiologist Carl Ludwig. On arriving in London he began researches with T. L. Brunton at St Bartholomew's Hospital, and from 1880 to 1884 published many valuable pharmacological papers which were representative of a new and accurate scientific approach to the elucidation of the actions of drugs. His elaborate and precise researches upon the various alkaloids of aconitum, begun prior to 1886, paved the way for his pioneer endeavours, by researches on the substituted ammonias and benzene compounds, to lay the foundations of a relationship between chemical constitution and pharmacological action; this investigation, published jointly with Brunton in the *Philosophical Transactions of the Royal Society* in 1884, indicated to synthetic chemists paths towards the discovery of new remedies. In the years that followed he made other communications to the Royal Society on this subject.

The high scientific standard of Cash's researches led to his appointment to the regius chair of materia medica and therapeutics in Aberdeen University in 1886 and to his election as a fellow of the Royal Society in the following year. He was a skilled experimentalist, ingenious in devising recording apparatus, and imbued with the axiom that in order to obtain true results the least disturbance of the tissues was of paramount importance. His gracious manner and cultured language as a lecturer inspired honourable work by his students and his scientific example encouraged Arthur Robertson Cushny to adopt pharmacology as his life work.

Cash was dean of the faculty of medicine at Aberdeen University and from 1911 to 1919 a member of the General Medical Council when he took a large share in editing the *British Pharmacopœia* of 1914. He received the honorary degree of LLD from the universities of Edinburgh and Aberdeen.

Cash's chief recreation was a passionate devotion to salmon and trout fishing: he was an expert on the pathology of diseases of the salmon, and a particular salmon fly bears his name. The opening of the salmon fishing season could always be dated by his disappearance from the laboratory after months of continuous research. He retired from his chair in 1919 and settled at Hereford where, on the Wye, he enjoyed his favourite pastime but continued to be keenly interested in pharmacological researches. Cash died at his home, Albyn House, Broomy Hill, Hereford, on 30 November 1936 and was buried at Hereford.

W. J. Dilling, *rev.* M. P. Earles

Sources C. R. Marshall, *Obits. FRS*, 2 (1936–8) [incl. bibliography] · *WWW*, 1929–40 · W. J. Dilling, 'John Theodore Cash', *Aberdeen University Review*, 24 (1936–7), 133–6 · *BMJ* (12 Dec 1936), 1238 · *The Lancet* (12 Dec 1936), 1429 · *Nature*, 138 (1937), 1087 · W. F. Bynum, 'Chemical structure and pharmacological action: a chapter in the history of 19th century molecular pharmacology', *Bulletin of the History of Medicine*, 44 (1970), 518–38, esp. 532 · *CGPLA Eng. & Wales* (1937)
Likenesses portrait, repro. in Marshall, *Obits. FRS*
Wealth at death £45,768 9s. 9d.: resworn probate, 24 Feb 1937, *CGPLA Eng. & Wales*

Cash, Joseph (1826–1880). *See under* Cash, John (1822–1880).

Cashmore, Hilda (1876–1943), university teacher and welfare worker, was born on 22 August 1876 at Norton House, Norton Malreward, Somerset, the fifth of a family of six sisters. Her father was Samuel Cashmore, a merchant, and her mother was Mary, formerly Edmunds. She early became interested in political and social issues, her father being a Liberal and a free-trader. The sisters discussed politics as children and were active in local election campaigns. After an education at home in Barrow Gurney in Somerset, to which she moved as a young girl, Hilda Cashmore was educated at Cheltenham Ladies' College and went as an exhibitioner to Somerville College, Oxford (1899–1902), where she gained a second class in modern history.

After Oxford, Hilda Cashmore took the Cambridge teachers' diploma and went to work as a teacher at the Chesterfield Pupil Teacher Centre. In 1904 she became a history tutor at the Day Training College of University College, Bristol, where she was a charismatic lecturer. A lifelong supporter of the Labour Party, trade unions, and the Workers' Educational Association, she was impelled by her political persuasion, together with her Quaker faith, to an interest in establishing a university settlement, a building where staff and students could provide educational and welfare facilities in areas of social deprivation. At the same time students could be trained in social work. She inspired her students at the Day Training College with an enthusiasm for social work—by 1911 more than a hundred of them were enrolled in the Women's Guild for Social Service. In that year the university authorities allowed her to make a study tour of provision in the USA and Canada, where she visited the Columbia University Settlement in New York and the North-Western University Settlement in Chicago. On returning to England she became the first warden of the Bristol University Settlement at Barton Hill and was lecturer in local government and responsible for the supervision of practical work for the Bristol diploma in social study, an early university training course for social workers. She left this post in 1926 to become the warden of the Manchester University Settlement, also combined with teaching for the Manchester social study diploma. Homesick for her rural Somerset in the rundown slums of Ancoats, she returned to Bristol in 1934. Her influence in community social work was more than local. She was a member of the executive committee of the British Association of Residential Settlements from its foundation in 1920 and became its president in 1926. For many years she was also an active member of the tobacco, corsets, and toy manufacturing trades boards. She was a strong proponent of providing community centres on new housing estates and of using local schools as neighbourhood centres for community care.

A pacifist by conviction and a leader by temperament, Hilda Cashmore was the secretary of the Society of Friends relief mission to France from November 1914 to May 1915, working in Paris, Vitry, Épernay, and Châlons-sur-Marne. During the Polish-Russian war in 1920 she worked in Galicia, Poland, with the Friends' War Victims Relief Committee as an anti-typhus team member. In the early 1930s she joined a group interested in conciliation between the British government and the Indian National Movement. As a result she visited Bombay, Delhi, and Calcutta in 1932, and included in her travels some time at the Friends Mission Centre in Itarsi in the Central Provinces. This encouraged her to spend from 1934 to 1938 creating a settlement in Itarsi 'to which', in her words, 'educated young Indians and English people from different parts of the country who are interested in the new social problems can freely come for study, for meditation, for thinking' (Hilda Cashmore, 75). While in India she travelled widely, including speaking at the All India Women's Conference in Karachi in 1934. She lectured to teachers and welfare workers in many parts of India on schooling, neighbourhood schools, and community centres.

Back in Bristol after 1938 Hilda Cashmore lived at 107 Church Road and continued to be active in the university settlement. From 1940 she worked for the Bristol Council for Refugees, developing the work of both the Non-Aryan Relief Committee of the Bristol Council of Churches and the Jewish Relief Committee. She was a member of the Bristol Committee of the Friends' Relief Service and from 1941 to her death the district service organizer of the Women's Voluntary Service in east Bristol.

Hilda Cashmore's life was one of dedicated Quaker service. She regarded herself as physically plain, and could be reserved and detached. In a memoir printed after her death by her closest friends they describe her sense of fun, her love of people, and most of all her dedication. She was a prolific letter writer and wrote some poetry for her private enjoyment. A friend (Violet Markham) described her as born in the wrong century: 'in the 13th or 14th century Hilda Cashmore would have tuned in naturally to the wavelength of an ordered community, vowed to poverty, chastity and obedience' (Hilda Cashmore, 12). Hilda Cashmore died at the British Hospital for Mothers and Babies at Woolwich, London, where her sister was matron, on 15 November 1943.   JOHN B. THOMAS

Sources Hilda Cashmore, 1876–1943 [n.d., c.1950] • The Times (25 Feb 1976), 7b [Hilda Cashmore memorial fund] • W. T. Sanigar, Leaves from a Barton Hill notebook, 1 (1954) • Somerville College register, 1879–1971 [1972] • b. cert.

Likenesses photograph, 1934, repro. in Hilda Cashmore, 1876–1943, frontispiece

Wealth at death £2360 4s. 6d.: probate, 29 Dec 1943, CGPLA Eng. & Wales

Casley, David (1681/2–1754), librarian, was probably born in the West Riding of Yorkshire, perhaps near Sowerby, the son of Robert Casley. He attended Meadowlane School in Leeds, and in 1707, aged twenty-five, entered Trinity College, Cambridge, as a sizar, and took his BA degree in 1711. In 1718 he was appointed deputy to Richard Bentley, who was the keeper of the Royal Library and of the Cotton Library. Because of the ruinous state of Cotton House, Westminster, where the two libraries were installed, the board of works took a seven-year lease on Essex House in Essex Street, the Strand, and when this expired the libraries were moved in 1730 to Ashburnham House, Little Dean's Yard, Westminster.

Between 1720 and 1725 Casley visited Humfrey Wanley on a number of occasions to consult volumes of the Harley manuscripts on behalf of Bentley, and to borrow manuscripts for Bentley's use. These visits sometimes resulted in Wanley's making uncomplimentary references in his diary to Casley. The latter also collated manuscripts in the Harley collection for Jacques Philippe D'Orville (1696–1751), the classical scholar from the Netherlands. In 1722 Casley had in his care the manuscripts of John Walker of Trinity College, Cambridge, and he asked Wanley if Lord Oxford was interested in buying them for the Harley collection.

On 30 March 1728 Casley married Mary Martin at Dry Drayton, Cambridgeshire. According to William Cole she was the daughter of Mrs Martin, the letter-carrier of Cambridge. In October of that year Casley became a member of the Gentlemen's Society of Spalding, Lincolnshire. At this time he was transcribing documents in the Cotton collection for the Revd Thomas Rutherfurth, rector of Papworth St Agnes, Cambridgeshire. Cole later acquired Rutherfurth's manuscripts and wrote that, though Casley was 'an ingenious man, and understood old writings and ancient hands well' (BL, Add. MS 5846, fol. 85), there were many mistakes in his transcripts.

The Royal Library and the Cotton manuscripts were damaged by a fire which broke out in Ashburnham House on 23 October 1731. Bentley had in 1725 transferred the office of keeper of these libraries to his son Richard, but the elder Bentley was staying at Ashburnham House when the fire occurred, and helped with the salvage work, as did Casley. Robert Freind, headmaster of Westminster School, stated that the famous Codex Alexandrinus (Royal MS I.D. V–VIII) was saved by Dr Bentley, but the report of the committee which investigated the fire gave Casley the credit for this. Casley was a member of this committee and compiled the list of damaged and destroyed Cotton manuscripts which was printed in an appendix to the committee's report, published in 1732.

Casley published in 1734 his Catalogue of the manuscripts of the King's Library: an appendix to the catalogue of the Cottonian

Library; together with an account of books burnt or damaged by a late fire. He had produced proposals for printing by subscription such a catalogue before 1730 when the library was still in Essex House (BL, Add. MS 44919, fol. 103). Warner and Gilson wrote that, though it was not a good catalogue, it was better than Edward Bernard's descriptions in his catalogue of 1697, and the preface was not 'quite devoid of palaeographical interest' (Warner and Gilson, xxxi). Between 1733 and 1736 Casley wrote descriptions of Harley manuscripts 2408 to 5709, which were included in the catalogue of this collection published by the British Museum between 1759 and 1763. The preface to this catalogue (vol. 1, p. 28) described Casley's entries as 'extreamly concise', which is not surprising, considering the speed with which they were produced.

On 23 September 1742 Casley wrote to Lord Hardwicke, the lord chancellor, asking to be appointed keeper of the Cotton Library, of which he had been deputy keeper for twenty-five years. Three years later Richard Bentley the younger, who was often in financial difficulties, sold the office of keeper of the Royal Library to Claudius Amyand. Writing to John Ward at Gresham College on 26 November 1745, Casley complained that Bentley and Amyand had kept him in ignorance of their negotiations—'they have strugled with me for the keys, but I have got the better of them, Mr. Amyand consenting, when he could not help it, that I should have the sole keeping of all the keys' (BL, Add. MS 6209, fol. 314).

When the British Museum was founded in 1753 the Cotton manuscripts were incorporated in its collections (the Royal Library was presented to the museum by George II in 1757), and in February 1754 a committee of the trustees of the museum inspected them in the old dormitory of Westminster School. They found that Casley was disabled by age and infirmity from carrying out his duties, so the care of the library had devolved on his wife, with the occasional help of the Revd Richard Widmore, keeper of the library of Westminster Abbey. By July Casley was so old and deaf that he could not go out of doors, and on 20 September he died, probably at home (the announcement of his death in the *Gentleman's Magazine* gave his name as Castelle). He had made his will on 26 July 1752, giving his address as the Bowling Alley, Westminster, where he had lived since at least 1742. He left £1500 to his daughter Elizabeth, who later married Richard Pownall, and £1500 to his wife, Mary. The residue of his estate was to be shared equally between them. He was buried in the churchyard of St Margaret's, Westminster, on 23 September 1754.

P. R. HARRIS

Sources W. W. Rouse Ball and J. A. Venn, eds., *Admissions to Trinity College, Cambridge*, 3 (1911) · *The diary of Humfrey Wanley, 1715–1726*, ed. C. E. Wright and R. C. Wright, 2 vols. (1966) · G. F. Warner and J. P. Gilson, *Catalogue of Western manuscripts in the old Royal and King's collections*, 1 (1921) · Nichols, *Illustrations*, 4.446–8 · W. Cole's MSS, vol. 45, BL, Add. MS 5846, fol. 85 · will, PRO, PROB 11/811, sig. 268 · minutes of trustees' general meetings, 13 Feb 1754, BM, CE 1/1, 25 · *GM*, 1st ser., 24 (1754), 435 · parish register, Westminster, St Margaret's [burial], 23 Sept 1754 · W. A. Shaw, ed., *Calendar of treasury books*, 32/2, PRO (1957), 64 · *IGI* · D. Casley, 'Prospectus for printing a catalogue of the MSS of H. M. Library', BL, Add. MS 44919, fol.

103 · Casley to Lord Hardwicke, 23 Sept 1742, BL, Add. MS 36269, fol. 1 · Casley to John Ward, 26 Nov 1745, BL, Add. MS 6209, fol. 314 · *An account of the Gentlemen's Society at Spalding, being an introduction to the Reliquiae Galeanae* (1784), no. 20 [3/1] of *Bibliotheca topographica Britannica*, ed. J. Nichols (1780–1800), account of the Gentlemen's Society of Spalding · 'A report from the committee appointed to view the Cottonian Library', *Reports from Committees of the House of Commons*, 1 (1732), 443–536
Archives BL, Add. MSS
Wealth at death at least £3000; incl. £1500 to wife; £1500 to daughter; residue to them jointly: will, PRO, PROB 11/811, sig. 268

Caslon [*née* Cartlich], **Elizabeth** (1730–1795), typefounder, was born in Foster Lane, London, on 31 May 1730, the daughter of William Cartlich, refiner, of Foster Lane, and his wife, Elizabeth. She was baptized on 4 June at St John Zachary, London. On 25 June 1751 she married William *Caslon (1720–1778) [*see under* Caslon, William (1692–1766)], typefounder, of Chiswell Street; they had two sons, William and Henry. When her husband died intestate, on 17 August 1778, Elizabeth and her sons each inherited one third share of the typefounding business, which she continued, trading as Elizabeth Caslon & Sons. She was a talented businesswoman, having assisted her husband during his lifetime in the management of the foundry. In 1785 the firm produced an extensive type specimen book on sixty-four leaves, dedicated to George III. With Edward Fry & Co., Vincent Figgins, Simon Stephenson, and Miles Swinney she was an active member of the Society of Typefounders, which she helped to establish in 1793, on one occasion being one of a deputation of two founders who conferred with printers on the price of type. One son, Henry, died in 1788, leaving his share of the foundry to his widow, Elizabeth, and in 1792 the other son, William, sold his share for £3000 and acquired Jackson's foundry.

Elizabeth Caslon died in London on 24 October 1795 from the effects of a paralytic stroke. The management of the Chiswell Street foundry was taken over by her daughter-in-law **Elizabeth Caslon** [*née* Rowe; *other married name* Strong] (*c*.1755–1809), typefounder, who was the daughter of William Rowe of Higham Hill, Walthamstow, Essex. She married Henry Caslon (*c*.1755–1788), typefounder, of 62 Chiswell Street; they had a son, Henry (1786–1850). On her husband's death in 1788 Elizabeth inherited his share of the foundry with her son, then aged two. On 24 August 1799 she married Jonathan Strong (*d*. 1802), a doctor of medicine, but she retained the name Caslon for business purposes. The terms of her mother-in-law's will caused a dispute, as a result of which the estate was thrown into chancery and, by order of the court, the foundry was put up for auction in March 1799. Elizabeth purchased it on behalf of her son, Henry, for £520, a sum which in part reflects the decline of the foundry in the face of competition since 1792. Despite suffering from ill health—she was a prey to pulmonary attacks—she determined to revive the foundry, and took into partnership a distant relative, Nathaniel Catherwood, in 1799; together they produced a specimen sheet in 1800. Elizabeth commissioned the foundry's first modern face types from the engraver John Isaac Drury. These featured prominently in a type specimen of 1805 but modern faces already appear

Elizabeth Caslon (1730–1795), by William Satchwell Leney (after Charles Catton the elder)

on surviving single-leaf specimens of 1796 and 1799; a further specimen appeared as a supplement to Stower's *Printer's Grammar* in 1808.

In the spring of 1808 Elizabeth Caslon went to live at Hotwells in Bristol for the sake of her health. She died there on 3 March 1809 and was buried in Bristol Cathedral on 9 March. Her business partner, Nathaniel Catherwood, died on 6 June 1809, aged forty-five, and the foundry was continued by her son, Henry, in partnership with John James Catherwood, Nathaniel's brother.

IAN MAXTED

Sources T. B. Reed, *A history of the old English letter foundries*, rev. A. F. Johnson, 2nd edn (1952), 244–8 · W. T. Berry and A. F. Johnson, *Catalogue of specimens of printing types … 1665–1830* (1935), 12, 19–23 · J. Batt, *William Caslon* (1973), 372–3 · I. Maxted, *The London book trades, 1775–1800: a preliminary checklist of members* (1977), 40 · IGI · *Bristol Cathedral registers*, ed. C. R. Hudleston (1933), 45 · J. Mosley, *British type specimens before 1831: a hand-list* (1984)
Likenesses W. S. Leney, stipple (after C. Catton the elder), NPG [*see illus.*] · engraving, repro. in *Freemason's Magazine* (March 1796)

Caslon, Elizabeth (*c*.1755–1809). *See under* Caslon, Elizabeth (1730–1795).

Caslon, William, the elder (1692–1766), typefounder, was born at Cradley, Worcestershire, the son of George Caslon (*d*. 1709), shoemaker, of nearby Halesowen, and Mary Steven. George was the son of William Castledowne, also a shoemaker of Halesowen, and an earlier form of the family surname, recorded in Worcestershire in 1593, was Castelldon. The traditional date for his birth is 1692, but one biographer (Johnson Ball) argued for the following year on the grounds that the date of birth is not likely to

have been more than a few weeks earlier than the record of his baptism on 23 April 1693.

Education, early work, and marriage Caslon was apprenticed in London on 17 May 1706 to Edward Cookes, loriner (metalworker), who according to John Nichols specialized in the engraving of ornaments on gun barrels. Cookes was also under contract from 1707 to 1715 to the Board of Ordnance to engrave the maker's name, the broad arrow, and the royal cipher on the locks of guns supplied to them. Nichols gives Vine Street, Minories, a district favoured by gunsmiths, as Caslon's first residence. From 1716 (which in the Caslon foundry's type specimen book of 1851 was given as the date of the establishment of the firm) to 1719 Caslon's name appears as an engraver of muskets in the records of the Board of Ordnance, a contract that appears to have been terminated in favour of a cheaper supplier. About 1980 the lock of a ship's musketoon in the armouries, Tower of London, having been removed for refurbishment, was found to be stamped on the reverse with Caslon's name.

There are some inconsistencies in accounts of Caslon's introduction to typefounding. That of John Nichols, assistant and later successor to the younger William Bowyer, has the authority that is due to information obtained from the family of Caslon's first major patron. According to Nichols,

one considerable branch of his employment was to make tools for bookbinders and for the chasing of silver plate. Whilst he was engaged in this employment, the elder Mr. *Bowyer* accidentally saw in the bookshop of Mr. *Daniel Browne*, bookseller, near Temple-Bar, the lettering of a book uncommonly neat; and enquiring who the artist was by whom the letters were made, Mr. *Caslon* was introduced to his acquaintance, and was taken by him to Mr *James's* foundery in *Bartholomew Close*. *Caslon* had never before that time seen any part of the business; and being asked by his friend if he thought he could undertake to cut types, he requested a single day to consider the matter, and then replied he had no doubt that he could. From this answer, Mr. *Bowyer* lent him 200*l*. Mr. *Bettenham* lent the same sum, and Mr. *Watts* 100*l*.; and by that assistance our ingenious artist applied himself assiduously to his new pursuit, and was eminently successful. The three printers above-mentioned were of course his constant customers.   (Nichols, 585n.)

T. C. Hansard gave a different account, in which the printer who noticed the quality of Caslon's bookbinding tools was John Watts, printer in Little Queen Street, not Bowyer. Hansard's version appears to be the result of an attempt to conflate the earlier narratives of Edward Rowe Mores with Nichols, and although later writers such as Charles Henry Timperley and Talbot Baines Reed accepted it—though the latter also complained of 'confusion' in stories about Caslon's early career (Reed, 230n.)—it appears to have no contemporary foundation.

On 29 August 1717 Caslon married Sarah Pearman (*bap.* 1689, *d*. 1728), at St Peter Cornhill, London; she was the daughter of Thomas Pearman, a butcher of Clent, Staffordshire, and Mary Cookes, whose son John, like Caslon, was an apprentice of Edward Cookes. It is likely, as Ball suggests, that this marriage provided the capital that enabled Caslon to establish his business. The first child,

William Caslon the elder (1692–1766), by John Faber junior (after Francis Kyte, 1740)

named William [*see below*], was born in 1720 and baptized at St Botolph, Aldgate, on 23 June; two, possibly three, further children were baptized between 1722 and 1726.

New types The first type by Caslon for which there is any substantial contemporary record is the Arabic that he cut for the Society for Promoting Christian Knowledge (SPCK), an episode for which Edward Rowe Mores gives a brief but accurate account. The SPCK approached Samuel Palmer to print a psalter and New Testament in Arabic to be sent to Christian communities in the East. Palmer, whose printing office in Bartholomew Close adjoined the typefoundry of John James, made an estimate based on the use of a seventeenth-century Great Primer Arabic in the James foundry. When it was calculated that this size would make the books too expensive, the SPCK commissioned a smaller Arabic for an English body from Caslon, who was recommended to them in 1722 by Thomas Guy. Caslon's cutting of the type was delayed by illness and his inexperience, but it was completed in 1724 when payment was made for 355 punches, 366 matrices, and a mould. The psalter was printed in 1725 and the New Testament in 1727. Mores relates that Caslon cut his name in pica roman and set it below a specimen of his Arabic. Palmer encouraged him to complete the type, and

> as the performance exceeded the letter of the other founders of the time, *Mr. Palmer*, whose circumstances required credit with those which by this advice was now obstructed, repented the advice and discouraged *Mr. Casl*[on] from any further progress. *Mr. Casl*[on] disgusted applied to Mr. Bowyer, and was encouraged to proceed by *Mr Bowyer* and *Mr Bettenham*. (Mores, 60)

This story (misquoted by Nichols in 1785, and also by Reed and later historians) indicates that Palmer depended on

credit with the established typefounders, including James. The deteriorating relationship between Palmer and Caslon is corroborated by an anecdote of George Psalmanazar, who claimed that Palmer, having been asked to use a new Hebrew cut by Caslon and also to obtain some special roman characters, was unable to pay for it and was also probably afraid of the reaction of the James foundry. He therefore blackened Caslon's character by calling him 'an idle, dilatory workman' who 'hated work, and was not to be depended upon' (Nichols, 537n.).

However the connection was made, the suggestion that Bowyer was an early patron of Caslon's typefounding is confirmed by observation of the use that his printing office made of types from Caslon's new foundry. Caslon's pica, of which the first known use is an *Anacreon* printed by Bowyer in 1725, was based very closely indeed on a pica roman and italic that appears on the specimen sheet of the widow of the Amsterdam printer Dirck Voskens, *c.*1695, and which Bowyer had used for some years. Caslon's pica replaces it in his printing from 1725. This use of the pica is the first that has been traced of all Caslon's roman types. Nichols (in his supplement to Mores's narrative) asserted that Caslon's Hebrew and English roman were used by Bowyer for his part of an edition of Selden's works in 1722–6. The Hebrew in this work may be Caslon's; however, the roman and italic, as A. F. Johnson showed, are not.

Adoption of Caslon's types Caslon's other roman and italic types, although they are less evidently modelled on existing types, are seen coming into use during the following years in the printing of Bowyer and his contemporaries. Caslon's Great Primer roman, first used in 1728, a type that was much admired in the twentieth century, is clearly related to the Text Romeyn of Voskens, a type of the early seventeenth century used by several London printers and now attributed to the punch-cutter Nicolas Briot of Gouda. However, certain of Caslon's other sizes, notably the Long Primer no. 1, which is ubiquitous in London-printed works in small formats during the half-century following its appearance in the specimen of 1734, are intelligent adaptations of the pica, made to work on its smaller body. According to Mores, the Canon roman which appears in Caslon's specimens was acquired from the Andrews foundry. It is a type that appeared on Joseph Moxon's type specimen of 1669 and was probably originally cut by him. It was in common use for title-pages and headings for about a century. The Canon italic is Caslon's.

In 1727 Caslon moved his workshop, first of all to 'a small house' or 'a garret' in Helmet Row, and shortly afterwards to Ironmonger Row, the streets lying on either side of St Luke's churchyard, Old Street (Nichols, 317n.; Mores, 231). After the death of his first wife in 1728, Caslon married Elizabeth Long on 11 September 1729 in St Giles Cripplegate; the couple had three children. His first known complete type specimen sheet, bearing the address Ironmonger Row, is dated 1734. Some earlier undated fragments of it survive. The sheet shows fourteen roman and italic types, seven two-line or titling types, black letter, Anglo-Saxon, and Gothic; the non-Latin types are Greek,

Hebrew, Coptic, Armenian, Samaritan, and the Arabic made for the SPCK. There are also some ornaments. By 1737 the foundry had moved to Chiswell Street, where it remained until 1936. The specimen sheet of 1734, incorporating the new address, appears in Chambers's *Cyclopaedia* from the second edition (1738) to the fifth (1752–3); Caslon is also shown holding it in the portrait by Francis Kyte (1740). Later specimen sheets were issued in 1742 and 1746; two separate sheets showing non-Latin and roman and italic types were issued in 1748 and 1749; an associated specimen sheet of ornaments, of which no copy is known, was issued about this time.

Growing reputation In 1733 Henry Newman of the SPCK sent a specimen of Caslon's types to Edward Hutchison of Boston with the comment that they were the work of 'that Artist who seems to aspire to outvying all the Workmen in his way in Europe, so that our Printers send no more to Holland for the Elzevir and other Letters which they formerly valued themselves much on' (W. O. B. Allen and E. McLure, *Two Hundred Years: the History of the Society for Promoting Christian Knowledge*, 1898, 57). This prescient remark was confirmed in practice. For the next fifty years the types of the Caslon foundry are prominent in printing done in Britain and British North America, and for some years the rival foundries established in London, like those of Cottrell and Jackson (former Caslon apprentices), made types that were modelled on Caslon's. The new Bristol foundry of Joseph Fry, which initially made types following the new style of John Baskerville, also found it useful to make a set of types that was claimed, with justice, to be indistinguishable from those of the Caslon foundry. Echoing the claim of Newman, John Nichols wrote that Caslon

> arrived to that perfection, as not only to free us from the necessity of importing types from *Holland*, but in the beauty and elegance of those made by him so far surpassed the best productions of foreign artificers, that his types have not unfrequently been exported to the continent. (Nichols, 317n.)

With the exception of the special case of British North America, where Benjamin Franklin made extensive use of Caslon's types and where they figure largely in Dunlap's printing of the Declaration of Independence (1776), there is very little evidence to support this loyal claim. A small Caslon italic appears in the *Sallust* of Joachin Ibarra in Madrid in 1772, Caslon titling types have been noticed in Portuguese printing, and the edition of the Diderot and D'Alembert *Encyclopédie* that was printed at Leghorn between 1769 and 1779 is set wholly in Caslon types; however, Leghorn, as a free port much used by British ships, is another special case.

Retirement and death Caslon married his third wife, Elizabeth Warter (*d.* in or after 1760), on 9 July 1741 at Lincoln's Inn chapel, Holborn. He retired in 1750 to a house in the Hackney Road, where he was a justice of the peace for Middlesex. Soon after he removed to his 'country house' on Bethnal Green, he died there on 23 January 1766 (Reed, 241). He was buried in St Luke's churchyard, Old Street, London, where his name and those of other members of

the family appear on a monument. His will, dated 22 January 1760 and proved on 31 January 1766, left the business to his son William, and shared his personal estate between his wife, Elizabeth, and his children, William, Mary, and Thomas.

In his *General History of the Science and Practice of Music* (1776), Sir John Hawkins describes Caslon's hospitality and the musical entertainments and monthly concerts that took place in Caslon's house in Chiswell Street, where the concert room was fitted with an organ and the refreshments included ale brewed by Caslon himself. The *Universal Magazine* for June 1750 contains a folding-plate headed 'A True and Exact representation of the Art of Cutting and Preparing Letters for Printing', which, according to John Nichols, represents the interior of Caslon's foundry and some of its workmen.

William Caslon the younger and successors William Caslon the younger (1720–1778) followed his father as a punch-cutter, and his first types, an Ethiopic and a Greek, are dated 1738. He signed five roman and italic types which appear on the foundry's sheet dated 1742. The quality of his punch-cutting is not generally held to match that of his father. The specimen of 1746 was issued in the name of the partnership William Caslon & Son, and the younger Caslon increasingly took over the management of the business, eventually inheriting the foundry upon his father's death. It was to him that one of the most gifted of the foundry's apprentices, Joseph Jackson, 'expecting to be rewarded for his ingenuity', took a punch that he had made after secretly watching his masters at work, and received a blow and the threat of gaol (*GM*). Some years later, a request for an increase of wages having been sent to the elder Caslon, who was already in retirement, Jackson and a fellow journeyman Thomas Cottrell were both dismissed as the supposed ringleaders. They both became typefounders.

During the administration of the younger Caslon the specimens of the foundry, the contents of which exceeded what could be shown on a single sheet, began to be issued as books, a format already used by Dutch and French typefounders. The earliest, known only from a fragment, is dated 1764; other printings followed in 1764 and 1766. On 25 June 1751 Caslon married Elizabeth Cartlich (1730–1795) [*see* Caslon, Elizabeth], only daughter of William and Elizabeth Cartlich, at St Mary-le-Bow, London. His wife, who brought with her a fortune of £10,000, assisted in the management of the letter-foundry up to the death of her husband in 1778, after which she continued to manage it jointly with her two sons, William Caslon (1754–1833) and Henry Caslon (*c.*1755–1788). The former, having sold his share of the Chiswell Street foundry in 1792, bought that of Joseph Jackson in Salisbury Square, and traded under his own name, so that between 1792 and 1818 there were two distinct Caslon foundries in London. In 1799 Elizabeth *Caslon [*see under* Caslon, Elizabeth], widow of Henry, acquired the original foundry, taking Nathaniel Catherwood into partnership. From 1796 she began to acknowledge the changing taste in typography by ordering new types from John Isaac Drury to replace those supplied by the foundry since its establishment. The foundry passed to her son Henry (1786–1850), and to his son Henry William Caslon (d. 1874), the last descendant of the elder Caslon, after whose death his manager, Thomas White Smith, acquired the firm, retaining its style of H. W. Caslon & Co. With his encouragement, Smith's sons took the surname Caslon, which passed to their descendants. JAMES MOSLEY

Sources ordnance minute books, PRO, WO 47/25–8, WO 48/56 · minute books, CUL, SPCK MSS, vols. 9–10 · letters and papers concerning Arabic Testament, CUL, SPCK MSS · minutes relating to Arabic impressions (extracts), CUL, SPCK MSS · W. Caslon, *A specimen of printing types* (1766); facs. edn J. Mosley, ed., *Journal of the Printing Historical Society*, 16 (1981–2) [whole issue] · J. Hawkins, *A general history of the science and practice of music*, 5 (1776), p. 127 · E. R. Mores, *A dissertation upon English typographical founders and founderies* (1778), with, *A catalogue and specimen of the typefoundry of John James* (1782), ed. H. Carter and C. Ricks (1961); repr. with corrections (1963) · J. Nichols, *Biographical and literary anecdotes of William Bowyer, printer, FSA, and of many of his learned friends* (privately printed, London, 1782) · 'Memoirs of Mr. William Caslon, the celebrated letter-founder: with his portrait engraved by James Heath', *Universal Magazine of Knowledge and Pleasure*, 84 (1789), 169–70 · 'The art of cutting, casting, and preparing of letter for printing', *Universal Magazine of Knowledge and Pleasure*, 6 (1750), 274–8 · T. B. Reed, *A history of the old English letter founderies* (1887); new edn, ed. A. F. Johnson (1952) · J. Mosley, 'The early career of William Caslon', *Journal of the Printing Historical Society*, 3 (1967), 66–81 · J. Ball, *William Caslon, 1693–1766* (1973) · H. L. Blackmore, 'William Caslon, gun engraver', *Journal of the Arms and Armour Society*, 10/3 (1981), 103–7 · J. Mosley, *British type specimens before 1831: a hand-list* (1984) · J. Mosley, 'The Caslon foundry in 1902', *Matrix*, 13 (1993), 34–42 · J. Howes, 'Caslon's punches and matrices', *Matrix*, 20 (2000), 1–7 [with 'Caslon's old face: an inventory', pp. i–viii] · T. C. Hansard, *Typographia: an historical sketch of the origin and progress of the art of printing* (1825), 348 · IGI · will, PRO, PROB 11/915, sig. 6 · GM, 1st ser., 62 (1792), 92

Archives PRO, ordnance minute books, WO 47/25–8; 48/56

Likenesses F. Kyte, oils, 1740, Monotype Corporation; repro. in Ball, *William Caslon*, frontispiece · J. Faber junior, mezzotint (after F. Kyte, 1740), BM, NPG [*see illus.*] · J. Heath, engraving (after mezzotint by Faber?), repro. in 'Memoirs of Mr. William Caslon' · J. Lee, wood-engraving, repro. in Hansard, *Typographia*, facing p. 348 · engraving (after mezzotint by Faber?), repro. in T. F. Dibdin, *The bibliographical decameron*, 2 (1819), 380

Caslon, William, the younger (1720–1778). *See under* Caslon, William, the elder (1692–1766).

Cass, Sir John (*bap.* 1660, *d.* 1718), politician, was baptized on 28 February 1660 at St Botolph, Aldgate, London, the son of Thomas Cass (d. 1699), a Hackney carpenter who made a fortune from ordnance contracts and became master of the Carpenters' Company, and his wife, Martha, née Johnson. On 7 January 1684 he married Elizabeth, née Franklin; she died on 7 July 1732. He was a relative and the intended heir of Sir John *Friend, the Jacobite conspirator; the Cass family were suspected of Jacobitism during the 1690s. In 1700 Cass recovered £1300 from Friend's forfeited estate.

Cass rose to an influential position in the commercial world of the City, which enabled him to build and endow a school in his native parish to educate the young in 'the knowledge of the Christian religion according to the principles of the Church of England'. It was opened with much

publicity, and a thanksgiving service was conducted by Dr Henry Sacheverell. A year earlier Cass had been elected an alderman of Portsoken ward and also returned to parliament for the City on the church and tory interest. On 25 June 1711 he was chosen sheriff, 'to the great joy of the high church party', and on 14 June 1712, on presenting the loyal address of the City to Queen Anne in favour of the peace, he was knighted. In spite of his undoubted toryism and membership of the extremist October Club, he voted against the ministry in June 1713 over the treaty of commerce with France, probably on economic grounds. He lost his parliamentary seat in 1715, a casualty of the whig triumph at the general election, and died at his home in Grove Street, Hackney, on 5 July 1718. He was buried at St Mary, Whitechapel, on 15 July. In his will, dated 6 May 1709, he had left £1000 to found another charity school in Hackney. In 1732 this bequest was greatly enlarged by a decision of chancery, in conformity with Cass's intention as set out in an unfinished codicil. The income from the Cass estate was eventually used to build an elementary day school in the borough.

THOMAS SECCOMBE, *rev.* D. W. HAYTON

Sources HoP, *Commons, 1690–1715* [draft] · D. A. Brunning, 'A short account of Sir John Cass', GL · A. B. Beaven, ed., *The aldermen of the City of London, temp. Henry III–*[1912], 1 (1908), 185; 2 (1913), 122 · G. S. De Krey, *A fractured society: the politics of London in the first age of party, 1688–1715* (1985), 227–9 · J. B. Hollingworth, *A sermon preached before the trustees of the charity schools founded by… Sir J. Cass* (1817) · S. J. Farthing, *Sir John Cass and his school* (1910) · parish register, London, St Botolph, Aldgate, 28 Feb 1660 [baptism] · parish register, London, St Mary Whitechapel, 15 July 1718 [burial] · will, PRO, PROB 11/566, sig. 210

Archives GL, MS 21742/1

Likenesses L. F. Roubiliac, lead statue, 1751, Cass Institute, London

Cassan, Stephen Hyde (1789–1841), ecclesiastical biographer, son of Stephen Cassan, barrister, and his wife, Sarah, daughter of Captain Charles Mears, was born at Calcutta, where his father was sheriff. He was educated at Magdalen Hall, Oxford, from May 1811 and took his BA degree on 14 January 1815. He received deacon's orders on 26 March 1816, and was ordained priest in 1817. While curate of Frome, Somerset, in 1820, he made a 'stolen marriage' (GM, 550) with Fanny, third daughter of the Revd William Ireland (deceased at the time of the marriage), former vicar of that parish. This marriage occasioned considerable scandal, and led to legal proceedings, of which an account is given in two pamphlets published at Bath in 1821—*A report of the trial, Cassan v. Ireland, for defamation* and *Who Wrote the Letters, or, A Statement of Facts*, the latter by Cassan.

Cassan then held the curacy of Mere, Wiltshire, where his literary interests were encouraged by Sir Richard Hoare of Stourhead. In 1831 Hoare presented him to the living of Bruton with Wyke Champflower. He was also chaplain to the earl of Caledon and to the duke of Cambridge. His family was large, and he was constantly in financial difficulty, from which he sought to free himself by publishing books by subscription and by seeking for promotion. He was elected a fellow of the Society of Antiquaries in 1829.

Cassan published several notable series of episcopal biographies on: the bishops of Sherborne and Salisbury (3 vols., 1824), the bishops of Winchester (2 vols., 1827), and the bishops of Bath and Wells (2 vols., 1829–30). These he laced with appendices on the condition of the clergy which remain of interest. Though publishing pamphlets against the repeal of the Test and Corporation Acts and against Catholic emancipation which show a high-church character, he encouraged elimination of clerical corruption.

Cassan was an obsessive genealogist, especially of his own family, and incurred further debts by having its pedigree privately printed. He was a frequent contributor to the *Gentleman's Magazine*. Always vehement in his mode of expression, Cassan became mentally ill about 1839 and was removed from his benefice. He died on 19 July 1841 of 'apoplexy'. His wife survived him.   H. C. G. MATTHEW

Sources *GM*, 2nd ser., 16 (1841), 550 · Foster, *Alum. Oxon.* · G. F. A. Best, *Temporal pillars: Queen Anne's bounty, the ecclesiastical commissioners, and the Church of England* (1964)

Likenesses Day and Haghe, lithograph, NPG

Cassel, Sir Ernest Joseph (1852–1921), merchant banker and financier, was born on 3 March 1852 in Cologne, Germany, the youngest of the three children of Jacob Cassel (1802–1875) and Amalia, *née* Rosenheim (*d.* 1874). Jacob Cassel had a small banking business, founded by his father, Moses Cassel, which provided a modest but comfortable income. Since at least the late seventeenth century the Cassels had been active in financial affairs in the Rhineland; several of them were advisers or agents for the prince electors. Ernest had a brother, Max Cassel, born in 1848, who died in 1875, and a sister, Wilhelmina Cassel (later Schoenbrunn), to whom he remained close and who managed his household in England in later years. In later life Cassel gave entirely conflicting accounts of the atmosphere of his early home life and the truth is difficult to establish.

Ernest was educated in Cologne until the age of fourteen, when he started work with the banking firm of Eltzbacher. In 1869 he emigrated to Liverpool, where he is said to have arrived with a bag of clothes and a violin, and no evident promise of a job. He soon started work with a firm of German grain-merchants in Liverpool, but a little over a year later he moved to a clerkship with the Anglo-Egyptian Bank in Paris. The outbreak shortly afterwards of the Franco-Prussian War forced him, as a German subject, to return to England, this time to a clerkship at the London merchant bank, Bischoffsheim and Goldschmidt, where he was closely associated with Henri Bischoffsheim. This move was probably facilitated by an introduction from the powerful but mysterious European financier Baron Maurice de Hirsch. Cassel was linked with the independent and enterprising businessman until the latter's death in 1896, and he may have modelled his career on Hirsch's.

Early career and marriage Within a year Cassel, aged only nineteen, had demonstrated his flair by rapidly saving the

Sir Ernest Joseph Cassel (1852–1921), by Anders Leonard Zorn, 1909

affairs of a Jewish firm in Constantinople in which Bischoffsheims had an interest. In 1874 he was appointed manager, at an unusually early age, at a salary said to have been £5000 a year, following a series of further highly successful negotiations, especially in connection with South American loans. In addition to his salary he obtained substantial commission from the rescue or liquidation of troublesome ventures on Bischoffsheims' behalf. Such activities gained for him international contacts through whom he became profitably involved on his own account in American and other overseas enterprises. When his father died in 1875, leaving Ernest a half share with his sister of RM 91,286 (£4500), Cassel could afford to settle more than his own half (£3000) upon his sister, who was now divorced, and her two children. When he married in 1878 he was able to put aside capital of £150,000.

In 1878 Cassel married Annette (*d.* 1881), daughter of Robert Thompson Maxwell, of Croft House, Croft, Darlington, and on the day of his marriage he became a naturalized British subject. His wife died of tuberculosis three years later, to his great grief. They had one daughter, Maud. Mrs Cassel had been converted to Roman Catholicism and by her wish Cassel, never devoutly Jewish, was received into the Roman Catholic church shortly after her death. His devotion to his new religion was never very evident, nor was his conversion widely known until, at his appointment to the privy council in 1902 he chose, to general surprise, to be sworn in on the Catholic Bible. He never remarried and is not known to have had any intimate relationships for the remainder of his life. He was known as a warm and sociable man, devoted to his daughter and to what remained of his family, and he sustained a number of close and lasting friendships. Margot Asquith described him as 'a man of natural authority ... dignified, autocratic and wise; with a power of loving those he cared for'. She added that 'he had no small talk and disliked gossip' (Adler, 328). Others who knew him less well described him as kind but cold. He was a very private man who left no intimate record of his life or feelings and destroyed most of his personal papers. After his wife's death his sister and her children, Anna (later Anna Jenkins) and Felix (later knighted, and a prominent barrister and Conservative assistant attorney-general) moved to live with him, and they adopted the name Cassel. First Wilhelmina and then Anna acted as his official hostesses.

Expansion of financial affairs Thereafter Cassel's main preoccupations, other than his family, were with international finance and entry into high society. He increased his fortune vastly and rapidly through investment in the mining, transportation, and processing of Swedish iron ore (he was responsible for introducing the Gilchrist–Thomas processing technique into Sweden) and in the rapidly expanding American railways. In the early 1880s his association with Bischoffsheims was on a profit-sharing rather than a salaried basis, but he never formally became a partner. In 1884 he left the firm, though he continued to occupy part of their offices until 1898 while working on his own account. He did not join another finance house until 1910, preferring to work independently or to associate in consortia with other financiers for specific projects.

International finance in the fast-growing international economy of the late nineteenth century was risky, requiring a cool head, good contacts, and a shrewd capacity to keep on good terms with powerful people in many countries. At this Cassel was adept. He was known for the sharpness of his dealing and he aroused considerable suspicion, antagonism, and jealousy, though no proof of actual dishonesty was ever disclosed. His great wealth endowed him with a useful capacity for flexibility in his dealings when necessary. In Sweden, for example, he countered the hostility of influential men to the degree of economic power he wielded by allowing Swedish representatives to dominate the board of his company (the Grangesborg-Oxelsund Traffic Company Ltd) and by selling many of its fast-rising shares to Swedish bankers, politicians, and journalists at below the market price, though still at considerable profit. His enemies referred to these tactics as 'Cassel's greasing system' (Grunwald, 131). He played an important role in the economic development of Sweden.

At least as important in determining Cassel's great success as any dubious dealing in Sweden and elsewhere was his immense, unremitting capacity for hard work. He was constantly in touch with a multitude of simultaneous transactions, delegating effectively yet never losing control, always available for the key meeting or decision, yet rarely working from his office, constantly travelling among business locations or entertaining contacts. He never neglected to keep in contact with the world of influence wherever it was to be found, whether at the card table, the dinner table, or at Cowes. Also important was his capacity to choose shrewd people to assist him with his affairs or to run specific projects. From 1902 he employed the influential Reginald Brett, Viscount Esher, who was succeeded in 1904 by Sir Sidney Peel. He appointed the talented former public servant Sir Henry Babington-Smith to head the National Bank of Turkey in 1909. They remained close friends and associates and Babington-Smith was an executor of Cassel's will. But the essential ingredients of Cassel's success were his own keen observation and judgement of international and financial affairs, which drew on information from his huge range of contacts worldwide.

From his earliest days with Bischoffsheims, Cassel had been profitably involved with American enterprises, notably the disentanglement of the affairs of the New York, Pennsylvania, and Ohio Railway. In the course of such activities he had become a close and lasting friend of Jacob H. Schiff of the banking house of Kuhn, Loeb & Co., through whom he became profitably interested on his own account in other American enterprises. One of his first operations after becoming independent of Bischoffsheims was the reorganization of the Louisville and Nashville Railway, which he carried through in conjunction with Kuhn, Loeb and with Wertheim and Gompertz of Amsterdam.

From the late 1880s Cassel's interests expanded into South America. He arranged the finances of the Mexican Central Railway for some time and in 1893 he issued the Mexican government's 6 per cent loan. In 1896 he issued the Uruguay government's 5 per cent loan. To a lesser extent he was also active in China, still concentrating on transport and mining, and also in 1895 issuing a 6 per cent government loan. Between 1890 and 1910 he was also involved in arranging loans for Japan, Egypt, Turkey, and Russia. He took relatively little interest in domestic investment, though he did play a part in financing the building of the London underground from 1894, through participation in the Electric Traction Company. However, this did not prove to be a profitable investment. From 1897 Cassel began a long and more rewarding association with Vickers, Sons & Co., the shipbuilding and armaments firm. He organized their purchase of the Barrow Naval and Shipbuilding Construction Company and of the Maxim Gun and Nordenfelt companies. For some years he underwrote the financial issues for Vickers and its subsidiaries.

Cassel was an early investor in gold and diamond mining in South Africa, and this was an important source of his increasing fortune in the 1890s and 1900s. In 1897 he agreed to finance the Aswan Dam and Asyut barrage on the upper Nile, another successful intervention in an underdeveloped economy. He later moved, also profitably, into financing the development of sugar production and marketing (through the Daira Sanieh Company) and also of railways in Egypt. In 1898 he established the

National Bank of Egypt and the Agricultural Bank of Egypt, which played an especially important role in financing agricultural development. So also did the Société Anonyme de Wadi Kom Ombo, which he played a leading role in establishing for the purpose of irrigating the great desert plain from the Nile to Gebel es Silsila. A similar attempt to stimulate the economic development of Morocco by establishing the State Bank of Morocco, which Cassel reluctantly undertook in 1906 at the urging of the British and French governments, was less successful. The National Bank of Turkey, which he established in association with other London bankers at the urging of the Turkish government in 1909 with the aim of expanding British commercial and financial involvement in Turkey (in particular for the development of mineral resources), was also unsuccessful. It proved impossible to defeat the strength of French financial and commercial interests in Turkey.

Characteristically Cassel calmed the potential for opposition in Egypt by winning the friendship of the khedive of Egypt. He arranged for him to meet Cassel's other good friend, King Edward VII, in 1903 and in 1904, and he made him a loan of £500,000 at the low rate of 2.5 per cent, in return for commercial and land concessions. This infuriated the consul-general, Lord Cromer, who had encouraged Cassel's initial ventures in Egypt as a means of increasing British influence, but who had the thankless task of attempting to curb the khedive's expenditure. In 1903 Cassel also donated £341,000 to equip and operate travelling eye hospitals in Egypt. This may have been motivated by a desire to mollify opposition. His motives were probably mixed, as he also gave generously to philanthropic causes in Britain. Whatever the motive, the outcome was a major contribution to combating the ravages of eye diseases such as trachoma in poverty-stricken rural Egypt.

Cassel was suspected of demanding honours in return for services to governments and this was a persistent theme in London society gossip of the time. There is certainly an interesting congruence between his progress through the honours lists of the world and his financial services. He became KCMG in 1899, following his major Egyptian deals, and was sworn of the privy council in 1902, after the accession of Edward VII. He had been the friend and companion of the prince of Wales at racing and cards, and as Edward's financial adviser (in succession to Hirsch) he was reputed to be responsible for the surprising fact that Edward ascended the throne free from debt. He became a commander of the Légion d'honneur and received the British GCVO in 1906, following the establishment of the State Bank of Morocco. He was made GCB in 1909, following his agreement to a Foreign Office request to put a further £500,000 into the ailing Bank of Morocco. His collection of decorations, of which he was immensely proud, came to include: commander, first class, of the royal order of Vasa, Sweden (1900); the grand cordon of the Imperial Ottoman order of the Osmanieh, conferred by the khedive in 1903; the crown of Prussia, first class (1908); the grand cross of the Polar Star, Sweden (1909); the order of the Rising Sun, first class, Japan (1911); and the Red Eagle of Prussia, first class, with brilliants (1913).

High society, politics, and philanthropy Cassel penetrated the élite with the same determination and with some of the same methods by which he achieved business success. From the time of his marriage he cultivated, at a succession of rented and, later, personally owned country houses, the social and political élites—on the hunting field, with the shooting party, at the racecourse, and at the card table. By the 1890s he was an accepted house-guest of the Devonshires at Chatsworth. He took up hunting despite a certain dislike of horses and his incompetence at riding them. He started to own and breed racehorses in 1889, and continued until 1894 in company with Lord Willoughby de Broke, and thereafter alone. Among the chief stallions owned by him were Cylgad and Hapsburg; among his mares were Gadfly, Sonatura, and Doctrine. He had some successes on the course, though the nearest he came to winning the Derby was to come second with Hapsburg in 1914. It took him thirteen years to achieve election to the Jockey Club, in 1908. The patronage of Edward VII enabled his entry to circles otherwise closed to a largely self-made German Jew, but it could not win him entire acceptance.

Some prominent politicians were more welcoming to Cassel. Both Randolph and Winston Churchill were his good friends, as were the Asquiths. Cassel's own politics appear to have been Conservative, but he was never active in the political world. Like other prominent financiers his advice was sought on financial matters by politicians of both parties and by civil servants. He was described in 1903 by Sir Edward Hamilton, joint permanent secretary at the Treasury, as 'one of the representative men—Natty Rothschild, John (Lord) Revelstoke (the head of Barings) and Cassel, whom I now regard as my first counsellors' (Hamilton diaries, BL, Add. MS 48658, 16 Nov 1903). Cassel was consulted by Sir Michael Hicks Beach and by Asquith when they were chancellors of the exchequer. Lloyd George dined with him while he held the office but was more reserved. A certain aloofness towards party politics was one of the keys to Cassel's business success; in 1909, at the height of the budget crisis, when the City was organizing against Lloyd George's proposed taxes, Cassel wrote to his son-in-law, Wilfred Ashley, stressing his 'absolute loyalty to whatever government I happen to be serving, and if whoever happened to be in power could not be certain of this he would not give me, and I certainly would not wish, his confidence' (Cassel to Ashley, 18 Aug 1909, Broadlands Archive, Cassel MS, folder X6). He did not sign the City's anti-budget petition, though he did cautiously arrange to shift funds to the United States to avoid the new taxes. He was an early, though anonymous, contributor to the Tariff Reform League. Also in the 1900s he opposed the City's Jewish-led boycott of Russian finance in retaliation for the persecution of the Jews. He argued that negotiation and alliance with Russia were more likely to mute their anti-semitism than was a boycott.

Especially in his earlier years Cassel mixed widely in theatrical and artistic circles. Alma-Tadema and Burne-

Jones were both grateful for his friendship and patronage. He amassed an impressive collection of old masters, including important works by Van Dyck, Franz Hals, Romney, Raeburn, Reynolds, and Murillo, and he acquired French and English furniture, Renaissance bronzes, Dresden china, Chinese jade, and old English silver. He gave away at least £2 million in charitable donations, including £200,000 in 1902 for the founding of the King Edward VII Sanatorium for Consumption at Fenhurst, near Midhurst, with a further £20,000 in 1913; £10,000 in 1907 to the Imperial College of Science and Technology; in 1909 a half share of £46,000 with Lord Iveagh for founding the Radium Institute; £210,000 in 1911 for setting up the King Edward VII British–German Foundation for the aid of distressed people in Germany; £30,000 for distressed workers in Swedish mines; £50,000 to Hampshire hospitals in memory of his daughter; in 1913 £10,000 to Egyptian hospitals; and £50,000 for the sick and needy of Cologne.

Despite his formal conversion to Roman Catholicism, Cassel still regarded himself as Jewish and devoted a considerable amount of money and effort to the international attempts of wealthy Jews to acquire a national home for Jews fleeing from Russia, a movement in which Hirsch had been prominent. During the First World War, Cassel gave at least £400,000 for medical services and the relief of servicemen's families. In 1919 he donated £500,000 for an educational trust fund which was used to establish a faculty of commerce at the London School of Economics, to support the Workers' Educational Association, to finance scholarships for the technical and commercial education of working men, to promote the study of foreign languages by the establishment of professorships, lectureships, and scholarships, and finally to support the higher education of women. He gave £212,000 for the founding of a hospital at Penhurst, Kent, for functional nervous disorders.

Personal grief, winding down, and death In 1910–11 Cassel came to a turning point in his life, for a mixture of personal and political reasons. He felt great personal grief at the death of Edward VII, as well as losing much of his social and political influence, to the undisguised and often openly antisemitic glee of certain members of high society. The friendship between Edward and 'Windsor-Cassel' was close and strong. The two had met at the racecourse about 1896, possibly introduced by Hirsch, and were friends thereafter. They even looked somewhat alike: substantially built, bearded, and moustached in similar style.

Equally tragically, in 1911 his only daughter died after a long battle with tuberculosis. Cassel devoted much care to her in her last year. In 1901 she had married Lieutenant-Colonel Wilfred Ashley, grandson of the great earl of Shaftesbury and great-grandson of Lady Palmerston, through whom he had inherited Broadlands House in Hampshire. Ashley had been Conservative MP for Blackpool since 1906; he served as minister of transport in 1924–9, and was created Baron Mount Temple of Lee in 1932. He was on friendly terms with Cassel, who provided him with financial advice. After his daughter's death

Cassel's affection centred upon his two granddaughters, especially the elder, Edwina.

Having decided to reduce the volume of his activity, in 1910 Cassel became a partner in the merchant bank of S. Japhet & Co., but he kept up independent interests and an office close to his sumptuous new home, Brook House in Park Lane. He had previously lived at 48 Grosvenor Square. Brook House had six marble-lined kitchens; an oak-panelled dining room, designed to seat one hundred in comfort; and the entrance hall was panelled in lapis lazuli alternating with green-veined cream-coloured marble and was described as the 'giant's lavatory' by Edwina's friends. Until his death Cassel lived there much of the time. He also had a flat in Paris, a Swiss villa (Villa Cassel, at Riederfurk, in the canton of Valais), another villa in the south of France, a stud farm at Moulton Paddocks, Newmarket, bought in 1899, and three country houses bought between 1912 and 1917. These were the Six Mile Bottom estate, Cambridgeshire, purchased in 1912; Branksome Dene, Bournemouth, bought in 1913; and Upper Hare Park, Cambridgeshire, which he acquired in 1917.

The more general curtailment of Cassel's activities may have been due to anticipation of that great disrupter of international finance, a major war. Certainly his personal investments were safely concentrated in North America by 1914. He was strongly aware of the danger of war with Germany as early as 1908. Between 1908 and 1912 he and the German shipowner Alfred Ballin made secret efforts to bring together German and British political leaders to try to avert conflict. When war came he made one of the largest contributions to the war loan and was a member of the Anglo-French financial mission to the USA in 1915, which resulted in a large American loan. Such activities did not prevent Cassel from suffering constant attack in Britain for his German birth, including an unsuccessful attempt to remove him from the privy council.

Thereafter Cassel confined his attention to a limited amount of American business and to racing and shooting parties with old friends, and he was cared for by Edwina. He died on 21 September 1921, sitting at his desk at Brook House, and was buried at Kensal Green cemetery, London, according to Roman Catholic rites. Shortly afterwards Edwina married Lord Louis Mountbatten (Earl Mountbatten of Burma), bringing Broadlands House, which she inherited, into the Mountbatten family. Cassel left an estate worth £7,333,411 gross (with a probate value of £6 million), most of it to his immediate family. He left small items from his art, china, and jade collections to a list of old and valued friends who included the Asquiths, Mr and Mrs Winston Churchill, Lord Birkenhead, Mrs Keppel, Lord Revelstoke, Lord and Lady Reading, and the marchioness of Winchester, as well as some banking friends.

PAT THANE

Sources P. Thane, 'Cassel, Sir Ernest Joseph', *DBB* · P. Thane, 'Financiers and the British state: the case of Sir Ernest Cassel', *Business History*, 28 (1986), 80–99 · K. Grunwald, 'Windsor Cassel: the last court Jew', *Yearbook of the Leo Baeck Institute*, 14 (1969), 119–61 · M. Kent, 'Agent of empire? The National Bank of Turkey and British foreign policy', *HJ*, 18 (1975), 367–389 · C. Adler, *Jacob H. Schiff* (1928), 2. 328 · diaries of Sir Edward Hamilton, BL, Add. MS

48658, 16 Nov 1903 · Cassel to Wilfred Ashley, 18 Aug 1909, Broadlands Archive, Hampshire, Cassel MSS, Folder X6 · d. cert. · *DNB*
Archives Broadlands House, Hampshire · CAC Cam. · U. Southampton L., corresp. and papers | American Jewish Archive, Cincinnati, Ohio, Jacob H. Schiff MSS · Trinity Cam., corresp. with Sir Henry Babington Smith · U. Durham L., corresp. with the khedive of Egypt
Likenesses P. de Laszlo, portrait, 1900? · A. L. Zorn, etching, 1909, NPG [*see illus.*] · W. Stoneman, photograph, 1917, NPG · Spy [L. Ward], chromolithograph caricature, repro. in *VF* (7 Dec 1899)
Wealth at death £6,000,000: probate, 7 Oct 1921, *CGPLA Eng. & Wales*

Cassel, Sir Felix Maximilian Schoenbrunn, first baronet (1869–1953), lawyer, was born in Cologne, Germany, on 16 September 1869, the only son of Louis Schoenbrunn Cassel. The philanthropist Sir Ernest Joseph *Cassel (1852–1921) was his uncle. He was educated at Elstree School and Harrow School (1883–8), and in 1888 he won a scholarship at Corpus Christi College, Oxford, where he obtained firsts in classical moderations (1892) and jurisprudence (1892). After being called to the bar at Lincoln's Inn in 1894, he appeared as a junior at the notable trial of the fraudster Whitaker Wright in 1904. He took silk in 1906 and became a leading Chancery practitioner and, in 1912, a bencher of his inn. On 18 November 1908 he married Lady Helen (*d.* 1947), third daughter of James Walter Grimston, third earl of Verulam; they had three sons (one of whom predeceased his parents) and two daughters.

In 1907 Cassel entered politics, standing successfully as Municipal Reform (conservative) candidate for the West St Pancras constituency of the London county council. At the general election of February 1910 he was defeated as Unionist candidate for Hackney Central, but he was elected in December 1910 for West St Pancras. As an officer in the 19th battalion, the London regiment, between 1914 and 1916, he served in France until posted back to England in August 1915, when his association with the judge advocate general's office began.

On the death in September 1916 of Sir Thomas Milvain, Cassel became judge advocate general, resigning his seat in the House of Commons. The judge advocate general ('neither a judge, nor an advocate, nor a general', as Voltairian critics not wholly accurately complained) was the senior civilian lawyer responsible, primarily, for overseeing the proper administration of military law. Cassel became head of a small department with civilian lawyers in London and military lawyers representing him at military headquarters. His office advised on court martial prosecutions and appropriate charges but during the war usually left prosecuting itself to regimental or court martial officers (the pre-trial and prosecuting function). Second, Cassel supplied judge advocates in more serious cases to provide legal guidance during trials, to sum up at the end of the hearing, and to advise on sentencing rules (the judicial function). Third, he or his deputies provided legal advice to commanders on whether to confirm finding and sentence, on post-confirmation review of findings, or on convicted soldiers' petitions against finding or sentence (the post-trial function). He presided over an enormous increase in the workload of the department and in the variety of issues to be addressed. The creation of the Royal Air Force in 1918 and the post-war troubles in Ireland also expanded his responsibilities.

Providentially for Cassel, his office attracted nothing like the attention, and therefore the condemnation, both at the time and for decades subsequently, visited upon army commanders such as Haig who had the final authority to confirm death sentences imposed by field general courts martial on British soldiers convicted of military offences such as cowardice or desertion during the First World War. In the various books published since the 1970s which deal with the First World War executions (and which prompted both an unsuccessful private member's bill in 1995 to secure pardons for the executed soldiers and a Ministry of Defence re-examination of the cases in 1998), Cassel's name does not feature, though the post-war committee of inquiry into the law and procedure of courts martial chaired by Sir Charles Darling stated that death sentences were only carried out 'after the Judge Advocate General or his Deputy had advised upon their legality' ('Committee … courts-martial', para. 106). When Cassel was criticized by name in parliament in July 1918 by the Irish nationalist MP for Donegal, John Gordon Swift Mac-Neill, it was in respect of his alien origins (he had long since stopped using his middle names).

The Darling committee, whose members included Cassel's deputy in France and Flanders, Sir Gilbert Mellor, and the deputy adjutant general, Sir Wyndham Childs, reached the general conclusion that the military law system had worked well during the war. It was not a view shared by three other committee members, including Horatio Bottomley, who believed that the committee had not fully investigated alleged miscarriages of justice. Cassel did recognize that there were structural problems with his department, especially that the pre-trial and prosecution function had not been formally separated from the (civilian) judicial and post-trial side. Until the formation of the military and air force department of his office in 1923, which became organizationally separate from the judicial branch, a 'Chinese walls' system was constructed with a view to preventing improper influence being exerted by the military prosecution branch on the judicial branch. (It was only in April 1997 that the military prosecution side itself was, in consequence of the requirements of the European convention on human rights, separated from the military chain of command.) That there remained confusion over the structural independence of his office from the War Office was apparent in press reporting of the 'officer in the Tower' case in 1933, when Second Lieutenant Norman Baillie-Stewart was convicted by court martial of offences under the Official Secrets Act (1911).

With parliamentary controversy also stoked up by a further court martial, that of Colonel Herbert Sandford in 1934, the government in 1938 set up another committee, chaired by Sir Roland Giffard Oliver, to enquire into military law, and Cassel was again appointed to serve on it. Yet while the Oliver committee was also asked to consider the possibility of creating a civilian court of appeal from courts martial (which was eventually established in 1951), the status of the judge advocate general and his office were not within its remit. Nevertheless the committee's main recommendation was, precisely, that the judicial branch of the office should now be shifted from the War Office and the Air Ministry to the Lord Chancellor's Office, to which the judge advocate general would become responsible, in order to emphasize the independence of the judicial branch from the military departments of state, and that the judge advocate general should no longer have even nominal control over the military and air force departments with their pre-trial and prosecution functions. Again, these changes were only effected after several years' delay and after yet another committee, under Sir Wilfrid Hubert Poyer Lewis, had been set up in 1946.

It would be a mistake to conclude that Cassel's tenure represented a constant struggle in the face of adverse criticism. (Indeed he possibly felt that deflecting the claims to his office space of rival departments, such as the public trustee office, was a stiffer challenge.) But his influence on the day-to-day practice of military law, a reflection of his forceful personality, continued long after his formal retirement in 1934. His successor, Sir Henry Foster Mac-Geagh, often sought his advice on particularly difficult military law questions, and Cassel was more than happy to be asked.

Cassel was created a baronet in January 1920 and became a privy councillor in 1937. He was appointed chairman of the Board of Trade committee on compulsory insurance which sat between 1935 and 1937 and addressed compulsory insurance questions relating among other things to road traffic accidents and employment in the coal industry. Cassel became treasurer of Lincoln's Inn in 1935, an honorary fellow of Corpus Christi College, Oxford, in 1942, and a member of the Council of Legal Education in 1943.

Cassel took part in his wealthy family's philanthropic work, chairing the Cassel educational trust, and the management committee of the Cassel Hospital for functional nervous disorders, and belonging to the council of the King Edward VII Sanatorium, Midhurst, Sussex. On retiring in 1945 as master of the Worshipful Company of Musicians he made a donation for the encouragement of military music, and also endowed three annual Cassel scholarships at Lincoln's Inn. He was a justice of the peace for Hertfordshire and in 1942–3 high sheriff of the county. In his later years he owned a country residence at Putteridge Bury, Luton, which was subsequently acquired by the University of Luton. Cassel died in hospital at Midhurst on 22 February 1953.　　　　　　　　　　　G. R. Rubin

Sources G. R. Rubin, 'The status of the judge advocate general of the forces in the United Kingdom since the 1930s', *Military Law and Law of War Review*, 33 (1994), 243–71 · 'Committee constituted by the army council to inquire into … courts-martial', *Parl. papers* (1919), 10.163, Cmd 428 · *The Times* (23 Feb 1953) · *Hansard 5C* (1918), 108.2158–9 · PRO, WO 32/11656 · PRO, HO 45/11020/395948 · Marquess of Reading [G. R. Isaacs], *Rufus Isaacs, first marquess of Reading*, 2 vols. (1942–5) · Burke, *Peerage* (2000) · P. A. Hunt, *Corpus Christi College biographical register*, ed. N. A. Flanagan (1988)
Wealth at death £294,757 (duty paid £210,522): *The Times*

Cassell, John (1817–1865), publisher, was born on 23 January 1817 in the Ring o' Bells inn, Old Churchyard, Manchester, the youngest child of Mark Cassell, landlord of the inn, and his wife, Hannah Slingsby (d. 1865), a farmer's daughter. His father died when John was still very young; probably as a result, his education at a British and Foreign Society day school was basic, and he worked as a child labourer in a local cotton mill and a velveteen factory. From the age of sixteen to nineteen years he was bound as an apprentice to a joiner in Salford; during these years he came under the influence of the temperance campaigner Thomas Whittaker. Possibly as a reformed alcoholic, he took the pledge in July 1835. On the completion of his indentures he set out on a temperance lecturing tour (and in search of employment), reaching London in October 1836. By April 1837 he was an official agent of the National Temperance Society: he toured East Anglia on foot, taking 550 pledges in two months, and also visited the north, the home counties, and the west country. Known (somewhat predictably) as the Manchester Carpenter, Cassell was an impressive figure: gaunt, dark, with bright, fanatical eyes, he appeared in the apron of his profession and spoke in a broad Lancashire accent. In later years a cigar habitually hung from his lips, no doubt a compensation for his abstinence from alcohol.

In 1841 Cassell married Mary Abbott (d. 1885), a cultivated woman some years his senior; they had one surviving daughter, Sophia (d. 1912). With his wife's patrimony he established a company selling tea, coffee, and cocoa in Budge Row, London; in 1845 he started a separate business selling vegetable restorative pills. In March 1849 he opened a coffee establishment at 80 Fenchurch Street. Cassell was an effective advertiser, and the slogan 'Buy Cassell's shilling coffee' became a familiar phrase. Meanwhile Cassell had found another field of action for his temperance campaigns. In March 1846 there appeared the first number of the *Teetotal Times*, of which Cassell was the anonymous proprietor; it was absorbed into the organ of the National Temperance Society.

From July 1848 Cassell published the *Standard of Freedom*, which advocated religious, political, and commercial emancipation and reflected his radical politics: an admirer of Richard Cobden and Joseph Hume, he was committed to the pursuit of free trade and universal suffrage. He also published for a short time the *London Mercury* and several spin-off publications, including *The Emigrant's Almanack and Directory* (1849). In January 1850 he launched a new periodical, the *Working Man's Friend, and Family Instructor*, for which he claimed a circulation of 100,000 by 1851. It was followed by *The Freeholder*, the organ of a freehold land society. The Great Exhibition of 1851 was met with the *Illustrated Exhibitor*, a four-volumed publication in which Cassell made his first large-scale use of illustrations, including wood-engravings for which he had paid £50; he also arranged an artisan lodging-house register for working-class visitors during the exhibition.

As an up-and-coming publisher of newspapers and periodicals Cassell joined the radical wing of the campaign against stamp duty, which he deplored both as a 'tax on knowledge' and as an attack on his profits. Cassell was inspired by an enthusiasm for the education and 'improvement' of the working classes similar to that of Charles Knight, publisher of the *Penny Magazine*: 'I entered into the publishing trade', he declared in his evidence before the select committee on newspaper stamps in May 1851, 'for the purpose of issuing a series of publications which I believed were calculated to advance the moral and social well-being of the working classes' (Nowell-Smith, 22). But—like George Stiff of the *London Journal* and G. W. M. Reynolds of *Reynold's Miscellany*—Cassell had a keen commercial instinct for what sold, opining that working people 'will not take namby-pamby' (ibid., 22). *Cassell's Popular Educator* and *Cassell's Magazine*, both launched in 1852, each reflected one aspect of his publishing practice; in *Cassell's Illustrated Family Paper*, which first appeared in December 1853, both were combined—'instruction' was mixed with 'amusement' in a publication which was intended to reach the middle as well as the working classes. Thomas Frost, who worked for Cassell as a sub-editor, rightly described the *Family Paper* as 'a judicious combination of the pictorial newspaper with the popular periodical' (Frost, 227): it contained a serialized novel, short stories, current news, educational pieces on history and geography, answers to correspondents' queries, solutions to chess problems, fashion news, and recipes, all profusely illustrated with wood-engravings reproduced by mechanized stereotype printing. The *Family Paper* quickly gained a high circulation, at least partially owing to its extensive pictorial coverage of the Crimean War; it survived under different titles until 1932.

Despite its serious features the *Family Paper* tended to lean more towards entertainment than education. By contrast the *Popular Educator*, which provided a course of formal lessons in the sciences, the arts, and languages (some later were reprinted as textbooks), represented Cassell's strong commitment to self-education. An autodidact himself, he even funded evening classes for working men anxious for self-improvement, and got up an unsuccessful petition for the admission of the self-educated to the University of London. He had also published (from May 1850) *Cassell's Library*, periodical serializations of geographical, historical, and biographical works, and (from 1852) the *Illustrated Magazine of Art*, which achieved steady publication only in the 1880s; contributors to the latter included Eliza Meteyard and Anna Maria Howitt.

Cassell's flair for publicity and marketing was not matched by bookkeeping skills. Initially based at 335 Strand, from 1851 he rented premises at the Belle Sauvage inn for his publishing activities, and by the summer of 1854 he was planning to expand further. But—with no insurance and no sinking fund—he was heavily in debt to his paper supplier, who was now demanding payment; a take-over by Thomas Dixon Galpin and George William Petter ensued. Shouldering his liability in return for sole use of his name, they retained Cassell as editor (although later admitting him as a partner in 1858). The two young printers initially controlled all the editorial and managerial business, and embarked on a programme of retrenchment, working with a reduced editorial department and discontinuing some comparatively unremunerative publications. Few new projects were undertaken until 1856, when *Cassell's Illustrated History of England* and *John Cassell's Educational Course* both began publication. In later years Cassell's influence was most apparent in the religious publications of the firm: *The Quiver*, which started in the early 1860s, carried religious articles combined with serialized novels, which included Mrs Henry Wood's *The Channings*. In 1859 Cassell visited America to set up a New York branch of the firm; an account of his visit appeared in the *Family Paper*.

In his later years Cassell's largely prosperous condition (he and his family were comfortably established in St John's Wood, London, and enjoyed foreign holidays) did not erode either his commitment to radical causes or his flair for spotting a marketable product. After a visit to America in 1852 he had published the first English edition of Harriet Beecher Stowe's enormously popular novel *Uncle Tom's Cabin*, exhibiting his support for the abolition of slavery in America; illustrated by George Cruikshank, it was accompanied by an almanac. Active in the Newspaper and Periodical Press Association, he continued to campaign for the repeal of paper duty, which was finally abolished in 1861. Henry Vizetelly recalled a visit with Cassell and John Francis to Ireland and Scotland in autumn 1859 to stir up support for the repeal: he remarked, with his customary sourness, that Cassell's delivery was poor, commenting that 'his orations sorely needed a few flashes of logic to render them at all tolerable' (Vizetelly, 2.54). Cassell also supported campaigns for the relief of the victims of the Lancashire cotton famine of 1862, and in 1865 adroitly secured the right to publish the first English translation of Napoleon III's biography of Caesar. Meanwhile his grocery business continued to trade, and he started several oil and lamp companies.

By 1864 Cassell had stomach cancer; he died on 2 April 1865 at 25 Avenue Road, Regent's Park, London, and was buried in Kensal Green cemetery on 8 April. Among mid-nineteenth-century popular publishers he ranks with Charles Knight and William and Robert Chambers as one of the most significant and innovative. Indeed his publishing endeavours were ultimately more successful, both financially and educationally, than those of Knight and the Chambers brothers: more of a publicist with an eye for the market than Knight, more attuned to both working-class and middle-class radicalism than the Chambers brothers, Cassell's range of publications appealed to an extraordinarily wide audience of mid-century readers. The firm of which he was the founder still survives.

ROSEMARY MITCHELL

Sources G. H. Pike, *John Cassell* (1894) · S. Nowell-Smith, *The house of Cassell, 1848–1958* (1958) · *Cassell's Illustrated Family Paper* (20 May 1865), 262–4 · *The Bookseller* (29 April 1865), 225 · *The Bookseller* (31 May 1865), 291–2 · T. Frost, *Forty years' recollections: literary and political* (1880), 226–38 · H. Vizetelly, *Glances back through seventy years:*

autobiographical and other reminiscences, 2 (1893), 41–60 • P. Anderson, *The printed image and the transformation of popular culture, 1790–1860* (1991) • H. Curwen, *A history of booksellers, the old and the new* (1873), 267–75

Archives BL, corresp. with Richard Cobden, Add. MS 43668 • W. Sussex RO, corresp. with Richard Cobden
Likenesses photograph, repro. in Pike, *John Cassell*, frontispiece • print, Cassell and Collier Macmillan Publishers, London
Wealth at death under £25,000: probate, 23 June 1865, *CGPLA Eng. & Wales*

Cassels, Sir (Archibald) James Halkett (1907–1996), army officer, was born in Quetta, India, on 28 February 1907, the only son of General Sir Robert Archibald *Cassels (1876–1959), army officer, and his wife, Florence Emily, daughter of Lieutenant-Colonel Halkett Jackson. Jim Cassels, as he was invariably known, was educated at Rugby School and the Royal Military College, Sandhurst, where he won the sword of honour. He was commissioned second lieutenant in the Seaforth Highlanders in 1926. In 1930 (having been promoted lieutenant the previous year) he served with the 2nd battalion at Jhansi and then took part in operations in the North-West Frontier Province on the Khajauri plain. He moved with the battalion to Haifa in 1931, was appointed adjutant, and was involved in the Arab disturbance of 1933. In 1934 he returned to England but soon went back to India to become aide-de-camp to his father, first when the latter was general officer commanding, northern command, and later when he was commander-in-chief of the army of India. On 29 October 1935 he married Joyce Emily (*d.* 1978), daughter of the late Brigadier-General Henry Kirk, and his wife, Mrs G. A. McL. Sceales, of Clifts End Hall, Thanet, Kent; they had one son, Robert James (*b.* 1941).

At the outbreak of war in 1939 Cassels (who had been promoted captain the previous year) was at the regimental depot on the Moray Firth; from here he was posted to the Staff College, Camberley, in 1940 for the wartime course. He then saw a short period of active service in France where he was appointed brigade major to Brigadier Sir John Laurie of 157th infantry brigade, in the 52nd Lowland division, which was sent to France after the Dunkirk evacuation. The aim of this operation was to assist the French to hold a line along the Somme and the Aisne against the advancing Panzers. However, the French regarded the position as hopeless and surrendered, leaving the 157th brigade to fight its way back to Cherbourg, from where it was lucky to be evacuated on 17 June 1940.

Between 1940 and 1944 Cassels held a number of staff appointments but in June 1944 he took command of the 152nd infantry brigade, 51st Highland division, on the beachhead east of the River Orne. He led the brigade with distinction, liberating St Valéry, capturing Le Havre, and taking it through the operations in the Netherlands, the Ardennes battle, the Rhine crossing, and the final advance into Germany. He was made DSO and was mentioned twice in dispatches. In 1945 he was promoted temporary major-general commanding the 51st Highland division, which was then occupying the Bremen district. In 1946 he

took command of the 6th airborne division, which was sent to Palestine to engage in anti-terrorist duties, where he was again mentioned in dispatches.

In 1947 Cassels attended the course at the Imperial Defence College (IDC) and in 1948 he became director of land/air warfare at the War Office, with the full rank of major-general. This was followed by a year as chief liaison officer, UK liaison staff, in Australia. His next assignment was to form and command the 1st British Commonwealth division in Korea in 1951. The division consisted of troops from Britain, Canada, Australia, and New Zealand, but was quickly welded by him into an excellent fighting formation. Cassels's informal style, combined with his habit of visiting soldiers in forward, isolated positions, made him extremely popular and successful. He was awarded the American Legion of Merit. In 1953 he became commander of 1st (British) corps in Germany, and after returning to England in 1954 (when he was promoted lieutenant-general) he was director-general of military training (1954–7). He was then appointed director of emergency operations in the Federation of Malaya, a post he held for two years, and in which he was noted for his perception and drive in bringing the operations to a successful conclusion.

Having been promoted general in 1958, Cassels was general officer commanding, eastern command (1959–60); commander-in-chief, British army of the Rhine and commander, NATO northern army group (1960–63); adjutant-general to the forces (1963–4); and chief of the Imperial General Staff (CIGS) (1965–8). He was promoted field marshal on retirement in 1968. His period as CIGS (the word 'imperial' was later dropped) came at a particularly difficult time for, although the Soviet forces greatly outnumbered those of the West in men, guns, tanks, and aircraft, the British government was determined to cut down on defence expenditure. At the same time Cassels was convinced that some members of the House of Commons regarded the expansion of Soviet power as no threat to Britain and were even prepared to assist the Russians, openly or secretly, but as his information about Soviet intentions and domestic subversion was classified he was unable to reveal it. He was unable to prevent drastic reductions in the Territorial Army and the truncation or amalgamation of regiments of the regular army. He was also unable to prevent Britain's being weakened by the loss of aircraft-carriers, and by inadequate provision for the future of the RAF. Nevertheless his influence and prestige undoubtedly prevented much more damaging reductions. He also helped restrain the government from precipitate actions such as military intervention against the declaration of independence in Rhodesia.

Tall and good-looking, Cassels was an inspiring commander, who could be stern when necessary, but was popular with troops owing to his cheerfulness and approachability. An enthusiast for what was then called 'dance music', he would often enliven the mess by singing the latest tune to the accompaniment of his own guitar. He also played the clarinet. An exceptional all-round sportsman in his youth, Cassels played cricket, fives, and rugby football for Rugby for several years and continued to show outstanding sporting prowess at Sandhurst. He was a good shot and a skilled fisherman, and a first-class polo player, cricketer, and golfer; he was a member of the MCC committee and president of the company of veteran motorists.

Cassels was appointed CBE in 1944, CB in 1950, KBE in 1952, and GCB in 1961. His first wife, Joyce, died in 1978, and later that year he married Joy, widow of Kenneth Dickson. Cassels died in Newmarket on 13 December 1996, and was survived by his second wife and the son of his first marriage.

PHILIP WARNER

Sources *The Times* (17 Dec 1996) · *The Independent* (16 Dec 1996) · *Daily Telegraph* (16 Dec 1996) · L. F. Ellis and others, *Victory in the West*, 2 vols. (1962–8) · *WWW* · *Rugby School who's who* · Archives of the Royal Military Academy, Sandhurst · Burke, *Peerage* · private information (2004) · C. N. Barclay, *The first commonwealth divison: the story of the British commonwealth land forces in Korea, 1950–53* (1954) · J. Gray, *The commonwealth armies and the Korean War* (1988)
Likenesses photograph, repro. in *The Times* · photograph, repro. in *The Independent* · photograph, repro. in *Daily Telegraph*
Wealth at death £314,410: probate, 21 March 1997, *CGPLA Eng. & Wales*

Cassels, Sir Robert Archibald (1876–1959), army officer, was born at Bandra, near Bombay, on 15 March 1876, the son of John Andrew Cassels, merchant, of Red Litten, Prince's Risborough, Buckinghamshire, and his wife, Helen, daughter of Thomas White. He was educated at Sedbergh School and the Royal Military College, Sandhurst, was commissioned in 1896, and went to India in the following year, before joining the 32nd Lancers in 1901. He acted as aide-de-camp to his divisional commander (1906–7), was brigade-major (1909–11), and general staff officer, grade 2 (GSO2) in 1911–13. He had married on 9 June 1904 Florence Emily, daughter of Lieutenant-Colonel Halkett Jackson, and they had one son, the army officer Sir James Halkett *Cassels.

In 1915 Cassels became deputy adjutant-general at the headquarters of the force, the nucleus of which had landed in Mesopotamia late in 1914. Before the end of 1915, however, he became GSO1 with the 3rd Indian army corps; he moved to the 14th division in May 1916, and by August 1917 had served in the same capacity with the small cavalry division and as brigadier-general, general staff, of the expeditionary force. When in early April 1917 Sir Stanley Maude advanced north astride the Tigris, Cassels manoeuvred with masterly skill on the left flank, and on 22 April at Istabulat he was sharply engaged.

By now regarded as a coming man, Cassels took command of the 11th cavalry brigade in November 1917. When his great opportunity came in the final offensive of 1918 he revealed himself as an even more outstanding cavalry leader than his promise had foretold. His orders were to reach with his brigade the Little Zab River 25 miles above its junction with the Tigris. He marched 77 miles in 39 hours, but unexpectedly found about a thousand Turks holding the ford for which he was making. None the less he decided to cross, managing to do so by another ford about a mile downstream. Ismael Hakki, his flank turned,

Sir Robert Archibald Cassels (1876–1959), by Walter Stoneman, 1935

skilfully crossed to the right bank of the Tigris and broke up his floating bridge. On 25 October the brigade received orders to cross the river next day above Sharqat and cut off the enemy. Cassels decided he must find a ford near Huwaish, but had to go farther north before one was discovered, all three channels of which were highly dangerous. Most of the horses had to swim; Cassels led the way and rode at a gallop to Huwaish. He had ordered another regiment to join him, but the ford could not be crossed in darkness, so he was isolated and in considerable danger. He estimated the Turkish force nearest to him, 2½ miles south of Huwaish, at four hundred or more.

Early on 27 October, Cassels took the bold decision to attack, mainly to disguise his weakness. The action disclosed the Turkish strength to be between eight hundred and a thousand. Cassels therefore drew back and dug in. The Turkish main body facing the infantry under Sir A. S. Cobbe was doing the same thing at Sharqat. In the early hours of 28 October, Cassels was reinforced by an infantry brigade which had marched 33 miles to join him, and he felt encouraged to try a bluff. A considerable force of the enemy was moving towards him from the south and he sent the 7th hussars, less two squadrons, to meet it. A brilliant dismounted attack drove the enemy back, and though they came on again and forced the hussars to retire, they showed no further signs of attacking. The brigade suffered about a hundred casualties and lost many more horses. In the course of the action the 7th cavalry brigade arrived, and a few more reinforcements came up later.

On 29 October the 13th hussars carried out a dashing attack, first galloping into dead ground unscathed, then dismounting, swarming up a height known as Cemetery Hill, driving off the Turks, and taking 730 prisoners. 29 October was the day of the battle of Sharqat. How great was the part played by Cassels is made clear by the fact that, although the British infantry attack was repulsed, nevertheless next morning white flags fluttered all down the Turkish line.

Cassels next led his forces north to occupy Mosul, but could not induce the Turks to abandon the place until they received the terms of the armistice. He was appointed CB and DSO in 1918 and promoted major-general in 1919. In June of that year serious unrest in southern Kurdistan disturbed the tribes north and north-east of the Mosul vilayet. His commander, Sir Theodore Fraser, being absent, Cassels took immediate steps to prevent the spread of the rebellion. He acted with his usual vigour, with the consequence that after some months of fighting the Kurds had been so handled that they scarcely stirred in the subsequent general Arab revolt.

Cassels was cavalry adviser in India (1920–23), commandant of the Peshawar district (1923–7), and adjutant-general in India (1928–30), being promoted lieutenant-general in 1927 and general in 1929. He next held the Indian northern command (1930–34) in the course of which he became colonel of the 7th light cavalry. (He was appointed colonel of his regiment, which had become the 13th (DCO) Lancers, in 1939.) In 1935 came his final promotion to commander-in-chief of the army of India and member of the executive council of the governor-general, an appointment lasting until 1941 when he went on retired pay. Within a few weeks of taking over Cassels had to face one of the familiar troubles on the north-west frontier. Afridi bands, set in motion by the 'Red Shirt' movement, which in its turn was coached by Russian agents, penetrated to Peshawar, and one Indian battalion refused duty. Cassels speedily restored order. Later he undertook the building of a series of blockhouses across a plain which actually lay outside the administrative borders of India. The creation of these defences brought another threat of frontier war but this he succeeded in averting.

The outbreak of war in 1939 brought a host of problems, foremost among them the expansion of the Indian army, which grew with a rapidity so great that it far outstripped the available equipment. One of the strategic factors Cassels had already anticipated when in May 1936 he had been directed to examine road and rail facilities for moving a division to the Burma frontier and its maintenance there. He estimated that the programme would take eight years, or five if sole reliance were placed in a road from Manipur. He was eager to go ahead at once, but this project was not accepted. Many officers of promise served under Cassels, but the protégé who seemed to excel them all was Claude Auchinleck, a close friend to whom he acted to some extent as mentor and who served with him in Mesopotamia and on his staff in India. Auchinleck, who was to succeed him as commander-in-chief, for his part thought Cassels had certain of the characteristics of Rommel.

Cassels was appointed KCB in 1927, GCB in 1933, and GCSI in 1940. After his retirement he lived at Copthorne, in Sussex, where he took a prominent and useful part in local affairs. He was always very uncommunicative about his military experiences and never spoke of them even to his son, who was to become General Sir James Cassels, chief of the general staff, Ministry of Defence (1965–8).

Cassels's greatest assets were his determination and his *coup d'œil* on the battlefield. He was prepared to gamble, as he did at Sharqat, and gambling boldly and skilfully is proverbially a necessity for the successful leader, but he did not make a single mistake in that campaign and was never abandoned by fortune. His sense of duty and probity equalled his extreme modesty. Cassels died at Ticehurst House, Ticehurst, Sussex on 23 December 1959. Lady Cassels survived her husband.   CYRIL FALLS, *rev.*

Sources F. J. Moberly, ed., *The campaign in Mesopotamia, 1914–1918*, 4 vols. (1923–7), vols. 3–4 · E. W. C. Sandes, *The Indian sappers and miners* (1948) · C. Mackenzie, *Eastern epic*, 1 (1951) · private information (1971) · personal knowledge (1971) · *WWW* · Burke, *Peerage* (1949) · *CGPLA Eng. & Wales* (1960)
Archives FILM BFI NFTVA, home footage
Likenesses W. Stoneman, photograph, 1935, NPG [*see illus.*]
Wealth at death £43,930 16s.: probate, 4 March 1960, *CGPLA Eng. & Wales*

Cassels, Walter Richard (1826–1907), religious controversialist, fourth son of Robert Cassels, for many years British consul at Honfleur, and his wife, Jean, daughter of John Scougall of Leith, was born in London on 4 September 1826. The family, which liked to trace its pedigree to Alfred the Great, was of mercantile capacity.

Walter, who early showed literary ability, with two volumes of poetry published (1850, 1856), became partner with his brothers Andrew and John in the firm of Peel, Cassels & Co. at Bombay. That position he held until 1865, publishing *Cotton: an Account of its Culture in the Bombay Presidency* (1862). From 1863 to 1865 he was an active member of the legislative council of Bombay. Referring to a debate in the council on 8 September 1864, the *Bombay Gazette* distinguished Sir William Rose Mansfield and Cassels as 'men known not only throughout India but in England for the knowledge and ability they have shown in discussing the most important questions of commercial law and practice'. Returning to England, Cassels lived in London, save for an interval spent in the neighbourhood of Manchester.

In 1874 Cassels published anonymously two volumes entitled *Supernatural Religion: an Inquiry into the Reality of Divine Revelation*, in which he impugned the credibility of miracles and the authenticity of the New Testament. This publication, which was calculated to provoke antagonism, was a *succès de scandale*. The wildest conjectures as to its author were rife; it was attributed among others to a nephew of E. B. Pusey, and to Connop Thirlwall. Joseph

Barber Lightfoot, moved by what he deemed its 'cruel and unjustifiable assault ... on a very dear friend', began in the *Contemporary Review* a series of nine articles entitled 'Supernatural religion', which appeared at intervals up to May 1877; though left unfinished, these articles materially reduced the anonymous writer's pretensions to scholarship, and were regarded as giving new strength to the defence of the New Testament canon; they were collected into a volume of *Essays* in 1889.

Meanwhile Cassels's book passed through six editions by 1875; in 1877 a third volume was added; a revised edition of the complete work appeared in 1879; popular editions in one volume, after compression and further revision, were issued in 1902 and 1905. To Lightfoot's first essay the author had replied anonymously in the *Fortnightly Review* (January 1875); this and other rejoinders he collected in *A Reply to Dr Lightfoot's Essays by the Author of 'Supernatural Religion'* (1889). Lightfoot reverted to the controversy in a paper in the *Academy*, the last he wrote (21 September 1889), to which Cassels replied anonymously in the *Academy* (28 September). In 1894 appeared *The Gospel According to Peter: a Study by the Author of 'Supernatural Religion'*. The secret of this authorship was marvellously well kept: Lightfoot wrote in 1889 that he knew neither his name nor 'whether he is living or dead'. On the appearance in the *Nineteenth Century* (April 1895) of an article, 'The Diatessaron of Tatian', signed Walter R. Cassels, the statement was made in the *Manchester City News* (20 April 1895) that Cassels (described as 'a Manchester poet') 'has now avowed himself the author of "Supernatural religion"'. There was no public avowal. Further articles appeared in the *Nineteenth Century* entitled 'The virgin birth of Jesus' (January 1903) and 'The present position of apologetics' (October 1903) and signed Walter R. Cassels, yet the public was slow to connect them with the author of *Supernatural Religion*.

Cassels was long a collector of pictures. Five were sold at Christies on 30 June 1906; they had cost him £1685 5s., and they realized £8547. Among them was Turner's *Rape of Europa*, which he had bought in 1871 for 295 guineas and which sold for 6400 guineas, and the portrait of John Wesley by Romney. Cassels died, unmarried, at his house, 43 Harrington Gardens, South Kensington, London, on 10 June 1907.

ALEXANDER GORDON, *rev.* H. C. G. MATTHEW

Sources R. Cassels, *Records of the family of Cassels* (1870) · *The Times* (1 July 1906) · *The Times* (20 June 1907) · *Annual Register* (1906–7) · *CGPLA Eng. & Wales* (1907)
Wealth at death £52,798 3s. 10d.: probate, 20 June 1907, *CGPLA Eng. & Wales*

Cassie, James (1819–1879), painter, born at Keithhall, near Inverurie, Aberdeenshire, and baptized on 12 February, was one of at least two children of James Cassie, a tea merchant, and his wife, Catherine, *née* Dawnie. In his childhood he met with an accident which left him permanently lame, and he decided to devote his life to painting. He became a pupil of James Giles, a painter of highland scenery and animals, and settled in Aberdeen, where the local fishing community and the seascape were his favourite subjects. Characterized by a simple, unfinished style, most of his paintings were of a modest size. He also painted numerous portraits and domestic subjects and was a competent animal painter. He exhibited works at the Royal Scottish Academy, the Royal Academy, the British Institution, and the Suffolk Street Gallery in London. In 1869 he was elected an associate of the Royal Scottish Academy and moved to Edinburgh, where he lived until his death. In February 1879 he was elected an academician, but he had been ailing for some time, and died at his home, 7 Castle Terrace, Edinburgh, on 11 May of that year. Cassie often signed his works with a monogram; many of his works are in the Aberdeen Art Gallery.

L. H. CUST, *rev.* ROMITA RAY

Sources *The Scotsman* (12 May 1879) · *Art Journal*, 41 (1879), 156 · baptismal cert. · d. cert. · Wood, *Vic. painters*, 3rd edn · J. Halsby and P. Harris, *The dictionary of Scottish painters, 1600–1960* (1990) · W. D. McKay, *The Scottish school of painting* (1906) · J. L. Caw, *Scottish painting past and present, 1620–1908* (1908); repr. (1975) · W. Hardie, *Scottish painting, 1837 to the present* (1990) · R. Brydall, *Art in Scotland, its origin and progress* (1889) · Graves, *Artists* · A. Graves, *A century of loan exhibitions, 1813–1912*, 1 (1913) · private information (1886) · CCI (1880)
Likenesses J. Phillip, oils
Wealth at death £4380 1s.: confirmation, 27 April 1880, CCI · £1604 12s. 7d.: eik additional inventory, 17 May 1880, CCI

Cassilhas. For this title name *see* Thornton, Sir Edward, count of Cassilhas in the Portuguese nobility (1766–1852).

Cassillis. For this title name *see* Kennedy, Gilbert, second earl of Cassillis (*c*.1492–1527); Kennedy, Gilbert, third earl of Cassillis (*c*.1517–1558); Kennedy, Gilbert, fourth earl of Cassillis (*c*.1541–1576); Fleming, Jean, countess of Cassillis (1553/4–1609); Kennedy, John, fifth earl of Cassillis (1574/5–1615); Kennedy, John, sixth earl of Cassillis (1601x7–1668); Kennedy, John, seventh earl of Cassillis (*c*.1646–1701).

Cassivellaunus (*fl.* 54 BC), king in Britain, has been characterized as the 'first British personality' because of his mention by Caesar (Stevens, 3). He may be described as the king of a powerful tribe in the patchwork of Celtic peoples inhabiting south-east Britain in the first century BC, and although his people is not named by Caesar it is generally held to be the Catuvellauni, inhabiting the rich cornlands of modern Hertfordshire. Certainly, Caesar places his kingdom north of the Thames, some 80 miles from the channel coast. The origin of his subjects is uncertain: they may have been indigenous or part of the attested migration of Belgic peoples from Gaul on either side of 100 BC. Cassivellaunus's own name may be broadly translated as 'great leader' and that of the Catuvellauni as 'great warriors', a point of some significance. Even before the coming of the Roman army, Caesar records their bellicosity, in particular against the neighbouring Trinovantes of modern Essex; Cassivellaunus had threatened their king, Mandubracius, having already killed his father (named by some as Imanuentius, but this is an uncertain restoration of an interpolation in some Caesarean manuscripts). Mandubracius fled to Gaul and put himself under the protection of Caesar, who was to use him later as a negotiating ploy.

Caesar's narrative records the events of the summer of 54 BC, after the brief raid in 55 BC. He landed in Kent about 7 July and advanced rapidly westwards, subduing the Celtic stronghold at Bigbury, near Canterbury. Meanwhile, his fleet anchored off the coast was damaged by a sudden storm, which compelled a pause while he arranged for the ships to be beached inside a defensive earthwork; he was then able to resume his advance to the west to a crossing of the Thames, possibly in the area of what is now Wandsworth. Against this threat the British tribes composed their differences and appointed Cassivellaunus as their overall leader. He assembled a large force on the north bank of the river with a strong contingent of charioteers, a favourite Celtic tactic. The light two-wheeled vehicles (*esseda*) carried a crew of two, a driver and a warrior. They would drive rapidly into the enemy's lines, the warrior would leap down and inflict such damage as he could, while the driver retired a short distance ready to rescue the warrior as he fled the scene. Caesar successfully forced a crossing of the river with his cavalry in the lead; the story that they were headed by an armoured elephant is probably apocryphal since Caesar makes no mention of it. The Roman infantry followed and the dispirited Cassivellaunus abandoned the field and dispersed his army, retaining about 4000 charioteers, with which to harass Caesar as he moved north into Catuvellaunian territory. But his main allies now abandoned him, and in particular the Trinovantes appealed to Caesar for protection and the return of Mandubracius. Caesar quickly agreed in return for hostages and a supply of corn, while five other tribes of the area to the north of the Thames surrendered to the Romans and gave Caesar details of the location of Cassivellaunus's stronghold. Caesar names them as the Cenimagni, Segontiaci, Ancalites, Bibroci, and Cassi; their tribal areas are uncertain though the Cenimagni may possibly have been the Iceni of Norfolk.

Opinion varies about the location of Cassivellaunus's stronghold, but pre-war excavation established the general view that it was at Wheathampstead above the River Lea (here possibly the boundary between the Catuvellauni and the Trinovantes) and about 6 miles north-east of the later Catuvellaunian capital at Verulamium (St Albans), destined to become a major town of Roman Britain. Caesar attacked the stronghold and again defeated Cassivellaunus, inflicting heavy casualties and seizing his herds of cattle. As a diversion Cassivellaunus appealed to four kings in Kent, Cingetorix, Carvilius, Taximagulus, and Segovax, to make a raid on Caesar's beachhead, but the Roman defenders threw back the attack with heavy casualties and the capture of one of their leaders, Lugotorix. Cassivellaunus now yielded and sued for peace, using the Gaul Commius as his intermediary. Caesar requested hostages, the payment of an annual tribute, and warned Cassivellaunus not to attack Mandubracius and the Trinovantes. The Roman army withdrew to the naval camp early in August, and then safely crossed to Gaul with the hostages and a large number of prisoners. The whole campaign may have been over in four weeks of fighting, perhaps followed by a week for the imposition of terms, and was clearly a remarkable success for Caesar.

The later life of Cassivellaunus is unknown, but it seems likely that he remained as king of the Catuvellauni, and that the dynasty continued under a son, or more probably grandson, Tasciovanus. The date of Cassivellaunus's death is also unknown, but it may have occurred in the 40s or 30s BC.

F. H. THOMPSON

Sources *The battle for Gaul: Julius Caesar*, ed. and trans. A. Wiseman and P. Wiseman (1980), 85, 91–8 · C. Hawkes, 'Britain and Julius Caesar', *PBA*, 63 (1977), 125–92 · R. E. M. Wheeler and T. V. Wheeler, *Verulamium: a Belgic and two Roman cities* (1936), 6–24 · S. S. Frere, *Britannia: a history of Roman Britain*, 3rd edn (1987), 11–29 · P. Salway, *Roman Britain* (1987), 33–8 · C. E. Stevens, '55 BC and 54 BC', *Antiquity*, 21 (1947), 3–9 · A. Holder, *Alt-Celtischer Sprachschatz* (1896–1913) · H. Meusel, *Lexicon Caesarianum*, 2 (Berlin, 1914), 1, 54 · Polyaenus, *Strategica*, ed. E. Wolfein and J. Melber (1887), viii.23, 5

Casson, Sir Hugh Maxwell (1910–1999), architect, was born on 23 May 1910 at 4 Grossfield Road, London, the second of two children of Randal Casson (1879–1972), colonial civil servant, and his wife, May Caroline (*d.* 1962), daughter of Edward Garnett Man and his wife, Catherine. Randal Casson was posted in Burma and his son's first three years were spent there, before being sent back to Britain with his sister for safety during the First World War, where they were looked after by their maternal grandparents at Sandgate, Kent. Hugh Casson's ability to charm people by conversational wit enabled him to adapt to changing households of relations until his parents' permanent return in 1923. His uncle Lewis Casson was an actor, married to Dame Sybil Thorndike.

After a conventional preparatory school Casson went to Eastbourne College. He was small (5 feet 4 inches) and light in build, out of place in a philistine atmosphere, and left the college early in 1927. After a year at home he entered St John's College, Cambridge, to read architecture, for which his private pursuit of drawing over many years had demonstrated his aptitude, proven when his course began in 1929. In his second year one of the young tutors was Christopher Nicholson, the brother of the painter Ben Nicholson, the most prominent among several members of staff who were engaged in the early stages of modern architecture in Britain. Outside the school Casson was cox for the college boat and painted scenery for the festival theatre. After graduating with a first in 1932, Casson was awarded a travel grant to spend three months at the British School at Athens, studying Byzantine brickwork, the subject of his RIBA final thesis, part of the completion of his qualification at the Bartlett School of Architecture, London, in 1934. The most significant aspect of the Bartlett was Casson's meeting, on the first day, his future wife, Margaret MacDonald Troup [*see below*]. They were married at St Margaret's, Westminster, on 19 November 1938.

Casson went to work for Christopher Nicholson in 1935. His talent in perspective drawing, nurtured at Cambridge,

Sir Hugh Maxwell Casson (1910–1999), by David Ashdown, 1976

and his personal skills with clients were valued. Casson's attitude to modern architecture was one of acceptance without the exclusive commitment demanded by zealots. A small house which he designed speculatively in 1937 was traditional in style, and his early writings, such as the guidebook *New Sights of London* (1937), are surprisingly inclusive. The Nicholson office tempered its modernism with a sense of fun and accepted some bizarre commissions, such as the transformation of Monkton House for the surrealist patron Edward James. As a journalist on *Night and Day* magazine (1937–8), and as the main contributor to the gossip column 'Astragal' in the *Architects' Journal*, Casson was influential in creating a fashionable but undidactic climate of opinion around modern architecture which was absent from the earlier 1930s. His contact with the *Architects' Journal* and its sister magazine the *Architectural Review* gave him a platform in what became, after the war, an alternative to the 'establishment' and, eventually, an establishment of its own.

The Cassons were visiting South Africa when war broke out in 1939, but soon returned. Casson joined the camouflage service of the Air Ministry in July 1940, based near Cheltenham, where the first two of his three daughters were born, and his writing and illustrating activities continued. In April 1944 Casson went to the Ministry of Town and Country Planning to work under William Holford. He

co-wrote two books on prefabricated housing as well as continuing a stream of journalism and illustration, before rejoining Nicholson in practice in 1946. Their work consisted mainly of design consultancy for British European Airways and Ferranti, with exhibition stands. Nicholson died following a gliding accident in 1948, shortly after Casson had accepted an invitation from Sir Gerald Barry to become director of architecture for the Festival of Britain in 1951. This was a transformative moment, as Casson, recovering from the loss of a close friend as well as professional partner, took over the practice, joined by two younger architects, Neville Conder and Patience Clifford, with whom he had worked closely at the ministry.

The festival dominated Casson's working life for three years. He proved ideal for a job which required team-building, public relations, and skill in overcoming perpetual obstacles and opposition with last-minute improvisation. The 'design group' consisted of Casson, Misha Black, Ralph Tubbs, and James Holland. His own contribution to the eventual outcome was not limited to the relatively minor sections which he personally designed, but was manifested in the selection of architects for individual buildings, most of whom were relatively young. The chief task was the south bank site, for which Casson and Holland produced the basic plan idea, based on asymmetrical subdivisions of the space, acknowledging the existing irregularities on the ground, and making dramatic views outwards from this then unfamiliar vantage point. Casson's theatrical flair was combined with the revival of picturesque theory and landscaping technique, involving informality and surprise, described in the 1940s as 'Townscape'. Cues were taken from earlier exhibition designs from pre-war Europe for decorative effects achievable within the constraints of the modern style and limited budgets, including a prodigal use of colour and a preference for lightweight, nautically inspired buildings. Landscaping, with living plants and with permanent materials, was fully integrated to create a festive and domestic atmosphere. Sculpture and murals by a mixture of modern and unknown artists provided points of interest. A special lettering panel recommended piquant versions of Victorian 'Egyptian' and shadowed faces which can be traced back to the taste of the *Architectural Review* in the 1930s. The experience was kinetic, with people moving around spaces and objects themselves in motion. It was most effective at night, with skilful illumination and dancing couples out of doors, as represented in the short film *Brief City*, in which Casson appeared as a commentator. Other festival sites, such as the pleasure gardens at Battersea and the 'Live Architecture' exhibition at Lansbury, in Poplar, were moulded by Casson less directly in the appointments of architects and designers made under his guidance.

Casson was knighted in 1952 for his work on the festival. In the following year he designed the coronation decorations for the city of Westminster. His architectural practice Casson Conder & Partners henceforth formed one aspect of his life, but his personal involvement was less than appearances might have suggested, despite Neville

Conder's attempts to engage him more closely in the activity of designing buildings. His versatility and originality in conceptual planning, his worldly wisdom, and his skill in handling people none the less contributed to the success of buildings such as the Sidgwick Avenue arts faculty buildings at Cambridge, the Faculty Club for Birmingham University, and, in the 1970s, the Ismaili Centre in South Kensington. The principal buildings attributable to Casson personally were the beach house for Lord Montagu of Beaulieu (1957) and the elephant house at London Zoo (1963–4), which made effective use of bush-hammered concrete. He was professor of environmental design at the Royal College of Art from 1953 to 1975, and his wife was senior tutor. Casson's own interior commissions included the *Time Life* building in London, private rooms in Buckingham Palace, the royal yacht *Britannia*, and RMS *Canberra*. The association with the royal family developed into a series of lasting friendships. Casson also designed a number of theatre and opera productions for Glyndebourne and the Royal Opera House, Covent Garden. His drawings were reproduced on decorative ceramics typical of the 1950s.

Casson was a member of the Royal Fine Arts Commission (1960–83) and was thus able to influence the choice of architects for major commissions during a period when the commission was eager to promote modern architecture in place of traditional survival. In 1975 he was elected president of the Royal Academy, and brought all his energy and charm to making it more popular and commercially enterprising during his nine-year term, rescuing the academy from a position of near insolvency a few years earlier and embracing modern artists more comprehensively than before. At the same time he became a public figure for a new generation, and was identified with his lightweight pen and wash sketches which were widely exhibited and published, individually or in book form. Casson's illustrated letters of thanks and persuasion were legendary. His verbal wit, cultivated in early life on the basis of paradox and word play, was freely dispensed on public and private occasions, deflecting the possibility of deeper analysis. Casson's willingness to appear as an expert witness for the demolition of historic buildings was seen by many as an opportunistic abuse of his reputation.

From 1992 onwards Casson's health began to decline, and in his last years he suffered from loss of eyesight and of memory. He died in St Charles Hospital, Kensington, on 15 August 1999, and was buried nine days later. His wife, whose personal support was crucial to his career, outlived him by less than three months and they were commemorated jointly in a memorial service at St Paul's Cathedral. They were survived by their three daughters. Writing in 1986, Sir John Summerson described Casson as 'the gentle knight, compact but slightly shaggy, reflective but also ambitious, a tiger for work, observing everything, absorbing much, sometimes grave, often witty' ('Foreword' to *Casson: Architect etcetera*, 4).

Casson's wife, **Margaret** [Reta] **MacDonald Casson** [*née* Margaret Troup], Lady Casson (1913–1999), architect and designer, was born on 26 September 1913 in Pretoria, South Africa, the second daughter of James MacDonald Troup, medical practitioner, and his wife, Alberta, *née* Davis. She was educated at Wychwood School, Oxford, and the Bartlett School of Architecture at University College, London. 'When I saw her in the studio I thought she was of surpassing beauty', Hugh Casson later said (*The Times*, 30 Nov 1999). Following their marriage she supported her husband in all his activities. She was also a talented architect, designer, and photographer in her own right. From 1952 to 1974 she was a tutor in design at the Royal College of Art; she also acted as design consultant to a number of companies and accepted posts on a number of public bodies, including the Design Council (1967–73), the design committee of London Transport (1980–88), and the stamp advisory committee of the Post Office (1980–95). She held a series of exhibitions of her photographs in London, Bath, New York, and Tokyo, under the name Margaret MacDonald. She died at her home, 6 Hereford Mansions, Hereford Road, London, on 13 November 1999.

ALAN POWERS

Sources J. Manser, *Hugh Casson: a biography* (2000) · *Hugh Casson: architect etcetera* (1986) [exhibition catalogue, 18 Sept – 25 Oct 1986, Heinz Gallery] · *The Guardian* (17 Aug 1999), 16 · *The Independent* (17 Aug 1999), 6 · *Daily Telegraph* (17 Aug 1999) · *The Times* (17 Aug 1999) · *Hugh Casson's diary* (1983) · C. Olmo, ed., *Dizionario dell'archititura del XX secovo*, 2, 33–4 · M. Emanuel, ed., *Contemporary architects* (1994), 163–4 · b. cert. [Hugh Casson] · m. cert. · d. certs · *Daily Telegraph* (18 Nov 1999) · *The Times* (30 Nov 1999)

Archives NL Wales, letters to Kyffin Williams · Tate collection, transcript of interview for TV South West | SOUND BL NSA, National Life Story Collection

Likenesses D. Ashdown, photograph, 1976, Hult. Arch. [*see illus.*]

Wealth at death £367,839: probate, 20 April 2000, *CGPLA Eng. & Wales* · £488,027—Margaret Casson: probate, 2000, *CGPLA Eng. & Wales*

Casson, John (1909–1999), naval officer and management consultant, was born on 28 October 1909 at 75 St George's Square, Pimlico, London, the first of the four children of Sir Lewis Thomas *Casson (1875–1969), the actor-manager, and his wife, Dame (Agnes) Sybil *Thorndike (1882–1976), the actress. While his two sisters, Mary and Ann, were destined for the stage, John and his brother, Christopher (1912–1996), chose naval careers. Both received early education at King's College School, Wimbledon, after which Christopher was accepted for the Royal Naval College, Dartmouth, but John was by then too old and was sent instead to the nautical training ship *Worcester*, moored in the Thames at Greenhithe. He later entered the Royal Navy as a special entry cadet in 1926, while Christopher proved unsuited to naval life and later became an actor and an Irish citizen.

Casson loved the navy, first serving in the battleship *Emperor of India*. In 1931, while a sub-lieutenant in the destroyer *Velox*, he applied for flying training, to be told by his commanding officer that he should understand that that would only hamper his naval career; ten years later this commanding officer, then Vice-Admiral Sir Tom Phillips, was lost with his two capital ships, *Prince of Wales* and

Repulse, to Japanese air attack. Casson persevered, qualified as a pilot in the Fleet Air Arm, and flew for the next eight years, particularly enjoying aerobatics and writing poetry celebrating the joys of flight.

While serving in the Far East as a pilot in the aircraft-carrier *Eagle*, Casson took part in air operations against Chinese pirates. In Shanghai in 1933 he met his future wife, Patricia Mary Chester-Master (1914–1992), and they were married in London on 7 June 1935; during the next four years a son and two daughters were born.

Before the outbreak of the Second World War in 1939 Casson was flying Walrus flying boats from the cruisers *Glasgow* and *Southampton*, which was to be damaged by air attack. Promoted lieutenant commander in April 1940, he was appointed to command 803 squadron, flying Skua dive-bombers from the carrier *Ark Royal*, then operating in support of the failing campaign in Norway. After the sinking of the carrier *Glorious* by the German battlecruisers *Scharnhorst* and *Gneisnau*, two squadrons of Skuas were sent to attack the former and the heavy cruiser *Hipper*, lying in Trondheim Fjord. German fighters were waiting over the target, and eight of the fifteen Skuas—including Casson's—were shot down, having been unable to damage the enemy ships. Casson then began five years as a prisoner of war.

In two prison camps—Dulag Luft and Stalag Luft 111—Casson worked as a clandestine code master, passing messages in cipher via the prisoners' mail to MI9 in London, the department of military intelligence dealing with prisoners of war, escapers, and evaders. In the latter camp he helped to mount what became known as the 'great escape', after which fifty of those recaptured were shot on Hitler's orders. He produced plays in the camp's theatre and studied German, Russian, and philosophy. He returned home in May 1945 and was appointed to the Order of the British Empire (military) for his coding work.

Having missed most of the war, Casson decided that his naval career was at an end, so he resigned in 1946 and followed his parents, brother, and sisters into the theatre. After beginning as an assistant stage manager at the Citizens' Theatre, Glasgow, he became its producer–manager, working closely with James Bridie, the Scottish playwright, and directing his own parents for a season. In 1951 he was appointed senior producer for J. C. Williamson Theatres in Australia and moved to Melbourne. Over the next seventeen years he became well known in Australia: first in the theatre, then in television, and after 1956 as a management consultant.

Combining his experiences in the navy and the theatre (and, perhaps, something of his family's socialist ideals), Casson was an immediate success, instructing business management in communication and presentation. Some of his advice was included in his book *Using Words: Verbal Communication in Industry*, published in London by Duckworth in 1968. After returning to England in the following year he ran management training courses in a variety of industries, including banking, insurance, accountancy, and shipbuilding.

Casson continued this work until he was past eighty, also giving readings of prose and poetry in joint recitals, often with one of his daughters or his niece. He was asked to read at memorial services, most notably that of his cousin Sir Hugh Casson (1910–1999), the architect and former president of the Royal Academy, in St Paul's Cathedral a month before his own death. Having learned conjuring as a young naval officer and become a member of the Magic Circle, he continued to delight children with his sleight of hand. In 1972 his memoir of his parents, *Lewis and Sybil*, was published by Collins.

Casson was a strikingly handsome, vigorous man with a commanding presence and sonorous voice. After his wife's death in a swimming accident in 1992, he continued living in London, where he was a member of the Garrick Club, until his sudden death in the Lister Hospital, Westminster, from a kidney infection on 24 December 1999; he had been looking forward to celebrating the millennium. He was cremated at Mortlake crematorium on 7 January 2000. He was survived by his children, and at the time of his death had five grandchildren and five great-grandchildren.

TOM POCOCK

Sources personal knowledge (2004) · private information (2004) [family] · J. Casson, *Lewis and Sybil* (1972) · b. cert. · m. cert. · d. cert. · *The Times* (7 Jan 2000) · *Daily Telegraph* (2 March 2000) **Archives** priv. coll., family papers · Theatre Museum, London, corresp. and papers, incl. papers as POW in Stalag Luft 111 **Likenesses** L. Kenyon, oils, *c.*1944, priv. coll. **Wealth at death** £339,539—net: probate, 27 March 2000, *CGPLA Eng. & Wales* · £370,000: Lee, Bolton and Lee, Solicitors

Casson, Sir Lewis Thomas (1875–1969), actor and theatre director, was born at 18 Alfred Road, Birkenhead, Cheshire, on 26 October 1875, the third of the seven children of Thomas Casson (1843–1911), bank manager and organ-builder, and his wife, Laura Ann (1843–1912), daughter of Lewis Holland-Thomas, a sea-captain from Talsarnau, in Merioneth, north Wales. The family settled in Denbigh and Lewis was educated at Ruthin grammar school. In 1891 his father turned his hobby of building church organs into a business. The family moved to London where, after a short apprenticeship, Lewis joined his father. When the business failed Lewis went to the City and Guilds Central Institution in South Kensington to study chemistry. However, his scientific ambition gave way to a determination to be an Anglican priest. Meanwhile he became a pupil teacher at St Augustine's Church school, Kilburn, winning in 1896 a queen's scholarship to St Mark's College, Chelsea, where he gained a teaching certificate and became assistant tutor. Here he grew interested in socialism and in literature, while his sense of ecclesiastical vocation and his Anglo-Catholic fervour faded. In 1900 his father started another church organ business, specializing in a small pipe-organ which he had invented for use in village churches. Lewis returned to work for his father for another four years.

From early childhood, Casson had acted in family plays and then in amateur theatre. He began to undertake semi-professional work, appearing in Shakespeare 'costume

Sir Lewis Thomas Casson (1875–1969), by W. Mear, 1906

recitals' and in productions by William Poel, the scholar of Elizabethan drama whose radical vision of authentic Shakespearian theatre was influential in changing the lavish Victorian approach to Shakespeare. In 1904 Casson left his father's business and became a professional actor. Besides Poel, his early theatrical influences included Harley Granville Barker, George Bernard Shaw, and Gilbert Murray. He joined the Vedrenne–Barker season at the Royal Court Theatre (1904–7), playing in the original production of Shaw's *Man and Superman* and in Murray's translation of Euripides' *Hippolytus*.

Casson shared Barker's vision of a national theatre and a network of regional companies, and in 1908 joined the first English repertory company, founded by Miss Annie Horniman at the Gaiety Theatre, Manchester. At the end of that year, on 22 December, he married another member of the company, (Agnes) Sybil *Thorndike (1882–1976). With her he appeared in Charles Frohman's repertory season in London, and soon after the birth of their first son, John *Casson (1909), they toured the USA with Frohman in Somerset Maugham's *Smith*. This long commercial run reaffirmed his belief in the repertory system. He was delighted to return to England as producer for Miss Horniman (1911–13). In Manchester, where his son Christopher was born (1912), his most successful productions included Stanley Houghton's *Hindle Wakes* (1912), a realistic Lancashire drama which caused moral outrage at the time, and an innovative interpretation of *Julius Caesar* (1913), performed continuously with a permanent set, played with

verve, speed, and excitement, which nevertheless displeased Miss Horniman and led to his resignation.

During the First World War, Casson joined the Army Service Corps, despite being over age. Later he joined the Royal Engineers (special brigade, poison gas), reaching the rank of major. He was awarded the Military Cross and sent home wounded in 1917. He ended the war as secretary of the Chemical Warfare Committee, but ever after regretted his part in the manufacture and release of gas. His family had been completed with the births of his daughters, Mary (1914) and Ann (1915).

From then on Casson's career was motivated as much by Sybil Thorndike's art as by his own, as she rose, with his support, to become one of the greatest actresses of her time. The zenith of both their careers was *Saint Joan* (1924) which Shaw wrote for her and which Casson directed alongside Shaw. Other artistic achievements included his productions of Gilbert Murray's Euripides translations, notably *The Trojan Women* and *Medea*, seasons of Grand Guignol at the Little Theatre in the early 1920s, and productions of *Henry VIII* (1925) and *Macbeth* (1926), in which he aimed to combine Poel's and Barker's approach with the more spectacular style West End audiences sought. He and Sybil Thorndike undertook tours of South Africa, Egypt, Palestine, and Australia. In 1939 he led an Old Vic tour around the Mediterranean. During the Second World War he ran tours for the Old Vic in the Welsh mining valleys. Bombed out of his London home, he spent time in the Casson family house in Portmadoc which he had inherited from an aunt. His last leading role was in J. B. Priestley's *The Linden Tree* (1947).

In later years Casson took part in numerous international recital tours with his wife. As an actor he was successful in classical and modern plays, having a mellifluous and powerful voice, a handsome face and sturdy bearing, and an ability in both comic and serious roles. As a director he was meticulous and often dictatorial, interested in moulding the performances to make a unified effect, especially vocally, and in creating strong effects through simple theatrical means. Though serious and dedicated, he was also humorous and not averse to playing practical jokes on stage.

Casson was energetic in promoting the organization of British theatre according to ideals formulated in his years with Barker. A founder member of the British Actors' Equity Association, established in 1929, he was its second president (1940–45). In the 1930s and 1940s he sat on the Shakespeare Memorial National Theatre Committee which eventually brought about the foundation of the National Theatre in 1963. In 1940 he became active in the Council for the Encouragement of Music and the Arts, forerunner of the Arts Council of Great Britain, and served as its drama director under Maynard Keynes (1942–5). In 1945 he was made a KBE for his services to the theatre. He received honorary degrees from the universities of Glasgow, Aberystwyth, and Oxford, and the fellowship of the Imperial College. His last appearance was in a tour of *Night must Fall* in 1968. He died in the Nuffield Nursing

Home in London on 16 May 1969. He was cremated at Golders Green on 19 May and his life was celebrated at a thanksgiving service at Westminster Abbey on 3 June 1969.

DIANA DEVLIN

Sources D. Devlin, *A speaking part: Lewis Casson and the theatre of his time* (1982) [incl. bibliography] · D. D. Graham, 'The dreamer and the maker: a study of Lewis Casson's work in the theatre', PhD diss., University of Minnesota, 1972 [incl. extensive bibliography] · J. Casson, *Lewis and Sybil: a memoir* (1972) · E. Sprigge, *Sybil Thorndike Casson* (1971) · b. cert. · personal knowledge (2004) · private information (2004)
Archives BL, letters to George Bernard Shaw, Add. MS 50531 · Bodl. Oxf., corresp. with Gilbert Murray | FILM BFI NFTVA, news footage · BFI NFTVA, performance footage | SOUND BL NSA, 'A man of many parts', BBC Home Service, 29 Oct 1965, NP933W C1 · BL NSA, 'Sir Lewis Casson', BBC Radio 4, 9 Sept 1969, P480W C1 · BL NSA, documentary recordings · BL NSA, performance recordings
Likenesses E. Jackson, drawing, 1905, priv. coll. · W. Mear, oils, 1906, Garr. Club [*see illus.*] · drawing, 1935, priv. coll. · W. Stoneman, photograph, 1946, NPG · G. Argent, photograph, *c.*1968, NPG · T. P. Andrew, photograph, NPG · A. Dearnley, bust, priv. coll. · E. Mear, watercolour drawing, Garr. Club · photographs, London, Mander and Mitchenson Collection
Wealth at death £17,321: probate, 3 Nov 1969, CGPLA Eng. & Wales

Casson, Margaret MacDonald, Lady Casson (1913–1999). *See under* Casson, Sir Hugh Maxwell (1910–1999).

Casson, (Agnes) Sybil. *See* Thorndike, Dame (Agnes) Sybil (1882–1976).

Casteels, Peter [*formerly* Pieter] (1684–1749), painter and designer, was born in Antwerp, Southern Netherlands, on 3 October 1684, the son of Pieter Casteels, painter. He was trained by his father and in 1708 arrived in London with his brother-in-law, Peter Tillemans, having been offered work by a picture dealer. He settled readily into London's artistic community, subscribing to Kneller's Great Queen Street academy in 1711 and becoming a member of the Rose and Crown Club. Although he returned briefly to Antwerp in 1716, Casteels settled permanently in England where he was a leading painter of flowers and exotic birds, chiefly for overdoors and chimney-pieces. His range as a decorative painter also encompassed small history pictures in architectural settings. But painting provided only a part of his income: he also imported fine pictures from the continent and sold them well, 'having had much business and reputation', including the patronage of James Stanley, tenth earl of Derby (Vertue, 3.148). Between September 1722 and May 1724 Derby spent just under £2500 on seventeen Italian and Flemish paintings supplied by Casteels and £10 on a flower piece by Casteels himself.

In 1726 Casteels successfully launched a subscription for a set of twelve prints of birds which he had etched after his own designs, 'this being the first work in that kind of his doing, (except some two or three other little plates as tryals)' (Vertue, 3.28–9). This undertaking encouraged him to take a third share in another publishing venture. *Twelve Months of Flowers* was backed by three entrepreneurs: the designer Casteels, the engraver Henry Fletcher, and the gardener Robert Furber from whose Kensington nursery

all the varieties depicted in the prints could be bought. Together they ventured £500 but found 457 people prepared to subscribe 2 guineas each for the set, allowing a handsome profit from the subscription edition alone. The *Flowers* provided a pattern for so many cheap copies by other printsellers that in 1735 Fletcher was called as a witness to give evidence to the parliamentary committee investigating the case for an engravers' copyright act, in which Hogarth was a prime mover. Casteels had already designed a companion set, *Twelve Months of Fruit* (1733), which he also helped to sell.

By advertising the usefulness of these sets of prints as patterns for workers in luxury industries, Casteels drew attention to his own potential as a textile designer. In May 1735 he retired from painting and spent his last fourteen years working for a calico manufacturer as a residential artist, first at Martin Abbey near Tooting, Surrey, and later, briefly, in Richmond, Surrey. He died in Richmond on 16 May 1749 after a lingering illness, and was buried there. A sale of his collections, including copperplates, was announced by the auctioneer Richard Ford in the *General Advertiser* on 6 March 1750 and the plates of his *Birds* were acquired by the printseller John Bowles. Examples of Casteels's etchings and the prints after his designs are in the British Museum, the British Library, and the Victoria and Albert Museum, London; some of his paintings are in the Bowes Museum, Barnard Castle, co. Durham; Leeds City Art Gallery; Yale Center for British Art, New Haven, Connecticut; and the Von der Heydt Museum, Wuppertal, Germany.

TIMOTHY CLAYTON

Sources Vertue, *Note books*, vol. 3 · F. Russell, 'The Derby collection (1721–1735)', *Walpole Society*, 53 (1987), 143–80 · T. Clayton, *The English print, 1688–1802* (1997) · I. Bignamini, 'George Vertue, art historian, and art institutions in London, 1689–1768', *Walpole Society*, 54 (1988), 1–148 · W. Hefford, *Design for printed textiles in England from 1750 to 1850* (1992) · *General Advertiser* (6 March 1750) · *A catalogue of maps, prints, copy-books &c. from off copper plates, printed for John Bowles and Son* [1753], 37 · Thieme & Becker, *Allgemeines Lexikon*

Castelin, Edward (*fl.* 1554–1578), merchant, was of a large and long-established family of Anglo-Iberian traders. With other London merchants Castelin was a member of several syndicates that financed English voyages to the Guinea coast in 1554, 1558, 1561, 1563, and 1564, to interlope upon the existing Portuguese trade to the region. He also invested in a further Guinea voyage, projected for 1555, which was abandoned under pressure from Queen Mary (herself responding to Portuguese pressure), albeit with compensation for the promoters' losses. In the same year he was a charter member of the Muscovy Company and, with Anthony Hickman, maintained two factors at Gran Canaria to trade in sugar. Also with Hickman he owned a ship of 800 tons, the *Great Christopher*, sold to the navy in 1560. With two others he jointly owned the *Primrose*, of 240 tons, which sailed in a Muscovy Company voyage in 1557.

In 1564 Castelin invested in and victualled John Hawkins's second slaving expedition. In 1574 and 1575 he was in Germany making attempts to secure a loan for the queen, even to the point of (unsuccessfully) wooing a widow who, it was rumoured, was prepared to lend 100,000 'dollars' at 5 per cent. In 1575 he became a charter member of the Mineral and Battery Works Company. A sometime cloth exporter, he was also a member of the Merchant Adventurers' Company.

From September 1578 Castelin became involved with (though he did not invest in) Martin Frobisher's north-west enterprise. At Deptford, as Michael Lok's deputy, he had responsibility for providing carts, lighters, and labourers for the unloading and storage of ore returned from Frobisher's second (1577) and third (1578) voyages, before its refining in a large, purpose-built complex there. He appears to have resigned this position shortly after 31 December (to which date his financial accounts are drawn), possibly following an incident in which Frobisher, imagining his own authority to have been side-stepped by Lok, took the Dartford workhouse keys forcibly from Castelin 'and reviled him, with villanous speech & threatenings' (BL, Lansdowne MS 100/1, fols. 9v, 11v; PRO, EKR E164/36, pp. 201–11). This is the last extant reference to Castelin. His place of residence in London, and details of his immediate family, are not known. The Muscovy merchant John Castelin may have been his brother, likewise Thomas Castelin; both men were London-based merchant adventurers and members of the Spanish Company upon its incorporation in 1577. In the same year a Francis Castelin sailed in William Towerson's final voyage to Guinea. All may have been sons or nephews of the brothers James and William Castelin, Anglo-Spanish and Levant traders active during the 1530s.

JAMES MCDERMOTT

Sources R. Hakluyt, *The principal navigations, voyages, traffiques and discoveries of the English nation*, 2, Hakluyt Society, extra ser., 2 (1903); 6, Hakluyt Society, extra ser., 6 (1904); 9, Hakluyt Society, extra ser., 9 (1904) · T. S. Willan, *The Muscovy merchants of 1555* (1953) · T. S. Willan, *Studies in Elizabethan foreign trade* (1959) · M. Lok, 'The doinges of Captaine Furbisher / amongest the Companyes busynes', BL, Lansdowne MS 100/1, fols. 1–14 · J. W. Blake, ed. and trans., *Europeans in west Africa, 1450–1560*, 2 vols., Hakluyt Society, 86–7 (1942) · PRO, EKR E164/36 [Michael Lok's financial accounts for Frobisher's north-west enterprise] · P. E. H. Hair and J. D. Alsop, *English seamen and traders in Guinea, 1553–1565: the new evidence of their wills* (1992) · G. Connell-Smith, *Forerunners of Drake* (1954) · M. Oppenheim, *A history of the administration of the Royal Navy* (1896) · J. A. Williamson, *Sir John Hawkins: the time and the man* (1927) · P. Croft, *The Spanish Company*, London RS, 9 (1973) · R. B. Outhwaite, 'Royal borrowing in the reign of Elizabeth I', *EngHR*, 86 (1971), 251–63

Castell, Edmund (*bap.* 1606, *d.* 1686), orientalist and lexicographer, was baptized on 4 January 1606 at East Hatley, Cambridgeshire, the second son of Robert Castell, a man of property and education, and his wife, Elizabeth, daughter of Edmund Alleyn of Hatfield Peverel, Essex. He matriculated a pensioner at Emmanuel College, Cambridge, on 6 May 1621, graduated BA in 1625, and proceeded MA in 1628 and BD in 1635. In 1635 he became vicar of Hatfield Peverel through the patronage of his cousin Edward Alleyn, but resigned in 1638. It seems probable that he held other livings in Essex or Cambridgeshire until 1647, when he was appointed rector of Woodham

Edmund Castell (*bap.* 1606, *d.* 1686), by William Faithorne the elder, pubd 1669

Walter, Essex, where his father had owned property. On 3 August 1648 he married Dorothy, sister of Charles Fytch, patron of the living, but she died with no children of the match surviving.

Castell's sister Elizabeth was married to the leading presbyterian minister Stephen Marshall, and his elder brother Robert was in 1643 a member of the committee for Cambridge appointed by the parliamentary commissioners for Essex. These connections may explain why Castell, although apparently always loyal to the king and the Church of England, suffered no persecution during the civil war and interregnum. Nor did he encounter any difficulties when he was in London, absent from his cure, for many years beginning in 1653. By this time Castell had acquired, by methods unknown, considerable expertise in Arabic and other oriental languages, and in that year he was recruited by Brian Walton as his chief assistant in supervising the printing of the polyglot Bible, a project that was to last until 1658. Castell was responsible for correcting the Samaritan, Syriac, Arabic, and Ethiopic versions, and he produced the Latin translations of the Canticles in Ethiopic, several books of the New Testament, and the Syriac version of Job. The polyglot Bible, which had been published by subscription, was a scholarly and commercial success. Encouraged by this Castell and another assistant on the project, Samuel Clarke, issued in 1658 a prospectus, *Lexicon linguarum orientalium*, for a

'Heptaglot Lexicon', named after the seven oriental languages represented in the polyglot—Hebrew, Samaritan, Chaldee, Syriac, Arabic, Ethiopian, and Persian. This was to be printed with the presses and types that Walton had specially made for the polyglot, and was intended as an aid to reading the polyglot, but also as a scholarly work in its own right. Castell was to spend the next twelve years of his life, enormous labour, and most of his patrimony on this disastrous project. He later claimed that he had been persuaded by Walton and other 'great men' to undertake it against his will, but in its early stages he was enthusiastic. Initially he had two partners in the enterprise, Clarke and Alexander Huish (also a polyglot contributor), who joined with him in petitioning Cromwell to be allowed to import paper free of duties, but Clarke and Huish soon departed for more congenial positions, and although the printer Thomas Roycroft (who had purchased the polyglot presses and types from Walton) became a partner for a while, by 1663 he too had withdrawn, and Castell was left with sole financial responsibility. Although a learned and hard-working man, he was, unlike Walton, utterly unfit by temperament and judgement to manage an enterprise requiring the co-ordinated work of numerous scholars, editors, and printers. A number of assistants were hired, including some, such as Thomas Hyde, J. M. Wansleben, Theodorus Petraeus, and William Beveridge, who made their mark in other fields, but only one, Martin Murray, a German from Greifswald, stayed with him for any length of time. One can see from the torrent of complaints in his surviving letters why Castell had difficulty retaining helpers. The following extract from a letter to Clarke of 1661 is typical:

> I have had not so fewe as 10. or 12. assistants … who have consumed mee great summs of mony, & stood mee in very little stead, less than you can wel imagine, makinge this crushing heavy ponderous burden upon mee, only their play & recreation. (BL, Add. MS 22905, fol. 48)

He made the mistake of starting to print as soon as there was material ready, but then the delays caused by his own vacillations and insistence on redoing his assistants' work caused the presses to stand idle, while the workmen still had to be paid.

Castell was soon beset by financial difficulties. Subscriptions were few, and some subscribers defaulted. He raised the price of subscriptions and later tried to profit from the presses by printing other books (such as Job Ludolf's *Ethiopic Lexicon*) in the intervals of printing the *Heptaglot*, but he was forced gradually to sell off the landed property he had inherited to cover expenses. By 1663 this property was all gone and Castell eventually claimed to have spent £12,000 of his own money on the *Lexicon*. In 1660 he tried to get support from another source by publishing *Sol Angliae Oriens*, a collection of poems in all the languages of the polyglot Bible, accompanied by Latin translations, that celebrated Charles II's Restoration with an explicit plea for the king to encourage the *Lexicon*. Charles (who had mandated the grant of DD at Cambridge to Castell that same year) did issue a letter recommending the work and he later appointed Castell to the sinecures of royal

chaplain (1665) and canon of Canterbury (1667). Archbishop Sheldon also recommended the work, but these appeals produced only £700 (most of it due to the efforts of Seth Ward, bishop of Salisbury).

Castell sustained other setbacks: 300 copies of volume 1 (substantially completed in 1661) were destroyed in the great fire of London (1666) and Castell himself was briefly imprisoned in July 1667 for the debts of his deceased brother Robert. Even when the *Lexicon* finally emerged from the press in 1669 further troubles awaited. Appeals in the *London Gazette* on 3 May 1669 and 27 December 1669 show that Castell waited many months at the warehouse in vain for subscribers to pick up their copies of the *Lexicon*. In 1673 he still had more than 1000 copies on his hands. At his death he still had at least 600 copies to bequeath, most of which were subsequently eaten by rats in a house at Merton, Surrey, owned by his executor, his brother's daughter Mary Crispe.

Castell's *Lexicon heptaglotton* is based on a wide range of literary sources in many languages and it embodies much excellent learning, but its form is so impractical as to render it largely useless. Disregarding the wise advice of the best Arabists in London, Castell insisted on grouping the entries for all the six Semitic languages under their supposed Hebrew root. Only the Persian (largely derived from a manuscript dictionary compiled by Jacobus Golius) was made into a separate section. The six languages are indeed related, but Castell, in imitation of the antiquated *Lexicon pentaglotton* of Schindler (Hanau, 1612), was following the dogma (almost universal in his time) that Hebrew was the 'mother' from which the others were derived. The resulting arrangement is confusing and makes looking up the meanings of words in the five related languages an exercise in frustration. Only when the words for the individual languages are extracted from the *Lexicon* and listed separately, as was done for Syriac by J. D. Michaelis (Göttingen, 1788) and for Hebrew by J. F. L. Trier (Göttingen and Leipzig, 1790–92), do the merits of Castell's work appear. Nevertheless, the *Lexicon*'s lack of commercial success was due less to its shortcomings than to the decline in interest in oriental studies in England, compounded by the delays in publication.

Castell was appointed professor of Arabic in Cambridge when the professorship was endowed by Sir Thomas Adams in 1666. He delivered his inaugural lecture, on the use of Avicenna's medical work in elucidating plants mentioned in scripture, and published it as *Oratio in scholis theologicis habita … cum praelectiones suas in secundum canonis Avicennae librum auspicaretur* (1667). Otherwise his tenure of the professorship had little effect: he visited Cambridge only as required by the weekly lecture in term time, staying with John Lightfoot at St Catharine's College until 1671, when he became a fellow-commoner at St John's College. He was excused from lecturing in some years in order to pursue his work on the *Heptaglot*, and even when his lectures were delivered they were sparsely attended, so that he once jokingly advertised a lecture by posting the announcement: 'Tomorrow the Arabic Professor will go into the desert' (Twells, 214). He complained that the £40 annual emolument of the Arabic lectureship was less than it cost him to maintain it. His only known pupil was Thomas Edwards, the scholar of Coptic.

Castell remained in London for much of 1669 and 1670 in a vain attempt to dispose of the stock of the *Lexicon*. He complained that to the hundred or so letters that he wrote to the bishops on the matter he received one reply, with the resultant sale of only five copies. From 1671 onwards he resided principally at his rectory of Higham Gobion, Bedfordshire, a living that he had held in plurality with Woodham Walter since 29 January 1663 (he resigned the latter in 1670). Apart from his desultory lectures on Arabic at Cambridge, and a failed attempt to obtain the library of Golius for that university, he made no further contributions to oriental scholarship. His last years were spent in comparative poverty (he had debts of over £1800 when the *Lexicon* was published). His sight, which was already bad in 1669, declined so much that by 1684 his letters had to be written by an amanuensis. He was elected a fellow of the Royal Society on 16 April 1674, on the recommendation of Bishop Ward, but did not participate in the society's activities and resigned in 1682.

Castell had married as his second wife Elizabeth Herris (b. 1610), widow successively of Sir Peter Bettesworth and of James Herris, some time before June 1666. The two had no offspring, but she already had several children from her second marriage. Castell died at Higham Gobion in January 1686, and on 5 January was buried in the church there, where in 1674 he had erected a funeral monument for himself and his wife, with a curious quotation in Arabic. He bequeathed his Hebrew books to Emmanuel College and his oriental manuscripts to Cambridge University, but the latter were taken back by his executor to pay the debts on Castell's estate. His other books were auctioned at Cambridge on 30 June 1686. He was survived by his wife and by members of the Crispe family, children of his niece Mary and Ellis Crispe.　　　　G. J. TOOMER

Sources E. Castell, *Lexicon heptaglotton* (1669), preface · letters from Castell to Samuel Clarke, BL, Add. MS 22905 · G. J. Toomer, *Eastern wisedome and learning: the study of Arabic in seventeenth-century England* (1996), 206, 225–65, 272 · J. E. B. Mayor, *Cambridge under Queen Anne* (1911), 487–530 · J. Lightfoot, *Works* (1822–5), 13.366–401 · H. T. Norris, 'Professor Edmund Castell ... and England's oldest Arabic inscription', *Journal of Semitic Studies*, 29 (1984), 155–67 · I. O'Dell, '"The gift of tongues": Edmund Castell of Higham Gobion', *Bedfordshire Magazine*, 2 (1949–51), 189–94 · will, PRO, PROB 11/382, fols. 16–17 · Nichols, *Lit. anecdotes*, 4.22–32, 693–9 · J. C. T. Oates, *Cambridge University Library: a history from the beginnings to the Copyright Act of Queen Anne* (1986), 448–50 · R. Newcourt, *Repertorium ecclesiasticum parochiale Londinense*, 2 (1710), 318, 685 · *Oratio in scholis theologicis habita ab Edmundo Castello ... cum praelectiones suas in secundum canonis Avicennae librum auspicaretur* (1667) · E. Castell, *Sol Angliae Oriens auspiciis Caroli II, regum gloriosissimi* (1660) · A. J. Arberry, *The Cambridge school of Arabic* (1948), 10–13 · *Bibliotheca Castelliana, sive, Catalogus variorum librorum plurimis facultatibus insignium R. Doct. V. Edm. Castelli* (1686) · W. C. Metcalfe, ed., *The visitations of Essex*, 1, Harleian Society, 13 (1878), 134, 371, 397 · J. Burke and J. B. Burke, *A genealogical and heraldic history of the extinct and dormant baronetcies of England, Ireland, and Scotland* (1854), 3–4 · M. Hunter, *The Royal Society and its fellows, 1660–1700: the morphology of an early scientific institution*, 2nd edn (1994), 192–3 · T. Birch, *The history of the Royal Society of London*, 4 vols. (1756–7), vol. 4, p. 144 · L. Twells and S. Burdy, *The lives of Dr Edward Pocock ... Dr Zachary Pearce ... Dr Thomas Newton ... and of the Rev Philip Skelton*, 1 (1816), 290–92 · BL, MS Egerton 2646, fol. 212 · 'Essex churches', *Essex Review*, 1 (1892), 95–6

Archives CUL, papers, MSS Dd vi 4, Dd vi 63, Dd xi 39, Dd xii 15, Kk ii 17, Dd iii 54 | BL, letters to Samuel Clarke and Bishop Compton, Add. MS 22905 · Bodl. Oxf., corresp. with Sancroft and papers, MSS Tanner 478, fol. 21, Tanner 448, fols. 4, 17

Likenesses W. Faithorne the elder, line engraving, pubd 1669, BM, NPG; repro. in Castell, *Lexicon heptaglotton*, frontispiece [*see illus.*]

Wealth at death see will, PRO, PROB 11/382, fols. 16–17; inventory, Nichols, *Lit. anecdotes*, 697–9

Castell, Thomas (c.1456–1519), prior of Durham, may have been a native of Newcastle upon Tyne. Already a professed monk at Durham in 1478, when he was dispensed to receive priest's orders at twenty-two years of age, he was soon to find himself a scholar and fellow of Durham College, Oxford, where he served as one of the two college bursars in 1484–5. After a brief return to his mother house, during which he held the influential office of monastic chancellor in 1487, he was dispatched to Durham College again, this time to serve as its warden from 1487 to 1494. Many of Castell's annual accounts for this term of office still survive at Durham: they testify not only to his success in managing the affairs of his college and its six fellows, but also to the amenities (including a private chapel as well as garden and stable) of the wardenship. In 1491–2 Castell received the degree of doctor of theology, and it was during this period that he became a familiar figure, not only in his university, but also in the Benedictine provincial chapters, by whom he was selected to conduct a visitation of Winchester Cathedral priory in June 1492.

It was therefore not at all surprising that on 6 May 1494, exactly a month after the death of Prior John Auckland on 6 April, the sixty-six members of the Benedictine community at Durham should decide to elect Thomas Castell as his successor. Their choice seems to have been a fortunate one. During his twenty-five years as prior Castell was confronted with the problem of having to forge and maintain amicable relations with no less than four very different and often absentee bishops (Richard Fox, 1494–1501; William Sever, 1502–5; Christopher Bainbridge, 1507–8; and Thomas Ruthall, 1509–23). Although tactful enough to appear obsequiously obedient—'I have none othir comforth of refuge and counsell bod onely in your good lordship' (*Historiae Dunelmensis scriptores tres*, cccxcvi)—Prior Castell was highly successful in preserving his convent's traditional liberties from interference, on the part of the bishops as well as of the lay magnates of the north. The financial state of the cathedral priory and its eight daughter houses seems to have improved under his management; and the membership of St Cuthbert's community had risen to as many as seventy-four at the time of his death. More impressively still, Prior Castell, who owned several printed books himself, took an active role in fostering learning within the cloister and at Durham College. Another (younger) Durham monk also named Thomas Castell was a graduate and warden there in the years immediately before 1511.

However, it was as the last great builder in the long line of priors of Durham that Thomas Castell was best remembered by the final generation of St Cuthbert's monks. His greatest visible memorial is still the east gatehouse into the abbey garth (now The College); remarkably well preserved and adorned with the prior's well-known device ('a winged heart pierced by a sword'), it originally incorporated a new chantry chapel of St Helen at first-floor level. Prior Castell was also responsible for the complete rebuilding and reglazing of the great 'window of the Four Doctors' in the north transept of the cathedral, for the repanelling of the monastic refectory, and for the construction of a magnificent new cathedral clock. He died on 27 November 1519, and was buried before his favourite altar in the cathedral, dedicated to Jesus, in the cathedral nave; here a memorial brass once recorded the 'humble stature but outstanding leadership' (*Historiae Dunelmensis scriptores tres*, 154) of a much venerated prior.

R. B. DOBSON

Sources Registrum, V, Registrum parvum, IV, Durham Cath. CL, muniments · obedientiary account rolls, 1494–1519, Durham Cath. CL, muniments · *Historiae Dunelmensis scriptores tres: Gaufridus de Coldingham, Robertus de Graystanes, et Willielmus de Chambre*, ed. J. Raine, SurtS, 9 (1839), 152–4, ccclxxx–ccccxxi · J. T. Fowler, ed., *Extracts from the account rolls of the abbey of Durham*, 3 vols., SurtS, 99–100, 103 (1898–1901) · [J. T. Fowler], ed., *Rites of Durham*, SurtS, 107 (1903) · R. B. Dobson, *Durham Priory, 1400–1450*, Cambridge Studies in Medieval Life and Thought, 3rd ser., 6 (1973), 32, 53, 219, 294–5 · H. E. D. Blakiston, ed., 'Some Durham College rolls', *Collectanea: third series*, ed. M. Burrows, OHS, 32 (1896), 1–76 · Emden, *Oxf.* · W. A. Pantin, ed., *Documents illustrating the activities of … the English black monks, 1215–1540*, 3 vols., CS, 3rd ser., 45, 47, 54 (1931–7) · A. Piper, 'The libraries of the monks of Durham', *Medieval scribes, manuscripts and libraries: essays presented to N. R. Ker*, ed. M. B. Parkes and A. G. Watson (1978), 213–49 · M. P. Howden, ed., *The register of Richard Fox, lord bishop of Durham, 1494–1501*, SurtS, 147 (1932)
Archives Durham Cath. CL, muniments: obedientiary account rolls; Registrum, V; Registrum parvum, IV

Castell, William (d. 1645), Church of England clergyman, of unknown background and parentage, was educated at Oxford University, graduating BA from Magdalen Hall in 1613 and MA from Lincoln College in 1615. In 1619 he secured appointment as rector of Harpsden, Oxfordshire, but failed to dislodge the sitting incumbent. This was his first resort to the courts, a habit he continued throughout the 1620s and 1630s. Between the mid-1620s and 1634 he and his wife, Cecil (d. 1661/2), became the parents of five children, the last stillborn.

Instituted rector of Courteenhall, Northamptonshire, on 13 April 1627, and of Dennington, Suffolk, in January 1629, Castell resigned the latter rectory in 1633 on receiving £260 compensation. As a pluralist he had also to surrender Courteenhall but was immediately reinstated on payment of a fee. Anti-Laudian and anti-Spanish, Castell was described in 1635 as an 'unruly simoniacal Puritan [who] bragged that at Northampton visitation he only and another sat with their hats on at divine service or sermon' (Northants. RO, MS ZB 134). Two years later, on 22 August 1637, during a visitation Castell refused to move and rail in the communion table, 'saying there should be no new

tricks upon him, and that he could live as well in New England as here'. When the apparitor tried to measure the table, Castell pushed him away and called him

disgraceful names. He said his parishioners did not come to the rails to take communion, nor should not, nor would he ever bring them to it, also that it was not fit to bow at the name of Jesus.

It was further alleged that he had made

diminutions and alterations in the service, never wore a surplice or hood, did not use the catechism in the prayer book, hindered the churchwardens from cancelling in the communion table, and was a quarreller and fighter on the bowling leys. (*CSP dom.*, 1637, 382)

Nevertheless, Castell survived as rector of Courteenhall and in his last years turned pamphleteer. In 1641 he published *A petition … to … parliament … for the propagating of the gospel in America, and the West Indies; and for the setling of our plantations there*; in 1642 *The Jesuits undermining of parliaments and protestants with their foolish phancy of a toleration, discovered and censured*; and in 1644 *A short discoverie of the coasts and continent of America, from the equinoctiall northward, and of the adjacent isles*. The final sentence of this last promised that 'The Southerne Description of America (God permitting) shall shortly be set forth in another Booke.' But Castell's death intervened; he was buried at Courteenhall on 4 July 1645. His widow was buried there on 4 January 1662.

Collectively Castell's three pamphlets offer nothing new. Anti-Catholic and anti-Spanish, in traditionally optimistic terms they describe the English colonies, and advocate the seizure of Spanish colonies and the conversion of the natives. What is new is the appeal to parliament, for which Castell had the support of seventy English clergymen of varied persuasions and of six Scottish pastors headed by Alexander Henderson.

DAVID R. RANSOME

Sources P. Gordon, 'William Castell of Courteenhall: a seventeenth century pioneer of missionary work', *Northamptonshire Past and Present*, 8 (1989–94), 354–62 · H. I. Longden, *Northamptonshire and Rutland clergy from 1500*, ed. P. I. King and others, 16 vols. in 6, Northamptonshire RS (1938–52), vol. 3, p. 55 · *DNB* · *CSP dom., 1637* · Foster, *Alum. Oxon.* · Northants. RO, MS ZB 134

Castellesi [da Castello, da Corneto], **Adriano** (c.1461–1521), cardinal and English agent in Rome, was born in Corneto (now Tarquinia) to 'a modest and almost servile family' (Paschini, 88). Castellesi began a career in the papal bureaucracy, and in 1488 was sent by Innocent VIII to intervene in the Scottish civil war. The killing of James III on 11 June forced his return to Rome, but not before he had met Henry VII, which probably helped to secure him the office of papal collector in England in 1490. It gave him enormous profits. On 10 May 1492 Henry granted him the prebend of Ealdland in St Paul's Cathedral and a week later Cardinal Morton presented him to St Dunstan-in-the-East. He was granted denization on 29 June. In a bull of 4 October 1494 he is called *officialis* of Canterbury. Alexander VI confirmed Castellesi as collector and also named him nuncio with powers to reform the clergy, but by mid-1494 he was back in Rome as Henry's proctor and later clerk of the papal treasury (2 December 1494). On 31

July 1496 he gave an oration before the pope in honour of Henry VII's signing of the league between the pope and Spain.

Created protonotary apostolic by the pope on 14 October 1497, in March 1498 Castellesi tried unsuccessfully to buy a cardinalate for 20,000 ducats. In 1499 he became a member of the English Hospice in Rome. Along with Silvestro Gigli, who would soon be his bitter rival, he helped to complete the treaty between Henry and the pope of 10 February 1500. The king gave him the bishopric of Hereford on 14 February 1502 with the pope serving as referee. Castellesi retained his collectorship, with Polydore Vergil as his deputy, but also became Alexander VI's right-hand man and on 31 May 1503 was created cardinal with the title of San Grisogono, probably in return for payment. On 6 August the new cardinal threw the famous banquet following which Alexander VI died, allegedly poisoned in a miscarried plot to murder Castellesi himself. The latter also fell violently ill and eventually his entire skin sloughed off, but he recovered sufficiently to be able to act in effect as cardinal protector of England during the brief reign of Pius III.

Honoured by Julius II, who immediately confirmed him as collector and several times defended him to the king, Castellesi claimed to be Henry's sole representative at Rome, shouldering Gigli aside. Castellesi already feared for his status, however, and demanded that the English mission sent to yield canonical obedience to Julius lodge with himself in order to make his standing clear. In March 1504 he put his unfinished palace (now Palazzo Torlonia in via della Conciliazione) at the disposal of the king, for occupation by his ambassadors or any other purpose, while intending to continue to inhabit it himself. The manoeuvre was so far successful that when obedience was rendered, the papal master of ceremonies recorded it as Castellesi's doing, even though Robert Sherborne had given the oration. Castellesi also presented Margaret Beaufort's request for a dispensation for John Fisher to be non-resident and serve as her confessor. But although he pressed for the marriage dispensation to Prince Henry and Katherine of Aragon, when this finally came through the pope attributed it solely to Gigli. Castellesi was also involved in a dispute over the authenticity of Sherborne's bulls for St David's, siding with Richard Fox against Archbishop Warham and Gigli, and claiming that Sherborne had bought forged bulls. Henry quashed the litigation, and, perhaps partly as a result of it, Castellesi lost much if not all of his standing in Julius II's court; on 6 July the pope's nephew replaced him as protector, probably through Gigli's machinations. Perhaps as a consolation prize, Henry translated him to Bath and Wells on 2 August 1504; he was installed by proxy (Vergil) on 20 October.

On a trip to Bologna in 1507 Castellesi may have drafted his *De sermone Latino*, a treatise on how to write Ciceronian Latin—the only sort that would do, insisted its author. Although not published until 1515, it enjoyed wide popularity. While in Bologna he also wrote his most important work, *De vera philosophia ex quattuor doctoribus ecclesiae*, first published in 1507. The dedication to Henry VII suggests that Castellesi developed an interest in scripture while in England. Castellesi's opinions emerge only in the section titles, but they reveal a strong scepticism about the powers of human reason and an equally marked preference for scripture. For example, three headings read: 'Spiritual matters cannot be proved by reason' (sig. Ciiir); 'Faith must precede understanding' (sig. Av); and 'the authority of holy scripture is sufficient for the world' (sig. Aiiir). Castellesi said in the dedication to the second edition of *De sermone Latino* (1515; repr., 1534) that at Trent he had begun work on a new translation of the Old Testament from Hebrew, and announced in a letter of early 1516 that he had completed the first two books. His friendship with Egidio da Viterbo and Johann Reuchlin's dedication to him of his *De accentibus et orthographia linguae Hebraicae* in 1518 further attest his interest in Hebrew.

On 1 September 1507 Castellesi inexplicably fled from Rome, although his motive may have been Henry's revelation to Julius of Castellesi's criticisms of the pope and his court. He returned briefly to Rome, but in October fled once more to Venice. Henry pleaded for mercy for him, and Julius promised in the following September that Castellesi had nothing to fear, but on 17 October Vergil was ordered to give up his sub-collectorship and his successor was instructed not to send funds to Castellesi. The latter ended up with Emperor Maximilian who thought highly of him and may have sent him back to Rome in 1511 to forward his plan to become pope-emperor. Meanwhile Castellesi apparently continued to draw the revenues of Bath and Wells and attempted to reconcile himself with Henry VIII, while Thomas Wolsey went so far as to recommend him as the English candidate should there be a conclave in 1511. In the winter of 1512–13 Henry asked Castellesi to help make peace between Venice and the empire.

In the conclave of March 1513 Castellesi voted for Cardinal Bainbridge on the second ballot, but an intense rivalry between the two men, fuelled by Gigli, soon developed and he switched to Cardinal Giovanni de' Medici. Elected pope as Leo X, the latter reappointed Castellesi collector and gave him back his palace. In the spring of 1514 Castellesi and Vergil began efforts to have Wolsey made cardinal, but these good relations did not last long. Gigli, in order to forward Henry's plan to replace Vergil with the king's Latin secretary, Andrea Ammonio, intercepted Castellesi's correspondence with Vergil and turned it over to Wolsey. As a result, on 31 October 1514 the sub-collectorship was transferred to Ammonio and Vergil was imprisoned in the Tower. Leo, who strongly supported Castellesi in the dispute, compensated him with a payment of 1272 gold ducats on 2 June 1515, but Castellesi could not obtain Vergil's release until early 1516, and then only by agreeing to Ammonio's appointment.

In May 1517, perhaps inspired by a prophecy that Leo would die young and be succeeded by an old man named Adriano of obscure birth but great learning, Castellesi was drawn into the Petrucci conspiracy against the pope. Subsequent investigations revealed him as Leo's bitter enemy, but unlike the principals, some of whom were executed, he was merely confined to his house and ordered to pay a large fine (originally 12,500 scudi, later doubled) upon a public confession. Castellesi's troubles in Rome and in England now coalesced. He was fiercely attacked by Wolsey for having failed to secure for him the bishopric of Tournai, even though it was Leo who was reluctant to agree to Wolsey's demand. Henry had already acceded to Wolsey's requests to press for Castellesi's deprivation not only as collector but also as cardinal, and after Castellesi once more fled to Venice in June 1517, the king and Wolsey had their chance, despite the protection of Giulio de' Medici, recently created vice-chancellor of the church. The Venetian ambassador to England tried to intervene on Castellesi's behalf but this only further enraged Wolsey, and in August 1517 the king repossessed Castellesi's palace.

Castellesi offered to resign Bath and Wells in exchange for a pension of 3000 scudi, but the olive branch was rejected. Leo was still inclined to clemency and dragged the case out as long as he could, until on 5 July 1518 Castellesi was simultaneously deprived both of his cardinalate and of Bath and Wells, which went to Wolsey *in commendam*. Wolsey's vendetta was implacable and when Lorenzo Campeggi came as legate to England in late 1518 he was offered the see of Salisbury as an inducement to undermine Castellesi further. Leo still hoped to get Castellesi into his hands, but no subterfuges could induce him to leave Venice where he continued to live almost in hiding, as he had done during his earlier retreats. But as soon as he heard of Leo's death, which took place on 1 December 1521, Castellesi set out for Rome, unaware that Leo may have pardoned him. He died later that month, probably murdered by a servant. His memory was still alive in 1550, nearly thirty years after his death, when punters at the interminable conclave of Julius III showed their frustration by placing wagers on Castellesi.

T. F. MAYER

Sources P. Paschini, *Tre illustri prelati del Rinascimento: Ermolao Barbaro, Adriano Castellesi, Giovanni Grimani* (Rome, 1957), 45–130 • W. E. Wilkie, *The cardinal protectors of England: Rome and the Tudors before the Reformation* (1974) • A. Castellesi, *De sermone Latino, et modis Latinae loquendi iam denuo restitutus* (1534) • A. Castellesi, *De vera philosophia ex quattuor doctoribus ecclesiae* (1507) • D. Cantimori, *Eretici italiani del Cinquecento: ricerche storiche* (Florence, 1939) • A. M. Ghisalberti and others, eds., *Dizionario biografico degli Italiani*, 56 vols. (Rome, 1960–) • Archivio di Stato, Florence, Archivio Medíceo del principato, 395, fol. 269r–v
Archives Apostolic Library, Vatican, Ottob. lat. 2377

Castelvetro, Giacomo (*bap.* 1546, *d.* 1616), writer and teacher of Italian, was born in Modena, Italy, and was baptized there at S. Barnaba, on 25 March 1546, the third son and ninth child of Niccolò Castelvetro (*d.* 1578), a wealthy banker, and his wife, Liberta Tassoni, a noblewoman. Apart from the fact that he described himself in autobiographical notes (BL, Harleian MS 3344) as a sickly child, a condition he attributed to his mother, nothing is known of his early life.

Apparently as a result of his unorthodox religious views, at the age of eighteen Castelvetro was smuggled out of Modena with his brother Lelio in two chests carried on a mule, to join his uncle Ludovico Castelvetro, the humanist critic, who lived in exile in Geneva. For the next seven years he lived with his uncle, moving to Lyon, Basel, Vienna, and Chiavenna, while studying with him Greek, Latin, French, German, Spanish, and English. Shortly after his uncle's death in late February 1571 he moved initially to Basel and then in 1574 visited England, where he became acquainted with Sir Roger North of Kirtling, Cambridgeshire, whose eldest son, John, had recently graduated from Cambridge. Castelvetro spent the next two years accompanying young North on an educational tour of Italy, before returning to Italy to claim his inheritance after his father's death in 1578.

By this time Castelvetro was clearly a protestant, and fearing difficulties with the Inquisition if he remained in Italy, he sold some of his property to his cousin and namesake, returning to England by the summer of 1580. During this period he was engaged in the publishing trade, enjoying the patronage of Sir Philip Sidney, Sir Christopher Hatton, and Sir Francis Walsingham, for whom he probably acted as a political agent. He made frequent trips to Europe, including to the great book fairs at Frankfurt and Basel, where in 1587 he married Isotta de Canonici (*d.* 1594), the wealthy and elderly widow of Thomas Lieber or Lüber (*d.* 1583), best known as Erastus, the distinguished physician and philosopher. Having edited a theological work by Erastus, *Explicatio gravissimae quaestionis utrum excommunicatio* (1589), in 1590 Castelvetro published a collection of medical works by Erastus which he had edited, explaining in an elegantly composed Latin introduction how his marriage had given him this opportunity. In 1591 it was at his expense that the very popular *Il pastor fido* was published in England.

In 1592 Castelvetro realized a long-held ambition of becoming Italian tutor to James VI of Scotland and Queen Anne. Two years later, following the death of his wife, who made her deathbed will on 7 March 1594, he travelled to Denmark and then Sweden, where he was on friendly terms with Duke Charles, who was to become king in 1599. In May 1598 he undertook a leisurely tour of Europe, encompassing France, Switzerland, and Germany. In the autumn of the following year he settled in Venice, editing and preparing contemporary manuscripts on Italian poetry and fiction for the publisher G. B. Ciotto. His brother Lelio, after a long imprisonment, was burnt at the stake as a relapsed heretic in 1609, and Castelvetro's own stay in Venice was brought to an abrupt end in 1611 when he was imprisoned by the Inquisition. Although it is not clear if he had become a subject of James VI and I, he had been closely involved with the activities of the English embassy in Venice and had enjoyed the friendship of Sir Henry Wotton, ambassador there until late 1610. The new ambassador, Sir Dudley Carleton, successfully intervened on his behalf to persuade the Italian authorities that the incarceration of someone at one time a servant of the king, and now described as a member of the diplomatic household, could lead to a diplomatic incident. Once released, Castelvetro set off on another tour round Europe in search of patronage.

By early 1613 Castelvetro was back in London, and that spring taught Italian for one term at Cambridge to a number of appreciative students including George Stanhope, but his poor health and financial impoverishment precluded him from obtaining more regular employment. Briefly at Oxford early in 1614, he lived otherwise in the household of Sir Adam Newton at Eltham, later moving with the family to their new mansion at Charlton, near Greenwich.

At this time Castelvetro compiled 'Brieve racconto di tutte le radici di tutte l'herbe e di tutte frutti, che crudi o cotti in Italia si mangiano' ('Brief account of all the vegetables, herbs, and fruit … in Italy') for which he was eventually best remembered. His text bore all the inaccuracies and misnomers of an enthusiastic amateur, but was an interesting and instructive critique of the gastronomic delicacies of Italy. This was not the first text on the subject, but was probably the most detailed. Sent to eminent potential patrons, it was dedicated to Lucy, countess of Bedford, at the request of her brother John Harington, and Castelvetro hoped that she would help him to secure work as a translator, editor, and teacher, but by 1614 the countess was in dire financial straits and his attempts to gain monetary assistance proved fruitless. He was later engaged to edit a manuscript by Tadio Duni of Zürich, but his hopes that the king or City of London might reward him for his translation of *A Remonstrance of James I … for the Right of Kings* (1615) were vain. He remained impoverished, dying after a long illness, probably at Charlton and soon after 21 March 1616, the date of his last autobiographical note.

During his lifetime Castelvetro achieved only limited recognition, but after John Florio, the first recorded teacher of Italian at Oxford, he was the most important promoter of his native tongue and national heritage in England at this period. It was only in the twentieth century, with reassessments of his career and the publication of his 'Brieve racconto' as *The Fruit, Herbs and Vegetables of Italy* (ed. G. Riley, 1989), that his significance as an advocate of the consumption of more fruit and vegetables was appreciated.   JOHN MARTIN

Sources G. Castelvetro, *The fruit, herbs and vegetables of Italy: an offering to Lucy, countess of Bedford*, ed. G. Riley (1989) · K. T. Butler, 'An Italian's message to England in 1614: eat more fruit and vegetables', *Italian Studies*, 2 (1938–9), 1–18 · K. T. Butler, 'Giacomo Castelvetro, 1546–1616', *Italian Studies*, 5 (1950), 1–42 · F. H. Morgan, 'A biography of Lucy countess of Bedford, the last great literary patroness', PhD diss., University of Southern California, 1956 · D. E. Rhodes, 'The Italian banquet, 1598, and its origins', *Italian Studies*, 27 (1972), 60–63 · *Dudley Carleton to John Chamberlain, 1603–1624: Jacobean letters*, ed. M. Lee (1972) · S. E. Dimsey, 'Giacomo Castelvetro', *Modern Language Review*, 23 (1928), 424–31 · T. Sandannini, *Ludovico Castelvetro e la sua famiglia* (1882) · R. J. Roberts, 'New light on the career of Giacomo Castelvetro', *Bodleian Library Record*, 13 (1988–91), 365–9 · BL, Harleian MS 7004, fol. 21 · BL, Harleian MS 3344

Archives BL, *Il Ragionamento di Carlo V. Imperadore*, trans. Castelvetro and dedicated to James VI, Add. MS 9282 and Sloane MS 912 · NHM, MS Banks 91 · NHM, *Il Ragionamento di Carlo V. Imperadore*, trans. Castelvetro and dedicated to James VI · NL Scot., Adv. MS 23-1-6 · Trinity Cam. · Trinity Cam., *Il Ragionamento di Carlo V. Imperadore*, trans. Castelvetro and dedicated to James VI, R.14.19; R.344a; R.344b

Wealth at death died in poverty and distress: Castelvetro, *The fruit, herbs and vegetables of Italy*

Castilians in Edinburgh (*act.* 1570–1573), armed political faction, were supporters of Mary, queen of Scots, who held Edinburgh Castle (hence 'castilian') between 1570 and 1573 and for much of this period controlled the town as well.

The assassination of the regent, James Stewart, earl of Moray, in January 1570 sparked off a civil war between the supporters of the government carried on in the name of James VI, and those who supported the restoration of his mother, Mary, who had been deposed in 1567. Edinburgh remained in the hands of the Marians until October 1572, and its strategically important castle was not surrendered until the end of May 1573.

Sir William *Kirkcaldy of Grange (*c.*1520–1573) was appointed commander of the castle by Moray in 1569, but transferred his allegiance to the queen's side, an action which particularly infuriated John Knox. The great reformer, who had been one of Kirkcaldy's colleagues and a fellow castilian in an earlier episode, the siege of St Andrews Castle in 1546–7, prophesied that Kirkcaldy's reward for his treachery would be to 'hang from a gallows in the face of the sun' (*Knox's History*, 2.157). Kirkcaldy was a resolute and experienced soldier who after his capture at St Andrews in 1547 had served with considerable distinction in the armies of Henri II of France before returning to Scotland to support the reformers. Kirkcaldy's principal ally was William *Maitland of Lethington (1525x30–1573), the former royal secretary, who, disapproving of Mary's deposition since he believed it would harm his efforts at closer links with England, had also changed sides. Under the threat of arrest by Moray's administration, he had welcomed Kirkcaldy's offer of protection and moved to Edinburgh Castle in September 1568. However, by November 1572 ill health greatly limited any contribution he might have made to the defence of the castle.

Other castilians included John *Maitland of Thirlestane (1543–1595), the former secretary's younger brother, who supported Mary's cause throughout the civil war. Another was Alexander *Home, fifth Lord Home (*c.*1525–1575), who had been badly wounded fighting as an ally of Moray at Langside in 1567, but who had transferred his allegiance to Mary in 1569. In the following year his main residence, Home Castle, was seized by the English, pursuing forces from the northern rising, and in 1571 Home joined the queen's followers in Edinburgh Castle. Another was Robert *Melville of Murdocairnie, later first Lord Melville (1527/8–1621). Melville, a Fife laird with a strong protestant background, was, like Maitland, an example of how support for Mary often had little to do with religious belief. Melville's diplomatic career was already well established; he had been Mary's ambassador at Elizabeth's court in the aftermath of the Darnley murder.

A further prominent figure among the castilians was **Robert Crichton** (*d.* 1585), bishop of Dunkeld. Crichton, the younger son of Sir Patrick Crichton of Cranstoun

Riddel, had become coadjutor bishop of Dunkeld in March 1543, assisting his uncle, Bishop George Crichton, and had opposed the nomination of John Hamilton as his uncle's successor in the see in January 1544. He also resisted Donald Campbell, nominated as Hamilton's successor in March 1548, and was in office as bishop of Dunkeld by 12 April 1554. At the August 1560 parliament he had, with Hamilton, hesitated over the confession of faith, but had acknowledged the presence of abuses in the church. He did not oppose the confession, but was never reconciled to the kirk. His loyalty to Mary probably stemmed from a combination of his Roman Catholicism and his family's general support for the queen.

The castilians held the upper hand in Edinburgh for two years. They established an alternative administration to that of the regent, John Erskine, earl of Mar, and dismissed the Edinburgh town council. They were sustained by a financial system supervised by Kirkcaldy and two Edinburgh goldsmiths, **James Mossman** (d. 1573) and his brother-in-law **James Cockie** (d. 1573). Both were well established, and Cockie had been deacon of the incorporation of goldsmiths of Edinburgh in 1563–4 and 1564–5. Mossman's large house on the High Street in Edinburgh has, since at least the nineteenth century, been misidentified as John Knox's house. Cockie had a network of aristocratic patrons, including the regent Mar for whom he crafted the 'Erskine ewer', an elaborate crystal vessel. Guaranteeing, arranging, and clearing loans was an established part of Mossman's business. Mossman and Cockie helped to keep the castilians afloat by advising in the evaluation of various items of royal jewellery which were pawned to sympathizers outside the castle. They probably also helped with the production of coins in Mary's name.

In June 1571 the castilians held their own parliament in the Tolbooth, the customary meeting place for Scottish parliaments. Maitland was able to boast to foreign courts that the Marian parliament consisted of the principal nobility of Scotland, while the regent's 'creeping parliament' in Canongate, under regular bombardment from Edinburgh Castle, was representative of only a faction of lesser men. However, the creeping parliament began the forfeiture of the principal Marians, including William and John Maitland and their brother Thomas *Maitland (d. 1572) [see under Maitland, Sir Richard, of Lethington], a process followed through in August by the regent's parliament at Stirling, where Crichton was among the forfeited, losing his see.

A truce between the two sides, negotiated in July 1572, was broken by the king's party, who used it to infiltrate Edinburgh and establish control of the town. When James Douglas, fourth earl of Morton, became regent in November 1572, only the castle remained in the queen's party's hands. Sir James Melville, Melville of Murdocairnie's brother, represented Morton at negotiations with the castilians, but Kirkcaldy was reluctant to yield the castle, even with a guarantee that the castilians' forfeited lands and possessions would be restored, without the restitution being extended to his allies in the rest of the country—principally the followers of the Hamiltons and the earl of Huntly. In January 1573 Morton resumed the bombardment of the castle, then containing 160 officers and men. None the less it was not until the Hamilton and Huntly families were persuaded to return to the fold at the pacification of Perth in February that the regent could direct all his attention towards the castilians.

In April, Kirkcaldy and his followers were presented with their last opportunity for an honourable surrender. On their rejection of this offer Morton brought into action the English army and its artillery, which had arrived at Leith the previous month. The bombardment began on 17 May, and Elizabeth's ordnance gave the regent a decisive advantage: Kirkcaldy was forced to surrender on 28 May. Most of the garrison were allowed to go free, many of them being recruited shortly afterwards for service in Sweden. On the other hand Kirkcaldy, the Maitland brothers, Home, Melville of Murdocairnie, Crichton, and a few others were to be 'reserved and kept where the regent shall appoint' (CSP Scot., 4.571), pending further discussions with Elizabeth. The latter, however, eventually agreed that Morton should have the final word on their fate.

Kirkcaldy of Grange, despite appeals for clemency, was hanged on 3 August, fulfilling Knox's prophecy. His brother Thomas, a prisoner since January 1573, was hanged on the same day, as were Mossman and Cockie. Mossman had been forfeited in April 1573 for assisting the rebels and for producing illegal currency. Most of the other leading castilians were given indefinite terms of imprisonment. Maitland of Thirlestane spent the next five years in various forms of confinement, but thereafter his fortunes greatly improved: once James VI assumed personal control of the kingdom he became royal secretary and subsequently chancellor. Home's life was spared only through the intercession of two of his kinsmen, the lairds of Cowdenknowes and Manderston, and he was not released from imprisonment until shortly before his death in 1575. Melville of Murdocairnie was reprieved at the instigation of Queen Elizabeth, but remained imprisoned for about a year. Crichton was committed for a period to Blackness Castle, and from December 1573 was bailed for £10,000 into the keeping of Sir Walter Ker of Cessford in Edinburgh. From May 1576 he was allowed to live at Seton or another property of Lord Seton, or else remain in Edinburgh. After securing financial support from his successor at Dunkeld, James Paton, he was restored to the bishopric of Dunkeld on 22 August 1584. He died a few days before 26 March 1585, when the town council of Edinburgh agreed to the request of James VI that Crichton be buried in the church of St Giles.

G. R. Hewitt

Sources CSP Scot., 1563–9, vols. 2–4 · D. Calderwood, The history of the Kirk of Scotland, ed. T. Thomson and D. Laing, 8 vols., Wodrow Society, 7 (1842–9), vol. 3 · Reg. PCS, 1st ser., vol. 2 · DNB · A diurnal of remarkable occurrents (1830) · [T. Thomson], ed., The historie and life of King James the Sext, Bannatyne Club, 13 (1825) · J. Melville, Memoirs of his own life (1827) · J. Knox, History of the Reformation in Scotland, vols. 1–2 of The works of John Knox, ed. D. Laing, Wodrow Society, 12 (1846–8), vol. 2 · M. Lynch, Edinburgh and the Reformation (1981) · G. Hewitt, Scotland under Morton, 1572–80 (1982) · C. Donnachie and G. Hewitt,

A companion to Scottish history (1989) • M. Lee, John Maitland of Thirlstane (1959) • B. P. Lenman, 'Jacobean goldsmith–jewellers as credit-creators: the cases of James Mossman, James Cockie and George Heriot', SHR, 74 (1995), 159–77 • G. Donaldson, All the queen's men: power and politics in Mary Stewart's Scotland (1983) • J. Dowden, The bishops of Scotland … prior to the Reformation, ed. J. M. Thomson (1912)

Castilians in St Andrews (act. 1546–1547), armed political faction, is the collective name given to the men who murdered Cardinal David Beaton in St Andrews Castle and then held it for fourteen months against government forces. Plots to assassinate Beaton had been current as early as 1544, but the grievance that brought many of the murderers together was the execution of the protestant reformer George Wishart on 1 March 1546. The principal driving force behind the murder was Norman *Leslie, master of Rothes (d. 1554), eldest son of George Leslie, fourth earl of Rothes, sheriff of Fife. Leslie claimed that Beaton had failed to honour his obligations under a bond of manrent they held. The Leslies had suffered from the expansion of Beaton's interest in Fife.

Among the other Fife gentry who joined Norman Leslie was his uncle **John Leslie of Parkhill** (d. 1585), second son of William Leslie, third earl of Rothes (d. 1513), and Janet (fl. c.1490–c.1520), daughter of Sir Michael Balfour of Montquhannie. His presence illustrates the high rank of many of the castilians. He had served in the household of James V from about 1534 until 1541, about which time he married Euphemia Moncrieff; they had two daughters. After being captured at the battle of Solway Moss on 24 November 1542, Leslie was released by the English under assurance. His presence among the conspirators owed little or nothing to English pressure; although characterized as 'rough and ready' (Sanderson, 223), he was committed to church reform and was one of the Fife lairds outraged by the execution of Wishart. Another Fife laird of protestant sympathies was **James Melville of Carnbee** (d. in or before 1550), who 'mourned Wishart as a friend' (ibid.). Other participants, like the Leslies and Melville, shared a dislike of Beaton's person and power: they were 'no artificial group merely thrown together by their grievances' but a 'closely-related and allied circle' (ibid., 224). William *Kirkcaldy of Grange (c.1520–1573) held protestant convictions; his father, Sir James *Kirkcaldy of Grange (d. 1556), who joined the castilians after the murder of Beaton, was also a protestant and had been removed as treasurer of the realm in 1543 by Beaton's influence. Peter Carmichael of Balmedie, another conspirator, was from a family with a history of dependence on Beaton, while David Monypenny of Pitmilly was Beaton's cousin. The exact number of conspirators is unknown, but there were probably between twelve and eighteen.

The murderers gained entrance to St Andrews Castle at about six o'clock in the morning of 29 May 1546, hiding among the 100 or so members of the garrison, masons, and members of the workforce engaged in rebuilding the castle as they walked across the lowered drawbridge. They seized the entrance, expelled the labourers, stole the keys from the gatekeeper, Ambrose Stirling, whom they then killed, and raised the drawbridge. The four principal assassins, Norman Leslie, William Kirkcaldy, James Melville, and John Leslie of Parkhill, made their way to Beaton's private chambers and with burning coals intimidated him into opening the door. According to John Knox, Beaton was stabbed twice by John Leslie and Peter Carmichael before James Melville declared that 'This work and judgment of God (although it be secret) ought to be done with greater gravity' (Knox's History, 1.77) and at swordpoint urged Beaton:

> Repent thee of thy former wicked life, but especially of the shedding of the blood of that notable instrument of God, Master George Wishart, which albeit the flame of fire consumed before men, yet cries it a vengeance upon thee, and we from God are sent to revenge it: For here, before my god, I protest, that neither the hetterent [hatred] of thy person, the love of thy riches, nor the fear of any trouble thou could have done to me in particular, moved, nor moves me to strike thee; but only because thou hast been and remains an obstinate enemy against Christ Jesus and his holy Evangel. (ibid., 1.78)

Melville then dealt the fatal blows by running Beaton through two or three times with his sword. The murderers dragged Beaton's body to the parapet to display to the townsfolk. One 'knaif' (Historie and Cronicles, 2.84), possibly Beaton's page Amand Guthrie, then urinated into the corpse's mouth.

The government of the regent, James Hamilton, second earl of Arran, was heavily entangled by a siege and negotiation at Dumbarton, but the conspirators chose not to escape the castle. Beaton had enough friends to make it unwise for Norman Leslie and his friends to hazard public exposure, and the castle was their protection and their safeguard. While the government was distracted the castilians were joined by other supporters including Norman Leslie's brothers William and Robert, and the diplomat Henry *Balnaves (d. 1570). A further advantage was the presence of James Hamilton, master of Arran, the regent's son, in the castle; this encouraged Arran to compromise with the castilians but they rejected his proposal that he arrange a papal pardon. The conspirators were forfeited by parliament on 16 August and that month a siege of St Andrews began.

William Kirkcaldy of Grange travelled to England in August to request support from Henry VIII. Kirkcaldy was gratefully received by the English king, who sent north essential supplies such as powder, food, and cannon. Despite English assistance, by December the castilians were severely weakened by disease and the lack of food. However, government forces had failed to overcome them. An impressive mine, hewn through solid rock, perhaps by Ayrshire miners, left a permanent monument to the siege but had not made an impact on the castilians' defences. The besiegers were also afflicted by plague. In December it was agreed that the government would seek a papal pardon for the castilians as long as they did not deliver the castle and the master of Arran to England. The castilians hoped that, while Arran negotiated with the pope and with France to secure the pardon, better weather would arrive and with it new supplies from England. For the next six months the castilians enjoyed relative freedom of access to the town of St Andrews and the surrounding country. They moved as an armed band for their own protection, but also as a gang of oppression. Robert Lindsay of Pitscottie recalled their riding wherever they pleased 'burnand and raissand fyre' (*Historie and Cronicles*, 2.86). He particularly highlighted how they 'wssit thair bodyis in leichorie witht fair wemen, servand thair appietyte as they thocht goode' (ibid., 2.86–7).

The death of Henry VIII of England in January 1547 seemed at first to confirm the castilians' hopes. In March the new English lord protector, Edward Seymour, duke of Somerset, formally made the principal castilians English pensioners and provided food and wages for their soldiers. The castilians agreed to hand over the castle to an English force and send the master of Arran into Somerset's custody in England, as part of the English plan to force the marriage of Mary, queen of Scots, to the new English king, Edward VI. The agreement may have encouraged the castilians to reject the papal pardon obtained by Arran in March or April, on the grounds that the clause *remittibus irremissibile* described the remitted crime as one that could not be remitted and thus suggested that the murderers of Beaton were not completely absolved. Several castilians, including Leslie of Parkhill and Balnaves, visited England in early 1547. In April, Balnaves supposedly delivered the signatures of twenty-three Scottish nobles who had pledged themselves to England. The castilians received in return the services of an Italian surveyor, Guillaume di Rossetti, as well as armaments and construction materials for the castle. Meanwhile, John *Knox (*c*.1514–1572) arrived in St Andrews in April, accompanied by three pupils. With Knox in St Andrews the castle became something of an evangelical city on a hill, Knox first engaging Catholics at the university in debate, and then preaching in the town itself.

The castilians' new concordat with England was immediately compromised by political changes in France following the death of François I in March 1547. The new king, Henri II, was politically aligned with the family of the Scottish queen dowager, Mary of Guise, and by May had agreed to send a French force to end the siege. This was unknown to the castilians and their English allies. A French fleet probably arrived off St Andrews on 16 July, and began a siege, led by an Italian mercenary, Leon Strozzi, which ended with the surrender of the castilians on 30 July. The castilians were first imprisoned in the castle, and then transferred to the holds of the French vessels.

The castilians became protestant martyrs, and Knox a galley slave. However, few of the castilians suffered excessively. Only James Melville of Carnbee died in captivity, in Brest Castle, Brittany, before Mary of Guise and the French agreed to the release of the last of the castilians in July 1550. Norman Leslie translated his imprisonment in France into service to Henri II. Knox was freed within nineteen months, thanks to English diplomatic pressure, and became a royal chaplain to Edward VI. Most of the castilians made their way home and were eventually restored to their property: Leslie of Parkhill was restored in 1563 and was formally discharged from his part in the murder of Beaton in 1575, before he died on 6 September 1585. William Kirkcaldy of Grange found preferment of France before returning to Scotland where he eventually became one of the *castilians in Edinburgh (act. 1570–1573).

MARCUS MERRIMAN

Sources M. Merriman, *The rough wooings: Mary queen of Scots, 1542–1551* (2000) · *The historie and cronicles of Scotland … by Robert Lindsay of Pitscottie*, ed. A. J. G. Mackay, 1–2, STS, 42 (1899) · *John Knox's History of the Reformation in Scotland*, ed. W. C. Dickinson, 2 vols. (1949) · M. H. B. Sanderson, *Cardinal of Scotland: David Beaton, c.1494–1546* (1986) · *Scots peerage*, 7.279–81

Castillo, John (1792–1845), stonemason, poet, and preacher, was born at Rathfarnham, near Dublin. When he was two or three years old his parents, who were Roman Catholics, emigrated to England, and on the voyage were shipwrecked off the Isle of Man. They settled in the hamlet of Lealholm Bridge, 9 miles from Whitby, Yorkshire. His father died when Castillo was eleven, and he left school to go into service in Lincolnshire. Two years later he returned and lived chiefly at Fryup, Yorkshire, working as a stonemason.

Castillo was admitted to the Wesleyan 'class' at Danby End chapel on 5 April 1818, and became an energetic revivalist preacher. He achieved considerable success in the Yorkshire dales, joining the Pickering circuit in 1838, when he wrote that he 'endeavoured as much as possible to keep out of the pulpits by holding prayer meetings and giving exhortations out of the singing pews or from the forms' (Castillo, *Poems in the North Yorkshire Dialect*, 13). He wrote verses suggested by Wesleyan subjects and incidents which occurred in the neighbourhood, and became known as the Bard of the Dales. His most notable poem is 'Awd Isaac', in the Cleveland dialect, said to be based on Isaac Hobb of Glaisdale. This poem has had many editions, not all attributed to Castillo. Another, 'T' Leealholm Chap's Lucky Dream', is a Yorkshire variant of a folk tale found earlier in the Persian poem called the 'Masnaví', written by Jalàuddin.

Castillo died of asthma at Pickering on 16 April 1845, and was buried in the graveyard of the Wesleyan chapel there. His collected writings were posthumously published as *The Bard of the Dales* (1850) with a second edition in 1858. *Poems in the North Yorkshire Dialect* was published with a biographical preface in 1878. One of Castillo's sermons, 'Jacob's ladder', was printed in pamphlet form in 1858.

W. E. A. AXON, rev. SARAH COUPER

Sources J. Castillo, *Poems in the north Yorkshire dialect*, ed. G. M. Tweddell (1878) [with a biographical preface by the ed.] · W. C. Newsam, *The poets of Yorkshire* (1845), 217 · W. Grainge, *The poets and poetry of Yorkshire*, 2 (1868), 366 · W. W. Skeat and J. H. Nodal, eds., *A bibliographical list* (1877), 118–19 · J. Castillo, *The bard of the dales … with a life of the author written by himself* (1858) · d. cert.

Castine, Thomas (*bap.* 1753?, *d.* 1793?), army officer and deserter, was apparently born at Ballyneille, in the parish of Loman, Isle of Man. He may have been the Thomas Castean baptized at St Peter's, Kirk German, Isle of Man, on 18 October 1753, the son of Thomas Castean and Catherine Dawson. He is stated by the Manx historian Joseph Train (1779–1852) to have enlisted in the 'king's own' regiment of foot (4th foot) and become a sergeant. On furlough after a few years, Train's account continues, he married about 1773 Helen Corlace. This is probably the marriage of Thomas Castean to Elinor Comish recorded at Arbory, Isle of Man, on 9 November 1771. Castine enjoyed the company of his old friends so much that he overstayed his leave. Fearing punishment as a deserter, he escaped in a smuggling lugger to Dunkirk, entered the French army, and served in America. At the outbreak of the French Revolution he was an infantry colonel. Train claims he was a prominent revolutionary army commander, executed in Paris in August 1793, apparently identifying him with the general of division Adam Philip de Custine, executed in Paris on 17 August 1793 for alleged treason at Mayence. Train states that Castine's wife stayed behind, and that their son was a twenty-year-old in 1793. The younger Castine enlisted in the Manx fencibles, was a sergeant in the Galloway militia, and in 1837 was working as a shopkeeper in the village of Auchencuir, Galloway. Believing his father had possessed property in France, he applied through Cutlar Fergusson, MP for Kirkcudbright, to Prince Talleyrand, when French ambassador in London; but an enquiry reported that evidence of such property, if it ever existed, had been lost in the confusion of 1793. The first and last parts of this story may be true, and possibly the Manx deserter Castine served in the French revolutionary army, but there is nothing to connect him with the general of division Custine.

H. M. CHICHESTER, rev. ROGER T. STEARN

Sources J. Train, *Historical and statistical account of the Isle of Man*, 2 vols. (1843), vol. 2, p. 349 · A. Alison, *History of Europe*, 9th edn, 20 vols. (1853–6) · L. M. Prudhomme, *Histoire générale et impartiale des erreurs, des fautes et des crimes pendant la révolution française*, 6 vols. (1797) · IGI

Castle, Edmund (1698–1750), college head and dean of Hereford, was born on 14 September 1698 at Newington, near Hythe, Kent, where he was baptized on 18 September. His parents were Edmund Castle and Ann Gibbs, who had married on 14 April 1696; he had at least two brothers, John and Henry, and one sister, Anne. Educated in Canterbury he was admitted into Corpus Christi College, Cambridge, in 1716; there he was appointed 'puer cubiculi' by the master, Bishop Greene, and to a Kentish scholarship on Archbishop Parker's foundation. He graduated BA in 1720, was made fellow in 1722, and proceeded MA (1723) and BD (1728). He was ordained deacon at Ely on 4 June 1721 and priest on 23 September 1722. He was public orator in 1727 but vacated the office in 1730 on being appointed to the vicarages of Elm and Emneth, in the Isle of Ely.

In 1731 Castle succeeded Thomas Herring as rector of Barley, in Hertfordshire. In October of that year he drew up his will, which shows that he was already married to Susanna. In 1744 he was made rector of St Paul's School, and on 20 February 1745 he was elected master of Corpus Christi College, Cambridge; he served as vice-chancellor of the university in 1746–7. In 1747 he was promoted to a

prebend at Lincoln, and in 1749 to the deanery of Hereford. Castle died at Bath on 6 June 1750; his widow survived him by about five years. He was buried at Barley, where there is a Latin inscription to his memory that describes him as a man of considerable learning and of great simplicity of manners.

T. F. HENDERSON, rev. S. J. SKEDD

Sources Venn, *Alum. Cant.* · Nichols, *Lit. anecdotes*, 6.78 · *Masters' History of the college of Corpus Christi and the Blessed Virgin Mary in the University of Cambridge*, ed. J. Lamb (1831), 235–9 · parish register, Kent, Newington, 18 Sept 1698 [baptism] · parish register, Kent, Newington, 14 April 1696 [marriage: Edmund Castle and Ann Gibbs] · will, PRO, PROB 11/788, fols. 137v–138r
Wealth at death bequests amounting to a few hundred pounds: will, PRO, PROB 11/788, fols. 137v–138r

Castle, George (1634/5–1673), physician, was born in London, the only son of John Castle (who was made a doctor of medicine at Oxford on 10 July 1644) and his wife, Grisagon. Castle first attended Thame grammar school in Oxfordshire under the tutelage of William Burt, and was then admitted as a commoner of Balliol College, Oxford, on 8 April 1652 at the age of seventeen. He was made BA on 18 October 1654 and MA on 29 May 1657. In 1654 he gained a probationary fellowship at All Souls, where he became DM on 21 June 1665. Castle then settled in London, practising (as his father had done) in the parish of St Margaret's, Westminster. Proposed by Christopher Wren, he was elected a fellow of the Royal Society in February 1669; he was not active in the society beyond the payment of his dues. Later, through the influence of his friend Martin Clifford, master of Sutton's Hospital at Charterhouse, Castle was appointed physician there.

While Castle was at Oxford he became a member of the Experimental Philosophy Club and associated with the 'Oxford Physiologists', an assemblage of virtuosi including George Ent, Robert Boyle, Francis Glisson, and John Locke. Castle showed an interest in anatomy, respiration, and several other medical topics. His sole publication, *The Chymical Galenist* (1667), assails contemporary iatrochemists who rejected anatomy and all of classical medicine in favour of the Paracelsian and Helmontian systems. His argument was directed specifically and sharply against the *Medela medicinae* (1665) of Marchamont Nedham (Needham). Castle (in his preface) says that Nedham 'flings dirt upon the learnedst Society of *Physicians* in the World, and libels the *Universities*' and then refers to Nedham as a 'bold and impertinent invader of Physick, and a plausible vender of very popular non-sense'. Castle defends the College of Physicians (of which he was not a member) and argues for a middle course in regard to medical philosophy, wherein the errors of ancient Galenic and Hippocratic medicine are to be corrected with new discoveries in natural philosophy and anatomy, yet their still-valuable 'Rules, Methods, and Medicins', which were gained by long experience, are to be preserved. Castle's only other appearance in print is a dedicatory poem, signed simply 'G.C. M.A. S.O.A.C., Oxon' to Samuel Austin's satirical *Naps upon Parnassus* (1658), a thin volume of satirical verses by several Oxford wits. In regard to this poem Wood remarks that Castle was 'better at lying and Buffooning' than at versifying.

Castle died of fever (brought on, according to Wood, by 'the liberty of too frequent indulgments') on 12 October 1673 and was buried in London, probably in the chapel of Charterhouse. His will, in which he is described as of the parish of St Martin-in-the-Fields, is dated 25 September 1673, and was proved by his widow, Anne, on 16 October.

LAWRENCE M. PRINCIPE

Sources Wood, *Ath. Oxon.* · G. Castle, *The chymical Galenist* (1667) · R. G. Frank, *Harvey and the Oxford physiologists* (1980) · M. Hunter, *The Royal Society and its fellows, 1660–1700: the morphology of an early scientific institution*, 2nd edn (1994) · Munk, *Roll* · C. Webster, *The great instauration: science, medicine and reform, 1626–1660* (1975) · will, 16 Oct 1673, PRO, PROB 11/343, sig. 122

Castle, Irene (1893–1969). *See under* Castle, Vernon (1887–1918).

Castle, Richard (*d.* 1751), architect and engineer, may have adopted his surname, which also appears as Castles, Cassel, and Cassels, to indicate a connection with Kassel in Germany. According to the biography in *Anthologia Hibernica* for October 1793, which is the principal source of information about him, he was born in Kassel of Huguenot parents. However, no record of his birth has been found in the registers of the Huguenot church in Kassel, and the three brothers to whom he left property in his will all bore the surname de Richardi and lived in Saxony. Castle became an officer in a regiment of engineers about 1715, and studied fortifications and canals in Germany, France, and the Netherlands: in his manuscript 'Essay on artificial navigation', he referred to his 'long application to the practical and speculative branches of the mathematics' (*c.*1730, NL Ire., MS 2737, fol. 1). By 1725 he was studying waterworks and architecture in England, where he was probably in contact with Lord Burlington's circle. In England he met Sir Gustavus Hume, who took him to Ireland to design his house at Castle Hume, co. Fermanagh, about 1727–8. On his arrival in Ireland, he was also employed by Edward Lovett Pearce as a draughtsman on the plans for the parliament house in Dublin.

Castle was as much an engineer as an architect in the early years of his Irish career. His 'Essay on artificial navigation' was addressed to the commissioners of inland navigation as proof that he was well qualified to be employed on the construction of the Newry Canal. He succeeded Pearce as engineer to the canal in 1733, and retained the position until he was discharged in 1736. In 1735 he was one of several experts consulted by the Dublin corporation about improving the city's water supply; his suggestions were published the same year as *An Essay toward Supplying the City of Dublin with Water*. It was, however, primarily as an architect that he made his name in Ireland. In 1728 Pearce had recommended him to the members of the Irish parliament, and this endorsement appears to have borne ample fruit. For over two decades until his death in 1751 Castle was the leading designer of country seats and Dublin houses for the protestant establishment; by 1743 he had taken on John Ensor as his clerk

and measurer. He is said to have been clear in his directions and exacting as to their execution.

Among Castle's surviving country houses are Hazlewood, Sligo (1731), Westport, co. Mayo (1731), Powerscourt, co. Wicklow (1731–40), Ballyhaise, co. Cavan (*c.*1733), Carton, co. Kildare (1739–45), Russborough, co. Wicklow (1742), and Bellinter, co. Meath (*c.*1750). Of the few churches which he is known to have designed, only one, Knockbreda parish church, Belfast (1737), is relatively intact. In Dublin, Castle's most substantial remaining works are Tyrone House (1740), Leinster House (1745–51), and the Rotunda Hospital, designed for his friend and drinking companion Dr Bartholomew Mosse in 1750 and completed by John Ensor. Of his various works for Trinity College, Dublin, only the printing house (1734) remains unaltered. Castle is often described as a Palladian architect: the regular Doric temple which he designed as the printing house, the robust massing of his country houses, flanked by pavilions and quadrant wings, and the rusticated ashlar façades of Leinster House and the Rotunda Hospital support this view. However, his use of detail was unorthodox: he tended to assemble niches, pediments, and oculi as centrepieces on a front, to use rusticated blocks of varying scales within one building, and to lean towards an almost mannerist conjunction of elements in the development of his interiors.

Castle is described as a man of the strictest integrity, though by temperament convivial, eccentric, and improvident. Intemperance and late hours were said to have caused the gout from which he suffered. He married Jane Truffet or Truphet (*d.* 1744) of Lisburn, co. Antrim, at the Huguenot church in Dublin on 28 June 1733, but there were no children of the marriage. He died suddenly of a fit, when he was 'between fifty and sixty years old' (*Anthologia Hibernica*), at Carton, co. Kildare, on 19 February 1751, and was buried in the churchyard at Maynooth, co. Kildare. In his will of 11 August 1750 he divided his property between his sister-in-law Anne Truffet and his three brothers in Saxony, Samuel, Daniel, and Benjamin de Richardi; his effects were sold at auction in 1752.

A. M. ROWAN

Sources 'History of the fine arts in Ireland: Richard Castles', *Anthologia Hibernica*, 2 (Oct 1793), 242–3 · D. Fitzgerald, 'Richard Castle, architect: his biography and works', *Quarterly Bulletin of the Irish Georgian Society*, 7/1 (1964), 31–8 · J. H. Farrington, ed., 'Richard Castle's "Essay on artificial navigation" 1730', *Transport History*, 5 (1972), 67–89, 155–67, pls. 114, 218, 219 · extracts from will of Richard Castle, Genealogical Office, Dublin, 424.187 · W. A. McCutcheon, *The canals of the north of Ireland* (1965), 18–20 · R. Castle, 'Essay on artificial navigation', *c.*1730, NL Ire., MS 2737, fol. 1
Archives Irish Architectural Archive, Dublin, Guinness collection

Castle, Roy (1932–1994), entertainer and charity campaigner, was born on 31 August 1932 in Holme Valley Memorial Hospital, Holmfirth, West Riding of Yorkshire, the only child of Hubert Castle, an insurance agent, and his wife, Eliza Alice Swallow, a mill worker. His childhood was spent in Scholes, a village near Huddersfield, from where he attended Honley grammar school. An early interest in music was encouraged by his mother—a keen member of the Huddersfield Choral Society—and he began receiving lessons in both singing and tap-dancing at the age of seven. When he was twelve his mother arranged for him to appear in a local variety show, *Youth on Parade*, run during the summer by Mildred Crossley, a dance instructor, and her husband Norman Teal, a performer and impresario. Two years later, in 1946, he left school aged fourteen in order to tour in a more ambitious Crossley and Teal production called *Happiness Ahead*.

National service interrupted Castle's fledgeling career in 1950, when he joined the RAF as a technical storeman, but it was resumed at the end of 1952, following demobilization, when he found employment in pantomime playing Dick Whittington's cat. A spell followed as the trumpeter in the Norman Teal Trio, before he branched out in the mid-1950s not only as a solo singer-dancer-musician, but also as a stooge to the northern comedian Jimmy James (from whom he learned the value of a sound technique and a steady temperament).

The year 1958 was the most important in Castle's career. First he was chosen by the influential impresario Val Parnell to appear in *New Look*, an ATV variety series designed as a showcase for fresh talent. Then, after impressing television executives with his initial performance in the (unscreened) pilot edition, he was added to the bill of that year's royal command performance. His subsequent contribution proved hugely successful, attracting reviews suggesting that he had stolen the show, and he later described the impact of his performance as his greatest moment in showbusiness.

Castle was taken promptly onto the books of the powerful Lew and Leslie Grade theatrical agency and was promoted vigorously as an exceptionally versatile entertainer. He could, it was noted, sing (in a bright tenor voice), dance (in every style but ballet), perform comedy, and play a wide range of instruments from the guitar and the drums to the vibraphone and the washboard. These varied talents, allied to his happy-go-lucky personality—he resembled, in both looks and demeanour, a smart Stan Laurel—ensured that his strong appeal traversed several different media. He continued to tour the club and variety theatre circuit, as well as make an increasing number of guest appearances on radio and television, and in 1961 he recorded an album of songs called *Castlewise*.

On 29 July 1963 Castle married the dancer (Joan) Fiona Dickson, daughter of William Walter Dickson, a doctor, one year on from the day when their mutual friend, the comedian Eric Morecambe, had introduced them to each other. ('This is Fiona', he had informed Castle, 'and she's in love with you.') They had two sons—Daniel and Benjamin—and two daughters—Julia and Antonia.

Castle stayed busy throughout the decade. In Britain he starred in his own BBC1 comedy sketch series, *The Roy Castle Show* (1965), acted in three films—*Dr Terror's House of Horrors* (1965), *Dr Who and the Daleks* (1965), and *Carry on up the Khyber* (1968)—and featured regularly in both summer seasons and pantomimes. In America—where his ebullient versatility was more eagerly appreciated—he made forty-two appearances on CBS Television's *The Garry Moore*

Show (1958–64), performed a solo set at the Sands Hotel in Las Vegas (1964), and received a Tony award nomination for his portrayal of Sam Weller in the Broadway production of the musical *Pickwick* (1965). Only his desire to see his children educated in England prevented him from establishing himself more firmly in the USA.

In 1972 Castle began a remarkable twenty-two-year run presenting the BBC1 television series *Record Breakers* (based on *The Guinness Book of Records*), and he ended up setting two records himself (one in 1985 for tap-dancing—completing one million taps in 23 hours and 44 minutes—and the other in 1990 for wing walking—3 hours and 23 minutes on a flight from Gatwick to Paris). He also starred in his own BBC Radio 2 series, *Castle's in the Air*, from 1974 to 1983, and appeared as Cosmo Brown in the 1983 stage version of *Singin' in the Rain* at the London Palladium.

Castle was diagnosed as having lung cancer in 1992 (despite never having smoked), but with characteristic fortitude and good humour he turned his struggle into a crusade, drawing attention to the dangers of passive smoking and, via a series of gruelling nationwide tours, promoting a £12 million appeal to establish an international lung cancer research centre in Liverpool. His efforts not only reminded people of his value as a performer but also highlighted his virtue as a person, and he was awarded the OBE in 1993. Castle, a committed Christian, died on 2 September 1994 at his home, Bearwood, 21 South Park View, Gerrards Cross, Buckinghamshire. His autobiography, *Now and Then* (1994), was published posthumously. The cancer research centre named after him opened in 1998.

GRAHAM McCANN

Sources R. Castle, *Now and then* (1994) · M. Craig, *Look back with laughter*, vol. 2 (1996) · personal knowledge (2004) · private information (2004) · *The Times* (3 Sept 1994) · *The Independent* (3 Sept 1994) · m. cert. · d. cert.
Likenesses photograph, 1961, Hult. Arch. · photograph, 1966, Mirrorpix · photograph, 1993, Mirrorpix · photograph, repro. in *The Times* · photograph, repro. in *The Independent*
Wealth at death £582,199: probate, CGPLA Eng. & Wales

Castle, Thomas (1805/6–1837), surgeon and botanist, was born in Kent, the youngest son of Slodden Castle, of Sandwich, Kent. After leaving school he became an apprentice of John Gill, a surgeon at Hythe; in his third year he began his first book, which he finished before going to London to continue his medical studies. In 1826 he entered Guy's Hospital, where he was a member of its Physical Society; in the year following he was elected a fellow of the Linnean Society. At that time he was living in Bermondsey Square, London. In 1830 he matriculated at Queen's College, Oxford. However, the next year he entered Trinity College, Cambridge. He does not appear to have graduated from either university.

Subsequently Castle moved to Brighton, and in the 1830s he signed himself 'M.D., F.L.S., consulting physician to St. John's British Hospital and memb. Trin. Coll. Camb.'. He published numerous botanical and medical works, including a translation of the pharmacopoeia of the Royal College of Physicians, *An Introduction to Systematical and Physiological Botany* (1829), *An Introduction to Medical Botany*

(1829), and *The Linnean Artificial Botany* (1837). He also edited *A Manual of Modern Surgery* (1828). Castle died by his own hand on 2 November 1837.

B. D. JACKSON, rev. PATRICK WALLIS

Sources Venn, *Alum. Cant.* · Foster, *Alum. Oxon.* · Desmond, *Botanists*, rev. edn · d. cert.

Castle, Vernon [*real name* Vernon William Blyth] (1887–1918), ballroom dancer, was born Vernon William Blyth on 2 May 1887 at Mill Hill Road, Heigham, near Norwich, Norfolk, the youngest in the family of four daughters and one son of William Thomas Blyth, public house manager, and his first wife, Jane Finley. His mother died when he was a child, and after attending local schools he studied civil engineering at Birmingham University. In the summer of 1906 he accompanied his sister, Coralie Blythe, and her husband, Lawrence Grossmith, to New York, where they had been engaged to act in a revue, *About Town*, the first Broadway show put on by the comedian Lew Fields at his Herald Square Theater. When the play went on tour, he became Grossmith's understudy, and back in New York he was given a small part in *The Girl behind the Counter* (1907), in which he was noticed for his elegant dancing. It was at this point that he took the name of Castle.

Castle played comic roles and danced in several more Lew Fields productions, including *The Midnight Sons* (1909), *Old Dutch* (1909), *The Summer Widowers* (1910), and *The Hen Pecks* (1911), which set off a craze for ragtime, with dances such as the turkey trot, the grizzly bear, and the bunny hug. Castle married Irene Foote [*see below*] in May 1911. He had persuaded Lew Fields to give her a very small part in the replacement cast of *The Summer Widowers* in November 1910 at the Majestic Theater in Brooklyn, her first professional engagement. After their honeymoon in England, she joined the cast of *The Hen Pecks* for its reopening.

Vernon and Irene Castle first appeared professionally as dancing partners in Paris in 1912. Vernon had been engaged to appear in a comic revue by a Paris manager who had seen him in *The Hen Pecks* in New York, in a famous slapstick scene in a barber's shop. Irene was given a small part, but they soon left to try out as dancers at the Café de Paris, dancing the grizzly bear and the Texas tommy. An overnight success, they spent six months there as cabaret entertainers.

On their return to New York the Castles were inundated with offers of work, and they set off a dancing craze which swept America. Turning their backs on the acrobatic animal dances, they popularized social ballroom dancing with dances such as the hesitation waltz and the Castle walk, and showed that dancing could be refined and graceful. Their most popular dance was the one-step, danced to ragtime music, and they introduced the tango to the ballroom in 1912, and the foxtrot in 1914. The Castles danced in C. B. Dillingham's Broadway production of *The Sunshine Girl* (1913), in which Vernon also had a comic role. They taught at Castle House, a school of modern dancing in New York—Vernon was an excellent teacher—and in 1914 they brought out *Modern Dancing*, showing people exactly how to dance the new dances:

'real dancing means graceful measures tripped to the lilting rhythm of fine music' (p. 37). Tea dances were held at Castle House, and the Castles danced most evenings at Castles in the Air, a rooftop dancing and supper establishment in New York, or at Castles by the Sea at Long Beach, Long Island, and they also owned a restaurant, Sans Souci, on 42nd Street, New York, where Vernon indulged in his passion for drumming. In 1913 they appeared in a film, *The Whirl of Life*: Irene continued to make films, and later went to Hollywood, where she starred in fifteen episodes of *Patria* for Pathé. With Jim Europe's band they went on a whirlwind tour of America in a special train in the spring of 1914. Their best, and last, work on stage together was for C. B. Dillingham in *Watch your Step*, advertised as 'the first Syncopated Musical', with music and lyrics by Irving Berlin, which opened on Broadway in December 1914, and then toured America.

The Castles were in France at the beginning of August 1914, engaged to dance for a month in the casino at Deauville, but with war imminent they went to England, where Irene persuaded Vernon not to enlist. But in December 1915, at the peak of his career, he left *Watch your Step* to train as a pilot at Newport News, Virginia, before sailing to England, where he was commissioned in the Royal Flying Corps. He flew 150 missions in France, and was awarded the Croix de Guerre, but after a flying accident in 1917 he was sent to Camp Mohawk, Deseronto, in Canada, as a flying instructor, and from there went with his squadron to winter quarters at Benbrook Field, near Fort Worth, Texas. Vernon Castle was killed in an air collision on 15 February 1918, while instructing a cadet. He was buried at Woodlawn cemetery, New York, five days later. Despite his success, he was a modest, unassuming man. When not performing, he liked to play polo near the Castles' home in Manhasset, Long Island, New York, and he showed German shepherd (Alsatian) dogs.

Irene Castle [*née* Foote] (1893–1969) was born on 7 April 1893 in New Rochelle, New York, the younger of the two daughters of Hubert Townsend Foote (*d.* 1912), a homoeopathic doctor, and his wife, Anne Elroy Thomas (*d.* 1922). It was thanks to Vernon Castle, whom she met at a swimming party, that she went on the stage, and after he joined the Royal Flying Corps she continued to perform in *Watch your Step*. She was in C. B. Dillingham's revue *Miss 1917*, which ran for only nine weeks after its opening in November 1917, and at the time of Vernon's death she was playing the leading role in Dillingham's *The Century Girl* at the Century Theater in New York. After his death she found a new dancing partner, Billy Reardon, and continued to act occasionally, coming out of retirement in 1939 to play the lead in Noël Coward's *Shadow Play*. She wrote about their partnership in *My Husband* (1919), and in *Castles in the Air* (1958). The Castles were much admired by Fred Astaire and Ginger Rogers, and it was they who were engaged to play the leading roles in the film *The Story of Vernon and Irene Castle* (1939), adapted from *My Husband*, with songs and dances from their heyday, including the Castle polka, danced to 'Little Brown Jug', and the Castle walk, to 'Too much Mustard'. Irene Castle was technical adviser to the film.

At the height of the popularity of the Castles, Irene set the fashions of the day. She was the first woman to bob her hair, and all America copied the Castle bob. Tall and elegant, she designed silk dresses for the Corticelli Silk Company in the 1920s, and later worked for the Formfit Company, promoting corsets in department stores. In 1928 she opened a dogs' home, Orphans of the Storm, in Illinois, and campaigned against cruelty to animals.

Irene Castle remarried three times. In 1919 she married Robert Treman. After their divorce in 1923 she married Frederic McClaughlin: there were two children from this marriage. After his death at the end of the Second World War she married George Enziger (d. 1959) in 1946. Irene Castle died on 25 January 1969 in Eureka Springs, Arkansas, USA.   ANNE PIMLOTT BAKER

Sources Mrs Vernon Castle [I. Castle], *My husband* (1919) · I. Castle, *Castles in the air* (1958) · A. Fields and L. M. Fields, *From the Bowery to Broadway: Lew Fields and the roots of American popular theatre* (1993) · I. Whitcomb, *Irving Berlin and ragtime America* (1987), 170–2 · G. Bordman, *American musical theatre*, enl. edn (1986) · F. Astaire, *Steps in time* (1960), 237–41 · T. Satchwell, *Astaire: the biography* (1987) · A. H. Franks, *Social dance: a short history* (1963) · *The Times* (27 Jan 1969) · *The Times* (16 Feb 1918) · *DAB* · *Who was who in America*, 4 (1968) · b. cert. · *IGI* · *CGPLA Eng. & Wales* (1920) · J. Malnig, 'Irene Castle and Vernon Castle', *ANB*
Archives NYPL, Robinson Locke collection, Billy Rose Theater Collection
Likenesses Mottett Studio, Chicago, photograph, 1915, repro. in Mrs Castle, *My husband*, facing p. 106 · C. Beaton, photograph, 1920–23 (Irene Castle), repro. in Castle, *Castles in the air* · double portrait, photograph (with Irene Castle), repro. in Mrs Castle, *My husband*, facing p. 14 · double portraits, photographs (with Irene Castle), repro. in Franks, *Social dance*, 39–44
Wealth at death £177 3s. 1d.: administration with will, 25 Oct 1920, *CGPLA Eng. & Wales*

Castlecomer. For this title name *see* Wandesford, Christopher, second Viscount Castlecomer (*bap.* 1684, *d.* 1719) [*see under* Wandesford, Christopher (1592–1640)].

Castlehaven. For this title name *see* Brydges, Anne, Lady Chandos [Anne Touchet, countess of Castlehaven] (1580–1647); Touchet, Mervin, second earl of Castlehaven (1593–1631); Touchet, James, third earl of Castlehaven (*bap.* 1612, *d.* 1684).

Castlemaine. For this title name *see* Palmer, Roger, earl of Castlemaine (1634–1705); Palmer, Barbara, countess of Castlemaine and *suo jure* duchess of Cleveland (*bap.* 1640, *d.* 1709).

Castlereagh. For this title name *see* Stewart, Robert, Viscount Castlereagh and second marquess of Londonderry (1769–1822).

Castner, Hamilton Young (1858–1899), industrial chemist, was born on 11 September 1858 in Brooklyn, New York, the second of three sons (there were no daughters) of Samuel Castner and his wife, Julia. His early education is unknown, but he attended the Brooklyn Polytechnic Institute before enrolling in 1875 in Columbia University

School of Mines. He left after three years without a degree, not from any lack of ability but because he selected from the course only those subjects—analytical and applied chemistry—which appealed to him.

In 1879 Castner and his elder brother, E. B. Castner, set up as consulting chemists in New York. The consultancy prospered, but some chemical processes which Castner developed were not successful commercially. About 1884 he sold his share and turned his attention to devising an improved process for manufacturing aluminium, a metal whose unique properties could not then be adequately utilized because of its high cost. Production at that time was by reducing aluminium chloride with sodium, which cost 14s. a pound. Castner devised a process, involving the reduction of caustic soda with carbon, by which the cost of sodium could be reduced to less than 1s. a pound. He failed to interest American industrialists and in 1886 travelled to England, thereafter the centre of his working life.

In England Castner aroused the interest of the Webster Crown Metal Company of Solihull, which was then manufacturing small quantities of aluminium at a cost of £3 a pound. Substantiation of Castner's claim led to the formation in 1887 of the Aluminium Company. Potential annual output was 100,000 pounds. After initial difficulties, they succeeded in producing aluminium of high purity but in 1889 the process was rendered obsolete by the advent of a much cheaper electrochemical process invented independently in France and the USA. With characteristic resource Castner developed new uses for his cheap sodium, his only asset. From it he manufactured sodium peroxide, a valuable bleaching agent, especially for straw hats, and sodium cyanide for the booming gold-mining industry, particularly in South Africa.

The now misnamed Aluminium Company flourished, and it was difficult to keep pace with the demand for sodium. In 1890 Castner devised a new process for its manufacture, based on the electrolytic decomposition of caustic soda. Difficulties arose because of the relative impurity of even the best available caustic soda, and this led to his greatest success—a process for manufacturing very pure caustic soda by the electrolysis of brine in a rocking cell containing mercury. Valuable by-products were chlorine (yielding bleaching powder for the textile and paper trades) and hydrogen. On seeking to patent his process, Castner discovered that a similar patent had been lodged in Germany by Karl Kellner and made over to the powerful Solvay Company in Belgium. To avoid expensive litigation, the two companies combined in 1895 to form the Castner-Kellner Alkali Company, with large works in Runcorn.

Castner's originality brought him little public acclaim, for the chemical industry was such that its products were largely the raw materials of other industries. Nevertheless, he ranked high among the pioneers of twentieth-century chemical technology. His life was clouded from the 1880s by the onset of tuberculosis, which led him to spend his winters in Florida. In spite of this, he had a remarkable record of achievement when he died, on 11 October 1899, at his home in Saranac Lake, Franklin county, New York state. He was unmarried.

TREVOR I. WILLIAMS, *rev.*

Sources A. Fleck, 'The life and work of Hamilton Young Castner', *Chemistry and Industry* (23 Aug 1947), 515–21 · *Fifty years of progress: the story of the Castner-Kellner Alkali Company*, Castner-Kellner Alkali Co. [1945]
Likenesses portrait, repro. in *Fifty years of progress*
Wealth at death £13,430 18s. 8d.: resworn probate, Sept 1900, CGPLA Eng. & Wales

Castro, Alfonso de (c.1495–1558), Franciscan friar and jurist, was born in Zamora (León), not far from the Castilian-Portuguese border, and in 1510 or 1511, at about the age of fifteen, he entered the friary of San Francisco in Salamanca. About 1516, or even earlier, he went to study at the University of Alcalá, recently founded with the intention of promoting humanist learning, where he studied under the distinguished canonist Martín de Azpilcueta. By 1520 he had returned to his fellow Franciscans in Salamanca as a professor of theology. His first trip outside Spain came in 1526, when he participated in his order's general chapter in Assisi. He also attended the coronation of Charles V by the pope in Bologna in 1530, and it is claimed that he wrote at the emperor's request an unpublished and now lost tract defending the marriage of Henry VIII and the emperor's aunt, Katherine of Aragon.

Castro first became acquainted with northern Europe about 1533, when he relocated to the Low Countries as pastor to the large Spanish business community in Bruges. He took the opportunity of travelling widely in Germany, visiting several cities including Cologne and Frankfurt, which allowed him to witness at first hand the dissemination of Lutheran ideas. After some years in Bruges he returned to Salamanca, probably in 1537, when the first of his two highly successful homiletic volumes on the Psalms were printed there. In 1545 he was nominated by the regency government in Spain to attend the first session of the Council of Trent. He took an active part in its meetings, and in March 1546 he was made a member of the commission which considered the relationship between the laity and scripture. He left after its findings were adopted on 13 January 1547. He returned in 1551 and strongly opposed the abrupt suspension of the council in March 1552.

Castro had been nominated because of his outstanding reputation as a theologian. He had completed, not long after his arrival in the Low Countries, the first of three great works in defence of Catholic orthodoxy and rightful punishment. Taken together, they synthesized theological thought with secular jurisprudence to lay the foundations for the equitable punishment of all transgressions, be they against the law of God or of man. The first of these works was *Adversus omnes haereses*, which appeared at Paris in 1534 and which was published another eleven times before his death, with the last edition being printed in Venice in the middle of the eighteenth century. The work listed in alphabetical order all the heresies which

the Catholic church had encountered down the centuries, along with its responses.

The second instalment in Castro's great project was published at Salamanca in October 1547. *De iusta haereticorum punitione* defended the church's right to punish heretics justly and appropriately. It revealed how his forensic sense of order had been profoundly disturbed by the fact that, though he had himself witnessed the decapitation of heretics, he also knew that in certain parts of the Low Countries they might have their arms and legs bound and be flung into a river to drown, whereas in the city of Bruges the punishment for disbelievers could involve being burnt alive in boiling oil. Six editions were published, of which all but two appeared in Castro's lifetime. A third work, in similar if much shorter vein, appeared in 1550 as *De potestate legis poenalis*, and again six editions were published, of which five are from the sixteenth century while the last, the only translation of any of Castro's works into Spanish, appeared in the 1930s.

Castro was at pains to show that the church could punish heterodoxy even to the point of death. Arguing against Duns Scotus's limited view that death could only be imposed for crimes expressly sanctioned by the Old Testament, Castro was of the opinion that it could be exacted whenever natural law deemed there to be just cause, claiming that the death penalty was sanctioned in the New Testament by Christ's words that those who lived by the sword should die by the sword (Matthew 26: 52). What was novel was that he rigorously applied to all offences, lay or religious, capital or otherwise, the same jurisprudential test. Was the sentence truly appropriate? Castro's organizing principle was that in the interests of justice sentence must always be mitigated wherever possible. As for punishment by death, he whittled down his argument to two essential criteria: the offence must be grave (and not just the killing of a royal deer, he suggested), and at the same time the delinquent must be incapable of correction by any other means. When *either* of these conditions did not obtain, then it was unjust to take human life. As for heresy, death was the only appropriate sentence if the beliefs involved endangered the soul of either the delinquent or of society, always provided that the transgressor remained incorrigible.

Castro's views on the condemnation of heretics became an English *cause célèbre* under Philip and Mary. He had been living and preaching at Philip's court since October 1553. In July the following year he accompanied the prince of Spain when he sailed to Southampton to marry Mary Tudor and assume the crown matrimonial of England. According to John Foxe, Castro gave a sermon at court on Sunday 10 February 1555. It allegedly provoked a temporary stay of execution for six protestant martyrs whose case had been heard by Bishop Bonner of London on the previous Friday, and who had been peremptorily sentenced by him the following day. Describing him as 'a very good friar', Foxe claimed that in the king's presence Castro 'did earnestly inveigh against the bishops for burning of men, saying plainly that they learnt it not in scripture, to burn any for his conscience: but the contrary—that they should live and be converted' (*Acts and Monuments*, 6.704–5). Foxe was clearly wrong-headed if he believed that Castro could deny that disbelievers might be executed. Heresy was, as Castro put it, a virus which could infect and plague society; he had even lamented the fact that, if Germany had only treated heresy with half the rigour to be found in Spain, then Lutheranism would not have taken hold. Preaching in either Spanish or Latin, Castro is more likely to have reminded the king of the requirement to seek an alternative to punishment by death wherever possible, implicitly attacking, perhaps, the swiftness of the condemnation of the six protestants. He may also have suggested that, since heresy was widespread in England, re-education would be more effective than exemplary punishment. As for the remarks about burning, Castro was almost certainly restating his long-held belief that there was no religious imperative for heretics to be punished this way. As he had already written, 'If you ask me if heretics should be burnt, I reply that this is by no fixed law, but only by custom' (*De iusta*, bk 2, chap. 1).

Whether Castro personally intervened on behalf of the six men condemned by Bonner is not known, but on 25 February he went with the king's confessor, Bernardo de Fresneda, to visit John Bradford in the Counter prison. A radical London priest, Bradford had been among the first five protestants to be condemned in the show-trial conducted by Lord Chancellor Gardiner a week before Bonner took over the persecution. Castro was apparently introduced as 'one Alphonsus who had written against heresies'. He tried to persuade Bradford of the doctrine of transubstantiation and that the wicked also received Christ's body (*Acts and Monuments*, 7.179). Despite a willingness to join with the condemned man in seeking out passages from the Bible, Castro failed to induce him to recant. That it was none other than the earl of Derby who persuaded Castro to visit the prisoner tells something of the contacts he made in England. It may be no coincidence that his great compendium of heresies was displayed (though with no more success) to another protestant martyr, George Marsh, who had also attracted the earl's interest.

Castro was an intimate friend of Bartolomé Carranza, the Dominican friar who also accompanied Philip to England. Along with Fresneda, they were ordered to remain behind in London when the king left for the first time at the end of August 1555. Both men knew Cardinal Reginald Pole from Trent and were influential in preparations for the synod which convened at Westminster in November that year. In a memorial composed in London at about this time which considered Philip's war in Italy against the pope, Castro demonstrated that, in his desire to improve the quality of the clergy in Spain, he was at one with Pole. He called for confirmation of everything that had been decided at Trent and that steps be taken to increase the number of trained theologians in Spanish cathedrals. His progressive stance is also evident in his support for another cause favoured by Pole. The former home of the London Greyfriars had been turned into Christ's Hospital,

a school for poor children. Headed by Friar William Peto, its former occupants campaigned for it to be returned to church ownership and Castro was brought to inspect the school. The plan backfired when Castro developed a 'very good liking of the training up of these children' and joined forces with other Spaniards to persuade the king and queen to preserve the school (*John Howes' MS, 1582*, 66).

Castro rejoined the king in the Low Countries either at the end of 1555 or early in 1556. He died in Brussels on 3 February 1558 and was buried there, awaiting the papal bulls which would have allowed him to take up the archbishopric of Santiago de Compostela.

GLYN REDWORTH

Sources M. de Castro, 'Fr Alfonso de Castro, OFM (1495–1558), consejero de Carlos V y Felipe II', *Salmanticensis*, 6 (1958), 281–322 · M. Rodríguez Molinero, *Origen español de la ciencia del derecho penal: Alfonso de Castro y su sistema penal* (Madrid, 1959) · C. Gutiérrez, *Españoles en Trento* (Valladolid, 1951) · *The acts and monuments of John Foxe*, ed. J. Pratt, [new edn], 8 vols. (1877) · *John Howes' MS, 1582*, ed. W. Lempriere (1904) · J. L. Nelson, 'Francisco de Enzinas (Dryander) and Spanish evangelical humanism before the Council of Trent', PhD diss., University of Manchester, 1999 · *Opera Alphonsi à Castro Zamorensi* (Paris, 1571)
Archives Archivo General, Simancas, papers

Castrucci, Pietro (1679–1752), violinist and composer, was born in Rome, the elder of the two known children of Domenico Castrucci (*d.* in or after 1709). Details of his early life are scarce, but his father was a violinist, and together they were in the employment of Francesco, Marchese Ruspoli, during Handel's periodic visits to Rome (*c.*1707–9). Together with his younger brother, the violinist Prospero Castrucci (1690?–1760), Castrucci was a pupil of Archangelo Corelli. Richard Boyle, third earl of Burlington, another Corelli pupil and an English patron of Handel, took the brothers to London. From their arrival in May 1715 until 1721 or later, they resided at his home in Piccadilly.

At his first public appearance in London (23 July 1715) Castrucci performed 'several Solos on the Violin, intirely New' (Avery, 1.363). By 1716 he had become a member of the orchestra at the King's Theatre, Haymarket. In 1718 Castrucci became leader of the newly established Royal Academy of Music, a post in which he remained until 1737. Handel became 'master of the orchestra' in November 1719, and many of his subsequent works featured the Castrucci brothers prominently. The operas *Sosarme* (1732), *Ezio* (1732), and *Orlando* (1733), together with the oratorio *Deborah* (1733), all indicate the involvement of an instrument called the *violetta marina*. This was probably a viola d'amore with sympathetic strings like that described by Leopold Mozart as an 'English violet' (Mozart, 12). Burney suggests that Castrucci invented this instrument, first playing it at his own benefit concert in 1732. Desirous of making an impression, Castrucci often included novelty attractions at his benefits. On 26 February 1731, for example, he advertised his intention to execute 'twenty-four notes with one bow' (Burney, *Hist. mus.*, 2.770), probably in the giga of his sonata op. 2 no. 2. This was parodied the following day in an advertisement which suggested that a solo would be played by 'the last violin of Goodman's Field's playhouse' including 'twenty-five notes with one bow' (ibid.).

Most contemporary commentators speak favourably of Castrucci's playing. Sir John Clerk of Penicuik, who attended the last night of *Orlando* on 5 May 1733, noted that the violins 'made a terrible noise & often drown'd the voices', but singled out the Castrucci brothers 'who play'd with great dexterity' (Dean and Knapp, 33). Sir John Hawkins likewise thought Castrucci 'an excellent performer on the violin' (Hawkins, 891), but Burney suggests that 'he was long thought insane … his compositions were too mad for his own age', but 'too sober for the present' (Burney, *Hist. mus.*, 2.1004). Burney's ascription of Castrucci as the subject of Hogarth's *Enraged Musician* is now considered unlikely by Hogarth experts, and the subject is more likely to be the German oboist and flautist John Festing although this identification has also been questioned.

Castrucci was extremely active outside the opera, performing frequently at various London concert venues and theatres. However, anecdotal accounts of his later years suggest that his playing declined significantly. In 1737 Handel seemingly decided to replace him as leader of the opera orchestra, Castrucci's reluctance leading Handel to devise a scheme to shame him into resignation:

Handel … composed a concerto, in which the second concertino was contrived, as to require an equal degree of execution with the first; this he gave to Clegg, who in the performance of it gave such proofs of his superiority, as reduced Castrucci to the necessity of yielding the palm to his rival. (Hawkins, 891)

This dismissal did not signal the end of his career, and on 28 August 1739 Castrucci became one of the original subscribers to the Royal Society of Musicians. Little is known of his activities during the 1740s, although he advertised a yearly benefit concert in the *General Advertiser* for 30 March 1748.

Burney observed 'that among the many passages of Corelli and Handel' in Castrucci's compositions, there are 'several of his own', but qualified this caustic comment with the statement that they nevertheless show Castrucci 'to have been a man of genius, well acquainted with the bow and finger-board of his instrument' (Burney, *Hist. mus.*, 2.1004). In collaboration with his friend Francesco Geminiani, a fellow Roman and pupil of Corelli, Castrucci produced *Six Sonatas or Solos … for a Flute and a Bass* (*c*.1720), of which he probably wrote the first four. His other significant extant published works include two further sets of twelve violin sonatas and a set of twelve concerti grossi which Hawkins described as 'hardly known' but having 'great merit' (Hawkins, 891). Castrucci's op. 1 sonatas, dedicated to his patron Lord Burlington, are remarkably similar to, but much shorter than, Corelli's op. 5 sonatas, and together with op. 2 call for a number of extended techniques including *bariolage*, multiple stops, scordatura tunings, and 'battute'. Many of the movements also have descriptive titles, such as 'Venetiana', 'Commodo alla francese', or 'Corni da cacci'. The concerti grossi op. 3 are much more simplistic, bearing a close resemblance to those by Geminiani. Some of Castrucci's music manuscripts are in the British Library and the Gesellschaft der Musikfreunde, Vienna.

In 1750 Castrucci went to Dublin, where he appeared at the Charitable Musical Society at the Fishamble Street Music Hall on 5 October. Two of his concertos were performed at the Philharmonic Society later that year, and he held a benefit concert on 21 February 1751. He died in Dublin between 7 February and 7 March 1752, probably of natural causes. His funeral took place on 10 March at St Mary's Church, Dublin, and despite his extreme poverty, it was a magnificent event. *Faulkner's Journal* reported that his cortège included 'the whole Band of Musick from the New Gardens in Great Britain St., who will perform the Dead March in Saul, composed by Mr Handel' (Highfill, Burnim & Langhans, *BDA*, 3.105). He was buried in St Mary's.   CLAIRE M. NELSON

Sources B. Boydell, *A Dublin musical calendar, 1700–1760* (1988) • D. D. Boyden, *The history of violin playing from its origins to 1761* (1990) • Burney, *Hist. mus.*, new edn • E. Careri, *Francesco Geminiani (1687–1762)* (1993) • W. Dean, 'Handel, George Frideric', *New Grove* • W. Dean, *Handel's dramatic oratorios and masques*, rev. edn (1990) • W. Dean and J. M. Knapp, *Handel's operas, 1704–1715* (1987) • J. Hawkins, *A general history of the science and practice of music*, new edn, 3 vols. (1853); repr. in 2 vols. (1963), vol. 1 • B. Matthews, ed., *The Royal Society of Musicians of Great Britain: list of members, 1738–1984* (1985) • W. S. Newman, *The sonata in the baroque era*, rev. edn (1983) • S. McVeigh, *The violinist in London's concert life, 1750–1784: Felice Giardini and his contemporaries* (1989) • W. C. Smith, *A bibliography of the musical works published by John Walsh … 1695–1720* (1948) • J. Uglow, *Hogarth: a life and a world* (1997) • L. Mozart, *A treatise on the fundamental principles of violin playing*, trans. E. Knocker, 2nd edn (1951); repr. (1990) • O. Edwards and S. McVeigh, 'Castrucci, Pietro', *New Grove*, 2nd edn • Highfill, Burnim & Langhans, *BDA* • E. L. Avery, ed., *The London stage, 1660–1800*, pt 2: *1700–1729* (1960) • A. H. Scouten, ed., *The London stage, 1660–1800*, pt 3: *1729–1747* (1961) • F.-J. Fétis, *Biographie universelle des musiciens, et bibliographie générale de la musique*, 8 vols. (Brussels, 1835–44) • H. Mendel and A. Reissmann, eds., *Musikalisches Conversations-Lexikon: eine Encyklopädie der gesammten musikalischen Wissenschaften*, 12 vols. (Berlin, 1870–83) • *Répertoire international des sources musicales*, ser. A/I, 9 vols. (Munich and Duisburg, 1971–81); addenda and corrigenda, 4 vols. (1986–99) • E. B. Schnapper, ed., *The British union-catalogue of early music printed before the year 1801*, 2 vols. (1957) • L. Baillie and R. Balchin, eds., *The catalogue of printed music in the British Library to 1980*, 62 vols. (1981–7) • P. Castrucci, *Sonate a violino e violone o cembalo* (Amsterdam, [n.d., 1730?]), op. 1

Wealth at death 'impoverished': Dean, 'Handel, George Frideric'

Caswall, Edward [*pseud.* Scriblerus Redivivus] (1814–1878), poet and Roman Catholic priest, the fourth of nine children of the Revd Robert Clarke Caswall (1768/9–1846), and the younger brother of Dr Henry Caswall, prebendary of Salisbury, was born on 15 July 1814 at Yateley, Hampshire, where his father was vicar. He was educated at Chigwell grammar school and Marlborough grammar school, before going on in 1832 to Brasenose College, Oxford, where he took a second-class degree in classics in 1836 and an MA in 1838. After ordination in 1839 he was presented to the perpetual curacy of Stratford-sub-Castle, Wiltshire, in the diocese of his uncle, Thomas Burgess, bishop of Salisbury.

In 1841 Caswall married Louisa Walker, the only child of

Edward Caswall (1814–1878), by Albin Roberts Burt, 1837

Oxon. • O. Shipley, preface, *Annus sanctus: hymns of the church for the ecclesiastical year* (1884) • J. Gondon, *Les récentes conversions de l'Angleterre* (1851), 227 • J. Gondon, postscript, *Conversions de soixante ministres anglicans*, 2nd edn (1847) • E. G. K. Browne, *Annals of the Tractarian movement*, 3rd edn (1861)

Archives Birmingham Oratory, corresp., diaries, journal, note-books, and papers

Likenesses A. R. Burt, pencil and watercolour, 1837, NPG [*see illus.*] • R. W. Thrupp, carte-de-visite, NPG

Wealth at death under £4000: probate, 18 Jan 1878, *CGPLA Eng. & Wales*

General Walker of Taunton. In 1845 he toured the continent with his wife and returned with a deep affection for the Roman Catholic faith. He resigned his church living in March 1846, and with his wife was received into the Catholic church in January 1847. Following her death from Asiatic cholera in 1849, Caswall joined the Oratory of St Philip Neri, at Edgbaston near Birmingham, under John Henry Newman, to whose writings he always partly attributed his conversion to the Catholic faith.

While at Oxford, Caswall had given evidence of his humour and literary skill in two pamphlets by Scriblerus Redivivus entitled *Pluck Examination Papers* (1836) and *A New Art, Teaching how to be Plucked* (1837); and before his conversion he published a thoughtful collection, *Sermons on the Seen and Unseen* (1846). Caswall then acquired distinction as a sacred poet. His translation of the breviary hymns was published in *Lyra catholica* (1849). He became a Roman Catholic priest on 18 September 1852, and a full member of the Oratory in 1854. In 1858 a number of devotional poems, both original and translated, were included in *The Masque of Mary* (1858). More than thirty of his hymns were adopted by the protestant compilers of *Hymns Ancient and Modern* (1861) and *The People's Hymnal* (1867).

Caswall died at the Oratory of St Philip Neri on 2 January 1878, and was buried at Rednal near Bromsgrove, in the private cemetery belonging to the Birmingham Oratory.

THOMPSON COOPER, *rev.* CHARLES BRAYNE

Sources E. F. Hatfield, *The poets of the church: a series of biographical sketches of hymn writers* (1884), 135–8 • *Birmingham Daily Post* (4 Jan 1878) • *The Guardian* (9 Jan 1878), 41 • *Weekly Register and Catholic Standard* (19 Jan 1878), 38 • Gillow, *Lit. biog. hist.* • Foster, *Alum.*

Caswell, Richard (1729–1789), surveyor and politician in America, was born on 3 August 1729 at Mulberry Point, a plantation overlooking Chesapeake Bay, near Joppa, Baltimore county, Maryland, the son of Richard Caswell, merchant and public official, and Christian Dallam (*b. c.*1690). He attended the local parish school, where he was taught by William Cawthorn and Joseph Hooper, priests of St John's Anglican Church. His father became ill in 1743, and young Richard and his older brother, William, took over the operation of the family farm and mercantile establishment to care for their parents and nine siblings. The decline of Joppa as a seaport led the family to follow many of their neighbours to North Carolina. The two brothers left first to prepare for the others. They reached New Bern, the capital of North Carolina, in 1745, bearing a letter of recommendation from the governor of Maryland to Governor Gabriel Johnston of North Carolina. William was employed in the office of the secretary of the province. The sixteen-year-old Richard was apprenticed to the surveyor-general, James Mackilwean, with whose family he lived for two years at the 850 acre plantation Tower Hill, near Stringer's Ferry on the Neuse River. Caswell made his home in this part of North Carolina for the remainder of his life. From time to time he also worked for Francis Stringer's business enterprises, where he gained additional experience.

In 1747 Caswell's formal training was completed, and when he reached the age of eighteen he was named deputy surveyor-general of the province. He then received a grant of land on which he built a home for his parents and the younger children who had remained with them. In the Mackilwean household Caswell was exposed to North Carolina politics—in addition to being the surveyor-general his host was also a member of the provincial assembly. Other politically active neighbours also contributed to Caswell's awareness of the significance of regional events. When Johnston county was created from the northern portion of Craven county in 1746, Caswell was commissioned an officer of the troop of horse. His father and brother were named deputy clerk and clerk, respectively, of the new county; the first county seat was established at Stringer's Ferry. There Richard was deputy clerk from 1749 to 1753, and for a very short time he also served as the first clerk of Orange county after it was formed from the upper part of Johnston county in 1752. A rising young man with a flair for politics, he was alert to new opportunities and soon became high sheriff, the chief county administrative officer.

At Tower Hill on 21 April 1752, when he was not quite

twenty-three, Caswell was married to Mary Mackilwean (c.1733–1757), daughter of his former surveying teacher. They became the parents of two daughters, who died young, and a son, William (b. 1754), who became a captain in the American army, a state militia brigadier-general, and a member of the legislature. After the death of his wife following childbirth, in 1757, Caswell married Sarah Heritage on 20 June 1758. They became the parents of eleven children, of whom eight lived to adulthood.

As a member of the colonial assembly during the years 1754–76, and as speaker of the assembly from 1770 to 1771, Caswell contributed to legislation concerning the court system, public defence, and humanitarian matters. He envisioned the creation of a system of free schools in each county through use of money reimbursed by the crown for support rendered by North Carolina in the French and Indian War. His desire for public aid for education was unsatisfied, however, until provision was made for it in the state's first constitution in December 1776.

During the dozen years after 1765, public sentiment against British management of affairs in the colonies was coalescing. Public needs and sentiment were disregarded by public officials, and people in many places sought personal solutions to common problems. Taxes seemed to be excessive, courts of justice appeared biased, and colonial government favoured the wealthier eastern counties. It was out of such dissatisfaction that the North Carolina regulator movement grew. When regulators threatened to burn New Bern, the colony's capital, in 1771, the governor, William Tryon, arrested and jailed the leader. Twice the grand jury, of which Caswell was foreman, refused to indict him. As colonel of the local militia, however, Caswell supported the royal governor in organizing an army to march against the insurgents. Caswell commanded the right wing of that army and the poorly equipped band of 3400 rural insurgents was defeated at the battle of Alamance (16 May 1771).

When the assembly was about to approve a popular boycott of British goods, Tryon dissolved it, but the members reassembled as a 'convention'—soon to become the provincial congress. Under Caswell's leadership the boycott was approved, and at the next assembly he became speaker. From 1760 until his death, twenty-nine years later, Caswell was almost constantly in the service of North Carolina. He served ten terms in the colonial assembly and eight in the state legislature, including several of which he was speaker. He was a delegate to two sessions of the continental congress and to four of the five meetings of the North Carolina provincial congress. He was appointed to a preliminary gubernatorial seat when that office was established in 1776, and thereafter was elected to four terms. He also served as a district treasurer in 1773–6 and comptroller in 1782–5. He was chosen to represent the state in the 1788 and 1789 federal constitutional conventions, but died before the last one convened. Caswell's military service during the war for independence was equally important and varied. As colonel of the partisan rangers he was effective in the victory at the battle of Moore's Creek Bridge, and as a major-general of the North Carolina militia he participated in the battle of Camden and in Nathanael Greene's southern campaign.

In the 1780s Caswell suffered headaches and dizziness until a fatal stroke on 8 November 1789, while he was presiding over the state senate at Fayetteville. He died two days later. He was an Anglican and a member of the masonic order. A funeral oration was delivered on 29 November 1789 at Christ Church, New Bern. Caswell's body was taken to Kinston for burial in the cemetery at his plantation, Red House, but the precise location is unidentified.   WILLIAM S. POWELL

Sources North Carolina Division of Archives and History, Raleigh, North Carolina, Caswell papers · W. L. Saunders and W. Clark, eds., *The colonial records of North Carolina*, 30 vols. (1886–1907), vols. 8–25 · C. R. Holloman, 'Caswell, Richard', *Dictionary of North Carolina biography*, ed. W. S. Powell (1979–96) · E. C. Brooks, 'Richard Caswell', *Biographical history of North Carolina*, ed. S. A. Ashe, 3 (1979), 65–79 · F. M. Hubbard, 'The life and times of Richard Caswell, the first governor of North Carolina: a lecture', *North Carolina University Magazine*, 7 (1857), 1–22 · 'An outline of the life of Gov. Caswell, with a selection of letters', *North Carolina University Magazine*, 4 (1855), 68–84 · J. L. Cheney, ed., *North Carolina government, 1585–1974: a narrative and statistical history* (1975)
Archives North Carolina Division of Archives and History, Raleigh, papers

Cat, Christopher (*fl.* 1688), pastry cook, became famous for his mutton pies, which were named Kit-cats after him, but little else is known about his life. He is said to have kept a pie shop near Temple Bar; this may have been, or been near, the Fountain in the Strand (no. 421 in Lillywhite, *London Signs* and *London Coffee Houses*). The prologue to Charles Burnaby's *Reform'd Wife* gives the first printed reference in 1700—'A Kit-cat is a Supper for a Lord'—and William King wrote in *The Art of Cookery* in 1708 (17),

> His Glory far, like Sir *Loyn's* Knighthood flies,
> Immortal made, as *Kit-cat*, by his Pyes.

What little is known about Cat derives almost entirely from accounts of the origin of the Kit-Cat Club—a whig society dedicated to poetry, politics, and good cheer—which alternately derive the name of the club from either the pieman or his pies. The Kit-Cat Club was at its height during the reign of Queen Anne (1702–14), but the whig historian John Oldmixon wrote in 1735 that it originated in private meetings before the revolution of 1688, and included Jacob Tonson, the bookseller, and John Somers, afterwards lord chancellor. They met, according to Oldmixon, for 'a little free and chearful Conversation in those dangerous Times' in a tavern near Temple Bar, with the famous mutton pies for their supper. Later, other 'Gentlemen of the same good *English* Principles' joined this original society (Oldmixon, 479). These obscure origins of the Kit-Cat Club were used as material for satire. Sir Richard Blackmore's poem *Kit-Cats* (1708) describes the first meetings at the Fountain of Tonson and his 'Poetic Tribe':

> Hence did th'Assembly's Title first arise,
> And *Kit-Cat* Wits sprung first from *Kit-Cat's* Pyes.

Edward Ward's *Secret History of Clubs* (1709) postulates an original friendship between Tonson and Cat, and a move from 'the end of *Bell-Court*, in Grays-Inn-Lane' (near Tonson's print shop) to 'a Pudding-Pye-Shop near the *Fountain-*

Tavern in the *Strand*'. Ward also attributes the name of the club to the sign outside Cat's shop, 'being the Cat and Fiddle', but this is probably an invention. Lady Mary Wortley Montagu was supposed to have been 'toasted' by the Kit-Cat Club when she was not yet eight; that is, in 1697 (*Remarks and Collections of Thomas Hearne*, 1.52). By January 1700, it was sufficiently well known for Matthew Prior to write of the 'Kit Katters' taking over a side-box to encourage a dramatic performance (*Bath MSS*, 3.394).

Certainly by the reign of Anne, the club was one of the most prestigious in London, comprising thirty-nine of the most influential whigs, and including literary men (Addison, Congreve, Steele, and Vanbrugh were members) as well as aristocrats and politicians. At any rate, in 1703 the club moved its main meeting place from public houses to a purpose-built room in Tonson's house in Barn Elms, Surrey. There portraits of the members of the club were hung, painted by Sir Godfrey Kneller on special 36 in. long by 28 in. wide canvases (known since as the kit-cat size of portrait) because the ceiling of the room was too low for half-lengths. These portraits are now in the National Portrait Gallery. The 1867 Exhibition of National Portraits at Kensington included a portrait of Cat and a scene supposedly set at his house in Chelsea Walk, both attributed to Kneller. The value of these paintings as historical evidence is doubtful, however. The portrait of Cat, showing a man with a white handkerchief on his head, a dark coat, and a glass of wine in his left hand, is reported to be not of kit-cat size, but rather 30½ in. by 25½ in. (*Catalogue*, no. 137).

There is no evidence of Cat's continuing association with the Kit-Cat Club and nothing is known about his death.   SYLVIA BROWN

Sources J. Spence, *Observations, anecdotes, and characters, of books and men*, ed. E. Malone (1820) · J. Oldmixon, *The history of England, during the reigns of King William and Queen Mary, Queen Anne, King George I* (1735) · *Remarks and collections of Thomas Hearne*, ed. C. E. Doble and others, 1, OHS, 2 (1885) · W. King, *The art of cookery* (1708) · R. Blackmore, *Kit-Cats: a poem* (1708) · E. Ward, *The secret history of clubs* (1709) · C. Burnaby, *Reform'd wife* (1700) · J. Caulfield, *Memoirs of the celebrated persons comprising the Kit-Cat Club* (1821) · B. Lillywhite, *London signs* (1972) · B. Lillywhite, *London coffee houses* (1963) · [R. H. Smith and others], *Catalogue of the second special exhibition of national portraits* (1867) [exhibition catalogue, South Kensington Museum, 1 May 1867] · R. J. Allen, *The clubs of Augustan London* (1933) · *The letters and works of Lady Mary Wortley Montagu*, ed. Lord Wharncliffe, 2 vols. (1893) [ed. by her great-grandson, Lord Wharncliffe. With … a memoir by W. Moy Thomas] · *Calendar of the manuscripts of the marquis of Bath preserved at Longleat, Wiltshire*, 5 vols., HMC, 58 (1904–80), vol. 3 · [M. Ransome], *The portraits of members of the Kit-Cat Club, painted during the years 1700–1720* (1945)
Likenesses portrait; formerly in possession of Mrs H. W. Hutton, 1867

Catcher [*alias* Burton], **Edward** (*c.*1585–1623), Jesuit, was born in London, the son of Thomas Catcher. Raised a protestant, he matriculated from Oriel College, Oxford, on 9 April 1597 and graduated BA from Balliol College on 14 February 1603. He was reconciled to the Catholic church in 1606, despite family hostility, and entered the English College, Rome, in October 1606 to complete his studies, particularly in theology. He took minor orders and the mission oath in 1607 and was sent to Valladolid for further studies. He was admitted there on 3 November 1608, but transferred to Flanders on account of ill health. He was ordained priest on 6 March 1610, and entered the Society of Jesus at the Louvain noviciate on 20 November 1610. In 1614 he took up the post of confessor at the English College at Douai, then the scene of a struggle by secular clergy to curtail Jesuit influence. His appointment fuelled the controversy, and a number of students protested against his alleged inexperience. When the college president's appeal to Rome resulted in the appointment of additional, secular, confessors, Catcher responded by denouncing any student who sought their counsel rather than his own. Eventually his withdrawal was secured as the college moved out of the Jesuit orbit. From 1617 he held a series of posts at the society's noviciate, now at Liège, before dispatch to the English mission in 1623. He translated and published (in 1616) at least one polemical work by the French Jesuit and distinguished controversialist François Véron, praising the text's 'brevity, simplicity and accessibility to the unlearned' (Clancy, 52–3) in tackling theological controversy through the medium of scripture alone. He also composed a Latin funeral oration for Cardinal Edward Farnese. He seems to have been the Father Burton who composed a treatise in defence of Mary Ward's Institute, also under attack by secular clergy. He died in London in 1623.

THOMPSON COOPER, *rev.* R. M. ARMSTRONG

Sources H. Foley, ed., *Records of the English province of the Society of Jesus*, 7 vols. in 8 (1875–83) · T. M. McCoog, *English and Welsh Jesuits, 1555–1650*, 2 vols., Catholic RS, 74–5 (1994–5) · P. Guilday, *The English Catholic refugees on the continent, 1558–1795* (1914) · Gillow, *Lit. biog. hist.* · E. H. Burton and T. L. Williams, eds., *The Douay College diaries, third, fourth and fifth, 1598–1654*, 1–2, Catholic RS, 10–11 (1911) · E. Henson, ed., *The registers of the English College at Valladolid, 1589–1862*, Catholic RS, 30 (1930) · A. Kenny, ed., *The responsa scholarum of the English College, Rome*, 1, Catholic RS, 54 (1962) · T. H. Clancy, *A literary history of the English Jesuits: a century of books, 1615–1714* (1996) · M. M. Littlehales, *Mary Ward: pilgrim and mystic, 1585–1645* (1998) · *Dodd's Church history of England*, ed. M. A. Tierney, 5 vols. (1839–43); repr. (1971)

Catchpole, Margaret (1762–1819), convict and author, was born on 14 March 1762, perhaps at Nacton, Suffolk, the illegitimate daughter of Elizabeth Catchpole and a farm labourer employed by a celebrated breeder of Suffolk carthorses. When Margaret was thirteen years of age the farmer's wife was suddenly seized with illness; Margaret mounted a Suffolk punch, and galloped, with only a halter round its neck, to Ipswich in order to fetch a doctor. After this she became a servant in the household of John Cobbold of Ipswich, and saved one of his children from drowning. Her biography, *The History of Margaret Catchpole* (3 vols., 1845) was based on her writings and letters, but both were heavily edited, altered, and distorted by Richard Cobbold, son of her employer, who, in particular, fabricated much about her private life. She is said to have fallen in love with William Laud, a sailor and smuggler, and to have left the Cobbolds' employment because of their dislike of Laud. Certainly, in May 1797, she stole John Cobbold's horse and rode it to London, 70 miles away, in

Margaret Catchpole (1762–1819), by Richard Cobbold, pubd 1845

ten hours. For the theft she was tried and sentenced to death on 9 August 1797. As a result of her comportment at the trial, and pressure from the Cobbolds, this sentence was commuted to seven years' transportation. She then boldly escaped from Ipswich gaol on 25 March 1800, letting herself down uninjured from the spikes on the top of its wall. She was soon recaptured, and a second time sentenced to death by the same judge, Chief Baron Macdonald. She had pleaded guilty at both trials, and her undaunted speech and demeanour a second time gained her many friends. The sentence was again commuted, but this time to transportation for life, and on 27 May 1801 she was sent to Australia.

Margaret Catchpole landed at Sydney on 14 December 1801. She worked for various families in New South Wales and established a good reputation. She was pardoned on 31 January 1814. However, she did not return to Britain, but opened a small store at Richmond, New South Wales. Her letters are among the best convicts' literary records, providing a vivid depiction of the variety of life in the colony, for which they remain an important early source. Margaret Catchpole was unmarried (Cobbold's account of

her marriage in Australia is a fiction). She died from influenza on 13 May 1819 and was buried the next day in what was to become the churchyard of St Peter's in Richmond, New South Wales.

M. G. WATKINS, *rev.* H. C. G. MATTHEW

Sources *AusDB* · R. Cobbold, *The history of Margaret Catchpole*, 3 vols. (1845) · G. B. Barton, *The true story of Margaret Catchpole* (1924) · B. M. Sanders, *The extraordinary Margaret Catchpole* (1966)
Likenesses R. Cobbold, etching, pubd 1845, NPG [*see illus.*]

Catchpool, (Egerton) St John Pettifor (1890–1971), social worker, was born in Leicester on 22 August 1890, the sixth child and fourth son in the family of five sons and two daughters of Thomas Kingham Catchpool, hosiery manufacturer, and his wife, Florence Emma Pettifor. He was educated at Quaker institutions: Sidcot School and Woodbrooke College, Birmingham, where he took the social studies course. During the First World War his pacifist convictions led him to serve with the Friends' ambulance unit in France and then with the Friends' war victims' relief committee in Russia. He returned to England and took up the post of sub-warden of Toynbee Hall, the universities' settlement in the East End of London, which he held from 1920 to 1929, and he served also as a co-opted member of the London county council education committee from 1925 to 1931. In 1920 he married Ruth Allason, daughter of Henry Lloyd Wilson, chemical manufacturer. Trained as a doctor, she never practised, devoting her life instead to the care of their son and four daughters and to support of her husband's work.

The years in east London gave Catchpool an insight into the restricted lives of inner-city youth, and when in 1930 he was invited to become the first national secretary of the newly formed Youth Hostels Association, he readily accepted. 'This seemed just the movement', he wrote in a letter, 'to give scope for all my enthusiasms and even hobby-horses'. He threw himself into the cause with immense energy, addressing meetings all over the country, persuading, lobbying, and begging for funds. He recruited G. M. Trevelyan, the historian, as president of the association, and William Temple, then archbishop of York, as vice-president. He secured financial support from the Carnegie Trust, the King George V Jubilee Trust, and, later, from the government's National Fitness Council. He acted as the focal point for the enthusiasm of many hundreds of volunteer workers of every social background up and down the country. Soon, tens of thousands of young city-dwellers, on bicycle or on foot, were enjoying their first taste of the countryside with the aid of the new network of youth hostels.

Catchpool also saw the importance of the youth hostels as centres of international contact and friendship among people. He worked closely with the German founder of the movement, Richard Schirrmann (later ousted by the Nazis), and with the idealists who were establishing youth hostels in other countries. In 1938 he was elected president of the International Youth Hostel Federation, an office which he held for the next twelve years. After his retirement as secretary of the English Association in 1950 he spent four years in India, encouraging the growth of youth hostels in that country, and subsequently paid two extended visits to Africa for the same purpose.

Catchpool (known to his friends as Jack and to his colleagues as Catch) combined the innocent enthusiasm of a child and the tenacity of purpose of a mature and deeply spiritual man, enlivened by a puckish sense of humour. Impatient with committee work, he was at his best when exploring new paths and communicating his enthusiasms to others. He was appointed chevalier of the Dutch order of Orange-Nassau in 1948 and CBE in 1951. Catchpool died in Welwyn Garden City, where his home was 17 Meadow Road, on 13 March 1971.

GRAHAM HEATH, *rev.*

Sources E. St J. Catchpool, *Candles in the darkness* (1966) · personal knowledge (1993) · *CGPLA Eng. & Wales* (1971)
Archives NL Wales, corresp. with Thomas Jones · Welwyn Garden City Central Library, corresp. with Sir Frederic Osborn
Wealth at death £11,770: probate, 14 May 1971, *CGPLA Eng. & Wales*

Catcott, Alexander (1725–1779), geologist and theologian, was born at Bristol on 2 November 1725, the eldest son of the Revd Alexander Stopford *Catcott (1692–1749), theologian and headmaster of Bristol grammar school. Catcott was educated at the grammar school before entering Winchester College in 1739 and Wadham College, Oxford, in 1744. He graduated BA in 1748, and later identified himself as MA, but Foster does not record this degree. After his graduation he became lecturer of St John's Church in Bristol, and then vicar of Temple Church (1767–1779). He was also a governor of Thomas White's hospital, where he preached twice a year.

Catcott was strongly influenced by the works of John Hutchinson, who developed an anti-Newtonian system of physico-theology which had as its basis the idea that the original unpointed Hebrew text of the Old Testament held the keys to understanding nature and the cosmos. Hutchinson and his adherents had strong religious motivations for adopting the system, for they felt that it offered the best intellectual basis for combating the naturalistic, and hence potentially anti-religious, implications of Newtonianism. Catcott's father had fallen under the spell of Hutchinson, and he influenced his son in that direction. By the time the younger Catcott was at Wadham, he was a firm believer in Hutchinsonianism. He was instrumental in causing others at Oxford, such as William Jones and George Horne, to study geology and accept Hutchinsonian explanations. William Jones told how Catcott was so dedicated that he made excavations near Wadham in search of fossils, and that he dug so deep that he was in peril of his life: one pit was so deep and precarious that it collapsed soon after Catcott climbed out. The friendships he made with the Hutchinsonians at Oxford lasted a lifetime, and he corresponded with them long after he left the university.

Catcott was a Hutchinsonian for his entire life. He first took a public stand for the system in 1756 when he published his *Remarks on the Lord Bishop of Clogher's 'Explanation of the Mosaic account of the creation and of the formation of the*

world'. The bishop had expressed doubts about the universality of the Noachian flood, and Catcott wrote to counter him. He wrote as a Hutchinsonian, but also from the perspective of one who had studied the geological record. And, indeed, Catcott's work as a geologist was extremely important. From 1748 until the 1760s, he roamed the country examining the ruins at Avebury and Stonehenge and geologic formations in the mines of Cornwall and Derbyshire. To be sure, his conclusions were always dependent upon his Hutchinsonian assumptions (which themselves were undoubtedly influenced by his religious values), but the calibre of his observations was superb. For this reason he, unlike many Hutchinsonians, garnered respect from many scientific scholars of the day. In 1761 he published his *opus magnum*, a *Treatise on the Deluge*, in which he attempted to prove not only that the flood was universal, but that it occurred when water which had been trapped under the earth's crust broke out. In a subsequent edition (1768), he included a 'Collection of the principal heathen accounts of the flood' and remarks on 'The time when, and the manner how, America was first peopled', both of which were acknowledged by Sir Charles Lyell to have been influential.

Catcott and his brother George, a merchant, were both bachelors and lived together in the parsonage of Temple Church. They gained notoriety in Bristol when they got into a row with the poet Thomas Chatterton, originally over whether Chatterton had been honest about his supposed discovery of an ancient manuscript. The brothers believed that Chatterton had forged it. From this point on, Chatterton took every opportunity to publicly humiliate Catcott with satirical writings. Catcott died in Bristol on 18 June 1779 after a serious illness and was buried in Bristol. His biographer, William Jones, complained that he may have been 'barked to death' and claimed that he was so irritated and disturbed by the constant barking of a dog chained up near his quarters that he succumbed to his illness (Jones, 1.27).   J. S. CHAMBERLAIN

Sources M. Neve and R. Porter, 'Alexander Catcott: glory and geography', *British Journal for the History of Science*, 10 (1977), 37–60 · E. H. W. Meyerstein, *A life of Thomas Chatterton* (1930), 306–13 · *The works of ... George Horne ... to which are prefixed memoirs of his life, studies and writings*, ed. W. Jones, 2 vols. (1846), vol. 1, pp. 25–76 · Foster, *Alum. Oxon.*
Archives Bristol Central Library, corresp., B 26063, SR43

Catcott, Alexander Stopford (1692–1749), Church of England clergyman and poet, was born in Long Acre in the parish of St Martin-in-the-Fields, Westminster, on 10 October 1692, the son of Alexander Catcott, gentleman, and his wife, Rebecca Scolfield. He was admitted to Merchant Taylors' School, London, on 3 May 1699 and subsequently matriculated from St John's College, Oxford, on 2 July 1709. He was elected a fellow of the college in 1712 and took the LLB degree on 6 March 1717.

Catcott decided not to pursue a career in the law. Instead he was ordained deacon on 8 June 1718 and priest on 15 March 1719 by John Potter, bishop of Oxford, and was elected headmaster of Bristol grammar school on 18 April

1722, the same year in which he resigned his Oxford fellowship. He was an outstanding principal, appreciably raising school numbers and including among his pupils Dr Thomas Fry, later president of St John's College, Oxford, and Richard Woodward, later bishop of Cloyne. Other appointments within the city followed. In June 1729 he was appointed reader in the mayor's chapel of St Mark, with an annual allowance of £20, having read prayers there for some years; in 1740 he held the lectureship of St John's, and on 2 January 1744 he was presented to the rectory of St Stephen's by Lord Chancellor Hardwicke, whereupon he resigned his headmastership.

Catcott's intellectual reputation originally rested on his verse. He published anonymously *The Poem of Musaeus on the Loves of Hero and Leander* (1715), dedicated to Lady Mary Wortley Montagu, and *The Court of Love: a Vision from Chaucer* (1717). There were other manuscript verses produced after he moved to Bristol, but by that date Catcott was increasingly preoccupied with his teaching. He was also immersed in the writings of the physico-theologian John Hutchinson, having initiated a correspondence with him in 1733 in which he sought elucidation of Hutchinson's often controversial views, such as an etymology of the cherubim in Genesis which saw there a covert disclosure of the Trinitarian godhead. He publicly announced his convictions on 16 August 1735 when he preached, on the day before the assizes, to a congregation that included Lord Hardwicke, lord chief justice and high steward of Bristol, on 'the supreme and inferior Elahim'. He focused on the typological importance of the Elahim in the Pentateuch, insisting that Moses taught the Trinity under that Hebrew name. Catcott took pride in his efforts:

> Providence has made it my lot, to have been the first clergyman, who published a defence of the fundamental article of Revealed Religion, grounded on the true construction of the Hebrew SS, in opposition to the inveterate prejudices of Christians, the unsuspected forgeries of the Jews, and the bold assertions of our omniscient and infallible freethinkers. (Catcott, *An Answer to the Observations on a Sermon Preached before the Corporation of Bristol on Sunday 16th Day of August 1735*, 1737, 87)

Catcott's sermon was printed at the expense of the corporation, reflecting the powerful preaching tradition that existed in Bristol. It set off a minor controversy that lasted many years. Another Bristol cleric, the Revd Arthur Bedford, produced *Observations* (1736), on Catcott's sermon, to which the latter replied. Other Hutchinsonians, including Julius Bate and Daniel Gittins, were also drawn in. Catcott himself went on, with Hutchinson's encouragement, to attempt a pamphlet summary of their belief system, but the end product, the *Tractatus* (1738), relating the causes of the earth's motion to the Hebrew scriptures, was written in Latin and was too technical to attract a wide audience. Catcott was disappointed but still did as much as anyone in the 1740s to draw attention to Hutchinsonianism, and indeed helped to turn it into a distinctive controversial system with Bristol as one of its foremost centres. He was never shy of acknowledging his debt to Hutchinson: 'I shall bless God, to my dying day, that His good providence ever brought me acquainted with that Gentleman's works

and person' (Catcott, *The Supreme and Inferior Elahim*, 1736, 37).

Catcott died in Bristol, after a long illness, on 23 November 1749, and was buried on 29 November in St Stephen's Church. He was a fine preacher as well as 'a good poet, profound linguist, well skilled in Hebrew and Scripture philosophy, and a judicious schoolmaster' (Barrett, 514). John Wesley, for one, was most impressed by Catcott's piety. Ten of his sermons were issued in 1752 and reprinted in 1753 in a collected volume edited by his son Alexander *Catcott (1725–1779) (reissued 1767). Works of the younger Catcott have often been attributed misleadingly to Alexander Stopford Catcott, and vice versa.   NIGEL ASTON

Sources H. B. Wilson, *The history of Merchant Taylors' School* (1814), vol. 2, p. 1072 · Foster, *Alum. Oxon.* · W. Barrett, *The history and antiquities of the city of Bristol* (1789), 512 · J. Latimer, *The annals of Bristol in the eighteenth century* (1893), 119, 126 · W. R. Barker, *St Mark's, or, The mayor's chapel, Bristol* (1892) · C. P. Hill, *The history of Bristol grammar school* (1951), 40–41, 43–4 · J. Barry, 'Bristol as a "reformation city", c. 1640–1780', *England's long reformation, 1500–1800*, ed. N. Tyacke (1998), 261–4 · R. Spearman, *Life of John Hutchinson* (1748) · C. D. A. Leighton, 'Hutchinsonianism: a counter-enlightenment reform movement', *Journal of Religious History*, 23 (1999), 168–84 · A. J. Kuhn, 'Glory or gravity: Hutchinson vs. Newton', *Journal of the History of Ideas*, 22 (1961), 303–22 · B. W. Young, *Religion and Enlightenment in eighteenth-century England: theological debate from Locke to Burke* (1998) · *Bristol Weekly Intelligencer* (29 Nov 1749) · *The journal of the Rev. John Wesley*, ed. N. Curnock and others, 6 (1915), 305–6 · DNB

Archives Bristol Reference Library, corresp., B 26063 | Bodl. Oxf., MS, Rawl. J. 4–5 fol. 209; fol. 16, fol. 352, 355 · Bristol RO, audit book, Bristol Corporation

Cates, Arthur (1829–1901), surveyor, was born on 29 April 1829 at 38 Alfred Street, Bedford Square, London, the son of James Cates and his wife, Susan, daughter of John Rose. After education at King's College School, London, he joined the office of Sydney Smirke RA as a pupil in 1846. From 1852 to 1859 he was an assistant to Sir James Pennethorne, and in 1870 succeeded him as architect to the land revenues of the crown under the commissioners of woods and forests, a position he held until 1898. This gave him considerable artistic control over the architecture of the crown estates in London. His temperament ideally suited him to this position. Cates's friends described him as pugnacious but professional, though sometimes 'a little too prone to show and use his strength'. Cates saw himself as a drill sergeant, and was never happier than when in charge (*RIBA Journal*, 353–4). His own architectural works were few but included St Mary, Cowes, Isle of Wight (1867), and a number of houses and commercial buildings in London. In 1887 as surveyor to the Honourable Society of the Inner Temple he designed the archway and gatehouse that lead from Tudor Street to King's Bench Walk.

Cates joined the Architectural Association in 1847, and became an associate of the Royal Institute of British Architects in 1856, a fellow in 1874, and a member of the council in 1879; he served as vice-president from 1888 to 1892. He was important in pressing for a systematic course of training for architects, with the particular aim of improving their practical knowledge. From 1882 to 1896 he was chairman of the institute's board of examiners, and under his guidance a system of progressive examinations (preliminary, intermediate, and final) was established. He was also a fellow of the Surveyors' Institution. From 1858 to 1892 Cates was honorary secretary of the Architectural Publication Society, and contributed to its six-volume *Dictionary of Architecture* (1852–92), edited by his friend Wyatt Papworth. He was first chairman of the tribunal of appeal under the London Building Act from 1894 until his death.

In 1881 Cates married Rosa, daughter of William Rose. They had no children. He died at his home, 12 York Terrace, Regent's Park, London, on 15 May 1901, and was cremated at Woking on 18 May. His wife survived him. He left an estate valued at over £197,000.

PAUL WATERHOUSE, *rev.* IAN DUNGAVELL

Sources *The Builder*, 80 (1901), 494 · *Building News*, 80 (1901), 658 · *RIBA Journal*, 8 (1900–01), 353–4 · *Building News*, 58 (1890), 658 · *WWW* · private information (1912) · *Dir. Brit. archs.* · *CGPLA Eng. & Wales* (1901)
Archives RIBA, drawings and MSS | RIBA, biography file · RIBA, nomination papers
Likenesses Bassano, photograph, repro. in *Building News*, 58 (1890), 326 · negative, RIBA BAL
Wealth at death £197,486 8*s*. 11*d*.: resworn probate, Oct 1901, *CGPLA Eng. & Wales*

Cates, William Leist Readwin (1821–1895), author, eldest son of Robert Cates, solicitor, of Fakenham, Norfolk, and his wife, Mary Ann Readwin, was born at Fakenham on 12 November 1821. He was educated for the law under a private tutor, and after passing his examinations at London University went to Chatteris, Cambridgeshire. He subsequently moved to Gravesend for about a year, but, failing to establish a practice, took an appointment in 1844 as articled clerk to John Barfield, solicitor, at Thatcham, Berkshire. On 25 July 1845 he married Catherine, daughter of Aquila Robins of Holt, Norfolk.

Cates did not enjoy his work and abandoned the legal profession, first for private tuition, and later on for literature. In 1848 he settled at Wilmslow, Cheshire, and some years later at Didsbury, near Manchester. In 1860 he moved to London, in order to co-operate with his friend Bernard Bolingbroke Woodward in the production of the *Encyclopaedia of Chronology*, which he completed in 1872 and which includes an essay of his own; in the interval he edited a *Dictionary of General Biography* (1867; 3rd edn, 1880). Cates's other works include *The Pocket Date Book* (1863; 2nd edn), with tables of dates, principal facts, and events 'from the beginning of the world' to the time of writing, and a *History of England from the Death of Edward the Confessor to the Death of King John*. He edited and largely rewrote S. Maunder's *Biographical Treasury* for its thirteenth edition (1866); he supervised the fourteenth edition in 1873, and another one in 1882. He also translated and edited volumes 6–8 of J. H. Merle d'Aubigné's *History of the Reformation in Europe in the Time of Calvin* (1875–8). Failing health compelled Cates to leave London in September 1887 for Hayes, near Uxbridge, where he died at his home, 2 Heath Villas on 9 December 1895.

B. B. WOODWARD, *rev.* MYFANWY LLOYD

Sources Allibone, *Dict.* · Boase, *Mod. Eng. biog.* · W. L. R. Cates, ed., *Dictionary of general biography* (1867)

Likenesses C. Pearson, pencil, NPG
Wealth at death £34 4*s*. 11*d*.: probate, 30 Dec 1895, *CGPLA Eng. & Wales*

Catesby family (*per. c*.1340–1505), gentry, came originally from a tenant family of Flecknoe, east Warwickshire. It was **William** [i] **Catesby** (*d.* 1383) and his son **John** [i] **Catesby** (*d.* 1404/5) whose land acquisitions started its rise into the front rank of local families. There were numbers of properties in Coventry, a town with which both William and John had strong ties, but most of the new land lay in east Warwickshire or the neighbouring counties of Leicestershire and Northamptonshire, especially the latter. It came by both purchase and marriage: William to Joan, daughter and heir of William Radbourne of Radbourne, and John to Emma, daughter and heir of Robert Cranford of Ashby St Ledgers, Northamptonshire. William, possibly a lawyer, had a lengthy official career from 1339, notably as MP for Warwickshire and escheator for several midland counties. John, definitely a lawyer, was JP in Warwickshire almost continuously from 1377. He too was steward of Coventry, to Edward, the Black Prince, as earl of Chester, but by 1389 he was close to Thomas Beauchamp, the appellant earl of Warwick. Warwick's support was important to Catesby in the protracted but eventually successful dispute over Ladbroke Manor, Warwickshire, between 1383 and 1399 and he narrowly evaded punishment when Richard II took his revenge on the appellants in 1397–9. From the time of John [i] the family divided its interests between Warwickshire and Northamptonshire. Initially there was a residence in each, at Ladbroke and Ashby respectively, but Ladbroke was eventually abandoned, probably under John [ii]. The changing balance of the estate is indicated by John [i]'s appointment as JP in Northamptonshire from 1392.

John's eldest son, William [ii], died in 1407 or 1408 leaving John's second son, **John** [ii] **Catesby** (*d.* 1437), as heir. This accident complicated the structure of the estate, as John [ii]'s future had already been secured by marriage to Margaret, granddaughter and heir of Richard Mountfort of Lapworth. Lapworth was in west Warwickshire, a long way from the area where the Catesbys had been so successfully building a compact estate. Some rationalization was achieved by giving peripheral manors to a third brother, Robert, founder of the line of Catesbys of Hopsford, Warwickshire, while the marriage of John [ii]'s heir, **Sir William** [iii] **Catesby** (*d.* 1478/9), to Philippa, the coheir of Bishopestone of Bishopton, Warwickshire, eventually brought lands that made the west Warwickshire estate geographically more coherent, including a second manor at Lapworth. John [ii], also a lawyer, followed his father into the service of the earls of Warwick, being retained by Richard Beauchamp, earl of Warwick, by 1417, although he seems to have been less central to the earl's affairs than some of the other Warwickshire gentry. This was perhaps because the Warwickshire–Northamptonshire border was not an area where Warwick had much direct influence. In fact John [ii]'s record as local officer shows that by the accession of Henry VI he was more a Northamptonshire than a Warwickshire man and, although he did have dealings with the dense local network around Lapworth, he was a key figure in the network that ran down the Warwickshire–Northamptonshire borders. If John's career was a relatively quiet one, this is a measure of his success: he contrived to avoid both political miscalculation and extended litigation.

William [iii] was still a minor at his father's death and was placed in the wardship of John Norreys of Berkshire, a rising member of the royal household. This was doubtless why Catesby himself was a king's esquire by 1442. By 1447–8 he was linked to John Talbot, first earl of Shrewsbury; these ties with the crown and the Talbots were to be a constant in his political life until 1461, and in 1453 he married as his second wife Joan, daughter of Sir Thomas Barre and Shrewsbury's niece. In 1449 he was made KB, the first of the family to be knighted. From 1443 he also served the king in all the major local offices. That he served in Warwickshire as well as Northamptonshire shows how the balance of the family's interests was shifting back across the border, chiefly because the death of William's Bishopestone father-in-law in 1444 had increased its Warwickshire weighting. Catesby avoided involvement in local upheavals in the 1450s and never entirely cut himself off from local associates linked to the Yorkists. Thus, although he may have fought for Henry VI at Towton—his uncle, Robert, did—and he was attainted by the Yorkists in 1461 and briefly in exile, he was soon pardoned and able to return.

In the 1460s, no longer attached to the royal household, Sir William became a substantial and fairly divisive force in local politics. He found himself at odds with various local landowners, most notably with John Brome of Baddesley Clinton, another former member of the Lancastrian household, who held one of the other manors at Lapworth, to which William now laid claim. William had clearly decided to make more of his west Warwickshire lands and he even established a residence at Lapworth. As Warwick's affinity crumbled around him in the early 1460s [see Mountford family], the earl struck up a surprising relationship with this former Lancastrian, who may indeed have gone north with him to fight Lancastrian resistance in 1463–4, and he supported him in his efforts to get Lapworth, while Brome gravitated towards the dissident group around Simon Mountford, Warwick's nominal retainer. In 1465–6 Catesby's return to respectability was completed with his reappointment as JP. In 1466 the Lapworth issue was settled by an arbitration that gave him the manor. The combination of his new patron, Warwick, and his old one, Henry VI, proved irresistible at the readeption and he was sheriff of Northamptonshire during Henry VI's brief second reign. He was again pardoned after this further misadventure and, perhaps chastened by this second near disaster, seems to have lived out a quiet old age, although he died in harness as sheriff of Northamptonshire.

It was William's son, William *Catesby (d. 1485), the notorious servant of Richard III, who took the family to its greatest political heights and almost to destruction. The mostly dubious land acquisitions he made in and around Northamptonshire under Richard caused him to refocus the estate back towards east Warwickshire and Northamptonshire, although he was local officer in several midland counties, including Warwickshire. His son **George Catesby** (c.1473–1505), who was given livery of his mother's Zouche lands in 1495, had his attainder reversed and was partially restored in 1496. George's marriage to Richard Empson's daughter Elizabeth must have helped his cause. The family thrived during the sixteenth century, especially in the lifetime of George's second son and heir Sir Richard Catesby (d. 1553), who was knight of the shire for Warwickshire in 1539 and 1553, and in the 1540s served twice as sheriff of Warwickshire and Leicestershire and once as sheriff of Northamptonshire. He was knighted in 1542. The recusancy of Richard's grandson and heir Sir William Catesby (1547–1598) brought financial pressure and exclusion from office, but it was only the involvement of William's son Robert *Catesby in the Gunpowder Plot, and his consequent forfeiture, that brought ruin upon the family.

Because of this confiscation, the Catesby records came into crown hands, which is why so many of them survive, although the archive was unfortunately broken up by the Public Record Office. In particular, the estate accounts are unusually good for a fifteenth-century gentry family. They reveal the Catesbys as painstaking managers and exploiters, who developed a centralized accounting and purchase system, especially as the properties became more widespread, and paid careful attention to the rentier side of the economy. But what differentiates them from most of the middling and upper gentry in the fifteenth century was their exploitation of the commercial possibilities of livestock farming well before the pastoral boom at the end of the century. They kept a flock for commercial wool production in the Warwickshire–Northamptonshire region, which was later to be a major centre for sheep farming, while in the 1460s and 1470s William [iii] began to graze cattle for the market, using the lands at Lapworth, which was in good cattle-raising country. In the family's use of its estate's resources, for both consumption and sale, there was specialization and careful integration which became especially marked right across the estate under William [iii].

For a rising family the Catesbys were surprisingly uninterested in making new religious foundations, perhaps because they inherited chantries on at least two of their acquired estates. They contributed to a bell-tower and bells for Ladbroke church but, as their residence moved to Ashby, so did their religious interests and it seems that, from at least John [ii], it was here that family members were buried.

The history of the family is of steady, careful ascent, accompanied by land acquisition and by careful husbanding and exploitation of the resources of the estate. On the way, cadet branches were established at Althorp, Northamptonshire, and Marston Waver, Warwickshire, as well as the one at Hopsford. Sir John *Catesby (d. 1487), justice of the common pleas, may have been related to the main line of the family—he was known as 'uncle' to William (d.

1485)—though in what degree is not known. He is almost certainly not identical with John Catesby of Althorp (d. 1486). Only occasionally was the family put in jeopardy by the political upheavals that could always endanger a high-profile family on the make. By the later years of William [iii] the Catesbys were a leading midland family that needed to do no more than maintain its position, and William's expert deployment of the resources of the entire estate meant that they were particularly favourably placed to do so. The inability of his son to resist the allure of still greater wealth and power in the service of Richard III, which would have been more appropriate at an earlier phase in the Catesbys' rise, was thus as foolish as it was almost disastrous. The arms of the Catesby family were argent two lions passant sable crowned or.

CHRISTINE CARPENTER

Sources C. Carpenter, *Locality and polity* (1992) · *A descriptive catalogue of ancient deeds in the Public Record Office*, 6 vols. (1890–1915) · W. Dugdale, *The antiquities of Warwickshire illustrated*, rev. W. Thomas, 2nd edn, 2 vols. (1730) · ministers' accounts, PRO, SC 6 · J. S. Roskell, 'William Catesby, counsellor to Richard III', *Parliament and politics in late medieval England*, 2 (1981), 307–36 · HoP, *Commons, 1386–1421* · J. B. Post, 'Courts, councils, and arbitration in the Ladbroke manor dispute', *Medieval legal records edited in honour of C. A. F. Meekings*, ed. R. F. Hunnisett and J. B. Post (1978) · *CClR* · *Calendar of the fine rolls*, 22 vols., PRO (1911–62) · *CPR* · C. Dyer, *Warwickshire farming, 1349–c.1520*, Dugdale Society, 27 (1981) · 'The status maneriorum of John Catesby, 1385 and 1386', *Miscellany I*, ed. R. Bearman, Dugdale Society, 31 (1977) · E. W. Ives, *The common lawyers of pre-Reformation England* (1983) · PRO, SC 12/41/8 · N. W. Alcock, 'The Catesbys in Coventry: a medieval estate and its archives', *Midland History*, 15 (1990), 1–36

Archives PRO, Catesby papers, SC 6, SC 11, SC 12

Wealth at death approx. £290: PRO, SC 12/41/8; SC 6/949/16; SC 6/1042/3

Catesby, George (c.1473–1505). *See under* Catesby family (*per. c.*1340–1505).

Catesby, John (d. 1404/5). *See under* Catesby family (*per. c.*1340–1505).

Catesby, John (d. 1437). *See under* Catesby family (*per. c.*1340–1505).

Catesby, Sir John (d. 1487), justice, was probably related to the main line of Catesbys of Ashby St Ledgers, Northamptonshire [*see* Catesby family]; he was known as 'uncle' to William Catesby, chancellor of the exchequer and councillor of Richard III. The family had been settled in Northamptonshire for some time, and also held the manor of Lapworth in Warwickshire. His father may have been Hugh Catesby of Arthingworth, Northamptonshire. He was a member of the Inner Temple, which was also known then as the Inner Inn, and his name first appears in the year-books in Michaelmas 1458. He received the coif in 1463, the same date as Richard Pigot, one of his executors, and was made king's serjeant on 18 April 1469. On 20 November 1481 he was appointed justice of the common pleas, and he was knighted in 1483. From the 1460s until his death he was regularly commissioned as a justice of gaol delivery, oyer and terminer, and of assize and inquiry; one of his inquiries investigated Lollardy in the west country in 1475. He served as a justice of the peace for

Northamptonshire from 1467, and for Surrey in 1466 and from 1469 to 1485. Throughout his career he acted as feoffee to uses and as an arbitrator, notably in the dispute between the city and priory at Coventry in 1481. A warden of the Fleet in 1480 and a member of William Hastings's council, Catesby was counsel to the queen mother in the 1470s, and was retained by the duchy of Lancaster, 1478–82. He was an executor of William Waynflete, bishop of Winchester, and his name appears in the Paston letters. He held lands in Buckinghamshire, Bedfordshire, and Warwickshire, and his will shows that he also held the manor of Whiston, Northamptonshire, which his family owned until 1699. At the accession of Henry VII his reappointment as a judge was delayed for about a month after that of his fellows, possibly in consequence of his close association with William Catesby, whose attainder and execution occurred shortly after the battle of Bosworth Field.

Catesby married Elizabeth, daughter of Walter Green of Hayes, Middlesex, exchequer clerk, justice of the peace, and member of parliament, who by his will excused Catesby 50 marks owed for the marriage of Elizabeth. By right of Elizabeth he held lands in Middlesex, Kent, and Westminster, and by the marriage he was related to John Arderne, probably the son of Peter Arderne, chief baron of the exchequer chamber, and to John Holgrave, baron of the exchequer. John and Elizabeth are known to have had eight sons and two daughters. One son, Humphrey, married the daughter of Richard Maryot of the Inner Temple and had a son Antony, who married the daughter of Thomas Pigot, serjeant. It is understood that on 23 January 1487 Catesby died, according to a year-book entry, eight leagues from London, while travelling to court. In his will he expressed his wish to be buried in the abbey of St James, Northampton but it is more likely that he was buried in Whiston, Northamptonshire.

NORMAN DOE

Sources E. W. Ives, *The common lawyers of pre-Reformation England* (1983) · Sainty, *Judges* · Baker, *Serjeants* · E. Foss, *Biographia juridica: a biographical dictionary of the judges of England … 1066–1870* (1870) · *The Paston letters, AD 1422–1509*, ed. J. Gairdner, new edn, 6 vols. (1904) · HoP, *Commons* · *Chancery records* · *CIPM, Henry VII*, 1, nos. 355–6, 374–5

Likenesses memorial, 1700, Whiston Church, Northamptonshire

Catesby, Mark (1683–1749), naturalist, was born, probably at Castle Hedingham, Essex, on 24 March 1683, the son of John Catesby (c.1642–1705), town clerk of Sudbury, Suffolk, and his wife, Elizabeth Jekyll (b. 1652). He seems to have been educated locally in spite of having affluent parents, forgoing a university education, but benefiting from the antiquarian and botanical knowledge of his grandfather Nicholas Jekyll, who was acquainted with the naturalist John Ray. Ray greatly influenced Catesby; Samuel Dale, an apothecary at Braintree, not far from Sudbury where Catesby lived, was also of great importance to him. Catesby raised the means for starting on a voyage in 1712 to Virginia where he stayed with his aunt Elizabeth Cocke and her physician husband. After an absence of several years spent in travelling in and around Carolina and the West Indies, Catesby returned to England in 1719 with a collection of dried plants, reported to have been the most perfect ever brought into the country, which attracted the attention of men of science, especially Sir Hans Sloane and Dr Sherard.

Catesby remained in England for some time, arranging and naming his specimens, a considerable number of which passed into Sloane's museum (thereafter into the British Museum and ultimately the Natural History Museum). With assistance from Sloane and others, Catesby went again to America in 1722 and sent from Carolina to his English subscribers large quantities of biological material. He also prepared for himself large drawings of birds, reptiles, fish, and plants, and explored the Bahama Islands in 1725.

In 1726 Catesby returned to England and at once set to work in preparing materials for his large and best-known work *The Natural History of Carolina, Florida, and the Bahama Islands*. This book included a new map drawn by Catesby showing the districts he had explored. Two volumes were published in parts from 1729 to 1747; volume one contained 120 plates and volume two 100 plates, all the figures of the plants and animals being drawn and etched by Catesby himself. He also coloured all the first copies, and the tinted copies required were executed under his inspection. During publication of this work, on 26 April 1733, he was admitted a fellow of the Royal Society. A second edition (revised by George Edwards, with an appendix) was issued in 1754; a German translation, with an introduction by Edwards, was printed in Nuremberg, as were several pirated editions. A third English edition appeared in 1771, to which a Linnaean index was appended. Catesby's *Hortus Britanno-Americanus* described eighty-five American trees and shrubs suitable for British gardens, with seventeen engravings. It was not published until 1763. Catesby takes credit for the first introduction to Europe of many such plants.

A West Indian shrub in the family Rubiaceae was named *Catesbaea* by Gronovius and validated by Linnaeus (*C. spinosa* L.), and a dozen other new plant species were named by Linnaeus based on Catesby's material.

On 5 March 1747 Catesby read a paper on birds of passage before the Royal Society which contained much new and striking evidence on the migration of birds (*PTRS*, 44, 1747, 435–44). His fame as an ornithologist has outlived his own preference for botany and horticulture.

Catesby had married, on 2 October 1747 at the age of sixty-four, Mrs Elizabeth Rowland (*d.* February 1753), a widow who already had one grown daughter. He died at his house in Old Street, London, on 23 December 1749; he was survived by his wife and her daughter, and by two children of his first marriage, of which nothing is known. He was buried in St Luke's churchyard, Old Street. Unfortunately, he was able to bequeath little more than a few copies of his *Natural History* and the plates, which his widow had to sell to relieve her need. This legacy probably included the original drawings by Catesby, bought by

George III in 1768 for £160, and now in the Royal Collection at Windsor. They are bound as a unique set of his *Natural History*, in three volumes instead of two.

F. NIGEL HEPPER

Sources G. F. Frick and R. P. Stearns, *Mark Catesby: the colonial Audubon* (1961) · J. Ewan, *The American Midland Naturalist*, 66 (1961), 510–12 [review] · Desmond, *Botanists*, rev. edn, 137–8 · B. Henrey, *British botanical and horticultural literature before 1800*, 2 (1975), 275–7 · H. M. Clokie, *An account of the herbaria of the department of botany in the University of Oxford* (1964), 144 · A. R. W. Meyers and M. B. Pritchard, eds., *Nature's empire: Mark Catesby's New World vision* (1998)

Archives BL, drawings and papers, Add. MSS 5267, 5271, 5283 · NHM, plant specimens · RS, letters and MSS · U. Oxf., department of plant sciences, plant specimens · University of Virginia, Charlottesville, papers

Catesby, Robert (*b.* in or after **1572**, *d.* **1605**), conspirator, was the third and only surviving son of Sir William Catesby (1547–1598) of Lapworth, Warwickshire [*see* Catesby family], and his wife, Anne, daughter of Sir Robert Throckmorton of Coughton in the same county. He was a direct descendant of that William *Catesby lampooned as Richard III's 'cat' in a famous fifteenth-century rhyme and executed at Leicester after the battle of Bosworth. Many works on Gunpowder Plot state that Robert Catesby was born at Lapworth in 1573, but no certain documentary proof for this detail seems to survive. The indenture for his marriage, dated 2 March 1593, notes that he was then under twenty-one years of age.

Essex rebel and Catholic conspirator Catesby's parents were prominent Roman Catholics, suffering the usual financial penalties dealt out to wealthy recusants in late Elizabethan England. Robert adhered to his parents' faith. He attended Gloucester Hall, Oxford, in 1586, the choice of a college noted for its Catholic intake being perhaps significant. In 1593 he married Catherine Leigh (*d.* 1598), daughter of Sir Thomas Leigh of Stoneleigh, and he inherited the Chastleton estate upon the death of his grandmother in the following year. His elder son, William, died young, and Catesby lost Catherine soon after, leaving him with an only surviving child, Robert, baptized on 11 November 1595.

On 8 February 1601 Catesby sided with the earl of Essex in the latter's doomed rebellion. He was wounded, imprisoned, and fined £3000 for his part in this affair. It has been supposed that his need of ready cash prompted the sale of Chastleton to Walter Jones, wool merchant of Witney, but the cause is in fact by no means certain. Catesby also owned, and occasionally lived in, houses in Hillingdon, Middlesex, and Lambeth, Surrey, while his mother held a life interest in the family home at Ashby St Ledgers, Northamptonshire.

Bitterness at the failure of Essex's design nevertheless seems to have sharpened an already well-honed neurosis; Catesby certainly attracted the attentions of a government all too wary of trouble from extremists in sensitive times. With his fellow Essex rebels John Wright and Christopher Wright, later participants in Gunpowder Plot, and also that perennial rowdy Sir Edmund Baynham, Catesby was placed under arrest at the death of Queen Elizabeth, William Camden contemptuously dismissing the group as men 'hunger-starved for innovation' (Smith, 347–8). It was about this time that Catesby used, occasionally, the alias Mr Roberts, particularly when visiting Jesuits and their followers at White Webbs and other safe houses. Though they were not to know this for some years, the government's suspicions were well founded. In 1602 a small group of Catholic gentlemen, Francis Tresham and Lord Monteagle prominent among them, had sent another future co-conspirator in the Gunpowder Plot, Catesby's cousin Thomas Winter, to Spain to negotiate for an invasion of England in support of domestic Catholics. Winter later confessed that Catesby had been involved in all these schemes.

According to Oswald Tesimond and John Gerard, two Jesuit priests who knew their man very well, Catesby was 'more than ordinarily well proportioned, some six feet tall, of good carriage and handsome countenance'. 'Very wild' in his youth, he was, so they say, 'reclaimed … and became a Catholic, unto which he had always been inclined in opinion, though not in practice'. In other words, the wayward young Catholic became, in maturity, a zealot (*Gunpowder Plot: the Narrative of Oswald Tesimond*, 61–2; *Catholics under James I*, 54–7). Both Tesimond and Gerard say that Catesby was loved by all for his generosity and affability, and it certainly appears that he did exercise some compelling hold over many co-conspirators in Gunpowder Plot, a hold sufficiently powerful to make them take his easy assurances at face value. Nevertheless, when reviewing the testimony gathered after 5 November 1605 it is important to reflect that prisoners seeking favour—seeking life itself—naturally placed blame and responsibility on the shoulders of a dead colleague.

Gunpowder Plot: planning and recruitment The date at which Catesby conceived the notion of destroying king and parliament with gunpowder remains uncertain, but it seems very likely that he had some such scheme in mind early in 1604. It may be that he, along with many co-religionists, had initially harboured hopes of better treatment under James I, but it is perhaps more likely that he had all along held James, his faith, and his religious policies in deep contempt. Catesby was more interested in establishing how Spain would react to the change of dynasty, sending his friend Christopher Wright to Madrid in order to sound out Philip III's government. Sensing correctly that the Spanish court was edging towards peace, Catesby dismissed further hopes of foreign military aid, reasoning that English Catholics would have to take matters into their own hands if they wished to rid the country of its protestant hierarchy. Others felt the same way, notably Thomas Percy, the scheming but capable constable of Alnwick Castle and cousin of the ninth earl of Northumberland. But whenever Percy and other more impetuous friends urged action Catesby would recommend caution, thinking through his plan. Eventually he revealed the idea to Christopher's brother John Wright and to his own cousin Thomas Winter, after swearing them both to secrecy.

Catesby's reasoning, as preserved in Winter's subsequent confession, was straightforward, and characteristic

of the man. 'In that place', he observed, 'have they done us all the mischeif, and perchance God hath desined that place for their punishment' (Salisbury MS 113/54). Further attempts to establish whether Spanish forces in the Low Countries might yet fight on behalf of English Catholics, which took the form of a visit to Flanders by Winter, were made without optimism, and seem to have had from the start a separate motive: it was on this visit that Winter sought out Guy Fawkes, and brought him back to England in order to join the conspiracy. Winter on his return told Catesby what he clearly both expected and wanted to hear, that although the Spanish authorities in the Low Countries had spoken 'good words' about supporting the English Catholics, he feared that 'the deeds would nott answere' (ibid.). In this he was right. Philip III made peace with England in August that year.

So Catesby, Wright, and Winter disclosed the plot to Fawkes and Thomas Percy. They did so early in May 1604 at Catesby's lodging in the Strand, the five men having first received communion from Father Gerard. From that moment the plot took on its own momentum, the pace dictated by subsequent prorogations of parliament and the providential availability of a ground-floor vault under the House of Lords, vacated by a coal merchant and swiftly rented by Percy. Fawkes, an unknown face after long service abroad, posed as his servant. Nothing deflected Catesby from his purpose. When a late recruit, Ambrose Rookwood, muttered on learning the secret that 'it was a matter of conscience to take away so much blood', Catesby replied briskly 'that he was resolved that in conscience it mought be done and wished this examinate so to satisfie himselfe'. It was even legitimate to see innocent men die, 'rather than the action should quaile' (PRO, SP 14/216/136). And Rookwood, admiring and docile, went along with this. He said afterwards in mitigation that he had 'loved and respected [Catesby] as his owne life' (PRO, SP 14/216/136).

Catesby seems to have enjoyed a wide circle of friends, beyond the list of embittered Catholic gentry and fugitive Jesuit priests. One anonymous piece of information that arrived on the earl of Salisbury's desk after the treason was discovered had him dining in October at the Mitre tavern in Bread Street with the Catholic peer Lord Mordaunt, the earl of Northumberland's brother Sir Josceline Percy, a servant of the archduke's ambassador, a Northamptonshire neighbour Mr Pickering, and Richard Hakluyt, presumably the chronicler of discovery and navigation (Salisbury MS 112/160). Another of Northumberland's brothers, Sir Charles Percy, had lived at Moorcrofts, Catesby's house at Hillingdon, rent-free for several months before taking a lease of the place in 1605. Catesby was certainly on close terms with Mordaunt during the summer of 1605, a circumstance which would count against the peer later that year. Conversations with another Catholic nobleman, Lord Montagu, made the authorities suspect that he too had been warned by Catesby to stay away from parliament on 5 November (PRO, SP 14/216/74, 86, 100). These suspicions were most probably groundless; in a revealing examination the plotter Robert Keys emphasized the contempt that had underpinned Catesby's dealings with the English nobility. When Keys asked that Mordaunt might be warned against attending parliament Catesby promised that he would 'put a tricke uppon him, but would not for the chamber full of diamonds acquaint him with the secret for that he knewe he could not kepe it'. While hoping to save 'nobles that were Catholiques', he 'said withall that rather then the project should not take effect, if they were as dere to him as his own sonne ... they should be also blowen uppe'. With far too few exceptions, the peers were nothing more than 'atheistes fooles and cowards' (PRO, SP 14/216/126).

The story of Gunpowder Plot is well enough known, and told fully elsewhere (see the articles on Guy *Fawkes and Thomas *Winter). At every stage Catesby was the moving spirit. He worked on the original mine, recruited the first additions to the inner ring of five, funded the accumulation of gunpowder, and schemed to raise the banner of rebellion upon the successful execution of the plot, assembling the Catholic gentry of the midlands under cover of a day's hunting and recruiting for the regiment pledged to serve the archduke in Flanders. The hope was, 'when the acte was done, that all the Catholiques and discontented persones would take their parts and proclaime the Lady Elizabeth being next heire', abducting the nine-year-old princess from the home of Sir John Harington, near Coventry (PRO, SP 14/216/126). Having cleared the matter with Thomas Percy in the summer of 1605, Catesby personally recruited three gentlemen with the means to finance this attempt, and the military struggle that would inevitably follow: Sir Everard Digby, Ambrose Rookwood, and Francis Tresham. Never persuaded that Catesby's cause was just, Tresham almost certainly betrayed the conspiracy by sending an anonymous warning letter to his brother-in-law, Lord Monteagle. The letter survives in the Public Record Office.

Failure and its aftermath When, early on the morning of 5 November, news spread round London that Guy Fawkes had been captured red-handed in the cellars at Westminster, Catesby and several fellow conspirators fled north, hastening as best they might up Watling Street to the appointed Northamptonshire rendezvous, Percy and John Wright casting their cloaks into the hedgerows in an effort to ride faster (PRO, SP 14/216/136). They stopped at Ashby St Ledgers only long enough for Catesby to call out his servant Thomas Bate, another sworn conspirator, who armed them all with pistols. Then they rode to Dunchurch. The Catholic gentry had enjoyed their day's hunting but when Catesby, with his dishevelled companions, arrived and told them even an optimistic version of what had occurred in London the majority vanished into the gloom of a November evening. Confusion and a sense of great peril held sway. George Prince, a servant at the Red Lion at Dunchurch, later remembered hearing a man speak 'owt at a casement in the ynne', saying 'I doubt wee are all betrayde' (Nicholls, *Investigating Gunpowder Plot*, 43).

There followed a protracted and miserable anticlimax.

Catesby, his fellow conspirators, and a few misguided Catholic gentlemen and their servants resolved to make the best of their lot and to see whether the country would rise for the Catholic cause. However, the country did not rise, and over the next two days even this meagre force dwindled, the ringleaders keeping a constant but not altogether successful watch to prevent desertions. Lacking any real plan of action—fatally torn between flight and resistance—the rebels plundered Warwick Castle for fresh horses late on the 5th, and then spent 6 and 7 November wandering from one Catholic house to another across Warwickshire and Worcestershire: from Norbrooks to Huddington, then to Hewell Grange, and then, finally, to Holbeach, the home of Stephen Littleton, just over the Staffordshire border. Here, as they rested on the evening of the seventh, the accidental explosion of gunpowder which they were drying in front of a fire injured some of the plotters, notably Ambrose Rookwood, Henry Morgan, John Grant, and Catesby himself.

This chance mishap, with its suggestion of divine condemnation, seems finally to have broken their nerve. According to Bate, John Wright:

> stept to Catesby, tooke him by the midle and sayd woe worth the time that wee have seene this day, and called for the rest of the powder, saying that he would have that also fired, that they might all togeather be blowen up. (PRO, SP 14/216/145)

Frightened out of his wits, Bate took horse and rode off into the night. He was not alone: even Catesby now began to suspect that the plotters had offended God. When Thomas Winter, who had been on a futile mission to raise the local gentry, returned to his companions he asked what they intended to do. Catesby informed him that they would fight to the death, and Winter, in his own version of events, declared that he would do the same. About eleven o'clock on the morning of 8 November the remaining rebels advanced out into the courtyard of the house, brandishing swords in a final gesture of defiance. Catesby was shot, perhaps by the same bullet that mortally wounded Thomas Percy, fired by John Street of Worcester. It is said that he crawled back inside the house, and that he died clasping an image of the Virgin. Thomas Lawley, who rode with the sheriff of Worcestershire against the insurgents, told the privy council in a letter dated 14 November how he had tried to revive the principal casualties, rightly reckoning that the king's interests would be better served by their preservation. But, he noted, the 'baser sort' among the sheriff's posse were quite out of hand. They stripped the wounded and countered any good he might have done (Salisbury MSS 113/4, 191/80). Ten other men, some of them wounded, were taken prisoner. Everyone else had fled.

The usual grim postscript followed: attainder for treason, and the forfeiture of estates and property. One Ralph Dobbinson, gentleman, of St Martin-in-the-Fields, sought allowance at the end of the year for 23s. 6d., the sum incurred by a blacksmith in making the ironwork which displayed the heads of Catesby and Percy on London Bridge. Catesby's son was taken by his servant to Ashby St Ledgers on 5 November. A pedigree in *The history and antiquities of Northamptonshire, compiled from the manuscript collections of … John Bridges* (1791, 1.17) has the boy subsequently marrying Thomas Percy's daughter.

MARK NICHOLLS

Sources PRO, SP14/216 · PRO, E178/4162 · Hatfield House, Hertfordshire, Salisbury–Cecil MSS · M. Nicholls, *Investigating Gunpowder Plot* (1991) · M. Nicholls, 'Sir Charles Percy', *Recusant History*, 18 (1986–7), 237–50 · personal information (2004) [Jennifer O'Brien] · M. Whitmore Jones, *The Gunpowder Plot and life of Robert Catesby, also an account of Chastleton House* (1909) · *The condition of Catholics under James I: Father Gerard's narrative of the Gunpowder Plot*, ed. J. Morris (1871) · *The Gunpowder Plot: the narrative of Oswald Tesimond alias Greenway*, ed. and trans. F. Edwards (1973) · G. B. Morgan, *The great English treason for religion known as Gunpowder Plot*, 2 vols. (1931–2) · T. Smith, ed., *V Cl Camdeni et illustrium virorum ad G Camdenum epistolae* (1691)

Archives priv. coll., papers, marriage settlement, and deeds

Likenesses C. van de Passe, line engraving, 1605 (*The Gunpowder Plot conspirators*), NPG · line engraving, pubd 1794 (after C. Passe), NPG · portrait, Syon House, Syon Park, Brentford, London · portrait, Brockhall Manor, Northamptonshire

Catesby, William (*d.* 1383). *See under* Catesby family (*per. c.*1340–1505).

Catesby, Sir William (*d.* 1478/9). *See under* Catesby family (*per. c.*1340–1505).

Catesby, William (*b.* in or before **1446**, *d.* **1485**), royal councillor, was the son of Sir William *Catesby (*d.* 1478/9) of Ashby St Ledgers [*see under* Catesby family] and his first wife, Philippa Bishopestone. Catesby followed his uncle Sir John *Catesby (*d.* 1487) to the Inner Temple, and in the course of the 1470s made a career for himself as a legal adviser and estate administrator for several local landowners, among them Elizabeth Beauchamp (the widow of George Neville, Lord Latimer), the Zouches of Harringworth, and his own wife's stepfather, John, Lord Scrope. His most important association, however, achieved through his uncle, John, was with Edward IV's close friend William, Lord Hastings (*d.* 1483). In 1481 Catesby became one of the apprentices-at-law retained as legal counsel by the duchy of Lancaster. He attained wider prominence in the events leading up to the usurpation of Richard III in 1483. On 14 May he was made chancellor of the earldom of March, an appointment that linked him with Henry Stafford, the duke of Buckingham, who had been given virtually vice-regal authority in Wales by the protector and for whom Catesby had been acting in the late 1470s. In June Catesby was the obvious choice to sound out Hastings over the possibility of Gloucester's taking the throne, a step that Hastings refused to countenance. Catesby's influence with the protector's circle was also recognized by Anthony, Earl Rivers, who named him one of his executors in his will drawn up before his execution at Pontefract.

Catesby benefited immediately from Richard's accession. He was an esquire of the king's body by the time of the coronation, and had also been made chancellor and chamberlain of the exchequer. He remained loyal to Richard in the rebellion of his former patron the duke of Buckingham, and was rewarded with extensive royal patronage, including three land grants and effective control

William Catesby (*b.* in or before 1446, *d.* 1485), memorial brass, *c.*1506 [with his wife, Margaret]

(without rendering account) of a block of Stafford estates to settle the duke's debts. He was one of a consortium of royal associates who paid £1000 for the custody and marriage of the young earl of Wiltshire, Edward Stafford. Catesby was a royal councillor, and with Richard Ratcliffe spoke out against the idea of Richard's marrying his niece, Elizabeth of York, after the death of Queen Anne in March 1485. His influence was recognized in William Collingbourne's famous couplet:

> The Cat, the Rat and Lovell our Dog
> Rule all England under the Hog.
> (Horrox, 222)

It was also demonstrated in the grants that Catesby received from men anxious to have the king's goodwill, among them Thomas, Lord Stanley, the abbots of St Albans and Selby, and the archbishop of Canterbury. Catesby's eminence is obliquely reflected in the number of times contemporaries described him as a knight, or a knight of the body, although he was never knighted.

Catesby was appointed speaker in the only parliament of Richard's reign, in January 1484, and he presumably contributed to the notably acquiescent tone of the assembly, which took the hitherto unprecedented step of granting tonnage and poundage for life to a new king in his first parliament. In September 1484 he was one of those commissioned to treat with Scotland. In the same month he was in Brittany, pursuing the negotiations that Richard hoped would lead to the surrender of Henry Tudor—negotiations that were aborted by Tudor's flight to France. In February 1485 Catesby was commissioned to treat for an extension of the truce with Brittany. He was present at the battle of Bosworth, where he was taken alive. He was executed, probably three days later, at Leicester. His will, made very shortly before his death, makes it clear that he had expected the Stanleys to intercede for him: 'My lords Stanley, Strange and all that blood help and pray for my soul, for you have not for my body as I trusted in you' (Roskell, 171). He made his wife sole executor, with the responsibility of restoring land that he had wrongfully acquired. He was buried, as he had requested, in the church of Ashby St Ledgers.

Catesby may have been something of a musician. A partial inventory of his goods, compiled in 1484, includes a pair of organs. He married, before December 1471, Margaret, the daughter of William, Lord Zouche of Harringworth, and his wife, Katherine Lenthall. Catesby was thus the brother-in-law of another of Richard III's allies, John, Lord Zouche. Margaret was also a cousin of Henry VII, though this did not prevent the dismembering of the family estate after Catesby's death and his attainder in Henry VII's first parliament. Even when the attainder was reversed in 1495 the existing grants were explicitly allowed to stand, and Catesby's heir, George, succeeded to a much diminished inheritance. With his 'dear and well beloved wife' ('to whom', he said in his will, 'I have ever been true of my body') Catesby had three sons and two daughters. Margaret died on 8 October 1494 and was buried with her husband.   ROSEMARY HORROX

Sources PRO · *Chancery records* · R. Horrox and P. W. Hammond, eds., *British Library Harleian manuscript 433*, 4 vols. (1979–83) · R. Horrox, *Richard III, a study of service*, Cambridge Studies in Medieval Life and Thought, 4th ser., 11 (1989) · J. S. Roskell, 'William Catesby, counsellor to Richard III', *Bulletin of the John Rylands University Library*, 42 (1959–60), 145–74 · E. W. Ives, *The common lawyers of pre-Reformation England* (1983) · M. Stephenson, *A list of monumental brasses in the British Isles* (1926) · D. Williams, 'The hastily drawn up will of William Catesby, esquire', *Leicestershire Archaeological and Historical Society Transactions*, 51 (1975–6), 43–51
Archives BL, Harley MSS, papers
Likenesses memorial brass, *c.*1506, Ashby St Ledgers church, Northamptonshire [*see illus.*]

Cathal mac Conchobair (*d.* 1010), king of Connacht, was a member of the Síl Muiredaig branch of Uí Briúin Aí. He was son of the Conchobar from whom the Uí Chonchobair of Connacht, who ruled as kings of that province for much of the rest of the middle ages, take their name; though, as Conchobar's son, he was not *ua* (or *Ó*) Conchobair (that is, grandson of Conchobar), but *mac* Conchobair. When Cathal's father, Conchobar son of Tadc, died in 973, the kingship of Connacht was assumed by a certain Cathal son of Tadc, a first cousin once removed according to an eighteenth-century king-list (O'Flaherty, 133). However,

he was killed by the Cenél nÉogain (line 5768 of the Book of Leinster says after a reign of three days) in the battle of Céis Corainn. Cathal himself then presumably succeeded to the kingship, although nothing whatever is known of him until 1001, when he and the reigning high-king, Máel Sechnaill mac Domnaill of the southern Uí Néill, built a causeway across the Shannon at Athlone. Máel Sechnaill invaded Connacht at least three times during Cathal's reign, in 985, 992, and 998, but only formally received the hostages of Connacht in 998, when they were handed to him by Brian Bóruma, king of Munster. In 1002, when Brian assumed the high-kingship, he himself is recorded as receiving the hostages of Connacht. Brian married Cathal's daughter, Dubchoblaig, who predeceased him in 1009, apparently childless. Cathal himself died in the following year. The annals say that he died in penitence, perhaps at Clonmacnoise, since the late king-list states that his death came two years after taking orders (*a dhul i nord crabhaidh*). He was succeeded as king of Connacht by his son, Tadc in Eich Gil.   SEÁN DUFFY

Sources *Ann. Ulster* · *AFM*, 2nd edn · M. A. O'Brien, ed., *Corpus genealogiarum Hiberniae* (Dublin, 1962) · W. Stokes, ed., 'The annals of Tigernach [8 pts]', *Revue Celtique*, 16 (1895), 374–419; 17 (1896), 6–33, 119–263, 337–420; 18 (1897), 9–59, 150–97, 267–303, 374–91; pubd sep. (1993) · M. C. Dobbs, ed. and trans., 'The Ban-shenchus [3 pts]', *Revue Celtique*, 47 (1930), 283–339; 48 (1931), 163–234; 49 (1932), 437–89 · R. I. Best and others, eds., *The Book of Leinster, formerly Lebar na Núachongbála*, 6 vols. (1954–83), vol. 6 · R. O'Flaherty, *A chronological description of west or h-Iar Connaught*, ed. J. Hardiman (1846) · F. J. Byrne, *Irish kings and high-kings* (1973)

Cathal mac Finguine (*d.* 742), king of Munster, was a member of the Éoganacht Glendamnach dynasty. Like his father, Finguine mac Con-cen-Máthair, and his son, Artrí mac Cathail, he was king of Munster, and he was the first to be involved in warfare against the dominant Uí Néill dynasties of the north of Ireland. Although he is of great significance on this account, his importance has been exaggerated by his reputation later in the middle ages. He was probably not the Cathal active in the midlands in 733, as claimed by some historians.

Cathal may have acceded to the kingship as early as 713, when Cormac mac Ailella, king of Munster, was killed. Although Eterscél mac Máele-Umai, also king of Munster, survived until 721, it seems that he had abdicated his office long before, probably even before the reign of Cormac mac Ailella. Therefore, when Murchad mac Brain, king of Leinster, led an army to Cashel (the seat of the kings of Munster) in 715, he may have been intending to subdue Cathal mac Finguine.

Six years later, Cathal's first appearance in the chronicles shows him devastating the plain of Brega in partnership with the same Murchad mac Brain. Brega was the homeland of the Uí Néill dynasty of Síl nÁeda Sláine and included Tara, the symbolic seat of those who claimed supremacy over Ireland. It may be that Cathal was the junior partner in this enterprise, if a possibly interpolated annal entry can be relied upon, which says that Fergal mac Máele-Dúin, the high-king of Ireland, undertook a revenge raid later that year against the Leinstermen (not the Munstermen). The annals of Inisfallen have their own view of this episode: they indicate that Cathal acted alone in the devastation of Brega, and state that Fergal mac Máele-Dúin submitted to Cathal, and that Cathal became king of Ireland. However, the entry is eleventh century and seems to be an artificial promotion of a favoured historical character.

The following year, 722, the battle of Allen, north of Kildare, took place between Fergal mac Máele-Dúin and Murchad mac Brain. In a twelfth-century version of a story about this battle, Cathal mac Finguine is given an obviously contrived role: he was angered by the battle having occurred in his absence and the Leinstermen brought Fergal's head to him in the hope of placating him. Cathal returned the head to the Uí Néill and appointed a new king for them.

The element of truth in this is that Cathal did not take part in the battle. Indeed, he does not reappear in the chronicles until 735, when, apparently in alliance with the Osraige and the Déisi, he was defeated in a battle against the Leinstermen (although the ever-favourable annals of Inisfallen and the tale of the battle of Allen claim that Cathal was victor). Two years later, he and Áed Allán, the Uí Néill high-king of Ireland, held a meeting at Terryglass (Tipperary), approximately where Munster bordered the Uí Néill territories. The two kings seem to have discussed the dues of the Patrician churches, for that same year the chronicles say that 'The Law of Patrick was in force in Ireland'. There may also have been an anti-Leinster pact, for the following year there was another major battle between the Uí Néill and Leinster, again without Cathal's involvement. It is possible that he later came to take hostages and treasures from the defeated king of Leinster, but the accounts of this are not consistent regarding the name of the king who submitted to Cathal, and the position and language of the entry give further grounds for reckoning it a late addition to the chronicles. The annals of Inisfallen do not report the incident, which may therefore be a misplaced and garbled version of Cathal's alleged victory over Leinster in 735.

Cathal was married to Caillech (or Cellach; *d.* 732), daughter of Dúnchad of the Uí Liatháin dynasty of Munster. He died in 742 and was buried in Emly (Tipperary).   PHILIP IRWIN

Sources *Ann. Ulster* · S. Mac Airt, ed. and trans., *The annals of Inisfallen* (1951) · F. J. Byrne, *Irish kings and high-kings* (1973) · P. Ó Riain, *Cath Almaine* (1978), xii–xxiv · W. Stokes, ed. and trans., 'The battle of Allen', *Revue Celtique*, 24 (1903), 41–70 · M. C. Dobbs, ed. and trans., 'The Ban-shenchus [pt 2]', *Revue Celtique*, 48 (1931), 163–234, esp. 185

Cathcart, Alan, of that ilk, first Lord Cathcart (*c.*1430–1496), landowner and courtier, was the eldest son of Alan Cathcart of that ilk; his mother's name is not known. Alan senior was a hostage in England for the ransom of James I from 1432 until exchanged for Alan junior in 1446, and is thought to have died shortly after his return to Scotland. The Cathcart genealogy in the middle ages is uncertain, as for 400 years from the early fourteenth century all the heads of the family except one were christened Alan, and references to the family before *c.*1450 are few. The

younger Alan was the first of his family to be raised to the peerage, in June 1452, when James II needed reliable allies in the tense aftermath of his killing of William Douglas, eighth earl of Douglas. That Cathcart's main estates lay in Renfrewshire, a region of Stewart lordship from the twelfth century, would have made him a member of the king's affinity, and so a man James could count on. These estates were now united into the barony of Cathcart; he also possessed lands in Ayrshire and Linlithgowshire.

Cathcart was seldom at court before 1469, but after that he attended parliament regularly, though he rarely witnessed crown charters. He obtained the minor office of mair of fee of Kyle-Regis, Ayrshire, in 1478, was appointed warden of the west marches against England in 1481, and by 1483 had become master of the king's artillery, suggesting that he had proved to be a valuable servant of James III, after whose death in battle in 1488 Cathcart disappeared from court. His health may have been poor, as there are references to his tutor or curator in 1489 and 1495. He married Janet Maxwell, perhaps of the Caldorwood or Pollok line, who was still alive in January 1503. She is presumed to have been the mother of his four sons and three daughters. Cathcart's eldest son, Alan (the name of whose spouse is not known), predeceased him about 1490 and the latter's son John succeeded him on his death in late 1496. He is said to have been buried in the Dominican convent in Ayr.   ALAN R. BORTHWICK

Sources J. M. Thomson and others, eds., *Registrum magni sigilli regum Scotorum / The register of the great seal of Scotland*, 11 vols. (1882–1914), vol. 2 · *APS, 1424–1567* · [T. Thomson] and others, eds., *The acts of the lords of council in civil causes, 1478–1503*, 3 vols. (1839–1993) · G. Burnett and others, eds., *The exchequer rolls of Scotland*, 23 vols. (1878–1908) · *RotS*, vol. 2 · G. Crawfurd, *The peerage of Scotland: containing an historical and genealogical account of the nobility of that kingdom* (privately printed, Edinburgh, 1716) · N. Macdougall, *James III: a political study* (1982) · priv. coll., Cathcart muniments
Archives priv. coll., Cathcart muniments

Cathcart, Charles, eighth Lord Cathcart (1685/6–1740). *See under* Cathcart, Charles Schaw, ninth Lord Cathcart (1721–1776).

Cathcart, Charles Murray, second Earl Cathcart [*formerly* Lord Greenock] (1783–1859), army officer, was born at Walton, Essex, on 21 December 1783, eldest surviving son of William Schaw *Cathcart, first Earl Cathcart (1755–1843), and his wife, Lady Elizabeth (*d.* 14 December 1847), daughter of Andrew Elliot, uncle of the first earl of Minto. He was educated at Eton College, entered the army as a cornet in the 2nd Life Guards on 2 March 1800, and served on the staff of Sir James Craig in Naples and Sicily during the campaigns of 1805–6. His father having been created a British peer on 3 November 1807 with the titles Viscount Cathcart and Baron Greenock, Charles Cathcart was from this time styled Lord Greenock. Having obtained his majority on 14 May 1807, he served in the Walcheren expedition in 1809 and the siege of Flushing, after which for some time he was disabled by illness contracted there.

After being made lieutenant-colonel on 30 August 1810, Lord Greenock embarked for the Peninsula, where he was present in the battle of Barossa, for which he received a gold medal on 6 April 1812, and the battles of Salamanca and Vitoria; during the latter he served as assistant quartermaster-general. He was next sent to assist Lord Lynedoch in the Low Countries as the head of the quartermaster-general's staff, and was afterwards present at Waterloo, where he distinguished himself, having three horses shot under him. He received the Russian order of St Vladimir, the Dutch order of St Wilhelm, and was made a CB on 4 June 1815. He married in France on 30 September 1818, and at Portsea on 12 February 1819, Henrietta (d. 24 June 1872), second daughter of Thomas Mather. They had two sons and three daughters.

Lord Greenock continued to act as quartermaster-general until 26 June 1823, at which date he became lieutenant-colonel of the Royal Staff Corps at Hythe. This corps was a scientific one, and had formed a museum of various objects collected by its several detachments, and in this way Lord Greenock became interested in a subject to which he subsequently devoted much attention.

After leaving Hythe on 22 July 1830, Lord Greenock lived in Edinburgh, and for some years was occupied in scientific pursuits. He attended university lectures, was active in the Highland Society, and was a member of the Royal Society of Edinburgh, to which he read several papers, which were published in its transactions. In 1841 he discovered a new mineral, a sulphate of cadmium, which was found in excavating the Bishopton Tunnel near Port Glasgow, and which received after him the name of Greenockite.

Lord Greenock held the appointments of commander of the forces in Scotland and governor of Edinburgh Castle from 17 February 1837 to 1 April 1842, and on 17 June in the following year succeeded his father as second earl and eleventh Lord Cathcart. He was commander-in-chief in British North America on 16 March 1846 and held the post until 1 October 1849; from March until September 1846 he was also governor-in-chief of British North America. On his return to England he was appointed to the command of the northern and midland district, and the resignation of this post in 1854 ended his active services.

He was colonel of the 11th hussars (1842–7), the 3rd dragoon guards (1847–51), and the 1st dragoon guards (1851 to his death), and a general in the army from 20 June 1854. Among other honours he was created a KCB on 19 July 1838 and a GCB 21 June 1859. In politics he was a Conservative.

In 1858 Cathcart's constitution gave way, and he died at St Leonards on 16 July 1859. A man of powerful mind, which was improved by industry and perseverance, he was kindly and generous, which threw a sunshine around the circle of his domestic life.

G. C. BOASE, rev. JAMES LUNT

Sources *Proceedings of the Royal Society of Edinburgh*, 4 (1857–62), 222–7 · *GM*, 3rd ser., 7 (1859), 306–7 · Burke, *Peerage* · Boase, *Mod. Eng. biog.* · GEC, *Peerage*
Archives NA Scot., report on the Isle De Leon · NRA, priv. coll., corresp. and papers | BL, corresp. with W. E. Gladstone, Add. MSS 44363–44364 · NL Scot., letters to Lord Lynedoch · U. St Andr. L., corresp. with J. Forbes

Wealth at death under £5000—in UK: probate, 10 Oct 1859, *CGPLA Eng. & Wales*

Cathcart, Charles Schaw, ninth Lord Cathcart

Cathcart, Charles Schaw, ninth Lord Cathcart (1721–1776), army officer and diplomat, was born in Edinburgh on 21 March 1721, the third but eldest surviving son of **Charles Cathcart**, eighth Lord Cathcart (1685/6–1740), and his first wife, Marion Schaw (1700–1733), the daughter of Sir John Schaw, first baronet, and his wife, Margaret, the daughter of Sir Hew Dalrymple, first baronet, a judge of the court of session as Lord North Berwick. His father, a prominent army officer, was the second son of Alan Cathcart, seventh Lord Cathcart (c.1648–1732), and his wife, Elizabeth (*bap.* 1653), the second daughter of James Dalrymple, first Viscount Stair, and became heir to the peerage on the death of his brother Alan in 1699. He served as a captain in Flanders in the War of the Spanish Succession from 1702 and was promoted major in the Scots Greys in 1709, afterwards becoming lieutenant-colonel. He fought on the government side during the Jacobite rising in 1715, and was largely responsible for the victory at Sheriffmuir on 13 November. In 1717 he became lieutenant-colonel of the 9th foot, and on 29 March 1718 he married Marion Schaw at St Mary Magdalen, Old Fish Street, London. Political appointments came his way; from 1725 to 1729 he was receiver-general for Scotland, and from 1727 to 1732 he was groom of the bedchamber to George II. His military career remained paramount, and he was promoted colonel of the 31st foot in 1728, moving to the 8th dragoons in 1731 and to the 7th horse or King's Carabiniers in 1733, a command which he held until his death. In 1734 he was elected a representative peer for Scotland. He was promoted brigadier-general in 1735, and at the outbreak of the War of Jenkins's Ear in 1739 he was appointed commander-in-chief of the force sent against the Spanish dominions in North America; however, he was taken ill with dysentery while sailing to the West Indies and died on board ship on 20 December 1740; he was buried on the beach at Prince Rupert's Bay, Dominica. He was survived by his second wife, Elizabeth (*née* Malyn; married names Sabine, Fleet; 1691/2–1789), whom he had married in 1739, and who later married an Irish army officer, Hugh Maguire.

Charles Schaw Cathcart's father's influence secured a flying start for his military career. He entered the foot guards at an early age and in 1742 was made captain of the 20th foot under his cousin John Dalrymple, second earl of Stair. The decisive influence upon his career was to be George II's favourite son, William Augustus, duke of Cumberland, whom he served as aide-de-camp in his campaigns in the Low Countries and Scotland during the War of the Austrian Succession (1740–48). He was severely wounded in the head at the battle of Fontenoy in May 1745, and proudly wore a black patch on his face for the rest of his life. It features prominently in the two portraits by Sir Joshua Reynolds (1761; 1773) and in the painting by Charles Philips of Cathcart and Cumberland at Culloden. The duke's patronage launched Cathcart on a career as a government loyalist. It even survived an episode in August

1746 when the two men fell into the River Thames when Cathcart's clumsiness overturned a boat as they were alighting. This important connection secured for him a series of significant offices. He was a representative peer of Scotland from 1752 to 1776 and high commissioner of the general assembly of the Church of Scotland from 1755 to 1763 and again from 1773 to 1776, while he also held a string of military positions: he became colonel and adjutant-general of the forces in north Britain in January 1750, rising to be lieutenant-general in December 1760, and was governor of Dumbarton Castle from 1761 to 1764. He became a knight of the Thistle in April 1763, and served as Scotland's first lord commissioner of police from 1764 to 1768. On 24 July 1753, at the Royal Naval Hospital, Greenwich, he married Jean Hamilton [**Jean Cathcart**, Lady Cathcart (1726–1771)], born in London on 19 August 1726, the daughter of Lord Archibald Hamilton (*bap.* 1673, *d.* 1754), governor of the hospital, and his second wife, Lady Jane Hamilton (*d.* 1753), mistress of Frederick, prince of Wales. Six of their children survived infancy.

Cathcart's diplomatic career was relatively brief and undistinguished. In 1768, when the government was experiencing the usual problems of persuading anyone to accept the distant and unattractive mission to St Petersburg, Cathcart accepted with the high rank of ambassador, though he was a diplomatic novice. It was plausibly claimed that, with a large family to support, he was attracted by the emoluments on offer (his financial situation was such that in 1763 he had sold an estate owned by the Cathcarts since 1376) and was able to secure an agreement that he would continue to enjoy them upon his return. Accompanied by Lady Cathcart, two of their sons, and the boys' tutor, William Richardson, he arrived in the Russian capital in August 1768 and remained there for four years, leaving in August 1772. This embassy saw further attempts by Britain to conclude the alliance which had been sought intermittently but unsuccessfully since the Seven Years' War (1756–63), and from 1768 to 1770 Cathcart was energetic in his pursuit of this will-o'-the-wisp. His enthusiasm, however, outran his discretion: his mission was the target of Horace Walpole's heartfelt remark about 'such simpletons as we have sent to Petersburgh' (Walpole, *Corr.*, 23.208). Disregarding his specific instructions, Cathcart promised Russia's foreign minister, Nikita Panin, a peacetime subsidy of £100,000 to conclude the political treaty, though the British government was determined not to pay it. When his actions were effectively disavowed by his superiors in London, Russian resentment was made clear to the ambassador. His remaining years in St Petersburg saw him politically redundant, as all prospect of an early alliance disappeared.

Cathcart was an inadequate if persevering ambassador, careless over cipher security, long-winded in his official dispatches, and relaxed about diplomatic etiquette, but he secured the friendship and even affection of the Russian empress, Catherine the Great (*r.* 1762–96). Catherine also befriended his wife, Jean, who introduced the empress to the antiquarian work of her brother Sir William

*Hamilton and acted as patron to Josiah Wedgwood in his attempts to find a market in Russia. Catherine's commission of the 'green frog' service in 1773 was partly the result of Lady Cathcart's efforts. Lord Cathcart, too, did his best to interest the empress and Russian nobility in British products. Lady Cathcart kept a journal of her period in Russia, which, although mainly an account of moral meditations, included observations on serfdom and a detailed pen-portrait of Catherine II. She died in childbirth in St Petersburg on 13 November 1771, and her body was taken back to Britain for burial at the Audley chapel, St George's, Hanover Square, London. Lady Cathcart's death cast a pall over Cathcart's final year as ambassador; on his voyage home the following autumn he read extracts from her journals to his children and urged them to follow her precepts. He was rector from 1773 to 1775 of Glasgow University, where he helped his sons' tutor Richardson become professor of humanities. He died, after a long illness, at his home in Grosvenor Place, London, on 14 August 1776, and was succeeded by his son William Schaw *Cathcart, later first Earl Cathcart (1755–1843). His other sons, Charles Allan Cathcart (1759–1788) and Archibald Hamilton Cathcart (1764–1841), became an army officer and MP, and a Church of England clergyman respectively. His daughters made marriages that underlined the Cathcarts' position in the Scottish ruling class: Jane (1754–1790) married John Murray, fourth duke of Atholl; Mary (1757–1792) married the army officer Thomas *Graham, later Baron Lynedoch; and Louisa (1758–1843), who married the diplomatist David *Murray, seventh Viscount Stormont and second earl of Mansfield, was herself from 1793 countess of Mansfield in her own right.

H. M. SCOTT

Sources Scots peerage · GEC, *Peerage* · H. M. Scott, *British foreign policy in the age of the American revolution* (1990) · DNB · Walpole, *Corr.* · A. Cross, *By the banks of the Neva: chapters from the lives and careers of the British in eighteenth-century Russia* (1997) · Burke, *Peerage* (1999) · GM, 1st ser., 11 (1741), 108

Archives priv. coll., corresp. and papers · PRO, official corresp. | Birm. CA, corresp. with J. Watt · Birm. CA, letters to J. Watt · BL, corresp. with R. Gunning, Eg MSS 2697–2702, *passim* · BL, corresp. with Sir A. Mitchell, Add. MSS 6810, 6826 · BL, corresp. with duke of Newcastle, Add. MSS 32702–33057, *passim* · BL, corresp. with secretaries of state, Add. MSS 24157–24158 · Hunt. L., letters to earl of Loudon · NL Scot., corresp. with Lord Barjarg · priv. coll., letters to A. Burnett · priv. coll., corresp. with Lord Stormont

Likenesses J. Reynolds, portrait, 1761, priv. coll. · J. Reynolds, portrait, 1773, priv. coll. · C. Philips, double portrait (with the duke of Cumberland), priv. coll.

Wealth at death see will, PRO, PROB 11/1022, sig. 353

Cathcart, David, Lord Alloway (1763–1829), judge, was born in Ayr on 30 December 1763, son of Elias Cathcart, a former provost, and his wife, Agnes Ferguson. He passed advocate at the Scottish bar on 16 July 1785. In 1793 he married Margaret Muir, daughter of Robert Muir of Blairston. They had at least one child. Cathcart was promoted to the bench as an ordinary lord of session on 8 June 1813, on the resignation of Sir William Honyman, baronet, and assumed the title of Lord Alloway. On the resignation of

Lord Hermand, in 1826, he was also appointed a lord of justiciary. He died at his seat, Blairston, near Ayr, on 27 April 1829, and was buried at Alloway.

T. F. HENDERSON, *rev.* ERIC METCALFE

Sources G. Brunton and D. Haig, *An historical account of the senators of the college of justice, from its institution in MDXXXII* (1832) · Irving, *Scots.* · Anderson, *Scot. nat.* · parish register (births and baptisms), Ayr, 30 and 31 Dec 1763
Archives Mitchell L., Glas., Glasgow City Archives, corresp.
Likenesses C. Smith, oils, Parliament Hall, Edinburgh, Faculty of Advocates
Wealth at death £38,699 5s. 11¾d.: inventory, 2 Oct 1829, NA Scot., SC 6/44/4, p.269

Cathcart, Edward Provan (1877–1954), physiologist, was born on 18 July 1877 in Ayr, Scotland, the son of Edward Moore Cathcart (*c.*1849–*c.*1886), merchant, and his wife, Margaret Miller. His father died at an early age, leaving the mother with three small children, of whom Edward, the eldest, was only nine. He was on the classical side in Ayr Academy and graduated MB, ChB, from the University of Glasgow in 1900. The following year he went to Germany to study bacteriology in Munich and chemical pathology in Berlin. In Munich he also attended lectures by Carl Voit, the foremost authority on human metabolism.

After returning to Britain, Cathcart spent three years (1902–5) in the Lister Institute of Preventive Medicine, London, as assistant to S. G. Hedin. For his work on enzyme activity and in bacteriology Cathcart received the MD of Glasgow (1904), with honours and a Bellahouston gold medal. In 1905 he was appointed to the Grieve lectureship in physiological chemistry in Glasgow, which he held until 1915. During those years Cathcart conducted many experiments on protein metabolism, including a study of human starvation, for which he received the degree of DSc in 1908. In 1912 he published his *Physiology of Protein Metabolism*.

In 1908 Cathcart spent five months in Ivan Pavlov's laboratory in St Petersburg and in 1912 a year with F. G. Benedict in Boston at the nutritional laboratory of the Carnegie Institution. With Benedict, Cathcart studied the efficiency of a trained cyclist, using the technique of indirect calorimetry, which involves collecting and analysing expired air.

In 1913 Cathcart married Gertrude Dorman (1876–1960), daughter of Henry Bostock (1833–1923), shoe manufacturer of Stafford, and his wife, Alice Susannah. She graduated in science, then in medicine, at Glasgow; and their three daughters all graduated in medicine from the same university.

In 1915 Cathcart became professor of physiology in the London Hospital medical school, but gave much of his time to war service, first in anti-gas duties, then as lieutenant-colonel, Army Medical Services, engaged on special work in connection with the feeding of the army. He employed indirect calorimetry during and after the war to assess the food requirements of recruits, the most efficient rate of marching, and the weight of equipment that troops should be expected to carry, and in tests of

new designs of army clothing. The later projects were carried out under the Army Hygiene Advisory Committee, of which Cathcart was a member from 1919 to 1944.

In 1919 Cathcart returned to Glasgow to the new Gardiner chair of physiological chemistry; in 1928 he transferred to the regius chair of physiology, a transfer which did no violence to his interests, which continued to be centred on the human scene. Indeed, in his later years he was out of sympathy with much conventional physiological experimentation on animals.

As a member, and later chairman, of the Physiology of Muscular Work Committee of the Industrial Fatigue (later Health) Research Board (of which he also became a member, and then chairman), Cathcart became concerned with industrial physiology. He supervised a study of weight carrying by women and the physique of women in industry, which was published in 1928, and which was followed by a study on the physique of men in industry, published in 1935.

In his views on industrial and political problems, Cathcart showed no sympathy with what he regarded as the sentimental attitudes of the political Left; nor did he approve of the growing trends towards automation. In *The Human Factor in Industry* (1928), and elsewhere, Cathcart emphasized that workers should not be reduced to 'machine-tickling aphids'.

Cathcart became increasingly interested in human dietary habits. He supervised five dietary studies of different parts of Great Britain, which were published between 1924 and 1940 and funded by the Medical Research Council, on which he served. These studies employed methods pioneered in Britain by Cathcart's predecessor in the regius chair, D. N. Paton. Cathcart, like Paton, attempted to assess 'maternal efficiency' and to explore its relationship to the adequacy of household diets and the nutritional condition of children. He also followed Paton in being sceptical about the practical value of vitamins, and during the 1930s offered an alternative viewpoint on nutrition to that of vitamin-enthusiasts such as F. G. Hopkins, and E. Mellanby. Cathcart's view that such nutritional problems as existed were caused mainly by ignorance rather than poverty, and could be tackled most effectively by education, was also counter to the position of his former student and colleague J. B. Orr. During the 1930s Cathcart was a member of the Ministry of Health's advisory committee on nutrition, of the committee on nutrition in the colonial empire, and of several committees of the League of Nations which were concerned with nutrition.

Cathcart also served on the Agricultural Research Council during the 1930s, and as honorary interim director (1928–30) of the Hannah Dairy Research Institute.

In 1933 Cathcart was appointed to the Scottish health services committee, of which he became chairman. The Cathcart committee published one of the most complete official surveys of the country's health services and gave information of value in the framing of the National Health Service. From 1933 to 1945 Cathcart represented his university on the General Medical Council; and he served as assessor of the senate on the court of the university. He inevitably had less time for teaching and research; and yet, to the day when he retired in 1947, he shouldered the responsibility for the majority of the lectures in physiology to the elementary medical class.

Cathcart was elected FRS in 1920 and FRSE in 1932. In 1924 he was appointed CBE. He received the honorary degree of LLD from St Andrews in 1928 and Glasgow in 1948.

Cathcart was tall, dark-haired, and swarthy, with light steel-grey eyes. His voice was deep and resonant and his accent showed his origins in south-west Scotland. He could be grim and gloomy, especially when confronted with lazy or dishonest work, but could arouse deep emotion and enthusiasm in his undergraduate audiences (*Obits. FRS*). He was remarkably fit until struck down with coronary thrombosis at the age of seventy. He played no sport but loved literature, the theatre, and good talk, sometimes physiological 'shop', more often not. He attended the university chapel regularly; he was a friend and admirer of J. S. Haldane, with whose philosophical outlook he had sympathy. Cathcart died in Glasgow on 18 February 1954.   R. C. GARRY, *rev.* DAVID F. SMITH

Sources G. M. Wishart, *Obits. FRS*, 9 (1954), 35–53 · R. C. Garry, *Life in physiology*, ed. D. Smith (1992) · personal knowledge (1971) · *WWW* · *CGPLA Eng. & Wales* (1954)

Archives PRO, Medical Research Council MSS · U. Glas. L., papers | CAC Cam., corresp. with A. V. Hill

Likenesses W. Stoneman, photograph, 1932, NPG · T. and R. Annan & Sons Ltd, photograph, 1948, Wellcome L. · N. N. Gray, oils (*Study in scarlet*), U. Glas. L., Institute of Physiology · photograph, repro. in Wishart, *Obits. FRS* (1954) · photographs, U. Glas.

Wealth at death £31,166 2s. 9d.: confirmation, 13 May 1954, *CCI*

Cathcart, Sir George (1794–1854), army officer, third surviving son of William Schaw *Cathcart, first Earl Cathcart (1755–1843), and his wife, Elizabeth, *née* Elliot (*d.* 14 December 1847), was born at Albemarle Street, London, on 12 May 1794. Educated at Eton College and Edinburgh University, he received his first commission as a cornet in the 2nd Life Guards on 10 May 1810, and was promoted lieutenant into the 6th dragoon guards or Carabiniers on 1 July 1811. In 1813 he succeeded his elder brother as aide-de-camp and private secretary to his father on his embassy to Russia, when Lord Cathcart was both ambassador and military commissioner with the Russian army. As aide-de-camp Cathcart repeatedly carried dispatches from his father to the British officers with the different Russian armies. He was present at all the main battles in 1813, was the first to raise Moreau from the ground when he received his mortal wound at the battle of Dresden, and entered Paris with the allied armies on 31 March 1814.

Cathcart was aide-de-camp to Wellington in 1815 at the battles of Quatre Bras and Waterloo, and in Paris until 1818. He was then promoted to a company in the 1st West India regiment without purchase, and at once exchanged into the 7th hussars, of which he became lieutenant-colonel in May 1826. On 12 May 1824 Cathcart married Lady Georgiana Greville, daughter of Louisa, countess of

Sir George Cathcart (1794–1854), by Sir Francis Grant

Mansfield, and her second husband, the Hon. Robert Greville. She died on 12 December 1871. They had one son and six daughters. In 1828 he exchanged to the lieutenant-colonelcy of the 57th regiment, in 1830 to that of the 8th hussars, and in 1838 to that of the 1st dragoon guards, and was promoted colonel on 23 November 1841. In 1846 he gave up the command of this regiment, becoming deputy lieutenant of the Tower of London, where he resided until his promotion to major-general on 11 November 1851.

Cathcart was quite unknown to the general public, except from his excellent *Commentaries on the War in Russia and Germany in 1812 and 1813* (1850), and his appointment to succeed Sir Harry Smith as governor and commander-in-chief at the Cape was received with surprise in January 1852, and questions were asked in both houses of parliament about the appointment, for which Wellington was really responsible. Smith had lost the confidence of the colonial secretary, Earl Grey, and was in effect superseded by Cathcart—Wellington's choice despite his disagreeing with Smith's removal. Cathcart was sent out to establish a colonial parliament and revive the dying loyalty of the colonists, and also to crush the Sotho and Xhosa ('Kaffirs'). On his arrival he summoned the first Cape parliament and granted them a constitution, and then marched against the Xhosa and Basuto chiefs. The Xhosa under Sandile and Macomo were subdued, and in November 1852 he marched against the Sotho. He pursued them right into the recesses of the mountains, to which no English general had ever before penetrated, and in December 1852 the Basuto Mosesh surrendered. The war was over and the chiefs Sandile and Macomo were granted residences within the Cape Colony. Cathcart received the thanks of both houses of parliament, and in July 1853 was made KCB.

On 12 December 1853 Cathcart was appointed adjutant-general at the Horse Guards, and in April left the Cape. When he reached London he was sent to the Crimea as commander of the 4th division, with a dormant commission to succeed Lord Raglan as commander-in-chief should an accident befall the latter. His division was hardly engaged at all at the battle of the Alma, and his advice to storm Sevastopol at once was rejected by the allied generals. He finally became bitterly incensed against Raglan for not paying more attention to him, and on 4 October addressed him a note complaining of the influence of Sir George Brown and Major-General Airey, and alluding to the dormant commission. Raglan undoubtedly behaved coldly towards Cathcart, who regarded himself as badly treated, until a private letter from the duke of Newcastle, dated 13 October 1854, directed the cancelling of the dormant commission, which Cathcart accordingly surrendered on 26 October.

On the morning of 5 November 1854 Cathcart heard the heavy firing which announced the attack upon Mount Inkerman. He collected his 1st brigade and led them to where the battle was raging. There is a considerable conflict of evidence as to the later course of events. A dispatch from Sir Charles Windham, first published in *The Times* on 8 February 1875 by Lord Cathcart, should be compared with Kinglake's narrative. The duke of Cambridge sent, requesting Cathcart to fill the 'gap' on the left of the guards and thus prevent them from being isolated, and Airey soon conveyed Lord Raglan's orders that Cathcart should 'move to the left and support the brigade of guards, and not descend or leave the plateau'. Great confusion prevailed, many contradictory messages were sent, and it is disputed whether Cathcart ever received these orders. Cathcart ordered General Torrens to lead his 400 men down the hill to the right of the guards against the extreme left of the Russian column. Torrens was immediately struck down, and Cathcart rode down to take the command, but before he had gone far he perceived that a Russian column had forced its way through the gap and had isolated the guards. Cathcart then attempted to charge up the hill with some fifty men of the 20th regiment to repair his fault; his last words to his favourite staff officer, Major Maitland, were, 'I fear we are in a mess', and then he fell dead from his horse, shot through the heart. A tablet was erected to him in St Paul's Cathedral, though his body rests under the hill in the Crimea which bore his name, and it was announced in the *London Gazette* (5 July 1855) that if he had survived he would have been made a GCB. Despite Christopher Hibbert's criticism of Cathcart as being 'Touchy, inexperienced, stubborn and tactless' (Hibbert, 14), J. W. Fortescue rated Cathcart highly, and he certainly showed to advantage in South Africa.

H. M. STEPHENS, *rev.* JAMES LUNT

Sources Fortescue, *Brit. army*, vols. 12–13 · A. W. Kinglake, *The invasion of the Crimea*, [new edn], 5 (1877) · Boase, *Mod. Eng. biog.* · C. Hibbert, *The destruction of Lord Raglan* [1961] · J. H. Lehmann, *Remember you are an Englishman: a biography of Sir Harry Smith* (1977) · A. J. Smithers, *The Kaffir wars, 1779–1877* (1973) · Burke, *Peerage* · *Correspondence of Lieut.-General the Hon. Sir George Cathcart* (1856)

Archives NRA, priv. coll., corresp. and papers | BL, corresp. with A. J. Fraser, Add. MS 44912 · NAM, corresp. with Lord Raglan · U. Southampton L., letters to first duke of Wellington

Likenesses F. Grant, portrait, priv. coll. [*see illus.*] · wood-engraving (after daguerreotype by Claudet), NPG; repro. in *ILN*, 20 (1852), 125

Cathcart, Jean, Lady Cathcart (1726–1771). *See under* Cathcart, Charles Schaw, ninth Lord Cathcart (1721–1776).

Cathcart, William Schaw, first Earl Cathcart (1755–1843), army officer and politician, was born on 17 September 1755 at Petersham, Surrey, the eldest child of Charles Schaw *Cathcart, ninth Lord Cathcart (1721–1776), diplomat, and Jean (1726–1771), daughter of Lord Archibald Hamilton and Jane Hamilton, and sister of Sir William *Hamilton (1731–1803), diplomat.

Education and military career in America, 1766–1780 Sent to Eton College in 1766, Cathcart moved to St Petersburg in 1768 when his father was appointed ambassador to Russia. There he learned Russian and studied classics under William Richardson, the University of Glasgow's future professor of humanities. He returned to Scotland in 1773. During the next three years he studied for the bar privately and at the universities of Dresden and Glasgow. In 1776 he was admitted to the Faculty of Advocates and published his *disputatio juridica*. He became tenth Lord Cathcart upon his father's death in August 1776. He purchased a cornetcy in the 7th dragoons in 1777.

Obtaining leave later in the year, Cathcart went to the American colonies to participate in the British army's offensive against the colonial rebellion. His first post was as extra aide-de-camp to Major-General Sir Thomas Spencer Wilson, bt. He was then appointed as aide-de-camp to Sir Henry Clinton, commander-in-chief of the British forces in America. Under Clinton he participated in the Hudson highlands initiative by storming forts Clinton and Montgomery on 6 October 1777; he was rewarded with the captaincy of the 17th light dragoons late in the year. In 1778 he was made major-commandant of the Caledonian Volunteers. He was also given permission to form the British Legion, one of five provincial regiments to be made part of the American establishment between 1779 and 1781. This regiment incorporated the Caledonian Volunteers and consisted of six cavalry troops and six companies of infantry.

On 10 April 1779 in New York, Cathcart married Elizabeth Elliot (d. 1847), the daughter of the lieutenant-governor of New York, Andrew Elliot, of Greenwells, Roxburghshire, and Elizabeth Plumstead. In the same year he was appointed major of the 38th regiment and quartermaster general to the forces in America, and was also raised to the provincial rank of lieutenant-colonel of the British Legion. The last appointment caused consternation among some officers and exacerbated the enmity often experienced between the provincial and British regiments. As part of his new responsibilities, he had to deal with insubordination and criminal conduct among his troops. His most pressing concern was the raising of provincial troops. To this end he placed advertisements in local newspapers such as *The Royal Georgia Gazette* and garnered infantrymen from recently disbanded corps like Emmerick's chasseurs.

Savannah was taken by the British in the autumn of 1779 and Cathcart took the British Legion there in December to collect new recruits. His intent was to command the regiment in Clinton's imminent siege of Charles Town. After Clinton sailed from New York, however, his ships were blown off course. He landed in February 1780 and took Charles Town in May. Cathcart commanded the British Legion in this initiative until April, at which time he was forced to sail back to New York on account of his ill health. Ordered to choose between his provincial and British commands, Cathcart chose the latter and gave the command of the British Legion to Colonel Banastre Tarleton. He then returned to his post as a major in the 38th British regiment of Long Island. His health briefly recovered and allowed him to command the 38th against Springfield and Elizabeth Town. By October of 1780, however, his health had failed again and he returned to England where George III gave him a captaincy and a lieutenant-colonelcy in the Coldstream Guards.

Politics and domestic issues Cathcart now occupied himself with Scottish issues, family matters, and politics. Like his father before him he served as president of the Scottish board of police. His growing family took up more of his time: five children were born in the 1780s, the first of whom, Louisa, died soon after her birth in New York on 25 January 1780. Five more children were still to come, including Sir George *Cathcart, army officer; the last, Adolphus Frederick, was born on 28 June 1803. In politics, Cathcart sought election as one of the sixteen Scottish peers to sit in the House of Lords. In January 1788, a by-election was held to fill the seat of the recently deceased Lord Dalhousie, and with the unequivocal support of Pitt's government, he was elected by twenty-eight votes to twenty-seven on 10 January. His opponent, Lord Dumfries, immediately challenged the election by claiming that the vote cast by Lord Rutherford was illegitimate. A heated debate ensued between the government and the opposition and served to highlight the difficulties created by the Scottish representative-peer system. His election was eventually legitimated by only one vote. Such a narrow election did not discourage him from playing an active role in the upper house. In 1788 he supported Dolen's Slave Regulation Bill and in 1789 he was appointed lord chairman of committees. During his absence from London, his unofficial deputy lord chairman, the bishop of Bangor, presided over the committees. These absences were especially frequent during the 1792–3 session when Cathcart presided over 58 private committees while Lord Bangor presided over 102. He remained lord chairman until 1794, when the French Revolutionary Wars called him back to military duty.

Military advancement, 1789–1805 Cathcart's time in parliament did not prevent him from accumulating military appointments. In 1789 he transferred his lieutenant-colonelcy from the Coldstream Guards to the earl of Harrington's 29th regiment, stationed at Windsor. In 1790 he was made colonel by brevet and in 1792 he was appointed to the colonelcy of the 29th when Harrington transferred to George III's 2nd Life Guards. In 1793 he was appointed brigadier-general under the earl of Moira. From 1793 to 1798 Lady Cathcart served as lady of the bedchamber to the younger princesses and established a long-standing relationship with Queen Charlotte. Military duties caused Cathcart to relinquish his parliamentary duties to his deputy in 1794. He then sailed for the continent with Lord Moira's army to participate in the relief of Ostend. Experiencing failure at Quiberon, the army was ordered to assist the duke of York in the Netherlands. Cathcart was placed under the command of Sir David Dundas and successfully commanded a brigade against the French at Brommel; he was made major-general in September. He went on to command the 27th and 28th foot regiments in the battle of Buren during January 1795. He drove them beyond Geldermalsen before having to retreat to Buren. The French eventually proved to be too strong and the British army was forced to evacuate the Netherlands. He took his squadrons to Wesen, released his Hanoverian troops, and then returned to England in December 1795 where he was made vice-admiral of Scotland and head of the court of Admiralty.

In 1797 Cathcart succeeded Lord Amherst as colonel of the 2nd Life Guards, an appointment which made him an official member of the king's household. His favour with the court was furthered when he was sworn of the privy council on 28 September 1798. In 1801 he was promoted lieutenant-general and Lady Cathcart was made lady-in-waiting to Queen Charlotte. In October 1803 he became commander-in-chief of the military forces in Ireland. While he was in this position, his eldest son, William, died of yellow fever while commanding the frigate *Chlorinde* off the coast of Jamaica in June 1804. In 1805, upon the advice of Castlereagh, Pitt removed Cathcart from his Irish post and appointed him lord lieutenant of Clackmannanshire, knight of the Thistle, and ambassador-extraordinary to both the Russian and Prussian courts. He was not installed in the latter position on account of both monarchs being in the field. Instead, Pitt sent him to Hanover and made him commander-in-chief of British forces in northern Europe, a command that included Russian, Swedish, and Prussian troops. In this capacity, he made Bremen his headquarters, fought a small battle at Munkaiser, and corresponded with Castlereagh, the duke of York, and others concerning the state of the war and the possible role of the northern army.

The siege of Copenhagen Following the battle of Austerlitz and Pitt's death, Cathcart returned home in February 1806 and was made commander-in-chief of the forces in Scotland. Although he held this position until 1814, events on the continent occupied his time during much of his tenure. In the summer of 1807 it became clear to Lord Castlereagh that the French might commandeer the Danish fleet stationed in Copenhagen. To prevent this, Castlereagh sent Admiral Gambier and Cathcart to take control of the fleet and the city. The British arrived at the end of August and immediately tried to negotiate a surrender with Major-General Peiman, the commander of Copenhagen's military forces. This proved ineffectual and by 1 September they had placed mortar and gun batteries around the city and had blockaded Stralsund, the nearest Danish port capable of assisting Copenhagen. Having strengthened their position, Gambier and Cathcart once again asked Peiman to surrender the city and the fleet. He refused and emphasized his resolution by not allowing the women and children to leave the city. The British batteries began to shell Copenhagen on 2 September. This pounding continued until 6 September and articles of surrender were signed on the next day. The British forces then took control of the citadel and arsenal and began to repair the naval vessels that the Danish had tried to scuttle.

Cathcart returned home and, despite the controversial siege, was honoured with a British peerage on 3 November 1807. He was given two titles: Baron Greenock of Greenock, after his mother's family, the Schaws of Greenock, and Viscount Cathcart of Cathcart in the county of Renfrew. Additionally, he and Gambier split an estimated £300,000 prize money. Cathcart returned to Scotland on 7 November where he resumed his role as commander-in-chief. Edinburgh conferred the freedom of the city upon him on 17 November. Although his Copenhagen victory had enabled the British army to impound naval supplies and vessels, the British public remained divided in its opinion of the episode. Opponents of the attack were especially appalled by the number of women and children who died in the siege. As the war continued, however, it became clear that the siege had greatly strengthened Britain's control in the Baltic and in northern Europe. Because of this, both houses of parliament voted their support of the measure in March 1808.

Ambassador to Russia, 1812–1820 Upon his return from the Baltic, Cathcart concentrated on Scottish military matters, paying special attention to finding accommodation for several thousand French prisoners of war. On 1 January 1812 he was promoted to the rank of full military general. In July Castlereagh recalled him again from his Scottish post and appointed him both ambassador to the Russian court in St Petersburg and the British military commissioner to Tsar Alexander's army. These appointments were motivated by Alexander's personal request and by the fact that Cathcart was conversant in both the language and the politics of Russia. He took two of his sons with him: Captain Frederick Macadam Cathcart served as his private secretary and Lieutenant George Cathcart functioned as his aide-de-camp.

In August Cathcart participated in the Swedish diet of Orbero, met Alexander at Abo, and travelled with him to St Petersburg. In September Napoleon's forces captured Moscow and, as a result, Cathcart dispatched Lord Walpole to the Viennese court to negotiate a formal military alliance. Alexander commissioned Cathcart to take the Russian fleet to England should the French forces come any closer to St Petersburg. Despite Walpole's failure to obtain Austria's help, the Russian army forced the French to retreat from Moscow the next month. In February Cathcart left St Petersburg to accompany Alexander on the battlefield and he travelled with the Russian army for the next year and a half. He kept the government informed by letters written from the battlefield and via his contact with Lord Walpole and Sir Robert Wilson.

After the Silesian armistice, signed on 4 June 1813, Cathcart personally negotiated treaties with Russia's emissaries, Count Nesselrode, Baron Anstedt, and Baron d'Alopeus, in which Britain pledged well over £1 million to support the maintenance of an army of 160,000 men in the field. He then went to Prague and arranged for £250,000 to be given to Austria, thereby inducing her to take to the field against Napoleon. He continued to accompany Alexander until Napoleon's army was defeated. Alexander honoured him for these services by giving him three Russian knighthoods; that of the military order of St George (fourth class), the order of St Anne, and the order of St Andrew. Likewise, on 16 July 1814, he was given the British title of Earl Cathcart. He served as joint minister-plenipotentiary to the Congress of Vienna and then remained ambassador to Russia until 1820. In addition to negotiating commercial and political treaties, he spent the rest of his time in Russia closely monitoring Alexander's increasing emotional instability and the rebalancing of post-Napoleonic Russian, Prussian, and Austrian military powers.

Later years After returning to Britain in 1820 Cathcart spent his time principally at his family seats: Schaw Castle, Clackmannanshire, and Cathcart House, outside Glasgow. In 1830 he was made governor of Hull. He remained an active supporter of the tory party until 1832 when the turbulent political and social events surrounding the passing of the Reform Bill seemed to sour his interest. His personal correspondence from the late 1820s to the early 1840s indicates that he remained indirectly involved with politics (especially in Scotland) and that he spent his time entertaining guests, monitoring the careers of his sons, improving the productivity of his farms and collieries, and pursuing his interest in natural history. During the last years of his life he was the oldest member of the Faculty of Advocates. He retained this distinction until he died at Cartside, Renfrewshire, on 16 June 1843. Charles Murray *Cathcart (1783–1859), army officer, assumed both his Scottish and his British titles. Lady Cathcart died four years later on 14 December 1847 at Cathcart House, Renfrewshire.   M. D. EDDY

Sources G. Cathcart, *Commentaries on the war in Russia and Germany in 1812* (1850) · M. W. McCahill, 'The Scottish peerage and the House of Lords in the eighteenth century', *Peers, politics and power*, ed. C. Jones and D. L. Jones (1986), 283–307 · *Memoirs and correspondence of Viscount Castlereagh, second marquess of Londonderry*, ed. C. Vane, marquess of Londonderry, 12 vols. (1848–53) · Anderson, *Scot. nat.* · W. S. Cathcart, 'Letter from Lord Cathcart to Lord Castlereagh', *LondG* (25 May 1813) · W. James, *The naval history of Great Britain, from the declaration of war by France in 1793, to the accession of George IV*, [5th edn], 6 vols. (1859–60), vol. 4 · *Scots peerage* · A. N. Ryan, 'The Copenhagen expedition, 1807', MA diss., U. Lpool,

1951 • *Scots Magazine*, 50 (1788), 68–71 • C. K. Webster, *The foreign policy of Castlereagh, 1815–1822: Britain and the European alliance* (1925) • C. A. Cathcart, *Notes on the Cathcart family with special reference to the Cathcarts of Brockloch and Drumgrange* (1936) • *The American rebellion: Sir Henry Clinton's narrative of his campaigns, 1775–1782*, ed. W. B. Willcox (1954) • *DNB* • GEC, *Peerage*

Archives NL Scot., Earls Cathcart MSS, diaries, corresp., and estate papers • NRA, priv. coll., corresp. and MSS | BL, corresp. with Lord Castlereagh, Add. MSS 43073–43077 • BL, letters to Lord Hardwicke, Add. MS 35719 • BL, corresp. with G. Rose, Add. MS 42792 • Durham RO, Londonderry MSS, corresp. with Lord Stewart • NL Scot., corresp. with Lord Lynedoch, MSS 3590–3624 • PRO, Pierrepont MSS, corresp. with H. Pierrepont, FO 334 • PRO NIre., corresp. with Lord Castlereagh, D3030 • Sandon Hall, Staffordshire, Harrowby Manuscript Trust, Harrowby MSS, letters to Lord Harrowby • U. Mich., Sir Henry Clinton MSS

Likenesses H. Meyer, mezzotint, pubd 1807, BM, NAM, NPG • L. Clennell, pencil and watercolour drawing, NAM, Scot. NPG • silhouette, NAM, NPG

Catherine. *See also* Katherine.

Catherine [Catherine of Valois] (**1401–1437**), queen of England, consort of Henry V, was the youngest daughter of Charles VI of France (*r.* 1380–1422) and Isabella of Bavaria. She was born at the Hôtel St Pol in Paris on 27 October 1401. Her childhood was clouded by the impoverishment of the royal family and political divisions between the Armagnac and Burgundian factions in France. Stories later circulated that Isabella rejected her and that, along with other royal siblings and her mentally deranged father, Catherine was left in conditions of squalor only redeemed by the devotion of pitying servants, but this cannot now be verified. She was provisionally betrothed by 18 June 1403 to Charles, grandson and heir of Louis, duke of Bourbon, but little is otherwise known with certainty about her upbringing.

In 1408 *Henry IV suggested that to promote peace between England and France his son Henry [see Henry V] should marry a French princess. Catherine's name was first mentioned in 1409, and recurred frequently in Anglo-French diplomacy during the next decade. A match between her and Henry V was formally discussed in November 1413, and in January 1414 Henry promised to marry no one else before 1 May. At first English demands were excessively high, and though these were later moderated—helped, perhaps, by a portrait of Catherine brought from France in February 1415—the Agincourt campaign of that year led to marriage plans being shelved for some years. They were resumed in October 1418, however, and Henry and Catherine finally met at Meulan on 2 June 1419. The meeting was deemed highly successful, with Henry gallantly kissing Catherine, who blushed modestly. The rest of their courtship, delightfully rendered in Shakespeare's words and Sir William Walton's music for the film *Henry V*, was conducted from afar; a present from Henry of jewellery worth 100,000 écus was allegedly seized by enemy troops in August 1419. But Henry was now so smitten with Catherine that he was prepared to marry her at no cost to her relatives. He promised to give her a dower in England of 40,000 écus p.a. (10,000 marks) and agreed to renounce the style 'king of France', provided he was recognized as regent during Charles VI's

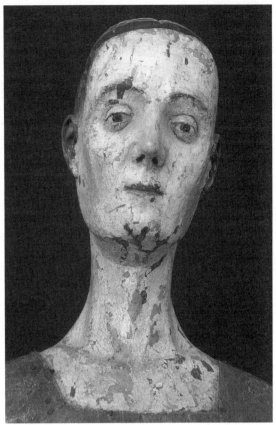

Catherine [of Valois] (**1401–1437**), wooden funeral effigy

lifetime and as heir to the kingdom of France thereafter. Further hard bargaining was needed to secure acceptance of these terms, but on 20 May 1420 Henry arrived at Troyes to seal the peace. The treaty was confirmed in the cathedral on the following day, the succession to the French throne being invested in him and his heirs by Catherine. Betrothal immediately followed, and on Trinity Sunday (2 June) their marriage was celebrated in the humbler surroundings of the parish church of St John at Troyes.

Military needs meant that the honeymoon was spent in a succession of sieges; Catherine was present at the surrender of Sens on 11 June and then stayed with her parents at Bray and Corbeil while Henry besieged Melun, from where he made short visits to his new bride. A domestic note is struck by an entry in royal accounts for expenses incurred in bringing two harps from England for the couple in October 1420, but the subjugation of his enemies was Henry's main concern. At the beginning of December they made a ceremonial entry into Paris, and held Christmas in magnificent state at the Louvre Palace. Observers ruefully commented on the stark contrast with the poverty-stricken circumstances of Charles VI in the nearby Hôtel St Pol.

On 27 December Henry and Catherine left for Rouen, into which they also made a ceremonial entry on 31 December. In mid-January 1421 they set off, via Amiens and Calais, for England. At Dover the barons of the Cinque

Ports waded into the sea to carry them ashore. The king and queen then made their way slowly towards London where another magnificent formal reception (minutely described in city chronicles) was provided on 21 February and Catherine was crowned by Archbishop Chichele in Westminster Abbey on the 23rd. Henry had absented himself from the coronation (as the liturgy permitted) in order not to detract from Catherine's glory on that day. But then perambulating the country to rekindle enthusiasm for his military ventures, he also seized the opportunity to display Catherine to her English subjects. Travelling via St Albans, she joined the king at Kenilworth on 15 March and they kept Easter (23 March) at Leicester, then went north via Nottingham and Pontefract to York (2 April), before returning south through Lincoln (15 April). When Henry left for France in June his wife's pregnancy was well established, and she gave birth to a son at Windsor on 6 December 1421.

Plans for Catherine to rejoin Henry, but without her baby, were soon made, though it was May 1422 before she crossed with John, duke of Bedford (d. 1435), to Harfleur. They were at Rouen by 14 May and found Henry at Vincennes on 26 May. A few days later the couple watched the mystery of St George at the Hôtel de Nesle in Paris and visited the abbey of St Denis on 11 June, before travelling on to Senlis. Once again military duties called Henry away, but as the gravity of the illness he had contracted at Meaux became plain, Catherine remained at Senlis, and was absent from his deathbed at Vincennes on 31 August 1422.

The serious constitutional crisis which Henry's death created was compounded when Charles VI followed him to the grave on 21 October 1422, for this left the nine-month-old *Henry VI as their joint heir and necessitated two regency councils. Catherine was only twenty-one; in the immediate aftermath, her primary functions were ceremonial and maternal: in official records she is usually styled 'Queen of England, the King's mother'. But within a few years her remarriage became a matter of debate though she never played a major political role. She accompanied Henry's body on its slow journey for burial in England. The cortège had reached Rouen by 24 September; on 5 October it set out via Abbeville, Hesdin, Montreuil, and Calais for Westminster, where the funeral was held with great pomp on 7 November. Two days later parliament assigned her a generous dower of over £6000 p.a. Because many traditional dower lands were already in the hands of Henry IV's widow, *Joan of Navarre, Catherine's were largely settled on duchy of Lancaster estates or the Lancastrians' Bohun inheritance. Among the most profitable were Anglesey, Flintshire, Leicester, and Knaresborough, while her castles and manor houses included Wallingford, Hertford, Leicester, and Waltham.

In the early days of her widowhood, when her household was almost entirely made up of English servants, Catherine normally appears in contemporary records on ceremonial occasions, accompanying the infant king to sessions of parliament, for example, or entertaining guests such as James I of Scotland (r. 1406–37), still a prisoner in England, at the major ecclesiastical festivals. But by 1425 rumours began circulating about an amorous attachment to Edmund *Beaufort, the nineteen-year-old nephew of the chancellor, Bishop Henry Beaufort. A petition by the commons in the Leicester parliament of 1426, asking the chancellor to allow 'widows of the king' to marry as they wished upon payment of an appropriate fine, probably alluded to Catherine rather than to the ageing Joan of Navarre. The government's response, a statute enacted in the parliament of October 1427 – March 1428, which forbade marriage to a queen without royal consent on pain of forfeiture of lands for life, may be regarded as expressing the council's concern over Catherine's liaison with Beaufort, since it was feared, as one contemporary put it, that she was unable 'to curb fully her carnal passions' (Incerti scriptoris chronicon, 17). Catherine continued to appear on public occasions, such as her son's English coronation on 6 November 1429, but for the next three years she had no separate household, instead contributing £7 a day to Henry VI's household towards her upkeep. However, in her own letters she continued to style herself proudly 'Catherine, queen of England, daughter of King Charles of France, mother of the king of England, and lady of Ireland' (U. Nott. L., department of manuscripts and special collections, Mi D 2563/6, 6 June 1430).

Nevertheless, in spite of the council's precautions, some time between 1428 and 1432 Catherine did contract a morganatic marriage, though this only became known after her death. Her new husband was a young Welsh squire, Owen *Tudor. Where and when they first met is unknown. Many later legends developed to explain their remarkable romance: that Owen had been in Henry V's service in the wars in France or in the royal household, that he had first attracted attention by falling into the queen's lap in an inebriated state at a dance or when she and her ladies had espied him swimming, but nothing is certainly known to explain the start of their relationship. It has even been suggested that she may have taken Tudor as her husband to prevent her true love, Edmund Beaufort, suffering the penalties of the statute of 1428, since Owen had so few possessions to forfeit. The naming of their first child, Edmund *Tudor, has also led to serious speculation on whether Henry VII, Edmund Tudor's son, descended from Beauforts on both sides of his pedigree, though this seems improbable.

Within court circles Catherine's second marriage was known by May 1432 when Owen Tudor was given the rights of an Englishman, to protect him from earlier anti-alien legislation; in March 1434 Catherine openly granted him various favours on her Flintshire lands. She also gave birth to two other children whose paternity is certain: Jasper *Tudor, later earl of Pembroke (d. 1495), and a daughter, Margaret, who died young. The tradition that another son, Owen, died as a monk of Westminster in 1502 appears to be a later invention, perhaps conflating another unsubstantiated story that Edward Bridgewater, who entered the monastery in 1465–6 and died in the course of 1471–2, was also a son of Catherine and Owen Tudor. Perhaps weakened by successive pregnancies, or by the congenital frailty that afflicted so many members of the Valois family, Catherine's last months were passed (in the words of her will) in 'grievous malady, in the which I have been long, and yet am, troubled and vexed' (Strickland, 2.153–4). She retired to Bermondsey Abbey where she died on 3 January 1437.

Catherine was buried in Westminster Abbey. Henry VII replaced the original inscription on his grandmother's grave, which made no mention of her second marriage, with one that did, and, about 1503 during rebuilding work, her body, loosely wrapped in lead, was placed in Henry V's tomb. By then it had become strangely embalmed, and from the sixteenth to the eighteenth century it was often displayed as a curiosity. On 23 February 1669 Pepys 'by perticular favour' took Catherine's body into his hands and planted a kiss on her mouth, 'reflecting upon it that I did kiss a Queen, and that this was my birthday' (Pepys, 9.457). In 1776 the dean of Westminster ordered her reburial but the corpse was still visible in 1793; in 1878 it was moved to its current resting place in Henry V's chantry. A striking wooden painted effigy used for the queen's first funeral is in the abbey museum, and a book of hours that she owned (BL, Add. MS 65100), with some prayers possibly in her own hand, also survives.

MICHAEL JONES

Sources P. Chaplais, *English medieval diplomatic practice*, 1, PRO (1982) · J. A. Giles, ed., *Incerti scriptoris chronicon Angliae de regnis trium regum Lancastrensium* (1848) · *Annales monasterii S. Albani a Johanne Amundesham*, ed. H. T. Riley, 2 vols., pt 5 of *Chronica monasterii S. Albani*, Rolls Series, 28 (1870–71) · calendars, PRO · N. H. Nicolas, ed., *Proceedings and ordinances of the privy council of England*, 7 vols., RC, 26 (1834–7) · *RotP* · Rymer, *Foedera* · Pepys, *Diary*, 9.457 · C. Allmand, *Henry V* (1992) · F. Autrand, *Charles VI* (1986) · P. Bonenfant, *Du meurtre de Montereau au traité de Troyes* (1958) · R. C. Famiglietti, *Royal intrigue: crisis at the court of Charles VI, 1392–1420* (1986) · R. A. Griffiths, 'Queen Katherine of Valois and a missing statute of the realm', *Law Quarterly Review*, 93 (1977), 248–58; repr. in R. A. Griffiths, *King and Country: England and Wales in the fifteenth century* (1991) · R. A. Griffiths, *The reign of King Henry VI: the exercise of royal authority, 1422–1461* (1981) · R. A. Griffiths and R. S. Thomas, *The making of the Tudor dynasty* (1985) · G. L. Harriss, *Cardinal Beaufort: a study of Lancastrian ascendancy and decline* (1988) · A. Strickland and [E. Strickland], *Lives of the queens of England*, new edn, 2 (1851), 106–61 · J. H. Wylie and W. T. Waugh, eds., *The reign of Henry the Fifth*, 3 vols. (1914–29) · A. Vallet de Viriville, 'Notes sur l'état civil des princes et princesses nés de Charles VI et d'Isabeau de Bavière', *Bibliothèque de l'École des Chartes* (1858), 473–82

Archives BL, Add. MS 65100 · PRO

Likenesses wooden funeral effigy, Westminster Abbey, London [see illus.]

Wealth at death see extracts from will; Strickland, *Lives*, vol. 2, pp. 153–4

Catherine [Catherine of Braganza, Catarina Henriqueta de Bragança] (**1638–1705**), queen of England, Scotland, and Ireland, consort of Charles II, was born on 25 November 1638 NS at the Vila Viçosa in Alentejo, Portugal, the third but only surviving daughter of the five children of John (João) de Bragança, eighth duke of Bragança, later King John IV (the Fortunate) of Portugal (1604–1656), and his wife, Luiza Maria (1613–1666), daughter of Juan Manuel

Catherine (1638–1705), by Jacob Huysmans, c.1664 [as a shepherdess]

Domingo Perez de Guzman, eighth duke of Medina Sidonia. In 1640 a rebellion against the Spanish, who ruled Portugal, established Bragança on the Portuguese throne and the family moved to the royal palace in Lisbon. Four years later only the English had recognized John IV as king of Portugal and he immediately proposed marriage between the infanta, Catherine, and Charles Stuart, prince of Wales, later *Charles II (1630–1685). The proposal was rejected. Little is known of Catherine's childhood but she was probably brought up in the royal palace rather than a convent as is sometimes suggested. She was later reported by the English consul in Lisbon to have been 'bred hugely retired. She hath hardly been ten times out of the palace in her life' (Rosenthal, 'Notes', 2.70).

A marriage treaty John IV died in 1656 and his widow was appointed regent. In 1660, having unsuccessfully tried to secure the French king, Louis XIV, for her daughter, the queen regent revived the proposal to marry Catherine to Charles II. This time the English were willing to listen and the negotiations were conducted by Francisco de Melo, Catherine's godfather. The Spanish vigorously opposed the match but the French supported it and after a year of discussions it was agreed, Charles announcing at the opening of parliament on 8 May 1661 his intention to marry Catherine, and signing a marriage treaty on 23 June 1661. Under the treaty Catherine was to bring Charles the huge portion of 2 million cruzados (about £300,000), the important strategic and trading posts of Tangier in north Africa and Bombay in India, and free trade with Brazil and the East Indies. In return England would give military assistance to help protect Portugal from Spain, while Catherine was to have an income of £30,000 and, as a Roman Catholic, a private chapel in any palace where she might reside, and the right to practise her religion freely. The usual proxy marriage was not conducted before Catherine set off from Portugal on 13 April 1662, probably because Portuguese independence was still not recognized by the pope and any papal dispensations for the marriage would have described Catherine as the daughter of a duke rather than a king. On 14 May 1662 Catherine landed at Portsmouth, where she stayed until Charles II arrived a week later. They were married on 21 May at Portsmouth in both a secret Roman Catholic ceremony, conducted by Catherine's chief almoner, Ludovic Stuart, Lord d'Aubigny, and a public Anglican one, conducted by Bishop Gilbert Sheldon. Charles wrote to his lord chancellor that Catherine's 'face is not so exact as to be caled a beuty, though her eyes are excelent good, and not any thing in her face that in the least degree can shoque one' (Hartmann, 43). A later report claimed that Charles privately told one of his companions that he thought they had brought him a bat rather than a woman. The king's contemporaries also concluded that Catherine was not a beauty: she had rather protruding teeth 'wronging her mouth' and was very short and slight, but they agreed that her large, dark eyes were, as one observer put it, 'angelic' (Evelyn, 3.320; *Lorenzo Magalotti*, 29).

On 29 May Catherine arrived at Hampton Court with Charles II. Crowds came 'streaming in' from London hoping for a glimpse of the new queen and the following day they were able to see her and the king dining in public, but the hall became so crowded and hot that Catherine hurriedly left the room, her make-up being 'about to run off with sweat' (*Journal of William Schellinks' Travels*, 90). At Hampton Court the king admired Catherine's wit and was 'extremely fond, and spends all his time with her', while Catherine was 'of extraordinary piety, full of sweetness and goodnese'. In an indication of future conflicts she was also concerned that the ladies of the court 'spend soe much time in dressing themselves, she feares they bestow but little on God Almighty, and in housewivry' (*Beaufort MSS*, 52–3). The marital harmony soon disappeared. The king had decided to give his mistress, Barbara Palmer, countess of Castlemaine, a place as lady of the bedchamber in Catherine's household but when the two were introduced the queen, who by some means had heard of Castlemaine and resolved never to see her, caused a public scene by bleeding from the nose and fainting. For some weeks thereafter Catherine put up a vigorous resistance, displaying an unexpectedly fierce temper: she erased Castlemaine's name from the list of household servants presented to her by the king, argued passionately with him against the appointment and told the lord chancellor that she would never agree to the king's request. Charles's sister Henriette Anne wrote to him from France on 22 July

NS, 'it is said here that she [Catherine] is grieved beyond measure, and to speak frankly I think it is with reason' (Hartmann, 51). The quarrel was resolved only when, after threats by Charles II that all her Portuguese attendants would be sent away, Catherine gave way in late August, just before she went to Whitehall.

Catherine's arrival by barge at Whitehall Palace on 23 August 1662 was the occasion of spectacular celebrations on the Thames. The diarist Samuel Pepys was among the crowds but his first sighting of Catherine was at the queen mother Henrietta Maria's residence, Somerset House, on 7 September when he thought that 'though she be not very charming, yet she hath a good modest and innocent look' (Pepys, 3.191). Once at Whitehall, Catherine appeared determined to please the king by being gracious not only to Lady Castlemaine but also to the king's eldest illegitimate son James Scott, later duke of Monmouth. She was seen sharing a coach with both of them and 'was merry' with Castlemaine and 'talked kindly of her' (*Life of … Clarendon*, 2.194). To add to her difficulties Catherine at first spoke very little English and as late as 1668 it was reported that she understood the language with some difficulty. Another source of friction was the continuing difficulty over the payment of her portion which, as might have been predicted, was beyond Portugal's resources. Half the portion had accompanied Catherine to England but much of it had not been in cash as agreed but, to the great annoyance of the English, in commodities such as sugar and in bills of exchange. Negotiations over the remainder continued for years and it was never fully paid.

Disappointed hopes Despite Catherine's appeasement of the king she did not gain much influence at court, mainly due to her failure (in marked contrast to Charles's mistresses) to have children. She apparently suffered from dysfunctional uterine bleeding; a visitor to the court in 1668 heard that 'the extraordinary frequency and abundance of her menses' (*Lorenzo Magalotti*, 30) made it unlikely that she would have children, while Sir John Reresby also recorded that she had 'a constant flux upon her' (*Memoirs of Sir John Reresby*, 40–41). In September 1662 Charles II was heard joking to his mother that Catherine was pregnant, to which Catherine responded, 'you lye' (Pepys, 3.191). Not long afterwards the situation was recognized as serious and already by December that year there was speculation that Catherine was infertile and that the king might legitimate Monmouth. In July 1663 Catherine began the first of several summer visits to the waters of Tunbridge Wells and then Bath in hopes of a cure. Returning to Whitehall without the desired result Catherine fell ill of a fever in October and, revealing the pressure she was under, talked deliriously of the three children she believed she already had. Her misfortunes were increased by Charles's obsession with her maid of honour Frances Stuart, which began in early 1663 and continued until Frances's marriage in 1667.

In 1665 the plague forced the court to leave London, going first to Salisbury and then moving to Oxford. In

Oxford Catherine probably suffered a miscarriage in January or February 1666, but it seems that Charles II may not have been present at the time, having already returned to Whitehall, and according to the earl of Clarendon he refused to believe that it had occurred. Indeed, when a pregnancy in 1668 ended in miscarriage at about ten weeks, on 7 May the king wrote to his sister that at least it was proof that she could conceive, 'which I will not deny to you till now I did feare she was not capable of' (Hartmann, 208–9). A year later, in May 1669, another pregnancy was announced but ended in early miscarriage by 7 June. According to one report the miscarriage was caused by a fright Catherine received when a tame fox owned by the king jumped on her bed and ran across her face. Thereafter the attempts at conceiving an heir seem to have been largely abandoned. Catherine's failure to produce children had serious implications for the royal succession. Already in 1667 the rumour circulated that Charles would divorce Catherine, the first of many such suggestions. In 1669 the duke of Buckingham claimed to have discussed divorcing Catherine with the king and in March 1670 the notorious divorce case of Lord Roos came before parliament. Charles II displayed an interest and was said to support Roos's desire for a divorce. Catherine was annoyed by Charles's close attention to the case and reportedly declared that if in conscience she could retire to a convent she would be very pleased to do it.

Catherine found some pleasure in the fashionable entertainments of the court. She enjoyed playing cards, shocking protestants such as Pepys and the duke of Ormond by playing on Sundays. She also organized a number of masques and was very fond of dancing. The poet Edmund Waller credited her with making tea a fashionable drink. In 1666 she was said to be considering leading the way in wearing shorter dresses which showed the feet. On one occasion, while staying at Audley End in 1670, Catherine and two of her ladies attended a nearby fair disguised as country women but were soon discovered and, the crowds becoming so great, were forced to make a hasty retreat. Her favourite painter was Jacob Huysmans, a Dutch Catholic. About 1664 he painted her as St Catherine, apparently prompting a fashion for women to be painted in the same guise as a compliment to the queen. Even in her artistic patronage, however, the queen was overshadowed, the countess of Castlemaine setting the fashionable court look and patronizing the most successful court painter, Peter Lely.

No doubt Catherine's deep faith sustained her, the English remarking with some amazement on her manifest piety. Before she arrived Charles II rebuilt the Catholic chapel at St James's Palace for her use, and invited six English Benedictine monks from Douai to staff it. In her own household there were between four and six priests. In December 1663 the king requested his sister to send some pictures to put in prayer books for Catherine. They would be a 'greate present to her, and she will looke upon them often, for she is not only content to say the great ofice in the breviere every day, but likewise that of our Lady too, and this is besides goeing to chapell' (Hartmann, 89).

When the pictures arrived Charles wrote that 'they are very fine ones and she never saw such before' (ibid., 94). About 1665 Catherine decided to build a religious house east of the chapel at St James's, to be occupied by thirteen Portuguese Franciscans of the order of St Peter of Alcantara. The convent, which no longer exists, was known as The Friary, and was completed and being lived in by January 1667. The order chosen to inhabit it occasioned some criticism of their lack of sophistication but their simplicity may have appealed to the queen. Her attendance at mass before seven o'clock in the morning on St Katherine's day in 1666 provoked one contemporary to remark that 'he never saw anything have so much zeale … much beyond the bigotery that ever the old Queen-mother had' (Pepys, 7.384). In 1668 she was reported to have publicly rejoiced at the news of the French Marshal Turenne's conversion to Catholicism, while the protestant women of the court wept. Eager to establish cordial relations with the pope and gain recognition for Portuguese independence she sent Richard Bellings, later her principal secretary, to Rome in October 1662 with letters for the pope and several cardinals. In 1669 she interested herself in the relief of Candia in Crete, which was under siege by the Turks and whose cause was promoted by Rome, although she could not persuade the king to take any action. In 1670 she requested and received devotional objects from the pope.

Increasing difficulties Catherine had been given Somerset House on the death of Henrietta Maria in August 1669 and in 1671 she moved her chapel, priests, and monks there. The move caused some confusion with many reports that she was going to live permanently at Somerset House, but this did not happen. Continuing to fulfil her role as queen consort Catherine usually accompanied the king on his journeys outside London. In September 1671 they made a tour of Norfolk, visiting Norwich, where Catherine was praised for being 'infinitely gratious' and allowing many the privilege of kissing her hand, so 'our whole inhabitants … sing of nothing else but her prayses' (T. C., 16). In February 1673 Catherine suffered a serious illness and told one of her ladies that she had been poisoned. She seems to have become genuinely afraid of further 'attempts', her fears probably stimulated by repeated moves, which increased in urgency after the conversion of the duke of York (later James II) to Catholicism became generally known in 1673, to convince Charles II to abandon her. Throughout the 1673–4 session of parliament the earl of Shaftesbury, by this time in opposition to the court, was known to be offering a reconciliation with Charles if only he would consent to divorce. Charles again refused to countenance the suggestion, but after a summer spent at Windsor in 1674 royal relations seem to have reached a low ebb. That autumn Catherine did not go to Newmarket and instead spent some weeks at Hampton Court 'in retirement'. According to the Venetian ambassador, 'Contrary to her usual custom, stifling the pangs of jealousy by which she is tormented, her Majesty made an effort to amuse herself during the whole of this last season with hunting and dancing', and she returned 'unwillingly to

London where the customary freedoms of the king and even more the flaunting of his mistresses dispirit her and render her incapable of disguising her sorrows' (*CSP Venice, 1673–5*, 305). Undoubtedly the presence of the latest royal mistress, Louise de Kéroualle, duchess of Portsmouth, affected Catherine's mood. She was again seriously ill in March 1675, which her doctors believed was due as much to mental as physical causes, in particular the stress of a possible revival of the divorce project and the increasing measures against Catholics.

In 1675 all English and Irish Catholic priests were ordered to leave the country, making Catherine thenceforth rely on her foreign priests. Other Catholics in the queen's entourage also caused concern. In 1670 Francisco de Melo returned to England privately and was shown great favour by the queen. When he was appointed ambassador to England in 1671 it was left to Catherine to uphold the honour of Portugal and pay his expenses, part of his salary (despite protests in the privy council), and insist that he be allowed to make a formal entry to London. In 1675 Catherine appointed the ambassador as her lord chamberlain, an unusual and controversial move, for which the king, wishing to please Catherine and perhaps demonstrate the futility of moves for divorce, gave his permission. De Melo was dismissed a year later after it was discovered that he had ordered the printing of a Catholic book.

Catherine herself did not seek any active role in the religious politics of the country although she inevitably had some interest in the support of her religion. In 1672 she was said to be pressing her claims for a place in the first promotion of cardinals based on the advantages Catholics in England had by her presence. She renewed her claims for a cardinal's place in 1675 and, taking an interest in the government of Catholics in England, apparently supported the idea of appointing a bishop to England who would resolve the internal disputes among Catholics. Despite orders to the contrary her chapel continued to be attended by English Catholics and in 1671 the Venetian ambassador had reported that 'she causes the free exercise of the Roman Church to glow amid the fog of these heresies' (*CSP Venice, 1671–2*, 62).

The Popish Plot of 1678 directly threatened Catherine's position, as she and her household were immediately under suspicion of involvement in the alleged conspiracy to kill the king. Catherine's Catholic servants were accused by William Bedloe of murdering the magistrate Sir Edmund Berry Godfrey at Somerset House, which was searched for evidence on 8 November. Titus Oates then accused the queen of high treason, claiming that Catherine knew and approved the plot, her motive supposedly being revenge for the king's infidelities and desire to bring in Catholicism. Under questioning it was clear that both had invented their stories but on 28 and 29 November 1678 Bedloe and Oates made their depositions against the queen before parliament and such was the belief in the plot that the House of Commons voted for an address calling for Catherine and her household's banishment from Whitehall. The address did not pass the Lords but the accusations continued and further depositions were made against her.

Catherine's peril prompted Charles to new displays of affection. After the 1678 Test Act restricted the queen to nine Catholic servants besides her Portuguese attendants she quickly reappointed the duchess of Portsmouth (the king's mistress) as one of her ladies because, it was said, she 'out of civility thinkes shee could do no less; since the king stuck to her and showed so much concerne for her' (*Beaufort MSS*, 83). The pressure on the king to remove all Catholics from his presence seemed inexorable, however, and in a letter to her brother on 17 March 1679 Catherine subtly criticized her husband's decision to send away the duke of York and highlighted the apparent precariousness of her own position. Charles II:

> hath seemingly clos'd his Eyes … and taken a Step soe contrary to the affection he bears toward this Brother to whom he owes soe much. Such Decision evokes alarm that were others to support his [the duke of York's] attitudes they must suffer the same fate. (Rau, 'Letters', 564)

She protested her innocence of all accusations against her and wrote that the king believed her innocent. A special envoy, the marquez de Arronches, arrived from Portugal in April 1679 with the proposal that she return to Portugal for her own safety, but she refused. In July there was renewed speculation that Charles would now consent to divorce her but the case against her largely collapsed the same month when Catherine's physician Sir George Wakeman was acquitted of preparing the poison that was to kill Charles. Bedloe died in August saying that she was indeed innocent. On 15 August 1679 the countess of Sunderland wrote, 'The king and queen, who is now a mistress, the passion her spouse has for her is so great, go both to Newmarket the 18th of September, together with the whole court' (*Henry Sidney's Diary*, 1.86). At the end of the year Catherine wrote to her brother praising 'the loving kindness' with which the king supported her (Rau, 'Letters', 565–7). Charles again rejected proposals by Shaftesbury at the end of the year that he divorce Catherine. The unpopularity of Catholics led to Catherine being publicly insulted as she went to her chapel at Somerset House and in January 1680 it was decided that she would go back to the chapel at St James's, the access to which was more private. The earl of Shaftesbury made a final attempt to convince the king to abandon Catherine, introducing a divorce bill in the House of Lords on 17 November 1680 but, the bill finding few supporters, it was soon dropped. Afterwards Charles signalled his support for his wife by going immediately to tell her the news and sleeping for some time in her chamber after dinner, something he usually did at the duchess of Portsmouth's.

End of the reign, last years in England Catherine had survived as England's queen but thereafter seems to have become more withdrawn. In March 1681 she was at Newmarket when one of her dressers reported that although the other ladies of the court went out riding every day, 'our good Mistres entertaines better thoughts in her solitude, being retired most part of the day at her devotions and reading' (Lady Tuke to Mary Evelyn, 20 March 1681[–

2], BL, Evelyn MS ME6). She was also not playing cards, something that she usually did a great deal. The dominance of the duchess of Portsmouth increased to unbearable proportions for Catherine who in 1683 complained to Charles in the course of an argument about her servants' privileges that 'the queen mother did a great deal more [than she], but that now the mistresses governe all' (*CSP dom.*, 1683, pt 1, 202). In April 1684 she chose Lord Halifax as her new lord chancellor, apparently because of his opposition to that faction at court which included the duchess of Portsmouth. Catherine suffered 'many swoons and nervous attacks' during Charles II's last illness, but remained at his bedside as much as possible until the night before his death on 6 February 1685 when she was taken back to her own room (Rau, 'King Charles', 517). She had no role in arranging the king's deathbed conversion to Catholicism but probably knew of it at the time. She ordered an elaborate marble bust of Charles II and fell into a 'profound depression and melancholy' which lasted for some months (ibid., 519). After a year she recovered somewhat, took an interest in her household affairs, and resolved firmly to maintain her recent weight loss through diet and exercise.

In the reign of James II, Catherine lived at Somerset House and had a summer residence in Hammersmith, Middlesex. She experienced fewer difficulties regarding her religion under the Catholic James II and established a community of nuns at Hammersmith but, as a former queen consort, her public role was negligible. An increasingly isolated figure, from at least 1687 Catherine wished to return to Portugal, but she had still to depend on the whims of kings, and in letters to her brother Pedro II pleaded with him to give her permission to leave England. She wrote revealingly that there was little purpose in remaining now that 'the Almighty hath seen fitt to set me free'. She offered to live some distance away from him so that she would not cause jealousy among courtiers who might fear her influence, and wrote:

> there remains nothing more to say than, if Hermitages were not forbidden to Women, or were I of the other Sex, it wd. be no longer necessary for the World to take account of me, certain it be I shd. no longer be Here.   (Rau, 'Letters', 570–71)

Pedro II, however, seemed reluctant to act and Catherine was still in England when the revolution of 1688 took place. She remained carefully neutral but her presence seems to have been an irritation to the protestant William and Mary, the former requesting, unsuccessfully, that she might move to somewhere less conspicuous than Somerset House. She seems to have spent the summers from 1689 at a house in Islington.

Homecoming and conclusion Catherine remained in England until 30 March 1692, when she left for Portugal, travelling overland across France and Spain. She reached Lisbon in January 1693 and after residing at palaces at Alcantara, Santa Marta, Moinho de Vento, and Belem, in and near Lisbon, settled at Bemposta near Lisbon, where she had a new palace and chapel built. Her court was much reduced and in 1700 an observer wrote of her retired life; 'there is now no noise, nor Ostentation of Grandeur about

her House but all things are quiet and still' (Rosenthal, 'Notes', 2.74). There seems little to indicate that she had anything to do with the Methuen treaty between England and Portugal in 1703. In 1704, however, she came out of retirement, being appointed regent to Pedro II due to his ill health. Portugal had a series of military victories against Spain under Catherine and she remained regent until her death on 31 December 1705 at the palace at Bemposta. She was buried in the monastery at Belem, near Lisbon. In the twentieth century her body was moved to the Bragança mausoleum of St Vincent, Lisbon.

Catherine had not been unwilling to fulfil her role as the British queen consort but circumstances conspired to make her success unlikely. Her 'ordinary mind' and lack of beauty and sophistication disappointed her court, and while she came to love her husband, who for his part welcomed her non-interference in politics and praised her goodness, his mistresses were the bane of her life, and her childlessness the cause of great misery (*Lorenzo Magalotti*, 31). Looking back in 1687 on her marriage Catherine wrote with some bitterness, 'There were then Reasons for my coming to this Kingdom, solely for the advantage of Portugal, & for this cause & for the interests of our House I was Sacrific'd' (Rau, 'Letters', 567).   S. M. WYNNE

Sources L. C. Davidson, *Catherine of Bragança: infanta of Portugal* (1908) · A. Strickland, *Lives of the queens of England*, rev. edn, 6 vols. (1889), vol. 4 · *The journal of William Schellinks' travels in England, 1661–1663*, ed. M. Exwood and H. L. Lehmann, CS, 5th ser., 1 (1993) · *Lorenzo Magalotti at the court of Charles II: his Relazione d'Inghilterra of 1668*, ed. and trans. W. Middleton (1980) · *The manuscripts of the duke of Beaufort ... the earl of Donoughmore*, HMC, 27 (1891) · C. H. Hartmann, *Charles II and Madame* (1934) · Evelyn, *Diary*, vol. 3 · *The life of Edward, earl of Clarendon ... written by himself*, new edn, 3 vols. (1827) · E. Rosenthal, 'Notes on Catherine of Bragança, queen consort of King Charles II of England', *The Historical Association: Lisbon branch. Annual Report and Review*, 1 (1937), 14–17 · E. Rosenthal, 'Notes on Catherine of Bragança, queen of Charles II of England and her life in Portugal', *The Historical Association: Lisbon branch. Annual Report and Review*, 2 (1938), 68–75 · V. Rau, ed., 'Letters from Catherine of Bragança, queen-consort of Charles II to her brother, Dom Pedro II, king of Portugal (1679–1691)', *The Historical Association: Lisbon branch. Annual Report and Review*, 9 (1945), 559–72 · V. Rau, ed., 'King Charles and Queen Catherine: two letters', *The Historical Association: Lisbon Branch. Annual Report and Review*, 8 (1944), 514–21 · S. Wynne, 'The mistresses of Charles II and Restoration court politics, 1660–1685', PhD diss., U. Cam., 1997 · *CSP Venice, 1666–8, 1671–5* · BL, Evelyn MS, ME6 · A. S. Barnes, 'Catholic chapels royal, III: St James' Palace and Catherine of Braganza', *Downside Review*, new ser., 1 (1901), 232–49 · A. S. Barnes, 'Catholic chapels royal, IV: the later years of Charles II and the reign of James II', *Downside Review*, new ser., 2 (1901), 40–55 · *The manuscripts of his grace the duke of Rutland*, 4 vols., HMC, 24 (1888–1905), vols. 1–2 · *Sixth report*, HMC, 5 (1877–8) · *Bishop Burnet's History* · PRO, PRO 31/3/124, fol. 66; 31/3/147, fols. 33–42 · [T. Carte], *The life of James, duke of Ormond*, new edn, 6 vols. (1851), vol. 4, p. 704 · *Henry Sidney's diary of the times of Charles II*, ed. R. Blencowe, 2 vols. (1843) · [T. C.], *Narrative of the visit of his majesty King Charles the Second to Norwich*, ed. D. Turner (1846) · *The poems of Edmund Waller*, ed. G. Thorn Drury, new edn, vol. 2 (1901) · Pepys, *Diary* · *Memoirs of Sir John Reresby*, ed. A. Browning (1936)

Archives BL, corresp., Add MS 17020 · Lincs. Arch., accounts of the queen; privy purse | BL, corresp. with her brother Pedro II, Egerton MS 1534

Likenesses oils, mid 17th cent. (aged ten), Museu Regional de Evora, Portugal · oils, *c*.1660–1661 (after D. Stoop), NPG; version,

NPG · W. Hollar, etching, 1661, BM · N. Munier, etching, pubd 1662, BM · P. Lely, oils, c.1663–1665, Royal Collection · J. Huysmans, oils, c.1664, Royal Collection [see illus.] · attrib. studio of J. Huysmans, oils, c.1670, NPG · B. Gennari, oils, c.1675–1685, Goodwood House, West Sussex · G. Bower, medals, BM · S. Cooper, miniature, Royal Collection · J. Roettier, medals and badges, BM

Catherlough. For this title name *see* Wharton, Thomas, first marquess of Wharton, first marquess of Malmesbury, and first marquess of Catherlough (1648–1715).

Catley, Ann (1745–1789), singer and actress, was born in an alley off Tower Hill, London, the daughter of a washer-woman and a hackney coachman, Robert Catley. According to *The Life and Memoirs of the Late Miss Ann Catley* (1789–90) she was a pretty and sexually precocious girl who earned money singing at public houses and to officers at the Tower of London. At the age of fifteen she was bound apprentice to the theatre composer and singing teacher William Bates. In 1762 she sang at Vauxhall Gardens and then joined the Covent Garden Theatre company, making her début as the pastoral nymph in Thomas Arne's *Comus* on 8 October. The high-spirited girl rebelled against Bates's control and left to live with a lover, the dissolute baronet Sir Francis Blake Delaval (1727–1771). Delaval arranged for her apprenticeship to be transferred to himself and recompensed Bates for his loss of earnings from her engagements. Ann's father, supported by his Quaker employer, who was shocked by the immorality of the transaction, brought a law suit in May 1763 against Delaval, Delaval's lawyer, and Bates, but Ann remained with Delaval and sang that summer at Marylebone Gardens. The love affair ended and she was engaged by the Smock Alley Theatre, Dublin, on the recommendation of Charles Macklin, who was giving her acting lessons. On 31 December 1763 the *Dublin Journal* printed a poem in praise of her performance as Rosetta in Isaac Bickerstaff's *Love in a Village*. Her impudent charms and accomplished singing drew crowded houses and, according to *The Thespian Dictionary*, she was paid 40 guineas a night. Her favourite roles included Polly (and occasionally Macheath) in John Gay's *The Beggar's Opera*, Sally in *Thomas and Sally*, Fanny in Bickerstaffe's *Maid of the Mill*, Mandane in Arne's *Artaxerxes*, Laura in *The Chaplet*, and Euphrosyne in *Comus*. According to Macklin she was pregnant in February 1764 and there was gossip about numerous lovers, but the Irish public warmed to her personality. When she performed gratis at a concert for the lying-in hospital in May 1765 the takings were £66 13s. as against an average of £6. About 1768 she met Lieutenant-Colonel Francis Lascelles (1744–1799); they became a mutually devoted couple and lived together until her death, when her will divided her estate between their eight surviving children.

Catley returned to the London stage in October 1770. She sang at Marylebone Gardens in summer 1771, visited Dublin in 1773, 1775–6, and 1777, spent a few weeks at the Edinburgh Theatre in 1776, but sang mainly at Covent Garden, with breaks for the birth of children and, increasingly, for ill health. As the vulgar Juno in Shane O'Hara's burlesque *The Golden Pippin* (6 February 1773) she both

Ann Catley (1745–1789), by William Evans, pubd 1807 (after William Lawranson, in or before 1777) [as Euphrosyne in *Comus*, music by Thomas Arne]

delighted and shocked audiences. In November 1773 Horace Walpole commented that, when playing a British virgin in *Elfrida*, 'she looked so impudent and was so big with child, you would have imagined she had been singing the "Black Joke"' (Walpole, 28.109–10). But she succeeded in the vocally demanding soprano role of Mandane and *ABC Dario Musico* found her voice 'prodigiously fine, of wonderful extent and power' (p. 51). At least eight different engraved portraits survive of her as Euphrosyne, a role 'in which she delighted, and astonished with her vocal powers' (*Morning Post*, 8 Oct 1776). After a long indisposition she had two final years on stage from February 1780. She was suffering from consumption and although James Boaden remembered her as 'the ghost of her former self, gasping even for breath' (Boaden, 1.113) she was still highly paid and had successful benefits. After her last appearance, on 28 May 1782, she lived in her country house at Little Ealing, where she showed herself generous to the poor and was considered an excellent wife and mother and a 'truly good woman' (*Court and Private Life*, 2.159). She died at Little Ealing on 14 October 1789 and was buried on 21 October at St Mary's, Little Ealing, Middlesex, as Mrs Ann Lascelles, although her will makes it clear that she was not married. Ann Catley was thin, with a brown, freckled face, but John O'Keeffe wrote 'she was one of the most beautiful women I ever saw: the expression of her eyes, and the smiles and dimples that played round her lips and cheeks, enchanting' (O'Keeffe, 2.22). For Boaden 'no other female singer ever gave the slightest notion of her.—She was bold, volatile, audacious; mistress of herself, of her talent, and her audience' (Boaden, 1.115).

OLIVE BALDWIN and THELMA WILSON

Sources G. W. Stone and C. B. Hogan, eds., *The London stage, 1660–1800*, pts 4–5 (1962–8) · Miss Ambross, *The life and memoirs of the late Miss Ann Catley* [1789–90] · 'Memoirs of Colonel Las-lles and Miss C-tl-y', *Town and Country Magazine*, 2 (1770), 569–72 · *GM*, 1st ser., 59 (1789), 962, 1049–50 · *European Magazine and London Review*, 16 (1789), 299–300 · parish register, St Mary, Ealing · copy of the will of Ann Catley (Cateley), Family Records Centre, London, 11/1183, fol. 373 · W. Blackstone, *Reports of cases determined in … Westminster-Hall, from 1746 to 1779*, 2nd edn, 2 vols. (1828) · B. Boydell, *Rotunda music in eighteenth-century Dublin* (Dublin, 1992) · T. J. Walsh, *Opera in Dublin, 1705–1797: the social scene* (1973) · *The thespian dictionary, or, Dramatic biography of the eighteenth century* (1802) · J. T. Kirkman, *Memoirs of the life of Charles Macklin*, 1 (1799) · W. Cooke, *Memoirs of Charles Macklin, comedian* (1804) · Walpole, *Corr.*, vol. 28 · *ABC dario musico* (privately printed, Bath, 1780) · *Court and private life in the time of Queen Charlotte, being the journals of Mrs Papendiek*, ed. V. D. Broughton, 2 (1887) · J. O'Keeffe, *Recollections of the life of John O'Keeffe, written by himself*, 2 vols. (1826) · J. Boaden, *Memoirs of Mrs Siddons*, 1 (1827) · M. Sands, *The eighteenth-century pleasure gardens of Marylebone, 1737–1777* (1987) · J. C. Dibdin, *The annals of the Edinburgh stage* (1888) · *Smithfield Rosciad* (1763) · *The Courtesan* (1765) · *The Drama* (1775) · W. Hawkins, *Miscellanies in prose and verse, containing candid and impartial observations on the principal performers belonging to the two Theatres-Royal, from January 1773 to May 1775* (1775) · W. T. Parke, *Musical memoirs*, 2 (1830) · M. J. Young, *Memoirs of Mrs Crouch*, 2 (1806)

Likenesses R. Dunkarton, engraving, 1777 (as Euphrosyne in *Comus*; after W. Lawranson), BM, Harvard TC · J. Jones, engraving, pubd 1777 (after W. Lawranson, in or before 1777), BM, Harvard TC, NPG · engraving, 1777 (as Euphrosyne in *Comus*), BM, Harvard TC · engraving, 1781 (as Kitty), BM, Harvard TC · engraving, 1789, repro. in Ambross, *Life*, frontispiece · W. Evans, engraving, pubd 1807 (as Euphrosyne in *Comus*; after W. Lawranson), BM, Harvard TC [see illus.] · T. Bonnor, engraving (as Leonora in *The padlock*; after T. Bonnor), BM, Harvard TC · W. Read, engraving (as Euphrosyne in *Comus*; after W. Lawranson), Harvard TC · J. Roberts, coloured drawing (as Polly in *The beggar's opera*), BM · G. Terry, engraving (as Rachel in *The jovial crew*), repro. in R. Brome, *The jovial crew* (1780) · J. Thornthwaite, engraving (as Euphrosyne in *Comus*; after J. Roberts), repro. in J. Bell, *Bell's British theatre* (1777) · J. Thornthwaite, engraving (as Rachel in *The jovial crew*; after J. Roberts), repro. in J. Bell, *Bell's British theatre* (1781) · W. Walker, engraving (after R. Dighton), repro. in *The new English theatre*, 12 vols. (1776–7) · engraving, repro. in 'Memoirs', *Town and Country Magazine* (Nov 1770) · engraving (as Rosetta in *Love in a village*), repro. in *Lady's Magazine* (1770) · engraving, repro. in *Oxford Magazine* (April 1773) · engraving (as Euphrosyne in *Comus*), repro. in *Hibernian Magazine* (1775) · engraving (as Euphrosyne in *Comus*), Harvard TC · engraving (as Leonora in *The padlock*), BM, Harvard TC

Wealth at death considerable; at least £5000: *GM*, 59 (1789), 962, 1049–50; copy of will, Family Records Centre, London 11/1183, fol. 373

Catlin [Catlyn], **Sir Robert** (*c*.1510–1574), judge, was born at Thrapston, Northamptonshire, the son of Thomas Catlin of Thrapston, who was the second son of Thomas Catlin of Raunds. He has sometimes been confused with his cousin, Richard Catlin (*d*. 1556) of Norwich and Lincoln's Inn, who became a serjeant-at-law in 1552 and was appointed queen's serjeant in the same year as Robert. He is also liable to be confused with his uncle Robert, who was seated at Raunds; and there was a prominent merchant of the same name. An autograph note on the flyleaf of a year-book records that he spent a year in Clement's Inn in 1530–31 before proceeding to the Middle Temple in Lent 1531, and that he also served a pupillage with John Jenour, protonotary of the common pleas. He was already 'of the Temple' when he appeared as counsel in the duchy chamber in 1531. It was doubtless the same Robert Catlyn whose name occurs as an attorney of the common pleas in the mid-1530s. When he became a bencher of the Middle Temple in 1547 he read on the 1540 Statute of Fines; there is a text of the reading in Exeter College, Oxford.

In November 1555 Catlin was created a serjeant-at-law, his patrons at the ceremony being the earl of Shrewsbury and the marquess of Winchester. A year later he was appointed one of the queen's serjeants, in succession to his cousin Richard, and after two years in the royal service became a justice of the common pleas on 27 October 1558. He was reappointed by Elizabeth I in November, but sat in the common pleas for only one term before his promotion on 22 January 1559 to be chief justice of the queen's bench in the place of Sir Edward Saunders. Shortly afterwards he was knighted at the coronation. He was generally accounted a good and impartial judge, though in 1566 a disgruntled litigant was indicted for contempt in slandering him by saying that 'My lord chief justice Catlin is incensed against me, I cannot have justice, nor can be heard; for that court now is made a court of conscience' (*Lost Notebooks*, 345).

Catlin was a justice of the peace for Leicestershire from 1547 until 1554, and presumably lived in the county. He obtained the manor of Beby from the crown in 1553, and his will referred to a lease of St Nicholas Shambles and Drapery Shambles in the town of Leicester. From 1554, however, he was a justice of the peace for Bedfordshire, and according to Plowden was living in that county when he took the coif in 1555. Although he was described in the pardon of 1559 as of Dunton, his eventual home was at the dissolved priory of Newnham, where he died; his will mentions the red chamber next to the chapel there, hung with red say, the prior's chamber, the gallery, and a convent grove and gardens. He had a town house in the parish of St Bartholomew-the-Great, Smithfield, where there were hangings with the stories of Actaeon and Diana and of King David. He married Anne, daughter of John Boles of Wallington, Hertfordshire, and widow of Thomas Burgoyne, esquire, and had an only child, Mary.

Catlin's later years were much occupied with the proceedings following the Ridolfi plot. He was the only judge who dissented from the opinion that the attempts to rescue the queen of Scots, by Sir Thomas Stanley and others, did not amount to treason inasmuch as Mary was not then reputed a traitor or enemy. He attended the trial of the duke of Norfolk, which, as he recorded in his notebook, lasted all day from eight o'clock in the morning until half past six in the evening. His speech before passing sentence on Hickford gives a taste of his eloquence:

> As for them that seek fame by treason, and by procuring the destruction of princes, where shall sound that fame? Shall the golden trump of fame and good report, that Chaucer speaketh of? No; but the black trump of shame shall blow out their infamy for ever. (*State trials*, 1.1046)

After fifteen years as lord chief justice, Catlin died on 16 September 1574 at Newnham near Bedford, and in accordance with his wishes was buried at Sutton, Bedfordshire, on 30 September. Among other bequests, he left £3 6s. 8d. 'to the worshipfull company of Serjeauntes Inne in Fleetestreete … to be bestowed by their wysdomes'; his arms were set in the hall windows there. The only book mentioned in his will is his 'greate abridgement of Mr Fitzharberte with the table to the same lately imprinted by Richard Tottle' (referring to the 1565 edition), which he left to his cousin Robert Catlin of Raunds. His notebook, which is of a very miscellaneous character and ends with precedents concerning treason trials, is now at Alnwick Castle (MS 475); the year-book containing notes in his hand is now in private possession in New York. His daughter Mary married Sir John Spencer, to whom the chief justice left his collar of SS 'to make him a cheyne at his pleasure', and from this match issued in later generations the earls of Sunderland, the dukes of Marlborough, and the earls Spencer of Althorp. J. H. BAKER

Sources Foss, *Judges*, 5.471–4 · will, PRO, PROB 11/57, fol. 35–7 · *The reports of Sir John Spelman*, ed. J. H. Baker, 2, SeldS, 94 (1978), 2.128, 130 · Baker, *Serjeants*, 169–170, 434, 504 · Sainty, *King's counsel*, 15 · Sainty, *Judges*, 10, 73 · *Reports from the lost notebooks of Sir James Dyer*, ed. J. H. Baker, 2, SeldS, 110 (1994), 308, 345 · *Les commentaries, ou, Les reportes de Edmunde Plowden* (1571), fol. 164 · W. C. Metcalfe, *A book of knights banneret, knights of the Bath and knights bachelor* (1885), 116 · PRO, DL 5/5, fol. 483v · *State trials*, 1.1046 · Exeter College, Oxford, MS 108, fol. 84 · R. Catlin, notebook, Alnwick Castle, Northumberland, MS 475 · PRO, C 142/176/1

Archives Alnwick Castle, Northumberland, commonplace book

Catnach, James (1792–1841), broadsheet publisher, was born on 18 August 1792 in Alnwick, Northumberland, the son of John Catnach (1769–1813), printer, and his wife, Mary Hutchinson. His father was ahead of his time in publishing cheap attractively illustrated books, including children's books, but was a poor businessman. Working in Newcastle, he was imprisoned for debt, and in an attempt to mend his fortunes by moving to London with his family in 1808 he only sank deeper into poverty. In 1813 he died, broken in spirit, of an infected leg. James was left in charge of his mother and sisters, and set about supporting them with energy. He installed his father's old wooden press in cramped quarters at 2 Monmouth Court, St Giles, then an impoverished quarter of London. Cannibalizing his father's stock, which included fine blocks by the master woodcutter Thomas Bewick, he began publishing broadsheets and duodecimo chapbooks for children. As canny with money as his father had been inadequate, he overcame the active hostility from John Pitts and other established rivals to become the leading broadsheet seller of his day.

Catnach's career came at an important phase in the development of popular literacy. The turbulent Napoleonic period created a demand for information, but books and even newspapers were too expensive for any but the élite few. The 'literature of the poor' since the seventeenth century had been the broadsheet, but the popular ballad tradition was largely rural, and the urban masses demanded more immediate and grittily realistic reading matter. Catnach in particular set about satisfying this demand, and commissioned a constant stream of sensational ephemera on the interests of the day. On occasion he would write ballads himself, and hack his own woodcuts. He bridged between the oral and printed ballad, keeping a fiddler on hand and insisting on hearing an item before accepting it for printing. Many of his broadsheets were sold by 'patterers', who would perform as well as selling their wares.

Printed crudely on the cheapest paper available, on sheets measuring approximately 502 mm x 375, the broadsheets were paid for in the pennies that Catnach would take to the bank weekly in sacks, and he was reputed to have paved his parlour with counterfeit coins. His sheets capitalized on the sensational, and were sometimes hoaxes. In 1818 he was imprisoned for libel when a print suggesting a Mr Pizzey of Clare Market, London, made his sausages from human flesh caused a riot. Crime was his best-selling subject. In 1823 when John Thurtell and his accomplices murdered William Weare, Catnach was claimed to have printed 250,000 broadsheets on the trial, working day and night on four presses, and making over £500 profit. He commissioned 'last dying confessions' to be sold under the drop at public executions, causing disappointment if there was a last-minute reprieve.

Catnach's broadsheets, like those of his rivals, were often crude and opportunistic. Nevertheless they played a significant role in developing a literate public at the beginning of the nineteenth century. He specialized in a wide variety of crude but attractive children's books and alphabets, priced between a farthing and a penny, contributing to popular education. Reacting to the events and fashions of the moment, he made broadsheets the popular chronicles of the times, in some respects more informative than newspapers, for journals recorded events, while his sheets reflected popular reactions to them. Developments such as public transport, the Metropolitan Police Act of 1829, Princess Victoria's 1837 accession, and the fashions of the day, all took their place alongside accounts of sensational murders, sheets of religious reflections, and plain invention in his inexhaustible output. The historian Thomas Babington Macaulay was an avid collector of ballads as a source of popular history, and the broadsheet format was imitated by religious tract societies and other middle-class reform propagandists.

Catnach prepared the way for the change in popular readership that took place by the 1840s, when cheaper print and a higher level of literacy brought in the modern era of circulation newspapers, and sales of broadsheets dwindled. This Catnach did not live to see. In 1839, aged forty-six, he retired to Dancer's Hill, South Mimms, Barnet, reputedly with a modest fortune of £10,000. When visiting his Seven Dials shop at 2 Monmouth Court, St Giles, London, on 1 February 1841 he collapsed and died of jaundice; his property was bequeathed to his surviving sister, Anne Ryle. He was buried in Highgate cemetery, Middlesex.   LOUIS JAMES

Sources D. Buchan, *The ballad and the folk* (1972) · R. Collinson, *The story of street literature* (1973) · W. Henderson, ed., *Victorian street ballads* (1937) · C. Hindley, *The Catnach Press* (1869) · C. Hindley, *The life and times of James Catnach* (1878); repr. (1970) · 'The poetry of Seven Dials', *QR*, 122 (1867), 382–406 [review] · H. Mayhew, *London labour and the London poor*, ed. J. Ginsberg, 1 (1983), 234–317 · V. E. Neuberg, *The penny histories* (1968) · V. E. Neuberg, *Popular literature: a history and guide* (1977) · L. Shepard, *The broadside ballad* (1962) · L. Shepard, *The history of street literature* (1973) · 'Street ballads', *National Review*, 26 (July 1861) · D. Vincent, *Literacy and popular culture: England, 1750–1914* (1989)
Archives BL, collections of broadsheets · Bodl. Oxf., collections of broadsheets · CUL, collections of broadsheets
Wealth at death £6000–£10,000: Hindley, *Life and times*

Cato Street conspirators (*act.* **1820**) plotted the mass assassination of the British cabinet from a loft in Cato Street, Marylebone, London, in 1820. Of the ten tried for high treason, five were transported and five executed. The latter comprised the leader, Arthur *Thistlewood, and four impoverished tradesmen: **John Thomas Brunt** (1782–1820), a bootcloser, born on Union Street, off Oxford Street, London; an unemployed cabinetmaker, William *Davidson; **James Ings** (*bap.* 1794, *d.* 1820), a butcher, recently arrived in London from Waltham, Hampshire; and **Richard Tidd** (*bap.* 1773, *d.* 1820), born at Grantham, Lincolnshire, a shoemaker. The conspiracy was wider and of longer maturation than the trials established. The prosecution, anxious to reveal neither the scope of government intelligence sources nor the extent of political unrest, offered only limited evidence. The defence mainly sought to establish the conspiracy as the work of an *agent provocateur*, George *Edwards, a Fleet Street model maker.

A government spy since arriving in London from Windsor early in 1818, Edwards certainly helped precipitate the affair by colluding in the fiction that the cabinet would dine at the Grosvenor Square home of the earl of Harrowby, lord president of the council, on 23 February 1820. Police and guardsmen raided the Cato Street loft early that evening. In the fight that ensued Richard Smithers, a Bow Street officer, was stabbed and killed by Thistlewood. Though he and other conspirators initially escaped, all who had been present in the loft were eventually captured. Two turned king's evidence: Robert Adams (a shoemaker) and a baker, **John Harrison** (*b.* 1786, *d.* after 1830). This eliminated any need for Edwards, on watch in Grosvenor Square on the night of the 23rd, to appear at the trial.

The conspirators had deep roots in London ultra-radicalism. Tidd had allegedly been involved in the Despard conspiracy of 1802. Nearly all the others had been involved in the Spencean Philanthropists, admirers of the agrarian revolutionary Thomas Spence. After he died in 1814 they were consistently at the heart of political conspiracy in the capital and maintained an extensive correspondence with provincial ultra-radicals. It was the Spenceans who organized the great radical meeting at Spa Fields on 2 December 1816, which they intended as the signal for a general rising. During the autumn they had made a concerted play to win over the London trades and secure Henry Hunt as a speaker to attract a capacity crowd. Hunt, however, insisted that Spencean sentiments be removed from resolutions presented to the meeting, causing purists in the society to secede and leaving the 'Spencean conservative committee' in the hands of Thistlewood, James *Watson, and Thomas *Preston. Preston, a shoemaker born on 22 February 1774 in a slum court (Huggin's Alley, Paul's Court) off Cheapside, London, was severely lame, the consequence of childhood neglect by a nurse to whom he was farmed out by his mother and stepfather. This, though, had not impeded a picaresque career which had taken him to Ireland (where, about 1790, he led a Cork shoemakers' strike) and in 1797 to the West Indies, evading arrest at the time of William Pitt's suppression of London radicalism.

Expectations for the Spa Fields meeting ran high in both capital and provinces. 'In the course of the Day', it was reported from Lancashire on 2 December, 'the Tower in London was taken by the Rioters … all agree in expressing the fullest determination to have mustered and armed immediately, in case the disturbance in London had been attended with Success' (PRO, HO 40/4/1[2], 3 Dec 1816). Though the meeting dissolved into widespread rioting, the intended assault on prisons and the Tower was aborted. The most serious violence occurred during the looting of City of London gunsmiths, at one of which a customer was shot, possibly by James Watson's son. Only at nightfall was order fully restored.

The events of 2 December 1816 were pivotal to the evolution of Cato Street. They suggested that a mass meeting, however large, would not alone generate the momentum necessary to destabilize the capital, and that the authorities would always be prepared for unrest. Thereafter the Spenceans favoured covert tactics. It was reported that they 'cherished some desperate project' for a further Spa Fields rally on 10 February 1817, a rumour given force by meetings they held with provincial delegates a few days before (PRO, HO 42/158, 29 Jan and 7 Feb 1817). This meeting passed peaceably, but from its platform Hunt pointedly dissociated himself from the Spenceans. The effect was to incline them further to the politics of conspiracy: 'They … say the Philanthropy and Benevolence of Spencean Principles will never effect any Change, and that Luddism is best calculated for the times', reported an informer (PRO, HO 40/7[1], fol. 1929, report of J. Shegoe, 30 June 1817). Plans were devised for a *coup d'état* during Bartholomew fair in August. Under any circumstances this annual Smithfield fair tended to be riotous, and the plot was serious enough for the home secretary, Lord Sidmouth, to compare it to the Despard conspiracy. Preparations were called off at the last moment when the conspirators were confronted by hastily assembled official precautions. Thomas Preston, who had taken final leave of his family, 'declared he was so disappointed, that if he had had a Pistol by him, he thinks he should have blown his brains out' (PRO, HO 42/170, 9 Sept 1817).

The government, concerned to protect its intelligence sources, took no action against those involved. It was now Thistlewood who invoked Despard, suggesting that the mass assassination of the privy council should now be their objective. Another Spencean, Surrey paperhanger **John George** (1776/7–1842), also endorsed this tactic, 'the best signal … that would set all going' (PRO, HO 42/188, 30 June 1817). However, an attack on the Tower and Bank of England during the night of 11 October had to be abandoned when only eighty men mustered in the City. Further risings were mooted for 5 November and in January 1818, and again abandoned.

George Edwards was introduced to the group at about this time by his brother William (a City of London police officer and *bona fide* Spencean since 1812) and was commissioned to produce a bust of Thomas Spence. He quickly became a central member of the group and a keen proponent of the assassination tactic. The Spenceans, however, saw in the burgeoning politicization of the northern manufacturing districts an alternative route by which revolution might be instigated. Early in August 1819 Edwards reported to the Home Office that the conspirators looked 'with great Anxiety to the Manchr. Meeting on Monday, where they expect the Row to begin, and this they look upon as the Signal' (PRO, HO 42/191, 6 Aug 1819). The furious suppression of the Manchester meeting at St Peter's Field, which quickly led to its being named Peterloo, perhaps owed something to its association with the Spenceans in the government's mind. It galvanized the group, who immediately deemed it 'the revolution begun in blood'. 'For my own part I am ready now', declared the shoemaker Allen Davenport: 'I compare the present time to the French Revolution, we must arm ourselves as they did' (PRO, TS11/202, fol. 872; PRO, HO 42/197, 18 Oct 1819). In mid-October Thistlewood toured the provinces while the Spenceans worked the taprooms of London's poorest districts, particularly targeting Irish labourers. They contemplated using a rally on Clerkenwell Green on 1 November as the signal for an armed rising, but the subdued popular mood convinced them that more clandestine action was necessary. Shortly afterwards James Watson, the most inclined of the group to constitutional agitation, was imprisoned for debt. Without his restraining influence, the allure of attacking the cabinet dinner supposedly arranged for 23 February 1820 was hard to resist. James Ings even went so far as to prepare a placard to be displayed the following day, announcing the formation of a provisional government.

The full extent of the conspiratorial circles around Cato Street remains conjectural, but they clearly extended far beyond those who were tried. Viscount Sidmouth believed that 'a simultaneous explosion appears to be meditated at a early period' (Devon RO, Sidmouth papers, 152/M C1820/OH, 21 March 1820). When news of the Cato Street arrests reached the north, certain ultra-radicals 'were staggered and confounded' according to one observer (Richmond, 184–5). London shoemakers', coachmakers', tailors', and typefounders' trade societies lent active support, the latter by casting bullets. A number of arms caches were discovered, one at the home of John George's son, Robert, a discharged sailor.

The government, however, was primarily concerned to secure swift and exemplary verdicts upon Thistlewood and those with him when Richard Smithers was killed. Thus, Robert George and Preston avoided prosecution, even though the latter was known to have been preparing to seize cannon from the headquarters of the Honourable Artillery Company on 23 February. John George was another who escaped punishment, presumably in order not to expose the full extent of the government's informer network. George subsequently earned a living as a self-employed decorator but was reduced, possibly as a result of white lead poisoning, to manual labouring by the late 1830s. He died at Lambeth on 9 August 1842.

Brunt, Ings, Davidson, Tidd, and their leader were tried with high treason and murder, sentenced to death, and hanged at Newgate on 1 May 1820. Their corpses having been decapitated, they were all interred in quicklime inside the gaol later the same day. The crown witness Robert Adams was released without trial but almost immediately imprisoned for debt. His colleague John Harrison was transported to Australia, where he opened a bakery in Bathurst, New South Wales, and where Sir Roger Therry describes a meeting with him in 1830. Two other transported conspirators, John Strange and James Wilson, became police constables in New South Wales. A campaign led by the City radical Alderman Wood to bring Edwards to justice failed and the latter disappeared. Under the alias of George Parker, he settled in South Africa and died at Green Point, Cape Town, on 30 November 1843. The leading conspirator who lived longest was Thomas Preston, active in metropolitan radicalism until his death on 1 June 1850: at his funeral the coffin was draped with a red flag and accompanied by the banner of the Marylebone Chartists' Emmett League. The last surviving conspirator was almost certainly the unnamed 'master shoemaker' who, still insisting on anonymity, detailed his involvement in the autobiography he published at the age of eighty-one in 1879 (*Boot and Shoemaker*, 14 June – 6 Sept 1879).

MALCOLM CHASE

Sources M. Chase, *The people's farm: English radical agrarianism, 1775–1840* (1988) · G. T. Wilkinson, *An authentic history of the Cato Street conspiracy* (1820) · PRO, HO 42/136–202; HO 44/1–6; TS 11/197–208 · D. Johnson, *Regency revolution: the case of Arthur Thistlewood* (1974) · H. Mackey, 'The complexion of the accused: William Davidson, the black revolutionary in the Cato Street conspiracy', *Negro Educational Review*, 3 (1972), 132–47 · 'Preston, Thomas', *DLB*, vol. 8 · 'George, John', *DLB*, vol. 10 · [A Master Shoemaker], 'My life and adventures', *Boot and Shoemaker* (14 June–6 Sept 1879) · A. B. Richmond, *Narrative of the condition of the manufacturing population*, 2nd edn (1825) · Devon RO, Sidmouth papers · J. Stanhope, *The Cato Street conspiracy* (1962) · I. Prothero, *Artisans and politics in early nineteenth-century London* (1979) · IGI · *Northern Star* (13 Aug 1842)

Archives Essex RO, Colchester, papers relating to examination for the attempted murder of the cabinet [Arthur Thistlewood] |

PRO, prosecution MSS from the conspirators' trial, HO 42, 136–202, HO 44/1–6, TS 11/197–208
Likenesses engravings (after drawings by A. Wivell), repro. in Wilkinson, *Authentic history*

Caton, Lauderic Rex (1910–1999), guitarist and composer, was born on 31 August 1910 in Arena, Cedros, Trinidad, the fourth son and last among the eight children of Robert Caton, a merchant, and Margaret Caton, a baker. His father, who was of St Lucian descent, left soon after his birth and he was brought up by his mother, a Trinidadian. He learned tonic solfa at school and from the age of ten taught reading, writing, and arithmetic in elementary school. He also learned to play his brother-in-law's guitar and took violin lessons while studying diesel engineering in Palo Seco, but was otherwise a self-taught musician on several instruments, including saxophone and double bass. He played banjo in San Fernando with local bands before forming his own Caton Orchestra, then in 1937 he joined the Williams Brothers Orchestra, playing saxophone as a replacement for David 'Baba' Williams, who had left Trinidad to join Ken 'Snake Hips' Johnson's orchestra in England. In 1938 he went to Fort de France, Martinique, to work at the music school of the pianist and saxophonist Stanley Braithwaite (later known as Stanley Carter). They travelled together to Paris, where Caton played with Martiniquan musicians and the Argentinian guitarist Oscar Alemán before moving on to Belgium; there he worked with and arranged for Americans and prominent local bands. In May 1940, on the eve of the German invasion of Belgium, he left for England.

In London Caton worked at Soho bottle parties and at the exclusive Embassy nightclub, where he played Afro-Cuban rhythms with Don Marino Barreto. He also purchased an amplifier and, using a plectrum, began to play amplified guitar in the style of the American electric guitar innovator Charlie Christian. Amplification enabled the guitar to move from its hitherto primary function as a rhythm instrument, and Caton, influenced by Christian's single-string improvising, created a sensation with his modern ideas. He formed a band at Jig's Club in Wardour Street which attracted the attention of jazz enthusiasts, and it was recorded during a session held there in 1941. These exciting atmospheric 78 r.p.m. recordings, issued under the name of the band's trumpeter, Cyril Blake, are the only surviving evidence of such events taking place in a wartime London nightclub.

Already lauded in the jazz world, Caton reached a wider public through radio broadcasts and recordings with the popular clarinettist Harry Parry. His guitar solos were analysed in *B.M.G.*, the leading fretted-instrument publication, and he maintained his high profile in the co-operative West Indian Swing Stars and with the band of the progressive trumpeter Johnny Claes. In 1944 he formed a trio at the Caribbean Club with the German pianist Dick Katz and the Jamaican double bass player Coleridge Goode. Playing a repertory inspired largely by Duke Ellington, the Caribbean Trio attracted the positive attention of critics and serious jazz followers who heard them in concert, as well as from the club's habitués. When

Lauderic Rex Caton (1910–1999), by unknown photographer, *c*.1949 [centre, with young admirers]

in 1947 they joined forces with the drummer Ray Ellington to make up the Ray Ellington Quartet, they formed one of the most popular musical groups of the immediate post-war period. Caton left when the quartet's full touring schedule made him unwell, but he continued to operate as a freelance, leading his own band intermittently and playing whatever style of music was required. During this period he lived with Minnie Elam, then a hotel waitress named Esther Hollis.

A prolific composer and arranger, Caton wrote several improvisational vehicles, including *The Java Joint*, *Thrust and Parry*, *Blues in E*, and *Swinging on a Rusty Gate*. His most important work was the extended *Sepia Symphony* in C minor (1945); this, based around drum rhythms for Shango religious ceremonies he heard in Trinidad as a child, was to have a controversial fate. Its entry in the Italia prize competition of 1949 was solicited by the BBC, which had already accepted the work for performance, but a series of inexplicable misunderstandings led to the corporation advising its withdrawal from the competition. Caton interpreted this treatment as racial discrimination and, although he continued to compose and arrange for others, the incident was responsible for a deepening sense of frustration. He became depressed, a state that led to his growing immersion in yoga and the ascetic life.

In 1951 Caton formed a vocal trio, but when this failed to make an impact he returned to nightclub work. He played with musicians from the new wave of Caribbean settlers such as the trumpeter Shake Keane, but by 1952 he was more occupied building amplifiers for other guitarists. He took an electronics course that enabled him to construct radios and televisions, then on 25 February 1954 he married Maxina McDonell (*b.* 1931), a shorthand typist, and the daughter of Donald John McDonell, a consulting engineer. Soon afterwards he was reunited with Coleridge Goode in the Dominoes, another popular instrumental quartet. In 1956 he joined a Latin-American quartet for a Mediterranean cruise, but when his marriage broke up shortly afterwards he gradually abandoned music. He worked for the Red Cross as a driver and mechanic, and elsewhere as a chauffeur. He did photographic work for a studio, then, following his retirement, became a virtual recluse. He saw few visitors but valuably assisted Val Wilmer in recording important aspects of African-Caribbean musical and social history.

Caton was a master of the electric plectrum guitar and a major pioneer in its introduction in Britain. He was highly regarded by other instrumentalists for over two decades, yet many jazz histories failed to give him due recognition. By their own admission he exercised a significant influence on Pete Chilver and Dave Goldberg, the two jazz guitarists more generally credited as being the British pioneers of the amplified instrument, while his students, official and unofficial, ranged from jazz exponents to the Nigerian highlife specialist Ambrose Campbell and Hank Marvin of the Shadows. He died at University College Hospital, Camden, London, on 9 February 1999, of stomach cancer, and was buried later that month in Port of Spain, Trinidad.

VAL WILMER

Sources S. Adams, 'Lauderic Caton: guitarist extraordinary', *B. M. G.: a Journal Devoted to the Banjo, Mandoline, and Guitar* (Sept 1941), 223–4 · Boxman, 'With the Six-stringers', *B. M. G.: a Journal Devoted to the Banjo, Mandoline, and Guitar* (June 1944), 163 · V. Wilmer, 'I've created a monster!', *Mojo*, 44 (1997), 25–6 · V. Wilmer, 'How we met', *Independent Sunday Review* (7 Feb 1993), 61 · personal knowledge (2004) · private information (2004)
Likenesses G. Pype, photograph, 1940, priv. coll. · Yvonne, photograph, *c.*1943–1945, priv. coll. · I. Rich, photograph, 1945, priv. coll. · photograph, *c.*1949, priv. coll. [*see illus.*] · V. Wilmer, photographs, 1992–3, priv. coll.
Wealth at death under £200,000 gross; under £10,000 net: administration, 6 May 1999, *CGPLA Eng. & Wales*

Caton, William (1636–1665), Quaker preacher, details of whose parentage and early childhood are unknown, was probably brought up in north-west England in an orthodox Calvinist environment of prayer, sermon, and scripture. At fourteen he was taken by his father to Swarthmoor Hall, near Ulverston in Lancashire, home of Judge Thomas Fell, vice-chancellor of the duchy of Lancaster, to be educated by an ordained relation who was then tutor to Fell's children. Caton so impressed the Fell family that he was made companion to the eldest son and sent to join him at Hawkshead grammar school, near Windermere. In the summer of 1652 the Quaker George Fox arrived at Swarthmoor Hall on the invitation of Fell's wife, Margaret. Caton was convinced by Fox and immediately began to question the spiritual value of the humanist curriculum and the authority of his teachers at Hawkshead. Margaret Fell, whom Fox had also convinced, allowed Caton to leave school and act as her secretary. Caton refers to Fox at this time as his 'tender-hearted Father' and to Margaret Fell as his 'Nursing Mother', who together had 'begotten me thro the Gospel' (Caton, 1689, 8). Swarthmoor subsequently became an important Quaker headquarters during the early development of the movement and in his *Journal* Caton describes how the Fells frequently played host to Friends from across England.

In early 1655 Caton left Swarthmoor to become an itinerant preacher, making his way through the midlands, East Anglia, and London, where he was joined by John Stubbs, who became a regular travelling companion. Caton and Stubbs then proceeded to Kent, where among their successes was the conversion of Samuel Fisher, an Oxford-educated Baptist minister. Their activities in Kent, as well as their rough and violent treatment at the hands of the local authorities, are well documented in contemporary accounts. In the autumn of 1655 Caton and Stubbs made their first trip to the Netherlands. They had little success, having no knowledge of Dutch and finding their translators unreliable and sometimes malicious. On his return in December 1655 Caton went on a tour of Scotland, concluding that it was a 'barren and rude Country' and that the Scots '*could not endure sound Doctrine*' (Caton, 1689, 33). However, while in Edinburgh Caton had meetings with General Monck, whom he found 'seemingly *moderate*' (ibid., 28). It was to be on Monck's order that the army protected Quakers from assault by angry mobs at the Restoration. In October 1656 Caton returned to the Netherlands, following a route previously taken by Stubbs and William Ames, who had succeeded in founding a small Quaker community in Amsterdam. Caton still had no Dutch, but his brief grammar school education turned out to be useful after all, allowing him to communicate Quaker arguments in Latin and then have them translated for a wider audience. He was less well received in Middelburg, where he was arrested, imprisoned, and eventually deported. Nevertheless Caton arrived once more in Amsterdam in April 1657, staying this time for about a year and occupying himself with the printing, publishing, and dispersing of Dutch translations of Quaker books that he had brought with him from England. He wrote several pamphlets himself during this stay, including a long general defence of Quaker principles, *The Moderate Enquirer Resolved* (1658), translated into Latin in 1660 and into Dutch in 1669. Caton also had some contact with the Jewish community in Amsterdam, having been entrusted by Margaret Fell with the task of having several of her books translated into Hebrew. Letters from Caton to Fell describe how he employed an excommunicated Dutch Jew to translate her pamphlet *A Loving Salutation* (1657), which was issued in Hebrew in Amsterdam in 1658. Several scholars have argued that this excommunicated Jew was the young Spinoza, leading to speculation about the possible influence of Quaker theology on the development of Spinoza's thought.

In late 1659 Caton was back in Swarthmoor, where he copied out 170 letters that had been sent to Margaret Fell by Quakers throughout Britain and Europe during the previous five years, apparently with the intention of publication. These letters comprise the William Caton MSS in the Library of the Society of Friends, London. Most of Caton's own letters to Fell and other Friends are to be found in the Swarthmoor collection in the same library. His correspondence is generally of greater historical and literary interest than his published writings, which lack the rhetorical power of those of his mentor Fox. The letters, however, are characterized by the lucid and expressive personal voice that occasionally breaks through the repetitive prose of the *Journal*, which was none the less a popular text among Quakers in the nineteenth century. A letter of particular interest is Swarthmoor MS 4, fol. 241, in which Caton describes the 'fantastical' celebrations that greeted the entrance of Charles II into London and expresses his fears for the safety of Quakers under the new regime. Indeed, soon after the Restoration Caton published *An abridgement ... of the remarkable chronologies which are contained in that famous ecclesiasticall history of Eusebius* (1661), in which he sought to draw a parallel between the sufferings of the early Christians and the contemporary persecution of Quakers.

In October 1661 Caton went on a tour of Germany accompanied by William Ames. In Heidelberg Caton had meetings with the elector palatine, Charles Lewis, over the issue of religious toleration and in Frankfurt and Worms he again used his knowledge of Latin to communicate with Jews and Jesuits. However, in Frankfurt he was also attacked by Catholic priests, recalling how they 'left me bleeding in the Temple, where I left pretty much of my blood behind me, as a Testimony against the Idolatry of that place' (Caton, 1689, 69). Politely refusing Fox's request to go on a mission to eastern Europe, Caton returned to Amsterdam and married Annekin Dirrix, a Dutch Friend, in November 1662 (on the same day that his frequent companion Ames was buried). By now Caton had mastered High and Low Dutch and began to publish in the vernacular in Amsterdam. Copies of four of his Dutch tracts are in the British Library. Caton's last known letter is dated November 1665, and a letter sent to Margaret Fell in December 1665 refers to his death in Amsterdam, possibly from the plague which had been ravaging the city for some time and the victims of which Caton had recently been tending.　　　　NICHOLAS MᶜDOWELL

Sources W. Caton, *A journal of the life of ... Will. Caton*, ed. G. Fox (1689) · N. Penney, ed., *The first publishers of truth* (1907) · W. Caton, letters to M. Fell, RS Friends, Lond., Swarthmoor MS 4, fols. 28, 261 [17 April 1657; May 1660] · W. Caton, letter to M. Fell, March 1658, RS Friends, Lond., Caton MS 3, fol. 507 · R. H. Popkin and M. J. Signer, eds., *Spinoza's first publication? The Hebrew translation of Margaret Fell's 'A loving salutation'* (1987) · W. C. Braithwaite, *The beginnings of Quakerism*, ed. H. J. Cadbury, 2nd edn (1970) · I. Ross, *Margaret Fell: mother of Quakerism* (1949) · *DNB* · W. I. Hull, *The rise of Quakerism in Amsterdam, 1655–1665* (1938) · *A journal of the life of ... Will. Caton to which are now added some of his letters* (1845) · M. Watkins, letter to M. Fell, Dec 1665, RS Friends, Lond., Swarthmoor MS 2
Archives RS Friends, Lond., letters incl. some to M. Fell | RS Friends, Lond., Swarthmoor MSS, corresp.

Catroe [St Catroe, Kaddroe, Cadroe] (900/01–971), abbot of St Felix, Metz, is the subject of a life written by Reimann (or Ousmann) at the request of Immo, abbot of Gorze from *c*.984. Reimann claims to have been a disciple of Catroe. According to his life, Catroe was born of noble Scottish parents, Fochereach and Bania, who had a special devotion to a shrine of St Columba, probably at Dunkeld. He was also related to 'Dovenaldus king of the Cumbrians' (presumably Donald son of Owen, or Dyfnwal map Ywain,

king of Strathclyde and Cumbria (r. *c*.940–73), to St Bean (associated with Glen Almond), and to the wife of one of the Scandinavian kings of York in the 940s (perhaps Erik Bloodaxe or Olaf Guthfrithson). His name appears to be Bretonnic, or possibly Pictish. His parents originally intended him to have a secular career; but after a period in fosterage with a noble lay family, he was fostered by Bean and sent by him for education at Armagh. After studying there for a time, he returned to Scotland and taught at Bean's monastic school, possibly at Dunkeld. About his fortieth year, Catroe determined to go abroad on pilgrimage. The king of Scots, Constantine II (abdicated *c*.945), met him at a church dedicated to St Brigit, probably at Abernethy, and first tried to dissuade him from travelling abroad, but later relented on the advice of Abbot Maelodair (probably of Abernethy) and assisted him in his preparations. Catroe travelled through his relative Donald's kingdom of Strathclyde and Cumbria and on to York, where the king (named as Erik, perhaps erroneously—it may have been Olaf Guthfrithson) received him well because Catroe was related to his wife. Catroe proceeded to London, where part of the city was delivered from fire by his prayers; this brought him to the notice of the English king, Edmund (r. 939–46), at Winchester, who had him conducted to the channel by Oda, archbishop of Canterbury (941–58). He came to a channel port and sailed from there with other pilgrims to Boulogne. They proceeded from there first to the shrine of St Fursa at Péronne in Picardy.

The aristocracy of Lotharingia was at this time much influenced by the movement of monastic reform associated with the abbey of Gorze, near Metz. A noblewoman of the area called Hersent, wife of a nobleman called Eilbert, was impressed by the sanctity of the pilgrims and, being childless, proposed to bequeath her goods to them. A group of thirteen pilgrims was established at a place dedicated to St Michael in the forest of Thierache, where they enlarged the church and built dwellings. Catroe was elected superior, but declined; and the choice then fell on his companion Maccalan. Although the pilgrims were living as a religious community, they were not yet professed monks; so Hersent sent Maccalan to Gorze and Catroe to Fleury to make their monastic professions to the abbots of these houses. After a time Hersent recalled Maccalan to St Michael in Thierache; and when Catroe returned from Fleury, Hersent brought him to a place on the Meuse called Waulsort (Wassor), where she appointed him as prior (*c*.945). Soon after, Maccalan decided that the rule of both houses was too much for him, and persuaded Catroe to accept the title of abbot of Waulsort; his appointment was confirmed by King Otto I (later emperor). Monastic life increased and developed at Waulsort, and many new monks were received there. Catroe's fame spread, especially when it was reported that he had healed a monk called Girerus, wounded in the hand. Meanwhile his benefactress, Hersent, was moved to found a nunnery at Bucily; during the course of a visit Catroe cast out an evil spirit from one of the nuns. This brought him to the notice of Adalbero, the reforming bishop of Metz, who, on the advice of abbots Agenold of Gorze and Anstée de St Arnould of Metz, summoned him to the cathedral city. The bishop put Catroe in charge of the revival of a once famous but ruined abbey near Metz.

Catroe brought some of his monks from Waulsort to Metz. The remainder chose one of their number as his successor, and Catroe installed him as abbot there; but reportedly his successor fell away from 'the way of righteousness'. During Catroe's abbacy at Metz he travelled widely and performed a number of miracles, producing a spring of water at Waulsort, causing his abbatial staff to glow like the sun's rays, and healing the damaged eyes of a youthful companion. He healed John, abbot of Gorze, when he was sick and cast out a demon from one of the nuns of St Peter of Metz.

When Bishop Adalbero died in 964, his successor, Theodore, a member of the imperial family, transferred Catroe to the abbacy of St Felix of Metz. Catroe's fame reached the ears of the Empress Adelaide, mother of the future emperor, Otto II (r. 973–83), and he was summoned to meet her beside the Rhine. Before his departure he predicted that he would die before he could return, and he comforted all his friends in Metz. At the empress's court he performed his last living miracle, healing a man who had fallen from a height and broken many bones. His own body was now enfeebled with age and he besought the empress to let him return to his monastery and die there. Reluctantly she let him go; but he died, in 971, on the homeward journey between the Rhine and Metz. His remains were carried back and interred in his church of St Felix at Metz.   ALAN MACQUARRIE

Sources Reimann [Ousmann], 'De S. Cadroe abbate', Acta sanctorum: Martius (Antwerp, 1668), 469–81 · A. O. Anderson, ed. and trans., Early sources of Scottish history, AD 500 to 1286, 1 (1922), 431–43 · A. Macquarrie, The saints of Scotland, AD 450–1093 (1997), 199–210 · M. Coens, 'Le premier tome du legendier de Saint-Hubert', Analecta Bollandiana, 57 (1939), 109–22 · A. Dierkens, Abbayes et chapîtres entre Sambre et Meuse (1985) · DNB · W. F. Skene, ed., Chronicles of the Picts, chronicles of the Scots, and other early memorials of Scottish history (1867), 109–16

Cattanach, John (1885–1915), shinty player, was born at Newtonmore, Inverness-shire, on 2 February 1885, the youngest of the four children of William Cattanach, merchant, and his wife, Ann, née Kennedy. He was educated at Newtonmore and Kingussie public schools, George Watson's College, Edinburgh, and Edinburgh University, where he graduated in arts (MA 1907) and medicine (MB ChB 1912). His first medical appointment was at the Bangour Hospital, Linlithgow.

Cattanach was best-known in his native highlands as a shinty player; his peerless ability at the sport won him fame throughout the shinty-playing world. He is still held by many to have been the finest exponent of shinty ever, a tower of strength to the Newtonmore team, which he captained in a victorious season during a vintage period. Natural ability, superb physique, and a scientific approach to the playing of the ancient Celtic game marked him out from his many outstanding contemporaries. He trained hour after hour, with the ball on his camen (or club), darting round larch trees, catching the ball on his club before it touched the ground. On his way to play on the local field, the Eilan, he was said to run nearly a mile without letting the ball fall off his club. His most celebrated individual performance was when playing for Newtonmore against Furnace in shinty's premier event, the Camanachd cup final, at Glasgow in 1909. Newtonmore won 11–3, with Cattanach scoring eight goals, a cup final record which still stands. A controversial decision by shinty's ruling body in 1911 robbed Newtonmore of a cup final winning performance and left Cattanach, and many others in the Badenoch village, disillusioned. From then on he concentrated more on hockey and sprinting and he was capped for his country at both.

Cattanach was an accomplished all-round athlete, who excelled at the long jump and on the track. His aptitude with stick and ball extended to hockey, and while a member of the Carlton hockey club he was chosen as centre forward for Scotland in the international match with Wales in 1912. He also made his mark in Scottish amateur athletics. In 1909 and 1910 he won the long jump at Edinburgh University sports, and represented the university in the Scottish inter-university contests, 1909–11. In 1910 he was second in the 100 yards and long jump, and in 1911 he won the long jump (20 ft 10 in.) and an athletic international cap for Scotland against Ireland in Dublin. He reappeared on the track in 1913 and 1914, winning the Rangers Football Club 100 yards handicap (off 10 yards) in the fast time of 9.45 seconds.

In October 1914 Cattanach enlisted and obtained a commission as a lieutenant in the Royal Army Medical Corps. Attached to the 9th Royal Warwickshire regiment, he died in the Dardanelles in July 1915, of wounds sustained during the Gallipoli campaign. He was buried at Gallipoli.

HUGH D. MACLENNAN

Sources Badenoch Record (7 Aug 1915) · BMJ (14 Aug 1915), 271 · The Lancet (14 Aug 1915), 361 · graduation records, U. Edin. L., special collections division, university archives · J. E. MacKenzie, ed., University of Edinburgh roll of honour, 1914–1919 (1921) · registrar documents (birth record), Inverness · J. Richmond, 'Newtonmore', Shinty yearbook (1977–8), 32–4 · K. Maclean, 'Newtonmore', Book of remembrance (1939), 42

Likenesses photograph, repro. in Edinburgh University roll of honour, 1

Cattell, Clara Jane (1860–1923). See under Cattell, (Fanny) Maud (1857–1947).

Cattell, (Fanny) Maud (1857–1947), nurse, was born on 23 April 1857 at Sheldon, Warwickshire, the second of the ten children of John Cattell (bap. 1828, d. 1921), farmer, and his wife, Fanny Mary (bap. 1832, d. 1908), daughter of William Pate, farmer, of Haddenham, Cambridgeshire, and his wife, Mary. Known as Maud, she was probably educated at home by a governess. She learned housekeeping and cookery, and nursed family and friends, including her sister Emma Maria (1862–1932), who fell off a donkey, permanently injuring her leg.

In September 1886, aged twenty-nine, Cattell joined the Anglican evangelical Mildmay Mission and was trained as a deaconess by Mrs Pennefather at Mildmay Park, London. After several months at the Caledonian Road Mission, she went to the old Mildmay Mission Hospital, Turville Street, Bethnal Green. She was sent to train at the Middlesex Hospital for a year from September 1888 to take charge of a ward, and was considered 'excellent in every way and a most efficient nurse' (Middlesex Hospital, register of lady probationers, 1878–1905, 32). She returned to the old Mildmay Hospital, which was replaced in November 1892 by a new one with fifty beds, in Austin Street, Bethnal Green. She served as sister of the women's ward briefly, before becoming 'helper', and 'second in the staff' to the matron, Miss Goodwyn, whom she succeeded in November 1896, retaining this post until her retirement in 1919.

An able administrator and meticulous record-keeper, Cattell was responsible, under the medical superintendent, for her nurses and for the day-to-day running of the hospital, which provided patient services for the surrounding impoverished areas, and trained nurses for missionary work. It depended on charity and Maud recognized the importance of careful financial management. In her last years there she witnessed the decline of the Mildmay Mission through shortage of income. Only the mission's two hospitals survived, managed independently of the Mildmay Trust.

Maud's final years proved the most difficult. Staff shortages caused by the war effort were followed by problems with the drains, which closed the hospital in 1916. She helped to negotiate medical cover with the Elizabeth Garrett Anderson Hospital, to enable its partial reopening in 1917, and sought suitable hospitals to continue probationer training. During an air raid in 1917 the hospital received thirty-six casualties caused by the bombing. The closure of the trustees' offices in Mildmay Park in 1917 created extra administrative work. Cattell undertook the cooking, when there was no cook, for two months in 1918. When the war ended the hospital returned to full working order. Cattell felt that it needed a 'younger woman' to carry on the work (Mildmay Mission Hospital, council minute book, MM/A/2/1, 43). She stayed on to train Dora Woodhouse, who took up her duties on 12 August 1919.

Maud had an imposing and dignified presence. She was fairly tall and always slim, walking straight and upright. Her hair was originally dark, and she had a round face. As she got older, she wore glasses.

> During her thirty three years of service … she worked unremittingly for the good of all, and to the many who were privileged to serve under her she was not only 'Matron', but 'Mother' and friend. Her loving consideration for everyone under her care was a marked characteristic and the verse which constantly comes to mind in reference to her is, 'I am among you as he that serveth.' … She passed on to her nurses the habit of care over detail. For many years she [kept] … the accounts of the Hospital … most beautifully. It is impossible to estimate how much the Hospital owes to her guidance and to the faithful Christian witness of her life. (*Mildmay Mission Hospital Magazine*, 1)

In retirement Maud lived at Sheldon with her father and her sisters Clara and Emma. Latterly her married sister Hannah May Kemp (1866–1955) cared for her. She died on 25 June 1947 at home, at South Bank, Sheldon, Birmingham, and was buried at St Giles's Church, Sheldon, three days later.

Maud was assisted by her sister **Clara Jane Cattell** (1860–1923), who trained at the Brownlow Hill Infirmary, Liverpool, from 1883 to 1886. She worked abroad as a private nurse, mainly in Switzerland, becoming a registered nurse in 1890, when she joined the Mission Hospital, and became a deaconess. She was sister of the men's ward from November 1892 until 1907, when she left to care for her parents. Tougher than Maud, she 'gave herself unreservedly and whole heartedly to the task of nursing, teaching, and soul-winning in the wards with marked success' (Mildmay Mission Hospital, annual report, 1907, 7). She died on 23 January 1923 at Sheldon, and was buried there three days later.

J. HAMPSON

Sources Mildmay Mission Hospital, register of nurses, 1886–1909, Royal London Hospital Archives Centre, Mildmay archives, MM/N/1/1 · Mildmay Mission Hospital, register of nurses, 1908–36, Royal London Hospital Archives Centre, Mildmay archives, MM/N/1/2 · Mildmay Mission Hospital, annual reports, 1892–1900, Royal London Hospital Archives Centre, Mildmay archives, MM/A/8/2 · Mildmay Mission Hospital, annual reports, 1903–7, Royal London Hospital Archives Centre, Mildmay archives, MM/A/8/4 · Mildmay Mission Hospital, annual reports, 1912–21, Royal London Hospital Archives Centre, Mildmay archives, MM/A/8/6 · Middlesex Hospital, register of lady probationers, 1878–1905, Middlesex Hospital Archives, 32 · *Mildmay Mission Hospital Magazine*, 18/3 (Sept 1947), 1 [Mildmay Mission Hospital] · Mildmay Mission Hospital, council minute book, 1917–34, Royal London Hospital Archives Centre, Mildmay archives, MM/A/2/1 · Mildmay Mission Hospital, house committee minute book, 1917–21, Royal London Hospital Archives Centre, Mildmay archives, MM/A/3/2 · *Service for the king: a record of the Mildmay Missions*, 7th ser., 83 (Aug 1886), 191 [Mildmay Mission Hospital] · *The story of the Mildmay Mission Hospital*, Friends of Mildmay Mission Hospital [n.d.] · Liverpool Workhouse committee minutes, 13 Sept 1883, Lpool RO, 353 SEL 10/11 · register of nurses, entry 206, 7 March 1890, Royal British Nurses' Association archives · H. Burdett, ed., *Burdett's official nursing directory* (1899), 390 · private information (2004) · b. cert. · d. cert. · bur. cert., St Giles, Sheldon [1947] · baptism register, St Giles, Sheldon, no. 1, 1813–1861, Birm. CA, DRO 42/1 · b. cert. [Clara Jane Cattell] · d. cert. [Clara Jane Cattell] · burial register, St Giles, Sheldon, no. 2, 1900–39, Birm. CA, DRO 42/2

Archives Lpool RO, Liverpool Workhouse archives, Liverpool Workhouse committee minutes, 353 SEL 10/11 · Middlesex Hospital, archives, register of lady probationers · Mildmay Mission Hospital, London, Mildmay archives · Royal British Nurses' Association archives, London, register of nurses · Royal London Hospital Archives Centre, London, Mildmay archives

Likenesses group photograph, 1904 (with parents and siblings), priv. coll. · photograph, after 1904, Mildmay Mission Hospital, London; repro. in *Mildmay Mission Hospital Magazine*, 18/3 (Sept 1947)

Wealth at death £11,781 10s. 10d.: probate, 8 Oct 1947, CGPLA Eng. & Wales · £3410 18s. 5d.—Clara Jane Cattell: probate, 1923, CGPLA Eng. & Wales

Catterick [Ketterich], **John** (d. 1419), bishop of Coventry and Lichfield, was from Yorkshire, quite likely from near the North Riding village. His immediate origins are unknown, but in his will he remembered two sisters, Matilda and Margaret, and also the latter's two daughters. Robert Catterick, to whom he gave a prebend in Lichfield Cathedral, was his nephew and inherited all his books.

John Catterick was master of arts of Oxford by 1398, bachelor of both laws by 1401, and licentiate in canon law by 1406. Evidently he impressed his fellow student, Bishop Henry Beaufort of Lincoln, and had entered his service by 14 January 1400. His preferment came entirely from the bishop, notably as treasurer of the cathedral on 21 March 1403. When Beaufort was translated to Winchester, Catterick went with him as his chancellor in 1405, still holding this post in September 1408 when he made a visitation of the cathedral. He and Beaufort moved the emphasis of his preferments to Winchester too, notably as archdeacon of Surrey on 12 November 1410.

Although Catterick was called 'king's clerk' on 2 March 1403, this was simply for a visitation of a hospital in the king's jurisdiction. It was the need for the king to justify his execution of Archbishop Richard Scrope, and control the consequent vacancy at York, that elevated Catterick's career from local to national; while Archbishop Thomas Arundel was aghast, Henry's Beaufort kin rallied round: on 3 July 1405 Catterick set off 'in all haste' to help defend the king's position in the Roman curia, returning to London only on 3 February 1406. Beaufort then had him included in his own mission to Calais, from 26 March to 22 May 1406; from 6 October to 23 December he was touring trading centres in Germany and the Low Countries; and until October 1411 he was often engaged in lengthy embassies to France to try to keep the truce with France or turn it into something more secure. Possibly his continuing association with Beaufort in both diplomacy and diocese reduced his attraction to Henry IV at that point, but on 18 April 1412 he was preparing to go abroad once more, reason unspecified. On 1 July 1409 he had been appointed as a papal notary, not in itself demanding attendance in the curia but a signal that he had made his mark, and in 1413 was referred to as a notary in the papal chancery. More to the point, on 22 May 1413 the new king, Henry V, who had made Beaufort chancellor immediately after his accession, appointed Catterick his permanent proctor to the Roman curia.

On 27 April 1414 Catterick was papally provided to the see of St David's, was consecrated by John XXIII, perhaps at Bologna, and received the temporalities on 2 June. In a rare moment of public candour, the pope allowed him to retain some of his benefices until a 'fatter' see could be found for him. This became possible that same week, although distance meant the appointment to Coventry and Lichfield took time; he was elected by the chapter (perhaps on 23 July), received custody of the temporalities on 13 October, and was translated formally on 1 February 1415. Meanwhile, on 20 October 1414 he was appointed one of the king's representatives at the Council of Constance. He took part there in the deposition of his recent host, John XXIII, as one of the commissaries to take evidence against him. Shortly after 23 May 1415 he left for England, with a commission to collect papal revenues, but really to consult with his principals. He was home in time to receive French envoys at Winchester on 4 July and act as a witness to Henry V's will at Southampton on the 24th.

On 20 July 1416 Catterick was reappointed by the king as a proctor at Constance, although his commission on 5 August to discuss the council with the duke of Burgundy probably delayed his journey. On 21 December he had a wide commission to seek trading opportunities with Aragon, Genoa, the Hanse, and German princes, probably through contacts at Constance. On 18 July 1417 he was named by the king as one of the five bishops who were to direct all English delegates at the council, enabling Henry to control the vote of this 'nation'. The day after the death of Bishop Robert Hallum at Constance on 4 September, Cardinal des Ursins wrote to the king recommending Catterick for the vacancy at Salisbury, noting the judgment and learning he had shown during the council. In fact, because of the vacancy in the papacy and the king's absence in France, John Chaundler, the innocuous dean of Salisbury, had the promotion by election and without papal provision; possibly Archbishop Henry Chichele, no friend to Beaufort, had a hand in this peculiarity. Meantime Thomas Polton, another of the English bishops at the council, had met Beaufort at Ulm and brought him to Constance. There Beaufort dramatically swung the English delegation and, in turn, the whole council to making an election of a pope and in effect ending its own existence. Catterick then went with Martin V in early 1418 into Italy in his former role as king's proctor, and was with him, for example, on 5 May 1419 at Mantua. In the previous month he had been authorized to take all Normans in the curia into Henry V's obedience. It emerged years later that he had also been working and paying out money to gain Beaufort a personal and diocesan exemption from the jurisdiction of the archbishop of Canterbury, which would have outraged Chichele and Henry V, had it come to pass.

On 20 November 1419 he was elected to the see of Exeter, with royal assent. However, on 28 December he died at Florence, where the papal curia had been staying since February. In accordance with a codicil to his will, he was buried in the Franciscan church of Santa Croce there, in the centre of the nave near the choir. After some pious bequests to a few kin and of twelve cups to Beaufort, his residual estate went especially to 'poor land labourers who have lost animals by murrain and are otherwise depressed by misfortune' (*Register of Henry Chichele*, 2.179), especially on his own estates. He had probably never seen these people. Just possibly he may have managed a brief visit to his Lichfield diocese in 1416, but he had always left the administration to deputies. It is unsurprising that he expressed no wish for burial there. R. G. DAVIES

Sources Emden, *Oxf.* · R. G. Davies, 'The episcopate in England and Wales, 1375–1443', PhD diss., University of Manchester, 1974, 3.lxxv–viii · E. F. Jacob, ed., *The register of Henry Chichele, archbishop of Canterbury, 1414–1443*, 2, CYS, 42 (1937), 178–82 · *The register of John Catterick, bishop of Coventry, 1415–1419*, ed. R. N. Swanson, CYS, 77 (1990)

Cattermole, George (1800–1868), watercolour painter and illustrator, was born on 10 August 1800 in the village of Dickleburgh, near Diss, Norfolk, the youngest of seven

George Cattermole (1800–1868), by unknown artist

children, six sons and a daughter, of parents whose names are not known.

Early life and training, 1800–1820 Cattermole's mother died when he was very young and he was raised and taught by his father, a man of independent means. He was a great reader, familiar with Shakespeare and Scott from an early age. Cattermole knew history well, especially English history, was a good Latin scholar, and wrote in a correct and classic style. He may have served as an assistant at his father's school in Norfolk before his departure for London, where he arrived by 1819.

Soon thereafter, Cattermole began work as an architectural draughtsman for the antiquary John Britton and developed his skills of observation and accuracy, training congenial with his antiquarian and artistic interests.

Published illustrations, 1821–1844 With one of his brothers, the Revd Richard *Cattermole (1795?–1858), Cattermole contributed to two of Britton's most important series of publications: *Cathedral Antiquities of England* (14 vols., 1814–35) and *The Architectural Antiquities of Great Britain* (1807–26). Of the former Cattermole contributed to four volumes and Richard to three. Some of the most elaborate engraved drawings appear above the name of George Cattermole: nineteen in the volume on Canterbury and seven in that for Oxford, both published in 1821, twelve for Wells in 1824, and one drawing for Peterborough in 1828. Eighteen engravings after Cattermole's drawings appear in the fifth volume (1826) of *Architectural Antiquities*.

Cattermole illustrated numerous books. *Evenings at*

Haddon Hall (1832), edited by the baroness de Calabrella, contained twenty-four fancy subjects, which were 'supposed to be in a portfolio, turned over by a birthday party, confined to the house at Haddon by the snow' (Roget, 2.73). In the 1830s Cattermole travelled to Scotland to sketch localities mentioned in the Waverley novels by Walter Scott. Five drawings illustrating scenes from four of Scott's novels were exhibited between 1836 and 1850 at the Old Watercolour Society. Certain of Cattermole's drawings were engraved for illustrations to later editions of the Waverley novels. Twenty-one engravings after drawings by Cattermole were published in *Heath's Pictorial Annual for 1835: Scott and Scotland* by Leitch Ritchie. In his art Cattermole gave visual expression to Scott's evocation of a bygone age in Scotland. He also illustrated volumes 1 (1841) and 2 (1844) of Richard Cattermole's *The Great Civil War of Charles I and the Parliament*, with a total of twenty-eight engravings after his picturesque and vigorous sketches.

Bachelor days, 1819–1839 Cattermole enjoyed riding as a young man, and was an excellent carriage driver. His natural vivacity and good fellowship caused him to be a general favourite. He was a good conversationalist in both French and Spanish, and a man of literary tastes, who preferred intellectual associates of the more brilliant kind. An intimate of Count d'Orsay and Lady Blessington at Gore House, he was part of their circle of fashionable people from the worlds of art and literature in London. He was a member of the Garrick Club, and in 1838 was elected to the Athenaeum. In the late 1830s he moved into a suite of private chambers in The Albany, formerly occupied first by Lord Byron (of whom he made a posthumous drawing now in a private collection, after the portrait by Richard Westall, 1813) and later by Edward Bulwer-Lytton. Cattermole included among his close friends Robert Browning, Bulwer-Lytton, Charles Dickens, Benjamin Disraeli, Douglas Jerrold, Sir Edwin Landseer, Thomas Macaulay, Daniel Maclise, William Macready, Clarkson Stanfield, and William Makepeace Thackeray. In July 1839, as a result mainly of the positive reception to his drawing *Luther and his Adherents at the Diet of Spires* (1839; V&A), Cattermole was offered a knighthood, which he modestly declined. This was one of several incidents in which 'he thought fit to decline proposals the acceptance whereof might have been of advantage to him in the world' (Roget, 2.64).

Exhibition years, 1819–1850 Just before the publication of his first illustrations, Cattermole began to exhibit his architectural drawings. Two of Peterborough Cathedral appeared at the Royal Academy in 1819 and 1822, and a drawing of Wells Cathedral was shown at the Society of Painters in Water Colours in 1821. Altogether he exhibited 105 works between the years 1819 and 1850: six drawings at the Royal Academy between 1819 and 1827, two works at the British Institution in 1827, and, most importantly, from 1822 to 1850, ninety-seven drawings at the Society of Painters in Water Colours, which established his fame. He was elected an associate on 6 April 1822 and, having allowed his associateship to lapse, again on 9 February 1829, before becoming a full member on 10 June 1833. Cattermole became the foremost British historical painter in watercolours, influenced by the examples of two fellow countrymen in the same medium: the intimate historical subjects of Richard Parkes Bonington and the bold and loose handling of colour by David Cox.

Among the principal works Cattermole exhibited at the Old Watercolour Society were: *Sir Walter Raleigh Witnessing the Execution of the Earl of Essex in the Tower* (1839), *The Contest for the Bridge* (1844; V&A), and *Benvenuto Cellini Defending the Castle of St. Angelo* (1845). Although *The Diet of Spires* proved to be a great popular triumph in 1839, Cattermole considered it one of his least successful works, calling it laboured, because he was obliged to follow portraits and other authorities, when he abhorred copying from any sort of model.

In his earlier drawings Cattermole's practice had been to use transparent watercolours. However, in his more mature work he used body colour lavishly, painting with a loaded brush on thick absorbent paper, of a low tone and warm tint, prepared especially for him by Messrs Winsor and Newton and known by his name. Cattermole opposed the heavy gold 'exhibition' frames then in use by galleries, considering that his delicately coloured drawings were seen to better advantage surrounded by a white matt.

Cattermole's last large-scale exhibited work was *The Unwelcomed Return* (1846), deemed 'a work of such power as not to be equalled in its kind by the utmost effort of any living artist' ('Society of Painters', 1846, 190–91). An exhibition review of 1847 opened with a comment about the lack of paintings from certain members: 'others, to whom all lovers of Art have been accustomed to look with interest, are absent. Mr. Cattermole contributes nothing … there are blanks in the Exhibition which will not be readily filled up' ('Society of Painters', 1847, 201). Cox, a fellow member of the Old Watercolour Society, stated in a letter: 'The great man, Cattermole, has behaved rather shabby; he has not sent one drawing' (Solly, 148). Additionally, Cattermole enjoyed the society of Royal Academicians more than that of his fellow members of the Old Watercolour Society. From 1845 to 1850 he showed only small drawings, and he showed nothing at all in 1851. An announcement at the end of the exhibition catalogue drew attention to his serious illness. By 29 December 1851 Cattermole was so severely ill that relatives and friends were summoned to his bedside. In June 1852 he retired from the Old Watercolour Society, in part to become a painter in oils, but also because he appeared to be unsuited to the rigours of the exhibition schedule.

Marriage and family, 1838–1850 In 1838 Cattermole met Clarissa Hester, the daughter of James Elderton, a deputy remembrancer of the court of the exchequer and a distant maternal relation of Dickens; they were married on 20 August 1839 at St Marylebone, Middlesex. They lived in the rural suburb of Clapham Rise until 1863, and there brought up nine children, four sons and five daughters. They were a close family who lived on terms of great mutual affection.

Travelling from Charing Cross Station by omnibus to Clapham, Cattermole closely observed the driver, to whom he gave the sobriquet Sloppy. He imitated his Cockney accent, speaking 'in the gruff, hoarse accents of what seemed to be the remains of a deep bass voice wrapped up in wet straw' (Forster, 2.393), and related nonsense about the eccentricities of Sloppy's imaginary friend Jack. These stories encapsulated the driver's hard experiences before he became a convert to temperance and delighted both William Powell Frith and Dickens, who recorded some of them in dialect and incorporated them into his later novels. Cattermole had a keen sense of humour, was almost prudish in regard for the conventionalities of life, and was a tory in his politics. His speech was precise and measured and he had a horror of vulgarity. Few artists dressed as well as he. Cattermole was a member of the Portwiners and the Shakespeare Society, for whom he gave frequent dinner parties; these were served by white-gloved servants in their spacious dining-room, fitted with Byron's carved furniture from his Albany chambers and hung with wallpaper decorated with gold bars, designed by Cattermole himself (Cohen, 131). Those were 'red-letter days when Dickens, Thackeray, Landseer, et al. gathered at the Cattermole residence in Clapham Rise, on which occasions they retired to brew punch in the studio filled with picturesque armour, tapestry, carved furniture' (Kitton, 135).

Cattermole and Dickens, 1837–1845 John Forster describes Dickens's opinion of Cattermole, as one of his companions at Twickenham in the late 1830s:

> another painter-friend was George Cattermole, who had then enough and to spare of fun as well as fancy to supply ordinary artists and humourists by the dozen, and wanted only a little more ballast and steadiness to possess all that could give attraction to good-fellowship. (Forster, 1.104–5)

Dickens commissioned Cattermole as an illustrator for his fourth and fifth novels, *The Old Curiosity Shop* (1840–41) and *Barnaby Rudge* (1841). Both were first published in weekly part sets in *Master Humphrey's Clock*, illustrated with woodcuts dropped into the text. Dickens offered Cattermole sentimental, heartfelt, and picturesque subjects, especially those involving his heroine little Nell in *The Old Curiosity Shop*. Shortly after Cattermole completed these Dickens commissioned a pair of watercolours: *Little Nell's Home* (Dickens House Museum, London) and its companion *Little Nell's Grave* (V&A), both of which were in Dickens's possession until his death.

In 1845 Dickens asked Cattermole to play Downright in a production by his amateur theatrical company of Ben Jonson's comedy *Every Man in his Humour*. Cattermole turned Dickens down for the initial performance, but he did act with the company for two additional presentations, in the character of Well-Bred.

Later years, 1852–1868 Cattermole's oil painting was not successful. Although accustomed to the copious use of body colour, his hand felt weighted by the task of dragging the more viscid medium of oil. He soon longed for the freer play he enjoyed when working in watercolour and returned to that medium, working at the easel with intense and unremitting devotion from early dawn until past midnight. Few of these late watercolours were seen or exhibited, and they seem to have gone from his studio directly into the hands of collectors.

Yet Cattermole's greatest successes in public exhibition outside London followed his resignation from the Old Watercolour Society. The eleven works he exhibited at the Universal Exhibition in Paris in 1855 created a sensation, and he was awarded a medal of honour. He was appointed a member of the Academie voor Beelende Kunsten, Amsterdam, on 13 February 1856 and invited to join the Belgian Society of Watercolour Painters. He exhibited thirty-one works in the Manchester Art Treasures exhibition in 1857 and thirteen works at the International Exhibition of 1862 in London.

Increasingly frail and reclusive, Cattermole was concerned for the future of his family. In the summer of 1856 Dickens wrote of the 'unhappy Cattermoles' living in a seaside villa let by his landlord, who complained that the Cattermoles never paid their bills. In London the family moved from Clapham Rise to Clapham Common in the early 1860s, for reasons of economy. The unexpected deaths of two of their children were a huge shock to Cattermole and his wife. Their youngest daughter died from gastric fever in 1862, and in September 1863 their eldest son, Ernest George, an officer in the Bengal army, died. These losses, aggravated by financial anxieties and worsened by his self-imposed seclusion, caused Cattermole to retire completely from society and he fell into a severe depression. He died at his home, 4 Cedars Road, Clapham Common, on 24 July 1868, leaving a widow, three sons, and four daughters. He was buried at Norwood cemetery near his first mentor, John Britton.

Cattermole was remembered as 'the most affectionate of husbands and fathers' (Taylor, 93). Several efforts were made to provide for the bereaved Cattermole family: Dickens started a private appeal, whose funds were turned over to Mrs Cattermole in mid-April 1869. A petition to the Royal Academy failed. At the request of Cattermole's old friend Disraeli, Queen Victoria placed Mrs Cattermole on the civil list for a pension of £100 per year. An auction of Cattermole's paintings, drawings, and books was held at Christies on 9 March 1869. Following his death ten works by Cattermole were shown at the Royal Jubilee Exhibition at Manchester in 1887. In April of the same year the Royal Society of Painters in Water Colours assembled forty drawings for a solo exhibition. In March 1889 Messrs J. and W. Vokins showed 117 of his works.

There are numerous drawings by Cattermole in public collections, as well as signed autograph letters, sketches, and notebooks. The Victoria and Albert Museum, in the Ellison gift and the Ashbee, Dixon, Forster, Harrod, and Townshend bequests, holds the principal collection of his work.   DELLA CLASON SPERLING

Sources J. L. Roget, A history of the 'Old Water-Colour' Society, 2 vols. (1891) • F. G. Kitton, Dickens and his illustrators (1899) • R. Davies, 'George Cattermole (1800-1868)', Old Water-Colour Society's Club, 9 (1931-2), 25–37 • DNB • S. Wilcox, 'George Cattermole', The dictionary of art (1996), vol. 6, pp. 90–91 • J. R. Cohen, Charles Dickens and his original illustrators (Columbus, OH, 1980) • [T. Taylor], 'The late George Cattermole', Art Journal, 32 (March 1870), 92–3 • 'British artists: their style and character, no. XXVI: George Cattermole', Art Journal, 19 (July 1857), 209–11 • Art Journal, 30 (Sept 1868), 180–81 • J. Britton, The autobiography of John Britton, 3 vols. in 2 (privately printed, London, 1849–50) • The letters of Charles Dickens, 1833 to 1870, ed. G. Hogarth and M. Dickens, 2 vols. (1893) • J. Forster, The life of Charles Dickens, 3 vols. (1872–4) • N. N. Solly, Memoir of the life of David Cox (1873) • 'Society of Painters in Water Colours: forty-second exhibition—1846', Art Union, 8 (June 1846), 190–92 • 'The Society of Painters in Water Colours: forty-third exhibition—1847', Art Union, 9 (June 1847), 201 • Graves, RA exhibitors • Graves, Brit. Inst. • Graves, Artists • CGPLA Eng. & Wales (1868)

Archives Devizes Museum, Wiltshire, Wiltshire Archaeological and Natural History Society, sketches, plans and prints relating to John Britton's Illustrations of Fonthill Abbey | Hunt. L., letters to C. Dickens and others

Likenesses B. E. Duppa, black and white chalk drawing, exh. 1899, Vokins, London • G. Cattermole, self-portrait, chalk drawing, BM • G. Cattermole, self-portrait, pencil drawing, V&A • E. Chatfield, oils • L. Price, photograph, repro. in Kitton, Dickens and his illustrators, pl. 38, facing p. 121 • pencil and crayon drawing, NPG [see illus.]

Wealth at death under £1000: probate, 11 Sept 1868, CGPLA Eng. & Wales

Cattermole, Richard (1795?–1858), writer and Church of England clergyman, was a brother of George *Cattermole (1800–1868), the artist. As a youth he drew some illustrations for John Britton's volumes of the History and Antiquities of Cathedral Churches. He was admitted as a sizar at Christ's College, Cambridge, on 14 October 1819, matriculated at Lent 1830, and as a 'ten-year man' was allowed to proceed to the degree of BD in 1831.

Cattermole was a curate at St Matthew's Church, Brixton, Surrey, from 1825 to 1831, and it was during his tenure there, on 17 May 1825, that he married Maria Frances Giles. They had a son, George Richard Coleridge Cattermole, who was baptized on 28 August 1828, with Samuel Taylor Coleridge standing as godfather. Coleridge and Cattermole had become acquainted through their association with the Royal Society of Literature, as Cattermole had been elected secretary to the society at its first meeting, on 17 June 1823, and conscientiously carried out his duties until his retirement from the post in 1852. He was also one of the first one hundred members of the Society of British Authors, which was established in 1843 in order to protect authors' copyrights and their relationships with publishers, but which unfortunately achieved little during his lifetime. In addition to his work in the administration of literary institutions, his career in the church continued to develop. He was appointed perpetual curate of South Lambeth Chapel in 1838; he was preacher at Berkeley Chapel; and he was vicar of Little Marlow, Buckinghamshire, from 1848 to 1858.

Cattermole was a versatile author and editor of works on theology, literature, art, and history, and he was partly or wholly responsible for about fifteen substantial publications. One of his first assignments as a writer was to assist Jacques S. Spons in compiling his Doctrine of the Church of Geneva (1st and 2nd series, 1825–32). Like many contemporary clergymen, he published sermons: collections appeared in 1832 and 1839. As for his own literary creations, he wrote *Becket and other Poems* (1832); the work named in the title was described as 'an historical tragedy'. A little later he became one of the editors of the Sacred Classics, or, Select Library of Divinity, a compilation in thirty volumes published between 1834 and 1836. His artistic interests, which had begun in his youth (as mentioned earlier), were exemplified in *Book of the Cartoons* (of Raphael) (1837), in which engravings (by Warren) of the cartoons were systematically accompanied by his carefully considered aesthetic and religious commentaries. He edited anthologies of religious writing, including *Gems of Sacred Literature* (2 vols., 1841) and probably *Gems of Sacred Poetry* (1841). Among his historical books was *The Great Civil War of Charles I and the Parliament* (2 vols., 1841–4), illustrated by George Cattermole. One of his most ambitious works was *The literature of the Church of England, indicated in selections from the writings of eminent divines* (2 vols., 1844), which includes biographical and interpretative material on the chosen texts. All of Cattermole's writing, which not surprisingly is grounded in the orthodox teachings of the Church of England, is grave, precise, and informative. Although worthy in content and intention, it has largely been forgotten, with the possible exception of his book on Raphael. Nevertheless, the Royal Society of Literature is indebted to him for his years of work on their behalf and so he should at least be remembered for that contribution to the British literary world. Cattermole died on 6 December 1858 at 69 rue de la Paix, Boulogne, France.

DONALD HAWES

Sources DNB · L. S. Smith, 'Coleridge as godfather: a corrected text of his 14 August 1828 letter to Richard Cattermole', *N&Q*, 238 (1993), 468–9 · J. Peile, *Biographical register of Christ's College, 1505–1905, and of the earlier foundation, God's House, 1448–1505*, ed. [J. A. Venn], 1 (1910) · Venn, *Alum. Cant.*, 2/1 · Boase, *Mod. Eng. biog.*, vol. 1 · E. W. Brabrook, *The Royal Society of Literature of the United Kingdom. A brief account of its origin and progress* (1891) · BL, Add. MSS 29281, 25658, 25659 · W. Besant, *Essays and historiettes* (1903) · GM, 3rd ser., 6 (1859), 99 · d. cert. · 'Cattermole, George', *DNB* · IGI

Archives BL, corresp., Add. MSS 25658, fols. 43, 59; 25659, fol. 48; 29281, fols. 201–05; 34188, fol. 273; Egerton MS 2839, fol. 217; loan 96

Cattley, Charles Robert (1816/17–1855), diplomatist and intelligence officer in the Crimea, was born of English parents in St Petersburg, Russia: his father, Robert Cattley, had been a merchant in Russia since 1802. The Cattleys apparently traded with Cattley firms in England, including sawmills near York. Charles Cattley was educated in England at Sherborne School—with his brothers Edward (1814–1894) and Henry Richard (1818–1898)—and left there in 1832. He returned to St Petersburg and later moved to Odessa. From 1841 to May 1854 he was vice-consul at Kertch, an important Crimean port (Yenikale) on the Strait of Kaffa connecting the Sea of Azov and the Black Sea, where his brother Edward, a merchant, also resided. He was reported never to have married or had children. With Anglo-Russian relations deteriorating, Cattley was ordered to leave Russia, and reached England in mid-July 1854. In London a relative, George *Moberly (headmaster of Winchester College, 1835–66), wrote to Sidney Herbert (secretary at war), and Cattley was interviewed by several

key ministers: Lord Newcastle, Lord Clarendon, and Sir James Graham. While troops under Lord Raglan were poised in Bulgaria with allied French and Turkish armies to invade, on 29 July 1854 Cattley produced a memorandum about the Peninsula for the War Office. He noted that in 1846 there had been 'no fortifications on the Heights at the back of the town (Sevastopol)', the southern upland from which the allies would soon mount their siege. 'There can be no doubt', he claimed, 'artillery might be transported' from Balaklava to Sevastopol, but 'Balaklava Creek' was too narrow for a landing. He had not been to Eupatoria, some 30 miles north of Sevastopol, close to which the allies would descend, but was confident that cannon could be similarly conveyed over the 'undulating steppe'. Cattley believed that 70,000–80,000 Russian troops were in the Crimea, 40,000 of them at Sevastopol; a further 8000 cavalry and 'probably' a force of irregular 'Kazaks' near by. If Sevastopol were attacked, he recommended that the southern coast as far east as Kaffa and Kerth be assaulted to prevent troop reinforcements reaching the naval port. The population of the Peninsula totalled about 200,000, mostly Muslim Tartars speaking a Turkish dialect and hostile to the Russians, who might be useful foragers for supplies. 'Cattle and sheep would probably be found in plenty … but not corn. This latter probably might be seized at Beidiamsk or Taganrog in the Sea of Azov' (Raglan military papers, 6807/301).

Partly on the basis of this analysis, the government decided to send Cattley to assist Raglan. Newcastle realized his potential for the imminent Crimean campaign, and wrote to Raglan, 'I consider his information and knowledge so valuable that I propose to send him out to you' (Harris, 62). On 29 August 1854 Raglan confirmed he had joined the staff. Although a civilian, he was accepted by Raglan and those under him. That his services were officially valued was indicated by the payment he received: in addition to his consular £200 annual salary, 1 guinea a day plus expenses for food and travel. He spoke Russian, French, and Italian and his official status was initially as an interpreter, though before the allied invasion of the Crimea he began to serve also as an intelligence officer. His languages, ability, and local knowledge ideally qualified him for this. His role was foreshadowed in August 1854, when Lord Stratford de Redcliffe, British ambassador in Constantinople, recommended a Greek to him as a potential agent. He assumed the alias Charles Calvert as his family still resided in St Petersburg. The army had entered the war without any military intelligence organization, and Lintorn Simmons's improvised intelligence operation in the Balkans had failed. With the invasion of the Crimea the allies, Stephen Harris has written, 'were entering an intelligence void' (ibid., 22).

On 13 September, as the allied armada stood off-shore, Cattley acted as interpreter when Eupatoria was called upon to surrender. Shortly after the battle of the Alma (20 September 1854) the officer responsible for intelligence, Colonel J. A. H. Lloyd, died of cholera. Raglan chose Cattley, whom he trusted, to succeed Lloyd. Cattley's position was, as he wrote, 'anomalous': he was on Raglan's personal staff and his operation was largely unofficial. In late September his secret intelligence department began to function, and it soon became an effective intelligence-gathering organization, run from his office at Raglan's headquarters near Balaklava. He used deserters, especially Poles, and local Tartars. Apparently many of his contacts were made through his Tartar servant Ibrahim, who also acted as an interpreter. Cattley successfully deployed a Tartar agent in Sevastopol's northern suburb. Cattley provided data directly to Raglan, and Raglan cited or sent copies of Cattley's reports to Newcastle or Panmure. In March 1855 the duke of Newcastle, secretary of state for war in London, informed Queen Victoria that, although officially chief interpreter in the Crimea, 'Mr Cattley has charge of the department of intelligence' (Sweetman, 290). As well as gathering details of enemy troop deployments in and around Sevastopol, at Bakhchisaray, Yalta, and Simferopol, Cattley interrogated prisoners and deserters. His crucial contribution was his continual tracking of Russian forces. He submitted to Raglan a monthly summary: for example, in March 1855 he estimated that there were 130,000 Russian troops in the Sevastopol area, with a further 15,000 reinforcements expected soon. Under Cattley British intelligence was largely successful, and Raglan utilized it competently. As Stephen Harris has written, 'after Inkerman there were no more nasty surprises, while intelligence played an ever-increasing role in operational planning' (Harris, 67). Cattley was apparently little involved in counter-espionage.

On 21 October 1854 Cattley warned Raglan about the prospect of 'bleak winds, heavy rains, sleet [and] snow', which would replace pleasant sunshine the following month. Furthermore, every few years a fortnight of 'Russian cold' settled over the Peninsula, when 'if a man touches metal with an uncovered hand the skin adheres'. Enclosing Cattley's memorandum, Raglan wrote to Newcastle two days later: 'We must be prepared either for wet or extreme cold, and in neither case could our troops remain under canvas … the country hardly produces wood enough to cook the men's food' (Raglan military papers, 6807/301). Newcastle replied that Raglan must be 'greatly misinformed'; the Crimean climate was 'one of the mildest and finest in the world' (Hibbert, 211).

Cattley's data apparently contributed to the allies' decision to reinforce Eupatoria and their success at the battle there (17 February 1855). Cattley had a key role in the 1855 Sea of Azov campaign, described by Stephen Harris as 'an intelligence-driven operation' (Harris, 106). He advocated the operation, notably in his 'Memorandum regarding the Sea of Azov' (20 January 1855), provided intelligence, and accompanied the abortive first expedition (3–4 May 1855) against Kerch. His intelligence shaped the amphibious operations from May to November 1855, which destroyed large quantities of Russian supplies, and tied down many Russian troops. However, the campaign failed to achieve the aims Cattley had predicted and rapidly cause the fall of Sevastopol. Contemporaries and historians have disagreed on its effectiveness, and Andrew Lambert's claim

that it was 'among the finest achievements of the war … leading to the battle of Tchernaya and the fall of Sevastopol' (Lambert, 233) is disputed. After Raglan's death (28 June 1855) his successor, Lieutenant-General James Simpson, continued to employ Cattley.

Alexander William Kinglake, chronicler of the allied campaign, who knew Cattley in the Crimea, thought him 'a gentleman of much good sense and intelligence' (Kinglake, 4). He certainly worked hard to produce his frequent, detailed reports. Cattley died of cholera in the camp at Balaklava on 10 July 1855. Simpson wrote 'his loss is irreparable!' (Harris, 85), and Panmure that his death was 'a great loss' (ibid., 86). From its nature Cattley's work was known to few. Later histories of the war and of British military intelligence ignored or minimized his role, and the myth of British intelligence incompetence in the Crimea long continued, reinforced by the 1968 film *The Charge of the Light Brigade*. However, Stephen M. Harris's *British Military Intelligence in the Crimean War, 1854–1856* (1999) reappraised its subject, provided hitherto unpublished information on Cattley, and finally showed his achievement.

ROGER T. STEARN

Sources Gwent RO, Raglan military papers · S. M. Harris, *British military intelligence in the Crimean War, 1854–1856* (1999) · J. Sweetman, *Raglan: from the peninsula to the Crimea* (1993) · C. Hibbert, *The destruction of Lord Raglan* (1961) · A. W. Kinglake, *The invasion of the Crimea*, 4 (1868) · H. H. House, *The Sherborne register, 1823–1892* (1893) · *The Sherborne register, 1550–1937* (1937) · A. D. Lambert, *The Crimean War: British grand strategy, 1853–56* (1990) · P. Gibbs, *Crimean blunder* (1960) · P. Warner, *The Crimean War* (1972) · W. Baumgart, *The Crimean War, 1853–1856* (1999)
Likenesses group portrait, photograph, c.1854, repro. in Harris, *British military intelligence*, following p. 70

Catto, Thomas Sivewright, first Baron Catto (1879–1959), merchant and banker, was born at Newcastle upon Tyne on 15 March 1879, the fifth son and seventh child of William Catto (1835–1885), shipwright, of Peterhead, and his wife, Isabella, daughter of William Yule, sea captain. His father had moved to Tyneside with his family in search of steadier employment, but died within a year, and the family returned to Peterhead. Catto attended Peterhead Academy, but after a move back to Newcastle he won a scholarship to Heaton School (now Rutherford College). Catto's formal education ended at the pre-university stage, though in 1945 he was awarded an honorary LLD by the University of Manchester. Catto married in 1910, at Smyrna, Gladys Forbes, daughter of Stephen Gordon, a partner in MacAndrews and Forbes there and a native of Elgin in Morayshire. They had one son, Stephen Gordon (b. 1923), a partner in Morgan, Grenfell & Co., who succeeded to the title. They also had three daughters, the eldest of whom, Isabel, was elected president of the World YWCA in 1955.

Early career in shipping Catto's career began at the age of fifteen, when he entered the office of the Gordon Steam Shipping Company. Although by 1898 his wages had risen from 4s. to 10s. a week, Catto sought wider opportunities; through a newspaper advertisement he applied for, and he was employed in the organization of transporting supplies to Russia, and the same connection led to his becoming the British Admiralty representative on the Russian commission to the United States from 1915 to 1917. When Russia collapsed, he transferred to the British food mission in the United States, and in 1918 he became chairman of the allied provisions commission and head of the British Ministry of Food in the USA and Canada. In recognition of his war-time service, in 1918 he was appointed CBE, in 1919 a commander of the order of Leopold of Belgium, and in 1921 he received a baronetcy.

Catto never returned, as he had intended, to MacAndrews and Forbes. In 1917 Vivian Smith's firm, Morgan, Grenfell & Co., had acquired a predominating share in Andrew Yule & Co. of Calcutta and its associated business, George Yule & Co. of London, the great Indian commercial empire built by Sir David Yule, whom Catto was invited to succeed. With a young family, Catto had no mind to take up residence in India, but what decided him was that his mother's name was Yule (though no relationship was ever established). The position of head of Andrew Yule & Co., which he assumed in 1919, led to Catto's playing an active part in financial and economic affairs in India: he became president of the Bengal chamber of commerce, and served as a member of the Inchcape committee on Indian government retrenchment in 1922–3. Closer to home, he also served on the United Kingdom committee on coal-selling in 1926. In 1928 he became a partner in Morgan, Grenfell & Co., and retired from India. He remained chairman of Andrew Yule & Co., and of the London business, which became Yule, Catto & Co., until 1940.

Banking in London Established in London, Catto became a director of the Royal Exchange Assurance Corporation, the Mercantile Bank of India, the Tobacco Securities Trust Company Ltd, the Union Castle Mail Steamship Company Ltd, the Oriental Telephone and Electric Company Ltd, and the Royal Bank of Scotland. One other task he undertook in the 1930s was to act with Sir Ernest Harvey (deputy governor of the Bank of England) in reordering the affairs of the Royal Mail and the Elder Dempster shipping companies, an unpaid post to which he was drafted by Montagu Norman (1871–1950), the governor of the Bank of England. On 24 February 1936 he was created a baron, taking his territorial title from Cairncatto, a farm which he had purchased in Buchan, Aberdeenshire, whence his forebears had come.

On 3 April 1940 Catto became a director of the Bank of England, and until July 1941 he served on the bank's advances and discounts committee, staff committee, and securities committee, and paid supervisory visits to the bank's branch in Newcastle. These were, however, secondary activities, because, only a fortnight after his appointment as a director of the bank, Catto succeeded Lord Woolton as director-general of equipment and stores at the Ministry of Supply. In July 1941 he resigned his directorship of the bank and moved to the newly created post of financial adviser to the Treasury. Catto thus joined the influx of outside experts assembled to assist the Treasury war effort, working alongside, among others, John

Thomas Sivewright Catto, first Baron Catto (1879–1959), by Walter Stoneman, 1943

obtained, the post of secretary to W. H. Stuart, managing partner of F. A. Mattievich & Co. of Batumi, at a salary of £8 a month. He sailed from Cardiff, barely nineteen, with a small trunk, a bicycle, and £3 in cash. For six years he worked in Batumi and Baku, learned to speak Russian, and on his twenty-first birthday was made office manager. While working for Stuart, Catto met Vivian Hugh Smith (1867–1956), later Lord Bicester, who was to have an important influence on his subsequent career.

Among other friends made in Baku was David Forbes junior, a Scottish merchant, whose business was soon to be absorbed in MacAndrews and Forbes, Russian and Near Eastern merchants with headquarters in the United States. In 1904 Catto was offered the management of their new European selling agency and, with Stuart's goodwill, found himself organizing an office in London. He became a member of the Baltic Exchange and learned London ways of merchanting and the chartering of ships; but after two years he returned to the Near East as second-in-command to Forbes in Smyrna, a post entailing much travel in the Near and Middle East. In 1909 he was transferred to the New York office, becoming a vice-president. The United States was to provide his home base for the next eleven years.

First World War and India When war broke out in August 1914, Catto was in England. His lack of inches prevented military service, but on the introduction of Vivian Smith

Maynard Keynes. In this context, Catto represented commercial and banking experience, the kind of practical man of business Keynes had once scorned; he and Keynes, hitherto strangers, held widely contrasting economic views, but developed a strong mutual respect, and also friendship, and eventually became known to the press as lords 'Catto and Doggo'.

Governor of the Bank of England, 1944–1949 By the close of 1943 it had become evident that illness was about to end Montagu Norman's long reign at the Bank of England. In April 1944 Catto, then sixty-five, was chosen as Norman's successor and, having been released from his position at the Treasury, was elected on 18 April to the governorship in a brief ceremony held in Norman's room at the bank. Catto was in many respects well equipped by his merchant banking knowledge and by his recent experience in Whitehall to oversee the middle position which the bank occupied between government and the City, but he faced some important difficulties. Following Norman was in itself a problem, for the great man had occupied the governorship for twenty-four years and, during that time, had transformed the organization and outlook of the bank and had come to be regarded as the perfect partner for the 'Old Lady'. Moreover, in spite of his City background, Catto was initially regarded with some suspicion by senior bank staff, who felt that he had become too much a Treasury man. Most important, however, was the fact that Catto's tenure of the governorship coincided with the end of the war, the problems of domestic and international reconstruction, and the nationalization of the bank.

In dealing with these problems, Catto relied for the most part on the team that he inherited from Norman, which reassured those who had viewed him as a Treasury 'new broom'. In his first year he occupied himself with the main questions likely to arise in the post-war period, notably in the field of industrial finance, where he was much concerned with the establishment of the Finance Corporation for Industry and the Industrial and Commercial Finance Corporation—institutions designed to meet inter-war criticisms of the City's neglect of British industry. But he had been in office little more than a year when a Labour government was returned, pledged to an early nationalization of the Bank of England and ready to introduce new measures of control over the banking system as a whole; and it is with these questions that his name as governor is principally associated.

Catto accepted that the bank had already been converted, *de facto*, into a public institution, aligning its monetary policy with the general economic policy of the government of the day, and no longer seeking to provide for its stockholders more than a constant dividend. Accordingly he took the view that there was nothing in the proposal for public ownership which need diminish the utility or standing of the bank, provided its independence in thought and work was fully safeguarded. Similarly, he did not oppose the provision of a new measure of control over the banking system, provided that it was general in character and operated on the initiative of the bank. Catto's protracted negotiations with Hugh Dalton, the Labour

chancellor at the time of the bank's nationalization, bear ample testimony to the tenacity with which he sought to achieve these ends.

Catto judged correctly that he could best defend the bank's own position, and that of the banking world more generally, by not actively opposing the general policy of nationalization. As a result the bank was taken into public ownership with the minimum public controversy and the maximum retention of operational independence. Catto's own speeches in the House of Lords were important here, for they established some of the principles for future interpretations of the legal intention of the nationalization statute. His successor, Lord Cobbold, instructed bank staff to read these speeches as the best indications of the bank's position, and in the 1950s the Treasury solicitors accepted their significance when they undertook a detailed examination of the constraints on the government's limited powers over the bank. Catto was appointed as the first governor of the publicly owned bank in March 1946, and on 25 July 1947, midway through his term of office, he was sworn of the privy council. In his last years as governor Catto divided his time equally between consolidating the bank's new domestic role and involvement in the financial aspects of international post-war reconstruction; in the latter context he played a significant part in discussions on the role of the International Bank for Reconstruction and Development (World Bank). He resigned the governorship on 28 February 1949, two weeks before his seventieth birthday—by that time the statutory age limit for the office.

Retirement, reputation, and death In retirement, Catto served as chairman, in 1950–52, of a committee to report on the practicability of determining the financial and economic relations between Scotland and the rest of the United Kingdom. Scottish matters indeed, and particularly those of the county of Aberdeen, were a lifelong concern. In addition to the farm of Cairncatto, he had bought the nearby Schivas House, Ythanbank, which he restored fully on his return from India. In August 1957 he became the first freeman of Peterhead, an honour which gave him particular pleasure.

In appearance Catto was short of stature, with a fresh complexion and clear blue eyes. His open countenance and quiet manner perhaps tended to conceal his shrewdness and skill as a negotiator, so well displayed while he was governor of the bank. If there was occasion for controversy he avoided a head-on collision, and used his judgement to carry his objective without sacrificing any point of importance. As the head of a large organization he imposed his will with courtesy and with sensitivity towards his subordinates.

Catto's career formed a bridge between the pre-1914 world, in which informal business contacts and the presence of individual merchant companies, especially from Britain, were responsible for much of the world's commerce, and the post-1945 world, in which international financial institutions and conglomerates, and the emergence of world trading blocs, had become the engine of increasingly complex capital and trade flows and relationships. He was in the Middle East when the Baghdad to Berlin railway was projected, and when oil was discovered in Iran; he was still involved in business and economic development in the era of the International Monetary Fund, decolonization, and the emergence of the European Economic Community. Catto's business career is of intrinsic interest, but it is his period as governor of the bank that marks him out as a figure of historical importance. On a purely biographical level his ascent from humble Scots origins to the pinnacle of City, and ultimately national, financial rank is a story of great personal achievement. More broadly his brief period as governor of the bank witnessed a remarkable period of transition in international, national, and bank affairs.

Clement Attlee remarked with some justification on Catto's retirement that 'no governor has had to face such a difficult world situation' (Bank of England Archives, G 21) and Catto played a significant part in calming some of the turbulence which characterized post-war economic and financial reconstruction. But Catto's most important contribution to post-war history was his handling of the bank's nationalization. In the short term his adroit management of bank and City opinion indeed helped to ensure a minimum of public controversy. In the long term, however, his successful attempt to preserve much of the bank's independence was to prove crucial in shaping the future role of the financial sector and the governance of the post-war economy.

Catto suffered from Parkinson's disease and died in his sleep at his house, Holmdale, in Holmbury St Mary, Shere, Surrey, on 23 August 1959, at the age of eighty. A memorial service was held at St Margaret's Church, Westminster, on 23 October 1959. E. H. H. GREEN

Sources J. Fforde, The Bank of England and public policy, 1941–1958 (1992) · R. P. T. Davenport-Hines, 'Catto, Thomas Sivewright', DBB · The collected writings of John Maynard Keynes, ed. D. Moggridge and E. Johnson, 26 (1980) · record of C. Attlee's speech at Catto's retirement, Bank of England archives, G21 · d. cert.
Archives Bank of England archives, London, papers, G1, G2, G18, G21 | BL, letters to Lord Reading, MSS Eur. E 238, F 118 · BLPES, Dalton MSS · PRO, Treasury files
Likenesses W. Stoneman, photograph, 1943, NPG [see illus.] · D. Alison, portrait, c.1948, Bank of England, London · J. Gunn, portrait, 1952, Morgan, Grenfell & Co. Ltd, London; copies, priv. coll.
Wealth at death £501,805 6s. 9d.: probate, 2 Dec 1959, CGPLA Eng. & Wales

Catton, Charles, the elder (1728–1798), painter, was born in September 1728 at Norwich, and baptized on 8 October 1728 at St Mary-in-the-Marsh, Norwich, the son of Richard Catton and his wife, Hannah. He was one of a family of thirty-five children. Apprenticed to Thomas Maxfield, a London coach-painter, he found time also for some study in the St Martin's Lane Academy. He was highly regarded as a coach-painter, and according to Edward Edwards, he was 'the first herald-painter who ventured to correct the bad manner of painting the supporters of coats of arms' (Edwards, 259). He was a member of the Society of Artists, and exhibited various pictures in its exhibitions from 1760 to 1768. He received the appointment of coach-painter to

George III, and was one of the foundation members of the Royal Academy, where he exhibited from 1769 to the year of his death. In 1784 he was master of the Painter–Stainers' Company.

Catton is said to have painted the coaches of Sir Joshua Reynolds and the lord mayor. He worked as a decorative painter, mainly for Sir William Chambers, and executed works for the architect at Somerset House, Buckingham Palace, and Baron Clive's house at 45 Berkeley Square, London. He also painted portraits and animal subjects, but particularly landscapes in oils and in watercolours; examples of the last are found in the Victoria and Albert Museum, London, and the National Gallery of Scotland, Edinburgh. Some years before his death he gave up the practice of his art. He died at his house in Judd Place East, New Road, London, in August 1798, and was buried in the cemetery of St George's, Bloomsbury. His son Charles *Catton the younger (1756–1819) was a landscape painter and topographical draughtsman.

[ANON.], rev. MARTIN MYRONE

Sources E. Croft-Murray, Decorative painting in England, 1537–1837, 2 (1970) · E. Edwards, Anecdotes of painters (1808); facs. edn (1970) · will, PRO, PROB 11/1312, sig. 588 · Painter-Stainers' Company records, GL · RA · Farington, Diary · J. Harris, Sir William Chambers: knight of the polar star (1970) · W. A. D. Englefield, The history of the Painter–Stainers' Company of London (1950) · IGI
Likenesses G. Dance, drawing, 1793, RA · H. Singleton, group portrait, oils, 1793 (Royal Academicians, 1793), RA · C. Catton, jun. or C. Catton, sen., oils, Castle Museum, Norwich · J. Zoffany, group portrait, oils (Royal Academicians, 1772), Royal Collection
Wealth at death £200; plus property: will, PRO, PROB 11/1312

Catton, Charles, the younger (1756–1819), landscape painter and book illustrator, was born in London on 30 December 1756, the son of Charles *Catton the elder (1728–1798), also a painter. He was taught by his father, and was admitted to the Royal Academy Schools on 6 March 1775. He travelled widely in England and Scotland making sketches, some of which were later engraved and published. Catton was best known as a landscape painter and topographical draughtsman. Between 1775 and 1800 he exhibited thirty-seven paintings at the Royal Academy, including in 1776 a View of London from Blackfriars Bridge and Westminster from Westminster Bridge. He published Animals Drawn from Nature (1788), engraved by himself from his drawings of animals, and in 1793 he exhibited designs for John Gay's Fables, on which he had worked with E. F. Burney.

In 1804 Catton emigrated to the USA and settled on a farm on the River Hudson with his two daughters and a son. He died at New Paltz, New York, on 24 April 1819. The Victoria and Albert Museum has four Drawings of Animals for Book Illustrations and A View of Norwich from Mousehold Hill; there are also examples of his work in the British Museum, London, and the Ashmolean Museum, Oxford.

ANNE PIMLOTT BAKER

Sources Mallalieu, Watercolour artists, vol. 1 · Graves, RA exhibitors · Redgrave, Artists · S. C. Hutchison, 'The Royal Academy Schools, 1768–1830', Walpole Society, 38 (1960–62), 123–91 · L. Lambourne and J. Hamilton, eds., British watercolours in the Victoria and Albert Museum (1980) · DNB

Catton, Thomas (*bap.* 1758, *d.* 1838), astronomer, the son of Thomas Catton, was baptized on 30 July 1758 at West Dereham, Norfolk. After two years at a local school at Downham, where Horatio Nelson was a schoolfellow, he went to King's Lynn grammar school, thence in 1777 to St John's College, Cambridge. He obtained his BA in 1781 as fourth wrangler and first Smith's prizeman, won another prize in 1783 for Latin, and proceeded MA in 1784. He then spent three years as tutor in the family of Sir William Wake in Northampton, with whom he remained on friendly terms thereafter. After being ordained priest in 1790, he took his BD in 1791 and served as chaplain of Horningsea, Cambridge (1792–7), and rector of North Ockenden, Essex (1807–17).

Catton was a fellow and tutor of his college, and from 1791 to 1832 was responsible for the small observatory situated on one of its towers. It was furnished with a 3½ foot transit and a 46 inch telescope, which was replaced in 1832 by a Dollond 42 inch achromatic telescope. His observations of eclipses, occultations, and other phenomena were recorded in ten manuscript volumes. After his death these were edited by Sir George Airy, published in 1853, and also inserted in volume 22 of the *Memoirs of the Royal Astronomical Society*. Catton was one of the earliest members of the Royal Astronomical Society, and was elected a fellow of the Royal Society in 1821.

Catton's virtues were a quick apprehension, a powerful memory, and scrupulous attention to accuracy; his judgement was, however, often overruled by prejudice or passion, while excessive caution made it difficult for him to cope with everyday life. He shunned promotion, preferring a life of quiet social enjoyment within St John's College. During his last years he suffered a degeneration of his faculties. He died at St John's College on 6 January 1838, and was buried in the old college chapel.

A. M. CLERKE, *rev.* ANITA MCCONNELL

Sources Venn, *Alum. Cant.* · *GM*, 2nd ser., 9 (1838), 433–4 · R. T. Gunter, *Early science in Cambridge* (1937), 171, 194, 202 · A. C. Crook, *From the foundation to Gilbert Scott: a history of the buildings of St John's College, Cambridge, 1511 to 1885* (1980) · *Annual Register* (1838) · *Monthly Notices of the Astronomical Society of London*, 4 (1836–9), 110
Archives CUL, notes · St John Cam.

Catton, Walter. *See* Chatton, Walter (*d.* 1343/4).

Caudwell, Christopher. *See* Sprigg, Christopher St John (1907–1937).

Caudwell, Sarah. *See* Cockburn, Sarah Caudwell (1939–2000).

Caulfeild, James, first earl of Charlemont (1728–1799), politician, second but first surviving son of James Caulfeild, third Viscount Charlemont (1682–1734), politician, and Elizabeth Barnard (1703–1743) of Castle Barnard, Cork, was born on 18 August 1728 at Castle Caulfeild, co. Tyrone, and succeeded to the peerage as fourth Viscount Charlemont four months before his sixth birthday. Educated privately by a succession of tutors, of whom Philip

James Caulfeild, first earl of Charlemont (1728–1799), by Pompeo Batoni, 1753–6

Skelton was the most eminent and Edward Murphy the most influential, he was expected by family and friends to become 'the very first character of a peer in Ireland'. However, the young nobleman's discovery of 'cards and late hours' caused 'all thoughts of the university' to be put aside, and it was decided that he should embark early on a grand tour (*Charlemont MSS*, 1.178–9). Accompanied by Murphy he set out in 1746 on a journey that took him, as well as to the usual locations in the Low Countries, Italy, and France, to Germany, Spain, Turkey, Greece, and Egypt. He spent most of the nine years he was abroad in Italy, five of them in Rome, where he was part of a circle that included Joshua Reynolds, Robert Adam, and William Chambers, who subsequently became his architect. He also got to know David Hume, and Giambattista Piranesi, with whom he became embroiled in a dispute over the funding and dedication of his *Antichità Romane*. Charlemont wrote an account of his impressions of his visit to Greece and Turkey in 1749, which, as well as antiquarian descriptions, contains much contemporary sociological information. Charlemont believed correctly that this represented a new form of travel writing, but although he revisited and revised the manuscripts of his travels he did not publish them. However, their existence attests to the fact that his stay abroad achieved its purpose of steering him away from the life of dissipation and indolence into which he appeared to be descending in his teens.

Charlemont left Italy with a view to returning home in 1754. His journey was prolonged because of the circuitous route he chose, which resulted in lengthy visits to Barcelona, Paris, and London, and an encounter with Montesquieu. However, he was back in Ireland to receive an honorary doctorate of laws in July 1755 and to take his seat in the Irish House of Lords on 7 October. Shortly afterwards he was prevailed upon by the lord lieutenant, the marquess of Hartington, to mediate between the speaker of the Irish Commons, John Ponsonby, and the patriot politician Henry Boyle with a view to facilitating the conclusion of the money bill dispute. He successfully acquitted himself of this task, which brought him 'influence at the Castle' (*Charlemont MSS*, 1.6), but he found this uncongenial. A man of high principle, Charlemont was induced by the fact that he was 'sometimes obliged to oppose the measures of government' to conclude 'that in Ireland at least, a permanent and respectable opposition is absolutely and essentially necessary' (ibid., 1.7). He defined his political credo in patriot terms as that of 'emancipating my country', but when he took up the cause of jury reform in 1756 he was seized by such an acute attack of 'nervous diffidence', which precipitated a 'violent rheumatism' that 'totally disabled' him for two and a half years, that he never made a formal political speech thereafter (ibid., 1.8).

Charlemont had recovered from this debilitating affliction sufficiently, thanks in no small part to the ministrations of Charles Lucas, by February 1760 to conclude that as the governor of co. Armagh it was his duty to go to Belfast to help marshal that town's defences when Thurot captured Carrickfergus. Three years later he roused himself again to respond discreetly to the outbreak of agrarian unrest caused by the Hearts of Oak in south Ulster, as a result of which he was raised to the dignity of earl in the Irish peerage in December 1763. If this was a deserved honour, considering Charlemont's defence of the right of Irish peers to participate in the processions at George III's wedding and coronation in 1761, it was also one of the few he received during his lifetime. He let it be known on accepting the earldom that it 'should have no influence on my parliamentary conduct', and true to his promise he became the most steadfast representative in the House of Lords of the more assertive patriotism that emerged during the 1760s (*Charlemont MSS*, 1.22).

Like Henry Flood, with whom he built up a close political friendship during these years, Charlemont's political hero was William Pitt, and he was able to observe him at close quarters during the nine years (1763–73) that he kept a London house. He divided his time during these years between Dublin and London. In Dublin his continuing political involvement and ambitious architectural plans, which resulted in the neo-classical gem that was his suburban villa at Marino and the fine town house he built on the north side of what became Rutland Square, further enhanced his already high reputation as a man of principle and taste. In London his involvement with the Dilettanti Club allowed him to sustain his passionate interest in classical antiquity. Secure in his role and his political convictions, he was not cast down by the repeated rejection of the patriots' programme in parliament because he

was confident that virtue would triumph in the end: 'let no patriot', he wrote, 'be discouraged by defeat since, though repeated efforts may prove ineffectual, the time will come when the labours of the virtuous few will finally succeed against all the efforts of interested majorities' (*Charlemont MSS*, 1.27–8). Thus in every session from the early 1760s he entered 'protests', frequently written with Henry Flood and seldom endorsed by more than a handful of peers, against what he regarded as unprincipled and despotic actions of government. He had the satisfaction of an occasional triumph, such as the Octennial Act (1768), which provided for general elections every eight years, but the inability of the opposition to deflect Lord Townshend's plan to increase the power of the lord lieutenant and its numerical weakness in the early 1770s gave him little cause to anticipate more.

Though some set-backs, such as the acceptance, against Charlemont's strong advice, by Henry Flood of a vice-treasurership in 1775, upset him deeply, Charlemont's own conduct was unfailingly proper. A naturally sociable man, he and his wife, Mary Hickman (d. 1807), the daughter of Thomas Hickman of Brickhill, co. Clare, whom he married on 2 July 1768, entertained the cream of Dublin society in their splendid Dublin homes, amid his growing collection of fine books and *objets d'art*. It is a measure of the high esteem in which he continued to be held within the ranks of Irish patriotism that he was a prominent member of the main patriot social clubs of the day—the early 1770s' society of Granby Row and the Monks of the Order of St Patrick, commonly known as the Monks of the Screw, which was founded in 1779. By this date his main political confidant was Henry Grattan, whom he returned as MP for Charlemont borough in 1775 following the premature death of his brother Francis Caulfeild at sea in that year. As he had done with Henry Flood, Charlemont trusted Grattan explicitly and he was highly gratified both by Grattan's emergence as the leading patriot voice in the House of Commons and by the prospect of his achieving major commercial and constitutional reform for the country. Since the main focus of political activity was the House of Commons, Charlemont had to be content with an advisory role until his appointment as commander-in-chief of the volunteers in July 1780 put him at the head of one of the most important arms of patriot opinion.

Charlemont's involvement with the volunteers commenced in January 1779, when he became captain of the first Armagh company. Initially he had some reservations about the wisdom of arming civilian volunteers, but these were dispelled by the responsible conduct of the volunteers throughout the country and by their decisive contribution to the achievement of free trade in 1779. Indeed, following his acceptance of the invitation to become their commander-in-chief he devoted himself wholeheartedly to the role, attending reviews, providing prizes, and encouraging their activities in support of legislative independence. Charlemont was not unconscious of the challenge which their politicization posed to the authority of parliament, but he was sufficiently persuaded of the propriety of their motives and so disappointed by the failure of repeated attempts by Grattan and, following his dismissal in November 1781, by Flood to advance constitutional reform that it was in his house that Grattan, Flood, and he prepared the resolutions in support of legislative independence that were approved by the Ulster Volunteers at Dungannon in February 1782. The firm stand Grattan and he subsequently took in the face of enormous pressure from the Rockingham whigs to compromise ensured that the legislative changes that defined 'the constitution of 1782' were agreed unconditionally and without the 'final settlement' advocated by Charles James Fox.

Charlemont's moment of triumph was soured somewhat by Henry Flood's argument that it was not enough simply to repeal the Declaratory Act, but neither this nor his nomination to the Irish privy council in April 1783 inhibited his reformist commitment. He co-operated with Flood in advancing a measure of moderate parliamentary reform in 1783-4 and chaired the Grand National Convention, which was the parent of the reform legislation twice rejected by parliament. At the same time he encouraged the volunteers to oppose Catholic enfranchisement in the summer and autumn of 1784 in accordance with his belief that although Catholics should be accorded full toleration this did not extend to their admission to the constitution. In the following year he effectively took the volunteers out of politics by instructing them to 'be … quiet' when the Irish administration contemplated replacing them with a militia (Charlemont MSS, 2.17). His commitment to volunteering remained strong despite this, and his active opposition to William Pitt's plan for a commercial union between Britain and Ireland in 1785 and his support for an unlimited regency when George III fell ill in 1788-9 indicated that his politics also remained consistent. Indeed, he was a key figure in the Whig Club that was founded in Ireland in 1789.

The rise of the Catholic question and radicalism in the 1790s caused Charlemont some anxious moments, but although he advised the administration on the establishment of the yeomanry, his opposition to repression and to the proposed Act of Union, combined with his belated acceptance of Catholic emancipation, indicated that he retained his political integrity and sound political sense until his death, which took place at his house in Rutland Square, Dublin, on 4 August 1799. He was buried in the family vault in Armagh Cathedral six days later. He was survived by his wife and succeeded by the eldest of their three sons, Francis William Caulfeild, as second earl of Charlemont.

In his later years Charlemont devoted a considerable part of his time to the Royal Irish Academy (established in 1785), of which he was a founder member and president. He contributed four papers, mainly on classical subjects, to its transactions, but perhaps his greatest intellectual legacy was his political memoirs, which offer the profoundest insight into the life, character, and times of this learned, principled, and honourable man.

JAMES KELLY

Sources *The manuscripts and correspondence of James, first earl of Charlemont*, 2 vols., HMC, 28 (1891-4) · M. J. Craig, *The volunteer earl: being the life and times of James Caulfeild, first earl of Charlemont* (1948) · J. Kelly, 'A secret return of the volunteers of Ireland in 1784', *Irish Historical Studies*, 26 (1988-9), 268-9 · 'Lord Charlemont', *Public characters of 1798* (1799), 185-91 · T. G. F. Paterson, 'The county Armagh volunteers of 1778-1793', *Ulster Journal of Archaeology*, 3rd ser., 4 (1941), 101-27; 5 (1942), 31-61 · W. B. Stanford and E. J. Finopoulos, eds., *The travels of Lord Charlemont in Greece and Turkey, 1749* (1984) · GEC, *Peerage* · W. B. Stanford, 'The manuscripts of Lord Charlemont's Eastern travels', *Proceedings of the Royal Irish Academy*, 80C (1980), 69-90 · A. Blackstock, 'A dangerous species of ally: Orangeism and the Irish yeomanry', *Irish Historical Studies*, 30 (1996-7), 393-405 · F. Hardy, *Memoirs of the political and private life of James Caulfeild, earl of Charlemont*, 2nd edn, 2 vols. (1812) · *Journal of the House of Lords of the kingdom of Ireland*, 8 vols. (1783-1800)

Archives Royal Irish Acad., corresp. and papers | BL, letters to Henry Flood, Add. MS 22930 · CKS, corresp. with first marquess of Camden · PRO NIre., letters to Stewart of Killymoon · Sheff. Arch., corresp. with second marquess of Rockingham · Sheff. Arch., corresp. with Edward Burke

Likenesses J. Reynolds, group portrait, caricature, oils, *c.*1751 (with Sir Thomas Kennedy, Mr Ward, and Mr Phelps), NG Ire. · W. Cuming, oils, *c.*1751-1799, NG Ire. · P. Batoni, portrait, 1753-6, Yale U. CBA, Paul Mellon collection [*see illus.*] · W. Hogarth, oils, *c.*1764, Smith College, Northampton, Massachusetts · line engraving, *c.*1780, NG Ire. · J. Haynes, etching and stipple, pubd 1782 (after W. Hogarth), NG Ire. · R. Livesay, oils, *c.*1783, NG Ire. · line engraving, pubd 1783, NG Ire. · J. Dean, mezzotint, pubd 1785 (after R. Livesay), NG Ire. · T. Nugent, stipple, pubd 1790 (after N. Hone), BM, NPG · T. Nugent, stipple, pubd 1790 (after Hone), NG Ire. · M. Quadal, oils, 1790, NG Ire. · J. K. Sherwin, five group portraits, line engravings, pubd 1803 (*The installation banquet of the knights of St Patrick in the Great Hall, Dublin Castle, 17th March 1783*), NG Ire. · J. Heath, stipple, pubd 1810 (after Hone), NG Ire. · W. Daniell, etching, pubd 1814 (after G. Dance), BM, NPG · W. Daniell, soft-ground etching, pubd 1814 (after G. Dance), NG Ire. · B. Smith, stipple, pubd 1814 (after Hone), NG Ire. · J. Woodhouse, medal, 1820-29 (after W. Cuming), National Museum of Ireland, Dublin · W. Mossop, bronze medallion, National Museum of Ireland, Dublin · W. Mossop, wax relief, NG Ire. · L. Schiavanetti, engraving (after N. Hone), repro. in Hardy, *Memoirs* · portrait (after R. Livesay), NPG · two line engravings (after W. Hogarth), NG Ire.; repro. in *European Magazine* (Feb 1784)

Caulfeild, James Edward Geale, eighth Viscount Charlemont (1880-1949), politician in Ireland, was born in London on 12 May 1880, only son of the Hon. Marcus Piers Francis Caulfeild (1840-1895) CB, of the Admiralty and formerly a major in the mid-Ulster artillery militia, Dungannon, and Louisa Gwyn Williams (d. 1916).

James Caulfeild was educated at Cheam School, Surrey, and at Winchester College. He was gazetted to the Coldstream Guards in 1914. When found unfit for active service during the First World War he volunteered for work at Woolwich arsenal, and became inspector of munitions in 1916, a position he resigned in 1918. He was also involved in recruiting during the war. The eighth viscount succeeded to the title on the death of his uncle, James Alfred Caulfeild, in 1913. He married on 26 November 1914 Evelyn Fanny Charlotte Hull (d. 1940), daughter of E. C. P. Hull. She is said to have eloped with his chauffeur (Hyde, 168), and they were divorced in 1940; in the same year, on 25 July, he married Hildegarde, daughter of Mr R. Slock-Cottell, of Belgium. She had had a distinguished career with the Red Cross in the Balkan wars and the First World

James Edward Geale Caulfeild, eighth Viscount Charlemont (1880–1949), by Walter Stoneman, 1932

War, and was created a knight of the order of Leopold of Belgium and knight of the order of St Sava of Yugoslavia. Charlemont had no children and was succeeded by his cousin, Mr Charles Edward St George Caulfeild FSS.

The Caulfeild family had had a long-standing connection with Ulster, since Sir Toby Caulfeild (*bap.* 1565, *d.* 1627), a soldier of fortune in Elizabeth I's time, received large grants of the estates of the earl of Tyrone. After succeeding to the title, Charlemont settled in the family seat at Drumcairne, near Stewartstown, co. Tyrone, which remained the family home until 1936 when he moved to Newcastle, co. Down. Charlemont became involved in the Ulster unionist campaign against home rule, playing a prominent part in the Ulster volunteer movement in 1914.

Charlemont's main political significance lies in his activities after the establishment of the Northern Ireland state. He was elected to the senate of Northern Ireland in May 1925 but contributed little to debates until he succeeded Lord Londonderry as leader of the senate and minister of education in 1926. It fell to him to preside over a system of education established by legislation in 1923, under which state schools were non-denominational and voluntary schools poorly funded, a system disliked by both Catholics and protestants. Charlemont was confronted with an alliance of protestant clergy and the Orange order who sought to promote protestant influence in the state system. Their campaign led to the introduction of the 1930 Education Act, which required the provision of Bible instruction in state schools if requested by the parents of ten or more pupils, and facilitated the appointment of protestant teachers to state schools. In response to threats of legal action from Catholics, voluntary schools were granted half the cost of capital expenditure. Charlemont resisted appeals from the United Education Committee of protestant churches to permit clerical representation on the management committee of Stranmills Teacher Training College, a non-denominational, publicly funded institution. Nevertheless, the prime minister, Lord Craigavon, acceded to the demands when Charlemont was absent. Thus during Charlemont's ministry Northern Ireland's education system became increasingly denominational in character in response to pressure from the churches, though Charlemont was not in favour of such developments. He was also opposed to allowing sectarian prejudices to interfere in education matters. On a number of occasions he overruled regional education committees' decisions against Catholics, and met with protestant displeasure for his willingness to recognize Catholic schools. Privately he expressed exasperation with Catholic complaints, and also with protestant protests when any concessions were made to Catholics. Ultimately he won the respect and appreciation of nationalist MPs, who appreciated his fair-mindedness though rejecting the principles on which the education system was founded.

Apart from his work on education, Charlemont was vice-lieutenant of co. Tyrone from 1922 to 1939. In 1925 he was appointed district commandant of Cookstown area B special constabulary. He was sworn of the privy council of Northern Ireland in 1926, served as chairman of an advisory committee on ancient monuments in Northern Ireland, and as chairman on a commission to inquire into the resources of Northern Ireland and the development of its industry. He became honorary associate of the Royal Institute of British Architects, having earlier practised as an architect. Charlemont was awarded an honorary LLD by Queen's University of Belfast.

Charlemont sought to promote better relations between Catholics and protestants. He consciously employed Catholics and met with complaints for doing so. He opposed the gerrymander of Londonderry in 1936. He was consulted at length by Major-General Hugh Montgomery prior to the latter's foundation of the Irish Association in 1938. Charlemont, who was president of the Irish Association for eight years, saw its aims as being:

> to give effective expression to Irish opinion, to study business and commercial relations with a view to reconciling economic interests of North and South and to bring home the fact that every effort to eradicate misunderstanding and disseminate good feeling in Ireland is a definite contribution to international peace and security. (Bew, Darwin, and Gillespie, x)

As a goodwill gesture towards Presbyterians, Charlemont, a member of the Church of Ireland, presented a set of collecting plates to the First Stewartstown Presbyterian Church in 1935.

A man of wide-ranging enthusiasms, Charlemont had a

long association with the Royal Society for the Prevention of Cruelty to Animals. He was interested in folklore and fairies. While minister of education he attended wood-work classes and became a keen woodworker. He sketched, played the piano, and held memorable musical parties at Drumcairne. He was also renowned for his wit and keen sense of humour: once asked why an orchestra had not been provided from the members of Stormont, he is said to have suggested that there were plenty there ready to blow their own trumpets but none anxious to play second fiddle (*Belfast News-Letter*, 2 Sept 1949).

In poor health during much of his life, Charlemont died at his home, Carlton House, Newcastle, co. Down, on 30 August 1949, and was buried in St John's cemetery, Tully-brannigan, co. Down, on 2 September. His wife survived him. MARY N. HARRIS

Sources Burke, *Peerage* (1956) · M. Harris, *The Catholic church and the foundation of the Northern Irish state* (1993) · P. Bew, K. Darwin, and G. Gillespie, *Passion and prejudice: nationalist–unionist conflict and the founding of the Irish Association* (1993) · *Northern Whig and Belfast Post* (31 Aug 1949) · *Northern Whig and Belfast Post* (3 Sept 1949) · *Belfast News-Letter* (31 Aug 1949) · *Belfast News-Letter* (2 Sept 1949) · *Irish Times* (31 Aug 1949) · *The Times* (31 Aug 1949) · *MidUlster Mail* (3 Sept 1949) · PRO NIre., Charlemont MSS, D 1083 · D. H. Akenson, *Education and enmity: the control of education in Northern Ireland, 1920–50* (1973) · H. M. Hyde, *The Londonderrys: a family portrait* (1979), 168 · *CGPLA NIre.* (1949)

Archives PRO NIre., papers relating to Charlemont's family, D 1083 | PRO NIre., Ministry of Education records · PRO NIre., corresp. with Hugh Montgomery, D 2661/C

Likenesses W. Stoneman, photograph, 1932, NPG [*see illus.*]

Wealth at death £3489 7*s*. 2*d*.: probate, 7 Nov 1950, *CGPLA NIre.*

Caulfeild, Toby, first Baron Caulfeild of Charlemont (*bap.* 1565, *d.* 1627), soldier, politician, and landowner, was baptized on 2 December 1565 at Great Milton, Oxford-shire, a younger son of Alexander Caulfeild. Nothing is known of his early years or education, but from 1590 he pursued a military career, sailing on Sir Martin Frobisher's expedition to the Azores and on a similar expedition commanded by Lord Thomas Howard in 1591. On land he served in France at the siege of Dreux in 1593, in the Low Countries under Sir Francis Vere, and in 1596 as a captain of infantry in Essex's expedition against Cadiz. In May 1597 he captained men who were mustered and trained in Sussex in precaution against Spanish invasion, which by June involved preparation of another expedition, Essex's Islands voyage; in its aftermath he was responsible for all arms originally from Sussex. Early in 1598 he was made captain of a foot company to be transferred to Falmouth, Cornwall, where fortifications were then in plan.

The most significant phase of Caulfeild's military career took place in Ireland, where he was sent in September 1598 during the Nine Years' War as a captain of 150 soldiers from the Low Countries in Sir Samuel Bagenal's regiment. Stationed at first on the borders of Ulster or in the pale, his career rose from 1600 with the success of the newly appointed Lord Deputy Mountjoy, with whom he campaigned in south Armagh in that year. At the siege and battle of Kinsale in 1601 he was lieutenant-colonel of the regiment commanded by Sir Henry Foliott, and in the spring of 1602 he and his company formed part of the lord deputy's army in the field. A crucial opportunity for Caulfeild arose with Mountjoy's decision to campaign against O'Neill in Ulster in June 1602; with the building of Charlemont Fort at this time Caulfeild was placed there in command. After O'Neill's surrender Caulfeild was knighted in Dublin on King James's accession in 1603.

Under Lord Deputy Chichester, in the years after O'Neill's surrender and restoration, Caulfeild, as governor of Charlemont with fifty foot, was an important figure in, and beneficiary of, the attempt to establish a new order in Ulster. Payment to him towards the erection of a gaol and sessions house at Armagh symbolized the extension of English norms of authority; at the same time he was rewarded with a lease, in June 1607, of the estate of the dissolved monastery of St Peter and St Paul in Armagh as well as of the lands reserved to Charlemont Fort. His power grew in the locality with the flight of the earls in 1607. Thereafter he was charged with the collection of Tyrone's rents and duties until November 1610, and, among other responsibilities, had the custody of Tyrone's son, Conn O'Neill. With the implementation of plantation in Ulster in 1610 he was granted an estate as a servitor nearby in Tyrone, on which he built a residence. In 1610 and 1611 he was involved in the resolution of disputes over land in the counties of Armagh and Tyrone arising from the plantation in those counties, over which he exercised a continuing surveillance.

The transformation of Caulfeild's career from the military to a more political sphere was evident in his promotion to the Irish privy council on his return from England in 1613 (where he had represented the lord deputy) and by his election as MP for co. Armagh, where he also served as JP in the same year. By 1616 he had been promoted to central government office as master of the ordnance, when he was again in London to obtain military supplies following the appointment of his predecessor, Sir Oliver St John, as lord deputy. He had meanwhile extended his landholding in Ulster as tenant of part of the Trinity College estate in co. Armagh, and in 1618 he received a new patent of his Ulster land, having been compensated earlier for surrendering part of the monastic estate to enhance the co. Londonderry plantation. At this time also he acquired the south Armagh estate of the late Henry McShane O'Neill. In December 1620 Caulfeild, who was unmarried, was ennobled as Baron Caulfeild of Charlemont, with succession, should he die without male heirs, to his nephew Sir William Caulfeild, a son of his brother George (*d.* 1603), a London lawyer and Oxford MP.

In the wider context of European affairs, arising from events in the Palatinate, Charlemont was placed, as an Irish government officer, on the war committee established by the privy council in London in January 1621. In March 1622 he was appointed to the commission to investigate Irish affairs, and he became owner of Charlemont Fort in a money saving exercise in 1623. A benefit to share in the fines imposed for ploughing by the tail was due to expire at Michaelmas 1627. On his death in Dublin during August 1627, at a time of renewed uncertainty in Ireland with the Anglo-Spanish war, he was buried with a splendid funeral in the English style in Christ Church Cathedral, Dublin, in which city he had a house. An Elizabethan captain of Oxfordshire gentry background, formed by war with Spain and in the dangerous war of Ireland from 1598, he reaped the benefits of success not only as an Ulster landowner, but as a member of the Dublin government itself in the new Ireland of James I. He was succeeded by William Caulfeild, second Baron Caulfeild of Charlemont, who died in 1640. R. J. HUNTER

Sources APC, 1597–9, 1613–17, 1626 · Sir H. Wallop, treasurer at war in Ireland (per executor), PRO, AO 1/287/1080 · Lord Docwra (baron of Culmore), treasurer at war in Ireland, PRO, AO 1/291/1092 · CSP Ire., 1598–1625 · J. S. Brewer and W. Bullen, eds., Calendar of the Carew manuscripts, 6 vols., PRO (1867–73), vol. 6 · F. Moryson, An itinerary containing his ten yeeres travell through the twelve dominions, 2–3 (1907–8) · Calendar of the Irish patent rolls of James I (before 1830); facs. edn as Irish patent rolls of James I (1966) · J. P. Prendergast, 'Charlemont Fort', Journal of the Royal Historical and Archaeological Association of Ireland, 4th ser., vol. 6 (1883–4), 319–44 · V. Treadwell, Buckingham and Ireland, 1616–1628: a study in Anglo-Irish politics (1998) · R. B. Wernham, After the Armada: Elizabethan England and the struggle for western Europe, 1588–1595 (1984) · GEC, Peerage, 3.134–5 · IGI · Burke, Peerage · NL Ire., GO MS 68, 113–19 · DNB · R. Refaussé and C. Lennon, eds., The registers of Christ Church Cathedral, Dublin (1998), 91 · J. Lodge, The peerage of Ireland, rev. M. Archdall, rev. edn, 3 (1789), 134–5 · A. E. Vicars, ed., Index to the prerogative wills of Ireland, 1536–1810 (1897)

Archives PRO NIre., estate MSS
Likenesses portrait, repro. in C. Falls, The birth of Ulster (1936)
Wealth at death owned perhaps 20,000 acres of land; government salary (income £1000?)

Caulfeild, Toby, third Baron Caulfeild of Charlemont

(1621–1642), politician, was born in Dublin, the eldest child of the seven sons and three daughters of William Caulfeild, second Baron Caulfeild of Charlemont (bap. 1587, d. 1640), and Mary (d. 1663), daughter of Sir John King. One of his younger brothers was William *Caulfeild, first Viscount Charlemont. He was educated in England at Henley School before entering Christ's College, Cambridge, in April 1637 and then Lincoln's Inn in October 1637, and matriculating from Exeter College, Oxford, in June 1638. In early 1640 he was elected MP for County Tyrone, and he succeeded his father as third baron and as governor of Charlemont Fort in December 1640.

On the evening of 22 October 1641 Charlemont's neighbour and fellow MP Sir Phelim O'Neill called on a social visit and thus captured the fort and its store of arms, marking the beginning of the 1641 rising; that evening the Irish also captured Dungannon, and early the following morning they took Mountjoy and Castle Caulfeild. O'Neill kept Lord Charlemont and his mother, brothers, and sisters prisoner in the fort for about fifteen weeks. About the end of January 1642 the prisoners were separated and moved; the young lord, who did not speak Irish, was en route for Cloughouter Castle when he was taken to Kinard, the home of Sir Phelim O'Neill, about 1 February. As the prisoner was walking through the gate of the house he was shot in the back by Edmond Boy O'Hugh, servant and foster brother to O'Neill, apparently roused to anger by a

jest of one of the prisoner's guards. Charlemont died from his wounds. Sir Phelim was absent from his home at the time, and was furious at this breach of his hospitality; some days later he had up to six of those responsible hanged and beheaded in Armagh city. Charlemont was succeeded by his brother Robert, who died two years later. BRIAN MAC CUARTA

Sources J. Lodge, The peerage of Ireland, rev. M. Archdall, rev. edn, 3 (1789), 135–7, 140–42 · B. McGrath, 'A biographical dictionary of the membership of the Irish House of Commons, 1640–1641', PhD diss., University of Dublin, 1997, 1.102 · Venn, Alum. Cant., 1/1.309 · T. Ó Donnchadha, ed., 'Cín Lae Ó Mealláin' [Ó Mealláin's diary]', Analecta Hibernica, 3 (1931); 5 (1934); 7 (1935) [English translation: TCD, MS 1071] · A relation touching the present state and condition of Ireland (1641/2) [Thomason tract E 138(22)] · deposition of Alexander Creichtown, Feb 1642, TCD, MS 834, fol. 85 · M. Perceval-Maxwell, 'The Ulster rising of 1641, and the depositions', Irish Historical Studies, 21 (1978–9), 144–67, esp. 149 · CSP Ire., 1633–47, 250 · GEC, Peerage · examination of Patrick Dory, 21 Feb 1653, TCD, MS 836, fol. 163

Caulfeild, William, first Viscount Charlemont

(1625–1671), army officer and politician, was the third son of William Caulfeild, second Baron Caulfeild of Charlemont (bap. 1587, d. 1640), and his wife, Mary (d. 1663), daughter of Sir John King of Boyle Abbey, co. Roscommon. He was the brother of Toby *Caulfeild (1621–1642) and Robert (1623–1644), the third and fourth barons respectively. He fought in the parliamentary side in the English civil war and in 1644 was taken prisoner at the battle of Newbury, the year in which he came into his title, following the death of his brother Robert. When the New Model Army came into being the following year he was commissioned as a captain of horse. In 1653 he married Sarah (d. 1712), second daughter of Charles Moore, second Viscount Drogheda, and Alice, daughter of Adam Loftus, Viscount Loftus of Ely; of their children, at least three sons and three daughters survived infancy, including William *Caulfeild, second Viscount Charlemont. He was responsible for the capture of Sir Phelim O'Neill in 1653, subsequently executed for his part in the Ulster rising of 1641 and the murder of Caulfeild's brother Toby in 1642. He served with Sir Charles Coote's regiment until it was disbanded in 1655, but continued as garrison commander at his family fort of Charlemont on the Armagh–Tyrone border.

In 1660 Caulfeild represented Lifford, co. Donegal, in the general convention in Dublin. After the Restoration Caulfeild was appointed to the Irish privy council and to the commission responsible for executing the king's declaration and instructions for the Irish land settlement. He was designated governor and constable of Charlemont Fort for life, but its strategic significance was such that he agreed to sell it to the crown for £3500 on 13 April 1664. His loyal service was recognized by the king in 1665 when he was created Viscount Charlemont. Described by Archbishop Oliver Plunkett in 1670 as 'president' of the 'province of Armagh', Caulfeild not only intervened to prevent the Armagh magistrates from forcing Catholics to attend protestant church, but also protected Plunkett and offered him the use of his home to say mass and give confirmations. He died in April 1671 and was buried in Armagh Cathedral on 25 May. **M. A. CREIGHTON**

Sources GEC, *Peerage* · Burke, *Peerage* (1970), 1.521 · J. Lodge, *The peerage of Ireland*, rev. M. Archdall, rev. edn, 7 vols. (1789), vol. 3, pp. 142–6 · *CSP Ire.*, 1660–70, addenda 1624–70 · *The letters of Saint Oliver Plunkett, 1625–1681, archbishop of Armagh and primate of all Ireland*, ed. J. Hanly (Dublin, 1979), 151–2 · S. J. Connolly, *Religion, law and power: the making of protestant Ireland, 1660–1760* (1995), 11–12, 21 · A. Clarke, *Prelude to Restoration in Ireland: the end of the Commonwealth, 1659–1660* (1999) · P. J. Corish, 'The Cromwellian regime, 1650–60', *A new history of Ireland*, ed. T. W. Moody and others, 3: *Early modern Ireland, 1534–1691* (1976)

Caulfeild, William, second Viscount Charlemont (*b.* after **1653**, *d.* **1726**), army officer and politician, was the second, but first surviving, son of William *Caulfeild, fifth Baron Caulfeild of Charlemont and first Viscount Charlemont (1625–1671), and Sarah (*d.* 1712), second daughter of Charles *Moore, second Viscount Moore of Drogheda. Caulfeild's parents had married in 1653, and he became second viscount in 1671 on his father's death. He married, on 11 July 1678, Anne (*d.* 1729), daughter of James *Margetson, archbishop of Armagh; they had seven sons and five daughters, at least four sons and four daughters surviving their father.

Charlemont was active militarily against James II and as a consequence he was attainted on 7 May 1689 and his estates sequestrated by the Jacobite parliament in Ireland. His lands were restored by William III and he was named governor of the fort of Charlemont and custos of Tyrone and Armagh. Charlemont was commissioned a captain in the earl of Kingston's foot in 1689. He took his seat in the Irish House of Lords on 5 October 1692 and played an active role in the parliament of 1692, as he did in that of 1695. On 23 April 1694 he was commissioned colonel of the 36th foot which he was to raise. This regiment was disbanded in 1697 and Charlemont placed on half pay. He entered King's Inns in Dublin on 9 June 1697.

Charlemont was named colonel of the revived 36th foot regiment on 28 June 1701. The regiment served at Cadiz in 1702, then in the West Indies before returning to Ireland in 1703. Charlemont was promoted brigadier-general on 25 August 1704, and served with his regiment in Spain at Barcelona. In May 1706 he quitted the regiment, but he subsequently claimed that the commander in Spain, Charles Mordaunt, third earl of Peterborough, had forced him out, pretending that he had an order from Queen Anne for his replacement. Upon his appealing to the queen the matter was referred to the general officers who met on 15 December 1707: Peterborough claimed misconduct by Charlemont at Fort Montjuich and proceeded to delay matters. In February 1708 Charlemont was called as a witness against Peterborough's conduct in Spain, and a court martial to decide the dispute between the two met that month, but with no result. Charlemont never recovered his regiment, despite petitioning the queen again in December 1710.

Charlemont was sworn of the Irish privy council on 5 June 1726. He died at his home in College Green, Dublin, on 21 July 1726, and was buried on 26 July in the family vault in Armagh Cathedral. His widow died on 28 December 1729. **STUART HANDLEY**

Sources GEC, *Peerage* · C. Dalton, ed., *English army lists and commission registers, 1661–1714*, 3 (1896), 113; 4 (1898), 9; 5 (1902), 17, 159 · *The manuscripts of the House of Lords*, new ser., 12 vols. (1900–77), vol. 7, pp. 399, 466–7 · J. Lodge, *The peerage of Ireland*, 3 (1754), 97–102 · N. Luttrell, *A brief historical relation of state affairs from September 1678 to April 1714*, 6 (1857), 177–8, 265–8 · BL, Add. MS 61164, fols. 135–7 · BL, Add. MS 61515, fol. 127 · *Descriptive list of secretaries of state: state papers domestic, Anne*, 3 vols. (1995), 258–60 · N. B. Leslie, *The succession of colonels of the British army from 1660 to the present day* (1974), 75 · *The historical register*, 15 (1730), 4

Wealth at death legacies of over £2500; estate in co. Tyrone: will, 1726, Prerogative court of Armagh

Caulfield, James (1764–1826), author and printseller, was born in The Vineyard, Clerkenwell, on 11 February 1764, the son of a music engraver. He was brought up in Cambridge and educated by Christopher Sharpe, a print collector and amateur etcher who conveyed his passion to his pupil. In 1780 his father set Caulfield up with a small print shop in Old Round Court, in the Strand, where Dr Johnson was one of his customers. He was soon specializing in old English engravings and particularly in portraits, a market which boomed after the publication in 1769 of James Granger's *Biographical History of England*, which set a fashion for 'grangerizing' or pasting extra illustrations into historical or topographical books. He moved to a larger shop in Castle Street, Leicester Square, where he was patronized by the second generation of portrait collectors and grangerizers, Sir Charles Towneley, James Bindley, General Dowdeswell, Sir Philip Musgrave, Clayton Mordaunt Cracherode (whose collection is in the British Museum), and Alexander Hendras Sutherland (whose collection is in the Ashmolean Museum and the Bodleian Library, Oxford).

Many old English portrait prints were too rare and valuable to supply the extraordinarily large demand for them. To this end, many old plates were republished and many old prints were copied. Caulfield came to specialize in prints illustrating Granger's twelfth class of people— 'such as lived to a great age, deformed persons, convicts, &c.'—whose portraits were very often the hardest to come by. In 1788 he began his work *Portraits, Memoirs, and Characters of Remarkable Persons*, a series of reproductions of old portrait paintings and copies of rare old or popular prints accompanied by letterpress biographies. This was published in parts between 1790 and 1795. Most of his subsequent publications were in the same vein. About 1795 he republished Taylor the Water Poet's *Life of Old Parr* with new prints of the man who died aged 152. His plates for *Remarkable Persons* were reprinted with new ones in *The New Wonderful Museum* (1803–8), devoted to remarkable events, objects, and people. His *History of the Gunpowder Plot* (1804) and *Cromwelliana* (1810) deviated only slightly from the obsession with Granger's twelfth class, providing material for extra illustration. By this time Caulfield had married Mary Gascoigne (*d.* 1816) with whom he had seven children, four of whom survived him.

There was much speculation in 1814 as to the authorship

of the satirical poem *Chalcographimania, or, The portrait-collector and printsellers chronicle, with infatuations of every description*, containing lots of gossip on the insatiable headhunters who had provided Caulfield with a living. Caulfield denied authorship of this verse (also ascribed to William Henry Ireland and Thomas Coram) but very soon afterwards took advantage of the publicity to publish *Calcographiana: the printsellers chronicle and collectors guide to the knowledge and value of engraved British portraits*. For collectors and dealers this provided useful remarks on the value of old prints and the dangers of deceptive modern reprints and copies. It still affords insights into the extraordinarily inflated market for antiquarian portrait prints. Caulfield continued to deal from his shop in Wells Street, off Oxford Street, and to publish useful accessories such as his *Catalogue of Portraits of Foreigners who have Visited England* (1814) and *Gallery of British Portraits* (1814). He found a new use for his old plates and others in the *Eccentric Magazine* containing lives and portraits of his favourite misers, dwarfs, murderers, and idiots. In 1821 he edited *Memoirs of the Celebrated Persons Comprising the Kit-Cat Club* to illuminate the mezzotints by John Faber and similar portraits. He edited the fifth enlarged edition of Granger in 1824 and produced three parts of *Biographical Sketches Illustrative of British History* (1823–). This remained incomplete. His obituarist records that in later life he 'sacrificed too often at the shrine of Bacchus' and was 'excessively troublesome when inebriated' (G. S., 569). He died in St Bartholomew's Hospital on 22 April 1826, after breaking his kneecap, and was buried in Clerkenwell church.

TIMOTHY CLAYTON

Sources G. S. [G. Smeeton], *GM*, 1st ser., 96/1 (1826), 569 ff. · J. Caulfield, *Calcographiana: the printsellers chronicle and collectors guide to the knowledge and value of engraved British portraits* (1814) · *Chalcographimania, or, The portrait-collector and printsellers chronicle, with infatuations of every description* (1814) · J. Caulfield, *Portraits, memoirs, and characters of remarkable persons* (1790–95); 2nd edn (1813) · Nichols, *Illustrations*, 6.441 · *DNB* · M. Pointon, *Hanging the head: portraiture and social formation in eighteenth-century England* (1993)

Likenesses group portrait, line engraving, pubd 1798 (after *Sketches taken at Print Sales* by P. Sandby), BM · R. Cooper, stipple (after H. Walton), BM, NPG; repro. in Caulfield, *Chalcographiana* · engraving, repro. in Caulfield, *Portraits* (1790), frontispiece · etching (after A. Bengo), repro. in *Portraits from sketches made at rare print sales* (1814)

Caulfield, Richard (1823–1887), antiquary, was born in Cork on 23 April 1823, son of William Caulfield and Catherine Gosnell. His father was a merchant dealing in oils and colours in Cork city. He was educated by Dr Edward Browne at the Bandon endowed school. He was admitted a pensioner at Trinity College, Dublin, in 1841, and graduated BA in 1845, LLB in 1864, and LLD in 1866. He later acknowledged the influence of the lectures in ancient philosophy given by William Archer Butler. In 1864 he became librarian of the Royal Cork Institution, and in 1876 was appointed librarian to the Queen's College, Cork. As an archaeologist and genealogist he had few rivals, and his assistance was frequently sought. He was elected a fellow of the Society of Antiquaries in 1862, and

in 1882 was made an honorary member of the Real Academia de la Historia in Madrid. He was a member for many years of the Société des Antiquaires of Normandy, and an active member of the committee for rebuilding Cork Cathedral. In 1845 he had been elected a freeman of Cork city. In 1855 he was made a council member of the Cork Cuvierian Society. He died at the Royal Cork Institution on 3 February 1887, and was buried in the churchyard of Douglas, co. Cork. His wife, Dora Dowden, whom he married in 1869, survived him.

Caulfield's published work centred mainly on the records of the cathedral and churches of Cork, Cloyne, and Youghal, and the corporations of Cork, Youghal, and Kinsale. Of particular importance are his editions of the diary of Rowland Davies DD, dean of Cork (1689–90), published by the Camden Society, his discovery and subsequent publication of the autobiographical fragment by Sir Richard Cox, and a life of St Findbarr, which he found in the Bodleian Library and published in 1864. He wrote numerous articles for learned journals and was editor of the *Journal of the Royal Historical and Archaeological Association of Ireland*.

THOMAS SECCOMBE, *rev.* MARIE-LOUISE LEGG

Sources J. P. McCarthy, *Journal of the Cork Historical and Archaeological Society*, 2nd ser., 92 (1987), 1–23 · *The Times* (24 Feb 1887) · Burtchaell & Sadleir, *Alum. Dubl.* · *Cork Weekly News* (19 Feb 1887) · *The Athenaeum* (26 Feb 1887), 290

Archives Dublin City Library · NL Ire., notes relating to his family · Representative Church Body Library, Dublin, notebooks · TCD, antiquarian papers · U. Leeds · University College, Cork, notebooks | Archbishop Marsh's Library, Dublin, collections relating to the municipal affairs of Cork, sixteenth to eighteenth centuries · Dublin corporation, letters from Thomas Crofton Croker · U. Leeds, Brotherton L., letters to John Torrens Kyle

Caunt, Benjamin (1814–1861), pugilist, was born in the village of Hucknall Torkard, Nottinghamshire, on 22 March 1814 (some sources give 1815), the son of Robert Caunt, a labourer, and his wife, Martha. He was baptized on 15 May 1814. His father, a tenant of Lord Byron, worked on Byron's Newstead estate. Benjamin, according to his own account, was a gamekeeper; other people said he was a navvy or a miner. His height was 6 feet 2½ inches, and his weight 14 stone 7 lb; his size rather than his skill was the basis for his pugilistic aspirations. On 21 July 1835 Caunt lost to William Thompson, known as Bendigo. On 17 August 1837 he defeated William Butler in fourteen rounds for a stake of £20 a side. Caunt again fought Bendigo on 3 April 1838 on Skipwith Common, near Selby, when, after a fight of seventy-five rounds, lasting eighty minutes, a dispute arose, which was settled in favour of Caunt; the referee's decision notwithstanding, he had to ride for his life to escape Bendigo's partisans. On 26 October 1840 he beat John Leechman, known as Brassey, after 101 rounds. *Bell's Life* commented, 'We have seldom recorded a fight in which we experienced more difficulty to render the details interesting' (Miles, 3.68). In a fight with Nicholas Ward on 2 February 1841 Caunt was disqualified for a foul blow. At a match with the same opponent at Long Marston, near Stratford upon Avon, on 11 May, Ward gave in after the thirty-fifth round. Manoeuvring his opponents man who ever beat the famous Tom Sayers) on 23 September 1857; Langham was his brother-in-law, and family disputes enlivened the contest. After an unsatisfactory fight of sixty rounds, the men shook hands and no decision was given. Caunt was also well known as a pigeon-shooter, and while taking part in a match early in 1860 he caught a cold, from which he died at the Coach and Horses on 10 September 1861. He was buried in Hucknall Torkard churchyard on 14 September. Caunt was a big, unscientific fighter—known as Ursa Major and Goliath the Second; it was reported, 'he hits at random and has no idea of self-defence' (Dowling, *Fights*, 161, 187, 139). He found it very troublesome to fight such admittedly 'shifty' opponents as Ward, Langham, and Bendigo. The results were increasingly unedifying. It has been suggested that he had a more lasting claim to fame through having inspired the christening of the Palace of Westminster bell as Big Ben, though Sir Benjamin Hall remains the official candidate.

G. C. BOASE, *rev.* JULIAN LOCK

Sources H. D. Miles, *Pugilistica: being one hundred and forty-four years of the history of British boxing*, 3 vols. (1880–81), vol. 3, pp. 47–93 · [F. Dowling], *Fights for the championship; and celebrated prize battles* (1855) · B. Lynch, *Knuckles and gloves* (1922) · F. Dowling, *Fistiana* (1868) · Boase, *Mod. Eng. biog.* · D. Johnson, *Bare fist fighters of the 18th and 19th century: 1704–1861* (1987) · parish register, baptism, Hucknall Torkard, St Mary, 15 May 1814 · *IGI*

Likenesses engraving, NPG [*see illus.*] · portrait, repro. in Miles, *Pugilistica*, vol. 3, facing p. 48

Wealth at death under £100: probate, 2 Oct 1861, *CGPLA Eng. & Wales*

Benjamin Caunt (1814–1861), by unknown engraver

into fouls was Ward's main fighting skill. Having done so in the case of the (disputed) champion, 'Deaf' Burke, Ward might even have been champion; having now defeated both him and Bendigo, Caunt claimed the title.

In September 1841 Caunt went to the United States, taking with him the champion's belt. No fighting, however, took place in America. He exhibited himself in theatres, and returned to Britain on 10 March 1842. He brought back with him Charles Freeman, an American giant, 6 feet 10½ inches tall, weighing 18 stone, and with him made a sparring tour throughout the United Kingdom. Freeman died of consumption in the Winchester Hospital on 18 October 1845, aged twenty-eight, by which time his weight had fallen to 10 stone.

In 1843 Caunt became proprietor of the Coach and Horses public house, 90 St Martin's Lane, London, and married, his wife apparently being named Martha, like his mother. He went into training in 1845, and, having reduced himself from 17 stone to 14 stone, met Bendigo near Sutfield Green, Oxfordshire, on 9 September 1845, before over 10,000 spectators. The fight lasted over two hours, and in the ninety-third round the referee, George Osbaldiston, gave a decision (of doubtful correctness) in favour of Bendigo, who therefore claimed the championship. On 15 January 1851 a fire took place in the Coach and Horses, when two of Caunt's children were burnt to death. This calamity earned him great sympathy, and a ballad on the subject sold extensively. On his last appearance in the ring Caunt met Nathaniel Langham (the only

Caunter, John Hobart (1792–1851), writer, born at Dittisham, Devon, was the second son of George Caunter, governor of Penang, and his wife, Harriett Georgina, *née* Hutchings. He went to India about 1810 as a cadet with the 34th foot, but was soon disgusted with his situation and, 'having discovered, much to his disappointment, nothing on the continent of Asia to interest him', he returned home. He recorded his impressions of India in a poem entitled *The Cadet* (2 vols., 1814). Caunter then studied at Peterhouse, Cambridge, with the intention of being ordained. In 1828 he obtained the degree of BD. He was perpetual curate of St Paul's Chapel, Foley Place, London, from 1825 until 1844, and also of Portland Chapel, London, 1836–43. He was rector of Hailsham, Sussex, 1844–6, and minister of a proprietary chapel in Kennington, 1846–8, when he was appointed curate of Prittlewell, Essex. He was also chaplain to the earl of Thanet.

Caunter was well known in London as a fashionable preacher and was a minor author and poet of some substance. India remained a preoccupation, treated in several volumes including *India* (3 vols., 1836) (part of the Romance of History series). He published five volumes entitled *The Oriental Annual of Science* (1834–8). Caunter's other works include *The Island Bride* (1830), a poem in six cantos; *The Fellow Commoner* (3 vols., 1836), a novel; *St Leon: a Drama* (1835); and several works of theology. Caunter died at Edward Street, London, on 14 November 1851, survived by his wife and three daughters, for whom a public subscription was opened after his death.

His brother, **Richard McDonald Caunter** (1800–1879),

soldier and Church of England clergyman, had a similar career; he was born in Penang, served in the 16th lancers in India, went to Sidney Sussex College, Cambridge, in 1820, and was ordained in 1824. He held numerous curacies in London and the home counties, finally moving to Drayton about 1862. He was the author of a verse tragedy, *Attila* (1832), and died on 10 March 1879.

H. C. G. MATTHEW

Sources F. L. Caunter, *Caunter family records* (1930) · Venn, *Alum. Cant.* · *GM*, 2nd ser., 37 (1852), 627 · *The Times* (20 Nov 1851) · *N&Q*, 4th ser., 6 (1870), 274, 353, 445 · BL, Add. MS 24867, fol. 41

Caunter, Richard McDonald (1800–1879). *See under* Caunter, John Hobart (1792–1851).

Caus [Caux], **Isaac de** (1589/90–1648), garden designer and architect, was born in Dieppe. He was a relative (possibly a nephew) of Salomon de *Caus, and was, like him, a Huguenot. The date of his arrival in England is not known, but he was in the country by the early 1620s, and was naturalized in 1634.

Like Salomon, Isaac de Caus specialized in the design and construction of grottoes and waterworks. His earliest recorded work in England was the grotto in the basement of the Banqueting House in Whitehall, recently built to the designs of Inigo Jones, which he made in 1623–4. His most celebrated work of this kind was the grotto at Wilton House in Wiltshire, where it formed part of an elaborate formal garden designed by de Caus for the fourth earl of Pembroke in 1632–5. This, 'the greatest of English Renaissance gardens' (Strong, 151), featured statues and fountains set in parterres of *broderie*, flanked by arbours. The grotto was entered through a classical façade at the far end of the garden and contained spouting sea monsters, a table with hidden jets to wet the unwary, and hydraulically simulated birdsong. The whole was illustrated in a set of engravings published by de Caus entitled *Wilton Garden* (undated). He was also the author of a book entitled *Nouvelle invention de lever l'eau plus hault que sa source avec quelques machines mouvantes par le moyen de l'eau* (1644). This was closely based on the treatise *Les raisons des forces mouvantes*, published by Salomon de Caus in 1615, from which most of the copperplates were taken. An English translation was published in 1659 as *New and Rare Inventions of Water-Works*.

As an architect de Caus was involved in the fourth earl of Bedford's development on his Covent Garden estate in London (1631 onwards). Although Inigo Jones was responsible for the general scheme, there is evidence that de Caus supervised the building of some of the houses, and he himself lived in one of them for a time. At Wilton House the names of Inigo Jones and Isaac de Caus again appear together in connection with the rebuilding of the south front in 1636–40.

According to John Aubrey, this was to have been designed by Jones, but:

> having at that time ... engaged in his Majesties buildings at Greenwich, [he] could not attend to it: but he recommended it to an ingeniouse architect Monsieur ... de Caus, ... who performed it very well: but not without the advice and

approbation of Mr. Jones.   (J. Aubrey, *The Natural History of Wiltshire*, ed. J. Britton, 1847, 83–4)

That de Caus was in charge at Wilton is confirmed by documentary evidence, but precisely how the responsibility for the design of this celebrated building should be apportioned between Jones and de Caus is a problem to which the surviving evidence does not provide a categorical answer. Only one other building is known to have been designed by de Caus: an addition, long demolished without record, to Stalbridge Park, Dorset, for the first earl of Cork.

Isaac de Caus died in Paris, and was buried on 24 February 1648 in the Huguenot cemetery there. He was described in the register as 'Isaac de Caus, natif de Dieppe, agé de 58 ans, architeque'. His return to France may have been because of the civil war in England, but his family appears to have remained in London, for in July 1655 the will of Mary de Caus, widow, the lessee of a tenement on the Bedford estate in London, was proved by her elder son, Isaac. Other children mentioned in the will were Peter, Mary, and Magdalen.

HOWARD COLVIN

Sources Colvin, *Archs.* · R. Strong, *The Renaissance garden in England* (1979) · H. Colvin, 'The south front of Wilton House', *Essays in English architectural history* (1999), 136–57 · *The parish of St Paul, Covent Garden*, Survey of London, 36 (1970), 28 · P. Palme, *The triumph of peace: a study of the Whitehall Banqueting House* (1957), 66 · W. A. Shaw, ed., *Letters of denization and acts of naturalization for aliens in England and Ireland, 1603–1700*, Huguenot Society of London, 18 (1911), 53 · *The Lismore papers, first series: autobiographical notes, remembrances and diaries of Sir Richard Boyle, first and 'great' earl of Cork*, ed. A. B. Grosart, 5 (privately printed, London, 1886), 4 · *Catalogue of the drawings collection of the Royal Institute of British Architects: C–F* (1972), 80–81 · J. Harris and A. A. Tait, eds., *Catalogue of the drawings by Inigo Jones, John Webb and Isaac de Caus at Worcester College, Oxford* (1979), 47–53 · will of Mary de Caus, PRO, PROB 11/250, sig. 377
Archives Wilts. & Swindon RO, Earl of Pembroke MSS

Caus, Salomon de (*c.*1576–1626), engineer and architect, was born in the pays de Caux (whence derived the family name) in Normandy, probably in Dieppe. He was a relative (possibly an uncle) of Isaac de *Caus (1589/90–1648). In all probability Salomon's parents were Huguenots who took refuge in England. Knowledge about de Caus's youth is restricted to what he himself revealed in the dedications of his books. He studied such classical authors as Hero of Alexandria, Vitruvius, and Pliny, and was also familiar with the historical works of Diodorus Siculus and Diogenes Laertius. He derived his knowledge of mathematics from the first six books of Euclid and was acquainted with technical treatises by Jacques Besson and Agostino Ramelli.

From about 1595 until about 1598 de Caus journeyed through Italy, a tour which proved to be of great importance for his education. After his Italian travels, about 1598 he became an engineer in the service of the archdukes Albert and Isabella at Brussels. Here he became responsible for the construction of artificial grottoes and fountains in their gardens in Brussels and on their estate at Mariemont. On 21 January 1605 he received an official appointment as engineer to the archdukes, and on 10 April 1606 he married Hester Picart in the parish of St

Géry in Brussels. Their only son, William, was baptized on 24 February 1607, but died shortly afterwards.

In 1610 de Caus became an engineer in London at the court of James I. During his stay in Brussels he had already given some lessons in perspective to Henry, prince of Wales, and he was now attached to Henry's household at Richmond Palace. He supervised and transformed gardens for Queen Anne, the prince of Wales, and some of the principal courtiers. With his relative Isaac, he built the porticoes and loggias of Gorhambury and Campden House, Kensington. He must have known Cornelis Drebbel, who at that time—like de Caus—was in the service of Henry as an inventor. De Caus made a number of ingenious discoveries, which he later published in the second part of his *Les raisons des forces mouvantes*.

De Caus gave drawing lessons to Princess Elizabeth, Henry's youngest sister, and built a picture gallery at Richmond Palace for Henry, who was a great art lover; in 1612 he published the lessons he had given to Henry as *La perspective avec la raison des ombres et miroirs*. The death of the prince in November of that year marked the end of his employment. On 26 July 1613 he was paid £50 'for attendance on the late Prince' (*CSP dom.*, *1611–18*). In the year of Henry's death his sister Elizabeth married the elector palatine, Frederick V, and she asked de Caus to join her entourage. At her husband's residence, the castle of Heidelberg, de Caus designed a fabulous emblematic garden, for which the hillside had to be terraced; he later described the technical problems he had to conquer in his *Hortus palatinus, a Frederico rege Boemiae, electore palatino, Heidelbergae exstructus* (1620). On 14 July 1614 he became the elector's official engineer and architect. During his stay at Heidelberg he published two other works, *Institution harmonique divisée en deux parties: en la première sont monstrées les proportions des intervalles harmoniques, et en la deuxiesme les compositions d'icelles* and, his most important work, *Les raisons des forces mouvantes avec diverses machines tant utilles que plaisantes: aus quelles sont adjoints plusieurs desseings de grottes et fontaines*, both in 1615.

In 1619 Elizabeth became queen of Bohemia for one winter; she later settled at The Hague. De Caus did not follow her into exile, but returned to France. During the years 1618–20 he had vainly negotiated with the council of Rouen about the construction of a bridge over the Seine; in 1620 he was employed in public works in Paris, where his duties involved the transportation of water from the Seine into the city, both for drinking water and for cleaning the streets and the squares. In the last years of his life he occupied himself mainly with mathematical studies. His last book—which was on the subject of sundials—was published in 1624.

De Caus supplemented his income by producing air- and water-driven engines, which were used mainly to make emblematic figures to move. He used water, light, and artificial or solar heat as sources of energy. From *Les raisons des forces mouvantes*, it appears that he was an Aristotelian: he explained the action of his machines in terms of the four Aristotelian elements earth, water, fire, and air. Both artist and artisan, he attempted to place his inventions in a

magico-philosophical framework. He died in Paris, where he was living with his wife in the rue Poitou. On 15 January 1626 they made a mutual last will, from which it appears that they had no children. De Caus was buried at the protestant cemetery La Trinité at Paris on 28 February 1626.

H. A. M. SNELDERS

Sources C. S. Maks, *Salomon de Caus, 1576–1626* (1935) · A. Stöcklein, *Leitbilder der Technik: biblische Tradition und technischer Fortschritt* (1969) · A. G. H. Bachrach, 'The role of the Huygens family in seventeenth-century Dutch culture', *Studies on Christiaan Huygens*, ed. H. J. M. Bos and others (1980), 27–52 · E. Haag and E. Haag, *La France protestante*, 2nd edn, 6 vols. (Paris, 1877–88), vol. 3, p. 919 · K. M. Barañano-Letamendía, 'Der cartesianische Discours: eine plastische Geometrie', *Heidelberger Jahrbücher*, 32 (1988), 43–77
Likenesses portrait, Kurpfälzisches Museum, Heidelberg; repro. in Maks, *Salomon de Caus*

Causantín mac Cuilén. *See* Constantine III (*d.* 997) *under* Culen (*d.* 971).

Causantin mac Fergus. *See* Constantine mac Fergus, *under* Picts, kings of the (*act. c.*300–*c.*900).

Causton, Alice (*fl.* 1364). *See under* Women traders and artisans in London (*act. c.*1200–*c.*1500).

Causton, Richard Knight, Baron Southwark (1843–1929), politician, was born at 3 Pomeroy Terrace, Old Kent Road, Deptford, Kent, on 25 September 1843, the second son of Joseph Causton (1815–1871), wholesale stationer and sheriff of London, who was knighted in 1869, and his wife, Mary Anne (*d.* 1892), daughter of Edward Potter. Nothing is known of his education. He entered the successful family business, Sir Joseph Causton & Sons, printers and stationers, located in Eastcheap and Southwark, of which he became a partner and later chairman. On 10 August 1871 he married Selina Mary Chambers [*see below*]. They had no children.

Causton's family had a tradition of political involvement. His great-uncle Matthew Forster and Forster's son John had both been Liberal members for Berwick upon Tweed. Joseph Causton, before failing health robbed him of the opportunity, was considered likely to become lord mayor of London, gaining support from the City guild of the Company of Skinners, of which Richard, like his father and his brother before him, served as master (in 1877–8).

After Joseph Causton's death a 'political godfather' (Southwark, 92), Arthur B. Winterbotham, a wealthy Liberal cloth manufacturer in Gloucestershire, supported and facilitated Richard Causton's rising public career, which was assisted also by his father-in-law, Sir Thomas Chambers. Causton first stood, unsuccessfully, in 1874 as a Liberal candidate for Colchester. At his second attempt, in 1880, he topped the poll in the two-member constituency. In 1885, in the now single-member constituency, he was defeated by 166 votes. He lost again by a slightly larger margin in 1886.

The Liberal member for West Southwark in London resigned in 1888, and Causton, the 'comfortably-off gentleman reminiscent of Charles Dickens's Mr Pickwick' (Schneer, 233), returned to politics in the subsequent by-election. He gained political popularity through his opposition to a 'wheel and van' tax proposed on business vehicles, his campaign helping to defeat the proposal.

With the Liberal victory at the general election of 1892, when he retained his West Southwark seat, Causton was appointed as a junior lord of the treasury and a party whip. With the defeat of the government in 1895 he remained as an opposition whip, proving 'a most efficient slave-driver' (Southwark, 144). He was respected and liked by colleagues and opponents. Known from youth for his sporting prowess, especially in cricket and later golf, Causton was vice-president of the Surrey County Cricket Club, and he was remembered as also always having 'played the game' in his professional life (The Times, 25 Feb 1929, 17), with no deviousness or pretence, and as being a 'plainspoken' man (Schneer, 233).

After a narrow victory in 1895 Causton faced, as his Conservative opponent in the 'khaki' election of 1900, the lord mayor of London, Sir Alfred Newton; many predicted that Causton would be 'settled for good' as an MP by the contest (Southwark, 150). Newton ran a jingoistic campaign, largely based upon his role as founder of the City imperial volunteer force established for the South African campaign. In his poor south London constituency Causton identified the need for a different approach to the promotion of imperial greatness. In his addresses he strongly emphasized the need for social reform, so that 'the physical and intellectual well-being of our people, so truly essential to the prosperity of our Empire, be advanced' (Schneer, 233). He held on to the constituency by a similarly small margin to that in 1895. In the Liberal government after 1905 he served as paymaster-general, and became a privy councillor in January 1906.

Causton's wife carefully described him in his early political career as 'a Liberal, but not a Radical, candidate' (Southwark, 91), and his political philosophy was defined in Dod's Parliamentary Companion as of being for 'the policy of peace abroad, and of a safe and steady progress in those reforms at home much needed by agricultural and commercial interests' (Dod's Parliamentary Companion, 1900). In the general election of January 1910 he narrowly lost his seat. He wrote that he had been finally overwhelmed by a 'united combination of forces against me. Hops, Beer, Church, Roman Catholics (my opponent is a Catholic), Tariff Reformers amongst the poorest … together … they were too much for me' (Blewett, 331). But it has been suggested that Causton's defeat was due to his having 'lost popularity through having moved his own firm of wholesale stationers out the constituency' (Pelling, 51).

In July 1910 Causton was created Baron Southwark. In the House of Lords he took a particular interest in the issue of decimal currency, introducing the bill on that subject into the Lords in 1918 and serving on the royal commission inquiring into the matter. He also held a number of other public positions through political, business, and personal interest. He was president of the London chamber of commerce in 1913, and vice-president of the Association of British Chambers of Commerce, a lieutenant for the City of London, a fellow of the Statistical Society,

president of the Royal Eye Hospital, and vice-president of the Royal School for the Indigent Blind, as well as chairman of the London Liberal and Radical Union.

Continuing his earlier keen interest in sport and also in pastimes such as photography, Southwark 'retained his vigour well into old age' (The Times, 25 Feb 1929, 17). He died at his home, 12 Devonshire Place, London, on 23 February 1929, and was buried on 27 February.

Causton's wife, **Selina Mary Causton** [née Chambers], Lady Southwark (1852–1932), was born at 7 Great Cumberland Street, London, on 7 June 1852, the daughter of Sir Thomas *Chambers (1814–1891), a lawyer who became recorder of London and a Liberal MP, and his wife, Diana, née White (d. 1877). Her father discouraged her intellectual ambitions, and she had a casual education by a series of governesses, together with lessons in dancing and music. Her novel Claudius (1879), set in Rome during the reign of Domitian, was begun when she was fifteen. Since her mother's health was poor, she acted as her father's companion and had the opportunity to travel on the continent and to meet his political acquaintances. After her marriage in 1871 she also assisted her husband's political career, canvassing for him at elections, attending meetings, and sometimes addressing crowds of electors. Her Social and Political Reminiscences (1913) contains vivid accounts of late Victorian electioneering, together with anecdotes of the public figures whom she had met in London society. She also described changes in court life since the 1860s. A keen amateur artist, she persuaded many leading figures to sit for her sketches, which she reproduced along with her reminiscences. She was also a talented musician. She died in a nursing home, Maycroft, Shanklin, Isle of Wight, on 1 January 1932 and was buried at North Creake, Fakenham, Norfolk.

MARC BRODIE

Sources S. M. Causton, Lady Southwark, Social and political reminiscences (1913) • The Times (25 Feb 1929), 17; (2 Jan 1932), 12 • L. G. Pine, The new extinct peerage, 1884–1971 (1972) • b. cert. • b. cert. [Selina Mary Causton, Lady Southwark] • d. cert. [Selina Mary Causton, Lady Southwark] • A. T. C. Pratt, ed., People of the period: being a collection of the biographies of upwards of six thousand living celebrities, 2 vols. (1897) • A. T. C. Pratt, Men and women of the period (1899) • J. Schneer, London, 1900: the imperial metropolis (1999) • N. Blewett, The peers, the parties and the people: the general elections of 1910 (1972) • H. Pelling, Social geography of British elections, 1885–1910 (1967) • Dod's Parliamentary Companion (1900) • Walford, County families (1909) • F. W. S. Craig, British parliamentary election results, 1885–1918 (1974)

Likenesses double portrait, photograph (with Lady Southwark), repro. in Southwark, Social and political reminiscences, frontispiece • photograph, repro. in The Times (25 Feb 1929), 16

Wealth at death £21,282 12s. 2d.: probate, 3 May 1929, CGPLA Eng. & Wales • £3682 6s. 7d.—Selina Mary Causton, Lady Southwark: probate, 1932, CGPLA Eng. & Wales

Causton, Selina Mary, Lady Southwark (1852–1932). See under Causton, Richard Knight, Baron Southwark (1843–1929).

Causton, Thomas (d. 1570), composer, is of obscure origins; neither his parentage nor his date of birth is known. One Causton was a member, possibly a chorister, of Cardinal Wolsey's household in 1524–5; if this was the composer, his birth date was earlier than 1515 or thereabouts.

Causton the composer was a gentleman of the royal household chapel from about 1550 until his death. In one of her final acts of patronage Queen Mary solicited for him the freedom of the city of London in a letter to the mayor and aldermen, dated 29 October 1558. He died in London on 28 October 1570.

Causton's surviving compositions consist of English anthems, canticles, and metrical psalm settings published in John Day's collections *Whole Psalmes in Foure Partes* (1563) and *Certaine Notes* (1560/1565). Since over half the music contained in the latter compilation is of Causton's own composition, it appears likely that he exercised much influence over the selection of its contents. None of his surviving compositions was written for the Latin use of Salisbury, which was restored by Mary, but an anthem of which he claimed authorship, 'In Trouble and Adversity', is a recycling of an item of pre-Reformation music. It is a *contrafactum* of the 'In nomine' section of the Benedictus of John Taverner's mass *Gloria tibi trinitas* (composed c.1525). Although finally published in 1565, Causton's *contrafactum* appears to have been made during the reign of Edward VI, whose liturgical reforms necessitated the hurried composition (or recomposition) of vernacular repertory; another Edwardian *contrafactum* by Causton was included in the same collection. A similar adaptation of pre-Reformation practices to the needs of the 1549 prayer book is Causton's 'Service for men'; largely based on Salisbury psalm-tones and written in faburden style, this early Edwardian setting of morning prayer, communion, and evening prayer echoes pre-Reformation improvisatory techniques.

MAGNUS WILLIAMSON

Sources A. Ashbee, ed., *Records of English court music*, 9 vols. (1986–96), vols. 7–8 · A. Ashbee and D. Lasocki, eds., *A biographical dictionary of English court musicians, 1485–1714*, 2 vols. (1998) · J. Aplin, '"The fourth kind of faburden": the identity of an English four-part style', *Music and Letters*, 61 (1980), 245–65 · J. Aplin, 'The origin of John Day's *Certaine notes*', *Music and Letters*, 62 (1981), 295–9 · R. Bowers, 'The cultivation and promotion of music in the household and orbit of Thomas Wolsey', *Cardinal Wolsey: church, state, and art*, ed. S. J. Gunn and P. G. Lindley (1991), 178–218

Cautherley, Samuel (c.1747–1805), actor, was rumoured to be a love child of the great actor David *Garrick. Malicious gossip claimed Peg Woffington as his mother. A more plausible candidate is Jane *Hippisley (1719–1791) [*see under* Hippisley, John (1696–1748)], who had played Ophelia to Garrick's Hamlet at Goodman's Fields and who, in 1747–8, adopted the married name of Mrs Green without known recourse to a husband. The 1775 edition of *Theatrical Biography*, which published the rumour of this productive liaison between Garrick and Hippisley, is not, however, reliable, and Cautherley's parentage remains a mystery. What is clear is that, after his marriage in 1749, Garrick assumed the responsibilities of a guardian towards the boy.

Cautherley made his first appearance at Drury Lane on 28 April 1755, when Garrick's farce *Miss in her Teens* was given a novelty airing with a cast of children, but his serious début came on 23 October 1755, when he played the boy Duke of York to Garrick's Richard III. The fact that he made a handful of appearances in 1756 and 1757 suggests that Garrick considered him less than outstanding. We know from surviving letters that Cautherley was sent to board at a school in Bromley in 1759, and that Garrick had cause for concern about his charge's slow academic progress. The educational experiment was short-lived, and on 9 October 1760 Cautherley was billed as Prince Edward to Thomas Sheridan's Richard III at Drury Lane, where he made sporadic appearances during the next three seasons. From June 1763 to November 1764, at Garrick's expense, he was in Paris, probably with a tutor in attendance, but on 26 September 1765 he made his adult début at Drury Lane as George Barnwell in George Lillo's *The London Merchant*. The small theatrical success that Cautherley had over the next ten years at Drury Lane was owed to Garrick's indulgence. He was given his chance as Hamlet on 23 September 1766 and as Romeo seven days later, and failed to seize it. He was handsome, unintelligent, and vain enough to resent Garrick's wise decision to cast him in no more leading tragic roles.

On 4 July 1771, from Garrick's home in Hampton, Cautherley married Susanna Blanchard, the daughter of George III's wealthy cardmaker. Buoyed up by the new independence his wife had brought him, he began to pester Garrick for better parts. Eventually the exasperated actor–manager wrote a stinging letter, dated 7 October 1773, attacking Cautherley for his unjustified self-importance and desiring him to 'do your business or to leave it' (*Letters*, 2.902). Frightened into apology, Cautherley contained his bitterness for two years, but on 27 September 1775, the day after what proved to be his last appearance at Drury Lane, he sent Garrick a letter of resignation. Garrick's third-person response, dated 2 October 1775, ends chillingly: 'Mr Garrick said in a former letter, that Mr Cautherly [*sic*] could confer no favour upon him, which he now retracts; for he confesses, Mr Cautherly has found a Way to confer a very great one' (ibid., 3.1037).

The remaining ten years of Cautherley's undistinguished theatrical career were spent in provincial playhouses; he is known to have acted in Bristol, Hull, Dublin, Edinburgh, and York. There is no record of his response to Garrick's death in 1779, but in 1800 he wrote to Garrick's widow: 'The Gratitude I shall ever feel for the many kindnesses confer'd on me, while under your Hospitable Roof (for almost Twenty years) can never be effaced' (*Letters*, 1.305). Cautherley died at his home in Richmond, Surrey, on 15 November 1805. The affluence he owed to his wife now reverted to her as his widow. When she died, on 22 March 1820, her will listed South Sea annuities, Bank of England stock, various securities, and several properties. She was survived by three of their children. Two others had died in infancy.

PETER THOMSON

Sources Highfill, Burnim & Langhans, *BDA* · *The letters of David Garrick*, ed. D. M. Little and G. M. Kahrl, 3 vols. (1963) · G. W. Stone and G. M. Kahrl, *David Garrick: a critical biography* (1979) · G. W. Stone, ed., *The London stage, 1660–1800*, pt 4: 1747–1776 (1962)

Likenesses double portrait, engraving, c.1766 (as Romeo with Jane Barry as Juliet), repro. in Highfill, Burnim & Langhans, *BDA*, vol. 1

Cautley, **Sir Proby Thomas** (1802–1871), civil engineer and palaeontologist, was born on 3 January 1802 in Raydon, Suffolk, son of Thomas Cautley (c.1756–1817), rector of Raydon, and his second wife, Catherine Proby (c.1772–1830), daughter of the Revd Narcissus Charles Proby and his wife, Arabella Weller. There were two daughters from Thomas Cautley's first marriage. The first-born son of the second marriage died before Proby Thomas Cautley was born, leaving him as the eldest son; two more daughters and a son followed. The Cautleys originated in Cumberland. Thomas Cautley, after taking degrees at Trinity College, Cambridge, remained at Trinity as a fellow, holding various administrative posts before marrying and taking up residence in Raydon, a living he had held since 1791. The family was well off and the children were raised in an intellectually stimulating atmosphere.

Cautley was educated at Charterhouse School from 1813 to 1818, a school with strong connections with Indian service. Sponsored by his uncle, Archibald Impey, and James Pattison, a director of the East India Company, Cautley entered the company's Addiscombe College in July 1818, where he remained for less than a year, being one of those dispatched to India in response to an urgent request for artillerymen. He was commissioned second lieutenant on 19 April 1819, and was admitted into service on reaching Calcutta, on 11 September 1819. After several years on artillery duties he was sent early in 1825 to the foothills of the Himalayas to assist in the reconstruction of the Doab Canal. Apart from a single recall to military duty, later that year, he was committed to hydraulic engineering for his remaining years in India.

The Doab was one of two canals which took off from either bank of the Jumna. They had been created during the Mughal era by linking existing streams and rivers, and both had fallen into disrepair. Cautley joined Captain Robert Smith, who had begun work on the eastern canal some two years previously. The canal ran for 140 miles over difficult and varying terrain. Cautley and Smith cleared its bed and erected masonry bridges, sluices, and dams. The canal was formally opened in 1830, after which Smith returned to Europe, leaving Cautley to manage the canal during its first months. He was named superintendent in 1831, his assistant being Robert Napier, later to become commander-in-chief of the army in India. Cautley was directly responsible for the Doab Canal until 1843, remaining nominally in control thereafter as superintendent of canals in the North-Western Provinces. During the years 1837 to 1841 he designed several lesser canals in the Dehra Dun region, which served as important sources of irrigation and drinking water.

In 1832 a new dimension was added to Cautley's life through his friendship with Hugh Falconer, a Scottish surgeon on the Bengal establishment of the East India Company, whose passion for geology, and particularly fossils, had led to his appointment as superintendent of the company's botanic garden at Saharanpur. Cautley was living nearby; their shared interests soon led them to mount expeditions into the Siwalik hills where they hoped that

Sir Proby Thomas Cautley (1802–1871), by Charles Baugniet, 1846

the tertiary strata would yield animal remains. These expeditions, in which several of Cautley's friends and assistants took part, were extremely fruitful. Blasting exposed a rich and varied fauna of animals, birds, reptiles, and fish, in excellent condition. Careful measurements and drawings were made, and the most important findings published in Indian and British journals. Falconer and Cautley were awarded the Wollaston medal of the Geological Society in 1837. Eager to dispose of their huge collection to a national museum, they first offered it to the Geological Society of London, which was obliged to decline for lack of space. Cautley eventually persuaded the British Museum to accept it, and himself packed a total of 214 cases which were shipped back at the museum's expense, followed later by an additional twenty-two cases sent to India House.

On 20 September 1838, at Landour, in the foothills of the Himalayas, Cautley married Frances, third daughter of Anthony Bacon of Saharanpur. Their only child, Walter George, was born on 30 July 1840. His mother expressed concern for the child's health and they departed to England early in 1843, leaving Cautley engaged on his major project, begun in 1836: the Ganges Canal. This was to lead from the Ganges a few miles above Hardwar, past Roorkee to Nanu, with branches leading off along the way, and splitting at Nanu, one line returning to the Ganges at Cawnpore, the other discharging into the Jumna at Farrukhabad. The original proposal was for a channel of 255 miles with 73 miles of branches, but the plans were modified during construction. Cautley carried out much of the levelling himself, and was responsible for designing and building all the structures. Progress was slow to begin with, reflecting the lack of government interest and therefore funding; Cautley had few European staff to assist him, and, apart from brick making machinery and a canal-side tramway, little in the way of mechanical aids for his force of Indian labourers. His efforts to obtain well trained assistants eventually led to the setting up in 1848 of a college of engineering, where he later established the Cautley gold medal to be awarded annually to the best mathematician. This college eventually grew into the University of Roorkee.

Cautley took his three-year furlough in 1845, arriving in London in October to discover his wife having an affair with a Major Leonard Cooper, which resulted in the birth of twins in July 1846. Cautley was obliged to go through the then laborious and expensive business of taking action against Cooper, obtaining a divorce *a mensa et thoro* in the consistory court, then a full divorce by private act of parliament in 1850. To add to his grief, his own son died in October 1846.

For his palaeontology and his work on the Ganges Canal, Cautley was elected to the Royal Society on 2 April 1846. He returned to India via northern Italy, famed for its irrigation systems, though he saw nothing to match the scale of his own project. He continued to Egypt to view the barrage works under construction at the head of the Nile delta, arriving at Bombay in December 1847.

In April 1854 all was ready for the grand opening of the Ganges Canal. Vast crowds gathered and, amid much formal and informal celebration, Cautley led the official party to the steps at the top of the aqueduct where Lieutenant-Governor John Russell Colvin undid the first of the levers that kept the canal gates closed. All the gates were then opened, releasing the water to the strains of the national anthem and gunfire salvoes. Entertainment and speeches continued long into the night. It was a fitting end to Cautley's service and he was given permission to retire with effect from May 1854. News of the canal's opening had been transmitted by the new electric telegraph to Calcutta and, exceptionally, Cautley was given a thirteen-gun salute as his boat passed the ramparts of Fort William on the way to join the vessel that would transport him, with the various gifts that had been voted to him in Calcutta, to England. A knighthood was conferred on him on 29 July 1854, and in November that year he was raised to the honorary rank of colonel.

By an act of 1858 the government of India was transferred to the crown, exercised in London by a secretary of state and a council of fifteen members, of whom Cautley was one of the first appointed. It was no sinecure and Cautley attended weekly meetings in addition to his committee work. At the same time he was completing his *Report on the Ganges Canal*, published in 1860. In 1863 he became embroiled in a public debate over various faults in the canal's design. His adversary was Sir Arthur Cotton, himself the designer of a great irrigation system in Madras and now employed by the East India Irrigation Company to report on the Ganges Canal with a view to the Irrigation Company's purchasing it from the government.

Cautley admitted some of the proclaimed faults—indeed, it would have been remarkable if none had emerged in such a vast and novel project—but rejected other criticisms. Cautley and Cotton, backed by their supporters, battled it out, as was then customary, by privately circulated pamphlets, and publicly in *The Times*. Finally, the remedial works proposed by Captain James Crofton, who had been appointed by the public works department, were accepted, and by 1865 the matter had subsided.

Cautley participated in London social life, being a member of the Athenaeum and retaining a seat at the opera. He served on the council of the Geological Society in 1855-7. On 11 February 1865 at St John's Wood he married Julia Susannah Richards (1831/2–1916), who already had a son and a daughter, Ada Julia Gray, born on 3 December 1862, whom he adopted, giving her the name Cautley. In 1868 he retired to a large house called The Avenue, at Sydenham Park, London. He had suffered from asthma for some time and his declining years were troubled by bronchitis. He died at home after two weeks' illness on 25 January 1871.

ANITA MCCONNELL

Sources J. Brown, 'A memoir of Colonel Sir Proby Cautley, FRS, 1802–1871, engineer and palaeontologist', *Notes and Records of the Royal Society*, 34 (1979–80), 185–225 • J. Brown, 'Sir Proby Cautley (1802–1871), a pioneer of Indian irrigation', *History of Technology*, 3 (1978), 35–89 • parish register, Raydon, Suffolk
Archives BL, corresp., Add. MS 28599
Likenesses C. Baugniet, engraving, 1846, BL OIOC [*see illus.*] • photograph, repro. in Brown, 'Memoir of Colonel Sir Proby Cautley'
Wealth at death under £9000: probate, 1 March 1871, *CGPLA Eng. & Wales*

Caux [Caleto], **John de** (*c*.1205–1263), administrator and abbot of Peterborough, is said by Matthew Paris to have been of Norman birth, and the Peterborough chronicler Walter of Whittlesey confirms this, stating that John de Caux was professed in a Norman house at the age of seven, and thereafter went to Winchester. He may have been related to Geoffrey de Caux, a senior figure from around 1208 to 1221 in the household of Peter des Roches, bishop of Winchester (*d*. 1238). John de Caux was appointed prior of Winchester in 1247, and is recorded with the convent granting 'their town of Whitchurch', Hampshire, as a free borough. Late in 1249 the abbot of Peterborough, William Hotot, was deposed by Bishop Robert Grosseteste (*d*. 1253), and John de Caux was the royal nominee to replace him. Licence to elect was given on 27 December 1249 and royal confirmation on 15 January 1250. John de Caux found his new abbey in debt, and from the Purification (2 February) 1250 until the following harvest, supported it from his own resources. He earned a good reputation at Peterborough, even though he was often an absentee, by respecting the monks' susceptibilities. His predecessor, William Hotot, was recalled from the manor of Cottingham, and established in some comfort near the abbey at Oxney Grange. He protected the monks' privileges, in June 1253 purchasing a royal confirmation of the house's liberties for 570 marks. In 1255/6 he paid 540 marks towards the sum that Peter d'Aigueblanche, bishop of Hereford (*d*. 1268), had pledged at the papal curia in the name of the

English monasteries towards the costs of 'the Sicilian business'—Henry III's ruinously expensive attempt to strike a bargain with the papacy that would secure Sicily for his second son, Edmund. He built a new infirmary, and for the abbey church had made a great bell, which bore the inscription 'Ion de Caux Abbas Oswaldo contulit hoc vas' ('Abbot John de Caux gave this bell to St Oswald'). He gave five books to the library.

Abbot John was a conscientious administrator. Whenever he came to the abbey, he questioned the cellarer Robert of Sutton—his successor as abbot (1263–74)—and other senior monks. If they reported all was well, he would go immediately into the chapter house; if not, he would offer a gift, perhaps some good wine, or 'some other treat', and only then go to meet the community: 'in this way any difficulty was smoothed over' (Sparke, 129). On the national stage also he strove with some success for the same effect. He was chief justice on eyre from October 1254 until the summer of 1257, visiting thirteen counties in all. The eyre started in Bedfordshire, and Matthew Paris at St Albans named the abbot of Peterborough as typifying a number of monks whose secular activity was to the grave prejudice of their order. Having recently been on eyre in the northern counties, he was sent by Henry III as a royal commissioner to the Scottish parliament that met at Stirling at Easter 1258. He was appointed a papal chaplain on 23 July 1260.

The abbot and the monastery became closely involved in the period of reform and rebellion. Early in 1260 the king's son Edward, then estranged from his father, mortgaged the town of Grantham to the abbot, 'for a certain sum of money paid to merchants of Siena (*CClR, 1259–1261*, 448); this led to a serious quarrel with the king, who accused the abbot of treachery. In the parliament of October 1260, in which the interests of Edward and Simon de Montfort were strongly represented, John de Caux was appointed royal treasurer. A new chancellor and a new justiciar were appointed at the same time, but when these were replaced by the king in the summer of 1261, the treasurer remained in office. The king's official correspondence reveals that from this time on the abbot was fully involved in the work of the exchequer, and enjoyed the king's confidence. In June 1262 he discharged a variety of the king's debts, using in part money raised from Jewish financiers. Between August and October 1262 the king, now in Paris, bombarded the treasurer with letters: he was to advise on who should value the harvest of the bishopric of Winchester, a task for which he was well qualified; he was to send cash to Paris for the liveries of royal servants and the king's living expenses, and dispatch every penny he could to the Tower of London, 'for our needs' (*CClR, 1261–1264*, 157). The abbot died in London on 3 March 1263, it may be presumed suddenly, for an order to him to raise 165 marks for building works at Westminster was followed almost immediately by instructions to the custodian of the abbey in the vacancy to have its fish ponds drained of their stock. The abbot's body was taken to Peterborough and buried in the aisle on the south side of the choir, in front of the altar of St Andrew.

John de Caux is not to be identified with the John of *Peterborough said to have written or owned the Peterborough–Spalding annals in BL, Cotton MS Claudius A. v. fols. 2–45.   EDMUND KING

Sources J. Sparke, ed., *Historiae Anglicanae scriptores varii*, 2 vols. (1723) · *Chancery records* · Paris, *Chron.*, vol. 5 · H. R. Luard, ed., *Flores historiarum*, 3 vols., Rolls Series, 95 (1890) · D. Crook, *Records of the general eyre*, Public Record Office Handbooks, 20 (1982) · F. Liebermann, 'Ueber Ostenglische Geschichtsquellen des 12, 13, 14 Jahrhunderts besonders den falschen Ingulf', *Neues Archiv*, 18 (1892), 235–45 [demonstrates that John de Caux did not write 'The Chronicle of Abbot John'] · C. N. L. Brooke and M. M. Postan, eds., *Carte nativorum: a Peterborough Abbey cartulary of the fourteenth century*, Northamptonshire RS, 20 (1960), 224–5 · N. Vincent, ed., *Winchester, 1205–1238*, English Episcopal Acta, 9 (1994) [Caux family] · A. Harding, ed., *The roll of the Shropshire eyre of 1256*, SeldS, 96 (1981) · *CEPR letters*, vol. 1

Cavagnari, Sir Pierre Louis Napoleon (1841–1879), army and political officer in India, was born on 4 July 1841 at Stenay, *département* of the Meuse, France; he was the son of General Adolphe Cavagnari, an Italian of 'an ancient and noble Parmesan family' (*ILN*, 231), formerly an officer in Napoleon's army, and his wife, Caroline, third daughter of Hugh Lyons Montgomery of Laurencetown, co. Down, Ireland. He entered Christ's Hospital, London, in 1851, and after six years there passed the necessary examinations at Addiscombe, became a direct cadet of the East India Company on 9 April 1858, and was appointed ensign in the 67th Bengal native infantry on 21 June. He had on 7 December 1857 been naturalized as a British citizen (under the name of P. L. N. Cavagnaré, though he did not later use that spelling). On arriving in India on 12 July he joined the 1st Bengal European fusiliers and he served throughout the Oudh campaign (1858–9). Promoted lieutenant on 17 March 1860, in July 1861 he was appointed to the staff corps and appointed an assistant commissioner in the Punjab. He was ambitious, energetic, brave, charming, and 'self-confident to the point of arrogance, bold to the point of rashness' (Robson, 118). According to H. B. Hanna he was a man of rash and restless disposition and overbearing temper, consumed by the thirst for personal distinction (Hanna, 1.119–20). He distinguished himself in the frontier service, and had political charge of the Kohat district from April 1866 to May 1877, when he was appointed deputy commissioner of Peshawar. As chief political officer he served in several hill expeditions between 1868 and 1878, including the Afridi expedition, 1875–7, and in June 1877 was made CSI. He married on 23 November 1871 Mercy Emma, second daughter of Henry Graves MD, of Cookstown, co. Tyrone, Ireland; she survived her husband. Cavagnari met the new viceroy, Lord Lytton, gained his favour, and apparently influenced him, encouraging his forward policy, including domination of Afghanistan, to counter the perceived Russian threat from central Asia. Lytton advanced Cavagnari's career.

When the dispatch of a British mission to the amir of Afghanistan, Sher Ali Khan, in September 1878 under Sir Neville Chamberlain was decided upon, Cavagnari was attached to the staff, and he interviewed Faiz Mahomed Khan when the latter on 21 September 1878 refused to allow the mission to proceed. After the British invasion and defeat of Afghan forces, the death of the amir (21 February 1879), and the succession of his son Yakub Khan, Cavagnari met the new ruler and negotiated the treaty of Gandamak (26 May 1879), by which the amir agreed to a British envoy at Kabul and British control of foreign policy. For this Cavagnari was made a KCB on 19 July. Cavagnari himself favoured breaking up Afghanistan. Lytton appointed him envoy resident at Kabul: both Lytton and Cavagnari intended he should bring Afghanistan more under British influence. Reportedly Cavagnari told his friends that the chances were four to one that he would never return, though according to Roberts he went 'in the best of spirits' (Roberts, 381). He entered Kabul on 24 July, and resided in the Bala Hissar. His reception by Yakub Khan was friendly, but on 3 September 1879 several Afghan regiments mutinied and attacked the citadel where Cavagnari and the other members of the embassy were living. Cavagnari fought until wounded or killed, then the burning building collapsed and presumably his body was burned. His Guides escort, commanded by Lieutenant Walter Hamilton (*b.* August 1856), fought until all were killed.   G. C. BOASE, rev. JAMES LUNT

Sources B. Robson, *The road to Kabul: the Second Afghan War, 1878–1881* (1986) • H. B. Hanna, *The Second Afghan War*, 3 vols. (1899–1910) • Lord Roberts [F. S. Roberts], *Forty-one years in India*, 2 vols. (1897) • K. Kaliprasanna, *Life and career of Major Sir Louis Cavagnari* (1881) • *Annual Register* (1879) • 'Afghan revolt and murder of the British envoy at Cabul', *ILN* (13 Sept 1879), 229, 231, 234 • 'The death of Prince Louis Napoleon', *The Graphic* (5 July 1879), 2 • 'Our illustrations: Major Cavagnari', *The Graphic* (5 July 1879), 3 • 'The last photograph of Major Cavagnari—a conference with Yakoob Khan at Gundamak', *The Graphic* (27 Sept 1879), 303–4 • M. M. Kaye, *The far pavilions* (1978) • H. Hensman, *The Afghan war of 1879–80* (1881)
Archives BL OIOC, corresp. with Sir Alfred Lyall, MS Eur. F 132
Likenesses J. Burke, albumen print photograph, 1878–9, NPG [*see illus.*] • wood-engravings, *c.*1879, NPG; repro. in *ILN* • J. Burke, photograph, NAM • portrait, repro. in Kaliprasanna, *Life and career* • portrait, repro. in *Illustrated News* (1879), 262–70 • portrait, repro. in Robson, *Road to Kabul* • portraits, repro. in *The Graphic*, 20 (1879), 4, 29, 261, 304

Cavalcanti, Alberto de Almeida (1897–1982), film director and producer, was born in Dona Marciana Street, Rio de Janeiro, Brazil, on 6 February 1897, the youngest son of Captain Manoel de Almeida Cavalcanti (*d. c.*1920) and his wife, Dona Ana Olinda do Rego Rangel (*d.* 1945). His father, of Italian descent, taught mathematics at the military school of Praia Vermelha. His mother came from an artistic family; an uncle, Alberto Rangel, was a leading novelist of the period.

Like his elder brothers, Cavalcanti was sent to military school in Rio de Janeiro, but he showed little aptitude for army life. Nor did law suit him: in 1913 he was enrolled at the law faculty of the Rio de Janeiro Polytechnic College, but after less than a year he quarrelled with his professor and quit. Aged seventeen, he left for Geneva to study architecture, and spent three years there before moving to Paris and the École des Beaux-Arts in 1918. Having graduated, he joined an architectural practice, but found the work boring and poorly paid. On both counts the cinema offered greater attractions. Around this time Cavalcanti's father died. He had always been closer to his mother, who now became his frequent companion until her death in 1945. Thirty years later he dedicated his book *Film and Reality* to her memory. A homosexual, Cavalcanti never married.

Cavalcanti entered films as art director on Marcel l'Herbier's unfinished version of Tolstoy's *Resurrection* (1922), and made his directorial début with *Le train sans yeux* (1925). This was impounded when the producers ran out of money. To replace it, Cavalcanti hastily improvised *Rien que les heures* (1926), an impressionistic study of twenty-four hours in the life of Paris. Poetic, quirky, and humorous, it made his reputation and influenced other 'city films' of the period, such as Walter Ruttmann's *Berlin: Symphony of a Great City* and Dziga Vertov's *The Man with a*

Sir Pierre Louis Napoleon Cavagnari (1841–1879), by John Burke, 1878–9 [centre, with the sirdars]

Movie Camera. Cavalcanti followed it up with *En rade* (1927), a feature about a young man wandering through a busy seaport which in mood and treatment anticipated the 'poetic realism' of the 1930s. Now rated one of the foremost avant-garde directors, he completed several more features and short films before the coming of sound disrupted his career.

'The producers thought that [sound] films should be made by stage directors', Cavalcanti later recalled. 'The results were pitiful and we were called back to the studios very quickly' (Hillier, Lovell, and Rohdie, 36). But the only work he could find was at Paramount's Paris studios, directing French and Portuguese-language versions of Hollywood comedies. After a few years of this soulless toil, 'I did what I have done many times in my long life, I said I was sick and I came to London to recover' (ibid.). There he met John Grierson, leader of the British documentary school and head of the General Post Office (GPO) film unit. Cavalcanti's stint at Paramount had given him expertise in sound technique, which the GPO unit lacked; Grierson invited him to join them at their Blackheath studio 'for a few months'. In the event he stayed for seven years, working as director, producer, and, above all, mentor to the other film-makers in the unit.

According to Harry Watt, the arrival of Cavalcanti was 'the turning point of British documentary. If I've had any success in films I put it down to my training from Cavalcanti and I think a lot of other people should say the same thing' (Sussex, 'Cavalcanti', 207). Others who benefited from Cavalcanti's enthusiasm and professional expertise included Humphrey Jennings, Basil Wright, Len Lye, and Norman McLaren. Exact credits for the films Cavalcanti contributed to are hard to establish, since the GPO unit worked collaboratively; besides, Cavalcanti later claimed, he was often denied credit by the aesthetically austere Grierson, who looked with suspicion on Cavalcanti's playful, surrealist-tinged approach. Relations between the two men were edgy: according to Cavalcanti, Grierson 'only came to the studios to upset my work' (ibid.).

None the less, Cavalcanti soon settled in. 'The GPO was a very nice place to work … The atmosphere was much better than it had been in France' (Hillier, Lovell, and Rohdie, 43). He took directorial credit on some of the unit's less remembered films: *Pett and Pott* (1934), a jokey fantasy supposedly promoting thrift; *Coalface* (1936), which with poetry by W. H. Auden and music by Benjamin Britten acted as a dry run for *Night Mail*; and *Line to Tcherva Hut* (1937), about phone services in the Alps. But Cavalcanti was closely involved, as producer and sound supervisor, on many of the unit's most famous productions, such as *Song of Ceylon* (1934) and *Night Mail* (1936). Basil Wright, credited director on both, paid him grateful tribute: 'His ideas about the use of sound were so liberating that they would liberate in you about a thousand other ideas' (Sussex, 'Cavalcanti', 207).

When Grierson left in 1937 to join the Film Centre (advising Commonwealth governments on film), Cavalcanti took over as head of the unit. Under his guidance the centre produced some fifteen films, including Harry Watt's best pre-war work, *North Sea* (1938), and the first of Humphrey Jennings's masterpieces of documentary poetry, *Spare Time* (1939). When war broke out the GPO unit was transferred to the Ministry of Information and renamed the Crown Film Unit. Since the ministry had little idea what the unit should do, Cavalcanti led his staff out into the streets to capture the sights and sounds of London as it adjusted to the coming of war. *The First Days* (1939), with its quiet, understated air of determination, set the tone of 'the people's war' that would become the main theme of British wartime propaganda.

Unfortunately Cavalcanti, who lacked Grierson's skill at dealing with officialdom, found himself in an equivocal position as a foreign national. Pressure was put on him to relinquish his Brazilian citizenship; instead he quit the unit in 1940, and accepted an invitation from Michael Balcon to join Ealing Studios. Though a commercial studio, Ealing was to Cavalcanti 'an absolute parallel to the GPO' (Hillier, Lovell, and Rohdie, 45). Under Balcon's benevolent rule he continued to direct and produce documentaries such as *Yellow Caesar* (1941), a virulent attack on Mussolini. He also resumed directing feature films for the first time since leaving France. *Went the Day Well?* (1942), based loosely on a short story by Graham Greene, vividly imagined a sleepy English village taken over by undercover German paratroopers. By contrast, *Champagne Charlie* (1944) celebrated the robust culture of the Victorian music-halls. Cavalcanti masterminded, and part-directed, *Dead of Night* (1945), a chilling anthology of ghost stories. His last feature for Ealing, *Nicholas Nickleby* (1946), was a workmanlike adaptation of Dickens that paled beside David Lean's two masterpieces.

As at the GPO, Cavalcanti's significance at Ealing extended far beyond the films he himself directed; the character of the studio in its most famous manifestation was as much his creation as Balcon's. Several members of the unit followed him to Ealing, notably Harry Watt and Robert Hamer, and he acted as mentor to other young recruits such as Charles Crichton, Charles Frend, and the cinematographer Douglas Slocombe. His influence on Ealing's wartime output was crucial: the switch from the stilted, stagey films produced early in the war to gritty, realist works such as *Next of Kin* and *San Demetrio London* owed much to his inspiration. Monia Danischewsky, Ealing's publicity officer turned producer, wrote 'If Mick [Balcon] was the father figure, Cavalcanti was the Nanny who brought us up … a natural if inarticulate teacher' (Danischewsky, 134). At moments of excitement, Cavalcanti's strong Brazilian accent and fractured syntax could run wild; on one occasion, accused of underlighting a scene, he retorted, 'I 'ave been making films in France for years and years when nobody could see nothing and everybody was delighted' (ibid.).

Balcon, generous with opportunities, was frugal with money, and in 1946 Cavalcanti left Ealing, hoping for richer pickings as a freelance film-maker. His first independent film, *They Made me a Fugitive* (1947), was a remarkably tough crime drama about a bored former serviceman (Trevor Howard) drawn into the Soho gang world, a rare example of British *film noir*. But his next two films—*The First Gentleman* (1947), a costume drama about the prince regent, and another crime drama, *For them that Trespass* (1948)—did poorly. When a deal with the Rank Organisation fell through in 1950, Cavalcanti accepted an invitation from Brazil to lecture at the Museum of Modern Art in São Paulo.

There followed what Cavalcanti called 'an unhappy adventure' (Sussex, 'Cavalcanti', 211). Hoping to create his native country's first film industry, he became production chief of the newly formed Vera Cruz film company. But he encountered hostility and obstruction on all sides, not least from powerful Hollywood interests who whispered that he was a communist. He struggled on for four years, directing three films—of which the best was *O canto de mar* (*The Song of the Sea*, 1954), a compassionate study of impoverished peasants—before giving up and returning to Europe. From then on Cavalcanti worked as a peripatetic filmmaker in Austria, East Germany, Romania, Britain, Israel, and France. His films included: a Brecht adaptation, *Herr Puntila und sein Knecht Matti* (1955), which Brecht called the only faithful version of his work ever filmed; a children's film in Britain, *The Monster of Highgate Pond* (1960); and *Thus Spake Theodor Herzl* (1967), a tribute to the founder of Israel. In his later years Cavalcanti settled in Paris, where he directed for television and the stage. He died there, at a clinic in rue de Passy, from a cardiac seizure on 23 August 1982.

PHILIP KEMP

Sources L. Pellizzari and C. M. Valentinetti, *Alberto Cavalcanti* (1988) · E. Sussex, *The rise and fall of British documentary* (1975) · H. Watt, *Don't look at the camera* (1974) · M. Danischewsky, *White Russian, red face* (1966) · J. Hillier, A. Lovell, and C. Rohdie, 'Interview with Alberto Cavalcanti', *Screen* (summer 1972), 36–53 · E. Sussex, 'Cavalcanti in England', *Sight and Sound*, 44 (1974–5), 205–11

Cavalier, Jean (1681–1740), army officer and leader of the Camisard rising in France, was born on 28 November 1681 at Mas Roux, Ribaute, near Anduze, Languedoc, subsequently in the département of Gard, the son of Antoine Cavalier, a small farmer, and his wife, Elisabeth Granier. Following local schooling his father apprenticed him, after a time herding cattle at Vezenobres, to a baker at Anduze. Brought up ostensibly a Catholic, he was secretly taught protestant doctrines by his mother, and to escape persecution for non-attendance at mass he made his way, aged nineteen, to Geneva, where he worked as a baker. The imprisonment of his parents induced him to return to Ribaute where he found his parents released.

Cavalier took part in the assassination of the abbé du Chayla which began the revolt in the Cévennes in autumn 1702, and joined the insurgents. His bravery, tactical skill, and outstanding leadership qualities led to his election as one of the five commanders of the rising. The region assigned to him was the plain of Lower Languedoc stretching to the sea, though he made frequent forays in the hill country of the Cévennes. In less than two years he became the most conspicuous of the insurgent Camisards. With few intermissions his guerrilla warfare was successful and

Cavalier, whose band grew to 1300 men, won major victories against the superior numbers of the French royal forces at the Tour de Billot and Martignargues in 1703. His fame spread throughout Europe. Attempts to extend the war into the Vivarais, where he was repelled, and Rouergue, failed, partly owing to lack of communication with Sir Cloudesley Shovell's English fleet. On 16 April 1704 he was defeated with great slaughter, being surrounded by a superior force under Marshal Montrevel, who commanded in Languedoc, in a series of engagements near Nages. This defeat, followed by the betrayal to government troops of the caverns in which the Camisards had concealed their stores, led to Cavalier's negotiation with Montrevel's successor, the great Marshal Villars, especially after the failure of English military intervention. On 16 May the 22-year-old Cavalier had a conference with Villars in a garden in Nîmes. Villars bore testimony to the firmness, good sense, and good faith displayed by Cavalier throughout the negotiation, as well as to his military capacity. Ultimately an agreement was signed, in which Villars made some concessions to the protestants of Languedoc. Cavalier accepted the offer of a colonel's commission and a pension of 1200 livres. But the agreement satisfied neither the other leaders of the insurrection nor Cavalier's own band. Cavalier travelled with 100 men, under military escort, to Paris. At Versailles a secret interview with Louis XIV took place in July. According to his own account, Cavalier pleaded the cause of the protestants of Languedoc, sought to gain the king's recognition of his treaty with Villars, and refused the king's invitation to become a Catholic.

In August, Cavalier received orders from the French authorities to proceed with his men under escort to the Rhine fortress of Neu Breisach. Alarmed by reports that he was to be detained there for life, he daringly escaped from his escort and, with his followers, took refuge in Switzerland. Introduced by Richard Hill, the English envoy in Turin, he entered the service of Victor Amadeus II, duke of Savoy, who had joined the league against France. At the beginning of 1706 he raised in the Netherlands a regiment of foot, one-third of the expenses of which were to be paid by the Dutch, the other by the English government. After visiting England, and having an interview with the lord high treasurer, Sidney Godolphin, first earl of Godolphin, his regiment was assigned to the expeditionary force under Richard Savage, fourth Earl Rivers, whose invasion of France was aborted by bad weather. They proceeded instead to Spain where at the battle of Almanza on 25 April 1707 Cavalier's Camisards were drawn up against a French regiment with whom they fought with bayonets, so desperately that fewer than 300 survived. Cavalier was severely wounded, and before escaping lay for some time among the killed. In the final attempt to revive the rebellion in the Cévennes Cavalier was landed at Fréjus in July but had to withdraw with his men when the duke of Savoy's troops were driven back over the Alps. At The Hague thereafter he drew up the first of several affidavits, in which he denounced as liars and impostors three of the so-called 'French prophets' in London, who pretended to the possession of supernatural gifts and to have exercised them in the Cévennes. In 1710 he made an unsuccessful attempt to gain support in England and the Netherlands for an incursion from Catalonia into the Foix region and thence into the Languedoc (PRO, SP 341/12; E 351/192). During this stay at The Hague, encouraged by her mother, a marriage was arranged with a young woman called Olympe du Noyer (who some years later captivated the young Voltaire). The proposed marriage was broken off by Cavalier. The duke of Marlborough, though an admirer of Cavalier's, threatened to 'complain of him to the Queen, that she may have justice done her out of his pension', if he did not comply with Madame du Noyer's 'just requests' for the return of the dowry (J. Churchill, *Letters and Dispatches of John, Duke of Marlborough*, ed. G. Murray, 1845, 5.269).

Cavalier, with a British pension, spent most of the remainder of his life in The Hague, in London, and with the French colony in Ireland founded at Portarlington, Queen's county, by Henri de Massue de Ruvigny, earl of Galway. He married, before 1718, Elizabeth Marguerite, daughter of Captain Charles de Ponthieu and his wife, Marguerite de la Rochefoucauld, and, though the marriage was said to have been unhappy, one of her relatives helped him financially. His *Memoirs of the War of the Cévennes* was probably written in London in 1708–9, with the help of Pierre Gally de Gaujac, a refugee pastor. Translated into English, it was first published in Dublin in 1726, perhaps as a riposte to the 1722 edition of Daniel's *Histoire de France* (in English in 1726) which belittled the Camisards and misreported his role. The *Memoirs* is written with animation, and is full of military detail, but as a contribution to the history of the revolt in the Cévennes it is very fragmentary. Some of its most startling stories seem to be confirmed by the testimony of hostile witnesses, contemporaries of the events recorded (Peyrat, 2.52n.; 3.135–6n.). The inaccuracies in it are comparatively unimportant, with the exception of a grave misrepresentation of the spirit in which his companions opposed the treaty with Villars. The *Memoirs* breathe a strongly protestant spirit.

In 1727 Cavalier went to England with a recommendatory letter to Thomas Pelham-Holles, duke of Newcastle, from Hugh Boulter, archbishop of Armagh. He was made a brigadier on 27 October 1735, and in March 1738 lieutenant-governor of Jersey, where he presided at several meetings of the estates. He was appointed a major-general on 2 July 1739. In his last extant letter, from Jersey, he wrote to a cousin in Ribaute that his health and strength were failing but he would take the waters in England and would go to war against Spain if it did not behave itself. He ended by quoting the 74th psalm, a Camisard battle hymn. He died in Chelsea and on 18 May 1740 was buried in St Luke's churchyard there. Voltaire, who had known him, described him as 'a slight, fair man with a pleasant and refined expression'. Hill encapsulated his person and achievements in 1704 thus:

> a very little fellow, son of a peasant, bred to be a baker, at 20 years of age, with 18 men like himself, began to make war on the King of France. He kept the field about 18 months against

a Marischal of France and an army of 10,000 men, and made an honourable capitulation at last with the mighty Monarch. (*Diplomatic Correspondence*, 1.459)

FRANCIS ESPINASSE, *rev.* RANDOLPH VIGNE

Sources J. Cavalier, *Mémoires sur la guerre des Cévennes*, ed. F. Puaux (1918) · J. Cavalier, *Memoirs of the wars of the Cévennes* (1726) · M. Pin, *Jean Cavalier* (1936) · H. Bosc, *La guerre des Cévennes, 1702–1710*, 6 vols. (1958–93) · A. P. Hands, 'Jean Cavalier: notes on the publication of the *Memoirs*', *Proceedings of the Huguenot Society*, 20 (1958–64), 341–71 · N. Peyrat, *The pastors in the wilderness*, 3 vols. (1852) · D. C. A. Agnew, *Protestant exiles from France in the reign of Louis XIV, or, The Huguenot refugees and their descendants in Great Britain and Ireland*, 2nd edn, 3 vols. (1871–4) · E. Haag and E. Haag, *La France protestante*, 2nd edn, 6 vols. (Paris, 1877–88) · *The diplomatic correspondence of the Right Hon. Richard Hill*, ed. W. Blackley, 2 vols. (1845) · *Nouveaux mémoires pour servir à l'histoire des trois camisars ou l'on voit les déclarations du Col. Cavallier* (1708) · Voltaire, *Le siècle de Louis XIV* (1751) · A. P. Grubb, *Jean Cavalier: baker's boy and British general* (1931) · G. Charvet, *Nouveaux documents inédits* (1884) · parish register (burial), St Luke's, Chelsea, Middlesex, 18 May 1740

Archives Archives Départementales de Gard, Nîmes, MSS · Archives Départementales de l'Herault, Montpellier, MSS · Les Eglises Wallonnes, Leiden, MSS · Musée du Desert, St Jean-du-Gard, Gard, memorabilia · Société de l'Histoire du Protestantisme Français, Paris, MSS · UCL, Huguenot Library, MSS · UCL, memoir of the war in the Cévennes

Wealth at death many debts: Pin, *Jean Cavalier*, 442

Cavallo, Tiberius (1749–1809), natural philosopher, was born on 30 March 1749 in Naples, the son of a physician in the same city. Nothing further is known of his parents or childhood. In 1762 he went to London, where he devoted himself to the investigation of natural phenomena. During the 1770s he lodged with Mr Davies, a Catholic clergyman in Islington, and subsequently he rented a house of his own at 8 Little St Martin's Lane. In London he moved easily in cultivated circles and developed an interest in electrical experiments, in particular on atmospheric electricity. His experimental skill and inventiveness brought him quickly to the notice of some of the leading natural philosophers of the day. He designed an ingenious electrometer for detecting and measuring the smallest quantity of electricity in the atmosphere, and in 1777 he published *A Complete Treatise on Electricity in Theory and Practice with Original Experiments*. The manuscript of the work was corrected by the electrician William Henley, who recommended it for publication to the London publisher Charles Dilly. In 1782 a second edition followed; a fourth, in three volumes, was published in 1795. The work was a compendium of contemporary understanding of electricity, and in it Cavallo emphasized the importance of experiments for the advancement of natural knowledge and identified possible directions for further investigation, both practical and theoretical. The *Treatise* was well received, and it earned him a high reputation within the Royal Society of London, of which he was elected a fellow on 9 December 1779.

Pursuing his interests in electricity and its possible applications, Cavallo published *An Essay on the Theory and Practice of Medical Electricity* (1780; 2nd edn, 1781), which was concerned with the medical uses of the electric 'fluid'. In the *Essay* he described the methods and instruments in use at the time and reported cases of diseases that had

Tiberius Cavallo (1749–1809), by unknown artist, c.1785

been treated by electricity. He admitted, however, that further research was needed in order for medical electricity to be seriously distinguished from the practices of quacks and charlatans, and, in his private correspondence with James Lind, physician to George III, he alluded to his reservations about the value of electricity as a medical therapy.

In May 1781 Cavallo became a member of the Chapter Coffee House Society in London, and there he discussed a number of subjects related to medical electricity and demonstrated an elegant method of freezing water by evaporation. In the same year he published a quarto volume entitled *A Treatise on the Nature and Properties of Air and other Permanently Elastic Fluids*. At about the same time his interest in gases and their properties resulted in a number of experiments carried by small balloons, which he described in his *History of Aerostation* (1784).

In 1782 Cavallo was appointed Bakerian lecturer at the Royal Society. Holding the position until 1792, he lectured on a wide range of subjects, including natural and artificial electricity, magnetism, experiments on 'inflammable airs', and instruments such as the air-pump, blowpipe, pyrometer, telescope, and micrometer. The lectures reflected his gifts as an inventor of philosophical instruments and a notable experimenter. In line with his interests and skills he designed and improved apparatus for various branches of natural philosophy, from electricity to astronomy, while acting as an agent between London instrument makers and the purchasers of instruments abroad, especially in Italy. His lectures also demonstrated his qualities as a communicator, which he displayed not only in his *Complete Treatise on Electricity* but also in other works, such as *A Treatise on Magnetism in Theory and Practice* (2nd edn, 1800) and *Elements of Natural and Experimental Philosophy* (1804).

Cavallo maintained an extensive network of correspondents, with whom he shared interests ranging from natural philosophy to politics and music. A particularly important contact with the Italian scientific community was made in 1782, when he met the physicist Alessandro Volta, who visited London in that year. Ten years later it was through Cavallo that Volta's memoirs on Galvani's experiments on muscular motion were published in the Royal Society's *Philosophical Transactions*. Another notable correspondent was General Pasquale Paoli, the champion of Corsican independence. Like Paoli, Cavallo welcomed the French Revolution, but was later disappointed by the authoritarian nature of the terror. Throughout his life Cavallo maintained a keen interest in music and was an accomplished musician. An article by him on the temperament of fretted instruments appeared in the *Philosophical Transactions* in 1788.

On 4 July 1804 Cavallo received a royal licence from George III allowing him to reside 'in any part of the Kingdom' without any restriction of time. His house, where he kept a notable collection of manuscripts, prints, and mineralia, was at 54 Wells Street, London (the number was 51 before 1797). He never married. As he wrote to his friend Rackett: 'I very well perceive in myself a deficiency of most qualities, which may attract a female heart. I have, neither flattery, nor beauty, nor riches, nor &c. &c.' (Solly MSS, fol. 145).

Cavallo spent the last months of his life at Spetisbury in Dorset, where Thomas Rackett, an antiquarian who had been his friend for thirty years, offered him hospitality. He suffered from respiratory problems for most of his life, and asthma was the cause of his death, at his London house, on 22 December 1809. He was buried that month in the churchyard of St Pancras Old Church, London, in a tomb next to Paoli's, after a Catholic funeral. At his death, his belongings were sold at auction. The £250 so obtained was invested in stocks and partly used to pay his debts. He left no will, and it was only after inquiries lasting almost twenty years that his legitimate heir was found in Naples: in 1826 his nephew, Girolamo Cavallo, a resident of Naples, inherited the sum of £77 6s. 6d.

PAOLA BERTUCCI

Sources BL, Add. MSS 22897, 22898 [letters to J. Lind] · Dorset RO, Solly MS DRAC 1452149 · *Epistolario de Alessandro Volta*, ed. [F. Massardi], 5 vols. (Bologna, 1949–55), vol. 3 · RS, Canton MSS, fols. 103, 107 · election certificate, RS, 4.33 · MHS Oxf., Gunther MS 4 · *GM*, 1st ser., 79 (1809), 1239 · *DNB* · Yale U., Beinecke L., Osborne collection, drawer 44 · A. M. Ghisalberti, ed., *Dizionario biografico degli Italiani*, 1, 22 (Rome, 1960–79)

Archives Dorset RO, corresp. and papers · RS, letters and papers | BL, letters to J. Lind, Add. MSS 22897–22898 · Hollandsche Maatschapij, Wetenschappen, Haarlem, letters to M. van Marum · Yale U., Beinecke L., Osborne files, 44

Likenesses T. Trotter, stipple, 1785, BM, NPG · oils, c.1785, NPG [see illus.] · W. Daniell, soft-ground etching, pubd 1809 (after G. Dance, 1799), BM, NPG, Wellcome L. · stipple, Wellcome L. · two engraved silhouettes, BM, NPG

Wealth at death £250: Solly MSS, J.10, Dorset RO

Cavan. For this title name *see* Lambart, Charles, first earl of Cavan (*c.*1600–1660); Lambart, Richard Ford William, seventh earl of Cavan (1763–1837); Lambart, (Frederic) Rudolph, tenth earl of Cavan (1865–1946).

Cavanagh, John [Jack] (*d.* **1819**), fives player, was born in Ireland but moved to London and earned his living as a house painter. Ireland was the home of handball, the game from which fives originates; it was established in England by the mid-eighteenth century as a working-class sport played for wagers or rewards. According to William Hazlitt, his sole memorialist, Cavanagh was incomparably the most skilful player of his time: 'His eye was certain, his hand fatal, his presence of mind complete' (Hazlitt, 'Death', 94). His service was prodigious: in a match against two top-class English players, Woodward and Meredith, he once scored twenty-seven successive aces. On court he was remarkable for his coolness and economy of effort. In his *Table Talk* Hazlitt calls him 'the best *up-hill* player in the world' (Hazlitt, 'Indian jugglers', 87) because of his capacity to recover from a position of disadvantage. A peculiarity of his style of play was that he never volleyed the ball, but he was unerring on the half-volley.

Cavanagh lived in Buckbridge Street (now part of New Oxford Street) in the parish of St Giles-in-the-Fields, then a predominantly Irish community. He usually played at the fives court in St Martin's Street, Leicester Fields, where crowds would pay to watch him, or at the Copenhagen House, a public house in Islington. Hazlitt records one occasion when Cavanagh went, smartly dressed, to another tavern, the Rosemary Branch at Peckham, merely 'for an afternoon's pleasure', but was persuaded by a stranger to play for a wager of half a crown and a bottle of cider. Cavanagh won eleven games in a row, but in the middle of the twelfth, while the other player was leading, his identity was revealed by chance; at this point his opponent refused to go on, saying 'What! have I been breaking my heart all this time to beat Cavanagh?' Cavanagh, repeating this story, swore that he played all through with his fist clenched (Hazlitt, 'Death', 95).

Cavanagh was described by Hazlitt as 'a young fellow of sense, humour, and courage', and portrayed as a zealous Roman Catholic, open in manner and upright in character. Two or three years before his death a burst blood vessel stopped him from playing. He was recovering well until he suffered another stroke and died at home on a Friday, 5 February 1819 or earlier.   KARINA WILLIAMSON

Sources W. Hazlitt, 'Death of John Cavanagh', *The Examiner* (7 Feb 1819), 94–5 • W. Hazlitt, 'Essay IX: The Indian jugglers', *Table talk, or, Original essays*, 2 vols. (1821); repr. in *The complete works of William Hazlitt*, ed. P. P. Howe, 8 (1931), 86–9 [an expanded version of the *Examiner* obit.] • *Horwood's new plan of London*, 4th edn (1819)

Cave, Alfred (**1847–1900**), Congregational minister, born in London on 29 August 1847, was the fourth son of Benjamin Cave and his wife, Harriet Jane, daughter of the Revd Samuel Hackett. He was educated at the Philological School, Marylebone Road, Middlesex, and originally intended to study medicine. However, in 1866, having resolved to become a minister, he entered New College, London, from which he graduated BA at London University in 1870. On leaving New College in 1872 he became minister at Berkhamsted, moving in 1876 to Watford. In 1873 he married Sarah Rebecca Hallifax Fox.

In 1880 Cave resigned his pastorate and became professor of Hebrew and church history at Hackney College. Two years later he was appointed principal and professor of apologetic, doctrinal, and pastoral theology, offices which he retained until his death. He was the author of a number of theological works, including *The Scriptural Doctrine of Sacrifice and Atonement* (1877) and the highly conservative *The Battle of the Standpoints: the Old Testament and the Higher Criticism* (1890). In 1898 he published a history of the foundation of Hackney College.

In 1888 Cave was chosen Congregational Union lecturer, and took as his subject 'The inspiration of the Old Testament inductively considered'; the lecture was published in 1888 and reissued the following year. In 1889 he received the honorary degree of DD from the University of St Andrews. In 1888 and 1898 Cave was chairman of the London Board of Congregational Ministers, and in 1893–4 he was merchants' lecturer. He was also a director of the London Missionary Society and of the Colonial Missionary Society. He died on 19 December 1900 at his home, Hackney College House, Hampstead, and was buried on 24 December.   E. I. CARLYLE, *rev.* DAVID HUDDLESTON

Sources WW (1901) • *Congregational Year Book* (1902) • *The Times* (20 Dec 1900) • W. B. Glover, *Evangelical nonconformists and higher criticism in the nineteenth century* (1954) • R. Tudur Jones, *Congregationalism in England, 1662–1962* (1962) • *CGPLA Eng. & Wales* (1901)
Archives DWL, commonplace book and papers
Likenesses T. Fall, photograph?, 1890–1899?, repro. in *Congregational Year Book*
Wealth at death £5998 4s. 1d.: probate, 6 Feb 1901, *CGPLA Eng. & Wales*

Cave, Sir Ambrose (*c.*1503–1568), knight of the hospital of St John of Jerusalem and administrator, was the fourth or fifth son of Richard Cave (*d.* 1542) of Stanford, Northamptonshire, and his second wife, Margaret, daughter of John Saxby of Northampton. He satisfied the criteria of nobility of birth necessary for admission as a knight of the English *langue* branch of St John of Jerusalem, and also had a family wealthy enough to pay the considerable 'passage' fees. Put forward by the chapter in England on 3 October 1524, when he would have reached the statutory age of twenty, he left for the mandatory five-year period in the convent in Europe and from April 1525 to October 1529 was among those signing attendance lists at meetings of the English *langue*. He was knighted in 1525. Presumably he undertook the three 'caravans'—a year's service on the galleys—which were required of a knight before he was eligible to put himself forward for a commandery. Whether before this he had attended either Cambridge or Oxford, as has been claimed, is doubtful. The only evidence lies in his establishment in his will of four scholars in divinity, two at Oxford and two at Cambridge, the choice of college being left to his executors.

By 1528 Cave was already putting himself forward for commanderies as they became available, and in 1529 was

Sir Ambrose Cave (c.1503–1568), by unknown artist

the candidate most eligible for that of Yeaveley and Barrow in Derbyshire because his place of birth was the nearest. From 1530 he was evidently back in England. A knight could move from one commandery to a more prestigious one after five years if he had improved his holding, and as early as 1532 he was asking for visitors to assess him. In 1534 he was claiming improvement so that he could shift to Shingay, Cambridgeshire, even though he had not held Yeaveley for five years. By now procurator-general of the common treasure in England, he was summoned back to Malta in 1535 and received licence from Henry VIII to leave the realm. When he reached Vienne, however, the newly elected grand master Didier de Sainct-Jailhe sent him back to England for an urgent interview with Henry. Concerned that he might be personally disadvantaged by this in his search for betterment, he complained in a long letter to Sir Thomas Dingley, the commander of Badsley and Mayne whom he had made his proctor, that he was always 'put to charges without reward' (*LP Henry VIII*, vol. 10, no. 882). Cave obtained consent from the convent for his transfer to Shingay but in the meantime Dingley, under a privilege from Didier, had been instituted by his uncle, the English grand prior, Sir William Weston. The order overthrew this, but despite Cave's approaches to Cromwell, Henry VIII confirmed it in April 1537, although in September Weston still thought it might be reversed. The order did not anticipate dissolution, for Henry, formally their protector, was known to admire their fighting prowess, and in 1538 sent a charter suggesting that if they took the oath of allegiance and paid him first fruits and tenths all would be well. Several of the knights, however, refused

and were executed, and the dissolution of the order was confirmed by act of parliament in April 1540.

Unlike his brethren Cave conformed and became committed to the reformed religion. He received a pension of 100 marks and the use of a house in London, and became the king's servant. He began to acquire property, including the former preceptory of Rothley in Leicestershire, and concerned himself with the family estates and wool business. In 1544 he held a subsidiary command in the army sent to France under Lord Grey of Wilton. In 1545 he sat in parliament for Leicestershire. In 1546 when a naval fleet was being prepared, as a former Rhodian he was given command of the galliots and chaloupes. When former religious were permitted to marry he espoused a wealthy woman, Margaret (*d*. in or before 1561?), daughter and coheir of William Willington of Barcheston, Warwickshire, and widow of Thomas Holte (*d*. 1546) of Duddeston, with whom he had a daughter. Fully established as a county gentleman, and a JP for Leicestershire, he sat for that county in both of Edward's parliaments, was sheriff for Warwickshire and Leicestershire in 1548–9, and served on numerous local commissions. By 1553 Cave was attached to Princess Elizabeth's household as one of the managers of her estates. His position under Mary was difficult, as she reinstated most of his surviving brethren to their lost positions, but he remained on the quorum for Warwickshire, avoided confrontation and sat in her last parliament for Warwickshire.

Following the accession of Elizabeth, Cave was one of the small group who met at Hatfield and signed the first official documents of the reign. No doubt it helped him that he was a kinsman of Sir William Cecil, and that he was on good terms with Lord Robert Dudley, later earl of Leicester, with whom he was appointed jointly to the lord lieutenantcy of Warwickshire in 1559. He was immediately appointed to the privy council and made chancellor of the duchy of Lancaster, whose administration was giving some cause for concern. In 1561 he undertook a protracted visit to the north to investigate the problems, and his report resulted in administrative changes in 1564 which increased revenues. As a committed protestant, he served on all the commissions to enforce the Acts of Uniformity and Supremacy, to eliminate papists and the disaffected from positions of power, preventing them attending the mass. With the earls of Leicester, Warwick, and Huntingdon and other leaders of the godly he took out letters patent of incorporation as 'governors of the possessions of the preachers of the gospel' in Warwickshire. In 1559 and 1563 he sat in parliament for Warwickshire, in 1559 clashing with Sir Thomas White over the Book of Common Prayer. He also served on miscellaneous other commissions concerning matters such as the state of armour and munitions, counterfeiting, the issue of a new coinage, and measures to combat plague in Westminster.

A portrait of Cave shows him wearing on his left arm a yellow garter, said to have been dropped by Elizabeth while dancing, which he had sworn to wear as long as he lived. His wife probably died before 17 October 1561, when he made formal arrangements with royal agreement for the custody of his only child, Margaret, now named as his heir apparent, should he die before she reached her majority. She was married to Henry Knollys, the eldest son of Sir Francis Knollys, on 16 July 1565 at a stunning ceremony in Durham House, London, which was attended by the queen and which involved a ball, a tourney, and two masques. It nearly provoked a diplomatic incident between the French and Spanish ambassadors over precedence; Cave having unsuccessfully attempted to defuse it, the queen was obliged to intervene.

Cave's household at the Savoy was increased by the daughters of his brothers who predeceased him and other children of relatives whose wardship he obtained. By the time of his death on 2 April 1568 at the Savoy he had become the family patriarch, and he made appropriately careful arrangements for his extended family. His funeral, at which Sir Francis Knollys was chief mourner, took place at the Savoy chapel on the 19th. But in accordance with his request he was buried at Stanford, where a memorial was erected in the church. His will has a long religious preamble stressing his desire to see Christ his only Saviour, and to hear Him pronounce the long thirsted-for sentence of all His elect and chosen, the members of His holy catholic church.   SYBIL M. JACK

Sources R. Somerville, *History of the duchy of Lancaster, 1265–1603* (1953) • *LP Henry VIII*, vols. 4–21 • *CSP for., 1547–68* • *CSP dom., 1547–80* • H. P. Scicluna, ed., *The book of deliberations of the venerable tongue of England, 1523–1567* (1949) • A. Mifsud, *Knights hospitallers of the ven. tongue of England in Malta* (1914) • BL, Add. MSS 36901; 36902; 35830 • PRO, C142/148/4; E150/1164/1; Wards 11/74 • will, PRO, PROB 11/54, sig. 9 • *CSP Spain, 1558–67* • HoP, *Commons, 1509–58*, 1.594–5 • HoP, *Commons, 1558–1603*, 1.563–4
Archives BL, Add. MSS 36901–36902
Likenesses oils, Stanford Hall, Leicestershire [*see illus.*]
Wealth at death £1500 plus annuities of £100: PRO, C 142/148/4; will, PRO, PROB 11/54, fols. 66r–67r

Cave, Beatrice Mabel Cave-Browne- (1874–1947), applied mathematician, was born on 30 May 1874 at 7 Kempshott Road, Streatham Common, London; her sister Evelyn [*see below*] was also born there. They were respectively the second and third daughters of Sir Thomas Cave-Browne-Cave (1835–1924), civil servant, sometime deputy accountant-general for the army, and his wife, Blanche Matilda Mary Anne Milton (d. 1928). The composite surname of the family came about as the result of marriage and acquisition of property over several centuries, while a baronetcy in the family was created by Charles I. Both sisters tended to use the single surname Cave professionally (Beatrice adopted it also for some publications).

All three sisters were educated at home. In 1895 Beatrice and Evelyn took the entrance examination to Girton College, Cambridge, and were accepted together: Jeanette, the eldest, chose to remain at home. The family was completed by two younger brothers, both of whom went into the engineering branch of the navy, and transferred to the Royal Air Force on its formation in 1918: neither attended a university. However, the career of Thomas Reginald, the elder, occasionally impinged on the distinct interests of

his sisters—first as an aeronautical engineer in the services, and then, when the airship branch of the RAF closed down in 1930, as professor of engineering at the University College of Southampton.

Beatrice gained the title of a second-class degree in the mathematical tripos part one in 1898; she went on in 1899 to take part two, and was placed in the third class. She taught mathematics at Clapham high school for eleven years and then in 1913 started work in the Galton Laboratory at University College, London, under Professor Karl Pearson. There, co-operative work was customary, and she contributed to two joint papers for *Biometrika* (in which her sister's work of 1904 was cited). She also produced statistical analyses for the Board of Trade and the Treasury. In 1916 she carried out research of her own into the mathematics of aeronautics for the Admiralty air department, the Air Board of the Air Ministry, and the aircraft production department, for whom she wrote reports, and two confidential information memoranda of significance—'Loads on tail planes in high speed flight' and 'Loads on wing structure in flight' (June 1917)—whose publication was prohibited by the Official Secrets Act for fifty years. It may have been to compensate for this non-recognition of her originality that she was appointed MBE in 1920, 'for services in connection with the War'. On her application form for election to (associate) fellowship of the Royal Aeronautical Society in 1919 she listed aircraft stability and performance, and propeller efficiency among her research interests. Though her brother Thomas joined the society about the same time, there is no evidence of any mutual interaction between Beatrice and Thomas, whose expertise in aeronautics was certainly more practical.

After the war Beatrice moved to Imperial College, University of London, where she was appointed assistant to the Zaharoff professor of aviation, Leonard Bairstow, and collaborated with him on two Royal Society publications examining fluid motion. However, her later work did not show the intensity she had brought to independent investigations under wartime conditions. She retired in 1937 and continued to live at 36 North Side, Streatham Common, where she died on 9 July 1947.

(Frances) Evelyn Cave-Browne-Cave (1876–1965), mathematician, was born at the family home on 21 February 1876. She obtained the title of a first-class degree in part one of the Cambridge mathematical tripos in 1898, placed between fourth and fifth wranglers, and in part two in 1899. Independently, and then as a research student at Girton in 1901–3, she carried out statistical research directed by Pearson and published two papers (the first jointly with Pearson) in *Proceedings of the Royal Society* (70, 1902, and 74, 1904–5) on patterns in barometric measurements. She undertook no further research: in 1903 she was appointed resident lecturer in mathematics at Girton, and in 1918 she succeeded Miss Meyer as director of studies. During discussions concerning his academic appointment in 1930, Thomas confirmed that his sister believed the primary function of a university was to teach, and that trouble taken with weaker students was more rewarding because one could make a proportionately greater improvement. Evelyn was a gifted teacher who was especially talented in helping less able students: a stammer that affected her normal speech completely disappeared when she was teaching.

Cavey, as she was sometimes affectionately known, was an archetypal Girtonian of austere and old-fashioned tastes. She was fond of gardening and a former student particularly remembered the zest with which she chopped wood for her sitting-room fire. She was mainly responsible for drafting the original college statutes in 1924. She retired in 1936 to live with her siblings in Southampton, and died in Shedfield Lodge Nursing Home, Shedfield, Hampshire, on 30 March 1965.   A. E. L. DAVIS

Sources K. T. Butler and H. I. McMorran, eds., *Girton College register, 1869–1946* (1948) [student list, 1895; staff list, 1903] · Lady Jeffreys, *Girton Review*, Easter term (1965), 32–4 · Burke, *Baronetage and knightage* · Debrett's Peerage · J. Foster, *The peerage, baronetage, and knightage of the British empire for 1883*, 2 [1883] · *LondG* (26 March 1920) [3rd suppl.] · A. W. Thorp, ed., *Burke's handbook* (1921) · *War Office Lists* (1879) · *War Office Lists* (1900) · PRO, AIR 1 2427/305/29/1001 · private information (2004) · correspondence, Girton Cam. · *CGPLA Eng. & Wales* (1947) · *CGPLA Eng. & Wales* (1965) [Frances Evelyn Cave-Browne-Cave]
Wealth at death £13,068 12s. 8d.: probate, 8 Oct 1947, *CGPLA Eng. & Wales* · £22,682—Frances Evelyn Cave-Browne-Cave: probate, 23 June 1965, *CGPLA Eng. & Wales*

Cave, Edward (1691–1754), printer and magazine proprietor, was born on 27 February 1691 at Cave's Hole on Watling Street in Newton, near Rugby, Warwickshire, the son of Joseph Cave (1667–1747), who, having lost an entailed family estate, had become a shoemaker in Rugby, and his wife, Esther (1665–1734). Lennart Carlson, however, claims that Cave was born on 27 February 1692 and was baptized in the nearby village of Clifton on 7 March 1692. Joseph also had two younger sons, William and Joseph, and a daughter, Mary. Edward Cave was admitted to Rugby School in 1700 and, according to his biographer and the sole source for his early life, Samuel Johnson, showed promise of academic abilities, but forfeited any prospect of entering university by alienating the school's head with his unruly independence of spirit. Compelled to leave, Cave at first worked as a clerk to a travelling excise man. He gave up this picaresque life to settle in London, working for a Bankside timber merchant. His superior education subsequently drove him to seek employment in the trade of printing. He was indentured to the deputy alderman and printer Freeman Collins on 6 February 1710, and was sent in 1712 by his master to run the Red Well print shop in Norwich and publish a local paper, the *Norwich Post*. On Collins's early death in 1713 Cave was recalled to London, but after disagreements with Collins's widow, Susanna, he left her employ 'upon a stipulated allowance' (Johnson, 'Life', 314) to work as a journeyman for the distinguished tory printer (and future mayor of London) John Barber. Barber's interests would have associated Cave with some of the day's leading tory controversialists and

Edward Cave (1691–1754), by Thomas Worlidge, pubd 1754 (after Francis Kyte, 1740)

newsletter writers. Cave was given copywriting assignments on *Mist's Weekly Journal* at this time, where he would have been collaborating with Defoe.

Following his marriage on 18 September 1716 at St Dunstan's in Stepney to Susannah Newton, *née* Milton (1683/4–1750), a widow of some means and eight years his elder, with whom he lived in Bow, Cave became free of the Stationers' Company on 4 March 1717. His wife's connections enabled him to procure a post as a sorter at the Post Office's inland office in Lombard Street in February 1721. He was rapidly promoted until his appointment in 1723 as the inspector of franks. Samuel Johnson's comment about Cave that by 'the correspondence which his place in the Post-office facilitated, he procured country news-papers, and sold their intelligence to a journalist in London' (Johnson, 'Life', 313) massively underestimates the extent of traffic in newsletters, newspapers, and other unpaid correspondence through the Post Office, both into and out of the capital. Cave and his fellow Post Office appointees farmed their positions to earn generous incomes. In addition, the inspector of franks, ostensibly defending state revenues, carried out routine surveillance of the mail for his political masters. Having started with tory associates, Cave later became a mild whig, although as an editor he never put politics before profit. In March 1727 he was arraigned before the House of Commons for distributing newsletter accounts of its proceedings to the *Gloucester Journal*. Despite his eleven days of detention, his news dealing went on largely unabated, as similar recurrences of the offence testify.

Cave did jobbing work and printed many catchpenny pamphlets and newsbooks in the 1720s, taking his first apprentice (Richard Newton jun., possibly a stepson) in 1722, and his name appears in imprints from 1727 onwards. He set up as a printer in Aldermanbury and then near Smithfield's, before making his final move, probably in late 1729, to a large printing office located in the arch and west tower of St John's Gate, Clerkenwell, that had formerly been owned by the widow printer Sarah Holt. This London landmark, originally the grand south gate to the priory of St John of Jerusalem, became Cave's trademark: his plate, coach, and most famous publication all bore its image. As a natural development of his dealings in news and ephemera, Cave began the *Gentleman's Magazine* in January 1731, thus giving birth to one of the major publishing forms of the modern era, the magazine. It began modestly as a digest of London newspapers and periodicals for country customers (an orientation signalled in Cave's editorial pseudonym, Sylvanus Urban), but it went on to prosper and survive until 1922. At 6*d*. and seven octavo half-sheets it truly gave 'more in quantity, and greater variety, than any Book of the kind and price' (Bavius). The proprietors of the papers extracted by Cave were enraged by these appropriations, but the hazy status of abridgements, like that of translations, made it more attractive to compete with an interloper than to seek legal redress. Powerful metropolitan bookselling and newspaper interests therefore set up the *London Magazine* in 1732. These two journals fought bitterly and often underhandedly against each other throughout Cave's life, both achieving considerable circulations, with Hawkins claiming that the *Gentleman's Magazine* reached sales of 15,000 copies a month during Walpole's fall. Cave's success at first took him by surprise; he was compelled to reprint magazines from the first two years to match demand for back numbers and volumes.

The *Gentleman's Magazine*'s prodigious success may well have rested as much upon distribution advantages that Cave enjoyed with the provincial book trade through the Post Office as upon editorial policy, but he was certainly a shrewd innovator. Newspaper extracts, commercial information, and later parliamentary reports launched the magazine, but they did not wholly sustain it. Regular imputations of literary piracy led Cave to seek original contributions and to cultivate a wide circle of customer–correspondents, particularly lovers of poetry. His poetry columns contained a mixture of licensed and unlicensed extracts from celebrated writers like Thomson and Savage, together with the work of amateur and provincial poets, and gave a number of younger poets such as Johnson, Elizabeth Carter, Mark Akenside, and John Hawkesworth their first chance. Valuable publicity (and copy) for the columns was achieved by poetry competitions, eight in all, throughout the 1730s, and better magazine contributors were often engaged as editorial assistants as a result. The uneven quality of this verse often exposed the magazine to censure from those indifferent to the realities of running a contributory mass circulation miscellany. Nor did they appreciate the emergence of a new kind of mercantile patronage, where an educated provincial middle class could achieve literary visibility in the face of a trade dominated by metropolitan booksellers. As the magazine reached a circulation of about 8000 to 10,000 in

the late 1730s, poetry declined in significance as the events following the declaration of war with Spain in October 1739 until the peace of Aix-la-Chapelle in 1748 brought politics and hard news to greater prominence in the magazine. The parliamentary reports that had begun in July 1732 and thereafter been printed during the parliamentary recess became longer, more literate, and more dangerous at this time. Cave adopted the subterfuge of 'Debates in the senate of Magna Lilliputia' in 1738, and Samuel Johnson was engaged to write them for three years from July 1741. Exciting political affairs were supplemented by innovative reporting of military campaigns; Cave pioneered the use of maps and charts to make sense of various theatres of war. He also popularized science, particularly in the fields of astronomy and mathematics. He had a businessman's appreciation that the proper application of astronomy was in navigation and that of physics and chemistry in new technologies. The magazine abounded in new machines and schemes for improving commerce. Cave himself published Benjamin Franklin's *Experiments and Observations on Electricity* (1753) and had one of Franklin's lightning conductors rigged up on St John's Gate. His own substantial investment in the cotton-spinning inventions of Lewis Paul, and his setting up of a cotton spinning mill in Northampton in 1743, employing over fifty workers, came within a few small technical improvements of mechanizing textile production in the generation before Arkwright and Hargreaves. Although he discontinued spinning cotton in 1747, he never sold the mill, and after his death it was leased to other entrepreneurs by his brother William. This venture became emblematic of Cave's 'innumerable projects' (Johnson, 'Life', 314), not one of which, Johnson claimed, ever succeeded and which impaired his fortune.

Another such project was Cave's edition of Jean-Baptiste du Halde's *A Description of the Empire of China* (1737–42), a lavish serial publication which met with serious book trade opposition and indifference from the public. A departure from Cave's usual practice of low-cost, low-risk publishing for a mass audience, this work nevertheless was a pioneering work in geography, challenged Europeans' complacency about their advancement, and established the orthographic conventions by which Chinese has been represented in English until very recently. The financial losses he sustained as a result made him more cautious about future projects, many abandoned at the proposal stage. His subsequent successes, like Johnson's *Rambler* (1750–2) and Hawkesworth's *Adventurer* (1752–4), were more rooted in the world of periodical publications that he knew better. But he never declined a profitable occasional publication, including a large proportion of Johnson's early work. In all, some 220 known titles were printed or published by him.

Hawkins draws Cave as a chill and peremptory figure, a niggardly paymaster, and insensitive to literary merit. He is characterized as offhand with his workers and unintentionally brusque with his equals. Johnson qualifies this impression by paying greater attention to his qualities of perseverance, courage in challenging entrenched interests, loyalty to friends, and conviviality. Anecdotes survive of his affability and hospitality at table with Johnson and others, his modestly referring to himself as Ned Cave the Cobbler, and his belonging to literary clubs like the one in Butcher's Row in 1747 where pieces for the magazine were selected and improved. The great arch of St John's Gate saw the presses drawn back to permit games of battledores and shuttlecock, and on one occasion David Garrick performed *The Mock Doctor* with Cave's journeymen reading the minor roles. A number of etchings of Cave's likeness were published after his death, and a portrait by Hogarth is said to have existed.

Cave's health was poor for the last ten years of his life. He resigned from the Post Office in February 1745 for this reason, but not before he had already secured a generous annuity from his successor and posts for two of his ex-apprentices. Although a bulky six-footer and vigorous in his youth, he came to suffer from gout and gave up both meat and alcohol for long periods. He made regular trips to Bath to take the waters, sponsored the building of a pump room in 1750 for the reputedly 'miraculous' Glastonbury waters, and has been identified as the 'honest man' who told Johnson that he had once seen a ghost (Boswell, *Life*, 2.178). Johnson dates his final decline from his wife's death from asthma at the end of 1750, a curious assertion since he must have identified Susannah Cave to Boswell as the woman who made a deathbed confession of squirreling away amounts of her husband's money but expired before she could reveal their whereabouts. After two years of recovery and relapse and weakened by diarrhoea, Cave fell into a lethargy and died at home at St John's Gate aged sixty-two, with Johnson at hand, on 10 January 1754, and was buried a week later in the Vestry Place of St James's, Clerkenwell. At his death he had a personal fortune of £8708, including £3000 invested in the *Gentleman's Magazine*, of which he was sole owner. His estate passed to his sister Mary Henry, his brother-in-law David *Henry, and his nephew Richard Cave. Effectively, the *Gentleman's Magazine* was run by Cave's family until John Nichols took it over in 1778, with Henry continuing to own St John's Gate until his own death in 1792.

ANTHONY DAVID BARKER

Sources S. Johnson, 'Life of Cave', *Biographia Britannica, or, The lives of the most eminent persons who have flourished in Great Britain and Ireland*, ed. A. Kippis and others, 2nd edn (1784), vol. 3, pp. 313–15 · J. Hawkins, *The life of Samuel Johnson, LL.D.*, 2nd edn (1787), 27–30, 43–160 · Boswell, *Life* · J. G. Nichols, 'The autobiography of Sylvanus Urban', *GM*, 3rd ser., 1 (1856), 1–9, 131–40, 267–77; 2 (1857), 3–10, 149–57, 282–90, 379–87 · A. D. Barker, 'Edward Cave, Samuel Johnson and the *Gentleman's Magazine*, 1731–54', DPhil diss., U. Oxf., 1981 · B. Foster, *Ye history of ye priory and gate of St. John* (1851), 35–66 · C. L. Carlson, *The first magazine* (1938) · T. Kaminski, *The early career of Samuel Johnson* (1987) · *The letters of Samuel Johnson*, ed. R. W. Chapman, 3 vols. (1952) · D. F. McKenzie, ed., *Stationers' Company apprentices*, [3]: 1701–1800 (1978), 68, 82, 178 · D. Stokes, 'Edward Cave and the *Norwich Post*', *University of East Anglia Bulletin*, 7/2 (1973), 1–5 · Bavius, editorial, *The Grubstreet Journal* (22–9 Dec 1737) · J. D. Fleeman, *A bibliography of the works of Samuel Johnson*, vol. 1 (2000) · *IGI* · administration, PRO, PROB 6/130, fol. 166v · R. Hovenden, ed., *A true register of all the christenings, mariages, and burialles in the parishe of St James, Clerkenwell, from … 1551 (to 1754)*, 4, Harleian Society, register section, 17 (1891), 294; 6, Harleian Society, register section, 20 (1894), 320

Archives BL, corresp., Stowe MS 748 | BL, letters to T. Birch, Add. MS 4302, Add. Ch. 5972, 5973 · Finsbury Public Library, London, poor rate books for Clerkenwell · Royal Mail Heritage, London, minute books

Likenesses J. Basire, engraving, repro. in Nichols, *Lit. anecdotes*, vol. 5, frontispiece · attrib. Hogarth, portrait; formerly in possession of Benjamin Foster, occupant of St John's Gate, Clerkenwell, London · E. Scriven, engraving (after oil painting by Kyte, 1740), repro. in Boswell, *Life*, following p. 84 · T. Worlidge, engraving (after F. Kyte), NPG; repro. in *GM* (1754), 55 [*see illus.*]

Wealth at death £8708, incl. share value of *GM* (£3000) and £900 stake in *Daily Advertiser*: Boswell, *Life*, vol. 1, p. 256 n. 1 · administration, PRO, PROB 6/130, fol. 166v

Cave, (Frances) Evelyn Cave-Browne- (1876–1965). *See under* Cave, Beatrice Mabel Cave-Browne- (1874–1947).

Cave, George, Viscount Cave (1856–1928), lawyer and politician, was born on 23 February 1856 at 67 Cheapside, London, the second son of Thomas Cave (1825–1894), a City of London merchant, and his wife, Elizabeth (1827/8–1925), daughter of Jasper Shallcrass of Banstead, Surrey, who were married in 1849. Cave's father was sheriff of London and Middlesex in 1863–4 and Liberal MP for Barnstaple from 1865 to 1880; his mother outlived her husband by thirty years, dying at the age of ninety-seven. His elder brother, Thomas, became a solicitor, and of his two younger brothers Edmund became a master of the Supreme Court and Basil was consul-general in Zanzibar and was knighted. In 1866, Cave was sent to the Lycée Impérial de Caen, where he stayed for three years. He then went to Merchant Taylors' School, London. In 1874 he gained a closed scholarship to St John's College, Oxford, where he also held a Pitt Club exhibition and a Taylorian exhibition in French. Cave was a successful scholar: he obtained first-class honours in classical moderations in 1875 and went on to be in the first class in Greats in 1878. In 1916 he was made an honorary fellow of his college. He attempted an All Souls fellowship but was unsuccessful.

In May 1876 Cave was admitted to the Inner Temple, and in June 1880 he was called to the bar and took up practice in chambers at 26 Old Buildings, Lincoln's Inn. He soon gained a steady if not brilliant practice at the Chancery bar. By 1890 he was earning £1000 a year and by 1904 between £4000 and £5000. On 6 January 1885 he married (Anne) Estella Sarah Penfold Mathews (d. 1938), daughter of William Witney Mathews of Chard, Somerset. They had one child, who died at birth.

Cave's father had been active in local government in Richmond-on-Thames, Surrey, and in 1886 George Cave was elected to Richmond vestry. In 1890, after Richmond was incorporated, he was elected to the new Richmond borough council. He went on to be a member of Surrey county council. In 1892 he was made alderman and in 1897 became deputy lieutenant of Surrey. Cave became chairman of Surrey quarter sessions in 1894. Here his advice was influential in the nomination of candidates to the

George Cave, Viscount Cave (1856–1928), by Sir Gerald Kelly, exh. RA 1924

magistracy. In 1904 he took silk and became a bencher of his inn in 1912. He was appointed attorney-general to the prince of Wales in 1914.

Conservative politician, home secretary, and law lord Cave was elected to parliament in 1906 as Conservative MP for Kingston upon Thames and was re-elected subsequently until he was elevated to the peerage. His parliamentary style was quiet, unemotional, and persuasive and he was valued for his tactful approach to difficult problems. He made his name in 1908 with his speech opposing the Licensing Bill, where his experience as a licensing justice in Surrey was of considerable value. From 1905 to 1909 he was a member of the royal commission on land transfer. In 1913 Cave moved the minority report of the select committee which inquired into the circumstances surrounding the purchase of shares in the American Marconi Company by Sir Herbert Samuel, Lloyd George (then chancellor of the exchequer), and Sir Rufus Isaacs. This condemned their conduct as a 'grave impropriety'. Cave emphasized the concern that the head of the Treasury, who 'desires the respect of the City of London', was unwise to engage in such transactions (Heuston, 413).

In the debates on the 1913 Home Rule Bill, Cave followed the Unionist view that Ulster must either be persuaded to be included under the terms of the bill or be excluded by parliament. He went further than his party in claiming

that such an important change in the constitution of Ireland required the assent of the electors, saying that if the Liberal government failed to hold a referendum before the bill was passed, the king would be entitled to dissolve parliament without the consent of the prime minister. Here he was supported by both Dicey and Anson, who argued that the king had power to dissolve parliament in order to secure the consent of electors to fundamental change. Lord Esher dissented, pointing out that Cave's view was contrary to the provisions of the Act of Settlement 1701 and would bring the king into party politics, which 'No loyal subject could contemplate without misgivings'. In a letter to Asquith, Birrell thought it was 'odd that a mouldy Equity draftsman and conveyancer should be so *bold*' (Heuston, 414). The issue of the king's prerogative arose later, in 1923, when Cave was lord chancellor. On the ground that the king must be kept out of political debates, he advised Stamfordham that the king could not be bound to grant a dissolution to Ramsay MacDonald if the minority Labour government were defeated in the house.

In 1915, unusually for a back-bencher, Cave was sworn of the privy council and was knighted. That autumn Carson resigned as attorney-general and F. E. Smith secured the succession for himself, with Cave as solicitor-general. They appeared for the crown in the prosecution of Roger Casement for high treason in 1916. In a contentious decision, F. E. made a formal request to Cave to support his decision not to allow Casement to appeal to the House of Lords, with which Cave concurred. Cave became home secretary in December 1917. In that capacity, he agreed that the chief secretary for Ireland could allow 'a Roman Catholic dignitary' to examine the controversial Casement diaries. One of his first acts as home secretary was to steer through the bill which doubled the size of the electorate, reduced seven franchise qualifications to three, and gave the vote to women over thirty. During the passage of the bill he was offered the mastership of the rolls, to which as a Chancery lawyer he would have been well suited, but he declined it. In June 1918 he led a mission to The Hague to negotiate an agreement with the German government over the exchange of prisoners of war. In August that year, he offered his resignation when the commissioner of the Metropolitan Police resigned in the wake of a police strike. It was refused.

On 13 November 1918 Cave was appointed a lord of appeal in ordinary and was created a viscount. He did not surrender the seals as home secretary until 14 January 1919 which created the odd situation of a law lord discharging the duties of a cabinet minister.

In 1919 Cave led a commission to South Africa to decide on the appropriate compensation to be awarded to the British South Africa Company for the loss of investment in Southern Rhodesia. The question had been who owned the land: the British South Africa Company, the Matabele (Ndebele) people, the white settlers, or the British crown. Originally referred to the judicial committee in 1914, the case was heard in 1918. The judicial committee held that the unoccupied lands were held by the crown, and the question remained of compensation to the British South Africa Company for developing the land. Cave's commission set the compensation at £4.5million, half the company claim. Cave received the GCMG for this task.

Lord chancellor On the formation of the Bonar Law cabinet in October 1922 Cave was made lord chancellor. His appointment was due to the refusal of the post by Pollock, who had opposed Bonar Law at the Carlton Club meeting of the Conservative Party on their continued membership of the coalition. Cave was reappointed by Baldwin in 1923, and served as lord chancellor until the election of January 1924. When Haldane, who was in failing health, was made lord chancellor, Cave helped him by continuing to perform his judicial duties during Haldane's ten-month tenure. Cave resumed office as lord chancellor in November 1924, and held it until his death in March 1928.

Cave's approach as lord chancellor was orthodox. He made reforms to advisory committees responsible for appointing magistrates, making members retire by rotation every three years and fixing their term of appointment to six years. He was instrumental in seeing through the Law of Property Act 1925, and its six ancillary statutes, which together modernized and simplified the law governing the ownership and transfer of land in England and Wales. They were the fruit of many years' work by many hands and much debate. They were opposed by large sections of the legal profession, and Cave himself had spoken against the reforms when Birkenhead promoted them in 1922. But when they were reintroduced later the same year, after Cave had taken office as lord chancellor, he accepted that they must pass. All seven acts became law in 1925. Cave also presided over the passing of the Supreme Court of Judicature (Consolidation) Act 1925 clarifying and reforming the law governing the administration of the courts. In 1926 Cave was criticized for his handling of a debate on the Trades Disputes Bill in the wake of the general strike. When Labour peers tried to filibuster, and the leader of the house moved the closure, Cave accepted the motion without a debate. A debate followed over the next four days on the propriety of Cave's judgment; Lord Ullswater, who had been speaker from 1910 to 1913, questioned Cave's decision, but Cave refused to admit he was wrong.

In 1925 Cave was approached to stand as chancellor of the University of Oxford. He was very reluctant, as he and others felt that should he lose against the other candidate, Asquith, it would reflect badly on the Conservative Party, and only after considerable persuasion did he accept. Cave was elected, owing to the votes of people described by Asquith as 'cavemen': 'half literate followers in rural parsonages' (Koss, 275).

Cave died at his Somerset home, St Ann's, Burnham-on-Sea, on 29 March 1928, and was buried at St Mary's, Berrow. He had sent his resignation to Baldwin a week earlier and the day before he died he was told that he had been made an earl; his widow was subsequently granted the title Countess Cave of Richmond. For a successful barrister, he left surprisingly little money, and Hailsham arranged for a number of people to subscribe to an annuity to support his widow.

THOMAS S. LEGG and MARIE-LOUISE LEGG

Sources R. F. V. Heuston, *Lives of the lord chancellors, 1885–1940* (1964) · C. Mallet, *Lord Cave: a memoir* (1931) · S. Koss, *Asquith* (1985) · J. Campbell, *F. E. Smith, first earl of Birkenhead* (1983) · G. B. Grundy, *Fifty-five years at Oxford: an unconventional autobiography* (1945) · GEC, *Peerage*

Archives BL, corresp. and MSS, Add. MSS 62455–62516 | Bodl. Oxf., corresp. with Viscount Addison · HLRO, corresp. with Bonar Law · HLRO, letters to David Lloyd George | FILM BFI NFTVA, news footage

Likenesses W. R. Symonds, oils, 1911, County Hall, Kinston upon Thames, Surrey · G. Kelly, oils, exh. RA 1924, Merchant Taylors' School, Northwood, London [*see illus.*] · F. Dodd, chalk drawing, 1925, NPG · R. G. Eve, oils, 1925, Inner Temple, London · F. Dodd, oils, St John's College, Oxford · cartoons, local history archives, Richmond-on-Thames · photographs, local history archives, Richmond-on-Thames

Wealth at death £27,832: resworn probate, 7 June 1928, *CGPLA Eng. & Wales*

Cave [*married name* Winscom], **Jane** (*b.* 1754/5, *d.* in or before 1813), poet, was born in Wales, probably at Talgarth in Brecon, where her father, John Cave (*b.* 1712/13), was an exciseman. He was later converted to Methodism by the religious reformer Howel Harris (1714–1773), an associate of the Wesleys. He worked as an excise officer in Talgarth and as a glover in Brecon. Jane wrote on the deaths of Harris and of George Whitefield, and on the consecration of chapels for the sect known as the Countess of Huntingdon's Connexion; she also attended Anglican services. Her mother, who died on 6 February 1777, must have been a Miss H—, as was an aunt to whom her daughter addressed verse letters. Jane Cave had more than one sister. She addressed to her mother, not her father, a poem of farewell to her own maiden name.

From her childhood Cave had a taste for books and poetry. She lived in several places before her marriage, probably in employment. In Bath she had friends who were like parents to her, and she wrote a poem for two young women being bound apprentices to a milliner. She moved to Winchester in November 1779. In 1783 she had printed by subscription there, 'for the Author', *Poems on Various Subjects, Entertaining, Elegiac, and Religious*. It bore her birth-name and a portrait showing her pen in hand. It had a lengthy list of subscribers, arranged by their places of residence. This work became the basis of her publishing career. The next edition, published in Bristol in 1786, added 'Now Mrs. W—' to her name.

Thomas Winscom, whom Cave married on 18 May 1783, was an exciseman like her father. They had two sons, and perhaps other children who did not survive. Her husband's job entailed moving to a new place every four years: they were at Chagford in Devon before moving in 1792 to Bristol, where he was still working in 1797. A family named Cave were bankers in Bristol, but their family tree gives no evidence of connection; nor is there any evidence of relationship with Edward Cave (1691–1754), founder of the *Gentleman's Magazine*, which printed an obituary notice of Jane Cave. She enjoyed a network of links all over the west country, though it was not of her own building, since she says she had not the honour of being known to most of her subscribers. Those to her first volume (whose names fill fifty-two closely printed columns) come from towns like Oxford, Woodstock, Abingdon, Whitchurch, Newbury, Southampton, and Portsmouth, several places in the Isle of Wight, Salisbury, Winchester, and Bath. The next edition expands the list to draw from Windsor and from Sussex. Further editions appeared at Shrewsbury in 1789 and at Bristol again in 1794 (listing the names of newly acquired noble subscribers only). The number of subscribers, and the continual addition of new ones, suggests that Cave was skilled in operating the patronage system.

The first edition is dedicated in a poem 'To the Subscribers', and mentions the author's humble admiration for the 'Celebrated Poetesses' Anna Seward, Anne Steele, and Hannah More, whom Cave does not presume to emulate. The poems are arranged more or less by genre: occasional poems (many written at some specific request), pieces on love, marriage, and family affection, elegies, epitaphs, and hymns. The second edition breaks up this generic ordering, adds new poems, and drops others which might be considered low, like 'Written by Desire of a Lady, on an Angry, Petulant Kitchen-Maid'. Cave writes advice to unborn children, an address to her baby son, poems on religious topics, and about her own relationship to poetry (notably of being too busy with domestic duties to give proper attention to the muses when they make a social call). She also addresses the perennial topic of a reader who disbelieves that she can, as a woman, really have written her works herself. Poems in her last collection relate how in 1791 she rescued a poor woman from debtors' prison by getting up a subscription, and how she has treated her persistent headaches, for which doctors' prescriptions proved useless, both by sea-bathing and by drinking the waters of Bristol.

On 25 May 1793, the year before her final volume appeared, Cave published 'The Head-ach, or, An Ode to Health' in a Bristol newspaper, including a request for suggestions from any readers who might know of a remedy. From the 1780s onwards, she says, she was losing twelve days every month to excruciating headaches, which a modern scholar diagnoses as migraines, and felt that her effectiveness as wife and mother was seriously impaired. She was scathing about the best efforts of the medical profession. When she first tried sea-bathing she found it terrifying, but later she came to revel in the experience. It did not cure her headaches, but she may have persisted in the practice none the less, for her *Gentleman's Magazine* obituary says that two years before she died she had a 'miraculous escape from a watery grave'. This obituary pays tribute to Cave's genius, intellect, writings, and virtues as a wife and mother. She died aged fifty-eight in Newport, Monmouthshire, by January 1813 (the date of the obituary). ISOBEL GRUNDY

Sources E. Poole, *The illustrated history and biography of Brecknockshire* (1886) · Blain, Clements & Grundy, *Feminist comp.* · *DWB* · *History of banking in Bristol* (1899) [Cave family tree, pp. 224–5] · A. E. McKim, 'Jane Cave Winscom and the poetry of pain' [unpubd article] · *GM*, 1st ser., 83/1 (1813), 88

Cave, John (*d.* 1657), Church of England clergyman, was born at Pickwell, Leicestershire, the third son of John Cave, gentleman, and his wife, Elizabeth Brudenell. He subscribed to the Thirty-Nine Articles at Oxford on 23 April 1613 and was at some date admitted to Lincoln College, where he was said to have shared a room for eight years with the future Leicestershire clergyman and Restoration bishop of Lincoln Robert Sanderson, at that time a fellow. Cave graduated BA on 24 April 1616 and proceeded MA on 28 January 1619. Three weeks later, on 21 and 22 February, he was ordained deacon and priest at Peterborough. In 1629 he was presented by his father to the rectory of Pickwell. Before 1637, when his younger son William was born, he had married his wife, Elizabeth.

With the outbreak of the civil war Cave and his family suffered a series of assaults and mistreatments at the hands of parliamentary troops, according to the account later given by his son William *Cave (1637–1713) to John Walker. Complaints to JPs about the misbehaviour of soldiers billeted in the rectory went unheeded. Cave was falsely accused of theft, and having been taken to the regional headquarters was 'tried at a Council of War for his Life' (Walker, 2.220–21). Just as the council was ready to pass sentence, Colonel Henry Ireton unexpectedly arrived and, 'suspect[ing] (as later proved) villainy', halted the proceedings. Cave's persistence in loyalty to the king and his unshaken zeal for the episcopal Church of England led to several violent incidents in his church involving soldiers. After an abortive journey to London to argue his case and the failure of his kinsmen, MPs Sir William Armyne and Sir Arthur Hesilrige, to lend him promised support, he was ejected from his living, probably late in 1644; John Weld held it from 1645.

Cave, his wife, and six children at first stayed with neighbours, but not being 'suffered long to continue there, nor … to teach school there or elsewhere' (Walker, 2.220–21), they moved to near Stamford. On 17 January 1646 the county committee fined Cave £40 for being at Leicester, then held for the king, but on 10 November the following year, following his appeal, the committee for sequestrations discharged the sequestration of his temporal estates. At some point the family moved to London. Cave's only publication was a contribution (as from a *humillimus servus*) to *Lachrymae musarum* (1650), a collection of elegies written on the death of Henry, Lord Hastings, heir of the earl of Huntingdon, which had taken place in the city the previous year.

By the time Cave drew up his will on 20 January 1657, he was living at Bunhill, in the parish of St Giles Cripplegate, London, with his wife, Elizabeth. He still held land at Pickwell, but his books and manuscripts were at Eason, Northamptonshire. After his wife's death the land, or profits from its sale, were to go to his elder son, John; his son William and daughters Elizabeth and Bridget were each to have £40, while his second (married) daughter, Mary Woodriffe, was to have £20. Cave died, probably in London, 'about the beginning of November 1657' (Walker, 2.221). His widow, as executor, proved the will on 4 December. VIVIENNE LARMINIE

Sources J. Walker, *An attempt towards recovering an account of the numbers and sufferings of the clergy of the Church of England*, pt 2 (1714), 220–21 • *Walker rev.*, 233 • Foster, *Alum. Oxon.* • J. Nichols, *The history and antiquities of the county of Leicester*, 2 (1795–8), 771, 773; facs. edn (1971) • H. I. Longden, *Northamptonshire and Rutland clergy from 1500*, ed. P. I. King and others, 16 vols. in 6, Northamptonshire RS (1938–52), vol. 3, p. 65 • ESTC • will of John Cave, PRO, PROB 11/271, fols. 205r–205v • *DNB*

Cave, Sir **Lewis William** (1832–1897),

judge, was born on 3 July 1832 at Desborough, Northamptonshire, the eldest son of William Cave, a small landowner there, and his wife, Elizabeth. He was educated at Rugby School before matriculating on 26 March 1851 at Lincoln College, Oxford, where he was Crewe exhibitioner and graduated BA with a second-class degree in *literae humaniores* in 1855 and MA in 1877.

After leaving university, Cave was admitted in 1856 as a student of the Inner Temple. On 5 August 1856 he married Julia, daughter of the Revd C. F. Watkins, vicar of Brixworth, Northamptonshire; they had at least one child. Cave was called to the bar on 10 June 1859 and elected bencher on 15 June 1877, joining the midland circuit before moving to the north-eastern circuit, where he had built a large general practice. He also acted as joint editor of Stone's *Practice of Petty Sessions* (1861) and *Reports of the Court for the Consideration of Crown Cases Reserved* (1861–5).

Cave's career ambitions began to be realized: in 1865 he was appointed revising barrister, in 1873 recorder of Lincoln, and on 28 June 1875 was gazetted queen's counsel. He also continued to edit legal texts, including sixth and seventh issues of Addison's *Treatise on the Law of Contracts* (1869; 1875) and the fifth edition of Addison's *Law of Torts* (1879). He was commissioner for the autumn assize in 1877 and was placed on the Oxford election commission on 10 September 1880.

In 1881 Cave was raised to the bench as justice of the High Court, Queen's Bench Division (14 March), and knighted (1 April). The appointment was unexpected, as Cave's reputation was greater on circuit than in London, but proved justified by the unusual vigour and soundness of judgment he displayed. Burly in person and bluff in manner, he had a businesslike approach which shortened his cases. He seized points very rapidly, and frequently cut short argument with sharp questions of counsel, such as: 'That won't do, you know. Have you anything else?' or 'What do you say to that?' He was as competent in criminal as in civil cases. His knowledge of business made him an especially good bankruptcy judge in the Queen's Bench Division under the act of 1883. Had he retired when he resigned the bankruptcy jurisdiction in 1891, his reputation would have remained high. His vigour flagged thereafter, however, and signs of decay were plain for some

time before his death of paralysis at his home, the Manor House, Woodmansterne, Epsom, on 7 September 1897. He was buried at St Peter's, Woodmansterne, on 10 September. J. M. RIGG, *rev.* HUGH MOONEY

Sources *Law Magazine*, 4th ser., 23 (1897–8), 39–42 • *The Times* (8 Sept 1897) • *Annual Register* (1897) • *Law Journal* (11 Sept 1897) • *Law Times* (11 Sept 1897) • *Solicitors' Journal*, 41 (1896–7), 756 • J. Foster, *Men-at-the-bar: a biographical hand-list of the members of the various inns of court*, 2nd edn (1885) • Foster, *Alum. Oxon.* • J. Foster, *The peerage, baronetage, and knightage of the British empire for 1881*, [2 pts] [1881] • *LondG* (10 Sept 1880) • *VF* (7 Dec 1893) • A. Birrell, *Sir Frank Lockwood, a biographical sketch* (1895), 84 • 'Royal commission to inquire into … corrupt practices in the city of Oxford', *Parl. papers* (1881), vol. 44, C. 2856 • *CGPLA Eng. & Wales* (1897)

Likenesses Lock & Whitfield, woodburytype photograph, NPG; repro. in T. Cooper, *Men of mark: a gallery of contemporary portraits* (1883) • Spy [L. Ward], chromolithograph caricature, NPG; repro. in *VF* (7 Dec 1893)

Wealth at death £31,380 15s. 4d.: probate, 25 Nov 1897, *CGPLA Eng. & Wales*

Cave, Sir **Richard Guy** (1920–1986),

industrialist, was born on 16 March 1920 in Bickley, Kent, the youngest in the family of two sons and three daughters of William Thomas Cave, London solicitor, and his wife, Gwendoline Mary Nicholls. The already very tall Richard Cave (Dick to his many friends from an early age) was educated at Tonbridge School, where he was captain of the rowing four and of swimming, and was in the rugby fifteen. In 1938 he went to Gonville and Caius College, Cambridge, to read mechanical engineering. His course was interrupted by the outbreak of the Second World War in 1939.

From 1940 Cave served with the 44th battalion of the Royal Tank regiment in north Africa (taking part in the battle of El Alamein), Sicily, and mainland Italy. Landing in Normandy on D-day plus three (9 June 1944), he commanded A squadron of the 44th battalion with great distinction throughout the campaign in north-west Europe, being awarded the MC (1944). His tank was among the first to cross the Rhine. His brigade commander, Michael Carver, described him as 'a splendid squadron commander, brave, sensible, level-headed, always calm and resolute and unfailingly cheerful'. After the war Cave decided not to return to Cambridge to complete his degree and instead joined Smiths Industries in 1946. The drive, intelligence, insight, and all-round competence of this big man—Cave stood a good 6 feet 5 inches—were recognized from the outset. He was appointed export director of the motor accessory division in 1956 and managing director of that division in 1963, joining the main board at the same time. In 1967 he became managing director of the firm, in 1968 chief executive, and in 1973 chairman. Under his steady, firm, forceful, and also imaginative direction, Smiths achieved remarkable progress and success, and diversified considerably.

In 1976 Cave left Smiths to become chairman of Thorn Electrical Industries, taking over from its founder, Sir Jules Thorn. Cave's outstanding leadership qualities—humanity, humour, and warmth, combined when necessary with toughness and directness—were equal to the challenge. He quickly won the loyalty of the staff, recognizing at the same time that Thorn was perhaps unduly dependent on the home market and that too many of its businesses were in comparatively low-level technologies. His major achievement at Thorn was the merger with EMI in 1979, which, despite much criticism at the time from the newspaper press and the City, secured the twin objectives of establishing a truly international company and strengthening Thorn's technological base. Notwithstanding major lung surgery in 1980, Cave characteristically continued as an active chairman of Thorn until late in 1983.

Cave also played a positive and valuable role in many other companies. He served as non-executive chairman of Vickers from 1984, during a period in the company's history of significant divestments and some important acquisitions. He was also deputy chairman of British Rail (1983–5), and his directorships included those of Thomas Tilling (1969–76), Tate and Lyle (1976–86), Equity and Law (1972–9), and Thames Television (1981–4).

Throughout his business career Cave left a distinctive and personal mark on wider industrial policy. He had a long-standing belief in training, having created a training college for young entrants to Smiths Industries. He also had a deep interest, from the wider national viewpoint, in export promotion, as shown by his membership of the British Overseas Trade Board (1977–80), and in employment matters, as demonstrated by his chairmanship of the Confederation of British Industry's steering group on unemployment (1981–3). His active membership, from 1970 until his death, of the Industrial Society, of which he was chairman from 1979 to 1983, bore witness to his lasting concern for better industrial relations. He was knighted in 1976.

Cave was a many-sided man with several interests. He was a keen supporter of the arts, in particular of the Aldeburgh festival close to his much-loved home in Suffolk, being chairman of the successful Aldeburgh appeal. He loved opera and ballet and, perhaps even more, sailing, and was commodore of the Aldeburgh Yacht Club (1975–6) and a member of the Royal Yacht Squadron. In 1957 he married Dorothy Gillian, daughter of Henry Kenneth Fry, of Adelaide, a general physician who later specialized in psychiatry and neurology. They had two sons and two daughters. Cave, a devoted family man, died of cancer at his home in Aldeburgh on 5 December 1986 after a long period of illness. GEORGE JELLICOE, *rev.*

Sources *The Times* (6 Dec 1986) · personal knowledge (2004) · private information (2004) · *WWW* · *CGPLA Eng. & Wales* (1987) **Wealth at death** £775,472: probate, 14 May 1987, *CGPLA Eng. & Wales*

Cave, Sir Stephen (1820–1880), politician, eldest son of Daniel Cave (*d.* 1872) of Cleeve Hill, near Bristol, and his wife (whom he married on 15 April 1820), Frances, only daughter of Henry Locock MD of London, was born at Clifton on 28 December 1820. He was educated at Harrow School and at Balliol College, Oxford, where he graduated

BA with a second class in 1843, and MA in 1846. Called to the bar at the Inner Temple on 20 November 1846, he began his career by going on the western circuit. On 7 September 1852 he married Emma Jane (*d.* 13 Nov 1905), eldest daughter of the Revd William Smyth of Elkington Hall, Lincolnshire; they had no surviving children.

Cave published pamphlets on slavery and the 1846 Sugar Bill in 1849, on crime prevention and reformatory institutions in 1856 and 1857, and on free labour and the slave trade in 1861. He was elected as a tory for Shoreham on 29 April 1859 and held the seat until 24 March 1880, uncontested save in 1865 and 1874. He was sworn of the privy council on 10 July 1866, and served as a paymaster-general and vice-president of the Board of Trade from that date to December 1868; in 1866 he was appointed chief commissioner for negotiating a fishery convention in Paris. Disraeli made Cave both judge-advocate and paymaster-general in his second government formed in February 1874. In November 1875 Cave was offered the presidency of the Board of Trade, but his insistence on membership of the cabinet lost him the offer, and he then resigned as judge-advocate. At this time he was in poor health. Later in November, it was decided to send him on a special mission to Egypt, to report on its financial condition. He exceeded his instructions and the cabinet considered recalling him, Derby noting that he was 'mixing himself up more than might be wished with the plans of speculators who are trying to make a good thing out of the Khedive's difficulties' (*Diaries*, 273). He returned in March 1876. His report played a part in the establishment of the Dual Control in Egypt later in 1876. Cave was made GCB on 20 March 1880 and left office as paymaster on 20 April 1880.

Cave was a fellow of the Society of Antiquaries, of the Zoological Society, and of other learned societies, and he was chairman of the West India Committee, and a director of the Bank of England and of the London Dock Company. He lived at 35 Wilton Place, London; Cleeve Hill, Mangotsfield, Gloucestershire; and Sidbury Manor, near Sidmouth in Devon, but died at Chambéry, Savoy, on 6 June 1880. G. C. BOASE, *rev.* H. C. G. MATTHEW

Sources *Law Times* (19 June 1880), 146 · *The Graphic* (11 Dec 1875), 574, 589 · *ILN* (11 Dec 1875), 501 · R. Shannon, *The age of Disraeli, 1868–1881: the rise of tory democracy* (1992) · A. Schölch, *Egypt for the Egyptians: the socio-political crisis in Egypt, 1878–1882* (1981); trans. of *Ägypten den Ägyptern! Die politische und gesellschaftliche Krise der Jahre 1878–1882 in Ägypten* (1972) · P. Smith, *Disraelian Conservatism and social reform* (1967) · *The diaries of E. H. Stanley, 15th earl of Derby, 1869–1878, CS*, 5th series, 4 (1994) · *Dod's Parliamentary Companion · CGPLA Eng. & Wales* (1880)
Likenesses Ape [C. Pellegrini], chromolithograph caricature, NPG; repro. in *VF* (3 Oct 1874) · Lock & Whitfield, woodburytype photograph, NPG; repro. in T. Cooper, *Men of mark: a gallery of contemporary portraits* (1878) · portrait, repro. in *The Graphic* · portrait, NPG; repro. in *ILN*
Wealth at death under £350,000: probate, 19 July 1880, *CGPLA Eng. & Wales*

Cave, Sydney (1883–1953), Congregational minister, missionary, and theologian, was born at 2 Park Place, Regent's

Park, London, on 18 November 1883, the second of the five sons of William Cave (1843–1910), a trunk maker, and his wife, Sarah (1851–1939), who also had two daughters. He was a nephew of Dr Alfred Cave. Growing up in Fulham he was educated at St Mark's School, Chelsea, and the City of London School (1899–1902), at both of which he won several prizes. In 1902 he entered Hackney College, a school of divinity of the University of London, to study under P. T. Forsyth who, according to a memoir, 'helped him find the cross in the centre of his thinking' (Jones, 454). He proved to be an outstanding student, gaining firsts in his BA and BD (honours) degrees, being awarded college scholarships, and becoming a Dr Williams's scholar. After four months' study in Germany he was ordained at Dawes Road Congregational Church, Fulham, on 8 October 1908.

Having offered for service with the London Missionary Society, Cave was appointed to India and stationed at Nagercoil, Travancore, where he served as acting principal of Scott Christian College (1909–11 and 1916), and principal of Duthie Divinity College (1911–15) training the local ministry.

Cave's fiancée, Elizabeth Jane Baxter (1880–1950), originally from Aberdeen, arrived in Madras in November 1909 and they were married there on 25 November. A daughter and son were born in India, and a second son in Bristol. Following their recurrent illnesses, doctors decided that the children could not live in India. They returned to England with Mrs Cave in 1914, but Sydney was not allowed to follow until his furlough, which was due in 1916. On 16 April 1918, having been inducted as minister of Henleaze Congregational Church, Bristol, he resigned from the society.

Although Cave's years in India were to influence all his subsequent work, his studies of Hindu thought found early expression in his thesis 'Redemption: Hindu and Christian' for which in March 1917 he was awarded the DD degree (London).

In 1920 his scholarship and experience led to his appointment as president of Cheshunt College, Cambridge. Recognizing his academic ability, Cambridge University awarded him in 1925 an honorary MA, and he became a member of Emmanuel College. In 1949 he was select preacher before the university. The Cheshunt governors' report for 1922 records that the president 'has quickly proved his competence, being eagerly welcomed by the churches, commanding the complete confidence of the Governors and having gained the trust and affection of the students'. Under his presidency the educational standard was raised, the curriculum widened, and many of his books were written.

In 1933 Cave became principal of New College, London, which had been formed in 1924 from the union of New and Hackney colleges. He held this position for the rest of his life, and it was here, in the building where he had once been a student, that full recognition came: the award by the University of Glasgow of an honorary DD (1934); professor of theology in the University of London (1936–49)

and emeritus professor until his death; chairman of the board of studies in theology (1938–44); dean of the faculty (1944–8); and member of the collegiate council (1937–53).

In both Cambridge and London, Sydney Cave concentrated on his college work, serving the denomination in ways for which his position and experience peculiarly fitted him: director of the London Missionary Society from 1920, serving on the India and candidates' committees; member of the council of the Congregational Union of England and Wales, serving on the ministerial committee (sometimes as chairman) and the 'special' committee (concerned with the recognition of ministers and churches); but consistently declining nomination as chairman of the union lest it interfere with his college work.

Cave's writings were on the doctrines of the Christian faith—his last book, *The Christian Way* (1949), being an exploration of current ethical issues—or on other religions and their relation to Christianity. His concern that all his students should be acquainted with the tenets of other faiths was then somewhat unusual but far sighted. His sensitive understanding of other religions also found expression in his Carew lectures at Hartford (1929) and Haskell lectures at Oberlin, Ohio (1939), the latter being published as *Hinduism or Christianity?*. Elsewhere, in works such as *The Doctrines of the Christian Faith* (1931), he demonstrated that although he regarded strict Calvinism as a 'hollow doctrine' he also believed in the 'inadequacy' of theological liberalism (Jones, 454). He took the part of Nathaniel Micklem in the 'Blackheath controversy' of 1933, after being provoked by accusations of having taught his students the rationalized Christianity promoted by the Blackheath group (Grant, 329). In March 1939 he put his name to the manifesto drafted by Micklem and Bernard Manning, calling for a revival of faithfulness to the word of the gospel (Jones, 455).

Sydney Cave was concerned to provide the church with well-educated, competent ministers. He sought no glory for himself, but his influence upon generations of students was of lasting importance. Colleagues sometimes found this shy man remote, but students found him approachable and sympathetic. In the post-war New College there were few rules, for he depended upon the Christian commitment of all. His slight stutter led him to adopt a steady tone when preaching, but his sense of the holiness and grace of God was inescapable.

After never having to miss giving a lecture, Cave was struck down by leukaemia in 1953, and died on 8 September at the Middlesex Hospital, London. He was cremated at Golders Green three days later. His wife had predeceased him, on 7 December 1950. The way he faced his last days confirmed his teaching.   RONALD BOCKING

Sources register, City of London School, record no. 13645 · SOAS, Archives of the Council for World Mission (incorporating the London Missionary Society) · candidate's application, DWL, Hackney College MSS · Cheshunt College, committee minutes and annual reports, Westminster College, Cambridge · New College board and committee minutes and annual reports, DWL · personal knowledge (2004) · private information (2004) · R. Tudur Jones,

Congregationalism in England, 1662–1962 (1962) · J. W. Grant, Free churchmanship in England, 1870–1940 [1955]
Archives DWL, collection
Likenesses photograph, c.1920, Trinity-Henleaze United Reformed Church, Bristol · photograph, c.1950, DWL · photograph, repro. in Congregational Yearbook (1954)

Cave, William (1637–1713), Church of England clergyman and patristic scholar, was born on 30 December 1637 at Pickwell in Leicestershire, where his father, John *Cave (d. 1657), was rector of the parish. John Cave remained a staunch royalist during the civil war, and as a result was expelled from his parish and home for a time, with his wife, Elizabeth, and six children. William Cave was educated at Oakham School, then in 1653 entered St John's College, Cambridge, from where he graduated BA in 1656 and MA in 1660. He was admitted DD at Cambridge in 1672 and incorporated as DD at Oxford in 1681. Cave was the vicar of Islington in Middlesex from 1662 to 1691, and the rector of All Hallows-the-Great, Upper Thames Street, London, from 1679 to 1689 (he was collated to this position by William Sancroft, archbishop of Canterbury, to whom Cave later dedicated his *Ecclesiastici*). Cave's most prestigious positions were chaplain in ordinary to Charles II (which he took up some time after becoming the vicar of Islington) and canon of Windsor (installed between 1681 and 1684).

Early works Cave is known for his written works of patristic scholarship and church history. His first book was *Primitive Christianity, or, The Religion of the Ancient Christians in the First Ages of the Gospel* (1673). The first part of this work discusses 'things charged against early Christians', the second 'the virtue of primitive Christians with respect to themselves', and the third 'the virtue of primitive Christians with respect to others'. In the preface Cave laments the impious state of Christians in his own world, but writes that he

> could not think that this had always been the unhappy fate and portion of Christianity, and that if the footsteps of true Christian Piety and Simplicity were any where to be found, it must be in those Times, When (as S. [Jerome] notes) The Blood of Christ was yet warm in the breasts of Christians, and the Faith and Spirit of Religion more brisk and vigorous.

His declared purpose in *Primitive Christianity* is to outline the 'pure' condition of the early church in order to provide an exemplar for pious life in his own time. He includes a chronological index of the authors cited, together with an account of editions of their works that he was using (Cave clearly owned most of these works himself, but he assures his readers that the reason for this index is scholarly: 'not that I had a mind to tell the world … how many books I had'). Finally he concludes with a list of councils, emperors, and recently deceased writers.

Cave's interest in charts and tables continued throughout his life. In his short work *Tabulae ecclesiasticae* (tables of ecclesiastical writers; 1674), organized according to centuries (*saecula*) beginning with the birth of Christ and ending in 1517, he lists all of the Christian writers with whom

he was acquainted, together with the most basic information about their nationality, occupation, birth, and death.

Contributions to Christian biography and church history, 1675–1683 In 1649 Jeremy Taylor published *The great exemplar of sanctity and holy life … described in the history of the life and death of the ever blessed Jesus Christ the saviour of the world*. This is a biography of Christ, together with discourses and prayers to enable readers to follow Christ's example. The fifth edition of this work was published in 1675 as *Antiquitates Christianae, or, The history of the life and death of the holy Jesus: as also the lives, acts and martyrdoms of his apostles … the first part, containing the life of Christ, written by Jer. Taylor, late lord bishop of Down and Connor, the second, containing the lives of the apostles, with an enumeration, and some brief remarks upon their first successors in the five great apostolical churches, by William Cave, D.D. chaplain in ordinary to his majesty*. Cave wrote an introduction to this work on 'the Three Great Dispensations of the Church, Patriarchal, Mosaical and Evangelical'. The work was dedicated to Nathanael Crewe, bishop of Durham and clerk of the king's closet (to whom Cave had also dedicated *Primitive Christianity*, when Crewe was bishop of Oxford). Although Cave's *Lives of the Apostles* purports to be a continuation of Taylor's *Life and Death of … Jesus*, the two works are actually quite different. Rather than providing a meditation upon the lives as Taylor does, Cave is following much more closely in the footsteps of the first church historian, Eusebius of Caesarea (c.260–340), who included the lives of the apostles and earliest church fathers as a substantial part of his *Church History*. Cave published his portion of the work (*Antiquitates apostolicae*) independently several times; it includes the lives of the twelve apostles as well as Paul, Mark, and Luke and ends with an account of the first 200 years of the 'five great churches' founded by the apostles.

The *Antiquitates apostolicae* set the stage for Cave's next two historical works, which were chronological continuations of this one: *Apostolici, or, The history of the lives, acts, death, and martyrdoms of those who were contemporary with, or immediately succeeded the apostles, as also of the most eminent of the primitive fathers for the first three hundred years* (1677) and *Ecclesiastici, or, The history of the lives, acts, deaths, & writings of the most eminent fathers of the church, that flourisht in the fourth century, wherein among other things an account is given of the rise, growth, and progress of Arianism, and all other sects of that age descending from it, together with an introduction, containing an historical account of the state of paganism under the first Christian emperours* (1683). The main objective of these two works, which together comprise a history of the church in the first 400 years after Christ, is to give the biographies of famous fathers of the church. In each case Cave begins with a cameo picture of the subject, then relates his life in narrative form, and ends with a list of his writings: extant, lost, and spurious. By organizing his work in this way Cave was following the method of Eusebius's *Church History*, which also lists subjects' writings in this manner; indeed, Cave acknowledges Eusebius as the primary inspiration for his work. Both *Apostolici* and *Ecclesiastici* conclude with a chronological table that lists for each year the emperors, consuls, and ecclesiastical affairs. In this practice Cave is once again following the precedent set in the early church by the Eusebius–Jerome *Chronicon*, a chronological table which includes political events alongside lives of famous people—especially authors.

Later works—and crowning achievement Cave's interest in pagan as well as Christian writers is evident throughout his works. In 1685 Cave published an expanded version of his earlier *Tabulae ecclesiasticae*, this time calling it *Chartophylax ecclesiasticus* (a 'written vanguard' which identifies writers as pagan, Christian, or heretical). This work was clearly a preparation for Cave's crowning achievement: the *Scriptorum ecclesiasticorum historia literaria* (a literary history of the writers of the church; 1688, rev. 1698). Written in Latin for a wider European audience, this work carefully catalogues the writers of the church from the birth of Christ to the rise of Luther in 1517. This type of Christian bio-bibliography closely imitates the work of Jerome's *De viris illustribus*. Now Cave gives names to each of the *saecula* (*apostolicum, gnosticum, arianum,* and so on), and organizes his literary history accordingly (in this, Cave was probably following the work of his countryman John Bale, whose *Catalogus*—also clearly inspired by Jerome's work—provided a literary history organized according to *saecula*). At the end of the *Historia literaria* Cave includes a defence of Eusebius against the charge of Arianism—a defence which elicited a controversy with Jean le Clerc. For this mammoth work of scholarship, Cave was assisted for several months in 1686 by the young cleric Henry Wharton, who worked on the project in exchange for a salary and access to Cave's impressive library. Cave was ill during this time, and when he set Wharton to work on the final two *saecula*, Wharton believed that he should have received authorial credit, which perpetuated a long-term argument. The final three *saecula* (1300–1517) were, in fact, published in Wharton's name as the appendix to the *Historia literaria*.

Of Cave's six other works, three are sermons (two preached before the king, and one before the lord mayor); one is a historical work, *A dissertation concerning the government of the ancient church, by bishops, metropolitans, and patriarchs* (1683); and two relate to the controversies of his own day, *A serious exhortation, with some important advices, relating to the late cases about conformity, recommended to the present dissenters from the Church of England* (1683) and *A Discourse Concerning the Unity of the Catholick Church* (1684). These works also argue for the validity of the current church because of a precedent set by the early church—a form of argumentation made popular by the reformers in the sixteenth century, and which Cave was anxious to continue.

On 19 November 1690 Cave took up his final post as vicar at Isleworth; he remained there until his death at Windsor on 4 August 1713. He was buried at St Mary's Church in Islington, where a monument erected in his memory recorded the only information that is known about his family: on 11 September 1660 he married in London Anna (1637–1691), daughter of the Revd Walter Stonehouse; she died on 10 January 1691, and was buried at Islington

church, as were four of their sons and two of their daughters.

Assessment The influence of Cave upon subsequent writers and thinkers is difficult to trace. He was clearly well known and respected for a century or more after his death; his works (especially *Antiquitates apostolicae* and *Primitive Christianity*) were republished frequently, including several times on the continent during his lifetime without his knowledge. After the *Historia literaria* was republished in Geneva in 1705 without his permission Cave made alterations and additions to this work, and wrote a new prolegomenon, but it was not published in his lifetime (this celebrated version of the *Historia literaria* was sold by subscription from 1740 to 1743). *Apostolici* and *Ecclesiastici* were edited and published as a three-volume set by Henry Cary in 1840 (who also edited *Primitive Christianity* together with *A Dissertation*). In 1846 John Fleetwood published a work that included three parts: his own life of Christ and lives of the apostles and evangelists, Cave's *Lives of the most Eminent Fathers and Martyrs, and the History of Primitive Christianity*, and then *A Concise History of the Christian Church* by Thomas Sims. However, since the mid-nineteenth century there has been little interest in Cave, and no other published edition of his works.

In his preface of 1840 to Cave's works Cary writes that 'The writings of Cave, especially his *Lives of the Fathers*, are so well known and appreciated, that the Editor is persuaded a lengthened preface of his own would not add at all to their value.' Interestingly Cave has always been known by his works, and thus comparatively few details are known about his life. What is significant about Cave's writings is that they follow the tradition of Christian bio-bibliography that in late antiquity and into the medieval period had such a long and rich history, and which was revived in the Reformation. Cave's works provide valuable evidence for the interest in patristic scholarship at the end of the seventeenth century, and for an interest in literary history that continues today.

GRETCHEN E. MINTON

Sources A. Kippis and others, eds., *Biographia Britannica, or, The lives of the most eminent persons who have flourished in Great Britain and Ireland*, 2nd edn, 5 vols. (1778–93), vol. 3 · H. J. Rose, *A new general biographical dictionary*, ed. H. J. Rose and T. Wright, 12 vols. (1848), vol. 6 · J. McClintock and J. Strong, eds., *Cyclopaedia of biblical, theological, and ecclesiastical literature* (1968) · Wing, *STC* · *DNB* · Allibone, *Dict.* · S. M. Jackson and L. A. Loetscher, eds., *The new Schaff-Herzog encyclopedia of religious knowledge*, 15 vols. (1952–7) · P. Schaff and S. M. Jackson, eds., *A religious encyclopedia, or, Dictionary of biblical, historical, doctrinal, and practical theology* (1894) · G. D'Oyly, *The life of William Sancroft, archbishop of Canterbury* (1821) · J. Walker, *An attempt towards recovering an account of the numbers and sufferings of the clergy of the Church of England*, 2 pts in 1 (1714)
Archives St George's Chapel, Windsor, literary MSS and annotated books

Cavell, Edith Louisa (1865–1915), nurse and war heroine, was born on 4 December 1865, the first child of the Revd Frederick Cavell (1825–1910), Church of England clergyman, and his wife, Louisa Sophia (1835–1918), *née* Warming, in Swardeston vicarage, Norfolk. Her father, a graduate of King's College, London, met his future wife in the

Edith Louisa Cavell (1865–1915), by unknown photographer, 1915

Islington parish of St Mary, where he was curate. The Cavells had three other children, Florence, Louisa, and Jack. Life at Swardeston was dominated by the family's strict evangelical beliefs. The children were educated at home, taught mostly by their mother: Edith showed a talent for drawing, as is evident in a surviving sketchbook. In her early teens she was sent to boarding-school to prepare her for earning a living. She attended Belgrave House School, Clevedon, Somerset (1883–4), and then schools in the Kensington area of London (1884) and in Peterborough (1884–5). The latter school, Laurel Court, had a good reputation for finding suitable employment for its pupils, and she became governess to the family of the vicar of Steeple Bumpstead, Essex. After a short time money from a legacy offered her the opportunity to travel on the continent. In 1889 Miss Gibson, the headmistress of Laurel Court, provided her with an introduction for the post of governess to the children of the François family in Brussels, with whom she remained for six years. She was liked and appreciated by the family, but religious and cultural differences, and her reserved nature, were always in evidence.

Cavell returned to England in 1895 to help nurse her father, who was seriously ill, and then decided to train as a nurse. After gaining experience at Fountains Fever Hospital, Tooting, she registered at the London Hospital

school of nursing on 3 September 1896. The London Hospital was a leading voluntary hospital, situated in the East End, whose matron, Eva Luckes, was later opposed to state registration for nurses, preferring to keep control of training and accreditation in the hands of the matron and governors. After an initial period at the recently opened preliminary training school in Bow, Cavell moved to the hospital in Whitechapel. Reports indicate that, though she had a competent and intelligent approach to her work, she did not adapt easily to the hospital community. She seems to have been most successful when working outside the hospital, caring for wealthy private patients in their homes (the London Hospital had a private nursing staff), or for victims of a typhoid epidemic in Maidstone.

Cavell spent only a brief time as a staff nurse at the London Hospital before moving, in 1901, to be night superintendent at the St Pancras Infirmary, a poor-law hospital. She then moved, in 1903, to be assistant matron of Shoreditch Infirmary, where she took on both training and managerial responsibilities. When she left Shoreditch in 1906 she had a reputation as someone with a great sense of duty, a kind but very reserved person. She left to join her friend, and former Londoner, Eveline Dickinson, on a trip to continental Europe. Not long after their return, Dickinson married and went to live in Ireland, leaving Cavell without a close friend or a job. She took a temporary position as head of the Queen's Nursing Institute (district nurses) in Manchester, but left this after a short time to take up a post, in 1907, as director of a nurses' training school in Brussels.

The school, the first of its kind in Belgium, and one of the first in Europe, was being set up by Dr Antoine De Page, an acquaintance of the François family, one of the leaders of a movement for change among the medical profession in Belgium. De Page and his associates wanted to diminish the influence of the religious orders on the care of the sick. He saw that they had a role to play, but believed that they were too powerful: they distrusted modern medicine, and this was preventing the introduction of new techniques. The institution that Cavell took on was not only a training school, but also a clinic. It was financed by funds raised by De Page and his associates, and was governed by them and a group of their wives. Although Cavell was the director, she was answerable to committees and above all to De Page who, though professionally effective, was arrogant and quick-tempered. She remained in constant contact with Eva Luckes, depending on her for professional advice and personal support, and recruited former Londoners to help her. (Her only constant companion was her dog, Jack, a Jack Russell terrier, later to become an exhibit at the Imperial War Museum.) Her main obstacle was to recruit the right sort of trainee. She required educated middle-class laywomen, in a country where nursing was carried out by members of religious orders, assisted by members of the working class. She had to convince her potential recruits, and members of her committee, that nursing was a respectable profession that required professional training. She showed skill and tact in doing this and in working with the committees. In 1910 the first certificates of competence were awarded; at the same time a new hospital opened in the St Gilles district of Brussels and state registration of nurses was introduced.

Cavell's reputation, and that of the school, spread, and the number of recruits, from Germany as well as France and Belgium, began to grow. In 1912 plans were drawn up for a new building, and a site was found close to the new hospital at St Gilles. The building programme and the expansion of the training programme were, however, halted in late 1914 by the German occupation of Belgium. The work of the clinic continued but Cavell was frustrated in her plans for the school. Her energies, however, were soon redirected towards assisting in the escape of allied soldiers. A network of opposition to the German occupation, and of assistance to prisoners of war, centred on the aristocratic De Croy family. Members of the Brussels bourgeoisie were involved, and through Cavell's contact with them the training school and the clinic came to be part of the network. The organization provided soldiers with hiding places and with false papers, and facilitated their escape into allied territory. Use was made of the clinic, with soldiers often disguised as patients. During this period Edith Cavell was correspondent of the *Nursing Mirror* and had accounts published of the impact of the war on Belgium.

In a short space of time the work with the escape organization took over Cavell's life. Many of those working for her were uneasy, and aware that they were at risk; the Germans became suspicious and began to pay frequent visits to the clinic. Her arrest on 5 August 1915, together with that of one of her assistants, was not unexpected, coming shortly after that of Philippe Baucq, one of the leaders of the organization. Cavell was detained and on 7 August put in solitary confinement in the prison at St Gilles. Others involved in the escape organization were also arrested and imprisoned, but the Germans were careful to keep them too in solitary confinement while evidence was assembled for their trial. Each prisoner made a statement: Edith Cavell's amounted to a confession, and it named several of her accomplices. It is not known why she agreed to sign this statement; nor is it evident that she was aware of its likely consequences. It was clear from her past, and from her very strong religious belief, that she was unwilling to lie, and it may be that she underestimated the Germans' intentions.

Nine people were court-martialled on 7 October 1915, and the following day five were sentenced to death, the remaining four to periods of hard labour. All were accused of assisting the enemy and of trying to damage the German war effort. Three of those condemned to death had their executions adjourned while pleas of clemency were heard, but Cavell and Baucq were ordered to be executed immediately. Cavell remained outwardly calm, and prepared for her death by praying and reading, and by writing to her family and nurses. In spite of intense diplomatic activity across Europe, particularly on the part of the Americans through the tireless efforts of the US minister in Brussels, Brand Whitlock, and an international outcry against the Germans, she was shot at dawn on 12 October 1915.

Initial shock at Cavell's death was quickly succeeded by international protest, and to many she became, overnight, a heroine and martyr. For the Germans her death provided an opportunity to show how tough they were prepared to be with those judged to be traitors and spies. The fact that Cavell confessed and was not willing to defend herself seemed to justify their actions. A propaganda war followed, leading to increased recruitment for the allies. The Kaiser later ordered no more women to be shot without his permission.

Edith Cavell's memory was immortalized in statues: the most famous, by Sir George Frampton, situated in London at the junction between Charing Cross and Trafalgar Square, in St Martin's Place, was erected in the early 1920s. It was inscribed with the words 'Patriotism is not enough', part of her final message from prison. Roads, bridges, streets, and institutions in Belgium and throughout the British empire were also named after her. Her death was the subject of a famous painting by the American war artist George Wesley Bellows whose *Murder of Edith Cavell* was the most famous in his War Series of 1918. She clearly showed personal courage and humanity in her willingness to help wounded soldiers in enemy territory. She also undertook pioneering work in establishing the clinic and training school, and in shaping the profession of nursing in Belgium and neighbouring countries. But it was the timing of her death, the manner of it, the reaction to it, and the fact that she was a woman and a nurse that secured her lasting reputation as a heroine. After the war there was a funeral service at Westminster Abbey, and on 15 May 1919 her body was buried in Norwich Cathedral.

CLAIRE DAUNTON

Sources A. E. C. Kennedy, *Edith Cavell: pioneer and patriot* (1965) · R. V. Ryder, *Edith Cavell* (1975) · M. M. Bihet, *Histoire de nursing* (1947) · A. A. Hoehling, *Edith Cavell* (1958) · London Hospital, *Edith Cavell: her life and her art* (1991) · N. Boston, *The dutiful Edith Cavell* (1962) · S. T. Felstead, *Edith Cavell: the crime that shook the world* (1940) · C. Sarolea, *The murder of Nurse Cavell* (1915) · E. Protheroe, *A noble woman: the life story of Edith Cavell* (1916) · parish register (birth), Swardeston, Norfolk, 4 Dec 1865 · parish register (burial), Swardeston, Norfolk, 10 June 1910 and 17 June 1918 · London Hospital Archives · *The Times* · K. Adie, 'Nurse heroes of the century', *Nursing Times* (17 Nov 1999) · 'Correspondence with the United States ambassador respecting the execution of Miss Cavell at Brussels', *Parl. papers* (1915), 84.703, Cd 8013

Archives IWM, copies of corresp., diary, and papers relating to her work, arrest, trial, and execution · Royal London Hospital, Whitechapel, London, manuscripts

Likenesses photograph, 1915, NPG [*see illus.*] · G. W. Bellows, lithograph, 1918 (*Murder of Edith Cavell*), National Gallery of Art, Washington, DC · G. Frampton, marble statue, 1920, St Martin's Place, London · G. Frampton, bust, IWM · photographs, IWM · photogravure photograph, postcard, NPG · statue, outside Norwich Cathedral

Cavendish [*married name* Marshall], **Ada** (1839?–1895), actress, born by some accounts in 1839, by others in 1847, was a pupil of Walter Lacy, and made her first appearance in London at the New Royalty Theatre on 31 August 1863, as Selina Squeers in a burletta called *The Pirates of Putney*.

Ada Cavendish (1839?–1895), by unknown photographer

the Broadway, again as Mercy Merrick. She toured as Rosalind, Juliet, and Lady Teazle to San Francisco, Chicago, and St Louis. After returning to England in 1881 she was seen in *Lady Clare* on 24 April 1883 by W. E. Gladstone, who had been invited by the author, R. W. Buchanan, and who commented in his diary on the 'excellent female acting'. On 2 May 1885 she married the playwright Francis Albert *Marshall (1840–1889) and virtually retired from the stage, though she appeared in William Creswell's farewell benefit on 29 October 1885 at Drury Lane. She had become a Roman Catholic in this year. After her husband's death on 28 December 1889 she acted occasionally in the provinces. Latterly she was a drama teacher. During her stage career Ada Cavendish was variously described as a sprightly, fair-haired burlesque actress with good gifts in comedy and serious drama, especially Shakespeare; dignified and refined, she earned many laudatory notices. She returned to the protestant church in 1895, a week before her death, from cirrhosis of the liver, on 5 October, at her home, 34 Thurloe Square, London. She was buried at Kensal Green cemetery. JOSEPH KNIGHT, *rev.* J. GILLILAND

Sources Adams, *Drama* · H. B. Baker, *The London stage: its history and traditions from 1576 to 1888*, 2 vols. (1889) · *The life and reminiscences of E. L. Blanchard, with notes from the diary of Wm. Blanchard*, ed. C. W. Scott and C. Howard, 2 vols. (1891) · J. Hollingshead, *Gaiety chronicles* (1898) · C. E. Pascoe, ed., *The dramatic list* (1879) · D. Cook, *Nights at the play* (1883) · C. Scott, *The drama of yesterday and today*, 2 vols. (1899) · S. D'Amico, ed., *Enciclopedia dello spettacolo*, 11 vols. (Rome, 1954–68) · A. Davies and E. Kilmurray, *Dictionary of British portraiture*, 4 vols. (1979–81) · Hall, *Dramatic ports.* · *The Athenaeum* (12 Oct 1895) · Boase, *Mod. Eng. biog.* · m. cert. · d. cert. · Gladstone, *Diaries*

Likenesses photograph, 1878, repro. in *Enciclopedia dello spettacolo* · Barraud, Elliott & Fry, and Southwell Bros., photographs, NPG · A. Bean, photograph, repro. in Scott, *Drama of yesterday and today* · photograph, NPG [*see illus.*] · photographs, Harvard TC · prints, Harvard TC · two prints, NPG

Wealth at death £1603 13s. 10d.: probate, 29 Nov 1895, *CGPLA Eng. & Wales*

Next, as a pupil of Mrs Charles Selby, she played Venus in F. C. Burnand's *Ixion*. On 15 February 1866, at the Haymarket, she essayed comedy for the first time in *A Romantic Attachment*. She distinguished herself as the original Mrs Pinchbeck in T. W. Robertson's adaptation *Home* at the same theatre on 8 January 1869. She then played at the opening of the Vaudeville (as the original Mrs Darlington in Halliday's *For Love or Money*), at the Globe, the Royalty, the Gaiety, and the Court. She managed the Olympic in 1872, having renovated and redecorated the theatre to make it one of the most elegant houses of the period, and there she gained the approval of large audiences. Her greatest success was here, as Mercy Merrick in Wilkie Collins's *New Magdalen* (19 May 1873), which she also produced. Her acting in this melodrama of a fallen woman made the subject matter palatable to Victorian audiences. She also played several original parts, and was seen as Juliet at her benefit in September 1873. Lady Clancarty, an original role in Tom Taylor's piece about Mary, queen of Scots, was given on 9 March 1874, when her acting was considered to be forced, but powerful and intelligent. At the Globe on 15 April 1876 she was the heroine of Wilkie Collins's *Miss Gwilt*. She opened the St James's as Lady Teazle in 1877.

In 1878 Ada Cavendish went to America, and opened at

Cavendish, Sir Charles (1595?–1654), mathematician, was the youngest son of Sir Charles Cavendish (1553–1617), of Welbeck Abbey, Nottinghamshire, and his second wife, Catherine Ogle, Baroness Ogle (d. 1629). Sir William *Cavendish (1508–1557) was his grandfather, and William *Cavendish, first duke of Newcastle upon Tyne (d. 1676), was his brother. From his youth he inclined to learning. According to John Aubrey 'he was a little weake crooked man, and nature having not adapted him for the court nor campe, he betooke himselfe to the study of the mathematiques, wherein he became a great master' (*Brief Lives*, 1.153). In March 1612 he may have joined his brother in accompanying Sir Henry Wotton to France.

Cavendish inherited a good estate from his father, and devoted himself to the collection of mathematical works and the patronage of mathematicians. He was knighted at Welbeck on 10 August 1619 during a visit of the king to his brother. On 23 January 1624 he was returned to parliament for the borough of Nottingham. He was also returned for the same place to the third parliament of

Charles I on 18 February 1628, and to the Short Parliament on 30 March 1640. His surviving manuscript collections reflect the range of his interests: they include copies of mathematical works by Thomas Harriot, translations of works of Galilean mechanics, and extensive notes on his reading in psychology, physiology, optics, ethics, and poetics. Cavendish was not an original thinker; his importance lay in his sponsorship of research and his promotion of communication between English and European intellectuals. During the 1630s he and his brother William, along with their chaplain, Robert Payne, conducted experiments and held correspondence about mathematics, optics, and mechanics with Thomas Hobbes, Walter Warner, William Oughtred, and the French scholars François Derand, Claude Mydorge, and Marin Mersenne. Prompted by the optical researches of René Descartes, in the summer of 1641 Cavendish and John Pell set the London craftsman Richard Reeve, already an experienced lens grinder, about the difficult and expensive task of grinding hyperbolic lenses for telescopes. Reeve's efforts yielded much broken glass, but no lenses. These endeavours to match technology to optical theory were cut short by the deterioration of the political situation in England, but following flight to the continent, Cavendish continued in his quest for adequate lenses, re-establishing links with Pell, then in the Low Countries, and pursuing information about the telescopes of Johann Wiesel of Augsburg, one of whose instruments Cavendish might have purchased. During his exile he was also in contact with Joachim Jungius of Hamburg, and with Hobbes and Mersenne in Paris. The works dedicated to him attest to the affection and esteem in which he was held: these included Mydorge's *Prodromi catoptricorum* (1631), Mersenne's *Harmonicorum libri* (1636), and Margaret Cavendish's *Poems and Fancies* (1653).

On the outbreak of the civil war Cavendish, with his brother Newcastle, entered the king's service, serving under his brother as lieutenant-general of the horse. He behaved with great gallantry in several actions, particularly distinguishing himself at Marston Moor. After that battle, despairing of the royal cause, he repaired to Scarborough and embarked with his brother for Hamburg, where he arrived on 8 July 1644. He accompanied his brother to Paris in 1645 and then, in the summer of 1648, to the Spanish Netherlands, settling in Antwerp.

Cavendish was noted for his mathematical knowledge as well as for his love of mathematicians. Aubrey relates that:

> he had collected in Italie, France, &c., with no small chardge, as many manuscript mathematicall bookes as filled a hoggeshead, which he intended to have printed; which if he had lived to have donne, the growth of mathematicall learning had been thirty yeares or more forwarder than 'tis. (1.153)

On 4 May 1649 Cavendish petitioned the committee for compounding, to be permitted to compound his delinquency in the first war, and on 27 August, his fine having been paid, an order was made for discharging his estate.

On 4 January 1651, however, the committee for Staffordshire informed the committee for compounding that Sir Charles had been beyond seas at the time of his composition, and that he was a very dangerous person. On 27 and 28 March the sequestration of his estates was ordered on account of his adherence to Charles Stuart and of his being abroad without leave. Cavendish was disinclined to make any concession by returning to England, but as the revenue from his estates was serviceable to his family, his brother Newcastle induced Clarendon to persuade him to make his submission. He accordingly repaired to England in the beginning of November with Lady Newcastle. They stayed in Southwark and afterwards in lodgings at Covent Garden, in great poverty. He was finally admitted to compound, and succeeded in purchasing Welbeck and Bolsover, which had been confiscated from his brother. The proceedings in regard to his estates were not completed at the time of his death. He died, unmarried, on 4 February 1654 and was buried at Bolsover in the family vault on 25 February. Aubrey claims that his executor, an attorney of Clifford's Inn, died, leaving Cavendish's manuscripts in the custody of his wife, who sold them as waste paper; some of his notes and correspondence survive, however, in the British Library.

E. I. CARLYLE, *rev.* TIMOTHY RAYLOR

Sources J. Jacquot, 'Sir Charles Cavendish and his learned friends', *Annals of Science*, 8 (1952), 13–27, 175–91 · G. Trease, *Portrait of a cavalier: William Cavendish, first duke of Newcastle* (1979) · *The correspondence of Thomas Hobbes*, ed. N. Malcolm, 2 vols. (1994) · H. Hervey, 'Hobbes and Descartes in the light of some unpublished letters of the correspondence between Sir Charles Cavendish and Dr. John Pell', *Osiris*, 10 (1952), 67–90 · C. von Brockdorff, 'Des Sir Charles Cavendish Bericht für Joachim Jungius über die Grundzüge der Hobbes'schen Naturphilosophie', *Veröffentlichungen der Hobbes-Gesellschaft*, 6 (1937), 7–23 · R. H. Kargon, *Atomism in England from Hariot to Newton* (1966) · Margaret, duchess of Newcastle [M. Cavendish], *The life of William Cavendish, duke of Newcastle*, ed. C. H. Firth, 2nd rev. edn (1906) · C. Cavendish, notes and memoranda, BL, Harley MS 6083 · J. Pell, correspondence, BL, Add. MSS 4278–4280 · *Brief lives, chiefly of contemporaries, set down by John Aubrey, between the years 1669 and 1696*, ed. A. Clark, 2 vols. (1898) · Clarendon, *Hist. rebellion* · M. A. E. Green, ed., *Calendar of the proceedings of the committee for compounding … 1643–1660*, 5 vols., PRO (1889–92)

Archives BL, Harley MSS 6001–6002, 6083, 6796 · BL, corresp. with J. Pell, Add. MSS 4278, 4280, 4422

Likenesses G. P. Harding, drawing, AM Oxf. · school of Van Dyck, oils, Welbeck Abbey, Nottinghamshire; repro. in A. S. Turberville, *A history of Welbeck Abbey and its owners*, 1 (1938)

Wealth at death £2000 p.a. (est.); composition fees est. at £5000: Margaret, duchess of Newcastle, *Life of William Cavendish*; Green, ed., *Calendar of the proceedings of the committee for compounding*

Cavendish, Charles (1620–1643), royalist army officer, was born at Chatsworth House, Derbyshire, on 20 May 1620, the second son of William *Cavendish, second earl of Devonshire (1590–1628), and his wife, Christian [*see* Cavendish, Christian (1595–1675)], daughter of Edward Bruce, first Lord Kinloss. He was named after his godfather Prince Charles, the future Charles I. In 1638 he was sent on the grand tour and travelled into France and Italy; he then went further afield, reaching Cairo and seeing a large part of Turkey. According to John Aubrey the tour was ended only by his governor's protests and by practical difficulties. Cavendish

> was so extremely delighted in travelling, that he went into Greece, all over; and that would not serve his turne but he would goe to Babylon, and then his governour would not adventure to goe any further with him; but to see Babylon he was to march in the Turks' armie. (Brief Lives, 1.154)

Having returned to England in May 1641 Cavendish then served in Europe under the prince of Orange. On the outbreak of civil war he joined the king's troop of guards as a volunteer under Lord Bernard Stuart, in contrast with his elder brother William *Cavendish, third earl of Devonshire, who spent the war on the continent. After the battle of Edgehill, Cavendish was given command of the duke of York's troop, left vacant by the death of Lord Aubigny. He expanded the troop to a regiment, recruiting largely in the West Riding of Yorkshire and in Lincolnshire, and was commissioned colonel in December 1642. He also took up duties on the commission of array for Lincolnshire, where his seat at Wellingore lay. At Newark he took command of the royalist forces in Lincolnshire, under the earl of Newcastle, with the rank of colonel-general. On 23 March 1643 he captured Grantham and on 11 April defeated Yorkshire parliamentarians under Captain John Hotham at Ancaster. Queen Henrietta Maria having moved south with an ammunition train, Cavendish and Henry Hastings joined forces with her at Newark; the combined force stormed Burton upon Trent on 2 July. On 20 July a parliamentarian force under Lord Willoughby of Parham captured Gainsborough, an important river-crossing on the Trent. Cavendish immediately laid siege to the town. A relieving force under Oliver Cromwell and Sir John Meldrum clashed with Cavendish's cavalry a mile out of the town on 28 July. Three of the royalist regiments were scattered but Cavendish's own regiment in reserve stood firm until Cromwell's troopers broke it and forced Cavendish and his men down the hill into a marsh. He was struck from his horse with a bad headwound. Thereafter accounts of his death diverge. The royalist newsletter *Mercurius Aulicus* claimed that he was then shot 'with a brace of bullets' (*Brief Lives*, 1.155); Cromwell's official report states that his captain-lieutenant, James Berry, stabbed Cavendish in the side, and that the royalist commander died of the wound two hours later. According to William Naylour, chaplain to Cavendish's mother, his death was the consequence both of his own courage—'he knew not how to flie away—he knew not how to ask quarter'—and the treachery of his enemies: 'the rebels surround him, and take him prisoner; and after he was so, a base raskall comes behind him, and runs him through' (*Brief Lives*, 1.156).

Cavendish, who died unmarried, was initially buried at Newark, but thirty-two years later, on 18 February 1675, he was reburied, in All Saints', Derby, beside his mother. Edmund Waller composed his epitaph.

MARTYN BENNETT

Sources E. Waller, *Poems on several occasions*, 10th edn (1722), 153 • *Brief lives, chiefly of contemporaries, set down by John Aubrey, between the years 1669 and 1696*, ed. A. Clark, 1 (1898), 154–7 • P. R. Newman, *Royalist officers in England and Wales, 1642–1660: a biographical dictionary* (1981) • D. Lloyd, *Memoires of the lives … of those … personages that suffered … for the protestant religion* (1668) • *The writings and speeches of Oliver Cromwell*, ed. W. C. Abbott and C. D. Crane, 1 (1937), 240–42 • GEC, *Peerage* • W. Kennet, *Memoirs of the family of Cavendish* (1708) • J. Rushworth, *Historical collections*, new edn, 5 (1721), 274 • P. R. Newman, *The old service: royalist regimental colonels and the civil war, 1642–1646* (1993)
Archives Northants. RO, Finch Hatton 133
Likenesses attrib. A. Hannerman, oils, Hardwick Hall, Derbyshire

Cavendish [née Bruce], Christian [Christiana], countess of Devonshire (1595–1675), royalist noblewoman, was born on 25 December 1595, the daughter of Edward *Bruce, first Lord Bruce of Kinloss (1548/9–1611), master of the rolls, and his wife, Magdalen Clerk, daughter of Alexander Clerk of Balbirnie, Fife. Her birth on Christmas day inspired her name, and as Lord Bruce's only daughter she was destined for a superior match. Her marriage portion, £10,000—part of which was contributed by James VI and I—made her an attractive prospective daughter-in-law for William *Cavendish, first earl of Devonshire (1551–1626). Cavendish's son and heir, William *Cavendish (1590–1628), was persuaded reluctantly to marry the twelve-year-old girl on 10 April 1608. He promptly departed on an extensive tour of Europe, accompanied by his tutor, Thomas Hobbes. Despite the ill-omened beginning of the marriage (William preferred an older bride), Christian was devoted to him and together they had four children: William *Cavendish (1617–1684), Charles *Cavendish (1620–1643), Henry, and Anne. In 1626 William became second earl of Devonshire, but he died on 20 June 1628, ostensibly of over-indulgence, and was succeeded by the eleven-year-old William as third earl.

Her husband's death catapulted Lady Devonshire into a very different kind of life, as *de facto* head of her family. She took great care with her sons' education, keeping Hobbes as their tutor, and sending them on long European tours. More important for the family, however, was her stewardship of the Cavendish estates. The second earl died deeply indebted and Christian spent years fighting some thirty lawsuits filed by disgruntled creditors. She allegedly won all of them, provoking a wry comment from Charles I: 'Madam, you have all my judges at your disposal, as what courts would not be influenced by such commanding charms to do justice?' (Pomfret, 27–8). She personally lobbied members of parliament and won the passage of an estate bill allowing her to sell land and pay down her husband's debts. Her determination to protect her sons' interests was fierce. In 1637 she earned the enmity of Dorothy Percy, countess of Leicester, because of her hard dealing in a projected match between her eldest son and Leicester's daughter. She was 'full of sivilitie, craft, and coldnes' (*De L'Isle and Dudley MSS*, 6.101).

A firm royalist during the civil wars, Lady Devonshire lost her younger son, Charles, killed in a Lincolnshire skirmish in 1643. About 1647 she moved to Ampthill, Bedfordshire, where she lived for three years with her brother, Thomas Bruce, first earl of Elgin. Her nephew Robert *Bruce (later first earl of Ailesbury) was an active plotter and drew her into the world of royalist conspiracy. Her

Christian Cavendish, countess of Devonshire (1595–1675), by Sir Anthony Van Dyck, c.1632

home at Roehampton, Surrey, which she bought about 1650, became a centre of surreptitious activity on behalf of the exiled Charles II. She sent the king money, and narrowly avoided arrest by means of a well-placed bribe in the late 1650s.

The Cavendish family fortunes revived following the Restoration and Lady Devonshire presided over an elaborate establishment at Roehampton, welcoming wits, authors, and politicians to her home. John Evelyn was a particular favourite of hers, Edmund Waller dedicated his *Epistles* to her, and John Donne wrote in her praise. The Italian visitor Lorenzo Magalotti described her in 1667 as living 'in a magnificent house in the style of something more than a great princess' (*Lorenzo Magalotti*, 117). She died in Southampton Buildings, Middlesex, aged seventy-nine on 16 January 1675 and was buried in All Saints' Church, Derby:

> … a lady above the common strain,
> In whom all vertues did United Reign.
> (*An Elegy on the … Countesse of Devonshire*)

VICTOR STATER

Sources T. Pomfret, *Life of the right honourable and religious Lady Christian late countess-dowager of Devonshire* (1685) • GEC, *Peerage* • *Report on the manuscripts of Lord De L'Isle and Dudley*, 6, HMC, 77

(1966) • *Lorenzo Magalotti at the court of Charles II: his Relazione d'Inghilterra of 1668*, ed. and trans. W. E. K. Middleton (1980) • *An elegy on the truly honorable and most virtuous, charitable, and pious lady countesse of Devonshire* (1675) • F. Bickley, *The Cavendish family* (1914) • *The manuscripts of the duke of Somerset, the marquis of Ailesbury, and the Rev. Sir T. H. G. Puleston, bart.*, HMC, 43 (1898)

Archives Chatsworth House, Derbyshire, papers | BL, corresp. with Robert Rich and Francis Rich • U. Nott., letters to earl of Newcastle

Likenesses attrib. P. Somer, oils, 1619, North Carolina Museum of Art, Raleigh • A. Van Dyck, oils, c.1632, Columbus Museum of Art, Ohio [see illus.] • attrib. G. Houthorst, group portrait, oils (with her children), Chatsworth, Derbyshire • funeral monument, All Saints' Church, Derby

Cavendish [*née* Hervey; *other married name* Foster], **Elizabeth Christiana**, duchess of Devonshire (1757–1824), society hostess and patron of the arts, was the middle daughter of Frederick Augustus *Hervey, fourth earl of Bristol (1730–1803), and his wife, Elizabeth Davers (1730–1800), and was known for most her life as Lady Elizabeth Foster, Bess to her friends. She was born in November 1757 at Horrenger, Suffolk, and baptized there on 13 May 1758. She was initially educated at home, but spent her formative years in semi-poverty abroad and in Ireland, where her father was the bishop of Derry. A brief, unhappy marriage in 1776 to the Revd Dr John Thomas Foster (*d.* 1796) produced two boys, Frederick (*b.* 1777) and Augustus (*b.* 1780). She later said that she had been forced to marry Foster, a respectable Irish MP, but there is no evidence to support this. The reasons for their separation in 1780 have never been clear, and each party blamed the other. Many years later Elizabeth Foster justified her subsequent actions by her youth and poverty:

> I was without a guide; a wife and no husband, a mother and no children … by myself alone to steer through every peril that surrounds a young woman so situated; books, the arts, and a wish to be loved and approved. (Foster, 199–200)

During the summer of 1782, while lodging with her aunt in Bath, she met William Cavendish, fifth duke of Devonshire, and his wife, Georgiana. After only a few weeks of acquaintance she moved in with them.

Foster's relationship with the duke and duchess mystified society. There were many who assumed that she was at one time the lover of both, and there is circumstantial evidence to support this (Foster to Georgiana, duchess of Devonshire, 17 Jan 1784 and February 1785, Chatsworth MSS, n.584 and 667.1). Others, including Fanny Burney, believed that Foster was primarily the duke's mistress, and was using the duchess's vast debts to blackmail her into agreeing that she live with them as a permanent house guest. In December 1784 she became pregnant with the duke of Devonshire's child. Using her health as a pretext for leaving the Devonshires, she went to Naples and gave birth in secret to Caroline Rosalie on 16 August 1785. Her unhappiness was tempered by a brief affair with John Sackville, third duke of Dorset. 'Misfortune', she confessed in her diary, 'cannot cure me of my vanity' (Stuart, 35). Leaving the child with foster parents, Foster travelled to Provence in France, where, for reasons which remain obscure, she persuaded the elderly Comte St Jules to accept paternity of Caroline. She then returned to Britain

Elizabeth Christiana Cavendish, duchess of Devonshire (1757–1824), by Sir Joshua Reynolds, 1787

in July 1786. Over the next two years Foster encouraged the duke to separate from the duchess, while remaining the latter's closest confidante. As a consequence, she was disliked and mistrusted by the duchess's family and friends. She again became pregnant and gave birth in France to Augustus *Clifford on 26 May 1788. There was some doubt as to Augustus's true paternity. At the time of conception Foster was also having an affair with Charles Lennox, eighth duke of Richmond. In 1790 Foster succeeded in having her children brought from France to live in the nursery with the three legitimate Cavendish children.

In the following year Foster's loyalty to Georgiana, duchess of Devonshire, was put to the test after the duke discovered that his wife was pregnant by Charles Grey. He ordered her to live abroad in exile, but gave Foster the opportunity to remain. She refused and travelled with the duchess until he relented in 1793. On her return the living arrangements continued but Foster resumed her affair with the duke of Richmond. The deaths of Mr Foster and the duchess of Richmond in 1796 led everyone, including Foster, to assume that she would become the next duchess. But violent objections from his family eventually made the duke cry off. The duchess of Devonshire died in 1806, making Foster her executrix and sole guardian of her papers. To the outrage of all, Foster married the duke of Devonshire on 19 October 1809. She was widowed a mere two years later and, after an embarrassing public row with the sixth duke over her late husband's will, lived by herself in Piccadilly Terrace, London. Styling herself Elizabeth, duchess of Devonshire, she entertained in a

regal manner and made several new friends, including Lord Byron. In 1816 she moved permanently to Rome and began a new career as a liberal patron of the arts, and of archaeologists in particular. Her final years were spent in the company of Cardinal Hercule Consalvi, secretary of state to the Vatican, who shared her passion for the arts. He advised Cavendish on her project to finance two new Italian translations of Horace and Virgil and in 1817 they helped to secure the return of the Stuart papers to Windsor. However, their real interest lay in Rome's archaeological antiquities: for eleven years Cavendish financed the excavation of the Forum, which led to the recovery of the Column of Phocas and the stones of the via Sacra. The city of Rome recognized her efforts with a medal struck in her honour. She died in Rome on 30 March 1824, and her body was interred in the Cavendish vault in Derby Cathedral.

Elizabeth Foster was a witness and participant in whig politics between 1784 and 1809 and, as Elizabeth Cavendish, an active patron of Rome's classical heritage between 1813 and 1824. Her diaries, although rewritten several times, provide valuable insight into the period. An acknowledged beauty, she was irresistible to a variety of men and women. She was frequently labelled artificial and duplicitous, but she retained the love and trust of Georgiana, duchess of Devonshire, for twenty-five years, and afterwards the unceasing companionship of Cardinal Consalvi. AMANDA FOREMAN

Sources A. Foreman, *Georgiana, duchess of Devonshire* (1998) · B. Fothergill, *The mitred earl* (1988), 84 · Lady E. Foster to Georgiana, duchess of Devonshire, 17/1/1784, Chatsworth House, Derbyshire, Chatsworth MSS, no. 584 · Lady E. Foster to Georgiana, duchess of Devonshire, 2/1785, Chatsworth House, Derbyshire, Chatsworth MSS, no. 667.1 · *The journals and letters of Fanny Burney (Madame D'Arblay)*, ed. J. Hemlow and others, 12 vols. (1972–84), vol. 1, p. 38 · V. Foster, *The two duchesses* (1974), 199–200 · D. M. Stuart, *Dearest Bess: the life and times of Lady Elizabeth Foster* (1955), 35 · A. Francis Steuart, *Diary of a lady-in-waiting* (1908), vol. 2, p. 18

Archives BL, journal, Add. MS 41579 · Chatsworth House, Derbyshire, corresp. · priv. coll., corresp. and papers | BL, letters to Lady Melbourne, Add. MSS 45548, 45911 · Castle Howard, Yorkshire, letters to Lady Carlisle · E. Sussex RO, letters to first earl of Sheffield · L. Cong., corresp. with Sir A. Foster · PRO NIre., corresp. with Foster family · RA, corresp. with T. Lawrence · Suffolk RO, Hervey MSS

Likenesses J. Downman, drawing, 1785 (with Georgiana), Ickworth House, Suffolk · A. Kauffmann, oils, 1786, Ickworth House, Suffolk · J. Reynolds, oils, 1787, Chatsworth House, Derbyshire [see illus.] · T. Lawrence, oils, 1803, NG Ire. · J. W. Chandler, oils, NPG · T. Lawrence, drawing, Royal Collection

Cavendish, Lord Frederick (1729–1803), army officer and politician, was born in August 1729, the third of the four sons of William Cavendish, third duke of Devonshire (1698–1755), and his wife, Catherine (d. 1777), the daughter of John Hoskins of Oxted, Surrey. Commissioned an ensign in the 1st foot guards on 29 April 1749, lieutenant and captain in the 2nd foot guards on 17 March 1752, and, after a secondment to the 29th foot as lieutenant-colonel in 1755, captain and lieutenant-colonel in the 1st foot guards on 1 June 1756, he accompanied William *Cavendish, marquess of Hartington, his elder brother and new lord lieutenant, to Ireland in 1755 and two years later served in Germany as aide-de-camp to the duke of Cumberland. On 7 May 1758 he was appointed a colonel—but only after threatening to resign his commission should the duke of Richmond and earl of Pembroke be promoted over his head. He then took part in the descents on Cherbourg and St Malo before being caught up in the disaster at St Cast on 11 September 1758. Already wounded, he failed in his attempt to escape by swimming out to the boats when his heavy boots filled with water. It is reputed that as a prisoner he at first refused to go on parole, arguing that, as a member of parliament, he would have to vote supplies for war against France, whereupon the duc d'Aiguillon dismissed his objections, stating, 'Let not that prevent you, for we should no more object to your voting in parliament than to your begetting children lest they should one day fight against France' (Rose, 6.144). Cavendish informed his brother, however, that his scruples stemmed from the attempt of the French to have him undertake a diplomatic mission, with his parole contingent on its success. This notwithstanding, he soon returned home, was exchanged, and, after promotion to major-general on 7 March 1761, sailed to Germany the following month. In June 1762 Prince Ferdinand of Brunswick placed Cavendish at the head of a multinational brigade of light troops or chasseurs, and his command almost immediately distinguished itself in the victory at Wilhelmsthal. Asked by his brother why Prince Ferdinand had given command of chasseurs to him, Cavendish replied: 'I can't tell, but he certainly knew I loved hunting, and he has given us many a good chase' (Devonshire MSS, 397.122). His campaign nevertheless ended on a disappointing note when, in October 1762, Prussian hussars under his command were surprised during operations to cover the siege of Kassel.

Cavendish had been a member of parliament since 1751, sitting first for Derbyshire and between 1754 and 1780 for Derby borough. When his brother, now the fourth duke of Devonshire, was dismissed from government in October 1762, Cavendish went into opposition, a stance maintained by his family after the duke's death. Although the remaining three Cavendish brothers always voted together in the Commons, Horace Walpole drew attention to Lord Frederick's disquiet at the warmth exhibited by his younger brother, Lord John *Cavendish, over the Regency Bill in 1765. Lord Frederick, according to Walpole, also wished to moderate the hostility of his brothers towards Lord Bute, as he believed this to be the desire of the duke of Cumberland, to whom Cavendish was a lord of the bedchamber.

Cavendish was appointed colonel of the 67th foot in 1759, and between 1760 and 1797 he held the colonelcy of the 34th foot. Promoted lieutenant-general on 30 April 1770, he did not serve during the American War of Independence, belonging as he did to that section of parliament which was sympathetic towards the American claims; however, when, in March 1780, Lord Shelburne, an old comrade from St Cast, fought his political duel with William Fullarton, Cavendish acted as his second. On 20 November 1782 Cavendish was promoted general and on 30 July 1796 he was appointed field marshal. He died, unmarried, on 21 October 1803 at his home, Twickenham Park, Isleworth, Middlesex, which he had inherited under the will of the countess of Mountrath and where he had lived since 1788; his remains were interred in the family vault at All Saints' Church, Derby. He left the bulk of his considerable property—of which the personal estate alone was worth over £115,000—to his favourite nephew, Lord George Cavendish, afterwards first earl of Burlington.   ALASTAIR W. MASSIE

Sources family correspondence, 1754–1800, Chatsworth House, Derbyshire, Devonshire MSS, 397.0–136 · letters to Countess Spencer, 1779–88, BL, Althorp MSS, F121.2 · *GM*, 1st ser., 73 (1803), 995 · *Army List* · H. Walpole, *Memoirs of the reign of King George the Third*, ed. G. F. R. Barker, 4 vols. (1894) · Walpole, *Corr.* · letters to the duke of Portland, 1765–81, U. Nott. L., Portland MSS, PwF 2580–2598 · H. J. Rose, *A new general biographical dictionary*, ed. H. J. Rose and T. Wright, 12 vols. (1848), vol. 6, p. 144 · death duty registers, 1803, PRO, IR 26/80 · will, PRO, PROB 11/1399 · correspondence with the duke of Newcastle, 1763–8, BL, Add. MSS 32949–33072 · R. Savory, *His Britannic majesty's army in Germany during the Seven Years' War* (1966) · Burke, *Peerage* (1939)

Archives Chatsworth House, Derbyshire, family corresp. | BL, letters to Countess Spencer · BL, corresp. with duke of Newcastle, Add. MSS 32949–33072 · U. Nott. L., letters to duke of Portland

Wealth at death over £115,000: PRO, death duty registers, IR 26/80

Cavendish, Lord Frederick Charles (1836–1882), chief secretary for Ireland, was the second son of William *Cavendish, seventh duke of Devonshire (1808–1891), landowner and industrialist, and his wife, Blanche Georgiana Howard, fourth daughter of George, sixth earl of Carlisle, who were married on 6 August 1829. Cavendish's brother was Lord Hartington, the Liberal politician [see Cavendish, Spencer Compton]. He was born at Compton Place, Eastbourne, on 30 November 1836, and, after being educated at home, matriculated in 1855 from Trinity College, Cambridge, where he graduated BA in 1858, and then served as a cornet in the Duke of Lancaster's Own yeomanry cavalry. From 1859 to 1864 he was private secretary to Lord Granville. He travelled in the United States in 1859–60, and in Spain in 1860. He entered parliament as a Liberal for the northern division of the West Riding of Yorkshire on 15 July 1865, and retained that seat until his death.

After serving as private secretary to Gladstone, his wife's uncle by marriage, from July 1872 to August 1873, Cavendish became a junior lord of the Treasury, and held office until the resignation of the ministry. He was financial secretary to the Treasury from April 1880 to May 1882, favouring, but not pressing effectively, a land-purchase plan for Ireland. When W. E. Forster resigned as Irish secretary, Gladstone offered the post to A. M. Porter and, on his declining it, to Cavendish. In company with Earl Spencer, lord lieutenant, he proceeded to Dublin, and took the oath as chief secretary at Dublin Castle on 6 May 1882; but on the afternoon of the same day, while walking in Phoenix Park in company with Thomas Henry Burke, the under-secretary, he was attacked from behind by several men wielding knives, who murdered Burke and himself. His body was brought to England and buried in Edensor

Lord Frederick Charles Cavendish (1836–1882), by John D. Miller, pubd 1883 (after Sir William Blake Richmond, exh. RA 1874)

1912, as a member of the royal commission on education in 1894 (one of the first women to serve on a royal commission), and as president of the Friends of Armenia. She was a firm, public supporter of home rule. Her published diary is a useful source for the years 1841–82. The Cavendishes were childless. Lucy Cavendish died at her home, The Glebe, Penshurst, Tonbridge, on 22 April 1925, and was buried in her husband's grave. Lucy Cavendish College, Cambridge, was named for her in 1965.

G. C. BOASE, rev. H. C. G. MATTHEW

Sources The diary of Lady Frederick Cavendish, ed. J. Bailey, 2 vols. (1927) · Gladstone, Diaries · T. Corfe, The Phoenix Park murders: conflict, compromise and tragedy in Ireland, 1879–1882 (1968) · private information (2004) · GEC, Peerage · Burke, Peerage
Archives Chatsworth House, Derbyshire, corresp. | BL, corresp. with W. E. Gladstone, Add. MS 44124 · BL, letters to Sir Charles Dilke, Add. MS 43911 · Bodl. Oxf., corresp. with Lord Kimberley · W. Yorks. AS, Bradford, letters to W. S. Nichols relating to reform societies
Likenesses G. Richmond, oils, 1864, repro. in Bailey, ed., Diary of Lady Frederick Cavendish, vol. 2 · London Stereoscopic Co., cabinet photograph, 1882, NPG · J. D. Miller, mezzotint, pubd 1883 (after W. B. Richmond, exh. RA 1874), NG Ire., NPG [see illus.] · A. B. Joy, bronze statue, c.1884, Cavendish Square, Barrow in Furness · T. Woolner, marble effigy, 1885, Cartmel Priory, Cumbria · B. W. Bentley, photograph, NPG · John & Charles Watkins, carte-de-visite, NPG · photographs, repro. in Diary of Lady Frederick Cavendish, vol. 1
Wealth at death £19,265 8s. 9d.: administration, 4 Aug 1882, CGPLA Eng. & Wales · £11,056 19s. 8d.—Lucy Caroline Cavendish: probate, 5 June 1925, CGPLA Eng. & Wales

churchyard, near Chatsworth, on 11 May, when 300 members of the House of Commons and 30,000 other persons made up his cortège. The trial of the murderers in 1883 [see Carey, James] made it evident that the death of Cavendish was not premeditated, and that he was not recognized by the assassins. The plot was laid against Burke, and Cavendish was murdered because he happened to be in the company of a person who had been marked out for destruction. A window to Cavendish's memory was placed in St Margaret's Church, Westminster, at the cost of the members of the House of Commons.

Cavendish was known as an industrious administrator, who seldom spoke in the house except upon subjects of which he had official knowledge or special experience, but he took an interest in educational questions and in land purchase for Ireland. The Cavendish lisp made him a poor public speaker.

Cavendish's wife, **Lucy Caroline Cavendish** (1841–1925), whom he married on 7 June 1864, was born at Hagley Hall, Worcestershire, on 5 September 1841, the second daughter of George, fourth Baron Lyttelton, and his wife, Mary (Catherine Gladstone's sister). Known as Lady Frederick Cavendish, she was an assiduous diarist, was active in religious educational causes, and acted as intermediary between Gladstone and her whig relatives, especially in her widowhood. Before her marriage she was briefly a maid of honour. As a widow, she gave an impression of pious seclusion, declining the mistress-ship of Girton College, Cambridge, in 1884. But she was in fact quite active in the Girls' Public Day School Trust, as president of the Yorkshire Ladies' Council of Education, 1885–

Cavendish, George (b. 1494, d. in or before 1562?), biographer and poet, was born on 21 June 1494, the fourth child and eldest son of Thomas Cavendish (d. 1524), clerk of the pipe to Henry VII and Henry VIII, and Alice, daughter of John Smyth of Padbrook Hall, Suffolk. He studied at Cambridge (c.1510), but did not take a degree. He may have married an unidentified daughter of the family of Spring, in Pakenham, Suffolk, at some time before 1522; if so, she died within a short time of the marriage. He subsequently remarried, most probably in the early 1520s; his second wife was Margery Kemp, daughter of William Kemp and Mary Colt of Spains Hall, Essex, who survived him. They had at least two children.

At some point before 1522 Cavendish entered the service of Cardinal Thomas *Wolsey as gentleman usher. He remained an intimate member of Wolsey's household until the cardinal's death in 1529. Afterwards Cavendish declined to take service with Henry VIII and retired in 1530 to Suffolk, where he resided until his death, which probably took place before July 1562. He is recorded as a commissioner for Bedfordshire in 1535, and in the following year was a member of a committee to hear charges against William Ashwell, third prior of St Albans. His younger brother William *Cavendish went on to a career that brought him wealth and political prominence.

Towards the end of his life George Cavendish wrote his prose life of his patron, Thomas Wolsey, Late Cardinall, his Lyffe and Deathe. This was probably written between late 1554 and 24 June 1558; the date of completion is given by Cavendish himself, in the colophon to his holograph (BL,

Egerton MS 2402). Cavendish may have been drawn to compose his life as a response to the hostile portrait of Wolsey that appeared in Edward Hall's *Chronicle* (first published in 1548).

In his life of Wolsey, Cavendish draws on his observations and experiences in the cardinal's household to offer a portrait that has been acclaimed as the first major English biography. It remains the most important single contemporary source for Wolsey's life, as well as offering a detailed picture of early sixteenth-century court life and of political events in the 1520s, particularly the divorce proceedings against Katherine of Aragon.

The *Life* is also a work of high literary quality. Although Cavendish professes to 'lake wytt in my grosse old hede & Cunnyng in my bowelles' (Cavendish, *Wolsey*, 72), his artistry is in part evidenced in the cumulative detail of many of his descriptions and the dramatic vividness of the direct speech he grants to figures in his account. But it is in the larger formal design of his work that Cavendish achieves his greatest effects. His narrative does not simply describe but gives a tragic shape to Wolsey's rise from obscurity to:

> grete welthe, Joy tryhumphe & glory ... until Fortune (of whose favour no man is lenger assured than she is dysposed) began to wexe some thyng wrothe with his prosperous estate thought she wold devyse a means to abate his hyghe port. (ibid., 28–9)

He deals swiftly with Wolsey's rise to power (before he himself entered the cardinal's service), but offers a protracted account of his eclipse. Wolsey's fate is for Cavendish an exemplification of the power of fortune's wheel:

> Therfore lett all men to whome Fortune extendyth hir grace not to trust to myche to hir fikkyll favor and plesaunt promysis under Colour wherof she Cariethe venemous galle For whan she seyth hir servaunt in most highest auctorytie ... than tournythe she hir visage And plesaunt countenance unto a frownyng chere And utterly forsakyth hyme. (ibid., 13)

It is a fate that is realized most compellingly in the lingering pathos of Wolsey's failure and disgrace.

The popularity of the *Life* in the sixteenth and seventeenth centuries is demonstrated by the more than thirty manuscripts that have survived. In spite of their number, all these derive from a textual tradition differing from that of Cavendish's holograph manuscript, which contains a long, unique passage describing a boar hunt in France. Cavendish's evident Catholic sympathies may have been a factor in restricting the circulation of the *Life* to manuscript until 1641, when it was first printed in a garbled form. Before this it was used by a number of Elizabethan historians, including John Stow; one of the surviving manuscript copies is in his hand.

Cavendish also wrote a number of verse tragedies, which are included in his holograph in the Egerton manuscript. These were first published in 1825 by S. W. Singer under the title *Metrical Visions*. Written in rhyme royal, they comprise first-person laments for their fates by a number of contemporary figures, including some, like Wolsey himself, Anne Boleyn and her brother Viscount Rochford, who were known to Cavendish, as well as others including the poet earl of Surrey and Lady Jane Grey. These laments reveal Cavendish's careful reading of the *Fall of Princes* of John Lydgate, a work written in the 1430s, which provides the model for his poems and from which he borrows a number of passages. His verse does not seem to have enjoyed much popularity or circulation. Only one other manuscript survives (Bodl. Oxf., MS Dugdale 28), copied from Cavendish's holograph. It was as the author of the life of Wolsey that Cavendish claimed the attention of posterity. A. S. G. EDWARDS

Sources G. Cavendish, *The life and death of Cardinal Wolsey*, ed. R. S. Sylvester, EETS, original ser., 243 (1959) · G. Cavendish, *Metrical visions*, ed. A. S. G. Edwards (1980) · *LP Henry VIII*, vols. 8, 11 · *Missale secundum usum insignis ecclesie Sarisburiensis* (Rouen, 1497) [annotated copy with MS notes in calendar, BL, IC.43969] · J. Anderson, *Biographical truth: the representation of historical persons in Tudor–Stuart writing* (1984) · private information (2004) [J. Goldfinch] **Likenesses** oils, 16th cent., Hardwick Hall, Derbyshire

Cavendish [*née* Spencer], **Georgiana, duchess of Devonshire** (1757–1806), political hostess, was born in Wimbledon, Surrey, on 7 June 1757, the eldest daughter of John *Spencer, first Earl Spencer (1734–1783), and his wife, Margaret Georgiana *Spencer (*née* Poyntz) (1737–1814). Four more siblings followed, of whom two survived: George John *Spencer (1758–1834) and Harriet [*see* Ponsonby, Henrietta Frances].

Early life The Spencers travelled widely during Georgiana's childhood and, at home, entertained a variety of celebrated literary and political figures. As a consequence she developed an outward sophistication and charming manner with strangers which belied great emotional insecurity. During the summer of 1772, while staying with her family at Spa in the Southern Netherlands, she met William *Cavendish, fifth duke of Devonshire (1748–1811), and decided to marry him. The match was encouraged by her parents although both they and she were aware that she was unprepared for the duties inherent in being a duchess at the head of a powerful political family. Countess Spencer resisted the idea of her daughter's becoming a child bride, and several observers thought the lively and intelligent Georgiana and the uncommunicative and emotionally inexpressive duke of Devonshire ill matched. None the less both parties remained set on the union, the anticipation of which had generated a large amount of publicity; there had been no duchess of Devonshire for two decades and society looked forward to the great whig dynasty of Cavendish once more having a hostess to revive the splendour of Devonshire House. They were married on 7 June 1774 at Wimbledon parish church, two days earlier than advertised, in order to preserve the couple's privacy.

The early months of marriage rapidly revealed to Georgiana the difficulties she faced as wife and duchess. The duke showed little interest in providing her with guidance, and her mother was a vigorous and implacable critic. Georgiana's unhappiness was compounded by her seeming inability to bear a pregnancy to term, and she suffered multiple miscarriages during the first nine years of marriage. She sought and found diversion in fashionable

Georgiana Cavendish, duchess of Devonshire (1757–1806), by Sir Joshua Reynolds, 1784 [with her daughter Lady Georgiana Cavendish]

life. She was not beautiful in the conventional sense, being tall, large built, and heavy featured, but her charm and charisma made her compelling. Horace Walpole recorded: 'her youth, figure, flowing good nature, sense and lively modesty, and modest familiarity, make her a phenomenon' (Walpole, *Corr.*, 32.232). Almost overnight society began imitating her clothes and mannerisms. In 1774 Georgiana popularized the 3 foot ostrich-feather head-dress. The following year she initiated the craze for extravagant hair towers of preposterous designs. She introduced the 'picture hat' and, in 1783, again transformed women's fashion with the free-flowing muslin dress that was simply tied by a ribbon around the waist. But Georgiana's success was marred by heavy drinking and an insatiable addiction to gambling. The friends and hangers-on of the Devonshires, known collectively as the Devonshire House circle, included many celebrated politicians, wits, and literary figures, such as Thomas Grenville and Richard Brinsley Sheridan. But it also included most of the rakes, libertines, profligates, and notorious women of the era, including John Frederick Sackville, third duke of Dorset, Charles James Fox, Frances Villiers, countess of Jersey, and Elizabeth Lamb, Viscountess Melbourne. They perfected the 'Devonshire House drawl', a kind of aristocratic patois that was part affectation, part baby-talk. Sheridan satirized the circle in *The School for Scandal*, where Georgiana is one candidate for the original of the naïve but good-hearted Lady Teazle. Georgiana felt trapped by her lifestyle. 'When I first came into the world the novelty of the scene made me like everything', she wrote. 'But my heart now feels an emptiness in the beau monde which cannot be filled … nobody can think how much I am tired sometimes with the dissipation I live in' (Lynedoch MSS, Georgiana, duchess of Devonshire, to Mary Graham, *c*.1778). She also blamed herself for helping her beloved sister, Harriet, to become addicted to gambling. She expressed her discontent in an anonymous novel called *The Sylph*, a *roman-à-clef* about high society. *The Sylph* scandalized critics because it portrayed the aristocracy as, *inter*

alia, drunks, blackmailers, wife beaters, and adulterers. Although it was an open secret that Georgiana was the author, she was never publicly exposed. Indeed the press bent over backwards to print glowing stories about her. Such was her popularity with the nation that the mere association of her name with a performer, a play, a book, or piece of china could ensure success. Georgiana was also highly acclaimed in Paris and counted Queen Marie-Antoinette and the duchesse de Polignac among her intimate friends.

The political years, 1780–1789 A turning point came after Georgiana attracted the notice of the whig politician Charles James *Fox. During the French invasion scare of 1778 she had gained the whig party much-needed popularity by forming a female 'battalion' of leading whig women, who dressed in the style of their husbands' regiments and accompanied the men to the military training camps. Fox recognized a fellow populist in Georgiana and encouraged her to take a more active role in the whig party. Although Georgiana later denied that she was ever in love with Fox, circumstantial evidence suggests that they were sometime lovers between 1780 and 1784 (Chatsworth MSS, n. 533). In September 1780 Georgiana made her first election appearance on behalf of the whig party when she climbed the hustings at Westminster to support Charles James Fox. At the same time as she was bringing popularity to the party, Georgiana was also gaining influence through her friendship with the young prince of Wales, afterwards George IV. They were close enough to provoke rumours of an affair but Georgiana always denied that one ever took place. During the Fox–North coalition (1783–4) the prince's insistence that the government pay off his debts threatened to split the unstable ministry. Georgiana saved Fox from having to resign by persuading the prince to accept a vastly reduced sum. Georgiana was keenly aware that she held a privileged position in politics as an insider. 'I have been in the midst of action', she wrote in a memorandum. 'I have seen partys rise and fall—friends be united and disunited—the ties of love give way to caprice, to interest, and to vanity' (Chatsworth MSS, n. 433).

Georgiana's public campaigning for the whig party came to an abrupt end after the débâcle of the 1784 Westminster election. Fox was losing the election when Georgiana, her sister Harriet, and several other whig women and supporters descended on Westminster to canvass voters. George III and the new prime minister, William Pitt, were particularly anxious that Fox should lose his seat, and both sides poured money into the election. Georgiana's very success in wooing voters made her a target for the pro-government press which launched a vicious campaign of calumny against her. The *Morning Post* led the attacks against her, beginning on 31 March 1784, with the insinuation that she was exchanging kisses for votes. Thereafter Georgiana was hounded by cartoons, handbills, ballads, and newspaper articles, all of which portrayed her as a sexually depraved woman who was corrupting the voters of Westminster. Aristocratic society was appalled by the way Georgiana treated voters as if they were her equal, driving them to the polls in her carriage, visiting their homes, and sharing drinks with them. 'She is in the street, they tell me almost every day', wrote Mrs Boscawen to Lady Chatham. 'And this is her sole employment from morning till night. She gets out of her carriage and walks into alleys—many feathers and fox tails in her hat—many blackguards in her suit' (PRO, 30/8/21). Georgiana denied the kissing allegation and was in fact deeply embarrassed by the attacks made against her. Although Fox beat his opponent by 236 votes, the whig party as a whole fared badly and lost many seats to Pittite supporters.

The election was also a disaster for Georgiana, who was left with a tattered reputation and thousands of pounds worth of debts. Furthermore her private life was in turmoil. In 1782 she had befriended Lady Elizabeth Foster [see Cavendish, Elizabeth Christiana, duchess of Devonshire (1757–1824)], daughter of Frederick Augustus Hervey, fourth earl of Bristol. Lady Elizabeth, known as Bess, had separated from her husband, and was living almost destitute with her aunt in Bath. Clever, articulate, and ambitious, Bess insinuated herself into the Devonshire household, becoming Georgiana's best friend and the duke's mistress. Circumstantial evidence suggests that Georgiana and Bess may have been lovers too, and that there was considerable jealousy between all three. Georgiana's relationship with Bess was complex. Bess encouraged her to live a less self-destructive lifestyle which no doubt helped to ensure the successful birth of Lady Georgiana Cavendish (Little G; 1783–1858) and Lady Harriet Cavendish (Hary-O) (1785–1862) [see Gower, Henrietta Elizabeth Leveson-, Countess Granville]. On the other hand she used every means available to undermine Georgiana's position with the duke. She had two children with him, Caroline Rosalie St Jules and Augustus Clifford, whom Georgiana eventually agreed to have brought up on equal terms with her own children. In 1787 Bess seized on Georgiana's spiralling gambling debts to push the duke for a permanent separation. However, moved by her pleas, Bess relented and the uneasy *ménage à trois* continued. The writer Fanny Burney was not alone in assuming that Bess was blackmailing Georgiana. Georgiana was by now fatally ensnared by her gambling debts, and was indeed the victim of threats and blackmail from various loansharks. She constantly borrowed money from everyone, especially the prince of Wales. Her financial dependence on him had led her to becoming entangled in his determination to marry Maria Anne Fitzherbert. At one point he forced her to witness a secret ring ceremony and, although she was not present at his actual marriage, she was intimately involved in the events leading up to it. Mrs Fitzherbert always hated Georgiana because she advised the prince not to marry her. When the regency crisis of 1788–9 gave the whigs an opportunity to return to power, Georgiana was once again busy with party politics. Her diary of the intense squabbling and manoeuvring which took place remains the most quoted source material for the period. Georgiana jockeyed with Sheridan to advise the prince; she also acted as a party whip, cajoling and

pressing party members to remain loyal to Fox. But Fox badly miscalculated his strategy and the whigs were crumbling even before George III recovered his senses. Georgiana's attempts to maintain party morale and win public support for the whigs were blocked by Jane, duchess of Gordon, who was employed by William Pitt to counterbalance the weight of Devonshire House. However, it was Georgiana who received the most blame for dividing society down party lines. 'The acrimony is beyond anything you can conceive', wrote Thomas Townshend, Viscount Sydney (*Correspondence of … Cornwallis*, 1.406–7). As soon as it was practical to do so, the Devonshires and Bess went abroad to France to escape the atmosphere of blame and resentment at home.

The exile years, 1790–1800 While Georgiana was abroad she conceived and gave birth, in June 1790, to a son, William George Spencer *Cavendish, marquess of Hartington (1790–1858). The fact that the entire pregnancy took place out of England led some people to believe that there had been a switch or cover up. These rumours persisted during the marquess's lifetime until the diary of Georgiana's maidservant, Anne Scafe, who had been present at the birth, provided incontestable evidence. During her stay in France, Georgiana witnessed the harassment and imprisonment of her friends. She could not ignore the plight of Marie-Antoinette and, although she counted many aristocratic revolutionaries among her friends, she did not support the French Revolution *per se*. On her return to England she found the whig party in bitter disagreement over the revolution. Fox's enthusiastic support eventually caused the party to split, with William Cavendish Cavendish-Bentinck, third duke of Portland, taking the majority over to Pitt's side. Among those who deserted the whigs was her brother, Earl Spencer, who became first lord of the Admiralty. Georgiana played little part in these events. In 1787 she had become the object of the romantic attentions of the young whig politician Charles *Grey (1764–1845), and about 1789 they became lovers. In 1791 she became pregnant with Grey's child. Incensed, the duke offered her the choice between divorce and exile abroad. Georgiana chose exile for the sake of her three children and, when her illegitimate daughter Eliza Courtney (1792–1859) was born, gave her up to live with Charles Grey's parents. Georgiana was never allowed to acknowledge their true relationship and she felt tremendous guilt over Eliza's fate for the rest of her life. Lady Spencer, Harriet and her husband, and Bess accompanied Georgiana during her exile. They travelled through France, Switzerland, and Italy, eventually settling in Naples where they were lionized by Neapolitan society. During this time Georgiana wrote her best-known poem, *The Passage of the Mountain St Gothard*. After the duke recalled her in 1793 she promised to withdraw from society. The next few years were marred by illness and heartache. In 1795 Charles Grey married without first informing her. The following year she developed an infection in her right eye which spread to her left, leaving her scarred and three-quarters blind. Although initially unwilling to rebuild her life, Georgiana gradually overcame her handicap. She took a renewed interest in the world around her, increased her mineral collection at Chatsworth, and supervised the refurbishment of Chiswick House.

The triumphal return, 1801–1806 The resignation of William Pitt in 1801 lured Georgiana back into the political arena. She had recovered much of her self-confidence since her illness and had gained a sense of perspective which had been missing during the 1780s. Georgiana had finally stopped gambling, but she was never able to pay off her debts. They remained a source of extreme worry until the day she died. Georgiana's friends continued to find themselves importuned for money. However, two important friendships were rekindled as a result of Pitt's resignation—Charles James Fox and the prince of Wales were once more constant visitors to Devonshire House. Georgiana resumed her former role as one of the prince's closest advisers. She became convinced that the prime minister, Henry Addington, was no match against Napoleon and therefore dedicated herself to the formation of a 'broad-bottomed' coalition that could defeat him. She was instrumental in getting Fox and the prince of Wales to settle their differences. She also helped to nudge her brother Earl Spencer, George Canning, and Thomas Grenville into finding common ground with Fox and thus reunite the different whig factions into a force that could be co-ordinated. Although Pitt remained aloof from the coalition, many of his supporters joined with Fox to defeat Addington. The result was that Pitt returned as prime minister in 1804, although the opposition of George III kept Fox from office in the new government. In order to prevent Pitt from consolidating his power Georgiana used all her influence with the prince to keep him on Fox's side and thus maintain the hard-won unity of the whigs. Pitt struggled to remain in government until illness took him in January 1806. The new government, 'the ministry of all the talents', largely consisted of the coalition that Georgiana had helped to build. 'We are all statesmen and stateswomen and grown very dull and important', she joked to her daughter Georgiana, Lady Morpeth (Carlisle MSS J18/20/95). However, her triumph was short-lived. Georgiana died two months later, at Devonshire House, on 30 March 1806, of a liver abscess, and was buried on 8 April at All Saints', Derby. During her lifetime she had achieved a considerable number of political victories on behalf of the whig party. Although she was not the only woman to enjoy political influence and power, hers was one of the most enduring and publicly acknowledged. Her life exemplifies the robust and fluid relations between men and women during the late eighteenth century. She is remarkable for having attained so great a prominence in public life despite enduring great personal suffering. In her obituary the *Morning Chronicle* on 31 March 1806 wrote that '[she was] regarded as the glass and model of fashion, and amidst the homage which was paid to her, she moved with a simplicity that proved her to be unconscious of the charm which bound the world to her attraction'.

AMANDA FOREMAN

Sources A. Foreman, *Georgiana, duchess of Devonshire* (1998) · Chatsworth House, Derbyshire, Devonshire MSS, 433, 533, 584,

667.1, 937 · BL, Spencer MSS, Althorp · Castle Howard, Yorkshire, Carlisle MSS · PRO, 30/8/21 [Mrs Boscawen to Lady Chatham, 12 April 1784] · PRO, 30/29/6/7, fol. 5 [duchess of Devonshire to Fox, c.1803] · NL Scot., Lynedoch MSS · L. Dutens, *Memoirs of a traveller, now in retirement*, 5 vols. (1806) · Walpole, *Corr.* · *The correspondence of George, prince of Wales, 1770–1812*, ed. A. Aspinall, 8 vols. (1963–71) · J. Hartley, ed., *The history of the Westminster election* (1784) · *The journals and letters of Fanny Burney (Madame D'Arblay)*, ed. J. Hemlow and others, 12 vols. (1972–84) · *Correspondence of Charles, first Marquis Cornwallis*, ed. C. Ross, 2nd edn, 3 vols. (1859) · BL, Add. MS 47565, fol. 224

Archives priv. coll., corresp. · Yale U., Farmington, Lewis Walpole Library, letters | BL, letters to Lady Holland and Richard Fitzpatrick, Add. MSS 51454, 51723, 51799 · BL, letters to Lady Melbourne, Add. MSS 45548, 45911 · BL, Spencer MSS · Borth. Inst., letters to Mary Ponsonby, Countess Grey · NL Scot., corresp. with Mary Graham · priv. coll., corresp. with Lady Carlisle, journals, literary MSS · U. Mich., Clements L., letters to Alphonse Perregaux

Likenesses J. Reynolds, oils, c.1759 (with her mother), Chatsworth, Derbyshire · J. Reynolds, double portrait, oils, 1759–61 (with her mother), Althorp, Northamptonshire; *see illus.* in Spencer, (Margaret) Georgiana, Countess Spencer (1737–1814) · T. Gainsborough, oils, 1763, Althorp, Northamptonshire · R. E. Pine, oils, 1773, Althorp, Northamptonshire · A. Kauffmann, group portrait, oils, 1774, Althorp, Northamptonshire · J. Reynolds, oils, c.1775–1776, Hunt. L. · J. Reynolds, oils, c.1780, Chatsworth, Derbyshire · T. Gainsborough, oils, 1783, National Gallery of Art, Washington, DC · J. Reynolds, oils, 1784, Chatsworth, Derbyshire [*see illus.*] · J. Downman, drawing, c.1785, Ickworth House, Suffolk · D. Beauclerk, drawing, Royal Collection · R. Cosway, miniature, Royal Collection · C. Read, group portrait, pastel drawing, Althorp, Northamptonshire · C. Read, pastel drawing (as a child), Althorp, Northamptonshire · T. Rowlandson, ink and watercolour caricature (with Lady Duncannon), Yale U. CBA

Wealth at death debts of many thousands: Chatsworth MSS 1806

Cavendish, Henry (1550–1616), soldier and traveller, was the eldest son of Sir William *Cavendish (1508–1557) of Chatsworth, Derbyshire, administrator, and his third wife, Elizabeth [*see* Talbot, Elizabeth, countess of Shrewsbury (1527?–1608)], noblewoman, known as Bess of Hardwick, daughter of John Hardwick of Hardwick, Derbyshire, and his wife, Elizabeth. He was born on 17 December 1550.

Henry Cavendish's godparents were Princess Elizabeth and John Dudley, earl of Warwick. Little is known of his life until, on 9 February 1568, he married Grace, daughter of George *Talbot, sixth earl of Shrewsbury, and Gertrude, daughter of Thomas Manners, earl of Rutland. His sister, Mary, married Shrewsbury's heir, Gilbert *Talbot, at the same time. The matches resulted from Bess of Hardwick's dynastic ambitions, but Cavendish's marriage proved unsuccessful; Bess herself had already married Shrewsbury. Soon after his wedding, Cavendish, who attended Eton College in 1560, received private tuition, and was admitted to Gray's Inn in 1567, was sent on the 'grand tour' of the continent. It is tempting to see this as an early symptom of marital breakdown, but in fact Grace was only eight. Henry and his brother-in-law Talbot met in Germany, before going on to Padua and Venice. They did not return until early 1572, when Cavendish immediately took up the duties expected of him by his family: he was elected MP for Derbyshire, aged only twenty-two, and was soon serving on local panels such as commissions *post mortem*. He was again elected as MP in 1584, 1586, 1589, and 1593, and was sheriff of Derbyshire in 1582–3 and 1608–9.

A. C. Wood suggested Cavendish was 'fiery, turbulent and adventurous' (Wood, iv). He evidently found it hard to keep his attention focused on one thing for any length of time and had a violent temper, easily aroused when his will was thwarted. The first evidence of this was in 1574, when he was involved in an affray in Staffordshire. A man was killed and Cavendish came to the attention of the privy council—not for the last time. Cavendish did not become captain, then colonel, of a company in the Netherlands in 1574, as some historians have stated. In fact, it was in 1578 that he raised a regiment of some five or six hundred men from his own estates and joined the army of William of Orange. Since rumours indicated that he may originally have been looking for action in 'Scotch affairs ... to help Morton and his friends' (*CSP Spain*, 1509–25, 575), Cavendish may just have wanted to experience war rather than to aid the Dutch. In any event, he had a chance of action; but by March 1579 he had lost the stomach for the gruelling nature of the Dutch wars and came home, abandoning his regiment.

Later in 1579, Cavendish made a trip to Portugal. In March 1589, aged nearly forty, he left on a trip to Turkey, a journey planned well in advance and presumably made to satisfy his own taste for adventure. He went with Richard Mallory, a merchant with interests in Turkey, but Cavendish himself had no commercial interests in the Levant. Mallory replaced Cavendish's intended companion, the scholar Anthony Wingfield, at the last minute. Cavendish avoided the Netherlands and instead went via Germany and eastern Europe. One of his servants, Fox, left a memoir of the trip. Cavendish was back home by late 1591, when he became caught up in another violent feud, this time with William Agard. Both men used armed followers against each other, and Gilbert Talbot, now seventh earl of Shrewsbury, felt obliged to step in, asking the privy council on 30 May 1592 that the two men be obliged to agree that 'all matters of quarrell and pyke betwyxt them and theyrs' should be adjudicated by Robert Devereux, earl of Essex, and him (Talbot MS 2, fol. 102). The privy council did as he requested and the two earls duly resolved the dispute.

Cavendish avoided the privy council's attention again until December 1602, when he became caught up in (or even initiated) a plot to liberate his niece, Arabella Stuart, a potential heir to the throne, from the custody of her grandmother, Bess of Hardwick, in Hardwick Hall, Derbyshire. Cavendish and one Stapleton, a Yorkshire Catholic, gathered forty men to carry Arabella off, but when his mother refused his demand that she be given into his custody, he and the other conspirators simply faded away. Bess of Hardwick vigorously condemned her son's actions to the privy council, but fortunately for Cavendish his conduct seems to have got lost in the tumult of Elizabeth I's death and James VI and I's peaceful accession.

As the episode shows, however, Cavendish was not much of a leader. Part of his problem was an inability to handle money. Having raised his regiment for the Netherlands, he made insufficient provision for it to be paid and supplied, and the English ambassador, William Davison, had to use his own credit on Cavendish's behalf. Davison bitterly wrote home asking the secretaries of state 'to divert such gentlemen of our nation as are bending hitherwardes, for unless they come provided as Mr Candishe hath not ... they will find a cold wellcome' (PRO, SP 83/28, fols. 113r, 116r). When English colonels negotiated with the states general over unpaid wages, Cavendish was always accompanied by his lieutenant-colonel, Richard Bingham, as though not trusted by his officers to handle matters alone. However, part of his problem, as this hints, was a simple lack of leadership qualities. His regiment played a crucial role in the great victory over the Spanish at Rijmenam in August 1578, but it was commanded, 'in his absence', by Bingham (Churchyard, sig. Si); no contemporary source even attempts to explain where the colonel was.

The expedition to the Netherlands was a major factor in Cavendish's debts, which by 1584 totalled £3000, but he had started borrowing considerable sums at least as early as 1575. Yet his resources were great. His stepfather-in-law bestowed on him lands around Hardwick in Ashby in Nottinghamshire when he married, and on his twenty-first birthday, lands worth some £550 per annum, previously enjoyed by his mother, were settled on him. These did not include the splendid estate of Chatsworth, which was entailed on Henry, but which had been left to his mother in her lifetime. Bess was unimpressed by Henry's inability to produce an heir and thus help perpetuate her empire. What made it worse from her perspective was that Henry had at least four illegitimate sons and another four daughters. He was known among fellow MPs as 'the common bull of Derbyshire and Staffordshire' (HoP, *Commons, 1558–1603*, 1.556). Cavendish hated his wife, whom he referred to openly as a 'harlot' (Stone, 194). Despite this, he sided with his Talbot in-laws in their quarrels with his formidable mother. His attempt to liberate Arabella was the last straw for Bess of Hardwick, who notoriously added a codicil to her will, revoking all bequests to her eldest son. There was no reconciliation before her death in 1608.

Cavendish was now able to move into Chatsworth, having lived up to this point at Tutbury in Staffordshire. His debts, however, still troubled him and in 1610 he was obliged to sell the reversion of Chatsworth and most of his lands to his younger brother William *Cavendish, later first earl of Devonshire. Henry Cavendish lived in Chatsworth until his death on 12 October 1616. At some point, he settled the estate of Dovebridge in Derbyshire on his eldest bastard, Henry Cavendish, for he died intestate and administration of his estate was granted to Lord Cavendish, who was said to 'inherit £4,000 *p.a.* from the death of his brother' (*CSP dom., 1611–18*, 426). Lord Cavendish, the second son, was their mother's favourite and his descendants still live in Chatsworth. Bess of Hardwick, in a sense, got the better of Henry Cavendish in death, as in life. However, if his choleric and feckless personality made him a disappointment to her, it doubtless owed much to his having been brought up by such a mother. He was buried at Edensor in Derbyshire.   D. J. B. TRIM

Sources D. N. Durant, *Bess of Hardwick: portrait of an Elizabethan dynast* (1977) • A. C. Wood, ed., 'Mr Harrie Cavendish his journey to and from Constantinople 1589', *Camden miscellany, XVII*, CS, 3rd ser., 64 (1940) • L. Stone, *The crisis of the aristocracy, 1558–1641* (1965); repr. (1966) • HoP, *Commons, 1558–1603*, vol. 1 • J. Foster, *The register of admissions to Gray's Inn, 1521–1889, together with the register of marriages in Gray's Inn chapel, 1695–1754* (privately printed, London, 1889) • *CPR, 1572–5* • T. Churchyard, *A generall rehearsall of warres* (1579) • N. Japikse and H. H. P. Rijperman, eds., *Resolutiën der Staten-Generaal van 1576 tot 1609*, 14 vols. (The Hague, 1915–70), vol. 2 • M. A. S. Hume, *Calendar of letters and state papers relating to English affairs, preserved principally in the archives of Simancas*, 2, PRO (1894), 1568–79 • *CSP for.*, 1577–8 • *CSP dom.*, 1611–18, with *addenda, 1566–79* • PRO, SP 83/28 • PRO, SO3/1 • PRO, PROB 6/9, fol. 94v • *APC, 1591–2* • Longleat House, Wiltshire, Talbot MSS, vol. 2 • G. D. Squibb, ed., *The visitation of Derbyshire, begun in 1662*, Harleian Society, new ser., 8 (1989) • BL, Add. MS 6688

Archives BL, bill of sale of reversion of Chatsworth, Add. MS 6688, fol. 244 • Chatsworth House, Derbyshire, account of journey to Constantinople • LPL, letters from continent, MS 697

Likenesses oils, 1569–99, Hardwick Hall, Derbyshire; repro. in Wood, ed., 'Mr Harrie Cavendish'

Wealth at death land, allegedly worth £4000 p.a.: *CSP dom.*, 1611–18, 426 (Oct 1617)

Cavendish, Henry, second duke of Newcastle upon Tyne (**1630–1691**), politician, was born on 24 June 1630, the fourth but second surviving son of William *Cavendish, first duke of Newcastle upon Tyne (*bap.* 1593, *d.* 1676), and his first wife, Elizabeth (*d.* 1643), daughter of William Bassett of Blore, Staffordshire, and widow of Henry Howard. He was educated at home, and the principles that were to govern his life were instilled at an early age by his father. Before the battle of Marston Moor in 1644, Newcastle refused to send Lord Henry and his elder brother Charles Cavendish, Viscount Mansfield (1620–1659), to safety, for they 'should show their loyalty and duty to his Majesty in venturing their lives as well as himself' (Cavendish, 93). Lord Henry went into exile with his father, but returned in the autumn of 1647 to assist in the recovery of the family's estates. Over the next decade this was his main concern, but he was only able to make a financial contribution following the conclusion in May 1653 of the settlement on his marriage to Frances (1629/30–1695), eldest daughter of William *Pierrepont (1607/8–1678) and his wife, Elizabeth Harris. On the death of his elder brother in June 1659, he became Viscount Mansfield, and from March 1665 was styled earl of Ogle.

Before the elections for the Convention Parliament, Mansfield belatedly approached the earl of Clare, but finding him already committed to candidates for Nottinghamshire, sought a Derbyshire seat. His first election was declared void because of a trick in returning the writs. He arrived at a second poll to defend himself against any attacks by Anabaptists and was successfully returned. Elected the following year for Northumberland to the Cavalier Parliament, his most notable contributions were to defend the first charter to enfranchise Newark and to introduce a bill for the enfranchisement of Durham. Master of the robes at the coronation, he served from May

1660 until his resignation in March 1663, when he was appointed gentleman of the king's bedchamber, a post he retained until the end of the reign. Listed by his friend Danby among the court's supporters in the Commons, he became, as earl of Ogle and then, after the death of his father in December 1676, duke of Newcastle, a strong opponent of exclusion. In the Lords he argued 'it was not fitting to bee debated it is to Alter the succession' (Beer, 34).

It was as joint lieutenant (1670–77) and lieutenant of Northumberland (1677–88), as well as governor of Berwick (1675–86) and lieutenant of Nottinghamshire (1677–88), that Newcastle gave effective service to the crown. In Northumberland he attempted to govern by correspondence and the aid of the local élites. In Nottinghamshire, where he had previously served as a deputy lieutenant and which he claimed was the 'most factious' county in the kingdom (*CSP dom.*, *February–December 1685*, 105), Newcastle took an active role. After the defeat of his candidate (his brother-in-law Gervase Pierrepont) at the Nottinghamshire election in September 1679 it was not until the summer of 1681 that Newcastle began to promote petitions supporting the king's policies. He became the patron of the Nottingham townsmen who supported the surrender of its charter and their link with the crown. After the defeat of a determined opposition led by the Nottinghamshire whigs, the first elections under the new charter in September 1682 led to riots. Newcastle, by now recorder, was ordered to reside at the castle and to collect evidence to be used against the rioters and their whig supporters. He used news of the Rye House plot to attack the leading Nottinghamshire whigs and to search their houses. He attended the poll at the contested Nottingham parliamentary election of 1685, when for the first time tories were successful as they were in all the Nottinghamshire constituencies.

Reappointed by James II to his lieutenancies in 1685, Newcastle resolved to be loyal, even though he was concerned at the pace of the king's policies in favour of Roman Catholics. Rebuked for the slow return of answers to the three questions posed to lieutenants in February 1686, he sent his resignation with the replies. Pleas to his loyalty persuaded him to resume his duties and when in October 1686 he was appointed lieutenant of the three ridings of Yorkshire, the duke was in effect responsible for the security of the north-east. In September 1688 he was ordered to raise a regiment to secure Newcastle upon Tyne. After the prince of Orange landed at Torbay, Newcastle considered his regiment unnecessary, but his request to be 'employed where there is action' was refused (*Seventh Report*, HMC, 348). The support of the militias was essential, and Newcastle believed that the Yorkshire militia would accept a declaration of loyalty to James. When on 19 November he found a petition in favour of a freely elected parliament in circulation he refused to be affronted or overruled by deputies he had appointed, and to show his displeasure left York. He failed—though asked by Reresby, the governor of York—to dismiss the militias and this gave Danby an opportunity to take control.

Danby and the earl of Devonshire, who seized Nottingham, had falsely assured Newcastle of their loyalty. When Newcastle decided to take action the militias ignored his orders and he became a prisoner at Welbeck. James accepted that Newcastle's loyalty had left him isolated, and that without troops it was impossible 'to dissipate' the rebels. The duke's failure to take decisive action at York was censured and has been seen as a confirmation of his weak, often petulant, character, while his previously effective service has been ignored. In defeat Newcastle insisted he would 'always be loyall to the king, firm to his religion and act always according to lawe': consequently, he refused the oaths of allegiance to William and Mary and to hold office under them (ibid., 350; *Memoirs of Sir John Reresby*, 545).

Meanwhile Newcastle, whose thoughts were concentrated 'upon making his family great', had been dealt a sudden grievous blow when, on 1 November 1680, his only son, Henry Cavendish, Lord Ogle (*b*. 1663), died (*Life and Letters of Sir George Savile*, 244). The finding of suitable husbands and dowries for his five daughters had become a major concern. It was the cause of disputes and a separation from his wife who 'had had soe great a share of government in that family that she expected that everything should goe as she pleased' (*Memoirs of Sir John Reresby*, 437, 472). Sir John Reresby, who acted as an intermediary in a failed marriage negotiation, had an angry dispute with Newcastle, whom he considered was of an 'unsteady fickle humour' in these matters (*Memoirs of Sir John Reresby*). The provision of dowries made a substantial contribution to Newcastle's debts, which at his death exceeded £72,000 (U. Nott. L., PW I 655). He died at Welbeck on 26 July 1691, and was buried on 12 August at Bolsover. In his will of 26 May that year he tried to preserve the family name and estate. His estates were left to Lady Margaret Cavendish, his third surviving and favourite daughter, who had married in February 1690 John *Holles, fourth earl of Clare (1662–1711). The conditions were that the son or daughter of the marriage must, in honour of the first duke of Newcastle, retain the name of Cavendish, and the estate must pass undivided. The earl of Clare was to take the liabilities of the estate. Attempts made by his brothers-in-law the earls of Thanet and Montague to invalidate the will on the grounds that Newcastle was insane when it was made failed. Newcastle's wife survived her husband, and died in London on 23 September 1695.

P. R. SEDDON

Sources GEC, *Peerage* · U. Nott. L., department of manuscripts and special collections, Cavendish correspondence, PW I · Notts. Arch., DDP 1–6 · *CSP dom., 1660–91* · *Memoirs of Sir John Reresby*, ed. A. Browning (1936) · E. S. de Beer, 'The House of Lords in the parliament of 1680', *BIHR*, 20 (1943–5), 22–37 · M. W. Helms and E. R. Edwards, 'Cavendish, Henry', *HoP, Commons, 1660–90* · Margaret, duchess of Newcastle [M. Cavendish], *The life of William Cavendish, duke of Newcastle*, ed. C. H. Firth, 2nd rev. edn (1906) · *Seventh report*, HMC, 6 (1879) [Sir Frederick Graham] · A. Browning, *Thomas Osborne, earl of Danby and duke of Leeds, 1632–1712*, 3 vols. (1944–51) · D. H. Hosford, *Nottingham, nobles and the north: aspects of the revolution of 1688* (1976) · P. R. Seddon, 'The origins of the Nottinghamshire whigs: an analysis of the subscribers to the election expenses of Sir Scrope Howe and John White', *Historical Research*, 69 (1996), 218–

31 · G. Duckett, ed., *Penal laws and Test Act*, 2 vols. (1882–3) · *The life and letters of Sir George Savile … first marquis of Halifax*, ed. H. C. Foxcroft, 2 vols. (1898) · *The manuscripts of his grace the duke of Portland*, 10 vols., HMC, 29 (1891–1931) · M. A. E. Green, ed., *Calendar of the proceedings of the committee for compounding … 1643–1660*, 5 vols., PRO (1889–92)
Archives BL, Portland loan, corresp., Add. MSS 70499, 70500 [formerly loan 29/236–40] · Notts. Arch., Portland estates, legal and official, DDP 1–6 · U. Nott. L., corresp., PW I | BL, letters to Lord Danby, Egerton MSS 3328–3334 · BL, Spencer MSS, letters to first marquess of Halifax, C6 · Notts. Arch., DD SR 219/1
Likenesses G. Morphy, oils, Welbeck Abbey, Nottinghamshire; repro. in A. S. Turbeville, *A history of Welbeck Abbey and its owners*, 1 (1939), p. 206
Wealth at death £72,580 in debts: Cavendish correspondence, U. Nott., PW I, 400, 655 · £11,344 'clear' rental income in 1685

Cavendish, Henry (1731–1810), natural philosopher, was the eldest child of Lord Charles Cavendish (1704–1783), third son of William, second duke of Devonshire, an eminent whig politician and natural philosopher, and Anne De Grey (1706–1733), fourth daughter of Henry, duke of Kent. He was born on 10 October 1731 in Nice, where his recently married mother was convalescing. In June 1733 at the family home in Putteridge, Hertfordshire, she gave birth to a second son, Frederick, but died there three months later. In 1738 Charles Cavendish moved to 13 Great Marlborough Street in London. Henry was tutored there, then from 1742 at Hackney Academy, a school patronized by well-born whigs. On 24 November 1749 he entered Peterhouse, Cambridge, as a fellow-commoner and there absorbed Newtonian natural philosophy. In 1751 he contributed a banal Latin verse to a university collection commemorating Frederick, prince of Wales. Though he left the university in February 1753 without a degree, Cavendish established important Cambridge connections such as the physician John Hadley and the natural philosopher John Michell. Granted an annuity of £500 by his father, Cavendish settled at Great Marlborough Street. He first attended the Royal Society in June 1758, at his father's invitation, joined the Society of Arts in January 1760, was elected a fellow of the Royal Society on 1 May of that year, and two months later joined the Royal Society's dining club. In November 1765 he was elected to the Royal Society's council, on which he served regularly thenceforward. Though a principal member of London's philosophical clubland, Cavendish's shrill voice, shuffling gait, almost Trappist reticence, unfashionably plain dress, and pain at his increasing celebrity were all noted by more sociable contemporaries. However, these shortcomings did not prevent him from exercising a major public role in the sciences of later Georgian Britain.

Airs, waters, heats, 1764–1767 During the 1760s Cavendish became an expert chemical analyst using the principles of heat and phlogiston as guides. When in 1764 Hadley described the neutral arsenical salt (potassium arsenate) made by the French chemist Pierre-Joseph Macquer, Cavendish was prompted to prepare an unknown acid (arsenious oxide) and implicitly distinguished the two oxides of arsenic, then understood as dephlogisticated arsenic. In February 1764 he tested mineral samples from Tenerife

Henry Cavendish (1731–1810), by William Alexander, c.1800

his more private work on thermometry, Cavendish established a scale of specific heats, with water as standard. Sceptical that heat might be a material substance, Cavendish sought to match measured specific heats with the effects of evaporation and fermentation and with Newton's view that heat stemmed from strong short-range interparticulate forces. He assessed the heat absorbed in changing the state of matter: firstly in melting spermaceti, then more accurately by estimating the cooling when water turned to steam. He refined a trial designed by Black in which the specific heat of air was measured by determining temperature changes when air passed through a worm-tube encased in hot water. Impressed by Black's account of acidic fixed air (carbon dioxide), Cavendish also determined the relative heat changes when this air was released as alkalis dissolved in acids.

Cavendish followed this work with a series of public papers at the Royal Society on chemistry of 'airs' and waters, which won him the Copley medal for 1766. He showed there was a range of chemical airs or gases of different specific gravities. In a paper read in May 1766 Cavendish described using the gas jars designed earlier in the century by Stephen Hales to collect airs over water, measuring their specific gravity by weighing the water displaced. When metals (zinc, iron, or tin) were dissolved in acids—spirit of salt (hydrochloric acid) or dilute vitriol (sulphuric acid)—he collected the same inflammable air (hydrogen gas) in the same volume, an air he identified with phlogiston and found eleven times lighter than common air. He privately emphasized that phlogiston must be released when metals dissolved in acids. Air's combustibility was measured by the loudness of the explosion when detonated with inflammable air. In two further papers of November 1766 Cavendish reported on samples of Black's fixed air (carbon dioxide) collected over mercury, measured its specific weight, defined a numerical scale of acidity using the quantity of alkaline marble needed to saturate the acidic sample, and, following work of the Irish physician David Macbride, examined the fixed air generated in fermentation and putrefaction. The following February, prompted by Heberden's warnings of the dangers of common pump waters, he presented the society with his analysis, conducted in September 1765, of the large quantities of fixed air contained in and the chalky earth produced by samples from several London water-pumps, so confirming the findings of the Whitehaven physician William Brownrigg on acidic airs contained in spa waters.

Cavendish also soon took an active role in the Royal Society's plans for astronomical surveying. In June 1766 he sent the president a list of sites from which the imminent 1769 Venus transit could be observed to determine the solar parallax, and in November 1767 he joined the society's committee to plan these observations and correct likely errors. The following year Cavendish discussed with the new astronomer royal, Nevil Maskelyne, the gravitational pull of nearby mountains on the vertical plumb lines used earlier in the decade in American surveys by Charles Mason and Jeremiah Dixon. After trying to

for the London physician William Heberden, and examined the alkaline component of tartar (potassium tartrate) described by the German chemist Andreas Marggraf. After planning a treatise on Newtonian mechanics Cavendish wrote a commentary on the theory of motion using a principle of conservation of mechanical momentum, the product of mass and velocity. He included the hidden momenta contributed by elasticity and gravitation, and identified heat with the mechanical momentum of the vibrations of invisible particles. Mechanical momenta must be conserved in heat exchanges and were applied to sound, water waves, and the heating effects of light. However, Cavendish could not yet explain the heats involved in fermentation and combustion, nor the relation between mechanical heat and measurable temperature changes when bodies were in different physical states, so early in 1765 he started experiments on heat, drawing on work by the pre-eminent chemists Joseph Black and Hermann Boerhaave, and his own precision thermometry and pneumatics. Mixtures of hot and cold water and other chemicals, for which he designed a more accurate arrangement using a funnel and stirrer, showed that heating effects were not directly proportional to the reactants' weights.

In April 1766 at the Royal Society, Cavendish tried out a range of thermometers by London instrument makers to measure water's boiling point, finding discrepancies of as much as 3 degrees. Two years later he commissioned his favoured London instrument supplier, Edward Nairne, to build a large horizontal windmill to measure wind speeds in co-ordination with other atmospheric phenomena. In reconcile measures of pendulum rates with French data on the earth's shape published in the 1740s, Cavendish concluded that gravitational pull rather than meridional degrees would be a better guide to the earth's shape. The project typified his view that precise estimation of central forces held the key to rational mechanics and natural philosophy.

Electricity—artificial, animal, and atmospheric, 1767–1777
One concern of English natural philosophers absent from Cavendish's early mechanical programme was electricity, on which his father worked at the Royal Society in the 1750s. Principal electrical phenomena, as interpreted by Benjamin Franklin, were summarized in 1767 in a two-volume work by the natural philosopher Joseph Priestley, himself an admirer of Cavendish's pneumatic chemistry. Soon afterwards Cavendish made notes on an electrical fluid of mutually repellent particles to which he applied his understanding of heat and factitious airs. Cavendish rejected Franklin's model of electrical atmospheres round bodies, and distinguished between the fluid's variable compression (to account for degree of electrification) and its quantity (to describe electric charge). In December 1771 and January 1772 Cavendish presented the Royal Society with a paper on this fluid's mechanics. He knew Priestley's estimate that the electrical force law must be of the same form as gravitation, and stated that the repulsive force between electric particles must follow some power less than the cube of distance. The particles would attract those of common matter, which themselves must also be mutually repellent. Using trials by Franklin, Priestley, and John Canton, Cavendish referred to degree of electrification (variable compression of the fluid) and extent of saturation (normal state of fluid distribution) of bodies. His use of canals carrying incompressible fluids without resistance to model fluid distribution on variously shaped conductors was crucial in accomplishing such mechanical precision (a goal which he reckoned to have achieved more successfully than his predecessor, the St Petersburg mathematician Franz Aepinus).

During the early 1770s Cavendish performed many unpublished experiments on electrical force laws, condensation, and conduction. Most were done at Great Marlborough Street, though several were shown at Nairne's Cornhill instrument shop. In the winter of 1772–3, using separable concentric hemispheres and a pair of pith balls as a charge detector, Cavendish deduced from the absence of detectable charge inside a spherical electrified conductor that the electric force must vary with distance according to an inverse power of 2 ± 0.2. Cavendish corrected for electrical leak and the effect of his own body on measures of electrification. In 1773 he established a charge scale in terms of the dimensions of a conducting globe of given capacity and degree of electrification to estimate the capacitance of a range of conductors and condensers, including parallel foil-coated glass plates. By early 1775 he reckoned these plates were electrified proportionally to the ratio of the area coated and the glass thickness, measured with John Bird's fine dividing

engine. Cavendish concluded that each insulator possessed an electrical characteristic other than its conductivity because his model well accounted for air's capacitance but failed for glass condensers. He guessed that glass had alternately insulating and conducting layers, a model based on the account of optical transmission and reflection in glass developed by Michell and published in Priestley's optics treatise of 1772. Priestley had already tried to estimate the loss of force suffered when electricity discharged from condensers melted various wires. From late 1773 Cavendish started measuring these forces by determining the length of a tube of saturated salt which would yield the same shock through his body (delivered from an array of six Leyden jars) as would a test length of metal wire or chemical solution. Such estimates continued through the later 1770s, using fixed air as well as acids and salts. He judged that the force of resistance must be related to the length of the conductor, its intrinsic resistance, and the electric fluid's velocity.

Salt water conductivity and the behaviour of condensers were relevant to Cavendish's interest in the apparently electrical behaviour of marine eels and stingrays. Animal electricity preoccupied Cavendish and his colleagues from early 1773, when the East India merchant John Walsh reported on electrical torpedoes and asked Cavendish for advice on how they stored electricity. In March 1775 one of the Royal Society's fellows, William Henley, built an electrical model of the fish but found neither forces nor sparks. During the summer Cavendish followed suit with a model of thin pewter plates connected to four dozen thin Leyden jars covered in thick leather. The model delivered a large quantity of electrical fluid at low compression. Since humans conducted almost as well as sea water, they would feel a big shock even though only very weak sparks were produced. Cavendish invited Priestley, Nairne, and more sceptical witnesses to experience the force of his demonstration (and the model's shocks) at Great Marlborough Street in May 1775. In January 1776 he had a paper on the artificial torpedo read at the Royal Society itself. Cavendish also took a leading role in the long-running debate about Franklin's designs for lightning rods, chairing the society's committee to assess the defence of Purfleet arsenal from August 1772 and, in 1777, examining the dramatic model of the arsenal built by the hostile electrical philosopher Benjamin Wilson. Cavendish's experiments on electricity seem to have ceased in the early 1780s.

Towards a global physics, 1771–1781
Atmospheric electricity was only one part of what Cavendish saw as a universal science of climate and planetary mechanics. Although by the standards of his class and time he seemed unusually solitary, if not misanthropic, he energetically maintained metropolitan and international networks, involving astronomers, instrument makers, and navigators such as the East India Company hydrographer Alexander Dalrymple. These men helped link Cavendish's quantitative laboratory mechanics with meteorology, magnetism, and geodesy. In April 1771 Maskelyne and Cavendish discussed the attraction of particles by variously shaped solids, a

precedent for Cavendish's estimates of the electrical capacity of variously shaped conductors. Cavendish thence calculated tables of the variation in the compression of the earth with distance from its centre, and from older French pendulum data estimated the earth's mean density. Between July 1772 and January 1773 Cavendish advised Maskelyne on measures of plumb-line deviations near large mountains, to be funded with surplus money from the Venus transit expeditions. A year later the Royal Society chose Schiehallion in Perthshire as the best site, and until August 1775 Cavendish worked on correcting instruments and data for observations there. The results were eventually published, with Cavendish's help, by the mathematician Charles Hutton in 1778, yielding a mean density estimate of 4.5 times that of water, close to Cavendish's initial calculation made seven years earlier.

The Schiehallion scheme exemplified Cavendish's plans to combine instruments, travellers' reports, and precision measures. East India and Hudson's Bay Company agents provided information on temperatures, atmospherics, and ocean currents. His allies included the aristocratic mariner Constantine Phipps, who helped with the Schiehallion calculations and for whose 1773 Spitsbergen voyage Cavendish advised on sea water temperatures, magnetic observations, and a theory of the origin of icebergs. From 1773 a member of the Society of Antiquaries and, more actively, a trustee of the British Museum, Cavendish was also well placed to study metropolitan natural historical and antiquarian collections. In November 1773 he started a Royal Society meteorological recording system with barometers, thermometers, anemometers, and magnetic needles. From the winter of 1774 Cavendish learned of observations of extreme cold and the freezing of mercury by the Hudson's Bay agent Thomas Hutchins, and in early 1776 produced a temperature of 25 degrees below zero by mixing snow and aqua fortis. Cavendish made magnetic dip observations in his own garden, advised on the method for such observations for James Cook's third voyage, and in summer 1778 made regular magnetic observations with Nairne's needles during a tour of the midlands. With Nairne, Cavendish added telescopic sights to conventional variation needles for better accuracy. He started observations of the northern lights, including a computation of the corona of the aurora of February 1778.

Pneumatic tests also needed to be made more exact. In spring 1772 Priestley and Cavendish proposed treating metals with spirit of nitre (nitric acid) to make nitric oxide, which they called nitrous air. The 'nitrous air' was used to test phlogistication of airs by measuring diminution in volume of samples when they were shaken with this air, a technique soon turned into precision eudiometry. During 1776 Cavendish explained to Nairne how water vapour pressure would vitiate air pump gauges, in March of that year he published a full account of the society's instrument collection with details of his new methods for error calculation in measuring temperature, air pressure, and magnetic variation, and in November he

took over the Royal Society's committee on meteorological instruments. Cavendish was concerned with glaciation and temperature variation within the earth on the assumption of a purely solar heat source. In 1776–9 he planned a self-registering thermometer which would record maximum diurnal temperatures in air. When the Royal Society moved to more spacious premises in Somerset House in July 1781, Cavendish arranged its instrument collection and took over its meteorological journals. An important recruit for his work, and one of his rare intimates, was Charles Blagden, an Edinburgh-trained military physician whom in 1775 Cavendish instructed on measures of sea and air temperatures in the Atlantic for an early model of the Gulf Stream. Blagden eventually became the Royal Society's secretary under the presidency of Joseph Banks, whose expansionist regime, established in 1778, provided a stormy setting for Cavendish's new initiatives in pneumatic chemistry and, less enthusiastically, institutional politics.

The water controversies, 1781–1788 Cavendish's new chemical work of the early 1780s started with attempts to make meteorological chemistry precise, and culminated in 1787–8 with a remarkable global theory of heat, chemistry, and rational mechanics. At the start of the decade, with Banks's sponsorship, the Florentine naturalist Felice Fontana told the society of major errors in the nitrous air test for aerial phlogistication, and, despite Priestley's protests, that the composition of the atmosphere was uniform. Cavendish made eudiometric tests at Great Marlborough Street. He produced nitrous air from pure copper and acid, then bubbled the air in excess into a test sample over distilled water. The resultant gas was weighed using a fine chemical balance designed by William Harrison. Cavendish created a gravimetric scale of phlogistication, setting atmospheric air as unity and phlogisticated air (atmospheric nitrogen) as zero. Dephlogisticated air (oxygen gas) had a value of between 4.8 and 5, and made up almost one-fifth of the atmosphere, a proportion he judged constant. Cavendish also indicated the lack of relation between an air's smell and its degree of phlogistication.

Cavendish's eudiometry needed a new way of examining phlogistication of the atmosphere. In the later 1770s he learned that the Pavia natural philosopher Alessandro Volta tested for phlogistication by sparking samples with inflammable air (hydrogen gas). In March 1781 Priestley and his Birmingham colleague John Warltire determined the weight loss when they sparked atmospheric air with inflammable air in a glass vessel to check whether heat had weight, noting the production of some dew on the vessel. In June 1781 Cavendish reproduced the trial, found no loss of weight, but examined this dew. It was pure water condensed from inflammable air and from about one-fifth of the atmospheric air. He concluded that dephlogisticated air was water deprived of phlogiston and inflammable air was water united with phlogiston, and confirmed that the mephitic remnant of the atmosphere could not be fixed air. When dephlogisticated air was present in excess in the spark chamber, Cavendish found the liquid was not pure water, but nitrous acid.

The next four years involved Cavendish in uncharacteristic disruptions of his domestic and public life. In January 1782 he purchased a suburban house at 34 Church Row, Hampstead, and in the summer took over management of the family estate, raising his annual income and embroiling him with land disputes in Nottingham and Derbyshire. Hampstead was frequently used as a site for eudiometric work, results of which he published in the *Philosophical Transactions*. In May 1783, for example, Cavendish invited Blagden and Hutchins to Hampstead to witness the freezing of mercury at 39 degrees below zero. Cavendish then published comments on Hutchins's thermometry, artificial cold, and evidence against the materiality of heat. In the previous month Cavendish's father had died, leaving him almost £160,000; in the following year, having inherited a further £150,000 from his father's cousin Elizabeth Cavendish, he moved from Great Marlborough Street to 11 Bedford Square. There he established a laboratory, a museum, and a library of about 12,000 volumes open to learned guests. However, Cavendish himself never took a book from his own library without leaving a receipt. In September 1785 he moved his suburban base from Hampstead to Clapham Common, where he also owned a 15 acre estate purchased for £5000. Almost misanthropic in his reserve, Cavendish never received strangers at his residence, and ordered his dinner by leaving a note on the hall table. He seems to have had no other communication with any of his female domestic staff.

During these domestic changes, Cavendish's experiments on explosion of inflammable and dephlogisticated airs drew wide interest. In spring 1783 James Watt told Priestley that water must be dephlogisticated air united with inflammable air after the loss of latent heat. Cavendish denied the materiality of heat so rejected Watt's account. During the summer of 1783 versions of his trials were reproduced at the Royal Society by Priestley and in Paris by Antoine Lavoisier. Cavendish studied closely the new materialist heat theory announced by Lavoisier and Pierre Simon Laplace in June 1783. When later that year French schemes for hot-air balloons were copied in Britain, Cavendish and Blagden determined that gaseous rarefaction, not chemical change, was responsible for lift. At the end of 1783 this chemical work became entangled with major fights at the Royal Society between Banks and mathematicians led by Maskelyne and Hutton, who reckoned the president's imperium was inimical to the cultivators of mathematics and the exact sciences. Cavendish played a major role, as both doyen of the Royal Society's experimental philosophers and a circumspect mediator. In December 1783 he drafted a resolution he hoped would reconcile the factions, then on 8 January 1784 cautiously backed Banks's regime. The next week Cavendish's paper summarizing the condensation of water was read at the society. Its publication delayed by the conflict, the paper became the focus of controversy when in March 1784 the Swiss naturalist Jean-André Deluc convinced Watt that

Cavendish was a plagiarist, behaviour Watt initially linked with Cavendish's aristocratic politics. Watt's work was read at the society in April and May 1784, at the same time as Banks's triumph over his critics. Though Watt was eventually persuaded of Cavendish's good will, Cavendish now faced criticism from the Irish chemist Richard Kirwan, who held that at low temperatures fixed air was indeed present when common air was completely phlogisticated. Cavendish was forced publicly to answer Kirwan in March 1784 with demonstrations that the aerial remnant left after phlogistication did not contain this fixed air.

During the autumn of 1784 Cavendish encouraged the American balloonist John Jefferies to make eudiometric observations at various atmospheric heights. By December he had completed new experiments on Kirwan's problem of the remnant left when atmospheric air was phlogisticated. Cavendish identified phlogisticated air as nitrous acid combined with phlogiston, because all but a minute part of this remnant could be reduced to nitrous acid. Over a century later this remarkably acute observation of the minute gas bubble which could not be so reduced would be cited by the chemist William Ramsay, who identified it with the newly discovered inert gas argon. At the end of 1784 Cavendish himself went on to show that were phlogisticated air present when inflammable and dephlogisticated air were sparked together, nitrous acid rather than water would be produced. Neither Lavoisier, nor the Dutch natural philosopher Martin van Marum, could reproduce these claims once published in early 1785 in the *Philosophical Transactions* and publicized by the German chemist Lorenz Crell's *Chemische Annalen*, to which Cavendish was an active subscriber. Each summer between 1785 and 1787 Cavendish and Blagden toured the provinces, making geological, industrial, and chemical surveys in south Wales, the Lake District, and Cornwall and conducting barometric estimates of height in emulation of French techniques. During 1787 Cavendish studied Lavoisier's new chemical nomenclature, but firmly rejected French oxygen-based chemistry; during winter 1787–8, with Nairne's powerful electrical machine as a spark generator, he staged shows of the production of nitrous acid at the Royal Society.

About 1787, responding to the caloric theory of Lavoisier and Laplace, Cavendish drafted a long paper applying his early theory of mechanical momentum to thermal phenomena. He divided mechanical effect between visible motions and invisible vibrations. These vibrations were linked with active and latent heats, the latter due to repulsions between fundamental particles. The total heat of bodies, which Cavendish judged must be constant, would be distributed between these two components depending on such factors as the body's weight and the frequency of particle vibration. Changes in sensible heat would involve different changes in latent heat, since heating would change the distance between particles. During changes of state or chemical reactions the sensible heat of the reagents would also change. Here Cavendish ambitiously sought to extend his thermal mechanics to percussion, expansion, the electric heating of wires, and the conversion of mechanical into thermal effects. In Crell's journal he found evidence of heating rays to explain why hotter bodies shone. From John Michell, whom Cavendish visited in Yorkshire in summer 1786, he obtained data on the momentum of light particles to analyse the heating effects of sunlight on glass and metal plates. In 1788 he reported to the Royal Society on trials he had commissioned in Hudson's bay by the administrator John McNab on the freezing of acids. Further heat trials were conducted in the new laboratory Cavendish designed at his Clapham Common residence during the later 1780s.

Astronomical and terrestrial surveys, 1783–1810 Clapham Common also acted as an important site for astronomy and geodesy with observers such as Maskelyne and William Roy, who used Clapham as a base for their survey linking Paris and Greenwich observatories during the 1780s, and for whom Cavendish performed important error calculations. From May 1783 Cavendish's closest astronomical colleague, John Michell, sought to measure the retardation of light speed from a double star by passing one star's rays through a prism. Maskelyne and Roy guessed this retardation would be due to the larger gravitational pull of the star on emitted light particles. Cavendish judged lenses rather than prisms would work better, and in autumn 1783 made preparatory photometric observations of the double star Algol, newly identified by John Goodricke. Though Maskelyne tried measuring such changes in light speed, by April 1784 Michell and Cavendish agreed that there might be no star bulky enough to yield observable retardations. This abortive project did not lessen Cavendish's astronomical interests. He compiled, and after six years' delay published, observations of the aurora borealis of February 1784, to test his claim that the phenomenon was due to vertically projected light rays. From late 1785 at Clapham Common he tested the performance of the Royal Society's huge seventeenth-century aerial telescope and in spring 1786 he discussed with the pre-eminent astronomer William Herschel problems of aberration and the distinctness of vision in lenses and telescopic mirrors. From 1786 he also started working with Maskelyne on methods for computing cometary paths.

During the final two decades of his life Cavendish was the acknowledged leader of British experimental physics, a figure of enormous wealth and probity. His diffidence remained extreme—the sole extant portrait of him was secretly sketched without its subject's knowledge or permission by William Alexander while a dinner guest at the Royal Society Club. Cavendish's high status and expertise made him a welcome adviser on technical matters of precision measurement and design. In spring 1790 he advised Blagden on the best means for determining the specific gravity of alcohol to fix excise duties. During the French wars in June 1796 Cavendish acted as consultant on lightning rods to defend the Purfleet arsenal and in June 1801 advised on avoiding frictional electricity in powder magazines. During this period of conservative reaction his repute was not compromised by his continuing dynastic loyalty to Charles James Fox and the whig cause, nor by conflicts at the Royal Society during the 1790s involving Banks, Blagden, and Hutton. When Priestley fled Birmingham after riots there in 1791, Cavendish kept his distance from his erstwhile colleague.

Cavendish subscribed to *Asiatic Researches*, chief organ of English orientalism, in 1792 published on Sanskrit astronomy and calendrical theory, and pursued discussions with Hutton of the Schiehallion results and the earth's density. In summer 1797 Cavendish directed a series of experiments at Clapham to determine this density using an apparatus acquired via the Cambridge professor Francis Wollaston from Michell, who had died four years earlier. Cavendish's heroic experiments, whose design was derived from Charles Coulomb's measures of electrostatic force, involved measuring the gravitational torque on a 6 ft wooden rod carrying two small lead balls acting under the pull of two large weights nearby. The apparatus was isolated and its motions observed during more than two hours through a telescope focused on a vernier scale. Cavendish concluded that the earth's density was just under 5.5 times that of water. The results were published in 1798, and helped reinforce Cavendish's reputation for conscientious precision.

This reputation encouraged the tory government to employ Cavendish in 1798, after the suspension of gold payments, to work on problems of coin wear. With the young chemist Charles Hatchett and the instrument maker John Cuthbertson, Cavendish experimented until 1802 on coins' weight loss under repeated abrasion. In early 1800 he joined the managers of the new Royal Institution and in January 1803 was elected to the Institut de France. Among other new scientific groupings which flourished in Regency London, Cavendish at Hatchett's encouragement joined the Society for the Improvement of Animal Chemistry in spring 1809. The same year he published a paper on the division of circular scales using a beam compass and microscope, a study pursued with the instrument maker Edward Troughton, composed for the Royal Society committee overseeing the Royal Observatory.

Cavendish died of inflammation of the colon on 24 February 1810 at Clapham Common, and was buried on 12 March 1810 in the family vault at All Saints' Church, Derby. His executor, Lord George Cavendish, was left the bulk of the estate of almost £1 million, his lands were left to his brother Frederick, and small bequests were made to Blagden, Dalrymple, and others. Though his taciturnity was legendary and his work mainly unpublished, Cavendish's chemical and electrical achievements were at once lauded. The water controversy was violently revived in the 1840s by several critics who urged Watt's priority. The Cavendish Society, a chemical publishing venture founded in 1846, sponsored George Wilson's lengthy biography of Cavendish in 1851 as a hagiographic riposte. Publication of Cavendish's electrical papers by James Clerk Maxwell in 1879 helped change the terms of this sterile if symptomatic priority dispute. Subsequent biographers, with access to his private manuscripts, have formed a more balanced estimate of Cavendish's significance as the outstanding natural philosopher of late eighteenth-century Britain.

SIMON SCHAFFER

Sources C. Jungnickel and R. McCormmach, *Cavendish* (1996) · G. Wilson, *Life of the Honourable Henry Cavendish* (1851) · J. C. Maxwell, ed., *Scientific papers of Henry Cavendish: electrical researches*, 2nd edn (1921) · E. Thorpe, ed., *Scientific papers of Henry Cavendish: chemical and dynamical* (1921) · A. J. Berry, *Henry Cavendish* (1960) · J. Barrow, *Sketches of the Royal Society* (1849) · *Correspondence of the late James Watt on his discovery of the theory of the composition of water*, ed. J. P. Muirhead (1846) · R. McCormmach, 'Henry Cavendish on the theory of heat', *Isis*, 79 (1988), 37–67 · R. McCormmach, 'John Michell and Henry Cavendish: weighing the stars', *British Journal for the History of Science*, 4 (1968–9), 126–55 · W. V. Harcourt, 'Address', *Report of the British Association for the Advancement of Science* (1839), 3–68 · J. Dorling, 'Cavendish's deduction of the electrostatic inverse square law', *Studies in History and Philosophy of Science*, 4 (1974), 327–48 · R. A. Harvey, 'The private library of Henry Cavendish (1731–1810)', *The Library*, 6th ser., 2 (1980), 281–92 · H. Brougham, *Lives of men of letters and science who flourished in the time of George III*, 2 vols. (1845–6), vol. 1 · *A scientific autobiography of Joseph Priestley*, ed. R. E. Schofield (1966) · *DNB*

Archives Chatsworth House, Derbyshire, instruments · Chatsworth House, Derbyshire, scientific papers · NA Canada, rough draft and text of work on heat · Royal Institution of Great Britain, London, instruments · RS, letters and papers relating to experiments on air · Yale U., Beinecke L., corresp.

Likenesses W. Alexander, pencil and ink wash drawing, *c.*1800, BM [*see illus.*] · G. F. Skill, J. Gilbert, W. Walker, and E. Walker, group portrait, pencil and wash (*Men of science living in 1807–8*), NPG · oils, Peterhouse, Cambridge

Wealth at death £821,000 stocks; £18,000 stocks in trust; £48,000 mortgages; £11,000 cash; lands: Jungnickel and McCormmach, *Cavendish*, 355

Cavendish, Sir Henry, second baronet (1732–1804), parliamentary diarist and politician, was born on 29 September 1732, the eldest son of Sir Henry Cavendish, first baronet (1707–1776), of Doveridge Hall, Derbyshire, and his first wife, Anne (*b.* 1706/7, *d.* before 1748), daughter and heir of Henry Pyne of Waterpark, co. Cork. He was educated at Eton College and at Trinity College, Dublin, and on 29 August 1757 married Sarah (1740–1807), daughter and heir of Richard Bradshaw of Cork: they had four sons and four daughters. Cavendish was descended from an illegitimate branch of the Cavendish family headed by the dukes of Devonshire, and sat in the Irish House of Commons for the Devonshire-controlled borough of Lismore for the years 1766–8, 1776–91, and 1798–1800. When unseated there in 1791 he was brought in for the government borough of Killibegs (1791–7). He was given a Lostwithiel seat at Westminster by his relative Lord Edgcumb between 1768 and 1774.

Cavendish was a prodigious parliamentary diarist. When he entered the British House of Commons press reporting of debates was forbidden, and Cavendish intended to publish his diary. He had prepared for the undertaking by learning the recently invented system of Gurney's shorthand, making such alterations as were appropriate to the parliamentary situation. The original shorthand books seem to have disappeared, but almost all were transcribed by a clerk, and fifty longhand manuscript volumes survive in the British Library (BL, Egerton MSS 215–263, 3711). Despite some obvious gaps they contain altogether more than 15,700 pages, and the total length of the diary is nearly 3,000,000 words. When the clerk found the shorthand indecipherable, he left blanks. Cavendish meticulously started to fill these in, but found time to correct only twelve volumes. He probably stopped when he decided to suspend publication, not because from 1771 newspaper reporting was in full swing, but, according to his son George in 1839, 'whilst any of the speakers in the debate were living, from motives of delicacy' (BL, Egerton MSS 263X, fol. 2X). In the mid-nineteenth century J. Wright published portions of the diary, and in the late twentieth century R. C. Simmons and P. D. G. Thomas published those parts relating to North America.

Despite this decision Cavendish proceeded to compile a similar diary for the Irish House of Commons during the period from 1776 to 1789. Now in the Library of Congress, this comprises thirty-seven longhand volumes, amounting to more than 2,000,000 words, and forty-five of the original fifty-four shorthand notebooks: as with the British diary there are obvious omissions. The fullness and accuracy of both diaries, in so far as that can be established by comparison with other sources, is remarkable. Cavendish complained of his 'peculiar and inconvenient situation' in his Westminster seat, and of other handicaps, such as noise. Yet fewer than 100 omissions have been detected among the 12,000 speeches he noted at Westminster, and he seems to have captured much of the debating verbatim.

Remarkably Cavendish contrived to be an active parliamentarian himself. He made more than 160 speeches during his six years in the British House of Commons, nearly all somehow recorded by himself. Aligning with his Cavendish relatives, he soon made his mark in opposition, this declaration on 8 May 1769 about the Middlesex election being toasted as 'Mr. Henry Cavendish's Creed' at an opposition dinner two days later: 'I do from my soul abhor, detest, and abjure, as unconstitutional and illegal that damnable doctrine and position that a resolution of the House of Commons can make, alter, suspend abrogate or annihilate the law of the land' (Wright, *Sir Henry Cavendish's Debates*, 1.428n, 433n). Sometimes Cavendish's political opinions clashed with his strong sense of constitutional propriety, as when he walked out of debates in March 1771 concerning parliamentary reporting. He spoke frequently against government over the East India Regulating Bill of 1773, but in favour of both the North ministry's American legislation of 1774 and the Quebec Bill that followed. Yet at the general election of 1774 he was reckoned an opposition MP, and, since Lord Edgcumb was now a government supporter, forfeited his seat: the diarist Horace Walpole recalled him as 'hot-headed and odd' and 'a very absurd man' (Walpole, *Memoirs*, 3.145; *Journals*, 1.201).

Cavendish, who succeeded his father in title and estates on 31 December 1776, re-entered the Dublin parliament in 1776 as an opposition MP, but was won over to government in 1779 by a place on the Irish privy council and a promise of office. This never materialized, and he rejoined the opposition in 1782, being especially critical of government financial incompetence and corruption. He returned to support of government in 1784, though opposing Pitt's Irish Trade Bill of 1785, but reverted to opposition during the Regency crisis of 1788. His final political change, back to government, came in 1790 when Sir Henry, together with three sons also Irish MPs, was won over by a peerage for his wife, Lady Cavendish becoming Baroness Waterpark on 15 June 1792. Sir Henry's financial bent was acknowledged by appointment as an Irish treasury commissioner from 1793 to 1795, when he became receiver-general of the Irish revenue, until 1801. He was a staunch supporter of the Union. Never distinguished as a debater, Cavendish carved out specialist niches for himself as an expert on finance, and also on parliamentary procedure. The hostile Sir Jonah Barrington, who commented that 'Sir Henry Cavendish had changed his politics with different governments', allowed that he enjoyed 'a reputation of profound knowledge in parliamentary precedents and points of law, in both of which he acquired so much celebrity, that he had scarcely a competitor' (Barrington, 1.134–5). Especially during the 1790s did Cavendish infuriate opposition MPs by deploying his obstructive procedural expertise. The hot-headed opposition MP at Westminster had become the cool, evasive, government spokesman at Dublin. He died at Blackrock, near Dublin, on 3 August 1804. On the death of his widow in 1807 his eldest son, Sir Richard Cavendish, became Baron Waterpark.   PETER D. G. THOMAS

Sources P. D. G. Thomas, 'The debates of the House of Commons, 1768–1774', PhD diss., U. Lond., 1958 • HoP, *Commons, 1754–90* • P. D. G. Thomas, 'The authorship of the manuscript Irish parliamentary diary (1776–89) in the Library of Congress', *EngHR*, 77 (1962), 94–5 • parliamentary diary of Henry Cavendish, 1768–74, BL, Egerton MSS 215–263, 3711 • *Debates of the House of Commons in the year 1774 on the bill for making more effectual provision for the government of the province of Quebec*, ed. J. Wright (1839) • *Sir Henry Cavendish's Debates of the House of Commons during the thirteenth parliament of Great Britain*, ed. J. Wright, 2 vols. (1841–3) • R. C. Simmons and P. D. G. Thomas, eds., *Proceedings and debates of the British parliaments respecting North America, 1754–1783*, 3–5 (1984–6) • H. Walpole, *Memoirs of the reign of King George the Third*, ed. G. F. R. Barker, 4 vols. (1894) • *The last journals of Horace Walpole*, ed. Dr Doran, rev. A. F. Steuart, 2 vols. (1910) • J. Barrington, *Historic memoirs of Ireland*, 2 vols. (1833) • GEC, *Baronetage*
Archives BL, decipherment of shorthand passages in parliamentary diaries, Add. MS 64869 • BL, parliamentary diary, Egerton MSS 215–263, 3711 • L. Cong., Irish parliamentary diary | Derbys. RO, letters to Robert Wilmont
Likenesses F. Wheatley, group portrait, oils (*The Irish House of Commons, 1780*), Leeds City Art Galleries

Cavendish, Lady Jane. *See* Cheyne, Lady Jane (1620/21–1669).

Cavendish, Sir John (d. 1381), justice, was of unknown origins. Recorded links between him and the Suffolk village of Cavendish date from only 1358, when the manor of Overhall in Cavendish was conveyed by its lord, John Odyngseles, to John Cavendish, his wife Alice, and two other persons. By then Cavendish must have been married for several years to Alice, since their son Andrew is

said to have been aged thirty when his father died in 1381. John Cavendish is first recorded in a judicial capacity in May 1350, when he was appointed to an oyer and terminer commission for Essex. A year later he served as a keeper of the peace in Essex and Suffolk. Except during the period from January 1358 to February 1361, he was continuously appointed to commissions of the peace for a wide range of East Anglian and midland counties. He sat on numerous oyer and terminer commissions, acted as one of the collectors of the tenth and fifteenth for Essex and Suffolk in 1352, and was a justice of labourers in both counties. From the 1360s onwards he occasionally featured in commissions of sewers and of array. For his services as a justice of assize and gaol delivery he received £20 a year from 1370.

From early in his career Cavendish moved in the best circles; in January 1362 he was appointed one of the guardians for the young Humphrey (IX) de Bohun, who was a minor, together with the earl of Arundel and three other men. The beginning of his practice in the bench is obscure. He was firmly established as a serjeant-at-law by 1362, when he began to authorize final concords in the common bench. But the appearances in the year books for 1347 and 1355 of a pleader named Caund, or Cand, are suspicious, and cannot be regarded as secure evidence that Cavendish had practised as a serjeant before 1362. In 1361 Edward, the Black Prince, had retained him for 100s. per annum when he still was an apprentice of the law, but halved his stipend in 1363, because Cavendish's duties as a serjeant did not allow him to devote enough time to the prince's affairs. On 27 November 1371 Cavendish was appointed a puisne justice of the common bench, and on 15 July 1372 he became chief justice of the king's bench, and was knighted. Henceforth he regularly acted as a trier of petitions in parliament. In addition to his annual salary of 60 marks he was awarded a yearly allowance of 100 marks in December 1372. Immediately after the accession of Richard II, Cavendish was confirmed in his office of chief justice, on 26 June 1377.

Cavendish's judgments and opinions left their mark in the year books of the latter years of Edward's reign. In 1365, for instance, he engaged in a discussion with the chief justice of the common bench, Sir Robert Thorpe, about the difference between a statute to which the Commons had assented, and an ordinance which the king could make with the consent of the Lords alone, and rejected Thorpe's opinion that such an ordinance could become statute if the king commanded it. But his principal claim to fame in legal circles probably lies in his dictum in a land action in which he was invited to estimate a lady's age in court. Cavendish refused to do so, on the remarkable grounds that 'there is no man in England who can with certainty say whether a woman is of full age or not, for there are women of thirty who try to pass themselves off as eighteen' (year book 50 Edward III, Hilary, fol. 6, pl. 12).

Cavendish also attained fame through the manner of his death. During the peasants' revolt of 1381 his manor in Cavendish was looted on 12 June by a rebel band under the leadership of John Wraw. On the same day Cavendish was holding routine sessions of assize in nearby Bury St Edmunds. The inhabitants of Bury, habitually at odds with the abbey, were already in an explosive mood, in particular over the succession to the abbacy, when the rising reached their town. Against the strong opposition of the burgesses, Prior John Cambridge, supported by the majority of the convent, and very likely by John Cavendish too, nominated the sub-prior John Timworth as the new abbot. Links between the abbey and the judge dated back at least to 1357, when Cavendish was one of the justices appointed by the abbot to hear and terminate all pleas of the crown within the borough. At some stage he acquired a house in the town, and this was sacked by the rebels in 1381. Hearing of the approach of the insurgents, Cavendish and Cambridge fled from Bury. But on 14 June Cavendish was intercepted at Lakenheath, as he tried to escape in the direction of Ely. His capture was abetted by the villagers, who bore a personal grudge against him for having been one of the commissioners sent there in 1371 to deal with a riot against taxation. As soon as the rebels captured Cavendish they beheaded him, and stuck his head on a pole. Prior John Cambridge was captured in Newmarket and likewise killed. With both their victims' heads on poles, the rebels returned to Bury St Edmunds on 15 June, and there staged a ghastly 'puppet-play', vividly described by the almoner of the abbey: 'They put the head of the prior to the justice's head, now to his ear as though seeking advice, now to his mouth as though showing friendship, wishing in this way to make a mock of the friendship and counsel which was between them during their lives' (Arnold, 3.128).

Shortly before his death Cavendish had made his will, dated at Bury St Edmunds on 5 April 1381, in which he bequeathed his personal belongings to his son Andrew, Andrew's wife Rose, and their daughter Margaret, and to charitable purposes. His body was to be buried in Cavendish church beside his wife Alice, who had predeceased him. His son Andrew, who had been knight of the shire for Suffolk in 1371, and became sheriff of Suffolk and Norfolk in 1385, succeeded his father in the manor of Overhall, together with the advowson of Cavendish church, and the Suffolk manor of Fakenham Aspes.   HERBERT EIDEN

Sources Chancery records · CIPM, 4, 10, 15, 17, 19 · Year books Edward III, 1347, 1355, 1362, 1374, 1376 · M. C. B. Dawes, ed., Register of Edward, the Black Prince, PRO, 4 (1933) · F. Palgrave, ed., The antient kalendars and inventories of the treasury of his majesty's exchequer, RC, 1 (1836) · F. Devon, ed. and trans., Issue roll of Thomas de Brantingham, RC (1835) · G. O. Sayles, ed., Select cases in the court of king's bench, 7 vols., SeldS, 55, 57–8, 74, 76, 82, 88 (1936–71), vol. 6 · T. Arnold, ed., Memorials of St Edmund's Abbey, 3, Rolls Series, 96 (1896) · T. Ruggles, 'Notices of the manor of Cavendish, in Suffolk and the Cavendish family while possessed of that manor', Archaeologia, 11 (1794), 50–62 · Baker, Serjeants · Sainty, Judges · H. Eiden, 'In der Knechtschaft werdet ihr verharren …': Ursachen und Verlauf des englischen Bauernaufstandes von 1381 (Trier, 1995) · H. Eiden, 'Der Richter, der seinen Kopf verlor. Leben und Sterben des Sir John Cavendish († 1381), chief justice of the king's bench', Landesgeschichte als multidisziplinäre Wissenschaft: Festgabe für Franz Irsigler zum 60. Geburtstag, ed. D. Ebeling and others (Trier, 2001), 197–222 · M. M. Taylor, ed., Some sessions of the peace in Cambridgeshire in the fourteenth century, 1340, 1380–1383, Cambridge Antiquarian Society, octavo publications, 55 (1942) · Holdsworth, Eng. law, vol. 7 (2nd edn) · B. H. Putnam, The place in legal history of Sir William Shareshull (1950) · John, Lord Campbell, The lives of the chief justices of England, 1 (1849) · Foss, Judges

Wealth at death held the manor of Overhall in Cavendish, the advowson of Cavendish church, the manor of Fakenham Aspes, and some meadows and pastures in these villages: CIPM, 15, no. 476, 197–8 · items bequeathed: 'un lit de worstede … un lit vermayl … un coupe d'argent … un lit de saperye poudre de popyngays', £40 to the church of Cavendish, £20 to the poor people of his estates: will, Archaeologia, 11 (1794), 55–6

Cavendish, Lord John (1732–1796), politician, was born on 22 October 1732 at Berkeley House, Piccadilly (soon afterwards rebuilt as Devonshire House), the fourth son of William Cavendish, third duke of Devonshire (1698–1755), politician, of Chatsworth, Derbyshire, and Catharine (c.1700–1777), daughter and heir of John Hoskins, steward to the duke of Bedford, of Oxted, Surrey.

Early career Cavendish was educated in Hackney and, from 1750, at Peterhouse, Cambridge. On his graduation three years later his tutor, the Revd William Mason, addressed to him the elegy 'To a young nobleman leaving the university' (Works of William Mason, 1.93–6). As a member of one of the great English aristocratic families he was brought into parliament for the government borough of Weymouth and Melcombe Regis in 1754 and, as a court whig, he of course supported the premiership of his eldest brother, the fourth duke, from November 1756 to June 1757. Having been given a seat on the family interest at Knaresborough in 1761 he reprobated George III's removal of his brother's name from the list of the privy council late the following year. He spoke against the peace preliminaries on 10 December 1762 and soon became active in the opposition group of 'young friends' who gathered around the duke of Newcastle. Following Devonshire's death in 1764 he assumed the headship of the Cavendish dynasty, directing its political and electoral interests, and he remained the most prominent member of the family in national affairs, even after the fifth duke came of age in 1769.

Cavendish, who opposed the Regency Bill in May 1765, was in July of that year appointed a junior lord of the Treasury by the new first lord, the marquess of Rockingham; he was credited with making the introduction to the latter that was to ensure Edmund Burke's adhesion to the connection. Yet, suspicious of William Pitt, who replaced Rockingham as prime minister a year later, and having been 'a long time tired in the confinement of my employment' (BL, Add. MS 32976, fol. 269), as he informed Newcastle, he willingly resigned with his chief in July 1766. In the autumn, when the Rockinghams took alarm at the king's dismissal of Lord Edgcumbe, Cavendish urged that those who had stayed in office under the earl of Chatham (as Pitt had become) should now resign, and he made his farewell to administration in the Commons on 25 November 1766. During negotiations with other opposition groups in 1767 he was hostile to joining the Bedford whigs. Horace Walpole, who blamed him for the failure of the initiative, observed that he was the most 'intractable man of all' (Walpole, 3.128) and that he adversely influenced Rockingham with his 'violent and evil councils' (ibid., 167). After the collapse of his expensive attempt to contest Lancaster at the general election of 1768 Rockingham put him up for York, where he was returned unopposed.

Rockingham whig Supporting his colleagues on the Middlesex election, on 15 December 1768 Cavendish spoke with what Lady Mary Coke, who was present, described as 'a moderation, candour, & politeness, as is seldom practiced in that House' (*Letters and Journals*, 2.427). He was indeed a frequent and capable speaker, if apt to be pernickety in debate, and he was recognized as one of the principal spokesmen for the Rockinghamite opposition. In addition he usually divided with his colleagues, sometimes acting as a teller, and was involved in preparing motions and general party discussions. However, like his leader he was not immune to social distractions, and Burke had to write to Rockingham to beg him to summon Cavendish for the beginning of the 1770 session: 'He ought to be allowed a certain decent and reasonable portion of Foxhunting to put him into wind for the Parliamentary Race he is to run—but any thing more is intollerable' (*Correspondence*, 3.89). Wary of expressions of public opinion that might bind the party to unsavoury principles, Cavendish nevertheless helped to set up the county meeting held at York in September 1769, when he limited himself to calling for a redress of grievances by the king. A mainstream Rockinghamite, in parliamentary speeches about this time he defended the rights of electors against the growing power of the executive and vindicated party as a means of opposing the unconstitutional advisers of the crown. He declined to present a clerical petition calling for relief from the necessity of subscribing to the Thirty-Nine Articles but spoke in favour of wider religious toleration on 6 February 1772. He attacked the North ministry's proposed legislation on the East India Company on 18 December 1772 and 23 March 1773 but expressed guarded support for their actions in response to the Boston tea party on 14 and 25 March 1774.

Though in January 1774 Cavendish had commented to Rockingham that 'it is a comical state we are in' and that 'I see nothing to be wished for but an honourable retreat' (Rockingham MSS, R1-1478, 1479) he became the party leader in the Commons later that year, in place of the ailing William Dowdeswell, who died in 1775. On 5 December 1774 he therefore moved the amendment to the address, as he did at the start of the following two sessions, and steadily opposed the government's prosecution of the war against the American rebels, for instance in his speech on 29 February 1776 on the employment of German mercenaries. Suggesting privately to Rockingham that such issues should be raised outside parliament in order to strengthen the hand of opposition in the chamber, he observed that the 'evil consequences come on so gradually, & are so mixed with circumstances of a different nature, that they will not warm people soon enough' (Rockingham MS R1-1586). Though privy to the decision to secede formally in late 1776 he advocated returning to parliament early the following year, however ridiculous a figure the party would cut, as he thought that 'the nation had

a right to be informed of its true state, & that the account should be balanced like Debtor & Creditor of the good & evil accruing from the last year's transactions' (ibid., R1-1753). He vindicated the opposition's conduct in the Commons on 16 April 1777, when he attacked the scale of expenditure on the civil list. He seconded the amendment to the address on 18 November 1777 but by that time he had been superseded as leader in the Commons by the party's dynamic new recruit, Charles James Fox.

Chancellor of the exchequer Cavendish, who joined Brooks's Club in July 1779 and was later a founder member of the Whig Club, on 17 June moved for all British forces to be recalled from North America and again, on 25 November 1779, led the opposition to the address. At the Yorkshire meeting on 28 March 1780 he condemned the more radical reforms proposed by Wyvill's association, and in the house on 8 May he spoke against (but voted for) shorter parliaments. His refusal to bow to pressure from Mason and others to sign the association's petition for a time looked set to jeopardize his return for York at the general election that year. He stifled a similar campaign in Northamptonshire and, although he was a member of the Westminster association, he played almost no part in its activities. Having condemned the outbreak of war with the Netherlands, on 25 January, and having vindicated his friends' attitude to American independence, on 12 June 1781, he seconded the amendment for ending the war altogether, on 22 February 1782. It was he who on 8 March brought forward the resolutions censuring ministers, the first of which was defeated only by 226 votes to 216, thus precipitating North's resignation. Though reluctant to take office he was sworn of the privy council and was made chancellor of the exchequer (27 March) in Rockingham's brief second ministry. On 2 May he presented the king's message relating to alterations in the civil list—part of the government's economical reform programme—and on 22 May he announced several tax changes. After Rockingham's death on 1 July he resigned with those of his friends who were unable to work under his successor, Lord Shelburne, although had he been willing to become home secretary, Fox might have remained in office. He explained to the Commons on 9 July that he differed with the new ministerial system and he relinquished his position the following day. Chosen as one of the eight supporters on Rockingham's mausoleum at Wentworth Woodhouse, Yorkshire, it was noted by North in 1782 that he was 'more in the confidence of Lord Rockingham than any other person' (*Correspondence of George III*, 5.381).

A similar judgement was made in relation to the new leader the following year by Nathaniel Wraxall, who remarked that it was Cavendish 'whom Fox always selected for special and important occasions, as his high character for integrity and uprightness spread a sort of veil over the irregularities of his party' (*Historical and Posthumous Memoirs*, 2.424). Thus he successfully moved the amendment against the peace preliminaries (224 votes to 208) on 17 February 1783, and the government fell after being defeated on his censure motion (207 to 190) four days later. Despite what Burke's son called his 'extreme aversion to having any thing to do with Courts' (*Correspondence*, 5.53) he resumed his former office (2 April) under the duke of Portland (husband of his niece Dorothy) in the Fox–North coalition. In a measure inherited from his predecessor William Pitt he introduced on 16 April a loan bill to raise about £12.5 million by means of an annuity and a lottery. On opening his only proper budget, on 26 May, he raised new stamp taxes, including a controversial one on receipts. His additional duties on the register of births, marriages, and deaths, and even on quack medicines, earned him ridicule in several satirical prints. As well as other financial matters, notably in continuing the policy of substituting salaries for fees in public offices and reducing the number of sinecures, he held out against making extravagant provision for the prince of Wales. On 6 May he voted for Pitt's parliamentary reform proposals, but on 17 June he opposed the ensuing legislation and instead recommended on 4 July further measures of economical reform. He spoke in favour of Fox's India Bill on 20 November and left office with Fox after its defeat in the Lords the following month, justifying his party's policies in the Commons, in speeches on 19 December 1783 (his last day at the exchequer) and 3 February 1784.

Later life and career assessment One of the high profile 'Fox's martyrs', who lost their seats at the general election of 1784, Cavendish retired to his residence at Billing Hall, Great Billing, Northamptonshire; that year he received the attention of a published verse *Epistle* from Elizabeth Ryves. Although he wanted to keep out of politics and told Georgiana Cavendish, duchess of Devonshire, that it would 'kill him' to return to government (Bickley, 235) he would have become chancellor in the Foxite ministry that the prince of Wales intended to appoint under the—in the end abortive—regency in 1789. He did not return to the Commons until May 1794, when the death of his brother Lord George Augustus Cavendish created a vacancy for the seat that the family traditionally held in Derbyshire. He made little mark in this coda to his political career, during which, having broken with Fox, he followed Portland in supporting the Pitt ministry's war against revolutionary France. He died, unmarried, as the result of a stroke, at Twickenham Park, Middlesex, the house of his last surviving brother, Frederick, on 18 December 1796 and was buried in the family vault in All Saints', Derby, on 26 December. By his will he made Lord Frederick *Cavendish (1729–1803), army officer, his universal legatee, but he left a sizeable bequest to Burke, who was glad to have been reconciled to him shortly before his death.

Burke had latterly differed with Cavendish, who, in spite of admiring the *Reflections* (1790), doubted the existence of a Jacobin threat in Britain. Yet Burke left several eulogies of his old friend, whom he described as 'exactly what we conceive an English Nobleman of the old Stamp' to have been (*Correspondence*, 9.214). Without altogether excusing Cavendish for being 'unambitious almost to a fault' and 'cold in his exterior' (ibid., 213) he considered him:

a man who would have adorned the best of commonwealths at the brightest of periods. An accomplished scholar, and an excellent critic … with a sound judgment; a memory singularly attentive and exact, perfectly conversant in business, and particularly in that of finance; of great integrity, great tenderness and sensibility of heart, [and] with friendships few and unalterable. (Bickley, 236–7)

Walpole, who recorded that his 'fair little person, and the quaintness with which he untreasured as by rote the stores of his memory, occasioned George Selwyn to call him *the learned canary bird*', admitted his integrity and talents but sourly emphasized his arrogance and obstinacy, judging that to 'be first in however small a circle was his wish—but in that circle he must be absolute' (Walpole, 2.66). Yet neither the hyperbole of Burke nor the rancour of Walpole can mask the verdict of Cavendish as a decent and honourable politician who was a valuable member of the parliamentary opposition and an effective minister. However, he had a narrow conception of party; he once told Walpole that he 'wished the opposition was reduced to six or seven, who could depend on one another' (ibid., 2.127) and on another occasion he was reported to have stated a preference for Rockingham's party remaining a 'snug chaste corps' (Lock, 520). He certainly had only a limited desire to see his clan enter into executive coalitions, being reluctant to court fickle royal favour or to engage with developing public opinion. As he wrote to Burke in 1790, 'our original sett have allways contended for that temperate resistance to the abuse of power, as should not endanger the publick peace, or put all good order into hazard [sic]', and he found himself more and more taken with an aphorism of Tacitus: 'Between the extremes of bluff contumacy and repellent servility, to walk a straight road' (*Correspondence*, 6.161).

S. M. Farrell

Sources Chatsworth House, Derbyshire, Devonshire MSS · BL, Newcastle MSS, Add. MSS 32935–33070 · Rockingham MSS, Sheff. Arch., Wentworth Woodhouse muniments · *The correspondence of Edmund Burke*, ed. T. W. Copeland and others, 10 vols. (1958–78) · H. Walpole, *Memoirs of the reign of King George III*, ed. D. Jarrett, 4 vols. (2000) · *The correspondence of King George the Third from 1760 to December 1783*, ed. J. Fortescue, 6 vols. (1927–8) · Cobbett, *Parl. hist.*, vols. 15–24 · G. Thomas, earl of Albemarle [G. T. Keppel], *Memoirs of the marquis of Rockingham and his contemporaries*, 2 vols. (1852) · *Memorials and correspondence of Charles James Fox*, ed. J. Russell, 4 vols. (1853–7) · *The historical and the posthumous memoirs of Sir Nathaniel William Wraxall, 1772–1784*, ed. H. B. Wheatley, 5 vols. (1884) · *The letters and journals of Lady Mary Coke*, ed. J. A. Home, 4 vols. (1889–96) · *Autobiography and political correspondence of Augustus Henry, third duke of Grafton*, ed. W. R. Anson (1898) · *The works of William Mason M. A.*, 4 vols. (1811) · E. Ryves, *An epistle to the right honourable Lord John Cavendish, late chancellor of the exchequer* (1784) · F. Bickley, *The Cavendish family* (1911), 226–38 · F. O'Gorman, *The rise of party in England: the Rockingham whigs, 1760–1782* (1975) · J. Cannon, *The Fox–North coalition: crisis of the constitution, 1782–4* (1969) · F. P. Lock, *Edmund Burke*, 1 (1998) · *GM*, 1st ser., 2 (1732), 1030 · *GM*, 1st ser., 66 (1796), 1062 · *The Times* (21 Dec 1796) · *DNB* · *IGI* · Venn, *Alum. Cant.*

Archives Chatsworth House, Derbyshire, letters · Trustees of the Chatsworth Settlement, Chatsworth House, Derbyshire, letters | BL, letters to duke of Newcastle, Add. MSS 32935–33070 *passim* · BL, letters to Lady Spencer · Borth. Inst., Hickleton MSS A1.2.6 · Borth. Inst., letters to Lady Ponsonby · Sheff. Arch., corresp. with Edmund Burke · Sheff. Arch., letters to Lord Rockingham · U. Nott. L., letters to duke of Portland, PWF 2652–2676

Likenesses J. Reynolds, portrait, 1767 · J. Sayers, caricature, etching, pubd 1782 (after his earlier work), NPG · J. Grozer, mezzotint, pubd 1786 (after J. Reynolds), BM; repro. in Bickley, *Cavendish family*, facing p. 226 · J. Sayers, etching, pubd 1787, NPG · C. Bretherton, engraving, BM · J. Nollekens, bust, Rockingham Mausoleum, Wentworth Woodhouse · G. Tomlinson, oils (after J. Reynolds, 1767), Hardwick Hall, Derbyshire

Wealth at death see PRO, death duty registers, IR 26/4, no. 182

Cavendish, Louise Frederica Augusta, duchess of Devonshire [*née* Countess Louise Friederike Auguste von Alten; *other married name* Louise Frederica Augusta Montagu, duchess of Manchester] (1832–1911), society figure, was born on 15 January 1832, the second of the three daughters of Karl Franz Victor, Count von Alten, of Hanover, and his wife, Hermine de Schminke. On 22 July 1852 she married, in the palace chapel at Hanover, and subsequently at the British embassy, William Drogo Montagu (1823–1890), then Viscount Mandeville. They had two sons and three daughters.

Lady Mandeville, accounted one of the great beauties of the period, rapidly acquired a position of social pre-eminence and attracted admirers from across the political spectrum. Lord Granville wrote to her that 'you are irresistible for man, woman, and I should think beast. I can conceive, if it was not for your grande dame much-too-big-for-any-street-to-hold-me-look, being passionately in love with you' (Kennedy, 24). Duchess of Manchester from 1855, she served as mistress of the robes to Queen Victoria under Derby's ministry of 1858–9. Victoria, who had initially been pleased to have a German in her household, rapidly came to disapprove of the duchess, and urged the princess of Wales to drop the acquaintance, as she had 'done more harm to Society from her *tone*, her love of admiration and "fast" style, than almost anyone' (Magnus, 110). The duchess, however, remained one of the principal members of the Marlborough House set, sharing with the prince of Wales a passion for gambling and racing, and a willingness to overlook discreet infidelity.

Her liaison with Spencer Compton *Cavendish, marquess of Hartington (1833–1908), began in the early 1860s, when she reclaimed him from the embraces of the courtesan Catherine ('Skittles') Walters, and lasted until their marriage some thirty years later. The relationship was well-known in aristocratic society, but never drew public attention. The duchess was a convinced tory, though she cultivated politicians of differing opinions, including Lord Clarendon and Sir Charles Dilke, for the information they could provide. She devoted herself to inspiring political ambition in her notoriously indolent lover, and to fulfilling her own ambition of seeing him prime minister. Liberals regarded her with suspicion and Gladstone saw her influence as a barrier to Hartington's acceptance of his radical proposals. Of her intelligence, opinions differed: Dilke thought her lacking the 'clearness of head' necessary to make her useful to Hartington, but Baron von Eckardstein regarded her as 'one of the cleverest and most capable women that I ever met' (Eckardstein, 123).

Manchester died in 1890, and, with no show of

Louise Frederica Augusta Cavendish, duchess of Devonshire (1832–1911), by Franz Xaver Winterhalter, 1859

unseemly haste, on 16 August 1892 she married Hartington, who had become the eighth duke of Devonshire in the previous year. Widely referred to as 'the Double Duchess', she was one of the dominant figures of London society: awesome and formidable, she was admired and respected more than she was liked. Her entertainments at Chatsworth, at Devonshire House, and at the racecourses were lavish and spectacular, particularly the fancy-dress ball which was her contribution to the diamond jubilee celebrations of 1897. A passion for bridge in her later years earned her the unkind sobriquet 'Ponte Vecchio', though it is unlikely that anyone would have used it in her presence. Devonshire died in 1908; three years later Louise Devonshire had a seizure at the Sandown racecourse, and died the following day, 15 July 1911, at Sir Edgar Vincent's house, Esher Place, Esher, Surrey. She was buried on 18 July at Edensor, Derbyshire. K. D. REYNOLDS

Sources GEC, *Peerage* · A. L. Kennedy, ed., *My dear duchess: social and political letters to the duchess of Manchester, 1858–1869* (1956) · Baron von Eckardstein [Hermann Eckardstein], *Ten years at the court of St James* (1921) · A. Leslie, *Edwardians in love* (1972) · P. Magnus, *King Edward the Seventh* (1964) · Gladstone, *Diaries* · S. Gwynn and G. Tuckwell, *Life of Charles Dilke*, 1 (1917) · H. Blythe, *Skittles* (1970) · S. Murphy, *The duchess of Devonshire's ball* (1984) · *Dearest child: letters between Queen Victoria and the princess royal, 1858–1861*, ed. R. Fulford (1964)

Likenesses F. X. Winterhalter, portrait, 1859, Royal Collection [*see illus.*] · R. Thorburn, portrait, Chatsworth House, Derbyshire · drawing, repro. in Kennedy, *My dear duchess* · photograph, Hult. Arch. · photographs, repro. in Murphy, *Duchess* · two portraits, Royal Collection

Wealth at death £73,791 2s. 10d.: probate, 26 Aug 1911, CGPLA Eng. & Wales

Cavendish, Lucy Caroline [Lady Frederick Cavendish] (1841–1925). *See under* Cavendish, Lord Frederick Charles (1836–1882).

Cavendish [*née* Lucas], **Margaret, duchess of Newcastle upon Tyne** (1623?–1673), writer, was born at St John's Abbey, near Colchester, Essex, the youngest child of Thomas Lucas (*c.*1573–1625) and Elizabeth (*d.* 1647), daughter of John Leighton, of London. Her grandfather Sir Thomas Lucas (*c.*1531–1611) is often confused with her father, who bore no title, though the mistaken notion that he was earl of Colchester persists. Margaret in the autobiographical 'A true relation' firmly asserts that her father was only a gentleman and specifically denies that he purchased a title, even though he had the financial wherewithal to buy one. Margaret's oldest brother, Sir Thomas *Lucas (1597/8–1648/9), was born out of wedlock, as her father was banished in 1597 for duelling and was not able to marry Elizabeth Leighton until his return to England after James I ascended the throne.

Early life 'A true relation' paints a picture of a secure and harmonious family, whose happiness was shattered by civil war. Margaret's widowed mother is depicted as being 'of a grave Behaviour, and [of] such a Magestick Grandeur' that the common people held her in awe (Cavendish, 'True relation', 48). Her mother managed what came to her by jointure with little or no male help and provided Margaret with an example of how a woman might act to protect family interests. For instance, she was effective in shielding her son's inheritance from the court of wards by using the political connections of her son-in-law, Peter Killigrew. The family lived for about half the year in Colchester and the other half in London, enjoying the pleasures of 'Spring-garden, Hide-park, and the like places' (ibid., 45). Margaret's education was somewhat rudimentary; she had private tutors for 'all sorts of virtues, such as singing, dancing, playing on music, reading, writing [needle] working, and the like', but this may have been merely the 'ancient decayed gentlewoman', who taught her to read and write (Grant, 37). Her brother John *Lucas, later first Baron Lucas of Shenfield (1606–1671), seems to have been a contentious Colchester landowner rather than a carefree youth. His antagonism towards the lower orders may have provided the motivation for a raid on his home during the Stour valley riots on 22 August 1642 when he attempted to leave his house to join Charles I with men and supplies.

It may have been the dangers of war which caused Margaret to leave Colchester to live in Oxford with her sister Catherine Pye in the autumn of 1642. It is likely that her mother hoped that Margaret would find a place at court, then resident in Oxford. In 1643 Margaret became a maid of honour to Queen Henrietta Maria, and in 1644 accompanied the queen into exile in Paris.

Marriage In 'A true relation' Margaret says that she was bashful and painfully shy at court, qualities perhaps reflected in her plays, as with the character Lady Bashful in *Love's Adventures* (1662). Nevertheless, it was at court in Paris that Margaret met her future husband, William

Margaret Cavendish, duchess of Newcastle upon Tyne (1623?–1673), by Peter Ludwig van Schuppen, pubd 1668 (after Abraham van Diepenbeck, *c.*1655–8)

*Cavendish, marquess of Newcastle upon Tyne (*bap.* 1593, *d.* 1676), a widower whose first wife had died in 1643. He was also the defeated royalist commander at Marston Moor, and had left England in July 1644 and arrived in Paris in April 1645. After a courtship that was opposed by Henrietta Maria and many of his friends, they were married in late November or early December 1645 by the future bishop John Cosin, in the private chapel of the English resident at the French court, Sir Richard Browne. They had no children, though some effort was made by the physician Richard Farrer to treat her failure to conceive. The court physician, Sir Theodore Mayerne, examined her for 'general ill-health' and dissuaded Newcastle from further fertility treatments. Five of Newcastle's children from his first marriage had survived infancy, two of whom wrote *The Concealed Fancies* (*c.*1645), a comedy poking good-natured fun at the newly-weds. Margaret's marriage portion was £2000, but that could not be paid immediately. The bride and groom moved to Rotterdam, staying there for six months before moving to Antwerp and leasing a house from the widow of the painter Peter Paul Rubens. In

August 1648 her brother Sir Charles *Lucas (1612/13–1648) was summarily executed after the siege of Colchester. In November 1651 Margaret travelled to England with her brother-in-law, Sir Charles Cavendish, hoping to gain something from her husband's sequestered estates by appealing to the committee for compounding. The committee denied her request on 10 December 1651 because she had married her husband after he had become a delinquent and because he was, in their view, 'the greatest traitor to the state' (*Calendar of the Proceedings of the Committee for Compounding*). While in England, presumably awaiting the outcome of Sir Charles Cavendish's attempt to compound, Margaret published *Poems and Fancies* (1653; rev. edns, 1664 and 1668), the first edition containing verse descriptions of her atomic theory, which resembles that of Walter Charleton. Her atomism is derived from Epicurus and her use of poetry to explain her views aligns with Lucretius's notion that poetry can produce intellectual pleasure, the highest good. However, *Philosophical Fancies* (1653) repudiates her atomic theory. Her work certainly made an impact. In April 1653 Dorothy Osborne wrote to William Temple commenting on this event and Margaret's eccentric sense of dress: 'a book of Poems newly come out, made by Lady Newcastle ... tis ten times more Extravagant then her dresse' (Osborne, 75). The following month Osborne opined to the same correspondent that there were 'many soberer People in Bedlam' (ibid., 79).

After spending eighteen months in England, Margaret returned to Antwerp, where according to her later writings they endured some financial hardship. Nevertheless, Margaret continued to write and publish. *The World's Olio* (1655; repr. 1671) is a collection of brief observations on a wide variety of topics and includes caustic remarks on historical and mythological figures. *Philosophical and Physical Opinions* (1655; rev. edn, 1663) explains her materialist natural philosophy. Margaret agrees with Hobbes that incorporeal substance makes no sense and that all natural change involves change in motion. In her 'mature philosophy' she parts company with Hobbes, believing that change in motion is not caused by external forces but rather by 'vital agreement or sympathetic influence of parts, as within a single organism' (O'Neill, 261). In 1668 she reworked the second edition as *Grounds of Natural Philosophy* in a more tentative and plainer style than the original. *Nature's Pictures* (1656; rev. edn, 1671) is mostly a collection of love stories in verse and prose, which considers issues of sex and gender. There is, in addition, satire on disparate topics, such as the use of tobacco. The first edition contains the much-cited autobiography, 'A true relation', which was not reprinted in the second edition because she believed it lessened her dignity.

Newcastle followed Charles II back to England at the Restoration. She returned shortly afterwards and was evidently disappointed that her husband had failed to obtain the court office she thought he deserved. *The Lotterie* may have been written by Margaret at this time for a private royal performance, as part of a plan to secure royal favour. Margaret has been confused with the M. Cavendish who

was a member of Katherine Philips's Society of Friendship, but this was Lady Mary Butler, a daughter of the first duke of Ormond, who after her marriage to William, Lord Cavendish, in 1662 was known as Lady Mary Cavendish, until her husband succeeded as fourth earl of Devonshire in 1684. In September 1660 Newcastle secured the passage of an act restoring his estates. This improvement in Newcastle's finances allowed Margaret to secure the first of many improvements to her jointure to £1125 per annum and a life interest in Bolsover Castle. Margaret and her husband left London towards the end of 1660. Retirement in the country suited Margaret's temperament and accorded well with the image of voluntary seclusion that became a staple of her self-presentation.

More works were to follow from Margaret's country retreat. *Plays* (1662), like *Nature's Pictures*, considers issues of sex and gender, often in the context of courtship and marriage. It includes *Bell in campo* which contains a woman who goes to war and in so doing recalls the 'Assaulted and Pursued Chastity' found in *Nature's Pictures*. Margaret, according to Battigelli, thought of herself in terms of a military leader and understood Henrietta Maria to be an example of a woman who led an army. Margaret's *Orations of divers sorts* (1662; 2nd edn, 1668) contains exemplary speeches to be delivered on set occasions. It includes 'Female orations' in which she explores the following questions without resolving them. Are women in fact subordinate to men in society? If so, is the cause of this insubordination a natural inequality between the sexes or a lack of opportunity for women, particularly as regards education? *CCXI sociable Letters* (1664) contains readable, mostly fictional letters addressed by one woman to another, sometimes cast as brief essays and sometimes in the form of small narratives or dialogues. In many cases the letters function as commentary on marriage, infidelity, and divorce, and they frequently offer women warnings against marriage, similar to those to be seen in Margaret's other works. *Philosophical Letters* (1664) critiques the writings of René Descartes, J. B. van Helmont, Thomas Hobbes, and Henry More. Prior to this volume Margaret had not engaged in direct dispute with other philosophers. *Observations upon Experimental Philosophy* (1666; repr., 1668) attacks Robert Hooke's *Micrographia* and contains 'The description of a new blazing world', a much discussed work of science fiction notable for its depiction of Margaret as two separate but interacting characters: an empress and the duchess of Newcastle. This was published as a separate edition in 1668 entitled *The Description of a New World, called the Blazing-World*.

During the 1660s Margaret became more actively involved in the running of the ducal estate. She exerted her influence in part directly and in part through the management of Francis Topp, who had married her maid-in-waiting and confidante, Elizabeth Chaplain. The increase in estate revenues saw Margaret acquire further improvements to her jointure in January 1668, when the additions included the mansion at Clerkenwell, and two augmentations in 1670. Other family members, including Newcastle's daughter Lady Jane Cheyne, felt that this was a ploy to better herself financially in expectation of the duke's death.

In 1667 Margaret and Newcastle made a visit to London. Increasingly, he had become known as a playwright, with two pre-war plays being revived successfully in the 1660s. In spring 1667 his new play *The Humorous Lovers* was produced. Further, *The Life of William Cavendish* (1667; repr., 1675, and translated as *De vita et rebus gestis principis Guilielmi Duicis Novo-castrensis* in 1668) was due to come into print that year, and they both may have wanted to use the visit to call attention to its publication. The *Life* was a canny apologia for her husband's military career and a description of life in exile in Antwerp, which has been much used by historians. On 23 May she received an invitation to visit the Royal Society, duly attending on 30 May to watch the scientific demonstrations offered her by such notables as Robert Boyle and Robert Hooke, and generally impressing the members of the society. Margaret, more than Newcastle, was the centre of attention during the visit to London. Samuel Pepys compared her to Queen Kristina of Sweden, who was known for her cross-dressing. That comparison was apt, for Sir Charles Lyttelton, writing of a visit made by the duke and duchess of York to Nottinghamshire in August 1665, noted that Margaret 'was dressed in a vest, and instead of courtesies, made legs and bows' (Grant, 184). During the trip to London she met again Mary Evelyn, wife of the diarist and daughter of Sir Richard Browne, who 'was surprised to find so much extravagancy and vanity in any person not confined within four walls'. Evelyn found Margaret's speech full of 'oaths and obscenity' and suggested that she was a flirt, or at least 'more than necessarily submissive' where men were concerned. Margaret often wrote about her love of creating unusual fashions in dress for herself and there is ample evidence that she was taken to be a physically attractive woman throughout her life. Even Mary Evelyn admitted that she had 'a good shape, which she may truly boast of' (*Diary and Correspondence*, 731). Pepys concurred, spotting her on 26 April 1667 while in her coach 'naked necked, without anything about it, and a black juste-au-corps; she seemed to me a very comely woman' (Pepys, 8.186–7).

Margaret continued to publish work following her sojourn in London. *Plays Never before Printed* (1668) continues themes found in her first collection of plays. In addition, it sometimes ridicules the Restoration rake hero, rejecting this figure in favour of a less cynical and more sincere lover. Thus the crass Monsieur Take-Pleasure in *The Convent of Pleasure* is held up to scorn and the sincere, if cross-dressed, Prince is praiseworthy. Margaret, in this play, as elsewhere in her fiction and drama, inverts or transforms plots found in Shakespeare's plays. In the case of *The Convent*, the circumstances of the male and female *Love's Labour's Lost* are exchanged.

Margaret Cavendish died on 15 December 1673 at her home, Welbeck Abbey, Nottinghamshire, and was buried in London on 7 January 1674 in Westminster Abbey. In addition to ordering an elaborate funeral procession that wound through the streets of London, her husband arranged to have a volume of letters and poems published in her honour, *Letters and Poems in Honour of the Incomparable Princess, Margaret, Duchess of Newcastle* (1676).

Reputation It is difficult to gauge what Margaret's literary reputation was during her lifetime. Osborne says no more on the subject than is quoted above, and others, for the most part, discuss the writer but pay scant attention to the work. Bathsua Makin, writing in the year of Margaret's death, probably was more interested in the current state of education for women than in her achievements, when she wrote, 'the present Duchess of New-Castle, by her own genius, rather than any timely instruction, over-tops many grave Grown-men' (Makin, *An Essay to Revive the Antient Education of Gentlewomen*, 1673, repr. 1980, 10). *The Life of William Cavendish* was read carefully by some contemporaries. It was used as a source by the historian John Rushworth and was employed as a model by Lucy Hutchinson for her life of her own husband. Elizabeth Pepys recommended it to Samuel Pepys on 18 March 1668. It was reprinted once shortly after the death of the duke, and it is likely that the publisher expected to make a profit from sales rather than from any subsidy. Margaret's other books were not so reprinted.

By the middle of the eighteenth century a shift took place in the literary world by which Margaret came to be seen as a harmless, even delightful eccentric, who produced affecting verse on the subject of moods and fairy folk. Her scientific writing, when mentioned, was regarded from an amused distance, or occasionally ridiculed. In *The Connoisseur* (22 May 1755), George Colman the elder and Bonnell Thornton suggest that her poem on melancholy was used by Milton in 'Il penseroso', a suggestion qualified in later editions but often repeated in biographical notes elsewhere. George Ballard's *Memoirs of Several Ladies of Great Britain* (1752) popularized selected poems, and anthologists of women's poetry generally followed his lead until the end of the nineteenth century. Horace Walpole in *A catalogue of the royal and noble authors* (1758) treated her literary output with a good deal of scepticism, while Charles Lamb, writing in 'Mackery End', in *Essays of Elia* (1823), became known as the champion of what he took to be a delightfully fanciful poet.

Towards the end of the nineteenth century, Margaret, the poet of moods and fairy folk, was supplanted by the loyal wife who suffered with her husband in exile and who recorded his war years in *The Life of William Cavendish*. First M. A. Lower and soon afterwards C. H. Firth produced editions of the *Life*, both of which were frequently reissued. Firth's footnotes confirm Margaret's understanding of the facts of the civil wars in the details of dates and troop movements. At about the same time she became the subject of several biographies. Early twentieth-century treatments of the novel often note that studies of character found in *Sociable Letters* adumbrate what is to be seen in eighteenth-century fiction. It was customary for those who wrote about her during the twentieth century to remark that she was called Mad Madge of Newcastle during her lifetime, but it is more likely that the label developed later, perhaps by connection with Mad Madge Murdockson from Sir Walter Scott's *Heart of Midlothian*.

Today Margaret is read by three overlapping groups: those who have an interest in sex and gender in the seventeenth century, especially as the two connect to politics; historians of science; and historians of drama, particularly in performance. Many feminists find her writing to be a puzzling mix of proto-feminist and traditional positions, but feminists have become less likely in the last few years to see her as a bad writer whose bad writing derives from a patriarchal society. Rather, she is seen as a good writer who overcame the impediments of patriarchy to produce books that are ironic, suggestive, and discursive—as opposed to contradictory, vague, and lacking in structure. Historians of science and those who trace the relationship between science and literature also see her as an important writer. John Rogers believes that her connection to the vitalist movement is similar to Milton's, asserting that 'both writers find themselves in often untenable literary binds as they struggle to accommodate divergent and contradictory forms of sanctioned truth' (Rogers, 181). In the case of Margaret the contradiction (or perhaps ambivalence) that is most bothersome today is her unwillingness to decide whether women have essentially the same intellectual capacity as men or are naturally men's intellectual inferiors. Historians of drama have been intent on experimenting with the production and recording on videotape of her plays, which were once considered unactable. *The Blazing World* is widely available and read. Margaret's defence of Shakespeare (*Sociable Letters*, letter 123), the first extended treatment of that playwright by any writer, is also beginning to gain recognition.

JAMES FITZMAURICE

Sources D. Grant, *Margaret the First: a biography of Margaret Cavendish, duchess of Newcastle* (1957) • M. Cavendish, 'A true relation', *Nature's pictures* (1656), repr. in S. Bowerbank and S. Mendelson, eds., *Paper bodies: a Margaret Cavendish reader* (2000) • A. Battigelli, *Margaret Cavendish and the exiles of the mind* (1998) • R. Goulding, *Margaret Lucas, duchess of Newcastle* (1925) • J. Walter, *Understanding popular violence in the English revolution: the Colchester plunderers* (1999) • V. Woolf, *The common reader* (1929) • Pepys, *Diary*, vols. 8–9 • E. Hyde, earl of Clarendon, *Selections from 'The history of the rebellion' and 'The life by himself'*, new edn, ed. G. Huehns (1978) • C. Gallagher, 'Embracing the absolute: the politics of the female subject in seventeenth-century England', *Genders*, 1 (1988), 24–39 • *Diary and correspondence of John Evelyn*, ed. W. Bray, new edn, ed. [J. Forster], 4 vols. (1850–52) • M. Cavendish, *The life of William Cavendish, duke of Newcastle*, ed. C. H. Firth (1886) • G. Colman and B. Thornton, *The Connoisseur* (22 May 1755) • H. Walpole, *A catalogue of the royal and noble authors* (1758) • D. Osborne, *Letters to Sir William Temple*, ed. K. Parker (1987) • [T. Longueville], *The first duke and duchess of Newcastle-upon-Tyne* (1910) • *The collected works of Katherine Philips*, ed. P. Thomas (1990) • L. Hulse, '"The king's entertainment" by the duke of Newcastle', *Viator*, 26 (1995), 355–405 • J. Rogers, *The matter of revolution: science, poetry, and politics in the age of Milton* (1996) • E. O'Neill, *Routledge encyclopedia of philosophy*, 2 (1998) • H. Perry, *The first duchess of Newcastle and her husband as figures in literary history* (1918) • A. Bennett, *Bell in campo and The sociable companions* (2001) • M. B. Campbell, *Wonder and science: imagining worlds in early modern Europe* (1999) • GEC, *Peerage* • S. H. Mendelson, *The mental world of Stuart women: three studies* (1987), 1–61 • K. Whitaker, *Mad Madge: the extraordinary life of Margaret Cavendish, duchess of Newcastle, the first woman to live by her pen* (New York, 2002)

Archives BL, compendium of her philosophy, Sloane MS 1950, fols. 35–8 • BL, tracings of two signatures, Add. MS 41295 • Notts. Arch. • U. Nott., Portland MSS | Bodl. Oxf., MS Rawl. • Hunt. L., Ellesmere collection

Likenesses P. L. van Schuppen, etching, pubd 1668 (after A. van Diepenbeck, *c.*1655–1658), NPG [*see illus.*] • marble tomb effigy, *c.*1676 (with husband), Westminster Abbey, London • W. Greatbach, line engraving, pubd 1846 (after A. van Diepenbeck), BM, NPG • P. Clowet, etching (after A. van Diepenbeck), repro. in M. Cavendish, *Nature's pictures* (1656), frontispiece [1st edn only] • attrib. A. van Diepenbeck, oils, repro. in *Welbeck Abbey Pictures*, no. 37 • P. Lely, oils, National Gallery of Victoria

Cavendish, Michael (*c.*1565–1628), composer and courtier, was the youngest of three children of William Cavendish, landowner, and his wife, Ann Cox, and a grandson of George *Cavendish (*b.* 1494, *d.* in or before 1562?), the biographer of Cardinal Thomas Wolsey. The family, which can be traced back to the thirteenth century, lived at the manor of Cavendish Overhall, Suffolk, until the house and lands were sold in 1596 by William Cavendish, Michael's eldest brother. However, the dedication of Michael Cavendish's sole publication, *14. Ayres in Tabletorie to the Lute* (1598), is 'From Cavendish this 24 of July', so the family may have retained connections with the area.

Only one copy of Cavendish's book is extant, now in the British Library. It is dedicated to Lady Arabella Stuart, Cavendish's second cousin, and comprises twenty-eight compositions: fourteen songs for voice and lute or two voices and bass viol, six more lute songs with alternative versions for four voices alone, and eight madrigals for five voices—a range of performing options which justifies the claim in the dedication that the book 'hath in it humours variable for delights sake'.

The songs are tuneful and well crafted, sometimes delicate in expression. The madrigals, more clumsy and old-fashioned, look back to the models of Alfonso Ferrabosco the elder rather than forward to the looser, more expressive style of Thomas Morley; two of them (21 and 22) borrow musically as well as textually from Ferrabosco's settings, published by Nicholas Yonge in the influential second volume of *Musica transalpina* (1597). With 'Come gentle swains' (24) Cavendish has the distinction of being the first composer to introduce into a printed collection the English refrain which three years later concluded every composition in Morley's collection dedicated to Elizabeth I, *The Triumphs of Oriana* (1601):

then sang the shepherds and nimphes of Diana
Long live faire Oriana.

A heavily revised version of this madrigal was included in Morley's collection.

Little is known of Cavendish's life. The dedication contains the somewhat bitter generalization that 'the policie of times may hold it unfit to raise men humbled with adversities to titles of dearnesse', which could apply to Cavendish's own situation at the end of Elizabeth's reign. But his fortunes may have revived after the accession of James I, since a manuscript tracing the pedigree of the family states that Cavendish was 'Servant in the Bedchamber to Prince Charles', who was born in 1601 (BL, Add. MS 19122).

Whatever Cavendish's personal fortunes, it is likely that his connections with the more favoured branch of the family headed by William Cavendish, first earl of Devonshire and heir to Chatsworth and Hardwick, brought him into association with several other composers and musicians. His book of songs and madrigals has similarities in style with the *Songs of Sundrie Kindes* (1604) by Thomas Greaves, and both end with a group of five-part madrigals. Greaves was employed by Sir Henry Pierrepoint, whose wife, Frances Cavendish, was sister of the first earl and cousin to Michael's father. The madrigalist John Wilbye dedicated one set of published madrigals to Lady Arabella Stuart and the other to Sir Charles Cavendish, the earl's younger brother, who was himself connected by marriage to the Kytsons, Wilbye's patrons at Hengrave Hall. Lady Arabella was also the patron of Tobias Hume and the lutenist Francis Cuttinge. Two of the lyrics set by Cavendish (19 and 20) were later set by Michael East in his *Madrigales to 3. 4. and 5. Parts* (1604) and Cavendish's only other extant work, besides his published book, is a contribution to *The Whole Booke of Psalmes*, published in 1592 by Thomas East, thought to be the father of Michael East.

As a gentleman amateur with a place at court, Cavendish was not himself fully a member of 'a profession worthie some grace' (as he described music in his dedication). But the quality of his few compositions makes him not the least important of an influential group of musicians active around the turn of the century. Other than his service to Prince Charles, nothing is known of his later years. Cavendish's will was dated 5 July 1628 and proved six days later. He died, unmarried, in the parish of St Mary Aldermanbury, London.

CHRISTOPHER HOGWOOD, rev.

Sources E. Doughtie, *Lyrics from English airs, 1596–1622* (1970) · G. A. Philipps, 'John Wilbye's other patrons: the Cavendishes and their place in English musical life during the Renaissance', *Music Review*, 38 (1977), 81–93 · M. Cavendish, *14. ayres in tabletorie to the lute* (1598)

Cavendish, Richard (*c*.1530–1601), courtier, was the younger son of Sir Richard Gernon or Cavendish (*d*. 1554), landowner, of Trimley St Martin, Suffolk, and his wife, Beatrice Gould. His date of birth is estimated from the reference to his twenty-eight years of university study when granted his MA by Cambridge University in February 1573, and the comment of Robert Dudley, earl of Leicester, in September 1586, when sending 'this poor lame man' home from the Netherlands, that 'the time of the year is past for such a man to be in field' (*Correspondence*, 431–2). Sir Richard Cavendish, prominent in the Brandon and Wentworth connections in Suffolk, had an interest in military engineering, and was a principal officer of the Boulogne garrison in the later 1540s. His elder son, Richard's brother, William Cavendish (*c*.1530–1572), married Mary, daughter of Thomas Wentworth, first Baron Wentworth, and was the father of Thomas *Cavendish

(*bap*. 1560, *d*. 1592). William Cavendish succeeded his father as a pillar of Suffolk gentry protestantism.

Leicester was not the only man to refer to Richard Cavendish the younger's lameness in 1586, but the cause is unknown. No clearer is the basis of his reputation as a mathematician and intellectual. For all his supposed years of university study, only a vague connection to Corpus Christi College, Cambridge, can be traced. The only book he published was *The Image of Nature and Grace, Conteyning the Whole Course and Condition of Man's Estate* (two editions, 1571, 1574), a work of protestant apologetics. He has been claimed as a translator of Euclid, but the only printed translation is attributed to Henry Billingsley and was published as *The Elements of Geography* (1570). On the other hand, in October 1573 Cavendish did receive a patent of monopoly for his invention of an engine for draining mines. In 1575 he received a licence to travel abroad, but the purpose is unknown.

Cavendish gained a certain notoriety as a minor actor in the fall of Thomas Howard, fourth duke of Norfolk. Thanks to his 'long acquaintance' with Elizabeth Talbot, countess of Shrewsbury (probably through his family connection to her second husband, Sir William Cavendish), he had settled in Nottinghamshire by 1569, and in that year was carrying messages to the court from George Talbot, sixth earl of Shrewsbury. This brought him into contact with Leicester who informed Shrewsbury on 3 March 1569 that 'the more I am acquaynted with him [Cavendish] the better I lyke him' (Longleat, original (Talbot) letters, ii, fol. 87). According to Norfolk's self-serving confession in 1571 (in which he clearly tried to discredit Cavendish as Leicester's instrument), Leicester advanced 'your countriman' to him as a witness that Mary, queen of Scots, was greatly maligned. In May 1569 Leicester employed Cavendish to carry to Mary his proposals for her restoration to the Scottish throne following her marriage to Norfolk. Elizabeth I appears to have been aware of these journeys, though possibly not of their full import. Sir William Cecil, principal secretary, informed Shrewsbury on 25 May that although she approved of his 'preciseness' in viewing Cavendish's activities with suspicion, nevertheless 'hir Majesty findeth cause to allow so well of the gentilman as she is content that your lordship may use hym as your lordship was wont to do' (Arundel Castle, autograph letters, 1513–1585, art. 152).

Norfolk initially regarded Cavendish with suspicion as well—'I had no good liking to deal with that party because there was no goodwill betwixt me and his brother [William Cavendish]'—but appears to have changed his mind. When the intrigue was exposed in September 1569 and Cavendish was sought as one of those involved, he was living in Howard House in London, sick of an ague. He was the sole witness against Norfolk to testify in person at his trial in January 1572. He stated then that Norfolk had resolved to marry Mary in the summer of 1569 and had discussed his course of action should Elizabeth die. Norfolk dismissed him as 'a poor and abject fellow' (*CSP Scot.*, 4.32–40).

This episode did, however, solidify Cavendish's relations with Leicester, who in April 1570 described him (or possibly his brother) as 'my loving friend' (PRO, SP 46/28/198). In 1572 Leicester returned Cavendish as MP for Denbigh Boroughs, after the electors rejected his initial nominee. Cavendish continued as MP for Denbigh in 1584, but he was not a particularly active member and served on only two committees, one in 1576 and one in 1584. In March 1586 he joined Leicester in the Netherlands and remained there until September, when Leicester advised his recall. He wrote regularly and at length to Cecil (now Baron Burghley), but very much in support of Leicester's policies. Others reported him as one of four cronies who 'possessed' the earl.

Yet Cavendish was not completely dependent on Leicester; his 1573 patent styled him the queen's servant, and she too seems to have liked him personally. In June 1585 he received a more notorious patent, a seven-year licence for the issuing of writs of *supersedeas* by the court of common pleas. In April 1587 this patent caused a confrontation over the prerogative when the justices of common pleas refused to accept it on the ground that the existing officers of the court had a life interest in issuing the writs. In his later life Cavendish lived in Hornsey, Middlesex, where he was buried in 1601 with a funeral monument provided by Margaret Clifford, countess of Cumberland. He had been married and had at least three daughters, but they appear to have predeceased him. Beatrice married Thomas Denny of Mendlesham, Suffolk, Douglas (*d.* 1597) married Richard *Hakluyt (1552?–1616), while Margaret (*d.* 1595), who may have been a maid of honour, married Sir Robert Dudley about 1591.

The connection with Hakluyt is as frustrating as any aspect of Cavendish's life, for he was also a friend of John Dee, who dreamed of him in 1579. In 1590, after Dee returned to England, Cavendish brought his nephew Thomas Cavendish to see him, discussed alchemy, helped him financially, and used his access to Elizabeth to secure her protection for him. Cavendish clearly moved in mathematical and navigational circles, but his wider intellectual significance remains as enigmatic as his role in Leicester's entourage.   SIMON ADAMS

Sources J. Bruce, ed., *Correspondence of Robert Dudley, earl of Leycester*, CS, 27 (1844) • D. MacCulloch, *Suffolk and the Tudors: politics and religion in an English county, 1500–1600* (1986) • S. J. Gunn, *Charles Brandon, duke of Suffolk, c.1484–1545* (1988) • H. M. Colvin and others, eds., *The history of the king's works*, 3 (1975) • *CPR, 1558–82* • original (Talbot) letters, Longleat House, Wiltshire, Marquess of Bath MSS • autograph letters, 1515–85, Arundel Castle archives, West Sussex, manuscripts of the duke of Norfolk • *CSP Scot., 1547–1603* • W. Camden, *Annales: the true and royall history of the famous Empresse Elizabeth*, trans. A. Darcie (1625) • state papers miscellaneous, PRO, SP 46 • S. Adams, *Leicester and the court: essays on Elizabethan politics* (2002) • HoP, *Commons, 1558–1603*, 1.567–8 • *CSP for., 1558–89* • S. Adams, ed., *Household accounts and disbursement books of Robert Dudley, earl of Leicester, 1558–1561, 1584–1586*, CS, 6 (1995) • *The diaries of John Dee*, ed. E. Fenton (1998) • *DNB* • E. G. R. Taylor, *The mathematical practitioners of Tudor and Stuart England* (1954)

Cavendish, Spencer Compton, marquess of Hartington and eighth duke of Devonshire (1833–1908), politician, born on 23 July 1833 at Holker Hall, Lancashire, was the

Spencer Compton Cavendish, marquess of Hartington and eighth duke of Devonshire (1833–1908), by Sir Hubert von Herkomer, 1892

eldest son of William *Cavendish, second earl of Burlington and afterwards seventh duke of Devonshire (1808–1891), and his wife, Lady Blanche Georgiana (*b.* 1812), daughter of George Howard, sixth earl of Carlisle. His mother died on 27 April 1840, leaving also two younger sons, Frederick and Edward, and a daughter, Louisa.

Education, the turf, lovers, and early political career The sons were educated at home, chiefly by their father, a learned man particularly interested in science, who disapproved of the narrow and undemanding educational regime practised in most public schools. He was also devout, solemn, silent, and withdrawn, and an isolated, motherless upbringing in such circumstances may have contributed to some of the most striking characteristics of his eldest son, who remained self-contained and unemotional, prey to self-doubt, and uninterested in behaving or dressing to impress, in softening his remarks about others, or in social repartee. Known at first as Lord Cavendish, he was sent to Trinity College, Cambridge, at eighteen, in 1851. Without much reading he gained a second class in the mathematical tripos of 1854, graduating MA the same year. During the following three years he led the life of a young man of high social position. In January 1858 his cousin, the sixth duke of Devonshire, died. Cavendish's father succeeded to the dukedom and estates, and he himself became marquess of Hartington, the name by which he became famous (frequently shortened, in political gossip, to Harty or Harty-Tarty, though to his family he remained Cav or Cavvy).

Hartington quickly discovered an addiction to the turf, and many of his happiest hours were spent at Newmarket, where he later built himself a house. He spent lavishly on horse-breeding, but not with commensurate success, though horses of his won the One Thousand Guineas in 1877, the Gold Cup in 1891, and the Stewards' Cup three times. He was also a keen shot and bridge player. Hartington continued to indulge these tastes throughout life, playing bridge most days until the small hours at one of his clubs (the Turf, the Travellers', and Brooks were his favourites) and rising late. From a young age he was a member of the social circle of the prince of Wales, later Edward VII. His high social position worked together with his natural secretiveness to obscure from contemporaries and posterity much of his early private life, though he is known to have had a long and deeply felt affair with the young society courtesan Catherine *Walters (Skittles) (1839–1920) between 1859 and 1863.

His habits of life were not viewed favourably by his father, on whom Hartington remained financially dependent until he was fifty-eight (receiving a regular allowance and periodic debt settlements). Parental influence, in two senses, led to his return to parliament for North Lancashire as a Liberal and a supporter of Lord Palmerston in 1857. The leading men of the Liberal Party, concerned by the amount of recent middle-class criticism of the failings of the traditional governing classes and by the lack of able young aristocratic whigs interested in a political career, quickly identified Hartington as a man of promise. Despite having made only two major speeches he was appointed junior lord of the Admiralty by Palmerston in March 1863 and under-secretary at the War Office two months later. In the latter capacity he helped in promoting the organization of the volunteer force, in which he had participated keenly. Palmerston, who influenced Hartington's political outlook greatly, died in 1865. In February 1866 Hartington became secretary of state for war in Lord Russell's brief administration, thus entering the cabinet in his thirty-fourth year.

In the early 1860s Hartington formed a lifelong attachment to Louise Montagu, duchess of Manchester (1832–1911), the daughter of Count von Alten of Hanover [see Cavendish, Louise Frederica Augusta]. Her husband, the seventh duke of Manchester, whom she had married in 1852, did not die until 1890, and in 1892 she married her long-term lover. For nearly thirty years, therefore, Hartington combined a bachelor lifestyle with an adulterous affair which was common knowledge in aristocratic circles, though successfully shielded from the world at large at a time when it would almost certainly have damaged his political prospects. He sometimes accompanied the duke and duchess abroad, but in public in England he and she always addressed each other formally. This lifestyle both testified to, and deepened, Hartington's reserve. It gave him more time for politics and self-indulgence, though at the expense of not fathering an heir, of enduring many tedious social events unaccompanied, and of being unable to run a political salon.

Like a number of Lancashire Liberals, Hartington lost his seat at the general election of December 1868. Gladstone, the new Liberal leader, offered him the post of lord lieutenant of Ireland, which he declined. He accepted instead the office of postmaster-general, with a seat in the cabinet, and in early 1869 obtained a new seat from the Radnor boroughs in Wales. His chief work as postmaster-general was the nationalization of the telegraphs. In 1869 he was appointed chairman of the select committee appointed to investigate parliamentary and municipal electioneering. Following its report in 1870 he introduced the first of three government bills to establish voting by ballot. The proposal became law in 1872. He himself was a reluctant convert to the need for secrecy in voting.

Irish secretary At the end of 1870 Hartington, much against his will, became chief secretary for Ireland, a job which required him to spend long periods away from his mistress and from London society. His acceptance indicated the extent of his commitment to politics. It also brought him into daily contact with the Irish problem at a time when it was beginning to pose a severe strain on British, and especially Liberal, politics. The Devonshires owned 60,000 acres in Cork and Waterford, and Hartington was naturally conscious of the need to defend the security of Irish property. He never wavered in his belief that the firm administration of law was the prerequisite of peace, stability, and prosperity in Ireland, and the primary duty of Liberal government. His first major act as chief secretary was to urge the suspension of habeas corpus in co. Westmeath in early 1871 in response to the campaign of agrarian outrages known as Ribbonism. Anxious to prevent the extension of priestly control over Irish education, he staunchly defended the mixed national education system and the independence of the protestant Trinity College, Dublin. He strongly disliked Gladstone's proposal of 1873 to reform Irish university education by subordinating Trinity to a federal university examining board, which Roman Catholic colleges might dominate and which had the option to restrict the scope of examination in deference to Catholic susceptibilities. The scheme was defeated in parliament, leading to the government's temporary resignation. Hartington's view was that the future stability and prosperity of Ireland would best be secured by encouraging investment, and to that end he argued in vain that the state should purchase and run the Irish railway network.

Liberal leader in the Commons, and political creed The Liberal government was defeated at the general election of 1874. In early 1875 Gladstone announced his retirement as Liberal leader in the Commons, and on 3 February, despite his reluctance, Hartington was elected his successor at a party meeting held at the Reform Club. This was, not least, because he was almost the only cabinet minister to have enhanced his reputation during the 1868–74 government. Many Liberals also considered that Gladstone's Irish, religious, and foreign policy had alienated too many propertied voters and that a move in the direction of a more Palmerstonian approach would help to restore electoral confidence in the party. And Hartington's lack of clerical sympathies reassured those nonconformists who were hostile to the only serious rival candidate, W. E. Forster, on account of the privileges conferred on church schools by his 1870 Education Act.

Though at first characteristically doubtful about his qualifications for this new post, Hartington developed a quiet mastery of it by the same qualities of hard work, fair-mindedness, and independence of thought that he was to demonstrate in all the offices he held. He was not a natural orator; one wit dubbed him 'Lieder ohne Worte'. But his speeches quickly became effective; they were clear, incisive, unpretentious, and unvarnished, and they exuded trustworthiness. The years 1875–80, in opposition, were difficult for the Liberals, not least because of an internal difference of opinion about how to respond to the 1874 defeat. Some, like Hartington, argued that a Conservative spirit was dominant in the nation and that the Liberals would remain united and recover power only by patience and consolidation. But others believed that the Conservative victory did not reflect public feeling and that the Liberals could build a majority by arousing popular fervour. The young Birmingham radical Joseph Chamberlain took this view. So, though nominally in retirement, did Gladstone, and his behaviour, especially on foreign policy, was a severe trial to Hartington.

Disraeli's foreign policy aimed to strengthen imperial sentiment at home and British prestige abroad. Hartington did not object to these goals, and thought that opposition to them would be politically counter-productive. For this reason his criticism, in 1876, of the purchase of the Suez Canal shares and the bestowal on Queen Victoria of the title empress of India was limited. However, he did not approve of Disraeli's presentation of imperial policy, which he thought placed too much emphasis on empty pomp and display. His view was rather that the colonies were maturing, at various speeds, into a loose federation of progressive self-governing communities which would be beacons of commercial and constitutional liberalism, spreading 'all over the world the language, the civilisation, the laws and the customs of England'.

On the Eastern question, which dominated politics between 1876 and 1878, Hartington criticized Disraeli's pursuit of grandeur, taking the view that Britain should have co-operated with the European powers in order to force through reforms in Ottoman administration of her European provinces, rather than ostentatiously breaking ranks and so bolstering Constantinople's intransigence. But he could not accept Gladstone's suggestion that the European provinces should be given autonomy, believing that the mixture of races there would provoke conflict, perpetuate instability, and encourage Russian penetration. And he was alarmed at the agitation mounted by provincial Liberals against Turkish misrule in Europe (which Gladstone inflamed). In his eyes it elevated sentimental above informed and pragmatic judgements of British and European interests in the region, and it looked damagingly unpatriotic, especially after England's traditional *bête noire*, Russia, declared war on Turkey in April 1877. Both in May 1877 and in the spring of 1878 Hartington

refused to accept that there were no circumstances in which British military support of Turkey against Russia would be justified. The Liberal parliamentary party split at these times, a substantial number of MPs following Gladstone in a rigidly anti-Turkish viewpoint. However, Hartington regained control of the situation after the Congress of Berlin of 1878, taking the view that the government was unwise to commit Britain single-handedly to maintaining the integrity of the Ottoman empire, given the impossibility of forcing through administrative reforms, and that the only viable solution was for the powers to deal with Turkey in concert. This policy, balancing pragmatism and moralism, maintained party unity in the approach to the 1880 election. At that election Hartington also condemned the aggrandizing impulsiveness which he felt had led the government into the Second Anglo-Afghan War (1878–80), and developed a general critique of Conservative foreign policy—that it sought to dazzle voters with empty, foolish, and costly gestures. He claimed that the government had lowered the standing of parliament, both by marginalizing its input into foreign policy and by failing to maintain a regular diet of useful legislation to meet domestic grievances.

Though an electioneering gambit, this argument accurately reflected Hartington's constitutional outlook. He never deviated from the whig view in which he was educated, that a vigorous parliament, active in legislative reform, was the key to the working of the British constitution, forcing government to take account of public demands, but filtering those demands in the course of discussion by independently minded men of property and education. However, Hartington did not think that parliament was now the only important forum for discussion of reforms, in the light of the growth of the press, elected local authorities, voluntary bodies, and the professions, all of which played valuable roles in shaping opinion and demonstrated the welcome pluralism of British public life. In an inaugural address as lord rector of Edinburgh University in 1879 he argued that the health of the British polity depended on the continuation of this diffusion of effective power among a great variety of free associations of informed people, but that this placed a heavy responsibility on the universities to train future members of these agencies. He urged a training in scientific and philosophical method, as most likely to cultivate the independence of mind and disciplined imagination that the prominent men of the future would need in order to resist 'clamour and exaggeration' and to supply cogent, disinterested leadership.

Hartington was anxious that Liberals should commit themselves only to policy innovations which were rational or unmistakably advocated by public opinion, rather than those agitated by vocal but unrepresentative pressure groups within the party. In November 1877 he told the advocates of Scottish disestablishment and temperance reform that they must 'induce their Countrymen to agree' with them by a reasoned campaign of persuasion. Nor did he consider it his place, as leader of the whole parliamentary party, to associate with the National

Liberal Federation set up by Joseph Chamberlain, which at this stage represented a selection of the large borough constituencies and sought to generate a policy programme out of the views of local activists in those places. At the 1880 election Hartington sought to rally the Liberal Party by a three-pronged attack on landed complacency. The extension of household franchise to the counties would weaken the grip of the tory squirearchy and make more Commons seats available for representatives of landed Liberal families. The introduction of elected authorities would make rural local government more accountable, more efficient, and more active than most magistrates had been, so improving standards of education and health and increasing popular respect for the propertied classes. Measures to free land of the restrictions on its sale would assist encumbered landlords and might pump investment into the under-capitalized agricultural economy, checking the drift of labour to the towns and hence the rise in urban unemployment, and diminishing the appeal of protection.

Secretary for India, and for war The Liberals won the election and Queen Victoria invited Hartington, who had been returned MP for North-East Lancashire, to form a government. However, Gladstone, who had dominated press coverage of the election owing to his speeches in Midlothian, told him that, as a former prime minister, he would not serve in cabinet beneath him. At this moment, the most crucial in his career, Hartington's diffidence overcame him. Sensitive to the difficulties of disciplining the party at any time, he rejected the notion of leading a government of which Gladstone might well become a back-bench critic. Instead, Gladstone became prime minister on 23 April.

Hartington was appointed secretary of state for India. His most important work in this post was to help settle the Afghan question. Amir Abdurahman was installed in power and all the British forces were withdrawn from Afghanistan, except from the Sibi and Pishin frontier districts, which with Quetta were permanently added to the empire.

On 16 December 1882 Hartington became secretary of state for war—soon after the virtual establishment of the British protectorate over Egypt, for which he had argued vigorously. In January 1884 the British government decided to send General Charles George Gordon to superintend the Egyptian army's safe evacuation from the Sudan after it had encountered trouble from the forces of the Mahdi. Hartington, together with Lord Granville, the foreign secretary, was most responsible for this decision. Gordon's duties were defined imprecisely, partly because Hartington and Lord Wolseley, the adjutant-general, on whose military advice he relied heavily, doubted the practicability of the swift disengagement for which others in the government hoped. When it became apparent in March that peaceful evacuation had become impossible, and that Khartoum and Berber were threatened by the Mahdi, Hartington, supported by strong memoranda from Wolseley, repeatedly urged the prime minister and the cabinet as strongly as he could to prepare a relief expedition. Opposed throughout by Gladstone, he was unable to induce the cabinet to agree to do so until the end of July 1884, and then only by a threat of resignation. Consequently Wolseley's expedition—sent by the War Office up the Nile, contrary to the advice of those on the spot—arrived near Khartoum just too late to save that city from capture and Gordon from death on 26 January 1885. The government decided at first to retake Khartoum, and in parliament on 25 February Hartington pledged himself to this policy in the strongest terms, believing that the reputation of the empire, not least among its Muslim subjects, was affected by it. But the feeling died away; the momentary probability of a war with Russia in connection with the Afghan frontier enabled Gladstone to withdraw from the undertaking, which he had never liked; and Hartington had the mortification of seeing the complete abandonment of the Sudan, resisting in vain the proposal to evacuate even the province of Dongola, which had not as yet fallen to the Mahdi. In retrospect Hartington considered the Sudan episode to be the most shameful which he had ever witnessed in politics.

Domestic politics, distrust of Gladstone, and the Liberal split This imperial crisis intensified Hartington's unhappiness at the state of domestic politics, which had been manifest throughout the early 1880s; more than once he talked of retiring. One difficulty in these years was the impending democratization of the electoral system due towards the end of the government's term of office. Chamberlain exploited the uncertainty over the consequences, presenting himself as the exponent of a new programmatic politics capable of mobilizing and integrating the new electorate. Hartington was angry at Chamberlain's behaviour and tone, which he considered were creating unrealizable expectations among poorer voters, but he lacked confidence that his own brand of politics could compete. So from the early 1880s he was thrown back on the defensive, and was generally seen as the leader of a whiggish section of the party. In this guise he opposed, in late 1883, the proposal to separate the franchise and redistribution parts of the electoral reform package, fearing that the latter would then be determined by a more democratically elected parliament. This did not happen, but more small boroughs were disfranchised in the Redistribution Act of 1885 than he wished, despite his participation in the interparty discussions which led to it.

The dominance of the Irish question increased Hartington's defensiveness in these years. Indeed his anxiety about electoral reform in 1883–4 was largely caused by concern that the protestant minority in Ireland would be swamped in a more democratic representative system. Since 1880 Hartington had been a strong supporter of coercive measures to check agrarian crime and the power of the Land League. The regime of violence culminated in the assassination of his brother, Lord Frederick Cavendish, the new chief secretary for Ireland, on 6 May 1882. Though Hartington characteristically did not vent his feelings in public, this tragedy, and the serious threat of continuing agitation, strengthened his view that it would at present be 'madness' for Britain to diminish her responsibility for order in Ireland by granting significant power to locally elected bodies. In 1885 Hartington and his cabinet allies successfully resisted Chamberlain's scheme for a central board and elected county boards throughout Ireland.

Hartington's experience of Gladstone's attitude to imperial and Irish issues between 1880 and 1885 explains his view, expressed in March 1885, that Gladstone was 'in a fool's paradise about everything'. Yet throughout this government he appreciated that in general politics Gladstone was a conservative influence. One reason why Hartington never carried out his half-threats to resign was the fear that it would throw Gladstone, and the party, more into the hands of Chamberlainite elements. However, the situation changed by the end of 1885. Gladstone's administration was defeated in parliament and resigned in June; Lord Salisbury formed a minority Conservative government, upheld by Parnell's Irish nationalists; and an election late in the year removed the Liberals' majority. Chamberlain's exuberant radical rhetoric was largely blamed for this, and his position *vis-à-vis* Hartington (who was returned for the new division of Rossendale in Lancashire) was weakened. Meanwhile, the fact that the Parnellites held the balance of power enabled Gladstone to avoid retirement and instead to recover office by embarking on a policy of home rule for Ireland. Most of the members of the previous Liberal cabinet decided to follow him, but a minority, led by Hartington, declined to accept office in the government which he formed in February 1886 after defeating Salisbury in parliament. On the introduction of the Home Rule Bill (8 April), Hartington declared his opposition to it. He insisted that Britain had a responsibility to secure law and order in Ireland and to protect property—not least that of protestants with capital to invest in economic development. Gladstone claimed that his scheme guaranteed the continuing supremacy of the imperial parliament over Irish affairs, but Hartington regarded this as naïve. Hartington's opposition was assisted by Chamberlain, and on 8 June 1886 the bill was defeated on a second reading by a majority of thirty, with ninety-four Liberal MPs voting against it. Gladstone obtained a dissolution of parliament, leading the dissident Liberals to form a distinct Liberal Unionist group under Hartington's leadership and to fight the ensuing election in tandem with the Conservatives.

Liberal Unionism, dukedom, and marriage The 1886 election returned 316 Conservatives and 78 Liberal Unionists. Gladstone himself considered that Hartington had contributed most to the victory of the Unionist alliance, and that his political standing was extremely high. Salisbury, with Queen Victoria's warm encouragement, asked him to form a coalition government or, alternatively, to serve under him in one. Hartington was tempted, because he was worried that the Conservatives, governing alone, would be too weak to resist Irish pressure. But he feared that acceptance would split the Liberal Unionists and encourage Chamberlain and others to revert to the Gladstonian fold, imperilling the Union; while he had not

yet abandoned the hope that Gladstone might retire, allowing him to return to the Liberal Party as leader on a Unionist basis. Salisbury renewed the proposal in January 1887, after the crisis due to the sudden resignation of Lord Randolph Churchill; but Hartington again rejected it, for the same reasons. During the next five years Hartington continued with the strategy of keeping the Conservatives in power in order to uphold the Union, while hoping that this might force the Liberals to abandon home rule. However Gladstone did not retire, and the breach between the two Liberal factions widened owing to the government's strict public order policies in Ireland, which Gladstone opposed in an emotional and contentious manner. As a result, by 1891 the bond between Conservatives and Liberal Unionists was much stronger.

On 21 December of that year Hartington became eighth duke of Devonshire on his father's death and so left the House of Commons. He became leader of Liberal Unionism in the House of Lords, while Chamberlain led in the Commons. With Salisbury confirmed as leader of the whole coalition by the events of 1895, Devonshire's position was from now on that of an influential elder statesman. This was assisted by his marriage on 16 August 1892 to the dowager duchess of Manchester, because she developed Devonshire House and Chatsworth as prestigious social centres. Probably the most famous festivity was the historic fancy-dress ball given at Devonshire House in 1897, in celebration of the diamond jubilee, which was regarded as the most splendid London social event for over twenty years (the duke himself appeared as the emperor Charles V).

When, after three years in opposition to an ineffective Liberal government, the Unionists returned to power in June 1895, Salisbury offered five cabinet posts to the Liberal Unionists. A strong coalition government was formed, which lasted until Salisbury's resignation in 1902. The duke declined the foreign secretaryship. Instead he became lord president of the council, with particular responsibilities for the two political problems which most interested him for the remainder of his career, imperial defence and education.

In 1890 the duke had presided over a royal commission which identified weaknesses in defence planning. From 1895 he was chairman of a cabinet committee on defence set up in order to tackle these weaknesses, though its powers were inadequately defined, the service chiefs were not members, and it was unable to overcome obstruction in the individual defence departments. The duke also chaired the committee which oversaw the conduct of the Second South African War. The progress of the war intensified concern about the lack of co-ordination in defence matters, and the defence committee meeting that he chaired in December 1902 drew up proposals to strengthen itself. During 1903 and 1904 these ideas bore fruit and a new committee of imperial defence evolved, including military advisers from outside the cabinet and, by invitation, colonial governors and dominion ministers. Devonshire chaired the committee until he resigned from the government in October 1903. He was also president of the British Empire League, formed in 1894 to promote harmony between the countries of the empire through informal discussion of problems of defence, communications, and commerce.

As lord president of the council Devonshire was in charge of government educational policy. He headed that group which believed that the state must respond to international competition by establishing a systematic policy for secondary education, for which it had not taken responsibility up to that point. After several abortive attempts, local education authorities for secondary education were established by the 1902 Education Act. The duke was the politician most responsible for this act, and in particular for insisting that it should also deal with elementary education. As introduced, it encouraged the transfer of responsibility from school boards to local education authorities. In the interests of efficiency, authorities would, where established, also maintain the voluntary schools, which educated half of English schoolchildren. These had previously been funded not by the rates but by central government, because nonconformists had objected to paying from their rates for Anglican teaching. Characteristically, Devonshire rejected the argument of Chamberlain that the threat of agitation by partisan dissenters should obstruct the furtherance of a national interest. Indeed, during its passage the bill was amended in the direction of uniformity, so that all localities were required to set up local education authorities with these duties. After the Second South African War, Devonshire also became interested in the movement to investigate deficiencies in the physical condition of children, hoping that it would lead local authorities especially to address problems of overcrowding, nutrition, and physical education. He helped to establish an interdepartmental committee on physical deterioration, which reported in 1904, and he publicized its findings in a speech in the Lords in 1905.

Like his father, the duke was also anxious to encourage technical, scientific, and higher education. He was made FRS in 1892, and was president of the Royal Agricultural Society for 1893–4. He succeeded his father as chancellor of Cambridge University in 1891, and discharged his duties there with energy, being especially interested in promoting the teaching of applied science. He was, for example, responsible for securing funding from the Drapers' Company for a chair of agriculture, established in 1899. At a meeting under his aegis at Devonshire House leading members of the university decided to launch a public appeal to rectify the lack of funding for laboratories and professorships in modern subjects. Devonshire gave £10,000 and used his personal contacts to encourage other contributions. But the appeal was a failure, raising only £100,000 in all. He discovered that successful businessmen were reluctant to support the university financially, believing that its education was of little relevance to their world. He came to the opinion that a wide-ranging royal commission should be established, with a view to changing the content and tone of the courses by diverting

powers and financial resources from the colleges to university teachers. He also remained interested in the university extension movement and, at the privy council, facilitated the grant of charters to Birmingham, Manchester, and Liverpool universities. He was chancellor of Manchester University from 1907.

Many honours and responsibilities devolved on the duke in consequence of his political and social standing. He was made KG by Queen Victoria in 1892, lord lieutenant of Derbyshire in the same year and of Waterford in 1895, and GCVO in 1907. In the control and management of his large estates in England and Ireland he was recognized as an excellent landlord and public-spirited benefactor; he took a particularly close interest in the development of Eastbourne. He presided over the successful restructuring of the family's finances, which had been hit by the agricultural depression and by the collapse of demand for the ships and steel produced in Barrow in Furness, in which his father had invested over £2 million. He took advantage of the Land Purchase Acts to sell a lot of his Irish land and reinvested the proceeds in the stock market. By these means the family debt was reduced from £2 million to £0.5 million. He also continued the family tradition of opening Chatsworth to the public; there were 80,000 visitors a year by the end of his life, testifying in some degree to the respect in which he and his order were held.

Free trade, tariff reform, and death Devonshire believed very strongly that the survival of the Unionist coalition government was the best safeguard of the political ideals which he upheld—the defence of the Union and empire, and the pursuit of educational reform and other measures of national efficiency through thoughtful administration. Yet his hopes for its longevity were dashed soon after the retirement of Lord Salisbury in July 1902 and the succession of Arthur Balfour to the premiership (Devonshire himself became leader in the Lords). Moreover the cause, in Devonshire's eyes, was a manifestation of the problem which had alarmed him since the 1880s, the irrational impulsiveness to which democratic politicians were prone. The crisis was created by Chamberlain's campaign for the introduction of preferential duties on imported goods, which he launched in the spring of 1903. The duke, schooled in the principles of political economy by his father, was an instinctive advocate of free trade, unlike the majority of government supporters. Moreover, his involvement in the City encouraged him in the view that invisible earnings, which protection might jeopardize, would continue to underpin British economic success. He was willing to accept an inquiry into the merits of protection, in view of the damage then being suffered by elements of British industry. But careful consideration of the economic arguments did not change his mind, nor that of a minority of his cabinet colleagues. Three of them resigned after the cabinet meeting of 14 September. The duke would have followed suit, had not Balfour informed him that Chamberlain had also resigned. Conscious of the supreme importance of holding the government together, and of his own indispensability, as leader of the

Liberal Unionist forces, in that task, he allowed himself to be persuaded by Balfour to stay in office. But Balfour's strategy depended on leading the party some way down the road of fiscal reform, and as this quickly became clear Devonshire soon found that his position in cabinet was untenable. On 2 October he resigned, taking advantage of strong expressions in favour of a change in fiscal policy used by Balfour in a speech at Sheffield. The government never recovered from these events. The duke strongly opposed the new policy of tariff reform in the House of Lords. In May 1904, recognizing that the Chamberlainites controlled the party's constituency organization, he resigned his chairmanship of, and connection with, the Liberal Unionist Association, over which he had presided since its formation in 1886.

But the duke was not among those free-traders sympathetic to an association with the reviving Liberal Party, believing that the Union was an even more important cause than that of free trade. So, having been a supporter of the dominant governing force during his entire political life, Devonshire's last years were spent out of sympathy with both major parties. In June 1907 he suffered a sudden collapse of health through weakness of the heart. Having recovered to some degree, he left England on 24 October and went to Egypt for the winter. On his way home, on 24 March 1908, he died almost suddenly at the Hotel Metropole at Cannes. His body was brought to Derbyshire and buried at Edensor, close to Chatsworth. He left no children, and the title and estates passed to his nephew Victor, son of the late Lord Edward Cavendish.

Assessment Hartington's success in hiding his feelings disguised from most observers how wholeheartedly he was devoted to the game of politics. Without it he would have been bored to distraction, for he had little taste for society, few cultural interests, and, for most of his existence, an undemanding private life. He was far from unambitious, and his refusal of the premiership on a unique three occasions should not be taken to imply that he was uninterested in political eminence on the right terms. But his overriding commitment was to the defence of a certain approach to politics, which he embodied better, and did more to safeguard, than any man of his generation. He inherited the whig belief in the duty of political leadership, afforced by the intellectual notions characteristic of well-educated, propertied early to mid-Victorian Liberals: a confidence that the application of free trade, rational public administration, scientific enquiry, and a patriotic defence policy would promote Britain's international greatness—in which he strongly believed—and her economic and social progress. Though no intellectual, and affecting indolence, his powers of industry and of unprejudiced insight into practical problems were undoubted, and allowed him to live up to the ideal of a safe, high-minded, disinterested, equable Liberal administrator. He worked slowly and steadily to make himself master of the issues with which he was charged; never swayed by received opinion or sentiment, he read and enquired doggedly until he had made up his own mind. His speeches set out his reasoning clearly, bluntly, and logically; he was

never caught dissembling or romanticizing. He knew he was not an exciting speaker and disliked the limelight; so he was diffident about his ability to compete for a popular following with colleagues such as Gladstone and Chamberlain. But he distrusted the democratic impulse in both of them, and blamed the consequences of their behaviour for the destruction, in turn, of the two great propertied governing coalitions to which he devoted his political life.

None the less, the span of Hartington's period of real political power, at over thirty years, was remarkable. His rank, his character, and his reputation for pragmatic and patriotic common sense gave him unique public standing; many regarded him as representing the middle ground of opinion. Despite his unorthodox private relationships and his indifference to his public appearance (W. H. Smith, meeting him at Cannes, thought he looked like 'a shabby seedy sailor'), he became a model of the dutiful aristocrat. His integrity and public-spiritedness were undoubted; as Hartington himself noted, with mock puzzlement, 'whenever a man is caught cheating at cards the case is referred to me'. It was said of him, late in life, that he was 'the best excuse that the last half-century has produced for the continuance of the peerages'. To bolster the position of the traditional governing classes was his most important, and most intentional, achievement.

JONATHAN PARRY

Sources B. H. Holland, *The life of Spencer Compton, eighth duke of Devonshire*, 2 vols. (1911) · P. Jackson, *The last of the whigs: a political biography of Lord Hartington* (1994) · H. Leach, *The duke of Devonshire: a personal and political biography* (1904) · Marquis of Hartington [S. C. Cavendish], *An address, delivered before the University of Edinburgh, on his inauguration as lord rector* (1879) · Lord Hartington [S. C. Cavendish], *Election speeches in 1879 and 1880* (1880) · G. D. L. [G. D. Liveing], *PRS*, 82A (1909), xi–xvii · J. E. B. Munson, 'The unionist coalition and education, 1895–1902', *HJ*, 20 (1977), 607–45 · T. A. Jenkins, *Gladstone, whiggery and the liberal party, 1874–1886* (1988) · T. A. Jenkins, 'Hartington, Chamberlain and the unionist alliance, 1886–1895', *Parliamentary History*, 11 (1992), 108–38 · D. Cannadine, *Lords and landlords: the aristocracy and the towns, 1774–1967* (1980) · *The Red Earl: the papers of the fifth Earl Spencer, 1835–1910*, ed. P. Gordon, 2 vols., Northamptonshire RS, 31, 34 (1981–6) · Viscount Esher [R. B. B. Esher], *Cloud-capp'd towers* (1927) · Gladstone, *Diaries* · P. Jackson, 'Skittles and the marquis: a Victorian love affair', *History Today*, 45/12 (1995), 47–52

Archives BL OIOC, corresp. and papers relating to India, MS Eur. D 604 · Chatsworth House, Derbyshire, corresp. and papers | Balliol Oxf., letters to Sir Louis Mallet · BL, corresp. with Arthur James Balfour, Add. MSS 49769–49770 · BL, letters to John Bright, Add. MS 43387 · BL, corresp. with Sir Charles Dilke, Add. MS 43891 · BL, corresp. with W. E. Gladstone, Add. MSS 44143–44148 · BL, letters to Lord Halsbury, Add. MS 56371 · BL, corresp. with Sir Edward Walter Hamilton, Add. MS 48613 · BL, corresp. with Lord Ripon, MSS 43565–43569 · BL, letters to Lord Ritchie, Add. MS 53780 · BL OIOC, letters to Sir Owen Burne, MS Eur. D 951 · BL OIOC, corresp. with Sir James Fergusson, MS Eur. E 214 · Bodl. Oxf., letters to Lord Clarendon · Bodl. Oxf., letters to Benjamin Disraeli · Bodl. Oxf., corresp. with William Harcourt · Bodl. Oxf., letters to Lord Kimberley · Bodl. Oxf., corresp. with Lord Selborne · CAC Cam., corresp. with Lord Randolph Churchill · CKS, letters to Aretas Akers-Douglas · CUL, corresp. relating to University of Cambridge · CUL, Royal Commonwealth Society collection, corresp. with Hugh Childers · CUL, letters to Catherine Walters · FM Cam., letters to Catherine Walters · Glos. RO, corresp. with Sir

Michael Hicks Beach · HLRO, corresp. with John St Loe Strachey · Hove Central Library, Sussex, letters to Lord Wolseley and Lady Wolseley · ICL, letters to Lord Playfair · LPL, corresp. with Lord Selborne · NA Scot., corresp. with A. J. Balfour and G. W. Balfour · NL Scot., corresp., incl. with Lord Rosebery · PRO, corresp. with Lord Granville · PRO NIre., corresp. with Lord O'Hagan, reference D2777 · U. Birm. L., corresp. with Joseph Chamberlain · U. Durham L., corresp. with third Earl Grey · UCL, corresp. with Sir Edwin Chadwick

Likenesses G. F. Watts, portrait, 1882 · C. A. Tomkins, mezzotint, pubd 1883 (after H. T. Munns), BM · J. E. Millais, oils, 1886, Chatsworth House, Derbyshire · Lady Abercromby, watercolour, 1888, NPG · Violet, duchess of Rutland, lithograph, 1888, NPG · A. S. Cope, portrait, 1889 · H. von Herkomer, oils, 1892, NPG [*see illus.*] · Ape [C. Pellegrini], caricature, watercolour study, NPG; repro. in *VF* (1869) · Barraud, photograph, NPG; repro. in *Men and Women of the Day*, 1 (1888) · Bassano, photograph, NPG; repro. in *Our conservative and unionist statesmen*, 2 vols. [n.d., c.1898] · M. Beerbohm, drawing, University of Indiana, Bloomington, Lily Library · L. C. Dickinson, group portrait, oils (*Gladstone's cabinet of 1868*), NPG · A. Drury, statue, Eastbourne · F. C. Gould, two sketches, NPG · S. P. Hall, pencil sketch, NPG · H. Hampton, bronze statue, Whitehall, London · John and Charles Watkins, photograph, NPG · A. Legros, photogravure, NPG · London Stereoscopic Co., photograph, NPG · E. Scriven, stipple (after J. Lucas), BM, NPG; repro. in *Miss Fairlie's Children of the nobility* · Spy [L. Ward], caricature, watercolour study, NPG; repro. in *VF* (1888) · Spy [L. Ward], chromolithograph caricature, NPG; repro. in *VF* (1902)

Wealth at death £1,164,960 14s. 9d.: probate, 16 July 1908, *CGPLA Eng. & Wales*

Cavendish, Thomas (*bap.* 1560, *d.* 1592), explorer, was baptized on 19 September 1560 in St Martin's Church, Trimley St Martin, Suffolk, the third son of William Cavendish (*d.* 1572) of Grimston Hall, Trimley St Martin, and his wife, Mary Wentworth (*d.* 1611?). William Cavendish was a puritan sympathizer, and at his death left Thomas Wentworth of Nettlestead, Suffolk, to be Thomas's legal guardian and had arranged for Robert Norgate, the moderate protestant master of Corpus Christi College, to tutor him at Cambridge from Easter 1576. Cavendish matriculated as a fellow-commoner at Easter 1576 but left in November 1577 without graduating. He then entered Gray's Inn, London, possibly moving to the Middle Temple in the 1580s, where he had access to Richard Hakluyt's circle, the royal court, and the temptations of London life.

While at Gray's Inn, Cavendish lent money to Thomas Gresham, and in 1581 he collaborated with courtiers Thomas Perrot and Richard Skipwith to venture £1000 to send Sir Francis Walsingham's agent George Gifford to Constantinople. Though possibly a wager, the recognizance was redeemed in 1591 and may have been a secret part of Walsingham's plan to revive the Levant trade. Between 1581 and 1583 Cavendish was taken to court for non-payment of debts, and his reputation as a spendthrift grew. At the age of seventeen, with Wentworth's consent, Cavendish gained control of leasehold lands in Levington; Dyke's suggestion (Dyke, 109) that these and other Suffolk deals were investments in Gilbert's voyage of 1583 has been refuted by recent evidence that they were courtly debts.

Virginia, 1585 Cavendish sought advancement at court under Ralegh's patronage. In the early 1580s he was tutored by Thomas Harriot, with other sea captains, in the theory and practice of navigation at Ralegh's Durham House, Westminster. Through Ralegh, Cavendish secured the earl of Pembroke's patronage as MP for the borough of Shaftesbury, Dorset, in 1584. He supported Ralegh's application to parliament to take over Sir Humphrey Gilbert's patent to colonize America. Despite his lack of nautical or military expertise, Cavendish was appointed high marshal of the Virgina expedition of 1585 as second in command to Richard Grenville, and was provided with notes to guide him on matters of military and judicial government.

The appointment sparked a vigorous round of financial deals organized by Cavendish's newly appointed land steward Henry Seckford, resulting in the purchase or fitting-out of the pinnace *Elizabeth*, which sailed from Plymouth on 9 April 1585 with Grenville's fleet, bound for Virginia. The fleet was scattered by a ferocious storm and Cavendish, alone of the 'many choise and principall gentlemen' (Strachey, 143), met Grenville eight days later at the Puerto Rican rendezvous: '[we] discerned him as laste to be one of our consorts, for joy of whose comming our ships discharged their ordnance' (Quinn, *Roanoke Voyages*, 1.182). This achievement of a novice navigator proved the effectiveness of Harriot's training, and demonstrated Cavendish's worth—he was noted in January 1586 as suitable for royal naval command.

In Puerto Rico, Cavendish befriended Ralph Lane, governor designate of Virginia, and he subsequently intervened on Lane's behalf in a public quarrel with Grenville which threatened the colony's viability. Lane later wrote warmly about Cavendish's enthusiasm, probably in the forays from the fort, 'Yt ys not possible for men to beehave themselves more fayethfully and more industryously in an Accion especially Master Candysshe our High Marshall' (PRO, CO 1/1, 6). Cavendish and Grenville returned on the *Tyger*, and while Grenville sailed a rich Spanish prize home, Cavendish entered Falmouth without profit but having acquired several close friends.

Circumnavigation, 1585–1588 'Fleshed and somewhat hardened to the sea … immediately after his coming home [Cavendish] began to take in hand a voyage to the South Sea' (Hakluyt, 1589, 809). Queen Elizabeth sanctioned this voyage, possibly originally for Bernard Drake, as a foil to Francis Drake's planned Caribbean attacks. Cavendish ordered two new ships: *Desire*, a galleon of 120–140 tons, and the pinnace *Hugh Gallant*, or *Galliot*, probably constructed on the River Orwell and paid for by complex sales and mortgages of Lincolnshire and Suffolk lands. The Aldeburgh MP and merchant John Foxe contributed the pinnace *Free Pryson*; Ralegh ventured the pinnace *Dorothy*, a veteran of the earlier Virginia voyage.

The fleet was commissioned on 23 May 1586, Cavendish paying a £2000 bond to the high court of admiralty to ensure that *Desire* only attacked Spanish vessels. By this time other powerful backers had been found: Walsingham, the admiralty judge Julius Caesar, Lord Hunsdon, cousin to the queen, Sir George Carey of Cockington, and some London merchants. Problems arose on Foxe's death: the *Free Pryson* was to be sold to build Aldeburgh's new quay. The *Content* replaced her, and the *Dorothy* transferred to the fleet under George Clifford, third earl of Cumberland, hence the confused Spanish reports of a joint venture.

Aware of the value of good planning and benefiting from mistakes made on Edward Fenton's south sea voyage of 1582, Cavendish obtained copies of all available charts that might be of use to him. He consulted and enlisted several of Drake's veterans, among them Francis Pretty of Eye (one of Drake's gentlemen pensioners), Buteres (a Dutch pilot), Captain Mellis, Captain John Brewer (or Bruer), who knew the west African coast well, and Stephen Hare, who had sailed to Brazil in 1582. He recruited Robert Hues, the Oxford mathematician, and, according to Spanish reports, also employed Dom Antonio's Portuguese pilots. Other crew members were local: Captain Havers from Trimley, Thomas Fuller, an Ipswich pilot who left a detailed rutter, and Thomas Eldred, an Ipswich wax-chandler who celebrated his return with an elaborate mantelpiece now at Christchurch Mansion, Ipswich.

Leaving London on 10 June, Cavendish loaded provisions at Harwich, Essex, before reaching Plymouth on 27 June. Pretty reported:

> We departed out of Plimmouth on Thursday the 21 of July 1586 with three sayles ... in which small fleete were 123 persons of all sortes with all kinde of furniture and victuals sufficient for the space of two yeeres of the charges of the worshipful Master Candish.   (Hakluyt, 1598, 11.290)

Cavendish's month-long wait for Cumberland ensured that he received the good news that a fortified colony which Pedro Sarmiento de Gamboa had endeavoured to set up at the Strait of Magellan had failed; he sailed some four days before Cumberland reached Plymouth.

Planning to follow Drake's course (south-west to the Strait of Magellan, north to California, across the Pacific to the spice islands, and home via the Cape of Good Hope), Cavendish wanted to develop Drake's contacts in the Far East and explore possible locations for colonies on the southern coasts of South America, mooted by Grenville in the 1570s. Above all he wanted to open a new English trade with China and Japan, breaking the Spanish monopoly. Hakluyt printed two accounts of this voyage. The first, a terse narrative by the unknown N. H. in 1589 to accompany the account of Francis Drake's circumnavigation, was replaced with Pretty's fuller description and Fuller's rutter. These well-known descriptions provided most of the knowledge about Thomas Cavendish until the twentieth century, when they were complemented and augmented, largely from Spanish archives.

Five days out from Plymouth they met five Spanish fishing vessels returning from Newfoundland; these they shot at, but did not capture. This minor incident was to prove important on the homeward voyage as it may have provoked the charge of piracy in 1589 on the pilot, Fuller. Touching at Sierra Leone to reprovision, Cavendish carved a signal for Cumberland, alongside that left by Drake. By 21 October, when Cumberland landed, Cavendish had reached Brazil, refitted, and built a stowable pinnace. On

reaching Patagonia he visited the inaptly named Port Desire, marking it with other places on a south Atlantic chart based on a Spanish original. By 6 January 1587 he had entered the Strait of Magellan and picked up a survivor of Sarmiento's colony, Tomé Hernandez, who reported the storm damage inflicted on the *Hugh Gallant* before she entered the strait, 'owing to which two ships [*Desire* and *Content*] anchored in the bay, taking the southern side where there are soundings' (Markham, 365). Cavendish remarked on another entrance to the strait but ignored it because 'it was in a higher latitude, and that as there were many islands he did not wish to run the risk of entering by another mouth' (ibid., 369). This possibly explains why Cavendish did not profit from Drake's discovery that Tierra del Fuego was an island.

Cavendish was also criticized for callously abandoning the remnants of Sarmiento's colony, hastily making sail when the weather turned favourable, despite having earlier offered them passage to Peru. They cleared the strait by 24 February, drew ahead of the storm-damaged *Hugh Gallant*, but were reunited 700 miles to the north, on 15 March, off Mocha Island. Revictualling, and running unmolested up to Quintero Bay, north of Valparaiso, Cavendish encountered the first signs of the Spanish early warning defence system emplaced along the Pacific coast since Drake's visit. A goatherd alerted the Spanish authorities to Cavendish's presence; during subsequent negotiations with an advance party Hernandez managed to escape. He reported what then took place, 'By this time the corregidor of Santiago had received tidings of the arrival of the enemy and came with his troops' (Markham, 366). Cavendish's foraging party was attacked by 200 Spaniards, who killed 12, including Hugh Blackenals, master of the *Gallant*. Cavendish exacted a devastating retribution. '19 sailes of ships great and small, All the villages and townes that ever I landed at, I burned and spoiled: and had I not been discovered upon the coast, I had taken great quantitie of treasure' (Letter, Cavendish to Hunsdon, 9 Sept 1588, Hakluyt, 1598, 11.377).

At earthquake-damaged Arica, Cavendish was able to take over the bark *George* and a larger vessel he unsuccessfully tried to barter for prisoners. Later he took a Greek, Jorge Caradino, 'a reasonable pilot for all the coast of Chili' (Hakluyt, 11.309), and an elderly Fleming, torturing them for intelligence. In May the pilot of the leaking coaster *Lewis*, Gonsalvo de Ribas, and a negro, Emannuel, provided useful information on capture. The fleet looted and burnt two Spanish ships illicitly trading from the River Plate to Peru laden with sugar, conserves, and merchandise estimated by Pretty at £20,000 if sold in Europe. Both Spanish ships were 'compelled to sail away with the corsairs for the space of 29 days' to prevent an alarm being raised, 'after which they returned to Buenos Aires' (Haring, 140). When the English fleet landed on Puná Island, close to the equator, to careen, Emannuel escaped, returning with 100 Spanish soldiers. After casualties on both sides, Cavendish sacked and burnt the town and four great ships building on the stocks. On 9 July a new 120 ton ship was looted. Cavendish hanged two crew members, detaining six others. The Marseillais pilot, Miguel Sanchez, who disliked Spaniards, warned of the approach of another small vessel and of the impending arrival of the annual Manila galleons off the Californian coast.

At Huatulco, having ignored the well-defended port of Acapulco, Cavendish captured a damaged, partly off-loaded 50 ton bark, *Nuestra Senora de la Candelaria*, anchored in the bay. The pilot and ship's boy, fishing nearby, identified his ships as pirates by the unusual costume of their crews. Hernando de Ribas Thabuado, master and part owner of the *Candelaria*, negotiated its release, noting Cavendish's pride in *Desire*, its armaments, a detailed map of the coast (possibly similar to one now in The Hague), and the strength and actions of the crew. Cavendish justified his destructiveness 'because the king [of Spain] has declared war by fire and blood against them and they are Christians too and perhaps better' (Conway, 16–17), an arrogance noted also by Hernandez. Before releasing Ribas, Cavendish informed him that he was authorized to return with a larger fleet and to visit Mexico's viceroy with fifty armed men.

At Navidad on 24 August, Cavendish careened his ships at leisure, the pursuing fleet having been delayed by arguments over command. He destroyed two more ships under construction, killed a sleeping dispatch rider, then found time to go pearl-fishing. The fleet patrolled for two weeks off Agueda Segura awaiting the Manila galleons. One escaped in the fog but the 700 ton *Santa Ana* was taken. Cavendish selected the best of her silks, satins, spices, and specie, which later accrued £900 in duty: Quinn estimated the total value as nearly £90,000 (Quinn, *Last Voyage*, 16) whereas the contemporary value was £125,000. Her loss badly damaged the Manila economy for some years and delayed the annual Spain-bound flotilla owing to panic. Once useful charts, pilots, and personnel were safely on board *Desire* she made one of the fastest crossings of the Pacific at that time, aided by the *Santa Ana*'s Spanish pilot whom he hanged near the Philippines for attempting to inform the Spanish authorities of the *Content*'s attempted voyage to the Straits of Amàn. She had left *Desire* off the Californian coast, quarrelling over her share of the spoil, and subsequently disappeared in a storm (Bawlf, 68, 88).

Cavendish spent some time exploring the Philippines, promising disaffected natives support against their Spanish rulers; he was prevented from destroying a new galleon under construction at Panay only by quick-thinking workmen. He sent a letter to the bishop of Manila, provoking the description:

> An English youth of about twenty-two years, with a wretched little vessel of a hundred 'toneladas', dared come to my place of residence, defy us, and boast of the damage that he wrought. He went from our midst laughing, without anyone molesting or troubling him: neither has he felt that the Spaniards are in this land to any purpose. (Blair and Robertson, 7.68)

At some time during this period Cavendish explored the Chinese coast, and captured a Chinese junk with a Portuguese merchant passenger, who may be the source for the 'Great Map of China' (described by Hakluyt but now lost), which Cavendish carried to England.

Cavendish was back in Plymouth by 9 September 1588 after a largely uneventful return, although he was the first Englishman to explore the mid-Atlantic island of St Helena. A ferocious storm in the channel was the worst encountered by the expedition, the *Desire* being almost wrecked off the Lizard Point (*CSP dom.*, *1619–23*, 51; *1623–5*, 159), and he limped into port escorted by John Clerke, bringing in a prize brazilman. The defeat of the Spanish Armada overshadowed his triumph; though he received Elizabeth at Greenwich in November, on board *Desire* dressed overall with silken sails and with ballads written in Cavendish's honour, he did not receive the knighthood mistakenly credited to him by later historians. Elizabeth remarked '[Spanish] ships loaded with gold and silver from the Indes come hither after all' (Quinn, *Last Voyage*, 17).

Cavendish, undeterred by sickness, immediately contacted his patrons, summarizing his achievements, but sensitive material was retained for Walsingham alone. Walsingham reciprocated by offering his physician to treat a grateful Cavendish, 'for whose coming unto me I am most highly bound unto your honoure' (BL, Harley MS 286/92, fol. 16). Other activities followed: refurbishing *Desire*, buying the 240 ton fly-boat *Roebuck* in Plymouth, and sitting for a costly court portrait. After meeting customs dues, repaying creditors, generously rewarding his crew, and recovering his estate, there was little left: 'although his great welthe was thought to have sufficed for hym for his whole lyffe yet he sawe it out thereof within verie shorte time' (Vowell, book 51).

Cavendish was again backed as MP for Wilton, Wiltshire, on 1 October 1585 by Pembroke. Judge Julius Caesar's annoyance at Cavendish's delay in paying his profit led him to threaten court action in 1589, only withdrawn after John Clerke intervened. Cavendish had made a powerful enemy, who was probably behind the impounding of *Desire* in the Thames until December 1589, the accusation of piracy against her pilot Thomas Fuller, and the forfeiture of *Desire*'s good-behaviour bond of £2000. These actions, coupled with Burghley's general stay on shipping, thwarted the restless Cavendish's hopes of an immediate return to the Far East. He bought the *Galleon Dudley* initially with that intention, but in February 1590 she and *Roebuck* (known as *Woolf* in some documents) were commissioned as privateers, their two £2000 bonds paid for by Cavendish's cousin John Cock and his friend John Clerke. In March the *Dudley* illegally attacked the *White Horse*, a disguised English ship in a Dutch convoy off Portugal. The ship was dismasted and sinking fast, and Clerke had to rescue her crew. *Roebuck* later captured other vessels, for which actions Cocke, and Cavendish as owner, were charged with piracy and had to pay restitution. Meanwhile Cavendish had bought Henry Seckford's privateering pinnace *Discharge*, which later became involved in the lucrative capture of the rich Venetian argosy *Uggera*

Salvagina. His links with the south-west were strengthened when he became a burgess of Portsmouth in September 1590 and of Southampton in the following July, allowing him to trade from those towns.

Last voyage, 1591–1592 Robert Parkes's *Historie of the Great and Mighty Kingdom of China* (1588), dedicated to Cavendish, Hakluyt's *Principal Navigations*, and the production of Hues's globes between 1589 and 1591 celebrated Cavendish's achievements, and in 1591 Elizabeth was finally persuaded to commission him to return east. Cavendish intended to take five ships: *Galleon Leicester* (formerly Fenton's ship) and *Roebuck* for their firepower and capacity to stow loot, *Desire* and *Black Pinnace* for inshore work, and an unnamed pinnace, which however sank in the Thames with all hands. Unfortunately support from the court and the London merchants was half-hearted. Cavendish had to share both leadership and financial burdens with a reluctant John Davis (c.1550–1605), the Arctic explorer, who joined him against his friends' advice, on Cavendish's promise to hand over a pinnace on reaching the Pacific for Davis's own planned voyage in search of the north-west passage.

Problems abounded: in April the imprisonment of Thomas Andrewes, a circumnavigation veteran who was now overseeing the fitting out of Cavendish's ships in the Thames, where he accidentally killed a cooper, crucially deprived Cavendish of good-quality supplies and rigging. Cavendish complained to Richard Hawkins in Plymouth Sound how he lost £1500 to absconding impressed sailors, their replacement delaying his departure until 26 August. This late start pressured Cavendish to risk sailing directly to Brazil, without stopping for fresh supplies, a bad decision as, becalmed for twenty-seven days in the doldrums, crews succumbed to fever and scurvy, leading to discontent.

In November 1591 the fleet was becalmed off the Brazilian coast at Cape Frio where plans were laid to capture Santos. The foray there proved to be the turning point of this expedition and was the cause of quarrels between Davis, Cavendish, Cocke, and the crews. Davis's ship *Daintie* reconnoitred disguised as a trader, loaded a valuable cargo of sugar, and requested permission to return home. Her eventual departure forced Cavendish to order a two-month delay to build a replacement stowable pinnace, the *Crow*, and load new stores. In his reports Anthony Knivet gave these delays as the cause of the expedition's failure; Davis's supercargo, John Jane, accused Cavendish of negligence, while Cavendish accused Davis of treachery.

Near the River Plate strong offshore winds severely damaged the fleet; *Crow* was lost, *Leicester* and *Roebuck* collided, both losing ship's boats and leaving *Leicester*'s crew without change of clothing, the vessel shipping water and with few sails. The captainless *Daintie* headed home after the storm. A weakened *Roebuck* was escorted by *Desire* to Port Desire, the agreed rendezvous, where they were joined by Cavendish on *Leicester*, manned by an increasingly rebellious crew.

The damaged fleet, beset by severe storms, entered the Strait of Magellan in mid-April. Blizzards and hard frosts signalled winter's arrival; scavenging for meagre supplies from land and sea, forty men died each week and seventy more weakened on *Leicester* alone. With such an insupportable loss, Cavendish decided to turn back and make for the Philippines via the Cape of Good Hope, a plan that Davis strongly opposed. Cavendish left eight sick men on shore before a violent storm drove them back into the Atlantic and north to Port Desire. 'Roebucke and myself held our course for Brasile and kept together' until reaching the Plate. 'Davys in the Desier and my Pinnis lost me … but I synce understood Davis his intention was ever to run awaye' (Quinn, *Last Voyage*, 26). It is unclear what really happened, but Davis refitted *Desire* at Port Desire for another attempt on the straits, and Cavendish never saw them again, as *Leicester* lost *Roebuck* in the storm, Cavendish resorting to violence to keep order as they headed for Santos, the agreed rendezvous. Raiding San Vincente, north of Buenos Aires, for vital fresh food, his men were routed by settlers through disobeying Cavendish's orders. A dismasted *Roebuck* appeared, and both ships limped up to Santos seeking revenge on the Portuguese, in which they were unsuccessful, gathering a little food in recompense. Moving on to Espirito Santo, where they were wrongly assured they could cross the entrance bar, their attempt to capture two moored ships was delayed, costing them fifty-five lives.

Cavendish's secret plan, to strip and destroy *Roebuck* and return to the strait with the refurbished *Leicester*, now leaked out. Robert Tharlton, having replaced Cocke who was mortally sick on *Leicester* as *Roebuck*'s master, reacted by sailing back to England. *Leicester* began repairs off San Sebastian, abandoning sick crewmen, but was forced to sail before the refit was complete, when attacked by Portuguese settlers and natives. Shortage of food prevented both Cavendish's desired return to the strait and a visit to St Helena, while the near mutinous crew refused even to consider Ascension Island, preferring Brazil. Cocke's death near the equator was the last straw. 'The strain of constantly asserting himself against his men and his failure to make them obey him had destroyed … his will to live' (Quinn, *Last Voyage*, 32). By now suicidal, Cavendish dictated his will, witnessed by Hues and others. He died—legend says of a broken heart, but possibly from natural causes—in May or June 1592; *Leicester* reached Plymouth in March 1593.

Sequel and reputation *Leicester* delivered Cavendish's will with its detailed instructions to Tristram Gorges, his executor, and Cavendish's account of the voyage, including a vitriolic attack on Davis, used in a now lost admiralty inquiry. The will sparked off a family row. Anne Dudley, one of his two surviving sisters, was the only one to benefit, gaining the residue from the sale of *Leicester* and *Roebuck*; the *Desire*, which limped into Ireland in 1593, was bequeathed to Sir George Carey. Beatrice Denny, the other sister, had signed away rights to the estate before 1591, but she contested the will, a plea rejected in 1596 when the high court accepted Cavendish's documents.

Further challenges followed from a group of sailors

deprived by the will of their customary rewards, and from John Chambers, Cavendish's cook, who petitioned for non-payment of four years' wages at the court of requests. He claimed that Cavendish was worth £3000 at his death, although the Suffolk lands subsequently sold for £13,000. Cavendish's mother, reduced to penury, spent the rest of her life unsuccessfully attempting to recover £2000 that her son had owed her since 1589. Cavendish's demise split up the estate: the Cornwallis family bought the Suffolk lands, while the Lincolnshire manors went to his cousin Augustine Cavendish, who had unsuccessfully challenged Seckford's stewardship in 1587.

Some of his contemporaries hailed Cavendish's navigation skills, shown graphically in the contemporary and seventeenth-century engravings by Jodocus Hondius and C. de Passe. The Spaniards noted his new nautical invention in 1588, and the Dutch East India Company prized his charts and the pilots he trained on the circumnavigation, recruiting them to establish their trade to the Philippines early in 1598. Ralegh called Cavendish and Drake 'children of fortune': the privateering havoc wrought on the South American coast prevented the development of a proper trading policy as it encouraged freebooters to seek short-term personal wealth, not natural growth. Comments that Cavendish was 'lucky' in the circumnavigation of 1586 ignore his excellent planning and personal navigation skills; others, that he was 'merely repeating Drake's voyage', ignore his attempts at establishing trade round the River Plate, in Brazil, and in the Far East, his investigations about China, and the 'Great Map' given to Walsingham.

Cavendish's penchant for gambling—wagering his whole estate for greater profit—yielded great gains in 1588. His youthful reputation as a spendthrift resurfaced, however, revived by the extravagant portrait commissioned and his overgenerosity to his circumnavigation crew, to the detriment of important investors like Sir Julius Caesar. Thus his reputation was diminished commercially and potential merchant backers shied away from the venture of 1591, leaving him without the courtly support provided earlier by Ralegh and Walsingham. His rapid mental deterioration during the last voyage, brought about by divided command, poor food, bad weather, and gradual loss of confidence in his ability to command, may have been a recurrence of the illness seen in 1588 and was not helped by the absence of a surgeon on board.

Dyke and Quinn, writing in the last half of the twentieth century, have highlighted Cavendish's achievements and his influence. Recent research reinforces his importance as East Anglia's major Elizabethan seafarer, backed by local and London enterprise. His voyages were part of Elizabeth's strategy for independent expansion overseas, working in tandem with Drake and as a foil to the activities of the Devon seafarers. His vision of a trade based in the Philippines attracted the Dutch, and only belatedly the English merchants, and was largely overlooked by historians.   SUSAN M. MAXWELL

Sources R. Hakluyt, *The principal navigations, voyages, traffiques and discoveries of the English nation*, 2nd edn, 3 vols. (1598–1600); repr. 12 vols., Hakluyt Society, extra ser., 1–12 (1903–5) · R. Hakluyt, *The principall naviggations, voiages and discoveries of the English nation* (1589) [facs. ed. D. B. Quinn and R. A. Skelton, 2 vols. (1965), vol. 1, pp. 808–15)] · S. Purchas, *Hakluytus posthumus, or, Purchas his pilgrimes*, 20 bks in 4 vols. (1625); repr. 20 vols., Hakluyt Society, extra ser., 14–33 (1905–7), 472–3 · D. B. Quinn, ed., *The Roanoke voyages, 1584–90*, 2 vols., Hakluyt Society, 2nd ser., 104, 105 (1995), vol. 1, pp. 62, 163–5, 210–14 · D. B. Quinn, ed., *The last voyage of Thomas Cavendish, 1591–2* (1975) · S. M. Maxwell, *The first Virginia voyage: the Cavendish connection*, The Durham Thomas Harriot Seminar, Occasional paper no. 23 (1996) · S. M. Maxwell, 'Henry Seckford: Elizabethan courtier, merchant and privateer', *Mariner's Mirror*, 82 (1996), 387–97 · G. Dyke, 'The finances of a sixteenth century navigator, Thomas Cavendish of Trimley in Suffolk', *Mariner's Mirror*, 44 (1958), 108–15 · R. F. Hitchcock, 'Cavendish's last voyage: the charges against Davis', *Mariner's Mirror*, 80 (1994), 259–69 · E. H. Blair and J. A. Robertson, eds., *The Philippine islands, 1493–1898*, 7 (1903–9), pp. 52–111 · J. Callender, ed., *Terra Australis cognita, or, Voyages to the Terra Australis or southern hemisphere during the sixteenth, seventeenth and eighteenth centuries*, 3 vols. (1766–8), vol. 1 · Cumberland's journal, 1586, BL, Lansdowne MS 100/23 · C. R. Markham, ed., *Narratives of the voyages of Pedro Sarmiento de Gamboa*, Hakluyt Society, 91 (1895), 209, 341, 352–74 [Hernandez's narrative] · D. Sowerbuts, partial abridgement and translation of transcript by G. R. C. Conway of documents relating to Thomas Cavendish, Oaxaca, 1587, Ag. G. N. Mexico, inquisicion, vol. 1A, relation of Hernando de Ribas Thibuado, priv. coll. [copies of Conway's transcript in U. Aberdeen L. and CUL] · P. Gerhard, *Pirates of the Pacific, 1575–1742* (1990) · *The naval tracts of Sir William Monson*, ed. M. Oppenheim, 3, Navy RS, 43 (1912), 359; 4, Navy RS, 45 (1913), 281 · L. de Alberti and A. B. Wallis Chapman, *English merchants and the Spanish Inquisition in the Canaries: extracts from the archives in possession of the most hon. the Marquess of Bute*, CS, 3rd ser., 23 (1912) · W. W. Borah, 'Early trade and navigation between Mexico and Peru', *Iberoamericana*, 38 (1954) · Bodl. Oxf., MS Tanner 313, fol. 22 [quitclaim, Thomas, Anne, and Beatrice Cavendish, n. d.] · E. Sluiter, ed., *New light from Spanish archives on the voyage of Olivier van Noort: the vice-admiral ship the Hendrick Frederick, on the west coast of the Americas* (1600) (1937) · Alnwick Castle, Duke of Northumberland MSS, SH at ACY 111, 1 and bundle 5 [recognizances, Thomas Cavendish, Thomas Perrott, and Richard Skipwith] · will, PRO, PROB 10/Box 163 [Thomas Caundish, original will] · P. Edwards, ed., *Last voyages: Cavendish, Hudson, Ralegh—the original narratives* (1988) · DNB · W. Strachey, *The historie of travell into Virginia Britannia*, ed. L. B. Wright and V. Freund, Hakluyt Society, 2nd ser., 32 (1953) · C. H. Haring, *Trade and navigation between Spain and the Indies in the time of the Hapsburgs* (1918); repr. (1964), 140–41 · commonplace book of John Hooker, chamberlain of the city of Exeter, ECR, book 51, s.a. 1588 · S. Bawlf, *Sir Francis Drake's secret voyage to the northwest coast of America, AD 1579* (2001), 68, 88 · *CSP dom.*, 1619–23, 51; 1623–5, 159

Likenesses M. Gheeraerts, oils, Berkeley Castle, Gloucestershire · C. Passe, line engraving, BM; repro. in C. de Passe, *Effigies Regum … in re nautica* (Cologne, 1598) · Passe, line engraving, BM, NPG; repro. in H. Holland, *Heröologia* (1620) · oils, Longleat House, Wiltshire

Wealth at death Suffolk lands later sold for £13,000; also lands in Lincolnshire, plus three ships

Cavendish, Victor Christian William, ninth duke of Devonshire

Cavendish, Victor Christian William, ninth duke of **Devonshire** (1868–1938), politician and governor-general of Canada, was born on 31 May 1868, the eldest son of Lord Edward Cavendish (1838–1891) and his wife, Emma Elizabeth Lascelles (1838–1920). He was educated at Eton College and Trinity College, Cambridge, from where he graduated BA in 1891. After leaving university he trained for several months in an accountant's office and studied law in the Inner Temple chambers of Judge Lush-Wilson. This pioneering form of management training prepared him for his responsibilities on the board of such family businesses as the Barrow Hematite Steel Company and the Furness Railway. Following the death of his father, who was Liberal Unionist MP for West Derbyshire, he was returned unopposed in June 1891 for the constituency, which he held until March 1908, when he succeeded his uncle (Spencer Compton Cavendish, marquess of Harting-ton and eighth duke of Devonshire) in the dukedom. On the death in December 1891 of his grandfather William Cavendish (the seventh duke), he inherited the Holker Hall estate in north Lancashire. On 30 July 1892 he married Lady Evelyn Emily Mary (1870–1960), elder daughter of Henry Charles Keith Petty-*Fitzmaurice, fifth marquess of Lansdowne. They had two sons and five daughters.

As a politician who preferred listening to speaking, Cav-endish was treasurer of the royal household (1900–03) in the last Salisbury government. Under Balfour he was a painstaking financial secretary to the Treasury (1903–05). He became a privy councillor after losing office in 1905, and was created GCVO in 1912, but rued his exclusion from the Commons after 1908. 'The Duchess says he can't think what to do in the evenings and that he writes all sorts of needless letters to kill time' (*Crawford Papers*, 108). However, he became an assiduous and influential mem-ber of the Lords during the tense years of the Asquith administration. His political opponent John Morley con-sidered his interventions 'simple, direct, weighty and bal-anced' (FitzRoy, 460). In 1912 he was recruited to Bonar Law's shadow cabinet where he had a deserved reputation as a 'safe man' (*Crawford Papers*, 348).

Devonshire assumed numerous responsibilities after succeeding to the dukedom, together with some 186,000 acres. He was lord lieutenant of Derbyshire and high stew-ard of Derby from 1908, honorary colonel of the 5th bat-talion of the Sherwood Foresters (the Nottinghamshire and Derbyshire regiment) from 1908, mayor of East-bourne (1909–10) and of Chesterfield (1911–12). He was also chancellor of the University of Leeds from 1910, and high steward of the University of Cambridge from 1923 (sitting on the council of Selwyn College). From 1908 he was presi-dent of the British Empire League. He was twice elected president of the Royal Agricultural Society (1908, 1932).

The duke, who was vice-president of the Navy League from 1909, returned to government in the wartime coali-tion as civil lord of the Admiralty (1915–16). His replies on behalf of the Admiralty in the upper house were 'capital' (Sandhurst, 325). He received the Garter in January 1916, and in June succeeded the duke of Connaught as governor-general and commander-in-chief of Canada. He was created GCMG in July, and after landing in Canada in November during a critical phase of the war, consistently strove to sustain patriotic morale. The imposition of con-scription had been resented, especially among the Qué-becois, and the wartime upheaval was followed by eco-nomic dislocation and social unrest. Devonshire's skilful treatment of different sections of Canadian opinion was widely acknowledged. His interventions in the intricacies

of post-war Canadian party politics were deft and harmo-nious. He enjoyed discussing political tactics with his aide-de-camp Harold *Macmillan, who married his daughter Dorothy Evelyn Cavendish in 1920. The prince of Wales, touring the dominion in 1919, thought the duke was 'a damned good fellow and has no side', although stuck in a 'hopelessly narrow groove' (Davenport-Hines, 163). His appointment expired in August 1921.

Devonshire's sale of Devonshire House in Piccadilly for £750,000 in 1920 inspired Siegfried Sassoon's 'Monody on the Demolition of Devonshire House'. His refusal in March 1922 to serve as secretary of state for India under Lloyd-George damaged the prestige of the coalition gov-ernment. An evolved whig rather than a tory die-hard, he supported the Irish settlement of 1922. After the fall of the coalition Devonshire joined Bonar Law's cabinet as secre-tary of state for the colonies in October 1922. As colonial secretary he issued the Devonshire declaration of 1923 that the interests of African natives must be paramount over those of immigrant settlers in Kenya colony. This announcement was pregnant with significance for future colonial policy, and was generally unexpected. It accorded with Devonshire's generous whiggish inclinations, and he withstood pressure to withdraw or amend the prin-ciple of paramountcy. Sir Maurice Hankey, the cabinet secretary, observed that Devonshire resembled 'an apo-plectic idol and gives little counsel' (Roskill, 2.323). Craw-ford, however, described him in 1923:

> what a solid person he is—uncouth in gesture, ponderous in appearance, slow in style—yet giving the impression of saying all that requires statement and doing so without any effort to score a success. There is a massive imperturbability about him which gives confidence. He will never let one down, never play for his own advantage, never do anything brilliant. (*Crawford Papers*, 486)

In cabinet he resisted attempts by Amery and other pro-tectionists to extend safeguarding of industry. Baldwin's handling of the American debt question disquieted him, and he deplored the new prime minister's decision to go to the country on a protectionist platform. He left the Colonial Office in January 1924, and was not invited to hold office when Baldwin resumed power in November. It was believed that Baldwin contemplated offering him the lord presidency of the council until Curzon insisted on that office.

Devonshire in middle life resembled a solemn, ruddy-complexioned walrus with a strong jaw. Despite looking stolid and even sleepy, he was shrewd, tactful, observant, and clear-headed. His authority rested on real though unostentatious ability. During 1924–5 he served as chair-man of the British Empire Exhibition held at Wembley and unobtrusively became one of its financial guarantors. In 1925 he accepted further public responsibilities, includ-ing the chairmanship of both a privy council committee to enquire into the Channel Islands' contributions to the imperial exchequer and the Sadler's Wells theatre trust. He went for the Easter holidays to Lismore Castle, where on 12 April 1925 he suffered a paralytic stroke. This changed him from a calm, impassive, and patient man into at best a querulous, morose invalid and at worst a ferocious bully. Although he relished the presence of his grandchildren, his domestic rages became increasingly unpleasant. The cold, authoritarian, and frugal duchess had anxiously reorganized the management of the Devonshire properties after 1908, and rose to greater ascendancy as her husband's mental condition deteriorated. She introduced nettle soup to Chatsworth menus to save expense, had Sir Joseph Paxton's great conservatory there dynamited in 1920, and replanted his garden with rhododendrons and bamboo. The duke continued to fulfil certain public duties until shortly before his death on 6 May 1938, at Chatsworth. On 9 May he was buried at Edensor church. RICHARD DAVENPORT-HINES

Sources The Times (7 May 1938) · The Times (9–12 May 1938) · J. Pearson, Stags and serpents: the story of the house of Cavendish and the dukes of Devonshire (1983) · R. Davenport-Hines, The Macmillans (1992) · H. Macmillan, Winds of change, 1914–1939 (1966) [vol. 1 of autobiography] · The Crawford papers: the journals of David Lindsay, twenty-seventh earl of Crawford … 1892–1940, ed. J. Vincent (1984) · A. Fitz-Roy, Memoirs (1925) · Viscount Sandhurst, From day to day (1928) · S. W. Roskill, Hankey, man of secrets, 2 (1972) · R. Churchill, Lord Derby (1959) · Venn, Alum. Cant. · J. M. Brown and W. R. Louis, The twentieth century (1999), vol. 4 of The Oxford history of the British Empire

Archives Chatsworth House, Derbyshire, diaries and political MSS; papers · NA Canada | Bodl. Oxf., letters to Herbert Asquith · Bodl. Oxf., corresp. with Lord Selborne · Bodl. RH, corresp. relating to Kenya · HLRO, corresp. with Andrew Bonar Law · NL Aus., corresp. with Viscount Novar · NRA, priv. coll., corresp. with Lord Balfour of Burleigh · U. Nott. L., letters to E. M. Wrench · Wilts. & Swindon RO, corresp. with Viscount Long | FILM BFI NFTVA, news footage

Likenesses photograph, c.1900, Hult. Arch. · W. Rothenstein, pencil drawing, 1916, NPG · W. Stoneman, photograph, 1923, NPG · P. A. de Laszlo, oils, 1928, Chatsworth House, Derbyshire · H. Furniss, ink caricature, NPG · R. S. Sherriffs, ink caricature, NPG

Wealth at death £112,808 18s. 7d.: probate, 24 June 1938, CGPLA Eng. & Wales

Cavendish, Sir William (1508–1557), administrator, was born on 1 May 1508, a younger son of Sir Thomas Cavendish (c.1480–1524) of Cavendish, Suffolk, and his wife, Alice, daughter of John Smith or Smyth of Padbrook Hall, Cavendish. Historians of his family like White Kennett and Edmund Lodge were ill-informed about this progenitor of the great Cavendish dynasties, surmising that it was he, rather than his brother George *Cavendish, who was gentleman usher (and biographer) to Wolsey, and that William was sworn of the privy council when he became treasurer of the chamber. In fact the latter's career was based upon his work as an agent of crown finance. Thomas Cavendish had been a senior clerk in the clerk of the pipe's office in the exchequer, and William followed in his father's footsteps, making his fortune as an auditor. By the early 1530s he was an accepted financial expert. In December 1530 he was authorized to receive the surrender of Sheen Priory. Having become one of Thomas Cromwell's trusted clerks he was empowered in 1532 to deal with Holy Trinity Priory, Aldgate, and in 1533 with the temporalities of Ely sede vacante. He already had the confidence to face down opponents, but he took risks, and his

Sir William Cavendish (1508–1557), attrib. John Bettes the elder

reputation was far from spotless. He was one of Cromwell's principal agents in the dissolution of the monasteries, which gave him additional bargaining power at a time when he had recently set up house in Hertfordshire and was starting to acquire leases. But he was accused of adding to the rewards allocated to commissioners like himself without the knowledge of his clerks, prompting an expensive but ultimately inconclusive inquiry into his conduct. It was not until January 1546, moreover, that he obtained a discharge for Ely revenues totalling £2033 0s. 6d. which he was said to have paid to Cromwell for the king's use.

By 1534 Cavendish had married Margaret, daughter of Edward Bostock of Cheshire, with whom he had five children; only two daughters survived infancy. He was desperately anxious at this time to accumulate offices in order to improve his 'poor living'. In 1536 he was touting to become auditor to the earl of Shrewsbury and to the hospital of St John of Jerusalem, persisting in pursuit of the latter office even when it was granted elsewhere: 'It would be high advancement for him for he would have continually meat and drink for himself and his two servants with their liveries and chamber' (LP Henry VIII, 10, no. 425). From 28 April 1536 he held the desirable auditorship of the home counties circuit of the court of augmentations, which did not prevent his becoming auditor of Lord Beauchamp, and therefore having to cope with conflicting demands upon his energies, later in the year. In February 1540 he bought the manor of Northaw, Hertfordshire, formerly leased by him from St Albans Abbey. On 9 June his wife died.

Cavendish enhanced his reputation by his performance

as a commissioner in Ireland, where he arrived on 8 September 1540, appointed to investigate the administration of Lord Deputy Grey, along with the vice-treasurer's accounts and the surveys for the dissolution of the Irish monasteries. He won praise for:

> his painstaking (he journeyed as far as Limerick, where no English commissioners have been this many years, and that in such frost and snow as the writer never rode in) and for being a man that little feareth the displeasure of any man, in the King's service. (*LP Henry VIII*, 17, no. 304)

Following his return to England he received licence on 26 October 1541 for a settlement of his estates before his marriage to Elizabeth Parys, widow, the daughter of Thomas Parker of Poslingford, Suffolk. They were married at the London Blackfriars on 3 November 1542, but their three daughters all died young, and Elizabeth was dead by 1547.

Cavendish paid £1000 for the position of treasurer of the chamber, granted to him on 19 February 1546. A month later he was in trouble with the privy council for failing to bring the declaration of his accounts before the chancellor, but he was still knighted on 23 April. He may have owed this promotion to Sir William Paget, or to Edward Seymour, earl of Hertford, whose auditor he was, but he had clearly been acquiring a wide range of patronage, for his marriage to Elizabeth Barley, *née* Hardwick (d. 1608), which took place secretly at 2 a.m. on 20 August 1547 at the Greys' manor house at Bradgate, Leicestershire, seems to have been promoted both by the Greys and the Brandons. They had three sons and five daughters. Cavendish had arrived. In 1547 he sat in parliament for Thirsk, was a JP for Hertfordshire, and furnished great horses, light horses, and demi-lances for the wars, under an assessment of £100.

Cavendish had also been appointed treasurer of the court of general surveyors, but he lost this position in 1547. The office of treasurer of the chamber was losing importance, moreover. He received it in a state of disorder, and complained that after the death of Henry VIII he had lost 5000 marks through the earl of Warwick's withholding his dues. He struggled through Edward VI's reign without much regular income. His receipts in his first year were £46,555 0s. 5d., but there had been a sharp drop by 1549, and by 1553 they came to only £9924 12s. 1d., insufficient to meet the fixed payments. He supported Mary in 1553 at a cost to himself of 1000 marks, so he claimed, and she reappointed him to the office. But the receipts continued to decline and had to be supplemented from other treasuries. In 1555 he also became deputy chamberlain of the exchequer. By 1557 his accounts were under examination. As always with unexpected audits, utter confusion was alleged but not really substantiated. The report on Cavendish's debts submitted to Lord Treasurer Winchester on 12 October 1557 shows an initial assessment of his debt as £5237 0s. 0½d., but he put forward various counter-claims, including the dishonesty of his clerk Thomas Knot, who ran away leaving him £12,031 1s. 8d. in debt. Cavendish wrote a grovelling appeal for clemency, describing himself as 'a humble pore man standing without her highnes great mercy' (PRO, E101/424/10), and listing his resources as 500 marks in land and £440 in fees and life annuities. He died on 25 October 1557 and was buried on the 30th. By 14 December following his widow had married Sir William Saintloe, captain of the queen's guard. They were duly pursued for Cavendish's debts, in proceedings which became a *cause célèbre*, with a major debate at the bar of the exchequer over the liability of his lands. Warned that the law was against him and his wife, Saintloe compounded with the queen for £1000 and had a release and pardon for the residue.

Following his third marriage Cavendish reorganized his estates, selling property in Hertfordshire and buying in Derbyshire, where he began the building of Chatsworth House. On 5 April 1557 he entailed lands in Derbyshire and Staffordshire to his eldest son Henry *Cavendish, aged six, and also conveyed property to his younger sons Charles Cavendish and William *Cavendish. His widow, who remarried after Saintloe's death in 1565 and died as Elizabeth *Talbot, countess of Shrewsbury, arranged prestigious marriages for her children. Although Henry, who married his own stepsister Grace Talbot, died without issue, William became first earl of Devonshire and Charles the father of the first duke of Newcastle. Elizabeth Cavendish married Charles Stuart, earl of Lennox, and was the mother of Arabella Stuart, making William the grandfather of a possible queen. Frances, who married Sir Henry Pierpoint of Holme Pierpoint, Nottinghamshire, was the mother of the first earl of Kingston upon Hull. Mary married her stepbrother Gilbert Talbot. Cavendish's other daughters did not marry.   SYBIL M. JACK

Sources HoP, *Commons, 1509–58*, 1.597–9 · GEC, *Peerage*, new edn, vols. 4, 9, 11 · *The diary of Henry Machyn, citizen and merchant-taylor of London, from AD 1550 to AD 1563*, ed. J. G. Nichols, CS, 42 (1848) · *LP Henry VIII*, vols. 3–21 · APC, 1542–63 · PRO, chancery, inquisitions post mortem, second series, C142/111/22 · PRO, exchequer, king's remembrancer, accounts various, E101/424/10 · PRO, king's remembrancer, memoranda rolls, E159 · PRO, E101/424/9; E101/426/5; E101/637/1 · PRO, exchequer, augmentations office, miscellaneous books, E315/439; E315/541 · PRO, king's remembrancer, modern deeds, series B, E216/658, 659 · *Whissale secundum usum insignis ecclesie Sarisburiensis* (Rouen, 1497) [missal formerly at Chatsworth, now in BL (IC 43969) with family notes in calendar] · private information (2004) [John Goldfinch] · *DNB*
Likenesses attrib. J. Bettes the elder, oils, Hardwick Hall, Derbyshire [*see illus.*]
Wealth at death claimed 500 marks in land: PRO, E 101/424/10; PRO, C 142/111/22

Cavendish, William, first earl of Devonshire (1551–1626), nobleman, was born on 27 December 1551, the second son of Sir William *Cavendish (1508–1557), administrator, of Chatsworth, Derbyshire, and his third wife, Elizabeth [see Talbot, Elizabeth, countess of Shrewsbury (1527?–1608)], noblewoman, daughter and coheir of John Hardwick of Hardwick, Derbyshire, and his wife, Elizabeth. His godparents were Elizabeth Parr, marchioness of Northampton, William Paulet, first marquess of Winchester, and William Herbert, first earl of Pembroke. His two

William Cavendish, first earl of Devonshire (1551–1626), by unknown artist, 1576

brothers were Henry *Cavendish (1550–1616), soldier and traveller, and Sir Charles Cavendish (1553–1617), of Welbeck Abbey, Nottinghamshire. However, William Cavendish was his mother's favourite, especially from the 1580s onwards when she was disillusioned with his elder brother.

Sir William Cavendish died on 25 October 1557, and his widow married Sir William Saintloe on 14 December. Saintloe had William and Henry Cavendish educated at Eton College from 21 November 1560. William Cavendish matriculated from Clare College, Cambridge, on 29 September 1567. His mother, again a widow, married George *Talbot, sixth earl of Shrewsbury (c.1522–1590), magnate, about this time. In the marriage settlement Shrewsbury agreed to pay his new wife's debts and promised considerable sums to William and Charles Cavendish when they reached the age of twenty-one.

When Cavendish turned twenty-one Shrewsbury, because of the cost of the guardianship of Mary, queen of Scots, was not in a strong financial position. The countess of Shrewsbury agreed to absolve her husband from what he had promised to pay her and her children if he would legally return the lands she had originally brought to the marriage and give them to William and Charles Cavendish, with a discretionary life interest in them for herself. On 22 April 1572 Shrewsbury signed the deed of gift, something he was to regret later. During the same year William Cavendish was admitted to study law at Gray's Inn. He was possibly knighted in 1580, but the evidence is ambiguous.

On 21 March 1581 he married Anne (d. before 1619), daughter and coheir of Henry Keighley of Keighley, Yorkshire, and his wife, Mary. The couple had three sons, including William *Cavendish, second earl of Devonshire (1590–1628), nobleman, and three daughters. By 1584 the earl and countess of Shrewsbury were in conflict, and he claimed the rents from his wife's tenants in Derbyshire and Somerset. He raided Chatsworth, Derbyshire, and Cavendish barred the great doors while his mother fled. Cavendish, armed and surrounded by his loyal servants, faced his stepfather as he prepared to fight for his family's honour and inheritance. Elizabeth I commanded that they call off their feud, and royal officials took Cavendish to London, where he was briefly imprisoned in the Fleet. The queen then insisted on a full inquiry conducted by the lord chancellor, Sir Thomas Bromley, with Robert Dudley, earl of Leicester, acting as an informal mediator.

On both occasions when Cavendish was returned to parliament (for Liverpool in 1586 and for Newport in Monmouthshire in 1588), it was from boroughs remote from Derbyshire. This may have been because of Shrewsbury's enmity, the earl effectively blocking any local patronage for his stepsons. Quite possibly in 1585, at the height of the quarrel between the earl and countess of Shrewsbury, she considered it would be potentially helpful to have her son in parliament, and Sir Ralph Sadler arranged the election in 1586 as a favour. A royal commissioner investigated but trod warily because of Shrewsbury's power. The earl died in 1590 and the situation eased. Cavendish was named of the quorum about 1583. Chatsworth was legally entailed to Henry Cavendish and reverted to him at Shrewsbury's death. He was not on speaking terms with his mother, and she bought lands for William Cavendish valued at £15,900 by 1584. William Cavendish had little interest in life at court, but from 1595 to 1596 he was sheriff of Derbyshire, his local consequence being based on his status as a great landowner.

Cavendish became more prominent after the accession of James I in 1603. He was elevated to the peerage as Baron Cavendish of Hardwick on 4 May 1605. He inherited the bulk of his mother's land and property when she died on 13 February 1608 and bought Chatsworth from his elder brother in the following year. Cavendish managed his estates very carefully, promoted industrial enterprise, had a thorough understanding of finance, continued to purchase land, and was one of the first investors in Virginia and a co-grantee of the Bermuda Islands, with one of Bermuda's nine parishes named Devonshire after his most senior title. He also invested in the Russia Company, Somers Island Company, and North-West Passage Company, and very heavily but successfully in the East India Company. His local importance grew. He was named bailiff of Tutbury Castle, Staffordshire, *custos rotulorum* for Derbyshire in 1615, and, jointly with his heir, lord lieutenant of Derbyshire from 1619. Cavendish succeeded his elder brother on 12 October 1616, acquiring more property, and was promoted earl of Devonshire on 7 August 1618. This title was acquired after some unedifying petitioning of Arabella Stuart and cost Cavendish £10,900 in total. Devonshire married again by 1619, his second wife being Elizabeth (d. c.1642), daughter and heir of Edward Boughton of Cawston, Warwickshire, and his wife, Susanna, and widow of Sir Richard Wortley. They had one son. Devonshire died at Hardwick Hall on 3 March 1626 and was buried in the parish church at Edensor. Leaving his heir about 100,000 acres, he had consolidated his own inheritance and laid the foundation for one of the greatest estates of the seventeenth century.   CAROLE LEVIN

Sources F. Bickley, *The Cavendish family* (1911) • A. Collins, *Historical collections of the noble families of Cavendishe, Holles, Vere, Harley and Ogle* (1752) • D. N. Durant, *Bess of Hardwick: portrait of an Elizabethan dynast* (1977) • HoP, *Commons, 1558–1603*, 1.565–6 • J. Pearson, *The serpent and the stag* (New York, 1983) • M. S. Rawson, *Bess of Hardwick and her circle* (1910) • L. Stone, *The crisis of the aristocracy, 1558–1641*, abridged edn (1967) • C. Jamison, G. R. Batho, and E. G. W. Bill, eds., *A calendar of the Shrewsbury and Talbot papers in Lambeth Palace Library and the College of Arms*, 2 vols., HMC, JP 6–7 (1966–71) • GEC, *Peerage*
Archives Chatsworth House, Derbyshire, Devonshire MSS • LPL, corresp. and papers | Folger, MS Xd 428
Likenesses portrait, 1576, Hardwick Hall, Derbyshire [*see illus.*]
Wealth at death estate of 100,000 acres: Pearson, *The serpent and the stag*

Cavendish, William, second earl of Devonshire (1590–1628), nobleman, was the second son of William *Cavendish, first earl of Devonshire (1551–1626), and his first wife, Anne Keighley. He was educated by Thomas Hobbes the philosopher, who resided at Chatsworth as his private tutor for many years and accompanied him in a tour through France and Italy before his coming of age. Hobbes states that he was his pupil's friend for twenty years, and eulogizes his learning in the dedication of his translation of Thucydides. Cavendish was admitted to Gray's Inn on 14 May 1602, and it is asserted that he was created MA at Cambridge, incorporated at Oxford on 8 July 1608. He was knighted at Whitehall in 1609. He married, allegedly against his will, on 10 April 1608; his wife was Christian Bruce (1595–1675) [*see* Cavendish, Christian], daughter of Edward, Lord Bruce of Kinloss, and later a notable royalist. Cavendish was after this a leader of court society, and an intimate friend of James I. He was MP for Bishop's Castle in 1610 and for Derbyshire in 1614, 1621, 1624, 1625, and 1626, and lord lieutenant of Derbyshire, jointly with his father in 1619 and alone after the latter's death. In April 1622 he introduced to audiences with the king ambassadors from the emperor Ferdinand, Venice, and the United Provinces.

Devonshire was a leading member of the Virginia and Somers Island companies, frequently lobbying the crown on their behalf. His role in overseas adventure led, in 1623, to conflict with Robert Rich, earl of Warwick; a duel was arranged, but prevented by the privy council. In 1625 he was present at Charles I's marriage with Henrietta Maria. Styled Lord Cavendish from 1616, early in 1626 he inherited his father's title and his seat in the House of Lords: there he resisted Buckingham's attempt to interpret a speech of Sir Dudley Digges as treasonous (13 May 1626). His lavish hospitality strained his ample resources in his last years, and in 1628 a private act of parliament

enabled him to sell some of the entailed estates in discharge of his debts. Devonshire's London house was in Bishopsgate, on the site afterwards occupied by Devonshire Square. He died there (from excessive indulgence in good living, it is said) on 20 June 1628, and was buried on 11 July in All Saints' Church, Derby. He and his wife had three sons: William *Cavendish, third earl of Devonshire, Charles *Cavendish, army officer, and Henry, who died in youth. His daughter Anne, a well-known patroness of literature, married Robert, Lord Rich, heir of the earl of Warwick.   SIDNEY LEE, rev. VICTOR STATER

Sources CSP dom., 1619–28 • GEC, *Peerage* • APC, 1621–3 • S. M. Kingsbury, ed., *The records of the Virginia Company of London*, 4 vols. (1906–35) • S. Glover, *The history and gazetteer of the county of Derby*, ed. T. Noble, 2 (1833), 222–53 • T. K. Rabb, *Jacobean gentleman: Sir Edwin Sandys, 1561–1629* (1998), 234 • *Dudley Carleton to John Chamberlain, 1603–1624: Jacobean letters*, ed. M. Lee (1972), 167, 308, 311 • L. L. Peck, *Northampton: patronage and policy at the court of James I* (1982), 173 • R. T. Spence, *Lady Anne Clifford: countess of Pembroke, Dorset and Montgomery, 1590–1676* (1997), 19
Likenesses oils, 1625, Hardwick Hall, Derbyshire • attrib. D. Mytens, oils, Hardwick Hall, Derbyshire • attrib. P. van Somer, oils, North Carolina Museum of Art, Raleigh • monument, All Saints' Church, Derby

Cavendish, William, first duke of Newcastle upon Tyne (*bap.* 1593, *d.* 1676), writer, patron, and royalist army officer, was born at Handsworth Manor, Yorkshire, and was baptized in the parish on 16 December 1593. He was the second of three children, the first having died in infancy, of Sir Charles Cavendish (1553–1617) MP, the youngest son of Bess of Hardwick [*see* Talbot, Elizabeth, countess of Shrewsbury] and her second husband, Sir William *Cavendish of Chatsworth, Derbyshire, and his second wife, Catherine (1570–1629), daughter of Cuthbert, Baron Ogle, of Ogle Castle, Northumberland.

Education and early career In 1597 Gilbert Talbot, seventh earl of Shrewsbury, passed over the lease of Welbeck Abbey, Nottinghamshire, to his stepbrother and brother-in-law, Sir Charles Cavendish, and it was here that William spent his formative years. Initially he was tutored at home but he was also 'partly bred' along with his younger brother the mathematician Charles *Cavendish (1595?–1654) in the Shrewsbury household (Cavendish, *Life*, 1). William Cavendish entered St John's College, Cambridge, as a fellow-commoner in 1608. Mary, countess of Shrewsbury, was a benefactress of St John's and in recognition of her generosity Cavendish presented a statue of his aunt by the sculptor Thomas Burman to the college in 1671. Since he had little aptitude for academic pursuits Cavendish's tutors 'could not persuade him to read or study much, he taking more delight in sports, than in learning' (ibid., 104). Sir Charles Cavendish encouraged William to 'follow his own genius', and was delighted when his son spent £50 each on a singing boy and a horse instead of investing his money in land as a young kinsman had done, declaring, 'if he should find his son to be so covetous, that he would buy land before he was twenty years of age, he would disinherit him' (ibid., 105).

In contrast to many of his contemporaries Cavendish eschewed the inns of court, preferring instead to enter the Royal Mews. Here in the company of Prince Henry he was trained by the French riding instructor St Antoine in the art of *manège*, a passion that he pursued throughout his life. He later wrote, 'I have practised ever since I was ten years old, have rid with the best masters of all nations' (R. Strong, 65). Cavendish was one of twenty-five youths who attended Henry at his investiture as prince of Wales on 4 June 1610. On the eve of the ceremony he was created knight of the Bath, and on the following day he participated in a tilt staged to mark the event. In March 1612 Cavendish and his younger brother joined the diplomat Sir Henry Wotton on his mission to Italy to discuss a possible match between the prince of Wales and the duke of Savoy's daughter. Wotton described Cavendish as 'so sweet an ornament of my journey, and a gentleman himself of so excellent nature and institution' (Trease, 33). Moreover Duke Charles was so impressed that he wanted to detain Cavendish, promising to 'confer upon him the best titles of honour he could' (Cavendish, *Life*, 3), but he returned to England that summer.

As the seventh earl of Shrewsbury's nominee, Cavendish was elected MP for the Nottinghamshire seat of East Retford in 1614. It was probably about this time that he became a disciple of the poet and playwright Ben Jonson, for whom he had a 'particular kindness' (Langbaine, 386), and whose works had a profound influence on his own literary endeavours. Following the death of his father on 4 April 1617, William inherited the Cavendish estates, including Bolsover Castle in Derbyshire, which Sir Charles had acquired from Gilbert Talbot, seventh earl of Shrewsbury, in 1608. Passionate about architecture, Sir Charles had set about constructing a miniature version of a medieval castle with the help of the master mason and architect Robert Smythson and his son, John.

Career up to the civil war On or shortly before 24 October 1618 Cavendish married the heiress Elizabeth Howard (1599–1643), only daughter of William Bassett of Blore in Staffordshire and his wife, Judith Austin, and widow of Henry Howard, third son of the earl of Suffolk. In the same year he planned a visit to London to consider the 'furneshinge paynting and carving' of the Little Castle at Bolsover (Worsley, *Bolsover Castle*, 15). The building has been described as 'a superb instance of that blend of romance, chivalry, and pageant merged with classical myth and legend that informed the court masques and tournaments of the late Renaissance' (Raylor, '"Pleasure Reconciled to Virtue"', 403). Cavendish was largely responsible for the decorative scheme of the Little Castle which contains the most extensive and important surviving wall paintings from Jacobean England. Influenced by the palace of Fontainebleau and the Palazzo del Te, the interior depicts the humours (anteroom), the labours of Hercules (hall), the five senses (pillar chamber), Old and New Testament figures (star chamber), the virtues (marble closet), Christ's ascent into heaven and Elysium (first floor closets). The couple entertained James I at Welbeck on 10 August 1619. Cavendish's close affinity with the royal family was further cemented when Prince Charles agreed to be godfather to his second son. Jonson wrote an entertainment to mark the christening, which was celebrated at Blackfriars.

In 1616 Cavendish had been appointed executor to the seventh earl of Shrewsbury and he was involved subsequently in a lengthy dispute over Talbot lands that the countess had promised to him. In order to resolve their differences Shrewsbury's heirs proposed raising William to the peerage and on 29 October 1620 he became Viscount Mansfield. However, he was precluded from sitting

William Cavendish, first duke of Newcastle upon Tyne (*bap.* 1593, *d.* 1676), by Abraham van Diepenbeck [with Bolsover Castle in the background]

in the House of Lords for much of 1621 by his wife's failing health. In the following year she gave birth to a daughter, Jane (1622–1669). It was about this time that the famous riding school designed by John Smythson was built at Welbeck. Here on 10 August 1624 James I was entertained once again during his final hunting-trip to Sherwood. Mansfield was appointed lord lieutenant of Nottinghamshire on 6 July 1626 and was assiduous in the execution of his duties. The office had remained vacant since 1590 because of gentry hostility towards the local magnate, the seventh earl of Shrewsbury, but Mansfield's loyalty to the duke of Buckingham ensured his success in obtaining the post. Probably in the same year Elizabeth gave birth to their third, but first surviving, son, Charles (1626?–1659), followed quickly by a daughter, Elizabeth (1627?–1663).

On 7 March 1628 Mansfield was created earl of Newcastle upon Tyne, a title which acknowledged his growing prestige in the north of England, and Baron Cavendish of Bolsover. At the death of his cousin William Cavendish, second earl of Devonshire, in June of that year Newcastle assumed the role of lord lieutenant of Derbyshire, and he retained that office until the third earl achieved his majority in 1638. With the death of his mother on 18 April 1629 the barony of Ogle, which had been revived for her and her heirs, along with vast estates in the north, passed to Newcastle. As a consequence the earl could trace his nobility back to the reign of Edward IV. About 1630 he began work on a London town house, built by John Smythson, or possibly his son Huntingdon, on the site of a former Benedictine nunnery on the east side of Clerkenwell Close. On 24 June 1630 Elizabeth bore their second surviving son, Henry *Cavendish (1630–1691), who would eventually succeed to his father's titles.

Newcastle was vying for a court appointment, a desire which later prompted Lucy Hutchinson to remark 'a foolish ambition of glorious slavery carried him to the court, where he ran himself much into debt to purchase neglects of the King and Queen, and scorns of the proud courtiers' (Hutchinson, 84). By the end of 1631 rumours were spreading around court that Newcastle might become lord president of the council in the north in place of Sir Thomas Wentworth who had been appointed lord deputy of Ireland. Nothing came of the gossip, but in a letter dated 13 December 1632 Lord Cottington informed Newcastle of his appointment to attend the king into Scotland, 'which I Conceaue wyll be a good motiue for your frendes to putt it to a period' (BL, Add. MS 70499, fol. 156). Newcastle's attendance consisted in providing safe passage for Charles I through Nottinghamshire on his journey north for his Scottish coronation, and in the hope of currying royal favour the earl resolved to entertain the monarch at Welbeck on 21 May 1633. Clarendon later recorded, 'both King and Court were received and entertained by the earl of Newcastle, and at his own proper expense, in such a wonderful manner, and in such an excess of feasting, as had never before been known in England' (Clarendon, *Hist. rebellion*, 1.104).

The visit is reputed to have cost the earl between £4000 and £5000. Newcastle turned to his old friend Ben Jonson to provide the text of *The King's Entertainment at Welbeck*. By the early 1630s Jonson had lost his commanding position both in the public theatre and at court. He was sick and infirm and suffering financial hardship. He was therefore indebted to Newcastle, 'next the King, my best Patron', describing himself as 'Your truest beadsman & most thankefull seruant' (BL, Harley MS 4955, fols. 203, 204). Jonson celebrated the earl's consummate skill in horsemanship and his expertise as a swordsman in two epigrams (*The Underwood*, 1641, LIII and LIX), and several of his works, including masques and poems, are preserved in the 'Newcastle manuscript' (BL, Harley MS 4955), compiled for the earl some time before 1640. The influence of Newcastle's patronage is evident in Jonson's late plays. For example, Lovel, the hero of *The New Inn*, is to some extent modelled on the earl and shares his enthusiasm for fencing and riding as well as his interest in science.

Newcastle's own political views are voiced in Jonson's *A Tale of a Tub* and in the unfinished pastoral *The Sad Shepherd*, both of which uphold rural hospitality, traditional customs, and country sports. Similarly the text of *The King's Entertainment at Welbeck* introduces local references into the framework of a dramatized equestrian show designed to appeal to the king. William Lawes's setting of Jonson's dialogue 'What softer sounds than these' (BL, Add. MS 31432, fols. 20v–21) may have been the one sung at the banquet. Newcastle's hospitality failed to achieve the desired effect. He complained to Wentworth on 5 August, 'I have hurt my estate much with the hopes of it' (Trease, 68). Charles hinted that the queen, who had not attended the Welbeck entertainment, would enjoy a similar spectacle on their midlands progress the following summer. Despite his financial difficulties Newcastle decided to gamble once again, this time spending between £14,000 and £15,000 on 'a more stupendous entertainment; which (God be thanked), though possibly it might too much whet the appetite of others to excess, no man after imitated' (Clarendon, *Hist. rebellion*, 1.105). The court was feasted at Welbeck for six days. An account of the royal visit is preserved in the manuscript poem 'Carmen basileuporion' (BL, Harley MS 4345), dedicated to Newcastle's brother by the Cambridge student John Westwood of Mansfield, Nottinghamshire. Newcastle had begun work on the riding house and the terrace range at his Derbyshire seat. Here on 30 July 1634 the king and queen were entertained by Jonson's *Love's Welcome at Bolsover*, inspired by the cult of platonic love which flourished around Henrietta Maria. Following a banquet of the senses given in the pillar chamber of the Little Castle, the royal couple retired to the garden where they were met by the surveyor Colonel Vitruvius, a satirical portrayal of Jonson's rival Inigo Jones, and his attendant tradesmen involved in the construction of the new wing. The entertainment closed with a second banquet given by the quarrelling twin sons of Venus whose reconciliation is attributed to the setting which is described as an academy of love. Jonson was grateful for Newcastle's second commission, writing 'your Lordships timely gratuity … fell like the dewe of heauen on my necessities, it came so oportunely & in season' (BL, Harley MS 4955, fol. 203).

Acting on Wentworth's advice, Newcastle accompanied Charles for two or three days following his removal from Welbeck in order to pursue his desire for a court appointment. No sign was forthcoming; however, both royal visits did much to enhance Newcastle's status as a literary patron. In *The Chronicle History of Perkin Warbeck* (1634) the dramatist John Ford commented, 'The custom of your Lordship's entertainments, even to strangers, is rather an example than a fashion' (Ford, 5). The following year James Shirley 'confesse[d] his guilt of a long ambition, by some Service to be knowne to you' (Shirley, *The Traytor*, sig. A2), a desire soon to be realized in connection with Newcastle's plays written for the public stage. William Sampson's elegies on the local gentry and nobility, *Virtus Post funera vivit, or, Honour Triumphing over Death*, published the following year, attested to the earl's status among the midlands ruling élite. Newcastle shared Charles's love of art and in the same year as the visit to Bolsover he presented the king with a landscape by the Antwerp artist Alexander Keirincx. It was about this time that the earl sat for Van Dyck. Writing to the artist from Welbeck in February 1637 he recalled 'the Blessinge off your Coumpanye & Sweetnes off your Conuersation', praising the artist's skill and describing himself uncharacteristically for a nobleman at this time as 'your moste Humble Seruant' (BL, Add. MS 70499, fol. 218).

By the early 1630s Newcastle and his brother were 'at the forefront of the new philosophy in England, promoting theoretical research and practical experiments on optics, mathematics and mechanics' (Raylor, 'Newcastle ghosts', 94). The Cavendish circle included Robert Payne, Walter Warner, and Thomas Hobbes. Payne, the earl's chaplain from 1632 to 1638, assisted the brothers in their experiments and translated Italian works on mechanics including a section of Benedetto Castelli's *Della misura dell'acque correnti* (1628) and Galileo's *Della scienza mecanica* (BL, Harley MS 6796, fols. 309–39). Payne and not Hobbes was the author of the seminal work *A Short Tract on First Principles* (BL, Harley MS 6796, fols. 297–308), written while Payne was in Newcastle's employment. Furthermore the earl's writings on horsemanship allude to Payne's essay 'Considerations touching the facility or difficulty of the motions of a horse' (in S. A. Strong, 237–40). Payne was also responsible for undertaking a number of revisions to the earl's literary works 'intended for some kind of public appearance' (Raylor, 'Newcastle ghosts', 110). Warner did not hold a post at Welbeck but he corresponded with the brothers on optics and psychology and received money from them. Hobbes had been in service to Newcastle's cousins the earls of Devonshire since the 1610s, and in autumn 1636 he toyed with the idea of moving to Welbeck. In 1640 he presented Newcastle with *The Elements of Law*, noting 'the principles fit for such a foundation, are those which I have heretofore acquainted your Lordship withal in private discourse, and which by your command I have here put into method' (ibid., 99).

According to Clarendon, Newcastle 'was amorous in poetry and music, to which he indulged the greatest part of his time' (Clarendon, *Hist. rebellion*, 3.381). Newcastle inherited his father's 'great love and favour of Musicke' (Wilbye, *First Set of English Madrigals*). Sir Charles was a patron of the composer John Wilbye and dedicatee of his *First Set of English Madrigals* (1598). Moreover he was almost certainly the anonymous translator of Nicholas Yonge's *Musica transalpina* (1588), England's first printed anthology of translated Italian madrigals, dedicated to the seventh earl of Shrewsbury. Throughout his life Newcastle 'cherish[ed] and maintain[ed] such as are excellent in [music]' (Simpson, sig. A2), and is reputed to have been a skilled practitioner. Nothing is known of his musical education, though his writings on the use of music in the training of horses suggest that he may have been a lutenist. During the 1630s Newcastle employed at least five musicians, including one or possibly two members of the royal household. Maurice Webster, who had been appointed to 'the three lutes' under James I in 1623, served on a temporary basis and was in charge of the earl's musical possessions until his death at Nottingham in December 1635. Newcastle's keyboard player Mr Tomkin or Tomkins may have been related to or was one of the famous Tomkins brothers, John and Giles, who accompanied Charles I during his Scottish royal progress, stopping at Welbeck in 1633. 'A note of seuerall instruments and setts of bookes' compiled at Welbeck on 9 November 1636 reveals much about Newcastle's musical taste. The sets of madrigals, canzonets, and chansons by the late sixteenth- and early seventeenth-century composers Wilbye, Thomas Morley, Giacomo Gastoldi, Antonio Mortaro, Orazio Vecchi, and Jean de Castro are indicative of his cosmopolitan upbringing. It is highly unlikely that the liturgical prints in Latin by William Byrd, including his mass for three voices, and the Spanish theologian Fernando de las Infantas formed part of Newcastle's household devotion. But their existence suggests that the Roman Catholic rite was practised at Welbeck during the lifetime of his father who in 1592 was branded a notorious papist and dangerous recusant (*CSP dom.*, 1591–4, 174).

Four harpsichords, a virginal, an organ, and a claviorganum (a double- or triple-strung full-size harpsichord incorporating a positive organ), eleven wind and twenty-two plucked and bowed stringed instruments, including twelve viols, four by the highly esteemed English maker John Rose the younger, are listed at Welbeck in 1636. Newcastle particularly admired the viol and its repertory, and owned four books of divisions by the leading exponents of the genre including Webster, Daniel Norcombe, and Alfonso Ferrabosco II. Furthermore his passion for the instrument places in context his relationship with the composer and violist Christopher Simpson who served as quartermaster in the troop of horse commanded during the civil war by the earl's younger son. Simpson may have joined Newcastle's household prior to 1642. His early career is shrouded in mystery, but there is reason to believe that the musician and Christopher Sampson or

Simpson, a Jesuit educated abroad who returned to England about 1639 to join the English mission at Durham, are one and the same person. The Jesuit Simpson taught the sons of several protestant noblemen and therefore he could have been employed as a tutor to the earl's sons. Newcastle's relations with English and continental Roman Catholics were 'cordial and relaxed' (Chaney, 309). His intellectual circle numbered several priests and lay papists including, among others, Richard Flecknoe whose *Enigmaticall Characters* (1658) contains commendatory verses by Newcastle, Endymion Porter, Sir Kenelm Digby, Marin Mersenne, René Descartes, François Derand, and Beatrix de Cusance.

A substantial proportion of Newcastle's literary works in verse and prose date from the Caroline period. *Witts Triumvirate, or, The Philosopher* (BL, Add. MS 45865), devised unusually for an all-male cast, is probably Newcastle's 'earliest attempt at full-scale drama' (Kelliher, 152). This comedy of humours, which echoes Jonson's *The Alchemist* (1612), was written for performance before the king and queen in the winter of 1635–6; however, there is no record of its being staged either in the public theatre or at court. Preserved among the earl's papers (U. Nott. L., MSS Pw V 25–6) are several dramatic fragments, including a dialogue on 'Progectes … for the Good off the Common welth', a scene from 'The Cutpurse', a prologue and epilogue to 'a newe playe & a maske', and a Christmas masque presented at Welbeck during the mid- to late-1630s (Hulse, *Dramatic Works*, 1–33). Two of Newcastle's plays were performed by the King's Men at the Blackfriars Theatre: *The Varietie*, c.1639–1641, and *The Country Captaine*, May–August 1641. According to Anthony Wood, Shirley assisted Newcastle 'in the composure of certain plays which the [earl] afterwards published' (*Country Captain*, ed. Johnson, xxv). In 1641 Shirley was paid for 'several reformations' made to *The varietie* (Bawcutt, 209), and may have had a similar hand in *The Country Captaine*. For example, the lyric 'Come let us cast the dice' was first printed in Shirley's *Poems &c* (1646). The text was set to music by William Lawes who composed several play songs for the King's Men during the years 1630–41. A copy of *The Country Captaine* containing annotations in Newcastle's hand survives among the Harley papers (BL, Harley MS 7650). The play was printed in The Hague in 1649 and published with *The Varietie* in London in the same year as *Two comedies, written by a person of honor*.

Newcastle's Blackfriars plays are significant in that they publicly express the earl's political view and foreshadow his advice to Charles II. Newcastle was devoted to the concept of monarchy, seeing in its authority the 'foundation and support of his own greatness'. However, reflecting later on the causes of the civil war, he believed that the king's failure to maintain ceremony and degrees of honour had ultimately weakened the nobility and brought them into contempt. He blamed Charles I's downfall on 'mean People' close to the royal couple who jeered and despised those noblemen who could not make 'le Bon Reverance & coulde nott dance a Sereban with castenettes

off their fingers' (S. A. Strong, 213). In *The Varietie* Newcastle voiced his discontent with the Frenchified atmosphere of Whitehall. Monsieur Galliard claims that dancing to the French fiddle is the basis of good government for it quells any thought of rebellion and instils obedience to the monarchy. Manley, a patriotic gentleman of honour modelled on Newcastle himself, is the antithesis of Galliard. Dressed in Elizabethan costume after the style of the earl of Leicester, he launches a vicious attack on the dancing master in which he looks back with nostalgia to the reign of the virgin queen. Newcastle also expressed his criticism of continental foppishness through his preference for native customs. In *The Country Captaine* Monsieur Device, a frivolous gallant who admits to being 'an English Monsier made vp by a Scotch taylor that was Prentice in France' (p. 11), mocks country-dancing and ballad-singing, thereby striking at the heart of noble hospitality and denigrating the importance of traditional pastimes which Newcastle saw as part of the foundation of a stable monarchy.

By 1636 Newcastle had set his sights on the governorship of Prince Charles, but on 8 April he wrote to his wife

> I finde a Great dell of venum Agaynste mee, butt both the kinge & the Queene hath vsed mee very Gratiusly … They saye absolutly an other shall bee for the Prince & that the kinge wonderde att the reporte & sayde hee knewe no sutch thinge & tolde the queen so. (BL, Add. MS 70499, fol. 196)

He returned to the midlands by the summer in preparation for the visit of the palatine princes, Charles Louis and his brother Rupert, and their uncle Charles I, who were entertained by the earl in the park at Welbeck. Newcastle's apparent lack of religious conviction had threatened his appointment. Rumours spread round Whitehall that he was not fit to attend the prince, being 'off no religion neyther fearde God nor the Diuell beleued Heauen or Hell' (BL, Add. MS 70499, fol. 198v). George Conn, papal agent to the court of Henrietta Maria, reported as much to Cardinal Franceso Barberini at Rome on 17 September 1638, adding that the earl hated puritans. Newcastle's antipathy towards the godly clergy is evident in his Christmas masque which contains a satirical portrayal of Francis Stevenson, the puritan vicar of the local parish church of Norton Cuckney. Conn wrote to Barberini five months later, 'il mondo hoara commincia à sospettarlo per Cattolico, et egli mostra di rallegrarsi di esser tenuto di qualche religione, perche viene assai sospettato d'una totale indifferenza' (Chaney, 310). But Newcastle was not a papist. He disliked any form of recusancy, declaring himself to be a practising member of the 'true Reformed Religion … as it was professed and practised in the purest times of peerlesse Queen *Elizabeth*' (Cavendish, *Declaration … for his Resolution*, 13).

Newcastle realized his ambition in 1638; on 21 March he was appointed sole gentleman of the bedchamber and on 4 July governor to the prince of Wales, spending £40,000 of his own money in the execution of his office. He took charge of Charles's equestrian training, his academic instruction being entrusted to Dr Brian Duppa, bishop of Chichester. Newcastle set out his principles on education in a letter of instruction, advising the prince, 'I would rather have you study things than words ... for too much contemplation spoils action'; however, he recommended the study of history, 'so you might compare the dead with the living'. He cautioned Charles to be wary of flatterers and to be mindful of his status but not so much as to lose sight of his subjects. In matters of religion he warned, 'Beware of too much devotion for a King, for one may be a good man, but a bad King' (Cavendish, *Life*, 184–7). The threat of war from Scotland following the government's attempt to impose divine right episcopacy and a service book composed by the Scottish bishops forced Newcastle temporarily to curtail his duties to the prince. He raised at his own expense a force of 120 knights and gentlemen, which he named the prince of Wales troop, and contributed £10,000 to the king. Newcastle joined the army at Berwick under the command of the earl of Holland. Affronted by the latter's decision to place the prince of Wales's troop in the rear of the cavalry advance on the covenanters, Newcastle challenged Holland to a duel, but the king intervened. On 29 November 1639 Newcastle was made a privy councillor. He became joint constable and high steward of Pontefract with his son, Charles, Viscount Mansfield, on 13 July 1640. The following year he was implicated in the first army plot to rescue the earl of Strafford from execution for high treason. On 29 May 1641, two weeks after Strafford was beheaded, Newcastle was summoned to the House of Lords. He was never charged, but with suspicion mounting against him he was forced to resign his office as governor despite being made gentleman of the robes to the prince on 17 July 1641. Five days later his daughter Elizabeth married John Egerton, earl of Bridgewater, at St James's Clerkenwell, after which Newcastle retired to Welbeck, intent on managing his estate and enjoying family life. On 17 August 1641 he was made steward and warden of Sherwood Forest.

Civil war commander As the country moved ever close to civil war Charles I secretly instructed Newcastle on 11 January 1642 'to repair with all possible speed and privacy' to the magazine at Hull (Cavendish, *Life*, 8) and to assume the role of governor. However, Newcastle wrote to the king four days later, 'the town will by no means admit of me, so I am very flat and out of countenance' (*CSP dom.*, *1641–3*, 256). Parliament soon got wind of Charles's plan. The king was forced to recall Newcastle, and Sir John Hotham was installed in his place. On 29 June the earl was appointed governor of Newcastle upon Tyne and given jurisdiction over the four northern counties of Northumberland, Durham, Cumberland, and Westmorland. The lands and influence he inherited as Baron Ogle enabled him to raise troops and his regiments were soon training in preparation for war. Lacking confidence in the leadership of the fifth earl of Cumberland, the Yorkshire royalists appealed to Newcastle for help in the autumn of 1642. He marched south with about 8000 men, including his own recently formed regiment known as the Whitecoats or Newcastle's Lambs, famous for their valour in battle. Newcastle defeated Hotham at Piercebridge on 1 December, and entered York two days later, receiving the keys of the city from the governor, Sir Thomas Glemham. He became commander-in-chief in the north. On 7 December, 10 miles away at Tadcaster, he attacked Ferdinando, Lord Fairfax, and though the battle itself was indecisive, the parliamentarian commander was forced to retreat.

Newcastle proceeded to garrison Pontefract and to dispatch troops to occupy Newark in order to maintain a line of communication with the king who had set up his court at Oxford. With the repulse of the royalist forces in the West Riding at Bradford on 17 or 18 December and Sir Thomas Fairfax's recapture of Leeds on 23 January 1643, Newcastle recalled his troops from Newark and retreated from Pontefract back to York. The following month the earl published *A Declaration ... in Answer to Six Groundlesse Aspersions Cast upon him by the Lord Fairefax* in which he debated the rights of kings and subjects and defended his employment of Roman Catholics. He was criticized by his enemies for accepting so many northern recusants that his force was dubbed by hostile propagandists as the 'Popish army'. In answer to his critics Newcastle claimed, 'I have received them not for their Religion, but for their Allegiance which they professe' (Cavendish, *Declaration ... for his Resolution*, 13).

On 22 February the queen landed at Bridlington where she was received by Newcastle and escorted to York. Lord Goring's victory over Sir Thomas Fairfax at Seacroft Moor on 30 March paved the way for a second royalist attack in the West Riding. Newcastle abandoned the idea of entering Leeds but retook Wakefield on 2 April. With little time to mourn the loss of his wife who died at Bolsover on 17 April he stormed the town of Rotherham early in May, capturing arms and £5000 in cash, and went on to take Sheffield. The fall of Wakefield to Sir Thomas Fairfax on 21 May prevented Newcastle from attending the queen beyond Pontefract on her journey to Oxford. He stormed the parliamentarian stronghold of Howley House on 22 June and defeated the Fairfaxes at Adwalton Moor eight days later. With the successful bombardment of Bradford, Newcastle subjected Yorkshire, except for Wressel Castle and Hull, to the king's authority. In the following month he entered Lincolnshire, retaking Gainsborough on 30 July, occupying Lincoln, and threatening to raise the siege of Lynn. At the beginning of August he demanded the surrender of Nottingham but Colonel John Hutchinson refused to yield 'on any terms to a papistical army led by an atheistical general' (Trease, 120).

On 19 August Newcastle was made lieutenant-general in the counties of Lincoln, Rutland, Huntingdon, Cambridge, and Norfolk. The earl's orders were to march on London via Essex in a three-pronged attack on the capital. But Newcastle decided instead to secure Yorkshire and promised the king that he would march south once Hull had fallen to the royalists. However, the six-week assault on the town scarcely dented the roundheads' resolve. This setback, coupled with Cromwell's defeat at Winceby of the troops left to protect Lincolnshire, made the earl decide to abandon the siege and fall back on York. Newcastle was created a marquess on 27 October 1643. He set off for Derbyshire in early November with the intention of reducing all the parliamentarian garrisons in the area from his headquarters at Chesterfield. On 19 January 1644 the Scots under the command of Alexander Leslie, earl of Leven, invaded England. Newcastle returned to York where on 28 January Dr John Bramhall, bishop of Derry, preached at York Minster before the marquess, 'Being then ready to meet the Scotch Army' (Bramhall). He departed for Newcastle the same day, reaching the town on 2 February, the night before the Scots. Lulled into a false sense of security by the atrocious weather, Newcastle lowered his guard, thus allowing Leven to cross the Tyne and march south into Sunderland. The marquess gave pursuit, but it was not until 24 March that he finally engaged the Scots in battle. Disheartened by his inability to defeat Leven and by 'the impertinent and malicious tongues' of his critics at court, Newcastle tendered his resignation to the king, but Charles refused to accept it (Trease, 127).

The defeat of the royalist army at Selby on 11 April forced Newcastle to withdraw to York. Fairfax, Manchester, and Leven laid siege to the city, outnumbering the royalists six to one, but the marquess held out until Prince Rupert successfully raised the siege on 1 July. Newcastle's plea to wait for reinforcements fell on deaf ears and the prince set off the following day in pursuit of the enemy. Learning of Rupert's desire to fight, the allied generals retreating towards Tadcaster made a volte-face. The opposing armies met at Marston Moor where the royalists suffered their most crushing defeat of the civil war. Against all the odds Newcastle's whitecoats stood their ground, but 4000 of their number were slaughtered in the field. Without an army to command Newcastle was unwilling to 'endure the laughter of the court' (Trease, 141). He retired to the Netherlands. His enemies were quick to seize upon his departure from the stage of war. One pamphleteer commented, 'the brave Marquess of Newcastle, which made the fine plays, he danced so quaintly, played his part a while in the North, was soundly beaten, shew'd a pair of heels, and exit Newcastle' (Trease, 143). Moreover his allies disparaged his skills as a military commander. Clarendon, for example, recognized Newcastle's courage in the field, but criticized him for his limitations:

> He liked the pomp, and absolute authority of a general well, and preserved the dignity of it to the full ... But the substantial part, and fatigue of a general, he did not in any degree understand, (being utterly unacquainted with war) nor could submit to; but referred all matters of that nature to the discretion of his lieutenant general King ... In all actions of the field he was still present, and never absent in any battle; in all which he gave instances of an invincible courage and fearlessness in danger; in which the exposing of himself notoriously did sometimes change the fortunes of the day, when his troops began to give ground. Such articles of action were no sooner over, than he retired to his delightful company, music or his softer pleasures, to all which he was so indulgent, and to his ease, that he would not be interrupted upon what occasion soever; insomuch as he sometimes denied admission to the chiefest officers of the army, even to general King himself [his principal military adviser, James King, a veteran of the Thirty Years' War], for

two days together; from whence many inconveniences fell out. (Clarendon, *Hist. rebellion*, 3.382–3)

Newcastle in exile Newcastle set off immediately for Scarborough in the company of his brother, his two sons and their tutor Mark Anthony Benoist, Lieutenant-General King, Major General Sir Francis Mackworth, Sir William Carnaby (treasurer of the army), Sir Arthur Basset (colonel of Newcastle's own infantry), Captain John Mazine (master of his horse), colonels Francis Carnaby and Walter Vavasour, the Scottish peer Lord Carnwath, Lord Falconbridge, and the bishop of Derry. The party arrived in Hamburg on 8 July. Meanwhile at home the garrison at Welbeck fell to the earl of Manchester on 2 August and Bolsover surrendered to the enemy ten days later. On 16 February 1645 Newcastle travelled to Paris by way of Rotterdam and Brussels to join Henrietta Maria's court, reaching his destination on 20 April. It was here that he met his second wife, Margaret Lucas (1623?–1673) [*see* Cavendish, Margaret], a maid of honour to the queen. She was the eighth child of Thomas Lucas of Colchester, Essex, and sister of Sir Charles Lucas, Newcastle's lieutenant-general of the horse. The marquess professed his love for Margaret in a series of verses entitled *The Phanseys*. The couple were married some time in November or December 1645 in the chapel of Sir Richard Browne, the king's English resident in Paris.

Newcastle and his brother resumed their philosophical and scientific researches in the French capital. The marquess compiled a book of 'rare minerall receipts collected at Paris from those who hath great experience of them', including the Paracelsian physician Theodore Turquet de Mayerne (U. Nott. L., MS Pw V 90). The Cavendish circle included among others Hobbes, Mersenne, Descartes, and Pierre Gassendi, professor of mathematics at the Collège Royal. Hobbes's discussions with Bishop Bramhall on the problem of determination, which he later published as *Of Libertie and Necessitie* (1654), were instigated by Newcastle in August 1645. Hobbes also undertook at the marquess's behest a treatise on optics, *A minute, or, First Draught of the Optiques*, which he dedicated to Newcastle in 1646. According to Margaret, her husband had developed a new method 'in the art of weapons ... beyond all that ever were famous in it, found out by his own ingenuity and practice' (Cavendish, *Life*, 112–13). Newcastle set down his 'method' in 'The truth off the sorde' (BL, Harley MS 4206). This unpublished treatise, which is addressed to his two sons and dedicated to Charles II, was begun during the period spent in Paris. Hobbes provided a brief essay entitled 'The mathematicall demonstration off the sorde' (BL, Harley MS 5219), intended for insertion near the beginning of the work.

Since his departure from England, Newcastle had suffered financial hardship, but his credit improved considerably when the queen reimbursed nearly £2000 of the money she had borrowed from him in Yorkshire. In spring 1648 the marquess was summoned to a conference at St Germain to discuss the possibility of rekindling the royalist campaign. Before the end of June, Rupert travelled to

The Hague in the company of Prince Charles to take command of the navy which had defected from parliament, with the intention of rescuing the king from the Isle of Wight and sailing up the Thames to London. The queen implored Newcastle to follow her son but he arrived after the prince had set sail. Nothing came of the venture, and the marquess finding life in Rotterdam too expensive, decided to move to Antwerp towards the end of 1648. Newcastle took up residence in the house of Peter Paul Rubens, converting the artist's second studio, a circular room, into a riding school. On 12 January 1650 he was made a knight of the Garter and he became a privy councillor three months later. Newcastle found the council deeply divided over the issue of brokering a deal with the Scots. He supported the proposition and was desirous to accompany the king, but the covenanters refused to countenance his involvement. Instead he was sent as ambassador extraordinary to the king of Denmark with the purpose of seeking help for the invasion of England. During the rest of his exile in Antwerp, Newcastle seems to have taken no part in political transactions. In November 1651 Sir Charles returned to England in the company of his brother's wife in order to save Welbeck and Bolsover from confiscation. Margaret returned to Antwerp early in 1653, but Sir Charles died in England on 4 February 1654.

Newcastle spent the greater part of his time abroad in training horses. His equestrian skill was famous throughout Europe and his riding school at Antwerp attracted visitors from all over the continent. In 1658 he published his treatise on horsemanship, *La méthode nouvelle et Invention extraordinaire de dresser les chevaux*. The volume contains forty plates by Clouet, de Jode, and Vorsterman after drawings by Van Diepenbeck. The printing alone cost in excess of £1300, and he was obliged to borrow money to see the book through the press. Newcastle also indulged his muse. The *Kingdom's Weekly Intelligencer* for 23 February–2 March 1647 reported that the marquess had written for a company of English actors: 'in the ruins of his country and himself he can be at leisure to make Prologues and Epilogues for players' (Trease, 154). Newcastle's literary papers contain several dramatic works written in exile, including a dialogue on the origin of names which draws on real and fictitious characters, a prologue and part of a pastoral written at Antwerp and a comic interlude entitled 'A Pleasante & Merrye Humor off a Roge'. In February 1658 he collaborated with the exiled court musician and composer Nicholas Lanier on a royal entertainment staged in the Cavendishes' lodgings at Antwerp in which the actor Michael Mohun, 'made a speech in verse of his lordship's own poetry, complimenting the King in his highest hyperbole'. Alice, Viscountess Moore of Drogheda, sang a song 'of the same author's set ... by Nich. Lanier', and Mohun 'ended all with another speech, prophesying his Majesty's re-establishment' (*CSP dom.*, 1657–8, 311).

Life during the Restoration Newcastle travelled to The Hague shortly after Charles II was proclaimed king on 8 May 1660. He sailed to London independently of the royal party and was present in the House of Lords on several occasions throughout June and July. Some time before the autumn Newcastle devised a private royal entertainment for Charles II which drew on events in the monarch's recent past and alluded to his affair with Barbara Villiers (Hulse, 'King's entertainment', 355–405).

Newcastle's lengthy advice for Charles II, 'For your most sacred matie', was written in or shortly before the Restoration. Reflecting on the mistakes of the king's father, he warned Charles II to take command of the army, 'for withoute an Armeye In your owne handes you are butt a kinge Upon the Courteseye of others' (S. A. Strong, 176), and to ensure that the crown was never again insolvent and dependent upon parliament to vote supplies. On the subject of religion Newcastle believed that the Church of England was the only true faith, for 'Popery, & Presbetery, though they looke divers wayes, with their heads, yett they are tied together like Samson Foxes by theyr Tayles Careinge the same firebrandes of Covetusnes & Ambition' (ibid., 183). On a lighter note he recommended the return of all the court ceremonies and festivities.

On 13 September the bill for restoring unto the marquess all the honours, lands, and tenements which he had enjoyed before October 1642 received royal assent. Margaret estimated that the civil war and interregnum had lost her husband nearly £1 million in land revenue. Welbeck and Bolsover were in need of repair. Newcastle's townhouse in Clerkenwell had been sold in 1654 in payment of his debts. He was therefore obliged to occupy lodgings first in Aldgate then at Dorset House on his return from exile. Legal wrangling prevented the Clerkenwell property reverting to the family until after Michaelmas 1662. Newcastle presumed that Charles would grant him a major office in recognition of his past loyalty and services but he was denied such an honour. Disillusioned, he took leave of the king following his reappointment as gentleman of the bedchamber on 21 September 1660 and lord lieutenant of Nottinghamshire ten days later. Newcastle did not return to London for his installation as knight of the Garter on 15 April 1661, but sent his son Henry as proxy. Moreover he did not attend Charles's coronation on St George's day though he travelled south during the summer and is listed among the persons of quality present at the first reading of the English liturgy in the French church at the Savoy on 14 July 1661. In the same month he was made chief justice of eyre north of the Trent. On 16 March 1665 he was created duke of Newcastle upon Tyne. His retirement from public life was taken up with breeding horses. He laid out a 5-mile racetrack at Welbeck, holding meetings six times a year in which his neighbours competed for a silver cup. Newcastle began work on his second treatise on horsemanship, *A New Method, and Extraordinary Invention, to Dress Horses* (1667), which he described as 'neither a translation of the first, nor an absolutely necessary addition to it' (Trease, 196). A partial draft of this work entitled 'The epitomey of the new method ...' is preserved among the duke's papers (U. Nott. L., MSS Pw V 21–2).

Newcastle continued to patronize music after the Restoration. On 2 November 1661 he paid wages of £15 to 'Mr

Young the Violist' (U. Nott. L., MS Pw V 1/670), possibly the composer William Young (*d.* 1671) who returned briefly to England in the early 1660s. In the second edition of his theoretical treatise *A Compendium of Practical Musick*, dedicated to the duke in 1667, Simpson refers to 'some things which I formerly composed for your Grace's recreation'. At least one of his three-part pavans, inscribed 'at Welbeck' (Bodl. Oxf., MSS Mus. Sch. C59–60, p. 59), must have been composed during the period December 1643–mid-January 1644 when Newcastle marched 'to his own House and Garrison, in which parts he stayed some time, both to refresh his army, and to settle and reform some disorders he found there' (Cavendish, *Life*, 32).

Pepys, who saw a revival of *The Country Captaine* on four occasions in 1661, 1667, and 1668, described the comedy as 'so silly a play as in all my life I never saw, and the first that ever I was weary of in my life' (Pepys, 2.202). Newcastle's Restoration comedies *The Humorous Lovers* (1677) and *The Triumphant Widow, or, The Medley of Humours* (1677), both of which are indebted to Jonson, were staged by the duke of York's company at Lincoln's Inn Fields in 1667 and the Dorset Garden Theatre in 1674 respectively. Newcastle's friendship with the company's founder, Sir William Davenant, pre-dated the civil war. Together they had been implicated in the first army plot. Davenant later served as lieutenant-general of ordnance in Newcastle's army and like the duke was forced into exile at Henrietta Maria's French court. Matthew Locke, who may have met Newcastle in the Netherlands in 1648, collaborated in the production of *The Triumphant Widow*; two songs in the composer's hand are preserved among the duke's papers (U. Nott. L., MS Pw V 23). In August 1667 Davenant's company performed *Sir Martin Mar-All*. Based on Molière's *L'Etourdi*, the play was 'made by my Lord Duke of Newcastle, but as everybody says corrected by Dryden' (Pepys, 8.387).

According to Mary Evelyn the duke also collaborated with Dryden on the lost comedy *The Heiress*, which the king saw on 29 January 1669 (Trease, 200). Throughout his writing career Newcastle reworked material from his earlier compositions. Several verses from *The Phanseys* were reused in *The Humorous Lovers* while a substantial proportion of *The Triumphant Widow* is based on 'A Pleasante & Merrye Humor off a Roge' and 'The king's entertainment' of 1660. Following Newcastle's death his protégé Thomas Shadwell supervised the printing of both plays, for which he received £22, and was largely responsible for rewriting the scenes from the royal entertainment. The dramatist was a regular visitor to Welbeck. He enjoyed considerable favours from the duke and dedicated four of his plays to him, *The Sullen Lovers* (1668), *Epsom Wells* (1673), *The Virtuoso* (1676), and *The Libertine* (1676). Newcastle contributed commendatory poems and several passages in verse and prose to Margaret's literary works both before and after the Restoration, including among others *Natures Pictures Drawn by Fancies Pencil to the Life* (1656) and *Plays* (1668). A series of poems or songs dated 30 September 1675 to 27 October 1676 (U. Nott. L., MSS Pw V 25, fols. 56a–103) reveals that he continued to write verse up until his death.

On 16 May 1670 Charles II granted Newcastle's request for burial in Westminster Abbey. Three years later on 15 December Margaret died unexpectedly. The duke was too old to make the journey south for the funeral. He wrote the inscription for her tomb and collected together all the letters, addresses, dedications, and elegies written in praise of his wife which he published in 1676 as *Letters and Poems in Honour of the Incomparable Princess, Margaret, Duchess of Newcastle*. At the beginning of the Restoration, Newcastle had bought Nottingham Castle and in the 1670s he set about building a residence on the site. The work was undertaken by Samuel Marsh who had rebuilt the state rooms at Bolsover in the previous decade. The duke recorded in his will, dated 4 October 1676, 'I earnestly desire [it] may be finished to the form and model by me laid and designed' (Trease, 211). The castle was completed in 1679 at a cost of over £14,000. Newcastle died at Welbeck Abbey on Christmas day 1676 and was buried on 22 January 1677 alongside Margaret in Westminster Abbey.

Newcastle's dominant position among the ruling élite in the midlands was founded on his landed wealth and public office in which he discharged his duties as lord lieutenant with diplomacy and understanding. His unswerving loyalty to the crown during his command of the royalist forces in the north won him the respect of his officers and troops alike. However, except for a brief period as governor to the prince, Newcastle remained on the fringes of the court. Both in his dramatic works and in his advice to Charles II he was an outspoken critic of the growing remoteness of the Caroline monarchy. Fifteen years after his death Newcastle was described by Gerard Langbaine as '*our English Mecoenas*' (Langbaine, 386). Throughout his life he patronized many of the leading exponents in the fields of literature, art, music, and science, and was a major contributor to the development of the English baroque.

LYNN HULSE

Sources G. Trease, *Portrait of a cavalier: William Cavendish, first duke of Newcastle* (1979) · M. Cavendish, duchess of Newcastle, *The life of William Cavendish, duke of Newcastle*, ed. C. H. Firth (1907) · L. Hulse, ed., *Dramatic works by William Cavendish*, Malone Society Reprints, 158 (1996) · *The country captain by William Cavendish, earl of Newcastle*, ed. A. Johnson, Malone Society Reprints, 162 (1999) · W. Cavendish, marquess of Newcastle, *The country captaine and The varietie, two comedies, written by a person of honor* (1649) · L. Hulse, '"The king's entertainment" by the duke of Newcastle', *Viator*, 26 (1995), 355–405 · W. Cavendish, 'Witts triumvirate, or, The philosopher', BL, Add. MS 45865 · W. Cavendish, duke of Newcastle, *The humorous lovers* (1677) · W. Cavendish, duke of Newcastle, *The triumphant widow* (1677) · W. Cavendish, marquess of Newcastle, *The phanseys*, BL, Add. MS 32497 · D. Grant, ed., *The phanseys of William Cavendish marquis of Newcastle, addressed to Margaret Lucas, and her letters in reply* (1956) · W. Cavendish, earl of Newcastle, *A declaration ... for his resolution of marching into Yorkshire* (1642) · W. Cavendish, earl of Newcastle, *A declaration ... in answer to six groundlesse aspersions cast upon him by the Lord Fairefax* (1643) · J. Bramhall, bishop of Derry, *A sermon preached in York Minster* (1643) · W. Cavendish, marquess of Newcastle, 'Rare minerall receipts collected at Paris', U. Nott. L., MS Pw V 90 · W. Cavendish, marquess of Newcastle, *La méthode nouvelle et invention extraordinaire de dresser les chevaux* (Antwerp, 1658) · W. Cavendish, marquess of Newcastle, *The Ld Marquis of Newcastle ... articles for his new course* (1662) · W. Cavendish, duke of Newcastle, *A new method, and extraordinary invention, to dress horses* (1667) · W. Cavendish, duke of Newcastle, 'The epitomey of the new method', U. Nott. L., MSS Pw V 21–22 · W. Cavendish, duke of Newcastle, literary works in verse and prose, U. Nott. L., MSS Pw V 23–26 · S. A. Strong, *A catalogue of letters and other historical documents exhibited in the library at Welbeck* (1903) · W. Cavendish, duke of Newcastle, corresp., BL, Add. MSS 70499–70500 · W. Cavendish, duke of Newcastle, correspondence, U. Nott. L., MS Pw I · L. Hulse, '"Apollo's Whirligig": William Cavendish, duke of Newcastle, and his music collection', *Seventeenth Century*, 9/2 (1994), 213–46 · L. Hulse, 'The duke of Newcastle and the English viol', *Chelys*, 29 (2001), 28–43 · T. Raylor, '"Pleasure reconciled to virtue": William Cavendish, Ben Jonson, and the decorative scheme of Bolsover Castle', *Renaissance Quarterly*, 52 (1999), 402–39 · L. Hulse, 'Matthew Locke: three newly discovered songs for the Restoration stage', *Music and Letters*, 75/2 (1994), 200–13 · T. Raylor, 'Newcastle ghosts: Robert Payne, Ben Jonson, and the "Cavendish Circle"', *Literary circles and cultural communities in Renaissance England*, ed. C. J. Summers and T. L. Pebworth (2000), 92–114 · P. R. Newman, 'The royalist army in northern England, 1642–5', DPhil diss., University of York, 1978 · P. R. Newman, *The battle of Marston Moor, 1644* (1981) · Clarendon, *Hist. rebellion* · H. Kelliher, 'Donne, Jonson, Richard Andrews and the Newcastle manuscript', *English Manuscript Studies, 1100–1700*, 4 (1993), 134–73 · 'The Newcastle manuscript', BL, Harley MS 4955 · N. Rowe, '"My best patron": William Cavendish and Jonson's Caroline drama', *Seventeenth Century*, 9/2 (1994), 197–212 · C. C. Brown, 'Courtesies of place and arts of diplomacy in Ben Jonson's last two entertainments for royalty', *Seventeenth Century*, 9/2 (1994), 147–71 · T. Raylor and J. Bryce, 'A manuscript poem on the royal progress of 1634: an edition and translation of John Westwood's "Carmen Basileuporion"', *Seventeenth Century*, 9/2 (1994), 173–95 · S. Clucas, 'The atomism of the Cavendish circle: a reappraisal', *Seventeenth Century*, 9/2 (1994), 247–73 · T. Raylor, 'Thomas Hobbes and "The mathematical demonstration of the sword"', *Seventeenth Century*, 15/2 (2000), 175–98 · T. Raylor, 'Hobbes, Payne, and *A short tract on first principles*', *HJ*, 44 (2001), 29–58 · L. Worsley, *Bolsover Castle* (2000) · C. Simpson, *A compendium of practical musick* (1667) · G. Langbaine, *An account of the English dramatick poets* (1691) · *CSP dom.*, 1591–4; 1657–8 · K. Jones, *A glorious flame: the life of Margaret Cavendish, duchess of Newcastle, 1623–1673* (1998) · G. Parry, 'Cavendish memorials', *Seventeenth Century*, 9/2 (1994), 275–87 · R. Strong, *Henry prince of Wales and England's lost renaissance* (1986) · M. Butler, 'Entertaining the palatine prince: plays on foreign affairs, 1635–1637', *English Literary Renaissance*, 13 (1983), 319–44 · M. Butler, *Theatre and crisis, 1632–1642* (1984) · C. Condren, 'The date of Cavendish's advice to Charles II', *Parergon*, 17/2 (2000), 147–50 · J. Ford, *The chronicle history of Perkin Warbeck* (1634); P. Ure, ed. (1968) · J. Shirley, *The traytor* (1635) · W. Sampson, *Virtus post funera vivit, or, Honour triumphing over death* (1636) · R. Flecknoe, *Enigmaticall characters* (1658) · T. Shadwell, *The sullen lovers* (1668) · T. Shadwell, *Epsom wells* (1673) · T. Shadwell, *The virtuoso* (1676) · T. Shadwell, *The libertine* (1676) · R. Payne, 'A short tract on first principles', BL, Harley MS 6796, fols. 297–308 · R. Payne, trans., Benedetto Castelli, *Della misura dell'acque correnti* and Galileo Galilei, *Della scienza mecanica*, BL, Harley MS 6796, fols. 309–39 · T. Hobbes, *The elements of law* (1640) · M. Cavendish, marchioness of Newcastle, *Natures pictures drawn by fancies pencil to the life* (1656) · M. Cavendish, duchess of Newcastle, *Plays* (1668) · L. Hutchinson, *Memoirs of the life of Colonel Hutchinson* (1995) · M. Girouard, *Robert Smythson & the Elizabethan country house* (1983) · T. Mowl, *Elizabethan & Jacobean style* (1993) · A. Wells-Cole, *Art and decoration in Elizabethan and Jacobean England* (1997) · B. Jonson, *Workes* (1641) · J. Shirley, *Poems &c* (1646) · *Letters and poems in honour of the incomparable princess, Margaret, duchess of Newcastle* (1676) · N. Yonge, *The first set of English madrigals* (1598) · E. Chaney, *The grand tour and the great rebellion* (Geneva, 1985) · N. W. Bawcutt, *The control and censorship of Caroline drama: the records of Sir Henry Herbert, master of the revels, 1623–1673* (1996) · Pepys, *Diary* (1970–83) · L. Worsley, 'The architectural patronage of William Cavendish, 1st duke of Newcastle, 1593–1676', 2 vols., DPhil diss., U. Sussex, 2001 · J. Knowles and L. Hulse, eds., *Fornicating with the*

nine muses: William Cavendish, 1st duke of Newcastle and his patronage [forthcoming]

Archives BL, Add. MSS 70499–70500 · U. Nott., Portland MSS, Pw I and Pw V series | BL, Harley MSS · BL, letters to first marquess of Halifax and James, duke of York, C6

Likenesses A. Van Dyck, oils, 1637, Welbeck Abbey, Nottinghamshire · marble tomb effigy, *c*.1676, Westminster Abbey · S. Cooper, miniature (after A. Van Dyck), Buccleuch estates, Selkirk · A. van Diepenbeck, portrait, BM [*see illus.*] · W. Hollar, engraving, NPG · engravings, repro. in W. Cavendish, *Méthode et invention extraordinaire de dresser les chevaux* (Antwerp, 1658) · miniatures, Welbeck Abbey, Nottinghamshire; repro. in Trease, *Portrait* · oils (after A. Van Dyck), Althorp, Northamptonshire · portrait (after A. Van Dyck), Palace of Westminster, London; repro. in Trease, *Portrait*

Cavendish, William, third earl of Devonshire (1617–1684), politician, was born on 10 October 1617, either at Chatsworth, Derbyshire, or Devonshire House, London, the eldest son of Sir William *Cavendish, later second earl of Devonshire (1590–1628), and his wife, Christian *Cavendish (1595–1675), daughter of Edward, first Lord Bruce of Kinloss. He was dubbed knight of the Bath at Charles I's coronation in 1625. Like his father before him and his own sons in later years, William's education was directed by Thomas Hobbes. In dedicating his translation of Thucydides to the second earl, Hobbes described William as 'the image of your father', whom he praised for his learning and ability (Hobbes's *Thucydides*, 3–4). He conducted the young earl upon a tour of Europe from 1634 to 1637, in the course of which, at Florence, Devonshire met Galileo. Having inherited his title in June 1628 William returned from the continent to assume his father's social and political position. Charles I named him lord lieutenant of Derbyshire upon his coming of age in 1638, an appointment he held to 1642 and again from the Restoration until his death. He married, on 4 March 1639, Elizabeth Cecil (1620–1689), second daughter of William *Cecil, second earl of Salisbury.

In the House of Lords, Devonshire showed himself a friend of the court from early on, voting against Strafford's impeachment. Queen Henrietta Maria met him in October 1641 in her effort to build a royalist faction in parliament. In the summer of 1642 he was named to Leicestershire's commission of array, and withdrew from London to the court at York, promising to raise 100 horse for the king's army. In July parliament expelled him from the Lords and ordered his imprisonment. Although his younger brother Charles *Cavendish, a royalist officer, was killed in a skirmish in Lincolnshire, Devonshire did not bear arms for the king, but withdrew to Europe. His estates were sequestrated and he remained on the continent until 1645, when he returned to England and compounded with parliament, paying a £5000 fine. On 13 October 1645 Charles stayed overnight with him at his house at Latimers, Buckinghamshire, although the visit seems to have done little to bestir the earl on the king's behalf. He spent most of the interregnum living in retirement with his mother, Christian, the dowager countess, to whom he remained very close: 'evry one perseavs that he dairs not eate or drinke but as shee apoints' as one of

Christian's critics complained (*De L'Isle and Dudley MSS*, 6.101). Although he supported the exiled court financially and his mother was an active royalist plotter Devonshire seems to have avoided active conspiracy during the interregnum, claiming in 1659 to be a 'perfect lover of sports' (Bickley, 59) rather than politics. He also cultivated relationships with some of the period's most formidable intellects; he remained Hobbes' patron until the old man died aged ninety-two at Hardwick in 1679. He befriended John Evelyn and was an original member of the Royal Society.

Following the Restoration, Devonshire returned to his Derbyshire lieutenancy and added the stewardships of Tutbury (1660) and the High Peak (1661) to his responsibilities. But apart from a brief term as a commissioner of trade from 5 March 1668 to 1669, the earl was not politically active. He attended the Lords irregularly, preferring to remain in the country, husbanding his estates and entertaining gentlemen such as Sir John Reresby, who in September 1679 enjoyed dinner and 'excellent buck hunting' with Devonshire at Chatsworth (*Memoirs of Sir John Reresby*, 187). He was, for example, absent from the house when it voted on exclusion in 1680. The earl's apparent political indifference was probably a further source of friction with his heir, William *Cavendish, who, in addition to being 'the most dissolute man in London' (*Lorenzo Magalotti*, 117), was also a strong whig. Father and son clashed more frequently, however, on financial matters. In 1680 the king encouraged Devonshire to pay his son's debts and allow him a larger income in hopes of returning Lord Cavendish 'to his duty … to the King as well as to his father' (*CSP dom.*, *1680–81*, 37). The earl and his son remained estranged despite the king's good offices and the intervention of their kinsman, the duke of Newcastle. Despite these difficulties, however, when the earl died aged sixty-seven at Roehampton, Surrey, on 23 November 1684, he left his son an ample income to support his title. He was buried at Edensor, Derbyshire.   VICTOR STATER

Sources GEC, *Peerage* · T. Pomfret, *Life of the right honourable and religious Lady Christian late countess-dowager of Devonshire* (1685) · F. Bickley, *The Cavendish family* (1914), 45–59 · *Report on the manuscripts of Lord De L'Isle and Dudley*, 6, HMC, 77 (1966) · Evelyn, *Diary*, vol. 3 · *Lorenzo Magalotti at the court of Charles II: his Relazione d'Inghilterra of 1668*, ed. and trans. W. E. K. Middleton (1980), 117 · *Memoirs of Sir John Reresby*, ed. A. Browning, 2nd edn, ed. M. K. Geiter and W. A. Speck (1991), 187 · *CSP dom.*, *1680–81*, 37–9, 308 · *Calendar of the manuscripts of the marquess of Ormonde*, new ser., 8 vols., HMC, 36 (1902–20), vol. 2, p. 397; vol. 6, p. 380; vol. 7, pp. 105–6 · *Hobbes's Thucydides*, ed. R. Schlatter (New Brunswick, 1975), 3–4
Archives Chatsworth House, Derbyshire, MSS; privy purse accounts
Likenesses oils, 1638, Hardwick Hall, Derbyshire · attrib. P. Lely, oils, Burghley House; version attrib. to P. Lely, Hardwick Hall, Derbyshire · A. Van Dyck, oils, Chatsworth, Derbyshire
Wealth at death left £10,000 p.a. after his legacies were paid: HMC, Portland, vol. 3, p. 383

Cavendish, William, first duke of Devonshire (1641–1707), politician, was born on 25 January 1641. He was styled Lord Cavendish until the death of his father, also William *Cavendish, third earl of Devonshire (1617–1684).

William Cavendish, first duke of Devonshire (1641–1707), by Isaac Beckett (after Sir Godfrey Kneller, c.1680–85)

His father was a royalist supporter but personally reclusive; his mother was Lady Elizabeth Cecil (1620–1689), second daughter of William *Cecil, second earl of Salisbury.

Education, travels, and marriage Despite significant family sacrifices on behalf of the royalist cause Cavendish himself grew up in an environment largely protected from the upheavals of the English civil wars and the interregnum. His father, who made his peace with parliament in 1645, took an active interest in his son's education and first turned for advice to Thomas Hobbes, once his own tutor and still a family retainer. Writing from St Germain in 1648 Hobbes recommended a curriculum focused on the 'latine tonge and the Mathematiques' (*Correspondence of Thomas Hobbes*, 1.170). The study of men and manners, the nature of government, and history and the poets would then follow naturally when the boy was more mature. Over the next several years a succession of tutors passed through the household, including Dr Henry Killigrew, sometime chaplain to the duke of York and later master of the Savoy, Henry Oldenberg, and François du Prat, who was engaged to accompany Cavendish on the grand tour. In May 1657 the two young men—du Prat was only five or six years older than his charge—left for Paris, and by the beginning of the following year they had arrived safely in Florence, despite reports about their capture by Turks while crossing from France to Italy by sea. Before finally returning to England in 1661 Cavendish and his tutor were said by the latter to have visited most of Europe. Always regarded by his contemporaries as a person of taste and sophistication, the subsequent rebuilding of Chatsworth alone suggests how important this experience was in terms of shaping Cavendish's appreciation of architecture and the visual arts.

At a ceremony presided over by Charles II, Cavendish and Mary (1646–1710), second daughter of James Butler, first duke of Ormond, were betrothed on 5 March 1661. Because of her youth they did not marry until 26 October 1662, at Kilkenny Castle, Ireland, at a lavish event marred only by the fact that the groom's wedding clothes failed to arrive in time. There were five children born to the marriage but two died before their parents: Charles, the first-born son, in 1670 and Henry in 1700. The surviving children included two sons—William and James—and a daughter, Elizabeth. Cavendish also had other children with his long-term mistress, the actress Mrs Heneage, as well as a daughter born to Anne Campion, an aspiring thespian with whom he formed a liaison in the year before his death.

On 23 April 1661 Cavendish served as one of four aristocratic scions chosen to carry the train of Charles II at his coronation, and that same year he was first elected to a seat in the Commons as a member from Derbyshire, despite the fact that he was not yet of age. During his early years in parliament, however, he made little mark other than in the spirited debate in 1667 about the fate of the earl of Clarendon after the latter's fall from power. Cavendish strongly advocated impeachment rather than banishment in a speech so well received that he was then named one of the members to negotiate the matter with the House of Lords, until Clarendon's flight abroad rendered the issue moot. Given his youth and a reputation for sowing wild oats perhaps it is not surprising to find his interest so little focused on the political arena. In October 1662 he went to Ireland for his marriage and stayed there until the following summer. Two years later he served, apparently briefly, as a gentleman volunteer in the Second Anglo-Dutch war. Sir Thomas Clifford reported that at the battle of Lowestoft in 1665 Cavendish comported himself well on the *Young Rupert*, a shallop with six guns and a crew of twenty. Then in 1669 he spent time in Paris with Ralph Montagu, the English ambassador, supposedly for reasons of health but actually to escape his creditors, who were threatening legal action. There he received a good press in the newsletters by showing great forbearance after an unprovoked assault by three drunken members of the royal guard, even going so far as to intercede on their behalf when they were about to be cashiered.

Country party Generally counted a court supporter in the 1660s, Cavendish began early in the following decade to associate actively with the opposition. Bishop Burnet and others attributed this change of heart to disappointment arising from failure to secure a military commission resigned by his brother-in-law, the earl of Ossory, in 1672 but such was at most catalyst rather than cause. Cavendish's change in viewpoint, which mirrors that of others gravitating toward formation of what would eventually become the country or first whig party, reflects a revival of concern within the political nation about three traditional bogeymen: the French, Roman Catholics, and,

ultimately, the Stuarts themselves. During the three sessions of parliament in 1673 and 1674 he became a frequent participant in the debates of the day and made several verbal attacks on members of the cabal, especially Clifford and Lauderdale. He also served on the committee that drew up the Test Bill but strongly opposed trading the grant of a large supply to Charles II for the king's repudiation of the declaration of indulgence and assent to the legislation in question. He was in fact firmly opposed to providing any additional funds to meet the cost of the Third Anglo-Dutch war and also opposed to continued alliance with France. In 1675 Cavendish was a leader in the movement to secure the ouster of Lauderdale and served as one of the tellers for the majority when the house divided on the issue of whether to send an address on the subject to the king. That same year he also played an active role in preparing articles of impeachment against the earl of Danby, who had replaced Clifford as lord treasurer, but in this matter he and the other strong critics of the earl were ahead of the curve and failed even to secure the full backing of opposition colleagues when the matter came to a vote. He was more successful, however, in agitating for passage of a resolution asking the king to recall all English soldiers in the service of Louis XIV but almost came to blows with Sir John Hanmer in a dispute about the count of the tellers when the house divided on the question of sending a second and even more pointed address on the subject. By June 1675 a newsletter noted that 'several of our briske House-of-Commons men, who made so bold with his ma. in the time of Parlement, are now forbidden the Court, particularly the Ld. Cavendish & Mr. Newport' (*Bulstrode papers*, 302–3). Such clear evidence of royal displeasure notwithstanding, later that autumn Cavendish also helped to engineer the defeat of a supply bill intended to remove the anticipations on customs revenues used to finance the Third Anglo-Dutch war when parliament had refused to do so.

In the largely fruitless sessions of 1677 Cavendish became involved in complicated manoeuvring initiated by the earl of Shaftesbury to have the Cavalier Parliament declare itself dissolved. The obvious intent was to force new elections but the Commons refused to take up the issue when it was raised by Lord Russell, both friend and political associate of Cavendish, and seconded by the latter. For his part in the scheme Shaftesbury was sent briefly to the Tower, and Cavendish's name appears among those of opposition members who made a point of visiting him there. He also tried, again with no success, to interest the house in a debate about the role of the speaker in ordering adjournment without consent of the Commons after Charles prorogued parliament at the end of May. By this time he had clearly emerged as one of the leading and most vocal members of the opposition, along with William Garroway, Sir Thomas Lee, Sir Thomas Meres, Richard Newport, Lord Russell, and William Sacheverell but the group was more of a coalition—a collective point of view—than a political party in the modern sense. Indeed relationships remained sufficiently fluid in the parliamentary arena that his father-in-law, Ormond, still hoped that after all his late 'mistakes and misadventures' Cavendish might prove useful to the crown (*Ormonde MSS*, 4.58).

Popish Plot and exclusion During the first session of parliament in 1678 Cavendish was active on committees considering the issue of French aggression against the Dutch and, when it appeared later that spring that peace might break out, the need to pay off and disband the army and reduce both the size and cost of the fleet. Then the political atmosphere was transformed dramatically by the revelations of the Popish Plot, and a sense of crisis pervaded the Commons when it reassembled in October. Cavendish was immediately placed on committees to provide for the safety of the king, to investigate the murder of Sir Edmund Berry Godfrey, to consider the removal of all Catholics from London, to bring in a bill prohibiting Catholics from sitting in parliament, and to examine the letters of Edward Coleman, which supposedly implicated the duke of York. On 4 November he seconded a motion by Lord Russell urging the king to send his brother away. While apparently convinced that James had not been party to the plot Cavendish argued in the house that the very fact of his Catholicism rendered him incapable of serving in government and, accordingly, he also opposed the proviso introduced in the House of Lords to exempt the duke from a bill aimed at excluding Catholics from parliament. Cavendish took part as well in the continuing attack on the army, noting that 'it is but of late that we have heard of assassinations. We may fear them, especially when the Papists are encouraged by a Popish successor and a standing Army' (Grey, 6.236). He also joined in the general assault on the king's ministers and in particular took aim at the earl of Danby and his management of public funds. Although Cavendish had had little success in securing votes to proceed against the lord treasurer three years earlier, by December the Commons agreed to appoint a committee to bring in articles of impeachment, a move then forestalled by the dissolution of parliament in February 1679.

Returned without opposition from Derbyshire to all three exclusion parliaments Cavendish played a more moderate role than the rhetoric of his earlier speeches might have suggested. He was, however, never a supporter of the pretensions of the duke of Monmouth and, perhaps with a bit of pressure from his father-in-law, willing initially to consider solutions to the problem of James's Catholicism other than that of barring his succession to the throne. At the instigation of the king he allowed himself to be brought to court by the earl of Ossory in March 1679 and he then agreed to accept appointment to a reconstituted privy council, on which he was joined by three other members of the Commons associated with the nascent whig party: Lord Russell, Sir Henry Capel, and Henry Powle. It was an interesting if unlikely experiment, the brainchild of Sir William Temple, aimed at bridging the gap between Charles and a discontented and obstructive majority in the lower house. It certainly failed to deter Cavendish from continuing to assist in pursuing impeachment of the earl of Danby or indeed advocating for a bill of attainder when it appeared

that Danby might not surrender for trial. During the debate on this matter Cavendish argued that Charles had exceeded his authority by granting the lord treasurer a pardon, since parliamentary consent was required in a case where the public trust had been violated. This and other related issues were, however, only the prelude to the consideration of the first bill of exclusion brought before the Commons in May 1679. In the only recorded vote ever taken on the question Cavendish—joined by Powle and Capel but not by Russell—voted against the measure. Their opposition notwithstanding the bill passed by a margin of almost two to one, with none of the three even able to influence the vote of other members from their respective home counties. Prorogation and dissolution of parliament followed quickly. Thereafter Cavendish's position on the privy council and that of his whig cohorts became increasingly untenable. Their continuing complaints about Lauderdale and their advice about how to handle the uprising that had broken out in Scotland were ignored, leading Cavendish to sit on his hands when given a commission that summer to raise a regiment of foot. More galling yet was the deaf ear turned to their urging that parliament be called into session immediately after new elections were held early that autumn. Instead Charles temporized with a series of prorogations—eight in all—stretching over more than a year.

In January 1680 Cavendish and the three other whigs on the council finally resigned as a group, to the surprise of some outsiders who thought that they had been co-opted by the court party but much to the satisfaction of the king, for whom their presence on the council had been little more than an irritant from the very first. The specific occasion for leaving was yet another prorogation of parliament coincident with Charles's decision to let his brother return from abroad. The consequence was that Cavendish finally became persuaded that exclusion was a necessity. That March, while at Newmarket, he went out of his way to offend conspicuously by ignoring the presence of the duke of York on several occasions and, as a consequence, he was once again forbidden attendance at court. A month later Sir John Reresby noted in his diary that Cavendish had been seen going to meetings of the opposition leadership, and in June he numbered among a dozen prominent whigs who attempted to use the Middlesex grand jury as the vehicle by which to present the duke of York as a Catholic recusant. An interesting gambit forestalled by Chief Justice Scroggs, it was followed up a few days later when most of the same group went to Windsor and tried to give Charles a petition calling for parliament to meet, a particular bit of effrontery on Cavendish's part that enraged the king. When in October parliament was finally allowed to assemble he joined the ranks of the exclusionists in rushing through a bill in little more than two weeks. He and other supporters of the measure then thrashed around rather aimlessly after it was rejected equally decisively and even more rapidly in the House of Lords. Cavendish did use the opportunity to push for impeachment of Scroggs for having dismissed the Middlesex grand jury early but, to his credit, he refused to engage in the effort to find a pretext for attacking the marquess of Halifax for his role in defeating exclusion in the upper house. Toward the end of the session, which was prorogued in early January, Cavendish suggested the alternative of creating a protestant association to protect the life of the king and the established church, but in the debate that ensued it is clear that neither he nor anyone else believed that such an expedient would do the job.

When the Oxford parliament met in March 1681 Cavendish was named to the committee in the Commons entrusted with bringing in a new bill of exclusion but the session was too short for him to have left other significant footprints in the record. Thereafter, however, he backed away quickly from the more extreme elements in the whig party. The first rumours to that effect were circulating as early as May, and by the beginning of October he had been admitted to kiss the king's hand while at Newmarket. Consistent in his rejection of the duke of Monmouth as a viable candidate for the throne, Cavendish was apparently a sufficient realist to accept the fact that the cause had failed for lack of a suitable alternative. In this regard his thinking may also have been influenced by pressure from his father-in-law and his father, combined with a financial package to rescue him from creditors no longer being held at bay by the protective shield of parliamentary privilege. In any event the rapprochement with the Stuart regime was of sufficient substance to protect Cavendish from any suspicion of complicity in the Rye House plot. It did not, however, prevent him from taking a public stand against surrender of London's charter, nor from providing a character witness at the treason trial of his longtime friend Lord Russell and then proposing, if whig mythology is to be believed, a quixotic scheme to rescue him from captivity before his execution. When Cavendish's father died late in the autumn of 1684 he ordered a funeral appropriate for a duke, apparently to serve as a reflection on the fact that Charles II had failed properly to reward a loyal and faithful supporter, no matter how wayward the son. The royal response, hardly unexpected given the general remodelling of local government in progress, was to remove the lord lieutenancy of Derbyshire from the almost hereditary grasp of the family.

The revolution of 1688 The new earl of Devonshire played a minor ceremonial role at the coronation of James II. He took his seat in the House of Lords with the opening of the first and only parliament to meet in the king's reign but was not a conspicuous participant in the session held that spring. When parliament was reconvened in November, however, he signalled his discontent with the direction of royal policy almost immediately, suggesting ironically that the traditional vote of thanks for the speech from the throne was particularly appropriate in view of the fact that James had been so forthright in declaring his intention of maintaining a standing army and of retaining the Catholic officers commissioned during the Monmouth rebellion. Devonshire then proposed that a date be set aside for serious reconsideration of the king's speech, a motion supported in a compelling speech by the bishop of London as well as by the marquess of Halifax, the earl of

Nottingham, and others but ultimately frustrated by an immediate prorogation. Having made himself no friends at court the earl then put his reputation for political independence in jeopardy early in 1687 as a consequence of striking Thomas Colepeper within the precincts of the palace at Whitehall when the latter refused to accept a challenge to a duel. The final chapter in a dispute that had first broken out into the open two years earlier, when Colepeper had assaulted the earl, Devonshire's bad judgement in responding in kind resulted in his being brought to trial in the court of the king's bench on a charge of breach of the peace. A plea of privilege of parliament was quickly overruled and on 15 June he was found guilty and ordered to pay a fine of £30,000, an enormous amount of money and a figure set by the judges at the behest of Lord Chief Justice Jeffreys. In fact the fine never was paid and the earl managed to avoid imprisonment temporarily by retreating to the relative isolation of Chatsworth while attempts were made to negotiate a settlement, but eventually he was forced out of seclusion and by the end of October he gave the king a bond for the full amount as guarantee of future good conduct.

Coming just at the time when James II was intensifying his efforts to secure repeal of the Test Act and challenging the power of the traditional protestant élite on virtually every front, Devonshire's surrender was regarded by the diarist Roger Morrice as a disaster equivalent to the Magdalen College affair. He feared that the two represented 'no lesse then the submission of the University and really the Clergy of England, and of the house of Lords for Devonshire … was the only man that had reputation enough to have been a back to the Peeres in that house' (DWL, Roger Morrice, Ent'ring Book, MS Q, fol. 182). To the earl himself, however, his mistreatment at the hands of the king and the judiciary simply reinforced opposition in principle with a strong sense of personal grievance. He had in fact already been in contact with William of Orange's emissary Dykvelt, sent to London in the spring of 1687 to establish a line of communication with those disaffected with the regime, and the threat of financial reprisal notwithstanding he engaged in a series of meetings with other opponents of the government and began a correspondence with the prince. By late spring 1688 Devonshire became convinced that William needed to intervene in English affairs, and on 30 June—the very day that the seven bishops were acquitted—he was one of the seven men who affixed their ciphers to the famed invitation. A cautious statement of what support the prince could expect, it was followed by advice favouring a northern descent because of the local base of power that he and two of his co-conspirators, the earl of Danby and Lord Lumley, possessed in that part of the world. In fact this may have been the occasion when it was agreed that Devonshire and Danby would take the lead in organizing risings at Nottingham and York, respectively, to be triggered by news of the prince's landing.

The earl apparently remained in the south as late as 23 August, when he attended the installation of the duke of Ormond as chancellor of Oxford University, and then withdrew into the country after sending his eldest son off to Brussels and presumably out of harm's way. During September and again just at the beginning of October, Devonshire met twice with the earl of Danby to concert plans for the risings at Nottingham and York. The first of these meetings was also occasion for him to make amends for the rough political treatment that he and the whigs had accorded Danby in the 1670s. In the latter part of September, Devonshire also met with Bishop Compton of London, who brought him word of others who had engaged in the rapidly expanding conspiracy. When James II finally began to take seriously the dimensions of the threat confronting him Devonshire's absence from court and his politics made him an obvious suspect but the king took no action against him and indeed several newsletters reported that he had returned the earl's £30,000 bond in a conciliatory gesture. None the less there followed several weeks of great uncertainty for all the conspirators, first when in mid-October William's fleet was held back by bad weather, and then because of the news that the prince had landed at Torbay rather than in the north. Within less than a week, however, Devonshire and Danby had agreed on a new timetable for action which called for them and their supporters to seize control of both cities by 21 November.

On 17 November Devonshire arrived at Derby with a considerable troop of horse raised from among his tenantry and household staff, even including a number of artisans then employed on the reconstruction of Chatsworth. There he was also joined by Sir Scrope Howe and Sir William Russell, each accompanied by about fifteen men on horse, and a declaration was issued calling for the meeting of a free parliament and enumerating the grievances making a resort to arms necessary. Meeting no organized opposition of any kind, three days later Devonshire moved on to Nottingham, where he found the earl of Stamford already waiting with a small party of supporters and where he was joined on 21 November by Lord Delamer and a troop of 300 or so horse. Tensions quickly developed between the two. Delamer was intent on joining the prince of Orange as quickly as possible, while Devonshire wanted to pursue a more cautious strategy, taking the time to raise and organize additional men and seeking specific direction rather than striking out independently. At the end of the day a joint declaration urging assembly of a freely elected parliament was issued, and at the Saturday market on 25 November both men delivered energetic speeches about the defence of protestantism and traditional English liberties. Delamer, now accompanied by his cousin the earl of Stamford, then left immediately on his way to join forces with William, carrying a message from Devonshire that he would follow suit in due course. The last few days of the month found the earl and his principal associates engaged in raising additional men in Derby, Nottingham, and Leicestershire, organizing the beginnings of a regiment of eight or nine troops of fifty horse each, and seizing tax receipts in local hands to help finance the venture. On 29 November several other peers, the earls of Manchester, Northampton, and Scarsdale, and

Lord Grey of Ruthin, joined Devonshire at Nottingham, as had been originally planned but subsequently delayed by the confusion growing out of the prince's landing at Torbay. With their arrival the fledgeling army at Nottingham swelled to almost a thousand men in arms, a number limited at this point by the decision not to raise foot soldiers.

Although Nottingham had proved a safe and convenient staging area Devonshire was still intent on marching south until news arrived that Princess Anne had fled London and was on her way to join the northern insurgents. Her arrival at Nottingham on 2 December was not an unmixed blessing for the earl. On the one hand her presence gave some stamp of legitimacy to what many had regarded as simple rebellion, and as a consequence it enabled Devonshire to raise the Derbyshire militia and, subsequently and in association with others, militia units in Leicester, Northampton, and Warwickshire. On the other hand it blurred the political focus of the rising as various members of the nobility and gentry rallied to provide a protective escort for a member of the royal family but clearly not to support the larger objective of boxing James II into a corner if not removing him from power altogether. Further, the wishes of the princess obviously took precedence over those of the earl, and they were translated through the bishop of London, who had engineered her escape from the Cockpit and who thus became a major voice in the decision-making process. In the final analysis Anne sought direction from the prince of Orange before deciding what to do next, and William ordered a rendezvous at Oxford. Accordingly the entire assemblage at Nottingham departed on 9 December, with Devonshire in command of a regiment of horse, Sir Scrope Howe in command of another, and a variety of other independent troops of horse and militia units. In his autobiography Colley Cibber (whose father, the sculptor Caius Gabriel Cibber, had been working at Chatsworth) described the march as something of a triumphal progress through Leicester, Coventry, Warwick, Banbury, and Woodstock, and into Oxford on 15 December. However, a surviving autobiographical fragment of the earl of Chesterfield suggests something of the deep divisions of political viewpoint among the principals in arms and the limits of Devonshire's ability to influence the situation.

By the end of the month Devonshire was back in London and a participant in the meeting of peers on 23 December that decided upon the strategy of summoning a convention parliament. At a similar gathering the following day he openly tipped his hand in favour of William by opposing strongly the suggestion that the princess of Orange be immediately declared queen on the grounds that her father's flight constituted an act of abdication, and he continued to support the prince's interest when parliament actually assembled in late January. It was Devonshire, for instance, who manoeuvred a delay in the debate in the House of Lords that permitted the whig majority in the Commons to act first and declare the throne vacant. He also played a key role in promoting informal discussions aimed at creating an alliance between those who supported William and those, led by the earl of Danby, who advocated the claims of Mary. As a consequence, on 29 January the whig peers, in combination with Danby's group, defeated a proposal to establish a regency, with Devonshire serving as a teller for the majority. However, meeting as a committee of the whole two days later and again in a session held on 4 February, the upper chamber refused to declare the throne vacant or to name William and Mary as king and queen, both times by a narrow majority and with the earl serving as teller for the minority view. On two occasions he also served as a member of conference committees appointed to reconcile the differences between the two houses but it was not until William finally set his price and several tory peers, including both the earl of Chesterfield and Lord Ferrers (who had complicated life for Devonshire after Anne's arrival at Nottingham), abstained from voting that a majority was finally secured to ratify the revolution already accomplished.

Later years Devonshire was suitably and substantially rewarded for his role in the revolution and for his steadfast support for the new regime. On 14 February 1689 he was sworn of the privy council and continued a member until his death in 1707. The lord lieutenancy of Derbyshire was restored to the Cavendish family on 16 March, and at William and Mary's coronation on 11 April Devonshire was appointed lord high steward of England for the day, an honour again accorded him at the coronation of Queen Anne in 1702. During the spring of 1689 he was elected and installed as a knight of the Garter and given a commission as colonel of the regiment of horse that he had raised during the revolution and that was soon to see service in Ireland. He was also appointed lord steward of the household, a ministerial position of no great administrative importance but one which provided good opportunities for profit and political patronage. In 1690 a real sinecure came his way when he was named chief justice in eyre of all royal chases, parks, and warrens north of Trent, and between 1692 and 1694 he briefly added the lieutenancy of Nottinghamshire to his portfolio. As early as 1691 Narcissus Luttrell records a rumour to the effect that William intended to make Devonshire a duke, although it was not until 12 May 1694 that he was actually created marquess of Hartington and duke of Devonshire, probably at the instigation of the earl of Sunderland as the latter manoeuvred a whig ministry into place. Devonshire was also twice included in the cabinet council appointed to assist Queen Mary when she acted as regent during William's absences from the country. After her death the king resorted to a collective regency—the lords justices—in such a situation, and between 1695 and 1701 the duke served all six times that the king used the device by virtue of his position as lord steward.

The trappings of power and position aside, Devonshire does not emerge as a major player in the politics of the later Stuart era. Unlike a number of his contemporaries he took out no insurance policy at St Germain, and attempts by Lord Preston in 1690 and the informer John Taaffe in 1694 to link his name with the exiled king were simply unbelievable. His loyalty aside, however, Devonshire lacked the energy and appetite to carve out a leadership role in the kaleidoscope of ministries during William and Mary's reign. The queen did turn to him and the earl of Pembroke in 1690 to sort out what needed to be done in the aftermath of the battle off Beachy Head yet on other occasions she characterized Devonshire as 'weak and obstinate' (Browning, *Thomas Osborne*, 1.479) and—a sentiment echoed by others—too easily distracted by his desire to be a 'courtier among ladies' (Dalrymple, 2, app, pt. 2, 134). In 1691 Devonshire was part of the large entourage that accompanied William to The Hague for a meeting of leaders allied against Louis XIV. For a brief moment there was speculation that the king intended to tap him for a diplomatic mission to Vienna afterwards, although the report proved false and his part in the proceedings was essentially limited to that of social ornament. Two years later the earl was numbered among the whig leaders whom Sunderland brought together at Althorp in the summer of 1693 to lay plans for taking control of the government but he did his ministerial colleagues no favours when the Sir John Fenwick affair erupted in the summer of 1696. In his capacity as a lord justice Devonshire had been approached with the offer of a confession from Fenwick in exchange for immunity from prosecution for the latter's part in Jacobite plotting against the life of William III. The duke was dilatory and less than skilful in dealing with what soon escalated into a political crisis as rumours began to emerge about allegations that Fenwick had made against several members of the government, and witness tampering then made it necessary to resort to a bill of attainder rather than pursuing conviction under the terms of the newly enacted treason statute. Thought by many to have badly mishandled the situation, Devonshire did at least stick with personal principle, and at the end of the day he cast a futile no vote when the attainder bill was approved by the House of Lords on its third reading.

J. P. Kenyon has not unfairly described Devonshire as one of a handful of wealthy but otherwise unremarkable peers who provided ballast for the government in the years following the revolution—a well-connected patrician, predictable in viewpoint, and a reassuring symbol to certain constituencies. Perhaps his greatest value to the king was his unwavering support of William's efforts against the French, and that very steadiness led Marlborough, in particular, to press him to stay on as lord steward when Queen Anne ascended the throne. The duke's views about religion were also firmly fixed and relatively moderate. Early on he is supposed to have reminded William that he came to England to defend protestants rather than to persecute Catholics, and in January 1689 he was instrumental in arranging access to the prince for a delegation of Presbyterian, Congregationalist, and Baptist leaders to bring their thanks for his coming. Again at the beginning of Anne's reign Luttrell reports that he introduced a large group of dissenting ministers to offer congratulations on her accession. He was moreover a leading opponent of the occasional conformity bills in 1702 and 1703 but remained convinced throughout his life of the necessity of retaining the Test Act. In other legislative debates where his name figures prominently, such as the part he played in securing defeat of the place bill in 1693 or in opposing the resumption bill in 1699 before William threw in the towel, the duke's views tended to mirror those of the government of the day, with an occasional bow to whig principle. Devonshire had been an active participant in the work of the commission for the union of England and Scotland, and the passage of that statute in March 1707 marked, for all practical purposes, his disappearance from the political arena nearly a half-century after first being elected to the Commons. He died at Devonshire House, Piccadilly, London, on 18 August 1707, of complications arising from kidney stones and strangury, and was buried on 5 September in the family vault at All Saints', Derby. His widow died on 31 July 1710 and was buried with her parents in Westminster Abbey on 6 August.

Achievements As might be expected Lord Macaulay saw Devonshire as one of the great whig heroes of the age—certainly something of an exaggeration if one considers only the later years in his political career. By virtue of wealth and class he was almost predetermined to figure prominently in the annals of the period, although he did not emerge as a talent of the first order and indeed lacked the ambition to take on a sustained leadership role. Well suited by temperament and skill to the hit-and-run tactics of the opposition before the revolution, Devonshire seems to have understood unconsciously the limits of his ability and not to have pressed for office or influence beyond that for which he was suited in the years thereafter. Some contemporary observers, with modern echoes, voiced criticisms of his lifestyle. It is certainly true that he gambled substantial sums on the races and on cockfights at Newmarket. He also had a litigious nature and a quick temper that led to several duels. And he was personally dissolute, as John Dunton recounts in *The Hazard of a Death-Bed-Repentance*, a vastly popular and amusing antidote to the bromides of White Kennet's funeral sermon. None the less, the pattern of behaviour is not exceptional for the period, including a habit of extravagance limited only by the caution of his creditors and the strictures of the trust that his father had created to protect the Cavendish estates. What is more to the point, however, is the fact that Devonshire made two truly significant contributions to the development of English civilization. The first was his transformation of Chatsworth into an architectural masterpiece and its furnishing with some superb works of art. The duke's original intention was to do no more than add a south wing to Bess of Hardwick's large Elizabethan house, but between 1687 and 1706 it was totally reconstructed in several different phases. During the process Devonshire called on the services of architects William Talman (whom he sacked in 1696) and, later, Thomas Archer, while employing leading artists such as the decorative painters Antonio Verrio and Louis Laguerre, and the sculptor Caius Gabriel Cibber, but the vision and energy behind the overall project were his. Defoe makes the point nicely:

> The House had indeed received Additions as it did every Year and perhaps would to this Day, had the Duke liv'd, who had a Genius for such Things beyond the reach of the most perfect Masters and was not only capable to design, but to finish. (Defoe, 2.582)

Other travellers, such as Celia Fiennes, who saw the house while building was still in progress, were also much taken with the new Chatsworth, its wonderful gardens, and substantial reconfiguration of the surrounding landscape to create an appropriate setting. It was, again in the words of Defoe, 'a Palace for a Prince, a most magnificent Beauty, and in spite of all the Difficulties or Disadvantages of the Situation … a perfect Beauty' (ibid., 581).

Devonshire's second and perhaps better known contribution was the part that he played in both bringing about and determining the outcome of the revolution of 1688. Convinced of the necessity of what he was doing, the duke was among the handful of aristocratic leaders whose efforts enabled the success of William of Orange. In the epitaph that he composed Devonshire describes himself as a faithful subject to good sovereigns, inimical and hateful to tyrants. It is a turn of phrase that speaks to an age and a conception of state that, in fact, his actions unwittingly helped to end. DAVID HOSFORD

Sources A. Grey, ed., *Debates of the House of Commons, from the year 1667 to the year 1694*, 10 vols. (1763), vols. 2–8 · *CSP dom.*, 1673–1704 · *Report on the manuscripts of his grace the duke of Buccleuch and Queensberry … preserved at Montagu House*, 3 vols. in 4, HMC, 45 (1899–1926), vol. 2, pt 1 · *The manuscripts of the Earl Cowper*, 3 vols., HMC, 23 (1888–9), vols. 2–3 · *Report on the manuscripts of the marquis of Downshire*, 6 vols. in 7, HMC, 75 (1924–95), vols. 1–2 · *Report on the manuscripts of Allan George Finch*, 5 vols., HMC, 71 (1913–2003), vols. 2–3 · *Seventh report*, HMC, 6 (1879), pt 1 [Sir F. Graham; Sir H. Verney] · *The manuscripts of the House of Lords*, new ser., 12 vols. (1900–77), vol. 2 · *The manuscripts of S. H. Le Fleming*, HMC, 25 (1890) · *Calendar of the manuscripts of the marquess of Ormonde*, new ser., 8 vols., HMC, 36 (1902–20), vols. 1–4 · *The manuscripts of his grace the duke of Portland*, 10 vols., HMC, 29 (1891–1931), vol. 3 · *The manuscripts of his grace the duke of Rutland*, 4 vols., HMC, 24 (1888–1905), vol. 2 · J. Dalrymple, *Memoirs of Great Britain and Ireland*, 3 vols. (1771–8) · *Bishop Burnet's History*, vols. 1–2 · N. Luttrell, *A brief historical relation of state affairs from September 1678 to April 1714*, 6 vols. (1857), 1–5 · *Memoirs of Sir John Reresby*, ed. A. Browning (1936) · W. Kennet, *The duke of Devonshire's funeral-sermon with some memoirs of the family of Cavendish* (1708) · [J. Dunton], *The hazard of a death-bed-repentance* (1708) · *Memoirs of Thomas, earl of Ailesbury*, ed. W. E. Buckley, 2 vols., Roxburghe Club, 122 (1890) · *The correspondence of Thomas Hobbes*, ed. N. Malcolm, 2 vols. (1994) · *State trials* · *The correspondence of Henry Hyde, earl of Clarendon, and of his brother Lawrence Hyde, earl of Rochester*, ed. S. W. Singer, 2 (1828) · *Private and original correspondence of Charles Talbot, duke of Shrewsbury*, ed. W. Coxe (1821) · *Works of the earls of Rochester, Roscomon, and Dorset: the dukes of Devonshire, Buckinghamshire, etc.* (1789) · *The collection of autograph letters and historical documents, formed by Alfred Morrison*, 2nd ser., [vol. 7]: *The Bulstrode papers, 1667–1675* (1897) · A. Browning, *Thomas Osborne, earl of Danby and duke of Leeds, 1632–1712*, 3 vols. (1944–51) · T. B. Macaulay, *The history of England from the accession of James II*, new edn, ed. C. H. Firth, 6 vols. (1913–15), vols. 2–4 · J. P. Kenyon, *The Stuarts: a study in kingship* (1958) · D. H. Hosford, *Nottingham, nobles and the north: aspects of the revolution of 1688* (1976) · F. Thompson, *A history of Chatsworth* (1949) · F. Bickley, *The Cavendish family* (1911) · *Derbyshire*, Pevsner (1978) · D. Defoe, *A tour thro' the whole island of Great Britain*, 2 vols. (1927), vol. 2 · *The journeys of Celia Fiennes*, ed. C. Morris (1949)

Archives Chatsworth House, Derbyshire, MSS | BL, corresp. with Lady Fenwick, Add. MS 47608 · BL, Middleton papers, Add. MS 41805 · Bodl. Oxf., Le Fleming newsletters, donated MSS C/38,

C/39 • DWL, Roger Morrice, ent'ring book • Hunt. L., Hastings MSS • U. Nott., Portland (Welbeck Abbey) MSS
Likenesses J. Hoskins, watercolour miniature, 1644, Burghley House, Peterborough • I. Beckett, mezzotint (after G. Kneller, c.1680–1685), BM, NPG [see illus.] • attrib. G. Kneller, oils, Hardwick Hall, Derbyshire • G. Kneller, oils, Chatsworth House, Derbyshire • A. F. van der Meulen, oils, Chatsworth House, Derbyshire • P. Pelham, mezzotint (after G. Kneller), NG Ire. • J. Riley, oils, Chatsworth House, Derbyshire • P. Schenk, mezzotint (after G. Kneller), BM, NPG • J. M. Wright, oils, Hardwick Hall, Derbyshire • group portrait, engraving (The Cavendish family; after Riley), repro. in Bickley, Cavendish family • oils (after G. Kneller), Chatsworth House, Derbyshire

Cavendish, William, fourth duke of Devonshire (bap. 1720, d. 1764), prime minister, was baptized at St Martin-in-the-Fields, Westminster, on 1 June 1720, the eldest of the four sons of William Cavendish, third duke of Devonshire (1698–1755), politician and landowner, and his wife, Catherine (c.1700–1777), the eldest daughter of John Hoskins, of Oxted, Surrey, steward to the duke of Bedford. Styled marquess of Hartington from 1729, when his father succeeded to the dukedom, he was probably educated at home before undertaking the grand tour to France and Italy in 1739–40, accompanied by his tutor, the Revd Arthur Smyth.

The Cavendish family was at the heart of the whig party that had dominated politics since the Hanoverian succession, and a career in politics was the inevitable destiny for Hartington, as heir to one of the premier dukedoms in the country. As soon as he came of age he was elected to the House of Commons in May 1741 as MP for Derbyshire, the family seat, and adopted his father's allegiance to the prime minister, Sir Robert Walpole. After Walpole's resignation in 1742 Hartington sided with Walpole's political heirs, the Pelham faction, led by Henry Pelham and his brother the duke of Newcastle, and strongly supported their attempts to fashion a viable administration over the next four years. Pelham highly valued both his abilities and his loyalty; as he informed Devonshire in 1743, Hartington was 'our mainstay amongst the young ones, of themselves liable to wander' (Sedgwick, 538).

On 27 March 1748 Hartington married Lady Charlotte Elizabeth Boyle, Baroness Clifford of Londesborough (1731–1754), the third yet only surviving daughter of Richard Boyle, third earl of Burlington (1694–1753), and his wife, Dorothy Savile (1699–1758). The match had been planned during the couple's childhood, although Hartington's mother, who had married for love, refused to approve the arranged marriage and remained estranged from her son and his family for the rest of her life. Despite her fears, the marriage proved to be happy and loving, albeit short, for Charlotte died six years later, on 8 December 1754 at Uppingham. They had four children: William *Cavendish, later fifth duke of Devonshire (1748–1811); Dorothy (1750–1794), who married William Bentinck, third duke of Portland; Richard (1752–1781), MP for Lancaster and then Derbyshire; and George (1754–1834), MP for Knaresborough, then Derby, who became first earl of Burlington of the second creation in 1831. It was certainly a

politically advantageous marriage, as Charlotte's inheritance on her father's death in 1754 included vast estates in Yorkshire and Ireland, as well as electoral interests over the two parliamentary seats at Knaresborough and the Irish parliamentary constituency of Lismore Town. Burlington's valuable art collection, his villa at Chiswick, and Burlington House in Piccadilly also passed into the Devonshire family.

With his political standing enhanced by his marriage, Hartington took his seat in the Lords in his father's barony of Cavendish on 13 June 1749, which enabled him to accept the mastership of the horse and a cabinet seat from Pelham; he had earlier declined the governorship of the new prince of Wales, the future George III. He was appointed to these offices and sworn of the privy council on 12 July. Following Pelham's death in 1754 he adhered closely to Newcastle, who appointed him lord lieutenant of Ireland in March 1755, in succession to the first duke of Dorset. He was ideally qualified for the post, not only by his landed and political interests in Ireland, but also by his family connections with some of the principal political players in the country, namely Henry Boyle (his late wife's uncle) and William and John Ponsonby (both of whom were married to his sisters). Crucially, his closeness to Henry Fox at Westminster made him acceptable to Fox's brother-in-law, the earl of Kildare, who opposed the Ponsonby faction. Furthermore his father had been a popular lord lieutenant in Ireland from 1737 to 1745, and Hartington's own easy-going temperament seemed suited to the difficult job of reconciling the Irish patriot factions, led by Boyle and Kildare, with the Dublin Castle administration, headed by George Stone, archbishop of Armagh, and his Ponsonby allies.

Hartington arrived in Dublin in May 1755 to find Boyle and Kildare demanding Stone's removal from office as chancellor of exchequer and the restoration of offices to Boyle and his supporters. A common source of strife was the appointment of lords justice to govern Ireland in the absence of the lord lieutenant, which Hartington deliberately side-stepped by resolving to remain in Ireland. He outlined his policy of reconciling the rival factions in a letter to Newcastle, dated 4 October 1755: 'My scheme is if possible to govern this country without a party and make those that receive favours from the Crown think themselves obliged to it and not to their party here' (J. C. D. Clark, 282). In spring 1756 he made a bolder attempt to neutralize the friction between the patriots and the Dublin Castle administration when in March he procured Boyle's resignation as speaker of the Irish Commons for the price of a pension and a peerage, and replaced him with John Ponsonby. He followed this up by appointing Kildare sole lord justice in May and by persuading Stone to withdraw his claim to be considered as a lord justice. Hartington left Ireland in the autumn, having won a tactical victory by wrong-footing the patriots and by adopting an 'anti-party ideology'. Though it proved only a temporary success in breaking the Irish undertakers' dominance, his policy paved the way for the decisive viceroyalty of the fourth Viscount Townshend in the 1760s.

On 5 December 1755 Hartington succeeded on his father's death as fourth duke of Devonshire. He returned to England in October 1756 at a time of conflict with France and political instability at home. Fox's resignation that month triggered the end of Newcastle's administration, which had been worn down by military failures, such as the loss of Minorca earlier that year and the French capture of Fort Oswego on Lake Ontario. Pending a more permanent arrangement, whereby William Pitt could be reconciled with Newcastle, George II summoned Devonshire to form an interim ministry to avert government collapse and to manage the war with France. On 6 November, Devonshire was appointed first lord of the Treasury and Pitt succeeded Fox, who had been unable to form a viable ministry, as secretary of state for the south. The virtues of tact, affability, and honesty that Devonshire had used to good effect as lord lieutenant were now needed to bring about the desired reconciliation between Pitt and Newcastle; as Newcastle commented on 13 November, Devonshire was the 'great engine, on whom the whole turns at present' (J. Clark, 287). As in Ireland, Devonshire attempted to utilize Pitt's patriot credentials to create a ministry that was devoid of party allegiances but as a consequence lacked a secure political base. Despite the notorious court martial and execution of Admiral Byng, which dominated politics early in 1757, there were definite achievements. It was under this administration that America was set forth as a strategic priority, a militia for home defence was established, a continental army was assembled, and naval raids against the French coast were organized; however, these policies owed more to Pitt than to Devonshire.

As predicted, the Devonshire–Pitt ministry proved short-lived, and it was fatally damaged in April 1757 when Pitt resigned, along with his cousin Temple. After two months of protracted negotiations the Newcastle–Pitt coalition succeeded to office on 29 June, a coalition that led Britain to victory over France. Although Devonshire had played a vital role in forging the coalition, he was far from complacent about its chances of survival. He wrote to Lord Mansfield on 20 June of the proposed ministry:

> the plan is undoubtedly the best that could be formed, the only difficulty will be to make it hold … the utmost of my abilities are to see an administration settled that will endeavour with firmness and unanimity to extricate this country out of the dangerous situation it is in at present. (J. Clark, 442)

With no desire for high office, Devonshire became lord chamberlain in the coalition but retained a seat in the inner cabinet, where his integrity, family standing, and friendship with leading whigs allowed him to calm the rancour of party politics and personality differences. This was especially important after the accession of George III in October 1760 and the advent of his mentor, Lord Bute, whose rapid advancement threatened to undermine whig hegemony and destabilize governmental politics. Throughout 1761 and 1762, during the peace negotiations with France, Devonshire was a key factor in maintaining the ministerial harmony necessary for achieving peace. During the momentous months from September 1759 to October 1762 he kept a diary which offers keen insights into the decision-making process and general diplomatic affairs of the time. Fascinatingly, Devonshire's diary reveals his unalterable view that Britain should be governed by an aristocratic oligarchy while at the same time testifying to his own resolution to remain an onlooker rather than a principal actor in the political arena.

When Newcastle resigned in May 1762 Devonshire did not follow him out of office but showed his solidarity by refusing to attend cabinet. This anomalous situation, whereby he retained his office yet absented himself from the business of government, could not be tolerated for long. Disagreement with Bute over the final peace treaty led to his resignation as lord chamberlain on 28 November 1762. George III expressed his extreme displeasure at his conduct a few days later when, with his own pen, he struck Devonshire's name from the list of privy councillors, a rare gesture that emphatically ended Devonshire's political career. Devonshire took part in the opposition to the Cider Tax Bill that brought about Bute's downfall in April 1763. Perhaps as a punishment, Devonshire was further disgraced when in October 1764 the king dismissed him as lord lieutenant of Derbyshire, an office that had been held continuously by the Cavendishes since George I's accession. His last months were spent at Spa, Germany, in a state of deteriorating health. He died there on 2 October 1764, aged forty-four, and was buried next to his wife in All Saints', Derby.

Devonshire was a man of solid if not outstanding abilities. He was endowed with the qualities—devotion to friends and duty, patriotism, and unswerving integrity—which made him the ideal sounding board and factotum among the prominent politicians of his day. Unlike Pitt or Fox he lacked a brilliant mind, and his diary provides evidence of devotion to king, country, and duty rather than quickness of intellect. A political broker rather than a leader, he exploited his personal popularity and family prestige to mediate between the factious and egotistical individuals who dominated Dublin and Westminster politics in the 1750s and early 1760s.

KARL WOLFGANG SCHWEIZER

Sources Collins peerage of England: genealogical, biographical and historical, ed. E. Brydges, 9 vols. (1812) • GEC, Peerage • R. Eccleshall and G. Walker, Biographical dictionary of British prime ministers (1998) • The Devonshire diary: memoranda on state of affairs, 1759–1762, ed. P. D. Brown and K. W. Schweizer, CS, 4th ser., 27 (1982) • J. Clark, The dynamics of change: the crisis of the 1750s and English party systems (1982) • The memoirs and speeches of James, 2nd Earl Waldegrave, 1742–1763, ed. J. C. D. Clark (1988) • Letters from George III to Lord Bute, 1756–1766, ed. R. Sedgwick (1939) • R. R. Sedgwick, 'Cavendish, Lord William', HoP, Commons, 1715–54 • H. Walpole, Memoirs of King George II, ed. J. Brooke, 3 vols. (1985) • H. van Thal, ed., The prime ministers (1974) • J. C. D. Clark, 'Whig tactics and parliamentary precedent: the English management of Irish politics, 1754–1756', HJ, 21 (1978), 275–301 • N. J. Powell, 'The reform of the undertaker system: Anglo-Irish politics, 1750–1767', Irish Historical Studies, 31 (1998–9), 19–36 • IGI

Archives Chatsworth House, Derbyshire, corresp. and papers • PRO, letters on dismissal as lord chamberlain of the household, PRO 30/47/29/1 | BL, letters to Lord Hardwicke, Add. MSS 35593–

35597 · BL, corresp. with Lord Holdernesse, Egerton MS 3432 · BL, corresp. with Lord Holland, Add. MSS 51381–51384 · BL, Liverpool MSS · BL, Mitchell papers · BL, corresp. with duke of Newcastle, Add. MSS 32712–33068 · Derbys. RO, corresp. with R. Wilmot and others · Mount Stuart Trust, Isle of Bute, corresp. with Lord Bute · PRO, Chatham papers, PRO 30/8 · PRO, Egremont MSS, PRO 47/26 · Royal Arch., Cumberland papers · Sheff. Arch., letters to the second marquess of Rockingham · Suffolk RO, Ipswich, Barrington MSS · Woburn Abbey, Bedfordshire, Bedford MSS

Likenesses W. Hogarth, oils, 1741, Yale U. CBA · attrib. T. Hudson, oils, *c.*1757, Chatsworth, Derbyshire · A. Ramsay, oils, 1759, NPG · attrib. G. Knapton, oils, Hardwick Hall, Derbyshire · J. Reynolds?, oils, J. B. Speed Art Museum, Louisville, Kentucky

Cavendish, William, **fifth duke of Devonshire** (1748–1811), nobleman, was born on 14 December 1748, the eldest of the four children of William *Cavendish, fourth duke of Devonshire (*bap.* 1720, *d.* 1764), politician, and his wife, Charlotte Elizabeth Boyle, Baroness Clifford (1731–1754), daughter and heir of Richard Boyle, third earl of Burlington. He was known by the courtesy title Lord Cavendish until his mother's death, when he succeeded her as seventh Baron Clifford; from his father's accession to the dukedom in 1755 he was known as marquess of Hartington. He attended a school before becoming duke, but it is unknown which one. On his father's death on 3 October 1764 he became fifth duke of Devonshire and inherited vast estates in England, principally in Derbyshire and Yorkshire, and in Ireland valued at over £36,000 a year. These included the properties of Chatsworth House and Hardwick Hall in Derbyshire, Londesborough House and Bolton Abbey in Yorkshire, Lismore Castle in co. Waterford, Chiswick House in Middlesex, and Devonshire House and Burlington House in Piccadilly, London. Further family estates were settled on his brother George, later first earl of Burlington (1754–1834). After the deaths of his parents Devonshire was brought up by his three bachelor uncles—lords Frederick, George, and John Cavendish—and was presented at court in the spring of 1765. His uncles abandoned an idea that he should attend Cambridge University for fear people there would 'pay dirty court' to him and that he would contract 'unbecoming friendships' (Lord John Cavendish to Richard Newcome, 11 Oct 1764, Chatsworth MS 428.12). He travelled on the continent in 1767–8, and his uncles kept him informed of their management of his interest at the 1768 general election.

On 7 June 1774 Devonshire married the gregarious Lady Georgiana Spencer [*see* Cavendish, Georgiana, duchess of Devonshire (1757–1806)], eldest daughter of John, first Earl Spencer, at Wimbledon parish church, Surrey, despite rumours that he was to wed Lady Betty Hamilton. Earlier in the year he had fathered an illegitimate daughter, Charlotte Williams, by a London milliner, Charlotte Spencer (*d.* 1781). Georgiana bore him three children: Georgiana (1783–1858), Harriet (1785–1862) [*see* Gower, Henrietta Elizabeth Leveson-, Countess Granville], and William George Spencer *Cavendish, the future sixth duke (1790–1858). In contrast to his extravagant wife, Devonshire was reserved and insular, prone to heavy drinking

William Cavendish, fifth duke of Devonshire (1748–1811), by Pompeo Batoni, 1768

and gambling, and he possessed a greater affection for dogs than for people. As Nathaniel Wraxall described him:

> He seemed to be incapable of any strong emotion, and destitute of all energy or activity of mind. As play became indispensable in order to rouse him from this lethargic habit and to awaken his torpid faculties, he passed his evenings usually at Brookes's, engaged at whist or faro. Yet beneath so quiet an exterior he possessed a highly improved understanding, and on all disputes that occasionally arose among the members of the club relative to passages of the Roman poets or historians, I know that appeal was constantly made to the Duke, and his decision or opinion was regarded as final. (*Historical and Posthumous Memoirs*, 3.344)

Devonshire came from one of the wealthiest and most powerful whig families. However, he possessed no great ability or political ambition. He was lord high treasurer of Ireland and governor of Cork from 1766 to 1793, and lord lieutenant of Derbyshire from 1782 to his death, but three times refused cabinet office: once during the formation of the Fox–North administration in 1783, again during the regency crisis of 1788–9 when Charles James Fox told him any post was his for the asking, and again in 1806 when he was invited to join the 'ministry of all the talents'. He took his duties seriously: in 1778 he became colonel of the Derbyshire militia, and he spent summer the next year in camp with his men rather than go to Spa with his wife and her family, although this decision also reflected a measure of estrangement between Devonshire and the duchess. He made the first of his two recorded speeches in the House of Lords on 6 March 1780, when he opposed the dismissal of Francis Osborne, marquess of Carmarthen, and Henry Herbert, earl of Pembroke, from their lord lieutenancies. He was appointed KG on 19 April 1782, an honour he allegedly said he would no more ask the king for 'than I would ask him for a blue great coat' (*Last Journals of Horace Walpole*, 2.427). On 3 July 1793 he was created DCL by the University of Oxford.

In May 1782 the Devonshires met Lady Elizabeth Christiana Foster [see Cavendish, Elizabeth Christiana, duchess of Devonshire (1757–1824)], daughter of Frederick *Hervey, fourth earl of Bristol, bishop of Derry, and estranged wife of John Thomas Foster MP. Together the three formed a bizarre love triangle whose conspicuous interdependence provoked much gossip and speculation. Georgiana and Lady Elizabeth nicknamed the duke Canis because of his obsessive love of dogs. Lady Elizabeth gave birth to two children fathered by the duke: Caroline St Jules (1785–1862), who married George *Lamb, and Augustus William James *Clifford (1788–1877), later a naval officer and a baronet. The irregularity of their domestic arrangements lent colour to Devonshire House, which remained the focus for the Foxite whigs through the 1790s. Neither Devonshire's hostility to the radicalism favoured by Fox and Georgiana's lover Charles Grey, nor his opposition to the policy of peace with France favoured by Fox's circle, threatened its status, which was guaranteed by the personal qualities of Georgiana, and by the willingness of the duke to divert his estate income towards the financial support of Foxite candidates and impoverished members of the circle.

Devonshire regarded himself as bound to the whig tradition by heredity. He was not a natural leader, and those who thought he could succeed Fox as the focus of the whig party when Fox temporarily retired from politics were disappointed: John Nichols dismissed him as 'a mere sensualist' (Foreman, 309). His sympathy towards some of the Pitt ministry's measures in the face of revolutionary agitation and invasion from France led him to make his second recorded speech in the Lords, supporting an address to the king on Irish affairs on 15 June 1798. It was said that when he voted with the government on an anti-Jacobin measure, his whig nominees as members for Knaresborough in Yorkshire arrived at Devonshire House the next day to submit their resignations; Devonshire responded: 'I never interfere with your vote—I don't see why you should interfere with mine' (Thorne). Although a tolerant borough patron where his members were concerned, Devonshire jealously protected his rights as the proprietor of the majority of the burgesses in Knaresborough. At the general election of 1806, when the inhabitants attempted to disrupt the voting of the burgesses in the hope of overturning the limited franchise, he sent in 300 lead miners and soldiers of the Scots Greys to take on the disaffected residents.

From middle life Devonshire increasingly suffered from bouts of ill health, the consequence of excessive drinking, and spent less and less time in London, preferring Chatsworth, Chiswick, or visits to Bath. The death of Georgiana in 1806 shook his life both personally and politically. Lady Elizabeth Foster took over as female head of the household, to the fury of his unmarried daughter Harriet. It was only at this point that he made a great effort to know his children, and considered it a great expression of affection when in November 1807 he presented Harriet with a puppy, attempting to pass on his mania for dogs. Harriet wrote:

> he really thinks of little else and the whole time of dinner and supper he feeds and watches them, laughs excessively every time they squeak or run and listens to no conversation with half the pleasure as he does when these puppies are the subject. (*Letters of Lady Harriet Cavendish*, 232)

His cohabitation with Lady Elizabeth Foster was regularized on 19 October 1809 when they married at Chiswick House, although the marriage seems to have scandalized society more than Lady Elizabeth's previous status as his mistress, and fewer people than before called at Devonshire House.

Devonshire died at Devonshire House, Piccadilly, London, on 29 July 1811, of 'water on the chest' (GEC, *Peerage*), and was buried at All Saints' Church, Derby. He left an estate estimated at £125,000, but expenditure on the acquisition of land and on property development during his lifetime, including The Crescent at Buxton, Derbyshire, as well as the burden of Georgiana's gambling losses and the other demands of the Devonshires' expensive lifestyle, had burdened the estate with debts calculated at £593,000 in 1814, an unpromising legacy to his successor. Nevertheless most of his contemporaries would have agreed with Wraxall's assessment: 'if not a superior man, he was an honourable and respectable member of society' (*Historical and Posthumous Memoirs*, 3.344).

MICHAEL DURBAN

Sources A. Foreman, *Georgiana, duchess of Devonshire* (1998) · R. Adair, *Sketch of the character of the late duke of Devonshire* (1811) · GEC, *Peerage*, new edn, vol. 4 · *The historical and the posthumous memoirs of Sir Nathaniel William Wraxall, 1772–1784*, ed. H. B. Wheatley, 5 vols. (1884) · *The last journals of Horace Walpole*, ed. Dr Doran, rev. A. F. Steuart, 2 vols. (1910) · *The letters and journals of Lady Mary Coke*, ed. J. A. Home, 4 vols. (1889) · Earl of Bessborough, ed., *Lady Bessborough and her family circle* (1940) · H. Walpole, *Memoirs of the reign of King George the Third*, ed. G. F. R. Barker, 4 vols. (1894) · A. Calder-Marshall, *The two duchesses* (1978) · B. Masters, *Georgiana* (1981) · D. M. Stuart, *Dearest Bess: the life and times of Lady Elizabeth Foster afterwards duchess of Devonshire* (1955) · H. Stokes, *The Devonshire House circle* (1917) · *The Devonshire diary: memoranda on state of affairs, 1759–1762*, ed. P. D. Brown and K. W. Schweizer, CS, 4th ser., 27 (1982) · G. M. D. Howat, 'The duke of Devonshire', *The prime ministers*, ed. H. van Thal, 2 vols. (1978) · F. Bickley, *The Cavendish family* (1911) · J. Bunting, *The earls and dukes of Devonshire* (1996) · Duchess of Devonshire, *Chatsworth: the home of the duke and duchess of Devonshire* (1986) · B. Masters, *The dukes: the origins, ennoblement and history of 26 families* (1975) · J. Pearson, *Stags and serpents: the story of the house of Cavendish and the dukes of Devonshire* (1976) · L. J. Proudfoot, *Urban patronage and social authority: the management of the duke of Devonshire's towns in Ireland, 1764–1891* (1995) · Foster, *Alum. Oxon.*, 1715–

1886 • *Hary-O: the letters of Lady Harriet Cavendish, 1796–1809*, ed. G. Leveson-Gower and I. Palmer (1940) • D. Cannadine, 'The land-owner as millionaire', *Aspects of aristocracy* (1995), 165–83 • R. G. Thorne, 'Knaresborough', HoP, *Commons, 1790–1820*, 2.450–52

Archives Chatsworth House, Derbyshire, MSS | Castle Howard, North Yorkshire, letters to his daughter, countess of Carlisle • U. Nott. L., letters to third duke of Portland

Likenesses P. Batoni, oils, 1768, Chatsworth House, Derbyshire [*see illus.*] • J. Reynolds, oils, exh. RA 1776, Althorp, Northampton-shire • W. Lane, group portrait, chalk, *c.*1810 (*Whig statesmen and their friends*), NPG • W. T. Hulland, mezzotint (after J. Reynolds), NPG, BM • A. van Maron, oils, Chatsworth House, Derbyshire

Wealth at death approx. £125,000 p.a.: Calder-Marshall, *The two duchesses*, 167

Cavendish, William, seventh duke of Devonshire (1808–1891), landowner and industrialist, was born on 27 April 1808, in Charles Street, Berkeley Square, London, the eld-est of the four children of William Cavendish (1783–1812) and his wife, the Hon. Louisa O'Callaghan (*d.* 1863), eldest daughter of Cornelius O'Callaghan, first Baron Lismore. His grandfather was George Augustus Cavendish, first earl of Burlington (1754–1834); William Cavendish, fourth duke of Devonshire, was his great-grandfather. William's father was killed in a carriage accident in 1812. He was edu-cated at Eton College and Trinity College, Cambridge, and took his BA and MA in 1829, when he was second wrangler to Henry Philpott as senior wrangler, and first Smith's prizeman to Philpott's second. In June 1829 he was returned as MP for Cambridge University, and two months later he married his relative, Lady Blanche Georgiana (1812–1840), fourth daughter of George *Howard, sixth earl of Carlisle, and favourite niece of William George Spencer Cavendish, sixth duke of Devonshire. Blanche, almost a child bride, was as serious, earnest, and devout as her husband. They had three sons and one daughter. A well-matched pair, they were happiest when reading Wes-ley's sermons together. When her uncle, the bachelor duke, took to religion in the 1830s after a lifetime of profli-gacy, Blanche was a source of support and encouragement to him in his new-found sense of sin. When she died in 1840 (her doctors said of 'great nervous debility', but more probably of tuberculosis since she had been coughing blood) her uncle was almost as desolated as her husband.

For a few years Cavendish pursued a desultory parlia-mentary career; ejected by Cambridge University in 1831 because he had taken the family whig line in supporting the Reform Bill, he was immediately found another seat in the Fitzwilliam borough of Malton, and he was then trans-lated to the Cavendish family Derbyshire seat when the incumbent, his grandfather, was created earl of Burling-ton later that year. He had no political talent or ambition, and was rarely heard from again in parliament after suc-ceeding to the Burlington title and estates in 1834. Those estates, in north Lancashire and Sussex, had come to the fourth duke of Devonshire by marriage (along with vast Irish estates in Cork and Waterford), and had been left by him to his third, but second surviving, son, a fairly regular disposition of an heiress's estate in an attempt to preserve a separate identity for her family's inheritance. The ploy

William Cavendish, seventh duke of Devonshire (1808–1891), by George Frederic Watts, 1883

did not work in this instance, for the Cavendish and Bur-lington (Boyle) estates were reunited in 1858 when Caven-dish succeeded his cousin as seventh duke of Devonshire. It had, however, succeeded in the sense that the duke and duchess became greatly attached to the houses on the Bur-lington properties—Holker Hall in north Lancashire and Compton Place in Eastbourne. These remained the duke's favourite residences, perhaps out of attachment to his wife's memory, throughout the long period after Blanche's death, even after he had inherited the greater and magnificent Chatsworth.

The death of his adored wife at first turned Cavendish into a recluse at Holker, looking after its famous herd of shorthorns and resisting his kinsman's suggestion that he should move to Chatsworth with his four young children. Very soon he threw himself into the serious and useful work of the personal management of his estates which was to occupy the rest of his life. Furness was the first to absorb his attention, when he and the other great land-owner in the neighbourhood, the duke of Buccleuch, played leading parts in launching the Furness Railway in 1843; this was designed to facilitate the transport of their slate and iron ore to the coast at the village of Barrow. Then from 1848 Cavendish became interested in the development of Eastbourne, and over the next forty years his investments in waterworks, gasworks, pier, and park, along with his patronage and the measures of his estate office to control the tone of development, were held to have been largely responsible for making Eastbourne into 'the Empress of watering places' (*Eastbourne Chronicle*, 4 June 1904). 'The Duke can do without Eastbourne, but

Eastbourne cannot do without the Duke' (*Eastbourne Gazette*, 10 April 1878), it was said—implying, by chance correctly, not only that the swelling income from Eastbourne was of no great consequence to the duke with his other and much larger sources of income, but also that from his point of view the whole enterprise was self-financing, with ducal investment financed by ploughing back the profits from ground rents. Later he contributed in a similar way to the development of Buxton as a watering place.

Furness was a different story. There nothing less was afoot than the creation, virtually from scratch, of a whole new industrial district, and the duke found himself, sometimes reluctantly, drawn into the leadership of this process. The rise of Barrow as an industrial town, which began with the establishment of the Haemetite Steel Company in 1859, was most directly associated with the enterprise and capital of the major industrialists, H. W. Schneider, Robert Hannay, and Sir James Ramsden. Behind them lay the capital and commitment to the economic expansion of the region manifested by the seventh duke. He never adopted a rentier attitude towards this part of his possessions; far from simply pocketing his mineral royalties and railway dividends he regarded it as a matter of self-interest and moral duty to use them to finance the further development of the region; and this continuing stream of investment, coupled with his close attention to all the businesses with which he became involved, made him into a regional entrepreneur of the first rank. The Park-Vale iron ore and Furness Railway ventures led on, with convincing economic logic, to his active involvement in the steel company and in the Barrow docks, once more in partnership with the duke of Buccleuch; and thence to the shipbuilding company which became the Naval Construction and Armaments Company (eventually sold to Vickers in 1896). He also invested in a shipping company and, using the growing pool of potential female labour created by the growth of Barrow and its male-dominated industries, in a flax and jute company.

Even before he succeeded to the dukedom Cavendish had committed more than £100,000 to Barrow enterprises. He then discovered that the sixth duke, a bachelor, in a dazzling display of extravagant projects at Chatsworth and at Lismore Castle in Waterford, and egged on by the costly genius of Sir Joseph Paxton, had left the Devonshire estates saddled with debts of £1 million. A resolve to put an end to irresponsible frivolity led to the instant departure of Paxton and the consideration of the wisdom of reducing the debt by selling parts of the estates. Persuaded that this would lead to loss of influence and social humiliation, the seventh duke was saved from this fate, as it seemed, by his own exertions in nurturing the great Barrow boom of the 1860s and early 1870s. Investment in the Barrow ventures increased steadily and for a while the dividends from them soared, so that at the peak in 1874 the duke, with a gross income of more than £300,000, was probably the richest individual in the land, with more than half of his income coming from Barrow. Some of the

inherited debt was cleared, but unhappily the Barrow investments necessitated some fresh borrowing, so that the overall debt remained much the same. Then, after 1874, misfortune struck. First, the whole British economy suffered a setback, and second, Barrow was hit especially hard by the ending of the 'Bessemer boom' in the steel industry (stimulated by Sir Henry Bessemer's process). The duke's income from the Barrow enterprises collapsed from £150,000 a year in the early 1870s to barely £8000 a year at the end of the 1880s; in the same period he poured money into 'his' firms in a frantic effort to prop up the ailing steel, shipbuilding, shipping, and jute companies, so that at his death he left debts of some £2 million, all sunk in what had turned into unproductive investments. His eldest son, Spencer Compton *Cavendish, eighth duke, was left to sort out this financial mess, and though as marquess of Hartington he had not exactly established a reputation for prudence or sound business sense he was astonishingly successful in the task.

The contemporary view of the seventh duke as the prime example of the industrious, abstemious, virtuous, public-spirited, mid-Victorian aristocrat was formed at the time of his, and Barrow's, greatest material prosperity. It was during this period that W. E. Gladstone attended the opening of the Barrow docks, in 1867, and that the duke was elected first president of the Iron and Steel Institute on its foundation, in 1868. In 1869 Cavendish became president of the Royal Agricultural Society of England. Twenty years later, amid the ruins of Barrow's industrial pretensions, the public spirit remained; however, the great entrepreneurial saviour of the family fortunes had been transformed into the source of embarrassments much more severe than those caused by the sixth duke's wonderful conservatory and Emperor fountain at Chatsworth and the great Pugin alterations at Lismore.

The seventh duke never appeared in society in London, reserving his public life for more serious and uplifting pursuits, notably the support of higher education. He was the first chancellor of the University of London, from 1836 to 1856, and an important influence on its early development. He was chancellor of Cambridge University from 1862 until his death; he was chairman of the royal commission on scientific instruction and the advancement of science, which sat from 1871 to 1874; and as an earnest of his commitment to the cause, he provided for the Cavendish Laboratory at Cambridge in 1874. He was a considerable benefactor of Owens College, Manchester, and of the Yorkshire College of Science, Leeds; when these colleges became part of the new federal Victoria University in 1880 he was its first chancellor.

Cavendish supported Irish disestablishment in 1869 but opposed home rule and became a Liberal Unionist in 1886. Elected FRS on 10 December 1829, he was made an honorary LLD of Cambridge, as well as being nominated KG in 1858 and sworn of the privy council in 1876. He died at Holker Hall on 21 December 1891 and was buried at Edensor, close to Chatsworth, on 26 December. He was survived by his eldest son and his only daughter, Lady Louisa Caroline (*d.* 1907), who married Rear-Admiral Francis

Egerton in 1865. His two younger sons, Lord Frederick Charles *Cavendish (1836–1882) and Lord Edward Cavendish (1838–1891), predeceased him.

F. M. L. THOMPSON

Sources D. Cannadine, 'The landowner as millionaire: the finances of the dukes of Devonshire', *Agricultural History Review*, 25 (1977), 77–97 · *The Times* (22 Dec 1891) · *The Times* (28 Dec 1891) · S. Pollard, 'Barrow-in-Furness and the seventh duke of Devonshire', *Economic History Review*, 2nd ser., 8 (1955–6), 213–21 · J. G. Pearson, *Stags and serpents: the story of the house of Cavendish and the dukes of Devonshire* (1983) · D. Cannadine, 'The Devonshires and Eastbourne', *Lords and landlords: the aristocracy and the towns, 1774–1967* (1980), 229–388 · *Eastbourne Chronicle* (4 June 1904) · *Eastbourne Gazette* (10 April 1878) · G. D. L., *PRS*, 51 (1892), xxxviii–xli · *Journal of the Iron and Steel Institute* (1869), 5–28 · *Journal of the Iron and Steel Institute*, 1 (1872), 213–9 · *Journal of the Iron and Steel Institute*, 2 (1891), 120–7 · Burke, *Peerage*
Archives Chatsworth House, Derbyshire, corresp. and diaries · Keele University Library, letters, incl. his wife's | BL, letters to W. E. Gladstone, Add. MSS 44405–44788, *passim* · Trinity Cam., letters to William Whewell
Likenesses W. Tweedie, oils, before 1856, U. Lond. · H. T. Wells, oils, 1872, Iron and Steel Institute, London · G. F. Watts, portrait, 1883, FM Cam. [*see illus.*] · W. G. John, bronze statue, 1901, Devonshire Place, Eastbourne · Barraud, photograph, NPG; repro. in *Men and women of the day* (1889), vol. 2 · G. Haiter, group portrait, oils (*The House of Commons, 1833*), NPG · Maull & Polyblank, carte-de-visite, NPG · W. Roffe, stipple, BM · W. Walker & Sons, carte-de-visite, NPG
Wealth at death £1,782,239 8s. 5d.: resworn probate, Dec 1894, *CGPLA Eng. & Wales* (1892)

Cavendish, William George Spencer, sixth duke of Devonshire

Cavendish, William George Spencer, sixth duke of Devonshire (1790–1858), whig grandee and connoisseur of the arts, only son and youngest of three children of William *Cavendish, fifth duke of Devonshire (1748–1811), and Georgiana *Cavendish (1757–1806), elder daughter of John Spencer, first Earl Spencer, was born in Passy, Paris, on 21 May 1790, and was baptized in St George's, Hanover Square, London, on 21 May 1791. He and his sisters grew up in the curious *menage à trois* of their parents and Lady Elizabeth Foster. His early education was supervised by Selina Trimmer, daughter of the evangelical Mrs Sarah Trimmer, and he subsequently attended Harrow School before proceeding to Trinity College, Cambridge, whence he graduated BA in 1811.

Hart (as he was known to his family) succeeded to the dukedom on 29 July 1811, shortly after reaching his majority. In the House of Lords, he was a consistent supporter of the whigs, although he seldom spoke there, perhaps on account of his deafness which was an increasing handicap. Despite his youth, he rapidly stepped into the role of elder statesman and party grandee, advancing the political careers of the whig cousinhood through his extensive political patronage, and using his influence with William IV in the interests of reform in the 1830s.

In 1826 the duke was sent to St Petersburg for the coronation of Nicholas II, on which occasion he spent £26,000 of his own money on his entourage, and was decorated by the tsar with the orders of St Andrew and St Alexander Nevsky in recognition of his liberality. The duke was sworn of the privy council in April 1827 and was made KG

William George Spencer Cavendish, sixth duke of Devonshire (1790–1858), by Sir Edwin Landseer, exh. RA 1832

in the following May. He served as lord chamberlain to George IV from May 1827 to February 1828, and to William IV from November 1830 to December 1834. He was lord lieutenant and *custos rotulorum* of Derbyshire and high steward of Derby.

The duke never married, despite being one of the country's most eligible bachelors and his pursuit by many mothers ambitious for their daughters. As a youth he had planned to marry his cousin, Lady Caroline Ponsonby, and was devastated by her marriage to William Lamb, later Viscount Melbourne. In November 1827 he began an alliance with Eliza Warwick, about whom little else is known, which remained a well-kept secret throughout its ten-year duration.

Devonshire's principal interests were cultural and literary. He acquired a number of important libraries, including those of Thomas Dampier (bishop of Ely), the duke of Roxburghe, and John Kemble, and owned a collection of coins and medals, which he sold for a loss of almost £40,000. He engaged in a vast programme of redevelopment at Chatsworth, spending a commensurate sum of money in the creation of his showcase, to the dismay of his heir presumptive, Lord Burlington. Indeed, the duke's habits of expenditure put his estates heavily into debt, and some had to be sold. The duke is perhaps most remembered as the patron of Joseph Paxton, the gardener and architect whose designs were realized at Chatsworth. The great conservatory, 300 feet long by 145 feet wide and 60 feet high, was seen by Victoria and Albert during their visit in 1843, and served as a model for the Crystal Palace which Paxton built to house the Great Exhibition of 1851.

The duke suffered a paralytic seizure in 1854, from which he never fully recovered, and died at Hardwick Hall, Derbyshire, on 18 January 1858. He was buried at Edensor, Derbyshire. K. D. REYNOLDS

Sources J. Lees-Milne, *The bachelor duke* (1991) · P. Mandler, *Aristocratic government in the age of reform: whigs and liberals, 1830–1852* (1990) · GEC, *Peerage* · D. Cannadine, 'The landowner as millionaire: the finances of the dukes of Devonshire', *Agricultural History Review*, 25 (1977), 77–97
Archives Chatsworth House, Derbyshire, corresp. and papers | BL, letters to Mary Berry, Add. MS 37726 · BL, corresp. with Prince Lieven and Princess Lieven, Add. MSS 47289–47293, 47374–47376 · BL, letters to Lord Spencer [p 9] · Castle Howard, Yorkshire, letters to countess of Carlisle · Keele University Library, letters to Ralph Sneyd, 1248 · PRO, letters to Countess Granville, PRO 30/29 · U. Durham L., corresp. with second Earl Grey
Likenesses H. Howard, oils, exh. RA 1799, Althorp House, Northamptonshire · M. A. Shee, oils, exh. RA 1806, Hardwick Hall, Derbyshire · J. Nollekens, marble bust, 1812, Royal Collection · G. Sanders, oils, 1812–13, Chatsworth House, Derbyshire · G. Hayter, oils, 1816, Chatsworth House, Derbyshire · R. Dighton, coloured etching, pubd 1820 (after his portrait), NPG · T. Campbell, bust, 1823, Chatsworth House, Derbyshire · T. Lawrence, oils, *c.*1824, Royal Collection · E. Landseer, oils, exh. RA 1832, Chatsworth House, Derbyshire [*see illus.*] · E. Landseer, pen-and-wash caricature, *c.*1835, NPG · G. Hayter, group portrait, oils, 1838 (*Coronation of Queen Victoria*), Royal Collection · F. Grant, oils, exh. RA 1850, Chatsworth House, Derbyshire · G. Hayter, marble bust, 1858, Chatsworth House, Derbyshire · G. Hayter, group portrait, oils (*The trial of Queen Caroline, 1820*), NPG
Wealth at death under £500,000: probate, 15 June 1858, CGPLA Eng. & Wales · under £45,000: probate, 20 July 1858, CGPLA Ire.

Caverhill, John (*d.* 1781), physician, a Scot, was admitted a licentiate of the Royal College of Physicians in 1767. In 1769 he was elected FRS and was awarded his MD by Marischal College, Aberdeen. He published a *Treatise on the Cause and Cure of Gout* in the same year. In this book he put forward the theory that the matter of nerves was earthy, and descended through the nerves to form the bones, and that the friction of this earthy substance, on its way to the bones, gave rise to animal heat. He followed this by *Experiments on the Causes of Heat in Living Animals* (1770), in which he attempted to prove his theory by a large number of barbaric experiments on rabbits, destroying various nerves or portions of the spinal cord and awaiting the death of the animals. He also wrote a *Dissertation on Nervous ganglions and Nervous plexus* (1772), and an *Explanation of the Seventy Weeks of Daniel* (1777). He died at Old Melrose, Roxburghshire, on 1 September 1781.

G. T. BETTANY, rev. RACHEL E. DAVIES

Sources Munk, *Roll* · *Fasti academiae Mariscallanae Aberdonensis: selections from the records of the Marischal College and University, MDXCIII–MDCCCLX*, 2, ed. P. J. Anderson, New Spalding Club, 18 (1898); 3, ed. J. F. K. Johnstone, New Spalding Club, 19 (1898) · *The record of the Royal Society of London*, 4th edn (1940)

Caw, Sir James Lewis (1864–1950), museum director and art historian, was born on 25 September 1864 at Craigie Terrace, St Quivox, Ayr, the son of James Caw, draper, and his wife, Eliza Murray, *née* Greenfield. Educated at Ayr Academy, he undertook an apprenticeship in engineering at the West of Scotland Technical College, Ayr (1883–7). Caw worked as an engineering draughtsman in Glasgow (1887–9) and in Edinburgh (1889–95), where he also studied science part-time at Heriot-Watt College. During this time he attended night classes at Glasgow School of Art and at the Royal Scottish Academy School of Art, becoming an accomplished watercolour painter. Between 1887 and 1922 he exhibited thirty-one land- and seascapes at the Royal Scottish Academy.

Well-read and with a keen intellect, Caw published his first article on art in 1884, at the age of twenty. From 1883 his close friendship with the pioneering Glasgow school artist and future president of the Royal Scottish Academy, Sir James Guthrie (1859–1920), combined with his emerging position as a knowledgeable art critic, gained him the attention and friendship of some of the most important modern Scottish painters. These included Sir James Lawton Wingate, president of the Royal Scottish Academy, the Glasgow Boys Edward Arthur Walton and Alexander Roche, both Royal Scottish Academicians, and William McTaggart, also a Royal Scottish Academician. Almost thirty years McTaggart's junior, Caw brilliantly understood and supported this highly independent and original artist, who by the 1880s had pioneered Scotland's own interpretation of impressionism. Such insight was prescient.

Appointed curator of the Scottish National Portrait Gallery, Edinburgh (SNPG), in 1895, Caw enriched the somewhat haphazardly formed collection with what has been described as 'a history of Scotland in portraits from the beginning of the sixteenth century to recent times' (*123rd Annual Report of the Council of the Royal Scottish Academy of Painting, Sculpture, and Architecture*). For the first time, portraits by Scottish artists spanning three centuries were included. In 1907 Caw was appointed the first director of the National Galleries of Scotland (NGS) and the SNPG; the artist Stanley Cursiter became curator at the SNPG. It was the beginning of a new era for the arts in Scotland. Cursiter continued Caw's policy of expanding the gallery's collection of portraits by Scottish artists. As director of the National Galleries of Scotland, Caw was later described as bringing to the task 'the outlook of a private collector rather than that of an official, he gave to the NGS the intimate and kindly character which is its charm' (ibid.). This comment does him an injustice. Unusually for a museum director in the early twentieth century, Caw's appreciation of art extended from the early Renaissance through Victorian art to post-impressionism; his buying policy was in fact wide-ranging. He acquired an interesting range of Italian primitive paintings, Scottish art, and modern French art. For example, in 1925 Paul Gauguin's *The Vision after the Sermon* (*Jacob and the Angel*; NGS) and Claude Monet's *Poplars on the Epte* (NGS) comprised very modern additions to the collection. On 6 October 1909 Caw married Anne Mary (Annie; 1864–1949), the eldest daughter of William *McTaggart. There were no children.

In his generation, Caw championed appreciation of

Scottish art as an important expression of national identity. He was the first writer to document Scottish art in an intellectual and critical way and, above all, to celebrate it with pride rather than to apologize for it. His *Scottish Painting, 1620–1908* (1908) and his publications on Sir Henry Raeburn (1901, 1909), William McTaggart (1917), Sir James Guthrie (1932), Allan Ramsay (1937), and Sir David Y. Cameron (1949) each became standard works of reference. Described as having a 'kindly and helpful personality and a lifelong devotion to cultural interests, devoid of any personal motive' (*The Scotsman*), Caw played a leading role in bringing art appreciation to the general Scottish public. He published at least five works on how to enjoy the paintings in the national galleries and portrait gallery, and he was the art critic for *The Scotsman* newspaper from 1916 to 1933. Caw was knighted in 1931, and Edinburgh University conferred on him the honorary degree of LLD in 1933. He retired from the national galleries in 1939, but continued to be active in the arts; notably, in collaboration with Stanley Cursiter, he organized the exhibition of Scottish art at the Royal Academy, London, in 1939. Caw contributed articles to the *Dictionary of National Biography* and was a member of several committees, including those of the *Burlington Magazine* and the Walpole Society. He died, aged eighty-six, at his home, Edinkerry, Lasswade, Midlothian, on 5 December 1950. Caw's will includes a schedule of pictures that he left to the National Galleries of Scotland, and eight paintings by him are in the Scottish National Gallery of Modern Art.   JILL C. MACKENZIE

Sources WWW, 1941–50 · *The Scotsman* (6 Dec 1950) · *123rd annual report of the council of the Royal Scottish Academy of Painting, Sculpture, and Architecture* (1950), 8–9 · C. B. de Laperriere, ed., *The Royal Scottish Academy exhibitors, 1826–1990*, 4 vols. (1991), vol. 1, pp. 291–2 · J. L. Caw, *Scottish painting past and present, 1620–1908* (1908); repr. (1975) · [J. Lloyd Williams], *National Gallery of Scotland: concise catalogue of paintings* (1997) · H. Smailes, *The concise catalogue of the Scottish National Portrait Gallery* (1990) · L. Errington, *William McTaggart, 1835–1910* (1989) [exhibition catalogue, Royal Scot. Acad., 11 Aug – 29 Oct 1989] · b. cert. · m. cert. · d. cert. · will, SC 70/4/981, fols. 123–52

Archives Royal Scot. Acad., letters; notes and drafts on speeches for opening of art exhibitions; notes on sailing round Scotland | NL Scot., Blackwood MSS, T. J. Honeyman MSS, McTaggart MSS, etc.

Likenesses R. Bryden, bronze medallion, 1928, Scot. NPG · B. Schotz, bronze bust, c.1928, Scot. NPG · group portrait, photograph (with family), repro. in Errington, *William McTaggart*, 95 · photographs, NL Scot., Taggart MSS

Wealth at death £7184 14s. 4d.: confirmation, 2 May 1951, CCI

Caw, John Young (c.1810–1858), banker and author, was born at Perth about 1810. He was educated at St Andrews, then at Trinity College, Cambridge, where he matriculated in 1830, but did not stay to take a degree. His first thoughts were of the Anglican ministry, but this design was abandoned and he found employment as cashier in the Commercial Bank of England, moving to become head cashier, and later sub-manager, in the new Manchester and Salford Bank, which opened in 1836. In 1848 Caw married Martha Anne, daughter of Rowland Harpur, surgeon, of Etwall, Derbyshire. Caw's leisure was devoted to literary and archæological studies, and to the extension of

the offertory system in the Church of England. He was a fellow of the Society of Antiquaries of Scotland, a member of the Royal Society of Literature, and of various local associations, notably the Literary and Philosophical Society of Manchester, to whose *Proceedings* he contributed. His writing reflected his professional work and his diverse other interests, as in the case of his pamphlet, 'Remarks on "The Deserted Village" of Oliver Goldsmith' (1852), where he surveyed the poet's work from the standpoint of a political economist. Caw had the reputation of an earnest-minded man of liberal disposition and intellectual sympathies. He died at his home, Fountain Villa, Cheetham Hill, Manchester, on 22 October 1858, and was buried at St Luke's, Cheetham Hill. A memorial to him was set up in the church of St Andrew, Ancoats, in Lancashire, of which he was a benefactor. He was survived by his wife.   W. E. A. AXON, *rev.* ANITA McCONNELL

Sources L. H. Grindon, *Manchester banks and bankers: historical, biographical, and anecdotal* (1877), 282, 284 · Venn, *Alum. Cant.* · *Manchester Courier* (30 Oct 1858) · *Proceedings, Manchester Literary and Philosophical Society* (1858) · *Catalogue of the books in the Manchester Free Library*, 3 vols. (1864–81) · d. cert. · m. cert.

Wealth at death under £5000: probate, 6 Nov 1858, CGPLA Eng. & Wales

Cawarden, Sir Thomas (c.1514–1559), courtier, was the son of William Cawarden, shearman and fuller of London, and his wife, Elizabeth. Apprenticed in 1528 to Owen Hawkins, mercer of London (a date which suggests he was born c.1514), he later became free of the Mercers' Company. He was probably identical with the Thomas 'Hawarden' admitted to Gray's Inn in 1528.

Cawarden probably attracted Henry VIII's favour through Thomas Cromwell. In 1539 or 1540 he became a gentleman of the privy chamber, a post he retained under Edward VI. A committed evangelical, he and his wife, Elizabeth (whom he had married by 1542; her surname is unrecorded), were accused of heresy in March 1543 with the 'Windsor martyrs', but in September they were pardoned. In 1544 Henry appointed him keeper of the tents and master of the revels; in the former capacity Cawarden helped to organize the Boulogne expedition of 1544, to which he brought a retinue of fifty-one horse and 200 foot, and was knighted for his services on 30 September. He was licensed to keep forty liveried retainers in 1545. Between 1538 and 1547 Henry granted him lands in Bedfordshire, Kent, Sussex, Warwickshire, and especially Surrey. He became Anne of Cleves's steward for Blechingley in 1540, acquired the manor itself in 1547, and represented the borough in parliament in 1542, 1545 (probably), and 1547. He became keeper of numerous royal manors, most notably Nonsuch Palace in 1544. In his will Henry left him £200 and lands worth 100 marks per annum.

Protector Somerset made Cawarden a Surrey JP and he was also sheriff of Surrey and Sussex in 1547/8. He was elected Surrey's senior knight of the shire in a 1548 by-election and was returned again (at the council's recommendation) in March 1553. He served on Surrey commissions for the subsidy (1547–51), dissolution of chantries (1547), musters (1548), and seizure of church goods (1553). Following Somerset's fall the council entrusted Cawarden with the Tower of London garrison. In 1550 he became steward of Hampton Court and was granted the site of the London Blackfriars, to which he removed the revels office from Warwick Inn. He turned the parish church of St Anne's (part of the Blackfriars complex) into a store for tents, having ordered the parishioners to remove the sacrament over the altar before he did so himself. He also enjoyed good relations with the duke of Northumberland, and Princess Elizabeth addressed him in a letter as 'loving friend'. With Sir Christopher and William More of Loseley, Cawarden headed a gentry faction in Surrey which was at odds with a rival group led by William, Lord Howard of Effingham. He was a contentious figure in other ways too, arousing hostility over enclosures during the 1549 insurrection, quarrelling with his fellow JP William Sackville, and in 1550 suing Philip Paris for implicating him in the murder of Robert Paris, killed that year at Newbury. Cawarden was an active supporter of Northumberland's unsuccessful scheme to secure the throne for Lady Jane Grey in 1553. He seems to have tried to raise men on Jane's behalf among the royal tenants at Wimbledon, and in his capacity as master of the tents was ordered by the duke of Suffolk on 16 July to provide tents for the garrison appointed to secure the tower for his daughter. Three days later Jane herself sent a warrant directing Cawarden to deliver four tents to her 'beloved father and counsellor the Duke of Suffolke' (*Seventh Report*, HMC, 610). He was also suspected of involvement in Sir Thomas Wyatt's rising at the beginning of 1554. On 25 January Lord Howard arrested him; the following day Bishop Stephen Gardiner questioned Cawarden and then released him to raise forces against the rebels. Acting without Gardiner's knowledge, Howard then rearrested Cawarden on the 27th, detaining him at Reigate until the 30th while the sheriff of Surrey confiscated eighteen wagonloads of his equipment, including sixteen pieces of ordnance. Finally the council placed Cawarden under house arrest at Blackfriars until the rising was suppressed.

Cawarden escaped punishment, was elected a knight of the shire in November, and was restored as a JP in 1555. But in the latter year he had to pay Mary £1000 for an unspecified offence and was cited in king's bench for leaving parliament early. He clearly remained suspect in government eyes, and in March 1556 he was arrested on suspicion of involvement in the Dudley conspiracy. But though his servant John Dethicke was executed, Cawarden himself was not indicted. Nevertheless a year later he was briefly in the Fleet prison, and he lost the keepership of Nonsuch to the twelfth earl of Arundel. No doubt his religious stance was largely responsible for his difficulties. Mary's regime forced him to provide the parishioners of St Anne's with another place of worship—according to Stow he gave them only 'a lodging chamber above a staire', which later fell down (Stow, 1.341)—but it was unable to win him for Catholicism, for he maintained a secret protestant conventicle in his own house near by.

Elizabeth restored Cawarden's fortunes, appointing him lieutenant of the Tower in 1558. He was again elected knight of the shire for Surrey in 1559 and helped Thomas Browne win a contested election for the county's other seat. He died on 25 August that year at Horsley, probably at John Agmondesham's house, and was buried on 29 August in Blechingley church beneath a prominent monument. His heir was his brother Anthony's son William; his executors were his wife (who was buried beside him after her death on 20 February 1560) and William More. Having kept house 'right bounteously' (*DNB*), with a hundred servants and retainers, he left an estate valued at £1611 14*s*. 8*d*., though debts and legacies perhaps consumed it.

As master of the revels (a position he was the first to hold) Cawarden was a significant figure in the development of mid-Tudor court culture. His activities took a variety of forms. In 1551 he was involved in the construction of a substantial banqueting house (possibly modelled on Nonsuch) for the reception of French ambassadors in Hyde Park, being responsible for its interior decoration. But he is more often recorded in the context of court entertainments. He was later described as 'skilfull and delightinge in matters of devise' (Colvin, 1.93), and there is evidence that he played a part in the choice of entertainments, notably a letter which William Baldwin sent him during Mary's reign concerning the latter's play *Love and Lyve*, in which, according to its author, Cawarden had expressed an interest three years earlier. But he is more often recorded as an enabler than as a deviser of revels, being called on to provide costumes and other necessary gear, often both elaborate and expensive. It cost nearly £300 to enable the courtier George Ferrers to make his state entry into London as the lord of misrule for the Christmas season of 1551/2.

Cawarden was particularly active in Edward VI's last years, for instance with the five masques he helped stage between 7 January and 12 February 1553 to distract the sickening king—'a Maske of Greek Woorthyes, a Maske of Medyoxes, beinge halfe deathe, halfe man, a Maske of Bagpypes, A Maske of Cattes, a Maske of Tumblers goinge upon theyre handes with theyre feet upward' (*Seventh Report*, HMC, 606). But he also provided costumes for a play at Queen Mary's coronation feast, for entertainments later in her reign by Nicholas Udall, and finally for London citizens preparing to greet Elizabeth when she in turn processed through the city on her way to be crowned. Cawarden sometimes had to be pressed to deliver what was needed for such occasions, but no one seems to have doubted his competence, suggesting that in this respect, at least, he earned the dedication of Robert Burrant's translation of Cato's *Preceptes*, praising his 'politique wisdom'. WILLIAM B. ROBISON

Sources Loseley MSS, Folger · Surrey HC · HoP, *Commons, 1509–58*, 1.599–602 · W. B. Robison, 'The national and local significance of Wyatt's rebellion in Surrey', *HJ*, 30 (1987), 769–90 · W. B. Robison, 'The justices of the peace of Surrey in national and county politics, 1483–1570', PhD diss., Louisiana State University, 1983 · S. Brigden, *London and the Reformation* (1989) · *DNB* · E. K. Chambers, *Notes on the history of the revels office under the Tudors* (1906) · A. Feuillerat, *Documents relating to the revels at court in the time of King Edward VI and*

Queen Mary (1914) · T. Craib, 'Sir Thomas Cawarden', *Surrey Archaeological Collections*, 28 (1941), 7–28 · U. Lambert, *Blechingley: a parish history*, 2 vols. (1921) · *VCH Surrey* · J. Foster, *The register of admissions to Gray's Inn, 1521–1889, together with the register of marriages in Gray's Inn chapel, 1695–1754* (privately printed, London, 1889) · *Seventh report*, HMC, 6 (1879), 596–681 [W. More-Molyneux] · S. Anglo, *Spectacle, pageantry and early Tudor policy* (1997) · H. M. Colvin and others, eds., *The history of the king's works*, 3–4 (1975–82) · E. K. Chambers, *The Elizabethan stage*, 4 vols. (1923) · J. Stow, *A survay of London*, rev. edn (1603); repr. with introduction by C. L. Kingsford as *A survey of London*, 2 vols. (1908); repr. with addns (1971) · D. M. Loades, *Two Tudor conspiracies* (1965)

Archives Folger, Loseley MSS, corresp. and papers · Surrey HC, Loseley MSS, letters and papers

Wealth at death personalty of £1611 14s. 8d., with debts and legacies totalling £1768 17s. 7d., according to executor William More: will, 4 Aug 1559, PRO, PROB 11/43/4, printed Craib, 'Sir Thomas Cawarden'; lengthily discussed Lambert, *Blechingley*

Cawdell, James (*bap.* 1749, *d.* 1800), actor and theatre manager, was baptized at Baldock, Hertfordshire, on 6 February 1749, the eldest son and second of seven children of John Caudel (*d.* 1771), a cooper, and his wife, Mary Bates (*bap.* 1718, *d.* 1771), a carrier's daughter. He is said to have been a ploughboy, but was well enough educated to compose passable verses at the age of thirteen when his mother was gravely ill. His uncle Thomas Bates (baptized at Baldock in 1725) became a comic actor, and by 1763 was manager of a stock company touring the north-eastern circuit at North Shields, Sunderland, Durham, Darlington, Stockton, Whitby, Scarborough, and, from 1763 to 1766, Newcastle. As a youth Cawdell harboured theatrical ambitions, encouraged by Joseph Younger, the prompter at Covent Garden, 'the kindest patron of my youthful toil' (Cawdell, 20), but was forced to relinquish the stage 'for the dry Drudgeries of a Mercer's Shop' (ibid., 46). Estrangement from his parents followed, and by the age of twenty he had joined Bates, his first recorded role being Cupid in David Garrick's *Cymon* at North Shields in May 1769. At that period the company included the pastoral poet John Cunningham, the novelist Thomas Holcroft, and, as leader of the orchestra, the composer William Shield.

Cawdell widened his experience by spending one season 'with the best companies out of London' (*Newcastle Chronicle*, 19 July 1777), probably in Birmingham and Manchester, both places on Younger's circuit, and where he wrote poetry. In 1777 he rejoined his uncle in the north as male lead. At the end of 1781 he eloped to Gretna Green with fifteen-year-old Sarah Martin (*bap.* 1766, *d.* 1842), the daughter of a Sunderland innkeeper, but they returned and married with parental consent at Holy Trinity, Sunderland, on 19 January 1782. The couple settled there and had five children, of whom only two survived infancy. In 1782 Cawdell was taken into partnership, and when Bates retired in 1788 he left Cawdell in sole charge.

In 1789 Cawdell became involved in a long-running dispute with the mentally unbalanced landlady of his Durham theatre, and he moved into temporary premises until, with the assistance of local subscribers, a new playhouse was built nearby, which opened in 1792. Increasing deafness prevented him taking as active a role in management, and in 1799 the circuit was acquired by Stephen Kemble of the Newcastle and Edinburgh theatres. Cawdell died in Durham on 12 January 1800 and was buried in Holy Trinity churchyard, Sunderland, on 16 January. His widow lived until her death in 1842 at Houghton-le-Spring with their unmarried daughter. The only son, James Martin Cawdell (1784–1842), settled in Canada, where he was variously a soldier, teacher, author, publisher, and librarian.

Cawdell wrote several dramatic pieces and in 1785 published a selection of his poems and verse prologues. He is remembered neither as a literary man nor as an actor, though Tate Wilkinson thought highly of him, but as the able manager of a provincial circuit which survived his death, under his successor Kemble and later the Roxby-Beverly family, for another half century.

C. D. WATKINSON

Sources parish registers, Baldock · parish registers, Sunderland · J. Cawdell, *The miscellaneous poems of J. Cawdell, comedian* (privately printed, Sunderland, 1785) · *Newcastle Courant* (1763–1800) · *Newcastle Chronicle* (1764–1800) · 'James Cawdell', Sunderland Public Library, Corder MSS, 3, 156 · J. Winston, 'Theatrical tourist', Harvard TC [microfilm of MS notes] · R. L. Fraser, 'Cawdell, James Martin', *DCB*, vol. 7 · M. H. Dodds, 'The northern stage', *Archaeologia Aeliana*, 3rd ser., 11 (1914), 31–64 · D. Towland, *The Stockton Georgian theatre* (1991) · R. King, *North Shields theatres* (1948) · T. Wilkinson, *The wandering patentee, or, A history of the Yorkshire theatres from 1770 to the present time*, 4 vols. (1795) · K. E. Robinson, 'Stephen Kemble's management of the Theatre Royal, Newcastle-upon-Tyne', *Essays on the eighteenth-century stage: proceedings of a symposium sponsored by the Manchester University dept. of drama*, ed. K. Richards and P. Thomson (1972), 137–48

Likenesses Peltro, statue, repro. in Cawdell, *Miscellaneous poems* · T. Thwaites, drawing, repro. in Cawdell, *Miscellaneous poems*

Cawdor. For this title name *see* Campbell, John Pryse, first Baron Cawdor of Castlemartin (1755–1821) [*see under* Campbell family of Cawdor (*per.* 1511–1821)]; Campbell, Frederick Archibald Vaughan, third Earl Cawdor (1847–1911).

Cawdrey [Cawdry], **Daniel** (1587/8–1664), Church of England clergyman and ejected minister, was born in November 1587 or 1588 at South Luffenham, Rutland, the youngest of five sons of Robert *Cawdrey (*d.* in or after 1604), the rector, who was ejected in 1588 for opposition to the prayer book, and an unknown wife. He was admitted to Sidney Sussex College, Cambridge, in 1606, graduated BA in 1610, and proceeded MA from Peterhouse (following instruction from Alexander Richardson in Barking, Essex) in 1613. Ordained a deacon in London on 19 September 1613 aged twenty-five or in his twenty-fifth year, and a priest on 18 June 1614, he was presented to the rectory of Little Ilford, Essex, on 19 December 1617 by Barnard Hide.

In 1622 William Gouge invited Cawdrey to preach at Blackfriars, London. Cawdrey dedicated the resulting sermons, published as *Humilitie, the Saint's Liverie* (1624), to Sir Thomas Fanshawe, surveyor of lands to Prince Charles, and set forth the puritan division of society (predicated on Calvinist experimental predestinarianism) into the godly and the ungodly, almost corresponding with notions of the elect and the reprobate. Cawdrey served as preacher at St Lawrence Jewry, London, during 1623–5, and on 6

December 1625 the crown presented him to the rectory of Great Billing, Northamptonshire, whereupon he resigned from Ilford. A leading member of the godly community centred on Thomas Ball's Northampton, Cawdrey was chosen by Sir Edmund Hampden in 1627 to preach at his funeral.

During the 1630s Cawdrey contributed towards Samuel Hartlib's projected pan-protestant union, and probably about this time he married Catherine, a widow: they had two children. He opposed publicly Bishop William Laud of London—later claiming to have been present at his consecration of St Catherine Cree, London, in 1631—and preached without episcopal permission at Kettering that Laud barred the godly from court. Cawdrey did not directly disobey royal authority by refusing to read the anti-sabbatarian Book of Sports in 1633, but claimed to have written (with Herbert Palmer) a contemporary defence of sabbatarianism (*Sabbatum redivivum*) against John Pocklington, which was not published until 1645–52. The sabbath was portrayed as a Jacobean orthodoxy divinely ordained by scripture for the hearing of God's word; Cawdrey and Palmer claimed that their opponents' making its status derive from the church's authority invested excessive holiness in the bishops.

At William Laud's archiepiscopal visitation in 1635 Cawdrey was described as a leading nonconformist. Robert Woodford's diary shows Cawdrey dining with the godly Sir Christopher Yelverton and the conformist Sir Christopher Hatton, while an account of the execution of John Barker has his fellow ministers—Cawdrey and Ball—reaffirming his godliness. In 1637–8 Cawdrey took a stand against the Laudian altar policy; the churchwardens capitulated to church court instructions to rail in the communion table along the east wall of the chancel, but Cawdrey moved it outside the rails and placed it lengthways in the church during communion. His repudiation of the policy (*Superstitio superstes*) was obliged to wait until 1641 before achieving publication. Against John Pocklington's holy bishops, churches, altars, and ceremonies Cawdrey opposed the holiness of the godly saints and the word. On this view the conformists—by imposing indifferent worship as essential—polluted the sacraments with idolatry more so even than papists, who at least believed they were bowing towards the transubstantiated Christ. In 1638 the corporation of Northampton invited Cawdrey to read their lecture, and in 1639 to preach Sunday morning and afternoon, contrary to royal instructions. Cawdrey omitted to pay the clerical contribution towards funding the bishops' war, and preached at Kettering that the corruption of the times obliged people to arm themselves. His Northampton assize sermon of July 1640 (included in his *Three Sermons* (1641) and dedicated to Yelverton) was atypical of its pedestrian genre in openly denouncing persecutors of the saints. In August he attended a clerical conference at Kettering, which supported the aims of the invading Scots and rejected as illegal the oath legitimating the Laudian ecclesiastical canons.

In 1641 Cawdrey backed William Castle's proposal to the Long Parliament for a missionary expedition to convert Native Americans as part of a godly foreign policy. Cawdrey was a leading member of the Westminster assembly and active in the London presbyterian classis from October 1644 as minister of St Martin-in-the-Fields, into which living he was intruded by parliament. For the single year 1644 he was pastor of St Benet Gracechurch. He was among the most popular preachers at parliamentary fasts (preaching eleven times between 1644 and 1648), but published only his first sermon, *The Good Man a Publick Good* (1644), for which Yelverton was required to thank him. His solution to the military stalemate plaguing the civil war was for parliament to continue its work of religious reformation. The majority of his publications over the following sixteen years comprised disputes with the Independents (although he also argued with Giles Firmin and John Humfrey), beginning with *Vindiciae clavium* (1645) in response to John Cotton's writings. The period 1648–9 was a time of intense opposition to the revolutionary ideas of the army: Cawdrey preached four times before the Lords in 1648, and signed the London *Testimony* (1648) and *Vindication* (1649), defending presbyterianism and the person and authority of Charles I. In *The Inconsistencie of the Independent Way* (1651) he recapitulated the argument with Cotton and included a critique of Thomas Hooker. He was elected Sunday afternoon preacher at St Gregory's, London, in 1651, but about 1652–3 returned to Northamptonshire. A dispute with the conformist Henry Hammond began in 1654 with Cawdrey's *Diatribe triplex*, and lasted until 1658. Thomas Pierce, conformist tutor to the countess of Sunderland's son, attacked the core doctrine of predestination in 1655; the next year William Barlee, supported by presbyterians including Cawdrey, defended it. Cawdrey's open denunciation of Independency as schismatic in *Independencie a Great Schism* (1657) was regarded as a threat to the fragile unity of the orthodox godly in the face of sectarianism. John Owen publicly criticized Cawdrey's stance in 1657 and 1658, and Cawdrey responded with *Independency Further Proved to be a Schism* (1658).

The reprinting after the Restoration of the conformist Eleazer Duncon's 1633 defence of bowing towards the altar rekindled puritan fears of a projected reunification of the churches of England and Rome, provoking Cawdrey to publish *Bowing towards the Altar ... grossely Superstitious* (1661). Despite being recommended to the earl of Clarendon for a bishopric, Cawdrey was ejected from Great Billing by September 1662. He left behind a manuscript theological sourcebook drawing mainly on the works of William Perkins. Having retired to Wellingborough he died there in October 1664, it is claimed forty days before his seventy-sixth birthday. Vincent Alsop composed a funeral ode. Cawdrey's wife, to whom the administration of his goods was granted on 15 October, outlived him.

J. FIELDING

Sources A. J. Fielding, 'Conformists, puritans and the church courts: the diocese of Peterborough, 1603–1642', PhD diss., U. Birm., 1989, 22, 28, 124, 149, 159–60, 191, 205–12, 220, 248, 261 · T. Webster, *Godly clergy in early Stuart England: the Caroline puritan movement, c.1620–1643* (1997), 29, 55, 131, 226–8, 231, 233, 260 ·

Calamy rev., 105–6 · H. I. Longden, *Northamptonshire and Rutland clergy from 1500*, ed. P. I. King and others, 16 vols. in 6, Northamptonshire RS (1938–52), vol. 3, p. 67 · Tai Liu, *Discord in Zion: the puritan divines and the puritan revolution, 1640–1660* (1973), p. 55; p. 148, n. 6; pp. 162–3 · Tai Liu, *Puritan London: a study of religion and society in the City parishes* (1986), 93, 122, 131, 152 · P. S. Seaver, *The puritan lectureships: the politics of religious dissent, 1560–1662* (1970), 235, 279, 362, 371 · R. S. Paul, *The assembly of the Lord: politics and religion in the Westminster assembly and the 'Grand debate'* (1985), 547, 556 · W. A. Shaw, *A history of the English church during the civil wars and under the Commonwealth, 1640–1660*, 2 (1900), 403 · bishops' register, GL, MS 9531/14, fol. 219v · *VCH Essex*, 6.171–3 · P. Lake, 'The Laudian style: order, uniformity and the pursuit of the beauty of holiness in the 1630s', *The early Stuart church, 1603–42*, ed. K. Fincham (1993), 161–86 · *DNB* · W. J. Sheils, *The puritans in the diocese of Peterborough, 1558–1610*, Northamptonshire RS, 30 (1979), 64 · D. Cawdrey, *Bowing towards the altar … grossely superstitious* (1661), 22

Archives Northants. RO, parish records, record book, 31P/21

Cawdrey, Robert (*b.* 1537/8?, *d.* in or after 1604), Church of England clergyman and lexicographer, was born in 1537 or 1538; his parentage is unknown. Although four of his five sons are recorded as having studied at Cambridge— Anthony, Thomas, and Zachary (father of Zachary *Cawdrey) as sizars at Christ's College, Daniel *Cawdrey at Sidney Sussex College—and he was vigorously to deny the charge of 'Want of Learning' (Strype, 131–3), Robert himself received no university education. From *c.*1563 to 1571, however, he 'taught the Grammer Schoole at Okeham', Rutland (R. Cawdrey, *Table Alphabeticall*, 1604, 'Epistle'). Having been ordained deacon in 1565 and priest in 1570, he was presented to the living of South Luffenham, Rutland, by Lord Burghley and instituted as rector on 22 October 1571.

An uncompromising puritan, Cawdrey fell foul of the church authorities from at least 1576 (in which year he was said to be aged thirty-eight), when he was presented for not reading either injunctions or homilies in church, to September 1586, when he argued from the pulpit for the equality of Christian ministers, maintaining that lords spiritual should not lord it over their brethren, and fiercely attacked the Book of Common Prayer, 'a Vile book' and 'Fy upon it' (Strype, 134). This led to a short period in ward and what Strype was to describe (at some length) as 'a tedious suit' (ibid., 147); it ended in the Star Chamber in June 1591, when the right of ecclesiastical courts to proceed upon ecclesiastical law, even in matters touched by statute law, was established, and the legality of sentences of deprivation of benefice (1585), and degradation from the priesthood (1590), confirmed. Throughout this time Cawdrey's patron Burghley, 'who had a Compassion for the Man, having a Wife and eight Children' (ibid., 132) and who was regularly petitioned by him, stood by him, intervening both directly and through the attorney of the court of wards. However, Cawdrey, having for four and a half years stubbornly refused to accept the legality of the decisions of the ecclesiastical courts, also spurned repeated attempts at conciliation by Burghley, Bishop Aylmer, and Archbishop Whitgift (including offers of a pension and even reinstatement).

After his ejection Cawdrey continued to express his puritan beliefs in *A Treasurie or Storehouse of Similies* (1600), a revised edition (1601) of his *Short and Fruitful Treatise of the Profit and Necessity of Catechisms* (1580), and (probably) *A Godlie Forme of Householde Government* 'gathered by R.C' (1598). He is best known for *A table alphabeticall, conteyning and teaching the true writing, and understanding of hard usuall English wordes, borrowed from the Hebrew, Greek, Latine, or French etc with the interpretation thereof by plaine English words, gathered for the benefit & helpe of ladies, gentlewomen, or any other unskilfull persons, whereby they may the more easilie and better understand many hard English wordes, which they shall heare or read in scriptures, sermons, or elsewhere, and also be made able to use the same aptly themselves* (1604). It was the first monolingual English dictionary ever published. This work, containing 2543 lemmas, 'long ago for the most part', Cawdrey explains, 'was gathered by me, but lately augmented by my sonne Thomas', a schoolmaster in London (*Table Alphabeticall*, 'Epistle'), and it was Thomas who revised the second edition in 1609 (3009 lemmas). However, subsequent editions, dated 1613 and 1617 (3086 and 3264 lemmas), do not name the reviser—though they do remove the reference to women as their prime 'unskilfull' target.

Cawdrey's *Table* is heavily derivative, taking over 90 per cent of the 1368 lemmas contained in the similarly named 'table' of hard English words which concludes Edmund Coote's *Englishe Schole-Maister* (1596), and also drawing on Thomas Thomas's Latin–English dictionary, Rastell's law dictionary, and at least three other specialist glossaries. The 1617 edition incorporates material (and part of its expanded title) from John Bullokar's *English Expositor* (1616). Cawdrey's *Table* was, in its 1613 edition, a major source for Bullokar, and it was used also by Henry Cockeram. Thomas Cawdrey died in Grantham in 1640. Robert himself is last heard of in Coventry in June 1604. Perhaps significantly, his personal epistle dedicatory is omitted from editions of the *Table* after 1609.　　JANET BATELY

Sources BL, Lansdowne MSS, part 1, Burghley MSS, MSS 53, 55, 58, 61, 64, 68, 115 · BL, Lansdowne MSS, part 2, Kennett MSS, MS 982 · J. Strype, *Historical collections of the life and acts of … John Aylmer* (1701), chap. 8, pp. 129–48 · E. A. Irons, 'Sir Robert Cawdrie: rector of South Luffenham, 1571–87', *Annual Report and Transactions of the Rutland Archaeological and Natural History Society*, 14 (1916), 23–33 · J. Schäfer, *Early modern English lexicography*, 1 (1989) · De W. T. Starnes and G. E. Noyes, *The English dictionary from Cawdrey to Johnson, 1604–1755*, new edn, ed. G. Stein (1991) · R. C. Alston, *A bibliography of the English language from the invention of printing to the year 1800*, 5 (1966) · Venn, *Alum. Cant.* · visitation book, Northants. RO, Peterborough diocesan records, Arch 4, fol. 110v [Archdeacon of Northampton's visitations for 1574–1577]

Archives BL, Lansdowne MSS, letters to Lord Burghley

Cawdrey [Cawdry], **Zachary** (1618–1684), Church of England clergyman, was born at Melton Mowbray, Leicestershire, where he was baptized on 23 August 1618. His parents were Zachary Cawdrey (1577/8–1659), the vicar there, and his wife, Anne Withers. His grandfather was the clergyman and lexicographer Robert *Cawdrey; his uncle Daniel Cawdrey became a presbyterian and was ejected from his living in 1662.

The younger Zachary Cawdrey was educated locally at the free school in Melton Mowbray, and subsequently matriculated sizar at St John's College, Cambridge, on 7 May 1635, aged sixteen. He graduated BA in 1639, was made a fellow of St John's in 1641, and proceeded MA in 1642. Cawdrey continued at St John's, and entered the ministry, being ordained deacon at Lincoln on 16 June 1644 and priest the following day. Cawdrey's royalism and commitment to the rites of the Church of England brought him into trouble at Cambridge. On 30 October 1647 the vice-chancellor of the university presented an array of charges against him to the House of Lords. Cawdrey had read the Book of Common Prayer in service time, and used the ring in the marriage ceremony and the sign of the cross at baptism; he had refused to obey an order of the Lords and protested when the master and fellows of St John's did so; he had prayed in the college chapel for the success of the king and confusion to all who opposed him. On 4 December 1647 the Lords deprived Cawdrey of his proctorship, and his antagonists used the opportunity to attempt to deprive him of his college place; despite the Lords' later clarification that they had intended that he lose only the proctorship, they were evidently successful in driving Cawdrey from Cambridge. He was admitted as rector of Barthomley in Cheshire, where he compounded for first fruits on 1 April 1649. Memories of the notorious massacre in the parish church by royalist soldiers at Christmas 1643 were perhaps still too raw to allow for easy acceptance of a man of Cawdrey's political sympathies, and later that year he was sequestered by the county committee because of his Cambridge royalism; his attempt to have the sequestration reversed was thrown out by the exchequer barons in 1652. He was minister at Langar, Nottinghamshire, in 1650. Thereafter he managed to be appointed vicar of the strongly parliamentarian parish of Woodford, Essex, in 1654, but at the Restoration he was content to return to Barthomley and regain his living there.

After 1660 Cawdrey ministered to his Cheshire parishioners, and it may have been here that he met and married his wife, Helen, who died before him. Increasingly he was also keen to indulge a passion for scholarship which had been hindered by his experiences in the late 1640s and 1650s. In 1675 he published *A Discourse of Patronage*, a lengthy and detailed account of ecclesiastical patronage and tithes. Increasingly Cawdrey also seems to have tried to maintain links between the worlds of moderate dissent and the Church of England. He kept up monthly lectures at Tarvin and Nantwich and wrote two works which overtly attacked the tory reaction of the early 1680s and its values, *A Preparation for Martyrdom* (1681) and *A Calm Answer to a Bitter Invective* (1683). On 9 September 1684 he delivered the funeral sermon of George Booth, first Lord Delamere, at Bowdon church, Cheshire. About the same time, he appears to have become seriously unwell. He died on 21 December 1684 at Barthomley, where he was buried three days later 'near his wife, Helen, and his very dear pupil, John Crewe' (*DNB*). The leading nonconformist Philip

Henry remembered Cawdrey as 'a conformist, and formerly a great sufferer for the King, but in his latter times much maligned and reproached by some people for his moderation towards dissenters' (Henry, 277).

S. J. GUSCOTT

Sources Venn, *Alum. Cant.* · *Walker rev.* · *DNB* · M. Henry, *The life of the reverend Philip Henry*, ed. J. B. Williams (1825), 277 · W. Urwick, ed., *Historical sketches of nonconformity in the county palatine of Cheshire, by various ministers and laymen* (1864), 142–3 · *IGI* · *Sixth report*, HMC, 5 (1877–8), 202 · *Seventh report*, HMC, 6 (1879), 105

Cawdry, Daniel. *See* Cawdrey, Daniel (1587/8–1664).

Cawdry, Zachary. *See* Cawdrey, Zachary (1618–1684).

Cawley, William (*bap.* 1602, *d.* 1667), politician and regicide, the eldest son of John Cawley (*d.* 1621), a brewer of Chichester who was three times mayor, and his third wife, Catherine, was born in Chichester and baptized on 3 November 1602 at St Andrew's Church there. He was educated at Chichester grammar school, then went on to Hart Hall, Oxford, in 1621 and Gray's Inn in 1622. He was evidently the first member of his family to receive such a formal education, although he received no degree and was not called to the bar. On his father's death Cawley established an almshouse for aged tradesmen in Chichester, in accordance with the dictates of John Cawley's will. The building was completed in 1626, when its chapel was consecrated by the then bishop of Chichester, George Carleton. Cawley's own financial security is indicated by the privy seal loan directed to him for £20 in 1625, and by his having compounded for his knighthood at £14. About 1625 he married Catherine (*d.* 1650), daughter of William Walrond of Isle Brewers in Somerset.

Cawley's social standing in Chichester enabled him to gain one of the town's seats in the parliament of 1628, in an election which broke the influence of local magnates such as the ninth earl of Northumberland and the fourteenth earl of Arundel. Although he made little impression at Westminster, an early sign of his political zeal in opposition to the government of Charles I was provided by his role in organizing a protest against the billeting of soldiers at Chichester in the same year, for which he was briefly detained on the orders of the privy council. He subsequently refused to pay his ship money assessment in 1635 and 1636. Although not returned in the Short Parliament, Cawley was able to represent another Sussex constituency, Midhurst, after 15 February 1641, following a double return and a successful challenge to the claim of the Arminian civil lawyer Richard Chaworth.

During the civil wars Cawley was an active parliamentarian, albeit largely in a civilian, rather than a military, capacity. When Chichester was surprised by a party of royalists in November 1642 he informed parliament of the news and the successful expedition of Sir William Waller into Sussex followed, in which Chichester was retaken on 29 December 1642 after a siege lasting eight days. In the months and years that followed Cawley emerged as one of the most zealous parliamentarian activists in Sussex, and one of the most energetic members of the county committee. His aggressive methods of dealing with delinquents, not least in seizing their property, alarmed men such as the tenth earl of Northumberland. Cawley was also accused of financial corruption by rival parliamentarians, in a bitter row with parliament's committee for taking the accounts of the kingdom. Although he was not cleared of impropriety until 1649 or 1650 his position of influence in Sussex was not affected, and he was active in suppressing the club-men, and was appointed governor of Cowdray House in October 1645.

Cawley was one of the members of the high court of justice appointed by parliament in 1649 to try the king for treason. He attended every meeting of the court in Westminster Hall and signed the death warrant [see also Regicides]. During that year his parliamentary career began in earnest, with his nomination to many of the most important standing committees such as the army committee, the committee for the advance of money, the committee for plundered ministers, and the committee for compounding. His political allies were republicans such as Thomas Scot, Henry Marten, and Thomas Chaloner, although he baulked at the views of tolerationists such as Thomas Harrison. In religion Cawley favoured congregationalist Independents, but was active in opposing men such as the Seeker, William Erbury. Although frustrated by the conservatism of the Rump, Cawley's election to the council of state in February 1651 reflected a wave of republican enthusiasm after the battle of Dunbar. He also served on a later council of state, to which he was elected in December 1652. In both parliament and council he continued to display his zeal for seizing and selling the lands of delinquents, including those of the royal family.

Cawley probably felt little sympathy for the protectorate and played no part in central or local government for most of the later 1650s, although there is no evidence of active opposition to Cromwell. Instead he concentrated on developing his estate, engaging in extensive property speculation, purchasing the manors of Oldberry and Seabeach, Wartling, and Lancing, all in Sussex. About two years after Cawley's first wife died in 1650 he married again; his second wife's name was Mary. He returned to Westminster upon the recall of the Rump in May 1659, when he worked alongside the civilian republicans once again. By February 1660, as political events began to indicate growing sympathy for the return of Charles II, he was largely absent from the Commons, and after the Restoration he was excepted from pardon, and faced arrest and trial for his complicity in the trial of Charles I. He therefore fled to the continent for refuge, travelling first to the Southern Netherlands and afterwards to Switzerland, where he joined at least two other *Regicides, Edmund Ludlow and Nicholas Love. He died in Vevey on 6 January 1667 and was buried there in the church of St Martin.

Cawley had three sons and a daughter from his first marriage. His eldest son, William Cawley, who represented Chichester in 1659 and the convention of 1660, claimed to have opposed his father's role in the regicide, and petitioned in 1660 for the restitution of the family estate,

which had been forfeited to the crown. He claimed that most of his father's property had been settled on him at his own marriage, and that his father-in-law's estate had been sequestered for his loyalty to Charles I. The petition, however, does not seem to have been successful, and most of Cawley's property was bestowed on the duke of York, afterwards James II. Another son, John Cawley, was archdeacon of Lincoln in 1667–1709.   J. T. PEACEY

Sources F. H. Arnold, 'Cawley the regicide', *Sussex Archaeological Collections*, 34 (1886), 21–38 · *CSP dom.*, 1640–60 · *JHC*, 2–8 (1640–67) · C. H. Firth and R. S. Rait, eds., *Acts and ordinances of the interregnum, 1642–1660*, 3 vols. (1911) · *The manuscripts of his grace the duke of Portland*, 10 vols., HMC, 29 (1891–1931), vol. 1, pp. 72–4, 159, 289 · PRO, SP 28/255–6 · J. G. Muddiman, *The trial of King Charles the First* (1928), 76, 88–9, 96, 103, 197–228 · E. Ludlow, *A voyce from the watch tower*, ed. A. B. Worden, CS, 4th ser., 21 (1978), 195–6, 304–5 · E. H. W. Dunkin, ed., *Sussex manors*, 2 vols., Sussex RS, 19–20 (1914–15), 14, 376, 477 · *APC, 1628–9*, 188, 197 · A. Fletcher, *A county community in peace and war: Sussex, 1600–1660* (1975) · W. Sussex RO, Cap I/12/2, 327–63 · BL, Add. MS 33058 · *The Clarke papers*, ed. C. H. Firth, 4 vols., CS, new ser., 49, 54, 61–2 (1891–1901)

Likenesses oils, *c*.1620, Council House, Chichester, Sussex; repro. in Arnold, 'Cawley the regicide', facing p. 21

Cawood, John (1513/14–1572), printer, came from the de Cawood family of Cawood, Yorkshire, but his parents are unknown. He was apprenticed to the London stationer and bookbinder John Reynes; in 1541 he was noted as keeping shop in St Paul's Churchyard with a fellow stationer, John Birckman. Reynes died in 1544, and Cawood seems to have taken over his business. On 1 January 1548 he took over the lease of Henry Tab's bookshop in St Paul's Churchyard. He appears to have done a little printing as early as 1550, when an English and Latin New Testament ascribed to him appeared.

The decisive moment of Cawood's career, however, was the accession of Mary Tudor in 1553. Richard Grafton, the king's printer under Edward VI, printed a proclamation declaring the succession of Jane Grey to the throne, in which he styled himself queen's printer. With the swift resolution of the crisis in Mary's favour, Grafton was imprisoned; his role was taken over by Cawood, who was printing official publications by the end of July 1553. In December he was formally appointed as queen's printer, and was also granted the reversion of Reyner Wolfe's 1547 royal patent to print items in Latin, Greek, and Hebrew (which he never enjoyed, as Wolfe outlived him). It was also in 1553 that the name of Cawood's shop in St Paul's Churchyard, the Holy Ghost, first appeared in book imprints. It appears that the sudden expansion of Cawood's business in 1553 may have been managed partly through the appropriation of the stock of Steven Mierdman, an evangelical printer who fled the country in the wake of Mary's accession. In any case, the appointment quickly made Cawood's fortune. By 1556 he was the wealthiest member of the Stationers' Company, and was maintaining an appropriately large number of apprentices. Several hundred imprints appeared over his name in the nineteen years of his appointment. As Cawood also leased premises on the eastern edge of the churchyard with an exceptionally long frontage of 73 feet, Peter Blayney has suggested that this obviously well-illuminated property would have been ideal for a printing-house, with the Holy Ghost serving as his main bookshop.

There is no direct evidence of Cawood's religious views, but on 28 July 1556 he was named as one of the wardens for the refounded fraternity of the Holy Name of Jesus, based in a chapel under the choir of St Paul's Cathedral. (Cawood continued to lease the chapel after the guild was again dissolved in 1559.) He was also later associated with several committed Catholics: the future martyr William Carter was Cawood's apprentice from 1563, and Cawood's own son Gabriel was to become one of the most prominent supporters of Catholicism within the book trade. Cawood was also, inevitably, responsible for printing the key texts of the Marian restoration of Catholicism, including Bishop Bonner's *Homilies* and the official editions of Archbishop Cranmer's recantations. In 1555 a protestant exile in Strasbourg paid him the backhanded compliment of falsely ascribing the tract *A Supplicacyon to the Quenes Maiestie* to Cawood; an ascription which, in Miles Hogarde's eyes, libelled a true Catholic. This may have been overstating the case. Despite a new year's gift of books to the royal couple, Cawood was certainly non-partisan enough for the privy council to order his premises to be searched for illegal books in September 1557, although nothing incriminating seems to have been found. Nor was he so closely associated with Mary's regime as to fall with it in 1558. The proclamation which declared Elizabeth's accession was printed by Richard Jugge, and by the end of December 1558 the privy council was referring to Jugge as the queen's printer. However, in January 1559 Jugge and Cawood produced a printed statute jointly, and in March 1560 they were formally named as joint royal printers, with Jugge as the senior; by this time they were renting a room together at Stationers' Hall. This arrangement endured until Cawood's death.

In keeping with his new dignity, Cawood was one of the wardens of the Stationers' Company from 1554 onwards. When the company was granted its royal charter on 4 May 1557, Cawood, as upper warden, was named second in the charter. He remained as upper warden until July 1558. In 1560, although not an office-holder, he was instrumental in the company's successful efforts to become a livery company. For 1561–3, and again for 1566–7, he served as master of the company, and he remained a member of the company's governing body, the court of assistants, until his death. He was also a substantial benefactor of the company. His more significant gifts included a magnificent hearse cloth in 1556; two glass windows in Stationers' Hall, in honour of himself and of his former master John Reynes, also in 1556; portraits of himself and Reynes, and a stone-engraving of the royal arms, both before 1561; and an ornate door in 1569–70. He was blacklisted by the company only once, in the summer of 1565, when he and sixteen others were fined 16s. 8d. 'for Stechen [Stitching] of bookes which ys contrary to the orders of this howse' (Arber, *Regs. Stationers*, 1.277).

Cawood married three times, but his first wife is the only one whose name—Joan—is recorded, and all his seven children were with her. John, the eldest, was a bachelor of laws and a fellow of New College, Oxford, but also a member of the Stationers' Company, to which he was admitted in 1565; he predeceased his father, dying in 1570. There followed two daughters, Mary and Isabel, both of whom married stationers (George Bishop and Thomas Woodcock respectively); a second son, Gabriel (d. 1602), who became a bookseller and took over his father's lease of the Holy Ghost in 1559; two more daughters, Susanna and Barbara; and a third son, Edmund, who also died in 1570. Cawood himself died in London on 1 April 1572 aged fifty-eight. He was probably buried in St Faith's under St Paul's, where Gabriel had an epitaph inscribed to him in 1591.   ALEC RYRIE

Sources STC, 1475–1640 · Arber, *Regs. Stationers*, vol. 1 · W. Dugdale, *The history of St Paul's Cathedral in London*, 2nd edn (1716), 127 · C. Clair, *A history of printing in Britain* (1965) · *APC, 1556–8* · L. Rostenberg, *The minority press and the English crown: a study in repression, 1558–1625* (1971) · *CSP dom.*, 1547–80, 116, 549 · C. Blagden, *The Stationers' Company: a history, 1403–1959* (1960) · E. G. Duff, *A century of the English book trade* (1905) · J. Ames, *Typographical antiquities, or, An historical account of the origin and progress of printing in Great Britain and Ireland*, ed. W. Herbert, 3 vols. (1785–90) · J. Nichols, *The progresses and public processions of Queen Elizabeth*, new edn, 1 (1823), xxiv n. 2 · D. Loades, *Mary Tudor: a life* (1989), 365–6 · P. W. M. Blayney, *The bookshops in Paul's Cross churchyard* (1990) · DNB

Cawood, Sir Walter (1907–1967), chemist and civil servant, was born on 28 April 1907 in York, the son of Walter Cawood, civil servant, of New Earswick, York, and his wife, Elizabeth McSall, the daughter of a Lincolnshire farmer. He had one sister. He was educated at Archbishop Holgate's Grammar School, York, and at the University of Leeds, where he took his PhD degree in chemistry (1932), having obtained an external BSc from London in 1929. He was a Ramsey memorial fellow (1931–3), and a Moseley scholar of the Royal Society (1933–8). His early research was concerned with the properties of aerosols and the theory of coagulation, and he always maintained an interest in physical chemistry. In 1934 he married Molly, daughter of Fred Johnson, a schoolmaster of York. They had one son and a daughter.

In 1938 Cawood joined the Air Ministry, working with a team investigating chemical warfare. This involved him in the design of proximity fuses but, from 1942, his most valuable work was in instrumentation. He was responsible for the development of bomb and torpedo sights and for synthetic training aids, particularly for night flying. He improvised a simple pre-set rangefinder for use in aircraft attacking the V1 flying bomb, and to improve this device flew in operations as an honorary wing commander.

Cawood was deputy director at the Royal Aircraft Establishment, Farnborough, from 1947 to 1953 and during this time he acquired his interest in aviation and avionics. From 1953 to 1959 he was at the headquarters of the Ministry of Aviation, where he was responsible for the aeronautical research programme. In 1954 he enthusiastically supported the creation of the Advisory Group for Aerospace Research and Development, which did much to restore European aeronautical collaboration. During the group's early years he served as national delegate.

Cawood was a scientist who believed in identifying the few important growth points from a wide range of promising alternatives, and single-mindedly supporting them. He foresaw the potential of vertical take-off and as early as 1958 provided support for Sir Sydney Camm's deflected thrust aircraft, the forerunner of the Harrier jump jet, which later served with the Royal Air Force. He understood the need to supplement wind-tunnel measurements with actual flight trials. He encouraged the investigation of light weight-lifting engines in experimental aircraft, and of low-speed handling properties of slender wings which did so much to validate the design of the revolutionary supersonic passenger aircraft Concorde.

In 1959 Cawood became the first chief scientist of the War Office and later, in 1964, the first scientist to be a member of the army board. His wide experience in rationalizing research and development was invaluable in unifying the various scientific and engineering organizations within the War Office, and in building up relationships between scientists and their military colleagues. His knowledge of aviation technology was particularly useful to the army, which was beginning to invest in helicopters and air transportability, and his training as a chemist found application in the affairs of the Chemical Defence Establishment at Porton and the ordnance factories.

In 1964 Cawood returned to the Ministry of Aviation as chief scientist and became involved in the integration of the Ministry of Aviation into the new Ministry of Technology. His particular concern was to extend the mandate of the defence establishments so that their resources would be more directly available to civil industry. He suffered poor health during his last year, but continued to carry his heavy responsibilities. He died at the Cambridge Military Hospital in Aldershot on 6 March 1967, survived by his widow.

Cawood was an enthusiastic yachtsman and crewed in many offshore races as well as sailing single-handed in his own boat, *Cobber*. He was an active member of the Royal Ocean Racing Club, of the Royal Southern Yacht Club, and of the Royal Aeronautical Society, of which he was a fellow. He was appointed CBE in 1953, CB in 1956, and KBE in 1965. ROBERT COCKBURN, *rev.*

Sources *Nature*, 214 (1967), 217 · *New Scientist* (16 March 1967) · *Journal of the Royal Aeronautical Society*, 71 (1967), 310 · personal knowledge (1981)

Wealth at death £15,896: probate, 22 June 1967, *CGPLA Eng. & Wales*

Cawston, George (1851–1918), stockbroker and financier, was born on 13 February 1851 at Barrington Road, Brixton, Surrey, the second son of Samuel William Cawston, gentleman, and Elizabeth Rosa Cawston, *née* Davis.

On 18 February 1873 Cawston married Mary Ellen, the twenty-year-old daughter of Richard Haworth, Manchester calico printer, at which time he described himself a stock dealer residing at Balham Hill, Surrey. The family firm was a member of the London stock exchange and Cawston had worked for it from the start of the previous year. By the 1880s he was head of the company that now bore his name. In July 1878 he was admitted a student of the Inner Temple, and he was called to the bar in May 1882. Noted for his 'remarkable combination of interests' (Galbraith, *Crown and Charter*, 54), Cawston was in addition a map maker and a keen fellow of the Royal Geographical Society.

Cawston first came to public prominence through his friendship and partnership with Eric Frederick Gifford, third Baron Gifford (1849–1911), former army officer and colonial official, who had won the Victoria Cross in 1874 in the Second Anglo-Asante War. Lord Gifford had long been interested in securing a mining concession in southern Africa, but what galvanized the two of them into action was the Moffat treaty (February 1888), which made Matabeleland a British sphere of influence. Although several years Gifford's junior and lacking his social status and connections, Cawston dominated the partnership and assembled the 'formidable financial combination' (Galbraith, 'Origins', 151) registered two months later as the Bechuanaland Exploration Company. Prominent among its backers were Baron Henry de Rothschild and Henry Oppenheim. In May 1888 Cawston sought Colonial Office support from Lord Knutsford, whose initial cool response warmed once the importance of the City interests became clear. By then, however, Cawston and Gifford faced powerful rivals, Cecil Rhodes and Charles Dunell Rudd. At Whitehall's insistence, the ensuing stalemate was broken by a judicious amalgamation of competing interests, out of which the British South Africa (BSA) Company emerged with a royal charter in October 1889. Included on its board of directors were Gifford and Cawston.

From the start Cawston was the most active of the chartered company's London-based directors. He played a key role in establishing the Central Search Association, later the United Concession Company, which unknown to the Colonial Office retained ownership of the Rudd concession [see Rudd, Charles Dunell (1844–1916)], the mineral grant on which the charter ostensibly rested and which was sold to the BSA Company only towards the end of 1893. This deal and others, some involving market rigging, were greatly to the benefit of the BSA Company's 'inner circle' and their friends. Cawston had earlier worked closely with Rhodes in allotting chartered shares to influential persons, particularly MPs and government officials. These contacts opened many doors, allowing Cawston to become the company's main interlocutor with both the Colonial Office and the Foreign Office, as well as its 'chief representative in great international commercial negotiations involving Katanga and Mozambique' (Galbraith, *Crown and Charter*, 156). None the less, the relationship between Rhodes and Cawston, always tinged with a degree of mutual irritation and incomprehension, soon deteriorated. Dismissed by Rhodes as 'too limp' over negotiations with Leopold II about Katanga, Cawston also had the ground cut beneath his feet when he tried to reach an accommodation with the Mozambique Company in 1891: 'while Cawston had been promoting a commercial union, Rhodes's energies had been directed to seizing by force what Cawston would have acquired by money' (Galbraith, *Crown and Charter*, 188). Less concerned with imperial expansion than with personal profit, Cawston found matters more to his liking in German-ruled Africa. Early in 1893 he became chairman of the recently formed South West Africa (SWA) Company. Based in the City and comprising German and a majority of British shareholders, the company brushed aside prior claims, including that of the shipping magnate, Sir Donald Currie, to win an exclusive concession over Damaraland in South-West Africa. It rapidly established a stranglehold over the territory's trade and development, but was careful not to upset German sensitivities. In November 1894 Cawston visited Berlin where he so 'favourably impressed' the German colonial department that the Reichstag was subsequently assured that the SWA Company had 'all along carried on its work most loyally and has undertaken nothing without first taking into consideration the intentions and wishes of the Imperial Government' (Dreyer, 282). He failed, however, to turn this success to advantage in east Africa, though his attempts to set up a central African syndicate 'for developing the Zambezi territories' did herald a rapprochement of sorts with Currie (Porter, 211). It also marked a deepening of his business relationship with the shady company promoter and City financier Edmund Davis (1861–1939), with whom he was already associated through the SWA Company.

Never much liking Rhodes's management of the BSA Company at the best of times, Cawston and Gifford used the fiasco of the Jameson raid to push for his resignation from the board of directors in April 1896. However, when Rhodes returned unbowed to the board in 1898, only Cawston resigned, on 27 June 1898. His objections were confined to Rhodes's methods. Himself the subject of criticism in the financial press for sharp practice, Cawston's business interests were increasingly focused on China. But even as the number of his companies multiplied, so their importance dwindled. Cawston lost control of both the Bechuanaland Exploration Company in 1899 and the SWA Company in 1904 to Davis. Desperate to the end to repair his fortune, he died alone of a heart attack in the Great Eastern Hotel, Liverpool Street, London, on 27 December 1918. He never visited Africa or China.

IAN PHIMISTER

Sources J. S. Galbraith, *Crown and charter: the early years of the British South Africa Company* (1974) · R. A. Voeltz, *German colonialism and the South West Africa Company, 1894–1914* (Athens, Ohio, 1988) · A. Keppel-Jones, *Rhodes and Rhodesia: the white conquest of Zimbabwe, 1884–1902* (1983) · 'Mr George Cawston', *African Review* (7 April 1894) · J. S. Galbraith, 'Origins of the British South Africa Company', *Perspectives of empire: essays presented to Gerald S. Graham*, ed. J. Flint and G. Williams (1973) · J. S. Galbraith, 'The British South Africa Company and the Jameson raid', *Journal of British Studies*, 10/1 (1970–71), 145–61 · R. Dreyer, 'Whitehall, Cape Town, Berlin and the economic partition of south-west Africa: the establishment of British economic control, 1885–94', *Journal of Imperial and Commonwealth History*, 15 (1986–7), 264–88 · P. Maylam, *Rhodes, the Tswana and the British* (1980) · A. N. Porter, *Victorian shipping, business, and imperial policy: Donald Currie, the Castle line and southern Africa*, Royal Historical Society Studies in History, 49 (1986) · *The Rialto* (27 Aug 1896) · *Directory of Directors* · *Stock Exchange Year Book* · L. Weinthal, ed., *The Anglo-African who's who*, [new edn] (1910) · J. Foster, *Men-at-the-bar: a biographical hand-list of the members of the various inns of court*, 2nd edn (1885) · GEC, *Peerage* · b. cert. · m. cert. · d. cert.

Archives Bodl. RH, papers | National Archives, Windhoek, Namibia, South West Africa Company papers

Likenesses photograph, repro. in 'Mr George Cawston', *African Review*

Wealth at death £7079: probate, 13 Feb 1919, *CGPLA Eng. & Wales*

Cawston [Causton], **Michael** (*d.* 1396), theologian and university principal, came from Norwich diocese (the village of Cawston is north-east of Norwich). His date of birth is unknown, but by 1354 he was a master of arts and in 1361 took his doctorate in theology at Cambridge. In the 1360s he may also have served as master of Michaelhouse, Cambridge, a college for theologians that was suppressed during the founding of Trinity College. Cawston was chancellor of the university from *c.*1361 to 1366. Nothing is known about his activities in that office, except that he travelled to Avignon in March 1363 to present university petitions at the court of Pope Urban V (*r.* 1362–70), who was known for his support of universities. The first petition on the roll was to dispense Cawston to hold incompatible benefices.

Cawston's generosity both to the university and to several colleges earned him a special thrice-yearly invocation during university processions, 'especially for the soul of Master Michael Causton, sometime chancellor of this university, who bestowed gifts on it and on all the colleges' (*Documents Relating to the University*, 1.401). His known benefactions included encasing the university processional cross in silver (it was sold during the Henrician Reformation) and donating manuscripts to Pembroke College, Gonville Hall, and Peterhouse. He is also recorded as having given £2 to the latter college. Cawston is not known to have written anything. His surviving volumes reflect the theological studies typical of his time: Scotus, Aquinas, and Richard of Media Villa on Peter Lombard's *Sentences*, Aquinas's *Prima* and *Secunda secundae*, Gregory the Great's *Moralia*, Hervey Natalis's polemic against Henri de Gand, Aristotle's *Logic*, Anselm, Boethius, and a Bible. Like many medieval university theologians Cawston also owned some legal texts, and he gave Justinian's *Code* and *Institutes* to Gonville Hall.

As was also typical for a senior university theologian of the fourteenth century, Cawston obtained considerable ecclesiastical preferment. Beginning in 1361, when he was presented the rectorship of Grundisburgh, Suffolk, by Michaelhouse, Cawston came to hold several livings, prebends, and canonries. He twice received permission to hold multiple and incompatible benefices. On his death in July 1396 he held a canonry at Salisbury, and canonries and prebends at Lincoln and Chichester, and may have been dean of the latter as well. Michael Cawston should not be confused with a man of the same name born in 1340, who was a bachelor of arts of Cambridge when he travelled to Avignon with his namesake in 1363. This other Michael Cawston later studied canon law and gave two copies of the *Liber sextus* to King's Hall. He has incorrectly been called a fellow of Pembroke College.

DAMIAN R. LEADER

Sources W. H. Bliss, ed., *Calendar of entries in the papal registers relating to Great Britain and Ireland: petitions to the pope* (1896), 404, 408, 415 · M. R. James, *Catalogues of the manuscripts in Peterhouse* (1899), 297 · Emden, *Cam.* · *Documents relating to the university and colleges of Cambridge*, Cambridge University Commission, 1 (1852), 401 · M. R. James, *A descriptive catalogue of the manuscripts in the library of Gonville and Caius College*, 2 vols. (1907–8), 15, 18, 315, 328, 348–52, 363–4, 527–8, 631–2, 640–41 · M. R. James, *A descriptive catalogue of the manuscripts in the library of Pembroke College, Cambridge* (1905), 14, 139 [incl. handlist of the printed books to the year 1500 by E. H. Minns] · CUL, Add. MS 7207 · A. L. Attwater, *Pembroke College, Cambridge: a short history*, ed. S. C. Roberts (1936), 14 · W. D. Peckham, ed., *The chartulary of the high church of Chichester*, Sussex RS, 46 (1946)

Cawston, (Edwin) Richard (1923–1986), documentary film-maker, was born on 31 May 1923 in Weybridge, Surrey, the elder child and elder son of Edwin Cawston, merchant, of Weybridge, and his wife, Phyllis, daughter of Henry Charles Hawkins. He always wanted to make films; as a boy at Westminster School he and a friend made a documentary of the school's evacuation to Lancing. In 1941 he joined the Royal Signals and then spent two terms at Oriel College, Oxford, doing an army short course in radio, electricity, and magnetism. He became a captain in 1945, and a major in 1946, while serving in the southern command in India. When he was demobilized in 1947, he took a post as assistant film librarian with the newly reopened BBC television service in Alexandra Palace.

Cawston did not stay a librarian for long. He soon became film editor and then the producer of the popular *Television Newsreel*. Between 1950 and 1954 he produced 700 editions and gained a depth of experience in the technicalities of film craftsmanship which few of his television contemporaries could equal. This early experience of volume production under pressure was the foundation of his success as one of Britain's (and later the world's) most respected television documentary producers over a period of thirty years. It is also a key to the kind of producer he became; he was a capable camera director, but he showed his greatest strengths in the cutting room and dubbing theatre after the film had been shot. The newsreel years gave him a grounding in the shaping and pacing of film, and the adding of commentary, music, and effects, which were to be of great value in guiding the work of younger producers as well as in developing his own.

In 1954 *Television Newsreel* lost its battle to stay independent of the BBC news division and Cawston left to join the talks department of the television service, as a documentary producer. The age of the old film documentary makers such as John Grierson and (F.) Humphrey Jennings was dead; Cawston was present at the birth of the new documentary on television. He produced a long series of major documentary films, many of which won national and international awards. He was especially interested in institutions and professions, with whom his frank and open approach, and high professionalism, created a trust which gained him an entrée that would have been refused to most producers. His films documented the worlds of lawyers, pilots, the National Health Service, the British educational system, and, perhaps most memorably, the

BBC itself in *This is the BBC* (1959). There was no 'typical Cawston' film because he did not impose his own views or slant on his subject matter. His aim was to let the subject speak for itself, usually with the minimum of narration or (as in the BBC film) none at all. The common factor was meticulous craftsmanship.

In 1965, just after the start of BBC2, he was made head of documentary programmes. It was here that for fourteen years he coached and developed a new generation of documentary makers. The sessions in which he looked at rough assemblies of their films were master-classes that refined the skills of many of today's leading documentary makers. But he did not stop making his own films; *Royal Family*, in which he recorded a year (1968–9) in the private and public life of the queen, was at that time the most popular and widely seen documentary in television history, and did much to restore the popularity the monarchy had lost in the mid-1960s. It led to his becoming the producer of the queen's Christmas day broadcast to the Commonwealth from 1970 to 1985, and to his appointment as CVO in 1972.

For most of his working life Cawston was an active and influential member of BAFTA, the television and film-makers' professional body; he was chairman from 1976 to 1979, and a trustee from 1971 until his death in 1986. It was largely through his energy and enterprise that BAFTA secured its home at 195 Piccadilly, and it was due to his advocacy that the queen made the initial major donation towards its funding out of the sales revenues of *Royal Family*.

Cawston left the BBC in 1979, having won almost all the major professional prizes, including the Italia prize (1962), three BAFTA awards, and the silver medal of the Royal Television Society (1961). He joined Video Arts Ltd as special projects director, but continued producing programmes for the BBC as an independent executive producer, and acting as consultant to the government and tourist board of Hong Kong.

Cawston was tall, clean-shaven, and well built; his dress was reassuringly conventional, more like that of a family solicitor than the usual image of a film-maker. In 1951 he married Elisabeth Anne (Liz), daughter of Richard Llewellyn Rhys, of St Fagans, canon of Llandaff. They had two sons. She died in 1977, and in 1978 he married Andrea, daughter of Michael Phillips, company director, of Cyprus. Cawston died of a heart attack in Cassis, France, on 7 June 1986.   ANTONY JAY, *rev.*

Sources BBC WAC · *The Times* (11 June 1986) · *The Times* (13 June 1986) · private knowledge (2004) · *CGPLA Eng. & Wales* (1987)
Archives BBC, BBC Research Library · BBC WAC
Wealth at death £390,674: probate, 28 Jan 1987, *CGPLA Eng. & Wales*

Cawthorn, James (1719–1761), poet and schoolmaster, was born in Sheffield, Yorkshire, on 4 November 1719, the son of Thomas Cawthorn, an upholsterer, and his wife, Mary, daughter of Edward Laughton of Gainsborough. James Cawthorn's will mentions a brother and three sisters. He attended Sheffield grammar school where, according to one of his sisters, he showed literary talents and attempted to begin a periodical, *The Tea-Table*—an attempt that she said was thwarted by their father (*GM*, 1791). He was then sent to the grammar school at Kirkby Lonsdale in 1735, and in the following year became an assistant teacher at Rotherham School. In September 1735 his poem 'Meditation on the Power of God', owing much to Pope's *Essay on Man*, appeared anonymously in the *Gentleman's Magazine* and around this time he also published his poem 'Perjured Lovers' in Sheffield, though this is now lost.

On 8 July 1738 Cawthorn matriculated from Clare College, Cambridge, but did not take up residence. Instead he became an assistant to Mr Clare, a schoolmaster of Soho Square, London. In 1743 he married his employer's daughter, Mary (*d.* 1747), and in the same year was chosen to be headmaster of Tonbridge grammar school, Kent (later known simply as Tonbridge School). There is some evidence that Cawthorn was a contentious choice, either because of his youth (he was only twenty-three when he took up the post) or because he had no apparent connections with the locality. On his appointment, more than half of the pupils left. However, by his death eighteen years later, the number of boys in the school had risen from twenty-six to sixty-seven. Cawthorn founded a library at the school.

According to the later account by his brother-in-law, the Revd Edward Goodwin—a Sheffield clergyman who married one of Cawthorn's sisters and who had eventual possession of his poetical manuscripts—Cawthorn had continued writing verse, much of it in Latin. His next known publication was a 'rhapsody' on the organization of a militia by Thomas Herring, archbishop of York, against the Jacobite rebels invading from Scotland. This appeared, anonymously, in the *Gentleman's Magazine* in October 1745. In the same year he also published a sermon, 'preach'd before the worshipful burgesses of Westminster'. It is notable for the high pitch of its tirade against contemporary metropolitan 'Lewdness and Luxury' (p. 19). The endpaper advertises 'An Essay on Education' by Cawthorn, to be published 'speedily'. There is no evidence of its ever appearing.

Cawthorn's wife died in 1747. In 1746 she had given birth to twin daughters, Anne and Mary, who both died two days later. They are remembered in Cawthorn's most personal poem, 'A Father's Extempore Consolation on the Death of Two Daughters, who Lived Only Two Days'. In the following year a third daughter, also called Mary, died soon after birth. In 1747 he published *Abelard to Eloisa*, anonymously. This dramatic monologue in heroic couplets, designedly a companion piece to Pope's 'Eloisa to Abelard', was Cawthorn's best-known and most frequently reprinted work. It was reissued in 1748 and published a number of times in collections of the early nineteenth century, sometimes together with Pope's poem. The first edition has an effusive, perhaps amorous, verse dedication 'To Miss — of Horsmanden in Kent', who is also the dedicatee of Cawthorn's humorous poem 'The Lottery'.

In 1748 Cawthorn published *Benevolence, the Source and*

Ornament of Civil Distinction, a sermon given to members of the Skinners' Company, founders of Tonbridge School. The title-page of this describes him as MA. In 1749 he appears to have sought the patronage of Lord Lyttleton, addressing to him his verse epistle 'The Vanity of Human Enjoyments' (Anderson). Some of the other poems by Cawthorn that have survived were originally composed for recitation by Tonbridge pupils during the annual visitation by representatives of the Skinners' Company.

On 15 April 1761 Cawthorn died after being thrown from his horse near Tonbridge. He was buried in Tonbridge church, where a marble slab with a Latin epitaph was erected by one of his sisters. Verses to his memory by Lord Eardley, a former pupil, appeared in the *Gentleman's Magazine*. A collection of Cawthorn's poems was eventually published by subscription in 1771. So many of the subscribers are from the Tonbridge area that it is likely that the organizer of the subscription was also local, perhaps connected to the school. Much of Cawthorn's verse is in Popean couplets and is conventionally sententious. The choice of public men that he praises reveals strong Whig sympathies.   JOHN MULLAN

Sources E. Goodwin, 'Memoir', *GM*, 1st ser., 61 (1791), 1081–3 · W Odom, *Hallamshire worthies* (1926) · *Poems, by the Rev. Mr Cawthorn* (1771) · W. G. Hart, ed., *The register of Tonbridge School from 1553 to 1820* (1935) · *GM*, 1st ser., 5 (1735) · *GM*, 1st ser., 15 (1745) · R. Anderson, *Poets of Great Britain* (1794) · will, PRO, PROB 11/865/163, fols. 136v–137r

Cawthorne, Sir Terence Edward (1902–1970), ear surgeon, was born in Aberdeen on 29 September 1902, the only child of William Cawthorne, a customs official, and his wife, Annie England. Cawthorne was educated at Denstone College and at the medical school of King's College Hospital, London. He qualified MRCS, LRCP, in 1924, and became FRCS in 1930. In 1929 he met Lilian Eve Blanche (1907–1975), daughter of William Southworth, musician, at the King's College Hospital annual ball, and they were married on 23 January 1930. They had one son and one daughter.

Cawthorne held a number of junior appointments at King's before becoming registrar to the ear and throat departments. He was appointed to the honorary consultant staff of the hospital as assistant surgeon to the now united ear, nose, and throat department in 1932, and became full surgeon in 1939. For a time he was also a consultant at the Metropolitan Hospital, the Royal Hospital, Richmond, and the East Surrey Hospital. In 1936 he became aural surgeon to the National Hospital for Nervous Diseases. In 1948 he was appointed consulting adviser in otolaryngology to the Ministry of Health, and he held this position until 1967.

At King's, Cawthorne began to concentrate on the problems of aural disease and the close relationship between some forms of deafness and vertigo with neurology, which made his appointment at the National Hospital peculiarly appropriate. Seeking to restore hearing by making a new fenestra for the entry of sound waves to the internal ear in certain types of deafness, he visited the pioneers in this field in various countries. He did much to introduce Lempert's fenestration operation to Europe, and was the first in this country to recognize the value of the operating microscope in ear surgery. It was a natural step for Cawthorne to become interested in the form of vertigo known as Ménière's disease, and with C. S. Hallpike he did much to further the understanding, diagnosis, and treatment of this condition. His third great neuro-otological interest was in the anatomically neighbouring facial nerve and in the various forms of paralysis of this. These matters, of which he made himself an authority, brought a constant stream of visitors, which must have been very wearing, but he received them all with characteristic patience and courtesy.

Although fully appreciative of the value of laboratory and clinical research and of the need to be closely associated with research workers, Cawthorne was essentially a clinical diagnostician and accurate technical surgeon. His influence attracted the Wernher research unit on deafness to King's and he was clinical director of this from 1958 to 1964. He was an excellent teacher of students and graduates, and was dean of the medical school at King's (1946–8). He was president of the Royal Society of Medicine (1962–4) and received its Dalby (1953) and W. J. Harrison (1961) prizes; and he was master of the second British Academic Conference in Otolaryngology in 1967.

A prolific contributor at gatherings and in learned journals, Cawthorne had numerous invitations to meetings all over the world. He delivered various endowed lectures and was awarded medals in the United Kingdom and other countries. He was particularly well known in the United States and Canada. He was created honorary MD of Uppsala in 1963, honorary LLD of Syracuse, New York, in 1964, and honorary FRCS, Ireland, in 1966. He was knighted in 1964.

Cawthorne was an imposing figure: he combined a calm, reassuring manner with being a good listener, traits which made easy his approaches to patients. The apparent solemnity of his later years covered an innate diffidence and schoolboyish sense of humour. As a graduate student he had worked for a time in an endowed dispensary in London's Drury Lane, meeting many of the odd characters connected with the stage and Covent Garden. No doubt these contacts stimulated his lifelong interest in the arts and led to his membership of the Garrick Club. Cawthorne also became interested in the history of his specialism and its relationship with famous figures. For instance, he wrote papers to show that Julius Caesar and Dean Swift suffered from Ménière's disease.

In 1964 Cawthorne had his first warning of the heart trouble of which ultimately he died. He was obliged to retire from King's, but he found it hard not to remain involved and he continued to travel. He died in Middlesex Hospital, St Marylebone, London, on 22 January 1970.

RONALD MACBETH, *rev.* ANITA MCCONNELL

Sources N. Weir, *Otolaryngology: an illustrated history* (1990) · K. B. Thomas, 'Pro memoria Terence Edward Cawthorne', *Proceedings of the Royal Society of Medicine*, 63 (1970), 799 · F. F. Cartwright, 'Sir Terence Cawthorne at King's College Hospital', *Proceedings of the Royal Society of Medicine*, 63 (1970), 805–6 · M. Ellis, 'Sir Terence Cawthorne', *Proceedings of the Royal Society of Medicine*, 63 (1970), 807 · personal knowledge (1981) · d. cert. · m. cert. · CGPLA Eng. & Wales (1970)

Likenesses Swan, portrait, Royal Society of Medicine, London

Wealth at death £19,296: probate, 4 June 1970, CGPLA Eng. & Wales

Cawton, Thomas (1605–1659), Reformed minister, was born at Rainham, Norfolk, of poor parents. Sir Roger Townshend became his patron and sent him to Queens' College, Cambridge, from where he matriculated in 1626, graduated BA in 1630, and proceeded MA in 1633. He was noted at the university for both his learning and his austere piety, which 'was so generally observed in the College, that it grew almost a proverb … that such and such a youth was poisoned by Cawton's faction, and was become a Cawtonist' (*Life*, 12). He then studied theology at the house of Herbert Palmer, the godly catechist and vicar of Ashwell, Hertfordshire, and was for four years chaplain to Sir William Armine of Orton, Northamptonshire.

In 1637 Cawton was presented by Townshend to the vicarage of Wivenhoe, Essex, a parish allegedly 'notorious for all manner of vice and wickedness, drunkenness and swearing' (*Life*, 16). He soon brought discipline to the community and persuaded his parishioners to observe the sabbath and discontinue their Sunday fish market. Some time after 1635 Cawton married Elizabeth, daughter of William Jenkyn (*d.* 1618), a preacher of Sudbury, Suffolk, sister of William *Jenkyn (*bap.* 1613, *d.* 1685), and granddaughter of Richard *Rogers (1551–1618). They had more than seven children.

In 1644 Cawton moved to London, and the following year, with the help of his friend Sir Harbottle Grimston, became minister of St Bartholomew by the Exchange, a very strongly presbyterian parish. Here he was 'deeply involved in the Presbyterian movement in the city' (Liu, 117). Opposed to the growth of sects, in 1647 Cawton signed *A testimony to the truth of Jesus Christ … against the errours, heresies and blasphemies of these times, and the toleration of them* (1648). In 1649 he signed *A Vindication of the Ministers of the Gospel in, and about London* against the radicalism of the army and the execution of Charles I. Admiration for his honest living and sincere preaching led to his being invited to preach before the lord mayor and aldermen of London at Mercers' Chapel on 25 February 1649. In his sermon Cawton discussed the authority of magistrates, 'Jesuits', and 'the killing of Kings'. He also prayed for the 'legal sovereign and the royal family' (ibid., 25, 117). This was seen as seditious and he was brought before the council of state in March, and twice refused to recant. He was committed to the Gatehouse prison, Westminster, until 14 August 1649 when, as a thanksgiving for Michael Jones's victory at Rathmines in Ireland, Cawton and others were released by order of the House of Commons.

In 1651, along with his brother-in-law William Jenkyn and others, Cawton was involved in Christopher Love's plot to send financial support for Charles in Scotland. A number of ministers were arrested and on 22 August 1651

Thomas Cawton (1605–1659), by unknown engraver, pubd 1662

Love was executed. Rather than face arrest Cawton fled to the Netherlands and was subsequently chosen pastor of the English church in Rotterdam. While on the continent he became acquainted with a number of scholars and developed contacts at various universities in the Netherlands. He also encouraged and assisted with Brian Walton's polyglot Bible (1698) and Edmund Castell's *Lexicon heptaglotton* (1669), and prepared his son Thomas for university by teaching him foreign languages. In 1658 Charles II was in Brussels and on 7 November he wrote to Cawton proclaiming his protestantism and his commitment to remain 'defender of the faith'. Charles asked that Cawton defend his protestant reputation among 'the ministers of the Dutch church, and others' in Rotterdam (*Life*, 79).

Cawton died at Rotterdam on 7 August 1659 and was buried there by Dutch ministers. He was survived by his wife. *The Life and Death of … Mr Thomas Cawton*, published in 1662 with commendatory prefaces by Arthur Jackson, Edmund Calamy, and others, has been attributed to his son, Thomas *Cawton, but internal evidence suggests otherwise. The biographer described this 'Saint' as 'of stature tall and thin, in countenance lean and pale, of a very weak constitution, yet very active and stirring'. He was 'of a courteous nature, very affable and easy to be entreated; in his fashions neither rude nor fantastic … and in all his actions graceful' (*Life*, 85).

MARK ROBERT BELL

Sources *The life and death of that holy and reverend man of God Mr Thomas Cawton* (1662) · B. Brook, *The lives of the puritans*, 3 (1813), 320–23 · DNB · J. Granger, *A biographical history of England from Egbert the Great to the revolution*, 5th edn, 3 (1824), 336–7 · Calamy rev. · Tai Liu, *Puritan London: a study of religion and society in the City parishes* (1986) · A. Kippis and others, eds., *Biographia Britannica, or, The lives of the most eminent persons who have flourished in Great Britain and Ireland*, 2nd edn, 3 (1784), 348–51 · Tai Liu, *Discord in Zion: the puritan divines and the puritan revolution, 1640–1660* (1973) · Venn, *Alum. Cant.* · R. Newcourt, *Repertorium ecclesiasticum parochiale Londinense*, 2 vols. (1708–10) · D. Neal, *The history of the puritans or protestant nonconformists*, 2 (1754), 537, 546 · W. Wilson, *The history and antiquities of the dissenting churches and meeting houses in London, Westminster and Southwark*, 4 vols. (1808–14), vol. 4, p. 60 · Foster, *Alum. Oxon.*
Likenesses line engraving, pubd 1801, BM, NPG · line engraving, BM, NPG; repro. in *Life* (1662) [*see illus.*] · woodcut, repro. in Brook, *Lives of the puritans*, vol. 3, facing p. 320

Cawton, Thomas (*bap.* 1642, *d.* 1677), orientalist and nonconformist minister, was baptized at Wivenhoe, Essex, on 23 September 1642, the eldest son of Thomas *Cawton (1605–1659), a distinguished divine and vicar of the parish, and Elizabeth, daughter of the preacher William Jenkyn. In 1644 the family moved to London, where the elder Thomas Cawton had been appointed vicar of St Bartholomew's. In 1651, however, as a consequence of his involvement in Love's plot to support Charles II in Scotland, the elder Cawton sought refuge in the Netherlands. Appointed minister of the English church in Rotterdam he was soon joined by his wife and children. After studying under his father's tuition the younger Thomas Cawton was taught Hebrew, Aramaic, Syriac, and Arabic by another English royalist in Rotterdam, Robert Sheringham.

The younger Cawton, who had assimilated his parents' presbyterianism, matriculated at the University of Utrecht in April 1657. His father accompanied him, entrusting him to one of his closest Dutch friends, Gisbertus Voetius, professor of theology and the foremost exponent of the orthodox Calvinism of which Utrecht was a bastion. At Utrecht, Cawton also met another friend of his father's, Johan Leusden, professor of Greek and Hebrew, who was impressed by his command of the Semitic languages.

Leusden was already working on the Syriac version of the New Testament. Under his supervision (and possibly even under his dictation), Cawton produced his first disputation on the authenticity, date, and merits of the Syriac versions of the Bible, and defended it on 14 December 1657. On 4 December of the following year he presented a second dissertation under the supervision of Voetius's son Daniel, professor of philosophy. A disquisition on whether God could create a perfect creature, it reflected the neo-scholastic (and anti-Cartesian) approach that prevailed at Utrecht. Finally, on 20 April 1659, he defended a third dissertation, again under Leusden's supervision, on the benefits of Hebrew for use by philosophers. The long lists of dedicatees in the three theses show that, besides the more distinguished refugees in the Netherlands such as Sheringham, James Nalton, Thomas Marshall, and Robert Paget, the young Cawton had the utmost esteem for those friends of his father who had remained in England—the elder Edmund Calamy, William Spurstowe, Roger Drake, and many others.

In 1660 Cawton, whose father had died in Rotterdam the previous year, joined Merton College, Oxford, on account of his father's friendship with the orientalist Samuel Clarke. With a certificate of his accomplishments signed by Leusden on 18 May 1659 and his three Utrecht dissertations (Bodl. Oxf., Mar. 148, 15–17), Cawton matriculated on 31 March and proceeded BA on 3 April. He exhibited his skills by composing some Hebrew verses celebrating the restoration of Charles II.

In 1661 Cawton was ordained by the bishop of Oxford, but refused to conform to the terms of the Act of Uniformity in May 1662. He consequently left the university to become chaplain to Sir Anthony Irby in London. In the same year he published his father's biography, *The Life and Death of that Holy and Reverend Man of God Mr Thomas Cawton*, dedicated to Irby and his wife. When in 1665 Irby withdrew to his Lincolnshire estates to escape the plague Cawton, whose health was never good, found that the climate did not suit him. He returned to London and settled in Westminster, where he acted as chaplain to Mary, Lady Armine, the widow of Sir William Armine, whom the elder Cawton had served as chaplain between 1633 and 1637. Lady Armine, noted for her piety and philanthropy, had been particularly generous to the ministers ejected in 1662. On 10 April 1668 Cawton, then living in the parish of St Martin-in-the-Fields and in possession of a copyhold estate at Great Bentley in Essex, was licensed to marry Anne Scutt of St Margaret's parish, Westminster. They had a son, Richard.

About 1670 Cawton gathered a dissenting congregation in Tothill Street. His single devotional publication, *Balaam's Wish* (1670), was dedicated to three of the numerous daughters of John Holles, second earl of Clare—Lady Anne Clinton (married to the earl of Lincoln) and Lady Eleanora and Lady Diana Holles—and suggests that Cawton, who preached close to the court, was popular among the nobility. A sermon on the subject of death in which he was prepared to accord some degree of merit to human effort, *Balaam's Wish* reveals a moderate presbyterianism. On 3 April 1672, following the declaration of indulgence, Cawton was licensed to preach in his house in St Anne's Lane as well as in a newly built meeting-house in the New Way, Westminster.

Despite his high reputation as a scholar and a linguist—Nathaniel Vincent referred to 'a miraculous gift' for languages both ancient and modern, 'somewhat like that vouchsafed the Disciples on the day of Pentecost' (Vincent, 32)—Cawton abandoned his learned pursuits after leaving Oxford. Declaring that 'he loves not to be in Print' (Cawton, *Balaam's Wish*, sig. A6v), he devoted his energies to his congregation. He had a special predilection for one of the wittiest dissenters, Vincent Alsop, whose attack on William Sherlock he admired.

Cawton's state of health had been declining steadily. He died in Kensington on 10 April 1677, after settling £400 on his son, and was buried at the new church in Tothill Street.

He was survived by his wife. Funeral sermons were delivered by Vincent and Henry Hurst; his death was much lamented by his congregation; and his last request, that Alsop should succeed him as its minister, was granted.

ALASTAIR HAMILTON

Sources *Calamy rev.* · T. Cawton, *The life and death of … Thomas Cawton* (1662) · *The nonconformist's memorial … originally written by … Edmund Calamy*, ed. S. Palmer, [3rd edn], 1 (1802); 3 (1803), vols. 1, 3 · Wood, *Ath. Oxon.*, new edn, vol. 3 · T. Cawton, *Balaam's wish: a sermon* (1670) · A. Kippis, 'Cawton, Thomas', *Biographia Britannica, or, The lives of the most eminent persons who have flourished in Great Britain and Ireland*, ed. A. Kippis and others, 3 (1784), 384–51 · W. Wilson, *The history and antiquities of the dissenting churches and meeting houses in London, Westminster and Southwark*, 4 vols. (1808–14), vol. 4 · *DNB* · N. Vincent, *Israels lamentation at the death of a prophet in a sermon preached at the funeral of … Mr Thomas Cawton* (1677) · *Album Studiosorum Academiae Rheno-Trajectinae, 1636–1886* (Utrecht, 1886) · Foster, *Alum. Oxon.*, 1500–1714, vol. 1 · T. Cawton, *Philologi mixti disputatio nona, quae est de versione Syriaca vet. et novi testamenti* (Utrecht, 1657) · T. Cawton, *Disputationum in theologia naturali selectarum decima septa, continens decisionem quaestionis: an deus creare possit creaturam perfectissimam* (Utrecht, 1658) · T. Cawton, *Dissertatio de usu linguae Hebraicae in philosophia theoretica* (Utrecht, 1659) · probate, City Westm. AC, act book 6, fol. 120v · will, City Westm. AC, filed wills, no. 621 · inventory, City Westm. AC, inventories 6, no. 295 · parish register, Wivenhoe, Essex, 23 Sept 1642, Essex RO, D/P227/1/1 [baptism]

Archives DWL, transcription of Hebrew texts, MS L4/3 | Bodl. Oxf., letter to Samuel Clarke, MS Rawl. D. 317 A, fol. 138

Wealth at death copyhold estate at Great Bentley, Essex; £400 settled on son: will, City Westm. AC, filed wills, no. 621; inventories, 6, no. 295

Caxton, Jeremy of (*d.* 1249), sheriff and justice, was probably a relative of Geoffrey of Caxton, a knight active in Cambridgeshire affairs in the 1230s and 1240s, perhaps a younger brother or cousin. Both took their name from the Cambridgeshire village of Caxton, where Jeremy was granted an estate by Geoffrey's sister Amphelisa and her husband in 1247, soon after Geoffrey's death. He was active by 1219, when he was the attorney of Geoffrey of Hatfield in a case in the bench. The early part of his career was apparently spent in administrative work in Cambridgeshire and Huntingdonshire, under Hatfield. The latter was sheriff of the two counties from 1224 to 1232; by 1231, and probably earlier, Jeremy was serving him as clerk or under-sheriff, and succeeded him as sheriff in 1232. He remained in office until 1236, although from later in 1232 until his fall in 1234 the titular sheriff was Peter de Rivaux, who held the same position in many other counties. After leaving office Caxton served as keeper of the temporalities of the bishopric of Norwich from 1237 to 1239, as well as performing other duties for the king, and then in 1240 served as a junior justice on the Norfolk eyre under William of York, Henry of Bath, and Roger of Thinkleby. Later that year he made an exhaustive inquiry into the chattels and debts of Jews in many counties in eastern England, before becoming a justice in the court *coram rege* early in 1241, possibly because of the ill health of Stephen of Segrave, who may have chosen him, since his interests in Cambridgeshire and Huntingdonshire probably meant that Caxton was known to him.

Despite minimal previous judicial experience, Caxton

continued as a justice there until his death, as one of the most senior judges in England, and with only a few short absences to undertake other government work. The latter included the keepership of the archbishopric of Canterbury, further Jewish and some forest inquiries, and some assize commissions, mainly in Cambridgeshire and Huntingdonshire. William of York and later Henry of Bracton and Henry de la Mare were his regular colleagues in the court, and he also held a London eyre in 1244 with York and Bath. An ordained clerk, the benefices he is known to have held were the Ramsey Abbey living of Warboys in Huntingdonshire, which he acquired in 1237; East Dereham in Norfolk, a rich living of the bishopric of Ely, which he held by 1245; and Godmersham in Kent, a church of Christchurch Priory, received in 1241. He is not known to have had any higher ecclesiastical ambitions, nor indeed to have attempted to acquire more extensive estates. He died in late November or early December 1249. In his obituary Matthew Paris described him as 'the king's special counsellor' (Paris, 5.94), but significantly did not credit him with being especially learned in the law, as he did several other senior judges. DAVID CROOK

Sources C. A. F. Meekings, *King's bench justices, 1239–58* [forthcoming] · Paris, *Chron.*, 5.85, 94 · H. M. Cam, 'Cambridgeshire sheriffs in the thirteenth century', *Liberties and communities in medieval England*, 2nd edn (1963), 36–7 · plea rolls, PRO, KB 26, JUST1 · lord treasurer's remembrancer pipe rolls, PRO, E372 · court of common pleas, feet of fines, PRO, CP 25/1 · *Chancery records* · *Curia regis rolls preserved in the Public Record Office* (1922–), vol. 8, p. 51

Caxton, William (1415×24–1492), printer, merchant, and diplomat, was the first Englishman to print books, bringing the printing press to England in 1475 or 1476.

Early years Nothing is known of Caxton's family or his place of birth. He was born in the weald of Kent; all suggestions identifying the actual place lack conviction. His parents sent him to school, where he may have learned Latin and rhetoric. He cannot have been highly educated, for he was apprenticed to Robert Large in London and his apprenticeship should have commenced when he was fourteen. The payment for his entry as an apprentice in the Mercers' Company is entered in their wardens' account book in 1438. This merely records when the payment was made, but many masters paid the fee late. This payment provides the sole basis for calculating his date of birth, which was between 1415 and 1424, possibly in the latter half of that period.

The mercers dealt in haberdashery, cloth, and luxury wares like silks. As the principal guild involved in trade with the Low Countries, the mercers formed the backbone of the Merchant Adventurers' Company, that loose association of merchants involved in the import–export trade. Mercers' Hall acted as its headquarters. Large, a prominent mercer, became successively a warden of the company in 1427, a sheriff of the City of London in 1430, and lord mayor in 1439. Caxton's father may have been a prosperous merchant, since it cannot have been easy to apprentice a son to an important man like Large. As an apprentice mercer he would learn how to handle money,

conduct negotiations, and mix with different people, including some from overseas.

By becoming a mercer Caxton was drawn into the overseas trade; and by being apprenticed to Large he became informed about and possibly involved in contemporary politics. The mercers provided finance for the government and the merchant adventurers were involved in politics concerning England, France, and Flanders (then part of the duchy of Burgundy). The dukes of Burgundy were among the richest and most fashionable aristocrats of the time; the source of their wealth and the centre of their operations lay increasingly in the Low Countries, where the cloth trade was fundamental to their financial well-being.

Caxton was still an apprentice in 1441 when Large died. Large's will, dated 11 April 1441, bequeathed Caxton 20 marks; as some apprentices received larger sums, Caxton may not have been a senior apprentice. The date of his issue from apprenticeship is uncertain, but was probably in the mid-1440s. He was involved in the overseas trade not long afterwards, for a document in Bruges from January 1450 records him acting as surety to a merchant of the staple. He was by this time of sufficient standing to act as surety to another merchant, and he was either living in Bruges or a regular visitor there. During the 1450s he took the livery of the Mercers' Company, though the records do not detail this process clearly. In 1453 a quitclaim in the close rolls records that he put all his goods in the hands of two merchants, and this may indicate that from then onwards his main home was in Bruges. At this period he would have learned to speak French and Dutch.

Established merchant and politician This quitclaim gave rise to lawsuits in 1454 and 1455, which involved dealings in pewter, wool, and cloth organized by Caxton in Ghent. By now he spent most of his time in the Low Countries and his business had expanded to embrace a variety of goods. Two documents in the 1450s record that a William Caxton was given a safe conduct to participate in Anglo-Burgundian negotiations in Bruges; if not our Caxton, they refer to the type of negotiations he was later to be involved in.

In the 1460s Caxton was permanently settled in Bruges and had become a respected and influential merchant. By April 1465 he was governor of the English nation in Bruges. All merchants in the Low Countries were organized into national fraternities under a governor who disciplined the members, negotiated with the local authorities on their behalf, and acted as the agent for their own government when required. That Caxton became governor in the 1460s reveals not only his wealth, skill as negotiator, and familiarity with affairs in the Low Countries, but also the confidence his fellow merchants had in him. Caxton was in regular communication with the merchant adventurers in London, and the period of his governorship was marked by delicate relations between England and Burgundy.

In 1463 trade relations between England and Burgundy deteriorated and a restriction on the sale of English cloth in the lands of the duke of Burgundy was imposed. So in

1464 the English merchants left Flanders and settled in Utrecht. Caxton may already have been governor at this time since he is referred to by name in the Dutch documents which gave the English merchants permission to trade there. While the English merchants traded from Utrecht, Caxton returned to Bruges to negotiate the end of the ban. A new treaty with Burgundy was finally agreed in 1467 and this was strengthened by the marriage of Charles, duke of Burgundy, to Margaret, the sister of Edward IV of England, in 1468.

Meanwhile, in England, partly to please the English merchants in London, Edward IV had taken discriminatory action against the Hanseatic merchants and this led to a breakdown in relations between England and the Hanse. Caxton was involved in the negotiations to restore commercial relations between them. The political situation became complicated when the earl of Warwick's rebellion led to the deposition of Edward IV and the reinstatement of Henry VI. In due course Edward IV fled to the Low Countries where he received support from Charles of Burgundy. By patching up his dispute with the Hanse, Edward was able in 1471 to return to England in Hanse ships and to regain his throne.

The last reference to Caxton as governor is from 1470. Presumably he gave up the governorship in that year, for in 1471 he went to Cologne. He remained a mercer and merchant adventurer, but he had decided to extend his business by dealing in printed books. He may already have traded in manuscripts, for English merchants shipped many manuscripts to London from Flanders, an important centre for the production of luxury manuscripts. It was this business which might have encouraged him to go into printed books.

Acquiring the printing press The register of aliens at Cologne records that William Caxton from England was given permission to reside there from 17 July 1471 until December 1472. Caxton himself, in his *History of Troy*, says that he had translated this book from French in Bruges, Ghent, and Cologne, where the translation was finished. Two conclusions arise from these facts: first, Caxton went to Cologne to acquire a printing press and the expertise to run a publishing business, and second, he embarked on the translation to provide material to be printed. The *History of Troy* was to become the first book printed in English. Caxton had decided on a publishing policy before he acquired a printing press, and set about the provision of appropriate material to achieve this policy. Everything that is known suggests that Caxton had done no translation before this one.

Some matters of dispute remain. In his prologue to the *History of Troy* Caxton dedicates the book to Margaret of Burgundy and refers to himself as 'her servant'. Some have taken this to mean that he left the governorship of the English nation to enter Margaret's employment as secretary or librarian. This is improbable since merchants did not act in such a capacity, and 'servant' here implies no more than general deference. He also notes that he had started the translation but, after completing a few quires, had put the work aside in despair. Two years later he had

shown this work to Margaret, who both approved the quality of the translation and commanded him to finish it. To some this has suggested that Margaret was the originator and patron of the project. But the acquisition of the printing press and the provision of translations show that Caxton had devised a strategy for the new venture. What may have interrupted the translation was the deposition of Edward IV and the resulting political uncertainty which this created in England. If the new venture was to succeed, books would have to be sold in England, for few on the continent were interested in buying books in English. Caxton's strategy involved selling printed books in English to people in England. In order to make these books attractive he would make translations of French texts which were fashionable in Flanders, and copies of many of the books he translated were found in the library of the duke of Burgundy. By issuing books in English he could achieve a monopoly of what was sold, for no one else provided this material; and by translating books popular in Flanders, he could appeal to the snobbery of English buyers who wanted to keep up with Burgundian fashion.

The acquisition of material would be no problem, since manuscripts of French texts were produced in abundance in Flanders, and Caxton knew scribes and booksellers there who supplied the ducal court and others with this kind of reading matter. What he needed were stable political conditions in England (which were re-established with the return of Edward IV) and a supply of English translations made by someone whose work was approved by the fashionable. Caxton could not get anyone to make the translations because the translator had to have recognized status. He decided to make the translations himself and to seek the support of someone influential. By writing that Margaret had approved the translation and commanded him to finish it, he was able to claim that his work carried the approval of the most fashionable Englishwoman of the time. No one would be able to call his style into question with that support. This story underlines Caxton's competence at marketing, for it is designed as an advertisement for his edition.

Printing had reached Cologne in 1464 and printed books from that city soon travelled down the Rhine to Flanders. Cologne was the Hanseatic town with the closest links to England and it had helped to settle the Hanse's dispute with Edward IV. Caxton may have had dealings with Cologne in his role as governor. It may be assumed that he had made arrangements with printers in Cologne to acquire a press before he went there, for when he arrived he entered into a partnership with Johannes Veldener, a printer and typecutter. Veldener was able to use the new capital that Caxton brought with him to print much larger volumes than before. Possibly the first book with which Caxton was associated as a co-publisher was Veldener's edition of Bartholomaeus Anglicus's *De proprietatibus rerum* (c.1472), for Wynkyn de Worde (d. 1535) mentions later that Caxton had learned printing in Cologne on this book. Caxton would have learned the art of printing and acquired a press, type, and men to run a workshop. But he should not be thought of as merely a printer; rather, he was a publisher who controlled the presses which produced his books. Wynkyn de Worde, Caxton's foreman in England, may have entered Caxton's employ in Cologne, for he was a German and knew about Caxton's work there.

At the end of 1472 Caxton returned to Bruges and was accompanied by Veldener and probably by de Worde. He set up his press and started to print the *History of Troy*. Veldener's hand has been detected in the initial compositorial work, but he left during the printing to move to Louvain. He did, however, continue to provide Caxton with new type. The *History of Troy* was finished in late 1473 or early 1474. It is a large work and would have taken time to complete. The finished books would be sent to England for sale. Caxton continued immediately with the printing of another of his translations, the *Game of Chess*, and that edition was completed on 31 March 1474.

When that was finished, there was a change in the material issuing from Caxton's press. The next four editions were all of French texts. This change may be explained by the difficulty Caxton found selling his books in England. To send a de luxe manuscript in French to be sold in London was one thing, but to dispose of two or three hundred copies of a printed edition in English was quite another. He may also have found it difficult to keep the press busy with translations in English, since he was himself the translator. He did not have sufficient time to make enough translations and yet he could not allow his men and presses to remain idle, because that would be expensive. He knew Flemish booksellers and scribes like Colard Mansion and he helped Mansion set up as a printer. He may have decided that as a temporary measure he would print and sell books in French, and this may have been done in partnership with Mansion. As a more permanent solution, he decided to return to England and set up his press there. In that way he could acquire material in English if he could not provide sufficient translated work and he could also oversee the sale of the books himself.

When Caxton returned to Bruges from Cologne, he did not cease to be a mercer or merchant adventurer. He was still engaged in diplomatic missions. In 1472 he received a full pardon from the king for any crimes committed until then. This may be merely a type of insurance to cover the period of political instability between 1470 and 1471 when Edward IV was deposed, but the implications of this pardon are not clear. After he had returned from Cologne, Caxton was employed by Edward in 1474 to negotiate with the Hanse, and in 1475 to provide the necessary shipping to transport the English army to the Low Countries. He also had some involvement in the provisioning of Calais at this time. He remained a trusted agent of the crown and a respected and influential person. He did not cease to enjoy the favour of those in power and he did not give up his merchant life to devote himself to books. Printing and publishing were an extension of his mercantile business; he was not a gentleman scholar–printer as some have portrayed him. Although an active and busy man, who would find it difficult to find time to make many translations, he

did not give up the printing and publishing venture. Unlike most printers of this time, he did not go bankrupt; he remained in business until he died. What he did do was adjust his strategy to conditions he encountered; and one of these adjustments involved a return to England.

Return to England and final years Probably in 1476, but possibly as early as 1475, Caxton brought his printing press to England. While an undated document, perhaps from early 1475, shows he was still abroad, the evidence of his printed output reveals he was established in England by the second half of 1476. He settled at Westminster rather than in London; he rented premises in Westminster Abbey at the sign of the Red Pale. Presumably he believed he could dispose of his books more easily from Westminster than from London; it was the home of the court and the administration. Many affluent and fashionable people came to Westminster and other tradesmen found them good customers for their wares.

The first book Caxton issued in England was the *editio princeps* of *The Canterbury Tales*. This was followed by a stream of printed material consisting of Caxton's own translations, works of English poets, English historical and chivalric prose, religious and didactic works, and a certain amount of jobbing printing which included material like indulgences. The bulk of this material was in English; work which was done to order might be in Latin. In England he published nothing in French. Over a hundred editions are attributed to Caxton, and some works were probably printed which have not survived. Lists of his editions are available in many sources. The various works he issued can be divided approximately as follows: eighteen he translated, printed, and published, though three works he translated he did not print; sixty-eight he printed and published, though these often included his own prologues and epilogues, and some were edited by Caxton; ten he printed; and a few texts printed abroad were published by him. The material he translated consists almost entirely of French works which had been written or printed recently in France or Flanders, for these could be presented as new and fashionable to his English buyers. The material he printed and published consisted of poetry in the Chaucerian style (rather than that in the alliterative style) and prose which was historical, religious, or chivalric, as well as works that had been translated by noblemen such as Anthony, Earl Rivers (*d.* 1483), the brother-in-law of Edward IV, or by clerics like John Trevisa (*d.* 1402).

Caxton continued to act as a merchant. He imported printed books from France and Flanders in bulk. He must have either sold these directly or passed them on to other booksellers. He had access to new foreign material from this extensive import business. As a bookseller many books and manuscripts passed through his shop. He sometimes experienced difficulty in acquiring a particular work, but probably much of what he printed came fortuitously to hand. If it was in his shop he might have chosen it to translate or print: what was important was that the text belonged to a certain type; it did not need to be a specific title. One ephemeral book could sell as well as another, provided it was new and fashionable. As a printer he accepted commissions to print documents and texts. Mostly these were small items like indulgences, though he did print works in Latin for authors like Guglielmo Traversagni or for those who wanted to use similar texts for pedagogical purposes. One or two books printed abroad were sold in England with his mark added to them, as though he had commissioned their printing.

Caxton continued to undertake commissions for the king, but these became less frequent as he got older. He was married and had at least one daughter, Elizabeth; but who his wife was and when his daughter was born are unknown. He participated in the life of the community and was a member of a fraternity in his local church, St Margaret's, Westminster. It is the churchwardens' accounts from St Margaret's which record his death, at Westminster Abbey. His burial is listed in the accounts for May 1491 to June 1492. From the position of the entry it is calculated that he died about March 1492. He left a will, but it is not extant. However, litigation arising from the will concerning his daughter Elizabeth and her husband, Gerard Crop, continued for several years after his death. Books bequeathed under his will to St Margaret's were still being disposed of in 1502.

The man and his work No authentic portrait of Caxton exists. What is known about the man and his character comes from his printed books. The documentary sources, which refer mainly to his early life, are formal and tell us nothing about him as an individual. They show him behaving as most merchants of his time did, for there is nothing in them to suggest that Caxton was any different from any other merchant. He was hard-working and ambitious. Few merchants of his time achieved as much as he did. He must have had stores of energy to accomplish what he did: he was sufficiently far-sighted to see the opportunities opened up by the printing press and sufficiently well-organized to plan and carry out the plans he devised. He was not put off by temporary set-backs, as when Edward IV lost his throne in 1470. It is important to see a continuity in his career. He may have been a part-time diplomat all his life, an accomplishment which was very important in cultivating the great and the good who might buy or commission his publications, but he was essentially a man who bought and sold goods for his livelihood. Printed books were simply a different type of merchandise from that which he had sold in his earlier career.

It is possible that Caxton suffered from a feeling of inferiority in his career. He was born in the weald in Kent, where people spoke an English which was not fashionable in contemporary London. He went to school locally and did not reach London until he was probably about fourteen. He may have felt like a country boy in comparison with those of metropolitan origins. He became a successful businessman, but started to meet members of the aristocracy only after his elevation to the governorship in Bruges. When he returned to Westminster he was on the fringes of court life. He was not a learned man, but he published the writings of those he regarded as great authors.

Throughout his work there is an element of fawning, both to the patrons whose names he used to sell his books and to authors he regarded as great creative artists. Some of this was required for his advertising; but it remains possible that though a successful entrepreneur he felt under the shadow of the nobility and recognized authors all his life.

Caxton certainly appreciated the importance of marketing. His prologues and epilogues are 'blurbs' intended to make his books attractive to potential customers. He cultivated the important people of his period, for they were able to influence the taste of others. Since much of the material he printed was ephemeral and fashionable, it was important that people should be encouraged to buy it in order to be seen to be in fashion. Patrons and patronage were essential for marketing purposes. His books had to be in a style which was acceptable to his buyers. The fifteenth century saw the acceptance of English as the major language in England, but its assumed poverty was such that it needed to be enriched in vocabulary and syntax from French and Latin. Hence Caxton imitated other translators of his time in keeping as close as possible to the original. He translated word for word rather than by sense, for in this way he could transfer the language of his source into his translation. He embellished his sources by creating doublets, consisting usually of the French word and an English word of similar meaning.

The question whether Caxton led or followed the taste of his time is irrelevant, because he was of his time and was influenced by prevailing attitudes. He introduced new material, but that material hardly deviated from what was typically being produced then. He was not a learned man, in that he may have learned some Latin at school and picked up French and Dutch. He was no scholar and his interest in literature was probably superficial and influenced by the prevailing taste. He did not seek learned works in Latin or English; he did not publish the writings of the English mystics or more technical works. He was not affected by the new humanism which was then sweeping through Europe. He was, however, a religious man of a traditional faith and there is no intimation that he was affected either by anti-clerical feeling or by Lollardy. In his translations he included stories of his visits to shrines and details of his religious reading. He was a man of the late medieval period, not of the Renaissance. His introduction of the printing press to England kept the old culture alive; it was not used in the service of the new learning.

N. F. BLAKE

Sources N. F. Blake, *Caxton and his world* (1969) · G. D. Painter, *William Caxton: a quincentenary biography of England's first printer* (1976) · L. Hellinga, *Caxton in focus* (1982) · W. J. B. Crotch, *The prologues and epilogues of William Caxton*, EETS, original ser., 176 (1928) · H. M. Nixon, 'Caxton, his contemporaries and successors in the book trade from Westminster documents', *The Library*, 5th ser., 31 (1976), 305–26 · L. Hellinga and W. Hellinga, 'Caxton in the Low Countries', *Journal of the Printing Historical Society*, 11 (1976–7), 19–32 · S. Corsten, 'Caxton in Cologne', *Journal of the Printing Historical Society*, 11 (1976–7), 1–18 · A. F. Sutton, 'Caxton was a mercer: his social milieu and friends', *England in the fifteenth century* [Harlaxton 1992], ed. N. Rogers (1994), 118–48 · N. F. Blake, *William Caxton* (1996), vol. 7 of *English writers of the late middle ages*, ed. M. C. Seymour (*c*.1996) · S. de Ricci, *A census of Caxtons* (1909) · N. F. Blake, *Caxton's own prose* (1973) · N. F. Blake, *Caxton: England's first publisher* (1976) · N. J. M. Kerling, 'Caxton and the trade in printed books', *Book Collector*, 4 (1955), 190–99 · P. Needham, *The printer and the pardoner* (1986) · L. Hellinga and H. Kelliher, 'The Malory manuscript and Caxton', *Aspects of Malory*, ed. D. S. Brewer and T. Takamiya (1981), 127–42 · L. A. Sheppard, 'A new light on Colard Mansion', *Signature*, 15, new ser. (1952), 28–39 · F. E. Penninger, *William Caxton* (1979) · E. G. Duff, *William Caxton* (1905) · W. Blades, *The life and typography of William Caxton, England's first printer, with evidence of his typographical connection with Colard Mansion, the printer at Bruges*, 2 vols. (1861–3) · N. Blake, *William Caxton and English literary culture* (1991) · C. E. Bühler, *William Caxton and his critics* (1960) · M. Kekewich, 'Edward IV, William Caxton and literary patronage in Yorkist England', *Modern Language Review*, 66 (1971), 481–7 · L. M. Matheson, 'Printer and scribe: Caxton, the *Polychronicon*, and the *Brut*', *Speculum*, 60 (1985), 593–614 · L. Lyell and F. D. Watney, eds., *Acts of court of the Mercers' Company, 1453–1527* (1936) · W. W. Stein, 'Die Merchant Adventurers in Utrecht', *Hansische Geschichtsblätter*, 9 (1899), 179–89 · M. R. Thielemans, *Bourgogne et Angleterre: relations politiques et économiques entre les Pays-Bas bourguignons et l'Angleterre, 1435–1467* (Brussels, 1966) · C. Ross, *Edward IV* (1974) · D. MacGibbon, *Elizabeth Woodville (1437–1492): her life and times* (1938) · M. J. Hughes, 'Margaret of York, duchess of Burgundy: diplomat, patroness, bibliophile and benefactress', *Private Library*, 3rd ser., 7 (1984), 3–17 · W. G. Hellinga and L. Hellinga, *The fifteenth-century printing types of the Low Countries*, 2 vols. (1966) · E. L. Eisenstein, *The printing press as an agent of change*, 2 vols. (1979) · E. G. Duff, *The printers, stationers, and bookbinders of London and Westminster in the fifteenth century* (1899) · J. Griffiths and D. A. Pearsall, *Book production and publishing in Britain, 1385–1475* (1989) · C. A. J. Armstrong, *England, France and Burgundy in the fifteenth century* (1983) · churchwardens' accounts, St Margaret's, Westminster

Archives city archives, Bruges · Historisches Archiv der Stadt Köln, Cologne · Mercers' Hall, London, acts of court of Mercers' Company and wardens' account book · Westminster Abbey Archives, London | GL, journal books of common council of city of London · PRO, close rolls, treaty rolls, patent rolls, warrants under the signet, early chancery proceedings, issue rolls of exchequer, treasury receipts, controlment rolls

Likenesses manuscript illumination, *c*.1475, Hunt. L.

Cay, Henry Boult (*d.* 1795). *See under* Cay, John (1700–1757).

Cay, John (1700–1757), legal writer, was the third son of John Cay of North Charlton, Northumberland, and his wife, Grace, daughter and coheir of Henry Wolff of Bridlington, Yorkshire. Intended for the legal profession, he was entered at Gray's Inn on 3 September 1719, called to the bar by that society on 20 June 1724, and subsequently made a bencher. In 1750 he was appointed steward and one of the judges of the Marshalsea. Cay married Sarah, daughter of Henry Boult of Gray's Inn; they had a son, Henry [*see below*], and two daughters.

Cay, as a classical antiquary, was admitted in August 1736 to the Society of Antiquaries. Together with his brother Robert, a merchant at Newcastle upon Tyne, who died on 22 April 1754, he was the friend and correspondent of John Horsley, the Northumberland archaeologist and antiquary. Following Horsley's death in January 1732, the brothers were indefatigable in their endeavours to promote the sale and collect the proceeds of *Britannia Romana* for Mrs Horsley's benefit. Cay died at his house in Essex Street, Strand, London, on 11 April 1757.

In the year following Cay's death there appeared his edition of *The Statutes at Large, from Magna Charta to the 30th Geo. II* (6 vols., 1758). This edition, which was justly praised for its learning and accuracy, was continued in three further volumes by Owen Ruffhead to 13 Geo. III (1769–73). Cay had previously published *Abridgment of the Publick Statutes, in Force and Use, from Magna Charta to the 11th Geo. II* (2 vols., 1739), which was continued in supplements by his son, Henry Boult Cay. In 1762 a second edition in two volumes was published, and in 1766 a supplemental volume, containing the statutes from 11 Geo. II to 1 Geo. III. Cay's *Abridgment* used to be continued by the abstracts of acts to 35 Geo. III, after which period they were not printed.

Henry Boult Cay (*d.* 1795), barrister, who completed his father's labours, was educated at Clare College, Cambridge, where he graduated BA in 1752 as second wrangler. He obtained a fellowship at Clare, which he vacated on his marriage, in August 1770, to Miss Stawel Piggot of Bassingbourn, Cambridgeshire. They had two daughters. Called to the bar at the Middle Temple, he afterwards filled several minor legal offices, and died at his residence in Cursitor Street, London, on 24 January 1795. His eldest daughter married the Revd William Adams, master of Pembroke College, Oxford, and friend of Dr Johnson.

GORDON GOODWIN, rev. ROBERT BROWN

Sources J. Foster, *The register of admissions to Gray's Inn, 1521–1889, together with the register of marriages in Gray's Inn chapel, 1695–1754* (privately printed, London, 1889) · J. Hodgson, *A history of Northumberland*, 3 pts in 7 vols. (1820–58) · Burke, *Gen. GB* (1858) · *GM*, 1st ser., 20 (1750), 429 · *GM*, 1st ser., 24 (1754), 243 · *GM*, 1st ser., 27 (1757), 189 · *GM*, 1st ser., 40 (1770), 392 · *GM*, 1st ser., 65 (1795), 171 · *GM*, 1st ser., 66 (1796), 166 · *The family memoirs of the Rev. William Stukeley*, ed. W. C. Lukis, 3 vols., SurtS, 73, 76, 80 (1882–7) · J. G. Marvin, *Legal bibliography, or, A thesaurus of American, English, Irish and Scotch law books* (1847) · W. Hutchinson, *A view of Northumberland*, 2 vols. (1776–8) · M. Lobban, *The common law and English jurisprudence, 1760–1850* (1991)

Archives St John's College, Oxford, business account book | BL, printed copy of a judgment by Henry Rolle with his MS notes and additions

Cayley, Arthur (1776–1848), biographer, was the son of Arthur Cayley and his wife, Anne Eleanor Shultz, and nephew of Sir George *Cayley, bt, of Brompton, Yorkshire. He was educated at Mr Robert's school, Wandsworth, then entered Trinity College, Cambridge, in 1792, where he received a scholarship in 1794 and graduated BA in 1796 as fourth wrangler. He was said to have been refused a fellowship on account of his political opinions. When the *Anti-Jacobin Review* was started in 1798, Cayley became an occasional contributor. He took orders in 1813, and in 1814 was presented to the rectory of Normanby, Yorkshire. He married Lucy, eldest daughter of his uncle, the Revd Digby Cayley, rector of Thormanby. Cayley wrote two works of historical biography: *The Life of Sir Walter Ralegh* (1805, 2nd edn, 1806), and *Memoirs of Sir Thomas More, with a new translation of his Utopia, also his History of King Richard III, and his Latin poems* (2 vols., 1808), neither of which was well regarded as a work of historical scholarship or biography. The work on More was particularly designed to reassert the integrity of the subject in reaction to Horace Walpole's *Historic Doubts* (1768). Cayley died at York on 22 April 1848, aged seventy-two.

GORDON GOODWIN, *rev.* MYFANWY LLOYD

Sources Venn, *Alum. Cant.* • [J. Watkins and F. Shoberl], *A biographical dictionary of the living authors of Great Britain and Ireland* (1816) • Allibone, *Dict.* • *A new biographical dictionary of 3000 cotemporary [sic] public characters, British and foreign, of all ranks and professions*, 2nd edn, 3 vols. in 6 pts (1825) • J. Foster, ed., *Pedigrees of the county families of Yorkshire*, 3 vols. (1874) • *GM*, 2nd ser., 30 (1848), 101

Cayley, Arthur (1821–1895), mathematician, was born on 16 August 1821 in Richmond, Surrey, the second son of five children of Henry Cayley (1768–1850), Russia merchant, and his wife, Maria Antonia Doughty (1794–1875). His parents lived in St Petersburg and Arthur was born on one of their summer visits to England. His grandfather John Cayley (1730–1795) served as consul-general in St Petersburg. Arthur Cayley was distantly related (fourth cousin) to Sir George Cayley FRS (1773–1857), inventor and aeronautical pioneer; his younger brother, Charles *Cayley (1823–1883), became a noted translator and scholar. The family returned to England permanently in 1828. Cayley's father, aged sixty, established himself at 29 York Terrace, Regent's Park, became a director of the London Assurance Corporation, and was active in the reorganization of the Baltic exchange.

Education and first mathematics After attending a private school at Blackheath, Cayley entered the senior department of King's College, London, at the unusually young age of fourteen. He consistently gained school prizes and in his final year won the chemistry prize in competition with specialist science students. He entered Trinity College, Cambridge, in October 1838 as a pensioner and continued his upward academic path by winning the college prizes. After the mathematical tripos examination in January 1842 he became senior wrangler and won a first Smith's prize, the result of a higher-level competitive examination taken by the most successful students in the tripos. He became a fellow of Trinity College the same year.

While an undergraduate Cayley published a paper on determinants, a subject connected with solving linear equations and one which was widely studied in the nineteenth century. Cayley introduced the array of coefficients within the now familiar vertical lines. His fresh choice of notation and his delight in coupling algebra with geometry indicates a rich vein in his work. Determinants became one of his favourite subjects and as a newly elected fellow of the Cambridge Philosophical Society he went on to describe *n*-dimensional determinants in a wide-ranging paper early in 1843. Although young, Cayley was familiar with the works of the European masters: Gabriel Cramer, Étienne Bezout, Pierre Simon Laplace, Augustin Cauchy, and his 'illustrious' Carl Gustav Jacob Jacobi.

In 1844 Cayley discovered the work of George Boole on linear transformations, and in correspondence with him made the first steps in what was to become his best-known contribution to mathematics—invariant theory,

Arthur Cayley (1821–1895), by Maull & Polyblank

as this subject became known in the 1850s. The general notion of an 'invariant' in mathematics is of a value or algebraic form dependent on variables subject to change but which itself does not change. For example, the area of a triangle in which a vertex is allowed to vary along a line parallel to its base is an invariant since it has the same value whatever the actual position of the vertex. Recognizing that a determinant was a special case of an invariant, Cayley introduced the term 'hyperdeterminant'. During the course of the nineteenth century there emerged two principal methods for generating invariants and it is significant that the seeds of both methods can be found in Cayley's early papers.

The year 1845 was an *annus mirabilis* in which Cayley published thirteen papers on a wide range of subjects. It was typical of his ability to recognize promising ideas that he was the first to write a paper on quaternions after their discovery by Sir William Rowan Hamilton in October 1843. Shortly afterwards, Cayley introduced the algebra of octonions as a generalization of quaternions. Invariant theory and quaternions became the two most intensively studied algebraic subjects in Britain during the second half of the century. Cayley made important contributions to each and was especially alive to the links between these two branches of mathematics.

In 1846 Cayley left Trinity College and entered Lincoln's

Inn as a pupil of the celebrated conveyancing counsel Jonathan Henry Christie. He was called to the bar on 3 May 1849. During this period he maintained his research in mathematics and met his lifelong friend James Joseph Sylvester, who was also studying for the bar. In 1850 Cayley's father died, leaving him effectively head of the family. His brother lost money through financial speculation and his sisters, Sophia and Henrietta Caroline, were (and remained) unmarried. On 3 June 1852 Cayley was elected to the Royal Society and after only one year was proposed for a royal medal. Charles Darwin won one that year, but Cayley was awarded the medal in 1859.

From his days as a young fellow of Trinity College, Cayley had published regularly in the continental publications *Journal des Mathématiques Pures et Appliquées* and *Journal für die Reine und Angewandte Mathematik*. He performed the invaluable service of summarizing achievements of continental mathematicians by publishing extracts in the *Cambridge Mathematical Journal* and other English journals. In this vein he outlined the theory of groups instigated by Évariste Galois about 1830 and, in a paper published in 1854, generalized it in the context of the calculus of operations. Cayley also published a major memoir on matrices in 1858. In this theory arrays of quantities called matrices are treated as single entities and the subject later became pivotal in the mathematics of the twentieth century. Other mathematicians had recognized that matrices were important, but Cayley felt the impetus to draw together the main ideas from which the theory could advance. He also discovered, independently of Hamilton, the striking theorem in the theory of matrices now known as the Cayley–Hamilton theorem.

Cayley's already wide knowledge of mathematics was matched by research qualities rarely found in one person. Apart from a sure grasp of algebraic principles and a refined geometrical intuition he was naturally inclined to the calculatory side of mathematics. This found expression in much of his algebra but especially in combinatorial mathematics (the subject then called 'tactic'). He showed great facility for dealing with generating functions and his expertise found applications in counting graphical structures. In the 1870s he applied these techniques to the enumeration of carbon/hydrogen molecules, results which were of considerable interest to chemists of that time. This same expertise in dealing with generating functions was fully utilized in invariant theory.

Work on invariant theory, 1850–1880 At the beginning of the 1850s Cayley entered a period of rich creativity. He had met Sylvester, and the two young mathematicians, in collaboration and in competition with each other, worked to establish invariant theory as a recognizable field of study. Cayley reworked his earlier ideas on hyperdeterminants and formalized the theory. In this, he focused on an invariant (the term replacing his earlier 'hyperdeterminant') and the more general notion of a covariant of a binary form (an algebraic form with two variables). He approached the subject through the study of differential operators in which he regarded invariants and covariants as those algebraic forms which were reduced to zero (annihilated) by two specific differential operators. The first paper read to the Royal Society on his assuming membership was an introductory memoir on quantics ('First memoir'). By introducing the term 'quantic', Cayley signalled his intention of formulating the theory afresh, synthesizing earlier results and promoting a new technical vocabulary. Some of the fanciful linguistic constructs employed by Cayley met with resistance from co-workers and have since passed into oblivion but others (for example, Sylvester's Hessian, Jacobian, invariant, covariant, annihilator) became established modern mathematical usage.

From 1854 to 1878 Cayley published a path-breaking series of memoirs on quantics in which he remodelled and extended his earlier work. He, Sylvester, and George Salmon from Dublin were dubbed the 'Invariant Trinity' by the mathematical community. In the period 1850–54, mathematicians from France, Italy, and Germany joined the study of invariant theory and an extensive body of knowledge soon developed.

Cayley's 'Second memoir' (1856) contained the algorithm by which invariants and covariants can be calculated. It is central to invariant theory and in subsequent memoirs Cayley put it to work in establishing miscellaneous results for binary forms. The importance of the 'Sixth memoir', published in 1859, overshadowed the computational gains of these earlier memoirs. In this paper he defined a notion of distance in projective geometry in terms of an absolute conic. This was a brilliant observation since projective geometry is a subject ostensibly free of metrical considerations such as size of angle and distance between points. Cayley's definition was later used as the basis for Felix Klein's schema for organizing non-Euclidean geometry (1872). Writing in 1859, Cayley had not realized the connection between the absolute and non-Euclidean geometry.

Marriage, teaching, and research In 1857 Cayley became a fellow of the Royal Astronomical Society. He was a council member for thirty-five years and editor of the *Monthly Notices*, 1859–81, except during 1872–4 when he served as president. Cayley specialized in mathematical astronomy and carried out research in lunar studies, a dominant subject of research in the 1860s. One of his most notable pieces of work was verifying a controversial conclusion reached by John Couch Adams on the secular acceleration of the moon's mean motion. Typically, the confirmation of Adams's work came at the end of extensive algebraic calculations.

Like many of his generation from Oxford and Cambridge, Cayley was a keen alpinist and member of the Alpine Club. Occasionally his love of mountaineering and hillwalking found expression in papers on topological ideas.

By the mid-1850s Cayley's natural inclination was for a life in academe. He was a successful conveyancing barrister but he made no attempt to establish a large legal practice. Suitable positions in higher education were few in the middle years of the century. He unsuccessfully applied for the Lowndean chair at Cambridge and the chair of natural philosophy at Aberdeen, and suffered other disappointments before, on 10 June 1863, he was elected first Sadleirian professor at Cambridge. On 8 September 1863 Cayley married Susan Moline (c.1831–1923). They had two children, Henry (1870–1949) and Mary (1872–1950). Henry Cayley studied mathematics at Cambridge (twenty-fourth wrangler in 1890), but he felt in the shadow of his father and turned from mathematics to become an architect. Both Henry and Mary Cayley died childless.

In 1868 Cayley was surprised to learn that the German mathematician Paul Gordan had proved that all binary quantics admit a finite system of covariants. This contradicted Cayley's earlier work published in his 'Second memoir'. The German school had developed a powerful calculus based on one of Cayley's earlier discarded methods. Their calculus was expressed in a succinct notation but it is notable that Cayley did not switch to the new method despite its success. In the light of Gordan's results Cayley completed his work on the binary quintic polynomial using his own methods and published it in the 'Ninth memoir' (1871).

In 1876 Cayley published his only book: *A Treatise on Elliptic Functions* (2nd edn, 1895). Sylvester had been appointed to the Johns Hopkins University in the same year and Cayley visited him there for six months in 1882. On his return he was awarded the Royal Society's Copley medal. For virtually all his life, Cayley had been England's leading pure mathematician. In 1883 he was president of the British Association for the Advancement of Science. Against the trend of popular lectures for such meetings, Cayley delivered an address in the 'severely scientific class' (Forsyth, xxi), and, with his encyclopaedic knowledge of mathematics, surveyed the mathematical accomplishments of the period.

During Cayley's years at Cambridge his influence was limited by the overbearing dominance in the examination system of the mathematical tripos. Student success depended on being well drilled in examination skills, and undergraduates perceived no need to learn mathematics which was not part of the curriculum. Cayley's lectures were few in number and sparsely attended, but several of the best British mathematicians were influenced by him. William Kingdon Clifford made a special study of Cayley's topics, and James Whitbread Lee Glaisher, son of the celebrated balloonist and a specialist in number theory and elliptic functions, was a protégé. J. J. Thomson, discoverer of the electron, remembered attending one of Cayley's lectures where the audience of three sat round a table and his lot was to follow Cayley's algebraic manipulations upside down. Andrew Russell Forsyth (1858–1942) was perhaps the student whose mathematical interests coincided most with Cayley's. He became adept at the manipulations and expertise in invariant theory and adopted Cayley's particular approach to the subject. He succeeded Cayley as second Sadleirian professor in 1895.

Cayley's view on the beauty of mathematics permeated all his thinking. He never relinquished his appreciation of Descartes and his introduction of co-ordinates. His admiration of Euclid, and in particular Euclid's *Elements*, Book 5 (on the theory of proportion), was unbounded, but his conviction that Euclid should be studied undiluted hindered the reform of geometrical teaching in England.

Cayley continued mathematical production during his last years. Postgraduate research began too late for him to found a school of mathematics as might have been expected of the doyen of British pure mathematics. Cayley was Britain's outstanding pure mathematician of the nineteenth century. An algebraist, analyst, and geometer, he was able to link these vast domains of study. More than fifty concepts and theorems of mathematics bear his name. By the end of his life he was revered by mathematicians the world over. He had published almost one thousand mathematical papers. Shoals of academic honours came his way. In addition to the Copley medal (1882) he was awarded the honorary degree of ScD at Cambridge (1887) and made a member of the French Légion d'honneur. He died at his home, Garden House, Cambridge, on 26 January 1895. He was buried on 2 February 1895 in Mill Road cemetery, Cambridge, but the headstone has not survived.

A. J. Crilly

Sources A. R. F. [A. R. Forsyth], *PRS*, 58 (1895), i–xliv · J. D. North, 'Cayley, Arthur', *DSB* · *The collected mathematical papers of Arthur Cayley*, ed. A. Cayley and A. R. Forsyth, 14 vols. (1889–98) · G. Salmon, 'Science worthies: Arthur Cayley', *Nature*, 28 (1883), 481–5 · T. Crilly, 'The rise of Cayley's invariant theory, 1841–62', *Historia Mathematica*, 13 (1986), 241–54 · T. Crilly, 'The decline of Cayley's invariant theory, 1863–95', *Historia Mathematica*, 15 (1988), 332–47 · K. H. Parshall, 'Towards a history of nineteenth-century invariant theory', *The history of modern mathematics*, ed. D. E. Rowe and J. McCleary, 1: *Ideas and their reception* (1989), 157–206, esp. 162–170 · J. Foster, ed., *Pedigrees of the county families of Yorkshire*, 3 (1874) · A. Macfarlane, *Lectures on ten British mathematicians of the nineteenth century* (1916) · C. A. Bristed, *Five years in an English university*, 2 vols. (1852) · C. B. Boyer, *History of analytical geometry* (1956) · S. Rothblatt, *The revolution of the dons: Cambridge and society in Victorian England* (1968) · *The Times* (28 Jan 1895) · *Manchester Guardian* (6 Feb 1895) · *Cambridge Review* (7 Feb 1895) · m. cert. · d. cert. · CGPLA Eng. & Wales (1895)

Archives CUL, papers · U. Reading L., papers relating to Hansen's lunar theory | Col. U., D. E. Smith MSS · CUL, letters to Lord Kelvin · CUL, corresp. with George Stokes · RAS, letters to Royal Astronomical Society · RS, corresp. with Sir J. F. W. Herschel · St John Cam., corresp. with James Sylvester · Trinity Cam., Boole-Cayley MSS · UCL, letters to Thomas Hirst · University of Göttingen, Klein-Cayley MSS

Likenesses portrait, 1842 (*The senior wrangler*), repro. in V. A. Huber, *The English universities*, 3 vols. (1843) · L. Dickinson, oils, 1874, Trinity Cam. · W. H. Longmaid, oils, 1884, Trinity Cam. · Maull & Polyblank, photograph, NPG [*see illus.*] · H. Wiles, marble bust, Trinity Cam.; plaster model, Philosophical Library, Cambridge · photograph, Trinity Cam., Wren Library · portrait (of Cayley?), repro. in *Scripta Mathematica*, 6, 32–6 · three photographs, RS

Wealth at death £23,979 2s. 6d.: resworn probate, June 1895, CGPLA Eng. & Wales

Cayley, Charles Bagot (1823–1883), translator, was born on 9 July 1823 near St Petersburg in Russia, son of Henry Cayley (1768–1850), a merchant, and his wife, Maria Antonia Doughty (1794–1875). He was the younger brother of Arthur *Cayley (1821–1895), mathematician. From Mr Pollecary's school, Blackheath, Charles Cayley went to

Trinity College, Cambridge, graduating in 1845 with a BA in the classical tripos. He also studied at King's College, London, under Gabriele Rossetti, who introduced him to his adult children: Maria, Dante Gabriel, William, and Christina *Rossetti. Cayley became a lifelong Rossetti family friend. An accomplished linguist, he based himself mostly in the British Museum, near which he always lodged. His four-volume *terza rima* translation of Dante's *Divina commedia* was published in 1851–5. Once he had learned Hebrew, his *Metrical Translations of the Psalms* appeared in 1860. Cayley was, however, a lamentable poet and the verse in his *Psyche's Interludes*, privately published in 1857, is forced and crude. He also translated Petrarch, Aeschylus, and Homer.

His work largely long forgotten, Cayley has the rare distinction (a neat reversal of the more usual situation) of being a nineteenth-century man remembered primarily for his long connection with a famous woman. The mid-1860s found Cayley—bald-headed, pink-cheeked, likeable, myopic, and legendarily absent-minded—growing increasingly close to Christina Rossetti. She addressed him affectionately in an 1864 poem as 'blindest buzzard' and 'special mole'. When, eventually, marriage was shyly discussed, she reluctantly turned it down, explaining that her profound religious devotion made total commitment to an agnostic impossible. But their lasting close friendship sustained them both until he predeceased her. The enduring love of Cayley and Christina is obliquely portrayed in his *Poems and Translations* (1880); in her *Il rosegar* poems, written (in Italian) in 1862–8, but published posthumously; and her *Monna innominata* sonnet sequence (1882).

Cayley died from heart failure at 4 South Crescent, Bedford Square, London, on 6 December 1883 and was buried at Hastings on 11 December. Rather than attend the funeral, Christina made a solitary journey to his grave three weeks later. As literary executor, she raised about £5 from Cayley's various books and translations in 1884, but sales quickly dwindled and there were no reprints.

SUSAN ELKIN

Sources J. Marsh, *Christina Rossetti: a literary biography* (1994) · K. Jones, *Learning not to be first: the life of Christina Rossetti* (1991) · F. Thomas, *Christina Rossetti* (1992) · *The poetical works of Christina Georgina Rossetti*, ed. W. M. Rossetti (1904) · *DNB* · d. cert.

Archives BL | Bodl. Oxf., letters to Christina Rossetti [copies]

Likenesses photograph, 1866, repro. in W. M. Rossetti, ed., *The family letters of Christina Rossetti* (1908)

Wealth at death £2890 11s. 11d.: probate, 31 Jan 1884, *CGPLA Eng. & Wales*

Cayley, Cornelius (1727–1779), Methodist preacher and writer, was born in Brompton, Yorkshire, on 23 April 1727, the son of Simeon and Elizabeth Cayley. He was educated at a public school for about four years and, when nineteen, he became a clerk in the prince of Wales's treasury through Lord Scarbrough's influence. Hoping for promotion, he learned foreign languages, music, and dancing, and applied unsuccessfully to go as under-secretary to the ambassador to Paris. After this disappointment he attempted to indulge in the gaieties of London life, but his

Cornelius Cayley (1727–1779), by Isaac Taylor, pubd 1778 (after J. J. Swanfelder, 1778)

temperament, and the deaths of his brother and mother within four months of each other in 1751, led him to religious pursuits. He became acquainted with the devotional writer James Hervey and through Hervey's influence he visited the tabernacle in Moorfields, London, where he was, for a time, in constant attendance. In the summer of 1752 Cayley began preaching in London. He printed a little treatise entitled *The Doctrine of Jesus Christ* for presentation. He lived for a while in Lady Cornelia Piers's house at Mill Hill, where he preached to very select company. He usually spent his autumn vacations travelling through the west country and Wales, preaching wherever opportunity offered. Cayley kept his place at the treasury until 1757, when he resigned on being told to stop preaching. He thereafter devoted himself entirely to religious work and moved to Norwich, where he published an account of his life and conversion in 1757–8, and a *Letter* (1758) in response to the publication of an anti-Methodist sermon by Robert Potter, prebendary of Norwich. He composed a Christmas anthem that was frequently sung to a fine piece of cathedral music.

In 1761 Cayley left Norwich. There is little information on him from this point, even in the third, expanded edition of his *Life* (1778), which does, however, contain his portrait, possibly by one of the Van Loo family, drawn by J. J. Swanfelder and engraved by I. Taylor. Cayley published a number of translations and poems between 1762 and

1772, including *The Seraphical Young Shepherd* (1762) and *A Small Bunch of Violets* (1762), that were reprinted together several times. He wrote an account of his tour through Holland, Flanders, and France in 1772, which was first printed serially in the *Leeds Weekly Newspaper* and later appeared separately. On returning from his travels he went to his house in Sowgate, Kingston upon Hull. In 1775 his translation of Miguel Molinos's *Spiritual Guide* appeared.

Cayley died in Kingston upon Hull in 1779, and was probably buried in St Mary's Church there. He left his house and over £2500, largely inherited from his wife, who predeceased him, to their children: Elizabeth, Cornelius, William (a clerk), John, Edward, and George. *An Evangelical Dialogue between Cornelius Cayley and Echo* (1780), in verse, appeared posthumously, as did *A Meditation on the Motto of the Rev. Mr John Wesley's Seal* (1781). Cayley is supposed to have written a work entitled *The Mystery of the Two Adams*, though the manuscript has been lost.

J. H. THORPE, rev. ADAM JACOB LEVIN

Sources C. Cayley, *The riches of God's free grace displayed in the life and conversion of Cornelius Cayley*, 3rd edn (1778) · C. Cayley, *Tour through Holland, Flanders, and part of France*, 2nd edn (1777) · IGI · GM, 1st ser., 49 (1779), 615 · will, PRO, PROB 11/1060, sig. 468 · K. Rowe, *A Methodist union catalogue: pre-1976 imprints*, 2 (1976), 354–5

Likenesses I. Taylor, line engraving, pubd 1778 (after J. J. Swanfelder, 1778), BM, NPG [*see illus.*]

Wealth at death over £2500; plus property, jewellery, etc.: will, PRO, PROB 11/1060, sig. 468

Sir George Cayley, sixth baronet (1773–1857), by Henry Perronet Briggs, 1840

Cayley, Sir George, sixth baronet (1773–1857), aeronautical designer, was born on 27 December 1773 in Scarborough, Yorkshire, the only son of Sir Thomas Cayley (1732–1792), and his wife, Isabella Seton (*d.* 1828); there were also four daughters. After brief schooling in York he was educated privately by George *Walker FRS in Nottingham and George Cadogan Morgan in Southgate, Middlesex, two nonconformist ministers selected by his mother. He succeeded his father as baronet in 1792, and lived at Brompton Hall, between Pickering and Scarborough, throughout his life. On 9 July 1795 he married Sarah (*d.* 1854), the daughter of his first tutor, the Revd George Walker; they had three sons and seven daughters, of whom three children died young.

As a landowner, Cayley was actively interested in agricultural improvements, and in 1800 he took a leading part in obtaining an act of parliament for the Muston drainage scheme, covering 10,000 acres frequently flooded by the rivers Derwent and Hertford. He was chairman of the directors of the scheme, which was executed by the engineer William Chapman, who developed a novel system using drainage ditches parallel to the main river channels.

Throughout his life Cayley showed keen interest in science and engineering developments, particularly in aeronautics. As early as 1799 he formulated the concept of the classical fixed wing aeroplane with separate mechanisms for generating lift and propulsion, and soon afterwards began experiments with a whirling arm rig to measure the lift of wings. In 1809 he experimented with a glider capable of lifting a person, and he published a paper in

Nicholson's Journal (November 1809–March 1810) setting out clearly the basic principles of aeroplane flight. This paper was thought sufficiently perceptive and important to be reprinted in England in 1876, in France in 1877, and in the USA in 1895.

Cayley also experimented with lighter-than-air flight: he wrote three papers on airships in the *Philosophical Magazine* (February 1816–July 1817) of Alexander Tilloch, and in 1820 he successfully flew a model airship at Brompton. In a period when ballooning was an activity only for itinerant showmen, any interest in flying invited ridicule, but he made several unsuccessful attempts to form a society to encourage aeronautical developments. He continued to speculate on the subject, and wrote letters to various journals, but seems to have done little further practical work until 1849, when a glider large enough to carry a small child was launched in free flight at Brompton. This was followed by a full-sized machine, reputedly piloted by his coachman, in 1853. Although the evidence for these flights is little better than anecdotal, sufficient information is available in his published and private papers to make possible the construction of a reproduction of the latter machine, which was successfully flown for a television film in 1972.

The aeronautical pioneers in the nineteenth century were constrained by the lack of a lightweight power source. Cayley was convinced that the steam engine would never be suitable, and he experimented from 1799 with hot air engines, and from 1807 with engines fuelled by gunpowder. Nothing came of the latter, but about 1838 he demonstrated a fairly successful hot air engine in London, suitable for a road vehicle.

Letters published in *Mechanics' Magazine* from 1826 to 1856 attest to Cayley's interest in many technical topics, including a projected caterpillar tractor, the safety of railway travel, projectile design, and an artificial hand made for one of his tenants. Convinced that the general public had an unsatisfied thirst for knowledge, he took an active part in several educational activities. He was president of the York Mechanics' Institute from its foundation in 1827, and was a founder member of the Yorkshire and Scarborough philosophical societies, and of the British Association, which first met in York in 1831.

In London, Cayley supported the formation of the Adelaide Gallery at the Strand, where lectures and demonstrations and an exhibition of machines and models were intended to educate and amuse the public. When it appeared that the intent to educate had been overwhelmed by the need to amuse, Cayley became chairman of the Royal Polytechnic at Regent Street, which from 1838 sought to do what the Adelaide Gallery had failed to do.

From early youth Cayley was a keen proponent of parliamentary reform, and he took an active part in local whig politics. He became president of the York Whig Club from 1821 to 1827, and was MP for Scarborough from 1832 to 1834. Among a wide circle of friends and correspondents Cayley seems to have been recognized as a generous and modest man of great personal charm. He died at Brompton Hall on 15 December 1857, and was buried at Brompton church. He was succeeded in the baronetcy by his only surviving son, Digby (b. 1807).   JOHN A. BAGLEY

Sources J. L. Pritchard, *Sir George Cayley* (1961) · C. H. Gibbs-Smith, *Sir George Cayley's aerodynamics* (1962) · G. Fairlie and E. Cayley, *The life of a genius* (1965) · P. Brett, *The rise and fall of the York Whig Club* (1989) · *The Times* (18 Dec 1857) · *PICE*, 18 (1858–9), 203 · *Debrett's Peerage* (1828)
Archives N. Yorks. CRO · Royal Aeronautical Society, London, corresp. and papers
Likenesses H. P. Briggs, oils, 1840, NPG [*see illus.*] · J. J. Penstone, stipple, pubd 1843, NPG · photograph, 1844, Sci. Mus. · E. Anes, photograph, NPG · G. Hayter, group portrait, oils (*The House of Commons, 1833*), NPG · bronze bust, Royal Aeronautical Society, London

Cayley, George John (1826–1878), traveller and writer, was born on 26 January 1826, the second son of Edward Stillingfleet Cayley (1802–1862), politician and economist, and his wife, Emma (d. 1848), the second daughter of Sir George *Cayley, bt, the aeronautics pioneer. He was educated at Eton College, but left early. He matriculated at Trinity College, Cambridge, in 1845, and he won the chancellor's gold medal for his poem *The Death of Baldur* (1848), but he did not graduate. He entered the Inner Temple in 1848 and was called to the bar in 1852. In 1849–50 he published *Some Account of Sir Reginald Mohun, Bt*, a poem in three cantos.

An early interest in his grandfather's aviation experiments was not sustained, and poor health obliged Cayley to journey in Spain in 1851–2, partly in the company of his friend, the Hon. Henry Coke (1827–1916). He published his travels in *Bentley's Miscellany* (August–December 1852) as *The Saddlebags, or, The Bridle Roads of Spain*, which was incorporated into *Las alforjas* (2 vols., 1853). The book is little read nowadays, but, as it deals with incidents rather than set-piece descriptions, it is an attractive work. In the preface to a second, slightly shortened, edition, renamed *The Bridle Roads of Spain* (1856), Cayley addressed complaints that the book contained fictions by identifying them, saying he was following other authors and also demonstrating 'how a seed of suggestion, picked up by the way side, germinated in the note-book, and finally expanded in printed leaves of florid narrative'.

In 1854 Cayley was a correspondent for the *Daily News* in the Crimea, and afterwards travelled in the Near East. He unsuccessfully contested Scarborough as a Conservative in a December 1857 by-election and at the general elections of 1859, 1865, and 1868. This borough was not usually promising territory for his party at this time, but his derisory poll in the 1859 election, when he obtained a mere sixty-six votes, may have been due to his unorthodox views. He advocated expanding the money supply to finance trade and industry in *The Working Classes; their Interest in Administrative, Financial and Electoral Reform* (1858), and in this and another, anonymous, pamphlet—*Indignant Rhymes* by An Illused Candidate (1859)—proposed extending the franchise to skilled workers, with an earnings qualification to prevent corruption. In the same spirit *The Service and the Reward: a Memoir of the Late Robert Wilson Roberts, RN* (1858) castigated the Admiralty for what he considered a failure to promote on merit. Between 1858 and 1862 he contributed articles to *Fraser's Magazine* on travel and craftsmanship, and from February to July 1864 he edited the short-lived pro-Conservative weekly *The Realm*. He was a skilled amateur artist—both editions of his Spanish travels published in his lifetime contain engravings after his drawings. He was also an accomplished gold- and silversmith, undertaking commissions from his friends.

Cayley was bearded and fair-skinned. His bohemian appearance, craftsmanship, versifying, and independent attitudes caused him to be regarded as an eccentric. He was a cigarette smoker before the habit became fashionable and, according to Lady Ritchie, 'had a high, harsh voice, with a chord in it' (Ritchie and Sickert, 15). Henry Coke remembers him as an 'always lively, and sometimes brilliant' conversationalist (Coke, 70–71). He was very selective in his friends, who included Thackeray, Caroline Norton, Stirling-Maxwell, Monckton Milnes, Millais, and A. J. Munby. In Yorkshire he lived at the family home, Wydale, and in London at 11 Dean's Yard, Westminster.

In 1860 Cayley married Mary Anne Frances Wilmot (d. 1908), of Osmaston, Derby; their children were Hugh (1861–1924), Arthur, and Violet. Hugh's and Cayley's own poor health caused the family to live in Majorca in 1869–70 and then to settle in Algiers. Here Cayley played tennis, *jeu de paume*, as long as his health permitted, and wrote 'Lusio Pilaris and lawn tennis' (*Edinburgh Review*, January 1875). He was returning to Algiers when he died, after a long illness but nevertheless rather suddenly, when visiting at Hunton rectory, near Maidstone, Kent, on 11 October 1878. THOMAS BEAN

Sources A. E. Ritchie and Mrs C. Sickert, 'Recollections of George John Cayley', in G. J. Cayley, *The bridle roads of Spain* (1908) · Venn, *Alum. Cant.* · H. J. Coke, *Tracks of a rolling stone*, 2nd edn (1905) · Burke, *Peerage* · *Wellesley index* · D. Hudson, *Munby, man of two worlds: the life and diaries of Arthur J. Munby, 1828–1910* (1972) · J. L. Pritchard, *Sir George Cayley* (1961) · Boase, *Mod. Eng. biog.* · *McCalmont's parliamentary poll book: British election results 1832–1918*, ed. J. Vincent and M. Stenton, 8th edn (1971) · G. Cayley, *The service and the reward* (1858)

Archives Strathclyde Regional Archive, Glasgow, Stirling (Keir) MS · Trinity Cam., Houghton MS

Likenesses photograph, repro. in Cayley, *Bridle roads of Spain*, frontispiece

Wealth at death under £3000: probate, 28 Dec 1878, *CGPLA Eng. & Wales*

Cayowaroco (*fl.* 1595–1596). *See under* American Indians in England (*act. c.*1500–1609).

Cayzer family (*per.* 1843–1999), shipowners and businessmen, first came to prominence with **Sir Charles William Cayzer**, first baronet (1843–1916). He was born on 15 July 1843 at Featherstone Buildings, Limehouse, London, the only son and third child of Charles Cayzer, a schoolmaster, and his wife, Mary Elizabeth Nicklin. Adept at mathematics, he gained occasional employment in his early teens in shipping offices along the Thames. At fifteen he got a job as the master's clerk in a sailing ship on a voyage to Japan. He did not remain long at sea and in 1861 became a clerk in the Bombay office of William Nicol & Co., shipping agents and merchants. He could not have chosen to move to India at a better time as demand for cotton was booming, because supplies from the United States were disrupted by the outbreak of the civil war. The collapse of the boom at the end of the war provided a salutary lesson that Charles Cayzer remembered for the rest of his life. In 1868 he married Agnes Elizabeth, daughter of William Trickey of Clifton, Bristol, who was visiting Bombay on her uncle's ship. They had nine children: six sons and three daughters. The eldest son was **Sir Charles William Cayzer**, second baronet (1869–1917), who was born in Bombay on 19 July 1869. His younger brothers included **Sir August Bernard Tellefsen** [Gus] **Cayzer**, first baronet (1876–1943), known as Gus, who was born at 2 Pellatt Grove, Wood Green, London, on 21 January 1876; and also **Herbert Robin** [Bertie] **Cayzer**, first Baron Rotherwick (1881–1958), known as Bertie, who was born on 1 January 1881.

By the time of his marriage Charles Cayzer was acting as keeper of stores for William Mackinnon's British India line. Although his career with Nicol & Co. was flourishing, he left India in 1873 because of his concerns about the effects of the climate on the health of his wife and young family. Back home, he went to work for Gray, Dawes & Co., the British India's London agents which had been set up by Mackinnon. When Mackinnon refused him a partnership, he resigned, warning him that in twenty years he would have a larger fleet than British India. In 1876 he became a shipowner in his own right by buying the old

wooden barque *Jalawar* while he looked for ways to finance the building of new tonnage. His enquiries took him to Glasgow, where he found support from Alexander Stephen, the head of the shipbuilding firm which bore his name, and John Muir of James Finlay & Co., East India merchants, who would have been known to him through the Bombay chamber of commerce. They agreed to back him in establishing a shipping business to compete with British India on the understanding that Finlays would be appointed the Bombay agents. Two ships were laid down in Stephen's Linthouse yard, the first of the Clan Line, and, in the spring of 1878, the ship management firm of Cayzer, Irvine & Co., in partnership with Captain Alexander Irvine, who had worked for British India.

In sharp contrast to Cayzer's arrival in Bombay, there could not have been a less opportune time to set up a new Glasgow-based enterprise. In October 1878 the City of Glasgow Bank collapsed and brought down a number of businesses in the city with Indian connections. Worse still for Charles Cayzer, his partner Captain Irvine died suddenly in January 1879. With credit hard to come by, relations with Muir and Stephen became strained. However, Muir was impressed with Cayzer's skill as a ship manager in the very difficult trading conditions and in 1880 he persuaded the fabulously rich Thomas Coats, and James Arthur, a Glasgow warehouseman and merchant, to support the formation of the Clan Line Association Steamers. The association was to be separate from Cayzer's Clan Line, but was to own vessels to be managed by Cayzer, Irvine & Co. Arthur was keen that the enlarged line should extend its services to South Africa, challenging the dominance of the Union and Castle Lines. Muir, with an eye to Finlay's Indian interests, wanted the Bombay service to be extended to include Calcutta, Madras, and Colombo, from which the London-based Queen Line had recently withdrawn.

Although a keen competitor with other shipping enterprises, Cayzer from the outset took care to work within the framework of the shipping conferences (cartels) which fixed freight prices and rebates for established customers. Between 1884 and 1885 he devoted much time and energy to secure the agreement of the lines operating between the United Kingdom and Bombay, Calcutta, Colombo, Karachi, and Madras to the formation of the Eastern Steam Trading Conference. He was assiduous in his efforts to maintain an alliance between his line and the City, Hall, and Anchor lines to ensure that they effectively dominated the Indian cargo trade. As a new entrant, he exploited the conferences to allow him a larger stake in the various trades and in this way won access to the lucrative market for shipping tea. Such tactics earned him the reputation of a 'bulldog', to which he bore a distinct resemblance, who set his competitors fighting among themselves instead of turning on him. For all his skill as ship manager, his business was not very profitable until 1884 and even then £1 million was owing to the banks. After a further dispute with Muir over this indebtedness, Cayzer resolved to form a limited company to acquire the ships of the Clan Line. Named Clan Line Steamers Ltd, it was formed in the summer of 1890 with an issued capital of just over £200,000.

Cayzer was by now a rich man, renting the sumptuous Ralston House between Paisley and Glasgow and owning a substantial holiday villa on the Clyde at Cove in the burgh of Kilcreggan. As provost he brought all his entrepreneurial energies to bear on this tiny burgh to improve the amenities for visitors while at the same time putting its finances in order. In 1891 he was persuaded to stand for parliament as a Conservative for the Barrow in Furness constituency and in the election of the following year ousted the sitting Liberal MP J. A. Duncan. During the 1890s he developed his South African trades, opened new routes to the Persian Gulf and to the Malabar coast, and was one of the first shipowners to make use of the newly built Manchester Ship Canal. The success of these initiatives demanded an increase in tonnage, partly by ordering innovative 'turret' ships from William Doxford & Sons.

In 1897 Cayzer was knighted. Since Ralston was fast becoming engulfed by Glasgow's urban sprawl and he had less time or inclination to go to Cove, at the end of the century he purchased the Gartmore estate in Perthshire from the extraordinarily eccentric R. B. Cunningham Graham, known in South America as Don Roberto. Sir Charles at once set about restoring and enlarging the house and improving the surrounding estate. Not content just with this estate, in 1902 he bought 4000 acres (later doubled) in Newtyle, Forfarshire, from the earl of Wharncliffe and built himself Kinpurnie Castle on Kinpurnie Hill. In 1902 Florence, his second daughter, married Captain John Jellicoe, the future Earl Jellicoe, and two years later Constance, his third daughter, married Captain Charles Madden, later admiral of the fleet. Both naval sons-in-law were appointed to the Clan Line board. These alliances were to give the Cayzers unique access to British naval thinking during the First World War. At the turn of the century John Ellerman emerged as a powerful competitor, buying both the City and Hall lines. Cayzer was quick to recognize his talents and to build offensive and defensive alliances with him.

By now Sir Charles had to consider the problem of succession. His eldest son, Charles, had trained as a barrister, but never practised, preferring instead to write verse in the manner of Tennyson. In 1893 he married Annie Mabel, daughter of Thomas Jennings White. They had one son and four daughters. After a few years and against his father's better judgement Charles Cayzer went to work in Cayzer Irvine's Liverpool office, moving to take charge of the London office in 1906. By this time three of his other brothers, Herbert, August, and Arthur, had also joined the firm. Charles, the eldest son, was outspoken in suggesting that the head office should move from Glasgow to London. In 1910 this led to Sir Charles forcing his eldest son out of the firm. Having inherited his father's baronetcy, the younger Charles Cayzer died on 20 July 1917 at 22 Lewes Crescent, Brighton. His wife survived him.

Sir Charles had lost his parliamentary seat in 1906 and two of his sons died in the next three years. He felt these blows keenly and in 1912 Sir Charles put the Clan Line on the market and entertained an approach from Sir Owen Philipps (later Lord Kylsant). On learning this news his two sons, who remained in the firm, were horrified and nothing more was heard of the matter, but the following year another son, Major Harold Cayzer, retired from the army to work alongside them. On the outbreak of war in 1914 his sons were all mobilized, leaving Sir Charles in sole charge of the company. The strain soon began to tell and he died on 28 September 1916 at Gartmore, Perthshire. The terms of his will, revised a fortnight before he died, led to continuing family disagreement. A family trust was created charged with controlling 'the business for themselves and their descendants who may succeed them' (M. Davies, *A Victorian Shipowner*, 1978, 298). August and Herbert Cayzer, both of whom had been released from war service, took the reins as chairman and deputy chairman. Together they were responsible for deploying the resources of the Clan Line to defeat the German U-boat campaign and in successfully navigating the fleet through the troubled waters of the inter-war years.

For his public and national service August Cayzer was created a baronet in 1921. He had married on 28 April 1904 Ina Frances, second daughter of William Stancomb of Blunt's Court, Potterne, Wiltshire. They had three children, the eldest of whom was **(William) Nicholas Cayzer**, Baron Cayzer (1910–1999), who was born on 21 January 1910 at Mauchline in Ayrshire, and educated at Eton College and Corpus Christi College, Cambridge, where he read history. Herbert Cayzer, who was a fastidious dresser, married on 18 January 1911 Freda Penelope, daughter of Colonel W. H. Rathborne, the scion of a great Liverpool merchant family, with whom he had four children. He entered parliament in 1918 as Conservative member for Plymouth. Also created a baronet, in 1924, he served as chairman of the Commons committee on shipping from 1923 until his elevation to the peerage as Lord Rotherwick in 1939. It was later commented of him that 'He believed profoundly in the causes he advocated and could, and did, advance them with forcefulness, sometimes tinged with a little acidity' (*The Times*, 18 March 1958).

These were difficult years for the British shipping industry, with government support through a number of schemes; Kylsant's Royal Mail Group, because it had drawn on such incentives, was the subject of parliamentary scrutiny after its collapse. Sir August died on 28 February 1943 at Roffey Park, Lower Deeding, Horsham, Sussex. After his death, Herbert, Lord Rotherwick, became chairman of Clan Line and was assisted by his nephew, Nicholas Cayzer. On graduation in 1931 Nicholas had immediately joined the family business, becoming a director in 1938. He married Elizabeth Catherine, daughter of Owain William, on 29 July 1935. They had two daughters. On the declaration of war he joined the colours but was quickly recalled to employ his shipping knowledge in the battle of the Atlantic, particularly in Liverpool, the Clan Line's home port. On the death of his uncle Major Harold in 1948, he succeeded to the vice-chairmanship of the family business. With the coming of peace the Clan Line had continued to cling tenaciously to its share of the South African trade despite strong competition from a revitalized Union Castle Line, which had been rescued from the wreckage of the Royal Mail Group by Sir Vernon Thomson. After Sir Vernon's death in 1952, the fortunes of the line began to wane and Lord Rotherwick launched a bid in 1955 against Harley Drayton, one of the wiliest financiers of the time. Almost immediately he fell ill and Sir Nicholas was left in charge of negotiations which were successfully concluded in October, when it was announced that the shares in both firms would be vested in a new holding company, British and Commonwealth Shipping, of which Lord Rotherwick became chairman. Rotherwick died on 16 March 1958 at Sedgwick Park, Nuthurst, Horsham, Sussex. He was succeeded as chairman by Sir Nicholas.

A shrewd entrepreneur, Sir Nicholas Cayzer had already grasped the need to shift the family's assets away from shipping. Recognizing the significance of containerization, he entered into a very successful joint venture with Ocean Transport and Trading in Overseas Containers Ltd (OCL). Using Caledonian Investments, the family holding company and successor of the Clan Line, as a vehicle, he invested in a variety of enterprises which offered growth potential including British United Airways, a competitive independent airline, Bristow Helicopters, a major player in the North Sea oil industry, the private Wellington Hospital in London, and Gartmore, an investment management concern named after his grandfather's Perthshire estate. His greatest success was the diversification of British and Commonwealth, now abbreviated to B and C, into a number of broking and investment businesses including the money-brokers Exco, which was managed by John Gunn. After Exco's acquisition Gunn joined the B and C board, soon becoming chief executive. In the expectation that he would release potential from the group, the share price rose dramatically, bolstering the Cayzer family's wealth. John Gunn daringly embarked on an aggressive take-over strategy. His acquisitions included Atlantic Computers, a leasing company, for the then colossal sum of £417 million. Sir Nicholas took fright and with perfect timing sold the family stake in B and C for £428 million only three days before the stock market crash on 'Black Monday' in October 1987. It subsequently emerged that as a result of dubious financial reporting Atlantic Computers was worthless and its collapse in April 1990 focused attention on the whole of B and C. Despite a brave disposal programme, B and C went into receivership in 1991. In the following year Sir Nicholas bought back Exco from the liquidators of B and C for £20 million. He retired as chairman of Caledonian Investments in 1994 and became president of the company.

A supporter of right-wing pressure groups, such as the Economic League and the Centre for Policy Studies, Cayzer was ennobled by Margaret Thatcher in 1982 as Baron Cayzer, of St Mary Axe in the City of London, but played little direct part in political life. In retirement he remained an enthusiastic golfer and a keen shot. Cayzer

died on 16 April 1999 at the Wellington Hospital, 8A Wellington Place, Westminster, London. His death brought to an end a remarkable business dynasty, whose involvement with shipping interests created considerable family wealth.   MICHAEL S. MOSS

Sources *The Times* (19 April 1999) · *The Independent* (21 April 1999) · Burke, *Peerage* (2000) · *CGPLA Eng. & Wales* (1917); (1943); (1958) · b. certs. · m. certs. · d. certs.
Archives NRA, priv. coll., plans and game books
Wealth at death £11,248,275—Sir (William) Nicholas Cayzer: probate, 1 July 1999, *CGPLA Eng. & Wales* · £2,204,148 9s. 3d.—Sir Charles William Cayzer: probate, 24 Jan 1917, *CGPLA Eng. & Wales* · £1,946,676 11s. 7d.—Sir Charles William Cayzer: further grant · £483,971 14s. 9d.—Sir August Bernard Tellefsen Cayzer: probate, 1 Nov 1943, *CGPLA Eng. & Wales* · £636,924 8s. 11d.—Herbert Robin Cayzer, Baron Rotherwick: probate, 5 Sept 1958, *CGPLA Eng. & Wales*

Cayzer, (Michael) Anthony Rathborne (1920–1990), shipowner and aviation company executive, was born on 28 May 1920 at Tylney Hall, Rotherwick, Hampshire, the second son in the family of two sons and two daughters of Major Herbert Robin Cayzer, first Baron Rotherwick [see under Cayzer family], shipowner and later chairman of the Clan Line, and his wife, Freda Penelope, daughter of Colonel William Hans Rathborne, of co. Cavan, Ireland. Anthony Cayzer grew up at Tylney and was educated at Eton College, from where, with the intention of becoming a professional soldier—his father had a distinguished military record—he went to the Royal Military College, Sandhurst, and was commissioned into the Royal Scots Greys in 1939.

Cayzer would probably have had a successful and happy army career, but while serving in the Middle East, where he was mentioned in dispatches, he contracted poliomyelitis and was invalided out in 1944. He entered the Cayzer family's shipowning and financial empire, and his business career was to span a period of great change in the shipping world. He was chairman of the Liverpool Steamship Owners' Association from 1956 to 1967. He was president of the chamber of shipping of the United Kingdom in 1967, and of the shipping and forwarding agents from 1963 to 1965. He was also deputy chairman of the British and Commonwealth Shipping Company and a director of Cayzer, Irvine & Co., and of Overseas Containers (Holdings) Ltd.

Professional involvement with shipping matters on this scale was to be expected in a grandson of Sir Charles Cayzer, founder of the Clan Line, one of the most prestigious of the later British merchant shipping concerns. Cayzer was fascinated by the complexities of the freight conferences, the collective monopolies by which potentially destructive competition between shipping concerns was avoided. His knowledge of these organizations and their workings found expression when, as chairman of the trustees of the National Maritime Museum from 1977 to 1987 (he had been a trustee since 1968), he personally inspired and organized a gallery which made this important aspect of maritime history intelligible to the lay visitor in a thoroughly attractive way.

This involvement in the National Maritime Museum's

development was typical of Cayzer's chairmanship. He was highly successful in this when as an academic institution it sought to interpret its themes to a mass public with accuracy and realism. Despite his interest and his background as an arbiter of power, he never sought to usurp the director's responsibility for initiating policy and managing its execution. He sought continuously for ways in which, with his immense circle of acquaintance and knowledge of the business world, he could further the aims of the museum. His association with it marked a considerable personal achievement. Cayzer broke away from his family business tradition by becoming deeply involved with civil aviation. He was fascinated by the element of risk enterprise and competition involved in the industry at this stage in its development, and by some of the more piratical business colleagues with whom he found himself working. A qualified pilot of multi-engined planes, he knew the handling characteristics of many of the aircraft his companies operated. He became deputy chairman of Air UK and of Aviation Services Ltd, chairman of Servisair (1954–87) and of Britavia, and a director of Bristow's Helicopter Group. In 1970 he was a moving force in the merger of British United with Caledonian Airways to form British Caledonian. He would have dearly liked to see the establishment of a national aviation museum to complement the National Maritime Museum.

A well-built, handsome man, Cayzer had all the social graces which went with his upbringing and considerable fortune. He held extensive shooting parties at his 1500-acre estate in Hertfordshire. He was not an intellectual, though he frequently expressed great respect for academic achievement. He was open-minded, flexible in his approach to problems, and always ready to enter into new worlds. He greatly enjoyed Glyndebourne as well as his motor yacht *Patra*. In his attitude to women he was intensely conservative. To him they were essentially private and social creatures. He could not accept them as suitable for higher professional responsibilities or as reliable participants in confidential business affairs. His very brave struggle with the after-effects of polio, which impeded his mobility, was at times painful to watch, and perhaps prevented him from reaching his full potential.

Cayzer married in 1952 the Hon. Patricia Helen Browne, elder daughter of Dominick Geoffrey Edward Browne, fourth Baron Oranmore and Browne; they had three daughters. She died in 1981 and in 1982 he married Baroness Sybille, daughter of Count de Selys Longchamps. Cayzer died of cancer in the Nuffield Hospital, Mayfair, London, on 4 March 1990.   BASIL GREENHILL, *rev.*

Sources A. Muir and M. Davies, *A Victorian shipowner: a portrait of Sir Charles Cayzer* (privately printed, London, 1978) · *The Times* (7 March 1990) · private information (2004) · personal knowledge (2004) · *CGPLA Eng. & Wales* (1990)

Wealth at death £12,590: probate, 15 Oct 1990, *CGPLA Eng. & Wales*

Cayzer, Sir August Bernard Tellefsen, first baronet (1876–1943). *See under* Cayzer family (*per.* 1843–1999).

Cayzer, Sir Charles William, first baronet (1843–1916). *See under* Cayzer family (*per.* 1843–1999).

Cayzer, Sir Charles William, second baronet (1869–1917). *See under* Cayzer family (*per.* 1843–1999).

Cayzer, Herbert Robin, first Baron Rotherwick (1881–1958). *See under* Cayzer family (*per.* 1843–1999).

Cayzer, (William) Nicholas, Baron Cayzer (1910–1999). *See under* Cayzer family (*per.* 1843–1999).

Cazalet, Edward (1827–1883), merchant and industrialist, was born on 9 November 1827 at Brighton, the youngest of the seven children of Peter Clement Cazalet (1785–1859), merchant and Russian consul, and his wife, Olympia (*d.* 1848). Of Huguenot extraction the Cazalets had established strong business connections in Russia in the late eighteenth century, and, after education in England, Edward Cazalet joined the family firm in St Petersburg in the mid-1840s. He became one of a closely knit group of English merchants who not only dominated the Baltic trade but increasingly invested in the domestic economy. The Cazalet firm, from its original base in silk weaving and rope manufacturing, grew under Edward's aegis to include a prosperous candle factory (with a monopoly contract for the imperial palaces), together with interests in the Neva Stearin Candle and Soap Factory, the Kalinkin brewery (one of Russia's largest), and a mineral water plant.

Following his father's death in 1859 and his own marriage on 15 March 1860 to Elizabeth Sutherland Marshall (*d.* 1888), daughter and heir of William Marshall, doctor and Danish consul at Edinburgh, Cazalet also joined William Miller & Co., a shipping firm controlled by his wife's uncle, the Russian merchant and future Liberal MP William Miller (1809–1887). Under Cazalet's guidance this firm exported herrings, coal, and Singer sewing machines from Scotland to Russia. Cazalet took a keen interest in working-class education in St Petersburg, and he also acted as treasurer of the Russia Company's 'English factory' from 1864 to 1865. His profitable ventures enabled him to leave Russia in 1870, having transferred his business concerns to managers under whom they continued to provide the basis of the family's fortunes until confiscation in 1917.

Back in Britain, combining generosity and broad sympathies, Cazalet made his mark in a number of diverse ways. First, he acquired the 1500 acre Fairlawne estate in Kent of Joseph Ridgway, paying in 1872 some £100,000 at the peak of nineteenth-century land prices. He not only transformed the house, gardens, and stables, but also the surrounding village of Shipbourne, raising much local discontent but leaving in its wake a new church, an inn, a modernized estate village, and improved schools. He also provided a building for the Plaxtol Working Men's Club and a ground for its cricket club at Fairlawne, and he was noted for his benevolence locally and nationally (contributing generously, for example, to Oxford's Indian Institute). Cazalet was soon accepted into county society; he acted as JP and deputy lieutenant for Kent, and in 1880 he contested (unsuccessfully) the mid-Kent seat for the Liberals. Untrammelled by local prejudices he supported the first channel tunnel scheme and provided £10,000 to modernize part of Tonbridge (Judd's) School. Cazalet later acquired 4 Whitehall Gardens, London, the former home of Sir Robert Peel, and, reflecting his growing interest in agriculture, he became one of the proprietors of the *Mark Lane Express*.

Secondly, Cazalet's experience of international trade, and perhaps especially the problems of the volatile currency of the Russian empire, led him to become an early advocate in Britain of the bimetallic (gold and silver) standard. Bimetallism, he believed, would provide monetary stability in the world and also help to promote harmony among nations, such that monetary arrangements between the powers would achieve more than 'the most successful foreign war' (E. Cazalet, *Bimetallism and its Connection with Commerce*, 1879, 35). Following private discussions at Fairlawne, Cazalet chaired the first meeting of the International Monetary Standard Association at the India Office on 12 November 1881, and it was from this influential group that the Bimetallic League later emerged.

Thirdly, Cazalet became a leading advocate of the Euphrates Valley Railway, a long-running scheme to complete the shortest route from Turkey to India and one whose construction would benefit the trade and security of British India while providing a bulwark against Russian expansionism. It was also to make Britain independent of the Suez Canal. Cazalet also saw this proposal in two wider contexts, for against the backcloth of the re-emergence of the Eastern question he believed that Britain and a liberalizing Russia could become natural allies. The latter would be allowed to expand at the expense of the Ottoman empire, while Britain would take responsibility for Syria, a country 'which possesses peculiar attractions for the minds and sympathies of the English race' (E. Cazalet, *The Eastern Question: an Address to Working Men*, 1878, 39). Cazalet believed that such a redirection of interest would deflect Britain from further intervention in Egypt, which might safely be left to Italian trusteeship. But even more imaginatively Cazalet proposed that the oppressed Jews of Europe, especially from Russia and Romania, should be resettled on either side of the railway, providing them with a homeland but also promoting the regeneration of Syria—a duty Britain had neglected since Palmerston's day. This scheme, like that of Laurence Oliphant, proved wholly visionary, but it acted as an important contribution to the projection of a Jewish homeland. Cazalet gained the interest of princes and working men, statesmen and diplomatists, notably that of Odo Russell, British ambassador at Berlin, where Cazalet canvassed his scheme in 1882. In partnership with Sir Thomas Selby Tancred (1840–1910), the future contractor for the Forth Bridge and builder of the Delagoa Bay Railway, he continued enthusiastically to seek support, and it was on his way to further the scheme with the Ottoman Porte that he caught typhus and died at the Hôtel d'Angleterre, Constantinople, on 21 April 1883, survived by his wife. He was buried at St Giles's Church, Shipbourne, Kent, on 7 May 1883.

Cazalet left a substantial fortune in Britain as well as assets in Russia and Villa Liserb, near Nice, from which he had campaigned against the gaming houses of Monte Carlo. His only child, William Marshall (1865–1932), was a talented real-tennis player (Cazalet had built a court at Fairlawne for the purpose). William was the father of Victor Cazalet (1896–1943), Conservative MP and political liaison officer to General Sikorski, of Peter Cazalet (1907–1973), the racehorse trainer, and of Thelma Cazalet-Keir (1899–1989), feminist and Conservative MP.

A. C. HOWE

Sources private information (2004) · *The Times* (23 April 1883) · *The Times* (3 May 1883) · *South Eastern Gazette* (23 April 1883) · A. Tupp, *The early proceedings of the Bimetallic League* (1897) · A. M. Hyamson, *British projects for the restoration of the Jews* (1917) · d. cert. · Burke, *Gen. GB* · *Tonbridge Free Press* (12 May 1883)
Archives CKS, family deeds, etc. | BL, genealogical collections of C. Boyce, vol. 2, Add. MS 45504 · PRO, Ampthill MSS · PRO, letters to Odo Russell, FO 918
Likenesses monument, St Giles's Church, Shipbourne, Kent · portrait, Plaxtol and Shipbourne village hall, Kent · portrait, priv. coll.
Wealth at death £346,414 9s. 7d.: probate, 5 June 1883, *CGPLA Eng. & Wales*

Cazalet, Peter Victor Ferdinand (1907–1973), racehorse trainer, was born on 15 January 1907 at Fairlawne, near Tonbridge in Kent, the fourth and youngest child and third son of William Marshall Cazalet (1865–1932) of Fairlawne and his wife, Maud Lucia Heron, daughter of Sir John Robert Heron-Maxwell, seventh baronet, of Springkell, Dumfriesshire. The Cazalets were a Basque family who came to England as Huguenot refugees. Peter Cazalet was educated at Eton College, where he developed as an excellent all-round player of ball games and made a century in the cricket match against Harrow at Lord's, and at Christ Church, Oxford, where he obtained a third-class degree in chemistry in 1930, a cricket blue, and half-blues for rackets, real tennis, and squash.

It was during his three years at Christ Church that the young man, who as a child used to hide whenever a pony was produced, suddenly took to riding. Determined, fearless, and superbly co-ordinated, he soon became a proficient amateur rider over fences and hurdles. After a brief unproductive flirtation with industrial chemistry, he spent two years improving his jockeyship and learning stable management with the successful Berkshire trainer Sonny Hall.

In 1932 Peter Cazalet inherited Fairlawne, a large William and Mary house, his eldest brother having been killed in the First World War and the second brother wishing to live elsewhere. He began to build up his own small string of jumpers with H. E. (Harry) Whiteman holding the trainer's licence. It was then, in the early thirties, that Anthony Mildmay, who had been in Cazalet's house at Eton, asked whether he could come and ride out in the mornings on his way to work in the City. Thus was born a friendship and sporting partnership which flourished until Mildmay's untimely death by drowning in 1950. Its saddest and best known moment, at least before the war, was when Mildmay's reins came unbuckled in the 1936 Grand National, allowing his horse Davy Jones, who had a clear lead and looked a certain winner, to run off the course before the last fence. Cazalet rode in that and four other Nationals but a bad fall in 1939 compelled him to give up riding and take out his own trainer's licence.

Cazalet spent the Second World War first in the Royal Artillery (1939–40) and then, with Mildmay as one of his platoon commanders, as a Welsh Guards company commander in the guards armoured division. The moment peace came the two friends returned to Fairlawne, determined to create a training stable run on the best possible lines and, above all, to win the Grand National, preferably with Mildmay in the saddle. That goal was thwarted for a second time when Mildmay finished a close third on Cromwell in 1948, having ridden blind over the last two fences with his head forced down on his chest by an attack of cramp (a similar attack almost certainly caused his death two years later). The friends never achieved a Grand National win but Mildmay—M'Lord as a devoted racing public knew him—was leading amateur in each of the post-war seasons leading up to his death, and did National Hunt racing a great service by communicating his enthusiasm to Queen Elizabeth and persuading her and her daughter Princess Elizabeth to have a horse in training with Cazalet. The partnership horse, Monaveen, won for the first time in 1949 but when Princess Elizabeth became queen she decided to concentrate on flat racing, so it was in the queen mother's blue and buff colours that Dick Francis went out from the Cazalet stable to ride Devon Loch in the 1956 Grand National. Fifty yards from the winning post, with victory in his grasp, Devon Loch collapsed. That bitter disappointment did not diminish the queen mother's support for National Hunt racing and, of the 1100 winners Cazalet trained at Fairlawne, more than 250 carried her colours. They were ridden by several great stable jockeys including Bryan Marshall, Dick Francis, Bill Rees, Arthur Freeman, and, perhaps the most stylish of all, David Mould.

Three times leading trainer, Cazalet sent out what was then a record total of eighty-two winners in 1964–5. Fairlawne was run on old-fashioned lines but, though a strict disciplinarian with a merciless eye for detail, its master was also scrupulously fair. A high proportion of his stable lads stayed with him throughout their working lives and were both glad and proud to do so. They and the horses alike were always beautifully turned out and, even if some later trainers with all-weather gallops at their disposal might reckon the Fairlawne facilities barely adequate, the Cazalet horses were always as fit as horses can be made.

Himself rather shy and uninterested in what he considered pointless chit-chat, Cazalet was, by normal standards, a somewhat aloof figure on the racecourse. But, once formed, his friendships were very seldom broken and often a highly developed sense of humour warmed and brightened his attitude to life.

On 14 December 1932 Cazalet married Leonora, daughter of Leonard Rowley and stepdaughter of the author P. G. Wodehouse; they had a son and daughter. Their son, Edward, particularly delighted his father by becoming a first-rate amateur rider; having forsaken the turf for the

bar, he later became a QC and a judge. Leonora Cazalet died in 1944 while undergoing a minor operation and in 1949 Cazalet married Zara Sophie Kathleen Mary, daughter of Sir Harry Stapleton Mainwaring, fifth baronet, and former wife of Major (Alexander) Ronald George Strutt, later fourth Baron Belper, with whom she had one son. She and Cazalet had three sons, one of whom died in 1956.

Cazalet died at Fairlawne on 29 May 1973. Each January, weather permitting, the Anthony Mildmay Peter Cazalet memorial steeplechase is run over 3 miles 5 furlongs at Sandown. When it was first run, called simply the Mildmay memorial, Cazalet won it with Cromwell, Mildmay's favourite horse, ridden by Bryan Marshall.

JOHN OAKSEY, rev.

Sources private information (1986) · personal knowledge (1986) · *The Times* (30 May 1973) · *The Times* (7 June 1973) · *The Times* (14 June 1973) · Burke, *Peerage* (1907)

Wealth at death £626,454: probate, 27 June 1973, *CGPLA Eng. & Wales*

Cazalet, Victor Alexander (1896–1943), politician, was born at 4 Whitehall Gardens, London, on 27 December 1896, the second of the three sons of William Marshall Cazalet (1865–1932) of Fairlawne, Tonbridge, Kent, and his wife, Maud Lucia (d. 1952), daughter of Sir John Heron-Maxwell, seventh baronet, of Springkell, Dumfriesshire. Cazalet's younger sister was Thelma Cazalet-*Keir, later a Conservative MP.

The Cazalets were a wealthy and well-connected Kent family of Huguenot descent. Queen Victoria sometimes stayed at the family villa at Cimiez, Nice, and was godmother to Victor, who in 1909 was sent to Eton College. Although he excelled at games and became president of Pop, the self-electing society of boys that participated in the running of the school, Cazalet experienced deep unhappiness there. He found solace in the religion of Christian Science, and while never a proselytizer he became a lifelong adherent to this faith, which provided the bedrock to his character. Nicknamed Teenie by his friends because of his diminutive stature, Cazalet was unfailingly cheerful and preferred always to believe the best in others. His sister once remonstrated 'hotly' with him over this 'excess of credulity', but Cazalet replied that he would 'rather be taken in nine times out of ten than miss helping the tenth case' (Cazalet-Keir, 28).

Soon after leaving Eton in July 1915 Cazalet joined the Household battalion of the 1st Life Guards. He arrived in France early in November 1916, two months after his elder brother, Edward, had been killed at the front. Cazalet was promoted to captain early in 1917 and that November was awarded the Military Cross after leading an abortive attack against heavy odds. In February 1918 he was assigned to the staff of the supreme war council at Versailles, and in October he was sent to join the British mission in Siberia, an experience that left him strongly anti-bolshevik. He had a lifelong passion for foreign travel, which complemented his political interest in foreign affairs.

Cazalet returned to England in 1919 and in September

went up to Christ Church, Oxford, to read history. He took his studies seriously, but it was at games that he gained distinction, winning half-blues in tennis, real tennis, and squash rackets. He was later four times winner of the British amateur squash championship (1925–30). While at Oxford he decided upon a political career and cultivated friendships with the leading politicians of the day, including Winston Churchill, who had befriended him during the war. In February 1923 he was adopted as Conservative candidate for Chippenham, and though unsuccessful at the general election in that year he won the seat in the Conservative landslide of 1924, and held it until his death.

Cazalet was an effective speaker and he soon made his mark in the Commons, though he was criticized for showing 'too much cleverness in an Oxford Union kind of way' (James, 102). He served as parliamentary private secretary to Sir Philip Cunliffe-Lister, president of the Board of Trade, 1924–6, and gained a reputation as a broad-minded Conservative, concerned with social issues. He made friendships on both sides of the house, and notably with J. H. Thomas, serving as his parliamentary private secretary at the Dominions Office in 1931. By this date, though, Cazalet's early promise had faded and he was no longer thought of as a 'coming man'. He had spread himself too thinly to be identified with any particular piece of legislation, and in spite of his many connections he lacked a base of parliamentary support from which to lay claim to higher office. As late as 1942 his friend Harold Nicolson wrote of him:

> Victor cannot see a pie without wishing to have his finger in it. … But really he does rush in where angels fear to tread, and I have the feeling that his rushes are merely the roaming of a cow seeking fresh grass and getting into the flower-garden. (Nicolson, 224)

From the mid-1930s, though, under the influence of Chaim Weizmann and Blanche Dugdale, Cazalet found a more constant focus for his energies in the advocacy of Zionism. He became passionately concerned about this issue and its corollary, the plight of refugees, and especially Jews, from central Europe. On 29 July 1938 he gave a warning to the House of Commons of the possible consequences of antisemitism on the continent: 'Never since Milton immortalised the slaughter of the Albigenses has a whole community been in such danger' (Hansard 5C, 338, 1938, col. 3555). Such prescience, however, did not lead him openly to oppose appeasement, and this, together with his support for the government's white paper on India, led to a lasting breach with Churchill.

Excluded from any role in the wartime coalition, Cazalet found an outlet in the command of a light anti-aircraft battery; he was made major in August 1939 (becoming honorary colonel in April 1942). He was rescued from this relative obscurity after meeting the Polish leader, General Władysław Sikorski, in Paris in April 1940. Cazalet's first-hand knowledge of Polish affairs impressed Sikorski, who took an almost paternal interest in him, and on 9 July Cazalet was confirmed as British liaison officer to the free Poles. The great trust that Sikorski placed in Cazalet meant that he was able to reconcile the Polish forces more effectively with the wishes of the British government. But it also gave him the authority to lobby the government in defence of Polish interests, and this he did vigorously, notably in the run-up to the Anglo-Soviet treaty in the spring of 1942. Cazalet's suspicions about the expansionist intentions of the Soviet Union were unwelcome in ministerial circles, but in Sikorski at least they encouraged a more realistic appraisal of Soviet policy.

Cazalet's defence of Polish interests did not lead him to abandon the Jewish cause and in what proved to be his last speech in the Commons, on 19 May 1943, he raised again the issue of refugees, reporting on the stories circulating in Poland about 'the horrors of the massacres at a camp called Treblinka' (Hansard 5C, 389, 1943, col. 1157). Later that month he accompanied Sikorski on a visit to the Polish forces in the Middle East. On the return leg of this journey both men were killed, on 4 July 1943, when their plane crashed directly after take-off from Gibraltar. Cazalet's last public engagement had been at a large meeting in Jerusalem days before, presided over by David Ben-Gurion, at which he had proclaimed that 'I would gladly give my life for the establishment of a Jewish state in Palestine' (James, 286). He would not have been dismayed to have given it for a free Poland, and in his determined advocacy of these two great causes he exercised an influence that went well beyond the back benches of the Commons.   MARK POTTLE

Sources R. R. James, *Victor Cazalet: a portrait* (1976) • *WWW* • E. S. Craig and W. M. Gibson, eds., *Oxford University roll of service*, 3rd edn (1920) • *WWBMP*, vol. 3 • S. Koss, 'A charmed life', *TLS* (28 May 1976), review of R. R. James, *Victor Cazalet* • R. West, letter, *TLS* (11 June 1976), 706 • T. Cazalet-Keir, *From the wings* (1967) • H. Nicolson, *Diaries and letters*, ed. N. Nicolson, 2 (1967) • Burke, *Gen. GB* (1937) • b. cert.

Archives Bodl. RH, corresp. about African affairs

Cazenove, John (1788–1879), merchant and political economist, was born in London on 12 May 1788. He was the third son of James Cazenove (1744–1827), a merchant of French Huguenot origin, who emigrated from Geneva and married (1781) Marie-Anne Sophie Houssemayne Du Boulay, daughter of the pastor of the French church in Threadneedle Street, London. They had four sons and five daughters. John Cazenove, like his brothers, attended Charterhouse School in London. From 1813 he worked in his father's firm James Cazenove & Co. until its collapse in 1831. In 1832 he described himself as 'late a continental merchant' in 'a large commercial firm' with 'some sixty or seventy foreign correspondents'. Research by David Kynaston has revealed that the modern London-based stockbroking firm Cazenove & Co. was founded in 1823 by John Cazenove's younger brother Philip *Cazenove (1798–1880) and not, as previously thought, by their father's brother Philip Cazenove. There is no record of John Cazenove having been involved in that firm. He had become a member of Lloyd's in 1819, and from 1843 to 1858 was secretary to the Family Endowment Society. At one period he was manager of the London Institution.

Cazenove wrote at least nine books and pamphlets on

political economy, and contributed reviews to the *British Critic*. He was a particular friend of T. R. Malthus, who proposed him for membership of the Political Economy Club at its second meeting on 28 May 1821. He resigned in 1830, perhaps because of the difficulties being experienced by the family firm. There is strong evidence that Cazenove was the anonymous editor of the second (posthumous) edition (1836) of Malthus's *Principles of Political Economy*. Malthus described him as 'a very clever man, and good political economist', but their friendship did not prevent Cazenove from criticizing Malthus and adopting an independent line on some issues.

After Malthus's death in 1834, Cazenove applied unsuccessfully for Malthus's position at the East India College, but the position was awarded to Richard Jones, of whom Cazenove also became a great admirer and close personal friend. He was largely responsible for editing Jones's *Literary Remains* (1859), but declined William Whewell's invitation to be named as joint editor. His other interests included chess and music—his will made provision for the disposition of his harmonium and musical books; and an anonymous book of chess games (1817) has been attributed to a 'John Cazenove', president of the London Chess Club.

Cazenove married a Miss Gibson, and their only son, John Gibson Cazenove (1822–1896), educated at Marlborough grammar school and Brasenose College, Oxford, became subdean and chancellor of St Mary's Cathedral, Edinburgh, and published a number of theological works. John Cazenove died at his home, 13 Middleton Road, New Wandsworth, on 15 August 1879.   J. M. PULLEN

Sources Burke, *Gen. GB* · D. Kynaston, *Cazenove & Co.: a history* (1991) · H. D. Macleod, *A dictionary of political economy* (1863) · Boase, *Mod. Eng. biog.* · *CGPLA Eng. & Wales* (1879)

Archives priv. coll., letters to John Murray · Trinity Cam., letters to William Whewell

Wealth at death under £1000: probate, 13 Sept 1879, *CGPLA Eng. & Wales*

Cazenove, Philip (1798–1880), stockbroker, was born on 23 November 1798 at Walthamstow, Essex, the fourth son of James Cazenove (1744–1827), merchant, and his wife, Marie-Anne Sophie Houssemayne Du Boulay. Of Huguenot descent James Cazenove was born in Geneva and emigrated to England where he established his own business. He became a naturalized Englishman in 1778 and three years later married Marie-Anne, daughter of the pastor of the French church in Threadneedle Street, London. Four sons, one of whom was John *Cazenove, and five daughters made up their family. Philip Cazenove, like his three older brothers, was educated at Charterhouse School (from 1813 to 1815). As a young man he developed scholarly and literary tastes and a love of the classics which stayed with him throughout his life; 'many playful Latin epigrams issued from his pen on passing events in his family or in the world' (Kynaston, 14). No record survives of what he did in the three years between 1816 and 1819, but his three older brothers had all joined their father's business and it may well be that he gained some experience of the City by doing so.

Philip Cazenove (1798–1880), by unknown engraver, 1851

However, in 1819 Cazenove was introduced to the stock exchange as clerk to John Francis Menet, a man then in his forties and a stockbroker of only two years' standing. Menet was also of Huguenot descent and was Philip Cazenove's brother-in-law, married since 1805 to his elder sister, Louisa. In 1822 Philip married Emma (*d*. 1860), daughter of Edward Knapp, a banker. There was already a connection between the families, for Emma's sister Susan had married Philip's brother James two years earlier. Philip and Emma Cazenove had at least three sons.

On 19 March 1823 Cazenove became a member of the stock exchange and, shortly afterwards, Menet's partner. A considerable and prosperous business resulted from this partnership, which lasted until Menet's death in September 1835, and instrumental from its earliest days was a steady flow of work from N. M. Rothschild, then the most influential financier in the City. In 1836, following Menet's death, Cazenove formed a new partnership with two established stockbrokers, Joseph Laurence and Charles Pearce. Four years later Laurence's son, Sydney, joined the partnership along with Cazenove's elder brother, Henry, who had taken up stockbroking after the collapse of the Cazenove family business in 1831. By the 1840s the firm, with its five partners, was one of the largest on the stock exchange, and it seems that its business expanded commensurately. Henry Cazenove retired in 1852 and, probably because the next generation of all three families were looking for partnerships, the Laurence, Cazenove, and Pearce partnership was dissolved in 1854.

Next to be formed was Philip Cazenove & Co., with Cazenove taking as partners his nephew Edward (son of his brother James), and his own son, Henry. In the 1850s the firm's business, already large with a number of merchant banks as clients and a comfortable connection in money broking with Barings, widened as legislation made incorporation with limited liability easily accessible. Cazenove & Co. acted as broker to new issues and flotations of new joint-stock companies on the stock exchange, a business in which it continued to be significant for the rest of the century and indeed into the twentieth century.

After the death of his wife in 1860 Cazenove remained the titular head of the firm but now devoted more of his time and energy to good works and charitable activities. He acted as treasurer, and was himself a generous contributor, to a number of church charities, including the Society for the Propagation of the Gospel, the Society for the Propagation of Christian Knowledge, the National Society, and the Additional Curates' Society. He was an active member of the governing bodies of several hospitals (including Guy's Hospital, London, and St Luke's Hospital for the Insane) and philanthropic institutions. In 1872 Cazenove was elected a member of an influential if little-known association, the Club of Nobody's Friends. It comprised clerics and significant figures from the City of London, including the financier Henry Hucks Gibbs.

In 1873 Cazenove formally retired from the firm, leaving it in the hands of his son Henry; his nephew, Edward Cazenove, had died in 1857. Philip Cazenove continued to work for the Council of Foreign Bondholders, of which he had become a member in 1869, until his death in Clapham, London, where he had lived, on 20 January 1880. St Michael's Church, Clapham, which was consecrated in 1881, was built partly in memory of him.

Cazenove's sound business brain and sober working habits, combined with a degree of personal frugality, amassed for him a considerable fortune, enabling him to be 'one of the great Christian philanthropists of the age' (Kynaston, 14). The firm which he played such a large part in creating, known since 1954 as Cazenove & Co., continued to be a considerable force in the City of London. Cazenove was buried in the family vault in Hornsey churchyard, Middlesex.   JUDY SLINN

Sources D. Kynaston, *Cazenove & Co.: a history* (1991) · *The Guardian* (28 Jan 1880), 106 · *Church Bells* (24 Jan 1880), 123 · Boase, *Mod. Eng. biog.* · *CGPLA Eng. & Wales* (1880) · Foster, *Alum. Oxon.*
Archives Cazenove & Co., London · N. M. Rothschild, London, archives, letters | Cazenove & Co. · GL, stock exchange archives
Likenesses Lady Freyberg, two portraits, 1829–48, repro. in Kynaston, *Cazenove & Co* · engraving, 1851, Cazenove & Co. [*see illus.*]
Wealth at death under £250,000: probate, 9 Feb 1880, *CGPLA Eng. & Wales*

Ceadda [St Ceadda, Chad] (*d.* 672?), abbot of Lastingham and bishop of Mercia and Lindsey, generated a cult of which the principal centres were his cathedral at Lichfield and the monastery he founded nearby. This proved lasting in spite of the dearth of historical information about him. The principal source for his life is Bede's *Historia ecclesiastica*, complemented by the life of Wilfrid by Stephen of Ripon (Eddius Stephanus).

Ceadda was Northumbrian by birth. He had three brothers: *Cedd, Cynebill, and Caelin. All four became priests, and Cedd, like Ceadda, a bishop also. They were disciples of Áedán of Lindisfarne and Ceadda studied for a time in Ireland at 'Rathmelsigi' (probably Clonmelsh, co. Carlow). Áedán and other Irish saints who worked in Northumbria were admired by Bede for their simple and frugal way of life and Ceadda owed much to this tradition, as did his fellow Northumbrian Cuthbert; both also were monks who became bishops late in life for a comparatively few years. Ceadda took part in Cedd's foundation of the monastery of Lastingham, Northumbria, and became abbot in 664, on the death of Cedd, who had taken a notable part in the Synod of Whitby in that year, winning the respect of both sides in the complex dispute between adherents of Iona and Rome on the date of Easter and other matters. After the synod, Wilfrid, the principal speaker in favour of Northumbria and England celebrating Easter on the same day as the rest of the Christian church in Europe, was appointed bishop of Northumbria, with York rather than Lindisfarne as his seat. He went to Gaul for consecration, but delayed there so long that King Oswiu of Northumbria lost patience and appointed Ceadda in his place. In a time of dearth of bishops in England, Ceadda was indiscreet enough to accept consecration by Wine, a simoniacal bishop of Winchester, assisted by two British bishops not in communion with the apostolic see. However, Ceadda modelled his lifestyle on that of Áedán, devoting much time to both study and preaching, travelling on foot to villages and outposts.

After the death of Deusdedit, archbishop of Canterbury, in 664, one of his clergy, Wigheard, was sent by the king of Kent to Rome for consecration. But Wigheard and some of his followers died of the plague in Rome, and Pope Vitalian chose for the see of Canterbury a learned Greek monk, Theodore of Tarsus. This appointment was both unexpected and successful. Consecrated in Rome in 668, Theodore reached Canterbury in 669 and soon made a visitation of all the churches in England. He told Ceadda that his consecration had been irregular. According to Bede, Ceadda accepted this and resigned, saying 'I consented to receive it, however unworthy, in obedience to the commands I had received' (*Hist. eccl.*, 4.2). Theodore restored Wilfrid as bishop of York, but soon afterwards appointed Ceadda as bishop of the Mercians in succession to Jaruman, who had died in 667. Ceadda established his see at Lichfield, thenceforward Mercia's principal see. Here too he built a monastery for seven or eight monks, from which various details about Ceadda's prayer life and his death have come down to posterity. Ceadda's large diocese included Lindsey (modern Lincolnshire), for which the estate of 50 hides of land (about 6000 acres, probably at Barrow upon Humber), given by King Wulfhere of Mercia, provided a useful base. For travelling such long distances Ceadda agreed to ride a horse (against Áedán's custom); Bede records that Theodore ordered this and even lifted Ceadda onto a horse with his own hands.

Ceadda ruled his church for less than three years, until he caught the plague which had killed several of his clergy. It is recorded that in times of adversity, such as severe winds and storms, it was his custom to pray for God's mercy on the whole human race. In a violent thunderstorm he would go into the church and recite psalms until it ended. He would say that such storms were caused in order that people should 'respond to [God's] heavenly warning with due fear and love … implore his mercy, examining the innermost recesses of our hearts and purging out the dregs of our sins, and behave with such caution that we may never deserve to be struck down' (*Hist. eccl.*, 4.3). Ceadda's last days on earth, like those of other saints, were reportedly accompanied by heavenly voices. The monk Owine, a practical man rather than a scholar, heard these descend on Ceadda's room. A 'splendid guest' (believed to be Cedd) warned him of approaching death. Ceadda asked the monks to pray for him specially, and he died seven days later, on 2 March, probably in 672. He was buried near St Mary's Church, Lichfield, but when St Peter's Cathedral was later built, his body was translated to a shrine there which Bede describes as a wooden structure 'in the shape of a little house, having an aperture in its side, through which those who visit it out of devotion can insert their hands and take out a little of the dust' (*Hist. eccl.*, 4.3). When this was mixed with water and given to sick men or cattle, it was believed to heal them of their sickness.

The Synod of Hertford of 672 or 673 took place after Ceadda's death but it is extremely probable that he would have approved it. It was the first synod of the church in England as a whole and its decrees brought England into line with the rest of European Christianity. Under Theodore's guidance the church in England changed into a more settled, better organized and educated entity. Within it there was an important place and high esteem for men of holiness who espoused unity, like Ceadda and Cuthbert, even though their earlier Christian education had been in a different tradition. This esteem was expressed by Stephen of Ripon, the partisan biographer of Ceadda's 'rival' Wilfrid, when he described Ceadda as 'a most religious and admirable teacher … a true servant of God who in everything obeyed the bishops … who accomplished much good in his life and the Day of Judgment will have no terrors for him' (Eddius Stephanus, chap. 15). Another manifestation of this esteem was the cult of Ceadda, centred on his relics and shrine at Lichfield. To honour him, the splendidly illuminated St Chad's gospels were later given to Lichfield; probably written in eighth-century Wales or Mercia, they are comparable to the Lindisfarne gospels as a fine example of insular style and are still preserved at Lichfield. An Old English homily in Ceadda's honour, in ninth-century Mercian dialect, is evidence both for his cult and for vernacular preaching.

When the early Saxon cathedral church at Lichfield, where Ceadda was buried, had been rebuilt by the Normans, his relics were translated to a new shrine in 1148 and again, after Gothic alterations, in 1296. At some point his head was separated from his body and venerated by pilgrims in a gallery apart from the main shrine; it was kept initially in the lady chapel and later, when Walter Langton was bishop, in a new shrine behind the high altar,

which cost £2000. The sacrist's roll of 1345 lists the whole series of relics. The same source also records gifts offered at the shrine. Pilgrimages to 'St Chad' developed in the middle ages in a similar way to others elsewhere. Similar too was the fate of the shrine under Henry VIII. In spite of the pleas of the then bishop of Lichfield, Rowland Lee (1534–43), it was despoiled and destroyed. It is not known for certain whether or when the bones were subsequently reburied in the cathedral. Recusancy flourished in the area as late as the reign of Elizabeth I and in 1652 it was claimed in writing and with witnesses by Peter Turner SJ that a Henry Hodshead (d. 1615) possessed several bones of Ceadda, taken by prebendary Arthur Dudley (1531–1577) from Lichfield Cathedral and preserved in the original wrappings. These bones were venerated in Liège in 1671. Lost for some years, they were rediscovered at Aston Hall in 1837, described by Bishop Nicolas Wiseman in 1841 as a femur, two tibiae, and part of the humerus, and later venerated in the Roman Catholic cathedral of St Chad, Birmingham. A radiocarbon analysis and dating exercise, carried out at Oxford in 1995, concluded that at least three of these bones belonged to an individual who lived in the seventh century. One or more of them may well have been those of Chad.

Many ancient and recent churches are dedicated to Ceadda (usually spelt Chad); so too are several wells, one at Lichfield itself, believed to have been used for baptism. There is also some evidence for a cult in Ireland. The vernacular legend of Chad links his well with a thirsty stag and with the conversion of an otherwise unknown son of Wulfhere, king of Mercia, called Wulfhade. Whatever may be thought of this story, Ceadda is rightly remembered as a quiet, unambitious man of great faith and humility, who was a force for unity in a time of conflict. His name occurs frequently in medieval and modern calendars under 2 March.

D. H. FARMER

Sources Bede, *Hist. eccl.*, 3.28; 4.2, 3 · E. Stephanus, *The life of Bishop Wilfrid*, ed. and trans. B. Colgrave (1927); pbk edn (1985) · *Acta sanctorum: Martius*, 1 (Antwerp, 1688), 143–6 · *Propylaeum*, 83 · R. V. Vleeskruyer, *The life of St Chad* (1953) [homily] · *The kalendre of the newe legende of Englande*, ed. M. Gorlach (1994), 70, 199 · J. Austerberry, *Chad, bishop and saint* (1984) · J. Hewitt, 'The keeper of St Chad's head', *RIBA Journal*, 33 (1876), 72–82 · 'The relics of St Chad', *A history of St Chad's Cathedral, 1841–1904* (1904), 106–17 · M. W. Greenslade, *Saint Chad of Lichfield and Birmingham* (1996) · D. H. Farmer, *The Oxford dictionary of saints*, 3rd edn (1992), 94–5 · *Bibliotheca hagiographica latina antiquae et mediae aetatis*, 2 vols. (Brussels, 1898–1901) [suppls., 1911 and 1986]

Ceadwalla. *See* Cædwalla (c.659–689).

Ceallachan. *See* Cellachán mac Buadacháin (d. 954).

Ceannt, Éamonn [*formerly* Edward Thomas Kent] (1881–1916), Irish revolutionary, was born Edward Thomas Kent on 21 September 1881 at Ballymoe, co. Galway, the son of James Kent, an officer in the Royal Irish Constabulary, and his wife, Shauna Galway. At the age of ten he moved with his family to Dublin, where he was educated at the Christian Brothers' school on North Richmond Street and then proceeded to University College, Dublin. After leaving university he worked for Dublin corporation in the rates department and then the city treasury office. On 7 June 1905 he married Aine Bhraonain (otherwise Frances Brennan), the daughter of Francis Bhraonain, an auctioneer.

Ceannt was a committed Irish nationalist, and this belief manifested itself in a number of ways. In 1900 he joined the Gaelic League, becoming a proficient Irish speaker and adopting a Gaelic form of his name by which he was thereafter known. He immersed himself in Irish culture, especially music; he was an accomplished musician, setting up the Dublin Pipers' Club in 1910. Two years previously, at the jubilee celebrations in Rome for Pope Pius X, he had led the procession of Irish athletes, accompanying them on his uileann pipes. His political involvement began with Sinn Féin, which he joined in 1908; he then enrolled in the Irish Republican Brotherhood, being sworn in by Sean MacDiarmada, and subsequently became a member of its supreme council. He enlisted in and helped found the Irish Volunteers in 1913, and as director of communications on the headquarters staff was one of its key figures. He played a leading role in the Howth gun-running during the following summer. He helped to run, and wrote copy for, a number of advanced nationalist newspapers, including the *Irish Volunteer* and *The Spark* (the latter founded in 1915); he had also started his own political paper, published only in Irish, *An Barr Buadh*, but lack of money curtailed its life. By 1915 he was firmly committed to revolutionary nationalism; he was a member of the small secret military council which planned the Easter rising of 1916. Ceannt was one of the seven signatories of the 'Proclamation of the provisional government of the Irish republic', and during the rising was in command of the 4th battalion, which occupied the South Dublin Union (Cathal Brugha was his second in command). On 8 May 1916 he was executed by a firing squad in Kilmainham gaol, Dublin, for his role in the rising; he was buried in Arbour Hill cemetery, Dublin. He was survived by his wife and his ten-year-old son, Ronan. His brother William was killed in the following year in action with the Royal Dublin Fusiliers.

Ceannt has been described as being 6 feet tall, of a reserved temperament, and determined to pursue his chosen course of action. His fellow volunteer Edward Darrell Figgis recalled him as:

> a dark, proud, aloof man, of so extreme a sensitiveness that he had schooled himself to wear for mask a cold and rigid manner … He went into insurrection looking for victory because the thought of defeat chafed his intractable spirit. He spoke with cold contempt of Padraic Pearse's slow and moving eloquence as 'green flaggery'. He would have none of it. (Figgis, 86)

Ceannt's final written words are reported to have been: 'I leave for the guidance of other Irish revolutionaries who may tread the path which I have trod, this advice—never to treat with the enemy, never to surrender to his mercy, but to fight to the finish' (O'Donoghue, 196).

SALLY WARWICK-HALLER

Sources T. MacDonagh, radio broadcast, transcript, *c.*1940, NL Ire., MS 33, 694/B • F. O'Donoghue, 'Ceannt, Devoy, O'Rahilly and the military plan', *Leaders and men of the Easter rising*, ed. F. X. Martin (1967) • www.rootsweb.com/~fianna/history/east1916.html, 26 April 2001 • M. Foy and B. Barton, *The Easter rising* (1999) • L. Ó Broin, *Revolutionary underground and the story of the IRB, 1858–1924* (1976) • M. Daly, *Memories of the dead — some impressions of Roger Casement, Eamonn Ceannt [and others]* (*c.*1920) • T. W. Moody and others, eds., *A new history of Ireland*, 6: *Ireland under the Union, 1870–1921* (1996) • D. Lynch, *The IRB and the 1916 rising*, ed. F. O'Donoghue (1957) • D. Figgis, *Recollections* (1927) • b. cert. • m. cert.
Likenesses S. O'Sullivan, *c.*1930–1934, National Museum of Ireland, Dublin • photograph, repro. in *Oidreacht, 1916–1966* [1966], vii [commemorative booklet] • photographs, Kilmainham gaol, Dublin • photographs and postcards, Kilmainham gaol, Dublin

Cearbhall. *See* Cerball mac Dúngaile (d. 888).

Ceawlin (*d.* 593), king of the Gewisse, was the son of *Cynric and the third recorded ruler of the Gewisse, later known as the West Saxons. He was remembered as one of the most powerful kings of his day. The dating of his reign presents particular problems, and like that of other sixth-century West Saxon rulers seems to have been deliberately lengthened, probably when the Anglo-Saxon Chronicle was compiled in the late ninth century. In the chronicle annals he is said to have come to the throne in 560 and to have been driven out of the kingdom in 592, though he may have ceased to rule in 591, when the accession of his successor (and nephew), *Ceol, was recorded. In the regnal lists Ceawlin is allotted a much shorter reign of either seven or seventeen years, which would imply accession in either 574–5 or 584–5. He may have been associated with his father's rule previously, and the chronicle records both men fighting the Britons at Barbury in 556. Ceawlin in turn seems to have shared power with Cuthwulf (who may have been his brother) and then with his son Cuthwine. In 568 Ceawlin and Cutha (probably Cuthwulf) are said to have put to flight Æthelberht of Kent at 'Wibbandun'. Cuthwulf fought against the British at 'Biedcanford' in 571, leading to the capture of the *tunas* ('estate centres') of Limbury, Aylesbury, Bensington, and Eynsham, while Ceawlin and Cuthwine are said to have killed three British kings, Conmail, Condidan, and Farinmail at Dyrham in 577 and to have taken their cities of Gloucester, Cirencester, and Bath. In 584 Ceawlin and Cutha fought the Britons at 'Fethanleag' (possibly in the north-east of modern Oxfordshire); Cutha was killed, but Ceawlin captured numerous unspecified *tunas* before 'returning in anger to his own land' (*ASC*, s.a. 584).

The reliability of these entries is hard to assess, and at the very least their dates must be suspect. The names of the three kings and their cities which fell to Ceawlin in 577 could have been taken from a Welsh triad, but whether they have been correctly allocated to Ceawlin's reign is another matter. Saxon settlement had begun in what is now Gloucestershire before 577, and the places said to have fallen to Cuthwulf in 571 are even less likely to have been still in British hands at that date, for these were areas with some of the earliest evidence for Anglo-Saxon settlement and the captured places all have Anglo-Saxon names. Bensington certainly, and possibly the other places in the 571 annal, were in dispute in the eighth century between Mercia and Wessex, and it has been suggested that the entry could have been constructed, or reconstructed, to help support the West Saxon cause by giving them a long-established claim to these local administrative centres. The impression given of Ceawlin as a successful and wide-ranging ruler does, however, receive some corroboration from his inclusion in Bede's *Historia ecclesiastica gentis Anglorum* as the second name in a list of kings who exercised substantial power in southern England. The Anglo-Saxon Chronicle is probably also correct in placing his activities in the upper Thames valley and beyond, for when King Cynegils was baptized in 635 he chose Dorchester-on-Thames for his episcopal see, which would suggest that the area was central to West Saxon interests. Ceawlin's reign appears to have ended with discord with rival members of the royal house after his nephew Ceol apparently seized the throne in 591. After 'a great slaughter' at Woden's Barrow on the Ridgeway, near Alton Priors in what is now Wiltshire, Ceawlin was driven out and his death is recorded the following year, 593, together with that of Cwichelm and Crida, who were presumably also members of the West Saxon royal house but are otherwise unknown (*ASC*, s.a. 592).

BARBARA YORKE

Sources *ASC*, s.a. 556, 560, 568, 571, 577, 584, 592, 593 · D. N. Dumville, 'The West Saxon genealogical regnal list and the chronology of early Wessex', *Peritia*, 4 (1985), 21–66 · P. Sims-Williams, 'The settlement of England in Bede and the *Chronicle*', *Anglo-Saxon England*, 12 (1983), 1–41 · Bede, *Hist. eccl.*, 2.5 · B. Yorke, *Wessex in the early middle ages* (1995)

Cecil, Alicia Margaret. *See* Amherst, Alicia Margaret (1865–1941).

Cecil [*née* Lake; *other married name* Rodney], **Anne**, **Lady Ros** (1599×1601–1630), noblewoman, was the daughter of the courtier and administrator Sir Thomas *Lake (*bap.* 1561, *d.* 1630) and his wife, Mary (*bap.* 1575, *d.* 1643), daughter of Sir William Ryder, alderman and former lord mayor of London. She may be the Anne Lake who was baptized in St Martin-in-the-Fields, Westminster, on 14 November 1599. On 12 February 1616, in the month after her father had been appointed secretary of state, Anne married William *Cecil, sixteenth Baron Ros (1590–1618). The match was no doubt a triumph for her father, connecting the Lakes to a powerful aristocratic family. Very quickly, however, the marriage turned sour, triggering a bizarre and sordid series of events that ruined Sir Thomas Lake and made Anne and her mother objects of widespread vilification.

The exact origins of the trouble are now impossible to discover, but by the end of 1616 two deep fractures marring the relationship between Lord and Lady Ros were visible. The first, between Anne and her husband, was probably sexual in origin. The second, between Lord Ros and his grandfather Thomas *Cecil, earl of Exeter, on the one hand, and Anne's parents on the other, concerned property. In the spring of 1616 Ros had been appointed ambassador-extraordinary to Spain, and in the months before Ros left England, Sir Thomas and Lady Lake pressured him to sign over to his wife and her heirs the manor of Walthamstow in Essex and to pawn other lands to Lake in order to raise funds for the embassy. The Lakes forced Ros to acquiesce in these arrangements through a combination of political pressure applied by Sir Thomas and

more personal threats made by Lady Lake and Lady Ros. According to John Chamberlain, Lady Ros and her mother blackmailed Ros, threatening to reveal that he was sexually impotent and then to sue for a humiliating nullity of the marriage. The Lakes's motives are unclear, but it seems likely that if their daughter's marriage was indeed doomed, their intention was to salvage some kind of permanent financial advantage from the once-promising match.

Ros left for Spain in November 1616 and returned the following spring to the same conflicts. His grandfather Exeter opposed the completion of the Walthamstow transaction, angering the Lakes, who still held the threat of humiliation over Ros's head. Late in May 1617 Ros attempted to take his wife from her parents' house, where she had long since retreated, only to be rebuffed in a brawl that spilled out onto the street and left several servants injured. Three months later Ros had had enough and fled the country in secret, making his way to Rome.

The affair was not over, however. Lady Ros and her parents next turned their attention to Ros's grandfather Exeter and his much younger second wife, Frances [*see* Cecil, Frances, countess of Exeter], both of whom were intent on protecting Ros's financial interests. The quarrel took a scandalous turn late in 1617, when Lady Ros and her mother publicly charged the countess of Exeter with carrying on an incestuous relationship with her stepgrandson Ros, and with attempting to poison his aggrieved wife. Lady Ros and Lady Lake also claimed to have sworn testimony and incriminating letters to back up their claims. The Exeters responded with an appeal to the king, who remanded the case to the privy council. Anne refused to co-operate with some of the council's inquiries and, late in February 1618, was committed to the bishop of London's house. Having moderated her stand she was released in early March, by which time the dispute had been removed to Star Chamber.

The investigation dragged on for a year. At the end of June 1618 Ros died in Naples, but his death settled nothing, and the terms of his will became yet another object of contention between the Exeters and the Lakes. At last, in February 1619, James I himself presided over the final determination of the case in Star Chamber. Anne, her parents, and her brothers were accused of slandering the Exeters and of suborning witnesses and forging documents to substantiate their slanders. Anne, her parents, one of her brothers, and one of her servants were sentenced to prison and heavily fined, with Anne incurring a fine of 10,000 marks.

In his censure on the case King James offered an analysis of the appropriate apportionment of guilt. Lady Lake, he asserted, was the root of the evil, the serpent in the garden; she had seduced her daughter, playing the role of Eve, and then they had both dragged the reluctant Sir Thomas Lake—Adam, in James's view—into the conspiracy. Contemporaries disagreed about whether Lady Lake or Lady Ros was the guiltier party, but all assumed that the women were at fault and that the Lake household suffered from an inversion of the appropriate balance of power between the sexes. Both mother and daughter were tarred with stereotypical misogynist allegations. Lady Anne Clifford recorded in her diary that 'there was spoken extraordinarie fowle matters of my Lady Ros' including reports of an incestuous relationship with her brother; she was 'counted a most odious woman' (Diary of Anne Clifford, 109). When Lady Ros was taken to the Tower after the verdict crowds in the street cursed her as she passed. The London newsmongers were hardly more favourable: pert and domineering, commented one; an imp and cockatrice, added another. One pornographic verse libel described the loss of the 'coronall', or crown, of Lady Ros's 'mirkin'—which seems to refer to the loss of her pubic hair or 'bearde'. The libel depicts her as sexually promiscuous—noting that her mirkin 'ne'er was foundered or made straye' in 'open waye', that is, during intercourse—and wonders what:

> tricke in dancinge could the devill produce
> to fitte her too a haire and make it loose.
> (Ches. & Chester ALSS, CR 63/2/19, fol. 20r)

Anne and her mother thus joined Frances Howard, countess of Somerset, and Mistress Anne Turner in the gallery of transgressive women associated with the Jacobean court during the 1610s.

Soon after her imprisonment Lady Ros began to co-operate with the authorities. She confessed to the king in May 1619 and supplied evidence further compromising her family. Late in June she made a formal confession in Star Chamber and in early July was released from the Tower to be confined in a place of her own choosing. By April of the following year Anne was ready to re-enter London society and in November 1621 John Chamberlain reported that she was to remarry, the intended husband being a 'young gentleman of small meanes as beeing a younger brother' (Letters of John Chamberlain, 2.408). This was probably George Rodney, second son of the Somerset gentleman Sir John Rodney. She moved with her husband to Somerset where she lived out the rest of her days. She died in 1630, aged twenty-nine or thirty, and was buried in the parish church of Stoke Rodney. The funeral monument erected to her by her second husband implicitly acknowledged her chequered past even as it celebrated 'the Memory of a Good Wife & a most penitent Christian' (Le Neve, Monumenta Anglicana, 1.128).

ALASTAIR BELLANY

Sources GEC, Peerage, new edn, 11.108–11 · Le Neve's Pedigrees of the knights, ed. G. W. Marshall, Harleian Society, 8 (1873), 243–4 · 'Lake, Thomas', DNB · F. T. Colby, ed., The visitation of the county of Somerset in the year 1623, Harleian Society, 11 (1876), 94 · The letters of John Chamberlain, ed. N. E. McClure, 2 (1939), 80, 92–3, 132, 134, 144–5, 148, 207, 220, 222, 235, 247, 302, 408 · [T. Birch and R. F. Williams], eds., The court and times of Charles the First, 2 (1848), 68–9, 135–6, 138–40, 165–6, 177–8 · CSP dom., 1611–18, 411, 472, 512, 523, 542–3; 1619–23, 13, 16 · APC, 1617–19, 46–7; 1619–21, 9 · Calendar of the manuscripts of the most hon. the marquess of Salisbury, 22, HMC, 9 (1971), 61–76 · S. R. Gardiner, History of England from the accession of James I to the outbreak of the civil war, new edn, 3 (1899–1901), 189–94 · The diary of Anne Clifford, 1616–1619, ed. K. Acheson (1995), 100, 109 · Report on the manuscripts of the marquis of Downshire, 6 vols. in 7, HMC, 75 (1924–95), vol. 6, pp. 464, 513 · W. Davenport, commonplace book, Ches.

& Chester ALSS, CR 63/2/19, fol. 20r · J. Le Neve, Monumenta Anglicana, 1: 1600–1649 (1717), 128 · IGI

Cecil, Arthur [real name Arthur Cecil Blunt] (1843–1896), actor, was born in Mayfair, Westminster, on 1 June 1843, the son of Joseph Blunt, a solicitor, and his wife, Mary, née James. He was intended for the legal profession, but his membership of an amateur dramatic club led to a professional acting career. He first played as an amateur at the Richmond theatre and elsewhere, and on Easter Monday 1869, as Arthur Cecil, made his first professional appearance at the Gallery of Illustration, as Mr Churchmouse in W. S. Gilbert's No Cards and Box in the musical version of Box and Cox, by F. C. Burnand and Arthur Sullivan. In 1874 he joined the company at the Globe, where he appeared as Jonathan Wagstaff in Gilbert's Committed for Trial and played Mr Justice Jones in James Albery's Wig and Gown. At the Gaiety he was Dr Caius in The Merry Wives of Windsor, and at the Opera Comique, in 1875, Touchstone in As You Like It. Among other parts in which he was seen were Sir Peter Teazle in The School for Scandal and Tony Lumpkin in She Stoops to Conquer. At the Globe in 1876 he was the first Dr Downward in Wilkie Collins's Miss Gwilt. For the next three years he played numerous roles at the Prince of Wales's, from Sir Woodbine Grafton in Peril to Sam Gerridge in Caste. At the opening by the Bancrofts of the Haymarket in 1880 he appeared as Graves in Bulwer-Lytton's Money.

From September 1881 Cecil began acting at the Court Theatre, in the management of which he was subsequently associated with John Clayton. He continued in such roles as Connor Hennessy in Pinero's The Rector, Vere Queckett in The Schoolmistress, also by Pinero, and Mr Guyon in G. W. Godfrey's The Millionaire. The theatre then closed. When, under Mrs John Wood (Matilda Charlotte Vining) and A. Chudleigh, the new house opened in September 1888, Cecil was the first Miles Henniker in Sydney Grundy's Mamma. In 1889 he played Pickwick in a cantata so named, at the Comedy. The remainder of his professional life was divided between regular performances at the Court Theatre and occasional appearances at such houses as the Comedy, Globe, and Avenue. One of his last successful roles was that of Lord Arthur Nugent in Vanity Fair at the Court (1895). Cecil suffered much from gout. He died at the Orleans Club, Brighton, on 16 April 1896, and was buried at Mortlake. In addition to his appearances on stage he gave private performances and wrote songs which had some vogue. He was a thorough artist and a clever actor, more remarkable for neatness than robustness or strength.

JOSEPH KNIGHT, rev. NILANJANA BANERJI

Sources Adams, Drama · C. E. Pascoe, ed., The dramatic list (1879) · C. E. Pascoe, ed., The dramatic list, 2nd edn (1880) · E. Reid and H. Compton, eds., The dramatic peerage [1891]; rev. edn [1892] · E. D. Cook, Nights at the play (1883) · The life and reminiscences of E. L. Blanchard, with notes from the diary of Wm. Blanchard, ed. C. W. Scott and C. Howard, 2 vols. (1891) · Hall, Dramatic ports. · J. Hollingshead, Gaiety chronicles (1898)

Likenesses A. Beardsley, V&A; repro. in Pall Mall Budget (23 Feb 1893) · A. Ellis, photograph, NPG; repro. in The Theatre (July 1895) · Fradelle & Marshall, four cartes-de-visite, NPG · W. G. Robertson, two watercolours, Garr. Club • Spy [L. Ward], chromolithograph, NPG; repro. in *VF* (28 Dec 1889) • Spy [L. Ward], watercolour study, Garr. Club • caricature, repro. in *Entr'acte* (12 Feb 1881) • caricature, repro. in *Entr'acte* (8 July 1876) • photograph, NPG

Wealth at death £14,198 18s. 6d.: probate, 20 May 1896, *CGPLA Eng. & Wales*

Cecil, Lord (Edward Christian) David Gascoyne- [*known as* David Cecil] **(1902–1986)**, author, was born on 9 April 1902 at 24 Grafton Street, Mayfair, London, the fourth and last child and the second son of James Edward Hubert Gascoyne-*Cecil, fourth marquess of Salisbury (1861–1947), politician, and his wife, Lady (Cicely) Alice Gore (1867–1955), second daughter of the fifth earl of Arran, descended on her mother's side from the Melbourne family. A delicate child, he was much at home and benefited in this from the company of his brilliant aunts and uncles, notorious for their eccentricities, wit, and zeal. Between 1915 and 1919 he was at Eton College, where the confidence fostered by this remarkable family carried him through an unfamiliar and in some ways uncongenial atmosphere. His experience of Oxford—he matriculated from Christ Church in 1920—was different. He loved the life and the place. His exceptionally quick, associative mind served him well in his final examinations where he took a first class in modern history (1924). Though he failed to win an All Souls fellowship, he was elected to a fellowship at Wadham in 1924 to teach mainly history. At the same time, with characteristic independence, he was writing a life of the poet William Cowper, *The Stricken Deer*, his first and one of his best books, which was published in 1929 and won the Hawthornden prize in 1930.

This success led to Cecil's decision to resign his fellowship in 1930 and take up the life of a writer in London. There he met and fell in love with Rachel, only daughter of Desmond *MacCarthy, literary critic, one of the original members of the Bloomsbury group. Their marriage took place in 1932. Virginia Woolf in a wry but affectionate entry in her diary describes 'David and Rachel, arm-in-arm, sleep-walking down the aisle, preceded by a cross which ushered them into a car and so into a happy, long life, I make no doubt' (*The Diary of Virginia Woolf*, ed. A. O. Bell, 4, 1982, 128). She was not to know how accurate her ironic prediction would prove. A remarkable woman in her own right, Rachel MacCarthy was the perfect match for her husband. Of a simpler, more practical nature, she shared his vivacity and his unfailing curiosity about people, literature, and life. Like him, she was instinctively religious and a practising Christian. They were perfectly happy together, drawing their many friends into that happiness, for fifty years.

As he now moved into the country near Cranborne, Dorset, David Cecil's new life, though congenial, showed him that he missed Oxford, especially the teaching. In 1939 he accepted a fellowship in English at New College and it was here as tutor and, from 1949, as Goldsmiths' professor that he exercised his widest influence and produced much of his best work. He had a genius for teaching, communicating enjoyment, and drawing out the best from others. A brilliant conversationalist, his wit consisted in verbal

Lord (Edward Christian) David Gascoyne-Cecil (1902–1986), by Augustus John, 1935

sharpness and accuracy, together with a peculiarly sympathetic humour that was always adapted to the company and the occasion. He was a celebrated lecturer, but his influence was most felt in tutorials, classes, or small, intimate groups. He and his wife, naturally hospitable, were eager to mix their friends and share them with young unknowns. Without condescension or pretension they spread over a wide circle of acquaintances and pupils the best-known cultural, political, and artistic influences of the mid-twentieth century.

In the 1960s Cecil began to feel that his particular concern for English literature was under attack in an increasingly professional age. He never avoided, indeed enjoyed, debate, and was confident of his position, but he shared his family's clear-sightedness about the signs of the times. Developments in graduate studies, and the insistence on advanced degrees as a qualification for university teaching, made him feel his way was out of favour. In 1969 he reached retirement age and went happily to Cranborne, where he continued to write and entertain until his wife's death in 1982, and, though less happily, with remarkable resilience and little diminished powers of enjoyment until his own death.

Cecil's writings, especially his biographies of William Cowper, Lord Melbourne (1955), Jane Austen (1978), and Charles Lamb (1983), are a substantial contribution to the understanding of different kinds of personality and period. As such they had a value beyond the academic, and reached a wide readership. His literary criticism came to be seriously underestimated. *Early Victorian Novelists* (1934) was ahead of its time in a subtle analysis and discussion of the structure of *Wuthering Heights*. *Hardy the Novelist* (1943) remains a classic exposition of the work of one of his favourite authors. His best essays, too often written off as *belles-lettres*, are as acute as they are sensitive. But most typical of his imagination is his response to extrovert, worldly figures like Melbourne, or balanced moral observers such as Jane Austen, and, on the other hand, to introverted, despondent, but gentle and humorous spirits, such as Cowper and Lamb. To their situation he was drawn by a sympathy typical of the depth and complexity of his own nature.

Cecil considered himself, with good reason, the most fortunate of men. Born into one of the first families in the land, gifted with intellectual and imaginative sympathies of a high order, professionally successful, idyllically happy in his marriage and family life, he might well have grown complacent and a figure of envy. But complacency was not in his nature or his background: he was self-critical and self-aware. As for enemies, he had few if any. He was greatly loved because of the unusual sweetness of his temper and his genuine humility. Naturally high-spirited and with some vanity, he felt most strongly an inherited impulse of service and purpose. Himself a devout Christian, what he possessed he wanted to share, and he had been given precisely the gifts to enable this. His appearance was extraordinary and memorable: elegant and at the same time spontaneously gauche, continually in motion from the twirling thumbs to the enthusiastic forward lurch. His voice, too, was rapid, stuttering, and spasmodic, with Edwardian pronunciation. David Cecil was one of the most influential cultural figures of his age.

Cecil was appointed CH in 1949 and CLit in 1972. He had honorary doctorates from London, Leeds, Liverpool, St Andrews, and Glasgow universities. He was a trustee of the National Portrait Gallery from 1937 to 1951. He died at his home, Red Lion House, Salisbury Street, Cranborne, Dorset, on 1 January 1986.   RACHEL TRICKETT, *rev.*

Sources W. W. Robson, ed., *Essays and poems presented to Lord David Cecil* (1970) · H. Cranborne, ed., *David Cecil: a portrait by his friends* (1990) [privately printed] · personal knowledge (2004) · private information (2004) [family] · *The Times* (3 Jan 1986) · P. Garland, interview, *The Listener* (24 Dec 1970), 867–9
Archives BL, corresp. with Society of Authors, Add. MS 63217 · Bodl. Oxf., letters to R. W. Chapman; corresp. with Barbara Pym · Herts. ALS, letters to Lady Desborough and Monica, Lady Salmond
Likenesses A. John, oils, 1935, Tate collection [*see illus.*] · S. Mrozewski, wood-engraving, 1935, NPG · E. Sergeant, oil on paper, 1982, NPG · H. Lamb, pencil, NPG
Wealth at death £206,650: probate, 1 May 1986, *CGPLA Eng. & Wales*

Cecil, David George Brownlow, sixth marquess of Exeter (1905–1981), athlete and politician, was born in the family's vast 350-year-old ancestral home, Burghley House, Stamford, Lincolnshire, on 9 February 1905. He was the second child and elder son in the family of four children of the fifth marquess, William Thomas Brownlow Cecil (1876–1956), and his wife, Myra Rowena Sibell (*b.*

David George Brownlow Cecil, sixth marquess of Exeter (1905–1981), by Sir Oswald Birley, 1926

1879), daughter of William Thomas Orde-Powlett, fourth Baron Bolton. Lord Burghley, as he was to be for more than fifty years, was educated at Eton College and from 1923 at Magdalene College, Cambridge, where he studied engineering and obtained a BA in 1926. He was selected for Britain's 1924 Olympic team but hurdled poorly. However, in 1925 this striking blond-haired, aquiline-featured young patrician emerged as the world's pre-eminent hurdler.

Burghley won both the high and low hurdles event in the inter-varsity sports against Oxford in 1925, 1926, and 1927 and became president of the Cambridge University athletics club in his last year. The time of 42.5 sec. recorded in Burghley's diary after he ran round the Great Court of Trinity College, Cambridge, before the twenty-third of the twenty-four noon-time chimes, was still unsurpassed half a century later. He went on to represent Great Britain in eleven full international matches and to win eight Amateur Athletics Association (AAA) titles and three British empire titles. He set English native records for the 120 yards high and 220 yards low hurdles with 14.5 and 24.7 sec. In 1927 he very briefly held the world's 440 yards hurdles record, set at 54.2 sec. at Stamford Bridge, London.

Burghley's greatest hour came in the 400 metres hurdles final at the 1928 Olympic games in Amsterdam where, by deliberately running for third place in the semi-final, he arrived quite fresh for the six-man final. He and

Britain's T. C. Livingstone-Learmonth drew the disadvantageous outside fifth and sixth lanes. Ranged against them were the world record holder and defending champion, F. Morgan Taylor (USA), Frank J. Cuhel (USA), the Italian Luigi Facelli, and Sweden's Sten Pettersson. Burghley went off seemingly too fast but reached the tenth and final flight of the all-wooden barriers just ahead of Cuhel. His finish was described as 'obstinate' and at the tape he won by a long yard in the Olympic record time of 53.4 sec., with Cuhel second and Morgan Taylor third, both in 53.6 sec. In that era before track suits he donned his greatcoat and confined his comment to 'The Americans are frightfully good losers'. In the fashion of the day his father, who sat alone at the back of the main stand, made no comment whatsoever, but his mother was later found to have kept a secret scrapbook of her son's many triumphs on the track.

Burghley's enjoyment of amateur athletics was such that four years later he defended his Olympic title in Los Angeles. By this time he was married, a father, and an MP. In the general election of 1931 he had won the Labour-held seat of Peterborough with a majority of 12,434. Under the California sun he ran his fastest ever time of 52.2 sec. but still finished behind his fellow Cambridge blue Robert Tisdall of Ireland (51.7 seconds) and the two Americans Glen Hardin and his old rival Morgan Taylor. In the 4 x 400 metres relay he ran an outstanding third stage for Great Britain in 46.7 sec. behind America's world record-breaking quartet, adding a silver medal to his collection. He was the British Olympic captain in both 1932 and 1936.

From 1933 to 1937 Burghley was chairman of the Junior Imperial League (president 1939). In the general election of 1935 he held his seat with a reduced majority. In the House of Commons, Burghley and Alan Lennox-Boyd (later Viscount Boyd of Merton) were the two fastest speakers and cherished their visits to the office of the *Hansard* shorthand writers, where they had to be permitted to improve rather than merely correct their speech proofs. Burghley, though a lieutenant in the Grenadier Guards until 1929 (when he resigned and obtained seats on the boards of a number of companies), was unable to take up combatant service in 1939 owing to a persistent leg injury. He was appointed a staff captain tank supply in 1940, and became assistant director with the rank of lieutenant-colonel in 1942. In August 1943 he left parliament to become governor of Bermuda, where he captivated many American and other allied visiting dignitaries. He was created KCMG in the same year.

Burghley was chairman of the organizing and executive committee of the fourteenth Olympiad, held in Wembley stadium in London in 1948. George VI adamantly refused to attend and the prime minister, C. R. Attlee, was obliged to intervene since Olympic protocol required that the head of state of the host nation declare the games open in person. Predictably the king's sense of duty prevailed, and on 29 July he performed the ceremony. Burghley, who had only two years, instead of the customary six, in which to organize these first post-war games, had worked tirelessly in surmounting all the difficulties in an era of rationing, bomb damage, and national austerity. The success of this quadrennial festival of what was then amateur sport was a credit to his zeal. Some of his team were less richly honoured for their heroic efforts to make the games a British success than might have been appropriate had not an honour of any kind been withheld from their chairman. Burghley was president of the AAA (1936–76), the International Amateur Athletic Federation (1946–76), and the British Olympic Association (1966–77, chairman 1936–66). His fervent, some thought naïve, belief that amateur and Olympic sport were a palliative in international strife brought him into conflict over the award in 1974 by the International Olympic Committee of the 1980 or twenty-second Olympiad to Moscow. He was obdurate in the face of mounting entreaties after the invasion of Afghanistan that Britain should pull out. Supported by lords Killanin and Luke, his defiance of the well-known wishes of the prime minister, Margaret Thatcher, resulted in his being ostracized by those who thought British participation would also demoralize the four millions imprisoned in Soviet gulags and be an insult to the captive peoples of eastern Europe.

Despite hip replacement operations, Burghley hunted with vigour, latterly with the Burghley hunt, up to 1967. He had succeeded to the marquessate in 1956. He often gave priority to local affairs over debates in the House of Lords because, as he said, 'They are of more importance to Mrs Buggins because it is her roof which is leaking'. In 1961 he was elected mayor of Stamford. He was honorary FRCS and had an honorary LLD from St Andrews University (of which he was rector from 1949 to 1952).

On 10 January 1929 Burghley married Mary Theresa, fourth daughter of John Charles Montagu-Douglas-Scott, seventh duke of Buccleuch and ninth duke of Queensberry, at a time when the announcement of her engagement to Prince Henry, later duke of Gloucester, was regarded as imminent in royal circles. They had a son and three daughters but the son died of tubercular meningitis at the age of thirteen months in 1934. The marriage was dissolved in 1946 and on 12 December that year Burghley married Diana Mary (d. 1982), widow of Lieutenant-Colonel David Walter Arthur William Forbes and daughter of the Hon. Arnold Henderson. The only child of his second marriage, Lady Victoria Leatham, was to become a vigorous and enterprising chatelaine of Burghley House, where he died on 21 October 1981. He was succeeded in the marquessate by his brother William Martin Alleyne Cecil (1909–1988).   NORRIS MCWHIRTER

Sources *The Times* (23 Oct 1981) · personal knowledge (2004) · Burke, *Peerage*

Archives Northants. RO, appointment diaries, 1920–56

Likenesses O. Birley, portrait, 1926, Burghley House, Stamford, Lincolnshire [*see illus.*] · two photographs, 1927–9, Hult. Arch. · photographs, 1930–31, repro. in P. Lovesey, *Official centenary history of the Amateur Athletic Association* (1979), 81–2 · photograph, 1976, repro. in P. Lovesey, *Official centenary history of the Amateur Athletic Association* (1979), 167 · A. Wysard, double portrait, watercolour (with H. C. Lowther), NPG

Wealth at death £1,813,782: probate, 6 Jan 1983, *CGPLA Eng. & Wales*

Cecil, Edgar Algernon Robert Gascoyne- [*known as* Lord Robert Cecil], **Viscount Cecil of Chelwood (1864–1958)**, politician and peace campaigner, always best-known as Lord Robert Cecil, was born on 14 September 1864 at 11 Duchess Street, Portland Place, London, the third son in the family of five sons and three daughters of Robert Arthur Talbot Gascoyne-*Cecil, third marquess of Salisbury (1830–1903), politician, and his wife, Georgina Caroline Alderson (*d*. 1899).

Education, the bar, and marriage As the son of a long-serving Conservative prime minister, Lord Robert Cecil inherited a party affiliation which, though reinforced by his devout high-Anglicanism, was in conflict with his progressive political instincts. As his nephew Lord David Cecil observed, he 'lacked his father's melancholy and scepticism', being instead 'sanguine and positive and impetuous like his mother' (D. Cecil, 294). He was educated by governesses and tutors at home until he was thirteen, a segregating experience which, though congenial, may have contributed to the individualism and propensity to resign which were to mark his political career. He then spent four not very agreeable years at Eton College, followed by another spell with a private tutor, after which, in January 1883, he went to University College, Oxford, where he flourished, becoming friendly with Edward Grey (the future Liberal foreign secretary), being elected to the Canning Club, speaking at the Oxford Union Society, playing real tennis against Cambridge, and taking a second in jurisprudence in 1886.

Cecil was employed for the next two years as his father's private secretary, during which time he was called to the bar (Inner Temple) in 1887. He established himself comfortably as a barrister, specializing in parliamentary work but also publishing a joint work on the principles of commercial law in 1891, and took silk in 1900. He also made a successful marriage in 1889 to Lady Eleanor Lambton (1868–1959), daughter of George Frederick D'Arcy Lambton, second earl of Durham: their relationship was always close, despite her almost complete loss of hearing from the age of about twenty-six; she died five months to the day after he did. In addition to maintaining a succession of London residences of increasingly fashionable location, of which 16 South Eaton Place was the apogee, they built a modest country house, which they called Gale on account of its exposed location, at Chelwood Gate, between East Grinstead and Uckfield, in Sussex: surviving a Luftwaffe bomb which fell just outside its front door in November 1940, it remained their best-loved home for more than half a century.

Unionist free-trader Cecil's political career began when he was returned as Conservative MP for Marylebone East at the 1906 general election. He soon made his mark as a diligent opposition back-bencher, though he was uneasy about the direction his party was taking: he was a free-trader, albeit of the moderate kind that accepted the case for retaliatory duties, and with a landowner's disdain for

Edgar Algernon Robert Gascoyne-Cecil [Lord Robert Cecil], Viscount Cecil of Chelwood (1864–1958), by Sir William Orpen, 1919

the rising commercial wing of his party dismissed tariff reform as 'a rather sordid attempt to ally Imperialism with State assistance for the rich' (R. Cecil, *All the Way*, 244). He was also a supporter of women's suffrage on the same basis as men's and of industrial co-partnership; and he disapproved of the rejection of the People's Budget by the House of Lords. Fear of opposition from tariff reformers within his constituency association caused him to quit East Marylebone; and at the two general elections of 1910 he unsuccessfully contested Blackburn and the Wisbech division of Cambridgeshire respectively, before winning a by-election for the Hitchin division of Hertfordshire in November 1911 as a Unionist free-trader.

War cabinet and the League of Nations Too old to enlist when the First World War broke out, Cecil worked for the Red Cross in France, helping to organize its department of wounded and missing, an experience which helped to persuade him that war prevention was 'the only political object worth while' (R. Cecil, *A Great Experiment*, 189). When Asquith broadened his Liberal government into a coalition in May 1915, Cecil entered it as parliamentary under-secretary of state for foreign affairs, a post he held for over four years, and was also sworn of the privy council. He joined the cabinet in February 1916 with the additional title of minister for blockade; and, despite disapproving of Lloyd George, who replaced Asquith as prime minister in December of that year, he remained in office under him, though the cabinet was replaced by a small war cabinet of which he was not a member. Cecil's experience of administering the blockade persuaded him that economic sanctions could prove a powerful yet non-military means of enforcing international law. The creation of a league of nations had become progressive opinion's leading war aim; and Cecil, who regarded his support for it as a logical development of the respect for the concert of Europe shown by his father, became the first ministerial convert to the league idea. He circulated a Foreign Office paper on the subject in September 1916, and thereafter pressed determinedly for a governmental commitment to it, though he did not join the League of Nations Society. He was promoted to the rank of assistant secretary of state for foreign affairs in June 1918, thereby becoming deputy to his cousin A. J. Balfour, but formally resigned from the government on 21 November 1918 because as a loyal Anglican—who indeed had co-authored a book entitled *Our National Church* in 1913—he opposed the disestablishment of the Welsh church, which was due to be implemented once the war was over.

None the less Cecil stayed in office on a caretaker basis and was re-elected at the December 1918 general election as a coalition Conservative. In January 1919 he finally left the Foreign Office to take up an appointment as adviser on league issues to Britain's delegation at the Paris peace conference, where he played an important part in establishing the League of Nations and shaping its covenant— unquestionably the most significant achievement of his career.

This work having been completed by the summer of 1919, Cecil severed his governmental links. He agreed to represent South Africa at the first three League of Nations assemblies (1920–22). With British politics in flux owing to the continuation of the coalition government, the Liberal split, and Labour's advance, he came close to changing parties. He sent a message of support to Asquith when he contested a by-election at Paisley in February 1920—a gesture which proved controversial when a coalition Conservative decided to stand and lost his deposit—and also tried to persuade Grey to offer himself as the leader of a new party of the centre. After Austen Chamberlain became Conservative leader in March 1921, Cecil lost the party whip and moved to the opposition benches. Moreover, although he was regarded as the official Conservative candidate in the 1922 general election, which followed the collapse of the coalition, he described himself in *Who's Who* as an independent Conservative.

League of Nations Union and Conservative cabinets Meanwhile, instead of returning to the law Cecil devoted an increasing amount of his time to the League of Nations Union (LNU), which had been formed in November 1918 as a merger of the League of Nations Society and a rival body, the League of Free Nations Association. Cecil became its acknowledged leader: he took over from Professor Gilbert Murray, with whom he was to develop a strong working relationship, as chairman of its executive committee in June 1919; and he made his first public appearance on an LNU platform the following month. As an influential Conservative, he brought the LNU authority and respectability, helping it to develop into one of Britain's most remarkable voluntary associations, with more than 400,000 paid-up members at its peak in 1931. Moreover, as

a political maverick with great confidence in his own judgement, he was willing to insist that the LNU do more than educate the public in league principles, as its general secretary Maxwell Garnett merely wished it to do. Cecil wanted the LNU to press successive British governments to be more supportive of the League of Nations even at the risk of being thought 'political'. In 1922, for example, he persuaded the LNU to oppose Lloyd George's proposed bilateral pact with France, as a relapse into the old diplomacy, and to support a strengthening of the league's security provisions through a draft treaty of mutual assistance instead.

Though omitted from Bonar Law's government in November 1922, Cecil was made cabinet minister responsible for league affairs, with the title of lord privy seal, when Baldwin took over as prime minister in May 1923, though he was not allowed to base himself in the Foreign Office. He handed the chairmanship of the LNU's executive committee back to Murray, but became its president in 1923, at first jointly with Grey, an office he held for the remainder of the LNU's existence (until 1945). The tension between his positions as minister and leader of a major pressure group did not have time to become acute in 1923: Baldwin failed to receive the mandate for protection which he sought in a general election in December, and resigned the following month. Cecil, who had refused to seek re-election on a protectionist programme, went to the House of Lords as the first—and, being childless, only—Viscount Cecil of Chelwood (24 December 1923).

Rumours that Viscount Cecil might join the first Labour government proved to be unfounded. But when Baldwin returned to office in November 1924, Cecil was reappointed to the cabinet, this time with the title of chancellor of the duchy of Lancaster, though once again excluded from the Foreign Office. Baldwin presumably hoped that Cecil would be tamed by office; but instead he was irritated by his lack of influence within the government, and by 21 March 1926 was complaining to the prime minister: 'I cannot remain as a kind of guarantee to supporters of the League in the country, that the policy they so much desire is safe, unless I am given some means of delivering the goods' (Middlemas and Barnes, 360). What Cecil saw as his colleagues' foot-dragging approach to arbitration and disarmament caused him to resign on 9 August 1927; and though, in response to entreaties from Austen Chamberlain, Cecil's resignation letter was progressively toned down in the course of five drafts, it none the less embarrassed the government. Moreover, he followed his resignation with an LNU campaign over the autumn and winter of 1927–8 which even Murray feared might seem anti-Conservative. And in the 1929 general election Cecil urged the electorate to ignore party considerations and vote only for pro-league candidates.

The Peace Ballot Cecil was rewarded by being appointed by the second MacDonald government as a British delegate to the League of Nations: he was given a room at the Foreign Office, and enjoyed excellent relations there with Arthur Henderson and his junior ministers Hugh Dalton and Philip Noel Baker (this last having at one time been

Cecil's private secretary). When this administration fell in the financial crisis of 1931 he felt obliged to support the National Government which replaced it, and so stayed on as a league delegate. However, in the light of the new ministry's half-hearted policy on the issue he declined to represent Britain at the World Disarmament Conference, which opened at Geneva in February 1932.

The collapse of that conference in October 1933, when Germany also gave notice of leaving the league, produced a vocal anti-Geneva reaction among both left and right in Britain. Cecil's challenge to this essentially isolationist response led to his most impressive campaigning achievement. The *Ilford Recorder*, whose editor was chairman of his LNU branch, had run a local poll which suggested that public opinion was more pro-league than politicians realized; and this result was confirmed by a number of other local newspapers. Cecil persuaded the LNU to hold a national poll on the same lines: a prodigious organizational feat as well as a major financial and political gamble, the National Declaration on the League of Nations Union and Armaments (or Peace Ballot, as it was colloquially known) secured responses from 38 per cent of the adult population between November 1934 and June 1935. These revealed not only overwhelming support for the league but also majority support for military sanctions, though Cecil later privately conceded that not enough emphasis had been placed on the latter in LNU propaganda prior to 1936. The success of the Peace Ballot encouraged the National Government to support the application of mild economic sanctions against Italy when it attacked Abyssinia and to take a pro-league line in the November 1935 general election. It also caused it to dismiss its foreign secretary, Sir Samuel Hoare, the following month when a leak of his discussions with his French opposite number revealed that he was privately seeking a deal with Mussolini.

International Peace Campaign and Nobel peace prize However, Cecil's greatest triumph led directly to his greatest frustration. The Peace Ballot highlighted the weakness of efforts to arouse pro-league sentiment in Europe. When, as an offshoot of popular-front politics, a collective security campaign known as the Rassemblement Universel pour la Paix was launched in France in the autumn of 1935, Cecil was determined that the British league movement support the continental initiative in order to lend it some of its own prestige. However, when extended to Britain in 1936 under the name International Peace Campaign (IPC), the Rassemblement ran into three difficulties. First, its timing was unlucky: the league was discredited in the spring of 1936 by its inability to stop Mussolini conquering Abyssinia, with the result that many former supporters of collective security began to advocate appeasement instead. Second, the IPC duplicated the LNU's work and drew funds away from it at a time when these were anyway drying up because of the league's unpopularity. Third, its communist links offended the labour movement and the Roman Catholic church in particular.

Cecil underestimated these difficulties, and hinted at resignation if the LNU did not co-operate with the IPC. The

LNU agreed to do so, but despite several attempts failed to work out a satisfactory constitutional relationship to the new body. Cecil grew irritated, and suggested that the Nobel peace prize which he was awarded in 1937 was a tribute to the IPC rather than to the LNU. At that year's LNU staff Christmas party he was further enraged by a satirical sketch written by a Catholic member of staff known to dislike the IPC which depicted him as not only fanatical about the IPC but also senile. In the ensuing row he forced the LNU's general secretary, Garnett, to resign.

However, for all Cecil's exertions, and those of loyal associates in the LNU such as Noel Baker, the IPC failed to make headway in Britain, either as a committee of the LNU, or as an independent body on which the LNU was represented on the same basis as other supportive associations, or even (in a desperate last throw) as a wholly separate organization. In 1939 Cecil wearily resigned as president of the IPC's British national committee (though he remained co-president with Pierre Cot of its parent body). He was to experience further disillusionment when as a result of the Molotov–Ribbentrop pact the IPC's communist element revealed its true loyalties by trying to turn the IPC against collective security in line with Soviet policy; and by the end of 1940 the IPC and its parent body had both, in effect, collapsed. Within Britain, Cecil's preoccupation with the IPC had thus hindered rather than helped the campaign for British rearmament and the containment of Germany, to which he was fully committed from 1936 onwards. And although on the continent the Rassemblement had made more political impact, it too ultimately failed.

Second World War and after A further tribulation for Cecil was that during 1939–40 the younger generation of British and American internationalists lost faith in confederal organizations such as the league and became converted to federalism. They therefore devoted their energies to a new organization, Federal Union, rather than to the LNU. Cecil remained doggedly loyal to the latter, however, and towards the end of the Second World War was rewarded by the revival of the confederal cause in the form of the allied agreement to replace the defunct league with a somewhat similar United Nations Organization. By his eightieth birthday in 1944 he was honoured by public praise from Winston Churchill, who also made a warm speech when the Royal Institute of International Affairs presented Cecil with a bust. He was invited to the final session of the league assembly at Geneva in the spring of 1946, where he ended his speech with the phrase: 'The League is dead; long live the United Nations'.

Thereafter Cecil's public work was virtually over. He was made an honorary life president of the United Nations Association, which succeeded the LNU without achieving anything like the same public support. In 1948 he wrote a pamphlet, *An Emergency Policy*, warning of the need for a western union against the Soviet threat. And on 23 April 1953, in what turned out to be his last speech in the House of Lords, he argued that 'Christian civilisation is the only real alternative to dialectical materialism'

(*Hansard 5L*, 181, 1953, 1159). In 1956 he was made a Companion of Honour.

Cecil, who from the late 1930s was increasingly deaf, was very tall, with a pronounced stoop, prominent eyes, a mobile and expressive face, an eagle-like profile, and a forehead which became more pronounced as his hair receded. Throughout his career he was in demand for honorific positions, and at various times served as chancellor of Birmingham University, rector of Aberdeen University, and visitor of St Hugh's College, Oxford. He died at the Lonsdale Nursing Home, Tunbridge Wells, Kent, on 24 November 1958. Paying tribute to him in the House of Lords two days later, the fourteenth earl of Home, whose father had been a league supporter prior to 1936, recalled of Cecil's visits to his home that

> many a time at dinner ... I would watch him, with his long figure, slide more and more under the table, until only the distinguished head was left above his plate, and he would tell us all of his plans for the future peace of the world. (*Hansard 5L*, 212, 1958, 838)

MARTIN CEADEL

Sources WW · BL, Cecil of Chelwood MSS · BLPES, League of Nations Union papers · Churchill College, Cambridge, Noel-Baker MSS · D. Cecil, *The Cecils of Hatfield House* (1973) · Viscount Cecil [R. Cecil], *A great experiment: an autobiography* (1941) · Viscount Cecil of Chelwood [R. Cecil], *All the way* (1949) · H. P. Cecil, 'The development of Lord Robert Cecil's views on securing a lasting peace, 1915–19', DPhil diss., U. Oxf., 1971 · M. Ceadel, 'The first British referendum: the Peace Ballot, 1934–35', *EngHR*, 95 (1980), 810–39 · K. Middlemas and J. Barnes, *Baldwin: a biography* (1969) · M. Cowling, *The impact of labour, 1920–1924: the beginning of modern British politics* (1971) · D. S. Birn, *The League of Nations Union, 1918–1945* (1981) · Bodl. Oxf., MSS Gilbert Murray · *The Times* [obit. of Eleanor Cecil, d. 24/4/1959]

Archives BL, corresp. and papers, Add. MSS 51071–51204 · Hatfield House, Hertfordshire, political and personal corresp. and papers · PRO, corresp., FO 800/195-8 | BL, corresp. with Arthur James Balfour, Add. MSS 49737–49738 · BL, corresp. with Lord Gladstone, Add. MSS 46476–46477 · BL, corresp. with Sir R. S. Paget, Add. MS 51254 · Bodl. Oxf., letters to Herbert Asquith · Bodl. Oxf., letters to Lady Milner · Bodl. Oxf., corresp. with Gilbert Murray · Bodl. Oxf., letters to Lord Ponsonby · Bodl. Oxf., corresp. with Rumbold · Bodl. Oxf., corresp. with second earl of Selborne · Bodl. Oxf., corresp. with second and third earls of Selborne and Maud, countess of Selborne · Bodl. Oxf., corresp. relating to Society for the Protection of Science and Learning · Bodl. RH, corresp. with Lord Lugard · CAC Cam., corresp. with Noel-Baker · CKS, letters to his brother, Lord Edward Cecil · HLRO, letters to R. D. Blumenfeld · HLRO, corresp. with J. C. C. Davidson and A. B. Law · HLRO, corresp. with David Lloyd George · HLRO, letters to Lord Samuel · HLRO, corresp. with John St Loe Strachey · IWM, corresp. with H. A. Gwynne · JRL, letters to *Manchester Guardian* · NA Scot., corresp. with Lord Lothian · NRA Scotland priv. coll., corresp. with Lord Balfour of Burleigh · Nuffield Oxf., corresp. with Lord Emmott · U. Newcastle, Robinson L., corresp. with Walter Runciman · Women's Library, London, letters to Dame Kathleen Courtney · Yale U., Sterling Memorial Library, corresp. with Edward House | FILM BFI NFTVA, news footage · BFI NFTVA, propaganda film footage (Hepworth Manufacturing Company)

Likenesses A. John, oils, 1919, Hatfield House, Hertfordshire · W. Orpen, oils, 1919, NPG [*see illus.*] · M. Beerbohm, pencil and wash caricature, 1921, AM Oxf. · W. Rothenstein, chalk drawing, 1922, NPG · W. Rothenstein, sanguine drawing, 1922, Man. City Gall. · F. H. Shepherd, group portrait, oils, 1928 (with family), University College, Oxford; version, Hatfield House, Hertfordshire · J. Mansbridge, oils, 1931, NPG · W. Stoneman, photograph, 1931, NPG ·

P. A. de Laszlo, oils, 1932, Hatfield House, Hertfordshire · P. A. de Laszlo, oils, 1932, U. Birm. · W. Stoneman, photograph, 1943, NPG · S. Charoux, bronze bust, 1945, Royal Institute of International Affairs, Chatham House, London · K. Pollak, three photographs, 1947, NPG · M. Beerbohm, wash caricature, Hatfield House, Hertfordshire · F. C. Gould, two ink caricatures, NPG · E. Kapp, lithograph, NPG · Spy [L. Ward], caricature, lithograph, NPG; repro. in *VF* (22 Feb 1906) · portrait, repro. in Cecil, *Great experiment* · portrait, repro. in Cecil, *All the way*

Wealth at death £28,997 8s. 3d.: probate, 23 April 1959, CGPLA Eng. & Wales

Cecil, Edward, Viscount Wimbledon (1572–1638), soldier and politician, was the third son of Sir Thomas *Cecil (1542–1623), created earl of Exeter in May 1605, and Dorothy (1546?–1609), daughter and coheir of John Neville, fourth and last Baron Latimer. He was born on 29 February 1572 at Burghley House near Stamford, Lincolnshire, the seat of his grandfather William *Cecil, first Baron Burghley. Nothing is known for certain about Cecil's education beyond his enrolment at Gray's Inn in 1591. In late 1594 he was given leave to travel abroad and two years later was in Florence. From there he wrote, in Italian, his earliest surviving letter, addressed to his uncle Sir Robert *Cecil (1563–1612), who had succeeded Burghley as Queen Elizabeth's principal minister. Cecil was proud of his connection with one of the greatest families in England and looked to his uncle to help advance him in the military career which he decided to pursue. He joined the English forces fighting to maintain Dutch independence and in 1600, thanks to Sir Robert's intervention, became a colonel of horse. Cecil's determination to uphold his family's honour had its darker side, for in 1601 he was accused of lying in wait in the Strand to kidnap 'and by presumption to have murdered' an unfortunate official who had offended his brother-in-law (*Salisbury MSS*, 11.561–2).

Although Cecil usually spent the summer months campaigning in the Netherlands he was in England in June 1601, when he married Theodosia (1583/4–1616), the daughter of Sir Andrew *Noel of Brooke in Rutland. Later that year he was a guest of his brother-in-law, the marquess of Winchester, at Basing House when the queen came to visit, and received a knighthood at her hands. Elizabeth died in March 1603 and Cecil's father, whose official residence as lord president of the council of the north was at York, sent him post-haste to Edinburgh to greet the new king, James VI and I. Cecil received a warm welcome, not only on his own behalf but as the nephew of Sir Robert, who had ensured James's peaceful accession to the English throne. James appointed him a gentleman of the privy chamber and also gave him the keepership of Putney park.

Military career and parliamentary experience On his return to the Netherlands, Cecil again requested his uncle's help, this time to secure him command of one of the four infantry regiments into which the British troops were divided. However, by 1607 his commitment to a military career was beginning to waver as the Dutch and their Spanish opponents began the negotiations that culminated in the twelve-year truce of 1609. Robert Cecil, now earl of Salisbury, resisted pressure from his nephew to appoint him lord president of Munster, but the desire to find new outlets for his talents may have prompted Cecil to put himself forward for election to parliament in 1609. He was not without experience in this arena since he had been selected as member for the Yorkshire borough of Aldborough in 1601, although he took no recorded part in the subsequent proceedings. In 1609 he was duly elected for the family borough of Stamford, replacing a deceased cousin, and not only took his seat but was named to a number of committees. However, he was called away from parliamentary duties when James chose him to lead the British contingent of an international force to be dispatched to the protestant Rhineland duchies of Julich and Cleve, where a succession dispute threatened to spark off a general war in Europe. The expedition was instrumental in resolving the dispute, and Cecil's stock rose accordingly.

As a professional soldier and convinced protestant Cecil had a natural affinity with James's eldest son, Prince Henry, and sent him letters from Julich as well as a gift of sycamore trees for Henry's park at Richmond. Unfortunately for Cecil the burgeoning friendship was cut short by the prince's death in November 1612. This blow came on top of a worse one, for in May of that year the earl of Salisbury had also died. The annuity of £200 which his uncle left him was little compensation for the loss of so powerful a protector. The next year James honoured Cecil by making him treasurer of the select band of nobles which accompanied James's daughter, Elizabeth, on her journey to Heidelberg following her marriage to Frederick, elector palatine. Two years later Cecil was back in the Netherlands but in March 1616 he suffered a personal tragedy when Lady Cecil died at the age of thirty-two. 'I must confess it inflicted a very strong sorrow upon me', he confided to one of his correspondents, 'for she was a dear and good wife to me' (PRO, SP 84/72.22). However, his widowerhood was short-lived for in February 1618 he married Diana Drury (d. 1631), daughter of Sir William Drury of Hawstead in Suffolk, whose substantial estate she inherited.

The Bohemian crisis A new crisis in European affairs arose in 1620 when the Elector Frederick, who had rashly accepted the crown of Bohemia, was not only driven out of his newly acquired kingdom by Habsburg forces but also threatened with the loss of his hereditary Rhineland possessions. English public opinion was strongly in favour of the 'King and Queen of Bohemia' and James authorized the dispatch of a volunteer force to defend the Palatinate. Cecil hoped to command this and was strongly supported by the marquess of Buckingham, James's favourite, but Baron Dohna, Frederick's ambassador in England, chose Sir Horace Vere, who had formerly commanded the British forces in Dutch service. Cecil was bitterly angry at this slight and made his feelings plain in a stormy interview with Dohna. However, there was no question of altering the decision, and Cecil therefore returned to the Netherlands where the struggle against Spain was about to be renewed.

Cecil was back in England in time to be elected to the 1621 parliament as member for Chichester. He took an active part in debates but was unable to persuade the Commons to accept a bill for the standardization of arms. He joined wholeheartedly in the attack on Edward Floyd, a Roman Catholic barrister accused of insulting Frederick and Elizabeth of Bohemia, and he helped draft a declaration that if the king was forced into war for the defence of the protestant religion and the rights of his children, members would support him with their lives and estates. Cecil acclaimed this declaration as 'come from heaven' and expressed the belief that it would 'work better effects with our enemies than if we had 10,000 soldiers on the march' (Nicholas, 2.169–70).

The death of Cecil's father in February 1623 meant that he now became the owner of the great house at Wimbledon which Thomas Cecil had constructed. It was damaged by an accidental explosion in 1628, and as part of its restoration Cecil commissioned the Dutch artist Francis Cleyne to paint frescoes on the exterior. He also added a family chapel to the south side of St Mary's Church. Wimbledon was some way from London, but Cecil possessed a house in the Strand and employed Inigo Jones to make additions to it. However, he preferred to let this property and instead to rent a house in Chelsea which had at one time belonged to William Cecil.

The Cadiz expedition Cecil was elected to the 1624 parliament, in which he represented Dover, and advocated breaking off negotiations with Spain. If this course of action led to war, as seemed likely, he was well placed for a senior command, but disillusionment set in when a foreign mercenary, Count Mansfeld, was put in charge of a joint Anglo-French expedition for the relief of the Palatinate. Writing to Buckingham from the Netherlands in December 1624, Cecil complained that now 'strangers get the command, and new soldiers are employed, which was never heard of before amongst men of our occupation' (Cabala, 170). As it happened Buckingham was already planning a combined naval and military expedition against Spain and in May 1625 he invited Cecil to command it. 'I have put into your hand', Buckingham reminded him, 'the first infinite trust and pawn of my goodwill that ever I had in my power to bestow' (PRO, SP 84/127.22). Cecil in reply assured Buckingham that he would 'have no cause to doubt, or repent you of your favours' (Cabala, 168).

Unfortunately for Cecil the perennial shortage of money that crippled early Stuart regimes meant that the expedition was ill prepared. The impressed men dispatched to Plymouth were drawn from the dregs of the population and lacked both discipline and training. Many of the ships designated for the expedition were in poor condition, and supplies of food and munitions came in only by fits and starts. Cecil's doubts about a successful outcome of the venture were indicated when he told Buckingham that 'if the journey beget nothing but experience, yet the cost is not cast away' (PRO, SP 16/6.31).

Cecil had been instructed to take advice from a council of war consisting of the captains and senior officers under him, and not to risk his ships unnecessarily. These instructions seem to have reinforced his natural caution, and although he eventually set sail on 5 October he returned to port the next day because of bad weather. He was rebuked by Sir John Coke, Buckingham's right-hand man in naval affairs, who pointed out that 'the wars require hazard, so it be with judgment, and if the safety of your ships had been most to be respected, the way had been to have kept them at Chatham' (PRO, SP 16/7.9). Cecil took the hint, and on 8 October the expedition finally set off for the Spanish coast. Its principal task, according to orders transmitted by Buckingham, was to watch out for the plate fleet which brought silver from the New World into Spanish harbours. Other objectives included the seizure of some major port so that the fleet and its projected successors could maintain a permanent presence in Spanish waters.

Despite suffering heavy damage in a violent gale the expedition reached the Spanish coast and took up position off Cadiz. Cecil summoned a council of war which decided the fleet should make for Puerto de Santa María, opposite Cadiz, where it could take in much-needed fresh water. He rejected calls for a plan of action to be drawn up, since so much depended on imponderables, but left it to the vice-admiral, the earl of Essex, to lead the way into the Bay of Cadiz. Essex did so, on 22 October, but instead of aiming for Puerto de Santa María he sailed towards a number of Spanish ships that were moored off the town of Cadiz. These promptly cut their cables and fled up the narrow channel that led to Puerto Real. Essex, who had outstripped the other ships in his squadron, thought it too dangerous to pursue the Spanish vessels unsupported and therefore came to anchor off Cadiz. He later alleged that he had been given no specific orders to engage the Spaniards.

Since no plan of action had been agreed Cecil summoned another council of war but in the meantime he received information from the captain of an English fishing boat that the arrival of the expedition had taken the Spaniards by surprise and that Cadiz was in no fit state to defend itself. Some members of the council argued in favour of an immediate attack upon the city, but Cecil went along with the majority view that they should first bombard Fort Puntal, which dominated the entrance to the harbour. The fort held out until the following day, 23 October, and only surrendered after troops had been landed. Its resistance had given time for reinforcements to be sent into Cadiz.

By the morning of 24 October the entire expeditionary force was on shore, commanded by Cecil in person. Cecil, whose strategic thinking had been conditioned by his experience of siege warfare in the Netherlands, ruled out a direct attack upon Cadiz. Instead he set out in the opposite direction, intending to seize the bridge which linked the city to the mainland and thereby cut off supplies and reinforcements. His troops were hot and tired and, looking for somewhere to rest, they came across deserted houses containing casks of new wine. Cecil had earlier issued explicit orders against the consumption of this potent brew but he now agreed that his men should be allowed to refresh themselves with it. The consequences, as he should have foreseen, were disastrous. The expeditionary force was abruptly transformed into a drunken rabble. When the officers attempted to restore control they were threatened and insulted. Even Cecil's authority was slighted, and 'base and contemptuous words' were used 'both against his person and place' (Glanville, 59).

Since the army had ceased to exist as a fighting force Cecil decided that the only option was to re-embark his men and put out to sea. One of the reasons for entering the Bay of Cadiz had been to take on water at Puerto de Santa María, but on 29 October the expedition left harbour without replenishing its supplies, even though they were running short. Cecil intended to remain at sea, waiting for the relief fleet that Buckingham had promised and keeping a look-out for Spanish treasure ships from the New World. A number of these were spotted making their way into Cadiz but the poor sailing capacities of the English ships, allied with bad weather, made interception impossible. In addition the crowding together of unwashed soldiers, combined with shortage of drinking water and bad food, had caused infection to set in and it quickly became apparent that the fleet would have to make all haste to England while there were still enough healthy mariners to manipulate the sails. The council of war gave its approval to this course of action on 17 November, but bad weather dispersed the fleet and each ship had to fend for itself. Cecil's flagship, the *Ann Royal*, suffered heavy storm damage and westerly winds pushed it towards Ireland. Not until 11 December did it limp into harbour at Kinsale.

Last years and reputation Before the expedition had set out from England, Cecil had been created Baron Cecil of Putney and Viscount Wimbledon, but it was only after his return that he began to use his title. There was widespread criticism of his conduct and he was lampooned as Viscount Sitstill, but although the council investigated the complaints made by Essex and others it took no action against him. He complained about being kept from the king's presence but his repeated protestations of loyalty to Buckingham saved him from further disgrace. When a new council of war was formed in May 1626 Wimbledon was a member, and in December of that year he was appointed lord lieutenant of Surrey. Just over a year later, in February 1628, he was sworn in as a privy councillor. It may be significant, however, that when Buckingham was planning the expedition to Ré in 1627 he did not invite Wimbledon to participate. Wimbledon remained nominally in Dutch service until June 1633 but in July 1630 he was appointed governor of Portsmouth and thereafter devoted himself to improving its defences.

In May 1631 Wimbledon's second wife died and was buried in the family chapel at St Mary's Church, Wimbledon. Wimbledon had four surviving daughters from his first marriage but no son to inherit his titles. In October 1635, therefore, at the age of sixty-three, he married Sophia (d. 1691), the seventeen-year-old daughter of Sir Edward Zouch. In January 1637 she gave birth to the longed-for son, but the child lived less than a year. On 16 November 1638 Wimbledon himself died, at Wimbledon House; he was buried in St Mary's Church, where his monument still stands.

Had Wimbledon not led the Cadiz expedition he would be remembered, rather like Sir Horace Vere, as a distinguished soldier who made his career fighting alongside the Dutch. In his campaigns in the Netherlands he had the advantage of employing troops who were experienced and highly trained. The raw levies of the 1625 expedition were another matter altogether, for they were soldiers only in name, but had they been led into an immediate assault upon Cadiz the town might well have been captured. It is noteworthy that, in his report to Buckingham, Wimbledon asserted that the English merchant who came on board the flagship immediately after the fleet's arrival in the Bay of Cadiz 'gave us intelligence of the great strength of the town' (PRO, SP 16/9.41v), whereas other accounts are unanimous in reporting him as saying that Cadiz was virtually undefended. This was an occasion when audacity and decisiveness might well have paid off, but as Sir William St Leger, who fought in the expedition, told Buckingham, Wimbledon 'hath not such abilities as I could wish in a General' (PRO, SP 16/12.32).

ROGER LOCKYER

Sources C. Dalton, *Life and times of General Sir Edward Cecil, Viscount Wimbledon* (1885) · J. Glanville, *The voyage to Cadiz in 1625*, ed. A. B. Grosart, CS, new ser., 32 (1883) · *Calendar of the manuscripts of the most hon. the marquis of Salisbury*, 24 vols., HMC, 9 (1883–1976) · HoP, *Commons* [draft] · PRO, SP 14 and SP 16 (domestic), SP 84 (Holland) · Rous journal, 1625, BL, Add. MS 48152, fols. 268v–270 · Bullock journal, 1625, BL, Add. MS 64885, fols. 101–2 · *Cabala, sive, Scrinia sacra: mysteries of state and government in letters of illustrious persons*, 3rd edn (1691) · *The letters of John Chamberlain*, ed. N. E. McClure, 2 vols. (1939) · [E. Nicholas], *Proceedings and debates of the House of Commons, in 1620 and 1621*, ed. [T. Tyrwhitt], 2 vols. (1766) · C. Knight, 'The Cecils at Wimbledon', *Patronage, culture and power: the early Cecils*, ed. P. Croft (2002), 47–66 · GEC, *Peerage*
Archives BL, letters, military journals, and treatises; charges against him
Likenesses M. J. van Miereveldt, oils, c.1610, Walker Art Gallery, Liverpool · M. J. van Miereveldt, oils, 1610, NPG · S. van de Passe, line engraving, 1618, BM, NPG · M. J. van Miereveldt, oils, 1631, NPG

Cecil, Lord Edward Herbert Gascoyne- (1867–1918), army officer and administrator, was born in London on 12 July 1867, the fourth son and sixth of eight children of Robert Arthur Talbot Gascoyne-*Cecil, third marquess of Salisbury (1830–1903), prime minister, and his wife, Georgina Caroline (1827–1899), daughter of Sir Edward Hall Alderson and his wife, Georgina Drewe. Known to his family as Nigs, and to friends as Ned, Edward Cecil was educated privately and at Eton College, and was commissioned in the Grenadier Guards in 1887. On 18 June 1894 he married Violet Georgina [see Milner, Violet (1872–1958)], the brilliant daughter of Admiral Frederick Augustus Maxse. He was aide-de-camp to Lord Wolseley in Ireland and from 1896 to Sir Horatio Kitchener, then sirdar (commander-in-chief) of the Egyptian army, who valued the intermediary role Cecil could play with his father in pressing for the reconquest of the Sudan. Cecil served in the Dongola campaign and, in 1897, accompanied the Rodd mission to Abyssinia. He was present at Kitchener's decisive victory over the Sudanese Mahdists at Omdurman in September 1898. His ensuing service in South Africa was spent almost entirely under siege at Mafeking. Sir Reginald Wingate, newly appointed to succeed Kitchener as sirdar and governor-general of the Sudan, thereafter persuaded Cecil to join the Egyptian army and the Sudan government, and appointed him to the important if ill-defined post of Sudan agent in Cairo. There Cecil's administrative abilities were recognized by Lord Cromer, the famous pro-consul, who made him successively under-secretary for war and under-secretary for finance in the Egyptian government.

Between 1907, when Cromer was succeeded by Sir Eldon Gorst, and 1911, when Kitchener returned to Egypt as agent and consul-general, Cecil endured a disagreeable eclipse. In 1912, however, his years of efficient administration were rewarded with his appointment as financial adviser to the Egyptian government, the second position in the byzantine hierarchy of British Egypt. With the outbreak of war in 1914 Cecil's personal authority was further enhanced; during the interregnum caused by Kitchener's appointment as secretary of state for war and, indeed, during the ensuing high commissionership of Sir Henry McMahon, who was without Egyptian experience, Cecil was pre-eminent.

The death of Kitchener in 1916 and succession of Wingate as high commissioner led to Cecil's departure from Egypt. Wingate challenged the powerful financial adviser who, after repeated political and personal disagreements, finally resigned in 1918, ostensibly for war service in Europe. But Cecil was ill in any case, with what was eventually diagnosed as tuberculosis. He spent most of the last year of his life in a sanatorium at Leysin in Switzerland, where he died in the Grand Hotel at midnight on 13–14 December 1918.

Edward Cecil was an important figure in Anglo-Egyptian history. Willingly overshadowed by a succession of imperial grandees—Cromer, Kitchener, Wingate—he epitomized the competent stewardship that has since been hailed as Britain's most notable achievement in Egypt. That he was unhappy in his personal life—his marriage soon broke down, and the couple lived apart for most of their marriage—may account for a single-minded devotion to his work. He found fault more easily than pleasure in his eastern postings, though ironically is remembered for *The Leisure of an Egyptian Official*, the sometimes smug and acerbic sketches written only for his own and his friends' amusement, which was published by his widow in 1921. There were two children of the marriage: George, who was killed in action during the First World War, and Helen, who married the second Baron Hardinge of Penhurst.

M. W. DALY

Sources K. Rose, *The later Cecils* (1975) · *DNB* · Cecil MSS, Hatfield House, Hertfordshire · private information (2004) · m. cert. · CGPLA Eng. & Wales (1919) · *The Times* (16 Dec 1918), 11e
Archives BL, corresp. and orders, Add. MSS 46848–46855 · Bodl. Oxf., corresp. and papers · Hatfield House, Hertfordshire | Bodl.

Oxf., corresp. with Lady Selborne, MSS Selborne add; Eng. hist. a 23–24, b 231–236, c 975–1031, d 442–480, e 338, f 27–29, g 25–27; lett c 454–456, d 422–433, e 152; misc c 685–691, d 997–998 · CUL, corresp. with Lady Hardinge · NRA, priv. coll., letters from daughter Lady Hardinge and drafts of literary works · U. Durham L., corresp. with Sir R. Wingate

Likenesses Spy [L. Ward], lithograph caricature, NPG; repro. in *VF* (9 Nov 1899) · A. Vollon, group portrait (as a child; with family), Hatfield House, Hertfordshire

Wealth at death £10,059 16s. 5d.: probate, 22 March 1919, *CGPLA Eng. & Wales*

Cecil, Lady Elizabeth. *See* Hatton, Elizabeth, Lady Hatton (1578–1646).

Cecil, Evelyn, first Baron Rockley (1865–1941), politician, was born on 30 May 1865 at 32 Eccleston Square, London, the elder son and first of three children of Conservative MP Lord Eustace Brownlow Henry Gascoyne-Cecil (1834–1921), fourth son of the second marquess of Salisbury, and his wife, Lady Gertrude Louisa Scott (d. 1919). Evelyn went to Eton College and New College, Oxford (1884–7). He took a second in jurisprudence and made a world tour before reading for the bar at the Inner Temple and joining the western circuit in 1889. Two years later, however, he gave up the law to become assistant private secretary (1891–2, 1895–1902) to the prime minister, who was his uncle, Lord Salisbury (even though his father viewed Salisbury as a betrayer of true Conservatism).

While the Conservatives were in opposition, Cecil wrote a scholarly study of primogeniture (seen by him as a path to the ideal of refinement) and won a seat on the London school board (1894–9), where he made his name as a champion of religious education. A high-church Anglican like all the Cecils, he would have liked denominational divinity lessons to be available to all. The Hon. Alicia Margaret Tyssen-*Amherst (1865–1941), garden historian, became his wife on 16 February 1898. They had three children.

Evelyn Cecil, the first parliamentary candidate to use a motor car, secured a narrow victory at the Hertford by-election of 22 June 1898. A cogent speaker, with pleasant features and a thick moustache, he continued to specialize in educational and church issues, and could always be relied on to oppose legalization of marriage with deceased wife's sister. Less predictably he soon emerged as a fervent imperialist after visiting South Africa in 1899–1900. His book *On the Eve of War* (1900) argued that peace had been impossible with a corrupt Boer oligarchy intent on turning the Transvaal into a hotbed of pan-Afrikaner conspiracy. After Britain overran the Boer states Cecil endorsed Alfred Milner's plan to flood the new colonies with English-speaking immigrants. Concern about German penetration of east Africa inspired him to propose the select committee on foreign steamship subsidies and their effect on British trade, which he chaired in 1901–2.

Cecil, who had transferred to the safe seat of Aston Manor, near Birmingham, in 1900, agreed to serve on the executive council of the Tariff Reform League at its launch on 21 July 1903. Imperial preference joined church schools, empire migration, and merchant shipping as one of his primary interests; Joseph Chamberlain had few stauncher Conservative disciples.

New Liberal reforms provoked fierce condemnation from Cecil, who contended that free school meals would check the flow of charity, encourage irresponsible parental behaviour, and sap the foundations of national independence. Passive resistance by taxpayers and a flight of capital abroad might be the result of the 1909 budget. He attacked women's suffrage and the payment of MPs. His own income came from directorships: of the Foreign and Colonial Investment Trust Company (1896–1940), the London and South Western Railway (1902–23), and the Southern Railway (1923–41). A member of many international railway congresses between 1905 and 1937, he could speak with knowledge on railway legislation.

Though never as prominent in the House of Commons as his cousins Lord Hugh Cecil and Lord Robert Cecil, Evelyn Cecil took part in all the debates on disestablishing the Welsh church between 1912 and 1914. The theme of his political life throughout the ensuing decade, however, was the need to economize: the Liberals had let loose a spirit of reckless expenditure, and war added urgency to his calls to minimize waste. A member of the committee on public retrenchment, set up in July 1915, he campaigned doggedly for an increase in the postal rate from 1d. to 1½d. until its enactment in May 1918. He was sworn of the privy council on 13 June 1917 and attended the inter-allied parliamentary committee (1916–18), at which British MPs and peers met French and Italian deputies and senators. Consciousness of the war debt burden made him persist in urging thrift after 1918, when his recommendations included scrapping labour exchanges, replacing super-tax with graduated income tax, and strengthening the powers of the Treasury.

A senior back-bencher, Cecil was chairman of the select committee on the telephone service (1921–2) and the Home Office committee on young offenders (1925), and he served on the royal commission on honours (1921–2). Wartime charity work as secretary-general of the order of St John of Jerusalem (1915–21) largely accounted for his own knighthood in January 1922. The greatest legislative achievement of his career came at the third attempt in December 1926, when the Judicial Proceedings (Regulation of Reports) Act outlawed salacious press coverage of divorce cases. Still eager to encourage dominion settlement, Sir Evelyn visited Australia with an empire parliamentary delegation in 1926. (He had been shortlisted for the governor-generalship the previous year.)

In 1929 Cecil did not seek re-election for Aston (the name of his constituency since the boundary changes of 1918), yet his public life continued in an undramatic way. He was chairman of a Board of Trade committee on deaths by coal gas poisoning in 1930, and the new year honours of 1934 brought him a peerage, as Baron Rockley of Lytchett Heath. He had inherited Lytchett Heath House near Poole in Dorset from his father in 1921 and purchased picturesque Rockley Sands on the shores of Poole harbour to preserve them from factory development.

Rockley introduced a Life Peers Bill in 1935 in accordance with his long-standing interest in cautious reform of the House of Lords (which predated his participation in the second chamber conference chaired by James Bryce in 1916–17). The Lords passed it, but the Commons found no time. On 14 December 1935 he took on his final major assignment: the chairmanship of the royal commission on safety and health in coalmines, set up to consider revision of the Coal Mines Act of 1911 in the light of the Gresford disaster of 22 September 1934, when 266 men were killed in a pit explosion. The Rockley report of 1938 ('Safety in coal mines', *Parl. papers*, 1938–9, 13, Cmd 5890) suggested greater powers for mines inspectors (but legislation had to wait until 1954). Evelyn Cecil made his last speech in the Lords in March 1939 on the subject of pit-head baths. After retiring to Dorset, he died on 1 April 1941 at Lytchett Heath, where his funeral took place at the family's private chapel (later St Aldhelm's Church) on 5 April. His wife, Alicia, survived him by only a few months, dying on 14 September 1941. He was succeeded as second Baron Rockley by his son, Robert William Evelyn.

JASON TOMES

Sources Hansard 4 (1898–1908) · Hansard 5C (1909–41) · *The Times* (3 April 1941) · 'A MP for nearly 30 years', *The Times* (28 March 1934) · E. Cecil, *On the eve of war* (1900) · J. Amery, *The life of Joseph Chamberlain*, 6: *Joseph Chamberlain and the tariff reform campaign, 1903–1968* (1969) · S. Williamson, *Gresford—the anatomy of a disaster* (1999) · *The Leo Amery diaries*, ed. J. Barnes and D. Nicholson, 1 (1980) · E. Cecil, *Notes of my journey round the world* (1889) · E. Cecil, *Primogeniture: a short history of its development in various countries and its practical effects* (1895) · GEC, *Peerage*
Archives NRA, press cuttings and papers
Likenesses photograph, repro. in *Times* (1 Jan 1934)
Wealth at death £92,780 1s. 10d.—save and except settled land: probate, 26 May 1941, CGPLA Eng. & Wales · further grant, 3 July 1942, CGPLA Eng. & Wales

Cecil [née Brydges; *other married name* Smith], **Frances, countess of Exeter** (1580–1663), noblewoman, was the daughter of William Brydges, fourth Baron Chandos (d. 1602), and his wife, Mary (d. 1624), daughter of Sir Owen Hopton. Some time before 1604, she married Thomas *Smith (c.1556–1609), former secretary to the second earl of Essex and, from 1587 to 1605, clerk of the privy council. The circumstances of the match—as well as the precise wedding date—are unknown, but Smith had long known the bride's family; his selection as MP for Cricklade in 1589 was most likely the work of Frances's uncle, Giles *Brydges, third Baron Chandos [see under Brydges, Edmund]. Smith was knighted in May 1603; he became Latin secretary the following month and master of requests in 1608. Sir Thomas's duties brought Frances into court society; the couple lived at his house in Westminster and his estate in Parsons Green, Fulham. They had two children: Robert, baptized in the summer of 1605, and Margaret.

Sir Thomas died in November 1609 and was buried in Fulham, his widow erecting a simple but substantial monument to his memory. He left his relatively modest estate to his son, but Frances, whom he named executor, was to enjoy the profits during her lifetime. She did not, however, remain a widow for long. Late in 1610 she married Thomas *Cecil, first earl of Exeter (1542–1623), a man nearly forty years her senior. The earl was a member of the privy council, the son of William *Cecil, Lord Burghley,

and the brother of Robert *Cecil, earl of Salisbury, chief minister to James I. Her marriage to Exeter connected Frances to one of the kingdom's most influential families. As mistress of the earl's palatial house at Wimbledon she entertained monarchs and ambassadors. When her only child with the earl, Georgi-Anna, was baptized in July 1616, the bishop of London officiated while the earl of Worcester and Queen Anne stood as witnesses. But her marriage to Exeter also dragged Frances into the strange and sordid events surrounding the unhappy marriage of the earl's grandson, William *Cecil, Lord Ros.

Early in 1616 Ros married Anne Lake [see Cecil, Anne, Lady Ros], daughter of Sir Thomas *Lake, secretary of state, but the marriage foundered almost immediately. By December 1616, when Ros was abroad as ambassador-extraordinary to Spain, news of a serious rift had reached the London newsmongers. The problem was a nasty combination of the sexual and the financial. In the months before leaving for Spain, Ros had been pressed by Sir Thomas and Lady Lake to sign over to his wife and her heirs the lucrative manor of Walthamstow in Essex. The Lakes pushed Ros to acquiesce in this unusual financial arrangement through a combination of political pressure and the threat of public humiliation. According to John Chamberlain, Lady Ros and her mother essentially blackmailed Ros, threatening to 'publish' his sexual impotence and 'so come to a nullitie' (*Letters of John Chamberlain*, 2.80). Matters degenerated further on Ros's return from Spain, and in August 1617 he suddenly fled the country for Italy, where he died the following summer.

Even before Ros's flight the earl and countess of Exeter had been drawn into the conflict. They obstructed the Walthamstow transaction and, during 1617, continued to fight for Ros's interests. In retaliation Lady Ros and her parents publicly accused the countess of having an incestuous sexual relationship with her step-grandson and alleged that she had attempted to poison the aggrieved Lady Ros. The Lakes claimed that both charges were substantiated by letters, some in the countess's own hand, and by the sworn testimony of servants. Later Lady Lake also alleged that after her first husband's death the countess had contracted to marry Sir Francis Crane, but had broken the contract—and paid Crane off—in order to marry Exeter.

If the newsmongers are any indication, few believed the Lakes's allegations, yet the charges had some plausibility. The great age disparity between the earl and countess of Exeter no doubt encouraged the charge that she had been sexually involved with the much younger Ros; and at a time when the Overbury murder scandal was fresh in public memory, the possibility of an aristocratic woman's using poison to conceal a sexual transgression must have seemed real enough. Not surprisingly, the earl and countess fought vigorously to defend her honour, bringing their complaint to the king and eventually suing the Lakes in Star Chamber. Official investigations began early in 1618 and dragged on for a year. Finally, in January 1619 the king announced that the case would come to trial and that he himself would preside. For five days early in February 1619

James sat in Star Chamber to hear the evidence in the case and in a series of related suits and counter-suits. On the fifth day the censure was delivered and the countess of Exeter completely vindicated. Found guilty not only of slander but also of suborning witnesses and forging documents, the Lakes were imprisoned and ordered to pay heavy fines to the crown and the injured party.

Vindicated in Star Chamber, the countess of Exeter continued to enjoy prestige at court, especially after the marriage of the earl's granddaughter connected her to the family of the royal favourite Buckingham. The connection earned her lines of praise in Ben Jonson's *The Gipsies Metamorphos'd* (1621). 'An old man's wife', Jonson wrote, 'is the light of his life' (Jonson, 219). By now, however, the old man was fading fast. Their daughter Georgi-Anna died in 1621, and late in 1622 the earl became seriously ill. By the end of February 1623, Frances was a widow once again.

The countess of Exeter seems to have returned to Fulham, where she devoted great energy to finding a husband for her older daughter Margaret, eventually settling on Thomas Carey, second son of the earl of Monmouth. Early in 1626 Frances's son, Robert Smith, died, leaving his sister as heir to the Fulham estates. Frances may have lived on in Parsons Green until 1632, before giving up the house to Margaret and her husband, now one of Charles I's grooms of the bedchamber.

In the 1630s Van Dyck painted the countess of Exeter's portrait—a sombre study of an ageing woman, seated on a chair, dressed soberly in widow's black. She was to live another thirty years—long enough to see her daughter widowed in 1634 and married, in 1640, to Sir Edward *Herbert, and long enough to see the Herberts and the Brydges suffer for the royalist cause. She died in 1663 between 20 January, when she made her will, and 17 July, when it was proved, and although a space had been reserved for her on Exeter's grand monument in Westminster Abbey, she chose instead to be buried under the floor of Winchester Cathedral.　　　ALASTAIR BELLANY

Sources GEC, *Peerage*, new edn, 3.126–7; 5.216–18 · C. J. Fèret, *Fulham old and new*, 3 vols. (1900), vol. 1, pp. 221–2; vol. 2, pp. 90, 135–9 · A. Harding, 'Smith, Thomas', HoP, *Commons, 1558–1603*, 3.399 · *Calendar of the manuscripts of the most hon. the marquis of Salisbury*, 24 vols., HMC, 9 (1883–1976), vol. 17, pp. 368–9, 377, 379; vol. 22, pp. 61–76 · *The letters of John Chamberlain*, ed. N. E. McClure, 2 (1939), 80, 120, 123, 128, 132, 144–5, 153–4, 183, 207, 466, 477, 546, 630 · J. Nichols, *The progresses, processions, and magnificent festivities of King James I, his royal consort, family and court*, 3 (1828), 173–4, 1098 · *CSP dom., 1611–18*, pp. 512–13, 520, 524–5, 542–3 · [T. Birch and R. F. Williams], eds., *The court and times of Charles the First*, 2 (1848), 68–9 · S. R. Gardiner, *History of England from the accession of James I to the outbreak of the civil war*, new edn, 3 (1899–1901), 189–94 · *The diary of Anne Clifford, 1616–1619*, ed. K. Acheson (1995), 152 n. 57, no. 1 · E. Larsen, *The paintings of Anthony Van Dyck*, 2 vols. (Freren, 1988), vol. 2, p. 486, pl. 222 · B. Jonson, *Selected masques*, ed. S. Orgel (1970), 219–20

Archives CKS, letters to Lionel Cranfield

Likenesses A. Van Dyck, oils, 1630–39; missing since 1876 · A. Van Dyck, drawing, BM · oils (after A. Van Dyck), priv. coll.

Cecil, Lady **Gwendolen Gascoyne-** (1860–1945), biographer, was born on 2 July 1860 at 21 Fitzroy Square, London, the second of the eight children of Robert Arthur Talbot Gascoyne-*Cecil, third marquess of Salisbury (1830–

Lady Gwendolen Gascoyne-Cecil (1860–1945), by Lewis Carroll (Charles Lutwidge Dodgson)

1903), the leading Conservative statesman, and his wife, Georgina Caroline (1827–1899), daughter of Sir Edward Hall *Alderson, a baron of the exchequer. Lady Gwendolen had no formal education, but her home, Hatfield House, gave an exceptional schooling in history, religion, and politics. In her thirties, as her mother's health declined, she became increasingly her father's confidante and amanuensis and accompanied him on official trips. In 1906 she began work on her great achievement, his biography. Four volumes, lucid and magisterial, with stylistic echoes of Creighton and Macaulay, appeared between 1921 and 1932.

Although inevitably partial, the *Life of Robert, Marquis of Salisbury* is not hagiography. Its language is impersonal, its scholarship massive. Lady Gwendolen's analysis of Salisbury's religion is unequalled and she writes with the authority of one who often discussed with him and his colleagues such matters as the Eastern question, parliamentary reform, and imperial expansion. Her summings-up of the politics of Disraeli (in volume 1) and Chamberlain (in the final, unpublished volume) are invaluable. Subsequent research may uncover much more, but her *Life* will remain pre-eminent in the genre of family and contemporary biography.

Besides historical activities, religion and philanthropy were the centre of Lady Gwendolen's existence. She fought for the release of unnecessarily incarcerated mental patients and designed many cottages on the Hatfield estate. On the political scene, passionately though she felt—particularly where her brothers, James Edward Hubert Gascoyne-*Cecil, William Gascoyne-Cecil (1863–1936), Edgar Algernon Robert Gascoyne-*Cecil, Edward Herbert Gascoyne-*Cecil, and Hugh Richard Heathcote Gascoyne-*Cecil, were involved—about such topics as women's suffrage (which she favoured), she was more commentator than participant; but her judgements in her letters well deserve the historian's respect—for example on the Liberals' 1906 election victory and on the causes of the First World War.

Stories of Lady Gwendolen's eccentricities abound. Once she stood in front of her car to prevent it from running downhill and was run over by it. She never married. Devotion to her father and an over-close family circle fostered by her dominating mother may be one reason; her unfeminine appearance, noble and dignified with advancing years, another. In some ways she conformed to the type of the late-Victorian maiden lady, but it would be absurd to see the richly textured life of this humorous, much loved, and scholarly woman as unfulfilled. Lady Gwendolen Cecil died at her home, the Lodge House, Hatfield Park, on 28 September 1945 and was buried in Hatfield parish churchyard.   HUGH CECIL

Sources G. Cecil, 'Lord Salisbury in private life', *Salisbury: the man and his policies*, ed. Lord Blake and H. Cecil (1987), 30–59 · H. Cecil, 'Lady Gwendolen Cecil: Salisbury's biographer', *Salisbury: the man and his policies*, ed. Lord Blake and H. Cecil (1987), 60–89 · D. Cecil, *The Cecils of Hatfield House* (1973) · K. Rose, *The later Cecils* (1975) · d. cert.

Archives Hatfield House, Hertfordshire, muniments | Bodl. Oxf., letters to Lady Milner · Glos. RO, Michael Edward Hicks Beach, first Earl St Aldwyn MSS

Likenesses L. Carroll [C. L. Dodgson], photograph, priv. coll. [*see illus.*] · photographs, repro. in D. Cecil, *The Cecils of Hatfield House* (1973) · photographs, repro. in H. Cecil and M. Cecil, *Imperial marriage* (2002)

Cecil, Hugh Richard Heathcote Gascoyne-, Baron Quickswood (1869–1956), politician and educationist, was born at Hatfield House, Hertfordshire, on 14 October 1869, the fifth and youngest son of Robert Arthur Talbot Gascoyne-*Cecil, third marquess of Salisbury (1830–1903), and his wife, Georgina Caroline Alderson (d. 1899). Educated at Eton College and University College, Oxford, he laid the foundation of a life devoted to Anglican principles and Conservative politics in a family circle and historic house consecrated to both. Tradition has it that before he was seven he had indicted his nurse as a Socinian and admitted that for long he himself had not been quite orthodox.

Equipped with a first class in modern history and a prize fellowship at Hertford (1891), Cecil prepared to take holy orders like his brother William, later bishop of Exeter. Instead he was persuaded to become assistant private secretary to his father, who simultaneously held the offices of prime minister and foreign secretary. This apprenticeship led in 1895 to his election as Conservative member of parliament for Greenwich, a seat he held until his advocacy of free trade helped to ensure his defeat in the general election of 1906. Religion, nevertheless, remained the mainspring of his life; and even had the tenacity of his Conservative beliefs not deterred him from crossing the floor of the house in the wake of his lifelong friend Winston Churchill, the strength of nonconformity in the Liberal Party would no less surely have repelled him from so drastic a change of political faith. So his allegiance rested with the tories and in January 1910 he secured a congenial seat when elected unopposed as burgess for the University of Oxford which he retained until 1937. He received the honorary degree of DCL (1924) and was an honorary fellow of Hertford, Keble, and New colleges.

Cecil was perhaps the most accomplished classical orator of his generation. He was handicapped by a frail physique, restless mannerisms, and a voice pitched too high for sonority. But Lord Curzon, himself a majestic exponent of the art of eloquence, was not alone in holding that Cecil's words combined 'the charm of music with the rapture of the seer'. His most memorable speeches were delivered during debates on the Education Bill in 1902 and on the Welsh Church Bill in 1913. The intensity of his beliefs sometimes provoked him to less edifying interventions and the hysterical animosity which he and his friends bore against Asquith for daring to lay hands on the constitution in the Parliament Bill of 1911 earned them the style of 'Hughligans'.

Although well past the age of forty and never in robust health, Cecil joined the Royal Flying Corps in 1915. His intrepid manoeuvres while learning to fly eventually brought him his pilot's wings—on condition that he never again made a solo flight. In 1918 he was sworn of the privy council, an exceptional honour for a back-bench parliamentarian whose independence of mind and reverence for individual liberty unfitted him for the discipline of office.

During the years between the wars Cecil's interest was captured increasingly by the church assembly, which he had helped to create. As in the Commons, he relished an arena where Christian principles as he saw them could be defended by forensic logic and an artful grasp of procedure. In 1927, however, and again in 1928 he unexpectedly failed to persuade the Commons to accept the revised prayer book. Too often in controversy he spoke with the tongue of an ecclesiastical lawyer, not of an angel. The subtle magic of his eloquence fascinated as of old but did not convince; and many who thought themselves no less loyal churchmen than Cecil found his interpretation of Christian doctrine so rigid as almost to exclude the charity of Christ. In 1933–4 he exercised his authority in Anglican affairs by successfully challenging the right of a bishop (A. A. David) to admit Unitarian ministers to the pulpit of a cathedral. A later demand that the church assembly should pass a measure prohibiting the use of the marriage service to all divorced persons was overwhelmingly rejected.

In 1936 Cecil was appointed provost of Eton in succession to M. R. James. He delighted in the services in college chapel and as its ordinary would preface his sermons with the words, 'I speak as a layman to laymen without the authority of the priesthood', then go on to be very authoritative indeed. His tall swaying figure surmounted by a green eyeshade, his incisive and often provocative commentary on biblical texts, and his oblique anti-clericalism were all memorable. So too were his destructive *obiter dicta* on talks to the boys by distinguished visitors. 'I hope I am not boring you', one of them said nervously in the middle of an address. 'Not yet', the provost replied with a tigerish smile. He regarded the war as a vulgar intrusion on well-established routine and scorned to abandon his habit of dining in knee-breeches. As chairman of the governing body he amused some of his colleagues and exasperated others by insisting that under its statutes Eton was responsible only for educating the boys, not for providing air-raid shelters for their protection. The relentless analysis of a medieval schoolman to which he subjected human problems was not always appreciated. But fellows, masters, and boys alike loved him for the ingenuity of his fancy and the felicity of his phrase.

'Linky' Cecil, who had been best man at Churchill's wedding in 1908, was touched when in 1941 the prime minister recommended him for a peerage. He took the title Baron Quickswood but did not often speak in the Lords. Three years later he retired from Eton. 'I go to Bournemouth in lieu of Paradise', he told the assembled school, and there he bore the growing infirmities of age with cheerful courage. His last act before he died there, on 10 December 1956, was to dictate a characteristic letter in support of the local Conservative member of parliament whose political opinions he had not always shared but whose freedom of action he felt to be intolerably threatened by pressure from the constituency association.

Although Cecil never married and had no house of his own until appointed to Eton, he enjoyed unbroken domestic happiness. For most of his life he lived at Hatfield in rooms set aside for his private use. He took his meals, however, with the rest of the family, who readily forgave his unpunctuality in return for the sustained conviviality of his talk. At night he would retire early to read and to meditate. Unhappily he committed little to print except a small volume entitled *Conservatism*, published in the Home University Library in 1912 and embodying a personal creed which remained unchanged to the end of his days. Pageantry and ceremonial appealed to him as reminders of the past. To aesthetic experience, however, he was immune and when a friend once drew his attention to a glorious sunset he replied, 'Yes, extremely tasteful'. Until well into middle age he was an occasional but adventurous rider to hounds.　　　KENNETH ROSE, rev.

Sources *Eton College Chronicle* (7 Feb 1957) · *The Times* (11 Dec 1956) · private information (1971) · *CGPLA Eng. & Wales* (1957)
Archives Church of England Record Centre, corresp. and papers relating to Church Assembly · Hatfield House, Hertfordshire, corresp. and papers · Hertford College, Oxford, corresp. and papers relating to Hertford College trusts, his election as MP for Oxford, etc. | BL, corresp. with Lord Cecil of Chelwood, Add. MS 51157 · BL, corresp. with Lord Gladstone, Add. MSS 46061, 46078–46080 · BL, corresp. with Lord Northcliffe, Add. MS 62165 · BLPES, letters to Edwin Cannan · Bodl. Oxf., letters to Lady Milner · Bodl. Oxf., corresp. with second earl of Selborne · Bodl. Oxf., corresp. with third earl and countess of Selborne · Borth. Inst., corresp. with Lord Halifax · Chatsworth House, Derbyshire, letters to duke of Devonshire · CKS, letters to his brother, Lord Edward Cecil · Herts. ALS, letters to Lady Desborough and Lady Salmond · HLRO, corresp. with Bonar Law · HLRO, corresp. with John St Loe Strachey · LPL, corresp. with Edwin James Palmer · LPL, letters to Athelstan Riley · NL Scot., corresp., mainly with Lord Rosebery · PRO NIre., letters to Lady Londonderry · U. St Andr. L., corresp. with Wilfrid Ward
Likenesses G. C. Beresford, photograph, 1902, NPG · M. Beerbohm, wash caricature, 1913, Hatfield House, Hertfordshire · W. Stoneman, photograph, 1917, NPG · J. S. Sargent, charcoal drawing, 1920, Hatfield House, Hertfordshire · M. Beerbohm, pencil and wash caricature, 1921, AM Oxf. · M. Beerbohm, pencil and wash, 1926, Hatfield House, Hertfordshire · F. H. Shepherd, group portrait, oils, 1928, University College, Oxford; version, Hatfield House, Hertfordshire · W. Stoneman, photograph, 1931, NPG · P. A. de Laszlo, oils, 1934, Church House, Westminster · H. Coster, photographs, 1936, NPG · W. Stoneman, photograph, 1945, NPG · Spy [L. Ward], caricature, lithograph, NPG; repro. in *VF* (1900)
Wealth at death £44,194 8s. 10d.: probate, 24 Jan 1957, *CGPLA Eng. & Wales*

Cecil, James, third earl of Salisbury (*d.* 1683), politician, was the son of Charles Cecil, styled Viscount Cranborne (*bap.* 1619, *d.* 1660), and his wife, Lady Diana Maxwell (*c.*1623–1675), daughter of James, earl of Dirletoun. His father, the second but eldest surviving son of William, second earl of Salisbury, died in December 1660, leaving James heir to the earldom with the courtesy title of Viscount Cranborne. He may have been educated at St John's College, Cambridge, though the evidence for his admission there is unclear. He was a page of honour at the coronation of Charles II in April 1661, and served as a volunteer aboard the *Royal Charles* in the Second Anglo-Dutch War. In 1665 he married Lady Margaret Manners (*c.*1645–1682), daughter of John Manners, eighth earl of Rutland, and his wife, Frances Montagu. In 1668 Cecil became capital steward of Hertford, and in the same year he won a seat as knight of the shire for Hertfordshire in a by-election, spending £1200 and attracting the support of local Quakers. Cranborne sat in the lower house for only a short time; his grandfather's death on 3 December 1668 elevated him to the Lords as the third earl of Salisbury. While there, he marked himself as one of Shaftesbury's most vocal allies, and no friend of the court. In February 1674 he moved a bill for the protestant education of the duke of York's children. In February 1677 he supported the duke of Buckingham's claim that the Cavalier Parliament was illegally prorogued, an assertion that landed him a prisoner in the Tower. The king was reportedly very angry with him, and Salisbury's wife was convinced her husband would be executed. He was not; the king allowed him to return to Hatfield for the birth of one of his ten children, though his final release did not come until July 1677, after the earl formally apologized to both the king and the House of Lords.

Salisbury became a popular figure among the court's opponents. A false rumour appointed him the new lord treasurer in 1679, and the secretary of state received an anonymous letter accusing him of plotting against the monarchy in the same year. His prominence among Shaftesbury's allies led to his appointment to the reformed privy council in January 1679. Salisbury was an enthusiastic believer in the Popish Plot, and in January 1679 he joined several other peers in examining the hapless Lord Stafford, one of the plot's principal victims. His career peaked in August 1680, with his election as a knight of the Garter, but his attachment to exclusion and dislike of the duke of York hardly endeared him to the king. In October 1679 he deliberately snubbed the duke: on his way to his Scottish exile, James stopped at Hatfield to spend his first night on the road. Salisbury, expecting the duke's arrival, left home, leaving the house unprepared for its royal guest. The duke was forced to find food and candles in the village, and upon leaving he contemptuously left 8s. for the use of his host's bed.

Salisbury's career as a privy councillor ended dramatically in January 1681. He argued strenuously in council against a dissolution of parliament, which the king intended as a means to scotch exclusion. Charles roughly silenced the earl, and Salisbury asked permission to leave the council. 'The King answered he could not make any request that would be more easily granted, and ordered his lordship's name to be struck out of the Council Book' (*Ormonde MSS*, 5.555). By the summer of 1681 rumours of Salisbury's imminent arrest circulated. In August 1682 he and his wife travelled to France for their health, and in Paris the countess died. Cecil was gravely ill at Hatfield in March 1683, where some time later he received a visit from the duke of Monmouth and the earl of Essex. According to the later testimony of Lord Howard of Escrick, they successfully enrolled Salisbury in the Rye House plot. If true, he would have given little aid to the conspirators, for he died at Hatfield on 24 May 1683 and was buried there later that month. He left a heavily encumbered estate to his son James *Cecil, fourth earl of Salisbury (1666–1694), who succeeded him. 　　　　　VICTOR STATER

Sources GEC, *Peerage* · E. R. Edwards and G. Jagger, 'Cecil, James', HoP, *Commons, 1660–90*, 2.39–40 · *CSP dom., 1675–80*; *1682*; *Jan–June 1683* · N. Luttrell, *A brief historical relation of state affairs from September 1678 to April 1714*, 1 (1857) · *Calendar of the manuscripts of the marquess of Ormonde*, new ser., 8 vols., HMC, 36 (1902–20), vols. 5–6 · G. R. Dennis, *The Cecil family* (1914), 228–9 · *Calendar of the manuscripts of the most hon. the marquess of Salisbury*, 22, HMC, 9 (1971) · *Ninth report*, 2, HMC, 8 (1884), 42n · *The manuscripts of his grace the duke of Rutland*, 4 vols., HMC, 24 (1888–1905), vol. 2, p. 39 · Venn, *Alum. Cant.*
Archives Hatfield House, Hertfordshire, estate papers; papers
Likenesses G. Kneller, oils, *c*.1681, Hatfield House, Hertfordshire

Cecil, James, fourth earl of Salisbury (1666–1694), nobleman,

was born at Hatfield House, Hertfordshire, and baptized there on 25 September 1666, the second of ten children and eldest son of James *Cecil, third earl of Salisbury (*d.* 1683), and Margaret (*d.* 1682), daughter of John *Manners, eighth earl of Rutland, and his wife, Frances Montagu. He was educated at St John's College, Cambridge, in 1682.

When Cecil succeeded to the earldom, aged seventeen,

James Cecil, fourth earl of Salisbury (1666–1694), by Willem Wissing, *c*.1685

the Salisbury estates were already encumbered with debts and charged with paying £78,000 of legacies to his siblings. To rescue the family fortunes Salisbury's trustees negotiated a marriage for him, on 13 July 1683, with Frances (1670–1713), the thirteen-year-old daughter and coheir of Simon Bennett of Beachampton, Buckinghamshire, a wealthy tradesman. However, Bennett's will decreed that Frances would not inherit all her fortune if she married before the age of sixteen. The trustees could not wait, and, though Frances's income eased Salisbury's finances, he was never able to realize the full financial benefit of the match. Strict economy was needed to restore the family fortunes, but Salisbury was profligate.

From 1683 to 1688 Salisbury frequently travelled in France and Italy, leaving his child bride alone at Hatfield to be instructed in her role: she was so neglected that she went home until he returned. Contemporary reports portray Salisbury as obese: 'a mighty fat unwieldy man, so that he could scarce stir with ease about' (GEC, *Peerage*, 408); while Stone described him in 1973 as unintelligent and unfortunate in his allegiance (Stone, 157). In 1687, at Rome, he was converted to Roman Catholicism. He returned to England in 1688, a fervent supporter of James II. The king controlled borough parliamentary elections by new charters restricting franchise to holders of specified offices. Unlike most of his line, Salisbury did not enter parliament, but was appointed high steward of Hertford in August 1688. In September, as James feared invasion by William of Orange, Salisbury was appointed captain (later colonel) of one of the new regiments of horse recruited to defend the kingdom, and in November he was appointed a gentleman of the bedchamber. His triumph was very short-lived, as James fled London on 11 December. On the same day the emergency committee of peers ordered the seizure of Salisbury's possessions as he tried to remove them from his London home.

Salisbury was impeached for high treason and Roman Catholicism, and imprisoned in the Tower of London. He was released on bail in the spring of 1690, but was briefly imprisoned again in May 1692 after a letter, which later proved to be a forgery, implicated him in a plot to restore James II to the throne. In 1691 Salisbury was partly responsible for a family tragedy when he encouraged his younger brothers, William and Charles, to leave Eton College and go unsupervised to Paris. They quarrelled and fought, and William was killed.

Salisbury died at Hatfield House on 24 October 1694, and was buried beside his family at Hatfield church on 3 November. His steward, Samuel Percival, provided a suitable epitaph: 'An unhappy, self-willed man, (who) has put fair to undo himself, his relations, friends, all that had to do with him or for him' (Stone, 157). He had achieved very little, and left debts of more than £50,000. His will assigned his estate to trustees for ninety-nine years to pay his legacies and debts. Settlement took fifty years, despite land sales and severe economies during the long minority of Salisbury's son, James (*b.* 8 June 1691), who succeeded him as fifth earl.   JEAN MORRIN

Sources L. Stone, *Family and fortune* (1973), esp. 152–60 · PRO, PROB 11/423, sig. 237 · *CSP dom.*, 1687–9, 246, 341, 367, 371, 377, 379; 1689–90, 241–2, 304, 458; 1690–91, 18, 312; 1691–2, 280, 285, 329, 542 · *State trials*, 12.1234–8, 1051–1166 · H. Chauncy, *The historical antiquities of Hertfordshire* (1700); repr. in 2 vols., 1 (1826), 9 · GEC, *Peerage*, new edn · V. A. Rowe, 'Hertford borough charters of 1680 and 1688', *Hertford in history*, ed. D. Jones Baker (1971) · D. Cecil, *Hatfield House* (1997) · J. R. Western, *Monarchy and revolution* (1972) · E. Auerbach and C. Kingsley Adams, *Paintings and sculpture at Hatfield House* (1971) · G. R. Dennis, *The house of Cecil* (1914) · D. Cecil, *The Cecils of Hatfield House* (1973)
Archives Hatfield House, Hertfordshire, Salisbury archive
Likenesses J. M. Wright, group portrait, oils, *c.*1668–1669, Hatfield House, Hertfordshire · W. Wissing, two oil paintings, *c.*1685, Hatfield House, Hertfordshire [*see illus.*]
Wealth at death left debts of £52,000; £10,000 p.a. gross income from estates; annual charges on this £2210 to the dowager countess for her jointure; £1810 in annuities mainly to family; £1440 in land taxes and £2600 in interest on debts; £2240 to maintain household and pay off debts: Stone, *Family and fortune*, 158

Cecil, James Edward Hubert Gascoyne-, fourth marquess of Salisbury (1861–1947), politician and lay churchman, was born on 23 October 1861 at 21 Fitzroy Square, London, the eldest of the five sons and third of the eight children of Robert Arthur Talbot Gascoyne-*Cecil, successively Viscount Cranborne and third marquess of Salisbury (1830–1903), politician and later prime minister, and his wife, Georgina Caroline Alderson (1827–1899). With his similarly distinguished brothers (Rupert Ernest) William Gascoyne-Cecil (1863–1936), who became bishop of Exeter, Edgar Algernon Robert Gascoyne-*Cecil, Edward Herbert Gascoyne-*Cecil, and Hugh Richard Heathcote Gascoyne-*Cecil, and his two formidable sisters, (Beatrix) Maud [*see* Palmer, (Beatrix) Maud, countess of Selborne]

and Gwendolen Gascoyne-*Cecil, James Cecil obtained his principal intellectual, religious, and moral education from his parents.

Upbringing and political apprenticeship Contrary to contemporary aristocratic conventions, the Cecil children remained at home for most of their childhoods. From an early age their parents treated them as near equals and involved them in their own lives, expecting them to think for themselves, to justify their opinions, and to participate in the household's adult conversation. As their father was a leading politician and expert controversialist, whose many guests included statesmen, diplomats, churchmen, and intellectuals, this was an unusually bracing atmosphere which gave his children intellectual precision, robust dialectical skills, and an addiction to debate on public affairs as much between themselves as with others, continuing throughout their lives in a huge family correspondence. The children also absorbed a deep Christian faith and attachment to the Church of England, together with their father's sophisticated Conservative politics and elevated conception of aristocratic responsibilities. The effect was a distinctive practical idealism, fusing loyalty towards established institutions with a belief that privilege imposed duties, and tough-minded attention to public business with 'formidably developed social and political consciences' (Cecil, 259). While Lords Robert and Hugh Cecil became famously mercurial exemplars of these characteristics, James Cecil—'Jem' to his family and styled Viscount Cranborne from 1868—came to embody them with the diligence, deliberation, and dignity he thought necessary as heir to a great family tradition, to Hatfield House, and to his father's formidable legacy as prime minister, foreign secretary, and leader of the Conservative Party, the unionist alliance, and the House of Lords.

By comparison with his family upbringing, Cranborne learned little from his formal education at Eton College (1875–8) and University College, Oxford (1880–84), where he graduated BA with second-class honours in modern history—an education diversified by accompanying his father on diplomatic missions to Constantinople in 1876 and to the congress of Berlin in 1878. Cranborne had no interest in team games or field sports but became an enthusiastic volunteer soldier, 'the second dominant secular interest in his life' (*DNB*). He joined the 4th (militia) battalion of the Bedfordshire regiment while a student, was commissioned as major in 1887, and later commanded the battalion for nearly twenty years. In his primary secular interest of politics Cranborne's family advantages were manifest, but his father nevertheless expected him to serve an apprenticeship. He became candidate not for a safe Conservative parliamentary seat but for a marginal constituency, the Darwen division of north-east Lancashire. After intensive campaigning in the general election of 1885, he defeated the Liberal candidate by five votes. He increased his majority at the general election of 1886, and thereafter received further training as one of his father's links with House of Commons opinion and as a confidant on party and government business.

Only after he was defeated at Darwen in the general election of 1892 did he receive a secure seat. He was returned unopposed in 1893 in a by-election at Rochester, which he held until succeeding his father in the House of Lords in 1903.

Landowner and lay churchman While Lord Cranborne, and still more on becoming Lord Salisbury, Cecil conscientiously undertook the many local and county duties expected of the territorial aristocracy. Beginning with the eldest son's estate around Cranborne Manor in Dorset, then with the rest of the properties in Hertfordshire and Lancashire, he administered family estates totalling over 20,000 acres. He was an attentive and sympathetic landlord, who regularly visited his tenants, invested in improvements, and in Dorset and Hertfordshire built some 500 cottages, often to his own design. On receiving his full inheritance in 1903 he found that the family agents had allowed urban properties in Liverpool to degenerate into slum housing. He rejected advice to sell out to speculators, as Lord Derby was doing with neighbouring properties, because he felt this 'a cowardly way of evading one's responsibilities' (Jones, 2.192). Instead he spent about £40,000 on reconditioning the houses for the existing tenants, without raising their rents. Thereafter he retained a close interest in the problems of working-class housing, and until 1917 was president of the Garden Cities and Town Planning Association, the body dedicated to implementing Ebenezer Howard's progressive housing schemes. At Hatfield he restored the early Tudor bishop's palace, and created a muniment room for the considerable family archives. In 1919 he sold the family's London house at 20 Arlington Street which his father had enlarged for official entertainments, only to move next door to number 21, which became almost as significant as a political venue. He was a JP for Hertfordshire and chairman of its quarter sessions from 1896 to 1911, an alderman of Hertfordshire county council, a member of the visiting committee of St Albans prison, and president of numerous county associations. He was high steward of Westminster (1903) and of Hertford (1905).

Cranborne became a leading lay churchman, a dimension of his life he considered as important as his political career. He gave land and substantial funds for building churches and church schools. As a member of Hatfield parochial church council he served on St Albans diocesan conference, from which he was a representative in the house of laymen of Canterbury convocation and the Representative Church Council. As a founder member of the church parliamentary committee in 1893 and its chairman from 1895 to 1900, and from 1894 a member of Archbishop Benson's church committee for defence and instruction, he took a prominent part in defending and reforming the Anglican church establishments in the face of increasing radical nonconformist and secular pressures. In the House of Commons he helped organize efforts to secure increased public provision for church schools and the Unionist resistance to Welsh church disestablishment. In 1896 he introduced a private benefices bill to reform lay patronage and maintain worthy clergymen

in the parishes, some provisions of which were adopted by the Unionist government in 1898. He was chairman of the Canterbury house of laymen from 1906 to 1911, and a member of the standing committee of the body supervising Church of England schools, the National Society. To the end of his life successive archbishops of Canterbury consulted him as a matter of course on political and secular aspects of church affairs.

Cranborne was personally devout, notably courteous and considerate towards others, and sensitive to the religious and moral dimensions of public life. His

> whole life was dominated by his resolution to be a Christian. He believed that personal Christian endeavour was the only way of life and that it was worth while to take infinite trouble to achieve that end. If he had to make an important decision he wore himself out till he was sure that he was taking one that was right. (*The Times*, 17 April 1947)

This did not contribute to his personal ease, for all his wealth and privilege. An entirely unjustified sense of his own sinfulness and an exacting standard of public conduct aggravated a melancholic and hypochondriacal disposition, leading to periodic descents into nervous exhaustion and depression.

Marriage, peerage, and ministerial office Cranborne married Lady (Cicely) Alice Gore (1867–1955), the second daughter of Arthur, fifth earl of Arran, on 17 May 1887. High-spirited and a sympathetic conversationalist, she soothed her husband's self-doubts and as an energetic and popular hostess complemented his public life. She herself acquired political significance through friendships with and mediations between public figures—most notably as Lord Kitchener's unofficial channel of communication with the cabinet during his dispute with Curzon over Indian military arrangements in the early 1900s. She was appointed a lady of the bedchamber to Queen Alexandra in 1903. Cranborne and his wife had four children: Robert Arthur James Gascoyne-*Cecil, who succeeded to his titles and political prominence; Lord David Cecil, the literary critic [see Cecil, Lord (Edward Christian) David Gascoyne-]; Beatrice, who married the politician William Ormsby-*Gore, later fourth Baron Harlech; and Mary, who married the future tenth duke of Devonshire.

In the early 1900s Cranborne reaped the public advantages of being the prime minister's eldest son. Now a lieutenant-colonel, he led the 4th Bedfordshire battalion in February 1900 on campaign in the Second South African War. Although not involved in combat, he was mentioned in dispatches and created CB. He was recalled early, on being appointed under-secretary to the Foreign Office in November 1900—retaining a Cecil presence there on his father's relinquishing the foreign secretaryship (which he had previously held concurrently with the premiership). Cranborne's promotion was among those criticized as creating a government packed with the prime minister's relatives, satirized by Labouchere as 'the Hotel Cecil', and it caused particular comment because apart from his zealous churchmanship he had made little mark in the Commons. He soon attracted further criticism for tactlessness, especially in answering parliamentary questions, when personal honesty tended to prevail over departmental obfuscation in 'blazing indiscretions'. Nevertheless, after his father's political retirement in 1902 his advancement continued under his cousin the new prime minister, A. J. Balfour. In November 1903, following his father's death in August and his succession as fourth marquess of Salisbury, he was promoted by Balfour to the cabinet as lord privy seal in the government reshuffle caused by the tariff reform crisis. He soon proved more effective in the House of Lords' discursive exchanges than in the House of Commons' debating contests. Loyal to Balfour's efforts to create a fiscal *via media* that could hold the Unionist government together, he received the additional post of president of the Board of Trade in March 1905. He retained both offices until the government resigned in December 1905.

Political creed Salisbury's politics were rooted in tradition, and over three decades he was associated with three successive 'die-hard' movements. Nevertheless he was not a reactionary. His fundamental political creed was church-and-state Conservatism, linking religious establishment as the custodian of spiritual values, a balanced secular constitution as the check upon political excess, and a propertied and dutiful élite as the guarantee of freedom and stability. He remained loyal to his father's commitment to the union with Ireland, and adopted an imperialism conceived as an alliance of the dispersed British peoples and trusteeship over less developed peoples brought under their charge. He did not believe that democracy was necessarily good, nor that the most vocal 'public opinion' was automatically right or representative. While acutely conscious of social and political change, he neither accepted that his aristocratic rank distanced him from modern life nor assumed that the middle classes were better attuned to its demands. He was astounded when before the general election of 1923 Baldwin told him that 'his own social circumstances made him a better judge of popular opinion' than Salisbury, 'born in the purple', could be (Cowling, *Impact of Labour*, 415), and was not surprised when Baldwin was proved wrong. While regarding defence of property and private enterprise as obviously essential, he considered preservation of social solidarity no less vital and disliked the middle-class ethos of money-making as narrow, materialistic, and likely to provoke working-class resentment. He feared the labour movement as destructive, because socialistic and tending to incite class hatred, but was otherwise sympathetic towards working-class hardships and aspirations.

Salisbury did not oppose reform or state intervention in principle, but considered them matters to be judged according to circumstance and merits. On economic and social issues he was pragmatic, and even progressive if the purpose was to assist individual effort and avoid class conflict. He supported various ideas for a Unionist social policy, including contributory pensions and state-organized unemployment insurance, and in 1913 chaired a party agricultural committee which proposed a minimum wage. Nevertheless he believed that the ultimate solution for social problems was 'beyond the sphere of politics' and could not lie in 'public alms-giving', because they originated in 'moral evils and must be combatted with moral weapons' (Sykes, 669). He understood the Conservative and Unionist Party to have 'two main functions ... To defend certain capital institutions and in everything else to go slow' (4 Sept 1916, in Boyce, 196), and judged the party's natural strategy to be 'the rallying of cautious men' in resistance to 'restless change'.

Tariff reform and constitutional crisis Although Salisbury thought that limited preferential tariffs might have merits, he deplored the tariff reform movement for its clamorous radicalism and doctrinaire insistence on unpopular food taxes. In his view it jeopardized not simply Unionist electoral prospects but also the very principles and institutions that Conservatives and Unionists properly stood for:

> If it may be said to have finally made possible the destruction of the constitution, the prostitution of the Prerogative, the Repeal of the Union and the Disendowment of the Welsh Church, it will probably rank as the most costly policy in history.　(Salisbury to Bonar Law, 1 May 1912, in Blake, 108)

After the general election defeat of 1906 he tried to prevent tariff reform proscription of Unionist free-food MPs, including his brothers Robert and Hugh, but even his neighbouring East Hertfordshire Unionist Association succumbed to pressure from the tariff reform 'confederacy', and in 1909 he resigned as its president. Nevertheless he acquiesced in Balfour's modified version of tariff reform so far as this seemed to offer an alternative to the Liberal government's increasingly radical financial and social policies.

Salisbury's own efforts were concentrated on assisting Lord Lansdowne's use of the House of Lords to check Liberal measures, and Archbishop Davidson in opposing successive education bills which threatened the privileges of church schools. In 1909 he took a leading part in the House of Lords' defeat of Lloyd George's 'people's budget'. Personally sanguine about how the increased taxes would reduce his own wealth, his chief objection was to the government's transparent attempt to circumvent House of Lords power. After the Unionist defeat at the general election of January 1910 had created the prospect of legislation to limit the Lords' power, Salisbury's constitutional concerns became paramount. Seeking to defeat what he regarded as an attempt to erect single-chamber government, he paradoxically became an advocate of constitutional innovations. He supported proposed modifications in the composition of the House of Lords as a means to preserve its authority, and with his brother-in-law Lord Selborne, with whom he now began a close alliance in the House of Lords and in church affairs, he adopted the idea of a popular referendum as a further check on radical majorities in the House of Commons. As tariff reform had not secured election victory and so failed as a buttress for other Unionist purposes, Salisbury now pressed strongly for its abandonment and approved of Balfour's offer to submit it to a referendum. After the further general election defeat of December 1910, the Liberal introduction of the Parliament Bill, ending the House of Lords' veto on legislation, established a leading cause for the rest of Salisbury's life: House of Lords reform. During July 1911 he was among the shadow cabinet rebels who repudiated Balfour's and Lansdowne's advice to abstain on the Parliament Bill, and with Selborne he rallied the 'die-hard' Unionist peers who unsuccessfully voted against the bill. Afterwards, however, he sought restored party unity for the fight against further constitutional changes, and declined to join the organization of die-hard peers and MPs, the 'Halsbury Club'. Following Balfour's replacement as party leader by Bonar Law, Salisbury was a major figure in the prolonged House of Lords opposition to both the Irish Home Rule Bill and the Welsh Church Disestablishment Bill.

First World War On the outbreak of the First World War, Salisbury mobilized his Bedfordshire battalion for war service, and later at Kitchener's request took command of training a Territorial Army division, with the rank of major-general. He made Hatfield House Park available for secret trials of the original army tank, and chaired an advisory committee of the captain-general's office, supplying chaplains to the army. From June 1916 to September 1917 he chaired the central tribunal dealing with conscientious objectors' appeals for exemption from military service. On the creation of the Lloyd George coalition government in December 1916 Salisbury was offered the leadership of the House of Lords. He declined, however, ostensibly because he would have no cabinet or departmental position, but also because he retained his pre-war distrust of Lloyd George—'a windbag and a liar'. Instead, in June 1917 he succeeded Carson as chairman of the Unionist war committee, which expressed the independent views of back-bench Unionist peers and MPs, and made representations to ministers across a range of policies. Already made a GCVO in 1909, he was made KG in 1917.

Salisbury was active in several aspects of post-war reconstruction. He led Unionist peers in calling for enfranchisement of all soldiers on active service, but resigned from the speaker's conference on electoral reform in December 1916 when more radical changes were proposed. He chaired the Ministry of Reconstruction's advisory housing panel, which momentously recommended in August 1917 (*Parl. papers*, 1918, 26, Cmd 9087) that in order to remedy the war-induced shortage of houses the state and local authorities should take responsibility for building working-class houses—the origin of the Addison Housing Act (1919). He also chaired from 1917 to 1919 the ministry's advisory committee on the post-war disposal of surplus government property, and in early 1920 a committee which recommended (*Parl. papers*, 1920, 18, Cmd 658) a three-year extension of wartime rent control.

Salisbury was also important in reform of the Church of England's organization and constitutional position, following the report in 1916 of the archbishops' committee on church and state chaired by Selborne. He helped manage the parliamentary passage of the 1919 Enabling Act, which created an elected national assembly of the church with independent legislative powers. Salisbury was a member of the national assembly's house of laymen from its inception in 1920 until 1945, and served on its original standing committee. With Selborne chairing the house of laymen, and with Lord Hugh Cecil and Selborne's son Lord Wolmer and son-in-law the fifth Earl Grey as further leading members, the lay leadership of the church was substantially in Cecilian hands for the next twenty years.

Critic of the Lloyd George coalition During 1919 Salisbury declined invitations to chair the Church of England's central board of finance, and to become the British ambassador to the United States. He did so because he was increasingly concerned to prevent the Unionist Party's identity from being dissolved by its peacetime participation in the Lloyd George coalition government. In Salisbury's view Lloyd George and other Coalition Liberal ministers were not just indifferent or hostile to Unionist principles; they were also amoral, opportunistic, and a corrupting influence on their Unionist ministerial colleagues and on public life generally. He believed that the government was likely to alienate solid middle-class Unionist supporters, to create disillusion with existing institutions among new working-class voters, and to heighten class tension and strengthen the Labour Party and socialism.

Salisbury's preoccupation with public standards dated from pre-war Unionist campaigns against supposed misdemeanours under Asquith's Liberal cabinet, notably Lloyd George's entanglement in the Marconi scandal. In 1917 and 1918 he and Selborne publicly raised the issues of the proliferation and sale of honours and the appointment of newspaper owners to government posts. To them the 'honours scandal' of 1922, during which they helped force an inquiry, was a vindication. In August 1919 they opposed the archbishops as well as the government over a compromise settlement on disendowment of the Welsh church. They criticized concessions toward Indian and Irish nationalists, and were appalled when the Irish treaty of 1921 ended the Irish union. They criticized the levels of government expenditure—ironically, given Salisbury's wartime contributions to housing policy. They were also annoyed by the Unionist ministers' delay in proceeding with House of Lords reform, and the failure of their eventual bill in 1922.

Salisbury's vigilance over the coalition government was conducted through several channels. In March 1919 he and Selborne formed an association of independent Unionist peers. Sitting on the opposition benches in the House of Lords, they engaged in relentless verbal battles with Birkenhead, the lord chancellor, who later retaliated by satirizing them as 'the Dolly sisters', after the music-hall comediennes. Until March 1920 Salisbury remained chairman of the Unionist war committee's successors, the Unionist reconstruction committee and the Unionist parliamentary committee. In July 1920 he helped organize the People's Union for Economy, intended as a respectable alternative to Rothermere's Anti-Waste League. He also refined the art of using letters to newspapers as manifestos. In January 1920 he attacked the coalition's lack of principles, and from March began supporting Unionist candidates standing in by-elections against Coalition Liberals. Initially aiming only to preserve an independent unionism, in June 1921 he finally called upon all Unionist associations to support the replacement of the coalition government by a purely Unionist government.

Success came slowly, but Salisbury made a large contribution to the fall of the coalition government and the overthrow of the new Unionist Party leader, Austen Chamberlain. Although he disliked the fanaticism of the post-war breed of 'die-hard' MPs, Salisbury welcomed them as useful allies. In March 1922 he joined their leaders in a 'statement of conservative and unionist principles'—the 'die-hard manifesto'—and in July was elected leader of 'the conservative and unionist movement'. His real impact, however, lay less through these 'die-hards' than in his own authority as a highly respected public figure and embodiment of a central Conservative tradition, able to confer confidence upon diverse groups of Unionist dissidents and to cast doubt among coalition supporters. As he helped encourage a groundswell of constituency and back-bench discontent during 1922, so the coalition itself fragmented. Salisbury held a meeting in his Arlington Street house to steel dissident MPs before the decisive party meeting at the Carlton Club on 19 October 1922. His pivotal importance was indicated the following day, after the coalition cabinet's resignation, as a member of the deputation which asked Bonar Law to accept nomination as the Unionist Party leader.

Office under Bonar Law and Baldwin With the re-establishment of Unionist government Salisbury withdrew from his die-hard associations and rejoined the party leadership, as lord president of the council, deputy leader of the House of Lords, and, until May 1923, chancellor of the duchy of Lancaster. His brother Lord Robert Cecil was a cabinet colleague. Salisbury's main work was as chairman from March 1923 of a committee of imperial defence (CID) sub-committee appointed to consider the co-ordination of national and imperial defence. Its report, completed in August and published in 1924 (*Parl. papers*, 1924, 10, Cmd 2029), led to the creation of the chiefs-of-staff committee—vital in defence planning during the 1930s and in supervising British forces during the Second World War. The sub-committee also recommended an enlarged RAF as the vital defence force, and decided that the Fleet Air Arm should remain under RAF rather than Admiralty control. On Bonar Law's retirement in May 1923 Salisbury was asked to advise the king on his successor. He recommended Curzon, but was nevertheless content to serve under Baldwin's premiership. Difficulties arose, however, when in October Baldwin decided to call a general election on the issue of tariffs. As in the 1900s Salisbury thought the adoption of protection perverse, needlessly exposing fundamental public and Unionist Party interests to a large electoral risk, and probably to a

further socialist advance. He was also offended by Baldwin's reluctance to take himself and other ministers into his confidence, and by his apparent readiness to replace them with the former Unionist coalition leaders, Austen Chamberlain and, shockingly, Birkenhead, whom Salisbury considered 'disreputable'. Salisbury, Cecil and the other so-called 'free trade' ministers came close to resignation, but allowed themselves to be persuaded by Baldwin that the cabinet had to keep together.

In the aftermath of the general election in December 1923, which, as he had feared, led in January 1924 to the formation of a Labour government, Salisbury reluctantly acquiesced in reunion with Chamberlain, Birkenhead, and the other Unionist coalitionists. He was now conscious of a new need: to offer a positive contrast to socialism, appealing to the idealism of new voters and distinguishing Conservatism from any 'hard-shelled defence of the Haves against the Have-nots'. In two statements—'Conservative policy' (*The Times*, 18 and 19 March 1924) and 'An outline of Christian anti-socialism' (*The Nineteenth Century and After*, 97, 1925)—Salisbury presented the Conservatives as the truly national party, concerned with all classes, seeking mutual trust in industry, and promoting the values of service and self-sacrifice.

In Baldwin's second government, from November 1924 to June 1929, Salisbury was lord privy seal and, after Curzon's death in April 1925, leader of the House of Lords. He chaired or served on numerous committees of the cabinet, CID, and Committee of Civil Research, on pensions, expenditure, imperial affairs, coal, and Ireland, though his visceral unionism baulked against signing the 1925 settlement on the Northern Irish boundary. Now considered a defence expert, he often chaired CID meetings and committees on naval limitation, disarmament, and belligerent rights. In 1926 and 1927 he visited Canada and Australia to review arrangements for imperial defence. Although much involved in disarmament policies, he shared only some of his brother Robert's confidence in the League of Nations, and felt only personal rather than political regret when Robert resigned from the government in October 1927. He had his own doubts on other matters, however. He was dismayed by the cabinet's wavering commitment to strengthen the House of Lords, and its abandonment of its own reform bill in 1927. Although he admired Baldwin's work in elevating public thinking after the coalition years, he was uneasy about what he judged to be concessions towards Liberal or Labour thinking. His colleagues received painfully fastidious notes of qualification, as he sought to square their policies with his sensitive political conscience. They were, he thought, 'without ballast or tradition', and he wondered 'if any of them know why they are Conservatives' (Salisbury to Selborne, 18 March 1929, Selborne papers, 7/203–5, Bodl. Oxf.).

Nevertheless, after the government defeat in the election of 1929 Salisbury continued as Conservative leader in the House of Lords. He persuaded Conservative peers to exercise restraint in dealing with Labour government measures, negotiating a compromise over the controversial Coal Mines Bill in early 1930. But he had growing reservations about the shadow cabinet's reversion to tariffs and acceptance of Indian constitutional reform, while remaining publicly loyal to Baldwin. When he retired from the collective leadership in June 1931 it was on the public grounds of ill health, though he privately noted to Baldwin that 'Alas, you and I do not belong to the same school of Conservatism' (Hatfield House archives).

Independent peer: India and Moral Re-Armament Once his health was restored, however, Salisbury resumed an active political role, independent of the Conservative-dominated national coalition governments of the 1930s. By now he was the most respected and influential peer in the House of Lords, where a remarkable family group accumulated: three of his brothers, two sons-in-law, Selborne, and his own and Selborne's eldest sons, both elevated by special dispensation in 1941. In March 1932 Salisbury assembled an unofficial joint committee of Unionist peers and MPs on House of Lords reform. Its report in October proposed that the House of Lords should have powers to refer legislation to the verdict of a general election, and should be composed of members elected from among the hereditary peers and by county councils. Although it obtained substantial Conservative Party support, although Salisbury's bill containing its recommendations obtained a second House of Lords reading in May 1934, and although he continued to make representations to ministers for three more years, the government judged the scheme too divisive to be adopted. From late 1931 Salisbury again became allied with Conservative 'diehards', now including Churchill, as a leading opponent of the government's policy of establishing native Indian responsibility in the central government of India. He felt deeply that this constituted an abdication of British moral obligations towards the Indian masses. Appointed by ministers in April 1933 to the joint select committee on their proposals in the hope of constraining his criticism, when the committee reported in November 1934 he led nine of its members in repudiating its principal recommendations. Defeated in the Conservative Party's central council in December, he persisted to the very end, breaching House of Lords conventions by opposing all three readings of the Government of India Bill during 1935. Salisbury was also associated with Churchill in directing attention to what they considered to be the inadequate rate of government rearmament against the military threat from Germany. In July and November 1936 he participated in deputations of privy councillors to express their disquiet to Baldwin and other ministers. During the abdication crisis, however, he advised and supported Baldwin, regretting Churchill's efforts to assist Edward VIII. At King George VI's coronation he was high steward, and bore St Edward's crown.

Salisbury was acutely anxious about the spiritual and ideological challenges of the 1930s: materialism, irreligion, communism, and fascism. Remarkably, this great upholder of establishment religion turned for an antidote to the unecclesiastical evangelism of Frank Buchman's Oxford Group, renamed Moral Re-Armament in 1938. While doubtful about several of its practices and never himself an adherent, he was much impressed by its apparent success in stimulating Christian belief among the young of all classes and among influential persons in many countries. From 1935 he became the most prominent British figure prepared to support the group. In October 1936 he invited other leading public figures to meet Buchman at Hatfield House; and in the House of Lords, in letters to newspapers, and in representations to ministers and bishops he promoted its appeal for wholehearted acceptance of guidance from God. Salisbury defended the group against its many critics, and when in 1941 the cabinet upheld a Ministry of Labour ruling that its workers were not exempt from conscription, he initiated a House of Lords debate in protest, though without success.

Anti-appeasement role, Second World War, and death Appalled during the late 1930s by the character and actions of the Nazi regime, Salisbury became increasingly critical of Neville Chamberlain's appeasement of Germany, especially after his son Cranborne, under-secretary at the Foreign Office since 1935, followed Eden in resigning from the government in February 1938. He disliked the Munich agreement and, sceptical of the cabinet defence preparations, joined public appeals late in 1938 for the introduction of national service. After the outbreak of war in 1939 he called for the formation of an all-party national coalition and a small war cabinet. Troubled by the apparent military inertia of the following months, he formed in April 1940 a secret group of non-ministerial peers and MPs, including Lord Cecil, Cranborne, and Wolmer, to act as a 'watching committee'. Its criticisms of the direction of the war meant that Salisbury was soon doing to Neville Chamberlain what he had done to Austen Chamberlain in 1922—contributing to the destruction of his leadership. During the political crisis of May he made representations to ministers on reconstruction of the government, and Churchill on becoming prime minister considered making him leader of the House of Lords. The watching committee remained in existence for the rest of the war, raising significant issues, on occasion criticizing Churchill's management of the war effort, and making proposals for reconstruction. In 1942 Salisbury published *Post-War Conservative Policy*, a pamphlet which recognized the inevitability of larger government, but argued the cases for individual freedom, private property, religious education, and a reformed House of Lords.

Salisbury was

> about five feet eight inches in height, clean shaved with moustache, well proportioned, and handsome in appearance. In London he was always immaculately dressed in the frock coat and top hat which had been *de rigueur* in his youth and which he was one of the last to wear. (*DNB*)

A long career as party grandee was formally recognized in his presidency of the National Union of Conservative and Unionist Associations from 1942 to 1945. His last letter to *The Times* in 1946 was on House of Lords reform. His last major House of Lords speech, in February 1947, was a protest against British abandonment of the care of 50 million

Indian 'untouchables'. His last public act was to lead a deputation to the archbishop of Canterbury calling for church union and a stand against post-war materialism and irreligion. He collapsed during the meeting and died a week later, at 25 Westminster Gardens, London, on 4 April 1947. He was buried in the family graveyard of St Etheldreda's Church, Hatfield. A bust of him was placed in the House of Lords 'by peers of all Parties in token of their affection and esteem'. PHILIP WILLIAMSON

Sources DNB · GEC, Peerage · The Times (5 April 1947) · The Times (17 April 1947) · D. Cecil, The Cecils of Hatfield House (1973) · K. Rose, The later Cecils (1975) · D. G. Boyce, ed., The crisis of British unionism: the domestic political papers of the second earl of Selborne, 1885–1922 (1987) · Hatfield House archives · Bodl. Oxf., MSS second earl of Selborne · A. Sykes, 'The radical right and the crisis of conservatism before the First World War', HJ, 26 (1983), 661–76, esp. 669 · R. Blake, The unknown prime minister: the life and times of Andrew Bonar Law, 1858–1923 (1955) · G. I. T. Machin, Politics and the churches in Great Britain, 1869–1921 (1987) · M. Cowling, The impact of labour, 1920–1924 (1971) · M. Cowling, The impact of Hitler, 1933–1940 (1975) · G. R. Searle, Corruption in British politics, 1895–1930 (1987) · T. Jones, Whitehall diary, ed. K. Middlemas, 3 vols. (1969–71) · S. W. Roskill, Hankey, man of secrets, 3 vols. (1970–74) · G. Lean, Frank Buchman (1985) · L. Witherell, 'Lord Salisbury's "watching committee" and the fall of Neville Chamberlain, May 1940', EngHR, 116 (2001) · CGPLA Eng. & Wales (1947)

Archives Hatfield House, Hertfordshire, corresp. and papers | BL, A. J. Balfour papers · BL, corresp. with viscount Cecil of Chelwood, Add. MSS 51085–51086 · BL, corresp. with P. V. Emrys-Evans, Add. MSS 58245–58246 · BL, corresp. with Lord Halsbury, Add. MS 56372 · BL OIOC, Marquess of Curzon papers · Bodl. Oxf., corresp. with second and third earls and countess of Selborne · Bodl. Oxf., corresp. with Viscount Addison · Bodl. Oxf., letters to Lord Hanworth · Bodl. Oxf., letters to Lord and Lady Milner · CAC Cam., corresp. with Lord Croft · CKS, letters to his brother, Lord Edward Cecil · CUL, Stanley Baldwin papers · Herts. ALS, letters to Lady Desborough and Lady Harlech · HLRO, corresp. with Andrew Bonar Law · HLRO, corresp. with J. St L. Strachey · LPL, Archbishop Davidson papers · LPL, Archbishop Lang papers · LPL, letters to Athelstan Riley · Lpool RO, corresp. with Lord Derby · NA Scot., corresp. with A. J. Balfour and G. W. Balfour · NL Scot., Balfour papers · PRO, corresp. with Lord Midleton, PRO 30/67 · PRO NIre., letters to Lord Belmore | FILM BFI NFTVA, news footage · IWM FVA, actuality footage

Likenesses pencil drawing, c.1867, Hatfield House, Hertfordshire · A. Bishop, oils, 1874, Hatfield House, Hertfordshire · W. B. Richmond, oils, 1882, Hatfield House, Hertfordshire · G. Philpot, oils, 1917, Hatfield House, Hertfordshire · W. Stoneman, photograph, 1917, NPG · Vivienne, photograph, 1940, NPG · B. Elkan, bronze bust, 1949, House of Lords, London · M. Beerbohm, group portrait, caricature (Cecils in conclave), Hatfield House, Hertfordshire; repro. in Cecil, Cecils of Hatfield House, 302 · Elliott & Fry, photograph, NPG; repro. in Our conservative and unionist statesmen, vol. 2 · G. Philpot, portrait, Church House, London · G. Richmond, double portrait, chalk (with his mother), Hatfield House, Hertfordshire · W. Richmond, portrait (at his coming of age), Hatfield House, Hertfordshire · F. H. Shepherd, group portrait, oils (with three of his brothers), University College, Oxford; copy, Hatfield House, Hertfordshire · Spy [L. Ward], watercolour caricature, Hatfield House, Hertfordshire

Wealth at death £317,457 7s. 6d.: probate, 29 Aug 1947, CGPLA Eng. & Wales

Cecil [alias Snowden], **John** (1558–1626), Roman Catholic priest and spy, was born at Worcester and educated at Trinity College, Oxford; he graduated BA in 1576 and MA in 1580. He and several other scholars left Oxford in August 1583 to attend the English Catholic seminary at Rheims. Cecil took minor orders there before moving to the English College at Rome, where he was ordained priest and where he spent much of 1587–8 as Latin secretary in the service of William Allen. Cecil next went to Spain to assist at the seminary of Valladolid, where the Jesuit Robert Persons was the director.

In 1591 Robert Persons sent John Cecil to England, but her majesty's ship Hope intercepted the vessel on which he was sailing, and Cecil and a companion priest became prisoners in England. Cecil then had to submit to interrogation before Lord Burghley, Queen Elizabeth's chief minister. He told Burghley that Persons had instructed him to assure English Catholics that the king of Spain, Philip II, desired only their benefit and the restoration of the true religion in their country; he did not seek to conquer England. Cecil, however, related that Persons actually wanted him to arouse English Catholics to support a Spanish invasion and to tell Philip II that large numbers of Catholics in his homeland were ready to do so. Cecil knew that was not the case, and he admitted it to Burghley. Moreover, he reported that Persons had planned to send seminary priests to England.

When Lord Burghley asked if Cecil would discuss doctrine with theologians of the established church who might correct his errors, the priest replied that he desired only to live in peace in his homeland and there to enjoy the freedom to practise his religion. Cecil contended that one could be a Roman Catholic and remain a loyal Englishman. He maintained that he opposed Spanish policy and that he tried to convince other English Catholics to do the same. He criticized Persons and Cardinal Allen, and he argued that their pro-Spanish posture only worsened conditions for Catholics in England. Cecil offered to work for the closure of the offensive English seminaries abroad, and by that assertion he effectively renounced Persons and Allen. He blamed Persons for deliberately exaggerating the extent of anti-Catholic measures in England, as when Persons had claimed that 30,000 people of his religious persuasion were in English prisons. Cecil concluded that the number did not exceed 200. In contradiction of Persons, Cecil affirmed that pro-Catholic sentiment was diminishing in England. He decried all efforts to overthrow the government of his homeland, and he denied that the king of Spain had just cause to invade it. Cecil indicated that he desired the end of Cardinal Allen's authority over English Catholics.

It is evident that Lord Burghley believed Cecil could be useful, so he accepted the priest's offer to become a secret agent for the crown on the condition that he would not be required to expose anyone who, even if a Catholic or a priest, was not engaged in subversion. Burghley then sent him to Scotland, where Cecil spent ten years as a missionary, while spying for the English, and as an adviser to and an agent of certain Roman Catholic noblemen.

Several Catholic earls in Scotland petitioned Philip II for

aid against Elizabeth I, thereby to encourage the conversion of their own monarch James VI to Roman Catholicism. They claimed that their ruler had no deep religious beliefs, but that he had allowed Elizabeth to intimidate him. Protestants intercepted the earls' messenger and informed the English government of the plot. James VI then responded to pressure from Elizabeth and began persecuting some of his Catholic subjects. The Scottish Catholic nobles then sent Cecil to Spain to present their cause to the king. The appeal Cecil gave to Philip II related that many Roman Catholic lords were eager to support an effort to regain their country for the true religion. Those earls asked for 3000 troops, funds, and weapons, and they claimed that with such aid they could seize both Edinburgh and Glasgow, after which they would subdue heretics across the land. They asked the king of Spain for a subsidy of 100,000 ducats. The nobles warned they would have to abandon Scotland to Elizabeth's domination if they did not receive the requested aid. Robert Persons wrote a letter of support for Cecil's proposal, and he asked the Spanish king to reward him monetarily. Several Catholic earls in Scotland also wrote to Philip II to urge him to comply with the request of John Cecil.

While engaged in his mission to Spain, Cecil kept Lord Burghley informed about his activities, and, thanks to the support of Persons, the Spanish official Juan d'Idiaquez paid for his passage back to Scotland. Cecil soon received another commission to go to Spain, this time from the earls of Erroll and Angus, who continued to plead for aid from King Philip. Once again Cecil reported the matter to English officials. In 1596 he undertook yet another journey to Spain on behalf of Scottish Catholic earls, this time to combat the influence of John Ogilvy of Poury (who claimed to represent James VI), who, he contended, sought an alliance with the Spanish monarch.

It appears that James VI had engaged Ogilvy as his agent to petition Philip II for aid against Elizabeth I, so that James could become king of England. As an inducement to the Spanish ruler, James would embrace Roman Catholicism and lead Scotland to restore its allegiance to the Roman church. Cecil joined Ogilvy in this project, but Cecil then was in league with some Catholic nobles who were rebelling against James, and it appears that he actually had their interests, not those of King James, in mind. William Crichton, a Jesuit missionary then in Flanders, naïvely thought that James was sincere about the Roman Catholic religion, and he supported the king's aspiration to replace Elizabeth on the throne of England. Crichton opposed the pro-Spanish position of Robert Persons, and he disapproved of Cecil's collaboration with rebellious earls against King James. Tensions between Crichton and Cecil produced an exchange of hostile writings. Cecil exposed the Jesuit to suspicion in Spain, and Crichton was arrested. Elizabeth I knew about the Scottish–Spanish negotiations, and when she confronted her Scottish counterpart with this matter, he denied that Ogilvy was his agent. By 1600 Ogilvy was back in Scotland in the pay of Burghley's son Sir Robert Cecil.

After a period in France in 1601, John Cecil became involved in a bitter and protracted dispute among Catholic clerics in England, a contention which pertained to the role of Arch-priest George Blackwell, who supervised the seminary priests there. The controversy was due to the death of Cardinal Allen in 1594, when Pope Clement VII appointed Blackwell and made him accountable to the papal nuncio in Flanders. With his commission as archpriest, Blackwell received instructions from the cardinal-protector for England to consult on all crucial matters with the Jesuits, an arrangement that offended a minority of clerics. Relations between secular and Jesuit priests became hostile, as the seculars assumed that Robert Persons would exercise decisive authority over them. A delegation of secular priests went to Rome to petition for the elimination of Blackwell's office, but the pope rejected their overture. The appellants then waged a pamphlet war against supporters of the arch-priest, and the bishop of London aided them in getting their material into print. The appellants claimed that the Jesuits sought to dominate their church in England. When Arch-priest Blackwell suspended some of the dissidents they again appealed to Rome for a bishop to replace the arch-priest. Persons opposed the appellants and thereby unwittingly gave credence to their argument against the Society of Jesus.

In 1602 a group of appellants went to Paris and there gained the support of King Henri IV, who regarded the Jesuits as pro-Spanish and therefore hostile to the interests of France. Cecil joined the appellants in France and accompanied them to Rome. He was very influential with them, although John Mush was their leader. It appears that the appellants knew nothing about Cecil's duplicitous career. It may be that they trusted Cecil because Persons had tried to enlist him in an effort to restore peace between the factions of priests in England. The Society of Jesus did not enjoy papal favour at the time the appellants pleaded their case, but the pope rejected their argument that Queen Elizabeth would grant toleration to her Catholic subjects if Rome would alter its policy towards England. In the course of the proceedings in Rome, Robert Persons accused John Cecil of being a spy.

When Cecil asked the pope to end all hostile political actions against the queen of England, he at the same time requested the abolition of the office of arch-priest, and he vaguely suggested the removal of the Jesuits from England. Cecil's only substantial successes in Rome were the pope's agreement to ban the writings of both parties in the arch-priest controversy, and the finding of a papal commission that the arch-priest should no longer consult the Jesuits in matters of church government.

Cecil's last effort to eliminate the office of arch-priest occurred in 1606, when he once more went to Rome and asked for the creation of an English episcopate. Robert Persons opposed this vigorously and slandered John Cecil as an enemy of the faith who often consorted with heretics and was therefore deserving of arrest, trial, and punishment for such offences. He did not obtain the arrest of his old adversary, but Persons did defeat the English priest's proposal for a change in church government. Cecil continued to serve in various ecclesiastical positions until his death on 21 December 1626 at Paris. He had resolutely argued against the Jesuit theories which justified resistance against and efforts to overthrow his protestant queen.   JAMES EDWARD MCGOLDRICK

Sources T. G. Law, ed., 'Documents illustrating Catholic policy in the reign of James VI', *Miscellany … I*, Scottish History Society, 15 (1893); repr. (1893) · M. A. S. Hume, ed., *Calendar of letters and state papers relating to English affairs, preserved principally in the archives of Simancas*, 4, PRO (1899); repr. (1971), 1587–1603 · *CSP dom.*, 1591–1594 · D. Calderwood, *The history of the Kirk of Scotland*, ed. T. Thomson and D. Laing, 8 vols., Wodrow Society, 7 (1842–9), vol. 5 · J. Cecil, 'A discoverye of the errors committed and injuryes don by a malitious mythologie', in J. Bucke and others, *Instructions for the use of the beades, 1589* (1971) · T. G. Law, ed., *The archpriest controversy: documents relating to the dissensions of the Roman Catholic clergy, 1597–1602*, 2, CS, new ser., 58 (1898) · T. Fuller, *The church history of Britain*, ed. J. S. Brewer, new edn, 6 vols. (1845), vol. 5 · J. H. Pollen, *The institution of the archpriest* (1916) · P. Renold, ed., *The Wisbech stirs, 1595–1598*, Catholic RS, 51 (1958) · E. L. Taunton, *The history of the Jesuits in England, 1580–1773* (1901) · *DNB* · T. G. Law, ed., *A historical sketch of the conflicts between Jesuits and seculars in the reign of Queen Elizabeth* (1889) · F. Medina de Borja, 'Escocia en la estrategia de la empresa de Inglaterra: la misión del P. William Crichton cerca de Felipe II (1590–1592)', *Revista de Historia Naval*, 17 (1999), 53–111 · F. Medina de Borja, 'Intrigues of a Scottish Jesuit at the Spanish Court: unpublished letters of William Crichton to Claudio Acquaviva (Madrid 1590–1592)', *The reckoned expense: Edmund Campion and the early English Jesuits*, ed. T. M. McCoog (1996), 215–45 · M. C. Questier, *Newsletters from the archpresbyterate of George Birkhead*, CS, 5th ser., 12 (1998) · G. Anstruther, *The seminary priests*, 4 vols. (1969–77) · W. Forbes-Leith, ed., *Narratives of Scottish Catholics under Mary Stuart and James VI* (1885) · *Collected essays and reviews of Thomas Graves Law*, ed. P. H. Brown (1904) · M. E. Williams, *St Alban's College, Valladolid: four centuries of English Catholic presence in Spain* (1986)
Wealth at death see City Westm. AC, act book 4, fol. 5v

Cecil [*née* Hill], **Mary Amelia** [Emily Mary], **marchioness of Salisbury** (1750–1835), political hostess and sportswoman, was born and baptized in Dublin on 16 August 1750, the eldest daughter of Wills *Hill, second Viscount Hillsborough and successively later first earl of Hillsborough and first marquess of Downshire (1718–1793), and his first wife, Margaretta Fitzgerald (1729–1766), sister of James Fitzgerald, first duke of Leinster. Baptized Mary Amelia, she always signed herself Emily Mary. She was at the very heart of the eighteenth-century political world by lineage as well as through her father's important political appointments in Ireland and England, which included that of secretary of state under Lord North during the American War of Independence. Given such a background, it is not surprising that she became a lifelong supporter of the monarchy or that her political sympathies were firmly with the king's ministers, particularly under William Pitt the younger. Nor should it be surprising that she grew up with a thorough understanding of eighteenth-century politics, including knowing how to use the social arena for political ends and secure patronage.

Emily Mary's marriage, on 2 December 1773, to James Cecil, Viscount Cranborne (1748–1823), the only son and heir of James Cecil, sixth earl of Salisbury (1713–1780), and his wife, Elizabeth Keet or Keate (*d.* 1776), enmeshed her yet more firmly into the British political establishment. She quickly became one of the North administration's

Mary Amelia Cecil, marchioness of Salisbury (1750–1835), by Sir Joshua Reynolds, 1780–81 [altered, 1787–9]

leading political hostesses, a position she went on to share with Mary Isabella Manners, duchess of Rutland, and Jane Gordon, duchess of Gordon, during Pitt's first premiership. Like her contemporary, Foxite political hostess Elizabeth Lamb, Lady Melbourne, Lady Salisbury (as she became on her husband's accession to the earldom in 1780) was a pretty, witty, intelligent, and outspoken young woman who understood people, politics, and social situations. She also easily outshone her sociable, if somewhat indolent, husband. Moreover, again like Lady Melbourne, she was ambitious. She used her social skills so adroitly that when Salisbury was made lord chamberlain in 1783 and then, in 1789, elevated to the rank of marquess, contemporaries assumed that he owed both appointments to her. The fact that she did not have her first child until thirteen years after her marriage allowed her to focus her attention on social politics. She then had three children in five years: Georgiana Charlotte Augusta in 1786, Emily in 1789, and James Brownlow William (later the second marquess) in 1791; a fourth, Caroline, was born in 1793 but died in childhood.

Lady Salisbury's political involvement was not limited to the drawing-room. While she did not have the same easy common touch as her younger political rival, Georgiana Cavendish, duchess of Devonshire, she was not above engaging in electoral politics. She was a canvasser to be reckoned with and was particularly active in the Westminster and St Albans elections of 1784. In St Albans, where Lord Salisbury supported her brother's candidature against the Spencer interest, Lady Salisbury canvassed so energetically and successfully that Margaret Georgiana Spencer, dowager Countess Spencer, feared losing the election. The Spencer interest won in the end, but only after Lady Spencer reluctantly realized that it would be necessary to have her daughters, the duchess of Devonshire and Henrietta Ponsonby, Lady Duncannon, abandon the Westminster election temporarily and canvass St Albans for the family interest. In the Westminster election of that year Lady Salisbury was one of the highest-ranking women to canvass for the ministerial candidates. She was the perfect foil to the duchess of Devonshire. Where the Pittite press vilified the duchess, it praised Lady Salisbury. She was portrayed as the model female canvasser: 'her proceedings have been marked with such *delicacy* and *dignity*, as to shame the *mobbing conduct* of her rivals' (Hartley and others, 258, n. v).

Dignity Lady Salisbury certainly had; whether she could ever have been described as delicate is debatable. Physically she was slight, but she had immense energy and vitality. When her husband's health forced him to give up the mastership of the Hertfordshire hounds in 1793, she took it over. Under her leadership, the kennels were moved to Hatfield House and the hunt accordingly became known as the Hatfield hounds. She led the field splendidly attired in her sky-blue habit with black collar and cuffs, and a hunting cap. In her late seventies she still could exhaust people half her age. Thomas Creevey, who referred to her kindly if irreverently as 'Old Sally', recorded a visit she paid to the earl and countess of Sefton, aged seventy-six. Not only did she drive the 20 miles from London herself in a stylish phaeton pulled by four excellent betasselled horses, but she also did so characteristically, all alone save for her two dogs. Nor was the usual combination of cards, gossip, and good company enough to keep her occupied. Each evening between ten and midnight the Seftons took her on a 10 mile drive before returning for several rubbers of whist. Only at about one thirty in the morning did she finally retire. What was most remarkable to Creevey, though, was that she was still an avid hunter: '*Sall* being the only one who mounted her horse like an arrow from the hand of her groom, the horse too being an uncommonly high one, milk white' (*Creevey Papers*, 216).

Lady Salisbury's love of hunting was lifelong. A keen sportswoman, she was also an avid archer. It was, however, her daring and skill in the field which most impressed her contemporaries. She continued to hunt until she was seventy-eight, when her eyesight and failing strength required her to be tied into her saddle and led by a groom. Even then, she thought that she was still good enough to hunt with the harriers.

She continued to live at the principal seat of the Salisburys, Hatfield House, Hertfordshire, until her death, aged eighty-five, in a terrible fire that destroyed the west wing of the house, on 27 November 1835. She was buried on 10 December 1835 at Hatfield.   E. H. CHALUS

Sources IGI · GEC, *Peerage*, new edn · *Collins peerage of England: genealogical, biographical and historical*, ed. E. Brydges, 9 vols. (1812), vol. 2, pp. 494–5 · N. W. Wraxall, *Posthumous memoirs of his own time*, 2nd edn, 3 (1836), 347 · *The Creevey papers*, ed. J. Gore, rev. edn (1963) · BL, Althorp MSS · *VCH Hertfordshire* · *Annual Register* (1835) · G. Cecil, *Life of Robert, marquis of Salisbury*, 4 vols. (1921–32) · *Sporting Magazine* (Oct 1793) · *Sporting Magazine* (Oct 1794) · *Sporting Magazine* (Jan 1796) · *Sporting Magazine* (Jan 1800) · C. Pigott, *The female Jockey Club* (1794) · J. Hartley and others, *A history of the Westminster election* (1784) · will, PRO, PROB 11/1862, sig. 325

Archives BL, letters to the third Lord Hardwicke, Add. MSS 35729 fols. 17, 254; 35764 fol. 24 · BL, corresp. with the second earl of Liverpool, Add. MSS 38264 fols. 144, 193; 38295 fol. 21 (draft); 38320 fol. 101 b; 38573 fol. 155; 38574 fols. 112 b, 113 b · BL, corresp. with Sir R. Peel, Add. MSS 40399 fols. 237, 238; 40416 fol. 233; 40419 fols. 300, 301 · BL, letters to Lord Wellesley, Add. MSS 37282 fols. 121, 147; 37300 fol. 357; 37308 fol. 272; 37309 fols. 154, 315

Likenesses A. Devis, group portrait, oils, *c*.1760 (1st marquess of Devonshire and family), NPG · J. Reynolds, oils, 1780–81 (altered 1787–1789), Hatfield House, Hertfordshire [*see illus.*] · G. Engelheart, miniature, *c*.1790, Hatfield House, Hertfordshire · A. Kauffmann, portrait, Downshire, Northern Ireland · engraving, repro. in *VCH Hertfordshire*, 1, facing p. 368 · mezzoprint (after Reynolds), NPG

Wealth at death left some estate; rents and profits used to fund bequests: will, PRO, PROB 11/1862, sig. 325

Cecil [*née* Cooke], **Mildred**, **Lady Burghley** (1526–1589), noblewoman and scholar, was born in 1526, the eldest of five daughters and four sons of Sir Anthony *Cooke (1505/6–1576), Edward VI's tutor, of Gidea Hall in Essex, and Anne (*d*. 1553), daughter of Sir William Fitzwilliam of Milton, Northamptonshire, and Gains Park, Essex, and widow of Sir John Hawes of London. She was educated at home by her father, himself a noted scholar. As well as undergoing a classical education equal to that offered to boys, she developed a long-lasting commitment to the puritan leanings of her father.

Mildred Cooke married William *Cecil as his second wife in December 1545, bringing with her important kinship links. Her first child was not born until nine years after her marriage, although she was involved in the upbringing of her stepson Thomas *Cecil. In total she had five children, of whom only Robert *Cecil was still living at the time of her own death. There is little direct evidence of her role in the household or her relationship with her children apart from what can be deduced from William Cecil's writings after her death, where he refers to strong affective ties. According to his eulogy on her monument in Westminster Abbey, Mildred was 'dearest above all' and 'far beyond the race of womankind'. For her part Mildred Cecil in a letter wrote of her happiness and 'everlasting comfort … living with this noble man in divine love and charity' (BL, Lansdowne MS 104, fol. 158r). Writing to his son Robert, William Cecil refers to 'the virtuous inclinations of thy matchless mother, by whose tender and godly care thy infancy was governed, together with thy education under so zealous and excellent a tutor' (Wright, 9).

Mildred Cecil [Cooke], Lady Burghley (1526–1589), attrib. Hans Eworth, c.1563

Wimbledon Manor was the chief home of the Cecils for ten years after 1550. Cecil continually added to the family property, buying land and building a great house in the Strand and subsequently further houses in the country. The household governed by Mildred Cecil was substantial, numbering at least fifty people, and grew in size as William Cecil became more significant politically; he was ennobled as Baron Burghley in 1571. The Cecils obtained several wardships, and a number of young men whose families sought advancement and connections for them were sent to live in the Burghley household. In addition, they were joined by the three daughters of the unhappy marriage of the Cecils' daughter Anne to Edward de Vere, earl of Oxford, after their father rejected them.

As Burghley's wife, Mildred Cecil was in a key position to exercise influence. She was known to have acted as an intermediary between petitioners and her husband, receiving at least one substantial payment of £250 in 1580. Her importance to her husband can be seen in letters to her in 1560 from three of the Scottish leaders negotiating the treaty of Edinburgh, including William Maitland, Lord Lethington. Cecil was urging the queen against her inclinations to commit herself to military involvement in Scotland. The letters were couched in terms indicating that Mildred Cecil had a considerable knowledge of the issues under discussion and could influence her husband in the attempt to secure English support against the French presence in Scotland. These political skills can be seen again in a single letter of advice, written in Latin and

dating from 1573, to her cousin William Fitzwilliam, the lord deputy of Ireland. The letter demonstrates that Mildred Cecil was not afraid to give advice even on public affairs at a high level.

By reputation among her contemporaries Mildred Cecil was supremely well educated. Strype later said she spoke Greek as easily as she spoke English, and she received three dedications of books. However, she left few manuscripts; those that do exist confirm her reputation for scholarship, revealing her fluency in both Greek and Latin and her interest in classical and religious authors. She made several lengthy translations including a sermon of Basil the Great from the Greek. Her preface reveals an appreciation of the art of translation while at the same time presenting the conventional modesty of intention. In a letter to the fellows of St John's College, Cambridge, written in Greek, she appears at ease, referring with gratitude to the hospitality she received on a visit with her husband and her desire to mark the occasion with an appropriate gift: the polyglot Bible she presented in 1580. Ballard adds that she also sent an epistle in Greek, written in her own hand. Having inherited only three books from her father, over a number of years Mildred Cecil built up an impressive library mainly in Latin and Greek; some thirty volumes still exist inscribed with her name. The titles indicate the breadth of her intellectual interests and the depth of her scholarship, covering medical texts, literature, history, religious commentaries, and church fathers; many of them were printed abroad. Seventeen of her books in Latin, Greek, French, and English remain at Hatfield House, which became her son's property. Lady Burghley was the owner of one of the finest private libraries of the day.

Mildred Cecil died at Burghley House in the Strand on 4 April 1589. Evidence of the extent of her concerns can be seen in the disposal of her property. She made a number of charitable bequests at her death, as well as gifts of books and money during her lifetime. Many of these she concealed even from her family by the use of intermediaries such as Dean Goodman of Westminster; in 1579 two scholarships were granted to St John's College, Cambridge, in this way. A number of gifts were structured in an attempt to create work. For example, in 1583 wool and flax were provided for the poor women of Cheshunt to process, and in 1586 she funded a scheme through the Haberdashers' Guild to provide loans for tradesmen. She also made more conventional donations, including provisions and money to the poor in Cheshunt. Mildred Cecil gave careful thought to the disposal of her library and divided her books between a number of institutions. In addition to her gift of the Bible to St John's, Cambridge, in 1587 she gave Christ Church, Oxford, eight volumes of Galen's works: three in Latin and five in Greek. She also gave two books each to St John's College, Oxford, and to Westminster School.

After Mildred Cecil's death, Lord Burghley arranged an impressive funeral involving 315 mourners as 'a testimony of my harty love which I did beare hir, with whom I lyved in the state of matrimony forty and tow yers contynually without any unkyndnes' (BL, Lansdowne MS 103, fol. 167r). A further indication of Burghley's devotion to his wife and their unfortunate daughter Anne can be seen in his joint memorial to them in the chapel of St Nicholas at Westminster Abbey. It is a substantial monument, containing more than the usual effigies; a lengthy eulogy testifies to the importance of his wife to him.

CAROLINE M. K. BOWDEN

Sources P. Hogrefe, *Women of action in Tudor England* (1977) · G. Ballard, *Memoirs of several ladies of Great Britain*, ed. R. Perry (1985) · M. Hannay, ed., *Silent but for the word* (1985) · S. Harvey, 'The Cooke sisters', PhD diss., Indiana University, 1981 · M. K. McIntosh, 'Sir Anthony Cooke: Tudor humanist, educator, and religious reformer', *Proceedings of the American Philosophical Society*, 119 (1975), 233–50 · T. Baker, *History of the college of St John the Evangelist, Cambridge*, ed. J. E. B. Mayor, 2 vols. (1869) · S. R. Jayne, *Library catalogues of the English Renaissance* (1956) · Mildred Cecil's translation of a sermon of Basil the Great, from the Greek, *c*.1550, BL, Royal MS 17.B.xviii · letter from Mildred Cecil, BL, Lansdowne MS 104, fol. 158 · *Advice to a son: precepts of Lord Burghley, Sir Walter Raleigh, and Francis Osborne*, ed. L. B. Wright (1962)

Likenesses attrib. H. Eworth, portrait, *c*.1563, Hatfield House, Hertfordshire [*see illus.*] · H. Eworth, portrait, Hatfield House, Hertfordshire · monument, Westminster Abbey, London

Cecil, Richard (1748–1810), Church of England clergyman, was born in Chiswell Street in the parish of St Luke's, Old Street, London, on 8 November 1748, and baptized at St Luke's on 30 November. He was the son of Thomas Cecil (*d.* 1779), who like his father before him was in the lucrative business of scarlet-dyer to the East India Company, and his wife, Tabitha Grosvenor (*d.* 1777), the pious daughter of a pious dissenting father, who was also an affluent London merchant. Richard was the youngest child of his parents, his mother being past fifty when she had him. Like John Wesley he narrowly escaped an early death when he was nearly drowned in one of the ponds attached to his father's business. Though destined for this family concern Cecil showed no inclination for it, his interests by contrast being directed with no mean level of proficiency towards poetry, music (he was an accomplished violinist), and especially painting. He frequented picture sales and made a clandestine visit to the continent. His father was prepared to support his going to Rome to develop his skills as an artist, but some unidentified circumstances intervened. During these years Cecil professed a militant atheism, apparently with some success in his influence on others. Though hearing George Whitefield had made no impression upon him, he was brought suddenly to consider his state by reflecting on the contrast between his own unsettled condition and the serenity his mother enjoyed, though deeply afflicted in mind and body. He experienced an evangelical conversion, somewhat to the consternation of his father who, however, agreed to support him on condition that he remained within the Church of England.

Cecil entered into residence at Queen's College, Oxford, on 19 May 1773 and graduated BA in Hilary term 1777. He had received both deacon's and priest's orders before graduation, the former from Bishop Green of Lincoln on 22 September 1776 and the latter on 23 February 1777. He received his title on becoming curate to John Pugh at

Richard Cecil (1748–1810), by Joseph Collyer the younger, pubd 1811 (after John Russell, 1798)

Rauceby, Lincolnshire, himself a prominent evangelical in whose vicarage the first discussions took place out of which the Church Missionary Society eventually emerged. After a brief stay with Pugh, Cecil moved to serve the parishes of Thornton-cum-Bagworth and Markfield, Leicestershire, during the minority of the potential vicar, a Mr Abbott, who himself underwent an evangelical conversion through Cecil's ministry. Early in 1777, through the interest of friends, Cecil obtained two small livings of All Saints and St Thomas of Canterbury at Cliff in Lewes, Sussex. It was here that in 1781 he married one of his parishioners (whose name is unknown); they had eleven children, of whom five died young. He kept this cure for twenty years, but did not reside for long, being afflicted by severe rheumatism in the head, a consequence of the dampness of his rectory. The livings were worth only £80 a year, and after his departure he allotted the whole of this sum to his curate.

Cecil returned to London and lived in Islington. He had already established his name as an effective evangelical preacher, and quickly found himself engaged in various lectureships. These included the uncomfortably early service at 6 a.m. at St Margaret, Lothbury, later to be served by Thomas Scott, and an evening lecture at Orange Street Chapel, where A. M. Toplady had preached. Besides these he undertook the Sunday evening lecture at Christ Church, Spitalfields, in September 1787 as well as that of the Long Acre Chapel, sharing both of them in three-year appointments with Henry Foster, Cecil serving in the periods beginning in 1787, 1793, and 1799, though ill health during the final tenure led to most of the duty being discharged by Josiah Pratt. Cecil's main work in London, however, was at St John's Chapel, Bedford Row, in the parish of St Andrew, Holborn, to which he was appointed in March 1780 by Sir Eardley Wilmot, acting for the trustees of Rugby School, the patrons, on the recommendation of Archbishop Cornwallis, and which he held until his death. It remained a centre of metropolitan evangelicalism until its demolition in the middle of the nineteenth century. The chapel was in bad repair when Cecil was invited to accept the charge, but a guarantee against any loss was provided by an aunt of William Wilberforce, though he himself went without remuneration from the pew rents for three years and paid interest on the debt for eighteen years until 1798, when friends contributed to reduce the principal. In his first few years at St John's he also had to contend with an unsympathetic congregation as he sought to persuade them of evangelical truths.

Cecil continued as minister of St John's until his death, but in 1798 he suffered the first of several seizures, losing the use of his right hand. In that year also he resigned his Lewes livings, but two years later Samuel Thornton, acting on behalf of his fellow members of the Thornton Trust, set up by his father, John Thornton of Clapham, offered Cecil the benefice of Chobham with Bisley, Surrey, valued at £235 a year but leaving only £150 after St John's had been supplied. In addition, it was necessary to build a new parsonage house which, incidentally, was not completed until 1811, after Cecil's death. He spent the summer months at Chobham, but his health continued to deteriorate under pressure of work. He suffered further seizures with increasing paralysis in 1807 and again in February 1808, after which he sought relief in visits first to Bath, then for six months from September 1808 to Clifton, and finally in May 1809 to Tunbridge Wells, returning to London in October 1809. He died after a fit of apoplexy at Belle Vue, Hampstead, on 15 August 1810.

Together with John Newton, Henry Foster, and the layman Eli Bates, Cecil in 1783 established the Eclectic Society, a group of evangelicals who met fortnightly in the vestry of St John's to discuss matters of spiritual interest. It was from a meeting of the Eclectics on 12 April 1795 at the Castle and Falcon inn, Aldersgate Street, though Cecil himself was absent through illness, that the Church Missionary Society took its origins. Josiah Pratt preserved the discussions of the Eclectics during the period 1798–1814 (subsequently published as *Eclectic Notes*, ed. John H. Pratt, 1856), and in them as in the generality of Cecil's writings one finds the qualities of precise address, clear statement, telling illustration, and broad sympathy. Thus he could argue for the width of God's mercy to the heathen and the value of the *via media* in doctrine, views not obviously characteristic of the evangelicals. Bishop Samuel Wilberforce considered him 'the one clerical genius of his party' (E. Stock, *History of the Church Missionary Society*, 1899, 1.43).

Cecil wrote memoirs of the painter John Bacon (1801), William Bromley Cadogan (1798), and John Newton (1808), of whom he also preached a funeral sermon published as *The Character and Commendation of a Faithful Minister* (1808).

A Friendly Visit to the House of Mourning (1792), a devotional manual for the bereaved, went through eight editions in Cecil's lifetime and several more posthumously up to 1861. His *Remains*, on a variety of topics from man's fallen nature and the need for grace to the question of visiting public exhibitions, are reminiscences of conversations collected by Josiah Pratt, displaying in J. H. Overton's words 'a scholarly habit of mind, a sense of humour, a grasp of leading principles, a liberality of thought and capacity of appreciating good wherever it may be found' (Abbey and Overton, 2.207). His *Works* were collected by Pratt and published with a memoir by him together with a portrait by John Russell in 1811.

Cecil, however, was more impressive as a preacher than a writer. He had the power of seizing the attention of his hearers, developing an argument and illustrating it vividly, and expressing it with what Daniel Wilson in his funeral sermon described as 'a lucid perspicuity'. Wilson continued:

> No one can form an adequate notion of his powers as a public speaker from his printed sermons. Like every true orator, the soul of his discourses lay, in a large degree, in that pathos, that touch of nature, that surprising originality, that sublimity and grandeur of expression, which must considerably evaporate with the affections which produced them … He was not merely one of the most eminent preachers of his day, but one of a totally different order from others—a completely original preacher.   (Wilson, 36)

ARTHUR POLLARD

Sources R. Cecil, *Works* (1811) [with memoir of his life by J. H. Pratt] · R. Cecil, *Remains*, 14th edn enlarged (1834) [with memoir by his wife and character by J. H. Pratt] · J. H. Pratt, ed., *The thought of the evangelical leaders: notes on the discussions of the Eclectic Society, London, during the years 1798–1814* (1856); facs. edn (1978) · M. Seeley, *The later evangelical fathers* (1879) · C. J. Abbey and J. H. Overton, *The English church in the eighteenth century*, 2 vols. (1878) · *DNB* · D. W. Bebbington, *Evangelicalism in modern Britain: a history from the 1730s to the 1980s* (1989) · D. B. Hindmarsh, *John Newton and the English evangelical tradition between the conversions of Wesley and Wilberforce* (1996) · D. Wilson, *The blessedness of the Christian in death* (1810)

Archives NRA, diary, sermons, and preaching notes; collections from his unpublished papers

Likenesses J. Collyer the younger, engraving, pubd 1811 (after J. Russell, 1798), BM, NPG [*see illus.*] · J. Russell, portrait, repro. in Cecil, *Works*

Cecil, Robert, first earl of Salisbury

Cecil, Robert, first earl of Salisbury (1563–1612), politician and courtier, was born on 1 June 1563 at Cecil House, Strand, Westminster, the second surviving child and only son of William *Cecil, first Baron Burghley (1520/21–1598), statesman, then secretary of state and from 1572 lord treasurer, and his second wife, Mildred (1526–1589) [see Cecil, Mildred, Lady Burghley], eldest daughter of Sir Anthony *Cooke of Gidea Hall, Essex, and his wife, Anne, *née* Fitzwilliam.

Education and early career Cecil was baptized at St Clement Danes, Strand, on 6 June. His parents had just moved to their new residence, Cecil (later Burghley) House, fronting the Strand and backing on to Covent Garden. A sickly child with splayed legs and a humpback, he was educated at home, first by his mother, an outstanding classicist and one of the most learned women of her generation, then

SERO SED SERIO

Robert Cecil, first earl of Salisbury (1563–1612), by John de Critz the elder

by tutors. Richard Howland, later master of St John's College, Cambridge, and bishop of Peterborough, was almost certainly one of them. The later claim by Thomas Fuller that the religious radical Walter Travers was also Cecil's tutor is unsubstantiated. He was taught Greek, Latin, French, Italian, and Spanish, together with music, mathematics, and cosmography. Cecil was thoroughly grounded in the Bible and the prayer book as well as in the classics, and in later life showed a marked interest in the new optics.

Burghley took care to converse over meals with his children and with the royal wards brought up in his household, to further their education. The Strand house was also a regular meeting place for privy councillors, and ambassadors were received there. Theobalds, the family's vast Hertfordshire mansion erected after 1563, was frequently used to entertain the queen and court on the summer progress, so Cecil from childhood would have known Elizabeth I. For at least ten weeks in 1577 Robert Devereux, the young second earl of Essex, another royal ward, lived with the Cecils. In 1580 Cecil was admitted to Gray's Inn, following his father, and received legal instruction while continuing to live at home. In July 1581 he was at Cambridge for the commencement, attending sermons and disputations, but there is no evidence that he completed an academic year, and he did not take a degree.

After further tutoring at home in 1582 by William Wilkinson, fellow of St John's College, Cambridge, Cecil spent the summer and autumn of 1583 in Paris. He returned to Paris in August 1584, attended disputations at the Sorbonne, and in company with the English ambassador, Sir Edward Stafford, visited Fontainebleau and

Orléans. After his return he sat in November 1584 for the first time in the House of Commons, for his birthplace, the borough of Westminster; he represented it again in 1586. In that parliament Elizabeth was under pressure to execute Mary, queen of Scots, for her part in the Babington plot, and on 24 November she addressed a delegation of both houses, assuring them only that she would pray for guidance. Shortly afterwards there appeared a brief tract, *The Copie of a Letter to the Right Honourable the Earle of Leycester*, ostensibly written to bring Leicester up to date with events that had occurred during his absence in the Low Countries. With a preface dated 25 November and signed 'R. C.', it contained the parliamentary petitions together with the queen's speech, and was translated into several languages, including French and Latin. A propaganda measure prepared by Robert Cecil for Sir Francis Walsingham and Burghley, it was intended to demonstrate to European public opinion how reluctant Elizabeth was to condemn the Scottish queen to death. Although both the title-page and the preface of *The Copie* emphasize that her answers were 'not expressed by the reporter with such grace and life, as the same were uttered by her Majestie', Elizabeth herself made detailed corrections to Cecil's draft report of the original speech, so the words in the tract were exactly what she wanted to convey. After 1585 Cecil was frequently in the presence chamber, and the tract of 1586 prefigures the later close collaboration between Elizabeth and her future secretary of state.

By 1587 Cecil was a JP for Hertfordshire, where Burghley was building up an estate for him around Theobalds. In February 1588 he accompanied the earl of Derby's embassy to Ostend for last-minute negotiations with the duke of Parma in the hope of averting war with Spain. Realizing that these were futile, Cecil left Derby and after being presented to Parma at Bruges travelled extensively around the Low Countries, visiting Antwerp, Amsterdam, Rotterdam, and Brielle before returning to Ostend. He sent detailed observations back to his father, particularly on the build-up of Parma's army for the intended invasion of England. Cecil returned to England in April but in July, as the Armada advanced, he abandoned his Italian lessons, intending to take a ship out into the channel for a better viewpoint. According to a later reminiscence by Lord Henry Seymour, in 1588 Cecil was an observer on Sir William Winter's *Vanguard*, one of the vessels in Seymour's Downs squadron.

In 1589 Cecil again sat in the Commons, Burghley having obtained for him the more prestigious place of senior knight of the shire for Hertfordshire. In August 1589 Cecil married Elizabeth Brooke (1562–1597), daughter of the tenth Lord Cobham. Six months older than Cecil, with a sister already a widow, she was a veteran of the privy chamber, serving her godmother the queen, and well beyond the usual age of first marriage for aristocratic girls. Nevertheless it seems to have been a love match, with Cecil taking the initiative. The ailing Lady Burghley was glad to know of their engagement before she died in

April. Both her daughters had predeceased her, and thereafter the bereaved widower and the only surviving son grew increasingly close, with Cecil acting as Burghley's aide.

First years in government After the death of Walsingham in April 1590 Burghley resumed the tasks of the secretary of state, for Elizabeth was reluctant to name a newcomer, in part because she was unwilling to confront her favourite, the young Essex. However, the knighting of Robert Cecil at Theobalds in May 1591 during her visit was preceded by an entertainment, a playlet in which the postman bringing letters for the queen asked for 'Mr Secretary Cecil' (J. Nichols, *Progresses and Public Processions of Queen Elizabeth*, 4 vols., 1788–1821, 4.76). The ambitious hint was not taken but in August 1591, at Nonsuch, Elizabeth elevated Cecil to the privy council, itself a remarkable honour for an inexperienced young man of twenty-eight who had held no previous government office. Insiders assumed that it was evidence of a tacit agreement between the queen and Burghley that Cecil would increasingly take over the workload while Burghley continued as acting secretary. Rumours continued to circulate that Cecil was about to be named to the office, but the queen left the situation unresolved. Cecil was an assiduous privy councillor, in his first year attending 112 meetings out of 164. In the same year he also became a JP for Middlesex and the high steward of Cambridge University, where Burghley was chancellor.

In 1592 Cecil was given his first major tasks, in spring sitting on the commission trying Sir John Perrot for treason, and in August overseeing the unloading of cargo from the great prize, the Spanish carrack *Madre de Dios*. Supported by Sir Walter Ralegh, who had been released from the Tower for the purpose, Cecil rode down to Dartmouth and roused local worthies—getting Sir Francis Drake out of bed—to stem the widespread private pilfering. He managed to obtain a decent return on the cargo for the exchequer and the episode probably triggered his interest in the profits obtainable from privateering. His first venture was with Lord Howard of Effingham in the winter of 1595–6, although his major investments were subsequently in Mediterranean voyages.

In January 1593 writs went out for another parliament and Cecil was on all the major committees. He made his maiden speech, indicating that he was becoming more than just his father's observer in the lower house. He was active in negotiating with the Lords when Burghley unexpectedly insisted upon three subsidies, not the two that the Commons had originally voted. The earl of Essex became a privy councillor in 1593, but meanwhile Cecil's grip on business tightened. He read dispatches from France to the queen and drafted her replies as well as reviving the intelligence work pursued by Walsingham. It was in this capacity that Cecil corresponded with certain English Catholic priests in the hope of discovering the plots of the more extreme element, and learned to distinguish between loyal English Catholics and those who sought foreign intervention, particularly from Spain.

Cecil was overwhelmed with work. Burghley was frequently indisposed, whereupon he would press his son relentlessly with orders for the prompt execution of secretarial business, insisting on replies that same day. In February 1594 Cecil was described as coming and going constantly to the court 'with his hands full of papers and head full of matter', so preoccupied that he 'passeth through the presence [chamber] like a blind man not looking upon any' (T. Birch, *Memoirs of the Reign of Queen Elizabeth*, 2 vols., 1754, 1.155).

The secretaryship of state Tensions with Essex were growing, particularly over the latter's abortive attempt to have his client Sir Francis Bacon made attorney-general. Burghley was increasingly absent for lengthy periods, so Cecil grew more prominent at court as his father's spokesman and factotum. In consequence the number of suitors begging his intervention in their affairs increased substantially. In February 1596 the death of the long-standing Latin secretary, Sir John Wolley, further concentrated affairs in Cecil's hands, and while Essex was abroad on the Cadiz expedition Elizabeth on 5 July 1596 at last bestowed the title of secretary of state on him.

Cecil's happy marriage to Elizabeth Brooke produced a son, William *Cecil, in 1591 and a daughter, Frances, in 1593. In January 1597, pregnant with her third child, Lady Cecil miscarried and died. Often at court after her wedding, she had remained a favourite of the queen, and her supportive influence probably contributed more to her husband's early career than can now be traced. She undoubtedly reinforced Cecil's position in the innermost circle of the regime. Elizabeth insisted on having her goddaughter buried at Westminster Abbey with the rank of a baroness. Cecil composed a moving epitaph for her simple tomb in the chapel dominated by the vast monument that Burghley had erected to his wife and elder daughter. Cecil was debilitated with grief, and although his name was to be linked with other women he resisted all future blandishments to remarry.

Cecil was attempting to maintain a working relationship with Essex, and in March 1597 the earl was made master of the ordnance, a sign of royal favour which balanced the elevation of Cecil to the secretaryship. Essex was then appointed chief commander of the fleet preparing against Spain. On 8 October Cecil became chancellor of the duchy of Lancaster, a valuable source of patronage and influence which also allowed him to move his residence into the duchy property of the Savoy. On 24 October the next parliament assembled. Cecil had been actively canvassing for seats, and was responsible for the return of about thirty members. As the most influential privy councillor in the Commons he took a leading role, and in a conference of the Lords and Commons on 19 January 1598 the parties were led by Burghley and Cecil respectively, a unique demonstration of their joint dominance. Cecil composed the preamble to the bill for three subsidies, speaking forcefully to it, but his private memoranda reveal that he was concerned at the impact of taxation, since the country was already suffering severe economic conditions. His support for the eventual acts on poor relief can be deduced from these papers, and he also tried to damp down the Commons' increasing irritation with patents of monopoly.

Regnum Cecilianum? The long-standing jibe that England 'was become regnum Cecilianum' (Croft, 'Reputation', 46), initially directed against Burghley alone, seemed after 1596 to relate to the lord treasurer's success in promoting his son to ensure the continuance of family power. Cecil was also becoming prominent on the international diplomatic scene. Late in 1597 negotiations began between Philip II and Henri IV, who had turned Catholic in order to consolidate his victory in the civil war that had broken out over his succession to the French throne. A separate peace between France and Spain broke the alliance made earlier between France, the Dutch, and England, and by January 1598, while the parliament was still in session, Cecil was preparing to be sent on an embassy.

Elizabeth hoped to prevent Henri from making peace with Philip II, but Cecil was resigned to failure, particularly after he had seen the war-ravaged state of the French countryside and sensed the overwhelming desire for an end to hostilities. However, Cecil thought that it would be valuable to probe the king's mind. Henri's sharp comment that the Dutch could not expect to be allowed to keep everyone else 'miserable in perpetuity' led Cecil to respond cautiously to the suggestion of a subsequent peace between England and Spain. 'So they (the Dutch) might not perish by it, it were less harmful'—less harmful than continuing the war (Croft, 'Brussels and London', 80). This showed greater flexibility than the attitude of the queen herself and was the germ of Cecil's future policy. He sailed to England in April, and went to his sick father's bedside before returning to court. Burghley recovered briefly in June but died in August 1598, leaving both Cecil and the queen bereft.

Little more than a year after the death of his wife, Cecil had also lost the father and mentor who had powerfully shaped his career. He remained devoted to the memory of both his remarkable parents, who had loved him dearly and displayed full confidence in his abilities, despite his deformities. When Cecil finished Hatfield House in 1611, a portrait of Burghley adorned the book-room or study in his private suite, and one of Lady Burghley hung in his bedroom. But after 1598 Cecil was an isolated figure, with only his two motherless children as close kin.

The last years of the Elizabethan regime In Burghley's will Cecil received Theobalds and the Hertfordshire estates, but the title, the great house at Burghley near Stamford, and the midlands estates all went to his half-brother, Thomas Cecil, Burghley's son from his first marriage. More importantly, the lord treasurer's death transformed the political scene. Cecil's enemies, particularly those among the retinue of Essex, hoped that his career would fade now that his father was no longer there to support him. Although Cecil had been high steward of the university since 1591, on Burghley's death Cambridge dons elected Essex as the new chancellor. In May 1599, as had long been assumed, the post of lord treasurer went to Lord

Buckhurst, while Essex hoped to be master of the court of wards, Burghley's other key office. However, the earl's position as the queen's favourite was growing increasingly uncertain after the climactic scene in July 1598 when Elizabeth boxed his ears for insolence. In March 1599 Essex left for Ireland on a military expedition he had no desire to lead, and in his absence Cecil became master of the wards on 21 May 1599, although he resigned the chancellorship of the duchy of Lancaster. The mastership was not a sinecure but an onerous task adding greatly to Cecil's already heavy burden of paperwork. It was a prize worth having, since it controlled a great array of patronage both at court and in the counties. However, by far the most significant aspect of his elevation was that it signalled unequivocally that the queen recognized his personal worth and ability. Her trust in Cecil was unaffected by Burghley's death.

Essex and his faction grew increasingly hostile to Cecil but the earl's reluctance to confront the earl of Tyrone's forces in Ireland, his precipitate return to England against Elizabeth's orders, and finally in January 1601 his chaotic revolt in London completed his self-destruction. Cecil was in charge of the preliminary collection and assessment of evidence against Essex and his followers, and on 13 January 1601 he spoke forcefully in Star Chamber, accusing the earl of devising in effect to be king of England. On 19 January Essex and the earl of Southampton were tried in Westminster Hall, and in his self-defence Essex in turn accused Cecil of favouring the right to the English throne of the Infanta-Archduchess Isabella, daughter of Philip II and co-regent with her husband Albert of the Spanish Netherlands. The problem of Elizabeth's successor was at the forefront of all political calculations, but any support for the infanta would immediately place Cecil among the enemies of James VI of Scotland. Cecil dramatically interrupted, stepping out from behind a tapestry to beg permission to defend himself from the wild charge. He demanded that Essex reveal his source for the statement. The earl, taken aback, replied that his uncle Sir William Knollys had told him so, but when Knollys was brought in, he cleared Cecil completely. The secretary, turning to Essex, told him that his malice proceeded from his passion for war, in contrast to Cecil's own desire for peace in the best interests of the country. He continued, devastatingly, 'I stand for loyalty, which I never lost: you stand for treachery, wherewith your heart is possessed' (*State trials*, 1.1351). Essex was condemned and went to the block on 25 February.

Recent research has fully upheld Cecil's claim that the differences between him and Essex stemmed not merely from a factional fight over patronage and power, but from a deep disagreement over foreign policy. By 1601 the costs of the revolt in Ireland were rising horrendously, while the threat from Spain elsewhere in Europe was receding. Essex wanted to escalate the continental war, aiming for outright victory over Spain, while Cecil aimed to wind it down as soon as possible.

The execution of Essex not only removed the chief advocate for further hostilities, but also brought Cecil a vital opportunity. James VI was by far the strongest claimant to the English throne, but Elizabeth could not be brought to acknowledge him openly as her heir. The king was growing increasingly restive, even to the extent of threatening force, and was building a party of supporters in England, of whom Essex had been the leader. The secret correspondence between them was legally treasonable, but Cecil sensed that such a link was the only practical way to ensure in advance that the transition of power, whenever it came, would be peaceful. James was willing to set aside his personal animosity, which stemmed from his conviction that Cecil's father had been responsible for the execution of James's mother, Mary, queen of Scots. He realized that after Essex's death there was no English privy councillor who could rival Cecil, who was 'king there in effect' (Croft, 'Robert Cecil and the early Jacobean court', 134). English public opinion shared the king's estimate, in a libel alleging that 'little Cecil ... rules both Court and Crown' (Croft, 'Reputation', 47). Cecil for his part recognized that reassuring James that his future accession was already accepted in England would be the safest way forward.

In May 1601 Cecil joined the group of men already in cipher correspondence with the king, led by Lord Henry Howard, whom James commended as entirely trustworthy. The king was at first cool, commenting that 'if your silence had continued any longer it might have bred some hazards to the fortunes of both the princes (besides your own particular)' (Letters of ... James VI & I, 181). However, his tone soon moderated and before long he was describing Cecil as 'so worthy, so wise and so provident a friend', assuring him moreover that these were not 'Italian complementoes' (ibid., 198–9). Cecil must have been reassured, but at the same time he knew that he faced other enormous administrative problems, not least the crushing of Tyrone's rebellion. 'God knoweth I labour like a Pack horse, and know that if success be nought it wilbe scorn to me', he wrote to his friend Sir George Carew in Ireland (Croft, 'Bureaucrat', 83).

After 1601, as the inevitable transition from Elizabeth to James pressed increasingly on his mind, Cecil threw himself into a fury of land speculation, becoming one of the half-dozen largest purchasers of crown estates then flooding on to the market to fund the costs of the Irish war. Besides spending about £30,000 in 1601–2, he borrowed heavily from London aldermen to enable him to snap up prime properties. At the same time he built himself a new mansion next to the Savoy on the Thames riverfront, proudly inviting Carew in 1602 to visit 'my new house (called Cecil House)' (Croft, 'Bureaucrat', 84). Cecil was acutely aware of the malleability of fortune, and his strategy was clear. If all went smoothly on James's accession, and his position in government continued, he would be well placed to entertain and impress the new king, with Theobalds in the country and a fine house in Westminster. But if, as was not unfeasible, Cecil should lose office under the new regime, he could retire to his newly acquired country properties. There he might indulge his passion for gardening and his enjoyment of hawking, while consolidating his land purchases gradually into a great estate to hand on to his son.

The accession of James VI and I The mutual trust between Cecil and the king of Scots grew steadily after 1601 and early in March 1603, with Elizabeth visibly failing, Cecil drafted the proclamation that would announce the king's accession and sent it north for prior approval. It was Cecil who read out the proclamation on 24 March 1603, first at Whitehall and then at the gates to the City of London. On learning of the queen's death James at once wrote from Edinburgh informally confirming all the privy council in their positions, adding in his own hand to Cecil, 'How happy I think myself by the conquest of so wise a councillor I reserve it to be expressed out of my own mouth unto you' (Letters of ... James VI & I, 209).

Cecil remained in London for a short time, to ascertain that there was no outbreak of trouble in the capital or elsewhere over the change of dynasty, and also to make arrangements for Elizabeth's funeral. Then in mid-April he rode north to meet James at York. Before leaving Holyroodhouse the king had temporarily confirmed Cecil as keeper of the privy seal and the signet. At York he obliquely intimated to Cecil's half-brother Thomas, currently president of the council in the north, that he intended to keep Cecil as secretary of state. 'He said', reported Thomas, 'he heard you were but a little man, but he would shortly load your shoulders with business' (Croft, 'Bureaucrat', 85). It was probably about this time that Cecil composed for the king his tract 'The state and dignitie of a secretarie of estates place, with the care and perill thereof', which circulated in manuscript before being printed in 1642. Cecil set out to explain the nature of his office, emphasizing the secretary's wide discretion— 'liberty to negotiate ... at home and abroad with friends and enemies in all matters of speech and intelligence'. Above all he underscored the need for complete trust on both sides. 'The prince's assurance must be his confidence in the secretary and the secretary's life his trust in the prince ... the place of a secretary is dreadful if he serve not a constant prince'. He concluded that 'he that lives at mercy ought to be careful in the choice of his master', a typically Cecilian touch of irony (Cecil, State and Dignitie, 1–4). Whether in response to the tract or not, James retained Cecil as his secretary of state until his death in 1612.

So Cecil continued in office, and was conspicuously honoured when in May 1603 at the end of his progress down from Edinburgh the king stayed for four nights at Theobalds. In October Cecil was also appointed lord high steward to the king's wife, Queen Anne of Denmark, in whose household he took care to place some of his female relatives and confidantes. Nevertheless it became clear that James was intent on widening the circle of Englishmen with access to power. The king particularly valued ancient nobility, as was made apparent by his promotion at Theobalds of Lord Henry Howard and his nephew Lord Thomas Howard to the privy council, and their creation as earls respectively of Northampton and Suffolk. The earl of

Northumberland also became a privy councillor, while the earl of Southampton was released from the Tower where he had been incarcerated since 1601. James brought both Englishmen and Scots on to the privy council, and he confirmed Cecil as master of the wards only after some indecision in which he apparently considered bestowing the lucrative office elsewhere. Although Cecil was ennobled on 13 May 1603 as Baron Cecil of Essendon, the Howard earls of Northampton and Suffolk outranked him and Southampton was given the Garter. The immediate rewards for his labours over the accession of the king were not outstandingly generous, and he seemed likely in future to be only one of a circle of half a dozen senior advisers.

The union and the peace of 1604 It was necessary to call a parliament, not least for an act to confirm the king's title, but a severe outbreak of plague in London in 1603 postponed the occasion. James desired above all else the success of his project for a union between England and Scotland. This was to be far more than the purely personal union of the two crowns which the king himself represented; although the details were deliberately left flexible, even vague, James envisaged a full legal, administrative, and parliamentary union. The project was carefully introduced in the first session, begun at Westminster in March 1604, but at once ran into deep suspicion and dislike in the Commons. By the third session of 1607 it was dead. The attitude of Cecil to the union was cautious. He offered enthusiastic lip-service but his own priority in 1604 was the urgently needed financial restructuring of the crown, a project he introduced with an innovative attempt to bargain away the royal rights of wardship in return for money. James at one point reportedly accused his English privy councillors of not backing him, but at the same time the king became aware that support for the union in Scotland was as limited as it was in England. Cecil escaped blame for the failure of the project.

Cecil was also faced with the prospect of accommodating himself to a monarch with a routine very different from that of the elderly Elizabeth, who in her later years had not travelled beyond the Thames valley. James embarked almost at once after arriving at Whitehall on an extensive progress of the south-east, visiting both Wilton and Winchester as well as several royal standing houses. The king's obsessive passion for hunting led him to spend increasing periods away from London, which in any case he disliked. By 1605 he was spending about half the year in the country, mostly at Royston and Newmarket. The privy council accompanied him only on major summer progresses, and even then not necessarily all the way. Much business was done by letter, and although the king was attentive to those matters which interested him, particularly foreign policy and the problems of religious faction, he left virtually everything else to his privy council. Cecil occasionally gave in to pangs of self-pity, comparing himself to the biblical Martha toiling in the kitchen, but the new style of governance gave him the chance once again to demonstrate his unparalleled administrative skills. The workaholism originally inculcated by Burghley stood

Cecil in good stead as he began to rebuild the pre-eminence that he had briefly enjoyed between 1601 and 1603.

In May 1604 formal negotiations began with the envoys of Philip III and the archdukes Albert and Isabella, to end the long Armada war begun in 1585. The sessions were led by Cecil, who completely dominated the other English commissioners; apart from him, only Henry Howard, earl of Northampton, is recorded as speaking, and then only on one occasion. James himself did not participate in the negotiations, coming to his capital city for the banquet that concluded the treaty, but on 20 August he conferred on Cecil the title of Viscount Cranborne, in recognition of his successful efforts. In the great group portrait *The Somerset House Conference*, probably by Pantoja de la Cruz, Cecil turns to the viewer from his position at the head of the English delegation, with an inkpot, a quill pen, and a file of papers on the carpeted table in front of him to signify his position as secretary of state.

The peace brought great benefits to English trade, despite occasional objections from English merchants trading to Spain, who found conditions there much harder than they expected. It enhanced the prosperity of both London and the outports, and considerably improved the yield from the customs. Cecil was always concerned to protect and foster trade, as his father had done before him, and he rejoiced in the expansion that peace made possible, particularly on the Mediterranean routes. Most importantly, by its studied ambiguities and deliberate silence on the Spanish claim to a monopoly of the New World, the 1604 treaty tacitly allowed Englishmen to trade and settle in the West Indies and North America. Cecil's personal insistence on leaving these contentious matters aside made a vital contribution to the growth of that later Atlantic world of commerce and colonies which the Elizabethans had dreamed of but which became a reality only after 1604.

Cecil also took the opportunity in 1604 to upgrade the customs' Book of Rates, which was lagging well behind inflation, and in consequence was able to win large increases in the terms offered by syndicates of London merchants for the farm of the customs. He also profited substantially from what might at best be termed consultancy fees offered to him by the winning syndicate. His interest in the profits of the customs had begun in January 1601, when he received a ten-year lease of the silk customs at a low rent, and while overseeing his own customs farm he acquired considerable expertise in the administration of the Customs House. In addition the silk farm increased his contacts among the great merchants of London. All this was put to good use both for the royal revenues and his own profit in 1604.

The early Jacobean years As England emerged from the isolation of the war years the size of the London diplomatic corps increased. James prided himself on firmly controlling the general direction of foreign policy, but ambassadors and envoys found the king's constant absences while hunting very irksome. They became increasingly accustomed to turning for information and decisions to Cecil.

His prestige was steadily enhanced by his growing day-to-day control of business, and it became widely known that the king and Cecil alone conducted diplomacy, rarely referring matters to the privy council. After 1604 a pattern of foreign-policy management emerged which endured to the last weeks of Cecil's life.

On the evening of 26 October 1605 Lord Monteagle brought to Whitehall a mysterious letter warning of a conspiracy and asked for a private word with Cecil. He and the other senior privy councillors present took the decision not to disturb the king until his return to Westminster, although further investigations began at once. After the discovery of Guy Fawkes in the cellar below the houses of parliament on the night of 4 November, Cecil led the commissioners entrusted with investigating the conspiracy and interrogating Fawkes. On 27 January 1606 he headed the commission at the trial of the plotters, and spoke at length to refute the allegation that the king himself was to blame because he had reneged on earlier promises of toleration for Catholics. By this time Cecil had already published the first of the tracts that emerged on the plot, *An answere to certaine scandalous papers, scattered abroad under colour of a Catholike admonition*. It discussed the death-threats that Cecil said he had received from other malcontents for his part in unmasking the conspiracy. The most significant feature of the tract, however, was Cecil's clear distinction between 'these late savage papists … some Infested spirits of that Profession' (Cecil, *Answere*, sig. F), as he described the plotters, and those other Catholics who had not wavered from their allegiance to their monarch. The distinction was not only one in which he personally believed, but it also characterized the attitude of the government, which took some pains to prevent the plot from triggering anti-recusant witch-hunts. However, in the inflamed atmosphere after November 1605, with wild accusations and counter-accusations being traded by religious polemicists, there were allegations that Cecil himself had devised the Gunpowder Plot to elevate his own importance in the eyes of the king, and to facilitate a further attack on the Jesuits. Numerous subsequent efforts to substantiate these conspiracy theories have all failed abysmally.

By 1605 any threat there might have been to Cecil's future under the new Stuart monarchy had vanished. On 4 May 1605 James elevated him to the earldom of Salisbury, giving him parity with the most senior aristocrats on the privy council. Cecil also became lord lieutenant of Hertfordshire, confirming his dominant position in the county. In 1606 he became a knight of the Garter, though with rumours of protests from the kings of Denmark and France that the honour should be confined to those of pre-eminent nobility. In response Salisbury devoted weeks to organizing for himself a magnificent procession from Westminster to Windsor for his elevation, reported as surpassing the coronation procession itself. James regarded Salisbury, Northampton, and Suffolk as his three senior councillors, his 'trinity of knaves' (*Letters of … James VI & I*, 257) as he jocularly called them, but Salisbury was easily the most powerful. In August 1606, when he suffered a distemper after a bitter dispute with the Spanish ambassador over the suspects in the Gunpowder Plot, the king came to Salisbury's bedside to instruct him to take better care of himself, 'for if he should once fail there were no more safe hunting for the King of England' (Croft, 'Bureaucrat', 86). The Venetian ambassador, who frequently commented on Salisbury's appalling workload, thoughtfully summarized his position:

> No-one seeks but to win his favour. It is thought that his power will last, for it is based not so much on the grace of His Majesty, as on an excellent prudence and ability which secures for him the universal opinion that he is worthy of his great authority and good fortune. (ibid., 87)

The ambassador realized that Salisbury was not a royal favourite but rather an indispensable bureaucrat.

Whatever his position, Salisbury could not afford to offend the king. After 1603 the great park at Theobalds became one of James's most visited hunting places, and in May 1607 Salisbury agreed to exchange the estate for a grant of other royal properties, most importantly the old palace of Hatfield built by Cardinal John Morton. It was not in any way comparable to Theobalds, but there are indications that Salisbury had found the great house a burden and he set out to build a new mansion that was far different in style from the sprawling palace that Burghley had erected. Compact, comfortable, and sumptuously decorated, Hatfield House marked a new departure in English domestic architecture. Meanwhile Salisbury compensated for his temporary inability to entertain the royal family in the country by devising lavish receptions in the capital. The most notable was the opening in 1609 of the New Exchange, a shopping centre built at his expense in the Strand, on recently acquired land close to the Cecil townhouses. It aimed to divert luxury retailing from the City of London (whose protests were ignored) to Salisbury's birthplace of Westminster, where like his father before him he served as high steward, exercising control through numerous appointees on the court of burgesses and in the administration of the abbey. The king, the queen, Prince Henry, Princess Elizabeth, and Prince Charles all attended the opening of the New Exchange, which began with the performance of a specially commissioned masque from Ben Jonson emphasizing the commodities of international trade which Salisbury was making available to consumers. The royal family were given lavish presents and encouraged to take whatever they wanted as Salisbury showed them round. James then announced that the exchange would henceforth be known as 'Britain's Burse', a name that pointed to the union with Scotland but was also a subtle compliment to Salisbury, who had done more than anyone else to smooth the king's accession in 1603. The festivities also underscored Salisbury's dominance of the developing area of the lower Strand, which was increasingly affluent and fashionable as the residential district of choice for politicians and courtiers anxious to be close to Whitehall. Westminster was an urban power base for the Cecils for over sixty years, providing them with considerable influence and patronage (including two burgess seats in the Commons), in a crucial area which contained not only the monarch's chief residence but also the office of the royal works. Many of the leading craftsmen of the works were regularly employed by both Burghley and Salisbury in their extensive building programmes. Britain's Burse was a pioneering venture which both symbolized and accelerated the steady movement of commerce westwards outside the older confines of the City.

Financial reform The most striking proof of Cecil's success after 1603 in regaining his earlier place as the pre-eminent councillor came in 1608. After the death of the elderly earl of Dorset, Salisbury on 4 May was given the post of lord treasurer, meanwhile retaining both the secretaryship of state and the mastership of the wards. This was an unparalleled accumulation of great office, greater even than his father's position under Elizabeth, and conveyed immense administrative and financial power as well as vast opportunities for patronage. Aware that the promotion had been criticized, since the secretaryship and the lord treasurership were usually regarded as so burdensome as to be mutually exclusive, James let it be known that he considered Salisbury's abilities sufficient to enable him to fill all three posts.

Not surprisingly, however, the concentration of office in Salisbury's hands exacerbated the hostility of such men as the earl of Northampton and Sir Francis Bacon, who both felt that their abilities should have ensured their advancement to greater power and profit. For Northampton, who during Salisbury's lifetime achieved only the empty title of lord privy seal, the king's choice of lord treasurer was a bitter blow, particularly as he considered his Howard ancestry vastly superior to that of the *arriviste* Cecils. The efficient working relationship between Salisbury and Northampton remained central to the smooth functioning of the regime, but after Salisbury's death, Northampton wrote a venomous series of letters in which he vented his anger at his late rival's overarching success and gloated at the thought of 'the little lord' in hell. Fortunately both the other Howard earls, Suffolk and Nottingham, enjoyed genuinely warm relationships with Salisbury, thereby averting any threat of serious factional animosities, although tensions simmered beneath the surface. The marriages of Salisbury's affectionate nieces, one to the earl of Derby and another to Sir Philip Herbert, brother of the earl of Pembroke and later created earl of Montgomery, also extended links with the older nobility. After 1603 Salisbury took pains to cultivate the earl of Dunbar, the most powerful of James's Scottish advisers and one of his oldest friends. In consequence, although Dunbar played the pre-eminent role in border affairs he made no attempt to challenge Salisbury's control of the administration of England.

Throughout his career Salisbury was fortunate to enjoy the support of an able and close-knit secretariat, which must have been crucial in the effective discharge of his onerous responsibilities. Several of his men had been trained up under Lord Burghley, but his own appointees tended to be more cosmopolitan and better travelled than the older generation. Sir Walter Cope, Sir Michael Hickes, Sir Julius Caesar, and the Netherlander Levinus Munck were all distinguished civil servants who worked devotedly for their master in his lifetime and defended his reputation after his death. They provided him with friendship and support as well as efficient service.

Salisbury proved to be an extremely vigorous lord treasurer. In 1605 it was he, not Dorset, who had led the English privy council in writing to the king to impress upon him that his bounty should be restrained, since the attempts to fund it by the increasing resort to fiscal feudalism bred 'great distraction and scandal' among the populace ('Collection', 255). Between 1606 and 1608 Salisbury also utilized a temporary disruption in the Levant trade to facilitate the introduction of additional levies on trade, known as the new impositions. One of London's leading importers of Levant currants, John Bate, refused at the quayside in 1606 to pay the levy then demanded by the crown. After Bate's condemnation by the barons of the exchequer, Salisbury used the verdict on currants as the vital precedent to support the imposition of additional charges on the importation of a wide range of luxury commodities. After 1608, when the new impositions were in place, they generated an additional revenue from trade of at least £70,000 per annum, not much less than a parliamentary subsidy and capable of rising steadily as trade increased.

Immediately on taking office as lord treasurer Salisbury sent for the chief officers of the exchequer to inform himself about the exact state of affairs. He was dismayed by the mess in which Dorset had left matters. According to the reminiscences of his close friend Sir Walter Cope, 'His Lordship found the Exchequer a chaos of confusion. He found the debts £300,000 or £400,000: but which were good, which were bad, which sperate, which desperate, no man knew' (Cope, 122). Thereafter he continued to pursue the two-pronged strategy he had already sketched out. On the one hand he worked tirelessly to effect economies and wherever possible to curb the king's reckless bounty. On the other he aimed to increase the exchequer's activities, and through the use of revenue commissions to enhance all streams of income.

Salisbury instituted surveys of the crown lands, and began to extract higher rents. At the same time he paid special attention to the valuable woodlands, tightening control over tree-felling and wood sales. He sold off some scattered and relatively unprofitable properties while making repeated attempts to devise unbreakable entails on the major part of the royal estates. The journal kept by Salisbury's other close friend, the chancellor of the exchequer Sir Julius Caesar, detailed the efforts of the new lord treasurer between May and July 1608. Caesar paid tribute to his master's whirlwind energies in galvanizing the exchequer administration into action, as well as to his 'longe and great patience' in sitting through complex cases in the exchequer court (Hill, 'Caesar's journal', 318).

Salisbury was well aware, however, that unless he could persuade the king to change his attitudes to expenditure there would be no lasting recovery. In a series of private treatises written for James he resorted to extraordinary bluntness in trying to bring him to a recognition that his extravagance was a fundamental cause of royal indebtedness. Using uncomfortable examples such as the Cornish tax revolt of 1497 and the disaster of the amicable grant in 1525, he emphasized that taxpayers' patience was not infinite, a clear condemnation of James's lavish distribution of largesse derived from the 1606 subsidy moneys to three of his favourite courtiers. Salisbury spelt out his admiration for the prudent, well-organized Henry VII, in pointed contrast to his condemnation of Henry VIII, a king who 'thought all things lawful' where money was concerned. James had been dazzled by the wealth of England, so much greater than that of Scotland, but Salisbury emphasized that by contrast with the continental monarchies England was not affluent. The costs of war had caused even the tight-fisted Elizabeth to fall into severe financial difficulties in the latter years of her reign. The treatises breathe a sense of urgency; at a time of mounting international tension between 1608 and 1610, there were no reserves. 'It is not possible for a king of England ... to be rich or safe, but by frugality ... this I write with dolour but have beheld with fear and terror'. His worst fear was that James would do lasting damage, leaving the English crown 'no better than a dotard tree'. It was the lord treasurer's responsibility above all others 'for showing you demonstrably how the storm comes before it breaks' ('Collection', 255–60).

Salisbury was driven to such dangerous frankness by a number of conflicting pressures. One was the increasing desire of Prince Henry to be granted the title of prince of Wales and thereafter to receive the estates due to him out of the crown lands. This would give him financial independence, and with it the means to create another lavish royal household. Salisbury despaired of Stuart household expenditure, describing it as 'Ignis Edax, a devouring fire' ('Collection', 257), and the limited establishment set up for the prince was already growing out of control. At the same time Salisbury was hoping to move the king to summon a parliament in 1610, and the promise that Henry might be created prince of Wales in an imposing parliamentary ceremony was intended to win the prince's support for a fresh session.

Since taking office as lord treasurer in 1608 Salisbury had devoted two years of grindingly hard work to the royal finances. He had driven down the debt, raised income, and improved the administration of the exchequer. He was thus in a position to impress on the Commons that the king's earlier irresponsibility over finance was changing. A parliament in spring 1610 might allow Salisbury to seize a unique window of opportunity to plead his case. The opportunity might soon pass, for the crisis over the succession to Cleves-Jülich-Berg was indicative of instability in Europe, which might involve expensive English intervention. Moreover it was anybody's guess how long James would tolerate Salisbury's restrictions on his generosity, and Henry's expenditures as prince of Wales might prove him as extravagant as his father.

The proposal Salisbury put to the parliament of 1610 was a complex design which emerged from researches undertaken by the lord treasurer and his team during 1609, but which was finalized only in the early weeks of the new year. Salisbury urged James not to rely on the 'sour and harsh supplies' of prerogative taxation, but to attend 'rather to what may be obtained in parliament upon divers propositions that may be thought of, wherein I have taken some pains' ('Collection', 264). He aimed to trade a number of the crown's more irksome prerogatives, mostly legal rights that brought in little revenue but were burdensome for the subject, for a lump sum to pay off the remaining royal debt. In addition he asked for an annual income raised in perpetuity thereafter, without any further parliamentary vote, to supply the regular expenditure of the crown.

Salisbury was well aware that the plan was likely to prove extremely contentious. The lump sum requested to cover the debt, £600,000, was greater than any of the heavy requests for supply that the crown had made during the Elizabethan war years. At the same time the permanent annual revenue, which Salisbury hoped would amount to £200,000 per annum, would require the Commons to abrogate their ancient control over regular taxation. However, Salisbury had no plans to put parliaments out of business. The new income would simply restore the ordinary revenues of the crown, ravaged by inflation and the sales of crown lands during the 1590s, to a reasonable level that was still far less than Henry VIII had enjoyed. Any war or international emergency would always require extraordinary supply that could come only from a parliament.

The great contract Even before winning the consent of the Commons, Salisbury had to obtain the agreement of the king to recall the parliament he had prorogued in 1607. By then James had become thoroughly jaundiced with what he saw as English time-wasting obstructionism. Salisbury won the king over, partly by impressing on him the seriousness of the financial situation, and partly by indicating that he personally would deflect the expected criticisms of the Scots, who had benefited so much from James's lavish bounty. He even dangled before the king the prospect of reviving discussions on the union, together with a plan for the grant of permanent pensions for leading Scottish courtiers. At the same time Salisbury could not resist the sideswipe that it had been 'the harsh effects and ill order' of the royal generosity to the Scots that had 'troubled' the passage of the union earlier. Moreover he was honest enough not to suggest that success would come easily. He 'would not be so idle as to move your Majesty to promise yourself any great fruits of that, which I can say (when all that all of us can say) must run his adventure' ('Collection', 267, 264).

The treatises strongly suggest that Salisbury was isolated in proposing the great contract. In urging the project on the king he spoke very largely for himself and not for the privy council as a whole. The evidence of the parliamentary session supports this view, for few other councillors offered much support and Salisbury bore almost the whole burden of negotiations. The treatises which he had written for the king also provide a startling comparative insight. In speaking in parliament Salisbury gave a very full account of the crown's financial difficulties. However, he substantially altered the balance of his financial analysis, stressing the problem of unavoidable expenditures such as the costs of Ireland while briskly dismissing the problem of the king's bounty. Yet in the Commons' blunt criticisms of royal fecklessness he could not have failed to hear echoes of his own confidential admonitions to James. The verdict of an anonymous member of parliament, 'that all theis courses would be to no purpose, except it would please the King to resume his pencions granted to cortiers out of the exchecquer, and to diminish his charge and expences' (Gardiner, 11), exactly mirrored Salisbury's own prescription.

Unfortunately for the success of the contract, during the parliamentary session some serious problems emerged that had not been foreseen. Amid the initial proposal of compensatory benefits, Salisbury offered the ending of purveyance (whereby the royal household was entitled to use compulsion to obtain foodstuffs at prices far beneath the going rate), but only a modification of the much-disliked system of wardship. His plan was that in future the crown would restrict sales of wardships to the family and friends, at fixed rates. The Commons did not much value the offer on purveyance, since in 1604 they had become convinced that it was in any case illegal; they refused to compensate the king for an abuse. In addition they rejected the proposed reform of wardship, wishing instead to abolish it completely. While discussion on these points of the contract was continuing, a third issue arose over the legality or otherwise of Salisbury's earlier impositions on trade. The Commons regarded these as extra-parliamentary taxation and refused to accept that the verdict in Bate's case had resolved the question. Running through all the debates was a pervasive distrust of the king, not merely over his use of any money they might offer but also over his trustworthiness. Would these objectionable features of the royal prerogative really be permanently abolished? 'The like may springe up againe the next yeare and so wee be forced to redeeme theym also', observed one member (Gardiner, 47).

In the circumstances Salisbury was remarkably fortunate to be able to conclude the first half of the contract, on the annual revenue, by the time that parliament was prorogued for the summer. He was assisted by the shocking news in May 1610 that Henri IV of France had been assassinated; this highlighted England's stability and good fortune in having both an adult monarch and an heir about to come of age. But the Commons drove a hard bargain, and during the summer recess their constituents showed little enthusiasm for Salisbury's grand scheme. At the same time support was ebbing at court, and James determined to remind the Commons that the contract had always been twofold: the agreement on the annual income must be followed by a vote of the large lump sum needed to pay off the recurring debt. On this rock the scheme was finally

shipwrecked, and anti-Scots feeling again began to surface in the Commons. Exasperated, the king adjourned the parliament for Christmas, then dissolved it.

Last years Salisbury was exhausted and distraught by the end of the year. Early in December James wrote him a savage letter, noting that 'in the perturbations of your mind, ye have broken forth in more passionate and strange discourses these last two sessions of Parliament than ever ye were wont to do'. But he continued with the command that 'it is now time for you to cast your care upon the next best means how to help my state', making clear that he had no intention of dismissing Salisbury (*Letters of … James VI & I*, 316–17). Nevertheless, the king made plain his view that the whole strategy of bargaining with the Commons had been misguided:

> There is no more trust to be laid upon this rotten reed of Egypt, for your greatest error hath been that ye ever expected to draw honey out of gall, being a little blinded with the self-love of your own counsel in holding together of this parliament, whereof all men were despaired (as I have oft told you) but yourself alone.   (ibid.)

Despite these harsh words James showed his appreciation of Salisbury's tireless efforts on his behalf. On 10 December 1610 the king renewed, for a further nineteen years, the extremely lucrative silk farm concession originally granted in 1601; to Salisbury it was worth a clear net income of £7000 per annum.

Salisbury responded to James in his last treatise, written on 23 January 1611. He made clear that he had little more to offer: 'I be not able to recover your estate out of the hands of those great wants to which your parliament hath now abandoned you'. However, he was too professional to despair completely, and sketched out for the king an account of the current situation, urging that his 'first work must be to settle an establishment as may prevent excess and amend defects' ('Collection', 313, 315). The exploitation of the traditional revenues of the crown would go ahead, but once again he begged James to restrain his bounty. Nor did Salisbury hide his deepest conviction, however displeasing it might be to the king. Parliament 'hath ever been the only foundation of supply to those princes whose necessities have been beyond the cares and endevours of private men' (ibid., 313). He was still convinced that the only long-term solution lay there.

Despite these sharp exchanges Salisbury continued to hold his three great offices, and by February 1611 the king had returned to his former practice of channelling virtually all privy council business through him. Salisbury the supreme bureaucrat was simply indispensable, and suitors continued to queue for hours in order to see him. At the same time the increasingly active negotiations between 1610 and 1612 to secure marriage partners for both Prince Henry and Princess Elizabeth reinforced his control over foreign policy and renewed his regular contacts with the king and the royal family. In November 1611 the ambassador of Savoy on his arrival with proposals for dowry immediately had an hour's private conference with the king, then another hour with Salisbury.

The pursuit of any plan that might increase revenue led

Salisbury in 1611 into the sale of baronetcies, which can clearly be demonstrated to have emerged from him and his exchequer circle. Between May and November 1611 the first round of sales saw eighty-eight baronets purchasing the new hereditary rank. The scheme was used not only as a revenue-raising device but also more imaginatively to enable well-affected Catholics to demonstrate their political support for the regime. Some twenty-six baronets came from recusant backgrounds, and at the centre of the cohort was an interlinked network of four families that had been deeply implicated in the Gunpowder Plot of 1605. From them emerged a group of men prepared to undertake the expensive honour as a sign of conspicuous loyalty that would distinguish them from their traitorous brothers and cousins. The sale of the baronetcies allowed Salisbury to put into practice that distinction between 'infested spirits' and reliable Catholic gentlemen that he had made in print immediately after the plot itself.

Failing health The spring and summer of 1611 brought the tragi-comedy of Lady Arabella Stuart's unsuccessful elopement, a matter of deep concern to the king since she was his nearest relative and had been a possible contender for the crown in 1603. Salisbury handled the whole affair, another indication that he had regained James's full confidence. All the signs are that by summer 1611 Salisbury had recovered his position after the failure of the great contract and was once again regarded as the single most powerful minister and privy councillor.

Nevertheless the political map was changing. On Monday 4 June 1610 the sixteen-year-old Henry was installed as prince of Wales in the midst of the Lords and Commons. The unique ceremony was devised with much effort by Salisbury, drawing on antiquarian researches he had specially commissioned for the occasion. It made a dazzling impression but failed in its aim of persuading the Commons to loosen their purse strings. Once given his new title, however, Henry was increasingly intent on making his views heard on matters of foreign policy, not least on the question of his marriage where he objected to his father's plans to marry him to a Roman Catholic princess. The conflict was bound to cause problems for Salisbury as secretary of state. Even more perturbing, the king by 1611 was publicly enamoured of Sir Robert Carr, a young Scot who showed every sign of becoming a favourite of much greater significance than the lightweight young men who had occasionally caught James's eye earlier. The disruption of relationships within the royal family, between the king and queen and also between the king and the prince, was the inevitable consequence. These new complexities seemed likely to test the sagacity even of a minister as experienced as Salisbury, but more significant was his own failing health.

Salisbury had never been robust and in August the royal doctor Sir Theodore Mayerne diagnosed two large tumours, though he could do little more than advise a healthy diet and moderate exercise. By December 1611 it became clear that Salisbury was seriously ill. He relinquished the day-to-day running of the exchequer to Sir Julius Caesar, a temporary expedient that rapidly became permanent. He was near death's door in February 1612, when government business nearly came to a standstill, but recovered sufficiently to receive visitors including the king, the queen, and the prince.

Still hoping for a cure, Salisbury in April 1612 left for Bath, where he had found relief in previous years. On the journey he frequently conversed and prayed with his chaplain, desperately anxious to be reassured about his salvation. He took great comfort in the parable of the lost sheep, exclaiming 'Oh that sheep am I, that sheep am I', after hearing an exposition of the text. Perhaps only a lord treasurer would have added 'My audit is made' (Croft, 'Religion', 794). Salisbury's increasingly high-church views mirrored those already visible in his circle of friends and chaplains, including Lancelot Andrewes and Richard Neile. The chapel he had just completed at Hatfield House was unique for its time in its lavish decoration, colourful interior, and exceptional stained glass, the first large window with a religious subject to be commissioned since the Reformation. It silently distanced him from the increasing visual austerity preferred by the godly wing of the Church of England.

At Bath, Salisbury immersed himself in the waters and commiserated with his old friend and fellow invalid Sir John Harington. To his great joy his son William hastened to him despite being forbidden to do so. Both the king and the queen sent him splendid gifts of jewellery, brought by the king's intimate Lord Hay, to testify to their enduring favour and affection. The last letter Salisbury wrote from Bath appears to have been his courteous Christian farewell to the earl of Northampton, who subsequently revealed that he had loathed his colleague. On the return journey, increasingly wracked with pain, Salisbury died at Marlborough, Wiltshire, on 24 May 1612.

Assessment Salisbury left his estates heavily encumbered with debt. He originally began to buy land soon after becoming master of the court of wards in 1599. Between 1601 and 1603 he invested heavily, and again after 1608 he made substantial purchases to consolidate his holdings around Hatfield House and Cranborne Manor in Dorset, a smaller estate originally purchased under Elizabeth. Despite a determined effort in 1611–12 to reduce his debts by selling unwanted estates, he still on his deathbed owed the huge sum of £37,867. He had borrowed a total of £61,000 over the previous four years, more than half from the leading merchants of London.

Salisbury spent heavily on conspicuous consumption, including royal entertainments that were intended to reinforce his political position. His chief extravagance, however, was his passion for building. Hatfield House, Salisbury (Cecil) House in the Strand, Britain's Burse, and additional works at Cranborne Manor amounted to the most astonishing building programme of his age. They caused his loyal man of affairs John Daccombe to despair: 'I beseech your Lordship to forbear buildings', he wrote towards the end of 1611 (Stone, 32). In addition Salisbury spent vast amounts on the splendid and innovative gardens that surrounded all his houses, and on their highly sophisticated, elaborate interiors; he was one of the earliest Englishmen to build up a major collection of paintings, antedating the earl of Arundel; he was the most notable musical patron of his day; he added extensively to his father's great library; and he commissioned Ben Jonson for the masques staged at his houses for the royal family. The range and quality of his taste and the discrimination implicit in his patronage were remarkable.

It was not surprising that all these luxury interests left his estate encumbered. However, by 1612 he had no outstanding family obligations, for he had already married off his two children, to whom he remained a conscientious father after their mother's early death. William was an unacademic youth who did little at Cambridge, and was subsequently dispatched on an improving tour of the continent. Salisbury pursued him with agitated, overprescriptive letters urging him to concentrate on his language studies and make every effort to grow taller. In December 1608 William married Catherine Howard, daughter of the earl and countess of Suffolk, in a match clearly designed to consolidate the political links between the two families. It proved an amicable and fecund partnership, though William did not relish the notoriety of his sister-in-law Frances Howard, the wife of Sir Robert Carr, when the couple were convicted of murder by poisoning in May 1616. Frances Cecil, who had inherited both her father's humpback and his love of music, was kept away from the court since Salisbury wished to shield her from the taunts that had made his own early years there a source of misery. In July 1610 she married Lord Clifford, heir of the earl of Cumberland. Salisbury paid Clifford a dowry of £6000, well above the average for his daughter's rank, suggesting that extra money was demanded to compensate for her deformity.

However, despite the daunting tally of unpaid loans in 1612, Salisbury had not seriously overstretched himself. By 1614 his executors had largely solved the financial problem, and by 1617 William was enjoying a regular income from land that placed him in the highest ranks of the English aristocracy. Between 1598 and 1612 Salisbury had turned his relatively modest inheritance from Burghley into one of the greatest estates in the realm. Both Hatfield House and Cranborne Manor remain almost unchanged, among the finest great houses to survive from one of the finest periods of English architecture. They are still lived in and cherished by Salisbury's direct descendants.

The political legacy of Robert Cecil was more ambiguous and remains hard to assess. He had made no attempt to train up his only son to follow in his footsteps as a pre-eminent administrator, and he left no cohesive political grouping behind him. It was nevertheless a tribute to Salisbury that the policies with which he was identified— co-operation with parliaments, restoration of sound royal finances, and pragmatic diplomacy aimed at upholding English commercial interests—continued to be widely advocated until the outbreak of the civil war.

Immediately after Salisbury's death there was an outpouring of libellous verses, depicting him as:

> Oppression's praiser,
> Taxation's raiser ...
> The country's scourger,
> the cities' cheater,
> of many a shilling

For good measure it went on:

> The king's misuser,
> The parliament's abuser,
> Hath left his plotting,
> ... is now a-rotting.
> (Croft, 'Reputation', 49, 53)

His humpback gave rise to invidious comparisons: 'here lieth Robin Crooktback, unjustly reckoned A Richard the Third: he was Judas the second' (ibid., 55). Lady Walsingham and Lady Suffolk, allegedly his mistresses, were said to have infected him with the pox. Sexual depravity was linked to his appalling sufferings from cancer and scurvy, with the ulcerous sores and fetid breath of his last days pitilessly pilloried by the libellers. The funeral, held at Hatfield on 10 June 1612, was a quiet affair for a man of Salisbury's eminence, but it was nearly interrupted by a symbolic protest which aimed to lay open the newly emparked grounds. The thrusting of his grand new house into a settled rural community had caused much local resentment.

Sir Francis Bacon, a more measured observer than the libellers, although admittedly a hostile witness since he thought Salisbury had blocked his promotion, told James that the lord treasurer 'was a fit man to keep things from growing worse but no very fit man to reduce things to be much better' (*The Works of Francis Bacon*, ed. J. Spedding, 14 vols., 1857–74, 11.280). Yet no other Jacobean lord treasurer achieved as much as Salisbury, and his successor Suffolk proved totally incompetent. Many of Salisbury's innovations were far-sighted. The new impositions were virtually inflation-proof, as well as being far more flexible and easier to collect than taxes on landed wealth. Constitutionally they proved unacceptable to parliament, but similar taxes on trade provided the most valuable source of crown income after the Restoration. Similarly it was not until the reign of William III that the great contract's concept of a permanent partnership between crown and parliament in raising annual state revenues was realized.

Salisbury can thus be credited with vision. There are other areas, too, where he made a major contribution to the politics of his day. First, between 1596 and 1603 he played the leading role in steering the enfeebled regime of Elizabeth through circumstances of great difficulty, with the Irish rising imposing immense fiscal burdens at a time when bad harvests, scarcity of coin, and widespread disruption of trade made it risky to levy taxation at home. He reacted promptly and coolly to Essex's rebellion, but was careful not to create a permanently disaffected faction by discreetly easing the punishments handed down to the lesser men who had been involved. Second, Cecil took great personal risks between 1601 and 1603 in smoothing the path for the trouble-free accession of James I, at a time when he could have been charged with treason. Of those

Englishmen who corresponded secretly with the king, he was the only one with sufficient political power to ensure that the necessary preparations had all been made before Elizabeth's death. Third, it was Cecil, effectively aided only by Northampton, who in 1604 conducted the negotiations with Spain which not only brought peace in Europe but also safely opened up to Englishmen the New World, with all its potential for the future.

Historians have tended to ignore the achievements while repeatedly debating how far Robert Cecil was corrupt. There can be no doubt that he used his official position for personal financial gain on an extraordinary scale. However, modern standards do not apply; in an era which did not pay adequate official salaries, it was expected that great servants of the state would reimburse themselves by exploiting their offices and seeking payment for favours that they were able to do for others. Cecil served Elizabeth for eleven years, carrying very heavy administrative burdens without much to show by way of reward. After 1603 he acquired a fortune, and was greedier than his father had been, but he debased his official position far less than did his successor Suffolk. The first area of grave concern must be his acceptance of a pension and substantial separate gifts from successive Spanish ambassadors after 1604. Yet he was never regarded at the Spanish court as a reliable friend or client of Spain; on the contrary, it was hoped that the pension might moderate his hostility and there was rejoicing in Madrid at his death. Second, his relationships with the great London merchants who farmed the customs were extremely close and he depended heavily on them for credit as he amassed his estate and funded his building programme. If Salisbury almost certainly did not extract from them the maximum price that might have been obtained for the great farm of the customs and other subsequent farms, he nevertheless ensured that customs revenue, and taxes on trade, contributed far more to the royal coffers than they had ever done before. Insofar as the merchants also generously contributed to his own coffers it might be argued that that was preferable to enriching himself directly from the crown.

Perhaps the most convincing defence of Salisbury was the one put forward by his friend Sir Walter Cope to James I:

> If this Lord's tomb could speak, it would assure us there were no gain to be gotten by defacing the monument of so worthy a Minister ... He lost the love of your people only for your sake, and for your service. (Cope, 121, 133)

Among all the drones and freeloaders at the Jacobean court, Salisbury stood out as a dedicated bureaucrat. In the service of the state he wore himself out, and if he was to blame for amassing too many great offices, the king was deeply misguided to think that any one privy councillor could carry the burdens of the wards, the secretaryship, and the treasury.

The tomb at Hatfield parish church, designed by Maximilian Colt and approved by Salisbury before his death, is a sombre masterpiece and the last item commissioned by him. A life-size effigy in Garter robes, holding the lord treasurer's staff in its right hand, lies on a black slab. The four cardinal virtues of Justice, Fortitude, Temperance, and Prudence, carved almost life-sized, hold up the slab, while a realistic skeleton lies beneath on a carved rolled mat. Extraordinarily for its time there is no epitaph extolling Salisbury's unparalleled tenure of the three great offices of state—a remarkable act of self-abnegation—and no mention of any family ties. On the other hand it seems a fitting monument for a man who years earlier had described himself to Sir John Harington as 'one that hath sorrowed in the bright lustre of a Court and gone heavily even on the best seeming fair ground' (J. Harington, *Nugae antiquae*, ed. H. Harington and T. Park, 2 vols., 1804, 263). It also expresses something of Salisbury's state of mind in the last year of his life. For all his remarkable frankness to James I, and his efforts over the great contract, Salisbury had not succeeded in impressing on the king 'how the storm comes before it breaks'. He probably went to his grave regarding that as his greatest failure.

PAULINE CROFT

Sources PRO, state papers domestic, Elizabeth I, SP 12 · PRO, state papers domestic, James I, SP 14 · Cecil MSS, Hatfield House, Hertfordshire · *Calendar of the manuscripts of the most hon. the marquis of Salisbury*, 24 vols., HMC, 9 (1883–1976), vols. 6–22 · 'A collection of several speeches and treatises of the late lord treasurer Cecil', ed. P. Croft, *Camden miscellany, XXIX*, CS, 4th ser., 34 (1987) · R. C. [R. Cecil], *The copie of a letter to the right honourable the earle of Leycester* (1586) · R. Cecil, *The state and dignitie of a secretarie of estates place, with the care and perill thereof* (1642) · R. Cecil, *An answere to certaine scandalous papers, scattered abroad* (1606) · *Letters of King James VI & I*, ed. G. P. V. Akrigg (1984) · P. Croft, 'The religion of Robert Cecil', *HJ*, 34 (1991), 773–96 · P. Croft, 'The reputation of Robert Cecil: libels, political opinion and popular awareness in the early seventeenth century', *TRHS*, 6th ser., 1 (1991), 43–69 · P. Croft, 'Robert Cecil and the early Jacobean court', *The mental world of the Jacobean court*, ed. L. L. Peck (1991), 134–47 · P. Croft, 'Can a bureaucrat be a favourite?', *The world of the favourite*, ed. J. Elliott and L. Brockliss (1999), 81–95 · P. Croft, 'The parliamentary installation of Henry, prince of Wales', *Historical Research*, 65 (1992), 177–93 · P. Croft, 'Brussels and London: the archdukes, Robert Cecil and James I', *Albert and Isabella: essays*, ed. W. Thomas and L. Duerloo (Brussels, 1999), 79–86 · W. Cope, 'An apology for the late lord treasurer', *Collectanea curiosa*, ed. J. Gutch, 1 (1781), 119–33 · L. M. Hill, 'Sir Julius Caesar's journal of Salisbury's first two months and twenty days as lord treasurer, 1608', *BIHR*, 45 (1972), 311–27 · L. Stone, *Family and fortune: studies in aristocratic finance in the sixteenth and seventeenth centuries* (1973) · P. E. J. Hammer, *The polarisation of Elizabethan politics: the political career of Robert Devereux, 2nd earl of Essex, 1585–1597* (1999) · L. M. Hill, *Bench and bureaucracy: the public career of Sir Julius Caesar, 1580–1636* (1988) · P. Croft, ed., *Patronage, culture and power: the early Cecils* (2002) · S. R. Gardiner, ed., *Parliamentary debates in 1610*, CS, 81 (1862) · St Clement Danes parish register, City Westm. AC [baptism] · C. Read, *Mr Secretary Cecil and Queen Elizabeth* (1955) · J. Foster, *The register of admissions to Gray's Inn, 1521–1889, together with the register of marriages in Gray's Inn chapel, 1695–1754* (privately printed, London, 1889) · BL, Sir Theodore Mayerne's MSS, Sloane MSS, vols. 2063, 2066 · J. Bowle, 'An account of the lord treasurer's last sickness', BL, Add. MS 34218, fols. 125–7

Archives BL, corresp. and MSS, Add. MSS 5664, 6177, 5503 · BL, Sloane MSS, corresp. and MSS · CKS, corresp. · Hatfield House, Hertfordshire, corresp. and MSS relating to Cambridge University · LPL, letters · Warks. CRO, letters | BL, letters to Sir J. Caesar, Add. MSS 11406, 36767 · BL, Cotton MSS, corresp. and MSS · BL, Harley MSS, corresp. and MSS · BL, register of corresp. with T. Parry, Add MS 38138 · BL, Stowe MSS, corresp. and MSS · BL, corresp. with W. Trumbull, Downshire II–III · CUL, corresp. relating to Cambridge University · Hunt. L., letters to Lord Chancellor

Ellesmere · LPL, corresp. with earls of Shrewsbury · Northants. RO, corresp. with R. Winwood · NYPL, corresp. with Mr Nicholson · PRO, SP 12, SP 14 · Stonyhurst College, Lancashire, letters to Sir Charles Cornwallis

Likenesses J. de Critz the elder, oil on panel, 1602, NPG · group portrait, oils, 1604 (*The Somerset House conference, 1604*), NPG · J. de Critz the elder, oils, *c*.1606, Hatfield House, Hertfordshire · M. Colt, tomb effigy, Hatfield church, Salisbury chapel · J. de Critz the elder, oils, Hatfield House, Hertfordshire [*see illus.*] · J. de Critz the elder, oils, Ingatestone Hall, Essex

Wealth at death £49,000 p.a. for 1608–12; heavily indebted on death: Stone, *Family and fortune*, 59–61 · by 1617 original estate was clear of debt and second earl lived in grand style

Cecil, Robert Arthur James Gascoyne-, fifth marquess of Salisbury (1893–1972), politician, was born on 27 August 1893 at Hatfield House, Hatfield, Hertfordshire. He was the elder son and second of the four children of the politician James Edward Hubert Gascoyne-*Cecil (1861–1947), who became the fourth marquess of Salisbury in 1903, and his wife, Lady Cicely Alice Gore (*d.* 1955), daughter of the fifth earl of Arran and a descendant of Lord Melbourne. As heir to the marquessate, he bore the name Viscount Cranborne. To his friends he was known all his life as Bobbety. His was a patrician inheritance, and his lengthy career in the Conservative Party and the House of Lords was nothing if not patrician. The irony was that the period in which he most famously defended his traditionalist values, the late 1950s and early 1960s, was also the time of his political marginalization within his own party.

Cranborne was educated at Eton College and Christ Church, but left Oxford for war service without completing his degree. Commissioned as a lieutenant in the Grenadier Guards, he saw action in France and won the Croix de Guerre. He was invalided home in September 1915 and on 8 December married Elizabeth Vere (*d.* 1982), daughter of Lord Richard Cavendish. In 1916 he served as personal military secretary to the earl of Derby, secretary of state for war.

After the war Cranborne joined a City billbroking firm, with which he stayed for some ten years. His entry to politics came at the general election of 1929, when he was returned as Conservative member for South Dorset. In 1934 he attained junior office, becoming parliamentary secretary to Anthony Eden (later the earl of Avon), who was at that time lord privy seal and minister without portfolio. Here began a long ministerial association. When Eden went to the Foreign Office in 1935, Cranborne accompanied him as under-secretary. When Eden resigned in February 1938 in protest against Neville Chamberlain's decision to parley with Mussolini, Cranborne resigned with him. In a personal statement to the Commons which angered Chamberlain, Cranborne described British policy towards Mussolini as a surrender to blackmail. The Munich agreement spurred him to a further attack; Chamberlain's achievement, he argued, was certainly not peace with honour, for the agreement had turned upon 'throwing [Czechoslovakia] to the wolves' (*Hansard 5C*, 339, 4 Oct 1938, 232–3).

Conservative peer Not surprisingly, Cranborne was brought back into office by Winston Churchill, who made him paymaster-general in May 1940 and then dominions secretary with a seat in cabinet in October. He was effective at the Dominions Office and soon acquired further responsibility. Churchill and Eden wanted him to speak for the government on foreign affairs in the upper house, and for this purpose he was raised to the Lords in January 1941 in his father's barony of Cecil of Essendon (though he continued to use the courtesy title of Lord Cranborne). In February 1942 he was appointed colonial secretary and leader of the House of Lords; the latter position was one his father had occupied as recently as 1925–9. He became at the same time Conservative Party leader in the Lords. Both his father and grandfather before him had held this office; he would retain it for fifteen years, the longest term since his grandfather's in 1881–1902. In November 1942 Cranborne left the Colonial Office and was for ten months lord privy seal, while continuing as leader of the Lords. Having declined an invitation to succeed Lord Linlithgow as viceroy of India, he returned to the Dominions Office in September 1943. He remained in charge of both dominions and the Lords until the 1945 election.

Cranborne was an influential figure in the reformulation of Conservative policy that followed the Labour victory. He was quick to acknowledge that the Conservatives would have to come to terms with a changing Britain. The age of unrestricted democracy, he wrote to Eden in 1946, had arrived, and power now lay in the hands of 'the small man'. The sensible option for the Conservatives was to give the voter 'a stake in the country … that he himself knows he will lose if, as an elector, he acts irresponsibly' (Ramsden, *Age of Churchill and Eden*, 175). He was thus an early advocate of the property-owning democracy, albeit for essentially paternalist and strategic reasons.

Throughout the Labour years Lord Salisbury (as he became in April 1947) was leader of the opposition in the Lords. Some have judged this the 'most effective' phase of his career (*DNB*). Leading a Conservative majority in the Lords but faced with the unprecedented situation of a Labour majority in the Commons, he devised guidelines, known unofficially as the Salisbury rules, under which the opposition would oppose while not rendering the system of government inoperable. In essence the Lords could choose to amend, but would not destroy or alter beyond recognition, the bills that comprised the government's declared programme. The gas and electricity nationalizations, for example, were treated in this way. But the government's plan to nationalize the profitable and efficient iron and steel industry was quite another matter. For Salisbury such a measure would constitute 'a definite step towards Communism' (*Hansard 5L*, 162, 24 May 1949, 1018), and was in any case in excess of the government's mandate since it had not been fully spelt out in the 1945 manifesto. Faced with intense Conservative opposition, the government in 1947 postponed the Iron and Steel Bill, and in January 1948 introduced a Parliament Bill with the aim of reducing the Lords' delaying power from two years to one. Having tried and failed to negotiate a compromise measure of upper house reform, Salisbury felt free to move the rejection of the Parliament Bill and did so in three successive sessions. It was eventually enacted against Conservative resistance in December 1949. The Iron and Steel Bill also became law late in 1949, but an amendment moved by Salisbury ensured that it would take effect only if Labour won the next election. Herbert Morrison spoke of Salisbury's intolerable interference; others said of Salisbury that he had political flair to match Morrison's, 'with the advantage of four centuries' start' (*The Times*).

Conservative cabinet minister Back in power in October 1951, Salisbury was reappointed leader of the House of Lords. He was Commonwealth secretary, serving his third term with the dominions, from March to November 1952, after which he became lord president of the council. In June 1953 it was he who carried the sword of state at the queen's coronation. Salisbury spoke for the right in Churchill's cabinet. He opposed any merging of British interests with European, argued for curbing non-white immigration, deplored a colonial policy of 'concessions under pressure' (Goldsworthy, 2.5), and regretted the changes in the Commonwealth, particularly the precedent established by the 1949 decision to let India remain a member after becoming a republic—for this undercut a principle he held dear, that allegiance to the crown should be a necessary element of Commonwealth membership. In foreign affairs and defence he was an implacable cold warrior; his reaction to Churchill's notion of a summit with the Soviet leadership in July 1954 was a resignation threat.

From June to October 1953, when Eden was hospitalized, Salisbury was acting foreign secretary. Churchill's incapacitation by a stroke in the same period brought Salisbury into consideration as a potential caretaker prime minister who could, if need be, keep the seat warm for Eden. When he became premier at last in 1955, Eden did not feel able to appoint Salisbury foreign secretary, but chose to keep him on as lord president and leader of the Lords. But during the Suez crisis of 1956 Salisbury was a member of Eden's innermost group, the Egypt committee. The support he gave Eden's policy reflected both his determination to crush Egypt's challenge to Britain's great-power status and his personal loyalty to Eden. After the collapse of the invasion he urged Eden to stay on as leader. But in January 1957 Eden resigned, and the queen turned to Salisbury for advice on the succession. He and the lord chancellor, Lord Kilmuir, interviewed each cabinet minister in turn in Salisbury's office, an experience which several ministers likened to being summoned to the headmaster's study. Here it was that Salisbury put his famous question: 'Well, which is it, Wab or Hawold?' (Kilmuir, 28).

Under the new prime minister, Harold Macmillan, Salisbury retained his position as lord president and leader of the Lords. At the end of March, however, he abruptly resigned from the government. The immediate occasion was the cabinet's decision to release Archbishop Makarios from detention; another relevant factor, not disclosed at the time, was Salisbury's exasperation at the government's continued dithering on immigration (Hennessy and Seldon, 111). Macmillan, who was related by marriage to Salisbury but found him a difficult colleague, wrote in his diary: 'The Cabinet, much as they all like him personally, feel like a man who has got rid of an inflamed tooth' (Horne, 2.38). Privately, Macmillan was relieved that Salisbury had chosen to resign over a containable issue.

Opponent of imperial retreat Two months later Salisbury took the government severely to task for agreeing to allow British ships to use the Suez Canal on Egypt's terms. His course as a die-hard opponent of the imperial retreat was now set. By the early 1960s he was increasingly focusing his attack on the government's policy of decolonization in Africa. To him this policy was doubly deplorable. First, in yielding to nationalist pressures it amounted to 'our old friend the policy of Appeasement through weakness in a new form' (*The Spectator*, 7 Feb 1964). Second, it entailed the betrayal of British settlers in Kenya and the Rhodesias. Early in 1961 he set up an informal 'watching committee' in the parliamentary party, with the aim of influencing the government's African policy in a rightward direction. His most biting public attack was launched in the Lords in March 1961, when he accused the colonial secretary, Iain Macleod, of setting out not to negotiate with the white settlers but to outwit them. He described Macleod as unscrupulous, and, in his most reverberant phrase, as 'too clever by half' (*Hansard 5L*, 229, 7 March 1961, 307). This was not just a political assault but a personal one; Sir Colin Coote may have had it in mind when he wrote later that Salisbury 'embodied the definition of a gentleman as one who never gives offence unintentionally' (*Daily Telegraph*).

Salisbury went on to resign from the presidency of his local Conservative constituency association in Hertfordshire, while accepting in 1962 the office of patron of the Monday Club, a group of younger Conservatives who shared his views on Africa. In the mid-1960s the Rhodesian rebellion became his last-ditch issue. He could not condone the illegal declaration of independence; he nevertheless sympathized with the Europeans' cause, and at the Conservative Party conferences of 1965 and 1966 spoke out against the imposition of penal sanctions. But although Salisbury had his following in the party's imperial wing and strong connections with the settlers, he did not now carry weight with the party's policy-making leadership, and indeed had not done so since his resignation. His convictions did not change, but the times did, and in most political quarters he came to be seen simply as a reactionary.

Certainly Salisbury was a deeply traditional Conservative. He was devoted to monarchy, church, country, and empire: institutions emblematic of order, hierarchy, and national pride. He defended his values with a strong will and, as his two resignations showed, independence of mind. If in the end it was the loss of empire that hurt him most, it was because empire was intrinsic to his notion of British identity. Empire signified national honour as well as national power. Further, he could not accept that its loss was inevitable. To him the essential problem, just as it had been in the appeasement era, was weakness at the core: a failure of British resolve.

Roy Jenkins judged Salisbury 'sour and malevolent' at the time of his attack on Macleod (Jenkins, 44). Generally Salisbury was known as a man of charm, wit, and courtesy. But when high principles were at stake, as his *Times* obituarist put it, 'passion could galvanize his slight frame and lift his light voice to icy disdain'. It was a bitterly disdainful Salisbury that his opponents saw much of in his later years. What also needs to be noted is that to have patrician values is to be motivated by an ethic—a paternalist one, to be sure—of public service. Salisbury had this; it no doubt had much to do with his Cecil heritage; and it probably played at least as great a part as personal ambition in leading him into a political career.

Salisbury also led a busy life outside politics. He served as chair of the Royal Commission on Historical Monuments in 1957, and from 1959 to 1966 was a trustee of the National Gallery. He was chancellor of Liverpool University from 1951 to 1971, a fellow of Eton College from 1951 to 1966, and, because of his work for science while lord president, a fellow of the Royal Society from 1957. Other honours included the high stewardship of Hertfordshire from 1947, the chancellorship of the Order of the Garter from 1960 (he had been appointed KG in 1946), and eight honorary degrees. After leaving government he returned to the business world in which he had begun his working life, taking on directorships with the British South Africa Company and the Westminster Bank.

Salisbury and his wife had three sons, the second of whom died in 1934 and the third in 1944, while on active military service. The eldest son succeeded as the sixth marquess when Salisbury died at Hatfield House on 23 February 1972.   DAVID GOLDSWORTHY

Sources *Daily Telegraph* (24 Feb 1972) · *The Times* (24 Feb 1972) · *DNB* · J. Ramsden, *The age of Churchill and Eden, 1940–1957* (1995) · J. Ramsden, *The winds of change: Macmillan to Heath, 1957–1975* (1996) · A. Horne, *Macmillan*, 2 vols. (1988–9) · J. Charmley, *A history of conservative politics, 1900–1996* (1996) · Lord Carrington, *Reflect on things past* (1988) · P. Hennessy and A. Seldon, eds., *Ruling performances* (1987) · P. Murphy, *Party politics and decolonisation: the conservative party and British colonial policy in tropical Africa, 1951–1964* (1995) · D. Goldsworthy, ed., *The conservative government and the end of empire, 1951–1957*, 3 vols. (1994) · Lord Kilmuir, *Political adventure: memoirs* (1962) · R. Jenkins, *Portraits and miniatures* (1993) · Burke, *Peerage*

Archives Hatfield House, Hertfordshire, papers · PRO, corresp., FO 800/296 | BL, corresp. with Lord Cecil, Add. MS 51987 · BL, corresp. with P. V. Emrys-Evans, Add. MSS 58240–58241 · Bodl. Oxf., corresp. with Viscount Addison · Bodl. Oxf., corresp. with H. A. Gwynne · Bodl. Oxf., letters to Lady Milner · Bodl. Oxf., corresp. with Lord Monckton · Bodl. Oxf., corresp. with third earl of Selborne · Bodl. Oxf., corresp. with Lord Simon · Bodl. Oxf., corresp. with Lord Woolton · Bodl. RH, corresp. with Sir R. R. Welensky · Borth. Inst., corresp. with Lord Halifax [copies in CAC Cam.] · CAC Cam., corresp. with Sir E. L. Spears · Carmarthenshire RO, Carmarthen, letters to J. P. L. Thomas · CUL, corresp. with Sir Samuel Hoare · HLRO, corresp. with Lord Beaverbrook · King's Lond., Liddell Hart C., corresp. with Sir B. H. Liddell Hart · NL Scot., corresp. with Lord Tweedsmuir · U. Birm. L., corresp. with Lord Avon and Lady Avon · U. Durham L., corresp. with Evelyn Baring, first Baron Howick of Glendale · University of Cape Town Library, Cape Town, letters, incl. of his wife, to C. J. Sibbert | SOUND BL NSA, current affairs recording

Likenesses W. Orpen, oils, *c.*1914–1919, Hatfield House, Hertfordshire · J. S. Sargent, chalk drawing, 1915, Hatfield House, Hertfordshire · J. S. Sargent, pencil drawing, 1915, Hatfield House, Hertfordshire · H. Coster, photographs, 1930–39, NPG · W. Stoneman, three photographs, 1936–54, NPG · H. Lamb, chalk drawing, 1950, Hatfield House, Hertfordshire · E. Halliday, group portrait, oils, 1951, Hatfield House, Hertfordshire · W. Bird, photograph, 1962, NPG · L. McKean, bronze bust, 1965, Hatfield House, Hertfordshire · D. Wynne, bronze head, 1966–7, Hatfield House, Hertfordshire · D. Hill, oils, 1967, Hatfield House, Hertfordshire · J. Ward, group portrait, line and wash, 1969 (*Directors of Westminster Bank, 1968*), National Westminster Bank, London · ivory miniature, Hatfield House, Hertfordshire

Wealth at death £1,486,724: probate, 28 March 1972, *CGPLA Eng. & Wales*

Cecil, Robert Arthur Talbot Gascoyne-, third marquess of Salisbury (1830–1903), prime minister, was born at Hatfield House, Hertfordshire, on 3 February 1830, the fifth of six children and third of four sons of James Brownlow William Cecil, second marquess of Salisbury (1791–1868), and his first wife, Frances Mary, only daughter of Bamber *Gascoyne of Childwall, near Liverpool. Lord Robert Cecil, as he was styled until 1865, was a direct descendant of Elizabeth I's ministers Lord Burghley and Robert Cecil, and his father revived the family's tradition of political service by holding office, respectively as lord privy seal and lord president of the council, in the Conservative cabinets of 1852 and 1858–9.

Childhood and youth Having lost his mother before he was ten, and lacking a brother or sister nearer than four years in age, Cecil was a solitary and sensitive child, with a passionate temper. At Eton College, from 1840, he was well grounded in French and German in addition to the classics, and showed unusual aptitude for theology, but was so enthusiastically bullied that he had to be taken away from the school in 1845. He found botanizing and reading at Hatfield a more congenial form of education, until he went in December 1847 to Christ Church, Oxford, where, though poor health restricted him to an honorary fourth class in mathematics conferred by nobleman's privilege after only two years, he became secretary and then treasurer of the Oxford Union.

Preparation for the bar was cut short by a voyage undertaken for the sake of his health from July 1851 to May 1853, during which he visited the Cape, Australia, and New Zealand, the only places outside western Europe he would ever visit (with the exception, briefly, of Constantinople). Beneficial though the stimulus to his physical and mental vitality was, it did not generate any enthusiasm for the possible careers of politics, religion, the law, or even journalism, about which he wrote to his father in September 1852, with the conclusion: 'all modes of life are equally uninviting' (Cecil, *Life*, 1.37). In August 1853 the influence of his cousin, the marquess of Exeter, returned him to parliament as Conservative member for Stamford, for which he sat for fifteen years without a contest. In the same year he competed successfully for a fellowship of All Souls, where he could claim the privilege of founder's kin. Ill health dogged his early steps in the House of Commons,

Robert Arthur Talbot Gascoyne-Cecil, third marquess of Salisbury (1830–1903), by Sir John Everett Millais, 1882

and until a late age he would be liable to the crises he called 'nerve storms', bringing depression, lassitude, and hypersensitiveness of touch and hearing.

Religion, marriage, and journalism Low animal spirits and bruising early experience left Cecil with little expectation of influence or popularity. He was rescued by his religion and his marriage. The critical and sceptical temper of his intellect was laid aside in what his daughter and biographer, Lady Gwendolen Cecil, called 'that personal surrender in love and trust to the living Christ, which lay at the heart of his religion' (Cecil, *Life*, 1.122). The core of religion, he insisted, was a mystery. Yet, if his faith was at bottom unreasoned and intuitive, it was not formless. He regarded a determinate creed as a precondition of firm belief and active zeal. No accommodation with other doctrines was acceptable to him which involved the dilution of the distinctive tenets of the Church of England, on the Tractarian wing of which he chose to lodge (Pusey House was to be launched at his London home in 1882). Religion was a sheet anchor of his personality, as the punctiliousness of his observance throughout his life suggested, but it was not a softening agent or a repository of guidance for the political fray. Cecil's combativeness made it hard for him to swallow the charitableness of Christian moral teaching except as an act of faintly grudging deference to divine authority. He wrote that 'the common sense of Christendom has always prescribed for national policy principles diametrically opposed to those that are laid down in the Sermon on the Mount' (*Saturday Review*, 17, 1864, 129–30).

The other sheet anchor was domestic life. Very tall, thin, stooped, and short-sighted, very shy, very serious, and deplorably dressed, Cecil was fortunate to find in Georgina Alderson (*d.* 1899), daughter of the judge Sir Edward *Alderson, a buoyant and forceful woman who could share his intellectual interests and encourage and facilitate his career. Married on 11 July 1857, they were to have five sons and three daughters, the eldest of whom, (Beatrix) Maud [*see* Palmer, (Beatrix) Maud, countess of Selborne], became president of the Conservative and Unionist Women's Franchise Association. The happiness of his family life at once enabled Cecil to work more effectively in the world and increased his tendency to seclusion from it. Almost all his intimacy was within his own home and family; few outsiders ever penetrated beyond the grave, courteous, but largely aloof exterior. Marriage estranged him from his father, who thought the Alderson connection a poor match. Since Cecil had only some £400 a year, mainly from the interest of his mother's fortune, and his wife £100 more, they were obliged to begin married life modestly, and the birth of a daughter in April 1858 increased the pressure on Cecil to supplement their income by the journalism on which he had embarked in December 1856, shortly after his engagement, in the weekly *Saturday Review*, owned by his brother-in-law Alexander Beresford-Hope. Between 1856 and 1868, he contributed 608 miscellaneous unsigned pieces to the paper, and he was soon adding to this output in the short-lived *Bentley's Quarterly Review*, in 1859–60, and the leading tory organ, Murray's *Quarterly Review*, to which he contributed twenty-four long, mostly political, articles between April 1860 and July 1866, with nine more to follow up to 1883 (his published writings, 1853–94, and speeches, 1848–68, are listed in Pinto-Duschinsky, 157–201). This grinding work raised his income probably by more than £300 a year in the early 1860s. Company directorships brought in more. Although in 1866 he was seriously embarrassed by the Overend Gurney crash, he had enough business acumen to make a successful chairman of the beleaguered Great Eastern Railway Company from 1868 to 1872.

Political ideas and polemics Journalism elicited from Cecil a more extensive elaboration of his political ideas than almost any other British statesman has set down. He was not given to theorizing, but it was his bent always to set the issues of the moment in the context of the broader tendencies and historic experience of human society. His Conservatism was not of the mystical or sentimental variety, and he did not believe that it could rest safely on mere custom or complacency. The questioning nature of his mind required that established institutions and arrangements should be capable of justification in rational and empirical terms. The test was their capacity to further the stability, security, and prosperity which Cecil identified with the greatest happiness of the greatest number—not least the security and prosperity of landed society, which he, 'essentially a squire' in Lady Gwendolen's perception, saw as fundamental to the national well-being. The political supremacy of the classes possessing property and education was justified as a natural product of social evolution and a necessary condition of political stability. Every community, he wrote in 1862, threw up 'natural leaders' and instinctively deferred to them, unless 'misled by the insane passion for equality'. Cecil acknowledged that they had to be 'checked by constitutional forms and watched by an active public opinion lest their rightful pre-eminence should degenerate into the domination of a class' (QR, 112, 1862, 547–8). He did not think mid-Victorian constitutional forms perfect: he did not care overmuch for representative government. But he did come to think that the 'accidental equilibrium of political forces' obtaining after 1832 'presented the highest ideal of internal government the world had hitherto seen' (QR, 130, 1871, 279–80). The destruction of that equilibrium by the introduction of a more democratic franchise was his predominant nightmare in the discussions of parliamentary reform which absorbed a large part of his polemical energies in the 1850s and 1860s.

Cecil argued that working men should not be given an electoral preponderance overwhelming the voice of other classes of society. Believing that political power should be proportioned to 'the magnitude of interests' not 'the number of noses' (Bentley's Quarterly Review, 1, 1859, 28), he dismissed as absurd and unjust any scheme in which 'two day-labourers shall outvote Baron Rothschild' (QR, 116, 1864, 266). His fear was partly that democracy would lower the tone of politics: men of integrity and refinement would stand aloof and careerists and professional organizers would take over. It was still more that numerical majority would lead the poor into spoliation of the rich, not because they were more vulnerable to the promptings of self-interest than the classes above them, but because they were no less so. This expectation rested on a highly schematic and materialistic interpretation of history as a process of class struggle. Cecil liked to think of himself as a political scientist, proceeding strictly upon empirical evidence to investigate 'the pathology of states' (QR, 110, 1861, 249). His conclusions about the dynamics of society and politics were more trenchant than subtle, embodying an almost Marxian view of the relations between economic and social substructure and political and ideological superstructure. Except when religious enthusiasm supervened, human beings were driven mainly by considerations of material interest and shaped their moral argumentation accordingly. Political contests found their most dramatic modern form in the struggle for power 'between the classes who have property and the classes who have none'. The struggle was not capable of final resolution: indeed it was a sign of vitality in a free state. 'We might as well hope', Cecil wrote in 1866, 'for the termination of the struggle for existence by which, some philosophers tell us, the existence or the modification of the various species of organized beings upon our planet are determined' (QR, 120, 1866, 273). If the 'comfortable classes' could never eliminate the forces of innovation,

however, they could at least temporarily halt their advance if they battled hard enough.

To frighten the 'comfortable classes' out of a fatal complacency was a main aim of Cecil's politics. The almost apocalyptic tone and the savage invective of some of his discourse served that purpose. They owed something, too, to the need to make a journalistic name so as to earn money. Most of all, they derived from the anger, only imperfectly modulated into sarcasm, produced in him by the wickedness of the enemies and the backsliding of the allies who imperilled his universe by their aggression or their cowardice. There was no desire to understand the alien force or argument, no inclination to concede virtue in opponents; only a determination to pulverize them with an intellectual violence that repaid the physical humiliation he had had to suffer in impotent rage as a boy. Some of Cecil's harshest words were reserved for those of the possessing classes who were laggardly in their own cause. The party system, he believed, prolonged a fatal division between Conservatives and whigs, natural allies in the defence of property, but in their attachment to historic antagonisms and their eagerness for office playing the game of the advanced Liberals and radicals, who could exact concessions from both. Their coalescence was Cecil's urgent political desire. The virulence of his feeling brought his language close to the scatological when he spoke of the rival party leaders' eating dirt and bearing the device of a rat before the radicals, and pictured Disraeli, whom he regarded as an unprincipled adventurer, as 'the grain of dirt' clogging the political machine (Bentley's Quarterly Review, 1, 1859, 346, 360).

This assault on his Commons leader, in July 1859, ensured Cecil's notoriety, but emphasized the dissonance between the latitude he could permit himself in formally anonymous articles and the demands of his party career. With his first child on the way, he had applied for a place to Derby when the latter came into office in February 1858, mentioning 'difficulty about the means of support' (Cecil, Life, 1.65). Refusal may have accounted for some of his acerbity in print, but he voted steadily with the ministry on major questions, even when it introduced a reform bill. Disraeli was sufficiently alive to the usefulness of a talented young Cecil to ignore his insults and, as the Conservative Party settled after 1859 into coexistence with Palmerston's essentially conservative regime, Cecil was able to devote his full combative vigour to resisting the advance of radicalism. His maiden speech, on 7 April 1854, had opposed interference with the ancient endowments of the universities. The land was defended against inequitable taxation, the Christian legislature against the admission of practising Jews, the Church of England against efforts to erode its privileges on the part of the nonconformists. The catastrophic results of democracy were sardonically illustrated from the experience of the United States. For Cecil, the American Civil War demonstrated how the despotism of a democratic majority would leave an oppressed minority with no alternative but rebellion. He pressed for Britain to recognize the Confederacy, and the emotional strain entailed by his passionate identification with its fortunes caused his wife to fear for his mental equilibrium. He was slow to come to the front in the Commons, but by 1864 he was making a mark with criticism of Palmerston's foreign policy, not least in its abandonment of Denmark in the Schleswig-Holstein crisis (he was for British intervention), and by his prominence in exposing the education department's censorship of school inspectors' reports, which led to the resignation of the responsible minister, Lowe, though the manner of it magnified the impression that he lacked 'kindly instincts or the spirit of fair play' (*The Parliamentary Diaries of Sir John Trelawny*, ed. T. A. Jenkins, 1990, 272). Awareness that the more hidebound tories were thinking of him as a possible Commons leader was perhaps an encouragement to his chiefs to take him into the inner councils of the party in that year, when Derby, anticipating office, put him down for the under-secretaryship for foreign affairs. Cecil's advance in political position no doubt helped, as it may have been helped by, the reconciliation with his father which in July 1864 brought him and his wife to Hatfield for the first time since their marriage, but still more effectual was the certainty, given the poor health of his unmarried elder brother, that he would eventually succeed to the title. He became Viscount Cranborne and heir to the marquessate when his brother died on 14 June 1865.

Parliamentary reform, 1865–1867 The revival of the parliamentary reform question in the mid-1860s brought Cranborne further into prominence. Although he was prepared to consider schemes of voting which offered working men 'a share of political power proportioned to the share which their labour gives them in the country's wealth' (*QR*, 117, 1865, 572), his fundamental instinct was not to move. 'The perils of change are so great', he wrote in 1865,

> the promise of the most hopeful theories is so often deceptive, that it is frequently the wiser part to uphold the existing state of things, if it can be done, even though, in point of argument, it should be utterly indefensible. (*QR*, 117, 1865, 550)

He took an enthusiastic part in 1866 in the Conservative Party's resistance to the Franchise Bill brought in by Russell and Gladstone, Lord Stanley classing him among those who 'abhor the idea of compromise, and enjoy a fight for its own sake' (J. Vincent, ed., *Disraeli, Derby and the Conservative Party*, 1978, 251). When the ministry fell, he became, on 6 July 1866, secretary of state for India in Lord Derby's third cabinet. He at once impressed the House of Commons with his characteristic rapidity in mastering a brief by successfully introducing the Indian budget after less than a fortnight in office, but his main concern was soon the efforts of the government to settle the reform question, despite its lack of a Commons majority. Cranborne was initially prepared to agree to the apparently radical proposal of household suffrage in borough constituencies, so long as it was restricted by the requirement of personal payment of rates and counterpoised by extra votes according to rateable value or house-tax payments. By February 1867, however, he had become convinced that

Disraeli was trying to hustle his colleagues into a dangerously large measure. He secured acceptance of a £5 rating franchise as the basis of the government's proposals, but three days later Derby and Disraeli reverted to the plan of rated household suffrage with plural voting as the likeliest ground of a settlement. When the cabinet discussed the plan on Saturday 23 February, Cranborne was already calculating its effects on the constituencies. Concluding on the Sunday that in the smaller boroughs plural voting would not counterbalance household suffrage, so that some three-fifths of the constituencies would be controlled by the new voters, he wrote a letter which obliged Derby to hold a cabinet next day, less than two hours before the proposed bill was to be outlined to a party meeting as a prelude to Disraeli's presenting it in the Commons. Threatened with the resignations of Cranborne, the earl of Carnarvon, and General Peel, the cabinet cobbled together a plan on a £6 rating basis; but it was soon clear that the Commons would not have it and that a substantial body of Conservative members thought household suffrage the only recipe for success. When household suffrage was reinstated at the cabinet of 2 March, Cranborne, Carnarvon, and Peel resigned.

Cranborne's fear that the exigencies of getting the bill through the Commons without a majority would lead Disraeli to whittle down its checks on household suffrage was fully realized, but the exhilaration of parliamentary triumph swept the Conservative Party along, and Cranborne made little attempt to organize a revolt. His gift was for the articulation of argument, not the leadership of men. In a lacerating *Quarterly* article in October 1867, he charged Derby and Disraeli with conspiring to betray their followers into a sweeping measure of reform in order to assure themselves of office. In precipitating an unparalleled experiment in 'placing a great empire under the absolute control of the poorest classes in the towns' (*QR*, 123, 1867, 534), they had ushered in a new political world in which Cranborne did not immediately see how he could function. There was no question of his responding to the feeler put out by Disraeli in February 1868, when the latter succeeded Derby as prime minister.

Hatfield and the House of Lords, 1868–1872 On his father's death on 12 April 1868, Cranborne became marquess of Salisbury and entered into the role of a great landed magnate, with restricted enthusiasm. The boy's distaste for outdoor exercise was translated in the man into a lack of interest in country pursuits, bar a little rabbit shooting, supplemented by occasional tennis. As lord of 13,000 acres around Hatfield, he learned what he had to about farming, but more than half his gross income of £50,000 to £60,000 a year was soon coming from the Cecil property in central London and from building development on the Gascoyne inheritance of land on the outskirts of Liverpool and on the Bifrons estate at Barking. Urban and suburban revenue cushioned Salisbury against the agricultural depression beginning in the late 1870s, and enabled him to pursue his paternalistic instincts by endowing Hatfield town with a variety of public buildings and improving the housing on his estate. Hatfield House underwent improvement too, driven not by its master's aesthetic taste, for he displayed none, but by his regard for practical convenience and his interest in science and gadgetry. From an early interest in photography, he had progressed to experiments in chemistry and electricity, and at Hatfield he established a laboratory with the guidance of Professor Herbert McLeod, and equipped the house with electric bells in 1869 and subsequently with electric lighting. Experiments with the telephone followed. Work on polarization, magnetism, and spectroscopy fed the appetite for precise empirical procedure often frustrated in politics, and in 1873 he published a paper entitled 'On spectral lines of low temperature' (*London, Edinburgh and Dublin Philosophical Magazine*, 45, 1873, 241–5). He became FRS in 1869, and as chancellor of the University of Oxford, a position he assumed in the same year, if his first anxiety was to preserve the Anglican character of the institution, his second was to encourage better provision for the physical sciences, new chairs for which were envisaged in the bill to establish a commission on Oxford which he introduced in 1876. Salisbury's imaginative interest in the social implications of science appears in his suggesting to the Institution of Electrical Engineers in 1889 that electricity, in enabling people 'to pursue in their own homes many industries which now require the aggregation of the factory', would help restore 'the integrity of the family upon which rest the moral hopes of our race' (*The Electrician*, 24, 1889, 13). He was president of the British Association in 1894, his address being printed in revised form as *Evolution: a Retrospect*.

At Hatfield and his London house in Arlington Street, Salisbury could insulate himself from the casual social intercourse which bored him (his excuse being that he would only bore others), and indulge his taste for working in soundless seclusion behind firmly shut double doors, often into the small hours. He not only felt no need of others' opinions but found them an annoying distraction from the business of thinking out his own. Paradoxically, this somewhat disdainful distancing, which might have seemed to unfit him for political leadership, formed a qualification for it. Aristocratic aloofness combined with ability and a reputation for integrity was what many Conservatives liked in a leader. When Disraeli's gamble with reform was followed in 1868 by electoral defeat, the tendency to look to Salisbury as a future leader was strengthened, despite the misgivings engendered by what Carnarvon in 1870 called his 'Wild elephant' mood (*The Diary of Gathorne Hardy*, ed. N. E. Johnson, 1981, 117). In 1869–70 strong support among Conservative peers for his taking the lead in the Lords was frustrated mainly because of the impossibility of his co-operating with Disraeli. Although he disclaimed any desire to come to the front, Salisbury's ambition was not insensitive to the expectations which centred on him, and translation to the House of Lords—which he had at first contemplated resisting—enabled him to take part in the politics of a more democratic era from a position detached from the necessity of intimate contact with the enlarged electorate or its representatives.

It was his concern that the House of Lords should be strong and self-confident enough to supply both an adequate platform for his exercise of high political authority and the essential Conservative brake on the activity of an otherwise unrestrained majority in the House of Commons. Salisbury argued that the Conservative Party's proper role was to 'act the part of the fulcrum from which the least Radical portion of the party opposed to them can work upon their friends and leaders', even if that meant 'the moderate Liberals enjoying a permanent tenure of office, propped up mainly by their support' (*QR*, 127, 1869, 560). In this self-denying strategy for the protection of religion, property, and the constitution, the Conservative majority in the Lords had a crucial place. Salisbury recognized that the Lords needed invigorating. In 1861 he criticized their poor attendance and feeble debates, and he was anxious to strengthen their influence by enlarging their representative character through the introduction of new blood from the business community, supporting Russell's bill for life peerages in 1869. He strongly backed their rejection of Gladstone's Paper Duties Bill in 1860, and one of his first actions on joining them in 1868 was to support the rejection of the bill suspending Irish church appointments with the assertion that to become 'a mere echo and supple tool' of the House of Commons was 'slavery' (*Hansard 3*, 193, 1868, 89). That they could not with safety reject a measure endorsed by the verdict of the constituencies he understood, and his role was vital in 1869 in securing the passage of the bill disestablishing the Irish church, for which the 1868 election had given Gladstone a mandate. That they should refer for the further consideration of the country any far-reaching measure hostile to Conservative interests which arguably lacked such endorsement, he was determined. Preparing to oppose the Ballot Bill in February 1872, he defined his strategy.

> The plan which I prefer is frankly to acknowledge that the nation is our Master, though the House of Commons is not, and to yield our opinion only when the judgement of the nation has been challenged at the polls and decidedly expressed. (Cecil, *Life*, 2.26)

He saw that approach as '(1) Theoretically sound, (2) Popular, (3) Safe against agitation, and (4) so rarely applicable as practically to place little fetter upon our independence' (ibid.).

Secretary of state for India, 1874–1878 Salisbury's recommended policy of bolstering the moderate Liberals against the radicals, until such time as the former's disillusionment should precipitate a reconstruction of political allegiances along the real lines of class interest, was nearly enough represented by Disraeli's post-1868 practice for Salisbury's sallies against his party leader to die away. When the Conservatives won the general election of 1874, it was inevitable that Disraeli should offer a cabinet place to the most powerful Conservative talent in the Lords. Unless he was to decline political responsibility and consign his career to the sidelines, it was inevitable that Salisbury, despite 'intense personal dislike', should accept. On 21 February 1874 he became again secretary of state for India.

Not everything in the conduct of the second Disraeli ministry met with Salisbury's approval. He had been assured that the government would not support measures against the ritualists in the church. Although he disliked their excesses, 'he sympathises', Derby told Disraeli, 'with a great deal of what they teach, and (like Gladstone) he attaches more importance, personally, to that class of questions than to all political or national considerations' (Shannon, *Disraeli*, 201). His high-churchmanship was offended by ministerial co-operation in Archbishop Tait's Public Worship Regulation Bill of 1874, and his refusal to endorse the measure in the Lords was the occasion of Disraeli's irritated but accurate characterization of him as 'a great master of gibes and flouts, and jeers' (*Hansard 3*, 221, 1874, 1358–9). In the same year he thought the interests of the church inadequately served in the Endowed Schools Bill, as he did later in the government's policy on elementary education. The labour legislation of 1875 went further in concession to the trade unions than he felt justified. But these were not resigning matters, and his attention was largely absorbed in the conduct of his office. His traits as a minister were quickly evident in his apprenticeship at the India Office, both in his eight-month tenure in 1866–7 and in 1874–8. Intellectual self-sufficiency placed strict limits on the usefulness to him of subordinates' advice. His first experience in the office caused him to begin in 1874 by reorganizing departmental procedures to enhance the secretary of state's independence of, and authority over, the permanent under-secretary, and by instructing the government of India to submit legislative proposals for his approval before they were considered by the viceroy's council. Successive viceroys and presidency governors were firmly guided in the direction he desired by private correspondence.

Salisbury was not a heedless imperialist. As a young man, he had seen that colonization all too easily involved exploitation (the white colonists' treatment of the New Zealand Maori was a case he cited) and that its advantages did not necessarily justify the expense and commitment incurred. But he did not escape conventional feelings of racial superiority, arguing in 1859 that some races needed the protection of stronger ones, and that India and Ireland were better off under English rule than they would be under their own. Derby recorded his saying ('truly enough') in cabinet in March 1878, when the occupation of a Mediterranean base was under consideration, that 'if our ancestors had cared for the rights of other people, the British empire would not have been made' (*The Diaries of Edward Henry Stanley, Fifteenth Earl of Derby*, ed. J. Vincent, 1994, 523). He was quite clear that, once made, it must be sustained by force, though the force might have its benevolent side. Appalled by the Orissa famine of 1866, he was angered by the Indian administration's deficiencies in famine relief and the callousness of the Anglo-Indian press, and he wanted to raise the condition of the peasantry—and lessen its potential for unrest—by promoting

cheaper credit and lower taxation. What he was determined not to see raised was 'a sort of bastard Home Rule cry' from the Anglo-Indians or any expectation of self-government in the native population. If England was to remain supreme, he told the viceroy, Lytton, in 1876, she must 'appeal to the coloured against the white as well as to the white against the coloured'. That meant some toleration of the political role of the Indian princes, and of participation by Indians in the administration, but Salisbury judged in 1877 that if the number of well-educated Indians able to secure posts by competition should increase, the government would face the 'indecent and embarrassing necessity' of closing that avenue to them (Blake and Cecil, 118, 140). The degree to which Indian interests were to be subordinated to British, and even to the electoral needs of the Conservative Party, was plain in his clash in 1875 with the viceroy, Northbrook, who sought to maintain the protective duties designed to foster an Indian cotton industry, which were bitterly opposed by the Lancashire cotton merchants.

The overriding preoccupation in Indian affairs was security against the threat posed by the southward pressure of Russia on Persia and Afghanistan. Salisbury doubted the ability of the tsarist empire to overrun the subcontinent, but wanted to provide, by maintaining a British envoy in Herat, against its acquiring a dominant influence in Afghanistan and stirring up the Indian Muslims—a policy which led to difficulties both with Northbrook, who opposed the idea of an Afghan client state, and with his successor as viceroy, Lytton, who was too inclined to adventure on the north-west frontier. When, however, revolts against Turkish rule in Bosnia and Herzegovina in 1875, and the atrocities of Turkish irregulars against insurgent Bulgarian Christians early in 1876, reopened the Eastern question, the defence of India became subsumed under the wider problem of British relations with Russia, if that state should attempt to capitalize on the disintegration of Turkey to advance its power in the Near East and menace the security of Britain's communications with India via the recently opened Suez Canal.

Foreign affairs, 1876–1880 In the tense cabinet discussions of foreign policy in 1876–8, Salisbury's high-churchmanship, like that of his close associate, Carnarvon, set him strongly against the continuance of Turkish government over the Christian peoples of the Balkans. In any case, he believed that the Ottoman empire in Europe could not be sustained. 'It is clear enough', he told Lord Beaconsfield (as Disraeli had just become) in September 1876, 'that the traditional Palmerstonian policy [of British support for Ottoman territorial integrity] is at an end' (Cecil, *Life*, 2.85): an understanding with Russia would have to be sought. He was given the chance to seek it, when Beaconsfield selected him as plenipotentiary to a conference of the powers convened on British initiative in Constantinople, with the view of forestalling any Russian military enterprise by bringing pressure to bear on the

Turks to concede administrative autonomy to the insurgent Balkan provinces. The conference, from December 1876 to January 1877, foundered on the refusal of the Turks to be coerced, which Salisbury was inclined to attribute to a conviction that they could always rely on British backing in the last resort. Throughout 1877, as Russia went to war with Turkey in April and, after early reverses, began to threaten complete military victory, he was anxious that Britain should not be drawn into what he regarded as a morally indefensible alliance with Turkey, but should rather sustain her interests, if need be, by securing a suitable vantage point in the Near East. In June he told the cabinet, according to Derby, 'that Russia at Constantinople would do us no harm: and that we ought to seize Egypt' (*Diaries of … Stanley … Earl of Derby*, ed. J. Vincent, 1994, 410). Beaconsfield grumbled to the queen that he was 'thinking more of raising the Cross on the cupola of St Sophia, than the power of England', and by June was conveying the queen's displeasure at the Indian secretary's 'wavering language', and envisaging his departure from the government (Millman, 274; W. F. Monypenny and G. E. Buckle, *The Life of Benjamin Disraeli*, 1910–20, 6.145–6). Salisbury shifted towards a more anti-Russian stance at the cabinet of 21 July, but continued sufficiently in line with the peace policy of the foreign secretary, Derby, to join him in December in opposing the prime minister's call for an immediate summoning of parliament to vote an increase in the armed forces and for the intervention of Britain as mediator between the now defeated Turks and the Russians. He told Beaconsfield on 26 December that the country was not prepared for war with Russia; and at the cabinet of 12 January 1878 apparently stood ready to resign with Derby had the latter not joined in accepting his compromise proposal to ask Turkey for permission for the British fleet to take station in the Dardanelles and Russia for an assurance that her troops would not occupy Gallipoli.

Yet Salisbury had no more patience than the prime minister with Derby's inability to impart a decisive tone to British diplomacy, inclining as always to think the firm and consistent execution of policy even more important than its content. By the beginning of 1878, with the Turks beaten and the Russians on the verge of taking Constantinople, it was possible to contemplate checking Russia without falling into a compromising alliance with Turkey. Beaconsfield thought Salisbury so far the key to bringing the cabinet round to a more assertive policy that he had made an appeal to him on 24 December: 'You & I must go together into the depth of the affair, & settle what we are prepared to do' (Millman, 348). At the cabinet of 15 January, Gathorne Hardy was 'much struck by Salisbury's resolution today' in standing for 'resistance to Russian encroachment' (*The Diary of … Hardy*, ed. N. E. Johnson, 1981, 349). Henceforth Beaconsfield and Salisbury worked in close accord. When Derby offered an abortive resignation on 23 January, it was Salisbury whom Beaconsfield proposed to the queen as his successor. On 27 March, when the cabinet, in order to enforce British interest in the revision of the terms of peace forced on Turkey by the Russians at San Stefano, discussed calling out the reserves and sending Indian troops to occupy Cyprus and Alexandretta (Iskenderun), Beaconsfield's assertion that peace could not be assured by 'drifting' bore the marks of concert with the Indian secretary, who supported warlike preparations partly in order to guard against an adverse swing of sentiment among the peoples of Asia if there were not a visible demonstration of British power. Derby's definitive resignation that day was followed by Salisbury's appointment as foreign secretary.

The determined tone Salisbury meant to give to the government's foreign policy was at once shown by his issuing on 1 April 1878, simultaneously to the European powers and to the public, a circular which insisted that the treaty of San Stefano, breaching as it did the treaty of Paris of 1856 and the treaty of London of 1871, must be submitted as a whole to the contracting powers, and castigated the provisions which, in infringing the independence of the Ottoman government, prejudiced vital British interests in the straits, the Persian Gulf, the shores of the Levant, and the region of the Suez Canal. In the ensuing months he negotiated the agreements which the Berlin congress of June–July 1878 would endorse, securing from Russia the reduction of the large Bulgarian state stipulated at San Stefano (seen as a Russian satellite), in return for her acquisition of Kars and Batumi and advance in Bessarabia; and from Turkey agreement to British occupation of Cyprus as a Mediterranean base and to reforms for the benefit of her Christian subjects, in return for a guarantee of her Asiatic possessions against Russia. At Berlin, Salisbury did the spadework, complaining wryly in letters home of Beaconsfield's lack of detailed grasp, and he received with his chief the Garter (30 July 1878) and the freedom of the City of London when they returned in triumph. Their policy secured British prestige, but the permanent gains were slender: the greater Bulgaria came into being in 1886, at the expense of the Turks, while Russia overturned the congress provisions by fortifying Batumi; and the system of installing special consuls in Asiatic Turkey to superintend the promised reforms proved futile.

Party leader, 1880–1884 The general election of April 1880 swept the Conservatives out of office and left Salisbury wondering whether this was 'the beginning of a serious war of classes' (Williams, 40). The Eastern crisis had made him the second man in the Conservative Party. Beaconsfield's death in April 1881 left him in ability and prestige the first, though the leadership of the opposition was split between him in the Lords and Sir Stafford Northcote in the Commons, and a good many still inclined to think him disqualified from the head of affairs by the impetuosity which led Gladstone to dub him 'Prince Rupert'. In his last *Quarterly Review* article, entitled 'Disintegration', in October 1883, Salisbury offered an alarmist analysis, both of the challenge posed to the integrity of the empire, in Ireland especially, by home-rule aspirations, and of the threat levelled at the social cohesion without which national power could not be sustained, by the alleged drive of radical extremists towards 'the equality not only of conditions but of possessions, and the extermination of religious dogma'. But his determination to frustrate radical designs led him into an approach with a radicalism of its own. Deriving a dubious authority from a mass electorate which gave attention to politics only 'partially and fitfully', its action distorted by the bargaining necessary to hold together the factions in the Liberal Party, and insufficiently disciplined by a weak executive, the House of Commons, he argued, was no longer capable of supplying that 'cool and deliberate judgement' of the 'generality of the nation' which was required to arbitrate between contending classes (*QR*, 156, 1883, 565–8, 576). Against the unchecked pretensions of the popularly elected chamber, Britain lacked the safeguards built into the constitution of the United States, of which Salisbury now wrote almost wistfully. The only body capable of ensuring that vital national questions were presented for the considered verdict of the people, and of checking an imperfectly representative House of Commons, was the House of Lords. It was the peers' duty, he said in October 1881, to reflect 'the permanent and enduring wishes of the nation as opposed to the casual impulse which some passing victory at the polls may in some circumstances have given to the decisions of the other House' (*The Times*, 12 Oct 1881).

Against the Liberals' Irish land legislation of 1881–2, which Salisbury was anxious to resist as infringing the rights of property in a manner he thought likely to form a precedent for Britain, the Lords proved a weak instrument. On the Arrears Bill of 1882, with the Irish landlords demoralized and some of his colleagues jibbing at his belligerence, Salisbury had angrily to acknowledge that he had been placed in a small minority on his own side. He was still feeling for an effective technique of leadership when, in 1884, the government's introduction of a bill for household suffrage in counties presented him with an issue in which the Lords could be made to play a decisive role. The assimilation of the county to the borough franchise was hard to resist indefinitely, but, scrutinizing the figures, Salisbury concluded that the Conservatives would suffer severely unless the new franchise were accompanied by a redistribution of seats which would enable what would otherwise be large Conservative minorities, especially in urban areas, to secure representation. The Conservative majority in the Lords rejected the bill in the absence of a redistribution scheme, but the pressure for a negotiated settlement exerted by the queen and his more cautious colleagues restrained Salisbury's original impulse to precipitate a general election on the existing franchise. Instead, he accepted Gladstone's offer to pass an Agreed Seats Bill following the franchise measure. In November 1884 he took the lead for the Conservatives in negotiating with Gladstone and Dilke in a series of private meetings the details of a redistribution scheme based on single-member constituencies, which, in facilitating the separation of rural from urban areas and middle-class from working-class districts of towns, much improved the

Conservative Party's electoral chances. In making the powers of his own house the key to the protection of Conservative interests in constitutional change, and in demonstrating his grasp of the details of electoral strategy, he made a large stride towards establishing himself as the first choice for the premiership if the Conservatives should regain office.

Salisbury was demonstrating at the same time his ability to embark on the direct appeal to the people that was the corollary of the referendal role he was giving to the Lords. 'Power', he told his eldest son in February 1881, 'is more and more leaving Parliament and going to the platform' (Adonis, 175). Before 1880 he had rarely spoken outside parliament and his own locality. Between 1880 and 1886 he spoke on more than seventy platforms all over the country. The man who shrank from recognition by strangers and from gawping admirers at railway stations could be warmed by the enthusiasm of great audiences, which he addressed in clear, unpatronizing, and hard-hitting language. Nor was the power of the press neglected: from June 1884 Salisbury was briefing Alfred Austin of *The Standard*, whom he would later make the most pedestrian of poets laureate. Salisbury's interest in the facts of electoral sociology and geography and his anxiety to achieve the most efficient mobilization of the Conservative forces led naturally to involvement in the oversight of party organization, but it was always organization from the top down. It was on the alleged manipulation of the Liberal Party by caucuses of log-rolling activists that he partly relied to discredit it and to deny true representative status to the measures of Liberal governments. He had no intention of countenancing in the Conservative Party anything analogous with the pretensions of the National Liberal Federation to influence policy, and hence no sympathy for Lord Randolph Churchill's efforts in 1883–4 to encourage the middle-class provincial stalwarts of the National Union of Conservative and Constitutional Associations to claim a voice in the party's inner councils and take over the functions of the central committee of whips and party officials and notables which directed party organization.

Churchill's use of the National Union was all the less welcome for forming part of the campaign to force himself to the front of the party that had begun with his subversion of Northcote's authority in the Commons through the activities of the 'Fourth Party', and was reaching its apogee in his proclamation of 'tory democracy', but the popularity that he was acquiring with the Conservative rank-and-file made a break with him inadvisable at a time when the Franchise Bill was dividing Conservative opinion. A compromise suited both Salisbury's and Churchill's interests, and it was reached between them on 26 July 1884. Informing Northcote, whom he had not consulted, Salisbury represented Churchill as having been willing 'to fall into line' in return for a very limited integration of the union's management with that of the parliamentary party (Shannon, *Salisbury*, 43). In fact, the arrangement included also the abandonment of the central committee, the recognition of the Primrose League, and a taking of Churchill into the confidence of the leadership which, by implication or possibly by express understanding, meant the relegation of Northcote's claims to leadership in a future Conservative administration. Salisbury had steadily expressed support of Northcote as a colleague; he does not seem to have felt compelled to resist Churchill's undermining of him as a rival.

The caretaker government and the home-rule crisis, 1885–1886
After the consolidation of his primacy in the party by the events of 1884, Salisbury's professed taste for weak Liberal government as a constitutional preservative had to contend with the knowledge that the overthrow of the ministry would establish him as the Conservative candidate for the premiership, as well as with his desire to wrest control of foreign policy from Liberal hands at a moment of renewed crisis over Bulgaria. A decision that the Conservatives would be prepared to govern Ireland without renewing the Crimes Act of 1881 made it possible to secure Parnellite votes to defeat the government in the Commons on 9 June 1885, and Gladstone resigned. With some appearance of reluctance, on 23 June 1885 Salisbury answered the queen's summons to form a caretaker ministry until an election on the new franchise and constituencies should be possible, embarrassedly accepting the necessity of dispatching Northcote to the Lords as earl of Iddesleigh in order to meet the terms of Churchill, who took the India Office. Salisbury joined the Foreign Office to the prime ministership, and quickly reinforced his credit by skilful maintenance of British interests in the Bulgarian crisis and dealings with Russia over Afghanistan, but by the end of the year the focal point of his administration was Ireland.

Salisbury's analysis of the problem of social and political unrest in Ireland was that it was spineless conciliation since 1780 that had fostered it. The Irish were irreconcilable to 'English' rule, and concession only stimulated their efforts to break free of it by teaching them what leverage they could exert by intransigence. Self-government was unacceptable, within a United Kingdom framework because the home-rulers would never accept the position of a permanent minority at Westminster, within a purely Irish framework because the permanent minority would then be the protestant, landlord, and loyalist contingents whom Salisbury was determined not to abandon, both on grounds of moral obligation and because that dereliction would signal across the empire England's lack of will to hold what she possessed. The alternative, the steady and masterful imposition of authority, was closest to Salisbury's natural bent. If he had an Irish policy, it consisted of dogged endurance, tinged with baffled exasperation.

However, a government which had come in with the help of Parnellite votes, had renounced the coercion embodied in the Crimes Act, and contained men like Carnarvon, Churchill, and Hicks Beach, who stood for constructive measures, could hardly rest on simple repression. Salisbury felt uncertainly for the means to keep Ireland quiet. Baling out the beleaguered landlord class and facilitating the emergence of a socially stabilizing peasant proprietary with state-assisted land purchase was an acceptably Conservative measure, pursued in the Ashbourne Act of 1885. Carnarvon was allowed to meet secretly with Parnell, and though the cabinet declined in October to endorse Carnarvon's inclination towards home rule, the interview, coupled with the cautious tone of Salisbury's public pronouncements, encouraged Parnell's hopes of the Conservatives sufficiently for him to throw the Irish vote in Britain against the Liberals in the general election of November–December 1885. Some dozen gains brought the Conservatives back 250 strong to face 334 Liberals, with Parnell's 86 Irish nationalists occupying a key position. Salisbury fended off the queen's and Churchill's promptings for a centre coalition with whigs, in which he would have been marginalized. His line was given definition by Gladstone's approach in December to discover whether the Irish problem could be disposed of by Liberal support for a Conservative measure of concession to Irish aspirations, which was followed immediately by the public revelation that action on Ireland was in Gladstone's mind. 'His hypocrisy makes me sick' (Marsh, 85) was Salisbury's reaction to what he evidently read as an invitation to take the risks of an initiative for which Gladstone could claim the credit. The precedents for Liberal assistance in Conservative settlement of contentious issues which weighed in Gladstone's mind, those of 1829, 1846, and 1867, weighed in Salisbury's too, as examples of breach of faith by tory leaders with their followers which both honour and expediency forbade him to emulate. Producing proposals likely to disrupt the Conservative Party had small attraction compared with forcing Gladstone to declare his own and disrupt the Liberal Party.

Salisbury now sought to move the cabinet towards a renewal of coercion in Ireland and a proscription of the National League, accepting Carnarvon's resignation, but defeat on the agricultural holdings issue supervened on 27 January 1886, and Salisbury resigned two days later. In the following weeks he began to concert with Goschen and Lord Hartington, leaders of the anti-home-rule Liberals, opposition to Gladstone's newly installed ministry, and on 14 April, the day of the first reading of Gladstone's Home Rule Bill, the three shared a London platform in denunciation of it. On 15 May, with a long-remembered reference to the Khoi-Khoi (Hottentots) among others, Salisbury told the National Union that:

> this,—which is called self-government, but is really government by the majority,—works admirably when it is confided to people who are of Teutonic race, but … does not work so well when people of other races are called upon to join in it; (Cecil, *Life*, 3.302)

and he called for twenty years of resolute and consistent government of Ireland. Any possibility that had existed of a bipartisan approach to the Irish question had been overwhelmed by the attraction for Salisbury of a ferocious defence of the union with Ireland which would affirm the Conservatives' claim to be the party of nation and empire, rally the widespread popular anti-Irish prejudice of the large towns which had proved a novel source of Conservative strength in the 1885 election, and precipitate the realignment of the whigs with the Conservative Party which would bring political life into line with his political logic. Conservatives and Liberal Unionists together defeated the Home Rule Bill in the Commons on 8 June 1886, and in the ensuing general election the two groups working in alliance secured an overwhelming anti-home-rule majority, 316 Conservatives and 79 Liberal Unionists being returned. Salisbury professed willingness to serve under Hartington in a Unionist coalition, but, designedly or not, he had defined his stance in terms too uncompromisingly tory for the Liberal Unionists to be able to enter the Conservative-dominated government, which he stipulated, and following Gladstone's resignation on 20 July he resumed the office of prime minister (25 July), which he would hold for thirteen of the next sixteen years.

The premiership and the Unionist alliance, 1886–1892 Salisbury never admitted to enjoying the premiership, complaining that its ostensible power was a sham, recoiling from what his wife called the 'exhibition of littleness' of the aspirants for office and reward who beset it, and bending under the incessant labour of combining it with the Foreign Office (as he did nearly the whole time), the official boxes pursuing him even to the Chalet Cecil, the family's holiday home near Dieppe, and later to Beaulieu, where he built his second French retreat. He was, one of his sons acknowledged, 'very averse to collaboration, and it was natural for him to think that his colleagues would equally dislike it' ('X' [Lord Robert Cecil], in *Monthly Review*, 13, 1903, 9). The latter, and even his own children, he might have difficulty in recognizing if coming on them unexpectedly, mental abstraction, aristocratic remoteness, and short sight combining in uncertain proportions. Masterful on paper and on the platform, he lacked stomach for imposing himself face-to-face, and ran his cabinets with so loose a rein that Cranbrook had to call upon him in November 1886 for 'your distinct *lead* and your just self-assertion' (Cecil, *Life*, 3.326). Hicks Beach recollected that he often allowed important matters to be decided by a small majority, even against his own opinion. That his knack was more for diplomacy than for leadership, however, was not always a disadvantage in the task of balancing the elements of the Conservative Party and managing its alliance with the Liberal Unionists. Less helpful was his aloofness from the party rank-and-file, accentuated by his being in the Lords, and his tendency to draw around him in government a narrow circle of friends and relatives, most conspicuously his nephew Arthur Balfour, who entered the cabinet in 1886. Salisbury was strongly conscious of the growing importance of the middle-class contingent in his party, and worked well with its leading representative, W. H. Smith, but he did not readily bring middle-class politicians to the fore. The self-importance of the party's constituency activists was judiciously flattered, but the National Union was kept well hobbled by the party managers, notably the chief whip, Akers-Douglas, and the principal agent, Captain Middleton, with both of whom Salisbury frequently indulged his interest in the details of organization and control, and

from whom he drew much of his sense of what the party and the country wanted. The after-effect of illness in 1880 was a gain in weight which turned his appearance from the lean and hungry to the portly and patriarchal and added physical mass to his reputation for ability and integrity, but the imposing combination, even when relieved by the negligence in dress which caused him to be refused admission to the casino at Monte Carlo, inspired respect more readily than affection. Middleton, in December 1886, thought that his personality was the great strength of the party among the 'uneducated', as Gladstone's was for the Liberals; but unlike Gladstone he never acquired a popular nickname, and even the caricaturists could find little to lighten the grave solemnity, or sombre resignation to duty, which appeared in his portraits, belying the charm and humour which he could display within his intimate circle.

The most significant challenge to Salisbury's command of the party was posed by the restless ambition of the chancellor of the exchequer and leader of the Commons, Lord Randolph Churchill, who by November 1886 was complaining petulantly to Salisbury about tory incapacity for legislation in a democratic constitution. The prime minister had no desire to see Churchill's association with Joseph Chamberlain, the leader of the radical wing of the Liberal Unionists, colour the character of the whole alliance, and Churchill made matters worse by conducting unofficial contacts with foreign powers and drafting a budget which seemed to Salisbury hostile to the landed interest. When in December Churchill took issue with the army estimates, and sought to enforce his point by offering to resign, Salisbury, characteristically conducting the whole affair by correspondence, presented so unyielding a front as effectively to accept the resignation. Churchill's position with the party was wrecked by his action, and the consent of Goschen to take over the exchequer enabled Salisbury to move further towards the development of the Unionist alliance on a fundamentally Conservative footing.

'We have so to conduct our legislation', Salisbury had explained in a vain attempt to teach Churchill the facts of Conservative life,

> that we shall give some satisfaction to both classes and masses. This is specially difficult with the classes—because all legislation is rather unwelcome to them, as tending to disturb a state of things with which they are satisfied. It is evident, therefore, that we must work at less speed, & at a lower temperature, than our opponents. Our bills must be tentative and cautious; not sweeping & dramatic. But I believe that with patience, feeling our way as we go, we may get the one element to concede, & the other to forbear. (Marsh, 80)

His acceptance of the need for some legislative concession by the 'classes' reflected the change of life from thirty-three years in which he had sat in parliament with a Liberal majority in the Commons for all but six of them, to an epoch in which it began to seem possible that the junction of all the Conservative elements of the country in defence of the union would deposit the legislative machinery in safe hands for most of the time. The conduct of opposition was giving way to the practice of government, and Salisbury had never held that government should be stationary or inert. The needs of the alliance counted for something in this evolution. An 'extra tinge of Liberalism in our policy', he had told Churchill in December 1885, would be part of the bargain with the whigs when the moment came (Cecil, *Life*, 3.275). When the alliance materialized, it included not only the whigs but the radical Unionists under Chamberlain, who had to be given the means to reassure his followers that he was not sustaining a reactionary regime. The Liberal Unionists were not in a position to impose terms, because Salisbury and his party managers had taken care to couch the electoral compact in terms that gave them no chance of increasing their numbers, and they were captive so long as Gladstone adhered to home rule, but their presence made it easier for Salisbury to persuade his 'classes' to concede when an 'extra tinge of Liberalism' seemed necessary for the health of the alliance and the safety of the union, as well as for the consolidation of the (to Salisbury startling) advance of Conservatism in the big urban electorates which had revealed itself in 1885–6.

Conventional Conservatism was appeased by Salisbury's efforts to aid the church, which he continued to regard as the only reliable agency for social as well as spiritual betterment. In October 1885, approaching the election, he had placed at the centre of his Newport speech the maintenance of church establishments and of religious education (an attraction not least to Catholic voters). His second ministry pursued legislation on tithes, patronage, and clerical discipline, and he took up free elementary education, enacted in 1891, largely in order to bring national taxation to the help of the Church of England's schools. Helping the clergy to gather their tithe, however, made that other reservoir of Conservative supporters, the landowners, feel more keenly the government's failure to shelter them against the agricultural depression. Profound though his conviction was of the crucial role of the landed interest in securing social and political stability, Salisbury did not think it feasible to bolster its position by measures which would expose the Conservatives to the reproach of being the party of protection, expensive food, and narrow class sympathies. The creation of the Board of Agriculture in 1889 was as much a gesture of goodwill as an earnest of practical assistance.

If tone deaf to Churchill's boisterous rendering of 'tory democracy', Salisbury was not committed against secular efforts at social and administrative improvement. He had no intention to undermine the responsibility of the individual or much to enlarge the sphere of action and of expenditure from direct taxation of a state theoretically controlled by a democratic electorate. Yet when he said in 1891 that the Conservative Party had 'always leaned—perhaps unduly leaned—to the use of the State, so far as it can properly be used for the improvement of the physical, moral and intellectual condition of our people' (*The Times*, 16 July 1891), he was sounding a note already evident in his Oxford Union days, his first election address at Stamford, and his early support for factory legislation and improved

treatment of paupers. He advocated the provision of cheap money for building working-class housing in a *National Review* article in 1883, secured in 1884 a royal commission on which he sat, and carried its recommendations into law in tandem with Sir Charles Dilke in 1885, increasing the availability of Treasury loans and taking new measures against slums. A second measure to facilitate slum clearance and rehousing received his backing in 1890. Though deeply disliking compulsory purchase of land to provide allotments for agricultural labourers, he swallowed the compulsory element of the bill of 1887, under pressure from back-benchers desperate for labourers' votes. If, at Newport, his support for a measure of popularly elected local government had been something of a sop to the provincial activists denied democracy in the management of the party, it was none the less implemented in the County Councils Act of 1888, which he justified on the safe tory ground of resistance to excessive centralization. A still larger concession to full democracy was not inconceivable to him after the enfranchisement of the agricultural labourer. 'When I am told that my ploughmen are capable citizens', he wrote to Lady John Manners in 1884,

> it seems to me ridiculous to say that educated women are not just as capable. A good deal of the political battle of the future will be a conflict between religion and unbelief: & the women will in that controversy be on the right side.
> (Smith, 18 n.)

In Ireland the Liberal tinge was evident mainly in the continuation in 1887 and 1891 of land purchase legislation and in the programme of rural economic development embodied in the congested districts legislation of 1890. But the government saw Ireland as an ongoing problem of firm administration rather than a question which might be susceptible of an answer. To implement the renewed coercion necessary to combat the National League and agrarian resistance, Salisbury chose as Irish secretary Balfour, whose hard-handedness with the militant Skye crofters while at the Scottish Office had won his approval ('Everything seems to be going on charmingly in Skye. By steady deliberate pressure … you will get them under surely enough'; Williams, 163). Salisbury's determination to get the Irish under caused him to make the most of the revelations about Parnell which *The Times* derived from the forger Piggott, and to lend his support to the paper even when their authenticity was challenged.

The Foreign Office, 1887–1892 Through its implications for imperial integrity and national defence, the Irish problem was part of the global picture which Salisbury surveyed from the Foreign Office, where he superseded Lord Iddesleigh in January 1887. He was to be foreign secretary for eleven of the next fourteen years. It was his post of predilection, where he could indulge his penchant for the conduct of politics as a detached intellectual pursuit little disturbed by the opinions of colleagues and only remotely hindered by parliament and public. 'We do not', he reminded the Lords in January 1887, 'usually discuss what goes on in the Foreign Office' (*Hansard 3*, 310, 1887, 34). In this sphere his proximate superior was the queen. If she was occasionally hard to manage, her experience and her European family connections made her a valuable source of advice and intelligence, and as her foreign secretary Salisbury came closest to what was perhaps his ideal of ministerial service, the relationship of his Cecil ancestors to Elizabeth I. He was not himself an easy chief to serve. He could not or would not delegate decision making, and he did not find discussion helpful. Behind his impenetrable courtesy lay the reluctance to direct human intercourse that made it hard for subordinates to know what he wanted. Ambassadors, apt to miss or misunderstand the element of ironic humour in his remarks, sometimes found him inscrutable.

Making his name as a polemicist on foreign affairs in the 1860s, Salisbury had stigmatized as a fatal confusion the attempt to apply to the relations of states, without a common law, the moral standards of civic and private life, and had castigated the reluctance of the 'commercial spirit' to meet the cost of the armaments required to secure British interests, which reduced the country to indulging popular pugnacity by bullying weak states like China and Brazil, while skirting confrontation with stronger ones. But he was convinced when he came to the helm that Britain, as a largely satisfied and so defensive power, found its highest interest in peace, and his conviction of the necessary egoism of state policy did not preclude a sense of international obligation. 'We are part of the community of Europe and we must do our duty as such', he declared in 1888, repudiating 'haughty and sullen isolation' (Cecil, *Life*, 4.90). The essence was to avoid truculence and to ensure that policy was backed by the necessary strength.

The latter condition was not easy to meet in the era of the 'scramble for Africa' and the emergence of two great continental alliances, the triple alliance of Germany, Austria, and Italy, completed in 1882, and the Franco-Russian alliance formed in 1891–4. Salisbury's most delicate skills were perhaps displayed in fending off without conflict German and French challenges in east and west Africa respectively, and in settling in the convention of 1891 the dispute with Portugal over territory north and south of the Zambezi. His Near-Eastern policy was the continuation of that which he had pursued alongside Beaconsfield, its kernel being the containment of Russia in the East and the control of the straits, working with the central powers, Germany and Austria, in the hope of averting any resumption of their old alignment with Russia in the Three Emperors' League and of securing their support in the imbroglio with France created by the British occupation of Egypt, from which Salisbury would have been glad to negotiate a withdrawal on suitable terms. The acceptance in 1885–6 of the union of the Turkish province of Eastern Roumelia with Bulgaria was part of this approach, Bulgaria now appearing as an obstacle to, rather than a tool of, Russian designs. Co-operation with the triple alliance involved concession to Bismarck's desire for British support of Italy in the Mediterranean, likely though that was to impede the improvement of relations with Italy's most direct competitor, France. The Mediterranean agreements of February–March and December 1887 linked Britain to the triple alliance in defence of the status quo in the Near East and secured Austro-German co-operation over Egypt. The mutual interest of Britain and Germany made it possible in 1890 for Salisbury to hand over Heligoland in return for recognition of British primacy in east Africa, including the Zanzibar protectorate. Britain's value as a partner, however, was lessened by doubts about her ability to fulfil her Near-Eastern role. The 'scare' over the adequacy of her naval power which was raised in 1888 led to Salisbury's sanctioning the formal adoption of the two-power standard and the establishment, in the Naval Defence Act of 1889, of a five-year construction programme protected against the ordinary budgetary control of parliament. In 1892, the Admiralty's unwillingness to face the risks of forcing the straits in the event of conflict with Russia drove him to complain that, if Constantinople could not be protected, 'our policy is a policy of false pretences' (Lowe, 89). The inauguration of the Franco-Russian alliance increased the desirability of a better understanding with France, but as he left office in August 1892 Salisbury explained that he was afraid of 'too hurried a rapprochement with France, involving the abandonment of the Triple Alliance by Italy—a reconstruction of the Drei-Kaiser-Bund and Russia on the Bosphorus' (ibid., 90).

Return to opposition, 1892–1895 Despite the parliamentary relief afforded by the split among the Irish nationalists at the end of 1890, government and party were by that time in the doldrums, not least because of what Salisbury registered as the muttering of 'our right wing' about such apparent concessions to radical Unionism as the measures on county government and free education. The prime minister baulked at further provocations, sounding in January 1892 his old, resistant note of conviction that 'I can get better terms for property out of office, than I can in office' (Williams, 390). The desire of Balfour and Chamberlain to respond to defeat in the general election of July 1892 by meeting parliament with a programme of social legislation encountered Salisbury's habitual reluctance to risk alienating 'a good many people who have always been with us' (ibid., 430), and his fear that 'these social questions are destined to break up our party' (ibid.). The Liberals and Irish, with a majority of forty, turned the government out in August. Salisbury resigned on 12 August. His private secretary at the Foreign Office noted that he 'shewed indecent joy at his release' (*The Diary of … Hardy*, ed. N. E. Johnson, 1981, 833).

In opposition to a Gladstone ministry bent on home rule Salisbury was better placed to control his party. Home rule was bound to pass the Commons and there was thus no need to make policy concessions to the Liberal Unionists in order to block it. The crucial decision would be taken in Salisbury's own arena in the Lords. He had pursued the strengthening of the representative claims of the Lords by bringing in more peers from commercial and industrial backgrounds, and by introducing in 1888 a bill to permit the creation of up to fifty life peers, though it was dropped to avoid major difficulties in the Commons. Now, in a

National Review article of November 1892 entitled 'Constitutional revision', he denied that the government's 'motley majority', based on a 'multiplicity of questions', and non-existent in England and Scotland, supplied a mandate for home rule, and contended that, in the absence of a referendum procedure, only the peers could ensure adequate consultation of the nation over proposals for organic change. Every effort was made to maul Gladstone's second Home Rule Bill in the Commons sufficiently to reduce the responsibility of the peers in rejecting it, but it was they who finally destroyed it by 419 votes to 41 in September 1893. Salisbury was anxious that the Lords should not seem to act along lines of class interest and warded them away from opposing Harcourt's death duties in 1894. He took out insurance against the election of another home-rule majority by declaring in April 1895 that a mandate for home rule would require 'a large majority of the nation in all its main divisions' (*The Times*, 8 April 1895), thus turning the heavy Unionist preponderance in England into an insuperable barrier. In the event, the general election of July 1895 returned a Unionist phalanx of 411, as against 259 Liberals and Irish nationalists.

The Unionist coalition, 1895–1900 Salisbury was already back in office (25 June 1895), having formed his third ministry after the defeat of the Liberal government in a Commons' vote on 21 June. He turned the Unionist alliance into coalition by introducing five Liberal Unionists into his cabinet, but there was no question this time of his offering the duke of Devonshire (as Hartington had become in 1891) the lead, though he did offer him the Foreign Office, which he eventually took himself. The overwhelming Unionist majority did something to dissipate Salisbury's fears of a democratic electorate, yet it lessened the degree of his authority, by moving the Unionist centre of gravity back into the Commons, where Balfour and Chamberlain were in charge, and by shifting the emphasis from a politics of resistance, at which Salisbury was adept, to the need for a creative response to the problems of a maturing industrial society and an increasingly challenged empire, which he showed little sign of supplying. He had recognized plainly, in two speeches of 1888 (*The Times*, 11 April 1888, 1 Dec 1888), the pressing difficulties of reconciling the claims of rich and poor, and of meeting the needs of a growing population in a cramped island, in a world of accelerating economic and imperial competition. But he was not enthusiastic about the nostrums canvassed among Unionists. In face of the threat to British trade from increasing protectionism, he openly sympathized with the fair-traders' demands for reciprocity agreements and retaliation, but feared the class and party divisions that they were likely to provoke. He accepted the necessity of further social legislation, and cautiously endorsed Chamberlain's promotion of social reform as the centrepiece of the Unionist campaign in the 1895 election, but his personal interest in such measures went little beyond his long-established concern for housing, though he supported Chamberlain in passing an Employers' Liability Bill in 1897. Salisbury's basic instincts were as usual to assist the church and the land, and he was disappointed by the failure of the Education Bill of 1896 to negotiate the hazardous waters of state aid for denominational schools, though there was better success the following year. Remission of half the farmers' rates by an act of 1896 was at least a token alleviation of the deepening agricultural depression, and in 1899 clergymen's tithes were relieved of rates. In Ireland, Salisbury sympathized with the landlords' dislike of the 1896 Land Act and did all he could to compensate them for the loss of influence arising from the local government reform of 1898. Conducted by Arthur Balfour and his brother, Gerald, appointed chief secretary in 1895, Irish policy emphasized both the departmentalization of Salisbury's third ministry and its generous allocation of office to his connections. His addition of his eldest son, Cranborne, to the three nephews and a son-in-law already in office was openly attacked in the Commons in December 1900, but Salisbury was undisturbed. The air of massive imperturbability and remoteness increased with the girth (he now took little exercise but tricycle rides). This enhanced Salisbury's aura but began to erode his authority, and from 1896 recurring bouts of influenza, preying on a constitution weakened by incessant overwork, forced him abroad for convalescence and interrupted his grip on affairs.

Foreign and imperial affairs, 1895–1902 The effects were nowhere more evident than in foreign policy, where new challenges were arising, with the extension of great power rivalry in Africa and the Far East, and in 1895–6 friction with the United States over Britain's boundary dispute with Venezuela, when Salisbury demurred to the too brusque application of the Monroe doctrine; feeling soon moderated, however, and by the Hay–Pauncefote treaty of 1900 Britain fell in with American plans for an Isthmian Canal. The prime minister's 'practice of holding few & far cabinets', Lord George Hamilton wrote in January 1896,

> enhances his difficulties as he nurses a policy until the time comes for expression or action & he then finds his cabinet against him & has to retrace his steps. This for a strong & proud man must be very unpleasant. (BL, Add. MS 49778, fols. 31–32)

Hamilton had specifically in mind 'The German alliance, & safeguarding of Constantinople … the two objects for which he has persistently worked during the last ten years' (ibid., fol. 32). To Salisbury's immense chagrin, the cabinet had refused to support him in the autumn of 1895 in overriding the fears of the admirals and forcing the straits in order to restrain Turkish massacres of Armenians, the effect of which on British opinion undermined the policy of sustaining the Ottoman empire, now in any case seen by Salisbury as beyond hope. Salisbury continued to want to 'lean to the Triple Alliance without belonging to it' (Grenville, 98), as he put it, but the Kaiser's telegram of congratulation to President Kruger on the repulse of Jameson's raid into the Transvaal emphasized the precariousness of Anglo-German understanding. Salisbury was obliged to look rather to permanent occupation of Egypt as security for British Mediterranean interests and the route to India, and hence to the management of relations with France and her ally, Russia. With France,

Salisbury hoped for what he called 'a mutual temper of apathetic tolerance' (ibid., 428)—which perhaps expressed his practical ideal of international relations. It was possible to patch up conflicts of interest in Siam and on the Niger in the hope of obtaining France's good offices with Russia in the Far East, where competition for concessions from China was exciting the apprehension of British imperialists. Salisbury's policy tended to the shoring up of China, like the Ottoman empire and Persia, as a buffer state between competing imperial powers, with an 'open door' to the trade of all nations. But the lack of return from his willingness to make concessions to the Russians, together with the forceful intervention of Germany in taking Kiaochow (Jiaozhou) in November 1897, raised criticism, not allayed by the acquisition of Weihaiwei, that British interests were not being adequately asserted. It took Kitchener's conquest of the Sudan and the repulse of French ambitions on the upper Nile in the Fashoda crisis of September–November 1898 to repair Salisbury's image of strength and emphasize his success in maintaining the British position in the partition of Africa without open collision.

From the spring of 1898, taking advantage of Salisbury's absences, which left Balfour in charge of the Foreign Office, Chamberlain and his cabinet allies set out to promote a new course which involved countering the supposed threat of the Franco-Russian bloc by alliance with Germany. The agreements with Germany on the future of the Portuguese colonies in Africa in August 1898 and on Samoa in 1899 have been taken to mark the influence of this group. Yet Salisbury was slow to give ground. His conviction of British commercial and imperial strength was, perhaps complacently, tougher than theirs. His references to the phrase 'splendid isolation', when it became current in 1896–7, were ironic rather than jubilant, but he did not think that Britain needed to commit herself to any alliance system. He did not expect that Russia and France would combine against Britain outside Europe. If favourable to accommodation with Germany, he believed that her long frontier with Russia would always predispose her to curry favour with her neighbour by throwing Britain over. Commitment to support the triple alliance powers against France and Russia would place a far heavier burden on Britain than the defence of Britain would impose on them. In any case, as he put it in a classic memorandum of 29 May 1901, using an argument he had often found convenient to repel importunity, binding commitments were excluded by the nature of parliamentary democracy: the British government 'cannot undertake to declare war, for any purpose, unless it is a purpose of which the electors of this country would approve', and there was no means of knowing 'what may be the humour of our people in circumstances which cannot be foreseen' (G. P. Gooch and H. Temperley, eds., *British Documents on the Origins of the War*, 1927–36, 2.68).

The outbreak of the Second South African War in October 1899 cast further doubt on Salisbury's command of the imperial scene. While favouring a strong line towards the Boer republics, he was uneasy to find the high commissioner in South Africa, Milner, and his 'jingo supporters' drawing the government into a major military effort 'for people whom we despise, and for territory which will bring no profit and no power to England' (Grenville, 267). He displayed his customary hardness towards obdurate opponents. 'You will not conquer these people until you have starved them out', he told Brodrick at the War Office in December 1900 (Marsh, 297). He defended the necessity of farm burning and of concentration camps, accepting the high mortality in the latter as inevitable, 'particularly among a people so dirty as the Boers' (Russell, 230–31). Yet war did not suit him. The early reverses of the campaign brought out his contempt for the military experts and 'that phase of British temper which ... has led detachment after detachment of British troops into the most obvious ambuscades—mere arrogance' (Grenville, 20–21). They also exposed the failure of his government to plan for the needs of imperial security, despite the establishment of a standing defence committee of the cabinet in 1895. The size of his victory in the 'khaki' election of October 1900 (called to confront the Boers with the national will to press on to victory) made him worry lest the Reform Acts should have exposed in the population 'a layer of pure combativeness' (A. E. Gathorne-Hardy, ed., *Gathorne Hardy*, 1910, 2.374), but he could no longer restrain the demands for increased defence expenditure which threatened the harsher taxation of property.

His wife's second stroke in July 1899 and death on 20 November had depleted Salisbury's resources. His sluggishness in responding to the Boxer uprising in the summer of 1900 convinced his colleagues of his loss of grip, and they imposed on him an agreement for Anglo-German co-operation in China in which he had no faith. Reluctantly, in November, he gave up the Foreign Office to Lansdowne, taking the privy seal. In January 1901 the death of Queen Victoria and the accession of Edward VII, to whose mistresses Hatfield had remained a closed house, emphasized the passing of his world. His foreign policy was beginning to be dismantled. He could still hamper moves for a German alliance, but in 1902 did not prevent a Japanese, much though he disliked the extent of the commitment involved. By now profoundly miserable in office, he saw the Second South African War to a successful conclusion, and resigned as prime minister on 11 July 1902.

Death and reputation Salisbury died at Hatfield House on 22 August 1903, after a fall from the chair in which the breathing difficulty caused by his great weight obliged him to sleep, and the development of blood poisoning from an ulcerated leg which exacerbated his heart weakness. 'It was just', his doctor said, 'that the machine was worn out' (Blake and Cecil, 69). He was buried in the family burial-ground at Hatfield churchyard beside his wife on 31 August, a memorial service taking place in Westminster Abbey on the same day.

In addition to the Garter in 1878, Salisbury received the GCVO in 1902. He was lord warden of the Cinque Ports from 1895. Three of his sons, James Edward Hubert Gascoyne-*Cecil (fourth marquess), Edgar Algernon Robert Gascoyne-*Cecil (Viscount Cecil of Chelwood), and Hugh Richard Heathcote Gascoyne-*Cecil (Baron Quickswood) followed him into Conservative politics; his fourth son, Lord Edward Herbert Gascoyne-*Cecil, became a civil servant in Egypt; and his second daughter, Lady Gwendolen Gascoyne-*Cecil, became his biographer, the intimate knowledge that only a member of the family could possess enabling her to paint an unrivalled portrait of the man, though the published volumes reach only 1892 (the manuscript of an unfinished final volume exists in the family papers).

Salisbury's reputation rests on his ranking as one of the greatest of British foreign secretaries and on the long predominance achieved by the Unionists under his leadership. If, towards the end of his career, he had to acknowledge that the Near-Eastern policy which had been the corner-stone of his as of most British diplomacy in the nineteenth century was no longer viable, and if he had no recipe, such as Chamberlain offered, for the consolidation and energization of the empire to meet intensifying international competition, he has none the less received recognition for performing with patient and undramatic skill the formidable task of defending the worldwide interests of a satiated power without open conflict with powers less replete or onerous commitment to any ally. Peace was an integral part of his matured strategy of Conservatism. It made it possible to contain the direct taxation which Salisbury feared would be levied with punitive incidence on property, not least landed property, in a democratic state. His hostile and pessimistic view of the approach of democracy contrasts with his record as the most electorally successful Conservative leader of the nineteenth century. If his political discourse, which has been analysed for its unusually sceptical and utilitarian presentation of Conservatism (Gladstone thought he had 'no respect for tradition'; *The Diary of Sir Edward Walter Hamilton, 1880–1885*, ed. D. W. R. Bahlman, 1972, 2.741), conveyed an uncompromising, though not reactionary, stance, the flexibility of the political practice which accompanied it has been remarked. Salisbury has been credited with high political skills in imposing himself with no little ambition and toughness as first Conservative and then Unionist leader, developing his own brand of tutelary populism to reach the enlarged electorate, guiding his party through the concessions necessary to meet the demand for social and administrative reform and to keep the Liberal Unionists in countenance, and turning a reinvigorated House of Lords into a decisive check on radical projects. A less admiring view is that the limited and immature democracy which he faced was skilfully managed by the Middleton machine, and that he was little more than the dexterous beneficiary of a well-established middle-class drift to Conservatism, and a Gladstonian thunderbolt over home rule, which delivered to him the realignment of parties he had always wanted and made easy the establishment of the Conservatives as the party of English nationalism which Disraeli had initiated. The domestic strategy was as

defensive as the foreign; it equally lacked the elements of creative imagination and hope of earthly betterment that were absent from Salisbury's nature.   PAUL SMITH

Sources G. Cecil, *Life of Robert, marquis of Salisbury*, 4 vols. (1921–32) · G. Cecil, *Biographical studies of the life and political character of Robert third marquis of Salisbury* (privately printed) · A. Roberts, *Salisbury: Victorian titan* (1999) · D. Steele, *Lord Salisbury: a political biography* (1999) · M. Bentley, *Lord Salisbury's world: conservative environments in late-Victorian Britain* (2001) · Lord Blake and H. Cecil, eds., *Salisbury: the man and his policies* (1987) · *Lord Robert Cecil's gold fields diary*, ed. E. Scott (1935) · *Salisbury–Balfour correspondence: letters exchanged between the third marquis of Salisbury and his nephew Arthur James Balfour, 1869–1892*, ed. R. H. Williams (1988) · P. Marsh, *The discipline of popular government: Lord Salisbury's domestic statecraft, 1881–1902* (1978); repr. (1993) · R. Shannon, *The age of Salisbury, 1881–1902: unionism and empire* (1996) · C. J. Lowe, *Salisbury and the Mediterranean, 1886–1896* (1965) · J. A. S. Grenville, *Lord Salisbury and foreign policy: the close of the nineteenth century* (1964) · C. C. Weston, *The House of Lords and ideological politics: Lord Salisbury's referendal theory and the conservative party, 1846–1922* (1995) · M. Pinto-Duschinsky, *The political thought of Lord Salisbury, 1854–68* (1967) · P. Smith, ed., *Lord Salisbury on politics: a selection from his articles in the Quarterly Review, 1860–83* (1972) · A. Adonis, *Making aristocracy work: the peerage and the political system in Britain, 1884–1914* (1993) · R. Shannon, *The age of Disraeli, 1868–1881: the rise of tory democracy* (1992) · R. Millman, *Britain and the Eastern question, 1875–1878* (1979) · A. Jones, *The politics of reform, 1884* (1972) · A. B. Cooke and J. Vincent, *The governing passion: cabinet government and party politics in Britain, 1885–86* (1974) · Viscountess Milner [V. G. M. Milner], *My picture gallery, 1868–1901* [1951] · *Malcolm MacColl: memoirs and correspondence*, ed. G. W. E. Russell (1914) · K. Rose, *The later Cecils* (1975) · GEC, *Peerage* · *The Times* (24 Aug 1903)

Archives Hatfield House, Hertfordshire, corresp. and papers | Balliol Oxf., corresp. with Sir Robert Morier · BL, corresp. with Arthur James Balfour, Add. MSS 49688–49691 · BL, corresp. with Sir Francis Bertie, Add. MSS 63013–63014 · BL, corresp. with Lord Carnarvon, Add. MSS 60758–60762 · BL, corresp. with Sir Charles Dilke, Add. MS 43876 · BL, corresp. with W. E. Gladstone, Add. MSS 44351–44508 · BL, corresp. with Lord Halsbury, Add. MS 56371 · BL, letters to Canon D. Hamilton, Add. MS 63178 · BL, letters to Sir Austen Layard, Add. MSS 39131–39139 · BL, corresp. with Florence Nightingale, Add. MS 45779 · BL, corresp. with Sir Stafford Northcote, Add. MSS 50019–50020 · BL, corresp. with Sir Augustus Paget, Add. MSS 51228–51229 · BL, corresp. with Lord Ripon, Add. MS 43519 · BL, corresp. with Lord Stanmore, Add. MS 49209 · BL OIOC, corresp. with Lord Curzon, MSS Eur. F 111–112 · BL OIOC, corresp. with Lord Northbrook, MS Eur. C 144 · BL OIOC, corresp. with Sir Richard Temple, MS Eur. F 86 · BL OIOC, corresp. with Sir Horatio Walpole, MS Eur. D 781 · BL OIOC, corresp. with Sir Philip Wodehouse, MS Eur. D 726 · Bodl. Oxf., letters to H. W. Acland and S. A. Acland · Bodl. Oxf., corresp. with A. J. Balfour · Bodl. Oxf., corresp. with Samuel Bickersteth · Bodl. Oxf., corresp. with Sir Henry Burdett · Bodl. Oxf., letters to Lord Edward Cecil and Lady Edward Cecil · Bodl. Oxf., letters to Benjamin Disraeli · Bodl. Oxf., corresp. with Lord Kimberley · Bodl. Oxf., corresp. with Lord Selborne · Bodl. RH, corresp. with Sir George Goldie · Bristol RO, letters to Mary Carpenter · CAC Cam., corresp. with Lord Randolph Churchill · CAC Cam., letters to W. T. Stead · CCC Cam., corresp. with sixteenth earl of Derby · Chatsworth House, Derbyshire, letters to duke of Devonshire · CKS, letters to Aretas Akers-Douglas · CKS, letters to Lord Brabourne · CKS, letters to Edward Stanhope · CUL, letters to Lord Hardinge · Glos. RO, corresp. with Sir Michael Hicks Beach · Hants. RO, letters to Sir A. B. Forwood · HLRO, letters to Lord Ashbourne · HLRO, corresp. with Lord Cadogan · Hunt. L., letters to Grenville family · Lancing College, Lancing, letters to Nathaniel Woodard · LMA, corresp. with Sir Willoughby Maycock · LPL, corresp. with Edward Benson · LPL, corresp. with Lord

Selborne · LPL, letters to A. C. Tait · Lpool RO, letters to fourteenth earl of Derby; corresp. with fifteenth earl of Derby · NA Scot., corresp. with A. J. Balfour · NL Scot., corresp. with Sir Henry Elliot · NL Scot., corresp., incl. with Lord Rosebery · NRA, priv. coll., letters to ninth duke of Argyll · NRA, priv. coll., corresp. with Lord Balfour of Burleigh · NRA, priv. coll., corresp. with Sir James Fergusson · NRA, priv. coll., letters to Sir Julian Pauncefote · Pembroke College, Oxford, letters to successive masters of Pembroke College · PRO, letters to Lord Cairns, PRO 30/51 · PRO, corresp. with Lord Cromer, vols. 2, 6 · PRO, corresp. with Sir Edward Malet, FO 343 · PRO, corresp. with Lord Midleton, PRO 30/67 · PRO, letters to William White, FO 364/1–11 · PRO, corresp. with Sir H. D. C. Wolff, FO 901 · PRO NIre., letters to duke of Abercorn · PRO NIre., corresp. with Edward Carson · PRO NIre., letters to Lord Dufferin · PRO NIre., letters to S. K. MacDonnell · Sandon Hall, Staffordshire, Harrowby Manuscript Trust, corresp. with Lord Harrowby · Suffolk RO, Ipswich, letters to Lord Cranbrook · Surrey HC, corresp. with Lord Onslow · Trinity Cam., letters to Lord Houghton · U. Birm. L., special collections department, corresp. with Joseph Chamberlain · UCL, corresp. with Sir Edwin Chadwick · University of Bristol Library, letters to Alfred Austin · W. H. Smith & Son Ltd, Swindon, corresp. with W. H. Smith · W. Sussex RO, letters to duke of Richmond · Warks. CRO, letters to Francis Alexander Newdigate Newdegate and Charles Newdigate Newdegate · Wilts. & Swindon RO, corresp. with Sir Michael Herbert | FILM BFI NFTVA, 'H.M. the queen at garden party, Buckingham Palace, June 1897', title ref. 505346

Likenesses G. Richmond, chalk drawing, 1861, Hatfield House, Hertfordshire · J. Griffiths, oils, 1865, V&A · London Stereoscopic Co., photograph, c.1870, NPG · G. Richmond, oils, c.1872, Hatfield House, Hertfordshire · W. Theed, marble bust, 1875, Hatfield House, Hertfordshire · A. von Werner, oils, 1878, Hatfield House, Hertfordshire · J. E. Millais, oils, 1882, NPG [see illus.] · G. F. Watts, oils, 1882, NPG · Horsburgh, oils, 1886, Hatfield House, Hertfordshire · E. Barnard, pencil drawing, 1887, Hatfield House, Hertfordshire · A. B. Joy, bronze bust, 1888, Hatfield House, Hertfordshire · duchess of Rutland, drawing, 1889, Hatfield House, Hertfordshire · lithograph, 1889, NPG · P. May, pen-and-ink caricature, 1893, NPG · H. von Herkomer, oils, exh. RA c.1894, Foreign Office, London · E. Fuchs, pencil drawing, 1901, Hatfield House, Hertfordshire · J. Russell & Sons, photograph, c.1901, NPG; repro. in *Our conservative and unionist statesmen*, vol. 4 · G. Frampton, bronze bust, 1903, Hatfield House, Hertfordshire · G. Frampton, statue, 1906, Hatfield House, Hertfordshire · H. Hampton, marble statue, 1909, Foreign Office, London · W. G. John, bronze effigy, exh. RA 1912, Salisbury Chapel, Hatfield House, Hertfordshire · Ape [C. Pellegrini], cartoon, NPG; repro. in *VF* (10 July 1869) · A. Bryan, pencil-and-ink drawing, NPG · H. Edwin, drawing, silhouette, NPG · Elliott & Fry, carte-de-visite, NPG · H. Furniss, caricatures, NPG · H. Furniss, pen-and-ink caricature, NPG · F. C. Gould, caricatures, NPG · Lock & Whitfield, woodburytype photograph, NPG; repro. in T. Cooper, *Men of mark: a gallery of contemporary portraits* (1877) · Spy [L. Ward], watercolour; related cartoon, NPG; repro. in *VF* (20 Dec 1900) · J. Tenniel, pencil caricature, V&A; repro. in *Punch* (8 March 1873) · J. Tenniel, pencil caricature, V&A; repro. in *Punch* (28 Nov 1885) · J. Tenniel, pencil cartoon, FM Cam.; repro. in *Punch* (23 April 1892) · J. Watkins, carte-de-visite, NPG · oils, Hatfield House, Hertfordshire · prints, NPG

Wealth at death £310,336 8s.: probate, 15 Sept 1903, *CGPLA Eng. & Wales*

Cecil, Thomas, first earl of Exeter (1542–1623), courtier and soldier, was born in Cambridge on 5 May 1542, the eldest son of William *Cecil, first Baron Burghley (1520/21–1598), and his first wife, Mary (c.1520–1544), sister of John Cheke. His mother died when he was less than two years old and he never seems to have aroused any affection in

Thomas Cecil, first earl of Exeter (1542–1623), by unknown artist, c.1610

his puritanical stepmother, Mildred *Cecil. His father was too concerned with affairs of state to have much time for him, and later admitted that he had never shown 'any fatherly fancy to him but in teaching and correcting' (*CSP for.*, 1561–2, 187). Thomas was educated at home by tutors, men such as the distinguished Dr Gabriel Goodman who during the 1550s looked after him and two young companions at the Cecil country retreat, The Parsonage, Wimbledon. The education was exacting—Latin, Greek, French, Italian, mathematics, cosmography (study of the universe), and religion—with gruelling general-knowledge tests set by the father. As occasional relief the boys went out riding and shooting with bows and arrows; they also learned to dance and play the virginals.

In 1561 Thomas's father sent him abroad to complete his education under the eye of his secretary, Thomas Windebank. He was armed with a long 'Memorial' telling him what prayers to say daily, how to study the Bible, and when to make a general confession of his sins. Once he reached Paris, however, the advice was soon forgotten. He began to enjoy life and neglect his studies. His father accused Thomas of being 'slothful in keeping his bed, rash in expenses, careless in his apparel, an unordinate lover of dice and cards; in study soon weary, in game never' (*CSP for.*, 1561–2, 491). On being told that 'my lewd son' had become involved with a young lady, he even thought of having him sent 'secretly to some sharp prison' before he could bring any more dishonour on his family (PRO, SP 12/22/49). Fortunately Thomas seems to have amended his ways. He finally completed his grand tour by visiting Antwerp, Speyer, Heidelberg, and Frankfurt, before returning home early in 1563 after an absence of nearly two years.

The following year his father arranged 'a good match' for Cecil with Dorothy Neville (1548–1609), daughter of Lord Latimer of Belvoir Castle. She was young and pretty, and was described by a relative, Sir Henry Percy, as 'very wise, sober of behaviour and womanly'. The marriage seems to have been happy. They had thirteen children, five sons and eight daughters. Two became famous: Edward *Cecil, who was made Viscount Wimbledon and led a disastrous attack on Cadiz in 1626, and Elizabeth [see Hatton, Elizabeth], whose marriage to the great lawyer Sir Edward *Coke 'was a *cause célèbre* before the law courts in 1617' (*DNB*). The parents' marriage, however, lasted until Dorothy's death. A year later, in 1610, Cecil married Frances Smith, *née* Brydges (1580–1663) [see Cecil, Frances, countess of Exeter], a thirty-year-old widow, less than half his age and younger than almost all his children. They had one daughter, who died in infancy.

Meanwhile, Thomas Cecil had become involved in Elizabethan politics. Through the influence of his father he became MP for Stamford, Lincolnshire, in 1563, represented the borough in two later parliaments, and then was elected for the county of Lincoln in 1584 and for Northamptonshire in 1592. But he was a man of action, not a politician, and wanted to be a soldier rather than a courtier. He helped to suppress the revolt of the northern earls in 1569. Four years later he volunteered to help the Scottish regent, Morton, storm Edinburgh Castle. In 1575 he was knighted by the queen during a tournament at Kenilworth. By now he was a brave and skilful officer. So when in 1585 the earl of Leicester was sent with an army to help the Dutch, Thomas Cecil was made captain of horse and governor of the English-controlled port of Brill, although he soon resigned on grounds of ill health. When the Armada sailed up the channel in July 1588, he was made colonel in an army set up to defend 'Her Majesty's person'. His final action came in 1601 when as colonel-general of the London foot he helped his half-brother Robert *Cecil smash the rebellion of the earl of Essex.

By now Cecil was also a leading courtier. In 1590 he had become the lord of the manor of Wimbledon and there built an impressive mansion, approached up a series of brick terraces on the slope of a hill, with a large garden and vineyard behind it. Here in the next ten years he entertained the queen on several occasions. The last, in July 1599, was notable for so many postponements that Thomas complained to Robert: 'Upon every change of coming I do nothing but give directions into the country for new provisions: most of the old thrown away by reason of the heat' (*Salisbury MSS*, 9.236). Still, he gained his reward, a commission as lord president of York (or president of the council of the north) with special orders to hunt down Catholic recusants. He was no ruthless persecutor, and does not seem to have been a committed protestant like his father, but he carried out the task conscientiously. He was soon able to tell Robert that 'since my coming, I have filled a little study with copes and mass books' (PRO, SP 12/272/112).

Further honours came his way. On the death of his father in 1598, Thomas Cecil became second Baron Burghley. For his part in crushing the Essex revolt he received the Garter. Then, when James I became king, he was first made a member of the privy council and in 1605, just before his sixty-third birthday, earl of Exeter, at the same time as Robert was created earl of Salisbury. His health, however, was now far from good. His letters to Robert are full of complaints about his gout and he had to make several visits to Bath. By the time the king paid him a visit at Wimbledon in June 1616, he had virtually retired from public life. But the following year he was forced back into prominence by accusations that his young wife, Frances, had plotted to poison Lady Lake, wife of one of the secretaries of state. The scandal became the talk of London. It was a very complicated affair, and the evidence was said to fill 17,000 sheets of paper. The earl appealed to the king, who took such an interest in the case that he presided in person in Star Chamber and then went down to Wimbledon to test the chief witnesses. Finally he pronounced the countess innocent and sentenced Lady Lake and her husband to the Tower for life.

The earl reached the ripe age of eighty. But in the 'very crasie winter' of 1622–3, with a flu epidemic raging, he became seriously ill. The letter writer Chamberlain reported: 'Some say he hath a gangrene in his foot or some other disease that will not let him last long' (*Letters of John Chamberlain*, 477). He died, probably at Wimbledon, on 7 February 1623 and was buried three days later under a splendid monument in the chapel of St John the Baptist, Westminster Abbey. Ever since, historians have followed his father's damning judgement: that he was 'meet only to keep a tennis court' (PRO, SP 12/20/20). Augustus Jessop in the *Dictionary of National Biography* claimed that he was 'a person of very ordinary abilities, and that if he had been born of other parentage we should have heard nothing of him'. Conyers Read, in his study of William Cecil, dismissed Thomas as 'quite undistinguished'. In fact he overcame a loveless childhood to become a kindly, upright man whose warmth of character made him far easier to get on with than his overbearing father or his astute half-brother. He also made a useful career for himself outside the court, despite attempts by his father to block it, and was highly thought of as a soldier. But perhaps the achievement that gave him greatest pleasure was to build at Wimbledon one of the finest prodigy houses in Elizabethan England, rivalling his father's palaces at Burghley and Theobalds, and then to entice the queen to honour it with several visits.

Cecil's will shows that he died one of the wealthiest men in England. He owned three great houses—Wimbledon, Burghley (after his father's death), and Exeter House in the Strand—as well as the plate and land that went with them. He was also very generous, remembering not only all his children and many grandchildren, but his servants (including 'the meaner servants in the kitchen that have no wages') and the poor in places connected with his manors. He also founded a hospital in Rutland for twelve poor men and two women and left money to Clare College, Cambridge.

The first earl of Exeter may not be one of the great figures in the annals of the Cecil family. His life has not attracted a single biographer, partly because most of his personal papers seem to have been destroyed in a fire at Exeter House, London, four years after his death. But he is certainly an interesting and influential personality.

RICHARD MILWARD

Sources R. J. Milward, *Tudor Wimbledon* (1972) · *DNB* · C. Read, *Mr Secretary Cecil and Queen Elizabeth* (1955) · G. R. Dennis, *The house of Cecil* (1914) · C. S. Higham, *Wimbledon Manor House under the Cecils* (1962) · *Calendar of the manuscripts of the most hon. the marquis of Salisbury*, 2, HMC, 9 (1888); 4 (1892); 9 (1902); 11–13 (1906–15) · *The letters of John Chamberlain*, ed. N. E. McClure, 2 vols. (1939) · will, PRO, PROB 11/141, sig. 23 · GEC, *Peerage*, new edn, vols. 2, 5 · R. Strong, *The Renaissance garden in England* (1979) · C. Dalton, *The life and times of Sir Edward Cecil, Viscount Wimbledon*, 1 (1885) · S. R. Gardiner, *History of England from the accession of James I to the outbreak of the civil war*, new edn, 3 (1885) · PRO, SP 12/20; 12/22; 12/272; SP 14/88 · court rolls of the manor of Wimbledon, 1589–1623, Northants. RO

Archives Beaulieu Archives, corresp. · N. Yorks. CRO, auditors' accounts of his estates · Northants. RO, corresp. and papers | PRO, letters to Lord Spencer, PRO 30/26/56

Likenesses oils on panel, *c.*1610, Burghley House, Lincolnshire [*see illus.*] · engraved effigy (after drawing by W. E. Wilkinson), Westminster Abbey · oils on panel, NPG

Wealth at death one of the richest men in England; Burghley House and estate, Wimbledon House and park, and Exeter House, London; plate and money, jewels, chains of pearl and gold, coaches with horses; bequests to all his children and many grandchildren, servants, the poor in places connected with his manors, prisoners, and those in hospital: will, PRO, PROB 11/141, sig. 23

Cecil, Thomas. *See* Cecill, Thomas (*fl. c.*1625–1640).

Cecil, William, first Baron Burghley (1520/21–1598), royal minister, son of Richard Cecil (*d.* 1553) and Jane, daughter of William Heckington of Bourne, Lincolnshire, and grandson of David Cecil, was born on 18 September 1520 or 1521. David Cecil, a member of a minor gentry family on the Welsh border, joined Henry of Richmond's army on his march through Wales. One of Henry VII's bodyguard, he served as yeoman of the chamber and serjeant-at-arms. A relative and patron, David Philips, himself a servant of Lady Margaret Beaufort, lived at Stamford in Lincolnshire, and it was this connection that led David Cecil to settle there. Established as a landowner, he flourished in local affairs, serving as sheriff of Nottinghamshire and five times as burgess in parliament for Stamford. He secured for his son appointment as page of the chamber to Henry VIII. Richard Cecil won promotion as groom and then yeoman of the wardrobe. He leased crown lands and advanced the family's local standing, serving as sheriff of Rutland and as a JP in Nottinghamshire. His marriage brought him the lordship of Burghley. William Cecil succeeded his father on 19 March 1553.

Education and early life Cecil was initially educated in local grammar schools in Stamford and Grantham. He entered St John's College, Cambridge, in 1535. In his six years there he benefited from the new curriculum enjoined by the royal injunctions of 1535, with its emphasis on humanistic studies and its inclusion of reformed authors. Although Cecil left without a degree, he had acquired a mastery of classical learning, both Latin and Greek, and,

William Cecil, first Baron Burghley (1520/21–1598), by unknown artist

then or later, competence in Italian, French, and Spanish. These Cambridge years, when the university was full of the ferment of humanist learning, shaped Cecil's thoughts about political society and his personal role in it. The influence of the classical treatises on citizenship and the conduct of public affairs, particularly Cicero's *De officiis*, was definitive to his outlook. From these authors he derived his concept of civil society as a compact of the various degrees of mankind, rationally and equitably governed by men self-disciplined in these classical virtues, indispensable to active participation in public life.

In Cecil these ideas blended with the contrasting native tradition of the subject, bound to obey the commands of a hereditary, divinely ordained ruler. For him his duties as councillor required that he take the initiative in developing independently informed, well-considered judgements of his own which, however unpalatable to her, he must tender to the queen. On one occasion at least he threatened retirement if she would not heed his advice, but in the long run he knew that after giving his advice, it was his duty as a subject to obey his sovereign even though she had rejected it.

It was among the humanist circles in the university that Cecil found his first wife. The distinguished Greek scholar John Cheke was a fellow of St John's and through him Cecil met his sister, Mary (*c.*1520–1544), who worked in the family wine shop and whom he married on 8 August 1541, a match neither socially nor financially suitable to Cecil's family background. His wife bore him a son, Thomas *Cecil, in May 1542 but died on 22 February 1544. Less than two years later, on 21 December 1545, Cecil married again. This time the lady was of suitable rank: Mildred Cooke

(1526–1589) [*see* Cecil, Mildred] was one of the four daughters of Sir Anthony Cooke, governor to Prince Edward, who were famous for their learning; a sister married Nicholas Bacon, future lord keeper.

Early career, 1547–1558 In 1541 Cecil had moved on to Gray's Inn. Richard Cecil now obtained for his son the reversion of the office of *custos brevium*, chief clerk of the court of common pleas, worth £250 a year (passed to his heir in 1548), his first step in crown service. In the new reign, Cecil made rapid advancement, helped by his Cambridge connections and his marital links. In 1547 he entered Protector Somerset's service and was present at the battle of Pinkie where he narrowly escaped injury. In the succeeding year he became the duke's secretary. That advancement proved unlucky. After Somerset's fall Cecil spent two months (November 1549–January 1550) in the Tower, but by September following he was a privy councillor and third secretary of state. In the temporary alliance between the former protector and John Dudley, earl of Warwick, Cecil acted as intermediary, enjoying the confidence of both. Somerset's second fall, however, left him untouched and at Dudley's creation as duke of Northumberland on 11 October 1551 Cecil was one of four knighted.

As junior secretary, Cecil was kept busy with routine tasks but he cultivated the career possibilities of the office, establishing wide contacts, particularly with protestant humanists at home or serving abroad as diplomats. He moved in a circle which mingled clergy of the reformed persuasion with sympathetic laity. It was such a group which met in his house in November 1551 for the first of two discussions on the nature of the sacrament, prefiguring the second Book of Common Prayer. It included a cluster of clerics and politicians, many of whom would be prominent in Elizabeth's reign. In the spring of 1553 he suffered a long illness which kept him away from court. Scenting the approaching crisis as Edward weakened, Cecil took precautions, making conveyances of his land and removing his valuables. Faced with the demand to sign the king's instrument shifting the crown to Jane Grey, Cecil had bouts of indecision before reluctantly giving in. Sent on a mission to Queen Mary by the council when it changed colours, he took the opportunity to defend his previous actions and to make peace with the new regime.

Declining offers from the Marian government, Cecil chose to retire from office on his own volition. His motives were religious; he would not have felt at ease as the executor of Catholic policy, but he remained on good terms with the new regime. In 1554 his services were called upon in a mission to bring Cardinal Pole to England. Later he attended Pole in a secretarial capacity in an attempted mediation between the emperor and France. This led to a three-week tour of the Low Countries, Cecil's sole experience of foreign travel. In 1555 he attended parliament as knight of the shire for Lincolnshire; he had previously sat in 1542 for an unknown constituency, in 1545 for

Stamford, and for Lincolnshire in 1553. He would represent Lincolnshire again in 1559, and in 1563 Northamptonshire. He was kept busy in shepherding several bills through the Commons, and voted against legislation penalizing exiles. Attendance at a dinner given by a group of the government's critics led to a summons before the council, where he was able to exonerate himself. For the remainder of Mary's reign he took no part in public business.

Secretary of state, 1558–1571 Cecil had, however, entered into another service, that of Princess Elizabeth. She had used his offices in Somerset's time and in 1550 appointed him her surveyor. He had links with her household through a distant relative, Sir Thomas Parry, her cofferer, and Roger Ascham, her tutor. By 1558 a personal relationship of confidence, trust, and mutual respect had grown up between the two. With her accession this became official. On 17 November 1558, the first day of her reign, she appointed him secretary of state. Returning to the post, Cecil made immediate use of the powers inherent in it and quickly took the lead in conducting all public business. This office, through which all official correspondence flowed—outgoing and incoming, foreign and domestic—offered an ambitious man the opportunity to become the centre to which all public business gravitated. Nothing would be done in which his voice had not been heard. Among his colleagues in council, a mixture of veteran courtiers, long-time civil servants, and some newcomers (including his wife's brother-in-law, Bacon, now lord keeper), none was likely to challenge his pre-eminence in business.

Cecil played an important role in the first two pieces of government business, the making of peace with France and Scotland and the re-establishment of a reformed polity in the church, the latter largely a matter of re-enacting Henrician and Edwardian statutes which repudiated Rome and replaced the mass with the English liturgy of 1552, slightly modified. Peace was achieved when the queen accepted a face-saving solution which decently veiled the loss of Calais. As for the second, Cecil's exact role in the struggle to pass the Uniformity Bill is unclear, but he clearly saw eye to eye with the queen as to the shape of the new ecclesiastical regime, firmly anti-papal but retaining enough of the formal structure of worship to conciliate those of conservative habits.

The first major challenge which would shape Cecil's role as a policy maker as well as his relations with his mistress, now that she was a sovereign and he was a minister of state, came in 1559. England stood in unprecedented danger; the ancient enemy, France, had an armed force in Scotland while the queen of that country (and of France) publicly laid claim to the English throne. In spring 1559 a band of Scottish nobles who had taken up arms against both the old religion and the alien regime appealed to the English government and specifically to Cecil for assistance. He responded with boldness and vision: boldness in his determination to oust the French, whatever the risks and cost, while displaying long-term vision in his perception that a reformed regime in Scotland would become the means for a permanent common interest between the kingdoms. He looked to a new era of British relations which would see the end of the 'auld alliance' and provide permanent insurance against future alien intrusions. He was laying the base of a 'British policy' which he would pursue for the long term in which the two kingdoms would stand together against intrusion in the island. More immediately it would serve as a united front against any papally inspired crusade against the new-founded protestant regime.

In implementing his policy, Cecil found his principal obstacle to be the queen herself. Elizabeth was strongly opposed to an enterprise which consumed so much of her scanty resources and threatened to shift crucial decisions from the court to the battlefield. In addition it meant giving aid to rebels against their sovereign. It required weeks of carefully managed manipulation and Cecil's threat of resignation to win her consent, first to a subsidy to the Scots lords, then a blockade, and finally an expeditionary force to assail the French entrenched in Leith. In the treaty of Edinburgh (July 1560) Cecil won, with some uncovenanted assistance from a winter storm which hurled back the French relief force, a complete victory for his policy: expulsion of the French and a native, protestant, regency, while acts of the Scottish parliament ended Roman jurisdiction and abolished the mass. Moreover Cecil had won for his queen the right to intervene in Scottish affairs in the future in order to sustain the terms of the 1560 treaties.

His triumph was dimmed by the queen's cold reception; courtiers commented on the lack of reward for his achievement. Worse still, the sudden death of Amy Robsart made the favourite Robert Dudley a probable royal husband. Cecil faced that possibility with dismay and seems to have contemplated withdrawal from public life. However, on 10 January the queen bestowed on him the lucrative office of master of the wards, a clear sign of her continuing confidence.

Cecil brought himself to give aid (or the appearance of it) to Dudley's scheme to enlist Spanish backing for his marriage to the queen. The bait held out was to be the reception of a papal nuncio bringing an invitation to the revived Council of Trent. Cecil speedily spiked this scheme by the timely discovery of a papist conspiracy and a few salutary arrests, while the nuncio was warned off. Dudley's marital prospects faded gradually, with intermittent spurts of revived hope. It was soon evident that the queen would stake him to a prominent political career— promotion to the privy council in 1562, earl of Leicester in 1564, and the landed endowment necessary to sustain his new dignity. Cecil had to adapt to the presence in council of a personal favourite of the queen. However, Elizabeth made it plain that Leicester's counsel on public matters weighed no more (and often less) than that of his fellows on the board.

There thus began a relationship between the secretary and the favourite which lasted to Dudley's death in 1588. It was probably not a welcome one to Cecil, but he quickly adapted to it. Relations between the men were flexible, adapted to circumstance, sometimes in opposition on a given question, often collaborating to attain a commonly agreed purpose. The basic difference between the two was one of personal goals. Cecil, although of course seeking personal gain and social advancement, pursued power for the promotion of public ends. Leicester, once his marital hopes faded, turned to the traditional ambitions of a nobleman: military fame, the glories of successful command in the field. Those ambitions became marked in the 1580s when he achieved command of the English army in alliance with the Low Countries. That policy decision clashed with Cecil's reluctance to enter into war with Spain. It did not, however, affect their collaboration in the conduct of the ensuing enterprise.

Leicester's first public appearance in a major political role came with the Newhaven (Le Havre) expedition of 1562–3. English aid to the French protestants was to be paid for by the retrocession of Calais, for which the French port was to be held in gauge. For the queen the purpose of the enterprise was the recovery of her lost possession. Cecil, for his part, had no doubt that the French protestants should be assisted, most immediately in order to check Guise ambitions and in the longer run to ensure continuing political instability in France. He did not show the enthusiasm he had displayed in 1559–60; there is a hint he would have preferred to limit English aid to money. For Dudley and his brother, Ambrose, earl of Warwick, commander of the English force, it was an opportunity for military adventure. All were disappointed. Bad faith on all sides wrecked English hopes. Calais remained French; the English, decimated by plague, surrendered to a reconciled French force of Catholics and protestants. Cecil at least could rejoice since an assassin had conveniently killed the duke of Guise, whom he saw as a prime enemy of England. Leicester, who had already been involved (along with the Scottish secretary Maitland) in the affairs of Mary Stewart in autumn 1561, now emerged fully onto the political stage.

By 1563, after the experience of the Scottish and French episodes, Cecil had laid down the outline of a foreign policy to which he would adhere in the future. He was acutely aware of the new dimension in inter-state relations. For the first time, ideology in the form of religion affected the dealings of one sovereign with another. Past experience offered little guidance. In Edward's reign the ferment of change had not yet disturbed either France or the Low Countries. How would neighbours live together when they differed so greatly on the fundamentals of man's salvation?

When the Scottish protestants appealed for help, Cecil responded readily. Assistance to the lords of the congregation not only advanced common faith but provided the means for resolving an acute political problem, the armed French presence on England's land border. It opened a way for a combined British front against any intruder in the island. Lastly, it offered the chance to end generations of hostility between the two island kingdoms. When the French protestants made their appeal, Cecil saw an opportunity to check the ambitions of the house of Guise for their niece. Yet behind them lurked a larger danger, a grand alliance of the Catholic powers in a crusade to exterminate English protestantism. In 1562 he painted a blood-chilling scenario in which France and Spain under papal sponsorship united in such an enterprise. This conviction became rooted in Cecil's mind and would shape his views henceforward.

In the Newhaven venture the English had burnt their fingers badly. Henceforward Cecil would oppose armed assistance to continental protestants. Unlike the Scottish scene, on the continent England lacked the armed power or political influence to sway events. Nevertheless it was essential in his view to encourage the French protestants—if necessary with money—in order to cripple the French monarchy in any move against the protestant English state. This humiliating exercise turned both the queen and Cecil against any more armed co-operation with continental brethren in the faith. Common religion had proved a weaker bond than traditional secular loyalties. What Cecil drew from the experience was a policy complementary to his established practice. Just as aliens were to be excluded from interference in British affairs, so should England abstain from any more continental adventures. He was happy to see the French preoccupied with their own domestic strife, and was prepared to intervene only if some urgent English interest was served.

At home the queen's nearly fatal smallpox attack in 1562 focused attention on the awkward problem of her marriage and the succession. It would absorb Cecil's attention for the next two decades and was from his point of view the gravest item on his list. The death of the queen without a settled succession would imperil everything for which he had worked. Worse still, the most obvious contender for the succession was a woman he feared and detested—Mary Stewart, who, backed by her Guise uncles, had flaunted her claims in the 1559 crisis.

Already in 1563 Cecil had given his support to a parliamentary petition to Queen Elizabeth that she marry. She had given her promise to do so—at a suitable time. Leicester still had lingering hopes. Cecil's private opinion of the earl as a prospective husband was put in a succinct memorandum of 1566: 'inflamed by the death of his wife … far in debt', Leicester was anxious 'to enhance only his particular friends to wealth, to offices, to lands' (Haynes, 444). Cecil put his hopes on the Archduke Karl, third son of the emperor. Pushing aside the awkward question of the archduke's religion, his advocates made his cause an active one in 1565. Led by Norfolk and Sussex, it dominated court politics for the next two years. Cecil supported the Austrian candidature wholeheartedly, but discreetly left open advocacy to others. Matters came to a head in parliament in 1566 when there was an organized move to petition Elizabeth either to marry or else to settle the succession. Cecil played a major but very discreet role in this move, personally drafting the petition. If the queen refused marriage, they should move a discussion of the succession. In the event the queen forbade discussion of the succession but reiterated her 1563 promise to marry.

The pressure generated in this move was sufficient to induce Elizabeth to send the earl of Sussex on a mission to Vienna. He departed in early 1567. There, finding the Habsburgs adamant that Karl should practise his own religion, he devised a scheme whereby the archduke could have private masses while attending officially at protestant public ceremonies. When that proposal reached England, the council divided, Cecil being among the supporters of such an arrangement, but the queen refused her consent. Whatever her motives, this sufficed to stifle the project. Anti-Catholic feeling in and outside council was too strong to be ignored. Cecil, too *politique* for popular opinion, had to live with the continued absence of a known successor to the throne.

In the meantime the English government had to cope the best it could with the schemes for Mary Stewart's remarriage following her widowhood in 1560. Her own efforts to secure a continental match, preferably with the Spanish heir, failed, and the English were able to press on her the choice of an English husband. Elizabeth took the matter into her own hands and offered Dudley (suitably elevated to the earldom of Leicester), a scheme for which it seems, so far as the evidence goes, Cecil was not an enthusiastic backer. Mary spiked the scheme by insisting on a recognition of her succession rights. She then made her own choice, marrying her cousin Henry, Lord Darnley, in July 1565, to the utter dismay of Cecil and his colleagues. The marriage spelt ruin to Cecil's whole British policy. England's interest at the Scottish court collapsed; her ally, the earl of Moray, fled to England in October. Mary's claims to the succession were strengthened, especially when a son was born in 1566, and English Catholics were encouraged at a moment when a survey of JPs found only a minority of them sound in the reformed faith. The panic-stricken English council contemplated armed intervention, but Cecil, surveying the whole scene, especially Ireland, where the menace of Shane O'Neill loomed large, rejected such a move.

Cecil soon had cause to rejoice in the shipwreck of Mary's fortunes. Darnley's murder in February 1567 was followed by her marriage to Bothwell and her forced abdication. Urged on by Cecil, Moray returned to Scotland to become regent for his infant nephew James. But by her flight to England in May 1568, Mary precipitated a new and even more perplexing set of problems. What was to be done with her? Elizabeth's initial reaction was one of sisterly indignation at the violation of Mary's regality and a resolve to replace her on the Scottish throne. This gradually cooled as the council urged delay. Cecil, surveying the situation, saw danger in any possible alternative: return to Scotland, departure for France, or detention in England. The first two he ruled out. How then to justify the detention of a sovereign person?

Cecil made use of the accusations against Mary by which the regent, Moray, defended his actions. With strong backing in the council, including that of Leicester, he persuaded Elizabeth she must hear these charges before determining Mary's fate. In August she appointed a commission (of Cecil's nominees) to sit at York to hear both Scottish parties put their case. Moray would appear as defendant but the purpose of the plan, as described to Mary, was a negotiated restoration to her throne. In fact Moray, assured of future support, was encouraged to present the so-called casket letters which contained evidence of Mary's compliance in Darnley's murder. This would put her on the defensive and compel her to answer the charges.

All went according to plan. The charges were made; proceedings were removed to London to be heard by the whole council, most of the earls, the archbishop of Canterbury, and the bishop of London. Mary refused to answer the allegations unless she was heard by Elizabeth in person; denied this, she was offered asylum in England and the dropping of the charges if she would renounce her throne. When she refused this offer, the council ordered her transfer to the custody of the earl of Shrewsbury. With Mary immured at Tutbury and Moray in power at Edinburgh, Cecil could take heart. Yet the problem of Mary's future remained unresolved. In spring 1569 Cecil drew up another proposal. He saw in the present situation an opportunity to recover the ground lost when Mary married Darnley. In sum, he proposed the restoration of Mary to her throne but bereft of royal power. That would be vested in Moray as regent, backed by a council of nobles, while Elizabeth retained the right to depose Mary if she violated the terms of this settlement. It would give the Scottish regime stability and also a gloss of legality. It would realize Cecil's own ideal of a British polity in which the alliance of the two kingdoms would present a solid front against outside aggression.

Mary's removal to Tutbury in January 1569 came at the opening of a momentous year, the most troubled in Cecil's career. There ensued a series of events, separate in themselves but convergent in their consequences. The first, which took place in the last days of 1568, was the seizure of Spanish ships, laden with specie borrowed from Genoese bankers, on their way to Flanders with pay for Alva's armies. Threatened by pirates, they sought refuge in English ports. Cecil persuaded the queen to seize the treasure. Alva responded by seizing English goods in the Low Countries, an act reciprocated by the English. The seizure risked war. Given the sparse documentation, Cecil's intentions are not wholly clear. War seemed to threaten, but both sides shied away from open conflict. Alva kept a cool head and dispatched an envoy who was treated to a barrage of complaints, but the temperature cooled and a diplomatic truce ensued. This violent and unpremeditated action did in fact reflect Cecil's changing view of the international scene. It is summed up in his state paper of early 1569, 'A short memorial of the state of the realm'. The fair weather of the early sixties was now, he wrote, superseded by gathering clouds. Spain, no longer distracted by Mediterranean problems, was concentrating on a new goal. United with France, she would, in obedience to papal command, attack England, restore the ancient faith, and crown Mary queen of England. These grim predictions coincided with worsening relations with Spain. The English ambassador at Madrid had been expelled; the current Spanish ambassador in London

was awkward and abrasive in relations with the English government. Alva's suppression of reform in Flanders and the precarious position of the French protestants all fed Cecil's fixed conviction of a Catholic crusade in the making, led by Philip. It had, he thought, been planned as long ago as 1565 when the French and Spanish queens met at Bayonne.

The immediate crisis over the treasure ships eased; one of a different complexion soon followed, in which the Scottish queen was again centre stage, but the principal actors were a clutch of English noblemen. The failure of the Habsburg match made the succession problem more urgent than ever; the only plausible English claimant, Lady Katherine Grey, had died a year earlier. The idea was now floated in several places that the disposition of the captive queen and the solution of the succession problem might be linked if she were married to an English nobleman. Assured of her future, Mary would settle down as a member of the English establishment. This was, of course, an alternative to Cecil's plan.

A promising candidate was Norfolk, sole duke, doyen of the English nobility. Recently widowed, he was amenable to the scheme. It was backed by Leicester, Arundel, Pembroke, and the northern earls of Northumberland and Westmorland. Significantly, the greater regional magnates, Derby and Shrewsbury, refused to have anything to do with it, as did Sussex, lord president of the north. Moray was pressured into a reluctant co-operation. By mid-July 1569 knowledge of the plot was widespread; almost certainly Cecil had more than an inkling of it; only the queen remained in the dark. In this same year there was what seems to have been an attempt to unseat Cecil or at least to clip his wings. The sources are in varying degrees unreliable, but all recount episodes in council. One is dated 1568, in which Norfolk in the royal presence accused Cecil of sending £100,000 to the French protestants besieged in La Rochelle. A second account, dated 1569, reports a similar scene, again in Elizabeth's presence, in which the duke and Leicester launched an attack on Cecil's monopoly of the royal confidence. A third story, even more lurid, tells of a plot to arrest the secretary, spearheaded by Norfolk and Arundel, in which he threw himself on the duke's mercy.

The sources are too unreliable and disjointed to give a coherent account. What is known from Cecil's own pen is that he did have a quarrel with Norfolk in May/June 1569. In a letter of 27 May to Sussex he laments the duke's unjust accusations, blames 'secret reports of evil doers', declares his innocence, and ends on a note of resignation. He looks forward to diminished power, 'I may percase use less diligence to serve and gain more quietness'. But in early June he was writing to an Irish correspondent, Rowland White, informing him that 'God has favoured me with His grace', and that divine goodness has preserved him 'from some clouds or mist whereof I trust my honest actions are proved to have been lightsome and clear'. He adds 'I find the queen's majesty my gracious good lady without any change of any part of her old good meaning towards me' (*Salisbury MSS*, 1.409; BL, Cotton MS Titus B II 336; BL, Lansdowne MS C II, fol. 143).

Cecil's triumph reflected the queen's abiding confidence, but he took trouble to mend broken fences. He saw that Norfolk's suit for the guardianship of the Dacre heir (his stepson) in the court of wards went as the duke desired. As always Cecil took pains to avoid turning political rivalry into personal animosity or policy disagreements into faction. Then, in September 1569, Norfolk himself was in deep trouble when the scheme for his marriage to Mary reached the queen's ears. Faced by the royal wrath, the duke took refuge in his Norfolk seat, Kenninghall. For a moment the prospect of open conflict loomed, but the duke quailed and was soon lodged in the Tower. The other parties to the plot (except Leicester, to whom all was forgiven) suffered various forms of restraint.

The sponsors of the match, largely courtiers, had sought support from a quite different group of malcontents outside the court circle. It was in the north, particularly the border counties, where loyalty to the old faith was strongest. Here a clutch of local gentry, led by the earls of Northumberland and Westmorland, saw Mary as their best hope for a Catholic restoration. They had collaborated with the Norfolk intrigue only half-heartedly, looking to their own force, aided by Spanish arms, to achieve their ends. Norfolk's surrender (when he told them a rising would cost his life) left them desperate; confusedly they stumbled into rebellion.

Cecil and the queen, disturbed by rumour and the revelations of Norfolk's associations, urged precautionary measures, but Sussex assured them all was well and advised leaving well enough alone. When revolt exploded, suspicion fell on the earl, cousin to Norfolk and enemy to Leicester. Cecil, however, retained his confidence in Sussex, with whom he had been on warm terms since the latter's days in Ireland. His trust was justified; Sussex's steadfastness rallied the lukewarm Yorkshire gentry to support the crown and the rising quickly fizzled. At this juncture the assassination of Moray in January 1570 revived the fortunes of the Marian party in Scotland. Cecil persuaded a reluctant queen, fearful of French intervention, to send Sussex over the border in a series of actions that summer which seriously weakened the Marian party. Sussex on his return to London entered the council, a steady ally of Cecil.

The latter needed support since Mary's friends at the English court, led by Leicester (who saw her as a probable successor), urged her restoration to the Scottish throne, a move to which Elizabeth assented. Cecil, who saw the Scottish queen as a deadly enemy, was able to gather control of negotiations with Mary into his own hands (and those of his trusted fellow councillor Mildmay) and eventually scuttled them. Cecil was no longer willing to let Mary free from English custody. Then in 1571 the government discovered the existence of yet another effort to marry Norfolk and Mary—the Ridolfi plot, which involved the Spanish ambassador and the papacy. Its discovery brought Norfolk to the scaffold, further blackened Mary's reputation, and drew her fangs.

The Anjou match and the Netherlands, 1571–1587 The turbulence which Mary's presence in England had induced was finally quieted. The Elizabethan regime, having weathered it, was now on firm foundations. Harmony at the centre was restored, while the failure of the northern earls laid to rest the haunting fear of Catholic resistance to the new order. After the fall of Edinburgh Castle in 1573 Scotland's protestant regency was again in place, the Marians crushed. Finally, there were overtures for an alliance from a French court where protestants had a strong voice.

For all these blessings Cecil could claim much credit, and he now received his reward. In 1570 Elizabeth reaffirmed her confidence in him by granting him power to stamp her signature on routine official documents; in the next year (25 February 1571) she elevated him to the peerage as Baron Burghley; in 1572 he relinquished the secretaryship, and on 15 July succeeded Winchester as lord treasurer while receiving the honour of the Garter. In the council an atmosphere of collegiality again prevailed. There would be disagreements between individuals, and alliances would be made and unmade, but open rifts were not repeated. The apparatus of the council was well lubricated and harmony would last until the 1590s.

Burghley's advancement to the treasury in 1572 altered the pattern of his public life. He now had direct responsibility for finance, but after Sir Francis Walsingham's appointment as second secretary to Sir Thomas Smith in December 1573, Burghley finally shed the heavy burden of the secretaryship. Attacks of the gout, increasingly frequent, forced two stays in Buxton Spa in 1575 and 1577 as well as briefer absences from council. Attendance at council fell from the 97 per cent of the 1560s to 80 per cent or even less. Nevertheless his weight in council and in the royal confidence remained undiminished. Smith was an ageing and insecure man who depended on Burghley for assistance in his office. But in Walsingham, whose appointment Burghley had backed, he had a strong and effective colleague, albeit with a voice of his own, not always in agreement with the treasurer. A deeply committed radical protestant, Walsingham pushed for co-operation with the continental brethren, not only on prudential grounds but out of loyalty to the international reformed corpus. He and Leicester often saw eye to eye on foreign policy issues, although for different reasons. The earl had now abandoned his matrimonial hopes and looked to a martial career, dreaming of fame in the field. These circumstances meant that there were now voices in council pressing for a proactive foreign policy.

For a time they had a hearing at court. In 1571 a new candidate for the queen's hand emerged, Henri, duke of Anjou, Catherine de' Medici's third son. Leicester pressed the match; Burghley, although wary of a foreign alliance, saw its advantages. It would deny Mary French aid and, if there was an heir (as Burghley desperately hoped), would cut her out altogether. He even proposed Anjou be allowed the private use of the mass, provided he conformed to the English service publicly. When the match foundered on the duke's refusal of such terms, an alliance was pushed as a substitute. Towards this Burghley was at first opposed, but when the Huguenot faction gained strength in the French court, he reluctantly agreed to an alliance, the treaty of Blois (April 1572). Deeply suspicious of French intentions in the Low Countries, he saw the alliance as a possible check on such ambitions. Nevertheless, he kept open contacts with Spain, looking to improved relations, which he accomplished with the reopening of trade in 1573.

The massacre of St Bartholomew threw French affairs, and correspondingly Anglo-French relations, into utter confusion. The English government played a wary game. On the one hand, they continued Burghley's policy of support so that the Huguenots remained strong enough to keep French affairs in constant flux. On the other, they made an attempt to maintain cordial relations with the French court, which now substituted Catherine's fourth son, François, duke of Alençon (after 1576 duke of Anjou) as a candidate for Elizabeth's hand. To this scheme Burghley gave reluctant approval, doubtful of the queen's seriousness. When Alençon entered into alliance with the protestants, English engagement became more serious. A combination of Alençon, Condé, Navarre, and the Montmorency brothers was canvassed. The queen was willing to give £15,000 to pay German mercenaries and to promise general support. For a moment it looked as though this *politique*-protestant combination might become dominant at court, as Coligny had been. With such a regime at Paris, co-operation, if not formal alliance, would be possible. The queen mother's success in patching up the peace of Monsieur in 1576 put paid to it, much to Elizabeth's disgust. Burghley (although absent from court because of illness) played an active role; when Navarre and Alençon were both prisoners in 1574 he suggested a source for bribing their guards. However, it was Leicester's followers who dealt with the French conspirators.

By 1576 the English government had to turn its attention elsewhere—to the Low Countries. In 1572 the rebel capture of Brill had set in motion civil war in the provinces. Burghley's immediate reaction was a fear of French intervention, and he was prepared to consider co-operation with the duke of Alva in suppressing the revolt if the French entered the scene. When that possibility receded in the wake of St Bartholomew, Burghley adopted a cautious policy reminiscent of his dealings with the French in the 1560s. Relations with Spain were repaired by agreements in 1573 and 1574 which reopened trade. Yet the rebels had easy access to English markets and ports, while English volunteers flocked to their assistance.

Burghley's fundamental views on the Netherlands problem are made clear in a series of memoranda in 1575–6 when the rebel cause faltered. Each posited the premise that either French or Spanish domination in the provinces was highly dangerous to English interests. But he weighed Spain as the more dangerous threat since Philip harboured plans to invade and conquer England in order to restore the old faith (and place Mary Stewart on the throne). Burghley's confidence that the rebels could win by their own efforts was slight. What should England do? Surveying the options available, he emphasized the crushing burden of cost and shied away from armed intervention. His hope was that somehow the *status quo ante* of the 1560s might be restored with some guarantee to protestants of exercise of their faith. Clear-sighted in his analysis, Burghley hesitated to face up to the implications of his own conclusions. In the end he fell back on English mediation, the queen's favourite recipe for action.

With the collapse of Spanish power in the Low Countries in 1576 power passed to the states general of the seventeen provinces. Their programme included the removal of Spanish troops and a return to the arrangements of Charles V's time. The English rejoiced in the prospective disappearance of an army whose presence on their doorstep aroused their alarm. When the states general appealed for a loan, the queen gave them £20,000 down with a promise of £80,000 more, while sending to Philip's new governor, Don John of Austria, her offer to act as a mediator with the states, urging him to accept their terms and warning him England would support them if he did not. Burghley hoped these strong words would be sufficient to persuade the governor. In fact a *modus vivendi* was reached between him and the states; for the moment the situation was calm.

Burghley's health kept him from court for a time, but by his return in autumn 1577 Don John was moving to a showdown with the states general which ended in his crushing victory at Gembloux in January 1578. This turn of events led Burghley to reconsider his commitment to neutrality; and even before that event, he came out for armed intervention on the states' behalf. After the battle, with backing from Leicester and Walsingham, he persuaded Elizabeth to provide funds to pay for a German mercenary force under Count Casimir of the Palatinate. She, however, hesitated and began to listen to signals from her long-time suitor, Anjou, who was now bidding for command of the states' forces. The duke, thwarted in his domestic ambitions, looked for a career in the Low Countries. By the time Elizabeth agreed to her councillors' scheme, he had made terms with the states. This met with the queen's approval. She hoped that lack of help from France would force him to turn to her. Thanks to his faithlessness, the arrangement was short-lived. The duke returned home. He now turned to a serious pursuit of Elizabeth's hand in marriage in order to win English backing for his military ambitions in the Low Countries.

From 1578 to 1581 English policy was shaped by a complex negotiation for a marriage of the duke of Anjou and Elizabeth which would resolve the Low Countries crisis. It was Sussex whom Elizabeth used as an intermediary to revive the match, but Burghley was a ready convert to the scheme. He made a persuasive case. While he shared fears of Philip's designs on England with Leicester and Walsingham, who opposed the match, he rejected their strategy of armed intervention. His solution was a peaceful one. England, by the marital link with France, would prevent independent French interference. The threat posed by the combined weight of the two kingdoms would be powerful enough to compel Philip to accept a restoration of the *status quo* of the 1550s with an accommodation for religious differences. But the Anglo-French combination must be bound by the marital tie; mere alliance, in Burghley's view, would not serve. Along with that argument there was a corollary. Blessed, as he continued to hope, by an heir, the marriage would bar Mary's road to the throne and lay at rest the grimmest of all spectres, a contested succession, with civil and religious war. Elizabeth gave enthusiastic co-operation to the scheme.

Neither Elizabeth nor the treasurer foresaw the storm of protest aroused by the prospect of a papist consort. Its manifestations were various, John Stubbs's pamphlet *The Gaping Gulf* being the most notorious, but the match's opponents also used the subtler arts of the masque and the pageant to drive home their message to Elizabeth. These protests strengthened opposition within the council, where Burghley and Sussex found themselves in a minority of supporters for the match. The most the body would offer was sullen acquiescence. Elizabeth reluctantly abandoned the marriage scheme. But in late 1580 the queen renewed proposals for an alliance with France, a move which automatically revived the marriage question. This was the opening play in extended negotiations for an Anglo-French alliance which would jointly back Anjou's role as commander of the army of the states general. Each side sought to bear as little of the costs as possible. Marriage was ruled out by the English, although Elizabeth, to the consternation of her ministers, momentarily upset the applecart in the famous exchange of rings in betrothal with the duke, a move cancelled the next morning, no doubt on the councillors' urging.

The French, during these negotiations, insisted on marriage. Burghley's views on this were plain. Marriage was an irreversible act. Elizabeth must have concrete evidence of real French commitment to an active role in the Low Countries' affairs, promises of action which would be profitable to Henri III and his brother and feasible in performance. His unspoken premise was that no such promises would be forthcoming. The lead in the whole negotiation with Anjou and with the French government was in the queen's hands. Burghley's role was shaped by the dilemma laid out in his memoranda. Of the Spanish menace to England he had no doubt. France he feared less, given her domestic troubles, although he distrusted her ambitions in the Low Countries. Whatever strategy was adopted must at all cost avoid English military involvement on the continent. Given these considerations the Anjou match was an attractive option and Burghley supported it; but when the marriage proved unacceptable domestically, he looked on mere alliance with growing doubt, which was borne out by events. The French did indeed withdraw altogether, leaving Elizabeth paymaster to the faithless duke, who destroyed himself. He retired ignominiously to France where he died in 1584.

Death removed Anjou from the Dutch scene, even as another death, that of Orange a month later, precipitated hard decisions which could no longer be avoided. The leaderless states general looked desperately for outside help for their survival. The success of the prince of Parma, the new governor, first in winning over the southern Catholic provinces and then in the reconquest of city after city, faced them with the total destruction of their cause. They turned first to France, but looming civil war in that distracted country ruled out any hope of French aid. If the Dutch were to be rescued, only England could be their saviour. Walsingham and Leicester pushed hard for intervention, the former because of his commitment to the reformed faith, the latter to satisfy his own martial ambitions. Burghley's views were expressed in a series of memoranda, all of which, while acknowledging the gravity of the Spanish threat, laid even heavier emphasis on the cost and dangers of intervention. Nevertheless he submitted a report which recommended assistance to the states (if French aid was not forthcoming), and proposed opening negotiations for a treaty. In the months before the treaty of Nonsuch was signed with the Dutch, Burghley came under fire from Leicester and Walsingham, partly for his degree of opposition, partly because of a personal grievance of the latter; but when the queen accepted the decision to intervene in arms, Burghley acknowledged the *fait accompli*. In the negotiations of July 1585 Burghley was fully involved in working out the exact terms of the treaty of Nonsuch. The responsibility for meeting the demands imposed on the realm fell on Burghley, ably assisted by Walsingham, with whom relations had warmed. He had other matters to deal with in the early 1580s besides the coming of war.

In 1583 Walsingham, with Burghley's involvement, had uncovered the so-called Throckmorton plot to murder the queen. This led him to devise an extraordinary measure, the bond of association, by which Englishmen individually pledged themselves to kill anyone who claimed the throne on the assassination of the queen. The association was clearly aimed against Mary Stewart. Parliament gave it statutory standing but left unresolved the awkward questions as to who should govern after the queen's death and how the successor should be chosen. Members of the council along with the higher judiciary anxiously discussed the situation; various draft proposals were drawn up, one almost certainly Burghley's. Like the others, it would have vested power in a council of notables who would summon parliament, on whom the task of selecting the successor would fall. Couched in typical Cecilian style, it canvassed the pro and con arguments, drew precedents from English and French history, and ended in doubtful uncertainty, weighted against action. It did, however, approve a draft bill which would have placed choice of the new sovereign with parliament. This measure echoed a similar proposal made in 1562 when Elizabeth nearly died from smallpox. The queen quashed the scheme. The episode throws an interesting light on the distance Burghley—and his contemporary councillors—had travelled from the personal-dynastic monarchy of Henry VIII towards an embryonic early modern state, built not on the interests of the sovereign, but of the commonwealth.

The threat to the queen's life was renewed in the

Babington plot of 1586 in which evidence was produced of Mary's consent to her cousin's murder. Burghley did not hesitate to strike at his old enemy. He played a leading role in the trial and condemnation of the Scottish queen and in parliament, where he helped draft the petition for the execution of the sentence. When Elizabeth, after signing the warrant, wavered in authorizing the execution, Burghley took the lead in dispatching it to Fotheringhay where the deed was done. He suffered four months' banishment from the royal presence as a punishment for his pains.

Meanwhile the campaign in the Low Countries went badly. Leicester forfeited the confidence of the Dutch leadership while offending the queen by assuming the office of governor. Burghley did his best to defend the earl, who finally returned home in December 1587. Invasion now impended. Burghley, partly to buy time, partly to satisfy a queen who desperately wanted to avoid open collision, entered into clandestine negotiations with Parma's agents which ended only as the Armada entered English waters. That he had any expectation of their success seems improbable.

In the months preceding the Armada's arrival Burghley was kept busy raising money for the war and supervising naval supplies. He could take pride in his long-term solicitude for the navy, notably his appointment of John Hawkins as treasurer of the navy in 1578. In 1584 Burghley outlined a strategy for dealing with the expected invasion fleet, which in its proposals largely corresponded to the course taken four years later.

The administrator The year 1588 was a landmark in the history of the reign, the end of an old and the beginning of a new (and for Burghley final) chapter in Elizabethan political history. In the aftermath of the Armada Leicester died; in 1589 Mildmay; in 1590 Walsingham; and in 1591 Hatton followed. Before examining the final decade of Burghley's life, it will be useful to pause and look retrospectively at other aspects of his many-sided career. Beside what might be termed his prime ministerial role as chief counsellor of the queen and initiator of grand policy, he was employed in other tasks. He was of course an omnicompetent administrator through whose hands passed almost every piece of government business, domestic and foreign. When parliament met, it was his business to draft, promote, and enact the crown's legislative programme. These responsibilities inevitably involved him in the affairs of the other body that Queen Elizabeth governed—the Church of England.

Burghley as secretary was a recipient of letters from ambassadors and agents abroad, as well as from foreign ambassadors in London. Likewise he handled correspondence with the deputy in Dublin, the regional presidents in Wales and the north, the wardens of the marches, and the new lord lieutenants and their deputies in the counties. He was also the recipient of private petitions. To all these items of business he had to respond and in many cases to make an appropriate decision. All this was done with a limited staff of a half-dozen assistants and required from him unremitting toil. Sheer industry alone would not

have sufficed without being disciplined by the ingrained habits which were a legacy of his university studies in the rigorous prescriptions of the classical rhetoricians. This mental discipline reflected itself in his systematic appraisal of each problem he faced. There are countless memoranda in his hand, each couched in the same form. A question is posed, for example, whether to make an alliance with the states general. There followed two lists, the first laying out the arguments in favour of an action, the second those opposed. This mode of analysis reflected the dispassionate clarity of vision Burghley sought to bring to his task: each problem dissected so as to display the consequences favourable and unfavourable.

Only rarely does the memorandum record a decision made and acted upon. Time and circumstance would play a role—the response of his volatile mistress, forever changeable, forever seeking to delay decisions—or the opposition of his colleagues in council. For Burghley, each decision, so far as he could influence it, rested on a set of broad long-term objectives, summed up in the interest of the realm, or as he would have put it, of the 'queen and the state'. The introduction of the latter term highlights the difference between Burghley and, say, Wolsey. For Elizabeth's minister the sovereign's personal interests were subordinate to those of the whole English body politic—hence Burghley's reproachful attitude towards her refusal to marry and beget an heir. In retrospect his long tenure of office stands out as a crucial moment in the process by which English dynastic monarchy slowly changed into the embryonic nation state of the next century.

The range and mixture of Burghley's responsibilities shifted when he relinquished the secretaryship in favour of the treasurership in 1572. He assumed his new office with the benefit of considerable experience in financial business in his Edwardian years and in the 1560s. In that decade he worked with Sir Thomas Gresham in the management of the crown debt in Antwerp. Accepting the latter's recommendation that a legalized interest rate of 10 per cent would shift royal borrowing to London, he pushed the necessary legislation through in 1571. From 1574 the crown raised all its loans in London. He inherited from his predecessor Winchester a conservative policy of rigorous economy, enforced by a penny-pinching monarch who watched anxiously over every item of expenditure. In some respects this strategy paid off. Burghley was able to accumulate £300,000 with which to face the war with Spain, but in the long term the pressure of royal parsimony on the one hand and the fear of offending the taxpaying classes on the other left the treasurer little room for manoeuvre. As a result major deficiencies in the crown's fiscal administration went unchecked or grew worse.

The subsidy (the land tax), one of the three pillars of royal finance (along with customs duties and crown lands), steadily declined in value because the self-assessed taxpayers consistently undervalued their worth. Burghley himself was among the sinners, reporting an annual income of £133 when in actual fact his yearly income was at least £4000, if not more. The return of a single subsidy fell from £140,000 to £80,000. When the pressures of war began to tell in the late 1580s Burghley expressed his concerns about these poor tax returns before the 1589 parliament and again in 1593. In the latter meeting he probably influenced the lord keeper's opening speech to the Commons in which he rebuked the practice of underassessment. When they offered a double subsidy, he weighed in strongly. Speaking at a conference between the houses, he insisted on a triple subsidy, to which the Lords had already consented. At the same time he rebuked them for the practice of underassessment. He demanded another conference and consent to a third subsidy. This aroused the lower house's indignation because it seemed to encroach on their sole right to initiate tax measures. The treasurer and his son took steps to heal the quarrel; the Commons granted the third subsidy. Some changes were made to raise the tax returns, but the problem of underassessment went unresolved. Yet he was responsible for one important change. Before Elizabeth's reign subsidies had been levied in wartime. Under Burghley they were routinely levied in peacetime, although of course national security was always advanced as a cause for taxation. An uncovenanted consequence was the much fuller body of information as to policy which the Commons now received.

In the case of the customs the same conservatism prevailed. Under Mary, Winchester had raised the valuation by which some commodities were assessed. Under Burghley, during a period of rising prices, no changes were made in the *ad valorem* rates. Other commodities continued to be taxed at quantity rather than at value. On one calculation the crown lost £500,000 in revenue as a consequence. The nature of the data makes impossible an estimate of income from crown lands, but in Burghley's own domain, the court of wards, revenue fell by half. He sought other sources in an effort to generate more income. One of these, grants of monopoly on the manufacture or export of certain goods, originally intended as a stimulus to innovation, became a device for increasing revenue in the war years and generated an outburst of protest which exploded only after Burghley's death.

Burghley can be faulted on his failure to reform the abuses in the fiscal system, but he laboured under tight constraints. It was neither in his power nor his inclination to challenge the landowning gentry or alienate the exporting merchants. From the early 1580s onwards he was under tremendous pressure to finance war in the Low Countries, France, and Ireland, and the naval assaults on Spain. He entered the war with a £300,000 nest egg; Elizabeth left to her successor the relatively modest debt of £350,000. All this stands in sharp contrast to continental experience, where suspension of debt repayment, debasement of the coinage, and the sale of office were common practice. In the short run Burghley had succeeded in finding the means to see England through the war, but he bequeathed a dysfunctional fiscal order which in turn raised larger, constitutional questions.

Patronage As the holder of high office and the trusted councillor of the queen, Burghley was constantly besieged by a throng of suitors, ambitious for employment under the crown, greedy for land grants, hopeful for the redress of grievance or of the great man's favourable countenance in the pursuit of their private enterprises. He had at his personal disposal a sizeable block of patronage in the offices which he controlled—his own staff as secretary, the personnel of the wards office, and, after 1572, of the treasury. Beyond that there was a vast but intangible realm in which his mere voice carried decisive weight.

Burghley's own secretarial staff was small, the wages offered modest. (His own secretaries served without pay.) They reaped their rewards in grants of land, appointment as feodaries, stewards, or to other minor but lucrative offices, or more profitably as the intermediaries for suitors, seeing that their petitions reached Burghley's desk. The treasury provided a host of such appointments in the management of royal lands scattered throughout the kingdom. Wards provided another stock of such offices, but its real importance lay in a different direction. In the course of the nearly forty years that Burghley served as master of the court, a high proportion of the landed families of England fell within its jurisdiction when ill fortune left a minor heir or heiress to the family estates. Such an occasion made them anxious suitors for control of the property and the destiny of the ward, male or female. This offered Burghley not only profit but the opportunity to cultivate the goodwill of a host of noble or gentle families in every county.

This squared with a larger but less tangible asset—his influence with the queen, his fellow councillors, and the political world at every level. Unlike Leicester, Burghley made no effort to develop an organized network of alliances and dependants, who regularly looked to him for protection and advancement. Instead he used his position to establish friendly relations with a broad range of courtiers, nobles, and gentry who came to owe him thanks for favours done.

The management of the economy Burghley's administrative responsibilities lay in the secretarial office, the court of wards and, later, the treasury. But he by no means limited his activities to these areas. His strong sense of the councillor's responsibilities for the welfare of the commonwealth, as well as practical problems such as securing adequate supplies of strategic materials or increasing customs revenue, led him to wide-ranging intervention in the regulation and stimulation of the economy. Some of this was achieved simply by welcoming and protecting refugees from religious persecution who brought with them their crafts which could be learned by English workers. Burghley supported such an exile community at Stamford. In other cases, however, he took the initiative in seeking out projectors who brought with them improved techniques of manufacture, offering them patents of monopoly, which guaranteed them sole right of production (and of profit) for a term of years. His known interest in turn led projectors to present themselves to him.

Historians argue as to how far in these activities Burghley was a convert to new bodies of thought which encouraged the pursuit of private profit as a means to securing the public good. Some see him as a practitioner of this nascent mercantilism; others insist on his rigid adherence to traditional views of a static social order. It is not easy to arrive at a solution. What is clear is that there was a generous issue of patents under his direction—thirty-one between 1558 and 1572, granted to foreign projectors who brought new manufacturing processes to England. The claimed advantage of these patents was the creation of new employment and the accumulation of new national wealth. A second consideration which much influenced Burghley was the benefit to national security in this age of profound danger.

In many cases the initiative came from the projector himself, but Burghley was active in searching out likely candidates. He worked through a group of economic advisers: officials in the treasury seconded for this purpose, London merchants, or freelance middlemen such as William Herle or Armigail Waad, men with contacts abroad. Burghley made use of these men both as contacts with likely projectors and as intermediaries who reported not only on the technical feasibility of the scheme but also on its effects on existing markets, on royal revenue, and on employment. In these matters he was meticulously careful, often withholding approval when he was not satisfied on one of these points. The introduction of woad, for instance, a commodity imported from Portugal with the encouragement of the government, aroused concerns about loss of customs revenue, labour shortage in traditional employment, and the exhaustion of the soil. Burghley sent an agent to investigate on the scene, who communicated with local JPs about the problem. He even received a treatise on the subject before finally establishing a licensing system to control the situation.

Burghley used other methods to promote change in the economy. He backed legislation to secure the transport of imports and exports in English shipping, while another act promoted the fishing industry and increased the number of seamen available to the navy. Proclamations encouraged the growth of new crops such as hemp or flax which increased tillage and employment of labour, and by securing a home-grown supply diminished imports. Considerations of national security played a major role in his actions. He had a vigorous interest (and personal investment) in mining, especially iron. Hemp and flax had naval uses; shipping and fishing had obvious importance for the same reason. Besides items directly connected with security there were other commodities, such as salt, necessary to the economy, which might be cut off in time of war. Items of a more general nature such as glass-making and new cloth-making processes were also favoured. The draining of the East Anglian fenland occupied Burghley's attention over a period of years when he was called in to mediate the quarrels between the inventor of a new pumping system and the local inhabitants.

In all these activities Burghley exhibited a characteristic pragmatism. He entertained—indeed sought out—innovative manufacturing processes or new crops which would increase employment and national wealth. But in many cases it was the domestic production of commodities vital to national defence or to the general economy which swayed his decision. Equally, if not more, important in his judgement was the effect of any project on the existing social and economic structure. Innovation was desirable to improve existing practice, but ought not to undermine an essentially unchanging order.

Councillor Burghley's role as the queen's chief minister was inextricably mixed with his concomitant role as a member of the privy council, a body which functioned as the principal executive branch of government. It had a second function, however, as the specially chosen, specially sworn, body of advisers to the only maker of decisions, the queen. When council was in this mode, Burghley's voice was one among others, respected and listened to, but challenged by his fellows. It was, certainly after the late 1560s, a collegiate body, working together smoothly. Burghley had his particular associates, such as Sussex or Mildmay, and a trusted collaborator in Walsingham.

Conciliar harmony reflected Elizabeth's strategy as a ruler in bestowing her confidence in a range of advisers, listening to all but accepting only that counsel which she chose to use. She was determined that all decisions were seen to be wholly the expression of her royal will, not reflecting the influence of any one councillor or group of councillors. This established a political order in which no one councillor could hope to monopolize the royal confidence or sway royal actions to compliance with his aims. It precluded the deadly virus of faction in which rivals sought each other's elimination.

Leicester and others had not quite learned that lesson, as the conspiracy of 1569 showed, but once the queen made clear she would not be panicked into repeating her father's behaviour in the fall of Thomas Cromwell, they fell into line. From 1570 to the early 1590s there prevailed in council an atmosphere which made possible a fluid give and take in the conduct of business, in which differences were aired but common ground found in carrying on their business. Alliances were made, unmade, and remade as the circumstance of each case obtained, thus barring the emergence of rigid factional divisions. This atmosphere prevailed even when the differences concerned the gravest matters of state.

This eased the situation when the council sat in its advisory capacity on those occasions when the queen required their explicit individual responses to her request for counsel. The decision was of course hers, their action purely advisory, so that divisions between majority and minority did not impair the body's unity. Hence Burghley found himself among minority voices on such matters as the Anjou match or the Dutch alliance without damage to his place in the inner circle of power or any diminution of his share of the royal confidence. Once the royal will was made known, even if he doubted its wisdom, he loyally accepted the responsibilities which the coming of war thrust on his shoulders. Thus he sat with Leicester,

Hatton, and Walsingham on the committee which negotiated the treaty of Nonsuch. Thomas Cecil's appointment as governor of the cautionary town of Brill was a token of his father's commitment to the war.

Burghley and parliament When parliament met a whole new set of responsibilities fell on Burghley's shoulders. As William Cecil he had sat in four parliaments before Elizabeth's accession. From 1559 on he was the crown's manager in all parliamentary business. First he had to fill the borough seats under his control. In 1559 these included Boston, Grantham, and Stamford, to which, following his establishment at Theobalds, he added St Albans. His influence weighed preponderantly in the county seats of Lincolnshire, Northamptonshire, Hertfordshire, and, late in the reign, Rutland. Beyond these he enjoyed varying degrees of influence, arising from his network of connections with nobles and gentry across the country. This led, for instance, to a collaboration in parliamentary patronage with the earl of Bedford in west-country seats. *The History of Parliament* credits him with a voice in the nomination of members varying from twelve to fourteen in the early years of the reign to twenty-six in 1584 and twenty-three two years later.

Burghley's next task was the preparation of the crown's legislative programme, framing and often shaping bills. He had been a prime promoter in the uniformity and supremacy bills of 1559, as of the Treason Acts of 1571 and the anti-recusancy measures of later years. One draft of the 1593 act is in his hand; the annotations are frequent. One regular item—usually the cause for summons—was the Subsidy Act. Now that it was no longer linked with actual hostilities, Burghley saw the necessity of giving the Commons a full account of the realm's relations with its neighbours, especially in the 1570s and thereafter. This task he delegated to his exchequer colleague Sir Walter Mildmay and later to Sir Christopher Hatton, for whom there is evidence of the treasurer's actual drafting of a key speech. As mentioned above, he himself intervened from the upper house to secure the triple subsidy of 1593. He was, in his years in the Lords, a systematic attender—as high as 91 per cent in 1576, and even in the last year of his life he was present at 66 per cent of the sittings. He was assisted in ensuring the passage of bills in the Commons and in monitoring the activities of the house by his fellow councillors, Sir Francis Knollys as floor manager in the early years of the reign and Sir Christopher Hatton in the later years.

Besides the subsidy bills and major acts of state, Burghley prepared in each session a programme of measures of his own devising, aimed at correcting a range of perceived public problems. Enactment of these measures was problematical. Pressure of time was great; the queen wanted a short session; the members pressed for time for their private bills. Moreover the queen's assent was by no means assured. In 1563 a bill proposed by Burghley for poor law funding and another for repairing Dover harbour failed to run the race, but the secretary was successful in pushing his pet measure, the establishment of a Wednesday fast day, aimed not at increased fish consumption but at increasing the pool of sailors for the navy. In 1571 he secured passage of a bill to restrict lawyers' fees only to see the queen veto it. Burghley continued to press such reform legislation until the 1580s when war measures began to pre-empt his attention.

Elizabeth's attitude towards parliament was, of course, a key element in checking its initiative; she refused to allow discussion of foreign policy, religion, or matters of state in general. Burghley was prepared to pressure the queen on matters which he saw as vital to the public interest. In the 1570s he and other privy councillors attempted to use parliament to push the queen into marriage—and, they hoped, the provision of an heir. They intended, if they failed in this purpose, to move to the succession issue. They did not succeed. Nor were they more successful in backing religious reform bills in 1571. The next year Burghley joined in an intensive campaign to secure Mary Stewart's condemnation, only to founder on a royal refusal. There was little to show for all their efforts from 1563 to 1572 other than a measure against simony and the confirmation of the Thirty-Nine Articles. They tried again in the 1580s to bring down Mary Stewart and at least succeeded in the act for Queen Elizabeth's safety of 1584–5, but in the end it was extra-parliamentary means which finally brought the Scottish queen to the block.

A continuing problem was the day-to-day management of an unwieldy Commons. Knollys and Hatton were delegated to use their authority as privy councillors, sitting on endless committees and speaking from the floor. Burghley also employed other means to keep in touch with parliamentary opinion. Such was his use of 'men of business', who served as advisers, the writers of 'white papers' on various subjects, as informants on public opinion and, of course, as active MPs on the floor of the house. They could act as spokesmen for measures which, because they were unpopular with the queen, were barred from public support by Burghley. They were especially useful in ensuring that public business was given priority. Here another device was at Burghley's disposal—appointment of the speaker, whose powers to guide legislation were considerable. He used his appointees, Robert Bell (1572) and John Puckering (1584–5 and 1586–7) to strike at Mary Stewart, taking care initially to secure them seats. When he was in the upper house he made use of the joint conference between both houses to exert his influence on the lower house. Burghley was, of course, solicited by corporate bodies, municipal, academic, or economic to advance bills they desired to pass. In 1571 he personally drafted a bill to cut a canal to the River Lea, just east of London. He took no reward for such services, but they clearly added to his political capital.

Burghley's duties did not end with the passage of a parliamentary statute or the implementation of a royal decision. The printing press was transforming English politics, its emergence coinciding with the existence of a new body of literate public opinion, deeply stirred by the politico-religious issues of the era. The opponents of the Anjou match had found a voice in Stubbs's famous pamphlet. The government now had to make its case in this and in other episodes. Burghley's talents were early employed in this new public relations world. In 1547 he had edited Katherine Parr's *The Lamentations of a Sinner*, and in Elizabeth's reign his pen was frequently in request. He had a hand in the published defence of the arrest of two of the bishops in the 1559 theological debate. In 1562 he defended in print the Newhaven expedition. Later, after the northern uprising, he wrote denying that subjects were punished for their religious beliefs. In 1585 (with Walsingham) he wrote to defend the Dutch alliance and in 1596 to explain why Elizabeth authorized the Cadiz expedition, but his most important piece was *The Execution of Justice in England* (1583), in which he masqueraded as a loyal English Catholic. This was translated into four languages—Dutch, French, Spanish, and Italian. There was in addition a clutch of unpublished pamphlets on the Scottish intervention of 1560, the bullion seizure of 1569, and other related subjects.

Burghley and religion Burghley's backing for the 1571 reform bills reflects his involvement in another large sector of public business—religion. Although Elizabeth's exercise of the supreme governorship was in her eyes a matter for herself alone, it proved impossible to maintain such a separation of function between religion and politics. Constant friction ensued and Burghley found himself very much a party in ecclesiastical issues. His personal commitment to the reformed faith was whole-hearted, but his determination to see it triumphant was conditioned by an acute awareness of the great risks involved in imposing a new religious order on a profoundly traditional society, always suspicious and fearful of change in any form. Resolved to achieve religious reform, he was equally determined to do this within the existing political and social order. It was to be a revolution but one strictly conditioned in its effects. Hence he embraced the Erastian and Henrician position in placing the institutional structure of the church and the regulation of public worship under royal control. The rejected authority of Rome must be replaced by an equally authoritative rule, that of the national monarch. The church could no more tolerate diversity of practice than the monarchy diversity of loyalties. Division within the church would be as fatal to civic order and social stability as open rebellion. A hierarchical authority descending from the supreme governor through the episcopate was essential, although the bishops' authority rested on secular rather than divine foundations. On so much sovereign and minister agreed.

They differed on two fundamentals. The queen saw her supreme governorship as an office separate from her regality. Burghley saw the two offices as blended together, with power shared between sovereign and the estates of the realm. Secondly, Elizabeth saw the clergy's duty as wholly static, enjoining obedience to the established order. For Burghley this was not enough. The people must be given popular instruction and stimulation in active piety; only a community of believers, not mere conformists, could be weaned from the old faith, rooted as it was in customs and habits. He was aware of serious defects in the ecclesiastical establishment which hindered this goal. In

practice this meant improving the quality of the clergy, making them effective and exemplary expositors of the gospel. Burghley strove to place clergy endowed with these qualities wherever he had influence. In 1566 and 1571 he backed bishops in pushing the so-called A–F bills, aimed at pluralities and simony. When the queen ordered the suppression of prophesyings, he attempted to persuade Archbishop Grindal to accept restriction to a wholly clerical audience. This conception of the church, however, ensured his hostility to reformers such as the presbyterians, who would set up a rival ecclesiastical authority against the state, or the sectaries who would turn religion into a wholly private matter. For him such views, breeding grounds of disunity, were wholly unacceptable.

Burghley played a role in the appointment of bishops in 1559, and worked closely with Archbishop Parker. He pressed Grindal's nomination to the primatial see on the queen, and tried to mediate between them when she demanded a ban on prophesyings. He backed Whitgift for Canterbury but fell out with him when the new archbishop tried to impose absolute conformity to the Book of Common Prayer and the Thirty-Nine Articles. In Burghley's view the procedures used to discipline the clergy savoured of the Spanish Inquisition. His distaste for Whitgift's policy was not shared by the queen and he was successively isolated from ecclesiastical business in the last years of the reign.

Towards the Catholics Burghley's policy was straightforward. In his personal perspective their beliefs were, in his usual terminology, 'the superstition'. In the earlier years of the reign he was content to check any hint of Catholic activity, but to turn a blind eye to private practice of the old faith. The coming of the Douai missionaries convinced him they were part of the grand Catholic crusade against England, and he vigorously promoted the body of statutes aimed at suppressing the practices of the old faith. In his *Execution of Justice in England* he defended this policy, arguing that the priests were traitors, not missionaries, and that their activities should be dealt with correspondingly.

Ireland Burghley's omnicompetence as administrator necessarily included the most intractable problem of Elizabethan government—Ireland. His interest dated from Edwardian times. He took care to inform himself with the help of maps and other materials on the state of the island, giving him a knowledge of Irish affairs far beyond that of his colleagues in council. Although his knowledge was wide and his concern was lively, however, he had no clearly defined policy. The career of Shane O'Neill in the 1560s aroused his indignation and may have toughened his views about the treatment of the Irish. He came to believe in the necessity of English colonization in the island (towards which he contributed), the adoption of English common law, and a check on the power of the great lords, Gaelic or Old English.

The low priority given Irish affairs by queen and council, plus the fiscal policy of strict economy, meant that the Irish administration was perpetually underfinanced. Burghley's early view that colonization should be self-financed gave way to a conviction that public moneys should be employed. He led the way in state intervention, personally devising the scheme for the plantation of Munster. Burghley was not without his moments of sympathy for the plight of the native Irish, but in practice he came down on the side of repression, albeit perpetually underfunded and rarely effective. He died in the midst of the Nine Years' War, an event which he had by his policy helped to provoke.

The private career Burghley's public career was paralleled by a private one, pursued with equal energy. He strove to raise the Cecils from country gentry to the élite community of the fifty-odd hereditary nobles. His own promotion came in 1571. He sought to cement the family's new status through the marriages of his children. His greatest catch was Edward de Vere, seventeenth earl of Oxford, for his daughter Anne [see Vere, Anne de], a marriage which brought nothing but misery for the couple. His other daughter, Elizabeth, married William Wentworth, eldest son of Lord Wentworth of Nettlestead. Thomas married Dorothy, daughter of the fourth Lord Latimer, and Robert *Cecil married Elizabeth, daughter of William Brooke, Lord Cobham.

The dignity of the peerage, Burghley well knew, required wealth to support it. He had begun the acquisition of land in his father's lifetime, under Edward VI. In 1549 he paid over £2000 for church lands in Lincolnshire and Northamptonshire, some of which he immediately sold. This was followed by more purchases, as well as by a number of grants from the crown. (His father was also buying lands and receiving royal grants.) With his inheritance and his own acquisitions, Burghley was already a considerable landowner before Elizabeth's accession. His appointment to the wards in January 1561 was followed by a substantial grant from the crown in May, again in his home counties of Lincolnshire, Rutland, and Northamptonshire. (Burghley was a JP in each of the parts of Lincolnshire and in Northamptonshire.)

In succeeding years grants continued, mingled with purchases and sales. In 1569 Burghley was granted land in Hertfordshire, six years after purchasing the old manor house of Theobalds at Cheshunt, and he subsequently built up his estate there. These properties had cost him £12,300 by 1583. He was also buying land in London, in Covent Garden and St Andrew's, Holborn. In 1572, in the wake of his promotion to the treasury, he had licence to buy 12,000 broad cloths and kerseys with the right to sell them, paying the city of London duty. In the same year he had another licence to export 4000 tuns of beer from London, Ipswich, and Sandwich. These rights he presumably sold to merchants. By his death Burghley had two major estates, one centred on his paternal inheritance at Stamford, the other on Theobalds, the former for Thomas, the latter for Robert. It is difficult to give a reliable figure for his total income. Stone lists him among the five wealthiest landowners in the realm, worth between £5400 and £7199 in landed income. One contemporary report at his death gave a figure of £5600, another £4000.

Wealth had to be displayed. As soon as Cecil inherited his ancestral home at Stamford, he set about improvements and additions to the house and garden which continued for the next thirty years. Having purchased Theobalds, he began a building programme which went on to 1585. Completed, Theobalds house consisted of three great courts, standing in a park 3 miles long with a circumference of 8 miles. It rivalled Longleat and Wollaton, not only in size but in architectural importance. The design was Burghley's own, and the house became a model consulted by Hatton and the builders of Audley End. Sited a convenient journey from London, it provided a venue for royal visits, eight in all, costing the host £2000–£3000 each.

Untiring in his determination to win and hold a great place in council and court, Burghley was equally determined to establish his family's position in his own home region. The estate which he built up centred on Stamford afforded not only the income necessary for a peer but also the base on which to erect a regional pre-eminence. To this end Burghley systematically accumulated local offices. He was steward and recorder of Stamford, steward of King's Lynn and Yarmouth, recorder of Boston, surveyor of royal lands in Lincolnshire, keeper of Rockingham Forest and Cliffe Park, *custos rotulorum* of Lincolnshire and Northamptonshire, and steward of numerous royal estates in the area. In the capital he was steward, escheator, bailiff, and clerk of the manor of Westminster. His local ambitions were fulfilled when he became lord lieutenant of Lincolnshire in 1587 and of Hertfordshire and Essex in the following year.

Burghley's role in these settings was by no means passive. He involved himself deeply in local business, the regulation of trade, and the provision of schools and almshouses. He arbitrated local disputes, and sat on the commission of sewers concerned with fen drainage. He was as important a figure in his own region as he was at court. All this led to competition with the established regional magnate, the earl of Lincoln. Civil relations were maintained, but by the 1590s the earl's blunders had opened the way for a Cecil lord lieutenancy. Many of these local offices were passed on to Thomas Cecil in his father's lifetime. Burghley also had interests elsewhere. He was from 1559 active chancellor of his old university, Cambridge (and steward of Trinity College lands). He served as steward to the bishoprics of Lichfield and Coventry, St David's, and Winchester.

Intellectual and cultural life Burghley's intellectual and cultural interests were shaped by his humanist education at Cambridge as well as by the need for practical knowledge demanded by his public responsibilities and a wide-ranging native curiosity. A great collector of books, he built a substantial library for his own use (unhappily no longer extant). Its core was a collection of the classical authors, Latin and Greek, many purchased from John Cheke. He continued reading in the ancient languages, and Latin (along with French) was one of the tools of his trade. Apart from the classical authors, his library contained medieval and modern works: Bede and the Anglo-Saxon Chronicle; Guicciardini; and Comines. There were also romances such as Amadis de Gaul. Besides the literary and historical works, there were books of medicine, law, mathematics, and architecture.

Burghley's special interest in history is evinced in his assistance to historians. Laurence Nowell, writing on Anglo-Saxon history, and John Clapham, writing on the Tudors, were members of his household. Grafton and Holinshed dedicated their works to him. He gave his support to William Camden in writing his history of the reign, a project which he hoped no doubt would secure his own place in posterity's retrospect of the age. Writers in the literary genre, however, found little favour from the treasurer. He showed no interest in the contemporary outpouring of poetry and drama. In fact he seems to have preferred to read continental authors. Similarly he showed no interest in music, but in practical bodies of knowledge he displayed a very active curiosity. His official interest in introducing new manufacturing techniques to England led to acquaintance with John Dee and Henry Billingsley, the translator of Euclid, both advocates of applied science.

Burghley had a particular interest in cartography and geography. He encouraged both Camden and Norden. The latter submitted his book on Kent to the treasurer's expert scrutiny. He annotated the 1579 edition of Saxton's maps and exhibited an encyclopaedic geographic knowledge, not only of England but of Europe and the overseas world. He shared the contemporary interest in astronomy and archaeology. Thomas Digges's book on the mathematics of astronomy was dedicated to him, and he studied Dee's plan to reform the calendar. Military science was another interest. He owned a French work on the art of war as well as Hood's *The Art of Shooting Great Ordonance*. Another contemporary interest which drew his attention was gardening. At all three of his houses he laid out extensive gardens. To those at Theobalds he gave special attention, importing fifty sorts of exotic seeds from Florence. John Gerard, the herbalist, advised him and chose him as patron for two learned botanical works. He gave the same care to the building of his great houses, collecting modern treatises on architecture and employing foreign craftsmen in buildings which blended English and continental styles.

Burghley had an active interest in education at different levels. He supervised very carefully the education of his two sons as well as that of the young men who fell under his control in the wards. Some of them were among the gentlemen retainers in his household, where they combined formal learning with training in aristocratic lifestyle. For their benefit and that of his sons he maintained a staff of teachers. He interested himself in a number of schools in his home region, at Stamford and in neighbouring towns, but he was not the founder of any. His role as chancellor of Cambridge University was that of an adjudicator of disputes among the academics; he showed no interest in curriculum matters. He gave a small endowment to St John's College.

The Cecils and Essex Leicester's death in September 1588 opened the final decade of Burghley's career. It removed a colleague who had been, after himself, the most conspicuous member of council. When Walsingham followed two years later (and Hatton in 1591), the treasurer enjoyed an eminence such as he had not known since the first years of the reign. The queen made no move to fill the vacant secretaryship; Burghley himself took over most of the work, assisted by his younger son, Robert, whose advancement to that office was his father's goal. Robert made a step forward with his promotion to privy councillor in 1591. Father and son were now assailed as makers of a *regnum Cecilianum*, a monopoly of favour and patronage.

The 1590s, sometimes referred to as Elizabeth's 'second reign', saw radical change, both in the climate and in the nature of high politics, and consequently in Burghley's role in that world. The court came to be faction ridden, one grouped around the Cecils, father and son; the other centred on Robert Devereux, second earl of Essex. In the latter Burghley faced for the first time a direct challenger for power. The earl set out to displace the treasurer's pre-eminent place in the royal confidence. The struggle for power involved not so much Burghley, whose imminent demise Essex took for granted, as the career of his son. The father's overriding ambition was that Robert Cecil should step into his shoes, in office as well as in the royal confidence. Essex, however, sought not only power but a radical reorientation of English foreign policy. He wanted to replace the defensive strategy of the Cecils with an aggressive stance which substituted outright victory for mere survival, a victory from which England would emerge as a leading European power and in which Essex would achieve martial glory.

Essex was brought to the queen's attention by his stepfather Leicester who surrendered to him the mastership of the horse. Burghley had been one of the young earl's guardians in his minority and relations between them were affable. Essex's ambitions were military and the treasurer, anxious that England support the new French king, Henri IV, promoted his appointment as commander of the English forces in Normandy in 1591. On his return Essex shifted activities to the court, realizing it was there that he would have to fight to achieve his ambitions. This put him in direct competition with Robert Cecil, privy councillor since 1591 and candidate for the vacant secretaryship, the duties of which he was already largely performing. The earl realized his first goal with promotion to the privy council in 1593. During these years and up to 1596, each side strove to avoid head-on collision, working together where possible, veiling their rivalry, and avoiding the widening of faction. They were initially in agreement on support for the French king; and on the most conspicuous case of patronage, Essex's sponsorship of Francis Bacon for the attorneyship, Cecil went out of his way to offer a compromise, which Essex refused.

When Henri IV's position became stabilized, Burghley pressed for withdrawal of English forces from France and their dispatch to Ireland. He won Elizabeth's agreement to this move, much to Essex's disappointment. The earl had hoped for an active alliance against Spain. He recovered ground when the threat of another Spanish assault on England compelled pre-emptive action and he was made joint commander, with Lord Admiral Nottingham, of the Cadiz expedition. He hoped to force the queen's hand by garrisoning Cadiz and establishing a base on the Spanish coast, thereby engaging her in an offensive war against Spain. He announced this plan to the queen and council in a letter delivered after his departure. A short time thereafter Elizabeth appointed Robert Cecil secretary, to the earl's fury.

Thrown on the defensive, Essex made one more bid for another assault which he hoped would swing the pendulum to continued war against Spain, a situation which would make him indispensable to Elizabeth. His failure in the Azores expedition weakened his position and led him to the bullying tactics which eventually poisoned his relationship with Elizabeth. By the time of Burghley's death in 1598, the balance was swinging decisively in the Cecils' favour. In the very month of his death, there occurred the famous council scene where the queen boxed Essex's ears, the first stage of his downfall. Burghley's last ambition had been fulfilled.

By contrast, Burghley's last years were personally unhappy. He greatly missed his wife, who died on 5 April 1589. Both his daughters predeceased him, Elizabeth childless and Anne, countess of Oxford, after a wretchedly unhappy marriage, leaving three daughters. His own health steadily worsened as the gout took hold. He died at his Westminster house on 4 August 1598 and was buried at St Martin's Church, Stamford Baron, Lincolnshire.

Perspective It is not easy to obtain a perspective on William Cecil's career. It would be tempting to fit him into a category of great ministers who served the early modern state-building process. Wolsey and Thomas Cromwell are obvious English examples, Richelieu and Olivares continental ones, but there were deep differences between them. The two English ministers were employed simply to implement the ambitions of their wilful master; the continental examples, servants in name, were masters in effect of their feeble sovereigns.

Burghley's career was shaped by the character of the royal lady he served. Elizabeth knew that the awesome power resident in the crown was visibly diminished when its wearer was a woman who was accordingly expected to rely on male guidance in her actions. From the first days of her reign she set out to quash those expectations, to make it clear that she alone was the maker of decisions. Yet Elizabeth was very different from her father. Henry had clearly defined ambitions, albeit fitfully pursued, and his servants' task was to fulfil them. His daughter, on the other hand, entertained no such programme for action. A pragmatist to the core, she waited on events, responding slowly and hesitantly, forever delaying and often reversing decisions. Uncertain as to action, she asked for and listened to councillors' advice, advice which she might or might not take.

Burghley's personality was an effective foil to that of his temperamental mistress: the clear-headed statesman, certain as to his long-term goals, but in any particular decision forced upon him by events, a pragmatist who before acting made a rigorous accounting of the advantages and disadvantages of any particular line of action. Acutely aware of England's weakness *vis-à-vis* her continental neighbours, he was cautious to a degree, yet prepared to take action—or risks—when he was convinced there was no other choice.

These two different personalities co-operated in a state of permanent but productive friction. Underlying the queen's exasperating indecision and her spurts of raw anger was a basic trust in the minister's judgement and an agreement on fundamentals. Burghley on his side never forgot his obligation of obedience to his sovereign, whatever reservations he may have entertained as to her particular actions. At the beginning of the reign he shared some of his contemporaries' doubts about female rule, but he soon came to have respect for Elizabeth's political acumen and sound judgement, even if his patience with her behaviour was sorely tried. Some of his exasperation comes through in private correspondence, even in threats of retirement. On one subject he was harsh in his judgement of his sovereign: her refusal to marry. In this cardinal neglect of the duty of her office she left at risk for decades the lives and fortunes of her subjects. Even as late as the last years of the 1570s Burghley clung to the hope of marriage—and an heir.

Beneath the frictions and frustrations of day-to-day dealings, subject and sovereign shared similar dispositions and similar responses to the flowing tide of events. Although in 1559–60 Cecil manoeuvred the queen into an action which she resisted, in the following years he found her responsive to his initiatives in foreign policy. From the 1570s onwards they both shared a deep unease in the face of the Dutch revolt. Equally apprehensive of either a Spanish or a French triumph, they shrank from the prospect of English armed intervention. They desperately sought some mediating solution which would turn the clock back to the 1550s while freezing out French involvement. Both reluctantly accepted the necessity of war in 1585. Both hoped to limit the English commitment to the bare necessities of defence.

Elizabeth's courtships posed an awkward problem for Burghley. On the one hand he desperately longed for the hoped-for heir, while on the other he deeply distrusted a dependence on foreign allies. The Anjou connection was acceptable to him only if bonded by the indissoluble marital tie. In the end he had to live with the acute worry of an unsettled succession to his dying day although he may have been cheered by the prospect of a British union.

From the beginning of the reign Cecil had a clear set of aims. At home he promoted the new religious settlement while preserving national unity under the strain of unwonted change which that settlement entailed. Within the British Isles he pressed for an Anglo-Scottish alliance, built on the common faith, a solid front against alien intrusion. On the continent he was willing to give encouragement, modest support, even money to foreign protestants in order to distract Catholic rulers from pursuing any designs against England. But he prepared to send soldiers only when the move was absolutely necessary to protect English interests.

All of Burghley's programme was informed by a profound sense of the vulnerability both of the regime and of the realm itself. The establishment of the new religious order was the work of a minority. How the community at large would respond, how far the old order would find spokesmen were constant concerns, especially with the example of the disorders of France and the Low Countries set before them. The English decision to opt for the reformed faith had driven a deep ideological gulf between the island kingdom and her continental neighbours. Would this create an orthodox hostility so intense that it could be purged only by the destruction of this heretic society? Burghley soon arrived at a deep conviction that a Catholic crusade against the heretic nation under papal inspiration was the ultimate goal of the Catholic powers. It informed all his thinking about relations with the world outside the realm. Yet, although uncompromising in his religious faith and contemptuously dismissive of what he termed the 'superstition', he was a pragmatist willing to sup with the devil provided the spoon was long enough, hence his willingness to support the queen's marriage with a Catholic husband. In these attitudes he was often divided from his more rigid colleagues whose world was starkly black and white. It also separated him from his sovereign lady's unwillingness to face the unpleasant realities of England's vulnerability.

On his deathbed Burghley had cause for satisfaction. His public goals were largely realized. The succession problem which had so long filled his thoughts was fading away as the English looked north; its solution would bring the added bonus of a British union, one of Burghley's key goals. The religious settlement was well grounded in the social consciousness and in the habits of Englishmen while the threat of a Catholic revival had steadily declined. On the continent, Dutch success and Henri IV's establishment in power wiped out the threat of a Catholic coalition against England, the spectre which had haunted Burghley. England's half-century of acute vulnerability was visibly drawing to a close by 1598.

Similarly Burghley's private ambitions were satisfied. His son Robert, ensconced in the secretary's office, was in a fair way to succeed to his father's eminence on the public stage. He left behind an estate large enough to support both sons in the premier rank of the landed aristocracy. From the standpoint of the twenty-first century, Burghley commands attention as the sixteenth-century English statesman who envisioned a changing English polity, one which moved away from the dynastic order of the early Tudor world, governed by the ambitions of the monarch for himself and his house, to a burgeoning perception of the public nature of the monarchy in which exercise of the executive will must be governed by calculations of public—of national—interest. Burghley has a rightful claim to a place among the architects and builders of the early-modern British nation state.

WALLACE T. MacCAFFREY

Sources *Elizabeth of England*, ed. E. P. Read and C. Read (1951) · *A collection of state papers ... left by William Cecill, Lord Burghley*, ed. S. Haynes, 1 (1740) · *Calendar of the manuscripts of the most hon. the marquis of Salisbury*, 24 vols., HMC, 9 (1883–1976) · M. Hickes, *The 'Anonymous life' of William Cecil, Lord Burghley*, ed. A. G. R. Smith (1990) · R. Naunton, *Fragmenta regalia* (1641) · W. Camden, *Annales: the true and royall history of the famous Empresse Elizabeth*, trans. A. Darcie (1625) · W. Camden, *Annales, or, The historie of the most renowned and victorious Princesse Elizabeth*, trans. R. N. [R. Norton], 3rd edn (1635) · C. Read, *Mr Secretary Cecil and Queen Elizabeth* (1955) · C. Read, *Lord Burghley and Queen Elizabeth* (1960) · B. W. Beckingsale, *Burghley: Tudor statesman* (1967) · M. A. R. Graves, *Burghley* (1998) · S. Alford, *The early Elizabethan polity* (1998) · HoP, *Commons, 1558–1603*

Archives BL, corresp., Stowe MSS · BL, corresp. and papers, Add. MSS 5754, 5843 · BL, corresp. and papers, Harley MSS · BL, corresp. and papers, Lansdowne MSS 1–22 · BL, corresp. and papers, Sloane MSS · BL, memorandum book, Royal MSS · Bodl. Oxf., corresp., Rawl. MS Lett 88 · Burghley House, Lincolnshire, letters, papers, private journal · CKS, letters and papers · GL · Hatfield House, Hertfordshire, diaries, memoranda, journal, etc. · Magd. Cam., corresp. | Arundel Castle, West Sussex, corresp. with earl of Shrewsbury · BL, letters to Sir Julius Caesar, Add. MSS 12497, 12505–12507 · BL, letters to Sir Christopher Hatton and William Davison, Egerton MS 2124 · BL, corresp. with Sir Ralph Sadleir, Add. MSS 33591–33594 · BL, corresp. with Sir Nicholas Throckmorton, etc., Add. MSS 35830–35831, 35837 · CUL, corresp. relating to Cambridge University · CUL, letters to Robert Cecil · Folger, letters to Richard Bagot · GL, letters to Peter Osborne · Hunt. L., Egerton MSS, corresp. with Lord Ellesmere · Lincs. Arch., corresp. with Lord Willoughby · Longleat House, Warminster, letters · LPL, corresp. with earls of Shrewsbury; corresp. with Archbishop Whitgift; letters · Sheff. Arch., corresp. with Archbishop of Canterbury, Walsingham, the Council, etc. [copies] · Staffs. RO, official corresp. with Sir John Leveson regarding Kent

Likenesses by or after A. van Brounckhorst, oils on panel, 1560?–1569, NPG · oils on panel, after 1572, NPG · oils on panel, after 1572, NPG · three portraits, oils on panel, after 1585, NPG · oils, 1590–99, NPG · G. Vertue, group portrait, line engraving, pubd 1747 (*A view of the court of wards and liveries, with the officers, servants, and other persons there assembled*), NPG · oils, Bodl. Oxf. [*see illus.*]

Cecil, William, sixteenth Baron Ros (1590–1618), courtier and ambassador, was born in May 1590 and baptized the following month, on 4 June, at Newark Castle, Nottinghamshire. He was the eldest son of William Cecil (1566–1640), Lord Burghley from 1605 until he succeeded as second earl of Exeter in 1623, and his wife, Lady Elizabeth Manners (1576–1591), only child of Edward *Manners, third earl of Rutland (1549–1587), from whom she inherited, *suo juro*, the barony of Ros. When his mother died in May 1591, William succeeded to the Ros title. His claim was challenged by his cousin Francis *Manners, sixth earl of Rutland, in 1616 on the grounds that the barony should not have descended in the female line, but the earl marshal's court adjudicated the dispute almost completely in Ros's favour.

At the age of fifteen Ros was granted a licence to travel abroad, and for the next decade he wandered Europe. From 1605 to 1607 he was in France, where he was presented to Henri IV and entertained by members of the French nobility, eager to honour the great-nephew of Robert *Cecil, earl of Salisbury and chief minister of James I. In 1606 Ros fell in love with the widow of a Huguenot nobleman; he wrote to his great-uncle for assistance and permission to pursue the match, but the affair came to nothing. Late in 1607 Ros left France for Italy—travelling with a tutor, John Mole, and with William Paulet, Lord St John, and his tutor as companions. In 1608 Ros decided to visit Rome. Both Mole and the English ambassador in Venice, Sir Henry Wotton, tried to dissuade him from making the potentially hazardous journey: his close tie to Robert Cecil, thought Wotton, made Ros a tempting target for Catholic intrigue. But Ros insisted, and the party arrived in Rome in the autumn of 1608. Almost immediately Mole, whose works included conventional anti-Catholic polemics, was arrested by the Roman Inquisition; he remained a prisoner for the next thirty years. Ros, however, left Rome safely and by November 1608 was in Venice, where he remained for several months. Early in 1610 he settled in Madrid, intending a year-long stay to learn the language, but at Robert Cecil's insistence he cut short his Spanish sojourn and was in France and the Low Countries in the winter and spring of 1611. A year later he was headed east, bearing James I's letters of congratulation to the newly elected Emperor Matthias. In August 1612 he arrived in Venice from Augsburg, and remained in Italy for three years before beginning his journey home, arriving back in England in the late spring of 1615.

Ros had spent a decade abroad, much of it in Italy and other Catholic countries. Not surprisingly, it was widely rumoured that he had converted. Wotton believed that the Inquisition had arrested Mole in hopes of converting the unprotected Ros, and when Dudley Carleton welcomed Ros to a protestant Christmas service in Venice in 1613 he was glad to note the young man's apparent religious soundness: the Catholics, Carleton noted, had been mistaken when they claimed Ros as one of their own. The actual state of Ros's religious sensibilities is difficult to discern. He returned to England still a protestant, at least outwardly, but with a distinct sympathy for the Spanish and Italian worlds, a Spanish servant, Diego de Silva, and friendships with Catholic or crypto-Catholic English travellers like the earl of Arundel and Tobie Matthew. He had also acquired one other Italian passion shared by Arundel—a connoisseur's interest in art: on his travels he accumulated a collection of classical sculpture, which he later gave to the earl.

On 12 February 1616 Ros married Anne Lake [see Cecil, Anne, Lady Ros], daughter of Sir Thomas *Lake, secretary of state. Two months later he was selected as an ambassador-extraordinary to Spain, charged with giving Philip III congratulations from James I on a marriage treaty with France. The planned embassy aroused widespread speculation. Many believed that Ros had been secretly charged to negotiate a marriage between the infanta of Spain and Prince Charles, and much was made of the great sums Ros spent to equip the embassy with the appropriate splendour. When Ros finally set sail in November 1616, however, he was specifically ordered not to meddle in marriage negotiations. He was instructed only to offer the king of Spain formal congratulations, and to urge him to desist from harassing the duchy of Savoy, whose interests James I had sworn to protect.

Ros left behind not only a great deal of diplomatic speculation but also a familial dispute that soon evolved into one of the tawdrier scandals of the Jacobean age. His marriage to Anne Lake had begun badly, apparently for both sexual and financial reasons. In the months before he left for Spain, Ros had been pressed by Sir Thomas and Lady Lake to sign over to his wife and her heirs the lucrative manor of Walthamstow and to pawn other lands to Lake in order to raise cash for the embassy. It seems that the Lakes forced Ros to agree to these financial arrangements through a combination of political pressure from Sir Thomas and more personal threats from Lady Lake and Lady Ros: according to John Chamberlain, Lady Ros and her mother blackmailed Ros by threatening to reveal that he was sexually impotent, a charge that could have led to a humiliating nullification of the marriage.

Ros returned from Spain in the spring of 1617 to a lukewarm royal reception and continued familial stress. In May 1617 he attempted to take his wife from her parents' house, an escapade that ended in a brawl during which a number of servants were hurt. Ros threatened to sue the Lakes for riot, but instead, in August 1617, he secretly fled the country, leaving behind a poorly written challenge to his brother-in-law, Arthur Lake. Some thought Ros had travelled to the continent to conduct the duel, while others speculated that he was fleeing his debts, many of them resulting from his Spanish embassy. Pursued by royal orders to return, Ros made his way to Italy, reaching Rome in November. His grandfather Thomas *Cecil, earl of Exeter, angrily accused the Spanish ambassador of facilitating Ros's flight, with the implication that the distressed aristocrat had been seduced to Catholicism.

Meanwhile, the dispute with the Lakes was escalating. Exeter and his much younger second wife, Frances [see Cecil, Frances, countess of Exeter], who had opposed the dealings over Walthamstow, intervened to protect Ros's financial interests. The Lakes responded by publicly accusing the countess of Exeter of conducting an incestuous affair with her step-grandson and then attempting to poison the aggrieved Lady Ros. The earl and countess appealed to the king and in 1618 brought suit against the Lakes in Star Chamber. From Italy Ros wrote to James, vigorously defending the countess's honour, apologizing for his flight, and confessing the mounting despair that had made him run. But at the end of June 1618, in Naples, he suddenly fell ill, and died on the 27th. Rumours of poison were rife—some implicated the Lakes, some Diego de Silva, some a group of unnamed Catholic companions. Archbishop Abbot reported that Ros had become 'very popish' in Rome and Naples, had shared a house with two friars, and received absolution on his death bed from a Jesuit (*Downshire MSS*, 6.559–60). The terms of Ros's will remained unclear, causing further friction between the earl of Exeter and the Lakes. English agents reported that Ros had left his property to his servant, Don Diego, and when the Spaniard was summoned to England to explain the circumstances of his master's death he was intercepted on the way by instructions to return immediately to Spain.

Contemporaries did not think highly of Ros. The Venetian ambassador, who found Ros 'by education and habit … entirely Spanish', judged him 'very light brained' (*CSP Venice, 1615–17*, 328); Henry Wotton blamed him for Mole's imprisonment; others thought his childish challenge to Arthur Lake an indication of his unfitness for serious responsibilities. Historians have dismissed him as shallow, vicious, even depraved. Yet much of his life—especially the circumstances of his relationship with Anne Lake—remains a mystery. Fittingly, five years after his death, a rumour circulated that Ros was still alive, and his father, who 'was best acquainted with his humours and tricks', believed it (*Letters of John Chamberlain*, 2.483).

ALASTAIR BELLANY

Sources GEC, *Peerage*, new edn, 9.108–11 · *Calendar of the manuscripts of the most hon. the marquis of Salisbury*, 24 vols., HMC, 9 (1883–1976), vol. 17, p. 564; vol. 18, pp. 130, 157–8; vol. 19, p. 283; vol. 22, pp. 61–76 · *The letters of John Chamberlain*, ed. N. E. McClure, 2 vols. (1939), vol. 1, pp. 233, 360; vol. 2, pp. 26–7, 35–6, 53, 80, 92–3, 120, 124, 128, 132, 152, 153–4, 192–3, 483 · *CSP dom., 1611–18*, 13, 16, 18, 28, 137, 381–2, 386–7, 411, 481, 482, 488, 542–3, 567, 596, 601 · *Report on the manuscripts of the marquis of Downshire*, 6 vols. in 7, HMC, 75 (1924–95), vol. 5, pp. 414, 487, 547; vol. 6, pp. 40, 113, 146, 258, 268–9, 292, 333, 350, 405, 419, 460, 559–60, 590, 625–6 · *The life and letters of Sir Henry Wotton*, ed. L. P. Smith, 2 vols. (1907), vol. 1, pp. 428–9, 440–41, 456–7; vol. 2, pp. 126–7, 473 · *Dudley Carleton to John Chamberlain, 1603–1624: Jacobean letters*, ed. M. Lee (1972), 132, 134, 154–5 · *APC, 1616–17*, 327, 400–01 · A. J. Loomie, ed., *Spain and the Jacobean Catholics* · *Report on the manuscripts of Lord De L'Isle and Dudley*, 6 vols., HMC, 77 (1925–66), vol. 5, pp. 292–3 · *Memorials of affairs of state in the reigns of Q. Elizabeth and K. James I, collected (chiefly) from the original papers of … Sir Ralph Winwood*, ed. E. Sawyer, 3 vols. (1725), vol. 3, pp. 103–4, 384 · S. R. Gardiner, *History of England from the accession of James I*, 10 vols. (1899–1901), vol. 3, pp. 189–94 · J. Le Neve, *Monumenta Anglicana*, 5 vols. (1717–19), vol. 1, p. 128 [1719] · *IGI*

Cecil, William, second earl of Salisbury (1591–1668), politician, was born in Westminster on 28 March 1591 and baptized on 11 April at St Clement Danes. He was the only son of Robert *Cecil, first earl of Salisbury (1563–1612), and his wife, Elizabeth (1563–1597), daughter of William Brooke, tenth Baron Cobham. His mother died when William was six years old and he and his only sister, Frances, were placed in the care of their aunt, Lady Frances Stourton, while their father attended to the boy's education. William attended Sherborne School and matriculated as a fellow-commoner in 1602 from St John's College, Cambridge, Sir Robert's former college.

Cecil inherited the title of Viscount Cranborne upon the creation of his father as first earl of Salisbury in 1605. In 1608 he was sent to France, but brought home to marry Catharine (d. 1673), daughter of Thomas Howard, first earl of Suffolk, on 1 December that year. He then returned to France, his father insisting that he should reside abroad for two years. However, in the arrangements made for the investiture of Henry, James I's eldest son, as prince of Wales, Salisbury, now lord treasurer, saw an opportunity for Cranborne to win royal favour and he was summoned home to share the privilege of holding the king's train at the ceremony on 4 June 1610. He then resumed his tour and travelled to Venice. He fell ill of a fever at Padua, left

Italy, and arrived in England resolved never to go abroad again.

Becoming second earl of Salisbury upon his father's death in 1612, the death of the prince of Wales in the same year left the new earl to his own resources. He became lord lieutenant of Hertfordshire in 1612 and his punctilious implementation of orders from the privy council impressed the king, who made him a knight of the Garter in 1624. Charles I was equally well disposed towards Salisbury and made him a privy councillor in 1626. During the period of Charles's personal rule Salisbury conformed. He was disappointed at being denied the mastership of the court of wards, but his ambitions were partially satisfied with the captaincy of the band of the king's gentlemen pensioners in 1635. Until 1639 he employed much of his time in improving his estates. He also made Hatfield House a centre of taste and culture, patronizing the painters George Geldrop and Peter Lely, the musicians Henry Oxford and Nicholas Lanier, and the gardener John Tradescant the elder.

In 1633 Salisbury accompanied Charles to his coronation in Edinburgh and became a member of the council of Scotland. But the king's failure to impose his ecclesiastical policy on Scotland and the tension between him and the English parliament in 1640 forced the earl to reconsider his position. He gradually inclined to the moderate party in the Lords while supporting the Commons in the removal of the instruments of arbitrary government. Since he did not commit himself unreservedly to any party he earned a reputation for political inconsistency, and had to confront the hazards of non-alignment when war broke out in 1642. While Hatfield was saved from depredation, the estate at Cranborne in Dorset suffered much damage. Salisbury's reaction at the end of hostilities was to seek security wherever it could be found. The House of Lords could offer none, since the victorious army was determined to suppress it. But that did not prevent Salisbury from acting as a member of the commission charged with negotiating an agreement with Charles in the Isle of Wight in 1648. When that failed he refused to approve the king's trial and execution.

With the disappearance of the old order Salisbury decided to support the republic. He found no difficulty in signing the engagement drawn up by parliament which bound him to be faithful to a Commonwealth without king and House of Lords. That two of his sons had fought for parliament may have played a part in this transfer of loyalty. He may also have been influenced by the favour shown by parliament to his friend, Philip Herbert, fourth earl of Pembroke, when it voted that he should be indemnified for his losses in the war. Many of his closest friends among the nobility, notably Algernon Percy, tenth earl of Northumberland, Salisbury's son-in-law, had declared for parliament, and this again may have encouraged him to join the new regime. He became a member of the council of state from 1649 to 1651, and its president for a while, and entered the Rump Parliament as MP for King's Lynn. The protectorate, however, led to a change in the official attitude towards him, and by 1656 he was ousted from public activities, being excluded from Oliver Cromwell's second parliament, though elected for Hertfordshire. Salisbury retired to Hatfield where he died on 3 December 1668, but not before Charles II had appointed him high steward of St Albans in 1663. He was succeeded in the earldom by his grandson James *Cecil (d. 1683), his eldest son, Charles, having died in December 1660.

G. D. OWEN, rev.

Sources *Calendar of the manuscripts of the most hon. the marquess of Salisbury*, 22, HMC, 9 (1971) · GEC, *Peerage* · L. Stone, *Family and fortune* (1973) · IGI · Venn, *Alum. Cant.*
Archives Hatfield House, Hertfordshire, corresp. and papers | Hants. RO, estate corresp. with Henry Sherfield and others

Cecil, William (1676–1745), Jacobite conspirator and agent, was born in December 1676 at Wakefield, the only son of John Cecil, of Northgate Hall in the West Riding of Yorkshire, and Anne Ogelthorpe (d. 1718). He was not, as has previously been suggested, a 'younger son of the family of the earl of Salisbury' (Jones, 159), a confusion which arose because of his later close friendship with Charles Boyle, fourth earl of Orrery, who married Lady Elizabeth Cecil, sister of John, the sixth earl of Exeter, of whom William Cecil was once thought to be a brother. He was in fact a descendant of a different branch of the Cecil family, his father being 'a near Relation of the Right Honourable the Earl of Salisbury' and 'lineally descended from Lord Burleigh, Earl of Exeter' (monument inscription in the Westbrook chapel, Church of St Peter and St Paul, Godalming, Surrey, quoted in Bott, appx 1, 42).

Details of Cecil's education and youth remain sketchy, although his murder of his landlord (for which he escaped sentence) suggests a somewhat rash individual. In 1702 he was commissioned cornet of the Royal regiment of dragoons and became ensign in Lord Mohun's regiment of foot later that year. The origin of his friendship with Orrery remains unclear; however, it was the earl's intercession which gained Cecil a captain's commission in his regiment in 1707, with which he saw action in Flanders during 1708–9 and was wounded at Malplaquet. Acquaintances afterwards lamented how Cecil was 'sadly mawled' and that 'his arme was all shattered to peeces' (Cartwright, 544–5). Elevated to colonel in 1712, he assisted Orrery in suppressing a mutiny involving the largely British garrison at Bruges, where Cecil presided over courts martial. Appointed major of Grant's regiment, Cecil was active in Scotland during the Jacobite rising of 1715 and thereafter subsisted on half pay and a small salary as an equerry to George I. He retained the appointment, which has wrongly been cited as the origins of his Jacobitism, until 1727.

Exactly when Cecil followed Orrery's example and embraced Jacobitism is unclear, though the earl's trip to Paris in 1720 to solicit support from the French court may provide early evidence of Cecil's involvement in a pro-Jacobite network which may also have included the British ambassador to Paris, Sir Robert Sutton. By mid-decade Cecil had assumed an important role in the communication of Orrery's correspondence with the Jacobite court in Rome, and first appears in the Stuart papers in 1724 when the earl endorsed his reliability. During Orrery's second visit to France in 1725 Cecil began his own correspondence with Rome, through which he emerged as a co-adviser on Jacobite affairs. By 1730 the Pretender wrote to Cecil directly. On Orrery's death in 1731 Cecil inherited *de facto* control of English Jacobite affairs, continuing negotiations for the Cornbury plot and maintaining links to the Boyle family through his less intimate, though still considerable, friendship with John, fifth earl of Cork and Orrery.

However, Cecil's record during the 1730s was one of incompetence and mismanagement. Despite clear instructions from Rome, he resisted efforts to encourage collaboration between Jacobite politicians and whigs opposed to the prime minister, Robert Walpole. In 1740 he very narrowly escaped arrest when he ignored contrary warnings and passed on a treasonous note to the duke of Argyll, which Argyll in turn presented to George II. There is no better evidence of Cecil's naïvety than his ongoing attempts to secure the defection of Walpole himself, despite the Pretender's repeated admonitions. For his part Cecil continued to discuss highly sensitive matters with the prime minister and was described by Walpole as his chief informant. By 1743 one Jacobite MP insisted on the exclusion from any new schemes of a man whom Lord Barrymore later described as 'not a traitor but a fool' (Cruickshanks, *Political Untouchables*, 39).

Cecil was arrested at his house on Masham Street, London, on 24 February 1744 on the charge of high treason. One possible explanation for his apprehension was the appearance of the Pretender's son, Charles Edward Stuart, in Paris. An inventory of Cecil's confiscated papers revealed ciphers and documents which incorrectly identified him as the Jacobite secretary of state and connected him with a request for a 16,000-strong French invasion force. After a privy council examination, Cecil was committed to the Tower on 27 February 1744 for having solicited men to join a rebellion. Disgraced, embarrassed, and in declining health, he was bailed for £4000 and several sureties on 11 May, ironically escaping a trial owing to his earlier collusion with Walpole. He was stripped of his half-pay status and spent his remaining months a penurious invalid. He died in the parish of St John, Westminster, on 9 December 1745 and was buried at St Peter's and St Paul's, Godalming, probably on the instruction of members of the Ogelthorpe family, to which he was related through his mother. His little remaining property was bequeathed to his attendant, Richard Clarkson.

LAWRENCE B. SMITH

Sources Royal Arch., Stuart papers · C. Dalton, ed., *George the First's army, 1714–1727*, 2 (1912) · J. J. Cartwright, ed., *The Wentworth papers, 1705–1739* (1885) · W. King, *Political and literary anecdotes of his own times*, 2nd edn (1818) · E. Cruickshanks, *Political untouchables: the tories and the '45* (1979) · A. Bott, *A guide to the parish church of Saint Peter and Saint Paul, Godalming*, 2nd edn (1987) · G. H. Jones, *The main stream of Jacobitism* (1954) · *Reports on the manuscripts of the earl of Eglinton*, HMC, 10 (1885) · C. Dalton, ed., *English army lists and commission registers, 1661–1714*, 6 vols. (1892–1904) · HoP, *Commons, 1715–54* · O. Manning and W. Bray, *History and antiquities of the county of Surrey*, 4 vols. (1804–14) · L. B. Smith, 'Charles Boyle, 4th earl of

Orrery, 1674–1731', PhD diss., U. Edin., 1994 · *GM*, 1st ser., 15 (1745) · Cobbett, *Parl. hist.*, vol. 13 · *Report on the manuscripts of the earl of Egmont*, 2 vols. in 3, HMC, 63 (1905–9) · countess of Cork and Orrery [E. C. Boyle], ed., *The Orrery papers*, 2 vols. (1903) · 'A copy of Charles earl of Orrery's marriage settlement with the Lady Elizabeth Cecil, anno 1705', Bisbrooke Hall, Leicestershire, MSS in the possession of Robert Boyle, esq. · *The official diary of Lieutenant General Adam Williamson: deputy lieutenant of the Tower of London, 1722–1747*, ed. J. C. Fox (1912) · E. Cruickshanks, 'The Ogelthorpes: a Jacobite family, 1689–1760', *Royal Stuart Papers*, 45 (1995) · will, PRO, PROB 11/646, sig. 236 [Charles Boyle, fourth earl of Orrery] · N. Luttrell, *A brief historical relation of state affairs from September 1678 to April 1714*, 6 vols. (1857)

Archives Royal Arch., Stuart papers

Cecilia. *See* Cecily, Viscountess Welles (1469–1507).

Cecill, Thomas (*fl. c.*1625–1640), engraver and draughtsman, was influenced by Dutch and Flemish engravers active in London; according to A. M. Hind he was stylistically close to the de Passe brothers. Cecill was much admired by his contemporaries, notably by John Evelyn, but his works were considered stiff and wanting in taste by nineteenth-century connoisseurs such as Samuel Redgrave. He engraved portraits of historical figures, courtiers, and clerics, often after his own drawings: among them are the full-length portrait of *Queen Elizabeth on Horseback*, a rare portrait of *Sir John Burgh Killed at the Isle de Rhé*, later reworked as *Gustavus Adolphus*, and the small full-length portrait of Charles I's court jester, *Archibald Armstrong*. He also engraved a number of often emblematical title-pages, including a frontispiece to Francis Bacon's *Sylva sylvarum* (1630), and one for a broadside, *A New Yeares Gift for Shrewes*.   ANNE PUETZ

Sources A. M. Hind, *Engraving in England in the sixteenth and seventeenth centuries*, 3, ed. M. Corbett and M. Norton (1964), 31–47 · S. Jenkins, 'Cecill, Thomas', *The dictionary of art*, ed. J. Turner (1996) · Bryan, *Painters* · *Engraved Brit. ports.*, 2.129, 150; 6.588 · Redgrave, *Artists* · J. F. Waller, ed., *The imperial dictionary of universal biography*, 3 vols. (1857–63) · H. Walpole, ed., *A catalogue of engravers, who have been born, or resided in England*, 2nd edn (1765) · H. Walpole, *Anecdotes of painting in England: with some account of the principal artists*, ed. R. N. Wornum, new edn, 3 (1849), 875 · [K. H. von Heinecken], *Dictionnaire des artistes dont nous avons des estampes*, 4 vols. (Leipzig, 1778–90) · Bénézit, *Dict.*

Cecily [Cicely; *née* Cecily Neville], **duchess of York** (1415–1495), Yorkist matriarch, was born on 3 May 1415, eighteenth child of Ralph *Neville, first earl of Westmorland (*c.*1364–1425), and the tenth from his second marriage, to Joan *Beaufort (*d.* 1440). Some time before 18 October 1424 she was betrothed to *Richard, duke of York, Neville's ward, and they married shortly before October 1429. This was one among what has been described as 'the most amazing series of child marriages in English history' (Lander, 121), designed to forge a network of aristocratic alliances. Between 1439 and 1452 Cecily gave birth to twelve children, of whom only six survived infancy. The first, Anne, and the last, the future *Richard III, were born at Fotheringhay Castle, Northamptonshire, which appears to have been her favourite residence. Another daughter, *Margaret, duchess of Burgundy, may also have been born there. Edward of March (later *Edward IV) and Edmund of Rutland were born at Rouen, while their father was governor of France, John at Westminster, and *George, future duke of Clarence, at Dublin, while Duke Richard was lieutenant of Ireland. In 1441 her husband made provision for her, granting her Marshwood, Dorset, Bisley, Gloucestershire, and Pirbright, Surrey, and nine properties in East Anglia; this was probably part of a more comprehensive settlement. On Richard's attainder in 1459 manors worth 1000 marks p.a. were assigned to her, and in June 1461 Edward IV granted her property worth 5000 marks p.a. in recompense for her jointure lands, and probably also gave her an annuity of £107 17s. 4d. In 1486 Henry VII ordered the payment of arrears, and also renewed her licence to export 250½ sacks of wool. Thus, throughout the political vicissitudes in which Cecily's husband and sons were the central figures, her financial security was guaranteed.

As the crisis developed in the 1450s, the fragility of the great marriage network became apparent. Even Cecily's brother, Richard *Neville, earl of Salisbury, was prominent among the supporters of Henry VI against York at Dartford in late February 1452. During this decade Cecily had no need to take a high-profile role akin to that of Margaret of Anjou, but when the conflict became open she could not avoid involvement. After Richard's flight from the 'rout of Ludford' in October 1459 she was captured by Lancastrian troops, and when her husband was attainted at the Coventry parliament in November, she apparently threw herself on Henry VI's mercy and intervened successfully for many of her people. She was assigned to the custody of her sister Anne, duchess of Buckingham. In late September 1460 she left London, where she was temporarily resident in John Paston's house rather than the Yorks' home at Baynard's Castle, to meet her husband on his return from Ireland, and the ceremonial nature of their reunion perhaps foreshadowed his ambitions for the throne. These were thwarted by his defeat and death at the battle of Wakefield on 30 December 1460. Cecily sent her two youngest sons to safety in Utrecht, but herself remained in London, where she must have felt extremely vulnerable after Queen Margaret's victory at the second battle of St Albans on 16 February 1461; but in the event eleven days later London opened its gates to the earl of Warwick and Cecily's son Edward, who on 4 March was recognized as king.

For the next twenty-four years, save for brief periods in 1470–71 and 1483, Cecily was mother of the reigning sovereign. In 1461 the papal legate was advised to communicate quickly with her, because of her great influence over her son. This, however, can seldom be documented. Her disapproval of Edward's marriage to Elizabeth Woodville [see Elizabeth (*c.*1437–1492)] was probably indicated by her absence from the new queen's coronation, on 26 May 1465. Later stories that in June 1469 she went to Sandwich to attempt to dissuade George of Clarence from rising with Warwick against Edward, and that as late as March 1470 she tried to reconcile the two brothers in a meeting at Baynard's Castle, may be apocryphal in their details, while still reflecting reality in showing Cecily as responsive to the extreme danger of division within the Yorkist family. It was now that the rumour of Edward IV's illegitimacy, due to his mother's adultery, was first circulated for political reasons. It re-emerged in 1483, when Richard of Gloucester began his attempt to wrest the crown from his young nephew. Mancini blames Richard for the calumny, and Vergil records that Cecily complained loud and long of the injury he had done her, but his campaign for the throne was launched from his mother's London house. Even after Richard III's death honourable provision was made for her by Henry VII, for she was the grandmother of his queen consort.

Because of the survival of her detailed will, made at Berkhamsted on 31 May 1495, a few days before her death, and also of a household ordinance book dating from after 1485, Cecily has been taken as a prime exemplar of late medieval female aristocratic piety. These sources document the dedicated regime of literate and ascetic piety practised by an old lady, but against this must be set the ostentatious dynastic religiosity displayed in the reburial of her husband's body at Fotheringhay in 1476, in the planning of which she surely played a part. The scene of her devotions was a lavishly decorated chapel, but her domestic religion was formulated by monastic precept. Her reading included the visions of Mathilde von Hackeborn, a thirteenth-century German Cistercian, the life of St Catherine of Siena, and the *Revelations* of St Bridget of Sweden—a clear indication of a common European religious culture. Her personal contact with the scriptures was made through Nicholas Love's translation of St Bonaventure's *Mirror of the Life of Blessed Jesu Christ*. One of her granddaughters was prioress of the Bridgettines of Syon, another a Dominican nun of Dartford, and she passed on her practical piety to her daughter Margaret, duchess of Burgundy, and, as is increasingly recognized, to Richard III.

Cecily's religion was, however, essentially conservative compared to that of her cousin, Lady Margaret Beaufort, in that she felt no compulsion to educational endowment as a means of strengthening the faith. Perhaps most revealing is her reading of Walter Hilton's *Epistle on the Mixed Life*, an exhortation to contemplation by those necessarily involved in worldly concerns; and most evocative is her bequest to Henry VII of an arras depicting the wheel of fortune, whose revolutions she had experienced so dramatically during her long life. She was buried at Fotheringhay, beside her husband, with a papal indulgence hung round her neck.

CHRISTOPHER HARPER-BILL

Sources J. G. Nichols and J. Bruce, eds., *Wills from Doctors' Commons*, CS, old ser., 83 (1863), 1–8 · *A collection of ordinances and regulations for the government of the royal household*, Society of Antiquaries (1790), 37–9 · C. A. J. Armstrong, 'The piety of Cicely, duchess of York: a study in late medieval culture', *England, France and Burgundy in the fifteenth century* (1983), 135–56 · *The usurpation of Richard the third: Dominicus Mancinus ad Angelum Catonem de occupatione regni Anglie per Ricardum tercium libellus*, ed. and trans. C. A. J. Armstrong, 2nd edn (1969) [Lat. orig., 1483, with parallel Eng. trans.] · *Three books of Polydore Vergil's 'English history'*, ed. H. Ellis, CS, 29 (1844) · *Chancery records* · A. H. Thomas and I. D. Thornley, eds., *The great chronicle of London* (1938); repr. (1983) · C. L. Scofield, *The life and reign of Edward the Fourth*, 2 vols. (1923) · P. A. Johnson, *Duke Richard of York, 1411–1460* (1988) · C. Ross, *Richard III* (1981) · J. R. Lander, 'Marriage and politics in the 15th century: the Nevilles and the Wydevilles', *BIHR*, 36 (1963), 119–52 · GEC, *Peerage*, new edn, 12/2.905–9

Cecily, Viscountess Welles (1469–1507), princess, was the third daughter of *Edward IV (1442–1483) and *Elizabeth, *née* Woodville (c.1437–1492). Born on 20 March 1469, she was presumably named after her paternal grandmother. In 1473 a marriage alliance between England and Scotland, by which Cecily was to marry James, the infant son of James III, was under consideration and the formal betrothal of the couple followed on 26 October 1474. Relations between the two countries subsequently worsened, however, with James III apparently condoning raids into England, and in 1480 Edward began preparing for an invasion of Scotland in the following year. In 1482 he agreed to back James's brother Alexander, duke of Albany, as claimant to the Scottish throne, and in the treaty of Fotheringhay (11 June 1482) it was agreed that Cecily should marry Albany, if he could make himself clear of his French wife, Anne de la Tour. Albany was shortly afterwards reconciled with his brother, but this did not have the effect of reviving the match with Prince James, which was formally broken off by Edward in October 1482.

Cecily, like her sisters, including *Elizabeth (1466–1503) and *Katherine (1479–1527), was thus unmarried at her father's death in April 1483. When Richard, duke of Gloucester, took possession of the young *Edward V at the end of the month, Elizabeth Woodville and her children took sanctuary at Westminster, where the sisters remained until 1 March 1484, when Richard, now Richard III, came to an agreement with Elizabeth Woodville. The king swore to treat them well and to marry them to gentlemen born, providing each bride with 200 marks p.a. in land. Only in Cecily's case was this promise fulfilled, and she was married to Ralph (c.1465–1515), the brother of Richard's ally Thomas, Lord Scrope of Upsall. The marriage was dissolved in 1486, after the accession of Henry VII, to free Cecily to marry the new king's half-uncle, John *Welles, Viscount Welles (d. 1499) [see under Welles, Leo]. That marriage had taken place by new year's day 1488. In the meantime Cecily played a prominent role in court ceremonial. She carried Prince Arthur to the font at his christening in Winchester Cathedral on 24 September 1486, and bore the train of Elizabeth of York at her coronation on 25 November 1487. Welles died on 9 February 1499, leaving Cecily a life interest in his lands. Henry VII initially respected the arrangement, but when in 1502 Cecily angered him by remarrying without permission, he seized the Welles estates. A settlement was negotiated the following year by Lady Margaret Beaufort, who had sheltered Cecily and her new husband, the Lincolnshire esquire Thomas Kyme of Friskney. Cecily surrendered some of the land in return for a life interest in the remainder, and she and her husband were allowed to keep the revenues they had already received from the estates.

Cecily died on 24 August 1507. In the seventeenth century there was a tradition, recorded by Sir John Oglander, that her last husband was a native of the Isle of Wight and that they had lived at East Standen until Cecily's death, when she was buried at Quarr Abbey. However, it is clear from the Beaufort accounts that Cecily died at Hatfield, Hertfordshire, after a stay there of three weeks. She was buried at 'the friars'. The house is unidentified, although the absence from the accounts of any payment for transporting her body suggests that burial was relatively local.

Cecily had two daughters, Elizabeth and Anne, with Welles. In 1498 a marriage was arranged between Elizabeth and the heir of George Stanley, Lord Strange, but Elizabeth died later that year. Anne, too, was dead by the time of Welles's own death in the following year, and was buried in the church of the Austin Friars in London. There is disagreement over whether Cecily and Kyme also had children. The claim that they did seems to derive entirely from the later tradition that misidentifies Kyme as a gentleman of the Isle of Wight, and it is likely that the marriage was childless. ROSEMARY HORROX

Sources C. Ross, *Edward IV* (1974) · R. Horrox, *Richard III, a study of service*, Cambridge Studies in Medieval Life and Thought, 4th ser., 11 (1989) · GEC, *Peerage* · M. K. Jones and M. G. Underwood, *The king's mother: Lady Margaret Beaufort, countess of Richmond and Derby* (1992) · *Joannis Lelandi antiquarii de rebus Britannicis collectanea*, ed. T. Hearne, [2nd edn], 6 vols. (1770), vol. 4 · *Chancery records* · RotP · F. Sandford, *A genealogical history of the kings of England* (1677) · S. F. Hockey, ed., *The charters of Quarr abbey* (1991)

Likenesses stained glass, Canterbury Cathedral · stained glass (of Cecily?), Little Malvern, Worcestershire · stained glass, panel, Burrell Collection, Glasgow

Cedd [St Cedd] (*d.* **664**), bishop of the East Saxons, was the eldest of four brothers who were Northumbrian and educated at Lindisfarne by Áedán and Finan. Cedd and the others, *Ceadda, Cynebill, and Caelin, all became priests and Ceadda also a bishop. Nearly all that is known of them comes from Bede's *Historia ecclesiastica* and the principal source for this section is named as the monastery of Lastingham, Northumbria, founded by Cedd with Lindisfarne's help near the end of his life. The bias of this source can be partially corrected by reference to other sources.

In 653 Cedd, together with Adda, Betti, and Diuma (later bishop of Mercia), was chosen to help evangelize the Middle Angles, an amalgam of small peoples under Mercian domination in the east and south-east midlands. This opportunity occurred in hitherto pagan Mercia because Peada, who ruled the Middle Angles for his father, Penda, had married Alhflaed, the daughter of the dominating King Oswiu of Northumbria, and had himself become a Christian. After a short and promising apostolate to all ranks of society Cedd was chosen by Oswiu and Finan, after a preliminary trial, as bishop of the East Saxons. These people lived in present-day Essex. Their king, Sigeberht II, had been converted by the articulate persuasions of King Oswiu. Cedd was consecrated at Lindisfarne in 654 and his two known centres of influence were the monasteries he built at Tilbury and Bradwell-on-Sea, while London was still dominated by Penda of Mercia. In spite of later claims, Cedd was not 'bishop of London'.

Cedd seems to have been a travelling missionary bishop, usually on the move and working closely with the local king, as Áedán had done. When King Sigeberht consorted with a thegn whom Cedd had excommunicated for an irregular marriage, Cedd's reproach and rebuke were believed to be the cause of Sigeberht's murder by his own family *c.*660. Cedd baptized the successor, Swithhelm, at Rendlesham, the vill of East Anglian kings, very close to Sutton Hoo.

On one of his visits to Northumbria, Cedd took a prominent part in the foundation of Lastingham. Æthelwald, sub-king of Deira, donated the remote moorland site for a monastery and a burial place. Cedd personally sanctified it by an austere Lenten fast each day, broken only by a boiled egg and a little bread and milk. When he was summoned elsewhere, a disciple continued the fast in his place.

Perhaps the most important achievement of Cedd's episcopate was his role as *interpres* at the Synod of Whitby. (The term seems to have its primary meaning as 'broker or negotiator' rather than 'interpreter'.) The synod had been summoned by King Oswiu in the interests of church unity, and in particular to agree on a single date for the celebration of Easter, the principal feast in the year. The choice of Cedd as an 'honest broker' says much for the respect in which he was held by both the Iona and 'Roman' parties. When the Synod of Whitby finally adopted the Easter calculation almost universal in the West (including southern Ireland), rather than the insular tradition of Iona, Cedd, with Ceadda and Cuthbert, accepted it although they had been brought up in the Iona tradition.

Cedd's church at Bradwell, called St Peter's-on-the-Wall, survives, though that at Tilbury does not. St Peter's is a stone structure in the Roman fort of Othona, which reused Roman materials; in style and size it closely resembles the stone churches built in Kent by Augustine and his successors. Soon after the Synod of Whitby, Cedd died at Lastingham, of the plague. He was buried first in the cemetery but his body was later translated to a fine tomb near the high altar of the stone church. This was the contemporary equivalent to canonization. Thirty monks from Bradwell-on-Sea travelled to Lastingham through devotion to their founder, but all except one died of the same plague. The 664 epidemic was particularly virulent and widespread: it contributed to a critical shortage of bishops in England, ended only by the appointment of Theodore of Tarsus to the see of Canterbury in 668. Both the Synod of Whitby and Theodore's appointment brought to an end the extraordinary dominance of Lindisfarne and marked the resumption by Canterbury of its role as effective metropolitan.

The principal feast day of Cedd is 26 October; the subsidiary feast of 7 January marks a translation, possibly that of his relics to Lichfield, where from the eleventh century they were venerated together with those of his brother St Ceadda (Chad). D. H. FARMER

Sources Bede, *Hist. eccl.* · H. M. Taylor and J. Taylor, *Anglo-Saxon architecture*, 1 (1965) · E. B. Fryde and others, eds., *Handbook of British chronology*, 3rd edn, Royal Historical Society Guides and Handbooks, 2 (1986) · F. M. Stenton, *Anglo-Saxon England* (1943), 55–7,

132–4 • R. Morris, *Churches in the landscape* (1989), 73, 115–16, 120 • D. H. Farmer, *The Oxford dictionary of saints*, 3rd edn (1992), 92, 94–5

Céitinn, Seathrún. *See* Keating, Geoffrey (*b. c.*1580, *d.* in or before 1644).

Celesia [*née* Mallet], **Dorothea** (*bap.* **1738**, *d.* **1790**), playwright and poet, was baptized on 11 October 1738 in the parish of Chiswick, Middlesex, the second of two children of David *Mallet (1701/2?–1765), playwright and poet, and his first wife, Susanna (*d.* 1742). Educated at home with her brother and her two half-sisters, in 1758 she married Pietro Paolo Celesia (*d.* 1806), a Genoese diplomat who was ambassador to England from 1755 to 1759. Celesia's former French mistress, Marianne Agnès Falques, published her *Mémoire* (1758) in which she criticized Dorothea Mallet as a protestant usurper of her place in Celesia's life. This ignored the fact that David Mallet had originally been a Roman Catholic.

In 1759 Dorothea Celesia moved with her husband to Genoa, where she lived with him for the remainder of her life. The Celesias had entertained the actor David Garrick when he visited Italy in 1761, and Dorothea Celesia came to brief prominence in London literary and dramatic circles when Garrick was instrumental in having her blank verse tragedy, *Almida*, which was a free translation of Voltaire's *Tancrède* (1760), performed at the Drury Lane Theatre from 12 January 1771 for ten nights, featuring Mrs Ann Spranger Barry. As her title *Almida* implies, Celesia pivoted the action on the characterization of the heroine rather than the valorous warrior Tancred, although generally she kept to the main plot of Voltaire's dramatization of an eleventh-century tale of ill-fated love. But whereas Voltaire used *vers croisés* she employed blank verse, and in contrast to Voltaire's neo-classical language she enlivened her dialogue with a vivid use of metaphor, such as in the lines: 'Fear's trembling pencil, ever dipped in black, / Paints to the mind strange images of woe'. Garrick told Elizabeth Griffiths that he admired Celesia's play: 'Mrs Celesia, Daughter of the late Mr Mallett … sent me from Genoa a very good Tragedy written by herself' (*Letters*, 680). In contrast, Arthur Murphy, Garrick's biographer, comments on Garrick's production of Celesia's *Almida*:

> Garrick thought himself bound to pay her all the respect in his power, and to introduce what she recommended to his care, with every advantage his theatre could afford … Mrs Barry, in compliance with the manager's request, made it a point to call forth all her powers in the part of *Almida*, and to her inimitable acting the piece owed its brilliant success during a run of twelve nights.   (Murphy, 309–10)

William Whitehead's 'Prologue' to *Almida* asserts Celesia's right to succeed her father as a dramatist: 'No Salick law here bars the female's claim, / Who pleads hereditary right to fame'. But David Erskine Baker criticized the quality of her translation: 'this play, though a very poor one, had a considerable run' (Baker, 2.97).

Celesia subsequently published a long poem in blank verse, *Indolence* (1772), in which she extolled the value of poetry and creativity, which for her were more important than the active pursuit of fame through ruling, warring, or exploring. She treated the imperial exploits of man ironically: 'Thus eager mortals toiling to be great, / With headlong steps anticipate their fate'. In foregrounding the importance of the contemplative life, Celesia is showing indirectly how women of her time could take a role in society as poets and thinkers. She praises, for example, Christina, queen of Sweden, who withdrew from her 'regal cares' to Italy in order to write poetry. Critics have dismissed this ambitious poem, although in it she foreshadows John Keats's *Ode on Indolence* (1819). Dorothea Celesia planned to translate Voltaire's heroic tragedy *Sémiramis* (1746) but this translation never appeared. Dorothea Celesia died in Genoa in September 1790. She is a significant figure in the history of women's drama in English in that she adapted Voltaire's *Tancrède* so as to foreground a psychological conflict—in relation to the notion of a daughter's right to choose her own partner in marriage— between an authoritarian father and a spirited daughter.

JENNIFER BREEN

Sources F. Dinsdale, 'Memoir', in D. Mallet, *Ballads and songs*, new edn (1857), 3–61 • *The letters of David Garrick*, ed. D. M. Little and G. M. Kahrl, 2 (1963), 283, 680, 735 • *The private correspondence of David Garrick*, ed. J. Boaden, 2nd edn, 1 (1835), 354, 379–80, 399–400, 415–16 • *GM*, 1st ser., 61 (1791), 381 • *Scots Magazine*, 53 (1791), 203 • Mme Fauques de Vaucluse [Marianne Agnès Falques], *Mémoire* (1758) • D. E. Baker, *Biographia dramatica, or, A companion to the playhouse*, rev. I. Reed, new edn, 1 (1782), 65; 2 (1782), 97 • D. Celesia, four letters to David Garrick, 1769–71, V&A NAL, F48.F33, 29.67–70 • D. Celesia, letter to Edward Gibbon, 1769–71, BL, Add. MS 34886, fol. 102 • A. Murphy, *The life of David Garrick*, 2 vols. (1801) • *DNB*

Céleste [*married name* Céleste-Elliott], **Céline** [*known as* Madame Céleste] (**1810/11–1882**), actress and theatre manager, was born in Paris. Contemporary biographers usually cite 1814 as the year of her birth, but a more likely date is 1810 or 1811. She showed acting and musical talent at an early age, and was enrolled as a pupil at the Paris conservatory, where she performed with François-Joseph Talma and Madame Pasta. Her first professional appearance was in 1827 at the Bowery Theatre in New York, in which she danced a *pas seul* with a Parisian dance troupe. During her visit to the United States, Céleste also performed in small ballets in theatres on the east coast. In 1828 she married Henry Elliott of Baltimore, with whom she had a daughter, born in 1829. Elliott died soon after their marriage.

In 1830 Madame Céleste arrived in Liverpool from New Orleans, and made her début in England as Fenella, the wronged mute sister of the Neapolitan fisherman hero, Masaniello, in Auber's opera of that name. Mute parts enabled Céleste to display her brilliant skills as a versatile and expressive mime artist, and also conveniently concealed her always halting command of the English language. At Easter 1831 she had her first metropolitan success, as the Arab Boy (alias Mathilde de Meric) in *The French Spy*, a topical military play about the French seizure of Algiers, written for her by J. T. Haines and staged at the Queen's Theatre in Tottenham Street. Haines was the first of several English dramatists, including J. B. Buckstone and Bayle Bernard, to create parts expressly for Madame Céleste.

After touring Italy, Germany, and Spain, Madame Céleste had brief engagements in Dublin and Edinburgh,

Céline Céleste (1810/11–1882), by Herbert Watkins, late 1850s

before appearing at Drury Lane in 1833 in *The Maid of Cashmere* and subsequently at Covent Garden, where she danced in *Gustavus the Third*. In her second tour to the United States, from 1834 to 1837, she became a theatrical sensation and box-office star, and returned with a small fortune, which she was later to lose in theatrical management in England. In America she became famous for her pantomimic roles in plays such as *The Wizard Skiff, or, The Tongueless Pirate Boy*, *The Wept of the Wish-Ton-Wish* (adapted from Fenimore Cooper's novel), and *The Dumb Brigand* as well as for her prowess as a dancer in the ballet of *La Bayadère*. She made three later tours to the United States, in 1842, 1851, and 1865.

In 1837 Madame Céleste reappeared at Drury Lane as the dumb boy Maurice in *The Child of the Wreck*, a play written for her by J. R. Planché, which had an impressive run of forty nights. *The Times* (9 October 1837) admired her performance, applauding her rapid transitions between 'the various passions of love, despair, indignation and joy'. In his domestic drama *Marie Ducange* (Haymarket, 1841), Bayle Bernard created for her the part of Marie, a Jersey woman who, in spite of conflicting feelings, flees with her lover to England, only to go mad when her husband deserts her and returns to his wife. With Benjamin *Webster, who became her lover and business partner, Madame Céleste then embarked on several periods as a theatrical manager, first at the Theatre Royal, Liverpool, in 1843, and subsequently at the Adelphi. There they produced a series of highly successful domestic dramas, many of which were written by Buckstone, with Madame Céleste in the leading role. Madame Céleste's liaison with Webster seems to have been both public and broadly accepted in

Victorian London, and it is likely that he was the father of her daughters, referred to by Charles Dickens in a letter of 1869. In *The Green Bushes* (Adelphi, 1845), a piece set at the time of the Irish rising of 1798, Madame Céleste played Miami, the graceful, wild, and restless huntress of the Mississippi, half Indian and half French. On discovering the infidelity of her Irish lover, Miami kills him in a moment of jealous passion, later atoning for her crime in Ireland (as Madame St Aubert) by reuniting her lover's child with its mother. Buckstone's subtle blend of sympathetic innocence and raw, almost anarchic energy made this Madame Céleste's most famous and most characteristic role. Other notable productions included Bernard's *St Mary's Eve* and Buckstone's *The Flowers of the Forest* (Adelphi, 1847), in which Madame Céleste played Cynthia, the Italian Gypsy queen, torn between loyalty to her race and compassion for an Englishman unjustly accused of murder.

In 1853 Madame Céleste played the sorrowful heroine in the first performance of Dion Boucicault's drama *Geneviève, or, The Reign of Terror*, and the following year she took the leading role of Ruth Ravensear in Tom Taylor's and Charles Reade's *Two Loves and a Life*. Other significant roles at the Adelphi in the 1850s included the callous Mademoiselle Marco in *The Marble Heart* (1854) and the title role in Boucicault's *Janet Pride* (1855). Having left the Adelphi after a serious disagreement with Webster, Madame Céleste was briefly the lessee of the Lyceum Theatre, where she opened with Taylor's dramatization of *A Tale of Two Cities*, in which she took the part of Madame Defarge. In 1860 she became the lessee of the Olympic Theatre, and created the character of Ernest de la Garde in *The House on the Bridge of Notre Dame*, a role which became one of her most famous impersonations.

After a long foreign tour between 1863 and 1868, including performances in America and Australia, Madame Céleste appeared in a series of farewell productions at the St James's Theatre, as Rudiga in Stirling Coyne's drama *The Woman in Red*. She nevertheless emerged from retirement several times to benefit Webster—with whom she was now reconciled—and who was struggling with financial difficulties. In 1869 she played Josephine Dubosc in the first performance of Boucicault's play *Presumptive Evidence* at the Princess's Theatre. She finally withdrew from the stage in 1874 after some final appearances as Miami in a revival of *The Green Bushes* at the Adelphi. Madame Céleste later retired to Paris, where she died, at 18 rue de Chapeyron, on 12 February 1882, from cancer.

Madame Céleste's highly successful career as a dancer and melodramatic performer (a success equalled in the United States only by Fanny Kemble and Jenny Lind) defied both language and national boundaries. In addition to her tragic expressiveness and mobility of feature, reviewers praised her eloquent black eyes and handsome face. Her most famous characters were wild, passionate, and often violent roles of 'half-untutored passion' (*The Examiner*, 25 March 1854). Her brilliance as a mime artist inspired those dramatists who created parts for her to explore the complex emotions of outcast figures such as Narramattah or Cynthia, divided from family and estranged from their ethnic pasts. In the dances incorporated into her roles, whether as a wild Arab boy or as an Eastern Gypsy, she tempered the fashionable sophistication of French ballet with a wild and exotic primitivism. Her characters dramatized in disturbing ways the conflicting politics and values of European and 'native' cultures. In several plays, such as *The French Spy* (in which she played Mathilde, the daughter of the General, later disguised as Henri, a French spy, who then masquerades as Hamet, an Arab boy), Madame Céleste's theatrical identities crossed the boundaries of both gender and ethnicity. Her mute characters, who expressed their ambivalent and sometimes tormented thoughts and emotions in the silent language of the body, accompanied by music, were significant for their theatrical insights into the inarticulate borders of rationality.　　　　　　　　　　　JANE MOODY

Sources *The Era* (25 Feb 1882) · *New York Herald* (29 Feb 1882) · *New York Times* (20 Feb 1882) · *Theatrical Times* (17 Oct 1846), 185–6 · C. E. Pascoe, ed., *The dramatic list* (1879) · H. B. Baker, *History of the London stage and its famous players, 1576–1903*, 2nd edn (1904) · G. C. D. Odell, *Annals of the New York stage*, 15 vols. (1927–49) · *Theatrical Journal* [reviews] · *The Athenaeum* [reviews] · W. B. Durban, ed., *American theatre companies, 1749–1887* (1986) · H. Simpson and Mrs C. Braun, *A century of famous actresses, 1750–1850* (1913) · R. J. Broadbent, *Annals of the Liverpool stage* (1908) · M. Webster, *The same only different* (1969) · H. P. Phelps, *Players of a century* (1880)

Likenesses H. Watkins, albumen print photograph, 1856–9, NPG [*see illus.*] · J. Fairburn, hand-coloured print (as dumb Arab boy in *The siege of Constantinople*), repro. in J. N. Ireland, *Records of the New York stage*, 1 (1866), 34 · Hollis, line-engraving (as Princess Katharine in *Henry V*; after a daguerreotype by J. E. Mayall), NPG · Mayall, carte-de-visite, NPG · D. J. Pound, engraving (after photograph by J. Norris), repro. in J. N. Ireland, *Records of the New York stage* (1867), 88 · engravings, repro. in J. N. Ireland, *Records of the New York stage*, 1 (1866), 37 · prints, BM, NPG · prints, Harvard TC

Cellach (*fl.* **6th–7th cent.**), bishop of Killala, was said to have been the elder son of Éogan Bél, king of the northern Uí Fhíachrach (in modern Carra, Ennis, and Tirawley in co. Mayo and Tireragh in co. Sligo). A highly literary version of his biography is preserved in the mixed prose and verse tale *Caithréim Cellaig* (also entitled *Betha Cellaig*), 'the martial career of Cellach' (or 'the life of Cellach'), probably dating from the thirteenth or early fourteenth century. A reworked version is preserved in the Yellow Book of Lecan, a manuscript associated with the Mac Firbhisigh family, the hereditary historians of the rulers of Tír Fhíachrach. A brief version of the story is preserved in the prose Dindsenchas on *Ard na Ríag* and also in the genealogies of the Uí Fhíachrach. Cellach does not appear as such in the calendars of saints, but Cellán Ua Fíachrach (1 May) in the martyrology of Gormán is thought to represent him. There are major chronological difficulties in the story; the annals place the death of Éogan Bél at 547 at the latest but the annals of Ulster put the death of King Gúaire, who instigated Cellach's death, at 663. It is clear that the tale is highly fictional, though there is a distinct message: the superiority of spiritual power over the secular. Furthermore, whenever the story was composed, the killing of a bishop by a king would probably have had a particular resonance.

The tale tells that when the Uí Néill attacked and plundered Éogan's territory, he defeated them at Sligo in 547 but was mortally wounded. Of his two sons, Cellach was studying to be a cleric at Clonmacnoise under Cíarán, while his younger son, Muredach, was too young to succeed. The followers of his dying father requested Cíarán to permit Cellach to leave the monastery and take up the kingship. When the request was refused, they approached Cellach directly and he left without permission. Cíarán cursed him and prophesied that he would suffer a violent death. But Cellach soon grew weary of being king and desired to return to Clonmacnoise. He was welcomed back by Cíarán who granted him forgiveness but said that he could not recall the curse. Cellach therefore took up his studies again, at the same time training his younger brother for the kingship. In due course he was received into holy orders and eventually consecrated bishop of Killala by the clergy of his own territory.

At this time Gúaire Aidne, son of Colmán, king of the southern Uí Fhíachrach (modern south-eastern co. Galway) had designs on Cellach's kingdom since there was no heir of suitable age to take over. One day Cellach was making an episcopal circuit when he encountered Gúaire near Durlus. Gúaire thought that Cellach had insulted him and summoned the bishop to appear before him. But since it was vespers on the Saturday and thus the beginning of the Lord's day, Cellach replied that he could do nothing until Monday. He then went to a lake called Claenloch where he found a deserted island, Oilean Etgair, where he decided to live as a hermit; and he dismissed all his retinue except for four students who were his kinsmen. Gúaire wanted to kill Cellach and planned to invite him to a feast and poison him. However, his invitation was refused. Gúaire therefore summoned Cellach's followers instead and persuaded them to murder Cellach by offering them the reward of the territory of Tirawley. They returned to the island to find Cellach holding his psalter in front of him and expecting death. They wounded him and carried him to the mainland into the forest between Lough Con and Lough Cuillen where they killed him the next morning. Cellach was left unburied but his brother Muredach eventually buried him at Escrecha after being refused burial in several other places. Muredach was forced to flee but eventually he returned and took vengeance on the four murderers, cutting off their limbs while they were still living.　　　　　　　　　　　PAUL RUSSELL

Sources K. Mulchrone, ed., *Caithréim Cellaig* (1978) · *Silva Gadelica*, ed. S. H. O'Grady, 2 vols. (1892), 1.49–65; 2.50–69 · W. Stokes, ed., 'The prose tales in the Rennes Dindsenchas: first supplement', *Revue Celtique*, 16 (1895), 135–67, item 133 · *Félire húi Gormáin / The martyrology of Gorman*, ed. and trans. W. Stokes, HBS, 9 (1895), 88–9 [1 May] · J. O'Donovan, ed. and trans., *The genealogies, tribes, and customs of Hy-Fiachrach, commonly called O'Dowda's country*, Irish Archaeological Society, 2 (1844) · *Ann. Ulster*

Cellach [St Cellach, Celsus, Celestinus] (**1080–1129**), archbishop of Armagh, was the son of Áed mac Máele Ísu meic Amalgada, *comarba Pátraic* ('successor or heir of Patrick'), that is head of the church of Armagh, 1074–91, and belonged to the hereditarily entrenched laicized ecclesiastical dynasty of Clann Sínaig, which had monopolized that office from 966. Following the death of Domnall mac Amalgada, in August 1105 Cellach succeeded as *comarba Pátraic* and took the decisive reform step of seeking priestly ordination, receiving orders on the feast of Adomnán, 23 September 1105. In 1106 Cáenchomrac Ó Baígill, bishop of Armagh, died, affording the possibility of uniting the abbatial and episcopal offices. In 1106 Cellach made a formal visitation of Munster and 'it was on that occasion that Cellach assumed the orders of a noble bishop by command of the men of Ireland' (*Ann. Ulster*, s.a. 1106). Visitations are recorded of Cenél nEógain in 1106, Munster in 1106 and 1120, Connacht in 1108 and 1116, and Mide in 1110. In 1107, 1109, and 1113 Cellach conducted negotiations between Muirchertach Ó Briain, king of Munster, and Domnall Ó Lochlainn, king of Cenél nEógain, who were in contention for the high-kingship.

In 1111 Cellach attended the reform Synod of Ráith Bressail, presided over by Muirchertach Ó Briain, at which a national diocesan constitution for the Irish church was drawn up. According to Bernard of Clairvaux, Cellach 'established anew another metropolitan see' ('Vita sancti Malachiae', 340) whose archbishop was subject to him as to a primate; that see must have been Cashel and the occasion almost certainly the Synod of Ráith Bressail. According to Eadmer and the annals of Ulster, on the death in 1121 of Bishop Samuel of Dublin, who had been consecrated by Anselm, archbishop of Canterbury, Cellach claimed Dublin for the see of Armagh, doubtless in pursuance of the decrees of the Synod of Ráith Bressail which had envisaged the absorption of Dublin into the newly created adjacent diocese of Glendalough. A party in the city, however, which wished to retain the link with Canterbury, sent a subdeacon, Gréne (or Gregorius), to Canterbury for consecration, which took place on 2 October 1121. Some agreement subsequently must have been reached, whereby Gréne was accepted as bishop of Dublin, probably in return for acknowledging the primacy of Cellach. Cellach's link with the see of Dublin is attested in later charters issued by his successors in the see of Armagh, Gilla in Choimded Ó Caráin, Tomaltach Ó Conchobair, and Echdonn mac Gilla Uidir, who confirmed 'terram Sancti Patricii que dicitur Balibachel' (Ballyboghill, Dublin) to St Mary's Abbey, Dublin, to hold as 'Kellach archiepiscopus … melius et liberius tenuit et habuit unquam' ('as well and freely as Archbishop Cellach ever had it'; Gilbert, 1.141–3). The place name suggests a portion of land set aside for the support of the *Bachall Ísu* ('staff of Jesus'), one of the principal insignia of the head of the church of Armagh.

In 1118 when crossing the River Blackwater, Cellach lost a substantial amount of vestments and was himself almost drowned. On 9 January 1125 he raised the protecting ridge on a new shingled roof on the church of Armagh. On 21 October 1126 he consecrated the stone church of Sts Peter and Paul at Armagh, which had been built by Abbot Imar Ó hÁedacháin. In 1128 Cellach and his retinue were attacked by Tigernán Ó Ruairc, king of Bréifne, and a cleric of his household killed. Bernard of Clairvaux assigned a formative role to Cellach in promoting the career of the reformer, Máel Máedóc Ó Morgair (St Malachy). It was Cellach who ordained Máel Máedóc as deacon, and priest, and charged him 'with his own office of sowing the holy seed' ('Vita sancti Malachiae', 315) when he was absent from Armagh, sent him to study under Bishop Máel Ísu Ó hAinmire at Lismore, and consecrated him as bishop of Connor in 1124. In 1126 the annals of Ulster described Cellach as absent from Armagh 'for a month and a year pacifying the men of Ireland', and in 1128 he negotiated a year's truce between the men of Munster and Connacht.

Before his death Cellach designated Máel Máedóc as his successor in the see of Armagh. Máel Máedóc was to be opposed first by Cellach's cousin, Muirchertach, and, even more ironically, by Cellach's own brother, Niall, in a bid to retain Clann Sínaig control of the church of Armagh. Cellach died on 1 April 1129 at Ardpatrick (Limerick) and was buried on 4 April at Lismore church (Waterford). The obituary notice in the annals of Ulster (s.a. 1129) states that he was 'the one head whom Gael and Gaill [Hiberno-Norse], laymen and clerics served', doubtless a reference to his assertion of primacy over the Hiberno-Norse see of Dublin, and possibly also Waterford and Limerick. In 1129 the silver chalice which Cellach had bestowed on the church of Clonmacnoise was stolen. In *The Vision of Tnugdal* he is one of four bishops said to be with St Patrick in paradise. His name was latinized as Celsus and Celestinus. He was commemorated on 1 April in the twelfth-century martyrology of Gormán, but his commemoration was entered under 6 April among J. Molanus's additions to the martyrology of Usuard, printed at Louvain in 1563, whence it passed into the Roman martyrology; hence also the insertion of Cellach in the *Acta sanctorum* under that date. His title of archbishop may be considered informal in the context of the contemporary reform movement within the Irish church since he was not in receipt of a pallium from the papacy.

M. T. FLANAGAN

Sources *Ann. Ulster*, s.a. 1080, 1105–1111, 1113, 1116, 1118, 1120–21, 1125–6, 1128–9 · S. Mac Airt, ed. and trans., *The annals of Inisfallen* (1951), s. a. 1111, 1120, 1129 · 'Vita Sancti Malachiae', *Sancti Bernardi opera*, ed. J. Leclercq and H. M. Rochais, 3 (Rome, 1963), 314–5, 317, 328–32, 340 · *Eadmeri Historia novorum in Anglia*, ed. M. Rule, Rolls Series, 81 (1884) · G. Keating, *Foras feasa ar Éirinn / The history of Ireland*, ed. D. Comyn and P. S. Dinneen, 3, ITS, 9 (1908), 298–306 · *The whole works of … James Ussher*, ed. C. R. Elrington and J. H. Todd, 17 vols. (1847–64), vol. 4, pp. 532–3 · W. M. Hennessy, ed. and trans., *The annals of Loch Cé: a chronicle of Irish affairs from AD 1014 to AD 1590*, 2 vols., Rolls Series, 54 (1871) · J. T. Gilbert, ed., *Chartularies of St Mary's Abbey, Dublin: with the register of its house at Dunbrody and annals of Ireland*, 2 vols., Rolls Series, 80 (1884–6) · *The vision of Tnugdal*, ed. and trans. J. M. Picard and Y. de Pontfarcy (1989) · *Félire húi Gormáin / The martyrology of Gorman*, ed. and trans. W. Stokes, HBS, 9 (1895), 68–9 · W. M. Hennessy, ed. and trans., *Chronicum Scotorum: a chronicle of Irish affairs*, Rolls Series, 46 (1866) · *Acta sanctorum: Aprilis*, 1 (Antwerp, 1675), 619–20

Cellach Cualann (*d.* 715), king of Leinster, was the last of his people to rule the province. He was of the Uí Máil (the eponym of the glen of Imaal on the west of the Wicklow Mountains); the territory of Cualu is coextensive with the later diocese of Glendalough. The dynastic name Uí Máil is unusual, deriving from *mál*, 'prince' or 'ruler'. Also, the symbols of the kingship of Leinster, the *cuirm Chualann*, 'the ales of Cualu', and the *cuirn buaball*, 'the drinking horns of wild oxen', are associated with them. This suggests that for long they had been regarded as the natural rulers of Leinster.

Cellach became king of Uí Máil on the death of his cousin, Fiannamail, in 680 and king of Leinster on the death of Bran Mut in 693. His first major challenge came in 704 when he defeated and killed Bodbcath mac Diarmata Déin of the Clann Cholmáin who was in alliance with Fogartach, grandson of Cernach, of the Lagore dynasty (both of the southern Uí Néill) at Clane in what is now co. Kildare. In 707 he submitted to the northern Uí Néill high-king Congal Cendmagair on the occasion of the traditional Uí Néill hosting on Leinster. In 709 he fought a battle at 'Selg' (unidentified but probably in the vicinity of the glen of Imaal) against the south Leinstermen in which he lost two sons, Fiachra and Fiannamail. He had employed British mercenaries (perhaps displaced warriors from the kingdom of Rheged) some of whom also fell. Cellach died in 715.

During the seventh century the Uí Máil faced strong challenges from the rising Uí Dúnlaige in north Leinster and the Uí Chennselaig in the south. Following Cellach's death, pressure from the Uí Dúnlaige intensified. In 719 his son Áed was killed in a conflict at Finnabair (Fennor near the Curragh of Kildare). Another son, Crimthann, was killed in the battle of 'Belach Licce' (unidentified) in 726 and in the following year his son Eterscél was killed in a battle on the River Burren in what is now co. Carlow, both at the hands of the Uí Dúnlaige. During his lifetime Cellach had clearly had to play astute politics in order to survive. This may be seen in his marriages and in the marriages of his daughters.

Cellach's first wife was Murgel, daughter of Muiredach of the Ciannacht of Glen Gemin (modern co. Londonderry). The second, Mugain, was daughter of Faílbe of the Uí Bairrche of south Leinster; her mother, Eithne, was daughter of Crundmáel, of the Uí Chennselaig (Síl Cormaic), king of Leinster, who died in 656. His third wife, Bé Fáil (d. 741), was daughter of the high-king *Sechnassach mac Blathmaic (d. 671) of the southern Uí Néill and the fourth was Caintigern, daughter of Conaing (d. 662), possibly of the Knowth branch of the southern Uí Néill. It is likely that Cellach's daughter Caintigern, or *Kentigerna, was a child of this last marriage. Scottish tradition claims that she was married to 'Feriacus', possibly the Dál Riata king Feradach (or Ferchar) hua hArtúir who (along with Cellach Cualann) was among the signatories to the *Lex innocentium* promulgated at the Synod of Birr in 697. She is said to have ended her days as a pious widow at Loch Lomond. Cellach's daughter with Mugain was Conchenn (d. 743), who married Murchad (d. 727) of the Uí Dúnlainge, king of Leinster; their son Muiredach (d. 760) was eponym of the Uí Muiredaig. Cellach's daughter Muirenn (d. 748) was wife of Írgalach of the Knowth branch of the

southern Uí Néill, who was killed by the Britons on Ireland's Eye (off Howth) in 702. Their son *Cináed mac Írgalaig was high-king and died in 728. It is possible that Muirenn was also married to the high-king *Loingsech mac Óenguso (d. 704) and that their son was the high-king *Flaithbertach mac Loingsig (abdicated 734) who died in Armagh in 765. This marriage must have taken place shortly after the death of Írgalach. Possibly another daughter was Derbforgaill, wife of the high-king *Fínsnechtae Fledach (d. 695).   CHARLES DOHERTY

Sources *Ann. Ulster* • W. M. Hennessy, ed. and trans., *Chronicum Scotorum: a chronicle of Irish affairs*, Rolls Series, 46 (1866) • W. Stokes, ed., 'The annals of Tigernach [8 pts]', *Revue Celtique*, 16 (1895), 374–419; 17 (1896), 6–33, 119–263, 337–420; 18 (1897), 9–59, 150–97, 267–303, 374–91; pubd sep. (1993) • *AFM* • S. Mac Airt, ed. and trans., *The annals of Inisfallen* (1951) • D. Murphy, ed., *The annals of Clonmacnoise*, trans. C. Mageoghagan (1896); facs. edn (1993) • A. P. Smyth, 'Kings, saints and sagas', *Wicklow: history and society*, ed. K. Hannigan and W. Nolan (1994), 41–111 • A. S. Mac Shamhráin, *Church and polity in pre-Norman Ireland: the case of Glendalough* (1996)

Cellach mac Ailella (d. 865). *See under* Iona, abbots of (*act*. 563–927).

Cellach mac Congaile (d. 815). *See under* Iona, abbots of (*act.* 563–927).

Cellach mac Máele Coba (d. 658), joint high-king of Ireland, belonged to Cenél Conaill, the branch of the Uí Néill settled in what is now Donegal. His mother may have been Croinsech, daughter of Áed Find, king of Osraige, and he may have been married to Dathnat (or Domnait). Cellach appears to have been joint ruler of Cenél Conaill with his brother **Conall Cóel mac Máele Coba** (d. 654) from the death of their uncle, Domnall mac Áeda, in 642. The brothers' authority over Cenél Conaill was challenged by their first cousin, Óengus mac Domnaill, but they defeated and killed him in 650. Their status as high-kings of Ireland was accepted by the main twelfth-century regnal lists but not in the late seventh-century text *Baile Chuinn* ('The frenzy of Conn'), a regnal list of Tara (the formal title of the high-kings) in the form of a prophecy. The silence of this source is, however, far from conclusive, since it was composed during the reign of Fínsnechtae Fledach (r. 675–95); he belonged to the Uí Néill of Brega and *Baile Chuinn* is notably hostile to the claims of the rival Cenél Conaill.

The chronicle of Ireland (the 'common stock' of the annals of Ulster, annals of Tigernach, and *Chronicum Scotorum*) was uncertain about this period, for it notes under 643: 'Here there is doubt as to who reigned after Domnall. Some historiographers say that four kings, namely Cellach and Conall Cóel and the two sons of Áed Sláine, namely Diarmait and Blathmac [Blaímac], ruled in shared reigns' (*Ann. Ulster*, s.a.).

At least broadly this may be accurate: these were the allies of Domnall mac Áeda in his great victory at Mag Roth in 637 and would be the natural heirs of his power after his peaceful death in 642. Diarmait mac Áeda Sláine was clearly the most active ruler in the midlands, winning a major battle against Guaire Aidne of the Connachta and his Munster allies in 649. The probability, therefore, is that, whatever the titular succession to the kingship of Tara, effective authority was shared between Cenél Conaill, led by the brothers Cellach and Conall Cóel, and Síl nÁeda Sláine (the Uí Néill of Brega), also led by two brothers, Diarmait and Blaímac (or Blathmac). Indeed, the alliance between these two branches of the Uí Néill, at opposite ends of the crescent of Uí Néill kingdoms stretching across the northern half of Ireland from the River Liffey to Donegal, dominated most of the seventh century.

Conall Cóel was killed in 654, probably by Diarmait mac Áeda Sláine; from then until his own death in 658 Cellach seems to have reigned alone. According to one set of annals, Cellach's death took place at Brug na Bóinne, the Neolithic passage grave at Newgrange on the Boyne (Meath).   T. M. CHARLES-EDWARDS

Sources W. Stokes, ed., 'The annals of Tigernach [8 pts]', *Revue Celtique*, 16 (1895), 374–419; 17 (1896), 6–33, 119–263, 337–420; 18 (1897), 9–59, 150–97, 267–303, 374–91; pubd sep. (1993) · *Ann. Ulster* · G. Murphy, 'On the dates of two sources used in Thurneysen's *Heldensage*: 1. *Baile Chuind* and the date of *Cin Dromma Snechtai*', *Ériu*, 16 (1952), 145–56, esp. 145–51 · M. C. Dobbs, ed. and trans., 'The Ban-shenchus [3 pts]', *Revue Celtique*, 47 (1930), 283–339; 48 (1931), 163–234; 49 (1932), 437–89 · W. M. Hennessy, ed. and trans., *Chronicum Scotorum: a chronicle of Irish affairs*, Rolls Series, 46 (1866) · M. A. O'Brien, ed., *Corpus genealogiarum Hiberniae* (Dublin, 1962) · K. Meyer, ed., 'The Laud genealogies and tribal histories', *Zeitschrift für Celtische Philologie*, 8 (1910–12), 291–338 · F. J. Byrne, *Irish kings and high-kings* (1973)

Cellachán mac Buadacháin (*d.* 954), king of Munster, was the son of Buadachán mac Lachtnai. He was a dynast of the powerful Éoganacht Chaisil, located round present-day Cashel, and was their last notable king until the twelfth century. His immediate family had not produced a king of Munster, however, since the seventh century. Cellachán is first noticed in the surviving records in 936 when he plundered the monastery of Clonmacnoise. In 939 he allied with the vikings of Waterford to plunder the southern Uí Néill of Meath as far as the monastery of Clonard; during that raid the Leinster monasteries of Killeigh and Clonenagh were attacked and their abbots were captured. His efforts to be recognized as king of Munster appear to have begun in earnest in 941 when he attacked his eastern neighbours, the Déisi, and in the ensuing slaughter more than 400 died beside their king Célechair mac Cormaic. The raid on the Déisi appears to have been in response to an invasion led against them and the neighbouring kingdom of Osraige by the northern Uí Néill prince Muirchertach mac Néill, better known as Muirchertach of the Leather Cloaks. Cellachán's raids on the Déisi provoked a counter-attack in the same year when he was defeated by them and their allies of Osraige. Muirchertach mac Néill, then on his famous circuit of Ireland, seized Cellachán and took him to the high-king Donnchad mac Flainn, where he remained a captive for some time.

Upon his return to Munster, Cellachán had to face a new threat, the emerging power of the kingdom of Dál Cais. In 944 he defeated their king, Cennétig mac Lorcáin, and killed two of his sons in the battle of Gort Rottacháin (also called the battle of Mag Dúine). There may have been

more hostilities than just this battle, for verses in Dál Cais records claim that Cellachán was defeated by Cennétig in the battle of Lough Saighlenn. His last known military action was in 951, when he and his son Donnchad (*d.* 963) attacked Clonfert, Gallen, Clonmacnoise, Síl nAnmchada, and Delbnae Bethra. Cellachán died in 954 and is known to have fathered only one child, the aforementioned Donnchad.

Beside the rather ordinary recitation of events that comprises the historical record of Cellachán's reign can be set the far more colourful account of *Caithréim Cellacháin Caisil* ('The martial career of Cellachán of Cashel'). This was composed in the mid-twelfth century by his distant Éoganacht kinsmen who wanted a semi-legendary figure as a rival to Cennétig's son, the great Brian 'Boru', ancestor of the powerful Uí Briain. In the twelfth century a rivalry between the Éoganachta and the Uí Briain had led to division of power in Munster between the north (Uí Briain) and south (Éoganachta); *Caithréim Cellacháin* was composed to promote the claims of the Éoganachta. It attempts to present Cellachán as the constant foe of the vikings, who comes forth in a time of crisis to lead the Irish to victory. This Cellachán of literature is credited with many of the attributes of the king-hero: the circumstances of his birth are irregular; he is proclaimed king after his mother supplies him with troops and precedes him to the assembly in order to announce his arrival; his claims are immediately recognized by the nobility; and during his career he can be defeated only through treachery. The first part of the *Caithréim Cellacháin* tells how Cellachán won the kingship of Munster and how he secured recognition as king throughout the province. The second part is a story of his capture by the vikings and his rescue. The vikings of Dublin offer Cellachán the hand in marriage of a viking princess named Bébinn; but this is a plot to seize him, to which the high-king Donnchad mac Flainn is party. Cellachán accepts, but before he enters Dublin the wife of the viking king (who secretly loves him) meets him outside the fortress in order to warn him of the treachery. Cellachán attempts to flee the territory of the vikings, but he is captured. The men of Munster come to his rescue and the story ends with Cellachán leading his troops home. The tale is important to the historian more as an indication of twelfth-century attitudes than as a record of tenth-century affairs. Especially interesting is the fiction of goodwill between Cellachán and Dál Cais, which completely ignores the warfare between the two, and the importance that control of the viking towns was given.   BENJAMIN T. HUDSON

Sources *Ann. Ulster* · S. Mac Airt, ed. and trans., *The annals of Inisfallen* (1951) · W. M. Hennessy, ed. and trans., *Chronicum Scotorum: a chronicle of Irish affairs*, Rolls Series, 46 (1866) · *AFM* · F. J. Byrne, *Irish kings and high-kings* (1987) · D. Ó Corráin, *Ireland before the Normans* (1972) · A. Bugge, *Caithréim Cellacháin Caisil* (1905) · T. W. Moody and others, eds., *A new history of Ireland*, 9: *Maps, genealogies, lists* (1984)

Cellán (*d.* 706), abbot of Péronne and writer, was an Irish monk who was sometime abbot of the monastery of Péronne in Neustria, known as 'Perrona Scottorum' from the fact that it housed numerous Irish monks from the time of its foundation. Virtually nothing is known of Cellán's life. If he was identical with an Irish Cellán *sapiens* whose death is recorded in the annals of Ulster *s.a.* 706, then his full name was Cellán mac Sechnasaig. According to Bede's *Historia ecclesiastica* (3.19), the church at Péronne was constructed by Erchinoald, mayor of the palace in the Frankish kingdom of Neustria from 640 to 657; it housed the relics of an earlier Irish pilgrim to the continent, St Fursa, who died *c*.650. It is not known when Cellán arrived at Péronne. William of Malmesbury, in his *Gesta pontificum*, preserves fragments of an epistolary exchange between Cellán and Aldhelm, then abbot of Malmesbury. In his letter to Aldhelm, Cellán describes himself as an exile 'born on the Isle of Ireland' but now 'concealed in the furthermost territory of the Franks' (*De gestis pontificum*, 337); he goes on to praise the eloquence of Aldhelm's Latin, and to ask Aldhelm to send him copies of his writings. Aldhelm's reply, of which William preserves only a sentence, expresses astonishment that Cellán should have heard of him. Cellán was also the author of a brief ten-line poem in hexameters ('Quid Vermendensis memorem tot milia plebis') to Transmarus, bishop of Noyon and hence of the people of Neustria, for he gives his name in lines 9–10 of the poem as follows:

> Haec modo Cellanus, venerandi nominis abbas
> Iussit dactilico discrivi carmina versu
> ('These poems Cellán, abbot of venerable title, commanded to
> be written in dactylic verse')

This poem occurs in a group of *tituli* in a ninth-century manuscript from Monte Cassino now preserved in Florence, and Ludwig Traube inclined to attribute to Cellán another *titulus* in the collection concerning a chapel dedicated to St Patrick ('Istam Patricius sanctus sibi vindicat aulam'); but in absence of any evidence for a chapel of St Patrick in Péronne, more modern scholars have been hesitant to accept Traube's attribution. Otherwise nothing is known of Cellán's life. The date given for the death of the Cellán in the annals of Ulster, 706, is confirmed by an independent notice for the same year in the *Annales Laureshamenses*. MICHAEL LAPIDGE

Sources *Aldhelmi opera*, ed. R. Ehwald, MGH Auctores Antiquissimi, 15 (Berlin, 1919) · Ann. Ulster, s.a. 706 · 'Annales Laureshamenses', [*Annales et chronica aevi Carolini*], ed. G. H. Pertz, MGH Scriptores [folio], 1 (Stuttgart, 1826), 22 · *Aldhelm: the prose works*, trans. M. Lapidge and M. Herren (1979) · L. Traube, 'Perrona Scottorum', *Vorlesungen und Abhandlungen*, ed. F. Boll, 3 vols. (1909–20), 3.95–119 · *Willelmi Malmesbiriensis monachi de gestis pontificum Anglorum libri quinque*, ed. N. E. S. A. Hamilton, Rolls Series, 52 (1870) · Bede, *Hist. eccl.*, 3.19

Cellier, Alfred (1844–1891), composer and conductor, the son of Arsène Cellier, a French master at Hackney grammar school, was born at Hackney, Middlesex, on 1 December 1844. He was educated at the grammar school there, and at the age of eleven he became a chorister at the Chapel Royal, where one of his contemporaries was Arthur Sullivan. He held several posts as organist, notably at All Saints', Blackheath (1862), Ulster Hall, Belfast (in succession to Dr E. T. Chipp), where he was also conductor of the Belfast Philharmonic Society (1866), and St Alban the Martyr, Holborn (1868). He soon, however, exchanged an organist's career for that of a composer and conductor.

Cellier was the first musical director of the Court Theatre (January 1871); from 1871 to 1875 he was director of the orchestra at the Prince's Theatre, Manchester, and from 1877 to 1879 director at the Opera Comique, London. In 1878–9 he was joint conductor, with Sullivan, of Gatti's Covent Garden Promenade Concerts, and he held similar appointments at several London theatres, including the Criterion, St James's, and the Savoy. Later, as a result of ill health, he resided abroad, notably in America and Australia, where he was a representative for the D'Oyly Carte Company.

Cellier's chief claim to fame rests upon his comic operas. The most successful of these was *Dorothy*, which had an extraordinary popularity when produced at the Gaiety Theatre on 25 September 1886, and its 931 performances made it the longest-running show of its time. The opera was a fresh arrangement of his music for an earlier work, *Nell Gwynne*, produced ten years before, although the libretto was new. The song 'Queen of my Heart', one of the most popular numbers in the opera, was one he had composed some time before. His other comic operas included *Charity Begins at Home* (Gallery of Illustration, 1872), *The Sultan of Mocha* (Prince's Theatre, Manchester, 1874), *The Tower of London* (Manchester, 1875), *Doris* (Lyric Theatre, 1889), and *The Mountebanks*, with a libretto by W. S. Gilbert (Lyric Theatre, 1892). His grand opera in three acts, *Pandora* (to words by Longfellow), was produced in Boston in 1881. He also set Gray's 'Elegy' as a cantata for the Leeds music festival of 1883, composed incidental music for *As You Like It* (1885), and wrote a suite symphonique for orchestra, a barcarolle for flute and pianoforte, and various songs and piano pieces, of which the *Danse pompadour* was particularly popular. However, his serious concert music was less successful than his stage works.

Cellier died at his home, 69 Torrington Square, Bloomsbury, on 28 December 1891, leaving a widow, Harriet Emily, and was buried in Norwood cemetery.

F. G. EDWARDS, rev. JAMES J. NOTT

Sources Boase, *Mod. Eng. biog.* · Brown & Stratton, *Brit. mus.* · *New Grove* · Adams, *Drama* · Grove, *Dict. mus.*
Likenesses photo-engraving, repro. in J. D. Champlin, ed., *Cyclopedia of music and musicians*, 3 vols. (1888–90) · woodcut, Harvard TC
Wealth at death £4594 17s. 11d.: resworn administration, June 1893, CGPLA Eng. & Wales (1892)

Cellier, Elizabeth (*fl.* 1668–1688), midwife, has been linked to the Dormer family of Buckinghamshire, while her enemies claimed that she was a brazier's daughter from Canterbury. Cellier said that she converted to Catholicism out of loyalty to the crown, after her father and brother died on the same day during the civil war. Nothing is known of her training as a midwife, although from her writings it appears that she owned Jacques Guillemeau's *Child-Birth, or, The Happy Deliverie of Women* (1612). Nor is it known whether Cellier was licensed; if, as is usually assumed, she served the Catholic nobility in London, a licence may have been irrelevant. The role of midwife enabled her to move freely about London by day or night, and it is known that Lady Powis used Cellier to carry messages. Although Cellier claimed that her advice had led to Mary of Modena's successful pregnancy in 1687–8, she was not present at the birth of the prince of Wales.

Cellier had either one or two husbands before marrying, some time between 1668 and 1676, Peter (Pierre) Cellier, a French merchant, who was listed in 1657 as a 'reputed Catholic' and husband of Margaret, of St Martin Orgar. The parish records of St Benet Fink record that Margaret, daughter of Peter and Elizabeth Cellier, was baptized on 21 February 1676. A daughter by an earlier marriage married a Catholic apothecary, Mr Blaredale of Arundel Street, London, and Cellier also mentions a son in her writings.

On 27 March 1678 three men of St Martin Ludgate were ordered to keep the peace after an incident in which five members of the Atterbury family seriously injured Elizabeth Cellier. This may have been one of many anti-Catholic incidents in the aftermath of the 1678 Popish Plot. Cellier's involvement in politics began while making charitable visits to the prisoners in Newgate; there she met Thomas *Dangerfield, also known as Willoughby. This plausible rogue claimed to have evidence that the Popish Plot had really been a Presbyterian conspiracy to seize the state. Cellier paid his fines, used him in collecting money owed to her husband, and introduced him to Lady Powis, who gave him access to the king. Dangerfield then changed his story, claiming that the 'Presbyterian conspiracy' hid a real Catholic plot to murder the king and the earl of Shaftesbury. Incriminating documents were duly discovered in Cellier's meal-tub. Cellier was tried for treason on 11 June 1680, but was acquitted after demonstrating Dangerfield's unreliability as a witness.

On her release Cellier quickly published *Malice Defeated* (1680), giving her version of events, but also alleging the torture of Catholic prisoners in Newgate. At a second trial, for libel, on 11 September 1680, she was found guilty. In November she was implicated in a plot to burn the fleet at Chatham, and on 10 December she was placed in the pillory three times, some of her books being burned on each occasion, and fined £1000, being confined to prison until it was paid. Catholic records claim that two of her accusers subsequently went mad, while of those who stoned her in the pillory one died a few days later and another was hanged and quartered. In 1682 Cellier complained of having spent two years in prison and asked for the fine to be remitted, but this did not happen until 10 May 1687. In June 1687 she published her plan for a royal college of midwives and associated foundling hospital, for which a patent was apparently granted on 26 November. *A Scheme for the Foundation of a Royal Hospital* proposed forming 2000 London midwives into a corporation, their fees supporting twelve parish houses, where any woman could be delivered, and a central hospital to educate foundlings. Medical practitioners who paid a registration fee could attend the midwives' instructional lectures, while the college would be run by a man-midwife. Bearing

in mind the Chamberlen family's unsuccessful attempts to incorporate London midwives, historians have speculated that one of the Chamberlens was behind Cellier's scheme. In January 1688 she defended the scheme in *To Dr —*, attacking male book-learning in favour of women's historical right to practise midwifery. Nothing is known of Cellier after this date and it has been assumed that she left the country following the revolution of 1688. There is, however, an antiquarian tradition which claims that Cellier is buried at Great Missenden, Buckinghamshire.

Cellier's verbal style was witty and vitriolic; she was a colourful, forthright character who made many enemies, who nicknamed her the 'Popish Midwife'. She combined a quick mind with some gullibility. The speeches she made in her defence consciously manipulated the jury's gender stereotypes; in *The Tryal and Sentence of Elizabeth Cellier* (1680) she asks that her boldness should not be 'thought too masculine' and veers from the pathos of 'I am a poor ignorant woman, and have erred out of ignorance' to the sophistry of 'I said it was my book, and so it was, because it was in my possession, but not that I writ it. This is my fan, but it does not follow that I made it'.   HELEN KING

Sources E. Cellier, *Malice defeated, or, A brief relation of the accusation and deliverance of Elizabeth Cellier, together with an abstract of her arraignment and tryal, written by herself* (1680) · *The tryal and sentence of Elizabeth Cellier for writing, printing and publishing a scandalous libel called Malice defeated, &c.* (1680) · E. Cellier, signed deposition, BL, Add. MS 17018, no. 153 · *The scarlet beast stripped naked, being the mistery of the meal-tub the second time unravelled* · *Thomas Dangerfield's particular narrative of the late Popish design* (1679) · *The complaint of Mrs Celiers and the Jesuits in Newgate, to the E of D and the lords in the Tower, concerning the discovery of their new sham-plot* · *A letter from Lady Creswell to Madam C. the midwife* (1680) · *A true copy of a letter of consolation sent to Nat. the printer … from the meal-tub midwife* (1681) · *CSP dom.*, 1660–85, p. 481 · W. A. Shaw, ed., *Calendar of treasury books*, 8, PRO (1923), 3, 1352 · *Calendar of the manuscripts of the marquess of Ormonde*, new ser., 8 vols., HMC, 36 (1902–20), vol. 5, pp. 237, 501; vol. 7, pp. 269–70 · H. Bowler, ed., *London sessions records, 1605–1685*, Catholic RS, 34 (1934), 132 · J. C. M. Weale, ed., *Registers of the Catholic chapels royal and of the Portuguese embassy chapel, 1662–1829*, Catholic RS, 38 (1941), 10 · R. North, *Examen, or, An enquiry into the credit and veracity of a pretended complete history* (1740), 260–64 · *State trials*, vol. 7 · H. Foley, ed., *Records of the English province of the Society of Jesus*, 5 (1879), 74–5 · C. Dodd [H. Tootell], *The church history of England, from the year 1500, to the year 1688*, 3 (1742), 329 · R. Halstead [H. Mordaunt, second earl of Peterborough], *Succinct genealogies of the noble and ancient houses* (1685), 434–7 · M. George, *Women in the first capitalist society: experiences in seventeenth-century England* (1988) · T. Dangerfield, *Answer to Malice defeated* (1680)

Celling, William. *See* Selling, William (*c.*1430–1494).

Celsus. *See* Cellach (1080–1129).

Cely [Sely] **family** (*per. c.*1450–*c.*1500), merchants, of London, are famous particularly because of the unique collection of letters written by family members (preserved in the Public Record Office, London) as a result of the case in chancery between the younger Richard Cely and the widow of his brother George; these provide an exceptionally intimate picture of late fifteenth-century family and business life. The Celys were typical staplers, carrying on a business of moderate size, though they were among the larger rather than smaller exporters of wool. Most of their exports were Cotswold fleeces or fells, brought on pack-horses or wagons to London, and then shipped overseas to Calais. There they were sold to visiting buyers from the Low Countries, preferably for cash, often for delayed payments. The trade at Calais, which was their main concern, also involved the Celys in visits to Bruges and the marts at Antwerp and Bergen op Zoom, which were frequented by English mercers acting as importers, and where it was possible to buy foreign goods and also to carry out exchanges between English and Netherlandish currencies. The Celys were therefore involved in a good deal of travel on the other side of the channel, and in a very complicated international trading system, which required expert knowledge of types of wool and currency values, as well as attention to the rules of the Calais staple. They themselves were commonly divided between London, from where business was controlled, and Calais, where the wool was received and sold to foreign buyers.

The elder **Richard Cely** (d. 1482) is first mentioned in 1449, when he was already a substantial stapler and was one of a group lending 2000 marks for the support of the Calais garrison. He was married to Agnes Andrew of Adderbury, Oxfordshire, the sister of Richard Andrew, secretary to Henry VI, dean of York, and first warden of All Souls College, Oxford. This established an ecclesiastical link which had some importance for his sons. His brother John was also a stapler. In 1455 Richard was in a group of leading staplers indenting with the victualler of Calais, and in 1460 he was accused, with other staplers, of helping the mayor of the staple to seize wool. In 1461 and 1474 he was joint constable at Calais. In 1481 he was an unsuccessful candidate for election as sheriff of London. He died in January 1482. The family correspondence suggests that he had been a careful, rather irritable businessman, evidently quite successful. His wife, Agnes, died a year later in January 1483, leaving to her son Robert money to be used as trading capital.

Richard and Agnes had three sons, Robert, Richard, and George. **Robert Cely** (d. 1485), the eldest, seems to have been a rather unsatisfactory person, devoted to good living, often in debt, and casual about the business. He was a stapler by 1474–5 and also married. There are reports of his buying hawks and horses and holding dinner parties at Calais. In 1478 he was in debt at Calais, and his brother Richard appears to have threatened to imprison him. His wife, whose name is unknown, and his child died in 1479. After his wife's death he was betrothed in 1480 to a lady named Joan Hart, but quickly quarrelled with her. He fled to Calais, but she sued for breach of promise, and he was compelled to flee further, to Bruges, to escape the ecclesiastical jurisdiction of Canterbury. A settlement was made with her by Robert's father and brothers. Back in London he fell sick and was in need of money, and apparently ceased to be a stapler. In 1484 he made a pilgrimage to Santiago de Compostela; he died in February of the following year.

The younger **Richard Cely** (d. 1493), the second son, was the effective manager of the business after his father's death. He established a partnership with his brother George in 1476 which lasted until George's death. He was patronized by Sir John Weston, the prior of the order of St John of Jerusalem in England, with whom he may have been acquainted because of the Andrew connection. He accompanied Sir John on an embassy to the French court in 1480, and on a trip to Gravesend to meet Margaret of Burgundy. In 1482 he was apparently wooing Elizabeth Limerick convivially at Northleach, but in the same year he in fact made an advantageous marriage with Anne, daughter of Richard Rawson, an alderman of London, who brought a dower of 500 marks. In 1486 Richard and George, together with William Maryon, bought a ship from a Breton, which they renamed the *Margaret Cely*; she was used to carry grain exported to the Low Countries and wool to Calais, and to import wine from Bordeaux. Richard was his father's executor, and usually remained in England, handling the purchase of wool in the Cotswolds and its dispatch abroad. After the death of his brother George in 1489 he tried to obtain repayment of debts owed to them jointly. He died, however, on 5 July 1493, fairly heavily in debt to his wife's family. He left three daughters, Margaret, Isabel, and Barbara. His widow married Walter Frost of West Ham and lived until 1527.

George Cely (c.1458–1489), the third son, appears from his surviving letters to have been an amiable person, and a rather casual and free writer. He is first mentioned in the records in 1472 as buying clothes in London. In 1474 he was learning music from a harpist at Calais, how to play 'Mine Heart's Lust' and 'O Freshest Flower'. In 1478 he was with the other two brothers in an excursion from Calais to Boulogne. In 1479 George appears to have been enjoying a love affair with a French lady at Calais, but later in the same year he fell seriously ill at Bruges, causing his relatives some anxiety. In 1482 he moved to London, remaining Richard's partner, and about 18 May 1484 married Margery, *née* Punt, the childless widow of Edmund Rygon, a prosperous draper; it was probably a very favourable match. George lived at Mark Lane, London. He died in 1489, leaving four sons, Richard, Avery, George, and John, and his wife pregnant with a fifth, Edmund. His widow married Sir John Haleghwell. There was afterwards a good deal of litigation between the widows Anne and Margery Cely and their new husbands, about the finances of the brothers Richard and George and lands that they had acquired, principally in Essex.   GEORGE HOLMES

Sources A. Hanham, ed., *The Cely letters, 1472–1488*, EETS, 273 (1975) · A. Hanham, *The Celys and their world: an English merchant family of the fifteenth century* (1985)
Archives PRO, E 122 · PRO, letters

Cely, George (c.1458–1489). *See under* Cely family (*per. c.*1450–*c.*1500).

Cely, Richard (d. 1482). *See under* Cely family (*per. c.*1450–*c.*1500).

Cely, Richard (d. 1493). *See under* Cely family (*per. c.*1450–*c.*1500).

Cely, Robert (d. 1485). *See under* Cely family (*per. c.*1450–*c.*1500).

Cenn Fáelad mac Blaímaic (*d.* 675), high-king of Ireland, was the son of *Blaímac mac Áeda (*d.* 665), joint high-king of Ireland. Blaímac and Diarmait, who both died in the great plague of 664–5, were first succeeded as high-king by Blaímac's son *Sechnassach, but he was killed late in 671 by one of his principal vassal kings, Dub Dúin, king of Cenél Coirpri. Cenn Fáelad's reign is not said by the annals to have started until the next year, 672, suggesting an interregnum of some months, and it was, to judge by these annals, serenely uneventful. He was married to Órlaith, daughter of Dúnlang, and was killed by his successor and first cousin, *Fínsnechtae Fledach mac Dúnchada, in 675. According to the annals of Tigernach, this occurred 'at the house of the descendant of Maine in Dál Celtra', perhaps on the west side of Lough Derg in the north-east corner of what is now Clare. If this is correct—and it is supported by the alternative name 'the battle of Aircheltra' given by the expanded regnal list in the Book of Leinster—he was probably ambushed while on his royal circuit (*cuairt ríg*) many miles to the west of his own territory. Cenn Fáelad's claim to be recognized as a king of Tara (the title of the high-kings of Ireland) is supported by the twelfth-century regnal lists, but also by the entry in the original chronicle of Ireland recording the beginning of his reign in succession to his brother Sechnassach, to whom the chronicle gave the title king of Tara. On the other hand, his name is not included in the late seventh-century *Baile Chuinn* ('The frenzy of Conn'), a regnal list of Tara in the form of a prophecy. *Baile Chuinn*, however, appears to reflect the particular interests of Cenn Fáelad's successor, Fínsnechtae Fledach, during whose reign it was composed.   T. M. CHARLES-EDWARDS

Sources W. Stokes, ed., 'The annals of Tigernach [8 pts]', *Revue Celtique*, 16 (1895), 374–419; 17 (1896), 6–33, 119–263, 337–420; 18 (1897), 9–59, 150–97, 267–303, 374–91; pubd sep. (1993) • *Ann. Ulster* • G. Murphy, 'On the dates of two sources used in Thurneysen's *Heldensage*: 1. *Baile Chuind* and the date of *Cin Dromma Snechtai*', *Ériu*, 16 (1952), 145–56, esp. 145–51 • M. C. Dobbs, ed. and trans., 'The Ban-shenchus [3 pts]', *Revue Celtique*, 47 (1930), 283–339; 48 (1931), 163–234; 49 (1932), 437–89 • R. I. Best and others, eds., *The Book of Leinster, formerly Lebar na Núachongbála*, 6 vols. (1954–83), vol. 1 • W. M. Hennessy, ed. and trans., *Chronicum Scotorum: a chronicle of Irish affairs*, Rolls Series, 46 (1866) • M. A. O'Brien, ed., *Corpus genealogiarum Hiberniae* (Dublin, 1962) • K. Meyer, ed., 'The Laud genealogies and tribal histories', *Zeitschrift für Celtische Philologie*, 8 (1910–12), 291–338 • F. J. Byrne, *Irish kings and high-kings* (1973)

Cennick, John (1718–1755), lay preacher and Moravian minister, was born in Reading on 12 December 1718, the son of a clothier who was of Quaker descent. Brought up in the established church, he experienced an evangelical conversion on 6 September 1737 in his parish church in Reading. Isolated by this experience he searched for support, and made contact with the Wesley brothers and George Whitefield. John Wesley visited him, and Cennick was invited to assist in the revival continuing at Kingswood, near Bristol. He preached in the open air, although not ordained, and so is sometimes claimed as the first Methodist lay preacher. A simple man trained as a shoemaker, it was his earnest exhortations and colourful illustrations which made him effective as a preacher. A gentle

and effective pastor and supervisor of the school at Kingswood, he had a deep impact on the Kingswood miners. His mission to Upton, Gloucestershire, in mid-1740 stirred up deep controversy.

Late in 1740 the evangelical revival was convulsed by disputes between Wesley and Whitefield over predestination and perfection. Cennick took Whitefield's side, and John Wesley expelled him on 6 March 1741. It was a fateful moment in the history of the revival. Cennick erected a Calvinist tabernacle in Kingswood in June 1741. That summer he went preaching along the Welsh border in one of the most opposed missions in the whole history of Methodism. In Swindon, Stratton, and Lyneham he was roughly treated by the mob, but there were many converts, who were organized into the Wiltshire Association, the first Calvinist Methodist body. He became a key preacher for many of Whitefield's chapels.

Meanwhile Cennick's contacts with Moravians were increasing (including a meeting with Zinzendorf in 1743), and he sought to encourage Whitefield to reach a rapprochement with them. His strong emphasis on imputed righteousness as the basis of spiritual life and universal salvation was viewed by other Calvinist Methodists as playing into the hands of the antinomians and Arminians. After an aborted mission to Ireland, where he hoped to establish his independence, he wrote on 20 November 1745 seeking admission to the brethren, subsequently offering his Wiltshire societies to the Moravians—an offer confirmed by the society stewards on 18 December 1745. His departure was a serious blow to Calvinist Methodism in England, and his former friends at Whitefield's tabernacle thereafter shunned him.

In December 1745 Cennick visited the Moravians in Germany. Zinzendorf permitted him to fulfil his dream of evangelizing Ireland, and he commenced on 3 June 1746. Nicknamed Swaddling John because he would adore only the infant Jesus, not images of the crucifixion, his preaching drew vast crowds, and aroused fervent support and opposition in Catholic circles. A society was formed in Dublin in March 1747. For the next five years he was based in Ireland, preaching not just in Dublin but also in Ballymena and throughout the northern counties. Perhaps 220 religious societies were formed through this work, although most had only a brief existence. He was finally ordained into Moravian deacon's orders in London in September 1749, and then returned to Ireland. He spent 1753 in Wales, and founded societies in Leominster and Haverfordwest. On 12 July 1747 he married Jane Bryant of Clack, Wiltshire. His extensive literary output of some fifty-seven works included vivid, gentle, and homely sermons, and one of the first hymnbooks of the revival, *Sacred Hymns for the Children of God* (1741). He wrote the widely used hymn 'Children of the heavenly king' and the grace 'Be present at our table Lord'.

Financial embarrassment, the growing attack on the brethren, and ill health strained Cennick's relations with the Moravians in the 1750s, and it was while on one of his visits to the brethren in London in 1755 that he died of a fever on 4 July. He was survived by two of his three children. He was one of the greatest evangelists of the revival, stirring up dramatic conversions and fierce opposition wherever he preached. His responsiveness to the language of religious experience (reflecting his temperament, although his Quaker background may have been a factor) drew him towards the Moravians, but his theology was more Calvinist than Moravian.

PETER J. LINEHAM

Sources J. Cennick, *The life of Mr. J. Cennick, with an account of the trials and temptations which he endured till it pleased our Saviour to shew him his love and send him into his vineyard*, 2nd edn (1745) · G. M. Roberts, ed., *Selected Trevecka letters (1742–1747)* (1956) · F. Baker, *John Cennick (1718–55): a handlist of his writings* (1958) · J. E. Hutton, *John Cennick: a sketch* [1906] · V. W. Couillard, *The theology of John Cennick* (1957) · T. Beynon, ed., *Howell Harris, reformer and soldier (1714–1773)* (1958) · *DNB* · D. M. Lewis, ed., *The Blackwell dictionary of evangelical biography, 1730–1860*, 2 vols. (1995)
Archives JRL, Methodist Archives and Research Centre · NL Wales, corresp. | Moravian House archives, Muswell Hill, London
Likenesses R. Purcell, mezzotint, 1754 (aged thirty-five; after Jenkins), BM, NPG · P. Dawe, mezzotint, pubd 1785 (after A. L. Brandt, 1785), BM, NPG

Centlivre [*née* Freeman; *other married name* Carroll], **Susanna** (*bap.* 1669?, *d.* 1723), playwright and actress, was probably the Susanna baptized on 20 November 1669 at the parish church of Whaplode, Lincolnshire, the daughter of William Freeman of Holbeach and his wife, Anne, the daughter of Mr Marham, a gentleman of Lynn Regis, Norfolk. Giles Jacob's brief account of Susanna's early life, which he claimed came from her hands and was published in 1719, paints a picture of a genteel family persecuted at the Restoration. Her father was apparently 'a Dissenter, and a zealous Parliamentarian' (Jacob, 31). The whig historian who published her early writing, Abel Boyer, thought in his short obituary for her that she had had 'a mean Parentage, and Education' (Boyer, 670). She was either orphaned at a young age or ran away from cruel step-parents and was 'married or something like it to a Mr. Fox, at age 16' (Mottley, 187). Jacob discreetly explains away two early marriages, of which no records exist, one:

> before the Age of Fifteen, to a Nephew of Sir Stephen Fox. This Gentleman living with her but a Year, she afterwards married Mr. Carrol, an Officer in the Army: And survived him likewise, in the space of a Year and a half.   (Jacob, 31)

She kept and wrote under the name Carroll for the early part of her career.

All biographers agree that Susanna's education was a matter of 'her own Industry and Application' (Jacob, 32). She could probably read French and was *au fait* with 'a great deal of poetry' (Mottley, 187). Mottley includes a picaresque story of her journey with Anthony Hammond to London via Cambridge, where she attended university lectures, disguised as 'Cousin Jack'. Although she certainly knew Hammond in later life, and contributed poems to his *New Miscellany* (1720), the educational value of this putative sojourn in Cambridge is suspect, as are many of the other romantic embellishments of Mottley's account. A more probable scenario comes from Chetwood, who thinks she endured an unhappy home until 'a company of

Susanna Centlivre (*bap.* 1669?, *d.* 1723), by Peter Pelham, 1720 (after D. Fermin)

stroling Players came to Stamford [near Holbeach] where she joined them with a little persuasion … having a greater inclination to wear the Britches, than the Petticoat, she stuck unto the Men's Parts' (Bowyer, 11). Satires on Susanna talk of her in the same breath as leading players.

Susanna's first writings were published in 1700, when she contributed a verse, as Polumnia, to a tribute volume on Dryden's death, *The Nine Muses*, alongside such women playwrights as Delariviere Manley (with whom she was to fall out over politics) and Mary Pix and the poet Sarah Fyge Egerton, who acted as her patron. She also contributed letters to volumes collected by Sam Briscoe (*Familiar and Courtly Letters*, 1700) and Boyer (*Letters of Wit, Politicks and Morality*, 1701). The letters, although witty fictions, reveal a connection with Farquhar, William Ayloffe, and other writers and playwrights. Boyer probably engineered the introduction of her first play, *The Perjured Husband*, to the company at Drury Lane. This was a strange play with a tragic main plot set in Venice at carnival time and a bawdy comic sub-plot, but it 'went off with general applause'. It was published under Susanna's name, and the prologue, spoken by Mrs Oldfield, proudly proclaimed that it had a female author. Susanna had found her métier in the theatre, and she wrote sixteen plays and three short afterpieces, as well as poems, letters, satire, and short prose. Susanna made a modest living over the next few years from witty and convoluted comedies, each judiciously dedicated to an open-handed whiggish patron (*The Beau Duel* and *The Stolen Heiress*, 1702; *Love's Contrivance*, 1703; *The Gamester* and *The Basset Table*, 1705). Although she complained that 'writing is a kind of lottery in this fickle age, and dependence on the stage as precarious as the cast of a die' (*Love at a Venture*, 1706), it was her gambling play, *The Gamester*, that found most success during this period. Susanna was established as part of a circle of playwrights who contributed prologues and epilogues to each other's work. George Farquhar, William Burnaby, Nicholas Rowe, Colley Cibber, Ambrose Philips, Thomas Baker, Thomas Burnet, and Richard Steele all provided material. But life was not always straightforward for the female playwright. Susanna's work was sometimes printed anonymously, or she was required to write a prologue which implied a male author—an injustice she railed against in the preface to *The Platonick Lady* (1707):

> A Play secretly introduc'd to the House, whilst the Author remains unknown, is approv'd by every Body: The Actor's cry it up, and are in expectation of a great Run; the Bookseller of a Second Edition, and the Scribler of a Sixth Night: But if by chance the Plot's discover'd, and the Brat found Fatherless, immediately it flags in the Opinion of those that extoll'd it before, and the Bookseller falls in his Price, with this Reason only, *It is a Woman's*.

In 1706 Susanna had been forced to tour with her *Love at a Venture*, a play rejected and then plagiarized by Cibber as *The Double Gallant*. The following year, allegedly while playing the breeches role of Alexander in Nathaniel Lee's *The Rival Queens* before Queen Anne at Windsor, she met Joseph Centlivre (d. 1724/5), a widower with a daughter and son by his first wife, Grace. Centlivre was yeoman of the mouth, a middle-ranking official in the queen's privy kitchen, earning £60 per annum. They were married on 23 April 1707 in London at St Benet Paul's Wharf and settled in some style at Buckingham Court as near neighbours of Colley Cibber. After her marriage Susanna was more financially secure, but she did not give up her writing. Indeed she returned to the stage in triumph on 12 May 1709 with *The Busybody*, which had a thirteen-night run and was revived by both patent companies the following season. Its witty, involved story follows the fortunes of Isabinda, who evades the Spanish rule of her father, and a Spanish match, to marry Charles Gripe. Charles's father, Sir Francis Gripe, has his eye on one of his wards, Miranda, who only narrowly escapes to marry Sir George Airy. The many plans of the pairs of lovers are continually thwarted by the ever-curious Marplot, whose attempts to help end in disaster and discovery. *The Busybody* became one of Garrick's favourite plays; it was performed more than 450 times before 1800 and ran into forty editions before 1884. Besides her income as author, including two benefit performances commanded by George I and the future George II, Mottley claimed that her dedication to William Bentinck, the earl of Portland, netted her 40 guineas. However, Susanna's sequel, *Marplot in Lisbon* (1710), did not meet with the same level of success.

Centlivre set her next comedy, *The Man's Bewitched* (1709), in the provinces and gave it a distinctly political twist. Laura, imprisoned by her tory guardian Sir David Watchum, liberates herself by feigning madness, recruiting for the army, and singing a rousing chorus of 'Give me liberty and love'. The *Female Tatler* for 12–14 December 1709 included an alleged conversation between Centlivre and the editor, where the author immodestly praised her own play and railed against the players. The company was outraged, and Susanna had difficulty in persuading them that it was a fiction and to play on. She attributed the incident to politically inspired malice on the part of the tory editors of the *Female Tatler*.

Centlivre was a writer who maintained close connections with the companies that performed her work: 'the Poet and the Player are like Soul and Body, indispensably necessary to one another; the correct Author makes the Player shine, whilst the judicious Player makes the Poet's fame immortal' (preface, *The Wonder*). This interaction was sometimes financial, as when she offered the 1703 publication rights of *Love's Contrivance* to the actress Mrs Knight. Indeed:

> she had much Vivacity and good Humour; she was remarkably good-natured and benevolent in her Temper, and ready to do any friendly Office as far as it was in her Power. She made herself some Friends and many Enemies by her strict Attachment to Whig Principles even in the most dangerous Times. (Mottley, 188)

Centlivre's political affiliation was marked in all her later work, notably through the characters of tory fathers or guardians, whose party fervour forms another obstacle to the happiness of the young lovers—always whiggishly inclined. Her afterpiece *A Bickerstaff's Burying* (1710) was a vicious political satire. While other whigs were retrenching as Queen Anne grew increasingly threatened by the issue, Susanna openly supported the Hanoverian succession. The epilogue she designed in 1712 to conclude *The Perplexed Lovers*, upholding the claim of Electoral Prince George Augustus to take his seat in the Lords as duke of Cambridge, was initially banned, and Anne Oldfield, who was to speak it, was threatened. When in 1714 the electoral prince's father became George I, Susanna gloated, as in her ironic autobiographical poem *A Woman's Case*:

> To GEORGE of WALES I dedicated,
> Tho' then at Court I knew him hated.
> Dick Steele was then in Reputation
> With all true Lovers of my Nation:
> Yet spight of Steel's Advice I did it
> Nay, tho' my Husband's place forbid it.

The Wonder: a Woman Keeps a Secret (1714) was dedicated to the new king. Like most of Centlivre's plays, it was based on an existing comedy, but her concentration of plot incidents, sharpened characterization, and topical comment remade it in popular form and assured it a long life. Garrick chose to make his farewell to the stage, on 10 June 1776, as Felix from *The Wonder*.

Centlivre made a respectable living from her writing later in life: Lintott paid £10 for the copyright of early work; Curll offered £21 each for *The Wonder*, *The Cruel Gift*, and *The Artifice*. Her admiring biographer records that she:

> could shew (which I believe few other Poets could, who depended chiefly on their Pen) a great many Jewels and Pieces of Plate, which were the Produce of her own Labour, either purchased by the Money brought in by her Copies, her Benefit-Plays, or were Presents from Patrons. (Mottley, 188)

Mottley lists the sums, gold snuff-boxes, and diamond

rings that she apparently accumulated in return for dedications and poems. She even made something from dedicating her unacted farce *The Gotham Election* to Secretary Craggs. He sent her 20 guineas via Mrs Bracegirdle as a consideration 'not so much [of] the Merit of the Piece, as what was proper to be done by a Secretary of State' (ibid., 190). *The Gotham Election* was the first English play to deal directly with electioneering and vote-rigging and was considered too inflammatory to be staged in the turbulent election year of 1715. It had its outing at the Haymarket in 1724.

In 1716 Centlivre collaborated with Nicholas Rowe on her only tragedy, *The Cruel Gift*, and defended herself from charges of having borrowed it all from him. *A Bold Stroke for a Wife* followed in 1718. Each earned their author a sixth night's income. Kemble kept *A Bold Stroke* in the repertory at Drury Lane. Centlivre fell ill in 1719 and produced only one more comedy, *The Artifice*, in 1722; it bears all of her hallmarks, being packed with comic set pieces and keenly observed buffoons, and takes a sideswipe at tories, Catholics, and Quakers. She continued to write laudatory poems, ballads, and short articles throughout her life.

Engravings of Centlivre's portrait, on sale in 1720, show a handsome woman and little sign of the 'small Wen on her left Eye lid, which gave her a Masculine Air' (Bowyer, 11) or a squint, according to some satirists. Although she made some political enemies, notably Pope, who dubbed her 'The Cook's Wife of Buckingham Court' (Pope, *A Further Account of the most Deplorable Condition of Mr. E. Curll*) or 'slip-shod Muse' (Pope, *The Dunciad*, 3.141), her plays remained firmly in the repertory for 150 years. Hazlitt's assessment goes some way to explaining the longevity of her work:

> Her plays have a provoking spirit and volatile salt in them, which still preserves them from decay … their interest depends chiefly on the intricate involution and artful denouement of the plot, which has a strong tincture of mischief in it, and the wit is seasoned by the archness of the humour and sly allusion to the most delicate points. (Hazlitt, 314)

Centlivre died on 1 December 1723 at Buckingham Court and was buried three days later in the actors' church at St Paul's, Covent Garden. Her husband survived her by little over a year.   J. MILLING

Sources J. W. Bowyer, *The celebrated Mrs Centlivre* (1952) · [J. Mottley], *A compleat list of all the English dramatick poets*, pubd with T. Whincop, *Scanderbeg* (1747) · F. P. Lock, *Susanna Centlivre* (1979) · A. Boyer, *The political state of Great Britain*, 26 (1723), 670–71 · W. R. Chetwood, *The British theatre* (1750), 140–41 · [G. Jacob], *The poetical register, or, The lives and characters of the English dramatick poets*, [1] (1719), 31–2 · N. Cotton, *Women playwrights in England, 1363–1750* (1980) · E. L. Avery, ed., *The London stage, 1660–1800*, pt 2: *1700–1729* (1960) · Genest, *Eng. stage* · W. Hazlitt, *English comic writers* (1930) · P. B. Anderson, 'Innocence and artifice, or, Mrs. Centlivre and *The Female Tatler*', *Philological Quarterly*, 16 (1937), 358–75 · R. Frushell, 'Biographical problems and satisfactions in Susanna Centlivre', *Restoration and Eighteenth-Century Theatre Research*, 7/2 (1992), 1–17 · J. H. Mackenzie, 'Susan Centlivre', *N&Q*, 198 (1953), 386–90 · J. Sutherland, 'Progress of error: Mrs C and the biographers', *Review of English Studies*, 18 (1942), 167–82 · J. Pearson, *The prostituted muse: images of women and women dramatists, 1642–1737* (1988) · J. Doran, *'Their majesties' servants': annals of the English stage*, 2 vols. (1864) · F. Morgan, *The female wits: women playwrights of the London stage, 1660–1720* (1981) · W. A. Littledale, ed., *The registers of St Bene't and St Peter, Paul's Wharf, London*, 2, Harleian Society, register section, 39 (1910), 67

Likenesses P. Pelham, mezzotint, 1720 (after D. Fermin), BM, Harvard TC [*see illus.*]

Centlivres, Albert van de Sandt (1887–1966), judge in South Africa, was born at Newlands, Cape Town, on 13 January 1887, the third son and seventh of the eleven children of Frederick James Centlivres, director of companies and mayor of Rondebosch, and his wife, Albertina de Villiers. Matriculating with distinction at the South African College School in 1903 he went on, at the South African College, to academic achievements which included honours in classics and a Rhodes scholarship. At New College, Oxford, he took his BA (with second-class honours in jurisprudence) in 1909, and the following year, with third-class honours, his BCL. He had joined the Middle Temple and was called to the bar in 1910. In 1911 he was admitted as an advocate of the Cape provincial division, South Africa.

At first Centlivres's was the usual fate of the young advocate and he had the time in which to edit *Juta's Daily Reporter* and so consolidate and extend his knowledge of procedure. His practice began to prosper after two interruptions: a brief interlude in Southern Rhodesia and the eruption of the First World War, in which he served in South-West Africa as a private and after which he returned to civil life with, it is believed, a military discharge recording his education as 'fair'. In 1916 he married Isabel, daughter of George Short, accountant and merchant of Cape Town; they had one son, who predeceased his father, and three daughters.

In 1927 Centlivres became a KC. It was as a lawyer rather than an advocate that he was achieving a reputation. His preparation was as comprehensive as it was thorough, his arguments were closely packed, yet precise, and he was considered an expert on the law of wills. He took part in a number of important cases, among them being the 'heresy trial', *Du Plessis v. Synod of the Dutch Reformed church*, and *Hofmeyr v. Badenhorst*, a defamation case resulting from an election at Riversdale. It was perhaps a portent that in 1920 he had been appointed parliamentary draftsman, a post which, during fourteen years, gave him a special insight into statute law. After acting as a judge of the high court of South-West Africa in 1922 and of the Cape provincial division in 1932, 1933, and 1934, he was appointed a puisne judge of the Cape provincial division in February 1935. Four years later, in 1939, he was elevated to the appellate division. He was appointed chairman of the public service inquiry commission in 1944 and his investigations into the salaries and conditions of service of civil servants were notable for their effective celerity. In 1950 he succeeded E. F. Watermeyer as chief justice and in 1957 he retired after a period in the appellate division which, in length, had been exceeded only by Sir William Solomon.

While, in other legal fields, Centlivres was responsible

for a number of notable judgments, as he was in the celebrated case *R*. v. *Milne and Erleigh* (1951), it is his pronouncements in the three most important constitutional cases in the history of South Africa which, in particular, have ensured for him the attention of posterity. These, *Harris* v. *Minister of the Interior* (1952), *Minister of the Interior* v. *Harris* (1952), and *Collins* v. *Minister of the Interior* (1956), represent a collision between cabinet and judiciary, and were the culmination of a government attempt to remove the coloured population from the common roll. Of the three cases the second is perhaps the most remarkable. Frustrated by the appellate division's insistence that the requirements for amending the entrenched clauses of the South Africa Act be respected, the house of assembly and the senate constituted themselves a superior high court of parliament. This was unanimously declared unconstitutional by the appellate division, the chief justice rejecting the contention that parliament could decide bicamerally that no previous court had the right finally to decide whether an act conformed with the requirements of the South Africa Act. His judgment in the first case was described by Professor E. N. Griswold, then dean of the Harvard law school, as 'a great judgement, deserving to rank with the best work of the judges who have contributed to the field of constitutional law' (*South African Law Journal*, 1957, 4). In the end the senate was 'packed' and the number of judges of the appellate division was increased from five to eleven without consultation with the chief justice, who endured political attacks with dignified restraint. It was during this turbulent period that the chief justice represented South Africa at, for instance, the seventh legal convention of the Law Council of Australia (1952) and the conference on government under law at Harvard (1955). In his address at Harvard, 'The South African constitution and the rule of law', he forcibly reaffirmed his faith in the rule of law and the rights and dignity of the individual, causes for which he fought unceasingly after his retirement.

In 1951 Centlivres had succeeded J. C. Smuts as chancellor of the University of Cape Town and, after his retirement as chief justice, was unremitting, through word and action, symbol, meeting, and procession, in his refusal to accept government insistence that, wherever possible, the university should be restricted to white students only. On his installation as chancellor he had emphasized his attitude in his *Inaugural Address*:

> To put it positively, academic freedom, as I understood it, means the unrestricted right on the part of a University to decide for itself what it shall teach, how it shall teach it and whom it shall admit to be taught, as well as the unrestricted right to select as its teachers the best men and women available, whether they happen to have been born in South Africa or elsewhere.

Sociable, unaffected, accessible, Albert Centlivres was typical of the English-speaking South African at his best. In action as well as word he was a democrat. Like Smuts, whom he knew well, he was happy climbing Table Mountain, and, when those days were over, his tall, craggy figure, with pipe, stick, and dog, could be seen ranging the walks of his neighbourhood. Honours burdened him little. He was an honorary DCL of Oxford, and an honorary LLD of the universities of Melbourne, Cape Town, and the Witwatersrand, and of Rhodes University. He was also an honorary fellow of New College and an honorary bencher of the Middle Temple. He died at Claremont, Cape Town, on 19 September 1966. A. LENNOX-SHORT, *rev.*

Sources 'Hon. Mr Justice A. V. de S. Centlivres', *South African Law Journal*, 52/4 (Nov 1935), 409–13 • 'Retirement of Mr Justice Centlivres, chief justice of South Africa', *South African Law Journal*, 74/1 (Feb 1957), 1–5 • A. van de Sandt Centlivres, *Inaugural address* [1951] • *Cape Argus* (19 Sept 1966) • *The Times* (20 Sept 1966) • *Cape Times* (20 Sept 1966) • A. Lennox-Short, ed., *Albert van de Sandt Centlivres, chancellor: University of Cape Town memorial ceremony, Jameson Hall, 13 October 1966* (Cape Town, 1966) • private information (1981) • personal knowledge (1981)

Likenesses N. Lewis, oils, University of Cape Town, South Africa, Jameson Hall • L. Rautenbach, bronze bust, University of Cape Town, South Africa, Jagger Library

Centwine (*d.* in or after **685**), king of the Gewisse, is said to have been the son of King *Cynegils. Cynegils was himself said to have been a son of *Ceolwulf, though he appears in genealogies to have been the son of Ceolwulf's brother, *Ceol. However, the similarity in the names of the two brothers could easily have led to confusion between them when the Anglo-Saxon Chronicle was compiled. Centwine came to power in 676, during what Bede characterized as a confused period of about ten years following the death of Cenwalh in 672, when the kingdom was divided between sub-kings. If Bede's ten years is taken literally it must have been Centwine who united the kingdom again under one ruler (though he does not seem to have been known to Bede). His reign can be seen as a restoration of the dominance enjoyed since the death of Ceawlin by his branch of the royal house. The Anglo-Saxon Chronicle records only one battle for Centwine, when he is said, in 682, to have 'put the Britons to flight as far as the sea' (*ASC*, s.a. 682); but Aldhelm, in a poem written for Centwine's daughter *Bugga, refers to his three great victories. These cannot be identified, but Centwine was presumably continuing Gewissan conquest of the south-west. Aldhelm also praises Centwine for his 'just' rule and for 'granting many estates to recently established churches' (Aldhelm, 47–9); there is a charter in his name granting land to Glastonbury, which also claimed it had been granted other estates by the king.

Among the foundations which benefited from Centwine's generosity was presumably the unnamed house to which he retired as a monk in 685. It is not clear if this withdrawal was forced on him by his successor Cædwalla, or if it was Centwine's decision to abdicate to follow a religious life which gave Cædwalla his opportunity. If the latter, as Aldhelm's poem perhaps suggests, it may be that Centwine, like several other Anglo-Saxon kings, had been influenced in his enthusiasm for Christianity by the charismatic Bishop Wilfrid. Centwine had received Wilfrid *c*.681 when he had been expelled from Northumbria by King Ecgfrith; but according to Wilfrid's biographer, Stephen of Ripon, the bishop was only allowed to stay in Wessex for a brief period because Centwine was married to a sister of Wilfrid's enemy, Queen Iurminburg of Northumbria, and so was obliged to require him to leave. It is not known when Centwine died, but he was no longer alive when Aldhelm wrote his poem for Bugga during the reign of King Ine (688–726).   BARBARA YORKE

Sources *ASC*, sa. 676, 682 • Aldhelm, 'Carmen ecclesiasticum III', *Aldhelm: the poetic works*, trans. M. Lapidge and J. Rosier (1985) • Bede, *Hist. eccl.*, 4.12 • *AS chart.*, S 237, 1667–9 • E. Stephanus, *The life of Bishop Wilfrid*, ed. and trans. B. Colgrave (1927), chap. 40 • C. Stancliffe, 'Kings who opted out', *Ideal and reality in Frankish and Anglo-Saxon society*, ed. P. Wormald, D. Bullough, and R. Collins (1983), 154–76 • B. A. E. Yorke, *Kings and kingdoms of early Anglo-Saxon England* (1990)

Cenwalh (*d.* 672), king of the Gewisse, was the son of King *Cynegils, whom he succeeded in 642. Three years after his accession he was driven into exile by *Penda of Mercia, because, according to Bede, he had previously repudiated his wife, Penda's sister. It is not known who ruled his kingdom during his absence. Cenwalh took refuge with another enemy of Penda, King Anna of the East Angles, and through his intervention was baptized in 646, for, unlike his father, brother, and nephew, he had apparently not been converted earlier by Bishop Birinus (*d.* 650). It is not known how Cenwalh reacquired his kingdom, but the first act recorded after his return in 648 is an accommodation with his nephew Cuthred, son of King *Cwichelm (*d.* 636) and presumably a rival candidate for the position of dominant king. This was in the form of control of a district of 3000 hides based on Ashdown, the Berkshire Downs—an area frequently in dispute between the Gewisse (or West Saxons, as they subsequently became known) and the Mercians.

Cenwalh appointed as second bishop of Dorchester-on-Thames a distinguished Frankish priest called Agilbert who had been studying in Ireland. His appointment is dated 650 in the Anglo-Saxon Chronicle. Some ten years later Cenwalh founded a new bishopric in Winchester and appointed Wine, an Anglo-Saxon who had been consecrated in Gaul, as its bishop. Bede attributes Cenwalh's actions to wanting to have a bishop who spoke his own language, but by 660 the Gewisse seem to have been having increasing trouble keeping control in the upper Thames valley and may have lost it altogether by 661 when Wulfhere of Mercia is recorded as harrying Ashdown. Whether in annoyance at having his diocese divided without being consulted, as Bede believed, or because the West Saxons could no longer provide protection, Agilbert returned to Francia and left Wine as the sole West Saxon bishop. A few years later Cenwalh expelled Wine from his diocese and his kingdom remained without a bishop for a while until Cenwalh invited Agilbert to return. Agilbert was by this time bishop of Paris, but arranged for his nephew Leuthere to be appointed instead and he was consecrated in 670 by Archbishop Theodore. Cenwalh naturally features prominently in Winchester tradition, but the generous grants attributed to him by the episcopal foundation of Old Minster, including the manor of Chilcomb which ringed the city and may have incorporated the *territorium* of the Roman town, are not supported by authentic surviving charters. However, the original church of Old Minster built during his reign has been recovered through excavation, and shown to be a stone church laid out with geometrical precision.

The establishment of the bishopric of Winchester is a sign of Gewissan interests gradually being concentrated to the south and west of their original homelands. The Anglo-Saxon Chronicle mentions major battles that were part of this process, though they cannot be fitted into a coherent narrative of conquest. Battles are recorded in 652 at Bradford-on-Avon, at 'Peonnan' in 658, when Cenwalh drove his British opponents 'in flight as far as the Parret' (*ASC*, s.a. 658), and in 661 at 'Posentesbyrig', which cannot be located with any certainty. Cenwalh was regarded as the founder of the monastery of Sherborne, but although this may be an authentic tradition, the charter which purports to be in his name is a forgery. It would appear that important advances into the Jutish province in what is now southern Hampshire and areas previously under British control in what would become west Wiltshire, Dorset, and Somerset were made during Cenwalh's reign. Close links with the Northumbrian court circle which had been established during the reign of his father were continued. Having a mutual enemy in Mercia was one factor bringing the courts together, but another link may have been Bishop Agilbert who seems to have had his own contacts with Northumbrian churchmen. Cenwalh is said to have been on friendly terms with King Alhfrith and recommended that he be reconciled with Bishop Wilfrid whom Agilbert subsequently advised at the Synod of Whitby in 664.

The last event that can be dated in the life of Cenwalh is his reception of Benedict Biscop on the latter's return from his fourth visit to Rome, some time in 672. According to the Anglo-Saxon Chronicle, Cenwalh died in the same year and was succeeded by his second wife, *Seaxburh, who, uniquely among Anglo-Saxon queens, apparently ruled in her own right for a year.   BARBARA YORKE

Sources *ASC*, s.a. 641, 644, 645, 648, 650, 652, 658, 660, 661, 672 • Bede, *Hist. eccl.*, 3.7 • *AS chart.*, S 227–9 • E. Stephanus, *The life of Bishop Wilfrid*, ed. and trans. B. Colgrave (1927), chap. 7 • 'Historia abbatum auctore Baeda', *Venerabilis Baedae opera historica*, ed. C. Plummer, 1 (1896), 364–87, esp. 367 • D. P. Kirby, *The earliest English kings* (1991) • B. Yorke, *Wessex in the early middle ages* (1995) • B. Kjølbye-Biddle, 'The 7th century minster at Winchester interpreted', *The Anglo-Saxon church: papers on history, architecture, and archaeology in honour of Dr H. M. Taylor*, ed. L. A. S. Butler and R. K. Morris, Council for British Archaeology Research Report, 60 (1986), 196–209

Cenwulf (*d.* 821), king of the Mercians, was the son of Cuthbert and, according to a contemporary genealogy, descended from Cenwalh, brother of King *Penda (*d.* 655). He succeeded the son of *Offa, *Ecgfrith [see under Offa], whose brief reign ended in December 796. Alcuin says that Offa shed much blood to secure Ecgfrith's position, and if this refers to a purge of the royal kindred it may explain why Cenwulf succeeded, despite being a distant relative.

Cenwulf's early years as king were troubled. Offa had

been overlord of much of southern England, but in 796 Kent rebelled under Eadberht Praen. In 798 Cenwulf attacked, captured Eadberht, and took him to Mercia, where his eyes were put out and his hands amputated. Cenwulf's brother Cuthred was made sub-king of Kent in the same year and they granted land there jointly and individually until Cuthred's death in 807. The coins of a King Eadwald precede Cenwulf's in East Anglia, and hint at another short-lived rising against Mercian overlordship. Relations with Essex are obscure until 811, when King Sigered first witnesses Cenwulf's charters; in 812 he is described as *subregulus* and in 814 as *dux*. Thus Cenwulf seems to have deprived him of royal status, as Offa did rulers of Kent and Sussex. Cenwulf's dealings with Sussex are witnessed only by a grant to the bishop of Selsey of 801. He had little power in other kingdoms. King Beorhtric of Wessex had married Offa's daughter and witnessed Ecgfrith's charters, which suggests some kind of association between the two. But there is no evidence of Cenwulf's influence in Wessex beyond a grant by Pope Leo III in 798 of Glastonbury Abbey to Cenwulf's son *Cynehelm, and a confirmation of it by Cenwulf himself, both of which may well be later forgeries. On Beorhtric's death in 802, which also saw the repulse of a Mercian invasion under Ealdorman Æthelmund, Wessex probably passed out of Cenwulf's orbit.

King Eardwulf of Northumbria attacked Mercia in 801, probably for sheltering political refugees, and a long campaign ended in a peace agreement. By 808 Eardwulf had been expelled from his kingdom, and Mercian involvement is suggested by a papal letter revealing that Cenwulf and the Northumbrian rebels had written to Charlemagne, to whom Eardwulf had fled. Nevertheless, he was reinstated by envoys of Charlemagne and Pope Leo III in 809. Cenwulf also fought the Welsh, presumably because the difficult situation which had necessitated the building of Offa's Dyke persisted. The Welsh annals record a battle at Rhuddlan, perhaps involving the Mercians, just after Offa's death in 796; in 816 they attacked Rhufoniog and Snowdonia, and in 818 Dyfed. Cenwulf was probably engaged in another Welsh campaign when he died near Chester.

Little is known of Cenwulf's administration, though charter witness lists suggest some continuity with previous regimes in the dozen or so ealdormen also present at grants of Offa and Ecgfrith. Coins, after c.805 bearing portraits derived from Roman models, were struck at Canterbury, Rochester (after c.810), London, and an East Anglian mint. Their royal title, 'COENVVLF REX M[ERCIORVM]', matches that of the charters. Although Offa may once have aspired to be 'king of the English', Cenwulf did not, and it is arguable, for all his control of southern England apart from Wessex, that Mercian power declined in his reign. In 825 the Mercians were heavily defeated by the West Saxons, and were subsequently unable to cope with viking raids. Sixty years after Cenwulf's death their monarchy no longer existed.

In 797 Alcuin wrote to Cenwulf praising his goodness and nobility and exhorting him to be a model Christian king. In 798 Cenwulf founded a monastery at Winchcombe, where a new church was dedicated in 811. Nevertheless, like his predecessors, Æthelbald and Offa, he had problems with the church, which was too powerful to be left uncontrolled, and Alcuin eventually felt obliged to commiserate with the abbess Æthelburgh, Offa's daughter, because ecclesiastics were ruled by tyrants not kings. Presumably as part of his attempt to rule Kent, Cenwulf gave the monastery of St Peter and St Paul, Canterbury, to his relative Cunred and the nunnery of Minster in Thanet to his daughter *Cwenthryth. He may also have obtained from popes Leo III and Paschal I privileges giving him control of all the monasteries he had acquired. Offa's difficulties with the archbishop of Canterbury had resulted in the creation of a Mercian archbishopric at Lichfield. Possibly pressed by his churchmen, Cenwulf reversed this. In 798 he suggested to Pope Leo III that the province of Canterbury be reconstituted and moved to London—a Mercian city. This Leo rejected, but after further negotiations he did suppress the archbishopric of Lichfield, and this was accepted by an English synod at 'Clofesho' in 803. For a time Cenwulf's relations with Canterbury were good, but by 808 a papal letter suggests that he and Archbishop Wulfred (d. 832) were in dispute. No more is known of this and in 814 and 815 Canterbury received a number of royal land grants; but in 816 a synod at Chelsea attempted to challenge lay control of monasteries. A dispute then arose between Cenwulf and Wulfred over the Kentish houses of Reculver and Minster in Thanet, and the pope seems to have suspended the archbishop at the king's request. He was probably not reinstated until 821.

Known relatives of Cenwulf are his brothers Ceolwulf and Cuthred, his queen, Ælfthryth, daughter Cwenthryth, Cuthred's son Cenwald, and Cyneberht and Abbot Cunwald, who appear in charters. Also his son Cynehelm who was evidently buried at Winchcombe and may be the Cynehelm who last witnesses a genuine charter in 811. By the late tenth century Cynehelm was venerated as St Kenelm, and an eleventh-century life claimed that he succeeded his father as a child but was murdered by Cwenthryth. Cenwulf died in 821, at Basingwerk, near Chester, according to the twelfth-century poet Geoffrey Gaimar, and was buried in Winchcombe. Contemporary sources say he was succeeded by his brother Ceolwulf. It may have been his association with St Kenelm which led John of Worcester to call Cenwulf a saint.   M. K. LAWSON

Sources ASC, s.a. 796, 819 · Alcuin, *Letters*, trans. S. Allott (1974), 57–60 · John of Worcester, *Chron.* · Symeon of Durham, *Opera*, 2.58–65 · *L'estoire des Engleis by Geffrei Gaimar*, ed. A. Bell, Anglo-Norman Texts, 14–16 (1960), 71 · William of Malmesbury, *Gesta regum Anglorum / The history of the English kings*, ed. and trans. R. A. B. Mynors, R. M. Thomson, and M. Winterbottom, 2 vols., OMT (1998–9) · *English historical documents*, 1, ed. D. Whitelock (1955) · C. E. Blunt and others, 'The coinage of southern England, 796–840', *British Numismatic Journal*, 32 (1963), 1–74 · N. Brooks, *The early history of the church of Canterbury: Christ Church from 597 to 1066* (1984) · D. N. Dumville, 'The Anglian collection of royal genealogies and regnal lists', *Anglo-Saxon England*, 5 (1976), 23–50 · S. Bassett, ed., *The origins* of *Anglo-Saxon kingdoms* (1989), 239–40 · D. P. Kirby, *The earliest English kings* (1991) · S. Keynes, 'The control of Kent in the ninth century', *Early Medieval Europe*, 2 (1993), 111–32, esp. 111–18

Cenwulf (d. 1006), abbot of Peterborough and bishop of Winchester, was chosen in 992 to succeed Ealdwulf (who had been appointed to the see of York) as second abbot of St Peter's (Peterborough). The late seventh-century monastery of Medeshamstede, founded on the same site, was later attacked by the vikings and was refounded as a Benedictine abbey c.996. The E version of the Anglo-Saxon Chronicle (copied at Peterborough some fifty years after the conquest) claims that it was Cenwulf who was 'the first to build a wall around the monastery and gave it the name of *Burg*, although formerly it had been known as Medeshamstede' (*ASC*, s.a. 963). In 1006, following the promotion of Ælfheah from Winchester to the archbishopric of Canterbury, Cenwulf was elected to Ælfheah's former see. The election can be seen as a move on the part of King Æthelred to strengthen links between the various parts of his kingdom. But Cenwulf died in the same year.

According to Hugh Candidus, the twelfth-century historian of Peterborough, Cenwulf added to the wealth and buildings of his community. In Hugh's chronicle, Cenwulf is described as a fine teacher and as remarkably learned and eloquent. He is also said to have carefully corrected the books belonging to the monastery. The destruction caused by a fire at Peterborough in 1116 makes it impossible fully to reconstruct the monastic library of Cenwulf's day but there is a list of the twenty-one books given to it by Æthelwold, the bishop and reformer under whose auspices the monastery had been refounded. Ælfric of Eynsham dedicated his life of Æthelwold to Cenwulf as bishop of Winchester. This dedication fixes the date of the work as 1006, the only year in which Cenwulf was bishop.　WILLIAM HUNT, *rev.* HENRIETTA LEYSER

Sources D. Knowles, C. N. L. Brooke, and V. C. M. London, eds., *The heads of religious houses, England and Wales*, 1: 940–1216 (1972) · M. Lapidge, 'Surviving booklists from Anglo-Saxon England', *Learning and literature in Anglo-Saxon England: studies presented to Peter Clemoes on the occasion of his sixty-fifth birthday*, ed. M. Lapidge and H. Gneuss (1985), 33–89 · *ASC*, s.a. 963 [text E]

Ceol [Ceola, Ceolric] (d. 597), king of the Gewisse, was the son of Cutha (probably Cuthwulf) and grandson of *Cynric (*fl.* 6th cent.). There are problems concerning the exact form of his name. He is presumably the Ceola who appears as the father of *Cynegils in the genealogy under the year 611 in the Anglo-Saxon Chronicle, since the West Saxon genealogical regnal list identifies Cynegils as 'the son of Ceolwulf's brother' and also states that *Ceolwulf (d. 611?) was the brother of Ceol. The form Ceola implies that Ceol had a dithematic name, and one manuscript of the chronicle supplies the name Ceolric; this may be the result of miscopying. Ceolwulf's name could also be abbreviated to Ceola, leading to a possible confusion of the two brothers, as may have occurred in the genealogy of Centwine in the chronicle under the year 676.

Ceol seems to have been responsible for the overthrow of his predecessor, his uncle *Ceawlin, and is recorded in the Anglo-Saxon Chronicle as beginning his reign in the year before Ceawlin was expelled following 'the great slaughter' at Woden's Barrow in Wiltshire, that is, in 591. Probably as a result of some uncertainty over exactly when his reign began sources differ over whether he ruled for five or six years. Nothing else is known of Ceol's activities as king. He died in 597 and was succeeded by Ceolwulf.　BARBARA YORKE

Sources *ASC*, s.a. 591, 592, 597 · D. N. Dumville, 'The West Saxon genealogical regnal list and the chronology of early Wessex', *Peritia*, 4 (1985), 21–66 · B. Yorke, *Wessex in the early middle ages* (1995)

Ceolfrid. *See* Ceolfrith (642–716).

Ceolfrith [St Ceolfrith, Ceolfrid] (642–716), abbot of Wearmouth and Jarrow, was born into an aristocratic family, his father being a member of the royal *comitatus* (band of companions) of Oswiu, king of Northumbria.

Early career as a monk In 660 Ceolfrith chose to become a monk and entered the minster of Gilling which had been ruled by his brother, Cynefrid. At the time of Ceolfrith's entry to the house, however, it was under the abbacy of their common kinsman, Tondbehrt, Cynefrid having withdrawn to Ireland. After an outbreak of plague in 664, the year of the Synod of Whitby where Bishop Wilfrid had zealously led the Northumbrian church to adhere to Roman orthodoxy concerning the calculation of Easter, Ceolfrith and Tondbehrt were invited to move to Wilfrid's foundation at Ripon. Here, at the age of twenty-seven, Ceolfrith was ordained to the priesthood by Wilfrid. Drawn more fully by the pull of Roman learning, he journeyed to Kent and then spent time in East Anglia at the minster of 'Icanho', Suffolk, which had been founded by St Botwulf. He returned to Ripon, where he held the office of baker while instructing the brethren in the observance of the monastic rule.

When in 674 Benedict Biscop founded a religious house at Wearmouth on land given to him by King Ecgfrith, he invited Ceolfrith to join him in its establishment and to serve as prior. The anonymous author of the life of Ceolfrith (written c.716, the earliest of the extant sources dealing with Ceolfrith's life) states that Benedict Biscop had to obtain Wilfrid's approval for Ceolfrith's transfer, a detail not recounted by Bede. Ceolfrith maintained close contact with Wilfrid and, having grown weary of his post as prior and suffered persecution from those who resented his regime, returned to Ripon. His relationship with Wilfrid must have further strengthened Ceolfrith's devotion to Rome, which was to form a central part of his ecclesiastical career.

If Wilfrid remained one formative influence on Ceolfrith's life, another was Benedict Biscop. He persuaded Ceolfrith to return to Wearmouth, anxious that it might be effectively governed during his frequent trips to Rome. During the period 678–80, Ceolfrith accompanied Benedict on one such trip, leaving behind Benedict's kinsman, Eosterwine, to rule Wearmouth and returning with John the Arch-Chanter, who instructed the brethren in Roman liturgical chant.

Abbot of Wearmouth and Jarrow A gift of more estates from King Ecgfrith enabled Benedict Biscop to found a sister house to Wearmouth at Jarrow in 681 or 682. Ceolfrith was assigned this task and the church there was dedicated to St Paul on 23 April 685. A stone preserved at Jarrow commemorates the dedication, naming Ceolfrith as the founder of the church. There is disagreement between the sources as to the size and status of Jarrow at its foundation. The life of Ceolfrith records that he took twenty-two brothers with him, of whom ten were tonsured while the remainder awaited tonsure. Bede, however, stated that seventeen monks accompanied Ceolfrith. The anonymous biographer paints a picture of Jarrow united with Wearmouth in 'brotherly accord' while Bede suggests that the two might be compared to the body and head, perhaps implying Wearmouth's superiority. Jarrow maintained the older house's discipline of regular observance. Ceolfrith attended the church at all canonical hours, diligently instructing the brethren. The anonymous biographer states that a plague almost destroyed the community in 685 or 686, leaving only Ceolfrith and a young boy (*parvulus*) behind. The latter has commonly been thought to have been Bede although it is more probable that the great scholar was received at Wearmouth and remained affiliated with the older site. Ceolfrith rebuilt his community, restoring the much-disrupted liturgy so that the psalms and antiphons were sung in their customary order. His authority was such that he was consulted by St Peter's, Wearmouth, to elect a replacement for Eosterwine while Benedict Biscop was again absent in Rome. The deacon Sigfrid was chosen but was to die soon afterwards. Accordingly, Ceolfrith was then summoned by Benedict to be the sole abbot of both houses and was appointed on 12 May 688; Benedict died in the following year on 12 January.

Ceolfrith was praised for his diligence in strictly ruling the two communities while painstakingly relieving poverty through the bestowal of alms. He sent envoys to Rome and obtained a letter of privileges from Pope Sergius I (r. 687–701), securing for the monks of Wearmouth and Jarrow the right to nominate their own abbot after the death of the founder and ensuring the community freedom from episcopal control (although confirmation of the monks' choice by the benediction of the bishop was still required). This privilege, drawing upon an earlier privilege obtained from Pope Agatho by Benedict Biscop, also enforced adherence to the Benedictine rule through its insistence that an abbot should be chosen for his spiritual qualities, not for his family connections. Ceolfrith laid the letter of privileges before a synod for its public confirmation by King Aldfrith and those bishops who were present.

Like Benedict Biscop, Ceolfrith was concerned to acquire ecclesiastical vessels, and, most notably, books for Wearmouth–Jarrow. His contribution to the libraries of the two houses is one of his most significant achievements. The life of Ceolfrith singles out three copies of the Bible (pandects) commissioned by him: one for each of the two houses and a third destined for St Peter's in Rome. Bede links these pandects (which were copies of the more recent translation of the Bible, the Vulgate) with a copy of the older translation, the *vetus Latina*, which Ceolfrith had brought back from Rome. It is possible that the text of the old translation used was that known as the *codex grandior* described in the *Institutiones* of Cassiodorus. One of the three pandects, the Codex Amiatinus, is the oldest surviving complete text of the Latin Bible. It places the books of the Bible in the order of the old translation as listed by Cassiodorus, yet uses the Vulgate translation of Jerome and was conceived as a papally organized text, further drawing Wearmouth–Jarrow into the orbit of Rome. The three pandects together would have required the skins of 1550 calves to provide the vellum, indicating the scale of Wearmouth–Jarrow's endowment and resources. The size of that endowment was increased when Ceolfrith gave a cosmography to King Aldfrith of Northumbria and received 8 hides of land in return.

Wearmouth–Jarrow's status as a scriptorium grew appreciably under Ceolfrith. Aside from the Codex Amiatinus, the Stonyhurst gospel of St John is thought to have been written during his abbacy. Fragments of one of the other pandects, of Gregory the Great's *Moralia in Job*, and of Bede's *De temporum ratione* are also associated with the scriptorium. Ceolfrith clearly had a keen sense of the importance of the written word in fostering and preserving monastic tradition. The manuscripts were written in a consistent capitular uncial script characteristic of that developed on the continent in the seventh and eighth centuries and derived from an ostentatiously Roman style developed in sixth-century Italy. Ceolfrith's devotion to Rome is further borne out by the Roman manner in which Wearmouth and Jarrow were built. The newly squared stones of the surviving east church at Jarrow may be the work of the Frankish masons whom Biscop had brought over, or of their trainees.

Ceolfrith's other notable achievement lay in establishing contact with Nechtan, king of the Picts. At Nechtan's request, Ceolfrith was said by Bede to have written a letter to the king in 710 concerning the disputed questions about Easter and the tonsure. It is possible that the letter may have been written by Bede himself but nevertheless it resulted in the adoption of Roman customs by the Picts. Ceolfrith then sent masons to build Nechtan a stone church.

Journey to Rome and death In 716, believing that age had diminished his powers, Ceolfrith decided to leave the community at Wearmouth–Jarrow and to head for Rome, bearing with him the Codex Amiatinus. While waiting to depart, he heard of the election of his successor, Hwætberht, and confirmed it. He crossed to Francia and travelled south with letters of recommendation from King Chilperic II. On his arrival at Langres he was met by the governor, Gangulf, but died there on 25 September, at the age of seventy-four. He was buried on the next day in the church of the holy triplets, the Tergemini. Some of his eighty devastated companions returned to carry news of his death to Wearmouth–Jarrow; a second party pressed on to Rome to deliver the Codex Amiatinus; and a third group stayed behind with the body. In the tenth century

Glastonbury claimed, probably spuriously, to have Ceolfrith's remains.

The anonymous life of Ceolfrith was composed after his death and is the fullest portrait of him. It has been argued that the author of the work may have been Bede, but the evidence is not fully conclusive. Bede's own *Historia abbatum* is a history of the community rather than of Ceolfrith alone and does not narrate his personal history before the death of Benedict Biscop. Ceolfrith heads the list of priest–abbots in the Durham *Liber vitae*, a list, perhaps begun in the eighth century, of royal persons and clergy to be prayed for at an unnamed church. The inclusion of Chilperic II, the only Frank to appear in the list of kings, may be a result of Ceolfrith's influence.

S. J. COATES

Sources 'Historia abbatum auctore anonymo', *Venerabilis Baedae opera historica*, ed. C. Plummer, 1 (1896), 388–404 [Vita Ceolfridi] • 'Historia abbatum auctore Baeda', *Venerabilis Baedae opera historica*, ed. C. Plummer, 1 (1896), 364–87 • Bede, *Hist. eccl.*, 4.18; 5.21, 24 • I. Wood, *The most holy abbot Ceolfrid* (1995) • J. McClure, 'Bede and the Life of Ceolfrid', *Peritia*, 3 (1984), 71–84 • M. B. Parkes, *The scriptorium of Wearmouth–Jarrow* (1982) • William of Malmesbury, *Gesta regum Anglorum | The history of the English kings*, ed. and trans. R. A. B. Mynors, R. M. Thomson, and M. Winterbottom, 2 vols., OMT (1998–9), vol. 1, pp. 50, 54, 58 • F. E. Warren, ed., *The Leofric missal* (1883), 31 • *The Bosworth psalter*, ed. F. Gasquet and E. Bishop (1908), 18, 21, 106 • *The early history of Glastonbury: an edition, translation, and study of William of Malmesbury's De antiquitate Glastonie ecclesie*, ed. J. Scott (1981) • [A. H. Thompson], ed., *Liber vitae ecclesiae Dunelmensis*, SurtS, 136 (1923), 1, 6 • J. Higgitt, 'The dedication inscription at Jarrow and its context', *Antiquaries Journal*, 59 (1979), 343–74 • S. Coates, 'Ceolfrid: history, hagiography and memory in seventh- and eighth-century Wearmouth–Jarrow', *Journal of Medieval History*, 25 (1999), 69–86
Archives Biblioteca Laurenziana, Florence, Codex Amiatinus • Stonyhurst College, Lancashire, Gospel of Saint John

Ceolnoth (d. 870), archbishop of Canterbury, faced two major political problems at the beginning of his pontificate in 833: he had to recognize and react to the new supremacy of the kings of Wessex, who had recently replaced the Mercian kings as the rulers of Kent; and he had to find means of protecting the Kentish church from viking attacks. He established an alliance with the kings of Wessex which acknowledged their power and he also sought to deal with the viking threat. Given the length of his pontificate, he may have been a young man when he was consecrated. There is no authentic evidence to indicate that he had any relations with either Canterbury or Kent before his consecration, and the nature of his policies suggests that he had powerful West Saxon connections.

The last year in which Ceolnoth attended a synod presided over by a Mercian king was 836, and henceforward he was to be found at the West Saxon royal court. In 838 he established an agreement with Æthelwulf, king of the West Saxons, who granted Canterbury the estate of Lyminge and a network of estates on the edge of the weald of Kent, as well as restoring a property at East Malling. In return, Ceolnoth ceded authority over the Kentish monasteries to Æthelwulf, who became their lord and secular patron. Under the agreement, the archbishop abandoned

claims to control the lands and incomes from the monasteries and to influence the election of abbots and abbesses. Æthelwulf henceforward was permitted to influence monastic elections, and as secular protector he may have exercised some authority over the temporalities of these churches. Although the king agreed to allow monasteries free elections after his own death, there was no guarantee that his successors would be willing to give up such powers. The net effect of the agreement in 838 was to establish the West Saxon monarchy as patron and protector of the see of Canterbury and its dependent monasteries. It would have served to stifle any potential re-emergence of Kentish independence. For Canterbury the alliance meant that the kings of Wessex were now directly responsible for the defence of the Kentish monasteries.

In the short term Ceolnoth's policies failed. Viking armies wintered on the islands of Sheppey and Thanet in 851 and 855 respectively, and by the end of his pontificate monastic life had ceased at Dover, Folkestone, Hoo, Lyminge, Sheppey, and Thanet. The exposed coastal positions of these monasteries (and the problems which the kings of Wessex faced in defending their own lands) meant that they were easily sacked and destroyed. In the Canterbury charters there is a noticeable difference between the first decade of Ceolnoth's pontificate, where the scripts have a majestic and simple clarity, and the work produced in the 850s and 860s, where there is a proliferation of misspellings and poorly formed characters. By the time of Ceolnoth's death, on 4 February 870, the church and kingdoms of England were approaching their nadir. Nevertheless the agreement of 838 formed the basis of future co-operation between the kings of England and the archbishops of Canterbury. Ceolnoth had recognized at a very early stage in his pontificate that the radical policies of his predecessor Wulfred were no longer viable. That the vikings made short shrift of his policies was something that even the most prescient of ecclesiastical statesmen could not have foreseen.

A. F. WAREHAM

Sources N. Brooks, *The early history of the church of Canterbury: Christ Church from 597 to 1066* (1984) • [H. Wharton], ed., *Anglia sacra*, 1 (1691), 53

Ceolred (d. 716), king of the Mercians, was the son of *Æthelred (d. after 704), king of the Mercians, and probably also of Æthelred's wife, *Osthryth (d. 697) daughter of the Northumbrian king *Oswiu. On Æthelred's abdication in 704, *Coenred, the son of King Wulfhere (d. 674), and Ceolred's cousin, had been designated king, perhaps in line with an existing arrangement. Ceolred himself succeeded to the kingship in 709, when Coenred resigned in order to go on pilgrimage to Rome. Early in his reign he summoned the ailing Bishop Wilfrid to a conference to discuss the position of the monasteries in Mercia which recognized Wilfrid's authority; the bishop complied, but died during the journey. A long-standing truce between Mercia and Wessex seems to have broken down in 715, when Ceolred and King Ine met in battle at a place called 'Woden's barrow' (which has been identified as Adam's

Graves at Alton Priors in the modern Wiltshire): the location of the battle suggests that the two kings were vying for control of the Vale of Pewsey.

Like his predecessors, Ceolred appears to have enjoyed a measure of authority in Middlesex and the kingdom of the Hwicce. He confirmed an earlier grant of land in Middlesex to the bishop of London (AS chart., S 65) and gave an estate in what is now Worcestershire to the abbess of Much Wenlock in Shropshire (AS chart., S 1800). This latter benefaction does not seem to have won the affections of the whole community at Much Wenlock. In a letter written between 716 and 719, Boniface describes a dreadful vision experienced by a monk of Wenlock at some point before Ceolred's death: among other terrors, the monk saw the king under assault from a party of demons, his angelic protectors having melted away after being informed of his crimes. In a much later letter, belonging to 746 or 747, Boniface held up Ceolred as a cautionary example to his successor, *Æthelbald. He describes how the earlier king fell raving mad at a feast and died, evidently as a consequence of a career of ravishing nuns and destroying monasteries, and he accuses Ceolred and his contemporary, Osred of Northumbria, of being the first Christian kings to violate the privileges of the church.

On his death in 716, Ceolred was succeeded by his distant cousin Æthelbald, who had previously lived in exile from Mercia; according to Felix's life of Guthlac, Æthelbald had been persecuted to the edge of endurance by Ceolred and it is possible that the denigration of Ceolred was in part intended to please Æthelbald. The Anglo-Saxon Chronicle mentions the death of Ceolred's wife, Wærburh, in 782. A much later source identifies her as the daughter of the earlier Mercian king Wulfhere (d. 674); but the dating would seem to make this unsustainable.

S. E. KELLY

Sources Bede, Hist. eccl., 5.19, 24 · E. Stephanus, The life of Bishop Wilfrid, ed. and trans. B. Colgrave (1927), 138 · ASC, s.a. 715, 716, 782 [Text E] · AS chart., S 65, 1800 · M. Tangl, ed., Die Briefe des heiligen Bonifatius und Lullus, MGH Epistolae Selectae, 1 (Berlin, 1916), nos. 10, 73 · The letters of Saint Boniface, trans. E. Emerton (1940), nos. 2, 57 · English historical documents, 1, ed. D. Whitelock (1955), no. 177 · Felix's life of Saint Guthlac, ed. and trans. B. Colgrave (1956), 148 · P. Sims-Williams, Religion and literature in western England, 600–800 (1990), 96–7, 243–72 · John of Worcester, Chron., 2.166, 172, 214

Ceolric. See Ceol (d. 597).

Ceolwulf (d. 611?), king of the Gewisse, was the son of Cutha (probably Cuthwulf), son of *Cynric. He ruled in succession to his brother *Ceol. The annals of the Anglo-Saxon Chronicle allot him a reign of fourteen years, but the West Saxon genealogical regnal list preserves a separate tradition of a reign of seventeen years, which may simply have resulted from a confusion between the Roman numerals XIIII and XVII. In the chronicle Ceolwulf was remembered as a powerful ruler who 'continually fought and contended either against the English, or the Britons, or the Picts, or the Scots' (ASC, s.a. 597). It is unlikely that Ceolwulf was involved with either of the last two northern peoples and it is tempting to see this as a misplaced entry for one of the Northumbrian kings. Nevertheless,

some of the foundations must have been laid in his reign for Gewissan expansion against British and Saxon peoples to their south and west. The chronicle records only a battle in 607 against the South Saxons, perhaps part of the competition between these two peoples for control of the Jutes of Wight and the south of what is now Hampshire. Ceolwulf was succeeded in 611 by *Cynegils, apparently his nephew.

BARBARA YORKE

Sources ASC, s.a. 597, 607 · D. N. Dumville, 'The West Saxon genealogical regnal list and the chronology of early Wessex', Peritia, 4 (1985), 21–66 · D. P. Kirby, The earliest English kings (1991) · B. A. E. Yorke, Kings and kingdoms of early Anglo-Saxon England (1990)

Ceolwulf [St Ceolwulf] (d. 764), king of Northumbria, was a descendant of *Ida, who had founded the kingdom of Bernicia (the northern part of Northumbria) in 547; but, whereas until 716 the only members of Ida's family to have reigned in Northumbria had been descendants of his son Æthelric, Ceolwulf and his brother Cenred were descendants of Ida's son Ocga and thus belonged to a collateral branch of the Bernician royal house. Following the murder of Osred in 716, Cenred became king; he died in 718 and was succeeded by Osric, who was of the main royal line (that of Æthelric). On Osric's death in 729 Ceolwulf became king, thus restoring the line of Ocga. The dynastic fluidity in Northumbria implied by these events may in part account for the political instability of Ceolwulf's reign. Virtually no details are known, but Bede noted in 731 that 'both the beginning and course of his reign have been filled with so many and such serious commotions and setbacks that it is as yet impossible to know what to say about them or to guess what the outcome will be' (Bede, Hist. eccl., 5.23). These troubles were apparently not of an external character, for Bede noted further that at the same time there was a treaty of peace in force with the Picts, the Irish were content, and the British were incapable of doing harm, so in that respect there were 'favourable times of peace and prosperity' (ibid.).

An annal in the early eighth-century Moore manuscript of Bede gives all the detail that exists of the internal troubles alluded to by Bede: it appears that Ceolwulf was seized by his enemies and forcibly tonsured, but that he managed to escape from what must have been an ecclesiastical prison and resume the kingship. (The event is mentioned in the Irish annals under 730, in a form which has caused some confusion between Ceolwulf and a prince of Dál Riata called Eochaid, who is quite unconnected.) Since Acca, bishop of Hexham, was expelled from his see in the same year, it has been conjectured that Ceolwulf's difficulties were connected with Acca's, and perhaps had something to do with Northumbrian diocesan organization; but this conjecture is weakened by the fact that Acca did not return to his see when Ceolwulf returned to his throne. Despite the apparent insecurity of Ceolwulf's position, Bede had high hopes of him, for he recommends him to Ecgberht, bishop (later archbishop) of York, as a very ready helper in the work of reforming and reorganizing the Northumbrian church, which Bede regarded as an urgent matter. Bede also saw Ceolwulf as a scholarly king, interested in holy scripture and in Northumbrian history; he sent him a draft of his *Historia ecclesiastica gentis Anglorum* for criticism, and then sent him the finished work for further study. It is not impossible that Ceolwulf influenced the content of the work at draft stage, and this may explain Bede's emphasis on how Osric designated Ceolwulf as his successor, and it may also have contributed to Bede's emphasis on the holiness of the church of Lindisfarne, which Ceolwulf favoured, as subsequent events showed.

In 737 (not 738 as given in some sources), the king abdicated in favour of his cousin *Eadberht and was again tonsured, apparently by his own volition, to become a monk of Lindisfarne, where he died in 764 and was buried. Durham writers of the eleventh and twelfth centuries remembered him as having given the estate of Warkworth, Northumberland, to that church, and as having permitted the monks to drink wine and beer. Ecgred, bishop of Lindisfarne (from 830 to 845), moved the church at least for a time to Norham, on the Tweed, and translated the king's body to it. When the former ecclesiastical community of Lindisfarne finally moved to Durham, Ceolwulf's head was among their relics, and is listed in Durham relic lists from the twelfth century, although the day of his death was not in Durham calendars.   DAVID ROLLASON

Sources Bede, *Hist. eccl.*, preface; 5.23 · *Venerabilis Baedae opera historica*, ed. C. Plummer, 2 vols. (1896) · Symeon of Durham, *Opera* · Symeon of Durham, *Libellus de exordio atque procursu istius, hoc est Dunhelmensis, ecclesie / Tract on the origins and progress of this the church of Durham*, ed. and trans. D. W. Rollason, OMT (2000) · D. P. Kirby, *The earliest English kings* (1991) · D. P. Kirby, 'King Ceolwulf of Northumbria and the *Historia ecclesiastica*', *Studia Celtica*, 14–15 (1979–80), 168–73 · C. F. Battiscombe, ed., *The relics of St Cuthbert* (1956) · F. Wormald, ed., *English Benedictine kalendars after AD 1100*, 2 vols., HBS, 77, 81 (1939–46)

Ceolwulf II (*fl.* 874–879), king of the Mercians, succeeded Burgred, who was driven out by the vikings in late 873 or early 874. The Anglo-Saxon Chronicle calls Ceolwulf 'a foolish king's thegn' who owed his kingship to the vikings. His only other appearance in English narrative sources is in 877, when the chronicle notes that a viking army retired into Mercia and divided it, sharing out part of it among themselves and leaving the rest for Ceolwulf. A regnal list from Worcester gives Ceolwulf a reign of five years: counting from his accession in 874, this suggests that he ruled the western part of Mercia, including Worcester, for another two years after the viking settlement. He was probably the leader of the 'English' force that killed Rhodri Mawr, king of Gwynedd, in 878, as reported in Welsh and Irish annals. Nothing is known of Ceolwulf after 879: the next Mercian leader on the Worcester regnal list was Æthelred. By 883 Æthelred was ealdorman in charge of Mercia under Alfred, who may by this stage have been recognized as king of the Anglo-Saxons and not just the West Saxons: the independent kingdom of the Mercians was no more.

Although the Anglo-Saxon Chronicle gibes that Ceolwulf was a foolish thegn and that he acted as steward for the vikings, holding the land 'ready for them on whatever day they wished to have it' (*ASC*, s.a. 874), contemporary evidence from charters and coins shows Ceolwulf acting independently as king of the Mercians. Two charters from 875 survive in his name (*AS chart.*, S 215 and 216), calling him *rex Merciorum* ('king of the Mercians') and witnessed by Mercian bishops and nobles. A later charter (*AS chart.*, S 361) refers to another grant of Ceolwulf, still called *rex*. Three types of penny survive in his name. Only a fragment survives of one; the other two, the two emperors and cross-and-lozenge, were also issued by King Alfred. The cross-and-lozenge penny was the product of a reform of the coinage, carried out by Alfred and Ceolwulf together. Alfred may have preferred dealing with his brother-in-law Burgred and later his son-in-law Æthelred, but it is clear that in the 870s both Mercians and West Saxons recognized Ceolwulf as the Mercian king. The fact that after the viking settlement of 877 Ceolwulf still held some part of Mercia may suggest that he was a shrewder negotiator than the composer of the Anglo-Saxon Chronicle chose to remember.   SEAN MILLER

Sources *ASC*, s.a. 874, 877 · *Hemingi chartularium ecclesiæ Wigorniensis*, ed. T. Hearne, 1 (1723) · *AS chart.*, S 215, 216, 218, 361 · S. Keynes, 'King Alfred and the Mercians', *Kings, currency and alliances: history and coinage of southern England in the ninth century*, ed. M. A. S. Blackburn and D. N. Dumville (1998), 1–46 · J. E. Lloyd, *A history of Wales from the earliest times to the Edwardian conquest*, 2nd edn, 1 (1912), 324–6 · J. Williams ab Ithel, ed., *Annales Cambriae*, Rolls Series, 20 (1860) · *Ann. Ulster*, 332 · M. A. S. Blackburn and S. Keynes, 'A corpus of the cross-and-lozenge coinage', *Kings, currency and alliances: the history and coinage of southern England in the ninth century*, ed. M. A. S. Blackburn and D. N. Dumville (1998), 125–50 · R. H. M. Dolley and C. E. Blunt, 'The chronology of the coins of Ælfred the Great, 871–99', *Anglo-Saxon coins: studies presented to F. M. Stenton*, ed. R. H. M. Dolley (1961), 77–95 · R. H. M. Dolley, 'An unpublished hoard-provenance for a penny of Ceolwulf II of Mercia', *British Numismatic Journal*, 32 (1963), 88–90 and pl. viii · H. E. Pagan, 'An unpublished fragment of a coin of Ceolwulf II', *British Numismatic Journal*, 41 (1972), 14–20 · P. Grierson and M. Blackburn, *Medieval European coinage: with a catalogue of the coins in the Fitzwilliam Museum, Cambridge*, 1: *The early middle ages (5th–10th centuries)* (1986), 311–13 · F. M. Stenton, 'Anglo-Saxon coinage and the historian', *Preparatory to 'Anglo-Saxon England': being the collected papers of Frank Merry Stenton* (1970), 371–82 · J. L. Nelson, '"A king across the sea": Alfred in continental perspective', *TRHS*, 5th ser., 36 (1986), 45–68 **Likenesses** coin, *c.*875 (two emperors type), Downham; repro. in Dolley, 'An unpublished hoard-provenance', pl. viii. 9 · coin, 875?–878 (cross-and-lozenge type), repro. in Dolley, 'An unpublished hoard-provenance', pl. viii.1-8 · three pennies (cross-and-lozenge type); discovered in 1996

Cerball [Cearbhall] **mac Dúngaile** (*d.* 888), king of Osraige, was the son of Dúngal (or Dúnlang) mac Fergaile (*d.* 842). Most information about him comes from a historical saga embedded in the late medieval (or early modern) 'fragmentary annals'. The early part of his career was involved with vikings. In 847 he defeated a viking force from Dublin, but in 852 he allied with a viking named Horm (who would be slain in Wales in 856) in order to fight against both other Irish and the vikings. Three years later he defeated a viking army which was ravaging Munster; in the course of the campaign he was captured, but escaped by slipping free from his fetters. In 858 Cerball joined with the viking chieftain Ívarr of Dublin in a campaign against the Gall-Gáedil; he would fight the vikings again in 860, 861, and 863.

To Cerball the vikings played only a secondary role as competitors or allies in his chief concern: the contest for control of Leinster and Munster. He attacked southern Leinster in 853 and was involved in the killing of Echtigern, the king of Uí Chennselaig. His interests in Munster were encouraged by the high-king Máel Sechnaill I (who was married to his sister Land), and in 854 Cerball took its hostages on his behalf. By 858, however, Cerball was collecting tribute from Leinster, which so alarmed Máel Sechnaill that he led an army against Cerball, whom he forced to submit; the saga embroiders this episode with a claim that witchcraft was used to put Cerball under a sleeping spell. This was a temporary setback for Cerball, who returned to Leinster and had his lordship reaffirmed. With viking allies, he attacked the lands of Máel Sechnaill in Meath in 859 and ravaged the region for three months. Once again the high-king brought Cerball to heel and at an assembly held at Rahugh (Westmeath), in the presence of the lords of northern Ireland and the abbots of Armagh and Clonard, Cerball not only submitted, but Osraige was moved into the political sphere of the northern half of Ireland (Leth Cuind).

After Máel Sechnaill died in 862, Cerball's sister Land married the next high-king, Áed mac Néill, and Cerball allied with his new brother-in-law. In 864 he again raided Leinster, but his victims retaliated by allying with the vikings and attacking Osraige. Some of the people of Osraige fled to their supposed friends the Eóganachta of Munster, who slaughtered them. Cerball first settled accounts with Leinster by means of a devastating raid, and then invaded southern Munster. The saga reveals the literary ideal for the character of a successful Irish prince when it credits Cerball with the statement that he was not angry at the barbarism of his enemies, because they were entitled to hate him. He returned to Leinster in 870 as an ally of Áed in the battle of Dún Bolg; and in 871 he allied with Munster for a raid into Connacht and then raided Munster. The remaining years until his death in 888 were largely uneventful.

Cerball's fame spread beyond Ireland and his death is recorded in the Welsh chronicle *Annales Cambriae*. His association with the vikings led to marriage alliances. In the Old Norse sagas he is called Kjarvalr Írakonungr, 'Cerball Irish-King', and *Landnámabók* records the names of three daughters and a son: Rafarta, Friðgerðr, Gormflaith, and Domnall. The 'Dream of Thorstein Side-Hall's Son' claims that Cerball also had a son named Bjaðmakr. The later lords of Osraige traced their lineage through his sons Diarmait (*d.* 928) and Cellach (*d.* 908).

BENJAMIN T. HUDSON

Sources *Ann. Ulster* • J. N. Radner, ed., *Fragmentary annals of Ireland* (1978) • Fróði Ari Þorgilsson, *Íslendingabók / Landnámabók*, ed. J. Benediktsson, 1 (Reykjavik, 1968) • M. C. Dobbs, ed. and trans., 'The Ban-shenchus [3 pts]', *Revue Celtique*, 47 (1930), 283–339; 48 (1931), 163–234; 49 (1932), 437–89 • F. J. Byrne, *Irish kings and high-kings* (1973) • B. T. Hudson, *Prophecy of Berchán* (1996) • J. H. Todd, ed. and trans., *Cogadh Gaedhel re Gallaibh / The war of the Gaedhil with the Gaill*, Rolls Series, 48 (1867) • M. A. O'Brien, ed., *Corpus genealogiarum Hiberniae* (Dublin, 1962) • D. Ó Corráin, *Ireland before the Normans* (1972) • T. W. Moody and others, eds., *A new history of Ireland*, 9: *Maps, genealogies, lists* (1984)

Cerdic (*fl.* **6th cent.**), king of the Gewisse, was believed to be the founder of the ruling dynasty of the Gewisse (or West Saxons, as they subsequently became known), and so the individual from whom all kings of the West Saxons are said to have traced their descent. In the Anglo-Saxon Chronicle Cerdic and his son *Cynric are said to have arrived with five ships at 'Cerdicesora' in 495; to have fought against a British king, called Natanleod, in 508; and to have become kings in 519 after defeating the British at Cerdicesford, identified in the tenth century with Charford in Hampshire. In 527 they appear fighting the Britons at 'Cerdicesleag', and in 530 are said to have captured the Isle of Wight and placed it under the control of their kinsmen Stuf and Wihtgar. Cerdic's death is recorded in 534.

There are insuperable problems to accepting these annals as an accurate historical record. The chronology cannot be correct, and certain events appear to have been duplicated nineteen years apart: for instance, Cerdic's arrival in 495 is a replication of an entry for 514 recording the arrival of the West Saxons at 'Cerdicesora'. Such duplication could be the result of miscopying or misinterpretation of events recorded after the conversion of the West Saxons in a Dionysiac Easter table, where entries would have been grouped in discrete cycles of nineteen years. Cerdic's accession in 519 and death in 534 is in keeping with a reign length of sixteen years allotted to him in the West Saxon regnal lists, but discrepancies between the Anglo-Saxon Chronicle annals and other regnal list entries for the sixth century suggest that his reign must have been placed too early, though it is difficult now to provide it with accurate dates.

The arrival of a pair of founders with alliterating names and a small number of ships recalls other Anglo-Saxon foundation myths, which are in turn part of a broader Indo-European tradition. Another sign of oral story telling is the apparent invention of individuals to explain place names; so *Natan leaga* (Netley Marsh, Hampshire) is said to take its name from the British king Natanleod who fell there, but in fact it seems to be a Germanic place name meaning 'wet wood'. A final problem is the name of Cerdic himself, which is not Germanic in origin but an Anglicization of the British name Caraticos. It is difficult to explain how Cerdic could have arrived straight from Germany with such a name, but it would become explicable if his family had already been established in Britain in a milieu where Germanic settlers mixed with Romano-British. The area of the upper Thames, where the first Gewissan or West Saxon bishopric was established at Dorchester-on-Thames and where Cerdic's grandson *Ceawlin appears to have been based, would meet these requirements, as it was one of the first areas in southern England to receive Germanic settlers in the fifth century. If Cerdic was indeed the first king of the Gewisse, he more likely to have come to power in the upper Thames than in what is now southern Hampshire and the Isle of Wight, which appear to have been under the control of separate Jutish dynasties in the sixth century. By the seventh century, descent from Cerdic seems to have been regarded as essential for claimants to the West Saxon throne and, even if no other genealogical information is given, the Anglo-Saxon Chronicle and regnal lists are likely to claim for a ruler that 'his kin goes back to Cerdic'. BARBARA YORKE

Sources ASC, s.a. 495, 508, 514, 519, 527, 530, 534 • D. N. Dumville, 'The West Saxon genealogical regnal list and the chronology of early Wessex', *Peritia*, 4 (1985), 21–66 • B. A. E. Yorke, 'The Jutes of Hampshire and Wight and the origins of Wessex', *The origins of Anglo-Saxon kingdoms*, ed. S. Bassett (1989), 84–96 • F. M. Stenton, *Anglo-Saxon England*, 3rd edn (1971) • K. Harrison, *The framework of Anglo-Saxon history* (1976) • B. Yorke, *Wessex in the early middle ages* (1995) • R. Coates, 'On some controversy surrounding *Gewissae/Gewissei*, *Cerdic* and *Ceawlin*', *Nomina*, 13 (1989–90), 1–11

Cérisantis, Mark Duncan de (d. 1648). *See under* Duncan, Mark (d. 1640).

Černý, Jaroslav (1898–1970), Egyptologist, was born on 22 August 1898 in Pilsen, Bohemia, the son of Antonín Černý, civil servant, and his wife, Anna Navrátilová. He was educated at Pilsen grammar school, where he first developed his lifelong passion for Egyptology, and from 1915 at the Charles University, Prague. He studied from 1917 under Bedřich Hrozný, the founder of Hittite scholarship, from 1919 under František Lexa, the most prominent Czech Egyptologist, and also for a time under Adolf Erman in Berlin. He completed his PhD in 1922.

From 1919 Černý had to support himself by working in the Živnostenská Banka (Trade Bank), but spent what time he could visiting Egyptian collections abroad, especially in Turin, which housed much of his thesis material. On these visits he made many international contacts, especially with French and Italian Egyptologists and also Alan Gardiner, whom he first met in London in 1925. He first visited Egypt in 1925 and 1926, as epigrapher for the excavations at Deir al-Medina by the Institut Français d'Archéologie Orientale. In 1927 a special scholarship from President Masaryk enabled him to leave the bank and spend two years in Egypt cataloguing the ostraca (limestone fragments used as writing material) in the Cairo Museum. From 1929, when he was appointed to a part-time lectureship in Prague, he spent his winters in Egypt engaged in epigraphy and cataloguing for both the museum and the institut, and his summers in Prague and London, where Gardiner employed him to catalogue his own ostraca (1934–9).

During the Second World War Černý was unable to return to Prague, but served in the Czech legations in Cairo (1940–42) and London (1943–5). Lack of prospects in Czechoslovakia after the war prompted him to accept the Edwards chair of Egyptology at University College, London, when it was offered him in 1946; he remained there until 1951, when he became professor of Egyptology at Oxford. On 14 June that year he married Marie (Manya) Sargant, *née* Hloušková (d. 1991), a fellow Czech. He was elected FBA in 1953. In the early 1960s he took part in the UNESCO mission to record the temples of Nubia, especially Abu Simbel, and later also supervised the recording

of the ancient graffiti in the Theban area. On his retirement in 1965 he was made emeritus professor and emeritus fellow of the Queen's College, Oxford. He also held visiting professorships at Brown University (1954–5), the University of Pennsylvania (1965–8), and Tübingen (1967), and lectured at the Collège de France (1968).

Černý's devotion to Egyptology was single-minded: once, when asked how he spent his weekends, he replied, 'I translate Coffin Texts in my pyjam[as]' (Janssen, 56). Egyptology had been his recreation since his schooldays, when he could already draw beautiful hieroglyphs, and learned German, Italian, French, and English because he had exhausted everything in Czech on the subject. His particular interest (starting with his doctoral thesis) was the community of workmen living at Deir al-Medina, who constructed and decorated the tombs in the Valley of the Kings. He became an expert at reading their records on ostraca, eventually publishing well over a thousand of these difficult texts, and editing many more in unpublished notebooks still frequently consulted by scholars in the Griffith Institute, Oxford. He also contributed greatly to the study of the Late Egyptian vernacular in which they are written, particularly by identifying its differences from contemporary literary idiom. His account of the tomb-workers' community, which provides valuable insights into social and economic life in ancient Egypt, was left unfinished at his death but published later as *The Community of Workmen at Thebes in the Ramesside Period* (1973); another important posthumous work was his *Coptic Etymological Dictionary* (1976). He died in Oxford on 29 May 1970. R. S. SIMPSON

Sources I. E. S. Edwards, 'Jaroslav Černý, 1898–1970', *PBA*, 58 (1972), 367–77 • Z. Žába, *Archiv Orientální*, 39 (1971), 385–8 • W. R. Dawson and E. P. Uphill, *Who was who in Egyptology*, 3rd edn, rev. M. L. Bierbrier (1995) • R. M. Janssen, *The first hundred years: Egyptology at University College London, 1892–1992* (1992), 54–63 • *Journal of Egyptology*, 54 (1968), 3–8 [bibliography of works] • *Journal of Egyptian Archaeology*, 57 (1971), 185–8 • *Expedition*, 12/4 (1970), 2–5 • *The Times* (30 May 1970), 10

Archives U. Oxf., Griffith Institute, papers, incl. copies, corresp., indexes, notebooks, photographs, and transcripts; notes relating to prices in ancient Egypt; notes relating to Egyptian linguistics

Likenesses photographs, c.1950, repro. in Janssen, *The first hundred years*, fig. 17 • photograph, 1951 (with his wife), repro. in Janssen, *The first hundred years*, fig. 18 • photograph, 1967?, U. Oxf., Griffith Institute • photograph, 1967?, repro. in *Journal of Egyptian Archaeology*, pl. xlii

Wealth at death £7256: probate, 17 Sept 1970, *CGPLA Eng. & Wales*

Cervetto, Giacobbe (1680/81–1783), cellist, was born in Italy, probably in Venice, in November 1680 or 1681, of Jewish parents. His real name was Basevi, but he adopted the name Cervetto before he settled in London between 1728 and 1738. He had made several visits to London as an instrument dealer, and it is said that he bought instruments from Stradivari. From 1742 to 1765 he performed regularly in London; he mounted a benefit concert on 5 May 1743. Engagements included musicians' fund benefits at the King's Theatre (14 April 1747 and 12 March 1761), oratorios at Covent Garden (spring 1777) and Drury Lane

(19 February – 26 March 1779), and work as 'featured violoncellist' (Highfill, Burnim & Langhans, *BDA*, 130) in the seasons of 1773–6 and 1778. He was well acquainted with the family of Charles Burney and played at their home. Burney wrote of him 'He was an honest Hebrew, had the largest nose, and wore the finest diamond ring on the forefinger of his bow hand' (*Memoirs*, 46 n. 2).

Cervetto, with Caporale, Pasqualini, and Lanzetti, was one of the first to popularize the cello in England, and he has been seen as the founder of the English school of cello playing. He performed in the theatre orchestra at Drury Lane for many years. It is said that the gallery cry 'Play up, nosey' owes its origin to his appearance; certainly the ribaldry from the upper gallery audience led Garrick to write a prologue in his defence given on 20 October 1753: 'Pursue your Mirth; each Night the Joke grows stronger, For as you fret the Man, his Nose looks longer' (Highfill, Burnim & Langhans, *BDA*, 131). Cervetto's compositions include solos, duets, and trios, mostly for the cello, and generally make limited demands on the player within a 'fluent *galant* style' (Sadler). His op. 1, six sonatas or trios, appeared in 1741 and his final six lessons or divertimenti for two cellos in 1767. He was a constant frequenter of the Orange Coffee House; in the early part of his London career he lodged 'at Mr. Marie's, tobacconist, in Compton Street, Soho' (*DNB*), but afterwards lived at 7 Charles Street, Covent Garden. Reputed to have been performing every summer at Vauxhall until he was 98, he died aged 101 or 102 at Friburg's snuff-shop in The Haymarket on 14 January 1783. By his will he directed that his body should be buried according to the rite of the Church of England. In the course of his long life Cervetto had amassed a large fortune, which is variously estimated at from £20,000 to £50,000; he bequeathed it to his son, the cellist James *Cervetto (1748–1837), who had been one of his pupils.

FIONA M. PALMER

Sources Highfill, Burnim & Langhans, *BDA*, 3.130–32 · G. Sadler, 'Cervetto, Giacobbe', *New Grove* · E. J. Semon, 'Ein Leben, ein Jahrhundert: Giacobo Basevi detto Cervetto (1682–1783), Cellist und Komponist', *Concerto: das Magazin für Alte Musik*, 15/138 (1988), 25–7 · V. Walden, *One hundred years of the violoncello: a history of technique and performance practice, 1740–1840* (1998) · *Memoirs of Dr Charles Burney, 1726–1769*, ed. S. Klima, G. Bowers, and K. S. Grant (1988) · [J. S. Sainsbury], ed., *A dictionary of musicians*, 2 vols. (1825); repr. (New York, 1966) · H. D. Johnstone and R. Fiske, eds., *Music in Britain: the eighteenth century* (1990), vol. 4 of *The Blackwell history of music in Britain*, ed. I. Spink (1988–95) · *The letters of Dr Charles Burney*, ed. A. Ribeiro, 1 (1991) · F. C. Petty, *Italian opera in London, 1760–1800* (Michigan, 1980) · T. B. Milligan, *The concerto and London's musical culture in the late 18th century* (1983) · *GM*, 1st ser., 53 (1783), 94 · C. Price, J. Milhous, and R. D. Hume, *Italian opera in late eighteenth-century London*, 1: *The King's Theatre, Haymarket, 1778–1791* (1995) · *DNB*
Likenesses M. Picot, mezzotint, pubd 1771 (after J. Zoffany), BM · portrait, BM
Wealth at death approx. £20,000 left to son: Highfill, Burnim & Langhans, *BDA*, 3.132

Cervetto, James (1748–1837), cellist and composer, was born on 8 January 1748 in London, the son of Giacobbe *Cervetto (1680/81–1783), and Elizabeth, about whom nothing is known. It is also unknown whether his parents were married. He was baptized on 31 January 1748 in the parish of St Martin-in-the-Fields, London. His father was a Venetian of Sephardi Jewish origin, and although James's will mentions many Jewish people, including the executor, his 'good friend' George Basevi (probably a relation), he was never an official member of a Jewish community. He learned the cello from his father, whom he soon excelled as a performer, his tone in particular being remarkably pure in quality. He and John Crosdill (with whom he was in friendly rivalry) were the foremost cellists of their generation in Britain. Cervetto's first appearance took place in a concert of child prodigies at the Little Theatre in the Haymarket on 23 April 1760. From 1761 to 1763 his father lodged at Mr Marie's, a tobacconist in Compton Street, Soho, and presumably James was also living there. Between 1763 and 1770 he travelled abroad, playing in most of the capitals of Europe; but he was in London in 1765, when he played at a concert given by the harpist Parry.

Cervetto was a member of the Concert of Ancient Music, the Royal Society of Musicians (from 1 September 1765), and the queen's private band (from 1771). He participated in the Salisbury festival (1773–81) and from about 1774 played at the King's Theatre. He was living with his father at 7 Charles Street, Covent Garden, in 1778, and in 1780 he joined the private orchestra of Willoughby Bertie, fourth earl of Abingdon. He inherited some £20,000 from his father in 1783, but continued to perform in London and the provinces. In 1784 he took part in the Handel commemoration, and on the institution of the Professional Concerts in 1783 he was engaged as soloist; he continued to play there until 1794, in which year he was living at 7 Newport Street, Soho. His last recorded concert, given by Frederick, duke of York, and at which George III was present, was held on 2 March 1795 at York House, Piccadilly. Other known London addresses for Cervetto are Marylebone High Street in 1821, and 65 Warren Street, Fitzroy Square, in 1828. Four extant portraits depict him as a distinguished, poised, and amiable man with an unmistakable aquiline nose. He composed six collections of cello music, all published in London: 6 *Solos*, op. 1 (1768), 12 *Divertiments*, op. 2 (1771), 6 *Solos*, op. 3 (1777), 12 *Sonatinas*, op. 4 (1781), 6 *Duetts*, op. 5 (c.1795), and 3[6] *Duetts*, op. 6 (c.1795). Opp. 5 and 6 are the most advanced, both compositionally and with regard to demands on the player. He died in London on Sunday 5 February 1837.

MARIJA ĐURIĆ SPEARE

Sources M. Đurić Speare, 'Cervetto, James', *New Grove*, 2nd edn · *Répertoire international des sources musicales*, ser. A/I, 9 vols. (Munich and Duisburg, 1971–81); addenda and corrigenda, 4 vols. (1986–99), vols. 2, 11 · G. W. Stone, ed., *The London stage, 1660–1800*, pt 4: *1747–1776* (1962) · parish register, London, St Martin-in-the-Fields, 1741–51, City Westm. AC, vol. 14 [baptism], vol. 14, 1741–51 · will, PRO, PROB 11/1872/120, fol. 159 · *Public Advertiser* (23 April 1760) · A. M. Hyamson, *The Sephardim of England: a history of the Spanish and Portuguese Jewish community, 1492–1951* (1951) · J. Doane, ed., *A musical directory for the year 1794* [1794] · M. Đurić, 'Giacobbe Basevi Cervetto and the violoncello in eighteenth-century England', BA diss., Colchester Institute, 1987 · M. Kelly, *Reminiscences*, 1 (1826), 324–5 · B. Matthews, ed., *The Royal Society of Musicians of Great Britain: list of members, 1738–1984* (1985) · J. H. Mee, *The oldest music room in Europe: a record of eighteenth-century enterprise at Oxford* (1911), 27 · *DNB* · *GM*,

1st ser., 53 (1783), 94 · C. Burney, *An account of the musical performances … in commemoration of Handel* (1785); repr. [1964] · *Public Advertiser* (12 Feb 1761) · *Mortimer's London universal directory* (1763) · Highfill, Burnim & Langhans, *BDA* · *Annual Register* (1837), 175 · H. Mendel and A. Reissmann, eds., *Musikalisches Conversations-Lexikon: eine Encyklopädie der gesammten musikalischen Wissenschaften*, 12 vols. (Berlin, 1870–83) · *Memoirs of Dr Charles Burney, 1726–1769*, ed. S. Klima, G. Bowers, and K. S. Grant (1988), 46 · *Musical World* (10 Feb 1837)

Likenesses J. Bretherton, etching, 1782 (*A Sunday concert*), BM · J. Nixon, pen and wash caricature, 1789 (*A bravura at the Hanover Square concert*), NPG · A. E. Chalon, drawing, 1832, BM · J. Zoffany, oils?, repro. in E. van der Straeten, *History of the violoncello* (1915); Christies, 19 Dec 1974, lot 9

Wealth at death will, PRO, PROB 11/1872 · inherited all father's possessions in 1783, apparently £20,000

Cetewayo ka Mpande. *See* Cetshwayo ka Mpande (*c*.1826–1884).

Céthech (*fl.* 5th cent.). *See under* Connacht, saints of (*act. c*.400–*c*.800).

Cetshwayo [Cetewayo] **ka Mpande** (*c*.1826–1884), king of the Zulu, the eldest son of King Mpande (*d*. 1872) and Ngqumbazi, daughter of the Zungu chief Mbondi, was born at his father's Mlambongwenya homestead near Eshowe.

As a young man Cetshwayo secured the succession to the Zulu kingdom (founded by his uncle Shaka) after the fratricidal battle at Ndondakusuka in 1856 in which he defeated and killed six of his brothers, including his chief rival, Mbuyazi. Thousands of Mbuyazi's followers were killed or fled southwards to Natal. In 1861, in an attempt to bolster his authority against possible usurpers from the south, Cetshwayo invited Natal's secretary for native affairs, Theophilus Shepstone, to recognize his future succession, and the colony became increasingly involved in Zulu affairs. From then Cetshwayo increasingly took control of the kingdom, although he only became king formally in 1872 when his father died. Cetshwayo had a considerable number of wives, many of whom he married to forge diplomatic ties. His chief wife was the daughter of Seketwayo, chief of the Mdlalose; but it was another spouse, Novimbi Msweli, a commoner, who gave birth in 1868 to the son who was to succeed him, *Dinizulu (sometimes spelt Dinuzulu).

At the time of Cetshwayo's accession, Zululand was still a comparatively self-sufficient, independent state, although it was beginning to feel pressures from traders and missionaries, and especially from Transvaal Afrikaners encroaching on the river valleys of the north-west in search of grazing. Hoping to secure Natal's support against the Transvaal and to stave off usurpers Cetshwayo invited Theophilus Shepstone to preside over his formal installation in 1873. Shepstone took the opportunity to impose unilateral 'guidelines' on the king; these provided the justification for the Anglo-Zulu War of 1879, when the British high commissioner, Sir Bartle Frere, who saw the kingdom as an obstacle to the confederation of southern Africa and believed Cetshwayo to be instigating a pan-African conspiracy to overthrow white rule, presented Cetshwayo with an ultimatum demanding *inter alia* the

Cetshwayo [Cetewayo] **ka Mpande** (*c*.1826–1884), by Bassano, 1882

disbanding of his army within thirty days, and the implementation of these coronation laws. Compliance would have spelt the destruction of the kingdom and on 11 January 1879 British troops invaded Zululand.

After a series of early British defeats, the most spectacular being that at Isandlwana, the Zulu were finally defeated on 4 July at the first battle of Ulundi, and Cetshwayo was captured and exiled to the Cape. Largely as a result of his brilliant diplomacy and the influence of carefully cultivated supporters, as well as the sympathy his imposing presence aroused when he appeared before Queen Victoria in mid-1882, at the beginning of 1883 the king was returned to a Zululand torn by civil war between his supporters and the chiefs the British had appointed in his stead.

Restored to a portion of his former kingdom, and confronted by a large number of powerful enemies, Cetshwayo was unable to re-establish peace. On 20 July 1883 his followers were defeated at the second battle of Ulundi and most of his senior councillors killed. Cetshwayo again fled but when British troops entered the country, he surrendered himself to the protection of the British resident commissioner. He died in captivity at Eshowe on 8 February 1884—of heart disease, according to the military doctor; his followers believed he had been poisoned. He was buried in a sacred grove in the Nkandhla forests, southern Zululand.

Cetshwayo was much maligned in his lifetime, but later

historians have generally seen him as a highly intelligent and dignified man, who ruled his people well. After his death continued turbulence led to the British annexation of Zululand in 1887 and its incorporation into Natal ten years later.

SHULA MARKS

Sources J. Guy, *The destruction of the Zulu kingdom* (1979) · C. T. Binns, *The last Zulu king: the life and death of Cetshwayo* (1963) · A. Duminy and B. Guest, eds., *Natal and Zululand from earliest times to 1910* (1989) · *The James Stuart archive of recorded oral evidence relating to the history of the Zulu and neighbouring peoples*, ed. and trans. C. de B. Webb and J. B. Wright, [5 vols.] (1976–) · *A Zulu king speaks: statements made by Cetshwayo ka Mpande on the history and customs of his people*, ed. C. de B. Webb and J. B. Wright (1978) · J. P. C. Laband, *Kingdom in crisis: the Zulu response to the British invasion of 1879* (1992) · A. Duminy and C. Ballard, eds., *The Anglo-Zulu War: new perspectives* (1981) [incl. N. A. Etherington, 'Anglo-Zulu relations 1856–1878', 13–52, and P. J. Colenbrander, 'The Zulu political economy on the eve of war', 78–97.] · E. H. Brookes and C. de B. Webb, *A history of Natal* (1965) · N. Etherington, 'The "Shepstone system", in the colony of Natal and beyond the borders', *Natal and Zululand from earliest times to 1910*, ed. A. Duminy and B. Guest (1989), 170–205 · P. Colenbrander, 'The Zulu kingdom, 1828–79', *Natal and Zululand from earliest times to 1910*, ed. A. Duminy and B. Guest (1989), 83–115
Likenesses photograph, *c.*1879, Cape Archives, Cape Town, South Africa · photograph, *c.*1879, Warae Archives · photograph, *c.*1879, Strange Africana Museum · photograph, *c.*1879, Hult. Arch. · Bassano, photograph, 1882, NPG [*see illus.*] · C. John, oils, *c.*1882, Old House Museum, Durban, South Africa; repro. in Binns, *Last Zulu king* · Spy [L. Ward], caricature, 1882, repro. in *VF* (26 Aug 1882) · photographs, repro. in Guy, *Zulu kingdom* · photographs, repro. in Webb and Wright, eds., *A Zulu king speaks* · photographs, repro. in Brooks and Webb, eds., *History of Natal*

Chabham, Thomas de. *See* Chobham, Thomas of (*d.* 1233x6).

Chabot, Charles (*bap.* 1815, *d.* 1882), graphologist, was born in Battersea, Surrey, and baptized on 19 March 1815 at St Mary's, Battersea, the second of the three children of Charles Chabot, a lithographer, and his wife, Amy (or Amey), *née* Pearson; the family was Huguenot. He began as a lithographer in Holborn, and on 3 August 1842 he married Sarah, *née* Nichols. From about 1855 Chabot acquired a large private practice as an expert in handwriting, while his undoubted integrity and professional skill made him in much request in the law courts. He gave evidence in the trial of William Roupell, the Lambeth MP convicted of forgery in 1862, and in the Tichborne trial. In some other important cases his testimony practically determined the decisions. In 1871 Chabot examined professionally the handwriting of the letters of Junius and compared it with the handwriting of those persons to whom the letters had at various times been attributed. His detailed reports, intended to confirm the identification of Sir Philip Francis with Junius, were published, with a preface and collateral evidence by Edward Twisleton, in 1871. Chabot died at his home, 26 Albert Square, Clapham, London, on 15 October 1882, leaving at least one son, Charles.

T. F. HENDERSON, *rev.* JOHN D. HAIGH

Sources E. Twisleton, preface, in C. Chabot, *The handwriting of Junius professionally investigated* (1871), xi–lxxviii · *Law Journal Reports*, 2nd ser., 17 (21 Oct 1882), 566 · *The Times* (17 Oct 1882) · Boase, *Mod. Eng. biog.*, 1.1965 · *ILN* (25 Nov 1882), 549 · 'Experts in handwriting', *Cornhill Magazine*, new ser., 4 (1885), 148–62 · *IGI* · m. cert. · d. cert. · *CGPLA Eng. & Wales* (1883)
Archives Harvard U., Houghton L., letters to Edward Twisleton
Likenesses etching, repro. in *ILN*, 549
Wealth at death £32,624 13*s.* 2*d.*: probate, 1883

Chaceporc, Peter (*d.* 1254), administrator, was born in Poitou, and had entered the service of Henry III by February 1240, when he was listed among those foreign-born royal clerks exempted from paying one-fifth of their revenues to the pope. Chaceporc was frequently employed as a royal messenger, initially to Poitou, and later to France, Aragon, and the papal court at Lyons. The focus of his administrative activity, however, was and remained the royal wardrobe. In July 1240 he was sent to inventory debts stored in the Jewish *archae* and to survey the royal demesne manors, work that may suggest he was already attached to the wardrobe. By January 1241 he was a wardrobe clerk, in company with the keeper William de Burgo, and from 28 October 1241 until his fatal illness in December 1254 Chaceporc was the sole keeper of the wardrobe. In this capacity he handled a wide variety of financial and administrative business with great skill, especially during the Gascon campaigns of 1242–3 and 1253–4, when the wardrobe became the chief financial office for the war effort. Although frequently referred to simply as 'treasurer', Chaceporc remained treasurer of the wardrobe, not the exchequer. Like others of Henry's household clerks, Chaceporc was a frequent witness to royal charters and writs, especially in 1253, when he acted as keeper of the great seal during the illness of the chancellor, Master William of Kilkenny (*d.* 1256).

In January 1243 Henry attempted to have Chaceporc elected bishop of Bath, but withdrew the recommendation. Thereafter Chaceporc became at various times dean of Tattenhall, Cheshire, constable of St Briavels and the Forest of Dean, Gloucestershire, archdeacon of Wells, Somerset, treasurer of Lincoln, dean of Tottenham, Middlesex, and custodian of the vacant bishoprics of Durham and Winchester. He died on 24 December 1254, while on pilgrimage with the king to the church of Ste Marie at Boulogne, where he was buried. His heir was his eldest brother, Hugh, whose marriage to one of King Henry's Poitevin relatives Chaceporc probably arranged. At his death he left 600 marks to found an Augustinian priory at Ravenstone, Buckinghamshire, for which King Henry became co-founder.

ROBERT C. STACEY

Sources *Chancery records* · Tout, *Admin. hist.*, vol. 1 · *Pipe rolls* · Dugdale, *Monasticon*, new edn · Paris, *Chron.*, vol. 5 · *CPR, 1247–58*, 388

Chacksfield, Sir Bernard Albert (1913–1999), air force officer and chief scout, was born at 28 Khartoum Road, Ilford, Essex, on 13 April 1913, son of Edgar Chacksfield, printers' reader, and his wife, Alice Annie, *née* Fairbeard. He was educated at Ilford county high school and, at age fifteen, joined the RAF as an apprentice engineer at RAF Halton and later at RAF Cranwell.

'Chacks' Chacksfield was one of only four from a field of 1000 students chosen for pilot and officer training, and between 1934 and 1937 he served in India as a pilot officer policing the north-west frontier in a Westland Wapiti biplane. On 29 May 1937, at the Vine Memorial Congregational Church, Ilford, he married Myrtle Elza Alexena (1911/12–1984), a nurse, daughter of Walter Matthews, a retired transport officer with the Indian state railways. They had three sons and two daughters.

Chacksfield's active RAF career from 1939 to 1945 was spent in the Far East, where he was posted to India, Burma, and Singapore. In India, Chacksfield was beginning to make a name for himself, being responsible for engineering, 226 group. After the fall of Burma in 1942 his success in maintaining aircraft ensured regular Dakota flights to supply Chiang Kai-shek's forces in China.

In 1944 Chacksfield received command of 910 wing's Thunderbolt squadron and in mid-March when General Slim's advance was held up outside Mandalay, Chacksfield's three squadrons of fighter bombers were called upon to engage the enemy in a low-level attack. Although initially unsuccessful, Chacksfield switched the direction of the attack on the second day. Acting as master bomber from his own Thunderbolt, he led his squadron in helping to breach the walls of Fort Dufferin that had resisted heavy artillery assaults from USA B-25 bombers. This action contributed vitally to hastening allied success in Burma. Although by war's end he had been mentioned in dispatches four times, it was a mystery to Slim that Chacksfield had not been awarded the DSO.

From 1945 to 1948 Chacksfield served with the Air Ministry, and between 1949 and 1951 he was at Fontainebleau with the Western Union (NATO). Promoted to group captain in 1951, Chacksfield spent the next two years at RAF Staff College. During this period he found time for sporting and athletic activities—particularly fencing—at which he excelled. Later he represented Britain at the Commonwealth games. Between 1954 and 1955 he was with Fighter Command in charge of a Meteor and Swift jet fighter station at Waterbeach, Cambridgeshire. Promoted to air commodore in 1956, he served as director, guided weapons (trials) at the Ministry of Supply, from 1956 to 1958, during which time he visited Australia to observe Fairey Fireflash rocket tests at the Woomera range. After introducing these air-to-air beam-riding guided missiles (the RAF's first) he returned to the mainstream in 1960 when, as acting air vice-marshal, he became senior air staff officer, technical training command. Between 1963 and 1968, when he retired, Chacksfield held the posts of commandant-general of the RAF regiment and inspector of ground defence.

Shortly before he retired Chacksfield flew supersonic in a single-seat Lightning fighter, gaining membership of the 1000 m.p.h. club, and relished a flight in a Vulcan nuclear deterrent bomber captained by his son, Christopher. Chacksfield was awarded an OBE (1945), and appointed KBE (1958) and CB (1961). He also held the Chinese order of cloud and banner with special rosette (1941).

Outside the RAF, Chacksfield had numerous interests. He was active in the Scout movement, organizing numerous gang shows; he would have made a creditable wartime armed forces' entertainer, specializing in impersonating

the Andrews Sisters. He was appointed chief commissioner for the Scout Association in 1970 and in 1975 was awarded the bronze wolf. In retirement he devoted himself to the Burma Star Association, of which he became chairman in 1977. He campaigned tenaciously on behalf of South-East Asia command veterans and former wartime prisoners of the Japanese. Tireless in community activities, he was chairman, board of management, Royal Masonic Hospital (1988–92); president, Bedstone College (from 1991); chairman of governors, Wye Valley School (1978–89); president, Bourne End Community Association (from 1995); president, British Model Flying Association (from 1965); president, RAF Pentathlon Association (1963–8), and chairman, RAF Small Arms Association (1963–8). In his spare time he enjoyed swimming, flying, sailing, and amateur dramatics, appearing with the Bourne End Operatic Society.

Following the death of his first wife in 1984, he married on 9 February 1985 a widow, Elizabeth Beatrice Ody, née Meek (b. 1912/13), who was his neighbour at Bourne End, Buckinghamshire. Chacksfield died from cancer at his home, 8 Rowan House, Blind Lane, Bourne End, on 27 December 1999, survived by his second wife, and two sons and two daughters from his first marriage. His memorial service, held at St Clement Danes, London, on 14 March 2000 drew a full house of over 300 people.

BRIAN WIMBORNE

Sources *Daily Telegraph* (9 Feb 2000) · *WW* (1990) · *WW* (2000) · *Debrett's People of today*, 327 · *Bucks Scouting Magazine*, 3rd ser., issue 4 (2000), 4 · *Debrett's handbook: distinguished people in British life* [n.d.] · *L. M. F. C. Newsletter* [Leatherhead Model Flying Club] (May 2000), 7 · b. cert. · m. certs. (2) · d. cert. · *RAF Thunderbolts over Burma*, British Forces site · *The Times* (1 Jan 1968) · *Round and About Bourne End Village News* [online], 11 Aug 2001 · *CGPLA Eng. & Wales* (2000)

Wealth at death under £200,000: probate, 2000, *CGPLA Eng. & Wales*

Chaderton, Laurence (1536?–1640), college head, was that rarity in early modern England, a centenarian who outlived trees that he himself, an enthusiastic gardener and herbalist, had planted. But whether he was born in 1536, or two or three years later, is uncertain.

Scholar and preacher Chaderton came from a family of minor Lancashire gentry, the son of Thomas Chaderton and Joan, daughter of Lawrence Tetloe of Oldham. Born at The Lees, Oldham, he grew up loving the sporting life, a wrestler who retained a lifelong zest for archery, tennis, and fives. His education began late, and was at first in the hands of Laurence Vaux, who as an exile from Elizabethan England would later write the standard English Catholic catechism. It can be assumed that when he went up to Christ's College, Cambridge, in his mid-twenties Chaderton was still a Catholic. When he experienced conversion to the deeply evangelical protestantism of that house, probably under the influence of the exemplary puritan divine Edward Dering, his father threatened to cut him off with the proverbial shilling. He was elected to a fellowship in 1568 as soon as he had proceeded BA, thanks it was said to Dering, who might have voted for one of his own pupils but acknowledged Chaderton's superior merit.

Chaderton acquired a formidable reputation as a learned trilingual biblical scholar and theologian. The annotations in the margins of several of his books which survive in the Wren Library of Trinity College suggest that he would have been an exacting tutor, not suffering fools gladly. He was even more famous as a preacher, and occupied the pulpit at St Clement's Church in Bridge Street for half a century. When he gave up this weekly lecture at the age of eighty-two, forty divines signed a testimonial to the effect that they owed their conversion to his teaching. His voice is first heard in a Paul's Cross sermon preached in 1579, an urgent call to national repentance appropriate for the place and the occasion, and an echo of the prophetic tones of Dering, who had died three years earlier, at about the time that Chaderton married. His bride was Cecily Culverwell, one of the daughters of the wealthy London haberdasher and benefactor Nicholas Culverwell. The marriage inducted Chaderton into the godly Culverwell clan and its many collateral connections, which soon included his Cambridge colleague William Whitaker, married to Cecily's sister Susan. As a married man Chaderton forfeited his fellowship, but continued to place promising students with suitably godly tutors, just as in later life he would make the whole Church of England, its parishes and schools, his chessboard. How did he live? Nicholas Culverwell had established a trust fund to support two poor and godly preachers in Christ's, and Chaderton was perhaps an early beneficiary of this charity. Later Nicholas's brother, the mercer Richard Culverwell, left £350 in trust to Chaderton, Whitaker, and other ministers to distribute to the most deserving, whether preachers or not. The trustees could, if they so chose, help themselves to this fund.

Master of Emmanuel College In 1584 an old Christ's man who had risen to greatness, Sir Walter Mildmay, founded a new college, Emmanuel, and Chaderton became its first master. The stipend was a niggardly £15 a year, and Chaderton, who is said to have been offered a living worth ten times as much, hesitated. Mildmay told him: 'if you won't be master, I certainly am not going to be founder of a college' (Shuckburgh, 7). It was unusual for a man in his late forties to become head of a house, and more unusual still that he should remain there for thirty-eight years. It was only in 1622 that by a cunning manoeuvre, which involved the fellows, the royal court where the duke of Buckingham was dominant, and perhaps Chaderton himself, the baton passed to John Preston, as great a pupilmonger as Chaderton and chaplain to Buckingham and Prince Charles. But Chaderton continued for another eighteen years to live across the street from the college, where he had always housed his family and sundry wellconnected student lodgers.

Emmanuel was a most peculiar foundation, not least in its statutes which the future archbishop William Sancroft would describe as 'very odd' (Bodl. Oxf., MS Tanner 48, fol. 52), and in its 'one aim', in the words of the founder, to serve as a seminary of godly preachers. Within forty years

Emmanuel grew to be the largest college in the university, outgrowing its endowment and accommodation. Oddly enough, it sent fewer men into the ministry than other colleges of a comparable size, and recruited a larger number of gentleman commoners. Although this was a matter of financial necessity, these prize pupils would become some of the great and good of early seventeenth-century England, whom Chaderton carefully cultivated, building up a benign country-wide alliance of magistracy and ministry.

Emmanuel under Chaderton's rule became notorious as a 'pure' house, renowned for the austerity of its chapel, where the surplice was never worn and communion was administered to those deemed worthy to receive it in a seated posture, according to a hostile report, 'one drinking as it were to another, like good fellows' (BL, Harley MS 7033, fol. 98). At the heart of the seminarian life of the college was a kind of conference, which resembled the exercises of 'prophesying' widely practised in the Elizabethan church at large. The prophesyings were not incompatible with episcopacy, and were normally sanctioned by the bishops. But at Emmanuel the formal censure of doctrine was collective, 'because the judgment is the judgment of all and not of any one alone' (*Statutes of Sir Walter Mildmay*, 110). Chaderton himself was a convinced presbyterian, and only Sancroft's dubious testimony indicates that he ever changed his mind or his ecclesiology, allegedly 'often' professing that 'they who dislike the government by bishops would bring in a far worse for Church and State' (Bodl. Oxf., MS Sancroft 79, p. 18).

Pillar of presbyterianism The evidence for Chaderton's presbyterianism is in some surviving lecture notes, dating from 1590–91, the marginalia and *adversaria* to be found in some of his books, and above all in *A Fruitfull Sermon* on the twelfth chapter of Romans, printed in 1584 and widely attributed to Chaderton. If the author was indeed Chaderton, then he 'loathed ... the calling of Archbishop, Bishop, Deans ... and all such as be rather members and parts of the whore and strumpet of Rome' (Lake, 30). Chaderton was actively involved in the so-called 'classical movement' of the 1580s, the holding of ministerial conferences approximating to the *classes* and synods of presbyterian church order. He was the principal correspondent in Cambridge of the organizer, John Field, and took part in meetings held in Cambridge in 1587 and 1589.

Yet like his brother-in-law, William Whitaker, Chaderton trod the delicate tightrope of the establishment puritan. He appears to have kept his presbyterianism under wraps, but in the 1590s he committed himself more publicly to the defence of Calvinist orthodoxy against its theological opponents. When William Barrett of Caius, a stalking horse for the Lady Margaret professor Peter Baro, began to advance 'Pelagian' opinions 'strongly savouring of the leaven of popery', Chaderton interviewed him and extracted a confession that his position was indeed that of the Church of Rome (LPL, MS 2550, fol. 164v). Chaderton continued to be in the van of the fight to make the university and the church at large waterproof against any deviation from Calvinist orthodoxy, and he would later publish the pronouncements that this crisis had provoked as *De justificationis perseverentia non intercisa* (1613).

The old radical Whether Chaderton could continue his balancing act, and whether there was a future for his kind of puritanism in the Church of England, were matters put to the test in the first two years of the new regime of James I, when the Elizabethan religious settlement was reviewed at the Hampton Court conference (1604), only to be energetically redefined and reimposed in Archbishop Bancroft's constitutions and canons, requiring subscription to a test of conformity. Chaderton was one of the four puritan spokesmen at Hampton Court, and, as his annotations show, took strong exception to the semi-official account of the conference, the *Summe and Substance* published by William Barlow. According to another version, Chaderton at Hampton Court was 'as mute as any fish' (Usher, 2.337), intervening only to ask for special indulgence for the nonconformist preachers of his native Lancashire. Evidently he understood himself to be in the business of damage limitation. In the aftermath of Hampton Court, with Emmanuel in the firing line, the nonconforming clergy facing suspension and deprivation looked to Chaderton for a lead. A Kentish minister wrote to say that 'many did talk of you', and were inclined to head for Cambridge to consult the oracle face to face. But Bancroft, a contemporary and sometime friend of Chaderton, told them that they would 'there meet to no good' (LPL, MS 2550, fols. 1r–2v).

Fortunately for the historian and biographer, Chaderton's views on the point at issue, technically a matter of Christian liberty in the use of 'things indifferent', were committed to paper. From material preserved at Lambeth Palace, and from his book annotations, emerges an unreconstructed radical whose pragmatic response to the necessity of conformity was hedged about with qualifications. The surplice, the sign of the cross, and kneeling were indeed matters of indifference and they ought not to be imposed by authority (for then they lost their indifference), but nor was it necessary, as a matter of conscience, in all circumstances to refuse them. To the argument that the surplice had been called indifferent 'falsely', Chaderton responded: 'Prove this "falsely" and take all' (Chaderton, annotations, in *Certaine Demandes*, 1605, Cambridge, Trinity College Library, C.9.126, sig. B4r). He was 'verily persuaded' that the ceremonies could be used 'without sin' (LPL, MS 2550, fol. 12v). But much depended upon local pastoral circumstances, especially for a presbyterian who believed in ecclesiastical devolution. Chaderton's own circumstances were favourable. Although James I suggested to the chancellor of the university, Sir Robert Cecil, that he should remove him 'if he continue obstinate' (*Salisbury MSS*, 16.367), and while he was no longer licensed to preach at St Clement's, which may be evidence that he himself had not subscribed, Chaderton was not disturbed. He had written: 'We may and ought to use [the ceremonies] to purchase and procure liberty to win souls by preaching the Gospel' (LPL, MS 2550, fol. 59r). That was the Emmanuel strategy which

would work for another thirty years, as the college continued to dispatch godly preachers into the country, and soon out of it, as far as Massachusetts.

As for Chaderton himself, he became one of the treasured antiquities of Cambridge, visited by royalty and fêted by such Emmanuel alumni as Henry Rich, earl of Holland, and John Finch, Charles I's chief justice and lord keeper. A visit in 1611 by Prince Charles and his brother-in-law, the elector palatine, was made the occasion for conferring on Chaderton, now aged over seventy, the degree of DD, which under the strict terms of the oddest of Emmanuel's statutes should have required him to leave the college for the pastoral ministry. He remained physically and mentally fit into extreme old age. The tradition that he could still read his Hebrew Bible without the aid of spectacles is borne out by a book that he annotated at the age of about a hundred. Chaderton's only daughter, Elizabeth, married Abraham Johnson, son of the wealthy founder of Uppingham and Oakham schools, Archdeacon Robert Johnson, and father of the Massachusetts pioneer, Isaac Johnson, who inherited his grandfather's wealth. As a widow, Elizabeth looked after her father until he died, at Emmanuel, of mere old age, on the eve of the English revolution, on 13 November 1640. After the Restoration his body was removed to the new college chapel built by Sancroft and Christopher Wren.

The fact that Chaderton published so little in his long life should not be surprising. The next three masters of Emmanuel, John Preston, William Sancroft the elder, and Richard Holdsworth, published nothing in their lifetimes, although Preston's works became best-sellers after his death, and Sancroft's manuscript remains, preserved by his nephew, Archbishop William Sancroft, are copious. Chaderton made his considerable mark in other ways.

PATRICK COLLINSON

Sources W. Dillingham, *Vita Laurentii Chadertoni* (1700) · E. S. Shuckburgh, *Laurence Chaderton, D.D.* (1884) · S. Bendall, C. Brooke, and P. Collinson, *A history of Emmanuel College, Cambridge* (1999) · *The statutes of Sir Walter Mildmay kt … authorised by him for the government of Emmanuel College founded by him*, ed. F. H. Stubbings (1983) · P. Lake, *Moderate puritans and the Elizabethan church* (1982) · A. Hunt, 'Laurence Chaderton and the Hampton Court conference', *Belief and practice in Reformation England*, ed. S. Wabuda and C. Litzenberger (1998), 207–28 · LPL, MS 2550 · DNB · *Calendar of the manuscripts of the most hon. the marquess of Salisbury*, 16, HMC, 9 (1933) · BL, Harley MS 7033 · Bodl. Oxf., MS Sancroft 79 · R. G. Usher, *The reconstruction of the English church*, 2 vols. (1910)

Archives LPL, corresp. and papers, MS 2550 · Pembroke Cam., notes on lectures · Trinity Cam., books annotated by subject, C. 9. 11, C. 9. 125, C. 9. 126, C. 9. 132, C. 26. 34

Chaderton, William (*d.* 1608), bishop of Lincoln, was the second of the three children of Edmund Chaderton (*fl.* 1529–1573) of Nuthurst near Manchester and his wife, Margaret Cliffe of Cheshire. He was entered at Magdalene College, Cambridge, in 1553, but matriculated as a pensioner at Pembroke College in 1555. He proceeded BA in 1558, MA in 1561, BTh in 1566, and DTh in 1568.

Early career, 1558–1579 Chaderton became a fellow of Christ's College in 1558, and was ordained deacon and

William Chaderton (*d*. 1608), by unknown artist, 1602

priest in London early in 1559 as the supremacy and uniformity bills were passing through parliament. In 1561 he contributed a commendatory Latin elegy 'to the reader' to Barnaby Googe's English translation of the first six books of the *Zodiacus vitae* of Marcellus Palingenius (Pietro Angelo Manzolli), and in August 1564 he was one of the philosophy disputants at Elizabeth I's visit to Cambridge, discussing whether monarchy was the best form of government and whether frequent changes in the laws were dangerous. In 1566 Chaderton was appointed a university preacher, and in 1567 Lady Margaret professor of divinity. In 1568 he was presented to the archdeaconry of York by the earl of Leicester and was elected president of Queens' College, Cambridge, writing a fulsome Latin letter of thanks to the secretary, Sir William Cecil, for the latter office. In 1569 he asked Leicester to approve his proposal to marry, and the earl's agreement was addressed 'to my loving chaplain Mr. Chaterton' from 'your loving friend and master' (Peck, bk 3, 3). He married Katherine Revell, daughter of John Revell of London, gentleman, but was later remembered for preaching at a Cambridge wedding that choosing a wife was like catching a fish in a barrel of serpents.

In 1569 Chaderton was appointed regius professor of divinity, having been recommended to Cecil by his fellow heads of house: he held the chair with his presidency until 1579. He was popular with students and, although he dealt firmly with disruptions at Queens', 'he did not affect any sour and austere fashion, either in teaching or government' (Harington, 81). On 11 June 1570 he wrote to Cecil, as chancellor of the university, complaining of the 'seditions, contention, and disquietude, such errors and schisms openly taught and preached' by Thomas Cartwright, Robert Some, and others (Mullinger, 2.215). Chaderton was by now a significant university administrator, sitting as an assessor in the vice-chancellor's court and hearing proceedings against nonconformists and presbyterians. But Edward Dering, who had been a colleague at Christ's, came to see him as a time-server, telling Cecil on 18 November 1570 that Chaderton and the master of St Catharine's had 'small constancy either in their life or their religion' (Strype, Appendix, 121).

In 1570 Chaderton became rector of Holywell, Huntingdonshire, and bought the estate of Moyne's Hall there. On 19 November 1572 he submitted an elegant but unsuccessful Latin application to Cecil for the vacant deanery of Winchester, which he hoped would free him from 'the wearisome duty of lecturing' (Searle, 308). In 1574 he became a prebendary of York, and in December exchanged the archdeaconry of York for a canonry at Westminster. By now he may have been looking for a bishopric, and was perhaps 'this chatterer' who in 1575 sought to discredit the bishop of Ely in hope of displacing him— to the annoyance of Archbishop Parker.

Bishop of Chester, 1579–1595 Chaderton was consecrated bishop of Chester on 8 November 1579. He presumably pleaded the poverty of the see, for on 5 June 1580 he was licensed to hold the wardenship of Manchester College *in commendam*. He also sought other commendams, including the rectory of Thornton-le-Moors, Cheshire, in 1581 and the rectory of Bangor, Flintshire, in 1584. Chaderton made Manchester his base, and from there supervised drives against Catholic priests and recusants in Lancashire and tried to improve protestant preaching throughout his diocese. With the earl of Derby he sat at quarter sessions and at hearings by the ecclesiastical commission, and was in frequent correspondence with Lord Treasurer Burghley and Secretary Walsingham about the treatment and punishment of Catholics. Although the problem of Lancashire Catholicism proved intractable, Chaderton's efforts were commended by the archbishop of York, the lord president of the council of the north, and the privy council. But he fell under suspicion in 1583, when he was accused by a troublesome tenant he called 'a malicious varlet' of detaining £3000 in fines levied by the ecclesiastical commission. Burghley warned him that 'to avoid doubtful reports made of you in this matter, you shall do well to make answer speedily' (Peck, bk 4, 16). Chaderton provided the exchequer with a meticulous account of all the fines imposed from June 1580, and demonstrated that only £757 had been demanded, of which no more than £40 had been paid: the council assured him that it had never doubted his probity!

In December 1582 the earl of Huntington praised Chaderton because 'your lordship doth esteem and encourage all the good ministers that are under you' (Peck, bk 4, 8). Chaderton co-operated closely with the leading preachers of his diocese: he took godly ministers into his diocesan administration and he seems to have been quietly tolerant of nonconformity. He encouraged a monthly preaching exercise for the clergy of Manchester deanery, but was warned by Archbishop Edwin Sandys of York on 2 May 1581 that 'you are noted to yield too much to general fastings, all the day preaching and praying' (ibid., bk 3, 29). In 1582 Chaderton endorsed a scheme for three exercises a year for the Lancashire clergy at Preston, but some of the preachers were more ambitious. They persuaded the privy council in 1584 to instruct Chaderton to organize more frequent exercises across his diocese, and a system of compulsory monthly meetings in each deanery was introduced in January 1585. Some ministers were slack in their attendance and attention, and in September 1585 the bishop introduced stiffer penalties for negligence, authorizing the moderators to suspend absentees.

Although leading preachers (including moderators of the exercises) were sometimes presented at visitation for nonconformity, there was no determined disciplinary action by Chaderton or his officers. But in 1590 a metropolitan visitation of the diocese of Chester revealed widespread reluctance by ministers to wear the surplice, especially in the deanery of Manchester. The archbishop's vicar-general ordered the offending ministers to appear before Chaderton, who gave them two months to conform. Chaderton then appealed to Archbishop John Piers on 30 September 1590 for some tolerance of the nonconformists but the response was brisk: 'I take it no good course to give men leave to do evil because they may do good'. Chaderton was instructed to enforce the surplice throughout his diocese, and to 'first begin with your own college at Manchester' (Raines, 'Visitation of the diocese of Chester', 15–16). On 22 January 1591 Chaderton ordered the churchwardens of each parish in the diocese to provide two surplices and to certify every three months that they were used, but thereafter he seems to have quietly forgotten the matter.

At Manchester, Chaderton was said to have been a frequent preacher and 'given to hospitality' (Hollinworth, 89). But towards the end of his episcopate he moved back to Chester, because of conflicts between his servants and the townspeople. In his will he left £50 to Manchester College and £40 to the poor of Manchester and Salford hundred—if the money could be obtained from debtors. Although recusancy among the Lancashire gentry complicated Chaderton's position, he seems to have been popular with and trusted by the protestant gentry of the diocese. On 15 October 1582 his eight-year-old daughter Joan was married to ten-year-old Richard Brooke, son of Thomas Brooke, esquire, of Norton in Cheshire. The young couple then lived with the bishop at his house in Manchester, and in 1586 the marriage was formally ratified by the diocesan chancellor after the couple had confirmed that this was their wish.

Chaderton's relations with the earl of Derby and the earl's son, Lord Strange, were close: he lent money to the family and was often a guest of the fourth earl, preaching to his household seven times in 1587–90; he also preached at the earl's funeral at Ormskirk on 4 December 1593. The earl of Leicester, as chamberlain of the palatinate of Chester, appointed Chaderton one of the assistant judges in the exchequer court at Chester in 1584. But the bishop's disciplinary work was conducted primarily through the diocesan ecclesiastical commission, and he rarely sat in his consistory or took part in visitations: these duties he left to his chancellor. He inherited Robert Leche as chancellor, but after Leche's death in 1587 appointed David Yale (who had been a fellow of Queens' when Chaderton was president). Chaderton had obtained licence from the queen for absence from parliament in 1581 so that he could continue his drive against Catholics, and was also absent in 1587, but he sat in the Lords for the sessions of 1585, 1589, and 1593.

Bishop of Lincoln, 1595–1608 In 1595 Chaderton was translated to Lincoln and was enthroned on 23 July. Promotion to a richer see may have been intended as a reward for his efforts against Lancashire Catholics, but Chaderton complained that episcopal revenues had been eroded by his predecessors' leases, and that he could not afford to maintain his houses and household. He resided mainly on the estate he purchased at Southoe in Huntingdonshire in 1598, and let the nearby episcopal palace at Buckden fall into ruin. It has been suggested that as bishop of Lincoln he was 'a remote and somewhat inscrutable figure' (Fincham, *Prelate as Pastor*, 90). He did not examine ordination and institution candidates personally, and rarely preached in the diocese. He was an active judge, however, and sat in his court of audience 214 times between 1597 and 1607. As he sought to exert his own authority from 1597, he came into conflict with diocesan officials who held their posts by patent, especially Thomas Rands, episcopal commissary for the archdeaconries of Lincoln and Stow. On 28 December 1601 Chaderton wrote a fierce letter to Rands, accusing him of negligence and failure to carry out instructions. As at Chester, Chaderton took little personal part in visitations, but his visitation articles were careful and influential. The articles compiled for the Chester visitation of 1581 were adapted for use in Lincoln in 1598, 1601, and 1604, but in 1604 the churchwardens of Ludborough, Lincolnshire, complained that the fifty-one articles were 'so many and so hard' (Foster, *State of the Church*, lxv–vi). Chaderton's articles, revised in the light of the canons of 1604 and divided into headed sections for the visitation of 1607, became a model version adopted by his successors and carried into other dioceses.

As James I travelled south from Scotland in 1603, Chaderton prepared to meet him as he entered the diocese. The bishop dressed his servants 'in tawny liveries, with facings of changeable taffeta yellow and red, being the colours now chiefly esteemed', and asked his archdeacons and officers to join him with their servants similarly attired (Foster, xlix). Chaderton preached before the king at Burghley, Northamptonshire, on Easter day 1603. But he was soon to face difficulties. As visitor of King's College, Cambridge, he was called in by the provost and senior fellows to deal with disputes and divisions in the college. Chaderton reported to Sir Robert Cecil on 8 May 1603 that the 'younger factious sort' had rejected his authority, chanted 'We appeal to the king, we appeal to the king!', and forced him to withdraw from the college in fear of violence (*Salisbury MSS*, 15.76).

Fairly or unfairly, Chaderton now acquired a reputation for weakness. On 16 January 1605 Sir Thomas Lake described him as 'aged and fearful ... old and weak' because of his timidity in dealing with nonconformity among his clergy (*Salisbury MSS*, 17.15). After the visitation of 1604, ninety-three ministers were called before Chaderton in his audience court at Huntingdon for their nonconformity. The king was determined that they should promise full conformity or be deprived of their benefices, but Chaderton proceeded cautiously, telling James he was uncertain of his authority and was waiting for a direct order from the archbishop and action by his fellow bishops—'which fearfulness the king much mislikes' (ibid., 16.379–80; 17.15).

The bishop gave the nonconformists every chance, postponing hearings, granting time for reflection, and even dropping prosecutions. For instance, on 23 October 1605 Simon Bradstreet, vicar of Horbling, Lincolnshire, was dismissed from Chaderton's court without any promise of conformity because of his hard work and honest conduct. After David Allen, rector of Ludborough, had appeared several times before Chaderton in 1604–5, the bishop gave him yet 'further time for reading and conference' on 6 November 1605, and on 6 June 1606 dropped the charges when Allen simply promised to 'endeavour to satisfy and conform himself therein' (Foster, cii–iii). But perhaps James was wrong, and Chaderton neither weak nor fearful: perhaps he was seeking to keep useful ministers in their posts, as he had done at Chester. He wrote to Robert Cecil, Viscount Cranborne, on 12 April 1605, arguing that the nonconformists maintained their stand only for fear of losing credit with their supporters, and explained that 'I will, by the grace of God use all the best means I can devise, by conference and brotherly exhortations, with mildness and discretion to win them' (*Salisbury MSS*, 17.133). Chaderton eventually deprived eight incumbents and suspended nine curates, but only under pressure from the king: the nonconformist John Jackson acknowledged Chaderton's 'general mild dealing with all my brethren' (Hajzyk, 56).

The first minister to be deprived was John Burges, rector of Waddesdon, Buckinghamshire, who had organized an address to the king by thirty Lincoln ministers in justification of their nonconformity. Burges was probably responsible for the publication in 1605 of *An Abridgement of that Booke which the Ministers of Lincoln Diocese Delivered to his Majestie*, which was answered in 1606 by William Covell in *A Briefe Answer unto Certaine Reasons*. Covell was born at Chadderton in Lancashire, had been ordained by Chaderton, and dedicated the answer to him—but the epistle dedicatory is noticeably cool and does not commend the bishop for action against nonconformity. As bishop of Lincoln, Chaderton attended the parliamentary sessions of 1601 and 1604, but was absent in 1597, 1605, and 1606–7. When Sir John Harington was writing his *Briefe View of the State of the Church of England* in 1608,

Chaderton was still living at Southoe 'in very good state' (Harington, 84), but he died there on 11 April 1608 and was buried next day in the parish church.

Bishop and man Chaderton appears to have been an administrator rather than a pastor, though this may be because the sources reflect his efforts against Catholicism in Lancashire and nonconformity in Lincoln. He certainly encouraged godly preachers, and in both of his dioceses he sought to protect nonconformists who were useful allies against popery and sin. In Whitney's *Choice of Emblemes* of 1586, Chaderton was commended with the motto 'Vigilantia & custodia' ('watchfulness and care'), an emblem of a church with a cock at its top and a lion at the door, and verses in praise of a pastor who was a cock to warn the world and a lion to fight off wolves. But Chaderton was also an ambitious careerist, chasing promotions and commendams, and he seems to have been thought avaricious. Harington mocked him for building up a fortune to pass on to his only grandchild, Elizabeth Sandys, to whom he allotted a dowry of £2000 and all his lands after his widow's death. Chaderton had no son to advance, but he deployed his patronage to the advantage of Roger Parker, his nephew. Through Chaderton's favour, Parker gained a prebend at Chester in 1587, a fellowship at Manchester College in 1594, a prebend at Lincoln in 1597, the precentorship in 1598, and the archdeaconry of Bedford in 1598. When Parker vacated a Lincoln prebend in 1598, Chaderton conferred it on his kinsman Lawrence Chaderton, master of Emmanuel College, Cambridge.

Chaderton presented the eight-volume Montanus polyglot Bible to the library of Queens' College, Cambridge, in 1589, but his generosity was usually confined to his family. He made his will on 31 March 1608, 'full of infirmity': he was a supralapsarian predestinarian, 'believing assuredly' in his own salvation (PRO, PROB 11/111, fol. 378*v*). He made careful arrangements for his property to pass to 'my loving and dear wife' Katherine, then to his granddaughter Elizabeth and her heirs, then to a string of Chaderton kinsmen in turn. Roger Parker was given a choice of his divinity books; his history books in English went to his widow; his other history books and works of philosophy and poetry went to Elizabeth Sandys's young husband; and to Elizabeth he left her dowry, a mass of plate, his set of viols, and his lute, bandora, recorders, and music books. Chaderton's public concerns had been the preaching of the gospel and the destruction of popery; in private, he was devoted to his family and to music.

CHRISTOPHER HAIGH

Sources F. Peck, ed., *Desiderata curiosa*, 1 (1732) · C. W. Foster, ed., *The state of the church in the reigns of Elizabeth and James I*, Lincoln RS, 23 (1926) · correspondence, Lincs. Arch., Cor/B · will, PRO, PROB 11/111, sig. 47 · W. G. Searle, *The history of the Queens' College of St Margaret and St Bernard in the University of Cambridge*, 2 vols., Cambridge Antiquarian RS, 9, 13 (1867–71), pt 1 · H. Hajzyk, 'The church in Lincolnshire, *c*.1595–*c*.1640', PhD diss., U. Cam., 1980 · K. Fincham, ed., *Visitation articles and injunctions of the early Stuart church*, 1 (1994) · W. P. M. Kennedy, ed., *Elizabethan episcopal administration*, 2–3, Alcuin Club, Collections, 26–7 (1924) · *Calendar of the manuscripts of the most hon. the marquess of Salisbury*, 15–17, HMC, 9 (1930–38) · C. Haigh, *Reformation and resistance in Tudor Lancashire* (1975) · F. R.

Raines, *The rectors of Manchester, and the wardens of the collegiate church of that town*, ed. [J. E. Bailey], 2 vols., Chetham Society, new ser., 5–6 (1885) • W. Ffarington, *The Derby household books*, ed. F. R. Raines, Chetham Society, 31 (1853) • J. Harington, *A briefe view of the state of the Church of England* (1653) • M. Palingenius [P. A. Manzolli], *The firste syxe bokes of … the zodyake of lyfe*, trans. B. Googe (1561) • register of bishop of Chester, 1579–1647, Ches. & Chester ALSS, EDA2/2 • JHL, 2 (1578–1614) • J. B. Mullinger, *The University of Cambridge*, 2 (1884) • J. Nichols, *The progresses and public processions of Queen Elizabeth*, 3 (1805); new edn (1823) • *Fasti Angl., 1541–1857*, [York] • *Fasti Angl., 1541–1857*, [Ely] • *Fasti Angl., 1541–1857*, [Lincoln] • *Correspondence of Matthew Parker*, ed. J. Bruce and T. T. Perowne, Parker Society, 42 (1853) • J. Strype, *The life and acts of Matthew Parker* (1711) • F. R. Hollinworth, *Mancuniensis*, ed. W. Willis (1839) • F. R. Raines, ed., 'A visitation of the diocese of Chester, by John, archbishop of York', *Chetham miscellanies*, 5, Chetham Society, 96 (1875) • K. Fincham, *Prelate as pastor: the episcopate of James I* (1990) • G. Whitney, *A choice of emblems* (1586) • J. W. Clay, ed., *The visitation of Cambridge … 1575 … 1619*, Harleian Society, 41 (1897) • *VCH Lancashire*, vol. 4 • S. Hibbert and W. R. Whatton, *History of the foundations in Manchester of Christ's College, Chetham's Hospital and the free grammar school*, 4 vols. (1828–48), vol. 2 • parish register, Southoe, 12 April 1608 [burial]

Archives Lincs. Arch., corresp. • NL Scot., copies of corresp.

Likenesses oils, 1602, Man. City Gall. [*see illus.*] • Woolnoth, engraving (after portrait, probably lost), repro. in Hibbert-Ware, *History of the foundations in Manchester*, vol. 2, pl. 16

Chads, Sir Henry (1819–1906), naval officer, born at Fareham, Hampshire, on 29 October 1819, was the son of Admiral Sir Henry Ducie *Chads (1788?–1868) and his wife, Elizabeth (d. 1861), daughter of John Pook of Fareham. Major-General William John Chads CB was his younger brother. After two years at the Royal Naval College, Portsmouth, Henry entered the navy in 1834, and served with his father in the *Andromache*, in the East Indies and against Malay pirates in the Strait of Malacca. In June 1841 he was promoted lieutenant, and as lieutenant of the *Harlequin* was, in 1844, severely wounded in an attack on pirate settlements in Sumatra. For this service he was specially promoted commander on 31 January 1845. From 1846 to 1848 he commanded the steam sloop *Styx* on the west coast of Africa with considerable success, and on 5 June 1848 was advanced to post rank. In 1863 he was appointed superintendent of Deptford Dock and victualling yards, from which, in April 1866, he was promoted to his flag. In 1869–70 he was second-in-command of the Channel Fleet; he was promoted rear-admiral in October 1872, and he was commander-in-chief at the Nore from 1876 to September 1877, when he reached the rank of admiral. On 27 October 1884, having reached the age of sixty-five, he was retired. He was made KCB in 1887. He settled at Southsea, where he devoted himself to naval charities, especially the Seamen and Marines' Orphanage, the committee of which he joined in 1868 in succession to his father. He died, unmarried, at his home, Portland House, Southsea, on 30 June 1906.

J. K. LAUGHTON, *rev.* ROGER MORRISS

Sources *The Times* (2 July 1906) • *Navy List* • W. L. Clowes, *The Royal Navy: a history from the earliest times to the present*, 7 vols. (1897–1903), vols. 6–7 • O'Byrne, *Naval biog. dict.* • *CGPLA Eng. & Wales* (1906)

Wealth at death £25,151 3s. 10d.: probate, 4 Aug 1906, CGPLA Eng. & Wales

Chads, Sir Henry Ducie (1788?–1868), naval officer, eldest son of Captain Henry Chads RN (d. 1799), and his wife, Susannah, daughter of John Cornell, entered the Royal Naval College at Portsmouth in 1800. From there he joined the *Excellent* in September 1803 (Captain Sotheron). He served for the next three years in the Mediterranean, and on 5 November 1806 was promoted lieutenant of the *Illustrious*, then blockading Cadiz. In 1808 he was appointed to the frigate *Iphigenia* (36 guns, Captain Henry Lambert), on the East India station, and in 1810 he took part in the operations leading to the capture of Mauritius. On 13 August Chads commanded the *Iphigenia*'s boats in the squadron attack on the Isle de la Passe; later, on the death of Lieutenant Norman, he succeeded to the command of the whole force. In reporting the attack Captain Pym erroneously described the command as falling to Lieutenant Watling (Chads's junior by two years), a mistake which caused the Admiralty to withhold the promotion which would otherwise have been conferred on the officer commanding.

The capture of the Isle de la Passe ended in misfortune for the British. In an attack on Grand Port on 24 August three of the ships got ashore and were taken or destroyed, while on 27 August the *Iphigenia* was beset in the narrow passage by a squadron of fourfold force, and next day was compelled to surrender, the officers and ship's company becoming prisoners of war. When Mauritius was captured, on 3 December 1810, the prisoners were set free, and Chads was again appointed to the *Iphigenia*, which was recovered at the same time. The ship was at once sent home, and was paid off in May 1811. In the following December, Chads was appointed to the *Semiramis*, in which he continued until August 1812, when Captain Lambert commissioned the *Java*, and at his request Chads was appointed her first-lieutenant.

The *Java* (38 18-pounder guns) was a fine frigate, taken from the French only the year before, and now under orders to carry the new governor, General Hislop, out to Bombay, together with a large quantity of naval stores. Her crew was exceptionally ill-suited to the voyage; an unusually large proportion had never been to sea before, and many had been drafted from prisons. She carried also sixty-eight supernumeraries, and when she sailed from Spithead on 12 November 1812 she had on board nearly 400 men all told. Owing to overcrowding, bad weather, and the rawness of the ship's company, drill was almost entirely neglected, and the guns were rarely, if ever, exercised. On 29 December 1812, off the coast of Brazil, in latitude 13° S, she met the United States frigate *Constitution*, a more powerful ship, with a numerous and well-trained crew. Lambert chose to attack, using the superior speed of his ship, but she was dismasted by the more powerful American guns. Thereafter her defence was highly creditable.

The action lasted for nearly three hours. Although, after about 90 minutes, Captain Lambert fell mortally wounded, and though the heavy, well-aimed broadsides of the *Constitution* racked the *Java* through and through, while the *Java*'s return was wild and produced little effect, her men stuck bravely to their guns to the last. Chads, though wounded, remained in command. It was only when the ship lay an unmanageable hulk, and the *Constitution* took up a raking position athwart her bows, that Chads gave the order to haul down the colours. The loss of the *Java* can be attributed to the size of the *Constitution*, the power of her armament, and the number of her crew. In addition the *Constitution*'s men had been trained to use their arms and the *Java*'s men had not. The *Constitution* lost thirty-four men killed and wounded, while the *Java* lost 150 men; the *Constitution* was scarcely damaged in hull or rigging, while the *Java* was entirely dismasted and sinking.

On 23 April 1813, after his return home, Chads, with the officers and men of the *Java*, was tried by court martial for the loss of the ship; he was honourably acquitted and specially complimented by the president of the court. He was promoted commander on 28 May, and appointed to the sloop *Columbia*, which he commanded in the West Indies until the final peace. Chads was paid off on 24 November 1815. Two days later he married Elizabeth Townsend (*d.* 1861), daughter of John Pook of Fareham, Hampshire. They had two daughters and two sons; their eldest son was Admiral Sir Henry *Chads (1819–1906).

Chads remained unemployed until November 1823, when he commissioned the *Arachne* (18 guns) for the East Indies, and in her was present during the operations in the Irawaddy, which he commanded for some time. His services were recognized by his promotion to captain on 25 July 1825 and his appointment to the frigate *Alligator* (28 guns), which he commanded until the end of the First Anglo-Burmese War; Chads signed the treaty, as senior naval officer. He returned to England and paid off his ship on 3 January 1827, having been nominated a CB on 26 December 1826. From 1834 to 1837 he commanded the *Andromache* (28 guns) on the East India station, and from 1841 to 1845 the *Cambrian* (36 guns), also in the East Indies, where he served as senior officer at Chusan (Zhoushan) and Amoy (Xiamen) during the later stages of the First Opium War.

On 28 August 1845, upon his return, Chads was appointed to the command of the *Excellent*, the School of Naval Gunnery, at Portsmouth. In this command he remained for more than eight years, earning an impressive reputation for the improvements which he introduced into the detail of gunnery exercise and gunnery instruction. He was frequently employed on committees and in the conduct of experiments; and, though repeatedly offered other employment, including a seat at the Admiralty board, he always begged to be allowed rather to stay in the *Excellent*. In 1848 he was selected to report on the *Blenheim*, the first screw line-of-battle ship, and at the same time to command a small squadron on the coast of Ireland during Smith O'Brien's 1848 uprising.

In September 1850 Chads was sent to witness a naval demonstration at Cherbourg, after which he made a confidential report on the strategic importance of Cherbourg, which he thought overrated, and on the French system of manning their ships, recommending the introduction into the Royal Navy of continuous service. He also pointed

out the dangerous situation of Portsmouth, then without any defence, and urged the construction of heavy forts. Chads's work on guns, coastal operations, and the French challenge culminated in the development of the 'Cherbourg strategy': the opening of any conflict with a large-scale bombardment of the enemy's naval bases, using steam gunboats.

On 12 January 1854 Chads attained the rank of rear-admiral; for the rest of the year he served as fourth in command in the Baltic, with his flag in the *Edinburgh*. His squadron was intended to carry out coastal bombardments. As the navy's leading gunnery officer Chads played a leading role in the capture of Bomarsund in August 1854, and he was made KCB on 5 July 1855. He was commander-in-chief at Cork from 1856 to 1858, after which he did not serve afloat, though in 1859 he was chairman of a committee on coast defence. He became vice-admiral on 24 November 1858, admiral on 3 December 1863, and was made GCB on 28 March 1865. The latter years of his life were passed at Southsea, Hampshire, where he was a county magistrate and known as a warm supporter of the local charities, especially of the Seamen and Marines' Orphan School. He died at Southsea on 7 April 1868.

Although Chads's career began with his being captured twice he became an outstanding seaman, leader, and gunnery officer. His work on board the *Excellent* brought the standard of naval gunnery with smooth bore muzzle-loading cannon to something approaching perfection. He was one of the most significant officers of his day.

J. K. LAUGHTON, *rev.* ANDREW LAMBERT

Sources M. Burrows, *Memoirs of Sir H. D. Chads* (1869) · C. N. Parkinson, *War in the eastern seas, 1793–1815* (1954) · W. S. Dudley, ed., *The naval war of 1812: a documentary history*, 1 (1985) · A. D. Lambert, *The Crimean War: British grand strategy, 1853–56* (1990) · O'Byrne, *Naval biog. dict.* · G. S. Graham, *The China station: war and diplomacy, 1830–1860* (1978) · G. S. Graham, *Great Britain in the Indian Ocean: a study of maritime enterprise, 1810–1850* (1967) · A. Phillimore, *The life of Admiral of the Fleet Sir William Parker*, 2 (1879) · C. J. Bartlett, *Great Britain and sea power, 1815–1853* (1963) · W. L. Clowes, *The Royal Navy: a history from the earliest times to the present*, 7 vols. (1897–1903), vol. 5 · *Experiments in H.M.s ship Excellent under Captain Sir T. Hastings & Sir H. D. Chads, from 1832 to 1854* · *Dod's Peerage* (1858) · Boase, *Mod. Eng. biog.* · *GM*, 4th ser., 5 (1868), 778–9 · *CGPLA Eng. & Wales* (1868)
Archives New York Historical Society, copy of report to Admiralty relating to naval action fought off Brazil | BL, letters to Sir Charles Napier, Add. MSS 40022–40044 · NL Scot., letters to Sir Thomas Cochrane · PRO, ADM · PRO, corresp. with Lord Ellenborough, PRO 30/12 · Wood MSS
Likenesses portrait, repro. in Burrows, *Memoirs*
Wealth at death under £9000: probate, 18 May 1868, *CGPLA Eng. & Wales*

Chadwick, David (1821–1895), accountant and company promoter, was born on 23 December 1821 at Macclesfield, Cheshire, the youngest of the nine children of John Chadwick, accountant, and his wife, Rebecca. His schooling was only brief and was terminated at an early age by employment in a warehouse. By attending evening classes, however, Chadwick eventually took up his father's occupation, and in 1843 he began to practise as an accountant. Between 1844 and 1860 he was treasurer to the corporation of Salford, and he also undertook that office for the town's gasworks, waterworks, and magistrates. In 1844 he married Louisa (d. 1877), youngest daughter of William Bow of Boughton, Manchester. The couple had a son and two daughters.

Chadwick's employment stimulated his interest in sanitary and educational questions. He began to publish widely in this field, and in a large number of papers and pamphlets he frequently combined a new and growing interest in statistics with the investigation of urban problems and conditions. In addition he also registered a series of patents for water meters, between 1853 and 1860. Chadwick's best-known statistical publication was *On the rate of wages in 200 trades and branches of labour in … the manufacturing district of Lancashire* (1859), which was first read as a paper to the Statistical Society of London. A member of the council of that society from 1865 to 1867, he also served as president of the Manchester Statistical Society.

Chadwick played a prominent role in the establishment of both the Salford Royal Free Library and Museum and the Salford Working Men's College. He subsequently served as treasurer of both institutions. His expertise was such that he advised the promoters of the act which enabled local authorities to establish public libraries and museums. One of his most important public achievements in Manchester occurred in 1868, when the city first appointed a medical officer of health. As an officer of local government it would seem that Chadwick became well acquainted with the middle classes of the industrial north-west; for when he returned to private accounting practice in Manchester, in 1860, all the evidence points to him providing a conduit for the savings of this social group to pass into the shares of industrial companies.

During the 1860s Chadwick's partnership was titled Chadwick, Adamson McKenna & Co.; and a London office was opened in 1864 or 1865. However, the frequent change of partner—Chadwick had ten associates between 1860 and 1892 and from seven he was separated by lawsuits— suggests he was not an easy man to work with. Indeed, it was later noted that he 'found excitement in litigiousness' rather than in the stock exchange, racing, betting, or gambling (Cottrell, *DBB*, 626). Notwithstanding such difficulties, between 1862 and 1874 Chadwick was responsible for the 'promotion' of at least forty-seven limited companies, transforming them from private partnerships to publicly owned companies. Many of these were already household names, such as Charles Cammell & Co., the Ebbw Vale Steel, Iron, and Coal Company, John Brown & Co., and Bolckow, Vaughan & Co. Chadwick's first industrial promotion concerned the Ashbury Carriage Company, a Manchester firm, but during the mid-1860s most of his energies were absorbed in the conversion of Sheffield and Cleveland manufacturing and mining companies. Generally these were private affairs, with large proportions of the shares being acquired by Chadwick's 'friends' in Manchester and Salford, while Chadwick charged the vendors a commission of 1 per cent for his services. He was also linked, increasingly, with a group of financiers associated with the private bank of Glyn Mills, as well as with the International Financial Society.

In his approach to company promotion Chadwick set the highest of standards by employing professional valuers; nor did he inflate the value of the assets in question through having them sold initially to 'dummy' vendors. By the 1870s his activities encompassed a wider range of financial securities; these included domestic and American railway shares and bonds, American land sales, shares of overseas mining, telegraph, and tramway companies, and domestic commercial and public utility companies. This broadening of his business interests led to a greater resort to the publication of prospectuses in order to attract subscriptions to his conversions, and between 1870 and 1875 he produced his own *Investment Circular*.

Chadwick's national importance as an industrial financier resulted in his giving evidence before a parliamentary committee in 1867 concerned with the operation of company law. In that year he was called before the select committee on the Limited Liability Acts, which met following the financial crisis of 1866. In the aftermath of the crash Chadwick's firm was involved in the rescue of four banks which had stopped trading: the Agra and Masterman's, the Bank of London, the Consolidated Bank, and the Preston Bank.

In 1868 Chadwick entered the Commons as the Liberal member for Macclesfield, and he acted there as a knowledgeable commentator on government measures to reform company law. He played a prominent role in 1876 when he introduced his own legislation in an attempt to place the legal framework for company conversions on a more satisfactory basis.

> Chadwick's concerns were to make the details of company flotation public knowledge, to ensure that companies had sufficient capital with which to commence business and to see that every company published uniform profit and loss accounts, balance sheets and annual reports. (Cottrell, *DBB*, 629)

Although his bill failed, his ideas were to be taken up by others in 1884 and again in 1887. However, Chadwick was unseated as an MP in 1880 following a successful petition, from a Conservative agent, which had alleged bribery and other electoral malpractices.

Chadwick remained an accountant throughout his life and during the 1880s acted largely for the companies that he had converted over the two previous decades. He also took a leading part in the professionalization of accountancy, being a founder member and fellow of the Institute of Accountants (London) and first president of the Manchester Institute of Chartered Accountants, established in 1871. A decade later Chadwick was one of the first council members of the Institute of Chartered Accountants in England and Wales. This interest was matched by his concern to provide public education, which in turn reflected his own, possibly bitter, experience of self-improvement through evening classes. In 1876 Chadwick gave a library of 10,000 books to his home town of Macclesfield. In addition he was involved with the creation of Royal Holloway College, London, and he later became a trustee of the estate and a governor of the college.

Chadwick was a busy 'high Victorian' with a wide range

of interests in public affairs. Privately he had little time for leisure, apart from the occasional game of billiards, and it was noted by his contemporaries that he gained the greatest excitement from his relentless pursuit of law cases. Chadwick's first wife died in 1877, and he then married, in 1878, Ursula, eldest daughter of Thomas *Sopwith FRS. Ursula Chadwick may have had a difficult time as during the last ten years of his life her husband became increasingly self-opinionated. This character trait certainly led him to dramatic public clashes, as with the boards of the companies that he had promoted, and the author of an obituary later discussed his character in terms of an 'aversion to criticism, advice or opposition, or even to listen to caution' (quoted in Cottrell, *DBB*, 630).

From the late 1870s the number of company flotations began to fall, and Chadwick was increasingly involved with his proposed company law reforms. He also fought a long series of actions arising from his promotion of the Blochairn Iron Company in 1873. In the event the action against him was dismissed, and he was awarded full costs. Although Chadwick continued to act as accountant for the companies he had floated, the 1880s witnessed a gradual decline of his entrepreneurial energy. He continued to write and publish occasional pamphlets on economic and financial matters, his final paper in 1890 being concerned with profit sharing.

Chadwick suffered from increasing deafness and blindness, and he finally died on 19 September 1895 at his home, The Poplars, 6 Herne Hill, London. He was survived by his second wife. PHILLIP L. COTTRELL

Sources P. L. Cottrell, 'Chadwick, David', *DBB* · P. L. Cottrell, *Industrial finance, 1830–1914: the finance and organization of English manufacturing industry* (1980) · *The Times* (1864–95) · *The Economist* (1864–78) · *Hansard 3* (1876–7) · R. H. Parker, ed., *British accountants: a biographical sourcebook* (1980) · T. S. Ashton, *Economic and social investigations in Manchester, 1833–1933* (1934) · *Chadwick's Investment Circular* (16 Aug 1875) · *CGPLA Eng. & Wales* (1895) · Boase, *Mod. Eng. biog.* · d. cert.

Archives Man. CL | Royal Holloway College, Egham, Surrey, corresp. with Thomas Holloway and Sir George Martin-Holloway · U. Hull, Mellors, Basden MSS

Likenesses photograph, repro. in Cotrell, 'David Chadwick'

Wealth at death £2726 6s. 4d.: probate, 7 Nov 1895, *CGPLA Eng. & Wales*

Chadwick, Sir Edwin (1800–1890), social reformer and civil servant, was born at Longsight, near Manchester, on 24 January 1800. Surprisingly little is known of his early life, and of his mother nothing, except that she died in the infancy of her only son. His father, James Chadwick, the son of a pioneering Lancashire Wesleyan, was a radical journalist who had spent heady days in Paris with Thomas Paine and is supposed to have taught botany and music to the scientist John Dalton.

A Benthamite education, c.1809–1832 Edwin Chadwick was educated at the village school in Longsight and then boarded briefly at Dr Wordsworth's school in Stockport, before moving with his father to London at about the age of ten. There James edited (and, it was said, rendered more moderate) David Lovell's paper *The Statesman* while its firebrand editor was in gaol for seditious libel. Upon Lovell's

Sir Edwin Chadwick (1800–1890), by unknown engraver, pubd 1889 (after Mayall & Co.)

release James Chadwick moved to Devon to edit the *Western Times*, leaving Edwin behind clerking in an attorney's office. About 1837 James emigrated to America with his second wife and their children (one of whom, Henry, became a pioneer of baseball). Edwin clerked until 1823, when he shifted his allegiance to the bar, was admitted to the Inner Temple, and took lodgings in Lyon's Inn, supporting himself by writing for newspapers. This combination of the law and the press drew him into an acquaintance with the social problems of prisons, hospitals, and slums, as well as with like-minded explorers of these problems in the circle of Jeremy Bentham. By 1824 he was already intimate with the Benthamite doctors Neil Arnott and (Thomas) Southwood Smith, and with John Stuart Mill, of whose London Debating Society he was a founder member.

Practically from the start Chadwick's passion was for the 'quick-fix' technical or administrative solution to deep-seated social problems. His first publications proposed means of extending life expectancy (*Westminster Review*, 9, 1828) and propagandized for the police as a deterrent force against crime (*London Review*, 1, 1829). These brought him to the attention of Bentham himself, who in 1830 engaged him as a private secretary to assist in the completion of the *Constitutional Code*. This work superseded Chadwick's legal career—he was called to the bar in 1830 but attempted only a single brief—and he moved into Bentham's Queen Square home in 1831. Bentham's death in June 1832 therefore left him peculiarly vulnerable, the more so as Chadwick had no sympathy for the populist (as opposed to the problem-solving) side of the Benthamites' cause. His ill-disguised contempt for the democratic 'agitators' of the day ultimately lost him a stopgap post as sub-editor of Albany Fonblanque's *Examiner* in the autumn of 1833.

Poor laws and factories, 1832–1839 Fortunately Chadwick had by then already found an alternative career as a kind of freelance civil servant. The new whig government needed young men with a social conscience, a taste for systematic investigation, and the administrative ability to help frame laws; Chadwick's distaste for democracy made him more acceptable than most Benthamites. Accordingly the political economist Nassau Senior, playing a leading role in the newly appointed royal commission on the poor laws, got Chadwick employment as an assistant in summer 1832. Chadwick's rapid accumulation of relevant evidence in London and Berkshire, his agreement with Senior on the principles of political economy that should guide a reform of the poor laws, and above all his ingenuity at devising administrative mechanisms to put those principles into practice soon won him a place at Senior's right hand. Though not (as he later claimed) the only begetter of the famous principle of the new poor law of 1834—that aid to an able-bodied male should be dispensed in a workhouse to ensure that his standard of living was 'less eligible' than that of a gainfully employed worker—he was undoubtedly responsible for artfully arranging the commission's evidence to point in this direction and for drawing up the administrative proposals sent to ministers that provided the basis of the new law. Senior confirmed his (otherwise undocumented) claim to have been made a full commissioner in April 1833 on the strength of this role.

In the midst of his poor-law work Chadwick was seconded to another inquiry, the royal commission on factories, which the government had hastily set up to sidetrack a humanitarian cry for a fixed ten-hour day in textile factories. On this comparatively ill-understood field Chadwick's influence was more direct and innovative than on the much debated poor laws. In a matter of a few months (April to July 1833) he drew up the terms of inquiry, directed the taking of evidence (in camera, to the disgust of the ten-hours lobby), and drew up a report which ingeniously recommended an eight-hour day for children under thirteen, complemented by three hours' education, appealing to humanitarian concerns for the young while avoiding the restrictions on adult labour that so horrified employers. Government seized on this compromise and rushed a modified version onto the statute books in August. Among its provisions the Factory Act of 1833 established what *The Times* called 'an important class of new officers, called "inspectors"'—as Chadwick saw it, a new field of employment for people like himself.

Meanwhile Chadwick had returned to the poor law, and with Senior set about writing the bulk of the royal commission's final report, published in February 1834. This, too, contained provisions for inspectors, specifically a central board of commissioners with travelling assistants. Chadwick was shocked not to participate in the drafting of the Poor Law Amendment Bill with ministers—this was directed by Senior—and even more so not to be appointed a central commissioner when the bill became law in the summer of 1834. Ministers considered Chadwick's 'station in society was not as would have made it fit that he should be made one of the Commissioners' (Finer, 109), and were concerned to maximize the acceptability of the new law among a jittery landed élite. They appointed more socially elevated and emollient commissioners, chaired by the mediocre tory landowner and politician Thomas Frankland Lewis. Chadwick was

offered the full-time secretaryship of the poor-law commission. Indignant at not receiving a commissionership, he initially refused, but was persuaded by Senior and Althorp, possibly given assurances as to the higher status he would enjoy in the commission that neither Senior nor Althorp was in a position to guarantee. Still hurt and suspicious, Chadwick became secretary, a post well suited to his talents for marshalling evidence and framing proposals, without requiring the higher political skills (which he decisively lacked).

Chadwick's time at the poor-law commission was not happy. His strong views on the need to impose the workhouse system immediately and nationally—if anything, first in the northern districts, where it was most unpopular—clashed with Lewis's more pragmatic reading of the political situation. For a time Chadwick became the focus of a storm of anti-poor-law hostility from working-class and localist interests, which saw the new law as inhumane, authoritarian, and over-centralized. This clash of method was exacerbated by a clash of style, between the stolid, snobby Lewis and the perfervid, prickly Chadwick. For both reasons Chadwick was progressively excluded from the policy-making work of the commission, although he continued to supervise the routine office work and to correspond with a network of sympathetic local officials and assistant commissioners, whose innovations he publicized in the annual reports of the commission. He also struck up a friendly relationship with Lord John Russell (home secretary, 1835–8), who proved willing to employ Chadwick's investigative talents in a variety of social inquiries. In October 1836 Russell appointed Chadwick with two others to a royal commission on rural police with a view to extending the experiment in professional policing initiated in London. Chadwick compiled a report (not issued until March 1839) containing horror stories of metropolitan crime migrating into the countryside and requiring a national system of police centrally controlled but locally funded, a formula guaranteed further to antagonize rural interests suspicious of centralization. The Rural Constabulary Act of 1839 bore closer resemblance to the views of Chadwick's fellow commissioners, Charles Rowan and Charles Shaw Lefevre, making the adoption of a rural police voluntary and leaving it almost wholly in the hands of county magistrates.

Though popular mythology also had Chadwick responsible for the new system of civil registration for births, deaths, and marriages—persons registered under this 1836 act were deemed 'Chadwicked'—in fact he had little to do with it; but he did help secure a key register office post for William Farr, and it may have been through Farr that he revived his old interest in preventing avoidable deaths. In any case by 1838 he was turning his attention to what came to be known as sanitary (or, later, public health) matters, and in the spring of that year he persuaded Russell to commission his medical friends Neil Arnott and Southwood Smith (along with a favoured poor-law assistant, James Kay-Shuttleworth) to inquire into the sanitary conditions of the metropolis. Despite this medical input, Chadwick's clear intention from the start was to focus public attention on the need for new administrative structures to address the problems of urban sanitation. This suited his natural inclinations but it also responded to his growing need to find a new sphere of employment. The new poor law required parliamentary reconfirmation in 1839, and a renewed outburst of popular agitation against it again focused on Chadwick, who must then, his biographer Samuel Finer thought, have been 'the most unpopular single individual in the whole kingdom' (Finer, 187). Furthermore, Lord John Russell had by now left the Home Office. Under such pressures Chadwick engineered a parliamentary motion for a wider inquiry into public health matters and in autumn 1839 secured his secondment to this inquiry, leaving even routine matters at the poor-law office to his assistant George Coode.

Private life and public health, c.1839–1854 The year 1839 thus marked the effective end of Chadwick's involvement in the poor-law system and the beginning of fifteen years' engagement with public health matters. It was also the year of his marriage to Rachel Dawson Kennedy, fifth daughter of John *Kennedy of Knocknalling, Kirkcudbrightshire, and Ardwick Hall, Manchester, a prominent textile manufacturer. She may have brought a substantial dowry, thus relieving slightly Chadwick's recurrent financial worries, although heavy investments in American securities seem to have been wiped out in a slump of the early 1840s. The couple moved to Stanhope Street, Hyde Park Gardens, London, and within the next few years produced Osbert (1842–1913), a civil engineer, and Marion (1844–1928), active in the women's movement. Apart from the possible financial impact, Chadwick's marriage had little effect on his public or perhaps even his private life; as his daughter noted, he had a high opinion of animals, children, and women (whose enfranchisement he supported), but did not enjoy close relations with any of them.

Instead Chadwick threw all of his considerable physical and mental energies into sanitary questions. Drawing on his now comprehensive network of poor-law, medical, factory, and prison informants, as well as his own extensive touring and reading, Chadwick produced by February 1842 one of the most celebrated (and best-selling) of all Victorian blue books, the *Report on the Sanitary Condition of the Labouring Population of Great Britain*, published as a House of Lords paper in July and credited to Chadwick. With graphic illustrations of filth and degradation among the lower classes, it connected the prevalence of disease and high mortality to grossly inadequate sanitary provisions, drainage, and water supply. Chadwick may have learned something from his misfortunes with poor law and police, in that he downplayed the centralized administrative solutions to which he still adhered (in private) as firmly as ever, and it was to elaborate on the administrative solutions to the problem that the new Conservative government then appointed (in 1843) a royal commission on the health of towns. Chadwick assisted this royal commission and at the same time completed a supplementary report on metropolitan interments, in this case recommending an ultra-centralized solution: the closure of metropolitan burial-grounds and the establishment of new exurban cemeteries under municipal control. Luckily little attention was paid to the interments report at the time, and in 1844–5, when the health of towns commission's reports appeared, Chadwick's public repute was probably at an all-time high. He gained much of the credit for publicizing the sanitary question and, for once, little of the opprobrium attached by vested interests to the necessary administrative changes.

While waiting for public health legislation that would provide him with a permanent post, Chadwick busied himself with the Towns Improvement Company, an experiment in providing sanitary works to municipalities by private enterprise. At the same time he agitated for closer government control of railway construction, and for a post for himself on a new railway commission. In the summer of 1846 he added further to his public reputation and revenged himself upon the poor-law commissioners by testifying damagingly against their conduct of the commission before the House of Commons select committee on the Andover Union, investigating cruel and corrupt practices in the administration of the law; its report in August endorsed his view of the commissioners' laxness.

In September 1847 Chadwick was appointed to a royal commission on the sanitary condition of the metropolis in order to begin the reform of London's many local sanitary bodies. Within a few months it had secured the supersession of the existing metropolitan sewer commissions and the appointment of a single board more favourable to Chadwick's views on sanitation. In the spring of 1848 government finally established a national public health authority, the General Board of Health, with a single paid commissionership intended for Chadwick. His peak period culminated in appointment as a CB, awarded at the instigation of Prince Albert on 27 April 1848.

In September Chadwick took up his post at the general board, alongside his friendly ministerial chief, Lord Morpeth, and unpaid commissioner Lord Ashley (later seventh earl of Shaftesbury, the evangelical and social reformer)—with whom, despite earlier disagreement on factory legislation, Chadwick worked amicably—and, later, an additional medical commissioner, Southwood Smith. Almost immediately cholera struck, and the board took emergency action to ensure the regular cleansing of streets and waste removal, cleaving to the then fashionable miasmatic theory of disease. It worked through poor-law boards and the local boards of health, which under the 1848 act could be instigated at ratepayers' initiative. Chadwick pressed upon them, and upon the new unitary commission for London, the replacement of the traditional brick sewers by his favoured comprehensive system of self-flushing, narrow diameter, glazed earthenware pipes, preferably conveying the sewage to farmers for use as manure. This dogma antagonized many engineers, as his earlier administrative dogmas had antagonized doctors. In autumn 1849, after a brief collapse brought on by overwork and possibly over-combativeness, Morpeth had to remove him from the metropolitan sewers commission. Chadwick continued to promote his system with the provincial boards. He also attacked metropolitan interests from a new angle by reopening the interments question, somewhat surprisingly inducing the government to empower the general board (via the Metropolitan Interments Act 1850) to close graveyards and replace them with its own exurban cemeteries. To this grandiose scheme Chadwick added in May 1850 a parallel plan to consolidate the metropolitan water supply under government direction.

By this point Chadwick had long since overreached himself, particularly as (from March 1850) he was deprived of the cabinet support of Lord Morpeth, replaced as the general board's chief by the hostile Lord Seymour. Between them Seymour and the Treasury blocked the general board's plan to buy up the graveyards, and by July 1852 new legislation was on the books giving government only a regulatory role in metropolitan interments and water supply. Now the board's opponents in the provinces began to mass against it as well. An outbreak of typhoid in Croydon in December 1852 led to an inquiry which, though co-authored by Chadwick's old comrade Neil Arnott, damned the Chadwickian pipe system installed there. When the general board came up for parliamentary renewal in July 1854, its enemies included leading engineers and medical men as well as ideological opponents of centralization; Chadwick's paid commissionership was abolished in a general reform and he was retired—permanently, as it turned out—on a £1000 per annum pension.

Retirement, death, and reputation Chadwick lived out his lengthy retirement first at 5 Montagu Villas, Richmond, Surrey, and then, from 1869 until his death, at Park Cottage (since demolished), near Richmond Park, East Sheen, Surrey, specially designed by him to feature modern heating and ventilation. He retained his massive build and long, dark hair, set over a dome-like forehead, into extreme old age, adding the straggling white beard characteristic of the Victorian patriarch. He continued to offer advice behind the scenes but it is doubtful whether any of these initiatives made much impact. His rationalizing and centralizing impulses were out of fashion in a period of legislative retrenchment, and became if anything more impetuous as he aged: free-market competition, which he used to regard as a necessary spur to efficiency in most spheres, he came to see more and more as productive of waste. He now advocated state consolidation of gas, tramways, railways, and telegraphs as well as interments and water supply, with the administration of these natural monopolies franchised out to competitive tender ('competition for the field' as opposed to 'within the field', a concept taken up by late twentieth-century economists seeking to dismantle rather than build up state ownership). For these views he was more respected on the continent—in Paris he was known as Le Père Sanitaire—than in England, where he came to be seen as an anachronistic crank. He made several embarrassingly abortive attempts

to find a parliamentary seat, two of which came to a poll—Evesham (1859) and Kilmarnock burghs (1868)—with fairly disastrous results. Among like-minded social reformers he was more effective, particularly as vice-president of the Society of Arts (almost continuously from 1872 to 1886), through which he agitated for the teaching of military drill in schools and on topics as diverse as fire prevention, omnibuses and tramways, and new methods of street paving (for which he held patents), as well as his old sanitary causes. His pioneering work in the latter field was recognized towards the end of his life, when in 1883 he was made president of the new Association of Sanitary Inspectors. In 1889, by which date his centralizing views had become harmless and in some quarters almost fashionable again, he was knighted on 4 March for achievements half a century old—just in time, for he died on 5 July 1890. He was buried on 9 July in Mortlake cemetery, Surrey. In his will he left £47,000 to a trust 'for the advancement of sanitary science and the physical training of the population' (Finer, 512).

Chadwick's reputation fluctuated in his own lifetime, and has done so since his death. For some time he remained the private hero of social reformers such as the Fabians. When the welfare state materialized after the Second World War, he was suddenly discovered as one of its forefathers and benefited from two major biographies in the same year, 1952, one of which (Samuel Finer's) remains the most exhaustive and readable treatment, though it takes its subject's heroic self-estimate too much at face value. Finer endorsed John Stuart Mill's description of Chadwick as one of the 'organizing and contriving minds of the age' (Finer, 2) and depicted him as an impetuous but tireless and disinterested public servant, dragged down by snobbery and corruption. Chadwick's reputation has declined *pari passu* with the welfare state, and several major revaluations have deemed him variously inept, ineffective, and authoritarian. Yet his passion for the public good still impresses and his achievements live on in every home and under every street in Britain.

PETER MANDLER

Sources S. E. Finer, *The life and times of Sir Edwin Chadwick* (1952) • UCL, Edwin Chadwick MSS • R. A. Lewis, *Edwin Chadwick and the public health movement, 1832–1854* (1952) • B. W. Richardson, *The health of nations: a review of the works of Edwin Chadwick, with a biographical dissertation*, 2 vols. (1887) • A. Brundage, *England's 'Prussian minister': Edwin Chadwick and the politics of government growth, 1832–1854* (1988) • *The life and times of Sir Edwin Chadwick, 1800–1890* (1990) [centenary exhibition catalogue, UCL] • E. Chadwick, *Report on the sanitary condition of the labouring population of Great Britain* (1842); repr. M. W. Flinn, ed. (1965) • R. B. Ekelund and E. O. Price, 'Sir Edwin Chadwick on competition and the social control of industry: railroads', *History of Political Economy*, 11 (1979), 213–39 • E. O. Price, 'The political economy of Sir Edwin Chadwick: an appraisal', *Social Science Quarterly*, 65 (1984), 975–87 • C. Hamlin, *Public health and social justice in the age of Chadwick: Britain, 1800–1854* (1998) • P. Mandler, *Aristocratic government in the age of reform: whigs and liberals, 1830–1852* (1990) • M. Poovey, *Making a social body: British cultural formation, 1830–1865* (1995)

Archives UCL, corresp. and papers; diary | BL, letters to Macvey Napier, Add. MSS 34617–34625 • BL, corresp. with Florence Nightingale, Add. MSS 45770–45771 • BL, corresp. with Sir Robert Peel, Add. MS 40537 • Bodl. Oxf., corresp. with Lord Kimberley • NL

Scot., letters to John Burton · PRO, corresp. with Lord John Russell, PRO 30/22 · RCS Eng., letters to Richard Owen · U. Durham L., corresp. with third Earl Grey · W. Sussex RO, letters to duke of Richmond
Likenesses wood-engraving, pubd 1848, BM, NPG · A. Salomon, marble bust, *c.*1863, NPG · woodcut, pubd 1889 (after photograph by Mayall & Co.), NPG [*see illus.*] · engraving, repro. in *ILN* (22 Jan 1848) · engraving, repro. in *Cassell's Illustrated Family Paper* (24 Nov 1860) · engraving, repro. in *House and Home* (March 1881) · photographs, UCL, Chadwick MSS · wood-engraving, NPG; repro. in *ILN* (22 Jan 1848)
Wealth at death £48,738 8s. 3d.: resworn probate, May 1892, *CGPLA Eng. & Wales* (1890)

Chadwick, Hector Munro (1870–1947), literary scholar, was born on 22 October 1870 at the vicarage, Thornhill Lees, Yorkshire, the third son of the Revd Edward Chadwick and his wife, Sarah Anne Bates, whose father had been in business in Oldham. Far the youngest child, he claimed that his sister, Dora, 'brought me up' (Navarro). From Wakefield grammar school he went, as Cave exhibitioner, to Clare College, Cambridge, in 1889, and became a scholar the following year. In 1892 he was placed in the third division of the first class of part one of the classical tripos. He had, however, been developing individually. As a day boy with an 8 mile trip into Wakefield and back each day, he had taught himself German on the train journeys, and his exceptional qualities began to appear when in 1893 he was placed in the first class of part two of the classical tripos, with distinction in the philology section, and was elected a fellow of his college. From 1895 he taught for section B of the medieval and modern languages tripos, the subjects of which ranged over the whole background of Old English.

In 1899 Chadwick's first book, *The Cult of Othin*, appeared, already exhibiting the highest linguistic and archaeological competence in collecting evidence, together with remarkable ability in discerning the significant patterns which evidence yielded in combination. *Studies on Anglo-Saxon Institutions* followed in 1905, and *The Origin of the English Nation* in 1907 (reprinted 1924). In 1909 the board of medieval and modern languages at Cambridge reported that 'it would be of advantage to the University and a fit recognition of the scholarship and learning of Mr. Chadwick' if a university lectureship in Scandinavian were created for him. Quite exceptional as such a step then was, the advice was taken and the appointment made in 1910. In 1912 Chadwick published *The Heroic Age*. Its main achievement was to bring together early Teutonic with Greek heroic poetry, to the better understanding of both. There were also 'Notes' on Slav and Celtic heroic poetry, indicative of the widening scope of Chadwick's studies. In 1912 he succeeded W. W. Skeat in the Elrington and Bosworth chair of Anglo-Saxon, which he occupied until 1941. He loved to recall the founder's wish that the subject should not be Anglo-Saxon only but 'the languages cognate therewith, together with the antiquities and history of the Anglo-Saxons'. The war years which followed gave opportunity to reconsider the studies carried on under the medieval and modern languages board. Modern linguists were declaring that Britain had been a

tight little island too long, and needed a living interest in other peoples rather than academic concentration on language. Chadwick saw in this both reason and opportunity for removing English studies from the school of modern languages, and, at the same time, reshaping the study of the origins and background of English literature, so as to make philological scholarship serve the knowledge of history and civilization. For this far-reaching reform of Cambridge studies, Sir Arthur Quiller-Couch declared, in the Senate House, nine-tenths of the credit was due to Chadwick.

On 4 May 1922 Chadwick married Norah (1891–1972), a former pupil, the daughter of James Kershaw, a cotton-mill owner of Farnworth, Lancashire, and his wife, Emma Clara, *née* Booth. (She was later, as Norah Kershaw *Chadwick, to become a fellow of Newnham College, Cambridge.) Their marriage established a most remarkable literary partnership, of which their *Growth of Literature* (3 vols., 1932–40) is an abiding monument. Meanwhile the study of modern English literature at Cambridge had greatly developed, and in 1927 Chadwick took the opportunity to transfer his department to the new faculty of archaeology and anthropology, where his group of studies might, like the classics, constitute an independent discipline. On reaching the age limit in 1940 he continued as head of the department until 1945. His last works were *The Study of Anglo-Saxon* (1941), *The Nationalities of Europe and the Growth of National Ideologies* (1945), and *Early Scotland*, which was unfinished when he died, at the Evelyn Nursing Home, Trumpington Road, Cambridge, on 2 January 1947, but was published by his widow in 1949. There were no children of the marriage.

Chadwick was elected FBA in 1925, and received the honorary degrees of DLitt from Durham University (1914) and Oxford (1944) and of LLD from St Andrews in 1919. His talent as a teacher is reflected in some thirty of his pupils who held university posts.

W. TELFER, rev. JOHN D. HAIGH

Sources J. M. de Navarro, 'Hector Munro Chadwick, 1870–1947', *PBA*, 33 (1947), 307–30 [incl. bibliography] · personal knowledge (1959) · private information (1959) · C. Fox and B. Dickins, eds., *The early cultures of north-west Europe: H. M. Chadwick memorial studies* (1950) · *WWW*, 1941–50 · m. cert. · d. cert. · *CGPLA Eng. & Wales* (1947)
Likenesses photograph, repro. in Fox and Dickins, eds., *Early cultures of north-west Europe*, frontispiece · photograph, repro. in de Navarro, 307
Wealth at death £26,883 7s. 8d.: probate, 13 Aug 1947, *CGPLA Eng. & Wales*

Chadwick, Helen Clare (1953–1996), artist, was born prematurely on 18 May 1953 at St Helier Hospital, Carshalton, Surrey, the only daughter and elder child of William Clare Chadwick, estate agent, and his Greek wife, Angeline, *née* Bardopoulou, of 4 Richmond Court, Richmond Road, Wimbledon, Surrey: the mother, with her daughter, featured in Chadwick's double portrait *Lofos nymphon* (1991). Her younger brother, David, became a South Downs shepherd and appeared in her 1987 installation, *Three Houses*, at the Hayward Gallery, London. The family soon moved to

In February 1977 she moved into 45 Beck Road, Bethnal Green, an East End street of Acme housing for artists, where she lived and worked for the rest of her life. Three sociological works followed: *Train of Thought* (1978–9) explored tube travel, *Model Institution* (1981–4) portrayed dole claimants, and a controversial art and industry residency with John Smith's Breweries culminated in the exhibition 'Fine art/fine ale' (Sheffield, 1982). Part-time visiting teaching at Cardiff, Sheffield, Brighton, Portsmouth, and later Chelsea and the Royal College of Art, provided some financial support, while involvement with the London Film Co-op (from 1977) led to her involvement in the selection for the 'Hayward Annual' (1979).

It was *Ego geometria sum* (touring 1983–5), which mixed autobiography with feminism, photography with sculpture, that first achieved national recognition for Chadwick and which led to the first purchase by the Arts Council. It also signalled what was to become a preoccupation with the body and identity. Blue photocopies of her body and dead animals surrounding large golden spheres in a faux rococo setting formed the basis for the *Oval Court* installation in the 'Of mutability' exhibition (Institute of Contemporary Arts, London, and touring 1986–7), which re-addressed the traditional genres of the self-portrait, nude, and vanitas. Another piece, *Carcass*, consisting of a column filled with household waste, which started to smell and then fractured, illustrated an increasing interest in unconventional materials. The exhibition was a critical success, leading to a purchase by the Victoria and Albert Museum, and to her short-listing—the first woman so honoured—for the 1987 Turner prize. An installation deploying a helium neon laser, *Blood Hyphen* (1988), in the Clerkenwell and Islington Medical Mission for Edge '88, became the basis for the exploration of cell structures using computers and microscopes in *Viral Landscapes* (1989–90).

Chadwick's major exhibition, 'Effluvia', at the Serpentine Gallery, London (also touring to Barcelona and Essen), opened in July 1994 and proved controversial but immensely popular, breaking the gallery's attendance record: it included a suggestive fountain of molten chocolate, *Cacao*, cibachrome photographs of flowers in Swarfega, Windolene, and Germolene, and *Piss Flowers*, twelve white-lacquered bronzes of casts made by herself and her partner, David Notarius, an American marine engineer whom she had met at the 1990 Fotofest in Houston, Texas, urinating in the snow during a residency at the Banff Centre for the Arts, Alberta, in March 1991. She then undertook a heavy programme of exhibitions and installations around the world, which ranged from the Aperto at the Venice Biennale (1984) to her representation of Great Britain at the São Paulo Bienal (1994) and her solo show at the Museum of Modern Art, New York (1995). She was also increasingly involved with the mass media—producing a film on the Mexican artist Frida Kahlo for the BBC *Artist's Journeys* series in 1992, a billboard project for the BBC 1992 (on sites in Birmingham, Bristol, Derry, Glasgow, London, and Newcastle), an AIDS awareness insert

Helen Clare Chadwick (1953–1996), by Liz Rideal, 1985

23 St Arvans Close, Chepstow Rise, East Croydon; the nearby Littleheath Woods later provided the source for her Common Ground project, *The Fox* (1987). Her childhood and adolescence were used in *Ego geometria sum* (Riverside Studios, London, 1983): images of her body were photographically mapped onto a plywood incubator, pram, wigwam, and vaulting-horse.

Chadwick attended Croydon high school from 1964 to 1971, studying geography, geology, and art, and was intending to pursue an academic career as an archaeologist. Instead, she followed a foundation course in art at Bristol Polytechnic, from 1971 to 1972. She returned to Croydon for a year and studied at Croydon College of Art, where she became involved in the activities of Fluxus and the Fluxshoe tour: she made self-portraits in jelly and chocolate, and co-authored *Door to Door* (1973) with David Mayor for the Beau Geste Press. In September 1973 she started to study for a fine art/sculpture diploma in art and design at Brighton Polytechnic, where she was taught by Gwyther Irwin, Richard Wentworth, Alison Wilding, and Derek Boshier. She graduated BA in July 1976 with first-class honours and a commendation in art history: her final exhibition was entitled 'Domestic sanitation', and was influenced by such feminist artists as Penny Slinger and Judy Clark. From September 1976 to September 1977 she worked for the degree of MA in fine art/painting at Chelsea School of Art under Ian Stephenson and Ron Bowen. She also encountered the punk scene of the King's Road, Chelsea. Her final show/performance was entitled *In the Kitchen*, which was again shown at Art Net, London.

for *Face* magazine in August 1994, and material for inclusion in the CD-ROM *Eve: the Music and Art Adventure* (1996) made by the musician Peter Gabriel.

Chadwick was well known on the London and international art scene for her Cleopatra hairstyle, bright red lipstick, rings on every finger, and dapper dress-sense, as well as for her vivacity, commitment, and enthusiasm for art and teaching. She had no commercial gallery until late on in her career, when she was represented by Maureen Paley of Interim Art, London, and the Friedman-Guinness Galerie, Frankfurt. Still working on a project with the assisted conception unit at King's College Hospital, London, which she had called *Stilled Lives*, and unknowingly suffering from myocarditis, she died suddenly of a heart attack at a private view at the Architect's Association on 15 March 1996. Her funeral took place at Randall's Park crematorium, Leatherhead, Surrey, on 23 March 1996. A memorial service was held at St Martin-in-the-Fields, London, on 21 September 1996. STEPHEN BURY

Sources M. Warner, L. Buck, and D. A. Mellor, *Stilled lives: Helen Chadwick* (1996) · H. Chadwick, *Enfleshings* (1989) · A. Beckett, 'What a swell party it was', *Independent on Sunday* (2 June 1996) · M. Haworth-Booth, interview, Aug 1994, BL NSA, Oral History of British Photography · H. Chadwick, *Effluvia* (1994) [exhibition catalogue, Essen, Barcelona, and London, 6 March – 29 Aug 1994] · 'A tribute to Helen Chadwick', BBC 2 film, 3 June 1996 · *The Guardian* (18 March 1996) · *The Independent* (18 March 1996) · *The Independent* (22 March 1996) · *The Times* (19 March 1996) · Chelsea College of Art and Design Archive, London · b. cert.
Archives FILM BBC WAC · BFI NFTVA, 'A tribute to Helen Chadwick', BBC2, 3 June 1996 | SOUND Audio Arts, London · BL NSA, Oral history of British photography, 1994, C 459/53/1–4 · BL NSA, 'A tribute to Helen Chadwick', BBC, 3 June 1996, V3728/2 · BL NSA, performance recordings
Likenesses L. Rideal, photograph, 1985, NPG [*see illus.*] · K. Brimacombe, photograph, 1994, repro. in *The Independent* (18 March 1996) · K. Matthews, photograph, repro. in Warner, Buck, and Mellor, *Stilled lives* · Vanity, self-portrait, cibachrome photograph, repro. in Chadwick, *Enfleshings* · photograph, repro. in *The Times*
Wealth at death £492,044: administration, 20 April 1998, *CGPLA Eng. & Wales*

Chadwick, James (1813–1882), Roman Catholic bishop of Hexham and Newcastle, was descended from an old Catholic family, the Chadwicks of Brough Hall, near Chorley. A great-uncle, John Chadwick, had been vicar-general of the northern district in the eighteenth century. John Chadwick, the bishop's father, emigrated to Ireland at the beginning of the nineteenth century, married Frances Dromgoole, of an old Catholic family of co. Louth, and settled in Drogheda, where James was born on 24 April 1813. He was educated at St Cuthbert's College, Ushaw, near Durham, from the age of twelve; he subsequently trained there for the priesthood, and was ordained at the college in December 1836. He then joined the staff of the college as general prefect, and later taught as professor of humanities, of philosophy, and finally of dogmatic theology.

In 1850 Chadwick left Ushaw to join Edward Consitt and Robert Rodolph Suffield in a community of secular priests established at St Ninian's, Wooler. For seven years he worked here as a diocesan missionary, conducting parochial missions throughout the diocese of Hexham and

Newcastle and also in Lancashire and Yorkshire, as well as giving retreats to convents of women religious in different parts of England. He was also gifted as a spiritual director. In 1857, following a fire which destroyed St Ninian's house and chapel, the community disbanded and James Chadwick returned to teach again at Ushaw College. In 1859 he left to become chaplain to Lord Stourton at Allerton Mauleverer, near Knaresborough, and while in Yorkshire was elected canon of the then diocese of Beverley. Four years later, Robert Tate, the new president of Ushaw, persuaded him to return once more to the college, where he resumed the teaching of philosophy and pastoral theology.

In 1866 Chadwick was appointed second bishop of Hexham and Newcastle in succession to William Hogarth, and was consecrated by Archbishop Manning at Ushaw College on 28 October 1866. He remained devoted to the interests of the college and was much loved by successive generations of students. In 1877, at a time of crisis in the history of the college, the northern bishops (its governors) asked him to be its eighth president, and on several occasions he was able to improve the living conditions of the students. However, finding himself unable to give full attention to the affairs of the college while supervising his diocese, he resigned the presidency in October 1878.

During the sixteen years of Chadwick's episcopate the number of churches in the diocese, covering Cumberland, Durham, Northumberland, and Westmorland, increased from 81 to 109, priests (both regular and secular) from 96 to 158, and convents of nuns (mostly engaged in teaching and care of the poor) from 11 to 26. His pastoral letters show that he was acutely aware of the social problems of the day. He felt a particular concern for orphaned and homeless children, and after his death the Bishop Chadwick Memorial School was established to meet their material and spiritual needs, while in his clergy addresses he emphasized the sanctity of the priesthood and dedication to pastoral work. He attended the First Vatican Council and voted consistently in favour of papal authority.

As a young man Chadwick published anonymously *Barabbas, a Jewish Tale and other Poems* (1834), and later edited Father Celestine Leuthner's *Coelum Christianum* (1871) and published *St Teresa's own words, or, Instructions on the Prayer of Recollection, arranged from the 28th and 29th chapters of her Way of Perfection* (1878). He is credited with the Christmas carol 'Angels we have heard on high'.

The bishop had suffered from ill health all his life, having to leave his studies as a student and later his work as a professor for several months to recover his strength. Indeed, on 29 January 1867, shortly after his consecration, he had received the last sacraments. He died at his home, 72 Rye Hill, Newcastle upon Tyne, on 14 May 1882, and was buried at Ushaw College on 16 May. He was survived by two brothers, John, sometime mayor of Drogheda, and Francis.

James Chadwick was recognized in his lifetime as a saintly man. In a sermon at his funeral, Edward Consitt, his lifelong friend and ecclesiastical colleague, described his qualities. He was a man of mild disposition and great humility, even diffident of his own powers, but nevertheless regarded by all as 'every inch a bishop'. He had a gift for personal friendship which endeared him to students, clergy, and, indeed, to all who sought his spiritual or practical advice. Consitt observed that his career 'had not been a very eventful one' but that all could testify 'to his fidelity and conscientiousness in the discharge of every duty'. Chadwick was not a crusader and avoided political and even religious issues. Consitt likened his life to the 'unruffled course of a beautiful inland river ... shedding light and gladness on every side, and making beautiful the landscape'.   ROBIN M. GARD

Sources W. M. Brady, *The episcopal succession in England, Scotland, and Ireland, AD 1400 to 1875*, 3 (1877), 414–15 · *Newcastle Daily Chronicle* (15 May 1882), 2–3 · *Newcastle Daily Chronicle* (18 May 1882), 2–3 · *The Tablet* (20 May 1882), 791–3 · *The Northern Catholic Calendar* (1883), 44–8 · Gillow, *Lit. biog. hist.* · *Records and recollections of St Cuthbert's College, Ushaw … by an old alumnus* (1889), 127–31 · G. A. Beck, ed., *The English Catholics, 1850–1950* (1950), 209–10 · D. Milburn, ed., 'Ushaw papers XVI', *Ushaw Magazine*, 70 (1960), 57–74 · D. Milburn, ed., 'Some correspondence of Bishop Chadwick, 1813–1882', *Ushaw Magazine*, 70 (1960), 57–74 · *Ushaw Magazine*, 71 (1961), 28–40, 96–105 · *Ushaw Magazine*, 72 (1962), 10–21 · D. Milburn, *A history of Ushaw College* (1964), 285–6

Archives Hexham and Newcastle diocesan archives, Bishop's House, Newcastle upon Tyne, papers · Northumbd RO, Morpeth, Hexham and Newcastle diocesan archives · Ushaw College, Durham, Ushaw archives

Likenesses photographs, Ushaw College, Durham · portrait, Ushaw College, Durham

Wealth at death £587 16s. 1d.: probate, 24 June 1882, *CGPLA Eng. & Wales*

Chadwick, Sir James

Chadwick, Sir James (1891–1974), nuclear physicist, was born on 20 October 1891 at Bollington, near Macclesfield, the eldest of the three sons and one daughter (who died young) of John Joseph Chadwick, cotton spinner, and his wife, Annie Mary Knowles. Chadwick's father moved to Manchester to establish a laundry and, when that failed, became a railway storekeeper. James meanwhile was left in the care of his grandmother and attended Bollington Cross School. About 1902 he rejoined his family in Manchester, finding the change in lifestyle difficult to adjust to. Unable to afford to take up a scholarship to Manchester grammar school, he attended the Central Grammar School for Boys instead, being greatly encouraged in mathematics by Mr Wolfenden.

Physics student At sixteen Chadwick won a scholarship to Manchester University where he enrolled as a physicist by mistake, but found himself fascinated by the professor, Ernest Rutherford, and his approach. In Chadwick's third year Rutherford asked him to devise a method of making accurate inter-comparisons of different radium sources, important for setting international standards. Chadwick was successful and graduated with first-class honours in 1911, publishing his work jointly with Rutherford in 1912 ('A balance method for comparison of quantities of radium and some of its applications', *Proceedings of the Physical Society*, 24, 141–51). Chadwick remained at Manchester as demonstrator, receiving his MSc in 1912 and being elected Beyer fellow of the university. He made the

Sir James Chadwick (1891–1974), by A. Barrington-Brown, 1953

first direct measurements of absorption of gamma rays by gases, pointing out incidentally that the concentration of ions in the upper atmosphere could not be 'wholly due to the radiation from the radioactive material in the earth' ('The absorption of gamma rays by gases and light substances', *Proceedings of the Physical Society*, 24, 152–6), and then, together with A. S. Russell, undertook a difficult series of measurements of the excitation of gamma rays by alpha and beta rays. The precision of his results, coupled with the elegance of his published accounts, established Chadwick as a first-class experimentalist. In 1913, on Rutherford's strong recommendation, he was awarded an 1851 scholarship to study for two years with Hans Geiger in Berlin. Here he learned German and met a number of eminent physicists, including Albert Einstein, Otto Hahn, and Lise Meitner. Using a new prototype electric counter he rapidly found that beta radiation gave a continuous, rather than a line, spectrum, contradicting the then generally accepted view and posing a theoretical problem that was not resolved until Fermi's postulation of the neutrino twenty years later ('Intensitatsverteilung im magnetischen Spektrum der Beta-Strahlen von Radium B + C', *Deutsches Physical Gesellschaft. Verh.*, 16, 383–91).

Chadwick's work ceased abruptly in August 1914 on the outbreak of the First World War, when he was interned as an enemy alien at Ruhleben racecourse near Spandau. Conditions were hard and food was appalling, but a number of societies were established, including a science circle of which Chadwick was the secretary. They set up a rudimentary laboratory, and here Chadwick continued some simple research using radioactive toothpaste. A fellow internee, Charles Ellis, was attracted to physics by Chadwick and became a long-term colleague. Chadwick returned home in 1918 having, as he considered, grown up, but with his digestive system shattered beyond recovery.

Nuclear research Rutherford immediately offered Chadwick a part-time teaching job at Manchester (for he was too debilitated to work more). Here he used an alpha-particle scattering technique to make the first direct measurements of the charge on atomic nuclei, demonstrating unambiguously that the nuclear charge was indeed equivalent to the chemical atomic number. He also showed that the electrostatic inverse square force law holds to a high degree of accuracy in the neighbourhood of the nucleus and concluded that there are no electrons in the region between the nucleus and the innermost electron ring—a hitherto untested assumption ('The charge on the atomic nucleus and the law of force', *Philosophical Magazine*, 40, 1920, 734–46). This work, begun in Manchester, was finished at the Cavendish Laboratory in Cambridge, to which Rutherford was appointed professor in 1919. Gonville and Caius College offered Chadwick a Wollaston research studentship and then, in 1920, the university awarded him the Clark Maxwell studentship. He was elected a fellow of Gonville and Caius in 1921 and in the same year gained one of the first of Cambridge's new PhD degrees; half of his thesis comprised an account of his work on alpha-particle scattering and half described his work with Etienne Bieler on the size and shape of the helium nucleus, work which has been cited as 'marking the birth of strong [nuclear] reactions' (A. Pais, *Inward Bound*, 1986, 240, cited in Brown, 51), for they provided direct evidence that electrostatic force alone could not explain the extremely strong forces present in and just around the nucleus.

Chadwick's *de facto* position as Rutherford's right-hand man and overseer of research at the Cavendish was officially recognized in 1923 when the Department of Scientific and Industrial Research appointed him assistant director of research at the Cavendish. Rutherford in 1919 had succeeded in the first artificial disintegration of an atomic nucleus, by bombarding nitrogen with alpha particles, and now the main thrust of research at the Cavendish was understanding the structure of the nucleus. Chadwick and Rutherford undertook a systematic study which established incontrovertibly the transmutation of light elements by incident alpha particles and provided further evidence for a, hitherto unknown, strong force within the nucleus. Their results were contested in 1924 by Hans Pettersson and Gerhard Kirsch, working in Vienna. The ensuing 'Vienna controversy' raged for four years and was resolved, largely in Rutherford's and Chadwick's favour, only when Chadwick travelled to Vienna and the two groups compared their particle counting procedures. It brought about a realization that visual scintillation counting was highly susceptible to observer bias, and prompted the Cavendish move to develop automatic counting techniques.

In 1925 Chadwick married Aileen Maud Stewart-Brown, daughter of a stockbroker and member of one of Liverpool's most prominent families. Vivacious and self-assured, she had a devastating effect on the shy, reserved Chadwick. Peter Kapitza, his best man, wrote to his mother in Russia, 'Chadwick is up to his ears in love and the crocodile [Rutherford] growls that he is not working enough' (J. W. Boag and others, eds., *Kapitza in Cambridge and Moscow*, 187–8). Twin daughters, Joanna and Judy, were born in 1927, the year in which Chadwick was elected a fellow of the Royal Society.

Through the 1920s Rutherford and Chadwick had speculated occasionally about the possibility of a neutral particle, which they initially thought of as a tightly bonded proton–electron pair, playing a fundamental role in nuclear structure. Chadwick sporadically tried two experimental approaches to finding these 'neutrons', either by synthesizing them from protons and electrons, or by knocking them out of an atomic nucleus. These experiments were minor adjuncts to his main experimental programme, and were hampered by his weak polonium source of alpha particles. By 1930, however, he had obtained a stronger polonium source, and had set a research student, Webster, to work on investigating the puzzling radiation from beryllium which was bombarded by alpha particles. When in 1932 the Joliot-Curies in Paris reported that gamma radiation from beryllium disintegration was sufficiently energetic to knock protons out of paraffin wax, Chadwick was in an excellent position to recognize what the radiation was: not gamma radiation but neutrons which, because of their lack of charge, were very penetrating and very difficult to detect by conventional methods. Working night and day for about three weeks Chadwick showed that the radiation from beryllium ejects particles from most of the light elements, and studied the tracks of target atoms as they recoiled from the collision. He published his results in a letter to *Nature*, 'Possible existence of a neutron', in February 1932, concluding that the difficulties of interpreting the radiation as gamma rays disappear 'if it be assumed that the radiation consists of particles of mass 1 and charge 0, or neutrons' (p. 312). He followed this up with a full paper, 'The existence of a neutron', in the *Proceedings of the Royal Society* (136, 1932, 692–708). Chadwick was awarded the Nobel prize in 1935 for his discovery. He was soon immersed in further investigations of protons, electrons, neutrons, and the newly discovered positrons, showing in 1935 (with Goldhaber) that the neutron was indeed an elementary particle ('The nuclear photoelectric effect', *Proceedings of the Royal Society*, 151, 479–93).

The Liverpool laboratory By then it was clear to Chadwick that further investigation of nuclear physics necessitated large-scale accelerators, particularly E. O. Lawrence's new cyclotron, and he was frustrated by Rutherford's inability to agree that the Cavendish should develop in this direction. When in 1935 the University of Liverpool offered Chadwick the Lyon Jones chair of physics he accepted with pleasure, for he was offered money and facilities to develop the moribund physics department in the direction he wanted. Aileen was glad to return to her native city as a professor's wife. They already had many friends there and Chadwick found the atmosphere more relaxing than at Cambridge. Chadwick galvanized the department and obtained an unprecedentedly large grant from the Royal Society to build a cyclotron, proposing a multidisciplinary research programme which looked not only at the structure of the nucleus, but also at the biological effects of neutrons and the use of radioactive isotopes in biochemistry. He also made his mark in the general affairs of the university. James Mountford, later the vice-chancellor, recalled that his

> disinterested devotion to excellence in any academic sphere inevitably demanded and gained attention, respect and eventual gratitude ... he stripped sloppy thinking of its pretensions and though invariably kind to individuals and sensitive to their difficulties, he was never deflected from his own high standards of judgement. (Brown, 138)

In the city, also, he became a member of a commission reporting on cancer research and treatment in Liverpool.

Military work: the nuclear bomb The Liverpool cyclotron was finally completed in 1939 a few months after the discovery of nuclear fission: uranium bombarded with neutrons split into two smaller atoms, and released sufficient neutrons to continue the process; a chain reaction could ensue. With the outbreak of the Second World War an atomic bomb was seen as a possible weapon. Chadwick, as a member of the Maud committee, was soon overseeing the collaborative efforts of a number of universities and Imperial Chemical Industries to investigate uranium fission and production. The Liverpool cyclotron did more war work than any outside Los Alamos. By the spring of 1941 Chadwick had realized that 'a nuclear bomb was not only possible—it was inevitable. Sooner or later these ideas could not be peculiar to us. Everybody would think about them before long, and some country would put them into action' (C. Weiner, 'Sir James Chadwick', oral history, 1969, American Institute of Physics, College Park, Maryland; cited in Brown, 205). So worried that he could not sleep, he resorted to sleeping pills, which he continued to take for most of his remaining years. He realized that full-scale production of a bomb would need North American help, but American nuclear research was still proceeding at a leisurely pace, aimed more at power plants than at bombs. The Maud report of July 1941, written largely by Chadwick, convinced both the British and, crucially, the USA, that a nuclear bomb was achievable in the current war. When, two years later, collaboration was finally agreed between the British efforts, now codenamed 'Tube Alloys', and the vast American Manhattan project, Chadwick became the scientific adviser to the British members of the Combined Policy Committee. He rapidly gained the confidence of General Groves, who was in charge of the joint effort, and became the only man apart from Groves and his second in command to have access to all the American research and production facilities. His support for Groves and his diplomacy in reconciling American and British interests during this period

ensured a continuing stake for Britain in the project and her future as a nuclear power after the war. In 1946 Chadwick persuaded a reluctant Groves to share future supplies of uranium with Britain, essential to her further nuclear development. Chadwick was a member of the government's advisory committee on atomic energy, and chairman of the nuclear physics subcommittee and his views both that production of independent nuclear weapons was essential to Britain's defence strategy, and on the related question of the types of nuclear power to develop, were influential in post-war policy. He was knighted on 1 January 1945.

On his return to Liverpool in the summer of 1946, Mountford recorded that he had never seen a man 'so physically, mentally and spiritually tired' as Chadwick, for he 'had plumbed such depths of moral decision as more fortunate men are never called upon even to peer into ... [and suffered] ... almost insupportable agonies of responsibility arising from his scientific work' (Brown, 323). Turning down the offer of the Jacksonian professorship at Cambridge, Chadwick plunged into rebuilding the Liverpool department, obtaining money from the Royal Society to build the new, high-energy synchrocyclotron now deemed necessary for investigating the mesons which had been found to mediate proton–neutron interactions. However, although he realized that it was inevitable in nuclear physics, the 'Big Science' and teamwork consequent on the Manhattan project held little appeal for Chadwick, and he found Liverpool, now launched on a downward economic spiral, depressing. In 1948 when his old Cambridge college, Gonville and Caius, invited him to be master, having failed to agree on an internal candidate, Chadwick felt duty-bound to accept, especially since his Liverpool department was now prospering. His main regret was having to resign as vice-president of the Royal Society because college meetings clashed with council dates; he thus forfeited the chance of becoming president.

Later years Chadwick's chief aim as master of Caius was to raise the academic standards of the college. His tenure saw a gradually increasing proportion of students accepted from state schools, a broadening of the fellowship to canvas the best available from other colleges and universities, and a great increase in the number of research fellows, all made possible by the improvement in the college finances that Chadwick engineered. However, the fellowship of Caius at the time were a contentious body in whom ultimate authority in the college rested and Chadwick was deeply upset by the antagonism engendered by the college's internal politics. He resigned the mastership in 1958.

The Chadwicks bought a house in north Wales, Wynne's Parc on the outskirts of Denbigh, where they spent ten happy years. Chadwick spent much of his time editing Rutherford's collected papers for publication. In 1968 they moved back to Cambridge to be near their daughters. Chadwick had received many honours: the Copley and Hughes medals of the Royal Society, the Faraday medal, and the Franklin medal. He held the American medal for merit and Germany's order of merit, the highest honours these countries can bestow on foreign citizens, and honours from universities and scientific societies all over the world. In 1970 the queen made Chadwick a Companion of Honour. Tall and dark, with a dry sense of humour, Chadwick was a very humble man who found public speaking so daunting that ill health often precluded him from delivering the lecture. Yet behind the reserve his students and colleagues detected a great kindness and an overriding concern for his duty. Chadwick died in his sleep on 24 July 1974.

ISOBEL FALCONER

Sources A. Brown, *The neutron and the bomb: a biography of Sir James Chadwick* (1997) · H. Massie and N. Feather, *Memoirs FRS*, 22 (1976), 11–20 [incl. list of publications] · M. Goldhaber, 'With Chadwick in the Cavendish', *Bulletin of Atomic Science*, 38/10 (1982), 12–13 · M. Oliphant, 'The beginning: Chadwick and the neutron', *Bulletin of Atomic Science*, 38/10 (1982), 14–18 · L. Arnold, 'A modest maker of modern physics', *Science*, 282 (1998), 422 · *The Times* (25 July 1974), 20g
Archives Atomic Energy Research Establishment, Harwell, corresp. and papers · CAC Cam., papers · U. Lpool L., corresp. | Bodl. Oxf., corresp. relating to Society for Protection of Science and Learning · CAC Cam., corresp. with Sir Edward Bullard · CUL, Rutherford collection, corresp. with Rutherford, MS 7653 · Nuffield Oxf., corresp. with Viscount Cherwell · Trinity Cam., corresp. with Egon Bretscher · University of Copenhagen, Niels Bohr Institute for Astronomy, Physics, and Geophysics, corresp. with Bohr
Likenesses A. Barrington-Brown, photograph, 1953, Daily Herald [*see illus.*] · J. Gunn, oils, 1953, Gon. & Caius Cam. · photograph, repro. in Massie and Feather, *Memoirs FRS* · photograph, NPG · photograph, Hult. Arch. · photographs, repro. in Brown, *Neutron and the bomb*, pl. 1–18 · photographs, U. Cam., Cavendish Laboratory
Wealth at death £33,146: probate, 4 Oct 1974, *CGPLA Eng. & Wales*

Chadwick, John (1920–1998), classical philologist, was born at 18 Christ Church Road, Mortlake, Surrey, on 21 May 1920, the younger son of Fred Chadwick, civil servant, and his wife, Margaret Pamela, *née* Bray. He was educated at St Paul's School and Corpus Christi College, Cambridge (1939–40), where he studied classics. After war service, including as a cryptographer in naval intelligence, he returned to Cambridge in 1945 to complete his degree, graduating in 1946. The same year he joined the staff of the *Oxford Latin Dictionary*. He retained an interest in lexicography all his life; his last book, *Lexicographica Graeca* (1996), was a forcefully argued study of the meaning of a number of Greek words. During his time in Oxford, Chadwick married, on 10 July 1947, Joan Isobel Hill, with whom he had a son.

In 1952 Chadwick was appointed to a lectureship at Cambridge, where he remained for the rest of his career. But it was another event that year that was to change Chadwick's life, and to bring him international celebrity. Early in July he heard a radio broadcast by a 29-year-old architect, Michael *Ventris, tentatively suggesting that the Linear B script found on clay tablets from Knossos in Crete and Pylos on the Greek mainland, and dating at latest to the thirteenth century BC, could be deciphered as Greek, and was thus much the earliest evidence for the language. Chadwick was already interested in Linear B,

and after further investigation was quickly convinced that Ventris's claim was valid. Writing to congratulate him, he offered his assistance as 'a mere philologist' (*The Times*, 2 Dec 1998). Thus began a partnership which ended only with Ventris's tragic death in a road accident in 1956.

Though it was Ventris (as Chadwick always stressed) who made the key breakthroughs in the decipherment, Chadwick, knowing as a linguist what Greek of this period would probably look like, played a vitally important role in the partnership as they worked to extend Ventris's results and translate more of the texts. During this process he himself established the sound-values of two previously undeciphered signs. When it came to publishing the first scholarly account of the decipherment in 1953, Ventris insisted that Chadwick's name should appear with his own at the head of the paper. In his best-selling *The Decipherment of Linear B* (1958), Chadwick gave a lucid account of the process of decipherment, and painted a charming and moving portrait of Ventris and of their work together. The book was translated into thirteen languages.

Ventris's and Chadwick's next collaborative venture was to produce, in an astonishingly short time, *Documents in Mycenaean Greek* (1956), a massive account of Linear B containing a full commentary on 300 selected texts. Though many of the details of *Documents* now need modification in the light of subsequent developments, it is remarkable how much of it remains valid: a tribute not only to the solidity of their scholarship but also to their caution and excellence of judgement. The same qualities characterized Chadwick's second edition of *Documents* (1973).

After Ventris's death Chadwick rapidly became established as one of the two or three leading scholars in the world working in the new field of Mycenaean Greek which the decipherment had opened up. He was a much respected figure at international conferences, and his presence in Cambridge made it a Mecca for younger scholars from many countries wanting to do advanced work in the subject. He became reader in Greek language in 1966, and Perceval Maitland Laurence reader in classics in 1969. Later in his career much of his writing continued to be on linguistic topics. But he was also an expert epigraphist, and published excellent editions of newly discovered texts, always with commendable speed. From the 1960s onwards he led an international group of collaborators working to produce a definitive edition of the Knossos tablets: the *Corpus of Mycenaean Inscriptions from Knossos* (4 vols., 1986–98). Chadwick never forgot that the tablets originally had a practical purpose, that they were the administrative records of Mycenaean kingdoms. He was superb at elucidating the bureaucratic function of tablets, and in his attractive *The Mycenaean World* (1976) summarized for non-specialist readers the results of his and others' work in reconstructing the geography, economy, and society of late Bronze Age Greece with the help of the documents.

Chadwick was also a fine teacher. His lecturing manner

was a little stiff and formal (eye-contact with the audience was a relatively rare event), but his audiences soon realized the quality of what they were hearing. His great forte, however, was supervising research students, over whom he took immense trouble. Many of them became his lifelong friends. He received many honours, particularly from abroad. At Cambridge he was made emeritus reader and an honorary fellow of his college, Downing, on retirement in 1984. He was elected a fellow of the British Academy in 1967 and was a foreign member of the Austrian, French, and Italian academies. In 1987–8 he served as president of the Swedenborg Society. Like his father, he was a Swedenborgian, and he compiled a lexicon of Swedenborg's neo-Latin and translated eight of his books.

Chadwick died suddenly of heart failure at the railway station in Royston, Hertfordshire, on 24 November 1998, and was cremated on 4 December; his ashes were later buried in the gardens at Downing College. He was survived by his wife and son. He was a rather private person, and on casual acquaintance could appear aloof. But he inspired great affection and admiration in those who knew him well, for his kindness and helpfulness, his absolute integrity and reliability, and his self-effacing modesty. It was entirely characteristic of him that in his *Dictionary of National Biography* notice of Ventris he made no mention of himself either as collaborator in the decipherment or as joint author of *Documents in Mycenaean Greek*.

J. T. KILLEN

Sources *The Times* (2 Dec 1998) · *Daily Telegraph* (3 Dec 1998) · *The Guardian* (3 Dec 1998) · *The Independent* (4 Dec 1998) · *Downing College Association newsletter and college record* (1999) · *Lifeline* (Feb 1999) · J. T. Killen and A. Morpurgo Davies, 'John Chadwick, 1920–1998', *PBA*, 115 (2002), 133–65 · J. Chadwick, *The decipherment of Linear B* (1958) · MS autobiographical sketches and private corresp., priv. coll. · private information (2004) · personal knowledge (2004) [Joan Chadwick] · b. cert.
Archives priv. coll., MSS · U. Cam., faculty of classics, papers, incl. MS autobiographical sketches and corresp. files
Likenesses photograph, *c*.1985, U. Cam., faculty of classics · photograph, repro. in *The Times* · photograph, repro. in *The Independent*
Wealth at death £96,164: probate, 16 June 1999, *CGPLA Eng. & Wales*

Chadwick [*née* Kershaw], **Nora** (1891–1972), literary scholar, was born on 28 January 1891 at Great Lever, near Bolton, Lancashire, the elder of the two children of James Kershaw, cotton manufacturer and mill owner, and his wife, Emma Clara, *née* Booth. Her given name was Norah, but she early on dropped the final 'h'. She had a sister, Mabel, who became a Catholic and a Carmelite sister, eventually living at the convent at Waterbeach.

Nora Kershaw was educated at Stoneycroft School near Southport and was admitted to Cambridge University in 1910 to read English at Newnham College. At Cambridge she became a pupil of her future husband, Hector Munro *Chadwick (1870–1947), professor of Anglo-Saxon. She took a second class in part one of the old medieval and modern languages tripos (English and Old English) in 1913

and a first class in part two (English literature) in 1914. On completing her degree she was appointed lecturer in English at St Andrews University where she taught herself Russian during the war years despite a heavy workload. Her father died in an accident in the war in France and her mother married a Dr Martin and settled at Houghton near St Ives, close to Cambridge, where Nora frequently visited her. The inheritance of money after the war enabled Nora to retire from St Andrews and live as a private individual in Cambridge.

On 4 May 1922 Nora married Hector Chadwick after a tour of Italy with him accompanied by her friend Enid Welsford; it was a happy marriage, though there were no children. Nora graduated MA from Cambridge in 1923. The Chadwicks lived initially at Paper Mills, Newmarket Road, and later in Cambridge where they entertained and educated students, and she frequently played the harp. They frequently visited archaeological sites around Britain and Ireland and co-authored several books, including *The Growth of Literature* (1932–40), a three-volume survey of heroic and oral literatures, and *A Study of Anglo-Saxon* (1955).

Nora Kershaw Chadwick, as she preferred to be called on the title-pages of her books (though she signed her name Nora Kershaw), wrote some fifty-nine books and articles. Her main interests were early Britain, Celtic culture, early Russian history, and oral literatures, especially oral epics in Russian and the Turkic languages of central Asia.

Nora Chadwick was an associate of Newnham College from 1923 to 1938 and a research fellow from 1941 to 1944. In 1950 she was appointed university lecturer in the early history and culture of the British Isles at Cambridge. She contributed a pioneering study of African literatures to *Cassell's Encyclopaedia of Literature* (1953) and published *Poetry and Letters in Early Christian Gaul* in 1955. In 1956 she was made a fellow of the British Academy and on retirement from her university post in 1958 was made an honorary fellow of Newnham. In addition to receiving honorary doctorates from the University of St Andrews, the University of Wales, and the National University of Ireland, she was, in 1961, made a commander of the British empire.

Nora Chadwick's survey of the vast corpus of Turkic oral literatures, *Oral Epics of Central Asia*, appeared in 1969. Most of her books and articles, however, focused on the Celtic cultures of ancient Britain where Welsh, Irish, Scottish, and Pictish were spoken before Latin, Norse, and English. *The Celts* (1971) continues to be a valuable introduction to the subject and remains in print. The fact that Cambridge did not establish a professorship of Celtic, to which she would willingly have contributed the bulk of her private means, was a source of great disappointment.

Nora Chadwick's warmth and generosity of character was attested at a dinner of her former students organized by Glyn Daniel on her eightieth birthday in 1971. Even in her old age, she haunted the Cambridge University Library assisted by her niece Dorothy. She died at the Hope Nursing Home, Brooklands Avenue, Cambridge, on 24 April 1972 after a series of strokes.

PAUL KNOBEL

Sources *PBA*, 58 (1972), 537–49 · *The Times* (26 April 1972) · *Newnham College Roll Letter* (1973) · Newnham College, Cambridge, register · *A list of the published writings of Hector Munro Chadwick and of his wife* (1971) · *CGPLA Eng. & Wales* (1972)

Wealth at death £35,057: probate, 7 Aug 1972, *CGPLA Eng. & Wales*

Chadwick, Roy (1893–1947), aircraft designer, was born at Farnworth, near Bolton, Lancashire, on 30 April 1893, the elder son of Charles Henry Chadwick, a mechanical engineer in Manchester, and his wife, Agnes Bradshaw. Educated at a school in Urmston and at the Manchester College of Technology, Chadwick was early fascinated with the idea of flying machines, and made model gliders and aeroplanes. Having decided to make aeronautics his career, in 1911 he became associated with Alliott Verdon-Roe, a pioneer of British aviation. With R. J. Parrott and Roy H. Dobson they dedicated their lives to the design and manufacture of aeroplanes, in the small concern known as A. V. Roe & Co. Ltd, later one of the largest aircraft companies. Chadwick was, therefore, from the beginning closely associated with the design of practical aircraft, including the famous Avro 504. During the First World War he worked on the design of several twin-engined biplanes and experimental fighters, and when hostilities ceased he was recognized as one of the youngest and most experienced aircraft designers. In 1920 he married Mary, daughter of Hubert Gomersall, head cashier of the English Sewing Cotton Company, Manchester; they had two daughters.

Roy Chadwick (1893–1947), by unknown photographer

Chadwick next designed several big military aircraft and also a number of light machines, including the Avro Baby, probably the first real light aeroplane in the world, to be followed later by the Avro Avian, famous for the record-breaking flights from England to Australia by H. J. L. Hinkler (1928) and Charles Kingsford Smith in 1930. He also devoted his energies to the development of the all-metal aeroplane.

Much of Chadwick's genius lay in an uncanny understanding of the need for perfect control in aeroplanes. This subtle characteristic was particularly noticeable in his trainer aircraft such as the Tutor which in 1932 replaced the 504, thus perpetuating the Avro tradition of training the Royal Air Force. Some years later, during the Second World War, another design by Chadwick, the Anson, was used extensively for training purposes. Already in 1935 events compelled him to turn his thoughts to military aviation. He designed the Manchester twin-engined heavy bomber which marked a gigantic step forward in aircraft design, although at first the project was almost abandoned on account of the failure of the engines to produce the power promised. Chadwick eventually proved the rightness of his design, however, and it was out of the Manchester that there emerged his greatest triumph, the four-engined Lancaster, capable of carrying a 10 ton bomb, and extensively used for night attack on Germany. Other wartime designs were the York and the Lincoln, followed after the war by the Lancastrian which, with the York, was used for civil aviation.

Chadwick's first true post-war aircraft, however, was the Tudor, the first pressurized civil aeroplane in the world. A national controversy arose over the Tudor design, but throughout Chadwick never lost faith in his aeroplane. Although production was greatly curtailed, the Tudor later proved its worth on the Berlin airlift. The Ashton, a Royal Air Force research aircraft, was a direct development of the Tudor. It was a tragic irony that it was in a Tudor that Chadwick was killed, when the plane crashed into a field at Shirl Fold Farm, Adlington, Cheshire, during a test flight on 23 August 1947.

Chadwick's death was an incalculable loss to the cause of British aeronautics which he had greatly served, particularly in the two wars. He designed some forty successful aircraft and the benefit of his last thoughts on design were seen in the Coastal Command Shackleton and the Avro delta-wing aircraft. Chadwick was friendly and good-humoured, but untiring in his quest for the better aeroplane. A combination of visionary and practical engineer, he could always see the next step clearly, and before he died he saw the enormous potential of jet propulsion, particularly in conjunction with the delta-wing form. He was appointed CBE and had received the honorary degree of MSc from Manchester University in 1944. He was a fellow of the Royal Aeronautical Society.   ROY DOBSON, *rev.*

Sources *Aircraft development and production* (1948) · *The Aeroplane* (29 Aug 1947) · private information (1959) · personal knowledge (1959) · d. cert.

Likenesses photographs, Royal Aeronautical Society, London [*see illus.*]

Wealth at death £19,912 15s. 1d.: administration with will, 17 Nov 1947, *CGPLA Eng. & Wales*

Chadwick, Samuel (1860–1932), Wesleyan Methodist minister, was born on 16 September 1860 at 8 Baldwin Street, Burnley, the elder son and eldest of the six children of William Chadwick (*d.* 1909), a cotton weaver, and his wife, Margaret Clayton. Margaret Chadwick's gift for incisive speech, combining 'the terseness of a telegram and the force of a catapult' (Howarth, 'Samuel Chadwick', 6) may have influenced her son, whose pithy 'Chadwickisms' were collected by biographers. After a rudimentary education at Red Lion Street infant school Chadwick began work with his father at the age of eight, staying at the Oak Mount Mill until he was twenty-one. During that time he sought to improve his education by studying at home for up to five hours a night.

Chadwick was converted at a Sunday school anniversary in 1870 and became a Wesleyan member in 1875. He was also a keen temperance advocate, and his forthright criticism of a non-abstaining local minister at a Band of Hope meeting perhaps contributed to the failure of his first attempt to offer as a candidate for the Wesleyan ministry: his superintendent refused to nominate him, on the ground that 'he would not add to the list of uncultured and uneducated men in the ranks' (Howarth, 'Samuel Chadwick', 11). While serving as a lay evangelist at Stacksteads (1881–3), Chadwick's exploration of the traditional Wesleyan doctrine of scriptural holiness, recast by J. D. Brash and others, led him to a new spiritual experience and to more effective evangelism. This 'personal Pentecost' was later described as 'the key to all my life' (Bowden, 8). Accepted as a candidate in 1883, Chadwick was sent to train at Didsbury College, Manchester. Besides the theology lectures of W. B. Pope, whose massive *Compendium of Christian Theology* he had read twice before entering college, Chadwick filled other gaps in his education, later claiming that he had worked through *Chambers' Dictionary*, word for word, four times. While at Didsbury he attended the first Southport Holiness Convention (1885) and established a lifelong friendship with F. L. Wiseman.

Chadwick was sent to Edinburgh in 1886, moving to Clydebank in 1887 for a three-year appointment in a new church. His four years in Scotland brought further mission experience, temperance battles, opportunities to hear prominent Scottish preachers, and a chance to observe the bitter disputes over biblical criticism. Although theologically conservative Chadwick expressed gratitude for the scholarship of critics like G. A. Smith and, in later life, avoided the polemics of ultra-conservative Wesleyans; his moderate stance during the controversy surrounding George Jackson and biblical criticism in the 1910s attracted recriminations from the fundamentalist Wesley Bible Union. Chadwick gave early indications of a breadth of sympathy and spirituality which coexisted with a basically conservative Wesleyan evangelicalism. In Edinburgh he introduced passion week services, a custom which he continued in other churches, and he was widely read in the devotional literature of the religious orders.

Chadwick moved from Clydebank to Leeds in 1890. Apart from one year (1893–4) in Shoreditch, he remained in Leeds until 1907, at the Central (1890–93) and Oxford Place (1894–1907) missions. He won a considerable reputation as a preacher, teacher, and evangelist, attracting large congregations, establishing a Bible class with over 800 members, and engaging in evangelism in the open air and at the Leeds Coliseum. He became editor of the quarterly holiness journal *Experience* in 1890 and of the weekly newspaper *Joyful News* in 1905. Chadwick published one volume of sermons, *Humanity and God* (1904); his other publications, *The Path of Prayer* (1931) and the posthumous *The Way to Pentecost* (1932), *The Gospel of the Cross* (1934), and *The Call to Christian Perfection* (1936), were collections of articles from *Joyful News*. During his early years in Leeds he met Sarah Elizabeth Crowther, daughter of Thomas Crowther of Boston Spa. They were married in the Wesleyan chapel at Boston Spa on 23 August 1893.

Chadwick's standing in Methodism was recognized by his election to the legal conference in 1902. He was elected chairman of the Sheffield district in 1911, president of conference in 1918, and president of the National Council of the Evangelical Free Churches in 1922. He visited the United States, Canada, and South Africa both as an official Methodist representative and as a Bible school and convention speaker. In 1903 the Wesleyan home mission committee acquired Hulmecliffe College at Calver, Derbyshire, near Sheffield, as a new base for the Joyful News Training Home and Mission, a venture in lay training founded in Rochdale in the 1880s. From 1904 Chadwick travelled from Leeds to give a weekly lecture at the new Cliff College (as Hulmecliffe had become), and in 1907 he was appointed to the staff as biblical and theological tutor. The death of the principal, Thomas Cook, shortly after Chadwick's appointment to the South Yorkshire Coalfields Mission in 1912, led to Chadwick's immediate return to Cliff as acting principal and to his confirmation as Cook's successor in 1913. Chadwick's lifelong quest to overcome his own early educational disadvantages and his commitment to evangelism and to Christian holiness encouraged him to maintain and develop the traditions he inherited at Cliff. He expanded the work of the college, building up its summer schools, establishing the Whitsun anniversary as a major event in the Methodist calendar, extending the premises, and sending students out on evangelistic 'treks' as 'Methodist friars'. Sam Chadwick was revered by many of his students and admired by most, although his authoritarian style and traditional theology did not suit everyone in the college or the Wesleyan Methodist Connexion: 'a born ruler: he liked to bend the intractable to his will' (*Methodist Recorder*, 5). Following several years of ill health, Chadwick died at Cliff College on 16 October 1932, survived by his wife. He was buried on 20 October in nearby Curbar churchyard.

MARTIN WELLINGS

Sources N. G. Dunning, *Samuel Chadwick* (1933) · D. H. Howarth, 'Samuel Chadwick and some aspects of Wesleyan Methodist evangelism, 1860–1932', MLitt diss., University of Lancaster, 1977 · D. H. Howarth, *How great a flame: the story of Samuel Chadwick* (privately printed, Cliff College, 1983) • K. F. Bowden, *Samuel Chadwick and Stacksteads* (1982) • *Methodist Recorder* (20 Oct 1932), 3, 5–6 • *The Times* (18 Oct 1932), 9 • *CGPLA Eng. & Wales* (1933) • b. cert. • m. cert.

Archives Cliff College, Calver, Sheffield, papers
Likenesses photograph, repro. in Dunning, *Samuel Chadwick*, frontispiece • photographs, repro. in *Methodist Recorder*
Wealth at death £748 5s. 11d.: probate, 10 May 1933, *CGPLA Eng. & Wales*

Chaffers, Richard (1731–1765). *See under* Chaffers, William (1811–1892).

Chaffers, William (1811–1892), authority on hallmarks and potters' marks, was born in Watling Street, London, on 28 September 1811, and was baptized on 25 October 1811 at St Antholin, Budge Row, London, the son of William Chaffers, and his wife, Sarah. He was educated at Margate, Kent, and at Merchant Taylors' School, London, where he was entered in 1824. He was descended collaterally from the family of **Richard Chaffers** (1731–1765), potter, the son of a Liverpool shipwright, who set up a pottery fabric in 1752 and made blue and white earthenware in Liverpool, mainly for the American colonies. After discovering a rich vein of soapstone at Mullion in Cornwall in 1755 he became a serious rival of Wedgwood as a practical potter until his premature death in December 1765. He was buried in the churchyard of St Nicholas in Liverpool.

William Chaffers was attracted to antiquarian studies while a clerk in the City of London by the discovery of the choice Roman and medieval antiquities in the foundations of the Royal Exchange during 1838–9. He began at the same time to concentrate attention upon the study of gold and silver plate and ceramics, especially in regard to the official and other marks by which dates and places of fabrication can be distinguished; and in 1863 he published two works by which he is remembered. Like Edward Hawkins's *Medallic Illustrations to the History of Great Britain and Ireland* (2 vols., 1895), both passed through several editions. The first—*Hall Marks on Gold and Silver Plate* (1863), illustrated—included in the eighth edition 'Histories of the goldsmiths' trade, both in England and France, and revised London and provincial tables' (with an introductory essay by C. A. Markham, 1896). An extended ninth edition was revised and published in 1905 by C. A. Markham. Chaffers's work on hallmarks has been superseded by more complete accounts, notably Sir Charles Jackson's *English Goldsmiths and their Marks* (1905; 2nd edn, 1921). Chaffers is better known for his second work, *Marks and Monograms on Pottery and Porcelain* (1863) which appeared under the title *Marks and Monograms on European and Oriental Pottery and Porcelain* from the seventh edition onwards. A ninth edition revised by F. Litchfield in 1900 included over 3500 potters' marks. A fifteenth revised edition appeared in 1965 edited by F. Litchfield, assisted by R. L. Hobson and G. Godden. The aim of the work was to be for the keramic art what François Brulliot's *Dictionnaire de monogrammes* (1917) was to painting, and it at once established Chaffers as the leading authority on his subject. Later revisions have kept it up to date, while Chaffers's

own observations continue to be of value, many of his original sources now being lost. He produced two further volumes: *The Keramic Gallery* (2 vols., 1872), with 500 illustrations, and *Gilda aurifabrorum* (1883), a history of goldsmiths and plate workers, and their marks. The latter has now been largely superseded by later works, notably A. G. Grimwade's *London Goldsmiths, 1697–1837* (1976). In addition Chaffers wrote a handbook in 1874 abridged from his *Marks and Monograms*, and a priced catalogue of coins.

The considerable talent Chaffers displayed in organizing the exhibitions of art treasures—at Manchester in 1857, South Kensington in 1862, Leeds in 1869, Dublin in 1872, Wrexham in 1876, and Hanley (at the great Staffordshire exhibition of ceramics) in 1890—also furthered his reputation. While this rests upon his two great works of reference, it is his work on ceramics that has remained of lasting value to students of that art.

Chaffers had been elected a fellow of the Society of Antiquaries in 1843, and was a frequent contributor to *Archaeologia*, to *Notes and Queries*, and to various learned journals upon the two subjects in which he maintained a specialist knowledge. He also dealt in antiques. About 1870 he retired from Fitzroy Square, London, to The Chestnuts, Willesden Lane, Middlesex, with his wife, Charlotte, son, William, and two daughters, Matilda and Louisa. He later moved to West Hampstead, where he died on 12 April 1892.
THOMAS SECCOMBE, *rev.* ANNETTE PEACH

Sources A. G. Grimwade, *London goldsmiths, 1697–1837: their marks and lives, from the original registers at Goldsmiths' Hall*, 2nd edn (1982) • *IGI* • private information (2004) [Michael Snodin] • census returns, 1881
Likenesses wood-engraving, NPG; repro. in *ILN* (30 April 1892)

Chafy, William (1779–1843), college head, was the eldest son of the Revd William Chafy (1746–1826), minor canon of Canterbury Cathedral, and Mary, the only daughter and heir of John Chafie (as he wrote the name) of Sherborne, Dorset. He was born on 7 February 1779 at Canterbury, and was sent in 1788 to the King's School in that city. He entered Corpus Christi College, Cambridge, on 1 January 1796, migrating to Sidney Sussex College, where his father had been a fellow, on 18 October of the same year. He graduated BA 1800 as eighth senior optime, and proceeded MA 1803, BD 1810, and DD (by royal mandate) 15 November 1813. He was elected fellow of Sidney Sussex on 4 June 1801, and in that year was also ordained and became curate of Gillingham in Kent. He was a tutor of his college. On 17 October 1813 he was elected master of Sidney Sussex, having been an unsuccessful candidate for the office in 1807, and held that position until his death. He married, on 4 December 1813, Mary, youngest daughter of John Westwood of Chatteris in the Isle of Ely. They had one child, a son, William Westwood (1814–1873).

During Chafy's mastership Sidney Sussex was refaced at his expense; many of his books were also presented by him to the college library. In 1813, and again in 1829, he was vice-chancellor of the university, and left his mark by his lavish hospitality. He was also chaplain-in-ordinary to George III, George IV, William IV, and Queen Victoria. He died at Cambridge on 16 May 1843, and was buried in the chapel of his college. He was known to be extremely wealthy, and left a considerable fortune.

W. W. WROTH, rev. M. C. CURTHOYS

Sources GM, 2nd ser., 20 (1843), 213 · Annual Register (1843) · Venn, Alum. Cant. · D. A. Winstanley, Early Victorian Cambridge (1940); repr. (1955) · C. W. Scott-Giles, Sidney Sussex College (1975) · private information (1886) [from his grandson Revd W. K. W. Chafy-Chafy] · J. S. Sidebotham, Memorials of the King's School Cambridge (1865), 94–5 · will, PROB 11/1985/618
Likenesses portrait, Sidney Sussex College, Cambridge
Wealth at death very wealthy

Chaigneau, William (1709–1781), novelist, was born in Dublin on 24 January 1709, the son of John Chaigneau, whose Huguenot father, Josias, had earlier settled in Ireland. Chaigneau was twice married; on 3 February 1738 he married Elizabeth Tige at St John's, Dublin. Chaigneau and his second wife had one daughter, Peggy, to whom he was devoted but who died in childhood. Chaigneau was 'agent to most of the regiments on the Irish establishment' and according to Tate Wilkinson, whom he and his wife generously befriended, 'a gentleman universally known, and whose memory is greatly respected' (Wilkinson, 1.11). In Dublin, the Chaigneaus lived principally in a house on Abbey Street.

In 1752 Chaigneau published, anonymously, a two-volume novel, *The History of Jack Connor*. Dedicated to Henry Fox, then secretary of war, the novel claims to be founded on the principles of 'INTEGRITY' and 'HONOUR' and designed for the reader's 'Amusement' and 'Improvement'. Conscious of the still contested respectability of the novel as a literary form, Chaigneau asserted his own status as a gentleman by declining to profit financially by his work, declaring that he sought no 'pecuniary indulgence' from his publisher. This fact was thought worthy of particular remark and commendation by the *Monthly Review* in a laudatory notice which declared the book to be 'a truly moral tale' (*Monthly Review*, 447). A picaresque novel, influenced by the examples of Le Sage's *Gil Blas* (1715–47) and Smollett's *Roderick Random* (1748), as well as by Fielding's *Tom Jones* (1749), *Jack Connor* offers glimpses of Ireland almost unparalleled in fiction of the period. Opening in co. Limerick, the novel ranges through co. Tipperary and co. Meath, and the city of Dublin, besides London, Paris, France, Flanders, and Spain. Chaigneau's protestant, colonial nationalism is much in evidence throughout. Besides direct comment on Irish political, economic, and social matters, Chaigneau offers an exemplary hero who is the son of a protestant father and Roman Catholic mother and who, after making his own fortune, returns to settle on what he eventually discovers to be his family estates in co. Limerick. Chaigneau's most insistent theme is perhaps that of English prejudice against the Irish—as an army officer in foreign service, an exiled descendant of the Wild Geese, declares: 'I love my Countrymen, the Irish, and I love the English well enough, but, Faith and Sowle, they are too hard upon us' (*Jack Connor*, Dublin, 1752, 1.322)—persuading London reviewers to acknowledge the justice of the author's 'smart reprizals upon the

English, for their national and vulgar prejudice against their brethren of Ireland' (*Monthly Review*, 447). Echoing this theme, *Jack Connor* has the bibliographical oddity of reflecting the hero's prudential change of name, designed to conceal his national identity, by a change of title: the running-head of the second half of the first volume and the title-page and running-head of volume two read *The History of Jack Connor, now Conyers*. Chaigneau's patriotic motivation in writing his only novel is reinforced by the inclusion, as a supplement to the second edition, of three discursive letters on Irish linen manufacture. Additionally noteworthy is *Jack Connor*'s use of mottoes (both borrowed and of Chaigneau's own devising) for chapter headings: the earliest example in English of a novel employing what would become a standard fictional device in the next century.

In the 1757–8 season Chaigneau helped Tate Wilkinson to make his stage début at Thomas Sheridan's theatre at Smock Alley in Dublin and induced Elizabeth Fitzhenry to perform alongside Wilkinson on the occasion of the latter's benefit night on 25 February 1758, when Nicholas Rowe's *Jane Shore* and Fielding's *Tom Thumb* were performed (Wilkinson, 1.147–8, 2.164–5). Chaigneau's assistance on this occasion extended to purchasing 40 guineas worth of tickets himself and to using his role as army agent to secure a large audience, especially of army officers, by paying personal visits to drum up support. Wilkinson's repeated expressions of gratitude to Chaigneau, whose kindness he contrasted with the indifference of Samuel Foote, acknowledged also the care given him during a severe illness and the loan of a house in Big Strand Street in Dublin, after he had been evicted by his landlord for disturbing a fellow lodger, the bishop of Llandaff, by his noisy rehearsing. William Chaigneau also adapted a farce from the French, under the title *Harlequin Soldier*, for a further benefit night for Wilkinson, this time on 22 March 1765 in Edinburgh.

In 1774 William Chaigneau travelled with his wife to France, where they spent almost a year, eventually returning from Montauban in June 1775. His final years were marked by sadness at the loss of many members of his family, including brothers, sisters, nephews, and a niece. Chaigneau died in Dublin on 1 October 1781.

IAN CAMPBELL ROSS

Sources N&Q, 3rd ser., 5 (1864), 507–8 · [W. Chaigneau], The history of Jack Connor, 2 vols. in 1 (1752); 2nd edn, 2 vols. (1753) [preface initialled] · T. Wilkinson, Memoirs of his own life, 3 vols. (1791) · Monthly Review, 6 (1752), 447–9 · I. C. Ross, 'An Irish picaresque novel: William Chaigneau's The history of Jack Connor', Studies: an Irish Quarterly Review, 71 (1982), 270–79 · IGI

Chaikin, Moses Avigdor (1852–1928), rabbi, was born in Shklov, in Mohilev province, Belorussia, then in the Russian empire, on 11 May 1852, the son of Rabbi Israel Shraga Chaikin and his wife, Chaya Dina. His parents were Hasidic Jews, adherents of the Lubavitch sect. Chaikin's father was appointed *shochet* (ritual slaughterman) to the Jewish community of St Petersburg, where Moses Chaikin began his religious education. He then studied at *yeshivot* (Talmudic colleges) in Volkovysk under Rabbi Abraham

Samuel Diskin, who bestowed on him the first of several *semichot* (rabbinical ordinations) in 1877, and in Kovno under the renowned Rabbi Isaac Elhanan Spektor. He also gained *semichot* from rabbis Yekutiel Salmon Landau and Isaac Woolf Olschwanger of St Petersburg as well as from Rabbi Jacob Vidrevitz of Moscow.

Some time during 1882–4, in the aftermath of the pogroms that followed the assassination of Tsar Alexander II, Chaikin went to Paris, where he became rabbi of the Russian and Polish Jews in the city and in 1887 established a Talmud Torah (traditional Jewish high school). He returned to Russia as rabbi of Rostov-on-Don, but was expelled in 1890 for reasons that are unclear. He emigrated to England to serve the Jewish community of Sheffield (1892–1901), as minister and *shochet* to the New Hebrew Congregation at West Bar, which largely consisted of new immigrants like himself. This was a breakaway from the old established synagogue at North Church Street, and Chaikin tried his utmost to unite the feuding community. He established a Talmud Torah and Sabbath Observance Society in Sheffield.

In July 1901 Rabbi Chaikin was selected to fill the post of chief minister of the Federation of Synagogues, which had been vacant since the departure of Rabbi Meyer Lerner in 1894, and he moved to London. Between 1902 and 1906 he was, with reluctance, permitted to participate in the work of the chief rabbi's *bet din* (ecclesiastical court). However, the title of *dayan* (judge) was withheld from him until 1911. This was on account of rivalry between the federation and the establishment United Synagogue which was under the chief rabbi's jurisdiction. Hermann Adler, the chief rabbi, was for a long time loath to appoint rabbis trained in eastern Europe to his court, which he preferred to maintain as a preserve of the 'native Anglo-Jewish ministry'—consisting of English-educated 'reverend gentlemen', not rabbis. This attitude was endorsed by the lay leaders of the United Synagogue, principally Lord Rothschild, but was increasingly resented by the Yiddish-speaking Jewish immigrants of east London, many of whom were members of synagogues of the Federation of Synagogues. In 1906 Chaikin's services were withdrawn from the *bet din* on the insistence of Samuel Montagu, president of the federation. Following Montagu's death, however, Chaikin served on the United Synagogue *bet din* from the end of 1911 until his retirement in August 1926.

Chaikin married, probably in Russia, Tony Rebecca Pinsker (1851–1923), a daughter of Rabbi Solomon Pinsker, *av bet din* (senior judge of the Jewish ecclesiastical court) of Kherson, who had also studied Latin and medicine at St Petersburg. A descendant of the seventeenth-century scholar Rabbi Yom Tov Lipmann Heller, Mrs Chaikin inherited a 'brilliant intellect' and was learned in rabbinics in her own right. The couple had two known children: a son, George, and a daughter. Mrs Chaikin died on 10 January 1923 and was buried the following day at the Federation Jewish cemetery, Edmonton.

Chaikin was a quiet, scholarly man who lacked the charisma of his fellow Hasidic contemporary in the East End

Rabbi Chaim Zundel Maccoby. He made his home at 47 White Lion Street, Aldgate, in the heart of the Jewish East End, and he worshipped, preached, and taught at the Old Castle Street *shtiebl* (Hasidic conventicle), known as Agudat Achim ('Society of brothers'). He published studies of biblical commentaries and compendia of rabbinical *responsa* in Hebrew. He also wrote in French and English on general Jewish history, including *Apologie des Juifs* (1887), and a work of biographical sketches entitled *The Celebrities of the Jews* (1899). In 1926 Chaikin retired to join his daughter's family in Tel Aviv, where he died on 17 June 1928.   SHARMAN KADISH

Sources *Jewish Chronicle* (19 Jan 1923) · *Jewish Chronicle* (22 June 1928) · *Jewish Encyclopedia* (1902) · J. Jung, *Champions of orthodoxy* (1974), 69–100 · S. Wininger, ed., *Grosse jüdische National-Biographie*, 1 (1926), 531 · G. Alderman, *The Federation of Synagogues* (1987), 35, 38–40, 46 · H. Rabinowicz, *A world apart: the story of the Chasidim in Britain* (1997), 51 · C. Roth, *The Federation of Synagogues: a record of twenty-five years, 1912 to 1937* (1937), 13

Likenesses D. MacPherson, sketch, 1901, repro. in *The Graphic* · D. MacPherson, sketch, 1901, repro. in V. D. Lipman, *A history of the Jews in Britain since 1858* (1990) · photograph, repro. in Jung, *Champions of orthodoxy*

Chain, Anne Ethel Beloff-, Lady Chain (1921–1991). *See under* Chain, Sir Ernst Boris (1906–1979).

Chain, Sir Ernst Boris (1906–1979), biochemist, was born on 19 June 1906 in Berlin, the only son of the two children of Dr Michael Chain, a Russian-born industrial chemist, and his wife, Margarete Eisner, who was related to Kurt Eisner, the socialist prime minister of Bavaria assassinated in 1919. Chain's parents were both Jewish, and faith played an important role in the house. His father died in 1919, leaving the family without an income; Chain's mother turned the family home into a guest house, but nevertheless their financial situation remained strained. The young Chain showed flair for both music and science, but the influence of his cousin (Mrs Sacharina, a widow twenty years his senior, who joined the household in 1923) turned him towards science.

Chain was educated in Berlin at the Luisengymnasium and the University of Berlin from which he graduated in chemistry and physiology in 1930. He then obtained a doctorate for research in the chemical department of the Institute of Pathology at the Charité Hospital. After graduation Chain dabbled with the idea of a musical career, performing on numerous Berlin platforms, writing as music critic for the newspaper *Welt am Abend*, and (unsuccessfully) attempting to organize exchanges of musicians between Russia, Germany, and Argentina (1930–31). However, contemporaries said that Chain now began to realize that, although a good pianist, he would never be a truly great one.

With the election of Hitler to power in 1933 Chain emigrated to Britain and sought to begin a scientific career. After a few months at University College Hospital, London, he obtained a place in the department of biochemistry at Cambridge. Chain worked under Sir Frederick Gowland Hopkins for a second PhD, believing a Cambridge

Sir Ernst Boris Chain (1906–1979), by Wolfgang Suschitzky, 1944

doctorate would advance an English career. During his years at Cambridge, Chain developed an irrational fear of being poisoned in the laboratory, which led to panic attacks and weakness. As a result, stomach pains were misdiagnosed as a psychological illness and he was temporarily placed in a specialist nursing home, from which he was released only by the combined efforts of a European acquaintance and his friend Ashley Miles. He was then seen by Mrs Sacharina's doctor in Paris, who diagnosed appendicitis.

The election of Howard Florey to the chair of pathology at Oxford in 1935 set the scene for Chain's subsequent life. Florey believed that experimental pathology would benefit from the collaboration of pathologists with chemists and offered him the chance to develop a department of biochemistry within the Sir William Dunn School of Pathology. In 1936 he became university lecturer and demonstrator in chemical pathology. At Florey's suggestion he began to study the mode of action of a bacteriolytic enzyme, lysozyme. This led him to read other accounts of the production of anti-microbial substances by microorganisms, and, during discussions with Florey in 1938, he suggested that they should jointly investigate some of these substances. Their decision to do this was motivated by scientific rather than medical interest, but fortunately penicillin (found by Fleming in 1928) was one of three substances chosen for study. Fleming had first believed that penicillin might be useful as an antiseptic, but he was quickly disheartened by its instability and did not realize that it might cure bacterial infections. Thus, for more than ten years, penicillin had aroused little medical interest.

Although Chain was confident that the problem of penicillin's instability could be overcome, little progress with its purification was made until N. G. Heatley suggested that it could be transferred from organic solvent into a neutral aqueous solution. In the spring of 1940 Florey, urged by Chain to begin his intended biological experiments, showed that preparations of penicillin no more than 1 per cent pure would protect mice from infections with streptococci and staphylococci when introduced

into the bloodstream. This dramatic result entirely changed the focus of research. High priority was given to the laboratory production of enough penicillin for a small clinical trial. With the success of this trial, even using only 3 per cent pure preparations, penicillin suddenly became a substance of major medical importance and of potential value in surgery during the Second World War.

Chain, together with Edward P. Abraham, showed some bacteria were resistant to penicillin because of their production of a penicillin-inactivating enzyme, penicillinase. They then began to purify penicillin and, early in 1943, joined with Sir Robert Robinson, Wilson Baker, and others to study its chemistry. Chain became a strong supporter of a β-lactam structure for penicillin, which was proposed in October 1943 but remained controversial until Dorothy Hodgkin and Barbara Low confirmed it two years later by X-ray crystallography. During these war years Chain played an active part in a major Anglo-American enterprise to produce penicillin by chemical synthesis. However, although this collaborative effort threw interesting light on the chemistry of penicillin it failed in its final aim, and, in the event, it was the increased yield obtainable by fermentation of *Penicillium chrysogenum* that enabled penicillin to be produced on a large scale.

Chain was a stimulus to Florey and for some years their relationship was amicable, but it deteriorated when Chain began to complain that he was receiving too little credit for his research and to believe that his failure to realize his ambitions in England was due to his foreign background. In 1948 he left Oxford for Rome to become director of a new international research centre for chemical microbiology at the Istituto Superiore di Sanità. Before leaving he married, on 7 October 1948, Dr Anne Ethel Beloff [see below], who was herself a biochemist; they subsequently collaborated in studies of the mode of action of insulin. They had a son (Benjamin) and then twins, a son and a daughter (Danny and Judy). Their married life was most contented.

In Rome, Chain faced no financial problems and set up a pilot plant for antibiotic production. He was strongly in favour of collaboration between academic and industrial institutions. He became a consultant to the Beecham Group and suggested that it should explore further the potential of penicillin. Two members of this company, G. N. Rolinson and F. R. Batchelor, were seconded to his laboratory in 1956 to become acquainted with penicillin fermentation. During their visit they made observations that later led to the isolation of the nucleus of the penicillin molecule and to the chemical synthesis from this nucleus of a series of new and clinically valuable penicillins.

In the 1950s Chain became anxious about the future of the Istituto Superiore di Sanità after its influential director-general, Domenico Marotta, had retired. In 1961 he accepted the chair of biochemistry at Imperial College, London, although he retained his position in Rome until 1964. His requirements were expensive and the return to England involved him in plans for a new department with a fermentation plant and the raising of relatively large sums of money to construct and maintain it. Despite a number of large grants, the financial base for his operations was not entirely secure.

At Imperial College, Chain worked with different colleagues on a variety of topics, ranging from a phytotoxin to an inducer of interferon production and the mode of action of insulin. But, as the time for his retirement in 1973 approached, he became deeply absorbed in an unsuccessful attempt to ensure that his successor would be in a field closely related to his own and would not be a molecular biologist.

Chain's role in the initiation of the work on penicillin in Oxford was his major contribution to medicine. He shared a Nobel prize with Fleming and Florey in 1945 and was elected to the fellowship of the Royal Society in 1949. He became an honorary fellow of the Royal College of Physicians in 1965 and was knighted in 1969. His many honours from other countries included the Paul Ehrlich centenary prize in 1954, appointment to the order of the Rising Sun, second degree, from Japan in 1976, and the grand decoration of honour in gold of the Federal Republic of Austria in 1973. In 1976 he became foreign member of the Academy of Sciences of the USSR.

Chain was a highly gifted and voluble man, with a jolly face, which was permanently adorned with a voluminous moustache. He was able to converse fluently in German, French, Russian, and Italian, as well as in English, and was socially engaging. Music always remained a major interest in his life and he played the piano with distinction. Throughout Chain's later life his Jewish identity became increasingly important to him. He became involved with the Weizmann Institute of Science at Rehovoth, becoming a member of the board of governors in 1954, and later a member of the executive council. He ensured his children were brought up securely within the Jewish faith, arranging much extra-curricular tuition for them. His views were expressed most clearly in his speech 'Why I am a Jew' given at the World Jewish Congress Conference of Intellectuals in 1965.

In 1971 Chain built a house at Mulranny in co. Mayo. He died there on 12 August 1979.

Chain's wife, **Anne Ethel Beloff-Chain** (1921–1991), biochemist, was born in Hampstead, Middlesex, on 26 June 1921, the youngest of the five children of Simon Beloff, export merchant, of Russian Jewish origin, and his wife, Marie, *née* Katzin. Max *Beloff, Baron Beloff (1913–1999), historian, and Nora *Beloff (1919–1997), journalist, were among her older siblings. She read chemistry at University College, London, graduating with first-class honours in 1942, and pursued her doctoral research on the biochemistry of skin burns at Oxford under Sir Rudolph Peters, and subsequently at Harvard Medical School with Dr Chris Anfinson and Dr Baird Hastings. In 1947 she returned briefly to Oxford as a tutor in biochemistry at Somerville College before marrying Chain and accompanying him to Rome. While raising their children she held the post of chief research scientist at the Istituto

Superiore di Sanità, investigating intermediate metabolism in animal tissues, especially the biochemistry of insulin and other hormones. On their return to London, both were employed at Imperial College, Anne as reader in biochemistry and, from 1983, professor of biochemistry. In 1986 she moved to the new University of Buckingham as professor to set up and direct an active research group in biochemistry, with funding from the Clore Foundation. She shared with her husband delight in their extended families and a concern with social and charitable causes. She was also involved with the Weizman Institute of Science in Israel, where she was a governor and member of its executive council. She died at her home in Camden, London, on 2 December 1991.   E. P. ABRAHAM, *rev.*

Sources E. Abraham, *Memoirs FRS*, 29 (1983), 43–91 · R. Clark, *The life of Ernst Chain* (1985) · personal knowledge (1986) · m. cert. · *The Independent* (25 Jan 1992) · *The Times* (17 Dec 1991)
Archives CAC Cam. · Wellcome L., corresp. and papers | Bodl. Oxf., corresp. relating to Society for the Protection of Science and Learning · Bodl. Oxf., letters to Dorothy Hodgkin · Bodl. Oxf., letters to Sir Rudolph Peters · RS, letters to Sir Robert Robinson · University of Sheffield, corresp. with Sir Hans Krebs
Likenesses W. Suschitzky, photograph, 1944, NPG [*see illus.*] · W. Suschitzky, photograph, 1944, NPG; *see illus. in* Robinson, Sir Robert (1886–1975) · W. Stoneman, photograph, *c.*1949, RS · G. Argent, photograph, *c.*1969, RS

Chair, Sir **Dudley Rawson Stratford de** (1864–1958), naval officer, was born in Lennoxville, Canada, on 30 August 1864, eldest son of Dudley Raikes de Chair, of French Huguenot descent, and his wife, Frances Emily, eldest daughter of Christopher Rawson, of The Hurst, Walton-on-Thames, Surrey. His parents returned to England in 1870 and in 1878 he joined the *Britannia* where Prince Edward and Prince George were also cadets.

As a midshipman de Chair attracted national attention through being captured by some of the Egyptian cavalry of Arabi Pasha when alone on a special mission. He was released after six weeks when Cairo was taken and was later selected by Sir Garnet Wolseley to take the dispatches to Alexandria.

With the exception of a short period as torpedo lieutenant in the flagship *Royal Sovereign* (1893–4), de Chair served as an instructor in the *Vernon*, the torpedo school at Portsmouth, from 1892 until his promotion to commander in 1897. In that year he was appointed commander in the flagship of his uncle, Sir Harry H. Rawson, at the Cape station. In 1899 he became commander in the *Majestic*, in which ship he remained until his promotion to captain in 1902.

In that year de Chair was appointed naval attaché at Washington, where his next three years were spent. Returning to seagoing duties, he next commanded successively the cruisers *Bacchante* and *Cochrane*. In 1908 he was brought into contact with Sir John Jellicoe, then controller of the navy, serving as his assistant controller until 1911. After a further spell of sea time as captain of the *Colossus* he returned to the Admiralty on promotion to flag rank in 1912 and on 1 March 1913 he succeeded David

Sir Dudley Rawson Stratford de Chair (1864–1958), by Walter Stoneman, 1933

Beatty as naval secretary to the first lord, Winston Churchill. He had met Churchill previously and had been impressed with his charm of manner and keen interest in naval affairs. But although Churchill had selected de Chair for this appointment, the latter was not as happy in it as Beatty had been. He found Churchill's ebullient zest and headstrong, sometimes impetuous, methods disturbing and had not the great wealth which Beatty had enjoyed to live fully in the circles which his chief frequented. In June 1914 he became admiral of the training squadron and at the outbreak of war he was moved to the cruiser *Crescent* in command of the 10th cruiser squadron.

The particular task of this squadron was the patrol of the North Sea from the Shetlands to the Norwegian coast as a blockade to Germany, and in his command of this task force until March 1916 de Chair made an important contribution towards the winning of the war. Owing to his efficient organization the number of ships which slipped through was negligible and as the war progressed the effect of the blockade became more apparent. For his services de Chair was appointed KCB in 1916.

De Chair relinquished his command to take up a post under the Foreign Office as naval adviser to the ministry of blockade. His experience made him eminently suitable for this work, as A. J. Balfour explained to him, but de Chair, as he revealed in his autobiography, was 'almost heartbroken' at giving up his command and active naval service. However he found the minister, Lord Robert Cecil, sympathetic and understanding.

De Chair's valuable work in this appointment continued until September 1917, when he was given command of the 3rd battle squadron, stationed in the channel, with the task of attacking the German high seas fleet, should it come out. That it never did was frustrating and disappointing to him, and he was further dismayed to learn of the dismissal of Jellicoe as first sea lord in December. When his successor, Sir Rosslyn Wemyss, asked de Chair to accept a post on the Board of Admiralty, he refused outright, telling Wemyss that he could not do so as he 'felt so keenly the disgraceful manner in which Jellicoe had been treated' (de Chair, 238). This outspokenness did de Chair no good and shortly afterwards he was relieved of his command and placed on half pay. He had been promoted vice-admiral in 1917. In July 1918 he was appointed admiral commanding coastguard and reserves; in 1920 he was promoted admiral; and in 1921–3 he was president of the inter-allied commission on enemy warships, and was then placed on the retired list.

The same year he was appointed governor of New South Wales, where he remained until 1930. During his term his determination and strength of character were fully tested in the political crisis of 1926, when the Labour premier, J. T. Lang, introduced a bill to abolish the legislative council, the state's second chamber. De Chair agreed to appoint twenty-five new Labour members to the council, but when the bill was defeated by forty-seven votes to forty-one he refused to appoint more. This led to strong attacks on his action by the Labour Party and to an examination of the powers of the state governors in Australia.

He married in 1903 Enid (*d.* 1966), third daughter of Henry William Struben, of Transvaal Colony; they had two sons and a daughter. The elder son, Henry Graham Dudley de Chair, became a commander in the Royal Navy; the younger, Somerset Struben de Chair, author of *The Golden Carpet* and other works, was for twelve years a member of parliament.

After his retirement Dudley de Chair lived mainly in London. He served in the Home Guard from 1940 to 1942. He died at his home, The Elms, Rottingdean, on 17 August 1958 and, after cremation, his ashes were scattered, in accordance with his wishes, in the English Channel from the *Hardy*.

In addition to the KCB, de Chair was appointed KCMG (1933), received the American DSM, and was a commander of the Légion d'honneur. McGill University conferred on him an honorary LLD.

Possessing much personal charm, de Chair was a man of great loyalty and integrity, direct in his manner and at times somewhat inflexible. As a leader some found him uninspiring, but Jellicoe termed him 'a very first-rate sea officer suited to any command afloat'. De Chair followed a code of ethics which frequently worked to his personal disadvantage and like Jellicoe, whom he greatly admired, he never allowed his judgement to be affected by personal considerations and never courted publicity.

G. K. S. HAMILTON-EDWARDS, *rev.*

Sources *The Times* (19 Aug 1958) · J. S. Corbett, *Naval operations*, 1 (1920); 3 (1923) · J. R. Jellicoe, *The Grand Fleet, 1914–1916: its creation,* development and work (1919) · D. De Chair, *The sea is strong* (1961) · A. J. Marder, *From the Dreadnought to Scapa Flow: the Royal Navy in the Fisher era, 1904–1919*, 5 vols. (1961–70), vol. 2 · Burke, *Gen. GB* (1965) · private information (1971) · *WWW* · *CGPLA Eng. & Wales* (1958)

Archives IWM, diaries, corresp., and papers | CAC Cam., corresp. with David Saunders | FILM BFI NFTVA, record footage · IWM FVA, actuality footage

Likenesses W. Stoneman, photographs, 1919–33, NPG [*see illus.*] · F. Dodd, charcoal and watercolour drawing, IWM · M. Spink, oils, priv. coll.

Wealth at death £1388 10*s.* 9*d.*: probate, 10 Nov 1958, *CGPLA Eng. & Wales*

Chalcombe [Chaucombe], **Hugh of** (*fl.* 1168–1209), justice, was probably born at Chalcombe in Northamptonshire; at least, it is certain that it was from that place that he received his surname. He was the heir of Matthew of Chalcombe. He is first mentioned in 1168, in the great roll of Henry II, as accounting for £30 for the relief of six knights' fees in the diocese of Lincoln, in which Chalcombe was then included. He next appears in the same record in 1184 as having been fined 1 mark to be released from an oath which he had taken to the abbot of St Albans. Fines reveal him acting as a royal justice between 1192 and 1194 and in the latter year he was a justice itinerant in the west midlands. Between 1194 and 1198 he was sheriff of Staffordshire, and was also involved in exacting tallages.

On the accession of John, Chalcombe was employed about the king's person, and accompanied him to Normandy. In June 1200 he witnessed a charter granted by John at Falaise, and in September he witnessed another charter at Argentan and sat as one of the justices in the king's court at Caen. In the same year the barons of the exchequer received instructions that a debt which Chalcombe owed to the king should be respited so long as he continued abroad in the royal service. In 1203 he was charged with the duty of making inquisition at the ports with regard to the persons who imported corn from Normandy. During the next two years he frequently accompanied the king on his journeys through England, and several charters granted at different places are witnessed by him. In 1205 he acted as justice itinerant in company with the king, fines being acknowledged before him in Yorkshire and Nottinghamshire, for example, and in July of that year he sat in the king's court at Wells. At Michaelmas 1205 and in 1206 and 1207 he accounted as custodian of Warwickshire and Leicestershire, jointly with one of the king's clerks named Hilary, and was entrusted with the care of the royal castle of Kenilworth. He was also appointed to manage the revenues of Kenilworth Priory during its vacancy, and again at this time was used to exact tallages.

In 1206–7 Chalcombe failed to appear for a suit brought against him by R. de Aungervile relating to the wrongful possession of some cattle, and orders were issued for his arrest. In the following July he was dismissed from his office of sheriff, being succeeded by Robert of Roppesley, to whom he was commanded to deliver up Kenilworth Castle. His dismissal may have been due to his failure to account for the profits of his office, and he had to make

fine for 800 marks to recover the king's favour. In 1209 he became a canon in the Augustinian priory he had founded at Chalcombe. Chalcombe and his wife, Hodierna, had one son, Robert, who by 1214 had become responsible for his father's debts to the crown, and two daughters, who were married to Hamund Passalewe and Ralph of Grafton.   HENRY BRADLEY, *rev.* JOHN HUDSON

Sources *Pipe rolls* · H. Hall, ed., *The Red Book of the Exchequer*, 3 vols., Rolls Series, 99 (1896) · F. Palgrave, ed., *Rotuli curiae regis: rolls and records of the court held before the king's justiciars or justices*, 2 vols., RC, 27 (1835) · D. M. Stenton, ed., *Pleas before the king or his justices*, 4 vols., SeldS, 67–8, 83–4 (1952–67) · T. D. Hardy, ed., *Rotuli litterarum patentium*, RC (1835) · T. D. Hardy, ed., *Rotuli litterarum clausarum*, 2 vols., RC (1833–4) · M. S. Walker, ed., *Feet of fines for the county of Lincoln for the reign of King John, 1199–1216*, PRSoc., new ser., 29 (1954) · D. Crook, *Records of the general eyre*, Public Record Office Handbooks, 20 (1982) · S. Painter, *The reign of King John* (1949)

Chalk, Sir James Jell (1803–1878), ecclesiastical civil servant, second son of James Chalk of Queensborough, Kent, and his wife, Mary, daughter of Edward Shove of the same place, was born in Queensborough and educated at Wye College, Kent. After passing several years of his early life in various occupations, including that of a strolling actor, on 4 October 1836 he joined the staff of the newly established ecclesiastical commission. He took the precaution of being called to the bar in November 1839, but rose to be assistant secretary of the commission. In 1849 his superior, Charles Knight Murray, was dismissed for embezzling the commission's funds and Chalk succeeded him as secretary. Chalk was a more orderly but less enterprising administrator than the buccaneering Murray. He restored the respectability of the commission and saw through the act of 1850 which established a full-time professional board known as the estates committee. He defended the commission effectively at several public inquiries. But his 'cautious and impassive demeanour' (*DNB*) fairly reflected his rather stolid approach. Chalk was knighted in July 1871 and retired from the secretaryship in October 1871. He was unmarried, and died at his home, 80 Warwick Square, Pimlico, London, on 23 September 1878.

H. C. G. MATTHEW

Sources *The Times* (27 Sept 1878) · G. F. A. Best, *Temporal pillars: Queen Anne's bounty, the ecclesiastical commissioners, and the Church of England* (1964) · *DNB*

Archives Georgetown University, Lauinger Library, corresp. relating to the building of St John the Evangelist Church, Clifton | LPL, corresp. with Archbishop Tait

Wealth at death under £8000: probate, 26 Oct 1878, *CGPLA Eng. & Wales*

Chalkhill, John (*d.* 1642), poet, was the son of Ion (or Ivon) Chalkhill (*d.* 1615), coroner of Middlesex, and his wife, Martha Browne (1566–1620), daughter of Thomas Browne, merchant tailor. The Chalkhill family was originally of Chalkhill House, Kingsbury, Middlesex, but the property was sold in 1606 to Thomas Gardiner, half-brother to John's mother. John's sister Martha (*d.* 1641) was the second wife of Thomas Ken, attorney, and stepmother of Ann Ken, the future wife of Izaak Walton. John matriculated as a pensioner from Trinity College, Cambridge, in December 1610 and was admitted as a scholar in April 1611.

Chalkhill wrote *Thealma and Clearchus: a Pastoral History in Smooth and Easie Verse*, posthumously edited by Izaak Walton (1683), who has been mistakenly identified as its author (Oliver, 24–37). Walton included two poems of Chalkhill's in *The Compleat Angler*: Coridon's song 'O, the sweet contentment', an eight-stanza appreciation of the life of a country man, and Piscator's six-stanza song to Coridon, 'O, the gallant fisher's life'. Two verse letters by Chalkhill survive, one addressed to 'his lovinge and kinde Coussen Mris Katherine Packerre at Mr John Packers house neere the Deanes yard in Westmister these be dd', and the other a mock love letter signed 'Penelope Trulove'. These and other works by Chalkhill are located at the Derbyshire Record Office among the family papers of the Gell family of Hopton Hall; they confirm Chalkhill's identity and differentiate him from John Chalkhill (*d.* 20 May 1679), fellow of New College, Oxford (1618–33), and later of Winchester College, the friend of Walton and of Chalkhill's brother-in-law Thomas Ken (Croft, 365). Chalkhill has also been confused with J. C., who wrote 'Alcilia, Philoparthen's Loving Follie', but A. B. Grosart, in his reprint of 'Alcilia' (1879), conclusively demonstrated that he was not the author.

Walton may not have known Chalkhill, whom he inaccurately identified as an acquaintance of Edmund Spenser. His preface to *Thealma and Clearchus*, dated 7 May 1678, offers the following description of him:

> And I have also this truth to say of the author, that he was in his time a man generally known and as well belov'd; for he was humble and obliging in his behaviour, a gentleman, a scholar, very innocent and prudent: and indeed his whole life was useful, quiet, and virtuous.

Chalkhill was buried on 8 April 1642 at St Margaret's, Westminster.   JEAN R. BRINK

Sources P. J. Croft, 'Izaak Walton's John Chalkhill', *TLS* (27 June 1958), 365 · I. Walton, *The compleat angler, 1653–1676*, ed. J. Bevan (1983), 28, 239–41, 331–3, 414 · A. B. Grosart, ed., *Alcilia, Philoparthen's loving follie (1595)* (1879), v–xxxi · H. J. Oliver, 'Izaak Walton as author of *Love and Truth* and *Thealma and Clearchus*', *Review of English Studies*, 25 (1949), 24–37

Archives Derbys. RO, family MSS, Gell family of Hopton Hall

Chalkley, Thomas (1675–1741), Quaker minister and master mariner, was born on 3 May 1675 in Southwark, London, the son of George Chalkley (*c.*1642–1725), a Quaker tradesman, and his wife, Rebecca, *née* Harding (*c.*1643–1694). The main source for a biography of Thomas Chalkley is his *Journal*, in which he recorded the events of his life from boyhood almost to his death. He was sent to a school run by Richard Scoryer, and in the streets boys taunted him because of his plain Quaker dress. Aged about fourteen he fearlessly determined to address everyone as 'thee' and 'thou', as he did at home. Aged sixteen he was apprenticed to his father, a trader in meal. He made his pacifist witness when, taken by a press-gang aboard a warship, he told the captain that he refused to fight and was released the next morning.

Chalkley early acquired the gift of ministry and undertook preaching tours in the west of England and to Scotland. He was locked out of the meeting-house, but the provost of Edinburgh returned the keys, saying that Quakers would do less harm preaching indoors than in the open air. In December 1697 he undertook his first visit to America and landed in Virginia in March of the following year, whence he went on a preaching tour as far as Massachusetts, where he met with considerable hostility. On 28 September 1699, a year after he had returned to England, he married Martha Betterton (*d.* 1712); the couple had four sons and one daughter, all of whom died in infancy.

In 1700 Chalkley and his family left Gravesend for Maryland, narrowly escaping shipwreck on the Goodwin Sands. Shortly after their arrival Chalkley purchased a piece of land in Philadelphia on the Delaware River, and in 1702 he commenced his long association with Barbados. The same year he visited Bermuda. From this time on Chalkley's life followed a regular pattern of business, in order to maintain his family, and missionary journeys, in the course of which he preached to Quakers and others who would listen to him. 1704 saw him in New England where, he observed, most Quakers upheld the peace testimony and would not fight against the Native Americans. Chalkley had contact with the Native Americans and, on remarking on the fact that women spoke in their councils, he was told that some women were wiser than men.

In 1707, when Chalkley was returning across the Atlantic, he narrowly avoided shipwreck on the Irish coast when the captain ran the vessel ashore to avoid privateers. Until June 1710 he preached in Ireland, Scotland, northern England, the Netherlands, and Germany, seeking out Quakers and making contact with Menonites; he also attended two London yearly meetings; he covered 14,300 miles and held nearly 1000 meetings. On his return to America he was accused of taking money for preaching, which he vigorously denied, averring that he had had to borrow money in London for his passage home. After his arrival in Maryland he spent a further two years travelling in the ministry.

On 30 March 1712 Chalkley's wife died; on 15 April 1714 he married Martha, widow of Thomas Brown, at a simple ceremony, for he deplored the growing habit of 'great entertainment' at weddings and funerals. After a second visit to Bermuda in 1716 his ship was delayed by calm weather and, food running short, he offered his body to be eaten. However, by divine intervention, as he thought, a dolphin was caught, which satisfied the sailors' hunger. In London in 1718 he visited his ageing father, his brother, and his cousins; at about this time also he acquired a brig, the *Hope*, which he sold in London, and purchased another.

The 1720s were a decade in which Chalkley did not prosper; in 1723–4 especially he suffered financial hardship, by the loss of three vessels. He was not reduced to poverty, however, for he was still able to purchase an estate at Frankford in Pennsylvania in 1723. Also at this time attempts were under way to tarnish Chalkley's reputation within the Quaker community. This attack was probably motivated by his criticism of wealthier merchants who, in his opinion, had discarded the simple living and fundamental testimonies of their Quaker forebears. These years also saw a period of 'dryness' and 'inward poverty', which reduced his ministry.

Chalkley was an empirical observer of natural phenomena but shared widespread eighteenth-century beliefs in miracles and prophetic dreams. A pragmatist in business he did not condemn slavery but declared forthrightly for humane treatment of slaves. He held firmly to simplicity and to the testimonies of early Friends. His writings were moralistic, chiding the young for frivolity and condemning especially dancing and tippling in alehouses. But the stern moralist showed a different side in his poetry, which was edited out of the printed *Journal*.

In 1729 Chalkley became master of a newly purchased vessel. Although wishing to curtail his business trips he undertook to satisfy all his creditors, a task he fulfilled on another journey to London in 1735. Thereafter his sea voyages diminished but in 1741 he went to Tortola in the Virgin Islands, where he died on 4 November and was buried later the same day. His donation of 111 volumes founded the Friends' Library of Philadelphia. Chalkley was regarded as one of the foremost Quaker ministers and his memory lived on, as witnessed by the poems of John Greenleaf Whittier and by frequent reprints of his *Journal*.   GERALD A. J. HODGETT

Sources DNB · *A collection of the works of Thomas Chalkley* (1749) · E. H. Beiswenger, 'Thomas Chalkley, pious Quaker businessman', PhD diss., U. Mich., 1969 · C. F. Jenkins, *Tortola: a Quaker experiment of long ago in the tropics* (1923) · *Encyclopedia of American Quaker genealogy*, ed. W. W. Henshaw (1938) · J. W. Frost, *The Quaker family in colonial America* (1973) · *Journal of the Friends' Historical Society*, 1–45 (1903–53) [indexes]

Archives Hist. Soc. Penn., journal MS pts 1 and 2 · RS Friends, Lond., letters and accounts of travels · Swarthmore College, Swarthmore, Pennsylvania, corresp.

Challans, (Eileen) Mary [*pseud.* Mary Renault] (1905–1983), novelist, was born on 4 September 1905 at Dacre Lodge, 49 Plashet Road, Forest Gate, West Ham, London, the first of two children born to Frank Challans (1875–1941), a physician, and his wife, Mary Clementine Newsome Baxter (1877–1960). Educated locally at Romford House School, she left home to attend Clifton high school in Bristol in 1920. In 1925 she went up to St Hugh's College, Oxford, receiving her bachelor's degree (a third in English) in 1928.

Mary Challans had always wanted to write, but her solitary and bookish childhood in an unaffectionate and unsympathetic family had given her neither the breadth of experience nor the discipline she needed to begin a literary career. Rejecting both marriage and teaching, the two paths generally open at this time to a young woman with a university education, she decided to return to Bristol, hoping to earn her living by odd jobs while trying to write in her spare time. She worked as a clerk and a factory worker while developing a friendship with a young man who introduced her to amateur theatre in Bath. Here she participated in a world which would influence all of her later writing, discovering a bohemian life in which gender as well as social roles were matters of performance. An attractive and athletic young woman with dark, curly

hair, she was beginning to develop the dedication to honesty and truthfulness that would shape her public persona and private values. Her writing, however, did not flourish and, pressed by economic circumstances, she developed rheumatic fever and was forced to return to her parents' home in 1932.

Recovering slowly, Mary Challans realized that her work on a novel set in medieval France was insubstantial and unmanageable. Abhorring dependence on her family, she decided on an unusual course which would enable her to earn her own living while giving her the vital contact with people for which she also longed. In 1933 she returned to Oxford to train as a nurse at the Radcliffe Infirmary, becoming a state registered nurse in 1937. Her experiences in hospital nursing gave her an understanding of the body which would inform all of her writing. She also now confronted directly issues of sexual orientation as well as gender and class. Few women with her education entered nursing in the 1930s, and most of her classmates were both younger and working-class. She found herself in an institution with strict hierarchies separating (female) nurses and (male) doctors, a setting in which she also recognized for the first time her own lesbian desire, falling in love in 1934 with a fellow student, Julie Mullard (b. 1911), who became her lifelong companion.

This important relationship both resolved and posed many problems for Mary Challans, not the least of which was how she was to write about issues at once intensely personal and socially challenging. Struggling with both her vocations (nursing, writing) and with her sexual identity in the social and moral context of English life in an atmosphere of war, she completed her first novel, *Purposes of Love*, in 1939. Drawing on her own hospital experiences, she chose the pseudonym Mary Renault to mask her identity and embarked on a literary career which would include five more accomplished novels with contemporary settings—*Kind are her Answers* (1940), *The Friendly Young Ladies* (1944), *Return to Night* (1947), *North Face* (1949), and *The Charioteer* (1953)—before she turned to the historical novels set in ancient Greece which established her reputation.

But Mary Challans was unable, despite the success of her first book, to leave nursing for writing. In 1939 she was called up by the Emergency Medical Service and assigned to Winford Hospital in Bristol where, assisted by conscientious objectors, she briefly worked with Dunkirk evacuees, an experience on which she would later draw both for setting and characters in *The Charioteer*, her moving novel about male homosexual relationships. By the end of 1940, she accepted a position as a nurse in the brain surgery ward of the Radcliffe Infirmary, where she continued to work until 1945.

Disillusioned with post-war England, Mary Challans was eager to leave nursing for literature when the war effort no longer required her skills. In part as a result of her good luck in winning an award of $125,000 for the rights to *Return to Night* from MGM film studios in 1946, she decided to leave England with Mullard for South Africa in 1948. She never returned. Settling first in Durban, then moving to Cape Town in 1959, she garnered many awards in later years, including an honorary fellowship from St Hugh's in 1982, but the end of the war, her two trips to the Mediterranean in 1954 and 1962, her physical distance from England, and intimacy with Mullard occasioned the shift from the early contemporary novels of manners to the mature historical novels of Hellenic life: *The Last of the Wine* (1956), an account of two male lovers during the Peloponnesian War; her two books about Theseus, *The King must Die* (1958) and *The Bull from the Sea* (1962); *The Mask of Apollo* (1966), a novel about the theatre and Greek politics; the first two books about Alexander the Great, *Fire from Heaven* (1970) and *The Persian Boy* (1972); her fictional biography of Simonides, *The Praise Singer* (1979); and the conclusion to the Alexander trilogy, *Funeral Games* (1981).

Expatriate life with Mullard in South Africa enabled Mary Challans to devote herself to literature. She was an active member of the PEN Club in Cape Town, serving as its president for many years, but she remained reticent about her personal life while she grew increasingly sure of herself as a writer. Her novels both obscured her life and allowed her to explore issues vital to her (war, peace, heroism, career-vocation, women's roles, sexual expression, and both male and female homosexuality). The clear shift in her work from contemporary to Greek settings has begun to receive important critical attention, for it divides her career in a way which may be obvious if simplistic: the meticulously researched classical settings allow her to mask material too explosive to deal with directly while simultaneously giving her an 'academic' freedom to write about her subjects with both personal and critical safety. Mary Renault's reception has been unfairly mixed: she is 'popular' with a sophisticated audience, yet only recently have readers begun to take her seriously as a consummate artist not only in her Greek novels but in her earlier work. There are many reasons for this reputation: one must certainly be her femaleness; others include her choice of genre (historical fiction), as well as her public representation in the press as a grey-haired and cardiganed matron. Her interest in sexuality and specifically in homosexuality and fluid gender roles and identities may also have contributed to her marginalization—yet these very interests warrant a re-evaluation of her achievement in an era more liberal than the one in which she began to write.

Mary Challans was at work on a new novel set in France at the time of the crusades when she died of cancer at a hospital near her home, 3 Atholl Road, Camps Bay, Cape Town, on 13 December 1983. After a funeral service at the Anglican cathedral in Cape Town on the 15th, her body was cremated and her ashes scattered at Ceres, near Cape Town, on the plateau above Camps Bay.

CAROLINE ZILBOORG

Sources D. Sweetman, *Mary Renault: a biography* (1993) · R. Hoberman, 'Masquing the phallus: genital ambiguity in Mary Renault's historical novels', *Gendering classicism: the ancient world in twentieth-century women's historical fiction* (1997), 73–88 · J. Abraham, 'Mary Renault's Greek drama', *Are girls necessary? Lesbian writing and modern histories* (1996), 61–78 · K. Kopelson, 'Friends and lovers: Yourcenar and Renault', *Love's litany: the writing of modern homoerotics* (1994), 104–28 · C. J. Summers, 'The plain of truth: Mary Renault's *The charioteer*', *Gay fictions: Wilde to Stonewall, studies in a male homosexual literary tradition* (1990), 156–71 · B. F. Dick, *The Hellenism of Mary Renault* (1972) · P. Wolfe, *Mary Renault* (1969) · C. Heilbrun, 'Axiothea's grief: the disability of the female imagination', *From Parnassus: essays in honor of Jacques Barzun*, ed. D. B. Weiner and W. R. Keylor (1976), 227–36 · L. C. Burns Jr., 'Men are only men: the novels of Mary Renault', *Critique*, 6 (winter 1963), 102–21 · H. Kenner, 'Mary Renault and her various personas', *New York Times Book Review* (10 Feb 1974), 15 · P. Green, 'The masks of Mary Renault', *New York Review of Books* (8 March 1979), 11–14 · J. Selby-Green, *The history of the Radcliffe Infirmary* (1990) · private information (2004)
Archives St Hugh's College, Oxford, corresp. · U. Reading L., corresp. and literary papers | Boston University, Jay Williams MSS · Yale U., corresp. with Bryher
Likenesses photographs, 1935–83, priv. coll. · photographs, 1950–83, priv. coll. · photographs, repro. in Sweetman, *Mary Renault*

Challice, Annie Emma (1821–1875). *See under* Challice, John (1815–1863).

Challice, John (1815–1863), physician, was born at Horsham, Sussex, and was educated at King's College, London. He qualified MD (Lond.) and was elected FRCP (Edin.), and he became a physician in London. Besides achieving some eminence in his profession he was an active liberal politician and a close friend of Sir William Molesworth and Admiral Sir Charles Napier. Well known as a public benefactor he was one of the first medical officers of health for Bermondsey, in which capacity he published various reports in 1856 and in subsequent years.

Challice wrote a number of medical advisory texts including *How to Avoid the Cholera* (1848), which as a cheap publication sold several thousand copies, as well as *Medical Advice for Mothers* (1851). He was also an active figure in the vociferous mid-nineteenth century debates surrounding public health practice, on which he published a number of texts including *Letter to Lord Palmerston on Sanitary Reform* (1854) and *Should Cholera Come, what Ought to be Done?* (1848).

Challice died suddenly on 11 May 1863, at 13 Cumberland Street, Hyde Park, London, following a brief paralysis. He was buried at Horsham, Sussex.

Challice's wife, **Annie Emma Challice** [*née* Armstrong] (1821–1875), author, was born in London. Her early publications included *The Village School Fête* (1847) and *The Sister of Charity* (1857). Her later works concentrated on French history and included *The History of the Court of France under Louis XV* (1861), *French Authors at Home* (1864), and *Illustrious Women of France* (1873). She died at 7 Upper Wimpole Street, Cavendish Square, London, on 11 January 1875.

[ANON.], *rev.* RICHARD HANKINS

Sources *The Lancet* (23 May 1863) · private information (1886) · *CGPLA Eng. & Wales* (1875)
Wealth at death under £5000: probate, 28 May 1863, *CGPLA Eng. & Wales* · under £1500—Annie Emma Challice: resworn will with codicil, Nov 1875, *CGPLA Eng. & Wales*

Challis, James (1803–1882), astronomer and physicist, was born on 12 December 1803 at Braintree, Essex, the fourth son of John Challis, a stonemason. After attending Braintree School, the Revd Daniel Copsey's school, Braintree, and Mill Hill School, Mill Hill, Middlesex, Challis matriculated at Trinity College, Cambridge, in 1821. Elected scholar of Trinity in 1824, he graduated in 1825 as senior wrangler and first Smith's prizeman, and was elected a fellow of Trinity in 1826. Ordained in 1830, he then held the college living at Papworth Everard, Cambridgeshire, until 1852. In 1831 Challis married Sarah Copsey of Braintree, the second daughter of Samuel Chandler of Tyringham, Buckinghamshire and the widowed daughter-in-law of his former schoolmaster.

Plumian professorship Challis examined for the mathematical tripos in 1831 and 1832, and on Airy's appointment as astronomer royal Challis was elected in February 1836 to succeed him as Plumian professor of astronomy and experimental philosophy. He became director of the Cambridge observatory at the same time. In April 1836 he was admitted a fellow of the Royal Astronomical Society (RAS), and in 1848 he was elected a fellow of the Royal Society of London. He and his wife lived at the Cambridge observatory, exercising a genial hospitality for twenty-five years. Challis once left his wife to guard an intruder at the observatory while he went for help. Stress, due to arrears of reductions derided by Airy, compelled him to resign direction of the observatory in 1861. He was replaced by J. C. Adams. Challis remained as Plumian professor, however, and in 1870 was re-elected to the Trinity fellowship which he had vacated upon his marriage.

As Plumian professor, Challis lectured on physical subjects covered by the mathematical tripos. By the time of his appointment in 1836 he had published some twenty papers on these subjects. His expertise in the area of hydrodynamics led the British Association for the Advancement of Science to invite him to write a report of the current state of research on the subject, which was published in the 1833 volume of the association's *Reports* and which he followed with a substantial 'Supplementary report' in 1836. In 1838 Challis published a syllabus for his course of experimental lectures on the equilibrium and motion of fluids and on geometrical and physical optics. Accepting the relatively new undulatory theory of light, the syllabus explained that light was transmitted through an unlimited elastic ether just as sound was conveyed through air. Challis rejected, however, the theory that light consisted of transverse ethereal vibrations. This theory was suggested by the phenomenon of the polarization of light and, in turn, implied that the ether (unlike air) possessed characteristics of a solid. Challis's views of the 1830s were central to his lifelong theoretical research, which mainly applied hydrodynamical principles to the physics of a fluid ether. Challis yielded teaching the subjects of light and fluids to Stokes in 1849 when the latter became Lucasian professor. Challis continued lecturing on practical astronomy, that is, on astronomical instruments and their use in making observations. He had published a syllabus for the lectures in 1843, and the lectures themselves appeared in 1879 as *Lectures on Practical Astronomy and Astronomical Instruments*. They emphasized instruments in the Cambridge observatory, some invented by Challis. The Plumian professor was one of four examiners

for the Smith's prizes, and in that role Challis evaluated the likes of Stokes, Cayley, Adams, William Thomson, Tait, and Maxwell. He wrote letters supporting Thomson's and Stokes's applications for professorships at Glasgow University in the 1840s and, in 1856, Maxwell's for the professorship of natural philosophy at Marischal College, Aberdeen. Challis published fourteen papers in the *Transactions of the Cambridge Philosophical Society*, mostly in the 1830s and 1840s, and was president of the society from 1845 to 1847. With Thomson, he set the subject and examined for the Adams prize which Maxwell won in 1857 with his groundbreaking analysis of Saturn's rings.

Observational astronomy Challis was best known as an observational astronomer. In his quarter century at the Cambridge observatory he emphasized determinations of the places of sun, moon, and planets, both to increase tabular accuracy and to test Newton's law of gravitation. He was the first in Britain to notice the division of Biela's comet on 15 January 1846, and he reobserved both nuclei in 1852. In fact, from the mid-1840s until the end of his directorship, he published some sixty papers reporting observations of comets and asteroids. He followed Airy's methods in his observations but improved the observatory's instrumentation. In 1848 he invented the meteoroscope, a kind of altitude-and-azimuth instrument in the form of a theodolite, designed for ascertaining the varying dimensions and positions of the zodiacal light, for measuring auroral arches, and for determining rapidly the points of appearance and disappearance of shooting stars. The next year he invented the transit-reducer, which was distinguished with a bronze medal at the Great Exhibition of 1851. Challis introduced the collimating eyepiece in 1850, and it was soon adopted at Greenwich and elsewhere. It was amended from Bohnenberger's design at his request by William Simms. From 1832 to 1864 Challis published twelve volumes of *Astronomical Observations Made at the Observatory of Cambridge*. Each volume contained an elaborate introduction, and the first two described instruments and methods.

In 1846 Challis failed to discover Neptune. Discussions of the episode, then and since, have often revealed more about the pride of nations and the wisdom of hindsight than about Challis as an observational astronomer. Adams communicated his unpublished theoretical prediction of the existence and location of an unknown planet to Challis and Airy in the autumn of 1845. Evidently, neither was entirely convinced by Adams's results, and both already had full workloads. Things changed only in June 1846 when Airy read U. Le Verrier's just published results that were similar to Adams's. By the end of July, Airy had persuaded Challis to use the Cambridge observatory's Northumberland telescope to search for the new planet. Lacking charts, Challis began plotting the positions of a few thousand stars in the appropriate part of the sky to determine which 'star' was moving and was therefore actually a planet. Before he finished, J. G. Galle at the Berlin observatory, using Le Verrier's prediction and an existing map of the stars in question, made the discovery in September 1846. Reviewing his observations, Challis found that he had observed the planet twice during August and once on 29 September, before learning on 1 October of its discovery. In November, Adams, Airy, and Challis read papers on the matter before the RAS, which published them in its *Memoirs*. Adams's was the first publication of his mathematical investigation; Airy's and Challis's explained their roles in the search for the new planet. Airy thought, given the simultaneous but independent theoretical and observational investigations in England and on the continent, 'that it will be found that the discovery is a consequence of what may properly be called a movement of the age' (Airy, 386). Challis's paper sounded the same theme as his report later that year to the Cambridge observatory syndicate, in which he stated: 'I lost the opportunity of announcing the discovery by deferring the discussion of the observations, being much occupied with reductions of comet observations, and little suspecting that the indications of theory were accurate enough to give a chance of discovery in so short a time' (Glaisher, 171). Airy's and Challis's accounts failed to disperse the cloud that shadowed their remaining careers for allowing such scientific glory to escape England.

Progress in physics In numerous papers and books Challis developed a comprehensive physical theory that was both unique and characteristic of Victorian physics. His earliest publications were mathematical studies of subjects he lectured on: hydrodynamics, light, and sound. His articles in the *Philosophical Magazine* in the 1840s brought him into conflict with Airy and Stokes. Challis later extended his investigations of fluids into a *Newtonian* theory of all physical phenomena. He followed Newton's rejection of the concept of action-at-a-distance forces, his insistence that nature's unobservable qualities resemble those that could be sensed, and his advocacy of 'a certain most subtle spirit which pervades and lies hid in all gross bodies' (*Sir Isaac Newton's Mathematical Principles*, 2.547). Newton's subtle spirit became Challis's ether. Challis's resultant vision pictured nature as consisting of two ultimate components: inert, spherical atoms and an elastic, fluid ether. Challis regarded these as *a priori* hypotheses whose truth was made highly probable through their predictions' agreement with quantitative observation. Mind acted through ether to cause bodily activity. Ethereal oscillations acted on atoms to cause the observable phenomena of gravity, light, electricity, magnetism, and heat. Though broadly similar to Victorian field theory, Challis's specific ideas gained no discernible support. He, however, regarded his theories as the only proper development of Newton's insights. Because they were so original, Challis thought that his theories' acceptance would take time, perhaps considerable time. In 1869 he published *Notes on the principles of pure and applied calculation; and applications of mathematical principles to theories of the physical forces*, which at nearly 700 pages was by far the fullest statement of his views. *An Essay on the Mathematical Principles of Physics* (1873) and *Remarks on the Cambridge Mathematical Studies* (1875) were much shorter summaries. In both he urged Cambridge's mathematical students to use the resources of the new Cavendish Laboratory to combine theory and experiment in pursuing physical research. He seemed to be in search of disciples.

Religious studies Challis's religious writings sought to harmonize modern science with a conservative view of the Bible. *Creation in Plan and Progress* (1861) responded to Goodwin's chapter in *Essays and Reviews*. Challis argued that Genesis was essentially God's 'antecedent plan' for creation, not a chronology of how he executed it. Even so, Genesis and science largely agreed. Light and heat from the primordial, self-luminous earth accounted for the light created on the first day as well as thick clouds of water vapour that constituted the water above the firmament that Genesis mentioned. As the earth cooled, rain fell, clouds dissipated, and the sun, moon, and stars appeared (on the fourth day). Genesis also agreed with much of the chronology of the appearance of plants and animals evident in the geological record. Though the geological record may have documented a vast period of time, human history extended only about 6000 years, back to Adam and Eve. *A Translation of the Epistle of the Apostle Paul to the Romans* (1871) maintained that Paul's use of the word 'law' was like modern science's use of the word. Hence, only now was it possible to realize what Paul meant by phrases like 'the law of faith' and 'the law of sin'. The inductive method of science guided Challis's close biblical exegesis in his *Essay on the Scriptural Doctrine of Immortality* (1880). He concluded, for example, that the eternal punishment of the Bible meant the eternal *effect* of punishment, that is, immortality. As needed, punishment would eventually make all men righteous and thus eligible for salvation.

Achievements Challis's genuine abilities won him a senior wranglership, a Cambridge professorship, a firm position in Cambridge's school of mathematics and mathematical physics, and undeniable accomplishments in observational astronomy. Thus assured a hearing, he articulated an elaborate physical theory as well as an intricate blend of religion and science. His desire to combine conservative religion and modern science was, in fact, not unlike that of Stokes. His unified physical theory mirrored the unifying aspects of Thomson's thermodynamics and Maxwell's electromagnetic theory of light. Even Challis's persistence in the face of stern opposition resembled that of Thomson, the difference being that Thomson was right often enough—and profoundly enough—that he enjoyed enormous acclaim. Challis's particular configuration of widespread Victorian ideas, by contrast, made little mark.

In the 1870s Challis continued his stream of articles, which numbered nearly 250 altogether, including four co-authored with Adams. He even pitted his version of physics against the striking phenomena of Crookes's radiometer, once again providing a peculiar explanation that he proclaimed a great success. He published books that summarized his physical theories and set forth his religious views. He hoped that his originality in physics would bring an appointment as emeritus professor, leaving lectures to younger men and more time to himself for

research. That did not happen, however. Ill health prevented his lecturing towards the end of his life, and in 1880 he appointed Alexander Freeman of St John's College as deputy to lecture for him. Challis died at his home, 2 Trumpington Street, Cambridge, on 3 December 1882 and was buried on 8 December beside his wife at Mill Road cemetery in Cambridge. A son and daughter survived him.
A. M. CLERKE, *rev.* DAVID B. WILSON

Sources J. W. L. G. [J. W. L. Glaisher], *Monthly Notices of the Royal Astronomical Society*, 43 (1882–3), 160–79 · *Catalogue of scientific papers*, Royal Society, 19 vols. (1867–1925) · R. W. Smith, 'The Cambridge network in action: the discovery of Neptune', *Isis*, 80 (1989), 395–422 · S. G. Brush, C. W. F. Everitt, and E. Garber, eds., *Maxwell on Saturn's rings* (1983) · G. B. Airy, 'Account of some circumstances historically connected with the discovery of the planet exterior to Uranus', *Memoirs of the Royal Astronomical Society*, 16 (1847), 385–414 · *Sir Isaac Newton's mathematical principles of natural philosophy and his system of the world*, trans. A. Motte, rev. F. Cajori, 2 vols. (1934); repr. (1962) · Venn, *Alum. Cant.* · D. B. Wilson, *Kelvin and Stokes: a comparative study in Victorian physics* (1987) · D. B. Wilson, *The correspondence between Sir George Gabriel Stokes and Sir William Thomson, Baron Kelvin of Largs*, 2 vols. (1990) · *The scientific letters and papers of James Clerk Maxwell*, ed. P. M. Harman, 1 (1990) · A. R. Hall, *The Cambridge Philosophical Society: a history, 1819–1969* (1969) · J. C. Adams, 'An explanation of the observed irregularities in the motion of Uranus, on the hypothesis of disturbances caused by a more distant planet; with a determination of the mass, orbit and position of the disturbing body', *Memoirs of the Royal Astronomical Society*, 16 (1847), 427–59 · M. Yamalidou, 'Molecular ideas in hydrodynamics', *Annals of Science*, 55 (1998), 369–400 · *CGPLA Eng. & Wales* (1883)
Archives RAS, letters to Royal Astronomical Society | CUL, Institute of Astronomy, Cambridge Observatory archives, corresp. · CUL, letters to Sir George Stokes · CUL, Kelvin collection, letters to W. Thomson · RAS, letters to Richard Sheepshanks · RS, corresp. with John Herschel · Trinity Cam., letters to William Whewell
Likenesses portrait, Trinity Cam.; repro. in Hall, *The Cambridge Philosophical Society*, 15
Wealth at death £781 14s. 8d.: administration, 9 Jan 1883, *CGPLA Eng. & Wales*

Challoner, Richard (1691–1781), religious writer and vicar apostolic of the London district, was born at or near Lewes, Sussex, on 29 September 1691, the only son of Richard Challoner (who died in the early 1690s), a wine cooper, and his wife, Grace Willard (1669–1731). Because his father, a 'rigid Dissenter' (Burton, 1.1), died when Challoner was a child, his mother went into service, first with Sir John Gage, a Roman Catholic landowner at Firle, near Lewes, then with another Catholic, George Holman, at Warkworth Manor, Northamptonshire, near Banbury, where the chaplain and religious writer John Gother received Challoner into the Roman Catholic church, possibly when he made his first communion at thirteen, and recommended him for education to the priesthood at the English College at Douai. He was entered there on 29 July 1705. Challoner took the college oath, preparatory to training for holy orders, on 3 November 1708. He was elected professor of poetry (to teach the classics) in 1711 and professor of rhetoric and then philosophy in 1712, and subscribed the anti-Jansenist bull *Unigenitus* in 1714. He was ordained deacon and priest in 1716 by J. E. von Löwenstein-Wertheim, bishop of Tournai, became prefect of studies in 1718, and took the degree of bachelor and

Richard Challoner (1691–1781), by unknown engraver

licentiate in theology in 1719, defending the controversial proposition 'that no Thomist could deny the Pope to be infallible' (ibid., 1.42). His alias at the college was his mother's maiden name, Willard. In 1720 he was appointed professor of theology and vice-president to the vigorous president, Robert Witham. He was unsuccessful in an attempt in 1721 to secure a chair at the University of Douai, which awarded him a doctorate of divinity in 1727.

In 1724 Challoner published the first of more than sixty works, *Aequitas constitutionis Unigenitus vindicata*, and another work, *Think well on't, or, Reflections on the great truths of the Christian religion for every day in the month*, appeared in 1728, but his career as a writer blossomed only after his appointment as a priest on the mission in London in 1730. His writings are 'clear, scriptural, tightly argued, but never original, the work of a first-rate jobbing carpenter in command of his tools but disapproving of imaginative frills' (Duffy, 11), his aim being merely to 'popularize and transmit the mainstream Douai tradition which he had received' (ibid., 90). In 1732 Challoner published *The Unerring Authority of the Catholic Church*, in which he appealed to protestants from their own Bible, and *A Profession of Catholic Faith*, later called *The Grounds of the Catholick Doctrine ... by Way of Question and Answer*, on the creed of Pope Pius IV. In 1733 there appeared his *A Short History of the First Beginning and Progress of the Protestant Religion*, which appealed to protestant authorities. His other polemical works included *A Roman Catholick's Reasons why he cannot Conform to the Protestant Religion* (1734); *The Touchstone of the New Religion* (1734), drawing in outline on Matthew Kellison's *The Touchstone of the Reformed Gospel*, and again invoking the protestant Bible; an edition of Gother's *Essay on the Change and Choice of Religion*, titled *The Sincere Christian's Guide in the Choice of Religion* (1734); *The Young Gentleman Instructed in the Grounds of the Christian Religion* (1735), against atheism, deism, and other forms of fashionable infidelity; and, under the pseudonym Philalethes, *A Specimen of the Spirit of the Dissenting Teachers* (1736) against the nonconformists John Barker and Samuel Chandler. In the Preface to *The Catholick Christian Instructed* (1737) Challoner attacked Conyers Middleton's argument in his *Letter from Rome* (1st edn, 1729) that popery was a revival of paganism. Challoner also translated *The Imitation of Christ* (1737) and St Augustine's *Confessions* (1739), and published a new folio edition of the Douai/Rheims New Testament (1738).

Challoner was elected to the clerical Chapter of the Old Brethren in 1732 and as their 'controversial writer' in 1736, holding the post until 1757. His works, however, were also an outgrowth of his favourite pastoral ministry to the poor, in the spirit of his favourite saints, Francis of Sales and Vincent de Paul. From about 1737 he undertook the administration of the diocese with its 25,000 Catholics as vicar-general to the absentee Benjamin Petre, vicar apostolic of the London district. In 1738 Challoner was appointed president of Douai, but Petre had Rome name Challoner as bishop of Debra and Petre's coadjutor with right of succession to the London district by papal briefs of 12 and 14 September 1739. Challoner resisted on the grounds that he had been raised an Anglican, but a dispensation was issued on 8 October 1740, and his election was effected by two further briefs of 24 November 1740. He was consecrated in the chapel of the Hammersmith convent on 29 January 1741 NS. Petre died in 1758 and Challoner became vicar apostolic of the London district; Challoner himself acquired a coadjutor-bishop, James Talbot, in 1759.

Challoner made an extensive visitation of the Catholics in his diocese in 1741–2, clearing the large backlog in confirmations left by his predecessors; he made another visitation in 1749–50. He lived austerely, with an hour's meditation at six, daily mass, and the reading of his breviary. He spent much of his time as an almoner, acting for Edward, ninth duke of Norfolk, for Catherine, Lady Stourton, the dowager Lady Arundell, and Mrs Southcote, as well as through the Benevolent Society for the Relief of the Aged and Infirm Poor. He founded a school in 1749 at Standon Lordship, Hertfordshire, which moved to Hare Street in 1767 and then to Old Hall Green in 1769. He was one of the three secular vicars apostolic whose differences with the regular clergy were resolved by Rome in favour of the former in 1753. He first opposed the take-over by the secular clergy of the Jesuit college at St Omer, on the dissolution of the Society of Jesus in France, but secured the endowments of the Jesuit English colleges at Seville and Madrid to the one at Valladolid in 1767, as well as the reform of the secular English College in Lisbon. He showed sensitivity towards former Jesuits in England and the American colonies when the pope dissolved the order in 1773.

In 1740 Challoner published *The Garden of the Soul*, which was strongly influenced by St Francis of Sales. It created the 'Garden of the Soul Catholic' as a spiritual type, devout but restrained, and even after 1850, with additions, it 'continued to be the staple devotional text for the vast majority of Catholics living in England' (Heimann, 76). It

was intended to supplement rather than supersede *A Manual of Prayers*, which Challoner republished in a revised edition in 1758. In the *Memoirs of Missionary Priests* (2 vols., 1741–2), largely based on Alban Butler's collections at Douai, Challoner renewed Catholic martyrology, while he recalled more ancient glories in *Britannia sancta* (2 vols., 1745) on the lives of the saints of Britain and Ireland. Challoner aspired to get Rome to raise the rank of some local feasts, as in 1749, and to restore a number of saints to the calendar, as in 1754 and 1774. *A Memorial of Ancient British Piety* (1760) is also devoted to British martyrology and hagiography. Challoner continued to defend the Catholic faith in *The Grounds of the Old Religion* (1742), which repudiated the Abbé Le Courayer's argument for Anglican orders (1st edn, 1723), and in *A Letter to a Friend Concerning the Infallibility of the Church of Christ* (1743) and *Remarks on Two Letters Against Popery* (1751). He attacked a more novel heresy in *A Caveat Against the Methodists* (1760), which Wesley described as 'an artful performance', one that concluded, if at all, 'not against the Methodists only but against the whole body of Protestants' (*Richard Challoner, 1691–1781*, 30). Challoner's pastoral writings included the *Instructions and Advice to Catholicks upon Occasion of the Late Earthquakes* (1750) and *Instructions for the Time of the Jubilee* (1751).

Challoner's main work was his updating in more modern idiom of the Rheims–Douai Catholic Bible, of which the New Testament appeared in 1749 and the whole Bible (5 vols.) in 1750. This removed the quaint Latinisms of its original and, in Cardinal Newman's words, 'is even nearer to the Protestant, than it is to the Douay' (Burton, 1.285); its Old Testament text remained unchanged into the twentieth century. Next in importance to the Bible and *The Garden of the Soul* were Challoner's *Meditations for every Day in the Year* (1754), 'for long the standard meditation book in every Catholic household' (1.346). His other additions to the Catholic spiritual armoury included: *The wonders of God in the wilderness, or, The lives of the most celebrated saints of the oriental desarts* (1755), drawing on the work of the Bollandists; an abridgement of Abraham Woodhead's translation of the *Life of … St Teresa* (1757); *The City of God of the New Testament* (1760), an abstract of church history; *The Morality of the Bible* (1762); and translations of St Francis of Sales's *An Introduction to a Devout Life* (1762), of F. J. Chrysostome's *A Short Treatise on the Method and Advantage of Withdrawing the Soul* (1765), and of H. M. Boudon's *God everywhere Present* (1766). He also wrote *Rules of Life for a Christian* (1766), *Abstract Histories* of the Bible and New Testament (1767), and the *Abridgement of Christian Doctrine* (1772).

Catholicism was not persecuted during Challoner's early episcopate, and he was perfectly open in his preaching in such public venues as the Ship tavern. The splendour of the Catholic embassy chapels, most notably the Sardinian, Challoner's cathedral, gave the old faith a certain Counter-Reformation public splendour. In 1765, however, the 'Protestant Carpenter' (Burton, 2.90) and informer William Payne initiated prosecutions against

Catholic priests and teachers. One cleric, John Baptist Maloney, was sentenced in 1767 to life imprisonment, later commuted to banishment, but further convictions were quashed or thwarted by the chief justice, Lord Mansfield, who required proof of ordination as well as of saying mass. The Catholic Relief Act of 1778 was followed by the Gordon riots of 1780, in which the London mob, whipped up by the Protestant Association led by a Scottish madman, Lord George Gordon, burnt Catholic chapels, houses, and businesses. Challoner narrowly escaped from his London house in Gloucester Street, Queen Square, taking refuge at the house of his friend the woollen merchant William Mawhood, in Finchley. He was gravely shaken by the destruction of the homes and chapels in which he had ministered for half a century, and had a stroke on 10 January 1781. His last word was 'charity', as he indicated to his chaplain Joseph Bolton his pocket containing money for the poor. He died at Gloucester Street on 12 January, in his ninetieth year, and was buried on 22 January with both Anglican and Catholic rites by his friend Briant Barrett in his family vault at Milton, in Berkshire. Public dirges were sung for him on 24, 26, and 30 January in the Bavarian, Portuguese, and Neapolitan embassy chapels, and in the Sardinian embassy chapel on 5 March. He had, in Cardinal Wiseman's words, 'supplied, in fact, almost the entire range of necessary or useful religious literature for his Catholic fellow-countrymen' (ibid., 2.280): the Bible, catechetical and apologetic works, prayer books, meditations, martyrologies, and controversy. All were written in plain, sound, instructive Augustan prose, often affective in tone, yet as sober as their century, and they ensured that Challoner's church did better than survive. His utterance that 'There will be a new people' (ibid., 2.214) was remembered in more prosperous days.

SHERIDAN GILLEY

Sources E. H. Burton, *The life and times of Bishop Challoner, 1691–1781*, 2 vols. (1909) · E. Duffy, ed., *Challoner and his church: a Catholic bishop in Georgian England* (1981) · *Richard Challoner, 1691–1781: the greatest of the vicars-apostolic* (1946) · L. E. Whatmore, 'The birthplace and parentage of Bishop Challoner: an enquiry', *Recusant History*, 12 (1973–4), 254–60 · M. Heimann, *Catholic devotion in Victorian England* (1995) · J. Barnard, *Life of the Venerable and Right Reverend Richard Challoner, D.D., bishop of Debra* (1784) · J. Milner, 'A brief account of the life of the late R. Rev. Richard Challoner', in R. Challoner, *The grounds of the old religion*, 5th edn (1798) · *Bishop Richard Challoner, 1691–1781* (1981) [exhibition catalogue, Westminster Cathedral north gallery, London, 1 July – 30 Sept 1981]
Archives Archivio Vaticano, Vatican City · Birmingham diocesan archives, MSS · Ushaw College, Durham, corresp. relating to Douai College · Ushaw College, Durham, MSS · Westm. DA, letterbook, *Liber baptizatorum*, literary MSS, material for Burton's *Life of Challoner*, and pastoral letters
Likenesses line engraving, NPG [*see illus.*] · oils, St Edmund's College, Old Hall Green, Hertfordshire; repro. in Burton, *Life and times*; copy, Cathedral Clergy House, Westminster · oils (Victorian), Ushaw College, Durham · print, repro. in R. Challoner, *Meditations*, ed. J. P. Coghlan (1784) · stipple, BM, NPG

Chalmers family (*per.* 1736–1876), newspaper proprietors and printers, established in Aberdeen what became the largest printing and publishing business in the north of

Scotland in the eighteenth and early nineteenth centuries. The family's prominence was founded on the *Aberdeen Journal*, among other newspapers and magazines, and on their succeeding as printers to the town and university of Aberdeen, in which capacity they were responsible for at least 40 per cent of works printed in Aberdeen from the 1730s to the end of the eighteenth century. The company remained the major regional printer and newspaper publisher during much of the nineteenth century, during which it faced markedly increased competition.

James [ii] **Chalmers** (*bap.* 1713, *d.* 1764), printer and newspaper proprietor, was born in Aberdeen and baptized on 8 January 1713 at Dyke, Morayshire, the eldest surviving son of James [i] Chalmers (*bap.* 1686, *d.* 1744), professor of divinity at Marischal College, Aberdeen (1728–44), and his cousin Jean Chalmers. He was apprenticed to James Nicol, printer to the town and university of Aberdeen, and thereafter, it is frequently stated, he continued his training in the office of John Watts, the respected London printer (Keith, 73). On Nicol's retirement in May 1736 Chalmers immediately made successful application to the town council to become its official printer, and shortly afterwards he was confirmed as printer to Marischal College. He also became official printer to the commissioners of supply for the county of Aberdeen; until 1752 his was the only printing house in the city. On 13 March 1739 he married Susan or Susanna Trail (1720–1791), daughter of James Trail, Church of Scotland minister at Montrose; they had seven children, including James [iii] [*see below*] and Alexander *Chalmers (1759–1834), literary critic and biographer. In November 1740 Chalmers's petition to the town council to become precentor of the East Church of St Nicholas was accepted. Contemporary sources state that in autumn 1745 Chalmers, a committed Hanoverian, produced some news sheets and that his printing shop and equipment were damaged by Jacobite sympathizers. In July 1746 he was appointed commissioner for the forfeited estates of Hallhead and Esslemont.

In January 1748, from his Castlegate premises, Chalmers launched the (then) weekly *Aberdeen Journal*, the first newspaper published north of Edinburgh and still extant in the late twentieth century as the *Press and Journal*. In 1797 the extension of the title to the *Aberdeen Journal and General Advertiser for the North of Scotland* reflected its success and commercial utility. Its avowed aim was respectability, and impartiality in reporting events. It had no enduring eighteenth-century rival, though Douglas and Murray's *Aberdeen Intelligencer* (1752–7) offered some competition. Pressure from the *Journal*, however, and protests upheld by the commissioners of supply over costs incurred in having to place advertisements in two newspapers, forced the cessation of the *Intelligencer*. In addition to his role as a newspaper publisher Chalmers produced works such as the 1762 edition of George Buchanan's *Rerum Scoticarum historia* (ed. James Man) for local booksellers; in his official capacity as university printer he also printed Alexander Gerard's influential *Plan of Education in Marischal College* (1755). Otherwise, his presses were given over to pamphlets on religious or civic subjects. He died in

Aberdeen on 25 August 1764 and was buried at St Nicholas's Church.

Shortly after James [ii] Chalmers's death his widow announced that the business would be continued by her son **James** [iii] **Chalmers** (1742–1810), printer and publisher. He was born in Aberdeen on 31 March 1742 and was educated (but did not graduate) at Marischal College between 1755 and 1757, with the aid of a Liddel bursary. He then entered the family business, for which he had been trained in London and Aberdeen. On 22 March 1769 he married Margaret Douglas (*d.* 1818); they had seven daughters and five sons, including James [iv] (1775–1831), later printer of the *Dundee Advertiser* (1801) and David [*see below*]. James [iii] faced greater business competition than his father and witnessed a marked increase in printing and publishing activity in a city that more than doubled in size from the 1750s to a population of 35,000 in 1811. Like his father he was not overly given to risky speculation; while more ambitious local printers attempted editions of the poets and Enlightenment texts James Chalmers & Co. (imprint adopted 1770) largely continued in its preferred, secure role as printers for the town council. Occasionally it adopted the conservative approach of publishing by subscription, and it remained the dominant local and regional printing business. As the owner of what was regarded as the most lucrative newspaper in Scotland James [iii] was a member of the Narrow Wynd and other respectable friendly societies. In 1787 he met Robert Burns, who described him as 'a facetious fellow' (Burns).

In the same year Chalmers began one of several unsuccessful new publishing ventures when he launched the *Northern Gazette*, which soon failed because of the burden of the stamp duty, and later reappeared as the *Aberdeen Magazine* (1788–91). Even the political preoccupations of the 1790s failed to provide sufficient stimulus to carry into print the *Aberdeen Courier*, due to have been published by Chalmers in partnership with two local booksellers. More successful was the *Aberdeen Almanack*, which first appeared in 1771 and sold throughout the north of Scotland. This annual finally ceased, with the 1955–6 edition, as the *Northern Year Book*. Chalmers's printing shop also provided stock for the chapbook trade, and several such works were produced by the company itself. Chalmers also acted as a local agent for newspapers published elsewhere. In 1803 he began a papermaking business with Alexander Brown, Aberdeen's principal bookseller, owner of the stamp office, and future tory provost, who in 1795 had married Chalmers's daughter Catherine. Contacts between Brown and Chalmers were undoubtedly of mutual benefit: the Chalmers family undertook most of the printing for Brown's many local publishing ventures. Notwithstanding the investment in steam-driven machinery the paper mill failed and in 1807 it closed. The first sustained challenge to the newspaper dynasty appeared in 1806 in the form of the *Aberdeen Chronicle*, though even its radical politics failed to draw any reaction at the time from the then stolidly neutral *Journal*.

James [iii] died in Aberdeen on 17 June 1810 and was buried at St Nicholas's Church; he was survived by his wife, who died on 14 August 1818, 'in her seventieth year'. The business was continued by their second son, **David Chalmers** (1778–1859), printer and publisher, who was born in Aberdeen on 19 October 1778. He was educated at Marischal College, and then began to work with his father on the *Aberdeen Journal*. On 27 February 1812 he married Ann Lamb Campbell (*d.* 1870), with whom he had seven sons and seven daughters. Under David Chalmers's control the business underwent significant changes, including a move to new premises at Adelphi Court, Aberdeen, in 1813 and the introduction of steam-powered presses for newspaper work about 1830. In other respects little changed and a considerable amount of civic printing was still undertaken. The political persuasion of the *Journal* became clearer with its support for tory interests in the 1832 election. That same year the *Journal* claimed the highest circulation of any newspaper in Scotland, a fact unhesitatingly drawn to the attention of advertisers. The appearance of a number of rival local newspapers (particularly the *Aberdeen Herald*, 1832, and the *Aberdeen Free Press*, 1853) helped consolidate the *Journal*'s own political stance. On Chalmers's retirement in 1854 the management passed to his two eldest sons, James [v] (*d.* 1896) and John Gray (*d.* 1890).

David Chalmers died on 24 April 1859 at his estate at Westburn, near Aberdeen (purchased in 1823), and was buried at St Nicholas's Church; his wife died, aged seventy-seven, on 20 March 1870. Six years later the family business was sold to form the North of Scotland Newspaper and Printing Co. Ltd, by which date the *Aberdeen Journal* had become a daily with conservative political principles. Late nineteenth-century competition for readers was intense, though the position of the *Journal* was made secure by John Gray Chalmers's bequest of £10,000, to be invested for the benefit of the paper. He also left a similar amount to endow the Chalmers chair of English literature at Aberdeen University. IAIN BEAVAN

Sources W. R. McDonald, 'Professional papers and research notes concerning Scottish bibliography, 1960s–1970s', U. Aberdeen, MS 3167 · A. A. Cormack, *The Chalmers family and Aberdeen newspapers* (1958) · I. Beavan, 'The nineteenth-century book trade in Aberdeen', PhD diss., Robert Gordon University, 1992 · J. M. Bulloch, 'Aberdeen periodicals: [a collection of newspapers cuttings]', U. Aberdeen · N. Harper, *Press and journal, the first 250 years: 1748–1998* (1997) · J. P. Edmond, *The Aberdeen printers: Edward Raban to James Nicol, 1620–1736* (1886) · G. Fraser and K. Peters, *The northern lights* (1978) · 'Genealogical tree [of the family of Chalmers]', U. Aberdeen, MS 2530 · W. R. McDonald, 'The *Aberdeen Journal* and the *Aberdeen Intelligencer*, 1752–7', *The Bibliotheck*, 5 (1967–70), 204–6 · Aberdeen Council, register, vol. 60, 1728–41, Aberdeen City Archives · R. M. W. Cowan, *The newspaper in Scotland: a study of its first expansion, 1815–1860* (1946) · 'Extracts from the diary of the Reverend John Bisset', *The miscellany of the Spalding Club*, ed. J. Stuart, 1, Spalding Club, 3 (1841) · W. Temple, *The thanage of Fermartyn* (1894) · A. Keith, *Eminent Aberdonians* (1984), 72–6 · R. Burns, *Tours of the highlands and Stirlingshire, 1787*, ed. R. Lamont-Brown (1973), 22 · *Scots Magazine*, 8 (1746), 343 · A. M. Munro, *Genealogical history of the family of Chalmers of Balnacraig and cadet branches* (1901), 118–35 · R. M. Lawrence, 'John Boyle, bookseller and bookbinder, Aberdeen', *Aberdeen Book-Lover*, 5/2 (1925), 43 · *Fasti academiae Mariscallanae Aberdonensis: selections from the records of the Marischal College and University, MDXCIII–MDCCCLX*, 2, ed. P. J. Anderson, New Spalding Club, 18

(1898) · family bible of James Chalmers, printer, Aberdeen and Margaret Douglas, married 1769, listing their descendants to 1825, U. Aberdeen, Historic collections, AU MS 3694
Archives U. Aberdeen
Likenesses portraits, repro. in Cormack, *Chalmers family*

Chalmers, Alexander (1759–1834), biographer and literary editor, was born on 29 March 1759 in Aberdeen and baptized that day at St Nicholas's in the city, the youngest son of James *Chalmers (*bap.* 1713, *d.* 1764), printer and publisher [*see under* Chalmers family (*per.* 1736–1876)], and his wife, Susan or Susanna, daughter of the Revd James Trail, minister at Montrose. His father had founded the *Aberdeen Journal*, which he edited until his death; his grandfather was the Revd James Chalmers (*d.* 1744), professor of divinity at Marischal College, Aberdeen.

Much of what is known about the life of Alexander Chalmers comes from a memoir written by John Bowyer Nichols, the son of Chalmers's good friend John Nichols, in the *Gentleman's Magazine* (Feb 1835) and reprinted in Nichols's *Illustrations*. According to this account, Chalmers left Aberdeen after receiving a classical and medical education. The institution from which he received his degree is not mentioned, but a footnote to a letter from Edmond Malone to Bishop Percy dated 9 December 1802 states that 'Chalmers was in the class of 1774–8 at Marischal College and University, where he took his M.A. degree' (*Correspondence of … Percy and … Malone*, 126 n. 31). When Chalmers left Scotland his plan was to serve as a surgeon in the West Indies, but on the way to Portsmouth to join his ship he changed his mind and went instead to London. According to John Taylor, a contemporary journalist and friend, he originally hoped to practise as a surgeon in London, but finding the city already well supplied with surgeons, he 'turned his attention to literary pursuits' (Taylor, 421). Thus began a long and successful career.

Chalmers first directed his attention to journalism. John Perry, also from Aberdeen, was on the staff of the *General Advertiser* in 1777, the approximate time of Chalmers's arrival in London. Deeply involved in London's journalistic scene, Perry became the conductor of the *General Advertiser*, *Gazetteer*, and *Morning Chronicle*, which he eventually bought. Although the accounts of Chalmers's life are vague on his early years in London, it was probably through Perry's efforts that he began his connection with the periodical press. He contributed to several newspapers and journals, and in 1788 began a relationship with the *Gentleman's Magazine* that was to continue throughout his productive years. His contributions included a monthly serial essay entitled 'The Projector' which ran for eight years, many miscellaneous pieces, and a thirteen-page memorial article to John Nichols. His well-known parody of James Boswell's *Life of Samuel Johnson, LL.D.*, 'Lesson in biography, or, How to write the life of one's friend', which has been described as the 'most exquisite and most neglected of prose parodies in our language' (Hollis, 164), first appeared in the *Morning Herald* (of which Chalmers had been editor) in July 1791. He also contributed to the *St James Chronicle*, *Morning Chronicle*, *Critical Review*, and *Analytical Review*.

Alexander Chalmers (1759–1834), by Richard James Lane, 1836

The details surrounding Chalmers's editorship of three London newspapers—the *London Packet*, *Morning Herald*, and *Public Ledger*—are meagre at best. In 1793, according to James Boswell, he was the editor of the *Public Ledger* and the former editor of the *London Packet*. He probably edited the *Packet* at some time during the American War of Independence. His tenure as editor of the *Morning Herald* ran from the latter part of 1781 to 1783, when the Revd Henry Bate, who later added Dudley to his name, resumed control of the newspaper.

It was as an editor and biographer that Chalmers made his most significant contributions to British literature. As John Bowyer Nichols noted, 'no man ever edited so many works for the Booksellers of London' (*GM*, 208). His major projects included Goldsmith's *An History of England in a Series of Letters from a Nobleman to his Son* (1793), Barclay's *A Complete and Universal Dictionary of the English Language* (1799), *The British Essayists* (1803) consisting of forty-five volumes with substantial biographical and critical prefaces written by Chalmers, Gibbon's *The Decline and Fall of the Roman Empire* (1807), and Cruden's *A Complete Concordance to the Holy Scriptures* (1805). He produced editions of the works of Pope, Burns, and Fielding, and of *The Tatler*, *The Spectator*, and *The Guardian*. During his lifetime he was perhaps best known for his contributions to an enlarged edition of the *General Biographical Dictionary* of 1798, which he revised and corrected, and to which he added almost 4000 lives. The subtitle, 'An historical and critical account of the lives and writings of the most eminent persons in every nation', gives some idea of its scope. In the preface he wrote, 'Of the lives retained from the last edition ... there are very few which are not, either in whole or in part, rewritten, or to which it has not been found necessary to make very important additions' (p. vi). Nichols calculates that Chalmers rewrote 2176 of the lives and wrote 3934 additional ones (*GM*, 209). The thirty-two volumes were published first monthly (vol. 1–4), and then every other month from May 1812 to March 1817. The dictionary remained standard for many years.

Another booksellers' project which remained, and remains, standard is the twenty-one volume *Works of the English Poets, from Chaucer to Cowper* (1810), an expanded version of the collection for which Samuel Johnson wrote the 'Prefaces, biographical and critical'. Chalmers was at liberty 'to form a collection of the more ancient poets to precede Dr. Johnson's series, and of the more recent authors to follow it' (preface, vi). He was responsible for all the new lives. Because many of the minor poets in this collection appear nowhere else, the work has become a valuable resource and continues to be reprinted.

Although he was regarded by some of his contemporaries as a retailer of minutiae and a booksellers' hack, Alexander Chalmers's extensive biographical and bibliographical research has been respected and cited by subsequent generations of students of British literature. For instance one biographer of James Beattie has written that Chalmers's account of Beattie in *The Works of the English Poets* is 'the best first hand account of Beattie and his writings' (King, 184), and according to Donald J. Greene, Chalmers was 'the assiduous corrector of Boswell' (Greene, 167). In *The British Essayists* Chalmers, who selected the periodicals for inclusion and wrote introductory prefaces for each, not only preserved many periodicals that might otherwise have been lost, but provided valuable analyses in the prefaces. Included in the original edition of 1803 are full runs of *The Tatler, The Spectator, The Guardian, The Rambler, The Adventurer, The World, The Connoisseur, The Idler, The Mirror, The Lounger,* and *The Observer*. The 1808 edition added *The Looker-On*. The collection went through numerous editions, and remains a valuable source for the lesser-known periodicals. Chalmers's original work on Samuel Johnson's essays *The Rambler, The Adventurer,* and *The Idler* is frequently cited in studies of those works. For instance, it was Chalmers who noted the thousands of alterations Johnson made for the second and third editions of *The Rambler*, of which Boswell, as well as earlier editors of Johnson's collected works, Sir John Hawkins and Arthur Murphy, appear to have been unaware. Also, Chalmers's estimate of the alterations that Johnson made to the *Idler* essays has since been confirmed by the editors of the Yale edition of that periodical. He also made valuable contributions to developing the canon of Samuel Johnson in his four editions of Johnson's works and edition of Boswell's *Life*.

Chalmers married in 1783 Elizabeth (*d.* 1816), the widow of John Gillett. Although baptized in the Church of Scotland he became a member of the Church of England. He died in Throgmorton Street on 10 December 1834 and was buried in a vault in the church of St Bartholomew, London, on 19 December. His will was proved in London on 31 December 1834. According to its terms Chalmers left £500 to his housekeeper and housemaid, and his house in Throgmorton Street and personal effects to his nephew David *Chalmers (1778–1859) [*see under* Chalmers family] of Aberdeen. BONNIE FERRERO

Sources *The correspondence of Thomas Percy and Edmond Malone*, ed. A. Tillotson (1944), vol. 1 of *The Percy letters*, ed. C. Brooks, A. N. Smith, and A. F. Falconer (1944–88) • W. L. Cross, *The history of Henry Fielding*, 3 (1918), 203 • B. Ferrero, 'Alexander Chalmers and the canon of Samuel Johnson', *British Journal for Eighteenth-Century Studies*, 22 (1999), 173–86 • *GM*, 2nd ser., 3 (1835), 207–10 • D. J. Greene, *Samuel Johnson: political writings* (New Haven, 1977) • C. Hollis, *Dr. Johnson* (New York, 1929) • E. H. King, *James Beattie* (Boston, 1977) • J. Taylor, *Records of my life*, new edn (New York, 1833) • L. Werkmeister, *The London daily press, 1772–1792* (1963) • E. P. Willey, 'The works of Alexander Chalmers, journalist, editor, biographer', *Bulletin of Research in the Humanities*, 86 (1983), 94–104 • *DNB* • *IGI* • will, PRO, PROB 11/1839, sig. 676
Archives NL Scot., papers
Likenesses R. J. Lane, lithograph, 1836, BM, NPG [*see illus.*] • G. P. Harding, lithograph, pubd 1837 (after W. Behnes), BM, NPG
Wealth at death £1000 bequests in will; also house on Throgmorton Street, London: will, PRO, PROB 11/1839, sig. 676

Chalmers, Archibald Kerr (1856–1942), medical officer of health, son of William Kerr Chalmers, a joiner, and Margaret Nichol, was born at Greenock, near Glasgow, on 10 April 1856. He entered Glasgow University in 1874 and graduated MB, CM, with high honours in 1879 and became houseman at the city's Belvidere Fever Hospital. Chalmers was in private practice for seven years before taking his MD with commendation in 1887 and the Cambridge diploma in public health in 1889. He was admitted to the fellowship of the Royal Faculty of Physicians and Surgeons of Glasgow in 1901. In 1892 he became full-time assistant to James Burn Russell, medical officer of health for Glasgow from 1872 to 1898. Russell joined the Scottish Local Government Board in 1898, and Chalmers was appointed Glasgow's medical officer of health, a position he occupied with distinction until his retirement in 1925.

Chalmers had a baptism of fire when, in 1900, Glasgow was struck with an outbreak of plague, which resurfaced in 1901. The plague was thought to have originated in Hong Kong about 1896 and had arrived, via Oporto, in Britain, where previously it had been absent since 1665. Despite his relative inexperience Chalmers, backed by the impressive sanitary organization built up by Russell, faced the difficulties well, perhaps in part because of his military experience, dating from the 1870s, with the local volunteer forces. Smallpox raged concurrently with plague, causing many deaths. However, apart from the rarity of plague, Glasgow's health problems were legion, stemming from overcrowded, insanitary living accommodation and poverty and hunger, and Chalmers met them all head on. It took time to improve housing and to increase environmental standards, but he made an early start on personal medical services such as those for mothers and children soon after the 1904 report of the interdepartmental committee on physical deterioration. The medical inspection of schoolchildren revealed the poor state of child health, against the backdrop of a crippling infant mortality in Glasgow of 14.9 per cent in 1901. Chalmers and some progressive councillors pioneered infant feeding by opening milk depots in 1904, based on Professor Budin's *Goutes de lait* in Paris. A female doctor employed in the city's health department began infant consultations. The child health movement grew and voluntary provisions followed on from Chalmers's initiative. Chalmers himself attended congresses in Paris on milk depots, to keep informed of European progress. By 1914 Glasgow had opened fourteen consultation centres with four doctors and ten trained health workers.

Strong leadership such as this was also echoed in the control of infectious disease and tuberculosis through the provision of new hospitals. Robroyston Hospital, for treating tuberculosis, opened in 1919, and Mearnskirk Hospital opened in 1922 specifically for children suffering from that disease. Chalmers carried out a positive onslaught on infectious diseases during his term of office, much of it aimed at protecting the health of the young. In 1920 he oversaw the reorganization of the city's sanitary department, when it became the public health department. This was no idle change of nomenclature. It was the point at which Glasgow accepted medical supervision of all medico-sanitary related provision. It was one of the last Scottish cities to do so.

Chalmers played a wide role in Scottish health policy. He was a member of the Belfast health commission in 1907 and a member of the Medical Research Committee from 1916 to 1918. He was an early member of the General Nursing Council and the Central Midwives' Board (Scotland), and of the consultative council of the Medical and Allied Services Committee (Scotland) shortly after the formation of the Scottish board of health in 1919. He was equally evident in academic and professional governance, being examiner for the Cambridge diplomas in public health, in hygiene, and in tropical medicine. He examined for the fellowship of the Royal Faculty of Physicians and Surgeons of Glasgow and for the degrees of public health and forensic medicine at the universities of Glasgow, Aberdeen, St Andrews, and Liverpool. He was deeply involved in the Royal Sanitary Association of Scotland and the British Medical Association. He wrote on a wide range of topics related to public health during his term of office, and he continued producing publications for many years after his retirement. He was made honorary LLD (Glasgow) in 1926.

Chalmers married Margaret Jessie, daughter of Henry Stewart, about 1879; the couple had two sons. Chalmers died in the Croydon Nursing Home, Bridge of Weir, Renfrewshire, on 24 January 1942.   BRENDA M. WHITE

Sources BMJ (7 Feb 1942), 202 · *Glasgow Herald* (7 Feb 1942) · *Glasgow Herald* (14 Feb 1942) · A. K. Chalmers, *The health of Glasgow, 1818–1925* (1930) · A. Macgregor, *Public health in Glasgow, 1905–1956* (1967) · A. K. Chalmers, Chalmers interests 1892–1925; press cuttings and photographs, Mitchell L., Glas., Glasgow City Archives, LP1/90 · *The Bailie* (7 June 1899) · *The Bailie* (13 Feb 1901) · G. E. Todd, *Who's who in Glasgow in 1909* (1909) · *Stothers's Glasgow, Lanarkshire and Renfrewshire Xmas and New Year annual* (1911) · *Report on certain cases of plague occurring in Glasgow in 1900, by the medical officer of health* (1901) · Medical officers' report on the plague in Glasgow (1901), *Annual report of the local government board Scotland for 1901* (1903) [CD 1521] · *Report of the Medical Officer of Health* [City of Glasgow] (1898–1925) · b. cert. · d. cert. · WW (1941) · WWW

Likenesses photographs, Mitchell L., Glas., Glasgow City Archives, LP1/90

Wealth at death £4191 10s. 1d.: confirmation, 16 April 1942, CGPLA Eng. & Wales

Chalmers [Chambers], **David, of Ormond** (c.1533–1592), historian and judge, was a younger son of Andrew Chalmers (*fl.* 1528–1554) of Strichen, Aberdeenshire, and his wife, Christine Fraser (*fl.* 1528–1554). He probably studied in Aberdeen (in the 1540s–1550s?) and certainly did so in Paris and Louvain (both in the 1550s); he also studied civil law at Bologna (in the 1550s). His uncle, Duncan Chalmers, chancellor of Ross, resigned his benefice to him about 1554, retaining a liferent. His uncle's resignation may have been connected with his attaining his majority about that time and taking holy orders. He was and remained a Catholic.

On the continent Chalmers entered the service of James Hepburn, fourth earl of Bothwell, thereby procuring the provostry of Crichton. He survived Bothwell's 1562 exile; on 26 January 1565 he succeeded his bishop, Henry Sinclair, as a judge of the court of session. Described as Bothwell's 'chief guyder' on the earl's rehabilitation in September, Chalmers was sent on an embassy to France (*CSP Scot.*, 1563–9, 211). After Riccio's murder he was forced on the unwilling burgh of Edinburgh as burgh clerk. He amassed property in the Black Isle, including the estate of Castleton or Ormond. Chalmers dedicated his manuscript 'Dictionary of Scots law' to the queen on 22 July 1566 (BL, Add. MS 27472). It was a digest under subject headings of medieval laws, statutes, and legal decisions, the first of its kind, antedating the better-known *Practicks* of his colleague Sir James Balfour.

Chalmers shared the downfall of Bothwell and Mary in June 1567 and by 27 October had fled to the Black Isle. He was forfeited in August 1568, his property passing to the Munros of Newmore. George Buchanan then propagated the untrue story that Bothwell had used Chalmers's house to facilitate an amorous encounter with Mary in 1566; Chalmers's enemies thereafter labelled him Bothwell's 'pandre' (*CSP Scot.*, 1571–4, 488).

Civil war resumed in January 1570, and Chalmers became a regular envoy from the queen's party to the Spanish Netherlands and France. He once acted for the Hamiltons alone, proposing that if Mary's deposition were confirmed, the family's head (James, duke of Châtelherault) should succeed to the Scottish throne. In 1570 or 1571 he settled at the French court as an adviser on Scottish affairs. He was accused in 1573 of co-authoring an anti-English squib, the *Treatise of Treasons*. Chalmers denied authorship in response to Lord Burghley's enquiries, thanked him for an offer of aid, and promised to repay any favours. He appears as a former English agent in 1584, grateful to Walsingham for past assistance; it is unclear which side he had been double-crossing. He went to Spain and the Netherlands in 1574–5, trying unsuccessfully to enter Spanish service. By February 1576 he had re-entered Mary's service. He annoyed her by his pro-Spanish views, but by 1578 was her master of requests. Mary was still writing to him in July 1581.

Chalmers also spent the 1570s renewing his scholarly pursuits. His *Histoire abbregée* (1572), written in French and dedicated to Charles IX, presented parallel narratives of the kings of France, England, and Scotland from earliest times to his own. In a second edition (1579) he added accounts of popes and emperors. The book was a small triumph of compilation, exposition, and typography. It placed Scotland in the mainstream of European history as seen by French readers, and emphasized the continuity of the Franco-Scottish alliance against England (dated by Chalmers to AD 792). Just to make sure, he included a description of that alliance as an appendix. Chalmers's history gains in interest from his assertion that he saw the mysterious chronicle of 'Veremund' from which Hector Boece had earlier claimed to derive his own mythical account of early Scottish history. In 1573 Chalmers published *Discours de la legitime succession des femmes*, a compliment to Mary, and also to Catherine de' Medici, the French queen mother, to whom it was dedicated. Finally, in 1579 he published *La recherche des singularitez plus remarquables concernant l'estat d'Écosse*, an introduction to Scotland's constitution and society. This stressed the civilized nature of the Scots, even the highlanders, and remarked (contrary to many received accounts of Scottish history) on the traditional harmony between Scottish kings and their subjects. The Francophile tone of these works does not conflict with Chalmers's pro-Spanish political leanings, since Frenchmen committed to the Counter-Reformation sought Spanish support.

In late 1582 Chalmers returned to Scotland from exile, allegedly bearing Spanish overtures to James VI. His forfeiture was rescinded on 4 September 1583. He still had to recover his property, and he acquired local allies by taking a wife, Christine, daughter of Alexander Ross of Balnagown, in 1585. Legal action and *force majeure* ejected the Munros, and on 21 July 1586 Chalmers regained his seat on the bench. Having finally settled down as a judge and royal administrator, he died on 18 October 1592 in the canonry of Ross, leaving three children, Elspeth, Christine, and William; his wife survived him.   JULIAN GOODARE

Sources *Calendar of the manuscripts of the most hon. the marquis of Salisbury*, 2, HMC, 9 (1888) [1572–82] · *CSP Scot.*, 1563–93 · 'Epistle', D. Chalmers, *La recherche des singularitez … concernant l'estat d'Ecosse* (1579) · G. Brunton and D. Haig, *An historical account of the senators of the college of justice, from its institution in MDXXXII* (1832) · *APS*, 1567–92 · *CSP for.*, 1569–74 · Baron Kervyn de Lettenhove [J. M. B. C. Kervyn de Lettenhove] and L. Gilliodts-van Severen, eds., *Relations politiques des Pays-Bas et de l'Angleterre sous le règne de Philippe II*, 11 vols. (Brussels, 1882–1900) · *Reg. PCS*, 1st ser., vol. 4 · Chalmers's 'Dictionary of Scots law', BL, Add. MS 27472 · privy seal register, NA Scot., PS1/55 · W. Forbes-Leith, ed., *Narratives of Scottish Catholics under Mary Stuart and James VI* (1885) · M. Lynch, *Edinburgh and the Reformation* (1981) · NA Scot., Cromartie MSS, GD305/1/167/1 · NA Scot., Ross of Pitcalnie MSS, GD199/20 · Edinburgh testaments, NA Scot., CC8/8/25, CC8/8/37 · G. Buchanan, *The tyrannous reign of Mary Stewart*, trans. W. A. Gatherer (1958) · *Correspondance diplomatique de Bertrand de Salignac de la Mothe Fénélon*, ed. A. Teulet, 5, Bannatyne Club, 67 (1840) · *CSP Spain, 1568–79* · *Lettres, instructions et mémoires de Marie Stuart, reine d'Écosse*, ed. A. Labanoff, 7 vols. (1844) · *CSP Rome, 1572–8* · *The correspondence of Robert Bowes, of Aske, esquire, the ambassador of Queen Elizabeth in the court of Scotland*, ed. [J. Stevenson], SurtS, 14 (1842) · books of sederunt, NA Scot., CS1/3/2 · J. M. Thomson and others, eds., *Registrum magni sigilli regum Scotorum / The register of the great seal of Scotland*, 11 vols. (1882–1914), vols. 3–4 · D. Calderwood, *The history of the Kirk of Scotland*, ed. T. Thomson and D. Laing, 8 vols., Wodrow Society, 7 (1842–9), vol. 4, pp. 2–3

Wealth at death £9592 Scots—incl. goods £437, debts owed to him £6343, and debts owed by him £395; supplementary testament incl. further debts £3207: Edinburgh testaments, NA Scot., CC 8/8/25, fol. 134v; Edinburgh testaments, NA Scot., CC 8/8/37, unfoliated (14 June 1603)

Chalmers, David (1778–1859). *See under* Chalmers family (*per.* 1736–1876).

Chalmers, George [styled Sir George Chalmers of Cults, fourth baronet] (c.1720×23–1791), portrait painter, was born in Edinburgh, the son of Sir George Chalmers (d. c.1764), who succeeded to the baronetcy in 1760 on the death of James Chalmers, brother of Sir Charles Chalmers who was apparently son and heir of Roderick Chalmers, Ross herald, who was recognized at the Lyon office c.1745 as the heir male of Cults. Cokayne noted that 'the succession to this Baronetcy is difficult to conjecture' (GEC, *Baronetage*, 3, 348–9). Although Cokayne lists Chalmers's entitlement to the baronetcy, this is questioned, the title having presumably become extinct after the death of the grantee (ibid.). Chalmers began his career as a heraldic painter and engraver. His earliest works date from 1738, and in 1739 he engraved two of his own portraits. Waterhouse noted that traces of his initial training persisted in his work, which was 'usually hard and wiry in outline' (Waterhouse, 75). After studying under Allan Ramsay in Edinburgh he travelled to Rome in the early 1750s; here he was patronized by the Jacobites the earl of Winton and Alexander Hay of Drummelzier. He also began a portrait of Isabella Lumisden and may have executed several history paintings (Ingamells, 193). After Rome, Chalmers travelled to Florence and then Minorca, where he painted a portrait of the governor of the island, General Blakeney, which was engraved by James McArdell.

On his return Chalmers settled first in Edinburgh, where on 4 June 1768 he married Isabella Alexander (d. 1784), daughter of John Alexander and sister of Cosmo Alexander, both painters and known Jacobites. They had one daughter, Isabella, who became a nun at York in 1796. In Edinburgh Chalmers enjoyed reasonable success. His most important commission came in 1771 from the Honourable Society of Edinburgh Golfers to paint their captain, William St Clair of Roslin (Hall of the Royal Company of Archers, Edinburgh); it is his most famous and accomplished work. The influence of Ramsay is evident in his portrait *Anne Kennedy* (1764, Blairquhan, Ayrshire) (McEwan, 123). J. L. Caw noted that his portraits, while competent, and showing considerable power of characterization, 'err in excessive projection of the features, and while fair in tone [are] rather hard in handling and negative in colour' (cited in McEwan, 123). Between 1775 and 1790 he exhibited at the Royal Academy, in 1775 and 1776 from addresses in London, between 1778 and 1780 from Hull, and between 1784 and 1790 in London. Of these pictures, twenty-three were portraits and one a Magdalen, exhibited in 1780. He died in Marylebone, Middlesex, and was buried on 15 November 1791 at St Pancras. Examples of his work may be found in the National Gallery of Scotland, the Scottish National Portrait Gallery, and the City of Edinburgh collection.

[ANON.], *rev.* DEBORAH GRAHAM-VERNON

Sources Redgrave, *Artists* · D. Irwin and F. Irwin, *Scottish painters at home and abroad, 1700–1900* (1975) · Waterhouse, *18c painters* · J. Ingamells, ed., *A dictionary of British and Irish travellers in Italy, 1701–1800* (1997) · D. Macmillan, *Scottish art, 1460–1990* (1990) · Graves, *RA exhibitors* · P. J. M. McEwan, *Dictionary of Scottish art and architecture* (1994) · GEC, *Baronetage*
Wealth at death under £300: administration, GEC, *Baronetage*, 3.349

Chalmers, George (*bap.* 1742, *d.* 1825), antiquary and political writer, was born in Fochabers, Bellie parish, Morayshire, and baptized there on 26 December 1742, the son of James Chalmers, postmaster at Fochabers, and his wife, Isabella Ruddock. He attended the parish school of Bellie and later appears to have studied at King's College, University of Aberdeen, before reading law at Edinburgh University. One of Chalmers's uncles was involved in a lawsuit in Maryland, in which it was felt that Chalmers's legal knowledge might be useful. Accordingly, Chalmers arrived in America on the *Chesapeake* in August 1763. He spent the next twelve years of his life in Maryland. On 18 December 1764 he purchased 1007 acres of land, which he called Fochabers, after his birthplace. However, he probably never intended to occupy it, because he sold it, at a considerable profit, on 23 June 1768. After 1768 he practised law in Baltimore. America at this time was experiencing the severe discontent which led to the War of Independence. A known and vocal loyalist, Chalmers became unpopular, and was sufficiently afraid of possible threats to carry pistols wherever he went. As America moved towards the break with Britain, the position of Chalmers and other loyalists became untenable, and, in September 1775 he left for England; he arrived in London in November.

It is unknown what Chalmers did during the next year and a half, but he may have visited Paris in 1777. However, in May of that year he was in London, where he published his *Answer from the Electors of Bristol to the Letter of Edmund Burke*. This was an attack on Burke's pro-American views, insisting that, far from having been too severe, the British government had been too lenient on the American colonists. This pamphlet showed all the features that would characterize Chalmers's later writings. His views can be described as broadly tory, in that he generally defended constituted government, particularly if monarchical, and regarded opposition to authority as sedition. These attitudes also emerged in the sentimental Jacobitism which influenced his views on Scottish subjects, especially Mary, queen of Scots. Although baptized in the Church of Scotland, he later changed to the Church of England, whose respectful attitude to authority was more compatible with

George Chalmers (*bap.* 1742, *d.* 1825), by Henry Edridge, 1809

his political views than Presbyterianism, which, historically, has often been notable for independence and opposition to government.

Like many loyalists who settled in England, Chalmers had financial trouble, and in June 1777 he applied for relief from government by sending a memorial to Sir Grey Cooper, secretary of the Treasury. This memorial was considered in August 1777, and Chalmers was awarded an immediate payment of £100 and £100 per annum thereafter. He evidently felt this to be inadequate, because he sent further memorials in 1782 and 1783. He also continued to agitate for general recompense for exiled loyalists.

Chalmers spent the early 1780s in literary projects designed to arouse opinion against the Americans and their British supporters. In 1780 he published his *Annals of the Present United Colonies*, in which he insisted that the American colonies had always had a subversive desire for independence and that parliament had the right to tax the colonies without their consent. In 1782 he produced his *Introduction to the History of the Revolt of the Colonies*, which was even more severe on the Americans, and highly critical of the weakness of the British government in dealing with them. The first volume, covering events up to the reign of George I, was printed by Baker and Galabin in 1782, but Chalmers immediately suppressed it. He was seeking employment from the government at the time, and probably felt that his chances would be weakened by a work criticizing governmental feebleness. Also in 1782 he published his *Estimate of the Comparative Strength of Great Britain during the Present and Four Preceding Reigns*, which took issue with the economic opinions of pro-American writers such as Richard Price, and stressed that gloomy predictions about declining British trade and population were ill founded. It stated that both trade and population had increased over the years, that Britain had always recovered from trade depressions, and that recent British history showed continuous expansion and progress. This proved to be a successful work: it went through seven editions in twenty-five years and was translated into most European languages. It also appealed to government, and George III personally ordered a copy from a bookseller.

Chalmers's efforts did not go unnoticed in official circles, and he was brought to the attention of Charles Jenkinson, later first earl of Liverpool, president of the committee of the privy council for the consideration of all matters relating to trade and foreign plantations. In August 1786 Chalmers was appointed chief clerk to this committee, at a salary of £500 per annum. He held this post until his death. In August 1792 the assembly of the Bahamas, remembering Chalmers's services to American loyalists, appointed him agent for the Bahamas in London. As agent, he saw himself as accountable to the assembly, which was often in conflict with the British government and its representatives, the various governors of the Bahamas, particularly over the issue of slavery. In 1815 he produced a pamphlet attacking a proposal to register slaves, in order to prevent the smuggling of new slaves from Africa into the colonies after the banning of the slave trade in 1807. This matter put Chalmers in an awkward position, because he was forced to use arguments about the rights of colonial legislatures similar to those that he had attacked in the 1770s and 1780s. He also used his position in the committee of trade to help his colonial employers. In 1817 the governor of the Bahamas complained that the assembly was receiving vital information and documents before he was, which could only have come from its agent in the committee. Chalmers was required to promise not to use official documents for such purposes again.

Chalmers's official duties were not onerous, and he had time to pursue his literary and antiquarian interests. He was elected to the Society of Antiquaries on 13 January 1791 and to the Royal Society on 5 May of the same year. On 20 November 1792 he was admitted to the Scottish Society of Antiquaries as a corresponding member. In 1794 he produced a life of the early eighteenth-century Scottish printer and antiquarian Thomas Ruddiman. This biography verges on panegyric: Ruddiman, an Episcopalian Jacobite, was a man after Chalmers's own heart. Chalmers's prejudices also led him to denigrate Ruddiman's contemporary James Anderson, whom he disliked as a Presbyterian, a whig, and a champion of George Buchanan, the sixteenth-century Scottish historian who had attacked Mary, queen of Scots, and disseminated the Scottish whig Presbyterian theory that monarchs can be justly resisted and deposed by their subjects. Chalmers even suggested that Anderson's important *Diplomata Scotiae* was largely the work of its editor, Ruddiman.

Between 1807 and 1824 Chalmers published what he regarded as his major work, *Caledonia*, an encyclopaedic regional survey of Scottish history and antiquities, which was not completed in his lifetime. His original plan called for six volumes, but only three were published before he died. Chalmers worked extremely hard on the project, and conducted exhaustive research. However, the work was for many years regarded as dated, erroneous, and even unoriginal, and was compared unfavourably with the efforts of English antiquaries. It has only recently been recognized that the *Caledonia* was in many ways a valuable piece of research into the remoter periods of Scottish history. As William Ferguson has pointed out, the work made a particularly important contribution regarding the identity of the Picts, whose origins have always been problematic. Chalmers stated that they were a non-Gaelic Celtic people, akin to the Britons and Gauls, which is the theory generally held by scholars today. This had been tentatively suggested by earlier historians, notably Buchanan and Thomas Innes, but Chalmers's work, in Ferguson's words, constituted 'a major breakthrough' and seriously challenged the influential but wholly inaccurate views of John Pinkerton and Malcolm Laing, who held that the Picts were Germanic rather than Celtic (Ferguson, 277).

In 1818 Chalmers published his *Life of Mary, Queen of Scots*, a work so saturated in sentimental Jacobitism and political prejudice that it has little value as an account. Chalmers took a view similar to that of John Whitaker, whose *Vindication* of Mary he admired and praised, and therefore saw Mary as the helpless and innocent victim of conspirators, and all her opponents as corrupt and evil. Any historian who took a different view of Mary was mercilessly attacked, from Buchanan onwards, and much of his work is given to criticizing the highly successful eighteenth-century Scottish Presbyterian historian William Robertson, for his supposedly hostile treatment of Mary. Chalmers's dislike of Presbyterianism also led him to take a severe view of the early Scottish reformers, especially John Knox, whose opinions on both Mary and the right of resistance to monarchs struck Chalmers as subversive.

Chalmers published numerous other works during his life. He was among the literati who were fooled by William Henry Ireland's Shakespeare forgeries and wrote several tracts on the controversy. He also wrote on Irish affairs, British economics and domestic policy, English jurisprudence, and the authorship of the Junius letters. He naturally opposed the French Revolution and wrote a highly critical biography of one of its greatest defenders, Thomas Paine, under the pseudonym of Oldys.

Chalmers never married, and died at his London house at 3 James Street, Buckingham Gate, on 31 May 1825. He was buried in the churchyard of St Margaret's Church, Westminster, on 6 June. Strangely for a lawyer, he made no will, and his brother James had to apply for admission to administer his estate, which was valued at £7000.

ALEXANDER DU TOIT

Sources G. A. Cockcroft, *The public life of George Chalmers* (New York, 1939) · Anderson, *Scot. nat.*, 1.620 · W. T. Lowndes, *The bibliographer's manual of English literature*, ed. H. G. Bohn, [new edn], 1

(1864), 403–4 · W. Ferguson, *The identity of the Scottish nation: an historic quest* (1998), 276–8 · C. Kidd, *Subverting Scotland's past: Scottish whig historians and the creation of an Anglo-British identity, 1689–c.1830* (1993), 253–4 · *DNB*

Archives BL, corresp. and papers, Add. MSS 14036, 15744–15747, 18901–18902, 22900–22903, 26694–26695, 27952, 32166, 32498, 33610 · BL, statistics relating to Church of Scotland stipends and collection relating to monastic history of Scotland, Add. MSS 15744–15747 · Bodl. Oxf., corresp. and papers · Bodl. Oxf., papers relating to Shakespeare · L. Cong., corresp. and papers · LUL, papers relating to Ireland · Montrose Museum, letters and notes for *Caledonia* · NL Scot., corresp., notes, and papers · NL Scot., notes on Scottish parliaments and British topography · NYPL, papers relating to American colonies · U. Edin. L., corresp., notes, and papers · U. Hull, Brynmor Jones L., corresp. and papers · V&A, papers · Yale U., Beinecke L., chronology of Scottish kings | BL, letters to Sir Joseph Banks, Add. MS 33982 · BL, corresp. with Lord Liverpool, Add. MSS 38218–38473; loan 72 · BL, letters to Arthur Young, Add. MSS 35127, 35130 · NL Scot., corresp. with Archibald Constable · NL Scot., letters to Edward Ellice · NL Scot., corresp. with G. Paton · NL Scot., letters to Charles Steuart · priv. coll., letters to Sir John Sinclair · U. Edin. L., letters to David Laing

Likenesses J. Tassie, paste medallion, 1796, Scot. NPG · H. Edridge, watercolour, 1809, NPG [*see illus.*] · J. Tannock, oils, 1824, Scot. NPG · A. Geddes, oils, Scot. NPG

Wealth at death £7000: Cockcroft, *George Chalmers* · £6190 11s.—value of library when sold by auction in 1841

Chalmers, George Paul (1833–1878), portrait and landscape painter, the son of Stewart Chalmers (1804–1848), seaman and captain of a coasting vessel, and Marjory Torrie (1810–1879), barmaid and innkeeper, was born in Montrose on 12 November 1833. He was educated at the burgh school and thereafter apprenticed to Alexander Thomson, general grocer and ship-chandler. As a schoolboy he took to sketching, and by about 1851 he was painting oil portraits of local people which helped to fund his move to Edinburgh in November 1853. He attended the Trustees' Academy under the inspirational teaching of Robert Scott Lauder for three sessions, winning prizes in his second and third years. He also made copies of old master paintings in the Royal Institution. In 1855 he had a painting accepted for the Royal Scottish Academy annual exhibition and thereafter was a regular exhibitor.

On completion of his studies Chalmers returned to Montrose. He joined a fellow student, William McTaggart, on a visit to the 'Fine art treasures' exhibition in Manchester in 1857. In addition to the old master paintings, he was particularly impressed by Turner's landscapes: these were to have a lasting impact for the rest of his career. In 1859 he settled in Edinburgh again and established a portrait painting practice. He visited Ireland in 1858, and from 1860 to 1861 attended the newly re-formed Royal Scottish Academy life school, winning a prize for his figure drawing. As his income increased, Chalmers travelled further afield visiting London, Kent, and Surrey in the 1860s, Brittany (with fellow artists John Pettie and Thomas Graham) in 1862, and Arran in 1867, a popular destination with Scottish painters of the day. He frequently returned to Montrose, and spent time in the remote Glen Esk in Forfarshire and also in Aberdeen. There Chalmers met the art connoisseur and collector John Forbes White, who became a close friend and supporter. White was an important collector of contemporary European painting, particularly of Corot and the Hague school. His collection was influential in the development of Chalmers's work and through him the painter met Joseph Israels in Aberdeen in 1870. In 1872 Chalmers paid a brief study visit to Paris and the Low Countries. By way of formal recognition he was elected an associate of the Royal Scottish Academy in 1867, and an academician in 1871.

Chalmers began his career as a self-taught painter of portraits. Although he studied in the formal art classes of the day he never became an accomplished draughtsman. Instead he concentrated on capturing the effects of light and colour, and employed gentle modelling against plain, dark backgrounds. His early works have a looseness of handling which conceals deficiencies in drawing. In his later paintings Chalmers aimed for a high degree of finish, without losing the harmony of pictorial effect. This striving for perfection often caused him to spend many years reworking paintings, the most notable being *The Legend* (1864–78; National Gallery of Scotland, Edinburgh) which remained unfinished at his death. This painting, of an old woman enthralling a group of children with her tales, is an example of the type of cottage subject that Chalmers painted in his mid-career. Later ones depict the bleakness of rural life, such as *The Eagle's Nest, Skye* (National Gallery of Scotland, Edinburgh) in which a shepherd drives his sheep through a dreich landscape under heavy, rain-filled clouds. Chalmers first visited Skye in 1867 and it was the rain, not the mountains, that impressed him. Late in his career he turned increasingly to landscape, especially rivers and lochs. He painted two versions of *Running Water* (1874 and 1875–7) from a platform directly above the North Esk River. A particularly fine late landscape, *The Head of Loch Lomond* (Dundee Art Galleries and Museums), is worked in soft greys, blues, and greens rather than the previously favoured browns. It evokes most subtly the effect of the mist rising from the loch, reminiscent of Turner's landscapes, and its silvery tones recall the landscapes of Corot.

On 15 February 1878 Chalmers attended the Royal Scottish Academy annual dinner. Afterwards he visited the Artists' Club where he spoke in praise of Corot's paintings: his views were not appreciated and he left soon afterwards. In the early hours of 16 February Chalmers was found in a doorway severely wounded; he died four days later in Edinburgh Royal Infirmary. Although he had lost his money, watch, and hat, the police never determined the exact circumstances of his death. His funeral on 23 February attracted great crowds as the coffin was taken in procession from St Stephen's Church to the Dean cemetery in Edinburgh.

A slight man, with light brown hair which gave way to baldness, Chalmers lived quietly and yet enjoyed the convivial company of his fellow artists. He never married and in later years looked after his ageing mother in Edinburgh. Chalmers was only forty-four when he died and his career as a painter was cut short by his premature death.

JOANNA SODEN

Sources E. Pinnington, *George Paul Chalmers and the art of his times* (1896) · A. Gibson and J. F. White, *George Paul Chalmers RSA* (1879) · E. Pinnington, 'George Paul Chalmers', *Art Journal*, new ser., 17 (1897), 83–8 · J. L. Caw, *Scottish painting past and present, 1620–1908* (1908), 244–7 · D. Irwin and F. Irwin, *Scottish painting at home and abroad* (1975), 344–8 · W. Hardie, *Scottish painting, 1837 to the present* (1990), 74–6 · R. Brydall, *Art in Scotland, its origin and progress* (1889), 382–4 · L. Errington, *Master class: Robert Scott Lauder and his pupils* (1983) [exhibition catalogue, NG Scot., 15 July – 2 Oct 1983, and Aberdeen Art Gallery, 15 Oct – 12 Nov 1983] · P. J. M. McEwan, *Dictionary of Scottish art and architecture* (1994), 123 · C. B. de Laperriere, ed., *The Royal Scottish Academy exhibitors, 1826–1990*, 4 vols. (1991), vol. 1, pp. 293–4 · *Annual Report of the Council of the Royal Scottish Academy of Painting, Sculpture, and Architecture*, 51 (1878), 270 · b. cert.
Archives Royal Scot. Acad., letter collection | NL Scot., letters to William McTaggart · Royal Scot. Acad., George B. Simpson collection
Likenesses J. Pettie, oils, 1862, Scot. NPG · J. G. Tunny, photograph, 1866, Royal Scot. Acad. · G. Reid, oils, 1878, Aberdeen Art Gallery · G. P. Chalmers, self-portrait, oils, Royal Scot. Acad. · G. P. Chalmers, self-portrait, oils, Scot. NPG · J. Farquharson, oils, Scot. NPG · J. Hutchinson, marble bust, Dean cemetery, Edinburgh
Wealth at death £5287 12s. 3d.: confirmation, 5 April 1878, CCI

Chalmers, James (*bap.* 1713, *d.* 1764). *See under* Chalmers family (*per.* 1736–1876).

Chalmers, James (1742–1810). *See under* Chalmers family (*per.* 1736–1876).

Chalmers, James (1782–1853), Post Office reformer, was born in Arbroath on 2 February 1782, and at an early age became a bookseller in Castle Street, Dundee, and was for some time the printer and publisher of the *Dundee Chronicle*. He married a Miss Dickson of Montrose and they had at least one son. He took a prominent part in public matters, first as dean and afterwards as convener of the nine incorporated trades. Later he was returned to the town council, and held the office of treasurer for several years. He was always eager to lend a helping hand in local charities. In 1825 he applied himself to the acceleration of the mails, and mainly through his efforts the time for a letter to travel between London and Dundee was lessened by a day each way.

Having become committed to the cause of Post Office reform, Chalmers was one of many who worked for change in the late 1830s. He presented his ideas to Robert Wallace, MP for Greenock and chairman of the fifth committee on Post Office reform, in December 1837, and he also corresponded on the subject with Joseph Hume MP, Henry Cole, and Rowland Hill himself, in 1839 and 1840. He was one of 2600 unsuccessful participants in the 1839 competition for stamp design sponsored by the Treasury. On 1 January 1846, at a public meeting of the citizens of Dundee, he was presented with a silver claret jug, a salver, and a purse of fifty sovereigns for his successful efforts in reducing the time required for the transit of the mails and for his plans for a uniform postage rate and an adhesive stamp. He was an excellent man of business, well known for his integrity and upright character in his commercial activities. He died at Comley Bank, Dundee, on 26 August 1853, aged seventy-one, and was buried in the old burying-ground on 1 September.

After the death of Sir Rowland Hill in 1879, Patrick Chalmers, son of James Chalmers, inserted advertisements and letters in newspapers, and published some forty pamphlets in which he argued that his father had invented the postage stamp in 1834, three years before Rowland Hill claimed to have done so. Patrick Chalmers went on to assert that his father had been fraudulently deprived of credit for his invention. A heated debate between Pearson Hill, Sir Rowland's son, and Patrick Chalmers ensued. While the ninth edition of the *Encyclopaedia Britannica* (1886) credited James Chalmers with the invention of the postage stamp, there is little evidence to support this judgement. Rowland Hill suggested use of postage stamps in the second edition of *Post Office Reform*, which appeared in February 1837. James Chalmers did not make his ideas publicly known until December of that year. As is the case with many 'inventions', exact moments of creation are difficult to fix. Adhesive revenue stamps, for example, had been used on patent medicine bottles before either Hill or Chalmers advocated the use of stamps for postage. [ANON.], *rev.* C. R. PERRY

Sources H. Robinson, *The British Post Office: a history* (1948) · P. Chalmers, *James Chalmers the inventor of the "adhesive stamp", not Sir Rowland Hill* (1884) · M. J. Daunton, *Royal Mail: the Post Office since 1840* (1985)
Archives BL, papers and papers relating to him, Add. MS 49383
Likenesses oils, Dundee City Art Gallery

Chalmers, James (1841–1901), missionary and explorer, was born at Ardrishaig, Argyll, on 4 August 1841, the son of John Chalmers (1802–1869), a stonemason from Peterhead. His mother, Mary, *née* Glen (1808–1876), came from Luss on Loch Lomond. Brought up in Ardrishaig, Lochgilphead, and Glenaray, with three younger sisters, one of whom was adopted, he was educated at the village schools. Of these the most important was that run by the Scottish Society for the Promotion of Christian Knowledge in Glenaray under John MacArthur, where Chalmers frequently won prizes. He then went to Inveraray grammar school. He also learnt much from Gilbert Meikle, the young United Presbyterian minister at Inveraray, who encouraged his parishioners' interest in home and overseas missions. A letter from a Fiji missionary read to his Sunday-school class made Chalmers seriously consider becoming a missionary in September 1855, and at about the same time he took up a clerical apprenticeship with the Inveraray lawyers Maclullich and Macniven. During the powerful religious revival of 1859, which swept Argyll in the autumn, Chalmers underwent a religious conversion, and he was formally admitted a member of the United Presbyterian church in the spring of 1860. In November he joined the Glasgow City Mission, to earn money for his further education and ministerial training. Persuaded by Dr George Turner, a well-known missionary from Samoa working for the London Missionary Society (LMS), he applied to that society in February 1862 and was admitted for ministerial instruction to Cheshunt College in Hertfordshire in September.

A boisterous student who found formal learning ever more difficult, Chalmers remained at Cheshunt until June

James Chalmers (1841–1901), by unknown photographer

1864. He then spent a final year acquiring a specific missionary training, chiefly at the LMS's Farquhar House, Highgate, in London, but also at Plumstead, learning the Rarotongan language under the missionary William Gill. In October 1865 he was ordained a Congregationalist minister. He married Jane K. Robertson Hercus (*d.* 1879), a schoolteacher, on 8 November 1865, and they set sail for the Pacific on 4 January 1866; they finally reached Rarotonga on 20 May 1867, after being shipwrecked on Niue and numerous other mishaps.

Like many volunteers inspired by David Livingstone, Chalmers had once thought of Africa, but from 1871 he was anxious to join the new LMS initiative in New Guinea. First, however, he spent ten years in Rarotonga, most of them in charge of the LMS institution and training Rarotongan agents. Recognizing the revolutionary impact of a European presence and the necessarily gradual penetration of Christian belief, he placed every confidence in his charges and was anxious to build up their independence rapidly in both church and state. 'They must act for themselves … Unless the natives are taught to look after their own Island and prepare for the future they will not be able to resist the pressure of the white faces', he wrote in his 1874 report (Hitchen, 26). His methods were often seen as casual and unconventional, for he avoided genteel living and Anglicization, preferring instead the assimilation of missionaries into indigenous conditions of diet or housing where possible; he also encouraged the inculcation of the gospel through the ordinary experiences of everyday life. This attracted criticism from some colleagues devoted to the formalities of 'civilized' life in 'raising' the islanders, as well as from others who either drew the line at Chalmers's ready enjoyment of whisky or simply feared for his own and his wife's survival. However, many others were devoted admirers of Tamate, as the Rarotongans called him, and his friendships especially with the local people were powerful and lasting.

New Guinea, with its reputedly wild and cannibalistic tribes, had long been the goal of LMS expansion in the Pacific, and Chalmers's offer to go there was finally accepted in December 1875. He left Rarotonga in May 1877, and visited W. G. Lawes in October at Port Moresby before settling himself for two years at Suau Island. Subsequently he lived at Port Moresby for nearly a decade, at Toaripi (1889–92; otherwise Motumotu), Saguane (1896–1900), and for the last months of his life at Daru. In New Guinea, Chalmers felt genuinely fulfilled as a missionary. Perhaps naturally restless, certainly relishing the pioneering aspects of his journeys, and able to satisfy his endless curiosity about new landscapes or peoples, he also believed theologically and practically that the true missionary should be constantly breaking new ground. There was for him no conflict between pioneering as a white person and the European missionary's role. He travelled endlessly, especially by boat, visiting village after village, often as the first European to be seen there. Establishing peaceful contact and fixing on potential stations were the essential complements of training the native agents, who were to be placed as soon as possible. However, this conception of his task, while acceptable to the LMS under Joseph Mullens in the 1870s, became much less so under Ralph Wardlaw Thompson's secretaryship.

Chalmers's contribution to European knowledge of Papua New Guinea is still debated but was undoubtedly considerable. He gathered botanical and geographical information, especially around the Gulf of Papua. His ethnographic work brought a close friendship with the anthropologist A. C. Haddon, which in turn refined both men's investigations. Firsthand information, Chalmers believed, was a vital basis for his missionary strategy. From the mid-1880s he began to publish widely in learned journals such as the proceedings of the Glasgow Philosophical Society and the Royal Geographical Society, as well as with the Religious Tract Society. His first book, *Work and Adventure in New Guinea, 1877–1885* (1885), and his *Pioneering in New Guinea* (1887), became especially well known. Although preferring English as the language of instruction, he nevertheless translated the synoptic gospels into Motu, which others like Lawes regarded as a potential lingua franca spreading out from Port Moresby.

His aim of 'New Guinea for the New Guineans' led him to cultivate good relations with the British naval and consular officials, many of whom became heavily dependent on his influence and advice. Naturally this won 'the tyrant missionary' enemies among some of the local traders and their supporters in the Australian press. Visiting Brisbane in 1883 he was active in the movement leading to the British imperial protectorate and to the official ending of Queensland's labour recruiting in New Guinea in 1885. He regretted the intrusion of outsiders while realizing its inevitability, and worked to minimize its impact, being as ready to help gold-diggers as government officials with advice which he believed would reconcile their interests and those of the Papuans.

Chalmers left New Guinea infrequently, visiting New Zealand in 1877 and again briefly after his wife's death in 1879. He hated the work of missionaries on furlough, referring to it in 1884 as 'the begging-friar business' with its 'telling of excited painted tales … lying reports, [and] salted statistics' (Hitchen, 61–2). Nevertheless, his visits to Britain in 1886–7 to publicize New Guinea's needs, and in 1894–5 during the LMS centenary, were regarded as missionary triumphs and made his a household name.

On 6 October 1888 Chalmers married Sarah Elizabeth (Lizzie) Harrison, *née* Large, old friend of his first wife and recently widowed. Happy enough with him she found the spartan conditions and loneliness during Chalmers's travels hard to bear. In the 1890s Chalmers attended particularly to the remote western districts on the Fly River, hoping to penetrate permanently well inland. He failed. With his energy and health declining, and his wife having died at Saguane, on 25 October 1900, he was forced to move to Daru. Finally, on 8 April 1901, on an expedition to Goaribari Island with the Revd Oliver Tompkins, Chalmers and his party were captured, clubbed, killed, and eaten.   ANDREW PORTER

Sources *James Chalmers: his autobiography and letters*, ed. R. Lovett (1902) · J. M. Hitchen, 'Formation of the 19th-century missionary worldview: the case of James Chalmers', PhD diss., 2 vols., U. Aberdeen, 1984 · D. Langmore, *Tamate, a king: James Chalmers in New Guinea, 1877–1901* (1974) · P. A. Prendergast, 'Chalmers, James', *AusDB*, vol. 3
Archives SOAS, letters and papers | Mitchell L., NSW, LMS Papua archives
Likenesses photograph, repro. in J. W. Lindt, *Picturesque New Guinea* (1887) · photographs, SOAS, Council for World Mission Archives · photographs, repro. in Langmore, *Tamate, a king*, 32, 112 · photographs, repro. in *James Chalmers*, ed. Lovett, frontispiece, 288 [*see illus.*]

Chalmers, Sir John (1756–1819), army officer in the East India Company, was a younger son of Patrick Chalmers of Balnacraig, near Aboyne, Aberdeenshire, and went to India as an ensign in the Madras infantry in 1775. He was promoted lieutenant in 1780, and won a reputation by his heroic defence of Coimbatore during the Third Anglo-Mysore War, in 1791. In the same year Charles, second Earl Cornwallis (1738–1805), the governor-general and commander-in-chief, finding it impossible to advance at once upon Seringapatam, the capital of Tipu, sultan of Mysore, ordered Major Cuppage to abandon the fortresses held by the British in the Mysore country, except Palgaut and Coimbatore, which commanded the passes of the Ghats, and even to abandon Coimbatore (captured in July 1790) if it could not be held. Cuppage therefore ordered Chalmers, who held Coimbatore with only 120 topasses (Indian soldiers of part Portuguese descent), to abandon it and to join him at Palgaut. Chalmers, finding that two 3-pounder and one 4-pounder barrels were serviceable, and improvising carriages for them, asked Cuppage to

send him 500 shot, and to allow him to defend the fortress. He was joined by a young Frenchman, Migot de la Combe, with 200 Travancoreans, of whom about half deserted while the others were 'extremely insubordinate' (Philippart, 333), and prepared for a siege. On 13 June 1791 Coimbatore was surrounded by one of Tipu's generals with about 2000 regular infantry, many irregulars, eight guns, and 'abundance of rockets' (ibid., 334), and was bombarded for nearly two months. On 11 August an assault was made but, owing to the improvised mines—small barrels of powder, with fuses—Chalmers used at the breach, it was repelled with loss. The defenders sallied out and captured two guns, and the Mysore army retreated. The gallant defence attracted the attention of Lord Cornwallis, who sent Lieutenant Nash, Madras infantry, with a company of sepoys to reinforce Chalmers, increasing the garrison to about 700 men. Tipu determined on a yet more vigorous attack. On 6 October Kummur-ud-deen, Tipu's most famous general, laid siege with about 8000 regular infantry, many irregulars, and fourteen guns and four mortars.

Again Chalmers made a protracted defence; but at last, when the ammunition was almost expended and both he and Nash were wounded, he capitulated on 3 November 1791, on condition he be allowed to march with his men to Palgaut. The fall of Coimbatore, though a set-back for the British, was not strategically important. It did not seriously interfere with Cornwallis's plans as his convoys were not using the southern route. The capitulation was violated by Tipu, and Chalmers and Nash were taken prisoners to Seringapatam in 1792. Tipu, however, treated them well, and when Cornwallis appeared before Seringapatam and demanded their release before he would enter negotiations, they were sent safe into his camp on 8 February 1792. Cornwallis had not approved of defending Coimbatore, but he acknowledged Chalmers's bravery, and recommended him to the court of directors for a financial reward. Chalmers was promoted captain on 3 October 1792, major on 27 July 1796, lieutenant-colonel in the company's service on 31 July 1799, colonel on 8 April 1808, and major-general on 1 January 1812, and was made a KCB when that order was first opened to the company's officers in April 1815. He commanded the subsidiary force at Travancore from 1803 to 1809, and the northern division of the Madras presidency from 1812 to 1817. He left India, after forty-two years' continuous service in the Madras presidency, and died on board the *Marquis of Wellington* on his way home to England on 31 March 1819.

H. M. STEPHENS, *rev.* ROGER T. STEARN

Sources Dodwell [E. Dodwell] and Miles [J. S. Miles], eds., *Alphabetical list of the officers of the Indian army: with the dates of their respective promotion, retirement, resignation, or death … from the year 1760 to the year … 1837* (1838) · J. Philippart, *East India military calendar*, 2 (1824) · M. Wilks, *Historical sketches of the south of India, in an attempt to trace the history of Mysoor*, 3 vols. (1810–17) · P. Moon, *The British conquest and dominion of India* (1989) · H. H. Dodwell, ed., *British India, 1497–1858* (1929), vol. 4 of *The Cambridge history of the British empire* (1929–59) · T. A. Heathcote, *The military in British India: the development of British land forces in south Asia, 1600–1947* (1995) · C. A. Bayly,

Indian society and the making of the British empire (1988), vol. 2/1 of *The new Cambridge history of India*, ed. G. Johnson

Chalmers, Sir **Mackenzie Dalzell** (1847–1927), judge and civil servant, was born on 7 February 1847 at Nonington, near Barham, Kent, the second son of the Revd Frederick Skene Courtenay Chalmers, rector of Nonington and his wife, Matilda, daughter of the Revd William *Marsh, honorary canon of Worcester Cathedral and perpetual curate of St Mary's, Leamington Spa. He was educated at King's College, London. His studies at Trinity College, Oxford, led to honours (second class) in the classical moderations in 1866, though he graduated in 1868 with only a pass degree. His connection with the college continued long after; indeed, in February 1907 some fellows approached him with a suggestion that he might succeed Professor H. F. Pelham as president of the college, though in the event nothing came of this. He made generous provision for the college in his will, leaving it the residue of his considerable personal estate, as well as his books and certain of his papers.

Sir Mackenzie Dalzell Chalmers (1847–1927), by Thomas Martine Ronaldson [posthumous]

After his call to the bar by the Inner Temple in 1869 and a short period as a member of the Indian Civil Service, Chalmers returned to London in 1872, joining the home circuit and taking chambers at 1 Paper Buildings. In 1875 he moved to the chambers of Farrer Herschell QC at 3 Harcourt Buildings. In 1880 he was appointed a revising barrister, and he followed Herschell in 1881 in a move to 11 New Court, Carey Street.

In 1882, through Herschell's influence, Chalmers was appointed as standing counsel to the Board of Trade. As such he did much work on the reforming bill which became the Bankruptcy Act 1883. About this time he also wrote *The Cost of Litigation* (1880), *Local Government* (1883), and, with E. Hough, *The Bankruptcy Act 1883* (1884).

In 1884 Chalmers became a county court judge at Birmingham, an office he held until 1896, apart from a short period in 1893 as acting chief justice of Gibraltar. In 1898 Herschell, then in his final year as lord chancellor, appointed Chalmers a commissioner of assize. His failure to promote him further, as it was said that he wished, may have been only through lack of opportunity, though transition from the county court bench to the High Court bench would then have been unprecedented. (Herschell's sole appointment to the Queen's Bench Division was in 1892, and went to William Rann Kennedy.)

In 1878 Chalmers published *A Digest of the Law of Bills of Exchange*, a work of considerable scholarship. Written as a step on the way to a codification of the area, it was cast in the form of numbered propositions with added notes, much as if it were an act and a commentary on that act. After presenting a paper on this intended codification to the Institute of Bankers in 1880, he was instructed by the institute and by the associated chambers of commerce to draft a bill. This bill rapidly became the Bills of Exchange Act of 1882. As well as the *Digest*, Chalmers wrote *The Negotiable Instruments Act 1881 (India)* (1882) and the briefer *The Bills of Exchange Act 1882* (1882). His next substantial task was the codification of the law of sale of goods. He produced a draft bill in 1888, 'an acknowledged masterpiece

of draftsmanship' (R. F. V. Henston, *Lives of the Lord Chancellors*, 1984, 108) which Herschell introduced to the House of Lords with the express purpose of eliciting criticisms, and in 1890 Chalmers published a text, *The Sale of Goods*. The bill was reintroduced to the house in 1891, and referred to a select committee of law lords. A proposal that the bill be extended to Scotland necessitated considerable delay, but it was eventually enacted as the Sale of Goods Act of 1893.

Marine insurance then claimed Chalmers's attention. In 1894 he produced a draft bill, which was introduced in the Lords and subjected to lengthy consideration in committee. In 1900 it was reintroduced, again considered in committee, and eventually passed by the Lords, but rejected by the Commons. In 1901 he produced (with Douglas Owen) *A Digest of the Law of Marine Insurance*. The Commons reconsidered the bill in 1906, when Lord Chancellor Loreburn's intervention secured its passage as the Marine Insurance Act of 1906.

Chalmers returned to India in 1896 as the legal member of the viceroy's council. His work included revisions to the code of criminal procedure, and an act aimed at legal touting. He was made a CSI in 1898. On his return to England in 1899 he was appointed assistant parliamentary counsel, in 1902 succeeding Courtenay Ilbert as first parliamentary counsel. In September 1903 he succeeded Sir Kenelm Digby as permanent under-secretary of state for the Home department. Here he handled petitions for clemency, in consultation with Lord Halsbury: together, they constituted a *de facto* criminal court of appeal prior to the formal constitution of this body in 1907. Chalmers was also on the standing committee for the revision of statute law: according to his *Times* obituarist he enjoyed pruning obsolete laws, but was bored by factory and social legislation. The same memoir described him as 'A man of the world with a wide, if not perhaps very profound, knowledge of human nature, and untrammelled by any belief in its essential goodness or ultimate perfection' (*The Times*, 23 Dec 1927). He was made a CB in 1904, and created KCB in 1906. He retired in 1908.

In 1910 and 1912 Chalmers served as the British delegate at conferences at The Hague about the international unification of the law of bills of exchange. In 1911 he served as a member of the royal commission on Maltese affairs, and in 1916 of the royal commission on the Easter rising in Ireland. During the First World War he served on the war risks commission, and he was chairman of the commission which investigated German violations of the laws of war in Belgium. He was a member of the council of the Royal Aeronautical Society and vice-president of the London Fever Hospital, and he was keenly interested in the affairs of the order of St John of Jerusalem. The last three bodies were the recipients of considerable bequests in his will.

Chalmers never married. In his later years he lived at Wimbledon, and was almost daily at the Athenaeum, where he had many friends. He was also a member of the Marylebone Cricket Club. In December 1927 he underwent a serious operation, and died at a nursing home at 4 Dorset Square, Marylebone, London, on 22 December. He was buried at his birthplace, Nonington.

STEVE HEDLEY

Sources *Journal of Comparative Legislation*, 3rd ser., 10 (1778), 124–5 · *DNB* · *The Times* (23 Dec 1927) · J. H. Baker, *An introduction to English legal history*, 3rd edn (1990) · G. R. R. [G. R. Rubin], 'Chalmers, Sir Mackenzie Dalzell', *Biographical dictionary of the common law*, ed. A. W. B. Simpson (1984) · *CGPLA Eng. & Wales* (1928)
Archives Trinity College, Oxford, MSS | BL, letters to Lord Gladstone, Add. MS 45993 · BL OIOC, letters to Arthur Godley, MS Eur. F 102 · CUL, corresp. with Lord Hardinge
Likenesses T. M. Ronaldson, oils (posthumous), Trinity College, Oxford [see illus.]
Wealth at death £107,379 15s. 10d.: resworn probate, 8 Feb 1928, *CGPLA Eng. & Wales*

Chalmers, Margaret (*b.* 1758), poet, was born at Lerwick in the Shetland Islands, and baptized there on 12 December 1758, the eldest child of William Chalmers, customs officer and landowner's steward, and his wife, Kitty Irvine. Her only brother, William, master of the *Royal Sovereign*, fell at Trafalgar, leaving his sisters and widowed mother in poverty. (The mother became bedridden about 1798, as did one of the sisters three years later.) Lord Collingwood petitioned the government for a pension for them, but without success. In 1813 Margaret (impelled, she said, 'by circumstances of severe domestic affliction'), published her *Poems* by subscription at Newcastle, through S. Hodgson. The volume was badly printed and publicized, and many subscribers were lost by delay. It did not attain the financial success which, for its literary panache and the interest of its subject matter, it deserved.

Chalmers calls herself 'the first British Thulian quill', though she shares that honour with Dorothea Primrose Campbell, who, more than a generation younger, was the first of the two to be published. Like Campbell, Chalmers expresses a mixture of pride and apology about her native land, enthusiastically describing its landscapes and customs while doubting that it is really a fitting environment for the poet. About herself as poet, too, she sounds ambivalent. She expresses vaunting literary ambition, but does so with self-deprecating wit; she calls herself 'a

hizzie', 'madam Thulia', or 'my Greenland Lady'. Much of her material is local: the place names of the island of Uist, scenes along the River Esk, a famine in the Faeroes relieved with British aid, the loss of a Shetland boat at sea. She provides prose notes in explanation of local matters such as handiwork and superstitions. More general topics include female friendship, British patriotism, the royal family, and local dignitaries. Her literary references are largely Scots: she quotes James Thomson, praises Walter Scott, and imitates Robert Burns.

Margaret Chalmers corresponded with Scott between 1814 and 1815, and sent him copies of some of her poems. In 1816, three years after her publishing venture, she appealed for financial help to the Royal Literary Fund, sending a poem 'To the Powerful Benevolent'. They responded with a grant of £10 but apparently did not keep the poem. It is not known when Margaret Chalmers died.

ISOBEL GRUNDY

Sources M. Chalmers, *Poems* (1813) · MSS, Royal Literary Fund [microfilm] · *Scots Magazine and Edinburgh Literary Miscellany* (1806) · Blain, Clements & Grundy, *Feminist comp.*
Archives NL Scot., letters to Sir Walter Scott

Chalmers, Patrick (1802–1854), antiquary, was born at Auldbar Castle, near Brechin, Forfarshire, on 31 October 1802, the elder son of Patrick Chalmers (*d.* 1826) and Frances, daughter of John Inglis, an East India director. His father was a merchant in London and did not reside much at Auldbar, which his own father had purchased in 1753, until 1819. Previous to that the younger Patrick Chalmers had lived little in Scotland, though (through the Chalmers of Balnacraig) he came of ancient Aberdeenshire stock, his forebears having been physicians in the county, and in later generations Gibraltar merchants. He was educated at Dr Coghan's school at Higham near Walthamstow, and entered Queen's College, Oxford, at sixteen, leaving before taking a degree to enter the 3rd dragoon guards, in which he was gazetted cornet in 1821 and served mainly in Ireland, before selling out, as a captain, on succeeding to the Auldbar estate in 1826. A fox-hunting laird who hunted his own hounds, he was drawn into local politics, contesting the Montrose burghs unsuccessfully in 1832, but being elected unopposed in 1835 and holding the seat for seven years. He was active on several parliamentary committees, particularly that on penny postage. From about 1840 he was much interested in the development of the Arbroath and Forfar Railway. In July 1839 he married Jessie Anne Letitia (*d.* 1840), younger daughter of John Herbert Foley of Ridgeway, Pembrokeshire, and widow of Thomas Taylor Vernon of Hanbury Hall, Worcestershire. She died on 7 April 1840, leaving two sons by her first marriage. Chalmers, who was by then suffering from a chronic disorder of the spine, resigned his parliamentary seat in spring 1842.

In his enforced retirement Chalmers took up the study of local antiquities, learning Latin and palaeography, building up a historical library, and corresponding with like-minded scholars. His circle included John Stuart, William Fraser, Cosmo Innes, W. B. D. D. Turnbull, Albert Way, and R. W. Billings. In 1848 he presented to the Bannatyne

Club a folio work entitled *The ancient sculptured monuments of the county of Angus, including those at Meigle in Perthshire, and one at Fordoun in the Mearns*. A quarto edition was later published, augmented by monuments from the Mearns and Aberdeenshire; the scale of the illustrations was large enough to give details of the sculptured symbols and thus to advance their archaeological study. Ill health interrupted his work on the Arbroath cartulary, *Liber S. Thome de Aberbrothoc* (Bannatyne Club, 1848–56) but he contributed largely to it in collaboration with Cosmo Innes. He also prepared from a manuscript owned by Lord Panmure much of the text of an edition of *Registrum episcopatus Brechinensis*, with illustrative charters. This, intended as his second presentation to the Bannatyne Club, was completed by his brother John Inglis Chalmers of Auldbar and published in two volumes in 1856, with the assistance of Innes, whose preface includes a memorial tribute to the donor. Chalmers was elected a fellow of the Society of Antiquaries of Scotland in 1846, and of the Society of Antiquaries (London) in 1850; he joined the British Archaeological Association in 1849 and contributed papers to the proceedings of all three societies. He was active in county business and in the improvement of his estate, and directed much rebuilding and modernizing work at Auldbar Castle in the 1840s, with Alexander Ross as his architect and A. M. Perkins as engineer. His health recovered sufficiently to allow him to venture again into society and in 1854 to undertake a continental tour with a stepson. He suffered an attack of smallpox, then a recurrence of his spinal complaint, and died at Rome on 23 June 1854. His body was brought back to Scotland for interment in the family chapel at Auldbar Castle. His name is perpetuated in the Chalmers–Jervise prize awarded by the Society of Antiquaries of Scotland. ALAN BELL

Sources P. Chalmers, J. I. Chalmers, and C. Innes, eds., *Registrum episcopatus Brechinensis*, 2, Bannatyne Club, 102 (1856) · *Journal of the British Archaeological Association*, 11 (1855), 164–70 · *Proceedings of the Society of Antiquaries of London*, 3 (1853–6), 182
Archives NL Scot., corresp. and papers
Likenesses engraving, repro. in Innes, *Registrum episcopatus Brechinensis*, vol. 1, frontispiece

Chalmers, Robert, Baron Chalmers (1858–1938), civil servant, was born at 14 Allen Road, Albert Town, Hornsey, Middlesex, on 18 August 1858, the only son of John Chalmers, a bookseller and publisher, originally from Aberdeen, and his wife, Julia, daughter of Robert Mackay. He was educated at the City of London School, where the headmaster, Dr Edwin Abbott, strongly influenced him in his commitment to scholarship and public service. In 1877 he entered Oriel College, Oxford, where he took a first class in classical moderations in 1878 and a second class in natural science (biology) in 1881. For a time he contemplated studying medicine at Edinburgh, but in 1882 he entered the open competitive examination for the upper division of the civil service and was placed first on the list with what was then a record total of marks.

Chalmers entered the Treasury as a second-class clerk on 14 August 1882 and rose steadily thereafter: from first-class clerk on 15 April 1894 to principal clerk on 25 February 1899, and to assistant secretary on 1 April 1903. For most of that time he served in the Treasury's finance division, and on 28 October 1907 he was appointed chairman of the Board of Inland Revenue, where he was largely responsible for the transfer of the excise from the Inland Revenue to a new board of customs and excise in 1908. In this role, and from 24 July 1911, when he succeeded Sir George Murray as permanent secretary of the Treasury, he was one of the principal advisers to successive chancellors of the exchequer: H. H. Asquith, David Lloyd George, Reginald McKenna, and Andrew Bonar Law. Chalmers had strong Liberal convictions and at first he got on well with Lloyd George, of whose 1909 budget he was one of the principal architects, but they fell out in 1913, when Chalmers believed that the chancellor had misled the House of Commons. On 26 September that year, apparently at his own suggestion, Chalmers was appointed governor of Ceylon, where he was able to indulge his hobby of the study of Pali, the ancient language of that country, on which he published several books.

Chalmers's period as governor was marred by riots in May and June 1915, arising from tension between native Buddhists and Muslim immigrants from India, and he was glad to be asked in December that year to return to the Treasury, which was sorely in need of his talents as it sought to cope with the problems of war finance. For two months he worked in the Treasury while on leave from Ceylon and on 4 March 1916 he was appointed joint permanent secretary (in conjunction with Sir John Bradbury and Sir Thomas Heath). From May to September 1916 he acted temporarily as under-secretary for Ireland during the troubles. He returned to the Treasury, where in July 1917 he and his junior colleague, John Maynard Keynes, clashed with the governor of the Bank of England, Walter Cunliffe, who claimed that the Treasury officials had taken over the bank's functions in relation to financing purchases in the United States. The chancellor, Bonar Law, supported Chalmers and Keynes, and Cunliffe had to concede the Treasury's primacy for the duration of the war. Chalmers was due to retire in August 1918, but at Bonar Law's request he agreed to stay on, and did not leave until 31 March 1919.

Chalmers had a reputation for tough efficiency and a sarcastic wit. However, behind a mask of pomposity and cynicism he hid a kind heart and a generous nature. As a young man he lived in the East End of London, where he worked under Samuel Barnett, then vicar of St Jude's, Whitechapel, giving up all the time not required by his work at the Treasury to helping by personal contact the poor and sick. As a senior official, he was a source of encouragement to younger members of his department, provided that they showed no fear of him (if they did he became irritated). He had a flair for bestowing nicknames: it was apparently he who first dubbed Lloyd George the Goat.

Chalmers combined public service with scholarship. As a Treasury clerk he persuaded the master of the rolls to unlock the gates of the Public Record Office in Chancery

Lane after dark, and there carried out the research that led to his *History of Currency in the British Colonies* (1893). As a member of the Pali Text Society he contributed to the translation and editing of a number of Buddhist texts published between 1895 and 1932. In 1919 he was appointed a member of the royal commission on the universities of Oxford and Cambridge, and, as a member of the commission, stayed for a time at Peterhouse, Cambridge, where his younger son had been an undergraduate, incorporating his Oxford degree at Cambridge and becoming a member of the college. He was elected master of Peterhouse in 1924, and during his seven years of office took a personal interest in the undergraduates, providing lavish hospitality and often helping poorer scholars unostentatiously from his own pocket.

Chalmers was appointed CB in 1900, KCB in 1908, and GCB in 1916, and on his retirement was made Baron Chalmers of Northiam in Sussex. He was elected an honorary fellow of Oriel College in 1918, and he received honorary degrees from the universities of Glasgow (1913), Oxford (1923), Cambridge (1924), and St Andrews (1930). He was a trustee of the British Museum (1924–31) and president of the Royal Asiatic Society (1922–5), and was elected a fellow of the British Academy in 1927.

Chalmers married Maud Mary, daughter of John George Pigott, a musician, on 2 July 1888; they had two sons, Ralph and Robert, and one daughter, Mabel. Ralph became a professional soldier, Robert a barrister. Both were killed while on active service in May 1915. His wife died in 1923, and on 1 June 1935 he married Iris Florence, elder daughter of Sir John Harvard Biles, professor of naval architecture at Glasgow University, and widow of Robert Latta, professor of logic at Glasgow University. Chalmers died on 17 November 1938 at his home, 14 Crick Road, Oxford. His funeral service was in Oriel College chapel, and there was a memorial service in the Chapel of the Order of the Bath, Westminster Abbey. As he died without surviving male children, the peerage became extinct. G. C. PEDEN

Sources P. E. Matheson, 'Lord Chalmers, 1858–1938', *PBA*, 25 (1939), 321–32, esp. 330 · *DNB* · *The Times* (18 Nov 1938) · *The Times* (26 Nov 1938) · *The Times* (28 Nov 1938) · treasury records, PRO · A. McFadyean, *Recollected in tranquillity* (1964), 44–7 · F. Leith-Ross, *Money talks* (1968), 21 · W. J. Braithwaite, *Lloyd George's ambulance wagon*, ed. H. N. Bunbury (1957), 67–8, 103, 272–3, 276, 303 · B. K. Murray, *The people's budget, 1909/10: Lloyd George and liberal politics* (1980), 79–80, 123–4, 136–8, 158–9, 165, 227 · R. Blake, *The unknown prime minister: the life and times of Andrew Bonar Law* (1955), 351–4 · A. Cairncross, *The Wilson years* (1997), 178–9 · b. cert. · m. certs. · d. cert.

Archives Bodl. Oxf., corresp. with Herbert Asquith · Bodl. Oxf., corresp. with Lewis Harcourt · CUL, corresp. with Lord Hardinge

Likenesses A. Cluysenaar, oils, *c.*1920, Gov. Art Coll. · O. Edis, photograph, *c.*1926, NPG · oils, Peterhouse, Cambridge · photograph, repro. in Matheson, 'Lord Chalmers', 320

Wealth at death £18,544 0s. 7d.: resworn probate, 17 Jan 1939, *CGPLA Eng. & Wales*

Chalmers, Thomas (1780–1847), Church of Scotland minister and social reformer, was born on 17 March 1780 in Anstruther, Fife, the sixth of fourteen children of John Chalmers (1740–1818), merchant and provost of Anstruther, and Elizabeth (1750–1827), daughter of George Hall,

Thomas Chalmers (1780–1847), by David Octavius Hill and Robert Adamson

wine merchant of Crail, Fife. He had nine brothers and five sisters, of whom all but one lived to adulthood. His father was a man of devout Calvinist faith and modest means, active in burgh politics. His mother engaged in charitable work among the poor, despite the pressures of raising a large family on limited resources.

Education, ordination, and early church career Thomas was educated at the Anstruther parish school, where he was remembered as physically strong and warm-hearted, but also idle. In 1791, at the age of eleven, he matriculated at nearby St Andrews University. Upon completing the arts course he entered the Divinity Hall at St Andrews, largely at the insistence of his father, and in 1799 he was licensed as a probationer minister in the Church of Scotland.

Chalmers was not, however, an enthusiastic student of theology: he found the lectures of the reformed theologian principal George Hill (1750–1819) to be dry and formal. His interests lay more in mathematics and natural philosophy, and in cutting a figure in the Scottish Enlightenment. Amid the unrest surrounding the French Revolution he was also drawn to politics, taking an advanced whig stance against the war with the French republic and the 'arrogant' pretensions of the local landed gentry. He was, a friend later recalled, 'full of heart and buoyant of spirit—an ardent lover of liberty' (Brown, 8). From 1799 to 1801 he continued his studies in natural philosophy at Edinburgh University, supporting himself by tutoring. In 1802, through the influence of his father's cousin, he was presented to the parish living of Kilmany in Fife by the patrons, the professors of the United College of St Andrews. He did not devote himself to his pastoral duties, but rather gave much of his time to lecturing on mathematics and chemistry at St Andrews, while he pursued an appointment to a university professorship. Although censured by his local presbytery for neglecting his parish, the ambitious young natural philosopher was unrepentant. Indeed, he argued in his first published pamphlet in 1805 that a parish minister's duties consisted of little more than preaching on Sunday, leaving the remainder of the week for whatever scholarly or scientific interests he wished to pursue.

In 1807 Chalmers left his parish for three months to make his first visit to London, staying with his elder brother, a merchant in the city. Fascinated by the political culture of the capital, and excited by the debates over what might happen if Napoleon succeeded in his aim of closing all British trade with the continent, Chalmers returned to Kilmany to write his first book, *An Inquiry into the Extent and Stability of National Resources*, which was published in 1808. In this work he rejected the idea that Britain's foreign trade was necessary to its economic welfare. Drawing on the writings of T. R. Malthus on population, Chalmers developed the argument that foreign trade only encouraged the growth of a 'surplus' population supported precariously by commerce and manufactures. Because foreign trade might be interrupted at any time by external factors such as war, the surplus population represented a danger to the stability of society. It would be better to tax the surplus agricultural wealth used to finance foreign trade and transfer the surplus population from precarious commercial pursuits to the service of the state—in an enlarged military and educational establishment. This would enhance both the stability and the permanent glory of the nation. In its criticism of the idea of unlimited economic growth through trade and industry, the *Inquiry* anticipated many of Chalmers's later economic and social theories. At the time, however, the *Inquiry* was either ignored or dismissed by reviewers, and Chalmers was devastated by the failure.

Conversion at Kilmany   In his parish of Kilmany declining church attendance testified to Chalmers's failure also as a parish minister. As a clergyman Chalmers had reflected the mood in Scottish religion known as moderatism. Embracing the ethos of the Enlightenment, moderate clergymen sought to take a leading role in the cultural life of the nation. Many moderates had moved quietly away from the Calvinist orthodoxy of the Westminster confession, the subordinate standard of faith in the Church of Scotland, and emphasized instead the moral teachings of Christianity. Chalmers had carried moderatism to an extreme, treating his parish ministry as little more than a sinecure while he pursued academic preferment. His ambitions, however, had been disappointed. In the winter of 1809–10 he became dangerously ill with consumption.

During his illness and the long months of convalescence that followed Chalmers turned to vital personal religion for consolation, reading the works of William Wilberforce (1759–1833), Thomas Scott (1747–1821), and other evangelicals. He was also drawn into the circle of several young whig evangelical clergymen and laymen, including David Brewster (1781–1868) and Andrew Thomson (1779–1831), who combined religious zeal with wide-ranging intellectual interests and commitment to political reform. The preparation of the article 'Christianity' for Brewster's *Edinburgh Encyclopaedia* brought Chalmers to a new appreciation for the evidences of the Christian faith. He experienced a conversion to an evangelical piety, and in January 1811 he returned to his duties in the Kilmany pulpit with a new religious fervour. His impassioned preaching of the 'peculiar' doctrines of the pervasiveness of sin, the emptiness of worldly ambition, and salvation through grace alone began to have a profound impact on his congregation. Stories of his dramatic conversion spread and attracted large crowds to Kilmany, while he was invited to preach at churches throughout the Scottish lowlands. He embraced the evangelical movement in Scotland, becoming a strong advocate of the overseas mission movement and especially of the British and Foreign Bible Society. His literary skills now found expression in religious pamphlets and articles in the evangelical press.

Chalmers also demonstrated a new commitment to the parish ministry. As a child in Anstruther he had known a strong sense of community, and his conversion now revived his attachment to a traditional communal sentiment as well as to a traditional Calvinist piety. In 1813 he began a programme of systematic visiting among the homes of his parishioners and took a more active role in the distribution of poor relief. He commenced a Saturday school for the religious instruction of children and he regularly visited the parish school to catechize. The aim of the programmes was to revive a sense of Christian community in the parish; the different social orders would be drawn together by a shared Christian ideal, emphasizing benevolence and mutual assistance. He became convinced that a reinvigorated parish system within the established church would be the most effective way to improve the spiritual, moral, and material condition of the country.

In November 1814 the town council and magistrates of Glasgow presented Chalmers to the city's Tron parish, in the hope that his preaching would fill the church and increase the pew rents which were a major source of income for the city churches. On moving to Glasgow in 1815 Chalmers confronted an environment very different from rural Kilmany. With a rapidly growing population of over 120,000, Glasgow was the largest city in Scotland. It was a commercial and manufacturing centre experiencing the excitement and the tensions of early industrialization. Chalmers's evangelical preaching soon made a powerful impression on the middle classes of the city, and the Tron Church attracted a congregation of wealth and talent. A series of Thursday afternoon lectures on science and Christianity, which he delivered in 1815 and 1816, were said to have filled the church with the urban élites, bringing the commercial districts to a standstill. When published, the *Astronomical Discourses* (1817) sold over 20,000 copies in nine months. His reputation was further recognized in 1816, when he was awarded the degree of DD by the unanimous vote of the senate of the University of Glasgow. In 1817 he visited London, where his preaching caused a sensation: 'All the world wild about Chalmers', Wilberforce noted in his diary (Brown, 110). His sermon for the benefit of the Hibernian Society visibly affected the cool and dignified Viscount Castlereagh and melted George Canning, the celebrated parliamentary orator, to tears. 'The Tartan beats us all', Canning exclaimed following the sermon. Thousands were turned away from one service after even the aisles of the church were packed, and Chalmers himself had to enter the church through a window.

While Chalmers's preaching brought him national fame, even admirers found it difficult to explain his power. He was, according to contemporary accounts, an ungainly figure in the pulpit: a heavy-set man with a sleepy, dishevelled appearance, who read his sermons with a broad Fife accent. But as he spoke congregations lost sight of his awkward presence and hung on his words. He preached the doctrines of human sin and saving grace with a conviction rooted in personal experience and an emotional intensity that appealed to the Romanticism of the times. Further, his evangelical commitments did not cause him to forsake his education in the language and thought of the Scottish Enlightenment. He consciously strove for an 'academic eloquence of style' in the pulpit, and flattered his congregations with references from natural and moral philosophy. And yet, observed the celebrated whig lawyer and author Henry Cockburn:

> neither devotional fervour, nor enlightened philosophy, nor vivid language, nor luminous exposition could produce the effect he does, without the aid of his manner. ... The magic lies in the concentrated intensity which agitates every fibre of the man ... and kindles the whole composition with living fire. (Brown, 58)

The St John's experiment From his arrival in Glasgow, Chalmers was disturbed by the social conditions that he encountered in the industrializing city. Glasgow was suffering acutely from the economic stagnation that followed the end of the Napoleonic wars. In the crowded Tron parish were scenes of profound human misery, while the vast majority of his parishioners attended no church. The parish system had largely broken down in Glasgow: there was no system of endowed parish schools and the care of the poor was largely in the hands of voluntary societies or of the Town Hospital, an institution supported by the combined church-door collections of the city churches and by an assessment on property. The majority of his largely middle-class congregation consisted of people who lived outside the parish and who resented their minister devoting time to the parishioners rather than to those whose pew rents helped pay his stipend. In 1816 Chalmers attempted to visit the homes of all his Tron parishioners, but found that he could not establish the same pastoral relationship with the Tron parish population of over 10,000 that he had known in Kilmany, with its 800 parishioners.

Chalmers became convinced that the fundamental problem in Glasgow and other Scottish cities was the breakdown of communal spirit. The middle and upper social orders had lost their sense of personal responsibility for the poor and unchurched. Moreover, many of the poor had become degraded to the status of 'paupers', dependent on institutional poor relief and suffering a loss of self-respect. His reading of Malthus convinced him that the major cause of poverty was the growth of population beyond the capacity of the country's agricultural resources to sustain it in decent comfort. This growth of population, in turn, was the direct result of the breakdown of communal responsibility—especially the tendency of the poor to have more children than they could support and then to rely on the state to provide for their needs. The growing pauper population threatened to overwhelm the nation with burgeoning poor-relief costs. Further, the growing numbers abandoned to poverty, ignorance, and irreligion were attracted to revolutionary politics and constituted a threat to the social order. For Chalmers the only way to preserve the social fabric was to revive what he perceived as the traditional communal responsibility of Scotland, by which the labouring poor would strive for independence through thrift, delayed marriage, and the limitation of child bearing, while communities would care for the 'worthy poor', the infirm, aged, and orphaned who fell into a dependent condition through no fault of their own. This communal sentiment, he further believed, could be revived only by restoring the parish system in the established church.

In 1819 Chalmers persuaded the Glasgow town council and magistrates to give him a free hand to conduct an experiment in urban ministry in a new parish, St John's, being created in a working-class district of the city. Permitted to pursue a parish ministry at St John's untrammelled by existing regulations regarding the care of the poor, he promised in return to eliminate gradually the need for any legal poor relief in the parish, taking all St John's paupers off the rolls of the Town Hospital and saving the city ratepayers over £300 per annum. This he would accomplish by reviving a traditional communal spirit, transforming his city parish into a stable and largely self-sufficient society, similar to the parish communities he had known in rural Fife.

Chalmers based his celebrated St John's experiment on two fundamental principles—'territoriality', or the territorial subdivision of the large urban parish into more manageable 'proportions', and 'aggression', or regular house-to-house visiting by a parish agency of church officers, designed to bring religious and moral instruction into each home. The parish of St John's was first subdivided into twenty-five proportions, each comprising a neighbourhood of about 400 inhabitants. Chalmers then organized a parish agency of elders and deacons to assist him in the work of visiting. The offices of elder and deacon had been established at the Reformation, and every parish was expected to have a kirk session of elders to provide moral and spiritual guidance and a session of deacons to care for the poor. During the eighteenth century, however, the eldership had declined into a mere formality, while most parishes had dispensed with the deaconship altogether. Chalmers now sought to restore the traditional powers of both offices. He assigned an elder to each proportion and instructed the elder to regard that neighbourhood as his field of operation, visiting each home on a regular basis. The elders were to fulfil their traditional responsibilities of moral and spiritual supervision, now by taking an aggressive line, visiting homes, seeking out cases of immorality and irreligion, serving as spiritual advisers, and bringing persistent offenders before the kirk session for discipline. A deacon was also assigned to each proportion and given the primary responsibility for poor relief. Deacons were to visit the households of their proportions regularly, in order to become familiar with the habits and moral character of the inhabitants. They were to work for the elimination of legal poor relief: first, by encouraging paupers to recover their independence through labour, thrift, and temperance; second, by encouraging families to assume responsibility for the care of impoverished relations; third, by appealing to neighbours and friends; and finally, by drawing assistance from the voluntary parish church-door collection for the poor. The aim was to replace institutional poor relief with a spirit of communal responsibility and self-help.

Chalmers introduced other programmes for the elevation of the St John's parishioners. He revived the parish school system in St John's, establishing four parish schools which offered inexpensive, quality primary education to the children of the parish, with fees waived for the very poor. He organized a Sunday school society, and assigned one or more Sunday school teachers to each proportion, with instructions both to set up a Sunday school and to visit the families regularly in order to interest them in their children's education. Further, he commenced a Sunday evening service, encouraging working-class parishioners to attend in their working clothes, while a new chapel, with its own minister, was built to provide additional church accommodation in the parish.

It was, however, the poor-relief programmes that most attracted public attention. Through careful investigations into the circumstances of paupers, encouragement to self-sufficiency, and appeals to neighbourhood charity the St John's deacons had by 1823 managed to remove all St John's paupers from the Town Hospital rolls and to reduce substantially the cost of poor relief in the parish. For the British governing orders Chalmers's St John's experiment seemed to offer a humane means to reduce the rising poor-relief costs. 'I consider you my ablest and best ally', T. R. Malthus wrote to Chalmers in 1822, seeing in Chalmers's programmes a practical means to limit population growth and avert social upheaval (Brown, 116). Chalmers described his programmes and their success in a remarkable three-volume work, *The Christian and Civic Economy of Large Towns*, published between 1819 and 1826, which was widely read in Britain and the United States.

At St John's, Chalmers had developed methods which would have a profound influence on the development of social work, including the territorial subdivision of cities, regular house-to-house visiting, and the collection of accurate information concerning both communities and individual cases for relief. There were, however, also serious weaknesses with the St John's system. Some of the deacons, an exclusively middle-class group, lacked empathy for the poor in their districts and often seemed more concerned to reduce the number of paupers receiving relief than to alleviate real suffering. As a result many parishioners grew to distrust the deacons and some paupers moved to other parishes, creating resentment among neighbouring ministers and congregations. Chalmers could be harsh in his regulations for the poor. For example, he insisted upon denying relief to unwed or deserted mothers, believing that this would force fathers to assume their responsibilities. Charity, he argued, should be restricted to the 'worthy' poor. His system betrayed an Enlightenment optimism concerning human nature: a belief that through religious and moral instruction or social engineering human character could be improved. None the less, for all its imperfections the St John's experiment pointed the way towards a more active response by the established Church of Scotland to the problems created by rapid industrialization and urbanization.

The champion of national religious establishments Late in 1823 Chalmers announced that he would leave the parish ministry and accept the chair of moral philosophy at St Andrews University. The St John's experiment, he believed, had been a success, and he proposed to devote his remaining years to training future ministers in the principles and programmes he had pioneered. He was also weary of the pressures of the urban ministry and of continued controversy with the town council and his fellow city ministers over the effects of his programmes. Perhaps most important, he wished to fulfil his youthful ambition of an academic career, and have time to devote to moral philosophy and political economy.

In his lectures on moral philosophy at St Andrews, Chalmers continued to demonstrate his intellectual roots in the thought of the Scottish Enlightenment. Influenced by the common-sense school of Scottish philosophy, he emphasized the central role of an internal moral regulator, or 'conscience', which enabled persons to perceive intuitively the imperatives of benevolence and social responsibility. Through conscience God had provided for humans to find their fulfilment in social relations and in striving for social improvement. Chalmers discerned a design in social life—a harmonious correlation between human nature, and especially conscience, and the organization of social institutions—a theme which he later explored at length in his Bridgewater treatise *The Adaptation of External Nature to the Moral and Intellectual Constitution of Man*, published in 1833. He did not, however, lose sight of his evangelical convictions. Conscience, in his view, not only directed the mind to social duties but it also revealed the inadequacy of human nature to fulfil the moral imperatives, and it awakened the heart to the need for revelation and the gospel of personal salvation.

Chalmers also became involved in questions of university reform and the proper use of university endowments.

This led him to explore the nature of national establishments in a treatise *On the Use and Abuse of Literary and Ecclesiastical Endowments*, published in 1827. It was, he argued, the national religious establishments of Scotland, England, and Ireland, with their parish churches and schools, and their universities, that formed the national character and provided for the transmission of Christian civilization. These establishments were by necessity supported by endowments and it was incumbent on the state to protect those endowments. Because of the weakness of human nature, religion and education could not be left to the laws of the market place. People had no natural desire for religion or education, as they had for such goods as wine or tobacco; on the contrary, the more irreligious or ignorant a person was, the less he or she would value religion or education. Nor could religion and education be left to the voluntary exertions of individuals, which would always prove inadequate because of the frailty of human nature. Only endowed national establishments, under the protection of the state, would have the power to break through corrupt human nature and reach the individual conscience with religious and moral truth. Only the establishments would have the permanent influence needed to preserve Christian civilization. Chalmers's work on endowments was well received, especially in England, where the establishment was coming under increasing attacks from radicals and dissenters. At the same time his defence of the establishment principle was largely free of intolerance, and during the later 1820s he took an active role in the campaign for Catholic emancipation. His speech at a packed public meeting in Edinburgh in support of the Catholic Emancipation Bill in March 1829 was one of his greatest oratorical moments. His establishment ideal included full civil rights for dissenters; competition from dissenters, he argued, would improve the efficiency of the establishment clergy, while freedom of speech and debate would serve the cause of truth.

In 1828 Chalmers was appointed to the chair of theology at Edinburgh University, which placed him in the legal and ecclesiastical capital of Scotland, and in 1830 he was made a chaplain-in-ordinary of the Scottish Chapel Royal. Following the death of Andrew Thomson in 1831 Chalmers was generally regarded as the leader of the evangelical party in the Church of Scotland; he was elected to the annual office of moderator of the general assembly in 1832.

The crisis of 1831–2 surrounding the Reform Bill for the expansion of the parliamentary franchise aroused Chalmers's fears for the condition of the country, and in 1832 he published *On Political Economy, in Connexion with the Moral State and Moral Prospects of Society*. The work opened on a note of urgency: the economy was unsettled by recurrent crises, the conditions for the labouring orders were deteriorating, the state was threatened with revolutionary violence. The cause of this unrest, he continued, would be found in the tendency of industrial society to press beyond the limits of its natural resources. His vision of society was gloomy, haunted by the Malthusian spectre of overpopulation. Population was pressing beyond the

limits of agricultural production, driving down wages, and increasing the cost of poor relief. Industry tended to produce more goods than hard-pressed home consumers could afford, and underconsumption in the home markets resulted in a glut of capital and chronic economic instability. Although he was a free-trader Chalmers did not believe that overseas trade or the exchange of industrial products for foreign foodstuffs would bring lasting prosperity. Such trade, he argued, would only encourage population growth, creating an enlarged, but no more prosperous, population dependent on foreign food and vulnerable to any interruptions of trade. He then proceeded to dismiss every proposal put forth by the politicians to alleviate the growing social distress, including poor-law reform, emigration schemes, reduced taxation, and expanded franchise. The only solution, he maintained, was to improve the character of the people through religious and moral instruction, teaching them the benefits of delayed marriage, thrift, moderate consumption, and communal responsibility. This reformation of national character, in turn, could be achieved only through the parish churches and schools of the endowed national establishments.

It was a well-argued exposition, and in its economic aspects one which anticipated many of the ideas of the economist J. A. Hobson on underconsumption and capital glut. In its defence of a stable, largely self-sufficient society it also bore many similarities to Chalmers's *Inquiry* of 1808. The work, however, was received with considerable disdain by leading political economists and Liberal politicians, who bristled at his rejection of the dominant ideas of social and economic progress through industrialization and political reform. Chalmers, however, became more than ever convinced that only a Christian communal ideal disseminated through the parochial structures of the national establishments could preserve the social fabric. He opposed the Reform Act of 1832 with its idea that more democratic politics would lead to social improvement, and he looked to the tory party under the leadership of Sir Robert Peel to champion the cause of the establishments.

Church extension In 1834 the evangelical party under Chalmers's leadership gained a working majority in the general assembly, the supreme legislative and judicial body in the Church of Scotland, overwhelming the moderate party which had dominated the church since the mid-eighteenth century. Chalmers now led a church beset with difficulties. The dissenters in Scotland had in the early 1830s organized a popular campaign for the disestablishment and disendowment of the Church of Scotland. In the growing towns and cities the established church was losing its hold as the parish system broke down under the weight of huge parish populations, of which only a small minority could find room in the parish church. The church itself was troubled internally by the revival of the patronage issue that had caused major secessions from the church in the previous century. Following the passage of the Parliamentary Reform Act of 1832 many evangelicals in the established church demanded that congregations be given the right to elect their ministers, rather than have them presented by wealthy patrons (about a third of the church patronages in Scotland were owned by the crown and nearly two-thirds by members of the landowning classes).

The evangelical majority in the general assembly of 1834 responded to these threats with two major acts, designed to restore both the internal harmony and the social influence and authority of the established church. First, the assembly dealt with the patronage issue by passing the Veto Act, which gave the majority of male communicant heads of family in a parish the right to veto a patron's presentation to the ministry of that parish if for any reason they were dissatisfied with the presentee. The patron would then be obliged either to present another candidate or to allow the congregation to elect its own candidate. The aim of the veto was to ensure that the right of parishioners to communicate a 'call' to a new minister, a right existing in civil law alongside of the patronage right, was respected by the church's procedures for the settlement of ministers. Chalmers supported the Veto Act, seeing it as a compromise that would both protect the property rights of patrons while recognizing the legitimate congregational voice in the selection of ministers. More importantly he believed the veto would be enough to silence the opponents of patronage and allow the church to get on with its work.

Second, the general assembly of 1834 called on Chalmers to head a church extension campaign, aimed at building hundreds of new parish churches and schools. The standing church accommodation committee was enlarged and given new powers. The assembly passed a Chapels Act, empowering the church to create new ecclesiastical parishes, with spiritual authority. Although Chalmers had suffered a serious stroke in January 1834, he threw himself into the work of church extension with a feverish activity—recognizing that this was the great opportunity of his life for realizing his social ideal. For years he had struggled to convince the nation that only an efficient established church, with a parochial system modelled on his St John's experiment, could restore Scotland to communal values and social harmony. Now he had the support of the general assembly for a national crusade aimed at transforming industrializing Scotland into a godly commonwealth.

Chalmers's campaign moved on two fronts. First, he created a national organization of local church extension societies, which were instructed to gather statistical information concerning the need for new churches and to collect money for building churches and schools. The aim was to create hundreds of new parishes in order to organize the whole of Scotland's expanding population into parish communities of no more than 2000 inhabitants. Each parish was to have a church and school, and a team of minister, elders, deacons, and Sunday school teachers, with parish programmes modelled on those of his St John's experiment. To achieve this aim he encouraged people of all social orders to contribute according to their means—penny-a-week subscriptions from the very poor

to donations of hundreds of pounds from wealthy landowners and merchants. He placed his greatest hope, however, on the penny subscriptions, or the 'power of littles'. Tens of thousands of penny-a-week subscriptions, he maintained, would translate into large sums, while at the same time involving the whole nation in the cause of the godly commonwealth. He demonstrated a considerable gift for organization: soon scores of new societies were formed across the country and new parish churches and schools began to be erected. In the Water of Leith district of Edinburgh, meanwhile, Chalmers organized a model operation to demonstrate how new parochial structures should be created in working-class districts in which there was little prior church attendance.

Second, Chalmers entered into negotiations with the government for a parliamentary grant to provide endowments that would pay part of the stipends of the new ministers and schoolmasters in the new parishes. Partial endowments were necessary, he maintained, to ensure that pew rents and school fees could be kept within the means of working-class families, while the parliamentary grant would demonstrate that the state was committed to maintaining the influence of the Scottish establishment amid the rapidly growing population. The grant, he argued, would be more than repaid by reduced poor-relief costs and diminished crime in the new parish communities.

The request for the state grant, however, encountered serious opposition. The dissenting denominations in Scotland resisted any grant of public money to an establishment the very existence of which they opposed. Scotland, they argued, already had enough churches for its population, if the dissenting churches were counted together with the established churches. Moreover, Chalmers's plan of reviving the authority of parish churches over education, poor relief, and moral discipline was a threat to the liberty of dissenters and would prove unworkable in a free society. If it were possible, asked the prominent dissenter and publisher Adam Black (1784–1874) in 1835, would it be desirable that the authorities in church and state 'should have the power of causing the inhabitants to form themselves into parishes, as the King of Prussia orders his troops to form themselves into squares?' (Brown, 248). The church extensionists were forced to respond in kind to the dissenters' challenges and Scotland was convulsed by the endowments question, with mass meetings and petitioning organized on both sides. In 1835 the whig government of Viscount Melbourne appointed a royal commission of inquiry to investigate church accommodation in Scotland, but the commission moved slowly about its work and angered Chalmers and the church extensionists by what they perceived as stalling methods and a bias towards the dissenters. In truth, the reformed parliament was in no mood to make new grants of public money to the established churches, while Melbourne's whig government was dependent for its survival on the support of dissenters.

Provoked by the delays, Chalmers began expressing his 'moral loathing' for the whigs and sought to unite the church against the whig government. In the 'moderatorship controversy' of 1837 Chalmers successfully blocked the election of the respected Edinburgh whig clergyman John Lee (1779–1859) to the moderatorship of the general assembly, claiming that Lee could not be trusted to press the claims of church extension with sufficient vigour. Many began to suspect Chalmers of vindictiveness and a desire for unquestioned personal authority. The crisis for church extension came in 1838. Early in the year the royal commission on church accommodation issued a preliminary report which vindicated the claims of the church extensionists for additional parish churches and schools. Then, in March 1838, the raised hopes of the church extensionists were dashed when Melbourne announced that his government would provide no grant to endow the new churches and schools in Scotland.

Chalmers was enraged at what he viewed as the government's abandonment of the established Church of Scotland. For years he had struggled to convince the nation that only an enlarged establishment, with parish structures modelled on the St John's experiment, could preserve the social fabric. Now, with most of the church united behind his godly commonwealth ideal, his plans were thwarted by the state's refusal of a modest endowment grant. The new parish churches and schools would have to support themselves through pew rents and fees which would, he believed, effectively exclude the labouring poor and thus undermine the larger communal aims of church extension. In the late spring of 1838 Chalmers appealed to English public opinion, travelling to London to present the celebrated *Lectures on the Establishment and Extension of National Churches* (1838). However, while his eloquent appeal received some sympathy from his fashionable audiences, it was not enough to reverse the government's decision. In Scotland, meanwhile, contributions dried up, the local societies were disbanded, construction of new churches and schools ceased, and in 1841 Chalmers resigned from his convenership of the church extension committee.

The achievements of the church extension campaign had been considerable. During the seven years of Chalmers's convenership, from 1834 to 1841, 222 new churches had been built, increasing the total number of churches in the Scottish establishment by over 20 per cent. It had been an impressive exhibition of national support for Chalmers's godly commonwealth ideal. The achievement was also a testimony to Chalmers's organizational gifts and to his ability to inspire philanthropic giving from all social orders. If he had been impatient and sometimes ill-tempered, he had also created a committed following in the church, especially among the younger evangelical clergy, many of whom had studied under him at St Andrews and Edinburgh. For all his achievements, however, he had failed in the main goal of convincing the state to support the extension of the establishment in response to the growing population.

The Disruption of 1843 As the church extension campaign was reaching its crisis, church and state in Scotland became embroiled in another, even more serious, conflict, this time over patronage. The Veto Act of 1834 was a compromise measure, but one which worked reasonably well to ensure peaceful settlements of ministers in vacant parish livings. On the whole, congregations exercised restraint in the use of the veto. However, difficulties emerged when a small number of vetoed candidates challenged the legality of the church's Veto Act in the civil courts.

In March 1838, in a case involving a disputed settlement in the parish of Auchterarder, the court of session, the supreme civil court in Scotland, decided in favour of a patron's candidate who had been vetoed by the congregation. In making its decision the court of session further declared that the church's Veto Act was an illegal infringement on the civil rights both of patrons and of candidates for the ministry. The church would have to set the Veto Act aside and enforce the rights of patrons without restriction. The general assembly of the church in May 1838 protested that the court of session, as a civil court, had no authority over the procedures of the church courts in the settlement of ministers, and it appealed against the decision to the House of Lords, the supreme court of the land. In May 1839, however, the House of Lords upheld the decision of the court of session that the Veto Act was illegal. Indeed, the house dismissed the idea that congregations should have any real voice in the settlement of ministers: the congregational call, it asserted, was a mere formality.

Until this point Chalmers had felt no strong commitment to the veto and was prepared to sanction its repeal in order to end the dispute. The House of Lords' Auchterarder decision of 1839, however, dramatically changed the situation. In his mind the civil law of patronage had always recognized that the patron's presentation must be accompanied by a call from the congregation. While the call had frequently been neglected, it remained the law. But in 1839 the House of Lords ruled against the call as well as the veto. Patrons' candidates were to be intruded on parishes, and there was nothing the church could do to recognize congregational opinion.

At the general assembly of 1839 Chalmers defined his positions in a three-hour speech. Church and state, he maintained, were two independent societies which had entered into a compact of mutual benefit—the church providing religious and moral instruction to the people; the state providing protection of the church's property. This compact, however, did not give the state the authority to interfere in the church's internal discipline or spiritual ordinances. For the church to accept state control in spiritual matters would render it nothing more than a department of state. In the Church of Scotland the settlement of ministers was a spiritual act, as indicated in the fact that the ordination of a minister took place concurrently with his settlement in his first parish charge. Therefore the church could not accept the power of the state to intrude ministers into parishes against the will of the congregations without sacrificing its spiritual independence. If the state persisted in its unwarranted claims, the church would be forced to withdraw from its compact with the state. Non-intrusion and spiritual independence now became the clarion calls of Chalmers's evangelical party.

Chalmers and his associates sought to negotiate with politicians of both parties in London in order to frame legislation that would legalize the veto and recognize the spiritual independence of the Church of Scotland. Chalmers, however, found little support at Westminster. The whigs were in no mood to help Chalmers's party after the bitter controversy surrounding church extension, while the whig leader disliked Chalmers intensely: 'I think him a madman', Melbourne wrote of Chalmers in 1840, 'and all madmen are also rogues' (Machin, 125). In early 1840 the tory Lord Aberdeen attempted to draft a bill that might satisfy all parties, but his negotiations with Chalmers soon broke down over the issue of the church's spiritual independence. In truth, neither the whig nor the tory party in parliament would contemplate placing any of the functions of the established Church of Scotland outside review by the civil courts. The sovereignty of the king-in-parliament was absolute, and no institution could claim to be outside the rule of civil law. This was especially true of an established church, which most politicians viewed as the creation of statute law.

Further disputed settlements continued to reach the court of session, which took an increasingly firm stand in enforcing the civil law of patronage against a recalcitrant church. For the most part the church courts maintained the Veto Act and resisted what they perceived as unwarranted encroachments by the civil courts. However, a sizeable minority of moderate clergymen showed themselves prepared to accept the authority of the civil courts, and divisions began to appear in the church. Chalmers grew more and more intractable, goaded on, some thought, by a group of zealous young evangelical clergymen led by R. S. Candlish (1806–1873) and William Cunningham (1805–1861). In May 1841, on Chalmers's motion, the general assembly deposed seven moderate ministers of the presbytery of Strathbogie in Aberdeenshire for obeying the court of session and ordaining a vetoed patron's candidate as minister of Marnoch, in defiance of the instructions of their ecclesiastical superiors. With the disciplining of the Strathbogie seven, all hopes of compromise faded. In May 1842 the general assembly sent to parliament a final appeal for the recognition of its spiritual independence. In January 1843 the tory government of Sir Robert Peel—in office since 1841—rejected the church's appeal while the court of session imposed a ruinous fine on the presbytery of Auchterarder for its continued refusal to ordain a vetoed candidate. The state made it clear that those refusing to accept the supremacy of civil law would have to leave the established church (though the government also believed that few ministers would actually relinquish their endowed incomes and manses).

In May 1843 Chalmers led some 470 ministers—over a third of the total—and perhaps half the lay membership out of the Scottish establishment to form the Free Church of Scotland. It was an impressive demonstration of sacrifice for a principle, and the size of the secession owed much to Chalmers's influence. He became the first moderator of the Free Church general assembly and his reputation helped to bring international support to the Free Church. The Disruption was in one sense a tragedy, breaking up the unity of the national Church of Scotland. But in another sense it was a glorious moment in the religious history of Scotland, a dramatic assertion of the rights of congregations to have a voice in the selection of their ministers and, more significantly, an assertion of the spiritual independence of the church under the sole headship of Christ.

The Free Church of Scotland Chalmers hoped to make the Free Church the true national church of Scotland, overwhelming the residual establishment. The Free Church was to include a presbyterian system of ecclesiastical courts and a parochial organization that would encompass the whole of Scotland's population. It would become a free national 'establishment' and carry on the work of achieving the godly commonwealth untrammelled by state interference. Money was needed for this ambitious goal, and Chalmers demonstrated again his organizational gifts as he set up the system for the financial support of a non-endowed national church. The basic principle was, once again, the 'power of littles', the appeal for penny-a-week subscriptions from the mass of Free Church members, with collectors visiting homes on a regular basis. Wealthier members were encouraged to give more, but Chalmers placed the greatest reliance on the small contributions. The results were impressive: within five years the Free Church had erected over 700 parish churches, over 500 parish schools, and over 400 manses, while it assumed an active role in overseas missions. It also created a college in Edinburgh for the education of its ministers, New College, over which Chalmers presided as principal and primary professor of divinity. Perhaps Chalmers's greatest organizational achievement had been the Sustentation Fund, a system by which wealthier congregations subsidized poorer congregations, thus ensuring a decent minimum stipend for all ministers.

Along with the organizational achievements, however, there was also a certain narrowing of aspirations. The Free Church quickly consolidated itself, but it failed to overwhelm the existing establishment and it was in danger of becoming simply another denomination, concerned primarily with the needs of its existing membership. Despite the successful organization of the new denomination, Chalmers agonized over the break-up of the national establishment and the waning of his godly commonwealth ideal. Amid the economic misery of the 'hungry forties', he also remained concerned for the impoverished and unchurched masses, especially in the growing cities. In 1844 he sought to revive his parish community ideal, now calling upon all the protestant denominations to join with him in a shared church and community-building campaign. Each existing church was to map out a territory in a deprived and irreligious district and develop a sense of Christian community there through regular visiting by volunteer workers and modest investments in religious and educational programmes. Through shared territorial missionary work the denominations would also draw more closely together in ecumenical co-operation. The Free Church must be prepared to risk its institutional achievements for the missionary ideal and the cause of church union. 'Who cares for the Free Church', he exclaimed in 1845, 'compared with the Christian good of the people of Scotland?' (Brown, 365). To show how the work could proceed, Chalmers devoted his remaining years to organizing a model territorial operation in the West Port, one of the most deprived districts of Edinburgh. With the aid of an agency of voluntary workers Chalmers established a church, school, Sunday schools, reading-rooms, and system of regular visiting for the moral, material, and spiritual elevation of the community. The West Port operation was not an unqualified success and the interdenominational campaign soon foundered. However, Chalmers managed to direct the Free Church to the work of territorial urban missions with considerable success during the 1850s and 1860s.

Character and death For all his fame Chalmers was a man of rustic manners who remained close to the small burgh life of eastern Fife—a man, according to his acquaintance Thomas Carlyle, 'of little culture, of narrow sphere, all his life'. He never lost his broad Fife accent, loved a humorous country story, and maintained the close friendships from his youth in rural Fife. On 4 August 1812 he had married Grace Pratt (1791/2–1850), a quiet woman with a practical head for business who looked after Chalmers's long-standing partnership with the publisher William Collins. They had six daughters, all of whom reached adulthood. His love for children was proverbial, and he enjoyed playful banter with his daughters, affecting a mock chivalry as they grew older. In appearance he was a heavy-set man, standing 5 feet 9 inches and weighing over 14 stone. He had a brisk walk and flourished his walking staff formidably. His eyes were his most distinctive feature, appearing drowsy, even vacant, much of the time, but beaming with merriment at a joke, narrowing in anger at a perceived injustice, or bulging in frenzy at the height of a sermon. He was quick to anger and suspicious by nature, which hampered his effectiveness as an ecclesiastical politician. In theology he remained attached to the orthodox Calvinism of the Westminster confession. His theological lectures, posthumously published as the *Institutes of Theology* (1849), revealed little originality of conception, while he had no interest in the new ideas in theology or biblical criticism coming from Germany.

Chalmers died quietly in his sleep, of heart failure, on 31 May 1847 in his Edinburgh home at 1 Churchill, Morningside. He was aged sixty-seven. He was buried with 'kingly honours' in Edinburgh, an estimated 100,000 turning out to witness the procession or attend the service in the Grange cemetery.

Chalmers has remained a controversial figure since his death. For some biographers, including his son-in-law, William Hanna, Chalmers was a saintly figure, a man of deep piety and evangelical conviction, whose main concern was the salvation of souls and who chose to lead a pure remnant out of a corrupt establishment in 1843. For others, such as the mid-twentieth-century historians Andrew Drummond and James Bulloch, he was the 'evil genius' of the nineteenth-century church, a middle-class ecclesiastical politician whose poor-relief programmes brought hardship to the labouring orders and whose ambition for power and unwillingness to compromise led to the unnecessary break-up of the national church. In the closing decades of the twentieth century there was a renewal of interest in Chalmers as a social theorist, especially in his communal ideas and his contributions to political economy, and a recognition that the Disruption was a personal tragedy for Chalmers, the break-up of the establishment which represented the greatest hope for achieving his godly commonwealth ideal.

STEWART J. BROWN

Sources S. J. Brown, *Thomas Chalmers and the godly commonwealth in Scotland* (1982) · W. Hanna, *Memoirs of Dr Chalmers*, 4 vols. (1849–52) · A. C. Cheyne, ed., *The practical and the pious: essays on Thomas Chalmers* (1985) · H. Watt, *Thomas Chalmers and the Disruption* (1943) · A. M. C. Waterman, *Revolution, economics and religion: Christian political economy, 1798–1833* (1991) · A. L. Drummond and J. Bulloch, *The Scottish church, 1688–1843* (1973) · G. I. T. Machin, *Politics and the churches in Great Britain, 1832–1868* (1977) · B. Hilton, *The age of atonement: the influence of evangelicalism on social and economic thought* (1988) · S. Mechie, *The church and Scottish social development, 1780–1870* (1960) · H. Watt, *The collected works of Thomas Chalmers: a descriptive list* (1943)

Archives Hunt. L., letters · Mitchell L., Glas., corresp. and papers · NL Scot., letters · U. Edin. L., corresp. · U. Edin., New Coll. L., corresp. and papers · U. St Andr. L., corresp.; private corresp. | BL, letters to Lord Aberdeen, Add. MSS 43237, 43240 · BL, corresp. with W. E. Gladstone, Add. MSS 44524–44527 · BL, corresp. with Sir Robert Peel, Add. MSS 40351–40598, *passim* · Edinburgh Central Reference Library, record of conversations with Joseph John Gurney · Edinburgh City Archives, letters to Wood family, etc. · NA Scot., corresp. with Fox Maule · NL Scot., letters to John Lee · NRA Scotland, priv. coll., letters to James Hog · NRA Scotland, priv. coll., letters to Sir George Sinclair · NRA, priv. coll., letters to Lord Moncreiff and Sir H. M. Wellwood · St Deiniol's Library, Hawarden, corresp. with Sir John Gladstone · Trinity Cam., letters to Thomas Babington · U. Edin. L., letters to James Brown; letters to A. L. Simpson · U. Glas. L., letters to William Buchanan; letters to Charles Peebles · U. St Andr. L., letters to Eliza Dalgleish

Likenesses S. Joseph, bust, 1820, U. Edin., New College · A. Edouart, silhouettes, 1830–43, Scot. NPG · J. Watson-Gordon, oils, 1837, Scot. NPG · D. O. Hill, calotypes, c.1840–1859, U. Edin. · D. Macnee, oils, 1843, Scot. NPG · D. O. Hill and R. Adamson, two calotypes, 1843–8, NPG · T. Duncan, oils, c.1845, Scot. NPG · J. Steell, bust, 1846, U. Edin., New College · K. Macleay, watercolour drawing, 1847, Scot. NPG · J. Faed, portrait, 1849 (posthumous), U. Edin., New Coll. L. · J. Steell, statue, 1878, George Street, Edinburgh · J. Steell, marble bust, 1883, Scot. NPG · W. Bonnar, oils, Scot. NPG · D. O. Hill, oils, Scot. NPG · D. O. Hill and R. Adamson, calotypes, Scot. NPG [*see illus.*]

Wealth at death £5193 10s. 4d.: inventory, 22 July 1847, NA Scot., SC 70/1/67, p. 883

Chalmers, W. A. (*b.* 1767/8?), watercolour painter, can possibly be identified with the William Chalmers who entered the Royal Academy Schools in London in December 1791, at the age of twenty-three. From 1790 to 1794 he exhibited nine pictures at the Royal Academy, including a *View in the Collegiate Church, Westminster* and *Mrs Jordan as Sir Harry Wildair* (both 1790), two interiors of Westminster

Abbey (both 1791), *The Interment of the Late President of the Royal Academy at St Paul's* (1792), *Inside the Henry VII Chapel with the Ceremony of the Installation* (1793), and *West Front of the Abbey, Bath* (1794). He last exhibited at the Royal Academy in 1798 and is thought to have died young.

[ANON.], *rev.* ANNE PIMLOTT BAKER

Sources Mallalieu, *Watercolour artists*, vols. 1–2 · Graves, *RA exhibitors* · Redgrave, *Artists* · S. C. Hutchison, 'The Royal Academy Schools, 1768–1830', *Walpole Society*, 38 (1960–62), 123–91

Chalmers, Sir William (1787–1860), army officer, was born at Castle Street, Dundee, the eldest son of William Chalmers of Glenericht, near Blairgowrie, Perthshire. He entered the army on 9 July 1803 as ensign in the 52nd foot, becoming lieutenant on 23 October of the same year. With the 1st battalion, of which he was at one time adjutant, Chalmers served in Sicily in 1806–7. When eleven British regiments stationed there were ordered to be augmented each by a company of Sicilians enlisted for seven years' service Chalmers, as senior subaltern, had to raise the regimental quota.

Chalmers became captain in the 2nd battalion in 1807. He served with his regiment in Portugal and Spain in 1808–9, in the Walcheren expedition (including the bombardment of Flushing), and subsequently as a regimental officer and brigade-major of various infantry brigades in the Peninsular campaigns from 1810 to 1814. In the course of these campaigns he was present in seventeen engagements, including the battles of Barossa, Salamanca, and Vitoria, various actions in the Pyrenees and on the Nivelle, and at the sieges of Ciudad Rodrigo, Badajoz, and San Sebastian; he had altogether six horses shot under him, and on one occasion—the attack on the entrenchments of Sarre in 1813—was himself severely wounded.

Chalmers received a brevet majority for service in the field in 1813, and a brevet lieutenant-colonelcy for Waterloo. During the latter period he was serving as aide-de-camp to his uncle, Major-General Sir Kenneth Mackenzie, afterwards Sir Kenneth Douglas, bt, of Glenbervie, who was commanding at Antwerp, which was in a very critical state, but got leave to join his regiment before the battle, where he commanded the right wing of the 52nd, and had three horses killed under him. He was also present at the capture of Paris, and with the army of occupation in France until 1817, when he retired from active military life.

Chalmers married, in 1826, the daughter (*d.* 1851) of Thomas Page. He became brevet colonel in 1837, and was made KCH and CB the following year. He became a knight-bachelor in 1844 and a major-general in 1846; he was colonel of the 20th foot from February to October 1853 and of the 78th highlanders in 1853, and became lieutenant-general in 1854. Chalmers died at Dundee, on 2 June 1860, and was buried at his seat, Glenericht, Perthshire.

H. M. CHICHESTER, *rev.* JAMES LUNT

Sources *Army List* · W. S. Moorsom, ed., *Historical record of the fifty-second regiment (Oxfordshire light infantry), from the year 1755 to the year 1858* (1860) · W. Leeke, *Lord Seaton's regt. at Waterloo* (1866) · C. R.

Dod, *The peerage, baronetage and knightage of Great Britain and Ireland* · *GM*, 3rd ser., 9 (1860), 104 · Boase, *Mod. Eng. biog.* · *Dod's Peerage* (1858)

Wealth at death £31,086 1s. 10d.: confirmation, 1860, Scotland

Chalon, Alfred Edward (1780–1860), portrait and subject painter, was born on 15 February 1780 at Geneva, Switzerland. His forebears were Huguenots who left France at the revocation of the edict of Nantes and settled in Geneva. Chalon's father, Jean Chalon, was a watchmaker who left Geneva in 1794, during troubles arising from the French Revolution; after briefly visiting Ireland, he resided in England with his wife, two sons, and a daughter, and was appointed professor of French at the Royal Military College, Sandhurst. The family later moved to London. Alfred Chalon was the younger brother of John James *Chalon (1778–1854). The Chalon brothers were intended by their father for a career in trade, and each was placed in a large commercial establishment. This was not successful, and shortly afterwards they became students at the Royal Academy Schools, John in 1796 and Alfred in 1797. Alfred first exhibited a picture at the Royal Academy in 1810; he was elected an associate two years later and Royal Academician in 1816. Before this, in 1808, the year after its foundation, he became a member of the short-lived Associated Artists in Water-Colours. Also in 1808 the Chalons with six other practising artists founded the Society for the Study of Epic and Pastoral Design, later known as the Bread and Cheese Society and then the Chalon Sketching Society. It held weekly evening meetings and survived until 1851.

Alfred Chalon's work is graceful yet vigorous. His watercolour portraits, usually about 10 to 15 inches high, depict in brilliant technique and colour the textures of fur, lace, velvet, silk, and jewellery in convincing detail. When he was living with his father, sister, and brother at 42 Great Marlborough Street in London, a neighbour, Mrs Newton, wrote in a letter of 12 May 1833:

> Next door to us are the Chalons. Alfred Chalon is the famous and fashionable watercolour painter; so fond of painting ladies in flowing silks and airy laces that some of the artists published an advertisement in one of the morning papers to the effect that 'muslins and laces would be done up equal to new at 19 Berners Street', which was his residence before he became our neighbour.   (Whitley, 262)

His work became fashionable, especially in court circles, and he was appointed painter in watercolour to Queen Victoria; he was the first artist to portray the queen after her accession in her robes of state, worn at the dissolution of parliament, in which he accentuated her youthful beauty (Royal Collection, Belgium). The portrait was copied by Edward Henry Corbould and from this the head and shoulders were engraved by William Humphrys, and were featured on many British colonial postage stamps. When asked by the queen whether he was worried by the new invention of photography, Chalon replied 'Ah non, Madame, photography can't flatter!' (Lambourne, *Chalon Brothers*, 66).

Alfred Chalon painted most of his miniatures early in his career. They are among the best miniatures painted during the Regency. Like his larger portraits they make the most of the elaborate dress of his sitters, who included

Alfred Edward Chalon (1780–1860), self-portrait, 1847

Mme Vestris, Mrs Peter DeWint, and Byron's daughter (Augusta) Ada, countess of Lovelace (priv. coll.). Chalon was noted for his studies of opera singers, actresses, and above all, ballerinas, which afforded poetic insights into the contemporary Romantic ballet. They include portrayals of Fanny Cerrito in *Giselle*, Marie Taglioni in *La sylphide*, and Taglioni, Cerrito, and Fanny Elssler in *The Three Graces*. These works were reproduced by leading lithographers, often in colour, and were sometimes used to decorate music covers. A set of six Chalon sketches of Taglioni in various roles, lithographed by R. J. Lee, and with poems by W. N. Bayley, was published in 1831.

Chalon was a gifted and witty caricaturist, depicting in such work the efforts and affectations of operatic performers such as *Pasta in 'Norma'* (1833), *Violante Camporese Singing an Aria by Rossini*, and *Zuchelli in 'Il Barbiere'* (both 1829; V&A). He painted also genre and history subjects, and could imitate the styles of other artists, especially Watteau. *The Opera Box* (BM) is among his genre subjects; originally painted as an illustration to Lady Blessington's poem *The Belle of the Season* (1839), it depicts a moment during the performance of a ballet, seen from a box.

Alfred Chalon and his brother John lived together and shared an unusually close fraternal relationship; each did everything possible to advance the interests of the other. Neither married. John died in 1854, and in 1855 Alfred mounted an exhibition of their work at the Society of Arts in the Adelphi. It attracted little public attention. Alfred had accumulated an extensive collection of pictures, sketches, and drawings by himself and his brother. He proposed to give this to Hampstead, but the authorities could not provide suitable accommodation. He then offered it to the nation, but died before arrangements

could be made. By a will discovered after his death, the collection was acquired by some relatives in Geneva, and was distributed at auction. In addition to his artistic gifts, Alfred Chalon was appreciated as an excellent and amusing raconteur, and was an accomplished musician. Alfred Chalon died, after a period of sickness, on 3 October 1860 at his Campden Hill house in Kensington. He was buried at Highgate cemetery, in the same grave as his brother, who had been interred six years previously.

RAYMOND LISTER

Sources J. L. Roget, *A history of the 'Old Water-Colour' Society*, 2 vols. (1891) · R. Loche, *Deux artistes: les Chalon* (Geneva, 1971) [exhibition catalogue, Museé Rath, Geneva] · L. Lambourne, *The Chalon brothers* (1981) [exhibition catalogue, V&A] · C. R. Leslie, *Autobiographical recollections*, ed. T. Taylor, 2 vols. (1860) · R. Redgrave and S. Redgrave, *A century of painters of the English school*, 2 vols. (1866) · W. T. Whitley, *Art in England, 1821–1837* (1930); repr. (1973) · M. Hardie, *Water-colour painting in Britain*, ed. D. Snelgrove, J. Mayne, and B. Taylor, 2: *The Romantic period* (1967) · L. Robson, *Masterpieces of engraving on postage stamps* (1943) · C. W. Beaumont and S. Sitwell, *The Romantic ballet in lithographs of the time* (1938) · R. Lister, *British Romantic art* (1973) · CGPLA Eng. & Wales (1860) · S. C. Hutchison, 'The Royal Academy Schools, 1768–1830', *Walpole Society*, 38 (1960–62), 123–91, esp. 157 · P. Conner, 'Chalon', *The dictionary of art*, ed. J. Turner (1996) · J. Hamilton, *The Sketching Society, 1799–1851* (1971) [exhibition catalogue, V&A] · L. Lambourne, *Victorian painting* (1999)

Archives V&A NAL, letters to C. F. Leslie

Likenesses A. E. Chalon, self-portrait, drawing, 1847, BM [*see illus.*] · C. R. Leslie, group portrait, pencil and wash, BM · J. Partridge, group portrait, pen, ink, and wash (*A Meeting of the Sketching Society*), BM

Wealth at death under £6000: administration, 16 Nov 1860, *CGPLA Eng. & Wales*

Chalon, John James (1778–1854), landscape and genre painter, was born at Geneva, Switzerland, on 27 March 1778, of a French protestant family resident there since the revocation of the edict of Nantes. In 1789 the family came to England and Chalon's father, Jean Chalon, who had been a watchmaker, was appointed professor of French language and literature at the Royal Military College, Sandhurst. He intended his two sons, John James and his younger brother Alfred Edward *Chalon (1780–1860) to become businessmen, but both had a bent towards the arts, and each attended the Royal Academy Schools, John James from 1796, and his brother from 1797. In 1800 J. J. Chalon exhibited at the academy his first picture, *Banditti at their Repast*, shortly followed by *A Landscape* and *Fortune Telling*. J. J. Chalon's early practice was in oil, but in 1806 he began to exhibit at the gallery of the Society of Painters in Watercolour, of which he became a member in 1808. But he was among those who in 1813 seceded and joined the rival society, Associated Artists in Water-Colours; he may also have been influenced in making this decision by a desire to become a member of the Royal Academy. In 1816 he exhibited an important work at the Royal Academy, *Napoleon on Board the 'Bellerophon'*, which he presented to Greenwich Hospital. This was followed by a fine painting, *A View of Hastings*, now in the Victoria and Albert Museum, London. In 1827 he was elected associate of the Royal Academy, and in 1845 Royal Academician. Among his later works are *Gil Blas in the Robbers' Cave*, a scene from Le Sage's picaresque romance (1843), and *The Arrival of the Steam-Packet at Folkestone* (1844). He published as a book *A Set of Twenty-Four Subjects, Exhibiting the Costumes of Paris*, which he had begun in May 1820, and lithographed himself. These were said to have been much admired by Thomas Stothard. Richard and Samuel Redgrave in their *Century of Painters* also praised Chalon's landscapes as 'beautiful studies from Nature', but noted his 'faults of colour that overtook him in later practice' (Redgrave and Redgrave, 2.471, 473).

With his brother and Francis Stevens in 1808 Chalon founded the Society for the Study of Epic and Pastoral Design, an evening sketching society later known as the Chalon Sketching Society, whose members included Clarkson Stanfield and C. R. Leslie RA. During meetings themes were set from the Bible, classical literature, Shakespeare, and English poetry for members' drawings. In 1842 Queen Victoria set the themes of 'Desire' and 'Elevation' as subjects for drawings. Leslie, who greatly respected J. J. Chalon's genius, said of him that few painters had such a range, or attained to so equal an excellence in so many departments of art.

The Chalon brothers were closely bonded: they lived together, and were inseparable throughout life. Sometimes they even collaborated on the same painting—John painting the background, Alfred the figures. Alfred exhibited more work than his brother, but he always did his best to promote John's interest. This happy fraternal relationship impressed all who met them. C. R. Leslie said of his own friendship with them that it was 'an intimacy I count among the best things of my life' (Leslie, 1.119). In 1847, while out walking with his brother, John suffered a paralytic seizure; this was followed by illness and mental decline. Alfred nursed him throughout but he died at his home, El Retiro, Campden Hill, Kensington, on 14 November 1854. He was buried in Highgate cemetery, Middlesex.

ERNEST RADFORD, rev. RAYMOND LISTER

Sources J. L. Roget, *A history of the 'Old Water-Colour' Society*, 2 vols. (1891) · R. Loche, *Deux artistes: les Chalon* (Geneva, 1971) [exhibition catalogue, Museé Rath, Geneva] · L. Lambourne, *The Chalon brothers* (1981) [exhibition catalogue, V&A] · R. Redgrave and S. Redgrave, *A century of painters of the English school*, 2 vols. (1866) · C. R. Leslie, *Autobiographical recollections*, ed. T. Taylor, 2 vols. (1860) · M. Hardie, *Water-colour painting in Britain*, ed. D. Snelgrove, J. Mayne, and B. Taylor, 2: *The Romantic period* (1967) · R. Ormond, *Early Victorian portraits*, 1 (1973), 97 · S. C. Hutchison, 'The Royal Academy Schools, 1768–1830', *Walpole Society*, 38 (1960–62), 123–91, esp. 157–8 · J. Hamilton, *The Sketching Society, 1799–1851* (1971) [exhibition catalogue, V&A] · P. Conner, 'Chalon', *The dictionary of art*, ed. J. Turner (1996)

Archives V&A

Likenesses J. Partridge, oils, 1836, NPG · C. R. Leslie, group portrait, pencil and wash, BM · J. Partridge, group portrait, pen and wash (*A meeting of the Sketching Society*), BM

Chaloner, Edward (1590/91–1625), Church of England clergyman, was born at Chiswick, Middlesex, the second of the four surviving sons of Sir Thomas *Chaloner (1563/4–1615), naturalist and courtier, and his first wife, Elizabeth (1568–1603), daughter of William Fleetwood, recorder of London. He matriculated at Magdalen College, Oxford, on 22 February 1605 and graduated BA on 8 July

1607, proceeding MA on 15 May 1610. On the occasion of the visit to Magdalen in August 1605 of Prince Henry (Chaloner's father was the young prince's tutor) he was among several undergraduates who took part in disputations before the prince, and later it was Chaloner who, in the name of the college, presented him with two pairs of gloves. He was elected a fellow of All Souls College in 1611, graduated BD on 30 May 1617, and was created DD on 6 November 1619.

By this time Chaloner had already risen to prominence as a preacher and a man of learning. In 1617, at the invitation of John King, bishop of London, he preached a sermon at Paul's Cross in London, perhaps the most public pulpit in England. He published *The Masse Displayed* (1619), a translation of *La messe en françois* (1610) by the French protestant Jean Bédé de la Gormandière. He preached sermons at several official university occasions, including the annual Oxford Act in 1620. By 1621 he was a royal chaplain, an appointment renewed with the accession of Charles I in 1625. A collection of his preaching, *Six Sermons*, appeared in 1623 (a further collection, also entitled *Six Sermons*, was published posthumously in 1629).

In October 1622 Chaloner resigned his fellowship at All Souls, and shortly afterwards married Elizabeth (*b.* 1604), daughter of George Hovenden, canon of Canterbury, and niece of the warden of All Souls. They had a son, Thomas, who died in infancy. Chaloner preached in Canterbury Cathedral on more than one occasion, presumably at the invitation of his father-in-law. At Oxford, Chaloner was a protégé of the chancellor, William, third earl of Pembroke, and when the headship of St Alban Hall fell vacant Pembroke chose Chaloner to fill it; he was admitted as principal on 29 December 1624.

Chaloner's polemical work *Credo ecclesiam sanctam catholicam: the authoritie, universalitie and visibilitie of the church* (1625; 2nd edn, 1638) was a contribution to the current debate about whether the antecedents of the Church of England were to be found inside or outside the Church of Rome. Dismissing the idea of a simple polarity, Chaloner skilfully argues for a complex synthesis—'our Church had in those dayes a twofold subsistencie, the one separate from the Church of Rome, the other mixt and conjoyned with it' (Chaloner, *Credo*, 91)—that is, separate in the persons of all the early reformers, and conjoined in the persons of all those who retained in their hearts the simple faith of the early church, and who were 'baptised into Christs Truth, and not the Popes errors' (ibid., 95). Published in the same volume with *Credo* was *Unde Zizania? The Originall and Progresse of Heresie*, a sermon that Chaloner had preached before James I at Theobalds in Hertfordshire in 1624.

In religion Chaloner was a Calvinist episcopalian very much in tune with the then prevailing orthodoxy of the Church of England establishment under Archbishop George Abbot. He charts a course between, on the one hand, the Arminians—'shall we feare … lest Altars and Images be taken away? … Neither our Prayers nor Sacrifices stand in need of such trimming' (Chaloner, *Six Sermons*, 321–2)—and, on the other, the puritans, who 'cannot brooke the Pope in the world, [but] would be glad, were they of the number, to have ten in a Parish' (ibid., 182–3).

Chaloner deplored obfuscation of any kind, and valued exposition through clear and precise language, of which his sermons are models. His knowledge of the church fathers, the schoolmen, and more recent theologians was compendious, and his interests also ranged beyond theology: he was, for example, conversant with contemporary developments in science. His respect for learning was great, as was his scorn of ignorance: 'I could wish them more charitie then to grudge that other men see with two eyes, because they can see but with one' (Chaloner, *Six Sermons*, 347). He was signally ready to accept what he felt to be essential truths whatever their immediate source, whether from the ancient philosophers and poets 'who had not those lights that wee have, and yet saw farre more then many of us doe' (ibid., 338), or even from the Church of Rome: 'Christian libertie ... ties us not to abrogate a good or indifferent thing for the abuse, but rather to preserve the substance, and to pare off the corruption' (Chaloner, *Masse*, preface).

Chaloner died at St Alban Hall on 25 July 1625, aged thirty-four, a victim of an outbreak of the plague. His body was hurriedly buried the same night in the churchyard of St Mary the Virgin. A monument was later raised to his memory.   ANTHONY ESPOSITO

Sources Wood, *Ath. Oxon.*, new edn · Wood, *Ath. Oxon.: Fasti*, new edn · W. D. Macray, *A register of the members of St Mary Magdalen College, Oxford*, 8 vols. (1894–1915) · R. Hovenden, *Genealogical memoranda relating to the family of Hovenden* (1872) · N. W. S. Cranfield, 'Chaplains in ordinary at the early Stuart court: the purple road', *Patronage and recruitment in the Tudor and early Stuart church*, ed. C. Cross (1996), 120–47, esp. 142 · E. Chaloner, *The masse displayed* (1619) · E. Chaloner, *Credo ecclesiam sanctam catholicam: the authoritie, universalitie and visibilitie of the church* (1625) · E. Chaloner, *Sixe sermons* (1623)

Chaloner, James (c.1602–1660), politician, was born in the parish of St Olave, Silver Street, London, the fourth son of Sir Thomas *Chaloner the younger (1563/4–1615) and Elizabeth Fleetwood (1568–1603). He matriculated from Brasenose College, Oxford, on 28 March 1617, and was admitted to the Middle Temple on 19 October 1619. On 28 September 1637 he married Ursula (d. 1650), daughter of Sir Philip Fairfax of Steeton, Yorkshire, with whom he had six children. With his elder brother Thomas *Chaloner (1595–1660) he pursued the Chaloners' claim against the crown over their 'alum rights', and in 1657 alleged that he had been 'extremely oppressed by the late king ... so that £6000 is owing to him' (*CSP dom.*, 1657–8, 60). He conceived another grievance against the crown in 1637, when he was imprisoned in the Tower for two months on suspicion of helping Thomas (who had been accused of writing an anti-Laudian tract) flee the country.

Chaloner seems to have lived in St Giles-in-the-Fields for most of the civil war, and with Thomas contributed £200 towards the parliamentarian war effort. Early in 1645 he wrote to his uncle by marriage, Ferdinando, second Lord Fairfax, expressing support for the self-denying ordinance and for new modelling of the parliamentarian armies.

During the autumn of 1645 Fairfax attempted to secure his election for Scarborough, but Chaloner's candidacy was successfully challenged by the local parliamentarian, Luke Robinson. Fairfax's son, Sir Thomas, then tried to use his influence as commander of the New Model Army to obtain a seat for Chaloner in Devon, but again his candidacy floundered in the face of local opposition. He finally secured a seat, on 10 April 1648, at Aldborough, Yorkshire—probably on the interest of Sir Thomas Mauleverer, a friend of the Fairfaxes.

Chaloner retained his seat at Pride's Purge, and on 20 December declared his dissent from the earlier vote of the Commons accepting the king's answers in the treaty of Newport as grounds for continuing negotiations. Appointed a commissioner to try the king, he attended only six sessions of the trial commission, and the first two days of the trial itself. Unlike his brother Thomas he did not sign the royal death warrant. In a vindication of his part in the king's trial written in 1660, he claimed that he had been opposed to the 'horrid and desperate actings' of the early months of the Rump, and had only continued to attend the house 'to keep things from falling into a worse condition' (BL, Add. MS 71448, fol. 67). He was 'the only instrument under God' (*Seventh Report*, HMC, 147) for saving the royalist plotter Sir John Owen from the scaffold in February 1649, and in April helped to draw up a declaration against the Levellers. He was named to numerous committees in the Rump for propagating the gospel, and was also active in settling 'godly orthodox ministers' (BL, Add. MS 71448, fol. 68) in vacant livings. His concern to promote godly religion may also explain his central role in the reform and regulation of the universities.

Chaloner was on close terms with Sir Thomas Fairfax, now third Lord Fairfax, and by February 1651 was lodging in Fairfax's York House residence in London. When that was sold by Fairfax in 1652 Chaloner moved to the lodge in the Middle Park at Hampton Court. In 1652 Fairfax appointed him one of three commissioners to report on the state of the Isle of Man (the Rump having granted Fairfax the lordship of the island), and he subsequently wrote a short treatise concerning its customs and topography, which he dedicated to Fairfax.

Chaloner played no significant part in national affairs under the protectorate, and in 1655 was suspected, probably wrongly, of trying to elicit Fairfax's support for the Yorkshire royalist rising. In 1656 Fairfax appointed him civil governor of the Isle of Man, and he apparently remained on the island for most of the period 1656–9. In December 1659 he attempted to secure the island for General Monck, but was imprisoned by order of the army leaders in London, 'who looked upon him as a person devoted to the royal interest' (*Seventh Report*, HMC, 147). The countess dowager of Derby later affirmed that he had performed many services to the royal party during his time on the island. On 27 December 1659 the Rump ordered Chaloner's release, and in January 1660 confirmed his governorship of the Isle of Man. Having fallen sick during his imprisonment and being of a 'tender and weak constitution' (ibid.) he died in July 1660, leaving a son and two daughters unprovided for. He was probably buried on the Isle of Man.   DAVID SCOTT

Sources HoP, *Commons, 1690–1715* [draft] · *JHC,* 2–7 (1640–59) · MSS relating to James Chaloner, BL, Add. MS 71448 · G. W. Johnson, ed., *The Fairfax correspondence: memoirs of the reign of Charles the First,* 2 vols. (1848) · R. Bell, ed., *Memorials of the civil war … forming the concluding volumes of the Fairfax correspondence,* 2 vols. (1849) · J. Chaloner, *A short treatise of the Isle of Man,* ed. J. G. Cumming, Manx Society, 10 (1864) · *CSP dom., 1636–61* · *Seventh report,* HMC, 6 (1879), 147 · J. G. Muddiman, *The trial of King Charles the First* (1928) · N. Yorks. CRO, ZFM/alum mines, 1.3, 5 · Wood, *Ath. Oxon.,* new edn, 3.50–53 · [W. Prynne], *A full declaration of the true state of the secluded members case* (1660) [Thomason tract E 1013(22)] · *Mercurius Pragmaticus* (12–19 Dec 1648) [Thomason tract E 476(35)] · *Heads of a Diarie, collected out of the Journalls of both Houses of Parliament* (26 Dec 1648) [TT E 536 (34)] · *Parliamentary Intelligencer* (26 Dec 1659–2 Jan 1660) [Thomason tract E 182(16)]

Archives BL, Add. MS 71448 · N. Yorks. CRO, MSS, Mic. 2050 · N. Yorks. CRO, MSS relating to alum mines, ZFM | BL, Add. MSS 18979, fol. 207; 36792, fols. 13, 57v, 62v, 69, 79v · Bodl. Oxf., Fairfax MS 32, fol. 179 · Bodl. Oxf., Nalson MS IV, fols. 90, 213, 244v, 317 · PRO, C181/6; E115/104/120; LR2/266, fol. 1; PSO 2/180

Chaloner, Richard (*d.* 1643), conspirator, is someone whose origins and parentage are as yet unknown. He was bound in London, perhaps between 1621 and 1628, as an apprentice to the Fishmongers' Company, to whose livery he was later admitted, but he set up in trade as a linen draper. In 1638 he and his partner Richard Norton were jointly rated at £40 (implying a full valuation of £115 for their premises at Finch Lane, St Michael Cornhill). Both Chaloner and Norton were active in the peace campaign of December 1642 by which moderates and conservatives in the City of London sought through petitions to halt the descent into war. Not all these men were royalists, and Chaloner himself appears to have been politically a moderate who continued to attend vestry meetings in St Michael Cornhill after the start of hostilities.

On 16 March 1643 Charles I issued a commission of array directed to leading citizens of London to raise money and recruit troops for the king in London, Westminster, Southwark, and the counties adjacent. The commission was let sleep while negotiations continued at Oxford, but after their collapse it was reactivated and taken to London on 19 May. The chief members of the conspiracy in London were the wealthy poet and MP Edmund Waller and his brother-in-law Nathaniel Tompkins, who had connections in both the City and the queen's household; after these, Chaloner ranked next in importance. While Waller carefully canvassed those in both houses of parliament whom he thought to be sympathetic to peace on the king's terms, Tompkins and Chaloner were involved in similar activity in the City. This may have originated separately from the military plans, as a renewal of the previous year's petitioning activity. An agitation was planned against high taxes occasioned by the war; complaints against assessments were to be encouraged, so as to deepen resentment of the government. Clarendon later claimed that this was the chief purpose of the plotters. But the City men were

also engaged in canvassing. Lists of supporters, opponents, and neutrals were drawn up and the results conveyed via Waller to Oxford: it may be assumed that this was not an opinion poll for its own sake.

John Pym was able to point to connections between peacemakers and insurrectionists, and his official account reported details of plans to seize strongpoints and arrest key men. All this was credible enough. But the plain fabric of the plot was elaborately embroidered by Pym and his followers. Claiming that the plotters 'would have left all the good Party, and good ministers, to be destroyed by the papists, and other ill affected Persons' (*JHC,* 1642–1644, 116) in a bloody massacre, they nevertheless withheld the news of this mortal danger for several days, releasing it on 31 May, when the plotters were already under arrest, at a time calculated to do the maximum damage to the peace party. The past activities of petitioners for peace such as Chaloner, they urged, were a mere cover for the ushering in of popery and destruction; the purpose, and the effect, was to stigmatize and silence efforts to end the war.

Nevertheless the military plot was real, and Chaloner was privy to it. It has been suggested that he and his circle may be distinguished politically from those around Tompkins with his mainly royalist links. Chaloner's own friends, and his own preference, may very well have been for a moderate and amicable solution, peacefully reached. But what if the government were in the hands of a party set on war, and immovable by peaceful means? Would this not justify forcible measures to remove the obstruction? In the House of Commons, on 6 June 1643, there was read 'a warrant from the King to Richard Challoner of London, Linen Draper signed C. R. dated 2 May, enabling him to receive moneys, plate, etc' (*JHC,* 1642–1644, 117).

On 9 June the House of Lords set the next Thursday as a day of public thanksgiving for deliverance. Essex was asked to appoint a council of war to try the defendants: their trial opened on 30 June and four days later Tompkins and Chaloner received sentence of death.

The chief conspirator, Waller, was able to use his wealth and connections to escape—by means of bribery, a short spell in prison, and a fine of £10,000—to freedom in France. Tompkins and Chaloner were left to shoulder responsibility for the plot, and for the terror which it had inspired among the citizenry. Both were executed near their homes. On 5 July, on the scaffold erected by his house in Cornhill by the Old Exchange, Chaloner admitted his guilt, objecting only to the accusation that he had engaged to help seize two of the magazines. Finally, he begged forgiveness and repeated that his death was deserved. 'Then his Father tendred him the King's pardon' to which Chaloner responded, 'Sir, I beseech you, trouble me not with it. Pray speak to my friends to take care of my corps and carry me home'—words which were surely intended to be his last. But there was a short, unexpected, delay. Hugh Peter asked whether there remained in his conscience anything which he wished to disburden. Chaloner replied:

Gentlemen, this is the happiest day that ever I had; I shall now, gentlemen, declare a little more of the occasion of this, as I am desired by Mr Peters, to give him and the world satisfaction in it. It came from Mr Waller under this notion, that if we could make a moderate party here in London, to stand betwixt, and in the gap to unite the King and the Parliament, it would be a very acceptable work, for now the three kingdoms lay a bleeding, and unless that were done, there was no hopes to unite them. Withal I made this reply: 'Sir, if I could assure you of three parts of London, none of them should stir, unless we had the countenance of the Lords and commons'. (Rushworth, 5.327)

Both Chaloner and the other convicted citizens had tried to hinge their involvement in the desperate measures planned upon the legitimacy conferred by parliamentary approval. But in this matter they had accepted Waller's assurances, and in almost his last sentence, Chaloner confirmed that 'As Mr Waller was the mouth from the Lords, as he did declare, so I was the unhappy instrument from Mr Waller to the rest' (Rushworth, 5.327). The parish register of St Michael Cornhill records the burial on 5 July 1643—the day of the execution—of 'Richard Shallener in the church, a linen draper' (Chester, 239). STEPHEN WRIGHT

Sources J. Rushworth, *Historical collections*, new edn, 5 (1721) · K. Lindley, *Popular politics and religion in civil war London* (1997) · I. Roy, 'A cavalier view of London', *London and the civil war*, ed. S. Porter (1996), 149–74 · *A discovery of the great plot for the utter ruine of the city of London … as it was at large made known by John Pym esq. on Thursday, being the eighth of June, 1643* (1643) [Thomason tract E 105(21)] · Clarendon, *Hist. rebellion*, vol. 3 · *Parliamentary diary of Sir Simonds D'Ewes*, BL, Harley MS 164, fols. 396–7 · *Parliamentary diary of Lawrence Whitacre*, BL, Add. MS 31116, fols. 22 and 55 · W. Haskett Smith, *The Worshipful Company of Fishmongers of the City of London: lists of apprentices and freemen in 1537 and 1600–50* (1916) · T. C. Dale, ed., *The inhabitants of London in 1638*, 2 vols. (1931) · T. C. Dale, 'The members of the City companies in 1641 as set forth in the return of the poll tax', 1935, U. Lond., Institute of Historical Research · J. L. Chester, ed., *The parish registers of St Michael, Cornhill, London*, Harleian Society, register section, 7 (1882) · J. Ashburnham, *A narrative by John Ashburnham of attendance on King Charles the First*, 2 vols. (1830), vol. 2, appx 1 · *JHC*, 3 (1642–4)

Chaloner, Robert (1547/8–1621), Church of England clergyman and educational benefactor, was born in Goldsborough, near Knaresborough, West Riding of Yorkshire, the second son of Robert and Ann Chaloner of Llanfyllin (possibly Llanfyllin, Montgomeryshire). He was elected to a studentship at Christ Church, Oxford—which held an estate at Meifod close to his parental home in Wales—on 9 August 1564, aged sixteen, and took his BA degree on 25 June 1566 and his MA on 19 June 1569. Chaloner held the positions of catechist (1573) and censor (1574) at Christ Church before he was presented by the duke of Bedford to the living of Amersham, Buckinghamshire, in 1576, the year in which he graduated BD. He resigned his studentship the following year and about this time married Christina Garbrand, in Oxford. She was probably the daughter of Garbrand Harkes, a friend of Chaloner, who was a bookseller in Oxford and rector of North Crawley, and his wife, Elizabeth; Harkes bequeathed his library to Chaloner. In 1584 Chaloner graduated DD and was appointed a canon of Windsor, where he served as chanter and auditor. He

appears to have been a man of considerable wealth and high connections; the duke of Bedford, his patron, was a frequent visitor to his home. Chaloner died, probably in Amersham, on 1 May 1621.

By the time of his death Chaloner's estate consisted of lands in East Oakley, Fyfield, Bray, Garsington, Ockenden, and Wavendon as well as urban property in Windsor. In his will, dated 20 June 1620, which is gently pious with suggestions of humour, he left the bulk of his estate to his wife but, as the couple were childless, there were substantial bequests to his sisters' children including his farm at Wavendon and most of his library, which was given to his youngest nephew, Gabriel Rolle. Abell Rolle was bequeathed Chaloner's lute, and his edition of Pellicanus's commentary on the Bible was left to the 'Library of Windsor College'. It is in his educational bequests, however, that Chaloner is best commemorated. £20 per year, derived from the estate at Wavendon, was to provide a stipend for the master at the grammar school (now King James's comprehensive school) which he had founded in Knaresborough in 1616. A small estate in Garsington, Oxfordshire, was left to Christ Church, Oxford, after Christina's death, to provide either a divinity lecture or an exhibition for three poor scholars, the lecturer or scholars to come from Amersham or Knaresborough. The writ of execution under the statute of charitable uses was signed on 16 February 1638, presumably soon after Christina's death, but the land in Garsington was so intermixed and confused that a lectureship (rather than the scholarships) was not constituted until 1750.

Chaloner also charged his friends and executors, William Tothill and William Penniman, to erect a free grammar school in Amersham 'as a testimony of my love to them and their children'. He provided property and another £20 from Wavendon as an annual stipend for the schoolmaster but Thomas Day, the husband of Chaloner's sister Ellen, ignored the terms of the bequest and refused to pay the rent charges necessary to fund the schoolmasters' stipends. Only after a chancery inquisition held on 16 September 1624 were the Days forced to make redress. The school, now Dr Challoner's Grammar School, Amersham, was opened later that month. (The school has used this spelling of his name since 1624.)

Robert Chaloner was buried, without a memorial, in St Mary's Church, Amersham. His funeral address was given by his neighbour, Richard Woodcock, vicar of Chesham, on the text 'I have fought a good fight, I have finished my course, I have kept the faith'. J. H. CURTHOYS

Sources F. R. Treadgold, 'Challoner's', *1624–1974* (1974) · *VCH Buckinghamshire*, vol. 2 · Christ Church Oxf., DPi.a.1 · will, PRO, PROB 11/138, sig. 69 · Foster, *Alum. Oxon.*
Wealth at death of considerable wealth: will, PRO, PROB 11/138, sig. 69

Chaloner, Sir Thomas, the elder (1521–1565), diplomat and writer, was born in London, the elder of three sons of Roger Chaloner (d. 1550), mercer and administrator, of London, and his first wife, Margaret, daughter of Richard Middleton. His younger brothers were John (b. before

Sir Thomas Chaloner the elder (1521–1565), by unknown artist, 1559

1526, d. 1581) and Francis (d. after 1565). He was educated at Cambridge, possibly at St John's College, and by 1538 was in the service of Sir Thomas Cromwell, king's secretary.

In 1540 Chaloner went to the imperial diet at Regensburg as the secretary of the ambassador, Sir Henry Knyvet. During the diet he became involved in an intrigue caused by a secret correspondence between Stephen Gardiner, bishop of Winchester, who was also ambassador, and Pope Paul III. Confused by the presence of two English ambassadors, an Italian merchant attached to Charles V's court mentioned these letters to Knyvet's other secretary, Wolfe. Knyvet sent Wolfe back to the merchant together with Chaloner who was told nothing about the affair. What Chaloner overheard and reported confirmed the information and began a controversy between the two English ambassadors which lasted two or three weeks and was finally stopped only by a letter from Henry VIII himself.

After the diet Chaloner accompanied Charles in his expedition against the Moors in Algeria. The imperial entourage set out from Regensburg on 29 July 1541 and travelled by way of Innsbruck, Trent, Genoa (where the emperor was met by Cosimo (I) de' Medici, duke of Florence), and Lucca (where he was ceremoniously received by the pope) to La Spezia, where he set sail for Africa with a large fleet towards the end of September. Because of violent storms the expedition failed, and Chaloner himself was shipwrecked off the coast of Algeria. Exhausted by swimming, he saved himself by clamping his teeth on a cable thrown from a nearby galley 'not without breaking and losse of certaine of his teeth' (Hakluyt, 5.99).

In November 1544 Chaloner and his father were granted the office of one of the tellers of the receipt of the exchequer. In December 1545 Thomas Chaloner was appointed clerk of the privy council with a salary of £10 a year. For the next six years his duties consisted mainly in delivering messages and money to leaders of the English army and to contingents of Italian, Spanish, and German mercenaries. He took musters of Spanish soldiers and made inventories of provisions; occasionally he presented Henry's rewards to foreign ambassadors. In November 1545 he was sent to the emperor's ambassador, Eustace Chapuys, to protest against the detention of certain English ships by the Spanish Inquisition at San Sebastián, Spain.

Chaloner was wooing Joan (d. 1557), daughter of William Cotton of Oxenhoath, Kent, and widow of Sir Thomas Leigh, by 1546 and making arrangements to marry her. They were married by October 1550. It is unknown whether they had any children or not but, if so, they were dead by 1563, when Chaloner described himself as childless. His wife died in January 1557 and was buried in Shoreditch church, Middlesex.

On 10 September 1547 Chaloner participated in the bloody English victory over the Scots at the battle of Pinkie. After the battle he was knighted by Edward Seymour, duke of Somerset and lord protector of Edward VI. On 26 October he became an MP for Lancaster. He was in good company among prominent Cambridge men and administrators, like William Cecil, Sir Thomas Cawarden, and John Cheke. Seven years later he was elected MP for Knaresborough in Yorkshire. He was JP for Middlesex from 1547 to 1554. He served on two commissions for Middlesex in 1550 and 1551: one responsible for collecting taxes, the other for regulating the prices of food.

On 18 January 1549, one day after the arrest of Thomas Seymour, Lord Seymour of Sudeley, the lord admiral, for high treason, Chaloner and two others were instructed to search Seymour's house at Bromham in Wiltshire. On 18 September, Chaloner, Sir John Mason, Cecil, and others testified in the trial for deprivation of Edmund Bonner, bishop of London. On 15 and 18 December 1550 Chaloner, Cecil, Cheke, Nicolas Udall, Sir Thomas Smith, principal secretary, and others testified in the trial for deprivation of Gardiner. From February to April 1551 Chaloner was treasurer of an expedition which was to sail around the southern coast of Ireland inspecting and fortifying harbours. In May and June he was one of the negotiators of a treaty with Scotland concluded at Norham. Later in the summer he returned to Scotland on business for the king. In 1552, from March to October, he was again a member of a commission sent to arrange a partition of the debatable land on the Scottish border.

In April 1553 Chaloner went to Poissy and was appointed special ambassador to France; in August, after the accession of Mary I, he was recalled. Although his name appears in a list of persons granted a general pardon in October

1553, he almost surely had no part in the plot of John Dudley, duke of Northumberland, since Chaloner was not in England while the conspiracy was in the making. Mary sent him to negotiate with Mary of Guise, dowager queen of Scotland, in February 1556. Moreover, he served Mary in her war with France (1557–8), both providing supplies and participating in the fighting.

After the accession of Elizabeth I, Chaloner was almost continuously busy as her ambassador in Germany, Flanders, and Spain. In 1558–9 he went to Augsburg as Elizabeth's ambassador to Ferdinand, holy Roman emperor. He shared in the delicate but unsuccessful negotiations for a marriage between Elizabeth and the emperor's eldest son Maximilian. In 1559–60 he was in Flanders as ambassador to Philip II and later to the duchess of Parma. During his stay in Flanders, Chaloner spent a few days at Bruges, a week or so at Ghent, about a month and a half (in two separate visits) at Antwerp, and the rest of the time in Brussels. He observed the solemnities of the order of the Golden Fleece, sounded out Gómez Suárez de Fingueroa, count de Feria, and Cardinal Antoine Perrenot de Granvelle, bishop of Arras, concerning Spain's policy toward England, had audiences with Philip and the duchess of Parma, interviewed Italian and German 'projectors' who offered to sell Elizabeth various schemes and inventions, undertook tedious negotiations to obtain an export licence for some horses the queen had purchased, and fretted about the late arrival of his funds.

In 1560 Chaloner was recalled, but in November 1561 he left England to become Elizabeth's ambassador in Spain. By 22 December, after a very uncomfortable journey through France, he reached the frontiers of Spain, or rather 'pain' as he called it. By 15 January 1562 he arrived in Madrid. He was robbed of almost £100 during his journey, and the delay of his baggage cost him 800 ducats. He learned that the funds of his predecessor, Sir Thomas Chamberlain, had arrived so late that he had been forced to borrow at ruinous rates of interest. Chaloner was outraged when he discovered that some of his coffers, which reached Bilbao before his arrival, had been broken open by inquisitors, who asserted that they contained forbidden books. Though he had a dispensation from Spanish religious laws, Chamberlain had had difficulties with the Inquisition, and Chaloner asked Sir John Mason to get the privy council to send him a written opinion about how he should adapt himself to religious practices in Spain.

Although he wished to travel in Spain, Chaloner was usually obliged to remain in Madrid in his house at Porte del Sol to be near the king. In September 1563 he accompanied Philip to the cortes at Monzón. Having spent some time at Saragossa, Barbastro, Monzón, Barcelona, Valencia, and Alcalá, he was back in Madrid by 6 April 1564. The necessity of Chaloner's stay in Spain was mostly nominal; the queen, Cecil, and his friends did not keep him posted on the latest news and this lack of information caused him serious embarrassment. The most important political struggles at this time were in France, and most of the news Chaloner wrote has more anecdotal than historical value. Like most English ambassadors of his time he complained bitterly and frequently about the late arrival of his funds. He was also almost continuously tormented by various illnesses: tertian agues, rheumatism, sharp stomach pains, kidney stones. He was recalled in December 1563, but by the time the revocation reached him there was new business to delay his departure. Finally, in May 1565 he embarked at San Sebastián and within four days landed totally exhausted at Exeter.

Chaloner married Audrey or Ethelreda (d. 1605), daughter of Edward Frodsham of Elton, Cheshire, in September 1565. Sir Thomas *Chaloner the younger (1563/4–1615) was his stepson, rather than his natural son, as generally believed, having been born between 19 November 1563 and 17 November 1564, a period when the elder Sir Thomas Chaloner was still in Spain. He refers to the 'sonne of the saide Audrie', never to his son (PRO, PROB 11/61, sig. 47). He made his stepson his heir and this explains the changes to his will immediately before his death.

To the Elizabethans, Chaloner's fame rested not on his English works, but on his Latin poetry, his military and diplomatic service to four Tudor monarchs, and his escape from drowning off the coast of Algiers. But today he is mostly remembered as the first translator into English of Desiderius Erasmus's *Praise of Folly* (1549). Chaloner's Latin writings include *In laudem Henrici octavi carmen panegiricum* (1560) and *De republica Anglorum instauranda* (1579), a long didactic epic in ten books which he composed in Spain; the volume also contains several short poems. He translated from Latin Gilbert Cousin's *Office of Servauntes* (1543) and Cheke's *An Homilie of Saint Iohn Crysostome* (1544). He translated into English verse Ovid's seventeenth heroic epistle, 'Helen to Paris', and nine metres of Boethius's *Consolations of Philosophy*. Some of his works which are no longer extant, including verses translated from Ariosto, are known only from letters.

Chaloner's share in the festivities of twelfth night 1552 shows that he moved in the same literary circles as William Baldwin, George Ferrers, and Thomas Phaer, the translator of the *Aeneid*. In 1555 Chaloner was one of the original seven gathered by Baldwin to begin work on the *Mirror for Magistrates*, to which he contributed the 'tragedy' of Richard II. Chaloner was a friend of Walter Haddon, Cheke, and other learned men of his time. Among his literary friends were Thomas Wilson, Barnaby Googe, Ferrers, and Thomas Sackville.

Some letters written in the last two years of Chaloner's life give a fleeting glimpse of the strife caused by his remarriage and his new will (13 October 1565), that disinherited his brothers John and Francis, who were understandably outraged. The will itself is really a codicil to two indentures made on 11 October 1565 between Chaloner and a group of his closest friends, including Cecil. The gist of the indentures was to give his property to this group and instruct them on the use and disposal of it. The general effect of the will was to give Steeple Claydon to the 'saide Thomas sonne of the saide Audrie', to commit the education of Thomas to the care of Cecil, to give 'his house nere St Johns' and some additional income to 'the saide Audrie my wife', and to make various smaller bequests, but it provides nothing for any of Chaloner's siblings (PRO, PROB 11/61, sig. 47). Chaloner died of fever on 14 October 1565 and was buried sumptuously in St Paul's Cathedral on the 20th. The brass plate on his monument was torn away but Haddon's fine epitaph, which was inscribed on it, has survived. CLARENCE H. MILLER

Sources 'The life of Sir Thomas Chaloner', *The praise of folie*, ed. C. H. Miller, EETS, 257 (1965), xxix–xlix • C. H. Miller, 'Sir Thomas Chaloner's translation of *The praise of folie*', PhD diss., Harvard U., 1955 • *LP Henry VIII* • *CSP dom.*, 1547–80 • *CSP for.*, 1547–65 • *APC*, 1542–58 • *CPR*, 1547–51; 1553–63 • G. Camdeno [W. Camden], *Annales rerum Anglicarum et Hibernicarum regnante Elizabetha* (1615), sigs. K3–3v, O3–3v • Cooper, *Ath. Cantab.*, vol. 1 • *CSP Spain*, 1558–67 • *CSP Scot. ser.*, 1509–89 • *CSP Ire.*, 1509–73 • Rymer, *Foedera*, 2nd edn, vol. 15 • HoP, *Commons*, 1509–58 • R. Hakluyt, *The principal navigations, voyages, traffiques and discoveries of the English nation*, 2nd edn, 3 vols. (1598–1600); repr. 12 vols., Hakluyt Society, extra ser., 1–12 (1903–5), 5.70–71 • will, PRO, PROB 11/61, sig. 47
Archives BL, Cotton MSS, corresp. with Queen Elizabeth • BL, Harley MSS, papers
Likenesses oils, 1559, NPG [*see illus.*] • copy of oil portrait of 1559, 17th cent., NPG • W. Hollar, line engraving (after unknown artist), BM, NPG • oils, priv. coll. • woodcut (after oils, 1559), BM, NPG; repro. in T. Chaloner, *De republica Anglorum instauranda* (1579)
Wealth at death a wealthy man; estates at St Bees in Cowpland, Cumberland (acquired 1546 and augmented in 1553); Guisborough, Yorkshire (1547; augmented in 1550 and 1558), Steeple Cleydon, Buckinghamshire (1557), and East Haddon, Northamptonshire, together with rectory of Cold Ashby in the same county (1561–2); since he served on commissions for Middlesex, he probably had establishment at Hoxton; salary as clerk of privy council was raised from £10 to £40 (1548) and £50 for life (1550); before leaving for Spain in 1561, had built himself fine town house within the close of Clerkenwell Priory: will of Sir Thomas Chaloner, preserved at Principal Registry of the Family Division, London, proved on 20 Nov 1579; *LP Henry VIII*

Chaloner, Sir Thomas, the younger (1563/4–1615), chemist and courtier, was the son of Audrey or Ethelreda Frodsham (*d.* 1605), and the stepson of Sir Thomas *Chaloner the elder (1521–1565), who married Ethelreda Frodsham in September 1565. After the death of his stepfather, a prominent English humanist and Elizabeth I's ambassador to Spain, his mother married Edward Brocket, son of Sir John Brocket, kt, of Wheathampstead, Hertfordshire. Chaloner was educated under the auspices of his stepfather's friend the leading Elizabethan statesman, William Cecil, first Baron Burghley, at St Paul's School and at Magdalen College, Oxford. As a student he was noted for his poetical abilities but he took no degree. In 1579 he honoured Lord Burghley with the dedication to his stepfather's poetical works, which he wrote himself.

Chaloner began his continental travels in 1580 and became friendly with many European scholars, especially in Italy. He returned home three years later to become a favourite at court, and married Elizabeth (1568–1603), daughter of William *Fleetwood, recorder of London, who was closely associated with Burghley's rival, Robert Dudley, earl of Leicester. Chaloner was MP for St Mawes in 1586 and for Lostwithiel in 1604. In 1588 he was a tutor to Robert Dudley, the son of the earl of Leicester, at Christ

Church, Oxford, and in 1591 he was knighted while serving with the English army in France. In 1592 he was appointed justice of the peace for Buckinghamshire. He again travelled abroad in 1596–7, corresponding (mainly from Florence) with the earl of Essex and with Anthony Bacon. With his wife Elizabeth he had eleven children, among whom were: Sir William Chaloner, created a baronet on 20 July 1620, who died unmarried at Iskenderun in Syria; Edward *Chaloner (1590/91–1625), a scholar of Magdalen College, Oxford, who became chaplain in ordinary to James I and VI, and then to Charles I; and Thomas *Chaloner and James *Chaloner, both of whom were strong opponents of royal government in the 1640s, and implicated in the execution of Charles I.

Chaloner was alert to the intellectual currents of his day and was especially interested in alchemy and chemical medicine. In 1584 he published *A shorte discourse of the most rare vertue of nitre, wherein is declared the sundry cures effected by the same*, promoting the medicinal properties of saltpetre. He was acquainted with John Dee, and had a notable collection of sixteenth-century chemical and alchemical manuscripts. He was also much involved with the development of economically applicable science, and was friendly with the Jacobean inventor Cornelis Drebbel.

During his travels on the continent Chaloner visited the pope's alum works at Puteoli, and later, about 1600, he discovered alum-stone at Belman Bank, on his estate of Guisborough, Yorkshire. It has been suggested that this discovery might have been due to his noticing the similarity of the vegetation around his Yorkshire estates to that at Puteoli. A number of legends surround this event, including a story that the pope anathematized both Chaloner and his workers.

Chaloner's mines form his main claim to historical importance. From 1605–8 they were managed by his cousin and namesake, Thomas Chaloner, the son of his uncle, John Chaloner. The company was practically bankrupt by 1608, but a deal was struck in which the king prohibited the importation of foreign alum after 1609. Before he died Chaloner had to petition the king for a continuance of the pension granted to him for discovering the mines. Later, in 1625, his children petitioned the crown for moneys due to their father from the alum works. Under Charles I the mines were confiscated for the crown, and brought the king considerable revenue.

Chaloner continued to benefit from his association with the family of Lord Burghley. Towards the end of Elizabeth's reign, Burghley's son Sir Robert Cecil (later the first earl of Salisbury) sent him to Scotland where he became acquainted with James VI, soon to be king of England. Chaloner became a favourite, and attended James on his journey to take possession of the English throne; even Sir Francis Bacon sought Chaloner's recommendation. Queen Anne gave him the management of her private estate, and the king appointed him governor of his eldest son, Henry, in 1603. The king expected Chaloner to maintain discipline in the prince's household, and to form it into a 'courtly college'. Reportedly, no gentleman was allowed to go out in the prince's company without

Chaloner's consent. In 1605 Chaloner was one of a number of favourites created MA during the king's visit to Oxford. As the head official of the prince's 420 servants his 'wages and diet' amounted to £66 13s. 4d. a year. In 1610, when Henry was created prince of Wales and duke of Cornwall, Chaloner was made his chamberlain.

After the death of his first wife in 1603, Chaloner married Judith (d. 1615), daughter of William Blunt of London, about 1605. They had four sons and three daughters. At court, he continued with his, not untypical, mix of interests in chemistry, alchemy, and applied science. He was put in charge of the repair of Kenilworth Castle and the development of its grounds, took part in courtly firework displays, and, with the prince of Wales's support, engaged in a scheme to extract silver from lead. He interested himself in improving the manufacture of water pipes, and was charged by the king with experiments on the improvement of shipbuilding.

Chaloner was a prominent figure in the Jacobean court, and seems to have had some influence, though when he tried to curb the expanding household of Prince Henry some applicants successfully petitioned the king for appointments. Some grants to him are mentioned in the public records: £100 a year in the lands of the duchy of Lancaster, and £36 a year in fee-farm of exchequer lands, in 1604. Subsequently he was also granted part of the manor of Clothall, Hertfordshire. The epigrammatist John Owen (1560–1622) addressed one of his epigrams to him, and Isaac Wake, in his *Rex platonicus* (1607), had a poem on him.

Chaloner died on 18 November 1615, leaving estates at Guisborough, Yorkshire, and Steeple Claydon, Buckinghamshire. He was buried at Chiswick church, Middlesex. A monument to him and his wife was built in the chancel of Chiswick church.

JOHN WESTBY-GIBSON, rev. KENNETH L. CAMPBELL

Sources C. Singer, *The earliest chemical industry* (1948) • C. Webster, 'Alchemical and Paracelsian medicine', *Health, medicine and mortality in the sixteenth century*, ed. C. Webster (1979), 301–31 • J. Nichols, *The progresses, processions, and magnificent festivities of King James I, his royal consort, family and court*, 1 (1828) • Wood, *Ath. Oxon.*, new edn • *CSP dom.* • C. V. P. Akrigg, *Jacobean pageant, or, The court of King James I* (1962) • *The manuscripts of the Earl Cowper*, 3 vols., HMC, 23 (1888–9), vol. 1 • *Report on the manuscripts of Lord De L'Isle and Dudley*, 3, HMC, 77 (1936) • *Calendar of the manuscripts of the most hon. the marquess of Salisbury*, 19, HMC, 9 (1965) • W. J. Jones, 'Ellesmere and politics, 1603–1617', *Early Stuart studies*, ed. H. S. Reinmuth (1970), 18–19 • *Memorials of affairs of state in the reigns of Q. Elizabeth and K. James I, collected (chiefly) from the original papers of … Sir Ralph Winwood*, ed. E. Sawyer, 3 vols. (1725), vol. 2

Archives LPL, letters to Essex and Bacon

Likenesses alabaster effigy on monument, Chiswick church

Chaloner, Thomas (1595–1660), politician and regicide, was born at Steeple Claydon, Buckinghamshire, the third son of Sir Thomas *Chaloner the younger (1563/4–1615) and Elizabeth Fleetwood (1568–1603), and elder brother of James *Chaloner (c.1602–1660). He matriculated at Exeter College, Oxford, on 7 June 1611, and was admitted to the Inner Temple in 1613. At some point in his youth he travelled into France, Italy, and Germany, returning to England 'a well-bred gentleman, but ting'd … with anti-

monarchical principles' (Wood, *Ath. Oxon.*, 3.531). His reverence for monarchy was unlikely to have been strengthened by the crown's failure to honour its agreement, on acquiring the family's alum mines at Guisborough, to pay Sir Thomas's children an annuity of £1000 after the death of their father. Charles I compounded their resentment by assigning the mines to a syndicate of courtiers. This was thought by some contemporaries to constitute Chaloner's main motive in seeking Charles's downfall (*Brief Lives*, 159).

Chaloner was probably the 'Mr Challoner' who played gentlemanly but irreverent parlour games with Bulstrode Whitelocke, Edward Hyde, and others in London in the late 1620s. His unorthodox opinions almost proved his undoing in 1637, when Archbishop Laud took exception to a treatise published in Brussels that his informants attributed to Chaloner (although he denied authorship). He was arrested, but escaped and fled abroad—probably joining his older brother William in Turkey. It was possibly this sojourn in Asia Minor that furnished him with material for a pamphlet he later published in mockery of formalized religion (*A True and Exact Relation of the Strange Finding out of Moses's Tombe*, 1657). He had returned to England by June 1644, when he was a witness at Laud's trial. He signed several of the northern association committee's letters to parliament in 1645 complaining about the 'oppressions' of the Scottish army, and on 20 October he was returned to parliament for the Yorkshire borough of Richmond, probably on the interest of Philip, Lord Wharton. At Westminster he was firmly aligned with the Independent faction, and was closely involved in the Commons' efforts to have the Scottish army removed from England. On 26 October 1646 he made a controversial speech in the Commons arguing that the Scots had no claim over Charles while he remained in England. He implied that parliament constituted the supreme authority in the kingdom, and that Charles's best interests were incompatible with those of the English people (*An Answer to the Scotch Papers*, 10 Nov 1646). By November 1647 he held the view that the king was 'bound in justice and by the duty of his office' to assent to all laws that 'the people represented in Parliament' deemed beneficial (Bodl. Oxf., MS Tanner 58B, fol. 569). From here it was but a short step to espousing the sovereignty of the Commons.

Following Charles's escape from Hampton Court in November 1647 contrary to the terms of his parole, Chaloner was consistently identified as one of the most 'bloody minded against the king' (Bodl. Oxf., MS Clarendon SPB 30, fols. 188–9). He was a vocal opponent of parliament's negotiations with Charles at Newport in 1648, while at the same time applauding the 'great modesty and good temper' of the army (*Mercurius Pragmaticus*, 3–10 Oct 1648, sig. Pp7). He retained his seat at Pride's Purge, and, having played a leading role in bringing the king to trial, signed the death warrant [see also Regicides]. He was a key figure in the establishment of the Commonwealth, and was elected to successive councils of state from February 1650. He was reputed a friend and drinking companion of republicans Henry Marten, Henry Neville, and Thomas

May—a group denounced by Cromwell, Vane, and others as debauched and irreligious. Chaloner was remembered as a devotee of 'the natural religion ... who loved to enjoy the pleasures of this life' (*Brief Lives*, 159). Nevertheless, his hostility to formalized religion does not appear to have been that of the atheist or debauchee, but rather of a man whose wide learning and experience made him unable to accept the often narrow, dogmatic piety of his day.

Chaloner has been widely credited with a major role in formulating the Commonwealth's foreign and commercial policy. Despite his endorsement in 1648 of a protestant crusade to free the Indians 'from Spanish yoke and Rome's idolatry' (T. Chaloner, *Upon the Worthy Work, of his most Worthy Friend the Author*, 1648), he was apparently more concerned with opening up new overseas markets, and thus saw the Dutch, not the Catholic powers, as England's principal foreign rivals. Indeed, by 1651 he, Marten, and Neville were pensioners of Spain, and intervened in council debates to frustrate policies harmful to Spanish interests. He was a founding member of the Rump's leading think-tank on commercial matters, the council of trade, and was also a key figure on council committees for trade and foreign affairs. Conciliar admiralty committees probably constituted his main powerbase—that is, until late 1652, when he and other advocates of war against the Dutch were discredited by a string of English naval defeats in the First Anglo-Dutch War.

Chaloner withdrew from public life after the dissolution of the Rump in 1653, and did not return to the national political stage until early 1659, when he was returned to the third protectorate parliament for Scarborough—possibly through the influence of his friends among the admiralty commissioners. At Westminster he joined other Commonwealthsmen in attempting to impede the passage of the bill recognizing Richard Cromwell's title as lord protector. As committed as ever to the sovereignty of the Commons, he would brook no 'negative voice upon the people' (*Diary of Thomas Burton*, 3.339, 538), either from the protector or the Cromwellian upper house. He took part in the negotiations between the Commonwealthsmen and the army that led to the restoration of the Rump in May 1659. He again emerged as a leading Rumper, and was active in the Commons and on the new council of state. When the army dissolved the restored Rump in October, he sided with Sir Arthur Hesilrige's faction in opposing the move and was imprisoned by Lieutenant-General Fleetwood. He was released late in December and elected to the Rump's last council of state. At the Restoration he surrendered himself in obedience to the royal proclamation, but when he was then excepted from the Act of Oblivion as to both life and estate he fled to the Netherlands, where he died at Middleburg. He was buried in the Old Church at Middleburg on 20 August 1660 under the alias George Sanders. He was remembered by his Dutch hosts as 'an old man, full of gray hairs; a thick, square man' (PRO, E 134/20CHASII/MICH38).

DAVID SCOTT

Sources HoP, *Commons* [draft] · *JHC*, 4–8 (1644–67) · *CSP dom.*, 1635–60 · Wood, *Ath. Oxon.*, new edn, 3.531–3 · *Aubrey's Brief lives*, ed.

O. L. Dick (1949) · B. Worden, *The Rump Parliament, 1648–1653* (1974) · *Diary of Thomas Burton*, ed. J. T. Rutt, 4 vols. (1828), vols. 3–4 · PRO, SP 22/2B; SP 18/12, 17, 27; SP 25/131–3; SP 28/70, 92; SP 16/354/94; SP 24/1, 2; LR 2/266; PSO 2/180; SP 16/516/6; E 134/20CHASII/MICH38 · J. G. Muddiman, *The trial of King Charles the First* (1928) · R. Brenner, *Merchants and revolution: commercial change, political conflict, and London's overseas traders, 1550–1653* (1993) · N. Yorks. CRO, ZFM/Alum mines, 1, 3, 4 · T. Chaloner, *An answer to the Scotch papers: delivered in the House of Commons in reply to the votes of both Houses of the Parliament of England* (1646) · *The justification of a safe and well-grounded answer to the Scottish papers ...* (1646), E 363(11) · *Lex Talionis, or a declamation against Mr. Challener* (1647) [E 396(20)] · newsletters [Thomason tracts: E 421(34); E 455(12); E 466(11); E 477(30); E 460(21)]
Archives Archivo General de Simancas, Cardenas's accounts, Estado 2532 · Bodl. Oxf., MS Clarendon SPB 30; MS Clarendon 34; MS Tanner 59A; MS Nalson IV; MS Rawlinson A224, A225 · PRO, SP 22/2B; SP 18/12, 17, 27; SP 25/131–3; SP 28/70, 92; SP 16/354/94; SP 24/1, 2; LR 2/266; PSO 2/180; SP 16/516/6; E 134/20CHASII/MICH38
Likenesses A. Van Dyck, oils, 1637, repro. in A. K. Wheelock, S. J. Barnes, and J. S. Held, eds., *Van Dyck's paintings* (1991)
Wealth at death £273 p.a.—estate at Steeple Claydon, Buckinghamshire; also estates in Yorkshire: PRO, LR 2/266, fol. 1

Chaloner [Challoner], **Thomas** (*c.*1600–1664), headmaster, was born at Llansilin near Oswestry in Denbighshire, the son of Jonas Chaloner, vicar of Much Wenlock, Shropshire, and later rector of Byfield in Northamptonshire. He was admitted to Shrewsbury School on 17 November 1614, and matriculated pensioner at Jesus College, Cambridge, on 5 July 1617, graduating BA in 1621 and proceeding MA in 1624. He was ordained priest at Peterborough on 26 February 1626.

About 1623, according to Chaloner's own account of 1658, he started teaching. In 1634 and 1635 a T. Chaloner is recorded as sending pupils from his school at Geddington, near Kettering in Northamptonshire, to St John's College, Cambridge. On 2 September 1635 the long-serving John Meighen retired from the headship of Shrewsbury School, and after a deal of controversy between the bailiffs of the town and the master and fellows of St John's, who legally had the right of nomination to the headship, Chaloner was finally confirmed in the post in 1637. He was twice married and had sons Thomas, John, and Samuel, who all attended Shrewsbury School, and David, and daughters Muriel, who married John Lloyd, and two called Mary, who died in infancy.

Having housed some of Charles I's court in the school during the king's brief stay in Shrewsbury in 1640, Chaloner was deprived of his headship when parliamentary forces took the town in 1645. There then followed a period of short-lived positions as a private schoolmaster, first at Ruyton, 15 miles north-west of Shrewsbury, then at Newnes and Birch Hall, both near Ellesmere, Shropshire, his tenure of the latter post lasting only a few months. In February 1647 he accepted the headship of Market Drayton grammar school, also in Shropshire, where, however, after only twenty days, he once again fell foul of the local representatives of the committee of plundered ministers. He thereupon took up the headship of a school at Hawarden on the borders of Flintshire and Cheshire, from which his pupils engaged in poetry contests with the boys of the King's School, Chester; in July 1647, the plague intervening, he moved yet again, this time to Overton in

Flintshire where he remained for nineteen months, moving to a school at Stone in Staffordshire in February 1649.

In June 1650 Chaloner gave up schoolmastering to become tutor to the sons of John Puleston of Emral near Bangor Is-coed, Flintshire, until August 1653, when he took up the headship of Ruthin grammar school, Denbighshire, where he stayed until November 1655. He was then invited to become the first head of Newport grammar school, which he opened in January 1657. In 1658 he composed two commendatory verses written for William Dugard's *Lexicon Graeci testamenti alphabeticum* (1660).

In 1663 Chaloner received a call to return to Shrewsbury. Throughout his period away he had carried with him the school register, in which he recorded in diary fashion his travels and various positions. Whether at or away from Shrewsbury he leaves the impression of a rather volatile personality who nevertheless accorded his pupils considerable care and attention. After only a few months back at Shrewsbury School, Chaloner died there; he was buried in the scholars' chapel of St Mary's Church in the town on 21 October 1664.   KENNETH CHARLTON

Sources J. B. Oldham, *A history of Shrewsbury School, 1552–1952* (1952) • G. W. Fisher, *Annals of Shrewsbury School*, rev. J. S. Hill (1899) • A. R. [A. Rimmer] and H. W. A. [H. W. Adnitt], *A history of Shrewsbury School* (1889) • J. E. Auden, ed., *Shrewsbury School register, 1636 to 1664* (1917) • Venn, *Alum. Cant.* • Cooper, *Ath. Cantab.*, vol. 3 • J. E. B. Mayor, ed., *Admissions to the College of St John the Evangelist in the University of Cambridge*, 1: *Jan 1629/30 – July 1665* (1882) • *Walker rev.* • *VCH Shropshire*, 2.154 • N. Carlisle, *A concise description of the endowed grammar schools in England and Wales*, 2 vols. (1818) • P. Addleshaw, *Thomas Chaloner, scholemaster* (privately printed, London, 1904)
Archives School register vol. II, 1636–64, Shrewsbury School

Chaloner, William (*d.* 1699), coiner and sham plotter, was born in Warwickshire, the son of a weaver; he had at least one brother and one sister involved in coining.

Early crimes Chaloner's father found him difficult to control and apprenticed him to a nailer in Birmingham, a town notorious for coining. After he had learned how to forge groats he left his master and walked to London, where he scraped a living by making and hawking dildoes before finding more success as a quack doctor. He may have been the William Chaloner who on 31 March 1684 married Katharine Atkinson at St Katharine by the Tower, and he certainly had several children. However, this relatively respectable period of Chaloner's life ended when he was suspected of robbery and forced to flee his lodgings. By early 1690 he was earning a poor living as a japanner, although he probably learned the gilding process as part of this trade. Subsequently he began to coat silver coins to appear as guineas. He was taught to coin by Patrick Coffee, a goldsmith, and by his own brother-in-law Joseph Gravenor. Chaloner had moulds made by Thomas Taylor, a Holborn engraver and printseller, and in 1691–2 produced his first coins, which were French pistoles. In the coining fraternity Chaloner was soon recognized as exceptionally skilled and he prospered accordingly. 'The trade went on busily, Chaloner's Guineas flew about as thick as some years ago did bad Silver' (*Guzman*, 5). He dressed as a gentleman, took a large house at Knightsbridge, and bought plate. By this time he had abandoned his family

and embarked upon a series of affairs with female coiners, the most significant of whom was Joan Porter (*fl.* 1692–1699).

In mid-1692 Chaloner had his first brush with the law over coining when William Blackford was condemned for passing out his guineas. Hoping to save his life Blackford denounced Chaloner to the authorities; Chaloner promptly absconded until his erstwhile colleague was hanged. About December 1692 Chaloner attempted to put his skills to another profitable use by putting forward to the Royal Mint a proposal to prevent coining by having shears and flatting mills (coiners' tools with limited legitimate uses) officially sealed and registered.

Discovering Jacobites Another possibility for profit appeared in the government's rewards for the discovery of Jacobite printers and presses. Chaloner duly laid a trap by paying the four journeymen printers of the main clandestine Jacobite press to print a fresh edition of James II's declaration of May 1693. When Chaloner entertained them on 1 June they were arrested while in possession of copies of the declaration and the press seized. Chaloner later claimed an extensive role in the government's anti-Jacobite drive, including the capture of another press and the seizure of thirty-six different titles, together with the discovery that a merchant, John Comyn, was remitting money to France. He spent five weeks in gaol to get further evidence from Jacobite prisoners, and allegedly expended £400 on spies and treating his dupes. However, he was assaulted by a printer's family, the prosecutions often failed, and rewards were not immediately forthcoming from the government.

More legitimately, in October 1693 Chaloner petitioned the privy council for a patent to make certain copper and silver-copper alloy coins, a project rejected by the Treasury in December. Undeterred, Chaloner hoped to repeat his anti-Jacobite success, proposing that Thomas Coppinger, an unscrupulous thief taker specializing in coining offences, write a treasonable satire, for which he himself would find a printer whom they would jointly denounce to the authorities. Coppinger, however, preferred to denounce Chaloner for coining and in May 1694 Chaloner was confronted by Coppinger before the lord mayor, Stamp, who sent him to Newgate. Chaloner turned the tables on his accuser testifying against Coppinger, who was executed on 27 February 1695. Later, he 'brought more Pupils [in coining] to the Gallows than all his Predecessors', gaining some informal immunity for his own activities (*Guzman redivivus*, 6–7).

The coinage and the mint As the debasement of the coin reached new depths the House of Commons in 1694–5 debated possible solutions. Chaloner published two sets of proposals addressed to the Commons. *Reasons Humbly Offered Against Passing an Act for Raising Ten Hundred Thousand Pounds* argued that it was a mistake to vote taxes in the hope of making up the weight of the coinage. *Proposals Humbly Offered, for Passing, an Act to Prevent Clipping and Counterfeiting of Money* (February 1695), suggested a swift recoinage to prevent further clipping, at only two-thirds of the face value, followed soon afterwards by a second recoinage once the clippers were powerless, which would restore the coin to full weight. To prevent future counterfeiting the coinage should be struck with an impression far deeper than coiners' tools or presses would allow, with a deep groove along the edge. Further safeguards against coining could be provided by extending the treason law, by adjusting the silver value, and by registering equipment.

Early in 1695 Chaloner petitioned the crown, setting out in detail his services in apprehending Jacobite suspects in 1693. His requests received support from Charles Mordaunt, earl of Monmouth (later third earl of Peterborough), who in May 1695 expressed his sense of Chaloner's potential usefulness. On 28 February 1696 William III ordered up to £1000 to be paid to Chaloner. Chaloner was now part of a bigger game in which Monmouth and other discontented but ambitious whigs with a record of unscrupulous tactics, such as Sir Henry Dutton Colt, his brother John Dutton Colt, and John Arnold, sought to force their way into office. One target was the mint. Chaloner had already written that 'The Minters have been a great cause of clipping and false coining' (Chaloner, *Proposals*, 1), and in late 1695 he had elaborated his accusations against mint officials to the privy council. The mint officials retaliated and the recorder of London, Sir Salathiel Lovell, and his thief takers brought the officials and some coiners he accused to testify against Chaloner, who was committed to Newgate. They certainly had plenty of material to work with as Chaloner was already deeply involved in two further criminal enterprises. He had begun to counterfeit the Bank of England's new £100 notes (not a felony until 1697), the first forgery being detected on 14 August 1695, two months after the notes began circulating. The forger who marbled the notes had denounced Chaloner, who immediately handed over his false notes to the bank. To protect himself further Chaloner exposed a major fraud against the bank, one presumably in which he was himself involved. Blank bills on the City orphans' fund were cut from the cheque book in the Chamber of London by Aubrey Price (d. 1698) and filled in, and the bank was tricked thereby into paying out sums up to £1000. John Gibbons, the notorious porter of Whitehall Palace, officially a pursuer (and privately an extortionate protector) of coiners who was known to Chaloner, arrested the swindlers, although Price escaped through bribery and compounded for his crime. Chaloner received a £200 reward. Hoping to capitalize on his enhanced credibility he then sent the bank a proposal to prevent counterfeiting of bank bills, which in November 1695 the directors referred to a committee. Chaloner impressed them sufficiently with his demonstrations that on 18 January 1696 a warrant was issued for him to be included in the next general free pardon of convicts in Newgate on the governor of the bank's representations. However, his release was blocked and Chaloner later claimed that the lord chief justice, Sir John Holt, and the recorder, Lovell, had refused to let his pardon pass unless he revealed what he knew about coining in the mint. Even after his release

it was never enrolled, with serious consequences for Chaloner in the future.

On 13 January 1696 Chaloner had petitioned the king and council from Newgate, claiming that the mint coined false guineas, struck debased blanks sent in from outside, and sent out stamps for coining (Chaloner boasted privately to have benefited from both), and regularly produced underweight coin. With Lovell threatening to prosecute him next session Chaloner asked to be examined by Charles Talbot, duke of Shrewsbury, secretary of state, and his under-secretary, James Vernon. He convinced Holt that 'there hath been great mystery or villainy at the Tower', the location of the mint (*Downshire MSS*, 1.667). On 3 February he testified in council, naming other coiners, Thomas Carter, John Abbot, and Coffee. He claimed that the stamps of the crypto-Jacobite chief engraver, John Roettier the elder, were loaned out of the Tower. While alleging that 'he himself never made a Guinea in his Life' (BL, Add. MS 35107, fol. 30v) he impudently included his alias, Chandler, in a list of guinea forgers. Yet on 26 March a committee of council reported that Chaloner was himself involved in coining and should remain a prisoner. After many delays caused by the plot to assassinate William, on 16 May the Treasury commissioners heard Chaloner's allegations on coining within the mint. However, from March 1696 Chaloner had been faced by a new adversary, the newly appointed warden of the mint, Isaac Newton, a man determined to protect its interests. In an audacious move Chaloner recommended Thomas Holloway (a long-term associate) to Newton as clerk to the warden, the official responsible for the prosecution of clippers and coiners. Chaloner was eventually released, but he had been impoverished by his imprisonment.

Chaloner's whig allies were keen to use parliament to secure for Sir Henry Dutton Colt the mastership of the mint. On 15 February 1697 Arnold, recently appointed chairman of a Commons committee on abuses in the mint, ordered Newton to assist Chaloner in preparing an experiment with guineas before them. However, the committee's wish that Chaloner be allowed to work in the mint to make an edger for grooving the guineas was thwarted because it contravened Newton's oath of office. The committee's report to the Commons on 8 April declared that Chaloner had shown a better method of coining to prevent counterfeiting and also recommended a bill to prevent abuses by the officers of the mint. Chaloner followed up the success of his allies in committee by presenting to the Commons *The Defects in the Present Constitution of the Mint*. This memorial stressed the mutual ignorance of the workmen outside their own processes and recommended the appointment of a supervisor (meaning himself) who knew all of them. Meanwhile Chaloner continued to experiment with coining. He taught Holloway a new method of coining, using small, easily concealed stamps. He also taught Aubrey Price how to counterfeit the new exchequer bills, by altering the denominations after a liquid, his invention, had removed the old ink.

Price was the main instrument of a sham plot which Chaloner hoped would be revealed to the authorities at a most auspicious moment through the agency of Sir Henry Colt. Price produced lists of Jacobites in various counties, which, as they mixed Jacobites with Williamites, were regarded with some incredulity by the lords justices. Nevertheless in mid-June 1697 they authorized him to investigate further. Chaloner encouraged Price saying that 'if he would be ruled by him they would bubble the government, who were the easiest to be cheated of any men in the world' (Vernon, 1.366). In late August another element of the sham plot appeared, with a story, supposedly told to Price by Kentish and London Jacobites, that Shrewsbury had tried to help Sir John Fenwick's escape in 1696 by providing a false pass. When confronted with this accusation Shrewsbury ordered Colt to inform the lords justices, which effectively destroyed the plot to blackmail him, although the government was obliged to follow up the allegations and arrest Jacobite suspects in order to forestall any recourse the accusers might have to parliament.

Newton's pursuit Meanwhile Newton had been collecting evidence against Chaloner for coining and forgery of exchequer bills. On the lords justices' orders Chaloner was sent to Newgate for high treason on 2 September 1697. Chaloner claimed to Colt that this was merely an act of revenge by Thomas Neale (master of the mint) and Newton for his exposing the state of the mint, but he testified to Newton that Price had tempted him to falsify exchequer bills. While implicating Price, Chaloner encouraged him to maintain his evidence against the Jacobites. Vernon believed that Chaloner was 'at ... Fenwick's game, and says he has a secret ... only fit to be communicated to the King, ... intimating as if some in power were not to be trusted' (Vernon, 1.348). However, Newton was unable to link Chaloner with exchequer bill forgeries, and could merely prosecute him for conspiracy to coin, using Thomas Holloway as his chief witness. Chaloner promptly bribed Holloway to flee with his family to Scotland. Thus, when the case against Chaloner was prosecuted at the Middlesex sessions in October 1697 the grand jury disbelieved the two remaining witnesses and he was acquitted.

Chaloner counter-attacked on 18 February 1698 with a petition to the Commons claiming that mint officials (evidently meaning Newton) had tried to procure his conviction and execution for having exposed their abuses to the Commons. The committee appointed to investigate included Sir Henry Colt, Vernon, and Arnold (as chair). Chaloner suborned the two witnesses from his trial to testify that Newton had made them tempt him to coin. However, the plan of Arnold and his supporters to produce a report hostile to Newton was thwarted by the attendance of Vernon and other government supporters who successfully defended Newton's commitment of Chaloner. Newton's testimony repeating Chaloner's boasts of 'funning' the government also damaged his reputation and the committee never reported.

Price's execution for further exchequer bill forgeries did not deter Chaloner. He now resumed coining crowns, half-crowns, and shillings, and had plans to coin English

money in the Netherlands, or Spanish currency aboard a merchant ship coasting off Spain. Meanwhile, 'resolved to be poor no more' (PRO, MINT 15/17, no. 119), he engraved a copperplate of tickets for the lottery on the malt duty. Though counterfeiting malt tickets was not a felony Chaloner was cautious enough to cover his tracks and to hide the main plate between printing sessions. In August 1698 another coiner, David Davis, betrayed the affair to Vernon and a warrant was issued for Chaloner on 6 October. In late October he was arrested by a messenger, at whose house Vernon had him detained to allow Newton more time to build a capital case against him. Chaloner immediately accused Carter (his favourite colleague) of engraving the plate and offered to surrender it in exchange for immunity. On 21 January 1699 Chaloner was committed to Newgate. He claimed to be a comparative innocent in the matter, but no assistance from his former patrons was forthcoming as neither the Colts nor Arnold now sat in parliament. Furthermore, his counterfeiting of every form of legal tender, old and new, threatened the government's war-weakened credit.

Trial and execution In Newgate, Chaloner became alarmed at the number of witnesses Newton was assembling. As he lacked the money to bribe them he pretended to be raving mad in an attempt to get his trial postponed, but this ploy failed. At the Old Bailey Middlesex sessions on 3 March 1699 he faced two indictments for treason. The first looked back to his 1692 coining of French pistoles, with Thomas Taylor and Mistress Coffee the witnesses (presumably the pardon he failed to have passed would have covered this charge). The other, for coining crowns and half-crowns in 1698, was supported by these witnesses and others including the coiner Abbot and the wives of Carter and Holloway. Chaloner claimed that their evidence, besides being perjured, related to acts in the City and Surrey and hence outside the jurisdiction of the Middlesex sessions. Otherwise, according to *Guzman Redivivus*, his defence was indifferent, but saucy, in affronting the recorder, Lovell.

'After his Condemnation, he was continually crying out they had Murder'd him, the Witnesses were perjur'd, and he had not had Justice done him. He struggl'd and flounc'd about for Life, like a Whale struck with a Harping-Iron' (*Guzman*, 11). In a letter to Newton he pleaded 'I shall be murdered the worst of all murders that is in the face of justice unless I am rescued by your mercifull hands', and 'O my offending you has brought this upon me' (*Correspondence of Isaac Newton*, 4.307–8). More practically he tried to save himself by further discoveries against others, and surrendered the copperplate for the malt tickets. When the government refused to pardon him Chaloner resumed howling that he was murdered, and continued doing so while being dragged to execution at Tyburn on 22 March 1699. The dying statement he had prepared was apparently too libellous for a printer to risk publishing. As his biographer concluded, Chaloner was 'a Man, who had he squar'd his Talents by the Rules of Justice and Integrity, might have been useful to the Commonwealth; But as he follow'd only the Dictates of Vice, was as a rotten member cut off' (*Guzman*, 12).

PAUL HOPKINS and STUART HANDLEY

Sources *Guzman redivivus: a short view of the life of Will. Chaloner, the notorious coyner, who was executed at Tyburn on Wednesday the 22d of March 1698/9* (1699) · *The correspondence of Isaac Newton*, ed. H. W. Turnbull and others, 7 vols. (1959–77), vol. 4 · Mint depositions, PRO, MINT 15/17 · Newton papers, PRO, MINT 19/1–3 · *CSP dom.* · *Letters illustrative of the reign of William III from 1696 to 1708 addressed to the duke of Shrewsbury by James Vernon*, ed. G. P. R. James, 3 vols. (1841) · Shrewsbury papers, Northants. RO, Buccleuch papers, vols. 46–7, 63 · *JHC*, 12–13 (1697–1702) · Chaloner's petitions to William III, 1695, BL, Add. MS 72568, fols. 47–54 · E. Southwell's privy council minutes, BL, Add. MS 35107 · papers of the first earl of Portland, Nottingham UL, PwA · W. A. Shaw, ed., *Calendar of treasury books*, [33 vols. in 64], PRO (1904–69), vols. 10–14 · Bank of England Archives, London, F2/160, G4/2, G4/4 · Middlesex sessions rolls, gaol delivery, LMA, MJ/SR/1821–1925 (1693–9) · sessions rolls and minute books, 1694–9, CLRO, City of London, SF402–39; SM 65–7 · F. E. Manuel, *A portrait of Isaac Newton* (1968) · R. S. Westfall, *Never at rest: a biography of Isaac Newton* (1980) · N. Luttrell, *A brief historical relation of state affairs from September 1678 to April 1714*, 6 vols. (1857) · W. Chaloner, *To the honourable, the knights, citizens and burgesses in parliament assembled: proposals humbly offered, for passing, an act to prevent clipping and counterfeiting of money* (1695) · W. Chaloner, *The defects in the present constitution of the mint, humbly offered to the consideration of the present House of Commons* [1697] · W. Chaloner, *To the honourable the knights, citizens and burgesses in parliament assembled. Reasons humbly offered against passing an act for raising ten hundred thousand pounds, to make good the deficiency of the clipt-money* [1694] · H. Haynes, 'Brief memoires relating to the silver and gold coins of England', 1700, BL, Lansdowne MS 801 · *Report on the manuscripts of the marquis of Downshire*, 6 vols. in 7, HMC, 75 (1924–95), vol. 1 · Sir W. Trumbull's diary, BL, Add. MS 72571 · J. M. Beattie, *Policing and punishment in London, 1660–1750* (2001) · [H. Fitzgerald's examination], 1699, BL, Add. MS 21136, fols. 71–2 · C. E. Challis, ed., *A new history of the royal mint* (1992) · J. Craig, *Newton at the mint* (1946) · Middlesex sessions papers, Feb. 1695, LMA, MJ/SP/1695/02/028–035, 02/006 · J. Redington, ed., *Calendar of Treasury papers*, 1–2, PRO (1868–71) · T. Wales, 'Thief-takers and their clients in later Stuart London', *Londinopolis: essays in the social and cultural history of early modern London*, ed. P. Griffiths and N. G. R. Jenner (2000), 67–84

Chamber, Anna [*married name* Anna Grenville-Temple, Countess Temple] (**1709?–1777**), poet, was probably born in Hanworth, Middlesex, the second daughter and coheir of Thomas Chamber, possibly a merchant, and Mary, daughter of the second earl of Berkeley. Having lost their parents at an early age, Anna and her sister, Mary, were brought up by their mother's younger sister Lady Betty Germaine, with whom Anna resided until her marriage. On 9 May 1737 she married Richard *Grenville (1711–1779), from 1749 Richard Grenville-Temple and from 1750 second Earl Temple, at Marble Hill, the Twickenham home of the widowed countess of Suffolk who in 1735 had married Anna's maternal uncle. Yet courtly connections hardly kept Anna from sharing her husband's anti-royalist manoeuvres in the 1760s: Temple's radical protégé John Wilkes, challenged to duel Earl Talbot, asked that Lady Temple superintend his daughter Mary's education if he died.

Anna was much admired by Horace Walpole as hostess

Anna Chamber (1709?–1777), by Allan Ramsay, 1760

at Stowe, Buckinghamshire, or at London's Buckingham House, 91 Pall Mall, even when gout confined her to a wheelchair. At the age of forty 'she discovered in herself a turn for genteel versification' in the wry anapaestic mode of Matthew Prior (*Catalogue of the Royal and Noble Authors*, 4.361). In 1764 Walpole's Strawberry Hill Press published under her maiden name 100 copies of her *Poems*, which included beast fables mocking contemporary manners and persons.

Though some slighter verse remains unpublished, her major poem, 'To the Earl Temple: on Gardening', reappeared in the 1768 and later editions of the *New Foundling Hospital for Wit* collection. This poem closely interprets the political manifesto inscribed by her husband's rededication in 1762 of Stowe's Grecian temple as the Temple of Concord and Victory, just as peacemaking in Paris curtailed their brother-in-law Pitt's 'Great War for Empire'. Lady Temple died at Stowe on 7 April 1777, and was buried there eight days later.   RICHARD QUAINTANCE

Sources Walpole, *Corr.* · *The Grenville papers: being the correspondence of Richard Grenville … and … George Grenville*, ed. W. J. Smith, 4 vols. (1852–3) · *A catalogue of the royal and noble authors of England, Scotland and Ireland … by the late Horatio Walpole*, ed. T. Park, 4 (1806) · A. T. Hazen, *A bibliography of the Strawberry Hill Press* (1942) · A. Collins, *The peerage of England: containing a genealogical and historical account of all the peers of England*, 4th edn (1768) · *Reminiscences written by Mr Horace Walpole in 1788*, ed. P. Toynbee (1924) · W. Petty, 'Character of Lord Temple', *Life of William, earl of Shelburne … with extracts from his papers and correspondence*, ed. E. G. P. Fitzmaurice, 3 (1876), 39–40 · J. V. Beckett, *The rise and fall of the Grenvilles: dukes of Buckingham and Chandos, 1710 to 1921* (1994) · A. Dyce, *Specimens of British poetesses*, 2nd edn (1827), 204

Archives BL, papers, Add. MSS 57805–57806 | Hunt. L., letters to George Berkeley, Henrietta, countess of Suffolk, Edward Jerningham, and Elizabeth Robinson Montagu
Likenesses A. Ramsay, oils, 1760, priv. coll. [*see illus.*] · H. D. Hamilton, pastel drawing, 1770, NPG · W. Birrell, engraving, pubd before 1798 (after H. D. Hamilton), repro. in A. Grenville, *Poems*, ed. T. Kirgate, new edn (*c.*1798)
Wealth at death dowry supposedly £50,000 in 1737: GEC, *Peerage*, s.v. Temple; copy of will, Hunt. L.; *Grenville papers*

Chamber [*née* Hall], **Grace** (1676–1762), Quaker minister, was born on 15 October 1676 at Monk Hesledon, co. Durham, the only child of James Hall and his second wife, Grace, widow of Anthony Pearson and daughter of Thomas and Grace Lamplough. Her father and his first wife, Frances Walker, had five other children. Brought up in an established Quaker household Grace was intelligent and 'endowed with an excellent understanding' (Testimony of Kendal monthly meeting). Although not formally educated she managed to acquire considerable medical skill, which she put to good use without ever asking for a fee or other reward. On 13 January 1704, when she was twenty-seven, Grace married Robert Chamber (*d.* 1753), a substantial Friend, and moved to his family home at Sedgwick, near Kendal, in Westmorland. At the age of thirty-five she was recognized as having a gift of ministry among Friends, although she did not speak frequently or at length. Her travel in the ministry was mainly local and in the company of her husband.

Grace Chamber had an extensive acquaintance among all classes in her local community and she concerned herself with the lives of her friends. She arranged for the widowed Abiah Sinclair, a fellow Quaker minister, to meet the ironmaster Abraham Darby (1711–1763), who became Abiah's second husband, and she remained a constant friend to the whole Darby family. There is no record that Grace and Robert had any children of their own but Grace acted as a mother, nurse, and friend to all who needed her. Robert supported her ministry and her benevolent and medical activities up to a point. After his death in April 1753 she said of him:

> [although] one of the best of husbands, he was very unwilling to want me, but I think he made that up as much as any man in his circumstance could have done in letting his house be free and open to sick and lame, poor and rich. If I were but there it was mostly well. (Grace Chamber to J. Wilson, 18 Oct 1753, RS Friends, Lond., MS 334/63)

Grace was aware of links between the physical, mental, and spiritual; she sent Thomas Story (1670?–1742), a travelling minister who visited the area in 1715, not only religious encouragement but a sample of a powder as a remedy for coughing and shortness of breath, which she thought he might need. Another who benefited from Grace's benevolence was Frances Henshaw (1714–1793), a convert to Quakerism from the established church. She was rejected by her family and became a Quaker minister, but was criticized by some Friends for her popularity. By 1743 she had reached a point of physical and mental collapse. Grace took Frances into her home for an extended period, giving her rest, good advice, and fresh- and salt-

water baths so that eventually she recovered and continued her ministry.

In her widowhood Grace Chamber continued to travel in the ministry, often with her lifelong friend Lydia Lancaster. Together they visited the Darby family at Coalbrookdale and attended local Quaker meetings. In 1760, at the very end of their lives, they went on a more extensive journey, first to Welsh yearly meeting, as they often had before, but then on to Bath, Bristol, and London. Contemporaries wondered at their taking on so much when so advanced in years but characterized them both as 'green in old age'. On her return Grace became more infirm, finding it difficult to get even to local Quaker meetings. She died on 22 September 1762, aged eighty-five, at Sedgwick, in the house to which she had come on her marriage nearly sixty years before; she was buried in the Quaker burial-ground at Preston Patrick, Westmorland.

Grace Chamber was not an eloquent minister or an extensive traveller in the ministry, and she wrote nothing for publication. She was notable as a companion and friend, one who tended the sick and cared for those who were sorrowful and troubled in mind. She shared her wisdom and her skills freely and was universally valued by her local and religious community. In the letters, diaries, and journals of contemporaries she emerges as 'dear Grace'—a fitting memorial.　　　GIL SKIDMORE

Sources 'Testimony of Kendal monthly meeting concerning Grace Chamber, deceased, 1763', *Journal of the Friends' Historical Society*, 7 (1910), 182–3 · 'Dictionary of Quaker biography', RS Friends, Lond. [card index] · J. J. Green, '"Bishop" John Hall (1662–1739) … his sister Grace Chamber (1676–1762) … with some account of their family', 1917, RS Friends, Lond. [typescript] · manuscript letters, RS Friends, Lond. · R. Labouchere, *Abiah Darby* (1988) · E. E. Moore, *Travelling with Thomas Story: the life and travels of an eighteenth-century Quaker* (1947) · M. H. Bacon, ed., *Wilt thou go on my errand? Three eighteenth-century journals of Quaker women ministers* (1994)
Archives RS Friends, Lond.

Chamber, John (1546–1604), Church of England clergyman and author, was born in May 1546, at Swillington in Yorkshire; nothing is known of his early life or parentage. He was educated at Merton College, Oxford, being admitted to the BA on 18 October 1568, and was elected a probationary fellow on 20 December 1569. Confirmed in his fellowship on 28 April 1571, he proceeded to the MA on 7 October 1573. He was appointed to lecture on grammar on 5 April 1574, and on Greek on 16 April 1576, and became the junior Linacre lecturer in medicine on 31 October 1576; he was reappointed to this position on 18 December 1579. He planned, but does not seem to have made, a trip to the continent in 1581; and being elected a fellow of Eton College in 1582, he vacated his position at Merton and moved from Oxford to Windsor. This did not prevent him from supplicating for a licence to practise medicine, however, which he did through the college on 5 November 1584. He became a prebendary of Netherbury in Terra, Salisbury, on 3 June 1593, and a canon of St George's Chapel, Windsor, on 17 June 1601.

Although described on his memorial as a distinguished theologian, physician, and mathematician, Chamber is best remembered today for his writings on astronomy and astrology. In 1600, he published *Barlaam monachi logistice*, translation and scholia of the *Logistica* of Barlaam of Calabria, a work that set out to provide a rigorous treatment of numbers and fractions, particularly as employed in astronomy. According to the preface, the Greek text was copied and sent to Chamber from overseas by Henry Savile; it must have reached him in 1581 or 1582, for he lamented the 'twice-nine' years it had taken him to publish it. Although dedicated to the queen, Chamber's text also contained a poem addressed to Henry Neville; and another former Mertonian, George Carleton, supplied verses lauding Chamber and Barlaam. In 1601 Chamber published his *Treatise Against Judicial Astrologie* and appended to it his *Astronomiae encomium*, an oration in praise of astronomy that he had delivered in Oxford, as the introduction to a course of lectures on the *Almagest*, twenty-seven years previously. (Savile had begun his own famous lectures on Ptolemy's text in 1570.) Chamber's critique of astrology, though uncompromising, seems not to have troubled all practitioners: the interleaved, annotated copy of the British Library may have belonged to an enthusiast, and William Lilly included Chamber in the catalogue of astrological authors in his *Christian Astrology* (1647). Nevertheless, the work sparked a brief controversy, provoking Christopher Heydon's *A Defence of Judicial Astrology* of 1603, in which Chamber was attacked at length for both reproducing the views of other critics, and misrepresenting or misunderstanding his authorities. Chamber's reply to Heydon, 'A confutation of astrological demonology, or, The divell's schole', is extant in a presentation manuscript (Bodl. Oxf., MS Savile 42), with a dedication to James I of 2 February 1604; however, since it came to Oxford in the collection of Savile, it was probably neither presented nor circulated. Perhaps for this reason, Carleton penned another response that year, *The Madnesse of Astrologers*, which was eventually published in 1624. Historians have described Chamber's *Treatise* as just one of a series of anti-astrological tracts written by English divines with Calvinist leanings; but this interpretation perhaps gives too little weight to Chamber's long association with Savile and real interest in astronomy. The fact that he served in 1583, alongside Savile and Leonard Digges, on a commission appointed by Lord Burghley to assess John Dee's proposal to introduce into England the Gregorian reform of the calendar, seems indicative of his ability, and offers some corroboration for Anthony Wood's claim that his learning was widely recognized.

Chamber died at Eton at the beginning of August 1604, and was buried at the entrance to the choir of St George's Chapel, Windsor. Savile and Neville, his executors, provided a memorial plaque; although no longer extant, its inscription was transcribed by Ashmole. This memorial noted that Chamber left £1000 to Merton College to endow two scholarships from Eton. He also bequeathed £50 to be used for the benefit of the poor of Windsor.

ADAM MOSLEY

Sources E. Ashmole, *The antiquities of Berkshire*, 3 (1719), 145–6 • J. M. Fletcher, ed., *Registrum annalium collegii Mertonensis, 1567–1603*, OHS, new ser., 24 (1976) • S. Bond, ed., *The chapter acts of the dean and canons of Windsor* (1966) • R. R. Tighe and J. E. Davis, *Annals of Windsor* (1858), vol. 2, pp. 66–7, 633 • Wood, *Ath. Oxon.*, new edn, 1.744–6 • Wood, *Ath. Oxon.: Fasti* (1815), 181, 193 • W. H. Jones, *Fasti ecclesiae Sarisberiensis, or, A calendar … of the cathedral body at Salisbury*, 2 vols. (1879–81), 408–9 • *Reg. Oxf.*, 1.272; 2/3.33 • W. S. Brassington, *Historic bindings in the Bodleian Library, Oxford* (1891), 42–5 • M. Feingold, *The mathematician's apprenticeship: science, universities and society in England, 1560–1640* (1984), 48, 128, 130
Wealth at death £1000 bequeathed to Merton: Ashmole, *Antiquities*, vol. 3, pp. 145–6 • £50 bequeathed to Windsor, of which £45 5s. was paid: Tighe and Davis, *Annals*, vol. 2, pp. 66–7

Chamber, Robert (*d.* 1489). *See under* Egremont, Sir John (*b.* 1459?, *d.* in or after 1505).

Chamberlain, Arthur (1842–1913), industrialist, was born on 11 April 1842 at 3 Grove Hill Terrace, Camberwell, Surrey, the third of six sons of Joseph Chamberlain (1796–1874), a wholesale shoe manufacturer, and Caroline, *née* Harben (1808–1875), daughter of a wealthy provision merchant. His eldest brother was Joseph *Chamberlain (1836–1914), the politician and tariff reformer; the other brothers were Richard, Herbert, Walter, and Frank, who died early. There were also three sisters.

Arthur and Joseph Chamberlain both spent two years at University College School in London. On leaving school at the age of sixteen, Arthur followed Joseph into the woodscrew business of Nettlefold and Chamberlain in Birmingham, in which, in 1854, his father, Nettlefold's brother-in-law, had invested an initial £10,000 and then more, adding his name to that of the firm. The family sold out in 1874, soon after Joseph entered politics in the late 1860s. Like others in his family Arthur Chamberlain married a Kenrick, namely Louisa, daughter of Timothy Kenrick, on 3 June 1870. They had two sons, Arthur (1880–1941) and John (1881–1917), who was killed in Flanders, and seven daughters, before Louisa died in 1892.

Arthur Chamberlain, while helping his brother in his political campaigns, remained a businessman all his life, building up a series of major Birmingham metal concerns. His arrival was not welcomed by Nettlefold and, in 1863, his father put him in charge of another of his interests in Birmingham, Smith and Chamberlain, brassfounders, which Arthur took into electric fittings. In 1883 Arthur himself (with partner George Hookham) developed Chamberlain and Hookham, next door in New Bartholomew Street. In 1886 the latter firm won the contract to install electric light in Birmingham Art Gallery but subsequently concentrated on the manufacture of meters, later becoming part of GEC. By 1891, when it was registered as a company, Chamberlain had entered the tube trade through the firm next door, Endurance Seamless Tube and Vial Company. As Endurance Tube and Engineering, this opened a factory in King's Norton in 1896. His co-directors were his son-in-law John Sutton Nettlefold and George Hookham, while his son John worked for Chamberlain and Hookham.

The big step in Chamberlain's expanding career was his rescue of Kynoch, a cartridge manufacturer, in Witton and Stirchley in Birmingham. Called in by the shareholders in 1888, he became chairman in 1889, remaining so for the rest of his life, and was succeeded by his son John. Chamberlain now showed his restructuring genius, making many redundant but sorting out the works, costs, stock, and purchasing, selling off operations not considered 'core' but also buying new rolling mills to ensure supplies. In eight years he doubled capacity in existing products and added many new lines, pushing into the munitions business in explosives and taking over several other firms. Employment rose from 2000 in 1892 to 6000 in 1904 in nine works scattered round the UK.

But expansion was too rapid and 1906–12 saw reduced profits, lost contracts, and redundancies and the tide turned in 1913, at the time of Chamberlain's death. However, he had laid the foundations of the metals and explosives division of what became ICI and survives, hived off, as Imperial Metal Industries (IMI).

Chamberlain was also director or chairman of other concerns, some bought through the Birmingham Investment Trust, in which the family were influential. In the mid-1890s he took over another ailing Birmingham firm, Weldless Tube, and merged it with others, only to be hit by the collapse of the cycle boom. These firms were reconstructed into Tubes in 1898, to form the nucleus of Tube Investments in 1919. His son and grandson, both called Arthur, were involved in the management into the 1950s. Other investments were made in Hoskins & Son, makers of ships' berths, though this was managed by his nephew Neville Chamberlain, and Elliotts Metal, makers of ships' sheathing.

In December 1900, when Joseph Chamberlain was advocating war, Lloyd George attacked the Chamberlains for holding shares in companies with government munitions contracts. Joseph defended the right of his family, not involved in political careers, to normal business ventures (Marsh, 569).

Arthur Chamberlain was also a business leader in the Birmingham chamber of commerce and the Association of UK Chambers of Commerce and the Empire in the 1900s. He became a JP in 1884 and was chairman of the licensing committee in Birmingham from 1893 to 1903, working to reduce drunkenness. His approach clashed with Joseph's views. Arthur Chamberlain was a free trader. After 1900 he also publicly opposed his brother's views on protection, a rift between them emerging from 1903 to 1906. Chamberlain preached to his employees and wrote in articles in the *Manchester Guardian* and *Birmingham Post* that competition promoted invention. He disliked state controls or indeed any red tape, and opposed both trade unions and employers' associations.

Two other activities make him an interesting man in a wider frame. First, he wrote *The Book of Business* (printed privately in 1899) for the confidential use of his children. This reveals his personal views on business management. Only a flavour of its wisdom can be included here. He wrote that 'the real interest of business … consists, not in money making, but its variety, and the constant call it makes on your courage, your judgement, your energy, or

your patience, at uncertain, and unexpected, but very frequent intervals' (Chamberlain, 1). A well-managed business was one that 'can support the unexpected absence of the principal'. His children were advised not to sit on 'addled eggs' (or lame ducks) but to expect 10 or 20 per cent return on capital.

The second activity was Chamberlain's interest in education and his involvement, with his brother Joseph (though more briefly), in the establishment of the faculty of commerce in the new University of Birmingham. In his *Book of Business* he recommended that commercial managers should pass the professional examinations in accountancy and master two languages (French and Spanish rather than German, as the Germans controlled no colonies), residing in each country for three months. They should spend six months in a machine shop to learn 'about the British workman, his habits and customs, his strengths and weaknesses, his vices and virtues' as he is 'the most important of all the machines' in the works (Chamberlain, 9, 16).

For the university, Arthur Chamberlain provided a practical business syllabus for a three-year course which may have influenced the faculty's first dean, William Ashley. He advised Ashley that 'if Tommy goes home and talks about balance sheets, father will think there is something' in the new courses (Chamberlain, 20n.).

He was himself a fair, strict, paternalist employer, putting wages up to 22s. a week for male workers in 1903, after the Rowntree inquiry showed that 21s. 8d. was a minimum living wage for a man, wife, and three children. He was one of the first to reduce the working week from sixty to forty-eight hours in 1890, and he gave clerks and foremen fourteen days paid holiday and a pension after ten years' service.

Chamberlain was a Unitarian like his brother and attended the church of the Messiah in Broad Street, Birmingham. He lived at Moor Green Hall in Moseley in Birmingham, his garden in those days adjoining that of his brother Joseph in Highbury Hall. After three or four years confined to a wheelchair, he died of cancer on 19 October 1913 at Cadhay House, Ottery St Mary, Devon, where he lived during the winter. BARBARA M. D. SMITH

Sources B. M. D. Smith, 'Chamberlain, Arthur', *DBB* · *Ironmonger* (July 1863) · *Ironmonger* (17 April 1866) · *Ironmonger* (Oct 1869) · *Ironmonger* (1 Aug 1881) · *Ironmonger* (28 Aug 1883) · *Ironmonger* (17 April 1886) · *Ironmonger* (8 June 1886) · *Ironmonger* (23 Aug 1886) · *Ironmonger* (30 June 1888) · *Ironmonger* (7 Nov 1891) · *Ironmonger* (3 Feb 1894) · *Ironmonger* (2 May 1896) · *Ironmonger* (10 Dec 1898) · *Ironmonger* (21 Jan 1899) · *Ironmonger* (27 May 1899) · *Ironmonger* (16 Dec 1899) · *Ironmonger* (8 Aug 1903) · *Ironmonger* (6 Feb 1906) · *Ironmonger* (3 Nov 1906) · *Ironmonger* (22 Dec 1906) · *Kynoch Journal* (1899–1900) · *Kynoch Journal* (1902–3) · *Under five flags: the story of Kynoch Works, Witton, Birmingham, 1862–1962* (privately printed, Birmingham, 1962) · P. T. Marsh, *Joseph Chamberlain, entrepreneur in politics* (1994) · 'Royal commission to inquire into … factory and workshop acts', *Parl. papers* (1876), vol. 29, C. 1443 · 'Departmental committee on income tax', *Parl. papers* (1905), vol. 44, Cd 2575 · B. M. D. Smith, *The Birmingham Business School: business education in the University of Birmingham, 1899–1965* (1990) · B. M. D. Smith, 'Bibliography of Birmingham industrial history', Birm. CL · *City of Birmingham Red Book and Reference Almanack* · *Directory of Directors* · *Stock Exchange Year Book* · *WW* · *Birmingham Daily Mail* (29 April 1899) ·

Birmingham Daily Post (25 May 1881) · *Birmingham Daily Post* (7 Sept 1886) · *Birmingham Daily Post* (18 Nov 1888) · *The Engineer* (24 Sept 1886) · A. Chamberlain, *The book of business* (privately printed, 1899)
Archives Birm. CL |FILM BFI NFTVA, 'Chamberlain the peacemaker', Gaumont British News, 19 Sept 1938; 'The Czech crisis from both sides', Gaumont British News, 22 Sept 1938; 'The man of the hour: the Rt Hon. Neville Chamberlain, M.P.', 1938; 'Personalities: a tribute to Mr Chamberlain and other items. Mr Chamberlain passes', British News, 20 Nov 1940; documentary footage; news footage; other footage |SOUND BL NSA, current affairs recordings; documentary recordings; news recordings; performance recordings
Likenesses photograph, Birmingham Reference Library; repro. in Smith, 'Chamberlain, Arthur'
Wealth at death £143,588 8s. 0d.: probate, 18 Dec 1913, *CGPLA Eng. & Wales*

Chamberlain, Sir (Joseph) Austen (1863–1937),

politician, was born on 16 October 1863 in Harborne Road, Edgbaston, Birmingham, the second child and only son of Joseph *Chamberlain (1836–1914), politician, and his first wife, Harriet (1838–1863), daughter of Archibald Kenrick of Berrow Court, Edgbaston. His mother died soon after his birth and his father subsequently remarried twice. In his second marriage Joseph Chamberlain fathered a second son, (Arthur) Neville *Chamberlain, the future prime minister. Austen was thus destined to be overshadowed at both the beginning and end of his life by a member of his own family.

Born into a political environment or, as Joseph once put it, into a red dispatch box, Austen Chamberlain's education was engineered with a political career in mind. His father was determined that he should follow him in public life, and that his progress up that greasy pole should be relieved of the impediments which the father had had to overcome. After preparatory school in Brighton, Chamberlain moved on to Rugby School shortly before his fifteenth birthday. At Trinity College, Cambridge, from 1882, he read history and graduated in 1885. Thereafter his father was anxious to continue the wider education of the future statesman. Experience of contemporary Europe would add to his understanding of the great issues of the day. Accordingly, Chamberlain spent nine months in Paris, where he attended the École des Sciences Politiques. His father's name secured access to leading political circles and he met figures such as Clemenceau, Gambetta, and Ferry. Early in 1887 he went to Germany. Though he stayed there for a year, he never took the country or its people to his heart as he had done in Paris. Lectures which he attended by von Treitschke on Prussian history filled him with alarm because of their repeated emphasis on the superiority of the German race. It is probably no exaggeration to suggest that many of the attitudes which Chamberlain displayed as foreign secretary in the 1920s were in part shaped by these early experiences of Europe.

Early political career Joseph Chamberlain now determined that his son should enter national politics, without the necessity of an apprenticeship on the municipal stage which had characterized his own career. Austen was formally adopted as Liberal Unionist candidate for the

Sir (Joseph) Austen Chamberlain (1863–1937), by H. Walter Barnett

Hawick district in the Scottish borders early in 1888 and set about nursing the constituency while awaiting the next general election. In 1892, however, he seized the opportunity of accepting the more attractive nomination as candidate for the vacant East Worcestershire seat, close to his father's Birmingham stronghold. His election to parliament, unopposed, in a by-election in March characterized the ease with which Chamberlain's early advancement was achieved. After retaining the seat with a comfortable majority in the general election later that year Chamberlain, already a junior whip for the Liberal Unionists, delivered his maiden speech in April 1893 on the second reading of the Liberal government's Home Rule Bill. It was an impressive performance which won the notice of his opponents, including Prime Minister Gladstone.

In the Unionist government of 1895 Chamberlain accepted the post of civil lord of the Admiralty. More importantly, his father took office as colonial secretary and rapidly emerged as the most powerful man in the government beneath the prime minister, Lord Salisbury. For Austen this transformation in his father's fortunes meant that for a further decade or more he would have to live in the shadow of his illustrious namesake, and see his own political career largely shaped by the causes which his father espoused. The five years which Chamberlain spent at the Admiralty were essentially a period of administrative experience rather than political decision making. It was not particularly exciting work, but Chamberlain found it congenial and progressively enhanced his reputation as a capable administrator and reliable parliamentarian. He could speak effectively, but at no time in his career developed into an orator who really stirred emotions. He was again returned unopposed at the general election of 1900, held during the Second South African War, and escaped largely unscathed from allegations that he and his father were making money out of the war because of their holdings in armaments firms which had contracts with the government.

In November 1900 Chamberlain was promoted to the position of financial secretary to the Treasury. Though outside the cabinet the post was an important one, and, as he was still only thirty-seven, his appointment was a clear indication that he was well regarded and destined for cabinet rank in the not too distant future. Promotion duly came on 8 August 1902 soon after Balfour succeeded Salisbury as prime minister. Chamberlain now entered the cabinet as postmaster-general to sit alongside his father.

The campaign for tariff reform The Second South African War served to highlight the twin problems of national finance and the isolated and potentially vulnerable position of Britain on the international stage. It also emphasized divisions inside the Unionist government. It was in this increasingly strained atmosphere that Joseph Chamberlain delivered his celebrated speech on tariff reform on 15 May 1903 in Birmingham. By proposing a route towards imperial unity while at the same time creating a new source of revenue, Chamberlain offered his solution to the nation's outstanding problems. Austen could not have known how important an event this speech was to prove for his own career. By September, in the face of irreconcilable differences within the cabinet, the elder Chamberlain determined to resign from the government, the better to educate the nation on the merits of tariff reform from the comparative freedom of the back benches. Balfour strove to maintain a balance of interests within his reorganized cabinet. But the fact that Austen stayed on, and indeed was promoted on 6 October to the senior post of chancellor of the exchequer, may indicate that Balfour himself accepted the broad thrust of the elder Chamberlain's tariff policy and that Austen would act as a bridge between Joseph and the prime minister. Austen himself clearly envisaged that his new role was to act as custodian of his father's cause, but over the years which followed he found it much more difficult than he had expected to induce Balfour to adopt a positive and committed attitude towards tariffs.

As chancellor Chamberlain was one of the few ministers to enhance his reputation while the government itself drifted indecisively towards the electoral catastrophe of 1906. Two competent, if orthodox, budgets were presented, but Chamberlain found his position inside the cabinet increasingly difficult as Balfour failed to commit the government to a full-blooded policy of tariff reform. He was probably relieved when the prime minister finally submitted the government's resignation in December 1905, making way for a minority Liberal administration under Sir Henry Campbell-Bannerman. The result of the general election of January 1906 was both decisive and yet ambiguous. On the one hand the Liberals secured a landslide victory in terms of seats in the House of Commons.

Many of the Unionist leadership, including Balfour himself, went down to defeat. Yet on the other hand those Unionists who were returned to parliament were overwhelmingly in favour of the Chamberlainite policy of tariff reform. Austen and his father were both among the victors and seemed set to dominate the internal dynamics of the Unionist Party. But in July 1906 the elder Chamberlain suffered a severe stroke from which he never fully recovered. For the remaining eight years of his life he was no more than a backstage observer of the political scene, still desperately anxious to see the fulfilment of his political dreams. In such a situation Austen was the obvious instrument through which the stricken statesman could still exert an influence upon national politics.

The younger Chamberlain thus found himself in the most difficult of positions. At a time when he was ready to carve out his own distinctive career in public affairs he was called upon to act as a sort of surrogate version of his father—to be even more his father's son than he had been before. Representing his father forced Chamberlain into uncharacteristic behaviour. The man who for most of his career was renowned for political rectitude found himself the object of scorn and vilification as a result of his actions. His behaviour was often inconsistent with his membership of the shadow cabinet and, in more recent times, would certainly have led to dismissal from such a body.

But for Austen Chamberlain tariff reform was never quite the crusade which it was for his father. His vision of the sort of socio-economic transformation which might result from the introduction of tariffs was always strictly limited. Furthermore, he failed to attract the unquestioning support of those who would have followed wherever his father had led. Deep down, Chamberlain probably wanted to play the role of mediator between the extremes of opinion within the Unionist ranks on the question of tariff reform rather than take the lead on one side of the debate, as his father's illness demanded. Not surprisingly, Balfour, successfully returned to the House of Commons at a by-election, found it possible to retreat once again into a cloud of ambiguities and imprecision as far as the issue of tariff reform was concerned. His character—'a locked Chinese box of paradoxes which seemed to defy penetration' (P. Brendon, *Eminent Edwardians*, 1980, 70)—proved, as it had done in the years 1903–5, too subtle for Chamberlain's more pedestrian mind.

None the less, as the country's economic situation deteriorated, Balfour became increasingly convinced of the merits of tariff reform on intellectual grounds until it was finally adopted as official party policy. So Chamberlain faced the general election of January 1910, precipitated by the House of Lords' rejection of the government's budget, with some optimism. His influence within the party in the whole period before the First World War was now at its height. For Chamberlain, perhaps even more than for the Unionist Party, the election represented a crucial test, for never before and not again until the 1920s was the cause of tariff reform so central to Unionist strategy. Against this background the outcome of the election must be seen as a considerable disappointment to him. Though the massive Liberal majority of 1906 was now wiped out, the government could still rely on a working majority in the new parliament because of the support of Labour and Irish MPs. Though Chamberlain was reluctant to admit it, the cause of tariff reform had suffered a severe set-back, and as the economic climate improved in the course of 1910 so its appeal diminished still further.

Later in the year Chamberlain was one of a four-man Unionist delegation to the constitutional conference called to try to resolve the impasse between the parties over the powers of the House of Lords. Its failure made another general election inevitable in December. During the course of the campaign Balfour substantially reduced the party's commitment to tariff reform by declaring that, in the event of a Unionist victory, no food taxes would be introduced until after a referendum had been held on this single issue. For Chamberlain this was a considerable blow, not relieved by the Unionists' failure once again to return to office.

At least Chamberlain could now seek refuge in a happy family life. On 21 July 1906, at the comparatively late age of forty-two, he had married Ivy Muriel Dundas (c.1879–1941), daughter of Colonel Henry Dundas of Datchet. This partnership lasted without blemish until broken by Chamberlain's death three decades later. The marriage produced two sons, Joseph and Lawrence, and one daughter, Diane. Chamberlain's private life was always a source of great joy, allowing him to put the cares of the political world into perspective and rescuing him from the many disappointments of his public career.

First chance of the leadership By the end of 1910 Balfour had led his party to defeat in three successive general elections. This fact, coupled with his equivocal leadership during the Parliament Bill crisis in the summer of 1911, gave rise to calls for his resignation. In November he decided to step down. Chamberlain, despite being a Liberal Unionist in a party dominated by Conservatives, and a Unitarian among Anglicans, was regarded as the front runner for the succession. But he was opposed by Walter Long, representative of the traditional tory landowning squirearchy. At this point Chamberlain suffered from a dual disadvantage of being his father's son. To Joseph Chamberlain's acolytes Austen lacked those qualities of fire and passion which made them unquestioning adherents to his father's cause. To those who held to a more traditional concept of Conservatism, Austen was tarred with his father's brush and stood as a symbol of the vulgar intrusion of 'Birmingham' and all it stood for into the party's ranks. In addition, Chamberlain's die-hard opposition to the Parliament Bill and his membership of the Halsbury Club were not likely, despite his professions of devotion to the outgoing leader, to endear him to Balfour loyalists. Even so, had he possessed his father's determination and ambition, he could probably have secured the leadership on a majority vote.

In the event, both Chamberlain and Long withdrew from the contest, allowing the little-known Andrew Bonar Law to emerge as a compromise candidate. Chamberlain's motivation was a combination of not wanting to split the party, an inner lack of conviction about his own leadership qualities, and a desire to live down his father's reputation as a man who had wrecked two political parties. This was a significant moment in his career. Thereafter, apart from the brief period of his own leadership in the 1920s, he found himself serving beneath men in the Conservative and Unionist Party whom he regarded as his juniors. He developed an exaggerated sense of his own importance and dignity which compounded an already stiff and unbending personal demeanour. With Bonar Law his relationship was never easy, especially when the new leader effectively abandoned tariff reform as a policy option for the foreseeable future.

Ireland and the war The years immediately before the outbreak of the First World War were dominated by the issue of Ireland. Chamberlain was never fully committed to the Unionist campaign of unyielding opposition to home rule and became increasingly concerned at the seemingly inexorable drift towards violence. His own preference was for a federal structure for the whole of the United Kingdom, or Home Rule All Round as it was usually called, but he failed to convert the Unionist Party to this cause. Joseph Chamberlain finally died at the beginning of July 1914, and Austen took over his West Birmingham seat in the House of Commons. More importantly, he now had the opportunity to carve out his own individual role in British politics, without the need to keep one eye on the wishes of his father. But he would do so against a background that was very different from anything he had so far experienced in public life. A month after Joseph Chamberlain's death, Britain and Germany were at war.

At the beginning of hostilities Chamberlain played an important part in persuading the Unionist leadership to bring pressure upon Asquith's government to stand by France and Russia and to assure the prime minister of the support of the Unionist Party. Though no coalition government was formed for the time being, the chancellor of the exchequer, David Lloyd George, invited Chamberlain as a former chancellor to hold a semi-official post at the Treasury. On one occasion Chamberlain even took over the chairmanship of a conference at the Treasury when Lloyd George had to leave for a meeting of the cabinet. Significantly, this represented a first step in Chamberlain's association with Lloyd George, a working partnership which would gradually evolve from a mood of suspicion and mistrust towards the feeling of deep loyalty which would cost Chamberlain dear in 1922. When Asquith's coalition was formed on 25 May 1915, Chamberlain entered the government as secretary of state for India, remaining in this post when Lloyd George took over as prime minister in December 1916.

As a passionate believer in the British empire Chamberlain took a keen interest in his new office. Though it did not seem central to the nation's war effort, he did inherit from his predecessor a small military campaign in Mesopotamia under the control of the government of India, designed in the first instance to protect oil fields at the head of the Persian Gulf. Over the following months the scope of the expedition was greatly extended, but by early 1916 it was becoming clear that provision for the sick and wounded had been hopelessly inadequate. The medical deficiencies of the campaign might not have attracted as much attention as they did had not the whole expedition turned sour after an initial run of military success. The decision to advance on Baghdad, which Chamberlain had supported in the cabinet, proved to be a grave mistake, and the Turks were far better prepared to meet the British advance than had been anticipated. After a series of setbacks Major-General Charles Townshend, commander of the 6th division which was besieged at Kut al-Amara, surrendered his 3000 British and 6000 Indian troops. 'In the whole history of the British Army there had never been a surrender like this' (A. J. Barker, *The Neglected War*, 1967, 266).

The combination of military disaster and medical scandal ensured that heads would have to roll. Asquith was obliged to set up a commission of inquiry under the chairmanship of Lord George Hamilton, a former secretary of state for India. Chamberlain's culpability was believed to be marginal. When, however, the commission reported in the early summer of 1917, Chamberlain faced criticism on two counts. He bore a share of collective responsibility for the advance on Baghdad, and over the question of medical provision it was argued that he had not brought his concerns sufficiently into his official correspondence with the viceroy and had not acted quickly enough to bring about an inquiry. The new prime minister, David Lloyd George, offered Chamberlain the chance of a move to the Paris embassy, but the latter determined to stay where he was. When, however, the cabinet decided to set up a court of inquiry to decide against which individuals action should be taken, Chamberlain determined to resign from the government on 12 July 1917. He accepted without hesitation—though many thought unnecessarily—the doctrine of ministerial responsibility.

The post-war coalition By the end of 1917 Chamberlain was again exerting political influence. From the back benches he voiced concern about Lloyd George's increasingly close association with the magnates of the press. The prime minister seems to have concluded that Chamberlain was too dangerous a critic to be left outside the government, and on 18 April 1918 he was appointed minister without portfolio with a seat in the war cabinet. He retained this office when it was decided to extend the life of the coalition beyond the armistice of November, before becoming chancellor of the exchequer again on 10 January 1919.

Chamberlain was apprehensive about returning to the Treasury, not least because of his expectation that the government was bound to confront severe financial problems and industrial unrest as a direct consequence of the war. The conflict had been largely financed through borrowing, so that the national debt stood at £7435 million by the end of the financial year 1918–19, compared to £650 million at the start of the war. His first budget announced a substantial reduction in planned public expenditure while reducing the rate of the excess profits duty. In 1920 there were violent fluctuations in the state of the British economy as an inflationary boom rapidly gave way to a severe recession marked by industrial stagnation and high unemployment. Though he has been much criticized for his management of the Treasury in this period, for first taking too long to respond to an overheating economy and then for making the slump more severe than it need have been by increasing the bank rate to 7 per cent, Chamberlain had little alternative but to pursue the chancellor's traditional role of exercising restraint over the spending plans of his ministerial colleagues. His budget of April 1920 increased both direct and indirect taxes, while at the same time he sought ever greater economies in the government's spending programmes. Overall it was to his credit that a deficit of £1690 million for the financial year 1918–19 was turned into a surplus of £238 million in 1920–21.

In a broader context the Chamberlain who emerged from the war was a subtly different figure from the politician of 1914. He was more conscious than most of his contemporaries that the political environment of Edwardian England could never be recreated. Gone was the somewhat reluctant radical of the pre-war era, replaced by someone who was determined to preserve the existing fabric of ordered society against what he saw as the new threat of socialism, and ready to abandon some of his earlier beliefs to secure this greater end. In other words, he now developed into a natural Conservative, a transition eased by the formal fusion of the Conservative and Liberal Unionist parties which had taken place in 1912. His inherent conservatism was emphasized by his appearance and dress. With his monocle and frock coat he readily gave the impression of being a relic from an earlier age. He was one of the last MPs to maintain the old tradition of wearing a top hat inside the chamber.

The evolution in Chamberlain's thinking shaped his attitude towards the coalition government and towards erstwhile political enemies in the Liberal Party. It was his long-term hope to combine in one party men of differing political traditions in order to avoid a peril more dangerous even than the war which had been so narrowly won. He did not believe that the Conservative Party standing alone would be able indefinitely to resist the challenge from the Labour Party. The maintenance of a coalition with Lloyd George's Liberals, even though the parliamentary strength of the Conservatives now gave them compelling claims to control a single-party government, was a necessary preliminary to such a political realignment. These calculations helped transform his attitude towards Lloyd George. His close association with the prime minister brought him a clear perception of the latter's qualities, and he developed a high regard for, and loyalty towards, Lloyd George which were ultimately to prove disastrous for him. It was an unlikely partnership between two men of vastly differing characters and public images, but it developed into the key axis of the coalition government.

Party leader Late in 1920 Chamberlain was offered, but turned down, the Indian viceroyalty. A few months later a different and unexpected prize fell into his lap. On 17 March 1921 Andrew Bonar Law was forced to resign from the government on the grounds of ill health, and Chamberlain faced no serious challenge for the succession to the leadership of the Conservative Party in the House of Commons. His election was proposed at the Carlton Club by Captain E. G. Pretyman, who in the course of his speech coined the idea that Conservative leaders 'emerge'. In Chamberlain's case the word helped to convey the breadth of support which he now enjoyed. He took on his new role, which involved leaving the exchequer and becoming lord privy seal and leader of the Commons, 'as a clear duty but I wish that the call of duty had not come' (Chamberlain MSS, AC 4/1/1204). Such reluctance reflected doubts about his own leadership qualities which events were to justify.

Chamberlain's elevation made him more than ever conscious of his dignity, while his lack of the common touch proved a serious handicap. He made few efforts to cultivate the support of Conservative back-benchers, many of whom had come into the Commons only since the war and knew very little of their new leader. More specifically, he proved a poor communicator. In this period he had developed into one of the more perceptive observers of the contemporary political scene. But he singularly failed to convey his understanding of the party-political struggle to those beneath him, most of whom were reluctant to submerge their identity inside a coalition headed by an increasingly unpopular prime minister. As a result, there developed a mutual failure of comprehension between leader and led.

The ending of the First World War brought the issue of Ireland back to the forefront of the political agenda. Chamberlain's involvement in this question did little to strengthen his position as Conservative leader, though he himself came to look upon it with a sense of pride and satisfaction. As has been seen, Chamberlain's views on Ireland had never been those of an orthodox Unionist, and during the war he had become ever more prepared to consider a radical departure in Britain's Irish policy. He was among the first to urge negotiations with the Sinn Féin leadership and was one of the government's delegation when talks began. Though it was Lloyd George who shaped the course of the negotiations, Chamberlain was an enthusiastic supporter of the articles of agreement which the Irish representatives signed on 6 December 1921. He had played an important part in moving his party from the absolutist stance on the Union with which it had been associated in the pre-war period. The Free State became a dominion under the crown, while the prospect of Irish unity receded into the distant future. Like many later British politicians, he tackled the Irish problem in a spirit of well-meaning compromise, but this approach was bound to disappoint those who held more extreme positions on this most contentious of issues. In particular, Chamberlain, by his part in the negotiations, succeeded in alienating a substantial number of right-wing Conservatives for whom the Union afforded no possibility of compromise. Thereby he further eroded his basis of support within the party.

By the beginning of 1922 attention was turning to the question of the next general election and, more specifically, the basis upon which the Conservative Party would contest it. Chamberlain remained one of the most committed advocates of maintaining the coalition. He was still convinced that, if it were to break up, the inevitable consequence would be to divide the moderate and constitutional forces into two hostile camps, leaving the Labour Party as the electoral beneficiary. Such thinking played its part when he declined Lloyd George's offer in February to step down from the premiership in his favour. Badly advised by those around him, Chamberlain seemed largely unaware of the strength of feeling against the continuation of coalition government which was now running through much of the Conservative Party. In private he may well have expected to succeed Lloyd George after the forthcoming election, but he found it difficult to articulate this in public, thereby giving the impression to many rank-and-file Conservatives that he was prepared to acquiesce indefinitely in a Lloyd George premiership. He could not understand, he told an audience at Oxford in March, 'the attitude of those who would desire needlessly to quarrel with our Liberal allies and to engage the constitutional forces in a fratricidal struggle' (Petrie, 2.179). At all events matters came to a head at a party meeting held at the Carlton Club on 19 October 1922.

Chamberlain badly misjudged the mood of the meeting. He gave an unimpressive performance which highlighted his deficiencies as party leader. But the key factor was the re-emergence of Bonar Law, apparently restored to good health, as the champion of independent Conservatism. Making the issue one of confidence in himself, Chamberlain forced Conservative MPs into a position where they had to choose between loyalty to the leadership and, as they saw it, loyalty to the party, and they chose the latter. A motion for independent Conservative action at the next general election was carried by a large majority. The coalition was at an end and Lloyd George resigned immediately. The king now invited Bonar Law, elected Conservative leader in Chamberlain's place, to form a new administration. Chamberlain, bitterly resenting what had happened, stayed aloof from the new government, although the appointment of his half-brother, Neville, to the position of postmaster-general caused some strains within the Chamberlain family. Though Bonar Law succeeded in securing a large parliamentary majority for the Conservatives at the general election of November 1922, Chamberlain did not alter his analysis of the longer-term political situation. Noting the rise in the Labour vote, he continued to believe in the desirability of fusion between Conservatives and Lloyd George Liberals.

Out of office Bonar Law's physical recovery proved short lived. By the spring of 1923 it was clear that he was a sick man, and in May he was obliged to resign, suffering from inoperable cancer. Had Chamberlain managed to reconcile himself to the verdict of the Carlton Club meeting, the party leadership, and therefore the premiership, would almost certainly have now reverted to him. In March Bonar Law, using Beaverbrook and Rothermere as intermediaries, had invited Chamberlain to return to the government as lord privy seal, with the expectation of succeeding him by the autumn. As it was, Chamberlain was still outside the government when Bonar Law resigned and had little chance of being considered for the succession, which passed to Stanley Baldwin. The latter did not feel able to offer Chamberlain a place in his government, and relations between the two men were badly damaged when the prime minister rather ineptly suggested that Chamberlain might like to consider becoming ambassador in Washington. Baldwin's decision to call a general election in December 1923 on the specific issue of tariffs brought about a partial reconciliation, and after the election, which resulted in Britain's first Labour government, Chamberlain resumed his place on the Conservative front bench. Neville played an important part in bringing Baldwin and his brother together, but Chamberlain still found it difficult to accept the new hierarchy of the Conservative Party. He remained a disgruntled and touchy colleague, looking down with some disdain from the eminence of his long parliamentary and ministerial career upon the inadequate efforts of the far less experienced Baldwin, whom chance and fate had installed as his leader.

The foreign secretaryship Lacking a majority in the House of Commons, Ramsay MacDonald's Labour government fell when Conservatives and Liberals combined to pass a vote of censure on its mishandling of a relatively minor legal case. The resulting general election of October 1924 produced an overwhelming Conservative victory. Baldwin was in a position to construct a government which would last its full term. Chamberlain, faced with a choice between the Foreign and India offices, inclined at first towards the latter, largely because it was a field of government where he already had experience. In the event he opted on 6 November for the more senior post. He did so with the diffidence and misgivings which accompanied most of the new initiatives of his career, but soon found his feet. Foreign affairs, in fact, now became the absorbing concern of the remainder of his life.

The most important issue facing the new secretary of state was the future of the Geneva protocol, an ambitious and somewhat idealistic agreement negotiated by the previous Labour government, which was designed to supplement and strengthen the covenant of the League of Nations. By creating an exhaustive machinery for the definition of aggression and automatic procedures to deal with it, the protocol might well have had the practical effect of making Britain, as the leading league power, the world's policeman with unlimited obligations to fulfil. Chamberlain was no isolationist. He saw the vital need for Britain to make a firm commitment to the continent of Europe. 'If we withdraw from Europe', he told a cabinet colleague, 'I say without hesitation that the chance of permanent peace is gone' (Chamberlain MSS, AC 52/38). But for him the most important point was to define the extent and limits of Britain's commitment. The other key element in Chamberlain's thinking was his appreciation that there would never be real stability in Europe until France acquired that sense of security which she had failed to derive from the treaty of Versailles. Indeed, Baldwin appointed Chamberlain to the Foreign Office at least in part to put right the damage done to Anglo-French relations under the last Conservative foreign secretary, Lord Curzon.

These factors made Chamberlain inherently hostile to the Geneva protocol, which was too wide-ranging in its ambitions, and led him towards a bilateral pact with France. Opposition within the cabinet towards Chamberlain's preferred option was, however, too strong, and, very much as a second best, the foreign secretary was obliged to take up proposals put forward by the German foreign ministry for a multilateral security pact in western Europe to guarantee the Franco-German and Germano-Belgian frontiers and the demilitarization of the Rhineland. Herein lay the seeds of the Locarno treaties, which were eventually concluded in October 1925 and for which Chamberlain's foreign secretaryship is best remembered. Though the agreements were not Chamberlain's in their origin, he adopted them with enthusiasm and played the key role through the spring and summer of 1925 in bringing his French and German opposite numbers, Aristide Briand and Gustav Stresemann, together.

The importance of Locarno At the time the Locarno treaties were widely hailed as the most significant contribution towards a lasting peace in Europe of the whole inter-war era, marking a final end to the divisions of the war years and, because it was now agreed that Germany should become a member, setting the League of Nations on a new and more hopeful course. 'This morning the Locarno Pact was signed at the Foreign Office', wrote George V in the privacy of his diary. 'I pray this may mean peace for many years. Why not for ever?' (H. Nicolson, *King George V*, 1952, 409). Chamberlain himself was well rewarded for his efforts. A knighthood of the Garter and the Nobel prize for peace were the most tangible of the accolades showered upon him. But, especially in the light of what happened in the 1930s when Locarno was violated with impunity, the verdict of history has been less enthusiastic. It must always be remembered that Locarno began life as an initiative of German foreign policy, whose overriding purpose was the revision of the Versailles peace settlement. Moreover, by defining those frontiers of Europe where Britain felt committed, Chamberlain was advertising the fact that there were other frontiers where Britain was less vitally involved and which might be subject to revision without British intervention. After Locarno, therefore, certain parts of the Versailles treaty were endowed with a greater degree of sanctity than others. Granted existing French commitments in eastern Europe, this had the potential to create problems for Britain, as the 1930s demonstrated.

Locarno's impact upon the League of Nations must also be considered. Chamberlain always maintained that the treaty should be seen as supplementing the league by adding specific obligations to the general ones inherent in the covenant. But this was true only in the context of the league as Chamberlain saw it—a limited body which had a useful role to play in international affairs but which had in no sense transformed the intrinsic nature of diplomacy. 'I am sometimes more afraid of the League's enthusiastic friends than its contemptuous opponents', he once told a meeting of the League of Nations Union (*The Times*, 17 March 1937). Objectively, Locarno may be viewed as a first step in Britain's abandonment of the sort of principles which underlay the covenant, with its belief in the indivisibility of peace, and a reversion to old-style foreign policy based on the priority of national self-interest.

To his credit Chamberlain saw that Locarno alone was not enough. He once said that it should be seen as the beginning of the work of European appeasement and reconciliation and not its end. Locarno did provide for arbitration conventions between Germany and her neighbours in eastern Europe, and Chamberlain clearly hoped that what had been done in relation to Germany's western frontiers could be replicated by comparable regional arrangements in the east. But it would be for other powers than Britain to take the lead in this respect. As he once memorably wrote, in a deliberate misquotation of Bismarck's famous words, the Polish corridor was something 'for which no British Government ever will or ever can risk the bones of a British grenadier' (Chamberlain MSS, AC 52/189). In the event these so-called Eastern Locarnos failed to materialize. What he could not have foreseen was the rise of a new generation of German politicians for whom the traditional norms of diplomatic conduct had no meaning, men who were prepared to use the loopholes which Locarno offered in the east to begin their assault on European peace. But for the rise of Hitler, it would be easier to view Locarno as Chamberlain's honest attempt to resolve the dilemma of limited resources and over-extended obligations which confronted all the custodians of British foreign policy in the inter-war period.

The Foreign Office after Locarno With what appeared to be the supreme accomplishment of Locarno behind him, Chamberlain became something of an elder statesman before his time. Locarno was his achievement and he revelled in it. But it is easy to forget that he remained foreign secretary for nearly four more years after its signature. Unhappily, the level of achievement was not maintained. He was the first British foreign secretary to attend meetings of the League of Nations on a regular basis. His primary purpose was to maintain personal contact with the other architects of the Locarno agreements. Thus began the so-called Locarno 'tea parties', a pattern of diplomacy whereby the representatives of the Locarno powers met in private in one another's hotel suites to discuss the outstanding international issues of the day. Though it has been argued that these meetings did not, in fact, divert business from its rightful forum in the league assembly, they did serve to emphasize the uniquely personal basis upon which the post-Locarno détente in European affairs was grounded. Personal chemistry, however, could not disguise the fact that serious differences remained between France and Germany. Even Germany's entry into the league was mishandled, with Chamberlain receiving much of the blame. Little of the spirit of Locarno survived

Stresemann's death and Chamberlain's loss of office in 1929.

In the years after Locarno the multiplicity of problems facing Britain in the international arena became far more apparent than it had been in the first twelve months of Chamberlain's foreign secretaryship, serving to remind him that Britain remained a worldwide and imperial power with interests across the globe. During the second part of his ministry he was confronted by serious problems relating to Britain's position in Egypt and in China and to the country's relations with the Soviet Union and the United States. The discovery that the All Russian Co-operative Society was a front organization for Soviet espionage led to the severing of diplomatic relations in May 1927. Relations with the Americans became particularly strained over the question of arms control and stand as one of the least distinguished aspects of his tenure of office.

Faced with the diversity of calls upon his time and attention, Chamberlain's energy and health began to fail. Never endowed with a robust constitution or an infinite capacity for work, he complained repeatedly of the strain and tiredness brought on by the demands of the Foreign Office. In 1928 he suffered a complete collapse, after which many observers believed that he was never quite the same man again. By the time of the 1929 general election his star was no longer in the ascendant. The hopes engendered by Locarno had begun to fade and there was widespread criticism of his performance which was not restricted to the ranks of the Labour opposition. He was generally believed to have been too indulgent towards French wishes, especially when these were expressed by Briand.

Elder statesman Chamberlain only narrowly held on to his West Birmingham seat in the election which brought the Labour Party back to power. In part this was testimony to his failings as a constituency MP. Certainly he never cultivated his Birmingham base as assiduously as did his father and half-brother. In opposition he became ever more critical of Baldwin's performance as party leader. He had never known 'so blunt a spearhead' or a man who 'left so large a gap between the recognition that he must act and action' (Self, 348). But by this stage of his career Chamberlain was careful to do nothing which might jeopardize Neville's claims to the succession. He had despaired when Neville had been persuaded to accept the party chairmanship in 1930 and had worked hard to extricate his brother from this commitment. He played no part in the crisis which led to the formation of the National Government in August 1931 but, with some reluctance, agreed to become first lord of the Admiralty without a seat in the cabinet. His official career would thus close with an odd symmetrical precision, as his first appointment thirty-six years earlier had been as civil lord of the Admiralty. In this position it fell to him to deal with the naval mutiny at Invergordon. He renounced any claim to further office after the general election in October, though he had some regrets about this decision when he saw the Foreign Office pass to the Liberal lawyer John Simon.

A ministerial career spanning three and a half decades thus came to an end. Early assessments of Chamberlain's public life tended to be shaped by two considerations—comparisons, generally unfavourable, with his father and half-brother, and attempts to attribute his failure to secure the premiership to some underlying character defect. He was the only Conservative leader of the twentieth century not to rise to this position. He might have found it easier to carve out his own political identity had it not been for a strong physical resemblance to his father, which he emphasized with his inevitable monocle and orchid. But there were physical differences between the two men which perhaps symbolized differences of character. Tall and slim like his father, his features were smooth and calm. His relaxed frame lacked the taut and wiry qualities of the older man. His appearance is well captured in portraits by I. M. Cohen, owned by the Cordwainers' Company but now hanging in committee room 6 of the House of Commons, and by Sir William Rothenstein at Reading University. Yet there is no need to consider him in terms of the post he did not attain or in comparison with members of his own family. He was a major figure in his own right. Only chance and his own decision stopped him becoming prime minister in 1922 or 1923. He played a significant role in the development of British political history from the turn of the century until shortly after the outbreak of the Second World War. He held the exchequer and Foreign Office at difficult periods and performed creditably in both posts. Leo Amery's assessment, written shortly after Chamberlain's death, remains balanced and fair: 'He just missed greatness and the highest position, but his was a fine life of honourable public service' (J. Barnes and D. Nicholson, *The Empire at Bay*, 1988, 437).

Though out of office, Chamberlain now embarked upon a last, and by no means undistinguished, phase of his long political career, emerging as one of the leading critics of the National Government. Ironically, in his last years his influence inside the House of Commons was probably greater than when he had held high office. He was now the most respected of Conservative back-benchers and it was to him that young members, particularly those who found themselves at odds with the foreign policy of the National Government, looked for leadership and guidance. It was a reflection of the authority which he still enjoyed that the government persuaded him to join the executive of the League of Nations Union in February 1932.

Whatever they later claimed, very few parliamentarians of the 1930s genuinely merited the description of 'anti-appeaser'. As far as Nazi Germany was concerned, Chamberlain belonged to this exclusive group. He wasted no time in drawing attention to the menace posed by Adolf Hitler after the latter became German chancellor on 30 January 1933. Fundamental to Chamberlain's assessment was his belief that Hitler's likely behaviour in the international arena could not be divorced from the nature of his domestic regime. He was adamant that the new German government was not one to which concessions could be granted. As early as 13 April 1933 Chamberlain declared:

> What is this new spirit of German nationalism? The worst of the old-Prussian Imperialism, with an added savagery, a racial pride, an exclusiveness which cannot allow to any fellow-subject not of 'pure Nordic birth' equality of rights and citizenship within the nation to which he belongs. Are you going to discuss revision [of the treaty of Versailles] with a Government like that? (Petrie, 2.392)

Outside interests Freed from the constraints of high office, Chamberlain had the time to develop his interests outside politics. Having already served when foreign secretary as rector of Glasgow University, he was chancellor of the University of Reading (1935–7) and chairman of the governors of Rugby School. He also took seriously his chairmanship of the London School of Tropical Medicine and of the governing body of the British Postgraduate Medical School. He held honorary degrees from the universities of Oxford, Cambridge, London, Birmingham, Glasgow, Toronto, and Lyons. Chamberlain was never a particularly rich man. The need to economize had already, in 1929, necessitated the sale of Twitt's Ghyll, the country home in Sussex which he had bought a decade earlier and whose garden had been a source of enormous pleasure and satisfaction to him. Sir Robert Vansittart described his last years, spent in 'straits and a small flat' from which he emerged 'immaculate in frayed white shirt and a shiny tail coat' (R. Vansittart, *The Mist Procession*, 1958, 549). But Chamberlain, always concerned for the financial security of his wife and children, may have exaggerated his own poverty. Out of office he found several lucrative sources of income. None the less, the expense involved was a compelling reason behind his decision to decline the sinecure post of lord warden of the Cinque Ports in October 1933. The desire to make some money provided an incentive to put together a volume of autobiographical essays, published in 1935 as *Down the Years*, though Chamberlain experienced some difficulty in spinning out the book to its required length. *Politics from Inside*, based on his letters to his stepmother during the period of his father's illness after 1906, appeared in 1936.

A volume of cultural reflections, *Seen in Passing*, based on Chamberlain's travels on the continent, was published posthumously in 1937. This book reflected the interests of a man for whom politics was never an all-consuming passion. 'There are moments', he once suggested, 'when I ask myself whether the game is worth the candle and whether any public duty calls upon me to slave and endure at so thankless a task' (Chamberlain MSS, AC 18/1/10). It was on the advice of his father that he had found himself a hobby. Rock gardening became one of the passions of his adult life. Even at the height of his political career in the 1920s he would absent himself from a League of Nations meeting at Geneva for a couple of hours in order to pursue a particular alpine plant. But the concepts of public service and civic duty were deeply embedded in his personality and help explain why he remained in politics for so long. Though born into a tradition of nonconformity, religion did not play a large part in his life and he found it difficult to conceptualize any notion of an afterlife.

Final years and death Though he was by then seventy-two years of age, there was serious speculation about Chamberlain's return to government at the end of 1935. His reaction was recognized to be crucial in determining whether the government could survive the parliamentary outcry which followed the disclosure of the details of the Hoare–Laval pact, by which the British foreign secretary hoped to defuse the crisis created by Italian aggression in Abyssinia. It seems that a strong hint from Baldwin that he would be asked to return to the Foreign Office encouraged Chamberlain to tone down his criticism of the government's conduct. The cabinet survived, but it was Anthony Eden and not Chamberlain who succeeded Hoare as foreign secretary. 'Poor man', reflected Winston Churchill, 'he always plays the game and never wins it' (M. Gilbert, *Winston S. Churchill*, 5, pt 2, 1981, 1363). A later offer of a non-departmental post in the cabinet to advise on foreign affairs and defence was unceremoniously rejected, with Chamberlain convinced that Baldwin was not looking for his experience and advice, but merely for his name to patch up the government's tarnished reputation. The following year saw Chamberlain and Churchill co-operating closely as vigilant critics of the National Government's foreign policy. The German remilitarization of the Rhineland in March 1936 left the former convinced that the independence of Austria was now the key to the European situation, for 'if Austria perishes, Czechoslovakia becomes indefensible' (Elleston, 264). Thereafter Germany would be left dominant in central Europe, with enormous consequences for the whole of the British empire. Chamberlain remained active to the end, before suffering a mild heart attack on 12 March 1937. He died at his London home, 24 Egerton Terrace, four days later after suffering a more serious attack. After a funeral service at St Margaret's, Westminster, he was buried in St Marylebone cemetery, East Finchley, on 19 March.

D. J. DUTTON

Sources U. Birm. L., Chamberlain MSS · D. J. Dutton, *Austen Chamberlain: gentleman in politics* (1985) · C. Petrie, *The life and letters of the Rt Hon. Sir Austen Chamberlain*, 2 vols. (1939–40) · *The Austen Chamberlain diary letters: the correspondence of Sir Austen Chamberlain with his sisters Hilda and Ida, 1916–1937*, ed. R. C. Self, CS, 5th ser., 5 (1995) · R. S. Grayson, *Austen Chamberlain and the commitment to Europe: British foreign policy, 1924–29* (1997) · *The Times* (21 Oct 1863) · *The Times* (17 March 1937) · A. Chamberlain, *Down the years* (1935) · A. Chamberlain, *Politics from inside: an epistolary chronicle, 1906–1914* (1936) · J. Jacobson, *Locarno diplomacy: Germany and the West, 1925–1929* (1972) · K. O. Morgan, *Consensus and disunity: the Lloyd George coalition government, 1918–1922* (1979) · D. J. Dutton, *His majesty's loyal opposition: the unionist party in opposition, 1905–1915* (1992) · D. H. Elleston, *The Chamberlains* (1966) · J. Ramsden, *The age of Balfour and Baldwin, 1902–1940* (1978) · N. Thompson, *The anti-appeasers* (1971) · M. Morris, '"Et l'honneur?" Politics and principles: a case study of Austen Chamberlain', *Warfare, diplomacy and politics: essays in honour of A. J. P. Taylor*, ed. C. Wrigley (1986), 80–92 · K. Middlemas and J. Barnes, *Baldwin: a biography* (1969) · R. Blake, *The unknown prime minister: the life and times of Andrew Bonar Law* (1955) · A. Sykes, *Tariff reform in British politics, 1903–1913* (1979) · J. L. Garvin, *The life of Joseph Chamberlain*, 1: *Chamberlain and democracy* (1932) · B. J. C. McKercher, *The second Baldwin government and the United States, 1924–1929: attitudes and diplomacy* (1984)

Archives BLPES, corresp. with tariff commission · Bodl. Oxf., Conservative party archives · PRO, corresp., FO 800/256–263 · U. Birm. L., corresp. and papers; letters | BL, corresp. with Arthur James Balfour, Add. MSS 49735–49736 · BL, corresp. with J. Burns, Add. MSS 46290–46291, 46298–46299 · BL, corresp. with Lord Cecil, Add. MSS 51078–51079 · BL, corresp. with Lord D'Abernon, Add. MS 48926 · BL, corresp. with Lord Long, Add. MS 62405 · BL OIOC, corresp. with Lord Chelmsford, MSS Eur. E 264 · Bodl. Oxf., corresp. with Viscount Addison · Bodl. Oxf., corresp. with Herbert Asquith · Bodl. Oxf., corresp. with H. A. Gwynne · Bodl. Oxf., letters to Lord Hanworth · Bodl. Oxf., letters to Lewis Harcourt · Bodl. Oxf., letters to Lady Milner · Bodl. Oxf., corresp. with Gilbert Murray · Bodl. Oxf., corresp. with Lord Ponsonby · Bodl. Oxf., corresp. with Sir Horace Rumbold · Bodl. Oxf., corresp. with second earl of Selborne · Bodl. Oxf., corresp. with third earl of Selborne · Bodl. Oxf., corresp. with Sir W. L. Worthington-Evans · Bodl. RH, corresp. with Lord Lugard · CAC Cam., corresp. with Sir H. Page Croft · CAC Cam., corresp. with David Lloyd George · CAC Cam., corresp. with Sir Eric Phipps and Lord Crewe · CUL, letters to Lord Hardinge · CUL, letters to Lord Kennet and Lady Kennet · CUL, corresp. with Sir Samuel Hoare · Cumbria AS, Carlisle, letters to Lord Howard of Penrith · Durham RO, letters relating to memoir of Lord Chaplin · Glos. RO, corresp. with Sir Michael Hicks Beach · HLRO, corresp. with Lord Beaverbrook · HLRO, letters to R. D. Blumenfeld · HLRO, corresp. with J. C. C. Davidson; papers relating to Genoa conference · HLRO, corresp. with Andrew Bonar Law · HLRO, corresp. with David Lloyd George and others · HLRO, letters to Herbert Samuel · HLRO, corresp. with J. St Loe Strachey · IWM, corresp. with H. A. Gwynne · Lpool RO, corresp. with seventeenth earl of Derby · NA Scot., corresp. with A. J. Balfour and G. W. Balfour · NA Scot., corresp. with Lord Lothian · NAM, letters to Earl Roberts · NL Scot., corresp. with Henry Craik · NL Scot., letters to Sir Charles Dalrymple · NL Scot., letters to F. S. Oliver · NL Scot., corresp. with Lord Roseby · Nuffield Oxf., corresp. with Lord Cherwell · PRO NIre., corresp. with Edward Carson, D 1507 · Shrops. RRC, letters to first Viscount Bridgeman · Trinity Cam., letters to Sir Henry Babington Smith · Trinity Cam., corresp. with Sir Joseph John Thomson · U. Birm., corresp. · U. Birm. L., letters to Lord Beaverbrook · U. Leeds, Brotherton L., letters to E. Gosse · U. Newcastle, Robinson L., corresp. with Walter Runciman · University of Sheffield, corresp. with W. A. S. Hewins | FILM BFI NFTVA, 'Austen Chamberlain wins at Birmingham', Topical Budget, 10 Dec 1923; 'Memoir: a great statesman's passing is mourned by his countrymen', British Movietone News, 16 March 1937; documentary footage; news footage; propaganda footage (ministry of health) · IWM FVA, documentary footage

Likenesses B. Stone, photograph, 1897, NPG · Spy [L. Ward], caricature, 1899, NPG · W. Stoneman, photograph, 1920, NPG · D. Low, chalk caricature, 1926, NPG · gravure, 1926 (after D. Low), NPG · B. Partridge, ink and watercolour caricature, 1927, NPG · W. Stoneman, photograph, 1931, NPG · S. de Strobl, bronze bust, 1935, NPG · S. Mrozewski, two wood-engravings, 1935–6, NPG · W. Rothenstein, oils, 1936, U. Reading · H. W. Barnett, photograph, NPG [*see illus.*] · Bassano, photograph, NPG · I. M. Cohen, oils, Palace of Westminster, London; version, Cordwainers' Company, London · T. Cottrell, cigarette card, NPG · O. Edis, photograph, NPG · P. A. de Laszlo, portrait, priv. coll. · J. Lavery, oils, Hugh Lane Municipal Gallery of Modern Art, Dublin · A. P. F. Ritchie, cigarette card, NPG · J. Russell & Sons, photograph, NPG · Stone, photograph, Birm. CL; repro. in Dutton, *Austen Chamberlain*

Wealth at death £45,044 18s. 1d.: probate, 24 May 1937, CGPLA Eng. & Wales

Chamberlain, Bartholomew (*bap.* 1545, *d.* in or after 1611), Church of England clergyman, was the eldest of at least three sons of Simon Chamberlain (*d.* 1597) and his wife, Joan (*d.* 1597); there were also at least two daughters.

He was baptized at Shipton under Wychwood, Oxfordshire, on 16 January 1545. His younger brother Thomas (1546–1628) was prosperous enough to guarantee half the first fruits for Chamberlain's first benefice in 1578. According to Wood the Chamberlains were an 'ancient and genteel' family (Wood, *Ath. Oxon.*, 1.583), but it is also possible that Simon Chamberlain kept The Crown inn at Shipton.

Chamberlain is recorded as entering Trinity College, Oxford, as a scholar in June 1563, and graduating BA in 1566. He became a fellow in 1567, supplicated for the degree of MA in 1570 (but incepted only in 1572), and proceeded BTh in 1576 and DTh in 1579. Cambridge incorporated him DTh in 1585. John Piers, bishop of Rochester, ordained him priest in June 1576, when he also supplicated at Oxford for a preaching licence. In 1578 he was one of those scrutinizing the doubtful views on predestination of Antonio del Corro, whom Robert Dudley, earl of Leicester, chancellor of the university, sought to have made DTh; with Thomas Bickley and Laurence Humphrey, he was appointed to examine the university's statutes against heresy.

In February 1578 a Worcestershire gentleman presented Chamberlain to the rectory of Abbots Morton. In November the crown gave him Burford vicarage, Oxfordshire, a more valuable benefice (necessitating resignation of his fellowship), which he held until 1586; and in December 1579 it added the rectory of Holywell-cum-Needingworth, Huntingdonshire. He gave up Abbots Morton by 1583; he had a curate at Holywell, but seems to have resided there increasingly.

Chamberlain's emerging status was underlined by his *Sermon Preached at S. James* to the privy council (1580, published 1584), dedicated to the lord chancellor, Sir Thomas Bromley, 'by whose meanes I enjoy for maintenance' (sig. A4r). It was reprinted in 1595 but became a best-seller when reissued as *The Passion of Christ and the Benefits Thereby* (1612, repr. 1613, 1615, 1620, 1623). The main difference was a section inserted just before the end, taking up the theme of the Corro affair by explicitly insisting on a doctrine of predestination involving supralapsarian and indefectible election:

> The devill cannot pluck them away finall from God, which are written in the book of life … We are in Christ by election before the world was made: we are called to Christ by the word after the world was made … We are justified by lively faith, the obedience of the Son of God being imputed to us. (*Passion*, sig. B8r–v)

However Calvinistic Chamberlain's theology, he was always considered ceremonially conformable, even if at Easter 1602 he gave communion 'without booke' (*Diary of John Manningham*, 86). He also published *A sermon preached at Farington in Barkeshire … at the buriall of … Anne countes of Warwicke* (1591) and in 1589 a sermon preached at St Paul's (of which only the title-page survives) dedicated to Elizabeth Powlett, widow of Trinity's founder, Sir Thomas Pope.

In 1593 Chamberlain was dispensed to hold Sandy rectory, Bedfordshire, along with Holywell. About 1601 he relinquished both when presented by Sir Thomas Gorges and his wife Helena, dowager marchioness of Northampton, to the rectory of Hemingford Abbots, Huntingdonshire. But when the bishop of Ely gave him the less valuable adjacent vicarage of Hemingford Grey he resided there. Perhaps he accepted a drop in income to reduce pastoral responsibility because of his age. He had apparently hoped for the presidency of Trinity after the death of Arthur Yeldard in 1599, and told John Manningham, the lawyer and diarist (whose family home was near Holywell and who joined with Chamberlain to convey some property), that the visitor, Thomas Bilson, bishop of Winchester:

> expelled such fellowes as he thought would be opposite, and placed such in their roomes as he knew would be sure unto him. By this meanes Dr Chamberlaine was defeated of his right, being an Oxfordshire man, whom by their statutes they are bound to preferr before anie other. (*Diary of John Manningham*, 85)

Other than Chamberlain's account, however, there is no sign that Ralph Kettell's election entailed such manipulation (private information).

Chamberlain relinquished Hemingford Grey by exchange in 1606, and apparently Hemingford Abbots in 1608. His wife, Joan, whom he had married before 1587, appeared on the conveyance made with Manningham in 1598; their known children were Elizabeth, named by Joan Chamberlain in her will, and William (1586/7–1625), born at Holywell, a student of Caius, Cambridge, and later rector of Wicken, Northamptonshire. The relationship of Henry Chamberlain, described as vicar of Hemingford Abbots in 1612–13, is unclear: no successor was regularly instituted until 1621. This date might represent Bartholomew Chamberlain's death after a period in incapacity; since Joan was buried on 28 November 1611 as his 'wife', not 'widow', he was presumably then still alive.

JULIAN LOCK

Sources Wood, *Ath. Oxon.*, new edn, 1.538ff · *Reg. Oxf.*, 1.264; 2/2.6, 24; 2/3.63 · Venn, *Alum. Cant.*, 1/1.316 · *The diary of John Manningham of the Middle Temple, 1602–1603*, ed. R. P. Sorlien (Hanover, NH, 1976) · *N&Q*, 12th ser., 12 (1923), 309–10, 353–4 · *N&Q*, 12th ser., 10 (1922), 166 · C. W. Foster, ed., *The state of the church in the reigns of Elizabeth and James I*, Lincoln RS, 23 (1926) · W. M. Noble, ed., 'Incumbents of the county of Huntingdon', *Transactions of the Cambridge and Huntingdon Archaeological Society*, 3 (1910–14) · A. Gibbons, *Ely episcopal records* (1890), 259 · T. Warton, *The life of Sir Thomas Pope, founder of Trinity College, Oxford*, 2nd edn (1780), 196 · *STC, 1475–1640* · exchequer first fruits composition books, PRO, E 334/9, 11, 12 · private information [Clare Hopkins, archivist, Trinity College, Oxford] · parish register, Shipton under Wychwood, Oxfordshire, Oxfordshire Archives · will of Simon Chamberlain, 1597, Oxfordshire Archives, MS wills Oxon. 187, fol. 343 · will of Joan Chamberlain, 1597, Oxfordshire Archives, MS wills Oxon. 187, fol. 398 · episcopal register of John Piers, bishop of Rochester, CKS, Drb/Ar 1/16, fol. 13v · J. Whitgift, episcopal register, Worcs. RO, BA 2648/10 (i), fol. 31r · archiepiscopal register of Edmund Grindal, LPL, fol. 357v · archiepiscopal register of John Whitgift, LPL, vol. 1, fol. 300v · faculty office register, LPL, F1/B, fol. 170

Chamberlain, Basil Hall [*called* Ōdō] (1850–1935), Japanologist, was born on 18 October 1850 in Southsea,

Hampshire, the eldest son of William Charles Chamberlain (1818–1878), an admiral in the British navy, and his wife, Eliza Jane (1825?–1856?), daughter of Captain Basil *Hall RN, travel writer. Houston Stewart *Chamberlain was his brother. His upbringing was cosmopolitan. He started travelling and learning a foreign language from the age of two. In 1856, after his mother's death, Chamberlain and his two brothers moved from England to Versailles, where his paternal grandmother lived. He was educated at the Lycée Impérial there and passed the *baccalauréat* examination. In Versailles he also received instruction from a German governess.

Due to a change in the family plans Chamberlain started working for Barings Bank in London in 1869, instead of going to Oxford University. Within a few months he had a nervous breakdown and left the bank. It was in the hope of regaining health that in November 1872 he boarded a sailer from the Thames, and started on a voyage which finally brought him to Yokohama, Japan, in May 1873. Japan in 1873 retained enough of her traditional civilization to fascinate Chamberlain. At the same time there were modernizing trends which ensured a strong demand for Western teachers, and Chamberlain remained in Japan as a teacher at the naval academy. Already a polyglot, he started learning Japanese with great enthusiasm. Within three years he knew enough Japanese to undertake serious work as a Japanologist.

With his numerous publications, such as 'The language, mythology, and geographical nomenclature of Japan viewed in the light of Aino studies' (*Memoirs of the Literature College, Imperial University of Japan*, 1887), *A Handbook of Colloquial Japanese* (1887), and 'Essay in aid of a grammar and dictionary of the Luchuan language' (*Transactions of the Asiatic Society of Japan*, 23, 1895, suppl.), Chamberlain made a pioneering and pivotal contribution to the study of the Japanese language. His translation of *Kojiki* ('Records of ancient matters'—Japan's oldest extant book dating back to AD 712), published in 1883, was also a very important contribution to the study of ancient Japanese history because of the rigorous critical scrutiny of the earliest Japanese records that appeared in his translator's introduction.

Chamberlain became professor of Japanese and philology of the Imperial University (later the University of Tokyo) in 1886. It was a reflection of the exceptionally high regard he had won from the Japanese that, still in his early forties and having taught at the university for only four years until 1890, he was made an emeritus professor in 1891.

From around 1890 the focus of his writing shifted to books for the general reader. *Things Japanese* (1890), for a long time the most handy and reliable guidebook on Japanese culture, and *A Handbook for Travellers in Japan* (a Murray's handbook originally written by E. M. Satow and A. G. S. Hawes, and revised by Chamberlain and G. B. Mason from the third edition published in 1891), were updated repeatedly. He also published several volumes of translations of Japanese fairy tales. He returned to Europe for good in 1911 and retired in Geneva, Switzerland. A few

months after completing the manuscript of the sixth edition of *Things Japanese* (published posthumously in 1939), he died, unmarried, at the Hôtel Richemond, Geneva, on 15 February 1935. He was buried in the St Georges cemetery on the 18th.

Chamberlain was one of the rare European intellectuals of real stature who devoted the best part of their lives to the study of Japan. He was not a rebel against his own civilization. His two French books published during his retirement, *Huit siècles de poésie française* (1927) and *... encore est vive la souris: pensées et réflexions* (1933), amply demonstrate how well he was grounded in European culture. His appearance—he was tall and wore a beard—was also that of a typical British gentleman. However, his remarkable command of Japanese, coupled with his kindly, tolerant, democratic personality, enabled him to establish a wonderful rapport, not only with intellectuals but also with common people of Japan, such as his servants. He also visited almost every prefecture in Japan. His solid knowledge and appreciation of Japan has tended to be underestimated because of the impression, more apparent than real, that he was Eurocentric. It is true that he candidly criticized some aspects of Japan, but awareness of the existence of more than one legitimate point of view made him free from any rigid Eurocentrism. His unpublished letters reveal that his attachment to Japan had an intensity hitherto unsuspected. His world was an ellipse with two foci—Japan and Europe. He became uprooted because he could not choose between Europe and Japan, both of which he loved, and he continued to swing between the two (he made six journeys to Europe during his years in Japan). Intense expressions of homesickness for Japan, found in his letters written after his retirement in Geneva, show that his return to Europe did not mean a renunciation of Japan and a spiritual return to Europe, as it was often interpreted. His unpublished letters, together with two volumes of his published letters to Lafcadio Hearn, a talented popular writer on Japan whom he befriended, document a fascinating drama of cultural contact played out in the soul of an individual.   YUZO OTA

Sources Richard Wagner Museum, Bayreuth, Germany, Houston Stewart Chamberlain MSS, letters to Houston Stewart Chamberlain and others · letters to Tōshirō Sugiura, Aichi University of Education, Japan, Chamberlain–Sugiura collection · H. S. Chamberlain, *Lebenswege meines Denkens* (1919) · K. Hanazono, 'Ōdō Chenbaren Sensei no tegami', *Gakutō* (Oct 1941), 7–10 [A letter of Professor Basil Hall Chamberlain] · N. Sasaki, ed., *Ōdō Chenbaren Sensei* (1948) [Professor Basil Hall Chamberlain] · K. Koizumi, ed., *Letters from Basil Hall Chamberlain to Lafcadio Hearn* (1936) · K. Koizumi, ed., *More letters from Basil Hall Chamberlain to Lafcadio Hearn* (1937) · H. S. Chamberlain, *Briefe, 1882–1924, und Briefwechsel mit Kaiser Wilhelm II*, 2 vols. (Munich, *c.*1928) · B. H. Chamberlain, *Things Japanese*, 6th edn, 1939 (1985), xi–xiv · Y. Ota, *Basil Hall Chamberlain: portrait of a Japanologist* (1998) · S. Kusuya, *Nezumi wa mada ikite iru: Chenbaren no denki* (1986) · 'Chamberlain, Houston Stewart', *DNB*
Archives Aichi University of Education [Aichi Kyōiku Daigaku], Japan, Chamberlain–Sugiura collection · Nihon University [Nihon Daigaku], Japan, faculty of arts and sciences [Bunri Gakubu], Ueda collection, Japanese books collected by him while in Japan, Kusuya 360 · Yokohama Archives of History [Yokohama Kaikō Shiryōkan], Japan, MSS | Glos. RO, letters to Lord Redesdale [Algernon Bertram Mitford] · PRO, letters to Ernest Mason Satow,

PRO 30/33 · Richard Wagner Museum, Bayreuth, Germany, letters to Houston Stewart Chamberlain and others related to him · Rutgers University, New Brunswick, letters to William Elliot Griffis **Likenesses** photographs, Yokohama Archives of History, Japan · photographs, Aichi University of Education, Japan

Wealth at death able to give financial assistance to brother and his wife from 1923: Chamberlain's letters to Eva Chamberlain; Chamberlain's letters to Sugiura

Chamberlain [*married name* Petts], **Brenda Irene** (1912–1971), painter and writer, was born on 17 March 1912 at 4 Euston Road, Bangor, Caernarvonshire, the elder child of Francis Thomas Chamberlain, originally from Hill Ridware, Staffordshire, and then employed as an inspector of bridges for the London, Midland, and Scottish Railway, and his wife, Elsie, *née* Cooil (*d.* 1972), who as a Labour councillor served as mayor of Bangor. Brenda Chamberlain was educated privately and at Bangor County School for Girls, where she showed such artistic ability that she was sent for lessons at the Royal Cambrian Academy in Conwy. On leaving school, she spent six months in Copenhagen, discovering the early work of Gauguin and exploring that fiercely independent style of living which she was to follow for the rest of her life. In 1931 she won a place at the Royal Academy Schools in London, where she met and, on 11 May 1935, married, the artist–craftsman John Petts (1914–1991); they shared a studio flat in Redcliffe Road, South Kensington.

The following year, drawn by their love of mountains, Chamberlain and her husband returned to Wales, making their home at Tŷ'r Mynydd, a pair of cottages high above the village of Rachub, near Llanllechid, in northern Caernarvonshire. Determined to live by their art, albeit frugally, they bought an Adana printing machine and founded the Caseg Press, originally producing hand-coloured greetings cards from their own woodcuts and engravings. Their first joint exhibition was held in Bangor in 1937. The coming of war in September 1939 and the growing rivalry between them as artists strained their marriage, particularly after John Petts became a conscientious objector and left to join a field ambulance unit in Europe and the Middle East; his wife remained in Snowdonia, working as a mountain guide for the Red Cross. Between November 1941 and June 1942, at the suggestion of the poet Alun Lewis, they printed (though not on the primitive Caseg Press) a series of six broadsheets in editions of 500 copies featuring poems by Dylan Thomas, Alun Lewis, Lynette Roberts, and Brenda Chamberlain; the story of this venture is told in her book *Alun Lewis and the Making of the Caseg Broadsheets* (1969). She and Petts separated in 1943 and were divorced three years later.

In 1946 Brenda Chamberlain paid a six-week visit to Germany, where she stayed with Karl von Laer, a German whom she had known in Bangor before the war. On her return to Wales she settled on Bardsey, a sparsely populated island a few miles off the extreme tip of the Llŷn peninsula in north-west Wales; her companion there was a Frenchman, Jean van der Bijl. She resumed painting and writing, determined to achieve recognition as an artist in her own right, painting canvases such as *Children on the Seashore*, *The Cristin Children*, and *Man with a John Dory*. Exhibitions of her work were held at the Gimpel Fils and Zwemmers galleries in London and she won the gold medal for fine art at the national eisteddfods of 1951 and 1953. Her first collection of poems, *The Green Heart* (1958), was dedicated to Karl von Laer, and was followed by *Tide-Race* (1962), a journal of life on Bardsey. The latter book, although a sympathetic portrait of the island, touches on the social tensions of the small community of crofter-fishermen and gave offence to some; when the writer eventually severed her connection with the place it was at the request of the owner, Lord Newborough.

In 1963 Brenda Chamberlain went to the island of Ydra in the Sardinia Gulf, where she was to live intermittently for the next five years; her time there was spent in the writing of a novel, *The Water-Castle* (1964), which draws on her relationship with Karl von Laer, and *A Rope of Vines* (1965), an account of her life on Ydra. The colonels' *coup d'état* of 1967 filled her with despair, and in November of that year she left Greece, although not before writing a play, *The Protagonists*, based on a visit to a detention centre for political prisoners. The play was performed in Bangor in October 1968, but her plans for taking it to London, together with an exhibition of the paintings she had done on Ydra, failed through lack of funds. Her last home was at 10 Menai View Terrace, Bangor.

Brenda Chamberlain was physically tough and self-sufficient; she had a small, boyish frame, a long bony jaw, heavy forehead, aquiline nose, and a childlike rather than feminine sensibility. Towards her friends she was kind, generous, and extremely loyal, and her nature was innocent, fervent, deeply fatalistic, and vulnerable. But she was also, towards the end of her life, frustrated in her artistic ambitions, desperately lonely, short of money, and given to bouts of depression. In 1969, shortly after the publication of *Poems with Drawings*, she suffered a nervous breakdown and spent some time in hospital. In 1970 her last exhibition, 'Word + image', work done on Ydra in collaboration with the composer Halim al-Dabh, was organized by the Welsh Arts Council. On 9 July 1971 she told a neighbour that she had done 'a very foolish thing' in taking eighteen sleeping tablets and that this was 'a *cri de coeur*'. She was rushed to Caernarfon and Anglesey Hospital but lost consciousness and died on 11 July. The coroner's verdict was accidental death, and after a service at St Peter's Church she was buried in Glanadda cemetery, Ffordd Caernarfon, Bangor, where her tombstone is inscribed with the words: 'I was born to live; I was born to die.'   MEIC STEPHENS

Sources K. Holman, *Brenda Chamberlain* (1997) · M. Stephens, ed., *Artists in Wales*, 1 (1971) [incl. autobiographical essay by B. Chamberlain] · personal knowledge (2004) · K. Holman, '"So near, so far, brother or lover": Brenda Chamberlain and the letters of Karl von Laer', *New Welsh Review*, 2 (1988), 45–50 · J. Jones, afterword, in B. Chamberlain, *Tide-race*, new edn (1996) · b. cert. · m. cert. · d. cert.
Archives NL Wales, corresp., journals, and literary MSS [journals: typescripts] · NMG Wales, MSS · State University of New York, Buffalo, letters and MSS | NL Wales, letters to Raymond

Garlick · NL Wales, letters to Gwyn Jones · NL Wales, letters to John Petts, sketches, and trial engravings · NL Wales, letters to Welsh Arts Council · TCD, letters to Seumas O'Sullivan
Likenesses B. Chamberlain, self-portrait, oils, 1938, NMG Wales

Chamberlain, Sir Crawford Trotter (1821–1902), army officer, was born in London on 9 May 1821, the third son of Sir Henry Chamberlain, first baronet, sometime consul-general and chargé d'affaires in Brazil, and his second wife, Anne Eugenia, daughter of William Morgan of London. Sir Neville Bowles *Chamberlain was an elder brother.

After education at private schools and under tutors Crawford obtained a cadetship in the Bengal army in 1837, and was posted to the 28th Bengal native infantry. He was transferred to the 16th Bengal native infantry, and with the outbreak of the First Anglo-Afghan War he began his active service. He was present at the siege of Ghazni (23 July 1839) and at the operations around Kandahar. In September 1841 he was appointed to command the 5th Janbaz cavalry, and in October he became adjutant of Christie's Horse. Until the end of the Afghan campaign he was engaged in constant and severe fighting. In 1843 he was sent to Sind with two squadrons of Christie's Horse as an independent command, to be known as Chamberlain's Horse.

In 1845 Chamberlain was invalided to the Cape, where he married Elizabeth, daughter of J. de Witt. She died on 19 January 1894. He returned to India in 1846 as second in command of the 9th irregular cavalry, into which his own regiment had been absorbed. During the Anglo-Sikh wars (1845–9) he was constantly in action. He was at the battle of Chilianwala on 13 January 1849. On 30 January he was again engaged in the neighbourhood; he was wounded, and was the subject of a special dispatch by Lord Gough (31 January). At the battle of Gujrat on 21 February, he had to be lifted into the saddle, where he remained throughout the day. He was mentioned in dispatches, and, being promoted captain and brevet major in November 1849, was given the command of the 1st irregular cavalry, formerly Skinner's Horse. He served with it in the Mohmand expedition of 1854.

On the outbreak of the mutiny in 1857 Chamberlain displayed courage and resolution. The force of his influence and the discipline in his regiment were manifest when his men, in the midst of mutiny, suspected and overt, volunteered to shoot condemned rebels at Jullundur (4 June 1857). Chamberlain, although not the senior officer on the spot, was entrusted with the dangerous duty of disarming the 62nd and 69th regiments at Multan. He did this on 11 June with 'an extraordinary mixture of audacity and skill'. Sir John Lawrence in his report declared that the disarming at Multan was a turning point in the Punjab crisis, second only in importance to the disarming at Lahore and Peshawar. At Cheekawutne in September Chamberlain was attacked by an overwhelming force, and was compelled to take the unusual course of securing his cavalry in a caravanserai. Chamberlain was sick, but he succeeded in

maintaining the defence, until he was relieved three days later.

For his services in the mutiny Chamberlain was promoted lieutenant-colonel, a reward generally regarded as inadequate. The oversight was admitted and rectified long afterwards. In April 1862 he was made colonel, in 1864 he was appointed honorary aide-de-camp to the governor-general, and two years later was made CSI, and was included in the first list of twelve officers for a good-service pension. In 1866, too, he was transferred to the command of the Central India horse, and the next year to the command of the Gwalior district with the rank of brigadier-general. In 1869 he was officiating political agent at Gwalior, and received the thanks of government. From October 1869 to February 1870 he was acting political agent at the court of Sindhia until his promotion to major-general.

During his unemployed time as major-general Chamberlain served on various commissions and courts of inquiry, and from 1874 to 1879 he commanded the Oudh division. He became lieutenant-general in October 1877 and general in January 1880. In that year he returned to England for the first time since 1837; with the exception of his visit to the Cape, he had never left India in the interval. In 1884 he was retired from the active list. In 1896 he married for the second time; his second wife was Augusta Margaret, daughter of Major-General John Christie. She survived him; there were no children from either marriage. In 1897 he was made GCIE. Sir Crawford, who retained his splendid physique until near the end, died at his residence, Lordswood, near Southampton, Hampshire, on 13 December 1902, and was buried at Rownhams.

REGINALD LUCAS, *rev.* JAMES LUNT

Sources Hart's Army List (1897) · Broad Arrow (30 Dec 1903) · Naval and Military Gazette (15 Feb 1896) · Naval and Military Gazette (20 Dec 1902) · O. Wilkinson and J. Wilkinson, Memoirs of the Gemini generals, 2nd edn (1896) · Lord Roberts [F. S. Roberts], Forty-one years in India, 30th edn (1898) · R. B. Smith, Life of Lord Lawrence, 7th edn, 2 vols. (1901) · T. R. E. Holmes, A history of the Indian mutiny, 5th edn (1898) · G. W. Forrest, Life of Field-Marshal Sir Neville Chamberlain (1909) · W. A. Watson, King George's own central India horse (1930) · C. E. Buckland, Dictionary of Indian biography (1906) · Burke, Gen. GB
Archives BL OIOC
Wealth at death £64,043 15s. 10d.: resworn probate, May 1903, CGPLA Eng. & Wales

Chamberlain, Elizabeth, Lady Chamberlain (1576–1635). *See under* Carey, Elizabeth, Lady Hunsdon (1552–1618).

Chamberlain [married name Garrington], **Elsie Dorothea** (1910–1991), Congregational minister and radio broadcaster, was born on 3 March 1910 at 30 Canonbury Park North, Islington, London, the third child of James Arthur Chamberlain (d. 1956), Post Office technician and clerk, and his wife, Annie Maria Hayward (d. 1975), clerk. Her father worked for the Post Office all his life and attended the local Anglican church while his wife, Annie, attended the nearby Congregational chapel in Islington. From her

Elsie Dorothea
Chamberlain
(1910–1991), by
Elliott & Fry

childhood, Elsie Chamberlain was immersed in two divergent ecclesial traditions. After four years at Dame Alice Owen School (1916–20), at ten she attended the Channing School for Girls, a fee-paying Unitarian foundation in Highgate. On leaving school in 1927 she took to dress design and maintained a full life in her local Congregational church. Chamberlain began to learn Hebrew and her minister inspired her to a clerical, nonconformist vocation.

With a view to becoming a Congregational minister, Chamberlain undertook a degree in theology at the (predominantly Anglican) King's College, London (c.1936–1939). During that time Dr Nathaniel Micklem, principal of Mansfield College, Oxford, assured her of a place to undertake two years of pastoral training. A fellow student at King's College was John Leslie St Clair Garrington (1912–1978), soon to be ordained in the Church of England. He was from sound Anglican stock, and in order to marry they had to endure a decade of struggle with church authorities. Her determination to become a minister complicated this relationship. In 1939, instead of going to Oxford University, Chamberlain accepted an offer to assist the Revd Muriel Paulden with her ministry in a run-down part of Liverpool. Then in 1941 she herself was called to be the minister at Christ Church, Friern Barnet, Middlesex. She was soon to be heard at Hyde Park Corner standing her ground with the best of soapbox speakers.

Elsie Chamberlain's friendship, while a theological student at King's College, with Margaret, Lady Stansgate, led to her appointment in 1946 as the first woman chaplain in the RAF. This was much to the irritation of Geoffrey Fisher, archbishop of Canterbury, who warned Viscount Stansgate, secretary of state at the Air Ministry, that 'under no conditions' should Church of England personnel 'either intentionally or by inadvertence attend Services at which she administers the sacraments' (Williams, 30). However, very soon severe arthritis struck and Chamberlain left the RAF.

Chamberlain's RAF appointment, while controversial in itself, arose from her impending marriage to John Garrington, then an Anglican curate in Kensington. The bishop of London, William Wand, unfortunately insisted that Garrington was unlikely to secure an incumbency so long as Chamberlain remained as a minister in a 'Free Church Pastorate' (Williams, 41). It was a conflict involving ecumenical relations and the place of women in the church: it was still felt that an Anglican clergyman's wife must devote her life to his ministry. It was also implied that Elsie Chamberlain could not serve two ecclesial masters.

Garrington described their marriage very neatly: 'we did it in the teeth of authority' (Williams, 48). They finally married amid huge publicity on 19 July 1947, Garrington having been appointed vicar of Hampton through the good offices of their supporter and friend Viscount Stansgate. Elsie Chamberlain undertook her role as 'vicar's wife' with gusto and enthusiasm. In November 1947 she became part-time minister of a Richmond congregation, combining both tasks: wife and minister across a deep confessional divide. They adopted a daughter, Janette, who later wrote an account of her mother's life.

In 1950 Chamberlain joined the BBC through which she was to become almost a household name. *Lift up your Hearts* was a daily morning radio talks programme (later renamed *Thought for the Day*) for which she was responsible as producer. Her aim was to 'win the ear of the people on the fringes of the Church to whom religion was only a word and not a very interesting word at that!' (Williams, 62). This was subsequently to be the leitmotif of her missionary endeavour. She was the first ordained woman to lead the *Daily Service*, which raised controversial issues for the BBC. However, Elsie Chamberlain resigned from the corporation in 1967. She felt increasingly out of sympathy with the BBC's religious policy, as it shifted away from her 'missionary' aims towards analysis rather than advocacy.

While still with the BBC, Chamberlain served in 1956–7 as chairman of the Congregational Union of England and Wales, and was the first woman to hold that post. After leaving the BBC she was on the staff of the City Temple in London (1968–70) with the Revd Kenneth Slack. He was in favour of, but Chamberlain was implacably opposed to, the union of the Congregational church with the English Presbyterians. This eventually took place in 1972 with the creation of the United Reformed church. Although she was subsequently involved with the ecumenical movement Chamberlain nevertheless defended those who wished to continue the ideals of congregationalism. It was therefore fitting that she helped lead the Nottingham-based splinter group, the Congregational Federation, that comprised about 300 independent Congregational churches.

Chamberlain's husband died in 1978 and in 1980 she moved to the west country to take charge of two federation churches, North Street Church in Taunton and the Congregational church in Chumleigh, north Devon. She later settled in Nottingham as warden of the revamped Castle Gate Congregational Church where her energies were directed to 'the least of my brethren' in the inner city. She supported women's causes, Amnesty International, and many other humanitarian projects. Her vigour seemed boundless but she fell ill and subsequently died on 10 April 1991 at the University Hospital, Nottingham.   KENNETH M. WOLFE

Sources J. Williams, *First lady of the pulpit* (1993) • *Lift up your hearts*, files, BBC WAC, R51/491, 492, 954, 955 • BBC WAC, R34 (policy: religion) • interviews, 1945–52, BBC WAC, RCONTI • b. cert. • m. cert. • d. cert. • *The Times* (12 April 1991)
Archives BBC WAC
Likenesses Elliott & Fry, photograph, NPG [*see illus.*]
Wealth at death £149,801: administration, 31 Jan 1992, CGPLA Eng. & Wales

Chamberlain, George (1576–1634), bishop of Ypres, was the second son of George Chamberlain, captain of Alderney, and grandson of Sir Leonard Chamberlain, governor of Guernsey [*see* Chamberlayne, Sir Leonard]. Chamberlain's father, a Catholic, went into exile for religion in 1571 and married the Flemish noblewoman Philippine L' Espinoy; George was born in Ghent in 1576, and as a child lived in St Omer. Between 1591 and 1600 he studied at the English colleges of Valladolid, Seville, and Rome, and he was ordained priest in the Lateran at Rome in 1600. He returned to the Low Countries as chaplain to Ottavio Mirto Frangipani, papal nuncio in Brussels, who valued him highly, nicknaming him Don Georgio, and in 1602 recommended him for a canonry in the cathedral of St Bavo in Ghent. While a canon Chamberlain graduated licentiate in canon law at the University of Louvain (1607), held various minor offices in the chapter in Ghent, and became in turn archdeacon (1614) and dean (1617). Several times he represented the clergy of the county of Flanders in the provincial estates and in deputations to Brussels. Chamberlain delivered an elegy on the Archduke Albert in Ghent Cathedral in 1622. In 1624 he aided the establishment of an English Benedictine convent in the city, and was deputized its visitor by the bishop, Antoine Triest, with whom he appears to have been on close terms.

In March 1627 Chamberlain was nominated to the bishopric of Ypres, but his installation was delayed until November 1628 by disputes about diocesan funds. As bishop Chamberlain immediately instituted reforms, most notably of preaching and education. At some point, as the last of his family in the male line, he travelled to England to confirm his sister's title to Shirburn Castle, Oxfordshire. Chamberlain was one of the lords spiritual of Flanders in the estates general of 1632–4, and in 1633 he and the duke of Aarschot travelled to Madrid to put the estates' case for peace with the Dutch following the near collapse of Habsburg authority and military power in the Netherlands. Chamberlain died of a stroke in Ypres on 19 December 1634 and was buried in the cathedral there. Although several contemporaries refer to his broad erudition, Chamberlain left no substantial writings to posterity.   PAUL ARBLASTER

Sources L. Jadin, 'Procès d'information pour la nomination des évêques et abbés des Pays-Bas, de Liège et de Franche-Comté d'après les Archives de la Congrégation Consistoriale', *Bulletin de L'Institut Historique Belge de Rome*, 8 (1928), 9, 118, 122, 136, 148, 161 •

F. Sweertius, *Athenae Belgicae* (1628), 273 • A. Louant, ed., *Correspondance d'Ottavio Mirto Frangipani, premier nonce de Flandre (1596–1606)*, 3 (Brussels and Rome, 1942) • B. de Meester, ed., *Correspondance du nonce Giovanni-Francesco Guidi di Bagno (1621–1627)*, 2 (Brussels, 1938) • C. Duhamel, 'Het Bisdom Ieper (1607–1646)', licence diss., Leuven, 1993 • J. J. De Smet, 'Chamberlain, Georges', *Biographie Nationale*, 3 (Brussels, 1872) • A. J. Loomie, *The Spanish Elizabethans* (1963) • L. Antheunis, 'The Right Rev. George Chamberlain, bishop of Ypres (1576–1634)', *Biographical Studies*, 2 (1953–4), 84–6 • M. Murphy, *St Gregory's College, Seville, 1592–1767*, Catholic RS, 73 (1992)
Archives Rijksarchief Gent, Archief van Sint-Baafs, accounts as receiver general, 1292–1294 • Rijksarchief Gent, Archief van Sint-Baafs, accounts for Ædium sacerdolalium, 3613–3616

Chamberlain, Houston Stewart (1855–1927), racialist writer, was born on 9 September 1855 in Southsea, the last of the four children (one daughter and three sons) of Rear-Admiral William Charles Chamberlain (1818–1878), and his first wife, Eliza Jane (1825?–1856?), daughter of Captain Basil *Hall RN and granddaughter of Sir James Hall. His brother was Basil Hall *Chamberlain, and he was nephew of Field Marshal Sir Neville Bowles Chamberlain, of General Sir Crawford Trotter Chamberlain, and of Major-General Thomas Hardy Chamberlain. Much of his early childhood was spent in Versailles, where he briefly attended the Lycée Impérial. From 1867 to 1869 Chamberlain went through a miserable period at Cheltenham College, and thereafter he saw as little as possible of England. In the years 1870–74 he was privately tutored by Otto Kuntze, a Prussian, during extensive travels and sojourns in France, Switzerland, and Italy. By the mid-1870s it was clear that nervous disabilities (which proved to be a lifelong affliction) would render him unfit for the military career otherwise almost dictated by his pedigree. On 9 April 1878 Chamberlain married Anna Horst, daughter of a Breslau lawyer, and then proceeded to study natural sciences at the University of Geneva (1879–84). Henceforth he survived on private family funds and through literary earnings, especially as author of works celebrating many aspects of Teutonic achievement. He lived in Dresden from 1885 to 1889 and began to produce articles about the Wagnerian cultural legacy. He then moved to Vienna, where he wrote not only his book on *Das Drama Richard Wagners* (1892) and a life of the composer (1896), but also a biological study of *Recherches sur la sève ascendante* (1897). During the latter part of this decade Chamberlain accepted a commission from the Munich publishing house of Bruckmann to prepare a historical work which, as the century reached its close, would take stock of the condition of civilization. It was this, *Die Grundlagen des neunzehnten Jahrhunderts* (2 vols., 1899), which made him famous.

The book, as Geoffrey Field observes, 'turned Chamberlain almost overnight into the prophet of race for educated laymen in Central Europe'. It was breathtaking in its range of scholarship, but also crude in its political intent. The treatise focused principally on Europe from classical times to the French Revolution, yet was never continued into that more detailed study of the nineteenth century itself which the author had originally envisaged. Chamberlain presented modern civilization as having been

Houston Stewart Chamberlain (1855–1927), by unknown photographer

shaped largely by five influences: the aesthetics and philosophy of Greece; the statecraft of Rome; the world-redeeming revelation of Christ; the alien and destructive influence of the Jew; and the regenerative power of *der Germane*, the hero of the Aryan–Teutonic races. These last, though initially deemed to embrace also the Celts and Slavs, become in the *Grundlagen* ever more emphatically equated with their most illustrious branch—that of *die Deutsche*, or Teutons in the narrower Tacitean sense of the term. The fulfilment of their racial destiny could not properly begin until the world-historical event of Christ's birth had converted the Graeco-Roman legacy into a form that they could exploit. Thus the Messiah who erupts into these pages is not merely non-Jewish, but also a haughty figure more akin to a Bismarckian Junker than to the conventional paragon of humility. This is a God well fitted to inspire the Teuton in his subsequent struggle against the Jew, fought for the survival both of Christian civilization and of racial virtue.

The *Grundlagen* places particular stress on the protestant Reformation, as a decisive Germanic act of liberation from the vacuous universalism of Catholic Rome. Even more strikingly, the Renaissance too is portrayed as a flowering of Teutonic genius, with artists such as Leonardo and Michelangelo being brought inside the fold of the great race. This exemplifies the way in which Chamberlain's 'method' depends on the opportunistic mixing of external physical qualities and inner spiritual ones, and thus on the process of validation by reference to 'intuition' whenever 'science' might seem to fail. Through such means he sought to present the most recent half-millennium of European history as a tale of progress. Yet he did so without implying that there was anything inevitable about this achievement. The Teutonic advances had been registered only in the face of an unrelenting Semitic peril. Therefore contemporaries must recognize the continuing challenge of *Volkwerdung*—not as a state of fulfilment already entirely attained, but as an ongoing struggle of racial *becoming*. This was something that Wilhelm II, among others, was pleased to hear. In a letter of 31 December 1901 he told Chamberlain that 'it was God who sent your book to the German people'. The Kaiser treated the imperial family to readings therefrom, and also organized subsidies for a popularly priced edition. By 1914 German sales had exceeded 100,000. Meanwhile, the first Baron Redesdale (A. B. F. Mitford) had produced an enthusiastic introduction for the English translation, issued as *The Foundations of the Nineteenth Century* (2 vols., 1911). It is perhaps particularly curious that, when the book received a predictably mixed reception in Britain, no one penned a warmer welcome than George Bernard Shaw.

In 1906 Chamberlain separated from his first wife. On his divorce two years later, he entered on 26 December 1908 into a similarly childless marriage with Eva Wagner, the composer's only daughter. He settled now at Bayreuth, 'the home of my soul'. There he wrote many further works, including *Goethe* (1912) and an intellectual autobiography called *Lebenswege meines Denkens* (1919). At the outbreak of the First World War he had also embarked on producing polemical essays against his native land. While German soldiers were able to admire these in a 'Trench Edition', the British turned the venture to their own propagandist purposes by publishing in 1916 an English translation tellingly titled *The Ravings of a Renegade*. Having been awarded the non-combatant's Iron Cross in 1915, Chamberlain at last took German citizenship in the following year. After the fall of the Wilhelmine regime he continued to correspond with the exiled Kaiser. Yet Chamberlain also began to forge ever closer links with the emergent Nazi movement. He celebrated his first meeting with its leader at Bayreuth in September 1923 by declaring in an open letter to Hitler in October: 'That in the hour of her deepest need Germany gives birth to a Hitler proves her vitality.' Two years later, on the seventieth birthday of the ailing author, the Nazis' official journal returned the compliment, praising the *Grundlagen* as 'the gospel of the Volkish movement'.

Chamberlain's final illness has been rather speculatively diagnosed as a form of multiple sclerosis. Certainly it was a condition of protracted weakening that took progressively heavier toll upon his energies from 1916 onward. He died in Bayreuth on 9 January 1927. His burial there, at the shrine of Wagnerism, was attended by Prince August Wilhelm, a son of the former Kaiser. However, far more significant for the posthumous cult of the author's reputation was Hitler's presence at the ceremony. A few months later Alfred Rosenberg, the principal 'philosopher' of Nazism, would publish a volume whose title hailed Chamberlain as the 'pioneer and founder of a German future'. As one of the earliest and most prominent intellectual promoters of the Hitlerite cause, this English renegade could hardly have been more deserving of such an ultimately damning panegyric.

MICHAEL BIDDISS

Sources G. G. Field, *Evangelist of race: the Germanic vision of Houston Stewart Chamberlain* (1981) · W. Schüler, *Der Bayreuther Kreis von seiner Entstehung bis zum Ausgang der Wilhelminischen Ära* (1971) · A. Chamberlain, *Meine Erinnerungen an Houston Stewart Chamberlain* (1923) · J. Réal, 'The religious conception of race: Houston Stewart Chamberlain and Germanic Christianity', *The third Reich*, ed. E. Vermeil (1955), 243–86 · M. Biddiss, 'History as destiny: Gobineau, H. S. Chamberlain and Spengler', *TRHS*, 6th ser., 7 (1997), 73–100 · E. Seillière, *H. S. Chamberlain: le plus récent philosophe du pangermanisme mystique* (1917) · *The Times* (10 Jan 1927) · H. S. Chamberlain, *Briefe, 1882–1924, und Briefwechsel mit Kaiser Wilhelm II*, 2 vols. (Munich, c.1928), vol. 2, pp. 126, 142
Archives Richard Wagner Gedenkstätte, Bayreuth, *Nachlass* | Glos. RO, letters to Lord Redesdale
Likenesses photograph, repro. in H. S. Chamberlain, *Briefe, 1882–1924*, 2 (1928), frontispiece [*see illus.*]

Chamberlain, Humphrey (*bap.* **1762**, *d.* **1841**). *See under* Chamberlain, Robert (*bap.* 1736?, *d.* 1798).

Chamberlain, Joan (*d.* **1504?**). *See under* Women traders and artisans in London (*act. c.*1200–*c.*1500).

Chamberlain, John (**1553–1628**), letter writer, was baptized on 15 January 1554 at St Olave Jewry, London, a younger son of Richard Chamberlain (*d.* 1566), alderman and sheriff of London and twice master of the Worshipful Company of Ironmongers, and his first wife, Anne (*d.* 1562), daughter of Robert and Margery Downe. In Richard Chamberlain's will, dated 18 October 1563, he made special provision for his son John:

> Because that he hath been tender, sickly, and weak, I would have him brought up to learning hereafter, when that he comes to some years either in the universities or else in some other place beyond the sea ... and I will commend him to my loving and friendly cousin Thomas Goore that he have the bringing of him up. (*Letters of John Chamberlain*, 1.3)

John was thirteen at the time of his father's death in 1566, but it is unclear where he resided until he matriculated at Trinity College, Cambridge, in 1570. He left without a degree. Almost certainly he was the John Chamberlain who entered Gray's Inn in 1575, but he was never called to the bar. Thanks to an inheritance from his father and later substantial legacies from two of his brothers, Chamberlain never had to earn a living, and he never married. Occasionally he visited a small circle of friends in the country and he went abroad twice, but mostly he was content to live in London in the immediate vicinity of St Paul's Cathedral. He was buried in St Olave Jewry on 20 March 1628.

The raucous, disorderly middle aisle of the Elizabethan St Paul's Cathedral was the best place in London to collect the latest news of court, city, and country, and to learn (in Shakespeare's words) 'who loses and who wins; who's in, who's out'. Chamberlain was an inveterate 'Paul's walker' and was so closely associated with St Paul's that he was appointed to a commission studying the repair of the cathedral in 1620. However, it was not until 1597, when he was forty-three, that it became habitual for him to write letters about what he daily learned in that grand concourse. He had become friendly with a promising young man, Dudley Carleton, some twenty years his junior, and for the rest of his life the two regularly exchanged long, detailed letters.

Some 452 of Chamberlain's letters to Carleton have survived as well as 27 written to others. Carleton, later Viscount Dorchester, was successively ambassador to Venice and The Hague, and ultimately secretary of state. Most of Chamberlain's letters were written to Carleton when he was in Europe and were designed to be useful to an ambitious diplomat eager to keep up with the latest English news and occasionally needful of sage worldly advice. Chamberlain was well equipped for that function because he socialized in a well-placed set that included among others Sir Henry Savile, provost of Eton, Bishop Launcelot Andrews, the antiquary William Camden, and his closest friend, Sir Ralph Winwood, who held various public offices including secretary of state. The advice was useful, but the main content of the letters is terse, accurate news items about the fortunes and misfortunes of what Chamberlain called 'the better sort of people'. Much of it is the announcement of their marriages, births, parties, promotions, scandals, deaths, and much of it reports court rumours and machinations. The more important matters get fuller descriptions: the trials of Essex and Southampton, the marriage of Princess Elizabeth, the execution of Ralegh, Queen Anne's funeral, the notorious trial of the earl of Somerset and Lady Frances Howard. In all, more than 1000 names are mentioned. That Shakespeare was not one of them is not surprising when Chamberlain says ironically in 1614, 'I heare much speech about this new playhouse [the rebuilt Globe], which is said to be the fairest that ever was in England, so that if I live but seven years longer I may chance to make a journey to see it' (*Letters of John Chamberlain*, 1.544). Indeed, Chamberlain did not pay much attention to any literature during its golden age in England. None the less, no diary of the period and no series of letters can equal Chamberlain's for its many-sided view of Elizabethan and Jacobean London and England.

P. J. FINKELPEARL

Sources *The letters of John Chamberlain*, ed. N. E. McClure, 2 vols. (1939) · W. Y. Notestein, *Four worthies* (1957) · *The Chamberlain letters*, ed. E. M. Thomson (1966) · *Dudley Carleton to John Chamberlain, 1603–1624: Jacobean letters*, ed. M. Lee (1972) · N. E. McClure, introduction, in *The letters of John Chamberlain*, 1 (1939), 1–25
Archives BL, Birch MSS · priv. coll., Winwood papers

Chamberlain, John Henry (**1831–1883**), architect, was born on 26 June 1831 at Leicester, the son of the Revd Joseph Chamberlain, minister at Leicester of a congregation of Calvinistic Baptists, and his wife, Jane. He was educated at schools in Leicester and in London. At an early age he was articled to Henry Goddard, a Leicester architect, with whom he remained for several years. On the completion of his articles there was a brief interval of further study in a London office. His growing admiration for Ruskin appeared in an essay on polychromy in architecture which won the Royal Institute of British Architects' silver medal in 1853. He toured Venice and other Italian cities and on his return to Britain in 1856 settled at Birmingham.

Not long after this he entered into a partnership with his lifelong friend William Harris, but, when the partnership was dissolved, he resumed practice on his own account. His chief works at this period were the Hollings memorial column at Leicester, and the Wesleyan chapel in Essington Street. In 1859 he married Anna Mary, daughter of the Revd George Abrahams. The same year he attracted the notice and the friendship of George William, fourth Baron Lyttelton, for whom he executed various works. In 1864, while the hopes of any real success in his profession were still very remote, he contemplated emigrating to New Zealand. That he did not, but instead became one of Birmingham's most successful architects, was owing to a web of friendships he had formed with a remarkable group of merchants, ministers, and civic leaders. These men, who included Joseph Chamberlain (no relation), John Thackeray Bunce, and George Dawson, enunciated a programme of municipal reform that they called the 'civic gospel'. Chamberlain became their preferred architect. In partnership with William Martin, who specialized in planning and construction, he designed such civic buildings as the Paradise Street addition to the Birmingham and Midland Institute (1881) and the Birmingham Municipal School of Arts and Crafts (1881). He erected libraries, pumping stations, and thirty board schools. He laid out Coronation Street in his capacity as surveyor for Birmingham's civic improvement plan. He designed homes for many of Birmingham's leading citizens, such as Highbury (1879–80) for Joseph Chamberlain. He also designed the Joseph Chamberlain memorial (1880), and possessed great skill in designing stained glass, metalwork in iron and brass, and domestic furniture. Chamberlain's architectural philosophy is set forth in his *Introductory Lecture on the Offices and Duties of Architecture* (1858) and in the essays on 'Gothic architecture and art' that he contributed to the *American Architect and Builder's Monthly* (Philadelphia) in 1870 and 1871.

In January 1867 he was appointed to the council of the Midland Institute and in the following year became its honorary secretary. When he undertook the management of the institute there were only a few hundred students, but through his incessant labour in developing the classes the number was advanced to four thousand. He was appointed chairman of the school of art in February 1874 and it too, under his fostering care, rapidly advanced in influence. He was elected a member of the Society of Artists in March 1861 and was appointed professor of architecture, and in 1879 became vice-president. For some years, while the arts department of the Queen's College was in existence, he was professor of architecture there;

he was one of the founders and one of the honorary secretaries of the Shakespeare Memorial Library; for some years he sat on the committee of the old library in Union Street; he was an original member of the Shakespeare Club; he was chosen by John Ruskin as one of the trustees of the St George's Guild; and finally, in 1880, he was nominated one of the justices of the borough.

On 22 October 1883 he delivered a lecture on exotic art at the Birmingham and Midland Institute, and died very suddenly of heart disease at 7 The Crescent, Birmingham, later in the day. He was buried in the Birmingham cemetery on 27 October. His wife survived him.

G. C. BOASE, rev. MICHAEL W. BROOKS

Sources *Birmingham Daily Post* (24 Oct 1883) · *Birmingham Daily Post* (29 Oct 1883) · *The Architect* (27 Oct 1883) · *The Architect* (3 Nov 1883) · *The Architect* (10 Nov 1883) · *The Times* (23–4 Oct 1883) · *The Times* (29 Oct 1883) · M. W. Brooks, *John Ruskin and Victorian architecture* (1989) · *CGPLA Eng. & Wales* (1884) · d. cert. · IGI
Archives RIBA BAL
Wealth at death £15,723 17s.: probate, 28 April 1884, *CGPLA Eng. & Wales*

Chamberlain, Joseph [Joe] (1836–1914), industrialist and politician, was born on 8 July 1836 at 3 Grove Hill Terrace, Camberwell, Surrey, the first of the nine children of Joseph Chamberlain (1796–1874), cordwainer and metal manufacturer, and his wife, Caroline (1808–1875), daughter of Henry Harben, brewer and provisions merchant. Joseph Chamberlain—the third member of the family, after his father and his grandfather, to bear that name—was the first industrialist to reach the highest tier of leadership in British politics. Though he never became prime minister, he was generally considered by the beginning of the twentieth century to be the first minister of the British empire. He was a Unitarian by conviction until the death of his second wife and remained so afterwards by proud allegiance. That allegiance accentuated his difference from the established élite in politics, and especially from his eventual Conservative allies with their loyalty to the established church. But it was the background of his family and his own experience in manufacturing industry that more profoundly shaped his politics.

Family background and education There was an imperial element in that background. For four generations, from the mid-eighteenth century, the Chamberlains had earned their living near the Guildhall in London as cordwainers or makers of new shoes. Their industry prospered in wartime because all those foot soldiers had to be shod. Accordingly the Chamberlains differed from their most prominent fellow Unitarian, the minister Joseph Priestley, in supporting the war against revolutionary France. They appreciated the blessings of a belligerent state. Joseph Chamberlain's grandfather was a staunch supporter of the Honourable Artillery Company and early in the war became captain of its north-western division.

Though the Chamberlains prospered from their industry, they continued to live modestly over their shop until young Joseph was about to be born, when they moved to a terraced house in Camberwell. The Chamberlains were an austere lot who stuck to business. But from his mother's

Joseph Chamberlain (1836–1914), by Eveleen Myers, early 1890s

side his family derived a richer literary culture, enjoyment of good food and drink, delight in the plays they put on for themselves at high days and family festivals—in which young Joseph shone—and, in an earlier age, involvement on the fringes of the world of high politics. His great-grandfather had managed the parliamentary constituency interests of two whig dukes, first for the elder Pitt's colleague the duke of Newcastle and then for the duke of Richmond. Young Joseph was a high-spirited boy and pugnacious as well as serious. He received the best education on offer for those destined for business. After early instruction at a dame-school in Camberwell and at a further school conducted by a Church of England clergyman in Islington, he was sent to University College School in London, an institution held in high esteem among Unitarians. He carried away prizes in Latin and French as well as mathematics and science. Upon graduation he was apprenticed to his father's business, briefly, to begin with, in the actual making of shoes but soon in bookkeeping, where the business was controlled. His horizons were broadened during this apprenticeship by a holiday trip to Belgium and France as translator for his uncle, another cordwainer.

Industrial career Although the family remained affluent, the business of cordwaining was flat in the comparatively pacific middle years of the nineteenth century. Joseph Chamberlain's father welcomed the opportunity to invest in a venture by his brother-in-law, J. S. Nettlefold, who manufactured wood screws in Birmingham. Nettlefold had been confronted at the 1851 exhibition in the Crystal Palace by machinery invented by an American for the

automated manufacture of wood screws with an improved design. Whoever purchased British rights to the patent could dominate the domestic market. The cost of the patent, together with a supply of machines and construction of a factory to house them, was high. Nettlefold sought help from Joseph Chamberlain's father, who invested £10,000 initially and more later. He sent young Joseph to Birmingham in 1854, shortly after his eighteenth birthday, to look after the investment. The new arrival and the industrious town took each other to heart.

In the course of the next fifteen years Joseph Chamberlain and his father, and J. S. Nettlefold and his son, yet another Joseph, turned themselves into the 'Screw Kings', as young Chamberlain called them. He began, as in his father's cordwaining business, on the accounting side. Moving up from that base, he assumed charge of marketing, leaving production to his cousin Joseph Nettlefold. The four men together made the decisions required to win monopoly control of the domestic market and carve out a commercial empire overseas. They extended their production vertically to include ironworks, the making of steel rods, and the drawing of the wire from which screws were made. On the accounting side Joseph Chamberlain scrutinized every category of cost, including the amount and kind of metal used, the steel cuttings from the nicks and threads of the screws which could be melted down with other steel to improve the quality of the mixture, and the processes involved, such as hot forging or the use of cold wire. He worked out percentages for the overhead costs at each mill as well as for packaging, warehousing, taxes, and the expenses of his sales organization. He took systematic note of the type of labour and the sex and age of the workers customarily employed to make each product. In this way he came to see that a shortened working day increased the productivity of labour. As a result he eventually introduced a nine-hour day, which earned the enduring gratitude of his employees and impressed the trade union movement nationally. He worked out a system of discounts, which prevailed throughout the industry into the next century, for cash payment or credit and for the sales organization, depending on the relationship of the sales agent to the firm and the nature of the competition in each particular market. He also paid attention to the idiosyncrasies of foreign markets, and produced an illustrated catalogue of the ever more varied wares of the firm.

To secure the co-operation he needed from other branches of commerce, Chamberlain joined the board of directors of the Midland Railway, and he helped turn the private banking firm of Lloyds in Birmingham into a public joint-stock company. Able in all these ways to reduce its intermediate costs and finance expansion, Nettlefold and Chamberlain, as the business was known, cut the price of its products in order to absorb or crush the domestic competition. Abroad Chamberlain marketed his goods so successfully that producers in the United States, though protected by a wall of tariffs, paid his firm a large annual sum to stay away—an achievement which left him long convinced of the compatibility of imperialism and free trade. He agreed with one French firm to divide continental Europe into spheres of influence, Nettlefold and Chamberlain taking the markets washed by the sea, leaving landlocked countries to the French company. He took advantage of the Franco-Prussian War to take over the markets of another French competitor.

Transfer into public life, and marriages The expansion of the firm, however, did not impress Chamberlain as much as its social impact in Birmingham. He was the first industrialist to recognize that large factory operations like his own, which were springing up around Birmingham, posed a threat to the comparative harmony between classes fostered by the prevalence hitherto of small workshops in which the distance between employer and employee was narrow. He explored some possibilities for restoring class co-operation within large business through company-sponsored education and recreational clubs for workers, and profit sharing with senior employees. But disappointed by or uneasy about these options, he turned, along with other concerned businessmen in Birmingham, to elementary education. In 1869 they founded the National Education League. Rapidly extended in alliance with the Central Nonconformist Committee across the English provinces, the Education League sought parliamentary legislation to create a national network of schools under civic control, fully funded by taxation, to instil into every child, unless educated elsewhere, basic literacy and numeracy and, if need be, nondenominational religious instruction. This initiative catapulted Chamberlain into national politics in 1870, though he did not enter parliament for another six years.

When the government of W. E. Gladstone met the demand with a measure which in effect retained the Church of England as the primary provider of elementary education, Chamberlain fomented a radical rebellion combining nonconformists and organized labour against the Liberal leadership. But the fruits of the rebellion indicated that he was as much out of touch with the Liberal rank and file as were the leaders of the party, and that divided from each other they would only incur defeat, which Disraeli duly inflicted in the general election of 1874. Standing for election at Sheffield, Chamberlain personally experienced the defeat to which he had contributed.

The major phases in Chamberlain's career were reinforced with happy marriages which, however, in the first two cases terminated tragically. In 1861 he married Harriet Kenrick (1838–1863), daughter of Archibald Kenrick of Berrow Court, Edgbaston, a Birmingham businessman and fellow Unitarian, and brother of William *Kenrick (1831–1919) [see under Kenrick family (per. c.1785–1926)]. This marriage introduced Chamberlain to the pleasures of life enjoyed by Birmingham's upper-middle class. He moved out of lodgings into a house on Harborne Road. There, from his father-in-law and in common with his younger partner, Joseph Nettlefold, he acquired a love of gardening which endured for the rest of his life. But two

years after their marriage, having already borne a daughter, Harriet died giving birth to her second child, (Joseph) Austen. Grief-stricken, Chamberlain fled from his home, eventually moving into the home of Harriet's parents, where her older sister could take care of the children. He threw himself frantically into his business and also into the educational activities which led him into public life. In 1868 he married Harriet's first cousin, Florence Kenrick (1847–1875), the daughter of Timothy Kenrick of Birmingham. Serious of spirit though never physically sturdy, Florence was an advocate of the franchise for women. She furthered her own education while she bore Chamberlain four more children, (Arthur) Neville, Ida, Hilda, and Ethel. Florence edited the articles Chamberlain wrote for the *Fortnightly Review* to proclaim the first of his radical programmes. She promoted the transformation of Southbourne, the home they acquired, into the after-hours headquarters for the radical captains of Birmingham. She looked forward to the political life of London once he gained election to parliament. But before that happened, in 1875, she died giving birth to a stillborn son. Once again Chamberlain fled, this time to the Mediterranean, after which he plunged himself deeper in work, now as mayor of Birmingham, to which he was first elected in 1873. He entered the House of Commons in 1876, but he never found the secure radical footing in parliamentary politics that Florence had helped him to find in the civic politics of Birmingham.

Civic achievement The defeat of the Liberals in the general election of 1874 concentrated Chamberlain's energies on the civic arena in Birmingham and on his role as mayor. In June he retired from business. After arranging for the rest of his family, he was left with capital of £100,000, enough to keep him affluent for the rest of his life.

Chamberlain devoted his talent for business to civic purposes. Taking over the local utilities, which were in private hands, first gas and then water, he consolidated and improved services, reduced costs, and at the same time broadened the town's revenue base. This remarkable financial accomplishment and its social benefits persuaded the town to extend its civic enterprise. Thus, early in his political career, Chamberlain constructed arguably his greatest and most enduring accomplishment, a model of 'gas-and-water' or municipal socialism widely admired in the industrial world. At his ceaseless urging, Birmingham embarked on an improvement scheme to tear down its central slums and replace them with healthy housing and commercial thoroughfares, both to ventilate the town and to attract business. This scheme, however, strained the financial resources of the town and undermined the consensus in favour of reform.

Radical Liberal Before his civic policy revived the partisan division of the town, Birmingham elected Chamberlain to be one of its members of parliament at a by-election in June 1876. He was sorry to leave the civic arena where he had performed so well. He never abandoned the belief that more good could be done in local politics than at the parliamentary level. He was almost forty when he secured election to parliament, and he knew that if he waited longer he would arrive too late to make his mark. Even so, after three years in the environs of Westminster, where his prospects for advancement looked good, he reaffirmed his attachment to Birmingham by building himself a new home there, much grander than Southbourne, on a crest of land at the southern edge of the town overlooking a still-rural valley. He named his new home Highbury after the district in London where he had spent his youth. He continued to lavish money on the building and its furnishings, to extend the attached greenhouses, and to elaborate the gardens in the 18 acres of grounds. Highbury was the centre of his universe, large enough to accommodate visiting colleagues from Westminster but away from its demands; it was close to his most intimate associates in Birmingham, with facilities for him to indulge in his favourite recreation of breeding orchids, and with space outside for the enormous garden parties that kept him in touch with his constituents. Once he became a cabinet minister he rented and then purchased a house on Princes Gardens in Knightsbridge, but it never became his residence of choice.

In appearance alone Chamberlain impressed parliament from the outset. Belying expectations of what a provincial mayor would look like, he wore his monocle like a gentleman, as the fastidious Disraeli observed. The monocle and an orchid—or three if they were small—in his buttonhole became his trademarks in politics. He was shorter than many of his aristocratic contemporaries, but that rarely provoked comment. He was clean-shaven in a bearded age. More remarkably, he looked young—as if he were in his twenties when he reached forty, in his forties when he passed sixty. Like his politics, he looked new.

Chamberlain's arrival in parliament coincided with a deepening downturn in the economy. It fortified the critics of his civic policy in Birmingham. Chamberlain did not have a ready political response either locally or nationally to what became known as the great depression. He understood industry's need for governmental action in the social sphere, but he remained confident that industry did not need assistance in the workshop or market place. His experience of overseas sales, particularly in the American market, left him contemptuous of tariffs. He did not see how to apply the principles of gas-and-water socialism at the national level. In any case, the issues with which the politicians and the public were preoccupied when he entered parliament were imperial and foreign rather than social or directly commercial.

Less interested in foreign affairs than in the set-back to radicals in common with all Liberals in the general election of 1874, Chamberlain sought to apply to the national party not the civic policy but the party organizational skills which he had helped to develop in Birmingham. The Birmingham Liberal Association mobilized its electoral support ward by ward through ascending levels of elective representation under the controlling leadership of Chamberlain and his lieutenants. He extended that model to industrial England with the establishment in 1877 of a National Federation of Liberal Associations. When Chamberlain presented the federation to Gladstone as a way to harness popular support for his agitation over the atrocities committed by the Ottoman empire in Bulgaria, the latter agreed to support the federation, and stayed with Chamberlain at his house, Southbourne, during the National Liberal Federation's inaugural meeting on 31 May 1877. Cautiously, Gladstone continued to defend the National Liberal Federation against its critics. For the next three years Gladstone and Chamberlain co-operated with each other, though always from a distance and with separate objectives, Gladstone reclaiming his leadership of the Liberal Party, Chamberlain climbing his way up towards its controlling echelons. There was little sign of the difference in imperial sentiment which would later divide them. Deterred by the cost of British imperial expansion in South Africa and south Asia, and delighted by the damage it did to Disraeli's government, for a while Chamberlain became a Little Englander.

The contribution the National Liberal Federation made to the Liberal victory in the general election of 1880 helped Chamberlain to push his way into the cabinet as president of the Board of Trade when Gladstone formed his second ministry. That ministry frustrated Chamberlain as it did each of its members, though in different ways. Like the rest of the cabinet, he entered office without a defined domestic agenda, and in any case they were all immediately distracted by upheavals in Ireland and Africa. His legislative accomplishments in his five years at the Board of Trade were for the most part measures already in the administrative pipeline of the board, in particular those on bankruptcy and patents. His chief initiative was intrinsically admirable, but he handled it with impetuous clumsiness and a disastrous lack of tact. He sought to prevent shipowners from insuring themselves against financial loss and occasionally even guaranteeing themselves a profit from the loss of life, sometimes heavy, among merchant seamen who were sent out in ill-equipped vessels. But his attack on shipowners for their negligence alienated conscientious owners as well as the callous; it frightened small investors as well as large, and failed to attract much support in the electorate, among whom merchant seamen were a negligible force.

The importance that affairs in Ireland and Africa acquired in the early 1880s might have diverted attention from Chamberlain, given his official responsibilities and known concerns for domestic matters. Yet from the outset of the ministry he assumed a prominent position on imperial issues. He responded with some sympathy to the agrarian unrest and accompanying nationalist agitation which erupted in Ireland. It gave him an opportunity to create a radical liaison between the cabinet and the Irish leader, C. S. Parnell, with whom he had sometimes co-operated in the previous parliament. But the intermediary upon whom in 1882 Chamberlain relied for this purpose, W. H. O'Shea, damaged Chamberlain's reputation and discredited the mediation. O'Shea wished to use his position as complaisant husband of Parnell's mistress to advance his personal ambitions in British politics, and his discretion was not equal to the demands of such an intrigue. These means nevertheless helped to release Parnell from gaol in 1882 and to give full effect to the previous year's transformation of Irish land law in the interest of the tenants.

Developments in Africa also had an ambivalent impact on Chamberlain. In common with most other radicals he was, on balance, repelled by Britain's deepening involvement in Egypt, with which he concerned himself only as a participant in cabinet discussion. But he was called upon to play a prominent role on South Africa, and the turn of events there ended his interlude as a Little Englander. R. W. Dale, his leading nonconformist lieutenant in Birmingham, had made him aware of the interest of British missionaries in southern Africa. From that time Chamberlain publicly endorsed the opposition which Gladstone proclaimed in the dying months of the Disraeli ministry to the annexation of the inland Boer republics by the British colonies along the southern coast. When the Liberals took office Gladstone asked Chamberlain to speak in the House of Commons for the government on South African issues, the colonial secretary being in the House of Lords. Gladstone then proved reluctant to cancel the annexation; but Chamberlain encouraged him to accept the Boer demand of internal autonomy for their republics, and he continued to press for this even after the humiliating defeat which the Boers inflicted on the British at Majuba Hill. He was accordingly among the most prominent advocates of the convention of Pretoria, in which Britain made the demanded concession. But the refusal of the Boers thereafter to confine themselves within the terms of the convention, and simultaneous encroachments upon the region by Bismarck's Germany, turned Chamberlain to defiance.

The prospect of a wide extension of the electorate in 1884 excited Chamberlain as promising a new chapter of domestic affairs in which his radicals could take charge. In the previous year, during a speech in Birmingham on 30 March, he had notoriously denounced the aristocracy as a class 'who toil not, neither do they spin' (J. Chamberlain, *Speeches of the Right Hon. Joseph Chamberlain MP*, ed. H. W. Lucy, 1885, 41). When the House of Lords resisted the government's Franchise Bill he orchestrated the popular outcry, and in doing so marked himself out as Liberal leader for the future. At the beginning of 1885, after the Franchise Bill became law, he proclaimed the most famous of his radical programmes to meet the needs and desires of the new electorate. In substance the programme was restrained. But the rhetoric Chamberlain employed, particularly his choice of the word 'ransom' to describe the social insurance which he wished the affluent to provide for the working class, raised fears among the propertied—and the new electors still had to be householders. In the ensuing general election campaign he reduced his demands to what he considered minimal proportions. But they still included free education—and that alarmed the supporters of Church of England schools, failed to satisfy the nonconformists who desired civic control of denominational schools, and repelled householders fearful of an increase in the rates. The results of the general election at the end of the year disappointed him. Although his proposals for small allotments of land, or 'three acres and a cow', attracted the new electors in the countryside, the Conservatives made headway in suburban constituencies and thus deprived the Liberals of their parliamentary majority outside of Ireland. The Irish nationalists under Parnell emerged with a much expanded Commons contingent, and thus gained decisive influence in the new house.

The home-rule crisis The ensuing parliamentary crisis distorted Chamberlain's partisan alignment and deprived the Liberal Party of power for twenty years, to say nothing of the impact on Anglo-Irish relations. Though the part Chamberlain played in the crisis was essentially self-defensive, it proved pivotal to the outcome in the kingdom.

At the beginning of 1885, giving his radical programme an Irish dimension, Chamberlain had offered Parnell a central board scheme framed to give Ireland an expanded version of the powers of local government that Birmingham had used to such good effect. But when, in the middle of the year, Conservatives indicated that they might be willing to make a more substantial bid for Irish nationalist support, Parnell turned Chamberlain down and, adding insult to injury, prevented him from receiving a civil reception in Ireland. Angered, Chamberlain dropped Ireland from his election programme.

Afterwards, in an attempt to minimize the significance of the losses which the Liberals sustained in the general election, Chamberlain advised the party to lie low and leave the Conservatives in office to be discredited by their tacit alliance with the Irish. But instead Gladstone returned to office in January 1886, and replaced Chamberlain's radical agenda with a proposal for internal self-government of Ireland on terms acceptable to Parnell. Before this reorientation of Liberal priorities became clear, Chamberlain, who bid for the Colonial Office, declined the Admiralty, and returned to office apprehensively as president of the Local Government Board, attempted to act on his own agenda by initiating an inquiry into the use of local public works to alleviate unemployment; this resulted in his circular of 15 March, which became a famous paper of governmental initiative. But at the same time he precipitated the disclosure of Gladstone's intentions on Ireland. Once their direction was clear, Chamberlain and G. O. Trevelyan resigned from the cabinet in a dramatic gesture on 26 March 1886: 'Trevelyan and myself again tendered our resignations and left the [Cabinet] room' (Chamberlain, *Political Memoir*, 199). Declining friendly advice to leave quietly, he threw himself into the fight against Gladstone's proposals, for a combination of reasons, imperial, domestic, and personal: because they threatened to weaken the central government of the United Kingdom, because they took precedence away from his radical programme, and because they undermined his own standing in the Liberal hierarchy. Still he hoped that Liberals would appreciate the conscientiousness of his opposition when it so obviously deprived him of office and that they would welcome him back when the Irish debate was resolved and Gladstone retired. The conflict, however, became bitterly personal. Most Liberals, including radicals and the National Liberal Federation, interpreted Chamberlain's behaviour as a blatant bid to supplant the Grand Old Man as leader of the party; and Gladstone, though already seventy-six, was destined to live for another decade.

Against Chamberlain's predilections and the grain of the major parties, he found himself allied not only with the Conservatives, led by the third marquess of Salisbury, whom he learned to respect, and Lord Randolph Churchill, whom he regarded as a kindred spirit, but also with whig defectors from the Liberal Party led by Lord Hartington, whom he disliked as a drag. This alliance of men who had denounced each other in vivid terms months earlier in the 1885 election was confirmed by the general election which Gladstone called in mid-1886 as soon as his Government of Ireland Bill was defeated in the House of Commons. The general election of 1886 hardened the split in the Liberal Party and necessitated an electoral compact between Liberal Unionists and Conservatives. The electoral survival of Hartington in Lancashire depended on support from Chamberlain as well as Conservatives, which both gave. Chamberlain had more independent strength in Birmingham. He turned the town into a bastion of radical Unionism, excluding Gladstonians from the parliamentary representation of the town and conceding only one of its seven seats to the Conservatives. He thus established himself as that rare phenomenon in English politics, a strong regional as well as national figure. He helped to preserve a substantial Liberal Unionist contingent in the new House of Commons, enough to keep the Conservatives from reaping all the fruits of the Unionist victory. Yet his place in the line-up of parties remained anomalous. Though Salisbury depended on Liberal Unionists for his majority in the Commons, he refused to form a ministry that included Chamberlain, nor would Chamberlain join a combined ministry led by Hartington. Chamberlain thus delayed the formation of a coalition for a decade.

Radical Unionist During that decade Chamberlain carved out a distinctive position for himself, innovative in both domestic and imperial affairs. The role he developed proved vital to the success of the Unionist cause and restored the prospect of his gaining high, though no longer the highest, office. He found the first year after the 1886 election discouraging. Churchill, the member of the Conservative ministry upon whom Chamberlain relied to make his wishes effective, resigned in December. Immediately Chamberlain proposed a round-table conference of leading Unionist and Gladstonian Liberals with a view to reunion. The conference was duly convened. But it exposed the impossibility of agreement so long as Gladstone insisted on, and Chamberlain refused to concede the prompt granting of, a generous measure of domestic autonomy for Ireland. The last real prospect of Liberal reunion thus vanished. Chamberlain looked to the alternative possibility of a centre party composed of Liberals

who would settle for less Irish autonomy and Unionists who would do more than defend the status quo. But this alternative depended on Churchill, who petulantly went his own way, and on Hartington, who shied away from any constitutional change. Against all expectation, the one reliable relationship to develop among the Unionist leaders was between Chamberlain and Salisbury. Both strong-minded men, though one wished to arrest and the other to accelerate the pace of change, they learned to trust each other even when they disagreed. Still, the end of the summer of 1887 found Chamberlain near despair, afraid that Gladstonians and the Irish would sweep all before them.

Chamberlain welcomed an opportunity for escape. Salisbury offered him the leadership of a diplomatic mission to Washington to deal with a fisheries dispute between Canada and the United States. The mission (November 1887 – March 1888) confirmed Chamberlain's Unionism. It also nourished his interest in imperial opportunities to strengthen Britain's international position, opportunities in pursuit of which he might also strengthen his personal position in British politics. He was gratified to discover that, belying Gladstonian reports, the leading men in American public life were closet Liberal Unionists. Though fear of the substantial and articulate Irish electorate in the United States made them unwilling to speak out, privately their memory of the hard fight to preserve the American Union inclined them to oppose the amount of autonomy Gladstone would give Ireland. When Chamberlain visited Canada he found that the governing Conservatives there shared his insistence on strong central government. He was still more impressed by the economic resources opened up by the Canadian Pacific Railway. At a banquet in Toronto, and then at Henry Adams's dinner table in Washington, Chamberlain began to preach an imperial mission for the English, unifying kindred races and 'working out ... the great problem of federal government' (W. Maycock, *With Mr Chamberlain in the United States and Canada, 1887–8*, 1914, 100 ff.).

Chamberlain secured two agreements in Washington: a *modus vivendi* with the American and Canadian governments to deal with the fisheries dispute, and an engagement to marry Mary Endicott (d. 1957), only daughter of William Crowninshield Endicott, secretary of the army in President Cleveland's cabinet. Less than half Chamberlain's age, Mary was a Massachusetts patrician who enjoyed the world of privilege and power. The wedding took place in November 1888, to the distress of Beatrice Potter, with whom he had had an association since 1883, though her passion for him was unrequited. When Mary joined Chamberlain in England she helped to settle him socially among the well-born Conservatives and whigs with whom he was now politically associated. The universality, none the less, with which he was known as Joe, not only on the streets of Birmingham but up to the royal family, reflected his sturdily popular associations. To the end of his life he refused any honour which would give him a title other than Mr.

On his return from the New World to the Old, Chamberlain made two lasting adjustments in his political course. He made himself indispensable to the Unionist cause through endlessly resourceful opposition to home rule; and he added policy initiatives on imperial issues to his programme while adapting and developing its social side to make the most of the Conservative interest in reform. Along the way he refined a lean and pointed style of speech, responsive to but never distracted by interjections, and in doing so established a new model of platform oratory. He also emerged, in the judgement of close observers, as the ablest debater in the House of Commons. His envenomed indictment of home rule provoked retaliatory personal attacks from English radicals and Irish nationalists, who could not forgive him for deserting them. But he earned the gratitude of Unionists as much as the hatred of the Irish for being the man who killed home rule. Sharp practice and scandal accompanied these controversies. Chamberlain made the most of what proved to be false charges in *The Times* in 1887 against Parnell for condoning crime, and he encouraged O'Shea to pursue the suit for divorce that finally ruined the Irish leader.

Meanwhile Chamberlain equipped Unionists with a constructive programme to enhance their essentially negative *raison d'être* of resistance to home rule. On the imperial side, he aimed to strengthen the central government of the empire and cultivate its economic resources. He turned his attention first to South Africa, where fabulous resources of gold had just been discovered and more seemed in store. In this case he was less concerned with these resources economically than with the political power which their development threatened to transfer from London to South Africa, and within South Africa to the Boer republics, particularly the Transvaal where the goldfields were situated. Suspicious of Cecil Rhodes, who used his enormous wealth from the diamond mines of Kimberley, and now the gold of the Rand, to promote his political ambitions at the Cape, Chamberlain wanted to limit the terms of the charter which Rhodes sought from Lord Salisbury's government for development to the north of the Transvaal. But the government gave way to Rhodes because it saw no other avenue for development which would avoid heavy imperial expenditure.

The economic developments Chamberlain wanted to promote lay elsewhere in the empire, and they usually involved the construction of railways. He was not in a position to make detailed proposals. But he drew the attention of working-class audiences, particularly after Gladstone's return to office in 1892, to the way in which markets and railway projects overseas could alleviate unemployment at home. Chamberlain himself invested heavily in a sisal plantation in the Bahamas. But his skill as an accountant had deteriorated with disuse. He made the initial investment against the advice of his brothers in business. When the returns proved disappointing, he deepened his investment; and he incurred further liabilities when he turned the business into a limited company, selling debentures. When the crop failed he lost so heavily that in the spring of 1895 he contemplated retiring from

public life. Yet this personal experience did nothing to diminish his enthusiasm for public investment in the empire.

On the domestic side, Chamberlain claimed and received credit for the Conservative government's extension of elective local government to the counties in 1888 and for the elimination of fees in state-aided elementary schools in 1891. Conservatives had reasons of their own for passing both measures, but Chamberlain undoubtedly increased their appetite for domestic reform. He took care wherever possible to encourage suggestions for reform made by Conservatives. It was through Sir John Gorst, the maverick Conservative MP for Chatham, that Chamberlain learned of the German scheme for insuring workmen hurt in industrial accidents. He placed workmen's compensation promptly on his Unionist platform and used the German model to undercut alternative Liberal proposals that pitted trade unions against employers. He always looked for ways to bring labour and capital together. In 1897, at last back in office now under Salisbury, Chamberlain saw to the enactment of a Workmen's Compensation Bill. The crowning domestic achievement of the Unionists at the end of the century, this act served its social purpose at little cost to the Treasury. The compensation was paid for by insurance which employers were required to take out.

Nothing comparable was to come of Chamberlain's more spectacular initiative in proposing old-age pensions. He first made the suggestion in 1891 in support of a Conservative candidate during a closely watched by-election at Aston on the borders of Birmingham. He pursued the suggestion after the narrow Liberal victory in the general election of 1892. But in spite of repeated attempts during the remainder of the decade, he could not find a scheme that offered much for what he liked to call the 'veterans of industry' without placing a heavier burden on the Treasury than Unionists were willing to impose. Once he launched his campaign for tariff reform a decade later, he suggested paying for old-age pensions from revenue raised through tariffs. But when the working class appeared to be more worried about raising the cost of living through a tariff on foodstuffs than they were attracted by benefits in old age, he dropped the suggestion, to the regret of some social reforming Conservatives.

In 1894, anticipating the fall of the beleaguered Liberal government, Chamberlain sought support from Lord Salisbury for his social programme by suggesting that parts of it be introduced through bills in the House of Lords. Salisbury evaded this proposal, as he did all other Liberal Unionist attempts to settle the terms for a coalition ministry with the Conservatives before the Liberals were removed from office. As a result Chamberlain's programme for Unionism remained unofficial, widely influential in some Conservative and Liberal Unionist circles but firmly opposed in others.

Colonial secretary Not until the Liberals fell from office in June 1895 did Salisbury call the duke of Devonshire (as Hartington had become) and Chamberlain into council to decide on the terms for and composition of a coalition Unionist ministry. The way in which Salisbury expressed himself on social policy, though vague, was flattering to Chamberlain, who did not ask for clarification. He disconcerted Salisbury, however, by choosing the post of secretary of state for the colonies for himself. Aside from gratifying Chamberlain's sense of imperial mission, the choice reduced the risks of confrontation with Conservatives on social and fiscal issues; but it encroached upon the responsibilities Salisbury chose for himself by becoming foreign secretary as well as prime minister.

That risk was averted for two years after the formation of the ministry and its triumphant confirmation at the polls by the basic agreement between Salisbury and Chamberlain on most imperial issues and by Chamberlain's distraction over the Jameson raid. Just after Christmas 1895 a lieutenant of Rhodes, Dr Starr Jameson, accompanied by a small force of men on horseback, invaded the Transvaal from a base under British control on its western border in an attempt to replace the Boer government of the republic with one sympathetic to Britain. The Boers crushed the raid without difficulty. Its defeat discredited the British inside the republic and out. It ruined Cecil Rhodes politically, though he preserved his economic might. It threatened to ruin Chamberlain, for he had given Rhodes's men possession of the strip of land from which Jameson launched his raid. Afterwards, for a year and a half, Chamberlain had to protect himself against the suspicion, which amounted among Rhodes's people to the knowledge, that he had known beforehand that the strip of land could be used for a raid—though he could never have conceived of one as ill supported as Jameson's. Chamberlain was saved by Rhodes's knowledge that the continuation of the British charter for his interests north of the Transvaal depended on Chamberlain's retention of office, and also by the preoccupation among Liberal investigators in Britain with the extent of Rhodes's guilt. Chamberlain escaped without discredit except among the Boers and their sympathizers in South Africa.

Amid the difficulties of these eighteen months Chamberlain canvassed the possibility of augmenting the trade between Britain and its self-governing colonies through creation of an imperial *Zollverein*; but the suggestion elicited little sympathy either in the colonies, which relied on tariffs for revenue and for protection of their nascent industries, or in free-trading Britain. He had a little more success with the crown colonies governed by Britain. Before the Jameson raid he asked the governors of these colonies for information to help expand trade with the mother country. The former marketing manager asked for specifics on everything from prices and freight rates to patterns and packaging, and for samples of each colony's imports and exports. At the same time he attempted to use the dividends which Britain earned from its shares in the Suez Canal to fund the construction of railways and other infrastructural improvements in the crown colonies. Resistance from the Treasury, however,

defeated this proposal and kept Chamberlain's subsequent achievement in 'cultivating the undeveloped estates' of the empire to modest proportions.

Chamberlain made arguably his most substantial contribution to the crown colonies by promoting research and education in the field of tropical medicine. Concern for education permeated Chamberlain's career in public life from its beginnings with the National Education League to the establishment of the University of Birmingham at the turn of the century. As colonial secretary he looked to education to address a problem that crippled imperial administration especially in tropical west Africa, where most men sent out from England were stricken with malaria before they could complete their assignments. He appointed Dr Patrick Manson, the best-known of the few experts in tropical medicine, to be the Colonial Office medical adviser. Chamberlain raised private as well as public money to found the London School of Tropical Medicine. He fostered the appointment of committees of British researchers to go to the tropics not only for on-site investigation but to make and execute policy. From the sanitary reforms he made as mayor of Birmingham to the transformation he brought about in the sanitation of the camps into which Boer women and children were herded during the Second South African War, even his opponents recognized that he knew how to deal effectively with public health. Before he left office he had made service in the tropical colonies a more attractive profession. One way and another, Chamberlain's administrative efforts as colonial secretary marked him out as the most outstanding holder of that formerly secondary office, while the importance of imperial issues at the turn of the century and his personal importance in the party politics of the day lifted his position to an eminence second only to the prime minister. Even his rivals treated him as the first minister of the empire.

Once the inquiry into the Jameson raid came to an end, Chamberlain invaded Salisbury's sanctuary at the Foreign Office by challenging his handling of the French in west Africa and his reluctance generally to seek an alliance with one of the other imperial powers. Salisbury had been dealing with the French over the Niger River in conciliatory fashion; he was anxious to save his diplomatic capital for a confrontation with them on the Nile. But Chamberlain insisted that Britain could not afford to diminish any of its colonial resources. To the embarrassment of the Foreign Office and its emissaries, he also demonstrated that the French would give way in face of stiffened British demands. His intransigent diplomacy, followed by the military activities of Frederick Lugard, extended the boundaries of what came to be known as Nigeria.

At the same time Chamberlain sought official recognition, and thus international confirmation, of the informal sway held by the British in the commerce of China, the market potential of which he was inclined to exaggerate. To this end he looked for some sort of alliance with the other industrial powers he admired, the United States and Germany. This co-operation would, he hoped, strengthen Britain more broadly in the imperial competition which prevailed among the great powers at the turn of the century. President Cleveland had provoked Chamberlain on the eve of the Jameson raid by asserting the interest of the United States in a boundary dispute between Venezuela and British Guiana. But Chamberlain welcomed the subsequent empire-building of the United States in the West Indies and the Pacific. Though his talk of an alliance disconcerted the Americans, republicans responded appreciatively to his expressions of sympathy and willingness to co-operate in the imperial arena. But Germany rebuffed his repeated, often clumsy, overtures over China, and drove him ultimately towards the French.

Chamberlain was distracted from these efforts by the onset of a war which he did not seek, but from which he did not recoil, to uphold British suzerainty over the Boer republics in South Africa. But at the end of 1898, with little idea that in less than a year he would lead Britain to war, he was preoccupied with founding and funding the University of Birmingham. In order to enhance the distinction of Birmingham and serve its industrial needs, he transformed Mason College into a university by adding an emphasis on the classics and humanities to its curriculum in the sciences, while applying higher education directly to business by adding a new faculty of commerce, Britain's first. He stimulated funding for the university by soliciting large grants from two expatriate Britons who had done well in North American business, Andrew Carnegie and Lord Strathcona. Manoeuvred by Chamberlain, the two men increased their offers and also made them contingent on matching funds, which he duly raised from the less wealthy business and professional élite of Birmingham. Chamberlain secured land for the new university from Lord Calthorpe, landlord of Edgbaston, the inner suburb of Birmingham beloved by its upper-middle class.

The Jameson raid had left Chamberlain more circumspect yet still erratic in his handling of South Africa. He remained ready to do what he could by rough means as well as fair to strengthen the imperial power there and resist the quest of President Kruger of the Transvaal for autonomy. Chamberlain's uncertainty about the right tactics to employ diminished his ability to control the man he sent out as high commissioner to South Africa, Alfred Milner, especially since they shared the same objective, to make Britain supreme in the region. Milner soon despaired of a peaceful solution to the conflict with Kruger and resolved to work up to war. Former colonial secretaries had often found themselves unable to control their distant emissaries, but there was no comparable excuse for Chamberlain's failure to make adequate military provision for a war the severity of which he occasionally foresaw.

Once the war broke out Chamberlain shrank from the role of war minister which was otherwise his for the taking—and the war demonstrated a crying need for better military management. The war nevertheless raised him to new heights of eminence in the government. It was Chamberlain who pulled the government out of the slump into which it fell after three British armies were defeated in South Africa within one week in December

1899. It was he who determined the timing of the general election (October 1900), which was called early once the British seemed assured of military victory. Almost alone among the members of the cabinet, he then strode into the electoral fray. Crudely identifying the partisan appeal of the Unionist coalition with the fortunes of the imperial war—'Every seat lost to the Government was a seat gained by the Boers'—he renewed the victory of 1895.

The fortunes of the government and of its most prominent member did not advance in step with his achievement. Lord Salisbury reconstructed the ministry in ancestral fashion, promoting the members of its leading families, including Chamberlain's son Austen, but adding little fresh blood to its tired forces. Meanwhile the eruption of guerrilla warfare in South Africa eroded the moral force of the electoral mandate. Still, the war seemed to validate Chamberlain's imperialism, just as the election seemed to prove its popularity. Nothing was more remarkable than the willingness, even eagerness, with which the self-governing colonies of Canada, Australia, and above all little New Zealand contributed contingent upon contingent of troops to fight for the imperial cause far away at the foot of Africa. Arthur Balfour, Salisbury's nephew and presumed political heir, heralded Chamberlain at a special presentation to him in the Guildhall towards the end of the war as 'the man who, above all others, has made the British Empire a reality'. Next day *The Times* (14 February 1902) greeted him as 'the most popular and trusted man in England'.

But the war and its rewards for Chamberlain ended together. The heroic fight put up by the Boer guerrillas and the 'methods of barbarism' employed by the British army to force them to make peace discredited Chamberlain's brand of imperialism. The war was scarcely concluded, at the end of May 1902, when Milner ruptured his relationship with Chamberlain by calling publicly for suspension of the Cape Colony's popular constitution in defiance of Chamberlain's injunctions. The obvious costs of the war in blood and treasure exceeded its apparent dividends, especially after the mine owners of the Rand indentured Chinese labour to meet their needs. The ending of the war allowed a backlog of domestic measures to the fore; and the most pressing of them, for improved funding and governance of elementary education, revived the denominational controversy that divided Chamberlain and nonconformist Unionists from their Anglican Conservative allies. The war also brought the government up against the limits of its fiscal resources. Finally, the termination of the war allowed Lord Salisbury to retire; and his retirement left the government under an uneasy dual leadership, with Balfour as prime minister and Chamberlain as first minister of the empire. The deterioration in Chamberlain's position as a result of these accumulating set-backs was not immediately apparent. But they were compounded as well as symbolized by the gash he sustained to his forehead a few weeks after the war from a falling pane of glass in a cab accident (7 July 1902). Though lean and vigorous, he had long been prone under stress to gout and neuralgia. He shunned exercise as a diversion from work, and he had been working under unremitting pressure for seven years. But he did not complain of fatigue until after this accident. It occurred just when Salisbury retired and when Balfour abandoned the one concession Chamberlain had secured in the terms of the Education Bill. Chamberlain forced himself back to work against doctors' orders before he had fully recovered.

The political situation from Chamberlain's standpoint continued to deteriorate. Still enthralled by his imperial assignment, he did not move to the exchequer which was his to take when Sir Michael Hicks Beach decided to accompany Salisbury into retirement; thus Chamberlain lost his best opportunity to determine the fiscal policy of the government, which was soon to be vital to him. Thereafter he had as little influence over Balfour's reconstruction of the ministry as over Salisbury's a year and a half earlier. The returns from by-elections turned sharply against the government, for which Chamberlain blamed the Education Bill. All that he could salvage from an unproductive conference with the premiers of the self-governing colonies (June 1902) was an informal agreement with the Canadians to lower their tariff against British goods if Britain amended its wartime corn tax to favour the Canadians; and Chamberlain was not sure that he could secure cabinet approval for this small step towards imperial preference. Balfour encouraged his proposal to visit South Africa as the first in a projected series of personal missions overseas to draw the empire together. But Chamberlain's departure towards the end of the year weakened him at home, while few of the agreements which he patched up between the recently warring factions in South Africa survived his return to England. On his way home he learned that the chancellor of the exchequer, C. T. Ritchie, would resign and precipitate a major governmental crisis unless Chamberlain abandoned the slight modification in the corn tax to which he had tentatively agreed with the Canadians. Once Chamberlain reached England (March 1903) he acquiesced but with evident irritation, as he did also when the cabinet, on grounds of expense, rejected his plan to station a division of the British army permanently in South Africa.

Tariff reform Frustration, not mature reflection, prompted the call that Chamberlain issued in Birmingham in May 1903 for 'a treaty of preference and reciprocity' with the colonies and for retaliatory tariffs against countries that threatened British imperial interests. His message nevertheless reflected deep-seated anxieties: about Britain's deteriorating industrial performance in comparison with the United States and Germany; about Britain's insecurity in the increasingly competitive world of the great political as well as economic powers; and, still, about the concern that first led him into public life, the social security of British industry unless it benefited labour as well as capital. He saw an opportunity to meet these concerns by cultivating the seed of imperial preference that Canada had sown. He elaborated his message rapidly under contradictory pressures: resistance in cabinet, but eager response from industrial and other Unionist interests.

Industrially his message shifted towards protectionism, without abandoning insistence on the primary importance of imperial preference. The importance to the colonies of agricultural production, and particularly to Canada of its wheat exports, forced Chamberlain to demand that Britain place a tariff on its imports of foodstuffs, to be lowered preferentially in favour of those colonies that offered a comparable preference to British exports. He thus offended the most deeply rooted popular sentiments attached to free trade. But industrially his proposals were conservative. He focused his offer of protection on Britain's increasingly uncompetitive staple exports in metals and textiles rather than on technologically more advanced infant industries such as chemicals. In the social sphere he raised but then dropped the possibility of funding old-age pensions through tariffs and dwelt instead on the ability of tariffs to guarantee remunerative employment.

At the same time Chamberlain created a formidable organization outside the regular channels of the government to promote his message. He worked from two bases. The avowedly non-partisan Tariff Reform League was set up in London, combining the talents of press magnates with the wealth of industrialists to flood the country with propaganda. The Tariff Reform Committee was set up in affiliation with the Liberal Unionist Association of Birmingham. Under close supervision by Chamberlain through his family and close friends it proceeded to capture control of the Unionist electoral machinery nationally. His most original organizational initiative came towards the end of the year when, in almost royal fashion, he appointed leading figures from industry and former governmental service to a tariff reform commission to make concrete proposals for a tariff after close industry-by-industry inquiry.

In September 1903, tired of the constraints of cabinet government and encouraged by the seeming sympathy of Balfour, Chamberlain resigned from the ministry to launch a nationwide campaign from the platform. His campaign teetered on the verge of success by the turn of the year. But thereafter it compounded the electoral woes of the government. Tariff reform fragmented the Unionist alliance, much as home rule had split the Liberals. For another two years Chamberlain and Balfour paralysed each other. Each was unwilling to do what the other wished yet unable to do without him. Each was strong where the other was weak. While Chamberlain captured the organization of both parties to the Unionist alliance, Balfour outmanoeuvred him in parliament. Balfour performed brilliantly in foreign and military affairs, but Chamberlain kept the initiative in colonial policy.

Chamberlain finally forced Balfour to resign in December 1905, thus precipitating a general election, which was held in January 1906 and brought in a Liberal government. The Unionists were overwhelmed by the allied forces of Liberals and Labour everywhere but in Birmingham, where Chamberlain and his men reversed the tide, increasing their already enormous majorities. The size of the majority the Liberals won in the new House of Commons destroyed Chamberlain's hopes of keeping their return to power brief. Still he fought back, struggling at least to commit the Unionist opposition to tariff reform.

To that end a protracted celebration of Chamberlain's seventieth birthday, which coincided with the thirtieth anniversary of his election to parliament, was conducted in Birmingham at the beginning of July. Over the past year Chamberlain had blacked out briefly two or three times under the strain of public speaking, and he sensed that the address he gave on this occasion could be his last. It was a true valediction. In contrast to the Manchester school, with its devotion to minimal government and free trade, he praised what he proclaimed as 'the Birmingham school' for its readiness to use the powers of the state to promote the welfare of the country and to strengthen the empire. Tariff reform as he presented it served both these ends. It would 'secure for the masses of the industrial population in this country constant employment at fair wages', and it would advance the power and prosperity of industrial England. 'England without an empire', he said scornfully, 'would be a fifth-rate nation, existing on the sufferance of its more powerful neighbours' (*Birmingham Daily Post*, 10 July 1906).

Chamberlain hastened afterwards to London to pursue his campaign, and there he suffered a stroke. It paralysed his right side, including his writing hand, and it muffled his voice. His active political life was over, though his family tried to disguise the fact for nearly a year while Mary struggled to secure a recovery. He survived for a further seven years, intervening when he was able through dictated letters and awkward conversation to keep Unionists faithful to tariff reform and opposed to home rule. He remained influential because no one else on the Unionist side matched his strength of conviction and his remembered force of personality. But in 1913 Balfour's successor as party leader, Bonar Law, virtually abandoned the Unionist commitment to food taxes and, with them, to imperial preference.

A year later Chamberlain, who had been re-elected in the two general elections of 1910, announced his intention to retire from the House of Commons at the next election. In mid-June he bid farewell to his faithful constituents, who saw him for the first time since his stroke being pushed along the footpaths of Highbury in a bath chair. He left Birmingham afterwards and returned to London, where he died at his home, 40 Princes Gardens, on 2 July 1914. Word of his death was overshadowed by the news of the assassination of Archduke Ferdinand at Sarajevo.

Governed by Chamberlain's wishes, his family declined burial in Westminster Abbey. His funeral was conducted with stark simplicity in Birmingham. He was buried on 6 July in a civic cemetery, Key Hill, in the heart of his West Birmingham constituency, not far from the factory where he had made his fortune, in a ground vault with his first two wives, surrounded by the graves of the industrialists and civic leaders among whom he had been chief. He left an estate valued at just over £125,000, reduced by his abandonment of business for politics but not out of line with the estates left by his brothers who had remained in business. He also left a political progeny: his only son by his first marriage, (Joseph) Austen *Chamberlain (1863–1937), foreign secretary; and his only son by his second marriage, (Arthur) Neville *Chamberlain (1869–1940), prime minister.

By 1914 Unionists had already given up one cause Joseph Chamberlain held dear. By the end of the summer they gave up another when they conceded home rule for Ireland. Only Birmingham remained true to his prescriptions in civic and national affairs for another thirty years. But his vision of empire continued to inspire Unionists at large, and his administrative policies at the Colonial Office were pursued by Labour as well into the mid-twentieth century. His willingness to use the powers of the state for domestic economic and social purposes has won more admirers among his political opponents than within his own party. PETER T. MARSH

Sources P. T. Marsh, *Joseph Chamberlain, entrepreneur in politics* (1994) · J. L. Garvin and J. Amery, *The life of Joseph Chamberlain*, 6 vols. (1932–69) · R. Jay, *Joseph Chamberlain* (1981) · *Mr Chamberlain's speeches*, ed. C. W. Boyd, 2 vols. (1914) · J. Chamberlain, *A political memoir, 1880–92*, ed. C. H. D. Howard (1953) · A. F. Hooper, 'Mid-Victorian radicalism', PhD diss., U. Lond., 1978 · E. P. Hennock, *Fit and proper persons: ideal and reality in nineteenth-century urban government* (1973) · A. Sykes, *Tariff reform in British politics, 1903–1913* (1979) · A. G. Gardiner, *The life of Sir William Harcourt*, 2 vols. (1923) · R. M. Kesner, *Economic control and colonial development* (1981) · *The diary of Beatrice Webb*, ed. N. MacKenzie and J. MacKenzie, 4 vols. (1982–5), vols. 1–2 · A. Chamberlain, *Politics from inside: an epistolary chronicle, 1906–1914*, 2nd edn (1936) · Gladstone, *Diaries* · M. Huron, *Joseph Chamberlain and liberal reunion* (1967) · J. Butler, *The liberal party and the Jameson raid* (1968)
Archives ICL, letters to *Playfair* · U. Birm. L., additional papers, incl. corresp. and diaries as colonial secretary; corresp. and papers; letters; political corresp., notebooks, and papers · Wellcome L., corresp. with Lister Institute | BL, corresp. with Arthur James Balfour, Add. MSS 49773–49774 · BL, letters to John Bright, Add. MS 43387 · BL, corresp. with Sir Charles Dilke, Add. MSS 43885–43889, 49610 · BL, letters to T. H. S. Escott, Add. MS 58777 · BL, corresp. with W. E. Gladstone, Add. MSS 44125–44126 · BL, letters to Lord Halsbury, Add. MS 56372 · BL, letters to Edward Hamilton, Add. MSS 48623–48624 · Bodl. Oxf., corresp. with Sir Henry Burdett · Bodl. Oxf., corresp. with Sir William Harcourt and Lewis Harcourt · Bodl. Oxf., letters to Lord Kimberley · Bodl. Oxf., corresp. with F. A. Maxse · Bodl. Oxf., corresp. with Lord Alfred Milner · Bodl. Oxf., corresp. with Sandars and Balfour · Bodl. Oxf., corresp. with Lord Selborne · Bodl. RH, corresp. with Lord Lugard · Brenthurst Library, corresp. with Lord Middleton · CAC Cam., corresp. with Lord Randolph Churchill · CAC Cam., corresp. with Lord Croft · CAC Cam., letters to G. Lloyd · CAC Cam., corresp. with Alfred Lyttelton · Chatsworth House, Derbyshire, letters to duke of Devonshire · CKS, letters to Edward Stanhope · Glos. RO, corresp. with Sir Michael Hicks Beach · Herefs. RO, Lord James of Hereford MSS · HLRO, corresp. with Andrew Bonar Law · HLRO, corresp. with John St Loe Strachey · Mitchell L., Glas., Glasgow City Archives, corresp. with J. P. Smith and letters relating to his biography; letters to J. P. Smith · NA Scot., corresp. with Arthur Balfour · NA Scot., corresp. with first Baron Lock · News Int. RO, corresp. with Moberly Bell · NL Aus., corresp. with Alfred Deakin · NL Ire., letters to A. S. Green · NL Scot., letters to Sir Henry Craik · NL Scot., letters to Sir Charles Dalrymple · NL. Scot., letters to Lord Minto · NRA, priv. coll., letters to the ninth duke of Argyll · NRA, priv. coll., letters to Sir Thomas Wrightson · PRO, letters to Lord Northcote, PRO 30/56 · Surrey HC, corresp. with Lord Onslow · U. Birm. L., corresp. with Mary Chamberlain · U. Birm. L., corresp.

with H. G. Fielder and Charles Harding · U. Birm. L., corresp. with E. R. Russell · University of Bristol Library, letters to Alfred Austin · University of Sheffield, corresp. with W. A. S. Hewins · University of Sheffield, letters to A. J. Mundella · University of Sheffield, letters to H. J. Wilson · W. Sussex RO, letters to F. A. Maxse · Warks. CRO, letters to Sir Francis Alexander Newdigate · Wilts. & Swindon RO, corresp. with fourteenth earl of Pembroke | FILM BFI NFTVA, documentary footage; news footage
Likenesses F. Holl, oils, 1886, NPG · E. Myers, platinum print, 1890–93, NPG [*see illus.*] · G. R. Halkett, wash drawing, 1893, Palace of Westminster, London · J. S. Sargent, oils, 1896, NPG · H. von Herkomer, oils, *c.*1900, Roveries Hall, Bishop's Castle, Shropshire · S. P. Hall, double portrait, oils, *c.*1902–1903 (with first earl of Balfour), NPG · H. von Herkomer, chalk drawing, 1903, NPG · W. Strang, chalk drawing, 1903, Chequers, Buckinghamshire · W. Strang, drypoint, 1903, NPG · W. Strang, etching, 1903, Roveries Hall, Bishop's Castle, Shropshire · C. W. Furse, oils, 1904, Cordwainers' Hall, London · J. S. Sargent, oils, 1907, NPG · J. Tweed, marble bust, 1916, Westminster Abbey · J. Tweed, marble statue, 1927, Palace of Westminster, London · F. S. Baden-Powell, silhouette, NPG · Barraud, photograph, NPG; repro. in *Men and Women of the Day*, 1 (1888) · Barraud, photograph, NPG · M. Beerbohm, caricature, Merton Oxf. · M. Beerbohm, caricature, U. Birm. L. · M. Beerbohm, caricatures, AM Oxf., V&A · O. Birley, oils (after C. W. Furse), Birmingham Museums and Art Gallery · A. Bryan, pen-and-ink drawing, NPG · F. C. Gould, cartoons, repro. in *Westminster Gazette* [and published volumes] (1895–1906) · F. C. Gould and H. Furniss, caricatures, NPG · S. P. Hall, pencil sketch, NPG · Histed, photograph, NPG · Lock & Whitfield, woodburytype photograph, NPG; repro. in T. Cooper, *Men of mark: a gallery of contemporary portraits* (1881) · London Stereoscopic Co., photograph, NPG · P. May, pen-and-ink caricature, NPG · C. Pollock, plaster bust, NPG · J. Russell & Sons, photograph, NPG · Spy [L. Ward], chromolithograph caricature, NPG; repro. in *VF* (1901) · B. Stone, four photographs, NPG · E. Ward, oils, Reform Club, London · H. J. Whitlock, photograph, NPG · Who, caricature, NPG; repro. in *VF* (29 Jan 1908)
Wealth at death £126,019 1s. 6d.: probate, 16 Oct 1914, CGPLA Eng. & Wales

Chamberlain, Sir Leonard. *See* Chamberlayne, Sir Leonard (*b.* in or before 1504, *d.* 1561).

Chamberlain [Chamberlen], **Nathaniel** (*bap.* 1612), linguist and physician, was the third son of the barber–surgeon Peter *Chamberlen the younger (1572–1626) [*see under* Chamberlen family] and his wife, Sara Delaune, daughter of William *Delaune (*c.*1530–1611). He was baptized at the French church in London on 23 August 1612, and was educated at Merchant Taylors' School (1620–24). He entered Pembroke College, Oxford, in 1634, graduating BM in 1636. In his sole publication, *Tractatus de literis et lingua philosophica* (1679?), he claimed to have conceived the idea of a universal language while at Oxford and to have had the benefit of advice from two of his contemporaries at Pembroke, William Hill (1619–1667) and Thomas Hunt (1611–1683).

Chamberlain's first known employment, to which he was directed in 1643 by order of the House of Commons, was as a physician to the parliamentary army. After the civil war he lived in London for a time on friendly terms with the royalist Sir Thomas Urquhart, with whom, as he explains in the dedicatory epistle to the *Tractatus*, he frequently discussed the topic of universal language, Urquhart urging him to publish his ideas, even if they were not yet fully worked out. Chamberlain later moved to Dublin, possibly to join his elder brother Peter, who

practised medicine there, and his former fellow student William Hill, now headmaster of the grammar school. The sixteen-page *Tractatus* appeared with no date or place of publication, but has been identified as almost certainly printed in Dublin in 1679.

The work consists of three parts: a dedicatory epistle containing biographical material, a section on orthography and pronunciation, and a third on the vocabulary and grammar of philosophical (that is, scientific) language. In the epistle, Chamberlain refers to some predecessors who had displayed an interest in universal language—Francis Bacon, Thomaso Campanella, and Thomas Urquhart—but he nowhere mentions the well-known *Essay towards a Real Character, and a Philosophical Language* by John Wilkins (1619–1672); and his ignorance of such an important work suggests that what he published in the *Tractatus* was the result of conversations with Urquhart which took place many years before Wilkins's *Essay* appeared in 1668. The work, however, is reasonably sophisticated, being more than a simplified version of an existing vernacular. Chamberlain intends to produce a language in which words are iconic, denoting in their structure the properties of the object signified. Chamberlain admits, however, that if every word must accord with the nature of the thing named, then the collaborative efforts of many learned men would be required, and the task would take them many years to complete. Thomas Hunt, however, suggested that Chamberlain should begin by producing a restricted vocabulary for the use of merchants who had to visit many different parts of the world, where a universal language would be so useful; but Chamberlain preferred a more theoretical approach, based on a limited number of 'radical' words supplemented by their derivatives.

The *Tractatus* is recorded as surviving in a single copy in Marsh's library in Dublin, and has not been translated or re-edited. The work is not of major significance in the universal language movement of the seventeenth century, but is of some importance in indicating that interest in the topic did not disappear after Wilkins's *Essay* was published in 1668. Nothing further is known about Chamberlain's life.   VIVIAN SALMON

Sources V. Salmon, 'Nathaniel Chamberlain and his *Tractatus de literis et lingua philosophica*', *Language and society in early modern England* (1996), 131–40 · J. H. Aveling, *The Chamberlens and the midwifery forceps* (1882) · Register of Oxford University · Register of Merchant Taylors' School

Chamberlain, (Arthur) Neville (1869–1940), prime minister, was born on 18 March 1869 at Edgbaston, Birmingham, the only son of Joseph *Chamberlain (1836–1914) and his second wife, Florence (1847–1875), the daughter of Timothy Kenrick of Birmingham. His childhood was by all accounts very happy, although the household in which he grew to maturity was affected by profound sadness. His father's first wife, Harriet Kenrick, had died while giving birth to Neville's elder half-brother, (Joseph) Austen *Chamberlain, in 1863, and his own mother died in similar circumstances in 1875, the child on this occasion also perishing. This unquestionably left its mark on Joseph

(Arthur) **Neville Chamberlain** (1869–1940), by Bassano, 1936

Chamberlain and imposed a certain strain on his relations with his children. Neville later recalled that for many years his feelings towards his father were characterized by respect and fear rather than love, noting that few could face his 'piercing eye' with composure (Feiling, 3). It is clear, though, that Joseph Chamberlain loved all his children equally, and that despite a busy life he spent considerable time with them and was in turn adored. Furthermore, the family remained remarkably close-knit and self-contained, providing Neville with a permanent haven of security and affection.

Youth Not unnaturally, age conferred a certain distance upon the relationship between the children of the first marriage—Beatrice (*b.* 1862) and Austen (*b.* 1863)—and those of the second: Neville, Ida (*b.* 1870), Hilda (*b.* 1872), and Ethel (*b.* 1873). This was later compounded by Austen's absence at Rugby School. Neville, however, emerged as the leader of a junior family group, and in the process formed particularly close relationships with his sisters Ida and Hilda. There was also a large cousinage, mostly female, spawned by the Chamberlains' intermarriage with other members of the Unitarian and Quaker industrial aristocracy of Birmingham, which completed Neville's family circle.

His Unitarian background and upbringing made Chamberlain aware of the need to promote progress and instilled in him a profound sense of duty. He also developed an understanding of the responsibilities that wealth and privilege incur. One of his cousins later wrote: 'You may say that Neville was a born social reformer, and

brought up in an atmosphere of precept and example' (Feiling, 13). Another cousin commented: 'We always understood as children that as our lives had fallen in pleasant places it behoved us all the more to do what we could to improve the lot of those less happily placed' (NCP (Neville Chamberlain papers, University of Birmingham Library), 11/15/44, Lady Cecily Debenham to Anne Chamberlain, 11 Sept 194[1]?). In this respect, Neville was much more like his father than was Austen, who styled himself Liberal Unionist out of sentiment and respect for his father, but was at heart a 'born Conservative' (Dilks, 25).

Neville Chamberlain, on the other hand, as he indicated on accepting the leadership of the Conservative Party, remained a Liberal Unionist from conviction. On 1 June 1937 he told the party that he:

> was not born a little Conservative. I was brought up as a Liberal and afterwards as a Liberal Unionist. The fact that I am here, accepted by you Conservatives as your leader, is to my mind a demonstration of the catholicity of the Conservative Party, of that readiness to cover the widest possible field which has made it this great force in the country, and has justified the saying of Disraeli that the Conservative Party was nothing if it was not a National Party. (Ramsden, *Age of Balfour*, 356)

For Neville Chamberlain, as for his father before him, issues such as slum clearance, urban development, and the provision of schools and hospitals were vital concerns and the proper preoccupations of politicians and statesmen. He never lost sight of these goals even during the most critical international crises of his premiership, informing a Conservative conference on 12 May 1938 that it was his observance of his father's

> deep sympathy with the working classes and his intense desire to better their lot which inspired me with an ambition to do something in my turn to afford better help to the working people and better opportunities for the enjoyment of life. (Chamberlain, 210)

The extent of his genuine concern for the quality of life of ordinary people is indicated in his shock at the condition of the working classes revealed by Birmingham evacuees during 1940, which no doubt would also have made clear to him the limitations of power. There can, however, be no gainsaying his anguish at his ignorance.

Chamberlain grew up to be a man of broad interests and avocations. In his youth a keen entomologist, he later developed an even keener interest in flowers, becoming eventually a fellow of the Royal Horticultural Society. Ornithology was another of his passions, which he advanced by rising at five in the morning to learn to distinguish the songs of the various species. Even during the frenetic years of the 1930s, when occupying the most senior offices, he found time to indulge these pursuits. In 1914 he added angling to his list of hobbies. His range of interests, however, was not confined to natural history. There is probably no prime minister who knew his Shakespeare better than Chamberlain; witness his quotation from Hotspur in *1 Henry IV* at Heston Airport on leaving for Munich in 1938: that he hoped to 'pluck from this nettle danger, this flower, safety'. Moreover, he read other authors widely. Finally, he inherited from his mother's side musicality and a deep love of music.

Education The only thing that disturbed Chamberlain's childhood happiness was school. He hated the preparatory school at Rugby and Rugby School itself, where he followed his brother in 1882. He was bullied and, perhaps as a result, became somewhat shy and withdrawn, not participating in the school debating society until the period of the home rule controversy in 1886, when he spoke in his father's defence. The real cause of his dislike of Rugby may, however, simply have been the reality of living away from the family and the associated loneliness. His father's decision that he be removed from the 'classical' to the recently introduced 'modern side' did nothing to endear him to the institution. A career in business had been predetermined for him by his father, who considered that the subjects taught in the modern curriculum would be more relevant. At the end of 1886 Neville left Rugby, but there was no question of his following Austen to Cambridge. Austen had been sent there by his father and thence on an extensive tour of Europe as preparation for a career in politics; but a university education was deemed an unnecessary expense for a career in business. In this Joseph Chamberlain, although unintentionally, did Neville a great disservice. A university education would in all probability have made him a better integrated, more self-confident, and poised personality, with a capacity to project his inner warmth beyond the confines of the family and intimate friends and an ability to appreciate that there were points of view as intellectually sound as his own. He certainly had the intelligence to benefit from the university experience, which his father later recognized. Comparing his two sons in 1902, Joseph Chamberlain observed that, while he thought Austen had a fair chance of leading a government, Neville was 'the really clever one' and that if ever he became interested in a political career he 'would back him to be Prime Minister' (Dilks, 86).

Chamberlain's education was completed at Mason College, Birmingham, which became the basis for the University of Birmingham. There he studied science, metallurgy, and engineering. These were, however, disciplines which did not fully absorb him and at which he did not excel. Nevertheless, it was at this time that he developed a profound interest in natural science, reading the works of Darwin, Huxley, and Wallace. On leaving Mason College he was apprenticed to a firm of chartered accountants, being so successful there that he was offered a permanency.

Business: failure By 1890 Chamberlain was a serious young man with a very strong sense of duty, a sharp intellect, and clarity of thought. He could also empathize with the distress of the less well-favoured sections of society and he understood their needs. With these qualities he combined resilience, determination, and obstinacy, which served him surprisingly well and immediately in 1890.

Having sold the family's business interests in 1874, Joseph Chamberlain was obliged to live off the profits of his investments in order to sustain his career in politics. By 1890 his South American investments had declined considerably, and he had not had a ministerial salary for four years. He was living off capital, and therefore susceptible to the suggestion that a fortune was to be made from growing sisal in the Bahama Islands. He instructed Neville to make his way to New York and proceed thence with Austen to the Bahamas to assess the profitability of sisal culture.

On returning to Birmingham in January 1891, the two brothers reported that profits of 30 per cent could be anticipated. Joseph Chamberlain decided to go ahead, despite words of caution from his brothers and other associates, and it was determined that Neville should supervise the entire undertaking. Back in the Bahamas in May 1891, Neville decided that the island of Andros would be the best location for the Chamberlain plantation, and he arranged the purchase of the land. Unfortunately, by 1896 the worst forebodings of Joseph Chamberlain's brothers were realized, and it was necessary to wind up the business at a personal loss to Joseph Chamberlain of £50,000. It was clear that Andros and the Bahamas in general were a poor location for the cultivation of sisal on a large scale, and that much of the fibre produced was of inferior quality. This and a catastrophic fall in the price of sisal forced Neville Chamberlain to inform his father in April 1896 that:

> there is only one conclusion to be drawn ... which I do with great reluctance and with the most bitter disappointment. I no longer see any chance of making the investment pay. I cannot blame myself too much for the want of judgment. You and Austen have had to rely solely on my reports but I have been here all the time and no doubt a sharper man would have seen long ago what the ultimate result was likely to be. (NCP, 1/6/10/114, Neville Chamberlain to Joseph Chamberlain, 28 April 1896)

There can be no doubting the personal sense of failure that Chamberlain felt, but the collapse of the enterprise could not be attributed to a lack of efficiency, skill, or determination on his part. Had the Andros Fibre Company ever had any prospect of success, the energy and single-mindedness of Neville Chamberlain would have ensured it. Merely to establish the plantation, he had had to endure demanding physical conditions and undertake substantial manual work himself. In truth, no amount of ingenuity on his part could have saved the plantation from the initial and critical misjudgement that sisal would grow on Andros. The responsibility for failure was as much that of his father and brother as it was his.

Nevertheless, there were gains. Chamberlain had had to be self-reliant and learn to be confident of his judgement: as a result he became altogether much tougher and more resilient. Andros had confirmed in him too the sense of social obligation and duty to his neighbour, genuinely expressed in the anguish he felt at abandoning his good works and leaving his workers to relapse into their previous state. The solitude of Andros and the lack of sophisticated company had been a disadvantage in one sense, but it enabled him to read extensively. He took with him to Andros works by Darwin, Bagehot, George Eliot, and the botanist John Lindley. The Bible and the complete Shakespeare followed, as did other scientific, historical, and biographical material. There were also the compensations of the local fauna, which absorbed him. In many respects, Andros was his university, although a more costly one than Cambridge. Nevertheless, so much solitude and experience of dissolute whites harmed his character: his shyness and reserve were reinforced and his sense of superiority and a certain conceit of himself confirmed. Yet at the same time he had become more tolerant and had learned to cope with human frailty. Even so, he still felt the need to prove himself: home and Birmingham provided him with that opportunity.

Business: success Between 1897 and 1916 Chamberlain established himself as a leading figure in the industrial life of Birmingham. Shortly after returning to Britain from the Bahamas he secured a directorship in Elliott's Metal Company. He soon acquired a reputation for his direct involvement in all aspects of the company's operations and his willingness to consult the workforce. His main business interest, however, until his semi-retirement from the world of commerce immediately before the First World War, was the Bordesley firm of Hoskins & Son, manufacturers of ships' berths, which he bought at the end of 1897 with the help of his family. He continued, however, to be a director of Elliott's, to which he devoted one day a week, eventually becoming chairman of that company too. Later he joined the board of the Birmingham Small Arms Company, with which there was a family connection through an uncle.

At Hoskins, Chamberlain added to his reputation as a hands-on manager. His practical involvement in the day-to-day running of the business was exceptional by the standards of the day. He was, nevertheless, prepared to entrust matters to proven and trusted subordinates and became an accomplished practitioner in the art of delegation. He was accessible to his workers and solicitous of their welfare to the extent of encouraging trade union membership, in which he was considerably in advance of his contemporaries. At Elliott's, Chamberlain introduced a surgery and welfare supervisors and, after 1914, instituted a scheme of war benefits for those too badly injured to resume work and their dependants. At Hoskins he was equally innovative in welfare and reform, devising a 5 per cent bonus on production and a pension plan. When business was slack he was reluctant to lay men off. Indeed, for his time he was an exemplary employer and could justifiably take pride in the fact that he never experienced a strike.

Emerging local politician Chamberlain's conspicuous success in business, besides enabling him to purge his sense of failure in Andros, gave him a base from which to involve himself in wider aspects of Birmingham life. He was an emphatic supporter of the creation of the University of Birmingham, which owed much to the determination of his father, who became its first chancellor in 1900. An indefatigable fund-raiser on its behalf, Neville was also on the university council. Perhaps more compelling,

though, was his concern for health care. He was a member of and eventually chaired Birmingham General Hospital's board of management, and was treasurer of the Birmingham General Dispensary. As evidence of the rigour that he brought to these voluntary duties, he devised a scheme to relieve the general hospital of trivial outpatient cases that foreshadowed Lloyd George's National Insurance Act. The acceptance of this scheme was a major success for Chamberlain, and the manner in which he promoted it—meticulous planning, close attention to detail, acute grasp of the complexities of the problem, and skill as a negotiator—demonstrated many of the attributes that made him a highly respected figure in local government.

There were inevitably rumours that Chamberlain's entry into municipal or national public life was imminent. He felt, however, that he had to succeed in business and restore the financial losses of Andros before embarking on a political career. But he did speak for his father and others during election campaigns, and when his father left the Unionist government in 1903 to campaign for tariff reform Neville became 'an ardent adherent', confessing that he had for many years been a convert to the cause (NCP, 3/9/18, Neville Chamberlain to F. B. Matthews, 31 Aug 1903). As a businessman he was naturally aware of the external threat to local manufacturers, and like his father and brother he favoured imperial preference. He also took a lively interest in international developments and recognized the threat from Germany before 1914. He did not believe that the ententes concluded with France in 1904 and Russia in 1907 would do much to deter Germany, and so he became very active in the Navy League in Birmingham. He deplored reductions in the size of the army.

The year 1911 was to be a significant turning point in Chamberlain's life. First, at the comparatively advanced age of forty-one he married, in January, Anne Vere, the daughter of William Utting Cole, an army officer, after a brief courtship and engagement. Until this time he had envisaged permanent bachelorhood, but to his everlasting joy he found in Anne Cole the perfect partner, although in many respects their characters were completely antithetical. He was precise, meticulous, and in control of his emotions; she was somewhat impulsive and volatile. Nevertheless, they were a devoted couple, and Neville later claimed that he owed everything to her. In 1911 their daughter, Dorothy, was born; in 1913 their son, Frank. Anne Chamberlain found immediate favour with her husband's family and particularly with Joseph Chamberlain, but her relationship with him was short-lived, for he died on 2 July 1914.

Anne Chamberlain emphatically supported her husband's entry into politics, preferably in the House of Commons, for which she, as did many others, thought him equipped. It was not, however, the stimulus of his wife that prompted this step, but rather the passage of the Greater Birmingham Bill in 1911 and the desire to participate actively in the development of the city which its provisions made possible. In November 1911, standing as a Liberal Unionist candidate, he was elected to Birmingham city council on a manifesto that emphasized town planning, the need to develop canals and inland waterways, and the importance of improved technical education.

Local government and political apprenticeship Chamberlain's rise to pre-eminence in local government was rapid. In 1914 he was elected as alderman, and in 1915 he became lord mayor. Lloyd George later jibed that Chamberlain was 'a good mayor of Birmingham in an off year' (Taylor, 256), but Chamberlain's actions and public statements throughout this period eloquently testify to his profound concern for social reform and for the welfare of ordinary people; it was even said that 'he should have been a Labour man' (Feiling, 52). To achieve his objectives, he became practised in the arts of persuasion and conciliation.

On election Chamberlain was immediately made chairman of the town planning committee. Under his leadership and direction the first two town planning schemes in Britain were passed into law by the end of 1913. In the same year he became chairman of a special committee charged with investigating the housing conditions of Birmingham's poorest citizens. Its interim report, although accepted by the council, was not immediately implemented because of the war, but the vision remained. On becoming lord mayor in November 1915 he spoke of the need to move 'the working classes from their hideous and depressing surroundings to cleaner, brighter and more wholesome dwellings in the still uncontaminated country which lay within [the city's] boundaries' (*Birmingham Daily Post*, 10 Nov 1915).

Chamberlain's assiduity in local government ensured that his reputation for industry and efficiency spread rapidly beyond Birmingham. In 1915 Lloyd George, the newly appointed minister of munitions in the Asquith coalition, invited him to serve on the liquor control board, set up to minimize the impact of alcohol consumption on arms production. Chamberlain accepted, but after a brief period of distinguished service felt compelled to resign because service on the board was incompatible with the duties of lord mayor. Despite the constraints of wartime, his record as lord mayor was exceptional. He was indefatigable in organizing the city for war, and his schedule was punishing. Within six weeks of assuming office he had persuaded the Ministry of Munitions to underwrite the costs of increasing Birmingham's electricity supply, begun rationalizing the purchase of coal for the gas and electricity industries in the city through a joint committee, and prevented a strike by the council's workers by mediating an agreement between their leaders and the labour committee.

The lasting monuments of Chamberlain's year as lord mayor, however, were the establishment of the Birmingham Symphony Orchestra and the Birmingham Municipal Bank. The former he proposed after a concert given in Birmingham in 1916 by the Hallé Orchestra. He felt that a city of Birmingham's stature should be endowed with an orchestra of a high standard and that it should be funded partly from the rates. There was, though, an additional agenda: such an orchestra, located in a large concert hall, would, through cheaper seats, make music both accessible to a wider audience and simultaneously more self-financing. In 1919 an annual grant from the rates was voted and made possible the creation of the city orchestra.

No less socially improving was Birmingham City Bank. The government was anxious by the end of 1915 to encourage investment in war loan by a population now enjoying high wages. The essence of the problem was to persuade those who had never before saved to invest. Chamberlain thought this could be done through municipal savings associations in which the workers could invest by means of regular contributions that would be deducted at source by employers; the deposited funds, not being generally available for withdrawal until the end of the war, would be available for war loan. Interest would be guaranteed by the municipalities. Despite petty obstruction from the Treasury and objections from the banks and trade unions, his tireless lobbying eventually ensured that his scheme for municipal savings banks became law in 1916. Such was the success of the Birmingham Municipal Bank that it was made permanent by an act of parliament in 1919 with the additional power to advance mortgages to depositors. It remained in existence until 1976, the only organization of its type in the country.

Chamberlain would have liked to have achieved much more, but he recognized the limitations that war imposed and that social advance must wait. He believed that the German government's 'wicked ambitions had stayed the march of progress and had set back for an indefinite period reforms that might have bettered the lot of generations to come' (*Birmingham Daily Post*, 10 Nov 1915). Even so, his undoubted achievements and popularity were such that he was elected lord mayor for a second term. He was, however, destined never to complete it.

Director-general of national service, 1916–1917 The need for the efficient organization of manpower for both the military effort and the industrial one that would sustain it had long been one of Chamberlain's convictions. When, therefore, in December 1916 the new prime minister, Lloyd George, on the suggestion of Austen Chamberlain, offered him the newly created post of director-general of national service, he was predisposed to accept the commission and resigned as lord mayor. His remit was to recruit *volunteers* for essential war work; but, beyond that, despite three interviews with Lloyd George, he had no detailed instructions or even terms of appointment. Moreover, it was decided that he did not need a seat in the Commons. Given these difficulties, he was in a hopeless position from the start. In eight months only a few thousand volunteers were placed in employment essential for war work. The underlying problem, however, was that Lloyd George took an instant dislike to him, dismissing him as a 'pin-headed incompetent' (*Amery Diaries*, 143); the contempt was reciprocated, Chamberlain later referring to Lloyd George as a 'dirty little Welsh Attorney' (Ramsden, *Age of Balfour*, 136).

On 8 August 1917 Chamberlain resigned. This was a bitter experience, redolent, as he himself recognized, of

Andros. He had made mistakes; he should have had experience of parliament before taking such a position; he should have insisted upon a seat in the Commons; and perhaps it had been imprudent to select as his principal assistant a man unversed in the intricacies of Whitehall, Birmingham's former town clerk. Chamberlain had, though, faced insuperable obstacles from the beginning. Both his successor, Sir Auckland Geddes, and the leader of the Conservative Party, Andrew Bonar Law, later publicly recognized the extent of his difficulties and acknowledged his contribution in very constrained circumstances.

This was a depressing period in Chamberlain's life, but with the support of his family he had within weeks determined upon a parliamentary future for himself. There was, though, a further sting in the tail of the year 1917 that intensified the mortification of failure in governmental office. In December his cousin Norman, for whom he had the highest regard and great affection, was reported missing in action, and his death was confirmed in the new year. This not only reinforced Chamberlain's hatred of war, but undoubtedly also contributed to the depression which followed his unsuccessful directorship of national service. He wrote: 'My career is broken. How can a man of nearly 50, entering the House with this stigma upon him, hope to achieve anything?' (NCP, 2/20, diary, 17 Dec 1917).

Election to parliament and advance to office, 1918–1923 Chamberlain was elected to parliament in the general election of 1918 as the member for Birmingham, Ladywood, and remained a radical while sitting in the Conservative and Liberal Unionist interest. His election address urged that reconstruction should be a national enterprise that disregarded party. The best monument to the war dead would be social improvement that embraced proper pension provision, a minimum wage where necessary, shorter working hours, and a programme of state-aided housing construction. This was all consonant with his enlightened and highly acclaimed speech to the Trades Union Congress in Birmingham in September 1916. This had urged partnership between unions and employers. He was not himself averse to workers being represented on boards of directors, and he keenly advocated steadiness of employment. Neville's radicalism soon brought about a brief clash with Austen Chamberlain, by then chancellor of the exchequer in the Lloyd George coalition. Whereas Austen thought Neville 'wild', Neville thought Austen 'unprogressive and prejudiced' (NCP, 18/1/196, Neville Chamberlain to Hilda Chamberlain, 4 Jan 1919).

As a back-bencher, Chamberlain made an immediate impression, precipitating an amendment to a bill in his maiden speech. It is said that he was lucid and penetrating in argument and had a style reminiscent of his father's. He dutifully supported the Lloyd George coalition government, but, already having declined a knighthood from Lloyd George, refused a junior post in the Ministry of Health when it was offered. His detestation of Lloyd George, which had its origins in the latter's criticisms of his father during the Second South African War, was now

complete after his experience of the department of national service.

His opportunity for ministerial advancement came with the fall of the coalition in 1922. Paradoxically, the Carlton Club meeting of Conservatives, which brought about the collapse of the coalition, also marked the end of his brother's leadership of the Conservative Party and the possibility of Austen's ever becoming prime minister, for he stood loyally by Lloyd George and paid the price. For Neville, who was in Canada and was spared the embarrassment of voting against Austen, it marked the threshold of his ministerial career. Bonar Law, who now became the prime minister of a Conservative government, offered Neville the post of postmaster-general outside the cabinet. After some hesitation, precipitated by fear of offending his brother, who—he felt—might have regarded his promotion as 'the last drop of bitterness in the cup' (NCP, 18/1/370, Neville Chamberlain to Hilda Chamberlain, 31 Oct 1922), he accepted with Austen's ultimately ungrudging approval. Simultaneously, Neville was sworn of the privy council.

The new government was confirmed in the general election of November 1922, which surprisingly opened up for Chamberlain the prospect of immediate advance. The minister of health, Griffith-Boscawen, lost two seats, one in the general election and another in a by-election, which turned on the issue of rent decontrol. Law, after offering Griffith-Boscawen's post, for political reasons, to a number of senior Conservatives, was finally compelled to turn to the man he thought ideally suited to the task, and Chamberlain became minister of health in March 1923. He even named his terms: he would have complete authority over the government's policy on control of rents and would supervise housing policy. By the summer recess he had successfully put the Rent Restriction Act on the statute book. This circumscribed landlords' power to evict and related rents to the state of repair of a property. He also provided, in the Chamberlain Housing Act of 1923, a government subsidy for the construction of homes completed by October 1925. The subsidy focused on smaller properties, for their unsubsidized construction by private enterprise, which he wished to promote, would have been uneconomic. In Chamberlain's thinking it was only thus that a start could be made in providing adequate housing for the working classes. Moreover, only by building new houses could an effective policy of slum clearance be inaugurated. This act was succeeded in 1924 by Labour's Wheatley Housing Act, which increased the subsidy and shifted the emphasis to municipal building.

Chamberlain and Baldwin In May 1923 Bonar Law could no longer continue in the premiership owing to ill health, and he was succeeded by Stanley Baldwin. There followed further elevation for Chamberlain, who, in Law's estimation, would have been a strong contender for the premiership itself had he possessed longer parliamentary experience. At first Baldwin continued as chancellor, combining the office with the premiership, while he endeavoured to induce a former Liberal, Reginald McKenna, to return both to the treasury and to the Commons. When he failed, he offered the post in August to Chamberlain, by whom he had already been greatly impressed. Baldwin's first government proved the beginning of a collaboration in government between Chamberlain and Baldwin which spanned a large part of the inter-war years.

Baldwin and Chamberlain shared a business background; both had been active in local government before entering the Commons, and both entered national politics relatively late in life. But whereas Chamberlain was ruthlessly efficient and instantly decisive, Baldwin was somewhat relaxed, overcontemplative, and disinclined to come to hasty decisions. For all that, Baldwin understood people as Chamberlain never did, had an intuitive feel for the mood of the House of Commons and public opinion, and exuded common sense and goodwill. As Chamberlain put it, Baldwin had 'a singular and instinctive knowledge of how the plain man's mind works' (Ramsden, *Age of Balfour*, 295) and was essential for retaining the floating vote. Yet Chamberlain was the dominant legislative and administrative inspiration in the governments over which Baldwin presided.

Their governmental collaboration in the short term, however, was brief and without significant consequence, for Baldwin chose on 25 October 1923 to call a general election on the issue of tariff protection. Chamberlain was naturally gratified by Baldwin's conversion to protectionism and loyally supported him. The election of December 1923 was, though, for the Conservatives a disaster. Although the tariffs Baldwin envisaged would not have added to the cost of food, the opposition parties were able to play on this fear, and the Conservatives lost. They were, however, back in office in October 1924, having dropped the idea of a general tariff, and as a fully united party.

Minister of health, 1924–1929 Chamberlain had been regarded from the moment he took office as a bridge to the disaffected coalition Conservatives, and his first act in opposition was to facilitate their re-entry into the shadow cabinet. Both Neville and Austen Chamberlain became members of Baldwin's cabinet of 1924–9. Neville did not, however, return to the Treasury. A place had to be found for Winston Churchill, now a Conservative again, and it was he who became chancellor of the exchequer. This was not a disappointment. Having triumphed over Oswald Mosley in the Ladywood constituency by only the narrowest of margins, Chamberlain was very conscious of Labour's growing electoral power and was convinced that only a programme of rigorous and conspicuous social reform would secure the future of the Conservatives in government.

Chamberlain's concern with social reform was not, though, merely pragmatic and tactical: it was the mainspring of his involvement in political activity. For him social reform was essential for the social progress he believed to be desirable. Significantly, he did not consider himself to be a Conservative, and neither was his mode of thought consonant with the Conservative mind or tradition. He cannot even be placed in the Disraelian tory radical mould: he disliked Disraeli and disdained the paternalism associated with him. On the contrary, his background of Liberalism and Liberal Unionism remained with him to the end and informed his attitude towards domestic politics, where he shared many of the beliefs of the Fabian socialists. Indeed, in the formal sense Chamberlain was never even elected as a Conservative member of parliament, but rather as a candidate of the Birmingham Unionist Association. Chamberlain was a politician of radical inclinations, who having drifted towards the Conservative Party later wanted to change its name. In the wake of the formation of the National Government and the general election of 1931, which presented both Chamberlain and Baldwin with the centrist, consensual opportunity they had long wanted, Chamberlain wrote of his desire for the creation of a truly national party, which would 'discard the odious title of Conservative' (Feiling, 197). Moreover, he welcomed the secession of the free-traders from the National Government in 1932 in the anticipation that it would facilitate the formation of a 'fused party under a National name' (ibid., 216). For Chamberlain the National Government, when it came, was not a means of pursuing narrow Conservative interests, but rather a vehicle for the realization of truly national and social reform objectives.

Given this mindset, Chamberlain was in 1924 not only content, but preferred, to return to the Ministry of Health. His four and a half years there witnessed a prodigious programme of legislation, all of it conceived by the beginning of the parliament. Of the twenty-five bills he proposed to enact over four years, twenty-one were on the statute book by the time parliament was dissolved in 1929.

The two most significant pieces of legislation were the Rating and Valuation Act of 1925 and the Local Government Act of 1929. The Rating and Valuation Act was the foundation of everything Chamberlain wished to achieve in social reform. Its four main provisions were to transfer rating powers from the poor-law guardians to the county, borough, and district councils, which he viewed as 'the real living bodies of to-day' (Macleod); to institute a single basis for rating valuation; to standardize the method of assessment; and to impose quinquennial valuations. An act of this type naturally affected the interests of some in his own party, and there was considerable resistance. The Local Government Act abolished the poor-law boards of guardians and transferred their responsibilities to the county and borough councils. It also recast the relationship between national and local government. Chamberlain's principal difficulty was with Churchill, who wished to combine poor-law reform with the abolition of the rate paid by business and agriculture. After some disputation it was eventually agreed that the rate paid by manufacturers should be set at a quarter of the general rate, while agriculture should pay none at all. The loss sustained by the local authorities would be made up by a block grant from the Treasury.

These two acts were very substantial accomplishments.

They were not demagogic and 'were designed, within the framework of financial discipline, to improve the condition of the people, not to win plaudits at party conferences' (Jenkins, 339). None the less, Chamberlain received many accolades from Conservatives in the Commons for the Local Government Act, and the press was fulsome. Such was Chamberlain's record in government that by 1929 he was, with Churchill, a serious contender for the premiership. He had been in the Commons for just over a decade.

Chamberlain's second term at the Ministry of Health involved close collaboration with Churchill. Their relationship was evidently cordial and is exemplified in the passage of the Widows, Orphans, and Old Age Pensions Act of 1925. This was launched by Churchill in his budget, but it was steered through parliament by Chamberlain, who won the praise of the king for his compassionate and skilful handling of the measure. This compulsory and contributory act, which arguably built upon the achievements of the pre-1914 legislation and pointed the way to Beveridge, illustrated Chamberlain's underlying commitment to the welfare of ordinary people. His attitude towards the trade unions at the time of the general strike also indicates moderation and sympathy with the working classes. He opposed the enactment of anti-trade union legislation during the strike and favoured generosity in the aftermath. He also held trade union leaders such as Ernest Bevin, secretary of the Transport and General Workers' Union, and Arthur Pugh, chairman of the general council of the TUC, in considerable esteem.

Yet from the mid-1920s onwards an acerbity entered into Chamberlain's relationship with Labour. This was connected with the measures he introduced to curb the practice of Poplarism, namely, setting rates of poor-law relief at levels beyond necessity. The Board of Guardians (Default) Act of 1926 and the Audit (Local Authorities) Act of 1927 engendered animus on both sides, which Chamberlain displayed too publicly for Baldwin's comfort. He was rebuked by the prime minister for treating the opposition as dirt, which Chamberlain thought intellectually they were, judged by the arguments the Labour leaders deployed. The mutual antipathy and bitterness was particularly poignant, for Chamberlain was by far the most progressive member of the government. It was on the basis of his act of 1923 and Wheatley's act of 1924, that 800,000 new homes were built during Baldwin's second government and fifty-eight slum clearance schemes approved.

Opposition and the Conservative leadership crisis, 1929–1931
Before parliament was dissolved in 1929 Baldwin speculated that Chamberlain might like to move to the Treasury if the government were returned. Chamberlain declined this suggestion and volunteered his candidature for the Colonial Office. In the event, he went to the Treasury, although not until he had spent two years in opposition and a further very brief spell at the Ministry of Health.

At the general election of 1929 Chamberlain moved from the marginal seat of Birmingham, Ladywood, to the safe Conservative constituency of Birmingham, Edgbaston, which he held until his death. Out of office as a result of Baldwin's defeat at the polls, Chamberlain spent the winter months of 1929–30 in east Africa as a frustrated colonial secretary. On his return from east Africa, however, he began looking to the future. Baldwin was prevailed upon in March 1930 to accept the formation of an inner shadow cabinet committee of business, and it was also agreed that Chamberlain should become the head of a new Conservative Party research department, of which he was the real founder. He retained the post until his death in 1940. In June 1930 he became chairman of the Conservative Party.

The years of opposition between 1929 and 1931 were a period of crisis for the Conservative Party, as the leadership of Baldwin was under constant attack. Baldwin's temperament and style were not suited to opposition, and Chamberlain himself was forced to alert him to the discontent at his lack of drive. Chamberlain's position was invidious, for many of Baldwin's critics would have liked him to replace Baldwin. The difficulty was compounded by the hostility of the press magnate Lord Beaverbrook, who underpinned his personal dislike for Baldwin with a campaign for empire free trade, which in essence meant tariffs and imperial preference. During the election of 1929 the Conservative government had committed itself to imperial preference, but with the proviso that protective taxation on food should be excluded. Beaverbrook, on the other hand, after the election, argued that there should be a referendum on the issue of food taxes, ran crusader candidates in by-elections to campaign for one, and for a brief period organized his own United Empire Party. Beaverbrook, in harness with the other great press magnate, Lord Rothermere, was a formidable adversary and even induced Baldwin in the end to concede the referendum. Even so, despite the mediation of Chamberlain, who was himself, of course, by no means averse to tariffs and imperial preference, Beaverbrook could not be induced to end his attacks. In June 1930, at Caxton Hall, Baldwin put his leadership to the test at a meeting of the Conservative Party. The overwhelming vote of confidence that Baldwin received was gratifying, but it did not bring the question of his leadership to a final determination.

On balance, Chamberlain conducted himself with great dignity throughout this crisis. He insisted that he would not play Lloyd George to Baldwin's Asquith, but was at the same time made aware that his position was strong. In July 1930 Rothermere plainly indicated to him that, if he were to become leader of the Conservative Party, he could rely upon his and Beaverbrook's complete support. The 'commonest loyalty' made it impossible for him to entertain such a suggestion, but the tragedy of it was 'that if S. B. would go the whole party would heave a sigh of relief' (Feiling, 180). From all sides Chamberlain was repeatedly alerted to the lack of confidence in Baldwin; so much so, that in February 1931 he felt compelled to confront his leader with a memorandum on the state of party opinion drawn up by the Conservatives' chief agent, Robert Topping. This argued that since the Caxton Hall speech Baldwin's position had steadily deteriorated and could not now be ignored. Given Chamberlain's own view of Baldwin, this memorandum could not have been totally unwelcome, for it also implied that he should be the next leader. After showing the document to senior Conservatives, on the rather disingenuous ground that he wanted to canvass their advice on whether Baldwin should see it, he sent it to him on 1 March 1931. On the afternoon of the same day he confirmed to Baldwin that the memorandum represented the views of his colleagues. Baldwin agreed that he should retire and that the announcement would be made at the shadow cabinet on the following day. *The Times* even prepared an appropriate leader.

The forthcoming by-election in the St George's division of Westminster had made it all the more necessary for Baldwin to see the Topping memorandum. This was particularly favourable ground for a Beaverbrook/Rothermere candidate, and if one had been elected it would have badly damaged Baldwin's leadership and the Conservative Party. By 1 March 1931 the press lords had an empire crusade candidate in place, but the official Conservative candidate had withdrawn. Having been dissuaded from retirement by his confidants, Baldwin informed Chamberlain on 2 March that 'he would go down fighting' and that he would do so by standing as the official candidate for St George's. To Chamberlain's remonstrance that he could not do this because of the effect upon his successor, he replied: 'I don't give a damn about my successor, Neville' (Jenkins, 42). This was a critical point, both for the defeat of Baldwin's opponents and for the future relationship between Baldwin and Chamberlain. Baldwin would retire when he was ready to do so and would not be pushed. As it happened, Baldwin did not have to resign his Bewdley constituency and Duff Cooper fought St George's as the official Conservative. To his credit, and whatever his personal feelings of disappointment, Chamberlain furnished Cooper with every support that the Conservative Party could provide. Baldwin, for his part, aided his own cause by a resounding speech at Queen's Hall in which he denounced the meretricious conduct of the press lords and asked the electors to reflect that they were not so much asked to consider who should lead the Conservative Party, but to determine who should appoint the leader. Duff Cooper was elected with a majority of 5000.

Economic crisis The internal wrangling within the Conservative Party was played out against the backdrop of the economic crisis that finally caused in 1931 the fall of Ramsay MacDonald's second Labour government. By that year unemployment had risen to two and a half million. Moreover, in July 1931 the loss of foreign confidence in the British financial and economic system was demonstrated by the withdrawal from the City of some £66 million in gold and foreign exchange. Chamberlain diagnosed the core of the problem in the growth of government expenditure over income. This was borne out by the report of the May committee on national expenditure, which recommended economies of £96.5 million, to be achieved by

reducing official salaries and unemployment expenditures. It was a programme that the Labour government could not put into effect. Neither could they devise any other strategy that would revive confidence and secure a foreign loan. The resources of the Conservative Research Department were fully employed by Chamberlain in preparing 'for debates in which Labour was impaled on a series of ever more difficult hooks of financial policy' (Ramsden, *Appetite for Power*, 280). Both Baldwin and Chamberlain had rejected earlier suggestions by MacDonald regarding the formation of a coalition government, but by the end of July Chamberlain had probably come round to thinking that a national government would be in the nation's best interests. The determination of Baldwin to continue his holidays at this critical juncture left the conduct of Conservative strategy in the hands of Chamberlain, who perhaps underestimated Conservative strength in persuading MacDonald to remain as prime minister. A national government under MacDonald was announced on 24 August 1931. Philip Snowden remained chancellor of the exchequer, while Chamberlain returned to the Ministry of Health. The fundamental objective of the government was the maintenance of the parity of the pound and the imposition of economies, after which parliament would be dissolved and party politics would resume as normal.

Events, however, ensured that the National Government became permanent for the duration of the 1930s. The parity of sterling had to be abandoned on 19 September, when the government abandoned the gold standard. Furthermore, the reaction to the economies introduced by the government—the Invergordon mutiny and demonstrations involving clashes with the police—convinced Chamberlain that the emphatic approval of public opinion should be sought through a general election for any further measures deemed necessary. Provided that MacDonald would accept tariffs, he was happy for him to remain prime minister, for the continuance of MacDonald in office would probably make it that much easier to gain the electorate's endorsement. The final appeal to the country, though, was a curious mixture. The parties fought for their own policies, while the government sought a 'doctor's mandate', or, more accurately expressed, a free hand. Given that the Conservatives were committed to tariffs, and given that they were the overwhelming beneficiaries of the election of October 1931, the government would henceforth be committed to tariffs.

Chancellor of the exchequer, 1931–1937: tariffs, reparations, and budgets In the Commons the National Government was now supported by 473 Conservatives, which meant that they could demand a larger number of cabinet posts. Chamberlain went to the Treasury, where he remained for five and a half years. He proved a powerful chancellor of the exchequer. Baldwin, who as leader of the Conservatives was happy to leave formal power in the hands of MacDonald, left the substance of power in Chamberlain's hands. From the beginning Chamberlain was in complete control of budgetary and economic policy and added to that social and industrial policy as well. Furthermore, once the international crisis of the 1930s deepened, he became a dominant voice in both rearmament and foreign policy. His was a formidable presence in the cabinet: not only did he read his own departmental briefs, but he seemed to read everyone else's as well. With considerable justification he confided to his diary in spring 1935: 'I am more and more carrying this government on my back. The P.M. is ill and tired, S. B. is tired and won't apply his mind to problems. It is certainly time there was a change' (NCP, 2/23a, diary, 8 March 1935).

Chamberlain took immediate steps to achieve the protection of the home market and with it the realization of his father's ambitions. First came the Abnormal Importations Act and then in February 1932 the general tariff of 10 per cent. This had several purposes: to improve the balance of payments deficit, to raise revenue, to stabilize sterling, and to decrease unemployment. This was an emotional occasion for Chamberlain, who made his feelings clear to the Commons. He stated:

> There can have been few occasions in all our long political history when the son of a man who counted for something in his day and generation has been vouchsafed the privilege of setting the seal on the work which the father began but had perforce to leave unfinished.   (*Hansard 5C*, 261.296)

Austen ventured to the Treasury bench to shake his brother's hand; the Commons gave him a tumultuous reception. Significantly, dominion goods were exempted from the tariff pending the Ottawa conference of July and August that year, when it was hoped to institute a regime of imperial preference. Baldwin led the delegation, but it was Chamberlain as usual who was the workhorse, subjecting his colleagues to endless preparatory seminars during the passage across the Atlantic. The dominion governments were, however, much less enthusiastic and more concerned with their national interests than with imperial economic unity. All that really emerged was a declaration of intent which affirmed the belief that the reduction or elimination of empire tariff barriers would increase trade and commended the agreements achieved at Ottawa as steps in the right direction. It could be said cynically that 'enough discrimination was achieved to give the Americans a running grievance, but not enough to produce any great stimulation of Empire trade' (Jenkins, 348).

In 1932 Chamberlain attended the Lausanne conference on reparations that ran from June to July. His favoured outcome was the cancellation all round of both reparations and war debts, for which he bid at the opening session. Here, however, he ran into the objections of the French. Yet he managed to establish good working relations with the French prime minister, Herriot, and with the Germans. Owing to his mediation, it proved possible in the end to achieve agreement on a final lump sum to be paid by the Germans and a political statement that stressed the importance of improved political relations for financial confidence.

The first of Chamberlain's budgets, introduced in April 1932, was castigated for its severity, although it could be argued that it merely continued the austerity introduced by Snowden's emergency budget of September 1931, with the addition of the 5 per cent cut in police pay that had been initially and accidentally omitted. His main purpose was to build up the gold and foreign currency reserves as a means of maintaining the stability of sterling, for which purpose he made provision to borrow up to £150 million to create the exchequer equalization account. The prospective deficit of £35 million he surmised would mostly be covered by the general tariff and the reimposition of the tax on tea. His strategy was to continue economies until expenditure and revenue were balanced. His caution was predicated on the prevailing economic orthodoxy, although it remains fashionable to criticize his lack of vision. Perhaps his major achievement in this year of frenetic activity was to save the exchequer £40 million in interest charges by converting £2000 million of war loan at 5 per cent to 3.5 per cent stock. This was an important prerequisite for the cheap money policy of the 1930s that greatly contributed to the decade's housing construction boom.

Similar budgetary discipline followed, until by 1934 Chamberlain spoke of the possibility of moving from *Bleak House* to *Great Expectations*. He reduced the standard rate of income tax by 6*d*. (2.5 per cent), restored the cut in unemployment benefit, and began restoring the cuts in the pay of state and local government employees. In the following year he confidently asserted that the nation had recovered 80 per cent of its prosperity. In essence, Chamberlain had aimed in his financial policy both at deflation sufficient to restore confidence and, by maintaining purchasing power in the economy, at inflation sufficient to promote recovery. He had done so with considerable courage and success, making his record as chancellor impressive. His economic policy was not, though, one of classic *laissez-faire*. He believed in the control of markets and in using the power of government to determine the structure of industry. Two examples of this were the protection and cartelization of the iron and steel industry, which led to increased production, and the creation of the London Passenger Transport Board, with a subsidy of £35 million from the public purse, which presided over what was then the world's most efficient underground system. Nevertheless, the entwined problems of unemployment, low wages, and poverty remained, and from within the Conservative ranks Harold Macmillan criticized the government for not doing enough. From outside the Conservative Party, the Next Five Years Group was also highly critical.

By 1935 Chamberlain felt that he was increasingly shouldering the burden of government and thought it was time for a change of leadership. He observed to his sister Hilda:

> As you will see I have become a sort of Acting P.M.—only without the actual power of the P.M. I have to say 'Have you thought' or 'What would you say' when it would be quicker to say 'This is what you must do'.   (NCP, 18/1/910A, Neville Chamberlain to Hilda Chamberlain, 23 March 1935)

The precipitous decline in MacDonald's ability to preside

over the government did not, however, result in Chamberlain's elevation to the premiership in June 1935, although that would have been favoured by many. Baldwin succeeded and led the government into the general election victory of 1935. But Chamberlain was the principal author of the government's manifesto, though he had not been able, as he wished, to put defence to the forefront as an issue in the election. At the same time Chamberlain recognized that Baldwin's ability to reassure the electorate was a major element in the result. The prime minister, though, was soon buffeted by the crisis created by the Hoare–Laval pact, and throughout 1936 his health so deteriorated that he announced that he would retire in May 1937. There was little doubt that Chamberlain would succeed him. Following the Conservative Party conference at Margate in October 1936, Chamberlain noted in his diary that his position as heir apparent and acting prime minister seemed to be generally accepted. In the abdication crisis of 1936 he showed himself very apprehensive of Edward VIII's succession, which he thought unsafe, and backed Baldwin in his handling of the issue.

Becomes prime minister, 1937 Thus when Chamberlain became prime minister on 28 May 1937 it was George VI's hands that he kissed. It had proved an effortless succession, but it proved a far from effortless premiership. Chamberlain brought instant control to the business of government. As chancellor of the exchequer he had assumed a certain responsibility for ensuring that ministers were appropriately active, and he could now do this with all the authority of his office. Almost his first prime ministerial act was to ask ministers to inform him of their departmental plans for the coming two years. He read all cabinet papers assiduously and chaired all the major cabinet committees, in particular the foreign policy committee and the committee of imperial defence. His mastery of government business was prodigious. His main aid in this was Sir Horace Wilson, who kept Chamberlain briefed of departmental actions and who rendered the mass 'of information to the coherence necessary for effective supervision' (Beattie, 223). Wilson's official role was that of chief industrial adviser to the government, but he had been brought into Downing Street by Baldwin in a general advisory capacity and was retained by Chamberlain in that role. Given, however, that the main problems that faced the Chamberlain government were external, he increasingly focused his attention on foreign affairs.

Chamberlain's management of the cabinet was not in fact authoritarian. He seldom spoke first, but was able to influence decisions by his capacity to reduce complex discussions to lucid conclusions in masterly summings-up—which led Lord Swinton to liken his mind to a searchlight. Chamberlain was also able to impress his views on the cabinet as a whole through an inner cabinet, which consisted of himself, Simon, Lord Halifax, and Hoare.

By the time he became prime minister, certain traits in Chamberlain's character had become marked. He was very averse to criticism, wanted to be in control, and was susceptible to flattery. The conviction that he was right undoubtedly contributed to his failure to court public and parliamentary support. Attention to public opinion and elections were low on his list of priorities, and he never socialized in the Commons smoking rooms. The importance of mollifying opposition with soothing language was not for him essential to the presentation of policy. He was, therefore, very easily misrepresented by opponents as cold, austere, and dictatorial.

Yet, at the same time Chamberlain was very concerned that government policy should be presented properly, as he saw it, by the media. He recognized the power of modern methods of communication and became an adept performer on contemporary newsreels. Moreover, he perceived radio's potential as a means of creating popular support for governmental policy. It could, however, also be used to stimulate opposition, and by broadcasting talks critical of other countries, most notably Nazi Germany, it could damage the outcome of foreign policy. Thus governmental pressure ensured that such talks were cancelled or redrafted in such a way as to make them quite anodyne. With regard to the press, Chamberlain was the first British prime minister to practise news management on a substantial scale. The primary objective of this activity was to suppress opposition to foreign policy and to facilitate its success. Through George Steward, head of the press office at 10 Downing Street, the political journalists at Westminster, who constituted the lobby, were gradually organized so that they became disseminators of the official line rather than journalists competitively seeking news and other stories.

Appeasement of Nazi Germany and fascist Italy In the wake of the Rhineland crisis in 1936, Chamberlain wrote to one of his sisters:

> If we could once get this trouble behind us and start Europe on a new basis we should I believe see a rapid expansion in trade for the undertone is firm and enterprise is just waiting for the restoration of confidence to go ahead. (NCP, 18/1/952, Neville Chamberlain to Hilda Chamberlain, 21 March 1936)

This was the agenda that Chamberlain would have preferred for his premiership; completion of recovery from the recession and further social reform on the basis provided by recovery. He could not, however, begin to contemplate such an agenda until the tensions in Europe provoked by the belligerence of Nazi Germany and fascist Italy had been resolved. In the past it has been suggested that he attempted to achieve this by introducing and pursuing the policy of appeasement.

Chamberlain did not, however, produce appeasement as a new policy initiative. On the contrary, appeasement had evolved steadily as the foreign policy of the National Government from 1931 until 1936, when it assumed its classic form. What Chamberlain did after 1937 was to inject the policy with some vigour in the hope all the sooner to end the crisis created in Europe by the Nazi clamour for revision of the treaty of Versailles. For Chamberlain and his colleagues appeasement implied the object of policy—namely, the pacification of Europe—to be achieved through negotiating a European and general settlement that would in almost all respects replace the treaty of Versailles and bring Germany into satisfactory treaty relations with all her neighbours. Appeasement was a policy that sought to bring about genuine peace in Europe by removing all sources of grievance in a Europe-wide agreement to which Germany would also make appropriate contributions. It was not a craven, cowardly policy of surrender and unilateral concession, or a sell out, as it was later described. The essence of this policy was first suggested by the Foreign Office officials Orme Sargent and Frank Ashton-Gwatkin in 1931 and received the full backing of the permanent under-secretary, Sir Robert Vansittart. It was, however, too ambitious to be pursued in the first instance in all its aspects. Not until 1935, when Hitler's unilateral denunciation of the disarmament clauses of the treaty of Versailles further deepened the European crisis, did the Foreign Office resume the recommendation of such a policy. It was subsequently adopted by the government in the early months of 1936.

The type of general settlement contemplated was the supplementation of the Locarno treaty arrangements with an air pact, in which France and Germany would guarantee Britain in addition to one another. As part of the deal, the demilitarized Rhineland zone would disappear. There would also be an arms limitation agreement. Provided that her aims were peacefully accomplished, Germany's preponderant interest in central and eastern Europe would be recognized. Finally, Britain would undertake not to impede the expansion of Germany's exports. For the time being it was deemed imprudent to raise the question of colonies or Germany's return to the League of Nations. On 6 March 1936, as an opening move, Anthony Eden, the foreign secretary, broached the issue of an air pact with the German ambassador, but on the following day Hitler remilitarized the Rhineland unilaterally. Although this denied Eden and the government a valuable concession, thereby placing them at a disadvantage in the negotiations they wished to start, it did not mean that those negotiations would not now be attempted. On the contrary, Eden thought them inevitable. Successive foreign secretaries—Simon, Hoare, and Eden—had all been complicit in the formulation of this policy, as had Chamberlain, on account of his dominating position in the cabinet and his office at the Treasury, where he had to bear in mind the financial implications of the rearmament necessary as long as Germany remained overtly dissatisfied and belligerent.

Chamberlain and foreign policy Chamberlain also played a critical role in the early stages of rearmament made essential by Japanese aggression in the Far East and the reality of Nazi rule in Germany. Given the absence of a co-ordinating defence ministry, he was the arbiter of the forces' competing claims on the meagre funds available. He was unable to allow the costs of the full programme recommended by the defence requirements sub-committee (DRC) in 1934 and determined that the bulk of the spending should be allocated to aerial rearmament. The strength of the Royal Air Force was, therefore, to be increased by 50 per cent. Connected with this decision

was his endorsement of the DRC's reversal of strategic priorities which now established Germany rather than Japan as the ultimate potential enemy. Chamberlain was, nevertheless, conscious of the threat posed to British interests in the Far East, and in agreement with the views of the head of the Treasury, Sir Warren Fisher, advocated the revival of the Anglo-Japanese alliance (1902–22), in substance though not necessarily in form. Here, however, he ran into the opposition of Vansittart, who deprecated the impact that such a course would have on American opinion.

As Chamberlain's private papers testify, the German menace remained a constant preoccupation, leading to a further revision of the defence estimates. The defence white papers of 1936 and 1937, of which he was the principal author, outlined a rearmament programme costing £1500 million over a five-year period, £400 million of which was to be found from borrowing. These statements contemplated substantial increases in the strength of all the armed forces, with the RAF having a front-line strength of 1750 aircraft. To pay for this Chamberlain raised income tax to 5s. in the pound in the budget of 1937, which he justified to the public at large in a Pathé newsreel item that for its time was a skilful performance. He was not so successful with his attempt to tax the *growth* in profits attendant upon rearmament. His proposed national defence contribution aroused firm opposition and had to be replaced with a straightforward tax on profits.

During the year before he became prime minister Chamberlain intervened decisively on three occasions in foreign policy. First, he gave a decisive lead in winding up sanctions against Italy, imposed during the Italo-Abyssinian War of 1935–6. On 5 May 1936 Italian forces entered Addis Ababa and the war was over. The lifting of sanctions posed a great moral problem as a member state of the League of Nations had been denied its independence. On the other hand, Germany, having taken advantage of the Abyssinian crisis to remilitarize the Rhineland in March 1936, continued to menace the peace of Europe. The maintenance of sanctions appeared in the circumstances gratuitous folly—a measure likely to increase Britain's number of enemies. Aware that Eden, the foreign secretary, had been persuaded of the intellectual case for dropping sanctions, Chamberlain elected to give a lead. In a speech on 10 June 1936 at the 1900 Club he spoke of the maintenance of sanctions as 'the very midsummer of madness' (Dutton, *Anthony Eden*, 73).

The other two occasions were not public, and both involved the nature of the response that Britain should make to Germany's claim for colonial equality of rights made in connection with her putative return to the League of Nations during the fallout from the remilitarization of the Rhineland. The committee chaired by Lord Plymouth to investigate the issue concluded that, while there were practical, legal, and economic difficulties in the way of returning colonies to Germany, the subject could not be avoided if a general settlement were to be achieved. Although Eden pleaded the case for a flat negative, Chamberlain's arguments in the cabinet committee on foreign policy were decisive, and in a Commons statement at the end of July 1936 the question was effectively left open.

In the following month Hjalmar Schacht, the German minister of economics, told French ministers that in return for colonial satisfaction Hitler would agree to arms limitation and a European settlement. The Foreign Office, however, was sceptical of this approach, arguing that, if Germany wanted to achieve a settlement, this should be negotiated through the established diplomatic channels. Subsequently, the department effectively stifled any further contact with Schacht without any explanation to the cabinet. Within the Treasury this had a devastating impression. Sir Frederick Leith-Ross, the chief economic adviser to the government, was, in the course of his duties, in regular contact with Schacht, and he learned from the latter that serious proposals had been frustrated by Eden and the Foreign Office. Sir Warren Fisher, for his part, was most disparaging of the competence of the Foreign Office, and Chamberlain was undoubtedly prompted towards a similarly unflattering view. Through Chamberlain it was decided that Leith-Ross should visit Schacht in Germany to explore the latter's suggestions more fully. Excitedly, Chamberlain wrote that he had 'a scheme in hand' which ultimately might restrain Hitler (NCP, 18/1/991, Neville Chamberlain to Ida Chamberlain, 6 Jan 1937). When the cabinet committee on foreign policy discussed Leith-Ross's visit to Badenweiler in March 1937, it was Chamberlain's voice again that moulded policy. He commented that he understood that Eden shared his view that, if a general settlement could be achieved on the back of a colonial deal, such a procedure should not be ruled out. With regard to the suggestions made by Schacht, he emphasized:

> Any government which turned down this invitation without at least exploring the possibilities sufficiently to make sure that there was no possible basis of agreement would incur a very heavy responsibility. Even a slight improvement in the international atmosphere may lead gradually to a general 'détente', whereas a policy of drift may lead to a general war. (Crozier, 201–3)

It was decided, therefore, to try to advance on the basis of the Schacht proposals. In the event, it proved impossible. The French were by spring 1937 less willing to proceed, and the reality anyway was that Schacht had exceeded his function.

First steps towards a general settlement By the time he became prime minister Chamberlain dominated the formulation of foreign policy. His involvement and interest were not new. He had been regularly informed by the foreign secretary about the international situation, and there was a strong identity of view between the two. Chamberlain continued the effort to secure a general settlement, but he doubted the willingness of the Foreign Office to play its part. He wrote that, in his opinion, 'the double policy of rearmament and better relations with Germany and Italy will carry us through if only the

F.O. will play up' (NCP, 18/1/1010, Neville Chamberlain to Hilda Chamberlain, 1 Aug 1937). Within the Treasury there was a firm conviction that the Foreign Office had missed an opportunity of coming to terms with Hitler, a major reason being the slow British response to the Schacht initiative. By August 1937 there was a feeling that the Foreign Office was 'frigid' and that a 'fresh start' was required (Crozier, 205). This was emphatically the opinion of Sir Warren Fisher and unquestionably that of Chamberlain, who was fortified in his views by Sir Samuel Hoare.

Chamberlain, therefore, wished to reinvigorate the policy of reaching a general settlement with Germany by himself taking, as prime minister, a more active role in foreign policy. Eden does not at first seem to have resented this. By December 1937, however, their relationship was undergoing considerable strain. For Chamberlain the principal object of foreign policy was to bring Germany, the main potential danger facing Britain, into a general European settlement. This ambition he believed would be achieved more easily if Britain and Italy were able to settle their differences, for such a development might also arrest the growing intimacy between Rome and Berlin. Finally, it would be important to complete the British rearmament programme, although within the necessary financial constraints. Germany was the central problem. As Chamberlain wrote: 'if only we could get on terms with Germany I would not care a rap for Musso' (Feiling, 329). It was, though, with Italy that he first attempted to improve relations.

Chamberlain and Eden, 1937–1938 During summer 1937, much to Chamberlain's annoyance, Eden continued to assess Italy as a greater threat to Britain than Germany and still hoped that the latter could be brought into a general settlement. It was, however, Eden who suggested to Chamberlain in July that a personal letter to Mussolini might be the way to start an improvement in Anglo-Italian relations. Eden thought he himself should write it, but Chamberlain pre-empted him, possibly because he thought the foreign secretary was showing insufficient urgency. But Eden resented this action, which he considered to be an interference, and the incident was the first breach in what had hitherto been a harmonious relationship. It was not, however, possible to make immediate progress in improving Anglo-Italian relations because the Nyon conference took firm measures to counter acts of Italian submarine piracy in the western Mediterranean connected with Italian intervention on the side of the nationalists in the Spanish Civil War.

An opening, however, to improved relations with Germany suggested itself when in November 1937 Lord Halifax, then lord president of the council, was invited by Göring to visit a hunting exhibition in Berlin. Far from opposing the visit, Eden in the first instance encouraged it, and Chamberlain was naturally enthusiastic. But, prompted by Foreign Office staff, Eden later raised objections, especially when it was learned that Hitler would receive Lord Halifax only at Berchtesgaden, an arrangement he felt redolent of servility if accepted. His differences over the Halifax visit eventually came to a heated disagreement with Chamberlain, but Eden eventually accepted that it might bring positive results.

An immediate consequence of this disagreement was that Chamberlain finally took the opportunity, as he put it, to stir up the Foreign Office 'with a long pole' (Crozier, 225). Vansittart, who had demurred at the prospect of the Halifax visit, was removed from the day-to-day running of the Foreign Office and elevated to the specially created rank of chief diplomatic adviser. He was replaced by Sir Alexander Cadogan, who was very enthusiastic for a policy of direct engagement with the dictators. Undoubtedly, the prime minister was determined that Vansittart should not inhibit contact with Göring as he had previously done with Schacht. Chamberlain, though, was a little unfair to Vansittart. The latter supported his policy towards Italy and had played a decisive part in formulating the government's policy towards Germany. He, therefore, had some justification for telling Chamberlain that he had always favoured his foreign policy, 'but had been obstructed by others!' (NCP, 18/1/1031, Neville Chamberlain to Ida Chamberlain, 12 Dec 1937). Chamberlain, however, did not believe him.

Lord Halifax concluded from his visit to Germany that Hitler and the German government might be amenable to a general settlement if Germany were conceded colonial satisfaction. Chamberlain was very satisfied; contact had been made and a picture of the German attitude obtained. It seemed that colonies had now assumed rather greater importance in the minds of the Germans, but nothing could be done without a German quid pro quo or French consent. At the end of November 1937 the French prime minister and foreign minister visited London for talks at which there was a large measure of agreement about the nature of a general settlement, and the French proved surprisingly compliant in the matter of colonies.

During December 1937 the cabinet also considered the financial implications of rearmament. It was decided to accept the £1500 million quinquennial estimate and not to exceed it, on the grounds that too lavish an expenditure on rearmament might damage the economy. Moreover, as British participation in any war against a major power was likely to result in a long-drawn-out war of attrition, it was thought best to maintain her financial resources intact. Finance now emerged as the fourth arm of Britain's defence preparations. During the same month the chiefs of staff reported that Britain's forces were still insufficiently developed to meet her global commitments: although Britain's forces could probably act as a deterrent to Germany, the nub of the problem was that a war with Germany would in all probability extend as well to war with Italy and Japan. This, therefore, emphasized the need to reduce the number of Britain's potential enemies.

On 24 January 1938 Chamberlain presented to the cabinet committee on foreign policy a scheme for a new approach to Germany in which the colonial question had been placed at the forefront. None the less, Chamberlain emphasized that the colonial question could not be settled independently of a general settlement; to meet the objections that other countries might raise to the renewal of German colonial activity he proposed the institution of a new colonial regime in Africa south of the Sahara and north of South Africa and the Rhodesias, in which all colonial powers would subscribe to a uniform code of colonial administration. Chamberlain's aim was to stimulate German interest in a general settlement by offering to negotiate in principle the prior settlement of the colonial question. It was agreed to accept this approach, and the British ambassador in Berlin was to broach this whole issue with Hitler in spring 1938.

By this time Eden had resigned. His resignation was not founded upon some great issue of principle connected with Germany. If his confidant, Oliver Harvey, thought that negotiations with Germany could only be beneficial, provided that they resulted in a general settlement, Eden's view would not have been that far distant. His resignation was based rather upon Chamberlain's rejection out of hand of a rather hazy proposal from President Roosevelt for a conference in Washington to discuss issues relating to world peace. Chamberlain felt this would cut across his own efforts to secure agreements with the European dictators, and, in any case, he doubted whether the United States government would contribute anything effective to world peace. Eden, who had throughout 1937 been pursuing the chimera of close Anglo-American co-operation, was furious with Chamberlain. Had the Roosevelt proposal not been secret, Eden would probably have resigned on that issue.

Eden was, however, provided with another opportunity when Chamberlain determined to press ahead with an Anglo-Italian agreement in February 1938. This was accompanied by some rather unorthodox manoeuvring involving contacts with the Italians via Lady Ivy Chamberlain, Sir Austen's widow, who was spending the winter in Rome, and Neville's angling companion, Sir Joseph Ball, a former MI5 official but now director of the Conservative Research Department. Eden was convinced that he was being sidelined. He also felt that Italy's position was worsening as a result of her involvement in Abyssinia and Spain and the threatened absorption of Austria by Germany. Thus it was unnecessary to court the treacherous Italians too assiduously. Chamberlain felt, however, that delay would result in yet another lost opportunity. On 20 February Eden resigned and was succeeded by Lord Halifax. On 16 April 1938 an Anglo-Italian agreement was concluded in which Britain undertook to recognize the Italian conquest of Abyssinia, while Italy agreed to accept a British scheme for the withdrawal of the so-called Italian volunteers assisting the nationalist forces in the Spanish Civil War. In the long run this agreement proved worthless, in the sense that it did nothing to deter Italy from ever closer involvement with Germany.

The offer to Germany of a general settlement and the Czechoslovakia crisis, 1938 The approach to Germany did not even produce an agreement. When Sir Nevile Henderson, British ambassador in Berlin, outlined to Hitler on 3 March 1938 the British proposals, it was to be the first and last occasion on which the offer of a general settlement was put directly to the German government. Henderson did not use the term, out of deference to Hitler's hostility to it, but that was what he clearly implied in both this interview and a previous one with Ribbentrop on 1 March. The interview was to prove a complete fiasco for British policy. The Führer bluntly rejected any possibility of being brought into a general settlement in exchange for a colonial settlement. This and the *Anschluss* of Austria and Germany effected by force a few days later were depressing results for Chamberlain's policy. Both the Foreign Office and Chamberlain were reconciled to the idea that it might not be possible to maintain Austria's independence in the long term, but the manner of its achievement was an ugly portent for the future. Furthermore, Chamberlain had failed to wrest the initiative from Hitler, who now proceeded to encourage the Sudeten German separatists in Czechoslovakia.

On 24 March 1938 Chamberlain, in a speech to the Commons, reviewed the situation following the *Anschluss*. After referring to the 'disturbance of international confidence' created by the German action, he mentioned the demands of the German minority in Czechoslovakia as one of the issues continuing to give rise to anxiety. A peaceful resolution of the problem could, however, do much to advance stability in central Europe. Reviewing Britain's defence commitments, he stated that a British guarantee of Czech independence would not be advisable, for it would effectively remove from the British government control over the decision on whether to go to war. But, he continued:

> Where peace and war are concerned, legal obligations are not alone involved, and if war broke out, it would be unlikely to be confined to those who have assumed such obligations. It would be quite impossible to say where it would end and what Governments might become involved. (*Hansard 5C*, 333.1405–6)

This was a clear warning to the German government of what might happen if they had recourse to force to solve the question of the German minority in Czechoslovakia. It also implied the threat of dragging Germany into a world war, a theme enlarged upon by Lord Lothian in a speech to Chatham House on the same day.

The situation in Czechoslovakia, however, continued to deteriorate. Chamberlain still aimed to bring Germany into a general settlement, but progress in that direction could not be achieved while uncertainty persisted in German–Czech relations. Lord Runciman was sent to mediate. On 5 September 1938 President Benes virtually conceded all the demands in the Karlsbad programme; this offer, though, was rejected by Henlein, the leader of the Sudeten Germans. On 12 September, in a speech at Nuremberg, Hitler demanded self-determination for the Sudetens and promised them all assistance. One central problem for Britain was the fact that France was pledged to defend the territorial integrity of Czechoslovakia. Chamberlain himself recognized that, if France became embroiled in a war with Germany over central Europe, Britain would be in a difficult and dangerous situation, for she could not afford to see France destroyed. Britain might, therefore, become involved in a war before she was

ready. On the other hand, Chamberlain suspected that the French were not prepared to honour their obligations to the Czechs, and this perception encouraged him in his belief that it was his duty to solve the Czech question. On 13 September he decided to activate a plan already conceived at the end of August; he would see Hitler personally, and on 15 September he flew to Germany, where he met Hitler at Berchtesgaden. It was the first time in his life that he had flown. At Berchtesgaden he accepted in principle the proposition of self-determination and secession of non-Czech areas, subject to endorsement by the cabinet, and Hitler agreed to refrain from using force.

Upon Chamberlain's return to London, the cabinet quickly agreed with the principle of secession combined with a guarantee of Czechoslovakia's new frontiers. Chamberlain informed his colleagues of his impression that Hitler's ambitions were limited and that he was sincere when he said that he wanted only a solution of the Sudeten problem. On 18–19 September the French prime minister and foreign minister flew to London and endorsed Chamberlain's proposals. The French subsequently informed the Czechs that the French government would not honour its alliance obligation to come to their assistance should a German attack follow Czech rejection of the Anglo-French proposals.

When, however, Chamberlain flew to Germany a second time and presented his hard-won concessions to Hitler, he was astonished by the Führer's reaction. There could be no further delay. There had to be a solution by 1 October, and German forces would start to occupy the Sudeten areas on 28 September. Moreover, Polish and Hungarian claims on Czech territory would also have to be settled. After a second meeting Hitler stated that German troops would only begin occupying Czech territory on 1 October and insisted that the document containing his proposals was a memorandum and not an ultimatum. Despite this depressing turn of events, Chamberlain felt bound to recommend to his colleagues, the French, and the Czechs the terms of Hitler's Godesberg memorandum. He now, however, began to face resistance. Lord Halifax felt it would be improper to coerce the Czechs into accepting the Godesberg terms, and the cabinet became divided, with Chamberlain's position supported by a minority. Furthermore, the French were now seemingly determined to stand by the Czechs, who rejected the Godesberg terms. War seemed inevitable, for Britain could not stand by with equanimity, whatever the formalities of treaty commitments, if France went to war in support of the Czechs and was in turn threatened with subjugation by Germany. The Royal Navy was mobilized, air-raid trenches were dug in Hyde Park, and gas masks were distributed.

The Munich conference With the agreement of the French, and on Chamberlain's suggestion, Sir Horace Wilson was sent to Berlin to make a further appeal to Hitler to settle the Sudeten dispute peacefully with instructions to state that, should Hitler be resolute in his determination to solve the crisis by force, then Britain would be obliged, if France took active measures in support of Czechoslovakia, to go to war with Germany. In the early morning of Monday 26 September 1938, Wilson made his appeal, but Hitler was adamant that he wanted Czech acceptance of the Godesberg terms by 2.00 p.m. on Wednesday 28 September. The German leader followed this with an intemperate broadcast to the German nation. After some hesitation, but fortified by Chamberlain, Wilson on 27 September warned Hitler of the consequences of a resort to force. Hitler merely replied that within six days all parties interested in the dispute would be at war. That same day Chamberlain broadcast to the British nation. It was, he said, 'horrible, fantastic, incredible' that Britain should be preparing for war on account 'of a quarrel in a far-away country between people of whom we know nothing' and he affirmed that he 'would not hesitate to pay even a third visit to Germany' if there were a prospect of success (Feiling, 372). That same evening the British ambassador in Rome was instructed to act on his own suggestion and propose to Mussolini that he use his influence with Hitler to persuade him to delay his proposed military action against Czechoslovakia.

This manoeuvre worked. At 3.00 p.m. on the afternoon of 28 September Chamberlain was opening a Commons debate on the European situation when an urgent message arrived from the Foreign Office informing the prime minister that Hitler had delayed mobilization by twenty-four hours and that he, the French prime minister, Daladier, and Mussolini had been invited to a conference the following morning in Munich. In a welter of tumult, Chamberlain informed the Commons of this development and said that he would accept the invitation. Neither the Czechs nor the Soviets were invited to the conference, where on 29–30 September the issue of the Sudetenland was disposed of in the Munich agreement, under which the Czech government was to evacuate specified areas by 10 October, an international commission was to determine Czechoslovakia's new frontiers, an international force was to occupy the areas subject to plebiscite, and the four signatory powers agreed to participate in a guarantee of the newly defined state.

After breakfast on the morning of 30 September, Chamberlain persuaded Hitler to sign the so-called Anglo-German declaration. Obtaining Hitler's signature on this document was undoubtedly a major aim of Chamberlain's visit to Munich, for it was in his mind a potential guarantee of future peace. Yet he had doubts, telling Lord Dunglass, his parliamentary private secretary, who accompanied him to Munich, that peace could not be a certainty, given Hitler's 'volatility'. He went further, opining that Hitler was 'without question the most detestable and bigoted man with whom it had been his lot to do business' and that Munich represented the 'last throw' (Home, 64–5). The Anglo-German declaration, therefore, had more than one dimension to it. As he informed Dunglass, it would also 'ensure that if war did break out the international community would know on which nation the responsibility' should fall (Thorpe, 83). This was of particular importance with regard to opinion in the United States.

The declaration emphasized the importance of Anglo-German relations for the future of European peace, recognized the Munich agreement and the Anglo-German naval agreement as symptomatic of the desire of the two nations never again to go to war with one another, and affirmed the determination of the two governments to remove further outstanding causes of difference. On landing at Heston Airport Chamberlain waved the Anglo-German declaration as he emerged from the aircraft and stated: 'The settlement of the Czechoslovakian problem which has now been achieved is, in my view, only the prelude to a larger settlement in which all Europe may find peace' (Parker, 180–81). For Chamberlain the Munich agreement and the Anglo-German declaration were, therefore, the essential preliminaries to the general settlement that since 1936 had proved so elusive. Later in the day, when he arrived at 10 Downing Street, Chamberlain appeared before the deliriously enthusiastic crowds at a first-floor window and against his better judgement declared that for the second time in British history peace with honour had been brought back from Berlin. He stated: 'I believe it is peace for our time' (Feiling, 381).

The relief that the Munich agreement brought to Britain cannot be overestimated, and Chamberlain's popularity soared. On the return from Munich, the drive from Heston Airport to Downing Street took one and a half hours because of the density of the crowds lining the route. There had been nothing like it since the armistice in 1918. In the words of the Scottish socialist James Maxton, Chamberlain had done 'something that the mass of the common people in the world wanted done' (Feiling, 379). He was effusively greeted by George VI and fêted on the balcony of Buckingham Palace to scenes of jubilant clamour. Downing Street was inundated with flowers, poems, and the icons of Chamberlain's public and private lives, umbrellas and fishing rods, as ordinary people sought to express their release from the abomination of war. A Mass-Observation survey reported that 54 per cent of the sample endorsed Chamberlain's actions, with only 10 per cent expressing outright opposition. In Germany, Chamberlain's contribution to peace was equally joyously received. In October 1938 a former German naval officer conveyed the following message: 'I feel like one having been condemned to death, and set free in the last minute … It is my fervent wish to let Mr. Chamberlain know that we will thank him and bless him, all our life long' (ibid., 380–81). Chamberlain's stock had reached its zenith. Had he decided to call an election in autumn 1938 his government would undoubtedly have been returned with a massive majority, despite the reservations of Conservative central office, which contributed to the prime minister's restraint.

The opposition of the Labour Party and a minority of Conservatives led by Churchill, and the resignation of Duff Cooper from the cabinet, did little immediately to dent the mood of optimism. But events proved that the quest for a general settlement was an increasingly forlorn aspiration. In November 1938 the disagreeable face of national socialism was brutally displayed in the anti-Jewish pogrom known as the *Kristallnacht*. For a time Britain seemed to fare better with Mussolini. During November 1938 the Anglo-Italian agreement was ratified, but the results of a visit by Chamberlain and Halifax to Rome in January 1939 were almost wholly negative. In the months after Munich, Halifax remained sceptical about the long-term prospects for peace, but Chamberlain still aspired to a general settlement, although that was contingent upon the Germans renouncing the use of force. In March 1939 Hitler demonstrated that such a renunciation was not imminent.

The policy of guarantees, spring and summer 1939 While Germany had at Munich agreed to participate in an international guarantee of Czechoslovakia, there was no intention on Hitler's part of honouring this commitment. On the contrary, he was preoccupied with destroying Czechoslovakia as soon as he could. In the separatist Slovak movement he had a willing ally. With the encouragement of Hitler, the Slovak parliament declared independence on 14 March 1939. The Czech president and the foreign minister subsequently requested a meeting with Hitler to persuade him to agree to the continued existence of Czechoslovakia. Hitler, however, bullied the Czech leaders into signing away their country's independence. On 15 March German forces entered Prague and the provinces of Bohemia and Moravia became protectorates of the Reich.

This created profound shock in Britain. Chamberlain's speech in the House of Commons on 15 March was rather bland in its condemnation, but two days later in Birmingham he displayed his anger in a number of rhetorical questions. Was the destruction of Czechoslovakia the beginning of a new phase of German policy? Would other small states now be attacked? More ominously, was this the first step in an advance towards domination of the globe? He warned that because Britain opposed war as absurd and barbarous it did not mean that Britain would flinch from resisting a challenge if it were made. On the same day a scare story was started by the Romanian minister in London that suggested an imminent German attack upon Romania. This proved ultimately to have been bogus, but it galvanized the attitude of the British government. On 18 March Chamberlain told the cabinet that he had come to the definite conclusion that 'Hitler's attitude made it impossible to negotiate on the old basis with the Nazi regime … No reliance could be placed on any of the assurances given by the Nazi leaders' (Colvin, 188) He thought that the next step should be to ascertain who would join Britain in resisting aggression. Poland, he felt, was the key to the situation. Two days later the cabinet again met and discussed a draft declaration of agreement to consult interested powers if the independence of European states was threatened further. Chamberlain emphasized that the central issue was to be able to confront Germany with war on two fronts if she really intended to attempt the domination of the world, and he said: 'We should attack Germany not in order to save a particular victim but in order to pull down the bully' (Colvin, 190). Herein lay the origins of the policy of guarantees pursued by the British government during the spring and summer of 1939. It was a commitment to go to war should Germany undertake a further unprovoked act of aggression; a commitment that was given public form the following month with the introduction of conscription.

Chamberlain's scheme for a declaration of agreement to consult was frustrated by the Polish refusal to be associated with the Soviet Union. By spring 1939 the Poles were in a desperate situation. In October 1938 the German government had suggested the resolution of all outstanding problems between the two countries. Danzig should be returned and there should be extra-territorial road and rail rights in the Polish corridor linking East Prussia with the Reich. The Poles refused to concede these demands, and neither a visit to Hitler by the Polish foreign minister, Beck, nor a visit to Warsaw by the German foreign minister, Ribbentrop, altered the situation. By March 1939 the Poles were not going to budge, however firm the pressure from Berlin. Moreover, they were determined to fight rather than surrender. The Poles concealed much of the reality of this from the British and the French. Nevertheless, scare stories at the end of March 1939 of an imminent German attack on Poland disseminated by the journalist Ian Colvin and a fear in London that the Poles might come to some agreement with the German government prompted Chamberlain into the offer of a guarantee to Poland on 30 March, for either eventuality was considered damaging for British policy, in that it would render resistance on a two-front basis difficult. The guarantee was accepted and made public on the following day. It was the measure that committed Britain to war five months later. Subsequently, the policy of guarantees was extended to Greece, Turkey, and Romania.

Outbreak of war and formation of war cabinet The seizure by Germany of the German-speaking Lithuanian city of Memel on 23 March had contributed to the anxieties that provoked the reversal that now gave Warsaw an influence over British policy. But further anxiety was occasioned by Mussolini's annexation of Albania on 7 April and by the conclusion of the so-called pact of steel between Germany and Italy. In addition, Hitler's denunciation of the Anglo-German naval agreement and the Polish–German non-aggression pact in a speech to the Reichstag of 28 April made it clear that German–Polish relations were reaching a point of crisis. Chamberlain was now persuaded by Halifax that the concept of the grand alliance, incorporating the Soviet Union, was the only remedy against the belligerence of Berlin. The problem here, though, was the reality that neither the Poles nor the Romanians wanted Soviet troops on their soil. The question of transit facilities for the Red Army bedevilled the negotiations from start to finish. Equally problematic were Soviet suspicions of the intentions of the Western powers, which prompted the Soviet government to conduct parallel negotiations with the Germans culminating in the Nazi–Soviet non-aggression pact of 23 August 1939. Hitler was evidently determined to destroy Poland and to realize German ambitions in Danzig by force, whatever the risk of war. Chamberlain's response on 25 August was finally to convert the guarantee of Poland into a formal, reciprocal military alliance. This gave Hitler some pause, and the attack on Poland was postponed from 26 August until 1 September.

When the invasion of Poland began the German government refused to comply with Anglo-French ultimata demanding withdrawal, and at 11.00 a.m. on 3 September a state of war was deemed to exist between Britain and Germany. In his broadcast to the nation announcing this, Chamberlain stated:

> Everything I have worked for, everything that I have hoped for, everything that I have believed in my public life, has crashed into ruins. There is only one thing left for me to do: that is, to devote what strength and powers I have to forwarding the victory of the cause for which we have sacrificed so much. (Feiling, 416)

Chamberlain immediately sought to widen the basis of his government, but neither the Labour nor the Liberal leader would agree to serve under him. None the less, Eden returned and, more importantly, Churchill, who went to the Admiralty, joined it. Chamberlain disliked the role of war leader. Nevertheless, his commitment to victory and what was tantamount to unconditional surrender was absolute. On 5 September 1939 he informed the archbishop of Canterbury: 'I pray the struggle may be short, but it can't end as long as Hitler remains in power' (Feiling, 419). While Chamberlain remained open to a negotiated settlement with Hitler right up to the outbreak of war, a point on which in the eyes of even favourably disposed critics he remains vulnerable, it is necessary to set against statements that he made to that effect the record of implacable opposition to a peace on any other than allied terms once the war had begun. He was certain that Britain 'ought to reject' any proposals that Hitler might make following the fall of Poland, convinced that the restoration of any civilized standards in Europe was contingent on putting 'an end to Nazi policy' (ibid., 424). When on 6 October 1939 Hitler suggested a European conference to resolve the problems arising from the collapse of Poland, despite the favourable American response, he excoriated Hitler's proposals in a letter to his sister Ida. There was 'no real advance in mind or spirit towards a reasonable peace'; no reliance could be placed on anything that Hitler said; and, finally, 'the only chance of peace is the disappearance of Hitler and that is what we are working for' (Macleod, 279). Such resolve proved crucial at the end of May 1940. In his determination the prime minister would have been fortified by the virtual unanimity of the empire in going to war with Germany. Both Australia and New Zealand declared war on 3 September. Although for constitutional reasons Canada did not declare war until 10 September, she was effectively at war as soon as Britain

was. Whatever the difficulties in other parts of the empire, such as South Africa and India, the reality was that, from the beginning, a large part of the earth's surface was hostile territory as far as Germany was concerned.

Given the absence of Labour and Liberal members, Chamberlain's war cabinet consisted of the old inner core—Halifax, Simon, and Hoare—together with Churchill, Lord Chatfield, Lord Hankey, Sir Kingsley Wood, and Leslie Hore-Belisha. The success of the team, however, depended upon the partnership that was soon forged between Chamberlain and Churchill. As early as the beginning of October 1939 the latter was informed by the prime minister that their relationship need not remain strictly formal, and thereafter their dealings were marked by a steadily increasing warmth. In February 1940 Churchill for the first time accompanied Chamberlain on a visit to Paris for a meeting of the supreme war council; two months later he was effectively presiding over the general running of the war by chairing the military co-ordination committee.

It did prove necessary, however, to reconstruct the cabinet in January 1940. Chamberlain greatly admired the 'courage, imagination and drive' (Macleod, 284) of Leslie Hore-Belisha, whom he had included in his cabinet as secretary of state for war in 1937; but the defects of his qualities soon became evident with the onset of hostilities. Hore-Belisha's self-confidence and lack of tact soon led to difficulties with Lord Gort, the commander-in-chief of the British expeditionary force (BEF) in France. The manner in which he criticized what he perceived to be the defensive inadequacies of the BEF was easily interpreted by Gort as outright condemnation of his ability as a general. Chamberlain correctly concluded that continuing friction of this kind was unsatisfactory and determined to reassign Hore-Belisha rather than lose him. But the latter would not accept a transfer to the presidency of the Board of Trade (the preferred option of the Ministry of Information having been vetoed by the Foreign Office), and he left the government. Oliver Stanley replaced him at the War Office and Sir Andrew Duncan went to the Ministry of Information. Further minor changes occurred in April 1940 when Lord Chatfield retired from the war cabinet.

Throughout the first six months of the war Chamberlain's eye was fixed firmly upon the defeat of Germany and the destruction of Hitler. This can be seen in his attitude towards the Russo-Finnish War that lasted from November 1939 until March 1940. Soviet motives were undoubtedly defensive and were connected with their desire to improve their strategic position in the Baltic. The Finns declined to respond to Soviet proposals for a territorial exchange that would have enhanced the defence of Leningrad, and Moscow elected to secure Soviet aims by recourse to war. Chamberlain, nevertheless, was not beguiled by the mood of public sentiment for the Finns that soon engulfed opinion in Britain, France, and the United States. He thought 'Stalin's latest performance ... no worse morally, and in its developments ... likely to be much less brutal' (Feiling, 427) than Hitler's attack on Poland. He could not allow his indignation against the Soviet action to blind him to the reality that it was not very likely to damage the allied war effort. Thus to conclude peace with Germany in order to pursue a crusade against Russia, as one correspondent urged, was not practical policy. He wrote:

> I still regard Germany as Public Enemy No. 1, and I cannot take Russia very seriously as an aggressive force … I am afraid that, although the Germans would like to make peace on their own terms, they are very far from the frame of mind which will be necessary before they are prepared to listen to what we should call reason.   (Feiling, 427–8)

The capitulation of the Finns on 12 March 1940 finally saved the British from madcap schemes, particularly from those elaborated by the French that would have involved military confrontation with the Soviet Union.

Although Chamberlain believed it prudent to remain on the defensive until Hitler attacked, he was convinced that Germany would ultimately be defeated by an economic pressure that would lead to economic failure and social collapse in Germany. This assumption was somewhat complacent, but there was intelligence information, though misguided, to support such an interpretation. He also believed that the longer Hitler delayed in taking the initiative the better it was for the allies. Nevertheless, it was unfortunate that he publicly declared on 4 April 1940 that 'Hitler missed the bus' (Taylor, 470), for within days the Wehrmacht overran Denmark and Norway. This had been prompted by German fears of allied interdiction of iron ore supplies from Sweden. While there was little that could be done to save Denmark, an allied expeditionary force endeavoured to eject the Germans from Norway, but without success.

Chamberlain's resignation as prime minister, May 1940
Although Churchill was the minister primarily responsible for the Norwegian fiasco, it was Chamberlain who incurred the odium for the failure. He won the Commons debate on the Norway campaign on 7–8 May by 281 votes to 200; but it was a Pyrrhic victory, for thirty-three supporters of the government had voted with the opposition and there had been more than sixty abstentions. There had also been many wounding words, not least from Leo Amery, a former colleague and fellow Birmingham MP of many years' standing, who, quoting Cromwell, said: 'You have sat here for too long for any good you have been doing. Depart, I say, and let us have done with you. In the name of God go!' (Macleod, 289). The previous September, on the eve of the outbreak of war, it had been Amery who had scathingly criticized his own government when he had urged the Labour leader, Arthur Greenwood, to 'speak for England!' (Cameron Watt, 579). What was critical was that Chamberlain himself realized that there must be now a full coalition government incorporating the Labour and Liberal opposition. As, however, the chancellor of the exchequer and his former parliamentary private secretary, Sir Kingsley Wood, advised him, he could not remain in office while Labour refused to serve under him.

On 10 May 1940, the day the 'phoney war' ended, as Hitler's forces attacked the Low Countries and France simultaneously, Chamberlain resigned. He had not been outstanding as a war leader and he knew it. There were, however, problems with his only really credible replacement, Winston Churchill, who was not popular in the Conservative Party. Chamberlain's preferred successor was Lord Halifax, but Halifax in effect declined on the grounds of his peerage and a self-recognition that his qualities did not match the hour. The premiership, therefore, passed to Churchill by default. Churchill, though, did not possess the immediate support of the Conservative Party, and Chamberlain continued as leader while remaining in the government as lord president of the council, in which post he served with distinction during the little time that was left to him.

It was as well that Halifax declined the premiership: he proved an appeaser for all seasons. At the end of May 1940, as France and western Europe were falling under the Nazi juggernaut, he argued the possibility of a negotiated peace, but he was opposed by Chamberlain, who was now in favour of seeing the struggle through to the bitter end. After relinquishing the premiership he had broadcast to the nation, stating:

> And you and I, must rally behind our new leader, and with our united strength, and with unshakeable courage, fight and work until this wild beast, that has sprung out of his lair upon us, has been finally disarmed and overthrown.
> (Feiling, 441)

Now, at crucial war cabinets on 26, 27, and 28 May, he lent Churchill his decisive support, as Halifax, following discussions with the Italian ambassador, Signor Bastianini, suggested that a European conference might achieve 'peace and security in Europe' and assure Britain's 'liberty and independence' (Lukacs, 109). Chamberlain agreed with Churchill that there were no terms which Hitler would endorse that Britain could accept. Had he sided with Halifax it is likely that Churchill's position would have been fatally weakened. It was a critical moment in British history and perhaps that of the world.

The excellent relations that had developed between Churchill and Chamberlain became more important following the latter's assumption of the premiership. On 10 May 1940 Churchill wrote the following to Chamberlain:

> my first act on coming back from the Palace is to write and tell you how grateful I am to you for promising to stand by me, and to aid the country at this extremely grievous and formidable moment … With your help and counsel, and the support of the great party of which you are the leader, I trust that I shall succeed … In these eight months we have worked together I am proud to have won your friendship and your confidence in an increasing measure. To a very large extent I am in your hands—and I feel no fear of that.   (Feiling, 442)

Following the war cabinet split at the end of May 1940 he informed Lloyd George, no friend of Chamberlain's: 'I have received a very great deal of help from Chamberlain. His kindness and courtesy to me in our new relations have touched me. I have joined hands with him and must act with perfect loyalty' (Lukacs, 121).

In his new role Chamberlain's position was far from

negligible. He was responsible for co-ordinating internal policy, while Churchill focused upon the elaboration of war policy. During the latter's absences he chaired the full cabinet. As chairman of the lord president's committee, in effect a subcommittee of senior cabinet ministers, he was responsible for determining a plethora of domestic issues. It was Chamberlain who was responsible for enacting the Emergency Powers (Defence) Bill. He also, at Churchill's behest and with the assistance of Malcolm MacDonald, attempted to secure the abandonment of Éire's neutrality. On the eve of his departure from public life, 'railway fares, rating problems of local authorities in coastal towns and war damage compensation' were listed by Churchill as issues on which he needed his predecessor's advice in addition to the fundamentals of general policy (Macleod, 295). War truly dissolved old enmities. In Clement Attlee's memoirs there appears the following encomium:

> He was Lord President. Very able and crafty, and free from any rancour he might well have felt against us. He worked very hard and well: a good chairman, a good committee man, always very businesslike. You could work with him. (Attlee, 37)

Death and reputation There can, however, be no gainsaying Chamberlain's mood of depression at the prospect of so much death and maiming. In a letter to his sister Hilda, he expressed his relief on retiring from the premiership, as he knew 'the agony of mind it would mean … to give directions that would bring death and mutilation to so many' (NCP, 18/1/1156, Neville Chamberlain to Hilda Chamberlain, 17 May 1940). Within a month the depression was accompanied by physical illness as he recorded the presence of abdominal pain. Following an X-ray on 24 July and an exploratory operation, terminal cancer of the large bowel was diagnosed. Chamberlain returned to 11 Downing Street on 9 September, as he put it, a partial cripple. He tendered his resignation as lord president on 22 September and resigned from public life on 3 October, having declined the Order of the Garter, preferring to remain simple Mr Chamberlain, like his father before him. He died on 9 November 1940 at Highfield Park, near the village of Heckfield, Hampshire. After a commemoration service in Westminster Abbey on 14 November, his ashes were interred beside the tomb of Andrew Bonar Law. On 12 November Churchill paid tribute to him in the House of Commons as a man who had 'acted with perfect sincerity according to his lights' and who had striven to save the world from the catastrophe into which it had fallen. 'This alone', he said, 'will stand him in good stead as far as what is called the verdict of history is concerned' (Macleod, 304).

In recent years Churchill's prophecy might well be said to have been fulfilled. But Chamberlain's reputation was severely damaged for many years after his death by the writings of men such as Sir Lewis Namier and Sir John Wheeler-Bennett. His entire career was encapsulated in the concept of the man of Munich, and foreign policy during his premiership was condemned as crass and craven.

Moreover, no opportunity was missed to stigmatize Chamberlain as a complete novice in foreign policy.

The process of vilification began in earnest with the publication in July 1940 of *Guilty Men* by the pseudonymous Cato. It was, in fact, written by three left-wing journalists who were then on the payroll of Beaverbrook newspapers—Peter Howard, Frank Owen, and Michael Foot. Its impact on Chamberlain's posthumous reputation is difficult to exaggerate. Published in the wake of Dunkirk and Hitler's conquest of France and western Europe, it caught a public mood agitated by the prospect of imminent invasion. The tract's central argument was that British defence policy during the 1930s left Britain ill-equipped and unprepared for war. Chamberlain was indicted as the first of the 'Guilty Men', who had inherited a 'great empire, supreme in arms and secure in liberty' and brought it to 'national humiliation' (Cato, 16, 19). More than that, he had wilfully ignored the sage advice of the Foreign Office in favour of the unaccountable Sir Horace Wilson, the second of the nominated guilty. In this way the myth was first disseminated that Chamberlain had preferred and acted upon 'the advice of shadowy figures such as Wilson and a small group of sycophantic ministers' (Dutton, *Chamberlain*, 76). With his scrawny neck inside a wing collar seemingly two sizes too big for him, and his umbrella, Chamberlain had always been an easy target for cartoonists; ridicule of him and the National Government that he effectively led for almost a decade was now *de rigueur*. It was perhaps most scathingly encapsulated in the stigmatization of the appointment in 1936 of Sir Thomas Inskip as minister for the co-ordination of defence as the most extraordinary 'since the Roman Emperor Caligula made his horse a Consul' (Cato, 76). Some wanted to go further, advocating the hanging of Chamberlain and his colleagues from the lamp-posts in Downing Street.

Guilty Men was followed by a series of imitation tracts, mostly published during the war, but the most cogent and sophisticated presentation of this view came in 1964 with the publication by Martin Gilbert and Richard Gott of *The Appeasers*. In the following year Professor Cameron Watt referred in the *Political Quarterly* to the rise of a revisionist school and asserted that the image of Chamberlain as a pro-German dupe, ignorant of foreign affairs, was less easy to sustain. In 1966 Martin Gilbert published a partial retraction of his earlier views in *The Roots of Appeasement*, which emphasized that appeasement had to be seen as a policy that was pursued before Chamberlain became prime minister, although he castigated Chamberlain for continuing it. He also pointed to the fact that appeasement was a policy of rather more sensible dimensions than sheer one-sided concession. In 1968 Keith Robbins published *Munich 1938*, which attempted to look at Munich in the context of fifty years of Anglo-German relations without the encumbering notion of appeasement. He indicated the identity of view between appeasers and anti-appeasers and rightly asserted that, at bottom, Munich was the consequence of the desire to avoid another Anglo-

German war, rather than an attempt to gain peace at any price.

Once the fifty-year rule regarding access to public archives was relaxed in 1968, the rehabilitation of Chamberlain could proceed and might be said to have started with Maurice Cowling's *The Impact of Hitler: British Politics and British Policy, 1933–1940* (1975). This curiously constructed work sought to interpret British politics in the 1930s in the context of British foreign policy, but it stressed the responsible nature of foreign policy under Chamberlain, which was designed to match British commitments with resources. Full rehabilitation might be said to have been achieved with John Charmley's *Chamberlain and the Lost Peace* (1989). According to Charmley, appeasement was justified to the last because Britain's involvement in war with Germany would be ruinous whether winner or loser. But he vitiates the argument for Chamberlain by concluding that the war itself was a mistake. Yet the degree to which Chamberlain's reputation has been enhanced is revealed in the way that post-revisionist critical works, such as R. A. C. Parker's *Chamberlain and Appeasement*, now recognize Chamberlain's intelligence, diligence, and administrative expertise.

The problem with all these accounts, though, is that they concentrate upon Chamberlain's premiership and foreign policy. This focus distorts the true image of Chamberlain's mission and contribution, which lay in domestic policy and social reform. He has, however, fared better at the hands of his principal biographers. The earliest official biography of Chamberlain, written by Keith Feiling, is still the best account of Chamberlain's entire life. Its interpretations have stood the test of time, as they have been steadily confirmed and buttressed by archival research. Iain Macleod's biography, concentrating as it does on presenting Chamberlain as a social reformer, is a valuable corrective to the mountain of literature on Chamberlain's foreign policy. The same can be said of David Dilks's first volume of an official life, which concentrates upon the years down to 1929.

On the eve of Chamberlain's becoming prime minister, Anthony Eden stated to a confidant that 'Neville Chamberlain had the makings of a really great Prime Minister' provided his health held out (*Diplomatic Diaries of Oliver Harvey*, 33–4). Chamberlain's problem, however, was not health, but Hitler. He had the misfortune to be in office when the European crisis that began with Hitler's appointment as German chancellor began to peak. Inevitably, he was diverted from focusing upon those issues, covered by social reform, which would probably have made his premiership distinguished. Indeed, his eagerness to bring Hitler to terms was rooted in a desire to return as quickly as possible to domestic issues. This was never a realistic prospect as long as Hitler remained in office. The central charge directed against Chamberlain has been that, had he adopted a more confrontational policy, war could have been avoided. This has been in recent years more sophisticatedly argued by R. A. C. Parker. The suggestion is that a policy of a close Franco-British alliance and collaboration with the USSR would effectively

have curbed the expansionist ambitions of Nazi Germany. Parker concludes: 'Led by Chamberlain, the government rejected effective deterrence. Chamberlain's powerful, obstinate personality and his skill in debate probably stifled serious chances of preventing the Second World War' (Parker, 347).

The problem with this view, and that of its supporters such as Michael Roi, is that it takes no account of the intentions of Hitler. Some historians, such as Klaus Hildebrand and Andreas Hillgruber, argue that Hitler had a foreign policy programme of phased expansion whatever the cost; others, such as Timothy Mason, argue that the domestic structures created by the National Socialists ensured that Germany would eventually have to embark upon a war of plunder; finally, others such as Professor Cameron Watt have argued simply that Hitler 'willed, wanted, craved war and the destruction wrought by war' (Cameron Watt, 623). If any of these interpretations is correct, and the truth probably lies in an amalgam of all three, no policy pursued by Chamberlain could have maintained peace. That he strove to avoid war, conscious of the vast human misery and material destruction it wrought, should redound to his eternal credit, for in doing so, as he told Hitler at Godesberg, he risked his political life.

Had Chamberlain retired with Baldwin in 1937 he would not have risked anything. He would still have been a considerable figure in British political history, his career a study in success. Like his father, Joseph Chamberlain, and his elder half-brother, Austen Chamberlain, he played a major part in British public life and, arguably, was more successful, for in 1937 he became prime minister. This was all the more noteworthy an achievement, for he had not entered the House of Commons until 1918 at the age of forty-nine. From then until the request by the crown that he form a government his political career might accurately be described as one of resounding achievement. The premiership, however, was to be the undoing of his reputation. He became prime minister precisely at the time when the international crisis of the 1930s, precipitated by the demands of Nazi Germany, was reaching its critical point and threatening to escalate into a major European war. In order to avert such a catastrophe, Neville Chamberlain attempted by an energetic policy of conciliation and redress of justified grievances to bring Germany into satisfactory and peaceable treaty relations with her neighbours. He did not succeed and war broke out in 1939, causing his premiership to be condemned as a failure for many years afterwards. His name became inextricably linked with the discredited, but much misunderstood, policy of appeasement and the shame and disgrace of the surrender to German demands at Munich in 1938. In short, he became the most maligned and vilified of twentieth-century British prime ministers. Foreign policy and war brought upon his premiership discredit for many years. Paradoxically, for his successor, Churchill, whose career up to 1939 has been described by Rhodes James as a study in failure, it was foreign policy and war that made his reputation.

On the other hand, Chamberlain had all the attributes of an outstanding peacetime prime minister and a radically reforming one at that. Even during the turbulent 1930s, the governments in which he played leading roles did not lose sight of social reform. The Unemployment Act of 1934 established the Unemployment Assistance Board, largely Chamberlain's creation. Its purpose was to remove the issue of relief from the political fray. Moreover, Chamberlain:

> saw the importance of 'providing some interest in life for the large numbers of men never likely to get work', and out of this realisation was to come the responsibility of the U.A.B. for the *welfare*, not merely the maintenance, of the unemployed.   (Bruce, 271)

What a Chamberlain government would have done had there been no war in 1939 will never be known, but an election was due in 1940, and the manifesto proposals outlined by the Conservative Research Department embraced family allowances and the inclusion of insured persons' dependants in health cover—about half the advances usually attributed to Beveridge. As Lady Cecily Debenham wrote to Chamberlain's widow, Anne, after his death:

> Neville was a Radical to the end of his days. It makes my blood boil when I see his 'Tory' and 'Reactionary' outlook taken as a matter of course because the Whirligig of Politics made him leader of the Tory party.   (NCP, 11/15/44, Lady Cecily Debenham to Anne Chamberlain, 11 Sept 194[1]?)

ANDREW J. CROZIER

Sources U. Birm. L., Neville Chamberlain MSS · K. Feiling, *The life of Neville Chamberlain* (1946) · D. Dilks, *Neville Chamberlain*, 1 (1984) · I. Macleod, *Neville Chamberlain* (1961) · R. Jenkins, *The chancellors* (1998) · R. A. C. Parker, *Chamberlain and appeasement* (1993) · A. J. Crozier, *Appeasement and Germany's last bid for colonies* (1988) · J. Ramsden, *The age of Balfour and Baldwin, 1902–1940* (1978) · J. A. Ramsden, *An appetite for power: a history of the Conservative Party since 1830* (1998) · J. A. Ramsden, *The making of Conservative Party policy* (1980) · D. Dutton, *Anthony Eden: a life and reputation* (1997) · D. Dutton, *Neville Chamberlain* (2001) · A. Beattie, 'Neville Chamberlain', *British prime ministers in the twentieth century*, ed. J. P. Mackintosh, 1 (1977) · I. Colvin, *The Chamberlain cabinet* (1971) · N. Crowson, *Facing fascism: the Conservative Party and the European dictators, 1935–1940* (1997) · P. Bell, *Chamberlain, Germany and Japan, 1933–4: redefining British strategy in the era of decline* (1996) · M. L. Roi, *Alternative to appeasement: Sir Robert Vansittart and alliance diplomacy, 1934–1937* (1997) · A. Roberts, *The holy fox* (1991) · Lord Home, *The way the wind blows* (1976) · D. R. Thorpe, *Alec Douglas-Home* (1997) · W. Wark, *The ultimate enemy* (1985) · D. Cameron Watt, *How war came* (1989) · R. Blake, 'How Churchill became prime minister', *Churchill*, ed. R. Blake and W. R. Louis (1993) · Lord Avon, *Facing the dictators* (1962) · Cato [F. Owen], *Guilty men* (1940) · M. Bruce, *The coming of the welfare state* (1968) · *Documents on British Foreign Policy* (1946–) · Lord Lothian, 'Issues in British foreign policy', *International Affairs*, 17 (1938) · J. Margach, *The abuse of power* (1978) · R. Cockett, *Twilight of truth* (1989) · *The Leo Amery diaries*, ed. J. Barnes and D. Nicholson, 1 (1980) · *Hansard 5C* (1931), 255.2497–506; (1932), 261.296; (1938), 101.778; 102.132; 255.2497–2506; 261.296; 333.1405–6 · G. Schmidt, 'The domestic background to British appeasement policy', *The fascist challenge and the policy of appeasement*, ed. W. J. Mommsen and L. Kettenacker (1983) · R. Rhodes James, *Churchill: a study in failure* (1970) · N. Chamberlain, *In search of peace* (1939) · A. J. P. Taylor, *English history* (1965) · Lord Swinton, *I remember* (1949) · A. Trotter, 'Tentative steps for an Anglo-Japanese rapprochement', *Modern Asian Studies*, 8 (1974) · *Documents Diplomatiques Français* (Paris, 1964–) · *The diplomatic diaries of Oliver Harvey*, ed. J. Harvey (1970) ·

J. Lukacs, *Five days in London: May 1940* (New Haven, 1999) · C. Attlee, *A prime minister remembers* (1961) · CGPLA Eng. & Wales (1941)
Archives NRA, priv. coll., papers · PRO, prime ministerial papers, cabinet conclusions, cabinet committee minutes and papers · PRO, corresp. and papers as lord president of the Council · U. Birm. L., corresp., diaries, and papers · U. Birm. L., letters | BL, corresp. with Lord Cecil, Add. MS 51087 · Bodl. Oxf., papers, incl. corresp. with Viscount Addison · Bodl. Oxf., corresp. with H. A. Gwynne · Bodl. Oxf., corresp. with Lord Ponsonby · Bodl. Oxf., corresp. with third earl of Selborne · Bodl. Oxf., corresp. with Lord Simon · Bodl. RH, corresp. with C. Walker · CAC Cam., corresp. with Lord Croft · CAC Cam., corresp. with Leslie Hore-Belisha · CAC Cam., corresp. with first Viscount Weir · CKS, letters to Lord Stanhope · CUL, Templewood papers, corresp. with Sir Samuel Hoare · CUL, letters to Lord and Lady Kennet · HLRO, corresp. with Lord Beaverbrook · HLRO, corresp. with Herbert Samuel · Lpool RO, corresp. with seventeenth earl of Derby · NA Scot., corresp. with Lord Elibank · NL Scot., letters to Seton Gordon · NMM, corresp. with Dame Katharine Furse · PRO NIre., letters to Lady Londonderry · Royal Entomological Society, London, letters to C. J. Wainwright · Shrops. RRC, letters to first Viscount Bridgeman · U. Birm. L., Austen Chamberlain papers · U. Birm. L., Joseph Chamberlain papers · U. Birm. L., letters to the MUCA · U. Glas., Archives and Business Records Centre, corresp. with first Viscount Weir · U. Newcastle, Robinson L., corresp. with Walter Runciman · U. Warwick Mod. RC, corresp. with Sir Leslie Scott | FILM BFI NFTVA, 'Neville Chamberlain', 18 Jan 1978 · BFI NFTVA, documentary footage · BFI NFTVA, news footage · BFI NFTVA, propaganda film footage · Pathé News | SOUND BL NSA, 'On his return from the Munich conference', 3 Sept 1938, 155 000 1489 D2 BD6 Rhino world beat, 155 000 2056 T2 S1 BD6 Rhino world beat · BL NSA, 'Speech at Heston Airport on his return from Munich', 3 Sept 1938, ICL 0015 2395 2C2, ICL 0015 2405 2C2 · IWM SA, 'British civilian prime minister speech at Heston', BBC, 30 Sept 1938, 4316 · IWM SA, 'British civilian prime minister speech on the outbreak of war with Germany', BBC, 3 Sept 1939, 4321 · IWM SA, 'British civilian prime minister on resigning premiership', BBC, 10 May 1940, 4323
Likenesses W. Stoneman, two photographs, 1921–37, NPG · O. Birley, oils, c.1933, Birmingham Museum and Art Gallery · F. May, gouache drawing, 1935, NPG · Bassano, photograph, 1936, NPG [see illus.] · Lady Kathleen Kennet, bronze bust, 1936, Birmingham Museum and Art Gallery · V. Demanet, bronze medal, 1938, NPG · J. Gunn, oils, c.1939, Carlton Club, London · H. Lamb, oils, c.1939, NPG · A. Maclaren, lithograph, 1940, NPG · T. Cottrell, cigarette card, NPG · P. Evans, pencil drawing, NPG · M. Hiley, bronze medallion, NMG Wales · D. Low, pencil caricature, NPG · W. Orpen, portrait, priv. coll. · B. Partridge, ink and watercolour caricature, NPG; repro. in *Punch* (1 Nov 1926) · B. Partridge, ink and watercolour caricature, NPG; repro. in *Punch* (22 June 1932)
Wealth at death £84,013 6s.: probate, 15 April 1941, CGPLA Eng. & Wales

Chamberlain, Sir Neville Bowles (1820–1902), army officer, was born at Rio de Janeiro on 10 January 1820, the second son of Henry Chamberlain, consul-general and chargé d'affaires in Brazil, and his second wife, Anne Eugenia (d. 28 Aug 1867), daughter of William Morgan of London. His father was created a baronet in 1828, and died on 31 July 1829. By his second marriage (his first had been dissolved in 1813) Henry Chamberlain had five sons and three daughters. The eldest son, William Charles (1818–1878), became an admiral; the other four entered the East India Company's service and distinguished themselves as soldiers. The third son, Sir Crawford Trotter *Chamberlain, was closely associated with Neville throughout his military career. The fourth son, Thomas Hardy (1822–1879), was major-general, Bombay staff corps. The fifth

Sir Neville Bowles Chamberlain (1820–1902), by unknown photographer

son, Charles Francis Falcon CB (1826–1870), was colonel in the Bombay staff corps.

At thirteen, on the nomination of Lord Beresford, Neville entered the Royal Military Academy as a cadet; but, more combative than studious, he was withdrawn at the end of his probationary year. On 24 February 1837, on the nomination of Mr Buckle, a director of the East India Company, he was commissioned as ensign in the company's army. He reached Calcutta in June and was posted to the 55th Bengal native infantry, joining it at Lucknow early in 1838. On 28 August he was transferred to the 16th Bengal native infantry, which was at Delhi. His brother Crawford was serving in the same regiment. Sir Henry Fane, the commander-in-chief and a friend of his father, wished the two sons to take part in the imminent invasion of Afghanistan.

The 16th formed part of the army of the Indus; at the end of June the army marched on Kabul and on 23 July Ghazni was stormed. Chamberlain distinguished himself in the fighting which preceded this assault. His regiment was left at Ghazni when the army moved on to Kabul, and the brothers became friendly with some of the sons of Dost Muhammad, who were on parole there. In June 1841 the 16th was relieved at Ghazni by the 27th, in which John *Nicholson was a subaltern. He and Neville Chamberlain became close friends.

On 25 August the 16th arrived at Kandahar, and on 8

November set out for India, but the outbreak at Kabul led to its immediate recall to Kandahar. During the next nine months General Nott's force had repeated encounters with the Afghans, in which Chamberlain was prominent. He was temporarily appointed to the 1st cavalry of Shah Shuja's force, and soon made a name for himself as a daring leader of irregular horse. In the action of the Arghandab (12 January 1842) he was wounded in the knee, but nevertheless took part in the pursuit. In March his men failed him, and he had to fight hard for his life. On 29 May he was again wounded, in the thigh. He was awarded a gratuity of twelve months' pay for his injuries.

In August 1842 Nott's force marched from Kandahar on Kabul. Chamberlain went with it, and took part in the capture and burning of Istalif on 28 September, which made him 'disgusted with myself, the world, and, above all, with my cruel profession' (Forrest, 149). The combined forces of Nott and Pollock left Kabul on 12 October. Chamberlain, with the rear-guard, was twice wounded, in the spine and in the leg. In nearly four years in Afghanistan he had been wounded six times. General Nott so praised him that on 2 January 1843 he was appointed to the governor-general's bodyguard. This did not remove him from his regiment (the 16th), in which he had become lieutenant on 16 July 1842.

Though still suffering from his last wound, Chamberlain took part in the Gwalior campaign and in the battle of Maharajpur on 29 December 1843. On 20 February 1845 he left Calcutta for England, very reluctantly, for the First Anglo-Sikh War was imminent, but this was regarded as his only chance of cure. He returned to India at the end of 1846, having partially recovered the use of his leg. He was military secretary to the governor of Bombay until May 1848, and was then employed for a few months at Indore; but on the outbreak of the Second Anglo-Sikh War he was appointed brigade major of a cavalry brigade.

In the operations preceding the passage of the Chenab Lord Gough called for a volunteer to swim the river and reconnoitre the right bank. Chamberlain swam across with a few men of the 9th lancers, found that the Sikhs had gone, and was greeted by Gough on his return as 'the bravest of the brave'. At Chilianwala his brigade was left to protect the baggage, but at Gujrat it was actively engaged. Chamberlain distinguished himself in the pursuit, and Gough promised him the command of a regiment of irregular cavalry. When he became captain in his regiment on 1 November 1849 he was given a brevet majority.

In May 1849 Chamberlain was appointed assistant adjutant-general of the Sirhind division, but he soon tired of office routine. In December he was made assistant commissioner in the Rawalpindi district, from where he was transferred to Hazara in June 1850 and organized the military police for the Punjab.

After a bad bout of malaria in late 1852 Chamberlain went to South Africa on sick leave and spent a year and a half hunting lion. He returned to India at the end of 1854 to take up the command of the Punjab irregular force, which Lord Dalhousie had reserved for him. This force, modelled upon the corps of Guides, numbered 11,000 men and had to guard 700 miles of frontier against turbulent tribes. Chamberlain was only a captain in his regiment, but he was made brevet lieutenant-colonel (28 November 1854) and was given the local rank of brigadier. 'That glorious soldier' (Barthorp, 51), as Lumsden called him, was liked and respected by all who knew him. He was thanked by government for his services on the frontier.

In May 1857, at the Indian mutiny, a column was formed to crush any outbreak in the Punjab, and Chamberlain was given command of it. But he soon handed this over to John Nicholson, being appointed adjutant-general of the Bengal army, and he joined the force before Delhi on 24 June. He took a leading part in repulsing the attacks of the mutineers on 9 and 14 July. In the latter action, seeing that the men hesitated before a wall lined by the enemy, he leapt his horse over it. They followed him, but he was shot in his shoulder, which partially disabled him for the rest of the siege. He helped, however, to stiffen the wavering purpose of the British commander during the storming of the city, and on 16 September he took temporary command of the force. He received the thanks of the governor-general, and was made CB on 11 November 1857.

Chamberlain was prevented by his wound from taking part in the relief of Lucknow, and had to decline Sir Colin Campbell's offer of command of the cavalry in the Rohilla campaign of 1858. He resigned the post of adjutant-general and was reappointed to the command of the Punjab irregular force with the rank of brevet colonel on 27 November 1857, and the local rank of brigadier-general. In August 1858 he crushed a dangerous conspiracy among the Sikh troops at Dera Ismail Khan. In December 1859 he led an expedition against the Kabul Khel Wazirs, and another in April 1860 against the Mahsuds, forcing his way to Kaniguram, which they boasted that hostile eyes had never seen. His force was composed entirely of native troops, including some men led by their own chiefs. On 11 April 1863 he was made KCB.

In the autumn of 1863 Chamberlain commanded a force of 5000 men against the Wahabi fanatics at Sitana. He decided to take one column from Peshawar over the Ambela Pass into the Chamla valley, while another column co-operated from Hazara. He reached the top of the pass on 20 October. During fierce fighting Chamberlain received a wound in the arm, which obliged him to hand over command. Lord Elgin the governor-general, died on the same day, and his council decided to withdraw the expedition. Chamberlain opposed this; eventually reinforcements were sent and under General Garvock the Yusufzai field force completed its task.

Chamberlain went home as soon as he was fit to travel, and joined his mother and sisters at Versailles in July 1864. He was promoted major-general on 5 August 1864, and was made KCSI on 24 May 1866. In 1869 he accompanied the duke of Edinburgh on his visit to India. He was promoted lieutenant-general on 1 May 1872, GCSI on 24 May 1874, and GCB on 29 May 1876. On 26 June 1873 he married Charlotte Cuyler, sixth daughter of Major-General Sir William *Reid; she died on 26 December 1896 without children.

Chamberlain returned to India in February 1876 to take command of the Madras army. When it was decided, in August 1878, to send a British mission to Kabul, he agreed to go as envoy, but the mission was stopped at Ali Masjid on 21 September by the amir's orders. Chamberlain agreed with Lord Lytton that this insult should be punished, and he acted for some months as military member of council. But he did not wholly approve of the treaty of Gandamak, still less of Lytton's policy of retribution after the second occupation of Kabul and the continuance of the army's commitments in Afghanistan. He opposed the retention of Kandahar in 1880.

Chamberlain's Madras command ended on 3 February 1881, and he left India. He spent the rest of his life at Lordswood, near Southampton. He had become general on 1 October 1877, was placed on the unemployed supernumerary list on 3 February 1886, and was made field marshal on 25 April 1900. He died at Lordswood on 18 February 1902, and was buried beside his wife at Rownhams near Southampton.   E. M. LLOYD, rev. JAMES LUNT

Sources G. W. Forrest, *Life of Field-Marshal Sir Neville Chamberlain* (1909) · *Hart's Army List* · *The Times* (19 Feb 1902) · Lord Roberts [F. S. Roberts], *Forty-one years in India*, 2 vols. (1897) · W. H. Paget, *A record of the expeditions against the north-west frontier tribes, since the annexation of the Punjab*, rev. A. H. Mason (1884) · J. Adye, *Sitana: a mountain campaign on the borders of Afghanistan in 1863* (1867) · B. Balfour, *Lord Lytton's Indian administration* (1899) · M. Lutyens, *The Lyttons in India* (1979) · B. Robson, *The road to Kabul: the Second Afghan War, 1878–1881* (1986) · H. C. B. Cook, *The Sikh wars: the British army in the Punjab, 1845–1849* (1975) · Fortescue, *Brit. army*, vol. 12 · M. Barthorp, *The north-west frontier: British India and Afghanistan, a pictorial history, 1839–1947* (1982) · *CGPLA Eng. & Wales* (1902)
Archives BL OIOC, corresp., MS Eur. C 203 · NAM, notes on Kabul massacre | CUL, corresp. with Lord Mayo · Hunt. L., letters to Grenville family
Likenesses portraits, repro. in Forrest, *Life of … Chamberlain*, frontispiece, 448 [see illus.]
Wealth at death £91,370 17s. 6d.: resworn probate, June 1902, *CGPLA Eng. & Wales*

Chamberlain, Sir Neville Francis Fitzgerald (1856–1944), army officer and inventor of snooker, was born at Upton Park, Upton, Buckinghamshire, on 13 January 1856, the only son of Lieutenant-Colonel Charles Francis Falcon Chamberlain (1826–1879), an Indian army officer, and his wife, Marianne Ormsby Drury. Field Marshal Sir Neville Bowles Chamberlain was his uncle. Chamberlain was educated abroad and at Brentwood School, Essex, before entering the Royal Military College, Sandhurst. On 9 August 1873 he was commissioned a second lieutenant in the 11th (Devon) regiment, in which he served between 1873 and 1876. He was promoted lieutenant in August 1874.

While serving at Jubbulpore in 1875 Chamberlain developed a new variation of black pool by introducing coloured balls into the game. It was dubbed snooker—a derogatory nickname given to first-year cadets studying at the Royal Military Academy at Woolwich that Chamberlain had heard about from a young Royal Artillery subaltern visiting the mess. Chamberlain later retorted to a fellow player who had failed to pot a coloured ball: 'Why, you're a regular snooker'. While explaining the term to his fellow officers Chamberlain, to mollify the officer concerned, remarked that they were all 'snookers at the game' and the name snooker or snooker's pool immediately stuck.

In 1876 Chamberlain transferred to the Indian Staff Corps and in August he was posted to the 1st Central India horse. During the Second Anglo-Afghan War (1878–80) he served on the staff of Sir Frederick Roberts, and was present during the fighting at the Peiwar Kotal, Sapari Pass, in the Khost valley, Charasiah, and the operations in and around the Sherpur cantonment. When it reached Kabul in September 1880 Chamberlain rejoined his regiment and was later wounded at the battle of Kandahar. For his services he was mentioned in dispatches and awarded the campaign medal with four clasps and a bronze star.

Chamberlain was an aide-de-camp to Sir Frederick Roberts when he served as commander-in-chief in Madras between 1881 and 1885. While residing at the hill station at Ootacamund, Chamberlain introduced snooker to members of the local club. It quickly became popular among members of the Ootacamund club, who worked out its rules in detail for the first time and posted them in the billiards room. It also gained widespread popularity among officers from military units stationed all over India who were introduced to the game while on leave. It also spread further afield. During a dinner with the maharaja of Cooch Behar and Chamberlain, John Ross, a professional billiards player, learned the rules and later introduced it to Britain, where it quickly became established.

Chamberlain was promoted captain in August 1885 and soon after major. On 1 September 1886 he married Mary Henrietta (d. 1936), daughter of Major-General Alexander Charles Hay of the Bengal staff corps. They had one daughter. For service in Burma between 1886 and 1887 he was awarded the campaign medal and a clasp. He was promoted lieutenant-colonel on 1 July 1887. Between 1890 and 1897 he served as military secretary to the Kashmir government and reorganized the Kashmir army, before being promoted temporary colonel in January 1894.

In February 1899 Chamberlain was promoted substantive colonel and commanded the Khyber force on the north-west frontier of India. During the Second South African War (1899–1902), he served as private secretary to Field Marshal Lord Roberts, was mentioned in dispatches, and awarded the campaign medal and five clasps. He was made CB in 1900.

In 1900 Chamberlain was appointed inspector-general of the Royal Irish Constabulary in an attempt to revitalize the senior ranks of the force. He was made a KCB in 1903 and KCVO in 1911. By the time of the home rule crisis in 1914, however, his reputation had fallen. Sir Matthew Nathan, the under-secretary for Ireland, regarded him as a blunderer (Ó Broin, 118). Unimpressed by the value of the intelligence gathered by the Royal Irish Constabulary, Major-General Sir Arthur Paget, general officer commanding Ireland, requested the appointment of a replacement for Chamberlain, whom he described as 'a man lacking in character and initiative', in the event of martial law being imposed (Paget to J. E. B. Seely, 23 March 1914, Beckett,

336). There were further moves to replace him early in 1916 as the situation in Ireland deteriorated, but he remained to lead the force at the time of the Easter rising. The Hardinge commission of inquiry commended Chamberlain's handling of the rising, but criticisms of the constabulary's intelligence failures continued, and he was replaced in July 1916.

Following his retirement Chamberlain enjoyed shooting and fishing as his main recreations and was an active member of the Naval and Military Club. He died of myocarditis at his home, The Wilderness, Ascot, Berkshire, on 28 May 1944.   T. R. MOREMAN

Sources WWW · *Quarterly Indian Army List* (1 July 1900) · C. Egerton, *The history of snooker and billiards* (1986) · W. A. Watson, *King George's own central India horse* (1930) · Burke, *Peerage* (1924) · Walford, *County families* (1919) · b. cert. · d. cert. · E. O'Halpin, *The decline of the union: British government in Ireland, 1892–1920* (1987) · L. Ó Broin, *The chief secretary: Augustine Birrell in Ireland* (1969) · I. F. W. Beckett, ed., *The army and the Curragh incident, 1914* (1986) · *Daily Telegraph* (23 March 2000), 31
Wealth at death £15,083 11s. 10d.: probate, 14 Aug 1944, CGPLA Eng. & Wales

Chamberlain [Chamberlane], **Robert** (1570/71–1636), Franciscan friar, was probably born at Niselrath, now Rathneestin, in the parish of Tallonstown, co. Louth, the son of Roger Chamberlain (Mac Artúir). His family had been in Ireland nearly four hundred years, had taken the Irish patronymic Mac Artúir, and were supporters of Irish culture; Robert Chamberlain was considered to be of old Irish stock. An informant in 1607 said, strangely, 'his right name is Edward Arthur, a Connaught man' (Jennings, *Wild Geese*, 533). Before the end of the sixteenth century Chamberlain appears to have obtained a doctorate in theology at Salamanca and was ordained there, although his name is not on the surviving list of students from 1595 at the Irish College in Salamanca.

Chamberlain wrote in Irish, English, Latin, and Spanish, and became confessor and counsellor to Hugh O'Neill, earl of Tyrone. In 1599 he was in Ireland with O'Neill, who, according to the earl of Essex, 'dare[d] not give the least show of conformity to Her Majesty's obedience' in the presence of Chamberlain or of Friar Peter Nangle (*CSP Ire.*, 1598–9, 475). In 1600 or 1601 Chamberlain was sent to Spain by Tyrone, probably as tutor to his son Henry at Salamanca, and at other times on important business. Both were in the Spanish Netherlands in 1605, and Chamberlain was said to have been in London in disguise in 1606, sending information back to the earls of Tyrone and Tyrconnell. In August that year Philip III granted him a salary of 30 crowns a month for his services to the army in Flanders, mentioning that five of Chamberlain's brothers had served in the war in Ireland with the loss of two. On 21 October 1607 he met the now exiled earls at Douai in company with Florence Conry OFM and probably accompanied them to Louvain, where Conry had just received permission for an Irish Franciscan foundation. When the earls set out for Rome in February 1608 Chamberlain went to Spain 'on business' (Jennings, *Wild Geese*, 102). In 1609 it was reported to the earl of Salisbury that, under Tyrone's direction, Chamberlain was writing an apologia 'attacking the State for the wrongs done to him [Tyrone] wherein are many passages slanderous to his Lordship', Salisbury (*CSP Ire.*, *1606–8*, 419). In June 1608 the Spanish authorities renewed the grant of 30 crowns a month to Chamberlain 'to continue his services at Louvain' (Jennings, *Wild Geese*, 108).

In February 1610 Chamberlain joined the order of Friars Minor at Louvain, being professed a year later, aged about forty. His will, then drawn up, mentioned the friars at Drogheda three times, which may mean that he was enrolled as an alumnus or son of that friary, and may have had close ties with it from his youth. He bequeathed his books to the friars there, his money to his relatives, and a small gold cross to Eoin MacMahon, bishop of Clogher. He appointed Bonaventure O'Hussey OFM his executor, and in 1611 wrote the official approval of O'Hussey's Irish catechism. He became a highly respected lecturer in theology at Louvain, but kept in touch with the Irish literary scene. In 1616–17 he contributed two poems to 'Iomarbhágh na bhFileadh' (the 'Contention of the bards'), a poetical dispute sparked off by Tadhg Mac Dáire Mac Bruaideadha, his declared aim being to put an end to controversy, 'the duty of one in my calling' (Mhág Craith, 2.76). He continued to help Tyrone: on 22 July 1622 William Trumbull, English representative at Brussels, reported that Chamberlain had just returned from Rome with an order from Tyrone concerning the gathering of ships for a descent on the Irish coast. On 14 September Trumbull wrote that Chamberlain had set out again for Rome 'with an errand of great secrecy' (Meehan, 427–8), perhaps to do with a projected Spanish marriage for a son of Tyrone. On the death of Hugh MacCaughwell OFM in 1626 Chamberlain refused to be considered for the archbishopric of Armagh, though his name was put forward by royal sponsors in France and the Spanish Netherlands, the papal nuncios there, the O'Neills and O'Donnells, and the clergy of Armagh; and though he may have been MacCaughwell's own choice, Chamberlain had had no experience of pastoral care in Ireland and had been banned by the English. A very careful writer, he left behind him two treatises on divine knowledge, 'De scientia Dei' and 'De futuris contingentibus'. Two Latin epitaphs, on Philip III of Spain and Archduke Albert, have been attributed to him, but may have been the work of his nephew, Christopher Chamberlain. Chamberlain died at St Anthony's College, Louvain, on 11 June 1636, aged sixty-five, and was buried there. IGNATIUS FENNESSY

Sources F. O'Brien, *Irish Ecclesiastical Record*, 5th ser., 40 (1932), 264–80 · T. G. F. Paterson, 'The Chamberlains of Nizelrath', *Journal of the County Louth Archaeological Society*, 10 (1944), 324–6 · L. Waddingus [L. Wadding], *Scriptores ordinis minorum*, [new edn] (1906), 205 · *CSP Ire.*, *1598–9*, 475; *1599–1600*, 63; *1603–6*, 569; *1606–8*, 419 · J. Brady, 'The Irish colleges in the Low Countries', *Archivium Hibernicum*, 14 (1949), 66–91 · C. P. Meehan, *The fate and fortunes of Hugh O'Neill, earl of Tyrone, and Rory O'Donel, earl of Tyrconnel*, 3rd edn (1886), 71–2, 255, 263, 427–8, 432, 444, 456 · B. Jennings, 'Irish names in the Malines ordination registers, 1602–1749', *Irish Ecclesiastical Record*, 5th ser., 75–6 (1951) · B. Jennings, ed., *Wild geese in Spanish Flanders, 1582–1700*, IMC (1964), 102, 532–3 · T. Sweeney, *Ireland and the printed word: a short descriptive catalogue of early books … relating to Ireland, printed, 1475–1700* (Dublin, 1997), no. 957–66 · C. Mhág Craith, ed., *Dán na mBráthar Minúr*, 2 vols. (1967–80), vol. 1, pp. 178–94; vol. 2, pp. 70–78, 199–203 · J. Leerssen, *The contention of the bards (Iomarbhágh na bhFileadh) and its place in Irish political and literary history*, subsidiary ser., ITS, 2 (1994), 46, 52n., 58–61 · L. McKenna, ed., *Iomarbhágh na bhFileadh*, 2 vols. (1918) · Franciscan Library, Killiney, Ireland, MSS A30, C11, D3/171–4, D9/341–2 · MSS, St Isidore's College, Rome · M. K. Walsh, *'Destruction by peace': Hugh O'Neill after Kinsale* (1986), 172–3, 174–5

Archives Franciscan Library, Killiney, co. Dublin, MSS · St Isidore's College, Rome, MSS

Chamberlain, Robert (*bap.* 1607), writer, was baptized on 13 April 1607 at Standish, Lancashire, the eldest child of Richard Chamberlain and Jennet, *née* Morris. He became clerk to Peter Ball, solicitor-general to Queen Henrietta Maria, and in 1637 Ball sent Chamberlain to study at Exeter College, Oxford, a kindness acknowledged in the fact that many of Chamberlain's dedications, starting with that of the first of his four jest books in 1635, are to members of the Ball family, including Ball's son William. At Exeter he probably trained for the clergy. There is no record of his having taken a degree, but in his commendatory verse to Thomas Jordan's *The Walks of Islington and Hogsdon* (1657, but first produced in 1641) he signs himself master of arts.

Chamberlain's friends, dedicatees, and those for whom or from whom he wrote or received commendatory verses included Thomas Nabbes, the London cleric Thomas Kendall, John Tatham, Richard Brome, Thomas Rawlins, Charles Gerbier, Edward Benlowes, and Humphrey Mills. Presumably because of the Exeter College connection, and because Peter Ball was a native of Devon who became recorder of Exeter in 1632, Chamberlain's poems also affectionately address, and in some cases claim kin with, a number of citizens of Exeter, as well as evidently borrowing from the Devon-based Robert Herrick. His first two jest books are entirely compilations, with only the third and fourth containing any original material: *Conceits, Clinches, Flashes, and Whimsies* (1639, and containing a joke about Shakespeare), and *Jocabella, or, A Cabinet of Conceits, whereunto are Added Epigrams, and other Poems* (1640, partially reproducing *Conceits*, and entirely lacking the promised epigrams).

Chamberlain's poetry, which is chiefly contained in *Nocturnall Lucubrations, or, Meditations Divine and Moral* (1638) and *The Harmony of the Muses* (1654), ostentatiously parades classical learning, and there are also a number of references to Asia which seem to suggest an interest in the continent; otherwise his verse is characterized mainly by the occasional rather heavy-handed metrical experiment and by conventional praise of private life over the cares of high public office.

Chamberlain's 1640 comedy *The Swaggering Damsell* seems to bear signs of having been written for the Phoenix. The dedicatory verses by E. B. (Edward Benlowes) praise it for its lack of bawdry and suitability for a female audience, and for the way it makes the figure of a female cavalier acceptable; and the chasteness of the lead characters' standards of honour and behaviour (even if not always their practice) do indeed accord with Henrietta Maria's emphasis on purity and platonic love. It is notable too for the fact that, in a plot which ingeniously and unpredictably combines elements of *Much Ado about Nothing* and of *The Taming of the Shrew*, its hero as well as its heroine cross-dresses, and it is indeed in this state of mutual disguise that they actually marry, with the groom's initial disgust at his bride's willingness to anticipate their wedding night eventually overcome and a happy ending secured.

It is now generally accepted that Chamberlain was the author of *Balaam's Asse Cudgeld* (1661), one of a number of texts responding to Lewis Griffin's *The asses complaint against Balaam, or, The cry of the country against ignorant and scandalous ministers* (1661) (the reference in the opening lines to Duke Humphrey's ghost does suggest an Oxford man, just as the explicit recollection of 1648 bespeaks an author with a long memory). It provides the last known indication of Chamberlain's literary activity or indeed existence.

LISA HOPKINS

Sources DNB · J. A. Gertzman, 'Robert Chamberlain and Robert Herrick', *N&Q*, 218 (1973), 182–4 · R. P. Fordyce, 'A diplomatic edition of Robert Chamberlaine's comedy *The swaggering damsell* (1640): the man and the play', PhD diss., University of Pittsburgh, 1972 · G. E. Bentley, *The Jacobean and Caroline stage*, 7 vols. (1941–68), vol. 3, pp. 152–4 · IGI

Chamberlain, Robert (1632?–1696), merchant and mathematician, may have been the Robert Chamberlain who attended Merchant Taylors' School for one year in 1645. If so, he was born on 13 June 1632 in Whitefriars, London, the youngest of ten children of Robert Chamberlain, 'Citizen and drawer of cloth', of Langbourne ward and Margery, his wife. There was, however, more than one Robert Chamberlain born in London near the same time, so his parentage is not certain. On 17 December 1663 a Robert Chamberlain married Catherine Wacom at the church of St Benet Paul's Wharf, London.

Having been in business in Virginia and in England, in 1678 Chamberlain was living in Northumberland Alley, Fenchurch Street, and described himself as an 'accomptant and practicioner of the mathematicks'. In 1679 he published *The accomptant's guide or merchant's book-keeper … with tables for the reducing of Flemish ells into English, and English into Flemish, … also … tables of exchange … with a journal or ledger*. The same year he also published *Chamberlain's arithmetick, being a plain and easie explanation of the most useful and necessary art of arithmetick in whole numbers and fractions … whereunto are added many rules and tables of interest, rebate, purchases, gaging of cask, and extraction of the square and cube roots, composed by Robert Chamberlain, accomptant and practicioner in the mathematicks*. The book was printed by John Clark of Mercer's Chappel, Cheapside; its frontispiece shows a portrait of Chamberlain engraved by W. Binneman as a man aged between thirty-five and fifty, with shoulder-length curled hair, large eyes, and aquiline

nose, together with a dedication to Thomas Lord Needham, and an anonymous laudatory poem to Chamberlain:

Ingenuous Chamberlain, brave soul, see heere,
In his Effigies, hee make appeare.
That cant withstand his wisdom, paines & skill
Which puzzled ages past, Numbers nor will
Triumph in their fam'd patron, Chamberlaine
Whose Art 'yond All, makes things abstruse most plaine.

H. Bromley, in his *Catalogue of Portraits*, states that Chamberlain died in 1696. No will or burial is recorded.

JOHN BRUNTON

Sources R. Chamberlain, *The accomptant's guide* (1679) · Mrs E. P. Hart, ed., *Merchant Taylors' School register, 1561–1934*, 1 (1936) · R. Chamberlain, *Chamberlain's arithmetick, being a plain and easie explanation* (1679) · 'Boyd's Inhabitants of London', Society of Genealogists, London, 1069 · H. Bromley, *A catalogue of engraved British portraits* (1793) · E. G. R. Taylor, *The mathematical practitioners of Tudor and Stuart England* (1954), 275 · IGI
Likenesses W. Binneman, engraving, repro. in Chamberlain, *Chamberlain's arithmetick*, frontispiece · W. Binneman, line engraving, BM, NPG; repro. in Chamberlain, *Accomptant's guide*

Chamberlain, Robert (*bap.* 1736?, *d.* 1798), enameller and porcelain manufacturer, may have been the 'base son' (baptismal register) of Sarah Chamberlain and an unknown father, baptized at St Michael's, Bedwardine, Worcester, on 1 August 1736. He was co-founder with his second son, **Humphrey Chamberlain** (*bap.* 1762, *d.* 1841), of the porcelain manufactory Chamberlains at Worcester. Robert Chamberlain was apprenticed to Richard Holdship of the Worcester Porcelain Company, about 1751, 'to learn pot painting' (enrolments of freemen, 26 Dec 1774). Tradition says that he was that company's first apprentice at Warmstry House (Green, 2.22ff) and he was employed there for some thirty years. He was probably the Robert Chamberlain who married a Mary Taylor (*bap.* 1734?) on 21 October 1753 at St Clement's, Worcester, by special licence, claiming to be over twenty-one years. They subsequently had eight children: Robert (1755–1832), Sarah (*b.* 1757), Mary (1759–1830), Humphrey (*bap.* 17 April 1762 at St Peter's, Worcester, *d.* 1841), Elizabeth (January–May 1775), Lucinda (January–May 1777), Ann (1779–1846), and George (1782–1836). The family lived in King Street, in St Peter's parish. Having enrolled as a freeman of Worcester in 1774, Chamberlain took his sons Robert and Humphrey as apprentices in 1775 and 1776 respectively. His importance to the Worcester Porcelain Company while in charge of the decorating department 'for many years' (Green, 2.23ff) has, in Frost's opinion, been seriously underestimated (Frost, 36). Chamberlain added to the family's income from 1779 by also holding the licence of an alehouse in St Peter's called The Chequer. After the Worcester Porcelain Company was sold to Thomas Flight of Hackney, Middlesex, in 1783, Chamberlain left and with his son Humphrey set up as independent decorators in Worcester, his reputation being such as to bring financial support from a prominent citizen, Richard Nash, and an agreement to decorate ware for Turner of Caughley. By 1789 they needed their own retail shop in Worcester High Street. Their gilding and enamelling was of such quality that as early as 1792 they decorated pieces of Caughley intended for the duke of York. George Davis, painter of Fancy Birds, became their senior decorator. Humphrey Chamberlain had married Ann Draycott (1763?–1851) about 1785 and she appears to have acted as the firm's secretary. It was probably Humphrey's ambition and business acumen that led them to manufacture hybrid hard paste porcelain from the early 1790s at Diglis in Worcester, thus becoming rivals not only to Flights but to Turner as well. Robert and Humphrey Chamberlain began as equal partners, but in 1796 Robert passed to his son Robert half his share in this expanding family firm which now manufactured wares for royalty. Chamberlain, the family founder, died on 19 December 1798 'This morning … much respected, after a lingering illness' (*Berrow's Worcester Journal*, 19 Dec 1798) and was buried at St Peter's on 21 December. From an estate valued at £2021 15s. 1d., he left 10 guineas to his grandson and apprentice Thomas Grainger, later founder of the third porcelain works in Worcester.

By 1801 Humphrey Chamberlain owned three-quarters of the business, and from 1804 to 1811 the brothers had Edward Grey Boulton as a sleeping partner. They prospered. The order books of the early 1800s which are held with other records of the firm at the Worcester Porcelain Museum read like a social register, the wares, and in particular the armorial table wares such as those Viscount Nelson ordered in 1802, suited opulent regency taste. In 1807 the firm received a royal warrant from the prince of Wales, in whose honour Humphrey Chamberlain named his Regent china body of 1811 from which superb dinner services were made, including those for Princess Charlotte and for the East India Company. From 1811 the business was in the indefatigable Humphrey's capable hands, Robert Chamberlain, junior, seemingly just drawing rent from a share of the properties. Humphrey employed his three sons, Henry (1790–1863), Humphrey (1791–1824), an outstanding ceramics painter, and Walter (1795–1868). When the Chamberlains' own London retail premises were opened in 1814 at 63 Piccadilly, Wedgwood's London manager feared Humphrey would prove 'a dangerous rival in our china trade' (Godden, 103). The showrooms moved to 155 New Bond Street in 1816, with Henry continuing in charge selling pretty trifles such as animal figurines, scent bottles, and miniature watering cans alongside the vases and tablewares, examples of which can be seen at the Worcester Porcelain and Victoria and Albert museums. Humphrey was mayor of Worcester, 1818–19, but the mid-1820s produced business and personal problems for him. There was keen competition from new Staffordshire firms, his son Humphrey died, and the irascible Henry left the firm having quarrelled with his formidable father over politics. Having 'amassed a considerable fortune' (Binns, 170), Humphrey retired in 1828, leaving Walter to run the manufactory with his brother-in-law, John Lilley. He lived long enough to see Walter organize the 1840 merger with the Worcester Porcelain Company in a joint stock company which traded as Chamberlain & Co.,

which ultimately manufactured only at Diglis, but, somewhat ironically, preserved the name of the Worcester Porcelain Company. Humphrey Chamberlain died of apoplexy at Park Place, parish of St Martin, Worcester, on 27 February 1841, and was buried at St Oswald's on 5 March.

SONIA F. G. PARKINSON

Sources S. F. G. Parkinson, 'Chamberlains of Worcester: the early years of a family enterprise', *Journal of the Northern Ceramics Society*, 8 (1991), 33–60 · R. W. Binns, *A century of potting in the city of Worcester* (1865) · H. E. Frost, 'Worcester porcelain: the forgotten years, 1774–1783', *The International Ceramics Fair and Seminar* [1991], 34–9 [exhibition catalogue, Park Lane Hotel, London] · Worcester Porcelain Museum, Chamberlain MSS, family and business · G. A. Godden, *Chamberlain–Worcester porcelain, 1788–1852* (1982) · V. Green, *The history and antiquities of the city and suburbs of Worcester*, 2 (1796) · affidavits and enrolments of freemen (Worcester City), Worcs. RO, X496.5 BA9360 A15 · parish registers, St Michael's Bedwardine, St Peter's, St Clement's, St Swithin's, St Martin's, St Oswald's, Worcestershire Library and History Centre, Worcester [microfilm] · leases, Worcester City Corporation, Worcs. RO, X496.5 BA9360 A21 · 'Mr. James Hickman and others to Mr. William Blew a trustee conveyance and declaration as to the interest of Messrs. Chamberlain in the premises', 20 Nov 1801, Worcs. RO · Humphrey Chamberlain, will, PRO [probate, 18 Nov 1841] · d. cert. [no. 106, Worcester Registration District, 4 March 1841] [Humphrey Chamberlain] · apprenticeship enrolments, Worcester City, 1742–1868, Worcs. RO, X496.5 BA9360 A11 [7 vols.] · recognizances of licensed victuallers (Worcester City), Worcs. RO, X496.5 BA9360 B9 · Dean and Chapter, Worcester, deeds, Worcs. RO, 009.1 BA2602, boxes 71, 72, 73 · Robert Chamberlain, will, Worcestershire Library and History Centre, X900.87 PG1015 [probate 12 June 1799, microfilm] · *Berrow's Worcester Journal* (19 Dec 1798)

Archives Worcester Porcelain Museum, Severn Street, Worcester, business and family MSS · Worcs. RO, family notes, 705.394 BA6335 | Worcs. RO, *Chamberlain pedigree notes* by Arthur Hill, 899.31 BA4380

Wealth at death £2021 15s. 1d.: Mr. James Hickman and others to Mr. William Blew, Worcs. RO · £300 p.a., £1500 in trust, household goods, and Park Cottage to widow; £3000 to each of three daughters; equivalent interest in porcelain business to two sons and to one daughter: Humphrey Chamberlain: will, PRO

Chamberlain, Sir Thomas (*c*.1504–1580), diplomat and financial agent, was the son of William Chamberlain of Hopton, Derbyshire, and his wife, Elizabeth Fleming of Dartmouth, Devon. He seems to have been distantly related to the gentry family of the same name in Oxfordshire, where his nephew, the judge Sir Thomas *Chamberlain (*d*. 1625), settled. His preparation for a career in diplomatic service probably began in 1539 with his first journey to Spain as a royal courier. In 1540 he may well have acted as messenger of Sir Thomas Wyatt the younger, during the envoy's sojourn in the Low Countries. Two years later Chamberlain was entrusted with the delivery of money to Spain, and in 1543 he acted as courier of Edmund Bonner, bishop of London, while the latter was accredited ambassador to the imperial court. By March 1542 Chamberlain had also become a groom of the chamber.

Chamberlain had clearly acquired a considerable reputation by 1544 when he assumed the dual role of royal agent in the Low Countries—Stephen Vaughan having asked for him to take over important negotiations for foreign loans—and governor of the Merchant Adventurers at

Antwerp, a key position in English foreign trade. He was also heavily involved in hiring German mercenaries, which led to embarrassing lawsuits against him in the Low Countries and a claim of diplomatic immunity. He assisted, and translated for, Thomas Thirlby and Sir William Petre in trade negotiations. Chamberlain organized an English boycott of Antwerp in 1548 in response to new customs duties, and then accompanied Sir Thomas Smith to Brussels wearing his diplomatic hat—though as a junior partner receiving £1 6s. 8d. a day to Smith's £2 13s. 4d. It was agreed that in return for customs concessions Chamberlain would resign as governor in favour of a 'peaceful, discreet man' (CSP Spain, 1545–6, 559). After leaving the Low Countries altogether he undertook in 1549 a trade-orientated embassy to Denmark and Sweden, and in 1550 he acted as interpreter for a reciprocal Swedish embassy.

Chamberlain was appointed vice-treasurer of the Bristol mint between 1549 and 1550 to clear up the confusion left by Sir William Sharington's malfeasance. Under Chamberlain 'Bristol was transformed into a highly efficient mint' (Challis, 259), with a higher-quality output than the Tower of London. The operation was none the less wound up, Chamberlain closing his accounts some £218 in surplus rather than with the usual deficit. While at the mint he started buying land in Gloucestershire with Richard Pate, paying the augmentations office £1134 for chantry property in and around Gloucester. In 1550 he was awarded a life pension of £133 6s. 8d.—the salary he had received at Bristol—but two years later it had apparently shrunk to £100.

In June 1550 Chamberlain was sent as ambassador to the regent of the Netherlands, Mary of Hungary. He was almost certainly knighted for the occasion, as his title first appears in his correspondence just after that date. Although still inclined to alarmism about imperial intentions towards England, he cultivated good local contacts and married Anne van der Zenny (d. 1556x8). They had no children. He complained of tactless blunders during personal audiences with the emperor, Charles V, by Sir Richard Morison in 1551 and Sir Andrew Dudley in 1553. However John Dudley, duke of Northumberland, accused Chamberlain of 'blind walking' (PRO, SP 10/15/74). Chamberlain's insistence on freedom to have protestant services in Brussels to counterbalance ambassadorial masses in London started the dispute over diplomatic immunity in 1551, though Morison did manage to exacerbate the situation.

The privy council conceded in September 1550 that Chamberlain 'hathe hadd no money as yet and hathe also great neede' (APC, 1550–52, 123). Chamberlain continued private cloth-trading activities as ambassador, saying that it was the only way to avoid a fraudulent exchange rate, but had mixed success. He was still able to lend money: after being fined heavily in 1552, William Paget, first Baron Paget, owed Chamberlain £204. Chamberlain was granted the barony of Churchdown, Gloucestershire, valued at £175 13s. od. per annum in June 1552 'in consideration of his services and the great charges which he has sustained therein', but apparently he later had to pay

£1200 to buy out the crown's residual interest (CPR, 1550–53, 357).

Chamberlain spent 1555–6 in Brussels, where he made financial arrangements for Edward Courtenay, earl of Devonshire, to go to Italy, but was also in contact with Mary I's ambassador in Spain, Sir John Mason. Although he was perhaps suspect on religious grounds, the stress of the war with France led to his employment in 1558 as a victualler. On the accession of Elizabeth I he was once again regarded as an official asset, notably by Sir William Cecil, principal secretary. In 1559 he was returned to parliament for the duchy of Cornwall borough of Camelford, where he took charge of a bill on probate, which, however, came to nothing. A testimony to the regard in which he was now held was the grand baptism in October 1559 at St Benet Paul's Wharf, London, of Chamberlain's son with his second wife, Joan Macham or Machell, née Ludington (d. 1563x7), widow of a sheriff of London, whom he had married a year earlier. This child—presumably John (d. 1617)—had John, duke of Finland (son of Eric XIV of Sweden), Sir Robert Dudley, and Elizabeth Parr, marchioness of Northampton, as godparents. Chamberlain and his wife also had another son, Edmund (1563–1634), and a daughter, Theophila (d. after 1580). Chamberlain's third wife, Anne Pierson, whom he was licensed to marry in October 1567, was another widow of a London worthy, but her father, Anthony Monck, was apparently of the Devon gentry. She was mother of at least two more sons, including Thomas (1568–1640).

Chamberlain left for Spain in January 1560 as professional assistant—and probably protestant watchdog—to Anthony Browne, first Viscount Montague. Their ticklish task of persuading Philip II to countenance the English invasion of Scotland was at least successful in protracting negotiations until the crisis was resolved. While Montague returned, Chamberlain was to 'reside there for a season, until … we may consider how to revocque you, and to place some other in your place' (Forbes, 1.445). Chamberlain inclined to 'warrant th'yndifferent frendship' of Philip and his 'inclination naturall to peax & quietnes' (PRO, SP 70/21, fols. 9r, 32r). Yet he considered Brussels as a more useful base for negotiation than Madrid, and his frustration was aggravated by a repeat of the religious trouble of 1551. Chamberlain more than anyone else in the period 'stated the privileges of an ambassador so clearly and so firmly' when it came to defending the embassy cook against the inquisition—an extension of privileges more often considered to be personal (Adair, 113).

Chamberlain responded to the delay in recalling him with a litany of complaints about his shortage of money and ill health—he finally escaped, overland via Paris, at the beginning of 1562. To clear his Spanish liabilities before his departure he required help from Gómez Suárez de Figueroa, count of Feria and husband of an Englishwoman, Jane Dormer, whose friendship he (unlike the later envoy John Man) managed to keep. The government tacitly admitted the inadequacy of a £3 diet by later increasing the normal daily allowance to £3 6s. 8d., but

Chamberlain was probably not economical—the 'plente' provided at the baptism in 1559 may have been typical (*Diary of Henry Machyn*, 225).

Whenever further service was proposed Chamberlain relied on the plea that Spain had broken his health. If he was proposed for another mission to Brussels in 1563 the entire idea was abandoned. He was appointed in 1571 to head a commission into corruption in the London customs but did not act in this capacity either, perhaps because it upset vested financial interests. He did act on less contentious commissions concerning coinage. His main interests were now local, with property in Gloucestershire south of Cheltenham at Compton Abdale, Churchdown, and Prestbury (where he was also keeper of the royal park), and in London at Cripplegate. Chamberlain was a JP for Gloucestershire from 1559 and for Middlesex from 1561, and he was promoted of the quorum for these counties in 1564 and 1569 respectively.

Chamberlain died some time between 27 July 1580, when he made his will, and 11 November 1580, when it was proved. It referred to mortgages on some of his lands and restricted charity largely to what the executors thought 'convenient', but still granted annuities of £44 and provided bequests of over £50 in cash. Theophila was basically disinherited, having 'in some sorte entangled hirself … withe a lewde felowe of base condicon called Richarde Webbe' (will, PRO, PROB 11/62, sig. 45). This *faux pas* aside, Chamberlain's children enjoyed the fruits of his valued government service and established position among the Gloucestershire gentry, and John Chamberlain became sheriff, knight, and MP.   JULIAN LOCK

Sources HoP, *Commons, 1558–1603*, 1.589–91 · G. M. Bell, 'Men and their rewards in Elizabethan diplomatic service, 1558–85', PhD diss., U. Cal., Los Angeles, 1974, 36–7, 47, 74, 106, 115, 122, 132ff., 144–5, 195–200 · *LP Henry VIII*, 14/1.15–20 · *APC*, 1542–52, 1558–70, 1575–7 · *CPR*, 1547–8; 1549–51; 1550–53 · PRO, State papers domestic, Edward VI, SP 10 · PRO, State papers domestic, Mary, SP 11 · PRO, State papers foreign, Edward VI, SP 68 · PRO, State papers foreign, Elizabeth, SP 70 · BL, Add. MSS 5753, 39866 · BL, Cotton MSS, Galba B xii, Vespasian C vii · PRO, REQ 2/17 · PRO, E 101/303/6 · *CSP Spain*, 1545–6; 1549–52; 1558–67 · *The diary of Henry Machyn, citizen and merchant-taylor of London, from AD 1550 to AD 1563*, ed. J. G. Nichols, CS, 42 (1848) · P. Forbes, *A full view of the public transactions in the reign of Queen Elizabeth*, 2 vols. (1740–41) · E. R. Adair, *The extraterritoriality of ambassadors in the sixteenth and seventeenth centuries* (1929) · will, PRO, PROB 11/62, sig. 45 · J. L. Chester and J. Foster, eds., *London marriage licences, 1521–1869* (1887), 259 · C. E. Challis, *The Tudor coinage* (1978) **Archives** BL, letter-book, Add. MS 39868 · PRO, diplomatic corresp., SP 1, SP 68, SP 70 | BL, diplomatic corresp., Cotton MSS Galba B xii, Vespasian C vii · BL, letters to privy council, Add. MS 5753 · Hatfield House, Hertfordshire, letters to Sir William Cecil and privy council **Wealth at death** £175 13s. 1d. p.a. from Churchdown barony, Gloucestershire; also Gloucester lands bought for £1134 in 1549 which might have brought in £45–£55 p.a. at 4–5 per cent of capital value; more than £50 cash given in will; plus £44 worth of annuities: *CPR*, 1547–9, 260–67, 1550–53, 357; PRO, PROB 11/62, sig. 45

Chamberlain, Sir Thomas (d. 1625), judge, was the son of William Chamberlain, who had settled in Ireland. Sir Thomas Chamberlain (c.1504–1580), sometime English envoy to the Netherlands, was his uncle. He entered Gray's Inn in 1578 and was called to the bar in 1585. His early practice was unspectacular, but he was steward to Lord Ellesmere and from 1591 he was retained as solicitor to Lord Berkeley, and his career was seemingly profitable enough to enable him to contribute substantially to building works in the inn. He was less enthusiastic about contributing to its less material aspects, and in 1606 he was fined £40 for refusing the office of reader. From the first decade of the seventeenth century Chamberlain invested heavily in lands in Oxfordshire. He had strong connections with the town of Banbury, whose puritan vicar he described as his loving friend, and where he served as recorder from 1608 to his death.

Chamberlain's life took a new direction in the second decade of the century. In 1612 he married Elizabeth, widow of Sir William Stafford, and in 1614 he was created serjeant-at-law. In 1615 he was appointed to the Welsh bench as justice of Anglesey, and in 1616 he was knighted and created chief justice of Chester. He held this office until 1620, when he was made a judge of the court of king's bench. He was spoken of as a candidate for the vacant position of master of the rolls in 1621, though he was not successful; in 1624 he was called back to his former position of chief justice of Chester after friction had arisen between the then chief justice, Sir James Whitelock, and the lord president of Wales. His first wife having died in 1620, in 1622 Chamberlain married Elizabeth, daughter of Lord Hunsdon and widow of Sir Thomas Berkeley, reputedly making her a jointure of £1000 per year. He died on 27 September 1625 leaving a daughter and three sons, the eldest of whom, also Thomas, was made a baronet. He was buried on 1 October 1625.

DAVID IBBETSON

Sources W. R. Prest, *The rise of the barristers: a social history of the English bar, 1590–1640* (1986), 349 · J. H. Baker, *An introduction to English legal history*, 2nd edn (1979), 504 · W. R. Williams, *The history of the great sessions in Wales, 1542–1830* (privately printed, Brecon, 1899), 33 · J. S. W. Gibson and E. R. C. Brinkworth, eds., *Banbury corporation records: Tudor and Stuart*, Banbury Historical Society, Records section, 15 (1977) · will, PRO, PROB 11/151, fol. 155v · *VCH Oxfordshire*, vols. 6, 9–10 · T. Wotton, *The English baronets*, 2 (1727), 374–7 · J. Foster, *The register of admissions to Gray's Inn, 1521–1889, together with the register of marriages in Gray's Inn chapel, 1695–1754* (privately printed, London, 1889) · R. J. Fletcher, ed., *The pension book of Gray's Inn*, 2 vols. (1901–10) · *The letters of John Chamberlain*, ed. N. E. McClure, 2 vols. (1939) · J. Smyth, *The Berkeley manuscripts: the lives of the Berkeleys … 1066 to 1618*, ed. J. Maclean, 3 vols. (1883–5) **Wealth at death** relatively wealthy: will, PRO, PROB 11/151, fol. 155v

Chamberlain, William (1770/71–1807), painter, was born in London. Of his parents, nothing is known. He registered with the Royal Academy Schools on 13 August 1790, aged nineteen. He subsequently studied under John Opie RA and submitted to the Royal Academy in 1794 from Opie's address in Berners Street, off Oxford Street, London. He established some reputation as a portrait painter, although no examples of his portrait work are known. Chamberlain's output, although small, constituted animal paintings such as *Portrait of a Newfoundland Dog* (exh.

RA, 1802) and subject pictures. He was an infrequent contributor, sending a modest total of six to the Royal Academy, where in 1803 he was entered as an honorary exhibitor. Between 1803 and 1807 he moved to Hull where his address was given as Robinson Row. Chamberlain died at Hull on 12 July 1807, leaving a widow and six children.

TINA FISKE

Sources GM, 1st ser., 77 (1807), 691 · Monthly Magazine, 24 (1807) · B. Stewart and M. Cutten, The dictionary of portrait painters in Britain up to 1920 (1997) · S. C. Hutchison, 'The Royal Academy Schools, 1768–1830', Walpole Society, 38 (1960–62), 123–91, esp. 151 · A. Earland, John Opie and his circle (1911) · Graves, RA exhibitors · Bénézit, Dict. · Redgrave, Artists · M. Pilkington, A general dictionary of painters: containing memoirs of the lives and works, ed. A. Cunningham and R. A. Davenport, new edn (1857) · Bryan, Painters (1886–9) · Battle's Hull Directory for the year 1807 (1807) · Hull Advertiser (18 July 1807), 3

Chamberlaine, John (c.1745–1812), antiquary, of whose parentage and place of birth nothing is known, had family connections in Wiltshire and his first home may have been there. He held an unidentified position in the royal household by 1772, as in April and September of that year he received payments from the privy purse 'for modelling various Fortifications' and a 'quarterly allowance for Drawing Plans etc' at '£80 per annum' (MS, Windsor Royal Archive, 17272, 17285). Following the death of Richard Dalton in February 1791, Chamberlaine was appointed keeper of the king's drawings and medals with a salary of £300. Chamberlaine held this appointment until his own death in 1812.

In 1764 Dalton had commissioned Francesco Bartolozzi to engrave plates after drawings by Guercino in the royal collection, and later proposed that the engraver make copies of the king's celebrated Holbein portrait drawings. Chamberlaine was responsible for publishing these latter engravings as *Imitations of original drawings, by Hans Holbein, in the collection of his majesty, for the portraits of illustrious persons of the court of Henry VIII, with biographical tracts* (1792–1800). The publication was intended to illuminate the subjects of the drawings rather than to illustrate Holbein's mastery of the pencil, and to that end the herald Edmund Lodge provided biographical notes. Bartolozzi's eighty-four stipple engravings, printed in colour, in folio, were of a high quality but were not entirely faithful to the Holbein originals; when Chamberlaine commissioned a young engraver, Frederick Lewis, to produce a trial plate for a smaller and cheaper edition he realized that Lewis's more accurate reproductions would expose the artistic licence of Bartolozzi's work, and he abandoned the idea. A quarto edition eventually appeared in 1812, reduced from Bartolozzi's plates rather than from the original drawings.

In 1796–7 Chamberlaine published two volumes of drawings by Leonardo da Vinci and the Carracci family, expanded and reissued in 1812 as *Original designs of the most celebrated masters of the Bolognese, Roman, Florentine, and Venetian schools; comprising some of the works of Leonardo da Vinci, the Caracci, Claude Lorraine, Raphael, Michael Angelo, the Poussins, and others, in his majesty's collection* (1812). He employed a number of engravers for these works, including Bartolozzi and his pupil P. W. Tomkins.

Chamberlaine was admitted to the Society of Antiquaries on 7 June 1792 and was for some years a member of the Society of Arts. He seems to have lived in London for at least the last twenty years of his life. He was married, and his wife, Anne, and four children survived him when he died on 12 January 1812 at Paddington Green, London. He was buried in the parish churchyard at Keevil, Wiltshire.

GORDON GOODWIN, rev. CHRISTOPHER MARSDEN

Sources The correspondence of George, prince of Wales, 1770–1812, ed. A. Aspinall, 8: 1811–1812 (1971), 323–4 · GM, 1st ser., 61 (1791), 188 · GM, 1st ser., 82/1 (1812), 92 · European Magazine and London Review, 61 (1812), 78 · A. W. Tuer, Bartolozzi and his works: a biographical and descriptive account of the life and career of Francesco Bartolozzi, R. A., 2nd edn (1885), 81–6 · W. T. Lowndes, The bibliographer's manual of English literature, ed. H. G. Bohn, [new edn], 1 (1869), 405 · will, LMA, DL/C/377, fols. 14–16 · letter of Anne Chamberlaine, 1812, Windsor Castle, Print Room [appended to a copy of J. Chamberlaine, Imitations of original drawings, by Hans Holbein, 1792] · Royal Arch., 17272–17285 · private information (2004) · death duty registers, PRO, IR 26/539, fol. 28 (1812)
Wealth at death approx. £3500: death duty registers, PRO, IR 26/539, fol. 28 (1812)

Chamberlane, Robert. See Chamberlain, Robert (1570/71–1636).

Chamberlayne, Sir Edward (1470–1541). See under Chamberlayne, Sir Edward (1480–1543).

Chamberlayne, Sir Edward (1480–1543), gentleman and soldier, was the first son of Sir Richard Chamberlayne of Coton, Northamptonshire, and Sybil, daughter of Sir Richard Fowler of Rycote, Oxfordshire, and was baptized at Weston on 22 December 1480. The Chamberlaynes traced their lineage back to the eleventh century and the Anglo-Norman house of Tancarville from whom the hereditary chamberlains to the duke of Normandy had been drawn. By the sixteenth century they held land in Bedfordshire, Buckinghamshire, Lincolnshire, Cambridgeshire, and Northamptonshire, as well as pursuing a claim against the duke of Buckingham to certain property in Kent. It was, however, in Oxfordshire that the greater part of the family's land was to be found, inherited by Edward upon his father's death on 28 August 1496. An important addition to his paternal inheritance was made in 1505 when his mother acquired the lease to the manor of Shirburn in Oxfordshire from her brother Richard Fowler which passed to her son upon her death in 1525. Chamberlayne married Cecily, daughter of Sir John Verney of Pendley, Hertfordshire.

It was as a leading member of the Oxfordshire gentry that Chamberlayne would perform his most important service to the crown. Between 1506 and 1539 he served as a commissioner of the peace for Oxfordshire. On at least six occasions his name was on the county's sheriff roll. In November 1523 and August 1524 he was chosen as a commissioner to collect the subsidy for Oxfordshire and Norfolk. In 1529 he represented Wallingford in parliament and in 1530 was one of those appointed to assess the value of Wolsey's possessions in Oxfordshire. Although mostly on the periphery of national affairs, Chamberlayne did take part in a number of the great events of Henry VIII's reign. He joined the funeral cortège of Henry VII as a squire for the body. In 1512 he accompanied the marquess of Dorset to Biscay, leading twenty men in the company of William, Lord Sandys, and the following year he took part in both the ill-fated naval expedition of Edmund Howard and the main invasion of France which culminated in the capture of Tournai. In recognition of his service he was included among those knighted by Henry in Tournai Cathedral on 24 September 1513. Nine years later he returned to France, this time serving in the earl of Surrey's expedition into Picardy between August and October 1522 which ended in the abortive siege of Hesdin. Chamberlayne was also involved in ceremonial diplomacy as a member of the king's entourage in his meetings with François I and Charles V in July 1520 at the Field of Cloth of Gold and Gravelines, and twelve years later, in October 1532, at the second Anglo-French summit held at Calais and Boulogne. On occasion he was resident at court, and was in attendance both at the 1517 banquet held at Greenwich and at the marriage celebrations of Henry and Anne Boleyn in May 1533.

Chamberlayne's energies were, however, mostly devoted to local responsibilities and the management of his Oxfordshire estates. These represented not only the greater part of his assets but also the lion's share of his liabilities. On an unspecified date Chamberlayne was charged in Star Chamber with using his position as lieutenant and keeper of Woodstock Park, granted to him in 1508, to extort money from his tenants. The case appears to have done him little harm since he, in tandem with his eldest son, Leonard *Chamberlayne, was reappointed to the office in 1532. At about this time Sir Edward faced further difficulties when this same son sued him for mismanagement of the Shirburn estates which had been entailed to Leonard in 1528. Chamberlayne was sixty-three when he died on 10 September 1543; he was buried at Woodstock, leaving three sons, Leonard, Edward, and Ralph, and at least three daughters.

This Edward Chamberlayne should not be confused with **Sir Edward Chamberlayne** (1470–1541) of Gedding, Suffolk, second son of Sir Ralph Chamberlayne. It was this Edward Chamberlayne who in company with Sir Edmund Bedingfield was entrusted with the captivity of Katherine of Aragon at Kimbolton in Huntingdonshire between May 1534 and her death on 7 January 1536.

Luke MacMahon

Sources LP Henry VIII · J. G. Nichols, ed., The chronicle of Calais, CS, 35 (1846) · HoP, Commons, 1509–58, 1.614–15 · W. H. Turner, ed., The visitations of the county of Oxford … 1566 … 1574 … and in 1634, Harleian Society, 5 (1871) · CIPM, Henry VII · G. Mattingly, Catherine of Aragon (1942) · monument, Woodstock parish church, Oxfordshire · DNB

Chamberlayne, Edward (1616–1703), writer, was born on 13 December 1616 at Oddington, Gloucestershire, the son of Thomas Chamberlayne and grandson of Sir Thomas Chamberlayne, ambassador to the Low Countries. He matriculated at St Edmund Hall, Oxford, in 1634 and proceeded BA on 20 April 1638 and MA on 6 March 1641, holding the office of rhetoric reader for part of the latter year.

During the whole of the civil war he was on an extended grand tour of northern and southern Europe, during which he visited France, Spain, Italy, Germany, Hungary, Bohemia, Sweden, and the Low Countries; he returned to live in England at the Restoration. In 1658 Chamberlayne married Susannah (d. 1704), daughter of Richard Clifford, with whom he had nine children, one of whom was the writer John *Chamberlayne. In 1669 he became secretary to Charles Howard, earl of Carlisle, and went to Stockholm to invest the king of Sweden with the Garter. At this time Chamberlayne brought out *Angliae notitiae, or, The Present State of England* (1669), his handbook to the social, historical, political, and religious condition of the country; it was modelled, without attribution, on *L'estat nouveau de la France* (Paris, 1661) and dedicated to his employer. Chamberlayne was made LLD at Cambridge in January 1671 and DCL at Oxford on 22 June 1672. About 1679 he was appointed tutor to Henry Fitzroy, illegitimate son of Charles II, and later became tutor to Prince George of Denmark. Chamberlayne was elected a fellow of the Royal Society on 3 December 1668.

Chamberlayne's *Angliae notitiae*, which describes the country's currency, exports, resources, weights and measures, inhabitants, classes of people, laws and customs, religion, and canon law, and lists the current holders of various courtly, judicial, and religious offices, argues that 'A good Historian by running back to Ages past, and by standing still and viewing the present times, and comparing the one with the other, may then run forward, and give a Verdict of the State almost Prophetic' (A3v). The work is a strongly monarchist panegyric on the wonders of Britain:

> O happy and blessed Britannie, above all other Countries in the World, Nature hath enricht thee with all the blessings of Heaven and Earth. Nothing in thee is hurtfull to Mankind, nothing wanting in thee that is desirable, in so much that thou seemest another World placed besides, or without the great World, meerly for the delight and pleasure of Mankind. (p. 8)

It was an immediate success with three editions in the first year of publication and a French translation of the second edition in 1669; and in 1682 there appeared *Scotiae judiculum, or, The Present State of Scotland*, by A. M. Philopatris. By 1689 *Angliae notitiae* had reached its sixteenth edition but Thomas Hearne declares that in it Chamberlayne failed to acknowledge the assistance of Andrew Allam of St Edmund Hall 'who drew up several sheets and communicated them … taking a journey on purpose to London for that End, where he got the small Pox and dyd of it' (*Remarks*, 1.130). In 1691 Guy Miege published *The New State of England*, which sought to profit from the popularity of Chamberlayne's handbook. In the following year Chamberlayne bitterly attacked him:

> in truth, for six lines he has piquaroon'd a hundred from Doctor Chamberlayne, in ipsissimis verbis; for as to the Historical part, 'tis little else but his Book, miserably Transpos'd and Mangl'd, meerly to elude the Law, and is an extravagant mass of Words, jumbl'd into a Hotch-Potch by a French Cook. (N&Q, 7th ser., 1.202)

Despite the competition, Chamberlayne's work reached

at least twenty issues or editions in his lifetime and, after his death, edited by his son John, it remained in print until 1755 with the thirty-fifth edition.

Chamberlayne wrote several other works of social and historical commentary. His historical studies included *The present war parallel'd, or, A brief relation of the five yeares' civil Warres of Henry the third* (1647) and *A Dialogue between an Englishman and a Dutchman Concerning the Late Dutch War* (1672). His socio-religious commentaries included *England's Wants* (1667); *The Converted Presbyterian* (1668); and *An academy or college: wherein young ladies and gentlewomen may at a very moderate expense be duly instructed in the true protestant religion* (1671). He also published *The rise & fall of the late … favourite of Spain, the count Olivares. The unparallel'd imposture of Michael de Molina executed at Madrid in … 1641. The right and title of the present king of Portugall Don John the fourth … Translated out of the Italian, Spanish, and Portuguez* (1653).

In his later lifetime, Chamberlayne lived in Chelsea and contributed £5 per annum so that a poor boy might be bound to a waterman, and, after his death, as a result of his wish, John Chamberlayne continued this benefaction, adding to it an additional £5 to educate the poor boys of the parish. Edward Chamberlayne died in May 1703 at Chelsea and was buried in the churchyard there on 27 May. His wife died on the following 17 December and was buried beside him. According to his friend Walter Harris, for the benefit of posterity he had some of his own books enclosed in wax and buried with him.   REAVLEY GAIR

Sources Wood, *Ath. Oxon.*, new edn, 4.789 · A. Kippis and others, eds., *Biographia Britannica, or, The lives of the most eminent persons who have flourished in Great Britain and Ireland*, 2nd edn, 3 (1784) · *N&Q*, 6th ser., 12 (1885), 189 · *N&Q*, 7th ser., 1 (1886), 123, 202, 462 · *Remarks and collections of Thomas Hearne*, ed. C. E. Doble and others, 1, OHS, 2 (1885), 130 · N. Luttrell, *A brief historical relation of state affairs from September 1678 to April 1714*, 5 (1857), 302 · T. Faulkner, *An historical and topographical description of Chelsea and its environs*, [new edn], 2 (1829) · *DNB* · M. Hunter, *The Royal Society and its fellows, 1660–1700: the morphology of an early scientific institution*, 2nd edn (1994)

Chamberlayne, Sir James, third baronet (*c.*1640–1694), poet, was the second son of Sir Thomas Chamberlayne, first baronet (*d.* 1643), of Wickham, Oxfordshire. He matriculated at Queen's College, Oxford, on 15 June 1657. He married Margaret Goodwin, of Bodicote, Oxfordshire; they had three sons and a daughter. Chamberlayne's elder brother, Thomas, the second baronet, had two daughters; when he died in 1682, Chamberlayne succeeded to the title, but not the estate (the family's considerable Oxfordshire holdings had been settled on his younger niece, Penelope).

Chamberlayne was the author of two volumes of religious verse. 'My only aim', he states in the preface to the first collection, 'was to compose some few things for my private devotion, and that I might not trifle away too much of that time, which God hath given me, having no calling to follow, nor Publick Concern to divert me' (Chamberlayne, sig. A3v). To that end, the work begins with a verse account of Christ's birth and ministry, includes paraphrases of eighteen of the psalms and the book of Lamentations, and concludes with a number of confessional 'Poems on Several Occasions'. He published

his second collection the following year. *Manuductio ad coelum* (1681) is a short volume which translates into verse Cardinal Bona's work of the same title, treating 'Of Joy and Sadness' and 'Of Patience'. Chamberlayne died in October 1694.   JONATHAN PRITCHARD

Sources GEC, *Baronetage*, 2.206–7 · *VCH Oxfordshire*, 6.223, 279, 9.20, 72, 10.47, 55–6, 234 · T. Wotton, *The baronetage of England*, ed. E. Kimber and R. Johnson, 1 (1771), 494–5 · T. Corser, *Collectanea Anglo-poetica, or, A … catalogue of a … collection of early English poetry*, 3, Chetham Society, 71 (1867), 266–70 · J. Chamberlayne, *A sacred poem* (1680) · *The life and times of Anthony Wood*, ed. A. Clark, 2, OHS, 21 (1892), 556 · *CSP dom., 1687–1689*, p. 415, no. 2345 · *DNB*
Wealth at death manor of Salford, Oxfordshire, and its 'messuages, lands, tenements and hereditaments' to wife: GEC, *Baronetage*, 2.207

Chamberlayne, John (1668/9–1723), translator and literary editor, was a younger son of Edward *Chamberlayne (1616–1703), author of *Angliae notitiae, or, The Present State of England*, and his wife, Susannah Clifford (*d.* 1704). He was probably born in Chelsea but may have spent part of his childhood in Oddington, Gloucestershire, where his uncle, Thomas Chamberlayne, was lord of the manor. On 7 April 1685, aged sixteen, he matriculated from Trinity College, Oxford, and in the same year published his first translation, from French and Spanish, *The manner of making coffee, tea, and chocolate as it is used in most parts of Europe, Asia, Africa, and America, with their vertues*. He followed this in 1686 with a translation from the Italian, *A Treasure of Health by Castor Durante Da Gualdo, Physician and Citizen of Rome*; this was dedicated to his uncle. Chamberlayne left Oxford without a degree but entered himself as a student at Leiden on 14 May 1688. His chief study seems to have been modern languages, of which he was reputed to be fluent in sixteen. After his return to England he filled some minor offices at court, including being gentleman waiter to Prince George of Denmark, and gentleman of the privy chamber to both Queen Anne and George I. He also served as secretary to the bounty commission of Queen Anne to the inferior clergy and was on the commission of the peace for Middlesex.

In 1702 Chamberlayne was elected a fellow of the Royal Society and contributed three minor papers to its *Transactions*: on the effects of a thunderstorm at 'Sampford Courtney in Devonshire on 7 Oct. 1711' (336, p. 528); on the 'Plague at Copenhagen' in 1711 (337, p. 279), and on the 'Sunk Island in the Humber' (361, p. 1014). In 1717 he translated from the French the *Lives of the French, Italian and German philosophers, late members of the Royal Academy of Sciences in Paris* and revealed a peripheral involvement in the great Newton/Leibnitz dispute as to who first discovered the differential calculus. Chamberlayne declares that 'Mr. Leibnitz did … acknowledge to me … that Sir Isaac Newton might be the first Inventor, but that he himself had luckily fallen about the same Time upon the same Notions' (dedication). In addition to his scientific interests, Chamberlayne was indefatigable in his zeal to defend protestantism against popery and by 1712 he was a member of the Society for Promoting Christian Knowledge. Most of his published translations were the product of his own zeal and his work for this society; they included Samuel

Puffendorf's *History of Popedom* (1691), Bernard Nieuwentijdt's *Religious Philosopher* (1718), Geeraert Brandt's *History of the Reformation* (1720), and Jacques Saurin's *Dissertations, Historical, Critical, Theological and Moral* (1723).

After his father's death Chamberlayne published, in 1704, the twentieth edition of *Angliae notitiae*, declaring that he felt 'bound in Gratitude to take care of those further Editions of it'. He continued his father's attack on Guy Miege who 'has rifled his Book, and with some insignificant and dry Additions of his own has set up for an author. An easy and cheap way to acquire Fame.' Miege defended himself in 1707 in *Reflections upon the Present State of England*, pointing out that: 'Though *Plagiarism* is not allowable, yet I hope an Author may make use of Books when he writes … Chamberlayne did not write his *Present State* by Inspiration … his Book is nothing but Sr. Tho. Smith's *De republica Anglorum* Disguised' (p. 31). While Miege is right, John Chamberlayne never wavered in his father's defence.

In his later life John Chamberlayne, a bachelor, lived in Petty France, Westminster, and died there on 2 November 1723; he was buried on 6 November in the family plot in Chelsea, where he had a residence, and where on the church wall a tablet was placed to his memory. He left money to provide for the education of five poor boys.

REAVLEY GAIR

Sources Foster, *Alum. Oxon.* · Strype correspondence, CUL, Add. MS 7 (47, 8, 9) · Wood, *Ath. Oxon.* · T. Faulkner, *Chelsea*, 1 (1829) · A. Boyer, *The political state of Great Britain*, 26 (1723) · additional personal correspondence in various British Library MSS · *DNB*
Archives BL, Sloane MSS, letters to Sir Hans Sloane · BL, Vernis collections, personal letters · BL, letters to Humphrey Wanley, Add. MSS 70474–70475 · CUL, Strype corresp., Add. MSS · LPL, corresp. as secretary of Society for the Propagation of the Gospel
Wealth at death house in Petty France, Westminster; left money to educate five poor boys

Chamberlayne [Chamberlain], **Sir Leonard** (*b.* in or before **1504**, *d.* **1561**), courtier and soldier, was the eldest son of Sir Edward *Chamberlayne (1480–1543) of Shirburn, Oxfordshire, and his wife, Cecily (*fl.* 1480–1540), daughter of Sir John Verney of Pendley, Hertfordshire. He was said to have spent his early years in riotous living, which may lie behind the pardon he received on 2 September 1529, but once the paternal estates had been entailed on him in 1528, probably on the occasion of his marriage to Dorothy Newdigate, he became a respectable courtier. By 1532 he had become an esquire of the body, and thereafter settled down to the life of a minor official who played a small part in the reception of important visitors and whose military skills were used in captaincies in the various armies sent to the continent. At Henry VIII's funeral he bore the banner of the king and Queen Katherine.

In 1532 his father associated Chamberlayne in the stewardship and lieutenancy of Woodstock manor and park. This was a favoured royal hunting lodge on which large sums were spent, and its charge was an office much coveted by others. On his father's death Chamberlayne became a leading Oxfordshire gentleman who served all the expected offices in the counties of Oxfordshire and

Berkshire: justice of the peace, escheator (1544–5), commissioner for musters (1546), sheriff (1546–7), and numerous miscellaneous commissions. His first wife, who may have been the mother of all his sons, had died by the early 1540s, when Chamberlayne was acting with Richard Andrews, the father of his second wife, another Dorothy, in a series of dealings in former monastic lands. In 1543 he received the keepership of Combe in Oxfordshire by Andrews's resignation.

During Edward VI's reign Chamberlayne was a trusted royal servant, suitable for temporary appointments in times of emergency, such as marshal of the army for the relief of Boulogne in 1549 and assistant to the lieutenant of the Tower in October 1549 (a position that implies support for the group against Somerset). He furnished great horses for various expeditions but was often ordered to stay in England to lead the defence if invasion occurred. In November 1552 he became sheriff of Oxfordshire and Berkshire for the second time and consequently on Edward's death was able to raise a sizeable number of troops in an official capacity to proclaim Mary queen.

Once Mary's accession was assured, the privy council instructed Chamberlayne to dismiss the soldiers and summoned him to the queen who commissioned him to provide her with a bodyguard. She then appointed him on 25 September 1553 to the difficult position of captain, keeper, and governor of Guernsey. The patent was reissued in December and in 1555 reissued to Chamberlayne and his eldest son, Francis. The almost self-governing position of the islands under their bailiffs and jurats (the royal court) made every captain's constitutional position debatable. Their patents gave them authority over advowsons, patronage, and fealty and empowered them to appoint to all offices and collect all issues, tolls, and customs, spending them on the island's needs without rendering account, but the returns were inadequate. Chamberlayne's first action was to persuade the council to permit the importation of provisions as the islands could not feed themselves. Alderney, Sark, Herm, and Jethou were also under his purview. In 1553 neither Sark nor Alderney were in English hands. In 1549 the French had taken and garrisoned Sark and only the English fleet under William Winter had stopped them taking Guernsey. Recovering the islands was to require the navy's assistance; defending them would require money which could not be raised locally.

Chamberlayne was knighted on 2 October, the day after Mary's coronation; he sat for Scarborough in her first parliament and for Oxfordshire in March–November 1554. His clear Catholic sympathies led to favours from the queen, for instance the sale to him of the site of Dunstable Abbey for only £300, and also to politically delicate jobs. He guarded Elizabeth during her imprisonment at Woodstock in 1554 and took part in the proceedings against Dr Rowland Taylor and John Bradford for heresy in January 1555. His third marriage in 1554 to Margery, herself thrice a widow, successively of Stephen Vaughan (*d.* 1549), George Rolle (*d.* 1552), and Henry Brinklow of London, brought him several lawsuits, as the couple sought to obtain from Vaughan's executors the money the chamber of London had advanced for her children from her first marriage.

In April 1555 Chamberlayne finally left for Guernsey. He did not stay continuously, periodically leaving Francis to manage the islands; as a new year's gift to the queen he brought back some of the knitted stockings that were the islands' main export. In 1557 his third wife died and he married another widow, Anne Conyers, daughter of Richard Blount of Iver, Buckinghamshire. On the eve of war with France in that same year he was ordered to return to his post, which he did, although he warned that the defences were in no state to withstand attack and that the islands were too weak to defend themselves. The privy council was unsympathetic to his requests for money to raise 100 troops in England, leading him to reply that if he were able to bear the charge himself the queen would not be charged with a penny. Much hampered by absence of money and the difficulty of obtaining ordnance, he began to improve the defences of Castle Cornet. He was involved in negotiations for the purchase of Sark, which a privateer had taken from the French, and helped Winter repel an attack on Alderney.

On Elizabeth's accession Chamberlayne wrote to Sir William Cecil seeking furtherance of his suit to the council over the island's costs, and sent him, too, 'such poor pleasures as this island affords' (Ewen, 'Essex Castle', 237). In January 1559 he was ordered to London to report on the state of the islands. It was not promising. For Alderney, he had to advise that it did not have a single piece of ordnance and was unable to repel pirates, so that the people were leaving it to live elsewhere. He returned to Guernsey in May 1559.

Chamberlayne made his will on 22 May 1560, asking that the Virgin pray for his soul and requesting that solemn exequies be sung and done for him according to the order of the holy Catholic church. He left the modest sum of 300 marks to each of his four unmarried children, provided for his servants and for the poor cottagers in Shirburn, bequeathed money for the augmentation of the living of Shirburn from the rental of its rectory, which he owned, and ordered the payment of the debts accumulated by his son-in-law Sir Francis Stonor. The will was proved on 29 August 1561, but Chamberlayne was not buried until the following October when his funeral procession had a strong military flavour. He asked to be buried by 'Dorothy my wife' in the chapel of St Mary Magdalen in Shirburn.   SYBIL M. JACK

Sources HoP, *Commons, 1509–58*, 1.614–17 • *Literary remains of King Edward the Sixth*, ed. J. G. Nichols, 2, Roxburghe Club, 75 (1857), 233 • *LP Henry VIII*, vols. 4–21 • *CSP dom., 1547–58* • A. J. Eagleston, *The Channel Islands under Tudor government, 1485–1642*, ed. J. Le Patourel (1949) • J. le Patourel, ed., *The building of Castle Cornet, Guernsey* (1958) • *Reports and Transactions* [Société Guernesiaise], 9 (1921–5); 10 (1926–9) • A. H. Ewen, 'Essex Castle, Alderney and the Chamberlain family', *Report and Transactions* [Société Guernesiaise], 16 (1955–9), 237 • *The diary of Henry Machyn, citizen and merchant-taylor of London, from AD 1550 to AD 1563*, ed. J. G. Nichols, CS, 42 (1848), 271 • F. B. Tupper, *History of Guernsey: its bailiwick*, 2nd edn (1876) • will,

PRO, PROB 11/44, sig. 28 • PRO, chancery, early chancery proceedings, C1/1339/16–20 • PRO, chancery, pleadings series 1, C 2/172 • *The acts and monuments of John Foxe*, new edn, ed. G. Townsend, 7 (1847), 162 • APC, 1542–70, 1–7

Wealth at death left c.1500 marks to be distributed; estate probably worth c.£150

Chamberlayne, Thomas (*fl.* 1609–1638), soldier and expert on Russia, began his eighteen-year military career as a sentinel and rose to the rank of captain; nothing is known about his birth, family, or education. In 1609, with the approval of the English government, he assisted Colonel James Spence in hiring 600 cavalry and 1800 infantry who sailed to Sweden and marched into Russia to aid Tsar Basil Shuysky against Russian rebels and a Polish army. Early in 1610 the mercenaries helped to neutralize the rebel threat to Moscow and were then attached to armies sent to stop the Polish invasion. In June, however, the Poles won a decisive victory at the battle of Klushino, which led to the overthrow of Tsar Basil. During the battle the mercenaries were betrayed and abandoned by their commanders, but they were spared by the Poles and allowed to return home.

In November 1610, while still in Poland, Chamberlayne wrote a letter to James I's secretary of state seeking employment and describing the military situation in Russia. He wrote follow-up letters describing the Polish occupation of Moscow and the dire threat that posed to Anglo-Russian commerce. Chamberlayne eventually joined forces with Sir Thomas Smith, governor of the Russia Company, to try to interest the king in the idea of English military intervention in north Russia. During the winter of 1612–13 he presented the king with a letter outlining the threats to English interests posed by Polish and Swedish armies operating in Russia. Claiming that Russian lords looked to the king for protection, he urged James to seize north Russia and emphasized the great wealth awaiting him there.

Chamberlayne also urged James to intervene in Russia in order to prevent the king of Poland and the Jesuits from forcing the Russians to convert to Catholicism. James became interested in Chamberlayne's proposal and referred the matter to Robert Carr, earl of Somerset, Sir Thomas Overbury, and Sir Henry Neville. Overbury and Neville became supporters of the project, and James himself discussed the matter frequently with John Merrick, chief agent of the Russia Company. By spring 1613 the king decided to pursue the project. He initially planned to send Overbury as his ambassador to negotiate final details with the Russians, and Merrick and Chamberlayne were instructed to accompany him as expert commissioners. When Overbury made the fatal mistake of arrogantly declining the king's offer and ended up in the Tower of London, James hastily put Merrick in charge of the embassy. At that point Chamberlayne became seriously ill and was unable to accompany Merrick to Russia, where the election of Michael Romanov as tsar put an end to Chamberlayne's plan and the king's fleeting dream of empire.

In the following years Chamberlayne continued to write

letters to the English government. In 1626, for example, he proposed various projects in Ireland and discussed potentially lucrative grain sales contracts. He also indicated his desire to be appointed 'chief commissary' and offered to quietly provide money to the king. In 1630 he secured letters from Charles I to Tsar Michael and Patriarch Filaret seeking permission for him to purchase a large quantity of Russian grain in order to relieve hunger in England. Tsar Michael turned down the king's request. In 1631 Chamberlayne sent the English government a long report about Russia and the war then being fought between Russia and Poland. He predicted the collapse of the Romanov dynasty and encouraged the king to consider military intervention in Russia in order to check Catholic Poland's expansion and to acquire great wealth. Charles wisely ignored his suggestions. Undeterred, in 1632 Chamberlayne again requested royal letters and offered money to the financially strapped king. By 1638 he apparently succeeded in gaining permission from the Russians to export grain to England. After that there is no trace of Captain Chamberlayne. Nothing is known about his death or place of burial.   CHESTER S. L. DUNNING

Sources C. Dunning, 'James I, the Russia Company, and the plan to establish a protectorate over north Russia', *Albion*, 21 (1989), 206–26 · C. Dunning, 'The fall of Sir Thomas Overbury and the embassy to Russia in 1613', *Sixteenth Century Journal*, 22 (1991), 695–704 · S. Konavolov, 'Thomas Chamberlayne's description of Russia, 1631', *Oxford Slavonic Papers*, 5 (1954), 107–16 · I. Lubimenko, 'A project for the acquisition of Russia by James I', *EngHR*, 29 (1914), 246–56 · *The manuscripts of the Earl Cowper*, 3 vols., HMC, 23 (1888–9), vol. 1 · PRO, SP 16/173, fol. 48; 16/398, fol. 17; SP 22/60, fols. 42, 43, 49; SP 88/2, fol. 246; 88/3, fols. 7–8v, 42–47v; SP 91/1, fols. 228–31; SP 91/2, fols. 174–5, 190–91v, 196–9, 204–5 · St John's College, Oxford, MS 253, fol. 9
Archives PRO, SP 16/173, fol. 48; SP 88/2, fol. 246; SP 88/3, fols. 7–8v, 42–7v; SP 91/1, fols. 228–31; SP 91/2, fols. 174–5, 190–91v, 196–9, 204–5
Wealth at death reasonably well off; offered money to King Charles in 1626 and 1632: *Manuscripts of Earl Cowper*, HMC, 23, vol. 1, pp. 272, 455–6

Chamberlayne, William (*c.*1619–1689), poet and playwright, was the second son of Warder and Mary Chamberlayne of Hindon, Wiltshire, later of Shaftesbury. Details of his education are unknown but he did practise as a physician in Shaftesbury. In 1644 the civil war saw Chamberlayne marching to Newbury for the king. His embryonic epic 'Pharonnida' accompanied him in manuscript, and several descriptive scenes within the poem are based on the campaigns in the south and west of England. Broadly based on Greek epic, the poem lacks narrative cohesion, yet is marked by the time of its composition. Chamberlayne certainly took part in the battles of Newbury, he may have taken a role in the rising of 1655, and certainly did in the plot of 1659. Following the Restoration, he featured strongly in the civic life of Shaftesbury, three times serving as mayor. All that is known of his wife is that her name was Margaret.

Besides *Pharonnida* (1659), Chamberlayne's literary output features a play, *Loves Victory* (1658), staged in 1677 in revised form as *Wits Led by the Nose*, printed in 1678, and an ode on the restoration of Charles II, *Englands Jubilee* (1660).

The play is massively endebted to Shakespeare, though it could not be performed because of the theatre closures at that time. As Chamberlayne says at the opening of the first version:

> The mourning Stage being silent, justly I
> May change a Prologue to Apologie

Described as a tragi-comedy, the play moves disconcertingly between the two moods scene by scene, creating an unsettling effect. The plot features the tribulations of a king who faces a rebellion, and a daughter who falls in love with the chief rebel. It utilizes the device of disguise quite heavily, and there is a marked penchant for ceremony. The second version is an attempt to bring it up to date, though the addition of lines against theatregoers detracts heavily. Apparently, strong abuse from country squires was driving the actors from the Theatre Royal, yet one can sympathize with the audience's evident impatience at such a wordy and disparate play. However, there are a few passages of genuine merit, as with the King's speech in act IV, which sees him alone on the stage, gazing at pictures of his wronged daughters:

> Be gone, and let me gaze my self to marble here.
> O have I lost the quiet of my soul,
> All peacefull harmony. My eyes have suckt
> A subtill poison, and disperst it through
> My souls oreflowing rivolet.

Another speech, this time spoken by Heroina, contains similarly strong echoes of Shakespeare, yet also reminds the reader of Chamberlayne's own experiences of war. In a like manner, in his epic, *Pharonnida*, completed at about the same time as the first version of the play published as *Loves Victory*, Chamberlayne evokes the mood of the battlefield with chilling precision.

Chamberlayne's work as a poet and playwright was interrupted by the civil war, an event that provided material for the poet, whose style is marked by a prolixity shared by his nineteenth-century advocate, Robert Southey. As with Southey, an interweaving of historical events and personal drama features significantly, though for Chamberlayne his own experiences were those of an active soldier. Direct experience, or close reworking of familiar Shakespearian themes, provides the basis for Chamberlayne's best work, which all too easily becomes repetitive and confused. The descriptive scenes contained in *Pharonnida*, directly drawn from civil war engagements in the south and west of England, are perhaps the best that Chamberlayne's limited talents produced, and it is these that offer the most to the modern reader. A romance based on the poem and entitled *Eromena, or, The Noble Stranger* appeared in 1683. Chamberlayne died at Shaftesbury in January 1689, and was buried there in the churchyard of Holy Trinity, where a monument was erected to him by his son Valentine Chamberlayne.   NICHOLAS JAGGER

Sources A. E. Parsons, 'A forgotten poet: William Chamberlayne and "Pharonnida"', *Modern Language Review*, 45 (1950), 296–311 · DNB
Likenesses A. Hertochs, line engraving, BM, NPG; repro. in W. Chamberlayne, *Pharonnida* (1659)

Chamberlen family (*per. c.*1600–*c.*1730), medical practitioners, practised medicine and midwifery in London during the seventeenth and early eighteenth centuries. Some were barber–surgeons, others physicians, and one—Paul—advertised as a vendor of an 'anodyne necklace' effective in labour. Connections to apothecaries existed through marriage, giving the family access to a further body of medical knowledge. Unusually for this period, the Chamberlens were often referred to by contemporaries as 'men-midwives'; several family members tried to extend their control over the London midwives, while challenging the established boundaries between the sphere of the surgeon and that of the physician.

The family originated in France, and may have sheltered in the Dutch republic before settling in England. William Chamberlen arrived at Southampton on 3 July 1569 with his wife, Genevieve (*née* Vingnon), and three children: Peter the elder, Simon, and Jane. A third son, James, was baptized on 26 July 1569; Peter the younger was born in 1572. William is assumed to have been a surgeon or apothecary; both Peters became barber–surgeons. William died before March 1596, and it appears that most of the family moved to London at some time between 1588 and this date.

Peter Chamberlen the elder (*c.*1560–1631) appears to have stayed in Southampton with his wife, Anne, until the death of his father, being admitted to the Barber–Surgeons' Company only in 1598. In London he was based in Mark Lane, and attended the queens of James I and Charles I. The first evidence of his reluctance to restrict his activities to surgery was in December 1609, when the College of Physicians summoned him to appear before the president and censors. He failed to attend, and was later fined 40s., which was halved at appeal in March 1610. In November 1612 he was again fined by the College of Physicians for usurping the role of a physician. Imprisoned in Newgate, he was released only after the intervention of the archbishop of Canterbury and the lord mayor, who may have been influenced by Thomas Chamberlen, Peter's cousin and the master of the Mercers' Company. He was listed in 1614 as a surgeon to Queen Anne; his will mentions a diamond ring which she gave him. He was the sole attendant to Henrietta Maria when she miscarried at Greenwich in 1628, and was present at the birth of the future Charles II in 1630, although this was managed by the French midwife Mme Péronne. He died in December 1631 and was buried in St Dionis Backchurch; at this time he seems to have been living mainly in Downe, Kent, where he owned land, and where his brother Simon also resided. His wife, Anne, predeceased him; his only child was a daughter, Esther.

Peter Chamberlen the younger (1572–1626), born on 15 February 1572 in Southampton and also a member of the Barber–Surgeons, shared his brother's interest in midwifery. In 1616 the brothers responded to a petition from the London midwives to form a college; in supporting this unsuccessful request, the Chamberlens stated that they both practised midwifery, although only Peter the younger appears to have held a licence from the bishop of London. Peter the younger shared his brother's disregard for the boundaries between surgical and medical practice, and also fell out with his fellow surgeons. When accused by the College of Physicians, in 1600, of treating syphilis by diet and purging, he confessed, but he was also fined by the Barber–Surgeons' Company for absence from lectures on a number of occasions between 1602 and 1606. He married Sara Delaune, the daughter of a French protestant minister and sister of Gideon *Delaune, the royal apothecary. In 1607 Peter was accused of prescribing medicines to three patients; in his defence, he claimed that he was following the advice of his father-in-law, William *Delaune, who was also licensed by the College of Physicians. He began the procedure of being examined for the college in 1610, but proceeded no further, and was threatened with imprisonment by the college in 1620 after altering a prescription written by Dr Argent. He died after 12 August 1626 and was buried at Downe on 16 August.

Peter the younger had eight children: Peter, Sarah, William, Ann, Henry, Robert, Nathaniel, and Marguerite. Of these Peter *Chamberlen (1601–1683) and Nathaniel *Chamberlain (*bap.* 1612) were physicians. Peter was usually known as Dr Peter not only to distinguish him from his father and uncle of the same name, but also to emphasize that he was qualified as a doctor of medicine rather than as a barber–surgeon. In the 1630s he too tried to organize the London midwives into a college, with himself as governor; a claim made in this context, that Dr Peter was particularly enthusiastic about the use of iron instruments in difficult cases, may be the first hint of there being a 'family secret' underpinning the Chamberlens' success in midwifery. Dr Peter was expelled from the College of Physicians in 1649 when, following the execution of Charles I, the college became more conservative and began to take action against empirics and others challenging its authority. He was reinstated as physician-in-ordinary by Charles II in 1660.

In *A Voice in Rhama* (1647) Dr Peter stated that his was an 'Asclepiad-family', to which he owed his knowledge of both medicine and drugs. The medical character of the family continued into the next generation: his daughter Elizabeth married Colonel William Walker, and their sons Chamberlen (d. 1731) and Middleton were both doctors, in Dublin and London respectively, while of his fourteen sons, four practised some form of medicine. The best-known of these is Hugh *Chamberlen the elder, whose own son (also Hugh) was also in practice. Nathaniel studied at Pembroke College, Oxford (BM 30 June 1636). John, who died in 1699 in the parish of St Clement Danes, was a physician who practised midwifery. Another son, **Paul Chamberlen** (1635–1717), born on 22 October 1635, was a quack doctor living in Great Suffolk Street, best known for the 'anodyne necklace' he sold for 5s. It came with liquid coral, which could be rubbed on to the gums to aid teething; the necklace was also marketed to ease pain in childbirth. When his brother Hugh left London for Scotland in 1699, Paul advertised in the *London Post* to assure his clientele that he remained in London, and had not deserted his practice. His patients included the duchess of Hamilton; unlike his brother, he appears to have been on good terms with midwives and, in 1706, he wrote to Hans Sloan recommending the midwifery skills of Mrs Bizzel. He died on 3 December 1717 and was buried in the church of St Martin-in-the-Fields; his wife, Mary (*née* Disbrowe), died in the following year.

It was through Hugh the elder that the claims of a family secret were first made public. In 1673, in the preface to *The Accomplisht Midwife*, his translation of François Mauriceau's *Traité des maladies des femmes grosses*, Hugh claimed that, with his father and two of his brothers, he possessed the secret of how to deliver a living child if it presented by the head but the birth was obstructed. He implied that the secret was a skill rather than a device, 'a Way to deliver Women in this Case, without any prejudice to them or their Infants'; however, this phrasing may have been intended to draw attention away from any suggestion that the secret was some form of instrument. Traditionally, surgeons used hooks in such deliveries, killing the child in the process if it were not already dead, so that their arrival was greeted with despair. In 1678 one of the family— either Hugh or his father, Dr Peter—proposed to the crown that the family secret could be passed on to '2 or more discreet persons in each county of England and Wales' (*CSP dom.*, *1678*, 610). The offer was not taken up; a petition by Hugh to the College of Physicians for 'a patent relating to midwifery' in 1687 also failed. It is possible that few believed in the secret, which smacked of typical quack methods more characteristic of Paul's practice; Hugh's political notoriety may also have contributed to the lack of wider interest in his claims at this time.

In 1694 Mauriceau's *Observations* gave his version of the events of 1670, when Hugh had met him in Paris, alleging that Hugh had offered to sell the secret for 10,000 crowns, and that he had then tested Hugh by allowing him to attempt to deliver a woman of whom he had previously despaired. Despite his boasts, Hugh had failed. But by the 1690s Hugh was working on other schemes; in particular, like his father in 1649 and his brother Paul in 1705–6, he was continually bombarding parliament with banking proposals.

The family midwifery practice meanwhile passed from Hugh to his son **Hugh Chamberlen the younger** (1664–1728) and to his cousin Middleton Walker. Hugh the younger held political and religious affiliations very different from those of his father, who was a whig and a Baptist. Hugh the younger—a tory and a member of the Church of England—was educated at Trinity College, Cambridge, studied medicine in Leiden, and became a fellow of the Royal College of Physicians on 2 April 1694. In striking contrast to the turbulent relationship of previous generations of the family to the college, he served as censor in 1707, 1718, and 1721. He married three times, his first wife being Mary Bacon and his third Mary, Lady Crew. He was a highly fashionable man-midwife, employed for example by the tory Stafford family; after the death of the duke of Buckingham, Hugh lived openly with his widow,

Catherine, parting from her in November 1727. He subscribed to books by tory authors including Thomas Hearne, Matthew Prior, and John Gay. On his monument in Westminster Abbey, erected in 1729 by Edmund, duke of Buckingham, the family medical tradition is represented by the snake of Asclepius, and reference is made to Hugh the elder and Dr Peter.

However, other English practitioners associated with the Chamberlen family used the forceps while the family was still active in midwifery. Among these was James Douglas, associated with Paul Chamberlen, and who attended Chamberlen patients when a family member was not available. Douglas used instruments unsuccessfully in a case he attended in 1702, and his own account of the event states that he was unable to fasten what he describes only as 'the thing' in such a way that he could exert traction with it. Douglas may have obtained the instruments while studying in the Dutch republic, possibly in Utrecht, or may have been taught their use by Hugh the elder. It is known that Hugh the elder sold two instruments to a group of Dutch surgeons, including Rogier van Roonhuysen, about 1694, and that they kept the knowledge secret until about 1750. As for France, a few French surgeons were using the forceps from 1717 onwards, employing them however not to deliver live children, but to extract a dead foetus.

As Hugh the younger had three daughters, his death in 1728, followed by that of Middleton Walker on 16 November 1732, marked the end of the Chamberlen family medical tradition; the design of the forceps was published in 1733. In the same period, three midwifery instruments emerged on the scene in England, France, and the Dutch republic: the forceps, the vectis, and the fillet. The forceps consisted of two blades by which the foetal head could be grasped and traction exerted; the vectis was a single curved blade which could be used to alter the position of the head; the fillet comprised a rigid handle and a flexible strip that could be looped around the head before exerting traction. But, in addition to Douglas, several practitioners in the London area were using the forceps before 1732; Hugh the younger, having no male heir, perhaps sold the secret for a fee to a few individuals in the period from about 1710 to 1720.

Nevertheless, it remained impossible to identify the forceps securely as the Chamberlen secret hinted at by Dr Peter and probably underlying the practice of his father and uncle; after 1733 some practitioners in England continued to suggest that the secret had been a manual technique rather than a medical instrument. The fillet was particularly difficult to use, so that part of the secret could have been instruction in the best technique. By 1750, opinion had generally settled on the forceps as the Chamberlens' device. But in 1813, Peter Chamberlen's own medical instruments were discovered under the floorboards of the attic at the house where he had died. These included not only three sets of the forceps, vectis, and fillet, with one example of what is apparently an earlier version of the forceps, but also the hooks used to remove a dead child. Wilson thus argues that 'all the three early-modern instruments for delivering a living child by the head originated with the Chamberlens' (Wilson, 57).

HELEN KING

Sources J. H. Aveling, *The Chamberlens and the midwifery forceps* (1882) · W. Radcliffe, *The secret instrument* (1947) · W. Radcliffe, *Milestones in midwifery* (1967) · A. Wilson, *The making of man-midwifery: childbirth in England, 1660–1770* (1995) · H. Chamberlen, *The accomplisht midwife* (1673) · J. H. Aveling, *English midwives* (1872) · M. Adrian, 'Les Chamberlen', medical faculty diss., Paris, 1923 · J. K. Horsefield, *British monetary experiments, 1650–1710* (1960), 156–79 · P. Chamberlen, *A voice in Rhama* (1647) · H. Brock, 'James Douglas of the pouch', *Medical History*, 18 (1974), 162–72 · H. Drinkwater, 'The modern descendents of Dr Peter Chamberlen', *Liverpool Medical and Chirurgical Journal*, 36 (1916), 98–105 · F. Stabler, 'The Chamberlen family', *University of Durham Medical Gazette* (1954), 48.3, 21–3 · J. T. Smith, 'The Chamberlen obstetrical instruments', *Bulletin of the Academy of Medicine of Cleveland*, 15/6 (1931), 13–14 · C. J. S. Thompson, 'William Chamberlen, the inventor of the midwifery forceps', *Medical Life* (July 1925), 247–53 · H. J. Cook, *The decline of the old medical regime in Stuart London* (1986) · R. Lee, *Observations on the discovery of the original obstetric instruments of the Chamberlens* (1862) · *CSP dom., 1678*, 610

Likenesses P. Scheemakers and L. Delvaux, tomb effigy, *c.*1730 (Hugh Chamberlen the younger), Westminster Abbey; terracotta model, V&A · T. Trotter, line engraving, pubd 1794 (Paul Chamberlen; after R. White), BM, NPG

Chamberlen, Hugh, the elder (*b.* 1630×34, *d.* after **1720**), physician and economist, the eldest son of Peter *Chamberlen (1601–1683), and his wife, Jane, eldest daughter of Sir Hugh Myddelton, was born in the parish of St Anne, Blackfriars, London, between 1630 and 1634. Peter *Chamberlen the younger (1572–1626) was his grandfather and Paul *Chamberlen (1635–1717) his brother [*see under* Chamberlen family (*per. c.*1600–*c.*1730)]. Nothing is known of his education; he held the bishop's licence to practise midwifery, but probably did not have a degree in medicine. He nevertheless appears as doctor of medicine in the state papers and on the lists of the Royal Society, to which he was elected a fellow on 6 April 1681. On 28 May 1663 he married Dorothy Brett, daughter of Colonel John Brett, at St Paul's, Covent Garden. They had three sons—Hugh *Chamberlen the younger (1664–1728) [*see under* Chamberlen family (*per. c.*1600–*c.*1730)], Peter, and Myddelton—and one daughter, Dorothy.

Chamberlen was one of the medical practitioners who stayed in London during the great plague; in a plan, published in 1666, to preserve the city from further outbreaks, he recommended the imposition of a national tax to fund preventative measures. In August 1670 he travelled to Paris. This may have been in order to try to sell the family secret (the obstetric forceps) to Jules Clement, who had been appointed court accoucheur in that year. While staying in Paris he met the surgeon François Mauriceau and—according to Mauriceau's later account of Chamberlen's time in Paris (*Observations*, 1694)—mentioned that he knew a secret enabling him to deliver a live child in difficult labours in a matter of minutes. However, an attempt to demonstrate this at the Hôtel-Dieu on 16 August failed miserably. In 1673 Chamberlen published as *The Accomplisht Midwife* an English translation of Mauriceau's treatise on midwifery, *Traité des maladies des femmes grosses,*

and in his preface made the first published claims for this family secret. In the same year, on the petition of his father, he was appointed physician-in-ordinary to Charles II. His court employment was not adversely affected by his whig politics, although he appears to have lost his position as physician to the king in 1682. In 1685 he joined Monmouth's rebellion, but was pardoned in June 1686.

Chamberlen wrote *Manuale medicum, or, A small treatise of the art of physick in general and of vomits and the Jesuits powder in particular* (1685) to send to a son in the East Indies. The advice given to patients in judging the skills of their physicians brought him into conflict with the Royal College of Physicians. In 1687 he tried to gain what was described as a patent relating to midwifery, but was unsuccessful. He subsequently faced the college on a charge of malpractice after treating the wife of John Willmer by vomiting, purging, and bleeding, shortly after which she had miscarried her pregnancy of six months, and then died. The college, on the information of Walter Charleton, claimed that Chamberlen's authority to practise medicine had lapsed with the death of Charles II, and fined him £10. This would explain why, at the birth of James II's son, James Francis Edward, later known as the Pretender, on 10 June 1688, Chamberlen was not called to apply the usual remedies to suppress the production of breast milk; however, he claimed that he had been sent for, only missing the event because he was seeing a patient in Chatham. In a letter written from The Hague on 4 October 1713 to the Electress Sophia of Hanover (BL, Sloan MS 4107, fol. 150), he strenuously denied claims that the prince was in fact an impostor smuggled into the birthing room in a warming pan. On 17 April 1692 he again attended a royal confinement, delivering, for a fee of 100 guineas, Princess Anne of Denmark of a son who died at birth.

Chamberlen's *A Few Queries Relating to the Practice of Physick, with Remarks upon some of them* (1694) includes 'A proposal for the better securing of health, intended in the year 1689 and still ready to be humbly offered to the consideration of the honourable houses of parliament'. This recommends an annual tax on each household to provide every family with medical and surgical services. He also proposed the revision of laws on the sale of bad food, and regular cleaning of streets and houses.

In order to solve the problem of public credit, Chamberlen proposed a land bank scheme; his father had put forward a banking scheme in 1649, and his brother Paul had his own such plans in 1705–6. From 1665 onwards Hugh was interested in 'Lumbard banks', which would give out £5 notes as credit for goods received, and eventually return the goods on the repayment of the notes, having levied charges beginning at a penny per week for each £5 note. He turned to land banks in 1689 (Bodl. Oxf., MS Locke b.3), and published the first draft of his proposal in November 1690, entitled *Dr. Hugh Chamberlen's Proposal to Make England Rich and Happy*. Landowners would be issued with paper money equivalent to the value of the land they held, in the assumption that, because all paper money corresponded to a piece of land, it would be secure. In 1690–91 he was involved in proposals for a country penny post, and between 1692 and 1697 he continued to issue many more pamphlets on land banks. He issued a newspaper—the *Old Post-Master*—and wrote to members of parliament asking for their support, his suggestions for the use of the capital raised including poor relief, military payments, and road repairs. His plans were mathematically flawed, as he thought that lending could occur on the basis of one hundred times the annual rent of the land, and he was not able to appreciate the inflationary effects. When the alternative measure, the Bank of England, was set up in 1694, other land bank campaigners—such as his friend and adviser John Briscoe—modified their schemes, but Chamberlen remained interested in a pure land bank. By 1699 he had gone into exile, possibly because of debt, settling first in Scotland, where he continued to issue pamphlets offering variations on a land bank and developed a plan to unify England and Scotland, and then in 1705 moving to the Netherlands, where he died after 1720.

HELEN KING

Sources J. H. Aveling, *The Chamberlens and the midwifery forceps* (1882) · W. Radcliffe, *The secret instrument* (1947) · W. Radcliffe, *Milestones in midwifery* (1967) · A. Wilson, *The making of man-midwifery: childbirth in England, 1660–1770* (1995) · F. Mauriceau, *The accomplisht midwife*, ed. and trans. H. Chamberlen (1673) [Fr. orig., *Traité des maladies des femmes grosses* (1668)] · Foster, *Alum. Oxon.* · W. A. Shaw, ed., *Calendar of treasury books*, 9, PRO (1931), 917, 1210 · J. K. Horsefield, *British monetary experiments, 1650–1710* (1960), 156–79 · BL, Sloane MS 4107, fol. 150 · Bodl. Oxf., MS Locke b.3 · D. Rubini, 'Politics and the battle for the banks, 1688–1697', *EngHR*, 85 (1970), 693–714 · Munk, *Roll* · CSP dom., 1670, 44, 133; 1678, 411, 429; 1682, 391, 546–7; 1686, 652; addenda 1660–85, 25; 1665, 140; 1668, 108; 1668–9, 498; 1670, 614 · S. Young, *The annals of the Barber–Surgeons of London: compiled from their records and other sources* (1890), 405

Chamberlen, Hugh, the younger (1664–1728). *See under* Chamberlen family (*per. c.*1600–*c.*1730).

Chamberlen, Paul (1635–1717). *See under* Chamberlen family (*per. c.*1600–*c.*1730).

Chamberlen, Peter, the elder (*c.*1560–1631). *See under* Chamberlen family (*per. c.*1600–*c.*1730).

Chamberlen, Peter, the younger (1572–1626). *See under* Chamberlen family (*per. c.*1600–*c.*1730).

Chamberlen, Peter (1601–1683), physician, was the eldest of eight children born to Peter *Chamberlen the younger (1572–1626) [*see under* Chamberlen family (*per. c.*1600–*c.*1730)] and Sara Delaune, the daughter of William *Delaune (*c.*1530–1611), and the sister of Gideon *Delaune (1564/5–1659). Chamberlen was born in the parish of St Anne, Blackfriars, London, on 8 May 1601, and baptized at the French church in Threadneedle Street on 12 May. He was educated at Merchant Taylors' School in London and Emmanuel College, Cambridge. He took his MD at Padua on 16 September 1619, and was afterwards incorporated at Oxford (1620) and at Cambridge (1621). He was admitted as a member of the College of Physicians in 1626, on his second attempt, and made a fellow in 1628. He gave the annual lecture to the barber–surgeons in 1642, and was made physician-in-ordinary to Charles I and, in 1661, to Charles II. He was married twice, to Jane Myddelton and

Ann Harrison, and in his lifetime had fourteen sons, including Hugh *Chamberlen the elder, four daughters, sixty-five grandchildren, including Hovenden *Walker, and fourteen great-grandchildren.

Chamberlen attempted to gain control over the London midwives by suggesting himself as the governor of a proposed college; he alleged that the midwives were ignorant and incompetent. In 1634 the midwives petitioned the College of Physicians against Chamberlen's bid, stating that his only knowledge of midwifery was through reading about it, and claiming that the English books they owned were a better guide to anatomy than the lectures Chamberlen proposed to deliver to them. They also complained that he had been expecting them to come to his house for regular lectures. As a physician, he should not in any case have been involved with midwifery, which was considered to be a surgeon's sphere in cases where normal delivery proved impossible. In his pamphlet *A Voice in Rhama, or, The Crie of Women and Children* (1647) Chamberlen defended his view that midwives should be formed into a college. He attacked the system of ecclesiastical licensing of midwives on the basis of patients' testimony, the taking of an oath, and the payment of a substantial fee, and claimed that 'Instruction and Order' were needed to save over three thousand lives a year in the London area alone. However, it is likely that many women practised as midwives without obtaining a licence; dioceses varied considerably in their attitude to enforcement. Chamberlen, who had been educated at the puritan-influenced Emmanuel College, Cambridge, also wrote in this pamphlet that 'Meum et tuum divide the world into factions, into atoms; and till the world return to its first simplicity or … to a Christian utopia … covetousness will be the root of all evil' (Hill, 115). Despite being a fellow of the College of Physicians Chamberlen had a relationship with it that was just as turbulent as those of the barber–surgeon members of his family. In 1634 complaints were made that he kept a French apothecary in his house, and the college's records show a series of charges that he had failed to attend its meetings.

Like other members of his family, Chamberlen produced a range of schemes, some of them related to social reform. He had patented an invention for bath stoves in the Netherlands, and applied for a patent in England in 1648. This was granted on condition that it was operated to provide the maximum accessibility to the poor of 'artificial baths and bath stoves' and 'hamacco beds and couches' (Webster, 298). The College of Physicians objected to the scheme partly on moral grounds and partly because it considered the English climate to be too cold. Chamberlen, who became an Independent and then a Baptist, also wrote *The Poor Man's Advocate* (1649), in which he put forward a joint-stock scheme to set 200,000 poor to work. Financed through the appropriation of church property, it was intended to establish colonies of the poor, who, in exchange for their labour, would receive their subsistence and have access to schools and hospitals. Their work would eventually make a profit for the subscribers to the scheme.

Chamberlen was expelled from the College of Physicians in 1649, having criticized it publicly, and having supported the Long Parliament and the army. During the Commonwealth he left London for Essex, letting his London house to Miles Woodshaw, but in 1660 he was reinstated as physician-in-ordinary by Charles II. In 1661 he was travelling in the Netherlands, but by 1662 was again in London, living in Coleman Street, where he wrote a pamphlet defending himself against a charge of madness. In April 1666 he returned to the Netherlands and worked on a scheme for wind-propelled sea and land transport, which would allow movement in a straight line even against a prevailing wind. He may also have visited Sweden and Denmark and obtained patents there for this idea. On his return to seek an English patent, he stated that the idea was already patented in the Dutch republic, France, and Venice; the patent granted in England was issued in 1668, to run for fourteen years. He also wrote on phonetic writing, receiving another patent in 1672 for his new invention of 'writing and printing true English' (*CSP dom.*, 1672–3, 229), and produced pamphlets on baptism. In 1670 he alleged that he had only been paid £100 in his last nine years as physician to Charles, and requested further payments. In 1680 he wrote defending himself against claims that he was a Jew, caused by his observance of the Jewish sabbath.

Chamberlen died on 22 December 1683 at Woodham Mortimer Hall, near Maldon in Essex, having purchased the property in 1638; his tomb is in the churchyard of that parish. His obstetric instruments were later discovered in the attic at Woodham Mortimer Hall. J. H. Aveling regarded him as a man ahead of his time, having 'great talent and wide celebrity, energetic and eccentric, but at the same time highly practical' (*English Midwives*, 28), but later revised this opinion, at least for Chamberlen's latter years, seeing him as being in a 'condition of religious exaltation, which bordered upon and sometimes reached lunacy' (p. 87). From Chamberlen's second marriage only one child survived, his son Hope, and it was he who erected his monument. The epitaph includes the couplet:

To tell his learning and his life to men
Enough is said, by here lyes Chamberlen.

HELEN KING

Sources J. H. Aveling, *English midwives: their history and prospects* (1872), chap. 2 · J. H. Aveling, *The Chamberlens and the midwifery forceps* (1882) · W. Radcliffe, *The secret instrument* (1947) · W. Radcliffe, *Milestones in midwifery* (1967) · A. Wilson, *The making of man-midwifery: childbirth in England, 1660–1770* (1995) · J. W. Ballantyne, 'Paul or Peter?', *Journal of Obstetrics and Gynaecology of the British Empire*, 13 (1908), 161–4 · *A paper delivered in by Dr Alston ... on Monday the 16th of October 1648 ... together with an answer thereunto by P. Chamberlen* (1648) · P. Chamberlen, *A voice in Rhama, or, The crie of women and children* (1647) · Foster, *Alum. Oxon.* · Munk, *Roll* · *CSP dom.*, addenda, 1660–85, 25; 1665, 140; 1668, 108; 1668–9, 498; 1670, 614 · *An answer to Dr Peter Chamberlaine's scandalous and false papers* (1650) · S. Young, *The annals of the Barber–Surgeons of London: compiled from their records and other sources* (1890), 405 · C. Webster, *The great instauration: science, medicine and reform, 1626–1660* (1975) · C. Hill, *The world turned upside down: radical ideas during the English revolution* (1972) · *DNB*

Likenesses T. Trotter, line engraving, pubd 1794 (after R. White; of Chamberlen?), BM, NPG

Chamberlin, Mason (*bap.* 1722, *d.* 1787), portrait painter, the son of Richard Chamberlain and his wife, Mary, *née* White, was baptized on 7 October 1722 at the Hand Alley presbytery, Bishopsgate, in the City of London. By 1737, when he was apprenticed for seven years at £100 premium to Jeremiah Pearce, a freeman of the Salters' Company, he was an orphan, but for most of his life he did not venture far from the parish of Bishopsgate Without where his parents had lived. The salters rented land to the dissenters for a meeting-place and City dissent is well represented among Chamberlin's portraits, for example those of Caleb Fleming (exh. RA, 1772; Dr Williams's Library, Gordon Square, London) and Samuel Chandler (exh. RA, 1775; Royal Society, London). Little is known about his artistic training but he is said to have been a pupil of Francis Hayman, at first producing conversation pieces in a similar style. His earliest signed work is a small oil on copper of the novelist Samuel Richardson, now in the National Portrait Gallery, London. Based at 7 Stuart Street, Spitalfields, he sent in two or three portraits annually for exhibition at the Society of Artists from 1760 until 1768 and thereafter until 1786 at the Royal Academy of Arts, of which he was a founder member. His name appears in the Society of Artists exhibition catalogue for 1760 as 'Chamberlayne'; some of his portraits are signed 'Chamberlain'. With his wife, Susanna, he had a son, Mason Chamberlin (*b.* 1767), who was also a painter, specializing in landscapes which he exhibited in London from 1786 to 1827.

Although Chamberlin won the second premium of 50 guineas for a history painting from the Society of Arts in 1764, he is best-known for his honest, unpretentious portraits of the merchant and professional classes, which resemble in many ways the early works of Joseph Wright of Derby and of John Singleton Copley in New England. Chamberlin's painting of Benjamin Franklin surrounded by his electrical experiments (1762), commissioned during the statesman's second mission to England by Philip Ludwell II, a Virginian living in London, now hangs in the Philadelphia Museum of Art. A portrait of the anatomist William Hunter was his presentation piece to the Royal Academy in 1769, while that of John Hunter, his brother, is in the Royal Collection. In 1771 he painted whole-length portraits of Prince Edward and Princess Augusta and some of his most distinctive compositions depict children in a refreshingly informal and unsentimental manner. His paintings of George, twenty-first earl of Crawford, with two of his children (exh. RA, 1775; priv. coll.), Captain Bentinck and his son (exh. RA, 1775; National Maritime Museum, Greenwich), and Master Simon Dendy (exh. RA, 1783; priv. coll.) number among his best work. Chamberlin died on 26 January 1787 at 10 Bartlett's Buildings, Holborn, London, where he had been living since 1785.

CELINA FOX

Sources E. Edwards, *Anecdotes of painters* (1808); facs. edn (1970) · W. T. Whitley, *Artists and their friends in England, 1700–1799*, 2 (1928) · *IGI* · Salters' Company, account of apprentices bound, 1706–1821, GL, MS Q1/1/2 · Graves, *RA exhibitors*

Archives GL, Salters' Company, account of apprentices bound, MS Q1/1/2
Likenesses J. Bacon, sculpture, NPG · J. Zoffany, group portrait, oils (*Royal Academicians, 1772*), Royal Collection

Chamberlin, Peter Hugh Girard [Joe] (1919–1978), architect and town planner, was born at the Waldorf Hotel, Aldwych, London, on 31 March 1919, the son of Hugh Noel Girard Chamberlin, an army officer of Sydney, New South Wales, Australia, and his wife, Eleanor Penelope, *née* Chamberlin, who died in childbirth. He was brought up by an aunt, Kitty Evershed, at 60 South Edwardes Square, Kensington.

Chamberlin was educated at Bedford School and Pembroke College, Oxford (1938–40), where he read politics, philosophy, and economics but left without a degree. During his youth he was an enthusiastic traveller: his jaunts included a trip on the Trans-Siberian Railway. A conscientious objector, he worked during the war years first as a farm labourer, then for civil defence in London. In 1940 he married Jean Evelyn Raper-Bingham (1912–1997), the daughter of a civil servant; they were close, but apparently agreed not to have children. It was she, always a strong influence on Chamberlin's career, who encouraged him to register as a student in the school of architecture at Kingston Polytechnic, then headed by Eric Brown. His talents were recognized and after qualifying in 1948 he became deputy head of the school and, for a time, Brown's professional partner.

It was at Kingston that Joe Chamberlin, as he was always known, met his fellow tutors Geoffry Powell and Christoph Bon. **Geoffry Charles Hamilton Powell** (1920–1999), architect, was born on 7 November 1920, in Bangalore, India, the son of Dacre Hamilton Powell, an army officer. He had been schooled at Wellington College and was expected to enter the army. Tuberculosis as a child rendered him unfit for the services, however, and he enrolled at the Architectural Association school. **Christoph Rudolph Bon** (1921–1999), architect, was born on 1 September 1921, at St Gallen, Switzerland. He had trained at the ETH (Swiss Federal Institute of Technology) in Zürich and worked briefly for Ernesto Rogers in Milan and for William Holford in London. His second visit to London, in 1949, was planned to last six weeks: he remained there for fifty years.

In 1951 all three men submitted entries to the competition for a public housing development at Golden Lane on the northern edge of the City of London. Powell was the winner. With his colleagues he formed the partnership of Chamberlin, Powell, and Bon in 1952 to develop the scheme. The Golden Lane estate, complete with shops, pub, sports centre, and community hall, was constructed in several phases between 1953 and 1963. The precise elegance and free use of colour seen in the earlier blocks at Golden Lane were echoed in the Cooper Taber seed warehouse at Witham, Essex (1955; dem.), and the Bousfield School in Kensington, completed in 1956, which confirmed Chamberlin, Powell, and Bon's high standing among the new post-war practices.

The success of Golden Lane led to the commission which was to dominate the work of the partnership for three decades: the Barbican. Its initial ideas for the development of the blitzed 35 acre site were submitted to the City of London corporation in June 1955. Chamberlin's report envisaged 'a district residential in character and with an identity of its own, surrounded by the quite different—but complementary—busy, commercial life of the City' (Chamberlin, 347–8). A dense development, with 300 residents to the acre, was advocated. The construction of the residential element of the scheme (with over 2000 flats) began in 1963 but the final component, the arts centre, was opened twenty years later. For a time the practice numbered over seventy people, with schools and housing work supplementing the principal projects. (The firm designed only one private house.)

The architecture of the Barbican, much heavier and more monumental in character than Golden Lane, with exposed concrete as the dominant material, reflected the influence on Chamberlin, in particular, of Le Corbusier's later work, with its strongly expressionistic and romantic qualities. This penchant for the monumental was shared by Powell, who was the finest draughtsman of the three, while Christoph Bon's sure grasp of detail contributed to the formation of a distinctive style, at once imposing and surprisingly decorative. It was Bon's talent for detail, reinforced perhaps by the time he spent working in Milan, which gave the firm's work its remarkably tactile and even sensual character.

In 1959 Chamberlin, Powell, and Bon were commissioned, on the recommendation of Leslie Martin, to prepare a master plan for the future development of the University of Leeds in tune with the projected expansion of student numbers. Le Corbusier was again a major influence on the project, constructed over the next fifteen years though never realized in its entirety thanks to spending cut-backs and the listing of some of the existing buildings scheduled for demolition. The aim was to connect the campus, which had developed piecemeal since the 1870s, with the city centre, using land made available by clearance of unfit housing and by roofing over, at the university's expense, the new Leeds inner ring road, then under construction. (This key move was the suggestion of Chamberlin.) As at Golden Lane and the Barbican, Chamberlin, Powell, and Bon demonstrated a conviction that modern architecture could have a civic dimension: the centrepiece of the redeveloped campus was a great square, ringed by social and residential, as well as teaching, accommodation. The lecture-theatre block, the work of Chamberlin, was a particularly bold composition, with stacks of lecture rooms arranged on a model—without central aisles but with rows of side doors for latecomers—subsequently developed at the Barbican arts centre. One of the residential buildings on the campus, designed by Bon, straddled the stone wall of a disused cemetery and was faced in red brick in deference to the solid Victorian houses of the neighbourhood.

The expressive and explicitly romantic qualities in the practice's work, seen vividly in the buildings at New Hall,

Cambridge, begun in 1962 (the project was never completed to the original designs), worried some critics: Pevsner found the Barbican towers 'wild and wilful' while the New Hall concrete domes were interpreted as covert historicism. Geoffrey Chaucer School in Southwark (1958–62) was contained under a striking, tent-like hyperbolic paraboloid roof. Though far removed, in intention and effect, from the excesses of postmodernism—a fashion for which none of the partners had any sympathy—this aspect of Chamberlin, Powell, and Bon's work reflected a realization of the shortcomings of the modern movement, in particular its rejection of the lessons of history and of traditional urban forms.

The firm had no sympathy with the 'towers in a park' vision of modernity epitomized by the London county council's Roehampton estate: its sympathies were firmly urban and were reflected in the planning scheme of 1958 for Boston Manor in west London. Ultimately unrealized, it was much publicized; Huw Weldon devoted an edition of the television programme *Monitor* to it. The Boston Manor project, developed by Chamberlin in collaboration with Graeme Shankland and David Gregory Jones, proposed a dense 'living suburb' where residential development, a mix of low- and high-rise, was integrated with offices, a shopping centre, and educational and entertainment facilities, all served by two underground stations. The development, housing 15,000, would be 'a different kind of new town: a suburban community within the city. A piece of metropolis on the inner edge of its green belt'. Boston Manor would have been a Barbican for the suburbs, the best of suburb and city, 'an architecture of towers and squares, paved promenades and green lanes' (Chamberlin, 347–8).

Chamberlin, Powell, and Bon was a practice where work was done collectively, with all the partners collaborating on projects, but it is clear that Chamberlin's abilities as strategist and planner contributed significantly to its success. He was appointed CBE in 1974. Joe Chamberlin's taste for travel—as well as for films, theatre, and large cars—continued until the end of his life. He was taken ill on a trip to the temples of Abu Simbel in 1978 and died on 23 May that year at his home on an island in the Thames, Mill House, Sonning, Berkshire.

Chamberlin's early death was a blow to the practice, which remained heavily involved in completing the Barbican, with added responsibilities falling on Powell and Bon. Geoffry Powell was married twice: first, on 24 July 1954, to Philippa Jane Cooper, an artist, with whom he had two daughters and a son (who died as an infant). The marriage was subsequently dissolved. Then in 1971 he married the radio producer and broadcaster Dorothy Louise Grenfell Williams (1934–1994), with whom he had a son. Powell, an enthusiastic traveller, amateur archaeologist, and coin collector, died at St Anthony's Hospital, North Cheam, Sutton, on 17 December 1999.

Christoph Bon, whose family background in the hotel business was reflected in his notable culinary abilities, remained single until he married Jean Chamberlin months before her death. Bon and the Chamberlins had always been close, sharing homes in London, Berkshire, and southern France, and Bon ended his days in Joe Chamberlin's childhood home at 60 South Edwardes Square, Kensington. It was there that he died on 21 October 1999.

With the retirement of Powell and Bon in 1985, the practice was renamed Chamberlin, Powell, Bon, and Woods, with Frank Woods as managing partner and Powell and Bon as consultants. In 1989 Woods merged the practice with that of Austin-Smith, Lord. Chamberlin, Powell, and Bon's significance in the history of post-war architecture lies in the practice's bold enlargement of the vocabulary of modernism, including its frank exploration of historical sources, and its determined pursuit of a modern architecture which addressed real urban, as well as social, issues and eschewed the destructive philosophy on which so much development after 1945 was based.

KENNETH POWELL

Sources *The Independent* (7 Feb 2000) · *The Guardian* (20 Dec 1999) · *The Times* (22 Dec 1999) · *The Times* (26 May 1978) [obit. of Joe Chamberlin] · *The Times* (16 Dec 1999) [obit. of Christoph Bon] · K. Powell, 'Golden years', *Building Design* (18 Feb 2000) · E. Harwood, *England: a guide to post-war listed buildings* (2000) · personal knowledge (2004) · P. H. G. Chamberlin, 'Report', *Architecture and Building* (Sept 1958), 347–8 · *DNB* · b. cert. [Chamberlin] · m. cert. [Powell] · d. cert. [Chamberlin] · d. cert. [Powell] · d. cert. [Bon] · *The Times* (27 May 1978) [obit. of Joe Chamberlin] · *CGPLA Eng. & Wales* (1978) [Peter Hugh Girard Chamberlin] · *CGPLA Eng. & Wales* (1999) [Christoph Rudolph Bon]

Wealth at death £297,994—Chamberlin: probate, 8 Jan 1979, *CGPLA Eng. & Wales* · £762,141—gross: Christoph Rudolph Bon: probate, 2000, *CGPLA Eng. & Wales*

Chambers, David. *See* Chalmers, David, of Ormond (*c.*1533–1592).

Chambers, David (*d.* 1641), Roman Catholic priest and college head, was the son of Patrick Chambers of Fintray. After studying at Aberdeen University he converted to Roman Catholicism and was ordained priest in Rome on 21 August 1612. From 1610 until 1623 Chambers was entrusted by the Holy See with various diplomatic missions which took him to Italy and Spain. It was during this period that he wrote to Rome from Paris requesting permission for a chapel in the Scots College, and for the privilege of ordaining students without dimissorial letters, both requests being granted by Pope Paul V on 27 May 1617. Chambers was the author of a doctrinal work, *De statu hominis veteris* (Chalons, 1627), and a historical work dedicated to Charles I of Great Britain, *De Scotorum fortitudine* (Paris, 1631), both of which contained comprehensive but inventive martyrologies of Scottish saints.

In 1631 Chambers went to work as a missionary in Scotland, whence he sent a report in 1633 to the *propaganda fide*, describing the state of the mission, and asking for the appointment of a bishop. On his return to France he was presented by Cardinal Richelieu to a French benefice, and on 9 September 1637 he was appointed principal of the Scots College, Paris. For the better management of the college he got the archbishop of Paris to amalgamate the foundation of David of Moray (1325) with that of Archbishop Beaton (1603), an action ratified by act of the Paris *parlement* in 1639. Chambers was notable in having remarkably good students. He died in office on 17 or 18 January 1641.   BRIAN M. HALLORAN

Sources G. Levi della Vida, *George Strachan: memorials of a wandering Scottish scholar of the seventeenth century*, Third Spalding Club (1956), 24–6 • M. V. Hay, *The Blairs papers, 1603–1660* (1929) • Archivio Vaticano, Vatican City, MS Barb. Lat. 8614, fols. 56, 57 • *Original letters relating to the ecclesiastical affairs of Scotland: chiefly written by … King James the Sixth*, ed. D. Laing, 2 vols., Bannatyne Club, 92 (1851), vol. 2, p. 447 • Avery collection of information about Scots College, Paris, Scottish Catholic Archives, Edinburgh, GC 13/1, fols. 85, 88, 91 • J. Durkan, 'Grisy burses at Scots College, Paris', *Innes Review*, 22 (1971), 50–52, esp. 51 • B. M. Halloran, *The Scots College, Paris, 1603–1792* (1997) • P. J. Anderson, *Studies in the history and development of the University of Aberdeen* (1906), 115 • J. F. Kellas Johnstone and A. W. Robertson, *Bibliographia Aberdonensis*, ed. W. D. Simpson, Third Spalding Club, 1 (1929), 233, 251 • *Liber ordinationes, 1609–17*, Archives of the Vicariate of Rome
Archives Archivio Vaticano, Vatican City, letters, MS Barb. Lat. 8614 | Scottish Catholic Archives, Edinburgh, Avery collection of information about Scots College, Paris, GC 13/1

Chambers, Dorothea Katharine Lambert [*née* Dorothea Katharine Douglass] (**1878–1960**), lawn tennis player, was born on 3 September 1878 at Ealing, Middlesex, the second daughter of the Revd Henry Charles Douglass (*d.* 1916), vicar of St Matthew's, Ealing Common, and his wife, Clara Collick. She learned to play tennis on the vicarage lawn, encouraged by her father, who was a constant support throughout her playing career. The game was not well catered for at her school, Princess Helena College in Ealing, but this did nothing to dampen her enthusiasm or her competitive spirit, and on one occasion she was given lines after getting into 'a very heated argument' with a mistress over a disputed line call (Lambert Chambers, 88). She joined the Ealing Common Lawn Tennis Club as a junior and won the club handicap singles as an eleven-year-old, the first of three successive victories. By taking every opportunity to play against the club's men, she developed into an all-rounder of 'immense skill, energy and intelligence' (Davidson and Jones, 10).

'Tall, lean, and always superbly fit' (*DNB*), Chambers became extremely hard to beat. Her strength lay in her forehand and in her steady and accurate driving, with the emphasis on flexibility rather than sheer pace. An excellent tactician, she could read her opponents extremely well, and her angled drop shot was a famous winner. Competing at first as Miss Douglass until her marriage (on 3 April 1907) to Robert Lambert Chambers, a merchant, of Ealing, after which she was known as Mrs Lambert Chambers, she had a long string of victories in many tournaments. She took part in her first Wimbledon in 1900 and won her first title in 1903 at the age of twenty-four, then made a successful defence in the following year. For the next three years she faced tough competition from the young American May Sutton, to whom she lost in 1905 and 1907, but whom she beat in 1906. Between 1903 and 1914 she won the Wimbledon singles title seven times and lost only once to a British player, in 1908 to Charlotte Sterry, who herself won Wimbledon five times. Her record of seven singles victories stood until the great Helen Wills-Moody won her eighth title in 1938, though it should be

Dorothea Katharine Lambert Chambers (1878–1960), by unknown photographer, 1904

noted that before 1922 the holder had to defend her title only in the final 'challenge' round.

Chambers also won the Wimbledon ladies' doubles at the championships in 1903 and 1907, and the mixed doubles in 1906, 1908, and 1910. In 1908 she won the Olympic gold medal in the ladies' singles. At badminton, her other game, she was all-England women's doubles champion in 1903, and mixed doubles champion in 1904; she also played hockey for Middlesex.

During her enforced break from the game in 1909, when she was expecting the first of her two sons, Chambers wrote *Lawn Tennis for Ladies* (1910). The book reflected the increasing participation of women in sport, a much observed phenomenon which Chambers regarded as wholly beneficial to 'the health and mind of the modern girl' (Lambert Chambers, 1). She dismissed the arguments against female athleticism and advocated not merely exercise for women, but strenuous competition: 'If you are skilled and well drilled in discipline and sportsmanship, you are bound to benefit in the strife of the world' (ibid., 5). She preferred the overhead serve to the underarm, and it was an axiom with her that only by constant repetition could a stroke be perfected. She recommended to her readers the example of one English champion who always practised in this way: 'If no friend were available for the purpose, the butler had to devote an hour a day to throwing the ball in the given direction' (ibid., 13).

Chambers's determination to win met indignation from

some of her opponents and one, who was repeatedly beaten by a short drop shot, complained afterwards: 'I cannot admire your length' (Lambert Chambers, 28). She did not take the reproach at all seriously and if she discovered a weakness in her opponent's game would ruthlessly exploit it. She returned to Wimbledon in 1910 and won the ladies' singles with relative ease, a feat that she repeated the following year. By this time she was probably at her peak and was acknowledged to be the best woman player in the world. Her second pregnancy prevented her from defending the Wimbledon title in 1912, but she made a triumphant return to the championships in 1913 and won her seventh, and last, title in 1914. On the latter occasion she defeated Ethel Larcombe on the centre court at the old Wimbledon, in Worple Road. In sweltering heat, which left both players exhausted, Chambers won two very hard-fought sets, 7–5, 6–4. She would certainly have added to her total of singles titles had the war not intervened.

When the championships were resumed in 1919 there was intense public interest, heightened by the appearance of the twenty-year-old Frenchwoman Suzanne Lenglen, who as a fifteen-year-old had won the world hard court championship in Paris before the war. From the moment that Lenglen appeared at Wimbledon crowds flocked to see her play and her wonderful progress through the opening rounds, together with her twenty years' advantage in age, made her a firm favourite to win. 'The only concession that Mrs Lambert Chambers had made to the passing of time since 1903 was that her long-sleeved blouse was open at the neck and her long skirt just a trifle shorter' (DNB). Lenglen won the first set 10–8 but Chambers counter-attacked strongly to take the second 6–4. In the final set Lenglen led 4–1 but Chambers fought back magnificently to take the lead. At 6–5 and 40–15 up she had two match points, but Lenglen kept her nerve and hit a lucky 'wooden' volley to save one match point, and then a sublime backhand to save the next. Lenglen went on to take the set 9–7 and win a brilliant and memorable victory. It was one of the finest women's matches ever seen at Wimbledon and the drama of the occasion was equalled by the high quality of the tennis. One contemporary commentator wrote: 'Viewed from any angle the struggle was memorable. The percentage of stroke error by both players was negligible; the net was rarely shaken by a mistimed drive' (Davidson and Jones, 13).

Chambers returned in the following year to seek revenge and reached the final comfortably, but Lenglen was now almost invincible and overwhelmed her 6–3, 6–0. This was the last singles match that Chambers played at Wimbledon, although she carried on competing in the doubles. In December 1922 she became the first woman to be elected a councillor of the Lawn Tennis Association. And in 1925 she was invited to captain the British team for the Wightman Cup match against America at Forest Hills, New York. Her victories in the singles and doubles enabled Britain to win the tie by four matches to three, and bearing in mind that she was then forty-six this must rank among her finest achievements. In the following year she

again captained the British team at Wimbledon, where she lost her doubles. She made her last playing appearance at Wimbledon in 1927, when she partnered the South African Billie Tapscott in the doubles and came through one round. She had played 161 matches at the championships and was nearly forty-nine years old: only Blanch Bingley and Martina Navratilova have played in more finals than her.

In 1928 Chambers became a professional coach and ceased to be a member of the All England Lawn Tennis Club, but after the war she was re-elected and thenceforward, until her death in London, on 7 January 1960, she was always to be seen in the members' enclosure at the championships.   MARK POTTLE

Sources DNB · D. Lambert Chambers, *Lawn tennis for ladies* (1910) · A. D. C. Macaulay and J. Smyth, *Behind the scenes at Wimbledon* (1965) · O. Davidson and C. M. Jones, *Great women tennis players* (1971) · A. Little and L. Tingay, *Wimbledon ladies: a centenary record, 1884–1984, the Single champions* (1984) · J. Huntington-Whiteley, ed., *The book of British sporting heroes* (1998) [exhibition catalogue, NPG, 16 Oct 1998 – 24 Jan 1999] · H. Gilmeister, *Tennis: a cultural history* (1990) · CGPLA Eng. & Wales (1960)
Likenesses photograph, 1904, Hult. Arch. [see illus.]
Wealth at death £18,215 9s. 8d.: probate, 28 April 1960, CGPLA Eng. & Wales

Chambers, Sir Edmund Kerchever (1866–1954), theatre historian and civil servant, was born at West Ilsley, Berkshire, on 16 March 1866. He was the son of the Revd William Chambers (b. 1826/7), curate, and fellow of Worcester College, Oxford, and his wife, Anna Heathcote, daughter of Thomas Kerchever *Arnold (1800–1853), the educational writer and theologian. After receiving his early education at Marlborough College, Chambers proceeded to Corpus Christi College, Oxford, as a classical scholar, took firsts in honour moderations (1887) and *literae humaniores* (1889), and in 1891 won the chancellor's English essay prize with an essay on literary forgeries. He was not awarded a fellowship, but before he left Oxford in 1892 for the education department, he had already acquired a bent for English studies and produced an edition of *Richard II* (1891). He went on to become a notable example of a man who followed two careers, both with distinction. On 5 September 1893 he married Eleanor Christabel (Nora) Bowman, the daughter of John Davison Bowman of the Exchequer and Audit Office. They had no children.

Chambers's duties in the education department were not at first onerous, but from 1903 he became a valued lieutenant of Robert Morant, permanent secretary to the newly constituted Board of Education. Chambers's contribution was most important in matters relating to day continuation schools and adult education. The day continuation schools were victims of the economies associated with the name of Sir Eric Geddes, but the Workers' Educational Association and other promoters of adult education were well aware of the debt of gratitude they owed to Chambers. He rose to be second secretary (1921), but perhaps because of his unaccommodating manner with deputations he was not offered the post of permanent secretary, and he resigned in 1926.

some extent on the liturgical and miracle plays, his was pioneer work. *The Elizabethan Stage* was more a work of consolidation than of discovery, but even so his originality appeared in the acuteness with which he balanced complicated evidence. His *Shakespeare*, completed in his days of leisure, was carefully composed, with due consideration given to all the material facts and problems. All three works showed the same grasp of all relevant evidence and the same lucidity in a prose that achieves a good expository level.

After his *Shakespeare* Chambers did not abandon Elizabethan studies (*Sir Thomas Wyatt and some Collected Studies*, 1933, and *Shakespearean Gleanings*, 1944) but in his biographies of Coleridge (1938) and Matthew Arnold (1947) he turned also to the Romantic poetry of which his own verses are late examples (*Carmina argentea*, privately printed, 1918).

Chambers's services to education and his scholarship earned him many honours. He received the honorary DLitt from Durham (1922) and Oxford (1939), and his election to an honorary fellowship at Corpus Christi (1934) gave him great pleasure. He was appointed CB in 1912 and KBE in 1925, and in 1924 was elected FBA. He also became a foreign member of the Royal Society of Letters of Lund (1928), and a corresponding fellow of the Medieval Academy of America (1933).

After his retirement Chambers lived at Eynsham, near Oxford, and there wrote *Sir Henry Lee* (1936), a life of the ranger of Woodstock, and *Eynsham under the Monks* (1936), his one work on medieval local history. In his *English Literature at the Close of the Middle Ages* (1945), a contribution to the Oxford History of English Literature, he returned to the subjects of medieval drama and lyric, the ballad and folk poetry, and Malory. In 1938 he moved from Eynsham to Bovey Coombe, Beer, Devon, where he died on 21 January 1954.   F. P. WILSON, *rev.* NILANJANA BANERJI

Sources F. P. Wilson and J. D. Wilson, 'Sir Edmund Kerchever Chambers, 1866–1954', *PBA*, 43 (1957), 267–85 · Foster, *Alum. Oxon.* · WWW
Archives Bodl. Oxf., papers | BL, corresp. with Society of Authors, Add. MS 56681
Likenesses W. Rothenstein, chalk drawing, 1924, NPG [*see illus.*] · W. Stoneman, photograph, 1926, NPG · photograph, repro. in *PBA*
Wealth at death £14,733 11s. 6d.: probate, 24 March 1954, *CGPLA Eng. & Wales*

Sir Edmund Kerchever Chambers (1866–1954), by Sir William Rothenstein, 1924

During his years as a civil servant Chambers also practised journalism and edited many editions of the English classics, especially Shakespeare. He was the first president of the Malone Society (1906–39) and contributed to its *Collections* valuable papers on dramatic records. Among the best of his publications were an anthology, *Early English Lyrics* (1907), chosen by him and Frank Sidgwick, and *The Oxford Book of Sixteenth-Century Verse* (1932). His interest in Arthurian studies, dating from his undergraduate days, resulted in *Arthur of Britain* (1927).

From the time Chambers left Oxford he was working at 'a little book about Shakespeare and the conditions, literary and dramatic, under which he wrote'. This 'little book' grew into his three chief publications, *The Mediaeval Stage* (2 vols., 1903), *The Elizabethan Stage* (4 vols., 1923), and *Shakespeare* (2 vols., 1930). A master of dramatic history, Chambers made no attempt in these works to evaluate plays as literature. He was convinced that any history of drama which does not confine itself solely to the analysis of genius must start from a study of the social and economic facts on which the drama rested, and these facts he presented with a fullness and accuracy not approached before. In *The Mediaeval Stage* the only well-trodden ground was the interlude; on minstrelsy and folk drama, and to

Chambers, Ephraim (1680?–1740), encyclopaedist, was born at Milton, near Kendal, Westmorland, where his father, Richard Chambers, occupied and owned a small farm. He was one of three sons and two daughters. Educated at Heversham grammar school, Westmorland, he was sent to London and ultimately apprenticed (1714–21) to John Senex, the map and globe maker, who encouraged his desire for the acquisition of knowledge. While an apprentice he formed the plan of compiling a cyclopaedia on a larger scale than that of John Harris's *Lexicon technicum* (1704). After he had begun the enterprise he left Senex's service and took chambers in Gray's Inn, where he remained until his death. In 1726 he published *Proposals* for a 'cyclopaedia', and it was this document that Samuel

Johnson later claimed had partly 'formed his style' (Boswell, *Life*, 1.218). The work was published by subscription and appeared in 1728 in two folio volumes as the *Cyclopaedia, or, An universal dictionary of arts and sciences … compiled from the best authors*. It cost 4 guineas, was dedicated to the king, and opened with an elaborate preface explaining the plan of the work, and attempting a classification of knowledge. Partly adapted from the work of B. Moreri and P. Bayle, it introduced cross-references, which proved indispensable to every subsequent lexicographer. Because of this, combined with inclusion of more of the humanities, Chambers's work became the first true general encyclopaedia. Dean Stanley later described Chambers as 'the Father of Cyclopaedias' (Boswell, *Life*, 1.219). Its value was at once recognized, and its compiler was elected a member of the Royal Society in 1729, the year after Senex.

A new edition being called for, Chambers resolved to recast the first on a plan explained in a paper entitled 'Considerations'. A clause in a bill introduced into parliament which would have obliged the publishers of an improved edition of a work to issue the improvements separately led to the abandonment of the recast. The bill was lost in the Lords; but in the event Chambers limited his ambitions to the issue of a second edition with some alterations and additions. In 1739 a third edition was advertised in London and published in Dublin. After the compiler's death a fourth, in 1741, was followed by a fifth in 1743, indicating a singularly rapid sale. A French translation of large parts of its content was used in the compilation of Diderot's and D'Alembert's *Encyclopédie*.

Chambers is said to have edited, and he certainly contributed to, the *Literary Magazine … by a Society of Gentlemen* (1735–7), which consisted mainly of reviews of new books. During 1726 and 1727 he translated from the French important works on perspective and chemistry and co-operated with John Martyn, the botanist, in an abridged translation of the *Philosophical History and Memoirs of the Royal Academy of Sciences at Paris* (5 vols., 1742). Martyn blamed Chambers's prolixity for its limited sale. During his later years Chambers paid a visit to France in an attempt to restore his health, and is said to have rejected a promising invitation to issue there an edition (or possibly a translation) of his *Cyclopaedia* dedicated to Louis XV. He left behind him a manuscript account of his French visit, which has never been published; but some letters to his wife descriptive of it and on other subjects were subsequently printed in the *Gentleman's Magazine* in 1787. As an author he was liberally, and as an invalid, most kindly treated by the first Thomas Longman, the founder of the publishing house of that name, who during Chambers's lifetime became the largest shareholder in the *Cyclopaedia*. Chambers was an avowed freethinker, irascible, kind to the poor, and extremely frugal. He died on 15 May 1740 at Canonbury House, Islington, and was buried in the cloisters of Westminster Abbey, where, in an epitaph of his own composition, reproduced in the original Latin in the *Gentleman's Magazine*, he described himself as: 'Heard of by many, known to few, who led a life between Fame and Obscurity, Neither abounding nor deficient in Learning, Devoted to Study, but as a Man who thinks himself bound to all offices of Humanity' (*GM*, 1st ser., 30). His will contained bequests to his two brothers, Nathanial and Zachary, to his two sisters, and to their respective children.

The *Cyclopaedia* has been described as 'judiciously, honestly and carefully done', but possessing 'many defects and omissions' (*Encyc. Brit.*). Chambers was himself well aware of these and at his death left materials for seven new volumes. These were utilized by Dr John Hill for a supplement published in 1753. Large parts of the original were also incorporated in a revised and enlarged edition by Dr Abraham Rees that appeared between 1778 and 1788.

FRANCIS ESPINASSE, *rev.* MICHAEL HARRIS

Sources *GM*, 1st ser., 10 (1740), 262 · *GM*, 1st ser., 57 (1787), 314–17 · *GM*, 1st ser., 55 (1785), 671–4, 938 · *Universal Magazine of Knowledge and Pleasure*, 76 (1785), 4–7 · Nichols, *Lit. anecdotes*, vol. 4 · R. V. Wallis and P. J. Wallis, eds., *Biobibliography of British mathematics and its applications*, 2 (1986) · PRO, PROB 11/702, sig. 136 · D. F. McKenzie, ed., *Stationers' Company apprentices*, [3]: *1701–1800* (1978) · Boswell, *Life* · *The letters of Samuel Johnson*, ed. B. Redford, 5 vols. (1992–4) · 'Encyclopaedia', *Encyclopaedia Britannica*, 11th edn (1910–11), vol. 9, pp. 369–82

Chambers, George (1803–1840), marine painter, was born on 23 September 1803 in Whitby, Yorkshire, the fourth of the eight children of John Chambers (*d. c.*1827), a mariner, and his wife, Mary Appleby (*d. c.*1825). The family lived in extreme poverty and Chambers began working at the age of eight, after having attended Whitby Free School. Two years later he went to sea. When thirteen he was bound apprentice and sailed on the brig *Equity* to the Mediterranean and the Baltic. Chambers was unusually small in stature and therefore often the target of ill-treatment by other crewmen. His diminutive size, however, led to his employment on lighter tasks such as painting and decorating and he was encouraged to make drawings for the captain and crew. His abilities as an artist developed and at the age of eighteen he was enabled to cancel his indentures and return to Whitby, where he became a house painter and decorator. In his spare time he practised drawing and painted ships' portraits. Although few have survived, most of these were done in oils on millboard. Finally, in 1825, aged twenty-one, he left Whitby and moved to London.

Chambers's first friend and patron in London was Christopher Crawford, who kept the Waterman's Arms in Wapping. Crawford employed him to embellish his premises with marine paintings and helped him to obtain commissions from sea captains. Wider recognition came when, in 1827, the British Institution accepted his *View of Whitby* for exhibition. In the same year he married, much against the wishes of Crawford, who later brought him to the attention of Thomas Horner. Horner, an entrepreneur, engaged him to help decorate the Colosseum in Regent's Park with a panorama of London, but the enterprise failed and Chambers was forced to return to Wapping without the wages due to him. Shortly afterwards, he and his wife, Mary Ann, had their first child, George William Crawford Chambers [*see below*].

The Royal Academy had shown a work by Chambers, *Sketch on the River Medway*, at its annual exhibition in 1828. His continued endeavours to develop his painterly skills were rewarded by purchases by distinguished naval clients. But, seeking new challenges, he became, in late 1829, the scenery painter at the Royal Pavilion Theatre in Whitechapel Road, London, quickly learning the new techniques of stage perspective painted in distemper and achieving acclaim for his work. But he left the theatre after about a year in order to devote himself to the demands of a growing circle of influential patrons. This was how he came to the notice of his most important aristocratic patron, Lord Mark Kerr, who ordered a series of paintings and encouraged him, also trying to help the young and diminutive painter to overcome his inherent shyness. In September 1831 Kerr obtained for Chambers an audience with William IV and Queen Adelaide at Windsor Castle, after which the king purchased a painting of his depicting the opening of London Bridge and one of a Mediterranean scene; the queen chose a view of Dover and one of the Royal Naval Hospital at Greenwich. (Three of these have remained in the Royal Collection.) Unfortunately this was followed by six months of illness which prevented Chambers from painting.

Most of Chambers's work prior to this date had been in oils, but he now began to develop a real talent as a watercolourist. His repeated sketching trips on the Thames and Medway, and a number of tours around the country, gave him ample scope to express in this medium his deeply felt romantic response to nature. While still showing regularly at the other societies, he first exhibited at the Old Watercolour Society in 1834. His immediate election to full membership was a significant accolade and a confirmation that watercolours were ranked among his best works.

Chambers owed his introduction to the Royal Naval Hospital at Greenwich to Edward Hawke Locker, a civil commissioner, who was building up its collection of paintings. *The Bombardment of Algiers* (1836), for which he was paid 200 guineas and which is widely regarded as his *chef-d'œuvre*, was one of the fruits of this patronage. In 1837 he made the first of two tours in the Netherlands: the wider horizons thus opened gave his art a new impetus. He continued to produce paintings and drawings of distinction which combined his romantic sensibility with a feeling for the sea and nautical truth, but he was not able to regain his earlier heights of patronage.

Chambers and his wife had another son, William Henry Martin, in 1832; a third son, born in 1837, died in 1839, the year in which a daughter, Emily, was born. The family lived at a number of addresses in the area of Regent's Park and Fitzrovia in London. In spite of his shyness, Chambers enjoyed the company of other artists and was particularly generous and helpful to young and struggling painters. His health had never been good and he was frequently unable to work. In 1840 he made a brief voyage to Madeira for his health, but died on 29 October at his home, 26 Percy Street, Rathbone Place, London, of an aneurysm of the aorta. He was buried in St James's Chapel, Pentonville, London.

George William Crawford Chambers (*b.* 1829, *d.* after 1863), marine painter, was born on 14 June 1829 at 11 Wapping Wall, London. Educated from 1840 at the Royal Naval Hospital school at Greenwich, Kent, he inherited his father's talent and benefited from his instruction to become a professional painter. His first painting was hung at public exhibition when he was eighteen and his work was accepted regularly by the Royal Academy and other societies over the next fifteen years—a total of fifty-four paintings. His subject matter was often similar to that of his father but his handling of oil paint was much more fluid. He did not exhibit at the watercolour societies. With such promising early success, it is strange that he disappeared so completely from the London scene after 1863, when he was only thirty-four years of age. He may have gone abroad, at least for a while, but random examples of his work in Great Britain have appeared, dated throughout the remainder of the century. Attribution is, however, often not secure and the rest of his life remains, for the time being at least, a mystery. ALAN RUSSETT

Sources A. Russett, *George Chambers (1803–40): his life and work* (1996) · J. Watkins, *Life and career of George Chambers* (1841) · d. cert. · parish register (baptism), London, Shadwell St Paul, 8 July 1829 [George William Crawford Chambers]
Likenesses A. Butler, lithograph, repro. in Watkins, *Life and career of George Chambers* · G. Chambers, self-portrait, pencil drawing, RA
Wealth at death £533 17s.—studio contents: Christies annotated catalogue, 1840?

Chambers, George William Crawford (*b.* 1829, *d.* after 1863). *See under* Chambers, George (1803–1840).

Chambers, Helen (1879–1935), pathologist and cancer research worker, was born on 18 July 1879 in Bombay, India, the only daughter of Frederick Chambers, of the Indian Civil Service. Her family returned to Britain and she was educated at the Jersey Ladies' College, and later at Park Street Girls' School in Cambridge; she studied chemistry and physics at Newnham College, Cambridge, and entered the London Royal Free Hospital School of Medicine for Women (LSMW) in 1898.

Chambers had a distinguished undergraduate career, gaining her medical degree from London University, MB (1903) and BS (1904); she was awarded first-class honours in obstetrics and the gold medal for forensic medicine. Chambers was determined on a career in pathology; in 1904 she was appointed as the clinical pathologist to the Royal Free Hospital, and lecturer in pathology at the LSMW. Four years later she gained her MD (London) for her thesis, 'Observations on pathology of the thyroid gland'. About the same time she won a newly founded scholarship in cancer research at the Middlesex Hospital where she worked with Sidney Russ, the professor of physics and radium expert. Between 1911 and 1913 they wrote a series of papers on the biological effects of radium, published in the *Proceedings of the Royal Society* and the *Archives of the Middlesex Hospital*, which established her reputation in cancer research.

Helen Chambers (1879–1935), by Reginald Haines, pubd 1920

During the First World War, Chambers took the post of consultant pathologist at the Military Hospital, Endell Street, in London. This hospital, which opened in 1915, was staffed entirely by women doctors and surgeons from the Women's Hospital Corps. Flora Murray, the commanding officer, described how 'a great deal of good team work' was done between the pathology department and Louisa Garrett Anderson, the chief surgeon, in treating thousands of cases of wound infection in injured soldiers. Chambers introduced a new antiseptic treatment, Bipp (bismuth-iodoform-paraffin-paste), which precluded the need for daily wound dressings, and which greatly reduced infection. When the hospital closed in 1920 Chambers was appointed CBE in recognition of her contribution to this work.

After the war Chambers returned to full-time cancer research with Professor Russ at the Middlesex Hospital; the Medical Research Council (MRC) appointed her as the radium research officer, a post she held for the rest of her life. During the early 1920s she contributed to several papers on the radiobiology and immunology of tumours, summarized in the *Proceedings of the Royal Society* (1921) and the *Journal of Cancer Research* (1926). Although always intrigued by the theoretical possibility of treating cancer immunologically (an advanced idea for that time), she turned all her attention to radiotherapy. She used a radium applicator to treat 168 cases of advanced cancers of all types—only 9 per cent survived, but she was impressed with the potential of radium for treating cancer of the cervix, which became the main target for her research. However, radium was in short supply and the MRC wanted to divide it among the major teaching hospitals for a trial to treat uterine cancer. In 1924 Chambers warned the Medical Women's Federation (MWF) in a lecture entitled 'Progress in cancer problems' that women doctors would lose their patients if they did not secure a supply of radium for treating their own cancer cases. She organized an MWF cancer research committee which persuaded the MRC to include their group in the trial, and obtained a supply of radium from the newly formed British Empire Cancer Campaign.

Helen Chambers, working with Elizabeth Hurdon, the MWF's research director, and four other women surgeons, improved the organization of the MRC radium trial; they adopted a new treatment technique from Sweden and introduced better long-term records and five-year survival statistics. By 1928 they had treated 300 cases at four women-run hospitals. However, transporting the radium was difficult and sometimes dangerous and it soon became apparent that there was a need for a special single centre for women's cancer. Chambers appealed for a new cancer hospital, indeed her obituary in *Nature* stresses that it was mainly due to her foresight and inspiration that the Marie Curie Hospital at Hampstead came into being in 1929.

The Marie Curie Hospital quickly established a reputation as the major centre for women's cancers, treating nearly a thousand cases in the first five years. The results were excellent; the 1933 MRC Special Report, *Medical Use of Radium*, described them as showing 'an astonishing difference in survival rates'. Chambers, in an important paper in *The Lancet*, published a few months before her death, reported a 42 per cent five-year survival rate in the Marie Curie Hospital's patients, compared with 20 to 30 per cent at other centres around the world. Chambers was justifiably proud of these results; her work at the Marie Curie was a major medical advance for the treatment of cervical cancer, and the high point of her own career. She was a gifted research worker, renowned for her careful methodology and detailed records, who combined her zeal for science with a strong desire for social service. Her life was totally devoted to cancer research and the promotion of women's interests in medicine; she never married and had few interests outside her work apart from gardening. A bibliography of her main publications can be found in the *MWF Quarterly Review* (January 1936). Although she never published a monograph on radiotherapy she contributed more than thirty papers on the subject to the medical literature.

Chambers's career was cut short by breast cancer; she died at Court Hall, Kenton, Devon, on 21 July 1935. It was a fitting memorial that the new pathology laboratory at the Marie Curie Hospital was named the Helen Chambers

Research Laboratory when it opened in 1937. Perhaps the greatest tribute came from Professor Henri Coutard, the radiotherapist at the Curie Institute in Paris whom she had visited a few months before her death, who stated that her results for the treatment of carcinoma of the cervix at the Marie Curie Hospital were the best in the world at that time.   PETER D. MOHR

Sources *The Times* (26 July 1935) · *The Lancet* (27 July 1935) · *BMJ* (3 Aug 1935), 234–5 · *Nature*, 136 (1935), 250 · 'Obituary and bibliography of Helen Chambers CBE MD BS', *Medical Women's Federation Quarterly Review* (Jan 1936), 58–61 · F. Murray, *Women as army surgeons* (1920) · M. A. Elston, 'Women doctors in the British health service: a sociological study of their careers and opportunities', PhD diss., U. Leeds, 1986 · P. D. Mohr, 'Women-run hospitals in Britain', PhD diss., University of Manchester, 1995 · L. Martindale, 'Recent advances in treatment of cancer of uterus and breast', *Medical Women's Federation Quarterly Review* (April 1936), 20–38 · R. J. Dickson, 'The Marie Curie Hospital, 1925–68', *BMJ* (16 Nov 1968), 444–6 · 'Elizabeth Hurdon, obituary', *Medical Women's Federation Quarterly Review* (April 1941), 59–62 · L. Leneman, 'Medical women at war, 1914–18', *Medical History*, 38 (1994), 160–77 · 'Opening of Helen Chambers Research Laboratory', *Medical Women's Federation Quarterly Review* (April 1937), 107–8 · H. Chambers, 'The Marie Curie Hospital', *Medical Women's Federation Quarterly Review* (July 1929), 19–23 · d. cert.
Archives Royal Free Hospital, London, medical school, details from application form and newspaper cuttings | Wellcome L., Medical Women's Federation
Likenesses R. Haines, photograph, repro. in Murray, *Women as army surgeons*, 136 [*see illus.*]
Wealth at death £2014 18s. 7d.: probate, 1 Oct 1935, *CGPLA Eng. & Wales*

Chambers, Humphrey (*bap.* 1599?, *d.* 1662), Church of England clergyman, was probably baptized on 27 May 1599, the son of Robert Chambers of Somerset. He matriculated from University College, Oxford, on 17 November 1615, graduated BA on 15 October 1618, and proceeded MA on 6 July 1621. Although noted for his oratorical skills he was 'put aside as insufficient' when standing for a fellowship at Merton (Wood, 3.610). Inducted as rector of Claverton, Somerset, in 1623, he married, by 1628, Anne, daughter of Bishop Richard *Brett (1567/8–1637) [*see under* Authorized Version of the Bible, translators of]. He proceeded BD in February 1631. Later he allegedly suffered two years' imprisonment when his defence of the morality of the sabbath incurred the wrath of both his diocesan bishop, William Piers, and Archbishop Laud.

Chambers supported parliament during the civil war, for a time maintaining a soldier and horse at his own expense. In 1643 he took the covenant, was invited as one of the assembly of divines, and published one of the earliest of his several fast sermons, *A Divine Ballance to Weigh Religious Fasts in*. Two years later he became rector of St Stephen Walbrook, London, but in 1646, in recognition of his good service, he was presented to the rich living of Pewsey, Wiltshire, worth £400 a year, by the moderately puritan Philip Herbert, earl of Pembroke. Having gained a DD from Oxford in 1648, Chambers published in the following year his sermon *A Motive to Peace and Love*. Other works in this period included, in 1653, a critical commentary on William Dell's *Crucified and Quickened Christian*, published interleaved with Dell's text, the *Apology for the*

Ministers of the County of Wiltshire (1654), written with Peter Ince, Adoniram Byfield, and John Strickland to defend their conduct at parliamentary elections, and a funeral sermon for John Graile, *Paul's Sad Farewell to the Ephesians* (1655). He also edited three works by Obadiah Sedgwick.

Appointed an assistant to the Wiltshire commission of triers and ejectors in 1654, Chambers became notorious for his uncompromising treatment of scandalous ministers. He was condemned in print by the ejected minister Walter Bushnell, and was obliged to publish a justification of his part in those proceedings; this appeared in 1660. Several sermons also appeared in 1660 and 1661. After the Restoration, Chambers was able to remain at Pewsey, there being no ejected minister to challenge him, but according to Calamy he 'quitted his living and his life together' at the Act of Uniformity. He wrote his will on 31 August 1662, a week after the act came into force. His son, Richard, received the larger portion of the estate, which included property in Barnet, Hertfordshire, while a small financial bequest was made to the poor of Pewsey, where he was buried 'with no other ceremony than we would use to a dog' (*Nonconformist's Memorial*, 3.370), on 8 September 1662. His wife survived him.   HENRY LANCASTER

Sources *The nonconformist's memorial … originally written by … Edmund Calamy*, ed. S. Palmer, [3rd edn], 3 (1803), 370–71 · *Calamy rev.*, 107–8 · Wood, *Ath. Oxon.*, new edn, 3.610–11 · E. Calamy, *A continuation of the account of the ministers … who were ejected and silenced after the Restoration in 1660*, 2 (1727), 864 · P. S. Seaver, *The puritan lectureships: the politics of religious dissent, 1560–1662* (1970) · W. A. Shaw, *A history of the English church during the civil wars and under the Commonwealth, 1640–1660*, 2 (1900), 325 · will, PRO, PROB 11/310, fol. 259 · D. Neal, *The history of the puritans or protestant nonconformists*, ed. J. Toulmin, new edn, 4 (1822), 343 · Foster, *Alum. Oxon.*
Wealth at death £216 in bequests, plus land in Barnet: will, PRO, PROB 11/310, fol. 259

Chambers [Borowe, Burgh], **John** (*d.* 1556), abbot and bishop of Peterborough, was a native of Peterborough, and is therefore sometimes named as Borowe or Burgh in the records. The suggestion that he was an illegitimate son of Richard Chambers cannot be confirmed. He studied at Cambridge, proceeding BTh in 1539, when he was said to have been studying theology for ten years. By then he had long been a Benedictine monk at Peterborough, possibly from the late 1490s, and was elected abbot in 1528, succeeding the aged and incompetent Robert Kyrton. Almost at once he received a demand for 1000 marks from Wolsey, to which he replied that he was 'so sore charged he cannot do it … The "livelode" of the house was never so far in decay, and he is fain to borrow' (*LP Henry VIII*, 4/2, no. 4279). Two years later, at Easter 1530, he received Wolsey at Peterborough, as the fallen minister made his way towards York. As abbot Chambers signed the letter of 1530 from English prelates to the pope, supporting Henry VIII's petition for a divorce, while in 1534 he and forty-one monks successively repudiated papal authority and acknowledged the royal supremacy. On 7 January 1536 he attended the funeral of Katherine of Aragon in his abbey church.

Chambers was attempting to defend his abbey's property in 1534, and he subsequently endeavoured to preserve the house for as long as possible. When the king's agents Richard Layton and Richard Cromwell were at Ramsey in January 1536 they looked next to Peterborough. Chambers appealed to Sir William Parr, later marquess of Northampton, in the vain hope of averting dissolution. He offered the king the abbey's entire income for a year, some 2500 marks, while promising Thomas Cromwell £300 'if he would bee good lorde to hym' (BL, Cotton MS Cleop. E. iv, fol. 205). But when these inducements failed he offered no further resistance. Chambers had the advantage of powerful friends, including John Russell, later earl of Bedford, Edward Lee, archbishop of York, and members of the Parr family, and when the abbey was surrendered to the king, on 29 November 1539, he was appointed guardian of the temporalities with an annual pension of £266 13s. 4d. and 100 loads of wood, and became a royal chaplain. Nearly two years later, on 4 September 1541, letters patent were issued converting the former abbey into a cathedral church, with Chambers as its first bishop; he was consecrated in his new cathedral on 23 October following by Bishop Thomas Goodrich of Ely. His stipend was set at £333, and as his official residence he was given his old home, the abbot's lodgings or abbot's side, together with the stone tower known as 'the Knyghtes chamber'. An endowment was also provided for a dean and a chapter consisting of six prebendaries.

Little can be said of the later years of Chambers's life. In 1542 he was one of the scholars involved in the abortive project to revise the Great Bible—with Bishop John Wakeman of Gloucester he was allotted Revelation. Nor can much be said of his position with regard to the subsequent religious reforms of the 1540s and 1550s, though his giving his proxy to Edmund Bonner and Nicholas Heath in the Lords' debate on the Book of Common Prayer in 1549 may well indicate conservative sympathies. But usually he seems to have acquiesced in the successive changes in religion. On 4 December 1553 Queen Mary granted him the collation of his cathedral prebendaries, but he does not appear to have tried to fill his chapter with committed Catholics. The fact that he permitted his diocesan registrar to accumulate offices may also point to a less than active episcopate. He died at Peterborough on 7 February 1556, and was buried in the choir of his cathedral, with great pomp, on 6 March.

Chambers's will, dated 31 December 1554, has an entirely traditional preamble, bequeathing his soul to the Trinity, the Virgin, and the whole company of heaven. He left £20 apiece to the poor, and to the repair of the parish church and the bridge of Peterborough. His cathedral was to receive a cope, a pyx, and two silver candlesticks, and his auditor was to surrender to his executors 'all maner of bookes courte rooles accomptes and other muniments whatsoever touchithe or concernythe the landes of the busshopp' (PRO, PROB 11/38, fol. 175). Numerous bequests of sheep suggest that he had been seriously engaged in pastoral farming. He seems to have remembered all his servants, along with his sister Emma and members of

leading midlands gentry families like Sir Thomas Tresham and Sir William Fitzwilliam (a godson). Chambers was commemorated by two monuments. One was a brass put up by him in his own lifetime, engraved with a laudatory epigraph with blanks left for the date of his death (never filled). The other, described as exquisitely carved, is recorded in a seventeenth-century manuscript drawing which shows a full-length recumbent effigy, robed, mitred, and holding a crozier, its feet resting on a lion. Both were destroyed in the civil wars.

ANDREW A. CHIBI

Sources Venn, Alum. Cant. · LP Henry VIII, vols. 4–21 · W. G. Searle, ed., Grace book Γ (1908) · L. B. Smith, Tudor prelates and politics, 1536–1558 (1953) · will, PRO, PROB 11/38, sig. 25 · C. H. Garrett, The Marian exiles: a study in the origins of Elizabethan puritanism (1938) · BL, Cotton MS Cleop. E. iv · S. Gunton, History of the church of Peterborough (1686) · Cooper, Ath. Cantab., 1.141–2 · Wood, Ath. Oxon., new edn, 2.773–4 · Rymer, Foedera, 1st edn, 11.731–6 · R. W. Dixon, History of the Church of England, 6 vols. (1878–1902) · T. Wright, ed., Three chapters of letters relating to the suppression of monasteries (1843) · J. Gereatrex, ed., Account rolls of the obedientiaries of Peterborough, Northamptonshire RS, 33 (1984) · W. T. Mellows, ed., Peterborough local administration: the last days of Peterborough monastery, Northamptonshire RS, 12 (1947) · W. T. Mellows, ed., Peterborough local administration: the foundation of Peterborough Cathedral, AD 1541, Northamptonshire RS, 13 (1941)
Archives BL, Add. MS 5828 · BL, Cotton MS Cleop. E. iv, fol. 205
Likenesses drawing (after effigy), repro. in Mellows, ed., Peterborough local administration: the last days of Peterborough monastery, facing p. xvi

Chambers, John (1780–1839), biographer and antiquary, was born in London in March 1780. After receiving a good preliminary education he was placed in the office of an architect, but having inherited an ample fortune on the death of his father, he determined to devote himself to the cultivation of art and literature as an amateur. In 1806 he became a member of the Society of Arts, and from 1809 to 1811 he acted as a chairman of the committee of polite arts. Chambers married, on 29 September 1814, Mary Foster, the daughter of Peter Le Neve Foster of Wymondham in Norfolk. A year after his marriage he left London for Worcester, and there planned and wrote most of his works. Besides occasional contributions to the *Gentleman's Magazine* and other periodicals (including a 'Life of Inigo Jones' to Arnold's *Magazine of the Fine Arts*), Chambers was the author of *A General History of Malvern* (1817), *A General History of Worcester* (1819), and *Biographical Illustrations of Worcestershire* (1820).

Chambers remained at Worcester for nearly eight years, before moving to his wife's home at Wymondham, and, after staying there for about two years, finally settled at Norwich so that his sons might attend the grammar school. At Norwich he published *A general history of the county of Norfolk … including biographical notices, original and selected* (1829). This was published anonymously, Chambers having received the assistance of contributors resident in the county. Chambers died in Dean's Square, Norwich, on 28 July 1839, leaving two sons and a daughter. The eldest son, John Charles *Chambers (1817–1874), theologian, was vicar of St Mary's and warden of the House of Charity, Soho, London, from 1856 until his death; the youngest son, Oswald Lyttleton, also entered into orders, and became vicar of Hook, Yorkshire, where he died in 1883. GORDON GOODWIN, *rev.* NILANJANA BANERJI

Sources GM, 2nd ser., 12 (1839), 430 · private information (1887) Archives RIBA BAL, MS of collections for a biography of English architects | Bodl. Oxf., corresp. with J. B. Nichols

Chambers, John Charles (1817–1874), Church of England clergyman, the son of John *Chambers (1780–1839), biographer and antiquary, and his wife, Mary, *née* Foster, was born at the Tything, Worcester, on 23 November 1817. He was educated at Norwich grammar school from 1824 to 1833 and then privately before entering Emmanuel College, Cambridge, in 1835, where he took his degree of BA in 1840, gaining a second class in classical studies, and his MA in 1843. In 1842 he obtained the Tyrwhitt Hebrew scholarship, and was ordained deacon, serving his title as curate of Sedbergh, Yorkshire.

On 1 October 1846 Chambers married Mary (*d.* 1873), daughter of James Upton, a merchant. In the same year he was ordained priest and moved as an Episcopalian missionary priest to Perth, where in 1850 he became canon and chancellor of the new cathedral of St Ninian's. In 1855, on his completion of the statutes and appointments at St Ninian's Cathedral, he became vicar of St Mary Magdalene's at Harlow. This living he exchanged in 1856 for the perpetual curacy of St Mary's, Crown Street, Soho, London, a benefice which he held until his death, together with the wardenship of the House of Charity, Soho, to which he was appointed in November 1856. Chambers turned St Mary's into a model for managing a parish along ritualist lines. He was one of the earliest ritualist priests to demonstrate a particular concern for ministry in poor areas of London. He built new schools and expanded the number of pupils to almost 1000, established a new clergy house, rebuilt the church, and achieved a fourfold increase in the income of the living, which had stood at £70 a year. He also established a refuge house for homeless men and women, and acquired and refurbished new premises in Soho Square for the House of Charity. He raised a large staff of volunteer workers to help with his educational and charitable work, and pioneered, with his friend J. M. Neale, the establishment of church guilds, such as the Guild of St Michael and All Angels founded in 1863 to encourage poor working women and girls to pursue an ideal of chaste Christian service. Chambers also played an important role in the founding and management of national Anglo-Catholic societies in the mid-nineteenth century. He was a founding member of the Confraternity of the Blessed Sacrament, a lay and clerical society formed in 1857 at St Mary's to promote more frequent celebration of holy communion. It was refounded by Chambers in 1862 after several of the founding priests converted to Roman Catholicism. He was one of the early members of the priestly Society of the Holy Cross, serving as its third master in 1862.

Sombre in manner and severe in personal discipline, Chambers was considerably learned in patristics, church history, and liturgiology. Like J. M. Neale, he stood for a Catholic Anglicanism which emphasized the Church of England's historic continuity with the Catholic church of East and West, but denied the universal claims of the Roman pontiff. The spirit of his scholarship and of its polemical use can be caught from various of his published lectures on ecclesiology, such as *The Witness of St Gregory the Great Against the Claims of the Roman Papacy* (1864). His published work consists mainly of sermons and lectures, including *Reformation, not Deformation* (1864) and *The Destruction of Sin, being Thirteen Addresses … Delivered in Advent, 1872* (ed. J. J. Elkington, 1874).

Chambers died at his home, 1 Greek Street, Soho, London, on 21 May 1874, and was buried in Kensal Green cemetery on 26 May. His name became notorious for a time through a posthumous controversy involving one of his works, *The Priest in Absolution*. It was published in two parts—the first, a treatise on moral theology, publicly in 1866, and the second, a manual for confessors, privately in 1872. Commissioned by the Society of the Holy Cross, the book was a rewritten version of a French Roman Catholic manual by Abbé Jean Gaume, and it attracted little attention until it was mentioned in a debate on ritualism in the House of Lords in 1877. Fuelling fears of the growth of the practice of private confession, the book was examined and condemned by the house of bishops.

JEREMY MORRIS

Sources J. Embry, The Catholic movement and the Society of the Holy Cross (1931), 15, 59, 97–111 · K. A. E. Warburton, Memories of a sister of S. Saviour's Priory (1912), 32–61,164–9 · The Guardian (27 May 1874) · G. T. S. Farquhar, The episcopal history of Perth, 1689–1894 (1894) · P. F. Anson, The call of the cloister: religious communities and kindred bodies in the Anglican communion (1955), 347–8 · archival deposit of the Confraternity of the Blessed Sacrament, LPL, MS 2889 · Venn, Alum. Cant. · d. cert. · CGPLA Eng. & Wales (1874) · m. cert.
Wealth at death under £3000: probate, 3 June 1874, CGPLA Eng. & Wales

Chambers, John Graham (1843–1883), sports administrator and journalist, was born on 12 February 1843, at Llanelli House, Llanelli, south Wales, the son of William Chambers, landowner, and Joanna Trant Speke Payne, daughter of Captain S. J. Speke Payne RN. He was educated first in France and then from 1856 at Eton College, before studying at Trinity College, Cambridge, between 1861 and 1865. By the time he left Cambridge a change in his family's financial circumstances required him to take paid employment, and he became a journalist, writing in the late 1860s for the sporting periodical *Land and Water*.

As a schoolboy and undergraduate Chambers had taken part in a variety of sporting activities, but it was as an organizer of sporting events that he was most influential. At Cambridge he was president of the university boat club, and closely associated with the organization of the first inter-university sports. The programme of these sports was hugely influential in succeeding athletic competitions, and Chambers was credited with giving it a particularly modern form. One contemporary recalled that Chambers gave the 'minutest attention to detail in measurement of height and length, while he encouraged the consistent use of the best stop watches available' (Croom). Chambers used a similar programme of events for the first championships of the Amateur Athletic Club (AAC), held in 1866. The club had been established by Chambers in London the previous year with the intention of establishing a leading authority for athletics, similar to the MCC in cricket, and one which could provide an 'established ground on which the numerous competitions in athletic sports and foot races may take place'.

From its inception there was a divide between the public and private roles of the AAC. Publicly, the AAC promoted an annual amateur championship which was remarkably liberal in its definition of an amateur; amateurism was seen in largely financial terms, and in the early 1870s the winners of amateur championship contests included bar workers and cart-drivers, who would have been barred from many of the other amateur sports of the period. Privately, the AAC was an exclusive club open to officers of the army and navy, members of the civil service, universities, the bar, and other London clubs, with a headquarters in Pall Mall. Its committee included many figures influential in the sporting world of the 1860s, but the club was driven by Chambers. The AAC followed a mid-Victorian understanding of the term amateur, where the distinction between a professional and an amateur was a social one, that followed unwritten rules. Unlike later amateur athletic bodies, the AAC was happy to promote professional athletic competitions, and saw no conflict between this and its promotion of the amateur championship. The club acquired a new ground at Lillie Bridge in 1869. As ground manager, Chambers promoted not only athletics but also cricket, cycling, wrestling, boxing, and football contests, including the 1873 FA cup final.

In addition to promoting sporting contests, Chambers became increasingly involved in the debates surrounding the development of rules for sports. In the 1860s and 1870s many sports were either being codified for the first time or were being reformed or refashioned. In 1867 the marquess of Queensberry donated a set of challenge cups for the first amateur boxing championship promoted by the AAC—and Chambers was involved in drawing up the Queensberry rules for the sport. Throughout the 1870s the issue of the definition of an amateur became increasingly controversial. Chambers was on the 1878 committee which drew up the exclusive Putney rules for rowing, barring 'mechanics, artisans and labourers' from competition with members of amateur rowing clubs—and he was a steward the following year when these rules were adopted for the Henley regatta. In athletics the London Athletic Club (LAC) argued against the AAC's liberal interpretation of amateurism for the amateur championships throughout the 1870s, and Chambers was attacked by some sections of the sporting press, and in particular by Walter Rye. In 1877 the LAC opened its new ground at Stamford Bridge, and in 1879 it promoted a rival championship meeting, to be held in summer rather than spring, in order to favour university athletes. This dispute was one of the major factors that led to the formation of the Amateur Athletic Association (AAA) in 1880 as a national governing body for the sport, accountable to its clubs or constituent organizations. At the meeting held in

Oxford in 1880 to form the new body Chambers donated the AAC championship cups to the AAA, but proposed that the new body should adopt a socially exclusive definition of amateurism based on the Putney rules for rowing. Clement Jackson, treasurer of Oxford University Athletic Club, opposed Chambers, and the definition accepted by the new body defined an amateur in financial rather than social terms.

Throughout the 1870s Chambers was active as a writer and sports coach. In 1871 he assumed the editorship of *Land and Water*; he coached Cambridge crews for the boat race, advised on long-distance pedestrian challenges, and rowed alongside Captain Webb as he swam the channel. In his last years he suffered from ill health, and died suddenly on 4 March 1883 at his home, 10 Wetherby Terrace, Earls Court, London, aged only forty—a death attributed by many contemporaries to overwork. He was buried at Brompton cemetery on 8 March, and his widow, Mary Rigby Chambers, was named as sole executor. According to a contemporary memoir, Chambers was missed by his friends 'not only on account of his athletic ability, but for his straightforwardness and kindliness' (*DNB*).

M. A. BRYANT

Sources P. Lovesey, *The official history of the Amateur Athletic Association* (1979) · H. F. Pash, ed., *Fifty years of progress, 1880–1930: the jubilee souvenir of the Amateur Athletic Association* [1930] · Oxford University Athletic Club minute book · M. Bryant, 'Ideas of amateurism in English sport c.1870–1920', diss. · A. C. M. Croom, ed., *Fifty years of sport at Oxford, Cambridge and the great public schools* (1913) · DNB · CGPLA Eng. & Wales (1883) · b. cert. · d. cert.
Wealth at death £6135 0s. 11d.: administration, 31 May 1883, CGPLA Eng. & Wales

Chambers, Oswald (1874–1917), missionary and author, was born on 24 July 1874 at Cherry Bank, Bon Accord Terrace, Aberdeen, the fourth of nine children of Clarence Chambers (1837–1925), pastor of Crown Terrace Baptist Church, Aberdeen, and his wife, Hannah Bullock (1840–1921). His father served the North Staffordshire Baptist Association (1877–81) before returning north to minister at the Baptist chapel in Perth. There Oswald attended Sharp's Institution, a private school, where his studies included the Bible, music, and art (his favourite subject). In 1889 the family moved to London, where his father worked for the Baptist Total Abstinence Association. After hearing C. H. Spurgeon preach Oswald Chambers was converted to Christ and baptized with his sister Gertrude in 1890.

After receiving his art master's certificate at the National Art Training School in South Kensington (which he attended 1893–5), Chambers began a two-year arts course at Edinburgh University. Torn between his love for art and a desire to be a minister, he heard the Lord's voice say (literally, he insists), 'I want you in My service—but I can do without you' (McCasland, 257). Yielding to this call he left Edinburgh in 1897 for the Gospel Training College, Dunoon, headed by the Baptist minister Duncan MacGregor. As well as studying, Chambers soon became tutor in philosophy. Few knew that he was undergoing a 'dark night of the soul' that ended in 1901 with the gift of assurance from the Holy Spirit.

Chambers left Dunoon in 1905 for an itinerant ministry at home and abroad before a 1907 appointment as missioner for the Pentecostal League of Prayer, which in 1911 opened the Bible Training College in London. With Chambers as principal enrolment rose steadily. Meanwhile, on 25 May 1910 he had married Gertrude Ann (1884–1966), daughter of the late Henry Hobbs, a London gas company clerk. Playfully called Biddy by Oswald, she joined the teaching staff, took down in shorthand all that Oswald taught there, and later published these notes in more than thirty posthumous volumes bearing his name and reflecting wide-ranging interests. Among the titles she gave them were *The Psychology of Redemption* (1922), *So Send I you* (1930), and *Biblical Ethics* (1946). Most noteworthy of all was *My Utmost for his Highest* (1927), offering one-page devotional readings for each day of the year. In numerous editions and languages this volume continues to be read by millions throughout the world and treasured almost as much as John Bunyan's *Pilgrim's Progress*.

Determined to do his part in the First World War, Chambers was appointed by the YMCA to work in the desert camps in Egypt. He sailed on 9 October 1915 and was stationed at Zeitun, 7 miles north-east of Cairo, at the base detail camp of the Australian and New Zealand forces. He was soon joined there by Biddy and two-year-old Kathleen, their only child. At Zeitun troop morale was particularly low. Wounded soldiers were streaming in, disillusioned and broken from the ill-fated Dardanelles campaign, while fresh troops were being sent there. 'Half will never return', remarked Chambers, 'and they know it. I never get used to the going-off scenes' (McCasland, 216).

Chambers stepped in to revitalize faith and restore a sense of human dignity. His down-to-earth approach put soldiers immediately at ease. If one of them said, 'I can't stand religious people', he might reply, 'Neither can I' (ibid., 227). Chambers's services, social gatherings, counselling sessions, open houses (with refreshments by the indefatigable Biddy), and mingling with the soldiers, coupled with his holiness of life, endeared him to everyone. Believers were strengthened, others converted. But he had a healthy suspicion of headcounting as the measure of Christ's victory. His artistic skill and whimsical humour produced eye-catching posters. Oswald Chambers groaned over those who read only the Bible and religious books; his own interests embraced Plato and Swedenborg, Balzac and Browning, and Ibsen.

Zeitun and other camps where Chambers was revered heard with profound sorrow that he had died unexpectedly in the Giza Red Cross Hospital, Cairo, on 15 November 1917, from a haemorrhage in the lungs after appendicitis. He was buried the next day with full military honours in the British military cemetery, Cairo. *Oswald Chambers: his Life and Work* was compiled by his widow in 1933.

WALTER A. ELWELL

Sources B. Chambers, *Oswald Chambers: his life and work*, 2nd edn (1938) • D. McCasland, *Oswald Chambers: abandoned to God* (1993) • b. cert. • m. cert. • d. cert.

Chambers, Sir (**Stanley**) **Paul** (1904–1981), civil servant and industrialist, was born at 3 Russell Road, Bowes Park, Southgate, London, on 2 April 1904, sixth of the eight children (six boys and two girls) of Philip Joseph Chambers, commercial clerk (later company secretary and finally cigar merchant), and his wife, Catherine Emily Abbott. He was educated at the City of London School and as an evening student at the London School of Economics, acquiring the degrees of BCom in 1928 and MSc (Econ) in 1934. His occupation was given as 'commercial teacher' at the time of his marriage, on 31 July 1926, to Dorothy Alice Marion (*b.* 1899/1900), a shorthand typist, daughter of Thomas Gill Baltershell Copp, printer. They had no children.

In 1927 Chambers joined the Inland Revenue tax inspectorate, initially based in Leeds and in London. His brilliance there was soon recognized and in 1935 he was selected for secondment to serve on the Indian income tax inquiry committee. In 1937 he was appointed income tax adviser to the government of India, with the rank of joint secretary, and he instituted a scheme for the deduction of income tax at source from salaries and wages.

On the outbreak of war in 1939 income tax in Britain needed to be sharply raised, which would create difficulty in paying it in two half-yearly lump sums. Chambers was therefore recalled from India and in 1940 appointed assistant secretary to set up a deduction scheme. With a small committee he devised a plan whereby each deduction was a proportion of the tax assessed for the previous year. The trade unions, however, soon began agitating for deductions to be related to current pay. This at first appeared impossible and Chambers wrote a white paper saying so, but the agitation continued. Meanwhile, in 1942, he was promoted to membership of the Board of Inland Revenue. Eventually A. G. T. Shingler, a principal inspector of taxes, devised a solution to the problem with the cumulative principle, which became the basis of the PAYE (pay as you earn) system. After working out the detailed operation of the scheme, which placed a burden of tax collection on employers, Chambers succeeded in winning the consent of the rest of his department, and of ministers, trade unions, and the employers' organizations. It took effect in 1943 and played a vital role in raising revenue during the war. Another achievement of his Inland Revenue days was the negotiation with the USA of the first double taxation agreement made by Britain, which has been described as 'a landmark in international fiscal cooperation' (*The Times*, 5 Jan 1982, 10h). In 1945 Chambers was seconded to the Allied Control Commission for Germany as finance director of the British element. His success in this post helped prepare the ground for the German 'economic miracle'.

In 1947 he resigned from the civil service and was appointed a director of Imperial Chemical Industries Ltd (ICI). In 1948 he became finance director, in 1952 one of three deputy chairmen, and from 1960 to 1968 he was chairman, the first to come from outside the company. He did much to modernize the organization and public image of ICI, and took it into Europe and America. The chemical industry was then undergoing great change as it moved from coal to oil as the basic raw material, and Chambers initiated a fundamental review of company policy. He concluded that ICI could best serve the public interest by satisfying its shareholders and concentrating on growth and profitability. The implications of this decision challenged the prevailing scientific ethos of the company, but Chambers intended to make it a major player in an increasingly competitive international market. He therefore increased borrowing to fund expanded production and oversaw a reorganization of the management structure, devolving power to divisional chairmen in order to free the directors to concentrate on the development of long-term strategy. He sought a company with a clear direction, but one capable of responding quickly to changing circumstances. In order to implement the necessary reforms Chambers called in the American management consultants McKinseys: the act of bringing in outsiders to remedy internal problems was another challenge to the corporate psychology.

During Chambers's time as chairman ICI's exports doubled in value, but his reputation was severely damaged by the failed take-over bid for Courtaulds in 1961–2. Chambers conducted the negotiations personally and his open style with the press ensured widespread publicity for the bid. He fatally misjudged, though, the price that would have to be offered to Courtaulds shareholders in order to persuade a majority to accept the merger: more than once he was forced publicly to raise his 'final' offer, which was finally made unconditional. This gave the Courtaulds directors, of whom he had been highly critical, valuable ammunition with which to resist the take-over. The proposal had been imaginative, indicative of ICI's ambitions under Chambers, but its failure damaged the image both of the company and of its chairman. A further blow came with a mismanagement of capital resources in 1966, which led to some expensive short-term borrowing. In 1968 he retired as chairman.

Chambers was a director from 1951 to 1974 of the National Provincial, later the National Westminster Bank, and, on leaving ICI, he was appointed chairman of three insurance companies, the Royal, the London and Lancashire, and the Liverpool and London and Globe. He was also a part-time member of the National Coal Board from 1956 to 1960. Between 1951 and 1972 he served, mostly as chairman, on committees reviewing the organization of the customs and excise department, departmental records, London Transport, and the British Medical Association. He also served various terms as president of the National Institute of Economic and Social Research, the British Shippers' Council, the Institute of Directors, the Royal Statistical Society, and the Advertising Association. In his later days he entered the academic world as vice-president of the Liverpool School of Tropical Medicine (1969–74), the first treasurer of the Open University (1969–75), and pro-chancellor of the University of Kent (1972–8).

Chambers's enormous energy and drive showed in his rapid movements and speech and his quick grasp of detail. He was always ready to delegate work; he pushed

people hard, but his generous appreciation of their efforts, his great personal charm, and his obvious mastery won him their support and affection. Despite being, as chairman of ICI, one of the highest-paid men in British industry at the time, Chambers lived simply. He was a keen gardener, and enjoyed music, Scrabble, and bridge, but read little. His first marriage was dissolved in 1955, and on 23 September of that year Chambers married Edith Pollack (b. 1917/18), whose previous marriage was also dissolved, second daughter of Robert Phillips Lamb, accountant, of Workington, Cumberland. They had two daughters.

Chambers was appointed CIE in 1941, CB in 1944, and KBE in 1965. He was awarded an honorary fellowship at the London School of Economics, and honorary degrees by the universities of Bristol (1963), Liverpool (1967), and Bradford (1967). The Open University gave him an honorary degree in 1975. He died at his home, 61 Northwick Avenue, Kenton, London, on 23 December 1981.

J. P. STRUDWICK, rev. MARK POTTLE

Sources personal knowledge (1990) · private information (1990) · *Financial Times* (29 Dec 1981) · *The Times* (29 Dec 1981) · *The Times* (5 Jan 1982) · M. Hodgson and C. Shaw, 'Chambers, Sir Stanley Paul', *DBB* · b. cert. · m. cert. [Dorothy Copp] · m. cert. [Edith Pollack] · d. cert.
Likenesses photograph, repro. in Hodgson and Shaw, 'Chambers, Sir Stanley Paul'
Wealth at death £339,873: probate, 3 Feb 1982, *CGPLA Eng. & Wales*

Chambers, Raymond Wilson (1874–1942), literary scholar, was born at Staxton, on the Yorkshire wolds, on 12 November 1874, the only son of Thomas Herbert Chambers, commercial traveller, and his wife, Annie, daughter of William Wilson. As a boy he knew privation. He was educated at the Grocers' Company's School and at University College, London, where he graduated in 1894 with a first class in English. After working in various libraries, among them the Guildhall Library, he returned in 1899 as Quain student to University College, where he remained thereafter. There he was in close contact over a period of years with such eminent men as A. E. Housman and W. P. Ker. His own contribution to the college, both as librarian and as teacher, was outstanding. He became a fellow in 1900, librarian in the next year, and assistant professor of English in 1904. In the First World War he served for a time as an orderly at a base hospital in France, and briefly with the YMCA in Belgium.

Although all Chambers's academic work came under the general heading of English studies, its range was nevertheless considerable, extending in time from early Germanic legend and history to Shakespeare and Milton, and occasionally beyond, and in kind from textual study to literary criticism and biography. His earliest book was *Widsith: a Study in Old English Heroic Legend* which was published in 1912, the same year in which he was awarded a DLitt degree from the University of London. This work, along with his edition of *Beowulf* (1914), which represented a very thorough revision of A. J. Wyatt's edition, and his

Beowulf: an Introduction to the Study of the Poem (1921) placed Chambers among the foremost Old English scholars.

In 1922 Chambers succeeded Ker as Quain professor of English language and literature, and he held the chair until 1941 when the college made him a special lecturer. He was elected FBA in 1927, and maintained close relations with the British Academy, lecturing before it on several occasions and becoming a member of its council in 1937. By this time his reputation as a scholar was widely recognized. He was made an honorary member of the Modern Language Association of America in 1930, and gave the Turnbull lectures at Johns Hopkins University in 1933 and the Clark lectures at Trinity College, Cambridge, in 1935. He was president of the Philological Society in 1933 and honorary director of the Early English Text Society from 1938 until his death.

Chambers also had a part in the facsimile edition *The Exeter Book of Old English Poetry* (1933), which was his last publication in this field; his contribution was recognized with honorary doctorates from the universities of Durham (1932) and Leeds (1936). Prior to any of this work, however, he had begun his study of *Piers Plowman*. Although the definitive edition, which was his aim, was never completed, he wrote and inspired a number of articles which contributed to the solution of some knotty problems. Another subject that long engaged his attention was the literary and historical significance of Sir Thomas More. The book that resulted, *Thomas More* (1935), made Chambers's name known outside academic circles and called forth the unusual tribute (to an Anglican) of a letter of thanks from Pope Pius XI. It was awarded the James Tait Black memorial prize. Included in it is Chambers's essay 'On the continuity of English prose from Alfred to Sir Thomas More', an important and influential corrective to current orthodoxies.

Chambers had great energy and untiring intellectual curiosity; he had, in addition, gifts of imagination, wit, and humour which enabled him to put life into a recondite subject. He was a generous and voluminous letter writer. He often engaged in controversy, but only to vindicate the truth as he saw it, and always with consideration for his opponents. Although his opinions have not always stood up to further investigation, much that he wrote is likely to remain of value, particularly as a stimulus to other workers. As he grew older, Chambers's reverence for the great men of the past became ever more prominent in his writings. He admired the courage and strength of mind, grounded in religious faith and submission to discipline, that he found in More. These qualities, in some measure, he himself possessed, as his colleagues and friends discovered during the early years of the Second World War. Beneath his reserve he was a man of generous affections and strong loyalties. His relations with his invalid father and his only sister, Gertrude, were the deeper manifestations of this; the public signs were his many friendships and his capacity for successful collaboration with other scholars.

Chambers was unmarried. He lived with his sister in north London for many years. His recreations included holidays in Switzerland, skiing in Norway, and visits to Florence. He served as secretary of St Christopher's Working Boys' Club. When in 1939, at the outbreak of the Second World War, University College migrated to Wales, Chambers went to Aberystwyth. He was taken ill in the course of a lecture tour to the scattered groups of the college, and died at 23 Sketty Road, Swansea, on 23 April 1942. DOROTHY EVERETT, *rev.* JOHN D. HAIGH

Sources C. J. Sisson, 'Raymond Wilson Chambers, 1874–1942', *PBA*, 30 (1944), 427–45 [incl. bibliography] · C. J. Sisson, *R. W. Chambers* (1951) · personal information (1959) · private information (1959) · *The Times* (24 April 1942) · CGPLA Eng. & Wales (1942)
Archives UCL, corresp. and papers | LUL, reminiscences of and corresp. with D. W. Wheeler about W. P. Ker · UCL, corresp. relating to W. P. Ker
Likenesses W. Stoneman, photograph, 1926, NPG · W. Stoneman, portrait, 1933, NPG · photograph, repro. in Sisson, *PBA*, facing p. 427
Wealth at death £15,720 16s. 9d.: probate, 11 Sept 1942, CGPLA Eng. & Wales

Chambers, Richard (*c*.1588–1658), merchant, whose origins and date of birth are unknown, is first encountered as a merchant of the Levant and East India companies, living in the parish of St Mary le Bow, in the western part of the City of London. The mainstay of the Levant Company was the commerce in raw silks, with an important subsidiary trade in currants brought from the Greek islands of Zante and Cephalonia. Chambers distinguished himself by his steadfast opposition to the unparliamentary levy of tonnage and poundage in 1628 and after, and to ship money in 1637. He thus merits the same attention as that which has traditionally been accorded to John Hampden and the five knights of 1627. In a petition of 1654 he described himself as 'the first man that opposed the pretended duties and the greatest sufferer' (Rushworth, 1.678). When he refused to pay duty on a case of silk grograms, which was then seized by the customs-house officers, he was summoned to appear in the council chamber on 28 September 1628. He was reported as saying 'the merchants are in no part of the world so screwed and wrung as in England … in Turkey they have more encouragement' (*CSP dom.*, *1628–9*, 539). Committed to the Marshalsea prison for contempt, he successfully applied to the king's bench for a writ of habeas corpus and was bailed by the judges on 23 October 1628 on the grounds that the response to the writ referred simply to 'contentious words at the Board' without specifying what these were.

The attorney-general then preferred an information against Chambers in the Star Chamber, where the case was tried on 6 May 1629. He was fined £2000, committed to the Fleet, and ordered to submit. Far from complying, he forcefully expressed his abhorrence of the form of submission tendered to him. He also brought an action in the exchequer chamber against the customs-house officers for the recovery of his goods, and applied to the same court to invalidate the decree of the Star Chamber on the ground that it had exceeded its statutory powers. In June 1629 it was ordered that neither he nor his goods should be released until he had paid both the tonnage and poundage of £364 2s. 2½d. and the Star Chamber fine. His imprisonment continued for six years, and the value of the goods seized for the tax was estimated by him at £7060. His undated petition of the early 1630s stressed the privations suffered by himself, his wife (the widow of Thomas Ferrer), and five children, due to his debts and enforced inactivity. His fidelity to constitutional principle may be contrasted with the resolutions of the majority of merchants, whose response to the common call to desist from trading if this involved payment of illegal duties was predictably short-lived.

In 1637 Chambers opposed the payment of ship money, was imprisoned in Newgate, and brought an unsuccessful action in the king's bench against the lord mayor for false imprisonment. On 13 July 1638 the lord mayor reported that Chambers had now paid his ship money contribution of £10. Following the dissolution of the Short Parliament in 1640, he was again arrested along with another Levant Company dissident, Samuel Vassall, for his part in organizing a citizens' petition of grievances. The Long Parliament ordered Chambers £13,680 in reparation of his losses, but this seems never to have been paid to him.

In 1640 Chambers was one of six representatives elected by Common Hall to negotiate with the lord mayor and aldermen over Common Hall's innovatory claim to the right to elect both sheriffs. His radical reputation and popularity secured his election as alderman of Walbrook ward in 1642 and sheriff in 1644. He also sat on the committee administering London's weekly assessment and on the radical City militia committee. In January 1643 this former opponent of unparliamentary tonnage and poundage was appropriately appointed as a parliamentary commissioner of customs. When in November 1642 the king went to Brentford, Chambers headed a troop of horse to oppose him. Like many former radicals his ardour had cooled by the later 1640s, when he appears to have espoused the parliamentary Presbyterian cause. In consequence of his refusal to attend the proclamation of the Commonwealth, he was dismissed both from the aldermanry (fined £800) and from the office of surveyor in the London customs house (worth £600 a year), to which he had been appointed in August 1648. He was even for a time imprisoned in the Gatehouse, but discharged on 30 April 1651 with the derisory gift of 20 nobles for his relief. His petitions received no attention and he died on 20 August 1658 at Hornsey, aged about seventy, and reduced, according to Rushworth (1.679), to a low estate and condition.

ROBERT ASHTON

Sources JHC, 1 (1547–1628), 929 · JHC, 2 (1640–42), 43, 122 · JHC, 6 (1648–51), 221–2 · W. Notestein and F. H. Relf, eds., *Commons debates for 1629* (1921) · State Papers Charles I, PRO, vol. 140, no. 24; vol. 141, no. 56 · CSP dom., 1628–9, 362, 529, 539; 1631–3, 222; 1637–8, 563 · J. Rushworth, *Historical collections*, new edn, 1 (1721), 655–6, 670–79; 2 (1721), 323–4 · APC, 1624–30, 66–7; 1628–9, 170–71 · R. Chambers, *To the right honourable the lords … in both houses of parliament: the humble petition of Richard Chambers* (1646) [Thomason tract 669.f.10(65)] · S. R. Gardiner, *History of England from the accession of James I to the outbreak of the civil war*, 7–10 (1884) · repertories of the court of aldermen, CLRO, vol. 59, fol. 419 · A. B. Beaven, ed., *The aldermen of the City of London, temp. Henry III–[1912]*, 2 vols. (1908–13), vol. 1, pp. 219, 351; vol. 2, p. 66 · *The obituary of Richard Smyth … being a catalogue of all such persons as he knew in their life*, ed. H. Ellis, CS, 44 (1849), 47 · V. Pearl, *London and the outbreak of the puritan revolution: city government and national politics, 1625–1643* (1961), esp. 314–15 · R. Ashton, *The city and the court, 1603–1643* (1979) · R. Brenner, *Merchants and revolution: commercial change, political conflict, and London's overseas traders, 1550–1653* (1993) · will, PRO, PROB 11/280, sig. 417

Archives LPL, proceedings against him in the Star Chamber, MS 1252 | BL, Thomason tracts, *To the right honourable the lords … the humble petition of Richard Chambers*, 1646

Wealth at death reduced to a low estate: Rushworth, *Historical collections*, vol. 1, p. 679

Chambers, Robert (1571–1628), Roman Catholic priest, was born in the diocese of York on 25 March 1571 and arrived at the English College, Rheims, in December 1582. On 9 June 1592 he set out from Rheims with other students for the English College at Valladolid, but was captured by Huguenot pirates and, after being ransomed and spending some days recuperating in Paris, he returned to Rheims on 25 August. He was admitted on 24 February 1593 into the English College at Rome, where he was ordained priest in 1594. In 1599 he was appointed confessor to the newly founded Benedictine convent at Brussels, with an annual stipend of 160 guilders.

After Chambers's departure from Italy his biblical allegorical romance *Palestina* was published at Florence (1600). His translation of Philip Numan's account of the miracles at Scherpenheuvel in Brabant was published at Antwerp in 1606 as *Miracles lately wrought by the intercession of the Glorious Virgin Marie at Mont-aigu, nere unto Siché in Brabant*, possibly by Richard Verstegan. In 1612 Chambers and Caesar Clement carried out a visitation of the English College, Douai, and drew up new statutes for the seminary.

From 1620 his relations with the convent were strained, partly due to personal differences with Lady Mary Percy, the abbess, and partly because his views on frequent communion were much stricter than those of his assistant, Ward. At the end of 1623 he was relieved of his position as confessor and was to have been sent to England, but was detained in Brussels for some years and continued to act as spiritual adviser to several of the nuns. He died in Flanders during 1628.   PAUL ARBLASTER

Sources Regulieren Brussel, Engelse Nonnen, letters Chambers, Mary Percy, Elizabeth Southcote, Margaret Curson, accounts for 1623, Aartsbisschappelÿk Archief Mechelen · Gillow, *Lit. biog. hist.*, 1.459 · T. F. Knox and others, eds., *The first and second diaries of the English College, Douay* (1878) · E. H. Burton and T. L. Williams, eds., *The Douay College diaries, third, fourth and fifth, 1598–1654*, 1–2, Catholic RS, 10–11 (1911) · G. Anstruther, *The seminary priests*, 1 (1969), 70

Chambers, Sir Robert (1737–1803), jurist and judge, was born in Newcastle upon Tyne on 14 January 1737 and baptized at St Nicholas's Church on 2 February 1737. He was the eldest of the four children of Robert Chambers (1698–1749), an attorney, and his wife, Anne (1713–1782), daughter of Richard Metcalfe of Newcastle.

Education and early career Chambers attended the Royal Grammar School in Newcastle. In May 1754 he was awarded a Crewe exhibition at Lincoln College, Oxford, and was admitted to the Middle Temple in the following month. A letter written by Samuel Johnson in November

Sir Robert Chambers (1737–1803), by Sir Joshua Reynolds, 1773

1754 regarding a transcription of a manuscript in an Oxford library indicates that Chambers and Johnson were already acquainted. Their acquaintance developed into an affectionate and enduring friendship that survived Chambers's departure for India and was ended only by Johnson's death in 1784. While arrangements for the institution of Vinerian scholars, fellows, and a professor of common law were in preparation in the spring of 1758, Chambers wrote to Johnson asking for his help in securing a scholarship. Johnson replied that he had little influence but wrote a recommendation none the less, and Chambers became one of two founding Vinerian scholars. He was called to the bar in 1761, starting a law practice in London and going on circuit. In the same year he was elected to a Percy fellowship at University College, Oxford. After becoming the first Vinerian fellow in 1762, Chambers succeeded Blackstone as the second Vinerian professor on 7 May 1766. He was nominated principal of New Inn Hall in December, which provided him with an abode in Oxford for the rest of his life.

Chambers had difficulty in meeting the deadlines for the lectures that he was required to give. His progress was made slow by the exceptional care that he took in choosing his words and by the calls of his practice. Johnson gave him considerable help in constructing and organizing the lectures, some of which were published in 1824 under the title *A Treatise on Estates and Tenures*. No comprehensive edition appeared until *A Course of Lectures on the English Law Delivered at the University of Oxford, 1767–1773* (ed. T. M. Curley, 2 vols., 1986). It was a demanding task to follow Blackstone, and Chambers met the challenge by focusing his attention on a conservative but thorough review of the British constitution.

A portrait of Chambers in his thirties by Sir Joshua Reynolds, commissioned by the Thrales for their library in Streatham, depicts a young man, somewhat frail in appearance, pensive and earnest, but with, perhaps, a hint of indecisiveness. In a poetic epistle to Johnson written in 1767 Chambers revealed deep uncertainties about the future direction of his life. This self-searching may have been prompted by the offer of the post of attorney-general of Jamaica, which he declined. The literary and artistic life of London, in which Chambers was a lively participant, became yet more open to him on 15 February 1768, when he was invited to be the twelfth member of the Literary Club. He was often visited by Johnson at New Inn Hall, but also had rooms at 6 King's Bench Walk in the Temple.

Appointment to the supreme court of judicature, Bengal In 1773 the East India Regulating Act was approved by parliament. Its intention was to reform and to rationalize the East India Company's administration, but it was flawed. It provided for a supreme council of Bengal, consisting of a governor-general and four councillors, and a supreme court of judicature, with a chief justice and three puisne judges appointed by the crown. Warren Hastings was nominated governor-general and Sir Elijah Impey chief justice; Chambers accepted appointment as second judge with a promise from Lord Bathurst, the lord chancellor, of succession to the chief justiceship should it become vacant. It was April 1774 before the judges, and those councillors not already in India, embarked for Calcutta. Shortly before, on 8 March, Chambers married Frances (1759–1839), the daughter of Joseph *Wilton, sculptor and a foundation member of the Royal Academy. She was then in her sixteenth year and described by Samuel Johnson in a letter to James Boswell as 'exquisitely beautiful' (*Letters of Samuel Johnson*, 2.127). They had seven children, two of whom died in India. Their eldest son was lost in the wreck of the *Grosvenor* on the coast of South Africa in 1782 at the age of five while on his way to England. Their eldest daughter, Maria (1774/5–1860), married John *Macdonald (1759–1831), military engineer and son of the Jacobite heroine Flora Macdonald. In all probability, Chambers was also the father of a natural daughter, Hannah Norris, born about 1764.

Councillors and judges landed in Calcutta in October 1774. An immediate polarization of the council into irreconcilable pro- and anti-Hastings factions, and a developing conflict between council and court, raised tensions and called for principled decision making in a climate of partisanship alien to an academically inclined legal mind. Chambers was cautious and scrupulous, acutely aware of his ill-defined position as an English judge in an Asian culture. Critics perceived in his diffidence an inherent weakness of character. His vacillations during the trial of Nandakumar, a Brahman, for forgery sprang from grave doubts about the justice of employing laws designed for Georgian England in the very different conditions obtaining in Bengal. He wrote: 'The Trial … was the most disagreeable Service I ever performed, and yet I must own I think the Jury gave a Verdict conformable to the Evidence when they found the Prisoner *guilty*' (BL, Add. MS 38401, fol. 7). Chambers had nothing to urge on Nandakumar's behalf 'but the general unfitness of punishing Forgery with Death in this country' (ibid., fol. 9). Yet, thirteen years later he was still regretting that the reasons for his equivocation at the trial were not better understood in England and that he had not registered his reservations more strongly at the time. Although the other judges had few inhibitions about pushing the jurisdiction of the supreme court to the limit, Chambers believed that 'Judges, appointed to act in a country of which the Sovereignty is not directly and openly assumed by the Power appointing them, ought to be more than ordinarily careful to keep within the intended Limits of their Jurisdiction' (ibid., fol. 11). In his observations on the judicial plan that Impey drafted for Hastings in 1776, Chambers favoured the open and direct assumption of sovereignty over Bengal by king and parliament to eradicate anomalies arising from the remnants of Mughal power and the uncertain administrative authority of the East India Company. By establishing a general judicial power the way would be cleared for a provincial legislature consisting of the governor-general, the supreme council, and the supreme court of judicature.

Middle years in India Chambers was knighted by patent on 7 June 1777, shortly after the three-year option that he had been granted on the resumption of his professorship had lapsed. He had clearly decided to stay in India and never seems to have contemplated seeking a post at home. On the death of a council member, Colonel George Monson, in September 1776, he sought patronage in England for the first of several unsuccessful attempts at nomination to council. He wrote: 'On account of my friendly Intercourse with each of the surviving Members of Council ... I am as likely as any man to become, what is here peculiarly desirable, a Peacemaker' (BL, Add. MS 38400, fol. 6). Nevertheless, with the passage of time, he turned increasingly towards Philip Francis and opposition to Hastings's policies. In October 1777 he welcomed an offer by Francis of 'a free and mutual Communication of Opinions and Advice' (BL OIOC, MS Eur. F 4, pp. 231–2). He also wrote that although he believed Impey to be well qualified for his office, he could not place his entire confidence in him in respect of some subjects. One outcome of this understanding with Francis was an exchange of documents. Francis permitted Chambers to see council minutes which were copied and forwarded to Charles Jenkinson in London, who was close to Lord North and secretary at war from 1778. Conversely, after the Grand affair trial in 1779 Chambers, who was on the bench, lent his notes to Francis, who was the defendant. Francis had been found guilty and fined for a criminal conversation with Madame Grand by a majority of the trial judges, Chambers dissenting on the grounds of insufficient evidence. In November 1779 Francis stood as godfather to Chambers's son Robert Joseph, and Chambers was one of the recipients of a valedictory letter in August 1780 immediately before Francis fought a duel with Hastings. Chambers was also one of Francis's sources of information on events in India after

Francis had returned to England in 1781 and was collaborating with Burke in his inquiries into Hastings's government.

Chief justice Two months before his return to England in 1799 Chambers wrote to his attorney in Calcutta: 'If you do not know already you will soon know that I am by no means a rich man' (BL OIOC, MS Eur. F 206/12). The councillors were paid £10,000 a year compared to £6,000 for the puisne judges, and Chambers pressed Jenkinson to recommend him for a seat on the council at every opportunity. In July 1781 he seemed to have found a way of supplementing his income by accepting the council's offer of the presidency of a court of justice that it established at Chinsura, the Dutch factory which had been seized on the outbreak of war with Holland. However, this new appointment was the subject of the fourth report of the Commons select committee which was inquiring into the administration of justice in Bengal. The house considered the report on 24 June 1782 and resolved that as the office was granted by and tenable at the pleasure of servants of the East India Company, it was contrary to the purposes of the Regulating Act. Chambers relinquished the appointment in November, but was not otherwise called to account.

Although structural reforms to the judicial system, and the departure of Francis, had improved the working relations between the supreme court and the supreme council, the early 1780s were a time of personal distress and worry for Chambers. He was incapacitated by fever for over a year and agitated lest his promised succession as chief justice might not be honoured following changes of prime minister and lord chancellor. In 1782 he suffered the loss of both his mother, who had accompanied the newly married couple to Calcutta, and his eldest son. Impey embarked for England in December 1783, recalled to explain his conduct to parliament. He did not, however, resign until 1787, and in the meantime Chambers was acting chief justice. Even then Chambers was not confirmed in office until 1791, when, for her health, his wife returned home with their youngest daughter.

While in India Chambers extended his literary and bibliophilic interests to oriental works. He was elected president of the Asiatic Society of Bengal in 1797 and a catalogue of the important collection of Sanskrit manuscripts that he formed during his residence was privately published in 1838.

Retirement and death Chambers retired to England in 1799. He was exhausted and worn out. Learned, virtuous, and amiable, a combination of characteristics rare enough in Hastings's Calcutta, he had discharged his judicial duties with integrity and percipience for a quarter of a century. He had made no great fortune in India, and although he owned property in Newcastle and Calcutta, and was granted a lump sum of around £6,000 by the East India Company, he was heavily dependent on a pension of £2,000 a year awarded him by the government. Shortly after his return he had the pleasure of becoming a bencher of the Middle Temple, but he also carried the burden of providing financial help for his bankrupted brother Richard. Chambers joined his wife, who was already residing at 56 Queen Anne Street East, Marylebone, but his health soon began to deteriorate. By September 1800 he was complaining of an inflammation of the lungs and other attacks followed. He set out for the south of France in the autumn of 1802 in search of relief. He halted in Paris, where he died on 9 May 1803 after a paralytic stroke. He was buried on 23 May in the Temple Church, London, and commemorated by a monument by Nollekens, which was destroyed in 1941.

T. H. BOWYER

Sources BL, Liverpool MSS, Chambers–Jenkinson correspondence · T. M. Curley, *Sir Robert Chambers: law, literature, and empire in the age of Johnson* (1998) · [R. Chambers], *A course of lectures on the English law … 1767–1773*, ed. T. M. Curley, 2 vols. (1986) · Chambers–Donald Macnabb correspondence, BL OIOC, Macnabb MSS, MSS Eur. F 206/12 · Chambers–Francis correspondence, BL OIOC, Francis MSS · *The letters of Samuel Johnson*, ed. B. Redford, 5 vols. (1992–4) · H. E. Busteed, *Echoes from old Calcutta*, 4th edn (1908) · *A history of Northumberland*, Northumberland County History Committee, 15 vols. (1893–1940), vol. 7 · B. D. Stevens, ed., *Register of the Royal Grammar School, Newcastle-upon-Tyne, 1545–1954* (1955) · F. Rosen, *Catalogue of the Sanskrit manuscripts collected by the late Sir Robert Chambers … with a brief memoir by Lady Chambers* (1838) · J. Boswell, *The life of Samuel Johnson*, 2 vols. (1791) · W. A. Shaw, *The knights of England*, 2 (1906)
Archives BL OIOC, corresp. and papers, Eur. MS D 491 · Victoria Memorial Hall, Calcutta, judicial notebooks | BL, corresp. with the earl of Liverpool, Add. MSS 38306–38470, *passim* · BL OIOC, diary of his wife, Lady Frances, MS Eur. A 172 · BL OIOC, corresp. with Sir Philip Francis, MSS Eur. K 46–106, J 772–773 · BL OIOC, Macnabb MSS · BL OIOC, letters to Raikes and Co., MS Eur. F 20 · Yale U., Beinecke L., letters to William and Thomas Raikes
Likenesses J. T. Seton, group portrait, *c*.1762 (with family), repro. in B. Stewart and M. Cutten, *Dictionary of portrait painters in Britain up to 1920* (1997), 416 · J. Reynolds, oils, 1773, priv. coll. [*see illus.*] · R. Home, oils, 1797, High Court, Calcutta, India · J. Flaxman, monument, 1803, University College, Oxford · J. Nollekens, monument, 1812, Temple Church, London; destroyed, 1941 · H. Dawe, portrait (after R. Home), University College, Oxford · attrib. A. W. Devis?, oils, Yale U. CBA · R. Home, oils, University College, Oxford · mezzotint (after J. Reynolds), BL · mezzotint (after J. Reynolds), BM
Wealth at death property in Calcutta, shares in old houses in Newcastle and several houses of small value in London (1801–2): BL OIOC, Macnabb MSS

Chambers, Robert (1802–1871), publisher and writer, was born on 10 July 1802 at Peebles, the second child and son of six children born to James Chambers (1778–1824), cotton manufacturer and merchant, and Jean Gibson (*c*.1781–1843).

Early years and education Robert Chambers received his education in Peebles parish school, conducted by James Gray, and at James Sloan's grammar school. He not only enjoyed studying Latin, but spent more time at it than other boys. He was born with six digits on each hand and foot, and those on his feet having been unsatisfactorily removed he could not play games but spent his time reading. His formal education was supplemented at home. James Chambers, a man especially interested in ideas,

Robert Chambers (1802–1871), by David Octavius Hill and Robert Adamson

brought home from the circulating library English classics for Robert and his brother William *Chambers (1800–1883) to read. At one time their father purchased the *Encyclopaedia Britannica*, which Robert read from cover to cover, finding the scientific articles particularly engrossing. He shared his father's love of music. Having heard him play the German flute and sing Scottish songs he recognized, at three years of age, no fewer than sixty old songs and ballads.

But the family fortunes changed. James Chambers was forced to declare bankruptcy, and in 1813 he moved the family from Peebles to Edinburgh, hoping that he could re-establish himself there. Robert remained behind to finish school. When he joined his family in August 1814 he was enrolled in the academy of Benjamin Mackay; the family thought his bookishness suited him for the ministry. At the academy he continued to excel in Latin. When the 1815 school year began he intended both to finish the sixth year at the academy and begin study at the University of Edinburgh, but his family could not afford the university fees.

First attempts at business and literary success When Chambers's formal education ended in May 1816, he attempted a variety of jobs. He worked as a copyist for a Russian merchant, as a clerk in the counting house of another merchant, and as a private tutor. Having no success at finding and keeping employment, with his brother William's encouragement he decided to try bookselling. He took the books that he and William had collected, as well as the few remaining to the family, and rented shop space on Leith

Walk. Much to his surprise he did 11 or 12 shillings' worth of business on the first day; in one week he made as much profit as originally he had in capital. In the meantime he also began practising various kinds of writing—poetry, prose, even a historical novel. When he and William joined their friend John Denovan in producing *The Patriot*, a weekly radical paper, Robert wrote poetry for it. Then in 1821 William suggested that they publish a weekly literary paper. He would set the type and print it if Robert would do the writing. The *Kaleidoscope*, however, lasted for only eight issues.

During the next decade Chambers, emulating Sir Walter Scott, wrote on Scottish subjects. At Archibald Constable's suggestion he copied out *The Lady of the Lake* in fine calligraphy and presented it to Scott, along with Constable's letter of introduction. His first attempt at historical writing was *Illustrations of the Author of Waverley* (1822), in which he drew upon his knowledge of border-country people and places to identify the originals of the novel's characters. History also inspired *Traditions of Edinburgh* (1824). Probably the last person to study the old, unaltered city of Edinburgh, he gathered anecdotes about people and manners of its past. Immediately successful, *Traditions* went into second and third editions and established Chambers's literary reputation; *Walks in Edinburgh* (1825) and *Popular Rhymes of Scotland* (1826) followed. For *Picture of Scotland* (1828) Chambers spent five months walking all over the country collecting topographical information, historical anecdotes, and old stories and poetry. Further historical research produced works for *Constable's Miscellany: History of the Rebellion of 1745* (1827), *History of the Rebellions in Scotland* (1828–9), and *Life of James I* (1830). Chambers also compiled two collections of Scottish poetry.

Chambers's Edinburgh Journal Chambers experienced increasing success in his life and work. In 1826 he moved his shop to Hanover Street, where business was more profitable, and on 7 December 1829 he married Anne (1808–1863), daughter of John Kirkwood and Jane Kirkland. He became editor of the Edinburgh *Advertiser* in 1830 and, in order to have more time for writing, turned over his retail business to his younger brother David. On 6 November 1830 his and Anne's first child and eldest daughter, Jane Gibson (Nina), was born. In all they had fourteen children, eleven of whom survived into adulthood.

In 1831 William Chambers proposed a project that became a landmark of nineteenth-century publishing. He suggested that they publish a low-priced, educational but entertaining, weekly paper. Initially sceptical, Robert agreed to write for it. On 4 February 1832 the first number of *Chambers's Edinburgh Journal* appeared. It sold 25,000 copies in Scotland alone. By April 1832, 30,000 copies were being printed weekly. Because William could not handle so large a task by himself Robert agreed to become joint editor of the journal and partner in the publishing firm of W. and R. Chambers. The journal was not enthusiastically received in all quarters, however. The minister of the church that Chambers and his family attended attacked it for being secular; the Edinburgh literary establishment thought cheap publications were 'low'.

Meanwhile Chambers continued his other writing. He estimated that by 1832 he had written twenty-three volumes, for which he earned £1050. He and William jointly prepared the *Gazetteer of Scotland* (1833). Independently he wrote *Life of Sir Walter Scott* (1832), *Biographical Dictionary of Eminent Scotsmen* (1833–5), and *Life and Work of Burns* (1834). At the same time he was writing an essay, as well as smaller pieces, for each number of the journal. For the Chambers Educational Course he wrote several early volumes: *History of the English Language and Literature* (1835), *History of the British Empire* (1836), *Exemplary and Instructive Biography* (1836), and *Introduction to the Sciences* (1836). The Educational Course, these texts, and much of Chambers's later thinking and writing were influenced by the concepts of phrenology, especially by its philosophy of improvability, to which George Combe had introduced him.

Major works These years of relentless writing took their toll; by the early 1840s Chambers was exhausted and depressed. To escape public attention and restore some tranquillity to his life he moved with his family to St Andrews in 1841. While there he undertook two projects for which he is best remembered. First was the *Cyclopaedia of English Literature*, in which Robert Carruthers assisted. Its two volumes (1840–43) were the first to treat writers of the day as well as those of the past. It provided biographical and historical background, extracts from literary texts, and illustrations. For nearly a century it was a standard resource for university courses and the foreign service examinations.

The second work engaging Chambers's attention at this period was *Vestiges of the Natural History of Creation*. Drawing upon his scientific reading, his interest in geology, and phrenological philosophy, he proposed that the universe had not been created in a single act by God, who then controlled all successive creative processes in the universe. Rather, scientific laws explained and governed not only the development of higher life forms but also the origin of life itself. Knowing that his theory, especially its dependence upon phrenological principles, would be controversial, Chambers arranged for the book's anonymous publication. His wife copied the manuscript, which was sent to his friend Alexander Ireland, who sent it on to the publisher. When the book appeared, in October 1844, discussion and controversy immediately ensued. Speculation about the author's identity ranged from Harriet Martineau to Prince Albert. Though attacked by scientists for factual errors and by the clergy for its materialism, *Vestiges* went through four editions in seven months. Chambers corrected errors in subsequent editions and ultimately wrote *Explanations: a Sequel* (1845). His seven-volume *Collected Writings* was published in 1847. During the remainder of the decade he continued geological excursions, writing *Ancient Sea Margins* (1848) and *Tracings of the North of Europe* (1849). Having returned to Edinburgh in the late 1840s he was nominated as a candidate for lord provost of the city; opposed by conservative religious and political factions because of his supposed authorship of the *Vestiges*, he was defeated. Probably his best business decision was not acknowledging his authorship of the *Vestiges*; had he done so he would have irreparably damaged the firm. Despite the claims of impiety and materialism brought against him by opponents of the *Vestiges* he had a deep spiritual sense. He rejected the Bible for its geological inaccuracy, but he believed in God as a divine reality, and frequently attended services of the Episcopal Church of Scotland.

In the 1850s Chambers gave his energies to the firm. William, tired of managing it, decided to return to his native Peeblesshire; a new partnership agreement gave Robert the majority of the firm's shares. Under his direction the firm began *Chambers's Encyclopaedia of Universal Knowledge for the People*. The first edition appeared between 1860 and 1868 and continued to be published until the 1960s. Chambers's own work on Scottish and geological interests continued. The *Life and Works of Burns* (1851) was written in part to raise money for Isabella Begg, Burns's youngest sister. Chambers collected new material from her and from others who had known the poet, and also drew upon his own knowledge of Scottish songs and ballads. *Tracings of Iceland and the Faroe Islands* (1856) and *Domestic Annals of Scotland* (1858) followed. During this time he became intrigued by spiritualism; he observed seances, took notes, and listened to testimony of enthusiasts in attempting to determine whether it was fraud or truth.

Final years　In 1860 William Chambers returned to Edinburgh and the firm. Robert Chambers and his wife travelled to America before he and his family moved to London so that he could oversee the firm's new London offices. At the same time he carried out research in the British Museum and the Athenaeum Library as he prepared the *Book of Days* (1864). Its assortment of historical figures and events, anecdotes, folklore, geographical oddities, and literary specimens associated with each day of the year has kept it on library shelves; but it was Chambers's last major work, for his productive life was coming to an end. His wife, Anne, became ill, and died in September 1863. In just a matter of weeks so did his daughter Janet. His own health suffered. Assistance that he had counted on for preparing the *Book of Days* did not materialize, and working on it mostly by himself took its toll; he called the book his 'death blow'. He returned to live in Scotland, where he built a home at 6 Gillespie Terrace, St Andrews, and in 1867 married the widow of Robert Frith. He did some writing, but his *Life of Smollett* (1867) was the only work published. Manuscripts from this period include 'Life and preachings of Jesus Christ' ('from the Evangelists'), a catechism for the young, private prayers and meditations, and several papers on spiritualism. Chambers's second wife died in 1870. Thinking that he would not live much longer himself, he selected his burial site, the ruined eleventh-century St Regulus's Tower, in St Andrews. He died at his home in St Andrews on 17 March 1871. Following a funeral at the Episcopal chapel, the provost and magistrates of the town and members of the Senatus Academicus escorted his body to the burial site. The memorial stone at the tower identifies him simply as Robert Chambers LLD, 'Author of the Traditions of Edinburgh and many other works'.

Robert Chambers was a man of insatiable curiosity, great energy, and astonishing memory. He read books of all kinds, studied Scottish poetry, history, and topography intensively, and questioned accepted truths, be they the facts of Burns's life, the origins of geological formations, or the source of spirit rappings. Needing only a few hours' sleep each night, he rose early, wrote and read before attending to the day's business, and went back to his books in the evening. Everything that he read or heard he seemed to remember—and use—in his writing. Family and friends admired his genial manner and generosity. His large circle of friends included writers and scientists from Scotland, England, and the United States. He was generous with advice and money, and many aspiring writers were encouraged by his gracious responses. Besides his publicized efforts on behalf of Burns's sister, his journals, letters, and will record many private charities. An advocate of life assurance, he invested in and served on the boards of several companies.

Like his brother William, Chambers was determined to overcome the family's early misfortunes. He forced his way to recognition; not only did such notables as Scott and J. G. Lockhart scoff at his early work but polite society dismissed the firm's publishing for the common reader. Ultimately, however, Robert Chambers was named a fellow of the Royal Society of Edinburgh, elected to the Athenaeum, and awarded an LLD by St Andrews University.　　　　　　　　　　SONDRA MILEY COONEY

Sources　W. Chambers, *Memoir of William and Robert Chambers*, 13th edn (1884) · S. M. Cooney, 'Publishers for the people: W. & R. Chambers, the early years, 1832–1850', PhD. diss., Ohio State University, 1970 · M. Millhauser, *Just before Darwin* (1959) · J. A. Secord, *Victorian sensation: the extraordinary publication, reception, and secret authorship of 'Vestiges of the natural history of creation'* (2000) · C. Layman, *Man of letters* (1990)
Archives　Hunt. L., letters · NL Scot., corresp. and papers · NL Scot., W. & R. Chambers archive, literary, historical, and personal papers, deposit 341 | BL, letters, as sponsor, to Royal Literary Fund · Edinburgh Central Reference Library, letters to C. K. Sharpe · Man. CL, Manchester Archives and Local Studies, letters to John Harland · NL Scot., letters to Blackwoods · NL Scot., corresp. with George Combe · NL Scot., letters to Archibald Constable · NL Scot., letters to Sir Walter Scott · priv. coll. · U. Edin. L., letters to D. Laing · U. Newcastle, Robinson L., letters to Sir Walter Calverley Trevelyan and Lady Pauline Trevelyan
Likenesses　D. O. Hill, calotype, 1840–49, Scot. NPG · R. Lehmann, crayon drawing, 1851, BM · R. C. Bell, line engraving (after J. R. Fairman), BM; repro. in W. Chambers, *Memoir of Robert Chambers* (1872) · D. O. Hill and R. Adamson, photograph, Scot. NPG [*see illus.*] · J. Horsburgh, oils, A. S. Chambers, Edinburgh · C. Lees, oils, Royal and Ancient Golf Club, St Andrews, Scotland · J. Watson-Gordon, oils, Alasdair R. M. Chambers, Inverness · bust, Chambers Harrap Publishers Ltd, Edinburgh
Wealth at death　£43,107: NA Scot., Fife county records, register of inventories in the commissariat of Fife, Cupar, 10 June 1871

Chambers, Robert (1832–1888), publisher, was born on 6 March 1832 at Edinburgh, the son of Robert *Chambers (1802–1871), publisher and writer, and Anne, *née* Kirkwood (1808–1863). William *Chambers, the publisher, was his uncle. Young Robert, who was known familiarly as Robert

Secundus to distinguish him from his father, was educated at Circus Place School, Edinburgh, and at Bruce Castle School, London. He additionally studied at the Edinburgh School of Arts, received tuition in French, and acquired practical experience in all departments of W. and R. Chambers, the family's publishing firm, in preparation for joining it as a partner in 1853. In 1856 he married Laura (d. 1904), daughter of Murray Anderson, of London. They had nine children, six of whom—three sons and three daughters—reached adulthood.

Robert Chambers took an active editorial role in producing the first edition of *Chambers's Encyclopaedia* (1860–68), corresponding with contributors, selecting illustrations, and writing the entry on golf. He helped in preliminary work for the revised edition of 1884. In 1874, on the resignation of James Payn, he became editor of *Chambers's Journal*, to which he occasionally contributed papers, and conducted the magazine with great success. On the death of his uncle William, in 1883, he took over direction of the Chambers firm, in which he was assisted during his last years by his eldest son, Charles Edward Stuart Chambers (1859–1936).

Besides the firm and his family Chambers's interests were outdoor pursuits, especially golf and the study of birds. These inspired his excellent book on golfing, *A Few Rambling Remarks on Golf* (1862), a poem about the St Andrews links (jointly written with his father), and his suggestion for including numerous engravings of birds in the first edition of *Chambers's Encyclopaedia*. He contributed to the supplementary chapter about his father and uncle that appeared in the twelfth edition of the *Memoir of William and Robert Chambers* (1883) and also helped Alexander Ireland to prepare the 1884 edition of the elder Robert Chambers's *Vestiges of the Natural History of Creation*.

Chambers was a member of the St Giles's Cathedral board and, like his uncle, took much interest in the church. He was liberal-minded, and his genial temperament made him very popular with his workmen and friends. Yet he was long in poor health and spent much of his time at his North Berwick home—St Baldred's Tower—and at his late father's St Andrews home. He died of heart failure on 23 March 1888 at his home—10 Claremont Crescent, Edinburgh—and was buried in Dean cemetery, Edinburgh.

G. A. AITKIN, rev. SONDRA MILEY COONEY

Sources NL Scot., W. and R. Chambers MS deposit 341 · family papers, priv. coll. · *The Athenaeum* (31 March 1888) · *The Scotsman* (23 March 1888) · *Glasgow Herald* (26 March 1888) · W. Chambers, *Memoir of William and Robert Chambers*, 13th edn (1884) · private information (2004)
Archives NL Scot., corresp. and papers · priv. coll., family papers
Wealth at death £25,947 2s. 6d.: estate inventory, NA Scot. commissariat of Edinburgh, SC70/1/266

Chambers [alias Mann], **Sabine** (c.1559–1633), Jesuit, was born in Leicestershire. He entered Broadgates Hall, Oxford, where he took his BA on 13 June 1580 and his MA on 30 April 1583. According to Anthony Wood 'he had the vogue of a good disputant' (Wood, 2.276). Dissatisfied with

protestantism he abandoned Oxford for Paris where he was received into the Roman Catholic church. Robert Parsons appointed him president of the English College in Eu recently founded by the duke of Guise. Chambers entered the Society of Jesus in France on 28 May 1588. On 19 December 1591 he matriculated at the University of Würzburg to pursue a doctorate in theology. Between 1593 and 1599 he taught at Jesuit colleges in Pont-à-Mousson, Fulda, and Hamburg. He completed his Jesuit formation in Trier in 1599. He also taught logic, physics, and metaphysics in Trier between 1601 and 1606. In 1607 and 1608 he was confessor and professor of cases of conscience at Dôle. On 24 June 1608 Father General granted his request to work on the English mission and he arrived in late 1609. He was professed of the four vows in London on 6 December 1618.

Because information available in Jesuit catalogues does not specify his location we do not know where he worked before the mission was reorganized as a vice-province. In 1621 and 1622 Chambers was stationed in Lincolnshire. He was transferred to the house of probation of St Ignatius (London) in 1623 and remained there until approximately 1628, when he moved to the College of St Francis Xavier (Wales). Most likely it was in that college that he died, probably on 16 March 1633. According to 'Summaria mortuorum', Chambers suffered from gout in his final years, but he bore the pain with great patience and resignation. He must have mellowed because he was characterized in earlier evaluations as being bad tempered (Clancy, 26).

Despite his reputation at Oxford and his subsequent doctorate and teaching experience, Chambers wrote no theological or controversial tome. His one publication, *The Garden of Our B. Lady* (1619) combined two themes, gardens and the Virgin Mary, then popular among Salesian writers.

THOMAS M. MCCOOG

Sources T. M. McCoog, *English and Welsh Jesuits, 1555–1650*, 1, Catholic RS, 74 (1994), 137–8 · T. M. McCoog, ed., *Monumenta Angliae*, 2: *English and Welsh Jesuits, catalogues, 1630–1640* (1992), 261 · H. Foley, ed., *Records of the English province of the Society of Jesus*, 7/1 (1882), 127; 7/2 (1883), 896 · Foster, *Alum. Oxon.* · S. Merkle, *Die Matrikel der Universität Würzburg*, 2 vols. (1922), 1.26 · Wood, *Ath. Oxon.*, new edn, 2.276 · 'The memoirs of Father Robert Persons', ed. J. H. Pollen, *Miscellanea, II*, Catholic RS, 2 (1906), 12–218, esp. 31 · A. F. Allison and D. M. Rogers, eds., *The contemporary printed literature of the English Counter-Reformation between 1558 and 1640*, 2 vols. (1989–94) · T. H. Clancy, *A literary history of the English Jesuits: a century of books, 1615–1714* (1996) · 'Summaria mortuorum', Archivum Romanum Societatis Iesu, Rome, Anglia, 7, p. 247
Archives Archivum Romanum Societatis Iesu, Rome | Archives of the British Province of the Society of Jesus, Stonyhurst College, Lancashire

Chambers, Sir Thomas (1814–1891), lawyer and politician, was born on 17 December 1814, the eldest son of Thomas Chambers (1784–1845) of Hertford, presumed to have been a linen draper, and his wife, Sarah (1783–1849), daughter of William Dean. He was admitted to Clare College, Cambridge, on 18 October 1837 but did not graduate LLB until 1846. He spent some years studying architecture. A student at the Middle Temple from 28 April 1837, he was called to the bar on 20 November 1840, became a bencher on 7 May 1861 and was treasurer in 1872.

Chambers collaborated on two law books in the 1840s, on the Metropolitan Buildings Act and railway companies respectively, and steadily worked up a lucrative practice in the common-law courts, taking silk on 25 February 1861. On 7 May 1851 he married Diana, daughter of Peter White of Brighton, who had been adopted by her uncle John Green of Hertford. They had a son and four daughters before her death on 14 January 1877. Chambers was elected common serjeant on 31 January 1857, was deputy recorder from 1866, and in 1878 was made recorder of the City of London, in preference to Fitzjames Stephen. Knighted on 15 March 1872, in 1884 he was elected steward of Southwark and was also a lieutenant for the City and president of the national chamber of trade from 1874 to about 1880.

First invited to stand for election by the Liberals at Hertford in 1847, Chambers did so in July 1852 and was elected, but lost his seat at the general election of March 1857. Returned on 12 July 1865 for Marylebone, he represented that constituency until the general election of November 1885. He was an active parliamentarian, especially in the 1850s and 1860s, and his low-church views made him a strong sabbatarian and an opponent of the liquor trade, though he was generally opposed to state regulation. He was best known for his persistent, if unsuccessful, advocacy of the inspection of convents and of the legalization of marriage with a deceased wife's sister. A cautious reformer in penal affairs, he addressed the Social Science Association in 1862 on punishment and reformation and spoke strongly in parliament against life sentences in 1867.

'Under middle height, with an apple rosy face and Victorian side whiskers' (Browne, 141), Chambers suffered from an eye condition which led to his nickname 'Weeping Tommy'. He was hospitable and convivial, and popular among the legal profession. He died suddenly and peacefully of bronchitis at his home, 63 Gloucester Place, Portman Square, London, on 24 December 1891 and was interred on 30 December in the family vault in All Saints' Church, Hertford.　　　　J. M. RIGG, rev. PATRICK POLDEN

Sources Venn, *Alum. Cant.* · J. E. Cussans, *History of Hertfordshire*, 2/1, 2/3 (1874) · *The Times* (25 Dec 1891) [obit.] · *Law Journal* (2 Jan 1892), 11 · *Law Times* (2 Jan 1892), 151 · H. J. B. Heath, 'Memoir', *Monthly Record of Eminent Men*, ed. G. Potter, 4 (1891), 68–78 · F. W. Ashley, *My sixty years in the law* (1936) · E. D. Purcell, *Forty years at the criminal bar* (1916) · J. H. B. Browne, *Forty years at the bar* (1916) · M. Williams, *Leaves of a life*, 2 vols. (1890) · C. Biron, *Without prejudice: impressions of life and law* (1936) · T. E. Crispe, *Reminiscences of a KC*, 2nd edn (1909) · Walford, *County families* (1888) · J. Foster, *Men-at-the-bar: a biographical hand-list of the members of the various inns of court*, 2nd edn (1885) · Boase, *Mod. Eng. biog.*, vol. 4 · H. A. C. Sturgess, ed., *Register of admissions to the Honourable Society of the Middle Temple, from the fifteenth century to the year 1944*, 2 (1949) · W. A. A'Beckett, *Recollections of a humourist* (1907) · W. A. Shaw, *The knights of England*, 2 vols. (1906) · J. Foster, *The peerage, baronetage, and knightage of the British empire for 1882*, 2 vols. [1882]

Likenesses Spy [L. Ward], chromolithograph caricature, repro. in *VF* (22 Nov 1884) · J. & C. Watkins, carte-de-visite, NPG; repro. in Heath, 'Memoir', facing p. 68

Wealth at death £7919 16s. 7d.: administration with will, 5 April 1892, *CGPLA Eng. & Wales*

Chambers, Walter (1824–1893), bishop of Labuan, Sarawak, and Singapore, was born in England and ordained at Lichfield as deacon in 1849 and priest in 1850. He served briefly as curate of Bentley in Derbyshire, before joining the Borneo Church Mission in Kuching, Sarawak, in March 1851. Founded in 1846 the struggling mission was led by a Kuching-based missionary doctor, Francis Thomas *McDougall (1817–1886), but other missionaries and teachers soon left.

Recruited to convert the newly pacified sea Dyaks of the second division, Chambers spent six months under the instruction of McDougall, who admired his energy, enthusiasm, and religious zeal, but deplored his obstinacy, prejudice, and lack of ear for foreign languages. Impatient to start work Chambers opened the first rural mission at Sekrang in September 1851, barely four months after peacemaking ceremonies between the Dyaks and the Brooke regime. Finding the tribe stubbornly unreceptive, in 1853 he moved his headquarters to less hostile territory at Banting. Chambers took his first four converts for baptism in Kuching on Christmas day 1853, but progress was slow, against a background of continuing violence and unrest.

In 1855 McDougall, newly appointed first bishop of Labuan and Sarawak, brought two women missionaries, a schoolmaster, and another clergyman from England, but none settled. Meanwhile Chambers drove himself hard, neglecting his comfort and health. McDougall feared he was 'going native' when he first saw him in Kuching, barefoot and shirtless, wearing a sarong and with a long unkempt beard, and looking 'more a pirate than a clergyman' (Saunders, 44). Mrs McDougall's formidable missionary cousin, Elizabeth Woolley (1814?–1875), a surgeon's daughter, transformed his disordered life. Having paid her own passage she arrived in December 1856; two months later, when Chinese miners burned Kuching and murdered some of the raja's men, Elizabeth, showing great spirit and courage, took charge of the mission house. Arriving from Banting, Chambers was enchanted by her personality, religious zeal, and capacity to produce order and comfort out of devastation. Married in Kuching on 27 August 1857, they had no children and made an incongruous couple, more like mother and son: Elizabeth at forty-three, ten years Chambers's senior and looking older than her years, was gaunt, angular, and beanpole thin. Unkindly dubbed Mrs Proudie by other wives, she was fiercely devoted to her husband and his missionary enterprise, accompanying Chambers on arduous journeys, sometimes gravely ill and near starvation, but keeping their house spick and span. By 1861 the Brookes had brought relative peace to the second division, and gradually Chambers and his wife built up a successful mission station. Toiling to commit sea Dyak to writing, Chambers translated prayers, hymns, and the gospels of Matthew and Mark. In 1863 a Dyak warrior chief sought baptism and then took Christianity back to his tribe. For the first time Elizabeth also coaxed Dyak women and girls to the mission. By 1867 the school boasted fifty pupils, boys and girls, some of them boarders, and the church had to be enlarged.

But in Kuching relations had soured between church and state, Chambers loyally supporting his bishop. While in England in July 1868 McDougall resigned, recommending Chambers, whom he had appointed archdeacon of Sarawak in May that year, as his successor. Chambers was duly consecrated bishop of Labuan on 29 June 1869 and formally installed as bishop of Sarawak on 5 June 1870. Meanwhile in 1869 the Straits Settlements diocese had been transferred from Calcutta, and the new diocese of Labuan, Sarawak, and Singapore was formed. Chambers made St Andrew's in Singapore the cathedral church of the united diocese and he visited it every year, although he met the extra expense himself since the diocese only funded a biennial visit. However, the Dyaks remained his priority. Appointing a resident chaplain for Kuching, he continued active missionary travel. His relationship with the government was less troubled than his predecessor's but there were still tensions. Rani Margaret Brooke called him a great friend of her husband Charles, but he refused to bury their unchristened stillborn child in the family cemetery. Although Brooke had known him from their pioneering bachelor days in the turbulent second division and respected his work among the Dyaks, both were solitary people. Their friendship had cooled when Chambers married and had worsened when he supported McDougall. Chambers's first sermon as bishop, critical of European ways, provoked an angry exchange between the raja, who preferred discreet liaisons to marriage among his officers, and Elizabeth Chambers, who upheld the bishop's ecclesiastical authority.

Relations mellowed after 1875, when Elizabeth died, aged sixty-one, while on leave in England. After returning to Kuching in July 1876 Chambers continued his tireless journeys despite increasing arthritis, but lack of funds, a dearth of suitable recruits, and the failure to train an Asian priesthood doomed his efforts. Too understaffed to attend the Lambeth conference in 1878, Chambers collapsed in August that year and was dispatched immediately to England to recuperate. In November 1879, unable to return, he told the archbishop of Canterbury that a complete failure of health compelled him to relinquish his loved work and people, and he formally resigned early in 1881, once a successor had been found. A disabled invalid, he eventually died at his home in London, 27 Bedford Gardens, Kensington, after a painful, lingering illness, on 21 December 1893.   C. M. TURNBULL

Sources G. Saunders, *Brookes and bishops, 1848–1941: the Anglican mission and the Brooke raj in Sarawak* (1992) · M. Saint, *A flourish for the bishop and Brooke's friend Grant: two studies in Sarawak history, 1848–1868* (1985) · B. Taylor, *The Anglican church in Borneo, 1848–1962* (1983) · M. Saint and A. Munan-Oettli, 'The second bishop's lady', *Sarawak Gazette*, 112/4 (Dec 1986), 1498 · S. St John, *Life in the forests of the Far East*, 2 vols. (1862); repr. (1974, [1975]) · *Mission Field* (1 Feb 1894) · C. N. Crisswell, *Rajah Charles Brooke* (1978) · Ranee Margaret of Sarawak [M. Brooke], *Good morning and good night* (1934) · Ranee of Sarawak [M. L. A. Brooke], *My life in Sarawak* (1913) · E. Green, *Borneo, the land of river and palm* (1910) · S. Runciman, *The white rajahs: a history of Sarawak from 1841 to 1946* (1960) · C. F. Pascoe, *Two hundred years of the SPG*, rev. edn, 2 vols. (1901) · H. P. Thompson, *Into all lands* (1951) · S. Baring-Gould and C. A. Bampfylde, *A history of Sarawak under its two white rajahs, 1839–1908* (1909) · R. Pringle, *Rajahs and rebels: the Ibans of Sarawak under Brooke rule, 1841–1941* (1970) · CGPLA Eng. & Wales (1894)

Likenesses photograph, repro. in Green, *Borneo*

Wealth at death £370 0s. 5d.: probate, 3 Feb 1894, CGPLA Eng. & Wales

Chambers, Sir William (1722–1796), architect, was born in December 1722 in Göteborg, Sweden, the son of John Chambers (d. 1735) and his wife, Sara Elphinstone (d. 1740) (there are portraits of his parents in the Göteborg Stadsmuseum). His father was a partner with William Pierson in the brokering firm of Chambers and Pierson. When William returned to Sweden in 1739 from schooling in Ripon, his father had been dead four years. In a letter dated July 1774 addressed to his namesake William Chambers, surgeon of Ripon, Yorkshire, he reflected nostalgically on his upbringing there: 'lovely bowers of innocence and ease, seats of my Youth' but 'where I know not a soul but my physical cousin, and two old women famous for telling long storys' (BL, Add. MS 41135, fols. 45–46v). In an 'Autobiographical note' compiled when he was informed that he was to be appointed by Gustav III of Sweden a *riddare* (or knight) of the order of the Polar Star, Chambers wrote, 'I was born in Gothenburg, was educated in England, and returned to Sweden when I was 16 years old. I made three journeys to Bengal and China in the service of the Swedish East India Company' (Uppsala University Archives x 222). Although his family can be traced back to the Scottish Chalmers and Forbes families on one side, and the Elphinstones of Glack on the other, Sir William's immediate forebears had lived in Ripon for more than a century, as can be read from the many memorials to the family in Ripon Minster. A Cuthbert Chambers was mayor in 1675 and a William Chambers died there in January 1689.

Eastern voyages On his return to Göteborg in 1739 Chambers found his mother, sisters Sara and Mary, and brother John. No doubt his future with the Swedish East India Company had long since been decided, for he set sail on the *Fredericus Rex Sueciae* in April 1740 destined for Bengal, with the rank of cadet to the assistant supercargoes. He was in business, and it was a profitable one. His mother died soon after he embarked. As Chambers explains in the 'Autobiographical note', 'I studied modern languages, mathematics and the liberal arts, but chiefly civil architecture', on these voyages. He returned to Göteborg in October 1742, and left again, on the *Riddarhuset*, in April 1743, bound for Canton (Guangzhou). His third voyage began in January 1748 on the *Hoppet*, again to China, from where he returned in July 1749 for the last time. Merchant adventuring was over, and architecture beckoned.

As an assistant supercargo on the China run, Chambers could amass great wealth, to which his portion of the family fortune would have been added. As the first European, albeit not yet an architect proper, to have studied Chinese architecture at first hand, Chambers saw his advantage.

Sir William Chambers (1722–1796), by Sir Joshua Reynolds, 1778?–80

Olof Torén, a fellow merchant, reported to the naturalist Carl Nilssohn Linnaeus that the young Chambers had already sent architectural memoranda, including drawings of Chinese houses, to 'First Commissioner Baron Harleman', Sweden's chief architect (O. Torén, *An East Indian Voyage*, 1771). That these drawings really did exist is proven by a nervous letter written by Chambers to his brother John in Göteborg in June 1756, before the publication of *Designs for Chinese Buildings* (1757), enquiring as to the whereabouts of his drawings of Chinese houses (Chambers correspondence, archives, RA). Chambers gained a reputation as a Sinologist through his 1757 folio, which served him well, not least with the Swedish minister in Paris, Count Carl Fredrik Scheffer, himself a Sinologist and physiocrat. Indeed, Scheffer, or a member of the Swedish chancellery, may have ensured that in the autumn of 1749 Chambers was recruited into Jacques François Blondel's celebrated École des Arts in the rue de la Harpe, Paris. His wealth enabled him to spend the next six years studying at leisure. In effect he was a gentleman, who would become the arch-professional and establishment architect in the England of George III.

Study in Paris Farewells were taken in Göteborg in the early summer of 1749. Chambers did not see the place again, or his family, except for brother John. But Paris was preceded by a summer interval in Britain, when two auspicious meetings must have taken place: first with Catherine More (*d.* 1798) of Bromsgrove, Worcestershire, his future wife; and perhaps through recommendations from Linnaeus in Sweden, with Frederick, prince of Wales, and

Princess Augusta, at Kew, where new gardens with exotic architecture were under consideration.

Architectural training in Sweden was based on a French curriculum. The French language was *de rigueur*. Swedish architects would seek to train on the Paris–Rome axis, whereas the English would go straight to Rome. So Chambers was behaving as any Swede would. Although by choosing Blondel's École he was departing from the Swedish norm, he was assured of a short but stringent and tough course, of a sort quite unknown in London. At the École he befriended C. de Wailly and M. J. Peyre, and belonged to a brilliant coterie that included C. N. Cochin, J. D. Leroy, F. D. Barreau de Chefdeville, J. G. Soufflot, G. F. Doyen, H. Robert, and A. Pajou, the future leaders of French neo-classical art and architecture of the 1760s and 1770s. Chambers also brought to his studies at the École an exceptional ability as a draughtsman. This is demonstrated by the beautiful drawings in his 'Franco-Italian Album' in the Victoria and Albert Museum. The course over, Chambers left for Italy late in September 1750, possibly in the company of Doyen, and arrived in Rome to meet Soufflot a few weeks before that architect left on 11 December. He returned twice to Paris: first in the summer of 1751, perhaps accompanied by C. F. Adelcranz, who became the comptroller of the Swedish royal works. This visit was not so much for professional reasons as to bring Catherine More back to Rome for the marriage that took place in his lodging at the Palazzo Tomati on 24 March 1752. In this year Chambers again returned to Paris, where he met the portrait painter Alexander Roslin and Baron Fredrik Sparre.

Study in Italy Although Chambers was not a *pensionnaire* at the French Academy in the Palazzo Mancini, he might just as well have been, so intimate was he in friendship with those who were. Indeed at this time he was fully French in inclinations and taste. He joined in all the *pensionnaires'* field studies. His site drawings in the 'Franco-Italian Album' can be matched to those by Pajou or Peyre. Piranesi's workshop at the Palazzo Tomati, where Chambers lodged, provided him with an opportunity to learn from this revolutionary the radical changes that were affecting architectural design. Piranesi had been at the centre of an international vortex spilling over from the French Academy since the early 1740s. It may be in this workshop that Chambers first encountered drawings by the enigmatic and brilliant Jean-Laurent Le Geay, whom he befriended in London in the late 1760s. The *pensionnaires* who embraced the theory and practice of architecture that emanated from the academy in the period 1740–60 included L. J. Le Lorrain, N. H. Jardin, G. P. M. Dumont, C. M. A. Challe, E. A. Petitot, and, among Chambers's Parisian colleagues, de Wailly and Peyre. If one design by Chambers can be singled out to represent these French alliances, it is that dated 1752 for the mausoleum of Frederick, prince of Wales, who had suddenly died in 1751. It supports the suggestion that Chambers met the prince in 1749, and is prophetic of his appointment in 1757 as architect to the dowager princess of Wales at Kew, and as architectural tutor to George, prince of Wales (later George III).

Practice in London Despite his Franco-Swedish education, and evidence that in 1752 he contemplated the possibility of employment with Frederick II of Prussia in Potsdam, Chambers decided to set up practice in London. This decision may well have been determined by the English *milordi* he met in Rome on their grand tour, nearly all of whom employed him in some capacity: lords Bessborough, Bruce, Charlemont, Huntingdon, Pembroke, and Tylney were there, as were Thomas Brand, Thomas Hollis, Thomas Kennedy, Thomas Scrope, Thomas Willoughby, and Robert Wood. Of his later artistic associates, Giambattista Cipriani, Simon Vierpyle, and Joseph Wilton were also resident in Rome. Shortly after Robert Adam arrived in February 1755, Chambers left in March or April. This brief overlapping was enough to cause the ambitious Adam heart-fluttering concern. Indeed it is through Adam that it is known that Chambers briefly had drawing lessons from C. L. Clérisseau and Laurent Pecheux. Adam wrote percipiently to his brother John on 18 April that

> All the English who have travelled for these five years …
> imagine him a prodigy for genius, for sense and good taste …
> But his taste for Bas reliefs, ornaments, & decorations of
> buildings, he both knows well and draws exquisitely … he is
> in such great esteem; so intimate and in such friendship
> with most of the English that have been in Rome that they
> are determined to support him to the utmost of their power
> … it will require very considerable interest to succeed
> against Chambers who has tolerable Friends & real merit.
> (J. Fleming, *Robert Adam and his Circle*, 1962, 160)

The pleasure that Adam derived from information that in London Chambers was 'drawing in a poor mean lodging up a long dark stair' (J. Fleming, *Robert Adam and his Circle*, 1962, 249), above Tom's Coffee House in Russell Street, Covent Garden, may imply that six years of study had somewhat depleted his fortune. Tom's was the convivial artistic meeting place where Chambers would have met Samuel Johnson, Oliver Goldsmith, James Paine, and Lord Clive. He and Catherine had brought with them from Italy their eldest daughter, Cornelia, leaving the youngest, Selina, in Italy in the charge of their nurse Rosa. Selina did not make the journey to London until May 1759, by which time Chambers had moved into 58 Poland Street, off Oxford Street.

Chambers's career in England might have struck society like a meteor had Edwin Lascelles accepted his design for Harewood House, Yorkshire, in November 1755. It was an uncompromising product of the French Academy in Rome. Its rejection in June 1756 was a sharp lesson for the Anglo-Swede with French tastes. In the mid-eighteenth century, after forty years of Palladian dominance, English patrons were not prepared to accept advanced French neo-classical architecture. This disappointment prompted Chambers to embark on a study tour of English Palladian architecture. Except for the uncompromising casino at Marino, Dublin, at the beginning of his career and the French-tinctured Somerset House at the end, he would 'establish a body of Sound Precepts'. His buildings would be 'Adapted to the Customs & Fashions of our Time, to the Climate and Manners of our Country, and to the wants & Feelings of its inhabitants' (W. Chambers, Royal Academy lecture notes, 2.4, RIBA). He would henceforth refine English Palladianism, sometimes lacing it with French decoration. In a measure reflecting his unostentatious and reserved personality, his architecture would be decoratively discreet. This was the language of his magnificent *Treatise on Civil Architecture* of 1759, a work of empirical and discriminating eclecticism, ranging selectively over the whole of the classical tradition. He revised this in 1791 adding more ornamental plates, and changing the title to *A Treatise on the Decorative Part of Civil Architecture*. He never wrote the 'constructive' part.

Publication In 1757 Chambers had recognized the need to promote himself by publication. He must already have made a comparison between the courses of academic tuition available in France and the lack of it in England. However, his *Proposals for Publishing by Subscription, Designs of Villas, Temples, Gates, Doors, and Chimney Pieces*, issued in April, smacks of a more traditional English design book, not an exegesis on architectural theory and practice. Instead, at first he had to take advantage of his unique experiences with Chinese architecture. In May 1757 he published *Designs of Chinese Buildings, Furniture, Dresses, Machines and Utensils*, dedicated to George, prince of Wales. Here for the first time Chinese architecture was presented as a subject worthy of the kind of serious study formerly reserved for Western antiquity. One of the handsomest architectural folios of the century, among its 164 subscribers were many of the *milordi* he had met in Italy. Nevertheless, its influence in Britain was less than Chambers might have hoped. The high fashion for Chinoiserie architecture in England was in the 1740s, a mongrel style made up from diverse ornamental sources. It lacked the authority of first-hand study. Oddly, Chambers himself at Amesbury, Wiltshire; Kew Gardens, Surrey; The Hoo, Hertfordshire; Blackheath, Kent; and perhaps Ingress Abbey, Kent, never used the authoritative detail of the very *Designs* he had published, except for his unexecuted design for a bridge for Frederick II at Sanssouci, Germany (1763). He may well have sensed that the Chinese architecture he had studied at first hand was an alien style in the Europe of rococo and early neo-classicism. Only after Chambers's death did the book come into its own in England as a model for Chinese decoration (for example at the Brighton Pavilion, 1815). However, on the continent circumstances were different, particularly in Germany and France, where the fashion did not reach a peak until the 1780s. There the book's plates had a profound effect throughout the century, particularly on garden architecture and interior decoration, for example at Drottningholm China House, Sweden (1760s), and Schloss Worlitz, Germany (1770s–1780s).

Chambers's essay 'Of the art of laying out gardens' had a different reception in Britain from the plates of *Designs*. It was reprinted in the *Gentleman's Magazine* in May 1757, again in the *Annual Register* in 1758, where Edmund Burke regarded it as 'much the best that has been written on the subject', and again in 1762 by Bishop Thomas Percy in *Miscellaneous Pieces Relating to the Chinese*. It recognized that nature must be improved by ingenious artifice and subtle deception (E. Harris, 156). The union of art and nature that Chambers saw as having a Chinese pedigree was one of the themes of his gardens at Kew, but was also the *cause célèbre* of his *Dissertation on Oriental Gardening* in 1772, a disguised attack on the landscape gardening of Capability Brown which misfired with the public. Chambers was forced to publish a second edition in 1773, to which he annexed an 'Explanatory discourse'. Nevertheless, the *Dissertation* contains some remarkably prescient suggestions, such as colour gradation in planting and the need for comprehensive country and urban planning. In essence, Chambers saw Chinese gardens as a union of art and nature, in which the gardener improved upon nature's beautiful irregularities. He believed that Capability Brown denied this in his 'natural' gardens based upon arboreal and landscape modelling.

Royal appointments Robert Wood's congratulations on 22 August 1757, 'upon the compliments paid you by the Prince & upon Lord Bute's friendship' (Chambers papers, RA archives), referred to the one event that would determine Chambers's future and his path to establishment success. He was appointed architect to the Princess Augusta at Kew, and architectural tutor to George, prince of Wales. 'The prince employs me three mornings a week to teach him architecture; the buildings (and) other decorations at Kew fill up the remaining time' (draft letter, RA archives). The appointment must surely have arisen out of their meeting at Kew in the summer of 1749 and the making of the Roman mausoleum design of 1752.

The architectural drawings made jointly by Chambers and the prince, conserved in the Royal Library at Windsor Castle, are a memorial to what must have been one of the most thorough courses of education in architecture ever received by any monarch. The appointment was a catalyst for Chambers to abandon his proposed design book of architecture, and to publish instead in the spring of 1759 the celebrated *Treatise on Civil Architecture*, a work whose

> aim is at once to simplify the study of architecture without sacrificing any of its richness, variety or precision, and to cultivate taste and increase pleasure not only by providing information and examples, but also by encouraging the development of critical judgement. (Eileen Harris in J. Harris, 130–31)

No other architect, not even François Blondel, had so subjected the literature of architecture to such an exegesis. To Horace Walpole it was the 'most sensible book and the most exempt from prejudices that ever was written on that science' (H. Walpole, *Anecdotes of Painting in England*, ed. R. Wornum, 1888, xiv). None would dispute this.

Chambers's achievement at Kew Gardens is commemorated by one of the most sumptuous folios ever produced on a single garden: *Plans, Elevations, Sections, and Perspective Views of the Gardens and Buildings at Kew in Surry* (1763), dedicated to Princess Augusta. Like the *Treatise*, it was paid for by George III. The role of John Stuart, third earl of Bute, at Kew is made clear in the specially composed manuscript volume that Chambers presented to Bute, with the inscription that the gardens were 'Plan'd by his Lordship, and executed under his direction' (department of prints and drawings, Metropolitan Museum of Art, New York).

Kew was a demonstration of the variety and contrast that Chambers presented as characteristic of Chinese gardens. It was a textbook on world architecture as first expounded in Fischer von Erlach's *Entwurff einer historischen Architectur* of 1725. It was also part of the prince's architectural education, for between 1757 and 1763 he was witness to the design and building of more than twenty structures, of which the Alhambra, Pagoda, and Mosque in their conjoined groves were perhaps the most famous trio of exotic buildings in Europe. The decision to isolate as a designed entity the horticultural buildings within an ornamental enclosure separate from, but adjacent to, the pleasure grounds, anticipated the innovations of H. Repton and J. C. Loudon.

Royal works Chambers's star was in the ascendant. Although Adam was supposed to have shared the post of architect to the office of works, an appointment made in November 1761, Chambers's friendship with the king ensured that Adam's contribution was minimal. There was no love lost between the two leading architects of the reign of George III. On the king's accession in 1760 it was Chambers who designed the resplendent state coach. Chambers refashioned Buckingham House (1762–73), built the observatory in Richmond Gardens (1768), and erected the pavilion for the reception there for Christian VII of Denmark in 1769, and he built the queen's lodge (1776) and the lower lodge (1779) at Windsor Castle. Architect to the king was a new post, and it is significant that in 1760 the new surveyor of the works, a political appointment, was Thomas Worsley, friend of both Bute and Chambers. For Chambers this was the first step towards the coveted comptrollership of the works in 1769, and in 1782 the combined office of comptroller and surveyor-general. As head of the royal works Chambers proved a most able, thorough, and humane administrator. Honours flowed in. In 1752 he had been made a member of the Florentine Accademia di Belle Arti. In 1763 he was a corresponding member of the French Académie de l'Architecture. In 1776 he was elected a fellow of the Royal Society.

Royal Academy of Arts Ever since his Paris days Chambers felt strongly that art and architecture could be improved by the provision of a forum for exhibition and discussion with a body of professional teachers. He had observed the squabbles and dissension within the Society of Arts and the Free Society of Artists. It was his determination that there should be a properly constituted Royal Academy of Arts. Surprisingly, Joshua Reynolds was not a signatory to the memorial that Chambers personally presented to the king on 8 December 1768, 'that the two principal objects we have in view are, the establishing of a well regulated School or Academy of Design … and an Annual Exhibition' (S. C. Hutchison, *The History of the Royal Academy, 1768–1968*, 1968, 43–4). On 10 December Chambers took the instrument of foundation to the king for his signature, and it was he who ensured that the king's prerogative was to appoint a treasurer (obviously to be Chambers himself) 'as a person in whom he places full confidence, in an office where his interest is concerned' (instrument of foundation, dated 10 Dec 1768, ibid., 209–13). On 14 December the new Royal Academy of Arts held its first meeting, with Reynolds being elected to the presidential chair. In May 1769 the Royal Academy held its inaugural summer exhibition, when the king knighted Reynolds as its first president. He would certainly have preferred to knight Chambers. But there was compensation. In 1770 Gustav III made Chambers a knight of the order of the Polar Star, to which George III later granted him permission to adopt the address of English knighthood. In Chambers's handling of the academy there were internal criticisms, but there is a parallel here with his strict autocratic but humane control of the office of works. Good and efficient administration was his recipe for success. Reynolds bemoaned, 'though he was President, Sir Wm was Viceroy over him' (Farington, *Diary*, 10 Dec 1804). But there was another side to Chambers, for at academy dinners he vied with Boswell in composing verses and sang Swedish love songs.

First works Chambers's first works in architecture are referred to by Barreau de Chefdeville on 5 May 1757, listing the Casina and Rock Bridge at Wilton for Henry Herbert, tenth earl of Pembroke, and stables at Goodwood for Charles Lennox, third duke of Richmond, and conveying 'mille compliments' from Pajou and Doyen. Also at Wilton he built a triumphal arch. The Casina paid homage to Giacomo Barozzi da Vignola, the arch was French-tinctured. Garden buildings became one of Chambers's specialities. He always enjoyed the challenge of designing small-scale units of design, and built more than fifty-two garden buildings, which he ornamented with exquisite and refined taste. Among those that survive the best are the Casina at Wilton (1757), the Pagoda (1761) and Temple of Bellona (1760) at Kew, the Temple of Romulus and Remus at Coleby, Lincolnshire (1762), and, of course, the Casino at Marino, Dublin (from 1758), a garden temple writ large.

Design of villas It may have been Fitz Foy at Castle Hill, Dorset, about 1760, who offered Chambers his first opportunity to design a country house. There he began to effect a rapid and complete development of a single refining theme: to take as a model the English Palladian villa of the generation of Colen Campbell and Lord Burlington and to elide inessentials. Castle Hill, Parksted (Roehampton), Surrey, and Duddingstone, Edinburghshire, were all conceived within two years. Teddington Grove, Middlesex, followed in 1765, as did Peper Harow, Surrey, but that last was much larger than the former, compact, villas. With Duddingstone, Mark Girouard's words cannot be bettered:

> Perhaps his most original and memorable design: just a cube, and a noble portico in front of it, with none of the gradations in the way of basement, string courses, and wings

which were the accepted hieratic structure of contemporary design. (M. Girouard, *RIBA Journal*, December 1970, 551)

Teddington may have been even more revolutionary. Loudon saw it as exceptional:

> a square mass, completely isolated, without the appearance of offices of any kind, and with nothing in it or about it, not even a servant's window in the basement which requires to be concealed. We could fancy it a temple in a wood. (J. C. Loudon, *The Gardener's Magazine*, 1839, 424–6)

Trent Place, Middlesex (c.1777), was also a temple in a wood, and astonishingly precocious, for it was a domed cube with a portico in the style of the Parisian architect Jean-François Neufforge.

The Casino at Marino was exceptional in so many ways. It began life as a garden temple, even if a very large one, but was also a villa in the sense of being a suburban residence. James Caulfeild, first earl of Charlemont, entrusted its design entirely to his friend Chambers, and originally intended to live in it. Drawings seem to have been made in 1758, and it was illustrated in the *Treatise* in 1759. However, its genesis must go back to at least 1755, as it features as one of the flanking pavilions of the Harewood design. Charlemont's implicit faith in Chambers enabled him to produce a design unsullied by interfering alterations by patron or building executant. Fully in the style of Franco-Roman neo-classicism, it was more revolutionary than anything in Europe at the time. As a perfect entity it must be judged in European architecture with Lord Burlington's Chiswick Villa or the Petit Trianon at Versailles.

Town houses Unlike Robert Adam, many of whose town house schemes have survived renovation, Chambers has suffered grievously owing to tragic losses. Melbourne House, Piccadilly, has been gutted and Gower House, Whitehall, demolished, as have his many houses in Berners Street. Of his internal urban domestic alterations, hardly an intact room survives. Unlike Adam's spatial pyrotechnics in planning, Chambers did not favour sequences of fluidly shaped rooms. He planned and decorated with reserve. But in the design of staircases he excelled as no other. We may witness this in the many plans among the tuition drawings for George III, where some staircases would do justice to Guarino Guarini or Filippo Juvarra in baroque Turin. The Gower House stair was an improvisation on Baldassare Longhena's celebrated staircase at the convent of San Giorgio Maggiore in Venice; the Melbourne House stair was a feat of engineering, a daring arrangement of cantilevers and landings; and the navy stair at Somerset House had no equal for spatial complexity.

The ornamental parts In both town and country Chambers's decoration is transparently by an architect who is passionately interested in ornament and ornamental subjects. This is demonstrated by nearly 500 ornamental drawings in the 'Franco-Italian Album', and a mass of miscellaneous record drawings, all gathered in France and Italy. Out of this vade-mecum Chambers was able to create his own personal vocabulary to apply to his compositions. What he achieved can today be best seen at Lord

Bessborough's Parksted (Roehampton), for which ceiling designs are dated 1763. Apart from the staircase, hall, and ground-floor rooms at Duddingstone, and Somerset House, this is the only surviving intact suite of rooms. The onlooker is struck by the clarity of compartition, with a subtle balance struck between the decorative and naturalistic plant ornament, aptly described by Joseph Gwilt as 'an easy flowing foliage and elegant imitation of such flowers and plants and other objects in nature as were best adapted to the purpose of architectural ornament' (J. Gwilt, in M. Jourdain, *English Decorative Plasterwork of the Renaissance*, 1926, 189). Among the lost interiors which might be said to be perfect expositions of Chambers's style would be the rooms at Castle Hill and the library at Barton Hall, Suffolk (1767).

Chambers was particularly innovative in the design of chimney-pieces. Hall chimney-pieces as at Peper Harow, Duddingstone, and Parksted evoke the theme of antique sarcophagi; the extraordinary chimney-piece at Thomas Brand's The Hoo, with an antique relief in the overmantel, may be said to reflect Brand's passion for antique marbles but, in the use of a scrolled pediment and lugged half pilasters, is deliberately designed in a style associated with the artisan mannerism of The Hoo's seventeenth-century interiors. In 1761 at The Hyde, Essex, for Brand's cousin Thomas Brand-Hollis, Chambers created a hall to be used as a receptacle for Brand's own marbles. Its singular feature was a sarcophagus set on neo-antique supports, itself supporting a *cippus* (or low column) with an eighteenth-century bust on top.

Chambers's work is distinguished from first to last by the high quality of craftsmanship. He had learned from Blondel the importance of the cutting and presentation of stone (stereotomy), and insisted on the employment of the best sculptors, including Joseph Wilton, the carver Sefferin Alken, the plasterer Thomas Collins, and for ormolu ornament Dietrich Anderson. Wilton almost certainly carved the monumental chimney-piece for the Great Drawing Room of Gower House (V&A), with antique terms that would do justice to the finest *goût grec* of Lalive de Jully, the patron of Chambers's friend Barreau de Chefdeville.

The Eating Room in Gower House, designed *c*.1767, had panelled walls with uprights with vine and medallion relief. It has been suggested that the remarkably beautiful ornamental French terms designed by Chambers about this time may have been intended for the recessed panels in the chimney recess (Snodin, 140–41). A version of this type of wall system appears first at Parksted, then Duddingstone, and later in the hall at Peper Harow. The design for the end wall of the Great Drawing Room at Gower House incorporates French furniture, tripod ornament, and candelabrum; that for the long chimney wall is also French, with bas-reliefs to the overdoors, and girandoles set against the larger panels. In contrast to these Gallic details, the decoration of the staircase was in the mid-Georgian Palladian style, although the ravishingly beautiful neo-classical plaster compositions on the wall could be by no other than Chambers, executed by Collins. The

main front of the house was conformably Palladian. This admixture of French Louis XVI and English Palladian is a characteristic of Chambers's greatest work: the building of public offices at Somerset House.

Somerset House Somerset House took up all Chambers's time from 1775 until the year before his death in 1796. When he confessed to Agmondesham Vesey on 2 April 1774 how 'heartily tired of the profession' he was (BL, Add. MS 41136, fol. 16*v*), little did he anticipate that he was only half-way through his professional career. Yet, even when writing this letter he knew that the condition of the palace at old Somerset House was causing concern, for his board of works had been compiling a damning report long before April. He must have been party to the idea of intended public offices on the site, and must have realized that the design of the new building would first be offered to William Robinson, who held the post of clerk of the works to Somerset House, but who was a deeply unimaginative architect.

Referred to in a letter to Thomas Worsley on 20 May 1774, Chambers without warning set out for Paris, 'where many great works have been done which I must examine with care and make proper remarks upon' (BL, Add. MS 41135, fols. 26*r*–26*v*). He wrote again to Worsley from Paris, 'where I come with a view to Observe and not to eat' (BL, Add. MS 41135, letter before fol. 27). As the watercolours in the 'Paris Album' (RIBA) reveal, he refreshed himself upon the frontier style of Parisian neo-classicism: Ledoux, de Wailly, Jacques Gondoin, and A. J. Gabriel. Later, on 15 September 1774, he recollected the old friends he met—Greuze, Doyen, Pajou, de Wailly, Le Roy, Vernet, Robert, Caffieri—as among those 'habiles artistes avec qui j'ai vécu à Paris' (15 Sept 1774; BL, Add. MS 41135).

Fortunately, Chambers's efforts to dispose of Robinson as architect were rendered unnecessary by the latter's death in 1775. Chambers was now free to set about the complexities of his design, bearing in mind Edmund Burke's recommendations that it be an 'ornament to the Metropolis', 'an object of national splendour as well as convenience', and 'a monument to the taste and elegance of His Majesty's Reign' (J. Baretti, *Guide through the Royal Academy*, 1981, 3–4). Naturally the first task was the demolition of old Somerset House, which comprised a Tudor palace, with exquisite additions by Inigo Jones and John Webb, and Georgian interiors by Henry Flitcroft and William Kent. Incorporation was impractical. Chambers was saddened by this necessary destruction. His first design for a new Somerset House was an ideal plan with a sensational vast oval concourse, and amazing staircases, that took no account of the 40 feet fall in the ground from the Strand to the River Thames, the necessary concentration of public offices on the site, and the incorporation of the Royal Academy of Art, Society of Antiquaries, and the Royal Society, known as the 'learned societies'.

In the executed design Chambers paid only lip service to France. As if to make amends for the loss of the Jonesian buildings, he sifted through the history of English Palladianism for the composition of his elevations. The general theme of his Strand front was Jonesian, and elsewhere he nods to the Jonesian Whitehall designs and William Kent's Palladian Treasury and Horse Guards, particularly in the use of rustication. Throughout, the building is invigorated by Chambers's masterful and subtle use of all the orders, as if the whole is a lesson in the *Treatise on Civil Architecture*. Perhaps deliberately, the palace front on the Strand hardly prepares the viewer for the excitement of the columned vestibule and the courtyard behind. Yet the effect of the courtyard is French, despite the elaborate and lavish Palladian entrances. French too is Chambers's use of ornamental sculpture. In this, as elsewhere, inside and out, Somerset House was intended to be a showcase for the finest in British craftsmanship.

Some of the most powerful architecture in Georgian London could be experienced on the river front: the vast rusticated terrace embanking the Thames, the dark, deep Piranesian chasms of river entries marked by powerful water gates, the pair of huge Palladian bridges that punctuate this long 700 foot elevation, and the Stygian blackness of the central king's bargemaster's entrance, where water flowed and barges entered.

For his interiors, particularly those in the Strand block, Chambers was untrammelled by precedent. His decoration is a subtle and learned fusion of English and French ornament. The Royal Society library would not look out of place in Paris, and the Royal Society council room ceiling anticipates the late classicism of James Wyatt and Henry Holland, and even C. R. Cockerell's rigorous decoration. The navy staircase hints of what might have been had Chambers carried out his 'ideal' plan.

Ornamental objects and furniture The ornamental beauty of the interior detail of Somerset House is a reminder that Chambers was an able designer of ornament, utensils, clocks, and furniture. Most of the silver is derived from French work, such as the Pembroke silver soup tureens of 1771 (priv. coll.) in the renovated Germain style. Perhaps the most celebrated ornamental object is the astronomical clock (Royal Collection) made by Christopher Pinchbeck in 1767 for George III, based on the Casino at Marino and an engraved plate in Chambers's *Treatise*. As he acknowledged of himself, Chambers was 'really a Very pretty Connoisseur in furniture' (Chambers to Lord Melbourne, August 1773, BL, Add. MS 41133, fol. 107). Much of his furniture still remains to be located and identified. His earliest piece is the Society of Arts president's chair (1759–60), which is among the earliest essays in neo-classical furniture design. Far more original is the table from the Great Drawing Room, Gower House (Courtauld Inst.), possibly carved by Sefferin Alken *c*.1768. It is an astonishing piece, prophetic of French Directoire design, that has no precedent in either England or France for so early a date. It is almost as if Chambers was inventing an alternative to the Parisian fashion for the *goût grec* of Lalive de Jully's furniture. The most exceptional piece was Lord Charlemont's medal cabinet (1767–8; Courtauld Inst.), designed to occupy a whole wall of his library pavilion in Charlemont House, Dublin. It is a perfect expression of Chambers's sobriety, his exquisite taste in ornament, his learned iconography, and, with the ormolu by Dietrich Anderson and the wood-carving by Sefferin Alken, his insistence on the highest level of craftsmanship.

Personal life and posthumous reputation In partnership with his favourite plasterer, and later executor, Thomas Collins, Chambers speculated in building at least twenty-five houses in Berners Street, north of Oxford Street. His own was no. 13, with his studio at the end of the garden. He moved there from Poland Street in 1766. The elevation to the garden must have been surprising, for it was executed in papier mâché in what has been described as a 'fanciful', perhaps Chinoiserie, style (C. Bielefeld, *On the Use of the Improved Papier-Mâché*, 1850, 7, 11). In July 1765 the duke of Argyll's estate at Whitton Park, Middlesex, was sold to Mr Gostling, from whom Chambers leased the Palladian villa and pleasure grounds designed by Roger Morris. Following his elevation to the comptrollership of the works in 1782, Chambers was now a grandee. Here in London and at Whitton he was a genial host, not least to his old friends from Paris and any Swede passing through London.

Chambers was a worthy person of rigid principles. This determined his relationship to his children. His beloved Cornelia (b. 1753), who married John Milbanke, died in 1795. Twin sons died in 1763. His son George (b. 1766) married Jane Rodney in 1784, and both became dissipated; by 1808 George was a vagabond. Chambers objected to Selina (b. 1754) marrying William Innes, a merchant in Jamaica, in 1778. Even in Lady Chambers's will, declared in March 1798, Selina was required to return to London within two years or be disinherited. In 1791 he regarded the terms of the marriage between Charlotte and Captain Harward as a 'vexatious business'. Such actions may suggest a strait-laced moralistic attitude that perhaps increased with age. This coloured his disciplined management of the Royal Academy of Arts in the later years. In 1791 he voted down a proposal that the academy contribute 100 guineas towards a monument to Dr Johnson. He observed that as there was to be no monument to Gainsborough or Wilson, the academy's revenues ought better to be spent on 'the education of young Artists' and 'to assist the Sick or distressed Artist' (Royal Academy archives). His initial refusal to allow the academy rooms to be used for Reynolds's lying-in-state in 1792 was seen by all, including the king, as an injustice. Yet from 1769 he had nursed the academy from strength to strength. He was the authoritarian sergeant-major who held the academy together. In despising his son George's wish to join the army in 1784, Chambers wrote:

> In my profession there is a very extensive power of doing good to others, as well as to ones self, which to me ... is a luxury of the highest sort. Whenever I see, as I do very often, five or six hundred industrious fellows supporting themselves and their families, many of them growing rich, under my command; I feel such a pleasure as no General ever felt in War, be the Victory what it might. (Chambers letters, 9 Dec 1784, RA archives)

Chambers had relinquished Whitton in 1790 and moved to 75 Norton (now Bolsover) Street, St Marylebone. On 12 March 1795 he wrote to the king resigning from Somerset

House, because of 'infirmities crouding on very fast' (Royal Library archives, Windsor Castle). A year later, on 10 March 1796, Chambers 'resigned his earthly post to sing hallelujahs' and died at his home in Norton Street. Two days later an extraordinary procession was seen walking down Whitehall to Westminster Abbey, where Chambers was that day buried. All the

> master workmen belonging to the Board of Works ... attended, unsolicited, to testify their regret for the loss, and their esteem for the memory of a man by whom their claims had ever been examined with attention, and decided with justice, and by whom themselves were always treated with mildness, courtesy, and affability. (*GM*, 1st ser., 66/1, 1796, 260)

He might have demurred had he known that he would find himself bedded down in the abbey between Robert Adam and James Wyatt! Lord Charlemont penned from his own sickbed a moving epitaph:

> Sir William Chambers, Knight. Etc,
> Fellow of the Royal Academy,
> And Professor of Architecture,
> The Best of Men, and the First of English Architects,
> Whose Buildings, Modelled From His Own Mind,
> Elegant, Pure, and Solid,
> Will Long Remain the Lasting Monuments
> Of That Taste,
> Whose Chastity Could Only Be Equalled
> By The Immaculate Purity of The Author's Heart,
> James Earl of Charlemont, His Friend, From Long Experience
>   of His Worth and Talents,
> Dedicates This Inscription To Him And Friendship.

Chambers's influence was widespread, not least on his subordinates in the office of works, many of whom were, or had been, assistants in his private office. These included Thomas Hardwick, John Yenn, and James Gandon, all of whom rose to distinction. His powerful position in the Royal Academy meant that pupils there in the architecture school came under his spell, and there were many Chambersian designs exhibited at the summer exhibitions. Chambers's architecture permeates that of John Nash and C. R. Cockerell. His *Treatise* was venerated: Joseph Gwilt produced an edition in 1825 and J. B. Papworth in 1826. Its supremacy as the textbook for the orders and the proportions of architecture was never challenged. Having extended its influence through the nineteenth century, it was taken up again in 1896 by Banister Fletcher in his *History of Architecture on the Comparative Method*. Even today every architectural student digests Banister Fletcher. Chambers was the role model for Edwardian architects working in a Georgian style in the first half of the twentieth century. Both Sir Reginald Blomfield and Sir Albert Richardson saw him as standing on Parnassus.   JOHN HARRIS

Sources J. Harris, *William Chambers, knight of the Polar Star* (1970) · H. M. Colvin and others, eds., *The history of the king's works*, 5 (1976) · E. Harris and N. Savage, *British architectural books and writers, 1556–1785* (1990) · Colvin, *Archs.* · M. Snodin, ed., *Sir William Chambers: catalogues of architectural drawing in the Victoria & Albert Museum* (1996) · J. Harris and M. Snodin, eds., *Sir William Chambers: architect to George III* (1996) · M. Olausson, ed., *Chambers and Adelcrantz* (Stockholm, 1997)

Archives BL, letter-books, Add. MS 41133–41136 · priv. coll., family archives · PRO, work letter-books · PRO, works, minutes, and proceedings · RA, corresp., notes, and bills · RIBA, corresp. and papers · Uppsala University, autobiographical note, no. X222 · Wilts. & Swindon RO, receipted account for building work at Wilton and Whitehall | PRO NIre., letters to Lord Abercorn · RA, corresp. relating to Society of Artists · Royal Irish Acad., letters to Lord Charlemont

Likenesses J. Reynolds, oils, *c.*1760, NPG · F. Cotes, chalk drawing, 1764, Scot. NPG · J. Reynolds, oils, 1778–1780?, RA [*see illus.*] · J. F. Rigaud, group portrait, oils, 1782, NPG · C. F. von Breda, portrait, 1788, RIBA · G. Dance, drawing, 1793, RA · P. E. Falconet, pencil drawing, BM · J. Meyer, miniature, NPG · H. Singleton, group portrait, oils (*Royal Academicians, 1793*), RA · J. Zoffany, group portrait, oils (*Royal Academicians, 1772*), Royal Collection · wash drawing (after Reynolds), NPG

Chambers, William (1724?–1777), Church of England clergyman, was probably born at Derby. He was the son of John Chambers of Derby (*b. c.*1693, *d.* 1751), who is variously described as 'Esq' and 'Gent.' (Venn, *Alum. Cant.*, 1.319; Glover, 2.469), and of his wife, Elizabeth (*b. c.*1700, *d.* 1785). He was educated at Derby School and, aged eighteen, matriculated at St John's College, Cambridge, as a pensioner on 5 March 1743; he graduated BA in 1747 and MA three years later. At Cambridge he formed a friendship with his fellow collegian Theophilus Lindsey, whose latitudinarian, and subsequently anti-trinitarian, theological opinions Chambers came to share. He was ordained deacon in the diocese of Ely on 5 June 1748 and priest in the diocese of Peterborough on 5 November of the same year. According to Lindsey he undertook a grand tour of the Netherlands, France, and Italy. His family was both wealthy and well connected. His aunt Hannah Sophia Chambers had married Brownlow Cecil, eighth earl of Exeter, in 1724 and their son Brownlow, from 1754 the ninth earl, was a contemporary of Chambers at St John's College. The earls of Exeter owned the advowson of the rectory of the church of St John the Baptist, Achurch, Northamptonshire, and it was through their patronage that Chambers was appointed rector of Achurch in 1748.

Chambers married Dorothy Rolleston (*d.* 1809) probably soon after his institution at Achurch; they had two sons and a daughter. Lindsey asserts that Chambers 'was endowed with a peculiar turn for medical knowledge, which he diligently cultivated by the preliminary studies of anatomy, chemistry &c' (Ditchfield, 'The Revd William Chambers', 9) and that he ministered diligently to the health of the poor of his parish. Though he appears to have published nothing he was awarded a DD by Cambridge in 1762. The endorsements that he wrote on his surviving manuscript sermons suggest that he was a conscientious priest. He developed a close sympathy with those clergymen, among them Lindsey's father-in-law, Francis Blackburne, who objected in principle to compulsory clerical subscription to the Thirty-Nine Articles. At Achurch, according to Lindsey, he experimented with the liturgy on lines previously suggested by Samuel Clarke: 'he never repeated any part of the service, where Jesus

Christ or the Holy Spirit were addressed and invoked, being persuaded that the God and Father of all, was the only true God and object of worship' (ibid., 4). That no disciplinary action was taken against him is a mark of the variety of liturgical practice that the eighteenth-century church tacitly accepted, as well as of the latitudinarian principles of Chambers's diocesan, John Hinchliffe, bishop of Peterborough.

In 1771–2 Chambers gave Lindsey full support in the organization of the Feathers tavern petition for the abolition of compulsory subscription to the articles. The petition was rejected by the House of Commons on 6 February 1772 and, more summarily, on 5 May 1774. On the latter occasion Chambers was present in the Commons gallery with Lindsey, Richard Price, and Joseph Priestley. By then Lindsey had resigned from the church and founded his own Unitarian chapel in London. On his way to London from his former parish of Catterick he resided with Chambers at Achurch. Only a very small number of clergymen followed Lindsey out of the church. For all his identification with Unitarianism Chambers was not among them, although his death from an apoplectic stroke shortly afterwards, at Achurch on 4 September 1777, leaves open the possibility that he might have seceded at a subsequent stage. On his death Lindsey wrote a eulogistic obituary. Chambers was buried at All Saints' Church, Derby.

Chambers bequeathed extensive real and personal estate and it is clear that his private fortune meant that he had no need to compromise his theological principles in a quest for ecclesiastical preferment. His historical significance lies in his association with a group of liberal Anglican clergymen, mostly Cambridge-educated, who helped to stimulate heterodox thought within the church and who contributed indirectly to the development of English Unitarianism.   G. M. DITCHFIELD

Sources Venn, *Alum. Cant.*, 1/1 · R. F. Scott, ed., *Admissions to the College of St John the Evangelist in the University of Cambridge*, 3: *July 1715 – November 1767* (1903) · G. M. Ditchfield, 'The Revd William Chambers, DD (*c*.1724–1777)', *Enlightenment and Dissent*, 4 (1985), 3–12 · S. Glover, *The history and gazetteer of the county of Derby*, ed. T. Noble, 2 (1833) · H. I. Longden, *Northamptonshire and Rutland clergy from 1500*, ed. P. I. King and others, 16 vols. in 6, Northamptonshire RS (1938–52) · B. Tacchella, ed., *The Derby School register, 1570–1901* (1902) · *GM*, 1st ser., 47 (1777), 565–6 · *GM*, 1st ser., 79 (1809), 1175 · *General Evening Post* (18–20 March 1773) · *General Evening Post* (21–3 Oct 1777) · *Northampton Mercury* (8 Sept 1777) · T. Belsham, *Memoirs of the late Reverend Theophilus Lindsey*, new edn (1873) · T. Lindsey, *An historical view of the state of Unitarian doctrine and worship from the Reformation to our own times* (1783) · GEC, *Peerage*, vol. 5 · G. M. Ditchfield, 'The subscription issue in British parliamentary politics, 1772–1779', *Parliamentary History*, 7 (1988), 45–80 · will, PRO, PROB 11/1046/393, fols. 118v–120v

Archives DWL, corresp. with Lindsey · JRL, corresp. with T. Lindsey

Wealth at death landed property in Derbyshire, Nottinghamshire, Surrey, and West Riding of Yorkshire; several thousand pounds in cash, and 4 per cent government stock: will, PRO, PROB 11/1046/393, fols. 118v–120v

Chambers, William (1800–1883), publisher, was born on 16 April 1800 in Peebles, Scotland, the first of six children

and the eldest son of James Chambers (1778–1824), cloth manufacturer and merchant, and Jean Gibson (*c*.1781–1843), the daughter of a local landowner. He spent the first thirteen years of his life in Peebles receiving the legendary Scottish education: dame-school for reading; burgh school for reading, writing, and arithmetic; and grammar school for Latin. He later complained that there was no instruction in history, geography, or the physical sciences. Fortunately family resources made up for this deficiency; because James Chambers subscribed to the local circulating library William had the opportunity to read classics of English literature. He read scientific and mechanical articles in the fourth edition of the *Encyclopaedia Britannica*, which his father purchased, and learned geography by studying a battered set of globes acquired at a sale.

When Chambers was thirteen the family's fortunes changed. Forced to declare bankruptcy, his father moved the family to Edinburgh so that he could find employment. William was apprenticed to John Sutherland, bookseller of Calton Street, on 8 May 1814. He continued to educate himself, reading books borrowed from Sutherland's shop and conducting scientific experiments with friends. During winter 1815–16 he read aloud Smollett and other novelists to a baker and his sons in Canal Street in the early mornings, and received 'a penny roll newly drawn from the oven' (*DNB*) for his trouble. Having completed his apprenticeship, in June 1819 he started his own business. His first shop, an open-air stall on Leith Walk, near the one that his brother Robert *Chambers (1802–1871) had started in 1818, consisted of trestles with boards on top for displaying books. In return for some assistance that he had offered an agent of Thomas Tegg he was given £10 worth of books on credit; his stock mostly consisted of editions that were inexpensively bound. He also acquired skills that were useful in his later work, and taught himself bookbinding. Having bought an old handpress and used type he taught himself composition and how to operate the press. He succeeded in producing 750 copies of a small edition of Burns, and he wrote, printed, and published several chapbooks, including *Exploits and Anecdotes of Scottish Gipsies*, a 6*d.* pamphlet. In addition, with the help of his brother Robert he attempted to publish a periodical. The first issue of the satirical *Kaleidoscope, or, Edinburgh Literary Amusement* appeared on 6 October 1821 but ceased publication on 12 January 1822. In spring 1823 Chambers moved to a shop in Broughton Street, Edinburgh. He attempted serious writing with the *Book of Scotland* (1830), an account of the machinery of Scottish government before the Union, and, with his brother Robert, *Gazetteer of Scotland* (1833). Though these publications did not make much financial sense he recalled that 'they were immensely serviceable as a training preparatory to the part which it was my destiny to take in the cheap literature movement of modern times' (Anderson and Rose, 84).

By this time Chambers was planning the publication that changed publishing history and made W. and R. Chambers a household name. He had become aware of the need for educational and entertaining reading material that the 'humbler orders'—to use his phrase—could afford to buy; influenced by the Society for the Diffusion of Useful Knowledge, he suggested to Robert Chambers that they publish a low-priced weekly paper for such readers. Initially sceptical, Robert agreed to provide literary assistance. *Chambers's Edinburgh Journal* appeared on 4 February 1832. William promised that among the wide range of essays and articles there would be a weekly story that would be 'no ordinary trash … but something really good' (Anderson and Rose, 85). Priced 1½d. per part, it became the first successful cheap weekly publication in Great Britain, a claim later rigorously defended by Chambers himself. By April 1832 30,000 copies were printed weekly. By issue 13 William had entered into an agreement with the publisher W. S. Orr to print a second edition in London (an association that ended in 1853 over complaints about the quality of Orr's paper and printing). Robert became joint editor after the fourteenth number. He oversaw the journal content and wrote articles, while William handled business matters. William ascribed their success to the fact that they never lost sight of their object 'to touch the heart—to purify the affections' (Anderson and Rose, 86), and they attracted many notable contributors, who in the early years included Maria Edgeworth, Thomas Hood, Harriet Martineau, David Masson, Hugh Miller, and Mary Russell Mitford. George Meredith published for the first time in the journal, as did many other major writers. William 'delighted in anecdotes' that percolated through the journal to 'the whole of society', from Glasgow millworkers to Cambridge schoolboys (ibid., 86–7).

Owing to the journal's success, William Chambers's bookselling business became a considerable and lucrative publishing firm. It soon moved to 19 Waterloo Place, and Robert joined William in officially founding W. and R. Chambers. The journal was followed by two non-fiction serials, *Chambers's Historical Newspaper* (1833) and *Chambers's Information for the People* (1833–5), which also was very popular. On 4 June 1833 William married Harriet Seddon, the only daughter of John Clark, engraver, of Westminster. They had three children, none of whom survived their day of birth.

The Chambers firm continued to introduce new publications. The Educational Course (1835–96) was a series of treatises and school textbooks that included the first on the physical sciences. In 1838 Chambers launched the People's Editions of standard authors such as Locke, Smollett, Burns, Scott, Crabbe, Addison, and Defoe; by 1840 the series of inexpensive reprints ran to thirty-two volumes. They also produced the *Miscellany of Useful and Entertaining Tracts* (1844), *Papers for the People* (1850), and ultimately *Chambers's Encyclopaedia: a Dictionary of Universal Knowledge* (1860–68). William, in his *Story of a Long and Busy Life* (1882), assessed the popular and profitable encyclopaedia as their 'crowning effort in cheap and instructive literature'. Edited by Andrew Findlater under the brothers' supervision, and based on the *Conversations-Lexikon*, the articles

were succinct and accessible, and the encyclopaedia distinguished itself from others by being easy to use. Subsequent editions have retained their reputation for thorough, erudite handling of subjects in the humanities, geography, and biography. The firm also ventured into dictionaries, of which *Chambers's English Dictionary* (1872) became a leader in the field.

Chambers also found time to write. *Tour in Holland and the Rhine Countries* (1839) was based on information gathered there; *Glenormiston* (1849) was about the estate that he bought for his home; *Fiddy: an Autobiography of a Dog* (1851) was produced for the national exhibition in Hyde Park; *Things as they are in America* (1854) and *American Slavery and Colour* (1857) recounted his journey to America; *History of Peeblesshire* (1864) was one of two books about his birthplace. Writing and the firm, however, did not take up all Chambers's energies. Asked by the poor law commissioner Edwin Chadwick to report on the sanitary condition of Edinburgh, he investigated the city carefully in the early 1840s. Comparing it with other cities in Great Britain and to cities on the continent, he concluded that Edinburgh was the dirtiest and had the foulest air of all. He also became a leading exponent of improved housing for the working classes and joined other city leaders in establishing the Pilrig Model Dwellings Company in 1849. By the end of the decade he had turned over the firm's management to Robert Chambers and purchased the estate of Glenormiston, near Peebles. He improved the estate extensively and built model houses for the farm labourers. In Peebles he acquired the Queensberry Lodging, which was remodelled to include a reading room, museum, art gallery, lecture hall, and 10,000-volume library; it was renamed the Chambers Institution. He was also associated with the Peebles Railway Company. But by 1860 he admitted in an unpublished memoir that 'the life of a country gentleman, fascinating as it appears, was not my rôle'.

During the remainder of his life Chambers's notable achievements were in Edinburgh. Having returned to manage the firm in 1860 he became involved again in housing reform and city improvement. He served as secretary of a committee proposing to restore Edinburgh's market cross to its original site. Elected lord provost of Edinburgh in 1865, he resolved to address sanitary improvements in the city, and personally inspected all the tenements, closes, and alleys in the Old Town. The City Improvement Act, passed in 1867, demolished old parts of the city south of the High Street. Since the work was unfinished when Chambers's term as lord provost expired he agreed to run again; re-elected, he retired once the work was completed. The act, at a cost of over a quarter of a million pounds, removed 2800 buildings and created many new streets, one of which—Chambers Street—was named in his honour. A statue of him, recognizing his contributions to the city, stands there today. While in office he also urged that Scotland be granted a national library, to be based on the Advocates' Library and open to public use.

On the death of his brother Robert in 1871, Chambers

once again became principal shareholder in the firm, and he thereafter assisted his nephew Robert in its direction. He wrote *Memoir of Robert Chambers* (1872), which included autobiographical material. A further edition was the joint accounts of the Chambers brothers. His major civic activity of the 1870s was restoring St Giles's Church, Edinburgh. During the seventeenth century its interior had been divided, serving four parishes. Both interior and exterior had been 'restored' early in the nineteenth century to suit neo-classical tastes; Chambers resolved to return it to something of its original grandeur. The four-stage renovation was to be financed through government, town council, and private donations. The project inevitably ruffled sectarian feathers and many pledges of support were withdrawn; Chambers therefore spent between £20,000 and £30,000 of his own money to carry the work to completion in 1883. He was not present for the service of reopening on 23 May 1883; he had died three days earlier, on 20 May, at his home, 13 Chester Street, Edinburgh. The first religious service in the newly designated high kirk of St Giles was William Chambers's funeral, on 25 May 1883.

William Chambers was of about middle height and dark-featured, with hair that greyed prematurely. He was rigorous and shrewd, and would not lend his name to projects in which he knew he could not take part. Naturally quiet and reserved, he was proud of his successes, adopting as his motto the Scottish proverb 'He that tholes overcomes'. Maintaining a policy of impartiality on controversial issues, he was considered a supporter of liberal governmental policies. He attended the Church of Scotland but was attached to the ritual of the Church of England. Awarded an honorary LLD by Edinburgh University in 1872, he rejected a knighthood offered by William Gladstone in 1881. Although he accepted a baronetcy in 1883 he did not live to receive it. His estate amounted to nearly £92,000, of which £58,000 accounted for his twenty shares in W. and R. Chambers. He was buried in Peebles on 25 May 1883 at the site of the original parish church, St Andrew's, whose tower he had restored as his memorial. At his death the directorship of W. and R. Chambers passed to Robert *Chambers (1832–1888), the son of his brother Robert. The firm was still a major force in reference works—for instance with *Chambers's Biographical Dictionary*—at the end of the twentieth century.

SONDRA MILEY COONEY

Sources W. Chambers, *Memoir of William and Robert Chambers*, 13th edn (1884) · W. Chambers, *Story of a long and busy life* (1882) · NL Scot., W. and R. Chambers MS deposit 341 · family papers, priv. coll. · P. J. Anderson and J. Rose, eds., *British literary publishing houses, 1820–1880*, DLitB, 106 (1991)
Archives NL Scot., corresp. and business papers
Likenesses J. W. Gordon, oils, c.1859, Chambers Institute, Peebles · J. Horsburgh, oils, c.1884, Chambers Harrap, Edinburgh · J. Horsburgh, oils, c.1884 (after lithograph?), Chambers Harrap, Edinburgh · R. C. Bell, double portrait, line engraving (with his brother, Robert; after J. R. Fairman), BM; repro. in W. Chambers, *Memoir of Robert Chambers* (1872) · D. J. Pound, line engraving (after photograph by Mayall), BM; repro. in D. J. Pound, *The drawing room portrait gallery of eminent personages* (1859–60) · chromolithograph, NPG · lithograph, repro. in M. Wood, *The lord provosts of Edinburgh*

(1932) · plaster bust, Chambers Harrap, Edinburgh · statue, Chambers Street, Edinburgh
Wealth at death under £92,000: confirmation, 22 June 1883, *CCI*

Chambers, William Frederick (1786–1855), physician, was born in India on 10 October 1786, the eldest son of William Chambers (d. 1793), a political servant of the East India Company and a distinguished oriental scholar, and his wife, Charity, daughter of Sir Thomas Fraser, of Balmain, Inverness-shire. Sir Robert Chambers (1737–1803) was his uncle. Chambers moved to England in 1793 and was educated at Bath grammar school and at Westminster School, where he was a king's scholar. He was elected to a scholarship at Trinity College, Cambridge, where he graduated BA (1808), MA (1811), and MD (1818).

After leaving Cambridge Chambers studied medicine in London at St George's Hospital and the Great Windmill Street school of medicine, and at Edinburgh. He was made inceptor candidate of the Royal College of Physicians, London, on 22 December 1813, candidate on 30 September 1818, fellow on 30 September 1819, censor in 1822 and 1836, *consiliarius* in 1836, 1841, and 1845, and elect in 1847. He became a fellow of the Royal Society on 13 March 1828.

On 20 April 1816 Chambers was elected physician to St George's Hospital, though the youngest of the candidates, and he held the post until 1839; his course of lectures on practical medicine was reported in the *Medical Gazette*. Between 1819 and 1835 he was also physician to the East India Company, and he was honorary physician to the Lock Hospital. For some time his private practice did not increase, and in 1820 his receipts were only about £200; however, from that year onwards he became more successful and began to acquire a large consulting practice among the upper classes. On 10 February 1821 he married Mary (d. 1839), daughter of William Mackinen Fraser, and moved to 10 Curzon Street, London.

Chambers was gazetted physician-in-ordinary to Queen Adelaide on 25 October 1836, and physician-in-ordinary to William IV on 4 May 1837. Ernest, the new king of Hanover, created him KCH on 8 August 1837; however, Chambers asked if he might decline the assumption of the ordinary prefix of knighthood and his request was granted. Chambers became physician-in-ordinary to Queen Victoria on 8 August 1837, and to the duchess of Kent in 1839. He continued to be the leading physician in London, with an income of between 7000 and 9000 guineas a year, until 1848, when he suffered a stroke which forced him to retire. Shortly after he had given up practising a notice of his death appeared in a medical journal, and was contradicted by himself.

Chambers was meticulous in his record keeping and left sixty-seven volumes of notes and prescriptions, all carefully recorded in Latin. His only contribution to medical literature was a series of papers on cholera, printed in *The Lancet* on 10 and 17 February and 3 March 1849. His manuscripts of cases in St George's Hospital between 1814 and 1828, in ten folio volumes, were preserved in the library of the Royal Medical and Chirurgical Society.

In 1834 a poisoned wound, occasioned during a post-mortem examination, had nearly cost Chambers his life, and he never fully recovered. On his retirement he took up residence on his estate at Hordlecliffe, near Lymington, Hampshire, where he died of paralysis on 16 December 1855.   G. C. BOASE, *rev.* KAYE BAGSHAW

Sources The Lancet (22 Dec 1855), 612 · The Lancet (25 May 1850), 632–8 · Munk, *Roll* · A. G. W. Whitfield, 'The gentle queen', *Journal of the Royal College of Physicians of London*, 20 (1986), 63–6 · H. Rolleston, 'William Frederic Chambers', *Annals of Medical History*, 3rd ser., 4 (1942), 89–94 · *GM*, 1st ser., 91/1 (1821), 181

Archives RCP Lond., corresp., notes, etc.

Likenesses H. Droehmer, mezzotint, pubd 1850 (after T. Hollins), BM, NPG · portrait, repro. in Rolleston, 'William Frederic Chambers'

Chambré, Sir Alan (1739–1823), judge, was born on 4 October 1739 at the New Inn, Highgate, Kendal, Westmorland, the eldest son of Walter Chambré, barrister, of Halhead Hall, Kendal, and his wife, Mary, daughter of Jacob Morland, of Capplethwaite Hall, Westmorland. After receiving an early education at the free grammar school of the town he was sent to Sedbergh School, and from Sedbergh he went to London, where he became a member of the Society of Staple Inn. He removed to Middle Temple in February 1758, and in November 1764 from the Middle Temple to Gray's Inn. In May 1767 he was called to the bar, and during term time he dined and slept at a villa taken by Lloyd Kenyon, later chief justice of king's bench, along with other rising barristers of the time, including John Dunning, James Mansfield, and Edward Thurlow. He went the northern circuit, of which he soon became one of the leaders. He was elected to the bench of Gray's Inn in June 1781, and in 1783 filled the annual office of treasurer.

In 1796 Chambré was appointed recorder of Lancaster. On the retirement of Sir Richard Perryn from the court of exchequer in early summer 1799 he was chosen as successor. By tradition all judges were required, prior to judicial appointment, to have become serjeants-at-law, and since serjeants could be called only in term, a special act of parliament (39 Geo. III c. 67) was passed authorizing for the first time the appointment of a serjeant in the vacation. Accordingly, Chambré received the degree of serjeant on 2 July 1799, and on the same day was appointed a baron of exchequer. He also received the customary knighthood. Lord Chief Justice Eyre dying five days after the special act had received the royal assent, the same difficulty again occurred, and a general act (39 Geo. III c. 113) was passed in the same session authorizing the appointment of any barrister to the degree of serjeant during the vacation if done for the purpose of filling a vacancy on the bench. On 13 June in the following year Chambré transferred to the court of common pleas as successor to Sir Francis Buller. Here he remained until December 1815 when he resigned his seat, receiving a pension of £2000 a year.

Chambré had a high reputation at the bar both for his legal knowledge and for the justness of his decisions. He was described by Lord Brougham as 'among the first ornaments of his profession, as among the most honest and amiable of men' (Brougham, 1.117). So extremely careful was he lest any of his actions should be misconstrued that,

it is said, he once refused an invitation to a house where the judges usually dined when on circuit, because the owner had been a defendant in one of the causes which had been tried at an assize at which he had lately presided. He conscientiously sought the opinion of his brother judges on issues that arose at trial if there was the least doubt. Thus at the Hereford spring assizes 1803 a woman was convicted of infanticide, but in the confusion of disposing a group of prisoners, Chambré accidentally omitted stating in open court the portion of the sentence calling for the woman's body to be dissected and anatomized. He therefore respited the woman's execution to take the opinion of the judges on the legal effect of his omission, and although he was of the opinion that the omission was not fatal, a majority of the judges thought otherwise, and the prisoner was reprieved (Russell and Ryan, 58).

Chambré was a close friend of Edward Law, later Lord Ellenborough. On his appointment to exchequer, Law wrote to Chambré: 'I feel a selfish regret for losing you upon the circuit—in matters of public and private conduct I have no longer an adviser to whom I can defer with confidence as I could to you' (26 June 1799, BL, Add. MS 21507, fol. 411). He died at The Crown inn, Harrogate, on 20 September 1823 in his eighty-fourth year, and was buried in the family vault in Kendal parish church, where a monument was erected to his memory. He never married, and his nephew, Thomas Chambré, succeeded to his estates.   JAMES OLDHAM

Sources H. Brougham, *Historical sketches of statesmen who flourished in the time of George III* (1839) · W. O. Russell and E. Ryan, *Crown cases reserved* (1825) · Foss, *Judges* · G. T. Kenyon, *The life of Lloyd, first Lord Kenyon* (1873) · J. Haydn, *The book of dignities: containing lists of the official personages of the British empire*, ed. H. Ockerby, 3rd edn (1894); repr. as *Haydn's book of dignities* (1969) · G. Atkinson, *The worthies of Westmorland*, 2 vols. (1849–50) · C. Durnford and E. H. East, *Reports of cases* (1811), vol. 8 · *GM*, 1st ser., 93/2 (1823), 469 · C. Nicholson, *The annals of Kendal* (1832) · A. Polson, *Law and lawyers, or, Sketches and illustrations of legal history and biography*, 2 vols. (1840)

Likenesses H. Meyer, mezzotint (after Allan), NPG

Wealth at death £2000 pension at retirement: Foss, *Judges*

Chambre, John (1470–1549), physician and cleric, was born in Northumberland. He studied at Oxford, where he was elected fellow of Merton College in 1492, and, after taking orders, became rector of Tichmarsh in Northamptonshire. Having obtained his MA, he visited Italy and studied medicine there, graduating at Padua in 1506. On his return to England he became physician to Henry VII, and later to Henry VIII.

When the College of Physicians was founded in 1518, Chambre was the first of six founders named in the charter. He became censor in 1523. In 1531 he received the degree of DM at Oxford. Chambre is also associated with the incorporation of surgery in England, for in Holbein's picture of the granting of a charter to the barber–surgeons in 1541, Chambre is depicted as the first of the three royal physicians on the king's right hand, witnessing the giving of the sealed charter into the hand of Thomas Vicary. He wears a gown trimmed with fur, and has a biretta-like cap on his head. He has a straight but somewhat short nose, well-marked eyebrows, a very long clean-shaven chin, and an almost severe expression of face.

Chambre left no medical publications, but some of his prescriptions for lotions and plasters were preserved in manuscript (BL, Sloane MS 1047, fols. 25–9, 84–6), and a letter signed by him on the health of Queen Jane Seymour after the birth of Prince Edward is extant.

Apart from medicine, Chambre pursued a successful career in the church. In 1508 he became vicar of Bowden in Leicestershire. From 1494 to 1509 he held the prebend of Coringham and from 1509 to 1549 that of Leighton Buzzard, both in Lincoln Cathedral; and in the same diocese as then constituted, he held the archdeaconry of Bedford from 1525 to 1549. He was also treasurer of Wells from 1510 to 1543, and in 1537 canon of Wiveliscombe, Somerset. He was precentor of Exeter from 1524 to 1549, canon of Windsor from 1509 to 1549, warden of Merton College, Oxford, from 1525 to 1544, archdeacon of Meath from 1540 to 1542, and dean of the collegiate chapel of St Stephen's, Westminster. Thus in 1540 Chambre was head of a college at Oxford, and held preferments in one Irish and three English dioceses.

Chambre built the beautiful cloisters of St Stephen's Chapel, Westminster, at his own cost, but lived to see them demolished during the Reformation, while he himself subscribed to the articles of faith in 1536. He died in 1549, and was buried in July in St Margaret's Church, Westminster.

NORMAN MOORE, rev. SARAH BAKEWELL

Sources Munk, *Roll* · Foster, *Alum. Oxon.*
Archives BL, Sloane MSS, MS 1047 fols. 25–9, 84–6
Likenesses H. Holbein, 1541 (*The granting of a charter to the barber-surgeons*) · H. Holbein, junior, oils, *c.*1541–1543, Kunsthistorisches Museum, Vienna, Austria · W. Hollar, etching, 1684 (after H. Holbein, 1543), Wellcome L. · attrib. P. Oliver, miniature (after H. Holbein), RCP Lond. · etching (after P. Oliver), Wellcome L. · line engraving (after H. Holbein), Wellcome L.

Chambre, William (*fl.* 1365?), supposed narrator of an account of Richard Bury, bishop of Durham, is recorded as its originator in only one of the three surviving copies preserved by the monks of Durham, all of the late fourteenth or early fifteenth century. In this copy, BL, Cotton MS Titus A.ii, fols. 132 and 133*v*, it is placed after the brief account of Bishop Bury (*d.* 1345), said to be on a board (*tabula*), which was most probably hung in Durham Cathedral; this was printed as the final paragraph of one of the chapters devoted to Bury in the edition of the Durham chronicles published by James Raine in 1839 (p. 130). The rest of that chapter is the account said to have been narrated by Chambre, with its final paragraph, concerning Bury's reaction to the death of the Durham chronicler Robert Greystones in 1334, preceded by a second attribution to Chambre.

One of the other medieval copies (Bodl. Oxf., MS Fairfax 6, fol. 133) is followed by an assemblage of materials relating to the bishops of Durham and the cathedral community down to the burial of Canon William Stevenson in

1575; there is good reason to think that the antiquary William Claxton (*d.* 1596/7) had a large hand in this, and also in a similar assemblage, where the materials added in the later sixteenth century begin with the accounts of Bishop Bury (Bodl. Oxf., MS Laud misc. 700). When Wharton came to print the Durham chronicles in his *Anglia sacra* in 1691, he put the entire final portion, from Bury down to 1575, under the name of Willelmus Chambre, although perhaps with some misgiving. In 1839 James Raine did the same, but after the preliminary matter to his edition had been printed, he discovered a copy of a grant for life, by the prior and monks of Durham, to one William Chaumbre of the office of the marshalcy of the hall in the abbey dated 1365; he printed the document in his preface, taking this William to be the author, and suggesting that he recorded occurrences down to the early fifteenth century.

The position of marshal of the guest hall at Durham Priory was not an elevated one: in 1365–6 the annual stipend was 10s., with clothing worth £1 also provided, and presumably board and lodging. None the less it is quite possible that Chambre had served in Bury's household, perhaps from about 1326, when the account begins to contain telling detail, that many years later he took employment with the Durham monks, and that they then recorded in Latin what he told them about his former master. This would chime well with the descriptions of grand occasions, the style of Bury's entourage, and the scale of his generosity. Chambre probably died and was buried in Durham.

A. J. PIPER

Sources [H. Wharton], ed., *Anglia sacra*, 1 (1691), 765–84 · *Historiae Dunelmensis scriptores tres: Gaufridus de Coldingham, Robertus de Graystanes, et Willielmus de Chambre*, ed. J. Raine, SurtS, 9 (1839), preface, xiv–xvi; 127–56 · hostillers account, 1365–6, Durham Dean and Chapter Muniments · N. Denholm-Young, 'The birth of a chronicle', *Bodleian Quarterly Record*, 7 (1932–4), 325–8 · A. I. Doyle, 'William Claxton and the Durham chronicles', *Books and collectors, 1200–1700: essays presented to Andrew Watson*, ed. J. P. Carley and C. G. C. Tite (1997), 335–55
Archives BL, Cotton MS Titus A.ii, fols. 132, 133*v* | Bodl. Oxf., MS Fairfax 6, fol. 133 · Bodl. Oxf., MS Laud misc. 700

Chamier, Anthony (1725–1780), financier and government official, was born on 6 October 1725 and baptized on 19 October 1725 at the French Huguenot chapel in Threadneedle Street, London, the fifth of the nine children of Daniel Chamier (1696–1741), merchant, and Susanne de la Mejanelle (1701/2–1787). His paternal grandfather, Daniel Chamier, was a Reformed minister from Neufchâtel who had sought refuge in 1691. After working as a stockbroker in Change Alley, Anthony Chamier became an influential financier and a trusted financial expert of the governments of Newcastle and Bute. At Chigwell, Essex, on 3 October 1753, he married Dorothy, the daughter and coheir of Robert Wilson, a merchant, of Woodford; they had no children. His sister-in-law Elizabeth Wilson married Thomas Bradshaw (1733–1774), a clerk successively in the war office and the Treasury, whose ministerial connections had aided Chamier's career.

In February 1763 Chamier was recommended by Lord Barrington as private secretary to the newly appointed ambassador to Madrid, Lord Sandwich; neither Chamier nor Sandwich travelled to Spain. Barrington then gave Chamier a position in the war office as secretary to the commander-in-chief. Chamier rose to become deputy secretary at war in 1772, and in 1775 he was named under-secretary of state for the southern department under Lord Weymouth. Weymouth's interest secured his election as MP for Tamworth in June 1778, but Chamier had no political ambitions and never spoke in the Commons. He seems to have preferred London's literary society; he was a founder member in 1764 of the Literary Club, and Samuel Johnson and Sir Joshua Reynolds were frequent visitors to his house at Epsom in Surrey. His portrait was painted three times by Reynolds.

Chamier died in Savile Row, London, on 12 October 1780, only a month after his re-election as MP for Tamworth. He was buried at St James's, Piccadilly, and he left his property to his nephew John Deschamps (1754–1831), on condition that he assume the name and arms of the Chamier family.   W. P. COURTNEY, rev. S. J. SKEDD

Sources J. Brooke, 'Chamier, Anthony', HoP, Commons, 1754–90 · GM, 1st ser., 50 (1780), 495 · W. P. Courthope, Memoir of Daniel Chamier, minister of the Reformed Church, with notices of his descendants (1852), 53–5 · C. E. Lart, Huguenot pedigrees, 2 vols. (1924–8), 2.25 · D. C. A. Agnew, Protestant exiles from France, chiefly in the reign of Louis XIV, or, The Huguenot refugees and their descendants in Great Britain and Ireland, 3rd edn, 2 vols. (1886) · C. R. Leslie and T. Taylor, Life and times of Sir Joshua Reynolds, 2 vols. (1865), 1.219, 228, 237, 250; 2.203, 286 · IGI · will, PRO, PROB 11/1069
Archives BL, letters to Sir Robert Keith, Add. MSS 35507–35518 · Suffolk RO, Bury St Edmunds, letters to duke of Grafton
Likenesses J. Reynolds, oils, exh. 1762, Pennsylvania Museum, Philadelphia · J. Reynolds, three portraits, 1762–77 · W. Ward, mezzotint (after J. Reynolds, exh. 1762), BM, NPG

Chamier, Frederick (1796–1870), naval officer, son of John Chamier (d. 23 Feb 1831), member of council for the Madras presidency, and Georgiana Grace, eldest daughter of Admiral Sir William *Burnaby, bt, was born in London in 1796. He entered the navy in June 1809, on board the Salsette, in which he served on the Walcheren expedition. He was afterwards midshipman of the Fame and of the Arethusa in the Mediterranean, and from 1811 to 1814 was in the Menelaus with Sir Peter Parker. During the Anglo-American War of 1812–14 the Menelaus went up the Chesapeake, and Chamier was ashore with Parker when the latter was killed at Bellair on 30 August 1814. On 6 July 1815 Chamier was promoted lieutenant, and continued serving in the Mediterranean, on the home station, and in the West Indies until 9 August 1826, when he was promoted to the command of the sloop Britomart, which he brought home and paid off in 1827. He had no further employment, and in 1833 was placed on the retired list, on which he was promoted captain on 1 April 1856.

In June 1832 Chamier married Elizabeth, daughter of John Soane of Chelsea and granddaughter of Sir John *Soane. They had one daughter. On his retirement he settled in the neighbourhood of Waltham Abbey (where he was magistrate for Essex and Hertfordshire) and devoted himself to literary pursuits. He was the author of several 'naval' novels, imitations of Marryat's, which had at one time considerable popularity: these included Life of a Sailor (1832) and Tom Bowline (1841). He also published some lesser works. Of greater value was his editing and continuing down to 1827 of William James's Naval History (1837); in his introduction Chamier good-humouredly disposed of disparaging criticism of the original work by Captain Edward Pelham *Brenton. He died in Paris on 29 October 1870, his wife surviving him.

J. K. LAUGHTON, rev. ROGER MORRISS

Sources O'Byrne, Naval biog. dict. · The Times (2 Nov 1870) · Boase, Mod. Eng. biog. · CGPLA Eng. & Wales (1870)
Likenesses S. Freeman, stipple (after L. Schmitz), BM, NPG; repro. in New Monthly Magazine, 52 (1838), cover
Wealth at death under £6000: probate, 5 Dec 1870, CGPLA Eng. & Wales

Chamier, Stephen Henry Edward (1834–1910), army officer, was born in Madras on 17 August 1834, of Huguenot descent, the fifth son of Henry Chamier of Upton Park, Slough, chief secretary to the Madras government and afterwards member of council, 1843–8, and his wife, Marie Antoinette Evelina, daughter of Thomas Thursby HEICS. His grandfather, Jean Ezéchiel Deschamps Chamier, was also a member of the Madras council. Captain Frederick Chamier was an uncle.

Educated at Cheltenham College and Addiscombe, Chamier was appointed on 11 June 1853 second-lieutenant in the Madras artillery, and joined artillery headquarters at St Thomas Mount on 8 October 1853. Posted to the 1st battery in March 1854, he went to Burma in July 1854. After commanding an outpost of artillery at Sittang on 3 August 1854, he was appointed station staff officer there on 16 November 1854. On 11 April 1856 he went on field service to the Karen hills in command of a mountain train of howitzers and rockets, and was engaged with hill Karens on 22 April.

After commanding B battery horse artillery for a few months at Bangalore, Chamier went in May 1857 to Madras en route for Burma, but following the news of the mutiny at Meerut he went with Major Cotter's horse battery to Calcutta and from there to Benares and Allahabad. Detached to Gopiganj with two guns and some infantry, he disarmed a part of the Bengal native infantry. Proceeding to Mirzapur and on towards Rewah, he held the Katra Pass, where he was joined by a Madras regiment and C battery Madras artillery, and was given command of a battery. Ordered to Cawnpore to aid General Windham's operations against the Gwalior contingent, the force was continuously engaged for three days, with heavy loss; of thirty-six men with Chamier's guns seventeen were killed or wounded. Chamier was thanked in dispatches. He also took part on 8 December 1857 in the rout of the Gwalior contingent mutineers by Sir Colin Campbell in the vicinity of Cawnpore.

At his own request Chamier, in February 1858, rejoined Major Cotter's horse battery and marched with General Franks from Benares through Oudh to Lucknow, engaging on the way in the actions of Chanda, Amirpur, Sultanpur, and various skirmishes. At Lucknow Chamier joined the 5th division of the army under Lord Clyde, and took part in the operations before and during the siege and capture of the city. After its fall Chamier's battery joined the force which went under Major-General Lugard to the relief of Azamgarh, being engaged against Kunwar Singh's rebel force and against other rebels near Jagdispur and Arrah. In June 1858 the campaign, during which, according to artillery orders, Chamier was engaged in nineteen actions, came to a close.

In September 1858 Lord Canning, the governor-general, appointed Chamier commandant of the 1st artillery battery, Hyderabad contingent. He was promoted second captain on 29 February 1864 and brevet major on 11 October 1864 for his actions in the field. After commanding a battery of horse artillery at home from 1872 to 1876, he was, on promotion to regimental lieutenant-colonel, put in command of two batteries at Barrackpore. From 1877 to 1881 he was deputy inspector-general and from 1881 to 1886 inspector-general of ordnance, Madras. During his tenure expeditions were sent to Malta, Afghanistan, and Upper Burma, and he received the thanks of the Madras government and of the viceroy. He retired in October 1886 with the rank of lieutenant-general, being made CB (1886) for his services during the Indian mutiny and receiving the reward for distinguished service. On 4 September 1858 Chamier married, at Dinapore, Dora Louisa, daughter of George Tyrrell MD, of Banbridge, co. Down, Ireland, and they had six daughters and three sons. Chamier was a good musician and played the violoncello. He graduated MusB of Trinity College, Dublin, in 1874. He was a fellow of the Huguenot Society. He died after a long illness at his residence, Brooke House, Camberley, on 9 June 1910. His wife survived him with two daughters and one son, George Daniel, lieutenant-colonel of the Royal Artillery.

H. M. VIBART, rev. JAMES LUNT

Sources The Times (11 June 1910) · Hart's Army List · J. W. Kaye and G. B. Malleson, Kaye's and Malleson's History of the Indian mutiny of 1857–8, new edn, 6 vols. (1897–8) · G. W. Forrest, Indian mutiny, 2 (1904) · W. J. Wilson, ed., History of the Madras army, 5 vols. (1882–9) · Kelly, Handbk · WWW
Archives Royal Artillery Institution, Woolwich, London, letters during Indian mutiny
Wealth at death £7678 9s. 6d.: probate, 22 July 1910, CGPLA Eng. & Wales

Chamot, Mary (1899–1993), art historian and museum curator, was born in Strelna, near St Petersburg, Russia, on 8 November 1899, the only child of Alfred Edward Chamot (1855–1934) and Elisabeth, née Grooten (1854–1935). Her English-born father was of French descent, her mother of Dutch and German origin. He was administrator of the imperial palace gardens, and belonged to the prosperous Anglo-Russian merchant community. Educated privately, Mary learned to speak English, French, Russian, and German with admirable fluency, and began her fine art studies at Dmitry Nikolayevich Kardowski's painting class at St Petersburg Academy (c.1915–16).

After the outbreak of the Russian Revolution Mary accompanied her parents to England, via Finland and Norway, in 1918, where she continued her studies at the Slade School of Fine Art, London, from 1919, gaining her diploma in 1922. Although talented as an artist, she trained in art history under Tancred Borenius and earned her living as a lecturer, first at the National Gallery (1922–4), then at the Victoria and Albert Museum (1924–39), and as an extension (extramural) lecturer for London University. Her first book, English Medieval Enamels (1930), was a popular introduction to the subject in a series edited by Borenius; it was followed by a pioneering work, Modern Painting in England (London and New York, 1937), and a complementary volume, Painting in England from Hogarth to Whistler (1939); she also translated books and organized exhibitions, notably one of Russian art in 1935. She wrote in an informed and easily accessible style, qualities characterizing her articles and reviews for Apollo and Country Life.

During the Second World War, Mary Chamot worked in postal and telegraph censorship, and her excellent linguistic skills were fully utilized when she served as an interpreter to the Allied Control Commission in Vienna from 1945 to 1949. In October 1949 she was appointed assistant keeper at the Tate Gallery, London, and compiled The British School: a Concise Catalogue (1953). This was the prelude to more detailed, scholarly publications on the Tate collections, and in 1964, in collaboration with Martin Butlin and Dennis Farr, she produced the two-volume Modern British School catalogue which contained much new information from the artists themselves and is an important reference book for twentieth-century British art. She collaborated with Sir John Rothenstein on the Early Works of J. M. W. Turner (1965), an artist whose work she greatly admired and which she had begun to catalogue before her retirement in 1965.

Mary Chamot's early days at the Slade had brought her a wide circle of artist friends and collectors, notably Stanley and Gilbert Spencer, the Carlines, Paul Methuen, Edward Bawden, and Jim Ede. Although she was gregarious, and had cousins and relations in every major European city, not to mention North America, she was in many ways a very private person. For many years she shared a house in Kensington (19 Gordon Place) with Helen (Lulette) Gerebzov, where they threw marvellously Russian parties, and she never lost her affection for Russia. In 1963 she published Russian Painting and Sculpture, and wrote the first monograph on her friend Natalya Goncharova, a leading pre-Revolution avant-garde artist and famous stage designer, which appeared first in Paris (1972), then in English in 1979. She contributed an essay to the Arts Council's 'Larionov and Goncharova' retrospective exhibition in 1961.

Mary Chamot was of medium height and stockily built; she had grace of character and indomitable spirit. Her schoolfriends had affectionately nicknamed her Marienka Verbliud ('Little Mary Camel')—a typically polyglot pun on the French word chameau. She could be devastatingly witty and direct, especially with Soviet bureaucrats, as those who accompanied her on the select tour parties she led with great verve to the USSR after her retirement soon discovered; but she could also be exceedingly kind and generous, and was much loved. In her later years she bore increasing deafness with great fortitude. She died at Weald Hall, Mayfield Lane, a nursing home near Wadhurst, Sussex, on 10 May 1993, and was cremated ten days later at Tunbridge Wells crematorium, Kent. She did not marry.   DENNIS FARR

Sources personal knowledge (2004) · private information (2004) [Colin Hutchinson, cousin] · *Geschichte der Familie Chamot* (privately printed, Germany, [n.d.]) · D. Farr, 'Mary Chamot', *The Independent* (17 May 1993), 20 · [R. Alley], *The Times* (21 May 1993), 19 · minutes of board meeting, 6 Oct 1949, Tate collection, 77 · *Who's who in art* (1934) · *Who's who in art* (1986) · *CGPLA Eng. & Wales* (1993)

Archives Tate collection, staff MSS

Likenesses black and white photographs, priv. coll.

Wealth at death £173,553: probate, 12 Nov 1993, *CGPLA Eng. & Wales*

Champain, Sir John Underwood Bateman- (1835–1887),

army officer and engineer in the East India Company, second son of Colonel Agnew Champain (*d.* 1876), of the 9th foot, was born in Gloucester Place, London, on 22 July 1835. Educated at Cheltenham College and for a short time in fortification and military drawing at the private Edinburgh military academy under Lieutenant (afterwards Colonel Sir) Henry Yule, he passed through Addiscombe College (1851–3), at the head of his term, receiving the Pollock medal. He obtained a commission as second lieutenant, Bengal Engineers, on 11 June 1853. He was promoted lieutenant on 13 July 1857, and then, successively, captain (1 September 1863), major (5 July 1872), lieutenant-colonel (31 December 1878), and colonel (31 December 1882). In 1872 he assumed the name Bateman in addition to his original surname of Champain on succeeding to the estate of Halton Park, Lancashire.

After the usual Chatham course Champain went to India in 1854. While he was acting as assistant principal of the engineering college at Roorkee the uprising of 1857 broke out, and he at once saw active service under Colonel Archdale Wilson, was adjutant of sappers and miners at the actions at Ghazi-ud-din-Nagar on the Hindan River on 30 and 31 May, at Badli-ki-sarai under Major-General Bernard on 8 June, and at the capture of the ridge in front of Delhi. During the siege of Delhi, Champain took his full share of general engineer work in addition to his duties as adjutant, and one of the siege batteries was named after him by order of the chief engineer in acknowledgement of his services. He was wounded by a grapeshot on 13 September, but, although still on the sick list, volunteered for duty on 20 September, and was present at the capture of the palace of Delhi.

Champain commanded the headquarters detachment of Bengal sappers during the march to Agra, at the capture of Fatehpur Sikri, and in numerous minor expeditions. He commanded a mixed force of nearly 2000 men on the march from Agra to Fatehgarh, where he joined the commander-in-chief in December 1857. He commanded the sappers during the march to Cawnpore and to the Alambagh, reverting to the adjutancy in March 1858, when he joined the force under Sir James Outram for the siege of Lucknow by Lord Clyde. After the capture of Lucknow he erected some twenty fortified posts for outlying detachments. In April he was specially employed under

Brigadier-General John Douglas in the Ghazipur and Shahabad districts, was present in fourteen minor engagements, and was thanked in dispatches for his services at the action of Ballia. He joined in the pursuit of the mutineers, who were driven to the Kaimur hills and finally defeated and broken up at Salia Dahar on 24 November 1858.

When the uprising was finally suppressed Champain became executive engineer in the public works department at Goudah, and afterwards at Lucknow, until February 1862, when he was selected to go with Major Patrick Stewart to Persia on government telegraph duty. At that time there was no electric telegraph to India. The attempt to construct one under a government guarantee had failed, and it was determined to make a line by the Persian Gulf route directly under government. Champain proceeded with Stewart to Bushehr and thence in June to Tehran, where negotiations were carried on with the Persian government. In 1865 the line was practically completed, and on Stewart's death in that year Champain was appointed to assist Sir Frederic Goldsmid, the chief director of the Indo-European government telegraph department. He spent the greater part of 1866 in Turkey, putting the Baghdad part of the line into an efficient state, and in 1867 went to St Petersburg to negotiate for a special wire through Russia to join the Persian system. This visit gave rise to close relations with General Lüders, director-general of Russian telegraphs, which proved of advantage to the service.

On his way out from England in September 1869, to superintend the laying of a second telegraph cable from Bushehr to Jask, Champain was nearly drowned in the wreck of the steamship *Carnatic* off the island of Shadwan in the Red Sea. After coming to the surface he assisted in saving lives. In 1870 he succeeded Goldsmid as chief director of the government Indo-European telegraph.

From 1870 to 1872 Persia suffered from a severe famine, and Champain took an active interest in the Mansion House relief fund, of which he was for some time secretary. He arranged for its distribution in Persia by the telegraph staff, and had the satisfaction of finding it very well done. His judgement, tact, and clear expression of his views enabled him to render important service at the periodical international telegraph conferences as the representative of the Indian government. Questions frequently arose which took him to many of the European capitals, and on his duties he made repeated visits to India, Turkey, Persia, and the Persian Gulf. In 1884 the shah of Persia presented him with a magnificent sword of honour. In October 1885 Champain went for the last time to the Persian Gulf, to lay a third cable between Bushehr and Jask, afterwards visiting Calcutta to confer with government. On his way home he went to Delhi to see his old friend Sir Frederick (later Earl) Roberts, from whom he learned that he had been made a KCMG (December 1885).

Champain married in 1865 Harriet Sophia, daughter of Sir Frederick Currie, first baronet (*d.* 1875). She survived her husband with six sons and two daughters; three sons went into the army and one into the navy. Champain was a member of the councils of the Royal Geographical Society and Society of Telegraph Engineers. He was an accomplished draughtsman. In the Albert Hall Exhibition of 1873 a gold medal was awarded to his painting of a Persian landscape. Many of the illustrations to Sir Frederic Goldsmid's *Telegraph and Travel* are from Champain's watercolour sketches. Champain died at San Remo, Italy, on 1 February 1887.					R. H. VETCH, rev. ROGER T. STEARN

Sources BL OIOC · W. Porter, *History of the corps of royal engineers*, 2 vols. (1889) · H. M. Vibart, *Addiscombe: its heroes and men of note* (1894) · F. J. Goldsmid, *Telegraph and travel* (1874) · R. M. Smith, *Royal Engineers Journal* (1887) · *The Times* (2 Feb 1887) · *Annual Register* (1887) · H. W. Norman, *A narrative of the campaign of the Delhi army* (1858) · J. W. Kaye, *A history of the Sepoy War in India, 1857–1858*, 9th edn, 3 vols. (1880) · G. B. Malleson, *History of the Indian mutiny, 1857–1858: commencing from the close of the second volume of Sir John Kaye's History of the Sepoy War*, 3 vols. (1878–80) · J. G. Medley, *A year's campaigning in India: from March 1857 to March 1858* (1858) · C. Hibbert, *The great mutiny, India, 1857* (1978) · Boase, *Mod. Eng. biog.* · D. R. Headrick, *The tentacles of progress: technology transfer in the age of imperialism, 1850–1940* (1988) · *CGPLA Eng. & Wales* (1887)
Wealth at death £1278 4s. 3d.: probate, 9 March 1887, *CGPLA Eng. & Wales*

Champernowne, Sir Arthur (*b.* in or before **1524**, *d.* **1578**), soldier and naval commander, was the second son of Sir Philip Champernowne (*d.* 1545), landowner of Modbury, Devon, and his wife, Katherine, daughter of Sir Edmund Carew of Mohun's Ottery, Devon, and his wife, Katherine. He entered royal service shortly after reaching adulthood, probably helped by his brother-in-law Sir Anthony *Denny (1501–1549), groom of the stool and first chief gentleman of the privy chamber. After Sir Philip Champernowne's death in 1545 he was head of the family for a time, as his elder brother, John Champernowne, had died in 1541 and John's son, Henry *Champernowne (1537/8–1570), was only an infant. His own inheritance (as a younger son) was not large, but he managed his nephew's patrimony well and the two remained close later in life.

Arthur Champernowne won praise from Edward Seymour, first earl of Hertford, for good service around Boulogne in 1546. A crucial step was his marriage by 1547 to Mary, daughter of Henry *Norris (*d.* 1536) of Bray, Berkshire, and his wife, Margery, and widow of Sir George Carew (*c.*1504–1545) of Mohun's Ottery. This union brought him her jointure of lands worth £65 per annum. He used this income as the basis for building up his estates and proved an adept manipulator of the land market. The couple had five sons and a daughter. In 1547 Champernowne stood successfully as MP for Barnstaple, Devon, in a by-election, and on 10 November 1549 he was knighted, after having helped to crush the western rebellion.

Champernowne was personally a zealous protestant, but he rallied support in Devon for the legitimate succession of Mary Tudor in July 1553 against Lady Jane Grey, and received a royal letter of thanks as a result. This was ironic, for the restoration of Roman Catholicism changed his views. In early 1554 he flirted with a conspiracy led by his cousin Sir Peter *Carew (1514?–1575). It came to nought and Champernowne let himself be arrested, but though he was released in May, after less than four months in prison, the Marian regime was suspicious of him and two years later, at the time of the more serious Dudley conspiracy, he was bound in a recognizance of £1000 to appear daily before one of the clerks of the privy council. This endured for two months before he was allowed to return home; he remained in disgrace for the rest of the reign. Despite this, his county standing remained high and he was appointed JP in 1555.

Elizabeth I's accession to the throne brought a reversal of fortune, reflecting Champernowne's protestantism and the fact that his sister-in-law was a gentlewoman of the new queen's privy chamber. Champernowne was elected MP for Plymouth, Devon, in the first Elizabethan parliament in 1559 and appointed sheriff of Devon for 1559–60. By 1563 he was vice-admiral for the county, reflecting a long-standing maritime interest. Throughout the 1560s Champernowne operated against pirates, yet at times he co-operated with the privateers licensed by Jeanne d'Albret, the Calvinist queen of Navarre, against the subjects of the Catholic kings of France and Spain. However, this did not affect his standing with Elizabeth, who in 1567 gave him the rectory of Bodecliste, Devon, 'for his service' (*CPR, 1566–9*, 4.55).

By this time the wars of religion in Europe were intensifying. In 1568 the third civil war broke out in France while William of Orange led a revolt in the Netherlands against Spanish oppression. At the end of the year Sir Arthur Champernowne's nephew, Henry, his eldest son, Gawine, and other English volunteers were fighting for the Huguenots in France, while a flotilla of ships carrying money raised from Italian merchants to pay the Spanish troops in the Netherlands was heading up the English Channel. In early December 1568, attacked by Huguenot and Dutch corsairs, the ships took refuge off Southampton and Plymouth, where they were taken into protective custody by Sir Arthur Champernowne and another protestant seadog, Edward Horsey.

The seizure of the treasure ships was one of the most controversial incidents in Elizabeth's reign. The queen took over the loan from the Italians and later repaid the Spanish, but to Champernowne it was a blow against the great Catholic threat. He wrote to the principal secretary, Sir William Cecil, describing the treasure (which he estimated at a greatly exaggerated £400,000) as 'most fytt for her Majestie', emphasizing that it had 'been gathered by the Pope [Pius V] for the fight against the Protestants' (Lettenhove, 5.197, 205). Meanwhile, Henry Champernowne won renown under Gabriel de Lorges, comte de Montgommery, a celebrated Huguenot general. His death on 28 May 1570, leaving an infant son, made his uncle head of the family once more. Sir Arthur Champernowne's son was evidently also on good terms with Montgommery, for in 1571 or early 1572, Sir Arthur Champernowne arranged that Gawine should marry Roberde, the count's third daughter. In 1572 he was asked to attend Henry Fiennes de Clinton, third earl of Lincoln, lord high admiral, on his embassy to Paris to ratify the treaty of Blois. Both Champernownes left early and went to Normandy, where the marriage was concluded in April. They joined Lincoln in

Paris in June. The Champernownes' connections were not lost on the French ministers and were even drawn to the attention of King Charles IX. Sir Arthur Champernowne dined in Paris with Gaspard de Coligny, admiral of France, the celebrated Huguenot leader, and also carried home with him a letter from Henri of Navarre to Elizabeth.

Two months later, during the St Bartholomew's day massacre, Coligny and four thousand other French protestants were murdered, and the last Huguenot bastion of La Rochelle was closely besieged. Champernowne was genuinely horrified, as were most Englishmen, but he went further than hand-wringing, urging Elizabeth to send troops to aid the Huguenots and arguing that she should disregard the treaty of Blois since those who had signed it were now clearly untrustworthy. Moreover, he wrote, if she 'needes yeet regard it', he would 'most willingly hazard lyfe, goodes, & credyt' to aid La Rochelle himself, ready to digest with 'settled mynd the infamy, the exile, the shewes of offens, that shuld be published against me, so that I wer the meane whiles sure they shuld be but shewes, and my sellfe sure of your majesties favor' (BL, Lansdowne MS 15, fol. 200v). As a vice-admiral Champernowne could scarcely be disavowed and so his request was denied, but he probably had an important role in aiding the Huguenots. Montgommery escaped the massacre and mounted a large relief expedition from Plymouth in early 1573. He was accompanied by his son-in-law, Gawine Champernowne, and used former royal ships and English troops, possibly provided by Sir Arthur Champernowne in his capacity as vice-admiral and through his influence as former sheriff of Devon. Sir Arthur Champernowne was appointed a commissioner for musters in the county in 1573. Montgommery and his Anglo-French force helped to ensure the survival of La Rochelle—and hence the protestant cause in France.

The wars of religion continued, and in early 1574 Champernowne's ships transported Montgommery to Normandy. The invasion was mistimed and he was soon cut off by Catholic armies. Champernowne and his brother-in-law Richard Grenville tried to rescue him, but before their squadron arrived Montgommery had been captured and executed. Champernowne still maintained an active interest in French affairs, trading to La Rochelle and keeping in contact with Huguenot captains. But after Montgommery's death he paid more attention to other matters. In 1574 he capitalized on his old ties to the Seymour family and arranged the marriage of his daughter, Elizabeth, to Edward Seymour (c.1563–1613), first son of Sir Edward Seymour of Berry Pomeroy, Devon. This marriage took place on 19 September 1576. Champernowne campaigned briefly in Ireland with Carew, and his appointment as vice-admiral of Monmouthshire, controlling the southern sea route to Ireland, probably reflects this Irish involvement.

By spring 1578 Champernowne was in poor health, and he made his will on 29 March, declaring his faith in 'Gods most holly word which never failes in any poinct', and in his salvation through 'the passion and sufferance of Jesus Christ my onely savior and Redemer' (PRO, PROB 11/60,

sig. 16). He died three days later, on 1 April. His will, proved on 10 April, left properties with annual rentals totalling nearly £100 to his four younger sons, Philip, Charles, George, and Edward, and the balance of the estate to Gawine. Sir Arthur Champernowne, an impoverished younger son, had made himself into an important provincial figure; though he was never a major player in the drama of Elizabeth's reign, he was nevertheless party to some of the great events of his time.   D. J. B. Trim

Sources APC, 1558–1575 · Baron Kervyn de Lettenhove [J. M. B. C. Kervyn de Lettenhove] and L. Gilliodts-van Severen, eds., *Relations politiques des Pays-Bas et de l'Angleterre sous le règne de Philippe II*, 11 vols. (Brussels, 1882–1900), vols. 5–6 · HoP, *Commons, 1509–58*, 1.620–21 · HoP, *Commons, 1558–1603*, 1.592–3 · will, PRO, PROB 11/60, sig. 16 · CSP for., 1572–7 · Bibliothèque Nationale, Paris, MS Français 5785; Fonds Clairambault, 1907 · *Calendar of the manuscripts of the most hon. the marquis of Salisbury*, 2, HMC, 9 (1888) · M. A. S. Hume, *Calendar of letters and state papers relating to English affairs, preserved principally in the archives of Simancas*, 2, PRO (1894) · N. M. Sutherland, *The massacre of St Bartholomew and the European conflict, 1559–1572* (1973) · D. M. Loades, *Two Tudor conspiracies* (1965) · G. D. Ramsay, *The queen's merchants and the revolt of the Netherlands* (1986) · Bodl. Oxf., MS Rawl. B. 66, 74 · F. T. Colby, ed., *The visitation of the county of Devon in the year 1620*, Harleian Society, 6 (1872) · J. L. Vivian and H. H. Drake, eds., *The visitation of the county of Cornwall in the year 1620*, Harleian Society, 9 (1874) · A. Emery, *Dartington Hall* (1970)
Archives BL, Lansdowne MS 15, fols. 197–200 · Hatfield House, Hertfordshire, Cecil papers, Salisbury MSS · PRO, state papers foreign, Elizabeth, SP 70
Likenesses portrait, Dartington Hall; repro. in Emery, *Dartington Hall*
Wealth at death left property sufficient for annuities totalling £80 and 20 marks and at least £200 of other property: will, PRO, PROB 11/60, sig. 16; CPR, 4, p. 55; A. J. Howard and T. L. Stoate, eds., *Devon muster roll for 1569* (1977), 215; HoP, *Commons, 1509–58*, 1.620–21

Champernowne, David Gawen (1912–2000), economist, was born on 9 July 1912 at 2 Keble Road, Oxford, the only child of Francis Gawayne Champernowne (1866–1921), a barrister and bursar of Keble College, Oxford, and his wife, Isabel Mary, daughter of George Rashleigh, of Riseley, Horton Kirby, Kent. He came from the Dartington line of the Champernowne family, who had lived in south Devon for over 500 years; Katherine Champernowne was the mother of both Sir Humphrey Gilbert and Sir Walter Ralegh. He went to Winchester College as a scholar and in 1931 won a scholarship in mathematics to King's College, Cambridge. There he was an exact contemporary of Alan Turing, who became a close friend and with whom he later developed an early chess-playing computer program. He completed the mathematics tripos in two years, obtaining a double first. While an undergraduate he published a scientific paper on 'normal numbers' in the *Journal of the London Mathematical Society* for 1933. In this paper he was the first to produce an actual example of such a number in base 10; this has since come to be known as Champernowne's constant and is obtained by concatenating positive integers from one upwards and interpreting them as decimal digits to the right of the decimal point: 0.123456789101112…

With the encouragement of John Maynard Keynes,

Champernowne switched to the economics tripos, and from October 1934 he was supervised by Keynes: again he obtained a first. He was an active member of Keynes's Political Economy Club, contributing papers on the theory of the rate of interest, on Marx, and on the conditions of short-period and long-period equilibrium. In 1935 he published an important review of Keynes's *General Theory* acknowledging the plausibility of Keynes's position, but only in the short run; he argued that in the long run, where price expectations are updated, workers' concern with money wages would be a temporary phenomenon and their primary focus would be on the maintenance of real wages.

After graduating, Champernowne was assistant lecturer at the London School of Economics (1936–8) and then university lecturer in statistics at Cambridge (1938–40). His research focused on the size distribution of people's incomes. His probabilistic model of the income-generating process was one of the first to show how an equilibrium distribution is related to the forces governing income mobility, and why the equilibrium distribution would conform to a characteristic shape. The work resulted in a prize fellowship at King's College in 1937. The essence of the model was eventually published in the *Economic Journal* in 1953, though the full version of the fellowship dissertation did not appear as a published monograph until 1973, as *The Distribution of Income between Persons*. It laid the foundations for the widespread application of stochastic process models to analysing income distributions.

During the Second World War, Champernowne served with F. A. Lindemann as assistant in the statistical section of the prime minister's office (1940–41). Later he worked with John Jewkes at the Ministry of Aircraft Production's department of statistics and programming. In 1945 he returned to academia and became a fellow of Nuffield College, Oxford, and director of the Oxford Institute of Statistics. He was appointed professor of statistics in 1948, and on 30 March the same year he married Wilhelmina Barbara Maria (Mieke) Dullaert, daughter of Petrus Ludovicus Dullaert, a merchant; she was from the Netherlands and worked at the institute. They had two sons. While at Oxford Champernowne pursued his pre-war interest in Frank Ramsey's theory of probability: this led to work on the application of Bayesian analysis to autoregressive series at a time when the Bayesian approach was intellectually unfashionable. The work culminated in the major trilogy, *Uncertainty and Estimation in Economics* (1969).

In 1959 Champernowne resigned his professorship at Oxford in order to return to Cambridge, taking a lower-ranking readership in order to do so. He became a fellow of Trinity College in the same year and was promoted to a personal chair in economics and statistics in 1970, the year in which he was made a fellow of the British Academy. He also acted as one of three co-editors of the *Economic Journal* from 1971 to 1975. In addition to his own output he acted as midwife to a number of major theoretical contributions. He provided an invaluable 'translation' to John von Neumann's seminal paper on multi-sector

growth, and his role as behind-the-scenes expert at Cambridge over many theoretical issues was legendary: A. C. Pigou's later writings on output and employment, Nicholas Kaldor's work on savings and economic growth models, and Dennis Robertson's *Principles* were all heavily indebted to his intellectual influence. Joan Robinson acknowledged the assistance of his 'heavy artillery' in underpinning and extending her major work on capital and growth; his early comment on her work encapsulated all the main points that subsequently emerged in the abstruse theoretical debate on capital theory.

After retirement in 1978 Champernowne's major project was to complete a monograph (with Frank Cowell of the London School of Economics), *Economic Inequality and Income Distribution* (1998). In many respects this brought together several lifelong concerns: the questioning of fundamental assumptions underlying market-orientated theories of production and distribution, the application of mathematical modelling to the analysis of income distribution, the desire for theoretical rigour in explaining the fundamentals of economic inequality (following his *Economic Journal* article of 1974), the application of ingenious numerical methods to solve analytically intractable problems (he had long shown a keen interest in applications of computer technology), and the concern for distributive justice (he was a long-time supporter of the Labour Party).

In his final years Champernowne suffered from Alzheimer's disease, and in 1995 he and his wife Mieke moved to Budleigh Salterton in order to be near their son Richard. He died at his home, Lower Eryl Mor, 22A Victoria Place, Budleigh Salterton, on 19 August 2000, of bronchial pneumonia. He was buried alongside his ancestors in the grounds of St Mary's Church, Dartington, where his grandfather, Richard Champernowne, had been rector. He was survived by his wife and two sons, Richard and Arthur.   FRANK A. COWELL

Sources *The Times* (25 Aug 2000) · *The Independent* (26 Aug 2000) · *The Guardian* (1 Sept 2000) · *Daily Telegraph* (4 Sept 2000) · WWW · Burke, *Gen. GB* · personal knowledge (2004) · private information (2004) · b. cert. · m. cert. · d. cert.

Archives BLPES, corresp. relating to Royal Economic Society and *Economic Journal* | BLPES, corresp. with J. E. Meade · Nuffield Oxf., corresp. with Lord Cherwell

Likenesses photograph, repro. in *The Times* · photograph, repro. in *The Independent* · photograph, repro. in *The Guardian* · photograph, repro. in *Daily Telegraph*

Champernowne, Henry (1537/8–1570), soldier, was the first son and heir of John Champernowne (d. 1541), soldier, of Modbury, Devon, and his wife, Katherine, daughter of William *Blount, fourth Baron Mountjoy, and his second wife, Agnes. He matriculated as a fellow-commoner at Pembroke College, Cambridge, on 29 September 1551 but it is unknown whether or not he received a degree. Several members of his extended family fought the Turks, including his father, who died at Vienna in 1541 while Henry Champernowne was still an infant. His mother then married Sir Maurice Berkeley, chief banner bearer of England. Katherine *Astley (née Champernowne) (d. 1565), chief gentlewoman of the privy chamber to Elizabeth I, was his aunt. In 1545 his grandfather Sir Philip Champernowne died; the boy, then aged seven, succeeded as lord of Modbury and numerous other manors in the west country. He married Katherine (*d.* in or after 1575), daughter of Sir Richard Edgcumbe of Mount Edgcumbe, Cornwall, and his wife, by 1563. They had four daughters, Mary, Elizabeth, Margaret, and Bridget, by 1568.

In 1566–7 a new war broke out against the Turks in Hungary. Champernowne, who until this time was known principally as a local landowner (he was JP for Devon from about 1561), followed his father's example and joined the imperialist army, along with a group of other young gentlemen, including Richard Grenville. In the words of one contemporary writer, these young aristocrats and gentlemen, who:

> for their naturall valour, thought themselves borne to live in Armes, and not in idlenes, seeing the Nobility of all parts, did rise at the report of the warre against the Turke, and carried their Armes and Courages into Hungarie. (Camden, 127)

The campaign of 1567 was short-lived, but the adventurers found a new opportunity for gallantry as they headed home via France, where the second war of religion began that autumn. Champernowne was a fervent protestant and wrote approvingly of the actions of iconoclasts in the Low Countries. Aiding fellow protestants against the papacy must have seemed equivalent to a crusade against the infidel to Champernowne and he led his friends into service with the Huguenots. They fought in the great but indecisive battle of St Denis on 10 November 1567, but Champernowne was home by 18 January 1568 and ensconced in local matters once more.

By November 1568 Champernowne led a small cavalry troop in the south of France after the third war of religion broke out. He had gone with licence from Elizabeth I (perhaps helped by his family's position at court). Elizabeth would not 'neglect the Protestants in France, their State beeing at that time wretched and deplorable: For the Princes of the same Religion having much importuned her … she … permitted Henry Champernoune to conduct into France a Company of … Noble voluntary Gentlemen' (Camden, 1.224). Among his men were Walter Ralegh and his own cousin Philip Buddockshide as lieutenant. Initially he was in the army of Gabriel de Lorges, comte de Montgommery, under whom he fought at the battle of Jazeneuil on 17 November. Shortly after, he moved into the army of Louis Bourbon, first prince de Condé, with whom he was soon on close terms. The prince even trusted Champernowne to organize a romantic liaison with a lady, which the gallant Englishman did to the best of his ability. However, on 13 March 1569, Condé engaged the royal army at Jarnac. The protestants were soundly defeated, the prince taken prisoner and killed. Champernowne's troop probably was badly mauled in the battle, because by April 1569 he was back in Devon, presumably in order to raise reinforcements.

However, as well as raising troops, Champernowne took care of family business. Worried about what would happen if he did not return, he assigned his manors of Dodbrooke, Godrington, Bridford, Challerley, Goodlong, Blackawton, Moreleighe, and Stancombe, Devon, to trustees to raise marriage portions for his daughters and a jointure for his wife. Champernowne was happy to venture his life in a good cause, but ensured his wife and daughters would be provided for in the event of his death. Immediately after concluding these arrangements, in September 1569 he made his will, leaving his arms and armour to his uncle Sir Arthur *Champernowne and to Buddockshide; 500 marks each to his daughters; and appointing his wife sole executor and residuary legatee. From the evidence of his will Champernowne's son, Richard, was not yet born.

Champernowne left England soon after with his new larger company. Its cornet (company flag) was all black with a Latin inscription *Det mihi virtus finem* ('My death is virtuous'; Popelinière, 363r). The Englishmen joined the protestant field army just after the great defeat at Moncontour on 10 October 1569. Champernowne and his men skilfully covered the retreat of the Huguenot army, his cornet attracting the notice of friend and foe alike. He and his men continued in service throughout the following winter, but suffered a steady attrition through casualties; these included, on 28 May 1570, less than three months before the war ended, the death of its captain. He was buried in France. Jeanne d'Albret, queen of Navarre, wrote to Elizabeth, requesting her 'favour for the widow and children of Mr. Champernoun' (*CSP for.*, 1569–71, 287). Elizabeth responded, granting the wardship of Richard Champernowne to his mother, who was also granted an annuity of £20, retrospectively from her husband's death.

Thomas Churchyard, soldier and popular Elizabethan writer, declared that:

> maister Henry Champernowne, as one desirous of renowne, and greedie of glorie gotten by service, remained till his death, where lively fame was to be wonne: and served so nobly and so gallantly, as the whole Campe where he was in sounded of his valliantnesse, and … augmented so muche his fame, that to this daie his deedes … are moste noblie spoken of, greatly to the honour of all our Englishe Nation. (Churchyard, sig. Kii v)

Nor did he exaggerate. One of Champernowne's Huguenot comrades-in-arms, the sieur de St Simon, declared that Champernowne 'was greatly honoured and esteemed by the whole army down to the day of his death' (*CSP for.*, 1569–71, 278). In 1572 his uncle, Sir Arthur Champernowne, was on the embassy to Paris led by Edward Fiennes de Clinton, first earl of Lincoln. One of the king's secretaries, briefing Charles IX, identified him by stating he was uncle of the Henry Champernowne who 'was in the late wars in France under the command of the late Prince of Condé, leading one hundred English cavaliers' (Bibliothèque Nationale, Paris, Manuscrits Français, 5785, fol. 17r). Contemporary French historians also write highly of Champernowne. Thus his fame did live on after death, though his contribution to the wars of religion seems small, in simple military terms. His rearguard action at Moncontour was a notable feat; but even more, in a society that prized chivalrous deeds of *prouesse*, the daring, courtesy, and apparently cheerful readiness for death of Champernowne and his followers won admiration from

Frenchmen, even on the enemy side. Champernowne attracted some of the best and brightest young gentlemen of Elizabethan England to his unique banner. His life and career exemplifies the chivalric revival, which was central to the recruitment of English and Welsh volunteers during the wars of religion. Whether Sir Philip Sidney or Edmund Spenser knew him is unclear, but they must have known of him—Sidney was also on Lincoln's embassy in 1572. Henry Champernowne may not have been a model for the knights-errant in the greatest verse of the English literary renaissance, but his honourable, courteous, and courageous life was the reality of Sidney's and Spenser's fiction.

D. J. B. TRIM

Sources CSP for., 1566–71 · will, PRO, PROB 11/52, sig. 33 · Bodl. Oxf., MSS Rawl. B. 66, 74, 285 · HoP, Commons, 1558–1603 · T. Churchyard, A generall rehearsall of warres (1579) · W. Camden, Annales: the true and royall history of the famous Empresse Elizabeth, trans. A. Darcie (1625) · Bibliothèque Nationale, Paris, manuscrits français 5785 and 23275 · Report on the Pepys manuscripts, HMC, 70 (1911) · [H.] L. de Voysin de la Popelinière, La vraye et entière histoire des troubles choses memorables, avenues tant en France qu'en Flandres, & pays circonvoisins, depuis l'an 1562 (La Rochelle, 1573) · J. de Serres, Mémoires de la troisième guerre civile et des derniers troubles de France (1571) · A. L. Rowse, Sir Richard Grenville of the Revenge (1937) · A. J. Howard and T. L. Stoate, eds., The Devon muster roll for 1569 (1977) · Devon RO, 269A/PF7 · J. L. Vivian and H. H. Drake, eds., The visitation of the county of Cornwall in the year 1620, Harleian Society, 9 (1874) · J. L. Vivian, ed., The visitations of the county of Devon, comprising the herald's visitations of 1531, 1564, and 1620 (privately printed, Exeter, [1895]) · M. Stoyle, Loyalty and locality: popular allegiance in Devon during the English civil war (1994) · CPR, 1569–72 · J. B. Wood, The king's army: warfare, soldiers and society during the wars of religion in France, 1562–1576 (1996)

Archives Devon RO | Bodl. Oxf., assignment of lands, MSS Rawl. B · Magd. Cam., Pepys MSS · PRO, State Papers foreign, Elizabeth, SP 70

Wealth at death at least 2000 marks; left 500 marks each to all of daughters; Modbury valued between 100 marks and £100 p.a. in April 1569: will, PRO, PROB 11/52, fol. 239; Howard and Stoate, eds., Devon muster roll, 216

Champion family (per. c.1670–1794), metal manufacturers and merchants, came to prominence with **Nehemiah [ii] Champion** (1649–1722), son of Nehemiah [i] Champion (b. 1614). As a merchant dealing countrywide in iron goods, and a Quaker from about 1670, Nehemiah [ii] became Bristol agent and largest customer of Abraham *Darby (1678–1717) of Coalbrookdale. He appears also to have represented Bristol interests in Newcomen's new atmospheric pump for mining. His sons included Nehemiah [iii] and Richard (1680–1764). He died on 1 May 1722 at Bristol.

Nehemiah [iii] Champion (1678–1747) is known to have been married three times. His first wife was Susanna, daughter of John Trueman, a Bristol Quaker. Their five children included John [i] (1705–1794) [see below], Nehemiah [iv] (1709–1782), William (1710–1789) [see below], and also Rachel (1712–1766), who, in 1731, married Quaker iron smelter Sampson [ii] Lloyd (1699–1779), it being his second marriage. Nehemiah [iii] made a second marriage, to Hannah Ball, and a third, in 1742, to Martha Vandewall, daughter of Quaker merchant William Goldney. Richard, younger brother of Nehemiah [iii], a merchant of Bisley,

Gloucestershire, briefly partnered Abraham Darby in 1711, providing capital for expansion at the Coalbrookdale ironworks, later becoming a leading partner of the Bristol brassworks after the death of Nehemiah [iii].

From 1706 Nehemiah [iii] Champion was purchasing Cornish copper ores on behalf of brassworks established in 1702 by Abraham Darby and his Quaker partners at Bristol. This company was to achieve success in establishing brass production in England as a thriving industry, whereas those before had failed under domination from exports from traditional European centres of manufacture. After Darby left Bristol for Coalbrookdale, some time between 1708 and 1710, Champion replaced him as manager, later becoming a partner, with responsibility for developing new technical expertise, particularly in adopting coal instead of charcoal as the main source of fuel.

Champion's new techniques in brass production and manufacture, patented in 1723 (no. 454), increased the output of alloy from its raw materials, copper and the zinc ore calamine. Included also were new methods of annealing—or heating—brass goods during manufacture to prevent cracking. A further patent, no. 567 in 1739, concerned overshot water-wheels, possibly for use in conjunction with the Newcomen pumping engine. Champion's methods brought the Bristol brass company to predominance throughout Britain and, later in the century, throughout Europe. He died on 9 June 1747.

Of Nehemiah's sons, **William Champion** (1710–1789), born on 26 April 1710, achieved greatest distinction, although he was often confused with his elder brother John [i]. William married Ann, daughter of George Bridges, on 18 June 1741. Travelling Europe as a young man, he became interested in producing zinc, which was only beginning to be understood and accepted as a metal rather than as a stone or earth which converted copper to brass. At that time its production was not possible on a large industrial scale in Europe. He returned home in 1730 and experimented for eight years until in 1738 he registered his patent (no. 564), which was obscurely worded for secrecy. The sound technical process he developed displayed a true understanding of problems previously encountered by others. To avoid the oxidization of zinc vapour at the high temperatures required for metal production, he built a large-scale distillation furnace, based on the Bristol glass cones and heated by coal. When the city fathers complained of the harmful 'smoke' from his Bristol furnaces, he moved in 1746 to Warmley, 5 miles away. An 80-acre site had been purchased by his father, Nehemiah [iii], who, shortly before he died, joined his son and other Quaker merchants in a new Warmley partnership.

William Champion established a large integrated works at Warmley, where, in addition to exploiting his new zinc smelting process, he incorporated the smelting of copper, together with brass production and manufacture. The output consisted mainly of hollowware—pots, pans, and vats—and wire, similar to the output of the Bristol company. Under such direct competition, antagonism soon developed between the two companies, which increased as the Warmley site was developed to capacity.

The principle of completely integrated production on one site was new to the industry, contrasting strongly with the Bristol company, which operated several separate manufacturing watermills in addition to two copper smelting sites. The water-wheels powering the Warmley hammers, rolling mills, wire mills, and other manufacturing equipment were kept working by recycling water with a large Newcomen pumping engine. This was the first time such an engine had been used in manufacturing processes. Zinc production proved less profitable than had been anticipated, however, especially after the refusal of an extension of patent rights; nevertheless, William Champion continually expanded his premises, plant, and processes, adding brass pin manufacture. By 1765 his business was still expanding, although he was forced to borrow heavily, and personal losses occurred after the failure of his dock improvements in the port of Bristol. He registered patent no. 867 for manufacturing brass and brass wire in 1767, but was bankrupt by 1769, his Warmley company premises eventually being purchased by the Bristol brass company. William Champion died on 22 May 1789 at Somerset Street, Bristol.

William and Ann Champion's five children included John [ii] Champion, born in Bristol in 1746, who was manufacturing metals at Cheese Lane, Bristol, at the end of the century. He corresponded in the 1790s with Matthew Boulton (1728–1809), through his Birmingham cousin Charles Lloyd, on the more efficient use of his rotative steam engine, with which he intended to operate a rolling mill for copper and lead in addition to producing iron and brass wire. He patented new methods of wire manufacture in 1798, but in the following year his premises were advertised for sale. He is known to have approached Lord Ribblesdale in 1806, in connection with purchasing calamine mined at Malham Moor for new zinc production in Yorkshire; but by 1810 at the age of sixty-four John [ii] Champion was declared a bankrupt.

William's elder brother **John** [i] **Champion** (1705–1794), who was born on 22 June 1705, developed separate interests in metals. His patent (no. 569) of 1739 involved antimony and arsenic to toughen metals; and no. 726, of 1758, registered brass production and the smelting of zinc from its sulphide ore, known as blende, instead of from calamine, the zinc carbonate used previously. Although receiving his father's share in the Bristol brass company and being agent for the Warmley company, he took no major part in either, but established his own brassworks at Holywell, north Wales, near local resources of blende and calamine. His production there appears to have been of a quality more suited to cast products, in contrast to the greater degree of purity required for the rolled-sheet goods, beaten hollowware, and drawn wire typical of the traditional Bristol processes. He relinquished the Holywell works in 1765 when under financial pressure.

His son John [iii] Champion (1754–1779), at the age of sixteen, was responsible for patent no. 950 (1770) for hatching eggs and rearing young domestic birds by artificial heat. He later worked on the extraction of sulphur during the roasting of copper sulphide ores, which his partner, William Roe of Macclesfield, patented in 1779, after John's early death at the age of twenty-five. During that same year his father was patenting another process for brass production in large sealed crucibles. Ten years later, aged eighty-four, John [i] Champion was writing to Matthew Boulton on coal gas, the 'inflammable matter for lighting' (Day, *Bristol Brass*, 120) he had produced, and which he thought suitable for lighthouse illumination. John [i] Champion died in Warwick Row, Pimlico, on 4 April 1794, aged eighty-eight.

Another member of the family, Richard *Champion (1743–1791), grandson of Richard Champion (1680–1764), became noted for collaboration with the Quaker William *Cookworthy (1705–1780), pioneer of hard-paste porcelain in England. Richard had shown interest in attempting to make porcelain before meeting Cookworthy in 1764, after Cookworthy's difficulty in establishing works in Cornwall. Successful manufacture was introduced to Bristol by the partners, with sole rights from Cookworthy's patent of 1768 being transferred to Champion by 1774. However, his petition to parliament, challenged by Josiah Wedgwood (1730–1795) and others, failed to obtain an extension of patent rights, and Champion's Bristol works proved unable to withstand the ensuing competition from other manufacturers.

The widespread contribution of members of the Society of Friends to eighteenth-century metal industries is well recognized, and the Champions, centred in Bristol, were deeply involved in the Quaker life of the city. Nevertheless, some members of the family were at times disciplined for un-Quakerly activities: their bankruptcies were not approved; Nehemiah [iii] Champion was proscribed for privateering; and Richard Champion (1743–1791) was admonished for irresponsible financial dealings. By marriage they were interrelated to many of the most prominent members of Quaker families, in the city and elsewhere, and in old age John [i] Champion particularly received support from the society.

The death of John [i] Champion in 1794 brought an end to the significant contributions of the Champion family to the technology of the eighteenth century. Their interests were widespread and of national significance, ranging from Cornish copper mining to manufacturing in Coalbrookdale, Swansea, Macclesfield, and Liverpool, but mainly concentrated on important developments in non-ferrous metal production.   JOAN DAY

Sources A. Raistrick, *Quakers in science and industry* (1950) · J. Day, *Bristol brass: a history of the industry* (1973) · A. Raistrick, *Dynasty of ironfounders: the Darbys of Coalbrookdale* (1953) · R. Jenkins, 'The zinc industry in England', *Transactions of Newcomen Society*, 25 (1945–6), 41–52 · R. Watson, *Chemical essays*, 4 (1786) · R. Champion and H. Owen, *Two centuries of ceramic art in Bristol* (1873) · J. Day, 'Copper, zinc and brass production', *The industrial revolution in metals*, ed. J. Day and R. F. Tylecote (1991), 131–99 · J. Morton, 'The rise of the modern copper and brass industry, 1690–1750', PhD diss., U. Birm., 1985 · J. Day, 'Brass and zinc in Europe from the middle ages until the 19th century', in P. T. Craddock, *2000 years of brass and zinc,*

British Museum Occasional Paper, 50 (1990), 123–50 · H. T. Ellacombe, *The history of the parish of Bitton* (1883)
Archives Bristol RO, Quaker records · Bristol RO, Coster family record books · Glos. RO, Bathurst papers · U. Lpool L., Rhys Jenkins papers

Champion, Anthony (1725–1801), poet and politician, was born at Croydon, Surrey, on 5 February 1725, the son of Peter Champion, a merchant of St Columb, Cornwall, and his wife, Catherine. He received his early education at Cheam School before attending Eton College from 1739 to 1742. While at Eton he met William Henry Lyttelton, later Lord Lyttelton, with whom he struck up a close and life-long friendship (indeed, Lyttelton followed Champion to St Mary Hall and the Middle Temple). On 28 February 1742 Champion matriculated at St Mary Hall, Oxford, where his tutor was Walter Harte, friend of Pope and Young and, at the time, vice-principal of the college. He left Oxford without taking his degree and in 1744 entered the Middle Temple, where he remained for the rest of his life, becoming a bencher (1779) and a reader (1785). Champion was MP for St Germans (1754–61) and Liskeard (1761–8), although he never spoke in the Commons, a fact attributed by Lyttelton to his 'great modesty and reserve' (*Miscellanies*). Champion died on 22 February 1801 at the Middle Temple and was buried in Temple Church on 3 March. Champion, who was unmarried, left bequests totalling over £30,000, as well as a number of estates in Essex. Included in his bequests were £1000 for the Middle Temple and £5000 for Lord Lyttelton, to whom he also left his large collection of books and papers. It was his 'great modesty and reserve' which not only caused him to remain silent in the House of Commons, but also, according to Lyttelton, 'prevented him from communicating to the world those effusions of his rich and luxuriant vein of Poetry'. From Champion's papers Lyttelton put together *Miscellanies, in Verse and Prose, English and Latin, by the Late Anthony Champion* which was published in 1801. The poetry, typical of the mid-century but without the subtlety of Collins, the larger sweep of Gray, or even the progressiveness of the Wartons, is unremarkable, Lyttelton's praises coming more from friendship than judgement.   HUGH REID

Sources 'Life', *Miscellanies, in verse and prose, English and Latin, by the late Anthony Champion*, ed. W. H. Lyttreton (1801) · J. H. Jesse, *Etonians* (1875) · Foster, *Alum. Oxon.* · *DNB* · *HoP, Commons, 1558–1603*, vol. 2 · will, PRO, PROB 11/1354, sig. 164
Archives BM, letters
Likenesses C. Turner, mezzotint, pubd 1807 (after B. Wilson, 1766), BM, NPG
Wealth at death bequests of £30,000; estates in Essex: will, PRO, PROB 11/1354, sig. 164

Champion, Harry [*real name* William Henry Crump] (1865–1942), music-hall entertainer, was probably the William Henry Crump born at 30 Grafton Street, Mile End, London, on 8 April 1865, the son of Walter Henry Crump, a tailor who was later a butcher and licensed victualler, and his wife, Louisa Ann, *née* Scantlebury. He had at least one brother and sister, who both outlived him. Few personal details are known about Champion's early life, as 'about his real name he was secretive' (*The Times*, 15 Jan 1942). He

was apprenticed to a boot clicker. Nevertheless his main interest was the music-hall, and he made his début at the Royal Victoria Music Hall in Old Ford Road, Bethnal Green, in July 1882, as 'Will Conray, comic'. He toured round the minor halls of London's East End, variously described as comic, character vocalist, and character comic and dancer, and the following year ventured into other parts of the capital. He probably appeared in these early days in 'blackface', at least in part when he sang plantation songs.

Late in 1886 Champion introduced a new act entitled 'From Light to Dark', in which he appeared alternately in black- and whiteface. This had some success, but a real change came in 1887 when he deserted the name of Will Conray for Harry Champion:

> Somebody gave it to me. It was all through a dislike the manager of the Marylebone took to me. I went on tour for a bit. When I came back, he told my agent he'd have nothing to do with me. 'Right', said the agent, 'but you might give a new man his chance.' 'Who is he?' asked the manager, and then and there my agent baptised me 'Harry Champion' and came and told me afterwards.   (Disher, 64–5)

Real success came in 1889 when Champion gave up the blackface part of his act and found the first song which came to be associated with his name: 'I'm Selling up the 'Appy 'Ome'. His network of engagements in the country widened and he made his West End début at the Tivoli in September 1890. Encores of his now famous song were often accompanied with a hornpipe dance. His renown throughout his career centred on his singing with verve and gusto songs which became closely associated with his name, one of the most notable being 'When the Old Dun Cow caught Fire', introduced in 1893.

On 30 November 1889, at St Peter's Church, Hackney, Champion married Sarah Potteweld (1869–1928), who accompanied him on many of his tours. They had three sons and a daughter, all of whom were alive at the time of their father's death. In 1914 Champion moved his home from the East End to 520 West Green Road, South Tottenham, and he lived in the Downhills area of Tottenham for the rest of his life.

His songs were in demand: 'Champion is a comic singer who is endowed with genuine humour, which is revealed in his several songs, of which the audience never seems to get enough' (*Entr'Acte*, 13 Jan 1894). He now had many songs in his repertory, a fact which may have prompted him early in 1898 to adopt the quickfire style of delivery which he retained for the remainder of his career: 'At one time I used to sing songs with plenty of patter but I changed the style for a new idea of my own, and started "quick singing". I think I am the only comedian who sings songs all in a lump, as you may say' (Barker, 35). With his eccentric make-up and outlandish clothes, he became known as the 'Quick-Fire Comedian'; he also tap-danced.

The titles of many of Champion's songs, supplied mainly by professional writers from his ideas, have become part of the British vocabulary. Those about food were an essential part of his repertory, so much so that about the time of the First World War it was possible to go into a cheap London restaurant and ask for 'a Harry Champion'; and be given a plate of boiled beef and carrots, echoing the title of one of his most famous songs. Other ditties praised cucumbers, pickled onions, piccalilli, saveloys, trotters, cold pork, and baked sheep's heart, all basic elements in the cockney's diet.

Champion's golden period was from 1910 to 1915, when he introduced successful new songs before an ever widening and appreciative audience ('Ginger you're Barmy' and 'I'm Henery the Eighth, I am', 1910; 'Any Old Iron', 1911; 'The End of my Old Cigar' and 'Wotcher, me Old Brown Son', 1914; 'Little Bit of Cucumber', 1915). He took part in the first royal variety performance at the Palace Theatre, London, in July 1912. 'Grow some Taters' (1915) was taken up by the government wartime publicity organization to encourage the home growing of vegetables.

However, the First World War changed tastes, and traditional music-hall went into a decline in comparison with other forms of entertainment; by 1918 Champion and his fellow entertainers from the previous century were no longer in demand. In 1920 he went into an enforced retirement and did not expect another engagement. He took this stoically, concentrating his interest on horses and on running livery stables and a taxi service. These he owned for decades, operated in conjunction with relatives, at Dalston, London.

The public mood had changed again by 1930 and the old-timers of music-hall once again became popular. Troupes of veterans were much in demand in the 1930s, and Lew Lake's 'Variety, 1906–1931—Stars who Never Failed to Shine' went on tour throughout the country early in the decade with Champion a leading member. 'He almost brought the house down with three of his typical ditties', reported *The Performer* on 6 May 1931.

Champion appeared at the royal variety performance in 1932 with other representatives of old-style music-hall, including Vesta Victoria, Fred Russell, and Marie Kendall. That same year he returned to the London Palladium, where he always sang 'Any Old Iron' to rapturous applause. Further royal variety performance appearances took place in 1935 and 1938, and he was seen in the successful *London Rhapsody* with the Crazy Gang at the Palladium in 1937–8.

Champion did not try anything new because that was not required by audiences in the 1930s. On stage the words shot out of him like bullets from a gun. He rattled off several songs in a monotonous voice, whirling his arms about with his foot tapping at the same time; he was always audible. He appeared grotesque, but was the embodiment of the spirit of the poorer parts of London; there was no refinement or sophistication in his performance, which was above all a vibrant evocation of working-class life. 'Like music hall itself, Harry Champion was of the people, he expressed the tastes of practically all his listeners, even those who would not openly admit it, and in World War 2 he sang to troops who found him a splendid tonic' (Pope, 406).

In the late 1930s Champion became a regular performer on the radio, and seemed indestructible. By late 1941, however, he had overtaxed his physical resources, and exhaustion forced him into a London nursing home, at 20 Devonshire Place, St Marylebone. He died there on 14 January 1942, having in a career of sixty years added several catchphrases to the English language. His most famous song, 'Any Old Iron', returned to popularity in the late 1950s, sung by Peter Sellers, to engage the attention of yet another generation. He was buried with his wife (who had predeceased him on 24 January 1928) in St Marylebone cemetery, East Finchley, on 24 January 1942.

ALAN RUSTON

Sources T. Barker, *Music Hall*, 26 (1982), ISSN 0143-8867 [Harry Champion issue] · 'Thanks for condolences', *Tottenham and Edmonton Weekly Herald* (30 Jan 1942), 7 · *The Times* (15 Jan 1942) · *Manchester Guardian* (15 Jan 1942) · *Evening Standard* (14 Jan 1942) · *Hackney Gazette* (16 Jan 1942) · *Daily Telegraph* (15 Jan 1942) · *Tottenham and Edmonton Weekly Herald* (16 Jan 1942) · M. W. Disher, 'Costers and cockneys', *Winkles and champagne: comedies and tragedies of the music hall* (1938), 64–6 · R. Busby, *British music hall: an illustrated who's who from 1850 to the present day* (1976), 32–3 · S. T. Felstead, *Stars who made the halls* (1946), 160 · W. M. Pope, *The melodies linger on* (1950), 406, 421 · C. Pulling, *They were singing: and what they sang about* (1952), 117, 224 · directories, Stamford Hill and Tottenham, 1913–15 · P. Davison, *Songs of the British music hall* (1971), 202–7 · P. Gambaccini, T. Rice, and J. Rice, *British hit singles*, 8th edn (1991), 258–9 · b. cert. [W. H. Crump] · m. cert. [W. H. Crump] · d. cert. [W. H. Crump] · b. cert. [Sarah Potteweld] · d. cert. [Sarah Crump]

Archives FILM BFI NFTVA, performance footage | SOUND BBC WAC · BL NSA, performance recordings

Likenesses prints, Harvard TC

Wealth at death £5681 8s. 11d.: administration with will, 1 Aug 1942, *CGPLA Eng. & Wales*

Champion, Henry Hyde (1859–1928), socialist and journalist, was born on 22 January 1859 in Poona, India, the son of Major-General James Hyde Champion and his wife, Henrietta Susan, *née* Urquhart. He was sent to England to be educated at Marlborough College before entering the Royal Military Academy at Woolwich. He was commissioned as a lieutenant in the Royal Artillery in 1878 and served in the Second Anglo-Afghan War before resigning his commission in September 1882 as a protest against the Egyptian campaign. On 9 August 1883 he married Juliet Bennett (d. 17 March 1886). After reading the work of Henry George, Karl Marx, and others, Champion embraced the socialist cause, to which he devoted his fortune and his many talents.

In 1883 Champion aligned himself with Henry Mayers Hyndman and the Democratic Federation (later the Social Democratic Federation or SDF). He served as the SDF's first secretary and invested £2000 in the Modern Press, which published *Justice*, the federation's mouthpiece. Having edited the *Christian Socialist* (1882–4) and *To-Day* (1884), Champion was ideally suited to edit *Justice*, which soon became a respected and influential socialist weekly. A major figure in the early history of the federation, Champion also played an important role in establishing and maintaining the dynamism of the Clerkenwell branch of the SDF. His reputation, however, was jeopardized in the 'tory gold scandal' of 1885, when he helped secure Conservative Party financial support for SDF candidates in the general election. On 8 February 1886, along with other SDF leaders, he participated in the demonstration of the unemployed in Trafalgar Square (for which he was arrested on charges of sedition and later acquitted) and managed in part to redeem his reputation.

By 1887 Champion had become disillusioned by Hyndman and the SDF, suggesting that the organization's abstract theory had converted few workers to the cause. In May he established a new monthly, *Common Sense*, in which he attacked Hyndman and suggested the need for a party that would appeal directly to workers' interests. He was expelled from the SDF in November 1888 and turned to the Labour Electoral Association in order to promote independent labour politics. Writing for a working-class readership in the *Labour Elector*, which he edited between 1888 and 1891, Champion argued in favour of immediate, practical reforms, particularly the eight-hour day. During the London Dock strike of 1889 he advised strikers on tactics and did much to secure sympathetic press coverage of the dispute.

Champion devoted his energy in the early 1890s to the cause of independent labour representation, and stood unsuccessfully for Aberdeen South in the general election of 1892. Although ill health prevented him from attending the conference that gave birth to the Independent Labour Party in 1893, Champion worked behind the scenes in shaping the new party. Nevertheless, many Independent Labour Party members remained suspicious of his background and tory financial connections, especially after he offered to fund the electoral campaigns of Labour candidates. By 1894 Champion's reputation was tarnished, and by choosing to emigrate to Australia, leaving behind few admirers, he ensured that the role he played in the formative days of the Independent Labour Party would soon be forgotten.

Champion settled in Melbourne, where he continued to promote socialist causes. Influenced by his second wife, Elsie Belle Goldstein (*d.* 1953), whom he married on 8 December 1898 and who was the younger sister of the noted Australian suffragist Vida Goldstein, he campaigned on behalf of women's suffrage. He also established the Australasian Authors' Agency in 1906 and published the work of aspiring Australian novelists. He suffered a stroke in 1901, was declared bankrupt in 1922, and died in South Yarra, Victoria, on 30 April 1928.

Although largely forgotten, Champion played a major role in the development of socialist thought and institutions in Britain. His many pamphlets, along with the articles he wrote between 1888 and 1892 for the *Nineteenth Century* (which he briefly edited), are evidence of his intellectual rigour, while his organizational and speaking skills were noted by many of his contemporaries. Nevertheless, his aristocratic demeanour and impetuous behaviour (he had an acerbic wit and temperamental personality), along with his dubious financial connections and his distrust of working-class ties to the Liberal Party, alienated many of his potential followers.　　CHRIS WATERS

Sources A. Whitehead, 'Champion, Henry Hyde, 1859–1928', *DLB*, vol. 8 · H. M. Pelling, 'H. H. Champion: pioneer of labour representation', *Cambridge Journal*, 6 (1952–3), 222–38 · H. H. Champion, '"Quorum pars fui": the autobiography of H. H. Champion', ed. A. Whitehead, *Bulletin of the Society for the Study of Labour History*, 47 (1983), 17–35 · S. Pierson, *Marxism and the origins of British socialism* (1973) · G. Serle, 'Champion, Henry Hyde', *AusDB*, vol. 7 · D. F. Bradshaw, 'Champion, Henry Hyde', *BDMBR*, vol. 3, pt 1
Archives Mitchell L., NSW, corresp. and autobiographical sketch | BL, John Burns collection

Champion, John (1705–1794). *See under* Champion family (*per. c.*1670–1794).

Champion, John George (1815–1854), collector of plants and insects, was born on 5 May 1815 at Edinburgh, the eldest son of Major John Carey Champion (*d.* 1825) of the 21st Royal North Britain fusiliers, and Elizabeth Herries, daughter of William Urquhart of Craigston Castle, Aberdeenshire. Educated at Sandhurst (1828–31), he was gazetted an ensign in the 95th regiment on 2 August 1831, and embarked for foreign service in 1838, having by then been promoted to the rank of captain. After a stay in the Ionian Islands, where he gathered and brought back a large collection of insects, Champion's duties took him to Ceylon. There too he collected a considerable number of insects, most of which were presented to the British Museum's natural history collection, and also devoted himself to botany, in which he was helped by correspondence with Dr George Gardner, and Sir William J. Hooker. In 1839 he returned to England after a severe fever. In 1841 he married Frances Mary, the eldest daughter of Captain David Carnegie. She returned to Ceylon with him.

In 1847 Champion was sent to Hong Kong, returning to England in 1850 with a collection of dried plants, including a number of new specimens that were described by the taxonomist George Bentham in *Hooker's Journal of Botany* (1849–55), and which served as part of the basis for Bentham's *Flora Hongkongensis* (1861). His entomological collections from Hong Kong were also varied and valuable. Before leaving for the Crimea in April 1854 Champion deposited his remaining specimens in Hooker's herbarium, which was later preserved in the Royal Botanical Gardens at Kew. He took part in the battle of the Alma and was wounded at Inkerman on 5 November 1854. He was then promoted to lieutenant-colonel and was made CB for his conduct in battle. Shortly afterwards, on 30 November 1854, he died at a hospital in Scutari from the effects of a gunshot wound in his chest. He was thirty-nine. His wife and a son and a daughter survived him. He is commemorated in a genus of African violet, *Championia* (defined by Gardner), and in the names of a number of plants, as well as in a red longicorn beetle, *Erythrus championi*.　　B. D. JACKSON, *rev.* P. E. KELL

Sources *A sketch of the life of the late Lieut.-Colonel Champion, of the 95th regiment, with extracts from his correspondence* (privately printed, London, 1854) · *Edinburgh New Philosophical Journal*, new ser., 1 (1855), 302–7 · G. Bentham, *Flora Hongkongensis* (1861), 8–9 · A. W. Kinglake, *The invasion of the Crimea*, 2 (1863), 329–30 · *Gardeners' Chronicle* (23 Dec 1854), 819–20 · *GM*, 2nd ser., 43 (1855), 218 · *Hart's Army List* (1840–53) · *Catalogue of scientific papers*, Royal Society, 1 (1867), 870 · *Botanische Zeitung*, 13 (1855), 488 · Desmond, *Botanists*, rev. edn

Archives Oxf. U. Mus. NH, notes relating to Chinese Coleoptera · RBG Kew, notes on Hong Kong plants · RBG Kew, Hong Kong plants · Oxford, Hong Kong plants · Cambridge, Sri Lankan plants

Champion, Joseph (*b.* 1709, *d.* in or before 1768), writing-master and accountant, was born in Chatham, Kent, the son of a wealthy Kent family who had been freeholders until they lost their property during the stock market crisis of 1720. Little is known of his early life except that he attended both St Paul's School and Sir John Johnson's Free Writing School, Foster Lane, London. At the latter he studied under the 'eminent' (Massey, 2.37) writing-master Charles Snell with whom he then served a regular apprenticeship. After completing this indenture he taught penmanship at a number of public schools while also working as a private tutor 'amongst the nobility and gentry' (ibid., 38). Over the following few years, Champion's increasing prosperity and success can be charted through a number of advertisements in the London press. At the age of twenty-two, he had set himself up as a 'writing-master and accomptant' (*The Craftsman*) at premises two doors away from his alma mater of St Paul's School. In the next year, an advertisement in the *Daily Journal* (17 January 1732) records that Champion had moved to a 'New Writing School, at the Golden Pen, Old Change Cheepside' and, in 1733, after another change of premises, he styled himself 'Master of the Boarding School, in King's Head Court, St Paul's Church Yard' where 'Writing & Accompts' were 'Taught as Applied in Business' in an 'airy and pleasant' house (Champion, *The Parallel*). During the remainder of his career Champion opened one other school in Bedford Street (1760) and ran, unsuccessfully, for the prestigious post of writing-master at St Paul's School in 1741.

Apart from his work as a schoolmaster, Champion 'was highly regarded by his contemporaries' (Whalley, 67) for the high quality of his several published copybooks and merchant primers. The first of these was entitled *Practical Arithmetick* (1733) and, as its title suggests, was a utilitarian exercise book teaching merchant accounts. By far the most important of Champion's works was *The Parallel* (1750) which was prefixed with a mezzotint portrait of this penman. This was unusual within the popular genre of engraved copybook as it not only combined practical business hands with other more ornamental styles of writing but it also made a point of reproducing the work of a number of foreign master penmen such as Lucas Materot and Louis Barbedor and prefaced the whole with 'An historical account of the art of writing'. Like all of Champion's publications, this work took as its distinctive motto 'Vive la Plume'—a phrase which he managed to incorporate into many of his, often decoratively flourished, exercises in calligraphy. His other published works include *New and Complete Alphabets in the Various Hands of Great Britain, with the Greek, Hebrew, and German Characters* (*c.*1760; *c.*1765; 1794; 1808); and *The Penman's Employment, a New Copy Book* (1762; 1765; 1798).

The exact date of Champion's death remains unclear but, according to Ambrose Heal, he must have died before April 1768 when he was described in one advert as the 'late' Joseph Champion. He was survived by a son, also called Joseph, who, in 1740, was living in the Old Jewry where he too was a writing-master.　　LUCY PELTZ

Sources J. Champion, *The parallel* (1750) · *Country Journal, or, The Craftsman* (16 Jan 1731) · *Daily Journal* (17 Jan 1732) · A. Heal, *The English writing-masters and their copy-books, 1570–1800* (1931) · W. Massey, *The origin and progress of letters: an essay in two parts* (1763) · M. McDonnell, ed., *The registers of St Paul's School, 1509–1748* (privately printed, London, 1977) · *Engraved Brit. ports.* · J. I. Whalley, *English handwriting, 1540–1853* (1969)
Archives Bath Central Library, examples of his lettering
Likenesses J. Hulett, engraving, 1750, repro. in Champion, *The parallel* · J. Hulett, line engraving (after H. Gravelot), NPG · mezzotint, BM, NPG

Champion, Nehemiah (1649–1722). *See under* Champion family (*per. c.*1670–1794).

Champion, Nehemiah (1678–1747). *See under* Champion family (*per. c.*1670–1794).

Champion, Richard (1743–1791), porcelain manufacturer, was born in Bristol on 6 November 1743, the second child and only son of Joseph Champion (1714–1794), merchant, and Elizabeth (*d.* 1745), daughter of Francis Rogers, merchant of Bristol. Through his great-grandfather Nehemiah *Champion (1649–1722) [*see under* Champion family (*per. c.*1670–1794)], Richard was related to the elder branch of the Champion family which played a prominent part in the brass industry. Little is known of his early years; in 1751 he was sent to London to live with his father who had remarried, but returned to Bristol in 1762 and worked for his merchant uncle, Richard 'Gospel' Champion. In 1764 he married Judith (Julia) Lloyd (1741–1790), with whom he was to have nine children.

About the same time Champion made the acquaintance of his fellow Quaker William *Cookworthy of Plymouth, who had for many years been experimenting with the production of true or hard-paste porcelain. In 1765 Champion records the existence in Bristol of a short-lived hard-paste porcelain factory which failed, but there is no evidence that Champion himself was involved in the ceramic industry before 1768, the year in which Cookworthy secured his patent for the protection of his discoveries and set up his factory in Plymouth. In the same year Champion entered into a partnership which has led to speculation that a hard-paste porcelain factory existed in Bristol from 1768. However, no other evidence has come to light to support this theory and it seems more likely that Champion was involved in Cookworthy's Plymouth undertaking. In 1770 the Plymouth works closed and production was transferred to Castle Green, Bristol, under Cookworthy's management and with Champion as one of the partners.

In 1773 Cookworthy sold his patent and interest in the factory to Richard Champion personally, while reserving to himself and his heirs a royalty for ninety-nine years. Although Champion had no practical experience of potting, under his management the quality of the ware improved markedly. The Bristol factory produced mainly figures and tea wares; these latter ranged in decoration from simple green husk ornament to lavishly decorated services for individuals, some of whom were partners in the firm, for example Edward Brice, and Joseph and Mark Harford. Champion's association with the statesman Edmund Burke, who was briefly MP for Bristol, gave rise to the finest of all Bristol services, the personal gift of Richard and Judith Champion to Mrs Edmund Burke (teapot, milk jug, and sugar bowl in the Royal Scottish Museum, Edinburgh). Major collections of Bristol porcelain can be seen in the Victoria and Albert Museum, London, and the Bristol City Museum and Art Gallery.

In 1775 Champion petitioned parliament for an extension of Cookworthy's patent for a further fourteen years. This petition was strongly opposed by Staffordshire potters, including Josiah Wedgwood. The act was passed, but in a modified form which was ultimately to play a part in Champion's failure.

The high costs of the porcelain venture, together with the decline in trade with America after 1776, led Champion into financial difficulties. In 1778 he came close to bankruptcy but the factory remained in limited production until 1781; the last dated piece is a figure of Grief commemorating Champion's eldest daughter, Eliza, who died on 13 October 1779 (Mint Museum of Art, Charlotte, North Carolina). In 1781 Champion disposed of his patent to a group of Staffordshire potters who formed the New Hall China Manufactory. Champion moved to Newcastle under Lyme but remained there only until April 1782 when, through the influence of Edmund Burke, he was appointed joint-deputy paymaster-general of his majesty's forces.

Champion participated actively in the politics of his city. He was treasurer of the Bristol Infirmary (1768–78), warden of the Society of Merchant Venturers (1772–3), and a founder member of the Bristol Library Society. In 1774 he played a major part in the election of Edmund Burke as MP for Bristol; the two became close friends and Champion, with trading and family connections in South Carolina, was able to keep Burke and other leading whigs informed of American feelings at a critical time. However, his involvement with politics, some of his business dealings, and the arming of his ships for protection, led to conflict with the Quakers and he ceased his association with them in 1778.

In 1784, on the collapse of the coalition government, Champion lost his post. He had hopes of being appointed consul-general to North America but was to be disappointed. Nevertheless, he and his family emigrated to South Carolina and settled on a plantation near Camden. He took naturalization and served briefly in the state assembly. In his latter years he wrote a pamphlet on the subject of free trade with America and a series of letters contrasting his gloomy view of Great Britain's future with his optimistic outlook for America. Richard Champion died on 7 October 1791 and was buried in the Quaker burial-ground at Camden.   KARIN M. WALTON

Sources H. Owen, *Two centuries of ceramic art in Bristol* (1873) · digest registers (births) in the library of the Society of Friends, Bristol RO, SF/R1/1, 3, 5 · F. S. Mackenna, *Cookworthy's Plymouth and Bristol porcelain* (1946) · F. S. Mackenna, *Champion's Bristol porcelain* (1947) · F. Hurlbutt, *Bristol porcelain* (1928) · Richard Champion's letter-books, Bristol RO, 38083 · minutes of the Men's Monthly Meeting, Bristol RO, SF/A1/11, 13 · [F. S. Mackenna], ed., *The F. S. Mackenna collection of English porcelain*, 3: *Plymouth and Bristol* (1975) · W. J. Pountney, *Old Bristol potteries* (1920) · A. D. Selleck, *Cookworthy, 1705–80, and his circle* (1978) · R. J. Charleston, 'The end of Bristol, the beginning of New Hall: some fresh evidence', *The Connoisseur*, 137 (1956), 185–8 · J. V. G. Mallet, 'Cookworthy's first Bristol factory of 1765', *Transactions of the English Ceramic Circle*, 9 (1973–5), 212–20 · D. M. Olsen, 'Richard Champion and the Society of Friends', *Transactions of the Bristol and Gloucestershire Archaeological Society*, 102 (1984), 173–95 · G. H. Guttridge, *The correspondence of a Bristol merchant, 1766–1776: letters of Richard Champion* (1934) · P. T. Underdown, 'Burke's Bristol friends', *Transactions of the Bristol and Gloucestershire Archaeological Society*, 77 (1958), 127–50 · *JHC*, 35 (1774–6), 138, 328, 364, 369, 382, 393–5 · D. Holgate, *New Hall*, 2nd edn (1987) · G. Munro Smith, *A history of the Bristol Royal Infirmary* (1917) · J. Latimer, *The history of the Society of Merchant Venturers of the city of Bristol* (1903) · J. Latimer, *The annals of Bristol in the eighteenth century* (1893); repr. (1970) · PRO, RG6/1655, fol. 142

Archives Bristol RO, letter-books, 38083 · NYPL, corresp. | Northants. RO, corresp. with Edmund Burke · Sheff. Arch., Wentworth Woodhouse Muniments, Burke MSS · Sheff. Arch., corresp. with marquess of Rockingham · U. Nott. L., letters to duke of Portland · Woodbrooke College archives, Birmingham, journal of Sarah (Champion) Fox [MS copy]

Likenesses miniature, priv. coll.; repro. in *British porcelain bicentenary 1770–1970* [exhibition catalogue, City Art Gallery, Bristol, 1970] · silhouette, Mint Museum of Art, Charlotte, North Carolina

Wealth at death almost bankrupt in 1778; made little or no money from porcelain; briefly earned salary as joint-deputy paymaster-general

Champion, William (1710–1789). *See under* Champion family (*per. c.*1670–1794).

Champion de Crespigny, Sir Claude, fourth baronet (1847–1935), military adventurer and sportsman, was born in Chelsea on 20 April 1847, the eldest son of Sir Claude Champion de Crespigny, third baronet (1818–1868), of Wivenhoe Hall, Essex, and his wife, Mary, second daughter of Sir J. Tyssen Tyrell, bt, MP. He attended Temple Grove School, East Sheen, until the age of thirteen, when he entered the navy, serving as a midshipman in the *Warrior* in 1862. In 1866 he transferred to the army as an ensign, and was with the King's Royal Rifle Corps (60th) in Ireland and India. In 1867 he won the first of the many steeplechases in a racing career spanning nearly fifty years. He succeeded to the baronetcy the following year. Sir Claude considered fighting, whether with fists or pistols, to be a manly occupation, and he engaged in fisticuffs until his seventies. He devoted his life to the maxim: 'Where there is a daring deed to be done in any part of the world, an Englishman should leap to the front to accomplish it' (Champion de Crespigny, *Sportsman's Life*, 221).

In 1870, irked by the restrictions of army life, Sir Claude resigned his commission to embark on the strenuous and dangerous pursuits he was to follow for the rest of his life. These included joining the Garde Cuirassiers, a German cavalry regiment, as a volunteer during the Franco-Prussian War, and being arrested as a spy three times by the French on his way home. He spent the next decade in the west country and Ireland, where his daring in the hunting field earned him the title of the 'Mad Rider'.

While training with the Limerick artillery militia he saved a man from drowning, a feat he had first performed at the age of fifteen. A fearless swimmer, canoeist, and single-handed sailor, he attributed his confidence in rough seas to his grandfather, a naval officer who had saved so many lives that he was known as the 'Newfoundland Dog'.

On 19 September 1872 Sir Claude married Georgiana Louisa Margaret (d. 16 Feb 1935), second daughter of Robert McKerrel of Hillhouse, and they had five sons and four daughters. In 1880 he returned to Essex, and combined serving as a captain in the Suffolk yeomanry with his steeplechasing career (he found flat racing too dull), often riding three or four races in a day. A fall in one race left him unconscious from a kick in the head. After two days in bed he rolled his cricket ground, took a Turkish bath the next day, and rode in two more races the day after. His distaste for heavy betting set him apart from other gentleman riders of the time, as did the strenuous physical regimen he followed all his life.

In 1882 Sir Claude took up ballooning, and in July 1883 became the first man to cross the North Sea, winning the Balloon Society's gold medal for this feat. In 1886 he caused considerable comment when he assisted at the execution of three murderers at Carlisle. Having been advised that he might shortly become high sheriff for Essex, and therefore responsible for executions within the county, he considered it his duty to ensure he knew what was involved.

Sir Claude became the first European to swim the Nile rapids in 1889 and, ten years later, he and his wife went out to join their three sons in the Second South African War. He saw action as a scout with Porter's cavalry, while his wife nursed the wounded. Another visit to Africa in 1905 enabled him to combine 'a certain amount of fighting' in the Sotik punitive expedition on the Uganda/Kenya border with big-game hunting, including shooting a charging rhinoceros at three paces.

In 1914, at the age of sixty-seven, Sir Claude rode in his last steeplechase, and thereafter devoted himself to the more leisurely pursuits, as he saw them, of sailing, swimming, high diving, and long-distance walking. Lean of face and of spare build, he was proud that his weight was still only 10½ stone.

Sir Claude published his *Memoirs* in 1896 and *Forty Years of a Sportsman's Life* in 1910 (new edn, 1925). He died at his home, Champion Lodge, Maldon, Essex, on 26 June 1935, and was buried in a mausoleum he had built in the grounds for his eldest son, who died in 1910. In the 1950s he was reburied in Hatfield Peverel churchyard.

N. T. P. MURPHY

Sources C. Champion de Crespigny, *Forty years of a sportsman's life*, new edn [1925] · C. Champion de Crespigny, *Memoirs* (1896) · C. Caulfield, *The emperor of the United States of America and other magnificent British eccentrics* (1981) · *The Times* (20 Feb 1886) · *The Times* (27 June 1935) · *Daily Telegraph* (27 June 1935) · *Daily Mail* (27 June 1935) · *Daily Express* (27 June 1935) · Burke, *Peerage* · Burke, *Gen. GB* · General Register Office for England · private information (2004)
Likenesses engraving?, repro. in Champion de Crespigny, *Memoirs*, frontispiece · photographs, repro. in Champion de Crespigny, *Forty years*, frontispiece, 300

Wealth at death £149,716—limited to settled land: probate, 30 Jan 1936, *CGPLA Eng. & Wales* · £10 0s. 0d.—save and except settled land: further grant, 2 Dec 1936, *CGPLA Eng. & Wales*

Champney, Anthony (1569–1644), Roman Catholic priest, was born in Cawthorne in the West Riding of Yorkshire. He was sometimes known as Percival Champney and occasionally used the alias of Forester. Nothing is known of his early life, but he was present at the execution of the Catholic priests John Amias and Robert Dalby at York on 16 March 1589. He soon went to Rheims, where the seminary at Douai was temporarily located, arriving there on 17 June 1590. A good classicist, he took minor orders on 24 February 1592 and went on to Rome on 19 January 1593 for further study. He entered the English College there, was ordained priest at St John Lateran on 21 September 1596, and on 16 September 1597 was sent to England, where he worked on the Yorkshire mission. He was soon arrested, and was imprisoned in the Marshalsea at the end of 1599. From there he was moved to Wisbech Castle, where he signed the appeal for the removal of the archpriest George Blackwell, and from that time he was to be associated with the anti-Jesuit appellants, writing *An Answere to a Letter of a Jesuited Gentleman*, published in 1601 under his initials A. C. He was one of the thirteen signatories to the declaration of allegiance to Elizabeth I on 31 January 1603, but was banished and moved to Paris, where, on 3 May that year, he signed the appeal to the pope on behalf of the appellants. He seems to have returned to England to pursue his ministry in Yorkshire for a short period and, in May 1606, he accompanied John Cecil to Rome to plead the appellants' case. That mission was no more successful than its predecessors, but Champney and Cecil returned to Paris with letters of commendation to the nuncio there.

Champney settled in Paris, becoming a BD and fellow of the Sorbonne, and in 1611 was appointed superior of Arras College, a small body of English priests engaged in writing works of apologetics. From there Champney played a leading role in the controversy over the government of Douai College from 1611 to 1613, was a strong supporter of the group seeking the appointment of a bishop for English Catholics, and was active in excluding the Jesuits from the Sorbonne. During his time at Arras College he was engaged in controversy, publishing in 1614 *A Manual of Controversies*, in which he set out to establish the scriptural grounds for all chief points of the Catholic faith, thereby meeting protestant critics on their own ground. This elicited a reply from Richard Pilkington, *The New Roman Catholick and Ancient Christian Religion Compared*, to which Champney published a further reply in 1620. His most important controversial work, however, was *A Treatise of the Vocation of Bishops, and other Ecclesiasticall Ministers*, published in 1616. This was a reply to Francis Mason's *A Vindication of the Church of England* (1613), which sought to establish the validity of episcopal orders in the English church. Champney dedicated his work to 'Mr George Abbot, called Arch-Bishop of Canterbury', who had commissioned Mason's work, but went much further than the question of episcopacy in the protestant churches by also challenging the works of Field and du Plessis on non-episcopal traditions. A Latin translation appeared at Paris in 1618 and Champney's book was, for a long time, a standard Catholic work on the disputed question of ecclesiastical orders. By this date Champney had become involved in an internal dispute over the administration of Arras College, and in 1619 he was appointed vice-president of Douai College, arriving there on 25 April. While at Douai he continued his apologetic writing, engaging in the controversy between Daniel Featley and George Fisher in a pamphlet published in 1623, but he also lectured in divinity to students. He was appointed chaplain to the English Benedictine nuns in Brussels in September 1628, despite the opposition of some Benedictine priests, who objected to his appellant past. He remained at Brussels until 1637 and a manuscript volume of sermons preached by him was formerly in the library of the convent there. In January 1637 he was elected dean of the London chapter and he returned to England, living in London and remaining in office until his death in 1644. He was described as 'very tall and lean; yet of a strong constitution, and able to endure labour' (*Dodd's Church History*, 3.81), and one of the more substantial testimonies to that ability is his manuscript 'History of the reign of Q. Elizabeth', now in the Westminster Cathedral archives, which was much used by Bishop Challoner for his *Memoirs of Missionary Priests* (1741–2).　　　　　　　　　　　　　WILLIAM JOSEPH SHEILS

Sources G. Anstruther, *The seminary priests 1: Elizabethan, 1558–1603* [1966] · P. Milward, *Religious controversies of the Jacobean age* (1978) · A. Milton, *Catholic and Reformed: the Roman and protestant churches in English protestant thought, 1600–1640* (1995) · *Dodd's Church history of England*, ed. M. A. Tierney, 5 vols. (1839–43) · M. C. Questier, *Newsletters from the archpresbyterate of George Birkhead*, CS, 5th ser., 12 (1998)

Archives Westm. DA, MS Annales Elizabethae Reginae

Champneys, Basil (1842–1935), architect and author, was born in Whitechapel, London, on 17 September 1842, the third of the five sons of (William) Weldon *Champneys (1807–1875), rector of St Mary's Church, Whitechapel, afterwards dean of Lichfield, and his wife, Mary Anne, fourth daughter of Paul Storr, of Beckenham, Kent. He was an elder brother of Sir Francis Henry *Champneys (1848–1930), obstetrician.

Champneys was educated at Charterhouse School, which was then in London, and at Trinity College, Cambridge, where he obtained a second class in the classical tripos of 1864. He then studied architecture under John Prichard, diocesan surveyor of Llandaff. He began private practice in 1867. Although trained in the tenets of the Gothic revival, Champneys soon advocated a more eclectic approach to style. He was one of the first to design in the new Queen Anne mode and he also worked in the late Gothic, neo-Jacobean, and early English Renaissance styles. He married in 1876 May Theresa Ella, second daughter of Maurice Drummond, a descendant of William Drummond, fourth Viscount Strathallan; they had two sons and two daughters.

The long list of Champneys's buildings at Oxford includes the Indian Institute (1883–96), Mansfield College

(1887–90), the Robinson Tower at New College (1896), new buildings for Oriel College (1908–11) and Merton College (1904–10), the library of Somerville College (1903), and the church of St Peter-le-Bailey (1872–4). His works at Cambridge include the Archaeological Museum (1883), the divinity and literary schools (1879), and Newnham College (at intervals from 1875 to 1910). His structures in London include the chapel at Mill Hill School (1898) and new buildings for Bedford College in Regent's Park (1910). He also designed King's Lynn grammar school in Norfolk (1910–13), the Butler Museum at Harrow School (1886), the museum at Winchester College in Hampshire (1898), and Bedford high school (1878–92). His churches include his father's parish church of St Luke's, Kentish Town (1867–70), the sailors' church of St Mary Star of the Sea, Hastings, Sussex (1878), and St Chad, Slindon, Staffordshire (1894). He was a surveyor to St Mary, Manchester, to which he added a west porch (1898) and a south annexe (1902–3). His domestic work includes his home, Hall Oak, in Frognal, Hampstead (1881).

Champneys's masterpiece was the John Rylands Memorial Library in Deansgate, Manchester, which took nine years (1890–99) to build and equip. This remarkable and costly monument was raised to the memory of John Rylands by the latter's widow, who admired the small library of Mansfield College, Oxford, and asked Champneys to develop it on a far more lavish scale. In spite of its cramped position on a mean street, the Rylands Library is a really noble design carried out in every detail with consummate skill in late Gothic style and with considerable regard for practical requirements.

The Royal Institute of British Architects awarded Champneys its royal gold medal for architecture in 1912, but he never became a member of that institute because he regarded architecture as an art allied to painting and sculpture rather than a profession. He supported younger architects who sought a unity of the arts and was an early member of the Century Guild. He was a sociable man with a wide circle of friends. He belonged to the Athenaeum, where he was a familiar face in the billiard-room, and to the Savile Club. He especially valued his connections with literary men, among them Walter Pater, Robert Louis Stevenson, Sidney Colvin, and the poet Coventry Patmore, whose *Memoirs and Correspondence* he published in 1900. He wrote an introduction to *Henry Merritt: Art Criticism and Romance* (1879). His papers on architecture include 'Churches about Queen Victoria Street' (*Portfolio*, 1871), 'Victorian art and originality' (*British Architect*, 1887), and 'The architecture of Queen Victoria's reign' (*Art Journal*, 1887). His papers on the then unfrequented district around Rye and Romney Marsh appeared first in *Portfolio* and later under the title *A Quiet Corner of England* (1875). In later life he published *A Retrospect and Memoir* (1915) of his mother-in-law, Adelaide Drummond. He died at his home, Hall Oak, 42 Frognal Lane, Hampstead, on 5 April 1935, at the age of ninety-two.

M. S. BRIGGS, rev. MICHAEL W. BROOKS

Sources *The Times* (6 April 1935), 14 · *Manchester Guardian* (8 April 1935), 5 · *The Builder*, 148 (1935), 682 · *The Architect*, 142 (12 April

1935), 31–2 · L. Stokes, 'The royal gold medal, 1912', *RIBA Journal*, 19 (1911–12), 585–92 · R. Blomfield, 'Basil Champneys', *RIBA Journal*, 42 (1934–5), 737–8 · M. Girouard, *Sweetness and light: the Queen Anne movement, 1860–1900* (1977) · *CGPLA Eng. & Wales* (1935)

Archives Bodl. Oxf., travel journal · JRL, corresp., plans, accounts, and specifications relating to the construction of the John Rylands Library · RIBA BAL | Essex RO, Chelmsford, plans, etc., of works at Havering church · Royal Holloway College, Egham, Surrey, corresp. and plans relating to Bedford College new buildings · UCL, letters to Sir Francis Galton

Likenesses Farren, carte-de-visite, NPG · photograph, RIBA BAL · portrait, repro. in *Building News*, 58 (7 Feb 1890), 202

Wealth at death £49,573 1s. 10d.: probate, 20 June 1935, CGPLA Eng. & Wales

Champneys, Sir Francis Henry, first baronet (1848–1930), obstetrician, was born on 25 March 1848 in Whitechapel, London, the fourth son of the Revd (William) Weldon *Champneys (1807–1875), rector of St Mary's Church, Whitechapel, afterwards dean of Lichfield, and his wife, Mary Anne, fourth daughter of Paul Storr, of Beckenham, Kent. The third son was the architect Basil *Champneys (1842–1935). Francis Champneys was educated at Winchester College, where he was a scholar (1860–66), and at Brasenose College, Oxford (1866–70), where he obtained a first class in natural science in 1870 and was captain of boats. He then proceeded as a medical student to St Bartholomew's Hospital, London, qualifying for the degrees of BM in 1875 and of MD in 1888. Elected to the Radcliffe travelling fellowship of Oxford University in 1872, Champneys spent half of each of the following three years in study at Vienna, Leipzig, and Dresden. He became a member of the Royal College of Physicians in 1876 and a fellow in 1882. In 1880 he was elected assistant obstetric physician to St George's Hospital and obstetric physician to the General Lying-in Hospital, York Road. In 1885 he became obstetric physician to St George's. In 1891 he succeeded James Matthews Duncan as physician accoucheur to St Bartholomew's Hospital, where he remained until his retirement in 1913.

Champneys had considerable success as a consultant and as a teacher. He also tried to influence medical practice through his writings, but his bias towards the medical aspects of obstetrics and gynaecology was out of step with a growing interest in the introduction of surgical procedures. His most important contribution to his profession was through his many public services. He was a fellow of the Royal Medical and Chirurgical Society of London and played an active part in the uniting of the various medical societies of London into the Royal Society of Medicine. He was elected president of the society in 1912. Although he had very decided convictions and a tendency towards conservatism, Champneys had an openness of mind and a breadth of outlook which meant that other medical professionals sought his help and advice. He is perhaps best known for the prominent part he took in the movement to raise the status of midwives which led to the Midwives Act of 1902 and for his chairmanship of the Central Midwives' Board (CMB), the regulatory body set up under the act.

First as a member (1882) of the board for the examination of midwives of the Obstetrical Society of London, later as its chairman (1891–5), and finally as president of the society (1895), Champneys advocated the legal recognition and registration of midwives. This drew the attention of the General Medical Council to the form of certificate issued under his signature, and led to its revision after mutual discussion. When the functions carried on by the Obstetrical Society were taken over by the CMB in 1903, Champneys became its first chairman and was re-elected annually until his death, twenty-seven years later. Champneys was a controversial chairman. He helped to advocate the vision of midwifery reform held by the well-educated, middle-class leaders of the Midwives' Institute, who believed that the practice of midwives should be limited in scope and that they should defer to doctors. This was not always shared by rank-and-file midwives who were disciplined by the CMB and who found the chairman harsh in his judgements and scathing towards those who were not submissive enough to the board.

Champneys was also crown nominee from 1911 to 1926 of the General Medical Council, where he strove to improve the training of medical students in practical midwifery. In 1929 he was involved in founding the British College of Obstetricians and Gynaecologists, despite at first being opposed to the bringing together of the disciplines of obstetrics and gynaecology. He became a foundation fellow of the college and was elected vice-patron.

Music was Champneys's chief relaxation and he was regarded in his day as the finest musician in his profession in London. He had a wide knowledge of sacred music, which he studied under Samuel Sebastian Wesley while at Winchester, and composed hymn tunes, anthems, and other metrical works. As a young man, under the name of Frank Champneys he contributed five tunes to *Hymns Ancient and Modern* (*BMJ*, 16 Aug 1930). He installed an organ in his house in London and took it with him to Sussex, where it became a very important part of his later life. For many years he was a member of the council of the Royal College of Music and of its executive committee.

Champneys married on 12 September 1876 Virginia Julian (d. 1922), the only daughter of Sir John Warrender Dalrymple, seventh baronet, of Luchie, North Berwick, with whom he had three sons and one daughter. Champneys was created a baronet in 1910. He died at his home, Littlemead, Nutley, Sussex, on 30 July 1930. He was buried on 2 August at Hampstead cemetery. The funeral was preceded by a requiem, and a memorial service was held on the same day at the church of St Bartholomew-the-Less. Champneys was succeeded, as second baronet, by his youngest and only surviving son, Weldon Dalrymple-Champneys (b. 1892).

J. S. FAIRBAIRN, rev. JUNE HANNAM

Sources J. Peel, *The lives of the fellows of the Royal College of Obstetricians and Gynaecologists, 1929–1969* (1976) · B. Heagerty, 'Class, gender and professionalisation: the struggle for British midwifery, 1900–1936', PhD diss., U. Mich., 1990 · J. Donnison, *Midwives and medical men: a history of inter-professional rivalries and women's rights*

(1977) · *Nursing Notes* (1886–1930) · private information (1937) · Burke, *Peerage* (1931) · *BMJ* (9 Aug 1930), 231–2; (16 Aug 1930), 271
Archives Royal College of Midwives, London
Likenesses J. P. Beadle, oils, Royal Society of Medicine, London · photograph, repro. in *BMJ* (9 Aug 1930) · photographs, Wellcome L.
Wealth at death £122,172 6s. 2d.: probate, 23 Oct 1930, *CGPLA Eng. & Wales*

Champneys, Sir John (d. 1556). *See under* Champneys, John (d. in or after 1559).

Champneys, John (d. in or after **1559**), religious radical, was by his own account a native of Somerset, near Bristol. A Champneys family has been traced in Somerset back to the reign of Henry II. Its later members included **Sir John Champneys** (d. 1556), the son of Robert Champneys of Chew, who joined the Skinners' Company in London and became sheriff in 1522 and lord mayor in 1534, when he was knighted. Three years later he bought Hall Place at Bexley, Kent, where he built himself a notable mansion, but he retained his position in London, serving as alderman of Cordwainer Street ward from 1534 until his death. In 1541 his estate in Tower Street ward was valued at 2000 marks. According to John Stow he owned a house near the west end of Tower Street, which he extended upwards with 'an High tower of Bricke, the first that ever I heard of in any private mans house to overlook his neighbours in this Citie. But this delight of his eye was punished with blindnesse some yeares before his death' (Stow, 1.133). Sir John Champneys married twice: his first wife was Margaret Hall (*née* Mirfine), who died before 1515, and his second Meriel Barret, who died in the year of his mayoralty and was the mother of his heir, Justinian. Sir John himself died on 3 October 1556 and was buried in Bexley church.

It seems unlikely that the London magnate would have acknowledged any connection with the evangelical agitator, who is doubtless to be identified with the John Champneys whose release from the Counter was ordered by the privy council in May 1543 in terms which suggest that he had been imprisoned for an offence against the Act of Six Articles. In 1548 this Champneys was living in London, in the parish of Stratford-le-Bow. In the same year he published a tract entitled *The Harvest is at Hand wherein the Tares shal be Bound, and Cast into the Fyre and Brent* (STC 4956). It was a characteristic product of a radical religious fringe that existed in London during the early years of the reign of Edward VI, when the city became 'a haven for Anabaptists and Libertines, sectaries who could be tolerated by no government in Europe; indeed many of those in London were exiles' (Brigden, 442). Champneys presents himself as a latter-day Elijah. He attacks all clergy as 'marked men', claiming that:

> not only because they [priests] are marked in their bodies [and] sometimes wear disguised monstrous garments, but because their doctrine is marked also, for … they wolde have the people to beleue it [the holy scripture] [and] receive it only as they do mark it [and] appoynt it out unto them. (B.ii. (v))

Champneys also offers in this work to come before King Edward and in open debate with the marked men prove the truth of his teaching. The origin of these extreme opinions is unclear. M. T. Pearse has argued that 'Champneys' thinking is best seen as a flowering of the Lollard-rooted tradition of English radicalism which, by the mid-century, was becoming increasingly heterogeneous' (Pearse, 111). John Davis, by contrast, has argued that the six articles Champneys adjured in 1548 'recall the antinomian heresy of the Dutch Libertines' (Davis, 103). It should be noted, however, that Champneys's use of term 'marked men' does not fit into the way this term is used in Lollard writing, while his beliefs are too idiosyncratic to be safely labelled as coming from any of the main doctrinal strands of radical European protestantism.

Whatever their background, his religious views quickly got Champneys into trouble, and on 27 April 1549 he was brought before Archbishop Cranmer at St Paul's and made to recant six heresies and 'damnable opinions'. He was accused of professing that after a man is regenerate in Christ he cannot sin, that the gospel had been so persecuted since the time of the apostles that no man might follow it, that those regenerate in Christ do not lose godly love and cannot break the commandments of Christ, that it is the principle of the marked men's doctrine to make people believe that men possessed no such spirit whereby they might remain righteous in Christ, and that God permits his elect people to enjoy fully all worldly things. Champneys recanted and was ordered to refrain from preaching or publishing. He was also instructed to gather as many copies of his book as possible and destroy them. Finally he was forced on the following day, which was a Sunday, to attend the sermon at Paul's Cross and to stand before the preacher with a faggot on his shoulder.

Although it is possible that Champneys was later ordained into the Edwardian church and then went into exile on the continent during Mary's reign, C. J. Clement has found evidence of Champneys being in England before the end of Mary's reign, in May 1557, and of his being ordained priest by Bishop Nicholas Bullingham of Lincoln at Lambeth on 10 March 1559. Thereafter he disappears from the historical record, and it is not known when he died. It is possible, however, during the early 1560s that Champneys was involved in a debate over predestination and free will with Jean Vernon and Robert Crowley. But the evidence for his authorship of a number of anonymous letters and tracts attacking the doctrine of predestination is sketchy and obscure—unsurprisingly, since what is known about these writings is derived from the works of Vernon and Crowley that were intended to refute them. It is also possible that Champneys was the author of an anonymous work entitled *Confutation of the Errors of the Careless by Necessity*, which seems to have been circulating in manuscript by the end of 1557, and which was attacked by John Knox in *The answer to a great number of blasphemous cavillations written by an Anabaptist and adversary to God's eternal predestination* (1589). However, Andrew Penny has persuasively argued that Henry Harte is the more likely author of this piece. TOM BETTERIDGE

Sources J. Champneys, *The harvest is at hand* (1548) · *LP Henry VIII*, 18/1, nos. 533, 578 · C. Wriothesley, *A chronicle of England during the reigns of the Tudors from AD 1485 to 1559*, ed. W. D. Hamilton, 2 vols.,

CS, new ser., 11, 20 (1875–7) · C. J. Clement, *Religious radicalism in England, 1535–1565* (1997) · M. T. Pearse, *Between known men and visible saints: a study in sixteenth-century English dissent* (1994) · D. A. Penny, *Freewill or predestination: the battle over saving grace in mid-Tudor England* (1990) · S. Brigden, *London and the Reformation* (1989) · J. F. Davis, *Heresy and reformation in the south-east of England, 1520–1559*, Royal Historical Society Studies in History, 34 (1983) · J. Stow, *A survay of London*, rev. edn (1603); repr. with introduction by C. L. Kingsford as *A survey of London*, 2 vols. (1908); repr. with addns (1971) · S. Robertson, 'Bexley: the church; Hall Place; and Blendon', *Archaeologia Cantiana*, 18 (1889), 369–82 · P. J. Tester, 'Hall Place, Bexley', *Archaeologia Cantiana*, 71 (1958), 153–61 · R. G. Lang, ed., *Two Tudor subsidy assessment rolls for the city of London, 1541 and 1581*, London RS, 29 (1993) · *DNB*

Champneys, (William) Weldon (1807–1875), dean of Lichfield, was the eldest son of the Revd William Betton Champneys (*d.* 1835), BCL, of St John's College, Oxford, and his wife, Martha, daughter of Montague Stable of Kentish Town. This branch of the Champneys family hailed from Essex and prospered in trade. Gaining respectability through the church and a name through marriage in 1731 into the family of John Weldon, the composer, they provided a succession of minor canons of Windsor and Westminster. Weldon, as he was known, was born in Camden Town, St Pancras, on 6 April 1807 and was educated by the Revd Richard Povah, rector of St James's, Duke's Place, City of London. In 1824 he was elected to a scholarship at Brasenose College, Oxford. Graduating with second-class honours in classics in 1828, he became a successful private tutor in Oxford, and was known as 'the BNC omnibus'. In 1832 he was elected a fellow of his college.

Champneys was ordained in 1830 to the title of Dorchester, where he is said to have had a conversion experience. He established the principles of his method for parochial ministry as assistant curate of St Ebbe's, Oxford, from 1831 to 1837, in succession to H. B. Bulteel. First he gathered round him a group of lay 'district visitors', many of whom were his pupils. Then he set up schools: he founded in 1834 the first national schools in the city and a Sunday school. In 1837 Brasenose College appointed him rector of St Mary's, Whitechapel, and on 20 March 1838 he married Mary Anne, daughter of Paul Storr, whom he described as 'the sharer of his joy and sorrow, the fellow pilgrim on the road'.

Whitechapel was a populous parish of 36,000 souls, of whom only about a hundred attended church. Champneys's first confirmation candidates became the nucleus of his Sunday school teachers. London City Missioners, converted Jews, and scripture readers formed his visiting teams. He simplified the liturgy and introduced evening holy communion services, the first in London. By the time of the 1851 religious census 10,000 were attending worship or Sunday school in the parish. He was instrumental in setting up the Whitechapel foundation school in 1860, and opened a girls' school and the first ragged schools in London. When in 1859 the government declined to renew the act which prohibited the hiring of coal whippers at public houses, he campaigned vigorously and successfully for its continuance. He had agitated for a

(William) Weldon Champneys (1807–1875), by D. J. Pound, pubd 1860 (after John Jabez Edwin Mayall)

comparable measure to protect ballast heavers in 1853. He formed unemployed boys into a shoe black brigade, and started a penny bank, maternity society, coal club, and young men's institute.

The area of the parish was too large to manage, so he set about the creation of three new parishes, each to have the traditional facilities of church, vicarage, and school: St Mark's, Goodmans' Fields; St Jude's, Commercial Street (partly financed by a rich West End parish); and St Paul's, Dock Street. He encouraged the parish to look outward through the Whitechapel Missionary Association, which supported the Church Missionary Society for Africa and the East, the Society for the Propagation of the Gospel, the London Society for Promoting Christianity among the Jews, and the Church Pastoral Aid Society. He encouraged a missionary link with a school in New Zealand. A reduction in the benefice income could have led to his removal from the parish in 1851 had he not been appointed a canon of St Paul's on the recommendation of Lord John Russell.

In 1860 the dean and chapter of St Paul's presented him to the vicarage of St Pancras, where his grandfather had previously served. He developed the schools, ragged schools, and Sunday schools and provided a daily soup kitchen and an invalid's dinner table. He continued Canon Thomas Dale's policy by completing the division of the original parish into more than twenty units. At the time of a cattle plague he called for a day of prayer; during an epidemic of cholera he circulated a broadsheet with advice on its prevention and cure.

To all Champneys gave 'the Gospel very simply

preached' through his teaching in church and lecture room, and in more than seventy published sermons, popular pamphlets, and scholarly tracts, including *The Path of a Sunbeam* (1845), *The Spirit of the Word* (1862), and *Things New and Old* (1869). But the parish was his base. It was said that he never left it, but he was not parochial in a restrictive sense. He was in the forefront of many evangelical societies, was one of the founders of the Church Association, and produced *A Simple Catechism for Protestant Children* (1877).

Champneys was appointed dean of Lichfield on 11 October 1868. Here he had the opportunity of sharing with the ordinands at the theological college his pastoral experience, crystallized in his *Parish Work* (1865). He restored the cathedral, revised the statutes, increased the stipend of his living at Tatenhill, and spoke with eloquence to those who had lost relatives in the Pelsall mining disaster (1873). He and the diocesan bishop (G. A. Selwyn) were close friends and Champneys asked to be buried beside him. He died at the deanery, Lichfield, on 4 February 1875, and was buried in the cathedral yard. His seven children included Basil *Champneys, the architect, and Francis Henry *Champneys, the obstetrician.

W. E. Gladstone called Champneys 'the most devoted parson and active clergyman who ever existed' (Champneys, 3/2.9), and Bishop Blomfield described him as 'the model working parson'. Although Queen Victoria referred to him in 1868 as 'an insignificant Low Churchman' (*Letters of Queen Victoria*, ed. A. C. Benson, Lord Esher, and G. E. Buckle, 2nd ser., 1926–8, 1.539), he may rightly be regarded as one of the foremost evangelical slum parsons of his generation.   H. E. C. STAPLETON

Sources C. Bullock, 'Biographical sketch', in W. W. Champneys, *The story of the tentmaker* (1875), 7–14 · Canon Champneys, 'William Weldon Champneys', *East London Church Chronicle*, 3/1 (Sept 1890); 3/2 (Dec 1890) · H. Stapleton, *The model working parson* (1976) · R. Reynolds, *The history of the Davenant Foundation grammar school* (1966) · *The Guardian* (10 Feb 1875), 168 · *The Guardian* (17 Feb 1875), 209 · M. Hennell and J. Root, 'Champneys of Whitechapel', *The Anvil*, 9/1 (1992) · private information (2004)

Archives deanery, Carlisle | LPL, corresp. with Tait

Likenesses D. J. Pound, line engraving, pubd 1860 (after photograph by J. J. E. Mayall), BM, NPG [*see illus.*]

Wealth at death under £18,000: probate, 18 March 1875, *CGPLA Eng. & Wales*

Chance, Alexander Macomb (1844–1917). *See under* Chance, Sir James Timmins, first baronet (1814–1902).

Chance, Sir James Timmins, first baronet (1814–1902),

glass manufacturer and lighthouse engineer, was born in Birmingham on 22 March 1814, the eldest of the six sons of William Chance (1788–1856), merchant and glass manufacturer, of Spring Grove, Birmingham, and his wife, Phoebe (*d.* 1865), fourth daughter of James Timmins of Birmingham. From a private school at Totteridge, James passed to University College School, London, where he gained high honours in languages, mathematics, and science. At seventeen he entered his father's mercantile business, but found the work distasteful and began to study for holy orders. In 1833 he entered Trinity College, Cambridge, where he made mathematics his chief study, won

a foundation scholarship, and graduated BA as seventh wrangler in 1838, after losing a year through insomnia brought on by overwork; he proceeded MA there in 1841, and MA *ad eundem* at Oxford in 1848. He had also begun the study of law, in 1836 entering as a student at Lincoln's Inn, but circumstances obliged him, on leaving Cambridge, to join his uncle, Robert Lucas Chance, and his father in their glassworks at Spon Lane, Smethwick, near Birmingham. Here he devoted himself to the manufacturing side of the business and to its scientific developments. He married, on 26 June 1845, Elizabeth, fourth daughter of George Ferguson of Houghton Hall, Carlisle; she died on 27 August 1887. They had three sons and five daughters.

While still at Cambridge, Chance had invented a process for polishing sheet glass so as to produce 'patent plate', but it was the production and perfection of lighthouse lenses which came to absorb his attention. This difficult manufacture, originally a French invention, was first carried on in England by Cookson & Co. of South Shields from 1831 to 1845, when it became again the monopoly of two firms in Paris. About 1850 the Chances started to make lighthouse lenses. They engaged a M. Tabouret, a French expert, to superintend the work but he left their service in 1853. Two years later manufacture began in earnest under James Chance's direction. Royal commissioners had been appointed in 1858 to inquire into the state of the lights, buoys, and beacons of the United Kingdom, and had soon detected grave defects in existing apparatus. On 23 December 1859 the commissioners visited the Spon Lane works, where they assessed Chance's technical competence and examined the production facilities. At the request of the commissioners, Sir George Airy, the astronomer royal, consulted with Chance and on 2 and 3 April 1860 examined at Spon Lane a large apparatus under construction for the government of Victoria. New principles formulated by Airy were first tried upon an apparatus which the company was constructing for the Russian government.

In the autumn of 1860 Chance joined Michael Faraday, acting for Trinity House, in experimenting with the firm's apparatus at the Whitby southern lighthouse. Faraday acknowledged his debt to Chance for the earnest and intelligent manner in which he co-operated in these trials, working and thinking out every point, and declared his confidence in the firm's capabilities. One thing that Chance discovered at Whitby was that it was not necessary to adjust lighthouse equipment *in situ* against the horizon itself, but that a graduated staff at a short distance from the light could be used. This important discovery enabled the apparatus to be adjusted accurately before it left the factory.

Chance effected permanent alterations in the Whitby light on the newly formulated scientific principles. A detailed paper dealing with all the questions at issue, which he sent to the commissioners in January 1861, formed part of their report. In May 1861, by request of Trinity House, Chance took part in an examination of all the dioptric apparatus in their charge. Most of the lights were of French manufacture, and in several cases Chance could remedy the defects only by reconstructing them, making the final adjustments mostly with his own hands. The old system of requiring the firm to make lights to prescribed specifications was abandoned, and Chance, with rare exceptions, was left to design them himself. He personally superintended every detail of the work, and from a sense of patriotism declined to patent improvements but made them public property. At the Paris Exhibition of 1867 his designs were demonstrably more efficient than similar apparatus of French manufacture. On 7 May in the same year he read before the Institution of Civil Engineers a paper entitled 'Optical apparatus used in lighthouses', which became a classic, and for which he was awarded a Telford medal and premium, and elected an associate of the institution. On 22 April 1879 he read before the institution a second important paper, 'Dioptric apparatus in lighthouses for the electric light'. Meanwhile, in 1872, he handed over responsibility for the lighthouse works to a new director, Dr John Hopkinson, and gradually retired from the management of the firm.

Chance was actively engaged in local and county affairs, and was prominent in directing the chief religious, educational, and philanthropic institutions in Birmingham. At a cost, including the endowment, of £30,000, in 1895 he gave the town West Smethwick Park. He was high sheriff of Staffordshire in 1868, and was mainly instrumental in forming the Handsworth volunteer rifle corps, the first corps in the midlands. He was a director of the London and North Western Railway from 1863 to 1874. In 1900 he endowed, at a cost of £50,000, the Chance School of Engineering in the University of Birmingham. He was created a baronet in the same year.

Chance lived at Brown's Green, Handsworth, Birmingham (1845–69), Four Oaks Park, Sutton Coldfield, Warwickshire (1870–79), and afterwards at 51 Prince's Gate, London, and 1 Grand Avenue, Hove, Sussex, where he died on 6 January 1902. He was buried, after cremation at Woking, in the Church of England cemetery, Warstone Lane, Birmingham. William, his eldest son, a barrister of the Inner Temple, succeeded as second baronet.

Alexander Macomb Chance (1844–1917), chemical manufacturer, was born on 28 June 1844 in Edgbaston, Birmingham, the ninth and youngest child of George Chance, hardware merchant, and his wife, Cornelia Maria, daughter of Arent Schuyler de Peyster of New York. George was a brother of Robert Lucas Chance, who had founded Chance Brothers & Co., glass makers of Smethwick, in 1824; Alexander was therefore a cousin of James Timmins Chance. Alexander was educated at King Edward's School, Birmingham, and then in Lausanne, subsequently joining the family firm.

Chance Brothers had established an alkali works at Oldbury in 1835, to supply the glassworks. Alexander Chance became managing director of the works in June 1868 and was made a partner of Chance Brothers in 1879. In 1870 he married Florence Hasted Mercer (d. 1903), daughter of Major Arthur Hill Hasted Mercer, of the 60th rifles. They

had eight children. When the alkali works were converted into the Oldbury Alkali Company Ltd in 1890, Chance was made deputy chairman as well as managing director. He decided not to take part in the creation of the United Alkali Company in 1890, but in 1898 amalgamated his firm with another Leblanc soda manufacturer, Hunt & Sons of Wednesbury, to form Chance and Hunt Ltd. He was chairman of Chance and Hunt from 1901 until his retirement in June 1912; Brunner, Mond & Co. (later part of ICI) acquired a majority shareholding in Chance and Hunt in 1917. In 1907, four years after his first wife's death, Chance married Agnes Elizabeth, daughter of William Fleming of Inverness. There were no children of this marriage.

Alexander Chance is chiefly remembered for the Chance process for the recovery of sulphur in the Leblanc method. This enabled the latter to weather, for another thirty years, the challenge from the ammonia–soda process used by the Solvay Company in Belgium and its British partner, Brunner Mond. The Leblanc process prepared soda (sodium carbonate) by heating salt with sulphuric acid, which formed salt-cake (sodium sulphate) and hydrochloric acid gas. The salt-cake was then converted into the desired soda by heating it with coal and limestone in large revolving furnaces. Unfortunately, impure calcium sulphide was a major by-product of this second step, and the Leblanc works were surrounded by mounds of evil-smelling waste called 'galligu'. In the 1880s Chance developed a method of pumping carbon dioxide gas through tanks of a slurry of galligu and water. The hydrogen sulphide gas thereby freed from calcium sulphide was burned to produce elemental sulphur, which was used to make sulphuric acid.

Chance built a convalescent home for his workers and set up a fund which quickly paid out compensation for industrial accidents on a no-fault basis. His concern about the evil effects of drunkenness led to the formation of the Langley Temperance Club, and he was also active in the social work of the Church of England. He presented the open space of Warley Woods to the city of Birmingham. Chance died at his home, Walcot, St Mark's Road, Torquay, Devon, on 22 November 1917.

CHARLES WELCH, rev. ANITA McCONNELL

Sources J. F. Chance, *The lighthouse work of Sir James Chance, baronet* (1902) · *PICE*, 149 (1901–2), 361–6 · *Birmingham Daily Post* (8 Jan 1902) · *Birmingham Weekly Post* (11 Jan 1902) · private information (1912) · *JCS*, 113 (1918), 307–9 [A. M. Chance] · K. M. Chance, 'The Chance memorial lecture', *Chemistry and Industry* (19 Aug 1944), 298–301 · P. J. T. Morris and C. A. Russell, *Archives of the British chemical industry, 1750–1914: a handlist* (1988), 54–65 · C. A. M. Press, *Worcestershire lives* · d. cert. · m. cert. · b. cert. [A. M. Chance] · m. certs. [A. M. Chance] · d. cert. [A. M. Chance]
Archives U. Birm. L., private ledger
Likenesses J. C. Horsley, portrait, 1854, repro. in Chance, *The lighthouse work*; formerly in the possession of George F. Chance, 1912 · Roden, portrait, c.1874; formerly in the possession of Sir William Chance, 1912 · H. Thornycroft, bronze bust, c.1894; formerly in the possession of Sir William Chance, 1912; photograph, repro. in Chance, *The lighthouse work* · J. Gibbs, oils, 1902, Smethwick town hall, Staffordshire · bronze bust (after H. Thornycroft, c.1894), West Smethwick Park, Birmingham

Wealth at death £246,654 7s. 2d.: resworn probate, Sept 1902, *CGPLA Eng. & Wales* • £45,557 5s. 11d.—A. M. Chance: probate, 9 March 1918, *CGPLA Eng. & Wales*

Chancellor, Sir **Christopher John Howard** (1904–1989), news agency executive, was born on 29 March 1904 in Cobham, Surrey, the elder son and eldest of three children of Sir John Robert *Chancellor (1870–1952), soldier and colonial administrator, and his wife, Elsie, daughter of George Rodie Thompson, barrister, of Lynwood, Ascot. He was educated at Eton College and at Trinity College, Cambridge, where he obtained a second class (division one) in part one of the history tripos (1924), and a first class (division two) in part two (1925). On graduation, friendship with the son of Ernest Debenham led Chancellor into the Debenham and Freebody drapery chain. But his hopes of rising to manage the business collapsed when the family sold out in 1927. In 1929 his wife wrote to Sir G. Roderick Jones, managing director of Reuters and a family friend, asking for a job for her husband. At interview, recollected Jones later, Chancellor revealed an 'executive outlook'— intelligence balanced by steadiness, energy and enthusiasm matched by prudence. These qualities, plus a necessary suave ruthlessness, were to serve Chancellor well throughout his business career. He was clean-cut and of medium build, with a distinctive, light voice. His piercing, enquiring eyes and expressive eyebrows gave him presence. After starting in 1930 in the editorial department of Reuters, Chancellor progressed rapidly. He was appointed general manager for the Far East at Shanghai from the beginning of 1932. Although not himself a regular journalist, Chancellor understood the news business. He was particularly effective in negotiating contracts, and in smoothly representing Reuters within ruling circles. Mixing duty with pleasure, the Chancellors became prominent figures within Shanghai society.

In 1939 Chancellor returned to London to become a third general manager. On Jones's enforced resignation in 1941 he became joint general manager, and sole general manager in 1944. Reuters could not make much profit out of selling general news, and money was always short. But at the end of the war Chancellor gave priority to negotiating supportive contracts with the news agencies of liberated western Europe. He also turned to the Commonwealth for new partners to join the Press Association and the Newspaper Proprietors' Association in the ownership of Reuters. In recognition of his work, he was appointed CMG in 1948, and knighted in 1951 at the time of Reuters' centenary.

After 1951 Chancellor found himself increasingly frustrated by an unenterprising board. Fortunately, the daily conduct of news reporting was in the hands of the management; and here, at the time of the 1956 Suez crisis, Chancellor was able to make one last and crucial contribution. He had long been sympathetic towards colonial nationalism, and he was a personal friend of several Labour politicians, including Hugh Gaitskell, who led the loud opposition to the Suez landings. Chancellor made sure that Reuters reported the Suez War from both sides, and in language which favoured neither side. Personally,

Sir Christopher John Howard Chancellor (1904–1989), by unknown photographer

he was disgusted by the British military intervention. But, as head of Reuters, he was motivated by a wider awareness. Under his guidance and just in time, Reuters successfully set out to end its British imperial role and become a supra-national news agency.

In 1959 Chancellor chose to step down. One of his successors later likened him at Reuters to Horatius defending the bridge, successful in holding his chosen ground but restricted in what he could otherwise attempt. Chancellor's underlying achievement was to keep Reuters in competition with the much more affluent American agencies. He became deputy chairman and then chairman of Odhams Press (1959–61). He found himself plunged uncomfortably into one of the most controversial takeover battles of the 1960s, between Thomson Newspapers and the Mirror group. After the Mirror's victory, Chancellor resigned. He disapproved of the new combined company gaining control of so many leading titles.

Chancellor next joined the Bowater Paper Corporation, becoming chairman in 1962. He pursued a necessary policy of drastic rationalization and decentralization. But when he retired in 1969 Bowaters was still vulnerable. Chancellor was chairman of Madame Tussaud's from 1961 to 1972, and of the Bath Preservation Trust from 1969 to 1976. With characteristic commitment to what he regarded as a moral duty of conservation, he successfully campaigned against proposals for the drastic modernization of the city.

In 1926 Chancellor married Sylvia Mary (d. 1996), daughter of Sir Richard Arthur Surtees *Paget, second baronet

(1869–1955), barrister and physicist. They had two sons and two daughters. Chancellor died on 9 September 1989 in Wincanton, Somerset.   DONALD READ, *rev.*

Sources *The Times* (11 Sept 1989) · *Daily Telegraph* (11 Sept 1989) · *The Independent* (11 Sept 1989) · C. Shaw, 'Chancellor, Sir Christopher John Howard', *DBB* · R. Jones, *A life in Reuters* (1951) · D. Read, *The power of news: the history of Reuters* (1992) · S. Underhill, interview, Reuters archive · *CGPLA Eng. & Wales* (1990) · *The Times* (29 Oct 1996)
Archives Reuters, London | BL, corresp. with Sir Sidney Cockerell, Add. MS 52709 | SOUND Reuters archive, speech, Reuters centenary dinner (11 July 1951)
Likenesses photograph, News International Syndication, London [*see illus.*] · photographs, Reuters archive
Wealth at death £290,927: probate, 12 Dec 1990, *CGPLA Eng. & Wales*

Chancellor, Sir John Robert (1870–1952), army officer and colonial governor, was born in Edinburgh on 20 October 1870, the second son of Edward Chancellor (1828–1907), writer to the signet, and his wife, Anne Helen (*d.* 1932), daughter of John Robert Todd, also a writer to the signet. He was educated at Blair Lodge, Polmont, and the Royal Military Academy, Woolwich, and was commissioned in the Royal Engineers in 1890. After a period of duty at home he served in India with the Dongola (1896) and the Tirah (1897–8) expeditions, and in the latter his courage and initiative earned him a mention in dispatches and appointment to the DSO in 1898. In 1903 he married Elsie, daughter of George Rodie Thompson, a barrister, of Lynwood, Ascot. They had one daughter and two sons, the elder of whom was Sir Christopher John Howard *Chancellor (1904–1989), general manager of Reuters.

Back in Britain, Chancellor attended the Staff College and in 1904 was appointed assistant military secretary to the committee of imperial defence. He showed such administrative ability and sound judgement that in 1906 he was made secretary of the colonial defence committee. He was promoted major in 1910. It was a tribute to Chancellor's qualities that, at the age of forty, a soldier with no experience of colonial administration, he was appointed to the important governorship of Mauritius where his term of office, 1911–16, was still recalled with admiration, more than thirty years later, by some who by then were leading personalities in the island. His success was rewarded by appointment to the governorship of Trinidad and Tobago, which he held from 1916 to 1921, and thereafter to the first governorship of Southern Rhodesia. This had to wait until 1923, when the territory was taken over from the Chartered Company, and during the interval he served as a principal assistant secretary to the committee of imperial defence. He had been promoted lieutenant-colonel in 1918.

Chancellor's term in Southern Rhodesia, 1923–8, more than justified his reputation as a capable and progressive administrator. The constitution which he helped to establish proved more durable than many such instruments and he opposed firmly any suggestion for the introduction of extreme forms of segregation. The ability which he showed in handling local politicians and in guiding the management of affairs led to his selection for the difficult

appointment of high commissioner for Palestine and Transjordan, from 1928 to 1931; he succeeded Lord Plumer, whose term of office had been noteworthy for its freedom from those serious disturbances so unhappily frequent during the British administration of Palestine. This tranquillity and reasons of economy led to the withdrawal of the British military garrison from Palestine and to the reduction and reorganization of the police force. In consequence the civil power was without military aid when in August 1929, following incidents at, and in connection with, the Wailing Wall at Jerusalem, Arab attacks were made on Jews in several large towns in Palestine.

Chancellor was then on leave and, although the parliamentary commission of inquiry under Sir Walter Shaw, reporting in March 1930, found no serious fault with the governmental handling of the riots, there were some in Palestine who felt that events might have taken a very different course had Chancellor been in the country. The principal recommendation of the Shaw commission was that the British government should issue a statement of policy defining clearly and positively the meaning which they attached to certain passages in the mandate and should make it plain that they intended to give full effect to the policy thus defined. That recommendation was, almost certainly, influenced by Chancellor's views and he must have been well satisfied when, after further investigations, including one of land and immigration problems by Sir John Hope Simpson, the government issued a statement on policy in October 1930 which went to what Chancellor undoubtedly regarded as the root of the Palestine problem. When in February 1931 the white paper was in effect reinterpreted by Ramsay MacDonald in a statement to Chaim Weizmann, Chancellor's faith in government policy in Palestine was badly shaken and his disappointment was made evident in his speech at a farewell banquet in Jerusalem when he said: 'I came hoping to increase the country's prosperity and happiness. I am leaving with my ambition unfulfilled. Conditions were against me' (private information).

Regarded as 'aloof and suspicious' (Sherman, 77), Chancellor was 'convinced that the entire Balfour Declaration policy had been "a colossal blunder", unjust to the Arabs and impossible of fulfilment in its own terms' (ibid., 85).

Though over sixty, Chancellor now embarked on a third career, serving as chairman or member of a number of governmental committees; on bodies such as the Royal Geographical, Royal Empire, and Royal African societies; and as a director of various companies.

Although not tall, Chancellor was impressive alike in appearance, in his carriage, and in the good taste with which he always dressed. He did not make friends quickly or easily but to his subordinates he showed a courtesy which commanded their devotion and, once his confidence had been won, his charm and sympathy made him excellent company. He held strong views on many issues of policy but after his retirement from Palestine he scrupulously avoided public controversy.

Chancellor was appointed CMG in 1909, KCMG in 1913,

GCMG in 1922, GCVO in 1925, and GBE in 1947. He died on 31 July 1952 at Shieldhill, Lanarkshire, an estate which his family had owned for nearly eight hundred years.

T. I. K. LLOYD, rev.

Sources *The Times* (2 Aug 1952) · *WWW* · private information (1971) · *CGPLA Eng. & Wales* (1952) · A. J. Sherman, *Mandate days: British lives in Palestine, 1918–1948* (1997) · personal knowledge (1971) · *The Society of Writers to His Majesty's Signet with a list of the members* (1936) · N. Shepherd, *Ploughing sand: British rule in Palestine, 1917–1948* (1999) · P. Ofer, 'The role of the high commissioner in British policy in Palestine: Sir John Chancellor, 1928–1931', PhD diss., SOAS, 1971 · B. Wasserstein, *The British in Palestine: the mandatory government and the Arab–Jewish conflict, 1917–1929* (1978) · G. Sheffer, 'Policy making and British policies towards Palestine, 1929–1939', DPhil diss., U. Oxf., 1971
Archives Bodl. RH, papers | Bodl. RH, letters to Sydney Moody
Likenesses W. Stoneman, photograph, 1919, NPG · H. Cecil, photographs, 1920–29, NPG · F. Wiles, oils, Legislative Assembly, Salisbury, Rhodesia
Wealth at death £33,057 4s. 3d.: probate, 26 Nov 1952, *CGPLA Eng. & Wales*

Chancellor, Richard (*d.* 1556), explorer, is of unknown origins; the scholar Clement Adams, who set down his Russian observations, claimed that he was brought up in the household of Sir Henry Sidney. In 1550 Chancellor sailed as an apprentice pilot under Roger Bodenham in the voyage of the bark *Aucher* to the Levant. Organized under the auspices of Sebastian Cabot, this was intended to provide much-needed experience of long-range voyaging to English mariners, who at that time lagged behind their Iberian and French counterparts in the application of the hydrographical sciences. Bodenham later claimed that of the *Aucher*'s crew of seventy men and boys, almost all had become ships' masters in the five years following their return.

In 1553 the search for new markets for English cloths gave rise to a project to find a passage to the Far East via the north-eastern seas. A large syndicate of noblemen, courtiers, and merchants financed the dispatch of an expedition of three ships—the *Bona Esperanza*, *Edward Bonaventure*, and *Bona Confidentia*—under the command of Sir Hugh Willoughby. Chancellor was appointed as pilot-general of the voyage and captain of the largest vessel, the *Edward Bonaventure*, of 160 tons. The vessels departed from Tilbury on 22 May 1553. At Harwich they were delayed for several weeks by reason of faulty casking and spoilage of some of their victuals, but departed thence on 23 June. The ships kept company northwards towards the Norwegian coast, but soon after a parley at the Lofoten islands on 30 July, where Willoughby and Chancellor agreed to meet at Vardö if they became separated, they were scattered by a storm. Chancellor duly made for the town, where he waited for seven days. Discounting the warnings of several Scottish traders there, who urged him not to attempt the dangerous navigation before him, Chancellor decided to press on in the *Edward Bonaventure*. Though neither his own account, nor that of Adams, mentions any discussions with local pilots, it is likely that he had obtained reasonably accurate plots of the coastline between Vardö and

the Russian port of St Nicholas, which he reached before the end of August 1553.

The town's inhabitants and governor, if perplexed at this apparition, were cautiously friendly, and Chancellor readily obtained victuals and rested his crew there. Lacking any information on Willoughby, he decided to travel to the court of the tsar rather than to sail on to the east. He reached Moscow some time during the winter of 1553–4, having written ahead to the court and been met thereafter by the tsar's emissaries. The details of Chancellor's discussions with the tsar's representatives are not known; however, in a letter to Edward VI written in February 1554 (by which time Edward was dead), Ivan IV refers to his request 'that we should grant unto your subjects, to goe and come, and in our dominions, and among our subjects, to frequent free Marts, with all sortes of marchandizes, and upon the same to have wares for their returne' (Hakluyt, 2.271–2). The tsar's acquiescence to these requests was the genesis of direct Anglo-Russian intercourse, and Chancellor delivered his letter to Queen Mary upon his return to England later in 1554.

In May 1555, as commander of the first expedition dispatched by the newly incorporated Russia Company, Chancellor returned to Muscovy with two ships, the *Philip and Mary* and the *Edward Bonaventure*, carrying merchants' factors and letters of privilege, drawn up by the company, to be ratified by the tsar. He journeyed overland to Moscow once more and remained there over the winter, though his ships returned to England. In the following year the Russia Company dispatched the same ships and a large pinnace, the *Serchthrift* (commanded by Stephen Borough, master of the *Edward Bonaventure* in 1553), which was to reconnoitre the hoped-for north-eastern passage east of the White Sea. The expedition was also to bring home the *Bona Esperanza* and *Bona Confidentia*, discovered intact with Willoughby's dead crews at Arzina in the Arctic, and to carry the tsar's embassy to England. With rich cargoes, the four ships departed from St Nicholas in July 1556.

Only one ship—the *Philip and Mary*—survived the passage to England. The unlucky *Bona Esperanza* and *Bona Confidentia* were lost at sea off Norway; the *Edward Bonaventure*, carrying Chancellor and the Russian ambassador, Osip Napeya, reached Scotland but was wrecked in Pitsligo Bay on the Aberdeenshire coast on 10 November 1556 with the loss of most of her crew. According to Napeya's later testimony, his own life was saved by Chancellor, who drowned in attempting to carry the ambassador and his entourage to shore in the *Edward*'s boat.

Clement Adams regarded Chancellor as 'of great estimation for many good partes of wit in him' (Hakluyt, 2.242). He also reported the words of Chancellor's guardian, Sir Henry Sidney, who recommended him to the backers of the 1553 expedition with protracted and fulsome praise:

> You know the man by report, I by experience, you by wordes, I by deedes, you by speech and companie, but I by the daily triall of his life have a full and perfect knowledge of him … wherefore in respect of the greatnesse of the dangers, and

the excellencie of his charge, you are to favour and love the man. (ibid., 2.242–3)

Chancellor's most valuable legacy lay in the minute observations of Muscovy that he gave to Clement Adams following his return to England in 1554, and in his own 'booke of the great and mighty Emperor of Russia, etc', a brief relation of his first audience with the tsar and observations on the country. In these pieces Chancellor described the topography of the country in detail; its principal cities—Moscow, Novgorod, Yaroslavl, Vologda, Pskov, and Kholmogory—and identified and named the rivers Volga, Ob, Don, Dnieper, and Dvina. More important, Chancellor observed life at the tsar's court, particularly its rituals, customs, and proscriptions, and the manner and methods of warfare practised by his armies. In effect, the data he supplied to his employers provided a manual of business etiquette for the English merchants who followed him. Too valuable to be disseminated widely (Richard Eden referred to their existence as early as 1556), the Russia Company jealously guarded Adams's handwritten notes until 1589, when Hakluyt reproduced them in the first edition of his *Principall Navigations*.

Details of Chancellor's personal connections are negligible. There are only two references to family: that of Clement Adams, who reported Chancellor's anxiety at his departure from England in 1553 that his death at sea would make orphans of his two sons; and Chancellor's dedication of his 'booke' to an uncle, Christopher Frothingham. One of Chancellor's sons, Nicholas, subsequently spent several years in Russia as an employee of the Russia Company. He later served as purser in Martin Frobisher's three voyages to Baffin Island (1576–8), as a merchant in Pet and Jackman's north-eastern voyage of 1580, and again as a purser in Edward Fenton's intended Moluccas voyage of 1582. On 29 September 1582, at Sierra Leone, he died of fever: 'a simple and honest man but timid … his father was an explorer in Muscovy' (Donno, 198 n. 2).

JAMES MCDERMOTT

Sources R. Hakluyt, *The principal navigations, voyages, traffiques and discoveries of the English nation*, 2, Hakluyt Society, extra ser., 2 (1903); 5, Hakluyt Society, extra ser., 5 (1904) · T. S. Willan, *The Muscovy merchants of 1555* (1953) · T. S. Willan, *The early history of the Russia Company, 1553–1603* (1956) · *An Elizabethan in 1582: the diary of Richard Madox, fellow of All Souls*, ed. E. S. Donno, Hakluyt Society, 2nd ser., 147 (1976)

PICTURE CREDITS

Capper, Joseph (1726/7–1804)—© National Portrait Gallery, London

Carausius (d. 293)—© Copyright The British Museum

Carden, Sir Sackville Hamilton (1857–1930)—© National Portrait Gallery, London

Cardew, Michael Ambrose (1901–1983)—© reserved; unknown collection; photograph National Portrait Gallery, London

Cardwell, Edward (1787–1861)—© National Portrait Gallery, London

Cardwell, Edward, first Viscount Cardwell (1813–1886)—© National Portrait Gallery, London

Carew, Bampfylde Moore (1693–1759)—© National Portrait Gallery, London

Carew, George, earl of Totnes (1555–1629)—© National Portrait Gallery, London

Carew, Sir Nicholas (b. in or before 1496, d. 1539)—in the collection of the Duke of Buccleuch and Queensberry KT

Carew, Sir Peter (1514?–1575)—National Gallery of Scotland

Carew, Richard (1555–1620)—by permission of the Trustees of the Carew Pole Family Trusts. Photograph: Photographic Survey, Courtauld Institute of Art, London

Carey, Henry, first Baron Hunsdon (1526–1596)—The Berkeley Castle Will Trust. Photograph: Photographic Survey, Courtauld Institute of Art, London

Carey, Henry, second earl of Monmouth (1596–1661)—The Metropolitan Museum of Art, Rogers Fund, 1949. (49.33) Photograph © 1994 The Metropolitan Museum of Art

Carey, James (1837–1883)—© National Portrait Gallery, London

Carey, William (c.1500–1528)—© National Portrait Gallery, London

Carey, William (1761–1834)—original owned by BMS World Mission, PO Box 49, Didcot, OX11 8XA, England

Cargill, Ann (c.1760–1784)—© reserved

Carleton, Dudley, Viscount Dorchester (1574–1632)—© National Portrait Gallery, London

Carleton, George (1557/8–1628)—unknown collection; photograph Sotheby's Picture Library, London / National Portrait Gallery, London

Carleton, Guy, first Baron Dorchester (1724–1808)—private collection

Carleton, Mary (1634x42–1673)—Ashmolean Museum, Oxford

Carleton, William (1794–1869)—© National Portrait Gallery, London

Carlile, Wilson (1847–1942)—© National Portrait Gallery, London

Carline family (per. c.1870–c.1975)—© Estate of the Artist. Picture destroyed. Photograph: Photographic Survey, Courtauld Institute of Art, London

Carline, Richard Cotton (1896–1980)—© Estate of Stanley Spencer 2004. All rights reserved, DACS; collection Rugby Art Gallery and Museum

Carlyle, Alexander (1722–1805)—Scottish National Portrait Gallery

Carlyle, Thomas (1795–1881)—© National Portrait Gallery, London

Carmichael, Richard (1779–1849)—Ashmolean Museum, Oxford

Carmichael, Thomas David Gibson, Baron Carmichael (1859–1926)—© National Portrait Gallery, London

Carnegie, Andrew (1835–1919)—© National Portrait Gallery, London

Carolan, Turlough (1670–1738)—by courtesy of the National Gallery of Ireland

Caroline (1683–1737)—© National Portrait Gallery, London

Caroline (1768–1821)—© National Portrait Gallery, London

Caroline Matilda, Princess (1751–1775)—Statens Museum for Kunst, Copenhagen

Carpenter, Alfred Francis Blakeney (1881–1955)—© National Portrait Gallery, London

Carpenter, Edward (1844–1929)—© National Portrait Gallery, London

Carpenter, (Joseph) Estlin (1844–1927)—© National Portrait Gallery, London

Carpenter, John Archibald Boyd-, Baron Boyd-Carpenter (1908–1998)—© National Portrait Gallery, London

Carpenter, Margaret Sarah (1793–1872)—© Copyright The British Museum

Carpenter, Richard (1604/5–1670?)—© National Portrait Gallery, London

Carpenter, William Benjamin (1813–1885)—© National Portrait Gallery, London

Carr, Sir Cecil Thomas (1878–1966)—© National Portrait Gallery, London

Carr, Edward Hallett (1892–1982)—© National Portrait Gallery, London

Carr, Sir (William) Emsley (1867–1941)—© National Portrait Gallery, London

Carr, Robert, earl of Somerset (1585/6?–1645)—The Royal Collection © 2004 HM Queen Elizabeth II

Carrington, Sir Codrington Edmund (1769–1849)—V&A Images, The Victoria and Albert Museum

Carrington, Dora de Houghton (1893–1932)—by permission of Luke Gertler; photograph National Portrait Gallery, London

Carroll, Charles [of Carrollton] (1737–1832)—courtesy of the Massachusetts Historical Society

Carron, William John, Baron Carron (1902–1969)—© National Portrait Gallery, London

Carruthers, Andrew (1770–1852)—© National Portrait Gallery, London

Carse, Alexander (bap. 1770, d. 1843)—Scottish National Portrait Gallery

Carson, Edward Henry, Baron Carson (1854–1935)—© National Portrait Gallery, London

Carson, Violet Helen (1898–1983)—Getty Images – John Madden

Carstairs, Joe (1900–1993)—Getty Images – Brooke

Carstairs, John Paddy (1910–1970)—© reserved; collection National Portrait Gallery, London

Carstares, William (1649–1715)—courtesy of the University of Edinburgh's Collections

Carte, Dame Bridget Cicely D'Oyly (1908–1985)—© Jane Bown

Carte, Richard D'Oyly (1844–1901)—V&A Images, The Victoria and Albert Museum

Carter, Angela Olive (1940–1992)—© News International Newspapers Ltd; collection National Portrait Gallery, London

Carter, Elizabeth (1717–1806)—reproduced by kind permission of Dr. Johnson's House Trust

Carter, Howard (1874–1939)—© Griffith Institute, Oxford

Carter, Robert (1663–1732)—National Portrait Gallery, Smithsonian Institution

Carter, Thomas Thellusson (1808–1901)—© National Portrait Gallery, London

Carter, (Helen) Violet Bonham, Baroness Asquith of Yarnbury (1887–1969)—© National Portrait Gallery, London

Carteret, John, second Earl Granville (1690–1763)—© National Portrait Gallery, London

Cartier, Sir George-Étienne, baronet (1814–1873)—© National Portrait Gallery, London

Cartland, Dame (Mary) Barbara Hamilton (1901–2000)—© Tom Hustler / National Portrait Gallery, London

Carton de Wiart, Sir Adrian (1880–1963)—© National Portrait Gallery, London

Cartwright, Edmund (1743–1823)—© National Portrait Gallery, London

Cartwright, John (1740–1824)—© National Portrait Gallery, London

Cartwright, Julia Mary (1851–1924)—© National Portrait Gallery, London

Cartwright, Dame Mary Lucy (1900–1998)—The Mistress and Fellows, Girton College, Cambridge

Cartwright, Sir Richard (1835–1912)—National Archives of Canada / PA-025546

Cartwright, Thomas (1634–1689)—© National Portrait Gallery, London

Cartwright, William (1606–1686)—by permission of the Trustees of Dulwich Picture Gallery

Cartwright, William (1611–1643)—Sterling Library, University College London; photograph © National Portrait Gallery, London

Carwardine, Penelope (1729–c.1801)—private collection. Photograph: Photographic Survey, Courtauld Institute of Art, London

Cary, Elizabeth, Viscountess Falkland (1585–1639)—Sarah Campbell Blaffer Foundation, Houston, TX; photograph © National Portrait Gallery, London

Cary, Francis Stephen (1808–1880)—© National Portrait Gallery, London

Cary, Henry, first Viscount Falkland (c.1575–1633)—by kind permission of the Viscount Cobham, Hagley Hall. Photograph: Photographic Survey, Courtauld Institute of Art, London

Cary, (Arthur) Joyce Lunel (1888–1957)—© National Portrait Gallery, London

Cary, Lettice, Viscountess Falkland (c.1612–1647)—© National Portrait Gallery, London

Cary, Lucius, second Viscount Falkland (1609/10–1643)—© National Portrait Gallery, London

Cary, Mary Ann Camberton (1823–1893)—National Archives of Canada / C-029977

Caryl, Joseph (1602–1673)—by permission of Dr Williams's Library

Casaubon, Isaac (1559–1614)—© National Portrait Gallery, London

Casaubon, (Florence Estienne) Meric (1599–1671)—© National Portrait Gallery, London

Case, John (1539/40?–1599)—The President and Fellows of St John's College, Oxford

Case, Thomas (bap. 1598, d. 1682)—Dr Williams's Library; photograph National Portrait Gallery, London

Casement, Roger David (1864–1916)—National Gallery of Ireland

Casey, Richard Gavin Gardiner, Baron Casey (1890–1976)—© National Portrait Gallery, London

Caslon, Elizabeth (1730–1795)—© National Portrait Gallery, London

Caslon, William, the elder (1692–1766)—© National Portrait Gallery, London

Cassel, Sir Ernest Joseph (1852–1921)—© National Portrait Gallery, London

Cassels, Sir Robert Archibald (1876–1959)—© National Portrait Gallery, London

Casson, Sir Hugh Maxwell (1910–1999)—Getty Images – Hulton Archive

Casson, Sir Lewis Thomas (1875–1969)—Garrick Club / the art archive

Castell, Edmund (bap. 1606, d. 1686)—© National Portrait Gallery, London

Caswall, Edward (1814–1878)—© National Portrait Gallery, London

Catchpole, Margaret (1762–1819)—© National Portrait Gallery, London

Catesby, William (b. in or before 1446, d. 1485)—reproduced by courtesy of H. M. Stuchfield, F.S.A., Hon. Secretary of the Monumental Brass Society